AF323618

AN

ELEMENTARY

DICTIONARY

OF THE

ENGLISH LANGUAGE.

BY

JOSEPH E. WORCESTER, LL.D.

A NEW EDITION,

REVISED AND ENLARGED.

———

BOSTON

SWAN, BREWER, AND TILESTON.

Entered according to Act of Congress, in the year 1860, by

JOSEPH E. WORCESTER,

In the Clerk's Office of the District Court of the District of Massachusetts.

ELECTROTYPED AT THE
BOSTON STEREOTYPE FOUNDRY.

PREFACE.

This Dictionary was first stereotyped and published in 1835; many impressions of it have since been issued; and it has now been carefully revised, and considerably enlarged.

The " Comprehensive, Pronouncing, and Explanatory Dictionary of the English Language," a work designed for the use of schools, academies, families, and individuals, contains not only a very full vocabulary of common English words, but also many words of rare occurrence, numerous technical terms used in the various arts and sciences, and a considerable number of such words from foreign languages as are often found in English books; and with respect to words of various, doubtful, or disputed pronunciation, the different modes in which they are pronounced by all the most eminent English orthoepists are exhibited, with the respective authorities annexed; and it also contains a notice of the principal synonymes of the language.

But a Dictionary is used, in common schools, for purposes in relation to which a more select vocabulary is preferable; and although the method adopted in the " Comprehensive Dictionary," with respect to words variously pronounced, adds much to the value of the work for teachers and the more advanced scholars, yet it may tend rather to embarrass than assist such pupils as are little accustomed to the use of a Dictionary.

(3)

This work is substantially a reduced form of the " Comprehensive Dictionary," and it has been brought to its present size by abridging a part of the definitions, by not retaining the notices of synonymes, and the various modes of pronunciation of words differently pronounced with their authorities annexed, and by the omission of most of such words as are obsolete or very rarely used, of many technical terms, and of some words from foreign languages. But notwithstanding these omissions, it contains a very full vocabulary of the common and well-authorized words of the language, which, together with the several vocabularies comprised in the volume, will, it is believed, render it a work well adapted to the use of common schools.

Active or transitive, and neuter or intransitive verbs are distinguished, irregular verbs are conjugated, and the plural forms of irregular nouns are exhibited.

Great care has been taken to give the pronunciation of the common words of the language, and also of the proper names contained in the several vocabularies, in accordance with the best usage and the most approved authorities.

With respect to orthography, the purpose has been to give that which is supported by the best usage in the United States and in England. Innovations which have no sanction from English usage, or the prevailing and best usage of this country, have been avoided as corruptions of the language. This small work, in its present state, will be found better adapted than heretofore to the use for which it was designed.

CAMBRIDGE, *November*, 1860.

CONTENTS.

PRINCIPLES OF PRONUNCIATION.

KEY

TO THE SOUNDS OF THE MARKED LETTERS.

VOWELS.

	Examples.		*Examples.*
1. Ā *long*	FĀTE, LĀCE, PLĀYER.	1. Ō *long*	NŌTE, FŌAL, TŌW.
2. Ă *short*	FĂT, MĂN, LĂD, CĂRRY.	2. Ŏ *short*	NŎT, DŎN, BŎRROW.
3. À *long before* R	FÀRE, PÀIR, BEÀR.	3. Ô *long and close*	MÔVE, PRÔVE, FÔÔD.
4. Ä *Italian or grave*	FÄR, FÄTHER, FÄRTHER.	4. Ö *broad, like broad* Â	NÖR, FÖRM, SÖRT.
5. Ȧ *intermediate*	FȦST, BRȦNCH, GRȦSP.	5. Ꝍ *like short* Ŭ	SꝊN, DꝊNE, CꝊME.
6. Â *broad*	FÂLL, HÂUL, WÂRM.	6. Ǫ *slight or obscure*	ACTǪR, CǪNFESS.
7. A̤ *slight or obscure*	LIA̤R, PALA̤CE, ABBA̤CY.		
		1. Ū *long*	TŪBE, TŪNE, PŪRE.
1. Ē *long*	MĒTE, FĒAR, KĒĒP.	2. Ŭ *short*	TŬB, TŬN, HŬRRY.
2. Ĕ *short*	MĔT, SĔLL, FĔRRY.	3. Û *middle or obtuse*	PÛLL, FÛLL, PÛSH.
3. Ê *like* À	HÊIR, THÊRE, WHÊRE.	4. Ü *short and obtuse*	FÜR, TÜRN, MÜRMUR.
4. Ė *short and obtuse*	HĖR, HĖRD, FĖRVID.	5. Ꝋ *like* Ō *in* MŌVE	RꝊLE, RꝊDE, BRꝊTE.
5. Ę *slight or obscure*	BRIĘR, FUĘL, CELĘRY.	6. Ꞟ *slight or obscure*	SULPHꞞR, FAMOꞞS.
1. Ī *long*	PĪNE, FĪLE, FĪND.	1. Ȳ *long*	TȲPE, STȲLE, LȲRE.
2. Ĭ *short*	PĬN, FĬLL, MĬRROR.	2. Y̆ *short*	SY̆LVAN, SY̆MBOL.
3. Î *like long* Ē	MÎEN, FÎELD, MARÎNE.	3. Ẏ *short and obtuse*	MẎRRH, MẎRTLE.
4. Ï *short and obtuse*	SÏR, FÏR, BÏRD, VÏRTUE.	4. Y̤ *slight or obscure*	TRULY̤, MARTY̤R.
5. I̦ *slight or obscure*	ELIXI̦R, RUI̦N, ABILI̦TY.		

ÖÏ *and* ÖY̆	BÖÏL, TÖÏL, BÖY̆, TÖY̆.
ÖÛ *and* ÖW̄	BÖÛND, TÖW̄N, NÖW̄.
EW̄ *like long* Ū	FEW̄, NEW̄, DEW̄.

CONSONANTS.

	Examples.			*Examples.*
Ç, ç, *soft, like* S	AÇID, PLAÇID.	CEA̤N } CIA̤N } *like* SHA̤N		{ OCEA̤N. OPTICIA̤N. }
Ꞓ, ꞓ, *hard, like* K	FLAꞒCID, SꞒEPTIC.	CIA̤L } SIA̤L } TIA̤L } *like* SHA̤L		{ COMMERCIA̤L. CONTROVERSIA̤L. PARTIA̤L, MARTIA̤L. }
ꞒH, ꞓh, *hard, like* K	ꞒHORUS, ꞒHASM.	CEOꞞS } CIOꞞS } TIOꞞS } *like* SHꞞS		{ FARINACEOꞞS. CAPACIOꞞS. SENTENTIOꞞS. }
ÇH, çh, *soft, like* SH	ÇHAISE, ÇHAGRIN.	ꞠEOꞞS } ꞠIOꞞS } *like* JꞞS		{ COURAꞠEOꞞS. RELIꞠIOꞞS. }
ꞒH (*unmarked*) *like* TSH	CHARM, CHURCH.	QU (*unmarked*) *like* KW		QUEEN, QUILL.
Ꞡ, ꞡ, *hard*	ꞠET, ꞠIVE, ꞠIFT.	WH (*unmarked*) *like* HW		WHEN, WHILE.
Ꞡ, ꞡ, *soft, like* J	ꞠENDER, ꞠIANT.	PH (*unmarked*) *like* F		PHANTOM, SERAꝒH.
Ș, ș, *soft, like* Z	MUȘE, DIȘMAL.			
X̧, x̧, *soft or flat, like* GZ	EX̧AMPLE, EX̧IST.			
ꞮH, Ɪh, *soft, flat, or vocal*	ꞮHIS, ꞮHEE, ꞮHEN.			
TH, th, (*unmarked*) *sharp*	THIN, THINK, PITH.			
TIǪN } SIǪN } *like* SHUN	{ NATIǪN, NOTIǪN. PENSIǪN, MISSIǪN. }			
ȘIǪN *like* ZHUN	CONFUȘIǪN, VIȘIǪN.			

REMARKS ON THE KEY.

1. The words which are used in the preceding Key as examples for illustrating the several sounds, exhibit accurately, when pronounced by correct speakers, the different sounds of the respective letters. Some distinctions are here made which are not found in other systems of notation ; they are, however, not intended to introduce any new sounds, but merely to discriminate such as are now heard from all who speak the language with propriety.

2. When the marks of pronunciation are affixed to words in their proper orthography, in this Dictionary, without respelling them, the vowels which are not marked are silent : thus, *a* in *bĕat, hĕar; e* in *āble, gĭve, härden; i* in *pāin, hĕıfer; o* in *māson, fāmous; u* in *thōugh;* and *w* in *fŏllŏw*, are not sounded. — To this rule there is an exception with respect to the first vowel in those proper diphthongs which are called *semi-consonant diphthongs*, as in *ocean, nation, assuage*. (See Sounds of the Diphthongs, No. 28, p. 12.)

3. The system of notation which is here used, while it makes a very exact discrimination of the different sounds of the letters, will be readily understood and easily applied to practice ; and it will also be much more easily remembered than a system in which the vowels are marked with figures. By applying the marks to the letters of the words in their proper orthography, the necessity of respelling most of them has been avoided ; and in this way considerable space has been saved, while the pronunciation is fixed with as much exactness as if the spelling of every word had been repeated.

4. It is an advantage of this method of notation, that it distinguishes the syllables which receive a secondary accent, or are pronounced with a distinct sound of the vowels, from those which are but slightly or indistinctly sounded. A great part of the words of the English language that have more than two syllables, have more than one syllable in some degree accented, or pronounced more distinctly than the rest ; yet this difference in distinctness is not made apparent by the usual modes of marking the words. In this notation, the vowels in the syllables which have either the primary or secondary accent, have a mark placed over them, denoting a distinct sound ; while those which are more feebly uttered, have a dot placed under them. Take, for example, the following words, which are thus noted : *sŭn'shīne, pā'pẹr, ăn'ẹcdōte, cär-ạ-văn', lĭt'ẹr-ạl, măn-ĭ-fẹs-tā'tiọn, ĭn-dĭvĭs-i-bĭl'ị-ty*. In these words, it will be readily perceived that all the vowels which have a mark placed over them, have a distinct sound, or are more or less accented, while those which have a dot under them are but slightly or indistinctly sounded ; and that the pronunciation is as clearly represented to the eye in their proper orthography, as it is, in other methods of notation, by respelling the words.

5. There are many cases in which the vowels are pronounced with so slight a degree of distinctness, that it may be a matter of indifference whether they are marked with the distinct or indistinct sound ; thus, for example, the last syllable of the words *consonant, difference, diffident, feebleness*, and *obvious*, might, with nearly equal propriety, have the vowel marked with a short or an indistinct sound.

SOUNDS OF THE VOWELS.

6. The *first*, or *long*, sound of each of the vowels, marked thus, *ā, ē, ī, ō, ū*, is styled its *alphabetic* or *name* sound, being the sound which is heard in naming the letter. The sound of the letter *y*, when used as a vowel, is the same as that of *i* ; but as a vowel it begins no properly English word now in common use.

7. The long sound of the vowels is generally indicated, in monosyllables, by a silent *e* at the end of the word, preceded by a single conso-nant ; as in *fate, mete, pine, note, tube, type*. The following words, however, are exceptions ; namely, *have, are,* and *bade*, the preterite of *to bid*. The vowels have regularly the long sound if final in an accented syllable ; as in *ba'sis, le'gal, tri'al, sono'rous, cu'bic, ty'rant*.

8. The *second*, or *short*, sound of the vowels is generally indicated, in monosyllables, by the absence of mute *e* at the end of the word ; as in *fat, met, pin, not, tub, hyp*. It is also the usual sound of a vowel in an accented syllable which ends with a consonant; as in *aban'don, atten'tive, ex-hib'it, lacon'ic, reluc'tant, lyr'ical.*

9. The *fourth* sound of the vowels, *a, e, i, o,* and *u,* and the *third* sound of *y,* (called, with respect to *e, i, u,* and *y, short and obtuse,*) marked thus, *ă, ĕ, ĭ, ŏ, ŭ, y,* are the *short* sounds of these several vowels when followed by *r* in a monosyllable or in an accented syllable; as, *far, hard; her, herd; fir, firkin; north, normal; fur, burden; myrrh, myrtle:* but when the succeeding syllable begins with *r,* or the *sound* of *r,* as in *pĕrry, pĕril,* the vowel has the proper short sound. Some orthoepists make no distinction between the sound indicated by this mark and the proper short sound of these vowels; others make a distinction in relation to a part of them only. The vowels having this mark are pronounced with as short a sound as they can readily receive when thus situated. The peculiar character of this sound, which distinguishes it from the proper short sound of the vowels, is caused by the letter *r;* and this letter, thus situated, has an influence peculiar to itself on the sound of all the vowels. The difference between the sound of the vowels when thus situated, and their proper short sound, will be readily perceived by the following examples: *măn, mărrow; mŭr, mărket; — mĕn, merry; hĕr, mĕrchant; — fĭn, mĭrror; fĭr, circle; — nŏt, bŏrrow; nŏr, bŏrder; — tŭn, hŭrry; fŭr, hŭrdle.* There is little or no difference in the sounds of the vowels *e, i, u,* and *y,* when under this mark; as, *hĕr, fĭr, fŭr, myrrh;* but their proper short sounds are widely different from each other, when they are followed by the sound of *r,* or by other consonants; as in *merry, peril, mirror, hurry.* — See remarks on the sound of the letter R, page 16.

10. Vowels marked with the dot underneath, thus, *ạ, ẹ, ị, ọ, ụ, y,* are found only in syllables which are not accented, and over which the organs of speech pass slightly and hastily in pronouncing the words in which they are found. It is to be observed that this mark is employed to indicate *a slight stress of voice* in uttering the appropriate sound of the vowel, rather than to note *any particular quality of sound.* If the syllables on which the primary and secondary accents fall, are uttered with a proper stress of voice, these comparatively indistinct syllables will naturally be pronounced right. In a majority of cases, this mark may be regarded as indicating an indistinct *short* sound of the vow-el; as in *tenable, mental, travel, peril, idol, forum, carry;* but in many cases it indicates a slight or unaccented *long* sound; as in *carbonate, sulphate, emerge, obey, ebony, follower, duplicity, educate, regulate, congratulate.* The letter *u,* in the last three words, is pronounced like *yu* slightly articulated. The vowels with this mark have, in some situations, particularly in the last syllable of words ending with *r,* no perceptible difference of sound; as in *friar, speaker, nadir, actor, sulphur, zephyr.* As Mr. Smart justly remarks, " the last syllables of *robber, nadir, author, sulphur,* and *satyr,* are quite undistinguishable in pronunciation."

A, unaccented, at the end of a word, approaches the Italian sound of *a* in *father;* as in the words *algebra, comma, idea;* and *ah,* final, partakes still more of the Italian sound, as in *Jehovah, Messiah.*

A.

11. The *third* sound of the letter *a,* marked thus *â,* is its *long* sound qualified by being followed by the letter *r;* as in *care, pare, fare.* The diphthong *ai,* followed by *r,* has precisely the same sound, as in *fair, pair;* so also, in some cases, has the diphthong *ea,* as in *bear, pear.* This sound of the letter *a* is the same as that of the letter *e* in *heir, there, where.* There is obviously a difference between the sound of *a* in these words, as they are pronounced by good speakers, and its sound in *pain* and *fate.* There is the same difference between the sound of *a* in the word *pair,* and its sound in the word *payer,* one who pays; also in the word *prayer,* a petition, and in the word *prayer,* one who prays.

12. The *fifth* sound of *a,* marked thus, *à,* is an *intermediate* sound of this letter, between its short sound, as in *fat, man,* and its Italian sound, as in *far, father;* this sound being somewhat shorter than the Italian sound of *a.* With respect to the class of words which, in this Dictionary, have this mark, there is much diversity among orthoepists. Most of these words are marked by Nares, Jones, and Perry, with the Italian sound of *a,* as in *fär* and *fäther;* but Walker, Jameson, Smart, Reid, and Craig, mark them, or most of them, with the short sound, as *a* in *făt, măn;* Fulton and Knight mark them as being intermediate between the short and the Italian sound; and Smart, though he gives to *a* in most of these words the short mark, says, in relation to it, " that when *a* is followed by *f, s,* or *n,* there is, in many words, a disposition to broadness in the vowel, not quite in unison with the mode of indication, as may be perceived in an unaffected pronunciation of *grass, graft, command.* This broadness is a decided vulgarism, when it identifies the sound with ŭ. The exact sound lies between the one indicated and the vulgar corruption."

The following list includes a considerable part of the class of words in which, in this Dictionary, *a* is marked thus, å ; and in which, according to Nares, Jones, and Perry, *a* has the *Italian* sound, as in *father;* according to Walker, Jameson, Reid, and Craig, the *short* sound of *a*, as in *fat, man;* and according to Fulton and Knight, an *intermediate* sound between these two sounds. This intermediate sound, marked thus, å, is in accordance with the remark of Mr. Smart, who says, that when this sound is identified with the Italian sound of ä, it "is a decided *vulgarism.*"

abaft	cast	glance	pastor
advance	castle	glass	pasture
aft	chaff	graff	pilaster
after	chance	graft	plaster
aghast	chandler	grant	prance
alas	chant	grasp	quaff
amass	clasp	grass	raff
answer	class	haft	raft
ant	contrast	hasp	rafter
ask	craft	lance	rasp
asp	dance	lass	repast
ass	dastard	last	sample
bask	disaster	mask	shaft
basket	draff	mass	slander
bastard	draft	mast	slant
blanch	draught	mastiff	staff
blast	enchant	mischance	surpass
bombast	enhance	nasty	task
branch	fast	pant	trance
brass	flask	pass	vast
cask	gasp	past	waft
casket	ghastly		

There is a considerable number of words in which *a* has the sound of short *o*, as in *not*, called by Walker " the short sound of broad *a.*" This sound occurs chiefly in words in which *a* is preceded by *qu, w,* or *wh;* as, *quadrangle* (quŏdrangle), *quality* (quŏlity), *swallow* (swŏllow), *wad* (wŏd), *wan* (wŏn), *what* (whŏt); also, *scallop* (scŏllop), *chaps* (chŏps).

E.

13. The letter *e* has, in several words, the same sound as *a* in *fare;* as in *heir, there, where;* but *were* is properly pronounced *wĕr.* In *clerk* and *sergeant,* it has, according to all the English orthoepists, the sound of *a* in *dark* and *margin;* yet in this country it is not uncommon to pronounce these words, more in accordance with their orthography, *clĕrk* and *sĕrgeant.*

14. When *e* precedes *l* or *n* in an unaccented final syllable, in some words it has an indistinct short sound, and in some it is entirely suppressed. In most of the words ending in *el*, the *e* is *sounded;* as, *flannel, travel, vessel,* &c. The following words are exceptions, and in these the sound of *e* before *l* is suppressed : *drivel, grovel, hazel, mantel, navel, ousel, ravel, rivel, shekel, shovel, shrivel, snivel, weasel.*

In most of the words ending in *en,* the sound of *e* is *suppressed;* as, *harden, heaven, often,* &c. The following words are exceptions : *abdomen, acumen, aspen, bitumen, catechumen, cerumen, chicken, flamen, hymen, hyphen, kitchen, latten, legumen, linen, marten, mitten, mynchen, omen, patten, platen, pollen, regimen, siren, sloven, specimen, sudden, ticken, woollen, women.*

15. The sound of the letter *e* is generally suppressed in the preterites of verbs, and in participles in *ed,* when the *e* is not preceded by *d* or *t;* as, *feared, praised, admired, tossed, suppressed,* pronounced *feard, praisd, admird, tost, supprest.* But adjectives ending in *ed,* unless they are participles as well as adjectives, commonly preserve the sound of *e* before *d,* as in *naked, ragged, striped, wicked, wretched,* &c. In the following words, *beloved, blessed, cursed, learned, picked,* and *winged,* the sound of *e* before *d* is suppressed when the words are used as verbs or participles, and it is sounded when they are used as adjectives; as, He was much *beloved;* he *blessed* the occasion ; he *cursed* the day ; he *learned* to read ; he *picked* his men ; he *winged* his flight : — A *belov'ed* son , a *bless'ed* day ; a *curs'ed* thing ; a *learn'ed* man , a *pick'ed* point; a *wing'ed* fowl. — *Picked,* however, used as a participial adjective, in the sense of *selected,* as, "*picked* men," is pronounced in one syllable.

I.

16. The long sound of the letter *i* is heard not only in monosyllables ending with a mute *e,* as in *file, time,* &c., but also in the word *pint,* and in the words *child, mild, wild;* also in *bind, blind, find, hind, kind, mind, rind,* &c.

17. There is a class of words, mostly derived from the French and Italian languages, in which *i* retains the sound of long *e;* as, *ambergris, antique, unique, bombazine, Brazil, capivi, capuchin, caprice, chagrin, chevaux-de-frise, critique, frize, gabardine, haberdine, quarantine, ravine, routine, fascine, fatigue, intrigue, invalid, machine, maga-*

zine, marine, palanquin, pique, police, recitative, tabourine, tambourine, tontine, transmarine, ultramarine, verdigris. In the word *shire, i* commonly has the same sound; and some orthoepists also give it the same in *oblige* and *oblique.*

18. In words which terminate in *ile* and *ine,* with the accent on the penultimate syllable, the *i* in the final syllable is generally short; as, *fertile, hostile, adamantine, intestine,* &c. The following are exceptions: *edile, exile, gentile, pentile, feline, ferine, confine,* and a few others. Also when the accent is on the antepenult, words ending in *ile* generally have the *i* short; as, *juvenile, puerile,* &c.; but it is long in *camomile, reconcile, eolipile.*

19. With respect to words ending in *ine,* and having the accent on the antepenultimate, there is much uncertainty as to the quantity of the *i;* and, in relation to a number of such words, there is much disagreement among orthoepists; yet the general rule inclines to the long sound of *i* in the termination of this class of words. In the following words, *i,* in the last syllable, is generally pronounced long: *adulterine, almandine, armentine, asinine, belluine, bizantine, brigantine, cannabine, celandine, colubrine, columbine, concubine, countermine, crystalline, legatine, leonine, metalline, muscadine, porcupine, saccharine, saturnine, serpentine, turpentine, vespertine, vituline.* — In the following words, *i,* in the last syllable, is short: *discipline, feminine, genuine, heroine, hyaline, jessamine, libertine, masculine, medicine, nectarine, palatine.* With respect to *alkaline, aquiline, coralline, sapphirine, uterine, viperine,* and some others, the orthoepists, as well as usage, are divided. In the termination *ine* in a class of chemical words, the *i* is short; as, *fluorine, iodine, nepheline,* &c. In the termination *ite,* the *i* is sometimes short, as in *respite, granite, favorite, infinite,* &c.; and sometimes long, as in *expedite, appetite, satellite,* &c. In a class of gentile nouns, and appellatives formed from proper names, it is long; as, *Hivite, Wicliffite;* also, generally, in names of minerals; as, *augite, steatite, tremolite.* In verbs which end in *ise,* the *i* is long; as, *advertise, exercise,* &c.; but *divertise, franchise, mortise, practise,* and their compounds, are exceptions; also, *promise.*

20. When *i* ends an initial syllable without the accent, and the succeeding syllable begins with a consonant, the *i* is generally short or indistinct, as if written *e;* as in *civility, divine, finance:* but the exceptions to this rule are numerous, among which are *biquadrate, chirogra-*

phy, biography, divaricate, librarian, primeval, tribunal, vitality, and many others, in which the *i* is pronounced long. There is also a considerable number of words with regard to which there is a diversity, in relation to the pronunciation of the *i,* among orthoepists and in usage; as, *dilate, diverge, virago,* &c.

O.

21. There is a class of monosyllables ending in *f, ft, ss, st,* and *th,* in which *o* is marked with the short sound in most pronouncing dictionaries, though some orthoepists give it the sound of broad *a,* as in *fall.* Mr. Nares gives the sound of broad *a* to *o* in the following words (as some others do in a part of them): *off, often, offer, coffee, scoff, aloft, loft, soft, cross, loss, toss, cost, frost, lost, tost, broth, cloth, froth, cough,* and *trough.* To these some others might, with equal propriety, be added; as, *offspring, dross, gloss, moss, moth, wroth.* Mr. Smart remarks, " that before *ss, st,* and *th,* the letter *o* is frequently sounded *âw; as* in *moss, gloss,* &c., *lost, cost,* &c., *broth, cloth,* &c. This practice is analogous to the broad utterance which the letter *a* [short] is liable to receive before certain consonants [see A, No. 12]; and the same remarks will apply in the present case, as to the one referred to, namely, that, though the broad sound is vulgar, there is an affectation in a *palpable* effort to avoid it in words where its use seems at one time to have been general. In such cases, a medium between the extremes is the practice of the best speakers." The sound of *o* is somewhat prolonged also in *gone* and *begone,* and in some words ending in *ng;* as, *long, along, prong, song, strong, thong, throng, wrong.*

There are a few words in which *o* has the mark of the long sound in all the pronouncing dictionaries, although it is in these words, by many, if not by most speakers in this country, somewhat shortened. Thus we hear the sound *o,* in the words *coat, home, hope, spoke, stone, whole, wholly,* and *wholesome,* pronounced with a sound a little shorter than its proper long sound, as heard in *goat, note, dome, hole, sole, holy,* and *dolesome.*

22. There are some words in which *o* has the same sound as *u* in *bull,* or *oo* in *good;* namely, *bosom, wolf, woman, Wolsey, Wolverhampton.* It has the sound of short *u* in *done, son,* &c.; and the sound of *u* as in *hurt* in *word, work, worth,* &c.

23. In many words ending in *on,* the sound of *o* is suppressed, as in *bacon, pardon, weapon, reason, cotton,* &c.

U.

24. *U*, at the beginning of words, when long, has the sound *yu*, as in *use*. — With respect to the manner of designating the sound of the vowel *u* when it comes immediately after the accent, as in the words *educate*, *nature*, *natural*, &c., there is much diversity among orthoepists. By Walker, the pronunciation of EDUCATE is thus noted — *ĕd'jū-kāt*; by Sheridan, Jones, Enfield, Fulton, and Jameson, thus — *ĕd'ū-kāt*; and by Perry, Knowles, Smart, and Reid, thus — *ĕd'u-kāt*. NATURE, by Walker, thus — *nā'chūr*; by Sheridan and Jones, thus — *nā'chŭr*; by Perry, Enfield, and Reid, thus — *nā'tur*; by Jameson and Knowles, thus — *nāt'yŭr*; by Smart, thus — *nā'tūr* or *nā'ch'ôr*. NATURAL, by Walker and Jones, thus — *năt'chū-răl*; by Sheridan, thus — *năt'chŭr-ăl*; by Fulton, Enfield, and Jameson, thus — *năt'ū-răl*; by Perry and Reid, thus — *năt'u-răl*; by Knowles, thus — *năt'yŭr-ăl*; by Smart, thus — *năt'chô-ral*.

There is a pretty large class of words with respect to which there is a similar diversity in the manner in which the pronunciation of *u* and *tu* is noted by the different orthoepists; but the difference is greater in appearance than in reality. The *u* thus situated may properly be regarded as having the slight sound of long *u*; and the sound may be noted by *yu*, slightly articulated. — Walker remarks, with respect to the pronunciation of *nature*, " There is a vulgar pronunciation of this word as if written *na'ter*, which cannot be too carefully avoided. Some critics have contended that it ought to be pronounced as if written *nate-yure*; but this pronunciation comes so near to that here adopted [*nā'chūr*], as scarcely to be distinguishable from it."

When *u* is preceded by *r* in the same syllable, it has the sound of *oo* in *fool*, and it is thus marked, as in *rule, true*. This sound is given to *u* thus situated, by Walker, Smart, and all the other principal English orthoepists.

In *busy* and *business*, *u* has the sound of short *i*; and in *bury*, the sound of short *e*.

Y.

25. *Y*, at the end of a word, preceded by a consonant, is commonly pronounced short and indistinct, like indistinct *e*; as, *policy, palpably, lately, colony*, &c. The exceptions are monosyllables; as, *by, cry, dry, fly, fry, sty, ply, try, wry*, with their compounds, *awry, hereby, whereby*, &c.: also, verbs ending in *fy*; as, *fortify, magnify, testify*, &c.: also, *ally, apply, comply, imply, supply, multiply, reply, occupy*, and *prophesy*; in all which it has the long sound.

SOUNDS OF THE DIPHTHONGS AND TRIPHTHONGS.

26. A diphthong is the union of two vowels, pronounced by a single impulse of the voice; as, *oi* in *voice*, *ou* in *sound*.

27. A triphthong is the union of three vowels, pronounced by a single impulse of the voice; as, *ieu* in *adieu*, *iew* in *view*.

28. A proper diphthong is one in which both vowels are sounded; as, *oi* in *voice*, *ou* in *sound*, *ow* in *now*.

PROPER DIPHTHONGS.

ea *in* ocean;	io *in* nation;	ua *in* assuage;
eu " feud;	oi " voice;	ue " desuetude;
ew " jewel;	ou " sound;	ui " languid;
ia " poniard;	ow " now;	uo " quote.
ie " spaniel;	oy " boy;	

The diphthongs which begin with *e*, *i*, or *u*, namely, *ea, eu, ew, ia, ie, io, ua, ue, ui*, and *uo*, differ from the rest; and they may, as Walker says, " not improperly be called *semi-consonant diphthongs*;" being pronounced as if *y* consonant was substituted in place of *e* or *i*; as, *ocean* (ose'yan), *poniard* (pon'yard), *question* (quest'-yon); and as if *w* consonant were substituted in place of *u*; as, *assuage* (as-swage'), *languid* (lan'gwid), &c.

29. An improper diphthong has only one of the vowels sounded; as, *ea* in *heat*, *oa* in *coal*.

IMPROPER DIPHTHONGS.

æ or ae *in* Cæsar;	ea *in* beat;	ie *in* friend;
ai " pain;	ee " seed;	oa " boat;
ao " gaol;	ei " either;	œ " œsophagus;
au " haul;	eo " people;	oo " soon;
aw " law;	ey " they;	ow " crow.
ay " bay;		

Æ.

30. This is a Latin diphthong, and is always pronounced like *e* in Latin. In English, it is used only in words of Latin origin or formation ; as, *aqua-vitæ*, *minutiæ*, *æsthetics* ; and it is commonly long, as in *pæan*, but sometimes short, as in *Dædalus.*

AI.

31. The usual sound of this diphthong is the same as long *a*; as in *pail*, *pain*, pronounced like *pale*, *pane.* The following are the principal exceptions. It has the sound of short *e* in *said* and *saith*, and in *again* and *against*; that of short *a* in *plaid* and *raillery*; that of long *i* in *aisle*; and, in a final unaccented syllable, it has the obscure sound of the indistinct short *i*, as in *fountain*, *mountain*, *curtain*, &c.

AO.

32. This diphthong occurs only in the word *gaol*, pronounced, as well as very often written, *jail.*

AU.

33. The common sound of this diphthong is the same as that of broad *a*, or *aw*, — *caul* and *haul* being pronounced exactly like *call* and *hall.* But when these letters are followed by *n* and another consonant, the sound is changed, in a number of words, to that of the Italian *a* in *far* and *farther*; as, by most of the orthoepists, in the following words : *aunt, craunch, daunt, flaunt, gaunt, gauntlet, haunch, haunt, jaunt, jaundice, laugh, launch, laundress, laundry, maund, paunch, saunter, staunch.* Some orthoepists pronounce a part of these words with the sound of broad *a*, as most of them do the word *vaunt*, and many of them the word *taunt.* In the word *draught*, this diphthong has, according to some orthoepists, the sound of *a* in *far*, and according to others the short sound of *a* in *fat*; in *gauge*, the sound of long *a* (as in *page*); in *hautboy*, the sound of long *o*; and in *cauliflower*, *laudanum*, and *laurel*, it is, by some orthoepists, pronounced with the sound of short *o*, and by others with the sound of broad *a*; as, *cŏl'iflower* or *câu'liflower*, &c.

AW.

34. This diphthong has the sound of broad *a*, — *bawl* and *ball* being pronounced exactly alike.

AY.

35. This diphthong has the sound of long *a*, as in *pay*, *hay*, &c. ; except in *quay*, which is pronounced *kē.* It has the sound of short *e* in *says*; and in *Sunday*, *Monday*, &c., the last syllable is pronounced as if written *Sundy*, *Mondy*, &c.

EA.

36. The regular sound of this diphthong is that of long *e*, as in *beat*, *hear*, pronounced like *beet*, *here*; but there are many words in which it has the sound of short *e*; as, *head*, *dead*, *ready*, &c. In some words it has the sound of short and obtuse *e*, as in *earn*, *heard*, *pearl*, &c. In a few words it has the sound of long *a*; as in *break*, *steak*, *great*, *bear*, *bearer*, *forbear*, *forswear*, *pear*, *swear*, *tear*, *wear.* In some words it has the sound of *a* in *far*; as in *heart*, *hearten*, *hearty*, *hearth*, *hearken*; and, when unaccented, it has only an obscure sound, as in *vengeance*, *sergeant.*

The proper diphthong *ea* is found in a very few words; as, *ocean*, *cetacean*, *testacean.*

EAU.

37. This triphthong is used only in words derived from the French. In *beauty* it has the sound of long *u*; but its regular sound is that of long *o*, as in *beau*, *bureau*, *flambeau*, &c.

EE.

38. This diphthong is almost always pronounced like long *e*; the principal exceptions are *been* and *breeches*, pronounced *bĭn* and *brĭtches.* The poetical contractions *e'er* and *ne'er*, for *ever* and *never*, are pronounced as if written *air* and *nair.*

EI.

39. This diphthong has most commonly the sound either of long *a* or of long *e*. It has the sound of long *a*, as in *deign*, *eight*, *feign*, *feint*, *freight*, *heinous*, *inveigh*, *neigh*, *neighbor*, *reindeer*, *skein*, *veil*, *vein*, *weigh*, *weight*, *heir*, *their*, &c. It has the sound of long *e* in *ceil*, *ceiling*, *conceit*, *conceive*, *deceit*, *deceive*, *inveigle*, *perceive*, *receipt*, *receive*, *seize*, *seizin*, *seignior*, *seigniory*, *seine*; commonly also in *either*, *neither*, and *leisure.* It has the sound of long *i* in *height*, *heighten*, and *sleight*; of short *e* in *heifer* and *nonpareil*; and, in an unaccented syllable, an indistinct sound of *i*, as in *foreign*, *foreigner*, *forfeit*, *forfeiture*, *sovereign*, *sovereignty*, *surfeit.*

EO.

40. This diphthong is pronounced like long *o* in *yeoman* and *yeomanry*, and like long *e* in *people*; like short *e* in *jeopard*, *jeopardy*, *leopard*, *feoffee*, *feoffer*, *feoffment*; like broad *o* (as in *nor*) in *georgic*; like long *u* in *feod*, *feodal*, *feodary* (which are now commonly written *feud*, *feudal*, and *feudary*); and, when unaccented, it has the indistinct sound of *u* or *o*, as in *bludgeon, cur-mudgeon, dudgeon, dungeon, gudgeon, luncheon, puncheon, truncheon, surgeon, sturgeon, scutcheon, escutcheon,* and the indistinct sound of *i* or *o*, as in *pigeon, widgeon.*

EU.

41. This diphthong is always sounded like long *u*, as in *feud, deuce.*

EW.

42. This diphthong is almost always sounded like long *u*, or *eu,* as in *few, hew, new;* but if *r* precedes it, it takes the sound of *oo,* or of *u* in *rule,* as in *brew, crew, drew.* In the words *shew* and *strew* (written also *show* and *strow*), this diphthong has the sound of long *o,* as it also has in the verb to *sew,* and commonly also in the word *sewer,* a drain.

EY.

43. This diphthong has the sound of long *a,* as in *bey, dey, grey, hey, prey, they, whey, convey, obey, purvey, survey, eyre, eyry.* In *key* and *ley,* it has the sound of long *e;* and, when unaccented, it has the slight sound of *e,* as in *galley, valley,* &c.

IA.

44. This diphthong, in the terminations *ial, ian,* and *iard,* often forms but one syllable, the *i* being sounded like consonant *y;* as, *Christian, filial, poniard,* pronounced as if written *Christ'yan, fil'yal, pon'yard.* In some words it has the obscure sound of indistinct short *i,* as in *carriage, marriage, parliament.*

IE, IO, IEU, IEW.

45. The regular sound of the diphthong *ie* is that of long *e,* as in *chief, fief, field, fiend, grenadier, grief, grieve, lief, liege, mien, thief,* &c. It has the sound of long *i* in *die, hie, lie, pie, vie,* &c.; and the sound of short *e* in *friend.* — The diphthong *io* occurs in many words in the termination *ion.* When *i,* in this termination, is preceded by a liquid, *ion* is pronounced like *yun,* as *million, minion.* The terminations *sion* and *tion* are pronounced like *shun,* as *version, nation;* but when the *t* is preceded by *s* or *x, ion* is pronounced *yun,* as *question, mixtion.*

The triphthong *ieu* is found only in a few words, which are derived from the French, as, *adieu, lieu, purlieu;* and it has the sound of long *u.* — The triphthong *iew* occurs only in *view, interview,* and *purview.*

OA.

46. The regular sound of this diphthong is that of long *o,* as in *boat, coat, coal, foal, loaf, moat,* &c.; but in *broad, abroad,* and *groat,* it has the sound of broad *a.*

Œ.

47. This diphthong is derived from the Latin; and it is retained in but very few words used in English. It is found in *assafœtida,* where it is pronounced like short *e;* and in *œdema, œsophagus, antœci,* also in *fœtus* (often written *fetus*), in which it has the sound of long *e.*

ŒU.

48. This triphthong is found only in the word *manœuvre,* and it has the sound of *oo* in *moon,* or of *u* in *rule.*

OI, OY.

49. The sound of these diphthongs is the same; and it is noted in this Dictionary, as it is in that of Walker, and in various other pronouncing dictionaries, by the combined sound of broad *o* (as in *nor*) and short *i* or *y,* as *bŏïl, bŏÿ.*

OO.

50. The regular sound of this diphthong is heard in *moon, food, stoop;* and it is the same as that of single *o* in *move, prove.*

51. This diphthong has a shorter sound (the same as the sound of *u* in *bull,* or of single *o* in *wolf*) in the words ending in *ook,* as *book, brook, cook, crook, look, rook, stook, took;* also in *foot, good, hood, stood, wood, wool,* and their compounds.

52. This diphthong has the sound of long *o* in *door, floor,* and *brooch;* and of short *u* in *blood* and *flood.*

OU.

53. This is the most irregular diphthong in the language. Its most common or regular sound is that in which both letters are heard, as in *bound, sound, cloud, loud, our, shout, south,* &c.

54. This diphthong has the sound of short *u* in *country, cousin, couple, accouple, double, trouble, southern, courage, encourage, flourish, nourish, nourishment, enough, chough, rough, tough, touch, touchy, young, youngster,* &c. It has the sound of *o* in *move,* or *oo* in *moon,* in *accoutre, aggroup, group, croup, bouge, amour, paramour, bouse, bousy, capouch, cartouch, rouge, soup, surtout, tour, contour, detour, tourney, tournament, through, uncouth, you, your, youth,* and also in various other words derived from the French. It has the sound of long *o* in *court, accourt, courtier, course, concourse, recourse, discourse, source, resource, four, fourth, pour, though, although, dough, mould, moult, mourn, shoulder, smoulder, poult, poultice, poultry, soul.* It has the sound of broad *a*, as in *ball*, or *o*, as in *nor*, in *bought, brought, fought, ought, nought, sought, besought, thought, wrought.* It has the sound of *u* in *bull*, or of *oo* in *good*, in *could, should, would.* It has the sound of short *o* in *hough;* also (or, according to some orthoepists, of broad *a*) in *cough* and *trough*, rhyming with *off* and *scoff.*

OW.

55. The regular sound of this diphthong, the same as the regular sound of *ou*, is heard in *how, now, down, town, tower*, &c. It has the sound of long *o* in *below, bestow, blow, crow, flow, flown, grow, grown, growth, glow, know, known, owe, own, owner, show, snow, sown, strow, throw, thrown;* also in the following words, in some of their senses: *bow, low, lower, mow, shower, sow.*

56. When this diphthong forms an unaccented syllable, it has the slight sound of long *o*, as in *borrow, follow, follower*

UA.

57. When both of the letters of this diph-thong are sounded, they have the power of *wa*, as in *equal, language, persuade, suavity.* In some words the *u* is silent, as in *guard, guardian, guarantee, piquant;* and in *victuals* and *victualling* both the letters are silent.

UE.

58. When these letters are united in a diphthong, and are both sounded, they have the power of *we*, as in *consuetude, desuetude, mansuetude, conquest.* In some words the *u* is silent, as in *guerdon, guess, guest.* When this diphthong is final, the *e* is in many words silent, as in *due, hue, pursue, value*, &c.; and in some words both letters are silent, as in *league, fatigue, harangue, tongue, plague, vague, fugue, brogue, antique, oblique, decalogue, demagogue, dialogue*, &c.—In the termination *ogue*, the *o* is short when preceded by *g* or *l;* as *demagŏgue*, *dialŏgue;* except *collŏgue :* but when any other consonant precedes *o*, it is long ; as, *brōgue, rōgue, vōgue, prorōgue.*

UI.

59. These letters, when they are united in a diphthong, and both are sounded, have the power of *wi*, as in *anguish, languid, vanquish.* In some words the *u* is silent, as in *guide, guile, build, guinea;* and in others the *i* is silent, as in *juice, pursuit, fruit*, &c.

SOUNDS OF THE CONSONANTS.

60. The consonants are divided into *mutes* and *semi-vowels.* The mutes cannot be sounded at all without the aid of a vowel. They are *b, d, k, p, t*, and *c* and *g* hard.

61. The semi-vowels have an imperfect sound of themselves. They are *f, l, m, n, r, s, v, x, z*, and *c* and *g* soft.

62. The four semi-vowels, *l, m, n*, and *r*, are also called *liquids*, because they readily unite with other consonants, flowing, as it were, into their sounds.

63. The following consonants are styled *dentals*, namely, *d, j, s, t, z*, and *g* soft, being pronounced chiefly by the aid of the teeth ; *d, g, j, k, l, n*, and *q* are called *palatals*, from the use made of the palate in pronouncing them ; *b, p, f, v*, and *m* are called *labials*, being pronounced chiefly by the lips ; *m, n*, and the digraph *ng*, are called *nasals*, being sounded through the nose; and *k, q*, and *c* and *g* hard, are called *gutturals*, being sounded by the throat.

64. The consonants *b, d, f, j, k, l, m, p, v*, also *w* and *y* when used as consonants, have each one uniform sound, except *d*, which in the termination *ed*, in many preterites and participles, takes the sound of *t*, as in *mixed*, pronounced *mixt*, and *f* in the preposition *of*, in which it has the sound of *v*.

C.

65. This letter is hard, and sounds like *k*, before *a, o*, and *u :* and it is soft, and sounds like *s*, before *e, i*, and *y ;* except in *sceptic* and *scirrhus* and their derivatives, in which it is hard, like *k*.

When *c* comes after the accent, and is followed by *ea, ia, io,* and *eous,* it takes, like *s* and *t,* under the same circumstances, the sound of *sh ;* as, *ocean, social, tenacious, cetaceous.*

In the words *discern, sacrifice,* and *suffice,* and in several words derived from them, and also in the word *sice, c* has the sound of *z.*

CH.

66. The regular English sound of this digraph is the same as that of *tch,* or *tsh ;* as in *chair, child, rich, church.*

In words derived from the Greek and Latin languages, the digraph *ch* is generally hard like *k ;* as in *anchor, character, chasm ;* and in words derived from the French, it has the sound of *sh,* as in *chaise, machine.*

G.

67: *G,* like *c,* has two sounds, one hard, and the other soft. It is hard before *a, o,* and *u ;* and before *e, i,* and *y,* it is sometimes hard and sometimes soft. It is generally soft before words derived from the Greek, Latin, and French, and hard before words from the Saxon ; and these last, being much the smaller number of the words of this sort, may be regarded as exceptions.

The *g* in *longer* (the comparative of *long*), *stronger, younger, longest, strongest,* and *youngest* must articulate the *e ;* and these words are pronounced as if written with *gg.* Thus *longer,* the comparative of *long,* is pronounced *long'ger ;* and *longer,* one who longs, *long'er.*

GH.

68. In this digraph, at the beginning of a word, the *h* is silent, as in *ghost, ghastly, gherkin ;* in *burgh, h* is silent at the end of the word ; at the end of words, both letters are commonly silent, as in *high, nigh,* &c. In some words this digraph has the sound of *f,* as in *enough, rough ;* in some, the sound of *k,* as in *hough, shough, lough.* In *slough* it is sometimes silent, and sometimes has the sound of *f.*

GHT.

69. In this termination, the letters *gh* are always silent ; as, *fight, right, height,* &c. , except in *draught,* which is pronounced, and in some of its senses usually written, *draft.*

H.

70. This letter is a note of aspiration, and it is silent at the beginning of a number of words ; as, *heir, heiress, honor, honesty, honorable, hostler, hour,* &c. In *hospital, humble, humor, humorous, humorsome, herb, herbage,* &c., according to some orthoepists, it is silent, and according to others, it is sounded. It is always silent after *r ;* as in *rheum, rhetoric, rhapsody,* &c.

N.

71. *N* has two sounds, one simple and pure, as in *man, not ;* the other compound and mixed, or nasal, called also by Walker its " ringing sound ; " which is heard in *king, angle, thank, concord, banquet, anxious.* This sound is given to *n* in many words, when this letter precedes *k, c* or *g* hard, *qu,* or *x.* It is accurately expressed as it is written, when *g* follows *n* at the end of a word, as *king, hang ;* but in other cases the sound of *g* is interposed between the *n* and the succeeding letter ; as, *angle* (ang'gle), *thank* (thangk), *concord* (cong'cord), *banquet* (bang'quet). In many words in which a syllable ending with *g* hard is followed by another syllable, the sound of *g* is given to the two syllables ; as, *stronger* (strong'ger), (see No. 67), *anger* (ang'ger), *finger* (fing'ger). But in *bringer, hanger, ringer, singer, slinger, springer,* and *stringer, g* is sounded only in the first syllable.

Q.

72. *Q* is always followed by *u,* and the digraph *qu* has commonly the sound of *kw,* as in *queen, quill, quart ;* but in many words, mostly derived from the French, it has the sound of *k,* as in *coquet, etiquette, mosque, liquor,* &c.

R.

73. The letter *r* has a jarring or trilling effect on the tongue, and is never silent. It has a peculiar influence both on the long and on the short sound of the vowels. It has the effect, under certain circumstances, to change the short sound of *a,* as in *man,* into its Italian sound, as in *far,* and the short sound of *o,* as in *not,* into its broad sound, like broad *a,* as in *nor ;* and it has a corresponding effect on the short sound of the other vowels. (See page 9.) When *r* is preceded by a long vowel, it has sometimes the effect of blending the syllables. Thus the monosyllables *hire, lore, more, roar, sore,* and *flour* are pronounced precisely like the dissyllables *higher, lower, mower, rower, sower,* and *flower.* These latter words, and also *bower, cower, dower, power, tower,* and some others, are regarded as dissyllables in prose, but are all commonly pronounced as monosyllables in poetry.

" *R* is a decided consonant when it begins a syllable with or without another consonant, as in *ray, pray* ; and also when it ends a syllable, if it should be so circumstanced that, ending one, it also begins the next, as in *arid, tarry, peril, berry, spirit, florid, hurry.* Here the *r* has the same effect on the previous vowel that any other consonant would have ; that is to say, it stops, or renders the vowel essentially short. But, under other circumstances, final *r* is not a decided consonant ; and therefore the syllables *ar, er, ir, or, ur* are not coincident, as to the vowel sound in each, with *at, et, it, ot, ut* ; neither do the vowel sounds in *fare, mere, ire, ore, ure, poor, our,* quite identify with those in *fate, mete, ide, ode, cube, pool, owl.*" *Smart.*

S.

74. The regular or genuine sound of *s* is its sharp, sibilant, or hissing sound, like *c* soft, as in *son, this.* It has also a flat or soft sound (called by some its *vocal* sound), the same as that of the letter *z*, as in *wise, his.* In the prefix *dis, s,* in some cases, has its flat, soft, or vocal sound ; as, *disarm, disdain, dismal,* &c.

S takes the sound of *sh* in words ending in *sion,* preceded by a consonant, as in *diversion, expulsion, dimension, passion,* &c. ; also in *censure, pressure, sure, nauseate, sensual,* &c.

S has the sound of *zh* in the termination *sion,* preceded by a vowel, as in *evasion, explosion,* &c. ; also in a number of words in which *s* is preceded by an accented vowel, and followed by the termination *ure,* as in *measure, pleasure,* &c. ; also in several words ending in *sier,* as *crosier, osier,* &c. ; also in *ambrosia, ambrosial, elysium, elysian ;* also in the words *abscission, scission,* and *rescission.*

T.

75. *T,* like *s* and *c,* is aspirated when it comes immediately after the accent, and is followed by the vowels *ia, ie,* or *io,* taking the sound, in these cases, of *sh ;* as in *partial, patient, nation,* &c.

TH.

76. This digraph has two sounds ; one hard, sharp, or aspirate, as in *thin, think, earth, breath,* &c. ; the other flat, soft, or vocal, as in *this, the, then, breathe,* &c.

In some nouns, it is sharp in the singular, as in *bath, lath, path, oath, mouth ;* and flat in the plural, as *baths, laths, paths, oaths, mouths.* In some words the *h* is silent, as in *Thomas, thyme.*

X.

77. The regular sound of *x* is its sharp sound, like *ks ;* as, *excellent, execute, expect, tax.*

It has a flat or soft sound, like *gz,* when the next syllable following begins with an accented vowel, as in *exalt, example,* &c.

Z.

78. *Z* has the same sound as flat or soft *s.* It is aspirated, taking the sound of *zh,* in a few words ; as, *glazier, azure, seizure.*

ACCENT.

79. All the words of the English language, of more than one syllable, have one accented syllable ; and most polysyllabic words have not only a syllable with a primary accent, but also one with a secondary accent.

80. It is the general tendency of the language to place the accent on the first syllable of dissyllables, and on the antepenultimate of polysyllables. The exceptions, however, are so numerous, that this is not to be regarded as a rule, but only as a general tendency of the language. With respect, however, to verbs of two syllables, the tendency is to place the accent on the second syllable.

81. Words which are adopted from the Latin language into the English without any change of orthography, generally retain the Latin accent, especially if they are terms of the arts and sciences, or words somewhat removed from common use. The following words have the accent on the penultimate syllable, both in Latin and in English : *abdomen, acumen, asylum, bitumen, curator, decorum, delator, dictator, horizon, spectator, testator.*

82. Some words, which have the accent on the penult in Latin, are conformed to the English analogy, and have the accent on the antepenult ; as, *auditor, character, orator,* &c.

83. Simple words of two syllables have only one syllable accented, except the word *amen·*

Many compound words of two syllables have both syllables more or less accented ; as, *back-slide, downfall, gainsay, henceforth, mankind, highway, waylay, windmill, almost,* &c.

84. Many words of three and of four syllables have only one accented syllable ; as, *sensible, occurrence, republic, celebrity,* &c. But some have a secondary accent almost as strong as the primary ; as, *advertise, artisan, caravan, animadvert,* &c.

85. Almost all words of more than four syllables have both a primary and a secondary accent, and some words of seven or eight syllables have one primary and two secondary accents; as, *indivisibility, incomprehensibility.*

86. There is a considerable number of dissyllables, which, when used as nouns or adjectives, have the accent on the first syllable, and when used as verbs, on the second; as, *con'-duct, con-duct'; pres'ent, pre-sent',* &c.

87. All words ending in *sion* and *tion* have the accent on the penultimate syllable ; as, *dissen'sion, declara'tion, medita'tion,* &c.

88. Words ending in *ia, iac, ial, ian, eous,* and *ious* have the accent on the preceding syllable; as, *rega'lia, demo'niac, impe'rial, merid'ian, sponta'neous, melo'dious.* If *c, g, s, t,* or *x* precedes the vowels *e* or *i,* in these terminations, these vowels are generally blended with the vowel or vowels which follow, being pronounced with them in one syllable ; as, *benefi'cial, magi'cian, farina'ceous, loqua'cious, dissen'sious, coura'geous, conta'gious, conten'tious, anx'ious.* The only exception to this rule, in relation to placing the accent, is the word *elegiac,* which is commonly pronounced *elegi'ac,* though some pronounce it, in accordance with the rule, *ele'giac.*

89. Words ending in *acal* and *ical* have the accent on the antepenultimate syllable ; as, *heli'acal, alphabet'ical, fanat'ical, geograph'ical, poet'ical,* &c. In words of this termination, the vowels in the accented syllables, if followed by a consonant, are short, except *u,* which is long ; as, *cu'bical, mu'sical, scorbu'tical.*

90. Words ending in *ic* generally have the accent on the penultimate syllable ; as, *algebra'ic, metal'lic, epidem'ic, scientif'ic, harmon'ic, paralyt'ic.* If a consonant immediately precedes the *i,* the vowels in the accented syllable are short, except the vowel *u,* which is long, if it is followed by a single consonant ; as, *cheru'bic, scorbu'tic, sulphu'ric, tellu'ric,* &c. But if *u* is followed by two consonants, it is sometimes short ; as, *fus'tic, rus'tic;* and sometimes long ;

as, *ru'bric, lu'bric.* The following words, which are exceptions to this rule, have the accent on the antepenultimate syllable : *ar'senic* (as a noun), *arith'metic, bish'opric, cath'olic, chol'eric, ephem'eric, her'etic, lu'natic, pol'itic, rhet'oric,* and *tur'meric.* The following words, *climacteric, empiric, phlegmatic, plethoric, splenetic,* according to some orthoepists, are conformed to the rule, and, according to others, they are exceptions to it.

91. Words of three or more syllables, ending in *eal,* have their accent on the antepenultimate syllable ; as, *bo'real, corpo'real, incorpo'real, cu'neal, empyr'eal, ethe'real, fune'real, homoge'neal, heteroge'neal, lac'teal, lin'eal, or'deal ;* except *hymene'al,* which has the penultimate accent.

92. Of words ending in *ean,* the following, being conformed to the English analogy, have the accent on the antepenultimate syllable : *cerbe'rean, ceru'lean, hyperbo'rean, Hercu'lean, marmo'rean, mediterra'nean, subterra'nean, Tarta'rean ;* but the following are pronounced by the principal orthoepists, in accordance with the best usage, with the accent on the penultimate : *adamante'an, antipode'an, Atlante'an, colosse'an, Epicure'an, Europe'an, hymene'an, pygme'an.*

93. Words ending in *tude, efy, ify, ety, ity, graphy, logy, loquy, athy, metry, tomy, meter, gonal, fluous, fluent,* and *parous,* have their accent on the antepenultimate ; as, *for'titude, rar'efy, diver'sify, vari'ety, liberal'ity, geog'raphy, geol'ogy, solil'oquy, sym'pathy, geom'etry, anat'omy, barom'eter, diag'onal, super'fluous, af'fluent, ovip'arous.*

94. Words of three or more syllables, ending in *ulous, inous, erous,* and *orous,* have the accent on the antepenultimate ; as, *sed'ulous, volu'minous, vocif'erous, carniv'orous ;* except *cano'rous* and *sono'rous.*

95. Words of three or more syllables, ending in *ative,* have the accent on the antepenultimate, or on the preceding syllable ; as *rel'ative, appel'lative, commu'nicative, spec'ulative.* The exceptions are *crea'tive, colla'tive, dila'tive.*

96. There is a class of words ending in *or,* which, when used, in law language, in connection with their correlative terms, have the accent on the last syllable. The following words, with their correlatives, are of this class : —

Appellor	appellee	Grantor	grantee
Assignor	assignee	Guarantor	guarantee
Bargainor	bargainee	Legator	legatee
Consignor	consignee	Mortgageor	mortgagee
Devisor	devisee	Obligor	obligee
Donor	donee	Recognizor	recognizee

RULES OF ORTHOGRAPHY.

1. A numerous class of words formerly written with the termination *ick*, as *musick, publick*, are now written, both in England and the United States, with the termination *ic*; as, *music, public*. But the verbs *to frolic, to mimic, to physic, to traffic, to bivouac*, though written without the *k* in the present tense, yet on assuming another syllable, in forming the past tense and participles, the *k* must be used in order to keep the *c* hard; as, *trafficked, trafficking*.

2. Verbs of one syllable, ending with a single consonant, preceded by a single vowel (as *plan*), and verbs of two or more syllables, ending in the same manner, and having the accent on the last syllable (as *regret*), double the final consonant of the verb on assuming an additional syllable; as, *plan, planned; regret, regretted*. But if a diphthong precedes the last consonant (as in *join*), or the accent is not on the last syllable (as in *suffer*), the consonant is not doubled; as, *join, joined; suffer, suffered*.

There is an exception to the last clause of the preceding rule, with respect to most of the verbs ending in the letter *l*, which, on assuming an additional syllable, are allowed, by general usage, to double the *l*, though the accent is not on the last syllable; as *travel, travelling, travelled, traveller; libel, libelling, libelled, libeller, libellous*. But the derivatives of *parallel* are written without doubling the final *l*; as, *paralleled, unparalleled.* — The nouns *petal, peril, novel, dial*, and *viol*, on assuming an additional syllable, do not double the *l*; as, *petalous, perilous, novelist, dialist, violist*.

The following list comprises the verbs ending in *l*, which, though they have not the accent on the last syllable, yet commonly double the final *l*: —

apparel	dishevel	handsel	model	rival
bevel	drivel	hatchel	panel	rowel
bowel	duel	imperil	parcel	shovel
cancel	embowel	jewel	pencil	shrivel
carol	enamel	kennel	peril	snivel
cavil	empanel	label	pistol	tassel
channel	equal	level	pommel	trammel
chisel	gambol	libel	quarrel	travel
counsel	gravel	marshal	ravel	tunnel
cudgel	grovel	marvel	revel	unravel

The derivatives of these verbs are spelt, in the Dictionaries of Perry and Webster, with a single *l*; and this mode is also more or less favored by the lexicographers Ash and Walker; and al-

though it better accords with the analogy of the language, yet the prevailing usage is to double the *l*.

3. Some words, having a secondary accent on the last syllable, double the last letter on assuming an additional syllable. The verb *to kidnap* always doubles the *p* on assuming an additional syllable; as, *kidnap, kidnapped, kidnapping, kidnapper*; — also the following words · *compromit, compromitted; carburet, carburetted; sulphuret, sulphuretted;* — also various compound words; as, *half-wit, half-witted; hare-lip, hare-lipped*, &c.

4. The verb *to bias* commonly doubles the *s* on assuming an additional syllable; as, *biassing, biassed, biasser;* as also the verb *to worship*, in like manner, commonly doubles the *p*; as, *worship, worshipping, worshipped, worshipper*.

5. Most of the words in the English language which end in *ise*, and almost all which end in *ize*, are verbs; and with regard to a number of these verbs there is a diversity in the English dictionaries, as well as in common usage, in relation to this termination, the same verbs sometimes ending in *ize* and sometimes in *ise*. With regard to this termination, the following rule is generally, though not invariably, observed: —

Verbs derived from Greek verbs ending in ιζω, and others formed after the same analogy, have the termination *ize*; as, *agonize, characterize;* — but words derived from the French *prendre*, have the termination *ise*; as, *apprise, surprise, enterprise*.

The following list comprises most of the English verbs which are generally written with the termination *ise*: —

advise	compromise	emprise	misprise
advertise	demise	enfranchise	premise
affranchise	despise	enterprise	revise
apprise	devise	exercise	supervise
chastise	disfranchise	exorcise	surmise
circumcise	disguise	franchise	surprise
comprise	divertise	merchandise	

In relation to the following words, *catechise* or *catechize, criticise* or *criticize, patronise* or *patronize, recognise* or *recognize*, the dictionaries and usage are divided, though the most of the dictionaries give the termination *ise* to these verbs. — There are other words with regard to which there is a want of uniformity in usage; as, *civilize, disseize, epitomize*, &c.

6. There are a few verbs which are derived

from *nouns* ending in *th* hard or sharp, as in *thin*, and which have *e* added to *th*, making the sound of *th* soft or vocal, as in *this*. Such are the following: from *bath, bathe;* from *breath, breathe;* from *cloth, clothe;* from *loath, loathe;* from *sheath, sheathe;* from *sooth, soothe;* from *swath, swathe;* from *wreath, wreathe* and *inwreathe;* but the following verbs are commonly written without a final *e*, viz., *to bequeath, to mouth,* and *to smooth.*

7. Verbs ending in *ie* change the *ie* into *y*, on adding *ing;* as, *die, dying; lie, lying; tie, tying; vie, vying.*

8. Verbs ending with a single *e* omit the *e* when *ing* is added; as, *place, placing; relate, relating.*

The following words are exceptions: *dye* (to color), *dyeing; hoe, hoeing; shoe, shoeing:*—and when *ing* is added to the verbs *singe, swinge,* and *tinge,* the *e* is properly retained, as, *singeing, swingeing,* and *tingeing,* in order to distinguish these participles from *singing, swinging,* and *tinging.*

9. All verbs ending in *y*, preceded by a consonant, retain the *y* on adding *ing;* as, *spy, spying; deny, denying;*—but when *ed* is added, the *y* is changed into *i;* as, *spy, spied; deny, denied;* and when *s* is added, *y* is changed into *ie;* as, *spy, spies; deny, denies.*

10. Verbs ending in *y*, preceded by another vowel, on adding *ing, ed,* or *s*, do not change *y* into *i;* as, *delay, delaying, delayed, delays.*

The following words are exceptions: *lay, laid; pay, paid; say, said; stay, stayed* or *staid.*

11. The greater part of verbal nouns end in *er*, as from *advertise, advertiser;* but many of them end in *or*, as from *imitate, imitator;* from *instruct, iustructor;* and some are seen in both forms, as *visitor, visiter.*—The verbal nouns from *beg* and *lie* are irregularly formed *beggar* and *liar.* From *peddle* the regular verbal noun would be *peddler;* but the noun is commonly written *pedler,* and sometimes *pedlar.*

12. There is a class of words, ending in *tre*, as *centre, metre,* &c., which are by some written *center, meter,* &c.; but the former mode is supported by the best usage.

13. Derivative adjectives ending in *able* are written without an *e* before *a;* as, *blamable, movable,* not *blameable, moveable;* except those of which the primitive word ends in *ce* or *ge;* in such the *e* is retained to soften the preceding consonant; as, *peaceable, changeable.*

14. Compound words, formed by prefixing a word or a syllable to a monosyllable ending in *all*, commonly retain the double *l;* as, *appall, befall, bethrall, downfall, forestall, fuzzball, headstall, install, inthrall, laystall, miscall, overfall, recall, saveall, thumbstall, waterfall, windfall;* but some of these words are very often, if not more commonly, seen with a single *l;* as, *appal, befal, bethral, inthral,* &c.—*Withal, therewithal,* and *wherewithal* end with a single *l.*

15. A class of other compound words commonly retain the final double *l* which is found in the simple words; as, *bridewell, downhill, uphill, molehill, watermill, windmill, handmill.*—With respect to *foretel, enrol,* and *unrol,* or *foretell, enroll,* and *unroll,* the authorities and usage are divided.

16. Nouns of the singular number ending in *ey* form their plural by adding *s* only to the singular; as, *attorney, attorneys; money, moneys; valley, valleys.* These plurals are often erroneously written *attornies, monies,* and *vallies.*

17. Nouns ending in *o*, preceded by another vowel, form their plural by the addition of *s;* as, *cameo, cameos; folio, folios;* but if the final *o* is preceded by a consonant, the plural is commonly formed by adding *es;* as, *cargo, cargoes.* The following nouns, however, *canto, cento, grotto, junto, portico, rotundo, salvo, solo, tyro, duodecimo, octavo, quarto,* and some others, commonly have their plural formed by the addition of *s* only to the singular; as, *canto, cantos.* Yet, with respect to the plural of some of these words, usage is not uniform; as the plural of *quarto,* for example, is sometimes seen written *quartos,* and sometimes *quartoes.*

18. There is a class of words which have, in their derivation, a twofold origin, from the Latin and French languages, and are indifferently written with the first syllable *en* or *in*, the former being derived from the French, and the latter from the Latin. With respect to some of these, it is difficult to determine which form is best supported by usage; as, for example, *inquire* or *enquire, insure* or *ensure.* A few of this class of words are found in the following Vocabulary.

19. There is a small class of words ending in *ped*, or *pede* (L. *pes*, foot); as, *biped, centiped, milleped, multiped, palmiped, plumiped, quadruped, soliped,* and a few others. Of these words, *biped* and *quadruped* are always written without the final *e*, but with respect to the others, the dictionaries and usage are divided; and although it has heretofore been the more common mode to write most of these words with a final *e*, yet there seems to be no good reason why they should not all be conformed to the same rule.

20. There is a class of chemical terms many of which signify that which contains the essence of the kind, as an extract, and which are variously written with the termination *ine* or *in ;* as, *asparagine, chlorine, olivine,* or *asparagin, chlorin, olivin ;* but the prevailing usage, with respect to most of these words, favors the use of the final *e ;* as, *asparagine, chlorine ;* but *tannin* is written without a final *e.*

21. The following words are generally written without an *e* after *g : abridgment, acknowledgment,* and *judgment ;* though many write them with it, — *abridgement, acknowledgement,* and *judgement,* — as Johnson and other lexicographers spell *lodgement.*

22. In some cases, words are so variously affected by etymology, analogy, and general usage, that it is difficult to determine what orthography is best supported ; as, for example, *connection* or *connexion, despatch* or *dispatch, hinderance* or *hindrance, jail* or *gaol, marquis* or *marquess, preterite* or *preterit, recognizance* or *recognisance, show* or *shew, sceptic* or *skeptic, sergeant* or *serjeant, thrash* or *thresh,* and various others.

VOCABULARY OF WORDS OF DOUBTFUL OR VARIOUS ORTHOGRAPHY.

The following Vocabulary contains only a few of the words which belong to the several classes referred to in the preceding remarks ; but, with the exception of these classes, it comprises nearly all the English words with regard to which a diversity of orthography is now often met with.

The orthography in the left-hand column is deemed to be well authorized, and in most cases preferable ; but with respect to the authority of that in the right-hand column, there is a great diversity. In some cases it is nearly or quite as well authorized as that on the left hand, and in some it has but a very feeble support. Both orthographies of some of the words are right, the words being differently spelt when used in different senses ; as, *draught* or *draft, forte* or *fort, subtle* or *subtile, abetter* or *abettor, canvass* or *canvas, caliber* or *calibre, caster* or *castor, controller* or *comptroller, neat* or *net, plain* or *plane,* &c.

A.

Abbey	Abby	Æsthetics	Esthetics	Amiability	Amability
Abettor, *and*	Abettor	Ætiology ; *see*	Etiology	Amice	Amess
Abnormal	Anormal	Affector	Affecter	Amortise	Amortize
Abreuvoir	Abbreuvoir	Affiliate	Adfiliate	Anademe	Anadem
Abridgment	Abridgement	Affiliation	Adfiliation	Ananas	Anana
Accessary, *and*	Accessory	Afraid	Affraid	Anapest	Anapæst
Accountant	Accomptant	Aghast	Agast	Anapestic	Anapæstic
Acetimeter	Acetometer	Agriculturist	Agriculturalist	Anbury	Ambury
Ache	Ake	Aide-de-camp	Aid-de-camp	Ancestral	Ancestrel
Achieve	Atchieve	Aisle, *church*	Isle	Ancient	Antient
Acknowledg-ment	Acknowledge-ment	Ajutage	Adjutage	Ancientry	Anchentry
Acronycal	{ Acronychal / Acronical	Alchemical	Alchymical	Andiron	Handiron
Addible	Addable	Alchemist	Alchymist	Anemone	Anemony
Adipocere	Adipocire	Alchemy	Alchymy	Angiography	Angeiography
Adjudgment	Adjudgement	Alcoran	Alkoran	Angiology	Angeiology
Admittible	Admittable	Alexipharmic	Alexipharmac	Angiotomy	Angeiotomy
Adscititious	Ascititious	Alkahest	Alcahest	Ankle	Ancle
Adulteress	Adultress	Alkali	Alcali	Annotto / Arnotto	{ Annotta / Arnotta
Advertise	Advertize	Allege	Alledge	Antechamber	Antichamber
Advoutry	Avoutry	Alloy	Allay	Antelope	Antilope
Advowee	Avowee	Almacantar	Almucantar	Antiemetic	Antemetic
Advowson	Advowzen	Almanac	Almanack	Apostasy	Apostacy
Adze	Adz, Addice	Almonry	Almry, Ambry	Aposteme	Apostume
Æolipile ; *see*	Eolipile	Alnager	{ Alnagar, Aulna-ger	Apothegm	Apophthegm
Aerie	Ayry, Eyry	Alum	Allum	Appall	Appal
Æsthetic	Esthetic	Amassment	Amasment	Appalment	Appalement
		Ambassador	Embassador	Appanage / Apanage	Appenage
		Ambergris	Ambergrise	Appraise	Apprize
		Ambs-ace	Ames-ace	Appraisement	Apprizement
		Amercement	Americiament		

Appraiser	Apprizer
Apprise	Apprize
Appurtenance	Appertenance
Apricot	Apricock
Arbitrament	Arbitrement
Archæolo- gical	Archeological Archaiological
Archæology	Archeology Archaiology
Archduchess	Archdutchess
Argol	Argal
Arquebuse	Arquebus Harquebuse
Arrack	Arack
Artisan	Artizan
Asbestos, *or*	Asbestus
Ascendency, *or*	Ascendancy
Ascendent, *or*	Ascendant
Askance	Askaunce
Askant	Askaunt
Askew	Askue
Assafœtida	Asafœtida
Assize	Assise
Assizer	Assiser
Assuage	Asswage
Athenæum	Atheneum
Auger	Augre
Aught	Ought
Autocracy	Autocrasy
Avoirdupois	Averdupois
Awkward	Aukward
Awn	Ane
Axe	Ax

B.

Baccalaureate	Baccalaureat
Bachelor	Batchelor
Bade, *from* bid	Bad
Balance	Ballance
Baldrick	Bawdrick
Balk	Baulk, Bauk
Ballister	Balister
Baluster	Banister
Bandanna	Bandana
Bandoleer	Bandolier
Bandore	Pandore
Bandrol	Bannerol [yan
Banian	Bannian, Ban-
Banns	Bans
Barbacan	Barbican
Barbecue	Barbacue
Barberry	Berberry
Bark	Barque
Barouche	Barouch
Baryta	Baryte
Barytone	Baritone
Basin	Bason
Bass, *Mus.*	Base
Bass-viol	Base-viol
Bastinado	Bastinade
Bateau	Batteau
Battledoor	Battledore
Bawble	Bauble
Bazaar	Bazar
Beadle	Beadel
Beaver	Bever
Befall	Befal
Behoove	Behove

Bellflower	Belflower
Belligerent	Belligerant
Bellman	Belman
Bellmetal	Belmetal
Bellwether	Belwether
Benumb	Benum
Bequeath	Bequeathe
Bergamot	Burgamot
Bergander	Birgander
Berth, *in ship*	Birth
Bestrew	Bestrow
Betel	Betle
Bevel	Bevil
Bezant	Byzant
Biassed	Biased
Biestings	Beastings Beestings
Bigoted	Bigotted
Bilge	Bulge
Billiards	Balliards
Billingsgate	Bilingsgate [cle
Binnacle	Binacle, Bitta-
Bistre	Bister
Bivouac	Biovac
Bizantine	Byzantine
Blanch	Blench
Blende, (*Min.*)	Blend
Blithely	Blithly
Blitheness	Blithness
Blithesome	Blithsome
Blomary	Bloomary
Blouse, Blowze	Blowse
Bodice	Boddice
Boil, *a tumor*	Bile
Bolt	Boult
Bombard	Bumbard
Bombast	Bumbast
Bombazette	Bombazet
Bombazine	Bombasin Bombasine
Borage	Burrage
Bourgeois	Burgeois
Bourn	Borne
Bourse	Burse
Bouse	Boose
Bousy	Boosy, Boozy
Bowlder	Boulder
Bowsprit	Boltsprit
Brakeman	Breakman
Bramin }	Brachman
Brahmin }	Brahman
Brawl	Broil
Brazen	Brasen
Brazier	Brasier
Brazil	Brasil
Brier	Briar [cage.
Brokerage	Brokage, Bro-
Bronze	Bronz
Brooch	Broach, Broche
Brunette	Brunet
Bryony	Briony
Buccaneer	Buccanier
Buffalo	Buffaloe
Buhrstone	Burrstone
Bulimy	Boulimy
Bumblebee	Humblebee
Bunn	Bun
Bunyon	Bunion
Burden	Burthen
Burdensome	Burthensome

Burganet	Burgonet
Burin	Burine
Burlesque	Burlesk
Burr	Bur
Buzz	Buz
By, *n.*	Bye

C.

Cabob	Kabob
Cacique	Cazique
Cæsura	Cesura, Cesure
Cag, *or*	Keg
Calcareous	Calcarious
Caldron	Cauldron
Calendar	Kalendar
Calends	Kalends
Caliber, *or*	Calibre
Calipers	Callipers
Caliph	Calif, Kaliph
Calk	Caulk
Calligraphy	Caligraphy
Calotte	Callot
Caloyer	Kaloyer
Caltrop	Calthrop
Calyx	Calix
Cameo	Camaieu [let
Camlet	Camblet, Came-
Camomile	Chamomile
Camphor	Camphire
Canal, Cannel	Candle, Kennel
Cannoneer	Cannonier
Canoe	Canoa
Cantilever	Cantiliver Cantaliver Canteliver
Canvas, *and*	Canvass
Capriole	Cabriole
Car	Carr
Carabine	Carbine
Carabineer	Carbineer
Carat	Caract, Carrat
Caravansary	Caravansera Caravanserai
Caravel	Carvel
Caraway	Carraway
Carcass	Carcase
Carle	Carl
Carnelian	Carnelion Cornelian
Carolytic	Carolitic
Cartel	Chartel
Cartridge	Cartrage
Cassada } Cassava }	Casava Cassavi
Cassimere	Kerseymere
Cassowary	Cassiowary
Caste, *class*	Cast
Castellan	Castellain
Caster	Castor
Castlery	Castelry
Catchpoll	Catchpole [up
Catchup	Catsup, Ketch-
Catechise	Catechize
Cauliflower	Colliflower
Causeway, *or*	Causey
Cavazion	Cavation
Caviare	Caviar, Cavier
Caw	Kaw

Cayman	Caiman	Commandery	Commandry	Daisied	Dazied
Cedilla	Cerilla	Commissariat	Commissariate	Damaskeen, v.	Damaskin
Ceiling	Cieling	Compatible	Competible	Damson	Damascene
Celt	Kelt	Complete	Compleat	Dandruff	Dandriff
Celtic	Keltic	Concordat	Concordate	Danegelt	Dangelt
Centiped	Centipede	Confectionery	Confectionary	Daub	Dawb
Cess	Sess	Confidant, n.	Confident	Dawdle	Daudle
Chalcedony	Calcedony	Congealable	Congelable	Dearn	Dern
Chaldron	Chalder	Connection	Connexion	Debarkation	Debarcation
Chalice	Calice	Connective	Connexive	Debonair	Debonnair
Chameleon	Cameleon	Consecrator	Consecrater	Decoy	Duckoy
Chamois	Shamois	Contemporary	Cotemporary	Decrepit	Decrepid
Champaign	Champain	Contra-dance	Country-dance	Defence	Defense
Champerty	Champarty	Contributory	Contributary	Defier	Defyer
Chant	Chaunt	Control	Controul	Deflection	Deflexion
Chap	Chop	Controller	Comptroller	Deflour	Deflower
Chaps	Chops	Conversable	Conversible	Delft	Delf, Delph
Char, or	Chare, Chore	Cony	Coney	Delphine	Delphin
Chase	Chace	Coomb, 4 bushs.	Comb	Deltoid	Deltoied
Chastely	Chastly	Copier	Copyer	Demain } Demesne }	Demean
Check, or	Cheque	Coping	Caping	Demarcation	Demarkation
Checker	Chequer	Copse	Coppice	Dependant, n.	Dependent
Cheer	Chear	Coquette, n.	Coquet	Dependence	Dependance
Chemical	Chymical	Coranach {	Coronach / Coranich }	Dependent, a.	Dependant
Chemist	Chymist	Corbel	Corbeil	Deposit	Deposite
Chemistry {	Chymistry / Chimistry }	Cordovan	Cordwain	Desert, n.	Desart
Chestnut	Chesnut	Corpse	Corse	Desolater	Desolator
Chiliahedron	Chiliaedron	Correlative	Corelative	Despatch, or	Dispatch
Chillness	Chilness	Cosey	Cosy, Cozey	Dessert, or	Desert
Chimb, or	Chine, Chime	Cot	Cott	Detecter	Detector
Chintz	Chints	Cotillon	Cotillion	Detorsion	Detortion
Chloride	Chlorid	Counsellor, and	Councillor [to	Detractor	Detracter
Choir	Quire	Courant	Corant, Couran-	Develop	Develope
Choke	Choak	Courtesan	Courtezan	Development	Developement
Choose	Chuse	Courtesy	Curtesy	Devest, or	Divest
Chorister	Quirister	Covin	Covine	Dexterous	Dextrous
Chyle	Chile	Covinous	Covenous	Diadrom	Diadrome
Chylifactive	Chilifactive	Cozen	Cosen	Diæresis	Dieresis
Cider	Cyder, Sider	Cozenage	Cosenage	Diarrhœa	Diarrhea
Cigar	Segar	Craunch	Cranch	Dike, or	Dyke
Cimeter / Scymitar {	Cimiter / Cymetar / Scymetar }	Crawfish	Crayfish	Dime	Disme
		Creak, v.	Creek	Diocese	Diocess
Cion; see	Scion	Crier	Cryer	Disburden	Disburthen
Cipher	Cypher	Croslet	Crosslet	Disfranchise	Diffranchise
Clam, v.	Clamm	Crowd	Croud	Dishabille	Deshabille
Clarinet	Clarionet	Crowfoot, or	Crow's-foot	Disinthrall {	Disenthrall / Disinthral }
Cleat	Cleet	Cruet	Crewet		
Clew	Clue	Crumb	Crum	Disk, or	Disc
Clinch	Clench	Crusade	Croisade	Dispatch, or	Despatch
Cloak	Cloke	Cruse, cruet	Cruise	Disseize	Disseise
Clodpoll	Clodpole	Crystal	Chrystal	Disseizin	Disseisin
Cloff, or	Clough	Cucurbit	Cucurbite	Disseizor	Disseisor
Clothe	Cloathe	Cue	Queue	Dissolvable	Dissolvible
Clothes	Cloaths	Cuerpo	Querpo	Distention	Distension
Cluck	Clock	Cuish	Cuisse	Distil	Distill
Clyster	Glister, Glyster	Cuneiform	Cuniform	Distrainor	Distrainer
Cobbler	Cobler	Cupel	Cuppel, Coppel	Diversely	Diversly
Cocoa	Cacao	Curb	Kerb	Divest, or	Devest
Coddle	Codle	Curb-stone	Kerb-stone	Docket	Doquet
Cœliac	Celiac	Curtain	Courtine	Doctress	Doctoress
Coif	Quoif	Cutlass	Cutlas	Dodecahedron	Dodecaedron
Coiffure	Quoiffure	Cyclopædia	Cyclopedia	Doggerel	Doggrel
Coke	Coak	Cyst	Cist	Domicile	Domicil
Colander	Cullender	Czar	Tzar, Tsar	Dory, Doree	Dorey
Colic	Cholic			Dote	Doat
Colliery	Coalery	**D.**		Doubloon	Doublon
Colter	Coulter, Culter	Dactyl	Dactyle	Dowry	Dowery
Comfrey	Cumfrey	Daily	Dayly	Downfall	Downfal
				Drachm, or	Dram

Dragoman	Drogoman / Druggerman
Draught, *or*	Draft
Dreadnaught	Dreadnought
Driblet	Dribblet
Drier	Dryer
Drought	Drouth
Dryly	Drily
Dryness	Driness
Duchess	Dutchess
Duchy	Dutchy
Dulness	Dullness
Dungeon	Donjon
Dunghill	Dunghil
Duress	Duresse
Dye, *color*	Die
Dyeing, *coloring*	Dying

E.

Eavesdropper	Evesdropper
Eccentric	Excentric
Echelon	Echellon
Economics	Œconomics
Ecstasy	Ecstacy, Extasy
Ecstatic	Extatic
Ecumenical	Œcumenical
Edile	Ædile
Eke	Eek
Embalm	Imbalm
Embank, *or*	Imbank
Embankment	Imbankment
Embargo	Imbargo
Embark	Imbark
Embarkation	Embarcation
Embase	Imbase
Embassy	Ambassy
Embed, *or*	Imbed
Embedded, *or*	Imbedded
Embezzle	Imbezzle
Embezzlement	Imbezzlement
Emblazon	Imblazon
Embody	Imbody
Embolden	Imbolden
Emborder	Imborder
Embosk	Imbosk
Embosom, *or*	Imbosom
Emboss	Imboss
Embowel	Imbowel
Embower	Imbower
Embrasure	Embrazure
Empale	Impale
Empanel, *or*	Empannel / Impanel
Empoison	Impoison
Empoverish, *or*	Impoverish
Empower	Impower
Empress	Emperess
Encage, *or*	Incage
Encenia	Encænia
Enchant	Inchant
Enchase	Inchase
Encircle	Incircle
Enclose, *or*	Inclose
Enclosure	Inclosure
Encroach	Incroach
Encumber	Incumber
Encumbrance	Incumbrance
Encyclopædia	Encyclopedia

Endamage	Indamage
Endict; *see*	Indict
Endite; *see*	Indite
Endorse, *or*	Indorse
Endow	Indow
Endue, *or*	Indue
Enfeeble	Infeeble
Enfeoff	Infeoff
Enfranchise	Infranchise
Engender	Ingender
Engorge	Ingorge
Engrain	Ingrain
Enhance	Inhance
Enigma	Ænigma
Enjoin	Injoin
Enlard	Inlard
Enlarge	Inlarge
Enlighten	Inlighten
Enlist	Inlist
Enquire, *or*	Inquire
Enquiry, *or*	Inquiry
Enroll	Enrol / Inrol
Enrolment	Inrolment
Enshrine	Inshrine
Ensnare, *or*	Insnare
Ensure, *or*	Insure
Entail	Intail
Entangle	Intangle
Enterprise	Enterprize
Enthrone	Inthrone
Enthymeme	Enthymem
Entice	Intice
Entire	Intire
Entirety	Entierty
Entitle	Intitle / Intitule
Entomb	Intomb
Entrance, *v.*	Intrance
Entrap	Intrap
Entreat	Intreat
Envelop, *v.*	Envelope
Envelopment	Envelopement
Eolipile	Æolipile
Epaulet	Epaulette
Epigraph	Epigraphe
Equerry	Equery
Equiangular	Equangular
Equivoke	Equivoque
Era	Æra
Eremite	Heremite
Escalade	Scalade
Shalot / Eschalot	Shallot
Escutcheon	Scutcheon
Estafette	Estafet
Esthetics, *or*	Æsthetics
Estoppel	Estopple
Etiology	Ætiology
Exactor	Exacter
Expense	Expence
Exsanguious	Exanguious
Exsect	Exect
Exsiccate	Exiccate
Exsiccation	Exiccation
Exsiccative	Exiccative
Exsuccous	Exuccous
Extrinsical	Extrinsecal
Exudation	Exsudation
Eyry	Ærie

F.

Fæces	Feces
Fagot	Faggot
Fairy	Faery
Fakir	Faquir / Faqueer
Falchion	Faulchion
Falcon	Faulcon
Fantasy	Phantasy
Farther, *or*	Further
Farthest, *or*	Furthest
Farthingale	Fardingale
Fattener	Fatner
Fearnaught	Fearnought
Fecal	Fæcal
Felly	Felloe
Felon	Fellon
Felspar	Feldspar
Ferrule, *or*	Ferule
Feud	Feod
Feudal	Feodal
Feudality	Feodality
Feudatory	Feodatory
Feuillemorte	Fueillemorte
Fie	Fy
Filanders	Felanders
Filbert	Filberd
Filigrane / Filigree	Filligrane / Filagree / Filligree
Fillibeg	Filibeg, Philibeg
Filly	Filley
Finery, *a forge*	Finary
Firman	Firmaun / Phirman
Fizgig	Fishgig
Flageolet	Flagelet
Fleam	Phleme, Flem
Flier	Flyer
Flotage	Floatage
Flotsam	Floatsam
Flour, *meal*	Flower
Fleur-de-lis, *or*	Flower-de-luce
Flugelman	Flugleman / Fugelman
Fluke	Flook, Flowk
Fluoride	Fluorid
Fœtus	Fetus
Forestall	Forestal
Foretell	Foretel
Forray	Foray
Forte, *strong side*	Fort
Fosse	Foss
Foundery, *or*	Foundry
Franc, *coin*	Frank
Frenetic	Phrenetic
Frenzy	Phrensy
Frieze	Frize
Frigate	Frigat
Frit	Fritt
Frizzle	Frizle
Frowzy	Frouzy
Frumentaceous	Frumentacious
Frumenty	Furmenty / Furmety
Frustum	Frustrum
Fuel	Fewel
Fulfil	Fulfill

Fulfilment	Fulfillment
Fulness	Fullness
Furlough	Furlow
Further, *or*	Farther
Furthest, *or*	Farthest
Fusee	Fusil
Fusileer	Fusilier
Fuze, *n.*, *or*	Fuse

G.

Gabardine	Gaberdine
Galiot	Galliot
Gallipot	Galipot
Galoche	Goloche
Gamut	Gammut
Gangue, *in ore*	Gang
Gantlet	Gantelope
Gaol, *or*	Jail
Garish	Gairish
Garreteer	Garretteer
Gauge, *or*	Gage
Gauger	Gager
Gault	Galt; Golt
Gauntlet, *glove*	Gantlet
Gayety	Gaiety
Gayly	Gaily
Gazelle	Gazel
Gear	Geer
Gelatine	Gelatin
Gelly; *see*	Jelly
Genet	Ginnet, Jennet
Gerfalcon	{ Gyrfalcon / Jerfakon }
Germ	Germe
Ghastly	Gastly
Ghibelline	Gibelline
Ghyll, *ravine*	Gill
Gibberish	Geberish
Gibe	Gybe, Jibe
Giglot	Giglet
Gimlet	Gimblet
Gimmal	Jymold
Gingle; *see*	Jingle
Girasole	Girasol
Girth, *or*	Girt
Glair	Glaire
Glave	Glaive
Glazier	Glasier
Glede	Glead
Gloar	Glour
Gloze	Glose
Glue	Glew
Gluey	Gluy, Glewy
Gnarled	Knarled
Gneiss	Gneis
Good-by	Good-bye
Gore	Goar
Gourmand, *or*	Gormand
Gormandize	Gourmandize
Governante	Governant
Graft	Graff
Grandam	Granam
Granddaughter	Grandaughter
Granite	Granit
Grasshopper	Grashopper
Gray, *or*	Grey
Grenade	Granade
Grenadier	Granadier
Greyhound	Grayhound
Griffin, Griffon	Gryphon
Grizzled	Grisled
Grocer	Grosser
Grotesque	Grotesk
Groundsill	Groundsel
Group	Groupe
Guarantee, *or*	Guaranty
Guild, *or*	Gild
Guilder, *or*	Gilder
Guillotine	Guillotin
Gulf	Gulph
Gunwale	Gunnel
Gurnet	Gournet
Gypsy	Gypsey, Gipsey
Gyre	Gire
Gyve	Give

H.

Haggard	Hagard
Haggess	Haggis
Ha-ha	Haw-haw
Hake	Haick
Halberd	Halbert
Hale, *healthy*	Hail
Halibut	Holibut
Halyards	Halliards
Halloo	Hollo, Holloa
Hame, *or*	Haum
Handiwork	Handywork
Hards	Hurds
Harebell	Hairbell
Harebrained	Hairbrained
Harem	Haram
Harrier	Harier
Harslet	Haslet
Hatchel } Hackle }	{ Hetchel, / { Heckle
Haul, *to drag*	Hale
Haum	Halm, Hawm
Haunch	Hanch
Haust, *cough*	Hoast
Hautboy	Hoboy
Havoc	Havock
Hawser	Halser
Hazel	Hazle
Headache	Headach
Hearse	Herse
Heartache	Heartach
Height	Hight
Heighten	Highten
Heinous	Hainous
Hemistich	Hemistick
Hemorrhoids	Emeroids
Heptamerede	Heptameride
Herpetology	Erpetology
Hexahedron	Hexaedron
Hibernate	Hybernate
Hibernation	Hybernation
Hiccough, *or*	Hickup
Hinderance, *or*	Hindrance
Hip, *v.*	Hyp
Hip, *n.*	Hep
Hippocras	Hippocrass
Hodge-podge	Hotch-potch
Hoiden	Hoyden
Holiday, *or*	Holyday
Holloo, Halloo	Holloa, Hollow
Holster	Holdster
Hominy	{ Homony / Hommony }
Homonyme, *or*	Homonym
Hone	Hoane
Honeyed	Honied
Hoop, *or*	Whoop
Hooping-cough	Whooping-cough
Hoot	Whoot
Horde	Hord
Horehound	Hoarhound
Hornblende	Hornblend
Hostler	Ostler
Household	Houshold
Housewife	Huswife
Howlet	Houlet
Hub, *or*	Hob
Hurrah	Hurra
Hydrangea	Hydrangia
Hypothenuse	Hypotenuse

I.

Icicle	Isicle
Illness	Ilness
Imbank; *see*	Embank
Imbitter	Embitter
Imbody, *or*	Embody
Imborder	Emborder
Imbosom	Embosom
Imbound	Embound
Imbrue	Embrue
Impanel	Empanel
Imparlance	Emparlance
Impassion	Empassion
Implead	Emplead
Imposthume	Impostume
Impoverish, *or*	Empoverish
Incage	Encage
Incase	Encase
Inclasp	Enclasp
Incloister	Encloister
Inclose, *or*	Enclose
Inclosure, *or*	Enclosure
Incondensable	Incondensible
Indefeasible	Indefeisible
Indelible	Indeleble
Indict	Endict
Indictment	Endictment
Indite	Endite
Inditer	Enditer
Indocile	Indocil
Indorsable	Endorsable
Indorse	Endorse
Indorsement	Endorsement
Indorser	Endorser
Indue, *or*	Endue
Inferrible	Inferable
Inflection	Inflexion
Infold	Enfold
Infoliate	Enfoliate
Ingraft	Engraft
Ingrain	Engrain
Ingulf	Engulf
Innuendo	Inuendo
Inquire, *or*	Enquire
Inquirer, *or*	Enquirer
Inquiry, *or*	Enquiry

Insnare, *or*	Ensnare
Install, *or*	Instal
Instalment	Installment
Instil	Instill
Instructor	Instructer
Insurance	Ensurance
Insure	Ensure
Insurer	Ensurer
Intenable, *or*	Intenible
Interlace	Enterlace
Interplead	Enterplead
Interpleader	Enterpleader
Inthrall	Inthral, Enthral
Intrinsical	Intrinsecal
Intrust	Entrust
Intwine	Entwine
Inure	Enure
Inurement	Enurement
Invalid, *n.*	Invalide
Inveigle	Enveigle
Inventor	Inventer
Inwheel	Enwheel
Inwrap, *or*	Enwrap
Inwreathe	Enwreathe
Isle	Ile

J.

Jackal	Jackall
Jacobin	Jacobine
Jag	Jagg
Jagghery	Jagary
Jail, *or*	Gaol
Jailer, *or*	Gaoler
Jalap	Jalop
Jamb, *n.*	Jam, Jaumb
Janizary	Janissary
Janty	Jaunty
Jasmine	Jessamine
Jaunt	Jant
Jelly	Gelly
Jenneting	{ Geniting / Juneating }
Jettee, Jetty	Jetta, Jutty
Jewellery, *or*	Jewelry
Jiffy	Giffy
Jingle	Gingle
Jointress	Jointuress
Jole, *or*	Jowl
Jonquille	Jonquil
Judgment	Judgement
Julep	Julap
Junket, *or*	Juncate
Just, *n.*	Joust
Justle, *or*	Jostle

K.

Kale	Kail, Cail
Kayle	Keel
Keelhaul	Keelhale
Keelson	Kelson
Keg, *or*	Cag
Kerseymere, *or*	Cassimere
Khan	Kan, Kann
Knapsack	Snapsack
Knarled, *or*	Gnarled
Knell	Knel

L.

Lackey	Laquey
Lacquer	Lacker
Lair	Lare
Lambdoidal	Lamdoidal
Lance	Launce
Landscape	Landskip
Landsman	Landman
Lantern	Lanthorn
Lanyard	Laniard
Launch	Lanch
Laundress	Landress
Laureate	Laureat
Lavender	Lavendar
Lea, *a plain*	Lee, Ley, Lay
Leach, *or*	Leech, Letch
Leaven	Leven
Ledger	Leger
Legging	Leggin
Lettuce	Lettice
License	Licence
Lickerish	Liquorish
Licorice	Liquorice
Lief	Lieve, Leef
Lilac	Lilach
Lily	Lilly
Linguiform	Lingueform
Liniment, *and*	Linament
Lintstock	Linstock
Litharge	Litherage
Llama, *animal*	Lama
Loadstar	Lodestar
Loadstone	Lodestone
Loath, *a.*	Loth
Loathe, *v.*	Lothe
Lode, *a vein*	Load
Lodgement	Lodgment
Lower	Lour
Luff	Loof
Luke	Leuke
Lustring, *or*	Lutestring
Lye, *from ashes*	Lie, Ley

M.

Maggoty	Maggotty [hem
Main, *or*	Mayhem, Ma'
Maize	Maiz
Maleadminis-tration, *or*	Maladminis-tration
Malecontent	Malcontent
Malefeasance	Malfeasance
Malepractice	Malpractice
Maltreat	Maletreat
Malkin	Maukin
Mall	Maul
Malanders	Mallenders
Mameluke	Mamaluke
Mandarin	Mandarine
Mandatary	Mandatory
Mandrel, *and*	Mandril
Manifestable	Manifestible
Manikin	Mannikin
Manœuvre	Maneuver
Mantle, *or*	Mantel
Mark	Marc
Marque, *license*	Mark

Marquee	Markee
Marquis, *or*	Marquess
Marshal	Marshall
Marten, *or*	Martin
Martingale	Martingal
Mask	Masque
Maslin, Meslin	Mastlin, Mislin
Mastic	Mastich
Matins	Mattins
Mattress	Matres, Mat-trass
Meagre	Meager
Mediæval	Medieval
Menagerie	Menagery
Merchandise	Merchandize
Mere, *a pool*	Meer
Metre, *and*	Meter
Mew	Meaw
Mewl	Meawl
Mileage	Milage
Milleped	Millepede
Millrea	Millree, Millreis
Miscall	Miscal
Misle, Mizzle	Mistle
Misspell	Mispell
Misspend	Mispend
Misy	Missy
Mistletoe	{ Misletoe / Misseltoe }
Mitre	Miter
Mizzen	Mizen
Moccason	{ Moccasin / Moggason }
Mocha-stone	Mocho-stone
Modillion	Modillon
Molasses	{ Melasses / Molosses }
Moneyed	Monied
Mongrel	Mungrel
Monodrame	Monodram
Mood, *or*	Mode
Moresque	Moresk
Morion	Murrion
Mortgageor	Mortgagor
Mosque	Mosk
Mosquito / Musquito	{ Moscheto / Mosquetto / Musketo / Musqueto / Musquitto }
Mould	Mold
Moult	Molt
Mulch	Mulsh
Mullein	Mullin
Multiped	Multipede
Mummery	Mommery
Murder	Murther
Murderous	Murtherous
Murky	Mirky
Murrhine	Myrrhine
Muscle, *and*	Mussel
Musket	Musquet
Mustache, *or*	Moustache

N.

Nankeen	Nankin
Naught	Nought
Negotiate	Negociate
Net, *a., clear*	Neat

Nib	Neb
Nobless	Noblesse
Nombles	Numbles
Novitiate	Noviciate
Nozle	Nozzle, Nosle
Nuisance	Nusance

O.

Oblique	Oblike
Octahedron	Octaedron
Œconomics; see	Economics
Œcumenical	Ecumenical
Offence	Offense
Offuscate	Obfuscate
Olio	Oglio
Opaque	Opake
Orach	Orache
Orison	Oraison
Osier	Ozier
Osmazome	Ozmazome
Osprey	Ospray
Ottar	Otto
Oxidate	Oxydate
Oxidation	Oxydation
Oxide	Oxyde, Oxyd
Oxidize	Oxydize
Oyes	Oyez

P.

Pacha	Pasha, Bashaw
Packet	Paquet
Painim	Paynim
Palanquin	Palankeen
Palette, or	Pallet
Palmiped	Palmipede
Pandore, or	Bandore
Panel	Pannel
Pansy	Pancy
Pantagraph ⎞ Pantograph ⎠	Pentagraph
Pappoose	⎧ Papoos ⎨ Papoose
Parallelopiped	Parallelepiped
Paralyze	Paralyse
Parcenary	Parcenery
Parol, a.	Parole
Paroquet	Parrakeet
Parral	Parrel
Parsnip	Parsnep
Partisan	Partizan
Patin	Patine
Patrol	Patroll, Patrole
Paver	Pavier, Pavior
Pawl	Paul
Pedler	Peddler, Pedlar
Pedlery	Peddlery
Peep	Piep
Penance	Pennance
Penniless	Pennyless
Pentahedral	Pentaedral
Pentahedron	Pentaedron
Pentile	Pantile
Peony	Piony
Perch	Pearch
Persistence	Persistance
Pewit	Pewet

Phantasm	Fantasm
Phantom	Fantom
Phenomenon	Phænomenon
Phial, or	Vial
Philibeg; see	Fillibeg
Philter	Philtre
Phlegm	Flegm
Phœnix	Phenix
Phthisic	Tisic
Picked, or	Piked
Picket, and	Piquet
Picturesque	Picturesk
Pie	Pye
Piebald	Pyebald
Pimento	Pimenta
Pincers	Pinchers
Placard	Placart
Plain, and	Plane
Plane-sailing	Plain-sailing
Plaster	Plaister
Plat, or	Plot
Plethora	Plethory
Pleurisy	Plurisy
Pliers	Plyers
Plough	Plow
Ploughman	Plowman
Ploughshare	Plowshare
Plumber	Plummer
Plumiped	Plumipede
Pluviameter	Pluviometer
Poise	Poize
Poltroon	Poltron
Polyanthus	Polyanthos
Polyhedral	Polyedral
Polyhedron	Polyedron
Pomade	Pommade
Pommel	Pummel
Pontoon, and	Ponton
Pony	Poney
Porpoise	⎧ Porpus ⎨ Porpess
Portray	Pourtray
Portress	Porteress
Postilion	Postillion
Potato	Potatoe
Pottage	Potage
Practise, v.	Practice
Præmunire	Premunire
Premise	Premiss
Pretence	Pretense
Preterite, or	Preterit
Pretor	Prætor
Prison-base	Prison-bars
Probate	Probat
Profane	Prophane
Protector	Protecter
Protractor	Protracter
Prunello	Prunella
Pumpkin	⎧ Pompion ⎨ Pumpion
Puny, and	Puisne
Pupillary	Pupilary
Purblind	Poreblind
Purlin	Purline
Purr	Pur
Purslain	Purslane
Putrefy	Putrify
Pygmean	Pigmean
Pygmy	Pigmy
Pyx	Pix

Q.

Quarantine	⎧ Quarantain ⎨ Carentane
Quartet	Quartett
Quatercousin	Catercousin
Quay, a mole	Key
Quinsy	⎧ Quinsey ⎨ Squinancy
Quintain	Quintin
Quintal	Kental, Kentle
Quoit	Coit

R.

Raccoon	Racoon, Rac-
Raillery	Rallery [koon
Ransom	Ransome
Rarefy	Rarify
Raspberry	Rasberry
Ratafia	Ratifia, Ratafee
Rattan	Ratan
Raven, prey	Ravin
Raze	Rase
Razure	Rasure
Real, coin	Rial, Ryal
Rear	Rere
Rearmouse	Reremouse
Rearward	Rereward
Recall	Recal
Recognizable	Recognisable
Recognizance	Recognisance
Recognize, or	Recognise
Recognizee	Recognisee
Recognizor	Recognisor
Recompense	Recompence
Reconnoitre	Reconnoiter
Redoubt	Redout
Redoubtable	Redoutable
Reenforcement	Reinforcement
Referable ⎞ Referrible ⎠	Referible
Reflection	Reflexion
Reflective	Reflexive
Reglet	Riglet
Reindeer	⎧ Raindeer ⎨ Ranedeer
Reinstall, or	Reinstal
Relic	Relique
Renard, or	Reynard
Rennet, or	Runnet
Reposit	Reposite
Resin, or	Rosin
Resistance	Resistence
Respite	Respit
Restive, or	Restiff
Restiveness	Restiffness
Retch, to vomit	Reach
Reverie, or	Revery
Reversible	Reversable
Rhomb, and	Rhumb
Ribbon	⎧ Riband ⎨ Ribband
Rider	Ryder
Rinse	Rince
Risk	Risque
Robbin	Robin
Rodomontade	Rhodomontade

Roquelaure	Roquelo
Route, *course*	Rout
Rummage	Romage
Runnet, *or*	Rennet
Rye	Rie

S.

Sag, *or*	Swag
Saic	Saik
Sainfoin	Saintfoin
Salic	Salique
Saltcellar	Saltseller
Sandarach	Sandarac
Sandiver	Sandever
Sanitary	Sanatory
Sarcenet	Sarsenet
Sat	Sate
Satchel	Sachel
Satinet	Satinett
Savin	Savine, Sabine
Saviour, *or*	Savior
Scallop	Scollop
Scath	Scathe
Scenery	Scenary
Sceptic	Skeptic
Sceptical	Skeptical
Scepticism	Skepticism
Schist	Shist
Schistose	Shistose
Scholium	Scholion
Schorl	Shorl
Sciagraphy, *or*	Sciography
Sciomachy, *or*	Sciamachy
Scion	Cion
Scirrhosity	Skirrhosty
Scirrhous	Skirrhous
Scirrhus	{ Schirrhus / Skirrhus }
Scissors	{ Cissors / Cizars / Scissars }
Sconce	Skonce
Scotfree	Shotfree
Scow	Skow
Screen	Skreen
Scrofula	Scrophula
Scymitar; *see*	Cimeter
Scythe	Sithe, Sythe
Seamstress	{ Sempstress / Semstress }
Sear	Sere
Searce	Sarse
Secretaryship	Secretariship
Seethe	Seeth
Seignior	Signior, Signor
Seine, *a net*	Sein, Seen
Seisin	Seizin
Sellenders	Sellanders
Selvage	Selvedge
Sentinel	Centinel
Sentry	Sentery, Centry
Sequin	{ Chequin / Zechin }
Sergeant, *or*	Serjeant
Sergeantry, *or*	Serjeantry
Sess, *or*	Cess
Sesspool, *or*	Cesspool
Sevennight	Sennight

Shad	Chad
Shard	Sherd
Shark, *or*	Shirk
Shawm	Shalm
Sheathe, *v.*	Sheath
Sheer, *pure*	Shear
Sheik	Sheikh, Sheick
Shemitic, *or*	Semitic
Sherbet	Scherbet
Sherry	Sherris
Shorling	Shoreling
Show	Shew
Showbread	Shewbread
Shrillness	Shrilness
Shroud	Shrowd
Shuttlecock	Shittlecock
Shyly	Shily
Shyness	Shiness
Sienite	Syenite
Silicious, *or*	Siliceous
Sill	Cill
Sillabub	Syllabub
Simar	Chimere, Cymar
Siphon	Syphon
Siren	Syren
Sirloin, *or*	Surloin
Sirocco	Scirocco
Sirup	Syrup, Sirop
Sit, *to incubate*	Set
Site	Scite
Sizar	Sizer
Size, *glue*	Cize, Cise
Skate	Scate
Skein	Skain
Skeptic; *see*	Sceptic
Skilful	Skillful
Skulk	Sculk
Skull	Scull
Slabber	Slobber
Slake, *to quench*	Slack
Sleight, *n.*	Slight
Sley, *a reed*	Slay, Slaie
Sluice	Sluce, Sluse
Slyly	Slily
Slyness	Sliness
Smallness	Smalness
Smirk	Smerk
Smooth, *v.*	Smoothe
Soap	Sope
Socage	Soccage
Socle	Sokle, Zocle
Solan	Soland, Solund
Solder, *or*	Soder
Soldier	Souldier
Soliped	Solipede
Solitaire	Solitair
Solvable	Solvible
Somerset } {	Somersault
Summerset } {	Summersault
Sonneteer	Sonnetteer
Soothe, *v.*	Sooth
Sorrel	Sorel
Souse	Sowse
Spa	Spaw
Spew	Spue
Spicknel	Spignel
Spinach	Spinage
Spinel	Spinelle, Spinell
Splice	Splise
Sponge	Spunge

Spongy	Spungy
Spright	Sprite
Sprightful	Spriteful
Spunk	Sponk
Spurt, *or*	Spirt
Stable	Stabile
Staddle	Stadle
Stanch	Staunch
Stationery, *n.*	Stationary
Steadfast	Stedfast
Steelyard	Stillyard
Sterile	Steril
Stillness	Stilness
Stockade	Stoccade
Strait, *n.*	Streight
Strake	Straik
Strap, *or*	Strop
Strengthener	Strengthner
Strew	Straw, Strow
Stupefy	Stupify
Sty	Stye
Style	Stile
Subtile, *thin*	Subtle
Subtle, *sly*	Subtile
Subtract	Substract
Subtraction	Substraction
Suit, *or*	Suite
Suitor	Suiter
Sulky, *n.*	Sulkey
Sulphuretted	Sulphureted
Sumach	Sumac, Shumac
Suretyship	Suretiship
Surloin, *or*	Sirloin
Surname	Sirname
Surprise	Surprize
Surreptitious	Subreptitious
Survivor	Surviver
Survivorship	Survivership
Swag, *or*	Sag
Swale	Sweale
Sward	Sord
Swath, *n.*	Swarth
Sweepstakes	Sweepstake
Swipple	Swiple
Swop, *or*	Swap
Sylvan	Silvan
Synonyme, *or*	Synonym
Syphilis	Siphilis
Systematize	Systemize

T.

Tabard	Taberd
Taffety	Taffeta, Taffata
Taffrail	Tafferel
Taillage	Tallage
Talc, *a stone*	Talk, Talck
Tallness	Talness
Talmud	Thalmud
Tambour	Tambor
Tambourine	Tambourin
Tarpauling	{ Tarpawling / Tarpaulin }
Tartan	Tartane
Tassel	Tossel
Tawny	Tawney
Tease	Teaze
Teazle, Teasel	Tassel, Tazel
Tenable	Tenible

Terrier	Tarrier			Waul	Wawl
Tether	Tedder			Wear, *v.*	Ware
Tetrastich	Tetrastick			Wear, *n.*	Weir, Wier
Theodolite	Theodolet	**U.**		Weasand	{ Wesand / Wezand
Thraldom	Thralldom			Welsh	Welch
Thrash, *or*	Thresh	Umbles	Humbles	Whang	Wang
Threshold	Threshhold	Unbiassed	Unbiased	Whelk	Welk
Throe, *a pang*	Throw	Unbigoted	Unbigotted	Whippletree	Whiffletree
Thyine, *wood*	Thine	Unroll	Unrol	Whippoorwill	Whippowill
Thyme	Thime	Until	Untill	Whiskey	Whisky
Ticking, *or*	Ticken			Whitleather	Whiteleather
Tidbit	Titbit			Whoop	Hoop
Tie	Tye	**V.**		Whooping-cough	Hooping-cough
Tier, *a row*	Tire			Widgeon	Wigeon
Tierce	Terce	Vaivode	Waiwode	Wilful	Willful
Tincal	Tinkal	Vales, *money*	Vails	Windlass	{ Windlace / Windlas
Tint	Teint	Valise	Vallise	Wintry	Wintery
Tiny	Tyny	Vantbrace	Vanbrass	Wiry	Wiery
Tippler	Tipler	Vat, *a vessel*	Fat	Witch-elm	Weech-elm
Tithe	Tythe	Vaudevil	Vaudeville	With, *n.*	Withe
Toilet	Toilette	Veil, *cover*	Vail	Withal	Withall
Toll, *to allure*	Tole	Vender, *or*	Vendor	Wizard	{ Wizzard, / Wisard
Tollbooth	Tolbooth	Veneer	Fineer	Woe	Wo
Ton, *or*	Tun	Venomous	Venemous	Woful	Woeful
Tonnage	Tunnage	Verdigris	{ Verdigrise / Verdigrease	Wondrous	Wonderous
Tormentor	Tormenter	Vermilion	{ Vermillion / Virmilion	Woodbine	Woodbind
Touchy, *or*	Techy	Vermin	Vermine	Woodchuck	Woodchuk
Tourmaline	Tourmalin	Verst	Berst, Werst	Woollen	Woolen
Trance	Transe	Vertebre, *or*	Vertebra	Wreathe, *v.*	Wreath
Tranquillity	Tranquility	Vervain	Vervane	Wreck	Wrack
Tranquillize	Tranquilize	Vial, *or*	Phial	Wriggle	Riggle
Transferable	Transferrible	Vice, *a screw*	Vise		
Transferrence	Transference	Vicious	Vitious		
Treadle	Treddle	Villain, *and*	Villein, Villan		
Treenail	{ Trenail, / Trunnel	Villanous	Villainous		
Trellis	Trellice	Villany	Villainy	**Y.**	
Trentals	Trigintals	Visitatorial	Visitorial		
Trestle	{ Tressel / Trussel	Visitor	Visiter	Yawl	Yaul
Trevet, *or*	{ Trivet / Trevit	Visor	Vizor	Yearn	Yern
Trousers	Trowsers	Vitiate	Viciate	Yeast	Yest
Truckle-bed, *or*	Trundle-bed	Vizter	Vizir, Visier	Yelk, *or*	Yolk
Tumbrel, *and*	Tumbril	Volcano	Vulcano	Yerk	Yark
Turkey	Turky			Yew	Eugh
Turkois	Turquoise				
Turnip	Turnep				
Turnsole	Turnsol	**W.**		**Z.**	
Tutenag	Tutenague				
Twibil	Twibill	Wagon, *or*	Waggon	Zaffre	Zaffir
Tymbal	Timbal	Waif	Waift	Zechin; *see*	Sequin
Tyro	Tiro	Waive, *to defer*	Wave	Zinc	Zink
		Wale	Weal	Zymology	Zumology
		Walrus	Walruss		
		Warranter, *and*	Warrantor		
		War-whoop	War-hoop		

3*

ABBREVIATIONS.

a. stands for . . . . . . Adjective.	*p. a.* . . . . Participial Adjective.
ad. . . . . Adverb.	*pl.* . . . . Plural.
comp. . . . . Comparative.	*prep.* . . . . Preposition.
conj. . . . . Conjunction.	*pron.* . . . . Pronoun.
imp. t. . . . . Imperfect Tense.	*sing.* . . . . Singular.
interj. . . . . Interjection.	*superl.* . . . . Superlative.
n. . . . . Noun.	*v.* . . . . Verb.
p. . . . . Participle.	*v. a.* . . . . Verb Active.
pp. . . . . Perfect Participle.	*v. n.* . . . . Verb Neuter.

A

DICTIONARY

OF THE

ENGLISH LANGUAGE.

A

A, *(pronounced ā as a letter, but ạ as a word.)* The indefinite article, put before nouns of the singular number; as, *a* man, *a* tree. Before words beginning with a vowel and *h* mute, it is written *an*; as, *an* ox, *an* hour. *A* is placed before a participle, or participial noun, and is considered as a contraction of *at* or *on*; as, I am *a* walking. *A*, prefixed to *many* or *few*, implies one whole number. *A* has also the signification of *each*, *every*; as, "The landlord has a hundred *a* year."

A-BĂCK', *ad.* Backwards; pressed against the mast by the wind, as a sail. [land.

ĂB'Ạ-CŎT, *n.* A cap of state once used in Eng-

ĂB'Ạ-CŬS, *n.* A counting instrument or table.

A-BĂFT', *prep.* Towards the stern of a vessel.

ĂB-ĀL'IEN-ĀTE, *v. a.* To transfer the title of to another, as of property; to alienate.

ĂB-ĀL-IEN-Ā'TIQN (ạb-āl-yen-ā'shụn), *n.* Act of transferring the title of property to another.

A-BĂN'DQN, *v. a.* To give up, desert, forsake.

A-BĂN'DQNED (ạ-băn'dụnd), *p. a.* Given up; corrupted in a high degree; very wicked.

A-BĂN'DQN-MĔNT, *n.* The act of abandoning.

A-BĀSE', *v. a.* To humble, depress, bring low.

A-BĀSE'MĔNT, *n.* State of being brought low.

A BĂSH', *v. a.* To make ashamed; to confuse.

A-BĂSH'MĔNT, *n.* Great shame or confusion.

A-BĀT'Ạ-BLE, *a.* That may be abated.

A-BĀTE', *v. a.* To lessen; to diminish.

A-BĀTE', *v. n.* To grow less, to decrease.

A-BĀTE'MĔNT, *n.* The act of abating; decrease.

A-BĀT'ER, *n.* One who, or that which, abates.

ĂBB, *n.* The yarn of a weaver's warp.

ĂB'BA, *n.* A Syriac word, signifying *father*.

ĂB'BA-CY, *n.* Rights and privileges of an abbot.

ĂB'BE, *n.* An abbot; an ecclesiastical title.

ĂB'BESS, *n.* The governess of a nunnery.

ĂB'BEY, *n.* A priory; a monastery; a convent.

ĂB'BQT, *n.* The chief of an abbey or convent.

AB-BRĒ'VĮ-ĀTE, *v. a.* To abridge; to shorten.

AB-BRĒ-VĮ-Ā'TIQN, *n.* A shortening; one or more letters of a word standing for the whole.

AB-BRĒ'VĮ-Ā-TQR, *n.* One who abbreviates.

AB-BRĒ'VĮ-Ạ-TŪRE, *n.* An abridgment.

ĂB'DĮ-CĂNT, *a.* Abdicating; renouncing.

ĂB'DĮ-CĀTE, *v. a.* To resign; to relinquish.

ĂB'DĮ-CĀTE, *v. n.* To relinquish or abandon an office; to resign.

AB-DĮ-CĀ'TIQN, *n.* Act of abdicating; resigna-

ĂB'DĮ-CĀ-TĮVE, *a.* Implying abdication. [tion.

AB-DŌ'MEN, *n.* The lower venter or belly.

AB-DŎM'Į-NAL, *a.* Relating to the abdomen.

AB-DŪCE', *v. a.* To draw from; to separate.

AB-DŪ'CENT, *a.* Drawing away; pulling back.

AB-DŬCT', *v. a.* To take away by force or fraud, as a person; to kidnap.

AB-DŬC'TIQN, *n.* A wrongful taking away.

AB-DŬCT'QR, *n.* A muscle which draws back.

Ā-BE-CE-DĀ'RĮ-AN, *n.* A teacher or learner of the alphabet. [the alphabet.

A-BĔD', *ad.* In bed; on the bed.

AB-ĔR'RANCE, *n.* Deviation from the right way.

AB-ĔR'RANT, *a.* Deviating from the right way.

ĂB-ER-RĀ'TIQN, *n.* The act of deviating.

A-BĔT', *v. a.* To assist; to set on; to incite.

A-BĔT'MENT, *n.* The act of abetting.

A-BĔT'TQR, *n.* One who abets; an accomplice.

A-BEY'ANCE (ạ-bā'ạns), *n.* Expectation of law.

AB-HŎR', *v. a.* To detest; to abominate.

AB-HŎR'RENCE, *n.* Hatred; detestation.

AB-HŎR'RENT, *a.* Odious; inconsistent.

AB-HŎR'RENT-LY, *ad.* In an abhorrent manner.

AB-HŎR'RER, *n.* One who abhors; a detester.

Ā'BĮB, *n.* First month of the Jewish year.

A-BĪDE', *v. n.* (*imp. t.* and *pp.* abode.) To stay in a place; to dwell; to remain; to continue.

A-BĪDE', *v. a.* To wait for; to expect; to attend.

A-BĪD'ER, *n.* One who abides or stays by.

A-BĬL'Į-TY, *n.* Power; skill; capacity; talent.

ĂB'JECT, *a.* Mean; low; despicable; vile.

AB-JĔC'TIQN, *n.* Want of spirit; baseness.

ĂB'JECT-LY, *ad.* Meanly; basely; vilely.

ĂB'JECT-NĔSS, *n.* Abjection; meanness.

AB-JŪ-DĮ-CĀ'TIQN, *n.* Rejection.

ĂB-JŲ-RĀ'TIQN, *n.* The act of abjuring.

AB-JŪRE', *v. a.* To recant; to renounce.

AB-JŪR'ER, *n.* One who abjures or recants.

AB-LĂC'TĀTE, *v. a.* To wean from the breast.

ĂB-LĂC-TĀ'TIǫN, *n.* Act of weaning from the breast : — a method of grafting.
ĄB-LĀ'TIǫN, *n.* The act of taking away.
ĂB'LĄ-TĬVE, *a.* Noting the sixth case in Latin.
Ą-BLĂZE, *ad.* In a blaze ; on fire.
Ā'BLE, *a.* Having strength, power, or skill.
Ā-BLE-BŎD-ĮED (ā'bl-bŏd-ĭd), *a.* Strong of body.
Ā'BLE-NĔSS, *n.* Ability ; vigor ;. force.
ĂB'LŲ-ĘNT, *a.* Washing clean ; purifying.
ĄB-LŪ'TIǫN, *n.* Act of cleansing or washing.
Ā'BLY, *ad.* In an able manner ; with ability.
ĂB-NĘ-GĀ'TIǪN, *n.* Denial ; renunciation.
ĄB-NŎR'MĂL, *a.* Irregular ; anomalous.
Ą-BŌARD' (ą-bŏrd'), *ad.* In a ship or vessel.
Ą-BŌARD', *prep.* On board of.
Ą-BŌDE', *n.* Habitation ; dwelling ; stay.
Ą-BŌDE', *imp. t.* and *pp.* from *abide.*
Ą-BŌDE'MĘNT, *n.* A secret anticipation.
Ą-BŎL'ĮSH, *v. a.* To annul ; to destroy.
Ą-BŎL'ĮSH-Ą-BLE, *a.* That may be abolished.
Ą-BŎL'ĮSH-ĘR, *n.* One who abolishes.
Ą-BŎL'ĮSH-MĔNT, *n.* The act of abolishing.
ĂB-ǫ-LĬ''TIǫN (ăb-ǫ-lĭsh'ųn), *n.* The state of being abolished ; the act of abolishing.
ĂB-ǫ-LĬ''TIǫN-ĬST, *n.* Promoter of abolition.
Ą-BŎM'Į-NĄ-BLE, *a.* Hateful ; detestable.
Ą-BŎM'Į-NĄ-BLE-NĔSS, *n.* Hatefulness.
Ą-BŎM'Į-NĄ-BLY, *ad.* Hatefully ; detestably.
Ą-BŎM Į-NĀTE, *v. a.* To detest ; to hate utterly.
Ą-BŎM-Į-NĀ'TIǪN, *n.* Hatred ; object of hatred.
ĂB-ǫ-RĬĠ'Į-NĄL, *a.* Original ; primitive ; first.
ĂB-ǫ-RĬĠ'Į-NĄL, *n.* An original inhabitant.
ĂB-ǫ-RĬĠ'Į-NĒŞ, *n. pl.* The earliest inhabitants.
Ą-BŎR'TIǫN, *n.* Miscarriage ; untimely birth.
Ą-BŎR'TĮVE, *a.* Immature ; unsuccessful.
Ą-BŎR'TĮVE-LY, *ad.* Immaturely ; untimely.
Ą-BŎR'TĮVE-NĔSS, *n.* The state of abortion.
Ą-BŎŪND', *v. n.* To be in great plenty.
Ą-BOŪT', *prep.* Around ; near to ; concerning.
Ą-BOŪT', *ad.* Circularly ; nearly ; around.
Ą-BŎVE' (ą-bŭv'), *prep.* Higher than ; more than ; greater than ; beyond ; too proud for.
Ą-BŎVE' (ą-bŭv'), *ad.* Overhead ; before.
Ą-BŎVE'BŌARD, *ad.* In open sight ; openly.
ĂB-RĄ-CĄ-DĂB'RĄ, *n.* A superstitious charm.
Ą-BRĀDE', *v. a.* To wear away ; to rub off.
Ą-BRĀ'ŞIǫN (ą-brā'zhųn), *n.* Act of rubbing off.
Ą-BRĔAST' (ą-brĕst'), *ad.* Side by side.
Ą-BRĬDĠE', *v. a.* To make shorter ; to contract.
Ą-BRĬDĠ'ĘR, *n.* One who abridges ; a shortener.
Ą-BRĬDĠ'MĘNT, *n.* A work abridged.
Ą-BRŌACH', *ad.* In a position to let the contents run out, as a cask ; broached.
Ą-BRŌAD' (ą-brȧwd'), *ad.* At large ; from home.
ĂB'RǪ-GĀTE, *v. a.* To repeal ; to annul, abolish.
ĂB-RǪ-GĀ'TIǪN, *n.* The act of abrogating.
ĄB-RŬPT', *a.* Broken ; sudden ; unconnected.
ĄB-RŬP'TIǪN, *n.* A violent or sudden separation.
ĄB-RŬPT'LY, *ad.* Hastily ; suddenly ; ruggedly.
ĄB-RŬPT'NESS, *n.* An abrupt manner.
ĂB'scĔss, *n.* A tumor containing matter.
ĄB-SCĬND' (ąb-sĭnd'), *v. a.* To cut or pare off.
ĄB-SCĬŞ'ŞIǪN (ąb-sĭzh'ųn), *n.* A cutting off.
ĄB-SCŎND', *v. n.* To hide or conceal one's self ; to withdraw secretly ; to steal away.
ĄB-SCŎND'ĘR, *n.* One who absconds.
ĂB'SĘNCE, *n.* The state of being absent ; want.
ĂB'SĘNT, *a.* Not present ; inattentive in mind.

ĄB-SĔNT', *v. a.* To keep away ; to withdraw.
ĂB-SĘN-TĒĔ', *n.* One absent from his station.
ĄB-SĬN'THĮ-ĄN, *a.* Of the nature of wormwood.
ĄB-SĬN'THĮ-ĀT-ĘD, *p.a.* Containing wormwood.
ĂB'SǪ-LŪTE, *a.* Complete ; not limited ; positive.
ĂB'SǪ-LŪTE-LY, *ad.* Fully ; unconditionally.
ĂB'SǪ-LŪTE-NĔSS, *n.* Completeness ; despotism.
ĂB-SǪ-LŪ'TIǪN, *n.* Act of absolving ; acquittal.
ĄB-SŎL'Ų-TǪ-RY, *a.* That absolves.
ĄB-SŎL'VĄ-TǪ-RY, *a.* Relating to pardon.
ĄB-SǪLVE', *v. a.* To clear ; to acquit ; to pardon.
ĄB-SǪLV'ĘR, *n.* One who absolves.
ĄB-SŎRB', *v. a.* To imbibe ; to swallow up.
ĄB-SŎR'BĘNT, *n.* Medicine that dries up.
ĄB-SŎR'BĘNT, *a.* Having power to absorb.
ĄB-SŎRP'TIǪN, *n.* The act of absorbing.
ĄB-STĀIN', *v. n.* To keep from ; to forbear.
ĄB-STĒ'MĮ-OŬS, *a.* Temperate ; abstinent.
ĄB-STĒ'MĮ-OŬS-LY, *ad.* Temperately ; soberly.
ĄB-STĒ'MĮ-OŲS-NĔSS, *n.* The being abstemious.
ĄB-STĔRĠE', *v. a.* To wipe ; to cleanse.
ĄB-STĔR'ĠĘNT, *a.* Having a cleansing quality.
ĄB-STĔR'SIǪN, *n.* The act of cleansing.
ĄB-STĔR'SĮVE, *a.* Cleansing.
ĂB'STĮ-NĔNCE, *n.* Forbearance of food or drink.
ĂB'STĮ-NĔNT, *a.* Practising abstinence.
ĂB'STĮ-NĔNT-LY, *ad.* In an abstinent manner.
ĄB-STRĂCT', *v. a.* To draw from ; to abridge.
ĂB'STRĂCT, *a.* Separate ; refined ; pure.
ĂB'STRĂCT, *n.* Concentration or essence : — an abridgment ; an epitome ; a summary.
ĄB-STRĂCT'ĘD, *p. a.* Separated ; inattentive.
ĄB-STRĂCT'ĘD-LY, *ad.* In an abstracted manner.
ĄB-STRĂCT'ĘD-NĔSS, *n.* The being abstracted.
ĄB-STRĂCT'ĘR, *n.* One who abstracts.
ĄB-STRĂC'TIǪN, *n.* Act of abstracting.
ĄB-STRĂC'TĮVE, *a.* Having power to abstract.
ĄB-STRŪSE', *a.* Hidden ; obscure ; difficult.
ĄB-STRŪSE'LY, *ad.* Obscurely ; not plainly.
ĄB-STRŪSE'NĘSS, *n.* Difficulty ; obscurity.
ĄB-SŪRD', *a.* Unreasonable ; inconsistent.
ĄB-SŪRD'Į-TY, *n.* Inconsitsency ; folly.
ĄB-SŪRD'LY, *ad.* Unreasonably ; injudiciously.
ĄB-SŪRD'NĘSS, *n.* The quality of being absurd.
Ą-BŬN'DĄNCE, *n.* Great plenty ; exuberance.
Ą-BŬN'DĄNT, *a.* Plentiful ; exuberant ; ample.
Ą-BŬN'DĄNT-LY, *ad.* In plenty ; amply.
Ą-BŪSE' *v. a.* To make an ill use of ; to revile.
Ą-BŪSE', *n.* Ill use ; injury ; reproach.
Ą-BŪS'ĘR, *n.* One who uses ill or reproaches.
Ą-BŪ'SĮVE, *a.* Containing abuse ; deceitful.
Ą-BŪ'SĮVE-LY, *ad.* By a wrong use ; rudely.
Ą-BŪ'SĮVE-NĔSS, *n.* Quality of being abusive.
Ą-BŬT', *v. n.* To end at ; border upon ; meet.
Ą-BŬT'MĘNT, *n.* That which joins another ; mass of masonry at the end of a bridge.
Ą-BŬT'TĄL, *n.* The butting or boundary of land.
Ą-BȲŞM' (ą-bĭzm'), *n.* A gulf ; an abyss.
Ą-BȲSS', *n.* A depth without bottom ; a gulf.
Ą-CĀ'CĮ-Ą (ą-kā'shę-ą), *n.* A plant ; a drug.
ĂC-Ą-DĒ'MĮ-ĄN, *n.* A member of an academy.
ĂC-Ą-DĔM'ĮC, *n.* An academic philosopher.
ĂC-Ą-DĔM'ĮC, } *a.* Belonging to an academy,
ĂC-Ą-DĔM'Į-CĄL, } or to the Platonic philosophy.
ĂC-Ą-DE-MĬ''CIĄN (ăk-ą-dę-mĭsh'ąn), *n.* A member of an academy ; a man of science.
Ą-CĂD'Ę-MY, *n.* A school of arts and sciences ; a school or seminary of learning.

ĂC-A-NĀ'CEOUS (ăk-a-nā'shus), a. Prickly.
A-CĂN'THUS, n. The herb bear's breech.
A-CĂT-A-LĔC'TIC, n. A complete verse.
A-CĂT-A-LĔP'TIC, a. Not discoverable.
AC-CĒDE', v. n. To comply; to assent.
AC-CĔL'ER-ĀTE, v. a. To hasten; to quicken.
AC-CĔL-ER-Ā'TIQN, n. A quickening.
AC-CĔL'ER-A-TĪVE, a. Increasing velocity.
AC-CĔN'SIQN, n. The act of kindling.
ĂC'CENT, n. Modulation or stress of voice; a mark on a syllable directing modulation or stress of voice; language; words.
AC-CĔNT', v. a. To express the accent of.
AC-CĔNT'U-AL, a. Relating to accent.
AC-CĔNT'U-ĀTE, v. a. To place the accent on.
AC-CĔNT-U-Ā'TIQN, n. Act of placing accent.
AC-CĔPT', v. a. To take; to receive; to admit.
AC-CĔPT-A-BĬL'I-TY, n. Acceptableness.
AC-CĔPT'A-BLE, a. Likely to be accepted; grateful; pleasing; welcome.
AC-CĔPT'A-BLE-NĔSS, n. A being acceptable.
AC-CĔPT'A-BLY, ad. In an acceptable manner.
AC-CĔPT'ANCE, n. Reception; acceptation.
ĂC-CEP-TĀ'TIQN, n. Acceptance; meaning.
AC-CĔPT'ER, n. One who accepts.
AC-CĔSS' or ĂC'CĔSS, n. Approach; admission.
ĂC'CES-SA-RY, n. (Law.) One who is guilty of a crime, not principally, but by participation.
ĂC'CES-SA-RY, a. Contributing. See ACCESSORY.
AC-CĔS-SI-BĬL'I-TY, n. State of being accessible.
AC-CĔS'SI-BLE, a. That may be approached.
AC-CĔS'SIQN (ak-sĕsh'un), n. Addition; enlargement; augmentation; approach; arrival.
ĂC'CES-SQ-RY, n. An accomplice; accessary.
ĂC'CES-SQ-RY, a. Joined; contributing.
ĂC'CI-DĔNCE, n. Book of rudiments of gram-
ĂC'CI-DĔNT, n. Casualty; chance; hap. [mar.
ĂC-CI-DĔNT'AL, a. Non-essential; casual.
ĂC-CI-DĔNT'AL-LY, ad. Casually; fortuitously.
AC-CLAIM', n. A shout of praise; acclamation.
ĂC-CLA-MĀ'TIQN, n. A shout of applause.
AC-CLĂM'A-TQ-RY, a. Pertaining to acclama-
AC-CLĪ'MĀTE, v. a. To inure to a climate. [tion.
AC-CLĬV'I-TY, n. Steepness reckoned upwards.
AC-CLĪ'VOUS, a. Rising with a slope.
ĂC-CQ-LĀDE', n. A blow given in knighting.
AC-CŎM'MQ-DA-BLE, a. That may be adapted.
AC-CŎM'MQ-DĀTE, v. a. To supply, fit, or adjust.
AC-CŎM-MQ-DĀ'TIQN, n. Provision of conveniences; fitness; reconciliation. [dates.
AC-CŎM'MQ-DA-TQR, n. One who accommo-
AC-CŎM'PA-NI-MĔNT, n. That which attends.
AC-CŎM'PA-NY, v. a. To attend; to go with.
AC-CŎM'PLICE, n. An associate in crime.
AC-CŎM'PLISH, v. a. To complete; to execute.
AC-CŎM'PLISHED (ak-kŏm'plisht), p. a. Complete in some qualification; refined; elegant.
AC-CŎM'PLISH-ER, n. One who accomplishes.
AC-CŎM'PLISH-MĔNT, n. Completion; full performance: — ornament of mind or body.
AC-COMPT' (ak-kŏunt'), n. See ACCOUNT.
AC-CŎRD', v. a. To make agree; to adjust.
AC-CŎRD', v. n. To agree; to harmonize.
AC-CŎRD', n. A compact; agreement; union.
AC-CŎRD'ANCE, n. Agreement; conformity.
AC-CŎRD'ANT, a. Consonant; corresponding.
AC-CŎRD'ANT-LY, ad. In an accordant manner.
AC-CŎRD'ER, n. An assistant; helper; favorer.

AC-CŎRD'ING TÔ, prep. Agreeably to; suiting.
AC-CŎRD'ING-LY, ad. Agreeably; conformably.
AC-CŎST', v. a. To speak to; to address.
AC-CŎST'A-BLE, a. Easy of access; familiar.
AC-CŎÛNT', n. A computation; reason; regard; rank; estimation; profit; narration.
AC-CŎÛNT', v. a. To esteem, reckon, compute.
AC-CŎÛNT', v. n. To reckon; to give an account.
AC-CŎÛNT-A-BĬL'I-TY, n. Accountableness.
AC-CŎÛNT'A-BLE, a. Amenable. [countable.
AC-CŎÛNT'A-BLE-NĔSS, n. State of being ac-
AC-CŎÛNT'ANT, n. One who keeps accounts.
AC-COŬP'LE (ak-kŭp'pl), v. a. To link together.
AC-COŬP'LE-MĔNT, n. A junction; a tie.
AC-CÔU'TRE (ak-kô'tur), v. a. To dress; to equip. [arms; equipage; equipments.
AC-CÔU'TRE-MĔNTS, n. pl. Military dress and
AC-CRĔD'IT, v. a. To give or procure credit to.
AC-CRĔD'IT-ED, p. a. Intrusted; empowered.
AC-CRĔS'CENT, a. Increasing; growing to.
AC-CRE'TIQN, n. Act of growing to another.
AC-CRE'TIVE, a. Increasing by growth.
AC-CRŬE' (ak-krŭ), v. n. To be added; to arise, as profits; to follow, as loss.
AC-CRŬ'MENT, n. Addition; increase.
ĂC-CU-BĀ'TIQN, n. Act of lying or reclining.
AC-CŬM'BEN-CY, n. State of being accumbent.
AC-CŬM'BENT, a. Leaning; reclining.
AC-CŪ'MU-LĀTE, v. a. To heap up; to pile up.
AC-CŪ'MU-LĀTE, v. n. To increase; to amass.
AC-CŪ-MU-LĀ'TIQN, n. The act of accumulating; increase; addition; augmentation.
AC-CŪ'MU-LA-TĪVE, a. That accumulates.
AC-CŪ'MU-LĀ-TQR, n. One who accumulates.
ĂC'CU-RA-CY, n. Exactness; correctness.
ĂC'CU-RATE, a. Exact; correct; precise.
ĂC'CU-RATE-LY, ad. Exactly; correctly.
ĂC'CU-RATE-NĔSS, n. Exactness; accuracy.
AC-CŬRSE', v. a. To doom to misery; to curse.
AC-CŬRS'ED, p. a. Cursed; execrable; hateful.
AC-CŪ'SA-BLE (ak-kū'za-bl), a. Blamable.
ĂC-CU-SĀ'TIQN, n. The act of accusing; that of which one is accused; charge.
AC-CŪ'SA-TĪVE, a. Noting the fourth case of Greek and Latin nouns.
AC-CŪ'SA-TQ-RY, a. Containing an accusation.
AC-CŪSE', v. a. To charge; to blame.
AC-CŪS'ER, n. One who accuses.
AC-CŬS'TQM, v. a. To habituate; to inure.
AC-CŬS'TQM-A-RY, a. Usual; customary.
AC-CŬS'TQMED (ak-kŭs'tumd), a. Usual.
ĀCE, n. A unit on cards or dice: — an atom.
A-CĔPH'A-LOŬS (a-sĕf'a-lŭs), a. Without a head.
A-CĔRB', a. Acid and astringent.
A-CĔR'BĀTE, v. a. To make sour.
A-CĔR'BI-TY, n. Sour taste; severity of temper.
A-CĔS'CENT, a. Tending to sourness or acidity.
ĂC'E-TĀTE, n. (Chem.) Neutral salt.
ĂC-E-TŌSE', a. Sour; sharp; acetous.
A-CĔ'TOUS, a. Having the quality of vinegar.
ĀCHE (āk), n. A continued pain.
ĀCHE (āk), v. n. To be in continued pain.
A-CHIĔV'A-BLE, a. Possible to be achieved.
A-CHIĔVE', v. a. To perform; to finish; to gain.
A-CHIĔVE'MENT, n. Performance; an exploit.
A-CHIĔV'ER, n. One who achieves.
ĀCH'ING (āk'ing), n. Pain; uneasiness.
ĂCH-RQ-MĂT'IC, a. Destitute of color.

MĪEN, SĬR; MŌVE, NÖR, SÖN; BŪLL, BŬR, RŪLE.—Ç, Ǥ, *soft*; Ð, Ǥ, *hard*; Ş *as* Z; Ҳ *as* gz; THIS.

ĂÇ'ĬD, *a.* Sour; sharp; like vinegar in taste.
ĂÇ'ĬD, *n.* An acid substance.
Ạ-CĬD'Ĭ-FĪ-Ạ-BLE, *a.* That may be acidified.
Ạ-CĬD-Ĭ-FĬ-CĀ'TIǪN, *n.* The act of acidifying.
Ạ-CĬD'Ĭ-FȲ, *v. a.* To convert into an acid.
Ạ-CĬD'Ĭ-TY, *n.* An acid taste; sourness.
ĂÇ'ĬD-NĔSS, *n.* Acidity; sourness.
Ạ-CĬD'Ụ-LĀTE, *v. a.* To tinge with acids.
Ạ-CĬD'Ụ-LOŬS, *a.* Sourish; somewhat acid.
ẠC-KNŎWL'ĘDǦE (ạk-nŏl'ej), *v. a.* To own;
to confess; to admit to be true; to grant.
ẠC-KNŎWL'ĘDǦ-MĔNT (ạk-nŏl'ej-mĕnt), *n.*
Concession; recognition; gratitude.
ĂC'MĘ, *n.* The highest point; the summit.
ĂC'Ǫ-NĪTE, *n.* The poisonous plant wolf's-bane.
Ā'CORN, *n.* The seed or fruit of the oak.
Ạ-CŎŬS'TĬC, *a.* Relating to hearing.
Ạ-CŎŬS'TĬCS, *n. pl.* The science of sounds.
ẠC-QUĀINT', *v. a.* To make familiar; to inform.
ẠC-QUĀINT'ẠNCE, *n.* Familiarity; knowledge;
a person with whom one is acquainted.
ẠC-QUĀINT'ĘD, *a.* Familiar; well known.
ẠC-QUĔST', *n.* Acquisition; thing gained.
ĂC-QUĬ-ĔSCE' (ăk-wę-ĕs'), *v. n.* To remain sat-
isfied; to comply; to assent; to agree.
ĂC-QUĬ-ĔS'CĘNCE, *n.* Compliance; assent.
ĂC-QUĬ-ĔS'CĘNT, *a.* Easy; complying.
ẠC-QUĬR'Ạ-BLE, *a.* That may be acquired.
ẠC-QUĪRE', *v. a.* To gain; to come to; to attain.
ẠC-QUĪR'ĘR, *n.* One who acquires.
ẠC-QUĪRE'MĘNT, *n.* Acquisition; attainment.
ĂC-QUĬ-ṢĬ''TIǪN (ăk-wę-zĭsh'ụn), *n.* The act
of acquiring or gaining; thing gained.
ẠC-QUĬṢ'Ĭ-TĪVE, *a.* Disposed to acquire.
ẠC-QUĬT', *v. a.* To set free; to discharge.
ẠC-QUĬT'TẠL, *n.* A judicial discharge.
ẠC-QUĬT'TẠNCE, *n.* A discharge from a debt.
Ā'CRE (ā'kụr), *n.* 160 square rods of land.
ĂC'RĬD, *a.* Of a hot, biting taste; pungent.
ĂC-RĬ-MŌ'NĬ-OŬS, *a.* Abounding with acrimony.
ĂC-RĬ-MŌ'NĬ-OŬS-NĔSS, *n.* Acrimony.
ĂC-RĬ-MŌ'NĬ-OŬS-LY, *ad.* With acrimony.
ĂC'RĬ-MǪ-NY, *n.* Sharpness; severity of temper.
ĂC'RĬ-TŪDE, *n.* An acrid quality or taste.
ĂC-RǪ-Ạ-MĂT'ĬC, *or* ĂC-RǪ-Ạ-MĂT'Ĭ-CẠL, *a.*
Pertaining to deep learning; abstruse.
ĂC'RǪ-BĂT, } *n.* A rope-dancer; a gymnast.
ĂC'RǪ-BĀTE, }
Ạ-CRŎN'Y-CẠL, *a.* Rising when the sun sets,
and setting when the sun rises.
ĂC'RǪ-SPĪRE, *n.* A shoot from the end of seeds.
Ạ-CRŎSS', *ad.* Athwart; transversely.
Ạ-CRŎS'TĬC, *n.* A poem in which the first or
first and last letters of the lines spell some
Ạ-CRŎS'TĬ-CẠL, *a.* Relating to acrostics. [name.
ĂCT, *v. n.* To be in action; not to rest.
ĂCT, *v. a.* To perform; to feign; to imitate.
ĂCT, *n.* A deed; an exploit; a part of a play.
ĂCT'ĬNG, *n.* Action; act of performing.
ĂC'TIǪN, *n.* Deed; battle; gesture; lawsuit.
ĂC'TIǪN-Ạ-BLE, *a.* That admits an action.
ĂC'TĬVE, *a.* Busy; nimble; agile; quick.
ĂC'TĬVE-LY, *ad.* In an active manner; busily.
ĂC'TĬVE-NĔSS, } *n.* The quality of being ac-
ẠC-TĬV'Ĭ-TY, } tive; nimbleness; liveliness.
ĂCT'ǪR, *n.* One who acts; a stage-player.
ĂC'TRĘSS, *n.* A woman that plays on the stage.
ĂCT'Ụ-ẠL, *a.* Real; true; effective; certain.

ĂCT-Ụ-ĂL'Ĭ-TY, *n.* The state of being actual.
ĂCT'Ụ-ẠL-LY, *ad.* In act; really; in fact.
ĂCT'Ụ-Ạ-RY, *n.* A clerk; a managing officer.
ĂCT'Ụ-ĀTE, *v. a.* To put into action; to excite.
ĂC'Ụ-ĀTE, *v. a.* To sharpen; to point.
Ạ-CŪ'LĘ-ẠTE, *a.* Having a point; prickly.
Ạ-CŪ'MĘN, *n.* Sharpness; quick perception.
Ạ-CŪ'MĬ-NĀT-ĘD, *p. a.* Sharp-pointed.
Ạ-CŪ-MĬ-NĀ'TIǪN, *n.* The act of sharpening.
Ạ-CŪTE', *a.* Sharp; keen; penetrating.
Ạ-CŪTE'LY, *ad.* Sharply; ingeniously; keenly.
Ạ-CŪTE'NĘSS, *n.* Sharpness; penetration.
ĂD'AǦE (ăd'ạj), *n.* A maxim; a proverb.
Ạ-DĀ'ǦĬ-Ō, *n.* (*Mus.*) A slow time.
ĂD'Ạ-MĂNT, *n.* A very hard stone; diamond.
ĂD-Ạ-MẠN-TĒ'ẠN, *a.* Hard as adamant.
ĂD-Ạ-MĂN'TĬNE, *a.* Made of adamant; hard.
Ạ-DĂPT', *v. a.* To fit; to suit; to accommodate.
Ạ-DĂPT-Ạ-BĬL'Ĭ-TY, *n.* Capability of adaptation.
Ạ-DĂPT'Ạ-BLE, *a.* That may be adapted.
ĂD-ẠP-TĀ'TIǪN, *n.* Act of adapting; fitness.
ĂDD, *v. a.* To join; to unite; to subjoin.
ẠD-DĔÇ'Ĭ-MĀTE, *v. a.* To take tithes of.
ĂD'DĘR, *n.* A viper; a venomous reptile.
ĂD'DĘR'Ṣ-GRĂSS, *n.* A species of plant.
ĂD'DĘR'Ṣ-TŌNGUE (ăd'dẹrz-tŭng), *n.* A plant.
ĂD-DĘR'Ṣ-WŎRT (-würt), *n.* Snake-weed.
ẠD-DĬ-BĬL'Ĭ-TY, *n.* Possibility of being added.
ĂD'DĬ-BLE, *a.* That may be added.
ĂD'DĬCE, *n.* A cutting tool. See ADZE.
ẠD-DĬCT', *v. a.* To devote; to apply.
ẠD-DĬCT'ĘD-NĔSS, *n.* State of being addicted.
ẠD-DĬC'TIǪN, *n.* The act of devoting; habit.
ẠD-DĬT'Ạ-MĔNT, *n.* Addition; thing added.
ẠD-DĬ''TIǪN (ạd-dĭsh'ụn), *n.* The act of add-
ing; increase: — a branch of arithmetic.
ẠD-DĬ''TIǪN-ẠL (ạd-dĭsh'ụn-ạl), *a.* Being added.
ĂD-DĬ''TIǪN-ẠL-LY, *ad.* In addition.
ĂD'DĬ-TǪ-RY, *a.* Having the power of adding.
ĂD'DLE, *a.* Barren; unfruitful. [Foolish.
ĂD'DLE-HĔAD'ĘD, *or* ĂD'DLE-PĀT'ĘD, *a.*
ẠD-DRĔSS', *v. a.* To speak, apply, or direct to.
ẠD-DRĔSS', *n.* A speech; petition; courtship;
skill; dexterity; direction, as of a letter.
ẠD-DRĔSS'ĘR, *n.* The person who addresses.
ẠD-DŪCE', *v. a.* To bring forward; to allege.
ẠD-DŪ'CĘNT, *a.* Drawing together.
ẠD-DŪ'CĬ-BLE, *a.* That may be adduced.
ẠD-DŬC'TIǪN, *n.* The act of adducing.
ẠD-DŬC'TĬVE, *a.* That brings forward.
Ạ-DĔMP'TIǪN, *n.* A taking away; privation.
ĂD-Ę-NŎG'RẠ-PHY, *n.* A treatise on the glands.
Ạ-DĔPT', *n.* One well versed in any art.
Ạ-DĔPT', *a.* Skilful; thoroughly versed.
ĂD'Ę-QUA-CY, *n.* Sufficiency; enough.
ĂD'Ę-QUẠTE, *a.* Equal; proportionate.
ĂD'Ę-QUẠTE-LY, *ad.* In an adequate manner.
ĂD'Ę-QUẠTE-NĔSS, *n.* State of being adequate.
ẠD-HĒRE', *v. n.* To stick; to remain fixed.
ẠD-HĒR'ĘNCE, } *n.* The quality of adhering;
ẠD-HĒR'ĘN-CY, } attachment; tenacity; fidel-
ẠD-HĒR'ĘNT, *a.* Sticking; adhering. [ity.
ẠD-HĒR'ĘNT, } *n.* One who adheres; a disci-
ẠD-HĒR'ĘR, } ple; a follower.
ẠD-HĒR'ĘNT-LY, *ad.* In an adherent manner.
ẠD-HĒ'ṢIǪN (ạd-hē'zhụn), *n.* Act of adhering.
ẠD-HĒ'ṢĬVE, *a.* Sticking; tenacious; viscous.
ẠD-HĒ'ṢĬVE-LY, *ad.* In an adhesive manner.

AD-HĔ′SĮVE-NĔSS, *n.* Tenacity ; viscosity.
ĂD-HǪR-TĀ′TIǪN, *n.* Advice ; act of advising.
ĂD-Į-ĂPH′Ǫ-ROŬS, *a.* Neutral ; indifferent.
Ą-DIEŪ′ (ą-dū′), *ad.* Farewell ; good-by.
Ą-DIEŪ′ (ą-dū′), *n.* A farewell ; a valediction.
ĂD′Į-PŌSE, *or* ĂD′Į-POŬS, *a.* Fat ; fatty.
ĂD′ĮT, *n.* A passage for water under ground.
AD-JĀ′CĘN-CY, *n.* The state of lying close to.
AD-JĀ′CĘNT, *a.* Lying near ; contiguous.
ĂD′JĘC-TĬV-ĄL, *a.* Pertaining to an adjective ; partaking of the nature of an adjective.
ĂD′JĘC-TĬVE, *n.* A word added to a noun, to express some quality ; as, *good, bad,* &c.
ĂD′JĘC-TĬVE-LY, *ad.* As an adjective.
AD-JŎĬN′, *v. a.* To join ; to unite or put to.
AD-JŎĬN′, *v. n.* To be contiguous ; to lie near.
AD-JOŬRN′ (ąd-jürn′), *v. a.* To put off, postpone.
AD-JOŬRN′MĘNT (ąd-jürn′męnt), *n.* A putting off till another time ; postponement ; delay.
AD-JŬDĢE′, *v. a.* To award ; to decree ; to deem.
AD-JŪ′DĮ-CĀTE, *v. n.* To pass judgment.
AD-JŪ′DĮ-CĀTE, *v. a.* To adjudge ; to sentence.
AD-JŪ-DĮ-CĀ′TIǪN, *n.* The act of adjudicating.
ĂD′JŬNCT, *n.* Something joined ; addition.
ĂD′JŬNCT, *a.* United ; joined ; adjoined.
AD-JŬNC′TIǪN, *n.* Act of adjoining ; addition.
AD-JŬNC′TĮVE, *n.* That which is joined.
AD-JŬNC′TĮVE, *a.* That joins ; joining.
ĂD-JŲ-RĀ′TIǪN, *n.* The act of adjuring.
AD-JŪRE′, *v. a.* To charge on oath or earnestly.
AD-JŬST′, *v. a.* To regulate ; to put in order.
AD-JŬST′MĘNT, *n.* Regulation ; settlement.
ĂD′JŲ-TĂN-CY, *n.* The office of an adjutant.
ĂD′JŲ-TĂNT, *n.* A military officer ; an assistant.
ĂD′JŲ-VĂNT, *a.* Helpful ; assisting ; useful.
AD-MĔAṢ′ŲRE-MĔNT (ąd-mĕzh′ụr-mĕnt), *n.* The act or result of measuring ; measure.
AD-MĔN-SŲ-RĀ′TIǪN, *n.* The act of measuring.
AD-MĬN′ĮS-TĘR, *v. a.* To supply ; to afford ; to direct ; to tender : — to act as administrator of.
AD-MĬN′ĮS-TĘR, *v. n.* To contribute ; to conduce ; to act as administrator of an estate. [tion.
AD-MĬN′ĮS-TRĄ-BLE, *a.* Capable of administra-
ĂD-MĮN-ĮS-TRĀ′TIǪN, *n.* Act of administering ; the executive part of government ; cabinet.
AD-MĬN′ĮS-TRĄ-TĬVE, *a.* That administers.
ĂD-MĮN-ĮS-TRĀ′TǪR, *n.* He who has the charge of the estate of a man dying intestate. [trator.
ĂD-MĮN-ĮS-TRĀ′TǪR-SHĬP, *n.* Office of adminis-
ĂD-MĮN-ĮS-TRĀ′TRĬX, *n.* She who administers.
ĂD-MĮ-RĄ-BĬL′Į-TY, *n.* Admirableness.
ĂD′MĮ-RĄ-BLE, *a.* Worthy of being admired.
ĂD′MĮ-RĄ-BLE-NĔSS, *n.* Admirable quality.
ĂD′MĮ-RĄ-BLY, *ad.* So as to raise wonder.
ĂD′MĮ-RĄL, *n.* The chief commander of a fleet.
ĂD′MĮ-RĄL-SHĬP, *n.* The office of an admiral.
ĂD′MĮ-RĄL-TY, *n.* The court or persons appointed for the administration of naval affairs.
ĂD-MĮ-RĀ′TIǪN, *n.* Act of admiring ; wonder.
AD-MĪRE′, *v. a.* To regard with wonder or love.
AD-MĪR′ĘR, *n.* One who admires ; a lover.
AD-MĬS′SĮ-BLE, *a.* That may be admitted.
AD-MĬS′SĮ-BLY, *ad.* In an admissible manner.
AD-MĬS′SIǪN (ąd-mĭsh′un), *n.* The act of admitting ; admittance ; entrance. [permit.
AD-MĬT′, *v. a.* To suffer to enter ; to grant ; to
AD-MĬT′TĮ-BLE, *a.* Capable of being admitted.
AD-MĬT′TĄNCE, *n.* Act of admitting ; entrance.

AD-MĬX′, *v. a.* To mingle ; to mix ; to blend.
AD-MĬX′TIǪN (ąd-mĭks′chụn), *n.* A mingling.
AD-MĬXT′ŲRE (ąd-mĭkst′yụr), *n.* Mixture.
AD-MŎN′ĮSH, *v. a.* To warn, reprove, advise.
AD-MŎN′ĮSH-ĘR, *n.* One who admonishes.
ĂD-MǪ-NĬ′′TIǪN (ăd-mǫ-nĭsh′un), *n.* The hint of a fault or duty ; gentle reproof or reprimand.
AD-MŎN′Į-TĬVE, *a.* Giving admonition.
AD-MŎN′Į-TǪ-RY, *a.* That admonishes.
AD-NĂS′CĘNT, *a.* Growing to something else.
Ą-DÔ′, *n.* Trouble ; difficulty ; bustle ; tumult.
ĂD-Ǫ-LĔS′CĘNCE, ⎰ *n.* The age between child-
ĂD-Ǫ-LĔS′CĘN-CY, ⎱ hood and manhood.
ĂD-Ǫ-LĔS′CĘNT, *a.* Relating to adolescence.
Ą-DŎPT′, *v. a.* To take as one's own.
Ą-DŎPT′ĘR, *n.* One who adopts : — a distilling
Ą-DŎP′TIǪN, *n.* The act of adopting. [vessel.
Ą-DŎP′TĮVE, *a.* That adopts or is adopted.
Ą-DŌR′Ą-BLE, *a.* Worthy of adoration ; divine.
Ą-DŌR′Ą-BLE-NĔSS, *n.* Worthiness of adoration.
Ą-DŌR′Ą-BLY, *ad.* In an adorable manner.
ĂD-Ǫ-RĀ′TIǪN, *n.* Divine worship ; homage.
Ą-DŌRE′, *v. a.* To worship ; to reverence ; to
Ą-DŌR′ĘR, *n.* One who adores ; a lover. [love.
Ą-DŌRN′, *v. a.* To dress, decorate, embellish.
Ą-DRĬFT′, *ad.* Floating at random, as a ship.
Ą-DRŎĬT′, *a.* Dexterous ; active ; skilful.
Ą-DRŎĬT′LY, *ad.* Dexterously ; skilfully.
Ą-DRŎĬT′NĔSS, *n.* Dexterity ; skill ; activity.
Ą-DRȲ′, *a.* Thirsty ; in want of drink.
ĂD-SCĮ-TĬ′′TIOŲS (ăd-sę-tĭsh′ụs), *a.* Additional.
ĂD-Ų-LĀ′TIǪN, *n.* Excessive flattery or praise.
ĂD′Ų-LĄ-TǪ-RY, *a.* Flattering ; complimental.
Ą-DŬLT′, *a.* Grown up ; of mature age.
Ą-DŬLT′, *n.* A person grown to maturity.
Ą-DŬLT′NĔSS, *n.* The state of being adult.
Ą-DŬL′TĘR-ĂNT, *n.* That which adulterates.
Ą-DŬL′TĘR-ĀTE, *v. a.* To corrupt ; to debase.
Ą-DŬL′TĘR-ĀTE, *a.* Corrupted ; spurious.
Ą-DŬL′TĘR-ĀTE-LY, *ad.* In an adulterate manner.
Ą-DŬL′TĘR-ĀTE-NĔSS, *n.* Spuriousness. [ner.
Ą-DŬL′TĘR-Ā′TIǪN, *n.* Act of adulterating.
Ą-DŬL′TĘR-ĘR, *n.* A person guilty of adultery.
Ą-DŬL′TĘR-ĔSS, *n.* She who commits adultery.
Ą DŬL′TĘR-ĪNE, *n.* A child of an adulteress.
Ą-DŬL′TĘR-ĪNE, *a.* Spurious ; adulterous.
Ą-DŬL′TĘR-OŬS, *a.* Guilty of, or tainted by, adultery ; spurious ; corrupt ; adulterate.
Ą-DŬL′TĘR-Y, *n.* Violation of the marriage bed.
AD-ŬM′BRĄNT, *a.* Giving a slight resemblance.
AD-ŬM′BRĀTE, *v. a.* To shadow out faintly.
ĂD-ŲM-BRĀ′TIǪN, *n.* A faint sketch ; a shadow.
Ą-DŪN′CĮ-TY, *n.* Crookedness ; form of a hook.
Ą-DŪST′, *or* Ą-DŬST′ĘD, *a.* Scorched.
Ą-DŪS′TIǪN, *n.* Act of burning up or drying.
AD-VĂNCE′, *v. a.* To bring forward ; to raise ; to heighten ; to propose ; to pay beforehand.
AD-VĂNCE′, *v. n.* To go forward ; to rise.
AD-VĂNCE′, *n.* A going forward ; progression ; improvement ; rise ; anticipation of time.
AD-VĂNCE′MĘNT, *n.* Improvement ; promotion.
AD-VĂN′CĘR, *n.* One who advances.
AD-VĂN′TĄGE, *n.* Superiority ; benefit ; gain.
AD-VĂN′TĄGE, *v. a.* To benefit ; to promote.
AD-VĂN′TĄGE-GROŬND, *n.* Ground or position that gives superiority ; vantage-ground.
ĂD-VĂN-TĀ′ĢEOŲS (ăd-vąn-tā′jụs), *a.* Affording advantages ; beneficial ; profitable ; useful.

MîEN, SĬR ; MÔVE, NÖR, SŎN ; BÛLL, BÜR, RÛLE.—Ç, Ģ, *soft* ; Ɛ, Ǥ, *hard* ; Ṣ *as* Z ; Ӿ *as* gz ; ŦHIS.

ĂD-VĂN-TĀ'ǴEOŲS-LỸ, *ad.* Profitably.
ĂD-VĂN-TĀ'ǴEOUS-NĔSS, *n.* Profitableness.
ĄD-VĒNE', *v. n.* To accede ; to come.
ĂD'VĘNT, *n.* A coming ; the coming of Christ ; the four weeks before Christmas. [dental.
ĂD-VĘN-TĬ''TIOŲS (ăd-vĕn-tĭsh'ŭs), *a.* Acci-
ĂD-VĘN-TĬ''TIOŲS-LỸ, *ad.* Accidentally.
ĄD-VĔN'TĪVE, *a.* Adventitious ; coming to.
ĄD-VĔNT'Ų-ĄL, *a.* Relating to the advent.
ĄD-VĔNT'ŲRE (ąd-vĕnt'yŭr), *n.* An accident ; a chance ; a hazard ; enterprise ; speculation.
ĄD-VĔNT'ŲRE, *v. n.* To try the chance ; to dare.
ĄD-VĔNT'ŲRE, *v. a.* To risk ; to hazard.
ĄD VĔNT'ŲR-ĘR, *n.* One who adventures.
ĄD-VĔNT'ŲRE-SŎME, *a.* Adventurous ; bold.
ĄD-VĔNT'ŲR-OŬS, *a.* Bold ; daring ; courageous.
ĄD-VĔNT'ŲR-OŬS-LỸ, *ad.* Boldly ; daringly.
ĂD'VĘRB, *n.* (*Gram.*) A word joined to a verb or adjective to modify its sense.
ĄD-VĔR'BĪ-ĄL, *a.* Pertaining to an adverb.
ĄD-VĔR'BĪ-ĄL-LỸ, *ad.* In an adverbial manner.
ĂD'VĘR-SĄ-RỸ, *n.* An opponent ; enemy.
ĂD'VĘR-SĄ-RỸ, *a.* Opposite to ; adverse.
ĄD-VĔR'SĄ-TĪVE, *a.* Noting opposition.
ĂD'VĘRSE, *a.* Contrary ; calamitous ; opposite.
ĄD-VĔR'SĪ-TỸ, *n.* Affliction ; misfortune.
ĂD'VĘRSE-LỸ, *ad.* Oppositely ; unfortunately.
ĄD-VĔRT', *v. n.* To turn or attend ; to regard.
ĄD-VĔR'TĘNCE, *or* ĄD-VĔR'TĘN-CỸ, *n.* Regard.
ĄD-VĔR'TĘNT, *a.* Attentive ; heedful.
ĂD-VĘR-TĪSE', *v. a.* To inform ; to give notice to ; to inform ; to announce ; to offer for sale.
ĄD-VĔR'TĪSE-MĔNT *or* ĂD-VĘR-TĪSE'MĘNT, *n.* Information ; admonition ; public notice.
ĂD-VĘR-TĪS'ĘR, *n.* One who advertises.
ĄD-VĪCE', *n.* Counsel ; instruction ; notice.
ĄD-VĪṢ'Ą-BLE, *a.* Prudent ; expedient ; fit.
ĄD-VĪṢ'Ą-BLE-NĔSS, *n.* Propriety ; fitness.
ĄD-VĪṢE', *v. a.* To counsel, inform, consult.
ĄD-VĪṢE', *v. n.* To consult ; to deliberate.
ĄD-VĪṢ'ĘD-LỸ, *ad.* Deliberately ; heedfully.
ĄD-VĪṢ'ĘD-NĔSS, *n.* Deliberation.
ĄD-VĪṢ'MĘNT, *n.* Counsel ; information.
ĄD-VĪṢ'ĘR, *n.* One who advises ; a counsellor.
ĂD'VŌ-CĀTE, *v. a.* To plead for ; to defend.
ĂD'VŌ-CĄTE, *n.* One who pleads for another.
ĂD-VŌ-CĀ'TIǪN, *n.* Act of pleading ; defence.
ĂD-VŎW-ĒĒ', *n.* He that has advowson.
ĄD-VŎW'ṢǪN (ąd-vŏŭ'zŭn), *n.* A right to present to a church or ecclesiastical benefice.
ĂDZE, *or* ĂD'DĪCE, *n.* A tool to cut surfaçes.
Æ'DĪLE (ē'dĪl), *n.* A Roman magistrate.
Æ'ǴĪL-ŎPS (ē'jĪl-ŏps), *n.* An abscess ; a plant.
Æ'ǴĪS (ē'jĬs), *n.* A shield : — affection of the eye.
Æ-Ō'LĪ-ĄN-HĂRP, *n.* A stringed musical instrument played upon by the wind.
Ā-Ē'RĪ-ĄL, *a.* Belonging to the air ; high ; lofty.
AĒ'RIĘ (ē're *or* ā'e-re), *n.* A nest of eagles, &c.
Ā'E-RĪ-FŌRM, *a.* Having the form of air.
Ā-Ē-RŎG'RĄ-PHỸ, *n.* A description of the air.
Ā'E-RŌ-LĪTE, *n.* A meteoric stone ; meteorite.
Ā-Ē-RŎL'Ọ-ǴỸ, *n.* The science of the air.
Ā'E-RǪ-MĂN-CỸ, *n.* Divination by the air.
Ā-Ē-RŎM'E-TĘR, *n.* A machine for weighing air.
Ā-Ē-RŎM'E-TRỸ, *n.* The art of measuring the air.
Ā'E-RǪ-NÂUT, *n.* One who sails in the air.
Ā-Ē-RǪ-NÂUT'ĬCS, *n.* Sailing in air ; ballooning.
Ā-Ē-RǪ-NÂUT', *a.* Pertaining to aëronautics.

Ā-Ē-RǪS-TĀ'TIǪN, *n.* The art or the science of weighing air : — aëronautics.
ÆS-THĔT'ĬCS (ęs-thĕt'ĭks), *n.* The science which treats of the beautiful, or of the fine arts.
Ą-FÄR', *ad.* At a great distance ; remotely ; far.
ĂF-FĄ-BĬL'Ĭ-TỸ, *n.* The quality of being affable.
ĂF'FĄ-BLE, *a.* Easy of access ; courteous.
ĂF'FĄ-BLE-NĔSS, *n.* Courtesy ; affability. [ly.
ĂF'FĄ-BLỸ, *ad.* In an affable manner ; courteous-
ĄF-FÀIR', *n.* Business ; concern ; transaction.
ĄF-FĔCT', *v. a.* To act upon ; to move.
ĂF-FĘC-TĀ'TIǪN, *n.* False pretence or show.
ĄF-FĔCT'ĘD, *p. a.* Moved : — full of affectation.
ĄF-FĔCT'ĘD-LỸ, *ad.* In an affected manner.
ĄF-FĔCT'ĘD-NĔSS, *n.* Quality of being affected.
ĄF-FĔCT'ĘR, *n.* One who practises affectation.
ĄF-FĔCT'ĮNG, *p. a.* Moving the passions.
ĄF-FĔCT'ĮNG-LỸ, *ad.* In an affecting manner.
ĄF-FĔC'TIǪN, *n.* Desire ; love ; tenderness. [kind.
ĄF-FĔC'TIǪN-ĄTE, *a.* Warm ; fond ; tender ;
ĄF-FĔC'TIǪN-ĄTE-LỸ, *ad.* Kindly ; tenderly.
ĄF-FĔC'TIǪN-ĄTE-NĔSS, *n.* Fondness ; tender-
ĄF-FĔC'TĮVE, *a.* That affects ; moving. [ness.
ĄF-FĔC'TĮVE-LỸ, *ad.* In an impressive manner.
ĄF-FĪ'ĄNCE, *n.* A marriage contract ; trust.
ĄF-FĪ'ĄNCE, *v. a.* To betroth ; to pledge.
ĄF-FĪ'ĄN-CĘR, *n.* One who affiances.
ĂF-FĮ-DĀ'VĬT, *n.* A written declaration on oath.
ĄF-FĬL'Ĭ-ĀTE, *v. a.* To adopt ; to associate with.
ĄF-FĬL-Ĭ-Ā'TIǪN, *n.* The adoption of a son.
ĂF'FĮ-NĄGE, *n.* Refining of metals by the cupel.
ĄF-FĬN'Į-TỸ, *n.* Relation by marriage ; likeness.
ĄF-FĬRM', *v. n.* To declare positively ; to assert.
ĄF-FĬRM', *v. a.* To ratify ; to assert ; to allege.
ĄF-FĬRM'Ą-BLE, *a.* Capable of being affirmed.
ĄF-FĬRM'ĄNCE, *n.* Confirmation ; declaration.
ĂF-FĬR-MĀ'TIǪN, *n.* A solemn declaration.
ĄF-FĬRM'Ą-TĪVE, *a.* That affirms ; positive.
ĄF-FĬRM'Ą-TĪVE-LỸ, *ad.* In an affirmative man-
ĄF-FĬRM'ĘR, *n.* The person who affirms. [ner.
ĄF-FĬX', *v. a.* To unite ; to subjoin ; to fix.
ĂF'FĮX, *n.* Something added to a word.
ĄF-FLĀ'TIǪN, *n.* The act of breathing upon.
ĄF-FLĀ'TŲS, *n.* Divine inspiration.
ĄF-FLĬCT', *v. a.* To put to pain ; to grieve.
ĄF-FLĬCT'ĘD-NĔSS, *n.* The state of affliction.
ĄF-FLĬCT'ĘR, *n.* One who afflicts. [grief.
ĄF-FLĬC'TIǪN, *n.* Calamity ; sorrow ; distress ;
ĄF-FLĬC'TĮVE, *a.* Painful ; calamitous.
ĄF-FLĬC'TĮVE-LỸ, *ad.* In an afflicting manner.
ĂF'FLŲ-ĘNCE, *n.* Riches ; plenty ; abundance.
ĂF'FLŲ-ĘNT, *a.* Abundant ; wealthy ; rich.
ĂF'FLŲX, *or* ĄF-FLŬX'IǪN, *n.* A flowing to.
ĄF-FŌRD', *v. a.* To yield or produce ; to grant.
ĄF-FŎR'ĘST, *v. a.* To turn into forest. [free.
ĄF-FRĂN'CHĪSE (ąf-frăn'chĬz), *v. a.* To make
ĄF-FRĂN'CHĪSE'MĘNT, *n.* Act of making free.
ĄF-FRĀY', *n.* A quarrel ; disturbance ; tumult.
ĄF-FRĪGHT' (ąf-frīt'), *v. a.* To alarm ; to terrify.
ĄF-FRĪGHT' (ąf-frīt'), *n.* Terror ; fear ; fright.
ĄF-FRŎNT' (ąf-frŭnt'), *v. a.* To insult ; to offend.
ĄF-FRŎNT' (ąf-frŭnt'), *n.* Insult ; outrage.
ĄF-FRŎNT'ĘR (ąf-frŭnt'ęr), *n.* One who affronts.
ĄF-FRŎNT'ĮVE, *a.* Causing affront ; abusive.
ĄF-FŪSE', *v. a.* To pour upon ; to sprinkle.
ĄF-FŪ'ṢIǪN (ąf-fū'zhun), *n.* Act of pouring upon.
ĄF-FỸ', *v. a.* To betroth ; to bind ; to join.
Ą-FĪELD' (ą-fēld'), *ad.* To the field ; in the field.

Ă,Ĕ,Ĭ,Ō,Ū,Ỹ, *long ;* Ă,Ĕ,Ĭ,Ŏ,Ŭ,Ў, *short ;* Ą,Ę,Į,Ǫ,Ų,Ỵ, *obscure.*— FÀRE,FÄR,FĂST,FÂLL ; HÊIR,HĔR ;

A-FLŌAT' (a-flŏt'), *ad.* In a floating state.
A-FOOT' (a-fůt'), *ad.* On foot; in motion.
A-FŌRE', *ad.* In time past; before; in front.
A-FŌRE'SAID (a-fōr'sĕd), *a.* Said before.
A-FŌRE'TIME, *ad.* In time past; formerly.
A-FRĀID' (a-frād'), *a.* Struck with fear.
A-FRĔSH', *ad.* Anew; over again; newly.
AFT, *ad.* Towards the stern of a vessel. [to.
AF'TER, *prep.* Later than; behind; according
AF'TER, *ad.* In succeeding time.—*a.* Succeeding.
AF'TER-CLAP, *n.* A subsequent event.
AF'TER-CROP, *n.* The second crop.
AF'TER-MATH, *n.* Second crop of grass.
AF'TER-NOON, *n.* Time from noon to evening.
AF'TER-PIECE (af'ter-pēs), *n.* A farce. [thought.
AF'TER-THOUGHT (af'ter-thawt), *n.* Later
AF'TER-WARD (af'ter-wurd),) *ad.* In succeed-
AF'TER-WARDS (af'ter-wurdz),) ing time.
AF'TER-WIT, *n.* Contrivance too late; after-
A'GA, *n.* A Turkish title of dignity. [thought.
A-GAIN' (a-gĕn'), *ad.* A second time; once more.
A-GAINST' (a-gĕnst'), *prep.* In opposition to;
in contradiction to; resting or leaning on.
A-GAPE' (a-găp'), *ad.* Staring with eagerness.
AG'ATE, *n.* A precious stone of a low class.
AG'A-TY, *a.* Pertaining to, or resembling, agate.
A-GĀ'VE, *n.* American aloe; century-plant.
AGE, *n.* A period of time; a generation of men;
a number of years; century; maturity; old age.
A'GED (ā'jed), *a.* Old; stricken in years.
A'GEN-CY, *n.* Action; action for another.
A'GENT, *n.* One who acts; a deputy; a factor.
AG-GE-LA'TION, *n.* Concretion into ice.
AG-GLŎM'ER-ĀTE, *v. a.* To gather up in a ball.
AG-GLŎM-ER-Ā'TION, *n.* A close gathering.
AG-GLŪ'TI-NANT, *a.* Uniting parts together.
AG-GLŪ'TI-NĀTE, *v. a.* To cause to adhere.
AG-GLŪ-TI-NĀ'TION, *n.* Union; cohesion.
AG'GRAN-DĪZE, *v. a.* To make great; to exalt.
AG'GRAN-DĪZE-MĔNT *or* AG-GRAN'DĪZE-
MĔNT, *n.* Act of aggrandizing; exaltation.
AG'GRAN-DĪ-ZER, *n.* One who aggrandizes.
AG'GRA-VĀTE, *v. a.* To make worse; to enhance.
AG-GRA-VĀ'TION, *n.* The act of aggravating.
AG'GRE-GATE, *a.* Formed of parts collected.
AG'GRE-GATE, *n.* The sum of parts collected.
AG'GRE-GATE, *v. a.* To accumulate. [ing.
AG-GRE-GA'TION, *n.* Collection; act of collect-
AG'GRE-GA-TIVE, *a.* Taken together. [olence.
AG-GRESS', *v. n.* To commit the first act of vi-
AG-GRES'SION (ag-grĕsh'un), *n.* The first injury.
AG-GRES'SIVE, *a.* Making the first attack.
AG-GRES'SOR, *n.* One who commences hostility.
AG-GRIE'VANCE (ag-grē'vans), *n.* Injury.
AG-GRIEVE', *v. a.* To give sorrow; to vex.
AG-GROUP' (ag-grōp'), *v. a.* To bring together.
A-GHAST', *a.* Struck with horror; amazed.
AG'ILE, *a.* Active; nimble; ready; brisk.
AG'ILE-NĔSS, *n.* Nimbleness; agility.
A-GIL'I-TY, *n.* Nimbleness; quickness; activity.
A'GI-Ō *or* AG'I-Ō, *n.* The difference between
the bank notes and current coin of any place.
AG'I-TA-BLE, *a.* That may be agitated.
AG'I-TĀTE, *v. a.* To put in motion; to discuss.
AG-I-TĀ'TION, *n.* Disturbance; violent motion.
AG'I-TĀ-TOR, *n.* One who agitates; disturber.
AG'NATE, *a.* Allied; akin from the father.
AG-NĀ'TION, *n.* Descent from the same father.

AG-NŌ'MEN, *n.* An additional name given to a
person from some event or illustrious action.
AG-NŎM-I-NĀ'TION, *n.* An additional name.
A-GŌ', *ad.* In time past; since; past.
A-GŎG', *ad.* In a state of desire. [*A low word.*]
A-GŌ'ING, *p. a.* Being in action; moving.
AG'O-NĬSM (ăg'o-nĭzm), *n.* Contention for a prize.
AG-O-NĬS'TIC,) *a.* Relating to prize-fight-
AG-O-NĬS'TI-CAL,) ing. [agony.
AG'O-NĪZE, *v. a. & n.* To afflict with, or be in,
AG'O-NY, *n.* Violent pain; suffering; anguish.
A-GRĀ'RI-AN, *a.* Relating to fields or grounds.
A-GRĒĒ', *v. n.* To be in concord; to concur.
A-GRĒĒ'A-BLE, *a.* Suitable; pleasing.
A-GRĒĒ'A-BLE-NĔSS, *n.* Quality of pleasing.
A-GRĒĒ'A-BLY, *ad.* Consistently; pleasingly.
A-GRĒĒD', *p. a.* Settled by consent; in concord.
A-GRĒĒ'MENT, *n.* Concord; compact; bargain.
A-GRĔS'TIC, *or* A-GRĔS'TI-CAL, *a.* Rustic.
AG-RI-CŬLT'U-RAL, *a.* Relating to agriculture.
AG'RI-CŬLT-URE (ăg're-kŭlt-yur), *n.* The art
of cultivating the ground; husbandry.
AG-RI-CŬLT'U-RIST, *n.* One skilled in agricul-
AG'RI-MO-NY, *n.* A perennial herb. [ture.
A-GROŪND', *ad.* On the ground, as a vessel.
A'GŪE (ā'gu), *n.* An intermitting fever, with
A'GU-ĬSH, *a.* Partaking of ague. [cold fits.
A'GŲ-ĬSH-NĔSS, *n.* Resemblance to an ague.
ÄH (ä), *int.* Noting dislike, surprise, or pity.
A-HÄ', *int.* Expressing triumph and contempt.
A-HĔAD', *ad.* Farther on; onward; on.
ĀID (ād), *v. a.* To help; to assist; to relieve.
ĀID (ād), *n.* Help; support; a helper.
AIDE-DE-CAMP (ād'de-kàwng'), *n.*; pl. AIDES-
DE-CAMP. A military officer employed under
AID'LĔSS (ād'les), *a.* Helpless. [a general.
AI'GRET (ā'gret), *n.* The egret or heron.
AI'GU-LĔT (ā'gu-let), *n.* A tag at the end of fringe.
ĀIL (āl), *v. a.* To pain; to trouble; to annoy.
ĀIL (āl), *v. n.* To be in pain or trouble.
ĀIL'ING (āl'ing), *p. a.* Sickly; morbid.
ĀIL'MENT (āl'ment), *n.* Pain; disease.
ĀIM (ām), *v. n.* To direct; to strive; to point.
ĀIM (ām), *v. a.* To direct, as a missile weapon.
ĀIM (ām), *n.* Direction; endeavor; design.
ĀIM'LĔSS (ām'les), *a.* Without aim or object.
ĀIR (âr), *n.* The element in which we breathe;
gentle wind:—mien of a person; aspect:—tune.
ĀIR (âir), *v. a.* To expose to the air; to warm.
ĀIR'-BAL-LOON, *n.* See BALLOON.
ĀIR'BUILT (âr'bilt), *a.* Constructed in the air.
ĀIR'DRÂWN, *a.* Drawn in air; visionary.
ĀIR'GŬN, *n.* A gun discharged by air.
ĀIR'I-NĔSS, *n.* Exposure to the air; gayety.
ĀIR'ING, *n.* Exposure to, or admission of, the air.
ĀIR'PŬMP, *n.* An apparatus by which the air is
exhausted from closed vessels.
ĀIR'SHÂFT, *n.* A passage for the air into mines.
ĀIR'Y, *a.* Relating to the air; gay; sprightly.
AISLE (īl), *n.* A walk or passage in a church.
ĀKE, *v. n.* See ACHE.
A-KĬN', *a.* Related; allied by nature; kindred.
ĂL'A-BĂS-TER, *n.* A kind of soft, white stone.
ĂL'A-BĂS-TER, *a.* Made of alabaster.
A-LĂCK', *int.* Alas; noting sorrow. [choly.
A-LĂCK'A-DĀY, *int.* Noting sorrow and melan-
A-LĂC'RI-TY, *n.* Cheerfulness; liveliness.
ĂL-A-MŌDE', *ad.* According to the fashion.

ĂL'Ạ-MŌDE, *n.* A thin silk stuff.
Ạ-LÄRM', *n.* A cry of danger; sudden terror.
Ạ-LÄRM', *v. a.* To call to arms; to excite fear in.
Ạ-LÄRM'-BĔLL, *n.* A bell rung noting danger.
Ạ-LÄRM'ĮNG, *p. a.* Terrifying; giving alarm.
Ạ-LÄRM'ĮST, *n.* One who excites an alarm.
Ạ-LÄ'RŲM, *n.* An alarm clock; alarm.
Ạ-LĂS', *int.* Expressing lamentation or pity.
ĀLB, *n.* A Roman Catholic priest's surplice.
ĂL'BẠ-TRÖSS, *n.* A large web-footed bird.
ÂL-BĒ'ĮT, *ad.* Although; notwithstanding.
ẠL-BĪ'NŌ, *n.* A person unnaturally white.
ĂL-BŲ-ĢĬN'Ẹ-OŬS, *a.* Like the white of an egg.
ĂL'BŲM, *n.* A book for inserting autographs, &c.
ẠL-BŪ'MĘN, *n.* The white of an egg. [wood.
ẠL-BÜR'NŲM, *n.* The white or softer part of
ẠL-CĀĪD', *n.* An officer in Barbary and Spain.
ẠL-ЄHĔM'Į-CẠL, *a.* Relating to alchemy.
ĂL'ЄHẸ-MĬST, *n.* One versed in alchemy. [mist.
ĂL-ЄHẸ-MĬS'TĮ-CẠL, *a.* Acting like an alche-
ĂL'ЄHẸ-MY, *n.* Occult chemistry; the pretended
  art of changing metals into gold and silver.
ĂL'CỌ-HŎL, *n.* Pure or highly-rectified spirit.
ĂL-CỌ-HŎL'ĮC, *a.* Relating to alcohol.
ĂL'CỌ-HỌ-LĪZE, *v. a.* To convert into alcohol.
ĂL'CỌ-RĂN, *n.* The Mahometan book of faith.
ĂL-CỌ-RĂN'ĮC, *a.* Relating to the Alcoran.
ẠL-CŌVE', *n.* A recess; a niche; an arbor.
ÂL'DĘR, *n.* A tree resembling the hazel.
ÂL'DĘR-MĂN, *n.* A magistrate in a corporation.
ĀLE, *n.* A fermented malt liquor.
Ạ-LĔC'TRY-Ọ-MĂN-CY, *n.* Divination by a cock.
ĀLE'HŎÔF, *n.* A species of ground-ivy.
ĀLE'HŎÛSE, *n.* A house where ale is sold.
Ạ-LĔM'BĮC, *n.* A vessel used in distilling.
Ạ-LĔRT', *a.* On guard; watchful; brisk; pert.
Ạ-LĔRT'NẸSS, *n.* Sprightliness; pertness.
ĀLE'WĪFE, *n.* A fish; a species of herring. [bles.
ĂL-ẸX-ĂN'DRĮNE, *n.* A verse of twelve sylla-
Ạ-LĔX-Į-PHÄR'MĮC, *a.* Counteracting poison.
Ạ-LĔX-Į-TĔR'ĮC,   *a.* Antidotal; counteract-
Ạ-LĔX-Į-TĔR'Į-CẠL,   ing poison.
ĂL'ĢẸ-BRẠ, *n.* A peculiar kind of arithmetic.
ĂL-ĢẸ-BRĂ'ĮC,   *a.* Relating to algebra;
ĂL-ĢẸ-BRĂ'Į-CẠL, performed by algebra.
ĂL'ĢẸ-BRĀ-ĮST, *n.* One versed in algebra.
ĂL'GỌ-RĬŞM,   *n.* The art of computation by
ĂL'GỌ-RĬTHM, numeral figures.
Ā'LĮ-ĂS, *ad.* [L.] Otherwise.—*n.* A kind of writ.
ĂL'Į-BĪ, *n.* [L.] (*Law.*) In another place.
ĀL'IĘN (āl'yẹn), *a.* Foreign; estranged.
ĀL'IĘN (āl'yẹn), *n.* A foreigner; a stranger.
ĀL'IĘN-Ạ-BLE (āl'yẹn-ạ-bl), *a.* Transferable.
ĀL'IĘN-ĀTE (āl'yẹn-āt), *v. a.* To transfer or
  deliver to another, as property; to estrange.
ĀL-IĘN-Ā'TIỌN (āl-yẹn-ā'shụn), *n.* The act of
  alienating; transfer: — mental derangement.
ĀL'IĘN-Ā-TỌR, *n.* One who transfers or alienates.
Ạ-LĪGHT' (ạ-līt'), *v. n.* To descend; to dismount.
Ạ-LĪKE', *a. & ad.* With resemblance; equally.
ĂL'Į-MĔNT, *n.* Nourishment; food; nutriment.
ĂL-Į-MĔNT'ẠL, *a.* Nutritious; nourishing.
ĂL-Į-MĔNT'Ạ-RY, *a.* Belonging to aliment.
ĂL-Į-MĘN-TĀ'TIỌN, *n.* Act of nourishing.
ĂL-Į-MŎ'NĮ-OŬS, *a.* Nourishing; supporting.
ĂL'Į-MỌ-NY, *n.* Allowance to a married woman,
  on a legal separation from her husband.
ĂL'Į-QUĂNT, *a.* Noting such parts of a number

as do not measure it exactly, or without a re-
  mainder; as, 3 is an aliquant part of 10.
ĂL'Į-QUŎT, *a.* Noting such parts of a number
  as will exactly measure it.
Ạ-LĪVE', *a.* Not dead; active; sprightly.
ĂL'KẠ-HĔST, *n.* A universal solvent.
ĂL'KẠ-LĮ *or* ĂL'KẠ-LĪ, *n.* (*Chem.*) A substance
  forming neutral salts with acids.
ĂL'KẠ-LĪNE, *a.* Having qualities of alkali.
ẠL-KĒR'MĘŞ, *n.* Confection made of kermes.
ÂLL, *a.* The whole; every one; every part.
ÂLL, *n.* The whole; every thing. [*All* is much
  used in composition: it adds force to the word;
  as, *all*-honored, *all*-conquering, &c.]
ÂLL, *ad.* Quite; completely; wholly; entirely.
ÂLL-FÔÔL'Ş-DĀY', *n.* The first of April.
ÂLL-FŌURŞ' (âl-fōrz'), *n.* A game at cards.
ÂLL-HĀĪL' (âl-hāl'), *int.* All health; a salutation.
ÂLL-HĂL'LỌWŞ (âl-hăl'lọz), *n.* All-saints-day.
ÂLL-HĂL'LỌW-MẠSS, ÂLL-HĂL'LỌW-TĪDE, *n.*
  All-saints-day, or the time near it.
ÂLL'-HĒAL (âl'hēl), *n.* A species of plant.
ÂLL-SĀĪNTŞ-DĀY' (âl-sāntz-dā'), *n.* The day
  for celebrating the saints; the first of November.
ÂLL-SŌULŞ-DĀY', *n.* The second of November.
ÂLL-WĪSE', *a.* Possessed of infinite wisdom.
ẠL-LĀY' (ạl-lā'), *v. a.* To quiet; to pacify.
ẠL-LĀY'. See ALLOY.
ẠL-LĀY'ĘR, *n.* The person or thing that allays.
ĂL-LẸ-GĀ'TIỌN, *n.* Affirmation; a plea.
ẠL-LĔĢE', *v. a.* To affirm; to declare; to plead.
ẠL-LĔĢE'Ạ-BLE, *a.* That may be alleged.
ẠL-LĔĢ'ĘR (ạl-lĕj'ụr), *n.* One who alleges.
ẠL-LĒ'ĢIẠNCE (ạl-lē'jạns), *n.* Duty of a subject.
ĂL-LẸ-GŎR'ĮC,   *a.* In the manner of an alle-
ĂL-LẸ-GŎR'Į-CẠL, gory; typical; figurative.
ĂL-LẸ-GŎR'Į-CẠL-LY, *ad.* In an allegorical
  manner; figuratively; typically.
ĂL-LẸ-GŎR'Į-CẠL-NĔSS, *n.* State of being alle-
  gorical.
ĂL'LẸ-GỌ-RĪZE, *v. a.* To turn into allegory.
ĂL'LẸ-GỌ-RĪZE, *v. n.* To speak allegorically.
ĂL'LẸ-GỌ-RY, *n.* A figurative discourse, im-
  plying something not literally expressed.
ĂL-LĒ'GRŌ. A sprightly motion in music.
ĂL-LẸ-LŪ'JẠH (ăl-lẹ-lū'yạ), *n.* A word of spir-
  itual exultation, signifying *praise God.* [lay.
ẠL-LĒ'VĮ-ĀTE, *v. a.* To ease; to soften; to al-
ẠL-LĒ-VĮ-Ā'TIỌN, *n.* Act of alleviating.
ĂL'LĘY (ăl'lẹ), *n.* A walk; a narrow passage.
ẠL-LĪ'ẠNCE, *n.* A union by treaty or marriage.
ĂL'LĮ-GĀTE, *v. a.* To join; to unite; to tie.
ĂL-LĮ-GĀ'TIỌN, *n.* A rule of arithmetic.
ĂL'LĮ-GĀ-TỌR, *n.* The American crocodile.
ẠL-LĪ''ŞIỌN (ạl-līzh'ụn), *n.* A striking against.
ẠL-LĬT-ĘR-Ā'TIỌN, *n.* The beginning of sev-
  eral connected words with the same letter.
ẠL-LĬT'ĘR-Ạ-TĬVE, *a.* Relating to alliteration.
ĂL-LỌ-CĀ'TIỌN, *n.* Act of placing or adding to.
ĂL-LỌ-CŪ'TIỌN, *n.* Act of speaking to; address.
ẠL-LŌ'DĮ-ẠL, *a.* Independent of any superior.
ẠL-LŌ'DĮ-ŬM, *n.* [L.] (*Law.*) A free manor.
ẠL-LŌNĢE' (ạl-lŭnj'), *n.* A thrust with a rapier.
ẠL-LÔÔ', *v. a.* To set on, as a dog; to incite.
ẠL-LŎT', *v. a.* To distribute; to parcel out.
ẠL-LŎT'MĘNT, *n.* A share; part appropriated.
ẠL-LŌW', *v. a.* To admit; to grant; to abate.
ẠL-LŌW'Ạ-BLE, *a.* Capable of being allowed.

ȦL-LÖW′Ȧ-BLE-NĔSS, *n.* State of being allowed.
ȦL-LÖW′Ȧ-BLY, *ad.* With claim of allowance.
ȦL-LÖW′ANCE, *n.* License ; abatement ; a grant.
ȦL-LÖŸ′, *n.* Baser metal mixed in coinage.
ȦL-LÖŸ′, *v. a.* To debase by mixing, as metals.
ÂLL′SPĪCE, *n.* Jamaica pepper or pimenta.
ȦL-LŪDE′, *v. n.* To refer ; to hint ; to insinuate.
ȦL-LŪ′MĮ-NǪR, *n.* A colorer or painter on paper.
ȦL-LŪRE′, *v. n.* To entice ; to decoy ; to lure.
ȦL-LŪRE′MENT, *n.* An enticement ; temptation.
ȦL-LŪR′ER, *n.* One who allures ; an enticer.
ȦL-LŪR′ĮNG, *a.* Tempting ; seducing ; enticing.
ȦL-LŪR′ĮNG-LY, *ad.* In an alluring manner.
ȦL-LŪR′ĮNG-NĔSS, *n.* Enticement ; seduction.
ȦL-LŪ′ŞĮǪN (ȧl-lū′zhųn), *n.* A reference to
  something known ; a hint ; an implication.
ȦL-LŪ′SĮVE, *a.* Hinting at something.
ȦL-LŪ′VĮ-ĂL, *a.* Pertaining to alluvion.
ȦL-LŪ′VĮ-ǪN, *n.* Alluvium ; alluvial land.
ȦL-LŪ′VĮ-ŬM, *n.* An accession of earth, gravel,
  &c., washed to the shore by rivers, &c.
ȦL-LŸ′, *v. a.* To unite by kindred or friendship.
ȦL-LŸ′, *n.* One allied ; a confederate.
ĂL′MȦ, *or* ĂL′ME, *n.* A dancing girl in the East.
ÂL′MȦ-NĂC, *n.* An annual register ; a calendar.
ÂL-MĪGH′TĮ-NĔSS, *n.* Unlimited power.
ÂL-MĪGH′TY (âl-mī′tę), *a.* Omnipotent.
ÂL-MĪGH′TY (âl-mī′tę), *n.* The divine Being.
ĂL′MǪND (ä′mųnd), *n.* Nut of the almond tree.
ĂL′MŲNDŞ (ä′mųndz), *n. pl.* Two round glands
  at the base of the tongue ; the tonsils.
ĂL′MǪN-ER, *n.* A distributer of alms.
ĂL′MǪN-RY, *n.* Place for distributing alms.
ÂL′MŎST *or* ÂL-MŎST′, *ad.* Nearly ; well nigh.
ÄLMŞ (ämz), *n.* A gift or benefaction to the poor.
ÄLMŞ′DĒĒD (ämz′dēd), *n.* An act of charity.
ÄLMŞ′ĠĬV-ER (ämz′ġĭv-ẹr), *n.* A giver of alms.
ÄLMŞ′HÖÛSE (ämz′hȯ̂ûs), *n.* A house devoted
  to the reception and support of the poor.
ÄLMŞ′MĂN, *n.* A man living upon alms.
ĂL′MŲG-TRĒĒ, *n.* A tree mentioned in Scrip-
ĂL′NȦĠE, *n.* Measurement by the ell. [ture.
ĂL′NȦ-ĠER, *n.* A measurer by the ell.
ĂL′ŌEŞ (ăl′ōz), *n.* A tree ; a cathartic juice.
ĂL-Ǫ-ĔT′ĮC,   } *a.* Consisting of aloes ; re-
ĂL-Ǫ-ĔT′Į-CĂL, }   lating to, or obtained from,
Ȧ-LŎFT′, *ad.* On high ; above ; in the air. [aloes.
Ȧ-LŌNE′, *a.* Single ; without company ; solitary.
Ȧ-LŎNG′, *ad.* At length ; forward ; onward.
Ȧ-LŎNG-SĪDE′, *ad.* By the side of, as of a ship.
Ȧ-LŌOF′, *ad.* At a distance ; cautiously.
Ȧ-LÖÛD′, *ad.* Loudly ; with a great noise.
ĂL′PHȦ, *n.* The first letter in the Greek alpha-
ĂL′PHȦ-BĔT, *n.* The letters of a language. [bet.
ĂL-PHȦ-BĔT′ĮC,   } *a.* In the order or nature
ĂL-PHȦ-BĔT′Į-CĂL, } of the alphabet. [manner.
ĂL-PHȦ-BĔT′Į-CĂL-LY, *ad.* In an alphabetical
ĂL′PĪNE *or* ĂL′PĬNE, *a.* Relating to the Alps.
ÂL-RĔAD′Y (âl-rĕd′dę), *ad.* Now ; at this time.
ÂL′SŌ, *ad.* In the same manner ; likewise.
ÂL′TȦR, *n.* A structure where offerings are
  laid : — the communion table in churches.
ÂL′TȦR-PIĒCE, *n.* A painting over the altar.
ÂL′TER, *v. a.* To change ; to make otherwise.
ÂL′TER, *v. n.* To suffer change ; to vary.
ÂL′TER-Ȧ-BLE, *a.* That may be changed.
ÂL-TER-Ā′TĮǪN, *n.* The act of altering ; change.
ÂL′TER-Ȧ-TĬVE, *a.* Producing a change.

ĂL′TER-CĀTE, *v. n.* To wrangle ; to contend
ĂL′TER-CĀ′TĮǪN, *n.* Angry debate ; wrangle.
ĂL′TER-NȦ-CY, *n.* Action performed by turns.
ȦL-TĔR′NȦTE, *a.* One after another ; reciprocal.
ȦL-TĔR′NȦTE, *n.* What happens alternately.
ȦL-TĔR′NȦTE, *or* ĂL′TER-NĀTE, *v. a.* To per-
  form alternately ; to change reciprocally.
ȦL-TĔR′NȦTE-LY, *ad.* In reciprocal succession.
ȦL-TĔR′NȦTE-NĔSS, *n.* The being alternate.
ĂL′TER-NĀ′TĮǪN, *n.* Reciprocal succession.
ȦL-TĔR′NȦ-TĬVE, *n.* Choice given of two things.
ȦL-TĔR′NȦ-TĬVE, *a.* Implying alternation.
ȦL-TĔR′NȦ-TĬVE-LY, *ad.* By turns ; reciprocal-
ȦL-TĔR′NȦ-TĮVE-NĔSS, *n.* Reciprocation. [ly.
ȦL-TĔR′NĮ-TY, *n.* Reciprocal succession.
ȦL-THĒ′Ȧ, *n.* A genus of flowering shrubs.
ÂL-THŌUGH′ (âl-thō′), *conj.* Though ; be it so.
ȦL-TĬL′Ǫ-QUĔNCE, *n.* Pompous language.
ȦL-TĬM′E-TRY, *n.* Measurement of heights.
ȦL-TĬS′Ǫ-NȦNT, *a.* Pompous or lofty in sound.
ĂL′TĮ-TŪDE, *n.* Height ; elevation ; loftiness.
ÂL-TǪ-ĠĔTH′ER, *ad.* Completely ; without ex-
ĂL′Ų-DĔL, *n.* A chemical vessel. [ception.
ĂL′ŲM, *n.* An astringent mineral salt.
Ȧ-LŪ′MĮ-NȦ, *n.* (*Chem.*) The oxide of aluminum.
Ȧ-LŪ′MĮ-NŬM, *n.* Metallic base of alumina.
Ȧ-LŪ′MĮ-NOŬS, *a.* Resembling alum : — clayey.
ĂL′VĪNE, *a.* Relating to the belly or intestines.
ÂL′WĀYŞ (âl′wāz), *ad.* Perpetually ; constantly.
ĂM. The first person of the verb *to be.*
ĂM-Ȧ-BĬL′Į-TY, *n.* Loveliness ; amiability.
Ȧ-MĀIN′, *ad.* With vehemence ; with vigor.
Ȧ-MĂL′GȦM, *n.* (*Chem.*) A combination of mer-
  cury with another metal.
Ȧ-MĂL′GȦ-MĀTE, *v. a.* To combine or unite, as
  metals ; to mix ; to mingle.
Ȧ-MĂL-GȦ-MĀ′TĮǪN, *n.* The act of amalgamat-
  ing ; mixture. [another dictates.
Ȧ-MĂN-Ų-ĔN′SĮS, *n.* A person who writes what
ĂM′Ȧ-RĂNTH, *n.* A plant the flower of which
  long retains its color ; a purplish color.
ĂM-Ȧ-RĂN′THĬNE, *a.* Consisting of amaranths ;
  undying ; imperishable ; undecaying.
ĂM-Ȧ-RŸL′LĮS, *n.* (*Bot.*) A genus of plants.
Ȧ-MĂSS′, *v. a.* To collect together ; to heap up.
Ȧ-MĂSS′MENT, *n.* A heap ; an accumulation.
ĂM-Ȧ-TEŪR′, *n.* A lover of any art or science.
ĂM-Ȧ-TŌ′RĮ-ĂL,   } *a.* Relating to love ; causing,
ĂM′Ȧ-TǪ-RY, }   or inciting to, love.
Ȧ-MĀZE′, *v. a.* To astonish, perplex, confuse.
Ȧ-MĀZE′MENT, *n.* Confusion ; astonishment.
Ȧ-MĀZ′ĮNG, *p. a.* Wonderful ; astonishing.
ĂM′Ȧ-ZǑN, *n.* A warlike woman ; a virago.
ĂM-Ȧ-ZŌ′NĮ-ȦN, *a.* Warlike ; relating to ama-
ĂM-BĀ′ĠEŞ, *n.* Windings ; circumlocution. [zons.
ĂM-BĀ′ĠĮ-OŬS, *a.* Circumlocutory ; tedious.
ĂM-BĂS′SȦ-DǪR, *n.* A person sent on public
  business from one sovereign power to another.
ĂM-BĂS′SȦ-DRĔSS, *n.* The wife of an ambas-
ĂM′BER, *n.* A fossil vegetable juice. [sador.
ĂM′BER-GRÎS, *n.* A fragrant, grayish sub-
  stance obtained from the spermaceti whale.
ĂM-BĮ-DĔX′TER, *n.* One that can use both
  hands with equal facility ; a double-dealer.
ĂM-BĮ-DĔX-TĔR′Į-TY, *n.* State of being able
  equally to use both hands ; double-dealing.
ĂM-BĮ-DĔX′TROŲS, *a.* Using either hand.
ĂM-BĮ-DĔX′TROŲS-NĔSS, *n.* Ambidexterity.

ĂM′BĬ-ENT, *a.* Surrounding; encompassing.
ĂM′BĬ-GŪ, *n.* [Fr.] A medley of dishes.
ĂM-BĬ-GŪ′Ĭ-TY, *n.* Uncertainty of signification.
ĄM-BĬG′Ų-OŬS, *a.* Of doubtful meaning.
ĄM-BĬG′Ų-OŬS-LY, *ad.* Doubtfully; uncertainly.
ĄM-BĬG′Ų-OŬS-NĔSS, *n.* Ambiguity. [sions.
ĄM-BĬL′Ọ-QUOŬS, *a.* Using ambiguous expres-
ĄM-BĬL′Ọ-QUY, *n.* Use of doubtful expressions.
ĂM′BĬT, *n.* Compass or circuit; circumference
ĄM-BĬ′′TIǪN (ạm-bĭsh′ụn), *n.* Eager desire of
 superiority, preferment, honor, or power.
ĄM-BĬ′′TIOŲS (ạm-bĭsh′ụs), *a.* Filled with am-
 bition; aspiring; eager after advancement.
ĄM-BĬ′′TIOŲS-NĔSS, *n.* The being ambitious.
ĂM′BLE, *n.* A pace of a horse; pacing.
ĂM′BLE, *v. n.* To move upon an amble.
ĂM′BLĘR, *n.* A horse that ambles.
ĄM-BRŌ′ŞĬ-Ą (ạm-brō′zhę-ạ), *n.* The imaginary
 food of the gods : — the name of a plant.
ĄM-BRŌ′ŞĬ-ĄL (ạm-brō′zhę-ạl),) *a.* Of the na-
ĄM-BRŌ′ŞĬ-ĄN (ạm-brō′zhę-ạn),) ture of ambro-
ĂM′BRY, *n.* An almonry. [sia; delicious.
ĀMBŞ-ĀCE′ (āmz-ās′), *n.* A double ace.
ĂM′BŲ-LĂNCE, *n.* A moving army hospital.
ĂM-BŲ-LĀ′TIǪN, *n.* Act of walking; a walk.
ĂM′BŲ-LĄ-TǬ-RY, *a.* Walking; movable.
ĂM′BŲ-LĄ-TǬ-RY, *n.* A place for walking.
ĂM′BŲ-RY, *n.* A bloody wart on a horse.
ĂM-BŲS-CĀDE′, *n.* A private station in which
 men lie to surprise others; an ambush.
ĂM′BŬSH, *n.* The place or act of lying in wait.
ĂM′BŬSHED (ăm′bŭsht), *p. a.* Placed in ambush.
Ą-MĒ′LIǪ-RĀTE (ạ-mēl′yǫ-rāt), *v. a.* To im-
 prove; to make better; to meliorate.
Ą-MĒ-LIǪ-RĀ′TIǪN (ạ-mēl-yǫ-rā′shụn), *n.* The
 act of making better; improvement.
Ā′MĔN′, *ad.* A term of assent; so be it.
Ą-MĒ′NĄ-BLE, *a.* Responsible; liable to account.
Ą-MĔND′, *v. a.* To correct; to reform, restore.
Ą-MĔND′, *v. n.* To grow better; to reform.
Ą-MĔND′Ą-BLE, *a.* Reparable; corrigible.
Ą-MĔND′MĘNT, *n.* Reformation; recovery.
Ą-MĔNDŞ′, *n.* Recompense; compensation.
Ą-MĔN′Ĭ-TY, *n.* Pleasantness; agreeableness.
Ą-MĔRCE′, *v. a.* To punish by fine; to mulct.
Ą-MĔRCE′Ą-BLE, *a.* Liable to amercement.
Ą-MĔRCE′MĘNT, *n.* Pecuniary punishment;
Ą-MĔR′CĘR, *n.* One who amerces. [fine.
Ą-MĔR′Ĭ-CĄN, *a.* Pertaining to America, or to
 the United States. [word, phrase, &c.
Ą-MĔR′Ĭ-CĄN-ĬSM, *n.* An American idiom,
ĂM′Ę-THȲST, *n.* A purple colored precious stone.
ĂM-Ę-THȲST′ĬNE, *a.* Resembling an amethyst.
Ā-MĬ-Ą-BĬL′Ĭ-TY, *n.* Loveliness; amiableness.
Ā′MĬ-Ą-BLE, *a.* Lovely; worthy to be loved.
Ā′MĬ-Ą-BLE-NĔSS, *n.* Loveliness; agreeableness.
Ā′MĬ-Ą-BLY, *ad.* In an amiable manner.
ĂM′Ĭ-ĂNTH, *or* ĂM-Ĭ-ĂN′THŲS, *n.* Earth-flax.
ĂM′Ĭ-CĄ-BLE, *a.* Friendly; kind; obliging.
ĂM′Ĭ-CĄ-BLE-NĔSS, *n.* Friendliness; good will.
ĂM′Ĭ-CĄ-BLY, *ad.* In an amicable manner.
ĂM′ĬCE, *n.* Part of a priest's habit.
Ą-MĬD′,) *prep.* In the midst; mingled with;
Ą-MĬDST′,) amongst; surrounded by.
Ą-MĬSS′, *ad.* Faultily; wrong; improperly.
ĂM′Ĭ-TY, *n.* Friendship; love; harmony.
ĄM-MŌ′NĬ-Ą, *n.* A gaseous volatile alkali.
ĄM-MŌ′NĬ-ĂC, *n.* A drug or gum-resin.

ĂM-MǪ-NĪ′Ą-CĄL, *a.* Containing ammonia.
ĂM-MŲ-NĬ′′TIǪN (ăm-mụ-nĭsh′ụn), *n.* Military
ĂM′NĘS-TY, *n.* A general pardon. [stores.
Ą-MŎNG′,) *prep.* Mingled with; in the
Ą-MŎNGST′,) midst of; making a part of.
ĂM′Ọ-ROŬS, *a.* Loving; inclined to love.
ĂM′Ọ-ROŬS-LY, *ad.* Fondly; lovingly.
ĂM′O-ROŲS-NĔSS, *n.* Fondness; lovingness.
Ą-MŎR′PHOŲS, *a.* Shapeless; without form.
Ą-MŎR-TĬ-ZĀ′TIǪN,) *n.* (*Law.*) The right, or
Ą-MŎR′TĬZE-MĔNT,) the act, of transferring
 lands to mortmain to a corporation.
Ą-MŎR′TĬŞE, *v. a.* To transfer in mortmain.
Ą-MÖÛNT′, *v. n.* To rise to; to come to.
Ą-MÖÛNT′, *n.* The aggregate or sum total.
Ą-MÖUR′ (ạ-môr′), *n.* Affair of love; intrigue.
ĄM-PHĬB′Ĭ-OŬS, *a.* Living in two elements.
ĄM-PHĬB′Ĭ-OŲS-NĔSS (ạm-fĭb′ę-ụs-nĕs), *n.* Ca-
 pability of living in two different elements.
ĂM-PHĬ-BŎL′Ọ-ĢY, *n.* Ambiguous discourse.
ĄM-PHĬB′Ọ-LOŬS, *a.* Tossed from one to another.
ĂM′PHĬ-BRĂCH, *n.* A foot of three syllables.
ĂM-PHĬ-THĒ′Ą-TRE (ăm-fę-thē′ạ-tẹr), *n.* A cir-
 cular building for public amusements, &c.
ĂM-PHĬ-THĘ-ĂT′RĬ-CĄL, *a.* Relating to exhi-
 bitions in, or to the form of, an amphitheatre.
ĂM′PLE, *a.* Large; wide; extended; diffusive.
ĂM-PLĬ-FĬ-CĀ′TIǪN, *n.* Enlargement; diffuse-
ĂM′PLĬ-FĬ-ĘR, *n.* One who amplifies. [ness.
ĂM′PLĬ-FȲ, *v. a.* To enlarge; to exaggerate.
ĂM′PLĬ-FȲ, *v. n.* To speak largely; to enlarge.
ĂM′PLĬ-TŪDE, *n.* Largeness; copiousness.
ĂM′PLY, *ad.* Largely; liberally; copiously.
ĂM′PŲ-TĀTE, *v. a.* To cut off, as a limb.
ĂM-PŲ-TĀ′TIǪN, *n.* The act of cutting off a limb.
ĂM′Ų-LĔT, *n.* A charm worn about the person.
Ą-MŪŞE′, *v. a.* To entertain; to divert.
Ą-MŪŞE′MĘNT, *n.* Recreation; diversion.
Ą-MŪŞ′ĘR, *n.* One who amuses; a diverter.
Ą-MŪŞ′ĬNG,) *a.* Affording amusement; pleas-
Ą-MŪ′SĬVE,) ing; entertaining; diverting.
Ą-MȲG′DĄ-LĄTE, *a.* Made of almonds.
Ą-MȲG′DĄ-LINE, *a.* Resembling almonds.
ĂN. The same with the article *a*; denoting one.
 The article *a* must be used before all words
 beginning with a consonant, and before the
 vowel *u* when long; and the article *an* must
 be used before all words beginning with a
 vowel, except long *u*, before words beginning
 with *h* mute, as, *an hour*, *an heir*, &c., or before
 words where the *h* is not mute, if the accent
 be on the second syllable, as, *an heroic action*,
 an historical account, &c. — See A. [tizing.
ĂN-Ą-BĂP′TĬST, *n.* One who holds to re-bap-
Ą-NĂCH′RǬ-NĬSM, *n.* An error in chronology.
ĂN-Ą-CLĂS′TĬCS, *n.* The doctrine of refract-
ĂN-Ą-CŎN′DĄ, *n.* A very large serpent. [ed light.
ĂN′Ą-GLȲPH, *n.* An ornament by sculpture.
ĂN′Ą-GRĂM, *n.* The transposition of the letters
 of a word, as *Amor* into *Roma.*
ĂN-Ą-GRĄM-MĂT′Ĭ-CĄL, *a.* Like an anagram.
ĂN-Ą-GRĂM′MĄ-TĬST, *n.* A maker of anagrams.
ĂN-Ą-LĔP′TĬC, *a.* Restorative; strengthening.
ĂN-Ą-LŎĢ′Ĭ-CĄL, *a.* Having analogy; analogous.
ĂN-Ą-LŎĢ′Ĭ-CĄL-LY, *ad.* In an analogical or
 analogous manner. [analogical.
ĂN-Ą-LŎĢ′Ĭ-CĄL-NĔSS, *n.* The state of being
Ą-NĂL′Ọ-GOŬS, *a.* Having analogy; analogical.

A-NĂL'O-ĢY, *n.* Resemblance, similarity, comparison, or proportion of one thing to another.
A-NĂL'Y-SĬS, *n.* ; pl. A-NĂL'Y-SĒṢ. The separation or solution of a thing into its elements.
ĂN-A-LȲT'ĬC, } *a.* Pertaining to analysis ; resolving into first principles.
ĂN-A-LȲT'Ĭ-CĂL, }
ĂN-A-LȲT'Ĭ-CĂL-LY, *ad.* In an analytical manner ; by means of analysis.
ĂN'A-LȲZE, *v. a.* To resolve into first principles or elementary parts ; to decompose.
ĂN'A-LȲZ-ĔR, ĂN'A-LȲST, *n.* One who analyzes ; that which has power of analyzing.
ĂN-A-MQR-PHŌ'SĬS, *n.* A distorted representation of an object ; change of form.
A-NĀ'NĄS, *n.* Plant producing the pineapple.
ĂN'A-PĔST, *n.* A metrical foot, containing two short syllables and one long one.
ĂN-A-PĔS'TĬC, *a.* Relating to the anapest.
ĂN'ARĊH, *n.* Author of confusion ; anarchist.
A-NĂR'ĊHĬC, } *a.* Confused ; without rule, order, or government.
A-NĂR'ĊHĬ-CĂL, }
ĂN'AR-ĊHĬST, *n.* Author or favorer of anarchy.
ĂN'AR-ĊHY, *n.* Want of government ; disorder.
ĂN-A-SĂR'COŲS, *a.* Pertaining to a general dropsy.
ĂN-A-STQ-MĂT'ĬC, *a.* Aperient ; opening. [sy.
A-NĂS'TRQ-PHĘ, *n.* (*Rhet.*) Inversion.
A-NĂTH'Ę-MĄ, *n.* An ecclesiastical curse.
ĂN-A-THE-MĂT'Ĭ-CĂL, *a.* Containing anathema.
A-NĂTH'Ę-MĄ-TĪZE, *v. a.* To pronounce accursed ; to excommunicate. [matizes.
A-NĂTH'Ę-MĄ-TĪZ-ĔR, *n.* One who anathe-
ĂN-A-TŎM'Ĭ-CĂL, *a.* Belonging to anatomy.
ĂN-A-TŎM'Ĭ-CĂL-LY, *ad.* In an anatomical manner ; according to anatomy.
A-NĂT'Q-MĬST, *n.* One skilled in anatomy.
A-NĂT'Q-MĪZE, *v. a.* To dissect, as an animal.
A-NĂT'Q-MY, *n.* The art of dissecting an animal body ; science of the structure of the body.
ĂN'CĘS-TQR, *n.* A progenitor ; a forefather.
ĂN'CĘS-TRĂL, *a.* Relating to ancestors.
ĂN'CĘS-TRY, *n.* Lineage ; a series of ancestors.
ĂNĊH'QR (ăng'kųr), *n.* An instrument for holding ships, &c., made generally of iron.
ĂNĊH'QR (ăng'kųr), *v. n.* & *a.* To cast anchor ; to place at anchor ; to fix ; to fasten.
ĂNĊH'QR-SMĬTH, *n.* A maker of anchors.
ĂNĊH'QR-AĢE, *n.* Ground for anchoring on.
ĂNĊH'Q-RĔSS (ăng'kǫ-rĕs), *n.* A female recluse.
ĂNĊH'Q-RĔT, *or* ĂNĊH'Q-RĪTE, *n.* A hermit.
AN-CHŌ'VY, *n.* A little sea-fish, used for sauce.
ĂN'CIĘNT (ān'shęnt), *a.* Old ; of old time.
ĂN'CIĘNTS (ān'shęnts), *n. pl.* Old men ; men who lived in old time ; — opposed to *moderns*.
ĂN'CIĘNT-LY (ān'shęnt-lę), *ad.* In old times.
ĂN'CĬL-LĄ-RY, *a.* Serving, as a handmaid.
ĂND, *conj.* A word which joins sentences.
AN-DĂN'TĘ, *a.* [It.] (*Mus.*) Equable ; exact.
ĂND'ĬR-ON (ănd'ī-ųrn), *n.* An iron utensil to support the ends of a spit or of wood.
AN-DRŎĢ'Y-NĂL, } *a.* Having two sexes ; hermaphroditical.
AN-DRŎĢ'Y-NOŬS, }
AN-DRŎĬ'DĔS, *n.* A machine in human shape.
ĂN'EC-DŌTE, *n.* A biographical fragment, incident, or fact ; a short story or narration.
ĂN-EC-DŎT'Ĭ-CĂL, *a.* Relating to anecdotes.
ĂN-E-MŎĢ'RA-PHY, *n.* Description of winds.
ĂN-E-MŎM'Ę-TĔR, *n.* An instrument to measure the force and velocity of the wind.

A-NĔM'Q-NĘ, *n.* A plant ; the wind-flower.
A-NĔM'Q-SCŌPE, *n.* A weather vane ; weathercock.
ĂN'EŲ-RĬṢM, *n.* Lesion of an artery. [cock.
A-NEW' (a-nū'), *ad.* Over again ; afresh.
ĂN'ĢĘL, *n.* A celestial spirit : — a gold coin.
ĀN'ĢĘL, *a.* Resembling angels ; angelic.
AN-ĢĔL'ĬC, } *a.* Belonging to angels ; partaking of the nature of angels.
A-N-GĔL'Ĭ-CĂL, }
ĂN'ĢĘ-LŎT, *n.* A musical instrument.
ĂN'ĢĘR (ăng'gųr), *n.* Resentment ; rage ; ire.
ĂN'ĢĘR, *v. a.* To make angry ; to enrage.
AN-GĪ'NĄ, *n.* Inflammation in the throat.
ĂN'GLE (ăng'gl), *n.* A point where two lines meet ; a corner ; a fishing-rod. [hook.
ĂN'GLE (ăng'gl), *v. n.* To fish with a rod and
ĂN'GLĘR (ăng'glęr), *n.* One who angles.
ĂN'GLĬ-CĬṢM, *n.* An English idiom or phrase.
ĂN'GLĬ-CĪZE, *v. a.* To make English.
ĂN'GLĬNG, *n.* Act or art of fishing with a rod.
ĂN'GQR, *n.* Acute bodily pain. [ner.
ĂN'GRĬ-LY (ăng'grę-lę), *ad.* In an angry man-
ĂN'GRY, *a.* Provoked ; affected with anger.
ĂN'GUĬSH (ăng'gwĭsh), *n.* Great pain or grief.
ĂN'GŲ-LAR, *a.* Having angles or corners.
ĂN-GŲ-LĂR'Ĭ-TY, *n.* Quality of being angular.
ĂN'GŲ-LĀT-ĘD, *a.* Formed with angles.
ĂN-HĘ-LĀ'TIQN, *n.* The act of panting.
A-NĬL'Ĭ-TY, *n.* The state of being an old woman.
ĂN-Ĭ-MĄD-VĔR'SIQN, *n.* Reproof ; censure.
ĂN-Ĭ-MĄD-VĔRT', *v. n.* To perceive ; to censure.
ĂN-Ĭ-MĄD-VĔRT'ĔR, *n.* One who animadverts.
ĂN'Ĭ-MĄL, *n.* A living corporeal creature.
ĂN'Ĭ-MĄL, *a.* That belongs to animals.
ĂN-Ĭ-MĂL'CŪLE, *n.* A minute animal.
ĂN'Ĭ-MĀTE, *v. a.* To quicken ; to make alive.
ĂN'Ĭ-MĄTE, *a.* Alive ; possessing animal life.
ĂN'Ĭ-MĀT-ĘD, *p. a.* Lively ; having life.
ĂN-Ĭ-MĀ'TIQN, *n.* Act of animating ; life ; spirit.
ĂN'Ĭ-MĀ-TQR, *n.* One that gives life.
ĂN-Ĭ-MŎS'Ĭ-TY, *n.* Extreme hatred ; malignity.
ĂN'ĬSE, *n.* A plant with medicinal seeds. [lons.
ĂNK'ĘR, *n.* A liquid measure of about 10 gal-
ĂN'KLE, *n.* The joint between the foot and leg.
ĂN'NAL-ĬST, *n.* A writer of annals ; historian.
ĂN'NALṢ, *n. pl.* History digested into years.
AN-NĒAL', *v. a.* To temper, as glass, &c. [&c.
AN-NĒAL'ĬNG, *n.* The art of tempering glass,
AN-NĔX', *v. a.* To unite to at the end ; to join.
ĂN-NĔX-Ā'TIQN, *n.* Conjunction ; addition.
AN-NĪ'HĬ-LA-BLE, *a.* Capable of annihilation.
AN-NĪ'HĬ-LĀTE, *v. a.* To reduce to nothing.
AN-NĪ-HĬ-LĀ'TIQN, *n.* A reducing to nothing.
AN-NĬ-VĔR'SA-RY, *n.* A stated day, on the annual recurrence of which an event is celebrated.
ĂN-NĬ-VĔR'SA-RY, *a.* Annual ; yearly. [brated.
ĂN'NQ-TĀTE, *v. n.* To make annotations.
ĂN-NQ-TĀ'TIQN, *n.* A note ; comment ; remark.
ĂN-NQ-TĀ'TQR, *n.* A commentator.
AN-NŌÜNCE', *v. a.* To publish ; to proclaim.
AN-NŌÜNCE'MĘNT, *n.* Declaration ; notice.
AN-NŌÜNÇ'ĘR, *n.* A declarer ; a proclaimer.
AN-NŌY', *v. a.* To incommode ; to vex.
AN-NŌY'ANCE, *n.* That which annoys or injures.
ĂN'NŲ-AL, *a.* Yearly ; living a year. [jures.
ĂN'NŲ-AL-LY, *ad.* Yearly ; every year.
AN-NŪ'Ĭ-TANT, *n.* One who has an annuity.
AN-NŪ'Ĭ-TY, *n.* A yearly rent or allowance.
AN-NŬL', *v. a.* To abolish ; to abrogate ; repeal.

ĂN′NŲ-LĂR, *a.* Having the form of a ring.
ĂN′NŲ-LĄ-RY, *a.* Having the form of a ring.
ĂN′NŲ-LĔT, *n.* A little ring : — a square mould-
ĄN-NŬL′MĘNT, *n.* Act of annulling. [ing.
ĄN-NŪ′MĘR-ĀTE, *v. a.* To add to a former
  number, or to something before mentioned.
ĄN-NŪ-MĘR-Ā′TIǪN, *n.* Addition to a number.
ĄN-NŬN′CĮ-ĀTE (ạn-nŭn′shẹ-āt), *v. a.* To bring
  tidings of ; to report ; to announce.
ĄN-NŬN-CĮ-Ā′TIǪN (ạn-nŭn-shẹ-ā′shụn), *n.* The
  act of announcing : — the 25th of March.
ĂN′Ǫ-DȲNE, *n.* Medicine which assuages pain.
ĂN′Ǫ-DȲNE, *a.* Mitigating or relieving pain.
Ą-NOÏNT′, *v. a.* To rub with oil ; to consecrate.
Ą-NOÏNT′ĘR, *n.* One who anoints.
Ą-NOÏNT′MĘNT, *n.* The act of anointing.
Ą-NŎM-Ą-LĬS′TĮC, ⎰ *a.* Irregular ; deviating
Ą-NŎM-Ą-LĬS′TĮ-CĄL, ⎱ from established rule.
Ą-NŎM′Ą-LOŬS, *a.* Irregular ; out of rule.
Ą-NŎM′Ą-LY, *n.* Irregularity ; deviation from
Ą-NŎN′, *ad.* Quickly ; soon ; shortly. [rule.
Ą-NŎN′Y-MOŬS, *a.* Wanting a name ; unknown.
Ą-NŎN′Y-MOŬS-LY, *ad.* Without a name.
ĂN′Ǫ-RĔX-Y, *n.* Want of appetite.
ĄN-Ŏ₸H′ĘR, *a.* Not the same ; one more.
ĂN′SWĘR (ăn′sẹr), *v. n.* To speak in return.
ĂN′SWĘR (ăn′sẹr), *v. a.* To reply to ; to suit.
ĂN′SWĘR (ăn′sẹr), *n.* A reply ; confutation.
ĂN′SWĘR-Ą-BLE (ăn′sẹr-ą-bl), *a.* Admitting
  an answer ; responsible ; amenable ; suitable.
ĂN′SWĘR-Ą-BLE-NĔSS,*n.* The being answerable.
ĂN′SWĘR-Ą-BLY, *ad.* In proportion ; suitably.
ĂNT, *n.* A small insect ; an emmet ; a pismire.
ĄN-TĂG′Ǫ-NĬŞM, *n.* Opposition ; contest.
ĄN-TĂG′Ǫ-NĬST, *n.* A contender ; an opponent.
ĄN-TĂG′Ǫ-NĪZE, *v. n.* To contend ; to oppose.
ĄN-TĂL′ĢĮC, *a.* Softening pain ; anodyne.
ĄNT-ĂRC′TĮC, *a.* Relating to the south pole.
ĂNT-ĄR-THRĬT′ĮC, *a.* Counteracting the gout.
ĂN′TE, A Latin particle signifying *before.*
ĂN-TĘ-CĒDE′, *v. n.* To precede ; to go before.
ĂN-TĘ-CĒ′DĘNCE, *n.* A going before.
ĂN-TĘ-CĒ′DĘNT, *a.* Going before ; preceding.
ĂN-TĘ-CĒ′DĘNT, *n.* That which goes before.
ĂN-TĘ-CĒ′DĘNT-LY, *ad.* Previously ; before.
ĂN-TĘ-CĒS′SǪR, *n.* One who goes before.
ĂN′TE-CHĂM-BĘR, *n.* A chamber or room that
  leads to a chief apartment ; anteroom.
ĂN-TĘ-CŬR′SǪR, *n.* A forerunner ; precursor.
ĂN′TĘ-DĀTE, *v. a.* To date before the true time.
ĂN-TĘ-DĮ-LŪ′VĮ-ĄN, *a.* Existing before the
  flood or deluge. [the flood.
ĂN-TĘ-DĮ-LŪ′VĮ-ĄN, *n.* One that lived before
ĂN′TE-LŌPE, *n.* An animal resembling deer.
ĂN-TĘ-LŪ′CĄN, *a.* Before daylight or dawn.
ĂN-TĘ-MĘ-RĬD′Į-ĄN, *a.* Being before noon.
ĂN-TĘ-MŬN′DĀNE, *a.* Before the creation.
ĂN-TĘ-PĂS′ꞒHĄL, *a.* Before Easter.
ĂN′TĘ-PĂST, *n.* A foretaste ; anticipation.
ĂN-TĘ-PĘ-NŬLT′, *n.* The last syllable but two.
ĂN-TĘ-PĘ-NŬL′TĮ-MĄTE, *a.* Relating to the
  last syllable of a word but two.
ĄN-TĒ′RĮ-ǪR, *a.* Going before ; prior.
ĄN-TĒ-RĮ-ŎR′Į-TY, *n.* Priority in time.
ĂN′TĘ-RÔÔM, *n.* A room before another.
ĂN-THĘL-MĬN′TĮC, *a.* Destroying worms.
ĂN′THĘM, *n.* A sacred song or hymn.
ĂN′THĘR, *n.* (*Bot.*) The part containing pollen.

ĂNT′-HĬLL, *n.* A hillock formed by ants.
ĂN-THǪ-LŎĢ′Į-CĄL,*a.* Relating to an anthology.
ĄN-THŎL′Ǫ-ĢY, *n.* Collection of flowers or
ĂN′THRĄ-CĪTE,*n.* A hard mineral coal.[poems.
ĂN-THRǪ-PŎL′O-ĢY, *n.* The doctrine of anat-
  omy : — a discourse on man or human nature.
ĄN-THRŌ-PǪ-MŌR′PHĪTE, *n.* One who believes
  that God has the form of a human being.
ĂN-THRǪ-PŎPH′Ą-ĢĪ, *n. pl.* Cannibals.
ĂN-THRǪ-PŎPH′Ą-ĢY, *n.* Cannibalism.
ĂNT-HYS-TĔR′ĮC, *a.* Good against hysterics.
ĂN′TĮ, in compound words, signifies *against.*
ĂN′TĮC, *a.* Odd ; ridiculously wild ; grotesque.
ĂN′TĮC, *n.* A buffoon ; trick ; odd appearance.
ĂN′TĮ-ꞒHRĬST, *n.* An enemy to Christ.
ĂN-TĮ-ꞒHRĬST′IĄN (ăn-tẹ-krĭst′yạn), *a.* Op-
  posed to Christianity. [of, Christianity.
ĂN-TĮ-ꞒHRĬST′IĄN, *n.* An enemy to, or opposer
ĄN-TĬC′Į-PĀTE, *v. a.* To take before ; to fore-
ĄN-TĬC-Į-PĀ′TIǪN,*n.* Act of anticipating.[taste.
ĄN-TĬC′Į-PĀ-TǪR, *n.* One who anticipates.
ĄN-TĬC′Į-PĄ-TǪ-RY, *a.* That anticipates.
ĂN-TĮ-CLĪ′MĂX, *n.* A sentence in which the
  last part expresses something lower than the
ĂN′TĮC-LY, *ad.* In an antic manner ; drolly.[first.
ĂN-TĮ-CǪŞ-MĔT′ĮC, *a.* Destructive of beauty.
ĂN′TĮ-DŌ-TĄL, *a.* Acting as an antidote.
ĂN′TĮ-DŌTE, *n.* A remedy for poison.
ĂN-TĮ-Ę-PĬS′CǪ-PĄL, *a.* Adverse to episcopacy.
ĂN-TĮ-FĔB′RĮLE, *a.* Good against fevers. [istry.
ĂN-TĮ-MĬN-ĮS-TĒ′RĮ-ĄL, *a.* Opposing the min-
ĂN-TĮ-MǪ-NĂRꞒH′Į-CĄL,*a.* Against monarchy.
ĂN-TĮ-MŎN′ĄR-ꞒHĬST, *n.* One who is opposed
  to monarchy ; a democrat ; a republican.
ĂN-TĮ-MŌ′NĮ-ĄL, *a.* Pertaining to, or resem-
  bling, antimony ; containing antimony.
ĂN′TĮ-MǪ-NY, *n.* A bluish-white, brittle metal.
ĂN-TĮ-NŌ′MĮ-ĄN, *n.* One of a religious sect
  who denied the obligation of the moral law.
ĂN-TĮ-NŌ′MĮ-ĄN, *a.* Relating to the antinomians.
ĂN-TĮ-NŌ′MĮ-ĄN-ĬŞM, *n.* Antinomian tenets.
ĂN′TĮ-NǪ-MY, *n.* Opposition of two laws.
ĂN-TĮ-PĀ′PĄL, *a.* Opposing the pope or papacy.
ĂN-TĮ-PĂR-Ą-LŸT′ĮC, *a.* Curing the palsy.
ĄN-TĬP′Ą-THY, *n.* Natural hatred ; aversion.
ĂN-TĮ-PĔS-TĮ-LĔN′TIĄL, *a.* Good against pes-
  tilence or plague.
ĂN-TĮ-PHLǪ-ĢĬS′TĮC, *a.* Counteracting or al-
  laying inflammation.
ĄN-TĬP′Ǫ-DAL, *a.* Relating to the antipodes.
ĄN-TĬP′Ǫ-DĘŞ, *n. pl.* Those people who live
  on the opposite side of the globe.
ĂN′TĮ-PŌPE, *n.* One who usurps the popedom.
ĂN-TĮ-QUĀ′RĮ-ĄN, *a.* Relating to antiquity.
ĂN-TĮ-QUĀ′RĮ-ĄN, *n.* An antiquary.
ĂN-TĮ-QUĀ′RĮ-ĄN-ĬŞM, *n.* Love of antiquities.
ĂN′TĮ-QUĄ-RY, *n.* A man studious of antiquity.
ĂN′TĮ-QUĀTE, *v. a.* To make old or obsolete.
ĂN-TĮ-QUĀT′ĘD-NĔSS, *n.* The being obsolete.
ĄN-TĮQUE′ (ạn-tēk′), *a.* Ancient ; very old.
ĄN-TĮQUE′ (ạn-tēk′), *n.* A piece of antiquity.
ĄN-TĮQUE′NĘSS, *n.* Quality of being ancient.
ĄN-TĬQ′UĮ-TY (ạn-tĭk′wẹ-tẹ), *n.* Old times ; the
  people of old times ; remains of old times.[vy.
ĂN-TĮ-SCǪR-BŪ′TĮC,*a.* Efficacious against scur-
ĂN-TĮ-SĚP′TĮC, *a.* Counteracting putrefaction.
ĂN-TĮ-SŌ′CIĄL, *a.* Adverse to civil society.
ĂN-TĮ-SPAŞ-MŎD′ĮC, *a.* Good against spasms.

ĂN-TĬ-SPLĔN'Ė-TĬC, *a.* Efficacious in diseases of the spleen, as a medicine. [strophe.

ĂN-TĬS'TRQ-PHĘ, *n.* The stanza opposed to the

ĂN-TĬTH'Ė-SĬS, *n.* ; pl. ĂN-TĬTH'Ė-SĒS. (*Rhet.*) Opposition of words or sentiments ; contrast.

ĂN-TĬ-THĔT'Ĭ-CĂL; *a.* Relating to antithesis.

ĂN'TĬ-TȲPE, *n.* The original, or that of which the type is the representation or prefiguration.

ĂN-TĬ-TȲP'Ĭ-CĂL, *a.* That relates to an antitype.

ĂNT'LĘR, *n.* A branch of a stag's horn.

ĂN'VĬL, *n.* The iron block which smiths use.

ĄNX-Ī'Ė-TY (ang-zī'ė-tę), *n.* Trouble of mind about the future ; concern ; solicitude ; care.

ĂNX'IOŲS (ăngk'shųs), *a.* Solicitous ; concerned.

ĂNX'IOŲS-LY (ăngk'shųs-lę), *ad.* With anxiety.

ĂNX'IOŲS-NĔSS (ăngk'shųs-nĕs), *n.* Solicitude.

AN'Y (ĕn'nę), *a.* Every ; whoever ; whatsoever.

Ā'Q-RĬST, *n.* An indefinite tense in the Greek.

Ą-ÖR'TĄ, *n.* The great artery or vessel which rises out of the left ventricle of the heart.

Ą-PĀCE', *ad.* Quickly ; hastily ; with speed.

Ą-PĂRT', *ad.* Separately ; distinctly ; aside.

Ą-PĂRT'MĘNT, *n.* A part of a house ; a room.

ĂP-Ą-THĔT'ĬC, *a.* Without feeling ; passionless.

ĂP'Ą-THY, *n.* Want of sensibility or feeling.

ĀPE, *n.* A kind of monkey : — an imitator.

ĀPE, *v. a.* To imitate, as an ape ; mimic. [ular.

Ą-PEAK', *ad.* In a posture to pierce ; perpendic-

Ą-PĒ'RĬ-ĘNT, *a.* Gently purgative ; laxative.

ĂP'ĘR-TŪRE, *n.* An opening ; a passage ; a hole.

Ą-PĔT'Ą-LOŨS, *a.* Without petals or corolla.

Ā'PĔX, *n.* ; pl. ĂP'Ĭ-CĘS *and* Ā'PĔX-ĘS. The summit or highest point, as of a cone ; tip.

Ą-PHĒ'LĬ-QN, *n.* That part of a planet's orbit in which it is most remote from the sun.

ĂPH'Q-RĬŞM, *n.* A maxim ; an adage ; a proverb.

ĂPH'Q-RĬST, *n.* A writer of aphorisms.

ĂPH-Q-RĬST'Ĭ-CĂL, *a.* Relating to aphorisms.

ĂPH-Q-RĬST'Ĭ-CĂL-LY, *ad.* With aphorisms.

Ā'PĬ-Ą-RY, *n.* A place where bees are kept.

Ą-PIECE', *ad.* To the part or share of each.

Ā'PĬSH, *a.* Like an ape ; foppish ; imitative.

Ā'PĬSH-NĔSS, *n.* Mimicry ; imitation ; foppery.

Ą-PŎC'Ą-LȲPSE, *n.* Disclosure ; Revelation.

Ą-PŎC-Ą-LȲP'TĬC, *a.* Relating to the Apoc-

Ą-PŎC-Ą-LȲP'TĬ-CĄL, alypse or Revelation.

Ą-PŎC'Q-PĘ, *n.* (*Gram.*) The cutting off or omission of the last letter or syllable of a word.

Ą-PŎC'RY-PHĄ, *n.* Books appended to the Old Testament, but of doubtful authority.

Ą-PŎC'RY-PHĄL, *a.* Not canonical ; uncertain.

ĂP'Q-GĒĒ, *n.* That point in the moon's orbit which is at the greatest distance from the earth.

Ą-PŎL-Q-GĔT'ĬC, *a.* Of the nature of an

Ą-PŎL-Q-GĔT'Ĭ-CĄL, apology ; excusing.

Ą-PŎL'Q-GĬST, *n.* One who makes an apology.

Ą-PŎL'Q-GĪZE, *v. n.* To make an apology.

ĂP'Q-LŎGUE (ăp'Q-lŏg), *n.* A fabulous story.

Ą-PŎL'Q-GY, *n.* A pleaded defence ; an excuse.

ĂP-Q-PHLĔG'MĄ-TĬC, *a.* Drawing away phlegm.

ĂP'QPH-THĔGM (ăp'Q-thĕm), *n.* A sententious saying ; a maxim. See APOTHEGM.

ĂP-Q-PLĔC'TĬC, *a.* Relating to an apoplexy.

ĂP'Q-PLĔX-Y, *n.* A disorder which suddenly takes away all sensation and voluntary motion.

Ą-PŎS'TĄ-SY, *n.* A departure from the principles which a man has professed ; defection.

Ą-PŎS'TĄTE, *n.* One who has apostatized.

Ą-PŎS'TĄTE, *a.* False ; traitorous ; recreant.

Ą-PŎS'TĄ-TĪZE, *v. n.* To forsake or renounce one's profession or principles. [aposteme.

Ą-PŎS-TĘ-MĀ'TIQN, *n.* The formation of an

ĂP'Q-STĒME, *n.* An abscess ; an imposthume.

Ą-PŎS'TLE (ą-pŏs'sl), *n.* A person sent ; *applied to those sent by our Saviour to preach the gospel.*

Ą-PŎS'TLE-SHĬP, *n.* The office of an apostle.

ĂP-QS-TŎL'ĬC, *a.* Relating to, or taught

ĂP-QS-TŎL'Ĭ-CĄL, by, the apostles of Christ.

ĂP-QS-TŎL'Ĭ-CĄL-NĔSS, *n.* Apostolic quality.

Ą-PŎS'TRQ-PHĘ, *n.* A digressive address ; a mark thus ('), showing that a word is contracted : the sign of the possessive case.

ĂP-QS-TRŎPH'ĬC, *a.* Denoting an apostrophe.

Ą-PŎS'TRQ-PHĪZE, *v. a.* To address by an apostrophe. [of medicines.

Ą-PŎTH'Ė-CĄ-RY, *n.* A compounder or vender

ĂP'Q-THĔGM (ăp'Q-thĕm), *n.* A sententious or remarkable saying ; a maxim ; a proverb.

ĂP-Q-THĔG-MĂT'Ĭ-CĄL, *a.* Containing apo-

ĂP-Q-THĒ'Q-SĬS, *n.* Deification. [thegms.

ĂP-PĂLL', *v. a.* To frighten ; to terrify.

ĂP'PĄ-NĄGE, *n.* Lands for younger children.

ĂP-PĄ-RĀ'TŲS, *n.* Tools, furniture, or necessary instruments for any trade or art ; utensils.

ĂP-PĂR'ĘL, *n.* Dress ; clothing ; vesture.

ĂP-PĂR'ĘL, *v. a.* To dress ; to clothe ; to adorn.

ĂP-PĂR'ĘNT, *a.* Plain ; seeming ; visible ; open.

ĂP-PĂR'ĘNT-LY, *ad.* Evidently ; seemingly.

ĂP-PĄ-RĬ''TIQN (ăp-pą-rĭsh'ụn), *n.* Appearance ; visibility ; the thing appearing ; spectre.

ĂP-PĂR'Ĭ-TQR, *n.* Messenger of a spiritual court.

ĂP-PĒAL', *v. n.* To refer to another tribunal.

ĂP-PĒAL', *n.* Application for justice to a superior tribunal ; recourse ; entreaty ; petition.

ĂP-PĒAL'Ą-BLE, *a.* That may be appealed.

ĂP-PĒAR', *v. n.* To be in sight ; to be evident.

ĂP-PĒAR'ĄNCE, *n.* Act of coming into sight ; semblance ; not reality ; show ; probability.

ĂP-PĒAR'ĘR, *n.* One who appears.

ĂP-PĒAŞ'Ą-BLE (ąp-pē'zą-bl), *a.* Reconcilable.

ĂP-PĒAŞ'Ą-BLE-NĔSS, *n.* Reconcilableness.

ĂP-PĒAŞE', *v. a.* To quiet ; to pacify ; to still.

ĂP-PĒAŞ'ĘR, *n.* One who appeases.

ĂP-PĔL'LĄNT, *a.* Relating to appeals ; having

ĂP-PĔL'LĄTE, cognizance of appeals.

ĂP-PĔL'LĄNT, *n.* One who appeals.

ĂP-PEL-LĀ'TIQN, *n.* Name ; title ; style ; term.

ĂP-PĔL'LĄ-TĬVE, *n.* A title ; a common noun.

ĂP-PĔL'LĄ-TĬVE, *a.* Common to many.

ĂP-PĘL-LĒĒ', *n.* One against whom an appeal in law has been made ; respondent. [pellant.

ĂP-PĘL-LÖR', *n.* The person appealing ; ap-

ĂP-PĔND', *v. a.* To hang or join ; to add.

ĂP-PĔN'DĄGE, *n.* Something added or joined.

ĂP-PĔN'DĄNT, *a.* Hanging ; annexed.

ĂP-PĔN'DĄNT, *n.* An adventitious part.

ĂP-PĔN'DĬX, *n.* ; pl. ĂP-PĔN'DĬ-CĘS *and* ĂP-PĔN'DĬX-ĘS. Something appended ; an adjunct ; a concomitant ; a supplement.

ĂP-PĘR-TĀIN', *v. n.* To belong ; to pertain.

ĂP'PĘ-TĔNCE, ĂP'PĘ-TĔN-CY, *n.* Desire.

ĂP'PĘ-TĪTE, *n.* Desire of food or of sensual pleasure ; longing ; hunger : — object of desire.

ĂP-PLÂUD', *v. a.* To praise ; to extol ; commend.

ĂP-PLÂUD'ĘR, *n.* One who applauds.

ĂP-PLÂUŞE', *n.* Approbation loudly expressed.

ĂP'PLE (ăp'pl), *n.* A fruit:—pupil of the eye.
ĂP'PLE-TREĒ, *n.* The tree producing apples.
ĂP-PLĬ-CĄ-BĬL'Ĭ-TY, *n.* Fitness to be applied.
ĂP'PLĬ-CĄ-BLE, *a.* Fit to be applied; suitable.
ĂP'PLĬ-CĄ-BLE-NĔSS, *n.* Fitness to be applied.
ĂP'PLĬ-CĄ-BLY, *ad.* Fitly; so as to be applied.
ĂP'PLĬ-CĂNT, *n.* One who applies; a suitor.
ĂP-PLĬ-CA'TIQN, *n.* The act of applying; so-
licitation; intense study; close attention.
ĄP-PLY̆', *v. a.* To put; to address; to busy.
ĄP-PLY̆', *v. n.* To suit; to have recourse.
ĄP-PÖÍNT', *v. a.* To fix; to settle; to establish.
ĄP-PÖÍNT'ĘR, *n.* One who appoints.
ĄP-PÖÍNT'MĘNT, *n.* Act of appointing; of-
fice; order; equipment; part assigned.
ĄP-PÕR'TIQN, *v. a.* To divide in just parts.
ĄP-PÕR'TIQN-ĘR, *n.* One who apportions.[tions.
ĄP-PÕR'TIQN-MĔNT, *n.* A dividing into por-
ĂP'PQ-ŞĬTE, *a.* Proper; fit; well adapted to.
ĂP'PQ-ŞĬTE-LY, *ad.* Properly; suitably; fitly.
ĂP'PQ-ŞĬTE-NĔSS, *n.* Fitness; adaptation.
ĂP-PQ-ŞĬ''TIQN (ăp-pǫ-zĭsh'ǔn), *n.* Addition:—
the putting of two nouns in the same case.
ĄP-PRĀIŞE', *v. a.* To set a price upon.
ĄP-PRĀIŞE'MĘNT, *n.* The act of appraising.
ĄP-PRĀIŞ'ĘR, *n.* One who appraises. [mate.
ĄP-PRĒ'CĬ-ĀTE (ąp-prē'shę-āt), *v. a.* To esti-
ĄP-PRĒ-CĬ-Ā'TIQN (ąp-prē-shę-ā'shun), *n.* Val-
uation; estimation. [ceive; to fear.
ĂP-PRĘ-HĔND', *v. a.* To lay hold on; to con-
ĂP-PRĘ-HĔN'SĬ-BLE, *a.* Conceivable.
ĂP-PRĘ-HĔN'SIQN, *n.* Act of apprehending; fear.
ĂP-PRĘ-HĔN'SĮVE, *a.* Sensible; fearful.
ĄP-PRĔN'TĮCE, *n.* One bound by indenture.
ĄP-PRĔN'TĮCE, *v. a.* To put out as an apprentice.
ĄP-PRĔN'TĮCE-SHĬP, *n.* State or term of service.
ĄP-PRIŞE', *v. a.* To inform; to give notice.
ĄP-PRŌACH' (ąp-prōch'), *v. n. & a.* To draw near.
ĄP-PRŌACH', *n.* Act of drawing near; access.
ĄP-PRŌACH'Ą-BLE, *a.* Accessible.
ĂP-PRQ-BĀ'TIQN, *n.* Act of approving; approval.
ĄP-PRŌ'PRĮ-ĀTE, *v. a.* To set apart; to annex to.
ĄP-PRŌ'PRĮ-ĄTE, *a.* Peculiar; fit; suitable.
ĄP-PRŌ'PRĮ-ĀTE-NĔSS, *n.* Fitness; propriety.
ĄP-PRŌ-PRĮ-Ā'TIQN, *n.* Application to a par-
ticular purpose; that which is appropriated.
ĄP-PRŌ'PRĮ-Ā-TQR, *n.* One who appropriates.
ĄP-PRŌV'Ą-BLE, *a.* Meriting approbation.
ĄP-PRŌV'ĄL, *n.* Approbation; commendation.
ĄP-PRŌVE', *v. a.* To like; to commend.
ĄP-PRŌV'ĘR, *n.* One who approves; commender.
ĄP-PRŌX'Į-MĀTE, *v. a. & n.* To draw near.
ĄP-PRŌX-Į-MĀ'TIQN, *n.* Approach to any thing.
ĂP'PŬLSE, *n.* The act of striking against.
ĄP-PŬR'TĘ-NĄNCE, *n.* That which appertains.
ĄP-PŬR'TĘ-NĄNT, *a.* Joined or belonging to.
Ā'PRĮ-CŎT, *n.* A fruit resembling a peach.
Ā'PRĮL, *n.* The fourth month of the year.
Ā'PRON (ā'pǔrn), *n.* A part of dress; a cover.
ĂPT, *a.* Suitable; ready; quick; dexterous.
ĂP'TĘ-ROŬS, *a.* Having no wings.
ĂP'TĮ-TŪDE, *n.* Fitness; tendency; disposition.
ĂPT'LY, *ad.* Properly; justly; readily; acutely.
ĂPT'NĘSS, *n.* Fitness; quick of apprehension.
ĂP'TŌTE, *n.* (*Gram.*) An indeclinable noun.
Ą-QUĄ-FÖR'TĮS, *n.* (*Chem.*) Nitric acid.
Ą-QUĀ'RĮ-ŬS, *n.* The 11th sign in the zodiac.
Ą-QUĄ-TĬN'TĄ, *n.* A species of engraving.

Ą-QUĂT'ĮC, *a.* Pertaining to, or living in, water.
ĂQ'UĘ-DŬCT (ăk'wę-dŭkt), *n.* An artificial
channel for conducting water; conduit; canal.
Ā'QUĘ-OŬS (ā'kwę-ŭs), *a.* Watery; of water.
ĂQ'UĮ-LĪNE (ăk'wę-lĭn), *a.* Like an eagle.
ĂR'Ą-BĔSQUE (är'ą-bĕsk), *a.* Arabic; Arabian.
Ą-RĀ'BĮ-ĄN, *a.* Pertaining to Arabia; Arabic.
ĂR'Ą-BĬC, *n.* Language of Arabia.—*a.* Arabian.
ĂR'Ą-BLE, *a.* Fit for the plough or tillage.
Ą-RĀ'NĘ-OŬS, *a.* Resembling a spider's web.
ĂR'BĮ-TĘR, *n.* A judge; an umpire. [choice.
ĄR-BĬT'RĄ-MĔNT, *n.* Will; determination;
ĂR'BĮ-TRĄ-RĮ-LY, *ad.* Absolutely; despotically.
ĂR'BĮ-TRĄ-RĮ-NĔSS, *n.* Despoticalness; tyranny.
ĂR'BĮ-TRĄ-RY, *a.* Despotic; absolute; unlimited.
ĂR'BĮ-TRĀTE, *v. a.* To decide; to determine.
ĂR'BĮ-TRĀTE, *v. n.* To give judgment; decide.
ĂR-BĮ-TRĀ'TIQN, *n.* Reference of a cause to
persons mutually agreed on by the parties.
ĂR'BĮ-TRĀ-TQR, *n.* An umpire; a judge.
ĂR'BĮ-TRĀ-TRĮX, *n.* A female judge; an arbitress.
ĂR'BĮ-TRĔSS, *n.* A female arbiter; arbitratrix.
ĂR'BQR, *n.* A bower:—spindle or axis. [to trees.
ĄR-BŌ'RĘ-OŬS, *or* ĂR'BQ-ROŬS, *a.* Belonging
ĂR'BQ-RĔT, *n.* A small tree or shrub.
ĂR-BQ-RĔS'CĘNT, *a.* Growing like a tree.
ĂR'BQ-RĬST, *n.* One who makes trees his study.
ĂR'BŬS-CLE (är'bŭs-sl), *n.* A little shrub.
ĂRC, *n.* A segment of a circle; an arch.
ĄR-CĀDE', *n.* A walk arched over; an arch.
ĄR-CĀ'NŲM, *n.*; *pl.* ĄR-CĀ'NĄ. A secret.
ĂRCH, *n.* Part of a circle or ellipse; a vault.
ĂRCH, *v. a.* To cover with an arch or arches:
—to form into an arch or arches; to vault.
ĂRCH, *a.* Waggish; mirthful; shrewd; princi-
pal; chief. *In composition* it signifies *chief.* [ogy.
ĂR-ℭHÆ-ŎL'Q-GĬST, *n.* One versed in archæol-
ĂR-ℭHÆ-ŎL'Q-G̣Y (är-kę-ŏl'ǫ-ję), *n.* The sci-
ence or doctrine which treats of antiquities.
ĂR-ℭHĀ'ĬC, *a.* Old; ancient; antique.
ĂRℭH'Ą-ĬSM, *n.* An ancient phrase or idiom.
ĂRℭH-ĂN'G̣ĘL (ärk-ān'jĕl), *n.* ·A chief angel.
ĂRℭH-ĄN-G̣ĔL'ĮC, *a.* Belonging to archangels.
ĂRCH-BĬSH'QP, *n.* The principal of the bishops.
ĂRCH-BĬSH'QP-RĬC, *n.* Province of an archbishop.
ĂRCH-DĒA'CON (ärch-dē'kn), *n.* Chief deacon.
ĂRCH-DĒA'CON-RY, *n.* Office of an archdeacon.
ĂRCH-DŪ'CĄL, *a.* Belonging to an archduke.
ĂRCH-DŬCH'ĘSS, *n.* Wife of an archduke.
ĂRCH-DŪKE', *n.* A sovereign prince of Austria.
ĂRCH-DŪKE'DQM, *n.* The territory of an arch-
ĂR'CHĘD, *p. a.* Formed like an arch. [duke.
ĂRCH'ĘR, *n.* One who shoots with a bow.
ĂRCH'ĘR-Y, *n.* The use of the bow. [fiends.
ĂRCH-FIĔND' (ärch-fēnd'), *n.* The chief of
ĂR-ℭHĘ-TY̆'PĄL, *a.* Belonging to the original.
ĂR'ℭHĘ-TY̆PE, *n.* The original; pattern.
ĂR-ℭHĮ-DĮ-ĂC'Q-NĄL, *a.* Belonging to an arch-
deacon, or to an archdeaconry. [bishop.
ĂR-ℭHĮ-Ę-PĬS'CQ-PĄL, *a.* Belonging to an arch-
ĂR-ℭHĮ-PĔL'Ą-GŌ, *n.* A sea abounding in isl-
ĂR'ℭHĮ-TĔCT, *n.* A builder; a chief builder.[ands.
ĂR'ℭHĮ-TĔCT-ŲRE (är'kę-tĕkt-yur), *n.* The art
or science of building; that which is built. [ure.
ĂR-ℭHĮ-TĔCT'Ų-RĄL, *a.* Relating to architect-
ĂR'ℭHĮ-TRĀVE, *n.* That part of the entablature
which lies immediately upon the capital.
ĂR'ℭHĪVĘS, *n. pl.* Records; a place for records.

Ā,Ē,Ī,Ō,Ū,Ȳ, *long;* Ă,Ĕ,Ĭ,Ŏ,Ŭ,Y̆, *short;* Ą,Ę,Į,Q,Ų,Y, *obscure.*—FĀRE, FÄR, FĀST, FÀLL; HÊIR, HĔR;

ÄRCH'LY, *ad.* Jocosely ; slyly ; shrewdly.
ÄRCH'NESS, *n.* Shrewdness ; sly humor.
ÄR'CHÖN (är'kön), *n.* A chief magistrate in
ÄRC'TIC, *a.* Northern ; lying far north. [Greece.
ÄRC'TIC–CÏR'CLE, *n.* The circle which forms
 the southern limit of the frigid zone.
ÄR'CU-ATE,*a.* Bent in the form of a bow ; curved.
ÄR-CU-BA-LÏS'TER, *n.* A crossbow-man.
ÄR'DEN-CY, *n.* Ardor ; eagerness ; heat.
ÄR'DENT, *a.* Hot ; fervid ; fierce ; vehement.
ÄR'DOR, *n.* Heat ; heat of affection ; zeal.
ÄR'DU-OŬS, *a.* High : — laborious ; difficult.
ÄR'DU-OŬS-NĔSS, *n.* Height ; difficulty.
ÄRE (är). The indicative mode, present tense,
 plural number of the verb *to be.*
Ä'RE-A, *n.* Superficial content ; open surface.
ÄR-E-FÄC'TIQN, *n.* The state of growing dry.
A-RĒ'NA, *n.* An open space for combat.
ÄR-E-NĀ'CEOŲS (är-e-nā'shŭs), *a.* Sandy.
A-RĒ'Q-LA, *n.* A colored circle round the nipple.
ÄR-E-ŎP'A-ĠĪTE, *n.* A judge in the Areopagus.
ÄR-E-ŎP'A-ĠŬS,*n.* The highest court at Athens.
ÄR'ĠENT, *a.* Silvery ; white, like silver.
ÄR'ĠENT, *n.* White color in coats of arms.
ÄR-ĠEN-TĀ'TIQN, *n.* An overlaying with silver.
ÄR'ĠEN-TĪNE, *a.* Pertaining to, or like, silver.
ÄR'ĠIL, *n.* Potter's clay ; white clay ; alumina.
ÄR-ĠIL-LĀ'CEOŲS (är-jil-lā'shŭs), *a.* Clayey.
ÄR'ĠUE (är'gŭ), *v. n.* To reason ; to dispute.
ÄR'ĠUE, *v. a.* To prove ; to reason ; to debate.
ÄR'ĠU-ER, *n.* A reasoner ; a debater. [discourse.
ÄR'ĠU-MĔNT, *n.* A reason alleged ; subject of
ÄR-ĠU-MĔNT'AL, *a.* Belonging to an argument.
ÄR-ĠU-MEN-TĀ'TIQN, *n.* The act of reasoning.
ÄR-ĠU-MĔNT'A-TĬVE, *a.* Consisting of argu-
AR-ĠŪTE', *a.* Subtle ; witty : — shrill. [ment.
Ä'RI-AN, *n.* One of the sect of Arius, who be-
 lieved Christ to be noblest of created beings.
Ä'RI-AN-ĬSM, *n.* The doctrine of the Arians.
ÄR'ĬD, *a.* Dry ; dried up ; parched with heat.
A-RĬD'I-TY, *n.* State of being arid ; dryness.
Ä'RI-ĒṢ, *n.* The Ram ; a sign of the zodiac.
A-RĬGHT' (a-rīt'), *ad.* Rightly ; correctly.
A-RĪṢE', *v. n.* [*imp. t.* arose ; *pp.* arisen.] To
 mount upward ; to ascend ; to get up ; to rise.
ÄR-IS-TŎC'RA-CY, *n.* A government by nobles ;
 the principal persons of a state or town, &c.
A-RÍS'TQ-CRÄT *or* ÄR'IS-TQ-CRÄT, *n.* One
 who favors aristocracy ; one of the aristocracy.
ÄR-IS-TQ-CRÄT'IC, *or* ÄR-IS-TQ-CRÄT'I-CAL, *a.*
 Relating to, or partaking of, aristocracy.
ÄR-IS-TQ-TĒ'LI-AN, *a.* Relating to Aristotle.
ÄR-IS-TQ-TĒ'LI-AN, *n.* A follower of Aristotle.
A-RÏTH'ME-TĬC, *n.* The science of numbers.
ÄR-ITH-MĔT'I-CAL, *a.* According to arithmetic.
A-RÏTH-ME-TÏ''CIAN (a-rĭth-me-tĭsh'an), *n.* One
 skilled in the art of numbers, or arithmetic.
ÄRK, *n.* A chest ; a coffer : — a ship ; a vessel.
ÄRM, *n.* A limb, as of the body ; inlet ; weapon.
ÄRM, *v. a.* To furnish with arms ; to fortify.
ÄRM, *v. n.* To take arms ; to arm one's self.
ÄR-MĀ'DA, *n.* An armament for sea ; a fleet.
ÄR-MA-DÏL'LÖ, *n.* A small South American
 quadruped covered with small bony plates.
ÄR'MA-MĔNT, *n.* A force equipped for war.
ÄR'MA-TŪRE, *n.* Armor : — a piece of soft iron
 applied to the opposite poles of magnets.
ÄRM'FŬL, *n.* As much as the arms can enfold.

ÄRM'HÖLE, *n.* Armpit ; hole of a sleeve.
ÄR'MI-ĠER, *n.* An armor-bearer ; an esquire.
AR-MÏĠ'ER-OŬS, *a.* Bearing arms or weapons.
ÄR'MIL-LA-RY, *a.* Resembling a bracelet.
ÄR'MIL-LÄT-ED, *a.* Having bracelets. [minius.
AR-MÏN'IAN (ar-mĭn'yan), *n.* A follower of Ar-
AR-MÏN'IAN, *a.* Relating to the sect of Arminius.
AR-MÏN'IAN-ĬṢM, *n.* The doctrine of Arminius.
AR-MÏP'Q-TĔNT, *a.* Powerful in arms.
ÄR'MIS-TĬCE, *n.* A cessation from arms ; a truce.
ÄRM'LET, *n.* A little arm ; a bracelet.
ÄR'MQR, *n.* Defensive arms for the body.
ÄR'MQR-BEÄR'ER (är'mur-bår'er), *n.* He who
 carries the armor of another ; an esquire.
ÄR'MQR-ER, *n.* One who makes or sells arms.
AR-MŌ'RI-AL, *a.* Belonging to armor ; heraldic.
ÄR'MQ-RY, *n.* A repository of arms ; armor.
ÄRM'PĬT, *n.* The hollow under the shoulder.
ÄRMṢ, *n. pl.* Weapons ; ensigns armorial.
ÄR'MY, *n.* A large body of troops : — multitude.
A-RŌ'MA, *n.* The odorant principle of plants.
ÄR-Q-MÄT'IC, { *a.* Containing aroma ; spicy ;
ÄR-Q-MÄT'I-CAL, } fragrant ; high-scented.
ÄR-Q-MÄT'ICS, *n. pl.* Spices ; fragrant drugs.
ÄR'Q-MA-TĪZE, *v. a.* To scent with spices.
A-RŌṢE', *imp. t.* of the verb *arise.*
A-RÖÜND', *ad.* In a circle ; on every side.
A-RÖÜND', *prep.* About ; encircling ; round.
A-RÖÜṢE', *v. a.* To wake from sleep ; to rouse.
ÄR'QUE-BŬSE, *n.* A sort of hand-gun.
AR-RÄCK', *n.* Spirit from the cocoa-nut, &c.
AR-RĀIGN' (ar-rän'), *v. a.* To call to answer to
 an indictment ; to charge ; to accuse.
AR-RĀIGN'MENT,*n.* The act of arraigning.
AR-RÄNĠE', *v. a.* To put in order ; to adjust.
AR-RÄNĠE'MENT, *n.* Order ; a putting in order.
ÄR'RANT, *a.* Bad in a high degree ; very vile.
ÄR'RAS, *n.* Tapestry or hangings for rooms.
AR-RĀY', *n.* Order of battle ; dress ; attire.
AR-RĀY' (ar-rā'), *v. a.* To put in order ; to deck.
AR-RĒAR', AR-RĒARṢ', *n.* That which is un-
AR-RĒAR'AĠE,*n.* Sum unpaid ; arrears. [paid.
AR-RĔCT', *a.* Erected ; upright ; attentive.
AR-RĔST', *n.* Seizure under legal process ; stop.
AR-RĔST', *v. a.* To seize ; to stay ; to obstruct.
AR-RĔT', *n.* Decision of a court, &c. ; arrest.
AR-RĪ'VAL, *n.* The act of arriving ; a coming.
AR-RĪVE', *v. n.* To come to a place ; to happen.
ÄR'RQ-GANCE, *n.* Haughtiness ; insolence.
ÄR'RQ-GANT,*a.* Containing arrogance ; haughty.
ÄR'RQ-GANT-LY, *ad.* In an arrogant manner.
ÄR'RQ-GĀTE,*v. a.* To claim proudly ; to assume.
ÄR'RÖW, *n.* A weapon shot from a bow.
ÄR'RÖW-Y (är'rq-e), *a.* Of, or resembling, arrows.
ÄR'SE-NAL, *n.* A magazine of arms, &c.
AR-SĔN'I-CAL, *a.* Containing arsenic.
ÄR'SE-NĬC, *n.* A very poisonous substance.
ÄR'SON (är'sn), *n.* The crime of house-burning.
ÄRT, 2d person singular of the verb *to be.*
ÄRT, *n.* A science ; a trade ; skill ; cunning.
AR-TĒ'RI-AL, *a.* Relating to an artery.
ÄR'TE-RY, *n.* A canal or tube conveying the
 blood from the heart to all parts of the body.
ÄRT'FŬL, *a.* Cunning ; dexterous ; crafty.
ÄRT'FŬL-LY, *ad.* With art ; skilfully ; craftily.
ÄRT'FŬL-NĔSS, *n.* Skill ; cunning ; craftiness.
AR-THRĬT'IC, { *a.* Relating to joints : — re-
AR-THRĬT'I-CAL, } lating to the gout ; gouty.

ÄR'TĮ-CHŌKE, *n.* An esculent plant.
ÄR'TĮ-CLE, *n.* A part· of speech; a clause; term; stipulation; a division; a substance.
ÄR'TĮ-CLE, *v. n. & a.* To bind by stipulation.
ĄR-TĬC'Ų-LĄR, *a.* Belonging to the joints.
ĄR-TĬC'Ų-LĄTE, *a.* Distinct; plain; jointed.
ĄR-TĬC'Ų-LĀTE, *v. a.* To utter; to speak. ·
ĄR-TĬC'Ų-LĀTE, *v. n.* To speak distinctly.
ĄR-TĬC'Ų-LĄTE-LY, *ad.* In an articulate voice.
ĄR TĬC-Ų-LĀ'TIǪN, *n.* Act of articulating; distinct utterance:—connection of bones by joints.
ÄR'TĮ-FĬCE, *n.* Trick; fraud; cunning; deceit.
ĄR-TĬF'Į-CĘR, *n.* An artist; a manufacturer.
ÄR-TĮ-FĬ''CIĄL (är-te-fĭsh'ạl), *a.* Made by art, not natural; fictitious; not genuine.
ÄR-TĮ-FĬ''CIĄL-LY, *ad.* By art; not naturally.
ĄR-TĬL'LĘR-Y, *n.* Weapons of war; ordnance.
ÄRT'Į-ŞÄN, *n.* A mechanic; handicraftsman.
ÄRT'ĮST, *n.* One skilled in the arts; an adept.
ÄRT'LĘSS, *a.* Unskilful; void of fraud; simple.
ÄRT'LĘSS-LY, *ad.* In an artless manner.
ÄRT'LĘSS-NĔSS, *n.* Want of art; simplicity.
Ą-RŬN-DĮ-NĀ'CEǪŲS (ạ-rŭn-de-nā'shụs), *or* ÄR-ŲN-DĬN'Ę-OŬS, *a.* Of, or resembling, reeds.
Ą-RŬS'PĘX,) *n.* A soothsayer; a diviner by
Ą-RŬS'PĮCE,) the entrails of victims.
ÄŞ, *conj.* In the same manner; like; equally.
ÄŞ-Ą-FŒT'Į-DĄ (äs-ạ-fĕt'e-dạ), *n.* A fetid gum.
ĄŞ-BĔS'TĮNE, *a.* Pertaining to asbestos. [stance.
ĄŞ-BĔS'TǪS, *n.* A fibrous incombustible sub-
ĄS-CĔND', *v. n. & a.* To rise; to move upwards.
ĄS-CĔND'Ą-BLE, *a.* Capable of being ascended.
ĄS-CĔND'ANT, *n.* Height; superiority.
ĄS-CĔND'ANT, *a.* Superior; above the horizon.
ĄS-CĔN'DĘN-CY, *n.* Influence; power; sway.
ĄS-CĔN'SIǪN (ạs-sĕn'shụn), *n.* Act of ascending.
ĄS-CĔN'SIǪN-DĀY, *n.* The day on which the ascension of our Saviour is commemorated.
ĄS-CĔNT', *n.* Rise; an eminence, or high place.
ÄS-CĘR-TĀIN', *v. a.* To make certain; to establish; to determine; to settle; to fix. [tained.
ÄS-CĘR-TĀIN'Ą-BLE, *a.* That may be ascer-
ÄS-CĘR-TĀIN'MĘNT, *n.* Act of ascertaining.
ĄS-CĔT'ĮC, *a.* Employed in devout exercises.
ĄS-CĔT'ĮC, *n.* A devout recluse; a hermit.
ĄS-CĔT'Į-CĬŞM, *n.* The state of an ascetic.
ĄS-CĬT'ĮC, *or* ĄS-CĬT'Į-CĄL, *a.* Dropsical.
ĄS-CRĪ'BĄ-BLE, *a.* That may be ascribed.
ĄS-CRĪBE', *v. a.* To attribute; to assign.
ĄS-CRĬP'TIǪN, *n.* The act of ascribing.
ÄSH, *n.* A tree; wood of the tree. [with shame.
Ą-SHĀM'ĘD (ạ-shämd' *or* ạ-shäm'ĕd), *a.* Touched
ÄSH'EŞ, *n. pl.* The remains of any thing burnt.
Ą-SHŌRE', *ad.* On shore; on land; aground.
ÄSH'-WĔDNEŞ'DĄY, *n.* The first day of Lent.
ÄSH'Y, *a.* Ash-colored; turned into ashes.
Ā-SĮ-ĂT'ĮC (ā-she-ăt'jk), *a.* Pertaining to Asia.
Ā'SĮ-ĂT'ĮC (ā-she-ăt'jk), *n.* A native of Asia.
Ą-SĪDE', *ad.* To one side; apart from the rest.
ÄS'Į-NĪNE, *a.* Belonging to, or like, an ass.
ÄSK, *v. a.* To beg; to request; to question.
ÄSK, *v. n.* To petition; to make inquiry.
ĄS-KĂNCE',) *ad.* Sideways; obliquely.
ĄS-KĂNT',)
ÄSK'ĘR, *n.* One who asks; a petitioner; inquirer.
Ą-SKEW', *ad.* Obliquely; askance; askant.
Ą-SLĂNT', *ad.* In a slanting manner; obliquely.
Ą-SLĒEP', *a. & ad.* Sleeping; at rest:—dead.

Ą-SLŌPE', *ad.* With declivity; obliquely.
ÄSP, *or* ÄS'PĮC, *n.* A poisonous serpent.
ĄS-PÄR'Ą-GŬS, *n.* An esculent plant.
ÄS'PĘCT, *n.* Look; countenance; air; view.
ÄS'PĘN, *n.* A poplar having trembling leaves.
ÄS'PĘR, *n.* A small Turkish coin. [ness.
ĄS-PĔR'Į-TY, *n.* Roughness; harshness; sharp-
ĄS-PĔRSE', *v. a.* To slander; to calumniate.
ĄS-PĔR'SIǪN, *n.* Detraction; censure; calumny.
ĄS-PHĂL'TĬC, *a.* Pertaining to asphaltum.
ĄS-PHĂL'TỤM, *n.* Compact native bitumen.
ÄS'PHǪ-DĔL, *n.* A genus of plants.
ÄS'PĬC, *n.* A venomous serpent. See ÄSP.
ĄS-PĪR'ANT *or* ÄS'PĮ-RĂNT, *n.* An aspirer.
ÄS'PĮ-RĀTE, *v. a.* To roughen in pronunciation.
ÄS'PĮ-RĄTE, *n.* A mark of aspiration.
ÄS-PĮ-RĀ'TIǪN, *n.* A breathing after; longing; pronunciation of a letter with rough breathing.
ĄS-PĪRE', *v. n.* To long; to desire eagerly.
ĄS-PĪR'ĘR, *n.* One who aspires; aspirant.
Ą-SQUĬNT', *ad.* Obliquely; not in a right line.
ÄSS, *n.* An animal of burden:—a dull fellow.
ĄS-SĀIL', *v. a.* To attack; to fall upon.
ĄS-SĀIL'Ą-BLE, *a.* That may be assailed.
ĄS-SĀIL'ANT,) *n.* One who assails or attacks;
ĄS-SĀIL'ĘR,) an aggressor; an assaulter.
ĄS-SĂS'SĮN, *n.* A secret or private murderer.
ĄS-SĂS'SĮ-NĀTE, *v. a.* To murder in secret.
ĄS-SĂS-SĮ-NĀ'TIǪN, *n.* The act of assassinating.
ĄS-SĂS'SĮ-NĀ-TǪR, *n.* One who assassinates.
ĄS-SÂULT', *n.* Attack; storm; hostile violence.
ĄS-SÂULT', *v. a.* To attack; fall upon violently.
ĄS-SÂULT'Ą-BLE, *a.* Capable of being assaulted.
ĄS-SÂULT'ĘR, *n.* One who assaults; assailer.
ĄS-SĀY', *n.* A trial; attempt; examination.
ĄS-SĀY', *v. a.* To try or prove, as metals; to test.
ĄS-SĀY', *v. n.* To try; to endeavor; to attempt.
ĄS-SĀY'ĘR, *n.* One who assays metals, &c.
ĄS-SĔM'BLĄGE, *n.* A collection; a group.
ĄS-SĔM'BLE, *v. a. & n.* To bring or meet together; to collect; to convene; to convoke.
ĄS-SĔM'BLY, *n.* A company; congregation.
ĄS-SĔNT', *n.* The act of agreeing; consent.
ĄS-SĔNT', *v. n.* To concede; to consent.
ĄS-SĔRT', *v. a.* To maintain; to affirm; to claim.
ĄS-SĔR'TIǪN, *n.* Act of asserting; affirmation.
ĄS-SĔR'TĮVE, *a.* That asserts; positive.
ĄS-SĔRT'ǪR, *n.* A maintainer; a vindicator.
ĄS-SĔSS', *v. a.* To charge with any certain sum.
ĄS-SĔS'SĄ-BLE, *a.* That may be assessed.
ĄS-SĔSS'MĘNT, *n.* A sum levied; act of assessing.
ĄS-SĔSS'ǪR, *n.* One who assesses for taxes.
ÄS'SĔTS, *n. pl.* Property or effects applicable to the discharge of debts, legacies, &c.
ĄS-SĔV'ĘR-ĀTE, *v. a.* To affirm; to aver.
ĄS-SĔV-ER-Ā'TIǪN, *n.* Solemn affirmation.
ÄS-SĮ-DŪ'Į-TY, *n.* Diligence; close application.
ĄS-SĬD'Ų-OŬS, *a.* Constant in application.
ĄS-SĬD'Ų-OŬS-LY, *ad.* Diligently; industriously.
ĄS-SĬD'Ų-OŲS-NĔSS, *n.* Diligence; assiduity.
ĄS-SĪGN' (ạs-sīn'), *v. a.* To mark out; to fix; to appropriate; to make over; to transfer.
ĄS-SĪGN', *n.* One to whom an assignment in law is made; an assignee. [assigned.
ĄS-SĪGN'Ą-BLE (ạs-sīn'ạ-bl), *a.* That may be
ÄS-SĮG-NĀ'TIǪN, *n.* An appointment to meet.
ÄS-SĮGN-ĒĒ' (äs-sę-nē'), *n.* One to whom any assignment is made; an assign; an executor.

Ā,Ē,Ī,Ō,Ū,Ȳ, *long;* Ă,Ĕ,Ĭ,Ŏ,Ŭ,Y̆, *short;* Ą,Ę,Į,Ǫ,Ų,Y, *obscure.*—FÀRE,FÄR,FĂST,FÂLL; HÊIR,HĒR;

Ąs-sĭGN′ẸR (ąs-sī′nẹr), } n. One who ap-
Ăs-sĭGN-ÖR′ (ăs-sẹ-nör′), } points or assigns.
Ąs-sĭGN′MẸNT (ąs-sīn′mẹnt), n. The act of as-
  signing; transfer of any property or right.
Ąs-sĭM′Ị-LĀTE, v. a. & n. To make or grow like.
Ąs-sĭM-Ị-LĀ′TIǪN, n. The act of assimilating.
Ąs-sĭST′, v. a. To help; to aid; to succor.
Ąs-sĭST′ẠNCE, n. Help; aid; succor; support.
Ąs-sĭST′ẠNT, n. One who assists; a coadjutor.
Ąs-sīZE′, n. A court, or the sitting of a court.
Ąs-sīZE′,v.a. To adjust,as weights,measures,&c.
Ąs-sīZ′ẸR, n. An officer who has the care of
  weights and measures : — in Scotland, a juryman.
Ąs-sō′CỊ-A-BLE (ąs-sō′shẹ-ạ-bl), a. Capable of
  being associated; sociable; companionable.
Ąs-sō′CỊ-ĀTE (ąs-sō′shẹ-āt), v. a. To join as
  follower, confederate, or companion ; to unite. ·
Ąs-sō′CỊ-ĀTE, v. n. To unite in company.
Ąs-sō′CỊ-ĀTE (ąs-sō′shẹ-ạt), a. Confederate.
Ąs-sō′CỊ-ĀTE, n. A partner; a companion.
Ąs-sō-CỊ-Ā′TIǪN (ąs-sō-shẹ-ā′shụn), n. Union;
  confederacy; connection; a society or body.
Ąs-sÖRT′, v. a. To arrange in order; to class.
Ąs-sÖRT′MẸNT, n. The act of assorting or
  classifying; a quantity selected or arranged.
Ąs-sUĀGE′ (ąs-swāj′), v. a. To soften; to ease.
Ąs-sUĀGE′MẸNT, n. Mitigation; abatement.
Ąs-sUĀG′ẸR, n. One who assuages; an appeaser.
Ąs-sUĀ′SỊVE (ąs-swā′sịv), a. Mitigating.
Ąs-sŪME′, v. a. To take; to claim; to arrogate.
Ąs-sŪME′, v. n. To claim more than is due.
Ąs-sŪM′ỊNG, p. a. Arrogant; haughty; proud.
Ąs-sŪMP′TIǪN (ąs-sŭm′shụn), n. The act of
  assuming; supposition; the thing supposed.
Ąs-sŪR′ẠNCE (ạ-shūr′ạns), n. Certain expecta-
  tion; confidence; courage; security; boldness.
Ąs-sŪRE′ (ạ-shūr′), v. a. To make sure.
Ąs-sŪR′ẸD-LY (ạ-shūr′ẹd-lẹ), ad. Certainly.
Ąs-sŪR′ẸD-NÈSS (ạ-shūr′ẹd-nĕs), n. Certainty.
Ąs-sŪR′ẸR (ạ-shūr′er), n. One who assures.
Ăs′TẸR-ĬSK, n. A star or mark in printing; as, *.
Ăs′TẸR-ĬSM, n. A constellation; an asterisk.
A-sTĖRN′, ad. Behind a ship; backward.
Ăs′TẸ-RŎĬD, n. A small planet.
Ăsth′MA (ăst′mạ), n. Difficulty of breathing.
Ąsth-MĂT′ĬC, ĄSTH-MĂT′I-CẠL, a. Relating
  to, or afflicted with, the asthma.
Ąs-TŎN′ĬSH, v. a. To amaze; to surprise.
Ąs-TŎN′ĬSH-ĬNG, a. Amazing; surprising.
Ąs-TŎN′ĬSH-MÈNT, n. Amazement; great sur-
Ąs-TÖÛND′, v. a. To astonish; to amaze. [prise.
A-sTRĂD′DLE, ad. With the legs across or open.
Ăs′TRẠ-GĂL, n. An ornament in architecture.
Ăs′TRẠL, a. Starry; relating to the stars.
A-sTRĀY′, ad. Out of the right way.
Ąs-TRĬCT′, v. a. To contract; to astringe.
Ąs-TRĬC′TIǪN, n. Restraint : — contraction.
A-sTRĪDE′, ad. With the legs apart; across.
Ąs-TRĬNGE′, v. a. To draw together; to bind.
Ąs-TRĬN′GEN-CY, n. The power of contracting.
Ąs-TRĬN′GENT, a. Binding; contracting. [tract.
Ąs-TRĬN′GENTS, n. pl. Medicines which con-
Ąs-TRŎL′Ǫ-GẸR, n. One versed in astrology.
Ăs-TRǪ-LŎG′ĬC, } a. Professing or relating
Ăs-TRǪ-LŎG′Ị-CẠL, } to astrology. [trology.
Ăs-TRǪ-LŎG′Ị-CẠL-LY, ad. According to as-
Ąs-TRŎL′Ǫ-GY, n. The foretelling future events
  by the position of the heavenly bodies.

Ąs-TRŎN′Ǫ-MẸR, n. One versed in astronomy.
Ăs-TRǪ-NŎM′Ị-CẠL, a. Belonging to astronomy.
Ăs-TRǪ-NŎM′Ị-CẠL-LY, ad. By astronomy.
Ąs-TRŎN′Ǫ-MY, n. The science which treats of
  the heavenly bodies,their motions,distances,&c.
Ąs-TŪTE′, a. Cunning; shrewd; clever.
Ạ-sŬN′DẸR, ad. Apart; in two parts.
Ạ-sȲ′LỤM, n. A sanctuary; a refuge; a shelter.
ĂT, prep. Denoting nearness or presence ; by.
ĂT′Ạ-BĂL, n. A kind of tabor used by the Moors.
ĀTE. Imp. t. from the verb eat.
ĂTH-Ạ-NĀ′SIẠN, a. Relating to Athanasius.
Ā′THẸ-ĬSM, n. Disbelief in the being of a God.
Ā′THẸ-ĬST, n. One who denies God's existence.
Ā-THẸ-ĬS′TĬC, } a. Pertaining to atheism;
Ā-THẸ-ĬS′TỊ-CẠL, } partaking of atheism.
Ā-THẸ-ĬS′TỊ-CẠL-LY, ad. In an atheistical man-
  ner; with atheism. [brary.
ĂTH-Ẹ-NÆ′ỤM, n. A public institution or li-
Ạ-THĬRST′, ad. or a. Thirsty; in want of drink.
ĂTH-LĔT′ĬC, a. Strong of body; vigorous; per-
  taining to wrestling or bodily exercise.
A-THWÂRT′, prep. Across; transverse; through.
A-TĬLT′, ad. In a tilted position. [gigantic.
ĂT-LĂN-TĒ′ẠN, a. Resembling the giant Atlas;
AT-LĂN′TỊC, a. Pertaining to the ocean which
  lies east of America. — n. Atlantic ocean.
ĂT′LẠS, n. A collection of maps; a large folio.
ĂT′MǪS-PHÈRE (ăt′mǫs-fēr), n. The air or elas-
  tic fluid which encompasses the earth.
ĂT-MǪS-PHĔR′ĬC, } a. Pertaining to, or con-
ĂT-MǪS-PHĔR′Ị-CẠL, } sisting of, the atmos-
ĂT′ǪM, n. An extremely small particle. [phere.
Ạ-TŎM′ĬC, or Ạ-TŎM′Ị-CẠL, a. Relating to atoms.
Ạ-TŌNE′, v. n. To expiate; to make satisfaction.
Ạ-TŌNE′MẸNT, n. Reconciliation; expiation.
Ạ-TŌN′ẸR, n. One who atones or reconciles.
ĂT-RẠ-MĔN′TẠL, ĂT-RẠ-MĔN′TOỤS, a. Black.
Ạ-TRŌ′CIOỤS (ạ-trō′shụs), a. Wicked in a high
  degree; villanous; outrageous; flagitous.
Ạ-TRŌ′CIOỤS-LY, ad. In an atrocious manner.
Ạ-TRŌ′CIOỤS-NÈSS, n. Enormous criminality.
Ạ-TRŎC′Ị-TY, n. Great wickedness; enormity.
ĂT′RǪ-PHY, n. Emaciation; a wasting. [seize.
AT-TĂCH′, v. a. To fasten; to bind; to take; to
AT-TĂCH′MẸNT, n. Adherence; liking; bond
  of affection. — (Law.) An apprehension.
AT-TĂCK′, v. a. To assault; to assail.
AT-TĂCK′, n. An assault; invasion; onset.
AT-TĀIN′, v. a. To gain; to obtain; to come to.
AT-TĀIN′, v. n. To reach; to arrive.
AT-TĀIN′Ạ-BLE, a. That may be attained.
AT-TĀIN′Ạ-BLE-NÈSS, n. The being attainable.
AT-TĀIND′ẸR, n. Act of attainting; taint.
AT-TĀIN′MẸNT, n. Acquisition; thing attained.
AT-TĀINT′, v. a. To disgrace; to taint, corrupt.
AT-TĀINT′, n. A stain; a spot; a kind of writ.
AT-TĀINT′MẸNT, n. The state of being attainted.
AT-TĔM′PẸR, v.a. To temper; to mingle; to adapt.
AT-TĔMPT′ (ąt-tĕmt′), v. a. To try; to endeav-
  or; to essay; to make experiment; to tempt.
AT-TĔMPT′, n. An essay ; a trial; endeavor.
AT-TĔMPT′Ạ-BLE, a. That may be attempted.
AT-TĔMPT′ẸR, n. One who attempts.
AT-TĔND′, v. a. To wait on; to accompany.
AT-TĔND′, v. n. To listen; to wait; to be near.
AT-TĔND′ẠNCE, n. Act of waiting on; a train.
AT-TĔND′ẠNT, a. Accompanying as subordinate.

ĂT-TĔND'ĂNT, n. One who attends.
ĂT-TĔN'TIŎN, n. The act of attending; civility.
ĂT-TĔN'TĪVE, a. Heedful; regardful; mindful.
ĂT-TĔN'TĪVE-LỲ, ad. Heedfully; carefully.
ĂT-TĔN'TĪVE-NĔSS, n. State of being attentive.
ĂT-TĔN'Ụ-ĀTE, v. a. To make thin or slender.
ĂT-TĔN-Ụ-Ā'TIŎN, n. Act of attenuating.
ĂT-TĔST', v. a. To bear witness to; to invoke.
ĂT-TĘS-TĀ'TIŎN, n. Testimony; formal witness.
ĂT'TĬC, a. Relating to Attica; elegant; upper.
ĂT'TĬC, n. A native of Attica: — a garret.
ĂT'TĬ-CĬŞM, n. An Attic idiom or phrase.
ĂT-TĪRE', v. a. To dress; to clothe; to array.
ĂT-TĪRE', n. Clothes; dress; the head-dress.
ĂT'TĬ-TŪDE, n. Posture; position; gesture.
ĂT-TÖR'NEỲ (ạt-tür'nẹ), n. One who is author-
  ized to act for another, as in matters of law.
ĂT-TRĂCT', v. a. To draw; to allure; to win.
ĂT-TRĂC'TIŎN, n. The power or act of drawing.
ĂT-TRĂC'TĪVE, a. Drawing; alluring; inviting.
ĂT-TRĂC'TĪVE, n. That which draws or incites.
ĂT-TRĂC'TĪVE-LỲ, ad. In an attracting manner.
ĂT-TRĂC'TĪVE-NĔSS, n. The being attractive.
ĂT-TRĂCT'ŎR, n. One that attracts.
ĂT-TRĬB'Ụ-TẠ-BLE, a. Ascribable; imputable.
ĂT-TRĬB'ỤTE, v. a. To ascribe; to impute.
ĂT'TRĬ-BŪTE, n. A quality; a thing inherent.
ĂT-TRĬB'Ụ-TĪVE, a. Expressing an attribute.
ĂT-TRĬ''TIŎN (ạt-trĭsh'ụn), n. Act of wearing.
ĂT-TŪNE', v. a. To make musical; to tune.
ÂU'BỤRN, a. Reddish-brown; chestnut color.
ÂUC'TIŎN (âwk'shụn), n. Public sale by bidding.
ÂUC-TIŎN-ĒĒR', n. One who sells by auction.
ÂU-DĀ'CIOỤS (âw-dā'shụs), a. Bold; impudent.
ÂU-DĀ'CIOỤS-LỲ, ad. Boldly; impudently.
ÂU-DĀ'CIOỤS-NĔSS, n. The being audacious.
ÂU-DĂÇ'Ĭ-TỲ, n. Effrontery; spirit; boldness.
ÂU'DĬ-BLE, a. Capable of being heard.
ÂU'DĬ-BLE-NĔSS, n. Capability of being heard.
ÂU'DĬ-BLỲ, ad. In an audible manner.
ÂU'DĬ-ĔNCE, n. A hearing; auditory; assembly.
ÂU'DĬT, n. The settling of accounts: — hearing.
ÂU'DĬT, v. a. To adjust, as an account.
ÂU'DĬ-TŎR, n. A hearer; a person employed
  and authorized to adjust an account.
ÂU'DĬ-TŎR-SHĬP, n. The office of an auditor.
ÂU'DĬ-TQ-RỲ, a. Relating to hearing.
ÂU'DĬ-TQ-RỲ, n. An audience; an assembly.
ÂU'GĔR, n. A tool to bore holes with.
ÂUGHT (âwt), n. Any thing; any part.
ÂUG-MĔNT', v. a. To increase; — v. n. To grow.
ÂUG'MĘNT, n. Increase; state of increase.
ÂUG-MĘN-TĀ'TIŎN, n. The act of increasing.
ÂU'GỤR, n. One who predicts by omens.
ÂU'GỤR, v. n. To guess; to conjecture by signs.
ÂU'GỤR, v. a. To foretell; to predict.
ÂU-GŪ'RĬ-ẠL, a. Relating to augury.
ÂU'GỤ-RỲ, n. Prognostication by omens.
ÂU'GỤST, n. The eighth month in the year.
ÂU-GŬST', a. Great; grand; awful; majestic.
ÂU-GŬST'NĘSS, n. Dignity; majesty; grandeur.
ÂU'LĬC, a. Belonging to an imperial court.
ÄUNT (änt), n. A father's or mother's sister.
ÂU'RẠ, n. A gentle current of air: — a vapor.
ÂU-RĒ'LĬ-Ạ, n. The chrysalis of an insect.
ÂU-RĒ'Q-LẠ, n. A circle of rays; halo of glory.
ÂU'RĬ-CLE, n. (Anat.) The external ear. [cret.
ÂU-RĬC'Ụ-LẠR, a. Within hearing; told in se-

ÂU-RĬF'ĘR-OŬS, a. Producing or yielding gold.
ÂU'RĬST, n. One who treats diseases of the ear.
ÂU-RŌ'RẠ, n. The dawn of day; morning.
ÂU-RŌ'RẠ-BŌ-RĘ-Ā'LĬS, n. The northern lights.
ÂUS-CỤL-TĀ'TIŎN, n. Act of listening.
ÂU'SPĬCE, n. Omen; protection; influence.
ÂU-SPĬ''CIOỤS (âw-spĭsh'ụs), a. Having omens
  of success; prosperous; propitious; fortunate.
ÂU-SPĬ''CIOỤS-LỲ, ad. Prosperously; happily.
ÂU-SPĬ''CIOỤS-NĔSS, n. Prosperous appearance.
ÂU-STĔRE', a. Severe; harsh; rigid; stern.
ÂU-STĔRE'NĘSS, n. Severity; rigor; sternness.
ÂU-STĔR'Ĭ-TỲ, n. Severity; rigor; mortified life.
ÂUS'TRẠL, a. Southern; towards the south.
ÂU-THĔN'TĬC, a. Not fictitious; genuine; true.
ÂU-THĔN'TĬ-CẠL-LỲ, ad. In an authentic man-
ÂU-THĔN'TĬ-CẠL-NĔSS, n. Authenticity. [ner.
ÂU-THĔN'TĬ-CĀTE, v. a. To prove authentic.
ÂU-THĘN-TĬÇ'Ĭ-TỲ, n. Authority; genuineness.
ÂU'THŎR, n. The first beginner or mover; the
  efficient; the writer or composer of a book.
ÂU'THŎR-ĔSS, n. A female author. [itive.
ÂU-THŎR'Ĭ-TẠ-TĪVE, a. Having authority; pos-
ÂU-THŎR'Ĭ-TỲ, n. Legal power; influence;
  power; rule; support; testimony; credibility.
ÂU'THŎR-ĪZE, v. a. To give authority to; to jus-
ÂU'THŎR-SHĬP, n. State of being an author. [tify.
ÂU-TQ-BĬ-ŎG'RẠ-PHỲ, n. The biography or
  life of a person written by himself.
ÂU'TQ-CRĂT, n. An absolute sovereign or ruler.
ÂU'TQ-GRĂPH, n. One's own handwriting.
ÂU-TQ-GRĂPH'Ĭ-CẠL, a. Relating to autography.
ÂU-TŎG'RẠ-PHỲ, n. A person's own writing.
ÂU-TQ-MĂT'Ĭ-CẠL, a. Belonging to an automaton.
ÂU-TŎM'Ạ-TŎN, n.; pl. ÂU-TŎM'Ạ-TẠ. A ma-
  chine so constructed as to appear to be self-
  moving; a self-moving machine.
ÂU'TỤMN (âw'tụm), n. The season of the year
  between summer and winter; fall of the year.
ÂU-TŬM'NẠL, a. Belonging to autumn.
ÂUX-ĬL'IẠ-RIĘS (âwg-zĭl'yạ-rẹz), n. pl. Foreign
  troops in the service of a nation at war.
ÂUX-ĬL'IẠ-RỲ (âwg-zĭl'yạ-rẹ), a. Assisting.
ÂUX-ĬL'IẠ-RỲ (âwg-zĭl'yạ-rẹ), n. A helper.
Ạ-VĀIL', v. a. To profit; to benefit; to assist.
Ạ-VĀIL', v. n. To be of use or advantage.
Ạ-VĀIL', n. Profit; advantage; benefit.
Ạ-VĀIL'Ạ-BLE, a. Profitable; powerful; useful.
Ạ-VĀIL'Ạ-BLE-NĔSS, n. Power; legal force.
Ạ-VĀIL'Ạ-BLỲ, ad. Powerfully; validly.
ĂV-Ạ-LĂNCHE', n. A body of sliding snow, &c.
Ạ-VĂNT'-GUÄRD (ạ-vänt'gärd), n. Van of an ar-
ĂV'Ạ-RĬCE, n. Inordinate desire of gain. [my.
ĂV-Ạ-RĬ''CIOỤS (ăv-ạ-rĭsh'ụs), a. Greedy of gain.
ĂV-Ạ-RĬ''CIOỤS-LỲ, ad. In an avaricious manner.
ĂV-Ạ-RĬ''CIOỤS-NĔSS, n. Covetousness.
Ạ-VĂST', interj. Hold, stop, stay; — a sea term.
Ạ-VÂUNT', interj. Expressing abhorrence; be-
Ạ-VĔNĢE', v. a. To revenge; to punish. [gone.
Ạ-VĔNĢE'MĘNT, n. Vengeance; punishment.
Ạ-VĔNT'ỤRE (ạ-vĕnt'ụre), n. (Law.) Mischance.
ĂV'Ę-NŪE (ăv'ẹ-nū), n. A passage; an entrance.
Ạ-VĔR', v. a. To declare positively; to assert.
ĂV'ĘR-AĢE, n. A medium; a mean proportion.
ĂV'ĘR-AĢE, v. a. To reduce to a medium.
ĂV'ĘR-AĢE, a. Medial; having a medium.
Ạ-VĔR'MĘNT, n. Affirmation; declaration.
Ạ-VĔRSE', a. Disinclined; not favorable.

A-VẼRSE′LY, *ad.* Unwillingly; backwardly.
A-VĚRSE′NĘSS, *n.* Unwillingness; dislike.
A-VĚR′SIQN, *n.* Hatred; dislike; abhorrence.
A-VĚRT′, *v. a.* To turn aside; to put away.
A-VĚRT′, *v. n.* To turn away; to turn aside.
Ā′VĮ-A-RY, *n.* A place to keep birds in.
A-VĬD′Į-TY, *n.* Eagerness; greediness; voracity.
ĂV-Q-CĀ′TIQN, *n.* Business that calls aside.
A-VOÏD′, *v. a.* To shun; to escape from; to an-
A-VOÏD′A-BLE, *a.* That may be avoided. [nul.
A-VOÏD′ANCE, *n.* Act of avoiding or annulling.
ĂV-OĮR-DŲ-POÏȘ′ (ăv-ẹr-dṳ-pöiz′), *n. & a.* A
  kind of weight of which a pound contains 16
A-VOÛCH′, *v. a.* To affirm; to declare. [ounces.
A-VÖW′, *v. a.* To declare openly; to affirm.
A-VÖW′A-BLE, *a.* That may be avowed.
A-VÖW′AL, *n.* Positive or open declaration.
A-VÖW′ĘD-LY, *ad.* In an open manner.
ĂV-Q-W-ĒĒ′, *n.* One with right of advowson.
A-VÖW′ER, *n.* One who avows or justifies.
A-VŬL′SIQN, *n.* The act of tearing away. [for.
A-WĀIT′, *v. n.* To expect; to attend; to wait
A-WĀKE′, *v. a.* [*imp. t.* awoke or awaked; *pp.*
  awaked.] To rouse from sleep; to excite.
A-WĀKE′, *v. n.* To break from sleep; to wake.
A-WĀKE′, *a.* Not sleeping; not being asleep.
A-WĀ′KEN (a-wā′kn), *v. a. & n.* To awake.
A-WÂRD′, *v. a. & n.* To adjudge; to decree.
A-WÂRD′, *n.* Judgment; sentence.

A-WÅRE′, *a.* Observant; mindful; cognizant.
A-WĀY′, *ad.* At a distance. — *interj.* Begone.
ÂWE (âw), *n.* Reverential fear; dread.
ÂWE (âw), *v. a.* To strike with reverence.
ÂWE′-STRŬCK, *p. a.* Impressed with awe.
ÂW′FÛL, *a.* That strikes with awe or dread.
ÂW′FÛL-LY, *ad.* In an awful manner.
ÂW′FÛL-NĔSS, *n.* Quality of being awful.
A-WHĪLE′, *ad.* For some time; for a time.
ÂWK′WĄRD, *a.* Unhandy; clumsy; unpolite.
ÂWK′WĄRD-NĔSS, *n.* Clumsiness; rudeness.
ÂWL (âl), *n.* An instrument to bore holes with.
ÂWN′ĮNG, *n.* Canvas spread over a boat, &c.
A-WŌKE′, *imp. t.* from *awake.* [versoly; wrong.
A-WRȲ′ (a-rī′), *ad.* Obliquely; asquint; per-
ĂXE, *n.* An instrument with a sharp edge.
ĂX′IQM (ăks′yum), *n.* A self-evident truth.
ĂX′ĮS, *n.*; pl. ĂX′ĘȘ. The line, real or imagi-
  nary, on which any thing revolves.
ĂX′LE (ăk′sl),   } *n.* Piece of timber on
ĂX′LE-TRĒĒ (ăk′sl-trē), }   which wheels turn.
ĀY (ăẹ), *ad.* Yes; — *a word expressing assent.*
ĀYE (āẹ), *ad.* Always; forever; to eternity.
ĂZ′ŌTE, *n.* A kind of gas; nitrogen.
A-ZŌT′ĮC, *a.* Relating to or containing azote.
Ā′ZŲRE (ā′zhụr *or* ăzh′ụr), *a.* Blue; faint blue;
  sky-colored; cerulean.
Ā′ZŲRE (ā′zhụr), *n.* Color of the sky; the sky;
  a blue pigment.

B.

B the second letter of the English alphabet,
  is a *mute* and a *labial.*
BĀA (bä), *n.* The cry of a sheep or lamb.
BĀA (bä), *v. n.* To cry like a sheep or lamb.
BĀ′AL, *n.* An ancient idol, representing the sun.
BĂB′BLE, *v. n.* To prattle like a child; to talk
BĂB′BLE, *n.* Idle talk; senseless prattle. [idly.
BĂB′BLĘR, *n.* An idle talker; a teller of secrets.
BĀBE, *n.* An infant; a baby; a young child.
BĀ′BE-RY, *n.* Finery to please a babe.
BA-BŌÔN′, *n.* A large kind of monkey.
BĀ′BY, *n.* A young child; an infant. [hood.
BĀ′BY-HOOD (bā′bẹ-hûd), *n.* Infancy; child-
BĀ′BY-ĬSH, *or* BĀ′BĮSH, *a.* Infantine; childish.
BĂC-CA-LÂU′RĘ-ATE, *n.* First degree in arts.
BĂC′ĊHA-NĂL, *or* BĂC-ĊHA-NĀ′LĮ-AN, *a.*
  Drunken; noisy; revelling. [drunkard.
BĂC′ĊHA-NĂL, *or* BĂC-ĊHA-NĀ′LĮ-AN, *n.* A
BĂC′ĊHA-NĂLȘ, *n. pl.* Drunken feasts or revels.
BAC-CĬF′ĘR-OÛS, *a.* Berry-bearing.
BĂCH′Ę-LQR, *n.* An unmarried man: — one who
  has taken his first degree in the liberal arts.
BĂCH′Ę-LQR-SHĮP, *n.* State of a bachelor.
BĂCK, *n.* The hinder part of the body in man,
  and the upper part in animals; the rear.
BĂCK, *ad.* To the place left; behind; again.
BĂCK, *v. a.* To mount; to justify; to second.
BĂCK′BĪTE, *v. a.* To censure when absent.
BĂCK′BĪT-ĘR, *n.* A privy calumniator.
BĂCK′BŌNE, *n.* The bone of the back.
BĂCK′DŌOR, *n.* A door on the back side of a
BĂCK-GĂM′MQN, *n.* A game with dice. [house.

BĂCK′PIĒCE, *n.* Armor to cover the back.
BĂCK-SĪDE′, *n.* The hinder part of a thing.
BĂCK-SLĪDE′, *v. n.* To fall off; to apostatize.
BĂCK-SLĪD′ĘR, *n.* An apostate.
BĂCK′STĂFF, *n.* A kind of quadrant.
BĂCK′STĀY, *n.* Rope to support a ship's masts.
BĂCK′SWŌRD (băk′sōrd), *n.* A one-edged sword.
BĂCK′WĄRD, *or* BĂCK′WĄRDȘ, *ad.* With the
  back forwards; towards the back; reversely.
BĂCK′WĄRD, *a.* Unwilling; sluggish; dull;
BĂCK′WĄRD-NĔSS, *n.* Dulness; tardiness. [late.
BĀ′CON (bā′kn), *n.* Hog's flesh salted and dried.
BĂD, *a.* Ill; not good; vicious; hurtful.
BĀDE (băd), *imp. t.* from *bid.*
BĂDGE, *n.* A mark or token of distinction.
BĂD′GĘR, *n.* A quadruped. — *v. a.* To tease.
BĂD′LY, *ad.* In a bad manner; not well.
BĂD′NĘSS, *n.* Want of good qualities. [feat.
BĂF′FLE, *v. a.* To elude; to confound; to de-
BĂG, *n.* A sack; a pouch; a purse; an udder.
BĂG, *v. a. & n.* To put into a bag; to load with
  a bag; to swell like a bag; to puff out.
BĂG-A-TĚLLE′ (băg-a-tĕl′), *n.* A trifle; a toy.
BĂG′GAGE, *n.* Luggage; a worthless woman.
BĂGN′IŌ (băn′yō), *n.* A bath: — a brothel.
BĂG′PĪPE, *n.* A musical wind instrument.
BĂG′PĪ-PĘR, *n.* One who plays on a bagpipe.
BĀIL, *n.* Surety given for another's appearance.
BĀIL, *v. a.* To give bail for; to admit to bail.
BĀIL′A-BLE, *a.* Capable of being bailed.
BĀI′LĮFF, *n.* A sheriff's deputy; a steward.
BĀIL′Į-WĬCK, *n.* The jurisdiction of a bailiff.

BĀIL'MĘNT, *n.* A delivery of things in trust.
BÀIRN, *or* BÄRN, *n.* A child. [*Scottish.*]
BĀIT, *v. a.* To put a bait on ; to refresh ; to
BĀIT, *v. n.* To take refreshment. [attack.
BĀIT, *n.* A lure ; a temptation ; a refreshment.
BĀIZE, *n.* A kind of coarse woollen stuff.
BĀKE, *v. a.* To harden ; to cook, as in an oven.
BĀKE, *v. n.* To be parched, heated, or baked.
BĀKE'HŌÛSE, *n.* A place for baking bread.
BĀK'ĘR, *n.* One whose trade is to bake.
BĀK'ĘR-Y, *n.* Place for baking ; bakehouse.
BĂL'ĄNCE, *n.* A pair of scales ; difference of
an account ; equipoise ; a sign in the zodiac.
BĂL'ĄNCE, *v. a.* To weigh ; to make equal.
BĂL'ĄNCE, *v. n.* To hesitate ; to fluctuate.
BĂL'CQ-NY, *or* BĄL-CŌ'NY, *n.* A frame pro-
jecting from a wall ; a projecting gallery.
BÂLD, *a.* Wanting hair ; bare ; plain ; mean.
BÂL'DĘR-DĂSH, *n.* A rude mixture ; jargon.
BÂLD'NĘSS, *n.* Want of hair or of ornament.
BÂLD'PĀTE, *n.* A head without hair.
BÂLD'RĮC, *n.* A girdle ; a belt ; the zodiac.
BĀLE, *n.* A bundle or package of goods ; mis-
BĀLE, *v. a.* To lade out ; to pack up. [ery.
BĀLE'FÛL, *a.* Full of misery, sorrow, or grief.
BĂL'ĮS-TĘR, *n.* A sort of crossbow. [ment.
BÂLK (bâwk), *n.* A great beam : — disappoint-
BÂLK (bâwk), *v. a.* To disappoint ; to heap.
BÂLL, *n.* A round body ; a bullet : — a dance.
BĂL'LĄD, *n.* A song ; a small, light poem.
BĂL'LĄST, *n.* Heavy matter to steady a ship.
BĂL'LĄST, *v. a.* To keep steady, as by ballast.
BĂL'LĘT, *n.* A kind of pantomimic dance.
BĄL-LŌÔN', *n.* A large round vessel ; a ball ;
a large hollow ball or bag filled with gas.
BĂL'LQT, *n.* A ball ; a ticket used in voting.
BĂL'LQT, *v. n.* To vote by ballot.
BÄLM (bäm), *n.* A fragrant resin ; a plant.
BÄLM'Y (bäm'ę), *a.* Having qualities of balm ;
soothing ; fragrant ; odoriferous ; aromatic.
BÂL'SĄM, *n.* A resinous liquid ; a tree.
BĄL-SĂM'ĮC, BĄL-SĂM'Į-CĄL, *a.* Like balsam.
BĂL'ŲS-TĘR, *n.* A small column or pilaster, as
of a rail to a flight of stairs. [rail.
BĂL'ŲS-TRĀDE, *n.* A row of balusters, with a
BĄM-BÔÔ', *n.* A plant of the reed kind.
BĄM-BÔÔ'ZLE, *v. a.* To deceive : *a low word.*
BĂN, *n.* Public notice ; a curse ; interdiction.
BĄ-NĀ'NĄ, *or* BĄ-NÄ'NĄ, *n.* A plant, and its fruit.
BĂND, *n.* Bandage ; cord ; ornament ; company.
BĂND, *v. a. & n.* To unite ; to bind ; to associate.
BĂND'ĄGE, *n.* A fillet ; a cloth for binding.
BĂN-DĂN'NĄ, *n.* A spotted silk handkerchief.
BĂND'BŌX, *n.* A slight box used far bands, &c.
BĂN'DĘ-LĔT, *n.* A flat moulding or fillet.
BĂN'DĮT, *n. ; pl.* BĂN-DĬT'TĮ. A robber.
BĂN-DĬT'TĮ (băn-dĭt'tę), *n.* A band of robbers.
BĂN-DQ-LĒĒR', *n.* A small case for powder.
BĂND'RŌL, *n.* A little flag or streamer.
BĂN'DY, *n.* A club for striking a ball.
BĂN'DY, *v. a.* To beat to and fro ; to exchange.
BĂN'DY-LĔGGED(-lĕgd), *a.* Having crooked legs.
BĀNE, *n.* Poison ; that which destroys or ruins.
BĀNE'FÛL, *a.* Poisonous ; destructive.
BĂNG, *v. a.* To beat ; to thump. — *n.* A blow.
BĂN-IĂN' (băn-yăn'), *n.* A tree of India : — a
Hindoo class : — a morning gown.
BĂN'ĮSH, *v. a.* To exile ; to drive away.

BĂN'ĮSH-MĔNT, *n.* The act of banishing ; exile.
BĂN'ĮS-TĘR, *n.* A corruption of *baluster.*
BĂNK, *n.* Any steep acclivity ; a shoal ; heap ;
a seat ; a place where money is laid up.
BĂNK, *v. a.* To enclose with banks ; to embank.
BĂNK'-BĬLL, *or* BĂNK'-NŌTE, *n.* A promis-
sory note issued by a banking company.
BĂNK'ĘR, *n.* One who carries on banking.
BĂNK'RŲPT, *a.* Unable to pay ; insolvent.
BĂNK'RŲPT, *n.* A trader unable to pay his debts.
BĂNK'RŲPT-CY, *n.* The state of a bankrupt.
BĂNK'-STŎCK, *n.* Stock or capital in a bank.
BĂN'NĘR, *n.* A military standard or flag.
BĂN'NĘR-ĔT, *n.* A knight made in battle-field.
BĂN'NQCK, *n.* A cake made of meal.
BĂN'QUĘT, *n.* A feast ; a grand entertainment.
BĂN'QUĘT, *v. a. & n.* To feast ; to give a feast.
BĂN'QUĘT-ĬNG, *n.* The act of feasting.
BĂN'TĄM, *n.* A species of dunghill fowl.
BĂN'TĘR, *v. a.* To play upon ; to rally ; to jeer.
BĂN'TĘR, *n.* Light ridicule ; raillery.
BĂNT'LĮNG, *n.* A little child ; an infant.
BĂP'TĬSM, *n.* A rite of the Christian church.
BĄP-TĬS'MĄL, *a.* Pertaining to baptism.
BĂP'TĬST, *n.* One of a Christian denomination.
BĂP'TĬS-TĘR-Y, *n.* A font or place for baptism.
BĄP-TĪZE', *v. a.* To administer baptism to.
BÄR, *n.* What is laid across a passage to hin-
der entrance ; a bank of sand or sunken rocks ;
a shoal : — a tribunal ; body of lawyers : — an
enclosed place in an inn, court-room, &c.
BÄR, *v. a.* To fasten ; to hinder ; to shut out.
BÄRB, *n.* Beard ; point : — a Barbary horse.
BÄR'BĄ-CÀN, *n.* An outward fortification.
BÄR-BĀ'RĮ-ĄN, *n.* A rude or uncivilized person.
BÄR-BĀ'RĮ-ĄN, *a.* Uncivilized ; savage.
BÄR-BĂR'ĮC, *a.* Foreign ; uncivilized ; rude.
BÄR'BĄ-RĮSM, *n.* Inhumanity ; ignorance of
arts ; brutality ; cruelty ; impropriety of speech.
BÄR-BÄR'Į-TY, *n.* Savageness ; cruelty.
BÄR'BĄR-ĪZE, *v. a.* To render barbarous.
BÄR'BĄR-OŬS, *a.* Rude ; uncivilized ; cruel.
BÄR'BĄR-QŲS-NĔSS, *n.* State of being barbarous.
BÄR'BĘ-CŪE, *n.* A hog, &c., dressed whole.
BÄR'BĘ-CŪE, *v. a.* To dress, as a hog.
BÄR'BĘD, *p. a.* Having barbs ; bearded.
BÄR'BEL (bär'bl), *n.* A river fish ; fleshy knot.
BÄR'BĘR, *n.* One whose trade is to shave.
BÄR'BĘR-RY, *n.* A shrub and its fruit.
BÄRD, *n.* A poet ; a minstrel : — caparison.
BÄRD'ĮC, *a.* Relating to bards or poets.
BÄRE, *a.* Naked ; plain ; simple ; poor ; mere.
BÄRE, *v. a.* To strip ; to uncover ; to divest.
BÄRE'FĀCED (bár'fäst), *n.* Shameless ; bold.
BÄRE'FOOT (bár'fůt), *n.* Having bare feet.
BÄRE'FOOT (bár'fůt), *ad.* With bare feet.
BÄRE'HĔAD-ĘD (bár'hĕd-ęd), *a.* With the head
BÄRE'LY, *ad.* Nakedly ; only ; merely. [bare.
BÄRE'NĘSS, *n.* Nakedness ; leanness ; poverty.
BÄR'GAĮN (bär'gin), *n.* A contract ; agreement.
BÄR'GAĮN (bär'gin), *v. n.* To make a contract.
BÄR-GAĮN-ĒĒ', *n.* One who accepts a bargain.
BÄR'GAĮN-ĘR, *n.* One who makes a bargain.
BÄRGE, *n.* A boat for pleasure or for burden.
BÄRGE'MĄN, *n.* The manager of a barge.
BÄRGE'MÄS-TĘR, *n.* The owner of a barge.
BÄRK, *n.* The rind of a tree : — a small ship.
BÄRK, *v. a.* To strip of their bark, as trees.

BÄRK, *v. n.* To make the noise of a dog.
BÄR'LĘY (bär'lę), *n.* A kind of grain.
BÄR'LĘY-CÖRN, *n.* A kernel of barley ; third
BÄRM, *n.* Yeast ; a leaven. [part of an inch.
BÄR'MY, *a.* Containing barm ; yeasty.
BÄRN, *n.* A storehouse for hay, corn, &c.
BÄR'NA-CLE, *n.* A shell-fish ; a kind of goose :
— instrument for holding a horse by the nose.
BA-RŎM'Ę-TER, *n.* An instrument to measure
pressure of the atmosphere ; weather-glass.
BÄR-O-MĔT'RĬ-CAL, *a.* Relating to a barometer.
BÄR'ŎN, *n.* A degree of nobility in England.
BÄR'ŎN-AĢE, *n.* Dignity or estate of a baron.
BÄR'ŎN-ĔSS, *n.* A baron's wife or lady.
BÄR'ŎN-ĔT, *n.* The lowest degree of nobility
that is hereditary in England. [nets.
BÄR'ŎN-ĔT-AĢE, *n.* The whole body of baro-
BA-RŌ'NĬ-AL, *a.* Relating to a baron or barony.
BÄR'O-NY, *n.* The lordship or fee of a baron.
BÄR'RACK, *n.* A building to lodge soldiers in.
BÄR'RA-TQR, *n.* One guilty of barratry.
BÄR'RA-TRY, *n.* Foul practice in law ; bribery.
BÄR'RĘL, *n.* A cask ; a tube ; a cylinder.
BÄR'RĘL, *v. a.* To put into a barrel or barrels.
BÄR'RĘN, *a.* Not prolific ; unfruitful ; dull.
BÄR'RĘN-NĔSS, *n.* Unfruitfulness ; sterility.
BÄR-RĬ-CĀDE', } *n.* Fortification made of trees,
BÄR-RĬ-CĀ'DŌ, } eaŕth, &c. ; an obstruction.
BÄR-RĬ-CĀ'DŌ, } *v. a.* To fortify ; to obstruct
BÄR-RĬ-CĀDE', } with fortification ; to block up.
BÄR'RĬ-ĘR (bär're-ęr *or* bär'yęr), *n.* A de-
fence ; a barricade ; a stop ; a bar ; obstruction.
BÄR'RĬS-TER, *n.* A counsellor at law. [hog.
BÄR'RŌW, *n.* A hand-carriage ; a hillock ; a
BÄR'-SHŌT, *n.* Two half bullets joined by a bar.
BÄR'TĘR, *v. n.* & *a.* To traffic by exchanging.
BÄR'TĘR, *n.* Traffic by exchanging wares.
BA-RŸ'TA, *n.* A heavy alkaline earth.
BÄR'Y-TŌNE, *a.* Noting a low pitch of voice.
BA-SÄLT', *n.* A species of volcanic rock.
BA-SÄLT'ĬC, *a.* Pertaining to, or like, basalt.
BĀSE, *n.* The bottom ; foundation ; pedestal ;
the lowest part in music. See BASS.
BĀSE, *a.* Mean ; vile ; contemptible ; of low
station or value. — (*Mus.*) Grave ; deep.
BĀSE, *v. a.* To found ; to lay the base of.
BĀSE'-BÖRN, *a.* Of illegitimate or low birth.
BĀSE'LĘSS, *a.* Without a base or foundation.
BĀSE'LY, *ad.* In a base or unworthy manner.
BĀSE'MĘNT, *n.* Ground floor of a building.
BĀSE'NĘSS, *n.* Meanness ; vileness ; badness.
BA-SHÂW', *n.* A Turkish viceroy ; a pacha.
BÄSH'FÛL, *a.* Modest ; shamefaced ; shy ; coy.
BÄSH'FÛL-LY, *ad.* Modestly ; in a shy manner.
BÄSH'FÛL-NĔSS, *n.* Modesty ; rustic shyness.
BÄṢ'ĬL, *n.* The angle of the edge of a tool.
BÄṢ'ĬL, *v. a.* To grind to an angle. [church.
BA-ṢĬL'Ĭ-CA, *n.* A large hall ; a magnificent
BÄṢ'Ĭ-LĬSK, *n.* A serpent ; a species of cannon.
BĀ'SĬN (bā'sn), *n.* A vessel ; a pond ; bay ; dock.
BĀ'SĬS, *n.* ; pl. BĀ'SĘṢ. The base or foundation.
BÄSK, *v. n.* & *a.* To lie in the warmth ; to warm.
BÄS'KĘT, *n.* A vessel made of twigs, &c.
BÄS'KĘT-HĬLT, *n.* A hilt covering the hand.
BÄSS, *n.* A kind of fish : — a tree and its wood.
BÄSS, *n.* The lowest part in music.
BÄSS, *a.* (*Mus.*) Grave ; deep ; low. See BASE.
BÄS'SĘT, *n.* A kind of game at cards.

BĄS-SÔÔN', *n.* A musical wind instrument.
BÄSS-RĘ-LIĔF', *n.* Sculpture, the figures of
which do not stand out far from the ground.
BÄSS'-VĪ'QL, *n.* A musical stringed instrument.
BÄS'TARD, *n.* A child born out of wedlock.
BÄS'TARD, *a.* Illegitimate ; spurious.
BÄS'TARD-ĪZE, *v. a.* To prove to be a bastard.
BÄS'TAR-DY, *n.* The state of being a bastard.
BĀSTE, *v. a.* To beat ; to drip ; to sew slightly.
BÄS-TÎLE', *n.* Formerly a state prison in France.
BÄS-TĬ-NĀDE', } *n.* Act of beating on the soles
BÄS-TĬ-NĀ'DŌ, } of the feet with a cudgel.
BÄS-TĬ-NĀDE', } *v. a.* To treat or punish with
BÄS-TĬ-NĀ'DŌ, } the bastinado.
BÄS'TIQN (bäs'chun), *n.* A huge mass of earth,
standing out from a rampart ; a bulwark.
BÄT, *n.* A heavy stick : — a small animal.
BÄTCH, *n.* Quantity of bread baked at once.
BĀTE, *v. a.* To lessen ; to abate ; to diminish.
BAT-EAU' (bät-ō'), *n.* A long, light boat.
BÄTH, *n.* ; pl. BÄTHṢ. A place to bathe in ;
act of bathing : — a Hebrew measure.
BĀTHE, *v. a.* & *n.* To wash in a bath ; to soften.
BĀT'ĬNG, *prep.* Excepting ; except ; without.
BÄT'LĘT, *n.* A piece of wood for beating linen.
BA-TON' (bä-tong'), *n.* A marshal's staff.
BA-TÔÔN', *n.* A marshal's staff ; a baton.
BAT-TÄL'ĬQN (bat-täl'yun), *n.* Body of troops.
BÄT'TEN (bät'tn), *v. a.* & *n.* To grow fat.
BÄT'TER, *v. a.* To beat down ; to wear out.
BÄT'TER, *n.* A mixture of several ingredients.
BÄT'TER-ĬNG-RÄM, *n.* Ancient military engine.
BÄT'TER-Y, *n.* A parapet ; line of cannon ; a
violent assault : — an electrical apparatus.
BÄT'TLE, *n.* A fight ; a combat ; an engagement.
BÄT'TLE, *v. n.* To contend in battle.
BÄT'TLE-AR-RĀY', *n.* Order of battle.
BÄT'TLE-ÄXE, *n.* A weapon of war, like an axe.
BÄT'TLE-DŌOR, *n.* An instrument, like a bat,
to strike a shuttlecock with in playing.
BÄT'TLE-MĔNT, *n.* A wall ; a breastwork.
BÂW'BLE, *n.* A gewgaw ; a trinket ; a trifle.
BÂWD, *n.* A procurer or a procuress.
BÂWD'Y, *a.* Filthy ; obscene ; lewd. [aloud.
BÂWL, *v. n.* & *a.* To hoot ; to shout ; to cry
BĀY, *a.* Inclining to a chestnut color ; reddish.
BĀY, *n.* An arm of the sea : — the laurel tree.
BĀY, *v. n.* To bark, as a dog at his game.
BĀY'Q-NĔT, *n.* A short dagger fixed to a musket.
BĀY'-SÂLT, *n.* Salt made from sea-water.
BĄ-ZÄAR', *n.* An Eastern market ; a market.
BĒ, *v. n.* [*imp. t.* was ; *pp.* been.] To have
some certain state ; to exist ; to remain.
BĒACH (bēch), *n.* The shore ; the strand.
BĒA'CON (bē'kn), *n.* Something raised on an
eminence for giving notice ; a signal-fire.
BĒAD, *n.* A small globe ; globule ; a moulding.
BĒA'DLE (bē'dl), *n.* A petty officer of a court.
BĒAD'RŌLL, *n.* List of persons to be prayed for.
BĒA'GLE (bē'gl), *n.* A small dog to hunt hares.
BĒAK, *n.* The bill of a bird ; a thing pointed.
BĒAK'ĘD (bē'kęd *or* bēkt), *a.* Having a beak.
BĒAK'ĘR (bē'kur), *n.* A drinking-cup.
BĒAM, *n.* Piece of timber ; a part of a bal-
ance ; the pole of a carriage : — a ray of light :
— the main horn of a stag : — width of a ship.
BĒAM, *v. n.* To shine forth ; to emit rays.
BĒAM'Y, *a.* Radiant ; shining ; having horns.

BĔAN, *n.* A species of pulse, of many varieties.
BEÀR (bár), *v. a.* & *n.* [*imp. t.* bɔre ; *pp.* borᴇe.] To carry ; to convey ; to endure ; to suffer.
BEÀR, *v. a.* [*imp. t.* bore *or* bare ; *pp.* born.] To bring forth, as a child ; to produce.
BEÀR, *n.* A savage animal ; a constellation.
BEÀR′-BĀIT-ING, *n.* Baiting bears with dogs.
BĔARD (bērd), *n.* Hair on the chin, &c. ; a barb.
BĔARD (bērd), *v. a.* To take by the beard ; to op-
BĔARD′ED, *a.* Having a beard. [pose.
BĔARD′LESS, *a.* Without beard ; youthful.
BEÀR′ER (bár′er), *n.* A carrier ; a supporter.
BEÀR′ING, *n.* Gesture ; mien ; situation.
BĔAST, *n.* An irrational animal ; a brutal man.
BĔAST′LY, *a.* Like a beast ; brutal ; brutish.
BĔAT, *v. a.* [*imp. t.* beat ; *pp.* beaten *or* beat.] To strike ; to bruise ; to tread ; to conquer.
BĔAT, *v. n.* To throb ; to dash, as a storm.
BĔAT, *n.* A stroke ; a pulsation ; striking.
BĔAT′EN (bē′tn), *pp.* from *beat.*
BĒ-A-TĬF′IC,   ) *a.* Affording heavenly bliss ;
BĒ-A-TĬF′I-CAL,) making completely happy.
BE-ĂT-I-FI-CĀ′TIQN, *n.* The act of beatifying.
BE-ĂT′I-FȲ, *v. a.* To bless ; to make happy.
BĔAT′ING, *n.* Correction by blows ; a drubbing.
BE-ĂT′I-TŪDE, *n.* Blessedness ; perfect felicity.
BEAU (bō), *n. :* pl. BEAUX. A man of dress.
BEAU′ISH (bō′ish), *a.* Like a beau ; foppish.
BEAŪ′TE-OŬS (bū′te-ŭs), *a.* Fair ; beautiful.
BEAŪ′TE-OUS-NĔSS (bū′te-us-nĕs), *n.* Beauty.
BEAŪ′TI-FŪL (bū′te-fŭl), *a.* Possessed of beauty.
BEAŪ′TI-FŪL-LY, *ad.* In a beautiful manner.
BEAŪ′TI-FȲ, *v. a.* To adorn ; to embellish.
BEAŪ′TY (bū′te), *n.* Pleasing assemblage of graces ; grace ; a beautiful person or thing.
BEAŪ′TY-SPŎT, *n.* A patch to heighten beauty.
BĒA′VER, *n.* A quadruped and his fur ; a hat.
BĔC-A-FĪ′CŌ, *n.* A bird, the fig-pecker.
BE-CĂLM′ (be-käm′), *v. a.* To still ; to calm.
BE-CĀME′, *imp. t.* from *become.*
BE-CÂUSE′, *conj.* For this reason ; for this cause.
BE-CHĂNCE′, *v. n.* To befall ; to happen.
BE-CHĂRM′, *v. a.* To captivate ; to charm.
BĔCK, *v. n.* To make a sign by a nod ; to beckon.
BĔCK, *n.* A sign with the head ; a nod.
BĔCK′ON (bĕk′kn), *v. n.* & *a.* To make a sign.
BĔCK′ON (bĕk′kn), *n.* A sign by a motion.
BE-CLÖŪD′, *v. a.* To cloud ; to dim ; to obscure.
BE-CŎME′ (be-kŭm′), *v. n.* [*imp. t.* became ; *pp.* become.] To enter into some state ; to be.
BE-CŎME′, *v. a.* To add grace to ; to befit.
BE-CŎM′ING, *p. a.* Graceful ; fit ; proper.
BĔD, *n.* A couch to sleep on ; a bank of earth ; bottom of a channel ; a layer ; stratum.
BĔD, *v. a.* To place in bed ; to sow, plant, lay.
BE-DĂB′BLE, *v. a.* To bespatter ; to besprinkle.
BE-DĂSH′, *v. a.* To besprinkle ; to bespatter.
BE-DÂUB′, *v. a.* To smear ; to daub over.
BE-DĂZ′ZLE, *v. a.* To make dim by lustre.
BĔD′CHĂM-BER, *n.* A chamber for a bed.
BĔD′DING, *n.* The materials of a bed.
BE-DĔCK′, *v. a.* To deck ; to ornament. [dew.
BE-DEW′ (be-dū′), *v. a.* To moisten, as with
BĔD′FĔL-LŌW, *n.* One who lies in the same
BĔD′HĂNG-INGS, *n. pl.* Curtains of a bed. [bed.
BE-DĪGHT′ (be-dīt′), *prep.* Adorned ; decked.
BE-DĬM′, *v. a.* To make dim ; to darken.
BE-DĪ′ZEN (be-dī′zn), *v. a.* To dress gaudily.

BĔD′LAM, *n.* A hospital for lunatics.
BĔD′LAM-ĪTE, *n.* A madman ; a lunatic.
BĔD′PŎST, *n.* The post of a bedstead.
BE-DRĂG′GLE, *v. a.* To soil in the dirt.
BE-DRĔNCH′, *v. a.* To drench ; to soak.
BĔD′RĬD, BĔD′RĬD-DEN, *a.* Confined to the bed.
BĔD′RÔÔM, *n.* An apartment for a bed.
BĔD′STĔAD (bĕd′stĕd), *n.* The frame of a bed.
BĔD′TĪME, *n.* The time to go to bed.
BĔE, *n.* An insect that makes honey and wax.
BĔE′HĪVE, *n.* A box or case for holding bees.
BĔECH, *n.* A well-known forest tree.
BĔECH′EN (bē′chn), *a.* Pertaining to beech.
BĔEF, *n.* The flesh of an ox, bull, or cow.
BĔEF′EAT-ER, *n.* Yeoman of the guard. [*Eng.*]
BEEN (bĭn), *pp.* from the verb *be.*
BĔER, *n.* Liquor made of malt and hops.
BĔET, *n.* A garden vegetable. [let.
BĔE′TLE, *n.* An insect : — a heavy wooden mal-
BĔE′TLE-HĔAD-ED, *a.* Wooden-headed ; stupid.
BĔE′TLE-STŎCK, *n.* The handle of a beetle.
BĔEVEȘ (bēvz), *n. pl.* of *beef.* Cattle ; oxen.
BE-FĂLL′, *v. a.* & *n.* [*imp. t.* befell ; *pp.* befallen.] To happen to ; to happen ; to occur.
BE-FĬT′, *v. a.* To suit ; to become.
BE-FÔÔL′, *v. a.* To make a fool of. [to.
BE-FŌRE′, *prep.* In front of ; prior to ; superior
BE-FŌRE′, *ad.* Sooner ; in time past ; previously.
BE-FŌRE′HĂND, *ad.* Before ; previously.
BE-FÔÛL′, *v. a.* To soil ; to pollute ; to foul.
BE-FRIĔND′ (be-frĕnd′), *v. a.* To be a friend to.
BĔG, *v. n.* To live upon alms ; to ask alms.
BĔG, *v. a.* To ask ; to crave ; to entreat for.
BE-GĔT′, *v. a.* [*imp. t.* begot, begat ; *pp.* begotten, begot.] To generate ; to procreate.
BĔG′GAR, *n.* One who lives by begging. [haust.
BĔG′GAR, *v. a.* To reduce to beggary ; to ex-
BĔG′GAR-LY, *a.* Mean ; poor. — *ad.* Meanly.
BĔG′GAR-Y, *n.* Indigence ; great want ; poverty.
BE-GĬN′, *v. n.* [*imp. t.* began ; *pp.* begun.] To enter upon something new ; to commence.
BE-GĬN′, *v. a.* To enter upon ; to commence.
BE-GĬN′NING, *n.* The first original or source ; the first part ; the rudiments, or first grounds.
BE-GĬRD′, *v. a.* [*imp. t.* begirded, begirt ; *pp.* begirt.] To gird ; to bind round ; to surround.
BE-GŎNE′ (be-gŏn′), *interj.* Exclamation of command ; go away ; haste away. [beget.
BE-GŎT′, BE-GŎT′TEN (be-gŏt′tn), *pp.* from
BE-GRŬDGE′, *v. a.* To envy the possession of.
BE-GUĪLE′ (be-ḡil′), *v. a.* To impose upon ; to
BE-GŬN′, *pp.* from *begin.* [deceive ; to amuse.
BE-HĂLF′ (be-häf′), *n.* Favor ; cause ; account.
BE-HĀVE′, *v. n.* & *a.* To conduct ; to demean.
BE-HĀV′IQR (be-hāv′yur), *n.* Manner ; conduct.
BE-HĔAD (be-hĕd′), *v. a.* To decapitate.
BE-HĔLD′, *imp. t.* & *pp.* from *behold.*
BĒ′HE-MŎTH, *n.* An animal described in Job.
BE-HĔST′, *n.* A command ; precept ; injunction.
BE-HĪND′, *prep.* At the back of ; inferior to.
BE-HĪND′, *ad.* In the rear ; backwards. [tardy.
BE-HĪND′HĂND, *ad.* In arrears ; backward ;
BE-HŌLD′, *v. a.* [*imp. t.* & *pp.* beheld.] To
BE-HŌLD′, *interj.* See ; lo. [view ; to see.
BE-HŌLD′EN (be-hōld′dn), *p. a.* Bound ; obliged.
BE-HŌLD′ER, *n.* One who beholds or sees.
BE-HÔÔF′, *n.* Profit ; advantage ; benefit.
BE-HÔÔVE′, *v. a.* & *n.* To be fit for ; to become.

BĒ'ING, n. Existence; a person or thing existing.
BẸ-LĀ'BỌR, v. a. To beat soundly; to thump.
BẸ-LĀT'ẸD, a. Benighted; too late. [fasten.
BẸ-LĀY', v. a. To block up; to besiege; to
BĔLCH, v. n. & a. To eject wind from the
BĔL'DẠM, n. An old woman; a hag. [stomach.
BẸ-LEĀG'UẸR (bẹ-lē'ḡẹr), v. a. To besiege.
BĔL'FRY, n. The place where a bell is hung.
BẸ-LĪE' (bẹ-lī'), v. a. To slander; to falsify.
BẸ-LIĔF' (bẹ-lēf'), n. Persuasion; creed; faith.
BẸ-LIĔV'Ạ-BLE, a. That may be believed.
BẸ-LIĔVE' (bẹ-lēv'), v. a. To credit; to trust.
BẸ-LIĔVE', v. n. To have belief or faith. [tian.
BẸ-LIĔV'ẸR, n. One who believes: — a Chris-
BĔLL, n. A hollow, sounding vessel of metal.
BĔLLE (bĕl), n. A handsome, gay, young lady.
BĔLLES-LĔTTRES (bĕl-lĕt'tr), n. Polite lit-
erature; rhetoric, poetry, criticism, &c.
BĔLL'FLOW-ẸR, n. A plant and its flower.
BĔLL'FOÙND-ẸR, n. One who casts bells.
BEL-LĬG'ẸR-ẸNT, a. Waging war.
BĔLL'MẠN, n. One who rings a bell.
BĔLL'-MĔT-AL (bĕl-mĕt'tl), n. An alloy of cop-
per and tin of which bells are made.
BĔL'LŌW (bĕl'lō), v. n. To roar, as a bull.
BĔL'LŌW, n. A loud, roaring noise; a roar.
BĔL'LOWS (bĕl'lụs), n. A machine for blowing.
BĔLL'-RĬNG-ẸR, n. One who rings bells.
BĔL'LỤ-ĬNE, a. Like a beast; beastly; brutal.
BĔLL'-WĔTH-ẸR, n. A sheep which carries a
BĔL'LY, n. Part containing the bowels. [bell.
BĔL'LY-ĀCHE, n. Pain in the bowels; colic.
BĔL'LY-FÛL, n. As much as fills the belly.
BẸ-LŎNG', v. n. To be property; to pertain.
BELOVED, p. a. (bẹ-lŭvd'). Loved. — a. (bẹ-
lŭv'ed). Much loved; dear. [ty.
BẸ-LŌW' (bẹ-lō'), prep. Under in place or digni-
BẸ-LŌW', ad. In a lower place; on earth.
BĔLT, n. A girdle; a cincture; a sash; a band.
BẸ-MĪRE', v. a. To drag or befoul in mire.
BẸ-MŌAN' (bẹ-mōn'), v. a. To lament; to bewail.
BĔNCH, n. A long seat; a tribunal; the court.
BĔNCH'ẸR, n. A senior in the inns of court.
BĔND, v. a. [imp. t. bent, bended; pp. bent,
bended.] To make crooked; to direct, incline.
BĔND, v. n. To be incurvated: — to yield.
BĔND, n. A curve; a crook; a flexure. [nity.
BẸ-NĒATH', prep. Lower in place, rank, or dig-
BẸ-NĒATH', ad. In a lower place; below.
BĔN-Ẹ-DĬC'TIỌN, n. A blessing; invocation
of happiness; expression of good wishes. [gift.
BĔN-Ẹ-FĂC'TIỌN, n. A good deed; a benefit; a
BĔN-Ẹ-FĂC'TỌR, n. One who confers a benefit.
BĔN-Ẹ-FĂC'TRẸSS, n. A female benefactor.
BĔN'Ẹ-FĬCE, n. An ecclesiastical living.
BĔN'Ẹ-FĬCED (bĕn'ẹ-fĭst), a. Having a benefice.
BẸ-NĔF'Ị-CENCE, n. Active goodness; bounty.
BẸ-NĔF'Ị-CENT, a. Kind; doing good.
BĔN-Ẹ-FĬ''CIẠL (bĕn-ẹ-fĭsh'ạl), a. Conferring
benefits; advantageous; useful; helpful.
BĔN-Ẹ-FĬ''CIẠL-LY, ad. Advantageously.
BĔN-Ẹ-FĬ''CIẠL-NĔSS, n. Usefulness.
BĔN-Ẹ-FĬ''CỊ-Ạ-RY (bĕn-ẹ-fĭsh'ẹ-ạ-rẹ), n. One
possessed of a benefice: — a person benefited.
BĔN'Ẹ-FĬT, n. A kindness; advantage; gain.
BĔN'Ẹ-FĬT, v. a. To do good to; to advantage.
BẸ-NĔV'Ọ-LĔNCE, n. Good will; kindness.
BẸ-NĔV'Ọ-LĔNT, a. Kind; having good will.

BẸ-NĪGHT' (bẹ-nīt'), v.a. To involve in darkness.
BẸ-NĪGN' (bẹ-nīn'), a. Kind; generous; gentle.
BẸ-NĬG'NẠNT, a. Kind; gracious; benign.
BẸ-NĬG'NỊ-TY, n. Graciousness; kindness.
BẸ-NĪGN'LY (bẹ-nīn'lẹ), ad. Favorably; kindly.
BĔNT, imp. t. from bend.
BĔNT, n. Flexure; inclination; tendency.
BẸ-NŬMB' (bẹ-nŭm'), v. a. To make numb.
BEN-ZŌÏN', n. A resinous substance.
BẸ-QUĒATH', v.a. To leave by will to another.
BẸ-QUĔST' (bẹ-kwĕst'), n. A legacy.
BẸ-RĒAVE', v. a. [imp. t. bereaved, bereft; pp.
bereaved, bereft.] To strip; to deprive; to
BẸ-RĒAVE'MẸNT, n. Deprivation. [take from.
BẸ-RĔFT', imp. t. & pp. from bereave.
BĔR'GẠ-MŎT, n. A sort of pear: — a perfume.
BẸR-LĬN', n. A coach of a particular form.
BĔR'RY, n. Any small fruit, with seeds.
BĔRTH, n. Station of a ship; a box to sleep in.
BĔR'YL (bĕr'rịl), n. A precious stone.
BẸ-SĒECH', v. a. [imp. t. & pp. besought.] To
entreat; to beg; to implore; to solicit; to pray.
BẸ-SĒEM', v. a. To become; to befit.
BẸ-SĔT', v. a. [imp. t. & pp. beset.] To be-
siege; to waylay; to embarrass; to attack.
BẸ-SHREW' (bẹ-shrū'), v. a. To call a curse on.
BẸ-SĪDE', prep. At the side of; over and
BẸ-SĪDEṢ', above; distinct from; out of.
BẸ-SĪDE', ad. More than that; moreover;
BẸ-SĪDEṢ', not in this number; out of.
BẸ-SĪEGE' (bẹ-sēj'), v. a. To lay siege to; to
BẸ-SĪEG'ẸR, n. One who besieges. [beset.
BẸ-SMĒAR', v. a. To bedaub; to soil.
BĒ'SỌM (bē'zụm), n. A broom of twigs.
BẸ-SŎT', v. a. To infatuate; to stupefy.
BẸ-SOUGHT' (bẹ-sâwt'), imp.t.& pp. from beseech.
BẸ-SPĂN'GLE, v. a. To adorn with spangles.
BẸ-SPĂT'TẸR, v. a. To soil by spattering.
BẸ-SPĒAK', v. a. [imp. t. bespoke; pp. be-
spoken.] To speak for beforehand; to betoken.
BẸ-SPRĔAD' (bẹ-sprĕd'), v. a. To spread over.
BẸ-SPRĬN'KLE, v. a. To sprinkle over.
BĔST, a. The superlative of good; most good.
BĔST, ad. In the highest degree of goodness.
BĔST'IẠL (bĕst'yạl), a. Like a beast; brutal.
BĔS-TỊ-ĂL'Ị-TY (bĕst-yẹ-ăl'ẹ-tẹ), n. Beastliness.
BẸ-STĬR', v. a. To put into vigorous action.
BẸ-STŌW' (bẹ-stōw'), v. a. To put; to give.
BẸ-STŌW'MENT, n. The act of bestowing.
BẸ-STREW' (bẹ-strū' or bẹ-strō'), v. a. [imp. t.
bestrewed; pp. bestrewed, bestrewn.] To
scatter; to strew; to sprinkle over.
BẸ-STRĪDE', v. a. [imp. t. bestrid, bestrode; pp.
bestridden.] To stride over; to ride on.
BẸ-STŬD', v. a. To set or adorn with studs.
BĔT, n. A wager. — v. a. To lay, as a wager.
BẸ-TĀKE', v. a. [imp. t. betook; pp. betaken.]
To have recourse to; to apply; to resort.
BĒ'TEL, or BĒ'TLE (bē'tl), n. Indian pepper.
BẸ-THĬNK', v. a. [imp. t. & pp. bethought.]
To recall to memory or reflection; to remind.
BẸ-TĪDE', v. n. & a. To happen; to happen to.
BẸ-TĪME', BẸ-TĪMEṢ', ad. Seasonably; early.
BẸ-TŌ'KEN (bẹ-tō'kn), v. a. To signify; to
BĔT'Ọ-NY, n. A genus of plants. [foreshow.
BẸ-TOOK' (bẹ-tŭk'), imp. t. from betake.
BẸ-TRĀY', v. a. To give up or disclose treach-
erously; to divulge; to discover; to entrap.

BĘ-TRĀY'ĘR, *n.* One who betrays; a traitor.
BĘ-TRŎTH', *v. a.* To give or receive a contract of marriage; to affiance; to pledge.
BĘ-TRŎTH'MĘNT, *n.* The act of betrothing.
BĚT'TĘR, *a.* The *comparative* of *good;* more good.
BĚT'TĘR, *ad.* More; rather; in a higher degree.
BĚT'TĘR, *v. a.* To improve; to advance. [gree.
BĚT'TĘR-MĚNT, *n.* Improvement.
BĚT'TŎR, *n.* One who bets, or lays wagers.
BĘ-TWĒĒN', *prep.* In the intermediate space of; from one to another; in the middle of.
BĘ-TWĬXT', *prep.* In the middle of; between.
BĚV'ĘL, *or* BĚV'ĬL, *n.* A kind of square rule.
BĚV'ĘL, *or* BĚV'ĬL, *v. a.* To cut to a bevel
BĚV'ĘR-ĄGE, *n.* Liquor to be drunk. [angle.
BĚV'Y, *n.* A flock of birds; a company. [plore.
BĘ-WĀIL', *v. a.* To bemoan; to lament; to deBĘ-WĀRE', *v. n.* To be cautious; to take heed.
BĘ-WĬL'DĘR, *v. a.* To perplex; to entangle.
BĘ-WĬTCH', *v. a.* To charm; to fascinate.
BEY (bā), *n.* A governor of a Turkish province.
BĘ-YŎND', *prep.* On the farther side of; past.
BĘ-YŎND', *ad.* At a distance; yonder.
BĘ-ZĂNT', *n.* A coin made at Byzantium.
BĚZ'ĘL *or* BĚZ'ĘL, *n.* That part of a ring in which the stone is set.
BĒ'ZŌAR (bē'zŏr), *n.* A sort of stone found in the stomach, &c., of ruminant animals.
BĪ'ĄS, *n.* Partiality; bent; inclination. [dice.
BĪ'ĄS, *v. a.* To incline to some side; to prejuBĬB, *n.* A piece of linen put on a child's breast.
BĪ-BĀ'CIOŲS (bī-bā'shŭs), *a.* Addicted to drinkBĬB'BĘR, *n.* A tippler; a toper; a sot. [ing.
BĪ'BLE, *n.* The volume of the sacred Scriptures.
BĬB'LĬ-CĄL, *a.* In, or according to, the Bible.
BĬB-LĬ-ŎG'RĄ-PHĘR, *n.* One skilled in books.
BĬB-LĬ-Q-GRĂPH'ĬC,   } *a.* Relating to the
BĬB-LĬ-Q-GRĂPH'Ĭ-CĄL, } knowledge of books.
BĬB-LĬ-ŎG'RĄ-PHY, *n.* Knowledge of books.
BĬB-LĬ-Q-MĀ'NĬ-ĄC, *n.* One who has a rage
BĬB'Ų-LOŬS, *a.* Absorbing; spongy. [for books.
BĬCK'ĘR-ĬNG, *n.* A quarrel; skirmish.
BĪ'CŎRN, BĪ-CŎR'NOŲS, *a.* Having two horns.
BĬD, *v. a.* [*imp. t.* bid, bade; *pp.* bidden, bid.] To command; to offer; to invite; to pronounce.
BĬD'DEN (bĭd'dn), *pp.* from *bid;* commanded.
BĬD'DĘR, *n.* One who bids, or makes an offer.
BĬD'DĬNG, *n.* Command; order; offer of price.
BĪ-DĚNT'ĄL, *a.* Having two teeth.
BĬ-DĚT', *n.* A little horse: — an article of chamber furniture for washing the person.
BĪ-ĚN'NĬ-ĄL, *a.* Occurring once in two years; living or continuing two years.
BĪ-ĚN'NĬ-ĄL-LY, *ad.* At the return of two years.
BIĘR, *n.* A frame for conveying the dead.
BIĔST'ĬNGŞ, *n.* First milk of a cow after calving.
BĪ-FĀ'RĬ-OŬS, *a.* Twofold; having two parts.
BĬF'ĘR-OŬS, *a.* Bearing fruit twice a year.
BĪ'FĬD,   } *a.* Divided into two; opening
BĬF'Ĭ-DĀT-ĘD, } with a cleft, as a leaf.
BĪ'FŌLD, *a.* Twofold; double; duplicate.
BĪ'FŌRM, *a.* Having a double form.
BĪ-FŪR'CĀT-ĘD, *a.* Having two forks or prongs.
BĬG, *a.* Great.; large; huge; pregnant; swollen.
BĬG'Ą-MĬST, *n.* One who commits bigamy.
BĬG'Ą-MY, *n.* The offence of having two wives or two husbands at once. [en vessel.
BĬG'GĬN, *n.* A child's cap; a can or small wood-

BĪGHT (bīt), *n.* A small bay; a coil of a rope.
BĬG'NĘSS, *n.* Bulk; size; dimensions.
BĬG'QT, *n.* One unduly devoted to some party.
BĬG'QT-ĘD, *a.* Unreasonably zealous.
BĬG'QT-RY, *n.* Blind zeal; great prejudice.
BĬL'BĘR-RY, *n.* A small shrub and its fruit.
BĬL'BŌ, *n.* A rapier; a sword. [the feet.
BĬL'BŌEŞ (bĭl'bōz), *n. pl.* A sort of stocks for
BĪLE, *n.* A thick, yellow, bitter liquor, separated in the liver: — a boil. See BOIL.
BĬLGE, *n.* The broadest part of a ship's bottom; the protuberant part of a cask.
BĬLGE, *v. n.* To spring a leak; to let in water.
BĬL'IĄ-RY (bĭl'yą-rę), *a.* Belonging to the bile.
BĬL'LĬNGŞ-GĀTE, *n.* Ribaldry; foul language.
BĪ-LĬN'GUĄL, *a.* Having two tongues.
BĬL'IOŲS (bĭl'yŭs), *a.* Partaking of bile.
BĬLL, *n.* A written paper; an account of money; beak of a fowl; a pickaxe; a battle-axe.
BĬLL, *v. n.* To caress, as doves, by joining bills.
BĬL'LĘT, *n.* A note; a letter; a piece of wood.
BĬL'LĘT, *v. a.* To place or quarter, as soldiers.
BĬLL'IARDŞ (bĭl'yardz), *n. pl.* A game played on a table with balls and cues or rods.
BĬLL'IQN (bĭl'yŭn), *n.* A thousand millions.
BĬL'LŌW (bĭl'lō), *n.* A wave; a surge.
BĬL'LQW-Y (bĭl'lǫ-ę), *a.* Swelling; turgid.
BĬN, *n.* A repository for corn, bread, or wine.
BĬN'NĄ-CLE, *n.* The compass-box of a ship.
BĪ'NĄ-RY, *a.* Two; dual; double; twofold.
BĬND, *v. a.* [*imp. t. & pp.* bound.] To confine with cords; to gird; to fasten; to tie; oblige.
BĬND, *v. n.* To contract its own parts together.
BĬND'ĘR, *n.* One who binds; a fillet.
BĬND'ĬNG, *n.* A bandage; the cover of a book.
BĪ-NŎC'Ų-LĄR, *a.* Having or using two eyes.
BĪ-NŌ'MĬ-ĄL, *a.* Composed of two parts.
BĪ-ŎG'RĄ-PHĘR, *n.* A writer of biography.
BĪ-Q-GRĂPH'Ĭ-CĄL, *a.* Relating to biography.
BĪ-ŎG'RĄ-PHY, *n.* A history or account of lives.
BĪP'Ą-ROŬS, *a.* Bringing forth two at a birth.
BĬP'ĄR-TĪTE, *a.* Having two correspondent
BĪ'PĘD, *n.* An animal with two feet. [parts.
BĬP'Ę-DĄL, *a.* Two feet in length, or having
BĪ-PĚN'NĄTE, *a.* Having two wings. [two feet.
BĪ-PĚT'Ą-LOŬS, *a.* Having two petals.
BĪ-QUĂD'RĄTE, *n.* The fourth power, arising from the multiplication of a square by itself.
BĪ-QUĄD-RĂT'ĬC, *a.* Relating to the fourth
BĬRCH, *n.* A well-known tree. [power.
BĬRCH'EN (bĭr'chn), *a.* Made of birch
BĬRD, *n.* An animal of the feathered kind.
BĬRD'-CĀGE, *n.* An enclosure for birds.
BĬRD'-CĀLL, *n.* A pipe for imitating the notes
BĬRD'LĪME, *n.* A glutinous substance. [of birds.
BĬRD'Ş'-EȲE (bĭrdz'ī), *a.* Seen from above, as by a bird; a word applied to pictures of places.
BĬRD'Ş'-NĚST, *n.* The place where birds deposit their eggs and hatch their young.
BĬRTH, *n.* Act of coming into life; extraction; rank by descent; lineage. See BERTH.
BĬRTH'DĀY, *n.* The day on which one is born.
BĬRTH'PLĀCE, *n.* Place where one is born.
BĬRTH'RĬGHT (bĭrth'rīt), *n.* The right or privilege to which one is entitled by birth.
BĬS'CUĬT (bĭs'kĭt), *n.* A small cake of bread.
BĪ-SĔCT', *v. a.* To divide into two equal parts.
BĪ-SĔC'TIQN, *n.* Division into two equal parts.

Ā,Ē,Ī,Ō,Ū,Ȳ, *long;* Ă,Ĕ,Ĭ,Ŏ,Ŭ,Y̆, *short;* Ą,Ę,Ĭ,Q,Ų,Y, *obscure.*—FĀRE,FÄR,FĂST,FÂLL; HÊIR,HĔR;

BĪ-SĔG′MENT, *n.* A part of a bisected line.
BĬSH′ǪP, *n.* A prelate; head of a diocese.
BĬSH′ǪP,*v. a.*To confirm; to admit to the church.
BĬSH′ǪP-RĬC, *n.* The diocese of a bishop.
BĬS′MUTH, *n.* A metal of a reddish-white color.
BĪ′SON (bī′sn), *n.* A kind of wild ox.
BĬS-SĔX′TĮLE, *n.* Leap year; every fourth year.
BĬ-SŬL′CǪŪS (bī-sŭl′kŭs), *a.* Cloven-footed.
BĬT, *n.* The iron of a bridle: — a small piece.
BĬT, *v. a.* To put the bit in the mouth of.
BĬTCH, *n.* The female of the canine kind.
BĪTE, *v. a.* [*imp. t.* bit; *pp.* bitten, bit.] To seize or crush with the teeth: — to cheat.
BĪTE, *n.* Seizure by the teeth; a cheat; a trick.
BĪT′ER, *n.* One that bites; a cheat; a deceiver.
BĬT′TEN (bĭt′tn), *pp.* from *bite.*
BĬT′TER, *a.* Acrid; sharp; cruel; painful.
BĬT′TER-LY, *ad.* In a bitter manner; sharply.
BĬT′TERN, *n.* A bird with long legs.
BĬT′TER-NĔSS, *n.* A bitter taste: — malice.
BĬT′TER-SWĒET, *n.* An apple sweet and bitter.
BĮ-TŪ′MEN, *n.* An inflammable mineral substance.
BĮ-TŪ′MĮ-NOŬS, *a.* Containing bitumen.
BĪ′VĂLVE, *a.* Having two valves or shells.
BĬV′Į-OŬS, *a.* That leads different ways.
BĬV′OUĄC (bĭv′wąk),*n.* A watch of an army at night.
BĬZ′ĄN-TĪNE, *n.* A great piece of gold.
BLĂB,*v. a. & n.* To tell, as secrets; to tell tales.
BLĂB, *n.* A telltale; a babbler; a tattler.
BLĂCK, *a.* Dark; cloudy; mournful; dismal.
BLĂCK, *n.* A black color; a blackmoor; a negro.
BLĂCK, *v. a.* To blacken; to make black.
BLĂCK′BER-RY, *n.* A plant and its fruit.
BLĂCK′BĬRD, *n.* A small, black, singing bird.
BLĂCK′CĂT-TLE, *n. pl.* Oxen, cows, and bulls.
BLĂCK′CǑCK, *n.* The heath-cock.
BLĂCK′EN (blăk′kn), *v. a.* To make black; to darken.
BLĂCK′EN (blăk′kn), *v. n.* To grow black.
BLĂCK′GUĂRD (blăg′gärd), *n.* A coarse fellow.
BLĂCK′ĮSH, *a.* Somewhat black.
BLĂCK′JĂCK, *n.* A leathern cup: — a mineral; blende.
BLĂCK-LĔAD′ (blăk-lĕd′),*n.* Mineral for pencils.
BLĂCK′MĀIL, *n.* A certain rate anciently paid to men allied with robbers for protection.
BLĂCK′-MǑN′DAY (-mŭn′dą), *n.* Easter-Monday.
BLĂCK′MÔÔR, *or* BLĂCK′A-MÔÔR, *n.* A negro.
BLĂCK′NĔSS, *n.* The quality of being black.
BLĂCK′SMĬTH, *n.* A smith that works in iron.
BLĂCK′THÖRN, *n.* The sloe, used for hedges.
BLĂD′DER, *n.* The vessel which contains urine.
BLĀDE, *n.* A spire, as of grass; sharp part.
BLĀD′ĘD, *a.* Having blades, or spires.
BLĀIN, *n.* A pustule; a sore; a blotch.
BLĂM′A-BLE, *a.* Faulty; culpable; reprehensible.
BLĀME, *v. a.* To censure; to charge with fault.
BLĀME, *n.* Imputation of a fault; censure.
BLĀME′LĘSS, *a.* Guiltless; innocent.
BLĀME′LĘSS-NĔSS, *n.* Innocence; guiltlessness.
BLĀME′WOR-ŦHY (blām′wür-thę), *a.* Culpable.
BLĂNCH,*v. a.* To whiten: — to strip or peel off.
BLĂNCH, *v. n.* To grow white; to shrink.
BLĬND, *a.* Soft; mild; gentle; pleasant.
BLĂN′DĮSH, *v. a.* To soothe; to flatter.
BLĂN′DĮSH-MĔNT, *n.* Soft words; caresses.
BLĂNK, *a.* White; without writing; pale.
BLĂNK, *n.* A void space; a paper unwritten.
BLĂNK, *v. a.* To confuse; to efface; to annul.
BLĂNK′ĘT, *n.* A woollen cover for a bed, &c.

BLĄS-PHĒME′, *v. a.* To speak evil of; to curse.
BLĄS-PHĒME′, *v. n.* To speak blasphemy.
BLĄS-PHĒM′ER, *n.* One who blasphemes.
BLĂS′PHĘ-MOŬS, *a.* Containing blasphemy.
BLĂS′PHĘ-MY, *n.* Indignity offered to God.
BLĂST, *n.* A gust of wind; a sound; a blight.
BLĂST, *v. a.* To wither; to blight; to blow up.
BLĀZE, *n.* A flame; a stream of light; a mark.
BLĀZE,*v. n. & a.* To flame; to publish.
BLĂ′ZON (blā′zn), *v. a.* To explain; to proclaim.
BLĂ′ZON (blā′zn), *n.* Blazonry; proclamation.
BLĂ′ZON-RY, *n.* Art of drawing coats of arms.
BLĒA (blē), *n.* The part of the wood of a tree which lies immediately under the bark.
BLĒACH, *v. a. & n.* To make white; to grow white.
BLĒACH′ER-Y, *n.* A place for bleaching.
BLĒAK, *a.* Exposed to the wind; cold; chill.
BLĒAK′NĔSS, *n.* State of being bleak; coldness.
BLĒAR, *a.* Dim with rheum or water, as eyes.
BLĒAR (blēr), *v. a.* To make dim, as eyes.
BLĒAR′EYĘD (blēr′īd), *a.* Having sore eyes.
BLĒAT (blēt), *v. n.* To cry as a sheep.
BLĒAT, BLĒAT′ĮNG, *n.* The cry of a sheep or lamb.
BLĒED, *v. n.* [*imp. t. & pp.* bled.] To lose blood.
BLĒED, *v. a.* To draw or let blood from.
BLĔM′ĮSH, *v. a.* To mark; to tarnish; to defame.
BLĔM′ĮSH, *n.* A mark of deformity; taint.
BLĔND, *v. a.* To mingle together; to mix.
BLĔNDE, *n.* An ore of zinc; blackjack.
BLĔSS, *v. a.* [*imp. t. & pp.* blessed, blest.] To make happy; to wish happiness to.
BLĔSS′ĘD, *p. a.* Happy; enjoying felicity; holy.
BLĔSS′ĘD-NĔSS, *n.* Happiness; divine favor.
BLĔSS′ĮNG, *n.* Benediction; divine favor.
BLĔST, *imp. t. & pp.* from *bless.*
BLEW (blū), *imp. t.* from *blow.*
BLĪGHT (blīt), *n.* A blasting; a mildew.
BLĪGHT,*v. a.* To injure by blight; to blast.
BLĪND, *a.* Destitute of sight; not seeing.
BLĪND, *v. a.* To make blind; to darken.
BLĪND, *n.* Something to obscure the light.
BLĪND′FŌLD, *v. a.* To hinder from seeing.
BLĪND′FŌLD, *a.* Having the eyes covered.
BLĪND′LY, *ad.* Without sight; implicitly.
BLĪND′NĔSS, *n.* Want of sight; ignorance.
BLĪND′SĪDE, *n.* A weakness; a weak part.
BLĪND′WORM (blīnd′würm), *n.* A small viper.
BLĬNK, *v. n.* To wink; to see obscurely.
BLĬNK, *n.* A glimpse; a glance; slight view.
BLĬNK′ARD, *n.* One who blinks or squints.
BLĬSS, *n.* The highest happiness; felicity.
BLĬSS′FŬL, *a.* Happy in the highest degree.
BLĬSS′FŬL-LY, *ad.* In a blissful manner.
BLĬSS′FŬL-NĔSS, *n.* Exalted happiness.
BLĬS′TER, *n.* A pustule; a vesicle; a plaster.
BLĬS′TER,*v. a. & n.* To rise in, or raise, blisters.
BLĪŦHE, *a.* Gay; airy; joyous; mirthful.
BLĪŦHE′NĔSS, *or* BLĪŦHE′SǪME-NĔSS,*n.* Gayety.
BLĪŦHE′SǪME, *a.* Gay; cheerful; merry.
BLŌAT,*v. a. & n.* To swell; to make or grow turgid.
BLŌAT′ĘD, *a.* Grown turgid; inflated; turgid.
BLǑB′BER-LĬPPED (-lĭpt), *a.* Having thick lips.
BLǑCK, *n.* A heavy piece of wood, &c.; pulley.
BLǑCK, *v. a.* To shut up; to obstruct.
BLǑCK-ĀDE′, *n.* A siege by shutting up a place.
BLǑCK-ĀDE′, *v. a.* To shut up by obstruction.
BLǑCK′HĔAD (blŏk′hĕd), *n.* A stupid fellow.
BLǑCK′HĔAD-ĘD (-hĕd-ęd), *a.* Stupid; dull.

MÎEN, SĬR; MÔVE, NÖR, SǑN; BŬLL, BÜR, RŪLE.—Ç, Ǧ, *soft;* Ꞓ, Ǥ, *hard;* Ş *as* Z; Ӿ *as* gz: ŦHĬS.

BLŎCK′-HŎÛSE, *n.* A military fortress.
BLŎCK-TĬN′, *n.* Tin in blocks ; pure tin.
BLÔÔ′MA̧-RY̧, *n.* The first forge of iron.
BLŎOD (blŭd), *n.* Red fluid that circulates in animals : — kindred ; descent ; birth. [der.
BLŎOD′GUĬLT-Į-NĔSS (blŭd′g̃ĭlt-ȩ-nĕs), *n.* Mur-
BLŎOD′HÔÛND, *n.* A fierce species of hound.
BLŎOD′Į-NĔSS (blŭd′ȩ-nĕs), *n.* A being bloody.
BLŎOD′LȨSS (blŭd′lȩs), *a.* Without blood ; dead.
BLŎOD′SHĔD, *n.* Murder ; slaughter.
BLŎOD′SHŎT (blŭd′shŏt), ⎱ *a.* Filled with
BLŎOD′SHŎT-TEN (-shŏt-tn), ⎰ blood ; red.
BLŎOD′SŬCK-ȨR, *n.* A leech ; a cruel man.
BLŎOD′THĬRS-TY̧, *a.* Desirous to shed blood.
BLŎOD′VĔS-SEL, *n.* A vein or an artery.
BLŎOD′Y̧ (blŭd′ȩ), *a.* Stained with blood ; cruel.
BLOOD′Y̧-FLŬX′ (blŭd′dȩ-flŭks′), *n.* Dysentery.
BLÔÔM, *n.* A blossom ; the opening of flowers ; prime of life ; native flush on the cheek.
BLÔÔM, *v. n.* To produce blossoms ; to flower.
BLÔÔM′ĬNG, *a.* Flourishing with blossoms.
BLŎS′SO̧M, *n.* The flower of a plant.
BLŎS′SO̧M, *v. n.* To put forth blossoms. [stain.
BLŎT, *v. a.* To efface ; to spot ; to disgrace ; to
BLŎT, *n.* Obliteration ; a blur ; a spot ; a stain.
BLŎTCH, *n.* A spot upon the skin ; a pustule.
BLŌW (blō), *n.* A stroke ; calamity : — egg of a fly.
BLŌW (blō), *v. n.* [*imp. t.* blew ; *pp.* blown.] To make a current of air ; to pant ; to flower.
BLŌW (blō), *v. a.* To drive or impel by wind.
BLŌW′ȨR (blō′ȩr), *n.* One who, or that which,
BLŌWN (blōn), *pp.* from *blow.* [blows.
BLŌW′PIPE, *n.* A tube used to produce flame.
BLŎW̃ZE, *n.* A ruddy, fat-faced wench.
BLŎW̃′ZY̧, *a.* Sunburnt ; tanned ; high-colored.
BLŬB′BȨR, *n.* The fat of whales. [cheeks.
BLŬB′BȨR, *v. n.* To weep so as to swell the
BLŬD′ĢEO̧N (blŭd′jụn), *n.* A cudgel ; a weapon.
BLŪE (blū), *a.* Sky-colored. — *n.* An original color. — *pl.* Low spirits ; melancholy. [belly.
BLŪE′BŎT-TLE, *n.* A flower ; a fly with a blue
BLŪE′NȨSS, *n.* The quality of being blue.
BLŬFF, *n.* A high, steep bank or shore.
BLŬFF, *a.* Pompous ; blustering ; surly.
BLŪ′ĬSH, *a.* Somewhat blue ; inclining to blue.
BLŬN′DȨR, *v. n.* To mistake grossly.
BLŬN′DȨR, *n.* A gross or hasty mistake.
BLŬN′DȨR-BŬSS, *n.* A gun with a large bore.
BLŬN′DȨR-ȨR, *n.* One who commits blunders.
BLŬN′DȨR-HĔAD, *n.* A stupid, careless fellow.
BLŬNT, *a.* Dull ; rough ; rude ; uncivil ; abrupt.
BLŬNT, *v. a.* To dull the edge of ; to repress.
BLŬNT′NȨSS, *n.* Want of edge ; coarseness.
BLŬR, *n.* A blot ; a stain : — disgrace ; reproach.
BLŬR, *v. a.* To blot ; to stain ; to obscure.
BLŬRT, *v. a.* To utter inadvertently.
BLŬSH, *v. n.* To redden in the face ; to color.
BLŬSH, *n.* A reddish color ; a glance ; glimpse.
BLŬS′TȨR, *v. n.* To roar as a storm ; to bully.
BLŬS′TȨR, *n.* Harsh noise ; roar ; boasting.
BLŬS′TȨR-ȨR, *n.* A swaggerer ; a bully.
BŌ, *interj.* A word of terror to frighten children.
BŌAR (bōr), *n.* The male of the swine.
BŌARD (bōrd), *n.* A flat piece of wood ; a table : — deck of a ship : — a council ; a court ; food.
BŌARD, *v. a.* To enter by force, as a ship ; to lay with boards ; to furnish with food.
BŌARD, *v. n.* To live at a certain rate for eating.

BŌARD′ȨR, *n.* One who boards ; a tabler.
BŌARD′ĬNG-SCHÔÔL (bōrd′ĭng-skôl), *n.* A school where scholars live with the teacher.
BŌAR′SPĒAR, *n.* A spear used in hunting boars.
BŌAST (bōst), *v. n.* To brag ; to vaunt one's self.
BŌAST, *v. a.* To brag of ; to magnify ; to exalt.
BŌAST, *n.* Vaunting speech ; cause of boasting.
BŌAST′ȨR, *n.* One who boasts ; a bragger.
BŌAST′FŬL, *a.* Ostentatious ; boasting ; vain.
BŌAT (bōt), *n.* A small vessel : — steam-packet.
BŌAT′MA̧N, *n.* One who manages a boat.
BŌAT′SWĀIN (bōt′swān *or* bō′sn), *n.* An offi-cer who has charge of a ship's rigging, boats,
BŎB′BĬN, *n.* A thing to wind thread upon. [&c.
BŎB′TĀIL, *n.* A short tail ; a tail cut short.
BŎB′TĀILED (bŏb′tāld), *a.* Having a short tail.
BŎB′WĬG, *n.* A wig made of short hair.
BŌDE, *v. a.* To portend ; to foreshow, presage.
BŎD′ĮCE (bŏd′ĭs), *n.* Short stays for women.
BŎD′ĮED (bŏd′ĭd), *a.* Having a body.
BŎD′Į-LĔSS, *a.* Incorporeal ; without a body.
BŎD′Į-LY̧, *a.* Corporeal ; relating to the body.
BŎD′Į-LY̧, *ad.* Corporeally ; completely.
BŎD′KĮN, *n.* A dagger : — an instrument to bore holes in cloth with : — a printer's tool.
BŎD′Y̧, *n.* The material substance of an ani-mal ; matter ; a person ; main part ; a system.
BŎD′Y̧-GUĀRD (bŏd′dȩ-gärd), *n.* A life-guard.
BŎG, *n.* A marsh ; a morass ; a quagmire.
BŎG′GLE, *v. n.* To start back ; to hesitate.
BŎG′ĢY̧, *a.* Full of bogs ; marshy ; swampy.
BŌ′GLE, *or* BŎG′GLE, *n.* A bugbear ; a spectre.
BŎG′TRŎT-TȨR, *n.* One living in a boggy coun-
BŌ-HĒA′ (bō-hē′), *n.* A species of black tea. [try.
BŎĬL, *v. n.* To be agitated by heat ; to bubble.
BŎĬL, *v. a.* To cook in boiling water.
BŎĬL, *n.* A painful or sore tumor. [boiled.
BŎĬL′ȨR, *n.* A vessel in which any thing is
BŎĬL′ȨR-Y̧, *n.* A place where salt is boiled.
BŎĬS′TȨR-ŎŬS, *a.* Loud ; noisy ; stormy ; furious.
BŎĬS′TȨR-OŲS-NĔSS, *n.* Turbulence ; noise.
BŌ′LA̧-RY̧, *a.* Pertaining to bole or clay.
BŌLD, *a.* Daring ; brave ; confident ; impudent.
BŌLD′-FĀCED (bōld′fāst), *a.* Impudent ; bold.
BŌLD′LY̧, *ad.* In a bold manner ; bravely.
BŌLD′NȨSS, *n.* Courage ; confidence ; impu
BŌLE, *n.* A kind of earth ; a measure. [dence.
BŌLL, *n.* The pod or capsule of a plant.
BŌL′STȨR, *n.* A long pillow or cushion ; a pad.
BŌL′STȨR, *v. a.* To support ; to swell out.
BŌLT, *n.* An arrow ; a pin or bar for fastening.
BŌLT, *v. a.* To fasten : — to blurt out : — to sift.
BŌLT, *v. n.* To spring out suddenly ; to start.
BŌLT′ȨR, *n.* One who bolts ; a sieve ; a kind
BŌ′LŲS, *n.* (*Med.*) A very large pill. [of net.
BŎMB (bŭm), *n.* A hollow iron ball or shell.
BŎMB′KĔTCH (bŭm′kĕtch), BŎMB′VĔS-SEL (bŭm′vĕs-sȩl), *n.* Vessel for throwing bombs.
BO̧M-BĀRD′, *v. a.* To attack with bombs.
BŎM-BAR-DIĒR′, *n.* Engineer who bombards.
BO̧M-BĀRD′MENT, *n.* An attack with bombs.
BŎM-BA̧-ZÎNE′, *n.* A slight twilled fabric.
BŎM-BĀST′, *or* BŎM′BĂST, *n.* Fustian ; inflated
BŎM-BĀST′, *a.* High-sounding ; inflated. [style.
BO̧M-BĂS′TĮC, *a.* Of great sound with little meaning ; turgid ; inflated ; high-sounding.
BO̧-NĀ′SŲS, *n.* A kind of wild ox ; the bison.
BŎND, *n.* Cord, or chain ; ligament ; union.

BŎND′AGE, *n.* Captivity; servitude; slavery.
BŎND′MĀID, *n.* A young female slave.
BŎND′MĂN, *n.* A man or male slave. [slave.
BŎND′-SĔR-VĂNT, *or* BŎND′-SLĀVE, *n.* A
BŎNDṢ′MĂN, *n.* A person bound or giving se-
　curity for another; a surety.
BŎND′WOM-ĂN (-wûm′ạn), *n.* A female slave.
BŌNE, *n.* Hard substance in an animal body.
BŌNE′LĀCE, *n.* Lace woven with bobbins.
BŌNE′-SĔT-TẸR, *n.* One who sets bones.
BŎN′FĪRE, *n.* A fire made for joy or triumph.
BŎN′NẸT, *n.* A woman's covering for the head.
BŎN′NY, *a.* Handsome; beautiful; gay; merry.
BŌ′NŲS, *n.* A premium given for a privilege.
BŌ′NY, *a.* Consisting of bones; full of bones.
BŎN′ZẸ, *n.* A priest of Japan, China, &c.
BŌÔ′BY, *n.* A dull, stupid fellow: — a bird.
BOOK (bûk), *n.* A volume for reading.
BOOK (bûk), *v. a.* To register in a book; to re-
BOOK′BĪND-ẸR, *n.* A binder of books. [cord.
BOOK′-CĀSE (bûk′kās), *n.* A case for books.
BOOK′ISH (bûk′ish), *a.* Given to books; studious.
BOOK′ISH-NĔSS, *n.* Devotion to books.
BOOK′KĒĒP-ẸR (bûk′kēp-ẹr), *n.* A keeper of
　a book of accounts; an accountant.
BOOK′KĒĒP-ĮNG, *n.* Art of keeping accounts.
BOOK′LĒARN-ẸD (bûk′lẽrn-ẹd), *a.* Versed in
BOOK′SĔLL-ẸR, *n.* A seller of books. [books.
BOOK′WORM (bûk′wûrm), *n.* A close student.
BÔÔM, *n.* A long pole used to spread a sail;
　a bar or chain laid across a harbor, &c.
BÔÔM, *v. n.* To make a roaring noise, as the
　waves; to rush with violence, as a ship.
BÔÔN, *n.* A gift; a grant; a favor; a present.
BÔÔN, *a.* Gay; merry; kind; bountiful.
BÔÔR, *n.* A lout; a clown; a rustic; a peasant.
BÔÔR′ISH, *a.* Clownish; rude; rustic.
BÔÔR′ISH-NĔSS, *n.* Clownishness; rusticity.
BÔÔT, *v. a.* To profit; to put boots on.
BÔÔT, *n.* Profit; gain: — covering for the legs.
BÔÔTH, *n.* A house for temporary purposes.
BÔÔT′HŌṢE, *n.* Stockings to serve for boots.
BÔÔT′LẸSS, *a.* Useless; without success.
BÔÔT′TRĒĒ, *n.* An instrument for stretching
BÔÔ′TY, *n.* Plunder; pillage; spoil. [boots.
BŌ-PĒĒP′, *n.* A play among children.
BŌ′RĂX, *n.* A salt of soda, used as a flux.
BŎR′DẸR, *n.* The outer part or edge; verge.
BŎR′DẸR, *v. n.* To be in contact; to approach.
BŎR′DẸR, *v. a.* To adorn with a border; touch.
BŎR′DẸR-ẸR, *n.* One who dwells on the
　borders; one who approaches another.
BŌRE, *v. a. & n.* To make a hole; to perforate.
BŌRE, *n.* A hole; the size of any hole; a borer:
　— rapid influx of the tide: — a tiresome person.
BŌRE, *imp. t.* from *bear.* [or north pole.
BŌ′RẸ-ĂL, *a.* Northern; tending to the north,
BŌ′RẸ-ĂS, *n.* The north wind.
BŎRN, *pp.* from *bear.* Brought forth.
BŌRNE, *pp.* from *bear.* Carried; conveyed.
BŎR′ŌUGH (bŭr′rō), *n.* A corporate town.
BŎR′RŌW (bŏr′rō), *v. a.* To take on credit.
BŎR′RŌW-ẸR (bŏr′rọ-ẹr), *n.* One who borrows.
‖BOṢ′ǪM (bûz′ọm *or* bô′zụm), *n.* The breast;
　any close or secret receptacle; enclosure.
‖BOṢ′ǪM, *v. a.* To enclose in the bosom.
BŎSS, *n.* A stud; a knob; a raised work.
BŎSSED (bŏst), BŎS′SY, *a.* Prominent; studded.

BǪ-TĂN′ĮC,　　 *a.* Relating to botany; con-
BǪ-TĂN′Į-CẠL, taining plants or herbs.
BŎT′A-NĬST, *n.* One skilled in botany.
BŎT′A-NY, *n.* The science of plants.
BŎTCH, *n.* A swelling on the skin; pustule;
　ill-finished work; a part clumsily added.
BŎTCH, *v. a.* To mend awkwardly; to patch.
BŎTCH′ẸR, *n.* One who botches; a bungler.
BŌTH, *a. & pron.* The two. — *conj.* As well.
BŎTH′ẸR, *v. a.* To perplex; to confound.
BŎTS, *n.* Small worms in the entrails of horses.
BŎT′TLE, *n.* A vessel to put liquor in.
BŎT′TLE, *v. a.* To enclose in bottles.
BŎT′TLE-SCREW (skrủ), *n.* A corkscrew.
BŎT′TǪM, *n.* The lowest part; ground; a ship.
BŎT′TǪM, *v. a.* To found or establish.
BŎT′TǪM-LĔSS, *a.* Being without a bottom.
BŎT′TǪM-RY, *n.* A borrowing of money by
　pledging the ship as security for payment.
BŌŪGH (bŏŭ), *n.* An arm or branch of a tree.
BOUGHT (bâwt), *imp. t. & pp.* from *buy.*
BŎŬNCE, *v. n.* To spring; to leap; to rebound.
BŎŬNCE, *n.* A heavy blow or thrust; a bound.
BŎŬN′CẸR, *n.* A boaster; a bully: — a lie; a
　falsehood: — any thing very large of its kind.
BŎŬND, *n.* A limit; boundary: — a leap; a jump.
BŎŬND, *v. a. & n.* To limit; to restrain; to re-
BŎŬND, *imp. t. & pp.* from *bind.* [bound.
BŎŬND, *a.* Destined; intending; tending.
BŎŬND′A-RY, *n.* A limit; a bound; a mark.
BŎŬND′EN, *pp.* of *bind.* Obliged; beholden to.
BŎŬND′LẸSS, *a.* Without bound; unlimited.
BŎŬND′LẸSS-NĔSS, *n.* Exemption from limits.
BŎŬN′TẸ-OŬS, *a.* Liberal; kind; bountiful.
BŎŬN′TẸ-OŬS-LY, *ad.* Liberally; bountifully.
BŎŬN′TẸ-OŲS-NĔSS, *n.* Munificence; bounty.
BŎŬN′TĮ-FÛL, *a.* Liberal; generous; kind.
BŎŬN′TĮ-FÛL-LY, *ad.* Liberally; bounteously.
BŎŬN′TY, *n.* Liberality; munificence; a pre-
BOUQUET (bô-kā′), *n.* A nosegay. [mium.
BOURN (bōrn *or* bôrn), *n.* A bound; a limit; a
BÔUṢE (bôz), *v. n.* To drink sottishly. [brook.
BÔU′ṢY (bô′zẹ), *a.* Drunken; intoxicated.
BŎŬT, *n.* A turn; a trial; a contest; a fight.
BŌW̑ (bŏŭ), *v. a.* To bend; to curve; to depress.
BŌW̑, *v. n.* To bend; to incline in respect.
BŌW̑, *n.* An act of reverence or respect: — the
　rounding part of a vessel's side forward.
BŌW (bō), *n.* An instrument for shooting ar-
　rows; a curve; an instrument to play on a viol.
BŌW̑′ẸL, *v. a.* To take out the bowels of.
BŌW̑′ẸLṢ, *n. pl.* The intestines: — compassion.
BŌW̑′ẸR, *n.* An arbor; an anchor at the bow.
BŌW̑′ẸR-Y, *a.* Shady; having bowers.
BŌWL (bōl), *n.* A vessel; hollow part; basin.
‖BOWL (bōl *or* bŏŭl), *n.* A round mass or ball
　which may be rolled along, as in play.
‖BŌWL *or* BŎW̑L, *v. a.* To roll as a bowl; to
‖BŌWL *or* BŎW̑L, *v. n.* To play at bowls. [pelt.
BŌWL′DẸR, *n.* A large round stone; an abraded
　fragment broken off a rock or cliff. [legs.
BŌW̑′LĔGGED (bō′lĕgd), *a.* Having crooked
‖BŌWL′ẸR *or* BŎW̑L′ẸR, *n.* One who bowls.
BŌW′LĮNE *or* BŎW̑′LĮNE, *n.* A ship's rope.
‖BŌWL′ĮNG *or* BŎW̑L′ĮNG, *n.* The rolling of,
　or playing at, bowls. [at bowls, or tenpins.
BŌW̑L′ĮNG-ĂL′LEY, *n.* A building for playing
BŌW̑L′ĮNG-GRĒĒN, *n.* Level ground for bowlers.

BŌW'MĄN (bō'mạn), *n.* An archer. [carry sails.
BŌW'SPRĬT (bō'sprĭt), *n.* A boom or spar to
BŌW-WĬN'DŌW, *n.* A projecting window.
BŎX, *n.* A case or chest made of wood, &c. ; a
  blow ; an evergreen plant ; a driver's seat.
BŎX, *v. a. & n.* To enclose in a box ; to strike.
BŎX'EN (bŏk'sn), *a.* Of, or pertaining to, box.
BŎX'ĘR, *n.* One who boxes ; a pugilist.
BŎY (bŏĕ), *n.* A male child ; a youth.
BŎY'HOOD (bŏĕ'hûd), *n.* The state of a boy.
BŎY'ISH, *a.* Belonging to a boy ; childish ; tri-
BŎY'ISH-NĚSS, *n.* Childishness. [fling.
BŎY'IŞM, *n.* Puerility ; the state of a boy.
BRĂB'BLE, *v. n.* To clamor. — *n.* A clamor.
BRĀCE, *v. a.* To bind ; to tie up ; to strain up.
BRĀCE, *n.* Bandage ; a timber ; a rope ; a pair.
BRĀCE'LĘT, *n.* An ornament for the arm.
BRĂCH'IĄL (brăk'yạl), *a.* Belonging to the arm.
BRĂCH'MĄN (brä'man), *n.* See BRAMIN.
BRĄ-CHȲG'RĄ-PHY, *n.* Short-hand writing.
BRĂCK'ĘT, *n.* A support for a shelf, &c.
BRĂCK'ISH, *a.* Saltish ; somewhat salt.
BRĂCK'ISH-NĚSS, *n.* Saltness in a small degree.
BRĂD, *n.* A sort of nail without a head.
BRĂG, *v. n.* To boast ; to vaunt. [*A low word.*]
BRĂG, *n.* A boast ; a game at cards.
BRĂG-GĄ-DŌ'CĮ-Ō (brăg-gạ-dō'she-ō), *n.* A boast-
BRĂG'GĄRT, *or* BRĂG'GĘR, *n.* A boaster. [er.
BRĀID, *v. a.* To weave together ; to plait.
BRĀID, *n.* A texture ; something braided.
BRĀIN, *n.* A soft whitish substance in the skull ;
  the seat of sensation and reflection.
BRĀIN'LĘSS, *a.* Silly ; foolish ; thoughtless.
BRĀIN'PĂN, *n.* The skull, containing the brain.
BRĀIN'SĬCK, *a.* Diseased in the understanding.
BRĀKE, *n.* An instrument for dressing flax : —
  fern : — a machine for retarding wheels.
BRĂM'BLE, *n.* A prickly or thorny shrub ; a
BRĂ'MĮN, *n.* A Hindoo priest. [bird.
BRĄ-MĬN'Į-CĄL, *a.* Relating to the Bramins.
BRĂN, *n.* The husk or outer coat of grain.
BRĂNCH, *n.* A bough ; a shoot ; offspring.
BRĂNCH, *v. a. & n.* To divide into branches.
BRĂNCH'ĘR, *n.* One that forms branches.
BRĂND, *n.* A piece of wood partly burnt ; a mark.
BRĂND, *v. a.* To mark with a brand or stigma.
BRĂND'ĪR-ON(brănd'Ī-urn),*n.*Iron to brandwith.
BRĂN'DĬSH, *v. a.* To flourish, as a weapon.
BRĂN'DY, *n.* A strong spirituous liquor.
BRĂN'GLE, *v. n.* To wrangle. — *n.* A wrangle.
BRĂNK, *n.* Buckwheat : — a bridle or halter.
BRĂSS, *n.* An alloy of copper and zinc ; impu-
BRĂSS'Y,*a.*Partaking of brass ; impudent.[dence.
BRĂT, *n.* A child ; — *so called in contempt.*
BRĄ-VĀ'DŌ, *n.* A boast ; an arrogant menace.
BRĀVE, *a.* Courageous ; gallant ; noble ; fine.
BRĀVE, *v. a.* To defy ; to set at defiance.
BRĀVE'LY, *ad.* In a brave manner ; finely.
BRĀ'VE-RY, *n.* Courage ; intrepidity ; heroism.
BRĂ'VŌ, *n.* A daring villain ; a murderer.
BRÂWL, *v. n.* To quarrel noisily ; to roar.
BRÂWL, *n.* A noisy quarrel ; uproar.
BRÂWL'ĘR, *n.* A wrangler ; a noisy fellow.
BRÂWN, *n.* Flesh of a boar ; muscular part.
BRÂWN'Į-NĚSS, *n.* Strength ; hardiness.
BRÂWN'Y, *a.* Muscular ; fleshy ; unfeeling.
BRĀY (brä), *v. a.* To pound or grind small.
BRĀY, *v. n.* To make a noise like an ass.

BRĀY, *n.* The noise of an ass ; a harsh sound.
BRĀZE, *v. a.* To solder with brass ; to harden.
BRĀ'ZEN (brā'zn), *a.* Made of brass ; impudent.
BRĀ'ZEN-FĀCE, *n.* An impudent person.
BRĀ'ZEN-FĀCED (brā'zen-fäst), *a.* Impudent.
BRĀZ'IĘR (brā'zhẹr), *n.* An artificer who
  works in brass : — a pan to hold coals.
BRĄ-ZÎL', *n.* A kind of wood for dyeing.
BRĒACH (brēch), *n.* The act of breaking ; a
  gap ; difference ; quarrel ; infraction.
BRĔAD (brĕd), *n.* Food made of ground grain.
BRĔADTH (brĕdth),*n.* Measure from side to side.
BRĒAK (brāk), *v. a.* [*imp. t.* broke ; *pp.* broken.]
  To burst by force ; to rend ; to infringe.
BRĒAK, *v. n.* To part in two ; to burst ; to open,
  as the morning ; to become bankrupt.
BRĒAK, *n.* A breach ; a pause ; the dawn.
BRĒAK'ĘR, *n.* One that breaks ; a wave.
BRĔAK'FĄST (brĕk'fạst), *n.* The first meal in
  the day. — *v. n.* To eat or take breakfast.
BRĒAK'WÂ-TĘR (brāk'wâ-tẹr), *n.* A wall or
  other obstacle raised at the entrance of a harbor.
BRĒAM (brēm), *n.* A small fresh-water fish.
BRĔAST (brĕst), *n.* Part of the body ; the heart.
BRĔAST (brĕst), *v. a.* To meet in front ; to face.
BRĔAST'KNŌT, *n.* A knot worn on the breast.
BRĔAST'PLĀTE, *n.* Armor for the breast.
BRĔAST'WORK (-würk), *n.* A kind of parapet.
BRĔATH (brĕth), *n.* Air drawn in and expelled
  by the lungs ; life ; respite ; pause ; breeze.
BRĒATHE, *v. n.* To respire ; to take breath.
BRĒATH'ĬNG, *n.* Aspiration ; vent ; an aspirate.
BRĔATH'LĘSS, *a.* Out of breath ; dead.
BRĔC'CIĄ (brĕt'chạ), *n.* A rock composed of
  angular fragments cemented together.
BRĔD, *imp. t. & pp.* from *breed.*
BRĒECH, *n.* The lower part of the body : — the
  solid part of a gun behind the bore. [men.
BREECH'ĘŞ (brĭtch'ẹz), *n. pl.* A garment for
BRĒED, *v. a.* [*imp. t. & pp.* bred.] To procre-
  ate ; to give birth to ; to educate ; to bring up.
BRĒED, *v. n.* To be with young ; to produce.
BRĒED, *n.* A race ; a kind ; a family ; progeny.
BRĒED'ĘR, *n.* The person or thing that breeds.
BRĒED'ĬNG, *n.* Education ; manners ; nurture.
BRĒEZE, *n.* A gentle gale ; a soft wind.
BRĒEZ'Y, *a.* Fanned with gales ; full of gales.
BRĔTH'REN, *n.* The plural of *brother.* [minims.
BRĒVE, *n.* (*Mus.*) A note of time equal to 4
BRĘ-VĔT' *or* BRĔV'ĘT, *n.* A commission to an
  officer in the army which entitles him to a
  rank above that for which pay is received.
BRĒ'VĮ-Ą-RY, *n.* An abridgment ; an epitome ;
  a book in the Roman Catholic church.
BRĘ-VIĒR' (brẹ-vĕr'), *n.* A small printing-type.
BRĔV'Į-TY, *n.* Conciseness ; shortness.
BREW (brū), *v. a. & n.* To make liquor ; to
BREW'ĘR (brū'ẹr), *n.* One who brews. [foment.
BREW'Ę-RY (brū'ẹr-ẹ), *n.* A place for brewing.
BREW'ĬS (brū'ĭs), *n.* Bread soaked in pottage.
BRĪBE, *n.* Reward given to corrupt the conduct.
BRĪBE, *v. a.* To give, or gain by, bribes.
BRĪB'ĘR, *n.* One who gives bribes. [bribes.
BRĪ'BĘR-Y, *n.* The crime of taking or giving
BRĬCK, *n.* A mass of burnt clay ; a small loaf.
BRĬCK, *v. a.* To lay or cover with bricks.
BRĬCK'-BĂT, *n.* A piece of a brick.
BRĬCK'-DŬST, *n.* Dust made by pounding bricks.

Ā,Ē,Ī,Ō,Ū,Ȳ, *long* ; Ă,Ĕ,Ĭ,Ŏ,Ŭ,Ў, *short* ; Ą,Ę,Į,Ǫ,Ų,Y, *obscure.*—FĀRE,FÄR, FĂST,FÂLL ; HÊIR,HĒR ;

BRĬCK′-KĬLN (-kĭl), _n._ A kiln to burn bricks.
BRĬCK′-LĀȲ-ẸR, _n._ A mason who lays bricks.
BRĬCK′-MĀK-ẸR, _n._ One who makes bricks.
BRĬCK′-WORK (brĭk′würk), _n._ Laying of bricks ; work or structure formed of bricks.
BRĪ′DẠL, _a._ Belonging to a wedding ; nuptial.
BRĪDE, _n._ A woman newly married.
BRĪDE′-CĀKE, _n._ Cake distributed at a wedding.
BRĪDE′-CHĂM-BẸR, _n._ The nuptial chamber.
BRĪDE′GRÔÔM, _n._ A newly married man.
BRĪDE′MĀID, _n._ She who attends on the bride.
BRĪDE′MĂN, _n._ He who attends the bride and bridegroom at the nuptial ceremony.
BRĪDE′WĔLL, _n._ A house of correction.
BRĬDĢE, _n._ A structure raised over water, &c., for passage :— part of the nose, of a violin, &c.
BRĪ′DLE, _n._ Harness for the head and mouth of a horse ; a restraint ; a curb ; a check.
BRĪ′DLE, _v. a._ To put a bridle on ; to restrain.
BRIĒF (brēf), _a._ Short ; concise ; contracted.
BRIĒF (brēf), _n._ A short writing ; a writ.
BRIĒF′LY, _ad._ In few words ; concisely; quickly.
BRIĒF′NẸSS, _n._ Conciseness ; shortness.
BRĪ′ẸR, _n._ A prickly shrub ; the bramble.
BRĪ′ẸR-Ȳ, _a._ Rough ; full of briers ; thorny.
BRĪ′ẸR-Ȳ, _n._ A place where briers grow.
BRĬG, _n._ A vessel with two masts.
BRĮ-GĀDE′, _n._ A small division of troops.
BRĬG-Ạ-DIĒR′, _n._ Commander of a brigade.
BRĬG′ẠND, _n._ A robber ; a freebooter ; a high-wayman.
BRĬG′ẠN-DĪNE, _n._ A coat of mail. [wayman.
BRĬG′ẠN-TĪNE, _n._ A light vessel. [dent ; witty.
BRĪGHT (brīt), _a._ Shining ; clear ; resplen-
BRĪGHT′EN (brī′tn), _v. a._ To make bright.
BRĪGHT′EN (brī′tn), _v. n._ To grow bright.
BRĪGHT′LY (brīt′lẹ), _ad._ In a bright manner.
BRĪGHT′NẸSS (brīt′nẹs), _n._ Lustre ; acuteness.
BRĬLL′IẠN-CȲ (brĭl′yạn-sẹ),_n._ Lustre ; splendor.
BRĬLL′IẠNT (brĭl′yạnt), _a._ Shining ; sparkling.
BRĬLL′IẠNT, _n._ A diamond cut into angles.
BRĬLLṢ, _n. pl._ Hair on the eyelids of a horse.
BRĬM, _n._ The upper edge of a vessel ; brink.
BRĬM′FŬL, _a._ Full to the top ; quite full.
BRĬM′MẸR, _n._ A bowl full to the top.
BRĬM′MĬNG, _a._ Full to the brim ; brimful.
BRĬM′STŌNE, _n._ Sulphur ; a yellow mineral.
BRĬN′DẸD, _a._ Of a varied color ; streaked.
BRĬN′DLED, _a._ Spotted ; brinded ; streaked.
BRĪNE, _n._ Water impregnated with salt ; the sea.
BRĪNE′PĬT, _n._ A pit of brine or salt water.
BRĬNG, _v. a._ [_imp. t. & pp._ brought.] To fetch ; to convey or carry to ; to lead ; to conduct.
BRĬN′ĬSH, _or_ BRĪ′NȲ, _a._ Saltish ; like brine.
BRĬNK, _n._ The edge, as of a precipice ; a border.
BRĬSK, _a._ Lively ; active ; quick ; sprightly.
BRĬSK′ẸT, _n._ The breast of an animal.
BRĬSK′LȲ, _ad._ Actively ; vigorously ; nimbly.
BRĬSK′NẸSS,_n._ Liveliness ; activity; nimbleness.
BRĬS′TLE (brĭs′sl), _n._ The stiff hair of a swine.
BRĬS′TLE (brĭs′sl), _v. a._ To erect in or fix bristles.
BRĬS′TLE (brĭs′sl), _v. n._ To stand erect, as bris-
BRĬST′LȲ (brĭs′lẹ), _a._ Set with bristles. [tles.
BRĬT′ĬSH, _a._ Relating to Britain ; English.
BRĬT′ỌN, _n._ A native of Britain ; an Englishman.
BRĬT′TLE, _a._ Easily broken ; fragile ; weak.
BRĬT′TLE-NĔSS, _n._ Aptness to break ; fragility.
BRĪZE, _n._ The gadfly :— land long uncultivated.
BRŌACH (brōch), _n._ A spit ; a bodkin or awl.

BRŌACH, _v. a._ To spit ; to tap ; to let out.
BRŌACH′ẸR, _n._ A spit ; an opener ; first author.
BROÂD (brâwd), _a._ Wide ; large ; open ; gross.
BROÂD′CLŎTH, _n._ A fine kind of woollen cloth.
BROÂD′EN (brâw′dn), _v. n._ To grow broad.
BROÂD′LȲ (brâwd′lẹ), _ad._ In a broad manner.
BROÂD′NẸSS, _n._ Breadth ; width :— grossness.
BROÂD′SĪDE, _n._ The side of a ship ; a discharge of all the guns, at once, from the side of a ship.
BROÂD′SWŌRD (brâwd′sōrd), _n._ A cutting sword with a broad blade. [breadth.
BROÂD′WĪṢE, _ad._ In the direction of the
BRỌ-CĀDE′, _n._ A kind of embroidered stuff.
BRỌ-CĀD′ẸD, _a._ Dressed in, or covered with,
BRŌ′CẠĢE, _n._ See BROKERAGE. [brocade.
BRŎC′CỌ-LĮ (brŏk′kọ-lẹ), _n._ A kind of cabbage.
BRŎCK, _n._ A badger ; a hart ; a brocket.
BRŎCK′ẸT, _n._ A hart two years old ; a brock.
BRŌ′GẠN, _n._ A thick, heavy, coarse shoe.
BRŌGUE (brōg), _n._ A brogan :— corrupt dialect.
BRŌÏL, _n._ A tumult ; a quarrel ; a disturbance.
BRŌÏL, _v. a._ To cook by laying on coals, as
BRŌÏL, _v. n._ To be broiled or heated. [meat.
BRŌKE, _imp. t._ from _break._
BRŌ′KEN (brō′kn), _pp._ from _break._ [grief.
BRŌ′KEN-HEÄRT′ẸD (brō′kn-), _a._ Crushed by
BRŌ′KẸR, _n._ A factor ; a commercial agent.
BRŌ′KẸR-ẠĢE, _n._ The percentage of a broker.
BRŌNZE _or_ BRŌNZE, _n._ A factitious metal compounded chiefly of copper and tin.
BRŌOCH (brōch), _n._ A jewelled ornament with a pin or clasp, to fasten a dress, &c.
BRŌÔD, _v. n._ To sit on eggs ; to watch anxiously.
BRŌÔD, _n._ Offspring ; progeny ; breed.
BROOK (brŭk), _n._ A running water ; a rivulet.
BROOK (brŭk), _v. a._ To bear ; to endure.
BRÔÔM, _n._ A shrub ; instrument to sweep with.
BRÔÔM′STĬCK, _n._ The handle of a broom.
BRÔÔM′Ȳ, _a._ Full of, or consisting of, broom.
BROTH, _n._ Liquor in which flesh is boiled.
BRŎTH′ẸL, _n._ A house for lewdness.
BRŎTH′ẸR, _n._ ; _pl._ BRŎTH′ẸRṢ _and_ BRĔTH′-RẸN. A male born of the same parents ; an associate ; a companion ; a fellow-creature.
BRŎTH′ẸR-HOOD (brŭth′ẹr-hûd), _n._ Fraternity.
BRŎTH′ẸR-LȲ, _a._ Like a brother ; affectionate.
BRŌUGHT (brâut), _imp. t. & pp._ from _bring._
BRŎW, _n._ The ridge of hair over the eye ; the forehead :— the edge of any high place.
BRŎW′BĒAT, _v. a._ To bear down ; to intimidate.
BRŎWN, _n. & a._ The name of a color.
BRŎW′NIE (brŏü′nẹ), _n._ A spirit formerly sup-posed to haunt old houses in Scotland.
BRŎW′NĬSH, _a._ Tending to brown ; somewhat
BRŎWN′NẸSS, _n._ Brown color. [brown.
BRŎWN′-STŬD-Y, _n._ Pensive musing ; revery.
BRỌWṢE, _v. a. & n._ To eat branches or shrubs.
BRỌWṢE, _n._ Tender branches or shrubs.
BRŪĬṢE, _v. a._ To crush or injure, as by a blow.
BRŪĬṢE, _n._ A hurt from a blow ; contusion.
BRŪĬṢ′ẸR, _n._ One who bruises ; a boxer.
BRŪĬT, _n._ Rumor ; report. — _v. a._ To report.
BRŪ′MẠL, _a._ Relating to the winter. [plexion.
BRỤ-NĔTTE′, _n._ A woman of a brown com-
BRŬNT, _n._ Shock ; violence ; blow ; stroke.
BRŬSH, _n._ An instrument to sweep or clean any thing ; a pencil :— assault :— a thicket.
BRŬSH, _v. a._ To rub with a brush ; to skim.

BRŬSH, *v. n.* To move with haste ; to fly over.
BRŬSH′WOOD (brŭsh′wŭd), *n.* Small bushes.
BRŬSH′Y, *a.* Rough or shaggy like a brush.
BRŪ′TAL, *a.* Like a brute ; savage ; cruel.
BRŲ-TĂL′I-TY, *n.* Savageness ; brutishness.
BRŪ′TAL-ĪZE, *v. n.* & *a.* To grow or make brutal.
BRŪ′TAL-LY, *ad.* In a brutal manner ; cruelly.
BRŪTE, *a.* Senseless ; savage ; bestial ; rude.
BRŬTE, *n.* An irrational animal ; a beast.
BRŬ′TI-FY, *v. a.* To make or render brutish.
BRŬT′ISH, *a.* Bestial ; savage ; ferocious ; gross.
BRŬT′ISH-NĔSS, *n.* Brutality ; beastliness.
BRȲ′Q-NY, *n.* A plant ; the wild hop.
BŬB′BLE, *n.* A water-bladder ; a cheat ; a hoax.
BŬB′BLE, *v. n.* & *a.* To rise in bubbles ; to cheat.
BŬB′BLER, *n.* A cheat ; a deceiver ; an imposter.
BŬB′BLY, *a.* Consisting of, or like, bubbles.
BŪ′BŌ, *n.* A tumor in the groin, armpit, &c.
BŲ-BŎN′Q-CĔLE, *n.* Rupture in the groin.
BŬC-CA-NĒĒR′, *or* BŬC′CA-NIĒR, *n.* A pirate.
BŬCK, *n.* Lye in which clothes are washed ; the male of deer, goats, &c. : — a dashing fellow.
BŬCK′-BĂS-KĘT, *n.* Basket for carrying clothes.
BŬCK′ĘT, *n.* A vessel for drawing or carrying
BŬCK′ING-STÔÔL, *n.* A washing block. [water.
BŬC′KLE, *n.* An instrument for fastening dress, &c. : — a curl of hair ; hair curled.
BŬC′KLE (bŭk′kl), *v. a.* To fasten with a buckle.
BŬCK′LER, *n.* A kind of shield for the arm.
BŬCK′MĂST, *n.* The fruit of the beech-tree.
BŬCK′RAM, *n.* A sort of stiffened linen cloth.
BŬCK′SKĬN, *n.* The skin of a buck.
BŬCK′THÖRN, *n.* A thorn ; a prickly bush.
BŬCK′WHĒAT, *n.* A plant ; a kind of grain.
BŲ-CŎL′IC, BŲ-CŎL′I-CAL, *a.* Pastoral.
BŲ-CŎL′IC, *n.* A pastoral poem or poet.
BŬD, *n.* The first-shoot of a plant ; a germ.
BŬD, *v. n.* & *a.* To put forth buds ; to inoculate.
BŬDGE, *v. n.* To stir ; to wag ; to move off.
BŬD′GĘT, *n.* A bag ; store, or stock.
BŬFF, *n.* A sort of leather ; a light yellow.
BŬF′FA-LŌ, *n.* A kind of wild ox in India ; in the U. S., a name given to the bison.
BŬF′FĘT, *n.* Blow with the hand : — cupboard.
BŬF′FĘT, *v. a.* & *n.* To strike with the hand.
BŬF′FLE-HĔAD′ED, *a.* Having a large head.
BŲF-FÔÔN′, *n.* A low jester ; a droll ; a mimic.
BŲF-FÔÔN′ER-Y, *n.* Low jests ; drollery.
BŬG, *n.* An insect of various kinds.
BŬG′BEAR, *n.* A frightful object ; a false terror.
BŬG′GY, *a.* Abounding with bugs.
BŬG′GY, *n.* A light four-wheeled carriage.
BŪ′GLE, *n.* A shining bead of glass ; a plant.
BŪ′GLE, BŪ′GLE-HÖRN, *n.* A musical wind instrument ; a hunting or military horn.
BUILD (bĭld), *v. a.* & *n.* [*imp. t.* & *pp.* built, builded.] To make an edifice ; to erect ; con-
BUILD′ER (bĭld′er), *n.* One who builds. [struct.
BUILD′ING (bĭld′ing), *n.* A fabric ; an edifice.
BŬLB, *n.* A round body or root, as of the onion.
BŬL′BOŲS, *a.* Having bulbs ; protuberant.
BŬLGE, *n.* Bilge ; protuberance ; broad part.
BŬLGE, *v. n.* To take in water ; to jut out.
BŬLK, *n.* Magnitude ; size ; mass ; a bench.
BŬLK′HĔAD (bŭlk′hĕd), *n.* Partition in a ship.
BŬLK′I-NĔSS, *n.* Greatness in bulk or size.
BŬLK′Y, *a.* Large ; of great size. [— a blunder.
BŬLL, *n.* The male of cattle ; edict of the pope :

BŬL′LACE, *n.* A sort of sour, wild plum.
BŬL′LA-RY, *n.* A collection of papal bulls.
BŬLL′-BĀIT′ING, *n.* A fight of bulls with dogs.
BŬLL′-DÖG, *n.* A dog remarkable for courage.
BŬL′LĘT, *n.* A round ball of metal ; shot.
BŬL′LĘT-ÎN, *n.* Official account of public news.
BŬLL′-FĀCED (bŭl′fāst), *a.* Having a large face.
BŬLL′-FĪGHT, *n.* A combat with a bull.
BŬLL′FĬNCH, *n.* A bird of the sparrow kind.
BŬLL′FRÖG, *n.* A large species of frog.
BŬLL′HĔAD, *n.* A fish : — a stupid fellow.
BŬLL′ION (bŭl′yun), *n.* Gold or silver in mass.
BŬLL′TRÖÜT, *n.* A large kind of trout.
BŬL′LQCK, *n.* An ox ; a castrated bull.
BŬL′LY, *n.* A noisy, quarrelsome fellow.
BŬL′LY, *v. a.* & *n.* To overbear ; to bluster.
BŬL′RŬSH, *n.* A large rush growing by water.
BŬL′TĘL, *n.* Bran of meal ; a bolter-cloth.
BŬL′WARK, *n.* A fortification ; a security.
BŬM′BLE-BĒĒ, *n.* Humble-bee ; a large bee.
BŬMP, *n.* A knock ; a protuberance. [strike.
BŬMP, *v. n.* & *a.* To make a loud noise ; to
BŬMP′ER, *n.* A cup or glass filled to the brim.
BŬMP′KĬN (bŭm′kĭn), *n.* A clown ; a rustic.
BŬNCH, *n.* A cluster ; a collection ; a lump.
BŬNCH, *v. n.* To swell out in a bunch.
BŬNCH′Y, *a.* Growing in, or full of, bunches.
BŬN′DLE, *n.* A parcel bound together ; a roll.
BŬN′DLE, *v. a.* To tie, or form, in a bundle.
BŬNG, *n.* A stopper for a barrel or cask.
BŬNG, *v. a.* To stop or close with a bung.
BŬNG′-HŌLE, *n.* The hole at which a barrel is
BŬN′GLE, *v. n.* & *a.* To perform clumsily. [filled.
BŬNG′LER, *n.* A bad or awkward workman.
BŬNG′LING, *a.* Clumsy ; awkward ; unhandy.
BŬNN, *n.* A kind of sweet bread ; a cake.
BŬNT′ING, *n.* A bird : — a thin cloth or stuff.
BUOY (bwŏy *or* bŏy), *n.* A piece of cork or wood floating on the water, tied to a weight ; an object for supporting any thing in water.
BUOY, *v. a.* To keep afloat. — *v. n.* To float.
BUOY′AN-CY (bwöĕ′an-se), *n.* Quality of floating.
BUOY′ANT (bwöĕ′ant), *a.* Floating ; light.
BŪR, *n.* A rough, prickly head of a plant.
BŬR′DEN, *or* BŬR′THEN, *n.* A load ; what is borne or carried ; cargo ; freight ; a grievance.
BŬR′DEN (bur′dn), *v. a.* To load ; to encumber.
BŬR′DEN-SŎME, *a.* Heavy ; grievous ; severe.
BŬR′DÖCK, *n.* A kind of plant with burs.
BŪ-REAU′ (bū-rō′), *n.* A chest of drawers : — an office ; department of government. [towns.
BŬR′GAGE, *n.* A tenure proper to cities and
BŬR′GA-MÖT, *n.* A species of pear ; a perfume.
BŬR-GEÖĬS′ (bur-jöĭs′), *n.* A kind of type.
BŬR′GESS, *n.* Citizen, representative, magistrate.
BŬRGH (bŭrg), *n.* A corporate town or borough.
BŬRGH′ER (bŭr′ger), *n.* Member of a borough.
BŬRG′LAR, *n.* One guilty of burglary.
BŬR-GLĀ′RI-OŬS, *a.* Relating to housebreaking.
BŬR′GLA-RY, *n.* The crime of housebreaking by night, with an intent to steal.
BŬR′GQ-MĂS-TĘR, *n.* A magistrate in a city.
BŬR′GRĀVE, *n.* A governor of a castle or town.
BŬR′GŲN-DY, *n.* Wine made in Burgundy.
BŬR′I-AL (bĕr′re-al), *n.* Act of burying ; a funeral.
BŪ′RĬN, *n.* An engraver's tool ; a graver.
BŬRL, *v. a.* To dress, as cloth. [comic.
BŲR-LĔSQUE′ (bụr-lĕsk′), *a.* Jocular ; ludicrous ;

BUR-LĔSQUE′, n. A ludicrous representation.
BUR-LĔSQUE′, v. a. To turn to ridicule.
BŬR′LY, a. Great in size; bulky; tumid :—loud.
BŬRN, v. a. [imp. t. & pp. burned, burnt.] To consume or affect with fire; to scorch.
BŬRN, v. n. To be on fire; to be inflamed.
BŬRN, n. A hurt or effect caused by fire.
BŬRN′ER, n. A person or thing that burns.
BŬR′NĘT, n. A plant of several species.
BŬRN′ING, n. Act of burning; inflammation.
BŬRN′ING, a. Flaming; vehement; powerful.
BŬRN′ING-GLĂSS, n. A glass which collects the rays of the sun, and produces intense heat.
BŬR′NĬSH, v. a. To polish.—v. n. To grow bright.
BŬR′NĬSH, n. A gloss; brightness; lustre.
BŬR′NĬSH-ER, n. A person or thing that bur- [nishes.
BŬRNT, imp. t. & pp. of burn.
BŬRR, n. The lobe or lap of the ear. [&c.
BŬR′RŌW, n. A hole in the ground for rabbits,
BŬR′RŌW, v. n. To lodge in holes in the ground.
BŬR′SĄR, n. A treasurer in universities, &c.
BŬRSE, n. An exchange where merchants meet.
BŬRST, v. n. & a. [imp. t. & pp. burst.] To break
BŬRST, n. A disruption; a rupture. [or fly open.
BŬR′THĔN (bŭr′thn), n. A load. See BURDEN.
BŬR′Y (bĕr′rę), v. a. To put into a grave; to hide.
BŬR′Y-ĬNG (bĕr′rę-ĭng), n. Burial; sepulture.
BŬSH, n. A young tree; a bough; a thicket.
BŬSH′ĘL, n. A dry measure containing 4 pecks.
BŬSH′Ĭ-NĔSS, n. The quality of being bushy.
BŬSH′Y, a. Thick like a bush; full of bushes.
BŬSILY (bĭz′zę-lę), ad. In a busy manner.
BŬSINESS (bĭz′nęs), n. Employment; trade; an
BŬSK, n. A piece of steel or whalebone. [affair.
BŬS′KĬN, n. A kind of half boot; a high shoe.
BŬS′KĬNED (bŭs′kĭnd), a. Dressed in buskins.
BŬSS, n. A kiss :— a fishing-boat.—v. a. To kiss.
BŬST, n. The upper part of a statue represent- ing a person down to the bottom of the breast.
BŬS′TĄRD, n. A large bird of the turkey kind.
BŬS′TLE (bŭs′sl), v. n. To be busy or active.
BŬS′TLE (bŭs′sl), n. A tumult; hurry; stir.
BŬS′TLĘR (bŭs′slęr), n. One who bustles.
BŬSY (bĭz′zę), a. Much employed; active; offi-
BŬSY (bĭz′zę), v. a. To employ constantly. [cious.
BŬSYBODY (bĭz′zę-bŏd-dę), n. A meddling person.
BŬT, conj. Except; except that; besides; only; unless; yet.—ad. No more than.—prep. Except.
BŬT, n. A boundary; a limit; end of a thing.

BŬT′-ĔND, n. The blunt end of any thing.
BÛTCH′ER, n. One who kills animals to sell.
BÛTCH′ER, v. a. To kill; to slaughter; to mur-
BÛTCH′ER-LY, a. Cruel; bloody. [der.
BÛTCH′ER-Y, n. Trade of a butcher; slaughter.
BŬT′LĘR, n. Servant intrusted with liquors, &c.
BŬTT, n. A mark to be shot at :—a push or blow : — object of ridicule :—a cask :—a kind of hinge.
BŬTT, v. a. To strike with the head, as a ram.
BŬT′TĘR, n. An oily substance made from cream.
BŬT′TĘR, v. a. To smear or spread with butter.
BŬT′TĘR-CŬP, n. The crow-foot, a yellow flower.
BŬT′TĘR-FLY, n. A beautiful winged insect.
BŬT′TĘR-MĬLK, n. Whey of churned cream.
BŬT-TĘR-PRĬNT, n. A stamp to mark butter.
BŬT′TĘR-TÔÔTH, n. A large, broad fore tooth.
BŬT′TĘR-Y, a. Having the appearance of butter.
BŬT′TĘR-Y, n. Room where provisions are kept.
BŬT′TOCK, n. The rump. [ing dress, &c.
BŬT′TON (bŭt′tn), n. A knob or ball for fasten-
BŬT′TON (bŭt′tn), v. a. To fasten with buttons.
BŬT′TON-HŌLE, n. A hole to admit a button.
BŬT′TON-MĀ′KĘR, n. One who makes buttons.
BŬT′TRĘSS, n. A prop; a support.—v. a. To prop.
BŪ-TY-RĀ′CEOŲS (bū-tę-rā′shŭs), a. Like butter.
BŬX′ŎM, a. Gay; lively; brisk; wanton; jolly.
BŬX′ŎM-LY, ad. Wantonly; amorously; briskly.
BŬX′ŎM-NĔSS, n. Gayety; amorousness.
BUȲ (bī), v. a. [imp. t. & pp. bought.] To pur- chase; to acquire by paying a price.
BUȲ (bī), v. n. To treat about a purchase.
BUȲ′ĘR (bī′er), n. One who buys; a purchaser.
BŬZZ, v. n. & a. To hum like bees; to whisper.
BŬZZ, n. The noise of bees; a whisper.
BŬZ′ZĄRD, n. A species of hawk :— a dunce.
BȲ, prep. At; in; near; for.—It denotes the means.
BȲ, ad. Near; beside; passing; in presence.
BȲ, BȲE, n. Something not direct or immediate.
BȲ, in composition, implies something out of the direct way, irregular, collateral, or private; as, a by-lane, a by-road, a by-path, a by-corner.
BȲ′-AND-BȲ′ (bī′and-bī′), ad. In a short time.
BȲ′-ĔND, n. Private advantage or interest.
BȲ′-LÂW, n. A private law or regulation.
BȲ′-PĂTH, n. A private or obscure path.
BȲ′-STĂND-ĘR, n. A looker-on; a spectator.
BȲ′-VIEW̄ (bī′vū), n. Self-interested purpose.
BY′-WĀY, n. A private and obscure way.
BȲ′-WORD (bī′wŭrd), n. A saying; a proverb.

C.

C, the third letter of the alphabet, has two sounds — one like k, before a, o, u, or a con- sonant; the other like s, before e, i, and y.
CĂB, n. A Hebrew measure :— kind of carriage.
CĄ-BĂL′, n. A junto; a set :— a plot; intrigue.
CĄ-BĂL′, v. n. To form intrigues; to plot.
CĂB′Ą-LĄ, n. pl. Jewish traditions; secret science.
CĂB′Ą-LĬST, n. One skilled in Jewish traditions.
CĂB-Ą-LĬS′TĬC, CĂB-Ą-LĬS′TĬ-CĄL, a. Secret;
CĄ-BĂL′LĘR, n. An intriguer; plotter. [occult.
CĂB′BĄGE, n. A genus of edible plants.
CĂB′BĄGE, v. a. To steal in cutting clothes.

CĂB′ĬN, n. A room in a ship; a cottage.
CĂB′ĬN-BÖY, n. A waiting boy in a ship.
CĂB′Ĭ-NĘT, n. A closet; a room; a set of draw- ers :— a collective body of ministers of state.
CĂB′Ĭ-NĘT-MĀK′ĘR, n. Maker of fine woodwork.
CĀ′BLE, n. A rope or chain to hold a ship at an-
CĄ-BÔÔSE′, n. The cook-room of a ship. [chor.
CABRIOLET (kăb′rę-ọ-lā), n. An open carriage.
CĄ-CHĔC′TĬC, CĄ-CHĔC′TĬ-CĄL, a. Ill in body.
CĄ-CHĔX′Y, CĂCH′ĔX-Y, n. Ill state of body.
CĂC′KLE, v. n. To make a noise like a hen.
CĂC′KLE, n. The noise of a fowl :— idle talk.

CĂCK′LĘR, *n.* A fowl that cackles : — a tattler.
CĄ-CŎPH′Ọ-NỴ, *n.* A bad or harsh sound.
CĄ-DĂV′ĘR-OŬS, *a.* Like a dead body ; ghastly.
CĂD′DĮS, *n.* A kind of tape : — a worm or grub.
CĂD′DỴ, *n.* A vessel for holding tea.
CĀDE, *a.* Tame ; bred by hand ; as, a *cade* lamb.
CĀ′DĘNCE, *n.* The fall of the voice : — a tone.
CĄ-DĔT′, *n.* A younger brother : — a volunteer in the army ; a pupil in a military school.
CĀ′DĮ (kā′dẹ), *n.* A judge among the Turks.
CĄ-DŪ′CĮ-TỴ, *n.* Frailty ; tendency to fall.
CÆ-ŞŪ′RĄ (sẹ-zū′rạ), *n.* A pause in verse.
CÆ-ŞŪ′RĄL, *a.* Relating to the pause of the voice.
CĂF′TĂN, *n.* A Persian or Turkish garment.
CĂG, *n.* A small barrel or cask ; a keg.
CĀĢE, *n.* An enclosure for birds or beasts.
CĀI′MĄN (kā′mạn), *n.* The American crocodile.
CĀIS-SÔN′ (kä-sôn′), *n.* A chest of bombs or CĀI′TĮFF, *n.* A mean villain ; a knave. [powder.
CĄ-JŌLE′, *v. a.* To flatter ; to soothe ; to coax.
CĄ-JŌL′ĘR, *n.* One who cajoles ; a flatterer.
CĄ-JŌL′ĘR-Ỵ, *n.* Flattery ; wheedling ; deceit.
CĀKE, *n.* A kind of delicate bread : — a mass.
CĀKE, *v. a.* To form into cake.—*v. n.* To harden.
CĂL′Ą-BĂSH, *n.* A species of large gourd.
CĂL-Ą-MĂN′CŌ, *n.* A kind of woollen stuff.
CĂL′Ą-MĪNE, *n.* An ore of zinc :—a mineral.
CĄ-LĂM′Į-TOŬS, *a.* Full of calamity or misery.
CĄ-LĂM′Į-TỴ, *n.* Misfortune ; misery ; disaster.
CĂL′Ą-MŬS, *n.* A sort of reed or flag.
CĄ-LĂSH′, *n.* An open carriage : — a head-dress.
CĄL-CĀ′RE-OŬS, *a.* Partaking of chalk or lime.
CĂL′CĘ-ĀT-ĘD (kăl′shẹ-āt-ẹd), *a.* Shod.
CĂL′CĘ-DỌ-NỴ, *n.* A stone. See CHALCEDONY.
CĂL′CĮ-NĄ-BLE, *a.* That may be calcined.
CĂL′CĮ-NĀTE, *v. a.* To calcine ; to powder.
CĂL-CĮ-NĀ′TIỌN, *n.* Act of pulverizing by fire.
CĄL-CĬN′Ą-TỌ-RỴ, *n.* Vessel used in calcination.
CĄL-CĪNE′, *v. a.* To burn to powder or ashes.
CĂL′CỤ-LĄ-BLE, *a.* That may be computed.
CĂL′CỤ-LĀTE, *v. a.* To compute ; to reckon.
CĂL′CỤ-LĀTE, *v. n.* To make a computation.
CĂL-CỤ-LĀ′TIỌN, *n.* A computation ; reckoning.
CĂL′CỤ-LĀ-TỌR, *n.* A computer ; a reckoner.
CĂL′CỤ-LŌSE′, CĂL′CỤ-LOŬS, *a.* Stony ; gritty.
CĂL′CỤ-LŬS, *n. ; pl.* CĂL′CỤ-LĪ. The stone in the bladder : — a method of computation.
CĂL′DRỌN, *n.* A pot ; a boiler ; a large kettle.
CĂL-Ę-FĂC′TIỌN, *n.* The act of heating.
CĂL-Ę-FĂC′TĮVE, *a.* That makes any thing hot.
CĂL-Ę-FĂC′TỌ-RỴ, *a.* That heats ; heating.
CĂL′Ę-FỴ, *v. n. & a.* To grow or make hot.
CĂL′ĘN-DĄR, *n.* A yearly register ; an almanac.
CĂL′ĘN-DĘR, *v. a.* To dress smooth, as cloth.
CĂL′ĘN-DĘR, *n.* Hot press; an engine to calender.
CĂL′ĘNDŞ, *n. pl.* The first day of each month in the ancient Roman calendar. [climates.
CĂL′ĘN-TŪRE, *n.* A febrile distemper in hot
CĂLF (käf), *n. ; pl.* CALVES (kävz). The young of a cow : — a dolt : — the thick part of the leg.
CĂL′Į-BĘR, *n.* The bore of a gun ; capacity.
CĂL′Į-CŌ, *n.* A kind of printed cotton cloth.
CĂL′Į-DŬCT, *n.* A pipe to convey heat.
CĄ-LĬĢ′Į-NOŬS, *a.* Obscure ; dim ; dark.
CĂL′Į-PĘRŞ, *n. pl.* Compasses with bowed shanks.
CĀ′LĮPH, *n.* A successor of Mahomet ; a vicar.
CĂL′Į-PHĀTE, *n.* The government of a caliph.
CĂL′Į-VĘR, *n.* A hand-gun ; an arquebuse.

CÂLK (kâwk), *v. a.* To stop or stuff with oakum and tar, as seams between planks of a
CÂLK′ĘR (kâwk′ęr), *n.* One who calks. [ship.
CÂLL, *v. a.* To name ; to summon ; to convoke.
CÂLL, *v. n.* To cry out ; to make a short visit.
CÂLL, *n.* An address ; a demand ; a short visit.
CĂL′LĘT, *n.* A trull ; a prostitute : — a scold.
CĄL-LĬD′Į-TỴ, CĂL′LĮD-NĔSS, *n.* Craftiness.
CĄL-LĬĢ′RĄ-PHỴ, *n.* Fine penmanship.
CÂLL′ĮNG, *n.* Vocation ; profession ; trade.
CĄL-LŎS′Į-TỴ, *n.* A hard swelling without pain.
CĂL′LOŬS, *a.* Hard ; indurated ; insensible.
CĂL′LOŬS-NĔSS, *n.* Hardness ; insensibility.
CĂL′LŌW (kăl′lō), *a.* Unfledged ; naked.
CĂL′LỤS, *n.* An induration ; a hardness.
CĂLM (käm), *a.* Quiet ; serene ; undisturbed.
CĂLM (käm), *n.* Serenity ; quiet ; repose.
CĂLM (käm), *v. a.* To still ; to pacify ; to soothe.
CĂLM′LỴ (käm′lẹ), *ad.* Serenely ; quietly.
CĂLM′NĔSS (käm′nẹs), *n.* Tranquillity ; mildness.
CĂL′Ọ-MĔL, *n.* A compound of chlorine and mercury, used in medicine; chloride of mercury.
CĄ-LŎR′ĮC, *n.* Principle or matter of heat ; heat.
CĂL-Ọ-RĬF′ĮC, *a.* Causing heat ; heating.
CĂL′TRỌP, *n.* An instrument with four spikes.
CĂL′Ụ-MĔT, *n.* The Indian pipe of peace.
CĄ-LŬM′NĮ-ĀTE, *v. a.* To accuse falsely.
CĄ-LŬM′NĮ-Ā-TỌR, *n.* A slanderer. [derous.
CĄ-LŬM′NĮ-Ą-TỌ-RỴ, CĄ-LŬM′NĮ-OŬS, *a.* Slan-
CĂL′ỤM-NỴ, *n.* Slander ; false accusation.
CĂLVE (käv), *v. n.* To bring forth a calf.
CĂL′VĮN-ĬŞM, *n.* The doctrine of Calvin.
CĂL′VĮN-ĬST, *n.* A follower of Calvin.
CĂL-VĮN-ĬS′TĮC, } *a.* Relating, or adhering, to
CĂL-VĮN-ĬS′TĮ-CĄL, } Calvin or to Calvinism.
CĂLX, *n. ; pl.* CĂL′CĘŞ. Residue of burnt lime.
CĀ′LỴX, *n.* (*Bot.*) A flower-cup :—shell of a shell-
CĂM′BĮST, *n.* One skilled in exchanges. [fish.
CĂM′BRĮC, *n.* A fine, thin linen or cotton fab-
CĀME, *imp. t.* from *come.* [ric.
CĂM′ĘL, *n.* A large animal common in Arabia.
CĄ-MĔL′Ọ-PĂRD, *n.* A tall African animal.
CĂM′Ę-Ō, *n.* An engraved stone or shell.
CĂM′Ę-RĄ-ỌB-SCŪ′RĄ, *n.* An optical machine.
CĂM-Į-SĀ′DŌ, *n.* An attack made at night.
CĂM′LĘT, *n.* A thin kind of cloth or stuff.
CĂM′Ọ-MĪLE, *n.* A genus of flowering plants.
CĂMP, *n.* The order of tents of an army.
CĄM-PĀIGN′ (kạm-pān′), *n.* The time an army keeps the field in one year :—open level ground.
CĄM-PĀIGN′, *v. n.* To serve in a campaign.
CĄM-PĂN′Į-FŎRM, *a.* In the shape of a bell.
CĂM′PHỌR, *n.* A fragrant concrete juice.
CĂM′PHỌ-RĀT-ĘD, *a.* Impregnated with cam-
CĂM′PHỌR-TRĔĒ, *n.* An evergreen tree. [phor.
CĂN, *n.* A metal cup or vessel for liquors.
CĂN, *v. n.* [*imp. t.* could.] To be able. [rabble.
CĄ-NĀILLE′ (kạ-nāl′), *n.* The lowest people ; the
CĄ-NĂL′, *n.* A watercourse made by art ; pas-
CĂN′ĄL-CŌAL, *n.* Cannel-coal. [sage.
CĄ-NĀ′RỴ, *n.* Wine from the Canaries : — a bird.
CĄ-NĀ′RỴ-BĬRD, *n.* A small singing bird.
CĂN′CĘL, *v. a.* To blot out ; to expunge ; to an-
CĂN′CĘL-LĀT-ĘD, *a.* Cross-barred. [nul.
CĂN′CĘR, *n.* The Crab ; the sign of the summer solstice : — a tumor terminating in an ulcer.
CĂN′CĘR-ĀTE, *v. n.* To become a cancer.
CĂN-CĘR-Ā′TIỌN, *n.* A growing cancerous.

CĂN'CER-OŬS, a. Having the qualities of a can-
CĂN'CRĬ-FÖRM, a. Formed like a cancer. [cer.
CĂN'DENT, a. White with heat; glowing.
CĂN'DĬD, a. Fair; open; frank; ingenuous.
CĂN'DĬ-DĀTE, n. A competitor; one who pro-
 poses himself, or is proposed, for some office.
CĂN'DĬD-LY, ad. Fairly; openly; frankly.
CĂN'DLE, n. A light made of tallow, &c.; a
CĂN'DLE–LĪGHT, n. Light of a candle. [light.
CĂN'DLE-MĂS, n. The feast of the purification
 of the Blessed Virgin, February 2.
CĂN'DLE-STĬCK, n. Instrument to hold candles.
CĂN'DOR, n. Frankness; openness; fairness.
CĂN'DY, v. a. To conserve with sugar. [serve.
CĂN'DY, v. n. To grow congealed.—n. A con-
CĀNE, n. A reed; sugar-cane; a walking staff.
CĀNE, v. a. To beat with a cane. [of reeds.
CĀNE'BRĀKE, n. A thicket of canes:—a genus
CA-NĬC'Ṳ-LAR, a. Belonging to the dog-star.
CA-NĪNE', a. Having the qualities of a dog.
CĂN'ĬS-TER, n. Box for tea, &c.; a small basket.
CĂNK'ER, n. An eating humor; a disease in trees.
CĂNK'ER, v. n. To grow corrupt; to decay.
CĂNK'ER, v. a. To corrupt; to corrode; to infect.
CĂNK'ERED (kăng'kerd), a. Crabbed; morose.
CĂNK'ER-OŬS, a. Corroding like a canker.
CĂNK'ER-WŎRM, n. A worm that injures trees.
CĂN'NEL-CŌAL, n. A hard, bituminous coal.
CĂN'NĬ-BAL, n. A man-eater; anthropophagite.
CĂN'NĬ-BAL-ĬṢM, n. The eating of human flesh.
CĂN'NON, n. A great gun, as for a battery.
CĂN-NON-ĀDE', v. a. To attack with cannon.
CĂN-NON-ĀDE', n. An attack by cannon.
CĂN'NON-BĂLL, n. A ball for a cannon.
CĂN'NON-PRŎŎF, a. Proof against cannon.
CĂN-NON-ĒER', n. One who manages cannon.
CĂN'NOT, v. n. Can and not, noting inability.
CA-NŌE' (ka-nô'), n. A small boat, paddled.
CĂN'ON, n. A rule; a law:—the books of Holy
 Scripture:—a dignitary in cathedrals.
CĂN'ON-ĚSS, n. A woman possessed of a prebend.
CA-NŎN'Ĭ-CAL, a. According to canon; regular.
CA-NŎN'Ĭ-CAL-LY, ad. In a canonical manner.
CA-NŎN'Ĭ-CAL-NĚSS, n. The being canonical.
CA-NŎN'Ĭ-CALṢ, n. pl. Full dress of a clergyman.
CĂN'ON-ĬST, n. A man versed in canon law.
CĂN-ON-Ĭ-ZĀ'TION, n. Act of making a saint.
CĂN'ON-ĪZE, v. a. To declare a saint.
CĂN'ON-RY,   } n. A benefice in some cathedral
CĂN'ON-SHĬP, } or collegiate church.
CĂN'O-PY, n. A covering over a throne, bed, &c.
CĂN'O-PY, v. a. To cover with a canopy.
CA-NŌ'ROŬS, a. Musical; tuneful; sonorous.
CĂNT, n. Whining tone; hypocritical speech;
 slang; dialect:—a throw; a turn; a jerk.
CĂNT, v. n. To speak with a whining tone.
CAN-TĀ'TA, n. (Mus.) A poem set to music.
CAN-TEEN', n. A vessel for carrying liquors.
CĂN'TER, n. An easy gallop:—a hypocrite.
CĂN'TER, v. n. To gallop easily or gently.
CAN-THĂR'Ĭ-DĚṢ, n. pl. Spanish flies.
CĂN'TĬ-CLE, n. A song; canto; Song of Solo-
CĂNT'LET, n. A piece; a fragment. [mon.
CĂN'TŌ, n.; pl. CĂN'TŌṢ. A section of a poem.
CĂN'TON, n. A division of a country; a clan.
CĂN'TON, v. a. To divide into little parts.
CĂN'TON-ĪZE, v. a. To divide into cantons.
CĂN'TON-MĔNT, n. Quarters for soldiers.

CĂN'VAṢ, n. Coarse cloth for sails, tents, &c.
CĂN'VAṢS, v. a. To examine; to debate; to so-
CĂN'VAṢS, v. n. To solicit votes. [licit votes from.
CĂN'VAṢS, n. Solicitation of votes:—discussion.
CĀ'NY, a. Full of canes; consisting of canes.
CAN-ZO-NĖT', n. (Mus.) A little song.
CAÔUT'CHÔUC (kô'chŭk), n. India rubber.
CĂP, n. A covering for the head:—the top.
CĂP, v. a. To cover the top or end of; to top.
CĀ-PA-BĬL'Ĭ-TY, n. Capableness; capacity.
CĀ'PA-BLE, a. Able to receive; able; equal.
CĀ'PA-BLE-NĚSS, n. The state of being capable.
CA-PĀ'CIOŬS (ka-pā'shus), a. Wide; large; vast.
CA-PĀ'CIOŬS-LY, ad. In a capacious manner.
CA-PĀ'CIOŬS-NĚSS, n. The power of holding.
CA-PĂÇ'Ĭ-TĀTE, v. a. To make capable.
CA-PĂÇ'Ĭ-TY, n. Room; ability; character.
CĂP-A-PIĒ', ad. From head to foot; all over.
CA-PĂR'Ĭ-SON, n. Ornamental dress for a horse.
CA-PĂR'Ĭ-SON, v. a. To dress showily, as a horse.
CĀPE, n. A headland; neck-piece of a coat, &c.
CĀ'PER, n. A leap; a skip:—a bud; a pickle.
CĀ'PER, v. n. To dance; to leap; to skip.
CA-PĬL'LA-MĔNT, n. A fine thread or fibre.
CĂP'ĬL-LA-RY, a. Like hair; small and slender.
CĂP'ĬL-LA-RY, n. A small tube or vein.
CĂP'Ĭ-TAL, a. Principal:—punishable by death.
CĂP'Ĭ-TAL, n. The upper part of a column; chief
 city; city or town in which a legislature meets:
 —stock invested:—a large letter.
CĂP'Ĭ-TAL-ĬST, n. One who has capital stock.
CĂP'Ĭ-TAL-LY, ad. In a capital manner. [tax.
CĂP-Ĭ-TĀ'TION, n. Numeration by heads; poll-
CĂP'Ĭ-TOL, n. A temple; a public edifice. [ter.
CA-PĬT'Ṳ-LAR, n. A statute; member of a chap-
CA-PĬT'Ṳ-LATE, v. n. To surrender by treaty.
CA-PĬT-Ṳ-LĀ'TION, n. The act of capitulating.
CA-PÎ'VĬ (ka-pē've), n. A tree and balsam.
CĀ'PON (kā'pn), n. A castrated cock.
CA-PŌUCH' (ka-pôch'), n. A monk's hood.
CĂP'-PĀ-PER, n. A coarse brown paper.
CA-PRĒ'O-LATE, a. Having tendrils; cirrous.
CA-PRĪCE', n. A freak; fancy; whim.
CA-PRĪ''CIOŬS (ka-prĭsh'us), a. Fickle; fanciful.
CA-PRĪ''CIOŬS-LY, ad. Whimsically; fancifully.
CA-PRĪ''CIOŬS-NĚSS (-prĭsh'us-nĕs), n. Caprice.
CĂP'RĬ-CÖRN, n. The Goat; a sign of the zodiac.
CĂP-RĬ-FĬ-CĀ'TION, n. The ripening of figs.
CĂP'RĬ-ŌLE, n. A leap without advancing.
CAP-SĪZE', v. a. To upset. [A nautical word.]
CĂP'STĂN, n. A machine for drawing. [chest.
CĂP'SṲ-LAR, CĂP'SṲ-LA-RY, a. Hollow, as a
CĂP'SŪLE, n. The seed-vessel of a plant. [&c.
CĂP'TAĬN (kăp'tin), n. Commander, as of a ship,
CĂP'TAĬN-CY, CĂP'TAĬN-SHĬP, n. Office of cap-
CĂP'TION, n. Arrest; a preamble or head. [tain.
CĂP'TIOŬS (kăp'shus), a. Cavilling; insnaring.
CĂP'TIOŬS-LY, ad. In a captious manner.
CĂP'TIOŬS-NĚSS, n. Inclination to find fault.
CĂP'TĬ-VĀTE, v. a. To take prisoner; to charm.
CĂP-TĬ-VĀ'TION, n. The act of captivating.
CĂP'TĬVE, n. A prisoner; one charmed.
CĂP'TĬVE, a. Made prisoner; enslaved.
CAP-TĬV'Ĭ-TY, n. Subjection; bondage; slavery.
CĂP'TOR, n. A taker of prisoners or prizes.
CĂPT'ŪRE (kăpt'yur), n. Act of taking; prize.
CĂPT'ŪRE (kăpt'yur), v. a. To take as a prize.
CĂP-Ṳ-ÇHÎN', n. A monk; garment; pigeon.

CÄR, *n.* A chariot; cart; a railway carriage.
CÄR′Ạ-BĪNE, *n.* A cavalry fire-arm; a petronel.
CÄR-Ạ-BĬN-ĒĒR′, *n.* A light-horseman.
CÄR′ẠT, *n.* A weight of four grains.
CÄR-Ạ-VĂN′, *n.* A company of travelling mer-chants, as in the East :—a travelling menagerie.
CÄR-Ạ-VĂN′SẠ-RY, *n.* A kind of inn in the East.
CÄR′Ạ-WĀY, *n.* A plant and its spicy seed.
CÄR′BĪNE, *n.* A small fire-arm; carabine.
CÄR′BŎN, *n.* (*Chem.*) Pure charcoal.
CÄR-BQ-NĀ′CEOŲS (-shụs), *a.* Having carbon.
CÄR′BQ-NẠTE, *n.* A chemical salt. [bon.
CAR-BŎN′ĮC, *a.* Relating to or containing car-
CÄR′BŬN-CLE, *n.* A gem; a hard tumor.
CẠR-BŬN′CỤ-LẠR, *a.* Like a carbuncle.
CÄR′CẠ-NĔT, *n.* A necklace or bracelet.
CÄR′CẠSS, *n.* A dead body; corpse :—a bomb.
CÄRD, *n.* A note; a message of civility; a painted paper :—a large comb for wool, &c.
CÄRD, *v. a.* To comb, as wool, &c.
CÄR′DẠ-MĪNE, *n.* The plant lady's-smock.
CÄR′DẠ-MQM, *n.* An aromatic seed.
CÄR′DĮ-NẠL, *n.* A dignitary in the Roman Catholic church, next in rank to the pope.
CÄR′DĮ-NẠL, *a.* Chief; principal; first.
CÄRD′-TÄ-BLE, *n.* A table for playing cards.
CÄRE, *n.* Solicitude; anxiety; caution; charge.
CÄRE, *v. n.* To be anxious; to be inclined.
CẠ-RĒĒN′, *v. a.* To lay on one side, as a vessel.
CẠ-RĒĒR′, *n.* A course; race; procedure.
CẠ-RĒĒR′, *v. n.* To run with swift motion.
CÄRE′FŬL, *a.* Anxious; provident; watchful.
CÄRE′FŬL-LY, *ad.* Heedfully; providently.
CÄRE′FŬL-NĔSS, *n.* Vigilance; anxiety.
CÄRE′LĔSS, *a.* Having no care; heedless.
CÄRE′LĔSS-LY, *ad.* In a careless manner.
CÄRE′LĔSS-NĔSS, *n.* Heedlessness; remissness.
CẠ-RĔSS′, *v. a.* To treat with fondness; to fondle.
CẠ-RĔSS′, *n.* An act of endearment.
CÄ′RĘT, *n.* This mark [ʌ], noting an omission.
CÄR′GŌ, *n.* The lading or freight of a ship.
CÄR′Į-CẠ-TŪRE, *n.* A ludicrous likeness.
CÄR-Į-CẠ-TŪRE′, *v. a.* To make a caricature of.
CÄR-Į-CẠ-TŪ′RĮST, *n.* One who caricatures.
CÄ′RĮ-ĒṢ, *n.* (*Med.*) Rottenness of a bone.
CÄ′RĮ-OŬS, *a.* Rotten; ulcerated, as a bone.
CÄRLE, *n.* A rude man :—a kind of hemp.
CÄR′MẠN, *n.* A man who drives a cart.
CÄR′MĔL-ĪTE, *n.* A mendicant friar; a pear.
CÄR′MĪNE, *n.* A bright red color or lake.
CÄR′NẠĢE, *n.* Slaughter; havoc; massacre.
CÄR′NẠL, *a.* Fleshly; not spiritual; lustful.
CẠR-NĂL′Į-TY, *n.* Fleshly lust; sensuality.
CÄR′NẠL-LY, *ad.* In a carnal manner.
CẠR-NĀ′TIQN, *n.* A flesh color; a fine flower.
CẠR-NĔL′IẠN (-nĕl′yạn), *n.* A precious stone.
CÄR′NĘ-OŬS, CÄR′NOŲS, *a.* Fleshy; like flesh.
CÄR′NĮ-FŸ, *v. n.* To form flesh from nutriment.
CÄR′NĮ-VẠL, *n.* A Catholic feast held before
CẠR-NĬV′Q-ROŬS, *a.* Flesh-eating. [Lent.
CẠR-NŎS′Į-TY, *n.* A fleshy excrescence.
CÄR′QL, *n.* A song of exultation or praise.
CÄR′QL, *v. n.* To sing; to warble.
CÄR′QL, *v. a.* To celebrate in song.
CẠ-RŎT′ĮD, *n.* An artery of the neck.
CẠ-RŎŨ′SẠL, *n.* A festival; a revelling.
CẠ-RŎŨSE′, *v. n.* To drink hard; to revel.
CẠ-RŎŨṢ′ĘR, *n.* A noisy, hard drinker.

CÄRP, *v. n.* To censure; to cavil.—*n.* A fish.
CÄR′PĘN-TĘR, *n.* A builder of houses, ships, &c.
CÄR′PĘN-TRY, *n.* The art of a carpenter.
CÄR′PĘT, *n.* A covering for a floor.
CÄR′PĘT, *v. a.* To spread with carpets.
CÄR′PĘT-ĬNG, *n.* Materials for carpets :—carpets.
CÄRP′ĮNG, *p. a.* Captious; censorious.
CÄRP′ĮNG, *n.* Cavil; censure; fault-finding.
CÄR′RIAĢE (kär′rij), *n.* The act of carrying; a vehicle; behavior; conduct; manners.
CÄR′RĮ-ĘR, *n.* One who carries; a sort of pigeon.
CÄR′RĮ-QN, *n.* Putrefying, dead flesh.
CÄR′RĮ-QN, *a.* Relating to, or feeding on, carrion.
CÄR′RQN-ĀDE, *n.* A very short piece of cannon.
CÄR′RQT, *n.* An esculent plant or root. [low.
CÄR′RQT-Y, *a.* Resembling carrots; reddish yel-
CÄR′RY, *v. a. & n.* To convey; transport, behave.
CÄRT, *n.* A carriage with two wheels.
CÄRT, *v. a. & n.* To carry or place in a cart.
CÄRT′AĢE, *n.* Act of carting, or charge for it.
CÄRT′-HÖRSE, *n.* A horse that draws a cart.
CÄRT′-LŌAD, *n.* Quantity sufficient to load a cart.
CẠR-TĔL′, *n.* An agreement between two states at war, relating to exchange of prisoners.
CÄRT′ĘR, *n.* A man who drives a cart. [stance.
CÄR′TĮ-LAĢE, *n.* Gristle; a tough, elastic sub-
CÄR-TĮ-LĂĢ′Į-NOŬS, *a.* Consisting of cartilage.
CẠR-TŌŌN′, *n.* A painting on strong paper.
CẠR-TÔUCH′, *n.* A case for balls and cartridges.
CÄR′TRĮDĢE, *n.* A paper case for gunpowder, &c.
CÄRT′-RŌPE, *n.* A strong cord, for carts.
CÄRT′-RŬT, *n.* Track made by a cart-wheel.
CÄRT′WRĪGHT (kärt′rīt), *n.* A maker of carts.
CÄR′ŲN-CLE, *n.* A fleshy protuberance.
CÄRVE, *v. a. & n.* To cut wood, stone, or meat.
CÄRV′ĘR, *n.* One who carves; a sculptor.
CẠS-CĀDE′, *n.* A small cataract; a waterfall.
CĀSE, *n.* A box; a sheath; a cover :—condition; state :—a cause in court :—inflection of nouns.
CĀSE, *v. a.* To put in a case; to cover. [outside.
CĀSE′HÄRD-EN (kās′här-dn), *v. a.* To harden the
CĀSE′-KNĪFE (kās′nīf), *n.* A large knife.
CĀSE′MĀTE, *n.* (*Fort.*) A vault in a bastion.
CĀSE′MENT, *n.* Window opening upon hinges.
CĀ′SĘ-OŬS, *a.* Resembling cheese.
CĀ′SĘRN, *n.* Small barracks for soldiers.
CĂSH, *n.* Money; ready money; coin; specie.
CĂSH, *v. a.* To pay money for. [money.
CẠ-SHIĒR′ (kạ-shēr′), *n.* One having charge of
CẠ-SHIĒR′, *v. a.* To dismiss from an office.
CĂSH′ÔÔ, *n.* An aromatic drug of Hindostan.
CĂS′ĬNG, *n.* The covering of any thing.
CĂSK, *n.* A barrel; a wooden vessel.
CĂS′KĘT, *n.* A small box for jewels, &c.
CĂSQUE (kăsk), *n.* A helmet; armor for the head.
CẠS-SĀ′TIQN, *n.* The act of annulling.
CẠS-SĀ′VẠ, *n.* Nutritious starch from a plant.
CĂS′SĮ-A (kăsh′ę-ạ), *n.* A spice; evergreen shrub.
CĂS′SĮ-DQ-NY, *n.* A plant :—chalcedony.
CĂS′SĮ-MĒRE, *n.* A sort of woollen cloth.
CĂS′SQCK, *n.* Under garment of a clergyman.
CĂS′SQ-WĀ-RY, *n.* A large bird of Java.
CĂST, *v. a.* [*imp. t. & pp.* cast.] To throw; to hurl; to compute; to found; to bring forth.
CĂST, *v. n.* To be formed in a mould; to warp.
CĂST, *n.* A throw; a mould; a shade; mien.
CĂS′TẠ-NĔT, *n.* A small piece of ivory or hard wood, used as an accompaniment to dances, &c.

CĂST′A-WĀY, *n.* A person lost or abandoned.
CĂSTE, *n.* An order or class of people.
CĂS′TEL-LĂN, *n.* The governor of a castle.
CĂS′TEL-LA-NY, *n.* The lordship of a castle.
CĂS′TEL-LĀT-ED, *a.* Having battlements.
CĂST′ER, *n.* One who casts; a phial; a wheel.
CĂS′TI-GĀTE, *v. a.* To chastise; to punish.
CĂS-TI-GĀ′TIQN, *n.* Punishment; chastisement.
CĂS′TI-GĀ-TQR, *n.* One who castigates.
CĂST′ING, *n.* Act of casting: — a thing cast.
CĂST′ING-NĔT, *n.* A net to be thrown.
CĂS′TLE (kăs′sl), *n.* A fortress or fortified house.
CĂS′TLED (kăs′sld), *a.* Furnished with castles.
CĂS′TQR, *n.* A beaver: — one of the *Gemini.*
CĂS′TQR-ÖĬL, *n.* A vegetable oil.
CĂS-TRA-ME-TĀ′TIQN, *n.* The act or the art of planning or tracing an encampment.
CĂS′TRĀTE, *v. a.* To geld; to emasculate.
CAS-TRĀ′TIQN, *n.* Act of gelding or castrating.
CĂṢ′U-AL (kăzh′u-al), *a.* Accidental; fortuitous.
CĂṢ′U-AL-LY (kăzh′u-al-le), *ad.* Accidentally.
CĂṢ′U-AL-TY (kăzh′u-al-te), *n.* An accident.
CĂṢ′U-ĬST (kăzh′u-ĭst), *n.* One who studies and resolves cases of conscience. [to casuistry.
CĂṢ-U-ĬS′TI-CAL (kăzh-u-ĭs′te-kal), *a.* Relating
CĂṢ′U-ĬS-TRY (kăzh′u-ĭs-tre), *n.* Science of a
CĂT, *n.* A domestic animal: — a ship. [casuist.
CĂT-A-CHRĒ′SIS, *n.* A harsh metaphor.
CĂT′A-CŌMBṢ, *n. pl.* Caverns for the dead.
CĂT-A-CÖŪS′TICS,*n.* Science of reflected sounds.
CĂT′A-LĔP-SY, *n.* A kind of apoplexy.
CĂT′A-LŌGUE (kăt′a-lŏg), *n.* A list or register.
CA-TĂL′PA, *n.* A large flowering tree.
CĂT′A-MÖŪNT, *n.* The North American tiger.
CĂT′A-PHRĂCT, *n.* A horseman in complete [armor.
CĂT′A-PLĂṢM, *n.* A poultice; a plaster.
CĂT′A-PŬLT, *n.* An ancient military engine.
CĂT′A-RĂCT, *n.* A waterfall:—a disease in the [eye.
CA-TĂRRH′ (ka-tär′), *n.* Cold in the head.
CA-TĂRRH′AL (ka-tär′ral), *a.* Relating to a
CA-TĂRRH′OŪS (ka-tär′rus), *}* catarrh or cold.
CA-TĂS′TRQ-PHE, *n.* A final event; calamity.
CĂT′CÂLL, *n.* A small squeaking instrument.
CĂTCH, *v. a.* [*imp. t.* & *pp.* caught, catched.] To-lay hold on; to seize; to stop; to insnare.
CĂTCH, *v. n.* To be contagious; to lay hold.
CĂTCH, *n.* Seizure; a clasp; a snatch; a song.
CĂTCH′ER, *n.* The person or thing that catches.
CĂTCH′PÖLE, *n.* A sergeant; a policeman.
CĂTCH′ŬP, *or* CĂT′SŬP, *n.* A sauce made from mushrooms, tomatoes, walnuts, &c.[of a page.
CĂTCH′WŎRD, *n.* A word under the last line
CĂT-E-CHĔT′I-CAL, *a.* Consisting of questions and answers; catechistical. [answers.
CĂT-E-CHĔT′I-CAL-LY, *ad.* By question and
CĂT′E-CHĪṢE, *v. a.* To instruct by questions and answers; to question; to interrogate.
CĂT′E-CHĬṢM, *n.* A form or book of instruction by questions and answers. [chism.
CĂT′E-CHĬST, *n.* One who teaches the cate-
CĂT-E-CHĬST′I-CAL, *a.* By question and answer.
CĂT-E-CHŪ′MEN, *n.* One yet in the rudiments of Christianity, or who is little advanced.
CĂT-E-GŎR′I-CAL, *a.* Absolute; positive.
CĂT-E-GŎR′I-CAL-LY, *ad.* Directly; positively.
CĂT′E-GQ-RY, *n.* An order of ideas; predica-
CĂT-E-NĀ′TIQN, *n.* Regular connection. [ment.
CĀ′TER, *v. n.* To procure or provide food.

CĀ′TER-ER, *n.* A provider; a purveyor.
CĀ′TER-ESS, *n.* A woman who provides food.
CĂT′ER-PĬL-LAR, *n.* Grub of an insect; a plant.
CĂT′ER-WÂUL, *v. n.* To make a noise as cats.
CĂT′FĬSH, *n.* A sort of fish; the horned-pout.
CĂT′GŬT, *n.* A string for musical instruments.
CA-THĂR′TIC, *n.* A purging medicine.
CA-THĂR′TIC, CA-THĂR′TI-CAL, *a.* Purgative.
CĂT′HĔAD, *n.* A piece of timber: — an apple.
CA-THĒ′DRAL, *n.* The head church of a diocese.
CĂTH′E-TER, *n.* Instrument to draw off urine.
CĂTH′Q-LĬC, *a.* Universal; general; liberal.
CĂTH′Q-LĬC, *n.* A Roman Catholic.
CA-THŎL′I-CĬṢM, *n.* Adherence to the Catholic church: — universality: — largeness of mind.
CA-THŎL′I-CĪZE, *v. n.* To become a Catholic.
CA-THŎL′I-CÖN, *n.* A universal remedy; a [panacea.
CĂT′KIN, *n.* A kind of inflorescence.
CĂT′MĬNT, *or* CĂT′NIP, *n.* A perennial plant.
CĂT-Q′-NĪNE′TĀILṢ,*n.* A whip with nine lashes.
CA-TŎP′TRQN, *n.* A kind of optic glass.
CĂT′S′-PÂW, *n.* A dupe used by another.
CĂT′SŬP, *n.* A sauce. See CATCHUP.
CĂT′TLE, *n.* Beasts of pasture not wild.
CÂU′CUS, *n.* A meeting for political purposes.
CÂU′DAL, *a.* Relating to the tail of an animal.
CÂU′DĀTE, CÂU′DĀT-ED, *a.* Having a tail.
CÂU′DLE, *n.* A mixture of wine, gruel, &c.
CÂUGHT (kăwt), *imp. t.* & *pp.* from *catch.*
CÂUL, *n.* A membrane covering the intestines.
CÂU-LĬF′ER-OŬS, *a.* Having a stalk.
CÂU′LI-FLÖW-ER, *n.* A fine species of cabbage.
CÂU′LIS, *n.* Stalk of herbaceous plants.
CÂU′ṢAL, *a.* Relating to or expressing a cause.
CÂU-ṢĂL′I-TY, *n.* The agency of a cause.
CÂU-ṢĀ′TIQN, *n.* The act of causing.
CÂU′ṢA-TĬVE, *a.* That expresses a cause.
CÂU′ṢA-TĬVE-LY, *ad.* In a causative manner.
CÂU-ṢĀ′TQR, *n.* One who causes; a causer.
CÂUṢE, *n.* That which produces an effect; reason; motive; suit; object; side; party.
CÂUṢE, *v. a.* To effect, as an agent; to produce.
CÂUṢE′LESS, *a.* Having no cause or reason.
CÂUṢ′ER, *n.* One who causes; an agent.
CÂU′ṢEY, *or* CÂUṢE′WĀY, *n.* A raised road.
CÂUS′TIC, *n.* A corroding application.
CÂUS′TIC, CÂUS′TI-CAL, *a.* Burning; corroding.
CÂUS-TĬÇ′I-TY, *n.* Caustic quality; causticness.
CÂUS′TIC-NĔSS, *n.* Quality of being caustic.
CÂU′TER, *n.* A searing hot iron.
CÂU′TER-ĬṢM, *n.* The application of caustics.
CÂU-TER-I-ZĀ′TIQN, *n.* Act of cauterizing.
CÂU′TER-ĪZE, *v. a.* To burn with a cautery.
CÂU′TE-RY, *n.* An iron for burning; a caustic.
CÂU′TIQN, *n.* Provident care; advice; warning.
CÂU′TIQN, *v. a.* To give notice of danger to.
CÂU′TIQN-A-RY, *a.* Given as a pledge; warning.
CÂU′TIOŬS (kâw′shus), *a.* Wary; watchful.
CÂU′TIOŬS-LY, *ad.* In a cautious manner.
CÂU′TIOŬS-NĔSS, *n.* Watchfulness; vigilance.
CĂV-AL-CĀDE′, *n.* A procession on horseback.
CĂV-A-LIĒR′, *n.* A horse-soldier; a knight.
CĂV-A-LIĒR′, *a.* Gay; brave: — disdainful.
CĂV-A-LIĒR′LY (kăv-a-lēr′le), *ad.* Haughtily.
CĂV′AL-RY, *n.* Soldiers or troops on horses.
CĀVE, *n.* A cavern; a grotto; a den.
CĀVE, *v. a.* To make hollow. — *v. n.* To fall in.
CĀ′VE-ĂT, *n.* (*Law.*) Process to stop proceedings.

CĂV'ERN, n. A hollow place in the ground.
CĂV'ERN-OŬS, a. Full of caverns; hollow.
CA-VÎARE' (ka-vēr'), n. The roe of the sturgeon.
CĂV'IL, v. n. To raise captious objections.
CĂV'IL, n. A false or frivolous objection.
CĂV'IL-LER, n. A captious disputant.
CĂV'I-TY, n. Hollowness; a hollow place.
CÂW, v. n. To cry as the rook or crow.
CĂY-ĔNNE', n. A pungent red pepper.
CA-ZÎQUE' (ka-zēk'), n. An Indian chief.
CĔASE (sēs), v. n. To leave off; to fail; to stop.
CĔASE'LESS, a. Without stop; incessant.
CĔ'DAR, n. An evergreen tree.
CĔDE, v. a. To yield; to resign; to give up.
CE-DĬL'LA, n. This mark [,] under the letter c, denoting that it sounds like s.
CĔ'DRINE or CĔ'DRINE, a. Belonging to cedar.
CĔIL (sēl), v. a. To overlay the inner roof.
CĔIL'ING, n. The covering of the inner roof.
CĔL'AN-DINE, n. A plant; swallow-wort.
CĔL'A-TURE, n. The art of engraving on metals.
CĔL'E-BRATE, v.a. To praise; to extol, honor.
CĔL-E-BRA'TION, n. Act of celebrating; praise.
CE-LĔB'RI-TY, n. Fame; renown; distinction.
CE-LĔR'I-TY, n. Swiftness; rapidity; speed.
CĔL'ER-Y, n. A species of parsley for salad.
CE-LĔST'IAL (se-lĕst'yal), a. Heavenly; ethereal.
CE-LĔST'IAL-LY, ad. In a heavenly manner.
CĔL'I-BA-CY, n. Unmarried state; single life.
CĔLL, n. A small, close room; a cavity; a cave.
CĔL'LAR, n. A room under a house.
CĔL'LAR-AGE, n. Room of a cellar; a cellar.
CĔL'LU-LAR, a. Having cells or cavities.
CĔL'TIC, a. Relating to the Celts, or Gauls.
CĔM'ENT, n. That which unites; mortar.
CE-MĔNT', v. a. To unite by something inter-
CE-MĔNT', v. n. To cohere; to unite. [posed.
CĔM-EN-TA'TION, n. The act of cementing.
CE-MĔNT'ER, n. The person or thing that ce-
CĔM'E-TER-Y, n. A burial-place. [ments.
CĔN'O-TĂPH, n. A monument erected to the memory of one buried elsewhere.
CĔN'SER, n. Vessel in which incense is burnt.
CĔN'SOR, n. An officer of Rome; a censurer.
CEN-SO'RI-AN, a. Relating to a censor.
CEN-SO'RI-OŬS, a. Addicted to censure; severe.
CEN-SO'RI-OŬS-LY, ad. In a severe manner.
CEN-SO'RI-OŬS-NĔSS, n. Disposition to censure.
CĔN'SOR-SHIP, n. The office of a censor.
CĔN'SU-RA-BLE (sĕn'shu-ra-bl), a. Culpable.
CĔN'SU-RA-BLE-NĔSS, n. Blamableness.
CĔN'SU-RA-BLY (sĕn'shu-ra-ble), ad. Culpably.
CĔN'SURE (sĕn'shur), n. Blame; reproach.
CĔN'SURE (sĕn'shur), v. a. To blame; to condemn; to reproach; to reprehend; to reprove.
CĔN'SUR-ER (sĕn'shur-er), n. One who blames.
CĔN'SUS, n. An enumeration of inhabitants.
CĔNT,n.A hundred : — an American copper coin.
CĔN'TAUR (sĕn'tàwr), n. A fabulous being, half man and half horse : — a southern constel-
CĔN'TAU-RY, n. A kind of shrub. [lation.
CĔN-TE-NA'RI-AN, n. A person 100 years old.
CĔN'TE-NA-RY, n. The number of a hundred.
CEN-TĔN'NI-AL, a. Completing a hundred years; occurring once in a hundred years.
CĔN-TĔS'I-MAL, a. Hundredth.
CĔN-TI-FO'LI-OŬS, a. Having a hundred leaves.
CĔN'TI-GRADE, a. Having a hundred degrees.

CĔN'TI-PĔD, n. A poisonous insect. [authors.
CĔN'TO, n. A collection of scraps from various
CĔN'TRAL, a. Relating to the centre; middle.
CĔN'TRAL-LY, ad. With regard to the centre.
CĔN'TRE (sĕn'ter), n. The exact middle.
CĔN'TRE (sĕn'ter), v. a. To place on a centre.
CĔN'TRE (sĕn'ter), v. n. To be in the centre.
CĔN'TRIC, CĔN'TRI-CAL, a. In the centre.
CĔN'TRI-CAL-LY, ad. In a centrical situation.
CEN-TRĬF'U-GAL, a. Flying from the centre.
CEN-TRĬP'E-TAL, a. Tending to the centre.
CĔN'TRY, n. A sentinel; a sentry.
CĔN'TU-PLE, a. Hundred fold.
CEN-TU'RI-ON, n. A Roman military officer, who commanded a hundred men.
CĔNT'U-RY, n. A period of one hundred years.
CE-PHĂL'IC, a. Relating to the head.
CĔ'RATE, n. A composition of wax, oil, &c.
CĔ'RAT-ED, a. Covered with wax.
CĔRE, v. a. To cover with wax; to wax.
CĔRE, n. Naked skin on the bill of some birds.
CĔR'E-BRAL, a. Relating to the brain.
CĔRE'CLOTH, } n. Cloth smeared with melted
CĔRE'MENT, } wax or with bitumen.
CĔR-E-MO'NI-AL, a. Relating to ceremony.[rite.
CĔR-E-MO'NI-AL, n. Outward form; external
CĔR-E-MO'NI-OŬS, a. Civil; formal; precise.
CĔR-E-MO'NI-OŬS-LY, ad. Formally; precisely.
CĔR-E-MO'NI-OŬS-NĔSS, n. Great formality.
CĔR'E-MO-NY, n. Outward rite; external form.
CE-RĬL'LA, n. Cedilla. See CEDILLA.
CĔR'TAIN (sĕr'tin), a. Sure; indubitable; some.
CĔR'TAIN-LY, ad. Indubitably; without fail.
CĔR'TAIN-TY, n. Assurance; real state; truth.
CER-TĬF'I-CATE, n. A testimony in writing.
CER-TĬF'I-CATE, v. a. To give a certificate to.
CĔR-TI-FI-CA'TION, n. The act of certifying.
CĔR'TI-FY, v.a. To give certain information to
CĔR'TI-TUDE, n. Freedom from doubt; certainty; real state; fact; truth.
CE-RÛ'LE-AN, a. Sky-colored; blue; azure.
CE-RÛ'MEN, n. The wax in the ear.
CĔ'RUSE, n. White lead; carbonate of lead.
CĔR'VI-CAL, a. Belonging to the neck.
CES-SA'TION, n. A stop; a rest; an armistice.
CĔS'SION (sĕsh'un), n. Act of ceding; surrender.
CĔS'TUS, n. The girdle or zone of Venus.
CE-TA'CEOŬS (se-tā'shus),a. Of the whale kind.
CHAFE, v. a. & n. To rub; to fret; to be rubbed or fretted; to be angry; to rage.
CHAFE, n. A fret; passion; a heat; a rage.
CHAF'ER, n. One who chafes : — an insect.
CHAF'ER-Y, n. A forge in an iron mill.
CHĂFF, n. The husks of grain; refuse.
CHĂF'FER, v.n.& a. To treat about a bargain.
CHĂF'FINCH, n. A small singing bird.
CHĂFF'Y, a. Full of chaff; light; worthless.
CHĂF'ING-DISH, n. A portable grate for coals.
CHA-GREEN', n. A rough-grained leather.
CHA-GRÎN', n. Ill humor; mortification.
CHA-GRÎN', v. a. To vex; to mortify.
CHÂIN, n. A series of links; a fetter; a bond.
CHÂIN, v. a. To fasten with a chain : — to en-
CHÂIN'-PUMP, n. A pump with a chain. [slave.
CHÂIN'-SHŎT, n. Bullets connected by a chain.
CHÂIR (chár), n. A movable seat; a sedan.
CHÂIR'MAN, n. The president of an assembly.
CHÂISE (shāz), n. A kind of light carriage.

A,E,I,O,U,Y, *long* ; Ă,Ĕ,Ĭ,Ŏ,Ŭ,Y̆, *short* ; A,E,I,O,U,Y, *obscure.*—FARE,FÄR,FÀST,FÂLL ; HÊIR,HĔR ;

ℭHĂL-CĔD′Q-NY, *n.* A kind of precious stone.
ℭHĂL-CŎG′RĄ-PHĘR, *n.* An engraver in brass.
ℭHĂL-CŎG′RĄ-PHỸ, *n.* Engraving in brass. [dea.
ℭHĂL-DĀ′ĮC, ℭHĂL′DĒĒ, *a.* Relating to Chal-
CHĂL′DRǪN *or* CHĂL′DRǪN, *n.* 36 bushels.
CHĂL′ĮCE, *n.* A cup; a communion cup.
CHĂL′ĮCED (chăl′ĭst), *a.* Having a cell or cup.
CHÂLK (chȧwk), *n.* A white fossil substance.
CHÂLK (chȧwk), *v. a.* To mark with chalk.
CHÂLK′Ỹ (chȧwk′ę), *a.* Consisting of chalk.
CHĂL′LĘNĢE, *v. a.* To call to answer; to defy.
CHĂL′LĘNĢE, *n.* A summons to combat.
CHĂL′LĘNĢ-ĘR, *n.* One who challenges.
ℭHĄ-LȲB′Ę-ĄTE, *a.* Impregnated with iron.
ℭHĂM, *or* KHĂN, *n.* Sovereign of Tartary.
ÇHĄ-MĀDE′, *n.* Beat of the drum for a parley.
CHĂM′BĘR, *n.* An upper room: — a cavity.
CHĂM′BĘR, *v. n. & a.* To be wanton; to shut up.
CHĂM′BĘR-CÖÛN′SĘL, *n.* A counsellor who
  gives his opinion or advice, but does not plead.
CHĂM′BĘR-ĪNG, *n.* Intrigue; wantonness.
CHĂM′BĘR-LAĮN, *n.* An English officer of state.
CHĂM′BĘR-MĀID, *n.* A female servant who
  takes care of chambers or bedrooms. [kind.
ℭHĄ-MĒ′LĘ-ǪN, *n.* An animal of the lizard
CHĂM′FĘR, *v. a.* To channel; to flute. [groove.
CHĂM′FĘR, *or* CHĂM′FRĘT, *n.* A furrow; a
ÇHĂM′OĮS (shăm′mę), *n.* A kind of antelope.
CHĂMP, *v. a. & n.* To bite frequently; to chew.
ÇHĂM-PĀGNE′ (shăm-pān′), *n.* A kind of wine.
ÇHĂM-PĀIGN′ (shăm-pān′), *n.* Flat, open country.
ÇHĂM-PĀIGN′, ÇHĂM-PĀIN′, *a.* Open; level.
ÇHĄM-PĪGN′ǪN (shąm-pĭn′yųn), *n.* A mushroom.
CHĂM′PĮ-ǪN, *n.* A single combatant; defender.
CHĂNCE, *n.* Fortuitous event; accident; fortune.
CHĂNCE, *v. n.* To happen; to fall out; to occur.
CHĂN′CĘL, *n.* The eastern part of a church.
CHĂN′CĘL-LǪR, *n.* A high judicial office; a
  judge of a court of chancery or other court.
CHĂN′CĘL-LǪR-SHĬP, *n.* Office of chancellor.
CHĂN′CĘR-Ỹ, *n.* A high court of equity.
ÇHĂN-DĘ-LIĒR′, *n.* A frame for candles.
CHĂND′LĘR, *n.* A seller of candles; a dealer.
CHĂN′DLĘR-Ỹ, *n.* Articles sold by a chandler.
CHĀNĢE, *v. a.* To make different; to exchange.
CHĀNĢE, *v. n.* To undergo change; to alter.
CHĀNĢE, *n.* Alteration; variety; small money.
CHĀNĢE′Ą-BLE, *a.* Subject to change; incon-
CHĀNĢE′Ą-BLE-NĔSS, *n.* Instability. [stant.
CHĀNĢE′LĮNG, *n.* A child changed; an idiot:
  — one apt to change; an inconstant person.
CHĀNĢ′ĘR, *n.* One who changes.
CHĂN′NĘL, *n.* The bed of running waters; a
  strait or narrow sea; a groove; a furrow.
CHĂN′NĘL, *v. a.* To cut in channels. [service.
CHĂNT, *v. n. & a.* To sing, as in the church
CHĂNT, *n.* A song; part of the church service.
CHĂNT′ĘR, *n.* One who chants; a singer.
CHĂN′TĮ-CLĒĒR, *n.* A cock; a loud crower.
CHĂN′T′RĘSS, *n.* A woman who chants. [in.
CHĂN′TRỸ, *n.* A chapel for priests to sing mass
ℭHĀ′ŎS, *n.* A confused mass of matter; con-
ℭHĀ-ŎT′ĮC, *a.* Like chaos; confused. [fusion.
CHĂP (chŏp), *v. a.* To cleave; to split; to crack.
CHAP (chŏp), *n.* A cleft; an aperture.
CHAP (chŏp), *n.* A part of a beast's mouth.
CHĂP, *n.* A boy; a dealer; a chapman.
ÇHĂP′EAU (shăp′pō), *n.* A hat; a cap or coronet.

CHĂP′ĘL, *n.* Place of worship; meeting-house.
CHĂP′ĘL-RY, *n.* The jurisdiction of a chapel.
ÇHĂP′ĘR-ŌN, *n.* A kind of hood or cap. [lic.
ÇHĂP′ĘR-ŌN, *v. a.* To attend, as a lady, in pub-
CHAP′FALLEN (chŏp′fȧln), *a.* Depressed; deject-
CHĂP′Į-TĘR, *n.* Capital of a column. [ed.
CHĂP′LAĮN, *n.* One who performs divine service.
CHĂP′LAĮN-CỸ,   } *n.* The office of a chaplain;
CHĂP′LAĮN-SHĬP, }   the revenue of a chapel.
CHĂP′LĘT, *n.* A garland or wreath for the head.
CHĂP′MĄN, *n.* A cheapener; dealer; seller.
CHAPS (chŏps), *n. pl.* The mouth, as of a beast.
CHĂP′TĘR, *n.* A division of a book: — an as-
  sembly of the clergy of a cathedral or collegiate
  church: — branch of a society or fraternity.
CHĂR, *v. a.* To burn to a black cinder, as wood.
CHĂR, *n.* A small job; in *America*, called *chore*.
ℭHĂR′ĄC-TĘR, *n.* A mark; a stamp; a letter:
  — a personage; personal qualities; reputation.
ℭHĂR-ĄC-TĘR-ĬS′TĮC, *n.* A mark of character.
ℭHĂR-ĄC-TĘR-ĬS′TĮC,   } *a.* Constituting or
ℭHĂR-ĄC-TĘR-ĬS′TĮ-CĄL, } distinguishing the
  character; noting or indicating character.
ℭHĂR′ĄC-TĘR-ĪZE, *v. a.* To give a character of.
ÇHĄ-RĀDE′ (shą-rād′), *n.* A species of riddle.
CHĂR′CŌAL, *n.* Coal made by burning wood.
CHARĢE, *v. a.* To load; to impute; to accuse;
  to enjoin; to commission; to attack; to assail.
CHĂRĢE, *v. n.* To make a charge or onset.
CHĂRĢE, *n.* Care; precept: — cost: — onset.
CHĂRĢE′Ą-BLE, *a.* Expensive; costly; imputa-
CHĂRĢ′ĘR, *n.* A large dish: — a war-horse. [ble.
CHĂR′Į-ǪT, *n.* A carriage of pleasure or state.
CHĂR′Į-ǪT-ĔĒR, *n.* One who drives a chariot.
CHĂR′Į-TĄ-BLE, *a.* Kind; bountiful; liberal.
CHĂR′Į-TĄ-BLE-NĔSS, *n.* Disposition to charity.
CHĂR′Į-TĄ-BLỸ, *ad.* Kindly; benevolently.
CHĂR′Į-TỸ, *n.* Benevolence; love: — alms.
ÇHĂR′LĄ-TĂN, *n.* A quack; a mountebank.
ÇHĂR-LĄ-TĂN′Į-CĄL, *a.* Quackish; empirical.
ÇHĂR′LĄ-TĂN-RỸ, *n.* Quackery; deceit. [tion.
CHĂRLEŞ′Ş-WĀIN, *n.* Great Bear, a constella-
CHĂR′LǪCK, *n.* A weed; a species of mustard.
CHĂRM, *n.* A philter; a spell; enchantment.
CHĂRM, *v. a.* To bewitch; to delight; to sub-
CHĂRM, *v. n.* To act as a charm. [due.
CHĂRM′ĘR, *n.* One who charms; an enchanter.
CHĂRM′ĮNG, *p. a.* Pleasing in a high degree.
CHĂRM′ĮNG-LỸ, *ad.* Delightfully; pleasingly.
CHĂRM′ĮNG-NĔSS, *n.* Delightfulness.
CHĂR′NĘL, *a.* Containing flesh or carcasses.
CHĂR′NĘL-HÖÛSE, *n.* Place for bones of the dead.
CHĂRT, *n.* A delineation of coasts, &c.; a map.
CHĂR′TĘR, *v. a.* To let or hire, as a sea vessel.
CHĂR′TĘR, *n.* A writing bestowing privileges
CHĂR′Ỹ, *a.* Careful; cautious; shy. [or rights.
CHĀSE, *v. a.* To hunt; to pursue; to drive.
CHĀSE, *n.* Hunting; pursuit: — that part of a
  gun in which the bore is: — frame for types in
CHĀS′ĘR, *n.* One who chases; a hunter. [pages.
ℭHĂŞM, *n.* A cleft; an opening; a vacuity.
CHĂSTE, *a.* Virtuous; pure; uncorrupt.
CHĂSTE′LỸ, *ad.* In a chaste manner; purely.
CHĂST′EN (chās′sn), *v. a.* To correct; to punish.
CHĂST′EN-ĘR (chās′sn-ęr), *n.* One who chast-
CHĂSTE′NĔSS, *n.* Chastity; purity. [ens.
CHĄS-TĪŞ′Ą-BLE, *a.* That may be chastised.
CHĄS-TĪŞE′, *v. a.* To punish; to chasten.

CHĂS′TĬSE-MĔNT, n. Correction; punishment.
CHĄS-TĪS′ĘR, n. One who chastises; a punisher.
CHĂS′TĬ-TY, n. Purity of the body; purity.
CHĂT, v. n. To prate; to converse at ease.
CHĂT, n. Idle or familiar talk; prate. [seat.
ÇHĂT′EAU (shát′tō), n. A castle; a country-
ÇHĂT′ĔL-LĄ-NÝ, n. Lordship of a castle.
CHĂT′TĘL, n. Any movable property.
CHĂT′TĘR, v. n. To make a noise like a mag-
pie; to chat; to prate; to talk idly. [talk.
CHĂT′TĘR, n. A noise, as of a magpie; idle
CHĂT′TĘR-BŎX, n. An incessant talker.
CHĂT′TĘR-ĘR, n. One who chatters.
CHĂT′TY, a. Chattering; conversing freely.
CHĂT′WOOD (chăt′wŭd), n. Little sticks; fuel.
CHÂW, v. a. To chew. See CHEW.
CHEAP (chēp), a. Bearing a low price; common.
CHEAP′EN (chē′pn), v. a. To attempt to buy;
to ask the price of; to lessen the value of.
CHEAP′LY, ad. At a small price.
CHEAP′NĘSS, n. Lowness of price.
CHEAT, v. a. To defraud; to impose upon.
CHEAT, n. A fraud; a trick; a deceiver.
CHEAT′ĘR, n. One who cheats; a cheat.
CHECK, v. a. To repress; to curb; to reprove.
CHECK, n. Stop; a reproof; order for money.
CHECK′ĘR, v. a. To vary; to diversify.
CHECK′MATE, n. A movement on a chess-board.
CHEĒK, n. The side of the face below the eye.
CHEĒK′BONE, n. The bone of the cheek.
CHEĒR, n. Entertainment; gayety; shout of joy.
CHEĒR, v. a. To incite; to encourage; to applaud.
CHEĒR′ĘR, n. One who, or that which, cheers.
CHEĒR′FŪL, a. Animated; lively; joyful.
CHEĒR′FŪL-LY, ad. In a cheerful manner.
CHEĒR′FŪL-NĔSS, n. Alacrity; animation.
CHEĒR′LĘSS, a. Without gayety or gladness.
CHEĒR′LY, CHEĒR′Y, a. Brisk; gay; cheerful.
CHEĒSE, n. Food made of the curd of milk.
CHEĒSE′-CAKE, n. A cake of curds, sugar, &c.
CHEĒSE′MŎN-ĜĘR, n. One who deals in cheese.
CHEĒSE′-PRĔSS, n. Engine for pressing curds.
ℭHĔM′Ĭ-CĄL, a. Pertaining to chemistry.
ℭHĔM′Ĭ-CĄL-LY, ad. In a chemical manner.
ÇHĘ-MÎSE′ (shę-mēz′), n. Under-garment of a wo-
ℭHĔM′ĬST, n. One versed in chemistry. [man.
ℭHĔM′ĬS-TRY, n. A science which investigates
the nature and properties of substances.
CHEQUER (chĕk′er). See CHECKER.
CHĔR′ĬSH, v. a. To support; to foster; to nurse.
CHĔR′ĬSH-ĘR, n. One who cherishes; a nurse.
CHĔR′RY, n. A tree and its fruit.
CHĔR′RY, a. Red; ruddy, like a cherry.
ℭHĔR′SŎ-NĒSE (kĕr′sǫ-nēs), n. A peninsula.
CHĔRT, n. A kind of flint; rock-flint.
CHĔR′ŲB, n.; pl. CHĔR′ŲBS and CHĔR′Ų-BĬM.
A celestial spirit; an angel; a figure.
CHĘ-RŪ′BĬC, CHĘ-RŪ′BĬ-CĄL, a. Angelic.
CHĔR′Ų-BĬM, n. The Hebrew plural of cherub.
CHĔR′ŲP, v. n. To chirp; to use a cheerful voice.
CHĔSS, n. A scientific game: — a kind of grass.
CHĔSS′-BOARD, n. A board for playing chess on.
CHĔSS′MĂN, n. A piece or man used in chess.
CHĔST, n. A large box; the breast; the thorax.
CHĔST′NŬT (chĕs′nŭt), n. Nut of a tree.
CHĔST′NŬT, a. Brown; colored like a chestnut.
ÇHĔV-Ą-LIĔR′, n. A knight; a cavalier.
CHĔV′ĘR-ĬL, n. Leather from the skin of the kid.

CHEW (chů), v. a. To crush with the teeth.
CHEW (chů), v. n. To ruminate; to meditate.
ÇHĬ-CANE′, n. Sophistry; chicanery. [try.
ÇHĬ-CAN′ĘR-Y, n. Mean arts; trickery; sophis-
CHĬCK, CHĬCK′ĘN, n. The young of a fowl.
CHĬCK′ĘN-HEÄRT-ĘD, a. Cowardly; timorous.
CHĬCK′ĘN-PŎX, n. A mild, eruptive disease.
CHĬCK′PĒA (chĭk′pē), n. A kind of pea.
CHĬCK′WEĒD, n. A small annual plant or weed.
CHĪDE, v. a. [imp. t. chid; pp. chidden, chid.]
To reprove; to reprimand; to censure; to re-
CHĪDE, v. n. To find fault; to scold. [buke.
CHĪD′ĬNG, n. Rebuke; scolding; noise; clamor.
CHIEF (chēf), a. Principal; most important.
CHIEF, n. A commander; head; leader.
CHIEF′LY, ad. Principally; eminently.
CHIEF′TAĬN, n. A leader; a commander; chief.
CHIEF′TAĬN-SHĬP, n. State of a chieftain.
CHĬL′BLAĬN, n. A sore made by cold.
CHILD, n.; pl. CHĬL′DRĘN. An infant or very
young person; offspring; progeny; issue.
CHĪLD′BEÄR-ĬNG, n. Act of bearing children.
CHĪLD′BĔD, n. State of a woman in labor.
CHĪLD′BĬRTH, n. The act of bearing children.
CHĪLD′HOOD (chīld′hŭd), n. State of a child.
CHĪLD′ĬSH, a. Like a child; trifling; puerile.
CHĪLD′ĬSH-LY, ad. In a childish, trifling way.
CHĪLD′ĬSH-NĔSS, n. Puerility; triflingness.
CHĪLD′LĘSS, a. Without children or offspring.
CHĪLD′-LĪKE, a. Like or becoming a child.
CHĬLL, a. Cold; depressed; not affectionate.
CHĬLL, n. Chilliness; cold; coolness. [ject.
CHĬLL, v. a. To make cold; to depress; to de-
CHĬLL′Ĭ-NĔSS, n. A sensation of cold.
CHĬLL′NĘSS, n. Chilliness; coldness.
CHĬL′LY, a. Somewhat cold. — ad. Coldly.
CHĪMB, or CHĪME, n. Edge of a cask.
CHĪME, n. A sound of bells; concord of sound.
CHĪME, v. n. To sound in harmony; to agree.
CHĪME, v. a. To move, strike, or sound in har-
CHĪM′ĘR, n. One who chimes. [mony.
ℭHĬ-MĒ′RĄ, n. A fabled monster; an odd fancy.
ÇHĬ-MERE′, n. Robe of a bishop. See SIMAR.
ℭHĬ-MĔR′Ĭ-CĄL, a. Imaginary; fanciful; unreal.
ℭHĬ-MĔR′Ĭ-CĄL-LY, ad. In a chimerical manner.
CHĬM′NĘY (chĭm′nę), n. A passage through
which smoke ascends; a fireplace; fireside.
CHĬN, n. The lowest part of the face.
CHĪ′NĄ, n. China ware; porcelain.
CHĬN′COUGH (chĭn′kŏf), n. Hooping-cough.
CHĪNE, n. Backbone or spine: — edge of a cask.
CHĪ-NĒSE′, n. Language and people of China.
CHĬNK, n. A small aperture; an opening.
CHĬNK, v. a. To shake so as to make a sound.
CHĬNK, v. n. To sound by striking each other.
CHĬNTZ, n. Printed cotton cloth. [crack.
CHĬP, v. a. & n. To cut into small pieces; to
CHĬP, n. A small piece cut or broken off.
ℭHĬ-RĀ′GRĄ, n. The gout in the hands.
ℭHĬ-RŎG′RĄ-PHĘR, n. A writer; a penman.
ℭHĬ-RŎG′RĄ-PHY, n. Handwriting. [hand.
ℭHĬ′RǪ-MĂN-CY, n. Art of foretelling by the
CHĬRP, v. n. To make a cheerful noise, as birds.
CHĬRP, CHĬRP′ĬNG, n. Voice of birds or insects.
ℭHĬ-RÜR′ĜĘ-RY, n. Art of a surgeon; surgery.
CHĬS′ĘL, n. A tool for cutting wood or stone.
CHĬS′ĘL, v. a. To cut or carve with a chisel.
CHĬT, n. A child; a baby: — a sprout of corn.

CHĬT′CHĂT, *n.* Prattle; idle talk or conversation.
‖ÇHĬ-VĂL′RĮC, *a.* Chivalrous; gallant.
‖ÇHĬV′ĄL-ROŬS, *a.* Relating to chivalry; gallant.
‖ÇHĬV′ĄL-RỴ *or* CHĬV′ĄL-RỴ, *n.* Knighthood.
CHĪVEŞ (chīvz), *n. pl.* Threads in flowers.
ĆHLŌ′RĮNE, *n.* A heavy, greenish-yellow gas.
ĆHLŌ′RQ-FŌRM, *n.* An anæsthetic liquid.
CHŎCK′-FŮLL, *a.* Entirely full; choke-full.
CHŎC′Q-LĄTE, *n.* A preparation of cocoa.
CHOĬCE, *n.* Act of choosing; the thing chosen.
CHOĬCE, *a.* Select; precious; excellent.
CHOĬCE′LỴ, *ad.* Carefully; excellently.
CHOĬR (kwīr), *n.* Band of singers :—part of a
CHŌKE, *v. a.* To suffocate; to stop up. [church.
CHŌKE, *v. n.* To be choked or obstructed.
CHŌKE′-FŮLL, *a.* As full as possible; chockful.
CHŌK′Ỵ, *a.* Tending to choke; suffocating.
ĆHŎL′ĘR, *n.* The bile :—anger; rage; wrath.
ĆHŎL′Ę-RĄ, *n.* A dangerous disease.
ĆHŎL′Ę-RĄ-MŌR′BŬS, *n.* A painful disease.
ĆHŎL′ĘR-ĬC, *a.* Full of choler; angry; irascible.
CHŌŌŞE, *v. a.* [*impt. t.* chose; *pp.* chosen.] To
prefer; to pick out; to select; to elect.
CHŌŌŞE, *v. n.* To have power of choice.
CHŌŌŞ′ĘR, *n.* One who chooses; an elector.
CHŎP, *v. a.* To cut with a quick blow; to mince.
CHŎP, *v. n.* To do any thing with a quick mo-
CHŎP, *n.* A piece cut off; a slice; a cleft. [tion.
CHŎP′FÂLLEN, *a.* Dejected. See CHAPFALLEN.
CHŎP′-HOŬSE, *n.* An eating or dining house.
CHŎP′ĮN, CHQ-PÎN′, *n.* A sort of clog or patten.
CHŎP′PĘR, *n.* One who chops :—a cleaver.
CHŎPS, *n. pl.* The mouth of a beast. See CHAPS.
ĆHŌ′RĄL, *a.* Belonging to, or singing in, a choir.
ĆHŌRD, *n.* The string of a musical instrument;
a certain combination of notes; a line.
CHŌRE, *n.* A small job of work. See CHAR.
ĆHŎR′ĮS-TĘR (kŏr′įs-tẹr), *n.* A singer in a
choir or concert :—a leader of a choir.
ĆHQ-RŎG′RĄ-PHĘR, *n.* Describer of a country.
ĆHŌ-RQ-GRĂPH′Į-CĄL, *a.* Descriptive of regions.
ĆHQ-RŎG′RĄ-PHỴ, *n.* Description of a place or
district, or the art of constructing maps of it.
ĆHŌ′RŲS, *n.* A number of singers; a choir;
verses of a song in which all join the singer.
CHŌŞE, *imp. t.* from *choose.*
CHŌ′ŞEN (chō′zn), *pp.* from *choose.*
CHOUGH (chŭf), *n.* A kind of sea-bird.
CHOŬSE, *v. a.* To cheat; to trick; to defraud.
CHOW′DĘR, *n.* Fish boiled with biscuit, &c.
ĆHRĬSM, *n.* Oil used in sacred ceremonies.
ĆHRĬS′TEN (krĭs′sn), *v. a.* To baptize and name.
ĆHRĬS′TEN-DŎM (krĭs′sn-dŭm), *n.* Regions in-
habited by Christians; whole body of Chris-
ĆHRĬS′TEN-ĬNG (krĭs′sn-ĭng), *n.* Baptism. [tians.
ĆHRĬS′TĮAN (krĭst′yạn), *n.* A disciple of Christ.
ĆHRĬS′TĮAN (krĭst′yạn), *a.* Pertaining to Christ.
ĆHRĬS′TĮAN-NÄME, *n.* A name given in baptism.
ĆHRĬS-TĮ-ĂN′Į-TỴ (krĭst-yẹ-ăn′ẹ-tẹ), *n.* The re-
ligion taught by Christ; religion of Christians.
ĆHRĬS′TĮAN-ĪZE, *v. a.* To convert to Christianity.
ĆHRĬST′MĄS (krĭs′mạs), *n.* The festival of
Christ's nativity, Dec. 25.   [presents.
ĆHRĬST′MĄS-BŎX, *n.* A box for Christmas
ĆHRQ-MĂT′ĮC, *a.* Relating to colors :—relating
to the scale of semitones in music.
ĆHRŌME, *n.* A whitish, brittle, infusible metal.
ĆHRŎN′ĮC, ĆHRŎN′Į-CĄL, *a.* Of long duration.

ĆHRŎN′Į-CLE, *n.* A register; a record; a history.
ĆHRŎN′Į-CLE, *v. a.* To record; to register. [rian.
ĆHRŎN′Į-CLĘR, *n.* A recorder of events; an histo-
ĆHRŎN′Q-GRĂM, *n.* An inscription in which
the date is expressed by numeral letters.
ĆHRQ-NŎL′Q-ĢĘR, ĆHRQ-NŎL′Q-ĢĬST, *n.* A
teacher of, or one versed in, chronology.
ĆHRŎN-Q-LŎĢ′ĮC,   ⎱ *a.* Denoting, or relating
ĆHRŎN-Q-LŎĢ′Į-CĄL, ⎰ to, chronology.
ĆHRŎN-Q-LŎĢ′Į-CĄL-LỴ, *ad.* By chronology.
ĆHRQ-NŎL′Q-ĢỴ, *n.* The science of computing
or ascertaining dates of events.
ĆHRQ-NŎM′Ę-TĘR, *n.* An instrument, or kind of
watch, for measuring time with great exactness.
ĆHRỸS′Ą-LĬS, *n.* Aurelia, or the last apparent
change of the larva of insects; pupa.
ĆHRỴS-ĂN′THĘ-MŬM, *n.* A genus of plants.
ĆHRỸS′Q-LĪTE, *n.* A yellowish precious stone.
ĆHRỸS′Q-PRĀŞE, *n.* A green precious stone.
CHŬB, *n.* A river fish; the cheven.
CHŬB′BĘD, CHŬB′BỴ, *a.* Short and thick.
CHŬCK, *v. n.* To make a noise like a hen.
CHŬCK, *v. a.* To call as a hen :—to pat; to pitch.
CHŬCK, *n.* The voice of a hen :—a pat or blow.
CHŬCK′-FÄR-THĮNG, *n.* A kind of play.
CHŬC′KLE, *v. n.* To laugh inwardly with triumph.
CHŬC′KLE, *v. a.* To call as a hen :—to fondle.
CHŬFF, *n.* A coarse, burly fellow; a clown.
CHŬFF′Ỵ, *a.* Blunt; fat; surly; clownish.
CHŬM, *n.* A chamber-fellow in a college, &c.
CHŬMP, *n.* A thick, short piece of wood.
CHURCH, *n.* The collective body of Christians;
a place of worship; ecclesiastical authority.
CHURCH, *v. a.* To return thanks in church for.
CHURCH′MĄN, *n.* An ecclesiastic; Episcopalian.
CHURCH′-WÂR′DEN, *n.* Officer of a church.
CHURCH′YÄRD, *n.* A burial-place near a church.
CHURL, *n.* A surly man; a rustic; a niggard.
CHURL′ĮSH, *a.* Rude; brutal; selfish; avaricious.
CHURL′ĮSH-NĚSS, *n.* Rudeness; niggardliness.
CHURN, *n.* A vessel used in making butter.
CHURN, *v. a.* To agitate; to make butter of.
CHURN′-STÄFF, *n.* A staff used in churning.
CHŪŞE. See CHOOSE.   [chyle.
ĆHỸ-LĀ′CEOŬS (kī-lā′shŭs), *a.* Belonging to
ĆHỸLE, *n.* A milky juice formed in digestion.
ĆHỸ-LĮ-FĂC′TĮQN, *n.* Process of making chyle.
ĆHỸME, *n.* Food digested in the stomach.
ĆHỸM′ĮS-TRỴ. See CHEMISTRY.
CĮ-BĀ′RĮ-OŬS, *a.* Relating to food; eatable.
CĬC′Ą-TRĬCE, *n.* A scar or mark left by a wound.
CĬC-Ą-TRĮ-ZĀ′TĮQN, *n.* The power of healing,
or skinning over, as in a wound.   [wound.
CĬC′Ą-TRĪZE, *v. a.* To heal or skin over, as a
CĬÇ-Ę-RŌ′NĮ-ĄN, *a.* Relating to Cicero.
CĪ′DĘR, *n.* The juice of apples fermented.
CĮ-GÄR′, *n.* A little roll of tobacco for smoking.
CĬL′ĮĄ-RỴ (sĭl′yạ-re), *a.* Relating to the eyelashes.
CĮ-LĮ″CIOŬS (sį-lĭsh′ŭs), *a.* Made of hair.
CĬM′Ę-TĘR, SCỸM′Į-TĄR, *n.* A short Turkish
CĮM-MĒ′RĮ-ĄN, *a.* Extremely dark.   [sword.
CĮN-ĆHŌ′NĄ, *n.* Peruvian or Jesuit's bark. [dle.
CĬNCT′ỤRE (sĭnkt′yụr), *n.* A belt; a band; a gir-
CĬN′DĘR, *n.* A small piece of matter remaining
after ignition or partial combustion; ashes.
CĬN-Ę-RĀ′TĮQN, *n.* Act of reducing to ashes.
CĮ-NĒ′RĘ-OŬS, *a.* Like ashes; ash-colored; gray.
CĬN-Ę-RĬ″TIOŬS (sĭn-ẹ-rĭsh′ŭs), *a.* Like ashes.

CĬN'GLE (sĭng'gl), _n._ See SURCINGLE.
CĬN'NA-BÀR, _n._ Red sulphuret of mercury.
CĬN'NA-MŎN, _n._ The spicy bark of a tree.
CĬNQUE (sĭngk), _n._ The number five in dice.
CĬNQUE'-FÖIL (sĭngk'föïl),_n._Five-leaved clover.
CĪ'ǪN, _n._ A sprout; a shoot ingrafted; scion.
CĪ'PHĘR, _n._ The arithmetical character [0]; a
  character or symbol:—a secret character.
CĪ'PHĘR, _v. n._ To practise arithmetic.
CĬR'CLE, _n._ A round figure; ring:—compass.
CĬR'CLE, _v. a. & n._ To move round; to enclose.
CĬR'CLĘT (sĭr'klęt), _n._ A little circle or ring.
CĬR'CUĮT (sĭr'kĭt), _n._ A circular space; a district.
CĮR-CŪ'Į-TOŬS, _a._ Round about; not direct.
CĮR-CŪ'Į-TOŬS-LY, _ad._ In a circuitous manner
CĬR-CŲ-LAR, _a._ Having the form of a circle.
CĬR-CŲ-LÄR'Į-TY,_n._ State of being circular.
CĬR'CŲ-LAR-LY, _ad._ In form of a circle. [spread.
CĬR'CŲ-LÄTE, _v. n. & a._ To move round; to
CĬR-CŲ-LÄ'TIǪN,_n._ Act of circulating; currency.
CĬR'CŲ-LA-TǪ-RY, _a._ Circular; moving round.
CĬR'CŲM-ÄM'BĮ-ĘN-CY,_n._ Act of encompassing.
CĬR-CŲM-ÄM'BĮ-ĘNT, _a._ Surrounding. [about.
CĬR'CŲM-ÄM'BŲ-LÄTE, _v. n._ To walk round
CĬR'CŲM-CĪ̶ṢE, _v. a._ To perform circumcision on.
CĬR'CŲM-CĪ̶Ṣ-ĘR, _n._ One who circumcises. [rite.
CĬR-CŲM-CĬ''ṢIǪN(sĭr-kųm-sĭzh'ųn),_n._ A Jewish
CĬR-CŲM-DŪCT', _v. a._ To contravene; to nullify.
CĮR-CŬM'FĘR-ĘNCE, _n._ A line bounding a circle.
CĬR'CŲM-FLĚX, _n._ An accent denoting a long
  syllable, marked in Greek [˜], in Latin [˄].
CĮR-CŬM'FLŲ-ĘNCE,_n._ An enclosure of waters.
CĮR-CŬM'FLŲ-ĘNT, _a._ Flowing round, as water.
CĮR-CŬM-FǪ-RÄ'NĘ-OŬS, _a._ Wandering about.
CĬR-CŲM-FŪṢE', _v. a._ To pour or spread round.
CĬR-CŲM-FŪ'ṢILE, _a._ That may be poured round.
CĬR-CŲM-FŪ'ṢIǪN, _n._ A pouring round. [ing.
CĬR-CŲM-JÄ'CĘNT, _a._ Lying round; surround-
CĬR-CŲM-LǪ-CŪ'TIǪN, _n._ A circuit or compass
  of words; periphrasis; indirect expression.
CĬR-CŲM-LŎC'Ų-TǪ-RY, _a._ Periphrastical.
CĬR-CŲM-NÄV'Į-GA-BLE, _a._ That may be sailed
CĬR-CŲM-NÄV'Į-GÄTE,_n.a._To sail round.[round.
CĬR-CŲM-NÄV-Į-GÄ'TIǪN, _n._ A sailing round.
CĬR-CŲM-NÄV'Į-GÄ-TǪR,_n._One who sails round.
CĬR-CŲM-PŌ'LAR, _a._ Round or near the pole.
CĬR-CŲM-RǪ-TÄ'TIǪN, _n._ Circumvolution.
CĬR-CŲM-RŌ'TA-TǪ-RY, _a._ Whirling round.
CĬR-CŲM-SCRĪBE', _v. a._ To enclose; to bound.
CĬR-CŲM-SCRĬP'TIǪN,_n._ Limitation; restriction.
CĬR-CŲM-SCRĬP'TĮVE,_a._ Marking the outline.
CĬR'CŲM-SPĔCT,_a._ Cautious; watchful; discreet.
CĬR-CŲM-SPĔC'TIǪN, _n._ Watchfulness; caution.
CĬR-CŲM-SPĔCT-LY, _ad._ Vigilantly; cautiously.
CĬR'CŲM-SPĔCT-NĔSS, _n._ Vigilance; caution.
CĬR'CŲM-STÄNCE, _n._ An adjunct of a fact;
  incident; event; condition; state of affairs.
CĬR'CŲM-STÄNCE, _v. a._ To place in situation.
CĬR-CŲM-STÄN'TIAL,_a._ Incidental; particular.
CĬR-CŲM-STÄN-TĮ-ÄL'Į-TY (sĭr-kųm-stän-she-
  äl'ę-tę), _n._ The state of being circumstantial.
CĬR-CŲM-VAL-LÄ'TIǪN, _n._ A kind of fortifica-
CĬR-CŲM-VĔNT',_v. a._ To deceive; to cheat.[tion.
CĬR-CŲM-VĔN'TIǪN,_n._ Fraud; deceit; imposture.
CĬR-CŲM-VĔN'TĮVE, _a._ Deluding; cheating.
CĬR-CŲM-VĔST', _v. a._ To cover round; to sur-
CĬR-CŲM-VǪ-LŪ'TIǪN,_n._ Rolling round. [round.
CĬR-CŲM-VŎLVE', _v. a._ To roll round; to whirl.

CĬR'CŲS, _n._ An area for sports, with seats round.
CĮS-ÄL'PĮNE,_a._ On this [Roman] side of the Alps.
CĬST,_n._ A chest; place of burial. See CYST.
CĬS'TĘRN, _n._ A vessel to hold water; a reservoir.
CĬS'TŲS, _n._ A genus of plants; the rockrose.
CĬT, _n._ A citizen, _in contempt or disparagement._
CĬT'A-DĔL, _n._ A fortress in or near a city.
CĪ'TAL, _n._ The act of citing; summons.
CĪ-TÄ'TIǪN, _n._ Summons to appear:—quotation.
CĪ'TA-TǪ-RY, _a._ In the form of a summons.
CĪTE, _v. a._ To summon to answer:—to quote.
CĬTH'ĘRN, _n._ A kind of harp or guitar.
CĬT'Į-ZEN,_n._ An inhabitant of a city; a freeman.
CĬT'Į-ZEN-SHĬP, _n._ The rights of a citizen.
CĬT'RĮNE, _a._ Like a citron or lemon; dark-yel-
CĬT'RǪN,_n._ A fruit of the lemon kind. [low.
CĬT'Y, _n._ A large town; a town corporate.
CĬT'Y, _a._ Relating to a city; of a city.
CĪVĘṢ, _n. pl._ A small species of leek or onion.
CĬV'ĘT, _n._ A perfume from the civet cat.
CĬV'ĮC, _a._ Relating to a city or to citizens.
CĬV'ĮL, _a._ Municipal; relating to society; in-
  testine; political:—complaisant; well-bred.
CĮ-VĬL'IAN (sę-vĭl'yąn), _n._ One versed in the
  civil law:—one employed in a civil capacity.
CĮ-VĬL'Į-TY, _n._ Refinement; politeness. [state.
CĬV-ĮL-Į-ZÄ'TIǪN,_n._ Act of civilizing; civilized
CĬV'ĮL-ĪZE, _v. a._ To reclaim from savageness.
CĬV'ĮL-LY, _ad._ In a civil manner; politely.
CLÄCK, _n._ Sharp, abrupt noise; click:—prate.
CLÄCK, _v. n._ To make a sudden, sharp noise.
CLÄD, _pp._ from _clothe;_ clothed; dressed.
CLÄIM, _v. a._ To demand of right; to require.
CLÄIM, _n._ A demand as of right; right; a title.
CLÄIM'A-BLE, _a._ That may be claimed:
CLÄIM'ANT, CLÄIM'ER, _n._ One who claims.
CLÄM, _n._ A small bivalve shell-fish.
CLÄM, _v. a._ To clog with any glutinous matter.
CLÄM'BER, _v. n._ To climb with difficulty.
CLÄM'MĮ-NĔSS, _n._ Viscosity; viscidity.
CLÄM'MY, _a._ Viscous; glutinous; adhesive.
CLÄM'ǬR, _n._ An outcry; noise; vociferation.
CLÄM'ǬR, _v. n._ To make outcries; to vociferate.
CLÄM'ǬR-OŬS, _a._ Vociferous; noisy; boisterous.
CLÄM'ǬR-OŬS-LY, _ad._ In a noisy manner. [other.
CLÄMP, _n._ A piece of wood or iron fixed to an-
CLÄMP, _v. a._ To bind or strengthen by a clamp.
CLÄN, _n._ A family; a race; a tribe:—cabal.
CLAN-DĔS'TĮNE, _a._ Secret; hidden; private.
CLÄNG, _n._ A sharp, ringing noise. [strike.
CLÄNG, _v. n. & a._ To make a shrill noise; to
CLÄN'GǬR, _n._ A loud, shrill, ringing sound.
CLÄNK, _n._ A shrill noise, as of a chain.
CLÄN'SHĬP,_n._ An association of persons. [plaud.
CLÄP, _v. a._ To strike; to pat; to put; to ap-
CLÄP, _v. n._ To make a noise by striking:—to
  strike the hands together in applause.
CLÄP, _n._ A loud explosion:—act of applause.
CLÄP'BŌARD,_n._ A narrow board to cover houses.
CLÄP'PĘR, _n._ One who claps:—tongue of a bell.
CLÄP'PĘR-CLÂW,_v. a._ To scold:—to revile.
CLARE-OB-SCŪRE',_n._ Light and shade in paint-
CLÄR'ĘT,_n._ A reddish kind of French wine.[ing.
CLÄR'Į-CHORD, _n._ A musical instrument.
CLÄR-Į-FĮ-CÄ'TIǪN,_n._ The act of making clear.
CLÄR'Į-FȲ,_v. a. & n._ To purify; to become clear.
CLÄR-Į-NĔT', _n._ A reed instrument of music.
CLÄR'Į-ǬN, _n._ A kind of shrill trumpet.

CLĂSH, *v. n.* To make a noise by collision :—to act in opposition ; to interfere ; to disagree.
CLĂSH, *v. a.* To strike against something.
CLĂSH, *n.* A noisy collision of two bodies.
CLĂSP, *n.* A kind of hook :—an embrace.
CLĂSP, *v. a.* To shut with a clasp :—to embrace.
CLĂSP′ER, *n.* One who clasps ; a tendril.
CLĂSP′KNĪFE, *n.* A knife which folds into the
CLĂSS, *n.* A rank ; an order ; a division.[handle.
CLĂSS, *v. a.* To arrange in a class ; to classify.
CLĂS′SĬC, } *a.* Relating to authors of the
CLĂS′SĬ-CAL, } first rank ; of the first order or rank in literature ; Greek or Latin ; elegant.
CLĂS′SĬC, *n.* An author of the first rank.
CLĂS′SĬ-CAL-LY, *ad.* In a classical manner.
CLĂS-SĬ-FĬ-CĀ′TĬON, *n.* Act of ranging into
CLĂS′SĬ-FȲ, *v. a.* To arrange in classes. [classes.
CLĂT′TER, *v. n.* To make a rattling noise.
CLĂT′TER, *n.* A rattling, confused noise.
CLÂUSE, *n.* Part of a sentence ; a stipulation.
CLÂUS′TRAL, *a.* Relating to a cloister.
CLÂUS′URE (klâw′zhur), *n.* Confinement.
CLĀVE, *imp. t.* from *cleave.*
CLĂV′Ĭ-CLE, *n.* A slender bone, the collar-bone.
CLÂW, *n.* The foot of a beast or of a bird.
CLÂW, *v. a.* To tear with claws ; to scratch.
CLÂWED (klâwd), *a.* Furnished with claws.
CLĀY (klā), *n.* A tenacious kind of earth.
CLĀY, *v. a.* To cover or mix with clay.
CLĀY′-PĬT, *n.* A pit where clay is dug.
CLĀY′EY (klā′e̱), *a.* Consisting of clay ; like
CLĀY′-MÄRL, *n.* A whitish, chalky clay. [clay.
CLĀY′MŌRE, *n.* A large, two-handed sword.
CLĀY′-STŌNE, *n.* An argillaceous limestone.
CLEAN (klēn), *a.* Free from dirt and impurity ; neat ; elegant ; dexterous ; entire ; innocent.
CLEAN, *ad.* Quite ; perfectly ; completely.
CLEAN, *v. a.* To free from dirt ; to purify.
CLEAN′LĬ-LY (klĕn′le̱-le̱), *ad.* In a cleanly man-
CLEAN′LĬ-NĔSS (klĕn′le̱-nĕs), *n.* Neatness.[ner.
CLEAN′LY (klĕn′le̱), *a.* Clean ; neat ; pure.
CLEAN′LY (klēn′le̱), *ad.* In a clean manner.
CLEAN′NĔSS, *n.* Neatness ; purity ; innocence.
CLEANS′A-BLE, *a.* That may be cleansed. [fy.
CLEANSE (klĕnz), *v. a.* To make clean ; to puri-
CLEANS′ER (klĕn′zer), *n.* One that cleanses.
CLEAR (klēr), *a.* Bright ; serene ; pure ; perspicuous ; indisputable ; manifest ; innocent.
CLEAR, *n.* Space from one wall to another.
CLEAR, *v. a.* To explain ; to justify ; to cleanse.
CLEAR, *v. n.* To grow bright or fair :—to sail from a port with a permit, as a vessel.
CLEAR′ANCE, *n.* The act of clearing ; a certificate of a ship given by the collector of a port.
CLEAR′ER, *n.* One who clears ; a purifier.
CLEAR′LY, *ad.* Brightly ; plainly ; evidently.
CLEAR′NĔSS, *n.* Transparency ; distinctness.
CLEAR′-SĪGHT-ED (klēr′sī-ted), *a.* Discerning.
CLEAR′STÄRCH, *v. a.* To stiffen with starch.
CLEAT, *n.* A piece of wood for fastening.
CLEAVE (klēv), *v. n.* [*imp. t.* cleaved ; *pp.* cleaved.] To adhere ; to be attached or united.
CLEAVE (klēv), *v. a.* [*imp. t.* clove, cleft ; *pp.* cloven, cleft.] To split ; to divide ; to part.
CLEAVE, *v. n.* To part asunder ; to separate.
CLEAV′ER, *n.* A butcher's instrument.
CLEF, *n.* A character on the staff in music.
CLĔFT, *imp. t.* & *pp.* from *cleave.* Divided.

CLĔFT, *n.* A space made by the separation of parts ; a crevice :—a disease in horses.
CLĔM′EN-CY, *n.* Mercy ; mildness ; leniency.
CLĔM′ENT, *a.* Mild ; compassionate ; merciful.
CLĔR′ĢY, *n.* The body or order of divines.
CLĔR′ĢY-A-BLE, *a.* Admitting benefit of clergy.
CLĔR′ĢY-MAN, *n.* A man in holy orders ; a divine :—an ordained Christian minister.
CLĔR′ĬC, CLĔR′Ĭ-CAL, *a.* Relating to the clergy.
CLERK (klärk *or* klĕrk), *n.* A secretary or bookkeeper ; a clergyman ; a reader ; a scholar.
CLERK′SHĬP, *n.* The state or office of a clerk.
CLĔV′ER, *a.* Dexterous ; skilful ; fit ; proper.
CLĔV′ER-LY, *ad.* Dexterously ; ingeniously.
CLĔV′ER-NĔSS, *n.* Dexterity ; skill ; ingenuity.
CLEW (klū), *n.* A ball of thread ; that which guides or directs ; a guide :—corner of a sail.
CLEW (klū), *v. a.* To direct ; to truss up, as sails.
CLĬCK, *v. n.* To make a sharp, small noise.
CLĬCK, *n.* The latch of a door :—sharp sound.
CLĬCK′ER, *n.* A servant to invite in customers.
CLĪ′ENT, *n.* A dependant ; one who employs
CLĪ′ENT-SHĬP, *n.* State of a client. [a lawyer.
CLĬFF, *n.* A steep rock ; a precipice ; a crag.
CLĬM-AC-TĔR′ĬC *or* CLĬ-MĂC′TER-ĬC, *n.* A critical period in human life ; the 63d year.
CLĪ′MATE, *n.* A zone or belt of the globe ; a region or tract of land ; temperature, wind, &c.
CLĬ-MA-TŌL′Q-ĢY, *n.* Science which treats of climates, or of the causes of a climate.
CLĪ′MĂX, *n.* (*Rhet.*) A gradual rising in a discourse to that which is more impressive.
CLIMB (klīm), *v. n.* & *a.* To ascend with labor.
CLIMB′ER (klīm′er), *n.* One who climbs :—a plant that creeps on some support, as ivy.
CLĪME, *n.* Climate ; region ; country. [to fix.
CLĬNCH, *v. a.* To grasp ; to contract ; to rivet ;
CLĬNCH, *n.* A pun :—holdfast :—part of a cable.
CLĬNCH′ER, *n.* One that clinches ; a clinch ; a holdfast :—a conclusive argument.
CLĬNG, *v. n.* [*imp. t.* & *pp.* clung.] To adhere.
CLĬN′ĬC, CLĬN′Ĭ-CAL, *a.* Pertaining to a bed.
CLĬN′ĬC, *n.* One confined on a bed of sickness.
CLĬNK, *v. a.* & *n.* To make a sharp ringing noise.
CLĬNK, *n.* A sharp, successive noise ; clank.
CLĬP, *v. a.* To cut, as with shears ; to curtail.
CLĬP′PER, *n.* One who clips ; a barber ; a vessel.
CLĬP′PĬNG, *n.* A part cut off, as with shears.
CLŌAK (klōk), *n.* An outer garment ; a cover.
CLŌAK, *v. a.* To cover with a cloak ; to hide.
CLŎCK, *n.* An instrument for measuring and indicating time :—an insect ; a sort of beetle.
CLŎCK′-MĀK-ER, *n.* One who makes clocks.
CLŎCK′WÖRK, *n.* The machinery of a clock.
CLŎD, *n.* A lump of earth or clay ; dolt ; clown.
CLŎD, *v. n.* To gather into a mass ; to clot.
CLŎD′DY, *a.* Consisting of, or resembling, clods.
CLŎD′HŎP-PER, *n.* A ploughman ; a clown.
CLŎD′PĀTE, CLŎD′PŌLL, *n.* A stupid fellow.
CLŎD′PĀT-ED, *a.* Stupid ; dull ; doltish ; obtuse.
CLŎFF, *n.* An allowance of weight. See CLOUGH.
CLŎG, *v. a.* & *n.* To encumber with a weight ; to obstruct ; to impede ; to be encumbered.
CLŎG, *n.* An impediment :—a wooden shoe.
CLŎG′GĬ-NĔSS, *n.* The state of being clogged
CLŎG′GY, *a.* Having the power of clogging up.
CLOÏS′TER, *n.* A monastery ; a nunnery.
CLOÏS′TER, *v. a.* To shut up in a cloister.

CLOÏS'TĘR-ĄL, *a.* Solitary ; recluse ; secluded.
CLOÏS'TĘR-ĘR, *n.* One belonging to a cloister.
CLŌSE, *v. a.* To shut, conclude, enclose, join.
CLŌSE, *v. n.* To coalesce ; to unite :—to end.
CLŌSE, *n.* Conclusion ; end · pause ; cessation.
CLŌSE, *n.* An enclosed place ; a field ; a passage.
CLŌSE, *a.* Shut fast ; compact ; solid ; secret ; trusty ; sly ; retired ; near ; penurious.
CLŌSE'-FÍST-ĘD, CLŌSE'-HÄND-ĘD, *a.* Penurious ; miserly ; stingy ; niggardly.
CLŌSE'LY, *ad.* In a close manner ; secretly.
CLŌSE'NĘSS, *n.* State of being close ; secrecy.
CLŌSE'STOÔL, *n.* A chamber convenience.
CLŎṢ'ĘT, *n.* A small private room ; cupboard.
CLŎṢ'ĘT, *v. a.* To shut up in a closet ; to conceal.
CLŌṢ'ING, *n.* Period ; conclusion ; end.
CLŌṢ'ŲRE (klō'zhųr), *n.* Act of closing or shutting up ; that which shuts ; enclosure ; end.
CLŎT, *n.* Any thing clotted ; coagulation.
CLŎT, *v. a.* To form into clots ; to coagulate.
CLŎT, *v. n.* To form clots ; to coagulate. [&c.
CLOTH, *n.;* pl. CLŎ[T]HṢ. Fabrics woven for dress,
CLŌ[T]HE, *v. a.* [*imp. t.* clothed ; *pp.* clothed, clad.] To cover with garments ; to dress.
CLŌ[T]HEṢ (klō[t]hz *or* klōz), *n. pl.* Garments for the body ; raiment ; dress ; vesture.
CLŌ[T]H'IĘR (klōth'yęr), *n.* A maker or seller of cloth ; a seller of clothes :—a fuller.
CLŌ[T]H'ING, *n.* Dress ; vesture ; garments; attire.
CLOÛD, *n.* A collection of vapors in the air ; that which obscures ; obscurity :—a multitude.
CLOÛD, *v. a. & n.* To cover or darken with clouds ; to grow cloudy ; to obscure ; to sully ;
CLOÛD'CĂPT, *a.* Topped with clouds. [to dim.
CLOÛD'I-NĚSS, *n.* State of being cloudy ; dark-
CLOÛD'LĘSS, *a.* Free from clouds ; clear. [ness.
CLOÛD'Y, *a.* Covered with clouds ; dark ; obscure.
CLOUGH (klŭf *or* klŏf), *n.* A cliff ; a cleft ; a glen :—an allowance of weight. See CLOFF.
CLOÛT, *n.* A cloth for any mean use ; a patch.
CLOÛT, *v. a.* To patch ; to cover with a cloth.
CLŌVE, *imp. t.* from *cleave.*
CLŌVE, *n.* A spice :—a weight :—a small bulb.
CLŌ'VEN (klō'vn), *pp.* from *cleave.*
CLŌ'VEN-FOOT'ĘD (klō'vn-fût'ęd), } *a.* Hav-
CLŌ'VEN-HÔÔFED (klō'vn-hôft), } ing the foot or hoof divided into two parts. [foil.
CLŌ'VĘR, *n.* A kind of grass ; a species of tre-
CLŎŴN, *n.* A rustic ; an ill-bred man ; a buffoon.
CLŎŴN'ISH, *a.* Coarse ; ill-bred ; clumsy.
CLŎŴN'ISH-NĚSS, *n.* Rusticity ; incivility.
CLŎY, *v. a.* To satiate ; to fill to loathing ; to glut :—to pierce ; to gore. [ciation suit of cards.
CLŬB, *n.* A heavy stick ; a society ; an asso-
CLŬB, *v. n. & a.* To join in a common expense.
CLŬB'-LÂW, *n.* The law of rude force ; compul-
CLŬB'-MĂN, *n.* One who carries a club. [sion.
CLŬB'-RÔÔM, *n.* Room in which a club assem-
CLŬCK, *v. n.* To call chickens, as a hen. [bles.
CLŬCK, *v. a.* To call, as a hen calls chickens.
CLŬMP, *n.* A shapeless mass ; a cluster of trees.
CLŬM'ṢI-LY, *ad.* In a clumsy manner.
CLŬM'ṢI-NĚSS, *n.* Awkwardness ; unhandiness.
CLŬM'ṢY, *a.* Awkward ; heavy ; unhandy.
CLŬNG, *imp. t. & pp.* from *cling.* [a crowd.
CLŬS'TĘR, *n.* A bunch ; a collection ; a body ;
CLŬS'TĘR, *v. a. & n.* To collect, or unite, in clusters ; to form or grow into clusters.

CLŬTCH, *v. a.* To gripe ; to grasp ; to hold fast.
CLŬTCH, *n.* Grasp ;—*pl.* The paws ; the hands.
CLŬT'TĘR, *n.* A clatter ; a confused mass.
CLŬT'TĘR, *v. a.* To scatter things over ; to litter.
CLŬT'TĘR, *v. n.* To make a noise or bustle.
CLŸS'TĘR, *n.* A liquid for injection. [state.
CŌACH (kōch), *n.* A carriage of pleasure or
CŌACH'-BŎX, *n.* Seat of the driver of a coach.
CŌACH'-HĪRE, *n.* Money for the use of a coach.
CŌACH'MĄN, *n.* The driver of a coach.
CŌACH'MĄN-SHIP, *n.* The skill of a coachman.
CŌ-ĂC'TIVE, *a.* Compulsory ; acting in con-
CŌ-ĂD'JŲ-TĄNT, *a.* Helping ; assisting. [currence.
CŌ-ĄD-JŪ'TQR, *n.* A helper ; an assistant.
CŌ-ĂG'Ų-LĄ-BLE, *a.* Capable of concretion.
CŌ-ĂG'Ų-LĂTE, *v. a. & n.* To run into concre-
tions ; to curdle ; to clot. [cretion.
CŌ-ĂG-Ų-LĀ'TIQN, *n.* Act of coagulating ; con-
CŌ-ĂG'Ų-LĄ-TĬVE, *a.* Causing coagulation.
CŌ-ĂG'Ų-LĂ-TQR, *n.* That causes coagulation.
CŌAL (kōl), *n.* A common fossil fuel ; charcoal : —a combustible substance ignited or charred.
CŌAL, *v. a.* To burn to charcoal, as wood.
CŌAL'-BLĂCK, *a.* Black as coal ; very black.
CŌAL'ĘR-Y, *n.* A place where coals are dug.
CŌ-Ą-LĚSCE' (kō-ą-lĕs'), *v. n.* To unite ; to join.
CŌ-Ą-LĚS'CĘNCE, *n.* Union ; concretion.
CŌ-Ą-LÏ''TIQN (-lĭsh'ųn), *n.* Union ; junction.
CŌAL'-MĪNE, *n.* A mine in which coals are dug.
CŌAL'-PĬT, *n.* A pit wherein coals are dug.
CŌAL'Y (kō'lę), *a.* Containing coal ; like coal.
CŌARSE (kōrs), *a.* Not soft or fine ; rude ; gross.
CŌARSE'LY, *ad.* In a coarse manner. [ness.
CŌARSE'NĘSS, *n.* Rudeness ; roughness ; gross-
CŌAST (kōst), *n.* An edge ; shore ; side ; frontier.
CŌAST, *v. n. & a.* To sail close by the coast.
CŌAST'ĘR (kōs'tęr), *n.* One that sails near the shore ; a small coasting or trading vessel.
CŌAT (kōt), *n.* An outside garment ; a covering.
CŌAT, *v. a.* To cover with a coat ; to invest.
CŌAT'-CÄRD, *n.* A pictured card, as the king,
CŌAX (kōks), *v. a.* To wheedle ; to flatter. [&c.
CŌAX'ĘR (kōks'ęr), *n.* One who coaxes.
CŎB, *n.* A pony :—a coin :—a spike of maize.
CŌ'BÂLT *or* CŎB'ĄLT, *n.* A reddish-gray metal.
CŎB'BLE, *v. a.* To mend or make coarsely.
CŎB'BLE, *n.* A fishing-boat :—a large pebble.
CŎB'BLĘR, *n.* A mender of old shoes.
CŎB'NŬT, *n.* A childish game ; a large nut.
CŎB'WĚB, *n.* The web of a spider ; a trap.
CŎB'WĚB, *a.* Fine, slight, or flimsy.
CQC-CĬF'ĘR-OŬS, *a.* Bearing berries.
CŎCH'I-NĚAL, *n.* An insect used to dye red.
CŎCH'LĘ-Ą-RY, *a.* In the form of a screw.
CŎCK, *n.* The male of birds ; a vane ; a spout ; conical heap of hay ; part of a gun-lock.
CŎCK, *v. a.* To set erect ; to fix the cock of.
CŎCK-ĀDE', *n.* A knot worn on the hat.
CŎCK-Ą-TÔÔ', *n.* A bird of the parrot kind.
CŎCK'Ą-TRĪCE, *n.* A kind of fabled serpent.
CŎCK'-BŌAT, *n.* A small boat belonging to a ship.
CŎCK'-CRŌW-ING, *n.* Time at which cocks crow.
CŎCK'ĘR, *n.* A cock-fighter :—a spatterdash.
CŎCK'ĘR-ĘL, *n.* A young cock or rooster.
CŎCK'ĘT, *n.* A ticket from the custom-house.
CŎCK'FĪGHT, CŎCK'FĪGHT-ING, *n.* A battle or match between game-cocks.
CŎC'KLE (kŏk'kl), *n.* A small testaceous fish.

CŎC′KLE, *v. a.* & *n.* To contract into wrinkles.
CŎCK′LŎFT, *n.* The top loft ; the garret ; attic.
CŎCK′NEY (kŏk′ne), *n.* A Londoner, *in contempt.*
CŎCK′PĬT, *n.* The area where cocks fight :—part of, or apartment in, a ship of war.
CŎCK′RŌACH, *n.* A troublesome insect.
CŎCK′S′CŎMB (kŏks′kŏm), *n.* A plant ; a flower.
CŎCK′SPŬR, *n.* A species of hawthorn.
CŎCK′SŪRE (kŏk′shur), *a.* Confidently certain.
CŎCK′SWAIN (kŏk′sn), *n.* The officer who has the command of a boat and its crew.
CŌ′CŌA (kō′kō), *n.* A species of palm-tree and its fruit :—a beverage made of the cocoa-nut.
CǪ-CÔON′, *n.* A ball made by the silk-worm.
CŎC′TĬLE, *a.* Made by baking, as a brick.
CŎC′TĬON, *n.* The act of boiling or digesting.
CŎD, *n.* A fish :—a case containing seeds ; pod.
CŎD′DLE, *v. a.* To parboil ; to boil slightly.
CŎD′LĬNG, *n.* A species of cooking apple.
CŌDE, *n.* A collection or digest of laws.
CŎD′ĢĔR, *n.* A miser :—a queer old man. [will.
CŎD′Ĭ-CĬL, *n.* An appendage or supplement to a
CŌ-ĔF′FĬ-CĄ-CY, *n.* Joint efficacy. [operation.
CŌ-ĔF-FĬ″CIĔN-CY (kō-ef-fĭsh′en-se), *n.* Co-
CŌ-ĔF-FĬ″CIĔNT (-ef-fĭsh′ent), *a.* Coöperating.
CŌ-ĔF-FĬ″CIĔNT, *n.* That which coöperates with something else :—a factor in algebra.
CŌ-Ē′QUĄL, *a.* Jointly equal ; of the same rank.
CŌ-E-QUĂL′Ĭ-TY (kō-e-kwŏl′e-te), *n.* Equality.
CŌ-ĔRCE′ (kō-ẽrs′), *v. a.* To compel ; to restrain.
CŌ-ĔR′CĬ-BLE, *a.* Capable of being coerced.
CŌ-ĔR′CIǪN (kō-ẽr′shun), *n.* Restraint ; check.
CŌ-ĔR′CĮVE, *a.* Restraining ; forcible ; checking.
CŌ-ĔS-SĔN′TIĄL, *a.* Partaking of the same essence ; having the same essence. [ner.
CŌ-ĔS-SĔN′TIĄL-LY, *ad.* In a coessential man-
CŌ-E-TĀ′NE-OŬS, *a.* Of the same age ; coeval.
CŌ-E-TĔR′NĄL, *a.* Equally eternal.
CŌ-Ē′VĄL, *a.* Of the same age with another.
CŌ-Ē′VĄL, *n.* One of the same age ; contemporary.
CŌ-ĔX-ĬST′ (kō-eg-zĭst′), *v. n.* To exist together.
CŌ-ĔX-ĬST′ĘNCE, *n.* Existence at the same time.
CŌ-ĔX-ĬST′ĘNT, *a.* Existing at the same time.
CŌ-ĔX-TĔND′, *v. a.* To extend to the same space.
CŌ-ĔX-TĔN′SIǪN, *n.* Joint or equal extension.
CŌ-ĔX-TĔN′SĮVE, *a.* Having the same extent.
CŎF′FEE, *n.* A berry, and drink made from it.
CŎF′FEE-HŎÛSE, *n.* House of entertainment.
CŎF′FEE-PŎT, *n.* A pot in which to boil coffee.
CŎF′FĘR, *n.* A chest ; a money-chest ; treasure.
CŎF′FĬN, *n.* A box in which a corpse is buried.
CŎF′FĬN, *v. a.* To enclose in a coffin. [cogs in.
CŎĢ, *v. a.* & *n.* To flatter ; to wheedle :—to fix
CŎĢ, *n.* The tooth of a wheel ; a little boat.
CŌ′ĢĘN-CY, *n.* Force ; strength ; power.
CŌ′ĢĘNT, *a.* Forcible ; powerful ; convincing.
CŎĢ′Ĭ-TĄ-BLE, *a.* Capable of being thought on.
CŎĢ′Ĭ-TĀTE, *v. n.* To think ; to meditate.
CŎĢ-Ĭ-TĀ′TIǪN, *n.* Meditation ; contemplation.
CŎĢ′Ĭ-TĀ-TĬVE, *a.* Thinking ; given to thought.
CŎĢ′NĀTE, *a.* Allied by blood ; akin ; kindred.
CǪĢ-NĀ′TIǪN, *n.* Relationship ; kindred.
CǪĢ-NĬ″TIǪN (kǫg-nĭsh′un), *n.* Knowledge.
CŎĢ′NĬ-ZĄ-BLE, *a.* Cognoscible; liable to be tried.
CŎĢ′NĬ-ZĄNCE (kŏg′nĭ-ząns), *n.* Observation ; knowledge ; judicial notice ; trial :—badge.
CŎĢ-NĬ-ZĒĒ′, *n.* (*Law.*) One to whom a fine in lands is acknowledged ;—opposed to *cognizor.*

CŎĢ-NĬ-ZŎR′, *n.* One who acknowledges a fine.
CǪĢ-NŌ′MĘN, *n.* A family name ; a surname.
CǪĢ-NŎM′Ĭ-NĄL, *a.* Belonging to the surname.
CǪĢ-NŎS′CĬ-BLE, *a.* That may be known.
CŎĢ′-WHEĒL, *n.* A wheel furnished with cogs.
CŌ-HĂB′ĬT, *v. n.* To dwell or live together.
CŌ-HĂB-Ĭ-TĀ′TIǪN, *n.* The act of cohabiting.
CŌ-HÊIR′ (kō-âr′), *n.* A joint heir with others.
CŌ-HÊIR′ĘSS (kō-âr′es), *n.* A joint heiress.
CŌ-HĒRE′, *v. n.* To stick together ; to adhere.
CŌ-HĒ′RĘNCE; *or* CŌ-HĒ′RĘN-CY, *n.* Cohesion.
CŌ-HĒ′RĘNT, *a.* Sticking together ; consistent.
CŌ-HĒ′SIǪN (kō-hē′zhun), *n.* State of cohering.
CŌ-HĒ′SĮVE, *a.* Having the power of sticking.
CŌ-HĒ′SĮVE-NĔSS, *n.* Quality of being cohesive.
CŌ-HǪ-BĀTE, *v. a.* To distil again ; to re-distil.
CŌ-HǪ-BĀ′TIǪN, *n.* Repeated distillation.
CŌ′HŌRT, *n.* Body of soldiers, in number about
CŌÏF, *n.* A head-dress ; a cap. [five hundred.
CŌÏF′FŪRE, *n.* A head-dress ; a coif.
CŎÏL, *v. a.* To gather into a circular form.
CŎÏL, *n.* A rope wound into a ring ; convolution.
CŎÏN, *n.* Metallic money bearing a legal stamp.
CŎÏN, *v. a.* To stamp money ; to make ; to invent.
CŎÏN′AĢE, *n.* Act of coining ; coin ; invention.
CŌ-ĬN-CĪDE′, *v. n.* To agree ; to concur.
CŌ-ĬN′CĮ-DĔNCE, *n.* Concurrence ; agreement.
CŌ-ĬN′CĮ-DĔNT, *a.* Agreeing ; concurring.
CŎÏN′ĔR, *n.* A maker of money :—an inventor.
CǪ-Ĭ″TIǪN (kǫ-ĭsh′un), *n.* Copulation.
CŌ-JŌÏN′, *v. n.* To be united ; to conjoin.
CŌKE, *n.* Fuel made by burning mineral coal.
CŎL′ĄN-DĔR, *n.* A sieve ; a strainer ; a cullender.
CŌLD, *a.* Not warm or hot ; chill ; frigid.
CŌLD, *n.* Privation of heat :—a disease.
CŌLD′-BLŌOD-ĘD (kŏld′blŭd-ęd), *a.* Having cold blood :—hard-hearted ; unfeeling. [sion.
CŌLD′-HEÄRT-ĘD, *a.* Wanting feeling or pas-
CŌLD′LY, *ad.* Without heat ; without concern.
CŌLD′NĔSS, *n.* Want of heat ; frigidity ; chillness :—want of ardor or affection ; indifference.
CŌLE, *n.* A general name for all sorts of cabbage.
CŌLE′WORT (kōl′würt), *n.* A species of cabbage.
CŎL′ĬC, *n.* A disorder of the bowels or abdomen.
CǪL-LĂPSE′, *n.* A falling together of the sides of a hollow vessel :—complete prostration.
CǪL-LĂPSE′ (kǫl-lăps′), *v. n.* To fall together.
CǪL-LĂPSED′ (kǫl-lăpst′), *a.* Withered ; closed.
CŎL′LĄR, *n.* A ring round the neck ; neck-band.
CŎL′LĄR, *v. a.* To bind with, or seize by, a collar.
CǪL-LĀTE′, *v. a.* To compare, examine, collect.
CǪL-LĂT′ĔR-ĄL, *a.* From, at, or on, the side ; indirect ; subordinate ; connected ; conjoined.
CǪL-LĂT′ĔR-ĄL-LY, *ad.* Side by side ; indirectly.
CǪL-LĀ′TIǪN, *n.* Act of collating :—a repast.
CǪL-LĀ′TǪR, *n.* One who collates or compares.
CŎL′LEAGUE (kŏl′lēg), *n.* A partner ; associate.
CǪL-LĔCT′, *v. a.* To gather ; to bring together.
CŎL′LĔCT, *n.* A short, comprehensive prayer.
CǪL-LĔCT′ED-NĔSS, *n.* State of being collected.
CǪL-LĔC′TIǪN, *n.* Act of collecting ; assemblage.
CǪL-LĔC′TĮVE, *a.* Tending to collect ; gathered.
CǪL-LĔC′TĮVE-LY, *ad.* In a general mass.
CǪL-LĔCT′ǪR, *n.* One who collects or gathers.
CǪL-LĔCT′ǪR-SHĬP, *n.* The office of a collector.
CŎL′LEĢE, *n.* A society of men set apart for learning, religion, &c. ; a seminary of learning.
CǪL-LĒ′ĢĬ-ĄL, *a.* Of a college ; collegiate.

CO̸L-LĒ'G̸I-ẠN, *n.* A student of a college.
CO̸L-LĒ'G̸I-ẠTE, *a.* Pertaining to a college.
CO̸L-LĒ'G̸I-ẠTE, *n.* A member of a college.
CŎL'LE̠T, *n.* The part of a ring in which the stone is set :—part of the axis of a plant.
CO̸L-LĪDE', *v. n.* To strike against each other.
CŎLL'IE̠R (kŏl'yẹr), *n.* A digger of coals :—a dealer in coals :—a coal-ship. [trade.
CŎLL'IE̠R-Y (kŏl'yẹr-ẹ), *n.* A coal mine :—coal
CŎL'LĮ-QUĀTE, *v. a. & n.* To melt ; to dissolve.
CO̸L-LĬQ-UE̠-FĂC'TIO̸N, *n.* A melting together.
CO̸L-LĬ''ṢIO̸N (-lĭzh'ụn), *n.* A striking together.
CŎL'LO̸-CĀTE, *v. a.* To place ; to put ; to arrange.
CŎL-LO̸-CĀ'TIO̸N, *n.* Act of placing ; disposition.
CŎL'LO̸P, *n.* A small slice of meat ; a rasher.
CO̸L-LŌ'QUĮ-ẠL, *a.* Relating to, or used in, common conversation ; conversational.
CŎL'LO̸-QUĬST, *n.* A speaker in a dialogue.
CŎL'LO̸-QUY, *n.* A dialogue ; a conversation.
CO̸L-LŪDE', *v. n.* To conspire or combine in a fraud ; to play into each other's hands. [ment.
CO̸L-LŪ'ṢIO̸N (kol-lū'zhụn), *n.* Deceitful agree-
CO̸L-LŪ'ṢĮVE, *a.* Fraudulently concerted.
CO̸L-LŪ'ṢĮVE-LY, *ad.* In a collusive manner.
CO̸L-LŪ'ṢĮVE-NĔSS, *n.* Fraudulent agreement.
CO̸L-LŪ'SO̸-RY, *a.* Containing collusion ; collu-
CŌ'LO̸N, *n.* A point [:] denoting a pause. [sive.
COLONEL (kür'nẹl), *n.* A commander of a regiment ; officer below a brigadier-general.
COLONELCY (kür'nẹl-sẹ), *n.* Colonelship.
COLONELSHIP (kür'nẹl-), *n.* Office of colonel.
CO̸-LŌ'NĮ-ẠL, *a.* Relating to a colony or colo-
CŎL'O̸-NĬST, *n.* An inhabitant of a colony. [nies.
CŎL-O̸-NĮ-ZĀ'TIO̸N, *n.* The act of colonizing.
CŎL'O̸-NĪZE, *v. a.* To establish a colony in.
CŎL-O̸N-NĀDE', *n.* Range of pillars or columns.
CŎL'O̸-NY, *n.* A body of people drawn from the mother country to inhabit, or settle in, a foreign country :—the country colonized.
CŎL'O̸-PHŎN, *n.* The conclusion of a book, where any device, or the printer's name, occurs.
CO̸-LŌPH'O̸-NY, *n.* A dark-colored resin.
CŎL'O̸R (kŭl'lụr), *n.* Hue or appearance of bodies to the eye ; pretence.—*pl.* A standard.
CŎL'O̸R, *v. a. & n.* To paint ; to tinge ; to dye :—to palliate ; to excuse :—to blush. [sible.
CŎL'O̸R-Ạ-BLE, *a.* Specious ; plausible ; osten-
CŎL'O̸R-Ạ-BLY, *ad.* Speciously ; plausibly.
CŎL-O̸R-ĬF'ĮC, *a.* Able to give or produce color.
CŎL'O̸R-ĬNG, *n.* An art in painting ; an excuse.
CŎL'O̸R-ĬST, *n.* One who excels in coloring.
CŎL'O̸R-LĔSS, *a.* Without color ; transparent.
CO̸-LŎS'SẠL, *or* CŎL-O̸S-Sē'ẠN, *a.* Like a colossus ; gigantic ; huge ; stupendous. [statue.
CO̸-LŎS'SŲS, *n.* ; *pl.* CO̸-LŎS'Sī. A gigantic
CŎLT, *n.* A young horse ; inexperienced person.
CŎLTS'-FOOT (kŏlts'-fůt), *n.* A medicinal plant.
CŎL'TE̠R, *n.* The cutting-iron of a plough.
CŎLT'ĮSH, *a.* Like a colt ; frolicsome ; frisky.
CŎL'U-BRĪNE, *a.* Relating to a serpent ; cunning.
CŎL'ŲM-BẠ-RY *or* CO̸-LŬM'BẠ-RY, *n.* A cot or house for doves or pigeons ; a dove-house.
CŎL'ŲM-BĪNE, *n.* A genus of perennial plants.
CŎL'ŲMN (kŏl'lụm), *n.* A cylindrical pillar or body ; a body of troops in files ; part of a page.
CO̸-LŬM'NẠR, *a.* Resembling columns in form.
CO̸-LŪRE', *n.* One of two imaginary great circles of the sphere, intersecting each other.

CŌ'MẠ, *n.* A morbid disposition to sleep.
CŌ-MĀTE', *n.* A companion ; a mate.
CŎM-Ạ-TŌSE', *a.* Lethargic ; drowsy ; dozing.
CŌMB (kōm), *n.* An instrument for the hair, &c. :—the crest of a cock :—cavities for honey.[hair.
CŌMB (kōm), *v. a.* To divide and adjust, as the
‖CŎM'BẠT *or* CŎM'BẠT, *v. n. & a.* To fight ; to contend ; to contest ; to oppose ; to conflict.
‖CŎM'BẠT, *n.* Contest ; battle ; fight ; duel.
‖CŎM'BẠT-ẠNT, *n.* One who combats ; a cham-
‖CŎM'BẠT-E̠R, *n.* One who combats. [pion.
CŌMB'E̠R (kōm'ẹr), *n.* One that combs.
CO̸M-BĪ'NẠ-BLE, *a.* Capable of being combined.
CŎM-BĮ-NĀ'TIO̸N, *n.* Union ; association.
CO̸M-BĪNE', *v. a. & n.* To unite, join, or agree.
CO̸M-BŬS-TĮ-BĬL'Į-TY, *n.* Quality of taking fire.
CO̸M-BŬS'TĮ-BLE, *a.* Susceptible of combustion.
CO̸M-BŬS'TĮ-BLE, *n.* A combustible material.
CO̸M-BŬS'TĮ-BLE-NĔSS, *n.* Aptness to take fire.
CO̸M-BŬS'TIO̸N, *n.* Conflagration ; a burning.
CŌME (kŭm), *v. n.* [*imp. t.* came ; *pp.* come.] To draw near ; to arrive ; to happen ; to fall out.
CO̸-MĒ'DĮ-ẠN, *n.* An actor, or writer, of comedies.
CŎM'E̠-DY, *n.* An amusing dramatic piece or play.
CŌME'LĮ-NĔSS, *n.* Grace ; beauty ; dignity.
CŌME'LY, *a.* Graceful ; becoming ; decent.
CŎM'E̠T, *n.* A heavenly body with a tail or train of light, and having eccentric motion.
CŎM'E̠-TẠ-RY, CO̸-MĔT'ĮC, *a.* Relating to a comet, or to the science of comets.
CŎM'FĬT, CŎM'FĮ-TŪRE, *n.* A dry sweetmeat.
CŎM'FO̸RT, *v. a.* To cheer ; to solace, console.
CŎM'FO̸RT, *n.* Support ; relief ; consolation.
CŎM'FO̸RT-Ạ-BLE, *a.* Having comfort ; cheerful.
CŎM'FO̸RT-Ạ-BLY, *ad.* In a comfortable manner.
CŎM'FO̸RT-E̠R, *n.* One who administers conso-
CŎM'FO̸RT-LĔSS, *a.* Wanting comfort. [lation.
CŎM'ĮC, *a.* Relating to comedy ; raising mirth.
CŎM'Į-CẠL, *a.* Diverting ; sportive ; droll ; odd.
CŎM'Į-CẠL-LY, *ad.* In a comical manner.
CŎM'Į-CẠL-NĔSS, *n.* Quality of being comical.
CŎM'ĮNG (kŭm'ĭng), *n.* Act of coming ; arrival.
CŎM'ĮNG, *p. a.* Future ; being about to come.
CŎM'Į-TY, *n.* Courtesy ; civility ; good breeding.
CŎM'MẠ, *n.* A point [,] noting a pause.
CO̸M-MĂND', *v. a.* To govern ; to order ; to lead.
CO̸M-MĂND', *v. n.* To have the supreme authority.
CO̸M-MĂND', *n.* Act of commanding ; order.
CŎM-MẠN-DĂNT', *n.* [Fr.] A commander.
CO̸M-MĂND'E̠R, *n.* One who commands.
CO̸M-MĂND'E̠R-Y, *n.* A district attached to a manor or chief messuage. [erful.
CO̸M-MĂND'ĮNG, *a.* Ordering ; directing ; pow-
CO̸M-MĂND'MENT, *n.* A mandate ; a command.
CO̸M-MĂND'RESS, *n.* A female who commands.
CŎM-MẠ-TĒ'RĮ-ẠL, *a.* Being of the same matter.
CO̸M-MĒAṢ'Ų-RẠ-BLE (ko̸m-mĕzh'ụ-rạ-bl), *a.* Of the same measure ; commensurable.
CO̸M-MĔM'O̸-RẠ-BLE, *a.* Memorable ; signal.
CO̸M-MĔM'O̸-RĀTE, *v. a.* To preserve in memory ; to celebrate publicly ; to solemnize.
CO̸M-MĔM-O̸-RĀ'TIO̸N, *n.* Act of commemorating.
CO̸M-MĔM'O̸-RẠ-TĬVE, *a.* Preserving in memory.
CO̸M-MĔNCE', *v. a. & n.* To begin ; to originate.
CO̸M-MĔNCE'MENT, *n.* Beginning :—the time when students in colleges receive degrees.
CO̸M-MĔND', *v. a.* To applaud ; to praise, extol.
CO̸M-MĔND'Ạ-BLE, *a.* Praiseworthy ; laudable.

CǪM-MĔND′A-BLE-NĔSS, *n.* Laudableness.
CǪM-MĔND′A-BLY,*ad.*Laudably ; praiseworthy.
CǪM-MĔN′DAM, *n.* [L.] A vacant benefice.
CǪM-MĔN′DA-TA-RY, *n.* Holder of a commen-
CŎM-MEN-DĀ′TIǪN, *n.* Recommendation.[dam.
CǪM-MĔN′DA-TǪ-RY, *a.* Serving to commend.
CǪM-MĔNS-Ų-RA-BĬL′Ị-TY,) *n.* Capacity of
CǪM-MĔNS′Ų-RA-BLE-NĔSS,) having a com-
mon measure, or of being measured by another.
CǪM-MĔNS′Ų-RA-BLE, *a.* Having a common
measure ; reducible to the same measure.
CǪM-MĔNS′Ų-RATE, *a.* Equal ; coëxtensive.
CǪM-MĔNS-Ų-RĀ′TIǪN, *n.* The state of hav-
ing a common measure ; proportion.
CŎM′MENT *or* CǪM-MĔNT′, *v. n.* To annotate ;
to make remarks ; to write notes or comments.
CŎM′MENT, *n.* Note ; explanation ; a remark.
CŎM′MEN-TA-RY, *n.* Book of comments ; anno-
tations :—a familiar narrative ; a memoir.
CŎM′MEN-TĀ-TǪR, *n.* An expositor ; annotator.
CŎM′MERCE, *n.* Trade ; traffic ; intercourse.
CǪM-MĔR′CIAL, *a.* Relating to commerce.
CǪM-MĔR′CIAL-LY, *ad.* In a commercial view.
CŎM-MĮ-NĀ′TIǪN, *n.* Threat ; a denunciation.
CǪM-MĬN′A-TǪ-RY, *a.* Denunciatory ; threaten-
CǪM-MĬN′GLE, *v. a.* To mix into one mass.[ing.
CǪM-MĬN′GLE, *v. n.* To unite one with another.
CŎM′MĮ-NŪTE, *v. a.* To grind ; to pulverize.
CŎM-MĮ-NŪ′TIǪN, *n.* Grinding ; pulverization.
CǪM-MĬS′ER-A-BLE, *a.* Worthy of compassion.
CǪM-MĬS′ER-ĀTE, *v. a.* To pity ; to compassion-
CǪM-MĬS-ER-Ā′TIǪN, *n.* Pity ; compassion.[ate.
CǪM-MĬS′ER-Ā-TǪR,*n.*One who has compassion.
CŎM′MĬS-SA-RĮ-SHĬP, *n.* Office of a commissary.
CŎM′MĬS-SA-RY, *n.* A commissioner ; an officer.
CǪM-MĬS′SIǪN (kǫm-mĭsh′ụn), *n.* A trust ; a
warrant of office ; charge ; employment; office.
CǪM-MĬS′SIǪN, *v. a.* To empower ; to depute.
CǪM-MĬS′SIǪN-ER, *n.* One empowered to act.
CǪM-MĬSS′ỤRE (kǫm-mĭsh′yụr), *n.* Seam ; joint.
CǪM-MĬT′, *v. a.* To intrust ; to consign ; to put ;
to deposit :—to imprison :—to perpetrate ; to do.
CǪM-MĬT′TAL, *n.* Commitment ; a pledge.
CǪM-MĬT′MENT, *n.* The act of committing.
CǪM-MĬT′TEE, *n.* A body of persons selected
to examine or manage any matter.
CǪM-MĬT′TER, *n.* One who commits. [mix.
CǪM-MĬX′, *v. a. & n.* To mingle ; to blend ; to
CǪM-MĬXT′IǪN, *or* CǪM-MĬX′IǪN, *n.* A mixture
CǪM-MĬXT′ỤRE (-mĭkst′yụr), *n.* A compound.
CǪM-MŌDE′, *n.* An article of furniture.
CǪM-MŌ′DĮ-OŬS, *a.* Convenient ; suitable.
CǪM-MŌ′DĮ-OŬS-LY, *ad.* Conveniently ; suita-
CǪM-MŌ′DĮ-OŲS-NĔSS, *n.* Convenience. [bly.
CǪM-MŎD′Į-TY,*n.* Interest ; profit ; merchandise.
CŎM′MǪ-DŌRE, *n.* The captain or officer who
commands a squadron of ships of war.
CŎM′MǪN, *a.* Belonging to more than one ; vul-
gar „ mean ; not scarce, public ; usual.
CŎM′MǪN, *n.* An open, public ground.
CŎM′MǪN-AL-TY, *n.* The common people.
CŎM′MǪN-CŎŬN′CĮL, *n.* The council of a city.
CŎM′MǪN-ER, *n.* One of the common people :—
a student of the second rank at Oxford, Eng.
CŎM′MǪN-LÂW′, *n.* Law established by usage.
CŎM′MǪN-LY, *ad.* Frequently ; usually ; jointly.
CŎM′MǪN-NĔSS, *n.* Usualness ; frequency.
CŎM′MǪN-PLĀCE, *a.*Ordinary; common ; usual.

CŎM′MǪN-PLĀCE, *n.* Usual or ordinary topic.
CŎM′MǪN-PLĀCE′-BOOK (-bûk), *n.* A book in
which things are ranged under general heads.
CŎM′MǪNS, *n. pl.* The common people ; the low-
er house of parliament :—food on equal pay.
CŎM′MǪN-WĔAL′, *n.* The public good. [state.
CŎM′MǪN-WĔALTH (-mǫn-wĕlth), *n.* A free
CǪM-MŌ′TIǪN,*n.*Tumult; disturbance; sedition.
CǪM-MŌ′TIǪN-ER, *n.* One causing commotions.
CǪM-MŪNE′, *v. n.* To converse ; to confer.
CǪM-MŪ′NĮ-CA-BLE, *a.* That may be imparted.
CǪM-MŪ′NĮ-CA-BLE-NĔSS, *n.* The state of be-
ing communicable. [ment.
CǪM-MŪ′NĮ-CĂNT, *n.* A partaker of the sacra-
CǪM-MŪ′NĮ-CĀTE, *v. a.* To impart ; to reveal.
CǪM-MŪ′NĮ-CĀTE, *v. n.* To partake of the sac-
rament :—to have connection or intercourse.
CǪM-MŪ-NĮ-CĀ′TIǪN,*n.*Conference; intercourse.
CǪM-MŪ′NĮ-CA-TĬVE, *a.* Ready to impart ; open.
CǪM-MŪ′NĮ-CA-TĬVE-NĔSS, *n.* Readiness to
impart ; inclination to give information.
CǪM-MŪN′IǪN (kǫm-mūn′yụn), *n.* Intercourse ;
fellowship :—celebration of the Lord's supper.
CǪM-MŪ′NĮ-TY,*n.* Common possession ; society.
CǪM-MŪ-TA-RĀ-BĬL′Į-TY, *n.* Interchangeableness.
CǪM-MŪ′TA-BLE, *a.* That may be commuted.
CŎM-MU-TĀ′TIǪN, *n.* Interchange ; alteration.
CǪM-MŪ′TA-TĬVE, *a.* Relating to exchange.
CǪM-MŪTE′, *v. a.* To exchange ; to change.
CǪM-MŪTE′, *v. n.* To bargain for exemption.
CǪM-MŪT′Ų-AL, *a.* Jointly mutual ; reciprocal.
CŎM′PĂCT, *n.* A contract ; a mutual agreement.
CǪM-PĂCT′, *v. a.* To join together with firm-
ness ; to unite closely ; to consolidate.
CǪM-PĂCT′, *a.* Firm ; solid ; close ; connected.
CǪM-PĂCT′LY, *ad.* In a compact manner ; close-
CǪM-PĂCT′NESS, *n.* Firmness ; closeness. [ly.
CǪM-PĂN′IǪN (kǫm-păn′yụn), *n.* A partner ; a
comrade ; an associate ; a fellow ; a mate.
CǪM-PĂN′IǪN-A-BLE, *n.* Social ; agreeable.
CǪM-PĂN′IǪN-A-BLE-NĔSS, *n.* Sociableness.
CǪM-PĂN′IǪN-SHĬP, *n.* Company ; fellowship.
CŎM′PA-NY, *n.* Persons assembled together ; fel-
lowship ; a band ; a firm ; a body corporate.
CŎM′PA-RA-BLE, *a.* Worthy to be compared.
CǪM-PĂR′A-TĬVE, *a.* Estimated by comparison.
CǪM-PĂR′A-TĬVE-LY,*ad.* In a comparative state.
CǪM-PĀRE′, *v. a.* To measure one thing by an-
other ; to illustrate ; to liken :—to form in
degrees of comparison, as an adjective.
CǪM-PĀRE′, *n.* Comparison ; similitude ; like-
CǪM-PĂR′ER, *n.* One who compares. [ness.
CǪM-PĂR′Į-SON, *n.* Act of comparing ; a simile.
CǪM-PĂRT′, *v. a.* To divide ; to mark into parts.
CŎM-PAR-TĬ″TIǪN,*n.* Act of dividing ; division.
CǪM-PĂRT′MENT, *n.* Division ; separate part.
CŎM′PĂSS, *v. a.* To encircle ; to grasp ; to obtain.
CŎM′PĂSS, *n.* A circuit ; grasp ; space ; extent ;
enclosure ; power ; an instrument. [eration.
CǪM-PĂS′SIǪN (kǫm-păsh′ụn),*n.* Pity ; commis-
CǪM-PĂS′SIǪN-ATE, *a.* Having compassion ;
inclined to pity ; merciful ; tender. [erate.
CǪM-PĂS′SIǪN-ĀTE, *v. a.* To pity ; to commis-
CǪM-PĂS′SIǪN-ATE-LY, *ad.* Mercifully ; ten-
derly ; with compassion or pity. [ness.
CǪM-PĂT-Į-BĬL′Į-TY, *n.* Consistency ; suitable-
CǪM-PĂT′Į-BLE, *a.* Suitable ; fit ; consistent.
CǪM-PĂT′Į-BLE-NĔSS, *n.* Consistency ; fitness.

CǪM-PẪT'Ǐ-BLY, *ad.* Suitably ; accordantly.
CǪM-PĀ'TRǏ-ǪT, *n.* One of the same country.
CǪM-PĀ'TRǏ-ǪT, *a.* Being of the same country.
CǪM-PĒĔR', *n.* An equal ; a companion ; mate.
CǪM-PĔL', *v. a.* To force; to oblige ; to constrain.
CǪM-PĔL'LA-BLE, *a.* That may be compelled.
CŎM-PĔL-LĀ'TIǪN, *n.* The style of address.
CǪM-PĔL'LĔR, *n.* One who compels.
CǪM-PĔN'DǏ-OŬS, *a.* Short ; brief ; summary.
CǪM-PĔN'DǏ-OŬS-LY, *ad.* Shortly ; in epitome.
CǪM-PĔN'DǏ-OǓS-NĔSS, *n.* Shortness ; brevity.
CǪM-PĔN'DǏ-ŬM, *n.* An abridgment ; summary.
CǪM-PĔN'SĀTE, *v. a.* To recompense ; to requite.
CŎM-PĔN-SĀ'TIǪN, *n.* Recompense ; amends.
CǪM-PĔN'SA-TĪVE, *a.* Of a compensating nature.
CǪM-PĔN'SA-TǪ-RY, *a.* Making compensation.
CǪM-PĒTE', *v. n.* To carry on competition.
CŎM'PĘ-TĔNCE, CŎM'PĘ-TĔN-CY, *n.* Suitableness ; ability ; sufficiency ; enough.
CŎM'PĘ-TĔNT, *a.* Suitable ; able ; fit ; sufficient.
CŎM'PĘ-TĔNT-LY, *ad.* Adequately ; sufficiently.
CŎM-PĘ-TǏ''TIǪN, *n.* Rivalry ; rivalship ; con-
CǪM-PĔT'Ǐ-TǪR, *n.* A rival ; an opponent. [test.
CŎM-PǏ-LĀ'TIǪN, *n.* Act of compiling ; a collection from various authors ; assemblage.
CǪM-PILE', *v. a.* To form by collecting parts or passages from various authors.
CǪM-PĪLE'MĘNT, *n.* The act of compiling.
CǪM-PĪL'ĘR, *n.* One who compiles.
CǪM-PLĀ'CĘNCE, CǪM-PLĀ'CĘN-CY, *n.* Gratification ; pleasure ; civility ; suavity.
CǪM-PLĀ'CĘNT, *a.* Civil ; affable ; courteous.
CǪM-PLĀ'CĘNT-LY, *ad.* With complacency.
CǪM-PLĀIN', *v. n.* To murmur ; to find fault.
CǪM-PLĀIN'ANT, *n.* A complainer :—a plaintiff.
CǪM-PLĀIN'ĔR, *n.* One who complains.
CǪM-PLĀINT', *n.* A lamentation ; accusation ; an allegation ; a malady ; a disease.
CŎM-PLAI-ŞĂNCE', *n.* Civility ; courteousness.
CŎM-PLAI-ŞĂNT', *a.* Civil ; courteous ; urbane.
CŎM-PLAI-ŞĂNT'LY, *ad.* Civilly ; politely.
CŎM-PLAI-ŞĂNT'NĔSS, *n.* Civility ; politeness.
CŎM'PLĘ-MĔNT, *n.* A full quantity or number.
CŎM-PLĘ-MĔNT'AL, *a.* Filling up ; completing.
CǪM-PLĒTE', *a.* Perfect ; full ; finished ; ended.
CǪM-PLĒTE', *v. a.* To perfect ; to finish ; to end.
CǪM-PLĒTE'LY, *ad.* Fully ; perfectly ; entirely.
CǪM-PLĒTE'NĔSS, *n.* Perfection ; entireness.
CǪM-PLĒ'TIǪN, *n.* Accomplishment ; end.
CŎM'PLĔX, *a.* Complicated ; of many parts.
CǪM-PLĔX'ĘD-NĔSS, *n.* State of being complex.
CǪM-PLĔX'IǪN (kǫm-plĕk'shųn), *n.* The color of the skin or face ; temperament of the body
CǪM-PLĔX'IǪN-AL, *a.* Pertaining to complexion.
CǪM-PLĔX'Ǐ-TY, *n.* State of being complex.
CŎM'PLĔX-LY, *ad.* In a complex manner.
CŎM'PLĔX-NĔSS, *n.* State of being complex.
CǪM-PLĪ'ANCE, *n.* Act of yielding ; acquiescence.
CǪM-PLĪ'ANT, *a.* Yielding ; complacent ; civil.
CǪM-PLĪ'ANT-LY, *ad.* In a compliant manner.
CŎM'PLǏ-CĀTE, *v. a.* To entangle ; to involve.
CŎM'PLǏ-CĀTE, *a.* Compounded of many parts.
CŎM'PLǏ-CATE-LY, *ad.* In a complicated manner.
CŎM'PLǏ-CATE-NĔSS, *n.* Intricacy ; perplexity.
CŎM-PLǏ-CĀ'TIǪN, *n.* A mixture of many things.
CŎM'PLǏ-MĔNT, *n.* An act of civility ; flattery.
CŎM'PLǏ-MĔNT, *v. a.* To flatter ; to praise.
CŎM'PLǏ-MĔNT, *v. n.* To use compliment.

CŎM-PLǏ-MĔNT'AL, *a.* Implying compliments.
CŎM-PLǏ-MĔNT'A-RY, *a.* Making compliments.
CŎM'PLŎT, *n.* A confederacy or union in a plot.
CǪM-PLŎT', *v. n.* To form a plot ; to conspire.
CǪM-PLY̆', *v. n.* To yield ; to accede ; to assent.
CǪM-PŌ'NĘNT, *a.* Constituting ; composing
CǪM-PŌRT', *v. n.* To agree ; to suit ; to bear.
CǪM-PŌRT', *v. a.* To bear ; to endure ; to behave.
CǪM-PŌRT'A-BLE, *a.* Consistent ; suitable.
CǪM-PŌRT'MĘNT, *n.* Behavior ; mien.
CǪM-PŌŞE', *v. a.* To form ; to put together ; to write, as an author ; to quiet ; to adjust.
CǪM-PŌŞED' (kǫm-pōzd'), *p. a.* Calm ; serious.
CǪM-PŌŞ'ĘR, *n.* One who composes ; an author.
CǪM-PŎŞ'ǏTE, *a.* Made up of parts ; compounded.
CŎM-PǪ-ŞǏ''TIǪN (kŏm-pǫ-zĭsh'ųn), *n.* A mixture ; a written work ; adjustment ; compact.
CǪM-PŎŞ'Ǐ-TǪR, *n.* One who adjusts types.
CŎM'PǪS MĔN'TǏS. [L.] Being of sound mind.
CŎM'PŎST, *n.* A manure ; any mixture. [der.
CǪM-PŎŞ'ŲRE (kǫm-pō'zhųr), *n.* Calmness ; or-
CŎM-PǪ-TĀ'TIǪN, *n.* A drinking together.
CŎM'PǪ-TĀ-TǪR, *n.* A drinker with another.
CǪM-PŎŬND', *v. a.* To mingle ; to combine.
CǪM-PŎŬND', *v. n.* To make an agreement.
CŎM'PŎŬND, *a.* Formed of different ingredients.
CŎM'PŎŬND, *n.* Mass of several ingredients.
CǪM-PŎŬND'ĔR, *n.* One who compounds.
CŎM-PRĘ-HĔND', *v. a.* To include ; to embrace ; to understand ; to apprehend.
CŎM-PRĘ-HĔN'SǏ-BLE, *a.* That may be comprehended ; intelligible ; conceivable.
CŎM-PRĘ-HĔN'SǏ-BLE-NĔSS, *n.* Intelligibleness.
CŎM-PRĘ-HĔN'SIǪN, *n.* A comprising ; capacity.
CŎM-PRĘ-HĔN'SǏVE, *a.* Extensive ; capacious.
CŎM-PRĘ-HĔN'SǏVE-LY, *ad.* In a comprehensive manner ; with comprehension.
CŎM-PRE-HĔN'SǏVE-NĔSS, *n.* Comprehension.
CǪM-PRĔSS', *v. a.* To press together ; to condense.
CǪM-PRĔS-SǏ-BǏL'Ǐ-TY, *n.* The state or quality of being compressible. [sion.
CǪM-PRĔS'SǏ-BLE, *a.* Susceptible of compres-
CǪM-PRĔS'SIǪN (kǫm-prĕsh'ųn), *n.* Act of compressing ; forcible contraction ; condensation.
CǪM-PRĔS'SǏVE, *a.* Having power to compress.
CǪM-PRĔSS'ŲRE (kǫm-prĕsh'ųr), *n.* Compression.
CǪM-PRĪŞE', *v. a.* To contain ; to include.
CŎM'PRǪ-MĪŞE, *n.* An agreement ; a compact in which mutual concessions are made.
CŎM'PRǪ-MĪŞE, *v. a.* To compound ; to adjust by mutual concessions ; to put to hazard.
CŎM'PRǪ-MĪŞ-ĘR, *n.* One who compromises.
CŎM'PRǪ-MĪT, *v. a.* To pledge ; to put to hazard.
CǪMP-TRŌL' (kǫn-trōl'), *v. a.* See CONTROL.
CǪMP-TRŌL'LĘR (kǫn-trōl'lęr), *n.* An examiner of accounts. See CONTROLLER.
CǪM-PŬL'SA-TǪ-RY, *a.* Compulsory ; forcing.
CǪM-PŬL'SIǪN, *n.* Act of compelling ; force.
CǪM-PŬL'SǏVE, *a.* Compelling ; forcing ; urging.
CǪM-PŬL'SǏVE-LY, *ad.* By force ; by violence.
CǪM-PŬL'SǏVE-NĔSS, *n.* Force ; compulsion.
CǪM-PŬL'SǪ-RY, *a.* Compelling ; constraining.
CǪM-PŬNC'TIǪN, *n.* Act of pricking :—remorse.
CǪM-PŬNC'TIOŲS, *a.* Repentant ; sorrowful.
CŎM-PŲR-GĀ'TIǪN, *n.* Act of establishing any man's veracity by the testimony of others.
CŎM'PŲR-GĀ-TǪR, *n.* One who bears his testimony to the credibility or innocence of another.

CŎM-PŪT′A-BLE, *a.* Capable of being computed.
CŎM-PŪ-TĀ′TIŎN, *n.* Act of reckoning; estimate.
CŎM-PŪTE′, *v. a.* To reckon; to calculate.
CŎM-PŪT′ER, *n.* A reckoner; a calculator.
CŎM′PŲ-TĬST, *n.* A computer; a calculator.
CŎM′RĀDE *or* CŎM′RĂDE, *n.* A companion.
CŎN, *ad.*, from the Latin *contra.* Against; as, to dispute *pro* and *con, for* and *against.*
CŎN, *v. a.* To study; to commit to memory.
CŎN-CĂM′E-RĀTE, *v. a.* To arch over; to vault.
CŎN-CĂT′E-NĀTE, *v. a.* To link together.
CŎN-CĂT-E-NĀ′TIŎN, *n.* A series of links.
CŎN′CĀVE, *a.* Hollow without angles, as the inner surface of a bowl ;—opposed to *convex.*
CŎN′CĀVE, *n.* Hollow place; cavity.
CŎN-CĂV′I-TY, *n.* A being concave; hollowness.
CŎN-CĀ′VŎ-CŎN′CĀVE, *a.* Concave on both sides
CŎN-CĀ′VŎ-CŎN′VĔX, *a.* Concave on one side and convex on the other side. [angles.
CŎN-CĀ′VOŲS, *a.* Concave; hollow without
CŎN-CĒAL′ (kŏn-sēl′), *v. a.* To hide; to secrete.
CŎN-CĒAL′A-BLE, *a.* That may be concealed.
CŎN-CĒAL′MENT, *n.* Secrecy :—hiding-place.
CŎN-CĒDE′, *v. a. & n.* To yield; to grant.
CŎN-CĒIT′ (kŏn-sēt′), *n.* Fancy; imagination; whim; opinion; idea :—vanity; pride.
CŎN-CĒIT′, *v. a.* To conceive; to imagine.
CŎN-CĒIT′ED, *p. a.* Proud; opinionative; vain.
CŎN-CĒIT′ED-NĔSS, *n.* Pride; opinionativeness.
CŎN-CĒIV′A-BLE, *a.* That may be conceived.
CŎN-CĒIV′A-BLE-NĔSS, *n.* The state of being conceivable; imaginableness. [ner.
CŎN-CĒIV′A-BLY, *ad.* In a conceivable man-
CŎN-CĒIVE′ (kŏn-sēv′), *v. a.* To admit into the womb :—to form in the mind; to imagine.
CŎN-CĒIVE′, *v.n.* To think :—to become pregnant.
CŎN-CĔN′TRĀTE, *v. a.* To bring together.
CŎN-CEN-TRĀ′TIŎN, *n.* Act of concentrating.
CŎN-CĔN′TRE (kŏn-sĕn′ter), *v. n. & a.* To tend or bring to one common centre; to concentrate.
CŎN-CĔN′TRĬC, *a.* Having one common centre.
CŎN-CĔP′TA-CLE, *n.* A receptacle :—a follicle.
CŎN-CĔP′TIŎN, *n.* The act of conceiving; idea.
CŎN-CĔP′TIVE, *a.* Capable of conceiving.
CŎN-CĔRN′, *v. a.* To belong to; to affect; to interest; to make anxious or uneasy.
CŎN-CĔRN′, *n.* Business; affair; interest; care.
CŎN-CĔRN′ĬNG, *prep.* Relating to; respecting.
CŎN-CĔRN′MENT, *n.* Concern; care; business.
CŎN-CĔRT′, *v. a. & n.* To settle; to contrive.
CŎN′CĔRT, *n.* Harmony; musical entertainment.
CŎN-CĔS′SIŎN (kŏn-sĕsh′un), *n.* Act of granting.
CŎN-CĔS′SIŎN-A-RY, *a.* Given by allowance.
CŎNCH (kŏngk), *n.* A marine shell. [conch.
CŎN′CHĪTE (kŏng′kīt), *n.* A petrified shell or
CŎN′CHŎÏD (kŏng′köïd), *n.* A kind of curve.
CŎN-CHŎÏD′AL, *a.* Resembling the conch shell.
CŎN-CHŎL′Ŏ-ĢY, *n.* The science of shells.
CŎN-CĬL′I-ĀTE, *v. a.* To gain; to win; to reconcile; to make satisfied; to pacify.
CŎN-CĬL-I-Ā′TIŎN, *n.* Act of conciliating; peace.
CŎN-CĬL′I-Ā-TŎR, *n.* One who conciliates.
CŎN-CĬL′I-A-TŎ-RY, *a.* Tending to conciliate.
CŎN-CĬN′NI-TY, *n.* Decency; fitness; neatness.
CŎN-CĬN′NOŲS, *a.* Becoming; agreeable; fit.
CŎN-CĪSE′, *a.* Brief; short; compendious, curt.
CŎN-CĪSE′LY, *ad.* Briefly; shortly; summarily.
CŎN-CĪSE′NĔSS, *n.* Brevity; shortness.

CŎN-CĪ′′SIŎN (kŏn-sĭzh′un), *n.* A cutting off; [excision.
CŎN-CĬ-TĀ′TIŎN, *n.* Act of exciting.
CŎN-CLA-MĀ′TIŎN, *n.* A general outcry or shout.
CŎN′CLĀVE, *n.* An assembly of cardinals, &c.
CŎN-CLŪDE′, *v. a. & n.* To determine, end, infer.
CŎN-CLŪ′SIŎN (kŏn-klū′zhun), *n.* Determination; final result or decision; inference; the end.
CŎN-CLŪ′SIVE, *a.* Decisive; ending debate or discussion :—having due logical form.
CŎN-CLŪ′SIVE-LY, *ad.* In a conclusive manner.
CŎN-CLŪ′SIVE-NĔSS, *n.* The being conclusive.
CŎN-CŎCT′, *v. a.* To digest; to mature; to devise.
CŎN-CŎC′TIŎN, *n.* Digestion; maturation.
CŎN-CŎC′TIVE, *a.* Having power to concoct.
CŎN-CŎM′I-TĂNCE, *n.* Accompaniment.
CŎN-CŎM′I-TĂNT, *a.* Accompanying; attending.
CŎN-CŎM′I-TĂNT, *n.* An attendant; companion.
CŎN′CŎRD, *n.* Agreement; union; harmony.
CŎN-CŎRD′ANCE, *n.* Index to the Scriptures, &c.
CŎN-CŎRD′ANT, *a.* Harmonious; agreeing.
CŎN-CŎRD′ANT-LY, *ad.* In an accordant manner.
CŎN-CŎR′DAT, *n.* A compact; a convention.
CŎN-CŎR′PŎ-RĀTE, *v. a. & n.* To unite in one
CŎN′CŌURSE, *n.* An assembly; meeting. [body.
CŎN′CRE-MĔNT, *n.* Mass formed by concretion.
CŎN-CRĔS′CENCE, *n.* Growth by union of particles, or by spontaneous union. [mass.
CŎN-CRĒTE′, *v. n. & a.* To unite into one
CŎN′CRĒTE, *n.* A mass formed by concretion.
CŎN′CRĒTE *or* CŎN-CRĒTE′, *a.* Formed by concretion :—*in logic,* not abstract.
CŎN-CRĒTE′LY, *ad.* In a concrete manner.
CŎN-CRĒ′TIŎN, *n.* Act of concreting; a mass.
CŎN-CRĒ′TIVE, *a.* Causing concretion.
CŎN-CŪ′BI-NAĢE, *n.* The act of living with a woman as a wife, though not married.
CŎN′CŲ-BĪNE, *n.* A woman kept in fornication.
CŎN-CŪ′PIS-CENCE, *n.* Carnal appetite; lust.
CŎN-CŪ′PIS-CENT, *a.* Libidinous; lecherous.
CŎN-CŪ′PIS-CI-BLE, *a.* Concupiscent; lustful.
CŎN-CŬR′, *v. n.* To come together; to agree.
CŎN-CŬR′RENCE, *n.* Conjuncture; agreement; aid.
CŎN-CŬR′RENT, *a.* Acting in conjunction or agreement; associate; concomitant. [ner.
CŎN-CŬR′RENT-LY, *ad.* In a concurrent man-
CŎN-CŬS′SIŎN (kŏn-kŭsh′un), *n.* Act of shaking; a shock; agitation; state of being shaken.
CŎN-CŬS′SIVE, *a.* Having the power of shaking.
CŎN-CŬS′SY, *a.* Noting certain kinds of knots on timber-trees. [*Local, U. S.*]
CŎN-DĔMN′ (kŏn-dĕm′), *v. a.* To find guilty; to doom to punishment; to censure; to blame.
CŎN-DĔM′NA-BLE, *a.* Blamable; censurable.
CŎN-DEM-NĀ′TIŎN, *n.* A sentence of punishment; blame; censure; cause of blame.
CŎN-DĔM′NA-TŎ-RY, *a.* Implying condemna-
CŎN-DĔM′NER, *n.* One who condemns. [tion.
CŎN-DEN′SA-BLE, *a.* Capable of condensation.
CŎN-DEN-SĀ′TIŎN, *n.* Act of condensing.
CŎN-DĔNSE′, *v. a. & n.* To make or grow dense.
CŎN-DĔN′SER, *n.* One who, or that which, condenses :—a vessel for condensing.
CŎN-DE-SCĔND′, *v. n.* To yield, submit, stoop.
CŎN-DE-SCĔN′SIŎN, *n.* Descent from superiority.
CŎN-DĪGN′ (kŏn-dīn′), *a.* Suitable; merited.
CŎN-DĪGN′NESS (kŏn-dīn′nes), *n.* Suitableness.
CŎN′DI-MĔNT, *n.* A seasoning, as salt, pepper, &c.
CŎN-DIS-CĪ′PLE, *n.* A schoolfellow.

CỌN-DĪTE', *v. a.* To pickle; to preserve.
CỌN-DĬ'ʹTIǪN (kọn-dĭsh'ụn), *n.* Quality; state; rank :—stipulation; article of agreement.
CỌN-DĬ'ʹTIǪN, *v. n.* To contract; to stipulate.
CỌN-DĬ'ʹTIǪN-ĄL, *a.* Containing conditions.
CỌN-DĬ'ʹTIǪN-ĄL-LY, *ad.* With limitations.
CỌN-DĬ'ʹTIǪNED (kọn-dĭsh'ụnd), *a.* Having conditions, qualities, or properties, good or bad.
CỌN-DŌLE', *v. n. & a.* To lament with others.
CỌN-DŌLE'MENT, *n.* Lamentation with others.
CỌN-DŌ'LENCE, *n.* Grief for another's sorrows.
CŎN'DǬR, *n.* The great vulture of the Andes.
CỌN-DŪCE', *v. n.* To tend; to contribute.
CỌN-DŪ'CĮ-BLE, *a.* Promoting; conducive.
CỌN-DŪ'CĮVE, *a.* That may forward or promote.
CỌN-DŪ'CĮVE-NĔSS, *n.* Quality of conducing.
CŎN'DŬCT, *n.* Management; economy; behavior.
CỌN-DŬCT', *v. a.* To lead; to direct; to manage.
CỌN-DŬCT'ǬR, *n.* A leader; chief; manager.
CỌN-DŬC'TRESS, *n.* A woman who directs.
CŎN'DUĮT (kŭn'dĭt), *n.* A water-pipe; a canal.
CŌNE, *n.* A solid body in the form of a sugar-loaf.
CỌN-FĂB'Ụ-LĀTE, *v. n.* To talk together; to chat.
CỌN-FĂB-Ụ-LĀ'TIǪN, *n.* Talk; conversation.
CŎN'FĄ-LŎN, *n.* One of a fraternity of seculars in the Roman Catholic church.
CỌN-FĔCT', *v. a.* To make up into sweetmeats.
CŎN'FĔCT, *n.* A sweetmeat; a confection.
CỌN-FĔC'TIǪN, *n.* A sweetmeat :—a mixture.
CỌN-FĔC'TIǪN-ER, *n.* A maker of sweetmeats.
CỌN-FĔC'TIǪN-E-RY, *n.* Sweetmeats; comfits; the making of sweetmeats, or a place for them.
CỌN-FĔD'ER-Ą-CY, *n.* League; federal compact.
CỌN-FĔD'ER-ĀTE, *v. a. & n.* To join in a league.
CỌN-FĔD'ER-ĄTE, *a.* United in a league; allied.
CỌN-FĔD'ER-ĄTE, *n.* An ally; an accomplice.
CỌN-FĔD-ER-Ā'TIǪN, *n.* League; confederacy.
CỌN-FĔR', *v. n.* To discourse; to consult.
CỌN-FĔR', *v. a.* To give; to bestow; to grant.
CŎN'FER-ĔNCE, *n.* Formal discourse; conversation; a meeting for discussion on some subject. [ject.
CỌN-FĔSS', *v. a.* To acknowledge; to own.
CỌN-FĔSS', *v. n.* To make confession.
CỌN-FĔSS'ED-LY, *ad.* Avowedly; indisputably.
CỌN-FĔS'SIǪN (kọn-fĕsh'ụn), *n.* The acknowledgment of a crime or a fault; avowal.
CỌN-FĔS'SIǪN-ĄL, *n.* A seat for confession.
CŎN'FĔSS-ǬR *or* CỌN-FĔSS'ǬR, *n.* One who confesses :—a priest who hears confessions.
CŎN-FĮ-DĂNT', *n.* One trusted with secrets.
CỌN-FĪDE', *v. n.* To trust.—*v. a.* To intrust.
CŎN'FĮ-DĔNCE, *n.* Firm belief; reliance; boldness.
CŎN'FI-DĔNT, *a.* Positive; trusting; bold; rash.
CŎN'FI-DĔNT, *n.* A confidant. See CONFIDANT.
CŎN'FĮ-DĔN'TIĄL, *a.* Private; trusty; faithful.
CŎN'FĮ-DĔNT-LY, *ad.* Without doubt or fear.
CỌN-FĬG-Ụ-RĀ'TIǪN, *n.* External form; figure.
CỌN-FĬG'ỤRE, *v. a.* To dispose into any form.
CỌN-FĪ'NĄ-BLE, *a.* Capable of being confined.
CŎN'FĪNE, *n.* Common boundary; edge. [limit.
CỌN-FĪNE', *v. n.* To border; to have the same
CỌN-FĪNE', *v. a.* To limit; to shut up; to restrain.
CỌN-FĪNE'MENT, *n.* Imprisonment; restraint.
CỌN-FĬRM', *v. a.* To put past doubt; to establish.
CỌN-FĬRM'Ą-BLE, *a.* Capable of being confirmed.
CŎN-FĮR-MĀ'TIǪN, *n.* Act of establishing; proof.
CỌN-FĬRM'Ą-TĬVE, *a.* Having power to confirm.
CỌN-FĬRM'Ą-TǬ-RY, *a.* That serves to confirm.

CỌN-FĬRM'ED-NĔSS, *n.* State of being confirmed.
CỌN-FĬRM'ER, *n.* One that confirms.
CỌN-FĬS'CĄ-BLE, *a.* Liable to confiscation.
CỌN-FĬS'CĀTE, *v. a.* To transfer to the government, as private property, for an offence.
CỌN-FĬS'CĄTE, *a.* Forfeited to the public.
CŎN-FĮS-CĀ'TIǪN, *n.* Act of confiscating; transfer of private property to public use. [ing.
CŎN-FLĄ-GRĀ'TIǪN, *n.* A general fire or burning.
CỌN-FLĬCT', *v. n.* To strive; to contend; to fight.
CŎN'FLĬCT, *n.* Collision; contest; struggle.
CŎN'FLỤ-ENCE, *n.* A flowing together; concourse
CŎN'FLỤ-ENT, *a.* Flowing together; meeting.
CŎN'FLŬX, *n.* Union of several currents; a crowd.
CỌN-FŌRM', *v. a. & n.* To make like; to comply.
CỌN-FŌRM'Ą-BLE, *a.* Agreeable; consistent.
CỌN-FŌRM'Ą-BLY, *ad.* Agreeably; suitably.
CŎN-FǬR-MĀ'TIǪN, *n.* Act of conforming; form; structure.
CỌN-FŌRM'ER, *n.* One who conforms. [structure.
CỌN-FŌRM'ĬST, *n.* One who complies with the worship of the Church of England.
CỌN-FŌRM' Į-TY, *n.* Accordance; resemblance.
CỌN-FÖŬND', *v. a.* To mingle, perplex, astonish.
CŎN-FRĄ-TĔR'NĮ-TY, *n.* A religious brotherhood.
CŎN-FRĮ-CĀ'TIǪN, *n.* Rubbing against; friction.
CỌN-FRŎNT' *or* CỌN-FRŌNT', *v. a.* To face; to oppose openly or to the face :—to compare.
CŎN-FRǪN-TĀ'TIǪN, *n.* Act of confronting.
CỌN-FŪṢE', *v. a.* To confound; to perplex.
CỌN-FŪṢ'ED-LY, *ad.* Indistinctly; not clearly.
CỌN-FŪ'ṢIǪN (kọn-fū'zhụn), *n.* Tumult; disorder.
CỌN-FŪ'TĄ-BLE, *a.* That may be confuted.
CŎN-FỤ-TĀ'TIǪN, *n.* Act of confuting; refutation.
CỌN-FŪTE', *v. a.* To convict of error; to disprove.
CỌN-FŪT'ER, *n.* One who confutes; a refuter.
CŎN'ĠĒ, *n.* Act of reverence; a bow; courtesy.
CŎN'ĠĒ, *n.* (*Arch.*) A moulding. [solid state.
CỌN-ĠĒAL', *v. a. & n.* To freeze or turn to a
CỌN-ĠĒAL'Ą-BLE, *a.* That may be frozen. [gealed.
CỌN-ĠĒAL'MENT, *n.* Congelation; a mass congealed.
CŎN-ĠE-LĀ'TIǪN, *n.* Act or process of freezing.
CỌN-ĠĔN'ER-OŬS, *a.* Of the same kind.
‖CỌN-ĠĒ'NĮ-ĄL *or* CỌN-ĠĒN'IĄL, *a.* Of the same nature; similar; kindred. [genial.
‖CỌN-ĠĒ-NĮ-ĂL'Į-TY, *n.* State of being congenial.
CỌN-ĠĔN'Į-TAL, *a.* Originating or existing at the time of birth; born with another; connate.
CŎN'ĠER (kŏng'ġer), *n.* A fish; the sea-eel.
CỌN-ĠĒ'RĮ-ĔṢ, *n.* A mass of small bodies.
CỌN-ĠĔS'TIǪN, *n.* Collection of matter or fluid.
CỌN-GLĂ'CĮ-ĀTE (kọn-glā'shę-āt), *v. n.* To congeal.
CỌN-GLŌ'BĀTE, *v. a.* To gather into a ball. [geal.
CỌN-GLŌ'BĄTE, *a.* Moulded into a firm ball.
CŎN-GLǬ-BĀ'TIǪN, *n.* Collection into a ball.
CỌN-GLŌBE', *v. a. & n.* To gather into a ball.
CỌN-GLŎM'ER-ĀTE, *v. a.* To gather into a ball.
CỌN-GLŎM'ER-ĄTE, *a.* Gathered into a round mass :—crowded together; clustered. [ball.
CỌN-GLŎM-ER-Ā'TIǪN, *n.* Collection into a
CỌN-GLŪ'TĮ-NĀTE, *v. a. & n.* To cement; to unite; to glue; to coalesce. [reunion.
CỌN-GLŪ-TĮ-NĀ'TIǪN, *n.* Junction; union;
CỌN-GLŪ'TĮ-NĄ-TĬVE, *a.* Tending to unite. [tion.
CỌN-GRĂT'Ụ-LĄNT, *a.* Rejoicing in participation.
CỌN-GRĂT'Ụ-LĀTE, *v. a.* To wish joy to; to felicitate upon any happy event.
CỌN-GRĂT-Ụ-LĀ'TIǪN, *n.* A wishing joy. [lates.
CỌN-GRĂT'Ụ-LĀ-TǬR, *n.* One who congratu-

CǪN-GRĂT'Ụ-LĄ-TǪ-RỴ, *a.* Wishing joy.
CŎN'GRẸ-GĀTE, *v. a. & n.* To collect together; to meet; to gather; to assemble. [bly.
CŎN-GRẸ-GĀ'TIǪN, *n.* A collection; an assem-
CŎN-GRẸ-GĀ'TIǪN-ĄL, *a.* Pertaining to a con-
gregation or to Congregationalists; general.
CŎN-GRẸ-GĀ'TIǪN-ĄL-ĬST, *n.* One of a religious
sect maintaining independence of churches.
CŎN'GRẸSS (kŏng'grẹs), *n.* A meeting; an as-
sembly :—the legislature of the United States.
CǪN-GRĔS'SIǪN-ĄL (kŏn-grĕsh'ụn-ạl), *a.* Re-
lating to congress; parliamentary. [assembling.
CǪN-GRĔS'SĪVE, *a.* Coming together; meeting;
CǪN-GRŪE' (kǫng-grū'), *v. n.* To agree; to suit.
CŎN'GRỤ-ĘNCE, *n.* Agreement; fitness; harmony.
CŎN'GRỤ-ĘNT, *a.* Agreeing; correspondent. [ness.
CǪN-GRŪ'Ĭ-TỴ, *n.* Suitableness; consistency; fit-
CŎN'GRỤ-OŬS, *a.* Agreeable; suitable; fit; meet.
CŎN'GRỤ-OŬS-LỴ, *ad.* Suitably; consistently.
CŎN'ĬC, CŎN'Ĭ-CĄL, *a.* Of the form of a cone.
CŎN'Ĭ-CĄL-LỴ, *ad.* In the form of a cone. [tured.
CǪN-JĔCT'Ụ-RĄ-BLE, *a.* Possible to be conjec-
CǪN-JĔCT'Ụ-RĄL, *a.* Depending on conjecture.
CǪN-JĔCT'ỤRE (kǫn-jĕkt'yụr), *n.* A guess; idea.
CǪN-JĔCT'ỤRE, *v. a.* To guess; to surmise.
CǪN-JĔCT'ỤR-ĘR (kǫn-jĕkt'yụr-ẹr), *n.* A guesser.
CǪN-JŌĬN', *v. a. & n.* To unite; to associate.
CǪN-JŌĬNT', *a.* Associated; connected.
CǪN-JŌĬNT'LỴ, *ad.* In union; together; jointly.
CŎN'JỤ-GĄL, *a.* Matrimonial; connubial. [verb.
CŎN'JỤ-GĀTE, *v. a.* To decline or inflect, as a
CŎN-JỤ-GĀ'TIǪN, *n.* Form of inflecting verbs.
CǪN-JŬNCT', *a.* Conjoined; concurrent; united.
CǪN-JŬNC'TIǪN, *n.* Union :—a connecting word.
CǪN-JŬNC'TĪVE, *a.* Closely united; uniting.
CǪN-JŬNC'TĪVE-LỴ, CǪN-JŬNCT'LỴ, *ad.* In
conjunction or union; jointly; together.
CǪN-JŬNCT'ỤRE (kǫn-jŭnkt'yụr), *n.* Combina-
tion of circumstances; occasion; critical time.
CŎN-JỤ-RĀ'TIǪN, *n.* Incantation; enchantment.
CǪN-JŪRE', *v. a.* To summon or enjoin solemnly.
CŎN'JỤRE (kŭn'jụr), *v. n. & a.* To practise charms.
CŎN'JỤR-ĘR (kŭn'jụr-ẹr), *n.* An enchanter.
CǪN-NĀTE', *a.* Born with another; kindred.
CǪN-NĂT'Ụ-RĄL, *a.* Participant of the same na-
CǪN-NĂT-Ụ-RĂL'Ĭ-TỴ, *n.* Union by nature. [ture.
CǪN-NĔCT', *v. a.* To join; to combine; to unite.
CǪN-NĔC'TIǪN, *n.* Union; junction; a relation.
CǪN-NĔC'TĪVE, *a.* Having power to connect.
CǪN-NĔC'TĪVE, *n.* (*Gram.*) A conjunction.
CǪN-NĔX'IǪN, *n.* Union. See CONNECTION.
CǪN-NĪ'VĄNCE, *n.* Voluntary blindness to an act.
CǪN-NĪVE', *v. n.* To wink; to pretend not to see.
CǪN-NĪV'ĘR, *n.* One who connives.
CǪN-NOĬS-SEŪR', *n.* A critical judge; a critic.
CŎN-NOĬS-SEŪR'SHĬP, *n.* Skill of a connoisseur.
CǪN-NŪ'BĬ-ĄL, *a.* Nuptial; matrimonial.
CŎ'NOÏD, *n.* A figure resembling a cone.
CŎN'QUĘR (kŏng'kẹr), *v. a.* To gain by con-
quest; to overcome; to vanquish; to subdue.
CŎN'QUĘR-Ą-BLE, *a.* Possible to be overcome.
CŎN'QUĘR-ǪR, *n.* One who conquers; victor.
CŎN'QUĘST (kŏng'kwẹst), *n.* The act of con-
quering; victory; acquisition by victory.
CŎN-SĄN-GUĬN'Ę-OŬS, *a.* Of the same blood.
CŎN-SĄN-GUĬN'Ĭ-TỴ, *n.* Relationship by blood.
CŎN'SCIĘNCE (kŏn'shẹns), *n.* The sense of
right and wrong; moral sense; moral faculty.

CŎN-SCĬ-ĚN'TIOỤS (kŏn-shẹ-ĕn'shụs), *a.* Scru-
pulous; upright; regulated by conscience.
CŎN-SCĬ-ĚN'TIOỤS-LỴ, *ad.* In a conscientious
manner; according to conscience.
CŎN-SCĬ-ĚN'TIOỤS-NĔSS, *n.* Scrupulousness.
CŎN'SCIǪN-Ą-BLE (kŏn'shụn-ạ-bı), *a.* Reasona-
CŎN'SCIǪN-Ą-BLỴ, *ad.* Reasonably; justly. [ble.
CŎN'SCIOỤS (kŏn'shụs), *a.* Knowing one's own
thoughts; knowing by mental perception.
CŎN'SCIOỤS-LỴ, *ad.* In a conscious manner.
CŎN'SCIOỤS-NĔSS (kŏn'shụs-nĕs), *n.* The per-
ception of what passes in one's own mind.
CŎN'SCRĬPT, *a.* Written; registered; enrolled.
CŎN'SCRĬPT, *n.* One enrolled for the army.
CǪN-SCRĬP'TIǪN, *n.* An enrolling or registering.
CŎN'SẸ-CRĀTE, *v. a.* To make sacred; to dedicate.
CŎN'SẸ-CRĀTE, *a.* Consecrated; sacred; devoted.
CŎN-SẸ-CRĀ'TIǪN, *n.* The act of consecrating.
CŎN'SẸ-CRĀ-TǪR, *n.* One who consecrates.
CǪN-SĔC'Ụ-TĪVE, *a.* Following in order; succes-
CǪN-SĔC'Ụ-TĪVE-LỴ, *ad.* By consequence [sive.
CǪN-SĔNT', *n.* Concord; agreement; compliance.
CǪN-SĔNT', *v. n.* To yield; to agree; to assent.
CŎN-SĔN-TĀ'NẸ-OŬS, *a.* Agreeable; consistent.
CŎN-SĔN-TĀ'NẸ-OŬS-LỴ, *ad.* Agreeably.
CŎN-SĔN-TĀ'NẸ-OŬS-NĔSS, *n.* Agreement.
CǪN-SĔN'TIĘNT (kǫn-sĕn'shęnt), *a.* Agreeing.
CŎN'SẸ-QUĔNCE, *n.* Event; effect; importance.
CŎN'SẸ-QUĔNT, *a.* Following naturally.
CŎN-SẸ-QUĔN'TIĄL, *a.* Following; important.
CŎN'SẸ-QUĔNT-LỴ, *ad.* By consequence.
CŎN-SĔR-VĀ'TIǪN, *n.* The act of preserving.
CǪN-SĔRV'Ą-TĪVE, *a.* Having power to pre-
serve :—adhering to existing institutions, &c.
CŎN'SĔR-VĀ-TǪR, *n.* One who preserves.
CǪN-SĔRV'Ą-TǪ-RỴ, *n.* A place for preserving.
CǪN-SĔRV'Ą-TǪ-RỴ, *a.* Preservative; preserving.
CǪN-SĔRVE', *v. a.* To preserve; to candy.
CŎN'SĔRVE, *n.* A sweetmeat; a preserve.
CǪN-SĬD'ĘR, *v. a.* To think upon; to ponder.
CǪN-SĬD'ĘR, *v. n.* To reflect; to deliberate.
CǪN-SĬD'ĘR-Ą-BLE, *a.* Respectable; important.
CǪN-SĬD'ĘR-Ą-BLE-NĔSS, *n.* Importance; value.
CǪN-SĬD'ĘR-Ą-BLỴ, *ad.* In a considerable degree.
CǪN-SĬD'ĘR-ĀTE, *a.* Thoughtful; prudent.
CǪN-SĬD'ĘR-ĀTE-LỴ, *ad.* Calmly; prudently.
CǪN-SĬD'ĘR-ĀTE-NĔSS, *n.* Calm deliberation.
CǪN-SĬD-ĘR-Ā'TIǪN, *n.* Act of considering;
prudence :—importance :—compensation.
CǪN-SĬD'ĘR-ĘR, *n.* One who considers.
CǪN-SĬD'ĘR-ĬNG, *prep.* If allowance be made for.
CǪN-SĬGN' (kǫn-sīn'), *v. a.* To give; to commit.
CŎN-SĬGN-ĒĒ' (kŏn-sẹ-nē'), *n.* A person to
whom merchandise, or a vessel, is consigned.
CǪN-SĬGN'MĘNT (kǫn-sīn'mẹnt), *n.* The act
of consigning; delivery; thing consigned.
CŎN-SĬGN-ǪR' (kŏn-sẹ-nör'), *or* CǪN-SĬGN'ĘR, *n.*
One who consigns or makes a consignment.
CǪN-SĬST', *v. n.* To subsist; to be composed.
CǪN-SĬST'ĘNCE, } *n.* Natural state; degree of
CǪN-SĬST'ĘN-CỴ, } density; form; congruity.
CǪN-SĬST'ĘNT, *a.* Conformable; firm; not fluid.
CǪN-SĬST'ĘNT-LỴ, *ad.* In agreement; agreeably.
CŎN-SĬS-TŌ'RĬ-ĄL, *a.* Relating to a consistory.
CŎN'SĬS-TǪ-RỴ, *n.* A spiritual court; assembly.
CǪN-SŌ'CĬ-ĀTE (kǫn-sō'shẹ-ạt), *n.* A partner.
CǪN-SŌ'CĬ-ĀTE (kǫn-sō'shẹ-āt), *v. a. & n.* To
unite; to join; to connect; to coalesce.

CŎN-SŌ-CĬ-Ā'TIǪN (kŏn-sō-she-ā'shṳn), n. Alliance; union; intimacy; association.
CǪN-SŌL'Ạ-BLE, a. That may be consoled. [ace.
CŎN-SǪ-LĀ'TIǪN, n. Comfort; alleviation; sol-
CǪN-SŌL'Ạ-TǪ-RY, a. Tending to give comfort.
CǪN-SŌLE', v a. To comfort; to cheer; to solace.
CŎN'SŌLE, n. (Arch.) A kind of truss or bracket.
CǪN-SŌL'ĘR, a. One that gives comfort. [solid.
CǪN-SŎL'Ĭ-DĀTE, v. a. & n. To make or grow
CǪN-SŎL-Ĭ-DĀ'TIǪN, n. Uniting into a solid mass
CǪN-SŌLṢ', or CŎN'SŌLṢ, n. pl. A sort of transferable stocks; consolidated annuities.
CŎN'SǪ-NANCE, n. Accord of sound; concord.
CŎN'SǪ-NANT, a. Agreeable; consistent; agreeing.
CŎN'SǪ-NANT, n. A letter not sounded by itself.
CŎN'SǪ-NANT-LY, ad. Consistently; agreeably.
CŎN'SŌRT, n. A companion; a wife or husband.
CǪN-SŌRT', v. n. & a. To associate:—to marry.
CǪN-SPĬC'Ṳ-OŬS, a. Obvious to the sight; eminent; distinguished; remarkable; noted. [bly.
CǪN-SPĬC'Ṳ-OŬS-LY, ad. Eminently; remarka-
CǪN-SPĬC'Ṳ-OUS-NĚSS, n. Eminence; celebrity.
CǪN-SPĬR'Ạ-CY, n. Combination for an ill design; a plotting:—concurrence; tendency.
CŎN-SPǏ-RĀ'TIǪN, n. A conspiracy. [acy.
CǪN-SPĬR'Ạ-TǪR, n. One engaged in a conspir-
CǪN-SPĪRE', v. n. To plot:—to concur; to tend.
CŎN'STẠ-BLE (kŭn'stạ-bl), n. A peace officer.
CŎN'STẠ-BLE-SHĬP, n. Office of a constable.
CŎN'STẠN-CY, n. Firmness; lasting affection.
CŎN'STẠNT, a. Fixed; faithful; unchanging.
CŎN'STẠNT-LY, ad. Perpetually; faithfully.
CŎN-STĚL-LĀ'TIǪN, n. A cluster of fixed stars.
CŎN-STĚR-NĀ'TIǪN, n. Astonishment; alarm.
CŎN'STĬ-PĀTE, v. a. To crowd:—to make costive.
CŎN-STĬ-PĀ'TIǪN, n. Condensation; costiveness.
CǪN-STĬT'Ṳ-ĘNT, a. Elementary; constituting.
CǪN-STĬT'Ṳ-ĘNT, n. He who deputes; elector.
CŎN'STĬ-TŪTE, v. a. To make, depute, appoint.
CŎN-STĬ-TŪ'TIǪN, n. The frame of body or mind:—laws of a state; form of government.
CŎN-STĬ-TŪ'TIǪN-ẠL, a. Relating to the constitution; according to the constitution.
CŎN-STĬ-TŪ-TIǪN-ĂL'Ĭ-TY, n. Accordance with the constitution or fundamental laws.
CŎN-STĬ-TŪ'TIǪN-ẠL-LY, ad. In a constitutional manner; agreeably to the constitution.
CŎN'STĬ-TŪ-TĬVE, a. Constituent; enacting.
CǪN-STRĀIN', v. a. To compel; to force; to press.
CǪN-STRĀIN'Ạ-BLE, a. That may be constrained.
CǪN-STRĀINT', n. Compulsion; confinement.
CǪN-STRĬC'TIǪN, n. Contraction; compression.
CǪN-STRĬC'TǪR, a. That which constricts:— a muscle that closes an orifice:—a very large serpent; the boa-constrictor.
CǪN-STRĬNGE', v. a. To compress; to contract.
CǪN-STRĬN'GĘNT, a. Binding or compressing.
CǪN-STRŬCT', v. a. To build; to form; to devise.
CǪN-STRŬCT'ĘR, n. One who forms or makes.
CǪN-STRŬC'TIǪN, n. Act of building; fabrication; structure:—meaning; interpretation:— disposition of words according to syntax.
CǪN-STRŬC'TĬVE, a. Relating to construction.
CǪN-STRŬC'TĬVE-LY, ad. By way of construc-
CŎN'STRŬE, v. a. To interpret; to translate. [tion.
CŎN-STṲ-PRĀ'TIǪN, n. Violation; defilement.
CŎN-SṲB-STĂN'TIẠL, a. Having the same substance or essence; being of the same nature.

CŎN-SṲB-STĂN'TĬ-ĀTE, v. a. To unite in one common substance or nature.
CŎN-SṲB-STĂN-TĬ-Ā'TIǪN (kŏn-sṳb-stăn-she-ā'shṳn), n. Substantial presence of the body of our Saviour with the sacramental elements.
CŎN'SṲL, n. A magistrate:—commercial agent.
CŎN'SṲ-LẠR, a. Relating to a consul.
CŎN'SṲ-LẠTE, n. The state, jurisdiction, or office of a consul; consulship. [sulate.
CŎN'SṲL-SHĬP, n. The office of consul; con-
CǪN-SŬLT', v. n. To take counsel together.
CǪN-SŬLT', v. a. To ask advice of:—to regard.
CŎN'SŬLT, n. The act of consulting; a council.
CŎN-SṲL-TĀ'TIǪN, n. A consulting; delibera-
CǪN-SŬLT'ĘR, n. One who consults. [tion.
CǪN-SŪM'Ạ-BLE, a. That may be consumed.
CǪN-SŪME', v. a. To waste; to spend; to de-
CǪN-SŪM'ĘR, n. One who consumes. [stroy.
CǪN-SŬM'MĀTE, v. a. To complete; to perfect.
CǪN-SŬM'MẠTE, a. Complete; perfect; finished.
CǪN-SŬM'MẠTE-LY, ad. Perfectly; completely.
CŎN-SṲM-MĀ'TIǪN, n. Completion; perfection.
CǪN-SŬMP'TIǪN, n. Act of consuming; a disease.
CǪN-SŬMP'TĬVE, a. Destructive; wasting.
CǪN-SŬMP'TĬVE-LY, ad. In a consumptive way.
CǪN-SŬMP'TĬVE-NĚSS, n. Consumptive state.
CŎN'TĂCT, n. Touch; juncture; close union.
CǪN-TĀ'ĢIǪN (kǫn-tā'jṳn), n. Infection; pestilence; propagation of any thing evil.
CǪN-TĀ'ĢIOUS (kǫn-tā'jṳs), a. Infectious; foul.
CǪN-TĀ'ĢIOUS-NĚSS, n. The state or the quality of being contagious; infection. [strain.
CǪN-TĀIN', v. a. To hold; to comprise; to re-
CǪN-TĀIN', v. n. To live in continence.
CǪN-TĀIN'Ạ-BLE, a. Possible to be contained.
CǪN-TĂM'Ĭ-NĀTE, v. a. To defile; to pollute.
CǪN-TĂM-Ĭ-NĀ'TIǪN, n. Pollution; defilement.
CǪN-TĔMN' (kǫn-tĕm'), v. a. To despise; to slight.
CǪN-TĔM'NĘR, n. One who contemns; scorner.
CǪN-TĔM'PĘR, v. a. To moderate; to temper.
CǪN-TĔM'PĘR-Ạ-MĚNT, n. Temperament.
CǪN-TĔM-PĘR-Ā'TIǪN, n. Act of moderating.
||CǪN-TĔM'PLĀTE, v. a. To consider attentively.
CǪN-TĔM'PLĀTE, v. n. To muse; to meditate.
CŎN-TEM-PLĀ'TIǪN, n. Meditation; study.
CǪN-TĔM'PLẠ-TĬVE, a. Studious; thoughtful.
CǪN-TĔM'PLĀ-TǪR, n. One who contemplates.
CǪN-TĔM'PǪ-RẠ-RY,   } a. Living at the
CǪN-TĔM-PǪ-RĀ'NĘ-OŬS, } same point of time, or in the same age; born at the same time.
CǪN-TĔM'PǪ-RẠ-RY, n. One who lives at the same time with another.
CǪN-TĔMPT' (kǫn-tĕmt'), n. Act of despising; scorn; disdain; disregard; disgrace. [vile.
CǪN-TĔMPT'Ĭ-BLE, a. Worthy of contempt;
CǪN-TĔMPT'Ĭ-BLE-NĚSS, n. Vileness; baseness.
CǪN-TĔMPT'Ĭ-BLY, ad. Meanly; basely; vilely.
CǪN-TĔMPT'Ṳ-OŬS, a. Scornful; apt to despise.
CǪN-TĔMPT'Ṳ-OŬS-LY, ad. In a scornful manner.
CǪN-TĔMPT'Ṳ-OŬS-NĚSS, n. Quality of being contemptuous; disposition to contempt. [vie.
CǪN-TĔND', v. n. To strive; to struggle; to
CǪN-TĔND'ĘR, n. One who contends.
CǪN-TĔN'Ę-MĚNT, n. (Law.) That which is held with a tenement, as its credit, lands, &c.
CǪN-TĔNT', a. Satisfied; quiet; contented.
CǪN-TĔNT', v. a. To satisfy; to please; to gratify.
CǪN-TĔNT', n. Satisfaction; rest:—capacity.

CŎN-TĔNT'ĔD, *p. a.* Satisfied ; not repining.
CŎN-TĔNT'ĔD-LY, *ad.* In a quiet manner.
CŎN-TĔNT'ĔD-NĔSS, *n.* State of being content-
CŎN-TĔN'TIŎN, *n.* Strife ; contest ; debate. [ed.
CŎN-TĔN'TIOŲS (kŏn-tĕn'shŭs),*a.*Quarrelsome.
CŎN-TĔN'TIOŲS-LY, *ad.* Quarrelsomely.
CŎN-TĔN'TIOŲS-NĔSS, *n.* Proneness to contest.
CŎN-TĔNT'MĔNT, *n.* Satisfaction ; content.
CŎN-TĔNTS' *or* CŎN'TĔNTS, *n. pl.* Heads of a
book; index : that which is contained.[bounds.
CŎN-TĔR'MĬ-NA-BLE, *a.* Capable of the same
CŎN-TĔR'MĬ-NATE, *a.* Having the same bounds.
CŎN-TĔR'MĬ-NOŬS,*a.* Bordering upon :—allied.
CŎN-TĔST', *v. a. & n.* To dispute ; to strive ;
to vie ; to contend :—to call in question.
CŎN'TĔST, *n.* Dispute ; debate ; quarrel ; fight.
CŎN-TĔST'A-BLE,*a.* Disputable ; controvertible.
CŎN-TĔS-TĀ'TIŎN, *n.* Act of contesting ; debate.
CŎN'TĔXT, *n.* The series of a discourse. [ure.
CŎN-TĔXT'ŲRE (-tĕxt'yųr), *n.* Structure ; text-
CŎN-TĬG-NĀ'TIŎN, *n.* A frame of beams joined.
CŎN-TĬ-GŪ'Ĭ-TY, *n.* Actual contact ; a touching.
CŎN-TĬG'Ų-OŬS, *a.* Meeting so as to touch.
CŎN-TĬG'Ų-OŬS-LY, *ad.* In a manner to touch.
CŎN-TĬG'Ų-OŬS-NĔSS, *n.* Close connection.
CŎN'TĬ-NĔNCE, *n.* Restraint ; chastity.
CŎN'TĬ-NĔNT,*a.*Chaste ; abstemious ; moderate.
CŎN'TĬ-NĔNT, *n.* A great extent of land.
CŎN-TĬ-NĔN'TAL, *a.* Relating to a continent.
CŎN'TĬ-NĔNT-LY, *ad.* In a continent manner.
CŎN-TĬN'ĢENCE, } *n.* The quality of being
CŎN-TĬN'ĢEN-CY, } casual or contingent.
CŎN-TĬN'ĢENT,*a.*Happening by chance ; casual.
CŎN-TĬN'ĢENT, *n.* Chance :—proportion ; quota.
CŎN-TĬN'ĢENT-LY,*ad.* Accidentally ; casually.
CŎN-TĬN'Ų-AL, *a.* Incessant ; uninterrupted.
CŎN-TĬN'Ų-AL-LY, *ad.* Without interruption.
CŎN-TĬN'Ų-ANCE, *n.* Duration ; permanence.
CŎN-TĬN-Ų-Ā'TIŎN,*n.* Uninterrupted succession.
CŎN-TĬN'Ų-Ā-TŎR, *n.* One who continues.
CŎN-TĬN'ŲE (-tĭn'yų), *v. n.* To remain ; to last.
CŎN-TĬN'ŲE, *v. a.* To protract ; to extend.
CŎN-TĬ-NŪ'Ĭ-TY, *n.* Uninterrupted connection.
CŎN-TĬN'Ų-OŬS, *a.* Closely joined together ; un-
interrupted ; connected ; continued.
CŎN-TÖRT', *v. a.* To twist ; to writhe ; to distort.
CŎN-TÖR'TIŎN, *n.* Twist ; wry motion ; distor-
CŎN-TÔUR', *n.* Outline of a figure. [tion.
CŎN'TRA. A Latin preposition used in compo-
sition, and signifying *against*, or *in opposition.*
CŎN'TRA-BĂND, *a.* Prohibited by law ; illegal.
CŎN'TRA-BĂND, *n.* Illegal traffic :—articles the
exportation or importation of which is illegal.
CŎN-TRĂCT', *v. a.* To lessen ; to narrow ; to
abridge ; to diminish :—to get :—to bargain.
CŎN-TRĂCT', *v. n.* To shrink up :—to bargain.
CŎN'TRĂCT, *n.* A covenant ; a bargain ; a
compact ; a uniting with terms of a bargain.
CŎN-TRĂCT'Ĭ-BLE, *a.* Capable of contraction.
CŎN-TRĂC'TĬLE, *a.* That may contract.
CŎN-TRĂC-TĬL'Ĭ-TY, *n.* Quality of contracting.
CŎN-TRĂC'TIŎN, *n.* A shrinking ; a shortening.
CŎN-TRĂCT'ŎR, *n.* One who contracts or bar-
gains ; a bargainer to perform any work. [deny.
CŎN-TRA-DĬCT', *v. a.* To oppose verbally ; to
CŎN-TRA-DĬCT'ER, *n.* One who contradicts.
CŎN-TRA-DĬC'TIŎN, *n.* A gainsaying ; opposi-
tion ; inconsistency ; incongruity ; contrariety.

CŎN-TRA-DĬC'TIOŲS, *a.* Inclined to contradict.
CŎN-TRA-DĬC'TO-RĬ-LY,*ad.*With contradiction.
CŎN-TRA-DĬC'TO-RĬ-NĔSS, *n.* Entire opposition.
CŎN-TRA-DĬC'TO-RY, *a.* Opposite ; contrary.
CŎN-TRA-DĬS-TĬNC'TIŎN, *n.* Distinction by
opposite qualities ; opposition ; difference.
CŎN-TRA-DĬS-TĬN'GUĬSH (-dĭs-tĭng'gwĭsh),*v. a.*
To distinguish by opposite qualities. [cy.
CŎN-TRA-RĪ'E-TY, *n.* Opposition ; inconsisten-
CŎN'TRA-RĬ-LY, *ad.* In a contrary manner.
CŎN'TRA-RĬ-WĪṢE, *ad.* Conversely ; oppositely.
CŎN'TRA-RY, *a.* Opposite ; inconsistent ; ad-
verse ; contradictory ; different :—refractory.
CŎN'TRA-RY, *n.* A thing of opposite qualities.
CŎN'TRĂST, *n.* Opposition of things ; difference.
CŎN-TRĂST', *v. a.* To place in opposition.
CŎN-TRA-TĔN'ŎR, *n.* (*Mus.*) Counter-tenor.
CŎN'TRĀTE-WHĒĒL, *n.* A wheel moved by
teeth or cŏgs which are parallel to its axis.
CŎN-TRA-VAL-LĀ'TIŎN, *n.* A counter-fortifica-
CŎN-TRA-VĒNE',*v. a.* To oppose ; to baffle.[tion.
CŎN-TRA-VĔN'TIŎN,*n.*Opposition ; obstruction.
CŎN-TRĬB'ŲTE, *v. a.* To give to a common
stock ; to bestow, as a part or share. [levy.
CŎN-TRĬ-BŪ'TIŎN, *n.* Act of contributing ; a
CŎN-TRĬB'Ų-TĪVE, *a.* Tending to contribute.
CŎN-TRĬB'Ų-TŎR, *n.* One who contributes.
CŎN-TRĬB'Ų-TO-RY, *a.* Contributing ; helping.
CŎN'TRĪTE, *a.* Broken-hearted for sin ; penitent.
CŎN'TRĪTE-LY, *ad.* In a penitent manner.
CŎN'TRĪTE-NĔSS, *n.* Contrition. [remorse.
CŎN-TRĬ''TIŎN (kŏn-trĭsh'ŭn), *n.* Penitence ;
CŎN-TRĪV'A-BLE, *a.* Possible to be planned.
CŎN-TRĪV'ANCE, *n.* Scheme ; plan ; plot ; art.
CŎN-TRĪVE',*v. a. & n.* To plan out ; to devise.
CŎN-TRĪV'ER, *n.* An inventor ; a schemer.
CŎN-TRŌL', *n.* Restraint ; power ; command.
CŎN-TRŌL', *v. a.* To govern ; to restrain ; to
CŎN-TRŌL'LA-BLE,*a.*Subject to control.[check.
CŎN-TRŌL'LER, *n.* One who controls or directs.
CŎN-TRŌL'LER-SHĬP, *n.* Office of a controller.
CŎN-TRŌL'MĔNT,*n.*Superintendence ; restraint.
CŎN-TRO-VĔR'SIAL, *a.* Relating to controversy.
CŎN-TRO-VĔR'SIAL-ĬST, *n.* A disputant.
CŎN'TRO-VĔR-SY,*n.* Dispute ; debate ; quarrel.
CŎN'TRO-VĔRT, *v. a.* To debate ; to dispute.
CŎN'TRO-VĔRT-ĬST, *n.* A controversialist.
CŎN-TŲ-MĀ'CIOŲS (kŏn-tṳ-mā'shṳs), *a.* Ob-
stinate ; stubborn ; intractable. [bornly.
CŎN-TŲ-MĀ'CIOŲS-LY, *ad.* Obstinately ; stub-
CŎN'TŲ-MA-CY, *n.* Obstinacy ; perverseness.
CŎN-TŲ-MĔ'LĬ-OŬS, *a.* Reproachful ; insolent.
CŎN-TŲ-MĔ'LĬ-OŬS-LY, *ad.* Insolently ; rudely.
CŎN'TŲ-MĔ-LY, *n.* Rudeness ; insolence ; re-
proach ; contemptuousness ; abusiveness.
CŎN-TŪṢE', *v. a.* To beat together ; to bruise.
CŎN-TŪ'ṢIŎN (-tū'zhŭn), *n.* Beating ; a bruise.
CO-NŬN'DRŬM, *n.* A sort of riddle ; a quibble.
CŎN-VA-LĔS'CENCE, *n.* Recovery of health.
CŎN-VA-LĔS'CENT, *a.* Recovering health.
CŎN-VĒNE',*v. n.* To come together ; to assemble.
CŎN-VĒNE',*v. a.* To call together ; to assemble.
CŎN-VĒN'IENCE, *n.* Fitness ; propriety ; ease ;
accommodation ; that which is convenient.
CŎN-VĒN'IENT, *a.* Fit ; suitable ; commodious.
CŎN-VĒN'IENT-LY,*ad.* Commodiously ; fitly.
CŎN'VENT,*n.* An abbey ; monastery ; nunnery.
CŎN-VĔN'TĬ-CLE, *n.* An assembly ; a meeting.

CON-VĔN'TĬ-CLĘR, *n.* Frequenter of conventi-
CON-VĔN'TIQN, *n.* Assembly :—contract. [cles.
CON-VĔN'TIQN-AL, *a.* Stipulated ; agreed on.
CON-VĔN'TIQN-ĬST, *n.* One who makes a contract, agreement, or convention.
CON-VĔNT'Ụ-AL, *a.* Belonging to a cònvent.
CON-VĔRĢE', *v. n.* To tend to one point.
CON-VĔR'ĢĘNT, *a.* Tending to one point from different places ; converging ; coming together.
CON-VĔR'SA-BLE, *a.* Free to converse ; sociable.
CŎN'VĘR-SĄNT, *a.* Acquainted ; familiar.
CŎN-VĘR-SĀ'TIQN, *n.* Familiar discourse ; talk.
CON-VĔRSE', *v. n.* To associate ; to discourse.
CŎN'VĘRSE, *n.* Conversation ; acquaintance.
CŎN'VĘRSE, *a.* Opposite ; reciprocal.
CŎN'VĘRSE-LY *or* CON-VĔRSE'LY, *ad.* By change of order ; reciprocally ; oppositely.
CON-VĔR'SIQN, *n.* Act of converting ; change of disposition, character, principles, or religion.
CON-VĔRT', *v. a.* To change ; to turn ; to apply.
CŎN'VĘRT, *n.* A person who is converted.
CON-VĔRT'ĘR, *n.* One who makes converts.
CON-VĔRT-Ĭ-BĬL'Ĭ-TY, *n.* The being convertible.
CON-VĔRT'Ĭ-BLE, *a.* Susceptible of change.
CŎN'VĔX, *a.* Rising in a spherical form.
CON-VĔX'Ĭ-TY, *n.* A spherical form ; rotundity.
CŎN'VĔX-LY, *ad.* In a convex form.
CŎN'VĔX-NĘSS, *n.* The state of being convex.
CON-VĔX'Q-CŎN'CĀVE, *a.* Convex on one side and concave on the other side.
CON-VEY' (kọn-vā'), *v. a.* To carry ; to send ; to transport ; to bear ; to transfer ; to impart.
CON-VEY'ANCE (kọn-vā'ạns), *h.* Act of conveying ; a vehicle ; a carriage ; transmission ; a deed for transferring property.
CON-VEY'AN-CĘR (kọn-vā'ạn-sęr), *n.* A lawyer who draws writings for transferring property.
CON-VEY'ANÇ-ĬNG (kọn-vā'ạns-ĭng), *n.* The business of a conveyancer ; transfer of property.
CON-VEY'ĘR (kọn-vā'ęr), *n.* One who conveys.
CON-VĬCT', *v. a.* To prove guilty ; to detect.
CŎN'VĬCT, *n.* One legally proved guilty. [tion.
CON-VĬC'TIQN, *n.* Detection of guilt ; confuta-
CON-VĬC'TĬVE, *a.* Having the power to convict.
CON-VĬNCE', *v. a.* To satisfy by proof ; to force to acknowledge ; to subdue by argument.
CON-VĬN'CĬ-BLE, *a.* Capable of conviction.
CON-VĬV'Ĭ-AL *or* CON-VĬV'ĬAL, *a.* Pertaining, or inclined, to festivity ; festive ; social.
CON-VĬV-Ĭ-ĂL'Ĭ-TY, *n.* Convivial disposition.
CŎN-VQ-CĀ'TIQN, *n.* An ecclesiastical assembly.
CON-VŌKE', *v. a.* To call together ; to summon.
CŎN-VQ-LŪ'TIQN, *n.* A rolling together.
CON-VŎLVE' (kọn-vŏlv'), *v. a.* To roll together.
CON-VŎL'VŲ-LŬS, *n.* A genus of plants.
CON-VŌY', *v. a.* To accompany for defence.
CŎN'VŌY, *n.* An attendance for defence ; defence.
CON-VŬLSE', *v. a.* To give violent motion to.
CON-VŬL'SIQN, *n.* Violent spasm ; disturbance.
CON-VŬL'SĬVE, *a.* Producing convulsion.
CŎN'Y (kŭn'ẹ), *n.* A rabbit :—a simpleton.
CŌÔ, *v. n.* To cry as a dove or pigeon.
COOK (kŭk), *n.* One who dresses victuals.
COOK (kŭk), *v. a.* To dress or prepare, as victuals.
COOK'ĘR-Y (kŭk'-), *n.* Art of dressing victuals.
CÔÔL, *a.* Somewhat cold ; not ardent or fond.
CÔÔL, *n.* A moderate degree or state of cold.
CÔÔL, *v. a. & n.* To make or grow cool ; to quiet.

CÔÔL'ĘR, *n.* That which cools ; a cooling vessel.
CÔÔL'NĘSS, *n.* Gentle cold :—want of affection.
CÔÔM, *n.* Soot collected over an oven's mouth.
CÔÔMB (kôm), *n.* A corn measure of 4 bushels.
CÔÔP, *n.* A barrel ; a cage ; a pen for animals.
CÔÔP, *v. a.* To shut up ; to confine ; to cage.
CÔÔP'ĘR, *n.* One who makes barrels, &c.
CÔÔP'ĘR-AĢE, *n.* The work or pay of a cooper.
CŌ-ŎP'ĘR-ĀTE, *v. n.* To labur for the same end.
CŌ-ŎP-ĘR-Ā'TIQN, *n.* Joint labor or operation.
CŌ-ŎP'ĘR-A-TĬVE, *a.* Promoting the same end.
CŌ-ŎP'ĘR-Ā-TQR, *n.* One who coöperates ; a joint operator ; fellow-laborer ; coadjutor.
CQ-ŎR'DĬ-NĄTE, *a.* Holding the same rank.
CŌ-ŎR'DĬ-NĄTE-LY, *ad.* In the same rank.
CÔÔT, *n.* A small water-fowl :—a simpleton.
CQ-PAÎ'BĄ, *n.* A balsam used in medicine.
CŌ'PAL, *n.* A resin used in varnishes.
CQ-PĂR'CĘ-NĄ-RY, *n.* Joint inheritance.
CQ-PĂR'CĘ-NĘR, *n.* A joint heir ; a coheir.
CQ-PĂR'CĘ-NY, *n.* Equal share of an inheritance.
CŌ-PĂRT'NĘR, *n.* A joint partner ; a partaker.
CŌ-PĂRT'NĘR-SHĬP, *n.* Joint partnership.
CQ-PĀY'VĄ (kọ-pā'vạ), *n.* See COPAIBA.
CŌPE, *n.* A priest's cloak :—a concave arch.
CŌPE, *v. n.* To contend ; to struggle ; to strive.
CQ-PĔR'NĬ-CAN, *a.* Relating to Copernicus.
CŎP'Ĭ-ĘR, *n.* One who copies ; a transcriber.
CŌ'PĬNG, *n.* The top or covering of a wall.
CŌ'PĬ-OŬS, *a.* Plentiful ; abundant ; ample.
CŌ'PĬ-OŬS-LY, *ad.* Plentifully ; abundantly.
CŌ'PĬ-OŲS-NĔSS, *n.* Plenty ; abundance.
CŎP'PĘD (kŏp'pęd *or* kŏpt), *n.* Rising to a top.
CŎP'PĘL, *n.* Instrument for purifying gold, &c.
CŎP'PĘR, *n.* A metal ; a vessel made of copper.
CŎP'PĘR-AS, *n.* Sulphate of iron ; green vitriol.
CŎP'PĘR-PLĀTE, *n.* A plate on which designs are engraved :—an impression from the plate.
CŎP'PĘR-SMĬTH, *n.* One who works in copper.
CŎP'PĘR-Y, *a.* Containing or like copper.
CŎP'PĬCE, CŎPSE, *n.* A wood of small trees.
CŎP'Ų-LĀTE, *v. a. & n.* To unite ; to embrace.
CŎP-Ụ-LĀ'TIQN, *n.* The act of copulating.
CŎP-Ụ-LĄ-TĬVE, *a.* Tending to connect or unite.
CŎP'Y, *n.* A manuscript ; an imitation ; pattern.
CŎP'Y, *v. a.* To transcribe ; to imitate ; to mimic.
CŎP'Y-BOOK (kŏp'ẹ-bûk), *n.* A book of copies.
CŎP'Y-HŌLD, *n.* A kind of tenure in England.
CŎP'Y-ĬST, *n.* One who copies ; a copier.
CŎP'Y-RĪGHT, *n.* The sole right to print a book.
CQ-QUĔT' (kọ-kĕt'), *v. a. & n.* To jilt ; to trifle.
CQ-QUĔT'RY (kọ-kĕt'rẹ), *n.* Deceit in love.
CQ-QUĔTTE' (kọ-kĕt'), *n.* A gay, airy girl ; a jilt.
CQ-QUĔT'TĬSH, *a.* Having the manners of a co-
CŎR'A-CLE, *n.* A boat used by fishers. [quette.
CŎR'AL, *n.* A hard, calcareous substance, growing in the sea like a plant :—a child's toy.
CŎR'AL-LĬNE, *a.* Consisting of, or like, coral.
CŎRB, *n.* An ornament in building ; a basket.
CŎR'BAN, *n.* An alms-basket ; a gift ; an alms.
CŎRD, *n.* A rope ; a sinew ; a measure of wood.
CŎRD, *v. a.* To tie or fasten with cords ; to pile.
CŎRD'AĢE, *n.* A quantity of cords ; ropes. [friar.
CŎR-DE-LIĒR' (kŏr-dẹ-lēr'), *n.* A Franciscan
‖CŎRD'IAL (kŏrd'yạl *or* kŏr'dẹ-ạl), *n.* Medicine.
‖CŎRD'IAL, *a.* Reviving ; sincere ; hearty.
‖CŎRD-Ĭ-ĂL'Ĭ-TY (kŏrd-yẹ-ăl'ẹ-tẹ), *n.* Sinceri-
ty ; affection ; heartiness ; warmth of feeling.

‖CÖRD′IAL-LY, *ad.* Sincerely ; heartily.
CÖR′DÖN, *n.* A ribbon or badge :—series of military posts to prevent egress or ingress.
CÖR′DO-VĂN, *n.* Spanish leather from Cordova.
CÖR-DU-RÖY′, *n.* A thick, ribbed, cotton stuff.
CÖRD′WĀIN-ER, CÖRD′I-NER, *n.* A shoemaker.
CÖRE, *n.* The heart :—the inner part of a thing.
CO-RI-Ā′CEOUS (kō-re-ā′shus), *a.* Consisting of leather ; resembling leather ; leathery.
CO-RI-ĂN′DER, *n.* A plant, and its spicy seed.
CÖRK, *n.* A tree and its bark :—a stopple.
CÖRK, *v. a.* To stop with a cork, as a bottle.
CÖRK′ING-PIN, *n.* A pin of the largest size.
CÖRK′SCREW, *n.* A screw for drawing corks.
CÖRK′Y, *a.* Consisting of, or resembling, cork.
CÖR′MO-RANT, *n.* A voracious bird :—a glutton.
CÖRN, *n.* Grain of wheat, &c. ; maize :—a tumor.
CÖRN, *v. a.* To preserve with salt :—to granulate.
CÖRN′CHĂND-LER, *n.* One who deals in corn.
CÖR′NE-A, *n.* The horny membrane of the eye.
COR-NĔL′IAN, *n.* A stone. See CARNELIAN.
CÖR′NE-OŬS, *a.* Horny ; resembling horn.
CÖR′NER, *n.* An angle :—a secret or remote place.
CÖR′NER-STŌNE, *n.* The principal stone.
CÖR′NET, *n.* A musical instrument :—an officer.
CÖR′NET-CY, *n.* The commission of a cornet.
CÖR′NICE, *n.* Upper projecting moulding.
CÖRN′-MĬLL, *n.* A mill for grinding corn.
CÖR-NU-CŌ′PI-A, *n.* Horn of plenty :—a plant.
COR-NŪT′ED, *a.* Having horns :—cuckolded.
CÖRN′Y, *a.* Horny ; producing grain or corn.
CÖR′OL, CO-RŎL′LA, *n.* The inner flower-leaves.
CÖR′OL-LA-RY, *n.* A consequence ; conclusion.
‖CO-RŌ′NAL *or* CÖR′O-NAL, *n.* A crown ; a garland ; a chaplet.—(*Anat.*) The frontal bone.
‖CO-RŌ′NAL, *a.* Belonging to the top of the head.
CÖR′O-NA-RY, *a.* Relating to, or like, a crown.
CÖR-O-NĀ′TION, *n.* The act of crowning.
CÖR′O-NER, *n.* An officer whose duty it is to inquire, by a jury, and a view of the body, how any violent or casual death was occasioned.
CÖR′O-NET, *n.* A crown worn by the nobility.
CÖR′PO-RAL, *n.* The lowest officer of infantry.
CÖR′PO-RAL, *a.* Relating to the body ; material.
CÖR-PO-RĀ′LE, *n.* Linen on which the sacramental elements are laid ; communion-cloth.
CÖR′PO-RAL-LY, *ad.* Bodily ; in the body.
CÖR′PO-RATE, *a.* Incorporated ; united ; general.
CÖR′PO-RATE-LY, *ad.* In a corporate capacity.
CÖR′PO-RATE-NĔSS, *n.* The quality or state of a body corporate. [porate.
CÖR-PO-RĀ′TION, *n.* A body politic, or cor-
COR-PŌ′RE-AL, *a.* Having a body ; not spiritual.
COR-PŌ′RE-AL-LY, *ad.* In a bodily manner.
CÖRPS (kör ; *pl.* körz), *n. sing. & pl.* A body of
CÖRPSE, *n.* A dead human body ; a corse. [forces.
CÖR′PU-LENCE, *n.* Fatness ; fleshiness ; obesity.
CÖR′PU-LENT, *a.* Fleshy ; very fat ; bulky.
CÖR′PUS-CLE (kör′pus-sl), *n.* A particle ; atom.
COR-PŬS′CU-LAR, *a.* Relating to corpuscles.
COR-RĔCT′, *v. a.* To amend ; to rectify, punish.
COR-RĔCT′, *a.* Free from faults ; right ; accurate.
COR-RĔC′TION, *n.* The act of correcting ; amendment ; improvement :—punishment.
COR-RĔC′TIVE, *a.* Having the power to correct.
COR-RĔC′TIVE, *n.* That which corrects.
COR-RĔCT′LY, *ad.* Accurately ; without faults.
COR-RĔCT′NESS, *n.* Accuracy ; exactness.

COR-RĔCT′OR, *n.* One that corrects.
COR-RĔG′I-DOR, *n.* A Spanish mayor.
COR-RĔL′A-TIVE, *a.* Having a reciprocal relation ; reciprocal. [ciprocal relation.
COR-RĔL′A-TIVE, *n.* One that stands in a re-
CÖR-RE-SPÖND′, *v. n.* To suit, write, answer.
CÖR-RE-SPÖND′ENCE, *n.* Suitableness ; fitting relation :—friendship ; intercourse. [fit.
CÖR-RE-SPÖND′ENT, *a.* Suitable ; adapted ;
CÖR-RE-SPÖND′ENT, *n.* One that corresponds.
CÖR′RI-DOR, *n.* Gallery or passage in a building.
CÖR′RI-GI-BLE, *a.* Capable of being corrected.
COR-RŎB′O-RANT, *a.* Strengthening ; confirming.
COR-RŎB′O-RĀTE, *v. a.* To confirm ; to establish.
COR-RŎB-O-RĀ′TION, *n.* The act of confirming.
COR-RŎB′O-RA-TIVE, *a.* Confirming.
COR-RŌDE′, *v. a.* To prey upon ; to eat away.
COR-RŌ′DI-BLE, *a.* That may be corroded.
COR-RŌ′SION (kor-rō′zhun), *n.* Act of corroding.
COR-RŌ′SIVE, *a.* Corroding ; consuming.
COR-RŌ′SIVE-LY, *ad.* In a corrosive manner.
COR-RŌ′SIVE-NĔSS, *n.* Quality of corroding.
CÖR′RU-GATE, *v. a.* To contract into wrinkles.
CÖR-RU-GĀ′TION, *n.* Contraction into wrinkles.
COR-RŬPT′, *v. a.* To infect ; to defile ; to bribe.
COR-RŬPT′, *v. n.* To become putrid or vitiated.
COR-RŬPT′, *a.* Spoiled ; tainted ; putrid ; vicious.
COR-RŬPT′ER, *n.* One that corrupts. [rupted.
COR-RŬPT-I-BĬL′I-TY, *n.* Possibility to be cor-
COR-RŬPT′I-BLE, *a.* Susceptible of corruption.
COR-RŬP′TION, *n.* Putrescence :—deterioration : —wickedness ; depravity :—bribery.
COR-RŬP′TIVE, *a.* Having the quality to taint.
COR-RŬPT′LY, *ad.* With corruption ; viciously.
COR-RŬPT′NESS, *n.* Putrescence ; corruption.
CÖR′SAIR (kör′sår), *n.* A pirate ; a piratical
CÖRSE, *n.* A dead human body ; a corpse. [vessel.
CÖRSE′LET, *n.* A light armor for the breast.
CÖR′SET, *n.* A woman's bodice ; stays.
CÖR′TES, *n.* The legislative body of Spain.
CÖR′TI-CAL, *a.* Belonging to the bark or rind.
CO-RŬS′CANT, *a.* Glittering by flashes ; flashing.
CO-RŬS′CATE, *v. n.* To glitter ; to flash, shine.
CÖR-US-CĀ′TION, *n.* A quick vibration of light.
COR-VĔTTE′, *n.* An advice-boat :—a sloop of war, with less than ten guns. [morant.
CÖR′VO-RANT, *n.* A voracious bird ; the cor-
CÖR-Y-PHĒ′US, *n.* The chief of a company.
COS-MĔT′IC, *n.* A wash to improve the skin.
COS-MĔT′IC, *a.* Increasing beauty ; beautifying.
CŎS′MI-CAL, *a.* Rising or setting with the sun.
COS-MŎG′O-NIST, *n.* One versed in cosmogony.
COS-MŎG′O-NY, *n.* The science which treats of the origin of the world or universe.
COS-MŎG′RA-PHER, *n.* A describer of the world.
CÖS-MO-GRĂPH′I-CAL, *a.* Describing the world.
CÖS-MO-GRĂPH′I-CAL-LY, *ad.* With cosmography ; in a cosmographical manner.
COS-MŎG′RA-PHY, *n.* The science which treats of the construction, figure, &c., of the world.
COS-MŎL′O-GY, *n.* The science of the world.
COS-MŎP′O-LITE, *n.* A citizen of the world ; one who is at home in every place.
CÖS′SET, *n.* A pet lamb :—a pet of any kind.
‖COST (kŏst *or* kâust), *n.* Price ; charge ; expense :—loss ; damage ; detriment. [for.
‖CÖST, *v. a.* [*imp. t. & pp.* cost.] To be bought
CŎS′TAL, *a.* Belonging to the ribs or side.

CŎS'TĄRD, n. A head :—a large kind of apple.
CŎS'TĮVE, a. Bound in the body ; constipated.
CŎS'TĮVE-NĔSS, n. State of being costive.[ness.
‖CŎST'LĮ-NĔSS, n. Sumptuousness ; expensive-
‖CŎST'LY, a. Expensive ; dear ; of great price.
CǪS-TŪME', n. Style or mode of dress.
CŎT, n. A small house ; a cottage :—a small bed.
CŌTE, n. A cottage ; a cot :—a sheep-fold.
CǪ-TĔM'PǪ-RĄ-RY, a. See CONTEMPORARY.
CŌ-TĘ-RIĒ' (kō-tę-rē'), n. A society ; assembly.
CǪ-TĬL'LǪN (kǫ-tĭl'yųn), n. A brisk, lively
dance, usually for eight persons.
CŎT'TĄǴE, n. A hut ; a cot ; a small dwelling.
CŎT'TĄ-ǴĘR, n. One who lives in a cottage.
CŎT'TĘR, CŎT'TIĘR (kŏt'tęr), n. A cottager.
CŎT'TON (kŏt'tn), n. A plant, and its down :—
cloth made of the down of the plant.
CŎÛCH, v. n. To lie down ; to stoop or bend.
CŎÛCH, v. a. To lay down ; to hide :—to in-
clude :—to remove, as cataracts from the eye.
CŎÛCH, n. A seat for reclining on ; a bed.
CŎÛCH'ĄNT, a. Lying down ; squatting.
‖COUGH (kŏf or kâuf), n. Convulsion of the
lungs, with noise. [vulsed.
‖COUGH (kŏf), v. n. To have the lungs con-
COULD (kûd), imp. t. from can. Was able.
CŌUL'TĘR (kōl'tęr), n. See COLTER.
CŎÛN'CĮL, n. An assembly for consultation.
CŎÛN'SĘL, n. Advice ; direction :—a counsellor.
CŎÛN'SĘL, v. a. To give advice to ; to advise.
CŎÛN'SĘL-LǪR, n. One who gives advice :—
a lawyer who advises a client.
CŎÛN'SĘL-LǪR-SHĬP, n. Office of a counsellor.
CŎÛNT, v. a. & n. To number ; to compute ; to
CŎÛNT, n. Number ; charge :—a title. [judge.
CŎÛN'TĘ-NĄNCE, n. The face ; air ; aspect ;
look :—support ; encouragement. [age.
CŎÛN'TĘ-NĄNCE, v. a. To support ; to encour-
CŎÛN'TĘ-NĄN-CĘR, n. One who countenances.
CŎÛN'TĘR, n. Base money :—a shop-table.
CŎÛNT'ĘR, ad. Contrary ; in a wrong way.
CŎÛN-TĘR-ĂCT', v. a. To act contrary to ; to
hinder ; to frustrate ; to defeat. [action.
CŎÛN-TĘR-ĂC'TIǪN, n. Contrary or opposite
CŎÛN-TĘR-BĂL'ĄNCE, v. a. To weigh against.
CŎÛN'TĘR-BĂL-ĄNCE, n. Opposite weight.
CŎÛN'TĘR-CHĂRM', v. a. To disenchant.
CŎÛN'TĘR-CHĔCK, n. A stop ; rebuke ; reproof.
CŎÛN'TĘR-ĔV'Į-DĘNCE, n. Opposite evidence.
CŎÛN'TĘR-FEĬT, v. a. To forge, imitate, copy.
CŎÛN'TĘR-FEĬT, a. Forged ; fictitious ; deceitful.
CŎÛN'TĘR-FEĬT, n. An imposture ; a forgery.
CŎÛN'TĘR-FEĬT-ĘR, n. A forger ; an impostor.
CŎÛN-TĘR-MĂND', v. a. To revoke or recall,
as a command previously given. [der.
CŎÛN'TĘR-MĂND, n. A repeal of a former or-
CŎÛN-TĘR-MĂRCH', v. n. To march back.
CŎÛN'TĘR-MĂRCH, n. A marching back.
CŎÛN'TĘR-MĂRK, n. An aftermark on goods.
CŎÛN-TĘR-MĪNE', v. a. To frustrate ; to defeat.
CŎÛN'TĘR-MŌVE'MĘNT, n. Opposite movement.
CŎÛN'TĘR-MŪRE, n. A wall behind another.
CŎÛN'TĘR-PĀNE, n. A coverlet for a bed.
CŎÛN'TĘR-PĂRT, n. Correspondent part ; copy.
CŎÛN'TĘR-PLĒA, n. (Law.) A replication.
CŎÛN-TĘR-PLŎT', v. a. To oppose by another plot.
CŎÛN'TĘR-PLŎT, n. A plot opposed to another.
CŎÛN'TĘR-PŌĬNT, n. A coverlet ; opposite point.

CŎÛN-TĘR-PŌĬSE', v. a. To counterbalance.
CŎÛN'TĘR-PŌĬSE, n. Equivalence of weight.
CŎÛN-TĘR-PŌĬ'SǪN, n. An antidote to poison.
CŎÛN'TĘR-RĔV-Ǫ-LŪ'TIǪN, n. A revolution
succeeding another, and opposite to it.
CŎÛN'TĘR-SCĂRP, n. A slope next the camp.
CŎÛN-TĘR-SĒAL', v. a. To seal with another.
CŎÛN-TĘR-SĪGN' (kŏûn-tęr-sīn'), v. a. To sign,
as an order of a superior, in quality of secretary.
CŎÛN'TĘR-SĪGN (-sīn), n. Military watchword.
CŎÛN'TĘR-SĬG-NĄL, n. A responsive signal.
CŎÛN-TĘR-SĬNK', v. a. To take off the edge
of, as of a hole to receive the head of a screw.
CŎÛN'TĘR-SĬNK, n. A hole to receive the head
of a screw :—a kind of carpenter's bit.
CŎÛN-TĘR-TĔN'ǪR, n. (Mus.) Second or con-
tralto part when sung by a male voice. [ance.
CŎÛN-TĘR-VĀIL', v. a. To be equal to ; to bal-
CŎÛN'TĘR-VIEW (kŏûn'tęr-vū), n. Contrast.
CŎÛN-TĘR-WORK', v. a. To counteract.
CŎÛNT'ĘSS, n. The wife of an earl or count.
CŎÛNT'ĬNG-HŎÛSE, n. A room for accounts.
CǪÛNT'LĘSS, a. Innumerable ; numberless.
CŎÛN'TRĮ-FĪED (kŭn'trę-fīd), a. Rustic ; rude.
CŎÛN'TRY (kŭn'trę), n. A region ; native
soil :—inhabitants ; people :—rural parts.
CŎÛN'TRY (kŭn'trę), a. Rustic ; rural ; rude.
CŎÛN'TRY-MĄN (kŭn'trę-mąn), n. One born
in the same country ; a rustic ; a farmer.
CŎÛN'TY, n. A shire ; a circuit, or district.
CŎÛP'LE (kŭp'pl), n. Two ; a pair ; man and
CŎÛP'LE (kŭp'pl), v. a. To join ; to marry. [wife.
CŎÛP'LE (kŭp'pl), v. n. To join in embraces.
CŎÛP'LĘT (kŭp'lęt), n. Two verses ; a pair.
CŎÛR'ĄǴE (kŭr'ąj), n. Bravery ; valor ; boldness.
CǪÛR-Ā'ǴEǪŲS (kųr-rā'jųs), a. Brave ; daring.
CǪÛR-Ā'ǴEǪŲS-LY (kųr-rā'jųs-lę), ad. Bravely.
CǪÛR-Ā'ǴEǪŲS-NĔSS, n. Bravery ; boldness.
CŎU-RĂNT' (kô-ränt'), n. A nimble dance :—any
thing that spreads quick, as a newspaper.
CŎÛ'RIĘR (kô'rēr), n. A messenger sent in haste.
CŌURSE (kōrs), n. Race ; career ; progress ; or-
der ; conduct ; service of food ; ship's track.
CŌURSE (kōrs), v. a. & n. To hunt ; to make
to run ; to pursue ; to run ; to rove about.
CŌURS'ĘR (kōrs'ęr), n. A race-horse :—a hunter.
CŌURS'ĬNG, n. Sport of hunting with hounds.
CŌURT (kōrt), n. Residence of a prince ; a hall ;
a narrow street ; seat of justice ; jurisdiction.
CŌURT (kōrt), v. a. To woo ; to solicit ; to seek.
‖CŎÛR'TĘ-ǪÛS (kŭr'tę-ŭs or kōrt'yųs), a. Po-
lite ; well-bred ; affable ; civil ; respectful.
‖CŎÛR'TĘ-ǪÛS-LY, ad. Politely ; respectfully.
‖CŎÛR'TĘ-ǪŲS-NĔSS, n. Civility ; complaisance.
CŎÛR-TĘ-ŞĂN' (kŭr-tę-zăn'), n. A prostitute.
CŎÛR'TĘ-SY (kŭr'tę-sę), n. Civility ; politeness.
CŎÛRTE'SY (kŭrt'sę), n. Act of civility made
by women by gently bending the body. [tesy.
CŎÛRTE'SY (kŭrt'sę), v. n. To make a cour-
CŌURT'-HĂND, n. Writing used in records, &c.
CŌURT'IĘR (kōrt'yęr), n. An attendant on a
CŌURT'LĮ-NĔSS, n. Elegance of manners. [court.
CŌURT'LY, a. Relating to a court ; courteous.
CŌURT'-MĂR'TIĄL, n. A military tribunal.
CŌURT'SHĬP, n. A making of love to a woman.
CŎÛŞ'IN (kŭz'zn), n. One collaterally related.
CŌVE, n. A small creek or bay ; a shelter.
CŎV'Ę-NĄNT, n. A contract ; agreement ; deed.

CŎV′Ę-NĂNT, *v. n.*   To bargain ; to contract.
CŎV-Ę-NĄNT-ĒĒ′, *n.*   A party to a covenant.
CŎV′Ę-NĄNT-ĘR,*n.* One who makes a covenant.
CŎV′Ę-NOŬS,*a.* Fraudulent ; collusive ; trickish.
CŎV′ĘR,*v.a.* To overspread ; to conceal ; to hide.
CŎV′ĘR, *n.*   A concealment ; a screen ; defence.
CŎV′ĘR-ĬNG, *n.*   Cover ; dress ; vesture.
CŎV′ĘR-LĔT, *n.*   The upper covering of a bed.
CŎV′ĘRT, *n.*   A shelter ; a defence ; a thicket.
CŎV′ĘRT, *a.*   Sheltered ; private ; insidious.
CŎV′ĘRT-LY, *ad.*   Secretly ; closely ; privately.
CŎV′ĘRT-ŪRE, *n.*   Shelter :—the state of a wife.
CŎV′ĘT, *v. a. & n.*   To desire eagerly or inor-
CŎV′ĘT-OŬS, *a.*   Avaricious ; greedy. [dinately.
CŎV′ĘT-OŬS-LY, *ad.*   Avariciously ; eagerly.
CŎV′ĘT-OŬS-NĔSS, *n.*   State of being covet-
ous ; avarice : –eagerness of desire.
CŎV′ĘY (kŭv′vę), *n.*   A hatch or brood of birds.
CŎV′ĬN, *n.*   (*Law.*) A fraudulent agreement.·
CŎV′ĬNG, *n.*   Exterior projection in a building.
CŎW, *n. ;* pl. CŎWŞ *or* †KĪNE.   Tȟe female of
the bull, or of bovine animals.   [awe.
CŎW (kŏû), *v. a.*   To depress with fear ; to over-
CŎW′ARD, *n.*   A poltroon ; one wanting courage.
CŎW′ARD-ĪCE, *n.*   Fear ; habitual timidity.
CŎW′ARD-LĮ-NĔSS, *n.*   Timidity ; cowardice.
CŎW′ARD-LY, *a.*   Fearful ; timorous ; mean. .
CŎW′ĘR, *v. n.*   To sink by bending the knees.
CŎW′HĔRD, *n.*   One who tends cows.
CŎWL, *n.*   A monk's hood : –a vessel for water.
CŎWL′-STĂFF, *n.*   The staff on which a cowl
or vessel is supported between two men.
CŎW′-PŎX, *n.*   The vaccine disease ; kine-pox.
CŎW′SLĬP, *n.*   A plant ; a species of primrose.
CŎX′CŌMB (kŏks′kōm), *n.*   A fop :—cockscomb.
CŎX′CŌMB-RY (kŏks′kōm-rę), *n.*   Foppishness.
CǪX-CŎM′Į-CĄL, *a.*   Foppish ; conceited ; vain.
CŎY, *a.*   Modest ; reserved ; not accessible.
CŎY′ĬSH, *a.*   Somewhat coy ; reserved ; shy.
CŎY′LY, *ad.*   With reserve ; modestly ; shyly.
CŎY′NĘSS, *n.*   Reserve ; shyness ; modesty.
CŎZ′EN (kŭz′zn), *v. a.*   To cheat ; to defraud.
CŎZ′EN-ĄĢE (kŭz′zn-ąj), *n.*   Fraud ; deceit.
CŎZ′EN-ĘR (kŭz′zn-ęr), *n.*   One who cheats.
,CRĂB, *n.*   A crustacean :—a wild apple :—a churl.
CRĂB′BĘD, *a.*Peevish ; morose ; harsh ; difficult.
CRĂB′BĘD-NĔSS, *n.*   Sourness of taste ; asperity.
CRĂCK, *n.*   A sudden noise ; a fissure ; a boast.
CRĂCK, *v. a. & n.*   To break into chinks ; to split.
CRĂCK′-BRĀINED (krăk′brāned), *a.*   Crazy.
CRĂCK′ĘR, *n.*   A charge of gunpowder, in a
roll :—a boaster :—a hard kind of biscuit.
CRĂC′KLE, *v. n.*   To make small, sharp, ex-
plosive sounds ; to decrepitate ; to snap.
CRĂCK′LĬNG, *n.*   A sharp and frequent noise.
CRĀ′DLE, *n.*   A movable bed for infants :—a
kind of scythe for mowing grain.
CRĀ′DLE, *v. a.*   To lay or rock in a cradle. [sel.
CRĂFT, *n.*   Trade ; art ; cunning :—sailing ves-
CRĂFT′Į-LY, *ad.*   Cunningly ; artfully ; skilfully.
CRĂFT′Į-NĔSS, *n.*   Cunning ; stratagem ; craft.
CRĂFTS′MĄN, *n.*   An artificer ; a mechanic.
CRĂFT′Y, *a.*   Cunning ; artful ; sly ; shrewd.
CRĂG, *n.*   A rough, steep rock :—the neck.
CRĂG′ĠĘD, *a.*   Rough ; full of prominences.
CRĂG′ĠY, *a.*   Rugged ; full of prominences.
CRĂM, *v. a. & n.*   To stuff ; to eat greedily.
CRĂM′BŌ, *n.*   A sort of play :—a rhyme.

CRĂMP, *n.*   A spasm :—restraint :—a crampiron.
CRĂMP, *v. a.*   To restrain ; to confine ; to bind.
CRĂMP′-FĬSH, *n.*   A kind of fish ; the torpedo.
CRĂMP′ĪR-ON, *n.*   A piece of iron, bent at the
ends, for fastening things together.
CRĂM′PĬT, *n.*   A thin plate or piece of metal at
the bottom of the scabbard of a broadsword.
CRĂN′BĘR-RY, *n.*   A red berry used for sauce.
CRĀNE, *n.*   A bird :—a machine :—a bent tube.
CRĂN-Į-Ǫ-LŎĢ′Į-CĄL, *a.*   Relating to craniology.
CRĂN-Į-ŎL′Ǫ-ĠY, *n.*   Phrenology.   [to turn it.
CRĂNK, *n.*   The end of an iron axis bent so as
CRĂNK, *a.*   Liable to lean over, as a ship :—jolly.
CRĂN′NĮED (krăn′nĭd), *a.*   Full of chinks.
CRĂN′NY, *n.*   A chink ; a fissure ; a crevice.
CRĀPE, *n.*   A thin stuff used in mourning, &c.
CRĂP′Ų-LĔNCE, *n.*   Sickness by intemperance.
CRĂSH,*v. n.* To make a loud, complicated noise.
CRĂSH, *n.*   A loud, mixed sound :—coarse cloth.
CRĂS′SĮ-TŪDE, *n.*   Grossness ; coarseness.
CRĂTCH, *n.*   A frame for hay ; a manger ; a crib.
CRĀTE,*n.* A sort of basket or wicker pannier.
CRĀ′TĘR, *n.*   The vent or mouth of a volcano.
CRĀUNCH (kranch), *v.a.*   To crush in the mouth.
CRĄ-VĂT′, *n.*   A cloth worn about the neck.
CRĀVE, *v. a.*   To ask earnestly for ; to long for.
CRĀ′VEN (krā′vn), *n.*   A cock conquered :—a
CRĀ′VEN (krā′vn), *a.*   Cowardly ; base.[coward.
CRÂW, *n.*   The crop or first stomach of birds.
CRÂW′FĬSH, CRĀY′FĬSH, *n.*   A crustaceous fish.
CRÂWL, *v. n.*   To creep ; to move as a worm.
CRĀY′ǪN (krā′ŭn), *n.*   A kind of pencil ; a de-
sign or drawing executed with a crayon.
CRĀZE,*v. a.* To break :—to impair in intellect.
CRĀ′ZĮ-NĔSS, *n.*   Shattered state :—insanity.
CRĀ′ZY, *a.*   Broken ; disordered in mind ; insane.
CRĒAK, *v. n.*   To make a harsh, grating noise.
CRĒAM, *n.*   The oily part of milk :—best part.
CRĒAM,*v. n. & a.* To be covered with some-
thing on the surface : –to take the best of.
CRĒAM′Y, *a.*   Having the nature of cream.
CRĒASE, *n.*   A mark made by doubling a thing.
CRĒASE, *v. a.*   To mark by doubling.
CRĘ-ĀTE′, *v. a.*   To make ; to cause ; to produce.
CRĘ-Ā′TIǪN, *n.*   Act of creating ; the universe.
CRĘ-Ā′TĮVE, *a.*   Having the power to create.
CRĘ-Ā′TǪR, *n.*   One who creates ; a maker :—
Supreme Being ; the Author of all things.
CRĒAT′ŲRE (krēt′yur),*n.* A created being ; man.
CRĒ′DĘNCE, *n.*   Belief ; credit ; reputation.
CRĘ-DĔN′DA, *n. pl.*   Things to be believed.
CRĒ′DĘNT, *a.*   Believing ; credulous :—deserv-
ing belief or credit ; not to questioned.
CRĘ-DĔN′TIĄL,*n.* That which entitles to credit.
CRĔD-Į-BĬL′Į-TY, *n.*   Claim to credit or belief.
CRĔD′Į-BLE, *a.*   Worthy of credit or belief.
CRĔD′Į-BLY, *ad.*   In a manner that claims belief.
CRĔD′ĮT, *n.*   Belief ; honor ; reputation ; trust.
CRĔD′ĮT, *v. a.*   To believe, trust, confide in.
CRĔD′ĮT-Ą-BLE, *a.*   Reputable ; honorable.[tion.
CRĔD′ĮT-Ą-BLE-NĔSS, *n.*   Reputation ; estima-
CRĔD′ĮT-ǪR, *n.*   One to whom a debt is owed.
CRĘ-DŪ′LĮ-TY, *n.*   Easiness of belief ; readi-
ness to believe ; credulousness.   [ceived.
CRĔD′Ų-LOŬS, *a.*   Apt to believe ; easily de-
CRĔD′Ų-LOŬS-LY, *ad.*   In a credulous manner.
CRĔD′Ų-LOŬS-NĔSS, *n.*   Credulity.   [of belief.
CREED, *n.*   A summary or statement of articles

CRĔĔK, *v. n.* To creak. See CREAK.
CRĔĔK, *n.* A small inlet or river ; a bay ; a cove.
CRĔĔK'Y, *a.* Full of, or having, creeks; winding.
CRĔĔP, *v. n.* [*imp. t.* and *pp.* crept.] To move slowly, or as a worm or insect :—to fawn.
CRĔĔP'ER, *n.* A plant; an insect :—a grapnel.
CRĔĔP'-HÖLE, *n.* A retreat ; a subterfuge ; ex-
CRĔ'NÁT-ĘD, *a.* Notched ; indented. [cuse.
CRĔ'ÖLE, *n.* A person born in Spanish Amer-ica or the West Indies,but of European descent.
CRĔ'Q-SÖTE, *n.* An antiseptic, oily liquid.
CRĔP'I-TĀTE, *v. n.* To make a crackling noise.
CRĔP-I-TĀ'TIQN, *n.* A small, crackling noise.
CRĔPT, *imp. t.* & *pp.* from *creep.* [mering.
CRĘ-PŪS'CU-LAR, *a.* Relating to twilight ; glim-
CRĔS'CĘNT, *a.* Increasing ; growing ; enlarging.
CRĔS'CĘNT, *n.* The moon in her state of increase.
CRĔSS, *n.* A name given to various plants.
CRĔS'SĘT, *n.* A beacon :—a cooper's frame.
CRĔST, *n.* A plume of feathers ; comb ; a tuft.
CRĔST'ĘD, *a.* Adorned with a plume or crest.
CRĔST'-FÂLLEN (krĕst'-fåln), *a.* Dejected.
CRĘ-TĀ'CEOŲS (krę-tä'shŭs), *a.* Having the qualities of chalk ; like chalk ; chalky.
CRĔV'ICE, *n.* A crack ; a cleft ; a fissure ; a gap.
CREW (krū), *n.* A company ; a ship's company.
CREW (krū), *imr. t.* from *crow.* [on a ball.
CREW'ĘL (krū'ęl), *n.* Yarn or worsted wound
CRĬB, *n.* A manger ; a stall ; a bin ; a child's bed.
CRĬB, *v. a.* To steal for a petty purpose :—to
CRĬB'BAĢE, *n.* A game at cards. [cage.
CRĬCK, *n.* Creaking:—cramp, as in the neck.
CRĬCK'ĘT, *n.* An insect :—a stool :—a game.
CRĪ'ĘR, *n.* One who cries goods for sale, &c.
CRĪME, *n.* An offence ; a great fault ; a felony.
CRĬM'I-NAL, *a.* Faulty ; contrary to law ; guilty.
CRĬM'I-NAL, *n.* One guilty of a crime ; a felon.
CRĬM-I-NĂL'I-TY, *n.* State of being criminal.
CRĬM'I-NAL-LY, *ad.* Wickedly ; guiltily.[crime.
CRĬM'I-NĀTE, *v. a.* To accuse ; to charge with
CRĬM-I-NĀ'TIQN, *n.* Accusation ; censure.
CRĬM'I-NA-TQ-RY, *a.* Accusing ; censorious.
CRĬMP, *a.* Friable ; brittle ; easily crumbled.
CRĬMP, *n.* An agent for coal-merchants. [plait.
CRĬMP, *v. a.* To curl, or crisp, as the hair ; to
CRĬM'PLE, *v. a.* To contract ; to corrugate.
CRĬM'ŞON (krĭm'zn), *n.* A deep red color.
CRĬM'ŞON (krĭm'zn), *a.* Of a deep red ; dark red.
CRĬM'ŞON (krĭm'zn), *v. a.* To dye with crimson.
CRĬNĢE, *n.* A servile bow ; mean civility.
CRĬNĢE, *v. n.* To bow servilely ; to fawn.
CRĬNĢ'ĘR, *n.* One who cringes ; a fawner.
CRĬN'KLE, *v. n.* & *a.* To run in flexures ; to
CRĬN'KLE, *n.* A wrinkle ; a sinuosity.[wrinkle.
CRĬN'Q-LĪNE, *n.* Stiff cloth for women's skirts : —an expansive skirt worn by women.
CRĬP'PLE, *n.* A lame person. [disable.
CRĬP'PLE, *v. a.* To lame ; to make lame :—to
CRĪ'SIS, *n.* ; *pl.* CRĪ'SĒŞ. A critical time or turn : —decisive point or period of a disease. [brisk.
CRĬSP, *a.* Curled :—brittle ; friable :—lively ;
CRĬSP, *v. a.* To curl ; to twist ; to make brittle.
CRĬSP'ING-ĪR-ON, *n.* An iron for crisping or
CRĬSP'NĘSS, *n.* Quality of being crisped.[curling.
CRĬSP'Y, *a.* Curled ; frizzled ; short and brittle.
CRĬ-TĒ'RI-QN, *n.* ; *pl.* CRĪ-TĒ'RI-A. A standard or mark by which any thing is judged of ; a test ; a measure.

CRĬT'IC, *n.* One skilled in criticism ; a judge.
CRĬT'I-CAL, *a.* Exact ; nice ;judicious ; decisive.
CRĬT'I-CAL-LY, *ad,* In a critical manner.
CRĬT'I-CAL-NĔSS, *n.* Quality of being critical ; exactness ; accuracy ; nicety. [judge.
CRĬT'I-CĪSE, *v. n.* & *a.* To act the critic ; to
CRĬT'I-CĬŞM, *n.* Art or act of judging ; critique.
CRI-TÎQUE' (krę-tēk'), *n.* A critical examina-tion ; critical remarks ; criticism ; review.
CRŌAK, *v. n.* To make a hoarse noise :—to mur-
CRŌAK (krōk), *n.* The cry of a frog, &c. [mur.
CRŌAK'ĘR, *n.* One who croaks ; a murmurer.
CRŌ'CEOŲS (krō'shŭs), *a.* Consisting of saffron.
CRŌCK, *n.* A cup or vessel made of earth ; soot.
CRŌCK'ĘR-Y, *n.* Earthen ware or vessels.
CRŎC'Q-DĪLE *or* CRŎC'Q-DĬLE, *n.* A large an-imal of the lizard tribe. [spring.
CRŌ'CŲS, *n.* A plant which flowers early in
CRŎFT, *n.* A little field adjoining a house.
CRŌNE, *n.* An old ewe :—an old woman.
CRŌ'NY, *n.* A bosom companion ; an associate.
CROOK (krŭk), *n.* A shepherd's hook :—a curve.
CROOK (krŭk), *v. a.* & *n.* To bend ; to pervert.
CROOK'ĘD (krŭk'ęd), *a.* Bent ; not straight.
CROOK'ĘD-NĔSS (krŭk'ęd-nĕs), *n.* Curvity.
CRŎP, *n.* Harvest :—the first stomach of birds.
CRŎP, *v. a.* To lop ; to gather, as fruit ; to plant.
CRŌ'ŞIĘR (krō'zhŭr), *n.* A bishop's staff.
‖CRŎSS (krŏs *or* kráus), *n.* A figure thus [+] , ensign of Christianity ; trial ; misfortune.
‖CRŎSS, *a.* Transverse ; peevish ; fretful.
‖CRŎSS, *v. a.* To lay athwart ; to thwart ; to vex.
‖CRŎSS'-BÄR, *n.* A transverse bar :—a lever.
‖CRŎSS'-BĬLL, *n.* Bill of a defendant :—a bird.
‖CRŎSS'BŌW, *n.* A weapon for shooting.
‖CRŎSS'-ĘX-ĂM'INE, *v. a.* To examine, as an opposite party ; to cross-question.
‖CRŎSS'-ĘX-ĂM-I-NĀ'TIQN, *n.* Examination of a witness of one party by the opposite party.
‖CRŎSS'-GRĀINED (krŏs'grānd), *a.* Having the fibres transverse :—ill-natured :—troublesome.
‖CRŎSS'-LĔGGED (-lĕgd), *a.* Having the legs crossed. [adversely ; peevishly.
‖CRŎSS'LY, *ad.* In a cross manner :—athwart ;
‖CRŎSS'-PŬR-PQSE, *n.* A kind of enigma.
‖CRŎSS'-QUĔS-TIQN, *v. a.* To cross-examine.
‖CRŎSS'-RŌAD, *n.* A road across the country.
‖CRŎSS'-WĀY, *n.* A path crossing the chief road.
‖CRŎSS'-WĬND, *n.* Wind blowing across.
CRŎTCH, *n.* A hook :—the fork of a tree.
CRŎTCH'ĘT, *n.* A note in music ;—*pl.* Marks [thus] ; hooks : — called also *brackets.*
CRŌÛCH, *v. n.* To stoop low ; to fawn ; to cringe.
CRŌUP (krôp), *n.* A disease affecting the throat.
CRŌW (krō), *v. n.* [*imp. t.* crew, crowed ; *pp.* crowed.] To cry as a cock ; to boast ; to vaunt.
CRŌW, *n.* A bird :—iron lever :—cock's voice.
CRŌWD, *n.* A confused multitude ; populace.
CRŌWD, *v. a.* To press close ; to urge ; to swarm.
CRŌWN, *n.* A royal diadem :—top of the head : —regal power ; honor :—a coin :—a garland.
CRŌWN, *v. a.* To invest with a crown ; to reward.
CRŌWN'-GLĂSS, *n.* A fine sort of window-glass.
CRŌWN'-ĮM-PĒ'RI-AL, *n.* A plant and its flower.
CRŌWN'ING, *n.* The finishing of any decoration.
CRŌWN'-WHĔĔL, *n.* A wheel of a watch.
CRŌW'Ş'-FĒĒT, *n. pl.* Wrinkles under the eyes.
CRŌW'Ş'FOOT (krŏz'fůt), *n.* A sort of plant.

CRŬ'CĮ-BLE, *n.* A chemist's melting-pot.
CRŬ'CĮ-FÍX, *n.* A representation, in painting or sculpture, of our Saviour on the cross.
CRŬ-CĮ-FÍX'ĮQN (krŭ-sẹ-fĭk'shṳn), *n.* Mode of putting to death by nailing to a cross.
CRŬ'CĮ-FÖRM, *a.* Having the form of a cross.
CRŬ'CĮ-FȲ, *v. a.* To nail or fasten to a cross:—to overcome by influence of Christian principles.
CRŬDE, *a.* Raw; harsh; unripe; undigested.
CRŬDE'LȲ, *ad.* In a crude manner; unripely.
CRŬDE'NĘSS, *n.* Rawness; unripeness; crudity.
CRŬ'DĮ-TȲ, *n.* Indigestion; unripeness.
CRŬ'ĘL, *a.* Inhuman; hardhearted; savage.
CRŬ'ĘL-LȲ, *ad.* In a cruel manner; savagely.
CRŬ'ĘL-NĔSS, *n.* Inhumanity; cruelty. [ness.
CRŬ'ĘL-TȲ, *n.* Inhumanity; barbarity; savage-
CRŬ'ĘT, *n.* A sort of vial for vinegar or oil, &c.
CRŬISE (krŭs), *n.* A small bottle; a cruet. [sel.
CRŬIŞE (krŭz), *n.* A voyage, as of an armed ves-
CRŬIŞE, *v. n.* To rove over the sea.
CRŬIŞ'ĘR, *n.* A person, or vessel, that cruises.
CRŬMB, CRŬM, *n.* A small particle, as of bread.
CRŬMB, *v. a.* To break into small pieces.
CRŬM'BLE, *v. a.* To break into small pieces.
CRŬM'MY, *a.* Soft; consisting of crumbs.
CRŬM'PLE, *v. a. & n.* To wrinkle; to rumple.
CRŬP'PĘR, *n.* A strap to keep a saddle right.
CRŬ'RAL, *a.* Belonging to the leg; like a leg.
CRŲ-SĀDE', *n.* Expedition against infidels:—a romantic enterprise:—a Portuguese coin.
CRŲ-SĀD'ĘR, *n.* One employed in a crusade.
CRŬ'SĘT, *n.* A goldsmith's melting-pot. [due.
CRŬSH, *v. a.* To squeeze; to bruise:—to sub-
CRŬSH, *n.* A collision; act of rushing together.
CRŬST, *n.* External coat; outer part of bread, &c.
CRŬST, *v. a. & n.* To envelop; to incrust.
CRŲS-TĀ'CEOŲS (krŭs-tā'shŭs), *a.* Shelly, with joints, as a lobster, &c. [jointed shells.
CRŲS-TĀ'CEOŲS-NĔSS, *n.* The state of having
CRŲS-TĀ'TĮQN, *n.* An incrustation.
CRŬST'Į-LȲ, *ad.* Peevishly; snappishly; testily.
CRŬST'Į-NĔSS, *n.* Quality of crust; peevishness.
CRŬST'Ȳ, *a.* Covered with a crust:—morose.
CRŬTCH, *n.* A support or staff used by cripples.
CRŬTCH, *v. a.* To support on crutches, as a cripple; to give support to. [claim.
CRȲ, *v. n. & a.* To call:—to weep:—to pro-
CRȲ, *n.* Outcry; shriek:—weeping:—clamor.
CRȲPT, *n.* A subterranean cell or cave; a tomb.
CRȲP-TŎG'RA-PHȲ, *n.* Art of writing in cipher.
CRȲS'TAL, *n.* A regular, solid, inorganic body:—a superior kind of glass:—a watch-glass.
CRȲS'TAL,   } *a.* Consisting of, or resem-
CRȲS'TAL-LĪNE, } bling, crystal; bright; pellucid; transparent; clear. [lizing.
CRȲS-TAL-LĮ-ZĀ'TĮQN, *n.* The act of crystal-
CRȲS'TAL-LĪZE, *v. a.* To form into crystals.
CRȲS'TAL-LĪZE, *v. n.* To be converted into crystals. [lization, or of crystals.
CRȲS-TAL-LŎG'RA-PHȲ, *n.* Science of crystal-
CŬB, *n.* Young of a beast, as of a bear or fox.
CŬB, *v. n.* To bring forth cubs, as a bear.
CŪ'BA-TŪRE, *n.* Measurement of cubic contents.
CŪBE, *n.* A square, solid body of six equal sides.
CŪ'BĘB, *n.* A small, spicy berry; Java pepper.
CŪ'BĮC, CŪ'BĮ-CAL, *a.* Having the form of a cube.
CŪ'BĮT, *n.* A measure from 18 to 22 inches.
CŪ'BĮ-TAL, *a.* Containing the length of a cubit.

CŬCK'ĮNG-STÔÔL, *n.* Engine to punish scolds.
CŬCK'QLD, *n.* The husband of an adulteress.
CŬCK'QL-DŎM, *n.* State of a cuckold; adultery.
CŬCK'ÔÔ, *n.* A well-known passerine bird.
CŲ-CŬL'LATE, *or* CŲ-CŬL'LĀT-ĘD, *a.* Hooded.
CŬ'CŲM-BĘR (kŭ'kṳm-bẹr), *n.* A plant, and fruit.
CŪ'CŲR-BĬT, *n.* A chemical distilling vessel.
CŬD, *n.* Food reposited in the first stomach of an animal in order to chew it again. [hug.
CŬD'DLE, *v. n. & a.* To lie close or snug; to
CŬD'GĘL, *n.* A short stick to strike with; a club.
CŬD'GĘL, *v. a.* To beat or punish with a cudgel.
CŪE (kū), *n.* The tail or end of any thing:—a hint:—a straight rod used in playing billiards.
CŬFF, *n.* A blow; a stroke:—part of a sleeve.
CŬFF, *v. n.* To fight; to box.—*v. a.* To strike.
CŲĮ-RĂSS' (kwẹ-răs'), *n.* A breastplate.
CUÎ-RAS-SIÊR', *n.* A soldier with a cuirass.
CUÏSSE, CUÏSH (kwĭs), *n.* Armor for the thigh.
CŪ'LĮ-NA-RȲ, *a.* Relating to the kitchen or cookery
CŬLL, *v. a.* To select from others; to pick out.
CŬLL'ĘR, *n.* One who picks or chooses.
CŬLL'ĮQN (kŭl'yṳn), *n.* A scoundrel; a wretch.
CŬL'LȲ, *n.* A mean dupe.—*v. a.* To befool, cheat.
CŬLM, *n.* A kind of fossil coal:—stem of grass.
CŲL-MĬF'ĘR-OŬS, *a.* Producing culms or stalks.
CŬL'MĮ-NĀTE, *v. n.* To be in the meridian.
CŬL-MĮ-NĀ'TĮQN, *n.* A coming to the meridian.
CŬL-PA-BĬL'Į-TȲ, *n.* Blamableness; faultiness.
CŬL'PA-BLE, *a.* Criminal; guilty; blamable.
CŬL'PA-BLE-NĔSS, *n.* Blamableness; guilt.
CŬL'PA-BLȲ, *ad.* Blamably; faultily; guiltily.
CŬL'PRĮT, *n.* A man arraigned; a criminal.
CŬL'TĮ-VA-BLE, *a.* Capable of cultivation.
CŬL'TĮ-VĀTE, *v. a.* To till; to labor; to improve.
CŬL-TĮ-VĀ'TĮQN, *n.* Act of improving soils, &c.
CŬL-TĮ-VĀ-TQR, *n.* One that cultivates.
CŬLT'ŲRE (kŭlt'yṳr), *n.* Cultivation; tillage.
CŬL'VĘR, *n.* A sort of pigeon or dove.
CŬL'VĘR-ĬN, *n.* A long kind of cannon.
CŬM'BĘR, *v. a.* To embarrass; to entangle.
CŬM'BĘR, *n.* Vexation; burdensomeness.
CŬM'BĘR-SŎME, *a.* Troublesome; burdensome.
CŬM'BRANCE, *n.* Encumbrance; hinderance.
CŬM'BROŲS, *a.* Troublesome; burdensome.
CŬM'ĮN, *n.* A plant with aromatic seeds. [mulate.
CŪ'MŲ-LĀTE, *v. a.* To heap together; to accu-
CŪ-MŲ-LĀ'TĮQN, *n.* Act of heaping together.
CŪ'MŲ-LA-TĬVE, *a.* Consisting of parts heaped
CŪ'NE-AL, *a.* Relating to, or like, a wedge. [up.
CŪ'NE-ÀT-ĘD, *a.* Made in form of a wedge.
CŲ-NĒ'Į-FÖRM, *a.* Having the form of a wedge.
CŬN'NĮNG, *a.* Skilful; artful; sly; subtle; crafty.
CŬN'NĮNG, *n.* Artifice; slyness; art; knowledge.
CŬN'NĮNG-LȲ, *ad.* Artfully; slyly; skilfully.
CŬN'NĮNG-NĔSS, *n.* Artifice; slyness; craftiness.
CŬP, *n.* A drinking vessel:—a part of a flower.
CŬP, *v. a.* To draw blood from by scarification.
CŬP'-BEÀR-ĘR (kŭp'bár-er), *n.* An officer of a king's household:—an attendant at a feast.
CŬP'BOARD (kŭb'hṳrd), *n.* A case with shelves.
CŪ'PĘL, *n.* A cup used in assaying metals.
CŲ-PĘL-LĀ'TĮQN, *n.* The assaying of metals.
CŲ-PĬD'Į-TȲ, *n.* Strong desire; avarice.
CŪ'PQ-LA, *n.* A dome; an arched roof; a small structure raised on a dome or on a roof.
CŬP'PĘR, *n.* One who cups; a scarifier.
CŪ'PRĘ-OŬS, *a.* Coppery; consisting of copper.

CŬR, *n.* A dog :—a snappish, mean person.
CŪR′A̱-BLE, *a.* Admitting a remedy or cure.
CŪ′RA̱-CY, *n.* Office or employment of a curate.
CŪ′RA̱TE, *n.* A parish priest or minister. [cure.
CŪ′RA̱-TĬVE, *a.* Relating to cure ; tending to
CY̱-RĀ′TǪR, *n.* Superintendent ; a guardian.
CŬRB, *n.* Part of a bridle :—restraint ; inhibition.
CŬRB, *v. a.* To restrain ; to check ; to bridle.
CŬRD, *n.* The coagulated part of milk. [agulate.
CŬR′DLE, *v. n. & a.* To change into curd ; to co-
CŪRE, *n.* Remedy ; a healing :—curate's office.
CŪRE, *v. a.* To heal; to restore to health:—to salt.
CŪRE′LESS, *a.* Without cure ; without remedy.
CŬR′E̱R, *n.* One who cures ; a healer.
CŬR′FEW̄, *n.* An evening bell :—a fireplate.
CŪ-RĬ-ŎS′Ḭ-TY̱, *n.* Inquisitiveness :—a rarity.
CŪ′RḬ-OŬS, *a.* Inquisitive :—rare :—accurate.
CŪ′RḬ-OŬS-LY̱, *ad.* In a curious manner ; exactly.
CŪ′RḬ-OŲS-NĔSS, *n.* Inquisitiveness :—nicety.
CŬRL, *n.* A ringlet of hair :—wave ; flexure.
CŬRL, *v. a. & n.* To turn in ringlets ; to twist.
CŬR′LEW̄ (kür′lu), *n.* A kind of water-fowl.
CŬRL′Ḭ-NĔSS, *n.* The state of being curled.
CŬRL′Y̱, *a.* Having curls ; tending to curl.
CY̱R-MŬD′GE̱ǪN (kŭr-mŭd′jŭn), *n.* A miser.
CŬR′RA̱NT, *n.* Name of a shrub and its fruit.
CŬR′RE̱N-CY̱, *n.* Circulation ; flow :—money.
CŬR′RE̱NT, *a.* Circulating ; common ; passing.
CŬR′RE̱NT, *n.* A running stream ; course.
CŬR′RE̱NT-LY̱, *ad.* In a current manner. [tion.
CŬR′RE̱NT-NĔSS, *n.* Circulation ; general recep-
CŬR′RḬ-CLE, *n.* An open chaise with two wheels.
CŬR′RḬ-E̱R, *n.* One who dresses leather. [pish.
CŬR′RḬSH, *a.* Like a cur ; brutal ; sour ; snap-
CŬR′RY̱, *v. a.* To dress, as leather ; to beat ; to
CŬR′RY̱, *n.* A highly-spiced Indian mixture.[rub.
CŬR′RY̱-CŌMB (kŭr′re̱-kōm), *n.* An iron comb.
CŬRSE, *v. a.* To wish evil to ; to execrate.
CŬRSE, *n.* A malediction ; affliction ; torment.
CŬR′SE̱D, *a.* Deserving a curse ; hateful ; unholy.
CŬR′SE̱D-LY̱, *ad.* Miserably ; shamefully.
CŬRS′E̱R, *n.* One who utters curses.
CŬR′SḬ-TǪR, *n.* A clerk in the court of chancery.
CŬR′SǪ-RḬ-LY̱, *ad.* Hastily ; slightly.
CŬR′SǪ-RY̱, *a.* Hasty ; quick ; slight ; careless ;
　desultory ; done rapidly. [abridge.
CY̱R-TĀIL′, *v. a.* To cut off ; to shorten ; to
CY̱R-TĀIL′E̱R, *n.* One who curtails ; an abridger.
CŬR′TAḬN (kür′tḭn), *n.* A cloth hanging round
　a bed, at a window, or in a theatre, &c.
CŬR′TAḬN, *v. a.* To furnish with curtains.
CŪ′RŪLE, *a.* Belonging to a chair ; magisterial.
CŬR′VĀT-E̱D, *a.* Bent ; crooked ; curved.
CY̱R-VĀ′TḬǪN, *n.* Act of bending or crooking.
CŬR′VA̱-TŪRE, *n.* Crookedness ; bent form.
CŬRVE, *a.* Crooked ; bent.—*n.* Any thing bent.

CŬRVE (kürv), *v. a.* To bend ; to crook.
CY̱R-VĔT′, *v. n.* To leap ; to bound ; to frisk.
CY̱R-VĔT′, *n.* A leap ; a bound ; a frolic ; a prank.
CŬR-VḬ-LĬN′E̱-A̱R, *a.* Consisting of a curved line.
CŬSH′IǪN (kûsh′ŭn), *n.* Pillow or pad for a seat.
CŬSH′IǪNED (kûsh′ŭnd), *a.* Seated on a cushion.
CŬSP, *n.* The point or horn of the moon, &c.
CŬS′PḬ-DA̱TE, CŬS′PḬ-DĀT-E̱D, *a.* Pointed. [&c.
CŬS′TA̱RD, *n.* Food made of eggs, milk, sugar,
CŬS′TǪ-DY̱, *n.* Imprisonment ; care ; security.
CŬS′TǪM, *n.* Habit ; habitual practice ; usage ;
　fashion :— duty ; impost ; toll ; tax ; tribute.
CŬS′TǪM-A̱-BLE, *a.* Common ; habitual, fre-
　quent :—chargeable with duties or impost.
CŬS′TǪM-A̱-RḬ-LY̱, *ad.* Habitually ; commonly.
CŬS′TǪM-A̱-RḬ-NĔSS, *n.* Frequency ; commonness.
CŬS′TǪM-A̱-RY̱, *a.* Conformable to custom ; usual.
CŬS′TǪM-E̱R, *n.* One in the habit of purchasing.
CŬS′TǪM-HÖÜSE, *n.* A house where the taxes
　on goods imported or exported are collected.
CŬT, *v. a. & n.* [*imp. t. & pp.* cut.] To make an
　incision ; to divide ; to hew ; to carve. [shape.
CŬT, *n.* Gash or wound :—a printed picture :—
CY̱-TĀ′NE̱-OŬS, *a.* Relating to the skin.
CŪ′TḬ-CLE, *n.* Thin, dry skin ; the scarf-skin.
CY̱-TĬC′Y̱-LA̱R, *a.* Belonging to the skin.
CŬT′LA̱SS, *n.* A slightly curved cutting-sword.
CŬT′LE̱R, *n.* One who makes or sells knives, &c.
CŬT′LE̱R-Y̱, *n.* A cutler's business or wares.
CŬT′LE̱T, *n.* A slice or small piece of meat.
CŬT′PŬRSE, *n.* One who steals by cutting purses.
CŬT′TE̱R, *n.* One who cuts :—a fast-sailing ves-
CŬT′THRŌAT, *n.* A murderer ; an assassin. [sel.
CŬT′TḬNG, *n.* A piece cut off ; a chop ; a branch.
CŬT′TLE, *n.* A mollusk :—a foul-mouthed fellow.
CY̆′CLE, *n.* A circle :—a periodical space of time.
CY̆′CLŌÏD, *n.* A kind of geometrical curve.
CY̆-CLǪ-PÆ′DḬ-A̱ (sī-klǫ-pē′de̱-a̱), *n.* A circle
　of the arts and sciences ; an encyclopædia.
CY̆G′NE̱T, *n.* A young swan.
CY̆L′ḬN-DE̱R, *n.* A long, round body ; a roller.
CY̱-LĬN′DRḬC, CY̱-LĬN′DRḬ-CA̱L, *a.* Like a cylin-
　der ; long and round, as a cylinder.
CY̱-MĀR′, *n.* A loose, light gown. See SIMAR.
CY̆M′BA̱L, *n.* A sort of musical instrument.
CY̆ME, CY̆′MA̱, *n.* A kind of inflorescence.
CY̱-NĂN′CHE̱, *n.* A disease of the throat.
CY̆N′ḬC, *n.* A follower of Diogenes ; a snarler.
CY̆N′ḬC, CY̆N′Ḭ-CA̱L, *a.* Snarling ; satirical.
CY̆′NǪ-SŪRE *or* CY̆N′Ǫ-SŪRE, *n.* The star near
　the north pole, by which mariners are guided.
CY̆′PRE̱SS, *n.* A tree ; an emblem of mourning.
CY̆′PRŲS, *n.* A thin, transparent, black stuff.
CY̆ST, *n.* A sac containing morbid matter.
CZÄR (zär), *n.* Title of the emperor of Russia.
CZA̱-RĬ′NA̱ (za̱-rē′na̱), *n.* The empress of Russia.

D.

D is a consonant nearly approaching in sound
　to *t*, but formed by a stronger appulse of
the tongue to the upper part of the mouth.
DĂB, *v. a.* To strike suddenly :—to touch gently.
DĂB, *n.* A lump :—a gentle blow :—an adept.

DĂB′BLE, *v. n.* To play in water :—to tamper.
DĂB′BLE̱R, *n.* One who dabbles or meddles :—
　a maker of slight and superficial essays.
DĂB′CHĬCK, *n.* A small water-fowl.
DĀCE, *n.* A small river-fish of the carp kind.

DĂC′TȲL (dăk′tĭl), *n.* A poetical foot consist-
ing of one long syllable and two short ones.
DĂD, DĂD′DY, *n.* A childish term for father.
DĂF′FǪ-DĬL, DĂF′FA-DĬL-LY, *n.* A plant and
flower ; a species of narcissus.   [mark [†].
DĂG′ĠĘR, *n.* A short sword ; a poniard :—
DĂG′ĠĘRṢ-DRĂW′ĮNG, *n.* A drawing of dag-
DĂG′GLE,*v. n.* To pass through wet or dirt.[gers.
D′ĂH′LĮ-A, *n.* A plant and beautiful flower.
DĀI′LY (dā′lẹ),*a.* Happening every day; diurnal.
DĀI′LY, *ad.* Every day ; very often.   [ly.
DĀIN′TĮ-LY,*ad.* Delicately ; nicely ; fastidious-
DĀIN′TĮ-NĔSS, *n.* Delicacy ; fastidiousness.
DĀIN′TY, *a.* Delicious :—nice ; squeamish.
DĀIN′TY, *n.* Something nice ǫr delicate.
DĀI′RY, *n.* A place for milk :—a milk-farm.
DĀI′RY-MĀID, *n.* A female who manages a dairy.
DĀI′ṢY (dā′zẹ), *n.* A plant and its flower.
DĀLE, *n.* A space between hills ; a vale.
DĂL′LĮ-ANCE, *n.* Mutual caresses ; fondling.
DĂL′LĮ-ĘR, *n.* One who dallies ; a trifler.
DĂL′LY, *v. n.* To trifle ; to sport ; to delay.
DĂM, *n.* A bank to confine water :—a mother.
DĂM, *v. a.* To confine or shut up, as water.
DĂM′AĢE, *n.* Mischief ; hurt ; detriment ; loss.
DĂM′AĢE, *v. a.* To injure ; to impair ; to hurt.
DĂM′AĢE-A-BLE, *a.* Susceptible of being hurt.
DĂM′ASCENE (dăm′zn), *n.* A plum ; damson.
DĂM′ASK, *n.* Cloth with flowers or figures.
DĂM′AS-KĒĒN, *v. a.* To ornament or inlay, as
iron, with gold and silver.   [rose.
DĂM′ASK-RŌṢE, *n.* Rose of Damascus ; a red
DĀME, *n.* A lady ; a mistress of a family.
DĂMN (dăm),*v.a.* To doom to eternal torments.
DĂM′NA-BLE, *a.* Most wicked ; pernicious.
DĂM-NĀ′TIǪN,*n.* Exclusion from divine mercy.
DĂM′NA-TǪ-RY,*a.* Containing condemnation.
DĂM′NĮ-FȲ, *v. a.* To endamage ; to injure.
DĂMP, *a.* Moist ; wet ; foggy ; dejected ; sunk.
DĂMP, *n.* Fog ; moisture ; vapor :—dejection.
DĂMP, *v. a.* To wet ; to moisten :—to depress.
DĂMP′ĘR, *n.* That which damps or checks.
DĂMP′ĮSH,*a.* Somewhat damp ; inclining to wet.
DĂMP′NĔSS, *n.* Moisture ; slight humidity.
DĂM′ṢĘL, *n.* A young maiden ; a girl.
DĂM′ṢON (dăm′zn), *n.* A small black plum.
DĂNCE, *v. n.* To move with measured steps.
DĂNCE,*n.* A motion of one or more in concert.
DĂN′CĘR, *n.* One who practises dancing.
DĂN′CĮNG, *n.* A moving with steps to music.
DĂN′CĮNG-MĂS′TĘR, *n.* A teacher of dancing.
DĂN-DE-LĪ′ǪN, *n.* The name of a plant.
DĂN′DĮ-PRĂT, *n.* A conceited little fellow.
DĂN′DLE,*v. n.* To fondle ; to treat like a child.
DĂN′DLĘR, *n.* One who dandles children.
DĂN′DRUFF, *n.* Scurf on the head.
DĂN′DY, *n.* A worthless coxcomb ; a fop.
DĀN′ĮSH, *a.* Relating to the Danes or to Den-
DĂN′ĠĘR, *n.* Risk ; hazard ; peril.   [mark.
DĂN′ĠĘR-OǓS, *a.* Full of danger ; perilous. [ger.
DĂN′ĠĘR-OǓS-LY, *a.* Hazardously ; with dan-
DĂN′ĠĘR-OǓS-NĔSS,*n.* Danger ; peril ; hazard.
DĂN′ĠLE, *v. n.* To hang loose ; to follow.
DĂN′ĠLĘR,*n.* One who dangles, or hangs about.
DĂNK, *a.* Damp ; humid ; moist ; wet.
DĂNK, *n.* Damp ; moisture ; humidity.
DĂPH′NĔ, *n.* A genus of diminutive shrubs.
DĂP′PĘR, *a.* Little and active ; spruce ; trim.

DĂP′PLE, *a.* Of various colors ; variegated.
DÀRE, *v. n.* [*imp. t.* durst ; *pp.* dared.] To have
courage or boldness ; not to be afraid.
DÀRE, *v. a.* [*imp. t.* & *pp.* dared.] To defy.
DÀR′ĘR, *n.* One who dares or defies.
DÀR′ĮNG, *a.* Bold ; adventurous ; fearless.
DÀR′ĮNG-LY, *ad.* Boldly ; bravely ; courageous-
DÀR′ĮNG-NĔSS, *n.* Boldness ; fearlessness. [ly.
DÄRK, *a.* Wanting light ; opaque ; obscure.
DÄRK, *n.* Darkness ; obscurity ; want of light.
DÄRK′EN (där′kn),*v. a.& n.* To make or grow
DÄRK′LY, *ad.* Obscurely ; blindly.   [dark.
DÄRK′NĔSS, *n.* Absence of light ; obscurity.
DÄRK′SǪME (därk′sụm), *a.* Gloomy ; obscure.
DÄR′LĮNG, *a.* Favǫrite ; dear ; much beloved.
DÄR′LĮNG, *n.* A favorite ; one much beloved.
DÄRN, *v. a.* To mend, as a rent or hole.
DÄR′NĘL, *n.* A genus of grasses ; ray-grass.
DÄRT, *n.* A weapon thrown by the hand.
DÄRT, *v. a. & n.* To throw or hurl rapidly ; to
shoot ; to fly rapidly, as a dart.
DĂSH, *v. a.* To strike :—to mix :—to ruin. [idly.
DĂSH,*v. n.* To rush impetuously :—to sketch rap-
DĂSH, *n.* A collision ; a stroke ; small admix-
ture :—mark of punctuation, thus [—].
DĂSH′ĮNG, *a.* Precipitate ; rushing carelessly.
DĂS′TARD,*n.* A mean coward ; a poltroon. [ery.
DĂS′TARD-LĮ-NĔSS,*n.* Cowardliness ; poltroon-
DĂS′TARD-LY, *a.* Cowardly ; meanly fearful.
DĂS′TARD-Y, *n.* Cowardliness ; poltroonery.
DĀ′TA, *n. pl.* Truths admitted. See DATUM.
DĀTE, *n.* The time of an event, or of some
writing :—a fruit of Arabia, &c.   [begin.
DĀTE, *v. a.* To note with the time.—*v. n.* To
DĀTE′LĔSS, *a.* Without any fixed term.
DĀ′TĮVE, *a.* (*Gram.*) The case that signifies
the person to whom any thing is given.
DĀ′TỤM,*n.* ; pl. DĀ′TA. [L.] A truth admitted.
DÂUB, *v. a.* To smear ; to paint coarsely.
DÂUB′ĘR,*n.* A coarse, low painter :—a flatterer.
DÂUB′ĮNG,*n.* Plaster; coarse painting :—flattery.
DÂUB′Y, *a.* Viscous ; glutinous ; smeary.
DÂUGH′TĘR (dâw′tẹr), *n.* A female child. [ter.
DÂUGH′TĘR-LY (dâw′tẹr-lẹ), *a.* Like a daugh-
DÂUNT (dänt), *v. a.* To discourage ; to fright.
DÂUNT′LĔSS (dänt′lẹs), *a.* Fearless ; bold.
DÂUNT′LĔSS-NĔSS, *n.* Fearlessness. [France.
DÂU′PHĮN, *n.* The heir-apparent to the crown of
DÂU′PHĮN-ĔSS, *n.* The wife of a dauphin.
DÂW′DLĘR, *n.* A trifler ; a dallier ; an idler.
DÂWN,*v. n.* To grow light ; to glimmer ; to open.
DÂWN, *n.* Break of day ; beginning ; rise.
DÂWN′ĮNG, *n.* Break of day :—beginning.
DĀY (dā), *n.* The time between the rising and
setting of the sun ; 24 hours :—life :—light.
DĀY′-BOOK (dā′bǔk),*n.* A tradesman′s journal.
DĀY′-BRĒĀK,*n.* Dawn ; first appearance of day.
DĀY′DRĒAM,*n.* A vision to the waking senses.
DĀY′-LĀ-BǪR, *n.* Labor by, or in, the day.
DĀY′-LĀ-BǪR-ĘR, *n.* A worker by the day.
DĀY′LĬGHT (dā′lĭt), *n.* The light of the day.
DĀY′-LĬL-Y, *n.* A kind of plant and its flower.
DĀYṢ′MAN, *n.* An umpire ; an arbitrator.
DĀY′SPRĬNG,*n.* Rise of the day ; the dawn.
DĀY′-STÄR, *n.* The morning star ; Venus.
DĀY′TĪME, *n.* Time in which there is light.
DĀY′-WORK, *n.* Work performed or imposed
by the day ; day-labor.

DĂZ′ZLE, *v. a.* To overpower with light; to dim.
DĒA′CON (dē′kn), *n.* An ecclesiastical officer.
DĒA′CON-ĔSS (dē′kn-ĕs), *n.* A female deacon.
DĒA′CON-RẎ,DĒA′CON-SHĬP,*n.*Office of deacon.
DĔAD (dĕd), *a.* Deprived of life ; inanimate.
DĔAD (dĕd), *n.* Dead persons :—still time.
DĔAD′-DRŬNK, *p. a.* Drunk and motionless.
DĔAD′EN (dĕd′dn), *v. a.* To deprive of vigor.
DĔAD′-LĬFT, *n.* A lift with main strength. [dow.
DĔAD′LĪGHT, *n.* A wooden port for a cabin win-
DĔAD′LẎ (dĕd′lę), *a.* Causing death ; fatal. [ity.
DĔAD′NĘSS (dĕd′nęs), *n.* Lifelessness ; inactiv-
DĔAD′-RĔCK′ON-ĬNG (dĕd′rĕk′kn-ĭng), *n.* Esti-
mation of the place where a ship is, by the log.
DĔAF (dĕf), *a.* Wanting the sense of hearing.
DĔAF′EN (dĕf′fn), *v. a.* To make deaf; to stun.
DĔAF′LẎ (dĕf′lę), *ad.* In a deaf manner.
DĔAF′NĘSS (dĕf′nęs), *n.* Want of hearing.
DĒAL (dēl), *n.* Part ; quantity :—fir or pine wood.
DĒAL, *v. a.* [*imp. t.* & *pp.* dĕalt, dēaled.] To
distribute ; to divide ; to bestow ; to throw
DĒAL, *v. n.* To traffic ; to transact ; to act. [about.
DĒAL′ĘR,*n.* One who deals; a trader, tradesman.
DĒAL′ĬNG, *n.* Practice ; intercourse ; traffic.
DĒAN, *n.* An ecclesiastical dignitary :—a clerk
or secretary of a faculty of a college, &c.
DĒAN′ĘR-Ẏ, *n.* The office or house of a dean.
DĒAN′SHĬP, *n.* The office or dignity of a dean.
DĒAR (dēr), *a.* Beloved ; precious ; costly.
DĒAR, *n.* A darling ; a person beloved.
DĒAR′BOUGHT (dēr′bȧwt),*a.* Purchased at a
high price ; costly ; expensive. [high price.
DĒAR′LẎ (dēr′lę), *ad.* In a dear manner ; at a
DĒAR′NĔSS, *n.* Fondness ; love :—costliness.
DĔARTH (dĕrth), *n.* Scarcity ; want ; famine.
DĔATH (dĕth),*n.* Extinction of life ; mortality.
DĔATH′-BĔD, *n.* Bed on which a person dies.
DĔATH′LĔSS, *a.* Immortal ; never-dying.
DĔATH′-LĪKE (dĕth′līk), *a.* Resembling death.
DĔATH′S′-DŌOR,*n.* A near approach to death.
DĔATHS′MĄN (dĕths′mąn), *n.* An executioner.
DĔATH′WATCH (dĕth′wŏch), *n.* A sort of insect.
DĘ-BĀR′,*v.a.* To exclude; to hinder; to prevent.
DĘ-BĀSE′, *v.a.* To degrade :—to adulterate.
DĘ-BĀSE′MĘNT, *n.* Act of debasing ; degrada-
DĘ-BĀS′ĘR, *n.* One who debases; degrader.[tion.
DĘ-BĀT′Ą-BLE, *a.* Disputable ; contestable.
DĘ-BĀTE′, *n.* A dispute ; a quarrel ; a contest.
DĘ-BĀTE′, *v.a.* & *n.* To controvert ; to dispute.
DĘ-BĀT′ĘR, *n.* One who debates ; a disputant.
DĘ-BÂUCH′,*v.a.* To corrupt ; to vitiate ; to ruin.
DĘ-BÂUCH′,*n.* Drunkenness ; excess ; lewdness.
DĔB-AU-ÇHĒĒ′ (dĕb-ǫ-shē′),*n.* A rake ; a drunk-
ard ; a libertine. [rupter.
DĘ-BÂUCH′ĘR, *n.* One who debauches ; a cor-
DĘ-BÂUCH′ĘR-Ẏ, *n.* Intemperance ; lewdness.
DĘ-BÂUCH′MĘNT, *n.* The act of debauching.
DĘ-BĔNT′ŲRE (dę-bĕnt′yųr), *n.* A certificate.
DĘ-BĬL′Ĭ-TĀTE,*v. a.* To weaken ; to make faint.
DĘ-BĬL-Ĭ-TĀ′TIǪN, *n.* The act of weakening.
DĘ-BĬL′Ĭ-TẎ, *n.* Weakness ; feebleness ; languor.
DĔB′ĬT, *n.* Money due for goods sold on credit.
DĔB′ĬT, *v. a.* To charge or register with debt.
DĔB-Ǫ-NÀIR′, *a.* Courteous ; affable ; gentle.
DĘ-BÔUCH′ (dę-bȯch′), *v. n.* To march out.
DĔBRIS (dā-brē′), *n.* [Fr.] Fragments ; ruins.
DĔBT (dĕt), *n.* What one man owes to another.
DĔBT′ǪR (dĕt′ǫr), *n.* One that owes money, &c.

DĔC′ĄDE, *n.* The sum or number of ten.
DĔC′Ą-GǑN, *n.* A plane figure having ten sides.
DĔC′Ą-LǑGUE (-ą-lŏg), *n.* Ten commandments.
DĘ-CĂM′Ę-RǑN, *n.* A volume having ten books
DĘ-CĂMP′, *v. n.* To shift a camp ; to move off.
DĘ-CĂMP′MĘNT, *n.* The act of decamping.
DĘ-CĂNT′, *v. a.* To pour off gently, as liquor.
DĔC-ĄN-TĀ′TIǪN, *n.* The act of decanting.
DĘ-CĂN′TĘR, *n.* Glass vessel for holding liquor.
DĘ-CĂP′Ĭ-TĀTE, *v. a.* To cut off the head of.
DĘ-CĂP-Ĭ-TĀ′TIǪN, *n.* The act of beheading.
DĘ-CĀẎ′, *v. n.* To lose excellence ; to waste
DĘ-CĀẎ′, *n.* A decline ; gradual failure. [away.
DĘ-CĒASE′, *n.* Death ; departure from life.
DĘ-CĒASE′ (dę.sēs′), *v. n.* To die ; to expire.
DĘ-CĒIT′ (dę-sēt′), *n.* Fraud ; cheat ; artifice.
DĘ-CĒIT′FŬL, *a.* Fraudulent ; full of deceit.
DĘ-CĒIT′FŬL-LẎ, *ad.* Fraudulently ; with deceit.
DĘ-CĒIT′FŬL-NĔSS, *n.* State of being deceitful.
DĘ-CĒIV′Ą-BLE, *a.* Liable to be deceived.
DĘ-CĒIV′Ą-BLE-NĔSS, *n.* Liableness to be de-
ceived ; ability to deceive or delude.
DĘ-CĒIVE′ (dę-sēv′), *v. a.* To cause to mis-
take ; to delude ; to impose on ; to beguile.
DĘ-CĒIV′ĘR, *n.* One who deceives ; a cheat.
DĘ-CĔM′BĘR, *n.* The last month of the year.
DĘ-CĔM′VĬ-RĄL, *a.* Belonging to a decemvirate.
DĘ-CĔM′VĬ-RATE, *n.* Government by ten rulers.
DĘ-CĔM′VĬ-RĬ, *n.* [L.] The ten magistrates of
ancient Rome having the whole government.
DĔ′CĘN-CẎ, *n.* Propriety ; decorum , modesty.
DĘ-CĔN′NĄ-RẎ, *n.* Tithing:—period of ten years.
DĘ-CĔN′NĬ-ĄL, *a.* Continuing for ten years :—
happening every ten years. [comely.
DĒ′CĘNT, *a.* Becoming ; fit ; suitable ; modest ;
DĒ′CĘNT-LẎ, *ad.* In a decent or proper manner.
DĘ-CĔPT-Ĭ-BĬL′Ĭ-TẎ,*n.*Liableness to be deceived.
DĘ-CĔPT′Ĭ-BLE, *a.* Liable to be deceived.
DĘ-CĔP′TIǪN, *n.* The act of deceiving ; fraud.
DĘ-CĔP′TĮVE, *a.* Having the power of deceiving.
DĘ-CHĂRM′, *v. a.* To counteract by a charm.
DĘ-CĪ′DĄ-BLE, *a.* Capable of being determined.
DĘ-CĪDE′, *v. a.* & *n.* To determine, end, settle.
DĘ-CĪD′ED-LẎ, *ad.* In a determined manner.
DĔÇ′Ĭ-DĔNCE, *n.* The act of falling off.
DĘ-CĪD′ĘR, *n.* One who decides or determines.
DĘ-CĪD′Ụ-OŬS, *a.* Falling off; not evergreen.
DĔÇ′Ĭ-MĄL, *a.* Numbered by ten ; pertaining
to a system of tenfold increase or decrease.
DĔÇ′Ĭ-MĀTE, *v. a.* To tithe :—to take the tenth.
DĔÇ-Ĭ-MĀ′TIǪN, *n.* A selection of every tenth.
DĔÇ′Ĭ-MĀ-TǪR, *n.* One who decimates.
DĘ-CĪ′PHĘR, *v. a.* To explain, unfold, unravel.
DĘ-CĪ′PHĘR-ĘR, *n.* One who deciphers.
DĘ-CĬ′′ŞIǪN (dę-sĭzh′un), *n.* Determination.
DĘ-CĪ′SĮVE, *a.* Conclusive ; final ; positive.
DĘ-ÇĪ′SĮVE-LẎ, *ad.* In a conclusive manner.
DĘ-CĪ′SĮVE-NĔSS, *n.* State of being decisive.
DĘ-CĪ′SǪ-RẎ, *a.* Able to determine. [adorn.
DĔCK, *v. a.* To cover ; to dress ; to array ; to
DĔCK, *n.* The floor of a ship :—a pack of cards.
DĔCK′ĘR, *n.* One who decks ; a dresser.
DĘ-CLĀIM′,*v.n.* To speak rhetorically, harangue.
DĘ-CLĀIM′ĘR,*n.* One who declaims; haranguer.
DĔC-LĄ-MĀ′TIǪN, *n.* The art of declaiming ;
a declamatory speech ; an harangue. [tion.
DĘ-CLĂM′Ą-TǪ-RẎ, *a.* Pertaining to declama-
DĔC-LĄ-RĀ′TIǪN,*n.* A proclamation; assertion.

DẸ-CLĂR'Ạ-TĬVE, *a.* Proclaiming; explanatory.
DẸ-CLĂR'Ạ-TQ-RY, *a.* Affirmative; expressive.
DẸ-CLĀRE', *v. a. & n.* To make known; to proclaim; to assert; to announce; to utter.
DẸ-CLĔN'SIQN, *n.* Descent; deterioration; degeneracy:—grammatical inflection of nouns,
DẸ-CLĪ'NẠ-BLE, *a.* That may be declined. [&c.
DĔC-LĮ-NĀ'TIQN, *n.* Descent; deviation. [&c.
DĔC-LĮ-NĀ'TQR, *n.* An instrument in dialing,
DẸ-CLĪNE', *v. n.* To lean:—to shun; to refuse:—to decay; to decrease; to diminish.
DẸ-CLĪNE', *v. a.* To refuse:—to vary or inflect.
DẸ-CLĪNE', *n.* A falling off; diminution; decay.
DẸ-CLĬV'Į-TY, *n.* A slope; gradual descent.
DẸ-CLĪ'VOỤS, *a.* Gradually descending; sloping.
DẸ-CŎCT', *v. a.* To boil; to digest; to inflame.
DẸ-CŎC'TIQN, *n.* Act of boiling; matter boiled.
DĔC-QL-LĀ'TIQN, *n.* The act of beheading.
DẸ-CŎL-QR-Ā'TIQN, *n.* Absence or privation of color. [pound; to resolve.
DĒ-CQM-PŌṢE', *v. a.* To dissolve; to decom-
DĒ-CQM-PŌṢ'ĮTE, *a.* Compounded a second time.
DĒ-CŎM-PQ-ṢĬ''TIQN, *n.* A separation of parts.
DĒ-CQM-PÖÜND', *v. a.* To compound anew.
DĒ-CQM-PÖÜND', *a.* Compounded a second time.
DĔC'Q-RĀTE, *v. a.* To adorn; to embellish.
DĔC-Q-RĀ'TIQN, *n.* Ornament; embellishment.
‖DẸ-CŌ'ROỤS *or* DĔC'Q-ROỤS, *a.* Decent; suitable to a character; becoming; proper; fit.
‖DẸ-CŌ'ROỤS-LY, *ad.* In a becoming manner.
DẸ-CŎR'TĮ-CĀTE, *v. a.* To divest of the bark.
DẸ-CÖR-TĮ-CĀ'TIQN, *n.* The act of peeling.
DẸ-CŌ'RỤM, *n.* Decency; order; propriety.
DẸ-CŌÝ', *v. a.* To lure; to entrap; to insnare.
DẸ-CŌÝ', *n.* Allurement; a lure; a snare.
DẸ-CŌÝ'-DŬCK, *n.* A duck that lures others.
DẸ-CRĒASE', *v. n. & a.* To grow or make less.
DẸ-CRĒASE', *n.* Decay; state of growing less.
DẸ-CRĒE', *v. a.* To doom or assign by a decree.
DẸ-CRĒE', *n.* An edict; a law:—determination.
DĔC'RẸ-MENT, *n.* Decrease; waste; diminution.
DẸ-CRĔP'ĮT, *a.* Wasted and worn with age.
DẸ-CRĔP'Į-TĀTE, *v. a.* To crackle in the fire.
DẸ-CRĔP-Į-TĀ'TIQN, *n.* A crackling noise.
DẸ-CRĔP'Į-TŪDE, *n.* The last stage of old age.
DẸ-CRĔS'CENT, *a.* Growing less; decreasing.
DẸ-CRĒ'TẠL, *a.* Appertaining to a decretal.
DẸ-CRĒ'TẠL, *n.* A book of decrees or edicts.
DĔC'RẸ-TQ-RY, *a.* Judicial; definitive; deciding.
DẸ-CRĪ'ẠL, *n.* Clamorous censure; condemna-
DẸ-CRĪ'ẸR, *n.* One who decries. [tion.
DẸ-CRÝ', *v. a.* To censure; to clamor against.
DẸ-CŬM'BENCE, DẸ-CŬM'BEN-CY, *n.* The act or posture of lying down; prostration.
DẸ-CŬM'BENT, *a.* Lying down; recumbent.
DẸ-CŬM'BĮ-TURE, *n.* Confinement to the bed.
DĔC'Ụ-PLE (dĕk'ụ-pl), *a.* Repeated ten times.
DẸ-CŪ'RĮ-QN, *n.* A commander over ten men.
DẸ-CŬR'SIQN, *n.* The act of running down.
DẸ-CŬS'SĀTE, *v. a.* To intersect at acute angles.
DĔC-ỤS-SĀ'TIQN, *n.* The act of crossing.
DĔD'Į-CĀTE, *v. a.* To consecrate; to inscribe.
DĔD'Į-CĀTE, *a.* Consecrate; devoted; sacred.
DĔD-Į-CĀ'TIQN, *n.* Consecration; an address.
DĔD'Į-CĀ-TQR, *n.* One who dedicates.
DĔD'Į-CẠ-TQ-RY, *a.* Relating to a dedication.
DẸ-DĬ''TIQN (dẹ-dĭsh'ụn), *n.* A surrender.
DẸ-DŪCE', *v. a.* To draw; to infer; to gather.

DẸ-DŪCE'MENT, *n.* Inference; thing deduced.
DẸ-DŪ'CĮ-BLE, *a.* Inferrible; consequential.
DẸ-DŬCT', *v. a.* To subtract; to take away.
DẸ-DŬC'TIQN, *n.* A deducting; inference.
DẸ-DŬC'TĮVE, *a.* Deducible; inferrible.
DĒED, *n.* Action; act; exploit:—fact.—(*Law.*) An instrument between parties able to contract.
DĒEM, *v. a. & n.* To judge; to think.
DĒEP, *a.* Descending far; profound:—artful:—absorbed; swallowed up; engrossed:—dark.
DĒEP, *n.* The sea; the main; the ocean.
DĒEP'EN (dē'pn), *v. a. & n.* To make or grow deep; to make more dark, as colors.
DĒEP'LY, *ad.* To a great depth; profoundly.
DĒEP'NESS, *n.* Depth; profundity; sagacity.
DĒER, *n.* A forest animal hunted for venison.
DẸ-FĀCE', *v. a.* To mar; to efface; to disfigure.
DẸ-FĀCE'MENT, *n.* Marring; razure; injury.
DẸ-FĀ'CER, *n.* One who defaces; a disfigurer.
DẸ-FĂL'CĀTE, *v. a.* To cut off; to lop; to take away a part of, as of public accounts.
DĔF-ẠL-CĀ'TIQN, *n.* Diminution; abatement; breach of trust by one having charge of money.
DĔF-Ạ-MĀ'TIQN, *n.* Slander; calumny; detraction.
DẸ-FĂM'Ạ-TQ-RY, *a.* Calumnious; libellous.
DẸ-FĀME', *v. a.* To slander; to calumniate.
DẸ-FĀM'ẸR, *n.* One who defames; a slanderer.
DẸ-FĂT'Į-GẠ-BLE, *a.* Liable to be weary.
DẸ-FÂULT', *n.* Omission; failure; fault; defect.
DẸ-FÂULT', *v. n.* To fail in performing a contract, or to appear in court; failure.
DẸ-FÂULT'ẸR, *n.* One that makes default.
DẸ-FĒA'SẠNCE (dẹ-fē'zạns), *n.* Act of annulling.
DẸ-FĒAṢ'Į-BLE, *a.* Capable of being annulled.
DẸ-FĒAT', *n.* An overthrow; frustration. [trate.
DẸ-FĒAT', *v. a.* To conquer; to undo; to frus-
DĔF'E-CĀTE, *v. a.* To clarify; to refine; to clear.
DĔF'E-CẠTE, *a.* Purged from lees or foulness.
DĔF-E-CĀ'TIQN, *n.* Purification; clarification.
DẸ-FĔCT', *n.* A fault; imperfection; a blemish.
DẸ-FĔCT'Į-BLE, *a.* Imperfect; deficient.
DẸ-FĔC'TIQN, *n.* Want; failure; apostasy; revolt from duty or allegiance. [faulty.
DẸ-FĔC'TĮVE, *a.* Full of defects; imperfect;
DẸ-FĔC'TĮVE-LY, *ad.* In a defective manner.
DẸ-FĔC'TĮVE-NĔSS, *n.* State of being imperfect.
DẸ-FĔNCE', *n.* Guard; vindication; resistance.
DẸ-FĔNCE'LESS, *a.* Unarmed; unguarded; weak; exposed. [unprotected manner.
DẸ-FĔNCE'LESS-LY, *ad.* In a defenceless or
DẸ-FĔNCE'LESS-NĔSS, *n.* Unprotected state.
DẸ-FĔND', *v. a.* To protect; to vindicate.
DẸ-FĔND'ẠNT, *n.* A person accused or sued.
DẸ-FĔND'ẸR, *n.* One who defends; an advocate.
DẸ-FĔN'SĮ-BLE, *a.* That may be defended.
DẸ-FĔN'SĮVE, *a.* Serving to defend; resisting.
DẸ-FĔN'SĮVE, *n.* A safeguard; state of defence.
DẸ-FĔN'SĮVE-LY, *ad.* In a defensive manner.
DẸ-FĔR', *v. a.* To put off; to delay; to refer.
DĔF'ẸR-ENCE, *n.* Regard; respect; submission.
DẸ-FĪ'ẠNCE, *n.* A challenge; contempt of opposition or danger; a setting at nought.
DẸ-FĪ'ẠNT, *a.* Bidding defiance; challenging.
DẸ-FĪ''CIEN-CY (-fĭsh'en-sẹ), *n.* Want; defect.
DẸ-FĪ''CIENT (-fĭsh'ent), *a.* Failing; wanting.
DĔF'Į-CĬT, *n.* [L.] Want; deficiency; lack.
DẸ-FĪ'ẸR, *n.* A challenger; a contemner.
DẸ-FĪLE', *v. a.* To make foul; to pollute.

DẸ-FĪLE', n. A narrow passage or way.
DẸ-FĪLE'MẸNT, n. Corruption ; pollution.
DẸ-FĪL'ẸR, n. One who defiles ; a polluter.
DẸ-FĬN'A-BLE, a. Capable of being defined.
DẸ-FĪNE', v. a. To explain ; to describe, limit.
DẸ-FĪN'ẸR, n. One who defines or describes.
DĔF'Ị-NĬTE, a. Certain ; limited ; exact ; precise.
DĔF'Ị-NĬTE-LY, ad. In a definite manner.
DĔF'Ị-NĮTE-NĔSS, n. Certainty ; exactness.
DĔF-Ị-NĬ''TIǪN (dĕf-ẹ-nĭsh'ụn), n. The act of
  defining ; meaning ; description ; explication.
DẸ-FĬN'Ị-TĪVE, a. Determinate ; positive.
DẸ-FĬN'Ị-TĬVE, n. That which defines ; final.
DẸ-FĬN'Ị-TĬVE-LY, ad. Positively ; decisively.
DẸ-FĬN'Ị-TĮVE-NĔSS, n. Decisiveness ; conclu-
DẸ-FLĀ'GRA-BLE, a. Combustible. [siveness.
DĔF'LA-GRĀTE, v. a. (Chem.) To set fire to ;
  to cause to burn suddenly.   [bustion.
DĔF-LA-GRĀ'TIǪN, n. Rapid or sudden com-
DẸ-FLĔCT', v. a. To turn aside ; to bend.
DẸ-FLĔC'TIǪN, n. Deviation ; a turning aside.
DĔF-LǪ-RĀ'TIǪN, n. Act of deflouring ; rape.
DẸ-FLOÛR', v. a. To ravish ; to destroy beauty.
DẸ-FLOÛR'ẸR, n. One who deflours ; a ravisher.
DẸ-FLŬX'IǪN, n. A flowing downward.
DẸ-FŌRCE', v. a. To keep out of possession.
DẸ-FŌRM', v. a. To disfigure ; to deface.
DĔF-ǪR-MĀ'TIǪN, n. A defacing ; a disfiguring.
DẸ-FŌRMED' (-fŏrmd'), p. a. Ugly ; disfigured.
DẸ-FŌRM'ẸD-NĔSS, n. Ugliness ; deformity.
DẸ-FŌRM'ẸR, n. One who defaces or deforms.
DẸ-FŌRM'Ị-TY, n. Ugliness ; defect ; distortion.
DẸ-FRÂUD', v. a. To rob by trick ; to cheat.
DẸ-FRÂUD'ẸR, n. One who defrauds ; a cheater.
DẸ-FRĀY', v. a. To bear, as charges ; to pay.
DẸ-FRĀY'ẸR, n. One who defrays.   [person.
DẸ-FŪNCT', a. Dead ; deceased.—n. A dead
DẸ-FȲ', v. a. To challenge ; to dare ; to brave.
DẸ-GĔN'ẸR-A-CY, n. A growing worse ; dete-
  rioration ; inferiority ; poorness.   [teriorate.
DẸ-GĔN'ẸR-ĀTE, v. n. To grow worse ; to de-
DẸ-GĔN'ẸR-ĄTE, a. Grown worse ; base.
DẸ-GĔN'ẸR-ĄTE-LY, ad. In a degenerate man-
DẸ-GĔN'ẸR-ĄTE-NĔSS, n. Degeneracy. [ner.
DẸ-GĔN-ẸR-Ā'TIǪN, n. Act of degenerating.
DĔG-LŲ-TĬ''TIǪN (dĕg-lụ-tĭsh'ụn), n. A swal-
  lowing ; the power of swallowing.   [ness.
DĔG-RA-DĀ'TIǪN, n. Act of degrading ; base-
DẸ-GRĀDE', v. a. To place lower ; to lower.
DẸ-GRĒĒ', n. Quality ; rank ; station ; step ;
  proportion :—360th part of a circle ; 69½ miles.
DẸ-HŌRT', v. a. To dissuade earnestly.
DĔ-HǪR-TĀ'TIǪN, n. Earnest dissuasion.
DẸ-HŌR'TA-TǪ-RY, a. Tending to dissuade ; dis-
DĔ-Ị-FỊ-CĀ'TIǪN, n. Act of deifying. [suading.
DĒ'Ị-FĪ-ẸR, n. One who deifies.
DĒ'Ị-FŌRM, a. Of a godlike form.
DĒ'Ị-FȲ, v. a. To make a god of ; to extol.
DEIGN (dān), v. n. To condescend ; to vouch-
  safe ; to think fit or proper.   [low.
DEIGN (dān), v. a. To grant ; to permit ; to al-
DĒ'ĬSM, n. The doctrine or creed of a deist.
DĒ'ĬST, n. One who believes in the existence
  of God, but disbelieves revealed religion.
DĒ-ĬS'TỊ-CAL, a. Belonging to deism or deists.
DĒ'Ị-TY, n. The Divine Being ; divine nature.
DẸ-JĔCT', v. a. To cast down ; to depress.
DẸ-JĔC'TIǪN, n. Lowness of spirits ; depression.

DẸ-LĀY', v. a. & n. To put off ; to hinder ; to
DẸ-LĀY', n. A deferring ; stay ; stop. [linger.
DĒ'LẸ, v. a. Blot out ; erase.
DĔL'Ẹ-BLE, a. Capable of being effaced.
DẸ-LĔC'TA-BLE, a. Pleasing ; delightful.
DĔL'Ẹ-GĀTE, v. a. To send on an embassy ;
  to depute ; to commission :—to intrust.
DĔL'Ẹ-GĄTE, n. A deputy ; a commissioner.
DĔL-Ẹ-GĀ'TIǪN, n. A sending away ; deputa-
  tion :—persons delegated.   [face.
DẸ-LĒTE', v. a. To blot out ; to erase ; to ef-
DĔL-Ẹ-TĒ'RỊ-OŬS, a. Deadly ; destructive.
DẸ-LĒ'TIǪN, n. Act of erasing or blotting out.
DĔLFT, n. Earthen ware resembling porcelain.
DẸ-LĬB'ẸR-ĀTE, v. a. & n. To weigh ; to con-
  sider any thing ; to ponder ; to reflect.
DẸ-LĬB'ẸR-ĀTE, a. Circumspect ; wary ; slow.
DẸ-LĬB'ẸR-ĄTE-LY, ad. In a deliberate manner.
DẸ-LĬB'ẸR-ĄTE-NĔSS, n. Circumspection.
DẸ-LĬB-ẸR-Ā'TIǪN, n. Act of deliberating.
DẸ-LĬB'ẸR-A-TĬVE, a. Containing deliberation.
DĔL'Ị-CA-CY, n. Daintiness ; nicety ; refine-
  ment ; a dainty:—gentle treatment ; tenderness.
DĔL'Ị-CĄTE, a. Nice ; dainty ; fine ; refined.
DĔL'Ị-CĄTE-LY, ad. In a delicate manner.
DĔL'Ị-CĄTE-NĔSS, n. Tenderness ; softness.
DẸ-LĬ''CIOŲS (dẹ-lĭsh'ụs), a. Highly pleasing ;
  very grateful ; sweet ; agreeable ; charming.
DẸ-LĬ''CIOŲS-LY, ad. In a delicious manner.
DẸ-LĬ''CIOŲS-NĔSS, n. Quality of being delicious.
DẸ-LĪGHT' (dẹ-lĭt'), n. Great pleasure or joy.
DẸ-LĪGHT' (dẹ-lĭt'), v. a. To please greatly.
DẸ-LĪGHT' (dẹ-lĭt'), v. n. To have delight.
DẸ-LĪGHT'FŬL (dẹ-lĭt'fŭl), a. Highly pleasing.
DẸ-LĪGHT'FŬL-LY, ad. In a delightful manner.
DẸ-LĪGHT'FŬL-NĔSS, n. Great pleasure ; joy.
DẸ-LĬN'Ẹ-ĀTE, v. a. To design ; to sketch ; to
  draw ; to represent ; to describe ; to portray.
DẸ-LĬN-Ẹ-Ā'TIǪN, n. Outline ; sketch ; drawing.
DẸ-LĬN'QUẸN-CY, n. A fault ; a misdeed ; crime.
DẸ-LĬN'QUẸNT (dẹ-lĭng'kwẹnt), n. An offender.
DĔL-Ị-QUĔSCE' (-kwĕs'), v. n. To melt in air.
DĔL-Ị-QUĔS'CẸNCE, n. A liquefying in the air.
DĔL-Ị-QUĔS'CẸNT, a. Liquefying in the air.
DẸ-LĬR'Ị-OŬS, a. Light-headed ; raving ; insane.
DẸ-LĬR'Ị-OŲS-NĔSS, n. The state of one raving.
DẸ-LĬR'Ị-ŬM, n. Alienation of mind ; insanity.
DẸ-LĬV'ẸR, v. a. To set free ; to release, utter.
DẸ-LĬV'ẸR-ANCE, n. Release ; rescue ; utterance.
DẸ-LĬV'ẸR-ẸR, n. One who delivers. [rescue.
DẸ-LĬV'ẸR-Y, n. Act of delivering ; release ;
DĔLL, n. A little dale or valley ; a dingle.
DẸ-LŪD'A-BLE, a. Liable to be deceived.
DẸ-LŪDE', v. a. To impose upon ; to cheat.
DẸ-LŪD'ẸR, n. One who deludes ; a deceiver.
DĔL'ŪGE (dĕl'lūj), n. A general inundation.
DĔL'ŪGE, v. a. To drown ; to overwhelm.
DẸ-LŪ'SIǪN (dẹ-lū'zhụn), n. Error ; deceit.
DẸ-LŪ'SĮVE, DẸ-LŪ'SǪ-RY, a. Deceptive ; fal-
  lacious ; deceitful ; fraudulent ; deluding.
DĔLVE, v. a. & n. To dig ; to open with a spade.
DĔM'A-GŌGUE (dĕm'a-gŏg), n. A ringleader
  of a faction ; a popular and factious orator.
DẸ-MĀIN', or DẸ-MĒSNE' (dẹ-mān', dẹ-mēn'),
  n. A freehold ; an estate in land ; a manor.
DẸ-MĂND', v. a. To claim with authority.
DẸ-MĂND', n. A claim ; a question ; exaction.
DẸ-MĂND'A-BLE, a. That may be demanded.

DẸ-MĂND′ẠNT, *n.* A plaintiff in a real action.
DẸ-MĂND′ẸR, *n.* One who demands; claimant.
DĔ-MẠR-CĀ′TIỌN, *n.* Division; boundary.
DẸ-MĒAN′, *v. a.* To behave; to carry or conduct one's self:—to debase; to disgrace.
DẸ-MĒAN′ỌR, *n.* Carriage; behavior; conduct.
DẸ-MĔR′ỊT, *n.* Desert of ill or blame; ill desert.
DẸ-MĔR′SIỌN (dẹ-mër′shụn), *n.* A drowning.
DẸ-MĒSNE′ (dẹ-mēn′), *n.* See DEMAIN.
DĔM′Ị (dĕm′ẹ). A prefix signifying *half.*
DĔM′Ị-JŌHN, *n.* A large glass vessel or bottle.
DẸ-MĪSE′, *n.* Death; decease:—lease; transfer.
DẸ-MĪSE′, *v. a.* To grant at one's death; to will.
DẸ-MŎC′RẠ-CỴ, *n.* Government by the people.
DĔM′Ọ-CRĂT, *n.* One devoted to democracy.
DĔM-Ọ-CRĂT′ỊC, } *a.* Pertaining to democracy, or government by the people; republican; popular. [manner.
DĔM-Ọ-CRĂT′Ị-CẠL, }
DĔM-Ọ-CRĂT′Ị-CẠL-LỴ, *ad.* In a democratical
DẸ-MŎL′ỊSH, *v. a.* To throw down; to destroy.
DẸ-MŎL′ỊSH-ẸR, *n.* One who demolishes.
DĔM-Ọ-LĬ′′TIỌN (dĕm-ọ-lĭsh′ụn), *n.* Destruction.
DĒ′MỌN, *n.* A spirit; an evil spirit; a devil.
DẸ-MŌ′NỊ-ĂC, } *a.* Belonging to evil spirits; devilish; infernal.
DĔM-Ọ-NĪ′Ạ-CẠL, }
DẸ-MŌ′NỊ-ĂC, *n.* One possessed by a demon.
DĒ-MỌN-ŎL′Ọ-GỴ, *n.* A treatise on evil spirits.
DẸ-MŎN′STRẠ-BLE, *a.* That may be demonstrated; that may be proved. [monstrable.
DẸ-MŎN′STRẠ-BLE-NĔSS, *n.* The being demonstrable.
DẸ-MŎN′STRẠ-BLỴ, *ad.* Evidently; clearly.
DẸ-MŎN′STRĀTE, *v. a.* To prove with certainty.
DĔM-ỌN-STRĀ′TIỌN, *n.* Indubitable proof.
DẸ-MŎN′STRẠ-TĪVE, *a.* Invincibly conclusive.
DẸ-MŎN′STRẠ-TĪVE-LỴ, *ad.* Clearly.
DĔM′ỌN-STRĀ-TỌR *or* DẸ-MŎN′STRĀ-TỌR, *n.* One who demonstrates. [als.
DẸ-MŎR-ẠL-Ị-ZĀ′TIỌN, *n.* Destruction of morals.
DẸ-MŎR′ẠL-ĪZE, *v. a.* To destroy the morals of.
DẸ-MŬL′CẸNT, *a.* Softening; mollifying.
DẸ-MŬR′, *v. n.* To doubt; to pause; to hesitate.
DẸ-MŬR′, *n.* Doubt; hesitation; pause.
DẸ-MŪRE′, *a.* Sober; grave; downcast; modest.
DẸ-MŪRE′LỴ, *ad.* In a demure manner; gravely.
DẸ-MŪRE′NĔSS, *n.* Affected modesty or gravity.
DẸ-MŬR′RẠGE, *n.* Delay of ships:—an allowance for delaying ships. [a lawsuit.
DẸ-MŬR′RẸR, *n.* One who demurs:—stop in
DẸ-MỸ′, *n.* A particular size of paper.
DĔN, *n.* A cavern; the cave of a wild beast.
DẸ-NĂ′′TIỌN-ẠL-ĪZE (dẹ-năsh′ụn-ạl-īz), *v. a.* To take away national rights from.
DẸN-DRŎL′Ọ-GỴ, *n.* Natural history of trees.
DẸ-NĪ′Ạ-BLE, *a.* Capable of being denied.
DẸ-NĪ′ẠL, *n.* Negation; refusal; abjuration.
DẸ-NĪ′ẸR, *n.* One who denies; a refuser.
DĔN′Ị-GRĀTE, *v. a.* To blacken; to make black.
DĔN-Ị-ZĀ′TIỌN, *n.* The act of enfranchising.
DĔN′Ị-ZEN, *n.* A citizen; one enfranchised. [to.
DẸ-NŎM′Ị-NĀTE, *v. a.* To name; to give name
DẸ-NŎM-Ị-NĀ′TIỌN, *n.* A name given to a thing.
DẸ-NŎM′Ị-NẠ-TĪVE, *a.* That gives a name.
DẸ-NŎM′Ị-NĀ-TỌR, *n.* The giver of a name:—term of a fraction denoting the number of parts.
DĔN-Ọ-TĀ′TIỌN, *n.* The act of denoting. [parts.
DẸ-NŌ′TẠ-TĪVE, *a.* Having power to denote.
DẸ-NŌTE′, *v. a.* To mark; to show, betoken.
DẸ-NŌŪNCE′, *v. a.* To threaten; to accuse.

DẸ-NŌŪNCE′MẸNT, *n.* Denunciation.
DẸ-NŌŪNÇ′ẸR, *n.* One who denounces.
DĔNSE, *a.* Close; compact; thick; condensed.
DĔN′SỊ-TỴ, *n.* Closeness; compactness.
DĔNT, *n.* A mark.—*v. a.* To make a dent in;
DĔN′TẠL, *a.* Belonging to the teeth. [to indent.
DĔN′TẠL, *n.* A letter pronounced by the teeth.
DĔNT′ẸD, *a.* Notched; indented. [point.
DĔN′TỊ-CLE, *n.* (*Arch.*) A small projecting
DẸN-TĬC′Ụ-LĀT-ẸD, *a.* Set with small teeth.
DẸN-TĬC-Ụ-LĀ′TIỌN, *n.* The state of being set with teeth, or with prominences like teeth.
DĔN′TỊ-FRĬCE, *n.* A powder for the teeth.
DĔN′TỊST, *n.* A tooth-surgeon or tooth-doctor.
DẸN-TĬ′′TIỌN, *n.* The breeding of teeth; teething:—the time of teething. [naked.
DĔN-Ụ-DĀ′TIỌN, *n.* A stripping or making
DẸ-NŪDE′, *v. a.* To strip; to make naked.
DẸ-NŬN′CỊ-ĀTE (-shẹ-āt), *v. a.* To denounce.
DẸ-NŬN-CỊ-Ā′TIỌN (dẹ-nŭn-shẹ-ā′shụn), *n.* The act of denouncing; menace; arraignment.
DẸ-NŬN′CỊ-Ā-TỌR (dẹ-nŭn-shẹ-ā′tọr), *n.* One who denounces:—a threatener. [own.
DẸ-NỸ′, *v. a.* To contradict; to refuse; to disown.
DẸ-ŎB′STRỤ-ẸNT, *n.* Removing obstructions.
DĒ′Ọ-DĂND, *n.* A thing given or forfeited to God.
DẸ-PĂRT′, *v. n.* To go away; to leave:—to decease; to die. [division.
DẸ-PĂRT′MẸNT, *n.* Separate office, part, or division.
DẸ-PĂRT′ỤRE (dẹ-pärt′yụr), *n.* A going away; abandonment; desertion:—death; decease.
DẸ-PĂST′ỤRE (dẹ-påst′yụr), *v. n.* To feed.
DẸ-PÂU′PẸR-ĀTE, *v. a.* To make poor.
DẸ-PĔND′, *v. n.* To hang; to rely; to adhere.
DẸ-PĔND′ẠNT, *n.* A subordinate; a relier.
DẸ-PĔND′ẸNCE, *n.* Connection; trust; reliance:—something hanging from a support:—connection:—an adjunct; a subject province.
DẸ-PĔND′ẸNT, *a.* Hanging down; subordinate.
DẸ-PĔND′ẸNT, *n.* One subordinate; dependant.
DẸ-PĬCT′, *v. a.* To paint; to portray; to describe.
DĔP-Ị-LĀ′TIỌN, *n.* A pulling off the hair.
DẸ-PĬL′Ạ-TỌ-RỴ, *a.* Taking away the hair.
DẸ-PLĒ′TIỌN, *n.* An emptying:—blood-letting.
DẸ-PLŌR′Ạ-BLE, *a.* Lamentable; calamitous.
DẸ-PLŌR′Ạ-BLE-NĔSS, *n.* The being deplorable.
DẸ-PLŌR′Ạ-BLỴ, *ad.* Lamentably; miserably.
DẸ-PLŌRE′, *v. a.* To lament; to bewail; to mourn; to bemoan. [bewailer.
DẸ-PLŌR′ẸR, *n.* A lamenter; a mourner; a
DẸ-PLŎỸ′, *v. a.* To unfold, as a body of troops.
DĔP-LỤ-MĀ′TIỌN, *n.* A plucking off feathers:—a disease or swelling of the eyelids.
DẸ-PLŪME′, *v. a.* To strip of feathers.
DẸ-PŌ′NẸNT, *n.* One who makes oath to a written statement. [ple.
DẸ-PŎP′Ụ-LĀTE, *v. a.* To dispeople; to unpeople.
DẸ-PŎP-Ụ-LĀ′TIỌN, *n.* Act of depopulating.
DẸ-PŎP′Ụ-LĀT-ỌR, *n.* One who depopulates.
DẸ-PŌRT′, *v. a.* To carry; to demean; to act.
DĔP-ỌR-TĀ′TIỌN, *n.* Removal; transportation; banishment; exile. [meanor.
DẸ-PŌRT′MẸNT, *n.* Conduct; bearing; demeanor.
DẸ-PŌ′SẠ-BLE, *a.* Capable of being deposed.
DẸ-PŌ′SẠL, *n.* The act of divesting of office.
DẸ-PŌSE′, *v. a.* To degrade; to dismiss.
DẸ-PŌSE′, *v. n.* To bear witness; to testify.
DẸ-PŌŞ′ẸR, *n.* One who deposes; a deponent.

DẸ-PŎṢ'ĬT, *v. a.* To lay up ; to drop ; to intrust.
DẸ-PŎṢ'ĬT, *n.* Any thing deposited ; a pledge.
DẸ-PŎṢ'Ĭ-TA-RY, *n.* One to whom a thing is intrusted.—(*Law.*)Receiver of another's goods.
DĔP-Ọ-ṢĬ''TIỌN (dĕp-ọ-zĭsh'ụn), *n.* The act of giving testimony on oath ; testimony in writing under oath :—dethronement. [thing.
DẸ-PŎṢ'Ĭ-TỌ-RY, *n.* A place for lodging any
DẸ-PŌT' (dẹ-pō'), *n.* A depository ; a storehouse ; a warehouse :—railway station.
DĔP-RA-VĀ'TIỌN, *n.* Corruption ; depravity.
DẸ-PRĀVE', *v. a.* To vitiate ; to corrupt ; to spoil.
DẸ-PRĂV'Ĭ-TY, *n.* Corruption ; a vitiated state.
DĔP'RẸ-CĀTE, *v. a.* To beg off ; to pray against.
DĔP-RẸ-CĀ'TIỌN, *n.* Prayer against evil.
DĔP'RẸ-CA-TỌ-RY, *a.* That serves to deprecate.
DĔP'RẸ-CA-TỌR, *n.* One who deprecates.
DẸ-PRĒ'CĬ-ĀTE (dẹ-prē'shẹ-āt), *v. a.* To undervalue ; to disparage ; to decry ; to malign.
DẸ-PRĒ-CĬ-Ā'TIỌN (dẹ-prē-shẹ-ā'shụn), *n.* Act of lessening the worth or value of any thing.
DĔP'RẸ-DĀTE, *v. a.* To rob ; to pillage ; to spoil.
DĔP-RẸ-DĀ'TIỌN, *n.* A robbing ; a spoiling.
DĔP'RẸ-DĀ-TỌR, *n.* A robber ; a devourer.
DẸ-PRĔSS', *v. a.* To cast down, humble, deject.
DẸ-PRĔS'SIỌN (dẹ-prĕsh'ụn), *n.* Dejection ; despondency ; melancholy :—a hollow. [down.
DẸ-PRĔSS'ỌR, *n.* One that keeps or presses
DĔP-RĬ-VĀ'TIỌN, *n.* The act of depriving ; loss.
DẸ-PRĪVE', *v. a.* To take from, bereave, debar.
DẸ-PRĪV'ẸR, *n.* He who, or that which,deprives.
DĔPTH, *n.* Deepness ; profundity ; sagacity.
DẸ-PŬL'SIỌN, *n.* A driving or thrusting away.
DĔP'Ụ-RĀTE, *v. a.* To purify ; to cleanse.
DĔP-Ụ-RĀ'TIỌN, *n.* The act of cleansing.
DĔP-Ụ-TĀ'TIỌN, *n.* Act of deputing :—vicegerency ; commission :—persons deputed.
DẸ-PŪTE', *v. a.* To send ; to empower to act.
DĔP'Ụ-TY, *n.* A delegate ; a substitute ; any one that transacts business for another.
DẸ-RĂÇ'Ĭ-NĀTE, *v. a.* To pluck up by the roots.
DẸ-RĂNǴE', *v. a.* To disorder ; to embarrass.
DẸ-RĂNǴE'MẸNT, *n.* Disorder :—disorder of mind ; delirium ; insanity. [saken.
DĔR'Ẹ-LĬCT, *a.* Purposely relinquished ; for-
DĔR-Ẹ-LĬC'TIỌN, *n.* Act of forsaking ; desertion.
DĔR'Ẹ-LĬCT, *n.* (*Law.*) Any thing purposely relinquished or forsaken. [scorn.
DẸ-RĪDE', *v. a.* To laugh at ; to mock ; to
DẸ-RĪD'ẸR, *n.* One who derides ; a scoffer.
DẸ-RĬ''SIỌN (dẹ-rĭzh'ụn), *n.* The act of deriding or laughing at ; contempt ; scorn ; mockery.
DẸ-RĪ'SĬVE, *a.* Containing derision ; mocking.
DẸ-RĪ'SỌ-RY, *a.* Mocking ; ridiculing ; derisive.
DẸ-RĪV'A-BLE, *a.* Coming by derivation.
DĔR-Ĭ-VĀ'TIỌN, *n.* Act of deriving ; a tracing.
DẸ-RĬV'A-TĬVE, *a.* Derived from another.
DẸ-RĬV'A-TĬVE, *n.* The thing or word derived.
DẸ-RĪVE', *v. a.* To deduce ; to draw ; to obtain.
DẸ-RĪV'ẸR, *n.* One that derives or draws.
DERNIER (dern-yár' *or* dĕr'nẹ-ẹr), *a.* Last ; final ;—used only in the phrase, *dernier resort.*
DĔR'Ọ-GĀTE, *v. a. & n.* To disparage ; to detract.
DĔR-Ọ-GĀ'TIỌN, *n.* A defamation ; detraction.
DẸ-RŎG'A-TỌ-RY, *a.* Detracting ; dishonoring.
DĔR'VĬS, *n.* A Turkish or Asiatic monk. [tion.
DĔS'CĂNT, *n.* A song ; a discourse ; a disputa-
DẸS-CĂNT', *v. n.* To sing ; to discourse, expatiate.

DẸ-SCĔND' (dẹ-sĕnd'), *v. n.* To come down.
DẸ-SCĔND'ĂNT, *n.* Offspring of an ancestor.
DẸ-SCĔND'ẸNT, *a.* Falling ; descending.
DẸ-SCĔND-Ĭ-BĬL'Ĭ-TY, *n.* The being descendible.
DẸ-SCĔND'Ĭ-BLE, *a.* Capable of being descended :—that may descend. [sion.
DẸ-SCĔN'SIỌN, *n.* A going downward ; declen-
DẸ-SCĔN'SIỌN-AL, *a.* Relating to descent.
DẸ-SCĔN'SĬVE, *a.* Descending ; having power to descend ; tending downward.
DẸ-SCĔNT', *n.* Declivity ; invasion ; extraction.
DẸ-SCRĪBE', *v. a.* To delineate ; to represent
DẸ-SCRĪB'ẸR, *n.* One who describes.[by words.
DẸ-SCRĪ'ẸR, *n.* A discoverer ; a detecter.
DẸ-SCRĬP'TIỌN, *n.* Act of describing ; delineation ; relation ; account ; representation.
DẸ-SCRĬP'TĬVE, *a.* Containing description.
DẸ-SCRŸ', *v. a.* To spy ; to detect ; to discover.
DĔS'Ẹ-CRĀTE, *v. a.* To divest of sacredness ; to profane :—to divest of sacred office.
DĔS-Ẹ-CRĀ'TIỌN, *n.* The act of desecrating.
DĔṢ'ẸRT, *n.* A wilderness ; a solitude ; waste.
DĔṢ'ẸRT, *a.* Wild ; waste ; solitary ; void.
DẸ-ṢĔRT', *v. a.* To forsake ; to abandon.
DẸ-ṢĔRT', *v. n.* To run away clandestinely.
DẸ-ṢĔRT', *n.* Claim to reward ; merit or desert. [merit.
DẸ-ṢĔRT'ẸR, *n.* One who deserts.
DẸ-ṢĔR'TIỌN, *n.* Act of deserting ; dereliction.
DẸ-ṢĔRVE', *v. n.* To be worthy of good or ill.
DẸ-ṢĔRVE', *v. a.* To be worthy of ; to merit.
DẸ-ṢĔRV'ĬNG, *a.* Worthy ; meritorious.
DẸ-SĬC'CẠNT, *n.* An application that dries up.
DẸ-SĬC'CĀTE, *v. a. & n.* To dry up.
DẸ-SĬC'CA-TĬVE, *a.* Having the power of drying.
DẸ-SĪD'ẸR-ĀTE, *v. a.* To want ; to desire.
DẸ-SĪD-ẸR-Ā'TỤM, *n.* ; *pl.* DẸ-SĪD-ẸR-Ā'TA. Something not possessed, but wanted.
‖DẸ-SĪGN' (dẹ-sīn' *or* dẹ-zīn'), *v. a.* To purpose ; to intend ; to plan ; to project. [a sketch.
‖DẸ-SĪGN' (-sīn'), *n.* Intention ; purpose ; plan ;
‖DẸ-SĪGN'A-BLE (-sīn'), *a.* Capable of being designed ; that may be marked out.
DĔS'ĬG-NĀTE, *v. a.* To point out ; to mark.
DĔS-ĬG-NĀ'TIỌN, *n.* Appointment ; direction.
‖DẸ-SĪGN'ẸD-LY (dẹ-sīn'ẹd-lẹ), *ad.* Purposely.
‖DẸ-SĪGN'ẸR (dẹ-sīn'ẹr), *n.* One who designs.
‖DẸ-SĪGN'ĬNG (de-sīn'ĭng), *p. a.* Insidious.
DẸ-SĪR'A-BLE, *a.* Worthy of desire ; pleasing.
DẸ-SĪR'A-BLE-NĔSS, *n.* Quality of being desirable ; needfulness ; eligibility. [joy.
DẸ-SĪRE', *n.* Wish ; eagerness to obtain or en-
DẸ-SĪRE', *v. a.* To wish or long for ; to covet.
DẸ-SĪR'ẸR, *n.* One who desires ; a wisher.
DẸ-SĪR'OỤS, *a.* Full of desire ; eager ; coveting.
DẸ-SĬST', *v. n.* To cease ; to stop ; to forbear.
DẸ-SĬST'ẠNCE, *n.* The act of desisting ; cessation ; forbearance ; a leaving off ; a stopping.
DĔSK, *n.* An inclined table to write on ; a pul-
DĔS'Ọ-LĀTE, *a.* Laid waste ; solitary. [pit.
DĔS'Ọ-LĀTE, *v. n.* To depopulate ; to lay waste.
DĔS'Ọ-LĀ-TẸR, *n.* One who causes desolation.
DĔS-Ọ-LĀ'TIỌN, *n.* Devastation ; sadness.
DẸ-SPAIR', *n.* Hopeless state ; despondence.
DẸ-SPAIR', *v. n.* To be without hope ; to de-
DẸ-SPAIR'ẸR, *n.* One without hope. [spond.
DẸ-SPAIR'ĬNG-LY, *ad.* In a despairing manner.
DẸ-SPĂTCH', *or* DĬS-PĂTCH', *v. a.* To send away hastily :—to expedite :—to kill.

DĘ-SPĂTCH', *n.* Speed :—an express :—message.
DĘ-SPĂTCH'ĘR, *n.* One who despatches.
DĔS-PĘ-RĀ'DŌ, *n. ; pl.* DĔS-PĘ-RĀ'DŌEŞ. One who is desperate ; a reckless man ; a robber.
DĔS'PĘR-ATE, *a.* Without hope ; rash ; reckless.
DĔS-PĘR-Ā'TIQN, *n.* Hopelessness ; despair.
DĔS'PI-CA-BLE, *a.* Contemptible ; vile.
DĔS'PI-CA-BLE-NĔSS, *n.* Meanness ; vileness.
DĔS'PI-CA-BLY, *ad.* Contemptibly ; meanly.
DĘ-SPĪŞE', *v.* To scorn ; to contemn ; to spurn.
DĘ-SPĪŞ'ĘR, *n.* A contemner ; a scorner.
DĘ-SPĪTE', *n.* Malice ; malignity ; defiance.
DĘ-SPĪTE'FŬL, *a.* Malicious ; full of spleen.
DĘ-SPOÏL', *v. a.* To rob ; to deprive ; to divest.
DĘ-SPŌ-LI-Ā'TIQN, *n.* The act of despoiling.
DĘ-SPŎND', *v. n.* To despair ; to lose hope.
DĘ-SPŎND'ĘN-CY, *n.* Despair ; hopelessness.
DĘ-SPŎND'ĘNT, *a.* Despairing ; hopeless.
DĘ-SPŎND'ĘR, *n.* One who is without hope.
DĔS'PQT, *n.* An absolute ruler ; a tyrant.
DĔS-PŎT'IC, DĔS-PŎT'I-CAL, *a.* Absolute.
DĔS-PŎT'I-CAL-LY, *ad.* In an arbitrary manner.
DĔS'PQT-ĪŞM, *n.* Absolute power ; tyranny.
DĘ-SPŬ'MĀTE, *v. n.* To foam ; to froth ; to work.
DĔS-PU-MĀ'TIQN, *n.* Scum ; frothiness.
DĔS-QUA-MĀ'TIQN, *n.* Act of scaling bones.
DĔŞ ŞĔRT', *n.* Service of fruits, &c., at table.
DĔS'TI-NĀTE, *v. a.* To design for any end.
DĔS-TI-NĀ'TIQN, *n.* End or ultimate design.
DĔS'TINE, *v. a.* To doom ; to appoint ; to devote.
DĔS'TI-NY, *n.* Fate ; invincible necessity ; doom.
DĔS'TI-TŪTE, *a.* Forsaken ; friendless ; in want.
DĔS-TI-TŪ'TIQN, *n.* Utter want ; indigence.
DĘ-STRŎŸ', *v. a.* To lay waste ; to ruin ; to kill.
DĘ-STRŎŸ'ĘR, *n.* One who destroys or ruins.
DĘ-STRŬC'TI-BLE, *a.* Liable to be destroyed.
DĘ-STRŬC'TIQN, *n.* A killing ; ruin ; overthrow.
DĘ-STRŬC'TIVE, *a.* That destroys ; ruinous.
DĘ-STRŬC'TIVE-LY, *ad.* With destruction.
DĘ-STRŬC'TIVE-NĔSS, *n.* Quality of destroying.
DĔS-U-DĀ'TIQN, *n.* A profuse sweating.
DĔS'UE-TŪDE (dĕs'wę-tūd), *n.* Cessation of use ; disuse ; discontinuance. [ical.
DĔS'ŬL-TQ-RY, *a.* Loose ; unsettled ; immethod-
DĘ-TĂCH', *v. a.* To sever ; to send off, as a party.
DĘ-TĂCH'MĔNT, *n.* A body of troops detached.
DĘ-TĀIL', *v. a.* To relate particularly.
DĘ-TĀIL', *n.* A minute account or narration.
DĘ-TĀIL'ĘR, *n.* One who relates particulars.
DĘ-TĀIN', *v. a.* To withhold ; to keep back.
DĘ-TĀIN'DĘR, *n.* Writ to detain one in custody.
DĘ-TĀIN'ĘR, *n.* One who, or that which, detains.
DĘ-TĔCT', *v. a.* To discover ; to find out.
DĘ-TĔC'TIQN, *n.* Discovery, as of guilt or fraud.
DĘ-TĔN'TIQN, *n.* Act of keeping ; restraint.
DĘ-TĔR', *v. n.* To discourage ; to hinder.
DĘ-TĔR'ĢĘNT, *a.* Having power of cleansing.
DĘ-TĔR'ĢĘNT, *n.* A substance that cleanses.
DĘ-TĒ'RI-Q-RĀTE, *v. a.* To impair ; to make worse.—*v. n.* To grow or become worse.
DĘ-TĒ-RI-Q-RĀ'TIQN, *n.* Act of making worse.
DĘ-TĔR'MI-NA-BLE, *a.* That may be determined.
DĘ-TĔR'MI-NATE, *a.* Definite ; decisive ; fixed.
DĘ-TĔR'MI-NATE-LY, *ad.* Definitely ; certainly.
DĘ-TĔR-MI-NĀ'TIQN, *n.* Resolution ; decision.
DĘ-TĔR'MI-NĀ-TQR, *n.* One who determines.
DĘ-TĔR'MINE, *v. a. & n.* To fix ; to settle ; to adjust ; to decide ; to purpose ; to influence.

DĘ-TĔR'SIQN, *n.* The act of cleansing a sore.
DĘ-TĔR'SIVE, *a.* Having the power to cleanse.
DĘ-TĔST', *v. a.* To hate ; to abhor, abominate.
DĘ-TĔST'A-BLE, *a.* Hateful ; abominable.
DĘ-TĔST'A-BLY, *ad.* Hatefully ; abominably.
DĔT-ĘS-TĀ'TIQN, *n.* Hatred ; abhorrence.
DĘ-TĔST'ĘR, *n.* One who hates or abhors.
DĘ-THRŌNE', *v. a.* To divest of sovereignty.
DĘ-THRŌNE'MĘNT, *n.* The act of dethroning.
DĘ-THRŌN'ĘR, *n.* One who dethrones.
DĔT'I-NŪE *or* DĘ-TĪN'UE, *n.* A kind of writ.
DĔT'Q-NĀTE, DĔT'Q-NĪZE, *v. n. & a.* To explode or cause to explode with a loud report.
DĔT-Q-NĀ'TIQN, *n.* An explosion with noise.
DĘ-TŎRT', *v. a.* To wrest from the design.
DĘ-TŎR'SIQN, *n.* A perversion ; a wresting.
DĘ-TRĂCT', *v. a. & n.* To derogate ; to defame ; to slander ; to depreciate ; to take away.
DĘ-TRĂC'TIQN, *n.* A taking away ; slander.
DĘ-TRĂC'TIVE, *a.* Tending to detract.
DĘ-TRĂCT'QR, *n.* One who detracts ; a defamer.
DĔT'RI-MĔNT, *n.* Loss ; damage ; mischief.
DĔT-RI-MĔN'TAL, *a.* Mischievous ; causing loss.
DĘ-TRŪDE', *v. a.* To thrust down. [loss.
DĘ-TRŬN'CĀTE, *v. a.* To lop ; to cut off.
DĔT-RUN-CĀ'TIQN, *n.* The act of cutting off.
DĘ-TRŪ'ŞIQN, *n.* The act of thrusting down.
DEŪCE (dūs), *n.* The two in cards or dice.
DEŪSE (dūs), *n.* A cant name for the devil.
DEŪ-TĘR-ŎG'A-MY, *n.* A second marriage.
DEŪ-TĘR-ŎN'Q-MY, *n.* The second law ; the fifth and last book of Moses. [waste.
DĘ-VĂS'TĀTE *or* DĔV'AS-TĀTE, *v. a.* To lay
DĔV-AS-TĀ'TIQN, *n.* Waste ; havoc ; desolation.
DĘ-VĔL'QP, *v. a.* To unfold, unravel, disclose.
DĘ-VĔL'QP-MĔNT, *n.* A disclosure ; an unfolding.
DĘ-VĔST', *v. a.* To strip. See DIVEST.
DĘ-VĔX'I-TY, *n.* A bending down ; declivity.
DĒ'VI-ĀTE, *v. n.* To wander ; to go astray.
DĒ-VI-Ā'TIQN, *n.* Act of deviating ; offence.
DĘ-VĪCE', *n.* A contrivance ; design ; emblem.
DĔV'IL (dĕv'vl), *n.* A fallen angel ; evil spirit.
DĔV'IL-ISH (dĕv'vl-ish), *a.* Diabolical ; wicked.
DĒ'VI-OŬS, *a.* Out of the common way ; erring.
DĘ-VĪŞ'A-BLE, *a.* That may be devised.
DĘ-VĪŞE', *v. a.* To contrive ; to invent :—to bequeath ; to grant or give by will. [plan.
DĘ-VĪŞE', *v. n.* To consider ; to contrive ; to
DĘ-VĪŞE', *n.* A gift of lands by will ; a bequest.
DĔV-I-ŞĒĒ', *n.* One to whom a thing is bequeathed ;—the correlative of *devisor.*
DĘ-VĪŞ'ĘR, *n.* A contriver. [queaths.
DĔV-I-ŞŌR' *or* DĘ-VĪŞ'QR, *n.* One who be-
DĘ-VOÏD', *a.* Empty ; vacant ; void ; free from.
DEVOIR (dĕv-wŏr'), *n.* [Fr.] An act of civility.
DĔV-Q-LŪ'TIQN, *n.* The act of rolling down.
DĘ-VŎLVE', *v. a. & n.* To roll down ; to fall.
DĘ-VŌTE', *v. a.* To dedicate ; to consecrate.
DĘ-VŌT'ED-NĔSS, *n.* State of being devoted.
DĔV-Q-TĒĒ', *n.* One entirely devoted ; a bigot.
DĘ-VŌ'TIQN, *n.* Piety ; worship ; prayer ; ardor.
DĘ-VŌ'TIQN-AL, *a.* Pertaining to devotion.
DĘ-VOÛR', *v. a.* To eat up ravenously ; to con-
DĘ-VOÛR'ĘR, *n.* One who devours. [sume.
DĘ-VOÛT', *a.* Pious ; religious ; earnest ; sincere.
DĘ-VOÛT'LY, *ad.* In a devout manner ; piously ; religiously ; sincerely. [piety.
DĘ-VOÛT'NĔSS, *n.* Quality of being devout ;

DEW̄ (dū), n. Moisture deposited at night.
DEW̄'DRŎP (dū'drŏp), n. A drop of dew.
DEW̄'LĄP, n. A membranous, fleshy substance
. hanging down from the throat of an ox, &c.
DEW̄'Y, a. Like dew ; partaking of dew.
DĔX'TĘR, a. [L.] The right ;—used in heraldry.
DĘX-TĔR'Į-TY, n. Readiness ; activity ; expert-
DĔX'TĘR-OŬS, a. Ready ; expert ; skilful. [ness.
DĔX'TĘR-OŲS-NĔSS (dĕk'stẹr-), n. Dexterity.
DĔX'TRĄL, a. The right ;—opposed to the left.
DEY (dā), n. Title of the governor of Algiers.
DĪ-Ạ-BĒ'TĘŞ, n. A morbid secretion of urine.
DĪ-Ạ-BŎL'ĮC, DĪ-Ạ-BŎL'Į-CĄL, a. Devilish ;
atrocious ; impious ; outrageous ; wicked.
DĪ-Ạ-BŎL'Į-CĄL-LY, ad. In a diabolical manner.
DĪ-Ạ-BŎL'Į-CĄL-NĔSS,n.Devilishness ; atrocity.
DĮ-ĂC'Ọ-NĄL, a. Pertaining to a deacon.
DĪ-Ạ-CÖŬS'TĮCS, n. Science of refracted sounds.
DĪ'Ạ-DĔM, n. A crown ; the mark of royalty.
DĪ'Ạ-DĔMED (dī'ạ-dĕmd), a. Crowned.
DĪ-ÆR'Ę-SĬS (dī-ĕr'ẹ-sĭs), n. ; pl. DĪ-ÆR'Ę-SĔŞ.
The mark [··], used to separate syllables.
DĪ-AG-NŎS'TĮC, n. A distinguishing symptom.
DĪ-ĂG'Ọ-NĄL, a. Reaching from angle to angle.
DĪ-ĂG'Ọ-NĄL, n. A line from angle to angle.
DĪ-ĂG'Ọ-NĄL-LY, ad. In a diagonal direction.
DĪ'Ạ-GRĂM, n. A geometrical figure ; a sketch.
DĪ'ĄL, n. An instrument for measuring time.
DĪ'Ạ-LĔCT, n. Peculiar form of a language.
DĪ-Ạ-LĔC'TĮC, DĪ-Ạ-LĔC'TĮ-CĄL, a. Logical.
DĪ-Ạ-LĔC-TĪ''CIĄN (-lẹk-tĭsh'ụn), n. Logician.
DĪ-Ạ-LĔC'TĮCS, n. pl. Logic ; art of reasoning.
DĪ'ĄL-ĬNG, n. The art of constructing dials.
DĪ'ĄL-ĬST, n. One who constructs dials.
DĪ-ĂL'Ọ-ĢĬST, n. A speaker or writer of dia-
logue ; an interlocutor. [logue.
DĪ-ĂL-Ọ-ĢĬS'TĮC, a. Having the form of a dia-
DĪ'Ạ-LŎGUE (dī'ạ-lŏg), n. A conference ; a con-
versation between two or more ; a colloquy.
DĪ'ĄL-PLĀTE, n. The plate of a dial on which
the hours are marked ; face of a clock or watch.
DĮ-ĂM'Ę-TĘR, n. A line which, passing through
the centre of a circle,divides it into equal parts.
DĪ-Ạ-MĔT'RĮ-CĄL, a. Describing a diameter ;
in the direction of a diameter ; direct.[rection.
DĪ-Ạ-MĔT'RĮ-CĄL-LY, ad. In a diametrical di-
DĪ'Ạ-MỌND or DĪA'MỌND, n. A precious gem.
DĪ-Ạ-PĀ'ŞỌN, n. (Mus.) An octave ; compass.
DĪ'Ạ-PĘR, n. Linen woven in flowers or figures.
DĪ-Ạ-PHĄ-NĒ'Į-TY, n. Transparency. [lucid.
DĮ-ĂPH'Ạ-NOŬS, a. Transparent ; clear ; pel-
DĪ-ĂPH-Ọ-RĔT'ĮC, or DĪ-ĂPH-Ọ-RĔT'Į-CĄL, a.
Causing profuse perspiration ; sudorific.
DĪ'Ạ-PHRĂGM (dī'ạ-frăm), n. A large separat-
ing muscle ; the midriff.
DĪ'Ạ-RĬST, n. One who keeps a diary or journal.
DĪ-AR-RHŒ'Ạ (dī-ạr-rē'ạ), n. A flux ; a purging.
DĪ-AR-RHŒT'ĮC (dī-ạr-rĕt'ĭk), a. Purgative.
DĪ'Ạ-RY, n. A daily account ; a journal.
DĪ'Ạ-STĔM, n. (Mus.) A simple interval.
DĪ-ĂS'TỌ-LĘ, n. (Rhet.) A figure by which a
short syllable is made long. [to tone.
DĪ-Ạ-TŎN'ĮC, a. (Mus.) Proceeding from tone
DĪ'Ạ-TRĪBE or DĪ-ĂT'RĮ-BĘ, n. A disputation.
DĬB'BLE, n. A gardener's planting tool.
DĪCE, n. pl. of die.—v. n. To game with dice.
DĪCE'-BŎX, n. Box from which dice are thrown.
DĪÇ'ĘR, n. A player at dice ; one who dices.

DĬC'TĀTE, v. a. To tell what to write ; to order.
DĬC'TĀTE, n. A precept ; maxim ; order ; rule.
DĮC-TĀ'TIỌN, n. The act of dictating ; order.
DĮC-TĀ'TỌR, n. A ruler ; a Roman magistrate.
DĬC-TĄ-TŌ'RĮ-ĄL,a.Authoritative ; overbearing.
DĮC-TĀ'TỌR-SHĬP, n. The office of dictator.
DĬC'TIỌN, n. Style ; language ; expression.
DĬC'TIỌN-Ạ-RY, n. A book in which words are
explained in alphabetical order ; a lexicon.
DĬD, imp. t. from do. [giving instruction.
DĮ-DĂC'TĮC, DĮ-DĂC'TĮ-CĄL, a. Preceptive ;
DĬD'ĄP-PĘR, n. A kind of aquatic bird.
DIE (dī), v. n. To lose life ; to expire ; to perish.
DIE, n. ; pl. DĪCE. A small cube to play with.
DIE (dī), n. ; pl. DĪEŞ. A stamp for coin.
DĪ'ĘT, n. Food ; victuals :—an assembly.
DĪ'ĘT, v. a. To supply with food ; to feed.
DĪ'ĘT, v. n. To eat by rule ; to eat sparingly.
DĪ'ĘT–DRĬNK, n. A medicated liquor. [diet.
DĪ-Ę-TĔT'ĮC, DĪ-Ę-TĔT'Į-CĄL, a. Relating to
DĬF'FĘR, v. n. To be unlike ; to vary ; to disagree.
DĬF'FĘR-ĔNCE, n. Dissimilarity ; dispute.
DĬF'FĘR-ĔNT, a. Distinct ; unlike ; dissimilar.
DĬF-FĘR-ĔN'TIĄL, a. Infinitely small.
DĬF'FĘR-ĔNT-LY, ad. In a different manner.
DĬF'FĮ-CŬLT, a. Hard ; not easy ; vexatious. [ty.
DĬF'FĮ-CŬL-TY, n. Hardness ; distress ; perplexi-
DĬF'FĮ-DĔNCE, n. Distrust ; want of confidence.
DĬF'FĮ-DĔNT, a. Distrustful ; not confident.
DĬF'FĮ-DĔNT-LY, ad. In a diffident manner.
DĬF'FŎRM, a. Unlike ; of two forms ; irregular.
DĮF-FŪŞE', v. a. To pour out, spread, scatter.
DĮF-FŪSE', a. Widely spread ; copious ; prolix.
DĮF-FŪSE'LY, ad. Extensively ; copiously.
DĮF-FŪŞ'Į-BLE, a. Capable of being diffused.
DĮF-FŪ'ŞIỌN (dĭf-fū'zhụn), n. Dispersion.
DĮF-FŪ'SĮVE, a. Scattered ; dispersed ; diffuse.
DĮF-FŪ'SĮVE-LY, ad. Widely ; extensively.
DĮF-FŪ'SĮVE-NĔSS, n. Extension ; dispersion.
DĬG, v. a. & n. [imp. t. & pp. dug, digged.] To
turn up or cultivate land ; to excavate.
DĪ'ĢĔST, n. A body of civil laws ; a pandect.
DĮ-ĢĔST', v. a. To arrange ; to dissolve, as food.
DĮ-ĢĔST'ĘR, n. He who, or that which, digests.
DĮ-ĢĔST'Į-BLE, a. Capable of being digested.
DĮ-ĢĔS'TIỌN, n. Act of digesting ; concoction.
DĮ-ĢĔS'TĮVE, a. Causing digestion ; dissolving.
DĬG'ĢĘR, n. One who digs or opens the ground.
DĬG'ĢĮNG, n. Place where ore is dug.
DĪGHT (dīt), v. a. To dress ; to deck ; to adorn.
DĬG'ĬT, n. Three fourths of an inch :—twelfth
part of the diameter of the sun or moon :—
one of the ten arithmetical symbols or figures.
DĬG'Į-TĄL, a. Pertaining to a digit or finger.
DĬĢ-Į-TĀ'LĮS, n. Foxglove ; a genus of plants.
DĬĢ'Į-TĀT-ĘD, a. Branched out like fingers.
DĬG'NĮ-FĪED (dĭg'nẹ-fīd), a. Invested with
dignity ; exalted ; honored ; noble ; stately.
DĬG'NĮ-FȲ, v. a. To advance ; to exalt ; to honor.
DĬG'NĮ-TĄ-RY, n. A clergyman of some rank.
DĬG'NĮ-TY, n. True honor ; rank ; grandeur.
DĪ'GRĂPH, n. A union of two vowels, or of
two consonants, representing a single sound.
DĮ-GRĔSS', v. n. To turn aside ; to wander.
DĮ-GRĔS'SIỌN (dẹ-grĕsh'ụn), n. Act of digress-
ing ; a turning aside ; an excursion. [ing.
DĮ-GRĔS'SĮVE, a. Tending to digress ; deviat-
DIKE, n. A channel ; a ditch ; a bank ; a mound.

DĬ-LĂÇ'ĔR-ĀTE, *v. a.* To tear apart; to rend.
DĬ-LĂÇ-ĔR-Ā'TIǪN, *n.* Act of rending in two.
DĬ-LĂP'Ĭ-DĀTE, *v. n.* To go to ruin; to fall.
DĬ-LĂP-Ĭ-DĀ'TIǪN, *n.* State of being dilapidated; waste; decay; destruction. [dation.
DĬ-LĂP'Ĭ-DĀ-TǪR, *n.* One who causes dilapi-
DĬ-LĀ-TĄ-BĬL'Ĭ-TȲ, *n.* Quality of being dilatable.
DĬ-LĀ'TĄ-BLE, *a.* That may be dilated or extended; capable of extension; extensible.
DĬL-Ą-TĀ'TIǪN, *n.* Expansion; extension.
DĬ-LĀTE', *v. a.* & *n.* To extend, spread; enlarge.
DĬ-LĀ'TǪR, *n.* That which widens or extends.
DĬL'Ą-TǪ-RĬ-LȲ, *ad.* In a dilatory manner.
DĬL'Ą-TǪ-RĬ-NĔSS, *n.* Slowness; sluggishness.
DĬL'Ą-TǪ-RȲ, *a.* Tardy; late; slow; loitering.
DĬ-LĔM'MĄ, *n.* A difficult, vexatious alternative.
DĬL'Ĭ-ĢĔNCE, *n.* Industry; assiduity; activity.
DĬL'Ĭ-ĢĔNT, *a.* Assiduous; not idle; sedulous.
DĬL'Ĭ-ĢĔNT-LY, *ad.* With assiduity; sedulously.
DĬLL, *n.* An annual aromatic plant.
DĬL'Ų-ĔNT, *a.* Making thin or more fluid.
DĬL'Ų-ĔNT, *n.* That which thins other matter.
DĬ-LŪTE', *v. a.* To make thin; to make weak.
DĬ-LŪTE', *a.* Thin; attenuated; weak; diluted.
DĬ-LŪT'ĔR, *n.* He who, or that which, dilutes.
DĬ-LŪ'TIǪN, *n.* Act of making thin or weak.
DĬ-LŪ'VĬ-ĄL, DĬ-LŪ'VĬ-ĄN, *a.* Relating to the deluge:—caused by a deluge or flood.
DĬM, *a.* Not seeing clearly:—obscure:—dull.
DĬM, *v. a.* To cloud; to darken; to obscure.
DĪME, *n.* A silver coin, value of ten cents.
DĬ-MĔN'SIǪN, *n.* Space; bulk; extent; measure.
DĬM'E-TĔR, *a.* Having two poetical measures.
DĬ-MĬN'ĬSH, *v. a.* To lessen; to decrease.
DĬ-MĬN'ĬSH, *v. n.* To grow less; to be impaired.
DĬM-Ĭ-NŪ'TIǪN, *n.* Act of making less; discredit.
DĬ-MĬN'Ų-TĪVE, *a.* Small; little; minute.
DĬ-MĬN'Ų-TĪVE, *n.* A thing little of the kind.
DĬ-MĬN'Ų-TĪVE-LY, *ad.* In a diminutive manner.
DĬ-MĬN'Ų-TĪVE-NĔSS, *n.* Smallness; littleness.
DĬM'Ĭ-TY, *n.* A cotton cloth of thick texture.
DĬM'LY, *ad.* In a dim manner; obscurely.
DĬM'NĔSS, *n.* Dulness of sight; obscurity.
DĬM'PLE, *n.* A hollow in the cheek or chin.
DĬM'PLE, *v. n.* To sink in small cavities.
DĬN, *n.* A loud noise.—*v. a.* To stun with noise.
DĪNE, *v. n.* & *a.* To eat or give a dinner.
DĬNG, *v. a.* [*imp. t.* & *pp.* dinged, dung.] To dash with violence; to impress with force.
DĬNG'-DŎNG, *n.* A word expressing the sound of
DĬN'ĢĬ-NĔSS, *n.* Quality of being dingy. [bells.
DĬN'GLE, *n.* A hollow between hills; a dale.
DĬN'ĢȲ, *a.* Dark brown; dun; dusky; soiled.
DĬN'ĬNG-RŎŎM, *n.* A room for dining in.
DĬN'NĔR, *n.* The chief meal of the day.
DĬNT, *n.* A blow; a mark:—power; force.
DĬNT, *v. a.* To indent or mark by a blow.
DĬ-NŪ-MĔR-Ā'TIǪN, *n.* A numbering one by one.
‖DĬ-ŎÇ'E-SĂN *or* DĬ-Ǫ-CĒ'SĄN, *n.* A bishop, as he stands related to his own clergy or flock.
‖DĬ-ŎÇ'E-SĂN, *a.* Pertaining to a diocese. [ric.
DĬ'Ǫ-CĒSE, *n.* A bishop's jurisdiction; a bishop-
DĬ-ŎP'TRĬCS, *n. pl.* Science of refracted light.
DĬ-Ǫ-RĀ'MĄ, *n.* A kind of optical machine.
DĬ-Ǫ-RĂM'ĬC, *a.* Relating to, or like, a diorama.
DĬP, *v. a.* & *n.* [*imp. t.* & *pp.* dipped, dipt.] To immerse; to put into any liquid; to wet.
DĬP, *n.* Depression; inclination downward.

DĬ-PĔT'Ą-LOŬS, *a.* Having two flower-leaves.
DĬPH'THŎNG (dĭp'thŏng), *n.* A union of two vowels in one sound; as in *vain, Cæsar, brow.*
DĬPH-THŎN'GĄL, *a.* Belonging to a diphthong.
DĬ-PLŌ'MĄ, *n.* A writing conferring a privilege.
DĬ-PLŌ'MĄ-CȲ, *n.* The art or practice of making negotiations between nations:—body of envoys:—political or artful management. [voys.
DĬP-LǪ-MĂT'ĬC, *a.* Respecting diplomacy or en-
DĬ-PLŌ'MĄ-TĬST, *n.* One versed in diplomacy.
DĬP'PĔR, *n.* One that dips:—vessel to dip with.
DĬP'PĬNG-NĒĒ'DLE, *n.* A magnetic needle.
DĬP'TǪTE, *n.* A noun having two cases only.
DĪRE, *a.* Dreadful; dismal; evil; horrible.
DĬ-RĔCT', *a.* Straight; right; open; express.
DĬ-RĔCT', *v. a.* To aim; to regulate; to order.
DĬ-RĔCT'ĔR, *n.* One who, or that which, directs; a superintendent; a director.
DĬ-RĔC'TIǪN, *n.* Aim; order; superscription.
DĬ-RĔC'TĬVE, *a.* Informing; showing the way.
DĬ-RĔCT'LY, *ad.* In a straight line; immediately.
DĬ-RĔCT'NĔSS, *n.* Straightness; straight course.
DĬ-RĔCT'ǪR, *n.* A superintendent; a guide.
DĬ-RĔC'TǪ-RȲ, *n.* Form of prayer:—a rule; a guide:—a book with addresses of individuals.
DĬ-RĔC'TǪ-RȲ, *a.* Guiding; commanding.
DĪRE'FŬL, *a.* Dire; dreadful; dismal; horrible.
DĪRE'FŬL-NĔSS, *n.* Dreadfulness; direness.
DĪRE'NĔSS, *n.* Dismalness; horror; direfulness.
DĬRĢE, *n.* A mournful ditty; a funeral song.
DĬRK, *n.* A kind of dagger or poniard.
DĬRT, *n.* Mud; filth; mire; dust; earth. [dily.
DĬRT'Ĭ-LY, *ad.* Nastily; foully; filthily; sor-
DĬRT'Ĭ-NĔSS, *n.* Filth; meanness; sordidness.
DĬRT'Ȳ, *a.* Foul; nasty; filthy; sullied; mean.
DĬRT'Ȳ, *v. a.* To foul; to soil; to disgrace.
DĬS-Ą-BĬL'Ĭ-TY, *n.* Want of power; weakness.
DĬS-Ā'BLE, *v. a.* To deprive of force; to weaken.
DĬS-Ą-BŪṢE', *v. a.* To undeceive; to set right.
DĬS-ĄC-CǑM-MǪ-DĀ'TIǪN, *n.* State of being unfit.
DĬS-ĄC-CŬS'TǪM, *v. a.* To destroy habit in.
DĬS-ĄD-VĂN'TAGE, *n.* Loss; injury to interest.
DĬS-ĄD-VĂN'TAGE, *v. a.* To injure in interest.
DĬS-ĂD-VĄN-TĀ'ĢEOŲS, *a.* Injurious; hurtful.
DĬS-ĂD-VĄN-TĀ'ĢEOŲS-LY, *ad.* With injury.
DĬS-ĂD-VĄN-TĀ'ĢEOŲS-NĔSS, *n.* Injury; loss.
DĬS-Ą-FĔCT', *v. a.* To alienate; to disorder.
DĬS-Ą-FĔCT'ĔD, *p. a.* Alienated; unfriendly.
DĬS-Ą-FĔC'TIǪN, *n.* Dislike; want of affection.
DĬS-Ą-FĬRM'ĄNCE, *n.* Confutation; negation.
DĬS-Ą-GRĒĒ', *v. n.* To differ in opinion; to dissent; to vary; to quarrel. [unfit.
DĬS-Ą-GRĒĒ'Ą-BLE, *a.* Unpleasing; offensive;
DĬS-Ą-GRĒĒ'Ą-BLE-NĔSS, *n.* Unpleasantness.
DĬS-Ą-GRĒĒ'Ą-BLY, *ad.* In a disagreeable manner; unpleasantly; offensively. [tude.
DĬS-Ą-GRĒĒ'MĔNT, *n.* Difference; dissimili-
DĬS-ĄL-LŌW', *v. a.* To deny; to refuse; to censure; to set aside; to reject. [bation.
DĬS-ĄL-LŌW'ĄNCE, *n.* Prohibition; disappro-
DĬṢ-ĂN'Ĭ-MĀTE, *v. a.* To deprive of life; to de-
DĬS-ĄN-NŬL', *v. a.* To annul; to make void. [ject.
DĬS-ĄP-PĒAR', *v. n.* To be lost to view; to van-
DĬS-ĄP-PĒAR'ĄNCE, *n.* Removal from sight. [ish.
DĬS-ĄP-PŎĬNT', *v. a.* To defeat of expectation.
DĬS-ĄP-PŎĬNT'MĔNT, *n.* Failure of expectation.
DĬS-ĄP-PRǪ-BĀ'TIǪN, *n.* A disapproval.
DĬS-ĄP-PRŎV'ĄL, *n.* Disapprobation; censure.

DĬS-AP-PRŌVE', v. a. To dislike; to censure.
DĬS-ÄRM', v. a. To spoil or divest of arms.
DĬS-AR-RÁNǴE', v. a. To put out of order. [ment.
DĬS-AR-RÁNǴE'MENT, n. Disorder; derange-
DĬS-AR-RÄY', v. a. To undress:—to overthrow.
DĬS-AR-RÄY', n. Disorder; confusion; undress.
DĬS-ÁS'TER, n. Misfortune; grief; calamity.
DĬS-ÁS'TROUS, a. Unlucky; calamitous; gloomy.
DĬS-ÁS'TROUS-LY, ad. In a disastrous manner.
DĬS-ÁS'TROUS-NÈSS,n. Unluckiness; misfortune.
DĬS-A-VŌW', v. a. To disown; to deny; to dis-
DĬS-A-VŌW'AL,n. A disowning; a denial. [claim.
DĬS-BÄND', v. a. & n. To dismiss or retire from
service; to unbind; to break up; to separate.
DĬS-BE-LIĒF' (dĭs-be-lēf'), n. Want of belief.
DĬS-BE-LIĒVE' (dĭs-be-lēv'), v. a. Not to believe.
DĬS-BE-LIĒV'ER, n. One who refuses belief.
DĬS-BÜR'DEN (dĭz-bür'dn), v. a. To unload.
DĬS-BÜRSE', v. a. To pay out, as money.
DĬS-BÜRSE'MENT, n. A disbursing; sum spent.
DĬS-BÜRS'ER, n. One who disburses. [off.
DĬS-CÄRD', v. a. To dismiss from service; to cast
DĬS-CÄSE', v. a. To strip; to undress; to divest.
DĬS-CÈRN' (dĭz-zërn'), v. a. To descry; to see;
to judge.—v. n. To make distinction; to judge.
DĬS-CÈRN'ER (dĭz-zër'ner),n. One who discerns.
DĬS-CÈRN'I-BLE (dĭz-zër'ne-bl), a. Perceptible.
DĬS-CÈRN'ING (dĭz-zër'ning), p. a. Judicious.
DĬS-CÈRN'MENT (dĭz-zërn'ment),n. Judgment.
DĬS-CHÄRǴE', v. a. To unload, pay, execute.
DĬS-CHÄRǴE', v. n. To deliver a charge; to fire.
DĬS-CHÄRǴE', n. Release; payment; execution.
DĬS-CĪ'PLE, n. A follower:—a pupil; a scholar.
DĬS-CĪ'PLE-SHĬP, n. The state of a disciple.
DĬS'CĪ-PLĬN-A-BLE, a. Capable of instruction.
DĬS-CĪ-PLĬ-NÄ'RI-AN, n. One strict in discipline.
DĬS'CĪ-PLĬ-NA-RY, a. Pertaining to discipline.
DĬS'CĪ-PLĬNE, n. Instruction; government.
DĬS'CĪ-PLĬNE, v. a. To educate, regulate, punish.
DĬS-CLÄIM', v. a. To disown; to renounce.
DĬS-CLÄIM'ER, n. One who disclaims; a denial.
DĬS-CLŌSE', v. a. To uncover; to reveal; to tell.
DĬS-CLŌS'URE (dĭs-klō'zhur), n. Discovery. [of.
DĬS-CÓL'OR, v. a. To stain, or change the color
DĬS-CÓL-O-RÄ'TIQN, n. Change of color; stain.
DĬS-CÖM'FĬT, v. a. To defeat; to vanquish.
DĬS-CÖM'FĬT-ŪRE, n. Defeat; overthrow; rout.
DĬS-CÖM'FORT, n. Uneasiness; sorrow; grief.
DĬS-CÖM'FORT, v. a. To disquiet; to sadden.
DĬS-COM-MÈND', v. a. To blame; to censure.
DĬS-COM-MÈND'A-BLE, a. Blamable.
DĬS-CÖM-MEN-DÄ'TIQN, n. Blame; censure.
DĬS-CÖM-MŌDE', v. a. To put to inconvenience.
DĬS-CQM-MŌ'DĬ-OÙS, a. Inconvenient.
DĬS-CQM-PŌSE', v. a. To disorder; to disturb.
DĬS-CQM-PŌS'URE (-kom-pō'zhur), n. Disorder.
DĬS-CON-CÈRT', v. a. To frustrate; to disturb.
DĬS-CON-FÖRM'I-TY, n. Want of conformity.
DĬS-CON-NÈCT', v. a. To separate; to disjoin.
DĬS-CON-NÈC'TIQN, n. Disunion; separation.
DĬS-CÖN'SQ-LATE, a. Comfortless; sorrowful.
DĬS-CÖN'SQ-LATE-LY, ad. In a disconsolate
manner; sorrowfully; sadly. [solate.
DĬS-CÖN'SQ-LATE-NÈSS, n. The being discon-
DĬS-CON-TÈNT', n. Want of content; uneasiness.
DĬS-CON-TÈNT'ED, p. a. Uneasy; dissatisfied.
DĬS-CON-TÈNT'MENT,n.Inquietude; discontent.
DĬS-CON-TĬN'U-ANCE,n.Cessation; intermission.

DĬS-CON-TĬN'UE, v. a. & n. To break off; to cease.
DĬS-CON-TI-NŪ'I-TY, n. Want of contact.
DĬS-CON-TĬN'U-OÙS, a. Interrupted; broken off.
DĬS'CÖRD, n. Disagreement; dissonance.
DĬS-CÖRD'ANCE, n. Disagreement; discord.
DĬS-CÖRD'ANT, a. Inconsistent; inharmonious.
DĬS'CÖÙNT, n. A deduction; an allowance.
DĬS-CÖÙNT', v. a. To pay back again; to deduct.
DĬS-CÖÙN'TE-NANCE, v. a. To abash; to dis-
courage; to show disapprobation of.
DĬS-CÖÙR'AǴE (dĭs-kür'aj), v. a. To depress;
to deprive of confidence; to deter; to dissuade.
DĬS-CÖÙR'AǴE-MÈNT,n.Determent; cause of fear.
DĬS-CŌURSE' (dĭs-kōrs'), n. Conversation; a ser-
mon; a speech; a treatise; a dissertation.
DĬS-CŌURSE', v. n.& a. To converse, talk, discuss.
DĬS-COÙR'TE-OÙS (dĭs-kür'te-ùs), a. Uncivil.
DĬS-COÙR'TE-SY (dĭs-kür'te-se), n. Incivility.
DĬS-CÖV'ER, v. a. To show, disclose, reveal.
DĬS-CÖV'ER-A-BLE, a. That may be discovered.
DĬS-CÖV'ER-ER, n. One who discovers.
DĬS-CÖV'ER-Y, n. The act of finding; disclosure.
DĬS-CRÈD'ĬT, n. Ignominy; reproach; disgrace.
DĬS-CRÈD'ĬT, v. a. To disgrace, distrust. [ful.
DĬS-CRÈD'ĬT-A-BLE, a. Disgraceful; reproach-
DĬS-CRĒET', a. Prudent; circumspect; cautious.
DĬS-CRĒET'LY, ad. Prudently; cautiously.
DĬS-CRĒET'NÈSS, n. Discretion; prudence.
DĬS'CRE-PANCE, n. Difference; contrariety.
DĬS'CRE-PANT, a. Different; disagreeing; unlike.
DĬS-CRĒTE', a. Distinct; disjoined; separate.
DĬS-CRĒ''TIQN (dĭs-krĕsh'un), n. Prudence;
wise management; liberty of acting at pleasure.
DĬS-CRĒ''TIQN-AL (-krĕsh'un-al), a. Unlimited.
DĬS-CRĒ''TIQN-A-RY (dĭs-krĕsh'un-a-re), a. Left
at large; unlimited; unrestrained; discretional.
DĬS-CRĒ'TIVE, a. Separate; disjunctive.
DĬS-CRĬM'I-NATE, v. a. To distinguish, separate.
DĬS-CRĬM-I-NÄ'TIQN, n. Act of distinguishing.
DĬS-CRĬM'I-NA-TIVE, a. Marking distinction.
DĬS-CÙM'BEN-CY,n. Recumbent posture at meals.
DĬS-CÙM'BER, v. a. To unburden; to disengage.
DĬS-CÜR'SIVE, a. Desultory; argumentative.
DĬS-CÜR'SIVE-LY, ad. In a discursive manner.
DĬS'CÙS, n. A quoit; a circular piece of iron.
DĬS-CÙSS', v. a. To examine, debate, disperse.
DĬS-CÙS'SIQN (dĭs-kùsh'un), n. Disquisition.
DĬS-CÙS'SIVE, a. Discussing; dissolving.
DĬS-DÄIN', v. a.& n. To scorn; to think unworthy.
DĬS-DÄIN', n. Contempt; scorn; indignation.
DĬS-DÄIN'FÙL, a. Contemptuous; scornful.
DĬS-DÄIN'FÙL-LY, ad. With haughty scorn.
DĬS-DÄIN'FÙL-NÈSS, n. Contemptuousness.
DĬS-ĒASE'(dĭz-ēz'), n. A distemper; a malady.
DĬS-ĒASE', v. a. To afflict with disease; to in-
DĬS-EM-BÄRK',v.a.&n. To land from a ship.[fect.
DĬS-EM-BÄR'RASS, v. a. To free from embar-
rassment; to disengage; to extricate. [dom.
DĬS-EM-BÄR'RASS-MÈNT, n. Liberation; free-
DĬS-EM-BĬT'TER, v. a. To free from bitterness.
DĬS-EM-BÖD'IED, a. Divested of the body.
DĬS-EM-BÖD'Y, v. a. To divest of the body.
DĬS-EM-BŌGUE', v. a. To pour out at the mouth.
DĬS-EM-BŌ'SQM, v. a. To disclose, as secrets.
DĬS-EM-BÖW'EL, v. a. To take out the bowels of.
DĬS-EN-CHÄNT', v. a. To free from enchantment.
DĬS-EN-CÙM'BER, v. a. To disburden; to free.
DĬS-EN-CÙM'BRANCE, n. Freedom; release.

DĬS-ĘN-GĀĢE′, *v. a.* To extricate, clear, free.
DĬS-ĘN-GĀĢE′MĘNT, *n.* Release from an obligation; freedom; vacancy. [list.
DĬS-ĘN-RŌLL′, *v. a.* To remove from a roll or
DĬS-ĘN-TĂN′ĢLE, *v. a.* To unravel; to set free.
DĬS-ĘN-TĂN′ĢLE-MĔNT, *n.* Act of disentangling.
DĬS-ĘN-THRŌNE′, *v. a.* To depose; to dethrone.
DĬS-ĘN-TRĂNCE′, *v. a.* To awaken from a trance.
DĬS-FĀ′VŎR, *n.* Discountenance; disesteem.
DĬS-FĀ′VŎR, *v. a.* To discountenance; to oppose.
DĬS-FĀ′VŎR-ĘR, *n.* One who disfavors.
DĬS-FĬG-Ŭ-RĀ′TIŎN, *n.* The act of disfiguring; injury to appearance; deformity.
DĬS-FĬG′URE, *v. a.* To deform; to deface.
DĬS-FĬG′URE-MĔNT, *n.* Defacement; marring.
DĬS-FRĂN′CHIṢE, *v. a.* To deprive of privileges.
DĬS-FRĂN′CHIṢE-MĔNT, *n.* Act of disfranchising.
DĬS-GŎRĢE′, *v. a.* To vomit; to eject; to give
DĬS-GRĀCE′, *n.* Ignominy; dishonor; shame. [up.
DĬS-GRĀCE′, *v. a.* To dishonor; to bring to shame.
DĬS-GRĀCE′FŬL, *a.* Shameful; ignominious; vile.
DĬS-GRĀCE′FŬL-LY, *ad.* In a disgraceful manner; ignominiously; shamefully; basely.
DĬS-GUĪṢE′ (dĭz-gīz′), *v. a.* To conceal by an unusual dress:—to feign; to dissemble.
DĬS-GUĪṢE′ (dĭz-gīz′), *n.* A counterfeit dress.
DĬS-GUĪṢ′ER (dĭz-gīz′er), *n.* One who disguises.
DĬS-GŬST′, *n.* Aversion; dislike; disrelish. [in.
DĬS-GŬST′, *v. a.* To offend; to produce aversion
DĬS-GŬST′FŬL, *a.* Nauseous; causing aversion.
DĬS-GŬST′ING, *p. a.* Offensive; nauseous.
DĬSH, *n.* A vessel for serving up food:—food.
DĬSH, *v. a.* To serve or put in a dish:—to cheat.
DĬS-HA-BĬLLE′ (dĭs-a-bĭl′), *n.* Undress; loose dress. [to depress; to dispirit.
DĬS-HEÄR′TEN (dĭs-här′tn), *v. a.* To discourage;
DĬ-SHĔV′ĘL (de-shĕv′vel), *v. a.* To spread loosely.
DĬS-HŎN′ĘST (dĭz-ŏn′ĕst), *a.* Void of honesty; faithless; wicked; fraudulent:—unchaste.
DĬS-HŎN′ĘST-LY (dĭz-ŏn′ĕst-le), *ad.* Wickedly.
DĬS-HŎN′ĘS-TY (dĭz ŏn′es-te), *n.* Want of probity.
DĬS-HŎN′ŎR (dĭz-ŏn′ur), *n.* Disgrace; shame.
DĬS-HŎN′ŎR (dĭz-ŏn′ur), *v. a.* To disgrace; to shame; to treat with indignity:—to violate.
DĬS-HŎN′ŎR-A-BLE (dĭz-ŏn′ur-a-bl), *a.* Shameful; reproachful; void of faith; ignominious.
DĬS-HŎN′ŎR-A-BLY, *ad.* Ignominiously.
DĬS-ĬN-CLI-NĀ′TIŎN, *n.* Want of inclination.
DĬS-ĬN-CLĪNE′, *v. a.* To excite aversion in. [sly.
DĬS-ĬN-ĢĔN′U-OŬS, *a.* Unfair; meanly artful;
DĬS-ĬN-ĢĔN′U-OŬS-LY, *ad.* Unfairly; artfully.
DĬS-ĬN-ĢĔN′U-OŬS-NĔSS, *n.* Unfairness; craft.
DĬS-ĬN-HĔR′I-ṢŎN, *n.* The act of disinheriting.
DĬS-ĬN-HĔR′ĬT, *v. a.* To deprive of an inheritance; to cut off from hereditary right. [cles.
DĬS-ĬN′TĘ-GRĀTE, *v. a.* To separate into parti-
DĬS-ĬN-TE-GRĀ′TIŎN, *n.* Separation into parti-
DĬS-ĬN-TĔR′, *v. a.* To take out of the grave. [cles.
DĬS-ĬN′TĘR-ĔST-ĘD, *a.* Free from self-interest.
DĬS-ĬN-TĔR′MĘNT, *n.* The act of unburying.
DĬS-ĬN-THRÂLL′, *v. a.* To set free; to liberate.
DĬS-JŌĬN′, *v. a.* To separate; to part; to sunder.
DĬS-JŌĬNT′, *v. a.* To put out of joint; to break.
DĬS-JŬNCT′, *a.* Disjoined; separate; apart.
DĬS-JŬNC′TIŎN, *n.* Disunion; separation.
DĬS-JŬNC′TĬVE, *a.* Separating; disjoining.
DĬSK, *n.* The face of the sun, &c.:—a quoit.
DĬS-LĪKE′, *n.* Disinclination; aversion; distaste.

DĬS-LĪKE′, *v. a.* To disapprove; to disrelish.
DĬS-LĪKE′NĘSS, *n.* Dissimilitude; unlikeness.
DĬS′LŎ-CĀTE, *v. a.* To put out of joint; to disjoint; to luxate:—to disarrange; to disorder.
DĬS-LŎ-CĀ′TIŎN, *n.* Act of displacing; luxation.
DĬS-LŌDĢE′, *v. a. & n.* To remove, or drive from.
DĬS-LŌY̆′AL, *a.* Not true to allegiance; faithless.
DĬS-LŌY̆′AL-LY, *ad.* Faithlessly; treacherously.
DĬS-LŌY̆′AL-TY, *n.* Want of allegiance or fidel-
DĬS′MAL, *a.* Sorrowful; gloomy; dire; dark. [ity.
DĬS′MAL-LY, *ad.* In a dismal manner; horribly.
DĬS-MĂN′TLE, *v. a.* To divest:—to unrig.
DĬS-MĂSK′, *v. a.* To divest of a mask; to uncover.
DĬS-MĂST′, *v. a.* To deprive of masts, as a ship.
DĬS-MĀY′, *v. a.* To terrify; to affright; to daunt.
DĬS-MĀY′, *n.* Affright; alarm; terror; fear.
DĬS-MĔM′BER, *v. a.* To divide limb from limb.
DĬS-MĔM′BER-MĔNT, *n.* Division; partition.
DĬS-MĬSS′, *v. a.* To send away; to discard.
DĬS-MĬS′SAL, *n.* Dismission; discharge.
DĬS-MĬS′SIŎN (dĭz-mĭsh′un), *n.* The act of sending away; leave to depart; discharge. [horse.
DĬS-MŎŬNT′, *v. a.* To throw off a horse; to un-
DĬS-MŎŬNT′, *v. n.* To alight from a horse.
DĬS-Ō-BĒ′DI-ĘNCE, *n.* Neglect or refusal to obey.
DĬS-Ō-BĒ′DI-ĘNT, *a.* Not observant of authority.
DĬS-Ō-BEY′ (dĭs-o-bā′), *v. a.* To refuse to obey.
‖DĬS-Ō-BLĪĢE′, *v. a.* To treat with unkindness; to displease; to give offence to; to offend.
‖DĬS-Ō-BLĪĢ′ER, *n.* One who disobliges.
‖DĬS-Ō-BLĪĢ′ING, *p. a.* Unfriendly; unkind.
DĬS-ŌRBED′ (dĭz-ŏrbd′), *a.* Thrown out of its orbit, as a star. [turbance:—sickness.
DĬS-ŎR′DER, *n.* ‘Irregularity; confusion; dis-
DĬS-ŎR′DER, *v. a.* To disturb, ruffle, make sick.
DĬS-ŎR′DERED (dĭz-ŏr′derd), *a.* Irregular:—ill.
DĬS-ŎR′DER-LY, *a.* Confused; irregular; lawless.
DĬS-ŎR′DER-LY, *ad.* Without rule; confusedly.
DĬS-ŎR-GAN-I-ZĀ′TIŎN, *n.* Act of disorganizing.
DĬS-ŎR′GAN-ĪZE, *v. a.* To destroy the organization of; to derange; to disorder; to disarrange.
DĬS-ŌWN′ (dĭz-ōn′), *v. a.* To deny; to renounce.
DĬS-PĂR′AĢE, *v. a.* To match unequally; to decry.
DĬS-PĂR′AĢE-MĔNT, *n.* Detraction; indignity.
DĬS-PĂR′A-ĢER, *n.* One who disparages. [ness.
DĬS-PĂR′I-TY, *n.* Inequality; difference; unlike-
DĬS-PÄRT′, *v. a.* To divide in two; to separate.
DĬS-PĂS′SIŎN-ATE, *a.* Cool; calm; impartial.
DĬS-PĂS′SIŎN-ATE-LY, *ad.* In a calm manner.
DĬS-PĂTCH′, DĘS-PĂTCH′, *v. a.* To send away.
DĬS-PĂTCH′, *n.* Speed:—an express; message.
DĬS-PĔL′, *v. a.* To drive away; to dissipate.
DĬS-PĔN′SA-BLE, *a.* That may be dispensed with.
DĬS-PĔN′SA-RY, *n.* A place for medicines.
DĬS-PĘN-SĀ′TIŎN, *n.* Distribution:—exemption.
DĬS-PĔN′SA-TO-RY, *n.* A book or directory for making medicines; a pharmacopœia. [direct.
DĬS-PĔN′SE, *v. a.* To deal out; to distribute; to
DĬS-PĔNS′ER, *n.* One who dispenses; a distrib-
DĬS PĔO′PLE (-pē′pl), *v. a.* To depopulate. [uter.
DĬS-PĔRSE′, *v. a.* To scatter; to drive away.
DĬS-PĔRS′ER, *n.* A scatterer; a spreader.
DĬS-PĔR′SIŎN, *n.* Act of dispersing; distribution.
DĬS-PĬR′ĬT, *v. a.* To discourage; to depress. [pose.
DĬS-PLĀCE′, *v. a.* To put out of place:—to de-
DĬS-PLĂNT′, *v. a.* To pluck up; to drive away.
DĬS-PLAN-TĀ′TIŎN, *n.* The act of displanting.
DĬS-PLĀY′, *v. a.* To spread wide:—to exhibit.

DĬS-PLĀY', *n.* Exhibition of any thing to view.
DĬS-PLĒASE', *v. a.* To offend ; to make angry.
DĬS-PLĔAŞ'URE (-plĕzh'ur), *n.* Offence ; anger.
DĬS-PLŌDE', *v. a.* To discharge with violence.
DĬS-PLŌ'ŞIǪN (dĭs-plō'zhun), *n.* An explosion.
DĬS-PŌRT', *n.* Play ; sport ; pastime.
DĬS-PŌRT', *v. a.* To divert ; to amuse :—to remove from a port.—*v. n.* To play ; to frolic.
DĬS-PŌŞ'A-BLE, *a.* Capable of being disposed.
DĬS-PŌŞ'AL, *n.* Regulation ; management.
DĬS-PŌŞE', *v. a.* To bestow, incline, adjust, sell.
DĬS-PŌŞ'ER, *n.* A distributer ; a giver ; director.
DĬS-PǪ-ŞĬ''TIǪN (dĭs-pǫ-zĭsh'un), *n.* Order ; method ; fitness ; quality :—temper of mind.
DĬS-PǪŞ-ŞĔSS', *v. a.* To put out of possession.
DĬS-PǪŞ-ŞĔS'SIǪN, *n.* A putting out of posses-
DĬS-PRĀISE', *n.* Blame; censure; dishonor. [sion.
DĬS-PRĀIŞE', *v. a.* To blame ; to censure.
DĬS-PRŌŌF', *n.* Confutation ; refutation. [ity.
DĬS-PRǪ-PŌR'TIǪN, *n.* Want of symmetry; dispar-
DĬS-PRǪ-PŌR'TIǪN, *v. a.* To join or unite unfitly.
DĬS-PRǪ-PŌR'TIǪN-AL, *a.* Without proportion.
DĬS-PRǪ-PŌR'TIǪN-ATE, *a.* Without proportion or symmetry ; unsuitable ; unsymmetrical.
DĬS-PRŌVE', *v. a.* To confute ; to prove false.
DĬS-PŬN'ISH-A-BLE, *a.* Without penal restraint.
DĬS'PŬ-TA-BLE, *a.* That may be disputed ; doubtful ; controvertible ; debatable.
DĬS'PŬ-TANT, *n.* A controvertist ; an arguer.
DĬS-PŬ-TĀ'TIǪN, *n.* Argumentation ; controversy ; debate ; dispute. [illing.
DĬS-PŬ-TĀ'TIOUS, *a.* Inclined to dispute ; cav-
DĬS-PŪTE', *v. n. & a.* To contend, argue, discuss.
DĬS-PŪTE', *n.* Contest in words ; controversy.
DĬS-PŪT'ER, *n.* One who disputes ; a disputant.
DĬS-QUAL-I-FĬ-CĀ'TIǪN (-kwŏl-e-fe-kā'shun), *n.* That which disqualifies ; incapacity. [unfit.
DĬS-QUAL'Ĭ-FȲ (dĭs-kwŏl'ę-fī), *v. a.* To make
DĬS-QUĬ'ET, *n.* Uneasiness ; vexation ; anxiety.
DĬS-QUĬ'ET, *v. a.* To disturb ; to make uneasy.
DĬS-QUĬ'ET-ER, *n.* A disturber ; a harasser.
DĬS-QUĬ'E-TŪDE, *n.* Uneasiness ; anxiety.
DĬS-QUĬ-ŞĬ''TIǪN (-kwę-zĭsh'un), *n.* Discussion.
DĬS-RE-GĀRD', *n.* Slight ; neglect ; contempt.
DĬS-RE-GĀRD', *v. a.* To slight, neglect, contemn.
DĬS-RE-GĀRD'FŬL, *a.* Negligent; contemptuous.
DĬS-RĔL'ISH, *n.* Dislike ; distaste ; aversion.
DĬS-RĔL'ISH, *v. a.* To make nauseous ; to dislike.
DĬS-RĔP'U-TA-BLE, *a.* Dishonorable ; disgrace-
DĬS-RE-PŪTE', *n.* Discredit ; dishonor. [ful.
DĬS-RE-SPĔCT', *n.* Incivility ; want of respect.
DĬS-RE-SPĔCT'FŬL, *a.* Irreverent ; uncivil. [illy.
DĬS-RE-SPĔCT'FŬL-LY, *ad.* Irreverently; unciv-
DĬS-RŌBE', *v. a.* To undress ; to uncover, strip.
DĬS-RŬP'TIǪN, *n.* Breach ; rent ; separation.
DĬS-SĂT-IS-FĂC'TIǪN, *n.* Uneasiness; discontent.
DĬS-SĂT-IS-FĂC'TǪ-RY, *a.* Unable to content.
DĬS-SĂT'IS-FȲ, *v. a.* To discontent ; to displease.
DĬS-SĔCT', *v. a.* To cut in pieces ; to anatomize.
DĬS-SĔC'TIǪN, *n.* Act of dissecting ; anatomy.
DĬS-SĔCT'ǪR, *n.* One who dissects. [fully.
DĬS-SĒIZE' (dĭs-sēz'), *v. a.* To dispossess wrong-
DĬS-SĒI'ŞIN, *or* DĬS-SĒI'ZIN (dĭs-sē'zin), *n.* Unlawful dispossessing of land, tenement, &c.
DĬS-SĒIZ'ǪR, *n.* He who wrongfully dispossess-
DĬS-SĔM'BLE, *v. a.* To disguise ; to pretend. [es.
DĬS-SĔM'BLE, *v. n.* To play the hypocrite ; to
DĬS-SĔM'BLER, *n.* One who dissembles. [feign.

DĬS-SĔM'I-NĀTE, *v. a.* To scatter, as seed; to sow.
DĬS-SĔM-I-NĀ'TIǪN, *n.* A scattering ; a sowing.
DĬS-SĔM'I-NĀ-TǪR, *n.* One who disseminates.
DĬS-SĔN'SIǪN, *n.* Disagreement ; strife ; quarrel.
DĬS-SĔN'SIOUS (dĭs-sĕn'shus), *a.* Quarrelsome.
DĬS-SĔNT', *v. n.* To disagree in opinion; to differ.
DĬS-SĔNT', *n.* Disagreement ; dissension.
DĬS-SĔNT'ER, *n.* One who dissents or disagrees.
DĬS-SĔN'TIENT, *a.* Dissenting ; not agreeing.
DĬS-SER-TĀ'TIǪN, *n.* A discourse ; a treatise.
DĬS-SĔRVE', *v. a.* To do injury to ; to hurt.
DĬS-SĔR'VICE, *n.* Injury ; mischief ; harm.
DĬS-SĔR'VICE-A-BLE, *a.* Injurious; mischievous.
DĬS-SĔV'ER, *v. a.* To part in two ; to divide.
DĬS'SI-DĔNT, *a.* Varying ; not agreeing. [der.
DĬS-SĬL'IENT (dĭs-sĭl'yent), *a.* Starting asun-
DĬS-SĬM'I-LAR, *a.* Unlike ; heterogeneous. [tude.
DĬS-SĬM-I-LĂR'I-TY, *n.* Unlikeness ; dissimili-
DĬS-SI-MĬL'I-TŪDE, *n.* Want of resemblance.
DĬS-SĬM-U-LĀ'TIǪN, *n.* A dissembling; hypocrisy.
DĬS'SI-PĀTE, *v. a.* To disperse ; to scatter ; to dispel :—to spend lavishly ; to squander. [ing.
DĬS-SI-PĀ'TIǪN, *n.* Dispersion :—dissolute liv-
DĬS-SŌ'CIAL, *a.* Disinclined to society ; unsocial.
DĬS-SŌ'CI-ĀTE (dĭs-sō'she-āt), *v. a.* To separate.
DĬS-SŌ-CI-Ā'TIǪN (-she-ā'shun), *n.* Division.
DĬS-SŌL-U-BĬL'I-TY, *n.* Liableness to dissolve.
DĬS'SǪ-LŪ-BLE, *a.* Capable of being dissolved.
DĬS'SǪ-LŪTE, *a.* Loose; unrestrained; debauched.
DĬS'SǪ-LŪTE-LY, *ad.* Loosely; without restraint.
DĬS'SǪ-LŪTE-NĔSS, *n.* Debauchery ; dissipation.
DĬS-SǪ-LŪ'TIǪN, *n.* Liquefaction :—death :—destruction ; disorganization ; ruin.
DĬS-ŞŎLV'A-BLE, *a.* Capable of dissolution.
DĬS-ŞŎLVE', *v. a.* To melt ; to separate.
DĬS-ŞŎLVE', *v. n.* To be liquefied ; to sink away.
DĬS-ŞŎLV'ENT, *a.* Tending to dissolve or melt.
DĬS-ŞŎLV'ENT, *n.* That which dissolves. [solves.
DĬS-ŞŎLV'ER, *n.* He who, or that which, dis-
DĬS'SǪ-NANCE, *n.* Discord ; disagreement.
DĬS'SǪ-NANT, *a.* Unharmonious ; incongruous.
DĬS-SUĀDE' (dĭs-swād'), *v. a.* To advise against.
DĬS-SUĀ'ŞIǪN (dĭs-swā'zhun), *n.* Dehortation.
DĬS-SUĀ'SIVE (dĭs-swā'siv), *a.* Dissuading.
DĬS-SUĀ'SIVE, *n.* An argument or reason employed to dissuade ; a dehortation.
DĬS-SYL-LĂB'IC, *a.* Consisting of two syllables.
DĬS-SȲL'LA-BLE *or* DĬS'SYL-LA-BLE, *n.* A word of two syllables.
DĬS'TAFF, *n.* The staff from which the flax is drawn off in spinning. [tarnish ; to soil.
DĬS-TĀIN', *v. a.* To stain ; to blot ; to sully ; to.
DĬS'TANCE, *n.* Remoteness in place or time :—ceremonious reserve :—aversion ; dislike.
DĬS'TANCE, *v. a.* To leave behind :—to outdo.
DĬS'TANT, *a.* Remote in time or place :—shy ;
DĬS-TĀSTE', *n.* Aversion; disrelish; dislike [cold.
DĬS-TĀSTE', *v. a.* To disrelish ; to dislike. [some.
DĬS-TĀSTE'FŬL, *a.* Nauseous ; offensive ; loath-
DĬS-TĔM'PER, *n.* A disease ; a malady ; ill humor.
DĬS-TĔM'PER, *v. a.* To disease; to disorder. [mor.
DĬS-TĔM'PER-A-TŪRE, *n.* Bad temperature ; illness.
DĬS-TĔND', *v. a.* To stretch out in breadth. [ness.
DĬS-TĔN'TIǪN, *n.* Act of stretching ; breadth.
DĬS'TICH, *n.* A couplet ; a couple of lines.
DĬS-TĬL', *v. n.* To drop ; to fall in drops. [solve.
DĬS-TĬL', *v. a.* To draw by distillation ; to dis-
DĬS-TĬL'LA-BLE, *a.* Capable of being distilled.

DĬS-TĬL-LĀ'TIǪN, n. Act or process of distil-
ling:—that which drops; a dropping. [tion.
DĬS-TĬL'LA-TǪ-RY, a. Belonging to distilla-
DĬS-TĬL'LER, n. One who distils. [tilled.
DĬS-TĬL'LER-Y, n. Place where spirits are dis-
DĬS-TĬNCT', a. Different; separate; unconfused.
DĬS-TĬNC'TIǪN, n. Difference; eminence; note.
DĬS-TĬNC'TĬVE, a. Marking a distinction.
DĬS-TĬNCT'LY, ad. Not confusedly; plainly.
DĬS-TĬNCT'NESS, n. Clearness; nice observation.
DĬS-TĬN'GUĬSH, v. a. To discern, divide, mark.
DĬS-TĬN'GUĬSH, v. n. To make distinction.
DĬS-TĬN'GUĬSH-A-BLE, a. Discernible; notable.
DĬS-TĬN'GUĬSHED (dĭs-tĭn'gwĭsht),p.a.Eminent.
DĬS-TÖRT', v. a. To writhe; to twist; to wrest.
DĬS-TÖR'TIǪN, n. Act of distorting; perversion.
DĬS-TRĂCT', v. a. To separate; to divide; to
vex; to disturb:—to make mad. [—madness.
DĬS-TRĂC'TIǪN, n. Confusion; perplexity:
DĬS-TRĂC'TĬVE, a. Causing perplexity.
DĬS-TRĀIN', v. a. To seize for debt, as goods.
DĬS-TRĀINT', n. A seizure of goods, &c. [ure.
DĬS-TRĔSS', n. Misery; misfortune; pain:—seiz-
DĬS-TRĔSS', v. a. To harass; to make miser-
able; to afflict; to trouble. [distressing.
DĬS-TRĔSS'FÜL, a. Miserable; full of trouble;
DĬS-TRĔSS'ĬNG, a. Harassing; afflicting.
DĬS-TRĬB'ŲTE, v. a. To divide among many; to
DĬS-TRĬB'Ų-TER, n. One who distributes. [allot.
DĬS-TRĬ-BŪ'TIǪN,n.A dealing out; dispensation.
DĬS-TRĬB'Ų-TĬVE, a. That distributes; divid-
DĬS-TRĬB'Ų-TĬVE-LY, ad. By distribution. [ing.
DĬS'TRĬCT, n. A circuit; province; territory.
DĬS-TRŬST', v. a. Not to trust; to disbelieve.
DĬS-TRŬST', n. Discredit; mistrust; suspicion.
DĬS-TRŬST'FÜL, a. Apt to distrust; diffident.
DĬS-TŬRB', v. a. To perplex, molest, interrupt.
DĬS-TŬRB'ANCE, n. Perplexity; confusion; tu-
DĬS-TŬRB'ER, n. One who molests. [mult.
DĬS-ŪN'IǪN (dĭs-yūn'yųn), n. Separation; dis-
junction; breach of concord. [arate.
DĬS-Ų-NĪTE' (dĭs-yu-nīt'), v. a. & n. To sep-
DĬS-Ū'NĬ-TY, n. Want of unity; separation.
DĬS-Ū'ȘAǴE, n. Cessation of use or custom.
DĬS-ŪSE', n. Cessation of use; desuetude.
DĬS-ŪSE', v. a. To cease to use; to disaccustom.
DĬŞ-VĂL'ŲE (dĭz-vǎl'yų), v. a. To undervalue.
DĬTCH, n. A trench cut in the ground; a moat.
DĬTCH, v. n. & a. To make a ditch; to sur-
round with a ditch; to make a ditch in.
DĬTCH'ER, n. One who digs ditches. [chus.
DĬTH-Y-RĂM'BĬC, n. A song in honor of Bac-
DĬTH-Y-RĂM'BĬC, a. Wild; enthusiastic. [said.
DĬT'TŌ, n. The same thing repeated:—as afore-
DĬT'TY, n. A poem to be sung; a song; a lay.
DĪ-Ų-RĔT'ĬC, a. Provoking discharge of urine.
DĪ-Ų-RĔT'ĬC, n. A medicine which increases
the secretion of urine. [formed in a day.
DĪ-ŬR'NAL, a. Relating to the day; daily; per-
DĪ-ŬR'NAL, n. A journal; a day-book; a diary.
DĪ-ŬR'NAL-LY, ad. Daily; every day.
DĬ-VĂN', n. The grand council of Turkey:—a
hall; a seat:—collection of poems. [into two.
DI-VĂR'Ĭ-CĀTE, v. n. & a. To divide or open
DĪ-VĂR-Ĭ-CĀ'TIǪN, n. Partition; division.
DĪVE, v. n. To plunge into water; to penetrate.
DĪV'ER, n. One who dives. [one point.
DĬ-VĔRǴE', v. n. To tend various ways from

DĬ-VĔR'ǴENCE, n. A receding from each other.
DĬ-VĔR'ǴENT, a. Separating from each other.
DĪ'VERŞ (dī'verz), a. Several; sundry; many.
DĪ'VERSE, a. Different; unlike; multiform.
DĪ'VERSE-LY, ad. In different ways; variously.
DĬ-VĔR-SĬ-FĬ-CĀ'TIǪN, n. Variegation; change.
DĬ-VĔR'SĬ-FȲ, v. a. To make different; to vary.
DĬ-VĔR'SIǪN, n. A turning aside; sport; game.
DĬ-VĔR'SĬ-TY, n. Difference; unlikeliness.
DĬ-VĔRT', v. a. To turn aside; to amuse.
DĬ-VĔRT'ER, n. One who, or that which, diverts.
DĬ-VĔR'TĬSE-MĔNT, n. Diversion; amusement.
DĬ-VĔR'TĬVE, a. Recreative; amusing.
DĬ-VĔST', v. a. To strip; to make naked. [ible.
DĬ-VĪD'A-BLE, a. That may be divided; divis-
DĬ-VĪDE', v. a. & n. To part, separate, sunder.
DĬV'Ĭ-DĔND, n. Share; number to be divided.
DĬ-VĪD'ER, n. One who, or that which, divides.
DĬ-VĪD'ERŞ, n. pl. A pair of compasses.
DĬV-Ĭ-NĀ'TIǪN, n. A foretelling of future events.
DĬ-VĪNE', a. Godlike; heavenly; not human.
DĬ-VĪNE', n. A priest; a clergyman; theologian.
DĬ-VĪNE', v. a. To foretell.—v. n. To conjecture.
DĬ-VĪNE'LY, ad. In a divine manner. [conjurer.
DĬ-VĪN'ER, n. One that practises divination; a
DĬ-VĬN'Ĭ-TY, n. The Deity; divine nature; god-
head:—science of divine things; theology.
DĬ-VĬŞ-Ĭ-BĬL'Ĭ-TY, n. Quality of being divisible.
DĬ-VĬŞ'Ĭ-BLE, a. Capable of being divided.
DĬ-VĬ''ŞIǪN (de-vĭzh'ųn), n. The act of divid-
ing; partition; a part; discord, difference.
DĬ-VĪ'ŞǪR, n. A number which divides. [wife.
DĬ-VŌRCE', n. Legal separation of husband and
DĬ-VŌRCE', v. a. To separate; to put away.
DĬ-VŌRCE'MĔNT, n. Divorce; separation.
DĪ-VŲL-GĀ'TIǪN, n. A publishing abroad.
DĬ-VŬLǴE', v. a. To publish; to reveal.
DĬ-VŬL'ǴER, n. A publisher; a proclaimer.
DĬ-VŬL'SIǪN, n. A plucking away; laceration.
DĬZ'ZĬ-NĔSS, n. Giddiness; whirl in the head.
DĬZ'ZY, a. Giddy; vertiginous; thoughtless.
DÔ, v. a. [thou dost, he does or doth; imp. t.
did; pp. done.] To practise, perform, execute.
DÔ, v. n. To act in any manner; to conclude;
DŎÇ'Ĭ-BLE, a. Tractable; docile. [to succeed.
DŎÇ'ĬLE, a. Teachable; easily taught. [ness.
DǪ-CĬL'Ĭ-TY, n. Aptness to be taught; teachable-
DŎCK, n. A plant:—yard or place for ships.
DŎCK, v. a. To cut short:—to put in a dock.
DŎCK'ET, n. A label; a list of cases in court.
DŎCK'ET, v. a. To mark with the titles.
DŎCK'-YĂRD, n. A yard for naval stores, &c.
DŎC'TǪR, n. A title in divinity, law, physic, &c.
DŎC'TǪR-AL, a. Relating to the degree of doc-
DŎC'TǪR-ATE, n. The degree of a doctor. [tor.
DŎC'TǪRŞ'-CŎM'MǪNŞ, n. College of civilians.
DŎC'TǪR-SHĬP, n. Rank of doctor; doctorate.
DŎC'TRESS, n. A female doctor or physician.
DŎC'TRĬ-NAL, a. Containing doctrine.
DŎC'TRĬ-NAL, n. A matter or part of doctrine.
DŎC'TRĬ-NAL-LY, ad. In a doctrinal manner.
DŎC'TRĬNE, n. A principle; precept; teaching.
DŎC'Ų-MĔNT, n. A written evidence; record.
DŎC'Ų-MĔNT, v. a. To teach; to direct, instruct.
DŎC-Ų-MĔNT'A-RY, a. Consisting of documents.
DŎD'DER, n. A twining, parasitical plant.
DǪ-DĔC'A-GǪN, n. A figure of twelve sides.
DŎDǴE, v. n. To start aside; to shift place.

DÔDǴE, *v. a.*   To evade by starting aside.
DŌE (dō), *n.*   A she deer ; the female of a buck.
DÔ'ĘR, *n.*   One who does a thing ; actor ; agent.
DŎĘŞ (dŭz).   The third person singular from *do.*
DŎFF, *v. a.*   To put off ; to strip ; to put away.
DŎǴ, *n.*   A domestic animal :—an andiron ; a
DŎǴ, *v. a.*   To hunt as a dog ; to follow. [hook.
DŎǴ'-CHĒAP, *a.*   Cheap as dog's meat ; cheap.
DŎǴ'DĀYŞ (dŏg'dāz), *n. pl.*   The days in which
the dog-star rises and sets with the sun.
DŌǴE, *n.*   The chief magistrate of Venice and
DŎǴ'ǴĘD, *a.*   Sullen ; sour ; morose.   [Genoa.
DŎǴ'ǴĘD-LY, *ad.*   Sullenly ; gloomily ; sourly.
DŎǴ'ǴĘD-NĔSS, *n.*   Gloominess ; sullenness.
DŎǴ'ǴĘR, *n.*   A small kind of fishing vessel.
DŎǴ'ǴERĘL (dŏg'grĕl), *a.*   Vile ; despicable.
DŎǴ'ǴERĘL (dŏg'grĕl), *n.*   Mean poetry.
DŎǴ'-KĔN-NĘL, *n.*   A little hut for dogs.
DŎǴ'MA, *n. ; pl.* DŎǴ'MAŞ *or* DŎǴ'MA-TA.
  Established principle ; a tenet ; a maxim.
DŎǴ-MĂT'ĬC, DŎǴ-MĂT'Ĭ-CAL, *a.*   Authorita-
  tive ; positive ; magisterial.   [tively.
DŎǴ-MĂT'Ĭ-CAL-LY, *ad.*   Magisterially ; posi-
DŎǴ'MA-TĬŞM, *n.*   Positiveness in opinion.
DŎǴ'MA-TĬST, *n.*   A dogmatical teacher. [tively.
DŎǴ'MA-TĪZE, *v. n.*   To assert or declare posi-
DŎǴ'MA-TĪZ-ĘR, *n.*   One who dogmatizes.
DŎǴ'RŌŞE, *n.*   Wild brier that bears the hip.
DŎǴ'Ş'-ĒAR, *n.*   Folded corner of a leaf.
DŎǴ'-STÄR, *n.*   The star Sirius, brightest of
  the fixed stars, giving name to the dog-days.
DŎǴ'-TÔÔTH, *n.*   A tooth next to the grinders.
DŎǴ'-TRĬCK, *n.*   An ill turn ; surly treatment.
DŎǴ'TRŎT, *n.*   A gentle trot, like that of a dog.
DŌ'ĬNǴŞ, *n. pl.*   Things done ; transactions ; acts.
DÖÏT, *n.*   A small piece of money :—a trifle.
DŌLE, *n.*   Any thing dealt out ; a share ; a lot.
DŌLE'FÛL, *a.*   Sorrowful ; dismal ; melancholy.
DŌLE'FÛL-LY, *ad.*   In a doleful manner.
DŌLE'SŎME (dōl'sŭm), *a.*   Melancholy ; gloomy.
DŎLL, *n.*   A child's puppet or baby.
DŎL'LAR, *n.*   A silver coin of Germany, Hol-
  land, Spain, and of the United States.
DŌ'LQR, *n.*   Grief ; sorrow ; complaint ; pain.
DŎL-QR-ĬF'ĬC, DŎL-QR-ĬF'Ĭ-CAL, *a.*   Causing
  pain ; inducing grief.   [painful ; dolorific.
DŎL'QR-OŬS, *a.*   Sorrowful ; doleful ; dismal ;
DŎL'PHĮN, *n.*   A fish :—a constellation.
DŌLT, *n.*   A heavy, stupid fellow ; a blockhead.
DŌLT'ĮSH, *a.*   Stupid ; foolish ; blockish ; dull.
DQ-MĀIN', *n.*   Dominion ; empire ; an estate.
DŌME, *n.*   A building ; a cupola ; an arched roof.
DQ-MĔS'TĮC, *a.*   Belonging to the house ; pri-
  vate ; tame ; not wild ; not foreign ; intestine.
DQ-MĔS'TĮC, *n.*   One kept in the house ; a ser-
  vant ; a menial.—*pl.*   Domestic manufactures.
DQ-MĔS'TĮ-CĀTE, *v. a.*   To make domestic.
DŎM'Ĭ-CĬLE, *n.*   A house ; a residence ; a home.
DŎM-Ĭ-CĬL'Ĭ-A-RY, *a.*   Relating to private houses.
DŎM-Ĭ-CĬL'Ĭ-ĀTE, *v. a.*   To render domestic.
DŎM'Ĭ-NANT, *a.*   Predominant ; prevailing.
DŎM-Ĭ-NĀ'TIQN, *n.*   Power ; dominion ; tyranny.
DŎM-Ĭ-NĒĒR', *v. n.*   To rule with insolence.
DQ-MĬN'Ĭ-CAL, *a.*   Relating to the Lord, or
  Lord's day ;—noting the Lord's prayer. [inic.
DQ-MĬN'Ĭ-CAN, *n.*   One of the order of St. Dom-
DQ-MĬN'IQN (dǫ-mĭn'yŭn), *n.*   Sovereign au-
  thority ; power ; predominance :—region.

DŎM'Ĭ-NŌ, *n.*   A kind of hood :—a long dress :
  —a piece of bone or ivory for playing with.
DŎN, *n.*   A title of honor in Spain.   [with.
DŎN, *v. a.*   To put on, as garments ; to invest
DQ-NĀ'TIQN, *n.*   Act of giving ; a gift ; a present.
DŌN'A-TĬVE, *n.*   A gift ; a largess ; a present.
DŎNE (dŭn), *pp.* from the verb *do.*
DQ-NĒĒ', *n.*   One to whom any thing is given.
DŎN'JQN (dŭn'jŭn), *n.*   The strongest tower of
  a castle ; a keep.   See DUNGEON.
DŎN'KEY, *n.*   A name for an ass or mule.
DŌ'NÖR, *n.*   One who gives ; a giver ; a bestower.
DÔÔ'DLE, *n.*   A trifler ; a simple fellow ; idler.
DÔÔM, *v. a.*   To judge ; to condemn ; to destine.
DÔÔM, *n.*   Judicial sentence ; judgment ; ruin.
DÔÔMŞ'DĀY, *n.*   The day of final judgment.
DŌOR (dōr), *n.*   The gate of a house ; entrance.
DŌOR'CĀSE, *n.*   A frame which encloses a door.
DŌOR'KĒĒP-ER (dōr'kēp-ęr), *n.*   One who has
  charge of a door or entrance ; a porter.
DŌOR'PŌST (dōr'pōst), *n.*   Post of a door.
DQ-RĀ'DŌ, *n.*   A southern constellation.
DQ-RĒĒ', *n.*   A fish, called *John Dory.*
DŌR'ĬC, *a.*   Noting an order of architecture.
DŌR'Ĭ-CĬŞM, *n.*   A phrase of the Doric dialect.
DŌR'MANT, *a.*   Sleeping ; not public ; concealed.
DŌR'MĮ-TQ-RY, *n.*   A place or room to sleep in.
DŌR'MŎŪSE, *n.*   A small animal, resembling
  the squirrel and mouse, that remains torpid in
DŌR'SAL, *a.*   Relating to, or in, the back. [winter.
DŌSE, *n.*   Enough of medicine, &c., for once.
DŌSE, *v. a.*   To proportion ; to give in doses.
DŎS'SĮL, *n.*   A pledget, or lump of lint for a sore.
DŎST.   The second person singular from *do.*
DŎT, *n.*   A small point or spot in a writing, &c.
DŎT, *v. a.*   To mark.—*v. n.*   To make dots.
DŌ'TAǴE, *n.*   Imbecility of mind ; silly fondness.
DŌ'TAL, *a.*   Relating to the portion of a woman.
DŌ'TARD, *n.*   One whose mind is impaired by
DŌTE, *v. n.*   To love greatly or foolishly.   [age.
DŌT'ĘR, *n.*   One who dotes ; a dotard ; driveller.
DŎTH.   Third per. sing. from *do.*   Same as *does.*
DŎT'TARD, *n.*   A tree kept low by cutting.
DŎT'TĘR-ĘL, *n.*   A bird ; a kind of plover.
DOŬB'LE (dŭb'bl), *a.*   Twofold ; two of a sort.
DOŬB'LE (dŭb'bl), *v. a.*   To add as much more
  to ; to repeat ; to fold ; to pass round, as a cape.
DOŬB'LE, *v. n.*   To increase to twice the quantity.
DOŬB'LE, *n.*   Twice as much ; a fold ; a turn.
DOŬB'LE-DĒAL'ĘR (-dēl'ęr), *n.*   A deceiver.
DOŬB'LE-DĒAL'ĮNG (dŭb'bl-dēl'-), *n.*   Artifice.
DOŬB'LĘT (dŭb'lęt), *n.*   A waistcoat :—a pair.
DOŬB'LE-TŎNGUĔD' (-tŭngd'), *a.*   Deceitful.
DOŬB'LĮNG (dŭb'lĭng), *n.*   An artifice ; a fold.
DOŬB-LŌÔN' (dŭb-lôn'), *n.*   A Spanish gold coin.
DOŬB'LY (dŭb'lę), *ad.*   In twice the quantity.
DOŬBT (dŏût), *v. a. & n.*   To suspect ; to hesitate.
DOŬBT (dŏût), *n.*   Hesitation ; suspense ; scruple.
DOŬBT'ĘR (dŏût'ęr), *n.*   One who doubts.
DOŬBT'FÛL (dŏût'fûl), *a.*   Dubious ; uncertain.
DOŬBT'FÛL-LY (dŏût'fûl-lę), *ad.*   Uncertainly.
DOŬBT'LĘSS (dŏût'lęs), *ad.*   Without doubt.
DÔU-CEÙR' (dô-sür'), *n.*   [Fr.]   A bribe ; a lure.
DŌUGH (dō), *n.*   Unbaked paste ; kneaded flour.
DŌÛGH'TY (dŏû'tę), *a.*   Brave ; valiant ; noble.
DŌUGH'Y (dō'ę), *a.*   Soft like dough.
DŎÛSE, *v. a. & n.*   To plunge or fall into water.
DŎVE (dŭv), *n.*   A tame or domesticated pigeon.

DŎVE′CŎT, DŎVE′HŎŪSE, n. House for doves.
DŎVE′-LĪKE, a. Resembling a dove; gentle.
DŎVE′TĂIL, n. A form of joining two pieces.
DŎVE′TĂILED (-tāld), a. Joined by dovetail.
DŎŴ′A-GĘR, n. A widow having a dower.
DŎŴ′DY, n. An awkward, ill-dressed woman.
DŎŴ′ĘR, or DŎŴ′ĘR-Y, n. Endowment; gift: —a wife's or widow's portion; a dowry.
DŎŴ′ĘR-LĔSS, a. Wanting a fortune or dower.
DŎŴ′LĄS, n. A coarse and strong linen cloth.
DŎŴN, n. Soft feathers or hair:—an open plain.
DŎŴN, prep. Along a descent.—ad. On the [ground.
DŎŴN′CĂST, a. Bent down; dejected.
DŎŴN′FĂLL, n. Ruin; calamity; sudden fall.
DŎŴN′FĂLL-EN (dŏŭn′fåln), a. Ruined; fallen.
DŎŴN′HĬLL, n. A declivity; a descent.
DŎŴN′HĬLL, a. Declivous; descending.
DŎŴN′RĪGHT (dŏŭn′rīt), a. Plain; open; direct.
DŎŴN′RĪGHT (dŏŭn′rīt), ad. Plainly; truly.
DŎŴN′WĄRD, DŎŴN′WĄRDȘ, ad. To a lower [place.
DŎŴN′WĄRD, a. Descending; dejected.
DŎŴN′Y, a. Covered with down; soft; tender.
DŎŴ′RY, n. A woman's portion; a dower.
DŎX-Q-LŎĞ′Ĭ-CĄL, a. Pertaining to doxology.
DQX-ŎL′Q-ĢY, n. A form of giving praise to [God.
DŎX′Y, n. A prostitute; a vile woman.
DŌZE, v. n. To slumber; to sleep lightly.
DŎZ′EN (dŭz′zn), n. The number of twelve.
DŌ′ZI-NĔSS, n. Drowsiness; sleepiness.
DŌ′ZY, a. Sleepy; drowsy; sluggish.
DRĂB, n. A strumpet; a slut:—a thick cloth.
DRĂB, a. Of a dun color, like fuller's earth.
DRĂCHM (drăm), or DRĂ€H′MĄ, n A coin.
DRĀ′CŌ, n. [L.] The Dragon; a constellation.
DRĂFF, n. Refuse; lees; dregs; sweepings.
DRĂFF′Y, a. Worthless; dreggy; mean; vile.
DRĂFT, n. A bill; a drawing. See DRAUGHT.
DRĂG, v. a. & n. To pull or draw along.
DRĂ€, n. A net:—a kind of sledge. [dragging.
DRĂG′GLE, v. a. & n. To make or grow dirty by
DRĂG′MĄN, n. A fisherman who uses a drag-net. [along the bottom.
DRĂG′-NĔT, n. A net to take fish, to be drawn
DRĂG′Q-MĂN, n. An interpreter in Turkey, &c.
DRĂG′QN, n. A large fabulous animal; a con-stellation:—a small, inoffensive lizard.
DRĂG′QN-ĔT, n. A little dragon; a kind of fish.
DRĂG′QN-FLY, n. A ferocious stinging fly.
DRĂG′QN'Ș-BLŎOD (-ŭnz-blŭd), n. A red resin.
DRĄ-GŎŌN′, n. A soldier riding on horseback.
DRĄ-GŎŌN′, v. a. To give up to the rage of sol-diers:—to compel to submit; to reduce. [dry.
DRĀIN, v. a. To draw off gradually; to make
DRĀIN, n. A channel for water or other liquid to flow off; a watercourse; a sink.
DRĀIN′Ą-BLE, a. Capable of being drained.
DRĀKE, n. The male of the duck:—a fly.
DRĂM, n. Eighth or sixteenth of an ounce:—a small quantity:—a glass of spirit.
DRĀ′MĄ, n. A composition accommodated to action, either tragedy or comedy. [the drama.
DRĄ-MĂT′ĬC, DRĄ-MĂT′Ĭ-CĄL, a. Pertaining to
DRĄ-MĂT′Ĭ-CĄL-LY, ad. In a dramatic manner.
DRĂM′Ą-TĬST, n. A writer of plays or dramas.
DRĂM′Ą-TĪZE, v. a. To represent in a drama.
DRĂNK, imp. t. from drink. [or drapery.
DRĀPE, v. a. To cover or ornament with cloth
DRĀ′PĘR, n. One who sells or deals in cloth.

DRĀ′PĘR-Y, n. Clothwork; curtains; hangings.
DRĂS′TĬC, a. Powerful; efficacious; vigorous.
DRĂUGHT (dråft), n. A quantity drunk at once; act of drawing; sketch; a bill. See DRAFT.
DRĂUGHTS (dråfts), n. pl. A game; checkers.
DRĂUGHTS′MĄN (dråfts′mąn), n. One who draws writings, pictures, plans, or maps.
DRÂW, v. a. [imp. t. drew; pp. drawn.] To pull; to attract; to win; to extract; to sketch.
DRÂW, v. n. To pull; to shrink; to move.
DRÂW, n. Act of drawing:—the lot drawn.
DRÂW′BĂCK, n. Loss of advantage:—money repaid:—repayment or remission of a duty.
DRÂW′BRĬDĢE, n. A bridge made to be drawn.
DRÂW-EĒ′, n. One on whom a bill is drawn.
DRÂW′ĘR, n. One who draws:—a sliding box.
DRÂW′ĘRȘ, n. pl. Under-garment for the legs.
DRÂW′ĬNG, n. Delineation; representation.
DRÂW′ĬNG-RŎÔM, n. A room for company.
DRÂWL, v. n. & a. To speak slowly and te-diously. [tone of voice.
DRÂWL, n. A protracted utterance; lingering
DRÂWN, pp. from draw. [for heavy loads.
DRĀY, DRĀY′-CĂRT, n. A low cart or carriage
DRĀY′-HŌRSE, n. A horse which draws a dray.
DRĀY′MĄN, n. A man who drives a dray.
DRĔAD (drĕd), n. Great fear; terror; awe.
DRĔAD (drĕd), a. Terrible; awful; venerable.
DRĔAD (drĕd), v. a. To fear; to be afraid of.
DRĔAD, v. n. To be in great fear. [ful.
DRĔAD′FŬL (drĕd′fŭl), a. Terrible; awful; dire-
DRĔAD′FŬL-LY (drĕd′fŭl-lę), ad. Terribly.
DRĔAD′LESS, (drĕd′lęs), a. Fearless; intrepid.
DRĒAM, n. Thoughts in sleep:—idle fancy.
DRĒAM, v. n. [imp. t. & pp. dreamt, dreamed.] To have ideas in sleep; to imagine; to idle.
DRĒAM (drēm), v. a. To see in a dream.
DRĒAM′ĘR, n. One who dreams; an idler.
DRĒAM′LĘSS, a. Free from dreams.
DRĒAR, a. Mournful; dismal; dreary; gloomy.
DRĒAR′Ĭ-LY, ad. Gloomily; dismally; horridly.
DRĒAR′Ĭ-NĔSS, n. Dismalness; gloominess.
DRĒAR′Y, a. Gloomy; dismal; horrid; mournful.
DRĔDĢE, n. An oyster net:—a machine for clearing canals and rivers:—mixture of grain.
DRĔDĢE, v. a. To scatter flour on:—to gather.
DRĔDĢ′ĘR, n. User of a dredge; dredging-box.
DRĔDĢ′ĬNG-BŎX, n. A box for dredging meat,
DRĔG′GY, a. Containing dregs; feculent. [&c.
DRĔGȘ, n. pl. Sediment of liquors; lees; refuse.
DRĔNCH, v. a. To wash; to soak; to physic.
DRĔNCH, n. A draught; liquid potion or dose.
DRĔSS, v. a. [imp. t. & pp. dressed, drest.] To clothe; to deck:—to prepare or fit, as leather, lamps, &c.; to trim:—to cover, as a wound.
DRĔSS, n. Clothes; garment; habit; finery.
DRĔSS′ĘR, n. One who dresses; kitchen table.
DRĔSS′ĬNG-RŎÔM, n. A room to dress in.
DRĔSS′Y, a. Showy in dress; attentive to dress.
DRĬB′BLE, v. n. To fall in drops; to slaver.
DRĬB′LĘT, n. A small quantity; a small sum.
DRĪ′ĘR, n. That which absorbs moisture.
DRĬFT, n. Design; aim; scope:—body of snow.
DRĬFT, v. a. & n. To throw or form into heaps.
DRĬLL, v. a. To bore; to train; to sow in rows.
DRĬLL, n. An instrument for making holes:— furrow for seed:—military exercise. [seed.
DRĬLL′-BŎX, n. A box for holding and sowing

DRĬNK. *v. a.* & *n.* [*imp. t.* drank; *pp.* drunk.]
 To swallow, as any liquid; to quench thirst.
DRĬNK, *n.* Liquor to be swallowed; beverage.
DRĬNK′A-BLE, *a.* Capable of being drunk.
DRĬNK′ER, *n.* One that drinks; a drunkard.
DRĬP, *v. n.* To fall in drops.—*v. a.* To let fall.
DRĬP, *n.* That which falls in drops; dripping.
DRĬP′PING, *n.* Fat gathered from roast meat.
DRĪVE, *v. a.* [*imp. t.* drove; *pp.* driven.] To
 force along; to urge; to compel; to send.
DRĪVE, *v. n.* To rush with violence; to tend.
DRĪVE, *n.* A course for, or ride in, a carriage.
DRĬV′EL (drĭv′vl), *v. n.* To slaver; to dote.
DRĬV′EL, *n.* Slaver; moisture from the mouth.
DRĬV′EL-LER (drĭv′vl-ler), *n.* A dotard; an
DRĬV′EN (drĭv′vn), *pp.* from *drive.* [idiot.
DRĬV′ER, *n.* One that drives; a charioteer.
DRĬZ′ZLE, *v. n.* & *a.* To fall in small drops.
DRĬZ′ZLE (drĭz′zl), *n.* A small rain; mist.
DRĬZ′ZLY, *a.* Shedding small rain; drizzling.
DRŌLL, *a.* Comical; odd; strange; queer.
DRŌLL, *n.* A jester; a buffoon:—a farce.
DRŌLL′ER-Y, *n.* Idle jokes; buffoonery; a show.
DRŎM′E-DA-RY, *n.* Sort of one-humped camel.
DRŌNE, *n.* The male bee:—an idler:—a hum.
DRŌNE, *v. n.* To live in idleness; to dream.
DRŎN′ISH, *a.* Idle; indolent; sluggish; lazy.
DRÔÔP, *v. n.* To sink or hang down; to de-
 cline:—to wither; to languish; to faint.
DRŎP, *n.* A globule of liquid:—an ear-ring.
DRŎP, *v. a.* To pour in drops; to let fall; to quit.
DRŎP, *v. n.* To fall in drops; to fall; to die.
DRŎP′LET, *n.* A little drop:—a small ear-ring.
DRŎP′PING, *n.* That which falls in drops.
DRŎP′SI-CAL, *a.* Diseased with, or like, dropsy.
DRŎP′SY, *n.* A collection of water in the body.
DRŎSS, *n.* The scum of metals; rust; refuse.
DRŎS′SY, *a.* Full of dross; worthless; foul.
DRÔÛGHT (drôût), *n.* Dry weather; thirst.
DRÔÛGH′TY (drôû′te), *a.* Wanting rain; dry.
DRŌVE, *n.* A number of cattle driven:—crowd;
DRŌVE, *imp. t.* from *drive.* [a collection.
DRŌ′VER, *n.* One that drives cattle to market.
DRŎẄN, *v. a.* To kill or suffocate in water.
DRŎẄN, *v. n.* To be suffocated in the water.
DRŎẄN′ER, *n.* He who, or that which, drowns.
DRŎẄSE, *v. n.* To slumber; to grow heavy.
DRŎẄ′SI-LY, *ad.* Sleepily; heavily; sluggishly.
DRŎẄ′SI-NESS, *n.* Sleepiness; sluggishness.
DRŎẄ′SY, *a.* Sleepy; heavy; lethargic; dull.
DRŬB, *v. a.* To thrash; to beat; to whip.
DRŬB, *n.* A thump; a knock; a blow.
DRŬB′BING, *n.* A beating; a thumping, flogging.
DRŬDGE, *v. n.* To work hard; to slave.
DRŬDGE, *n.* One who works hard; a slave.
DRŬDG′ER-Y, *n.* Mean labor; servile occupation.
DRŬG, *n.* A substance used in medicine, dye-
 ing, &c.:—thing unsalable. [ister drugs to.
DRŬG, *v. a.* To season with drugs; to admin-
DRŬG′GET, *n.* A coarse kind of woollen stuff.
DRŬG′GIST, *n.* A dealer in drugs or medicines.
DRŪ′ID, *n.* A priest of the ancient Britons.
DRŲ-ĬD′I-CAL, *a.* Pertaining to the Druids.
DRŪ′ID-ĬSM, *n.* The doctrines of the Druids.
DRŬM, *n.* An instrument of military music.
DRŬM, *v. n.* & *a.* To beat a drum; to beat.
DRŬM′-MĀ′JOR, *n.* Chief drummer of a regiment.
DRŬM′MER, *n.* One who beats a drum.

DRŬM′STĬCK, *n.* A stick for beating a drum.
DRŬNK, *a.* Intoxicated with liquor; inebriated.
DRŬNK, *pp.* from *drink.* [ety.
DRŬNK′ARD, *n.* One addicted to habitual ebri-
DRŬNK′EN (drŭng′kn), *a.* Intoxicated; drunk.
DRŬNK′EN-NESS (drŭng′kn-nĕs), *n.* The state
 of being drunken; intoxication; inebriety.
DRҮ, *a.* Arid; not wet; thirsty :—barren :—keen.
DRҮ, *v. a.* & *n.* To free from moisture; to grow
DRҮ′AD, *n.* (*Myth.*) A wood-nymph. [dry.
DRҮ′LY, *ad.* In a dry manner; coldly; wittily.
DRҮ′NESS, *n.* Want of moisture; aridity.
DRҮ′-NURSE, *n.* A nurse who does not suckle.
DRҮ′-RŎT, *n.* A disease incident to timber.
DRҮ′-SHŎD, *a.* Having the feet dry; with dry
DŪ′AL, *a.* Expressing the number two. [feet.
DŲ-ĂL′I-TY, *n.* The state of being two.
DŬB, *v. a.* To confer knighthood on; to entitle.
DŬB, *n.* A blow; a knock:—a pool; a puddle.
DŪ′BI-OŬS, *a.* Doubtful; uncertain; not clear.
DŪ′BI-OŬS-LY, *ad.* Uncertainly; doubtfully.
DŪ′CAL, *a.* Pertaining to a duke or dukedom.
DŬC′AT, *n.* A European coin struck by dukes.
DŬC-A-TÔÔN′, *n.* A silver coin of Holland, &c.
DŬCH′ESS, *n.* The consort or wife of a duke.
DŬCH′Y, *n.* Territory of a duke; a dukedom.
DŬCK, *n.* A web-footed water-fowl :—bow of
 the head :—a word of endearment :—a linen
 fabric lighter than canvas, for sails, &c.
DŬCK, *v. n.* & *a.* To dive or put under water.
DŬCK′ING-STÔÔL, *n.* A stool to duck scolds.
DŬCK′-LEGGED (dŭk′lĕgd), *a.* Short-legged.
DŬCK′LING, *n.* A young or small duck.
DŬCT, *n.* Guidance; a tube; a canal; passage.
DŬC′TILE, *a.* Docile; pliable; easily extended.
DŲC-TĬL′I-TY, *n.* Quality of being ductile; ca-
 pacity of extension; flexibility :—docility.
DŬD′GEON (dŭd′jụn), *n.* Anger; resentment.
DŪE (dū), *a.* Owed; proper; fit; exact.
DŪE (dū), *ad.* Exactly; directly; fitly; duly.
DŪE, *n.* A debt; right; just title; tribute ;.toll.
DŪ′EL, *n.* A combat between two individuals.
DŪ′EL, *v. n.* To fight a single combat.
DŪ′EL-LER, *n.* Fighter of a duel; a duellist.
DŪ′EL-LING, *n.* The custom of fighting duels.
DŪ′EL-LĬST, *n.* One who fights a duel.
DŲ-ĔN′NA, *n.* An old woman guarding a young-
 er :—a waiting-woman of the Queen of Spain.
DŲ-ĔT′, *n.* (*Mus.*) An air for two performers.
DŬG, *n.* A pap or teat of a beast; a breast.
DŬG, *imp. t.* & *pp.* from *dig.* [in England.
DŪKE, *n.* One of the highest order of nobility
DŪKE′DOM, *n.* Possessions or quality of a duke.
DŬL′CET, *a.* Sweet; luscious; harmonious.
DŬL-CI-FI-CĀ′TION, *n.* The act of sweetening.
DŬL′CI-FҮ, DŬL′CO-RĀTE, *v. a.* To sweeten.
DŬL′CI-MER, *n.* A kind of musical instrument.
DŬLL, *a.* Stupid; blunt; obtuse; sad; slow.
DŬLL, *v. a.* To stupefy; to blunt; to sadden.
DŬL′NESS, *n.* Stupidity; dimness; bluntness.
DŪ′LY, *ad.* Properly; fitly; in due manner.
DŬMB (dŭm), *a.* Mute; incapable of speech.
DŬMB′LY, (dŭm′le), *ad.* Mutely; silently.
DŬMB′NESS (dŭm′nes), *n.* Incapacity to speak.
DŬMPS, *n. pl.* Sorrow; melancholy; sadness.
DŬMP′ISH, *a.* Sad; dejected; melancholy.
DŬMP′ISH-NESS, *n.* Sadness; melancholy.
DŬMP′LING, *n.* A sort of paste or pudding.

DŬN, *a.* Of a dark color; brownish-black; fulvous brown:—dark; gloomy; obscure.
DŬN, *v. a.* To ask often for a debt.   [a debt.
DŬN, *n.* An importunate creditor:—demand for
DŬNCE, *n.* A thickskull; a dullard; a dolt.
DŬNG, *n.* The excrement of animals.
DŬN'GEQN (dŭn'jun), *n.* A close, dark prison.
DŬNG'HILL, *n.* A heap or accumulation of dung.
DŬNG'HILL, *a.* Sprung from the dunghill; mean.
DŬN'NER, *n.* One employed in soliciting debts.
DŪ-Q-DĔÇ'I-MŌ, *n.; pl.* DŪ-Q-DĔÇ'I-MŌES. A book having 12 leaves to a sheet:—also *adj.*
DŪPE, *n.* A person cheated or imposed on.
DŪPE, *v. a.* To trick; to cheat; to deceive.
DŪ'PLI-CĀTE, *v. a.* To double; to fold.
DŪ'PLI-CATE, *a.* Double; twofold; in pairs.
DŪ'PLI-CATE, *n.* A second thing of the same kind; a copy; a transcript; a counterpart.
DŪ-PLI-CĀ'TIQN, *n.* Act of doubling:—a fold.
DŪ'PLI-CA-TŪRE, *n.* A fold; any thing doubled.
DU-PLIÇ'I-TY, *n.* Deceit; dissimulation; artifice.
DŪ-RA-BĬL'I-TY, *n.* The power of lasting.
DŪR'A-BLE, *a.* Lasting; having long existence.
DŪR'A-BLE-NESS, *n.* Power of lasting; continu-
DŪR'ANCE, *n.* Endurance; imprisonment.[ance.
DU-RĀ'TIQN, *n.* Continuance; length of time.
DŪ'RĔSS, *n.* Constraint; imprisonment.   [of.
DŪR'ING, *prep.* For the time of the continuance
DŬRST, *pp.* from *dare.*   [darkish; dusky.
DŬSK, *a.* Tending to darkness; dark-colored;
DŬSK, *n.* Tendency to darkness; dark color.
DŬSK'I-LY, *ad.* With a tendency to darkness.
DŬSK'I-NĔSS, *n.* Incipient darkness or obscurity.
DŬSK'ISH, *a.* Inclining to darkness or blackness.
DŬSK'Y, *a.* Somewhat dark:—gloomy; sad.
DŬST, *n.* Earth, &c., reduced to powder; earth.
DŬST, *v. a.* To free from, or sprinkle with, dust.

DŬST'ER, *n.* That which frees from dust; a sifter.
DŬST'I-NĔSS, *n.* State of being covered with dust.
DŬST'MAN, *n.* One who carries away dust.
DŬST'Y, *a.* Filled or covered with dust.
DŬTCH, *n.* The people and language of Holland.
DŬTCH'ESS, DŬTCH'Y. See DUCHESS, DUCHY.
DŪ'TE-OŬS, *a.* Obedient; obsequious; dutiful.
DŪ'TI-A-BLE, *a.* Subject to duty or impost.
DŪ'TI-FÛL, *a.* Obedient; submissive; reverent.
DŪ'TI-FÛL-LY, *ad.* Obediently; submissively.
DŪ'TI-FÛL-NĔSS, *n.* Obedience; submission.
DŪ'TY, *n.* Whatever one is bound to perform:—service:—tax; impost; custom; toll.
DU-ŬM'VI-RATE, *n.* A government by two.
DWÂRF, *n.* One below the usual size.   [stunt.
DWÂRF, *v. a.* To hinder from full growth; to
DWÂRF'ISH, *a.* Below the natural bulk; small.
DWÂRF'ISH-NĔSS, *n.* Littleness of stature.
DWĔLL, *v. a.* [*imp. t.* & *pp.* dwĕlt, dwĕlled.] To remain; to inhabit; to live in a place.
DWĔLL'ER, *n.* One who dwells; an inhabitant.
DWĔLL'ING, *n.* Habitation; place of residence.
DWĔLL'ING-HOÛSE, *n.* A house in which one
DWĔLL'ING-PLĀCE, *n.* Place of residence.[lives.
DWĬN'DLE, *v. n.* & *a.* To grow or make less.
DȲE, *v. a.* To tinge; to color; to stain.
DȲE, *n.* Color; coloring matter; tinge; stain.
DȲE'ING, *n.* The art of coloring cloth, &c.
DȲ'ER, *n.* One who dyes cloth, &c.
DȲ'ING, *pres. part.* of *die.* Expiring; losing life.
DȲKE, *n.* A mound; a bank. See DIKE.
DȲ-NĂM'ICS, *n. pl.* Science of moving powers.
DȲ'NAS-TY or DȲN'AS-TY, *n.* A race of princes.
DYS-EN-TĔR'IC, *a.* Relating to dysentery.
DYS'EN-TĔR-Y, *n.* A looseness; bloody flux.
DYS'PEP-SY or DYS-PĔP'SY, *n.* Indigestion.
DYS-PĔP'TIC, *a.* Having bad digestion.

E.

E, the most frequent vowel in the English language, has two principal sounds — long, as in *mete*, and short, as in *met*.
ĒACH (ēch), *pron.* Either or one of two or more.
ĒA'GER (ē'ger), *a.* Keenly desirous; ardent.
ĒA'GER-LY (ē'ger-le), *ad.* Ardently; keenly.
ĒA'GER-NĔSS (ē'ger-nĕs), *n.* Strong desire.
ĒA'GLE (ē'gl), *n.* A bird of prey; a standard.
ĒA'GLE-EȲED (ē'gl-īd), *a.* Very sharp-sighted.
ĒA'GLET (ē'glet), *n.* A young eagle.   [corn.
ĒAR (ēr), *n.* The organ of hearing:—a spike of
ĒAR (ēr), *v. n.* To shoot into ears, as corn.
ĒARL (ĕrl), *n.* A title of English nobility.
ĒAR'LĂP (ēr'lăp), *n.* The tip of the ear.   [earl.
ĒARL'DQM (ĕrl'dum), *n.* The seigniory of an
ĒARL'LESS (ēr'les), *a.* Destitute of ears:—deaf.
ĒAR'LI-NĔSS (ĕr'le-nĕs), *n.* State of being early.
ĒAR'LY (ĕr'le), *a.* Being in season.—*ad.* Betimes.
ĒARN (ĕrn), *v. a.* To gain by labor; to obtain.
ĒAR'NEST (ĕr'nest), *a.* Ardent; zealous; eager.
ĒAR'NEST, *n.* Seriousness:—pledge; money ad-
ĒAR'NEST-LY (ĕr'nest-le), *ad.* Warmly.[vanced.
ĒAR'NEST-NĔSS (ĕr'nest-nĕs), *n.* Eagerness.
ĒARN'ING (ĕrn'ing), *n.* That which is earned.

ĒAR'PĬCK, *n.* An instrument for cleaning ears.
ĒAR'RĬNG (ĕr'rĭng), *n.* Ornament for the ear.
ĒARTH (ĕrth), *n.* Soil; ground; earthy matter:—the terraqueous globe; the world.[bury.
ĒARTH (ĕrth), *v. a.* & *n.* To hide in earth; to
ĒARTH'BŌARD, *n.* The board of a plough.
ĒARTH'-BŌRN (ĕrth'bōrn), *a.* Born of the earth.
ĒARTH'EN (ĕr'thn), *a.* Made of earth or clay.
ĒARTH'LI-NĔSS (ĕrth'le-nĕs), *n.* Worldliness.
ĒARTH'LY (ĕrth'le), *a.* Belonging to earth; vile.
ĒARTH'NŬT (ĕrth'nŭt), *n.* A pignut; a root.
ĒARTH'QUĀKE, *n.* A convulsion of the earth.
ĒARTH'Y (ĕrth'e), *a.* Consisting of earth; terrene.
ĒAR'WĂX (ēr'wăks), *n.* Cerumen of the ear.
ĒAR'WĬG (ēr'wĭg), *n.* An insect:—a whisperer.
ĒASE (ēz), *n.* Quiet; rest after labor:—facility.
ĒASE (ēz), *v. a.* To free from pain; to relieve.
ĒAS'EL (ē'zl), *n.* Frame for a painter's canvas.
ĒASE'MENT (ēz'ment), *n.* Ease; support; relief.
ĒA'SI-LY (ē'ze-le), *ad.* Without difficulty; readily.
ĒA'SI-NĔSS (ē'ze-nĕs), *n.* Readiness; ease; rest.
ĒAST (ēst), *n.* The quarter where the sun rises.
ĒAST, *a.* Being from, or towards, the rising sun.
ĒAST'ER, *n.* The feast of Christ's resurrection.

MÎEN, SÏR; MÔVE, NÖR, SŎN; BÛLL, BÜR, RÛLE.—Ç, Ģ, *soft;* Ɛ, Ǥ, *hard;* Ş *as* z; Ӿ *as* gz; ᵺHIS.

Ēast′ẹr-lỵ (ēst′ẹr-lẹ), *a. & ad.* Coming from the east :—towards the east. [ental.
Ēast′ẹrn (ēst′ẹrn), *a.* Being in the east ; ori-
Ēast′ward (ēst′wạrd), *ad.* Towards the east.
Ēa′sỵ (ē′zẹ), *a.* Not difficult ; quiet ; complying.
Ēat (ēt), *v. a. & n.* [*imp. t.* ate, eat ; *pp.* eaten.] To devour :—to corrode :—to take food.
Ēat′ạ-ble (ēt′ạ-bl), *a.* Capable of being eaten.
Ēat′ạ-ble, *n.* Any thing that may be eaten.
Ēat′en (ē′tn), *pp.* from *eat.* [corrodes.
Ēat′ẹr (ēt′ẹr), *n.* One that eats :—that which
Ēavẹṣ, *n. pl.* The edges of the roof of a house.
Ēavẹṣ′drŏp-pẹr,*n.* A listener under windows.
Ěbb, *n.* The reflux of the tide :—decline.
Ěbb, *v. n.* To flow back towards the sea :—to de-
Ěb′ọn, *a.* Dark ; black :—made of ebony. [cay.
Ěb′ọ-nỵ, *n.* A hard, black, valuable wood.
Ẹ-brī′ẹ-tỵ, *n.* Drunkenness ; intoxication.
Ěbb′-tīde, *n.* The reflux of the tide ;.the ebb.
Ẹ-bŭll′iẹnt (ẹ-bŭl′yẹnt),*a.* Boiling over. [ing.
Ěb-ụl-lĭ′′tiọn (ĕb-ụl-lĭsh′ụn), *n.* Act of boil-
Ẹc-cĕn′trĭc,) *a.* Deviating from the cen-
Ẹc-cĕn′trị-cạl,)   tre, or from the true line of a circle :—irregular ; anomalous ; odd.
Ẹc-cẹn-trĭç′ị-tỵ, *n.* State of being eccentric.
Ěc-clẹ-ṣị-ăs′tēṣ, *n.* A book of Holy Scripture.
Ěc-clẹ-ṣị-ăs′tịc, *n.* A clĕrgyman ; a priest.
Ěc-clẹ-ṣị-ăs′tịc,) *a.* Relating to the
Ěc-clẹ-ṣị-ăs′tị-cạl,) church ; not civil ; not secular. [the Apocrypha.
Ěc-clẹ-ṣị-ăs′tị-cŭs, *n.* One of the books of
Ěçh′ị-nate, Ěçh′ị-nāt-ẹd, *a.* Bristled ; cov- ered with sharp points or spines. [sound.
Ěçh′ō, *n.* ; pl. Ěçh′ōẹṣ. Reverberation of a
Ěçh′ō (ĕk′kō), *v. a. & n.* To send back a sound.
Ẹ-clàir′cịṣṣe-mĕnt (ẹ-klàr′sịz-mĕnt), *n.* Ex- planation ; the act of clearing up an affair.
Ẹ-clàt′ (ẹ-klä′), *n.* Splendor ; show ; lustre.
Ẹc-lĕc′tịc, *a.* Selecting ; choosing ; culling.
Ẹ-clĭpse′ (ẹ-klĭps′), *n.* Obscuration ; darkness.
Ẹ-clĭpse′, *v. a.* To darken, as a luminary ; to obscure ; to cloud ; to veil :—to degrade.
Ẹ-clĭp′tịc, *n.* A great circle of the sphere.
Ěc′lōgue (ĕk′lŏg), *n.* A pastoral poem.
‖Ěc-ọ-nŏm′ị-cạl *or* Ē-cọ-nŏm′ị-cạl, *a.* Fru- gal ; thrifty ; sparing ; saving.
‖Ěc-ọ-nŏm′ịcs, *n. pl.* Household management.
Ẹ-cŏn′ọ-mĭst, *n.* One who is thrifty or frugal.
Ẹ-cŏn′ọ-mīze, *v. a.* To employ with economy.
Ẹ-cŏn′ọ-mỵ,*n.* Thrifty management ; frugality.
Ěc′stạ-sỵ,*n.* Excessive joy ; rapture ; a trance.
Ẹc-stăt′ịc, Ẹc-stăt′ị-cạl, *a.* Ravished ; rapturous ; filling with ecstasy ; transporting.
Ěc-ụ-mĕn′ị-cạl, *a.* General ; universal.
Ěc′ụ-riẹ (ĕk′kụ-rẹ), *n.* A stable for horses.
Ẹ-dā′ciọụs (ẹ-dā′shụs), *a.* Eating ; voracious.
Ẹ-dăç′ị-tỵ, *n.* Voracity ; ravenousness.
Ěd′dẹr, *n.* Twigs binding hedge-stakes.
Ěd′dịsh,*n.* A second crop of grass ; aftermath.
Ěd′dỵ, *n.* A contrary current ; a whirlpool.
Ěd′dỵ, *v. n.* To move in an eddy or whirl.
Ědǥe (ĕj), *n.* Sharp part of a blade :—brink.
Ědǥe (ĕj), *v. a.* To sharpen ; to give an edge to.
Ědǥed (ĕjd *or* ĕd′jẹd), *p. a.* Sharp ; not blunt.
Ědǥe′-tôôl, *n.*. A tool with an edge ; cutting-
Ědǥe′wịṣe,*ad.* In the direction of the edge.[tool.
Ědǥ′ịng,*n.* A border; fringe; narrow lace-work.
Ěd′ị-ble, *a.* Fit to be eaten ; eatable.

Ē′dịct, *n.* A proclamation ; an order.
Ěd-ị-fị-cā′tiọn, *n.* Instruction ; improvement.
Ěd′ị-fĭce (ĕd′ẹ-fĭs), *n.* A structure ; a building.
Ěd′ị-fī-ẹr, *n.* One who edifies or enlightens.
Ěd′ị-fỵ (ĕd′ẹ-fī), *v. a.* To instruct ; to improve.
Ē′dīle, *n.* An ancient Roman magistrate.
Ěd′ịt, *v. a.* To superintend for publication.
Ẹ-dĭ′′tiọn, *n.* The impression or publication
Ěd′ị-tọr, *n.* One who edits. [of a book, &c.
Ěd-ị-tō′rị-ạl, *a.* Belonging to an editor. [tor.
Ěd′ị-tọr-shĭp, *n.* Office or function of an edi-
Ěd′ụ-cāte, *v. a.* To bring up ; to instruct. [tor.
Ěd-ụ-cā′tiọn, *n.* A bringing up ; instruction.
Ěd-ụ-cā′tiọn-ạl, *a.* Relating to education.
Ěd′ụ-cā-tọr, *n.* One who gives instruction.
Ẹ-dūce′, *v. a.* To bring or draw out ; to extract.
Ẹ-dŭc′tiọn, *n.* The act of bringing out.
Ẹ-dŭl′cọ-rāte, *v. a.* To sweeten ; to purify.
Ẹ-dŭl-cọ-rā′tiọn, *n.* The act of edulcorating.
Ēēl (ēl), *n.* A serpentine, slimy fish.
Ē′ēn (ēn), *ad.* Contracted from *even.* See Even.
E′er (àr). Contracted from *ever.* See Ever.
Ẹf-fàce′, *v. a.* To blot out, erase, obliterate.
Ẹf-fĕct′, *n.* Result ; issue ; consequence :— meaning ; reality.—*pl.* Goodṣ movables.
Ẹf-fĕct′, *v. a.* To bring to pass ; to produce.
Ẹf-fĕct′ị-ble, *a.* Feasible ; practicable.
Ẹf-fĕc′tiọn, *n.* Performance :—a problem.
Ẹf-fĕc′tịve, *a.* Efficacious ; efficient ; active.
Ẹf-fĕc′tịve-lỵ, *ad.* Powerfully ; with effect.
Ẹf-fĕct′ọr, *n.* He who, or that which, effects.
Ẹf-fĕct′ụ-ạl, *a.* Producing effect ; efficacious.
Ẹf-fĕct′ụ-ạl-lỵ, *ad.* In an effectual manner.
Ẹf-fĕct′ụ-ạl-nĕss, *n.* State of being effectual.
Ẹf-fĕct′ụ-āte, *v. a.* To bring to pass ; to effect.
Ẹf-fĕm′ị-nạ-cỵ, *n.* Womanish delicacy.
Ẹf-fĕm′ị-nate, *a.* Womanish ; soft ; feminine.
Ẹf-fĕm′ị-nāte, *v. a.* To make womanish.
Ẹf-fĕm′ị-nate-lỵ, *ad.* In an effeminate or unmanly manner. [effeminacy.
Ẹf-fĕm′ị-nate-nĕss, *n.* Unmanly softness ;
Ẹf-fĕn′dị (ẹf-fĕn′dẹ), *n.* A Turkish officer.
Ěf-fẹr-vĕsce′ (ĕf-fẹr-vĕs′), *v. n.* To work, as a liquid when fermenting ; to ferment. [tion.
Ěf-fẹr-vĕs′cẹnce, *n.* A bubbling ; fermenta-
Ěf-fẹr-vĕs′cẹnt, *a.* Effervescing ; bubbling.
Ẹf-fēte′, *a.* Barren ; worn out with age. [fect.
Ěf-fị-cā′ciọụs (-fẹ-kā′shụs), *a.* Producing ef-
Ěf-fị-cā′ciọụs-lỵ, *ad.* Effectually ; with effect.
Ěf′fị-cạ-cỵ, *n.* Ability to produce effects.
Ẹf-fị′′ciẹn-cỵ, *n.* Power of producing effects.
Ẹf-fị′′ciẹnt (ẹf-fĭsh′yẹnt),*a.* Causing effects.
Ẹf-fị′′ciẹnt-lỵ (-fĭsh′yẹnt-lẹ), *ad.* Effectively.
Ěf′fị-ǥỵ, *n.* Image ; likeness ; representation.
Ěf-flọ-rĕsce′ (ĕf-flọ-rĕs′), *v. n.* To form, or be covered with, dust or powder on the surface.
Ěf-flọ-rĕs′cence, *n.* Act of efflorescing :— eruption on the skin :—flowering of plants.[&c.
Ěf-flọ-rĕs′cent, *a.* Shooting out in flowers,
Ěf′flụ-ence, *n.* A flowing out ; efflux ; ema-
Ěf′flụ-ent, *a.* 'Flowing out ; issuing. [nation.
Ěf-flū′vị-ŭm, *n.* ; pl. Ěf-flū′vị-ạ. Invisible vapor, as from putrefying matter.
Ěf′flŭx, *n.* The act of flowing out ; effusion.
Ẹf-flŭx′iọn (-flŭk′shụn), *n.* Act of flowing out.
Ěf′fŏrt, *n.* A struggle ; exertion ; endeavor.
Ẹf-frŏn′tẹr-ỵ, *n.* Impudence ; shamelessness.
Ẹf-fŭl′ǥence, *n.* Lustre ; brilliancy.

EF-FŬL'ĢENT, a. Shining; bright; luminous.
EF-FŪSE', v. a. To pour out; to spill; to shed.
EF-FŪ'SIQN (-fū'zhun), n. A póuring out; waste.
EF-FŪ'SIVE, a. Pouring out; dispersing.
ĔFT, n. A species of salamander or newt.
ĔGG (ĕg), n. A body produced by the feathered tribe, and also by some other animals.
ĔG'LAN-TĪNE, n. A species of rose; sweetbrier.
Ē'ĢO-TĬŞM, n. Self-commendation; frequent use of the word I; speaking much of one's self.
Ē'ĢO-TĬST, n. One who talks much of himself.
Ē-ĢO-TĬST'Į-CĄL, a. Addicted to egotism; vain.
Ē'ĢO-TĪZE, v. n. To talk much of one's self. -
E-GRĒ'ĢIOŲS (e-grē'jus), a. Extraordinary.
E-GRĒ'ĢIOŲS-LY, ad. Eminently; remarkably.
Ē'GRĘSS, n. A going out; departure; egression.
E-GRĔS'SIQN (e-grĕsh'un), n. Act of going out.
Ē'GRĘT, n. A fowl of the heron kind:—down.
EI'DER, n. A large kind of northern duck.
EIGHT (āt), a. Twice four; seven and one.
EIGH'TĔEN (ā'tĕn), a. Twice nine.
EIGH'TĔENTH (ā'tĕnth), n. The next in order to the seventeenth; ordinal of eighteen.
EIGHTH (ātth), a. Next in order to the seventh.
EIGHTH'LY (ātth'le), ad. In the eighth place.
EIGH'TĮ-ĔTH (ā'te-ĕth), a. The ordinal of eighty.
EIGH'TY (ā'te), a. Eight times ten; fourscore.
ĒI'THER (ē'ther), prep. One or the other. [that.
ĒI'THER (ē'ther), conj. Or; as, either this or
E-JĂC'Ų-LĀTE, v. a. To throw; to hurl; to cast:—to utter suddenly. [pression.
E-JĂC-Ų-LĀ'TIQN, n. A darting:—a quick ex-
E-JĂC'Ų-LĄ-TQ-RY, a. Darted out; sudden; hasty.
E-JĔCT', v. a. To throw out; to cast forth, ex-
E-JĔC'TIQN, n. A casting out; expulsion. [pel.
E-JĔCT'MENT, n. Expulsion:—an action for the recovery of the possession of real property.
ĒKE, or ĒĔK (ēk), v. a. To supply; to protract.
ĒKE, ad. Also; likewise; beside; moreover.
E-LĂB'Q-RĀTE, v. a. To produce with labor.
E-LĂB'Q-RĄTE, a. Finished with great labor, and care; much labored or studied. [rate.
E-LĂB'Q-RĄTE-NĔSS, n. State of being elabo-
E-LĂB-Q-RĀ'TIQN, n. The act of elaborating.
E-LĂPSE', v. n. To pass away; to glide away.
E-LĂS'TĮC, a. Springing back; rebounding.
E-LĄS-TĬÇ'Į-TY, n. A property in bodies, by which they restore themselves to their original form; tendency to rebound. [spirits.
E-LĀTE', a. Flushed with success; high in
E-LĀTE', v. a. To elevate; to puff up; to exalt.
E-LĀ'TIQN, n. High spirits from success.
ĔL'BŌW (ĕl'bō), n. Curvature of the arm; angle.
ĔL'BŌW (ĕl'bō), v. a. & n. To push with the elbow; to crowd; to press. [chair.
ĔL'BŌW-CHÀIR, n. A chair with arms; arm-
ĔL'BŌW-RÔÔM, n. Room to extend the elbows.
ĔL'DER, a. Surpassing another in years.
ĔL'DER, n. A senior:—a ruler:—a tree or shrub.
ĔL'DER-LY, a. Bordering upon old age; old.
ĔL'DER-SHIP, n. Seniority; primogeniture.
ĔL'DEST, a. Oldest; most aged.
ĔL-E-CĂM-PĀNE', n. A large, herbaceous plant: —a sweetmeat of the root of the plant.
E-LĔCT', v. a. To choose for office; to select.
E-LĔCT', a. Chosen; taken by preference.
E-LĔC'TIQN, n. Act of choosing; choice. [tion.
E-LĔC-TIQN-ĒĒR', v. n. To use arts for an elec-

E-LĔC'TIVE, a. Having, or regulated by, choice.
E-LĔCT'QR, n. He who elects, or gives a vote.
E-LĔC'TQ-RAL, a. Pertaining to an elector or to an election. [an elector.
E-LĔC'TQ-RĄTE, n. Territory or the office of
E-LĔC'TRĮC, } a. Relating to, containing,
E-LĔC'TRĮ-CĄL, } or capable of, electricity.
E-LĘC-TRĬ''CIĄN, n. One versed in electricity.
E-LĘC-TRĬÇ'Į-TY, n. That property of bodies, first observed in amber, of attracting or repel- ling light bodies when excited by friction.
E-LĔC'TRĮ-FY, v. a. To communicate electrici- ty to:—to thrill; to charm; to enchant. [ment.
E-LĘC-TRŎM'E-TER, n. An electrical instru-
E-LĔCT'Ų-Ą-RY, n. A soft compound medicine.
ĔL-ĘE-MŎŞ'Y-NĄ-RY (ĕl-e-mŏz'e-na-re), a. Re- lating to alms or charity:—living on alms.
ĔL-ĘE-MŎŞ'Y-NĄ-RY, n. One living upon alms.
ĔL'E-GĄNCE, n. Beauty, propriety, grace, or symmetry, without grandeur; refinement.
ĔL'E-GĄNT, a. Having elegance; pleasing.
ĔL'E-GĄNT-LY, ad. With elegance; gracefully.
ĔL-E-ĢĪ'ĄC, a. Pertaining to, or like, elegy.
ĔL'E-ĢY, n. A mournful song or poem; a dirge.
ĔL'E-MĘNT, n. First or constituent principle of any thing:—suitable state or habitation.
ĔL-E-MĔNT'ĄL, a. Pertaining to elements; rude.
ĔL-E-MĔNT'Ą-RY, a. Primary; uncompounded.
ĔL'E-PHĄNT, n. The largest of quadrupeds.
ĔL-E-PHĄN-TĪ'Ą-SĬS, n. A species of leprosy.
ĔL-E-PHĂN'TĮNE, a. Pertaining to the ele- phant; huge; gigantic; colossal. [Ceres.
ĔL-EŲ-SĬN'Į-ĄN, a. Relating to the rites of
ĔL'E-VĀTE, v. a. To raise up; to exalt, dignify.
ĔL-E-VĀ'TIQN, n. A raising up; exaltation:—
E-LĔV'EN (e-lĕv'vn), a. Ten and one. [height.
E-LĔV'ENTH (e-lĕv'vnth), a. The next in or- der to the tenth; ordinal of eleven. [fairy.
ĔLF, n.; pl. ĔLVEŞ. A wandering spirit; a
ĔLF'LŎCK, n. A knot of hair twisted, as by elves.
E-LĬÇ'ĮT, v. a. To draw out; to educe, extract.
ĔL-Į-ĢĮ-BĬL'Į-TY, n. Worthiness to be chosen.
ĔL'Į-ĢĮ-BLE, a. Fit to be chosen; preferable.
ĔL'Į-ĢĮ-BLE-NĔSS, n. Worthiness to be chosen.
E-LĪ''SIQN (e-lĭzh'un), n. Act of cutting off a vowel or syllable, as at the end of a word.
E-LĬX'ĮR, n. A medicine; quintessence; cordial.
ĔLK, n. A quadruped of the stag kind.
ĔLL, n. A measure of length varying in differ-
EL-LĪPSE', n. An ellipsis. [ent countries.
EL-LĬP'SĮS, n.; pl. EL-LĬP'SĒŞ. An oval fig- ure:—an omission; a defect. [an ellipsis; oval.
EĿ-LĬP'TĮC, EL-LĬP'TĮ-CĄL, a. Pertaining to
ĔLM, n. The name of a large forest-tree.
ĔL-Q-CŪ'TIQN, n. Pronunciation; utterance.
ĔL'Q-ĢY, n. Panegyric; praise. See EULOGY.
E-LŎN'GĀTE, v. a. To lengthen; to draw out.
ĔL-QN-GĀ'TIQN, n. Act of lengthening; distance.
E-LŌPE', v. n. To run away, as a woman to be married; to escape privately. [parture.
E-LŌPE'MĘNT, n. Private or unlicensed de-
ĔL'Q-QUĔNCE, n. Oratory; art of speaking well.
ĔL'Q-QUĔNT, a. Having the power of oratory.
ĔL'Q-QUĔNT-LY, ad. In an eloquent manner.
ĔLSE, pron. Other; one besides.—ad. Otherwise.
ĔLSE'WHĔRE (ĕls'hwàr), ad. In another place.
E-LŪ'CĮ-DĀTE, v. a. To explain; to clear.
E-LŪ-CĮ-DĀ'TIQN, n. Explanation; exposition.

Ẹ-LŪ'CĮ-DĀ-TOR, n. An explainer ; expounder.
Ẹ-LŪDE', v. a. To escape by stratagem ; to evade.
Ẹ-LŪ'DĮ-BLE, a. That may be eluded. [sion.
Ẹ-LŪ'ŞIQN (ẹ-lū'zhụn), n. Act of eluding ; eva-
Ẹ-LŪ'ṢĮVE, a. Practising elusion ; evasive.
Ẹ-LŪ'SQ-RẎ, a. Tending to elude ; elusive.
Ẹ-LŪ'TRĮ-ĀTE, v. a. To purify by straining.
ĔLVEṢ (ĕlvz), n. The pl. of elf. See ELF.
Ẹ-LẎ''ṢĮ-ẠN (ẹ-lĭzh'ẹ-ạn), a. Very delightful.
Ẹ-LẎ''ṢĮ-ŬM (ẹ-lĭzh'ẹ-ŭm), n. The place assigned
  by the heathens to happy souls after death.
Ẹ-MĀ'CĮ-ĀTE (ẹ-mā'shẹ-āt), v. a. & n. To make
  lean ; to waste ; to deprive of flesh, attenuate.
Ẹ-MĀ-CĮ-Ā'TIQN, n. The act of making lean.
ĔM'Ạ-NĂNT, a. Issuing or flowing ; emanating.
ĔM'Ạ-NĀTE, v. n. To issue or flow ; to spring.
ĔM'Ạ-NĀ'TIQN, n. Act of issuing ; efflux.
ĔM'Ạ-NẠ-TĬVE, a. Issuing from ; emanant.
Ẹ-MĂN'CĮ-PĀTE, v. a. To set free from servi-
Ẹ-MĂN-CĮ-PĀ'TIQN, n. Act of setting free. [tude.
Ẹ-MĂN'CĮ-PĀ-TQR, n. One who emancipates.
Ẹ-MĀS'CŲ-LĀTE, v. a. To deprive of virility.
Ẹ-MĀS'CŲ-LẠTE, a. Unmanned ; vitiated.
Ẹ-MĀS-CŲ-LĀ'TIQN, n. Castration ; effeminacy.
ẸM-BĀLM' (ẹm-bäm'), v. a. To impregnate with
  aromatics to prevent putrefaction. [balms.
ẸM-BĀLM'ẸR (ẹm-bäm'ẹr), n. One who em-
ẸM-BĂR'GŌ, n. ; pl. ẸM-BĂR'GŌEṢ. Prohibi-
  tion to sail ; detention in port. [board.
ẸM-BĂRK', v. a. & n. To put or go on ship-
ĔM-BAR-KĀ'TIQN, n. The act of embarking.
ẸM-BĂR'RẠSS, v. a. To perplex ; to entangle.
ẸM-BĂR'RẠSS-MĔNT, n. Perplexity ; trouble.
ẸM-BĂS'SẠ-DQR, n. An ambassador ; a pleni-
  potentiary. [bassador :—legation.
ĔM'BẠS-SẎ, n. Message or function of an am-
ẸM-BĂT'TLE, v. a. To range in order of battle.
ẸM-BĀẎ' (ẹm-bā'), v. a. To enclose in a bay.
ẸM-BĔL'LĮSH, v. a. To adorn ; to beautify.
ẸM-BĔL'LĮSH-MĔNT, n. Ornament ; decoration.
ĔM'BERṢ, n. pl. Hot cinders or ashes.
ẸM-BĔZ'ZLE, v. a. To steal by breach of trust.
ẸM-BĔZ'ZLE-MĔNT, n. Act of embezzling.
ẸM-BLĀ'ZQN (ẹm-blā'zn), v. a. To adorn with
  figures of heraldry :—to deck glaringly.
ẸM-BLĀ'ZQN-ẸR (ẹm-blā'zn-ẹr), n. A blazoner.
ẸM-BLĀ'ZQN-RẎ, n. Blazonry ; heraldic or-
  naments ; pictures on shields. [inlaid work.
ĔM'BLẸM, n. A device ; a type ; a symbol :—
ĔM-BLẸM-ĂT'ĮC,) a. Pertaining to, or com-
ĔM-BLẸM-ĂT'Į-CẠL,) prising, an emblem ;
  allusive ; figurative ; representative. [emblems.
ĔM-BLẸM-ĂT'Į-CẠL-LẎ, ad. In the manner of
ẸM-BŎD'Ẏ, v. a. To form into a body ; to im-
  body :—to draw into one company or mass.
ẸM-BŌGU'ĮNG (ẹm-bōg'ĭng), n. A river's mouth.
ẸM-BŌLD'EN, ĮM-BŌLD'EN, v. a. To make bold.
ĔM'BQ-LĮṢM, n. Intercalation ; insertion of days.
ẸM-BŎSS', v. a. To engrave with rising work.
ẸM-BŎSS'MẸNT, n. A prominence ; jut ; relief.
ẸM-BŌW'ẸL, v. a. To take out the entrails of.
ẸM-BŌW'ẸR, v. n. To lodge or rest in a bower.
ẸM-BRĀCE', v. a. To hold fondly in the arms :
  —to enclose ; to comprise ; to contain ; to in-
ẸM-BRĀCE', v. n. To join in an embrace. [clude.
ẸM-BRĀCE', n. Clasp ; fond pressure in the arms.
ẸM-BRĀCE'MẸNT, n. Clasp ; hug ; embrace.
ẸM-BRĀ'CẸR-Ẏ, n. Attempt to corrupt a court.

EMBRASURE (ĕm-brạ-zhŭr' or ẹm-brā'zhụr), n.
  An opening made in a wall or parapet.
ĔM'BRQ-CĀTE, v. a. To moisten and rub, as a
  part diseased, with a liquid substance.
ĔM-BRQ-CĀ'TIQN, n. Act of embrocating. [work.
ẸM-BRŎÏD'ẸR, v. a. To adorn with figured
ẸM-BRŎÏD'ẸR-ẸR, n. One who embroiders.
ẸM-BRŎÏD'ẸR-Ẏ, n. Embroidered needle-work.
ẸM-BRŎÏL', v. a. To disturb, confuse, distract.
ẸM-BRŎÏL'MẸNT, n. Confusion ; disturbance.
ẸM-BRŪE', v. a. To soak. See ĬMBRUE.
ĔM'BRẎ-Ō, n. ; pl. ĔM'BRẎ-ŌṢ. Offspring not
  distinctly formed :—rudiments of any thing.
Ẹ-MĔND', v. a. To mend ; to amend ; to correct.
Ẹ-MĔND'Ạ-BLE, a. Capable of emendation.
ĔM-ẸN-DĀ'TIQN, n. Correction ; improvement.
ĔM'ẸN-DĀ-TQR, n. A corrector ; an improver.
Ẹ-MĔND'Ạ-TQ-RẎ, a. Contributing emendation.
ĔM'ẸR-ẠLD, n. A green precious stone.
Ẹ-MĔRGE', v. n. To emanate ; to rise ; to issue.
Ẹ-MĔR'GẸNCE,) n. A rising out :—sudden
Ẹ-MĔR'GẸN-CẎ,) occasion ; exigency.
Ẹ-MĔR'GẸNT, a. Rising into view :—sudden ;
ĔM'ẸR-ŎÏDṢ, n. pl. Hemorrhoids ; piles. [casual.
Ẹ-MĔR'SIQN, n. Act of rising out or into view.
ĔM'ẸR-Ẏ, n. A variety of sapphire, used for pol-
  ishing, and for cutting gems. [ing.
Ẹ-MĔT'ĮC, Ẹ-MĔT'Į-CẠL, a. Producing vomit-
Ẹ-MĔT'ĮC, n. A medicine producing vomits.
ĔM'Į-GRẠNT, n. One who emigrates.
ĔM'Į-GRĀTE, v. n. To leave one's native coun-
  try to reside in another ; to change residence.
ĔM-Į-GRĀ'TIQN, n. The act of emigrating.
ĔM'Į-NẸNCE, n. Height ; summit :—celebrity.
ĔM'Į-NẸNT, a. High ; exalted ; conspicuous.
ĔM'Į-NẸNT-LẎ, ad. Highly ; conspicuously.
Ē'MĮR, n. A title of dignity among the Turks.
ĔM'ĮS-SẠ-RẎ, n. One sent on a mission :—a spy.
Ẹ-MĬS'SIQN (ẹ-mĭsh'ụn), n. Act of emitting.
Ẹ-MĬT'; v. a. To send forth ; to vent ; to let fly.
ĔM'MẸT, n. An insect ; an ant ; a pismire.
Ẹ-MŎL'LIẸNT, a. Softening ; making supple.
Ẹ-MŎL'Ụ-MĔNT, n. Profit ; advantage ; gain.
Ẹ-MŌ'TIQN, n. A moving of the mind ; passion.
ẸM-PĀLE', v. a. To enclose :—to fix on a stake.
ẸM-PĀLE'MẸNT, n. Act of empaling :—calyx.
ẸM-PĂN'ẸL, v. a. To form, as a jury ; to enroll.
ẸM-PĂRK', v. a. To enclose in a park.
ĔM'PẸ-RQR, n. The sovereign of an empire.
ĔM'PHẠ-SĬS, n. ; pl. ĔM'PHẠ-SĒṢ. Particular
  stress laid on a word or sentence ; impressive
  utterance :—impressiveness ; significance.
ĔM'PHẠ-SĪZE, v. a. To place emphasis on.
ẸM-PHĂT'ĮC, ẸM-PHĂT'Į-CẠL, a. Forcible ;
  impressive ; significant ; striking ; strong.
ẸM-PHĂT'Į-CẠL-LẎ, ad. Strongly ; forcibly.
ĔM'PĪRE, n. Power :—dominion of an emperor.
ẸM-PĬR'ĮC or ĔM'PĮR-ĮC, n. A pretending or
  ignorant physician ; a quack ; a charlatan.
ẸM-PĬR'ĮC, ẸM-PĬR'Į-CẠL, a. Relating to ex-
  periments ; relying on experience :—charlatanic.
ẸM-PĬR'Į-CĬṢM, n. Quackery ; charlatanism.
ẸM-PLĂS'TẸR, v. a. To cover with a plaster.
ẸM-PLŎẎ', v. a. To occupy ; to exercise ; to use.
ẸM-PLŎẎ', n. Occupation ; employment.
ẸM-PLŎẎ'ẸR, n. One who employs ; a user.
ẸM-PLŎẎ'MẸNT, n. Business ; occupation ; of-
ẸM-PŎÏ'ṢQN, v. a. To poison, envenom. [fice.

Ā,Ē,Ī,Ō,Ū,Ẏ, long ; Ă,Ĕ,Ĭ,Ŏ,Ŭ,Ẏ, short ; Ạ,Ẹ,Į,Q,Ụ,Ẏ, obscure.—FĀRE,FĂR,FĂST,FĂLL ; HÊIR,HĔR ;

ẸM-PŌ'RỊ-ŬM, *n.* A place of commerce ; a mart.
ẸM-PŎV'ẸR-ĬSH, *v. a.* To make poor ; to exhaust.
ẸM-PŎV'ẸR-ĬSH-ẸR, *n.* One who empoverishes.
ẸM-PŎV'ẸR-ĬSH-MĔNT, *n.* Act of empoverishing.
ẸM-PŌW'ẸR, *v. a.* To authorize ; to enable.
ĔM'PRĘSS, *n.* Wife or consort of an emperor.
ẸM-PRĪ§Ẹ', *n.* Attempt of danger ; enterprise.
ĔMP'TỊ-NĔSS, (ĕm'tẹ-nĕs), *n.* Vacuity ; vacuum.
ĔMP'TY (ĕm'tẹ), *a.* Void ; not full ; unfurnished.
ĔMP'TY (ĕm'tẹ), *v. a.* To evacuate ; to exhaust.
ĔMP'TY (ĕm'tẹ), *v. n.* To become empty or void.
ẸM-PŬR'PLE, *v. a.* To make of a purple color.
ẸM-PŸR'Ẹ-ĄL, *a.* Formed of fire or light ; highly
 refined :—relating to the highest heaven.
ĔM-PY-RĒ'ĄN *or* ĔM-PŸR'Ẹ-ĄN, *n.* The highest
 heaven, of pure fire.   [heavenly.
ĔM-PY-RĒ'ĄN *or* ĔM-PŸR'Ẹ-ĄN, *a.* Empyreal ;
ĔM'Ụ-LĀTE, *v. a.* To rival ; to vie with :—to
 imitate ; to copy ; to resemble. [tion.
ĔM-Ụ-LĀ'TIỌN, *n.* Rivalry ; contest ; conten-
ĔM'Ụ-LĄ-TĬVE, *a.* Inclined to emulation.
ĔM'Ụ-LĀ-TỌR, *n.* A rival ; a competitor.
Ẹ-MŬL'ĢẸNT, *a.* Milking or draining out.
ĔM'Ụ-LOŬS, *a.* Rivalling ; desirous to excel.
Ẹ-MŬL'SIỌN, *n.* An oily, lubricating medicine.
Ẹ-MŬNC'TỌ-RY, *n.* (*Anat.*) An organ giving
 issue to matters ; an excretory duct.
ĔN, a prefix to many English words, identical
 with *em, im,* and *in,* chiefly borrowed from the
 French, and coinciding with the Latin *in.*
ẸN-Ā'BLE, *v. a.* To make able ; to empower.
ẸN-ĂCT', *v. a.* To perform ; to establish ; to de-
ẸN-ĂCT'ỌR, *n.* One who enacts or decrees. [cree.
ẸN-ĂCT'MẸNT, *n.* The passing of a bill into a
 law :—a law enacted ; a decree ; an act.
ẸN-ĂM'ẸL, *v. a.* To lay enamel on ; to inlay.
ẸN-ĂM'ẸL, *v. n.* To practise the use of enamel.
ẸN-ĂM'ẸL, *n.* A sort of semi-transparent glass :
 —hard, exterior surface of the teeth, &c.
ẸN-ĂM'ẸL-LẸR, *n.* One who enamels.
ẸN-ĂM'ẸL-LĬNG, *n.* The art or practice of an
 enameller ; the covering surfaces with enamel.
ẸN-ĂM-Ọ-RĂ'DŌ, *n.* One deeply in love.
ẸN-ĂM'OŲR, *v. a.* To inflame with love.
ẸN-CĀĢE', *v. a.* To shut up ; to coop up ; to cage.
ẸN-CĂMP', *v. n. & a.* To pitch tents ; to halt.
ẸN-CĂMP'MẸNT, *n.* Act of encamping ; camp.
ẸN-CĀSE', *v. a.* To enclose or hide, as in a case.
ẸN-CHĀFE', *v. a.* To chafe ; to enrage ; to irri-
 tate ; to fret.   [bind ; to fascinate.
ẸN-CHĀIN', *v. a.* To fasten with a chain :—to
ẸN-CHĂNT', *v. a.* To charm ; to bewitch ; to
 delight ; to captivate ; to enrapture.
ẸN-CHĂNT'ẸR, *n.* A magician ; a sorcerer.
ẸN-CHĂNT'MẸNT, *n.* Magic ; charm ; fascination.
ẸN-CHĂNT'RẸSS, *n.* A woman who enchants.
ẸN-CHĀSE', *v. a.* To infix ; to adorn ; to engrave.
ĔN-ÇHỊ-RĬD'Ị-ỌN, *n.* A little book ; a manual.
ẸN-CĬR'CLE, *v. a.* To surround ; to environ.
ẸN-CLŌSE', *v. a.* To surround ; to inclose ; to
ẸN-CLŌ§'ẸR, *n.* One who encloses. [wrap.
ẸN-CLŌ§'ỤRE (ẹn-klō'zhụr), *n.* Act of enclos-
 ing :—the thing enclosed, or which encloses.
ẸN-CŌ'MỊ-ĂST, *n.* A panegyrist ; a praiser.
ẸN-CŌ-MỊ-ĂS'TỊC,   } *a.* Laudatory ; panegyr-
ẸN-CŌ-MỊ-ĂS'TỊ-CĄL, } ical ; eulogistic.
ẸN-CŌ'MỊ-ŬM, *n. ;* pl. ẸN-CŌ'MỊ-ŬM§ *or* ẸN-CŌ'-
 MỊ-Ą. Panegyric ; praise ; commendation.

ẸN-CŎM'PĄSS, *v. a.* To encircle ; to surround.
ẸN-CŎM'PĄSS-MẸNT, *n.* Act of encompassing
EN-CŌRE' (äng-kōr'), *ad.* [Fr.] Again ; once
 more ; a word asking repetition. [tion of.
EN-CŌRE' (äng-kōr'), *v. a.* To call for repeti-
ẸN-COÛN'TẸR, *n.* Battle ; fight ; duel ; meeting.
ẸN-COÛN'TẸR, *v. a.* To meet ; to confront :—to
 attack ; to resist ; to oppose. [meet.
ẸN-COÛN'TẸR, *v. n.* To engage ; to fight ; to
ẸN-COÛR'AĢE (ẹn-kŭr'ạj), *v. a.* To incite ; to
 give courage to ; to stimulate ; to support.
ẸN-COÛR'AĢE-MẸNT, *n.* Incitement ; support.
ĔN'CRỊ-NĪTE, *n.* A fossil animal ; a species of
 star-fish, with a lily-shaped disk ; stone-lily.
ẸN-CRŌACH' (ẹn-krōch'), *v. n.* To make inva-
 sion ; to advance by stealth ; to infringe.
ẸN-CRŌACH'MẸNT, *n.* An unlawful intrusion.
ẸN-CŬM'BẸR, *v. a.* To clog ; to load ; to impede.
ẸN-CŬM'BRĄNCE, *n.* Clog ; load ; impediment.
ẸN-CỸ-CLỌ-PÆ'DỊ-Ą (ẹn-sī-klọ-pē'dẹ-ạ), *n.* A
 complete circle of sciences ; a cyclopædia.
ẸN-CỸ-CLỌ-PĒ'DỊST, *n.* One who compiles, or
 assists in compiling, an encyclopædia.
ẸN-CỸST'ED, *a.* Enclosed in a vesicle or bag.
ĔND, *n.* Conclusion ; termination ; period ; point :
 —death ; fate :—limit ; purpose ; design.
ĔND, *v. a.* To terminate ; to conclude ; to finish.
ĔND, *v. n.* To come to an end ; to cease ; to die.
ẸN-DĂM'AĢE, *v. a.* To injure ; to damage.
ẸN-DĀN'ĢER, *v. a.* To expose to danger ; to
 put to hazard ; to hazard ; to imperil.
ẸN-DEAR', *v. a.* To make dear ; to make beloved.
ẸN-DEAR'MẸNT, *n.* Cause of love ; affection.
ẸN-DĔAV'ỌR (ẹn-dĕv'ụr), *n.* Effort ; attempt.
ẸN-DĔAV'ỌR, *v. n.* To strive ; to exert one's self.
ẸN-DĔAV'ỌR, *v. a.* To attempt ; to essay.
ẸN-DĔC'Ą-GŎN, *n.* A figure of eleven sides.
ẸN-DEĪC'TỊC, *a.* Pointing out ; showing.
ẸN-DĔM'ỊC, } *a.* Peculiar to a country. [*Ap-*
ẸN-DĔM'Ị-CĄL, } *plied chiefly to diseases.*]
ẸN-DĔM'ỊC, *n.* An endemic disease.
ẸN-DĔN'Ị-ZEN (-dĕn'ẹ-zn), *v. a.* To naturalize.
ĔND'ỊNG, *n.* Conclusion ; termination. [INDICT.
ẸN-DĪTE', *v. n.* To compose. See INDITE and
ĔN'DĪVE, *n.* A plant used as a winter salad.
ĔND'LẸSS, *a.* Without end ; perpetual ; incessant.
ĔND'LẸSS-LY, *ad.* Perpetually ; without end.
ẸN-DŌRSE', *v. a.* To superscribe ; to sign by
 writing on the back of ; to indorse. [ance.
ẸN-DŌRSE'MẸNT, *n.* Superscription ; accept-
ẸN-DŌW', *v. a.* To furnish with a portion, &c.
ẸN-DŌW'MẸNT, *n.* Any thing bestowed ; a gift.
ẸN-DŪE', *v. n.* To supply ; to invest ; to endow.
ẸN-DŪR'Ą-BLE, *a.* Tolerable ; sufferable.
ẸN-DŪR'ĄNCE, *n.* Continuance ; sufferance.
ẸN-DŪRE', *v. a.* To bear ; to sustain ; to suffer
 without complaint ; to support ; to undergo.
ẸN-DŪRE', *v. n.* To last ; to remain ; to bear.
ĔND'WĪSE, *ad.* Erectly ; uprightly ; on end.
ĔN'Ẹ-MY, *n.* A foe ; an adversary ; an opponent.
ĔN'ẸR-ĢĔT'ỊC, } *a.* Forcible ; strong ; ac-
ĔN'ẸR-ĢĔT'Ị-CĄL, } tive ; vigorous.
ĔN'ẸR-ĢY, *n.* Power ; force ; vigor ; efficacy.
Ẹ-NĔR'VĀTE, *v. a.* To weaken ; to enfeeble.
ĔN'ẸR-VĀ'TIỌN, *n.* The act of weakening.
ẸN-FĒĒ'BLE, *v. a.* To weaken ; to enervate.
ẸN-FĔOFF' (ẹn-fĕf'), *v. a.* To invest with.
ẸN-FĔOFF'MẸNT, *n.* An instrument or deed.

ĔN-FĬ-LĀDE', n. [Fr.] (Mil.) Concatenation: —a direct fire raking the whole length.

ĔN-FĬ-LĀDE', v. a. (Mil.) To rake in a right line.

ĘN-FŌRCE', v. a. To incite; to urge; to compel:—to put in force, as a law; to execute.

ĘN-FŌRCE'MĘNT, n. Compulsion; sanction.

ĘN-FRĂN'CHĬṢE, v. a. To make free.

ĘN-FRĂN'CHĬṢE-MĔNT, n. Act of enfranchising.

ĘN-GĀGE', v. a. To enlist; to gain; to bind.

ĘN-GĀGE', v. n. To conflict; to fight:—to embark in any business:—to promise.

ĘN-GĀGE'MĘNT, n. Act of engaging; obligation; employment:—fight; conflict; battle.

ĘN-GĀG'ĬNG, a. Winning; attractive; attaching.

ĘN-GĔN'DĘR, v. a. To beget; to produce; to form; to generate; to cause. [ment.

ĔN'GĬNE (ĕn'jĭn), n. A machine; an instru-

ĔN-GĬ-NĒĔR', n. One who manages engines.

ĔN-GĬ-NĒĔR'ĬNG, n. Business of an engineer.

ĔN'GĬNE-RY, n. Engines of war; artillery.

ĘN-GĬRD', v. a. [imp. t. & pp. engirt, engirded.] To encircle; to surround; to environ; to gird.

ENG'LĬSH (ĭng'glĭsh), a. Belonging to England.

ĘN-GŌRGE', v. a. To swallow; to devour.

ĘN-GRĀIL', v. a. (Her.) To indent in curve lines.

ĘN-GRĀIN', v. a. To dye deep; to dye in grain.

ĘN-GRĂP'PLE, v. a. To grapple; to close with.

ĘN-GRĂSP', v. a. To seize hold of; to gripe.

ĘN-GRĀVE', v. a. [imp. t. engraved; pp. engraved, engraven.] To mark by incisions, as metal, wood, &c.:—to impress; to imprint.

ĘN-GRĂV'ĘR, n. One who engraves metals, &c.

ĘN-GRĂV'ĬNG, n. The work of an engraver.

ĘN-GRŌSS', v. a. To swallow up; to monopolize:—to copy in a large, fair hand.

ĘN-GRŌSS'ĘR, n. One who engrosses; monopo-

ĘN-GRŌSS'MĘNT, n. Act of engrossing. [lizer.

ĘN-GŬLF', v. a. To throw or absorb in a gulf.

ĘN-HĂNCE', v. a. To raise, advance, heighten.

ĘN-HĂNCE'MĘNT, n. Increase; augmentation.

Ę-NĬG'MA, n. A riddle; an obscure question.

Ĕ-NĬG-MĂT'ĬC, } a. Obscure; dark; ambig-
Ĕ-NĬG-MĂT'Ĭ-CAL, } uous; doubtful.

Ę-NĬG'MA-TĬST, n. One who deals in enigmas.

ĘN-JŌĬN', v. a. To direct; to order; to prescribe.

ĘN-JŌY', v. a. To possess:—to delight in.

ĘN-JŌY'MĘNT, n. Pleasure; happiness; fruition.

ĘN-KĬN'DLE, v. a. To set on fire; to inflame.

ĘN-LĂRGE', v. a. To make greater; to extend.

ĘN-LĂRGE', v. n. To expatiate; to be diffuse.

ĘN-LĂRGE'MĘNT, n. Increase; release; expan-

ĘN-LĪGHT'EN(-lī'tn), v. a. To make light. [sion.

ĘN-LĪGHT'EN-ĘR (-lī'tn-ęr), n. An illuminator.

ĘN-LĬST', v. a. To enroll or register, as troops.

ĘN-LĬST'MĘNT, n. Act of enlisting; enrolment.

ĘN-LĪ'VEN (ęn-lī'vn), v. a. To make alive; to quicken; to animate; to exhilarate; to cheer.

ĔN'MĬ-TY, n. Malevolence; hatred; malice.

ĘN-NŌ'BLE, v. a. To dignify; to exalt; to elevate.

ĘN-NŌ'BLE-MĔNT, n. Exaltation; elevation.

Ę-NŌR'MĬ-TY, n. Depravity; atrocious crime.

Ę-NŌR'MOUṢ, a. Irregular; excessive; prodigious:—atrocious; flagitious. [sively.

Ę-NŌR'MOUṢ-LY, ad. Beyond measure; exces-

Ę-NOŨGH' (ę-nŭf',) a. Sufficient; satisfying.

Ę-NOŨGH' (ę-nŭf'), n. A sufficiency; a plenty.

Ę-NOŨGH' (ę-nŭf'), ad. In a sufficient degree.

ĘN-QUĪRE', v. a. & n. To ask. See INQUIRE.

ĘN-RĀGE', v. a. To irritate; to make furious.

ĘN-RĂPT'ŪRE (ęn-răpt'yŭr), v. a. To transport with pleasure; to delight highly; to enchant.

ĘN-RĬCH', v. a. To make rich:—to fertilize.

ĘN-RĬCH'MĘNT, n. The act of making rich.

ĘN-RŌBE', v. a. To dress; to clothe; to invest.

ĘN-RŌLL', v. a. To register; to record; to enlist.

ĘN-RŌL'MĘNT, n. A register; writing; record.

ĘN-RŌŌT', v. a. To fix by the root; to implant.

ĘN-SĂN'GUĬNE (ęn-săng'gwĭn), v. a. To smear with blood or gore; to suffuse with blood.

ĘN-SCŎNCE', v. a. To cover as with a fort.

ĘN-SHIĔLD' (-shēld'), v. a. To shield; to cover.

ĘN-SHRĪNE', v. a. To preserve as a thing sacred.

ĔN'SĪGN (ĕn'sīn), n. National flag; standard; the officer who carries it:—a signal:—badge.

ĔN'SĬGN-CY (ĕn'sĭn-sę), n. The office of ensign.

ĘN-SLĀVE', v. a. To reduce to slavery or bondage; to deprive of liberty. [age.

ĘN-SLĀVE'MĘNT, n. Servitude; slavery; bond-

ĘN-SLĀV'ĘR, n. One who enslaves.

ĘN-SŪE' (ęn-sū'), v. n. To follow; to succeed.

ĘN-SŪRE'(ęn-shūr'), v. a. To secure. See INSURE.

ĘN-TĂB'LA-TŪRE, n. (Arch.) The whole of an order which is above the columns.

ĘN-TĀIL', n. An estate limited in its descent.

ĘN-TĀIL', v. a. To settle the descent of an estate, so that it cannot be bequeathed at pleasure.

ĘN-TĀIL'MĘNT, n. The act of entailing.

ĘN-TĂN'GLE (-tăn'gl), v. a. To inwrap; to twist, or confuse; to involve; to perplex; to puzzle.

ĘN-TĂN'GLE-MĔNT, n. Involution; perplexity.

ĔN'TĘR, v. a. To go into; to insert; to record.

ĔN'TĘR, v. n. To come in; to go in; to penetrate.

ĔN'TĘR-PRĪSE, n. A bold undertaking; energy

ĔN'TĘR-PRĪṢE, v. a. To undertake; to attempt.

ĔN'TĘR-PRĪṢ-ĬNG, a. Having enterprise; adventurous; energetic; bold; efficient.

ĔN-TĘR-TĀIN', v. a. To treat hospitably:—to treat at table:—to hold:—to amuse; to divert.

ĔN-TĘR-TĀIN'ĬNG, a. Amusing; diverting.

ĔN-TĘR-TĀIN'MĘNT, n. Treatment at table; hospitable reception; amusement; diversion.

ĘN-THRŌNE', v. a. To place on a throne; to invest with sovereign authority; to exalt.

ĘN-THŪ'ṢĬ-ĂṢM, n. Heat or ardor of mind; zeal.

ĘN-THŪ'ṢĬ-ĂST, n. One possessed of enthusiasm.

ĘN-THŪ-ṢĬ-ĂS'TĬC, } a. Having enthusiasm;
ĘN-THŪ-ṢĬ-ĂS'TĬ-CAL, } very zealous; ardent.

ĘN-TĪCE', v. a. To allure; to tempt; to seduce.

ĘN-TĪCE'MĘNT, n. Blandishment; allurement.

ĘN-TĪ'CĘR, n. One who entices or allures.

ĘN-TĪRE', a. Whole; undivided; complete; full.

ĘN-TĪRE'LY, ad. In whole; completely; fully.

ĘN-TĪRE'NESS, n. State or quality of being entire; totality; completeness; fulness.

ĘN-TĪRE'TY, n. Completeness; wholeness.

ĘN-TĪ'TLE, v. a. To give a title or a right to.

ĔN'TĬ-TY, n. Something which is; a real being.

ĘN-TŌMB' (ęn-tôm'), v. a. To put into a tomb.

ĔN-TQ-MŌL'Q-GY, n. Natural history of insects.

ĔN'TRĀILṢ (ĕn'trālz), n. pl. Intestines; bowels.

ĔN'TRANCE, n. Act of entering; avenue; ingress.

ĘN-TRĂNCE', v. a. To put into a trance; to charm; to enchant; to fascinate; to enrapture.

ĘN-TRĂP', v. a. To insnare; to catch in a trap.

ĘN-TRĔAT', v. a. To beg earnestly; to importune.

ĘN-TRĔA'TY (ęn-trē'tę), n. A petition; a prayer.

ĔN'TRY, n. Passage; act of entrance; ingress :
  —act of registering or recording ; record.
ĘN-TWĪNE', v. a. To twist round. See INTWINE.
Ę-NŪ'MĘR-ĀTE, v. a. To reckon up singly; to
  count ; to number ; to compute ; to relate.
Ę-NŪ-MĘR-Ā'TIǪN, n. Act of numbering.
Ę-NŬN'CĮ-ĀTE (ę-nŭn'shę-āt), v. a. To declare ;
  to utter ; to pronounce ; to express ; to relate.
Ę-NŬN-CĮ-Ā'TIǪN (ę-nŭn-shę-ā'shun), n. Decla-
  ration ; expression :—manner of utterance.
Ę-NŬN'CĮ-A-TĪVE (-shę-ạ-tĭv), a. Declarative.
ĘN-VĔL'ǪP (-vĕl'up), v. a. To inwrap ; to cover.
EN-VĘ-LŌPE' (äng-vę-lōp'), n. A wrapper.
ĘN-VĔN'ǪM, v. a. To taint ; to poison :—to make
  odious or hateful :—to enrage ; to exasperate.
ĔN'VĮ-A-BLE, a. Exciting envy ; desirable.
ĔN'VĮ-ĘR, n. One who envies ; a grudger.
ĔN'VĮ-OŬS, a. Full of envy ; jealous.
ĔN'VĮ-OŬS-LY, ad. With envy ; with jealousy.
ĘN-VĪ'RǪN, v. a. To surround ; to encompass.
ĘN-VĪ'RǪNŞ or ĔN'VĮ-RǪNŞ, n. pl. Places near.
ĔN'VŎȲ, n. A minister to a foreign government.
ĔN'VY, v. a. To grieve at another's good ; to
  dislike for success or excellence ; to grudge.
ĔN'VY, n. Pain or vexation at another's good.
Ē'PĂCT, n. The excess of the solar month or
  year above the lunar month or year.
ĔP-ÂU-LĔT', or ĔP-ÂU-LĔTTE', n. (Mil.) An
  ornament for the shoulder ; a shoulder-knot.
Ē'PHĄ, n. A Hebrew dry measure, containing
  about one and one ninth English bushels.
Ę-PHĔM'Ę-RĄ, n. Insect that lives only one day.
Ę-PHĔM'Ę-RẠL, a. Beginning and ending in a
  day ; continuing only a day :—short-lived.
Ę-PHĔM'Ę-RĬS, n. ; pl. ĔPH-Ę-ᴀMĔR'Į-DĘŞ. An
  account of the daily motions of the planets.
ĔPH'ǪD, n. Ornamental part of Hebrew dress.
ĔP'ĮC, a. Narrative ; not dramatic.
ĔP'Į-CĒNE, a. (Gram.) Common to both sexes.
ĔP'Į-CŪRE, n. One given to luxury, especially
  in eating ; a luxurious eater ; a voluptuary.
ĔP-Į-CŲ-RĒ'ẠN, n. One of the sect of Epicurus.
ĔP-Į-CŲ-RĒ'ẠN, a. Luxurious ; of Epicurus.
ĔP-Į-CŲ-RĒ'ẠN-ĬŞM, n. The doctrine of Epicurus.
ĔP'Į-CŲ-RĬŞM, n. Luxury ; voluptuousness.
ĔP-Į-DĔM'ĮC, n. A popular or general disease.
ĔP-Į-DĔM'ĮC,   ) a. Generally prevailing ; af-
ĔP-Į-DĔM'Į-CẠL,) fecting great numbers.
ĔP-Į-DĔR'MĮS, n. The scarf-skin of the body.
ĔP'Į-GRĂM, n. A pointed couplet or small poem.
ĔP-Į-GRẠM-MĂT'ĮC,   ) a. Dealing in or writ-
ĔP-Į-GRẠM-MĂT'Į-CẠL,) ing epigrams :—of
  the nature of an epigram ; pointed.
ĔP-Ĭ-GRĂM'MẠ-TĬST, n. A writer of epigrams.
ĔP'Į-GRĂPH, n. A citation placed at the com-
  mencement of a work :—an inscription.
ĔP'Į-LĔP-SY, n. A convulsion ; falling sickness.
ĔP-Į-LĔP'TĮC,   ) a. Affected with, pertaining
ĔP-Į-LĔP'TĮ-CẠL,) to, or like, epilepsy.
ĔP'Į-LŌGUE (ĕp'ę-lŏg), n. A concluding speech.
Ę-PĬPH'Ạ-NY, n. The 12th day after Christmas.
Ę-PĬS'CǪ-PẠ-CY, n. A government by bishops.
Ę-PĬS'CǪ-PẠL, a. Relating to episcopacy.
Ę-PĬS-CǪ-PĀ'LĮ-ẠN, n. An adherent to episco-
  pacy ; a church-man.   [manner.
Ę-PĬS'CǪ-PẠL-LY, ad. (Eccl.) In an episcopal
Ę-PĬS'CǪ-PẠTE, n. The office or rank of bishop.
ĔP'Į-SŌDE, n. Incidental narrative ; a digression.

ĔP-Į-SŎD'ĮC,   ) a. Pertaining to, or resem-
ĔP-Į-SŎD'Į-CẠL,) bling, an episode; digressing.
Ę-PĬS'TLE (ę-pĬs'sl), n. A letter ; a writing sent.
Ę-PĬS'TǪ-LẠ-RY, a. Relating to, or consisting
  of, letters :—having the form of letters.
ĔP'Į-TĂPH, n. An inscription on a monument.
ĔP'Į-THĔT, n. An adjective denoting a quality.
Ę-PĬT'Ǫ-MĘ, n. An abridgment ; a compendium.
Ę-PĬT'Ǫ-MĬST, Ę-PĬT'Ǫ-MĪZ-ĘR, n. An abridger.
Ę-PĬT'Ǫ-MĪZE, v. a. To abstract ; to abridge.
ĔP'ŎℭH or Ē'PŎℭH, n. The time or period from
  which dates are numbered ; era ; period ; date.
ĔP'ŌDE, n. The third or last part of an ode.
ĔP-Ǫ-PĒĒ', n. An epic poem :—epic poetry.
ĔP'Ų-LẠ-RY, a. Belonging to feasts or banquets.
Ē-QUA-BĬL'Į-TY, n. Evenness ; uniformity.
Ē'QUA-BLE, a. Equal to itself ; even ; uniform.
Ē'QUA-BLY, ad. Uniformly ; evenly ; steadily.
Ē'QUẠL, a. Like another ; even ; uniform ; just.
Ē'QUẠL, n. One of the same age, rank, or merit.
Ē'QUẠL, v. a. To make equal ; to be equal to.
Ę-QUẠL'Į-TY (-kwŏl'-) n. Likeness ; uniformity.
Ē-QUẠL-Į-ZĀ'TIǪN, n. State of equality.
Ē'QUẠL-ĪZE, v. a. To make even ; to make equal.
Ē'QUẠL-LY, ad. In the same degree ; uniformly.
Ē-QUA-NĬM'Į-TY, n. Evenness of mind.
Ę-QUĀ'TIǪN, n. Reduction to an equality :—
  statement of the equality of two quantities.
Ę-QUĀ'TǪR, n. A great circle which divides the
  world into two equal parts, north and south.
Ē-QUA-TŌ'RĮ-ẠL, a. Pertaining to the equator.
ĔQ'UĘR-RY (ĕk'wę-rę), n. A stable for horses :
  —an officer who has care of horses.   [knight.
Ę-QUĔS'TRĮ-ẠN, a. Relating to a horseman or
Ē-QUĮ-ĂN'GŲ-LẠR, a. Having equal angles.
Ē-QUĮ-CRŪ'RẠL, a. Having the legs equal.
Ē-QUĮ-DĬS'TẠNT, a. Being at the same distance.
Ē-QUĮ-LĂT'ĘR-ẠL, a. Having all sides equal.
Ē-QUĮ-LĮ-BRĀ'TIǪN, n. Equipoise ; even balance.
Ē-QUĮ-LĬB'RĮ-TY, n. Equality of weight. [weight.
Ē-QUĮ-LĬB'RĮ-ŬM, n. Equipoise ; equality of
Ę-QUĪ'NẠL, Ē'QUĪNE, a. Relating to horses.
Ē-QUĮ-NŎC'TIẠL, a. Pertaining to the equinox.
Ē-QUĮ-NŎC'TIẠL, n. An imaginary great circle
  of the heavens, under which the equator moves
  in its diurnal course ; equinoctial line.
Ē'QUĮ-NŎX, n. The precise time in which the
  sun enters into the first point of Aries or of
  Libra, making the nights and days equal.
Ę-QUĬP', v. a. To furnish ; to accoutre ; to dress.
ĔQ'UĮ-PĄĢE (ĕk'kwę-pāj), n. Furniture for a
  horseman ; carriage ; retinue :—habiliments.
Ę-QUĬP'MĘNT, n. Act of equipping :—furniture.
Ē'QUĮ-PŎĬŞE, n. The state of being balanced ;
  equality of weight ; equilibrium.
Ē-QUĮ-PŎL'LĘNCE, n. Equality of power.
Ē-QUĮ-PŎL'LĘNT, a. Having equal power.
Ē-QUĮ-PŎN'DĘR-ẠNCE, n. Equality of weight.
Ē-QUĮ-PŎN'DĘR-ẠNT, a. Of the same weight.
Ē-QUĮ-PŎN'DĘR-ĀTE, v. n. To be of equal weight.
ĔQ'UĮ-TẠ-BLE (ĕk'wę-tạ-bl), a. Just ; right ; im-
ĔQ'UĮ-TẠ-BLE-NĔSS, n. Justness. [partial ; fair.
ĔQ'UĮ-TẠ-BLY, ad. Justly ; impartially ; fairly.
ĔQ'UĮ-TY (ĕk'wę-tę), n. Natural justice ; natural
  right ; impartiality.   [ing, or worth.
Ę-QUĬV'Ạ-LĔNCE, n. Equality of power, mean-
Ę-QUĬV'Ạ-LĔNT, a. Equal in value, merit, or
  power :—of the same import or meaning.

E-QUĬV'A-LĔNT, n. A thing of the same value.
E-QUĬV'Q-CAL, a. Ambiguous; uncertain; doubt-
E-QUĬV'Q-CAL-LY, ad. Ambiguously. [ful.
E-QUĬV'Q-CĀTE, v. n. To use equivocal ex-
pressions; to prevaricate. [evasion.
E-QUĬV-Q-CĀ'TIQN, n. Ambiguity of speech;
E-QUĬV'Q-CĀ-TQR, n. One who equivocates.
ĔQ'UI-VŌKE, n. Ambiguous expression; quibble.
Ē'RA, n. An epoch; a period of time. [diate.
E-RĀ'DI-ĀTE, v. n. To shoot like a ray; to ra-
E-RĀ-DI-Ā'TIQN, n. Emission of radiance.
E-RĂD'I-CĀTE, v. a. To pull up by the roots;
to extirpate; to exterminate; to annihilate.
E-RĂD-I-CĀ'TIQN, n. Act of eradicating.
E-RĀSE', v. a. To expunge; to rub out; to efface.
E-RĀSE'MENT, n. Destruction; erasure.
E-RĀ'ȘIQN (e-rā'zhun),) n. Act of erasing; ra-
E-RĀȘ'URE (e-rā'zhur),) sure; obliteration.
ERE (ȧr), ad. Before; sooner than.—prep. Before.
ERE-LŎNG' (ȧr-lŏng'), ad. Before long; soon.
ERE-NŎW' (ȧr-nöû'), ad. Before this time.
ERE-WHĪLE' (ȧr-hwĪl'), ad. Some time ago.
E-RĔCT', v. a. To place upright, raise, build.
E-RĔCT', a. Upright:—firm; intent; bold.
E-RĔC'TIQN, n. The act of raising; elevation.
E-RĔCT'NESS, n. Uprightness of posture.
ĔR'GQT, n. A morbid excrescence in grain; spur.
ĔR'MINE, n. A species of animal, or its fur.
ĔR'MINED (ĕr'mind), a. Clothed with ermine.
E-RŌDE', v. a. To eat away; to córrode.
E-RŌ'ȘIQN (-zhun), n. The act of eating away.
E-RŎT'IC, E-RŎT'I-CAL, a. Relating to love.
ĔRR, v. n. To miss the right way; to mistake;
to depart or deviate from rectitude; to sin.
ĔR'RAND, n. A message; mandate; mission.
ĔR'RANT, a. Wandering; roving:—vile; bad.
ER-RĂT'IC,) a. Wandering; irregular; in-
ER-RĂT'I-CAL,) constant; abnormal.
ER-RĀ'TUM, n.: pl. ER-RĀ'TA. [L.] An er-
ror in printing or in writing. [untrue.
ER-RŌ'NE-OŬS, a. Being in error; incorrect;
ER-RŌ'NE-OŬS-LY, ad. By mistake; not rightly.
ER-RŌ'NE-OUS-NĔSS, n. Inconformity to truth.
ĔR'RQR, n. A mistake; blunder; sin; offence.
ĔR'RQR-ĬST, n. One who is in error.
ĔRST, ad. First; at first; formerly; till now.
ĔR-U-BĔS'CENCE, n. Redness; a blush.
ĔR-U-BĔS'CENT, a. Reddish; somewhat red.
E-RŬCT', E-RŬC'TĀTE, v. a. To belch; to vómit.
ĔR-UC-TĀ'TIQN, n. The act of belching; a belch.
ĔR'U-DĪTE or ĔR'U-DĬTE, a. Learned; instructed.
ĔR-U-DĬ''TIQN (-dĭsh'un), n. Learning; lore.
E-RŬ'GI-NOŬS, a. Partaking of copper; coppery.
E-RŬP'TIQN, n. A breaking forth; emission;
explosion; burst:—pimples, pustules, &c.
E-RŬP'TIVE, a. Bursting forth; having eruption.
ĔR-Y-SĬP'E-LAS, n. A disease affecting the skin.
ĔR-Y-SI-PĔL'A-TOŬS, a. Pertaining to erysipelas.
ĔS-CA-LĀDE', n. The act of scaling walls.
ESCAL'LQP (skŏl'lup), n. Shellfish:—indenture.
ES-CĀPE', v. a. & n. To shun; to flee from; to fly.
ES-CĀPE', n. Flight; a getting out of danger.
ESÇHA-LŎT' (shạ-), n. A small onion; a shallot.
ES-CHĒAT', n. A forfeiture by want of heirs.
ES-CHĒAT', v. n. To be forfeited by want of heirs.
ES-CHEW', v. a. To flee from; to avoid; to shun.
ĔS'CÖRT, n. A guard from place to place; a
convoy; safe conduct; protection; guard.

ĔS-CÖRT', v. a. To attend as a guàrd by land.
ESCOT (skŏt), n. A tax; a reckoning. See SCOT.
ĔS-CRI-TÖIRE' (ĕs-kre-twör'), n. A writing ap-
ĔS'CU-LĔNT, a. Good for food; eatable. [paratus.
ĔS-CŬTCH'EQN (es-kŭch'un) n. Armorial en-
signs; shield or arms of a family.
ĔS-Q-TĔR'IC, a. Secret;—opposed to exoteric.
ĔS-PĂL'IER (es-păl'yer), n. A tree on a lattice.
ĔS-PĔ''CIAL (es-pĕsh'al), a. Principal; chief.
ĔS-PĔ''CIAL-LY (es-pĕsh'al-le), ad. Principally.
ĔS'PI-Q-NĂ̄GE, n. The practice of a spy; spying.
ĔS-PLA-NĀDE', n. Open space between the for-
tifications of a citadel and those of a town.
ĔS-PÖÜ'SALS, n. pl. Contract to marry; mutual
promise to marry; betrothal. [defend.
ĔS-PÖÜSE', v. a. To betroth; to marry:—to
ĔS-PY', v. a. & n. To see at a distance; to watch.
ĔS-QUĪRE', n. A title of a magistrate, &c.
ĔS-QUĪRE', v. a. To attend; to wait on.
ĔS-SĀY', v. a. To attempt; to try; to endeavor.
ĔS'SAY, n. An attempt; a trial:—a shŏrt treatise.
ĔS-SĀY'ER (es-sā'er), n. One who essays.
ĔS'SAY-ĬST or ĔS-SĀY'ĬST, n. A writer of essays.
ĔS'SENCE, n. Substance of a thing:—perfume.
ĔS'SENCE, v. a. To perfume; to scent.
ĔS-SĔN'TIAL, a. Necessary; vital; important.
ĔS-SĔN'TIAL-LY, ad. In an essential manner.
ĔS-TĂB'LISH, v. a. To settle firmly:—to ratify.
ĔS-TĂB'LISH-MĔNT, n. Settlement; fixed state.
ĔS-TA-FĔTTE', n. [Fr.] A military courier.
ĔS-TĀTE', n. Condition; fortune; possession;
rank.—pl. Classes of people. [to think.
ĔS-TĒĒM', v. a. To value; to prize; to rate;
ĔS-TĒĒM', n. Estimation; high regard.
ĔS'TI-MA-BLE, a. Valuable; worthy of esteem.
ĔS'TI-MĀTE, v. a. To rate; to set a value on.
ĔS'TI-MATE, n. Computation; calculation;
value; valuation; estimation. [ation.
ĔS-TI-MĀ'TIQN, n. Opinion; esteem:—valu-
ĔS'TI-MĀ-TQR, n. One who estimates; a valuer.
ĔS'TI-VAL, a. Pertaining to the summer.
ĔS-TŎP', v. a. (Law.) To stop; to bar.
ĔS-TŎP'PEL, n. An act that bars a legal process.
ĔS-TŌ'VERS, n. pl. Necessaries allowed by law.
ĔS-TRĀNGE', v. a. To withdraw; to withhold:
—to disaffect; to alienate in affection.
ĔS-TRĀNGE'MENT, n. Alienation; removal.
ĔS-TRĀY', n. A beast lost or wandering; a stray.
ĔS'TU-A-RY, n. An arm of the sea; a frith.
ĔS'TU-ĀTE, v. a. To swell and rage; to boil.
ĔS-TU-Ā'TIQN, n. The act of boiling; agitation.
ET CÆTERA (ĕt sĕt'e-rạ), [L.] also the contrac-
tion etc. or &c. denote the rest or so forth.
ĔTCH, v. a. To engrave by nitric acid; to sketch.
ĔTCH'ING, n. An engraving etched. [lasting.
E-TĔR'NAL, a. Without beginning or end; ever-
E-TĔR'NAL, n. An appellation of God.
E-TĔR'NAL-LY, ad. Without beginning or end.
E-TĔR'NI-TY, n. Duration or existence without
beginning or end:—duration without end.
E-TĔR'NĪZE, v. a. To make eternal or endless.
E-TĒ'ȘI-AN (-zhe-ạn), a. Periodical, as winds.
Ē'THER, n. An element purer than air:—a fluid.
E-THĒ'RE-AL, a. Formed of ether:—celestial.
E-THĒ'RE-OŬS, a. Formed of ether:—heavenly.
ĔTH'IC, ĔTH'I-CAL, a. Moral; relating to mor-
als; treating of morals or moral philosophy.
ĔTH'I-CAL-LY, ad. In an ethical manner.

ĔTH′ĬCS, *n. pl.* The doctrine or system of morality ; moral philosophy ; morals.
ĔTH′NĬC,) *a.* Heathen ; pagan :—relating
ĔTH′NĬ-CĄL,) to races of mankind.
ĔTH′NĬ-CĬŞM, *n.* Heathenism ; paganism.
ĔTH-NŌ-GRĂPH′Ĭ-CĄL, *a.* Relating to ethnography, or races of mankind.　　　[or races.
ĘTH-NŌG′RĄ-PHY, *n.* A description of nations
ĔT-Ĭ-QUĔTTE′(ĕt-ę-kĕt′), *n.* Ceremonial code of polite life ; usages of good society ; ceremony.
ETUI (ą-twē′), *n.* [Fr.] A case for tweezers, &c.
ĔT-Y-MŎ-LŎG′Ĭ-CĄL, *a.* Relating to etymology.
ĔT-Y-MŎL′Ọ-GĬST, *n.* One versed in etymology.
ĔT-Y-MŎL′Ọ-GY, *n.* The derivation of words.
ĔT′Y-MŎN, *n.* An original or primitive word.
EŪ′ĆHĄ-RĬST (ū′ką-rĭst), *n.* The act of giving thanks :—the sacrament of the Lord's supper.
EŪ-ĆHĄ-RĬS′TĬC,) *a.* Relating to the eucharist or sacrament
EŪ-ĆHĄ-RĬS′TĬ-CĄL,) charist or sacrament
. of the Lord's supper.　　　[condition of body.
EŪ′ĆRĄ-SY, *n.* Good temperament, or healthy
EŪ-DĬ-ŎM′Ę-TĘR (yū-dę-ŏm′ę-tęr), *n.* An instrument to determine the purity of air or gas.
EŪ′LỌ-GĬST, *n.* One who eulogizes ; a lauder.
EỤ-LŌ′ĢĬ-ŬM, *n.* An encomium ; a eulogy.
EŪ′LỌ-GY, *n.* An encomium ; praise ; panegyric.
EŪ′LỌ-GĪZE, *v. a.* To commend ; to praise.
EŪ′NỤĆH (yū′nųk), *n.* A man castrated.
EŪ-PĔP′TĬC (yū-pĕp′tĭk), *a.* Easy of digestion.
EŪ′PHĘM-ĬŞM (yū′fęm-ĭzm), *n.* Description of an offensive thing by an inoffensive expression.
EŪ-PHŎN′ĬC,) *a.* Sounding agreeably ; having euphony ; euphonious.
EŪ-PHŎN′Ĭ-CĄL,) ing euphony ; euphonious.
EŪ-PHŌ′NĬ-OŬS, *a.* Harmonious ; euphonic.
EŪ′PHỌ-NY (yū′fọ-nę), *n.* Agreeable sound.
EŪ-RỌ-PĒ′ĄN, *a.* Belonging to Europe, or to its inhabitants ; living or found in Europe.
EŪ′RỤS, *n.* [L.] The east wind.
EŪ-THĄN-Ā′ŞĬ-Ą, *n.* An easy death ; euthanasy.
EŪ-THĂN′Ą-SY, *n.* An easy death.　　　[thartics.
Ę-VĂC′Ụ-ĄNTS, *n. pl.* Purgative medicines ; ca-
Ę-VĂC′Ụ-ĀTE, *v. a.* To void ; to eject ; to quit.
Ę-VĂC-Ụ-Ā′TIỌN, *n.* Discharge ; a withdrawing.
Ę-VĀDE′, *v. a. & n.* To elude ; to escape ; to equivocate ; to avoid by artifice or sophistry.
ĔV-Ą-GĀ′TIỌN, *n.* Act of wandering ; excursion.
ĔV-Ą-NĔS′CENCE, *n.* The act of vanishing.
ĔV-Ą-NĔS′CENT, *a.* Vanishing :—imperceptible.
‖Ē-VĄN-GĔL′Ĭ-CĄL *or* ĔV-ĄN-GĔL′Ĭ-CĄL, *a.* Agreeable to the gospel ; relating to, or contained in, the gospel.　　　[gospel.
‖Ē-VĄN-GĔL′Ĭ-CĄL-LY, *ad.* According to the
Ē-VĂN′ĢĘ-LĬŞM, *n.* Promulgation of the gospel.
Ē-VĂN′ĢĘ-LĬST, *n.* A preacher of the gospel.
Ē-VĂN′ĢĘ-LĪZE, *v. a.* To instruct in the gospel.
Ē-VĂP′Ọ-RĄ-BLE, *a.* Easily dissipated in vapor.
Ę-VĂP′Ọ-RĀTE, *v. n.* To fly away in vapors.
Ę-VĂP′Ọ-RĀTE, *v. a.* To disperse in vapors ; to convert into vapor ; to vaporize.　　　[vapor.
Ę-VĂP-Ọ-RĀ′TIỌN, *n.* Conversion of fluid into
Ę-VĀ′ŞIỌN (ę-vā′zhụn), *n.* Subterfuge ; artifice.
Ę-VĀ′ŞĬVE, *a.* Practising evasion ; elusive.
Ę-VĀ′ŞĬVE-LY, *ad.* By evasion ; elusively.
ĒVE, *or* Ē′VEN (ē′vn), *n.* Close of day ; evening.
Ē′VEN (ē′vn), *a.* Level ; uniform, equal ; flat.
Ē′VEN (ē′vn), *v. a.* To make even ; to level.
Ē′VEN, *ad.* Verily ; likewise ; so much as.
Ē′VEN-HĂND′ĘD, *a.* Impartial, equitable ; just.

Ē′VEN-ĬNG (ē′vn-ĭng), *n.* The close of the day.
Ē′VEN-LY (ē′vn-lę), *ad.* Equally ; uniformly.
Ē′VEN-NĔSS (ē′vn-nĕs), *n.* State of being even.
Ē′VEN-SŎNG, *n.* Song for the evening.
Ę-VĔNT′, *n.* Issue ; end ; incident ; consequence.
Ę-VĔNT′FỤL, *a.* Full of events ; momentous.
Ē′VEN-TĪDE (ē′vn-tīd), *n.* The time of evening.
Ę-VĔNT′Ụ-ĄL, *a.* Consequential ; ultimate ; final.
ĔV′ĘR, *ad.* At any time ; at all times ; always.
ĔV′ĘR-GRĒEN, *a.* Verdant throughout the year.
ĔV′ĘR-GRĒEN, *n.* A plant green all the year.
ĔV-ĘR-LĂST′ĬNG, *a.* Having no end ; eternal.
ĔV-ĘR-LĂST′ĬNG, *n.* Eternity :—God :—a plant.
ĔV-ĘR-MŌRE′, *ad.* Always ; perpetually.
ĔV′ĘR-Y, *a.* Each one of all ; all taken separately.—*Every where*, in all places.　　　[day.
ĔV′ĘR-Y-DĀY, *a.* Common ; occurring on any
Ę-VĬCT′, *v. a.* To dispossess by legal process.
ĔV′Ĭ-DĔNCE, *n.* Testimony ; proof :—a witness.
ĔV′Ĭ-DĔNCE, *v. a.* To prove ; to evince ; to show.
ĔV′Ĭ-DĔNT, *a.* Plain ; apparent ; notorious.
ĔV-Ĭ-DĔN′TIĄL, *a.* Affording evidence or proof.
ĔV′Ĭ-DĔNT-LY, *ad.* Apparently ; certainly.
Ē′VIL (ē′vl), *a.* Not good ; wicked ; bad ; corrupt.
Ē′VIL (ē′vl), *n.* Wickedness ; injury ; calamity.
Ē′VIL (ē′vl), *ad.* Not well ; injuriously.
Ē-VIL-DŌ′ĘR (ē-vl-dō′ęr), *n.* A doer of evil ; a malefactor ; a criminal.　　　[look.
Ē′VIL-EŸED (ē′vl-īd), *a.* Having a malignant
Ē′VIL-MĪND′ĘD (ē′vl-mīnd′ęd), *a.* Malicious.
Ē-VIL-SPĒAK′ĬNG (ē-vl-spēk′ing), *n.* Slander.
Ę-VĬNCE′, *v. a.* To prove ; to show ; to manifest.
Ę-VĬN′CĬ-BLE, *a.* Capable of being proved.
Ę-VĬS′CĘR-ĀTE, *v. a.* To take out the entrails of.
ĔV′Ĭ-TĄ-BLE, *a.* Capable of being shunned.
ĔV-Ọ-CĀ′TIỌN, *n.* The act of evoking.
Ę-VŌKE′, *v. a.* To call forth :—to remove.
ĔV-Ọ-LĀ′TIỌN, *n.* The act of flying away.
ĔV-Ọ-LŪ′TIỌN, *n.* Act of unfolding ; a displaying :—series of movements :—branch of arithmetic ; extraction of the roots of powers.
Ę-VŎLVE′ (ę-vŏlv′), *v. a.* To unfold ; to open ; to unroll ; to disclose ; to develop ; to detect.
Ę-VŬL′SIỌN, *n.* Act of plucking or tearing out.
EWE (yū), *n.* A female sheep.
EW′ĘR (yū′ęr), *n.* A kind of pitcher for water.
ĔX, *a Latin preposition*, often prefixed to compounded words ; sometimes meaning *out* ; as, *ex-minister*, a minister out of office.　　　[voke.
ĘX-ĂÇ′ĘR-BĀTE, *v. a.* To exasperate ; to pro-
ĘX-ĂÇ-ĘR-BĀ′TIỌN, *n.* Exasperation :—a paroxysm ; increase in symptoms of disease.
ĘX-ĂCT′, *a.* Nice ; accurate ; methodical.
ĘX-ĂCT′, *v. a.* To require ; to demand of right.
ĘX-ĂC′TIỌN, *n.* The act of exacting ; extortion.
ĘX-ĂCT′Ĭ-TŪDE, *n.* Exactness ; nicety.
ĘX-ĂCT′LY, *ad.* Accurately ; nicely ; precisely.
ĘX-ĂCT′NESS, *n.* Accuracy ; nicety ; regularity.
ĘX-ĂCT′OR, *n.* One who exacts ; an extortioner.
ĘX-ĂĢ′ĢĘR-ĀTE, *v. a.* To accumulate ; to heighten ; to overstate ; to overstrain.　　　[hole.
ĘX-ĂĢ-ĢĘR-Ā′TIỌN, *n.* Amplification ; hyper-
ĘX-ĂĢ′ĢĘR-Ą-TỌ-RY, *a.* Tending to exaggerate ; containing exaggerations.　　　[—to praise.
ĘX-ĂLT′, *v. a.* To raise ; to elevate ; to heighten :
ĘX-ĄL-TĀ′TIỌN, *n.* Act of raising ; elevation.
ĘX-ĂM′ĬN-Ą-BLE, *a.* Capable of being examined.
ĘX-ĂM-Ĭ-NĀ′TIỌN, *n.* The act of examining.

ĘX-ĂM'ĮNE (ęgz-), *v. a.* To try ; to question ; to search into ; to scrutinize ; to investigate.
ĘX-ĂM'ĮN-ĘR, *n.* One who examines ; inquirer.
ĘX-ĂM'PLE, *n.* A pattern ; model ; precedent ; case illustrating a general rule ; an instance.
ĘX-ĂN'Į-MĄTE, *a.* .Lifeless ; dead ; spiritless.
ĘX-ĂN-Į-MĀ'TIǪN, *n.* Deprivation of life.
ĘX-ĄN-THĚM'Ą-TĄ, *n. pl.* Eruptions ; pustules.
ĘX-ĄN-THĚM'Ą-TOŬS, *a.* Efflorescent ; eruptive.
ĚX'ĂRℭH (ĕks'ärk), *n.* A viceroy ; a prefect.
ĚX'ĄRℭHĀTE, *n.* The office of an exarch.
ĘX-ĂS'PĘR-ĀTE, *v. a.* To provoke ; to enrage.
ĘX-ĂS-PĘR-Ā'TIǪN, *n.* Great provocation; anger.
ĚX'CĄ-VĀTE *or* ĘX-CĂ'VĀTE, *v. a.* To hollow.
ĚX-CĄ-VĀ'TIǪN, *n.* Act of excavating ; cavity.
ĚX'CĄ-VĀ-TǪR, *n.* One who excavates.
ĘX-CĒĒD', *v. a. & n.* To excel ; to surpass.
ĘX-CĒĒD'ĮNG, *p. a.* Great in quantity,extent,&c.
ĘX-CĒĒD'ĮNG-LY, *ad.* To a great degree.
ĘX-CĚL', *v. a. & n.* To outdo in excellence ; to surpass ; to go beyond, exceed, transcend.
ĚX'CĘL-LĔNCE, } *n.* Good quality ; preëmi-
ĚX'CĘL-LĔN-CY, } nence ; dignity ; purity ; goodness :—title of honor of a governor, &c.
ĚX'CĘL-LĔNT, *a.* Eminent in any good quality.
ĚX'CĘL-LĔNT-LY, *ad.* Very well ; in a high degree ; extremely ; surpassingly.   [reject.
ĘX-CĔPT', *v. a.* To leave out; to exclude ; to
ĘX-CĔPT', *prep.* Exclusively of ; without including ; excepting.   [excluding.
ĘX-CĔPT'ĮNG, *prep.* With exception of ; except ;
ĘX-CĔP'TIǪN, *n.* Exclusion :—objection ; cavil.
ĘX-CĔP'TIǪN-Ą-BLE, *a.* Liable to objection.
ĘX-CĔP'TĮVE, *a.* Including an exception.
ĘX-CĔRPT', *n.* An extract from an author.
ĘX-CĔSS',*n.*Superfluity;surplus:—intemperance.
ĘX-CĔS'SĮVE, *a.* Beyond due bounds ; vehement.
ĘX-CĔS'SĮVE-LY, *ad.* Exceedingly ; extravagantly ; immoderately.   [change.
ĘX-CHĀNGE', *v. a.* To give for another ; to
ĘX-CHĀNGE', *n.* Act of bartering ; barter :— balance of money :—a place where merchants meet for the transaction of business.
ĘX-CHĀNGE'Ą-BLE, *a.* That may be exchanged.
ĘX-CHĔQ'UĘR (eks-chĕk'er), *n.* The court to which the public revenue in England is paid.
ĘX-CĪS'Ą-BLE, *a.* Liable to the duty of excise.
ĘX-CĪSE', *n.* A tax levied upon commodities.
ĘX-CĪSE', *v. a.* To levy a tax or excise.
ĘX-CĪSE'MĄN, *n.* An inspector of excised goods.
ĘX-CĪ''ṢIǪN (ęk-sĭzh'ųn), *n.* Extirpation ; ruin.
ĘX-CĪ-TĄ-BĬL'Į-TY, *n.* Capability of being excited ; proneness to excitement ; irritability.
ĘX-CĪ'TĄ-BLE, *a.* Susceptible of being excited.
ĚX-CĮ-TĀ'TIǪN, *n.* Act of exciting or rousing.
ĘX-CĪTE', *v. a.* To rouse ; to animate ; to stir up.
ĘX-CĪTE'MĘNT, *n.* Motive ; that which excites :—agitation ; commotion ; sensation.
ĘX-CĪT'ĘR, *n.* One who excites or animates.
ĘX-CLĀIM', *v. n.* To cry out ; to make an outcry.
ĘX-CLĀIM'ĘR, *n.* One who exclaims.
ĚX-CLĄ-MĀ'TIǪN, *n.* Vehement outcry ; clamor :—mark [!] indicating emotion or surprise.
ĘX-CLĂM'Ą-TǪ-RY, *a.* Containing exclamation.
ĘX-CLŪDE', *v. a.* To shut out, debar, prohibit.
ĘX-CLŪ'ṢIǪN (eks-klū'zhųn), *n.* A shutting out.
ĘX-CLŪ'SĮVE, *a.* Excluding ; debarring :—excepting ; not comprehending :—selfish.

ĘX-CLŪ'SĮVE-LY, *ad.* In an exclusive manner.
ĘX-CŎĢ'Į-TĀTE, *v. a.* To invent ; to contrive.
ĘX-CŎĢ-Į-TĀ'TIǪN, *n.* Invention ; thought.
ĚX-CǪM-MŪ'NĮ-CĀTE, *v. a.* To eject from the communion of the church.   [church.
ĚX-CǪM-MŪ'NĮ-CĄTE, *a.* Ejected from the
ĚX-CǪM-MŪ-NĮ-CĀ'TIǪN,*n.* Interdict ; exclusion from fellowship of the church. ·   [skin.
ĘX-CŌ'RĮ-ĀTE, *v. a.* To flay ; to strip off the
ĘX-CŌ-RĮ-Ā'TIǪN, *n.* Act of flaying :—robbery.
ĘX-CŎR-TĮ-CĀ'TIǪN, *n.* A pulling off the bark.
ĚX'CRĘ-MĔNT, *n.* Alvine discharges ; dung.
ĚX-CRĘ-MĔNT'ĄL, *a.* Relating to excrement.
ĚX-CRĘ-MĘN-TĪ''TIOŲS, *a.* Containing, or consisting of, excrement.   [berance.
ĘX-CRĔS'CĘNCE, *n.* Morbid growth or protu-
ĘX-CRĔS'CĘNT, *a.* Growing out of something.
ĘX-CRĒTE', *v. a.* To pass or eject by excretion.
ĘX-CRĒ'TIǪN, *n.* Ejection of animal substance.
ĚX'CRĘ-TĬVE, *a.* Able to eject excrements.
ĚX'CRĘ-TǪ-RY, *a.* Having power to excrete.
ĘX-CRŪ'CĮ-ĀTE(eks-krŭ'she-āt),*v.a.* To torture.
ĘX-CRŪ-CĮ-Ā'TIǪN, *n.* Torment ; torture ; vexation ; that which excruciates.   [cuse.
ĘX-CŬL'PĀTE, *v. a.* To clear from fault ; to ex-
ĚX-CŬL-PĀ'TIǪN, *n.* Vindication ; excuse.
ĘX-CŬL'PĄ-TǪ-RY, *a.* That exculpates ; clearing from imputed fault.   [ney.
ĘX-CŬR'SIǪN, *n.* A ramble ; digression ; jour-
ĘX-CŬR'SĮVE, *a.* Rambling ; wandering ; roving.
ĘX-CŪṢ'Ą-BLE,*a.* Admitting excuse; pardonable.
ĘX-CŪ'ṢĄ-TǪ-RY, *a.* Excusing ; apologetical.
ĘX-CŪ̧SE', *v. a.* To extenuate, exculpate, pardon.
ĘX-CŪ̧SE', *n.* Plea ; apology ; pardon ; pretext.
ĚX'Ę-CRĄ-BLE, *a.* Hateful; detestable; accursed.
ĚX'Ę-CRĀTE, *v. a.*- To curse ; to imprecate ill upon ; to abominate ; to detest ; to abhor.
ĚX-Ę-CRĀ'TIǪN, *n.* Curse ; imprecation of evil.
ĚX'Ę-CŪTE, *v. a.* To perform :—to put to death.
ĚX'Ę-CŪT-ĘR, *n.* One who performs or executes.
ĚX-Ę-CŪ'TIǪN, *n.* Performance :—seizure ; punishment ; death inflicted by forms of law.
ĚX-Ę-CŪ'TIǪN-ĘR, *n.* A person who inflicts capital punishment by law.   [ecuting.
ĘX-ĔC'Ų-TĬVE, *a.* Having the power to act ; ex-
ĘX-ĔC'Ų-TĬVE, *n.* Executive power or officer.
ĘX-ĔC'Ų-TǪR, *n.* He who is appointed by a testator to execute his will.   [utor.
ĘX-ĔC'Ų-TǪR-SHĬP, *n.* The office of an exec-
ĘX-ĔC'Ų-TǪ-RY, *a.* Relating to execution ; that
ĘX-ĔC'Ų-TRĬX, *n.* A female executor. [executes.
ĚX-Ę-ĢĒ'SĮS, *n.* Explanation ; interpretation.
ĚX-Ę-ĢĔT'ĮC,ĚX-Ę-ĢĔT'Į-CĄL, *a.* Explanatory.
ĘX-ĔM'PLĄR,*n.* A pattern ; an example ; a copy.
ĚX'ĘM-PLĄ-RĮ-LY, *ad.* In an exemplary manner ; in a worthy manner.   [monitory.
ĚX'ĘM-PLĄ-RY, *a.* Worthy of imitation :—
ĘX-ĔM-PLĮ-FĮ-CĀ'TIǪN, *n.* Illustration ; copy.
ĘX-ĔM'PLĮ-FĪ-ĘR, *n.* One who exemplifies.
ĘX-ĔM'PLĮ-FȲ, *v. a.* To illustrate by example : —to make a certified transcript or copy of.
ĘX-ĔMPT', *v. a.* To exonerate ; to free from.
ĘX-ĔMPT', *a.* Free by privilege ; not liable.
ĘX-ĔMPT', *n.* A person exempted from duty.
ĘX-ĔMP'TIǪN (ęgz-ĕm'shųn), *n.* Immunity.
ĚX'Ę-QUIĘ̧S, *n. pl.* Funeral rites or ceremonies.
ĚX'ĘR-CĪ̧SE, *n.* Labor ; practice ; performance : —a task or lesson required of a student.

ĔX′ẼR-CĪṢE, *v. a.* To employ, train, practise.
ĔX′ẼR-CĪṢE, *v. n.* To use exercise ; to labor.
EX-ẼR-CĪ-TĀ′TIǪN, *n.* Exercise ; practice ; use.
EX-ĔRGUE′ (egz-ẽrg′), *n.* A space on a coin, &c.
EX-ĔRT′, *v. a.* To use or urge with effort.
EX-ĔR′TIǪN, *n.* Act of exerting ; effort.
EX-FŌ′LĮ-ĀTE, *v. n.* To shell off ; to peel off.
EX-FŌ-LĮ-Ā′TIǪN, *n.* The act of shelling off.
EX-HĂL′A-BLE, *a.* Capable of being exhaled.
ĔX-HA-LĀ′TIǪN,*n.*Act of exhaling ; evaporation.
EX-HĀLE′, *v.* To send or draw out in vapors.
EX-HĀLE′MẼNT, *n.* Matter exhaled ; vapor.
EX-HÂUST′,*v. a.* To drain ; to draw out totally.
EX-HÂUST′ẼR, *n.* One that exhausts.
EX-HÂUST′Į-BLE, *a.* Capable of being exhausted.
EX-HÂUS′TIǪN (egz-hâws′chụn), *n.* An empty-
EX-HÂUST′LẼSS, *a.* Inexhaustible.   [ing.
EX-HĬB′ĮT, *v. a.* To offer to view ; to show ;
   to display :—to present to a court.
EX-HĬB′ĮT, *n.* A paper exhibited ; a statement.
EX-HĬB′ĮT-ẼR, *n.* One who exhibits or offers.
ĔX-HĮ-BĬ′′TIǪN (ĕks-ẹ-bĭsh′ụn), *n.* Act of ex-
   hibiting ; display :—public show :—a pension.
EX-HĬL′A-RĀTE,*v. a.* To make merry or cheer-
   ful ; to enliven ; to animate ; to inspire.
EX-HĬL-A-RĀ′TIǪN, *n.* Act of exhilarating.
EX-HÖRT′, *v. a.* To incite to any good action.
EX-HǪR-TĀ′TIǪN,*n.*Incitement to good ; advice.
EX-HÖR′TA-TǪ-RY, *a.* Tending to exhort.
EX-HÖRT′ẼR, *n.* One who exhorts. [terment.
ĔX-HỤ-MĀ′TIǪN, *n.* Act of unburying ; disin-
EX-HŪME′, *v. a.* To dig out of the earth.
ĔX′Į-ĢĔNCE, }*n.* Demand ; want ; need ; press-
ĔX′Į-ĢĔN-CY, } ing necessity ; occasion.
ĔX′Į-ĢĔNT, *n.* (*Law.*) Writ preparatory to an
   outlawry,when the defendant is not to be found.
ĔX′ĪLE, *n.* Banishment:—the person banished.
EX-ĪLE′, *v. a.* To banish from a country.
ĔX-ĪLE′, *a.* Small ; slendeř ; thin. [*Little used.*]
EX-ĬST′, *v. n.* To be ; to have a being ; to live.
EX-ĬST′ẼNCE, *n.* State of being ; a being ; life.
EX-ĬST′ẼNT, *a.* Having existence or being.
ĔX′ĮT, *n.* Departure ; a going :—passage out.
ĔX′Ǫ-DŬS, *n.* Departure :—2d book of Moses.
EX-ŎN′ẼR-ĀTE,*v. a.* To unload :—to exculpate.
EX-ŎN-ẼR-Ā′TIǪN, *n.* Act of exonerating.
ĔX′Ǫ-RA-BLE, *a.* That may be moved by en-
   treaty, or made to relent.   [travagance.
EX-ÖR′BĮ-TANCE, EX-ÖR′BĮ-TAN-CY, *n.* Ex-
EX-ÖR′BĮ-TANT, *a.* Enormous ; excessive.
EX-ÖR′BĮ-TANT-LY, *ad.* Beyond all bounds.
ĔX′ǬR-CĪSE,*v. a.* To drive away, as evil spirits.
ĔX′ǬR-CĪṢ-ẼR, *n.* One who exorcises ; an exor-
ĔX′ǬR-CĬṢM, *n.* Expulsion of evil spirits. [cist.
ĔX′ǬR-CĬST, *n.* A caster out of evil spirits.
EX-ÖR′DĮ-ŬM, *n.* Opening part of a speech, &c.
EX-Ǫ-TĔR′ĮC, }*a.* Public ; exterior ; not se-
EX-Ǫ-TĔR′Į-CAL, } cret ;—opposed to *esoteric.*
EX-ŎT′ĮC, *a.* Foreign ; not native or indige-
EX-ŎT′ĮC, *n.* A foreign plant or word. [nous.
EX-PĂND′, *v. a.* To spread ; to open ; to dilate.
EX-PĂNSE′, *n.* Wide extent :—the firmament.
EX-PĂN-SĮ-BĬL′Į-TY, *n.* Capacity of extension.
EX-PĂN′SĮ-BLE, *a.* Capable of being extended.
EX-PĂN′SIǪN,*n.* Act of spreading out :—extent.
EX-PĂN′SĮVE, *a.* Spreading ; being expanded.
EX-PĀ′TĮ-ĀTE (ek-spā′she-āt), *v.·n.* To range
   at large ; to enlarge in language ; to descant.

EX-PĀ′TRĮ-ĀTE, *v. a.* To banish or remove
   from one's country ; to exile.   [tion.
EX-PĀ-TRĮ-Ā′TIǪN, *n.* Banishment, or emigra-
EX-PĔCT′, *v. a.* To look for ; to wait for.
EX-PĔC′TAN-CY, *n.* Act or state of expecting.
EX-PĔC′TANT, *a.* Waiting in expectation.
EX-PĔC′TANT, *n.* One who waits in expectation.
ĔX-PẼC-TĀ′TIǪN, *n.* Act of expecting :—pros-
   pect :—object expected :—promising state.
EX-PĔC′TǪ-RANT, *a.* Promoting expectoration
EX-PĔC′TǬ-RANT, *n.* A medicine to promote
   expectoration.   [chest or lungs.
EX-PĔC′TǪ-RĀTE, *v. a.* To eject from the
EX-PĔC-TǪ-RĀ′TIǪN, *n.* The act of expecto-
   rating :—discharge by coughing, &c. [tion.
EX-PĔC′TǪ-RA-TĬVE, *a.* Promoting expectora-
EX-PĒ′DĮ-ẸNCE, }*n.* Fitness ; suitableness to
EX-PĒ′DĮ-ẸN-CY, } a good end ; convenience.
EX-PĒ′DĮ-ẸNT, *a.* Proper ; fit ; suitable ; useful.
EX-PĒ′DĮ-ẸNT, *n.* Means to an end ; resource.
EX-PĒ′DĮ-ẸNT-LY, *ad.* Suitably ; conveniently.
ĔX′PẸ-DĪTE,*v. a.* To faciliate ; to hasten.
ĔX-PẸ-DĬ′′TIǪN (ĕks-pẹ-dĭsh′ụn), *n.* Haste ;
   speed ; activity :—an enterprise ; undertaking.
ĔX-PẸ-DĬ′′TIǪUS (ĕks-pẹ-dĭsh′ụs), *a.* Quick ;
   nimble ; prompt ; ready ; punctual ; diligent.
ĔX-PẸ-DĬ′′TIǪUS-LY, *ad.* Speedily ; nimbly.
EX-PĔL′, *v. a.* To drive out ; to eject, banish.
EX-PĔND′, *v. a.* To lay out ; to spend.
EX-PĔN′DĮ-TŪRE, *n.* Expense ; disbursement.
EX-PĔNSE′, *n.* Cost ; charges ; money ex-
   pended ; expenditure ; price.   [costly ; dear.
EX-PĔN′SĮVE, *a.·* Given to expense ; lavish :—
EX-PĔN′SĮVE-LY, *ad.* With great expense.
EX-PĔN′SĮVE-NĔSS, *n.* State of being expen-
   sive ; extravagance :—costliness.   [edge.
EX-PĒ′RĮ-ẸNCE, *n.* Trial ; practical knowl-
EX-PĒ′RĮ-ẸNCE, *v. a.* To try ; to know.
EX-PĒ′RĮ-ẸNCED (ek-spē′re-ẹnst), *p. a.* Made
   skilful or wise by experience ; tried.
EX-PĔR′Į-MẼNT, *n.* Trial or proof of any thing.
EX-PĔR′Į-MĔNT, *v. n.* To make experiment.
EX-PĔR-Į-MĔN′TAL, *a.* Founded on experiment.
EX-PĔR-Į-MĔN′TAL-ĬST, *n.* An experimenter.
EX-PĔR-Į-MĔN′TAL-LY, *ad.* By experiment.
EX-PĔR′Į-MĔNT-ẼR, *n.* One who makes ex-
   periment.   [pert ; scientific witness.
EX-PĔRT′, *a.* Skilful ; dexterous.—*n.* One ex-
EX-PĔRT′LY, *ad.* In a skilful, ready manner.
EX-PĔRT′NẼSS, *n.* Skill ; readiness ; dexterity.
ĔX′PĮ-A-BLE, *a.* Capable of being expiated.
ĔX′PĮ-ĀTE, *v. a.* To make atonement for.
ĔX-PĮ-Ā′TIǪN, *n.* Act of expiating ; atonement.
ĔX′PĮ-A-TǪ-RY, *a.* Relating to expiation.
EX-PĮ-RĀ′TIǪN, *n.* A breathing out :—end ;
   termination ; close :—death.   [evaporate.
EX-PĪRE′,*v. a.* To breathe out ; to exhale ; to
EX-PĪRE′, *v. n.* To emit the last breath ; to die.
EX-PLĀIN′, *v. a.* To expound ; to illustrate.
EX-PLĀIN′A-BLE, *a.* Capable of explanation.
ĔX-PLA-NĀ′TIǪN, *n.* Act of explaining.
EX-PLĂN′A-TǪ-RY, *a.* Illustrative.
ĔX′PLẸ-TĬVE, *n.* A word used to fill a space.
ĔX′PLẸ-TǪ-RY, *a.* Filling up ; taking up room.
ĔX′PLĮ-CA-BLE, *a.* That may be explained.
ĔX′PLĮ-CĀTE, *v. a.* To explain ; to clear.
ĔX-PLĮ-CĀ′TIǪN, *n.* Explanation ; sense.
ĔX′PLĮ-CĀ-TĮVE, *a.* Tending to explain.

ᴇX-PLĬÇ'ĬT, *a.* Plain ; clear ; direct ; express.
ᴇX-PLĬÇ'ĬT-LY, *ad.* Plainly ; expressly ; directly.
ᴇX-PLĬÇ'ĬT-NĔSS, *n.* State of being explicit.
ᴇX-PLŌDE', *v. a. & n.* To drive out :—to burst.
ᴇX-PLŎÏT', *n.* A great action ; achievement.
ĔX-PLǪ-RĀ'TIǪN, *n.* Search ; examination.
ᴇX-PLŌRE', *v. a.* To search or pry into ; to examine by trial ; to inspect carefully.
ᴇX-PLŌ'ṢIǪN (ĕks-plō'zhụn), *n.* A sudden bursting with noise and violence ; a discharge.
ᴇX-PLŌ'ṢĮVE, *a.* Bursting ; causing explosion.
ᴇX-PŌ'NᴇNT, *n.* A term in algebra ; an index.
ĔX-PǪ-NĔN'TIAL, *a.* Relating to an exponent.
ᴇX-PŌRT', *v. a.* To carry or send out of a country, as merchandise. [market.
ĔX'PŌRT, *n.* Commodity sent to a foreign
ᴇX-PŌRT'A-BLE, *a.* Capable of being exported.
ĔX-PǪR-TĀ'TIǪN, *n.* The act of exporting.
ᴇX-PŌRT'ᴇR, *n.* One who exports commodities.
ᴇX-PŌṢE', *v. a.* To lay open :—to endanger.
ĔX-PǪ-SE' (ĕks-pǫ-zā'), *n.* [Fr.] An exposition.
ĔX-PǪ-ṢĬ''TIǪN (ĕks-pǫ-zĭsh'ụn), *n.* Explanation ; interpretation :—exhibition ; show.
ᴇX-PŎṢ'Į-TĮVE, *a.* Explanatory ; disclosing.
ᴇX-PŎṢ'Į-TǪR, *n.* An explainer ; interpreter.
ᴇX-PŎṢ'Į-TǪ-RY, *a.* Explanatory ; illustrative.
ᴇX-PŎST'Ụ-LĀTE, *v. n.* To reason, remonstrate.
ᴇX-PŎST-Ụ-LĀ'TIǪN, *n.* Debate ; remonstrance.
ᴇX-PŎST'Ụ-LA-TǪ-RY, *a.* Containing expostulation ; earnestly remonstrating.
ᴇX-PŎṢ'URE (-pō'zhụr), *n.* Act of exposing.
ᴇX-PŎÛND', *v. a.* To explain ; to interpret.
ᴇX-PŎÛND'ᴇR, *n.* An explainer ; an interpreter.
ᴇX-PRĔSS', *v. a.* To represent ; to utter ; to declare ; to designate :—to squeeze out.
ᴇX-PRĔSS', *a.* Plain ; manifest ; in direct terms.
ᴇX-PRĔSS', *n.* A messenger or message sent.
ᴇX-PRĔS'SĮ-BLE, *a.* That may be expressed.
ᴇX-PRĔS'SIǪN (ĕks-prĕsh'ụn), *n.* A phrase ; mode of speech ; representation :—a pressing.
ᴇX-PRĔS'SĮVE, *a.* Serving to express ; lively.
ᴇX-PRĔSS'LY, *ad.* In direct terms ; plainly.
ᴇX-PRŌ'BRA-TĮVE, *a.* Upbraiding ; reproaching.
ᴇX-PRŌ-PRĮ-Ā'TIǪN, *n.* The act of discarding.
ᴇX-PŪGN' (ĕks-pūn'), *v. a.* To conquer ; to take.
ĔX-PŲG-NĀ'TIǪN, *n.* Act of taking by assault.
ᴇX-PŬL'SIǪN, *n.* Act of expelling or driving out.
ᴇX-PŬL'SĮVE, *a.* Having power of expulsion.
ᴇX-PŬNǴE', *v. a.* To blot out ; to rub out, efface.
ᴇX-PŬR'GĀTE, *v. a.* To purify ; to cleanse.
ĔX-PŲR-GĀ'TIǪN, *n.* Act of expurgating or cleansing ; purification. [rifying.
ᴇX-PŪR'GA-TǪ-RY, *a.* Used for cleansing ; pu-
ĔX'QUĮ-ṢĬTE, *a.* Excellent ; consummate ; nice.
ĔX'QUĮ-ṢĬTE-LY, *ad.* Completely ; consum-
ᴇX-SCĬND', *v. a.* To cut off, separate. [mately.
ᴇX-SĬC'CANT, *a.* Drying ; having power to dry.
ᴇX-SĬC'CĀTE, *v. a.* To dry ; to exhaust of moist-
ĔX-SĮC-CĀ'TIǪN, *n.* The act of drying. [ture.
ĔX'TĂNT, *a.* Standing in view :—now in being.
ᴇX-TĔM-PǪ-RĀ'NE-OŬS,) *a.* Not studied ; un-
ᴇX-TĔM'PǪ-RA-RY,) premeditated.
ᴇX-TĔM'PǪ-RE, *ad.* Without premeditation.
ᴇX-TĔM'PǪ-RE, *a.* Extemporaneous ; unstudied.
ᴇX-TĔM'PǪ-RĪZE, *v. n.* To speak extempore.
ᴇX-TĔND', *v. a.* To stretch out ; to enlarge.
ᴇX-TĔND', *v. n.* To reach to any distance.
ᴇX-TĔN'DĮ-BLE, *a.* Capable of extension.

ᴇX-TĔN-SĮ-BĬL'Į-TY, *n.* The being extensible.
ᴇX-TĔN'SĮ-BLE, *a.* Capable of being extended.
ᴇX-TĔN'SIǪN, *n.* Act of extending ; dilatation.
ᴇX-TĔN'SĮVE, *a.* Wide ; large ; having great ex-
ᴇX-TĔN'SĮVE-LY, *ad.* Widely ; largely. [tent.
ᴇX-TĔN'SĮVE-NĔSS, *n.* Largeness ; diffusiveness.
ᴇX-TĔN'SǪR, *n.* A muscle which extends.
ᴇX-TĔNT', *n.* Space ; bulk ; compass ; length.
ᴇX-TĔN'Ụ-ĀTE, *v. a.* To lessen ; to palliate.
ᴇX-TĔN-Ụ-Ā'TIǪN, *n.* Palliation ; mitigation.
ᴇX-TĒ'RĮ-ǪR, *a.* Outward ; external ; extrinsic.
ᴇX-TĒ'RĮ-ǪR, *n.* Outward surface or appearance.
ᴇX-TĔR'MĮ-NĀTE, *v. a.* To root out ; to destroy.
ᴇX-TĔR-MĮ-NĀ'TIǪN, *n.* Destruction ; ruin.
ᴇX-TĔR'MĮ-NĀ-TǪR, *n.* One who exterminates.
ᴇX-TĔR'MĮ-NA-TǪ-RY, *a.* Causing extermina-
ᴇX-TĔRN', *a.* External ; exterior. [tion.
ᴇX-TĔRN', *n.* A day-scholar :—exterior form.
ᴇX-TĔR'NAL, *a.* Outward ; exterior :—visible.
ᴇX-TĔR'NAL-LY, *ad.* In an external manner.
ĔX-TĬL-LĀ'TIǪN, *n.* The act of falling in drops.
ᴇX-TĬNCT', *a.* Extinguished :—dead. [tion.
ᴇX-TĬNC'TIǪN, *n.* Act of quenching ; destruc-
ᴇX-TĬN'GUĮSH, *v. a.* To put out ; to destroy.
ᴇX-TĬN'GUĮSH-A-BLE, *a.* That may be quenched.
ᴇX-TĬN'GUĮSH-ᴇR, *n.* One that extinguishes.
ᴇX-TĬN'GUĮSH-MĔNT, *n.* Act of extinguishing.
ᴇX-TĬR'PĀTE, *v. a.* To root out ; to eradicate.
ĔX-TĮR-PĀ'TIǪN, *n.* Eradication ; destruction.
ᴇX-TĬR'PA-TǪR, *n.* One who roots out.
ᴇX-TŎL', *v. a.* To praise ; to magnify ; to laud.
ᴇX-TŎL'LᴇR, *n.* A praiser ; a magnifier ; a pan-
ᴇX-TŎR'SĮVE, *a.* Serving to extort. [egyrist.
ᴇX-TŎRT', *v. a.* To force away ; to wring from.
ᴇX-TŎR'TIǪN, *n.* Illegal exaction. [tortion.
ᴇX-TŎR'TIǪN-ᴇR, *n.* One who practises ex-
ĔX'TRA. [L.] A word often used in composition, meaning over and above, extraordinary ; as *extra*-pay, &c. ; or beyond, as *extra*-judicial.
ᴇX-TRĂCT', *v. a.* To draw out ; to abstract.
ĔX'TRĂCT, *n.* That which is extracted ; substance obtained by evaporation :—quotation.
ᴇX-TRĂC'TIǪN, *n.* Act of drawing out :—lineage.
ᴇX-TRĂCT'ǪR, *n.* One that extracts.
ĔX-TRA-JŲ-DĬ''CIAL (ĕks-tra-jụ-dĭsh'al), *a.* Being out of the regular course of legal procedure.
ĔX-TRA-MŬN'DĀNE, *a.* Beyond the world.
ᴇX-TRĀ'NE-OŬS, *a.* Foreign ; disconnected.
ᴇX-TRAÖR'DĮ-NA-RĮ-LY, *ad.* Uncommonly ; eminently ; remarkably ; unusually.
ᴇX-TRAÖR'DĮ-NA-RY, *a.* Not ordinary ; eminent ; remarkable ; uncommon ; unusual.
ĔX-TRA-PA-RŌ'ČHĮ-AL, *a.* Not within a parish.
ᴇX-TRĂV'A-GANCE, *n.* Irregularity ; prodigality.
ᴇX-TRĂV'A-GANT, *a.* Irregular ; wild ; waste-
ᴇX-TRĂV'A-GANT-LY, *ad.* Wastefully. [ful.
ᴇX-TRĂV'A-SĀTE, *v. a.* To force out of ducts.
ᴇX-TRĂV-A-SĀ'TIǪN, *n.* Act of forcing out of
ᴇX-TRĒME', *a.* Greatest ; utmost ; last. [ducts.
ᴇX-TRĒME', *n.* Utmost point ; extremity ; end.
ᴇX-TRĒME'LY, *ad.* In the utmost degree.
ᴇX-TRĔM'Į-TY, *n.* Utmost point ; necessity.
ĔX'TRĮ-CA-BLE, *a.* Capable of being extricated.
ĔX'TRĮ-CĀTE, *v. a.* To disembarrass ; to free.
ĔX-TRĮ-CĀ'TIǪN, *n.* The act of extricating.
ᴇX-TRĬN'SĮC,) *a.* External ; outward ; ex-
ᴇX-TRĬN'SĮ-CAL,) traneous. [wardly.
ᴇX-TRĬN'SĮ-CAL-LY, *ad.* From without ; out-

EX-TRŬDE', v. a. To thrust off; to drive off.
EX-TRŬ'ŞIQN, n. Act of thrusting out.
EX-TŪ'BER-ANCE, n. A swelling; protuberance.
EX-TŪ'BER-ANT, a. Swelled; standing out.
EX-TU-MĔS'CENCE, n. A swelling; a rising up.
EX-Ū'BER-ANCE, n. Overgrowth; luxuriance.
EX-Ū'BER-ANT (egz-yū'ber-ant), a. Abundant.
EX-Ū'BER-ANT-LY, ad. Abundantly.   [out.
EX-ŪDE' (ek-sūd'), v. n. & a. To sweat or force
EX-U-DĀ'TIQN (ĕk-su-dā'shun), n. A sweating.
EX-ŬLT' (egz-ŭlt'), v. n. To rejoice; to triumph.
EX-UL-TĀ'TIQN, n. Joy; triumph; rapture.
EYE (Ī), n. The organ of vision :— aspect; sight.
EYE (Ī), v. a. To watch; to view; to observe.
EYE'BÂLL (Ī'bâwl), n. The apple of the eye.

EYE'BRĪGHT (Ī'brīt), n. The name of a plant.
EYE'BRÖW (Ī'bröŭ), n. Hairy arch over the eye.
EYE'LĂSH (Ī'lăsh), n. Hair that edges the eyelid.
EYE'LĘT (Ī'lęt), n. A hole, as for the light, &c.
EYE'LĬD (Ī'lĭd), n. The membrane over the eye.
EYE'SHŎT (Ī'shŏt), n. A glance; transient view.
EYE'SĪGHT (Ī'sīt), n. Sight of the eye. [sight.
EYE'SŌRE (Ī'sōr), n. Something offensive to the
EYE'TÔÔTH, n. The tooth next to the grinders.
EYE'WĬT-NESS (Ī'wĭt-nęs), n. An ocular wit-
  ness or evidence; one who sees a transaction.
EYRE (âr), n. (Law.) A court of itinerant jus-
  tices :—circuit of the king's justices.
EYR'Y (âr'ę), n. The place where birds of prey
  build their nests and hatch; an aerie.

F.

F has, in English, one invariable sound, ex-
  cept in the preposition of.
FÄ, n. (Mus.) The fourth syllable of the scale.
FĀ'BLE (fā'bl), n. A feigned story; a fiction.
FĀ'BLE, v. a. & n. To feign; to tell falsely.
FĂB'RĬC, n. A building; an edifice :—texture.
FĂB'RĬ-CĀTE, v. a. To build; to construct;
  to make :—to forge; to feign; to invent [tion.
FĂB-RĬ-CĀ'TIQN, n. Act of building; construc-
FĂB'RĬ-CĀ-TQR, n. One who fabricates; forger.
FĂB'U-LĬST, n. A writer or author of fables.
FĂB'U-LOŬS, a. Feigned; full of fables; forged.
FĂB'U-LOŬS-LY, ad. In a fabulous manner.
FA-ÇÄDE', n. [Fr.] The front of an edifice.
FĀCE, n. Visage; countenance :—front; fore
FĀCE, v. a. & n. To meet or come in front. [part.
FĂÇ'ĘT, n. A little face; a small surface.
FA-CĒ'TIOŬS (fa-sē'shus), a. Lively; gay; witty.
FA-CĒ'TIOŬS-LY, ad. Gayly; wittily; merrily.
FA-CĒ'TIOŬS-NĔSS, n. The quality of being
  facetious; cheerful wit; mirth; gayety.
FĀ'CIAL (fā'shal), a. Relating to the face.
FĂÇ'ILE (făs'il), a. Easy; pliant; flexible.
FA-CĬL'I-TĀTE, v. a. To make easy or easier.
FA-CĬL-I-TĀ'TIQN, n. The act of making easy.
FA-CĬL'I-TY, n. Easiness; readiness; dexterity.
FĀ'CĬNG, n. A covering; ornamental covering.
FĂC-SĬM'I-LĘ, n. An exact copy or likeness.
FĂCT, n. A thing done; reality; action; deed.
FĂC'TIQN, n. Portion of a party :—dissension.
FĂC'TIOŬS (făk'shus), a. Given to faction; tur-
FĂC'TIOŬS-LY, ad. In a factious manner. [bulent.
FĂÇ'TIOŬS-NĔSS, n. Inclination to faction.
FĂC-TĬ''TIOŬS (făk-tĭsh'us), a. Made by art;
  artificial; not natural.   [of a quantity.
FĂC'TQR, n. A merchant's agent :—a divisor
FĂC'TQR-AGE, n. Commission allowed a factor.
FĂC'TQ-RY, n. House of factors :—manufactory.
FĂC-TŌ'TUM, n. A servant employed alike in
  all kinds of business; a doer of all work.
FĂC'UL-TY, n. Ability; power of mind or
  body; dexterity :—a body of professional men
FA-CŬN'DI-TY, n. Eloquence; easiness of speech.
FĂD'DLE, v. n. To trifle; to toy; to play. [Low.]
FĀDE, v. n. To lose color :—to wither; to decay.
FÆ'CĘŞ (fē'sēz), n. pl. [L.] Excrement; dregs.

FĂG, v. n. & a. To grow weary :—to beat.
FĂG-ĔND', n. End of a web of cloth :—refuse.
FĂG'QT, n. A bundle of sticks for fuel.
FĂG'QT, v. a. To tie up; to bundle together.
FĀIL, v. n. To be deficient or insolvent; to
  perish; to decay; to decline :—to miss.
FĀIL, v. a. To desert; to disappoint; to deceive.
FĀIL'ĬNG, n. Deficiency; imperfection; lapse.
FĀIL'URE (fāl'yur), n. Deficiency; cessation;
  omission; non-performance :—bankruptcy.
FĀIN, a. Glad; pleased.—ad. Gladly.
FĀINT, v. n. To decay; to sink motionless.
FĀINT, a. Languid; weak; cowardly; dejected.
FĀINT'-HEÄRT-ĘD (fānt'härt-ęd), a. Cowardly.
FĀINT'ISH, a. Somewhat or slightly faint.
FĀINT'ISH-NĔSS, n. A slight degree of faintness.
FĀINT'LY, ad. Feebly; languidly; timorously.
FĀINT'NĘSS, n. Languor; want of vigor.
FÂIR (fâr), a. Beautiful; white; clear; not
  foul :—favorable; equal; just; open; candid.
FÂIR, n. The female sex :—a stated market.
FÂIR'LY, ad. Justly; plainly; openly; candidly.
FÂIR'NĘSS, n. Beauty; honesty; clearness.
FÂIR'-SPŌ-KEN (fâr'spō-kn), a. Courteous.
FÂIR'Y, n. A fabled spirit; a fay; an elf.
FÂIR'Y, a. Given by, or belonging to, fairies.
FĀITH (fāth), n. Trust in God; belief; doc-
  trine believed :—fidelity; faithfulness; honor;
  confidence; sincerity.   [right; true.
FĀITH'FŬL, a. Firm to the truth; loyal; up-
FĀITH'FŬL-LY, ad. In a faithful manner.
FĀITH'FŬL-NĔSS, n. Fidelity; honesty; loyalty.
FĀITH'LĘSS, a. Without faith; perfidious.
FĀITH'LĘSS-NĔSS, n. Want of faith; perfidy.
FĀKE, n. A coil, as of a rope or cable.
FĀ'KĬR or FĀ'KĬR, n. A Mahometan monk. [hook.
FĂL'CĂT-ĘD, a. Hooked; bent like a reaping-
FĂL-CĀ'TIQN, n. Crookedness; a bending form.
FÂL'CHIQN (fâl'chun or fâl'shun), n. A broad
  sword with a curved point. [sport :—a cannon.
FÂL'CON (fâw'kn), n. A hawk trained for
FÂL'CON-ER (fâw'kn-), n. A trainer of falcons.
FĂL'CQ-NĔT, n. A sort of ordnance. [hawks.
FÂL'CON-RY, n. Art of training
FÂLL, v. n. [imp. t. fell; pp. fallen.] To drop
  down; to die; to decline; to ebb; to happen.

FÂLL, *n.* Act of falling ; overthrow :—autumn.
FAL-LĀ'CIOŲS (fal-lā'shŭs), *a.* Producing mistake ; misleading ; delusive ; false.
FAL-LĀ'CIOŲS-LY, *ad.* In a fallacious manner.
FAL-LĀ'CIOŲS-NĔSS, *n.* Tendenc⬤to deceive.
FĂL'LA-CY, *n.* Sophism ; deceitful argument ;
FÂLL'EN (fâl'ln), *pp.* from *fall.* [craft.
FĂL-LI-BĬL'I-TY, *n.* Liableness to be deceived or to err ; uncertainty ; frailty. [imperfect.
FĂL'LI-BLE, *a.* Liable to error ; frail ; uncertain ;
FĂL'LI-BLY, *ad.* In a fallible manner ; uncer-
FÂLL'ING-SĬCK'NĔSS, *n.* The epilepsy. [tainly.
FĂL'LOW (fál'lō), *a.* Pale red :—not tilled.
FÂLSE, *a.* Not true ; perfidious :—counterfeit.
FÂLSE-HEÄRT'ED (fâls-härt'ed), *a.* Perfidious.
FÂLSE'HOOD (-hûd), *n.* Want of truth ; a lie.
FÂLSE'LY, *ad.* In a false manner ; perfidiously.
FÂLSE'NĔSS, *n.* Want of truth ; deceit ; perfidy.
FĂL-SI-FI-CĀ'TIŌN, *n.* Act of falsifying. [feits.
FĂL'SI-FI-ER, *n.* One who falsifies or counter-
FĂL'SI-FY̆, *v. a.* & *n.* To counterfeit :—to lie.
FĂL'SI-TY, *n.* Contrariety to truth ; a lie ; error.
FÂL'TER, *v. n.* To hesitate in speech :—to fail.
FÂL'TER-ĬNG, *n.* Feebleness ; deficiency.
FÂL'TER-ĬNG-LY, *ad.* With hesitation.
FĀME, *n.* Celebrity ; renown :—report ; rumor.
FĀMED (fāmd), *p. a.* Renowned ; celebrated.
FA-MĬL'IAR (fa-mĭl'yạr), *a.* Domestic ; affable ; easy ; unceremonious ; free :—well known.
FA-MĬL'IAR, *n.* An intimate ; an associate.
FA-MĬL-I-ÄR'I-TY (fa-mĭl-ye-är'e-te), *n.* Intimate acquaintance ; easy intercourse.
FA-MĬL'IAR-ĪZE (fa-mĭl'yạr-īz), *v. a.* To make familiar ; to accustom ; to habituate. [sily.
FA-MĬL'IAR-LY, *ad.* In a familiar manner ; ea-
FĂM'I-LY, *n.* Household ; race ; generation ;
FĂM'INE, *n.* Scarcity of food ; dearth. [class.
FĂM'ĬSH, *v. n.* To starve ; to die of hunger.
FĂM'ĬSH-MĔNT, *n.* Extreme hunger or thirst.
FĀ'MOŲS, *a.* Renowned ; celebrated ; noted.
FĀ'MOŲS-LY, *ad.* In a famous manner.
FĂN, *n.* An instrument used by ladies to cool themselves :—a utensil to winnow grain.
FĂN, *v. a.* To cool with a fan :—to winnow.
FA-NĂT'ĬC, *n.* A wild enthusiast ; a visionary.
FA-NĂT'ĬC,] *a.* Excessively enthusiastic ;
FA-NĂT'I-CAL,} wild ; mad ; visionary.
FA-NĂT'I-CAL-LY, *ad.* In a fanatical manner.
FA-NĂT'I-CĬSM, *n.* Wild enthusiasm ; frenzy.
FĂN'CI-FŬL, *a.* Imaginative ; visionary.
FĂN'CI-FŬL-LY, *ad.* In a fanciful manner.
FĂN'CY, *n.* Imagination ; taste ; idea ; image ; thought :—inclination ; fondness ; whim.
FĂN'CY, *v. a.* To imagine ; to be pleased with.
FĂN'CY, *v. n.* To imagine ; to figure to one's self.
FAN-DĂN'GŌ, *n.* [Sp.] A lively Spanish dance.
FĀNE, *n.* A temple :—a weathercock ; a vane.
FĂN'FA-RŎN, *n.* [Fr.] A bully ; a blusterer.
FĂN-FA-RŌ-NĀDE', *n.* A bluster ; parade ; boast.
FĂNG, *n.* Tusk of an animal ; a talon ; a claw.
FĂNGED (făngd), *a.* Furnished with fangs.
FĂN'GLED (fáng'gld), *a.* Gaudy ; showy ; trifling.
FĂN'NEL, *n.* A priest's ornament, like a scarf.
FĂN-TĂS'TĬC,] *a.* Irrational ; imaginary ;
FĂN-TĂS'TI-CAL, } whimsical ; fanciful ; capricious ; indulging vagaries of the imagination.
FĂN-TĂS'TI-CAL-LY, *ad.* In a fantastic manner.
FĂN-TĂS'TI-CAL-NĔSS, *n.* Whimsicalness.

FĂN'TA-SY̆, *n.* Fancy ; imagination. See FAN-
FĀ'QUIR, *or* FÄ-QUEĒR', *n.* See FAKIR. [CY.
FÄR, *ad.* Remotely ; at a distance :—very much.
FÄR, *a.* Distant ; remote ; remoter of the two.
FÄRCE, *n.* A ludicrous dramatic representation.
FÄRCE, *v. a.* To stuff ; to cram ; to swell out.
FÄR'CI-CAL, *a.* Belonging to a farce ; ludicrous.
FÄR'CI-CAL-LY, *ad.* In a farcical manner.
FÄR'DEL, *n.* A bundle ; a pack ; a burden. [feed.
FÄRE, *v. n.* To pass ; to happen well or ill ; to
FÄRE, *n.* Price of passage :—food ; provisions.
FÄRE-WĔLL' *or* FÄRE'WĔLL, *ad.* Adieu.
FÄRE-WĔLL' *or* FÄRE'WĔLL, *n.* Departure.
FÄR'-FĔTCHED (fär'-fĕcht), *a.* Brought from a distance ; studiously sought :—strained.
FA-RĪ'NA, *n.* Pollen :—starch of the potato, &c.
FÄR-I-NĀ'CEOŲS (fär-e-nā'shŭs), *a.* Mealy.
FÄRM, *n.* Ground cultivated by a farmer.
FÄRM, *v. a.* To lease or let :—to cultivate, as land.
FÄRM'ER, *n.* One who cultivates a farm.
FÄRM'ĬNG, *n.* Husbandry ; tillage :—a renting.
FÄR'MŌST, *a.* Most distant ; remotest ; farthest.
FÄR'NĔSS, *n.* Distance ; remoteness.
FÄR-RĀ'GŌ, *n.* A confused mass ; a medley.
FÄR'RI-ER, *n.* A shoer of horses :—horse-doctor.
FÄR'RI-ER-Y̆, *n.* The art of the farrier.
FÄR'RŌW, *n.* A litter of pigs.—*v. a.* & *n.* To bring forth young ;—used only of swine.
FÄR'RŌW, *a.* Not producing young, as a cow.
FÄR'THER, *ad.* More remotely ; further.
FÄR'THER, *a. comp.* More remote ; further.
FÄR'THER, *v. a.* To further. See FURTHER.
FÄR'THEST, *a. sup.* Most distant ; furthest.
FÄR'THEST, *ad.* Most remote ; furthest.
FÄR'THING, *n.* The fourth part of a penny. [coat.
FÄR'THIN-GALE, *n.* A hoop to spread the petti-
FĂS'CI-A (fásh'e-a), *n.* [L.] A fillet ; a bandage : —belt of a planet :—expansion of a muscle.
FĂS-CĬC'U-LAR, *a.* Of or belonging to a bundle.
FĂS'CI-NĀTE, *v. a.* To bewitch ; to enchant.
FĂS-CI-NĀ'TIŌN, *n.* Enchantment ; witchcraft.
FĂSH'IŌN (fásh'ŭn), *n.* Form ; make , way ; custom ; general practice ; habit ; mode ; rank.
FĂSH'IŌN (fásh'ŭn), *v. a.* To form, mould, fit.
FĂSH'IŌN-A-BLE (fásh'ŭn-a-bl), *a.* Approved or established by custom ; modish ; genteel.
FĂSH'IŌN-A-BLE-NĔSS, *n.* Modishness; elegance.
FĂSH'IŌN-A-BLY, *ad.* In a fashionable manner.
FĂSH'IŌN-ER, *n.* One who fashions or makes.
FĂST, *v. n.* To abstain from food.
FĂST, *n.* Abstinence from food :—time of fasting.
FĂST, *a.* Firm ; strong ; fixed :—quick ; swift.
FĂST, *ad.* Firmly ; closely ; nearly :—swiftly.
FĂST'EN (fás'sn), *v. a.* To make fast or firm.
FĂST'EN-ĬNG (fás'sn-ĭng), *n.* That which fastens.
FĂST'ER, *n.* One who abstains from food.
FÄST'-HĂND-ED, *a.* Avaricious ; close-handed.
FAS-TĬD'I-OŬS, *a.* Disdainful ; squeamish ; nice.
FAS-TĬD'I-OŬS-LY, *ad.* In a fastidious manner.
FAS-TĬD'I-OŬS-NĔSS, *n.* Squeamishness. [place.
FĂST'NĔSS, *n.* Firmness ; strength :—a strong
FĂT, *n.* The oily part of animal bodies :—a vat.
FĂT, *a.* Plump ; fleshy ; coarse ; gross ; rich.
FĂT, *v. a.* & *n.* To make or grow fat ; to fatten.
FĀ'TAL, *a.* Mortal ; destructive ; inevitable.
FĀ'TAL-ĬSM, *n.* Doctrine of inevitable necessity.
FĀ'TAL-ĬST, *n.* An adherent of fatalism.
FA-TĂL'I-TY, *n.* Decree of fate ; cause of ill.

FĀ'TĄL-LY, *ad.* Mortally; destructively.
FĀTE, *n.* Destiny; destruction; cause of death.
FĀT'ED, *a.* Decreed or ordered by fate.
FÄ'THĘR, *n.* The male parent; ancestor; sire.
FÄ'THĘR-ĬN-LÂW,*n.*; pl. FÄ'THĘRŞ-ĬN-LÂW.
  The father of one's husband or wife.
FÄ'THĘR, *v. a.* To take; to adopt as a child.
FÄ'THĘR-LĔSS, *a.* Wanting a father; destitute.
FÄ'THĘR-LĬ-NĔSS,*n.* The tenderness of a father.
FÄ'THĘR-LY,*a.* Like a father; tender; paternal.
FÄ'THĘR-LY, *ad.* In the manner of a father.
FĂTH'ǪM, *n.* A measure of six feet in length.
FĂTH'ǪM,*v. a.* To sound; to find the bottom of.
FĂTH'ǪM-ĘR, *n.* One employed in fathoming.
FĂTH'ǪM-LĔSS, *a.* That cannot be fathomed;
  bottomless.   [toil; labor.
FĄ-TÎGUE' (fạ-tēg'), *n.* Weariness; lassitude;
FĄ-TÎGUE' (fạ-tēg'), *v. a.* To tire; to weary.
FĂT'LĬNG,*n.* A young animal, fed for slaughter.
FĂT'NĘSS, *n.* Quality of being fat; plumpness.
FĂT'TEN, *v. a. & n.* To make or grow fat.
FĂT'TY, *a.* Unctuous; oleaginous; greasy.
FĄ-TŪ'Ĭ-TY, *n.* Foolishness; weakness of mind.
FĂT'Ṳ-OŬS, *a.* Foolish; stupid; imbecile.
FÂU'CĘT, *n.* A pipe for drawing liquor.
FÂULT, *n.* Offence; mistake; defect; want.
FÂULT'Ĭ-LY, *ad.* Wrongly; defectively.
FÂULT'Ĭ-NĔSS,*n.* Badness; viciousness; defect.
FÂULT'LĘSS, *a.* Exempt from fault; perfect.
FÂULT'Y, *a.* Having faults; wrong; defective.
FÂUN, *n.* A kind of demigod or rural deity.
FĀ'VǪR, *v. a.* To support, assist, or resemble.
FĀ'VǪR, *n.* Kindness; regard; support; lenity.
FĀ'VǪR-Ą-BLE,*a.* Kind; propitious; friendly.
FĀ'VǪR-Ą-BLY, *ad.* Kindly; with favor.
FĀ'VǪRED (fä'vụrd), *p. a.* Aided :—featured.
FĀ'VǪR-ĘR, *n.* One who favors; a friend.
FĀ'VǪR-ÏTE, *n.* A person or thing beloved.
FĀ'VǪR-ÏTE, *a.* Beloved; regarded with favor.
FĀ'VǪR-ĬT-ĬŞM, *n.* Act of favoring; partiality.
FÂWN, *n.* The young of the fallow deer.
FÂWN, *v. n.* To court servilely; to cringe.
FĀY, *v. n.* To fit; to suit; to join.
FĀY, *n.* A fairy; an elf :–faith; troth.
FĒ'ĄL-TY,*n.* Duty to a superior lord; loyalty.
FĒAR (fēr),*n.* Dread; terror; awe; anxiety.
FĒAR, *v. a. & n.* To dread; to be afraid.
FĒAR'FŬL, *a.* Timorous; afraid; apprehensive;
  timid :—awful; dreadful; venerable.
FĒAR'FŬL-LY, *ad.* In a fearful manner.
FĒAR'FŬL-NĔSS,*n.* Timorousness; awe; dread.
FĒAR'LĘSS, *a.* Free from fear; intrepid; bold.
FĒAR'LĘSS-LY, *ad.* Without terror; intrepidly.
FĒAR'LĘSS-NĔSS, *n.* Courage; intrepidity.
FĒAR'NÂUGHT (fēr'nâut) *n.* A thick woollen
  stuff, used for warm garments, &c.   [ity.
FĒA-ŞĬ-BĬL'Ĭ-TY (fē-zẹ-bĭl'ẹ-tẹ) *n.* Practicabil-
FĒA'ŞĬ-BLE (fē'zẹ-bl), *a.* That may be done.
FĒAST (fēst), *n.* A sumptuous treat; a festival.
FĒAST (fēst), *v. n. & a.* To eat or entertain
  sumptuously :—to delight; to gladden.
FĒAT, *n.* An act; deed; action; exploit.
FĔATH'ĘR (fĕth'ẹr), *n.* The plume of birds.
FĔATH'ĘR (fĕth'ẹr), *v. a.* To dress in feathers.
FĔATH'ĘRED(fĕth'ẹrd),*a.*Clothed with feathers.
FĔATH'ĘR-Y, *a.* Clothed with, or like, feathers.
FĒAT'ỤRE (fēt'yụr),*n.* Form or part of the face.
FĒAT'ỤRED (fēt'yụrd), *a.* Having features.

FĔB'RĬ-FŪĢE, *n.* Medicine serviceable in fevers.
FĒ'BRĬLE *or* FĔB'RĬLE, *a.* Pertaining to fever.
FĔB'RṲ-Ą-RY,*n.* The second month in the year.
FĒ'CĄL, *a.* Relating to excrement, dregs, or lees.
FĒ'CĔŞ, *n. pl.* Dregs. See FÆCES.   [dregs.
FĔC'Ṳ-LĔNCE, *n.* Muddiness; lees; sediment;
FĔC'Ṳ-LĔNT, *a.* Foul; dreggy; excrementitious·
FĔC'ỤND, *a.* Fruitful; prolific; productive.
FĘ-CŬN'DĀTE, *v. a.* To make prolific.
FĔC-ỤN-DĀ'TIǪN, *n.* The act of making prolific.
FĘ-CŬN'DĬ-TY, *n.* Fruitfulness; prolificness.
FĔD, *imp. t. & pp.* from *feed.*
FĔD'ER-ĄL, *a.* Relating to a league or compact;
  confederate.   [eracy; banded.
FĔD'ĘR-ĀTE, *a.* Leagued; joined in confed-
FĔD-ĘR-Ā'TIǪN, *n.* A league; a confederacy.
FĔD'ĘR-Ą-TĪVE,*a.* Uniting; joining in a league.
FĔE, *n.* Reward; recompense :—a tenure.
FĒE, *v. a.* To reward; to pay; to bribe; to hire.
FĒE'BLE, *a.* Weak; debilitated; sickly; infirm.
FĒE'BLE-MĪND-ĘD, *a.* Weak of mind; imbe-
  cile :—irresolute; wavering.   [firmity.
FĒE'BLE-NĔSS, *n.* Weakness; imbecility; in-
FĒE'BLY, *ad.* Weakly; without strength.
FĒED, *v. a. & n.* [*imp. t. & pp.* fed.] To supply
  with food; to furnish; to take food; to eat.
FĒED, *n.* Food; that which is eaten; pasture.
FĒED'ĘR, *n.* One who feeds or gives food.
FĒEL, *v. a. & n.* [*imp. t. & pp.* felt.] To have
  perception by the touch; to touch; to handle :
  —to perceive mentally; to be affected.
FĒEL, *n.* The sense of feeling; the touch.
FĒEL'ĘR, *n.* One who, or that which, feels.
FĒEL'ĬNG, *p. a.* Expressive of sensibility; ten-
  der; sensitive.   [sibility.
FĒEL'ĬNG, *n.* Sense of touch; perception; sen-
FĒEL'ĬNG-LY, *ad.* In a feeling manner ; sensi-
FĒET, *n.* The plural of *foot.*   [tively.
FEIGN (fān), *v. a. & n.* To invent; to dissemble.
FEINT (fānt), *n.* False appearance :—mock as-
  sault :—a pretended thrust in fencing.
FĔLD'SPÄR, *n.* A mineral. See FELSPAR.
FĘ-LĬÇ'Ĭ-TĀTE, *v. a.* To make happy; to con-
FĘ-LĬÇ-Ĭ-TĀ'TIǪN,*n.* Congratulation.[gratulate.
FĘ-LĬÇ'Ĭ-TOŬS, *a.* Happy; skilful; ingenious;
  prosperous; successful.   [success.
FĘ-LĬÇ'Ĭ-TY, *n.* Happiness; prosperity; bliss;
FĒ'LĪNE, *a.* Like a cat; pertaining to a cat.
FĔLL, *a.* Cruel; inhuman; savage; bloody.
FĔLL, *n.* The skin; hide :—a hill; a mount.
FĔLL, *v. a.* To knock down; to cut or hew
FĔLL, *imp. t.* from *fall.*   [down.
FĔL'LŌW (fĕl'lō), *n.* A companion; an associ-
  ate :—an equal; peer :—a mean person.
FĔL'LŌW-FĒEL'ĬNG,*n.* Sympathy; agreement.
FĔL'LŌW-SHĬP, *n.* Companionship; society;
  association :—establishment in a college.
FĔL'LY, *ad.* Cruelly; savagely; barbarously.
FĔL'LY, FĔL'LŌE, *n.* Part of the rim of a wheel.
FĒ'LǪ-DĘ-SĒ', *n.* (*Law.*) He who commits felo-
  ny by murdering himself; a self-murderer.
FĔL'ǪN, *n.* One guilty of a crime :—a whitlow.
FĘ-LŌ'NĬ-OŬS,*a.*Wicked; villanous; malignant.
FĘ-LŌ'NĬ-OŬS-LY, *ad.* In a felonious way.
FĔL'Ǫ-NY, *n.* A capital, or punishable, crime.
FĔL'SPÄR, *n.* A silicious mineral in granite, &c.
FĔLT, *imp. t. & pp.* from *feel.*   [hide.
FĔLT, *n.* Woollen cloth or stuff for hats :—a

FĘ-LŬC′CẠ, n. [It.] A small vessel with two masts, and propelled by oars and sails.
FĒ′MĀLE, n. One of the sex producing young.
FĒ′MĀLE, a. Not male; feminine; soft. [cate.
FĔM′Ĭ-NĪNE, a. Relating to females; soft; deli-
FĔM′Ọ-RẠL, a. Belonging to the thigh.
FĔN, n. A marsh; a moor; a bog; a swamp.
FĔNCE, n. A guard; defence; hedge, wall, &c.
FĔNCE, v. a. To enclose; to secure; to guard.
FĔNCE, v. n. To practise the art of fencing.
FĔNCE′LĘSS, a. Without enclosure; open.
FĔN′CĘR, n. One who teaches or practises fen-
FĔN′CĬ-BLE, a. Capable of defence. [cing.
FĔN′CĬ-BLEŞ, n. pl. Soldiers raised for defence.
FĔN′CĬNG, n. The art of using the sword.
FĔN′CĬNG-MĂS′TĘR, n. A teacher of fencing.
FĔND, v. a. & n. To exclude, confine, dispute.
FĔND′ĘR, n. A guard before the fire, &c.
FĔN′NĘL, n. A plant used in medicine.
FĔN′NY, a. Marshy; boggy; moorish. [DAL.
FEO′DẠL (fū′dạl), a. Held by tenure. See FEU-
FĔOFF (fĕf), v. a. To invest with right or with a fee; to enfeoff.—n. A fief. [session.
FĔOF′FĒĒ or FĔOF-FĒĒ′, n. One put in pos-
FĔOF′FĘR (fĕf′-), n. One who gives possession.
FĔOFF′MĘNT (fĕf′-), n. Grant of a possession.
FĔR′Ę-TỌ-RY, n. A shrine or bier for relics.
FĘR-MĔNT′, v. a. & n. To work; to effervesce.
FĔR′MĘNT, n. Intestine motion; tumult:—yeast.
FĔR-MĔNT′Ạ-BLE, a. Capable of fermentation.
FĔR-MĘN-TĀ′TĬON, n. Working, as of liquors.
FĔR-MĔN′TẠ-TĬVE, a. Causing fermentation.
FĔRN, n. A plant of several species; a brake.
FĔRN′Y, a. Overgrown, or abounding, with fern.
FĘ-RŌ′CIOŬS (fę-rō′shụs), a. Savage; fierce.
FĘ-RŌ′CIOŬS-LY, ad. In a savage manner.
FĘ-RŎÇ′Ĭ-TY, n. Savageness; fierceness; wild-
 ness; barbarity. [made of iron.
FĔR′RĘ-OŬS, a. Containing iron; like iron;
FĔR′RĘT, n. A kind of weasel:—a narrow tape.
FĔR′RĘT, v. a. To drive out of lurking places.
FĔR′RĘT-ĘR, n. One who ferrets or hunts out.
FĔR′RĬ-ĄǴE, n. Fare for passage over a ferry.
FĘR-RŪ′ǴĬ-NOŬS, a. Partaking of iron.
FĔR′RỤLE, n. A ring put round any thing to keep it from splitting. [boat.
FĔR′RY, v. a. & n. To carry or pass over in a
FĔR′RY, n. Passage over which ferry-boats pass.
FĔR′RY-BŌAT, n. A boat for conveying passen-
gers over a ferry. [ferry.
FĔR′RY-MẠN, n. One who keeps or tends a
FĔR′TĬLE, a. Fruitful; abundant; productive.
FĔR′TĬLE-LY, ad. Fruitfully; abundantly.
FĘR-TĬL′Ĭ-TY, n. Fecundity; abundance; fruit-
fulness; plenteousness. [ductive.
FĔR′TĬL-ĪZE, v. a. To make fruitful or pro-
FĔR′ỤLE, or FĔR′Ụ-LẠ, n. An instrument or stick with which scholars are beaten on the hand for punishment.
FĔR′ỤLE, v. a. To chastise with the ferule.
FĔR′VĘN-CY, n. Heat of mind; ardor; eagerness.
FĔR′VĘNT, a. Hot; boiling; vehement; ardent.
FĔR′VĘNT-LY, ad. In a burning degree; eagerly.
FĔR′VĬD, a. Hot; vehement; eager; zealous.
FĔR′VĬD-NĔSS, n. Ardor of mind; zeal; passion.
FĔR′VOR, n. Heat; warmth; zeal; ardor.
FĔS′CŪE, n. A pin or wire to point with.
FĔS′TẠL, a. Relating to feasts; festive.

FĔS′TĘR, v. n. To rankle, corrupt, grow virulent.
FĔS′TĬ-VẠL, n. A day of feasting and joy.
FĔS′TĬ-VẠL, a. Relating to a feast; festive.
FĔS′TĬVE, a. Relating to feasts; joyous; gay.
FĘS-TĬV′Ĭ-TY, n. Social joy; gayety; joyfulness.
FĘS-TŌŌN′, n. A garland; a carved ornament.
FĔTCH, v. a. To go and bring; to derive, draw.
FĔTCH, n. A stratagem; an artifice; a trick.
FĔTCH′ĘR, n. One that fetches any thing.
FÊTE (fāt), n. [Fr.] A feast; a festival day.
FĔT′ĬD, a. Stinking; rancid; strong-smelling.
FĔT′LŎCK, n. Hair behind the pastern of horses.
FĒ′TOR, n. A stench; a strong, offensive smell.
FĔT′TĘR, n. A chain for the feet:—a restraint.
FĔT′TĘR, v. a. To bind; to enchain; to shackle.
FĒ′TỤS, n. An animal in the womb. See FŒTUS.
FEŪD (fūd), n. A tenure:—a quarrel; contention.
FEŪ′DẠL, a. Held by tenure, or of a superior.
FEŪ′DẠL-ĬŞM(fū′dạl-ĭzm), n. The feudal system.
FEŪ′DẠ-RY, a. Holding tenure under a superior.
FEŪ′DẠ-TỌ-RY, n. A feudal tenant; a vassal.
FĒ′VĘR, n. A disease characterized by an ac-
celerated pulse, increased heat, and thirst.
FĒ′VĘR-ĬSH, a. Diseased with a fever:—hot.
FĒ′VĘR-ĬSH-NĔSS, n. State of being feverish.
FEW (fū), a. Not many; not in a great number.
FEW′ĘL, n. Combustible matter. See FUEL.
FEW′NĔSS (fū′nęs), n. Smallness of number.
FĪ′ẠT, n. [L.] A peremptory order or decree.
FĬB, n. A lie; a falsehood:—v. n. To lie.
FĬB′BĘR, n. A teller of fibs; a liar.
FĪ′BRE (fī′bęr), n. A small thread-like sub-
stance, as of wood; filament of vegetables, &c.
FĪ′BROŬS (fī′brụs), a. Composed of fibres.
FĬB′Ụ-LẠ, n. The outer and lesser bone of the leg.
FĬC′KLE, a. Changeable; inconstant; wavering.
FĬC′KLE-NĔSS, n. Inconstancy; unsteadiness.
FĬC′TĬLE, a. Moulded into form by art.
FĬC′TĬON, n. An invented story; a fabrication; a tale; thing feigned. [tion.
FĬC-TĬ″TIOŬS (fĭk-tĭsh′ụs), a. Partaking of fic-
FĬC-TĬ″TIOŬS-LY, ad. Falsely; counterfeitly.
FĬD′DLE, n. An instrument of music; a violin.
FĬD′DLE, v. n. To play upon a fiddle; to trifle.
FĬD′DLE-FĂD′DLE, n. A trifle. [A cant word.]
FĬD′DLĘR, n. One who plays upon a fiddle.
FĬD′DLE-STĬCK, n. A bow used by a fiddler.
FĬD′DLE-STRĬNG, n. The string of a fiddle.
FĬ-DĔL′Ĭ-TY, n. Honesty; veracity; faithfulness.
FĬDǴ′ĘT, v. n. To move about uneasily.
FĬDǴ′ĘT, n. Restless agitation; restlessness.
FĬDǴ′ĘT-Y, a. Restless; impatient. [Low.]
FĬ-DŪ′CIẠL (fę-dū′shạl), a. Confident; firm.
FĬ-DŪ′CĬ-Ạ-RY, n. One who holds in trust.
FĪE (fī), interj. Expressing blame or contempt.
FIĔF (fēf), n. A fee; a manor; a possession.
FIELD (fēld), n. A tract of ground:—space.
FIELD′FĀRE, n. A bird; the gray thrush.
FIELD′-MĂR-SHẠL, n. A high military title.
FIELD′-MŌŪSE, n. A mouse living in fields, and burrowing in banks, &c. [tain.
FIELD′-ŎF-FĬ-CĘR, n. An officer above a cap-
FIELD′-PIĔCE, n. A small cannon. [&c.
FIELD′-SPŌRTS, n. pl. Diversions of hunting,
FIEND (fēnd), n. An enemy; a demon or devil.
FIERCE (fērs), a. Savage; ravenous; eager; violent; passionate; angry; furious.
FIERCE′LY, ad. Violently; furiously; angrily.

FIĔRCE'NESS, n. Ferocity; savageness; fury.
FĪ'ER-Į-NĔSS, n. Great heat; heat of temper.
FĪ'ER-Y, a. Consisting of fire; vehement; ar-
FĪFE, n. A shrill martial instrument. [dent.
FĪF'ER, n. One who plays on the fife.
FĬF'TĒEN, a. Five and ten, or nine and six.
FĬF'TĒENTH, a. & n. The ordinal of fifteen:—
one of fifteen equal parts of a thing.
FĬFTH, a. & n. Ordinal of five:—one of five
FĬFTH'LY, ad. In the fifth place. [equal parts.
FĬF'TĮ-ĔTH, a. The ordinal of fifty.
FĬF'TY, a. Five times ten; five tens.
FĬG, n. The fruit of the fig-tree:—a fig-tree.
FĪGHT (fīt), v. n. & a. [imp. t. & pp. fought.]
To contend in battle; to make war; to combat.
FĪGHT (fīt), n. A battle; a combat; a conflict.
FĪGHT'ER (fīt'er), n. A warrior; a combatant.
FĬG'-LĒAF, n. A leaf of the fig-tree; a flimsy
FĬG'MENT, n. An invention; a fiction.[covering.
FĬG'-TRĒE, n. Tree that bears figs. [ly formed.
FĬG'Ų-RĄ-BLE, a. Capable of being permanent-
FĬG'Ų-RĄTE, a. Having a certain form.
FĬG'Ų-RĄ-TĬVE, a. Full of figures; metaphori-
cal; typical; tropical:—ornate; flowery.
FĬG'Ų-RĄ-TĬVE-LY, ad. In a figurative manner.
FĬG'ŲRE (fĭg'yur), n. Shape; splendor; a statue:
—a character denoting a number:—a type.
FĬG'ŲRE (fĭg'yur), v. a. To form; to represent.
FĮ-LĀ'CEOŲS (-shųs), a. Consisting of threads.
FĬL'Ą-CER, n. An officer in an English court.
FĬL'Ą-MENT, n. A slender thread; a fibre.
FĬL-Ą-MĔN'TOŲS, a. Like a slender thread.
FĬL'BERT, n. The nut of a species of hazel.
FĬLCH, v. a. To steal; to take by theft; to pilfer.
FĬLCH'ER, n. A thief; a petty robber; a pilferer.
FĪLE, n. A line; a roll; a series; a catalogue:
—an instrument to rub down prominences.
FĪLE, v. a. To string; to smooth; to polish.
FĪLE, v. n. To march in a file or line.
FĬL'IĄL (-yąl), a. Relating to, or befitting, a son.
FĬL-Į-Ā'TĮON, n. Relation of a son to a father.
FĬL'Į-GRĀNE,) n. Delicate work, as of gold or
FĬL'Ą-GRĒE,) silver, in manner of threads.
FĬL'ĮNGS, n. pl. Particles rubbed off by a file.
FĬLL, v. a. To make full; to satisfy; to surfeit.
FĬLL, v. n. To give to drink; to grow full.
FĬLL, n. Fulness; satiety:—thill of a carriage.
FĬL'LET, n. A band; bandage:—a chine of meat.
FĬL'LET, v. a. To bind with a bandage or fillet.
FĬL'LĮ-BĔG, n. A loose dress. See PHILIBEG.
FĬL'LĮP, v. a. To strike with the nail of the
finger; thrown out from the ball of the thumb.
FĬL'LĮP, n. A jerk of the finger from the thumb.
FĬL'LY, n. A young mare, opposed to a colt, or
FĬLM, n. A thin pellicle or skin. [young horse.
FĬL'MY, a. Composed of membranes or pellicles.
FĬL'TER, v. a. To filtrate; to strain; to percolate.
FĬL'TER, n. A strainer for defecating liquors.
FĬLTH, n. Dirt; nastiness; grossness; pollution.
FĬLTH'Į-LY, ad. Nastily; foully; grossly.
FĬLTH'Į-NĔSS, n. Nastiness; foulness; dirtiness.
FĬLTH'Y, a. Nasty; foul; dirty; gross; polluted.
FĬL'TRĀTE, v. a. To strain; to filter.
FĬL-TRĀ'TĮON, n. The act of filtering liquors.
FĬM'BRĮ-ĀTE, v. a. To fringe.
FĬM'BRĮ-ĄTE, a. Fimbriated; fringed.
FĬN, n. Organ of a fish by which it swims.
FĪN'Ą-BLE, a. Admitting a fine; deserving a fine.

FĪ'NAL, a. Ultimate; last; conclusive:—mortal.
FĮ-NÄ'LE, n. (Mus.) The close; the last piece.
FĪ'NAL-LY, ad. Ultimately; lastly; decisively.
FĮ-NĂNCE', n. Income; public revenue.
FĮ-NĂN'CIAL (-shąl), a. Respecting finance.
FĬN-AN-CIĔR', n. One skilled in finance.
FĬN'Ą-RY, n. A sort of forge. See FINERY.
FĬNCH, n. A small bird of three kinds.
FĪND, v. a. [imp. t. & pp. found.] To obtain by
searching; to discover:—to furnish.
FĪND'ER, n. One who finds; a discoverer.
FĪND'ĮNG, n. Discovery:—verdict of a jury.
FĪNE, a. Not coarse; thin; clear; nice; gay.
FĪNE, n. A mulct; amercement; forfeit:—end.
FĪNE, v. a. To refine:—to amerce; to mulct.
FĪNE'DRÂW, v. a. To sew up with great nicety.
FĪNE'LY, ad. Beautifully; elegantly; nicely.
FĪNE'NESS, n. Elegance; beauty; delicacy.
FĪN'ER, n. One who purifies or refines.
FĪN'ER-Y, n. Show; splendor; gayety in dress;
trinkets:—a furnace in iron works.
FĪNE'SPŬN, a. Ingeniously contrived; minute.
FĮ-NĔSSE' (-nĕs'), n. [Fr.] Artifice; stratagem.
FĬN'-FOOT-ED (fĭn'fŭt-ed), a. Web-footed.
FĬN'GER (fĭng'ger), n. A member of the hand.
FĬN'GER, v. a. To touch lightly, handle, pilfer.
FĬN'GERED (fĭng'gerd), a. Having fingers.
FĬN'Į-CAL, a. Nice; foppish; showy; affected.
FĬN'Į-CAL-LY, ad. In a finical manner; showily.
FĬN'Į-CAL-NĔSS, n. Superfluous nicety; foppery.
FĬN'ĮNG-PŎT, n. A vessel for refining metals.
FĪ'NĮS, n. [L.] The end; the conclusion.
FĬN'ĮSH, v. a. To complete; to perfect; to end
FĬN'ĮSH, n. The last touch; last polish; end.
FĬN'ĮSH-ER, n. One who finishes or perfects.
FĬN'ĮSH-ĮNG, n. Completion; the last touch.
FĪ'NĬTE, a. Limited; bounded; not infinite.
FĪ'NĬTE-LY, ad. Only within certain limits.
FĪ'NĬTE-NĔSS, n. Limitation; confinement.
FĬN'NĮ-KĬN, n. A pigeon with a sort of mane.
FĬN'NY, a. Furnished with or having fins.
FĬR, n. A tree of several kinds for timber, &c.
FĪRE, n. The igneous element; flame; ardor.
FĪRE, v. a. To set on fire; to inflame; to ani-
mate; to kindle:—to discharge, as firearms.
FĪRE, v. n. To take fire; to discharge firearms.
FĪRE'ÄRMS, n. pl. Guns, muskets, pistols, &c.
FĪRE'BÂLL, n. A ball filled with combustibles.
FĪRE'BRÄND, n. Wood on fire:—an incendiary.
FĪRE'-ĔN-GĮNE, n. An hydraulic machine for
throwing water to extinguish fire.
FĪRE'LŎCK, n. A flint-lock gun; a musket.
FĪRE'MAN, n. An extinguisher of burning
houses:—a tender of the fire of a furnace, &c.
FĪRE'-ŎF-FĮCE, n. An office of insurance from
FĪRE'PĂN, n. A pan for holding fire. [fire.
FĪRE'PLĀCE, n. A place for fire in a house.
FĪRE'-SHĬP, n. A ship filled with combustible
matter to set fire to an enemy's ships.
FĪRE'-SHŎV-EL (fīr'shŭv-vl), n. An instrument
with which hot ashes and coals are taken up.
FĪRE'SĪDE, n. The hearth; chimney:—home.
FĪRE'-WOOD (fīr'wûd), n. Wood used for fuel.
FĪRE'WORKS (fīr'würks), n. pl. Shows of fire.
FĪR'ĮNG, n. Fuel:—discharge of firearms.
FĬR'KĮN, n. A vessel:—measure of nine gallons.
FĪRM, a. Strong; fast; hard; constant; solid.
FĬRM, n. A partnership carrying on business.

FĬR'Mᴀ-MĔNT, *n.* Region of the air; the heav-
FĬR-Mᴀ-MĔNT'ᴀL, *a.* Celestial; ethereal. [ens.
FĬR'MᴀN, *n.* A license or passport in Turkey, &c.
FĬRM'LY, *ad.* With firmness; strongly.
FĬRM'NᴇSS, *n.* Solidity; stability; steadiness.
FĬRST, *a.* Earliest in time; foremost; chief.
FĬRST, *ad.* Before any thing else; primarily.
FĬRST'-FRŪITS, *n. pl.* First profits of any thing.
FĬRST'LᴵNG, *n.* The first produce or offspring.
FĬRST'-RĀTE, *a.* Preëminent; superior; best.
FĬS'CᴀL, *a.* Belonging to a public treasury.
FĬS'CᴀL, *n.* Public revenue:—a treasurer.
FĬSH, *n.* An animal that inhabits the water.
FĬSH, *v. n. & a.* To catch fish:—to seek by art.
FĬSH'ᴇR, *n.* One employed in catching fish.
FĬSH'ᴇR-MᴀN, *n.* One employed in catching fish.
FĬSH'ᴇR-Y, *n.* The business of fishing:—a place
 where fishes are taken. [with.
FĬSH'HOOK (fĭsh'hûk), *n.* A hook to catch fish
FĬSH'ᴵNG, *n.* The art or practice of fishing.
FĬSH'-MŎN-ᴳᴇR, *n.* A dealer in fish.
FĬSH'-PŎND, *n.* A pond in which fish are kept.
FĬSH'-SPĒAR, *n.* A dart or spear for striking fish.
FĬSH'Y, *a.* Consisting of fish; like fish.
FĬS'SᴵLE, *a.* That may be split or cleft.
FᴵS-SĬL'Ĭ-TY, *n.* Quality of admitting to be cleft.
FĬS'SᴜRE (fĭsh'yᴜr), *n.* A cleft; a narrow chasm.
FĬST, *n.* The hand clinched or closed. [fist.
FĬS'Tᴵ-CŬFFS, *n. pl.* Blows or combat with the
FĬST'ᴜ-Lᴀ, *n.* A sinuous ulcer callous within.
FĬST'ᴜ-Lᴀʀ, *a.* Relating to, or like, a fistula or
 pipe; fistulous; hollow. [fistular.
FĬST'ᴜ-LoŬs, *a.* Having the nature of a fistula;
FĬT, *n.* A paroxysm; convulsion:—interval.
FĬT, *a.* Qualified; proper; convenient; meet.
FĬT, *v. a.* To accommodate; to suit; to adapt.
FĬT'FŬL, *a.* Varied by paroxysms; full of fits.
FĬT'LY, *ad.* Properly; justly; suitably.
FĬT'NᴇSS, *n.* Propriety; meetness; suitableness.
FĬT'TᴇR, *n.* One who, or that which, fits.
FĬTZ, *n.* A son; *used in names,* as *Fitzherbert.*
FĪVE, *a.* Four and one; half of ten.
FĪVE'FŌLD, *a.* Having five times as much.
FĪVᴇꜱ, *n.* A play with a ball:—disease of horses.
FĬX, *v. a. & n.* To make fast or stable; to settle.
FᴵX-Ā'TᴵON, *n.* Act of fixing; stability; firmness.
FĬX'ᴇD-LY, *ad.* Certainly; firmly; steadfastly.
FĬX'ᴇD-NĔSS, *n.* Stability; firmness; solidity.
FĬX'Ĭ-TY, *n.* Coherence of parts; fixedness.
FĬXT'ᴜRE (fĭxt'yᴜr), *n.* A thing fixed to a place.
FĬZ'ᴳᴵG, *n.* A harpoon:—a kind of firework.
FLĂB'BY, *a.* Soft; not firm; shaking.
FLĂB'Bᴵ-NĔSS, *n.* A soft, limber state.
FLĂᴄ'ᴄᴵD, *a.* Weak; limber; not stiff.
FLᴀᴄ-ᴄᴵD'Ĭ-TY, *n.* Laxity; limberness. [vigor.
FLĂG, *v. n.* To grow dejected or feeble; to lose
FLĂG, *v. a.* To let fall; to cover with flat stones.
FLĂG, *n.* A water plant; colors of a ship, &c.
FLĂᴳ'ᴇᴏ-LĔT, *n.* A small wooden wind in-
 strument, played with a mouth-piece.
FLĂG-ᴇL-LĀ'TᴵON, *n.* A whipping or scourging.
FLĂG'ᴳY, *a.* Weak; lax; limber; not tense.
FLᴀ-ᴳĬ''TIOᴜS (-jĭsh'ᴜs), *a.* Wicked; atrocious.
FLᴀ-ᴳĬ''TIOᴜS-NĔSS (-jĭsh'ᴜs-nĕs), *n.* Villany.
FLĂG'-ŎF'FĬ-CᴇR, *n.* Commander of a squadron.
FLĂG'ON, *n.* A sort of drinking vessel.
FLĀ'GRᴀN-CY, *n.* Burning; heat; fire; enormity.
FLĀ'GRᴀNT, *a.* Ardent; burning; notorious.

FLĀ'GRᴀNT-LY, *ad.* Ardently; notoriously.
FLĂG'-SHĬP, *n.* The ship which bears the ad
 miral or commander of a fleet.
FLĂG'STÄFF, *n.* Staff on which a flag is fixed.
FLĂG'-STŌNE, *n.* A flat stone for paving.
FLĀIL, *n.* An instrument for threshing grain.
FLĀKE, *n.* A stratum; layer; film; lamina.
FLĀKE, *v. a. & n.* To form or break into flakes.
FLĀ'KY, *a.* Consisting of flakes or layers.
FLĂM, *n.* A falsehood; a lie; illusory pretext.
FLĂM'BEAU (flăm'bō), *n.;* pl. FLAMBEAUX
 (flăm'bōz). [Fr.] A lighted torch; a flame.
FLĀME, *n.* Fire; blaze; heat; violence.
FLĀME, *v. n.* To shine as fire; to blaze.
FLĀ'MᴇN, *n.* [L.] A priest among the ancients.
FLĂM'ᴵNG, *a.* Brilliant; resplendent; gaudy.
FLᴀ-MĬN'GŌ, *n.;* pl. FLᴀ-MĬN'GŌEꜱ. A bird
 with very long legs and neck, and reddish plu-
FLĂM-Mᴀ-BĬL'Ĭ-TY, *n.* Inflammability. [mage.
FLĂ'MY, *a.* Inflamed; burning; blazing.
FLĂNK, *n.* Part of the side:—part of a bastion.
FLĂNK, *v. a.* To attack the flank:—to secure on
FLĂN'NᴇL, *n.* A soft woollen cloth. [the side.
FLĂP, *n.* A piece that hangs:—a blow.
FLĂP, *v. a. & n.* To beat:—to ply the wings.
FLĂP'DRĂG-ON, *n.* A play with sweetmeats.
FLĂP'-ĒARED (-ērd), *a.* Having pendent ears.
FLĂP'PᴇR, *n.* One who, or that which, flaps.
FLĀRE, *v. n.* To give a glaring or unsteady light.
FLĂSH, *n.* A sudden blaze:—burst, as of wit.
FLĂSH, *v. n.* To burst into flame; to blaze.
FLĂSH, *v. a.* To burst suddenly, as light, &c.
FLĂSH, *a.* Vile; low; as, *flash* language.
FLĂSH'Y, *a.* Showy, but empty; dashing.
FLĂSK, *n.* A bottle; a vessel; a powder-horn.
FLĂS'KᴇT, *n.* A vessel in which viands are
 served:—a sort of long, shallow basket.
FLĂT, *a.* Level; smooth:—insipid:—absolute.
FLĂT, *n.* A level; a plain:—a shoal:—a dunce.
FLĂT'-BŎT-TᴏMED, *a.* Having a flat bottom.
FLĂT'LY, *ad.* In a flat manner; peremptorily.
FLĂT'NᴇSS, *n.* Evenness; insipidity; dulness.
FLĂT'TEN (flăt'tn), *v. a.* To make flat or level.
FLĂT'TEN (flat'tn), *v. n.* To grow even or dull.
FLĂT'TᴇR, *v. a.* To soothe with praises; to
 compliment; to praise falsely:—to encourage.
FLĂT'TᴇR-ᴇR, *n.* One who flatters; a fawner.
FLĂT'TᴇR-ᴵNG, *a.* Artful; obsequious; pleasing.
FLĂT'TᴇR-Y, *n.* False, venal praise; adulation.
FLĂT'ᴜ-LᴇNCE, *n.* Windiness; emptiness.
FLĂT'ᴜ-LᴇNT, *a.* Turgid with air; windy;
 puffed out:—generating air or wind:—vain.
FLĀ'TᴜS, *n.* [L.] Wind; flatulence; a breath.
FLĂUNT (flänt), *v. n.* To make much display.
FLĂUNT, *n.* An ostentatious display or show.
FLĀ'VᴏR, *n.* Relish; taste; odor; fragrance.
FLĀ'VᴏRED (-vᴜrd), *a.* Having a fine taste.
FLĀ'VᴏR-OŬs, *a.* Delightful to the palate.
FLĀW, *n.* A crack; a breach; a fault; a defect.
FLĀW, *v. a.* To break; to crack; to violate.
FLĀW'Y, *a.* Full of flaws or cracks; defective.
FLĂX, *n.* A plant, and its fibres. [flax.
FLĂX'EN (flăk'sn), *a.* Made of flax:—resembling
FLĂX'Y, *a.* Like flax; flaxen; fair. [of.
FLĀY (flā), *v. a.* To skin; to strip off the skin
FLĀY'ᴇR (flā'-), *n.* One who strips off the skin.
FLĒA (flē), *n.* A small blood-sucking insect.
FLĒA'BĪTE (flē'bīt), *n.* The sting of a flea.

FLĒA'BĬT-TEN (flē'bĭt-tn), *a.* Stung or bitten by fleas :—mean ; worthless. [—a grate or hurdle.
FLĒAK (flēk), *n.* A small lock, thread, or twist :
FLĒAM, *n.* An instrument used to bleed horses.
FLĔC'TIQN, *n.* The act or power of bending.
FLĔC'TQR, *n.* A muscle, commonly called *flexor.*
FLĔD, *imp. t. & pp.* from *flee.* [ers.
FLĔDǴE, *v. a.* To furnish with wings or feath-
FLĒĒ, *v. n.* [*imp. t. & pp.* fled.] To run from danger ; to have recourse to shelter.
FLĒĒCE, *n.* The wool shorn from one sheep.
FLĒĒCE, *v. a.* To shear off ; to strip ; to plunder.
FLĒĒ'CĘR, *n.* One who strips or plunders.
FLĒĒ'CY, *a.* Woolly ; resembling a fleece.
FLĒĒR, *v. n.* To mock ; to gibe ; to jest ; to leer.
FLĒĒR, *n.* Mockery ; a deceitful grin ; a gibe.
FLĒĒT, *n.* A company of ships ; a navy.
FLĒĒT, *a.* Swift of pace ; quick ; nimble ; active.
FLĒĒT, *v. a. & n.* To skim the water ; to hasten.
FLĒĒT'LY, *ad.* Swiftly ; nimbly ; with swift pace.
FLĒĒT'NĘSS, *n.* Swiftness ; nimbleness ; celerity.
FLĔM'ISH, *a.* Relating to Flanders, or Flemings.
FLĔSH, *n.* The muscular part of the body :—animal food :—human race :—carnal state.
FLĔSH, *v. a.* To initiate ; to satiate. [tion.
FLĔSH'-CŎL-QR, *n.* The color of flesh ; carna-
FLĔSH'I-NĔSS, *n.* Plumpness ; fulness ; fatness.
FLĔSH'LY, *a.* Carnal ; lascivious ; not spiritual.
FLĔSH'-MĒAT, *n.* Animal food ; flesh of animals used for food. [pimp.
FLĔSH'MŎN-GĘR, *n.* A dealer in flesh :—a
FLĔSH'-PŎT, *n.* A vessel in which flesh is cooked :—diet of flesh :—abundance of flesh.
FLĔSH'Y, *a.* Full of flesh ; fat ; plump.
FLĔTCH'ĘR, *n.* A maker of bows and arrows.
FLEW (flū), *imp. t.* from *fly.*
FLĔX-I-BĬL'I-TY, *n.* Flexibleness ; pliancy.
FLĔX'I-BLE, *a.* That may be bent ; pliant.
FLĔX'I-BLE-NĔSS, *n.* Possibility to be bent.
FLĔX'ILE, *a.* Pliant ; easily bent :—obsequious.
FLĔX'IQN (flĕk'shun), *n.* Act of bending ; turn.
FLĔX'QR, *n.* A muscle which bends a part.
FLĔX'U-OŬS (flĕk'shu-ŭs), *a.* Winding ; bending.
FLĔX'URE (flĕk'shur), *n.* A bending ; a joint.
FLĬCK'ĘR, *v. n.* To waver :—to flap the wings.
FLI'ĘR, *n.* One who flies ; part of a machine.
FLĪGHT (flīt), *n.* Act of flying or fleeing ; escape.
FLĪGHT'I-NĔSS (flī'tę-nĕs), *n.* Flighty state.
FLĪGHT'Y, *a.* Wild ; of disordered imagination.
FLĬM'ŞY, *a.* Weak ; feeble ; mean ; slight.
FLĬNCH, *v. n.* To shrink ; to wince.
FLĬNG, *v. a.* [*imp. t. & pp.* flung.] To cast from the hand ; to throw ; to dart ; to cast with force.
FLĬNG, *v. n.* To flounce ; to wince ; to sneer.
FLĬNG, *n.* A throw ; a cast :—a gibe ; a sneer.
FLĬNT, *n.* A hard stone ; a stone for striking fire.
FLĬNT'Y, *a.* Made of flint :—hard ; cruel.
FLĬP, *n.* Liquor made of beer, spirits, and sugar.
FLĬP'PAN-CY, *n.* Loquacity ; pertness of talk.
FLĬP'PANT, *a.* Talkative ; loquacious ; pert.
FLĬP'PANT-LY, *ad.* In a flippant manner.
FLĬRT, *v. a. & n.* To toss :—to act with levity.
FLĬRT, *n.* Quick motion :—a pert girl ; coquette.
FLIR-TĀ'TIQN, *n.* The act of flirting ; coquetry ; desire or effort to attract notice or attention.
FLĬRT'I-GĬG, *n.* A wanton, pert girl ; coquette.
FLĬT, *v. n.* To fly away ; to remove ; to flutter.
FLĬTCH, *n.* The side of a hog salted and cured.

FLŌAT (flōt), *v. n.* To swim ; to move easily.
FLŌAT (flōt), *v. a.* To cover with water.
FLŌAT, *n.* A body swimming upon the water.
FLŎCK, *n.* A company of birds or sheep :—lock.
FLŎCK, *v. n.* To gather in crowds or companies.
FLŎG, *v. a.* To lash ; to whip ; to beat, chasten.
FLŎG'ĢING, *n.* A whipping ; chastisement.
FLŎOD (flŭd), *n.* The sea ; deluge ; inundation.
FLŎOD (flŭd), *v. a.* To deluge ; to overwhelm.
FLŎOD'GĀTE (flŭd'gāt), *n.* A gate to stop or let out water :—a passage ; an avenue ; vent.
FLŌOR (flōr), *n.* The bottom of a room or building ; a platform ; a story in a building.
FLŌOR (flōr), *v. a.* To lay with a floor.
FLŌOR'ING, *n.* Bottom ; materials for floors.
FLŎP, *v. a.* To clap the wings with noise.
FLŌ'RA, *n.* The botany, or various kinds of plants and trees, belonging to a country.
FLŌ'RAL, *a.* Relating to or consisting of flowers.
FLŎR'ĘN-TĪNE, *n.* A sort of silk.
FLŌ'RĘT, *n.* A diminutive flower. [red.
FLŎR'ID, *a.* Abounding in flowers ; flushed with
FLQ-RĬD'I-TY, *n.* Freshness of color ; floridness.
FLŎR'ID-LY, *ad.* In a florid manner ; showily.
FLŎR'ID-NĔSS, *n.* Freshness of color ; floridity.
FLQ-RĬF'ĘR-OŬS, *a.* Productive of flowers.
FLŎR'IN, *n.* A coin first made at Florence.
FLŌ'RIST, *n.* Cultivator of flowers.
FLŎS'CU-LOŬS, *a.* Composed of many florets.
FLŌT'AĢE, *n.* That which floats on water.
FLQ-TĬL'LA, *n.* A number of small vessels.
FLŎŬNCE, *n.* A sudden jerk or throw :—a frill or ruffle on a gown, and hanging loose.
FLŎŬNCE, *v. n. & a.* To move with violence ; to be uneasy :—to trim with flounces.
FLŎŬN'DĘR, *n.* A small, flat sea-fish.
FLŎŬN'DĘR, *v. n.* To struggle or move with violent and irregular motions. [meal.
FLŎŬR, *n.* The edible part of wheat, &c. :—
FLOUR'ISH (flŭr'-), *v. n.* To prosper ; to thrive.
FLOUR'ISH (flŭr'-), *v. a.* To adorn :—to brandish.
FLOUR'ISH (flŭr'-), *n.* A parade of words :— embellishment :—a musical prelude :—grace.
FLŎŬT, *v. a. & n.* To mock ; to insult ; to sneer.
FLŎŬT, *n.* A mock ; an insult ; a sneer ; a taunt.
FLŌW (flō), *v. n.* To run as water, melt, issue.
FLŌW (flō), *v. a.* To overflow ; to deluge.
FLŌW (flō), *n.* The rise of water :—fluency.
FLŌW'ĘR (flŏŭ'ęr), *n.* The blossom of a plant : —an ornament :—the most excellent part.
FLŌW'ĘR, *v. n.* To be in flower ; to bloom, blos-
FLŌW'ĘR, *v. a.* To adorn with flowers. [som.
FLŌW'ĘR-DĘ-LŪCE', *n.* A plant ; yellow flag.
FLŌW'ĘR-ĘT, *n.* A diminutive flower ; a floret.
FLŌW'ĘR-I-NĔSS, *n.* Floridness, as of speech.
FLŌW'ĘR-Y, *a.* Adorned with, or full of, flowers.
FLŌWN (flōn), *pp.* from *fly.* Gone away.
FLŪ'ATE, *n.* (*Chem.*) A kind of salt.
FLŬCT'U-ĀTE, *v. n.* To wave ; to be wavering.
FLŬCT-U-Ā'TIQN, *n.* The act of fluctuating ; alternate motion :—uncertainty ; doubt.
FLŪE (flū), *n.* Pipe of a chimney ; down or fur.
FLŪ'ĘN-CY, *n.* Flowing speech ; copiousness.
FLŪ'ĘNT, *a.* Liquid ; flowing ; copious ; voluble.
FLŪ'ĘNT-LY, *ad.* With ready flow ; volubly.
FLŪ'ID, *a.* Running as water ; not solid ; liquid.
FLŪ'ID, *n.* Any thing not solid ; a liquid ; juice.
FLU-ĬD'I-TY, *n.* The quality of flowing readily.

FLŪ′ĬD-NĔSS, *n.* The quality of being fluid.
FLŪKE, *n.* The broad part or arm of an anchor.
FLŪME, *n.* A channel for water of a mill.
FLŬM′MER-Y, *n.* Food made of flour, &c :—
FLŬNG, *imp. t. & pp.* from *fling.* [flattery.
FLŪ′ŎR, *n.* A fluid state :—fluate of lime.
FLŬR′RY, *n.* A gust or storm of wind :—bustle.
FLŬR′RY, *v. a.* To keep in agitation :—to alarm.
FLŬSH, *v. n.* To flow suddenly; to start; to glow.
FLŬSH, *v. a.* To color; to redden; to elate.
FLŬSH, *a.* Fresh; glowing; affluent; conceited.
FLŬSH, *n.* Flow; bloom; growth; abundance.
FLŬS′TER, *v. a.* To confound, heat, make rosy.
FLŬS′TER, *n.* Sudden impulse; agitation; bustle.
FLŬS′TERED (flŭs′tẹrd), *a.* Agitated; confused.
FLŪTE, *n.* A musical pipe:—channel in a pillar.
FLŪTE, *v. n. & a.* To play on a flute, cut hollows.
FLŬT′TER, *v. n.* To fly or move quickly.
FLŬT′TER, *v. a.* To drive in disorder; to agitate.
FLŬT′TER, *n.* Hurry; quick motion; confusion.
FLŪ-VĬ-ĂT′ĬC, *a.* Belonging to a river or rivers.
FLŬX, *n.* Act of flowing; dysentery; fusion.
FLŬX′ĬON (flŭk′shụn), *n.* The act of flowing:—
  an infinitely small, variable quantity.
FLȲ, *v. n.* [*imp. t.* flew; *pp.* flown.] To move
  with wings; to pass swiftly; to run away.
FLȲ, *v. a.* To shun; to quit:—to cause to fly.
FLȲ, *n.* A small winged insect :—balance of a
  jack, &c. :—part of a vane:—part of a flag.
FLȲ′BLŌW (flī′blō), *n.* The egg of a fly.
FLȲ′BLŌW, *v. a.* To taint with the eggs of flies.
FLȲ′FĬSH, *v. n.* To angle by baiting with a fly.
FŌAL (fōl), *n.* Offspring of a mare or she-ass.
FŌAL (fōl), *v. n.* To bring forth a foal or colt.
FŌAM (fōm), *n.* Froth; spume; bubbles.
FŌAM, *v. n.* To froth; to gather foam; to rage.
FŌAM′Y (fō′mẹ), *a.* Covered with foam; frothy.
FŎB, *n.* A small pocket for a watch :—a tap.
FŌ′CĂL, *a.* Belonging to the focus.
FŌ′CŲS, *n. ; pl.* FŌ′CĪ. [L.] (*Opt.*) The point
  where rays are collected by a lens or mirror.
FŎD′DER, *n.* Dry food stored up for cattle.
FŎD′DER, *v. a.* To feed with dry food.
FŌE (fō), *n.* An enemy; adversary; persecutor.
FŌE′MAN (fō′mạn), *n.* An enemy in war.
FŒ′TŲS (fē′tụs), *n.* [L.] A child in the womb.
FŎG, *n.* Thick mist; moist vapor :—aftergrass.
FŎG′GĬ-NĔSS, *n.* The state of being foggy.
FŎG′GY, *a.* Filled with fog; misty.
FŌ′GY, *n.* A dull man :—person averse to change.
FŎH, *interj.* Expressing contempt or abhorrence.
FŎÏ′BLE, *n.* A weakness; a failing; a fault.
FŎÏL, *v. a.* To defeat; to blunt; to dull, puzzle.
FŎÏL, *n.* A defeat :—leaf; gilding :—a blunt
  sword :—a coat of tin on a looking-glass.
FŎÏST, *v. a.* To insert wrongfully, interpolate.
FŌLD, *n.* A pen for sheep:—a plait, or double.
FŌLD, *v. a.* To shut in a fold :—to double.
FŌLD, *v. n.* To close over another of the same
FŌLD′ER, *n.* One that folds any thing. [kind.
FŌ-LĬ-Ā′CEOŲS (fō-lẹ-ā′shụs), *a.* Leafy.
FŌ′LĬ-AĠE, *n.* Leaves; tufts or cluster of leaves.
FŌ′LĬ-ĀTE, *v. a.* To beat into plates or leaves.
FŌ-LĬ-Ā′TIŌN, *n.* Act of beating into leaves.
FŌ′LĬ-Ō *or* FŎL′ĬŌ, *n. ; pl.* FŌ′LĬ-ŌS *or* FŎL′ĬŌS.
  A leaf or page :—book of two leaves to a sheet.
FŌLK (fōk) ; *modern,* FŌLKS (fōks), *n. pl.* People.
FŎL′LĬ-CLE (fŏl′lẹ-kl), *n.* A little bag or cyst.

FŎL′LŌW, *v. a.* To go after, pursue, imitate.
FŎL′LŌW, *v. n.* To be posterior; to result.
FŎL′LŌW-ER, *n.* One who follows; a disciple.
FŎL′LY, *n.* Foolishness; weakness; depravity.
FỌ-MĔNT′, *v. a.* To cherish with heat; to excite.
FŌ-MẸN-TĀ′TIŌN, *n.* Act of fomenting.
FỌ-MĔNT′ER, *n.* One who foments; encourager.
FŎND, *a.* Indulgent; weakly tender; doting.
FŎN′DLE, *v. a.* To treat with fondness; to caress.
FŎN′DLĬNG, *n.* A person or thing much fondled.
FŎND′LY, *ad.* Dotingly; with extreme tenderness.
FŎND′NĔSS, *n.* Foolish tenderness; affection.
FŎNT, *n.* A baptismal vessel :—a set of types.
FŌÔD, *n.* Victuals; any thing that nourishes.
FŌÔL, *n.* An idiot; a changeling; a buffoon.
FŌÔL, *v. n.* To trifle; to toy; to play; to idle.
FŌÔL′ER-Y, *n.* Habitual folly; an act of folly.
FŌÔL′HÄR-DĬ-NĔSS, *n.* Courage without sense.
FŌÔL′HÄR-DY, *a.* Madly adventurous.
FŌÔL′ĬSH, *a.* Void of understanding; indiscreet.
FŌÔL′ĬSH-LY, *ad.* Without understanding.
FŌÔL′ĬSH-NĔSS, *n.* Folly; foolish practice.
FŌÔLS′CĂP, *n.* A kind of paper of small size.
FOOT (fût), *n. ; pl.* FĒĒT. The part upon which
  an animal or thing stands :—twelve inches.
FOOT (fût), *v. n.* To dance; to trip; to walk.
FOOT′BĂLL (fût′-), *n.* A ball driven by the foot.
FOOT′BŎŸ (fût′bŏÿ), *n.* A menial; a runner.
FOOT′-GUÄRDS (fût′gärdz), *n. pl.* Foot soldiers.
FOOT′HŌLD (fût′hōld), *n.* Place for the foot.
FOOT′ĬNG (fût′ĭng), *n.* Ground for the foot :—
  support; foundation; state; condition.
FOOT′MAN (fût′mạn), *n.* A menial servant.
FOOT′-PĀCE (fût′pās), *n.* A slow pace; footstep.
FOOT′PĂD (fût′păd), *n.* A highwayman on foot.
FOOT′-PĂTH, *n.* A way for foot-passengers.
FOOT′-PŌST (fût′-), *n.* A post travelling on foot.
FOOT′-SŌL-DIER (fût′sōl-jẹr), *n.* Soldier on foot.
FOOT′STĔP (fût′stĕp), *n.* A mark of the foot.
FOOT′STÔÔL (fût′stôl), *n.* A stool for the feet.
FŎP, *n.* A beau; a dandy; a coxcomb.
FŎP′PER-Y, *n.* Coxcombry; showy folly.
FŎP′PĬSH, *a.* Vain in show; ostentatious.
FŎP′PĬSH-NĔSS, *n.* Showy or ostentatious vanity.
FŎR, *prep.* Because of :—with respect to; with
  regard to :—in place of; for the sake of.
FŎR, *conj.* Because; on this account that.
FŎR′AĠE, *n.* Food for horses and cattle.
FŎR′AĠE, *v. n.* To wander in search of forage.
FŎR-ĂS-MŬCH′, *conj.* In regard that; in con-
  sideration of; because that; inasmuch.
FỌR-BEÄR′ (fọr-bár′), *v. n.* [*imp. t.* forbore; *pp.*
  forborne.] To cease; to pause; to abstain.
FỌR-BEÄR′, *v. a.* To decline; to avoid; to omit.
FỌR-BEÄR′ANCE, *n.* Command of temper; lenity.
FỌR-BĬD′, *v. a.* [*imp. t.* forbade, forbid ; *pp.* for-
  bidden (fọr-bĭd′dn)]. To prohibit; to interdict.
FỌR-BĬD′DĬNG, *p. a.* Causing aversion; austere.
FỌR-BŌRNE′, *pp.* from *forbear.* [efficacy.
FŌRCE, *n.* Strength; vigor; power; might;
FŌRCE, *v. a.* To compel, press, urge, ravish.
FŌRCE′FŬL, *a.* Violent; strong; impetuous.
FŎR′CEPS, *n.* A surgical instrument; pincers.
FŌR′CER, *n.* He who, or that which, forces.
FŌR′CĬ-BLE, *a.* Strong; mighty; violent; valid.
FŌR′CĬ-BLY, *ad.* Strongly; powerfully; by force.
FŌRD, *n.* A shallow part of a river :—current.
FŌRD, *v. a.* To wade across or through.

FŌRD′A-BLE, *a.* That may be forded.
FŌRE, *a.* Anterior; not behind; coming first.
FŌRE, *ad.* Anteriorly; in the fore part.
FŌRE-ÄRM′, *v. a.* To arm beforehand.
FŌRE-BŌDE′, *v. n.* To prognosticate; to foretell.
FŌRE-CĂST′, *v. n.* To form schemes; to contrive.
FŌRE′CĂST, *n.* Contrivance beforehand; fore-
　sight; plan. 　　　　[sel before the foremast.
FŌRE′CĂS-TLE (fōr′kăs-sl), *n.* A part of a ves-
FŌRE-CLŌSE′, *v. a.* To shut up; to preclude.
FŌRE′DĔCK, *n.* Anterior part of a ship's deck.
FŌRE-DŌŌM′, *v. a.* To doom beforehand; to
　predetermine; to predestine; to foreordain.
FŌRE′ĔND, *n.* The anterior part; fore part.
FŌRE′FÄ-THER, *n.* An ancestor; a progenitor.
FŌRE-FĔND′, *v. a.* To prohibit; to avert.
FŌRE′-FĬN-GER, *n.* The finger next the thumb.
FŌRE′FOOT (fōr′fŭt), *n.* The anterior foot.
FŌRE-GŌ′, *v. d.* To quit; to resign. 　[figures.
FŌRE′GRŎŬND, *n.* Part of a picture before the
FŌRE′HĂND-ED, *a.* Early; timely; prosperous.
FŌREHEAD (fŏr′rĕd *or* fŏr′hĕd), *n.* The upper
　part of the face:—impudence; confidence.
FŎR′EIGN (fŏr′rin), *a.* Not of this country;
　alien; remote:—not to the point or purpose.
FŎR′EIGN-ER (fŏr′rin-er), *n.* One from another
　country; not a native; a stranger; an alien.
FŎR′EIGN-NĔSS (fŏr′rin-nĕs), *n.* Remoteness.
FŌRE-JŬDGE′, *v. a.* To prejudge. 　[to foresee.
FŌRE-KNŌW′ (-nō′), *v. a.* To know beforehand;
FŌRE-KNŎWL′EDGE (fōr-nŏl′ej), *n.* Prescience;
　knowledge of what has not yet happened.
FŌRE′LĂND, *n.* A promontory; a cape.
FŌRE-LĀY′, *v. a.* To lay wait for; to entrap.
FŌRE′LŎCK, *n.* Lock of hair on the forehead.
FŌRE′MAN, *n.* The chief person:—overseer.
FŌRE′MĂST, *n.* The forward mast of a ship.
FŌRE′MŌST, *a.* First in place, time, or dignity.
FŌRE′NĀMED (fōr′nāmd), *a.* Named before.
FŌRE′NŌŌN, *n.* The time from dawn to midday.
FŎ-RĔN′SĬC, *a.* Belonging to courts of law.
FŌRE-OR-DĀIN′, *v. a.* To ordain beforehand.
FŌRE′PÄRT, *n.* The anterior or previous part.
FŌRE′RĂNK, *n.* The first rank; the front; van.
FŌRE-RŬN′, *v. a.* To come before; to precede.
FŌRE-RŬN′NER, *n.* A harbinger; a predecessor.
FŌRE′SAID (fōr′sĕd), *p. a.* Spoken of before.
FŌRE′SAIL, *n.* The lower sail of the foremast.
FŌRE-SĒE′, *v.d.* To see beforehand; to foreknow.
FŌRE-SHŌW′, *v. a.* To show before it happens.
FŌRE′SIGHT (fōr′sīt), *n.* Foreknowledge.
FŎR′ĔST, *n.* A tract of land covered with trees.
FŌRE-STĂLL′, *v. a.* To anticipate:—to buy up.
FŎRE-STĂLL′ER, *n.* One who forestalls.
FŎR′ĔST-ER, *n.* A keeper, or inhabitant, of a
　forest:—a tree growing in a forest. 　[pate.
FŌRE-TĀSTE′, *v. a.* To taste before; to antici-
FŌRE′TĀSTE, *n.* Taste beforehand; anticipation.
FŌRE-TĔLL′, *v. a.* [*imp. t. & pp.* foretold.] To
FŌRE-TĔLL′ER, *n.* One who foretells. [predict.
FŌRE′THOUGHT (fōr′thawt), *n.* Provident care.
FŌRE-TŌ′KEN (fōr-tō′kn), *v. a.* To foreshow.
FŌRE′TŎP, *n.* The upper part in front.
FŎR-ĔV′ER, *ad.* Eternally; without end.
FŌRE-WÄRN′, *v. a.* To admonish beforehand.
FŎR′FEIT (fŏr′fit), *n.* A fine; forfeiture; mulct.
FŎR′FEIT (fŏr′fit), *v. a.* To lose by offence.
FŎR′FEIT-A-BLE (fŏr′fit-), *a.* That may be lost.

FŎR′FEIT-ŪRE (fŏr′fit-yūr), *n.* The act of for-
　feiting:—the thing forfeited; a mulct; a fine.
FOR-GĀVE′, *imp. t.* from *forgive.* 　　[smithy.
FŌRGE, *n.* A place where iron is worked; a
FŌRGE, *v. a.* To form; to beat:—to counterfeit.
FŌR′GER, *n.* One who forges or forms. 　[ing.
FŌRG′ER-Y, *n.* The act of forging or counterfeit-
FOR-GĔT′, *v. a.* [*imp. t.* forgot; *pp.* forgotten,
　forgot.] To lose the memory of; to disregard.
FOR-GĔT′FŬL, *a.* Apt to forget; heedless.
FOR-GĔT′FŬL-NĔSS, *n.* Loss of memory; fail-
　ure to remember:—remission; neglect.
FOR-GĪVE′, *v. a.* [*imp. t.* forgave; *pp.* forgiven.]
　To pardon; not to punish; to absolve.
FOR-GĪVE′NĔSS, *n.* The act of forgiving; par-
FOR-GŎT′, *imp. t. & pp.* from *forget.* 　　[don.
FOR-GŎT′TEN (for-gŏt′tn), *pp.* from *forget.*
FŌRK, *n.* An instrument with prongs:—branch.
FŌRK, *v. n.* To shoot into blades:—to divide.
FŌRK′ED, *a.* Opening into two or more parts.
FŌRK′Y, *a.* Forked; opening into parts.
FOR-LŌRN′, *a.* Forsaken; helpless; destitute.
FOR-LŌRN′NĔSS, *n.* Destitution; misery.
FŌRM, *n.* Shape; figure; beauty; order; show.
FŌRM *or* FŎRM, *n.* A long seat:—a class.
FŌRM, *v. a.* To fashion, model, plan, arrange.
FŌR′MAL, *a.* Ceremonious; precise; external.
FŌR′MAL-ĬST, *n.* An observer of forms. 　[der.
FOR-MĂL′I-TY, *n.* Ceremony; preciseness; or-
FŌR′MAL-LY, *ad.* In a formal manner.
FOR-MĀ′TION, *n.* The act of forming; creation.
FŌR′MA-TĬVE, *a.* Giving form; plastic.
FŌR′MER, *n.* One who forms; maker; author.
FŌR′MER, *a.* Before in time; preceding; past.
FŌR′MER-LY, *ad.* In times past; of old.
FŌR′MI-DA-BLE, *a.* Terrible; dreadful; terrific.
FŌR′MI-DA-BLE-NĔSS, *n.* Dreadfulness.
FŌR′MI-DA-BLY, *ad.* In a terrible manner.
FŌRM′LESS, *a.* Shapeless; having no form.
FŌR′MU-LA, *n.* ; *pl.* FŌR′MU-LÆ. [L.] A form;
　a ritual; a rule:—algebraic expression. [forms.
FŌR′MU-LA-RY, *n.* A book containing stated
FŌR′MU-LA-RY, *a.* Ritual; prescribed; stated.
FŌR-NI-CĀ′TION, *n.* Incontinence or lewdness.
FOR-RĀY′ *or* FŌR′RAY, *n.* An act of ravaging
　or pillaging; hostile incursion; invasion.
FOR-SĀKE′, *v. n.* [*imp. t.* forsook; *pp.* forsak-
　en.] To leave; to quit; to desert; to neglect.
FOR-SĀ′KEN (for-sā′kn), *pp.* from *forsake.*
FOR-SOOK′ (for-sŭk′), *imp. t.* from *forsake.*
FOR-SŌŌTH′, *ad.* In truth; indeed; certainly.
FOR-SWEAR′ (for-swâr′), *v. a.* [*imp. t.* forswore;
　pp. forsworn.] To deny upon oath; to abjure.
FOR-SWEAR′ (-swâr), *v. n.* To swear falsely.
FŌRT, *n.* A fortified post; a castle; a fortress.
FŌRTE, *n.* That in which one excels; a strong
FŌRTH, *ad.* Forward; abroad; out. 　　[side.
FŌRTH-CŎM′ING, *a.* Ready or about to appear.
FŌRTH-WĬTH′, *ad.* Immediately; without delay.
FŌR′TI-ĔTH, *a.* Ordinal of forty; fourth tenth:
　—noting one of forty equal parts of a thing.
FŌR-TI-FI-CĀ′TION, *n.* The act or the science
　of fortifying:—fortified place; a fort.
FŌR′TI-FY, *v. a.* To strengthen; to make strong.
FŌR′TI-TŪDE, *n.* Courage; strength to endure.
FŌRT′NĬGHT (fōrt′nīt *or* fōrt′nit), *n.* Two weeks.
FŌR′TRESS, *n.* A stronghold; a fortified place.
FOR-TŪ′I-TOŬS, *a.* Accidental; casual.

FŎR-TŪ'Ĭ-TOŬS-LY, *ad.* Accidentally ; casually.
FŎR-TŪ'Ĭ-TOŬS-NĔSS, *n.* Accident ; chance.
FŎRT'Ụ-NĄTE, *a.* Lucky ; happy ; successful.
FŎRT'Ụ-NĄTE-LY, *ad.* Happily ; successfully.
FŎRT'Ụ-NĄTE-NĔSS, *n.* Good luck ; success.
‖FŎRT'ỤNE (fŏrt'yụn), *n.* The good or ill that befalls man ; chance ; hap :—estate ; riches.
‖FŎRT'ỤNE-HŬNT'ẸR, *n.* One who seeks to marry a woman with a fortune or portion.
‖FŎRT'ỤNE-TĔLL'ẸR, *n.* A teller of fortunes.
FŎR'TY, *a.* Four times ten, or five times eight.
FŌ'RỤM, *n.* [L.] Roman market-place, in which discussions and courts were held :—a court.
FŎR'WĄRD, *ad.* Onward ; progressively. [rior.
FŎR'WĄRD, *a.* Warm :—bold :— early :—ante-
FŎR'WĄRD, *v. a.* To hasten ; to quicken :—to promote ; to further, help :—to send, transmit.
FŎR'WĄRD-NĔSS, *n.* Eagerness :—earliness.
FŎSSE, *n.* A ditch ; a moat ; an intrenchment.
FŎS'SĬL, *n.* A substance dug out of the earth.
FŎS'SĬL, *a.* Dug out of the earth, as shells.
FŎS'SĬL-ĬST, *n.* One who is versed in fossils.
FŎS'TẸR, *v. a.* To nurse ; to feed ; to support ; to rear :—to cherish ; to encourage. [breast.
FŎS'TẸR-BRŎTH-ẸR, *n.* One fed at the same
FŎS'TẸR-CHĬLD, *n.* A child nursed or bred by one who is not its mother or father.
FŎS'TẸR-FÄ-ŦHẸR, *n.* One who brings up another man's child. [of a foster-child.
FŎS'TẸR-MŎŦH-ẸR, FŎS'TẸR-DĂM, *n.* Nurse
FŎS'TẸR-SŎN, *n.* One fed and educated as a son.
FŎŦH'ẸR, *n.* A weight or load of lead.
FOUGHT (fàwt), *imp. t. & pp.* from *fight.*
FŎŬL, *a.* Not clean ; not clear ; not fair ; filthy ; dirty :—hateful ; ugly ; coarse ; gross.
FŎŬL, *v. a.* To daub ; to bemire ; to make filthy.
FŎŬL'LY, *ad.* Filthily ; odiously :—not fairly.
FŎŬL'MŎŬŦHED (fŏûl'mŏûthd), *a.* Scurrilous.
FŎŬL'NĔSS, *n.* Filthiness ; impurity ; ugliness.
FŎŬL'SPŌ-KEN (fŏûl'spō-kn), *a.* Contumelious.
FŎŬND, *imp. t. & pp.* from *find.* [cast.
FŎŬND, *v. a.* To lay ; to build ; to establish ; to
FŎŬN-DĂ'TIỌN, *n.* The basis of an edifice :— first principles or grounds; rise ; establishment.
FŎŬND'ẸR, *n.* One who founds ; a builder.
FŎŬN'DẸR, *v. a.* To cause great soreness, &c.
FŎŬN'DẸR, *v. n.* To sink to the bottom ; to fail.
FŎŬN'DẸR-Y, *n.* A casting-house ; place where founding is carried on :—art of casting.
FŎŬND'LĬNG, *n.* A child abandoned by its par-
FŎŬN'DRĔSS, *n.* A woman that founds. [ents.
FŎŬNT, FŎŬN'TAĬN, *n.* A well ; a spring :—a jet ; a spout of water :—first principles ; source.
FŌUR (fōr), *a.* Twice two.
FŌUR'FŌLD (fōr'fōld), *a.* Four times told.
FŌUR'FOOT-ẸD (fōr'fût-ẹd), *a.* Having four feet.
FŌUR'SCŌRE, *a.* Four times twenty ; eighty.
FŌUR'SQUÁRE (fōr'skwÁr), *a.* Quadrangular.
FŌUR'TĒEN (fōr'tēn), *a.* Four and ten.
FŌUR'TĒENTH, *a.* The ordinal of fourteen.
FŌURTH (fōrth), *a.* The ordinal of four.
FŌURTH'LY (fōrth'lẹ), *ad.* In the fourth place.
FŎŴL, *n.* A winged animal ; a bird.
FŎŴL, *v. n.* To kill birds for food or game.
FŎŴL'ẸR, *n.* A sportsman who pursues birds.
FŎŴL'ĬNG, *n.* The act of fowling ; falconry.
FŎŴL'ĬNG-PIĒCE, *n.* A gun for shooting birds.
FŎX, *n.* An animal remarkable for cunning.

FŎX'CHĀSE, *n.* Pursuit of the fox with hounds.
FŎX'GLŎVE (fŏks'glŭv), *n.* A plant ; *Digitalis.*
FŎX'HŎŬND, *n.* A hound for chasing foxes.
FŎX'HŬNT-ẸR, *n.* One who hunts foxes.
FŎX'TĀIL, *n.* A genus of grass of several species.
FŎX'TRĂP, *n.* A trap or snare to catch foxes.
FRĀ'CĄS, *n.* A noisy quarrel ; a disturbance.
FRĂC'TIỌN, *n.* A breaking :—part of an integer.
FRĂC'TIỌN-ĄL, *a.* Belonging to a broken num-
FRĂC'TIOỤS (fräk'shụs), *a.* Cross ; peevish.[ber.
FRĂCT'ỤRE (fräkt'yụr), *n.* A breach ; a rupture.
FRĂCT'ỤRE (fräkt'yụr), *v. a.* To break, as a bone.
FRĂG'ĬLE, *a.* Brittle ; easily broken :—weak.
FRĄ-GĬL'Ĭ-TY, *n.* Brittleness ; weakness ; frailty.
FRĂG'MẸNT, *n.* A part broken off ; a piece.
FRĂG'MẸN-TĄ-RY, *a.* Composed of fragments.
FRĀ'GỌR, *n.* A noise ; a crack ; a crash.
FRĀ'GRANCE, *n.* Sweetness of smell ; grateful
FRĀ'GRĄNT, *a.* Odorous ; sweet of smell. [odor.
FRĀIL, *a.* Weak ; infirm ; feeble :—liable to err.
FRĀIL'NĔSS, *n.* Weakness ; instability. [tion.
FRĀIL'TY, *n.* Weakness ; infirmity ; irresolu-
FRĀME, *v. a.* To form, make, compose, plan.
FRĀME, *n.* A fabric ; a structure composed of timbers or parts united :—order ; form.
FRĂNC, *n.* A French coin, value about 20 cents.
FRĂN'CHĬSE, *n.* Privilege ; immunity ; right.
FRĂN'CHĬSE, *v. a.* To enfranchise ; to free.
FRĂN'CHĬSE-MĔNT, *n.* Release ; freedom.
FRĂN-GĬ-BĬL'Ĭ-TY, *n.* State of being frangible.
FRĂN'GĬ-BLE, *a.* Fragile ; brittle ; easily broken.
FRĂNK, *a.* Liberal ; open ; ingenuous ; candid.
FRĂNK, *n.* A free letter :—a coin. See FRANC.
FRĂNK, *v. a.* To exempt from postage, as letters.
FRĂNK'ĬN-CĔNSE, *n.* An odoriferous resin.
FRĂNK'LĬN, *n.* A freeholder.
FRĂNK'LY, *ad.* Liberally ; freely ; openly ; readily.
FRĂNK'NĔSS, *n.* Openness ; liberality ; candor.
FRĂNK'PLĔDĢE, *n.* Pledge or surety for free-
men :—a decennary or tithing. [geous.
FRĂN'TĬC, *a.* Mad ; raving ; furious ; outra-
FRĂN'TĬC-LY, *ad.* In a frantic manner ; madly.
FRĂN'TĬC-NĔSS, *n.* Madness ; fury ; distraction.
FRĄ-TĔR'NĄL, *a.* Brotherly ; becoming brothers.
FRĄ-TĔR'NĄL-LY, *ad.* In a brotherly manner.
FRĄ-TĔR'NĬ-TY, *n.* A society ; a brotherhood.
FRĄ-TĔR'NĪZE, *v. n.* To agree, as brothers.
FRĂT'RĬ-CĪDE, *n.* The murder of a brother.
FRÂUD, *n.* Deceit ; a cheat ; a trick ; artifice.
FRÂUD'FŬL, *a.* Treacherous ; artful ; trickish.
FRÂUD'Ụ-LĔNCE, *n.* Deceitfulness ; trickery.
FRÂUD'Ụ-LĔNT, *a.* Full of artifice ; treacher-
ous ; deceitful ; fallacious ; trickish.
FRÂUD'Ụ-LĔNT-LY, *ad.* By fraud ; by artifice.
FRÂUGHT (frâwt), *pp.* from *freight.* Laden.
FRĀY, *n.* A battle ; a fight ; a quarrel ; a riot.
FRĒAK, *n.* A sudden fancy ; a humor ; a whim.
FRĒAK (frēk), *v. a.* To variegate ; to checker.
FRĒAK'ĬSH, *a.* Capricious ; whimsical.
FRĔC'KLE (frĕk'kl), *n.* A spot on the skin.
FRĔC'KLE (frĕk'kl), *a.* Spotted ; maculated.
FRĔC'KLY (frĕk'klẹ), *a.* Full of freckles.
FRĒE, *a.* Being at liberty ; not enslaved ; open ; ingenuous ; frank ; liberal :—innocent.
FRĒE, *v. a.* To set at liberty ; to rescue ; to clear.
FRĒE'BŎŎT-ẸR, *n.* A robber ; a pillager.
FRĒE'BŎRN, *a.* Not a slave ; inheriting liberty.
FRĒE'CŎST, *n.* Freedom from expense.

Ā,Ē,Ī,Ō,Ū,Ȳ, *long* ; Ă,Ĕ,Ĭ,Ŏ,Ŭ,Ў, *short* ; Ą,Ẹ,Ị,Ọ,Ụ,Y, *obscure.*—FÀRE,FÄR, FĂST,FÂLL ; HÊIR,HĔR ;

FRĒĒD'MĂN, *n.* A man freed from servitude.
FRĒĒ'DǪM, *n.* Liberty ; privileges ; license.
FRĒĒ'-HEÄRT'ĘD (-härt'ĕd), *a.* Open ;' liberal.
FRĒĒ'HŌLD, *n.* An estate held in free tenure.
FRĒĒ'HŌLD-ĘR, *n.* One who has a freehold.
FRĒĒ'LY, *ad.* With freedom ; frankly ; liberal-
FRĒĒ'MĂN, *n.* One who enjoys freedom. [ly.
FRĒĒ'-MĀ-SON (frē'mā-sn), *n.* One of the
  secret fraternity of masons. See MASON.
FRĒĒ'NĘSS, *n.* The state of being free ; liberty ;
  freedom ; openness ; candor. [pay.
FRĒĒ'-SǪHÔÔL, *n.* A school attended without
FRĒĒ'STŌNE, *n.* Sandstone used in building.
FRĒĒ'-THĬNK-ĘR, *n.* An unbeliever ; a sceptic.
FRĒĒ-WĬLL', *n.* Power of acting at pleasure.
FRĒĒZE, *v. n. & a.* [*imp. t.* froze ; *pp.* frozen.]
  To be congealed by cold ; to congeal by cold.
FREIGHT (frāt), *v. a.* [*imp. t.* freighted ; *pp.*
  fraught, freighted.] To load, as a ship, &c.
FREIGHT (frāt), *n.* The cargo or lading of a
  ship :—money due for transportation of goods.
FRĔNCH, *n.* The people and language of France.
FRĔNCH, *a.* Belonging to the French or France.
FRĔNCH'-HÖRN, *n.* A wind instrument.
FRĔNCH'Ǐ-FȲ, *v. a.* To make or render French.
FRĘ-NĔT'ǏC, *a.* Mad ; distracted ; frantic.
FRĘN'ZY, *n.* Madness ; distraction of mind.
FRĒ'QUĘN-CY, *n.* Occurrence often repeated.
FRĒ'QUĘNT, *a.* Often done, seen, or occurring.
FRĘ-QUĔNT', *v. a.* To visit often ; to resort to.
FRĘ-QUĘN-TĀ'TIǪN, *n.* Resort ; act of visiting.
FRĘ-QUĔNT'Ą-TĪVE, *a.* (*Gram.*) Denoting rep-
FRĘ-QUĔNT'ĘR, *n.* One who frequents. [etition.
FRĒ'QUĘNT-LY, *ad.* Often ; sometimes.
FRĔS'CŌ, *n.* [It.] Painting on fresh plaster.
FRĔSH, *a.* Cool ; not salt :—new :—ruddy.
FRĔSH'EN (frĕsh'shn), *v. a. & n.* To make or
  grow fresh ; to refresh :—to increase, as wind.
FRĔSH'ĘT, *n.* A flood of water or inundation
  caused by rains or melting snow. [ruddily.
FRĔSH'LY, *ad.* Coolly :—newly ; recently :—
FRĔSH'MĂN, *n.* A student of the first year.
FRĔSH'NĘSS, *n.* The being fresh ; newness.
FRĔT, *n.* Agitation of liquors :—irritation.
FRĔT, *v. a.* To vex :—to corrode ; to variegate.
FRĔT, *v. n.* To be irritated :—to be corroded.
FRĔT'FÛL, *a.* Angry ; peevish ; ill-humored.
FRĔT'TĘR, *n.* One who, or that which, frets.
FRĔT'TY, *a.* Adorned with raised or fretwork.
FRĔT'WORK, *n.* Masonry with protuberances.
FRĪ-Ą-BĬL'Ǐ-TY, FRĪ'Ą-BLE-NĔSS, *n.* The sus-
  ceptibility of being easily reduced to powder.
FRĪ'Ą-BLE, *a.* Easily reduced to powder.
FRĪ'ĄR, *n.* A religious brother of some order.
FRĪ'Ą-RY, *n.* A monastery or convent of friars.
FRĬB'BLE, *v. n.* To trifle :—to totter.
FRĬB'BLE, FRĬB'BLĘR, *n.* A frivolous person ;
  a trifler ; a coxcomb ; a beau ; a fop.
FRĬC-Ąs-SĒĒ', *n.* A fowl, &c., fried in sauce.
FRĬC-Ąs-SĒĒ', *v. a.* To dress in fricasee.
FRĬC'TIǪN, *n.* The act of rubbing ; attrition.
FRĪ'DĄY (frī'dą), *n.* The sixth day of the week.
FRIĔND (frĕnd), *n.* One joined to another by
  affection ; an intimate ; a confidant :—favorer.
FRIĔND'LĘSS (frĕnd'lĕs), *a.* Wanting friends.
FRIĔND'LǏ-NĔSS (frĕnd'lę-nĕs), *n.* Good will.
FRIĔND'LY, *a.* Kind ; favorable ; amicable.
FRIĔND'SHǏP, *n.* Intimacy united with affection.

FRIĒZE (frēz), *n.* A coarse woollen cloth :—a
  term for a part in ornamental architecture.
FRĬG'ĄTE, *n.* A ship of war with one covered
FRĪGHT (frīt), *n.* A sudden terror. [gun-deck.
FRĪGHT (frīt), *v. a.* To terrify ; to daunt.
FRĪGHT'EN (frī'tn), *v. a.* To terrify ; to daunt.
FRĪGHT'FÛL (frīt'fûl), *a.* Terrible ; dreadful.
FRĪGHT'FÛL-LY (frīt'fûl-lę), *ad.* Dreadfully.
FRĪGHT'FÛL-NĔSS (frīt'fûl-nĕs), *n.* Dread.
FRĬG'ĬD, *a.* Cold :—dull ; lifeless ; impotent.
FRĮ-GĬD'Ǐ-TY, *n.* Coldness ; want of warmth.
FRĬG'ĬD-LY, *ad.* Coldly ; dully ; without affec-
FRĬG'ĬD-NĔSS, *n.* Frigidity ; coldness. [tion.
FRĬG-Ǫ-RĬF'ǏC, *a.* Causing or producing cold.
FRĬLL, *v. n.* To quake or shiver with cold.
FRĬLL, *n.* A border or edging of linen or cot-
  ton, as on the bosom of a shirt ; ruffle. [margin.
FRĬNGE, *n.* Ornamental trimming ; edge ;
FRĬNGE, *v. a.* To adorn, or fit, with fringes.
FRĬNG'Y, *a.* Adorned with fringes ; like fringe.
FRĬP'PĘR-Y, *n.* Old clothes :—trumpery ; trifles.
FRĬSK, *v. n.* To leap ; to skip ; to dance in frolic.
FRĬSK, *n.* A frolic ; a fit of wanton gayety.
FRĬSK'ĘR, *n.* One who frisks ; a wanton. [ing.
FRĬSK'ĘT, *n.* A frame to confine paper in print-
FRĬSK'Ǐ-NĔSS, *n.* Gayety ; liveliness ; playfulness.
FRĬSK'Y, *a.* Gay ; airy ; frolicsome ; wanton.
FRĬT, *n.* The matter of which glass is made.
FRĬTH, *n.* A strait of the sea ; an estuary.
FRĬT'TĘR, *n.* A kind of fried cake :—a fragment.
FRĬT'TĘR, *v. a.* To cut or break into pieces.
FRĮ-VŎL'Ǐ-TY, *n.* Triflingness ; frivolousness.
FRĬV'Ǫ-LOŬS, *a.* Slight ; trifling ; of no moment.
FRĬV'Ǫ-LOŬS-LY, *ad.* Triflingly ; without weight.
FRĬV'Ǫ-LOŬS-NĔSS, *n.* Triflingness ; vanity.
FRĬZZ, FRĬZ'ZLE, *v. a.* To curl short ; to crisp.
FRĬZ'ZLE, *n.* A curl ; a lock of hair crisped.
FRĬZ'ZLĘR, *n.* One who frizzles hair. [fro.
FRŌ, *ad.* From :—contraction of *from* as, *to* and
FRŎCK, *n.* A dress ; a coat :—gown for children.
FRŎG, *n.* A small amphibious animal.
FRŎL'ǏC, *a.* Gay ; full of levity ; frolicsome.
FRŎL'ǏC, *n.* A wild prank :—a scene of mirth.
FRŎL'ǏC, *v. n.* [*imp. t. & pp.* frolicked.] To play
  wild pranks ; to be merry ; to act merrily.
FRŎL'ǏC-SǑME, *a.* Full of wild gayety ; sportive.
FRŎM, *prep.* Away ; out of ; noting distance.
FRŎND, *n.* A stem and leaf combined.
FRǪN-DĀ'TIǪN, *n.* A lopping of trees.
FRǪN-DĔS'CĘNCE, *n.* The time or the process
  of unfolding of leaves of plants. [fore part.
FRŎNT, *n.* The forehead ; the brow ; face :—van ;
FRŎNT, *v. a. & n.* To oppose ; to stand foremost.
FRŎNT'ĄL, *a.* Relating to, or of, the forehead.
FRŎNT'ĄL, *n.* A little pediment :—a frontlet.
FRŎN'TIĒR (frŏn'tēr), *n.* The utmost verge of
  any territory ; a border ; confine ; limit.
FRŎN'TIĒR, *a.* Bordering ; conterminous. [wine.
FRŎN-TĬN-IĂC' (frŏn-tįn-yăk'), *n.* [Fr.] A rich
FRŎN'TĬS-PIĒCE, *n.* A print or engraving which
  faces the title-page of a book. [bold.
FRŎNT'LĘSS, *a.* Unblushing ; wanting shame ;
FRŎNT'LĘT, *n.* A band worn on the forehead.
‖FRŎST (frŏst *or* frâust), *n.* The act or the
  process of the congelation of water or vapor :
  —frozen dew ; hoar-frost. [affected by frost.
‖FRŎST'BĬT-TEN (frŏst'bĭt-tn), *a.* Nipped or
‖FRŎST'ĘD, *a.* Covered with frost.

‖FRŎST′Ĭ-LY̆, *ad.* With frost or freezing ; with excessive cold ; coldly. [cold.
‖FRŎST′Ĭ-NĔSS, *n.* Cold ; frosty state ; freezing
‖FRŎST′-NĀIL, *n.* A nail driven into a horse's shoe to prevent his slipping on the ice.
‖FRŎST′Y̆, *a.* Very cold ; hoary ; like frost.
‖FRŎTH (frŏth *or* frâuth), *n.* Spume ; foam.
‖FRŎTH, *v. n.* To foam ; to throw out spume.
‖FRŎTH′Y̆, *a.* Full of froth or spume ; empty.
FRŎÛNCE, *v. a.* To curl ; to frizzle.—*n.* A curl.
FRŎÛ′ZY̆, *a.* Fetid ; ill-scented ; dirty. [*Low.*]
FRŌ′WARD, *a.* Peevish ; ungovernable ; angry.
FRŌ′WARD-LY̆, *ad.* Peevishly ; perversely.
FRŌ′WARD-NĔSS, *n.* Peevishness ; perverseness.
FRŌŴN, *v. n.* To express displeasure ; to look
FRŌŴN, *n.* A wrinkled or stern look. [stern.
FRŌZE, *imp. t.* from *freeze.*
FRŌ′ZEN (frŏ′zn), *pp.* from *freeze.* Congealed.
FRŲC-TĔS′CENCE, *n.* The ripening of fruit.
FRŲC-TĬF′ER-OŬS, *a.* Bearing fruit.
FRŬC-TĬ-FĬ-CĀ′TIQN, *n.* Act or process of fructifying ; fecundation. [fruitful.
FRŬC′TĬ-FY̆, *v. a. & n.* To make or become
FRŬC′TŲ-OŬS, *a.* Fruitful ; fertile ; productive.
FRŬ′GAL, *a.* Thrifty ; sparing ; economical.
FRŲ-GĂL′Ĭ-TY̆, *n.* Thrift ; prudent economy.
FRŬ′GAL-LY̆, *ad.* Economically ; thriftily.
FRŬG′ĠĬN, *n.* An oven fork or pole for stirring
FRŲ-ĠĬF′ER-OŬS, *a.* Bearing fruit. [ashes.
FRŬIT (frŭt), *n.* Product of the earth, trees, and plants ; profit ; effect :—offspring ; young.
FRŬIT′AĠE (frŭt′ąj), *n.* Fruit collectively.
FRŬIT′-BEÀR-ĬNG, *a.* Producing fruit ; fruitery.
FRŬIT′ER-ER, *n.* One who trades in fruit.
FRŬIT′ER-Y̆, *n.* Fruit :—a repository for fruit.
FRŬIT′FŬL, *a.* Productive ; bearing fruit ; pro-
FRŬIT′FŬL-LY̆, *ad.* In a fruitful manner. [lific.
FRŬIT′FŬL-NĔSS, *n.* Fertility ; productiveness.
FRŲ-Ĭ″TIQN (frų-ĭsh′ųn), *n.* Enjoyment ; use.
FRŬIT′LESS, *a.* Barren ; vain ; idle ; unprofitable.
FRŬIT′LESS-LY̆, *ad.* Vainly ; idly ; unprofitably.
FRŬIT′LESS-NĔSS, *n.* Unfruitfulness ; vanity.
FRŬIT′-TREĔ, *n.* A tree that produces fruit.
FRŬ′MEN-TY̆, *n.* Food of wheat boiled in milk.
FRŬS′TRĀTE, *v. a.* To defeat ; to disappoint.
FRŲS-TRĀ′TIQN, *n.* Disappointment ; defeat.
FRŬS′TRA-TĪVE, *a.* Fallacious ; disappointing.
FRŬS′TŲM, *n.* [L.] A piece of a solid cut off.
FRŸ, *n.* A swarm of little fishes :—a dish fried.
FRŸ, *v. a.* To cook in a pan on the fire.
FRŸ, *v. n.* To be cooked in a pan ; to cook. [&c.
FRŸ′ĬNG-PĂN, *n.* A pan used for frying meat,
FŬD′DLE, *v. a.* To make drunk ; to intoxicate ; to inebriate ; to muddle.—*v. n.* To tipple.
FŬDĠE, *interj.* An expression of contempt.
FŪ′EL, *n.* The matter or aliment of fire.
FŲ-GĀ′CIOŲS (fų-gā′shųs), *a.* Volatile ; flying.
FŲ-GĂC′Ĭ-TY̆, *n.* Volatility ; a flying away.
FŪ′ĠĬ-TĪVE, *a.* Flying away ; volatile :—per-
FŪ′ĠĬ-TĪVE, *n.* A runaway ; a deserter. [ishable.
FŪGUE (fūg), *n.* (*Mus.*) A repetition of parts.
FŪ′ĠUĬST (fū′ḡĭst), *n.* One who composes fugues.
FŬL′CĬ-MĔNT, *n.* A prop ; point of suspension.
FŬL′CRŲM, *n.* [L.] Support of a lever.
FŬL-FĬL′, *v. a.* To accomplish ; to perform.
FŬL-FĬL′MENT, *n.* Completion ; performance.
FŬL′ĠEN-CY̆, *n.* Splendor ; glitter ; effulgence.
FŬL′ĠENT, *a.* Shining ; dazzling ; bright.

FŬL′ĠĬD, *a.* Shining ; glittering ; dazzling.
FŲL-ĠĬD′Ĭ-TY̆, *n.* Splendor ; dazzling glitter.
FŬL′ĠQR, *n.* Splendor ; dazzling brightness.
FŲ-LĬĠ′Ĭ-NOŬS, *a.* Smoky ; sooty.
FŬLL, *a.* Replete ; without vacuity ; saturated ; impregnated ; large ; complete ; strong.
FŬLL, *n.* Complete measure ; the whole.
FŬLL, *ad.* Fully ; quite ; exactly ; directly.
FŬLL, *v. a.* To thicken and cleanse, as cloth.
FŬLL′AĠE, *n.* Money paid for fulling cloth.
FŬLL′ER, *n.* One whose trade is to full cloth.
FŬLL′ER'Ṣ-ĔARTH (fŭl′lerz-ĕrth), *n.* A kind of marl used for cleansing or fulling cloth.
FŬLL′ER-Y̆, *n.* The place where cloth is fulled.
FŬLL′ĬNG-MĬLL, *n.* A mill for fulling cloth.
FŬL′LY̆, *ad.* Completely ; without lack or de-
FŬL′MĬ-NĂNT, *a.* Thundering ; noisy. [fect.
FŬL′MĬ-NĀTE, *v. n.* To thunder :—to explode ; to detonate :—to utter censure. [plode.
FŬL′MĬ-NĀTE, *v. a.* To utter ; to cause to ex-
FŬL-MĬ-NĀ′TIQN, *n.* A thundering ; explosion.
FŬL′MĬ-NA-TQ-RY̆, *a.* Thundering ; striking
FŬL′NESS, *n.* Completeness ; satiety. [horror.
FŬL′SQME, *a.* Nauseous ; offensive ; disgusting.
FŬL′SQME-NĔSS (fŭl′ṣum-nĕs), *n.* Nauseousness.
FŬL′VĬD, FŬL′VOŬS, *a.* Of a dull yellow color.
FŬM′BLE, *v. n. & a.* To attempt or do awkwardly ; to act bunglingly :—to falter.
FŬM′BLER, *n.* One who acts awkwardly.
FŪME, *n.* Smoke ; vapor :—rage :—conceit.
FŪME, *v. n. & a.* To smoke :—to be in a rage.
FŪ′MĬD, *a.* Smoky ; vaporous ; fuliginous.
FŲ-MĬD′Ĭ-TY̆, *n.* Smokiness ; tendency to smoke.
FŪ′MĬ-GĀTE, *v. a.* To smoke ; to perfume.
FŪ-MĬ-GĀ′TIQN, *n.* Act of fumigating ; vapor.
FŪ′MOŬS, FŪ′MY̆, *a.* Producing fumes.
FŬN, *n.* Sport ; low merriment. [*Colloquial.*]
FŲ-NĂM′BŲ-LĬST, *n.* A rope-dancer.
FŬNC′TIQN, *n.* Employment ; office ; power.
FŬNC′TIQN-AL, *a.* Relating to some office.
FŬNC′TIQN-A-RY̆, *n.* One who has an office.
FŬND, *n.* An established stock ; capital.
FŬND, *v. a.* To invest in funds, as money.
FŬN′DA-MĔNT, *n.* The lower part of the body.
FŬN-DA-MĔNT′AL, *a.* Relating to the foundation or basis ; essential ; important ; radical.
FŬN-DA-MĔNT′AL-LY̆, *ad.* Essentially ; origi-
FŲ-NĒ′BRĬ-AL, *a.* Belonging to funerals. [nally.
FŪ′NER-AL, *n.* Burial ; interment :—obsequies.
FŪ′NER-AL, *a.* Relating to burial ; mourning.
FŲ-NĒ′RE-AL, *a.* Suiting a funeral ; dismal.
FŬN′GOŬS, *a.* Like a fungus ; excrescent.
FŬN′GŲS, *n.* ; pl. FŬN′ĠĪ *or* FŬN′GŲS-EṢ. A mushroom, toadstool, &c. ; an excrescence.
FŪ′NĬ-CLE, *n.* A small cord :—stalk of a seed.
FŲ-NĬC′Ų-LAR, *a.* Consisting of cord or fibre.
FŬN′NEL, *n.* A pipe or passage of communica-
FŬN′NY̆, *a.* Comical ; droll. [*Colloquial.*] [tion.
FŬR, *n.* Soft hair, or a skin with soft hair.
FŬR, *v. a.* To line or cover with fur, &c.
FŬR′BE-LŌW (fŭr′be-lō), *n.* A puckered flounce for ornamenting a woman's dress.
FŬR′BE-LŌW, *v. a.* To adorn with furbelows.
FŬR′BĬSH, *v. a.* To burnish ; to polish.
FŬR′BĬSH-ER, *n.* One who polishes any thing.
FŲR-CĀ′TIQN, *n.* State of being branched.
FŪ′RĬ-OŬS, *a.* Mad ; frantic ; raging ; violent.
FŪ′RĬ-OŬS-LY̆, *ad.* Madly ; violently ; ragingly.

FŪ'RĬ-OŲS-NĔSS, *n.* Frenzy ; madness ; rage.
FŪRL, *v. a.* To draw up, as sails ; to contract.
FŬR'LŎNG, *n.* The eighth part of a mile.
FŬR'LŌUGH (fŭr'lŏ), *n.* A leave of absence for a limited time from military service.
FŬR'NĄCE, *n.* A place for producing great heat.
FŬR'NĬSH, *v. a.* To supply ; to fit up ; to equip.
FŬR'NĬSH-ĔR, *n.* One who furnishes or fits out.
FŬR'NĬ-TŪRE, *n.* Movables ; goods in a house for use or ornament ; appendages ; equipage.
FŬR'RĬ-ĔR, *n.* One who deals in furs.
FŬR'RŌW (fŭr'rŏ), *n.* A long trench or hollow.
FŬR'RŌW (fŭr'rŏ), *v. a.* To cut in furrows.
FŬR'RY, *a.* Covered with, or made of, fur.
FŬR'THĔR, *a.* At a greater distance ; farther.
FŬR'THĔR, *ad.* To a greater distance. [assist.
FŬR'THĔR, *v. a.* To forward ; to promote ; to
FŬR'THĔR-ĂNCE, *n.* Promotion ; advancement.
FŬR'THĔR-ĔR, *n.* A promoter ; an advancer.
FŬR'THĔR-MŌRE, *ad.* Moreover ; besides.
FŬR'THEST, FŬR'THĔR-MŌST, *a.* Most distant.
FŬR'TĬVE, *a.* Stolen ; got by theft :—thievish.
FŪ'RY, *n.* Madness ; rage ; passion ; frenzy.
FŬRZE, *n.* A flowering evergreen shrub ; gorse.
FŬR'ZY, *a.* Overgrown with furze ; full of furze.

FŪŞE, *v. a. & n.* To melt ; to liquefy by heat.
FŲ-ŞĒĒ', *n.* A part of a watch, &c. ; a pipe for firing a bomb ; a musket ;— written also *fusil.*
FŪ-ŞĬ-BĬL'Ĭ-TY, *n.* Susceptibility of being melt-
FŪ'ŞĬ-BLE, *a.* Susceptible of being melted. [ed.
FŪ'ŞĬL, *a.* That may be melted ; fusible.
FŪ'ŞĬL (fū'zĭl *or* fŭ-zē'), *n.* A musket ; fusee.
FŪ-ŞĬ-LĒĒR', *n.* A soldier armed with a musket.
FŪ'ŞIQN (fū'zhŭn), *n.* Act of melting ; fluidity.
FŬSS, *n.* A tumult ; bustle ; noise. [*A low word.*]
FŬST, *n.* The shaft of a column :—mustiness.
FŬST'ĬAN (-yąn), *n.* A kind of cloth :—bombast.
FŬST'ĬĄN, *a.* Made of fustian ; pompous.
FŬS'TĬC, *n.* A sort of wood used in dyeing yellow.
FŬST'Y, *a.* Ill-smelling ; mouldy ; musty.
FŪ'TĬLE, *a.* Trifling ; worthless ; of no weight.
FŲ-TĬL'Ĭ-TY, *n.* Want of effect ; uselessness.
FŪT'URE (fūt'yŭr), *a.* That is to be hereafter.
FŪT'URE (fūt'yŭr), *n.* Time to come.
FŲ-TŪ'RĬ-TY, *n.* Future time or event.
FŪZE, *or* FŪŞE, *n.* A tube for blasting, &c.
FŬZZ, *v. n.* To fly out in small particles.
FŬZZ'BĂLL, *n.* A kind of fungus ; a puff.
FȲ, FĪE, *interj.* A word of blame and contempt.
FȲKE, *n.* Bow-net used for catching shad.

G.

G has two sounds ; one hard, as in *go, gun ;* the other soft, like *j*, as in *gem, ginger.*
GĂB, *n.* Idle talk ; loquacity. [*Vulgar.*]
GĂB-ĄR-DÎNE' (gäb-ąr-dēn'), *n.* A loose frock.
GĂB'BLE, *v. n.* To prate without meaning.
GĂB'BLE, *n.* Loud talk without meaning.
GĂB'BLĔR, *n.* A prater ; a chattering person.
GĀ'BLE, *n.* The triangular end of a house.
GĂD, *n.* An ingot of steel or iron : — a boss.
GĂD, *v. n.* To ramble about ; to rove idly.
GĂD'DĔR, *n.* One who gads or runs abroad.
GĂD'FLY, *n.* A fly that stings cattle and horses.
GĀE'LĬC (gā'lĭk), *n.* A Celtic dialect.
GĂFF, *n.* A harpoon, or large hook :—a spar.
GĂF'FĔR, *n.* An old word of respect for an old man.   [when he is set to fight.
GĂF'FLE, *n.* An artificial spur put upon a cock
GĂG, *v. a.* To stop the mouth of. [der speech.
GĂG, *n.* Something put into the mouth to hin-
GĀGE, *n.* A pledge ; a pawn :—a measure, rule.
GĀGE, *v. a.* To engage ; to measure. See GAUGE.
GĂG'GĔR, *n.* One who gags or stops the mouth.
GĂG'GLE, *v. n.* To make a noise like a goose.
GĀI'E-TY, *n.* Mirth. See GAYETY.
GĀIN (gān), *n.* Profit ; advantage ; interest.
GĀIN, *v. a.* To obtain ; to win ; to procure.
GĀIN, *v. n.* To grow rich :—to advance.
GĀIN'FŬL, *a.* Profitable ; lucrative ; productive.
GĀIN'FŬL-LY, *ad.* Profitably ; advantageously.
GĀIN'LESS, *a.* Unprofitable ; of no advantage.
GĀIN-SĀY' *or* GĀIN'SĀY, *v. a.* To contradict.
GĀIN-SĀY'ĔR *or* GĀIN'SĀY-ĔR, *n.* Contradictor.
GĀIN-SĀY'ĬNG *or* GĀIN'SĀY-ĬNG, *n.* Opposition.
GĂIR'ĬSH, *a.* Gaudy ; gay ; fine ; splendid.
GĂIR'ĬSH-NĔSS, *n.* Gaudiness ; showy finery.
GĀIT, *n.* March ; walk or manner of walking.

GĀIT'ĔRŞ, *n. pl.* A kind of spatterdashes.
GĀ'LĄ, *n.* [Sp.] A festival ; festivity.
GĂL'ĂX-Y, *n.* The milky way ; luminous tract.
GĂL'BĄ-NŬM, *n.* [L.] A resinous gum.
GĀLE, *n.* A strong wind ; a blast ; a gust.
GĀ'LE-ĀT-ĔD, *a.* Covered as with a helmet.
GĄ-LĒ'NĄ, *n.* Native sulphuret of lead.
GĂL'ĬQT *or* GĂL'Ĭ-QT, *n.* A small Dutch vessel.
GĂLL, *n.* The bile ; a bitter animal juice :—a hurt :—rancor ; malignity ; bitterness of mind.
GĂLL, *v. a. & n.* To rub off the skin of :—to tease ; to fret ; to irritate :—to be vexed. [fine.
GĂL'LĄNT, *a.* Brave ; high spirited ; daring ;
GĄL-LĂNT', *a.* Polite and attentive to ladies.
GĄL-LĂNT', *n.* A gay, sprightly man ; a wooer.
GĄL-LĂNT', *v. a.* To pay attention to, as ladies.
GĂL'LĄNT-LY, *ad.* Bravely ; nobly ; generously.
GĄL-LĂNT'LY, *ad.* In the manner of a wooer.
GĂL'LĄNT-RY, *n.* Valor ; bravery ; magnanim-ity :—courtship ; refined address to women.
GĂL'LE-QN, *n.* A large armed ship.
GĂL'LĔR-Y, *n.* A passage leading to several apartments ; a balcony or railed projection.
GĂL'LEY (gäl'le), *n.* A vessel with sails and oars :—a printer's frame for receiving types.
GĂL'LEY-SLĀVE, *n.* One condemned to the gal-
GĂLL'ĬARD, *n.* A gay man :—a dance. [leys.
GĂL'LĬC, GĂL'LĬ-CĄN, *a.* Relating to Gaul.
GĂL'LĬ-CĬSM, *n.* A French idiom or phrase.
GĂL-LĬ-GĂS'KĬNŞ, *n. pl.* Large, open hose.
GĂL-LĬ-MĀ'TĬ-Ą (gäl-lе-mā'she-ą), *n.* Nonsense.
GĂL-LĬ-MÂU'FRY, *n.* A hash ; an oglio ; a ridiculous medley ; a confused heap.
GĂL-LĬ-NĀ'CEOŲS (gäl-lе-nā'shŭs), *a.* Denoting an order of birds including the common hen.
GĂL'LĬ-PŎT, *n.* An earthen, glazed pot :—resin.

GẮLL′NŬT, *n.* Excrescence growing on an oak.
GĂL′LǪN, *n.* A liquid measure of four quarts.
GẠL-LŎŎN′, *n.* A kind of lace for binding, &c.
GĂL′LǪP, *v. n.* To move by leaps, or very fast.
GĂL′LǪP, *n.* The motion of a galloping horse.
GĂL′LǪ-WĀY, *n.* A species of horse of small size.
GĂL′LǪWS, *n.* ; *pl.* GĂL′LǪWS-ĘŞ. A beam laid over two posts, on which malefactors are hanged :—suspenders for pantaloons ; braces.
GẮLL′STŌNE, *n.* A concretion in the gall-bladder.
GẠ-LŌÇHE′(gạ-lōsh′), *n.* ; *pl.* GẠ-LŌ′ÇHĘŞ.[Fr.] A shoe worn over a boot or other shoe.
GẠL-VĂN′ĮC, *a.* Relating to galvanism.
GĂL′VẠN-ĬŞM, *n.* A species of electricity.
GĂL′VẠN-ĪZE, *v. a.* To affect with galvanism.
GẠM-BĀ′DŌĘŞ (-dōz), *n. pl.* Spatterdashes.
GẶM′BLE, *v. n.* To play or game for money.
GĂM′BLĘR, *n.* One addicted to gambling.
GẠM-BŌǴE′, *n.* A concreted gum-resin.
GĂM′BǪL, *v. n.* To dance ; to skip ; to frisk.
GĂM′BǪL, *n.* A skip ; a hop ; a leap for joy ; a
GĂM′BRĘL, *n.* The hind leg of a horse. [frolic.
GĀME, *n.* Sport ; merriment ; a play ; a match : —animals hunted :—a spectacular contest.
GĀME, *v. n.* To play for money ; to gamble.
GĀME′-CŎCK, *n.* A cock bred to fight.
GĀME′KĔĔP-ĘR, *n.* A person who protects game.
GĀME′SǪME (gām′sụm), *a.* Frolicsome ; gay.
GĀME′STĘR, *n.* One who games ; a gambler.
GĂM′ĮNG, *n.* The practice of gamesters.
GĂM′MǪN, *n.* The buttock of a hog salted and dried :—a play with dice :—humbug ; a hoax.
GĂM′ŪT, *n.* The scale or series of musical notes.
GĂN′DĘR, *n.* The male of the goose.
GĂNG, *v. n.* To go ; to walk. [*An old word.*]
GĂNG, *n.* A troop ; a company ; a ship's crew.
GĂN′GRĒNE(găng′grēn),*n.* (*Med.*) Mortification.
GĂN′GRĒNE, *v. n.* To become mortified ; to.
GẶN′GRĘ-NOŬS,*a.* Mortified; putrefied.[mortify.
GĂNG′WĀY, *n.* A passage, particularly in a ship.
GĂNT′LĘT, *n.* A military punishment.
G̦ĀOL (jāl), *n.* A prison ;—often written *jail.*
G̦ĀOL′-DĘ-LĬV′ĘR-Y, *n.* Delivery or release of prisoners from a gaol ; jail-delivery.
G̦ĀOL′ĘR (jāl′er), *n.* A keeper of a prison ; jail.
GĂP, *n.* An opening ; a breach ; a passage.
GĀPE, *v. n.* To open the mouth ; to yawn.
GÄRB, *n.* Dress ; clothes :—exterior appearance.
GÄR′BẠǴE, *n.* The bowels ; refuse ; offal.
GÄR′BLE, *v. a.* To part ; to pick out ; to mutilate.
GÄR′DEN (gär′dn *or* gär′dẹn), *n.* A piece of ground appropriated to plants, flowers, or fruits.
GÄR′DEN-ER (-dn-er), *n.* Cultivator of a garden.
GÄR′DEN-ĬNG (gär′dn-ĭng), *n.* Horticulture.
GÄR′GẠR-ĬŞM, *n.* A gargle ; a liquid medicine.
GÄR′GẠR-ĪZE,*v.a.* To wash or rinse with gargle.
GÄR′ǴĘT, *n.* A disease in the udders of cows.
GÄR′GLE, *v. a.* To wash the throat and mouth.
GÄR′GLE, *n.* Liquor for washing the throat, &c.
GÄR′LẠND, *n.* A wreath of branches or flowers.
GÄR′LĮC, *n.* A strong-scented, edible plant.
GÄR′MĘNT, *n.* Covering for the body ; dress.
GÄR′NĘR, *n.* A place for grain ; a granary.
GÄR′NĘT, *n.* A reddish mineral or gem.
GÄR′NĮSH, *v. a.* To decorate with appendages.
GÄR′NĮSH, *n.* Decoration :—fetters. [garniture.
GÄR′NĮSH-MĔNT,*n.* Ornament; embellishment ;

GÄR′NĮ-TŪRE, *n.* Embellishment ; ornament.
GÄR′RĘT, *n.* The uppermost room of a house.
GÄR-RĘT-ĔĔR′, *n.* One who lives in a garret.
GÄR′RĮ-SON (gär′rẹ-sn), *n.* Soldiers for the defence of a town or castle :—a fortified place.
GÄR′RĮ-SON, *v. a.* To secure by a garrison.
G̦ẠR-RŬ′LĮ-TY, *n.* Loquacity ; talkativeness.
GÄR′RỤ-LOŬS, *a.* Prattling ; prating ; talkative.
GÄR′TĘR, *n.* A band to hold up a stocking.
GÄR′TĘR, *v. a.* To bind with a garter.
GĂS, *n.* A permanently elastic aeriform fluid.
GĂS-CǪN-ĀDE′, *n.* A boast; a bravado; a vaunt.
GĂS-CǪN-ĀDE′, *v. n.* To boast ; to brag, bluster.
GĂŞ′Ę-OŬS, *a.* Having the form or state of gas.
GĂSH, *v. a.* To cut deep ; to make a gash in.
GĂSH, *n.* A deep cut ; a gaping wound.
GĂS′KĘTS,*n. pl.* Small cords to fasten sails with.
GĂS′KĮNŞ, *n. pl.* Wide. open hose ; galligaskins.
GĂS′-LĬGHT (-lĭt), *n.* The light produced by gas.
GĂS′-MĒ-TĘR, *n.* A gasometer ; a gas-holder.
GẠ-ŞŎM′Ę-TĘR, *n.* Instrument to measure gas.
GĂSP, *v. n.* To pant for breath :—to long, desire.
GĂSP, *n.* Convulsive catch of breath. [stomach.
GĂS′TRĮC, *a.* Belonging to, or contained in, the
GẠS-TRĬL′Ǫ-QUĬST, *n.* A ventriloquist.
GẠS-TRĬL′Ǫ-QUY, *n.* Ventriloquism. [passage.
GĀTE, *n.* The door of a city, building, &c. :—
GĀTE′WĀY, *n.* A way through a gate ; a gate.
GĂŦH′ĘR, *v. a.* To collect ; to pick up ; to glean.
GĂŦH′ĘR, *v. n.* To be collected ; to assemble.
GĂŦH′ĘR, *n.* A pucker ; a fold ; a wrinkle.
GĂŦH′ĘR-ĘR, *n.* One who gathers ; a collector.
GĂŦH′ĘR-ĬNG, *n.* An assembly ; a collection.
GÂU′DĮ-LY, *ad.* In a gaudy manner; showily ;
GÂU′DĮ-NĔSS, *n.* Showiness ; finery. [finically.
GÂU′DY, *a.* Showy ; ostentatiously fine.
GÄUǴE (gāj), *v. a.* To measure with respect to the contents, as a vessel :—to estimate.
GÄUǴE (gāj), *n.* A measure ; a standard :—cali-
GÄUǴ′ĘR (gā′jẹr), *n.* One who gauges. [bre.
GÄUNT (gänt), *a.* Thin ; slender ; lean ; meagre.
GÄUNT′LĘT, *n.* An iron glove formerly worn.
GÂUZE, *n.* A kind of thin, transparent stuff.
GĀVE. The *imp. t.* of *give.*
GĂV′ǪT, *n.* A kind of lively dance.
GÂWK, *n.* A cuckoo :—a foolish fellow. [clown.
GÂWK′Y, *n.* A stupid or awkward person ; a
GÂWK′Y, *a.* Awkward ; ungainly ; clownish.
GĀY, *a.* Airy ; cheerful ; merry ; fine ; showy.
GĀY′Ę-TY, *n.* Cheerfulness ; mirth ; finery.
GĀY′LY, *ad.* With gayety ; merrily ; finely
GĀY′NESS, *n.* Gayety ; showiness ; finery.
GĀZE, *v. n.* To look intently and earnestly.
GĀZE, *n.* Intent ; regard ; look of wonder, &c.
GẠ-ZĔLLE′, *n.* Small, swift species of antelope.
GẠ-ZĔTTE′ (gạ-zĕt′), *n.* A newspaper. [zette.
GẠ-ZĔTTE′, *v. a.* To insert or publish in a ga-
GĂZ-ĘT-TĒĔR′, *n.* A geographical dictionary.
GĂZ′ĮNG-STŎCK, *n.* A person gazed at with scorn :—an object gazed at. [ness.
G̦ĔAR (ǵēr), *n.* Furniture; dress ; goods ; har-
G̦ĔĔSE (ǵēs), *n.* The plural of *goose.*
G̦ĔL′Ạ-BLE, *a.* That may be congealed.
G̦ĔL′Ạ-TĬNE, *n.* A gelatinous substance.
G̦ĔL′Ạ-TĬNE,   } *a.* Of the nature of gelatine
G̦Ę-LĂT′Į-NOŬS, } or jelly ; viscous ; sticky.
G̦ĔLD, *v. a.* [*imp. t.* & *pp.* gelded, *or* gelt.] To castrate ; to emasculate.

ĢELD'ING, n. Castration :—castrated horse, &c.
ĢĔL'ID (jĕl'ĭd), a. Extremely cold ; frigid.
ĢĔL'LY, n. Viscous substance; viscidity ; glue.
ĢĔLT. The *imp. t.* & *pp.* of *geld.* [a bud.
ĢĔM (jĕm), n. A jewel ; a precious stone :—
ĢĔM, v. a. To adorn, as with jewels or buds.
ĢĔM-I-NĀ'TIǪN, n. Repetition ; reduplication.
ĢĔM'I-NĪ, n. pl. Twins, a sign in the zodiac.
ĢĔM'I-NOŬS, a. Double; existing in pairs.
ĢĔM'ME-OŬS, a. Pertaining to, or like, gems.
ĢĔM'MY, a. Resembling, or full of, gems.
ĢĔN'DER, n. Sex :—distinction of sex in words.
ĢĔN'DER, v. a. To beget ; to produce ; to cause.
ĢĔN'DER, v. n. To copulate ; to breed.
ĢĔN-E-A-LŎĢ'I-CAL, a. Pertaining to genealogy.
ĢĔN-E-ĂL'Ǫ-ĢIST, n. One who traces descents.
ĢĔN-E-ĂL'Ǫ-ĢY, n. Succession of families.
ĢĔN'ER-A, n. [L.] The plural of *genus.*
ĢĔN'ER-AL, a. Relating to the whole ; public ; extensive ; common ; usual ; compendious.
ĢĔN'ER-AL, n. Whole :—commander of an army.
ĢĔN-ER-AL-ĬS'SI-MŌ, n.; pl. GENERALISSI-MOES. The supreme commander of an army.
ĢĔN-ER-ĂL'I-TY, n. The main body ; the bulk.
ĢĔN-ER-ĂL-I-ZĀ'TIǪN, n. Act of generalizing.
ĢĔN'ER-AL-ĪZE, v. a. To render general.
ĢĔN'ER-AL-LY, ad. In general ; commonly ; usually, but not universally. [general.
ĢĔN'ER-AL-SHIP, n. The conduct or office of a
ĢĔN'ER-ĀTE, v. a. To beget ; to produce, cause.
ĢĔN-ER-Ā'TIǪN, n. Act of begetting :—a race : offspring :—a single succession ; an age.
ĢĔN'ER-A-TĬVE, a. Producing ; prolific ; fruitful.
ĢĔN'ER-Ā-TǪR, n. One that generates ; causer.
ĢE-NĔR'IC, } a. Embracing the genus; not-
ĢE-NĔR'I-CAL, } ing the kind or sort.
ĢE-NĔR'I-CAL-LY, ad. With regard to the genus.
ĢĔN-ER-ŎS'I-TY, n. Magnanimity ; liberality.
ĢĔN'ER-OŬS, a. Magnanimous ; liberal ; noble.
ĢĔN'ER-OŬS-LY, ad. In a generous manner.
ĢĔN'ER-OUS-NĔSS, n. Quality of being generous.
ĢĔN'E-SĬS, n. The first book of Scripture.
ĢĔN'ET, n. A small-sized Spanish horse :—a gray animal of the weasel kind. [gin.
ĢE-NĒ'VA, n. A distilled spirit, contracted to
ĢĒ'NI-AL, a. Causing production:—cheerful; gay.
ĢĒ'NI-AL-LY, ad. Naturally ; gayly ; cheerfully.
ĢE-NĬC-U-LĀ'TIǪN, n. Knottiness :—a kneeling.
ĢĒ'NI-Ō, n.; pl. ĢĒ'NI-ŌṢ. A genius.
ĢĔN'IT-ĬNG, n. An early apple. See JENNETING.
ĢĔN'I-TĬVE, a. Noting the second case of Latin and Greek nouns ; possessive.
ĢĔN'I-TǪR, n. A sire ; a father ; a progenitor.
ĢĔN'IUS or ĢĒ'NI-ŬS, n.; pl. ĢĒ'NI-ŬS-EṢ. Inborn bent of mind :—extraordinary mental power :—a person endowed with superior faculties :—peculiar character. [or evil.
ĢĒ'NI-ŬS, n.; pl. ĢĒ'NI-Ī. [L.] A spirit, good
ĢEN-TEĒL', a. Polite ; elegant ; civil ; graceful.
ĢEN-TEĒL'LY, ad. Elegantly; politely; gracefully.
ĢEN-TEĒL'NESS, n. Gracefulness ; politeness.
ĢĔN'TIAN, n. A plant of several varieties.
ĢĔN'TĪLE, n. A pagan ; a heathen. [or to a race.
ĢĔN'TĪLE, a. Belonging to pagans or heathens,
ĢĔN'TIL-ĬSM, n. Heathenism ; paganism.
ĢĔN-TI-LĪ''TIOUS (jĕn-te-lĭsh'ụs), a. Peculiar to a nation or people ; national :—hereditary.
ĢEN-TĬL'I-TY, n. Refinement ; politeness.

ĢĔN'TLE, a. Soft ; mild ; meek :—well-bred.
ĢĔN'TLE-FŌLKS (jĕn'tl-fōlks), n. pl. Persons distinguished from the vulgar. See FOLKS.
ĢĔN'TLE-MAN, n. A man raised above the vulgar ; a man of refined manners.
ĢĔN'TLE-MAN-LĪKE } a. Honorable ; becoming
ĢĔN'TLE-MAN-LY, } a gentleman ; polite.
ĢĔN'TLE-MAN-LI-NĔSS, n. Behavior of a gentleman ; breeding of a gentleman. [ness.
ĢĔN'TLE-NĔSS, n. Softness of manners ; mild-
ĢĔN'TLE-WOM-AN (jĕn'tl-wûm-ụn), n. A woman above the vulgar ; refined woman ; a lady.
ĢĔN'TLY, ad. Softly ; meekly; tenderly ; kindly.
ĢEN-TÔÔ', n. An aboriginal of Hindostan.
ĢĔN'TRY, n. A class of people above the vulgar.
ĢE-NU-FLĔC'TIǪN, n. Act of bending the knee.
ĢĔN'U-ĬNE, a. Not spurious ; pure ; real ; true.
ĢĔN'U-ĬNE-LY, ad. Really ; truly ; naturally.
ĢĔN'U-ĬNE-NĔSS, n. Freedom from adulteration.
ĢĒ'NUS, (jē'nus), n.; pl. ĢĔN'ER-A. A class of beings or things comprehending species. [tre.
ĢE-Q-CĔN'TRIC, a. Having the earth for the cen-
ĢE-ŎG'NO-SY, n. Geology, or a branch of it.
ĢE-ŎG'RA-PHER, n. One versed in geography.
ĢE-Q-GRĂPH'I-CAL, a. Relating to geography.
ĢE-Q-GRĂPH'I-CAL-LY, ad. In a geographical manner. [book describing the earth.
ĢE-ŎG'RA-PHY, n. A description of the earth :—
ĢE-Q-LŎĢ'I-CAL, a. Relating to geology.
ĢE-ŎL'Q-ĢIST, n. One versed in geology.
ĢE-ŎL'Q-ĢY, n. The science of the structure of the earth, as to its rocks, strata, minerals, &c.
ĢĒ'Q-MĂN-CER, n. A practiser of geomancy.
ĢĒ'Q-MĂN-CY, n. Divination by casting figures.
ĢE-Q-MĂN'TIC, a. Pertaining to geomancy.
ĢE-ŎM'E-TER, n. One skilled in geometry.
ĢĒ-Q-MĔT'RIC, } a. Pertaining to geometry ;
ĢĒ-Q-MĔT'RI-CAL, } consistent with geometry.
ĢĒ-Q-MĔT'RI-CAL-LY, ad. According to geometry ; in a geometrical manner. [etry.
ĢE-ŎM-E-TRĬ''CIAN, n. One skilled in geom-
ĢE-ŎM'E-TRĪZE, v. n. To act geometrically.
ĢE-ŎM'E-TRY, n. The science which teaches the dimensions of lines, surfaces, solids, &c.
ĢEÖR'ĢIC (jör'jik), a. Relating to agriculture.
ĢEÖR'ĢIC (jör'jik), n. A poem on husbandry.
ĢE-RĀ'NI-ŬM, n. A genus of plants ; cranes-bill.
ĢĔR'FÂL-CON (jër'fâw-kn), n. A bird of prey.
ĢĔRM, n. A sprout ; a shoot ; a bud :—origin.
ĢĔR'MAN, a. Akin:—cousin *german,* first cousin.
ĢĔR'MAN-DER or ĢER-MĂN'DER, n. A plant.
ĢĔR'MAN-ĬSM, n. Idiom of the German language.
ĢĔR'MI-NAL, a. Relating to a germ.
ĢĔR'MI-NĀTE, v. n. To sprout ; to shoot ; to bud.
ĢĔR-MI-NĀ'TIǪN, n. Act of sprouting ; growth.
ĢĔR'UND, n. A kind of verbal noun. [pregnancy.
ĢES-TĀ'TIǪN, n. Bearing of young in the womb;
ĢES-TĬC'U-LĀTE, v. n. & a. To use gestures; to act.
ĢES-TĬC-U-LĀ'TIǪN, n. Act of gesticulating.
ĢĔST'URE (jĕst'yụr), n. Action or posture expressive of sentiment ; movement of the body.
ĢĔT, v. a. [*imp. t.* & *pp.* got :—*imp. t.* gat, *obsolete* ; *pp.* gotten, *obsolescent.*] To procure ; to
ĢĔT, v. n. To attain ; to become. [obtain.
ĢEW'GÂW, a. Showy ; without value.
ĢHĂST'LI-NĔSS (ğăst'le-nĕs), n. Deathlike look.
ĢHĂST'LY, a. Like a ghost ; pale, dismal.
ĢHĔR'KIN (ğĕr'kin), n. A pickled cucumber.

ĠHŌST (ḡŏst), *n.* The spirit :—spectre; phantom.
ĠHŌST'LY, *a.* Spiritual ; relating to ghosts.
ĠHŸLL (ḡĭl), *n.* A mountain torrent :—ravine.
ĠĪ'ANT, *n.* A man of extraordinary size.
ĠĪ'ANT-ĔSS, *n.* A female giant ; a huge woman.
ĠĪ'ANT-LĪKE, ĠĪ'ANT-LŸ, *a.* Huge ; gigantic.
GIAOUR (jöûr), *n.* [Turkish.] A dog ; an infidel.
ĠĬB'BER, *v. n.* To speak inarticulately.
ĠĬB'BER-ĬSH, *n.* Unmeaning talk ; jargon.
ĠĬB'BER-ĬSH, *a.* Canting; unintelligible; fustian.
ĠĬB'BET, *n.* A gallows.—*v. a.* To hang.
ĠĬB-BŎS'I-TY, *n.* Convexity ; protuberance.
ĠĬB'BOUS, *a.* Convex ; protuberant ; swelling.
ĠĬB'BOUS-NĔSS, *n.* Gibbosity ; protuberance.
ĠĬB'CĂT, *n.* A male cat ; a tom-cat.
ĠĪBE, *v. a. & n.* To scoff at ; to deride ; to taunt.
ĠĪBE, *n.* A sneer ; a hint of contempt ; a taunt.
ĠĬB'LETS, *n. pl.* Gizzard, &c., of a goose, &c.
ĠĬB'STĂFF, *n.* A staff to gauge water, &c.
ĠĬD'DI-LY, *ad.* Inconstantly ; unsteadily.
ĠĬD'DI-NĔSS, *n.* State of being giddy ; vertigo.
ĠĬD'DY, *a.* Vertiginous ; whirling ; wild.
ĠĬD'DY-BRĀINED (ḡĭd'de-brānd), *a.* Thought-
ĠIĔR'ĒA-GLE, *n.* A kind of eagle. [less; volatile.
ĠĬFT, *n.* A thing given :—power ; faculty.
ĠĬFT'ED, *a.* Endowed with eminent powers.
ĠĬG, *n.* Any thing whirled round :—light chaise.
ĠĪ-GĂN-TĒ'AN, *a.* Like a giant ; gigantic.
ĠĪ-GĂN'TĬC, *a.* Like a giant ; huge ; enormous.
ĠĬG'GLE, *n.* A half-suppressed laugh ; a titter.
ĠĬG'GLE, *v. n.* To laugh sillily ; to titter.
ĠĬG'GLER, *n.* One who giggles ; a titterer.
ĠĬG'OT, *n.* A leg, or a slice, of mutton.
ĠĬLD, *v. a.* [*imp. t. & pp.* gilded, gilt.] To over-
lay with thin gold:— to adorn with lustre. [ER.
ĠĬLD'ER, *n.* One who gilds:— a coin. See GUILD-
ĠĬLD'ĬNG, *n.* Act of one who gilds :—gold
leaf laid on a surface, for ornament.
ĠĬLL, *n.* The fourth part of a pint : — a plant.
ĠĬLL, *n.* A mountain torrent. See GHYLL.
ĠĬLLS, *n. pl.* The apertures of a fish's head.
ĠĬL'LY-FLŎŴ-ER, *n.* A garden flower ; stock.
ĠĬLT, *n.* Gold laid on the surface of any thing.
ĠĬLT, *imp. t. & pp.* of *gild.* [pass.
ĠĬM'BALS, *n. pl.* Rings to suspend a sea-com-
ĠĬM'CRĂCK, *n.* A trivial mechanism ; a trifle.
ĠĬM'LET, ĠĬM'BLET, *n.* An instrument for
boring with a screw or worm at its point.
ĠĬMP, *n.* A kind of edging of silk twist.
ĠĬN, *n.* A trap :—a machine :—a distilled spirit.
ĠĬN, *v. a.* To catch in a trap:—to clear, as cotton.
ĠĬN'ĠER, *n.* A plant or root of a hot taste.
ĠĬN'ĠER-BRĒAD (jĭn'jer-brĕd), *n.* Sweet cake.
ĠĬNG'HAM, *n.* A checkered cotton cloth.
ĠĬN'GLE, *v. n.* To utter a sharp, tinkling noise.
ĠĬN'GLE, *v. a.* To cause a shrill, tinkling sound.
ĠĬN'GLE, *n.* A shrill, resounding noise ; tinkle.
ĠĬN'SĔNG, *n.* Aromatic root of a plant.
ĠĬP'SY, *n.* See GYPSY. [found in Africa.
ĠĬ-RĂFFE', *n.* The camelopard, a quadruped
ĠĬR'AN-DŌLE, *n.* A branched chandelier.
ĠĬR'A-SŌLE, *n.* A plant ; turnsole :—a mineral.
ĠĬRD, *v. a.* [*imp. t. & pp.* girded *or* girt.] To
bind round ; to invest ; to surround :—to gibe.
ĠĬRD'ER, *n.* A person who girds ; a binder :—
the largest piece of timber in a floor.
ĠĬR'DLE, *n.* A band ; a belt :—an enclosure.
ĠĬR'DLE, *v. a.* To bind:—to cut round, as a tree.

ĠĬR'DLE-BĔLT, *n.* A belt encircling the waist.
ĠĬRL, *n.* A young woman ; a female child.
ĠĬRL'HOOD (gĭrl'hûd), *n.* The state of a girl.
ĠĬRL'ĬSH, *a.* Suiting a girl, or girlhood ; like a
ĠĬRT, *imp. t. & pp.* from *gird.* [girl.
ĠĬRT, ĠĬRTH, *n.* A band by which the saddle
is fixed upon a horse:—a bandage :—compass.
ĠĬRT, ĠĬRTH, *v. a.* To bind with a girth ; to gird.
ĠĬST (jĭst), *n.* Main point ; essence ; substance.
ĠĪVE (ḡĭv), *v. a.* [*imp. t.* gave ; *pp.* given.] To
bestow ; to confer ; to yield ; to grant.
ĠĪVE, *v. n.* To relent :—to yield :—to melt, thaw.
ĠĬV'ER, *n.* One who gives ; a donor ; bestower.
ĠĪVES, *n. pl.* Fetters. See GYVE.
ĠĬZ'ZARD, *n.* The musculous stomach of a fowl.
GLĀ'CIAL (glā'shal), *a.* Pertaining to ice ; icy.
GLĀ'CI-ĀTE (glā'she-āt), *v. n.* To turn into ice.
GLĀ-CI-Ā'TĬON (glā-she-ā'shun), *n.* Ice formed.
GLĂÇ'I-ER (glăs'e-er), *n.* A field of ice and
snow in the elevated valleys of the Alps, &c.
GLĀ'CIOUS (glā'shus), *a.* Icy ; resembling ice.
GLĀ'CIS, *n.* [Fr.] (*Fort.*) A sloping bank.
GLĂD, *a.* Cheerful ; gay ; elevated with joy.
GLĂD, *v. a.* To make glad ; to exhilarate.
GLĂD'DEN (glăd'dn), *v. a.* To make glad.
GLĀDE, *n.* A lawn or opening in a wood.
GLĂD'I-Ā-TOR, *n.* A sword-player ; prize-fighter.
GLĂD-I-A-TŌ'RI-AL, *a.* Relating to prize-fighters.
GLĂD'LY, *ad.* Joyfully ; with gladness or joy.
GLĂD'NESS, *n.* Cheerfulness ; joy ; exultation.
GLĂD'SOME (glăd'sum), *a.* Gay ; delighted.
GLĂD'SOME-NĔSS, *n.* Gayety ; delight ; joy.
GLAIR (glâr), *n.* White of an egg :—a halberd.
GLAIR, *v. a.* To smear with the white of an egg.
GLĂNCE, *n.* A shoot of light :—a quick view.
GLĂNCE, *v. n.* To look with a quick cast of the
eye :—to glitter :—to fly off obliquely. [&c.
GLĂND, *n.* An organ composed of blood-vessels,
GLĂN'DERS, *n. pl.* A disease in horses.
GLĂN-DĪF'ER-OŬS, *a.* Bearing mast or acorns.
GLĂN'DU-LAR, *a.* Pertaining to the glands.
GLĂN'DU-LOŬS, *a.* Relating to, or having, glands.
GLĀRE, *v. n.* To shine so as to dazzle the eyes.
GLĀRE, *n.* Dazzling light, lustre, or splendor.
GLĀR'ĬNG, *a.* Blazing out : — notorious.
GLĂSS, *n.* A transparent substance :—a vessel :
GLĂSS, *a.* Vitreous ; made of glass. [—a mirror.
GLĂSS, *v. a.* To cover with glass ; to glaze.
GLĂSS'-BLŌW-ER, *n.* One who blows glass.
GLĂSS'FÛL, *n.* As much as a glass will hold.
GLĂSS'-HOÛSE, *n.* A house where glass is made.
GLĂSS'-MĔT-AL (-mĕt-tl), *n.* Glass in fusion.
GLĂSS'-WORK (-würk), *n.* Manufacture of glass.
GLĂSS'Y, *a.* Made of glass ; vitreous ; crystal.
GLÂU'BER-ĪTE, *n.* A sulphate of lime and soda.
GLÂU'BER'S-SĂLT, *n.* Sulphate of soda.
GLÂU-CŌ'MA, *n.* A fault or disease in the eye.
GLÂU'COUS, *a.* Of a dull green color.
GLĀVE, GLĀIVE, *n.* A broadsword.
GLĀZE, *v. a.* To furnish with glass or win-
dows :—to cover with a vitreous substance.
GLĀ'ZIER (glā'zher), *n.* One who glazes.
GLĀZ'ĬNG, *n.* Vitreous substance on potters'
ware :—the art or process of setting glass.
GLĒAM, *n.* Sudden shoot of light :—lustre.
GLĒAM, *v. n.* To shine ; to glitter ; to flash.
GLĒAM'Y, *a.* Flashing ; darting light or gleams.
GLĒAN, *v. a. & n.* To gather after the reapers.

Ā,Ē,Ī,Ō,Ū,Ȳ, *long;* Ă,Ĕ,Ĭ,Ŏ,Ŭ,Y̆, *short;* A,E,I,O,U,Y, *obscure.*—FĀRE,FĂR,FĂST,FÂLL ; HÊIR, HĔR ;

GLĒAN′ẸR, *n.* One who gleans or gathers.
GLĒBĒ, *n.* Turf; soil :—land belonging to a church :—piece of earth containing ore.
GLĒĒ, *n.* Joy ; merriment ; gayety ; mirth.
GLĒĒ′FŪL, *a.* Full of glee ; gay ; merry.
GLĒĒT, *n.* A thin matter running from a sore.
GLĔN, *n.* A valley ; a dale ; a vale ; a dingle.
GLĒNE, *n.* The cavity or socket of the eye.
GLĬB, *a.* Smooth ; slippery :—voluble ; fluent.
GLĬB′LẎ, *ad.* Smoothly :—volubly ; fluently.
GLĬB′NẸSS, *n.* Smoothness :—volubility.
GLĪDE, *v. n.* To flow gently ; to move smoothly.
GLĪDE, *n.* Lapse :—act of passing smoothly.
GLĪD′ẸR, *n.* One who, or that which, glides.
GLĬM′MẸR, *v. n.* To shine or appear faintly.
GLĬM′MẸR, *n.* Faint light ; gleam ; ray.
GLĬM′MẸR-ĬNG, *n.* A glimmer :—faint view.
GLĬMPSE, *n.* A gleam :—a glance ; short view.
GLĬS′TEN (glĭs′sn), *v. n.* To shine ; to sparkle.
GLĬS′TẸR, *v. n.* To shine ; to glitter ; to glisten.
GLĬS′TẸR, *n.* Glitter. See CLYSTER.
GLĬT′TẸR, *v. n.* To shine ; to exhibit lustre.
GLĬT′TẸR, *n.* Lustre ; bright show ; splendor.
GLŌAM′ĬNG, *n.* Morning or evening twilight.
GLŌAT (glōt), *v. n.* To stare with desire.
GLŌ′BĂT-ẸD, *a.* Spherical ; globular. [world.
GLŌBE, *n.* A sphere ; a ball :—the earth ; the
GLỌ-BŌSE′, *a.* Globular ; spherical ; round.
GLỌ-BŎS′Ị-TẎ, *n.* Sphericity ; sphericalness.
GLŌ′BOỤS, *a.* Spherical ; round ; globose.
GLŎB′Ụ-LẠR, *a.* In form of a globe or sphere; round ; spherical. [ter ; a little globe.
GLŎB′ŪLE, *n.* A small round particle of mat-
GLŎB′Ụ-LOŬS, *a.* In form of a sphere ; round.
GLŌME, *n.* A roundish head of flowers.
GLŎM′ẸR-ĀTE, *v. a.* To gather into a ball.
GLŎM-ẸR-Ā′TIǪN, *n.* Formation into a ball.
GLŎŌM, *n.* Dismalness ; obscurity ; dimness : —melancholy ; despondency. [fully.
GLŌŎM′Ị-LẎ, *ad.* Dimly ; dismally ; not cheer-
GLŌŎM′Ị-NĔSS, *n.* Want of light :—melancholy.
GLŌŎM′Ẏ, *a.* Almost dark ; dismal ; melan-
GLŌ-RỊ-FỊ-CĀ′TIǪN, *n.* Elevation to glory. [choly.
GLŌ′RỊ-FẎ, *v. a.* To honor ; to exalt to glory.
GLŌ′RỊ-OŬS, *a.* Noble ; illustrious , conspicuous ; resplendent ; very excellent. [triously.
GLŌ′RỊ-OŬS-LẎ, *ad.* Nobly ; splendidly ; illus-
GLŌ′RẎ, *n.* High honor; praise, renown; lustre.
GLŌ′RẎ, *v. n.* To boast ; to exult ; to be proud.
GLŎSS, *n.* Comment :—superficial lustre. [liate.
GLŎSS, *v. a.* To explain by comment :—to pal-
GLǪS-SĀ′RỊ-ẠL, *a.* Relating to, or like, a glossary.
GLŎS′SẠ-RĬST, *n.* Writer of a gloss or glossary.
GLŎS′SẠ-RẎ, *n.* Dictionary of uncommon words.
GLŎS′SỊ-NĔSS, *n.* Polish :—superficial lustre.
GLŎS′SẎ, *a.* Smooth and shining , polished.
GLŎT′TỊS, *n.* An oblong opening in the larynx.
GLOŬT, *v. n.* To pout ; to look sullen.
GLŌVE (glŭv), *n.* A covering for the hand.
GLŌVE (glŭv), *v. a.* To cover, as with a glove.
GLŌV′ẸR, *n.* One who makes or sells gloves.
GLŌW (glō), *v. n.* To shine with heat ; to burn.
GLŌW (glō), *n.* Shining heat ; incandescence : —vehemence of passion :—brightness.
GLŌW′-WORM (glō′würm), *n.* A shining insect.
GLŌZE, *v. n.* To flatter, wheedle.—*n.* Flattery.
GLUE (glū), *n.* A viscous substance ; a cement.
GLUE, *v. a.* To join with glue ; to cement.

GLŪ′EẎ (glū′ẹ), *a.* Having the nature of glue.
GLŬM, *a.* Sullen ; frowning ; stubbornly grave.
GLŪME, *n.* The calyx or husk of corn, grass, &c.
GLŬT, *v. a.* To swallow :—to cloy ; to satiate.
GLŬT, *n.* More than enough ; superabundance.
GLŪ′TẸN, *n.* An adhesive, elastic substance extracted from vegetable substances.
GLŪ-TỊ-NĀ′TIǪN, *n.* Act of joining with glue.
GLŪ′TỊ-NOŬS, *a.* Gluey ; viscous ; tenacious.
GLŬT′TON (glŭt′tn), *n.* One who eats to excess.
GLŬT′TON-OŬS, *a.* Given to excessive eating.
GLŬT′TON-Ẏ, *n.* Excess in eating ; voracity.
GLẎPH (glĭf), *n.* (*Arch.*) An engraved channel.
GLẎP′TỊC, *n.* The art of engraving figures on
GNÄRL′ẸD (närl′ẹd), *a.* Knotty ; twisted. [gems.
GNÄSH (näsh), *v. a.* To strike together ; to clash.
GNÄSH (näsh), *v. n.* To grind the teeth ; to fume.
GNÄT (năt), *n.* A small, winged, stinging insect.
GNÂW (nâw), *v. a. & n.* To bite off; to corrode.
GNŌME (nōm), *n.* An imaginary being.
GNŌ′MǪN (nō′mǫn), *n.* The hand or pin of a dial.
GNǪ-MŎN′ỊCS (nǫ-mŏn′ịks), *n. pl.* Art of dialing.
GŌ, *v. n.* [*impt. t.* went ; *pp.* gone.] To walk ; to move ; to travel ; to proceed ; to pass.
GŌAD (gōd), *n.* A pointed stick to drive oxen.
GŌAD, *v. a.* To prick with a goad :—to incite.
GŌAL (gōl), *n.* The end of a race :—end.
GŌAR, *n.* A triangular slip of cloth. See GORE.
GŌAT (gōt), *n.* A well known ruminant animal.
GŌAT′HẸRD, *n.* One who tends goats.
GŌAT′ỊSH, *a.* Resembling a goat :—rank :—lust-
GǪB, GŎB′BẸT, *n.* A mouthful ; a lump. [ful.
GŎB′BLE, *v. a.* To swallow hastily with noise.
GŎB′BLE, *v. n.* To make a noise, as a turkey.
GŌ′BẸ-TWĒĒN, *n.* One between two parties.
GŎB′LẸT, *n.* A bowl, cup, or drinking vessel.
GŎB′LỊN, *n.* An evil spirit ; a phantom ; fairy.
GŌ′-BẎ, *n.* Evasion ; a passing by ; omission.
GŌ′-CÄRT, *n.* A small frame with wheels, by which to teach children to walk. [idol.
GŎD, *n.* The Supreme Being ; the Creator :—
GŎD′CHĪLD, *n.* One for whom one becomes
GŎD′DẸSS, *n.* A female divinity. [sponsor.
GŎD′FÄ-THẸR, *n.* A male sponsor in baptism.
GŎD′HĔAD (gŏd′hĕd), *n.* Deity ; divine nature.
GŎD′LẸSS, *a.* Atheistical ; wicked ; impious.
GŎD′LĪKE, *a.* Divine ; supremely excellent.
GŎD′LỊ-NẸSS, *n.* Piety ; a religious life.
GŎD′LẎ, *a.* Pious towards God ; good ; religious.
GŎD′MŎTH-ẸR (gŏd′mŭth-ẹr), *n.* A female spon-
GŎD′SHĬP, *n.* Rank or character of a god. [sor.
GŎD′SŎN, *n.* He for whom one has become spon-
GŌ′ẸR, *n.* One who goes. [sor in baptism.
GŎFF, *n.* A foolish clown :—a game. See GOLF.
GŎG′GLE, *v. n.* To strain or roll the eyes ; to look asquint. [of glasses for the eyes.
GŎG′GLEȘ, *n. pl.* Blinds for horses :—a kind
GŎG′GLE-EȲED (gŏg′gl-īd), *a.* Large-eyed.
GŌ′ỊNG, *n.* The act of walking :—departure.
GOITRE (goï′tẹr), *n.* [Fr.] Tumor on the throat.
GOÏ′TROỤS, *a.* Partaking of, or like, the goitre.
GŌLD, *n.* A precious metal :—money.
GŌLD′BĒAT-ẸR, *n.* A beater of gold.
GŌLD′EN (gōl′dn), *a.* Of gold :—bright ; happy.
GŌLD′FĬNCH, *n.* A small singing bird.
GŌLD′LĒAF, *n.* Gold beaten into thin leaf.
GŌLD′SMĬTH, *n.* One who manufactures gold.
GŎLF, *n.* A game played with a ball and bat.

GŎN'DǬ-LA, *n.* A boat used in Venice :—a shell.
GŎN-DǬ-LIĒR', *n.* One who rows a gondola.
GŌNE, *pp.* from *go.* Advanced ; past.
GŎN'FA-LŎN, *n.* An ensign ; standard ; colors.
GŎN-FA-LǬ-NIĒR', *n.* A chief standard-bearer.
GŎNG, *n.* A sort of Chinese drum or cymbal.
GŌ-NĮ-ŎM'E̤-TE̤R, *n.* An instrument for measuring angles, as of crystals.
GOOD (gûd), *a.* [*comp.* better ; *sup.* best.] Not bad ; not ill :—proper ; fit ; useful :—sound.
GOOD (gûd), *n.* The contrary to *evil* ; benefit.
GOOD (gûd), *ad.* Well ; not ill ; not amiss.
GOOD-BȲ' (gûd-bī'), *interj.* Farewell ; adieu.
GOOD-HŪ'MǬR (gûd-yū'mu̧r), *n.* Cheerfulness.
GOOD'LĮ-NĔSS (gûd'le̤-nĕs), *n.* Beauty ; grace.
GOOD'LY (gûd'le̤), *a.* Beautiful ; graceful ; fine.
GOOD-NĀT'ŲRE (gûd-nāt'yu̧r), *n.* Benevolence.
GOOD-NĀT'ŲRED (gûd-nāt'yu̧rd), *a.* Benevolent.
GOOD'NE̤SS (gûd'ne̤s), *n.* Excellence ; kindness.
GOOD-WĬLL' (gûd-wĭl'), *n.* Benevolence.
GOODS (gûdz), *n. pl.* Movables ; merchandise.
GÔÔSE, *n. ; pl.* GĒĒSE. A large, web-footed waterfowl :—a tailor's iron. [fruit.
GÔÔSE'BE̤R-RY, *n.* A prickly shrub and its
GÔÔSE'QUĬLL, *n.* A quill of a goose. [obese.
GŌR'BĔL-LĮED (gör'bĕl-lįd), *a.* Fat ; big-bellied ;
GŌR'DĮ-AN, *a.* Relating to Gordius ; intricate.
GŌRE, *n.* Blood clotted :—piece of cloth or land.
GŌRE, *v. a.* To stab ; to pierce ; to penetrate.
GŌRGE, *n.* The throat ; the swallow ; the gullet.
GŌRGE, *v. a.* To glut ; to satiate :—to swallow.
GŌR'GEOŲS (gör'ju̧s), *a.* Fine ; splendid ; showy.
GŌR'GEOŲS-LY (gör'ju̧s-le̤), *ad.* Splendidly.
GŌR'GEOŲS-NĔSS (gör'ju̧s-nĕs), *n.* Splendor.
GŌR'GE̤T, *n.* Armor worn around the throat.
GŌR'GǬN, *n.* A monster ; any thing ugly.
GŌR'MAND, GŌR'MAND-E̤R, *n.* A greedy eater.
GŌR'MAN-DĪZE, *v. n.* To eat greedily or to excess ; to feed ravenously. [glutton.
GŌR'MAN-DĪZ-E̤R, *n.* A voracious eater ; a
GŌRSE, *n.* Furze ; a leguminous shrub.
GŌR'Y, *a.* Covered with clotted blood ; bloody.
GŎS'HĂWK, *n.* A hawk used in hunting.
GŎṢ'LĮNG, *n.* A young goose not full grown.
GŎS'PE̤L, *n.* History of Christ ; Christianity.
GŎS'SA-ME̤R, *n.* A fine film spun by spiders. [tial.
GŎS'SA-ME̤R-Y, *a.* Light ; flimsy ; unsubstan-
GŎS'SĮP, *n.* An idle tattler :—tattle ; trifling talk.
GŎS'SĮP, *v. n.* To chat ; to prate ; to be merry.
GŎT, *imp. t. & pp.* from *get.* [barian.
GŎTH'ĮC, *a.* Relating to the Goths ; rude ; bar-
GŎTH'Į-CĬṢM, *n.* A Gothic idiom ; barbarism.
GŎT'TEN (gŏt'tn), *pp.* of *get.* [*Obsolescent.*
GÔÛGE (gôûj *or* gôj), *n.* A sort of chisel.
GÔÛGE *or* GÔÛGE, *v. a.* To scoop out.
GOURD (gōrd *or* gôrd), *n.* A plant and its fruit.
GÔUR'MAND, *n.* [Fr.] A glutton. See GORMAND.
GÔÔT, *n.* A drop :—an inflammatory disease.
GÔUT (gô), *n.* [Fr.] A taste ; relish.
GÔÔT'Į-NĔSS, *n.* State of being gouty. [gout.
GÔÔT'Y, *a.* Diseased with, or relating to, the
GŎV'E̤RN, *v. a.* To rule ; to direct ; to manage.
GŎV'E̤RN-A-BLE, *a.* That may be governed.
GŎV'E̤R-NANCE, *n.* Government ; rule ; control.
GŎV'E̤R-NĂNT, GŎV-E̤R-NĂNTE', *n.* A govern-
GŎV'E̤RN-ĔSS, *n.* A tutoress ; instructress. [ess.
GŎV'E̤RN-MĔNT, *n.* Direction ; exercise of authority ; executive power ; management.

GŎV'E̤RN-ǬR, *n.* One who governs ; a ruler.
GŎŴN, *n.* A long garment ; a loose robe.
GŎŴNED (göûnd), *a.* Dressed in a gown.
GŎŴN'MAN, *n.* A man of letters ; a student.
GRĂB, *v. a.* To seize suddenly. [*Vulgar.*]
GRĂB'BLE, *v. n.* To grope ; to lie prostrate.
GRĀCE, *n.* Favor ; kindness ; virtue :—pardon ; mercy :—beauty :—a title :—a short prayer.
GRĀCE, *v. a.* To adorn ; to dignify, embellish.
GRĀCE'FÛL, *a.* Beautiful with dignity ; comely.
GRĀCE'FÛL-LY, *ad.* In a graceful manner.
GRĀCE'FÛL-NE̤SS, *n.* Elegance of manner.
GRĀCE'LE̤SS, *a.* Void of grace ; abandoned.
GRĀ'CE̤S, *n. pl.* Elegant manners :—favor.
GRĀ'CIOŲS (grā'shu̧s), *a.* Merciful ; kind ; good.
GRĀ'CIOŲS-LY (grā'shu̧s-le̤), *ad.* Mercifully.
GRĀ'CIOŲS-NĔSS (-shu̧s-nĕs), *n.* Mercifulness.
GRA-DĀ'TIǪN, *n.* Regular progress ; order ; series.
GRĂD'A-TǬ-RY, *n.* Flight of steps from cloisters.
GRĀDE, *n.* Rank ; degree :—rise and descent.
GRĀDE, *v. a.* To reduce to proper degrees of ascent and descent, as the bed of a railroad.
GRĀ'DĮ-E̤NT, *a.* Walking ; moving by steps.
GRĂD'Ų-AL (grăd'yu̧-al), *a.* Proceeding by degrees ; advancing or moving step by step.
GRĂD'Ų-AL-LY, *ad.* By degrees ; step by step.
GRĂD'Ų-ĀTE, *v. a.* To dignify with a degree or diploma :—to divide into degrees ; to proportion.
GRĂD'Ų-ĀTE, *v. n.* To receive a degree :—to proceed regularly or by degrees. [gree.
GRĂD'Ų-ATE, *n.* A man dignified with a de-
GRĂD-Ų-Ā'TIǪN, *n.* Regular progression :—the act of conferring academical degrees.
GRĂFT, *n.* A small shoot or scion of a tree.
GRĂFT, *v. a.* To insert, as a scion in another tree.
GRĀIN, *n.* All kinds of corn, as wheat, &c. ; a seed :—a minute particle :—a weight :—temper ; disposition :—fibre :—dye ; stain.
GRĀINED (grānd), *a.* Rough ; dyed in grain.
GRĀINS (grānz), *n. pl.* Husks of malt in brewing.
GRĂL'LĮC, *a.* Having long legs ; stilted.
GRA-MĬN'E̤-AL, GRA-MĬN'E̤-OŲS, *a.* Grassy.
GRĂM-Į-NĬV'Ǭ-ROŲS, *a.* Living upon grass.
GRĂM'MAR, *n.* Art of speaking or writing correctly :—book of grammatical principles.
GRAM-MĀ'RĮ-AN, *n.* One versed in grammar.
GRAM-MĂT'Į-CAL, *a.* Belonging to grammar.
GRAM-MĂT'Į-CAL-LY, *ad.* According to gram-
GRĂM'PŲS, *n.* A large cetaceous animal. [mar.
GRĂN'A-RY, *n.* A storehouse for grain.
GRĂND, *a.* Great ; splendid ; magnificent.
GRĂN'DAM, *n.* Grandmother :—an old woman.
GRĂND'CHĬLD, *n.* Child of a son or daughter.
GRĂND'DÂUGH-TER (grănd'dâw-ter), *n.* The daughter of a son or daughter. [a nobleman.
GRAN-DEĒ', *n.* A man of great power or dignity ;
GRĂND'EŲR (grănd'yu̧r), *n.* State ; splendor ; magnificence ; greatness ; majesty ; pomp.
GRĂND'FÄ-THER, *n.* A father's or mother's
GRĂND'-JŪ'RǬR, *n.* One of a grand jury. [father.
GRĂND'-JŪ'RY, *n.* A jury to decide on indictments. [ther's or mother's.
GRĂND'MŎTH-ER (grănd'mŭth-er), *n.* A fa-
GRĂND'SĪRE, *n.* A grandfather ; an ancestor.
GRĂND'SŎN, *n.* The son of a son or daughter.
GRĂNGE, *n.* A farm ; a farm-house :—granary.
GRĂN'ĮTE, *n.* A common hard rock. [ite.
GRA-NĬT'ĮC, *a.* Containing granite ; like gran-

GRẠ-NĬV'Ọ-ROŬS, *a.* Eating or living upon grain.
GRĂNT, *v. a.* To admit ; to allow ; to yield.
GRĂNT, *n.* Any thing granted ; a gift ; a boon.
GRĂNT'Ạ-BLE, *a.* That may be granted.
GRĂN-TĔĔ', *n.* One to whom a grant is made.
GRĂNT'ẸR, *n.* One who grants.
GRĂNT-ÖR' *or* GRĂNT'ǪR, *n.* (*Law.*) One who
  makes a grant ;—correlative to *grantee.*
GRĂN'Ụ-LẠR, GRĂN'Ụ-LẠ-RY, *a.* Having grains.
GRĂN'Ụ-LĀTE, *v. a. & n.* To form into grains.
GRĂN-Ụ-LĀ'TIǪN, *n.* Act of forming into grains.
GRĂN'ŪLE (grăn'yŭl), *n.* A small particle.
GRĂN'Ụ-LOŬS (grăn'yụ-lŭs), *a.* Full of grains.
GRĀPE, *n.* The fruit or berry of the vine.
GRĀPE'-SHŎT, *n.* A combination of small shot.
GRĀPE'STŌNE, *n.* The stone or seed of a grape.
GRĂPH'ĬC, GRĂPH'Ị-CẠL, *a.* Well delineated.
GRĂPH'Ị-CẠL-LY, *ad.* In a graphical manner.
GRĂPH'ĪTE, *n.* Black lead, a mineral substance.
GRẠ-PHŎM'Ẹ-TẸR, *n.* A surveying instrument.
GRĂP'NẸL, *n.* A small anchor for a boat, &c.
GRĂP'PLE, *v. a. & n.* To seize ; to lay fast hold.
GRĂP'PLE, *n.* Close fight :—iron instrument.
GRĂSP, *v. a.* To seize and hold ; to gripe.
GRĂSP, *n.* Gripe or seizure of the hand ; hold.
GRĂSS, *n.* The common herbage of the field.
GRĂSS, *v. a. & n.* To cover with, or breed, grass.
GRĂSS'HŎP-PẸR, *n.* An insect that hops or leaps.
GRĂSS'-PLŎT, *n.* A level spot covered with grass.
GRĂSS'Y, *a.* Covered with, or containing, grass.
GRĀTE, *n.* A partition or frame made with bars.
GRĀTE, *v. a. & n.* To rub ; to make a harsh sound.
GRĀT'ẸD, *a.* Having bars like a grate.
GRĀTE'FŬL, *a.* Thankful :—pleasing ; accepta-
GRĀTE'FŬL-LY, *ad.* In a grateful manner. [ble.
GRĀTE'FŬL-NĔSS, *n.* Gratitude ; thankfulness.
GRĀT'ẸR, *n.* A rough instrument to grate with.
GRĂT-Ị-FỊ-CĀ'TIǪN, *n.* Pleasure :—recompense.
GRĂT'Ị-FȲ, *v. a.* To indulge ; to please ; to de-
GRĀT'ĬNG, *n.* A partition made with bars. [light.
GRĀ'TĬS, *ad.* [L.] For nothing ; without pay.
GRĂT'Ị-TŪDE, *n.* Duty to benefactors ; thank-
  fulness for favors ; sense of kindness.   [ry.
GRẠ-TŪ'Ị-TOŬS, *a.* Bestowed freely ; volunta-
GRẠ-TŪ'Ị-TOŬS-LY, *ad.* In a gratuitous manner.
GRẠ-TŪ'Ị-TY, *n.* A present ; recompense ; gift.
GRĂT'Ụ-LĀTE (grăt'yụ-lāt), *v. a.* To congratu-
  late ; to felicitate.   [tion.
GRĂT-Ụ-LĀ'TIǪN, *n.* Congratulation ; felicita-
GRĂT'Ụ-LẠ-TǪ-RY, *a.* Expressing congratula-
  tion ; congratulatory.   [posited.
GRĀVE, *n.* A place in which the dead are re-
GRĀVE, *v. a.* [*imp. t.* graved ; *pp.* graven, graved.]
  To carve ; to cut ; to form ; to shape.
GRĀVE, *a.* Solemn ; serious ; important ; deep.
GRĂV'ẸL, *n.* Hard, rough sand :—a disease. [zle.
GRĂV'ẸL, *v. a.* To cover with gravel :—to puz-
GRĀVE'LẸSS, *a.* Wanting a tomb ; unburied.
GRĂV'ẸL-LY, *a.* Abounding with, or like, gravel.
GRĀVE'LY, *ad.* Solemnly ; seriously ; soberly.
GRĂV'ẸR, *n.* One who engraves :—graving tool.
GRĀVE'STŌNE, *n.* A stone placed over a grave.
GRĀVE'YĀRD, *n.* Place for burying the dead.
GRĂV'Ị-TĀTE, *v. n.* To tend to a centre.   [tre.
GRĂV-Ị-TĀ'TIǪN, *n.* Act of tending to the cen-
GRĂV'Ị-TY, *n.* Weight ; heaviness :—serious-
GRĀ'VY, *n.* Juice of roasted meat, &c.   [ness.
GRĀY, *a.* White mixed with black :—hoary.

GRĀY'BĒARD (grā'bērd), *n.* An old man.
GRĀY'ĬSH, *a.* Approaching to a gray color.
GRĀZE, *v. n.* To eat grass ; to supply grass.
GRĀZE, *v. a.* To supply with grass :—to touch
GRĀZ'ẸR, *n.* One that feeds on grass. [lightly.
GRĀZ'IẸR (grā'zhụr), *n.* One who grazes cattle.
GRĒASE (grēs), *n.* Animal fat in a soft state.
GRĒAṢE, *n.* A disease in the legs of horses.
GRĒAṢE, *v. a.* To smear or anoint with grease.
GRĒAṢ'Ị-NĔSS, *n.* Oiliness ; fatness ; unctuosity.
GRĒAṢ'Y (grē'zẹ), *a.* Oily ; fat ; unctuous ; gross.
GRĒAT (grāt), *a.* Large :—chief ; principal :—
  illustrious ; eminent ; noble ; magnanimous.
GRĒAT'LY (grāt'le), *ad.* In a great degree.
GRĒAT'NĔSS, *n.* Largeness ; dignity ; power ; state.
GRĒAVEṢ (grēvz), *n. pl.* Ancient armor for the
GRĒ'CIẠN (grē'shạn), *a.* Relating to Greece. [legs.
GRĒ'CĬṢM, *n.* An idiom of the Greek language.
GRĒĒD'Ị-LY, *ad.* Ravenously ; voraciously.
GRĒĒD'Ị-NĔSS, *n.* Ravenousness ; voracity.
GRĒĒD'Y, *a.* Ravenous ; voracious :—eager.
GRĒĒN, *a.* Verdant ; flourishing ; fresh ; unde-
  cayed ; new ; not dry ; unripe :—ignorant.—*pl.*
GRĒĒN, *n.* Green color :—a grassy plain.—*pl.*
  Leaves and stalks used for food.
GRĒĒN'GĀǴE, *n.* A species of green plum.
GRĒĒN'GRÖ-CẸR, *n.* A retailer of vegetables.
GRĒĒN'HÖRN, *n.* A raw, unpractised youth.
GRĒĒN'HÖÛSE, *n.* House for preserving plants.
GRĒĒN'ĬSH, *a.* Somewhat green ; tending to
  green.   [ness :—ignorance ; inexperience.
GRĒĒN'NĔSS, *n.* Viridity ; unripeness ; fresh-
GRĒĒN'RÔÔM, *n.* A room of a theatre.   [men.
GRĒĒN'SĬCK-NĔSS, *n.* A disease of young wo-
GRĒĒN'STÂLL, *n.* A stall to place greens on.
GRĒĒN'SWÂRD, *n.* Turf on which grass grows.
GRĒĒT, *v. a.* To address, salute, congratulate.
GRĒĒT, *v. n.* To meet and salute :—to weep.
GRĒĒT'ĬNG, *n.* A friendly salutation at meet-
GRẸ-GĀ'RỊ-OŬS, *a.* Going in flocks or herds. [ing.
GRẸ-GĀ'RỊ-OŬS-LY, *ad.* In a flock or company.
GRẸ-GĀ'RỊ-OŬS-NĔSS, *n.* State of being in herds.
GRẸ-NĀDE', GRẸ-NĀ'DŌ, *n.* Ball of iron filled
  with gunpowder, and thrown by the hand.
GRĔN-Ạ-DIĒR', *n.* A foot-soldier :—a fowl.
GREW (grū), *imp. t.* of *grow.*
GREY (grā), *a.* See GRAY. [used in the chase.
GREY'HOÛND (grā'hoûnd), *n.* A tall, fleet dog,
GRĬD'DLE, *n.* An iron pan for baking cakes.
GRĪDE, *v. n.* To cut or prick ; to smite.
GRĬD'ĪR-ON (grĭd'Ī-ụrn), *n.* A portable grate
  on which meat is laid to be broiled.
GRIĒF (grēf), *n.* Sorrow ; trouble :—grievance.
GRIĒV'ẠNCE, *n.* A wrong suffered ; an injury.
GRIĒVE, *v. a. & n.* To afflict :—to feel sorrow.
GRIĒV'OŬS, *a.* Afflictive ; painful ; heavy.
GRIĒV'OŬS-LY, *ad.* Painfully ; calamitously.
GRĬF'FĬN, GRĬF'FǪN, *n.* A fabled animal.
GRĬG, *n.* A small eel ; sand-eel :—health.
GRĬLL, *v. a.* To broil on a gridiron :—to scare.
GRĬM, *a.* Horrible ; hideous ; frightful ; ugly.
GRỊ-MĀCE', *n.* A distortion of the countenance.
GRỊ-MĂL'KĬN, *n.* A name for an old cat.
GRĪME, *v. a.* To dirt ; to sully deeply ; to daub
GRĪME, *n.* Dirt deeply insinuated. [with filth.
GRĪM'LY, *ad.* Horribly ; hideously ; sourly.
GRĬM'NĔSS, *n.* Horror ; frightful visage.
GRĬN, *v. n.* To show the teeth set together.

GRĬN, _n._ The act of one who grins.
GRĪND, _v. a._ [_imp. t._ & _pp._ ground.] To reduce to powder :—to sharpen :—to oppress.
GRĪND, _v. n._ To perform the act of grinding.
GRĪND′ẸR, _n._ One that grinds :—double tooth.
GRĪND′STŌNE, _n._ A stone for grinding tools.
GRĪPE, _v. a._ To hold hard ; to pinch, squeeze.
GRĪPE, _n._ A grasp ; hold.—_pl._ The colic.
GRĪP′ẸR, _n._ An oppressor ; an extortioner.
GRĬS′KĬN, _n._ The backbone of a hog. [ful.
GRĬS′LẎ, _a._ Dreadful ; horrible ; hideous ; fright-
GRĬST, _n._ Corn to be ground :—supply, provision.
GRĬS′TLE (grĭs′sl), _n._ A cartilage ; a tough, elastic, and compressible substance. [tle.
GRĬST′LẎ (grĭs′slẹ), _a._ Of, or containing, gris-
GRĬT, _n._ Coarse part of meal :—sand ; gravel.
GRĬT′TĬ-NĔSS, _n._ State of being gritty ; sandi-
GRĬT′TẎ, _a._ Full of grit ; consisting of grit. [ness.
GRĬZ′ZLE, _n._ Mixture of white and black ; gray.
GRĬZ′ZLED (grĭz′zld), _a._ Interspersed with gray.
GRĬZ′ZLẎ (grĭz′zlẹ), _a._ Somewhat gray. [pain.
GRŌAN (grōn), _v. n._ To breathe or sigh as in
GRŌAN, _n._ A deep sigh from sorrow or pain.
GROÂT (grâwt), _n._ A coin worth four pence.
GRŌ′CẸR, _n._ A dealer in tea, sugar, spices, &c.
GRŌ′CẸR-Ẏ, _n._ Commodities sold by grocers.
GRŎG, _n._ A beverage of spirit and water.
GRŎG′RẠM, _n._ A kind of stuff with a rough
GRŌĬN, _n._ The part next above the thigh. [pile.
GRŌŎM, _n._ One who tends horses ; a servant.
GRŌÔVE, _v. a._ To cut into channels or hollows.
GRŌÔVE, _n._ A furrow ; channel cut with a tool.
GRŌPE, _v. n._ To feel where one cannot see.
GRŌSS, _a._ Thick ; bulky ; indelicate ; coarse ; palpable ; impure ; unrefined ; stupid ; fat.
GRŌSS, _n._ Bulk or main body :—twelve dozen.
GRŌSS′LẎ, _ad._ Bulkily ; coarsely ; without art.
GRŌSS′NẸSS, _n._ Coarseness ; density ; fatness.
GRŎT, _n._ A cave ; a grotto ; a cavern. [odd.
GRỌ-TĔSQUE′ (-tĕsk′), _a._ Distorted ; fantastic ;
GRỌ-TĔSQUE′LẎ, _ad._ In a fantastical manner.
GRŎT′TŌ, _n._ ; _pl._ GRŎT′TŌṢ. A cave ; a cavern.
GRŌÛND, _n._ Earth ; land ; territory :—floor ; bottom :—first hint ; first principle.—_pl._ Lees.
GRŌÛND, _v. a._ To place on the ground :—to
GRŌÛND, _imp. t._ & _pp._ from _grind._ [found.
GRŌÛND′-ĀSH, _n._ A sapling of ash, taken from the ground ; young shoot of an ash-tree.
GRŌÛND′-BĀIT, _n._ A bait allowed to sink.
GRŌÛND′-FLŌOR (-flōr), _n._ The lower floor.
GRŌÛND′LẸSS, _a._ Void of reason ; unfounded ; ungrounded ; wanting ground. [nut.
GRŌÛND′NŬT, _n._ A plant and its fruit ; pig-
GRŌÛND′-PLŎT, _n._ Ground occupied by a build-
GRŌÛND′-RĔNT, _n._ Rent paid for ground. [ing.
GRŌÛND′SẸL, _n._ A plant ; ragwort :—a ground-
GRŌÛND′WŎRK, _n._ Ground; first principle. [sill.
GRŌÛP (grōp), _n._ A cluster ; a collection.
GRŌÛP (grōp), _v. a._ To form into a group.
GRŌÛSE, _n._ A kind of fowl ; a heathcock.
GRŌVE, _n._ A small wood ; place set with trees.
GRŌV′EL (grŏv′vl), _v. n._ To lie prone ; to be base.
GRŌV′EL-LẸR (grŏv′vl-ẹr), _n._ A mean person.
GRŌW (grō), _v. n._ [_imp. t._ grew ; _pp._ grown.] To vegetate :—to increase ; to extend ; to become.
GRŌW (grō), _v. a._ To cause to grow ; to produce.
GRŌW′ẸR (grō′ẹr), _n._ An increaser :—farmer.
GRŌŴL, _v. n._ To snarl ; to murmur ; to grumble.

GRŌŴL, _n._ A murmur, as of an angry dog.
GRŌWN (grōn), _pp._ from _grow._ Advanced.
GRŌWTH (grōth), _n._ The act or the process of growing ; vegetation :—product ; thing produced :—increase of stature :—advancement.
GRŬB, _v. a._ To dig up ; to root out, extirpate.
GRŬB, _n._ A kind of worm :—a dwarf. [ingly.
GRŬDGE, _v. a._ To envy ; to give or take unwill-
GRŬDGE, _v. n._ To murmur ; to be envious.
GRŬDGE, _n._ An old quarrel :—ill will ; envy.
GRŬ′EL, _n._ Food made by boiling meal in water.
GRŬFF, _a._ Sour of aspect ; harsh of manners.
GRŬFF′LẎ, _ad._ Harshly ; ruggedly ; sourly.
GRŬFF′NẸSS, _n._ Harshness of manner or look.
GRŬM, _a._ Sour ; surly ; severe ; harsh.
GRŬM′BLE, _v. n._ To murmur with discontent.
GRŬM′BLẸR, _n._ One that grumbles ; murmurer.
GRŬM′BLĬNG, _n._ A murmuring ; hoarse noise.
GRŬME, _n._ A thick, viscid consistence of a fluid.
GRŬM′LẎ, _ad._ In a grum manner ; morosely.
GRŬ′MOŲS, _a._ Thick ; clotted :—clubbed ; knot-
GRŬNT, _v. n._ To murmur like a hog. [ted.
GRŬNT, _n._ The noise of a hog :—a kind of fish.
GUĀ′IẠ-CŬM (gwā′yạ-kŭm), _n._ A medicinal wood.
GUÄR-ẠN-TĒĒ′ (gär-rạn-tē′), _n._ One who undertakes to see stipulations performed :—surety.
GUÄR′ẠN-TĒĒ, _or_ GUÄR′ẠN-TẎ (gär′rạn-tĕ), _n._ Surety for performance. [for performance.
GUÄR′ẠN-TĒĒ, _or_ GUÄR′ẠN-TẎ, _v. a._ To answer
GUÄRD (gärd), _v. a._ To protect ; to defend.
GUÄRD (gärd), _n._ A watch ; protection ; care.
GUÄR′DĬ-ẠN (gär′dẹ-ạn), _n._ One who has the care of an orphan ; a protector ; a warden. [or.
GUÄR′DĬ-ẠN, _a._ Performing the office of protect-
GUÄR′DĬ-ẠN-SHĬP, _n._ The office of a guardian.
GUÄRD′-RŌÔM (gärd′rôm), _n._ A room in which those who are appointed to watch assemble.
GUÄRD′SHĬP, _n._ A ship to guard the coast. [or.
GŪ-BẸR-NẠ-TŌ′RĬ-ẠL, _a._ Relating to a govern-
GŬD′GẸỌN (gŭd′jụn), _n._ A fish :—a man easily cheated :—a pin on which a wheel turns.
GUĔSS (gĕs), _v. n._ & _a._ To conjecture ; to judge.
GUĔSS (gĕs), _n._ A conjecture ; a supposition.
GUĔST (gĕst), _n._ One entertained by another.
GUĔST′-CHĂM-BẸR, _n._ A chamber of entertainment for guests. [ment ; conduct.
GUĪD′ẠNCE (gīd′ạns), _n._ Direction ; govern-
GUĪDE (gīd), _v. a._ To direct ; to regulate.
GUĪDE (gīd), _n._ One who directs ; a director.
GUĪDE′LẸSS (gīd′lẹs), _a._ Having no guide.
GUĪDE′PŌST (gīd′pōst), _n._ A directing post.
GUĪLD (gīld), _n._ A society ; a corporation.
GUĪLD′ẸR (gīld′ẹr), _n._ A Dutch coin.
GUĪLD′-HĂLL (gīld′hâl), _n._ A town-hall.
GUĪLE (gīl), _n._ Deceitful cunning ; artifice ; craft.
GUĪLE′FŪL (gīl′fûl), _a._ Wily ; insidious ; artful.
GUĪLE′LẸSS (gīl′-), _a._ Free from deceit ; honest.
GUĪLE′LẸSS-NĔSS (gīl′lẹs-nĕs), _n._ Honesty.
GUĬL′LẸ-MŌT, _n._ An Arctic aquatic fowl.
GUĬL-LỌ-TÎNE′ (gĭl-lọ-tēn′), _n._ [Fr.] A machine used for beheading in France.
GUĬL-LỌ-TÎNE′, _v. a._ To decapitate by the guil-
GUĬLT (gĭlt), _n._ Criminality :—a crime. [lotine.
GUĬLT′Ĭ-LẎ (gĭlt′ẹ-lẹ), _ad._ In a criminal man-
GUĬLT′Ĭ-NĔSS, _n._ State of being guilty. [ner.
GUĬLT′LẸSS, _a._ Innocent ; free from crime.
GUĬLT′Ẏ (gĭlt′ẹ), _a._ Criminal ; wicked ; corrupt.
GUĬN′ẸA (gĭn′nẹ), _n._ A gold coin, 21_s._ sterling.

GUĬN'E̲A-HĔN (gĭn'ne̲-hĕn), n. Species of fowl.
GUĬN'E̲A-PĬG (gĭn'ne̲-pĭg), n. A small animal.
GUĪṢE (gīz), n. Manner; mien; habit; dress.
GUI̱-TÄR' (g̱ĭt-tär'), n. An instrument of music.
GŪLE̲Ṣ (gūlz), a. Red. [*A term of heraldry.*]
GŬLF, n. A bay; an opening into land :—abyss.
GŬLF'Y̲, a. Full of gulfs or whirlpools.
GŬLL, v. a. To trick; to cheat; to defraud.
GŬLL, n. A sea-fowl :—a trick :—one easily
GŬL'LE̲T, n. The throat; œsophagus. [cheated.
GŬL'LY̲, n. A ravine formed by running water.
GŬL'LY̲, v. a. To wear away by water or friction.
GŬLP, v. a. To swallow eagerly; to suck down.
GŬLP, n. As much as can be swallowed at once.
GŬM, n. A substance exuding from trees :—the
hard, fleshy covering of the jaws.
GŬM, v. a. To close, or smear, with gum.
GŬM'MI̱-NĔSS, n. The state of being gummy.
GŬM'MOUṢ, GŬM'MY̲, a Of the nature of gum.
GŬN, n. The general name for fire-arms.
GŬN'-BŌAT, n. A small vessel of war.
GŬN'NE̲R, n. A cannoneer; one who shoots.
GŬN'NE̲R-Y̲, n. The art of managing guns.
GŬN'NY̲, n. A coarse kind of sack-cloth.
GŬN'PŎW-DE̲R, n. Powder for firing guns, &c.
GŬN'SHŎT, n. The reach or range of a gun.
GŬN'SHŎT, a. Made by the shot of a gun.
GŬN'SMĬTH, n A maker of guns.
GŬN'STŎCK, n. The wooden part of a gun.
GŬN'WALE, GŬN'NEL (gŭn'ne̲l), n. The upper
part of a ship's side, from the half deck to the
GŬRG̱E, n. A whirlpool; a gulf. [forecastle.
GŬR'GLE, v. n. To gush, as water from a bottle.
GŬSH, v. n. To flow or rush out with violence.
GŬSH, n. An emission of liquor with force.

GŬS'SE̲T, n. An angular piece of cloth.
GŬST, n. The sense of tasting :—blast of wind.
GŬST'A̱-BLE, a. Pleasant to the taste.
GUS-TĀ'TIO̲N, n. The act of tasting.
GŬS'TŌ, n. [It.] The relish of any thing; liking.
GŬST'Y̲, a. Stormy; tempestuous; windy.
GŬT, n. Internal passage for food :—a passage.
GŬT, v. a. To eviscerate; to draw; to exenter-
ate. [eye; drop-serene; amaurosis.
GŬT'TA̱-SE̲-RĒ'NA, n. [L.] A disease of the
GŬT'TE̲R, n. A passage for water; a channel.
GŬT'TE̲R, v. a. To cut in small hollows.
GŬT'TU̱-LOUṢ, a. In the form of a small drop.
GŬT'TU̱-RA̲L, a. Belonging to the throat; deep.
GUY̲ (g̱ī), n. A rope used for lifting in a ship.
GŬZ'ZLE, v. n. & a. To swallow any thing
greedily; to feed ravenously; to gormandize.
GŬZ'ZLE̲R, n. An immoderate eater or drinker.
GY̲M-NĀ'ṢI̱-ÄRCH, n. A master of a gymnasium.
GY̲M-NĀ'ṢI̱-ŬM (jim-nā'zhe̲-ŭm), n.; pl. GY̲M-
NĀ'ṢI̱-A, or GY̲M-NĀ'ṢI̱-ŬMṢ. [L.] A place
for athletic exercises :—a school; a seminary.
GY̲M-NĂS'TĬC, a. Pertaining to athletic exercises.
GY̲M-NĂS'TĬCS, n. pl. Gymnastic art or exercise.
GŶP'SE̲-OUṢ, GŶP'SĪNE, a. Relating to gypsum.
GŶP'SŬM, n. Plaster stone; sulphate of lime.
GŶP'SY̲, n. One of a wandering race of people.
GY̲-RĀ'TIO̲N, n. Act of turning about.
GŶRE, n. A circle described by any thing mov-
ing in an orbit; a circuit. [GERFALCON.
GY̲R'FÂL-CON (jër'fȧw-kn), n. A falcon. See
GŶ'RO̲-MA̱N-CY̲, n. A sort of divination.
GŶ'RO̲N, n. (*Her.*) One of the ordinaries.
GŶVE, v. a. To fetter; to shackle.
GŶVE̲Ṣ, n. pl. Fetters; chains for the legs̲.

H.

H is a note of aspiration, and is, by many gram-
marians, accounted no letter.
HÄ, *interj.* Expressing wonder, joy, or grief.
HĂB'E̲R-DĂSH-E̲R, n. A dealer in small wares.
HĂB'E̲R-DĂSH-E̲R-Y̲, n. Small wares or goods.
HA̱-BĒR'G̱E̲-ON, n. Armor for the neck and breast.
HA̱-BĬL'I̱-MĔNT, n. Dress; clothes; garment.
HĂB'I̱T, n. Dress; garb :—custom; inveterate use.
HĂB'I̱T, v. a. To dress; to accoutre; to array.
HĂB'I̱-TA̱-BLE, a. Capable of being dwelt in.
HĂB'I̱-TA̱-BLE-NĔSS, n. Capacity of being dwelt
HĂB'I̱-TA̱NT, n. A dweller; an inhabitant. [in.
HĂB-I̱-TĀ'TIO̲N, n. A place of abode; dwelling.
HĂB'I̱T-E̲D, a. Clothed; accustomed :—usual.
HA̱-BĬT'U̱-A̱L (ha̱-bĭt'yu̱-a̱l), a. Customary.
HA̱-BĬT'U̱-A̱L-LY̲, ad. Customarily; by habit.
HA̱-BĬT'U̱-ĀTE, v. a. To accustom; to familiarize.
HĂB'I̱-TŪDE, n. Long custom; habit :—state.
HĂCK, v. a. To cut; to chop; to cut clumsily.
HĂCK, n. A notch :—horse :—a hackney-coach.
HĂC'KLE, v. a. To dress flax :—to separate.
HĂC'KLE, n. A comb for dressing flax.
HĂCK'NE̲Y̲, n. A hired horse :—a hireling.
HĂCK'NE̲Y̲, a. Much used :—let out for hire.
HĂCK'NE̲Y̲, v. a. To use much; to accustom;
to habituate; to make common.

HĂCK'NE̲Y̲-CŌACH, n. A carriage let for hire.
HĂCK'NE̲Y̲ED (hăk'nĭd), p. a. Much used; worn
HĂD, imp. t. & pp. of have. [out.
HĂD'DO̲CK, n. A sea-fish of the cod kind.
HĂFT, n. A handle.—v. a. To set in a haft.
HĂG, n. A witch; a fury :—an old, ugly woman.
HĂG, v. a. To vex; to harass with vain terror.
HĂG'GA̱RD, a. Lean; rugged; pale; deformed.
HĂG'GA̱RD, n. A species of hawk not easily
HĂG'GLE, v. a. To chop; to mangle. [tamed.
HĂG'GLE, v. n. To be difficult in a bargain.
HĂGUE'BŬT (hăg'bu̱t), n. An arquebuse.
HÄH (hä), *interj.* Expressing surprise or effort.
HÄ-HÄ', n. A sunk fence.
HĀIL (hāl), n. Drops of rain frozen in falling.
HĀIL, v. n. To pour down hail.—v. a. To pour.
HĀIL, *interj.* A term of reverential salutation.
HĀIL, v. a. To salute; to call to; to greet.
HĀIL'SHŎT, n. Small shot scattered like hail.
HĀIL'STŌNE, n. A particle or single ball of hail.
HĀIL'Y̲, a. Consisting of hail; full of hail.
HĀIR (hȧr), n. Dry, elastic filaments arising
from the skin of animals :—a single hair.
HĀIR'BRĔADTH (hȧr'brĕdth), n. A very small
distance; diameter of a hair.—a. Very narrow.
HĀIR'CLŎTH, n. Stuff made of hair, very rough.

HÀIR'Ĭ-NĔSS, *n.* The state of being hairy.
HÀIR'LĘSS, *a.* Wanting hair; bald.
HÀIR'Y, *a.* Covered with, or consisting of, hair.
HĀKE, *n.* A kind of fish resembling the cod.
HĂL'BĘRD, *n.* A kind of spear :—a cross-bar.
HĂL-BĘR-DIĒR', *n.* One armed with a halberd.
HĂL'CY-ǪN (hăl'shę-ŭn), *n.* A sea-bird ; king-
HĂL'CY-ON (hăl'shę-ŭn), *a.* Placid; quiet.[fisher.
HĀLE, *a.* Healthy ; sound ; hearty ; uninjured.
HĀLE *or* HÂLE, *v. a.* To drag. See HAUL.
HĂLF (häf), *n.* ; *pl.* HĂLVEŞ. A moiety.
HĂLF (häf), *ad.* In part ; equally. [parent.
HĂLF'-BLŎOD (häf'blŭd), *n.* Relation by one
HĂLF'MÔÔN, *n.* The moon half illuminated.
HALF'-PĘN-NY (hā'pen-nę, hăp'pen-nę, *or* häf'-
pĕn-nę), *n.* ; *pl.* HALFPENCE. A copper coin.
HĂLF'-WĀY, *a.* Equidistant.—*ad.* In the mid-
HĂLF'-WĬT (häf'wĭt), *n.* A foolish fellow. [dle.
HĂLF'-WĬT-TĘD (häf'wĭt-ted), *a.* Foolish.
HAL'Ĭ-BŬT (hŏl'ę-bŭt), *n.* A large, flat sea-fish.
HÂLL, *n.* A court of justice :—a manor-house :
—a public room :—a large room :—a collegiate
body :—entrance of a dwelling-house.
HĂL-LĘ-LŪ'JĄH (hăl-lę-lū'yą), *n.* [Heb., *praise
ye Jehovah.*] A song of thanksgiving or praise.
HĂL-LŌO', *interj.* Expressing encouragement or
HĂL-LŌO', *v. n. & a.* To cry out ; to call to. [call.
HĂL'LŌW (hăl'lō), *v. a.* To consecrate or make
holy ; to dedicate ; to sanctify. [Souls.
HĂL'LŌW--MĂS (hăl'lǫ-măs), *n.* Feast of All-
HĄL-LŪ-CĬ-NĀ'TĬǪN, *n.* Error ; delusion.
HĀ'LŌ, *n.* ; *pl.* HĀ'LŌEŞ. A circle round the
sun or moon :—a circle round a nipple.
HÂL'SĘR (hâw'sęr), *n.* A rope. See HAWSER.
HÂLT, *v. n.* To limp ; to stop ; to hesitate ; to
HÂLT, *a.* Lame; crippled; limping. [falter.
HÂLT, *n.* Act of limping :—stop in a march.
HÂLT'ĘR, *n.* One who halts :—a rope :—a bridle.
HÂLT'ĘR, *v. a.* To bind or tie with a halter.
HĂLVE (häv), *v. a.* To divide into two parts.
HĂLVEŞ (hävz), *n.* The plural of *half.*
HĂM, *n.* Thigh :—the thigh of a hog salted.
HĂM'Ą-DRŶ-ĄD, *n.* A wood-nymph. [village.
HĂM'LĘT, *n.* A small village, or portion of a
HĂM'MĘR, *n.* An instrument for driving nails.
HĂM'MĘR, *v. a.* To beat or form with a hammer.
HĂM'MĘR-CLŎTH, *n.* Cloth covering a coach-
HĂM'MǪCK, *n.* Swinging bed, for sailors. [box.
HĂM'PĘR, *n.* A large basket :—a kind of fetter.
HĂM'PĘR, *v. a.* To shackle ; to entangle ; to
HĂM'STRĬNG, *n.* Tendon of the ham. [insnare.
HĂM'STRĬNG, *v. a.* [*imp. t. & pp.* hamstrung.]
To lame by cutting the tendon of the ham.
HĂN'Ą-PĘR, *n.* A hamper :—treasury.
HĂN'CĘŞ, *n. pl.* The ends of elliptical arches.
HĂND, *n.* The palm, with the fingers :—meas-
ure of four inches :—side :—person employed.
HĂND, *v. a.* To give or transmit ; to· guide or
HĂND'-BÂLL, *n.* Game played with a ball. [lead.
HĂND'-BĂR-RŌW, *n.* A frame carried by hand.
HĂND'-BĂS-KĘT, *n.* A portable basket. [bell.
HĂND'-BĔLL, *n.* A bell rung by the hand ; table-
HĂND'-BRĔADTH, *n.* Breadth of the hand; palm.
HĂND'CŬFF, *n.* A fetter for the hand or wrist.
HĂND'CŬFF, *v. a.* To manacle. [a handcuff.
HĂND'-FĔT-TĘR, *n.* A manacle for the hands ;
HĂND'FŬL, *n.* As much as the hand can grasp.
HĂND'-GĂL-LǪP, *n.* A gentle, easy gallop.

HĂND'GŬN, *n.* A gun wielded by the hand.
HĂND'Ĭ-CRĂFT, *n.* Work performed by hand.
HĂND'Ĭ-CRĂFTS-MĄN, *n.* A manufacturer. [sily.
HĂND'Ĭ-LY, *ad.* With skill ; with dexterity ; ea-
HĂND'Ĭ-NĔSS, *n.* Readiness ; dexterity. [facture.
HĂND'Ĭ-WǑRK, *n.* Work of the hand ; manu-
HĂND'KĘR-CHĬEF (hăng'kęr-chĭf), *n.* A piece
of cloth to wipe the face, or to cover the neck.
HĂN'DLE, *v. a.* To touch ; to manage ; to treat of.
HĂN'DLE, *n.* Part of a thing held in the hand.
HĂND'MĀID, *n.* A maid that waits at hand.
HĂND'MĀID-EN (hănd'mā-dn), *n.* A handmaid.
HĂND'MĬLL, *n.* A mill moved by the hand.
HĂND'SÂW, *n.* Saw used by one hand. [thing.
HĂND'SĘL (hăn'sel), *n.* The first use of any
HĂND'SĘL, *v. a.* To use or do for the first time.
HĂND'SǪME (hăn'sum), *a.* Beautiful with dig-
nity ; graceful ; elegant :—ample ; liberal.
HĂND'SǪME-LY, *ad.* Beautifully :—generously.
HĂND'SǪME-NĔSS, *n.* Beauty ; grace ; elegance.
HĂND'SPĪKE, *n.* A kind of wooden lever.
HĂND'-VĪCE, *n.* A vice to hold small work in.
HĂND'WRĬT-ĬNG (hănd'rīt-ing), *n.* A form of
writing peculiar to each hand ; chirography.
HĂND'Y, *a.* Ready ; dexterous :—convenient.
HĂNG, *v. a.* [*imp. t. & pp.* hung.] To suspend.
HĂNG, *v. n.* To be suspended ; to depend.
HĂNG, *v. a.* [*imp. t. & pp.* hanged.] To suspend
by the neck in order to put to death. [sword.
HĂNG'ĘR, *n.* One that hangs :—a sort of broad-
HĂNG-ĘR-ŎN', *n.* Servile dependant, parasite.
HĂNG'ĬNG, *n.* Drapery hung or fastened to the
walls of rooms ; tapestry :—suspension.
HĂNG'MĄN, *n.* A public executioner.
HĂNK (hăngk), *n.* Two or more skeins ; a tie.
HĂNK (hăngk), *v. n.* To form into hanks.
HĂNK'ĘR (hăngk'ęr), *v. n.* To long importu-
HĂNK'ĘR-ĬNG, *n.* Strong desire; longing.[nately.
HĂN-SĘ-ĂT'ĬC, *a.* Relating to the Hanse towns.
HĂP, *n.* Chance ; fortune.—*v. n.* To happen.
HĂP-HĂZ'ĄRD, *n.* Chance ; accident.
HĂP'LĘSS, *a.* Unhappy ; unfortunate ; luckless.
HĂP'LY, *ad.* Perhaps ; peradventure ; by chance.
HĂP'PEN (hăp'pn), *v. n.* To fall out ; to chance.
HĂP'PĬ-LY, *ad.* Fortunately; luckily :—skilfully.
HĂP'PĬ-NĔSS, *n.* Felicity ; good fortune. [ful.
HĂP'PY, *a.* Felicitous ; lucky ; fortunate :—skil-
HĄ-RĂNGUE' (hą-răng'), *n.* Declamatory speech.
HĄ-RĂNGUE' (hą-răng'), *v. n.* To make a speech.
HĄ-RĂNGUE', *v. a.* To address by a speech.
HĄ-RĂNGU'ĘR (hą-răng'ęr), *n.* A noisy speaker.
HĂR'ĄSS, *v. a.* To vex ; to weary ; to fatigue.
HĂR'BĬN-GĘR, *n.* A forerunner ; a precursor.
HĂR'BǪR, *n.* A port or haven :—asylum ; shel-
ter :—chest in glass-making. [to shelter.
HĂR'BǪR, *v. n. & a.* To lodge ; to sojourn :—
HĂRD, *a.* Firm ; not soft :—difficult ; laborious;
rigorous :—severe ; unkind ; obdurate.
HĂRD, *ad.* Close ; near :—diligently ; laboriously.
HĂRD'EN (här'dn), *v. n. & a.* To grow or make
hard ; to indurate :—to make unfeeling.
HĂRD'-FĬST-ĘD, *a.* Covetous ; close-handed.
HĂRD'-FOUGHT (härd'fàwt), *a.* Sharply or ve-
hemently contested. [verity.
HĂRD'-HĂND-ĘD, *a.* Coarse :—exercising se-
HĂRD'HEÄRT-ĘD (härd'härt-ęd), *a.* Cruel ; ob-
HĂR'DĬ-HOOD(här'dę-hûd), *n.* Audacity.[durate,
HĂR'DĬ-NĔSS, *n.* Firmness ; stoutness ; courage.

HÄRD'LY, *ad.* Not easily ; scarcely ; barely :—harshly ; rigorously ; painfully ; not tenderly.
HÄRD'-MÖÛ**Ŧ**HED (härd'möûthd), *a.* Disobedient to the rein ; not sensible to the bit.
HÄRD'NĘSS, *n.* Quality of being hard ; solidity.
HÄRDȘ, *n. pl.* The refuse of flax or hemp ; tow.
HÄRD'SHĬP, *n.* Severe labor ; want ; oppression.
HÄRD'WÅRE, *n.* Manufactures of metal.
HÄRD'WÅRE-MĄN, *n.* A dealer in hardware.
HÄRD' Y, *a.* Bold ; brave ; stout ; strong ; firm.
HÅRE, *n.* A small, swift, timid quadruped.
HÅRE'BĔLL, *n.* A plant bearing blue flowers.
HÅRE'-BRĀINED (hår'brānd), *a.* Volatile; wild.
HÅRE'FOOT (hår'fût), *n.* An herb :—a bird.
HÅRE'-HÖÛND, *n.* A hound for hunting hares.
HÅRE'LĬP, *n.* A divided lip, like that of a hare.
HÅRE'LĬPPED (hår'lĭpt), *a.* Having a harelip.
HÄ'RĘM *or* HÅ'RĘM, *n.* The apartment for women in a seraglio in Turkey, &c.
HÄR'Į-COT (här'ę-kō), *n.* [Fr.] A kind of ragout.
HÄR'Į-ĘR, *n.* A dog for hunting hares ; harrier.
HÄRK, *v. n.* To listen ; to give ear ; to hearken.
HÄRK, *interj.,* imperative of *hark.* List ! hear.
HÄRL, *n.* The filaments of flax :—mist ; fog.
HÄR'LĘ-QUĬN, *n.* A buffoon ; a merrry-andrew.
HÄR-LĘ-QUĬN-ĀDE', *n.* A feat of buffoonery.
HÄR'LŎT, *n.* A prostitute ; a strumpet. [tion.
HÄR'LŎT-RY, *n.* Trade of a harlot ; prostitu-
HÄRM, *n.* Injury ; mischief ; hurt :—crime.
HÄRM, *v. a.* To hurt ; to injure ; to damage.
HÄRM'FÛL, *a.* Hurtful ; mischievous ; injurious.
HÄRM'LĘSS, *a.* Innocent ; not hurtful :—unhurt.
HÄRM'LĘSS-LY, *ad.* Innocently ; without hurt.
HÄRM'LĘSS-NĔSS, *n.* A harmless quality.
HĄR-MŎN'ĮC,   } *a.* Relating to music or har-
HĄR-MŎN'Į-CĄL, } mony ; concordant ; musical.
HĄR-MŎN'Į-CÅ, *n.* A collection of musical glasses resembling goblets. [ner.
HĄR-MŎN'Į-CĄL-LY, *ad.* In a harmonical man-
HĄR-MŎN'ĮCS, *n. pl.* Science of musical sounds.
HĄR-MŌ'NĮ-OŬS, *a.* Concordant ; musical.
HĄR-MŌ'NĮ-OŬS-LY, *ad.* With harmony.
HĄR-MŌ'NĮ-OŲS-NĔSS, *n.* Concord ; musicalness.
HÄR'MQ-NĬST, *n.* A musician ; a harmonizer.
HÄR'MQ-NĪZE, *v. a.* To make harmonious.
HÄR'MQ-NĪZE, *v. n.* To agree ; to correspond.
HÄR'MQ-NY, *n.* Musical concord ; agreement.
HÄR'NĘSS, *n.* Armor :—furniture for horses.
HÄR'NĘSS, *v. a.* To put harness on ; to equip.
HÄRP, *n.* A stringed instrument :—constellation.
HÄRP, *v. n.* To play upon the harp :—to dwell.
HÄRP'ĘR, *n.* A player on the harp.
HÄRP'ĬNG-ĪR-ON (härp'ĭng-ī-ųrn), *n.* A bearded dart ; a harpoon. [with.
HÄR-PÖÖN', *n.* A barbed dart to strike whales
HĄR-PÖÖN', *v. a.* To strike with the harpoon.
HÄR-PÖÖN-ÉÉR', HĄR-PÖÖN'ĘR, *n.* One who throws the harpoon in whale-fishing.
HÄRP'SĮ-ℭHÖRD, *n.* A musical instrument.
HÄR'PY, *n.* A fabulous winged monster :—extortioner.
HÄR'RĮ-DĂN, *n.* A decayed strumpet. [tortioner.
HÄR'RĮ-ĘR, *v. a.* A dog for hunting hares ; harier.
HÄR'RŌW, *n.* A frame of timber set with teeth.
HÄR'RŌW (här'rō), *v. a.* To break or cover with the harrow :—to tear up ; to disturb.
HÄR'RŌW-ĘR, *n.* One who harrows :—a hawk.
HÄRSH, *a.* Austere ; rough ; crabbed ; morose.
HÄRSH'LY, *ad.* Sourly ; austerely ; severely.

HÄRSH'NĘSS, *n.* Roughness ; severity ; rigor.
HÄRS'LĘT, *or* HÄ'SLĘT, *n.* Liver, lights, &c.,
HÄRT, *n.* A stag or male deer. [of a hog.
HÄRTS'HÖRN, *n.* Horn of harts, and a drug from it ; salt of ammonia :—a plant or herb.
HÄR'VĘST, *n.* The season of reaping, &c. ; corn ripened and gathered :—product of labor.
HÄR'VĘST, *v. a.* To gather in, as grain, &c.
HÄR'VĘST-HŌME, *n.* Song, or time, of harvest.
HÄR'VĘST-MÖÖN, *n.* The lunation at harvest-time or near the autumnal equinox.
HĄȘ. The third person sing. of the verb *have.*
HĂSH, *v. a.* To mince ; to chop into small pieces.
HĂSH, *n.* Minced meat :—a mixture ; farrago.
HĂSP, *n.* A clasp folded over a staple ; a spindle.
HĂSP, *v. a.* To shut or fasten with a hasp.
HĂS'SQCK, *n.* A thick mat for kneeling upon.
HĂST. The second person singular of *have.*
HÄSTE, *n.* Hurry ; speed ; precipitation.
HÄSTE, HĀS'TEN (hā'sn), *v. n.* To make haste.
HĀS'TEN (hā'sn), *v. a.* To urge on, precipitate.
HĀS'TĮ-LY, *ad.* With haste ; speedily ; quickly.
HĀS'TĮ-NĔSS, *n.* Haste ; speed ; hurry. [fruit.
HĀST'ĮNGȘ, *n. pl.* Peas that come early ; early
HĀST'Y, *a.* Quick ; speedy ; vehement :—rash.
HĀST'Y-PŪD'DĮNG, *n.* A pudding made by boil-
HĂT, *n.* A cover for the head. [ing meal, &c.
HĂT'BĂND, *n.* A string tied round the hat.
HĂT'BŎX, HĂT'CĀSE, *n.* A box or case for a hat.
HĂTCH, *v. a.* To produce young from eggs.
HĂTCH, *n.* A brood :—door or opening in a deck,
HĂTCH'ĘL (hăch'ęl), *n.* A flax comb. [&c.
HĂTCH'ĘL, *v. a.* To clean or dress, as flax :—
HĂTCH'ĘT, *n.* A small axe. [to tease.
HĂTCH'ĘT-FĀCE, *n.* A prominent, ill-formed face ; a thin face. [deck.
HĂTCH'WĀY, *n.* The large opening in a ship's
HĀTE, *v. a.* To detest ; to abhor ; to abominate.
HĀTE, *n.* Hatred ; malignity ; detestation.
HĀTE'FÛL, *a.* Detestable ; odious :—malignant.
HĀTE'FÛL-LY, *ad.* Detestably ; malignantly.
HĀT'ĘR, *n.* One who hates ; an abhorrer.
HĀ'TRĘD, *n.* Enmity ; hate ; ill will ; malig-
HĂT'TĘR, *n.* One who makes hats. [nity.
HÂUGHT'Į-LY, *ad.* Proudly ; arrogantly ; dis-
HÂUGHT'Į-NĔSS, *n.* Pride ; arrogance. [dainfully.
HÂUGHT'Y (hâw'te), *a.* Proud ; arrogant ; disdainful ; supercilious ; assuming. [to tug.
HÂUL, *v. a.* To pull ; to draw ; to drag by force ;
HÂUL, *n.* A pull ; act of hauling :—draught.
HÂUNCH (hänsh), *n.* The thigh ; a hip ; rear.
HÄUNT (hänt), *v. a.* To resort to ; to frequent.
HÄUNT (hänt), *n.* A place much frequented.
HÄUNT'ĘR (hänt'ęr), *n.* One who haunts.
HAUT'BOY (hō'böę), *n.* A wind instrument.
HĂVE (hăv), *v. a.* [*imp. t. & pp.* had ; *ind. present,* I *have,* thou *hast,* he *has* ; we, you, they *have.*] To possess ; to enjoy ; to hold.
HÄ'VEN (hā'vn), *n.* A port ; a harbor :—shelter.
HĂV'QC, *n.* Waste ; devastation ; destruction.
HÂW, *n.* Berry of the hawthorn :—stammering.
HÂW, *v. n.* To speak slowly, with hesitation.
HÂWK, *n.* A voracious bird of prey.
HÂWK, *v. n.* To fly hawks at fowls :—to force up phlegm :—*v. a.* To cry and sell, as goods.
HÂWK'ĘR, *n.* A pedler ; news-carrier :—one who flies hawks ; a falconer. [eye.
HÂWK'-EȲED (hâwk'īd), *a.* Having a keen

HÂWK'ĬNG, *n.* The diversion of flying hawks.
HÂWS'ĘR, *n.* A rope or cable. See HALSER.
HÂW'THÖRN, *n.* A thorn that bears haws.
HĀY (hā), *n.* Grass dried for fodder :—a kind of
HĀY'CŎCK, *n.* A heap of fresh hay. [net.
HĀY'LŎFT, *n.* A loft to put hay in.
HĀY'-MĀK-ĘR, *n.* One employed in making hay.
HĀY'MŎW (hā'mŏŭ), *n.* A mow or mass of hay.
HAY'RĬCK (hā'rĭk), *n.* A rick of hay.
HĀY'STĂCK (hā'stăk), *n.* A stack of hay.
HĂZ'ĄRD, *n.* Chance ; danger :—a game at dice.
HĂZ'ĄRD, *v. a.* To expose to chance ; to risk.
HĂZ'ĄRD-OŬS, *a.* Dangerous ; exposed to haz-
HĀZE, *n.* Fog ; mist ; watery vapor. [ard.
HĀ'ZEL (hā'zl), *n.* A shrub bearing a nut.
HĀ'ZEL (hā'zl), *a.* Light brown ; like hazel.
HĀ'ZEL-NŬT, *n.* The nut or fruit of the hazel.
HĀ'ZY (hā'zę), *a.* Dark ; foggy ; misty.
HĒ, *pron.* The man ; the person :—sometimes
used adjectively for male ; as, a *he* goat.
HĔAD (hĕd), *n.* The part of an animal that
contains the brain :—chief ; fore part :—topic.
HĔAD (hĕd), *a.* Chief ; principal ; highest.
HĔAD (hĕd), *v. a.* To lead ; to direct ; to govern.
HĔAD'ĀCHE (hĕd'āk), *n.* Pain in the head.
HĔAD'BĂND (hĕd'bănd), *n.* A fillet ; a topknot.
HĔAD'DRĔSS (hĕd'drĕs), *n.* Dress of the head.
HĔAD'Ĭ-NĔSS (hĕd'dę-), *n.* Hurry ; rashness.
HĔAD'LĂND (hĕd'lănd), *n.* A promontory ; cape.
HĔAD'LĔSS (hĕd'lĕs), *a.* Having no head:—rash.
HĔAD'LŎNG (hĕd'lŏng), *a.* Steep :—thoughtless.
HĔAD'LŎNG (hĕd'lŏng), *ad.* Rashly ; hastily.
HĔAD'PIĔCE (hĕd'pēs), *n.* Armor for the head.
HĔAD'-QUÂR-TĘRS, *n. pl.* A general rendezvous.
HĔAD'STÂLL (hĕd'stâl), *n.* Part of a bridle.
HĔAD'STRŎNG (hĕd'strŏng), *a.* Ungovernable.
HĔAD'WĀY, *n.* (*Naut.*) Motion of advancing.
HĔAD'Y (hĕd'dę), *a.* Rash ; hasty ; violent.
HĒAL, *v. a. & n.* To cure ; reconcile, grow well.
HĒAL'Ą-BLE, *a.* Capable of being healed.
HĒAL'ĬNG, *p. a.* Tending to cure ; mild ; gentle.
HĔALTH (hĕlth), *n.* Freedom from bodily pain
or sickness ; a sound state ; purity ; goodness.
HĔALTH'FŬL (hĕlth'fŭl), *a.* Sound ; salubrious.
HĔALTH'FŬL-LY, *ad.* In a healthful manner.
HĔALTH'FŬL-NĔSS, *n.* State of being healthful.
HĔALTH'Ĭ-LY, *ad.* Without sickness or pain.
HĔALTH'Ĭ-NĔSS, *n.* The state of health. [firm.
HĔALTH'LĔSS (hĕlth'lĕs), *a.* Weak ; sickly ; in-
HĔALTH'Y (hĕlth'ę), *a.* Enjoying health ; hale ;
sound :—conducive to health ; wholesome.
HĔAP (hĕp), *n.* A pile ; accumulation ; cluster.
HĔAP, *v. a.* To throw ; to pile ; to accumulate.
HĔAP'Y (hē'pę), *a.* Lying in heaps or masses.
HĒAR (hēr), *v. n. & a.* [*imp. t. & pp.* heard.]
To perceive by the ear ; to listen ; to hearken.
HĒARD (hērd), *imp. t. & pp.* from *hear.*
HĒAR'ĘR (hēr'ęr), *n.* One who hears ; listener.
HĒAR'ĬNG, *n.* The sense of perceiving sounds.
HĒAR'KEN (här'kn), *v. n.* To listen ; to attend to.
HĒAR'KEN-ĘR (här'kn-), *n.* One who hearkens.
HĒAR'SĀY (hēr'sā), *n.* Report ; rumor. [dead.
HĒARSE (hērs), *n.* A carriage to convey the
HĒART (härt), *n.* Primary organ of the blood's
motion :—vital part ; courage ; spirit ; affec-
HĒART'-ĀCHE (härt'-āk), *n.* Sorrow ; pang. [tion.
HĒART'-BRŌ-KEN (härt'-brō-kn), *a.* Very sor-
HĒART'BŬRN, *n.* Pain in the stomach. [rowful.

HĒART'-BŬRN-ĬNG, *n.* Heartburn :—discontent.
HĒART'FĔLT (härt'fĕlt), *a.* Felt at heart.
HĒARTH (härth), *n.* A place for fire :—a home.
HĒÄR'TĬ-LY (här'tę-lę), *ad.* Cordially ; sincere-
HĒART'Ĭ-NĔSS, *n.* Cordiality ; sincerity. [ly.
HĒART'LĔSS, *a.* Void of affection ; spiritless.
HĒÄRT'LĔSS-LY, *ad.* Without courage ; faintly.
HĒART'LĔSS-NĔSS, *n.* Want of affection.
HĒART'-RĔND-ĬNG, *a.* Causing deep anguish.
HĒART'S'-ĒĄSE (härts'ēz), *n.* A plant:—quiet.
HĒART'-SĬCK, *a.* Pained in mind or heart.
HĒART'-STRĬNG, *n.* A tendon of the heart.
HĒART'Y (härt'ę), *a.* Cordial ; sincere ; zealous.
HĒAT (hĕt), *n.* The sensation caused by fire :
—caloric :—course at a race :—flush ; ardor.
HĒAT, *v. a.* To make hot ; to warm :—to rouse.
HĒAT'ĘR (hĕt'ęr), *n.* One that heats.
HĒATH (hĕth), *n.* A low shrub :—a wild tract.
HĒATH'-CŎCK, *n.* A species of grouse.
HĒA'THEN (hē'thn), *n.* A gentile ; a pagan.
HĒA'THEN (hē'thn), *a.* Gentile ; pagan ; savage.
HĒA'THEN-ĬSH (hē'thn-ĭsh), *a.* Pagan ; savage.
HĒA'THEN-ĬSM (hē'thn-ĭzm), *n.* Paganism.
HĒATH'Y (hĕth'ę), *a.* Covered with heath.
HĒAVE (hĕv), *v. a.* [*imp. t.* heaved *or* hove ; *pp.*
heaved.] To lift ; to raise ; to throw ; to cast.
HĒAVE, *v. n.* To breathe with pain ; to pant :
—to swell or toss :—to labor ; to struggle.
HĒAVE (hĕv), *n.* A throw :—an effort to vomit.
HĔAV'EN (hĕv'vn), *n.* Expanse of the sky :—
habitation of the blessed :—Supreme Power.
HĔAV'EN-BŌRN, *a.* Descended from heaven.
HĔAV'EN-LĬ-NĔSS, *n.* Supreme excellence.
HĔAV'EN-LY (hĕv'vn-lę), *a.* Angelic ; celestial.
HĔAV'EN-WÂRD, *ad.* Towards heaven.
HĔAVE'-ÖF-FĘR-ĬNG, *n.* An offering made
among the Jews. [oppressively.
HĔAV'Ĭ-LY (hĕv'ę-lę), *ad.* With weight or grief;
HĔAV'Ĭ-NĔSS (hĕv'ę-nĕs), *n.* Weight ; depression.
HĔAV'Y (hĕv'vę), *a.* Ponderous :—sorrowful ;
dejected ; depressed :—grievous :—sluggish.
HĘB-DŎM'Ą-DĄL, *or* HĘB-DŎM'Ą-DĄ-RY, *a.*
Weekly ; occurring every week. [pefy.
HĔB'E-TĀTE, *v. a.* To dull ; to blunt ; to stu-
HĔB'E-TŪDE, *n.* Dulness ; obtuseness ; blunt-
HĒ'BRĄ-ĬSM, *n.* A Hebrew idiom or phrase. [ness.
HĒ'BRĄ-ĬST, *n.* A man versed in Hebrew.
HĒ'BREW (hē'brū), *n.* A Jew :—Hebrew tongue.
HĘ-BRĬ''CIĄN (hę-brĭsh'ąn), *n.* A Hebraist.
HĔC'Ą-TŎMB (hĕk'ą-tôm), *n.* A sacrifice of a
HĔCK, *n.* A rack :—a latch. [hundred cattle.
HĔC'TĬC, } *a.* Habitual ; constitutional ;
HĔC'TĬ-CĄL, } protracted :—affected with con-
stitutional fever. [threaten.
HĔC'TŎR, *v. a. & n.* To bully ; to tease ; to
HĔC'TŎR, *n.* A bully ; one who teases. [&c.
HĔDGE, *n.* A fence made of thorns, shrubs,
HĔDGE, *v. n.* To enclose with a hedge :—to
obstruct :—to encircle for defence.
HĔDGE'HŎG, *n.* An animal set with prickles.
HĔDGE'RŌW, *n.* A hedge of bushes in a row.
HĔDGE'-SPÄR-RŌW (hĕdj'spär-rō), *n.* A bird.
HĒED, *v. a. & n.* To mind ; to regard ; to attend.
HĒED, *n.* Care ; attention ; caution ; regard.
HĒED'FŬL, *a.* Watchful ; cautious ; careful.
HĒED'FŬL-LY, *ad.* Attentively ; carefully.
HĒED'FŬL-NĔSS, *n.* The quality of being heed-
ful ; caution ; vigilance ; attention.

Ā,Ē,Ī,Ō,Ū,Ȳ, *long* ; Ă,Ĕ,Ĭ,Ŏ,Ŭ,Y̆, *short* : Ą,Ę,Ĭ,Ǫ,Ụ,Y, *obscure.*—FĀRE,FÄR,FĂST,FÂLL ; HÊIR, HĒR ;

HĔĔD′LĔSS, *a.* Negligent; inattentive; careless.
HĔĔD′LĔSS-LY̆, *ad.* Carelessly; inattentively.
HĔĔD′LĔSS-NĔSS, *n.* Carelessness; negligence.
HĔĔL, *n.* The hind part of the foot:—the foot.
HĔĔL, *v. n.* To dance:—to lean on one side.
HĔĔL, *v. a.* To arm a cock:—to add a heel to.
HĔĔL′-PIĔCE, *n.* A piece fixed upon the heel.
HĔFT, *n.* A handle; a haft:—weight; heaviness.
HE̱-G̱Ī′RA̱ *or* HĔG̱′I̱-RA̱, *n.* The Mahometan epoch or era, reckoned from July 16, A.D. 622.
HĔIF′E̱R (hĕf′fe̱r), *n.* A young cow.
HEĪGH′-HŌ (hī′hō), *interj.* Expressing languor.
HEĪGHT (hīt), *n.* Elevation; altitude; highness.
HEĪGHT′E̱N (hī′tn), *v. a.* To raise:—to improve.
HEI′NOY̱S (hā′ny̱s), *a.* Atrocious; very wicked.
HEI′NOY̱S-LY̆ (hā′ny̱s-le̱), *ad.* Atrociously.
HEI′NOY̱S-NĔSS (hā′ny̱s-nĕs), *n.* Atrociousness.
HÊIR (âr), *n.* One who inherits; an inheritor.
HÊIR′ĔSS (âr′e̱s), *n.* A woman who inherits.
HÊIR′LĔSS (âr′le̱s), *a.* Without an heir.
HÊIR′LÔÔM (âr′lôm), *n.* Any furniture or movable which descends by inheritance.
HÊIR′SHĬP (âr′shĭp), *n.* The state or privileges
HĔLD, *imp. t. & pp.* from *hold.* [of an heir.
HĒ′LI̱-ĂC, } *a.* Pertaining to the sun; rising
HE̱-LĪ′A̱-CA̱L, } or setting in the sun's rays.
HĔL′I̱-CA̱L, *a.* Spiral; having circumvolutions.
HĒ-LI̱-Ọ-CĔN′TRI̱C, *a.* Relating to the sun's
HĒ′LI̱-Ọ-TRŌPE, *n.* A plant; turnsole. [centre.
HĒ′LI̱X, *n.* Any thing spiral; a coil.
HĔLL, *n.* The place of the devil and wicked souls:—place of the dead; the grave. [plant.
HĔL′LE̱-BŌRE, *n.* The Christmas flower; a
HĔL′LE̱N-I̱SM, *n.* A Greek idiom; a Grecism.
HĔL′LE̱-NĬST, *n.* One skilled in the Greek language. [or to the Greek tongue.
HĔL-LE̱-NĬS′TI̱C, *a.* Relating to the Hellenists,
HĔLL′-HÖÜND, *n.* A dog of hell:—an agent of hell:—a recreant; a profligate. [able.
HĔLL′I̱SH, *a.* Relating to hell; infernal; detesta-
HĔLL′I̱SH-NĔSS, *n.* Extreme wickedness.
HĔLM, *n.* The apparatus by which a ship is steered:—place of direction:—a helmet.
HĔL′ME̱T, *n.* Armor for the head; head-piece.
HĔL′ỌT, *n.* A Spartan slave; a slave.
HĔLP, *v. a.* To assist; to support:—to avoid.
HĔLP, *n.* Assistance; aid; support; succor.
HĔLP′E̱R, *n.* One who helps; an assistant.
HĔLP′FŬL, *a.* Giving help; useful; salutary.
HĔLP′FŬL-NĔSS, *n.* Assistance; usefulness.
HĔLP′LĔSS, *a.* Wanting help or support; feeble.
HĔLP′LĔSS-LY̆, *ad.* Without help or succor.
HĔLP′LĔSS-NĔSS, *n.* Want of ability.
HĔL′TE̱R-SKĔL′TE̱R, *ad.* Confusedly. [*Vulgar.*]
HĔLVE (hĕlv), *n.* Handle of an axe. [zerland.
HE̱L-VĔT′I̱C, *a.* Relating to Helvetia or Swit-
HĔM, *n.* The edge of a garment:—margin.
HĔM, *v. a.* To form a hem on:—to border, skirt.
HĔM, *v. n.* To utter a noise expressed by *hem.*
HĔM′I̱ (hĕm′e̱), in composition, signifies *half.*
HĔM′I̱-PLĔG̱-Y̆, *n.* Paralysis of one side.
HĔM′I̱-SPHÊRE (hĕm′e̱-sfēr), *n.* Half of a globe.
HĔM-I̱-SPHĔR′I̱C, } *a.* Half round; contain-
HĔM-I̱-SPHĔR′I̱-CA̱L, } ing half a sphere.
HĔM′I̱S-TI̱CH *or* HE̱-MĬS′TI̱CH, *n.* Half a verse.
HĔM′LŎCK, *n.* A tree:—a poisonous plant.
HĔM′ỌR-RHĄG̱E (hĕm′ọr-rȧj), *n.* A flux of blood.
HĔM-ỌR-RHĄG̱′I̱C, *a.* Relating to hemorrhage.

HĔM-ỌR-RHÖĬD′A̱L, *a.* Relating to the hemor-
rhoids or piles. [disease; the piles.
HĔM′ỌR-RHÖIDṢ (hĕm′ọr-röĭds), *n. pl.* A painful
HĔMP, *n.* A plant, and its dressed fibres.
HĔMP′E̱N (hĕm′pn), *a.* Made of hemp.
HĔN, *n.* The female of the cock, or of any bird.
HĔN′BĀNE, *n.* A plant poisonous to poultry.
HĔNCE, *ad.* From this place, time, or cause.
HĔNCE′FŌRTH, *ad.* From this time forward.
HĔNCE-FŌR′WA̱RD, *ad.* From this time forward.
HĔNCH′MA̱N, *n.* A page; an attendant. [kept.
HĔN′-CÔÔP, *n.* A cage in which poultry are
HE̱N-DĔC′A̱-GŎN, *n.* A figure of eleven sides.
HĔN′-HEĂRT-E̱D (hĕn′härt-ed), *a.* Cowardly.
HĔN′PĔCKED (hĕn′pĕkt), *a.* Governed by a wife.
HĔN′-RÔÔST, *n.* A place where poultry roost.
HĔP, *n.* The fruit of the wild brier. See HIP.
HE̱-PĂT′I̱C, } *a.* Relating to the liver:—of a
HE̱-PĂT′I̱-CA̱L, } liver-brown color.
HĔP′TA̱-ℭHŌRD, *n.* A system of seven sounds.
HĔP′TA̱-GŎN, *n.* A figure with seven sides.
HĔP-TĂG̱′Ọ-NA̱L, *a.* Having seven angles.
HĔP′TĂR-ℭHY̆, *n.* A government by seven per-
HĔR, *prep.* Belonging to a female. [sons.
HĔR′A̱LD, *n.* An officer who adjusts coats of arms, &c.:—a harbinger:—a proclaimer, crier.
HE̱-RĂL′DI̱C, *a.* Relating to heraldry or blazonry.
HĔR′A̱LD-RY̆, *n.* The art or office of a herald.
HĔRB (ĕrb), *n.* A plant without a woody stem.
HE̱R-BĀ′CEOY̱S (he̱r-bā′shy̱s), *a.* Relating to
HĔRB′AG̱E (ĕr′baj), *n.* Herbs; grass. [herbs.
HĔRB′A̱L, HE̱R-BĀ′RI̱-ŬM, *n.* A book of plants.
HĔRB′A̱L-ĬST, *n.* One skilled in herbs; botanist.
HE̱R-BĬV′Ọ-ROŬS, *a.* Feeding on plants, &c.
HĔRB′Y̆ (ĕrb′e̱), *a.* Like herbs; full of herbs.
HE̱R-CŪ′LE̱-A̱N, *a.* Like Hercules; very strong.
HĔRD, *n.* A number of beasts together; a drove.
HĔRD, *v. n. & a.* To run or put in herds; to associate; to become one of a number.
HĔRDṢ′MA̱N, *n.* One employed in tending herds.
HĒRE, *ad.* In this place:—in the present state.
HĒRE′A̱-BÔÛTS, *ad.* About or near this place.
HĒRE-ĂF′TE̱R, *ad.* In time to come; in some future time; in some future state or time.
HĒRE-ĂF′TE̱R, *n.* A future state.
HĒRE-BȲ′, *ad.* By this. [ed; inheritable.
HE̱-RĔD′I̱-TA̱-BLE, *a.* Capable of being inherit-
HĒR-E̱-DĬT′A̱-MĔNT, *n.* (*Law.*) An inheritance.
HE̱-RĔD′I̱-TA̱-RI̱-LY̆, *ad.* By inheritance.
HE̱-RĔD′I̱-TA̱-RY̆, *a.* Descending by inheritance;
HĒRE-ĬN′, *ad.* In this. [transmissible.
HĒRE-ĬN′TŌ, *ad.* Into this.
HĒRE-ŌF′, *ad.* From this; of this.
HĒRE-ŎN′, HĒRE-ỤP-ŎN′, *ad.* Upon this. [esy.
HE̱-RĒ′ṢI̱-ĂRℭH (-zhe̱-ärk), *n.* A leader in her-
HĔR′E̱-SY̆, *n.* An opinion not orthodox:—sect.
HĔR′E̱-TI̱C, *n.* One who is given to heresy.
HE̱-RĔT′I̱-CA̱L, *a.* Containing heresy; heterodox.
HE̱-RĔT′I̱-CA̱L-LY̆, *ad.* In an heretical manner.
HĒRE-TỌ-FŌRE′, *ad.* Formerly; before this
HĒRE-TŌ′, HĒRE-ỤN-TŌ′, *ad.* To this. [time.
HĒRE′WĬTH, *ad.* With this; accompanying this.
HĔR′I̱-ỌT, *n.* A fine paid to the lord of a manor.
HĔR′I̱-TĄG̱E, *n.* An inheritance; an estate.
HE̱R-MĂPH′RỌ-DĪTE, *n.* One who is of both
HE̱R-MĂPH′RỌ-DĪTE, *a.* Of both sexes. [sexes.
HE̱R-MĂPH-RỌ-DĬT′I̱C, } *a.* Partaking of
HE̱R-MĂPH-RỌ-DĬT′I̱-CA̱L, } both sexes.

HĔR-MĘ-NEŪ'TIC, } *a.* Explaining ; inter-
HĔR-MĘ-NEŪ'TĬ-CĄL, } preting ; exegetical.
HĔR-MĘ-NEŪ'TĬCS, *n. pl.* Science of interpre-
tation ; exegesis ; interpretation.
HĘR-MĔT'ĬC, } *a.* Chemical :—completely
HĘR-MĔT'Ĭ-CĄL, } closing ; air-tight.
HĘR-MĔT'Ĭ-CĄL-LY, *ad.* Chemically :—closely.
HĔR'MĮT, *n.* An anchoret ; a devout recluse.
HĔR'MĮT-ĄGE, *n.* A hermit's habitation :—a
HĔR'MĮT-ĔSS, *n.* A female hermit.   [wine.
HĘR-MĬT'Ĭ-CĄL, *a.* Relating or suitable to a
HĔR'NĮ-Ą, *n.* [L.] (*Med.*) A rupture. [hermit.
HĒ'RŌ, *n.* ; pl. HĒ'RŌEȘ. A brave man.
HĘ-RŌ'ĬC, } *a.* Relating to, or like, a hero ;
HĘ-RŌ'Ĭ-CĄL, } brave ; noble ; illustrious.
HĘ-RŌ'Ĭ-CĄL-LY, HĘ-RŌ'ĬC-LY, *ad.* With her-
oism or valor ; bravely ; nobly.
HĔR'Ǫ-ĬNE *or* HĒ'RǪ-ĬNE, *n.* A female hero.
HĔR'Ǫ-ĬȘM *or* HĒ'RǪ-ĬȘM, *n.* Bravery ; valor.
HĔR'ǪN, *n.* A bird that feeds on fish, frogs, &c.
HĔR'RĬNG, *n.* A small sea-fish ; white-bait, &c.
HĔRȘ, *pron.* Possessive of *she* ; belonging to her.
HĔR'SCHĘL (-shĕl), *n.* A planet. See URANUS.
HĔRSE, *n.* (*Fort.*) A kind of lattice or portcullis.
HĔR-SĔLF', *pron.* A female individual.
HĔȘ'Ĭ-TĄN-CY, *n.* Uncertainty ; suspense.
HĔȘ'Ĭ-TĀTE, *v. n.* To be doubtful ; to pause.
HĔȘ-Ĭ-TĀ'TIǪN, *n.* Doubt :—a stopping in speech.
HĘS-PĒ'RĬ-ĄN, *a.* Western ; being in the west.
HĔT'ĘR-Ǫ-CLĬTE, *n.* An irregular noun.
HĔT-ĘR-Ǫ-CLĬT'ĬC, } *a.* Irregular ; deviat-
HĔT-ĘR-Ǫ-CLĬT'Ĭ-CĄL, } ing from the com-
mon rule.   [unsound in doctrine.
HĔT'ĘR-Ǫ-DŎX, *a.* Heretical ; not orthodox ;
HĔT'ĘR-Ǫ-DŎX-Y, *n.* Quality of being heterodox.
HĔT-Ę-RŌ-GĘ-NĒ'Ĭ-TY, *n.* Opposition of nature.
HĔT-Ę-RǪ-GĒ'NĘ-OŬS, *a.* Dissimilar in nature.
HEW (hū), *v. a.* [*imp. t.* hewed ; *pp.* hewn *or*
hewed.] To cut with an axe ; to chop ; to form.
HEW'ĘR (hū'ęr), *n.* One who hews wood, &c.
HĔX'Ą-ℭHŎRD, *n.* (*Mus.*) Scale of six notes.
HĔX'Ą-GŎN, *n.* A figure of six sides or angles.
HĘX-ĂG'Ǫ-NĄL, *a.* Having six sides or corners.
HĔX-Ą-HĒ'DRĄL, *a.* Relating to a hexahedron.
HĔX-Ą-HĒ'DRǪN, *n.* (*Geom.*) A cube.
HĘX-ĂM'Ę-TĘR, *n.* A verse or line of six feet.
HĘX-ĂN'GY-LĄR, *a.* Having six angles.
HĔX'Ą-STȲLE, *n.* A building with six columns
HEY (hā), *interj.* An expression of joy. [in front.
HEY'DĀY (hā'dā), *interj.* Expressing exultation.
HĪ-Ā'TỤS, *n.* [L.] An aperture ; a gaping breach.
HĪ-BĔR'NĄL, *a.* Belonging to winter ; wintry.
HĪ-BĔR'NĮ-ĄN, *a.* Relating to Ireland.
HĪ-BĔR'NĮ-CĬȘM, *n.* An Irish idiom ; a bull.
HĪ-BĬS'CỤS, *n.* A genus of showy plants.
‖HĬC'COUGH, HĬCK'ỤP (hĭk'kụp *or* hĭk'kŏf), *n.*
A spasmodic affection of the diaphragm and
glottis.   [cough.
‖HĬC'COUGH, HĬCK'ỤP, *v. n.* To utter a hic-
HĬCK'Ǫ-RY, *n.* A large North American tree.
HĬD, HĬD'DEN (hĭd'dn). See HIDE.   [man.
HĮ-DĂL'GŌ, *n.* [Sp.] A kind of Spanish noble-
HĪDE, *v. a. & n.* [*imp. t.* hid ; *pp.* hid *or* hidden.]
To conceal ; to cover ; to protect ; to lie hid.
HĪDE, *n.* Skin of an animal :—measure of land.
HĪDE'-ĄND-SEĒK', *n.* A play among children.
HĪDE'-BŌÛND, *a.* Having the skin close.
HĬD'Ę-OŬS, *a.* Horrible ; dreadful ; shocking.

HĬD'Ę-OŬS-LY, *ad.* Horribly ; dreadfully.
HĬD'Ę-OỤS-NĔSS, *n.* Horribleness ; dreadfulness.
HIE (hī), *v. n.* To hasten ; to go in haste.
HĪ'Ę-RĂRℭH, *n.* The chief of a sacred order.
HĪ-Ę-RĂRℭH'ĄL, } *a.* Relating to a hie-
HĪ-Ę-RĂRℭH'Ĭ-CĄL, } rarch, or a hierarchy.
HĪ'Ę-RĂRℭH-Y, *n.* Ecclesiastical government.
HĪ'ĘR-Ǫ-GLȲPH, } *n.* A symbolical charac-
HĪ-ĘR-Ǫ-GLȲPH'ĬC, } ter :—the art of writing in
picture ; sculpture-writing or picture-writing.
HĪ-ĘR-Ǫ-GLȲPH'ĬC, } *a.* Emblematical ; re-
HĪ-ĘR-Ǫ-GLȲPH'Ĭ-CĄL, } lating to, or consist-
ing of, hieroglyphics.   [ly.
HĪ-ĘR-Ǫ-GLȲPH'Ĭ-CĄL-LY, *ad.* Emblematical-
HĪ-Ę-RŎG'RĄ-PHY, *n.* Holy or sacred writing.
HĪ'Ę-RǪ-MĂN-CY, *n.* Divination by sacrifices.
HĪ-ĔR'Ǫ-PHĂNT, *n.* Expounder of sacred things.
HĬG'GLE, *v. a.* To chaffer ; to haggle :—to peddle.
HĬG'GLE-DY-PĬG'GLE-DY, *ad.* Confusedly.
HĬG'GLĘR, *n.* One who hawks or higgles.
HIGH (hī), *a.* Elevated ; exalted ; lofty :—dear.
HIGH (hī), *ad.* Aloft :—aloud :—profoundly.
HIGH'-BLŌWN (hī'blōn), *a.* Swelled with wind.
HIGH'-BŌRN (hī'börn), *a.* Of noble extraction.
HIGH'-FLĪ-ĘR, *n.* One extravagant in opinion.
HIGH'-FLŌWN (hī'flōn), *a.* Proud ; extravagant.
HIGH'LĄND (hī'lạnd), *n.* A mountainous region.
HIGH'LĄND-ĘR (hī'lạnd-ęr), *n.* A mountaineer.
HIGH'LY (hī'lę), *ad.* Aloft :—in a great degree.
HIGH'-MĬND-ĘD, *a.* Magnanimous :—proud.
HIGH'NĘSS (hī'nęs), *n.* Elevation ; dignity.
HIGH'-SĒA-ȘONED (hī'sē-znd), *a.* Piquant.
HIGH'-SPĬR'ĬT-ĘD, *a.* Bold ; daring ; insolent.
HIGH'-WÂ-TĘR, *n.* The utmost flow of the tide.
HIGH-WĀY' (hī-wā'), *n.* Great road ; public road.
HIGH'WĀY-MĄN (hī'wā-mạn), *n.* A robber.
HIGH'-WROUGHT (hī'râwt), *a.* Highly-finished.
HĮ-LĂR'Ĭ-TY, *n.* Mirth ; merriment ; gayety.
HĬLL, *n.* An elevation of ground less than a
HĬL'LǪCK, *n.* A little hill ; a knoll. [mountain.
HĬL'LY, *a.* Full of hills ; unequal in surface.
HĬLT, *n.* The handle of a sword, dagger, &c.
HĬM, *pron.* The objective case of *he.*
HĬM'SĔLF, *pron.* (emphatical). He or him.
HĬN, *n.* A Jewish measure of ten pints. [ward.
HĪND, *a.* [*comp.* hinder ; *sup.* hindmost.] Back-
HĪND, *n.* The female of the red deer :—a boor.
HĬN'DĘR, *v. a.* To obstruct ; to stop ; to impede.
HĬN'DĘR, *v. n.* To cause impediment.
HĬN'DĘR-ANCE, } *n.* That which hinders ; an
HĬN'DRANCE, } impediment ; an obstruction.
HĬND'ĘR-MŌST, *a.* Last. See HINDMOST.
HĪND'MŌST, *a.* Last ; that comes in the rear.
HĬN-DÔÔ', *n.* An aboriginal of Hindostan.
HĬNGE, *n.* A joint on which a door, &c., turns.
HĬNGE, *v. a.* To furnish with hinges :—to bend.
HĬNGE, *v. n.* To turn, as on a hinge ; to hang.
HĬNT, *v. a. & n.* To bring to mind ; to allude.
HĬNT, *n.* A remote suggestion ; an intimation.
HĬP, *n.* Joint of the thigh :—fruit of the brier.
HĬPPED (hĭpt), } *a.* [Corruption of *hypochondri-*
HĬP'PĬSH, } *ac.*] Low in spirits ; much
HĬP'PǪ-CĂMP, *n.* A sea-horse.   [dejected.
HĬP-PǪ-CĔN'TÂUR, *n.* A fabulous monster,
half horse and half man.
HĬP'PǪ-CRĂS, *n.* A medicated or spiced wine.
HĬP'PǪ-DRŌME, *n.* A course for horse-races.
HĬP'PǪ-GRĬFF, *n.* A fabulous winged horse.

Ā,Ē,Ī,Ō,Ū,Ȳ, *long* ; Ă,Ĕ,Ĭ,Ŏ,Ŭ,Y̆, *short* ; Ą,Ę,Į,Ǫ,Ụ,Y, *obscure.*—FĀRE,FÄR,FĂST,FÅLL ; HÊIR, HĔR ;

HĬP-PO-PŎT'Ā-MŬS, *n.* The river-horse.
HĬP'SHŎT, *a.* Sprained or dislocated in the hip.
HĪRE, *v. a.* To engage for pay :—to let ; to bribe.
HĪRE, *n.* Reward ; recompense ; wages.
HĪRE'LĬNG, *n.* One who is hired ; a mercenary.
HĪRE'LĬNG, *a.* Serving for hire ; mercenary.
HĬR-SŪTE', *a.* Rough ; hairy ; rugged ; shaggy.
HĬŞ (hĭz), *pron.* ; possessive of *he.* Of him.
HĬS'PĬD, *a.* Having stiff hairs or bristles.
HĬSS, *v. n.* To utter a noise as a serpent.
HĬSS, *v. a.* To condemn by hissing ; to disgrace.
HĬSS, *n.* The voice of a serpent, &c. :—censure.
HĬSS'ĬNG, *n.* The noise of a serpent, &c.
HĬST, *interj.* Exclamation commanding silence.
HĬS-TŌ'RĬ-ĂN, *n.* A writer of facts and events.
HĬS-TŎR'ĬC,) *a.* Relating to, consisting of,
HĬS-TŎR'Ĭ-CĂL,) or contained in, history.
HĬS-TŎR'Ĭ-CĂL-LȲ, *ad.* In the manner of history.
HĬS-TŌ-RĬ-ŎG'RĀ-PHĘR, *n.* Writer of history.
HĬS-TŌ-RĬ-ŎG'RĀ-PHȲ, *n.* Business of an histori-
HĬS'TO-RȲ, *n.* A narrative of past events. [an.
HĬS-TRĬ-ŎN'ĬC, HĬS-TRĬ-ŎN'Ĭ-CĂL, *a.* Relating
   to the stage ; theatrical ; dramatic.
HĬS'TRĬ-O-NĬŞM, *n.* Theatrical representation.
HĬT, *v. a.* & *n.* [*imp. t.* & *pp.* hit.] To strike ;
   to touch ; not to miss ; to reach ; to attain, suit.
HĬT, *n.* A stroke ; a chance ; a lucky chance.
HĬTCH, *v. a.* & *n.* To catch ; to move by jerks.
HĬTCH, *n.* A catch ; any thing that holds.
HĬTH'ĘR, *ad.* To this place :—to this end.
HĬTH'ĘR, *a.* Nearer ; towards this part.
HĬTH'ĘR-MŌST, *a.* Nearest on this side.
HĬTH'ĘR-TÔ, *ad.* To this time ; yet ; till now.
HĬTH'ĘR-WÂRD, HĬTH'ĘR-WÂRDŞ, *ad.* This
   way ; towards this place. [—a society.
HĪVE, *n.* A box or artificial receptacle of bees :
HĪVE, *v. a.* & *n.* To put into hives :—to reside.
HĪVEŞ, *n. pl.* The disease called croup.
HŌ, *interj.* Commanding attention ; attend !
HŌAR (hōr), *a.* White or gray with age or frost.
HŌARD (hōrd), *n.* A store laid up ; a treasure.
HŌARD, *v. a.* & *n.* To store ; to lay in hoards.
HŌAR'-FRŎST (hōr'frŏst), *n.* A white frost.
HŌAR'HŎÛND, *n.* A plant. See HOREHOUND.
HŌAR'Ĭ-NĔSS, *n.* The state of being hoary.
HŌARSE (hōrs), *a.* Having the voice rough.
HŌARSE'LȲ (hōrs'lę), *ad.* With a rough voice.
HŌARSE'NĘSS, *n.* Roughness of voice.
HŌAR'Ȳ (hōr'ę), *a.* White ; gray with age ; hoar.
HŌAX (hōks), *n.* An imposition ; a deception.
HŌAX (hōks), *v. a.* To deceive ; to impose upon.
HŎB, *n.* A clown :—a fairy :—part of a grate :
   —nave of a wheel ; a hub.—See HUB.
HŎB'BLE, *v. n.* To walk lamely ; to limp.
HŎB'BLE, *n.* Uneven, awkward gait :—difficulty.
HŎB'BȲ, *n.* A hawk ; a nag :—a favorite object.
HŎB'BȲ-HŌRSE, *n.* A stick on which boys
   ride astride :—a favorite object or pursuit.
HŎB-GŎB'LĬN, *n.* A frightful apparition.
HŎB'NĀIL, *n.* A nail used in shoeing a horse :
   —a clownish person, used in contempt.
HŎB'NŎB, *ad.* A familiar call in drinking.
HŎCK, *n.* The joint above the fetlock :—a wine.
HŌ'CŬS-PŌ'CŬS, *n.* A juggler :—a cheat :—trick.
HŎD, *n.* A trough used for carrying mortar.
HŎDGĘ'-PŎDGĘ, *n.* A mixed mass ; hotchpotch.
HŌ-DĬ-ĔR'NĂL, *a.* Of this day ; of to-day.
HŎD'MĂN, *n.* A laborer that carries a hod.

HŌE (hō), *n.* A tool used in gardening, &c.
HŌE (hō), *v. a.* To cut or dig with a hoe.
HŎG, *n.* The general name of swine :—a broom.
HŎG'CŌTE, *n.* A house for hogs ; a hogsty.
HŎG-GĘR-ĘL, HŎG'GĘT, *n.* A two-year-old
HŎG'GĬSH, *a.* Like a hog ; brutish ; selfish.[ewe.
HŎG'GĬSH-NĔSS, *n.* Brutality ; selfishness.
HŎG'HĔRD, *n.* A person who tends hogs.
HŎGŞ'HĘAD (hŏgz'hęd), *n.* A large barrel or
   cask :—sixty-three gallons, or half a pipe.
HŎG'-SHĔAR-ĬNG, *n.* Much ado about nothing.
HŎG'STȲ, HŎG'PĔN, *n.* An enclosure for hogs.
HŎG'WASH (hŏg'wŏsh), *n.* Draff given to swine.
HŎĬ'DEN (hŏĕ'dn), *n.* A rude, awkward girl.
HŎĬST, *v. a.* To raise or lift up ; to heave.
HŎĬST, *n.* A lift ; the act of raising ; a lifting.
HŎĬ'TȲ-TŎĬ'TȲ, *interj.* Noting surprise.
HŌLD, *v. a.* [*imp. t.* & *pp.* held *or* holden.]
   To grasp ; to keep ; to retain ; to contain.
HŌLD, *v. n.* To stand ; to last ; to refrain.
HŌLD, *n.* A grasp ; support ; power :—custody.
HŌLD'BĂCK, *n.* A let ; a hinderance ; obstacle.
HŌLD'ĘR, *n.* One that holds :—a tenant.
HŌLD'FĂST, *n.* A catch ; hook ; support ; hold.
HŌLE, *n.* A cavity ; a perforation ; a cell.
HŌL'Ĭ-DĀY, *n.* Anniversary celebration :—day
   for amusement. See HOLYDAY. [title.
HŌ'LĬ-NĔSS, *n.* Sanctity ; piety :—the pope's
HŌL-LŌ', HŌL-LŌA' (hŭl-lō'), *interj.* Noting a
   call ; a word used in calling. [Holland.
HŌL'LĄND, *n.* A fine sort of linen, made in
HŌL'LŌW (hŏl'lō), *a.* Excavated ; having a
   void within ; not solid :—noisy :—not faithful.
HŎL'LŌW (hŏl'lō), *n.* A cavity ; cavern ; hole ;
HŎL'LŌW (hŏl'lō), *v. a.* To make hollow. [pit.
HŎL'LŌW-NĔSS (hŏl'lo-nĕs), *n.* A cavity :—
HŎL'LȲ, *n.* An evergreen tree. [deceit.
HŎL'LȲ-HŎCK, *n.* A tall, flowering garden-plant.
HŌLM (hōm), *n.* A river isle :—evergreen oak.
HŌL'O-CÂUST, *n.* A whole burnt sacrifice.
HŌL'STĘR, *n.* A case for a horseman's pistol.
HŌ'LȲ, *a.* Religious ; pure ; immaculate ; sacred.
HŌL'Ȳ-DĀY, *n.* A festival day. See HOLIDAY.
HŌ'LȲ-GHŌST (hō'lę-gōst), *n.* The Holy Spirit.
HŎM'AGĘ, *n.* Service ; fealty ; duty ; respect.
HŎM'AGĘ, *v. a.* To reverence ; to pay honor to.
HŌME, *n.* One's house, dwelling, or country.
HŌME, *a.* Domestic :—close :—direct ; severe.
HŌME, *ad.* To one's home :—to the point or
   person ; pointedly ; directly ; closely.
HŌME'BŎRN, *a.* Native ; domestic ; not foreign.
HŌME'BRĔD, *a.* Native ; plain ; artless ; domestic.
HŌME'FĔLT, *a.* Felt within ; inward ; private.
HŌME'LĔSS, *a.* Wanting a home.
HŌME'LĬ-NĔSS, *n.* Plainness ; coarseness.
HŌME'LȲ, *a.* Plain ; not elegant ; coarse ; rude.
HŌME'MĀDE, *a.* Made at home ; plain.
HŌ'MĘR, *n.* A Hebrew measure of 11 bushels.
HŌME'SPŬN, *a.* Made at home ; plain ; homely.
HŌME'STĔAD, *n.* A house with its buildings.
HŌME'WARD, HŌME'WARDŞ, *ad.* Towards
HŎM-Ĭ-CĪ'DĂL, *a.* Murderous ; bloody. [home.
HŎM'Ĭ-CĪDE, *n.* Murder ; manslaughter :—one
   who kills a man ; a man-slayer. [tion.
HŎM'Ĭ-LȲ, *n.* A discourse read to a congrega-
HŎM'Ĭ-NȲ, HŎM'MO-NȲ, *n.* Food made of maize.
HŌ-MO-CĔN'TRĬC, *a.* Having the same centre.
HŌ-MO-GĒ'NĘ-ĂL, *a.* Homogeneous ; cognate.

HŎ-MQ-GĒ′NE-QŬs, *a.* Having the same nature.
HQ-MŎL′Q-GOŬs, *a.* Proportional to each other.
HQ-MŎN′Y-MOŬs, *a.* Equivocal; ambiguous.
HQ-MŎN′Y-MY, *n.* An equivocation; ambiguity.
HQ-MŎT′Q-NOŬs, *a.* Having the same sound.
HŌNE, *n.* A stone for whetting razors, &c. [just.
HŎN′EST (ŏn′est), *a.* Upright; true; chaste;
HŎN′EST-LY (ŏn′est-le), *ad.* Uprightly; justly.
HŎN′ES-TY (ŏn′es-te), *n.* Justice; virtue; purity.
HŎN′EY (hŭn′ne), *n.* Sweet produce of bees, &c.
HŎN′EY-BĂG, *n.* The stomach of the honey-bee.
HŎN′EY-CŌMB (hŭn′ne-kōm), *n.* Cells for hon-
HŎN′EY-DEW (-dū), *n.* A sweet substance. [ey.
HŎN′EY-MÔÔN, *n.* The first month after mar-
 riage. [woodbine; a fragrant flower.
HŎN′EY-SŬC-KLE, *n.* An ornamental plant;
HŎN′EYED (hŭn′nid), *a.* Covered with honey.
HŎN′QR (ŏn′nur), *n.* Dignity; high rank; repu-
 tation; fame; magnanimity; respect; a title.
HŎN′QR (ŏn′nur), *v. a.* To reverence; to dignify.
HŎN′QR-A-BLE (ŏn′nur-a-bl), *a.* Having honor;
 illustrious; noble; magnanimous; generous.
HŎN′QR-A-BLY (ŏn′nur-a-ble), *ad.* With honor.
HŎN′Q-RA-RY (ŏn′q-ra-re), *a.* Conferring honor.
HOOD (hŭd), *n.* A covering for the head. [hide.
HOOD′WĬNK (hŭd′wĭnk), *v. a.* To blind; to
HÔÔF, *n.* The horny part of a beast's foot.
HÔÔFED (hôft), *a.* Furnished with hoofs.
HOOK (hŭk), *n.* Any thing bent so as to catch.
HOOK (hŭk), *v. a.* To catch; to insnare.
HOOK (hŭk), *v. n.* To bend; to have a curve.
HOOKED (hŭk′ed *or* hŭkt), *a.* Bent; curvated.
HOOP (hûp *or* hôp), *n.* A band of wood or metal.
HOOP (hûp *or* hôp), *v. a.* To bind with hoops.
HÔÔP, *v. n.* To shout; to make an outcry.
HÔÔP, *n.* A shout:—measure containing a peck.
HÔÔP′ĬNG-CŎUGH′ (hôp′ĭng-kŏf′), *n.* A con-
 vulsive cough, so called from its noise;
 whooping-cough. [as an owl.
HÔÔT, *v. n.* To shout, as in contempt; to cry
HÔÔT, *v. a.* To drive with noise and shouts.
HÔÔT, *n.* A clamor; a loud shout; a noise.
HŎP, *v. n.* To jump; to skip; to leap on one leg.
HŎP, *n.* A plant:—a dance:—jump on one leg.
HŎP′-BĬND, *n.* The stem of the hop plant.
HŌPE, *n.* Desire united with expectation.
HŌPE, *v. n.* To live in expectation of some good.
HŌPE, *v. a.* To expect with desire; to long for.
HŌPE′FŮL, *a.* Full of hope; promising. [hope.
HŌPE′FŮL-LY, *ad.* In a hopeful manner; with
HŌPE′FŮL-NĔSS, *n.* Promise or prospect of good.
HŌPE′LESS, *a.* Wanting hope; despairing.
HŌPE′LESS-LY, *ad.* In a hopeless manner.
HŎP′PER, *n.* One who hops:—a box; a basket.
HŌ′RAL, HŌ′RA-RY, *a.* Relating to an hour.
HŌRDE, *n.* A clan; a migratory crew; a gang.
HQ-RĪ′ZQN, *n.* The line that bounds the view.
HŎR-Į-ZŎN′TAL, *a.* Parallel to the horizon;
 level :—near the horizon. [ner.
HŎR-Į-ZŎN′TAL-LY, *ad.* In a horizontal man-
HŎRN, *n.* A hard substance growing on the
 heads of some quadrupeds :—a wind instrument
HŎRN′BĒAM, *n.* A tree. [of music.
HŎRN′BLŌW-ER, *n.* One who blows a horn.
HŎRN′BOOK (hŏrn′bŭk), *n.* A child's first book
 of instruction; a primer.
HŎRN′ED, *a.* Having horns:—like a horn.
HŎRN′ER, *n.* One who works or deals in horn.

HŎR′NET, *n.* A very large sort of wasp.
HŎRN′PĪPE, *n.* A British dance :—a wind in-
 strument; a sort of pipe :—a tune.
HŎRN′STŌNE, *n.* A kind of blue stone.
HŎRN′Y, *a.* Made of horn :—hard; callous.
HQ-RŎG′RA-PHY, *n.* An account of the hours.
HŎR′Q-LŌĠE, *n.* A clock; a timepiece.
HQ-RŎL′Q-ĠY, *n.* Art of constructing timepieces.
HQ-RŎM′E-TRY, *n.* Art of measuring time.
HŎR′Q-SCŌPE, *n.* The aspect of the heavenly
 bodies at the hour of one's birth.
HŎR′RĮ-BLE, *a.* Dreadful; terrible; shocking.
HŎR′RĮ-BLE-NĔSS, *n.* Dreadfulness; terrible-
HŎR′RĮ-BLY, *ad.* In a horrible manner. [ness.
HŎR′RĮD, *a.* Terrible; dreadful; shocking.
HŎR′RĮD-LY, *ad.* Terrifically; shockingly.
HŎR′RĮD-NĔSS, *n.* Hideousness; enormity.
HQR-RĬF′ĮC, *a.* Causing horror; terrific.
HŎR′RQR, *n.* Terror mixed with hatred; dread.
HŎRSE, *n.* A quadruped :—a wooden machine.
HŎRSE′BĂCK, *n.* The back of a horse.
HŎRSE′BĒAN, *n.* A sort of bean given to horses.
HŎRSE′BLŎCK, *n.* A block, foot-stone, or step,
 used in mounting a horse.
HŎRSE′BŌAT, *n.* A boat moved by horses. [nut.
HŎRSE′CHĔST-NŬT, *n.* A flowering tree, and its
HŎRSE′FLY, *n.* Fly that stings horses; gadfly.
HŎRSE′GUĂRDŞ (hŏrs′gärdz), *n. pl.* Cavalry.
HŎRSE′HĂIR (hŏrs′hår), *n.* The hair of horses.
HŎRSE′LĂUGH (hŏrs′lȧf), *n.* A loud, rude laugh.
HŎRSE′LĒĒCH, *n.* A leech that bites horses.
HŎRSE′LĬT-TER, *n.* A carriage hung upon
 poles, and borne by and between two horses.
HŎRSE′LŌAD, *n.* As much as a horse can carry.
HŎRSE′MAN, *n.* One skilled in horses; a rider.
HŎRSE′MAN-SHĬP, *n.* Art of managing horses.
HŎRSE′MĂR-TEN, *n.* A large kind of bee.
HŎRSE′MĬLL, *n.* A mill turned by a horse.
HŎRSE′PLĂY (hŏrs′plā), *n.* Coarse, rough play.
HŎRSE′PŎND, *n.* A pond for horses.
HŎRSE′RĀCE, *n.* A race between horses.
HŎRSE′RĂD-ĮSH, *n.* A plant, and acrid root.
HŎRSE′SHŌE (hŏrs′shů), *n.* A shoe for horses.
HŎRSE′STĒAL-ER, *n.* A thief who steals horses.
HŎRSE′WĂY, *n.* A way for horses.
HŎRSE′WHĬP, *n.* A whip to strike a horse with.
HŎRSE′WHĬP, *v. a.* To strike with a horsewhip.
HŎR-TĀ′TIQN, *n.* Exhortation; act of exhorting.
HŎR′TA-TĬVE, } *a.* Encouraging; advising;
HŎR′TA-TQ-RY, } containing or expressing ex-
 hortation; persuasive. [ure.
HŎR-TĮ-CŬLT′U-RAL, *a.* Relating to horticult-
HŎR′TĮ-CŬLT-URE (hŏr′te-kŭlt-yur), *n.* The
 art of cultivating gardens; art of gardening.
HŎR-TĮ-CŬLT′U-RĬST, *n.* One skilled in horti-
 culture; a gardener. [garden.
HŎRT′U-LAN (hŏrt′yu-lan), *a.* Relating to a
HŎR′TUS SĬC′CUS, *n.* Specimens of plants dried.
HQ-SĂN′NA, *n.* An exclamation of praise to God.
HŌŞE, *n.* Stockings; covering for the legs :—a
 tube or pipe for conducting water.
HŌŞ′IER (hō′zher), *n.* Maker or seller of hose.
HŎS′PĮ-TA-BLE, *a.* Attentive or kind to stran-
 gers; entertaining strangers gratuitously.
HŎS′PĮ-TA-BLE-NĔSS, *n.* Kindness to strangers.
HŎS′PĮ-TA-BLY, *ad.* With kindness to strangers.
HŎS′PĮ-TAL (hŏs′pe-tal *or* ŏs′pe-tal), *n.* A build-
 ing for the sick, lunatics, the wounded, &c.

HŎS-PĪ-TĂL′Ĭ-TY, *n.* Quality of being hospitable.
HŎS-PĪ′′TĬ-ŬM (hŏs-pĭsh′ę-ŭm), *n.* A monastery serving as an inn for entertaining travellers.
HŎST, *n.* One who entertains another:—a landlord:—army:—multitude:—consecrated wafer.
HŎS′TĄĢE, *n.* One given in pledge as security for the performance of conditions; surety.
HŎST′ĘSS, *n.* A female host:—a landlady.
HŎS′TĬLE, *a.* Adverse; opposite; inimical.
HŎS′TĬLE-LY, *ad.* In a hostile manner.
HŎS-TĬL′Ĭ-TY, *n.* The practice of war; open war:—enmity; animosity; hatred; ill-will.
HŎS′TLĘR (ŏs′lęr), *n.* One who has the care of horses at an inn or stable. [eager.
HŎT, *a.* Having heat; fiery:—furious; ardent;
HŎT′BĘD, *n.* A bed of earth made hot, by the fermentation of dung, for rearing early plants.
HŎT′BRĀĬNED (hŏt′brānd), *a.* Violent; furious.
HŎT′-CŎC-KLĘS, *n. pl.* A kind of play or game.
HŎ-TĔL′, *n.* A genteel inn; a public house.
HŎT′HĔAD-ĘD, *a.* Violent; passionate.
HŎT′HŎŪSE, *n.* An enclosure kept warm for rearing tender plants, and ripening fruits.
HŎT′LY, *ad.* With heat; not coldly; violently.
HŎT′SPŬR, *n.* A violent, passionate man:—a kind of pea of speedy growth.
HOUGH (hŏk), *n.* The ankle joint of a horse.
HOUGH (hŏk), *v. a.* To hamstring:—to cut up.
HŎŪND, *n.* A sort of dog used in the chase.
HŎŪND, *v. a.* To set on the chase:—to hunt.
HŎŪR (ŏŭr), *n.* The 24th part of a natural day; 60 minutes:—particular time:—a goddess.
HŎŪR′GLĂSS (ŏŭr′glăs), *n.* A glass to show time.
HŎŪR′HĂND (ŏŭr′hănd), *n.* The hand of a clock or watch which points out the hour. [adise.
HŎŪ′RĬ (hŏä′rę), *n.* A Mahometan nymph of par-
HŎŪR′LY (ŏŭr′lę), *a.* Happening every hour.
HŎŪR′LY (ŏŭr′lę), *ad.* Every hour; frequently.
HŎŪSE, *n.* A place of human abode:—a family; a race:—a household:—a legislative body.
HŎŪSE, *v. a.* To harbor; to shelter; to cover.
HŎŪSE′BREĀK-ĘR (hŏŭs′brāk-ęr), *n.* A burglar.
HŎŪSE′BREĀK-ĬNG, *n.* Crime of breaking into a house for unlawful purposes by daylight.
HŎŪSE′HŌLD, *n.* A family living together.
HŎŪSE′HŌLD-ĘR, *n.* An occupier of a house.
HŎŪSE′HŌLD-STŬFF, *n.* Furniture of a house.
HŎŪSE′KĒĒP-ĘR, *n.* One who keeps a house.
HŎŪSE′KĒĒP-ĬNG, *n.* Management of a house.
HŎŪSE′LĒĒK, *n.* A plant tenacious of life.
HŎŪSE′LĘSS, *a.* Wanting an abode or a house.
HŎŪSE′MĀĬD, *n.* A female menial servant.
HŎŪSE′RŎŎM, *n.* Space in a house. [house.
HŎŪSE′WĂRM-ĬNG, *n.* A feast on entering a new
‖HOUSE′WIFE (hŭz′wĭf *or* hŏŭs′wīf), *n.* The mistress of a family; a female economist.
‖HOUSE′WIFE-RY (hŭz′wĭf-rę), *n.* Domestic or female management or economy.
HŎŪŞ′ĬNG, *n.* Houses collectively:—a saddle
HŎVE, *imp. t.* of *heave.* [cloth; horse-cloth.
HŎV′ĘL, *n.* A shed:—mean habitation; cottage.
HŎV′ĘR *or* HŎV′ĘR, *v. n.* To hang in the air:—
HŎW (hŏŭ), *ad.* In what manner. [to wander.
HŎW-BĒ′ĬT, *ad.* Nevertheless; notwithstanding.
HŎW-ĔV′ĘR, *ad.* In whatsoever manner, at all events; at least; nevertheless; yet.
HŎW′ĬTZ, HŎW′ĬT-ZĘR, *n.* A piece of ordnance of larger calibre than a cannon.

HŎWL, *v. n.* To cry as a wolf, or as one in distress:—to make a loud noise, as the wind.
HŎWL, *n.* The cry of a wolf or dog:—cry of distress.
HŎWL′ĬNG, *n.* The cry of one that howls. [tress.
HŎW-SQ-ĔV′ĘR, *ad.* Although; however.
HŎY, *n.* A small vessel, usually rigged as a sloop.
HŬB, *n.* The nave of a wheel:—a mark; target.
HŬB′BŬB, *n.* A confusion; a tumult. [*Vulgar.*]
HŬC′KLE-BĂCKED (hŭk′kl-bäkt), *a.* Crooked in the shoulders or back; crook-backed.
HŬCKS′TĘR, *n.* A retailer of small wares; pedler.
HŬD′DLE, *v. n. & a.* To crowd or press together.
HŬD′DLE, *n.* A crowd; a tumult; confusion.
HŬE (hū), *n.* Color; tint:—a clamor; shouting.
HŬFF, *n.* Swell of anger or arrogance:—a bully.
HŬFF, *v. n. & a.* To bluster; to storm; to swell.
HŬFF′ĬSH, *a.* Arrogant; insolent; petulant.
HŬFF′ĬSH-NĔSS, *n.* Petulance; arrogance.
HŬG, *v. a.* To embrace fondly:—to hold fast.
HŬG, *n.* Close embrace; a gripe in wrestling.
HŪĢE, *a.* Vast; very great; enormous.
HŪĢE′LY, *ad.* Immensely; enormously; greatly.
HŪĢE′NĔSS, *n.* Enormous bulk; vast extent.
HŪ′ĢUĘ-NŎT (hū′ĝe-nŏt), *n.* A French Calvinist.
HŬLK, *n.* The body of a ship:—an old vessel.
HŬLL, *n.* A husk; a covering:—body of a ship.
HŬLL, *v. a.* To peel:—to pierce the hull of.
HŬLL′Y, *a.* Having hulls; husky. [mock.
HŬM, *v. n. & a.* To sing low:—to buzz:—to
HŬM, *n.* A buzzing noise:—a jest; a hoax.
HŬM, *interj.* Implying doubt and deliberation.
HŪ′MĄN, *a.* Belonging to man or mankind.
HY-MĀNE′, *a.* Kind; civil; benevolent; tender.
HY-MĀNE′LY, *ad.* Kindly; with good nature.
HY-MĂN′Ĭ-TY, *n.* The nature of man:—mankind:—benevolence: philology:—polite literature.
HŪ′MĄN-ĪZE, *v. a.* To render humane. [ature.
HŪ-MĄN-KĪND′, *n.* The race of man; mankind.
HŪ′MĄN-LY, *ad.* After the manner of men.
‖HŬM′BLE (hŭm′bl *or* ŭm′bl), *a.* Not proud; modest; submissive; lowly of spirit; low.
‖HŬM′BLE, *v. a.* To make humble; to crush.
‖HŬM′BLE-BĒĒ, *n.* A large, buzzing, wild bee.
‖HŬM′BLY, *ad.* Without pride; with humility.
HŬM′BŬG, *n.* An imposition. [*Low.*]
HŬM′BŬG, *v. a.* To cheat; to impose upon.
HŬM′DRŬM, *n.* A stupid person; a drone.
HŪ′MĘ-RĄL, *a.* Belonging to the shoulder.
HŪ′MĘ-RŬS, *n.* Cylindrical bone of the arm.
HŪ′MĬD, *a.* Wet; moist; damp; watery.
HY-MĬD′Ĭ-TY, *n.* Moisture; dampness; wetness.
HY-MĬL-Ĭ-Ā′TĬQN, *n.* Act of humbling; descent from greatness; abasement; mortification.
HY-MĬL′Ĭ-TY, *n.* Freedom from pride; lowliness.
HŬM′MĬNG-BĬRD, *n.* A very small bird.
‖HŪ′MQR (yū′mŭr *or* hū′mŭr), *n.* Moisture:—disposition; turn of mind:—whim; fancy:—facetiousness; wit:—cutaneous eruption.
‖HŪ′MQR (yū′mŭr), *v. a.* To gratify; to indulge.
‖HŪ′MQ-RĄL (yū′mǫ-rąl), *a.* Relating to humors.
‖HŪ′MQ-RĬST (yū′mǫ-rĭst), *n.* A jester; a wag.
‖HŪ′MQ-RŎŪS (yū′mǫ-rŭs), *a.* Jocose; pleasant.
‖HŪ′MQ-RŎŪS-LY (yū′mǫ-rŭs-lę), *ad.* Jocosely.
‖HŪ′MQR-SŎME (yū′mŭr-sŭm), *a.* Petulant; odd.
HŬMP, *n.* Protuberance of a crooked back.
HŬMP′BĂCK, *n.* A crooked or hunched back.
HŬNCH, *v. a.* To jostle:—to crook, as the back.
HŬNCH, *n.* A hump; a bunch:—a push.

HŬN'DRĘD, *a.* Ten multiplied by ten. [county.
HŬN'DRĘD, *n.* The number 100 :—a part of a
HŬN'DRĘDTH, *a.* The ordinal of a hundred.
HŬNG, *imp. t. & pp.* of *hang.* Suspended.
HŬN'ĢĘR (hŭng'ġer), *n.* An eager desire or want
  of food ; a craving appetite :—violent desire.
HŬN'ĢĘR (hŭng'ġer), *v. n.* To feel hunger.
HŬN'ĢĘRED (hŭng'ġerd), *a.* Famished; starved.
HŬN'GRĮ-LY (hŭng'grę-lę), *ad.* With hunger.
HŬN'GRY (hŭng'grę), *a.* Being in want of food.
HŬNKS, *n.* A covetous, sordid wretch ; a miser.
HŬNT, *v. a. & n.* To chase ; to pursue ; to search.
HŬNT, *n.* A pack of hounds :—chase.; pursuit.
HŬNT'ĘR, *n.* One that hunts animals; huntsman.
HŬNT'ĮNG, *n.* The diversion of the chase ; hunt.
HŬNT'ĮNG-HÖRN, *n.* A horn used in hunting.
HŬNT'RĘSS, *n.* A woman that follows the chase.
HŬNTS'MĄN, *n.* One who practises hunting.
HŬR'DLE, *n.* A texture of sticks ; a crate.
HŬR'DLE, *v. a.* To hedge or close with hurdles.
HŬRDŞ, HÄRDŞ, *n. pl.* The refuse of flax.
HŬRL, *v. a.* To throw with violence ; to cast.
HŬRL, *n.* The act of throwing :—tumult ; riot.
HŬR'LY-BŬR'LY, *n.* Tumult; commotion; bustle.
HŬR-RÄH' (hŭ-rä'), *interj.* A shout noting joy,
  applause, encouragement, or triumph.
HŬR'RĮ-CÄNE, *n.* A violent storm ; a tornado.
HŬR'RY, *v. a. & n.* To hasten ; to move hastily.
HŬR'RY, *n.* Tumult; precipitation ; commotion.
HŬRT, *v. a.* [*imp. t. & pp.* hurt.] To harm ; to
  wound ; to injure; to damage ; to chafe, fret.
HŬRT, *n.* Harm ; mischief ; a wound ; injury.
HŬRT'FŬL, *a.* Mischievous ; injurious ; noxious.
HŬRT'FŬL-LY, *ad.* Injuriously ; mischievously.
HŬRT'FŬL-NĚSS, *n.* Injuriousness ; pernicious-
HŬR'TLE-BĚR-RY, *n.* A whortleberry. [ness.
HŬRT'LĘSS, *a.* Indecent ; harmless ; innoxious.
HŬŞ'BĄND, *n.* Correlative to *wife* ; a man mar-
  ried to a woman :—economist ;—farmer.
HŬŞ'BĄND, *v. a.* To manage frugally ; to till.
HŬŞ'BĄND-MÄN, *n.* A farmer ; a cultivator.
HŬŞ'BĄND-RY, *n.* Tillage :—thrift ; frugality ;
HŬSH, *interj.* Silence ! be still ! no noise ! [care.
HŬSH, *a.* Still ; silent ; quiet. [calm.
HŬSH, *v. a.* To still ; to silence ; to quiet ; to
HŬSH'MŎN-EY (hŭsh'mŭn-ę), *n.* A bribe to in-
  duce silence, or to hinder information.
HŬSK, *n.* The integument of fruits or seeds.
HŬSK, *v. a.* To strip off the integument of.
HŬSK'Į-NĚSS, *n.* The state of being husky.
HŬS'KY, *a.* Abounding in husks :—hoarse.
HŪ'SŌ, *n.* A large species of sturgeon.
HŬŞ-ŞÄR' (hŭz-zär'), *n.* A kind of horse-soldier.
HŬŞ'ŞY, *n.* A sorry or worthless woman.
HŬST'ĮNGŞ, *n.* A court :—place of meeting for
  electing a member of parliament *in England.*
HŬS'TLE (hŭs'sl), *v. a.* To shake ; to jostle.
HŬŞ'WĮFE (hŭz'zif), *n.* A female economist ; a
  thrifty woman or wife. See HOUSEWIFE. [RY.
HŬŞ'WĮFE-RY (hŭz'zif-rę), *n.* See HOUSEWIFE-
HŬT, *n.* A poor cottage :— temporary building.
HŬTCH, *n.* A chest :—a rabbit-box :—a rat-trap.
||HŬZ-ZÄ' *or* HŬZ-ZÄ', *interj.* An exclamation
  noting joy or triumph ; hurrah.
||HŬZ-ZÄ', *n.* A shout ; a cry of acclamation.
||HŬZ-ZÄ', *v. n.* To utter acclamation. [mation.
||HŬZ-ZÄ', *v. a.* To receive or attend with accla-
HȲ'Ą-CĬNTH, *n.* A flower :—a gem or mineral.

HȲ-Ą-CĬN'THĮNE, *a.* Of, or resembling, hya-
  cinths. [the Seven Stars.
HȲ'Ą-DĘŞ, HȲ'ĄDŞ, *n. pl.* A cluster of stars ;
HȲ'Ą-LĪNE, *a.* Glassy ; crystalline.
HȲ'BRĮD, *a.* Mongrel ; of different species.
HȲB'RĮ-DOŬS, *a.* Of different species ; hybrid.
HȲ'DRĄ, *n.* [L.] A monster with many heads.
HY-DRÄN'ĢĘ-Ą, *n.* A plant and its flower.
HȲ'DRĄNT, *n.* A pipe for discharging water.
HY-DRÂU'LĮC, *a.* Relating to hydraulics.
HY-DRÂU'LĮCS, *n. pl.* The science of the motion
  of liquids and of the effects they produce.
HȲ'DRQ-CĒLE, *n.* (*Med.*) Watery collection.
HȲ-DRQ-CĚPH'Ą-LŬS, *n.* Dropsy of the brain.
HȲ'DRQ-ĢĚN, *n.* A colorless gas, which, com-
  bined with oxygen, produces water. [raphy.
HY-DRŎG'RĄ-PHĘR, *n.* One versed in hydrog-
HȲ-DRQ-GRÄPH'Į-CĄL, *a.* Relating to, or par-
  taking of, hydrography. [earth.
HY-DRŎG'RĄ-PHY, *n.* Science of waters of the
HY-DRÖL'Q-ĢY, *n.* The science of water.
HȲ'DRQ-MĚL, *n.* A liquor of honey and water.
MY-DRŎM'Ę-TĘR, *n.* An instrument to meas-
  ure the specific gravity, density, &c., of liquids.
HY-DRŎM'Ę-TRY, *n.* Art of measuring liquids.
HȲ-DRQ-PHŌ'BĮ-Ą, *n.* Canine madness.
HY-DRŎP'ĮC, HY-DRŎP'Į-CĄL, *a.* Dropsical ;
  diseased with dropsy ; resembling dropsy.
HȲ-DRQ-STÄT'ĮC, } *a.* Relating or accord-
HȲ-DRQ-STÄT'Į-CĄL, } ing to hydrostatics.
HȲ-DRQ-STÄT'ĮCS, *n. pl.* The science which
  treats of the equilibrium and pressure of liquids.
HȲ'DRŲS, *n.* A water-snake :—a constellation.
HȲ-Ē'MĄL *or* HȲ'Ę-MĄL, *a.* Belonging to, or
  coming in, winter. [ter.
HȲ-Ę-MĀ'TIQN, *n.* Shelter from the cold of win-
HȲ-Ē'NĄ, *n.* A fierce animal, resembling a wolf.
HȲ-ĢĒ'IĄN, HȲ-ĢIĒ'ĄN, *a.* Relating to health.
HȲ-GRŎM'Ę-TĘR, *n.* An instrument to meas-
  ure the degrees of moisture of the atmosphere.
HȲ'MĘN, *n.* God of marriage :—a membrane.
HȲ-MĘ-NĒ'ĄL, HȲ-MĘ-NĒ'ĄN, *n.* A marriage
  song. [marriage.
HȲ-MĘ-NĒ'ĄL, HȲ-MĘ-NĒ'ĄN, *a.* Pertaining to
HȲMN (hĭm), *n.* A song of praise.
HȲMN (hĭm), *v. a.* To praise in song ; to sing.
HȲP, *v. a.* To make hypochondriacal. [*Vulgar.*]
HȲ-PĚR'BQ-LĄ, *n.* One of the conic sections.
HȲ-PĚR'BQ-LĘ, *n.* A rhetorical figure which
  expresses more than the exact truth.
HȲ-PĘR-BŎL'ĮC, HȲ-PĘR-BŎL'Į-CĄL, *a.* Per-
  taining to, or like, an hyperbole or an hyper-
  bola ; exaggerating or extenuating.
HȲ-PĘR-BŎL'Į-CĄL-LY, *ad.* With hyperbole.
HȲ-PĘR-BŌ'RĘ-ĄN, *a.* Far north ; cold ; frigid.
HȲ-PĘR-CRĬT'ĮC, *n.* Captious or uncandid critic.
HȲ-PĘR-CRĬT'Į-CĄL, *a.* Critical beyond reason.
HȲ'PHĘN, *n.* A mark of conjunction, thus [-].
HȲP-NŎT'ĮC, *n.* A medicine that induces sleep.
HȲP-Q-ℭHŎN'DRĮ-Ą, *n.* Melancholy ; dejection.
HȲP-Q-ℭHŎN'DRĮ-ĂC, *a.* Hypochondriacal.
HȲP'Q-ℭHŎN'DRĮ-ĂC, *n.* One afflicted with
  hypochondria ; one morbidly melancholy.
HȲP-Q-ℭHQN-DRĪ'Ą-CĄL, *a.* Melancholy ; dis-
  pirited ; affected with hypochondria ; gloomy.
HȲP-Q-ℭHQN-DRĪ'Ą-CĬŞM, *n.* Melancholy. [tion.
HȲP-Q-ℭHQN-DRĪ'Ą-SĬS, *n.* Hypochondriac affec-
HY-PŎC'RĮ-SY, *n.* Dissimulation ; false pretence.

HĬP'Ọ-CRĬTE, n. A dissembler in religion, &c.
HĬP-Ọ-CRĬT'ĬC,   } a. Dissembling; false; in-
HĬP-Ọ-CRĬT'Ĭ-CAL,   } sincere; counterfeit.
HĬP-Ọ-CRĬT'Ĭ-CAL-LY, ad. With dissimulation.
HY-PŎS'TA-SĬS, n.; pl. HY-PŎS'TA-SĒȘ. Per-
  sonality; person:—substance or subsistence:
  —element; principle.   [ent; personal.
HȲ-PỌ-STĂT'Ĭ-CAL, a. Constitutive; constitu-
HȲ-PŎTH'E-NŪSE, n. Longest side of a right-
  angled triangle, or line opposite the right-angle.

HY-PŎTH'E-SĬS, n.; pl. HY-PŎTH'E-SĒȘ. A
  supposition:—system assumed but not proved.
HȲ-PỌ-THĔT'ĬC,   } a. Including an hypothe-
HȲ-PỌ-THĔT'Ĭ-CAL,   } sis or supposition; im-
  plying supposition; conditional. [supposition.
HȲ-PỌ-THĔT'Ĭ-CAL-LY, ad. Conditionally; by
HȲ'SON, n. An excellent species of green tea.
HȲȘ'SOP or HȲS'SOP, n. A plant or herb. [fits.
HYS-TĔR'ĬC, HYS-TĔR'Ĭ-CAL, a. Troubled with
HYS-TĔR'ĬCS, n. pl. Fits peculiar to women.

I.

I a vowel, has two principal sounds; one
  long, as in *fine*; the other short, as in *fin*.
I, *pron.* of the first person; one's self.
Ĭ-ĂM'BĬC, a. Having a short and a long syllable.
Ĭ-ĂM'BĬC, n. A verse composed of iambic feet.
Ī'BĬS, n. An Egyptian bird like the stork. [sugar.
ICE, n. Water congealed by cold:—concreted
ICE, v. a. To cover with ice:—to freeze, chill.
ICE'BĔRG, n. A mountain or great mass of ice.
ICE'BLĬNK, n. A dazzling whiteness, caused by
  the reflection of light from a field of ice. [ited.
ICE'HŎŪSE, n. A house in which ice is repos-
ĬCH-NEŪ'MON (ĭk-nū'mon), n. A small animal.
ĬCH-NŎG'RA-PHY, n. A ground plan; a section.
Ī'ꞒHOR (ī'kọr), n. (*Med.*) A thin, watery humor.
Ī'ꞒHOR-OŬS (ī'kọr-ŭs), a. Serous; sanious; thin.
ĬꞒH-THY-ŎL'Ọ-ꞬY, n. The science of fishes.
ĬꞒH-THY-ŎPH'A-ꞬY, n. Practice of eating fish.
Ī'CĬ-CLE (ī'sĭk-kl), n. A pendent shoot of ice.
Ī'CĬ-NĔSS (ī'se-nĕs), n. The state of being icy.
Ī'CON, n. A picture; an image; a figure.
Ĭ-CŎN'Ọ-CLĂST, n. A breaker of images. [&c.
Ĭ-CỌ-NŎG'RA-PHY, n. A description of pictures;
Ĭ-CỌ-NŎL'Ọ-ꞬY, n. The doctrine of images, &c.
ĬC-TĔR'Ĭ-CAL, a. Good against the jaundice.
Ī'CY, a. Full of ice:—cold; frosty; frigid.
Ĭ-DĒ'A, n. A mental image; thought; notion.
Ĭ-DĒ'AL, a. Mental; intellectual; imagined.
Ĭ-DĒ'AL, n. Something imaginary; idea.
Ĭ-DĒ'AL-ĬSM, n. The doctrine of ideal existence.
Ĭ-DĒ'AL-LY, ad. Intellectually; mentally.
Ĭ-DĔN'TĬC, Ĭ-DĔN'TĬ-CAL, a. The same; not
  different; one and the same; self-same. [tity.
Ĭ-DĔN'TĬ-CAL-LY, ad. With sameness or iden-
Ĭ-DĔN'TĬ-CAL-NĔSS, n. Sameness; identity.
Ĭ-DĔN'TĬ-FȲ, v. a. To prove or make the same.
Ĭ-DĔN'TĬ-TY, n. Sameness; not diversity.
IDEȘ, n. The 15th day of March, May, July, and
  October, and the 13th of the other months.
ĬD-Ĭ-ŎC'RA-SY, n. Peculiarity of constitution.
ĬD-Ĭ-Ọ-CRĂT'Ĭ-CAL, a. Peculiar in constitution.
ĬD'Ĭ-Ọ-CY, n. State of an idiot.   [guage.
ĬD'Ĭ-ỌM, n. Mode of speech peculiar to a lan-
ĬD-Ĭ-Ọ-MĂT'ĬC, a. Peculiar to a language.
ĬD-Ĭ-Ọ-SȲN'CRA-SY, a. Peculiar temperament.
ĬD'Ĭ-ỌT, n. One devoid of understanding from
  birth; a natural fool.   [stupid; foolish.
ĬD-Ĭ-ŎT'ĬC, ĬD-Ĭ-ŎT'Ĭ-CAL, a. Like an idiot;
ĬD'Ĭ-ỌT-ĬSM, n. An idiom:—folly; idiocy.
Ī'DLE, a. Lazy; not employed; useless; trifling.
Ī'DLE, v. n. & a. To lose time:—to waste.

Ī'DLE-NĔSS, n. Laziness; sloth; trivialness.
Ī'DLER, n. A lazy or idle person; a sluggard.
Ī'DLY, ad. Without employment; lazily.
Ī'DOL, n. An image worshipped as a god.
Ĭ-DŎL'A-TER, n. A worshipper of idols; a pagan.
Ĭ-DŎL'A-TRĔSS, n. A female idolater.
Ĭ-DŎL'A-TRĪZE, v. a. & n. To worship idols; to
  practise idolatry; to adore; to idolize.
Ĭ-DŎL'A-TROŬS, a. Partaking of idolatry.
Ĭ-DŎL'A-TROŬS-LY, ad. In an idolatrous manner.
Ĭ-DŎL'A-TRY, n. The worship of idols or images.
Ī'DỌL-ĪZE, v. a. To deify; to love to adoration.
Ī'DYL (ī'dĭl), n. A short descriptive poem.
ĬF, *conj.* Used as a sign of condition; suppose
ĬG'NE-OŬS, a. Containing fire; fiery.   [that.
ĬG'NĬS FĂT'U-ŬS, n.; pl. ĬG'NĔȘ FĂT'U-Ī. [L.]
  A luminous meteor, called also *Will-with-a-
  wisp*, and *Jack-with-a-lantern*.   [fire.
ĬG-NĪTE', v. a. & n. To kindle; to set or be on
ĬG-NĪT'Ĭ-BLE, a. Capable of being ignited.
ĬG-NĬ''TĬON (ĭg-nĭsh'un), n. The act of igniting.
ĬG-NŌ'BLE, a. Of low birth; not noble; mean.
ĬG-NŌ'BLE-NĔSS, n. Want of dignity or splendor.
ĬG-NŌ'BLY, ad. Ignominiously; meanly; basely.
ĬG-NỌ-MĬN'Ĭ-OŬS, a. Mean; shameful.
ĬG-NỌ-MĬN'Ĭ-OŬS-LY, ad. Meanly; scandalously.
ĬG'NỌ-MĬN-Y, n. Disgrace; reproach; shame.
ĬG-NỌ-RĀ'MŲS, n. A vain pretender to knowl-
  edge; an ignorant person.   [ence.
ĬG'NỌ-RANCE, n. Want of knowledge; nesci-
ĬG'NỌ-RANT, a. Wanting knowledge; unlearned.
ĬG'NỌ-RANT-LY, ad. Without knowledge.
ĪLE, n. A walk in a church;—properly *aisle*.
Ī'LEX, n. [L.] A genus of plants or trees.
ĬL'Ĭ-ĂC, a. Relating to the lower bowels. [çolic.
ĬL'Ĭ-AC PĂS'SĬON (ĭl'e-ak păsh'un), n. Nervous
  ĬLL, a. Bad; not good; evil:—sick; not in health.
ĬLL, n. Wickedness; misfortune; misery.
ĬLL, ad. Not well; not rightly:—with difficulty.
ĬL-LĂPSE' (ĭl-lăps'), n. A gliding or falling in.
ĬL-LĀ'QUE-ĀTE, v. a. To entangle; to insnare.
ĬL-LĀ'TĬON, n. Inference; conclusion.
ĬL'LA-TĬVE, a. Relating to illation or conclusion.
ĬL-LĂU'DA-BLE, a. Not laudable; censurable.
ĬL-LĂU'DA-BLY, ad. Without deserving praise.
ĬLL'BRĔD, a. Not wellbred; impolite; uncivil.
ĬL-LĒ'GAL, a. Contrary to law; not legal; un-
ĬL-LE-GĂL'Ĭ-TY, n. Contrariety to law. [lawful.
ĬL-LĒ'GAL-LY, ad. In a manner contrary to law.
ĬL-LĒ'GAL-NĔSS, n. The state of being illegal.
ĬL-LĔꞬ-Ĭ-BĬL'Ĭ-TY, n. Incapability of being read.

ĬL-LĔǴ'Ĭ-BLE, *a.* That cannot be read.
ĬL-LĔǴ'Ĭ-BLY, *ad.* In a manner not to be read.
ĬL-LĘ-ǴĬT'Ĭ-MĄ-CY, *n.* State of bastardy.
ĬL-LĘ-ǴĬT'Ĭ-MĄTE, *a.* Contrary to law ; born out of wedlock :—unauthorized :—erroneous.
ĬL-LĘ-ǴĬT'Ĭ-MĀTE, *v. a.* To render illegitimate.
ĬL-LĔV'Ĭ-Ą-BLE, *a.* That cannot be levied.
ĬLL'FĀCED (ĭl'fāst), *a.* Having an ugly face.
ĬLL-FĀ'VQRED (ĭl-fā'vųrd), *a.* Deformed ; ugly.
ĬL-LĬB'ĘR-ĄL, *a.* Not liberal ; niggardly ; mean.
ĬL-LĬB-ĘR-ĂL'Ĭ-TY, *n.* Want of liberality.
ĬL-LĬB'ĘR-ĄL-LY, *ad.* Disingenuously ; meanly.
ĬL-LĬÇ'ĬT (ĭl-lĭs'sĭt), *a.* Unlawful ; illegal ; prohibited.
ĬL-LĬÇ'ĬT-NĔSS, *n.* Unlawfulness. [hibited.
ĬL-LĬM'ĬT-Ą-BLE, *a.* That cannot be limited.
ĬL-LĬT'ĘR-Ą-CY, *n.* Want of learning ; ignorance.
ĬL-LĬT'ĘR-ĄTE, *a.* Ignorant ; untaught ; unlearned.
ĬL-LĬT'ĘR-ĄTE-NĔSS, *n.* Waħt of learning. [ed.
ĬLL-NĀT'ŲRE (-nāt'yųr), *n.* Malevolence ; crabbedness ; moroseness ; sullenness. [morose.
ĬLL-NĀT'ŲRED (ĭl-nāt'yųrd), *a.* Cross ; peevish ;
ĬLL'NĔSS, *n.* Sickness ; a malady ; a disorder.
ĬL-LŎǴ'Ĭ-CĄL, *a.* Contrary to the rules of logic.
ĬL-LŎǴ'Ĭ-CĄL-LY, *ad.* In an illogical manner.
ĬLL'-STĂRRED (ĭl'stärd), *a.* Unlucky ; unfortunate.
ĬL-LŪDE', *v. a.* To deceive ; to mock. [nate.
ĬL-LŪME', *v. a.* To enlighten ; to illuminate.
ĬL-LŪ'MĬ-NĀTE, *v. a.* To enlighten ; to adorn.
ĬL-LŪ-MĬ-NĀ'TIQN, *n.* Act of giving light :—lights hung out as a token of joy :—brightness.
ĬL-LŪ'MĬ-NĄ-TĬVE, *a.* Affording illumination.
ĬL-LŪ'MĬ-NĀ-TQR, *n.* One that illuminates.
ĬL-LŪ'MĬNE, *v. a.* To enlighten :—to decorate.
ĬL-LŪ'ŞIQN (ĭl-lū'zhųn), *n.* False show ; deception ; deceptive appearance. [deception.
ĬL-LŪ'SĬVE, *a.* Deceiving by false appearance ;
ĬL-LŪ'SĬVE-LY, *ad.* In a deceptive manner.
ĬL-LŪ'SQ-RY, *a.* Deceiving ; fraudulent. [clear.
ĬL-LŬS'TRĀTE, *v. a.* To brighten ; to explain ; to
ĬL-LŲS-TRĀ'TIQN, *n.* An explanation ; elucidation.
ĬL-LŬS'TRĄ-TĬVE, *a.* Tending to illustrate. [tion.
ĬL-LŬS'TRĬ-OŬS, *a.* Conspicuous ; noble ; eminent ; distinguished ; famous. [nently.
ĬL-LŬS'TRĬ-OŬS-LY, *ad.* Conspicuously ; eminently.
ĬL-LŬS'TRĬ-OŲS-NĔSS, *n.* Eminence ; nobility.
ĬLL'-WĬLL', *n.* Disposition to envy or hatred.
ĬM'ĄǴE, *n.* A statue ; a picture ; an idol :—idea.
ĬM'ĄǴE, *v. a.* To copy by the fancy ; to imagine.
ĬM'Ą-ǴER-Y *or* ĬM'ĄǴE-RY, *n.* Sensible representation ; pictures ; show, &c. :—lively description ; figurative writing or language.
ĬM-ĂǴ'Ĭ-NĄ-BLE, *a.* Possible to be conceived.
ĬM-ĂǴ'Ĭ-NĄ-RY, *a.* Fancied ; visionary ; ideal.
ĬM-ĂǴ-Ĭ-NĀ'TIQN, *n.* Power of forming ideal pictures :—image in the mind ; idea ; fancy.
ĬM-ĂǴ'Ĭ-NĄ-TĬVE, *a.* Fantastic ; full of imagination ; forming mental images ; fancying.
ĬM-ĂǴ'ĬNE, *v. a.* To fancy, conceive, contrive.
ĬM-ĂǴ'ĬNE, *v. n.* To suppose ; to think.
ĬM-BĂNK', *v. a.* To enclose or defend with a bank ; to embank. [formation of a bank.
ĬM-BĂNK'MĘNT, *n.* A bank ; an embankment ;
ĬM-BĔÇ'ĬLE *or* ĬM-BĘ-CÎLE', *a.* Weak ; feeble.
ĬM-BĘ-CĬL'Ĭ-TY, *n.* Weakness ; feebleness.
ĬM-BĔD'DĘD, *a.* Laid in a bed. See EMBED.
ĬM-BĪBE', *v. a.* To drink in ; to draw in ; to admit or receive into the mind. [to madden.
ĬM-BĬT'TĘR, *v. a.* To make bitter ; to exasperate ;

ĬM-BŎD'Y, *v. a.* To form into a body ; to collect.
ĬM-BŌLD'EN (ĭm-bōl'dn), *v. a.* To embolden.
ĬM-BŎR'DĘR, *v. a.* To furnish with a border.
ĬM-BŎ'ŞQM, *v. a.* To hold in the bosom.
ĬM-BŌW' *or* ĬM-BŎŴ', *v. a.* To arch ; to vault.
ĬM-BŎŴ'ĘR, *v. a.* To shelter. See EMBOWER.
ĬM-BRĒĒD', *v. a.* To inbreed. See INBREED.
ĬM'BRĬ-CĄTE, *a.* Laid one under another, as tiles ; bent and hollowed like a roof.
ĬM'BRĬ-CĀT-ĘD, *a.* Indented with concavities.
ĬM-BRĬ-CĀ'TIQN, *n.* A concave indenture.
IMBROGLIO (ĭm-brōl'yẹ-ō), *n.* [It.] A perplexed and complicated plot, as of a drama.
ĬM-BRŎŴN', *v. a.* To make brown ; to darken.
ĬM-BRŪE' (ĭm-brų'), *v. a.* To steep ; to soak.
ĬM-BRŪTE', *v. a.* To degrade to brutality.
ĬM-BRŪTE', *v. n.* To sink down to brutality.
ĬM-BŪE' (ĭm-bū'), *v. a.* To tincture deeply ; to tinge ; to cause to imbibe. [itable.
ĬM-Ĭ-TĄ-BĬL'Ĭ-TY, *n.* The quality of being imitable.
ĬM'Ĭ-TĄ-BLE, *a.* Worthy or deserving to be imitated ; capable of being imitated.
ĬM'Ĭ-TĀTE, *v. a.* To follow the manner, way, or action of ; to copy ; to counterfeit.
ĬM-Ĭ-TĀ'TIQN, *n.* Act of imitating or copying : —copy ; likeness ; resemblance.
ĬM-Ĭ-TĀ'TIQN-ĄL, *a.* Implying imitation.
ĬM'Ĭ-TĀ-TĬVE, *a.* Inclined or tending to copy.
ĬM'Ĭ-TĀ-TQR, *n.* One who imitates or copies.
ĬM-MĂC'Ų-LĄTE, *a.* Spotless ; pure ; undefiled.
ĬM'MĄ-NĔN-CY, *n.* Quality of being immanent.
ĬM'MĄ-NĔNT, *a.* Intrinsic ; inherent ; internal.
ĬM-MĂN'Ĭ-TY, *n.* Barbarity ; savageness.
ĬM-MĂR'TIĄL (ĭm-mär'shĄl), *a.* Not warlike.
ĬM-MĄ-TĒ'RĬ-ĄL, *a.* Incorporeal :—unimportant.
ĬM-MĄ-TĒ'RĬ-ĄL-ĬŞM, *n.* Spiritual existence.
ĬM-MĄ-TĒ'RĬ-ĄL-ĬST, *n.* A believer in immateriality.
ĬM-MĄ-TĒ-RĬ-ĂL'Ĭ-TY, *n.* Distinctness from matter ; spirituality.
ĬM-MĄ-TŪRE', *a.* Not mature ; not ripe ; crude ; not perfect :—hasty ; early ; premature.
ĬM-MĄ-TŪRE'LY, *ad.* Too soon ; too early.
ĬM-MĄ-TŪRE'NĔSS, ĬM-MĄ-TŪ'RĬ-TY, *n.* Unripeness ; incompleteness ; crudeness.
ĬM-MĔ-Ą-BĬL'Ĭ-TY, *n.* Want of power to pass.
||ĬM-MĔAŞ'Ų-RĄ-BLE (ĭm-mĕzh'ų-rĄ-bl), *a.* Immense ; not to be measured ; indefinitely extensive.
||ĬM-MĔAŞ'Ų-RĄ-BLY, *ad.* Immensely. [tensive.
ĬM-MĒ'DĬ-ĄTE, *a.* Proximate :—acting without a medium :—instant ; present. [stantly.
ĬM-MĒ'DĬ-ĄTE-LY, *ad.* Without a medium :—instantly.
ĬM-MĔD'Ĭ-CĄ-BLE, *a.* That cannot be healed or cured ; incurable. [not remembered.
ĬM-MĘ-MŌ'RĬ-ĄL, *a.* Past the time of memory ;
ĬM-MĘ-MŌ'RĬ-ĄL-LY, *ad.* Beyond memory.
ĬM-MĔNSE', *a.* Unlimited ; unbounded ; infinite.
ĬM-MĔNSE'LY, *ad.* Infinitely ; without measure.
ĬM-MĔN'SĬ-TY, *n.* Unbounded greatness ; infinity.
ĬM-MĔNS'Ų-RĄ-BLE, *a.* Not to be measured. [ty.
ĬM-MĔRǴE', *v. a.* To put under water ; to dip.
ĬM-MĔRSE', *v. a.* To put under water ; to sink.
ĬM-MĔR'SIQN (ĭm-mĕr'shųn), *n.* The act of putting, or the state of being, below the surface.
ĬM-MĘ-THŎD'Ĭ-CĄL, *a.* Not methodical ; confused ; unsystematic ; irregular ; desultory.
ĬM-MĘ-THŎD'Ĭ-CĄL-LY, *ad.* Without method.
ĬM'MĬ-GRĂNT, *n.* One who immigrates.

ĬM′MĬ-GRĀTE, *v. a.*   To go into some country in order to dwell in it.
ĬM-MĬ-GRĀ′TIǪN, *n.*   The act of immigrating.
ĬM′MĬ-NĔNT, *a.*   Impending; threatening; near.
ĬM-MĬN′GLE (ĭm-mĭng′gl), *v. a.*   To mingle.
ĬM-MĬS′CĬ-BLE, *a.*   Not capable of being mingled.
ĬM-MĬS′SIǪN (ĭm-mĭsh′ǔn), *n.*   Act of sending in;
ĬM-MĬT′, *v. a.*   To send in; to inject. [injection.
ĬM-MĬT′Ĭ-GA-BLE, *a.*   Not to be mitigated.
ĬM-MǪ-BĬL′Ĭ-TY, *n.*   Unmovableness. [ordinate.
ĬM-MŎD′ĚR-ATE, *a.* Excessive; extravagant; in-
ĬM-MŎD′ĚR-ATE-LY, *ad.* In an excessive degree.
ĬM-MŎD-ĔR-Ā′TIǪN, *n.*   Want of moderation.
ĬM-MŎD′ĔST, *a.*   Wanting modesty or delicacy.
ĬM-MŎD′ĔST-LY, *ad.*   In an immodest manner.
ĬM-MŎD′ĔST-Y, *n.* Want of modesty or delicacy.
ĬM′MǪ-LĀTE, *v. a.*   To sacrifice :—to offer up.
ĬM-MǪ-LĀ′TIǪN, *n.*   Act of sacrificing; sacrifice.
ĬM′MǪ-LĀ-TǪR, *n.*   One who immolates.
ĬM-MŎR′AL, *a.*   Not moral; dishonest; vicious.
ĬM-MǪ-RĂL′Ĭ-TY, *n.*   Dishonesty; want of virtue.
ĬM-MŎR′TAL, *a.*   Exempt from death; perpetual.
ĬM-MǪR-TĂL′Ĭ-TY, *n.*   Exemption from death;
endless life :—exemption from oblivion.
ĬM-MŎR′TAL-ĪZE, *v. a.*   To make immortal.
ĬM-MÔV-A-BĬL′Ĭ-TY, *n.*   Immovableness.
ĬM-MÔV′A-BLE, *a.*   That cannot be moved. [able.
ĬM-MÔV′A-BLE-NĔSS, *n.*   State of being immov-
ĬM-MÔV′A-BLY, *ad.*   In a state not to be shaken.
ĬM-MŪ′NĬ-TY, *n.*   Privilege; exemption or free-
dom from service or performance.   [in.
ĬM-MŪRE′, *v. a.*   To enclose; to confine; to shut
ĬM-MŪ-TA-BĬL′Ĭ-TY, *n.* Exemption from change.
ĬM-MŪ′TA-BLE, *a.*   Unchangeable; unalterable.
ĬM-MŪ′TA-BLE-NĔSS, *n.*   Unchangeableness.
ĬM-MŪ′TA-BLY, *ad.* Unalterably; unchangeably.
ĬMP, *n.*   A subaltern or puny devil; a sprite.
ĬMP, *v. a.*   To lengthen; to enlarge :—to graft.
ĬM′PĂCT, *n.*   Communicated force; impulse.
ĬM-PĂCT′, *v. a.*   To drive close or hard. [worse.
ĬM-PÀIR′ (ĭm-pár′), *v. a.*   To injure; to make
ĬM-PĀLE′, *v. a.*   To enclose.   See EMPALE.
ĬM-PĂL-PA-BĬL′Ĭ-TY, *n.*   State of being impal-
pable.   [intangible; delicate.
ĬM-PĂL′PA-BLE, *a.* Not to be perceived by touch;
ĬM-PA-NĀ′TIǪN, *n.*   Consubstantiation.
ĬM-PĂN′ĚL, *v. a.*   To enroll.   See EMPANEL.
ĬM-PĂR′A-DĪSE, *v. a.* To put in a state of felicity.
ĬM-PĂR′Ĭ-TY, *n.*   Inequality; disproportion.
ĬM-PĂRK′, *v. a.*   To enclose in, or for, a park.
ĬM-PĂR′LANCE, *n.*   (*Law.*)   Delay of a cause.
ĬM-PĂRT′, *v. a.*   To grant; to give; to confer.
ĬM-PĂR′TIAL (-pär′shal), *a.*   Not partial; equi-
table; free from regard to party.   [bleness.
ĬM-PĂR-TĬ-ĂL′Ĭ-TY (-pär-she-ăl′e-tē), *n.* Equita-
ĬM-PĂR′TIAL-LY, *ad.*   With impartiality; justly.
ĬM-PĂR′TĬ-BLE, *a.*   Communicable; not partible.
ĬM-PĂS′SA-BLE, *a.*   Not to be passed; not ad-
mitting passage; impervious.   [sage.
ĬM-PĂS′SA-BLE-NĔSS, *n.*   Incapability of pas-
ĬM-PĂS-SĬ-BĬL′Ĭ-TY, *n.*   Exemption from suffer-
ĬM-PĂS′SĬ-BLE, *a.* Incapable of suffering. [ing.
ĬM-PĂS′SĬ-BLE-NĔSS, *n.*   Impassibility.
ĬM-PĂS′SIǪN (-păsh′ǔn), *v. a.*   To move with
passion; to affect stongly :—to excite.
ĬM-PĂS′SIǪNED (ĭm-păsh′ǔnd), *p. a.*   Animated.
ĬM-PĂS′SĬVE, *a.*   Exempt from suffering.   [on.
ĬM-PĀSTE′, *v. a.*   To knead; to paste :—to lay

ĬM-PĀ′TIĘNCE (ĭm-pā′shęns), *n.*   Want of pa-
tience; vehemence of temper; eagerness.
ĬM-PĀ′TIĘNT (ĭm-pā′shęnt), *a.*   Not able to en-
dure; uneasy; hot; eager; ardently desirous.
ĬM-PĀ′TIĘNT-LY (ĭm-pā′shęnt-lę), *ad.*   Eagerly.
ĬM-PÂWN′, *v. a.*   To pawn; to give as a pledge.
ĬM-PĒACH′ (ĭm-pēch′), *v.a.* To accuse; to arraign.
ĬM-PĒACH′A-BLE, *a.*   Accusable; chargeable.
ĬM-PĒACH′MĘNT, *n.* Public accusation; censure.
ĬM-PĒARL′ (ĭm-pĕrl′), *v. a.*   To form in resem-
blance of pearls :—to adorn as with pearls.
ĬM-PĔC-CA-BĬL′Ĭ-TY, *n.*   Exemption from sin.
ĬM-PĔC′CA-BLE, *a.*   Not liable to sin.
ĬM-PĒDE′, *v. a.*   To hinder; to let; to obstruct.
ĬM-PĔD′Ĭ-MĔNT, *n.* An obstruction; hinderance.
ĬM-PĔL′, *v. a.*   To urge forward; to press on.
ĬM-PĔL′LĘNT, *a.*   Impelling; urging onwards.
ĬM-PĔL′LĘNT, *n.*   A power that drives forward.
ĬM-PĔND′, *v. n.*   To hang over; to be at hand.
ĬM-PĔND′ĘNCE, *n.*   The state of hanging over.
ĬM-PĔND′ĘNT, *a.*   Imminent; hanging over.
ĬM-PĔND′ĬNG, *a.*   Hanging over; near at hand.
ĬM-PĔN-Ę-TRA-BĬL′Ĭ-TY, *n.*   The state of being
impenetrable.   [trated.
ĬM-PĔN′Ę-TRA-BLE, *a.*   That cannot be pene-
ĬM-PĔN′Ę-TRA-BLY, *ad.* With impenetrableness.
ĬM-PĔN′Ĭ-TĔNCE, *n.*   Want of penitence.
ĬM-PĔN′Ĭ-TĔNT, *a.*   Not penitent; obdurate.
ĬM-PĔN′Ĭ-TĔNT, *n.*   An obdurate sinner.
ĬM-PĔN′Ĭ-TĔNT-LY, *ad.*   Without penitence.
ĬM-PĔR′A-TĪVE, *a.* Commanding; authoritative.
ĬM-PĔR′A-TĪVE-LY, *ad.*   In a commanding style.
ĬM-PĔR-CĔP′TĬ-BLE, *a.*   Not to be perceived.
ĬM-PĔR-CĔP′TĬ-BLE-NĔSS, *n.* Imperceptibility.
ĬM-PĔR-CĔP′TĬ-BLY, *ad.*   Without being per-
ceived; so as not to be perceived.
ĬM-PĔR′FECT, *a.*   Not perfect; defective; frail.
ĬM-PĔR-FĔC′TIǪN, *n.* A defect; a failure, fault.
ĬM-PĔR′FECT-LY, *ad.* Not completely; not fully.
ĬM-PĔR′FECT-NĔSS, *n.*   A failure; a defect.
ĬM-PĔR′FǪ-RA-BLE, *a.* Not to be bored through.
ĬM-PĔR′FǪ-RĀT-ĘD, *a.*   Not pierced through.
ĬM-PĔR-FǪ-RĀ′TIǪN, *n.*   State of being closed.
ĬM-PĒ′RĬ-AL, *a.*   Relating to an empire or to an
emperor; royal; regal; monarchical.
ĬM-PĒ′RĬ-AL-ĬST, *n.* An adherent of an emperor.
ĬM-PĒ′RĬ-AL-LY, *ad.*   In an imperial manner.
ĬM-RĒ′RĬ-OǓS, *a.*   Authoritative; haughty.
ĬM-PĒ′RĬ-OǓS-LY, *ad.* In an imperious manner.
ĬM-PĒ′RĬ-OǓS-NĔSS, *n.*   Authority; arrogance.
ĬM-PĔR′ĬSH-A-BLE, *a.*   Not liable to perish.
ĬM-PĔR′MĘ-A-BLE, *a.* Not to be passed through.
ĬM-PĔR′SǪN-AL, *a.*   (*Gram.*)   Noting verbs used
only in the 3d person, with *it* for a nominative.
ĬM-PĔR-SǪN-ĂL′Ĭ-TY, *n.*   Want of personality.
ĬM-PĔR′SǪN-AL-LY, *ad.*   Without personality.
ĬM-PĔR-SPĬ-CŪ′Ĭ-TY, *n.*   Want of perspicuity.
ĬM-PĘR-SPĬC′Ṳ-OǓS, *a.*   Wanting clearness.
ĬM-PĘR-SUĀ′SĬ-BLE, *a.*   Not to be persuaded.
ĬM-PĔR′TĬ-NĔNCE, *n.*   Trifle :—irrelevance :—
intrusion; rudeness; insolence; impudence.
ĬM-PĔR′TĬ-NĔNT, *a.*   Intrusive; trifling; rude.
ĬM-PĔR′TĬ-NĔNT, *n.*   A meddler; an intruder.
ĬM-PĔR′TĬ-NĔNT-LY, *ad.*   Intrusively; rudely.
ĬM-PĘR-TÜRB′A-BLE, *a.*   That cannot be dis-
turbed; composed.   [lity; quietude.
ĬM-PĔR-TṲR-BĀ′TIǪN, *n.* Calmness; tranquil-
ĬM-PĔR′VĬ-OǓS, *a.*   Impenetrable; impassable.

ĬM-PĔR′VĬ-OŬS-LY, *ad.* Impenetrably.
ĬM-PĔR′VĬ-OŬS-NĔSS, *n.* The being impervious.
ĬM′PĘ-TRĀTE, *v. a.* To obtain by entreaty.
ĬM′PĘ-TRĀ′TIǪN, *n.* Act of obtaining by entreaty.
ĬM-PĔT-Ų-ŎS′Ĭ-TY, *n.* Violence ; vehemence.
ĬM-PĔT′Ų-OŬS (-pĕt′yu-ŭs), *a.* Violent ; forcible ; fierce ; vehement of mind ; passionate.
ĬM-PĔT′Ų-OŬS-LY, *ad.* Violently ; vehemently.
ĬM-PĔT′Ų-OŲS-NĔSS, *n.* Violence ; fury.
ĬM′PĘ-TŬS, *n.* [L.] Momentum ; force.
ĬM-PIĔRCE′A-BLE, *a.* Not to be pierced.
ĬM-PĪ′Ę-TY, *n.* Want of piety ; irreligion.
ĬM-PĬG′NǪ-RĀTE, *v. a.* To pawn ; to pledge.
ĬM-PĬNGE′, *v. a.* To strike against ; to clash.
ĬM′PĬ-OŬS, *a.* Irreligious ; wicked ; profane.
ĬM′PĬ-OŬS-LY, *ad.* Profanely ; wickedly.
ĬM′PĬ-OŲS-NĔSS, *n.* Impiety ; irreligion.
ĬM-PLĀ-CA-BĬL′Ĭ-TY, *n.* Irreconcilable enmity.
ĬM-PLĀ′CA-BLE, *a.* Not to be appeased. [cable.
ĬM-PLĀ′CA-BLE-NĔSS, *n.* State of being implacable.
ĬM-PLĀ′CA-BLY, *ad.* With malice ; inexorably.
ĬM-PLĂNT′, *v. a.* To plant ; to insert ; to ingraft.
ĬM-PLĂN-TĀ′TIǪN, *n.* The act of implanting.
ĬM-PLĀU′ŞĬ-BLE, *a.* Not plausible or specious.
ĬM-PLĀU′ŞĬ-BLY, *ad.* Without show of probability. [dict.; to arraign.
ĬM-PLĒAD′ (ĭm-plēd′), *v. a.* To accuse ; to indict.
ĬM-PLĒAD′ĘR, *n.* One who indicts another.
ĬM′PLĘ-MĔNT, *n.* An instrument ; a tool ; a vessel.
ĬM-PLĒ′TIǪN, *n.* Act of filling ; fulness. [sel.
ĬM′PLĔX, *a.* Intricate ; complicated ; complex.
ĬM′PLĬ-CĀTE, *v. a.* To entangle, infold, involve.
ĬM-PLĬ-CĀ′TIǪN, *n.* Involution ; entanglement : —tacit or implied inference.
ĬM-PLĬÇ′ĬT, *a.* Inferred ; tacitly comprised ; founded upon the authority of another.
ĬM-PLĬÇ′ĬT-LY, *ad.* In an implicit manner.
ĬM-PLĬÇ′ĬT-NĔSS, *n.* State of being implicit.
ĬM-PLŌRE′, *v. a.* To supplicate ; to entreat ; to
ĬM-PLŌR′ĘR, *n.* One who implores. [beg.
ĬM-PLŪMED′ (ĭm-plūmd′), *a.* Without feathers.
ĬM-PLȲ′, *v. a.* To involve by implication.
ĬM-PŎÏ′ŞON (ĭm-pŏï′zn), *v. a.* To poison ; to corrupt.
ĬM-PŎL′Ĭ-CY, *n.* Imprudence ; indiscretion. [rupt.
ĬM-PǪ-LĪTE′, *a.* Not polite ; rude ; uncivil.
ĬM-PǪ-LĪTE′NĘSS, *n.* Want of politeness.
ĬM-PŎL′Ĭ-TĬC, *a.* Imprudent ; indiscreet. [creetly.
ĬM-PŎL′Ĭ-TĬC-LY, *ad.* Without forecast ; indiscreetly.
ĬM-PŎN′DĘR-A-BLE, *a.* That cannot be weighed.
ĬM-PŎN′DĘR-OŲS, *a.* Void of perceptible weight.
ĬM-PǪ-RŌS′Ĭ-TY, *n.* Want of porosity ; closeness.
ĬM-PŌ′ROŬS, *a.* Free from pores ; close ; solid.
ĬM-PŌRT′, *v. a.* To bring from abroad, as merchandise :—to imply ; to signify. [ported.
ĬM′PŌRT, *n.* Moment ; meaning :—thing imported.
ĬM-PŌRT′A-BLE, *a.* That may be imported.
ĬM-PŌR′TANCE, *n.* Consequence ; moment.
ĬM-PŌR′TANT, *a.* Momentous ; weighty ; great.
ĬM-PŌR′TANT-LY, *ad.* Weightily ; forcibly.
ĬM-PǪR-TĀ′TIǪN, *n.* The act of importing.
ĬM-PŌRT′ĘR, *n.* One who imports. [pressing.
ĬM-PŌRT′Ų-NATE, *a.* Incessant in solicitation ;
ĬM-PŌRT′Ų-NATE-LY, *ad.* With importunity or urgent solicitation. [tion.
ĬM-PŌRT′Ų-NATE-NĔSS, *n.* Incessant solicitation.
ĬM-PǪR-TŪNE′, *v. a.* To tease ; to solicit earnestly ; to entreat. [pertinacity.
ĬM-PǪR-TŪ′NĬ-TY, *n.* Incessant solicitation ;

ĬM-PŌŞ′A-BLE, *a.* That may be imposed.
ĬM-PŌŞE′, *v. a.* To enjoin as a duty ; to lay on.
ĬM-PŌŞ′ĬNG, *p. a.* Exacting ; enjoining :—deceiving :—commanding ; impressive ; august.
ĬM-PǪ-ŞĬ′′TIǪN (ĭm-pǫ-zĭsh′ųn), *n.* Act of laying on ; constraint :—cheat ; imposture.
ĬM-PŎS-SĬ-BĬL′Ĭ-TY, *n.* That which cannot be.
ĬM-PŎS′SĬ-BLE, *a.* That cannot be ; not possible.
ĬM′PŎST, *n.* A tax ; a toll :—part of a pillar.
||ĬM-PŎST′HŲ-MĀTE (ĭm-pŏst′ų-māt), *v. n.* To form an abscess or cyst ; to gather. [abscess.
||ĬM-PŎST-HŲ-MĀ′TIǪN, *n.* Act of forming an
||ĬM-PŎST′HŪME (ĭm-pŏs′tūm), *n.* An abscess.
ĬM-PŎS′TǪR, *n.* A false pretender ; a deceiver.
ĬM-PŎST′ŲRE (ĭm-pŏst′yur), *n.* Deception ; fraud.
ĬM′PǪ-TĔNCE, *n.* Inability ; weakness ; defect.
ĬM′PǪ-TĔNT, *a.* Weak ; feeble ; wanting power.
ĬM′PǪ-TĔNT-LY, *ad.* Without power ; feebly.
ĬM-PŎŪND′, *v. a.* To enclose as in a pound.
ĬM-PŎV′ĘR-ĬSH, *v. a.* To make poor ; to exhaust.
ĬM-PŎV′ĘR-ĬSH-MĔNT, *n.* Reduction to poverty.
ĬM-PRĂC-TĬ-CA-BĬL′Ĭ-TY, *n.* State of being impracticable. [to be performed.
ĬM-PRĂC′TĬ-CA-BLE, *a.* Not practicable ; not
ĬM′PRĘ-CĀTE, *v. a.* To invoke evil ; to curse.
ĬM-PRĘ-CĀ′TIǪN, *n.* Invocation of evil ; curse.
ĬM′PRĘ-CA-TǪ-RY, *a.* Containing imprecation.
ĬM-PRĔG′NA-BLE, *a.* Not to be taken ; unmoved.
ĬM-PRĔG′NA-BLY, *ad.* In an impregnable manner ; invincibly. [lific.
ĬM-PRĔG′NĀTE, *v. a.* To make pregnant or prolific.
ĬM-PRĘG-NĀ′TIǪN, *n.* Act of impregnating.
ĬM-PRE-SCRĬPT′Ĭ-BLE, *a.* Not to be alienated.
ĬM-PRĔSS′, *v. a.* To stamp ; to fix deep ; to force.
ĬM′PRĔSS, *n.* A mark ; stamp ; figure ; device.
ĬM-PRĔS-SĬ-BĬL′Ĭ-TY, *n.* The being impressible.
ĬM-PRĔS′SĬ-BLE, *a.* That may be impressed.
ĬM-PRĔS′SIǪN (ĭm-prĕsh′ųn), *n.* A mark made by pressure ; a stamp ; effect :—an edition.
ĬM-PRĔS′SĬVE, *a.* Earnest ; making impression.
ĬM-PRĔS′SĬVE-LY, *ad.* In an impressive manner.
ĬM-PRĔSS′MĘNT, *n.* Act of forcing into service.
ĬM-PRĔSS′ŲRE (ĭm-prĕsh′ur), *n.* An impression.
ĬM-PRĔV′A-LĘN-CY, *n.* Incapability of prevailing.
ĬM-PRĬ-MĀ′TŲR, *n.* [L.] License to print. [ing.
ĬM-PRĪ′MĬS, *ad.* [L.] In the first place.
ĬM-PRĬNT′, *v. a.* To print :—to fix on the mind.
ĬM′PRĬNT, *n.* The designation of a place where and by whom a work is printed. [to confine.
ĬM-PRĬŞ′ON (ĭm-prĭz′zn), *v. a.* To shut up ;
ĬM-PRĬŞ′ON-MĔNT, *n.* Confinement ; duress.
ĬM-PRŎB-A-BĬL′Ĭ-TY, *n.* Want of probability.
ĬM-PRŎB′A-BLE, *a.* Unlikely ; hardly credible.
ĬM-PRŎB′A-BLY, *ad.* Without probability.
ĬM-PRŎB′Ĭ-TY, *n.* Want of honesty ; dishonesty.
ĬM-PRŎMP′TŲ, *ad.* Without previous study.
ĬM-PRŎP′ĘR, *a.* Not proper ; unqualified ; unfit.
ĬM-PRŎP′ĘR-LY, *ad.* Not fitly ; not properly.
ĬM-PRŌ′PRĬ-ĀTE, *v. a.* To put into the hands of laymen, as the possessions of the church.
ĬM-PRŌ-PRĬ-Ā′TIǪN, *n.* Act of impropriating.
ĬM-PRŌ′PRĬ-Ā-TǪR, *n.* A layman that has possession of the property of the church. [priety.
ĬM-PRǪ-PRĪ′Ę-TY, *n.* Unfitness ; want of propriety.
ĬM-PRŌV-A-BĬL′Ĭ-TY, *n.* The being improvable.
ĬM-PRŌV′A-BLE, *a.* Capable of improvement.
ĬM-PRÔVE′, *v. a.* To make better :—to increase.
ĬM-PRÔVE′, *v. n.* To advance in goodness.

ĬM-PRÔVE′MENT, n. Act of improving ; progress from good to better ; melioration ; amend-
ĬM-PRÔV′ER, n. One that improves. [ment.
ĬM-PRŎV′Ĭ-DĔNCE, n. Want of forethought.
ĬM-PRŎV′Ĭ-DĔNT, a. Wanting forecast ; careless.
ĬM-PRŎV′Ĭ-DĔNT-LY, ad. Without forethought.
ĬM-PRŬ′DĘNCE, n. Want of prudence ; rashness.
ĬM-PRŬ′DĘNT, a. Wanting prudence ; indiscreet.
ĬM-PRŬ′DĘNT-LY, ad. Without prudence ; rashly.
ĬM′PŲ-DĔNCE, n. Shamelessness ; immodesty.
ĬM′PŲ-DĔNT, a. Shameless ; immodest ; saucy.
ĬM′PŲ-DĔNT-LY, ad. Without modesty ; saucily.
ĬM-PŲ-DĬÇ′Ĭ-TY, n. Immodesty ; shamelessness.
ĬM-PŪGN′ (ĭm-pŭn′), v. a. To attack ; to oppose.
ĬM-PŪGN′ER (ĭm-pŭn′er), n. One who impugns.
ĬM-PŪ′ĬS-SĂNCE, n. Impotence ; weakness.
ĬM′PULSE, n. Communicated force ; impression.
ĬM-PŬL′SION, n. Act of impelling ; impulse.
ĬM-PŬL′SĬVE, a. Impelling ; moving ; impellent.
ĬM-PŪ′NĬ-TY, n. Exemption from punishment.
ĬM-PŪRE′, a. Not pure ; unholy ; foul ; lewd.
ĬM-PŪRE′LY, ad. With impurity; foully ; lewdly.
ĬM-PŪRE′NESS,) n. Want of purity or sancti-
ĬM-PŪ′RĬ-TY, (ty ; lewdness ; filthiness.
ĬM-PŬR′PLE, v. a. To color as with purple.
ĬM-PŪ′TA-BLE, a. That may be imputed.
ĬM-PŪ′TA-BLE-NĔSS, n. Quality of being im-
ĬM-PŲ-TĀ′TION, n. Act of imputing. [putable.
ĬM-PŪ′TA-TĬVE, a. That may impute. [cribe.
ĬM-PŪTE′, v. a. To charge ; to attribute ; to as-
ĬM-PŲ-TRĔS′CĬ-BLE, a. Not to be putrefied.
ĬN, prep. Noting presence in place, time, or state ; within ; not without :—according to.
ĬN-A-BĬL′Ĭ-TY, n. Impotence ; want of power.
ĬN-ĂC-CĔS-SĬ-BĬL′Ĭ-TY, n. State of being inaccessible. [unattainable.
ĬN-ĂC-CĔS′SĬ-BLE, a. Not to be approached ;
ĬN-ĂC-CĔS′SĬ-BLY, ad. So as not to be approached. [incorrectness.
ĬN-ĂC′CŲ-RA-CY, n. Want of accuracy ; error ;
ĬN-ĂC′CŲ-RATE, a. Not exact ; not accurate.
ĬN-ĂC′CŲ-RATE-LY, ad. Not correctly.
ĬN-ĂC′TION, n. Want of action ; idleness.
ĬN-ĂC′TĬVE, a. Not active ; indolent ; sluggish.
ĬN-ĂC′TĬVE-LY, ad. Without labor ; sluggishly.
ĬN-ĂC-TĬV′Ĭ-TY, n. Idleness ; rest ; sluggishness.
ĬN-ĂD′Ę-QUA-CY, n. Insufficiency ; defective-
ĬN-ĂD′Ę-QUATE, a. Not adequate. [ness.
ĬN-ĂD′Ę-QUATE-LY, ad. Defectively ; insuffi-
ĬN-ĂD′Ę-QUATE-NĔSS, n. Inadequacy. [ciency.
ĬN-AD-MĬS′SĬ-BLE, a. Not to be admitted.
ĬN-AD-VĔR′TĘNCE, n. Negligence ; inattention.
ĬN-AD-VĔR′TĘNT, a. Negligent ; careless.
ĬN-AD-VĔR′TĘNT-LY, ad. Carelessly ; negligent-
ĬN-ĂF′FA-BLE, a. Not affable ; reserved. [ly.
ĬN-ĀL′ĬEN-A-BLE (ĭn-āl′yen-a-bl), a. That cannot be alienated or granted to another.
ĬN-ĂM-O-RĂ′TA, n. A female in love ; mistress.
ĬN-ĂM-O-RĂ′TŎ, n. A man in love ; a lover.
ĬN-ĀNE′, a. Empty ; void ; useless.
ĬN-ĂN′Ĭ-MATE,) a. Void of life ; lifeless ;
ĬN-ĂN′Ĭ-MĀT-ĘD, (dead ; inert ; extinct.
ĬN-A-NĬ″TION (ĭn-a-nĭsh′un), n. Emptiness.
ĬN-ĂN′Ĭ-TY, n. Emptiness ; void space :—vanity.
ĬN-ĂP′PĘ-TĔNCE, n. Want of appetence or appetite. [purpose ; unsuitableness.
ĬN-ĂP-PLĬ-CA-BĬL′Ĭ-TY, n. Unfitness for the
ĬN-ĂP′PLĬ-CA-BLE, a. Not applicable ; unfit.

ĬN-ĂP-PLĬ-CĀ′TION, n. Indolence ; negligence.
ĬN-ĂP′PO-ṢĬTE, a. Not apposite ; unsuitable.
ĬN-ĂP-PRĒ′CĬ-A-BLE, a. That cannot be appreciated or estimated. [comprehensible.
ĬN-ĂP-PRĘ-HĔN′SĬ-BLE, a. Not intelligible ; in-
ĬN-ĂP-PRĘ-HĔN′SĬVE, a. Not apprehensive.
ĬN-AP-PRŎ′PRĬ-ATE, a. Not appropriate ; unfit.
ĬN-ĂPT′Ĭ-TŪDE, n. Unfitness ; unsuitableness.
ĬN-ĀRCH′, v. a. To graft by approach.
ĬN-AR-TĬC′Ų-LATE, a. Not distinct ; indistinct.
ĬN-AR-TĬC′Ų-LATE-LY, ad. Not distinctly. [ness.
ĬN-AR-TĬC′Ų-LATE-NĔSS, n. Want of distinct-
ĬN-AR-TĬC-Ų-LĀ′TION, n. Indistinct utterance.
ĬN-ĀR-TĬ-FĬ″CIAL (-tę-fĭsh′al), a. Plain ; artless.
ĬN-AṢ-MŬCH′, ad. Seeing ; seeing that. [lect.
ĬN-AT-TĔN′TION, n. Want of attention ; neg-
ĬN-AT-TĔN′TĬVE, a. Heedless ; careless.
ĬN-AT-TĔN′TĬVE-LY, ad. Without attention.
ĬN-ÂU′DĬ-BLE, a. That cannot be heard.
ĬN-ÂU′GŲ-RAL, a. Relating to inauguration.
ĬN-ÂU′GŲ-RĀTE, v. a. To consecrate ; to indust.
ĬN-ÂU-GŲ-RĀ′TION, n. Investiture by solemn rites ; installation. [tion ; inaugural.
ĬN-ÂU′GŲ-RA-TO-RY, a. Respecting inaugura-
ĬN-ÂU-RĀ′TION, n. Act of covering with gold.
ĬN-ÂU-SPĬ″CIOŲS (ĭn-âw-spĭsh′us), a. Unfortunate ; unfavorable ; unlucky. [ill omens.
ĬN-ÂU-SPĬ″CIOŲS-LY (-âw-spĭsh′us-), ad. With
ĬN-BĒ′ĬNG, n. Inherence ; inseparableness.
ĬN′BŎRN, a. Innate ; implanted by nature.
ĬN′BRĔD, a. Produced within ; innate.
ĬN-BRĒĒD′, v. a. To produce ; to cherish.
ĬN′CA, n. An ancient Peruvian king or prince.
ĬN-CĀGE′, v. a. To coop ; to shut up ; to confine.
ĬN-CĂL′CŲ-LA-BLE, a. That cannot be calcu-
ĬN-CA-LĔS′CENCE, n. State of warmth. [lated.
ĬN-CAN-DĔS′CENCE, n. A white, glowing heat.
ĬN-CAN-DĔS′CENT, a. White with heat.
ĬN-CAN-TĀ′TION, n. A charm ; an enchantment.
ĬN-CĂN′TA-TO-RY, a. Enchanting ; magical.
ĬN-CĀ-PA-BĬL′Ĭ-TY, ĬN-CĀ′PA-BLE-NĔSS, n. Incapacity ; inability. [unqualified.
ĬN-CĀ′PA-BLE, a. Not capable ; unable ; unfit.
ĬN-CA-PĀ′CIOŲS (ĭn-ka-pā′shus), a. Narrow.
ĬN-CA-PĂÇ′Ĭ-TĀTE, v. a. To disable ; to weaken.
ĬN-CA-PĂÇ-Ĭ-TĀ′TION, n. Disqualification.
ĬN-CA-PĂÇ′Ĭ-TY, n. Inability ; want of capacity.
ĬN-CĂR′CER-ĀTE, v. a. To imprison ; to confine.
ĬN-CĂR-CER-Ā′TION, n. Imprisonment. [flesh.
ĬN-CĂR′NĀTE, v. a. To clothe or imbody with
ĬN-CĂR′NATE, a. Clothed or imbodied in flesh.
ĬN-CAR-NĀ′TION, n. Act of assuming body or
ĬN-CĂR′NA-TĬVE, a. Generating flesh. [flesh.
ĬN-CĀSE′, v. a. To cover ; to enclose. [less.
ĬN-CÂU′TIOŲS (ĭn-kâw′shus), a. Unwary; heed-
ĬN-CÂU′TIOŲS-LY (-kâw′shus-lę), ad. Unwarily.
ĬN-CĔN′DĬ-A-RY, n. One who maliciously sets houses or towns on fire :—a fomenter of strife.
ĬN-CĔN′DĬ-A-RY, a. Enkindling strife, &c.
ĬN′CENSE, n. Perfume exhaled by fire. [fume.
ĬN-CĔNSE′, v. a. To enrage ; to provoke :—to per-
ĬN-CĔNSE′MĘNT, n. Rage ; heat ; fury. [Rare.]
ĬN-CĔN′SION, n. Act of kindling ; a burning.
ĬN-CĔN′SĬVE, a. That incites ; inflammatory.
ĬN′CEN-SO-RY or ĬN-CĔN′SO-RY, n. A vessel in which incense is burnt and offered ; censer.
ĬN-CĔN′TĬVE, n. An incitement ; motive ; spur.
ĬN-CĔN′TĬVE, a. Inciting ; encouraging.

IN-CĔP'TĮVE, a. Beginning; noting beginning.
ĬN-CĔR'TĮ-TŪDE, n. Uncertainty; doubtfulness.
ĮN-CĔS'SĄNT, a. Unceasing; continual; constant.
ĮN-CĔS'SĄNT-LY̆, ad. Without intermission.
ĬN'CĔST, n. Unnatural and criminal conjunction
of persons related within degrees prohibited.
ĮN-CĔST'Ų-OŬS (-sĕst'yų-ŭs), a. Guilty of incest.
ĮN-CĔST'Ų-OŬS-LY̆, ad. In an incestuous man-
ĬNCH, n. A measure; twelfth part of a foot. [ner.
ĬN'CHQ-ĄTE, a. Begun; commenced; entered
ĬN-CHQ-A'TIQN, n. Inception; beginning. [upon.
ĮN-CHŌ'Ą-TĬVE, a. Inceptive; noting beginning.
ĬN'CĮ-DĔNCE, n. The direction with which one
body falls upon or strikes another.
ĬN'CĮ-DĔNT, a. Casual; fortuitous; occasional.
ĬN'CĮ-DĔNT, n. Event; occurrence; casualty.
ĬN-CĮ-DĔN'TĄL, a. Casual; happening by chance.
ĬN-CĮ-DĔNT'ĄL-LY̆, ad. In an incidental manner.
ĮN-CĬN'ĘR-ĀTE, v. a. To burn to ashes.
ĮN-CĬN-ĘR-Ā'TIQN, n. Act of burning to ashes.
ĮN-CĬP'Į-ĔNT, a. Beginning; commencing.
ĬN-CĬR-CŲM-SPĔC'TIQN, n. Want of caution.
ĮN-CĪSE', v. a. To cut; to carve; to engrave.
ĮN-CĪ'/ŞIQN (ĭn-sĭzh'ụn), n. A cut; a gash.
ĮN-CĪ'SĮVE, a. Having the quality of cutting.
ĮN-CĪ'ŞOᴘ, n. A cutter; a fore tooth that cuts.
ĮN-CĪ'SQ-RY̆, a. Having the quality of cutting.
ĮN-CĪŞ'ŲRE (ĭn-sĭzh'ụr), n. A cut; an aperture.
ĬN-CĮ-TĀ'TIQN, n. Incitement; motive; impulse.
ĮN-CĪTE', v. a. To stir up; to animate, urge on.
ĮN-CĪTE'MĘNT, n. Motive; incentive; impulse.
ĮN-CĪT'ĘR, n. One that incites; an encourager.
ĬN-CĮ-VĬL'Į-TY̆, n. Want of courtesy; rudeness.
ĬN-CLĔM'ĘN-CY̆, n. Rigor; severity; roughness.
ĬN-CLĔM'ĘNT, a. Severe; rough; stormy; harsh.
ĮN-CLĬN'Ą-BLE, a. Willing; having a tendency.
ĬN-CLĮ-NĀ'TIQN, n. Tendency to a point; a
leaning; affection; regard:—disposition.
ĮN-CLĪNE', v. n. To bend; to lean; to be disposed.
ĮN-CLĪNE', v. a. To turn towards; to bend.
ĮN-CLĪNE', n. Regular ascent or descent.
ĮN-CLĪN'ĘR, n. (Dialing.) An inclined dial.
ĮN-CLÖĬS'TĘR, v. a. To shut up in a cloister.
ĮN-CLOŞE', v. a. To surround. See ENCLOSE.
ĮN-CLOŞ'ĘR, n. One that incloses; encloser.
ĮN-CLOŞ'ŲRE (ĭn-klō'zhụr), n. Act of inclosing:
—space inclosed; enclosure. [prise.
ĮN-CLŪDE', v. a. To inclose; to shut; to com-
ĮN-CLŪ'ŞIQN (ĭn-klū'zhụn), n. Act of including.
ĮN-CLŪ'SĮVE, a. Inclosing; comprehended.
ĮN-CLŪ'SĮVE-LY̆, ad. In an inclusive manner.
ĬN-CQ-ĂG'Ų-LĄ-BLE, a. Incapable of concretion.
ĬN-CŎG', ad. [Corrupted from incognito.] In
ĮN-CŎG'Į-TĄN-CY̆, n. Want of thought. [private.
ĮN-CŎG'Į-TĄNT, a. Inconsiderate; thoughtless.
ĮN-CŎG'Į-TĄ-TĬVE, a. Wanting thought.
ĬN-CŎG'NĮ-TŌ, ad. In a state of concealment.
ĬN-CQ-HĒ'RĘNCE,) n. Want of coherence or
ĬN-CQ-HĒ'RĘN-CY̆,) connection; incongruity.
ĬN-CQ-HĒ'RĘNT, a. Inconsequential; incon-
sistent; incongruous. [ner.
ĬN-CQ-HĒ'RĘNT-LY̆, ad. In an incoherent man-
ĬN-CQM-BŬS-TĮ-BĬL'Į-TY̆, n. Want of combus-
tibility. [fire; inconsumable.
ĬN-CQM-BŬS'TĮ-BLE, a. Not to be consumed by
ĬN'CŎME (ĭn'kŭm), n. Revenue; profit.
ĬN-CQM-MĔNS-Ų-RĄ-BĬL'Į-TY̆, n. State of be-
ing incommensurable.

ĬN-CQM-MĔNS'Ų-RĄ-BLE (-kọm-mĕns'u-rạ-bl),
a. Having no common measure.
ĬN-CQM-MĔNS'Ų-RĄTE (ĭn-kọm-mĕns'ụ-rạt), a.
Not having a common measure. [discommode.
ĬN-CQM-MŌDE', v. a. To be inconvenient to; to
ĬN-CQM-MŌ'DĮ-OŬS, a. Inconvenient.
ĬN-CQM-MŌ'DĮ-OŬS-LY̆, ad. Inconveniently.
ĬN-CQM-MŌ'DĮ-OŲS-NĔSS, n. Inconvenience.
ĬN-CQM-MŪ-NĮ-CĄ-BĬL'Į-TY̆, n. Impossibility
of being communicated. [communicated.
ĬN-CQM-MŪ'NĮ-CĄ-BLE, a. That cannot be
ĬN-CQM-MŪ'NĮ-CĄ-BLE-NĔSS, n. State of not
being impartible; incommunicability.
ĬN-CQM-MŪ'NĮ-CĄ-BLY̆, ad. In a manner not
to be imparted. [incommutable.
ĬN-CQM-MŬT-Ą-BĬL'Į-TY̆, n. The state of being
ĬN-CQM-MŬT'Ą-BLE, a. Not subject to change.
ĬN-CQM-PĂCT', ĬN-CQM-PĂCT'ĘD, a. Not com-
pact; not dense; loose. [less.
ĬN-CŎM'PĄ-RĄ-BLE, a. Very excellent; match-
ĬN-CŎM'PĄ-RĄ-BLE-NĔSS, n. Great excellence.
ĬN-CŎM'PĄ-RĄ-BLY̆, ad. Beyond comparison.
ĬN-CQM-PĂS'SIQN-ĄTE, a. Void of pity.
ĬN-CQM-PĂS'SIQN-ĄTE-LY̆, ad. Without pity.
ĬN-CQM-PĂS'SIQN-ĄTE-NĔSS, n. Want of pity.
ĬN-CQM-PĂT-Į-BĬL'Į-TY̆, n. Inconsistency.
ĬN-CQM-PĂT'Į-BLE, a. Inconsistent with an-
ĬN-CQM-PĂT'Į-BLY̆, ad. Inconsistently. [other.
ĬN-CŎM'PĘ-TĘNCE, ĬN-CŎM'PĘ-TĘN-CY̆, n. In-
ability; incapability. [quate.
ĬN-CŎM'PĘ-TĘNT, a. Not competent or ade-
ĬN-CŎM'PĘ-TĘNT-LY̆, ad. Inadequately.
ĬN-CQM-PLĒTE', a. Not perfect; not finished.
ĬN-CQM-PLĒTE'NĘSS, n. Unfinished state.
ĬN-CQM-PLĔX', a. Not complex; simple.
ĬN-CQM-PLĪ'ANCE, n. Want of compliance.
ĬN-CQM-PŎŞ'ĮTE, a. Uncompounded; simple.
ĬN-CŎM-PRĘ-HĔN-SĮ-BĬL'Į-TY̆, n. Inconceiv-
ableness; incomprehensibleness. [ceived-
ĬN-CŎM-PRĘ-HĔN'SĮ-BLE, a. Not to be con-
ĬN-CŎM-PRĘ-HĔN'SĮ-BLE-NĔSS, n. Inconceiv-
ableness; incomprehensibility.
ĬN-CŎM-PRĘ-HĔN'SĮ-BLY̆, ad. Inconceivably.
ĬN-CQM-PRĔSS-Į-BĬL'Į-TY̆, n. The quality of
being incompressible.
ĬN-CQM-PRĔSS'Į-BLE, a. Not to be compressed.
ĬN-CQN-CĒAL'Ą-BLE, a. Not to be concealed.
ĬN-CQN-CĒIV'Ą-BLE, a. Not to be conceived.
ĬN-CQN-CĒIV'Ą-BLE-NĔSS, n. The state of be-
ing inconceivable; incomprehensibleness.
ĬN-CQN-CĒIV'Ą-BLY̆, ad. Beyond conception.
ĬN-CQN-CLŪ'SĮVE, a. Not conclusive; inde-
cisive; not convincing. [ness.
ĬN-CQN-CLŪ'SĮVE-LY̆, ad. With inconclusive-
ĬN-CQN-CLŪ'SĮVE-NĔSS, n. Want of rational
force or cogency. [gested.
ĬN-CQN-CŎCT'ĘD, a. Immature; not fully di-
ĬN-CQN-CŎC'TIQN, n. State of being indigested.
ĬN'CQN-DĪTE or ĮN-CŎN'DĮTE, a. Irregular;
ĬN-CQN-FŎRM'Į-TY̆, n. Non-conformity. [rude.
ĬN-CQN-ĢĒAL'Ą-BLE, a. Not to be frozen.
ĬN-CQN-GRŬ'Į-TY̆, n. Unsuitableness.
ĬN-CŎN'GRŲ-OŬS (ĭn-kŏng'grụ-ŭs), a. Unsuit-
able; not fitting; inconsistent; absurd.
ĬN-CŎN'GRŲ-OŬS-LY̆, ad. Improperly; unfitly.
ĬN-CQN-NĔC'TIQN, n. Want of connection.
ĬN-CŎN'SCIQN-Ą-BLE (ĭn-kŏn'shụn-ạ-bl), a. Void
of conscience, or of the sense of good and evil.

ĬN-CŎN′SĘ-QUĔNCE, *n.* Want of just inference.
ĬN-CŎN′SĘ-QUĔNT, *a.* Not consequent; illogical.
ĬN-CŎN-SĘ-QUĔN′TIĄL, *a.* Not important.
ĬN-CǑN-SĬD′ĘR-Ą-BLE, *a.* Unimportant; trivial.
ĬN-CǑN-SĬD′ĘR-Ą-BLE-NĔSS, *n.* Small account.
ĬN-CǑN-SĬD′ĘR-ĄTE, *a.* Careless; thoughtless.
ĬN-CǑN-SĬD′ĘR-ĄTE-LY, *ad.* Thoughtlessly.
ĬN-CǑN-SĬD′ĘR-ĄTE-NĔSS, *n.* Thoughtlessness.
ĬN-CǑN-SĬD-ĘR-Ā′TIǬN, *n.* Want of thought.
ĬN-CǑN-SĬS′TĘN-CY,*n.* Contrariety; incongruity.
ĬN-CǑN-SĬS′TĘNT,*a.* Incompatible; incongruous.
ĬN-CǑN-SĬS′TĘNT-LY, *ad.* Absurdly; incongru-
ĬN-CǑN-SŌL′Ą-BLE, *a.* Not consolable. [ously.
ĬN-CŎN′SǪ-NANCE, *n.* Discordance of sounds.
ĬN-CǪN-SPĬC′Y-OŬS, *a.* Not conspicuous.
ĬN-CǑN′STĄN-CY, *n.* Unsteadiness; mutability.
ĬN-CŎN′STĄNT, *a.* Not firm; changeable.
ĬN-CŎN′STĄNT-LY, *ad.* Unsteadily; changeably.
ĬN-CǪN-SŪM′Ą-BLE, *a.* Not to be consumed.
ĬN-CǪN-TĔST′Ą-BLE, *a.* Not to be disputed.
ĬN-CǪN-TĔST′Ą-BLY, *ad.* Indisputably.
ĬN-CŎN′TĮ-NĔNCE, ĬN-CŎN′TĮ-NĔN-CY, *n.* Un-
chastity; lewdness.　　　　　　　[lascivious.
ĬN-CŎN′TĮ-NĔNT,*a.* Lewd; licentious; unchaste;
ĬN-CŎN′TĮ-NĔNT-LY, *ad.* Unchastely; lewdly.
ĬN-CǪN-TRŌL′LĄ-BLE, *a.* Not to be controlled.
ĬN-CǪN-TRŌL′LĄ-BLY, *ad.* Without control.
ĬN-CŎN-TRǪ-VĔRT′Į-BLE, *a.* Indisputable.
ĬN-CŎN-TRǪ-VĔRT′Į-BLY, *ad.* Indisputably.
‖ĬN-CǪN-VĔN′IĘNCE, ⎰ *n.* Unfitness; disad-
‖ĬN-CǪN-VĔN′IĘN-CY, ⎱ vantage; annoyance.
‖ĬN-CǪN-VĔN′IĘNT *or* ĬN-CǪN-VĔ′NĮ-ĘNT, *a.*
Incommodious; disadvantageous; annoying.
‖ĬN-CǪN-VĔN′IĘNT-LY, *ad.* Incommodiously.
ĬN-CǪN-VĔRS′Ą-BLE, *a.* Unsocial; stiff; formal.
ĬN-CǪN-VĔRT′Į-BLE, *a.* Incapable of change.
ĬN-CǪN-VĬN′CĮ-BLE, *a.* Not to be convinced.
ĬN-CŎR′PǪ-RĄL, *a.* Incorporeal; immaterial.
ĬN-CŎR′PǪ-RĄL-LY, *ad.* Without matter.
ĬN-CŎR′PǪ-RĀTE, *v. a.* To form into a body or
corporation; to unite; to associate; to embody.
ĬN-CŎR′PǪ-RĀTE, *v. n.* To unite or coalesce.
ĬN-CŎR-PǪ-RĀ′TIǪN, *n.* Act of incorporating.
ĬN-CǪR-PŌ′RE-ĄL, *a.* Immaterial; unbodied.
ĬN-CǪR-PŌ′RE-ĄL-LY, *ad.* Without body.
ĬN-CǑR-PǪ-RĒ′Į-TY, *n.* Distinctness from body.
ĬN-CǪR-RĔCT′, *a.* Not correct; inaccurate.
ĬN-CǪR-RĔCT′LY, *ad.* Inaccurately; not exactly.
ĬN-CǪR-RĔCT′NĘSS, *n.* Inaccuracy; error.
ĬN-CŎR′RĮ-ĢĮ-BLE, *a.* That cannot be corrected.
ĬN-CŎR′RĮ-ĢĮ-BLE-NĔSS, *n.* Hopeless depravity.
ĬN-CŎR′RĮ-ĢĮ-BLY, *ad.* Beyond amendment.
ĬN-CǪR-RŬPT′, *a.* Not corrupt; pure; good.
ĬN-CǪR-RŬPT-Į-BĬL′Į-TY, ⎰ *n.* Insusceptibility
ĬN-CǪR-RŬPT′Į-BLE-NĔSS, ⎱ of corruption.
ĬN-CǪR-RŬPT′Į-BLE, *a.* Incapable of corruption.
ĬN-CǪR-RŬP′TIǪN,*n.*Exemption from corruption
ĬN-CǪR-RŬPT′NĘSS, *n.* Integrity; incorruption.
ĬN-CRĂS′SĀTE,*v. a.* To thicken; to make thick.
ĬN-CRĄS-SĀ′TIǪN, *n.* The act of thickening.
ĬN-CRĔASE′ (ĭn-krēs′), *v. n.* To grow; advance.
ĬN-CRĔASE′, *v. a.* To make more; to augment.
ĬN′CRĔASE *or* ĬN-CRĔASE′, *n.* Augmentation.
ĬN′CRĘ-ĀTE, ĬN-CRĘ-ĀT′ĘD, *a.* Not created.
ĬN-CRĔD-Į-BĬL′Į-TY, ⎰ *n.* Quality of being in-
ĬN-CRĔD′Į-BLE-NĔSS, ⎱ credible. [credited.
ĬN-CRĔD′Į-BLE, *a.* Surpassing belief; not to be
ĬN-CRĔD′Į-BLY, *ad.* In an incredible manner.

ĬN-CRĘ-DŪ′LĮ-TY, *n.* Indisposition to believe.
ĬN-CRĔD′Y-LOŬS (ĭn-krĕd′y-lŭs), *a.* Hard of
belief; refusing credit; unbelieving; sceptical.
ĬN-CRĔD′Y-LOŬS-NĔSS, *n.* Hardness of belief.
ĬN′CRĘ-MĔNT, *n.* Increase; matter added.
ĬN-CRĘ-PĀ′TIǪN, *n.* Reprehension; a chiding.
ĬN-CRĔS′CĘNT, *a.* Increasing; growing.
ĬN-CRŬST′, *v. a.* To cover with a crust or coat.
ĬN-CRȖS-TĀ′TIǪN,*n.* Adherent covering; crust.
ĬN′CY-BĀTE, *v. n.* To sit upon eggs; to hatch.
ĬN-CY-BĀ′TIǪN, *n.* Act of sitting upon eggs.
ĬN′CY-BŬS, *n.* The nightmare :—fiend; demon.
ĬN-CŬL′CĀTE, *v. a.* To impress by admonition.
ĬN-CȖL-CĀ′TIǪN, *n.* The act of inculcating.
ĬN-CȖL′PĄ-BLE,*a.* Unblamable; irreproachable.
ĬN-CŬM′BĘN-CY, *n.* The keeping of an office.
ĬN-CŬM′BĘNT,*a.* Lying upon; imposed as duty.
ĬN-CŬM′BĘNT, *n.* One who possesses an office.
ĬN-CŬM′BĘR, *v. a.* To embarrass; to encum-
ber. See ĔNCUMBER.
ĬN-CŬR′, *v. a.* To become liable to; to bring on.
ĬN-CŪ-RĄ-BĬL′Į-TY, *n.* Impossibility of cure.
ĬN-CŪ′RĄ-BLE, *a.* Not to be cured; irremediable.
ĬN-CŪ′RĄ-BLE-NĔSS, *n.* State of being incurable.
ĬN-CŪ′RĄ-BLY, *ad.* Without remedy; hopelessly.
ĬN-CŪ′RĮ-OŬS, *a.* Negligent; inattentive.
ĬN-CŬR′SIǪN,*n.* An invasion; inroad; ravage.
ĬN-CŬR′VĀTE, *v. a.* To bend; to crook.
ĬN-CȖR-VĀ′TIǪN, *n.* Act of bending; curvity.
ĬN-CŬRVE′, *v. a.* To bow; to bend, incurvate.
ĬN-CŬR′VĮ-TY, *n.* Crookedness; a bending in-
ĬN-DĂRT′, *v. a.* To dart or throw in. [ward.
ĬN-DĔBT′ĘD (ĭn-dĕt′ĕd), *p. a.* Being in debt.
ĬN-DĔBT′MĘNT (ĭn-dĕt′mĕnt), *n.* State of be-
ing in debt; indebtedness. [decorum.
ĬN-DĒ′CĘN-CY,*n.* Any thing unbecoming; in-
ĬN-DĒ′CĘNT, *a.* Unbecoming; unseemly; im-
ĬN-DĒ′CĘNT-LY, *ad.* Without decency.[modest.
ĬN-DĘ-CĬD′Y-OŬS, *a.* Not falling yearly, as
leaves of trees; evergreen. [inconstancy.
ĬN-DĘ-CĬS′IǪN (ĭn-dę-sĭzh′yn), *n.* Irresolution;
ĬN-DĘ-CĪ′SĮVE, *a.* Not determining; inconclu-
sive. [tions.
ĬN-DĘ-CLĪN′Ą-BLE, *a.* Not varied by termina-
ĬN-DĘ-CLĪN′Ą-BLY, *ad.* Without variation.
‖ĬN-DĘ-CŌ′ROŬS *or* ĬN-DĔC′Ǫ-ROŬS, *a.* Inde-
cent; unbecoming; shameless; disreputable.
‖ĬN-DĘ-CŌ′ROŬS-LY, *ad.* In an indecorous
manner; indecently. [duct.
‖ĬN-DĘ-CŌ′ROŬS-NĔSS, *n.* Impropriety of con-
ĬN-DĘ-CŌ′RŬM, *n.* Indecency; a thing unbe-
coming; indecorousness. [truly.
ĬN-DĒĒD′, *ad.* In reality; in truth; in verity;
ĬN-DĘ-FĂT′Į-GĄ-BLE, *a.* Unwearied; untired.
ĬN-DĘ-FĂT′Į-GĄ-BLE-NĔSS, *n.* Unweariness.
ĬN-DĘ-FĂT′Į-GĄ-BLY, *ad.* Without weariness.
ĬN-DĘ-FĒĄ′ŞĮ-BLE, *a.* That cannot be defeated.
ĬN-DĘ-FĔCT-Į-BĬL′Į-TY, *n.* Exemption from de-
ĬN-DĘ-FĔCT′Į-BLE,*a.* Not liable to decay.[cay.
ĬN-DĘ-FĔN′SĮ-BLE,*a.* That cannot be defended.
ĬN-DĘ-FĪN′Ą-BLE, *a.* Not to be defined.
ĬN-DĔF′Į-NĪTE,*a.* Not determined; not limited.
ĬN-DĔF′Į-NĪTE-LY, *ad.* To a degree indefinite.
ĬN-DĔF′Į-NĪTE-NĔSS, *n.* The state of being in-
ĬN-DĘ-LĬB′ĘR-ĄTE,*a.*Unpremeditated.[definite.
ĬN-DĔL′Į BLE, *a.* Not to be effaced; inefface-
ĬN-DĔL′Į-BLY, *ad.* So as not to be effaced.[able.
ĬN-DĔL′Į-CĄ-CY, *n.* Want of delicacy or decency.

IN-DĔL'I-CATE, a. Wanting delicacy; indecent.
IN-DĔM-NI-FI-CĀ'TIQN, n. Reimbursement of
IN-DĔM'NI-FȲ, v. a. To exempt from loss. [loss.
IN-DĔM'NI-TY, n. Security; exemption from loss.
IN-DE-MŎN'STRA-BLE, a. That cannot be de-
monstrated. [to naturalize.
IN-DĔN'I-ZEN (-dĕn'e-zn), v. a. To make free;
IN-DĔNT', v. a. To notch:—to bind by contract.
IN-DĔNT', n. An incision; indentation; stamp.
IN-DEN-TĀ'TIQN, n. Act of indenting; a notch.
IN-DĔNT'URE (in-dĕnt'yur), n. A covenant; a
writing containing a contract or conveyance.
IN-DE-PĔN'DENCE, n. Freedom; exemption
from control or reliance. [respective.
IN-DE-PĔN'DENT, a. Not dependent; free; ir-
IN-DE-PĔN'DENT-LY, ad. Without dependence.
IN-DĔP'RE-CA-BLE, a. That cannot be entreated.
IN-DE-SCRĪB'A-BLE, a. That cannot be de-
scribed or defined. [ill-desert.
IN-DE-ŞĔRT' (ĭn-de-zĕrt'), n. Want of merit;
IN-DE-STRŬCT'I-BLE, a. Not to be destroyed.
IN-DE-TĔR'MI-NA-BLE, a. Not determinable;
not to be defined or fixed.
IN-DE-TĔR'MI-NATE, a. Not defined; indefinite.
IN-DE-TĔR'MI-NATE-LY, ad. Indefinitely.
IN-DE-TĔR'MI-NATE-NĔSS, n. Indefiniteness.
IN-DE-TĔR-MI-NĀ'TIQN, n. Want of determi-
nation or of fixed direction.
IN-DE-VŌ'TIQN, n. Want of devotion; irreligion.
IN-DE-VOÛT', a. Not devout; irreligious.
IN'DĔX, n.; pl. IN'DI-CĔŞ or IN'DĔX-EŞ. A
pointer out:—a hand that points:—table of
contents:—exponent in mathematics.
IN-DEX-TĔR'I-TY, n. Want of dexterity.
IN'DIAN (ĭnd'yan or ĭn'dĭ-an), a. Relating to
India or to the Indians. [cating.
IN'DI-CĂNT, a. Showing; pointing out; indi-
IN'DI-CĀTE, v. a. To show; to point out.
IN-DI-CĀ'TIQN, n. Mark; sign; note; symptom.
IN-DĬC'A-TĬVE, a. Showing; pointing out.
IN-DĬC'A-TĬVE-LY, ad. In such a manner as
indicates. [of the fore-arm.
IN'DI-CĀ-TQR, n. One that shows:—a muscle
IN-DĪCT' (in-dīt'), v. a. To impeach; to accuse.
IN-DĪCT'A-BLE (in-dīt'a-bl), a. Liable to be in-
dicted, or to be presented by a grand jury.
IN-DĪCT'ER (in-dīt'er), n. One who indicts.
IN-DĬC'TIQN, n. Declaration:—cycle of 15 years.
IN-DĪCT'MENT (in-dīt'ment), n. An accusation.
IN-DĬF'FER-ENCE, n. Neutrality; apathy.
IN-DĬF'FER-ENT, a. Neutral; unconcerned; in-
attentive; regardless; impartial:—passable.
IN-DĬF'FER-ENT-LY, ad. Impartially; passably.
IN'DI-GĔNCE, n. Want; penury; poverty.
IN-DĬG'E-NOŬS, a. Native; born in a country.
IN'DI-GĔNT, a. Poor; needy; necessitous.
IN-DI-GĔST'ED, a. Not digested; not concocted;
IN-DI-GĔS'TI-BLE, a. Not digestible. [crude.
IN-DI-GĔS'TIQN (ĭn-de-jĕst'yun), n. Want of
digestive power; dyspepsia. [dain.
IN-DĬG'NANT, a. Inflamed with anger and dis-
IN-DĬG'NANT-LY, ad. With indignation. [tempt.
IN-DIG-NĀ'TIQN, n. Anger mixed with con-
IN-DĬG'NI-TY, n. Contumely; contemptuous in-
IN'DI-GŌ, n. A drug used in dyeing blue. [jury.
IN'DINE, n. A substance from indigo.
IN-DI-RĔCT', a. Not direct; improper; not fair.
IN-DI-RĔC'TIQN, n. Oblique course or means.

IN-DI-RĔCT'LY, ad. Not directly; unfairly.
IN-DI-RĔCT'NESS, n. Obliquity; unfairness.
IN-DIŞ-CĔRN'I-BLE (ĭn-dĭz-zĕr'ne-bl), a. Not
perceptible; not discoverable. [parts.
IN-DIŞ-CĔRP'TI-BLE, a. Not to be separated into
IN-DĬS'CI-PLĬN-A-BLE, a. Incapable of disci-
pline; undisciplinable. [covered.
IN-DIŞ-CŎV'ER-A-BLE, a. That cannot be dis-
IN-DIŞ-CRĒĒT', a. Imprudent; incautious; un-
IN-DIŞ-CRĒĒT'LY, ad. Without prudence. [wise.
IN-DIŞ-CRĒTE', a. Not discrete or separated.
IN-DIŞ-CRĔ''TIQN (-krĕsh'un), n. Imprudence.
IN-DIŞ-CRĬM'I-NATE, a. Promiscuous; confused.
IN-DIŞ-CRĬM'I-NATE-LY, ad. Without discrim-
ination or distinction. [nation.
IN-DIŞ-CRĬM-I-NĀ'TIQN, n. Want of discrimi-
IN-DIŞ-PĔN'SA-BLE, a. Not to be dispensed with.
IN-DIŞ-PĔN'SA-BLY, ad. Necessarily.
IN-DIŞ-PŌŞE', v. a. To make unfit; to disincline.
IN-DIŞ-PŌŞED' (ĭn-dĭs-pōzd'), p. a. Disinclined;
averse:—disordered; unwell; ill. [ness.
IN-DIŞ-PŌŞ'ED-NĔSS, n. Indisposition; unfit-
IN-DIŞ-PQ-ŞĬ''TIQN (ĭn-dĭs-pq-zĭsh'un), n. Dis-
order of health; slight disease:—disinclination.
IN-DĬS'PU-TA-BLE, a. Not to be disputed.
IN-DĬS'PU-TA-BLE-NĔSS, n. Certainty; evidence.
IN-DĬS'PU-TA-BLY, ad. Without controversy.
IN-DĬS-SQ-LU-BĬL'I-TY, n. Firmness; stableness.
IN-DĬS'SQ-LU-BLE, a. Firm; stable; binding
forever; inseparable; indestructible.
IN-DĬS'SQ-LU-BLE-NĔSS, n. Indissolubility.
IN-DĬS'SQ-LU-BLY, ad. In a manner not to be
broken; inseparably. [solved.
IN-DIŞ-ŞŎLV'A-BLE, a. That cannot be dis-
IN-DIŞ-TĪNCT', a. Not plainly marked; confused.
IN-DIŞ-TĪNC'TIQN, n. Confusion; uncertainty.
IN-DIŞ-TĪNCT'LY, ad. Confusedly; uncertainly.
IN-DIŞ-TĪNCT'NESS, n. Confusion; uncertainty.
IN-DIŞ-TĬN'GUISH-A-BLE, a. Not plainly marked.
IN-DĪTE', v. a. To compose; to write:—to dic-
tate or direct. [one.
‖IN-DI-VĬD'U-AL (ĭn-de-vĭd'yu-al), a. Single;
‖IN-DI-VĬD'U-AL, n. A single person or being.
‖IN-DI-VĬD'U-AL-ĬSM, n. State of being indi-
vidual; individuality:—selfishness.
‖IN-DI-VĬD-U-ĂL'I-TY, n. Distinct existence.
‖IN-DI-VĬD'U-AL-ĪZE, v. a. To distinguish; to
separate; to consider individually. [ence.
‖IN-DI-VĬD'U-AL-LY, ad. With distinct exist-
‖IN-DI-VĬD'U-ĀTE, v. a. To distinguish or make
single; to individualize. [gle.
‖IN-DI-VĬD-U-Ā'TIQN, n. The act of making sin-
IN-DI-VĬŞ-I-BĬL'I-TY,) n. The state or quality
IN-DI-VĬŞ'I-BLE-NĔSS,) of being indivisible.
IN-DI-VĬŞ'I-BLE, a. That cannot be divided.
IN-DI-VĬŞ'I-BLY, ad. So as not to be divided.
IN-DŎC'I-BLE, a. Unteachable; not docible.
IN-DŎC'ILE, a. Unteachable; not docile.
IN-DQ-CĬL'I-TY, n. Unteachableness; dulness.
IN-DŎC'TRIN-ĀTE, v. a. To instruct in prin-
ciples; to teach; to educate. [ples.
IN-DŎC-TRI-NĀ'TIQN, n. Instruction in princi-
IN'DQ-LENCE, n. Laziness; idleness.
IN'DQ-LENT, a. Careless; lazy; idle; listless.
IN'DQ-LENT-LY, ad. Carelessly; lazily; listlessly.
IN-DŌRSE', v. a. To write upon; to endorse.
IN-DŪ'BI-TA-BLE, a. Undoubted; unquestion-
able; indisputable.

ĬN-DŪ′BĬ-TĄ-BLE-NĔSS,*n.*The being indubitable.
ĬN-DŪ′BĬ-TĄ-BLY, *ad.* Undoubtedly; certainly.
ĬN-DŪCE′, *v. a.* To influence, persuade, produce.
ĬN-DŪCE′MENT, *n.* Motive; that which induces.
ĬN-DŪ′CER, *n.* One who induces; a persuader.
ĬN-DŬCT′, *v. a.* To introduce; to bring in.
ĬN-DŬC′TIŎN, *n.* Entrance:—inference or con-
  clusion drawn from a number of facts. [tion.
ĬN-DŬC′TĬVE, *a.* Leading; proceeding by induc-
ĬN-DŬC′TĬVE-LY, *ad.* By induction; by infer-
ĬN-DŬCT′ŎR, *n.* The person who inducts. [ence.
ĬN-DŪE′ (ĭn-dū′), *v. a.* To invest; to clothe.
ĬN-DŪE′MENT (ĭn-dū′ment), *n.* Investment.
ĬN-DŬLGE′, *v. a.* To encourage by compliance;
  to humor; to gratify; to cherish; to favor.
ĬN-DŬLGE′, *v. n.* To give indulgence.
ĬN-DŬL′GENCE, *n.* Fondness; kindness; for-
  bearance; favor; compliance; gratification.
ĬN-DŬL′GENT, *a.* Kind; gentle; mild; favorable.
ĬN-DŬL′GENT-LY, *ad.* Without severity; mildly.
ĬN′DŪ-RĀTE, *v. n. & a.* To grow or make hard.
ĬN-DŪ-RĀ′TIŎN, *n.* Act of hardening; obduracy.
ĬN-DŬS′TRĬ-OŬS, *a.* Practising industry; dili-
  gent; laborious; assiduous. [uously.
ĬN-DŬS′TRĬ-OŬS-LY, *ad.* Laboriously; assid-
ĬN′DŬS-TRY, *n.* Habitual diligence; assiduity.
ĬN′DWĔLL-ĬNG, *a.* Dwelling within; internal.
ĬN-Ē′BRĬ-ĀTE, *v. a. & n.* To make drunk.
ĬN-Ē-BRĬ-Ā′TIŎN, *n.* Drunkenness; intoxication.
ĬN-ĔD′ĬT-ED, *a.* Not published; not edited.
ĬN-ĔF′FĄ-BLE, *a.* Unspeakable; unutterable.
ĬN-ĔF′FĄ-BLY, *ad.* In an ineffable manner.
ĬN-ĔF-FĔC′TĬVE, *a.* Producing no effect; in-
  effectual; not effective. [fectual; weak.
ĬN-EF-FĔCT′Ų-ĄL (ĭn-ef-fĕkt′yu-ạl), *a.* Not ef-
ĬN-EF-FĔCT′Ų-ĄL-LY, *ad.* Without effect.
ĬN-ĔF-FĬ-CĀ′CIOŲS (ĭn-ĕf-fę-kā′shụs), *a.* Unable
  to produce effects; weak; inefficient. [fect.
ĬN-ĔF′FĬ-CĄ-CY, *n.* Want of power; want of ef-
ĬN-EF-FĬ″CIEN-CY (ĭn-ef-fĭsh′ęn-sę), *n.* Want
  of efficiency; weakness.
ĬN-EF-FĬ″CIENT (ĭn-ef-fĭsh′ent), *a.* Ineffective.
ĬN-ĔL′E-GANCE, *n.* Want of elegance or beauty.
ĬN-ĔL′E-GANT, *a.* Not elegant; not beautiful.
ĬN-ĔL′E-GANT-LY, *ad.* Not beautifully; coarsely.
ĬN-ĔL-Ĭ-GĬ-BĬL′Ĭ-TY, *n.* The being ineligible.
ĬN-ĔL′Ĭ-GĬ-BLE, *a.* Incapable of being elected.
ĬN-ĔL′Ŏ-QUENT, *a.* Not persuasive; not ora-
  torical; not eloquent.
ĬN-ĔPT′, *a.* Trifling; foolish; useless; unapt.
ĬN-E-QUAL′Ĭ-TY (ĭn-ę-kwŏl′ę-tę), *n.* Difference
  of quantity, degree, or quality; unevenness.
ĬN-ĔQ′UĬ-TĄ-BLE, *a.* Not equitable; unjust.
ĬN-ĔR-RĄ-BĬL′Ĭ-TY, *n.* Exemption from error.
ĬN-ĔR′RĄ-BLE, *a.* Exempt from error; unerring.
ĬN-ĔRT′, *a.* Inactive; sluggish. [want of action.
ĬN-ĔR′TĬ-A (ĭn-ĕr′shę-ạ), *n.* [L.] Inactivity;
ĬN-ĔRT′LY, *ad.* Inactively; sluggishly; dully.
ĬN-ĔRT′NESS, *n.* Want of motion or activity.
ĬN-ĔS′TĬ-MĄ-BLE, *a.* Above all price; too val-
  uable to be estimated; invaluable.
ĬN-ĔS′TĬ-MĄ-BLY, *ad.* So as not to be estimated.
ĬN-ĔV-Ĭ-TĄ-BĬL′Ĭ-TY, *n.* State of being inevita-
  ble; impossibility of avoiding. [caped.
ĬN-ĔV′Ĭ-TĄ-BLE, *a.* Unavoidable; not to be es-
ĬN-ĔV′Ĭ-TĄ-BLE-NĔSS, *n.* Quality of being in-
  evitable; certainty; inevitability. [cape.
ĬN-ĔV′Ĭ-TĄ-BLY, *ad.* Without possibility of es-

ĬN-EX-ĂCT′ (-ęgz-), *a.* Not exact; incorrect.
ĬN-EX-CĬT′Ą-BLE, *a.* Not excitable; passionless.
ĬN-EX-CŪŞ′Ą-BLE, *a.* Not to be excused or pal-
  liated; not excusable. [excuse.
ĬN-EX-CŪŞ′Ą-BLE-NĔSS, *n.* Enormity beyond
ĬN-EX-CŪŞ′Ą-BLY, *ad.* To a degree beyond ex-
ĬN-ĔX-E-CŪ′TIŎN, *n.* Non-performance. [cuse.
ĬN-EX-HĀL′Ą-BLE, *a.* That cannot be exhaled
  or evaporated. [emptied.
ĬN-EX-HÂUST′ED, *a.* Unemptied; not to be
ĬN-EX-HÂUST′Ĭ-BLE, *a.* Not to be exhausted or
  spent; unfailing; exhaustless. [isting.
ĬN-EX-ĬST′ENT, *a.* Not having being; not ex-
ĬN-ĔX-Ŏ-RĄ-BĬL′Ĭ-TY, *n.* The being inexorable.
ĬN-ĔX′Ŏ-RĄ-BLE, *a.* Not to be moved by entreaty.
ĬN-ĔX′Ŏ-RĄ-BLY, *ad.* In an inexorable manner.
ĬN-EX-PĒ′DĬ-ENCE, } *n.* Want of fitness, pro-
ĬN-EX-PĒ′DĬ-ĔN-CY, }   priety, or expedience.
ĬN-EX-PĒ′DĬ-ĔNT, *a.* Not expedient; unsuitable.
ĬN-EX-PĒ′RĬ-ĔNCE, *n.* Want of experience.
ĬN-EX-PĒ′RĬ-ĔNCED (ĭn-ęks-pē′rę-ĕnst), *a.* Not
  experienced; not having experience. [ward.
ĬN-EX-PĔRT′, *a.* Unskilful; unskilled; awk-
ĬN-ĔX′PĬ-Ą-BLE, *a.* Admitting no satisfaction.
ĬN-ĔX′PĬ-Ą-BLY, *ad.* In an inexpiable manner.
ĬN-ĔX′PLĬ-CĄ-BLE, *a.* Incapable of being ex-
  plained; unaccountable. [plicable.
ĬN-ĔX′PLĬ-CĄ-BLE-NĔSS, *n.* The being inex-
ĬN-ĔX′PLĬ-CĄ-BLY, *ad.* So as not to be explained.
ĬN-EX-PLŌR′Ą-BLE, *a.* That cannot be explored.
ĬN-EX-PRĔSS′Ĭ-BLE, *a.* Not to be told; unspeak-
  able; unutterable. [ably.
ĬN-EX-PRĔSS′Ĭ-BLY, *ad.* Unutterably; unspeak-
ĬN-EX-PŬG′NĄ-BLE, *a.* Not to be taken by as-
  sault; impregnable; unconquerable.
ĬN-EX-TĬN′GUĬSH-Ą-BLE, *a.* Unquenchable.
ĬN-ĔX′TRĬ-CĄ-BLE, *a.* Not to be disentangled.
ĬN-ĔX′TRĬ-CĄ-BLE-NĔSS, *n.* The state of being
  inextricable.
ĬN-EȲE′ (ĭn-ī′), *v. a.* To inoculate, as a plant.
ĬN-FĂL-LĬ-BĬL′Ĭ-TY, } *n.* State of being infal-
ĬN-FĂL′LĬ-BLE-NĔSS, }   lible; inerrability;
  exemption from error or failure.
ĬN-FĂL′LĬ-BLE, *a.* Not fallible; certain; sure.
ĬN-FĂL′LĬ-BLY, *ad.* Without failure; certainly.
ĬN′FĄ-MOŬS, *a.* Notoriously bad; shameless.
ĬN′FĄ-MOŬS-LY, *ad.* With infamy; shamefully.
ĬN′FĄ-MOŲS-NĔSS, *n.* Infamy; shamefulness.
ĬN′FĄ-MY, *n.* Public reproach or disgrace.
ĬN′FĄN-CY, *n.* The first part of life:—beginning.
ĬN′FĄNT, *n.* A babe; a child under 7 years of age.
ĬN′FĄNT, *a.* Pertaining to infancy; young.
ĬN-FĂN′TĄ, *n.* In Spain and Portugal, the title
  of a princess of the royal blood.
ĬN-FĂN′TE, *n.* In Spain and Portugal, the title
  given to all the king's sons, except the eldest,
  or heir apparent. [infants.
ĬN-FĂN′TĬ-CĪDE, *n.* The murder, or a slayer, of
ĬN′FĄN-TĪLE, *a.* Relating to infants; childish.
ĬN′FĄN-TĪNE, *a.* Childish; young; infantile.
ĬN′FĄN-TRY, *n.* The foot soldiers of an army.
ĬN-FĂT′Ų-ĀTE (ĭn-făt′yu-āt), *v. a.* To strike with
  folly; to deprive of understanding; to besot.
ĬN-FĂT-Ų-Ā′TIŎN, *n.* A deprivation of reason.
ĬN-FĒA′ŞĬ-BLE (ĭn-fē′zę-bl), *a.* Not to be done.
ĬN-FĒA-ŞĬ-BĬL′Ĭ-TY, } *n.* State of being infea-
ĬN-FĒA′ŞĬ-BLE-NĔSS, }   sible; impracticability.
ĬN-FĔCT′, *v. a.* To taint; to corrupt; to pollute.

IN-FĔC'TIQN, n. Contagion; taint; poison.
IN-FĔC'TIOŲS (in-fĕk'shŭs), a. Contagious. [ly.
IN-FĔC'TIOŲS-LY (-fĕk'shŭs-lę), ad. Contagious-
IN-FĔC'TIOŲS-NĔSS, n. Quality of being in-
 fectious, or of communicating disease. [gion.
IN-FĔC'TIVE, a. Having the quality of conta-
IN-FĔC'ŲND, a. Unfruitful; intertile; sterile.
IN-FE-CŬND'I-TY, n. Want of fecundity.
IN-FE-LĬÇ'I-TY, n. Unhappiness; misery. [sions.
IN-FĔR', v. a. To deduce; to draw, as conclu-
IN-FĔR'A-BLE, IN-FĔR'RI-BLE, a. Deducible.
ĬN'FER-ENCE, n. A conclusion drawn from
 premises; a deduction; a corollary. [value.
IN-FĒ'RI-QR, a. Lower in place, station, or
IN-FĒ'RI-QR, n. One lower in rank or station.
IN-FĒ-RI-ŎR'I-TY, n. A lower state or quality.
IN-FĔR'NAL, a. Hellish; Tartarean; detestable.
IN-FĔR'TILE, a. Unfruitful; not productive.
IN-FER-TĬL'I-TY, n. Unfruitfulness; want of
 fertility; unproductiveness; sterility.
IN-FĔST', v. a. To harass; to disturb; to plague.
IN-FES-TĀ'TIQN, n. Molestation; annoyance.
IN-FĔS'TERED (in-fĕs'terd), a. Rankling.
IN-FĔS-TĪV'I-TY, n. Want of cheerfulness.
IN-FEŲ-DĀ'TIQN (in-fu-dā'shŭn), n. The act of
 putting one in possession of a fee or estate.
ĬN'FI-DĔL, n. A disbeliever of Christianity.
ĬN'FI-DĔL, a. Unbelieving; wanting belief.
ĬN-FI-DĔL'I-TY, n. Disbelief of Christianity;
 want of fidelity; perfidy.
IN-FĬL'TRĀTE, v. n. To enter by the pores.
ĬN'FI-NĪTE, a. Boundless; unlimited; immense.
ĬN'FI-NĪTE-LY, ad. Without limits; immensely.
ĬN'FI-NĪTE-NĔSS, n. Immensity; infinity.
IN-FĬN-I-TĔS'I-MAL, a. So small as to be less
 than any assignable quantity. [ited.
IN-FĬN'I-TĪVE, a. (Gram.) Undefined; not lim-
IN-FĬN'I-TŪDE, n. Infinity; immensity.
IN-FĬN'I-TY, n. Immensity; endless number.
ĬN-FĬRM', a. Not firm; weak; feeble; irresolute.
IN-FĬRM'A-RY, n. A residence for the sick.
IN-FĬRM'I-TY, n. Weakness; failing; fault; dis-
IN-FĬRM'NĔSS, n. Weakness; feebleness. [ease.
IN-FĬX', v. a. To drive in; to set; to fasten.
IN-FLĀME', v. a. To set on fire, provoke, irritate.
IN-FLĀME', v. n. To grow hot, angry, or painful.
IN-FLĀM'ER, n. He who or that which inflames.
IN-FLĂM-MA-BĬL'I-TY, n. Quality of being in-
 flammable; inflammableness.
IN-FLĂM'MA-BLE, a. Easy to be set on fire. [fire.
IN-FLĂM'MA-BLE-NĔSS, n. Quality of catching
IN-FLĂM-MĀ'TIQN, n. State of being in a flame:
 — a swelling and redness attended by heat.
IN-FLĂM'MA-TĪVE, a. That inflames.
IN-FLĂM'MA-TQ-RY, a. Tending to inflame.
IN-FLĀTE', v. a. To swell with wind; to puff up.
IN-FLĀ'TIQN, n. Act of inflating; flatulence.
IN-FLĔCT', v. a. To bend, turn:—to vary a noun,
IN-FLĔC'TIQN, n. Act of inflecting. [&c.
IN-FLĔC'TIVE, a. Having the power of bending.
IN-FLĔX-I-BĬL'I-TY, IN-FLĔX'I-BLE-NĔSS, n.
 Quality of being inflexible; stiffness.
IN-FLĔX'I-BLE, a. Not to be bent; stiff; firm.
IN-FLĔX'I-BLY, ad. With firmness; invariably.
IN-FLĬCT', v. a. To lay on; to apply; to impose.
IN-FLĬCT'ER, n. One who inflicts or punishes.
IN-FLĬC'TIQN, n. Act of inflicting; punishment.
IN-FLĬC'TIVE, a. Tending to inflict; imposing.

IN-FLQ-RĔS'CENCE, n. Mode of flowering in
 plants. [power.
ĬN'FLŲ-ENCE, n. An impulsive or directing
ĬN'FLŲ-ENCE, v. a. To act upon, bias, modify.
IN-FLŲ-ĔN'TIAL, a. Exerting influence or pow-
IN-FLŲ-ĔN'TIAL-LY, ad. With influence. [er.
IN-FLŲ-ĔN'ZA, n. An epidemic form of catarrh.
ĬN'FLŬX, n. Act of flowing in; infusion; power.
IN-FŌLD', v. a. To involve; to inwarp, enclose.
IN-FŌRM', v. a. To instruct; to acquaint; to tell.
ĬN-FŌR'MAL, a. Not in the usual form; irregular.
IN-FQR-MĂL'I-TY, n. Want of regular form.
ĬN-FŌR'MAL-LY, ad. Without attention to form.
IN-FŌRM'ANT, n. One who informs or accuses.
ĬN-FQR-MĀ'TIQN, n. Intelligence; notice given.
IN-FŌRM'ER, n. One who informs or accuses.
IN-FŌR'MI-DA-BLE, a. Not to be dreaded or
ĬN-FŌR'MOŲS, a. Shapeless; irregular. [feared.
IN-FRĂCT', v. a. To break; to violate, infringe.
IN-FRĂC'TIQN, n. The act of breaking; violation.
IN-FRĂCT'QR, n. One who infracts; a violator.
IN-FRĂN'GI-BLE, a. Not to be broken or violated.
ĬN-FRĒ'QUEN-CY, n. Uncommonness; rareness.
ĬN-FRĒ'QUENT, a. Rare; uncommon; unusual.
IN-FRĬNGE' (in-frĭnj'), v. a. To violate; to break.
IN-FRĬNGE'MENT, n. A breach; a violation.
IN-FRĬNG'ER, n. A breaker; a violator.
IN-FŪ'RI-ĀTE, a. Enraged; raging; furious.
IN-FŪ'RI-ĀTE, v. a. To render furious or insane.
IN-FŬS'CĀTE, v. a. To darken; to obscure.
IN-FŲS-CĀ'TIQN, n. The act of darkening.
IN-FŪSE', v. a. To pour in; to instil; to inspire.
IN-FŪ-SI-BĬL'I-TY, n. The being infusible.
IN-FŪ'SI-BLE, a. That may be infused:—not fu-
 sible; that cannot be melted.
IN-FŪ'SIQN (in-fū'zhŭn), n. The act of infusing;
 instillation; liquor made by infusion. [vest.
IN-GĂTH'ER-ĬNG, n. Act of getting in the har-
ĬN-GĔL'A-BLE, a. That cannot be congealed.
IN-GĔM'I-NĀTE, v. a. To double; to repeat. [in.
IN-GĔN'ER-ĀTE, v. a. To beget; to produce with-
IN-GĔN'ER-ATE, a. Inborn; innate; inherent.
||IN-GĒN'IOŲS or IN-GĒ'NI-OŬS, a. Skilful; in-
 ventive; possessed of ingenuity or genius.
||IN-GĒN'IOŲS-LY, ad. With ingenuity; with
 skill; cleverly; skilfully.
||IN-GĒN'IOŲS-NĔSS, n. Ingenuity; wittiness.
IN-GĔN'ITE or ĬN'GEN-ĪTE, a. Innate; inborn.
ĬN-GE-NŪ'I-TY, n. Power of invention; genius.
IN-GĔN'Ų-OŬS (in-jĕn'yŭ-ŭs), a. Open; frank;
 fair; candid; generous; noble:—freeborn. [ly.
IN-GĔN'Ų-OŬS-LY, ad. Openly; fairly; candid-
IN-GĔN'Ų-OŲS-NĔSS, n. Frankness; candor.
IN-GĔST', v. a. To throw into the stomach.
IN-GĔS'TIQN (in-jĕst'yŭn), n. Act of ingesting.
IN-GLŌ'RI-OŬS, a. Dishonorable; ignominious.
IN-GLŌ'RI-OŬS-LY, ad. With ignominy; meanly.
ĬN'GŎT, n. A mass or bar of gold, silver, &c.
IN-GRĂFT', v. a. To plant, as the sprig or scion
 of one tree in the stock of another; to fix deep.
IN-GRĂFT'MENT, n. Act of ingrafting a scion.
ĬN-GRĀTE', or ĬN-GRĀTE'FŬL, a. Ungrateful.
IN-GRĀ'TI-ĀTE (in-grā'she-āt), v. a. To put in
 favor; to recommend to kindness.
IN-GRĂT'I-TŪDE, n. Want of a sense of favors.
IN-GRĒ'DI-ENT, n. A part of any compound.
ĬN'GRĔSS, n. Entrance or power of entrance.
IN-GRĔS'SIQN (-grĕsh'ŭn), n. Entrance.

IN'GUI-NAL (ĭng'gwe-nal), a. Belonging to, or situated in, the groin.
IN-GŬLF', v. a. To swallow up, as in a gulf; to cast into a gulf. [ingulf.
IN-GŬR'GI-TĀTE, v. a. To swallow down; to IN-GŬR-GI-TĀ'TIQN, n. An intemperate swallowing. [apt; unqualified
IN-HĂB'ILE, or IN-HA-BÎLE', a. Unskilful; un-
IN-HĂB'IT, v. a. & n. To dwell or reside in; to occupy; to hold; to live; to abide.
IN-HĂB'IT-A-BLE, a. That may be inhabited.
IN-HĂB'IT-ANCE, IN-HĂB'IT-AN-CY, n. Residence; habitance.
IN-HĂB'IT-ANT, n. One who resides in a place.
IN-HĂB-I-TĀ'TIQN, n. Abode; act of inhabiting.
IN-HĂB'IT-ER, n. One who inhabits; a dweller.
IN-HĀLE', v. a. To draw in with air; to inspire.
IN-HAR-MŌ'NI-OŬS, a. Unmusical; discordant.
IN-HĒRE', v. n. To exist in something else.
IN-HĒ'RENCE,) n. Inseparable existence in
IN-HĒ'REN-CY,) something else; inhesion.
IN-HĒ'RENT, a. Existing in something:—innate.
IN-HĒ'RENT-LY, ad. In an inherent manner.
IN-HĔR'IT, v. a. To receive by inheritance.
IN-HĔR'IT-A-BLE, a. That may be inherited.
IN-HĔR'IT-A-BLY, ad. By inheritance. [session.
IN-HĔR'IT-ANCE, n. Patrimony; hereditary pos-
IN-HĔR'IT-OR, n. An heir; one who inherits.
IN-HĔR'IT-RĔSS, IN-HĔR'I-TRĬX, n. An heiress.
IN-HĒ'SIQN (in-hē'zhun), n. Inherence.
IN-HĬB'IT, v. a. To hinder, repress, prohibit.
IN-HI-BI''TIQN (ĭn-he-bĭsh'un), n. Prohibition.
IN-HŎS'PI-TA-BLE, a. Not hospitable; unkind.
IN-HŎS'PI-TA-BLY, ad. Unkindly to strangers.
IN-HŎS-PI-TĂL'I-TY, n. Want of hospitality.
IN-HŪ'MAN, a. Barbarous; savage; cruel.
IN-HU-MĂN'I-TY, n. Cruelty; barbarity.
IN-HŪ'MAN-LY, ad. Cruelly; barbarously.
IN-HŪ'MĀTE, IN-HŪME', v. a. To bury; to inter.
IN-HU-MĀ'TIQN, n. A burying; sepulture.
IN-ĬM'I-CAL, or IN-I-MĪ'CAL, a. Hostile; adverse; unfriendly; hurtful. [tated.
IN-ĬM-I-TA-BĬL'I-TY, n. Incapacity to be imi-
IN-ĬM'I-TA-BLE, a. That cannot be imitated.
IN-ĬM'I-TA-BLY, ad. In an inimitable manner.
IN-ĬQ'UI-TOŬS (-ĭk'we-tŭs), a. Unjust; wicked.
IN-ĬQ'UI-TY (in-ĭk'we-te), n. Injustice; sin.
IN-I''TIAL (in-ĭsh'al), a. Beginning; incipient.
IN-I''TI-ĀTE (-ĭsh'e-āt), v. a. To enter, introduce; to instruct in the rudiments:—to begin.
IN-I-TI-Ā'TIQN (in-ĭsh-e-ā'shun), n. Admission.
IN-I''TI-A-TĬVE (in-ĭsh'e-a-tĭv), n. The right or act of introducing or proposing measures.
IN-I''TI-A-TQ-RY (-ĭsh'e-a-tur e), a. Introductory.
IN-JĔCT', v. a. To throw in; to dart in. [ter.
IN-JĔC'TIQN, n. The act of throwing in; a clys-
IN-JU-DI''CIOŬS (-dĭsh'us), a. Not judicious;
IN-JU-DI''CIOŬS-LY, ad. Not wisely. [unwise.
IN-JU-DI''CIOŬS-NĔSS, n. Want of judgment.
IN-JŬNC'TIQN, n. A command; order; precept.
IN'JURE (ĭn'jur), v. a. To hurt; to wrong.
IN'JUR-ER, n. One who injures; a wronger.
IN-JŪ'RI-OŬS, a. Unjust; mischievous; hurtful.
IN-JŪ'RI-OŬS-LY, ad. Wrongfully; hurtfully.
IN-JŪ'RI-OŬS-NĔSS, n. Hurtfulness.
IN'JU-RY, n. Hurt; wrong; mischief; detriment.
IN-JŬS'TICE, n. Iniquity; wrong.
INK, n. A liquid for writing, printing, &c.

INK (ĭngk), v. a. To black or daub with ink.
INK'HÖRN, n. A vessel for ink; an inkstand.
INK'I-NĔSS, n. The quality of being inky.
IN'KLE, n. A sort of broad linen tape. [sire.
INK'LING, n. Hint; whisper; intimation:—de-
INK'STĂND, n. A vessel for holding ink.
INK'Y, a. Consisting of ink:—black as ink.
IN-LĀCE', v. a. To embellish, as with lace.
IN'LĂND, a. Interior; remote from the sea
IN'LĂND, n. Interior or midland parts.
IN-LĀY' (in-lā'), v. a. [imp. t. & pp. inlaid.] To diversify by insertion; to variegate.
IN'LĀY, n. Matter inlaid; matter cut to be inlaid.
IN'LĔT, n. Passage; place of ingress; entrance.
IN-LĬST', v. a. To enroll. See ENLIST. [other.
IN'MĀTE, n. One who dwells jointly with an-
IN'MŌST, a. Deepest within; most interior.
INN, n. A house of entertainment for travellers.
IN-NĀTE', a. Inborn; ingenerate; natural.
IN-NĀTE'LY, ad. Ingenerately; naturally.
IN-NĀTE'NĔSS, n. The quality of being innate.
IN-NĂV'I-GA-BLE, a. Not to be passed by sailing.
IN'NER, a. Interior; not outward; internal.
IN'NER-MŌST, a. Inmost; deepest within. [er.
INN'HŌLD-ER, n. A keeper of an inn; inn-keep-
INN'ING, n. The ingathering of corn or grain.
INN'INGS, n. pl. Lands recovered from the sea.
INN'KĒĒP-ER, n. One who keeps an inn. [ness.
IN'NQ-CĔNCE, n. Purity; integrity; harmless-
IN'NQ-CĔNT, a. Pure; without guilt; harmless.
IN'NQ-CĔNT-LY, ad. Without guilt or harm.
IN-NŎC'U-OŬS, a. Harmless; safe; innoxious.
IN'NQ-VĀTE, v. a. & n. To introduce novelties.
IN-NQ-VĀ'TIQN, n. The introduction of novelty.
IN'NQ-VĀ-TQR, n. An introducer of novelties.
‖IN-NŎX'IOŬS (ĭn-nŏk'shus), a. Harmless; pure.
‖IN-NŎX'IOŬS-LY, ad. Harmlessly; without
‖IN-NŎX'IOŬS-NĔSS, n. Harmlessness. [harm.
IN-NU-ĔN'DŌ, n.; pl. IN-NU-ĔN'DŌES. An oblique hint; indirect allusion; an insinuation.
IN-NŪ-MER-A-BĬL'I-TY, n. The state or quality of being innumerable.
IN-NŪ'MER-A-BLE, a. That cannot be numbered.
IN-NŪ'MER-A-BLY, ad. Without number.
IN-QB-SĔRV'ANT, a. Not observant; careless.
IN-ŎC'U-LĀTE, v. a. To bud, as a plant:—to infect with a disease, as the small-pox.
IN-ŎC-U-LĀ'TIQN, n. A grafting in the bud:— a method of communicating a disease; vaccina-
IN-ŎC'U-LĀ-TQR, n. One who inoculates. [tion.
IN-Ō'DQR-OŬS, a. Wanting scent or smell.
IN-QF-FĔN'SIVE, a. Giving no offence; harmless.
IN-QF-FĔN'SIVE-LY, ad. Without offence or
IN-QF-FĔN'SIVE-NĔSS, n. Harmlessness. [harm.
IN-QF-FI''CIAL (ĭn-qf-fĭsh'al), a. Not official.
IN-QF-FI''CIOŬS (ĭn-qf-fĭsh'us), a. Not officious.
IN-ŎP'ER-A-TĬVE, a. Not operative; inactive.
IN-QP-PQR-TŪNE', a. Unseasonable; inconven-
IN-QP-PQR-TŪNE'LY, ad. Unseasonably. [ient.
IN-ÖR'DI-NA-CY, n. Irregularity; disorder.
IN-ÖR'DI-NĀTE, a. Irregular; immoderate.
IN-ÖR'DI-NĀTE-LY, ad. Irregularly; excessively.
IN-ÖR'DI-NĀTE-NĔSS, n. Irregularity; excess.
IN-QR-GĂN'IC, IN-QR-GĂN'I-CAL, a. Void or destitute of organs. [tact.
IN-ŎS'CU-LĀTE, v. a. To insert; to join by con-
IN-ŎS-CU-LĀ'TIQN, n. Union by conjunction.
IN'QUĔST, n. A judicial inquiry or examination.

ĬN-QUĪ′Ḙ-TŪDE, n. Want of quiet; disquietude.
ĬN-QUĪR′Ḁ-BLE, a. That may be inquired into.
ĬN-QUĪRE′, v. n. To ask questions; to make search; to enquire;—written indifferently *inquire* or *enquire.* [enquire.
ĬN-QUĪRE′, v. a. To ask about; to seek out; to
ĬN-QUĪR′ḘR, n. One who inquires; enquirer.
ĬN-QUĪ′RY, n. Art of inquiry; enquiry.
ĬN-QUĬ-ṢĪ′′TĬQN (ĭn-kwḙ-zĭsh′un), n. Judicial inquiry; search :—an ecclesiastical tribunal.
ĬN-QUĬ-ṢĪ′′TĬQN-ḀL, a. Busy in making inquiry
ĬN-QUĬṢ′Ĭ-TĪVE, a. Curious; busy in search.
ĬN-QUĬṢ′Ĭ-TĪVE-LY, ad. In an inquisitive manner.
ĬN-QUĬṢ′Ĭ-TĬVE-NĔSS, n. Busy curiosity. [tion.
ĬN-QUĬṢ′Ĭ-TQR, n. Officer in the court of inquisi-
ĬN-QUĬṢ-Ĭ-TŌ′RĬ-ḀL, a. Relating to inquisition.
ĬN-QUĬṢ-Ĭ-TŌ′RĬ-OŬS, a. Making rigid inquiry.
ĬN-RĀIL′ (ĭn-rāl′), v. a. To enclose within rails.
ĬN′RŌAD (ĭn′rŏd), n. Incursion; invasion.
ĬN-SḀ-LŪ′BRĬ-OŬS, a. Unhealthy; unwholesome.
ĬN-SḀ-LŪ′BRĬ-TY, n. Unwholesomeness.
ĬN-SĂN′Ḁ-BLE, a. Incurable; irremediable.
ĬN-SĀNE′, a. Mad; distracted; delirious.
ĬN-SĂN′Ĭ-TY, n. Want of sound mind; madness.
ĬN-SĀ′TĬ-Ḁ-BLE (ĭn-sā′shḙ-ḁ-bl), a. Incapable of being satisfied; greedy beyond measure.
ĬN-SĀ′TĬ-Ḁ-BLḘ-NĔSS (ĭn-sā′shḙ-ḁ-bl-nĕs), n. Greediness not to be appeased. [greedily.
ĬN-SĀ′TĬ-Ḁ-BLY, ad. In an insatiable manner;
ĬN-SĀ′TĬ-Ḁ-ĀTE (-sā′shḙ-ḁt), a. Insatiable; greedy.
ĬN-SḀ-TĪ′Ḙ-TY, n. Insatiableness; greediness.
ĬN-SĂT′U-RḀ-BLE, a. Not to be saturated or filled.
ĬN-SCRĪBE′, v. a. To write on, address, assign.
ĬN-SCRĬP′TĬQN, n. A title, name, character, or address, either written or engraved.
ĬN-SCRŬ-TḀ-BĬL′Ĭ-TY,) n. Incapability of dis-
ĬN-SCRŬ′TḀ-BLE-NĔSS,) covery; unsearcha-bleness. [den; undiscoverable
ĬN-SCRŪ′TḀ-BLE, a. Unsearchable; deeply hid-
ĬN-SCRŪ′TḀ-BLY, ad. So as not to be traced out.
ĬN-SCŬLP′, v. a. To engrave; to cut or carve.
ĬN-SCŬLPT′URE (ĭn-skŭlpt′yur), n. Sculpture.
ĬN-SĒAM′ (ĭn-sēm′), v. a. To mark by a seam.
ĬN′SĔCT, n. A small creeping or flying animal.
ĬN-SĔC′TĬLE, a. Having the nature of insects.
ĬN-SĔC′TĬQN, n. An incision; a cutting in.
ĬN-SĔC-TĬV′Q-ROŬS, a. Feeding on insects.
ĬN-SḘ-CŪRE′, a. Not secure; not safe; dangerous.
ĬN-SḘ-CŪRE′LY, ad. Without certainty. [ard.
ĬN-SḘ-CŪ′RĬ-TY, n. Want of safety; danger; haz-
ĬN-SĔN′SḀTE, a. Stupid; foolish; wanting sense.
ĬN-SĔN-SĬ-BĬL′Ĭ-TY, n. Want of sensibility; torpor.
ĬN-SĔN′SĬ-BLE, a. Imperceptible; not discover-able by the senses; void of feeling; stupid.
ĬN-SĔN′SĬ-BLE-NĔSS, n. Want of sensibility.
ĬN-SĔN′SĬ-BLY, ad. Imperceptibly; torpidly.
ĬN-SĔN′TĬ-ḘNT (-sĕn′shḙ-ḙnt), a. Not sentient.
ĬN-SĔP-Ḁ-RḀ-BĬL′Ĭ-TY,) n. The quality of not
ĬN-SĔP′Ḁ-RḀ-BLE-NĔSS,) being separable.
ĬN-SĔP′Ḁ-RḀ-BLE, a. Not to be separated.
ĬN-SĔP′Ḁ-RḀ-BLY, ad. With indissoluble union.
ĬN-SĔRT′, v. a. To place or set in or among. [ed.
ĬN-SĔR′TĬQN, n. Act of inserting; thing insert-
ĬN-SHRĪNE′, v. a. To enclose. See ENSHRINE.
ĬN′SĪDE, n. Interior part;—opposed to the *outside.*
ĬN-SĬD′Ĭ-OŬS, a. Sly; crafty; diligent to entrap.
ĬN-SĬD′Ĭ-OŬS-LY, ad. In an insidious manner.
ĬN-SĬD′Ĭ-OŬS-NĔSS, n. Quality of being insidious.

ĬN′SĪGHT (ĭn′sīt), n. Introspection; deep view.
ĬN-SĬG′NĬ-Ḁ, n. pl. [L.] Badges of office or honor.
ĬN-SĬG-NĬF′Ĭ-CḀNCE, n. Want of importance.
ĬN-SĬG-NĬF′Ĭ-CḀNT, a. Unimportant; trifling.
ĬN-SĬG-NĬF′Ĭ-CḀNT-LY, ad. Without importance.
ĬN-SĬN-CĒRE′, a. Not sincere; not hearty; false.
ĬN-SĬN-CĒRE′LY, ad. Without sincerity; falsely.
ĬN-SĬN-CĔR′Ĭ-TY, n. Dissimulation; want of truth.
ĬN-SĬN′U-ĀTE, v. a. To introduce gently; to hint.
ĬN-SĬN′U-ĀTE, v. n. To creep or wind in.
ĬN-SĬN′U-Ā′TĬQN, n. Act of insinuating; a hint.
ĬN-SĬN′U-Ā-TQR, n. One that insinuates.
ĬN-SĬP′ĬD, a. Tasteless; vapid; flat; dull.
ĬN-SĬ-PĬD′Ĭ-TY,) n. Want of taste or spirit;
ĬN-SĬP′ĬD-NĔSS,) tastelessness; dulness.
ĬN-SĬP′ĬD-LY, ad. Without taste; without spirit.
ĬN-SĬST′, v. n. To persist in; to press; to urge.
ĬN-SĬST′ḘNT, a. Resting upon any thing.
ĬN-SĬ′′TĬQN (ĭn-sĭsh′un), n. A graft; insertion.
ĬN-SNĀRE′, v. a. To entrap; to ensnare. [ety.
ĬN-SQ-BRĪ′Ḙ-TY, n. Drunkenness; want of sobri-
ĬN′SQ-LĀTE, v. a. To dry or expose in the sun.
ĬN-SQ-LĀ′TĬQN, n. Exposure to the sun's rays.
ĬN′SQ-LĔNCE, n. Haughtiness or pride mixed with contempt; impudence; impertinence.
ĬN′SQ-LĔNT, a. Contemptuous of others; haughty.
ĬN′SQ-LĔNT-LY, ad. With insolence; haughtily.
ĬN-SQ-LĬD′Ĭ-TY, n. Want of solidity; weakness.
ĬN-SŎL-U-BĬL′Ĭ-TY, n. State of being insoluble.
ĬN-SŎL′U-BLE, a. Not to be dissolved or cleared.
ĬN-SŎLV′Ḁ-BLE, a. Not to be solved or explained.
ĬN-SŎL′VḘN-CY, n. Inability to pay all debts.
ĬN-SŎL′VḘNT, a. Unable to pay all debts. [less.
ĬN-SŎM′NĬ-OŬS, a. Troubled with dreams; rest-
ĬN-SQ-MŬCH′, conj. So that; to such a degree that.
ĬN-SPĔCT′, v. a. To look into for examination.
ĬN-SPĔC′TĬQN, n. Close examination; oversight.
ĬN-SPĔCT′QR, n. An examiner; a superintendent.
ĬN-SPHĒRE′, v. a. To place in an orb or sphere.
ĬN-SPĬR′Ḁ-BLE, a. That may be inspired.
ĬN-SPĬ-RĀ′TĬQN, n. Act of drawing in the breath; inhalation :—infusion of supernatural ideas into the mind. [hale the air.
ĬN-SPĬRE′, v. n. To draw in the breath; to in-
ĬN-SPĬRE′, v. a. To breathe into; to infuse into
ĬN-SPĬR′ḘR, n. One that inspires. [the mind.
ĬN-SPĬR′ĬT, v. a. To animate, excite, enliven.
ĬN-SPĬS′SĀTE, v. a. To thicken; to make thick.
ĬN-SPĬS-SĀ′TĬQN, n. The act of making thick.
ĬN-STḀ-BĬL′Ĭ-TY, n. Inconstancy; fickleness.
ĬN-STĀ′BLE, a. Inconstant; not stable; fickle.
ĬN-STĂLL′, v. a. To place in office; to instate.
ĬN-STḀL-LĀ′TĬQN, n. Act of installing; act of investing with an office,
ĬN-STĂL′MḘNT, n. Installation :—part of a sum of money to be paid at a particular time.
ĬN′STḀNCE, n. Importunity; urgency; solici-tation :—example; time; occasion; act.
ĬN′STḀNCE, v. a. To give or offer as an example.
ĬN′STḀNT, a. Urgent; immediate; present.
ĬN′STḀNT, n. A moment :—the present month.
ĬN-STḀN-TĀ′NḘ-OŬS, a. Done in an instant; speedy; immediate. [mediately.
ĬN-STḀN-TĀ′NḘ-OŬS-LY, ad. In an instant; im-
ĬN-STĂN′TḘR, ad. [L.] (Law.) Instantly.
ĬN′STḀNT-LY, ad. At the moment; immediately.
ĬN-STĀTE′, v. a. To place or establish; to install.
ĬN-STÂU-RĀ′TĬQN, n. A restoration; renewal.

ĬN-STÂU-RĀ'TQR, n. A renewer; a restorer.
ĬN-STĔAD' (-stĕd'), ad. In the place; in room.
ĬN-STĒĔP', v. a. To soak; to macerate in water.
ĬN'STĔP, n. The upper part of the foot. [to ill.
ĬN'STĬ-GĀTE, v. a. To urge, provoke, or incite
ĬN'STĬ-GĀ'TIQN, n. An incitement or impulse
ĬN'STĬ-GĀ-TQR, n. One who instigates. [to ill.
ĬN-STĬL', v. a. To infuse by drops; to insinuate.
ĬN-STĬL-LĀ'TIQN, n. Act of instilling or infusing.
ĬN'STĬNCT, n. A natural aptitude or faculty in
   animals, operating without instruction.
ĬN-STĬNC'TĬVE, a. Prompted by instinct; natural.
ĬN-STĬNC'TĬVE-LY, ad. By force of instinct.
ĬN'STĬ-TŪTE, v. a. To fix; to establish, found.
ĬN'STĬ-TŪTE, n. An established law; precept;
   maxim; principle:—a scientific body.
ĬN-STĬ-TŪ'TIQN, n. An establishment:—a law:
   —education:—the act of investing a clerk.
ĬN'STĬ-TŪ-TQR, n. An establisher:—instructor.
ĬN-STRŬCT', v. a. To teach; to direct, educate.
ĬN-STRŬC'TIQN, n. The act of teaching; infor-
   mation:—a precept:—direction; mandate.
ĬN-STRŬC'TĬVE, a. Conveying knowledge.
ĬN-STRŬC'TĬVE-LY, ad. So as to convey instruc-
ĬN-STRŬCT'QR, n. One who instructs. [tion.
ĬN-STRŬCT'RĔSS, n. A female who instructs.
ĬN'STRŲ-MĔNT, n. Tool:—agent:—a writing.
ĬN-STRŲ-MĔNT'AL, a. Conducive to some end.
ĬN-STRŲ-MĔN-TĂL'Ĭ-TY, n. Subordinate agency.
ĬN-STRŲ-MĔN'TAL-LY, ad. By way of an instru-
ĬN-SŲB-JĔC'TIQN, n. Disobedience. [ment.
ĬN-SŲB-ÖR-DĬ-NĀ'TIQN, n. Disobedience.
ĬN-SŲB-STĂN'TIAL, a. Not real; unsubstantial.
ĬN-SŬF'FĔR-A-BLE, a. Intolerable; insupporta-
ĬN-SŬF'FĔR-A-BLY, ad. Beyond endurance. [ble.
ĬN-SŲF-FĬ''CIĔN-CY (-fĭsh'ĕn-sę), n. Deficiency.
ĬN-SŲF-FĬ''CIĔNT (ĭn-sŭf-fĭsh'ĕnt), a. Not suf-
   ficient; inadequate; incapable; unfit. [ly.
ĬN-SŲF-FĬ''CIĔNT-LY (-fĭsh'ĕnt-lę), ad. Unfit-
ĬN'SŲ-LAR, a. Belonging to, or like, an island.
ĬN'SŲ-LĀTE, v. a. To make an island; to detach.
ĬN'SŲ-LĀT-ĘD, a. Not contiguous on any side.
ĬN'SŲ-LĀ'TIQN, n. The state of being insulated.
ĬN'SŲ-LĀ-TQR, n. One that insulates. [affront.
ĬN'SŬLT, n. An act of insolence; a gross abuse;
ĬN-SŬLT', v. a. To treat with insolence or abuse.
ĬN-SŬLT'ĘR, n. One who insults; an abuser.
ĬN-SŪ-PĘR-A-BĬL'Ĭ-TY, n. The being insuperable.
ĬN-SŪ'PĘR-A-BLE, a. Invincible; insurmounta-
ĬN-SŪ'PĘR-A-BLE-NĔSS, n. Invincibleness. [ble.
ĬN-SŪ'PĘR-A-BLY, ad. Invincibly.
ĬN-SŲP-PŌRT'A-BLE, a. Intolerable; insufferable.
ĬN-SŲP-PŌRT'A-BLE-NĔSS, n. Insufferableness.
ĬN-SŲP-PŌRT'A-BLY, ad. Beyond endurance.
ĬN-SŲP-PRĔS'SĬ-BLE, a. Not to be suppressed.
ĬN-SŬR'ANCE (ĭn-shŭr'ąns), n. Act of insuring.
ĬN-SŪRE' (ĭn-shŭr'), v. a. To secure; to make
   sure or secure;—written both *insure* and *ensure*.
ĬN-SŬR'ĔR (ĭn-shŭr'ęr), n. One who insures.
ĬN-SŬR'ĢĘNT, n. One who rises in open rebel-
   lion against the established government; rebel.
ĬN-SŬR'ĢĘNT, a. Rising in rebellion; rebellious.
ĬN-SŲR-MÖÜNT'A-BLE, a. Insuperable; invin-
   cible; unconquerable. [perably.
ĬN-SŲR-MÖÜNT'A-BLY, ad. Invincibly; insu-
ĬN-SŲR-RĔC'TIQN, n. A sedition; a rebellion.
ĬN-SŲS-CĔP'TĬ-BLE, a. That cannot admit or
   receive; not susceptible; not capable.

ĬN-TĂCT'Ĭ-BLE, a. Not perceptible to the touch.
ĬN-TĂGL'IŌ (ĭn-tăl'yō), n.; pl. ĬN-TĂGL'IŌŞ.
   [It.] A precious stone, having a figure en-
   graved on it. [impalpable.
ĬN-TĂN'ĢĬ-BLE, a. That cannot be touched;
ĬN'TĘ-ĢĘR, n. A whole; a whole number. [al.
ĬN'TĘ-GRAL, a. Whole; complete; not fraction-
ĬN-TĔĢ'RĬ-TY, n. Honesty; uprightness; entire-
ĬN-TĔĢ'Ų-MĔNT, n. Any thing that covers. [ness.
ĬN'TĘL-LĔCT, n. Intelligent mind; understand-
ĬN-TĘL-LĔC'TIQN, n. Act of understanding. [ing.
ĬN-TĘL-LĔC'TĬVE, a. Understanding; perceiving.
ĬN-TĘL-LĔCT'Ų-AL (-lĕkt'yu-al), a. Relating to
   the mind or understanding; mental; ideal.
ĬN-TĔL'LĬ-ĢĔNCE, n. Information; notice; skill.
ĬN-TĔL'LĬ-ĢĔN-CĘR, n. A conveyer of intelli-
   gence or news. [instructed; skilful.
ĬN-TĔL'LĬ-ĢĔNT, a. Knowing; understanding;
ĬN-TĔL-LĬ-ĢĔN'TIAL, a. Intellectual; intelligent.
ĬN-TĔL-LĬ-ĢĬ-BĬL'Ĭ-TY, } n. State of being un-
ĬN-TĔL'LĬ-ĢĬ-BLE-NĔSS, } derstood; compre-
   hensibility. [comprehensible; plain.
ĬN-TĔL'LĬ-ĢĬ-BLE, a. That may be understood;
ĬN-TĔL'LĬ-ĢĬ-BLY, ad. So as to be understood.
ĬN-TĔM'PĘR-ANCE, n. Want of temperance;
   excess; excessive indulgence of appetite.
ĬN-TĔM'PĘR-ATE, a. Immoderate in drink;
   drunken; gluttonous:—passionate; excessive.
ĬN-TĔM'PĘR-ATE-LY, ad. Immoderately; ex-
   cessively; with intemperance. [ance.
ĬN-TĔM'PĘR-ATE-NĔSS, n. Want of temper-
ĬN-TĔM'PĘR-A-TŪRE, n. Excess of some quality.
ĬN-TĔN'A-BLE, a. Indefensible; untenable.
ĬN-TĔND', v. a. To purpose; to mean; to design.
ĬN-TĔN'DANT, n. An officer who superintends.
ĬN-TĔND'MĔNT, n. (*Law.*) Intention; design.
ĬN-TĔN-ĘR-Ā'TIQN, n. Act of making soft or
   tender. [very attentive.
ĬN-TĔNSE', a. Vehement; excessive; ardent;
ĬN-TĔNSE'LY, ad. To a great degree; earnestly.
ĬN-TĔNSE'NĔSS, n. Vehemence; great attention.
ĬN-TĔN'SIQN, n. A straining or forcing.
ĬN-TĔN'SĬ-TY, n. State of being intense; excess.
ĬN-TĔN'SĬVE, a. Intent; assiduous; adding force.
ĬN-TĔN'SĬVE-LY, ad. In a manner to give force.
ĬN-TĔNT', a. Anxiously diligent; eager; earnest.
ĬN-TĔNT', n. A design; a purpose; meaning.
ĬN-TĔN'TIQN, n. Deep design; purpose; end; aim.
ĬN-TĔN'TIQN-AL, a. Designed; done by design.
ĬN-TĔN'TIQN-AL-LY, ad. By design; with choice.
ĬN-TĔN'TĬVE, a. Diligently applied; attentive.
ĬN-TĔNT'LY, ad. With close attention; eagerly.
ĬN-TĔNT'NĔSS, n. The state of being intent.
ĬN-TĔR', v. a. To cover under ground; to bury.
ĬN'TĘR-ĂCT, n. A short piece between others.
ĬN-TĘR-ĂM'NĬ-AN, a. Situated between rivers.
ĬN-TĔR'CA-LAR, ĬN-TĔR'CA-LA-RY, a. Inserted.
ĬN-TĔR'CA-LĀTE, v. a. To insert into the cal-
   endar, as an extraordinary day.
ĬN-TĔR-CA-LĀ'TIQN, n. Insertion of odd days.
ĬN-TĘR-CĒDE', v. n. To interpose; to mediate.
ĬN-TĘR-CĒD'ĘNT, a. Mediating; going between.
ĬN-TĘR-CĒD'ĘR, n. One that intercedes.
ĬN-TĘR-CĔPT', v. a. To stop; to seize, obstruct.
ĬN-TĘR-CĔPT'ĘR, n. One who intercepts.
ĬN-TĘR-CĔP'TIQN, n. A stoppage; obstruction.
ĬN-TĘR-CĔS'SIQN (-tęr-sĕsh'ųn), n. Mediation.
ĬN-TĘR-CĔS'SQR, n. A mediator; an agent.

ĬN-TĘR-CĔS'SǪ-RY, *a.* Containing intercessions.
ĬN-TĘR-CHĀIN', *v. a.* To chain ; to link together.
ĬN-TĘR-CHĀNĢE', *v. a.* To give and take mu-
ĬN'TĘR-CHĀNĢE, *n.* Mutual exchange. [tually.
ĬN-TĘR-CHĀNĢE'A-BLE, *a.* Given and taken
   mutually ; reciprocal.   [alternately.
ĬN-TĘR-CHĀNĢE'A-BLY, *ad.* By interchange ;
ĬN-TĘR-CHĀNĢE'MĘNT,*n.*Mutual transferrence.
ĬN-TĘR-CĬP'I-ĘNT, *a.* Obstructing ; stopping.
ĬN-TĘR-CĬP'I-ENT, *n.* An intercepting power.
ĬN-TĘR-CLŪDE', *v. n.* To shut from; to intercept.
ĬN-TĘR-CLŪ'ṢIǪN (-klū'zhụn), *n.* Obstruction.
ĬN-TĘR-CǪ-LŬM-NĮ-Ā'TIǪN, *n.* Space between
   two columns or pillars.   [table.
ĬN-TĘR-CŎM'MǪN, *v. n.* To feed at the same
ĬN-TĘR-CǪM-MŪN'IǪN, *n.* Mutual communion.
ĬN-TĘR-CǪM-MŪ'NĮ-TY,*n.*A mutual community.
ĬN-TĘR-CŌS'TAL, *a.* Placed between the ribs.
ĬN'TĘR-CŌURSE,*n.*Commerce; mutual exchange.
ĬN-TĘR-CŬR'RĘNCE, *n.* A passage between.
ĬN-TĘR-CŬR'RENT, *a.* Running or happening
   between ; intervening.
ĬN-TĘR-CŲ-TĀ'NĘ-OŬS, *a.* Within the skin.
ĬN-TĘR-DĬCT', *v. a.* To prohibit ; to inhibit :—
   to forbid communion.   [sacrament.
ĬN'TĘR-DĬCT, *n.* A papal prohibition of the
ĬN-TĘR-DĬC'TIǪN, *n.* Prohibition :—a curse.
ĬN-TĘR-DĬC'TǪ-RY, *a.* Serving to prohibit. [cite.
ĬN'TĘR-ĔST, *v. a.* To concern ; to affect ; to ex-
ĬN'TĘR-EST, *n.* Concern ; influence ; share ;
   feeling :—a premium for the use of money.
ĬN'TĘR-ĔST-ĘD,*p.a.* Having interest or concern.
ĬN-TĘR-FĒRE', *v. n.* To interpose, intermeddle.
ĬN-TĘR-FĒR'ĘNCE, *n.* An interposition ; a
   clashing.   [tween.
ĬN-TĘR-FŪṢED' (ĭn-tĕr-fūzd'), *a.* Poured be-
ĬN'TĘR-ĬM, *n.* The mean time ; intervening time.
ĮN-TĒ'RĮ-ǪR, *a.* Internal ; inner ; not outward.
ĮN-TĒ'RĮ-ǪR, *n.* That which is within ; inside.
ĮN-TĒ'RĮ-ǪR-LY, *ad.* Inwardly ; internally.
ĬN-TĘR-JĀ'CENCE, ĬN-TĘR-JĀ'CĘN-CY, *n.* A
   lying between.   [tween.
ĬN-TĘR-JĀ'CĘNT, *a.* Intervening ; lying be-
ĬN-TĘR-JĔCT', *v. a.* To put between; to throw in.
ĬN-TĘR-JĔC'TIǪN, *n.* An exclamation ; a word
   or part of speech expressing some emotion.
ĬN-TĘR-LĀCE', *v. a.* To intermix, put together.
ĬN-TĘR-LĀCE'MĘNT, *n.* Act of interlacing.
ĬN-TĘR-LĀRD', *v. a.* To lay lard between :—
   to interpose ; to insert between.
ĬN-TĘR-LĒAVE', *v. a.* To insert leaves between.
ĬN-TĘR-LĪNE', *v. a.* To write between lines.
ĬN-TĘR-LĬN'E-ĄR,   } *a.* Written or inserted
ĬN-TĘR-LĬN'E-A-RY, }   between lines.
ĬN-TĘR-LĬN-E-Ā'TIǪN, *n.* Act of interlining.
ĬN-TĘR-LĬNK', *v. a.* To connect by links. [other.
ĬN-TĘR-LŎCK', *v. n.* To communicate with each
ĬN-TĘR-LǪ-CŪ'TIǪN, *n.* Interchange of speech.
ĬN-TĘR-LŎC'Ų-TǪR, *n.* One that talks with
   another, or in dialogue.   [logue.
ĬN-TĘR-LŎC'Ų-TǪ-RY, *a.* Consisting of dia-
ĬN-TĘR-LŌPE', *v. n.* To run between parties ;
   to intrude ; to intermeddle.
ĬN-TĘR-LŌP'ER, *n.* Unauthorized intruder.
ĬN-TĘR-LŲ-CĀ'TIǪN, *n.* A thinning of a wood.
ĬN-TĘR-LŪ'CENT, *a.* Shining between.
ĬN'TĘR-LŪDE, *n.* A piece played in intervals
   of a play, or between stanzas of a hymn.

ĬN-TĘR-LŪ'NĂR,   } *a.* Belonging to the time
ĬN-TĘR-LŪ'NĄ-RY, } when the moon is invisible.
ĬN-TĘR-MĂR'RIĄĢE, *n.* Marriage between two
   families, where each takes one and gives an-
ĬN-TĘR-MĂR'RY,*v.n.* To marry mutually. [other.
ĬN-TĘR-MĔD'DLE, *v. n.* To interpose officiously.
ĬN-TĘR-MĔD'DLĘR, *n.* One who intermeddles.
ĬN-TĘR-MĒ'DĮ-ĄL, *a.* Lying between.
ĬN-TĘR-MĒ'DĮ-ĄTE, *a.* Intervening ; interposed.
ĬN-TĘR-MĒ'DĮ-ĄTE-LY, *ad.* In an intermediate
   manner ; by way of intervention.   [tion.
ĮN-TĔR'MĘNT, *n.* Burial ; sepulture ; inhuma-
ĮN-TĔR'MĮ-NA-BLE, *a.* Immense ; boundless.
ĮN-TĔR'MĮ-NATE, *a.* Unbounded ; unlimited.
ĬN-TĘR-MĬN'GLE, *v. a.* To mingle ; to mix.
ĬN-TĘR-MĬN'GLE, *v. n.* To be mixed or incor-
   porated ; to mingle ; to combine.
ĬN-TĘR-MĬS'SIǪN (-mĭsh'ụn), *n.* A cessation for
   a time ; a pause ; intervenient time ; rest.
ĬN-TĘR-MĬS'SĮVE, *a.* Coming by fits ; alternat-
   ing ; not continual.   [a time.
ĬN-TĘR-MĬT', *v. a.* & *n.* To forbear or cease for
ĬN-TĘR-MĬT'TENT, *a.* Ceasing at intervals.
ĬN-TĘR-MĬX', *v. a.* To mingle ; to put together.
ĬN-TĘR-MĬX', *v. n.* To be mingled together.
ĬN-TĘR-MĬXT'ŲRE (-mĭkst'yụr), *n.* Mixture.
ĬN-TĘR-MŬN'DĀNE, *a.* Being between worlds or
ĬN-TĘR-MŪ'RAL,*a.* Lying between walls. [orbs.
ĮN-TĔR'NAL, *a.* Inward ; interior ; not external.
ĮN-TĔR'NAL-LY, *ad.* Inwardly :—mentally.
ĬN-TĘR-NĂ''TIǪN-AL (ĭn-tęr-năsh'ụn-ąl), *a.* Re-
   lating to the mutual intercourse between dif-
   ferent nations ; common to nations.
ĬN'TĘR-NŌDE, *n.* Space between knots.
ĬN-TĘR-NŬN'CĮ-Ō (ĭn-tęr-nŭn'shę-ō), *n.* A mes-
   senger between two parties.   [point.
ĬN-TĘR-PLĒAD', *v. n.* To discuss a previous
ĬN-TĘR-PLĒAD'ER, *n.* Title of a bill in equity.
ĬN-TĘR-PLĒDĢE', *v. a.* To pledge mutually.
ĮN-TĔR'PǪ-LĀTE, *v. a.* To insert ; to foist in.
ĮN-TĔR-PǪ-LĀ'TIǪN, *n.* Act of interpolating.
ĮN-TĔR'PǪ-LĀ-TǪR, *n.* One who interpolates.
ĬN-TĘR-PŌṢ'AL, *n.* Interposition ; intervention.
ĬN-TĘR-PŌṢE', *v. a.* To place between ; to thrust
ĬN-TĘR-PŌṢE', *v. n.* To mediate ; to interfere.[in.
ĬN-TĘR-PŌṢ'ER, *n.* One who interposes ; a
   mediator ; an interceder.
ĬN-TĘR-PǪ-ṢĬ''TIǪN (ĭn-tęr-pǪ-zĭsh'ụn), *n.* Me-
   diation ; agency between parties ; intervention.
ĮN-TĔR'PRĘT, *v. a.* To explain ; to decipher.
ĮN-TĔR'PRĘT-A-BLE, *a.* That may be inter-
   preted or translated.   [sition.
ĮN-TĔR-PRĘ-TĀ'TIǪN, *n.* Explanation ; expo-
ĮN-TĔR'PRĘ-TA-TĬVE, *a.* Collected by interpre-
   tation ; explanatory ; expositive.   [tor.
ĮN-TĔR'PRĘT-ER, *n.* An explainer ; a transla-
ĬN-TĘR-RĒG'NŲM, *n.* Time between the death
   of one prince and the accession of another.
ĬN-TĘR-REIGN' (ĭn-tęr-rān'), *n.* Interregnum.
ĬN'TĘR-RĔX, *n.* A regent during an interregnum.
ĮN-TĔR'RǪ-GĀTE, *v. a.* To examine ; to question.
ĮN-TĔR-RǪ-GĀ'TIǪN, *n.* Act of interrogating ;
   a question :—this point [?].
ĬN-TĘR-RŎG'A-TĬVE, *a.* Denoting a question.
ĬN-TĘR-RŎG'A-TĬVE-LY, *ad.* In an interrogative
   manner ; in form of a question.
ĮN-TĔR'RǪ-GĀ-TǪR, *n.* An asker of questions.
ĬN-TĘR-RŎG'A-TǪ-RY, *n.* A question ; inquiry.

ĬN-TĘR-RŎG′A-TQ-RY, *a.* Containing a question.
ĬN-TĘR-RŬPT′, *v. a.* To hinder, obstruct, divide.
ĬN-TĘR-RŬPT′ĘR, *n.* One who interrupts. [stop.
ĬN-TĘR-RŬP′TIQN,*n.* Intervention ; hinderance ;
ĬN-TĘR-SĔCT′, *v. a.* To cut ; to divide mutually.
ĬN-TĘR-SĔCT′,*v.n.* To meet and cross each other.
ĬN-TĘR-SĔC′TIQN, *n.* A point where lines cross.
ĬN′TĘR-SPĀCE, *n.* An intervening space ; inter-
ĬN-TĘR-SPĔRSE′, *v. a.* To scatter among. [val.
ĬN-TĘR-SPĔR′SIQN, *n.* The act of interspersing.
ĬN-TĘR-STĔL′LAR, *a.* Intervening between the
 stars. [between things ; an interval.
ĬN′TĘR-STĬCE *or* ĬN-TĔR′STĮCE, *n.* A space
ĬN-TĘR-STĬ″TIAL (ĭn-tĕr-stĭsh′al), *a.* Contain-
 ing interstices ; intermediate.
ĬN-TĘR-TĔXT′ỤRE (ĭn-tĕr-tĕkst′yụr), *n.* A di-
 versification of things woven one among an-
 other. [tropics.
ĬN-TĘR-TRŎP′Į-CAL, *a.* Being between the
ĬN-TĘR-TWĪNE′,) *v. a.* To unite by twisting
ĬN-TĘR-TWĬST′,) one in another.
ĬN′TĘR-VAL, *n.* An interstice ; vacant space :
 —the time between two points :—low land.
ĬN-TĘR-VĒNE′,*v. n.* To come between interpose.
ĬN-TĘR-VĒ′NĮ-ENT, *a.* Being or passing between.
ĬN-TĘR-VĔN′TIQN, *n.* An interposition ; medi-
 ation ; interference. [ference.
ĬN′TĘR-VIEW (ĭn′tĕr-vū), *n.* A meeting or con-
ĬN-TĘR-VŎLVE′, *v. a.* To involve together.
ĬN-TĘR-WEAVE′, *v. a.* [*imp. t.* interwove *or* in-
 terweaved ; *pp.* interwoven.] To weave one
 with another ; to intermingle ; to intertwine.
ĬN-TĔST′A-BLE, *a.* Disqualified to make a will.
ĬN-TĔS′TATE, *a.* Dying without having made
 a will, without a will. [will.
ĬN-TĔS′TATE, *n.* One dying without leaving a
ĬN-TĔS′TĮ-NAL, *a.* Belonging to the intestines.
ĬN-TĔS′TĮNE, *a.* Internal ; inward :—domestic.
ĬN-TĔS′TĮNEŞ, *n. pl.* The bowels ; the entrails.
ĬN-THRÂLL′, *v. a.* To enslave ; to shackle.
ĬN-THRÂL′MĘNT, *n.* Servitude ; slavery.
ĬN′TĮ-MA-CY, *n.* Close familiarity or fellowship.
ĬN′TĮ-MATE, *a.* Inmost :—familiar ; near.
ĬN′TĮ-MATE, *n.* A familiar friend ; a confidant.
ĬN′TĮ-MĀTE,*v.a.* To hint ; to suggest obscurely.
ĬN′TĮ-MATE-LY, *ad.* Closely ; nearly ; familiarly.
ĬN-TĮ-MĀ′TIQN, *n.* A hint ; obscure suggestion.
ĬN TĬM′Į-DĀTE, *v. a.* To make fearful, overawe.
ĬN-TĬM-Į-DĀ′TIQN, *n.* The act of intimidating.
ĬN′TO, *prep.* Noting entrance :—noting inclusion.
ĬN-TŎL′ĘR-A-BLE, *a.* That cannot be tolerated ;
 not to be endured.
ĬN-TŎL′ĘR-A-BLE-NĔSS, *n.* Insufferableness.
ĬN-TŎL′ĘR-A-BLY, *ad.* Insupportably.
ĬN-TŎL′ĘR-ANCE, *n.* Want of toleration.
ĬN-TŎL′ĘR-ANT, *a.* Not enduring ; not tolerant.
ĬN-TQ-NĀ′TIQN, *n.* Manner of sounding.
ĬN-TŌNE′, *v. a.* To chant ; to sing.
ĬN-TŎRT′, *v. a.* To twist ; to wreathe ; to wring.
ĬN-TŎX′Į-CĀTE,*v. a.* To inebriate, make drunk.
ĬN-TŎX-Į-CĀ′TIQN, *n.* Inebriation ; drunkenness.
ĬN-TRĂCT-A-BĬL′Į-TY, *n.* Ungovernableness.
ĬN-TRĂCT′A-BLE, *a.* Stubborn ; unmanageable.
ĬN-TRĂCT′A-BLE-NĔSS, *n.* Obstinacy ; perverse-
 ness ; stubbornness. [bornly.
ĬN-TRĂCT′A-BLY, *ad.* Unmanageably ; stub-
ĬN-TRĂN′SĮ-TĬVE, *a.* (*Gram.*) Not transitive ;
 not passing over to an object.

ĬN-TRĂN′SĮ-TĬVE-LY, *ad.* Without an object
 following, as a verb. [stance.
ĬN-TRANS-MŪ′TA-BLE, *a.* Unchangeable in sub-
ĬN-TRĔNCH′, *v. a.* To furrow ; to fortify.
ĬN-TRĔNCH′, *v. n.* To invade ; to encroach.
ĬN-TRĔNCH′MĘNT, *n.* A fortification with a
ĬN-TRĔP′ĮD, *a.* Fearless ; daring ; brave. [trench.
ĬN-TRĘ-PĬD′Į-TY, *n.* Fearlessness ; courage ;
 boldness ; invincible resolution.
ĬN-TRĔP′ĮD-LY, *ad.* Fearlessly ; daringly.
ĬN′TRĮ-CA-CY, *n.* Perplexity ; complication.
ĬN′TRĮ-CATE,*a.* Perplexed ; complicated ; obscure.
ĬN′TRĮ-CATE-LY, *ad.* With intricacy ; obscurely.
ĬN′TRĮ-CATE-NĔSS, *n.* Perplexity ; involution.
ĬN-TRÎGUE′ (ĭn-trēg′), *n.* A plot ; an amour.
ĬN-TRÎGUE′ (ĭn-trēg′), *v. n.* To form plots.
ĬN-TRÎGU′ĘR (ĭn-trēg′ęr), *n.* One who intrigues.
ĬN-TRĬN′SĮC,) *a.* Internal ; solid ; natural ;
ĬN-TRĬN′SĮ-CAL,) real ; true ; not accidental.
ĬN-TRĬN′SĮ-CAL-LY, *ad.* Naturally ; really.
ĬN-TRĬN′SĮ-CATE, *a.* Perplexed ; entangled. [in.
ĬN-TRQ-DŪCE′,*v. a.* To bring, conduct, or usher
ĬN-TRQ-DŪ′CER, *n.* One who introduces.
ĬN-TRQ-DŬC′TIQN, *n.* A bringing in :—presenta-
 tion :—a preface ; a proem.
ĬN-TRQ-DŬC′TĮVE, *a.* Serving to introduce.
ĬN-TRQ-DŬC′TQ-RY, *a.* Serving to introduce.
ĬN-TRQ-GRĔS′SIQN, *n.* Act of entering. [psalm.
ĬN-TRŌ′ĮT *or* ĬN-TRŌÏT′, *n.* An introductory
ĬN-TRQ-MĬS′SIQN (ĭn-trq-mĭsh′ụn), *n.* The act
 of sending in. [admit.
ĬN-TRQ-MĬT′, *v. a.* To send in ; to let in ; to
ĬN-TRQ-SPĔC′TIQN, *n.* A view of the inside.
ĬN-TRQ-VĔR′SIQN, *n.* The act of introverting.
ĬN-TRQ-VĔRT′, *v. a.* To turn inwards.
ĬN-TRŪDE′, *v. n.* To come uninvited ; to inter-
 lope ; to encroach. [to dart in.
ĬN-TRŪDE′, *v. a.* To force or thrust in rudely ;
ĬN-TRŪD′ĘR, *n.* One who intrudes ; interloper.
ĬN-TRŪ′ŞIQN (-trụ′zhụn), *n.* Act of intruding.
ĬN-TRŪ′SĮVE, *a.* Intruding ; apt to intrude.
ĬN-TRŬST′,*v.a.* To deliver in trust ; to commit.
ĬN-TỤ-Ĭ″TIQN (ĭn-tụ-ĭsh′ụn), *n.* Intuitive per-
 ception ; immediate knowledge. [ly ; distinct.
ĬN-TŪ′Į TĬVE, *a.* Seen by the mind immediate-
ĬN-TŪ′Į-TĬVE-LY, *ad.* By immediate perception.
ĬN-TỤ-MĔS′CENCE, *n.* A swelling ; a tumor.
ĬN-TỤR-GĔS′CENCE, *n.* Act or state of swelling.
ĬN-TWĪNE′, *v. a.* To twist or wreathe together.
ĬN-ŬM′BRATE, *v. a.* To cover with shades.
ĬN-ŬNC′TIQN, *n.* Act of smearing or anointing.
ĬN-ŬN′DATE, *v. a.* To overflow with water.
ĬN-ŲN-DĀ′TIQN, *n.* Overflow of water ; deluge.
ĬN-ỤR-BĂN′Į-TY, *n.* Incivility ; rudeness. [tom.
ĬN-ŪRE′ (ĭn-yūr′),*v. a.* To habituate ; to accus-
ĬN-ŪRE′MĘNT, *n.* Practice ; habit ; use ; custom.
ĬN-ŬRN′, *v. a.* To intomb ; to bury ; to inhume.
ĬN-ŬS′TIQN (ĭn-ŭs′chụn), *n.* Act of burning.
ĬN-Ū-TĬL′Į-TY, *n.* Uselessness ; unprofitableness.
ĬN-VĀDE′, *v. a.* To attack ; to enter hostilely.
ĬN-VĀD′ĘR, *n.* One who invades ; an assailant.
ĬN-VĂL′ĮD, *a.* Weak ; of no weight or cogency.
ĬN-VA-LĬD′ (ĭn-va-lēd′), *n.* A soldier or other
 person disabled by sickness or wounds.
ĬN-VĂL′Į-DĀTE, *v. a.* To weaken ; to make void.
ĬN-VĂL-Į-DĀ′TIQN, *n.* The act of weakening.
ĬN-VA-LĬD′Į-TY, *n.* Weakness ; want of force.
ĬN-VĂL′Ụ-A-BLE (-văl′yụ-a-bl), *a.* Inestimable.

IN-VĀ'RĬ-Ạ-BLE, a. Unchangeable; constant.
IN-VĀ'RĬ-Ạ-BLE-NĔSS, n. Immutability; constancy; unchangeableness. [ly.
IN-VĀ'RĬ-Ạ-BLY, ad. Unchangeably; constant-
IN-VĀ'ŞIQN (ĭn-vā'zhụn), n. A hostile entrance.
IN-VĀ'SĬVE, a. Entering hostilely; aggressive.
IN-VĔC'TIQN, n. A railing; invective; abuse.
IN-VĔC'TIVE, n. A harsh censure; angry abuse.
IN-VĔC'TIVE, a. Satirical; abusive; censuring.
IN-VĔC'TIVE-LY, ad. Satirically; abusively.
IN-VEIGH' (ĭn-vā'), v. n. To utter censure.
IN-VEIGH'ER (ĭn-vā'ẹr), n. A vehement railer.
IN-VEI'GLE (ĭn-vē'gl), v. a. To wheedle, seduce.
IN-VEI'GLE-MENT (-vē'gl-mĕnt), n. Seduction.
IN-VEI'GLER (-vē'glẹr), n. A seducer; deceiver.
IN-VĔNT', v. a. To discover; to forge; to feign.
IN-VĔN'TIQN, n. Act or faculty of inventing; a thing invented; contrivance; forgery; fiction.
IN-VĔNT'IVE, a. Apt to invent; ingenious.
IN-VĔNT'QR, n. One who invents:—a forger.
IN-VEN-TŌ'RĬ-ẠL, a. Relating to an inventory.
IN'VEN-TQ-RY, n. An account or list of goods.
IN'VEN-TQ-RY, v. a. To register; to make a list
IN-VĔN'TRESS, n. A female who invents. [of.
IN-VĔRSE', a. Inverted; reciprocal; not direct.
IN-VĔRSE'LY, ad. In an inverted order. [&c.
IN-VĔR'SIQN, n. Change of order, time, place,
IN-VĔRT', v. a. To turn upside down; to change.
IN-VĔST', v. a. To dress, clothe, array, vest.
IN-VĔS'TĬ-GẠ-BLE, a. That may be searched out.
IN-VĔS'TĬ-GĀTE, v. a. To search out, find out.
IN-VĔS'TĬ-GĀ'TIQN, n. A searching into.
IN-VĔS'TĬ-GĀ-TQR, n. One who searches out.
IN-VĔST'Ĭ-TŪRE, n. Act of giving possession.
IN-VĔST'MENT, n. Act of investing; dress; clothes.
IN-VĔT'ER-Ạ-CY, n. Long continuance; confirmed obstinacy. [nate.
IN-VĔT'ER-ẠTE, a. Old; deep-rooted; obsti-
IN-VĔT'ER-ẠTE-NĔSS, n. Obstinacy formed by
IN-VĬD'Ĭ-OŬS, a. Envious; exciting envy. [time.
IN-VĬD'Ĭ-OŬS-LY, ad. Malignantly; enviously.
IN-VĬD'Ĭ-OŬS-NĔSS, n. Quality of provoking envy.
IN-VĬG'QR-ĀTE, v. a. To strengthen; to ani-
IN-VĬG-QR-Ā'TIQN, n. Act of invigorating. [mate.
IN-VĬN-CĬ-BĬL'Ĭ-TY, n. Invincibleness.
IN-VĬN'CĬ-BLE, a. Insuperable; unconquerable.
IN-VĬN'CĬ-BLE-NĔSS, n. Unconquerableness.
IN-VĬN'CĬ-BLY, ad. Insuperably; unconquerably.
IN-VĪ-Q-LẠ-BĬL'Ĭ-TY, n. Quality of being inviolable; inviolableness. [ken.
IN-VĪ'Q-LẠ-BLE, a. Not to be profaned or bro-
IN-VĪ'Q-LẠ-BLE-NĔSS, n. The state or the quality of being inviolable; inviolability.
IN-VĪ'Q-LẠ-BLY, ad. Without breach or failure.
IN-VĪ'Q-LẠTE, a. Unhurt; unprofaned; unbro-
IN'VĬ-OŬS, a. Impassable; not to be passed. [ken.
IN-VĬS'CĀTE, v. a. To lime; to daub with glue.
IN-VĬŞ-Ĭ-BĬL'Ĭ-TY, n. State of being invisible.
IN-VĬŞ'Ĭ-BLE, a. Not perceptible; not to be seen.
IN-VĬŞ'Ĭ-BLY, ad. Imperceptibly to the sight.
IN-VĬ-TĀ'TIQN, n. Act of inviting; solicitation.
IN-VĬT'Ạ-TQ-RY, a. Containing invitation.
IN-VĪTE', v. a. To bid, call, allure, persuade.
IN-VĪT'ING, p. a. Alluring; tempting; attrac-
IN'VQ-CĀTE, v. a. To invoke. [tive.
IN-VQ-CĀ'TIQN, n. Act of calling upon in prayer.
IN'VOICE, n. A list of goods with prices, &c., sent or shipped by a merchant.

IN VŌKE', v. a. To call upon; to supplicate; to entreat; to implore; to pray to.
IN-VŎL'ŲN-TẠ-RĬ-LY, ad. Not by choice or will.
IN-VŎL'ŲN-TẠ-RĬ-NĔSS, n. Want of choice or will
IN-VŎL'ŲN-TẠ-RY, a. Not voluntary; not willing.
IN-VQ-LŪ'TIQN, n. Act of involving.
IN-VŎLVE', v. a. To inwrap, comprise, blend.
IN-VŬL'NER-Ạ-BLE, a. Not to be wounded.
IN-VŬL'NER-Ạ-BLE-NĔSS, n. The state of being invulnerable. [wall.
IN-WÂLL', v. a. To enclose or fortify with a
IN'WẠRD, IN'WẠRDŞ, ad. Towards the inside.
IN'WẠRD, a. Internal; interior; placed within.
IN'WẠRD-LY, ad. In the heart; internally.
IN'WẠRDŞ, n. pl. The bowels; inner parts.
IN-WĒAVE' (ĭn-wēv'), v. n. [imp. t. inwove; pp. inwoven.] To mix in weaving; to intertwine.
IN-WRĂP' (ĭn-răp'), v. a. To infold; to involve.
IN-WRĒATHE' (ĭn-rēth'), v. a. To surround.
IN-WROUGHT' (-râwt'), a. Adorned or wrought in the texture. [ans.
Ī-ŎN'ĬC, a. Belonging to Ionia, or to the Ioni-
Ī-Ō'TẠ, n. A tittle; a jot; the smallest particle.
ĬP-Ē-CĂC-Ų-ĂN'HẠ (ĭp-ẹ-kăk-ụ-ăn'ạ), n. A plant and its root, used in medicine.
Ī-RĂS-CĬ-BĬL'Ĭ-TY, n. Propensity or disposition to anger; irritability. [sionate.
Ī-RĂS'CĬ-BLE, a. Prone to anger; irritable; pas-
Ī-RĂS'CĬ-BLE-NĔSS, n. State of being angry.
ĪRE, n. Anger; rage; passionate hatred; choler.
ĪRE'FŪL, a. Angry; raging; furious.
ĬR-Ĭ-DĔS'CENT, a. Colored like the rainbow.
Ī'RĬS, n. [L.] The rainbow:—the circle round the pupil of the eye:—the flower-de-luce.
ĪR'ĬSH, a. Relating to Ireland.
ĪR'ĬSH-ĬŞM, n. An Irish word, phrase, or idiom.
ĬRK, v. a. To weary;—used impersonally.
ĬRK'SQME (ürk'sụm), a. Wearisome; tedious.
ĬRK'SQME-LY (ürk'sụm-lẹ), ad. Wearisomely.
ĬRK'SQME-NĔSS (ürk'sụm-nĕs), n. Tediousness
ĪR'ON (ī'ụrn), n. A common, useful metal.
ĪR'ON (ī'ụrn), a. Made of iron:—harsh; hard.
ĪR'ON (ī'ụrn), v. a. To smooth with an iron.
ĪR'ONED (ī'ụrnd), a. Armed; dressed in iron.
Ī-RŎN'ĬC, } a. Expressing one thing, and
Ī-RŎN'Ĭ-CẠL, } meaning another; containing
Ī-RŎN'Ĭ-CẠL-LY, ad. By use of irony. [irony
ĪR'ON-MŎN-GER (ī'ụrn-mŭng-gẹr), n. A dealer in iron or hardware. [rust of iron
ĪR'ON-MŌULD, n. A spot on linen made by the
ĪR'ON-WOOD (ī'ụrn-wûd), n. A very hard wood
ĪR'ON-Y (ī'ụrn-ẹ), a. Made of, or like, iron.
Ī'RON-Y (ī'rụn-ẹ), n. A mode of speech in which the meaning is contrary to the words.
ĬR-RĀ'DĬ-ANCE, n. Beams of light emitted.
ĬR-RĀ'DĬ-ĀTE, v. a. To brighten; to illuminate
ĬR-RĀ'DĬ-ĀTE, v. n. To shine; to grow bright
ĬR-RĀ-DĬ-Ā'TIQN, n. Illumination; light.
ĬR-RĂ''TIQN-AL (ĭr-răsh'un-al), a. Not rational contrary to reason; absurd. [of reason
ĬR-RĂ-TIQN-ĂL'Ĭ-TY (-răsh-un-ăl'ẹ-tẹ), n. Wan
ĬR-RĂ''TIQN-AL-LY (-răsh'un-al-), ad. Absurdly
ĬR-RE-CLĀIM'Ạ-BLE, a. Not to be reclaimed.
ĬR-RE-CLĀIM'Ạ-BLY, ad. So as not to be reclaimed; irrecoverably.
ĬR-RĔC-QN-CĪL'Ạ-BLE, a. Not to be reconciled
ĬR-RĔC-QN-CĪL'Ạ-BLY, ad. In an irreconcilable manner; so as not to be reconciled.

ĬR-RĔC-ǪN-CĬL-Ĭ-Ā'TĬǪN, *n.* Want of recon-
ciliation; hostility.   [irreparable.
ĬR-RẸ-CŎV'ẸR-Ạ-BLE, *a.* Not to be regained;
ĬR-RẸ-CŎV'ẸR-Ạ-BLE-NĔSS, *n.* State beyond
recovery; irreparableness.
ĬR-RẸ-CŎV'ẸR-Ạ-BLY, *ad.* Beyond recovery.
ĬR-RẸ-DĒĒM'Ạ-BLE, *a.* Not to be redeemed.
ĬR-RẸ-DŪ'CĬ-BLE, *a.* Not to be brought or re-
duced.   [futation.
‖ĬR-RĔF-RẠ-GẠ-BĬL'Ĭ-TY, *n.* Incapacity of con-
‖ĬR-RĔF'RẠ-GẠ-BLE *or* ĬR-RẸ-FRĂG'Ạ-BLE, *a.*
Not to be refuted; indisputable; indubitable.
‖ĬR-RĔF'RẠ-GẠ-BLY, *ad.* Above confutation.
ĬR-RẸ-FŪT'Ạ-BLE *or* ĬR-RĔF'Ụ-TẠ-BLE, *a.* Not
to be overthrown by argument; irrefragable.
ĬR-RĔG'Ụ-LẠR, *a.* Not regular; immethodical.
ĬR-RĔG-Ụ-LĂR'Ĭ-TY, *n.* Deviation from rule.
ĬR-RĔG'Ụ-LẠR-LY, *ad.* Without rule or method.
ĬR-RĔL'Ạ-TĬVE, *a.* Not relative; unconnected.
ĬR-RĔL'Ạ-TĬVE-LY, *ad.* Unconnectedly.
ĬR-RĔL'Ẹ-VẠN-CY, *n.* State of being irrelevant.
ĬR-RĔL'Ẹ-VẠNT, *a.* Not applicable; not relevant.
ĬR-RẸ-LIĒV'Ạ-BLE, *a.* Not admitting relief.
ĬR-RẸ-LĬG'ĬǪN (ĭr-rẹ-lĭd'jụn), *n.* Want of relig-
ion; impiety; ungodliness.
ĬR-RẸ-LĬG'IOỤS (-lĭd'jụs), *a.* Impious; wicked.
ĬR-RẸ-LĬG'IOỤS-LY, *ad.* With irreligion.
ĬR-RẸ-MĒ'DĬ-Ạ-BLE, *a.* Not to be cured; incura-
ĬR-RẸ-MĒ'DĬ-Ạ-BLY, *ad.* Without cure. [ble.
ĬR-RẸ-MĬS'SĬ-BLE, *a.* Not to be pardoned.
ĬR-RẸ-MĬS'SĬ-BLY, *ad.* So as not to be pardoned.
ĬR-RẸ-MŎV'Ạ-BLE, *a.* Not to be moved.
ĬR-RẸ-MŪ'NẸR-Ạ-BLE, *a.* Not to be rewarded.
ĬR-RĔP-Ạ-RẠ-BĬL'Ĭ-TY, *n.* State of being irrep-
arable.   [ediless.
ĬR-RĔP'Ạ-RẠ-BLE, *a.* Not to be repaired; rem-
ĬR-RĔP'Ạ-RẠ-BLY, *ad.* Without recovery.
ĬR-RẸ-PLĔV'Ĭ-Ạ-BLE, *a.* Not to be redeemed.
ĬR-RĔP-RẸ-HĔN'SĬ-BLE, *a.* Exempt from blame.
ĬR-RĔP-RẸ-HĔN'SĬ-BLY, *ad.* Without blame.
ĬR-RẸ-PRĔSS'Ĭ-BLE, *a.* Not to be repressed.
ĬR-RẸ-PRŌACH'Ạ-BLE, *a.* Free from blame.
ĬR-RẸ-PRŌACH'Ạ-BLY, *ad.* Without blame or
reproach; blamelessly.   [right.
ĬR-RẸ-PRŎV'Ạ-BLE, *a.* Not to be blamed; up-
ĬR-RẸ-PRŎV'Ạ-BLY, *ad.* Beyond reproach. [tion.
ĬR-RẸ-SĬST-Ĭ-BĬL'Ĭ-TY, *n.* Force above opposi-
ĬR-RẸ-SĬST'Ĭ-BLE, *a.* Superior to opposition.
ĬR-RẸ-SĬST'Ĭ-BLY, *ad.* So as not to be opposed.
ĬR-RĔS'Ǫ-LŲ-BLE, *a.* Not to be broken or dis-
ĬR-RĔŞ'Ǫ-LŪTE, *a.* Not firm in purpose. [solved.
ĬR-RĔŞ'Ǫ-LŪTE-LY, *ad.* Without firmness of
ĬR-RĔŞ'Ǫ-LŪTE-NĔSS, *n.* Want of decision [mind.
ĬR-RĔŞ-Ǫ-LŪ'TĬǪN, *n.* Want of firmness of mind.
ĬR-RẸ-SPĔC'TĬVE, *a.* Regardless of circumstances
ĬR-RẸ-SPĔC'TĬVE-LY, *ad.* In an irrespective
manner.   [bility.
ĬR-RẸ-SPŎN-SĬ-BĬL'Ĭ-TY, *n.* Want of responsi-
ĬR-RẸ-SPŎN'SĬ-BLE, *a.* Not responsible or an-
swerable; not accountable.
ĬR-RẸ-TĔN'TĬVE, *a.* Not able to retain.
ĬR-RẸ-TRIĒV'Ạ-BLE, *a.* Not to be retrieved;
irrecoverable; irreparable.   [arably.
ĬR-RẸ-TRIĒV'Ạ-BLY, *ad.* Irrecoverably; irrep-

ĬR-RĔV'ẸR-ĔNCE, *n.* Want of reverence or ven-
eration; disregard.   [respect.
ĬR-RĔV'ẸR-ĔNT, *a.* Wanting in reverence or
ĬR-RĔV'ẸR-ĔNT-LY, *ad.* Without due respect.
ĬR-RẸ-VĔRS'Ĭ-BLE, *a.* Not to be recalled or
changed.   [reversible.
ĬR-RẸ-VĔRS'Ĭ-BLE-NĔSS, *n.* State of being ir-
ĬR-RẸ-VĔRS'Ĭ-BLY, *ad.* Without change.
ĬR-RĔV'Ǫ-CẠ-BLE, *a.* Not to be recalled or re-
versed.   [revocable.
ĬR-RĔV'Ǫ-CẠ-BLE-NĔSS, *n.* State of being ir-
ĬR-RĔV'Ǫ-CẠ-BLY, *ad.* So as not to be recalled.
ĬR'RĬ-GĀTE, *v. a.* To wet; to moisten; to water.
ĬR-RĬ-GĀ'TĬǪN, *n.* Act of irrigating or watering.
ĬR-RĬG'Ụ-OŬS, *a.* Watery; watered; dewy; moist.
ĬR-RĬ-TẠ-BĬL'Ĭ-TY, *n.* State of being irritable.
ĬR'RĬ-TẠ-BLE, *a.* Easily provoked or irritated.
ĬR'RĬ-TĀTE, *v. a.* To provoke; to tease; to fret.
ĬR-RĬ-TĀ'TĬǪN, *n.* A provocation; exasperation.
ĬR'RĬ-TẠ-TǪ-RY, *a.* Stimulating; irritating.
ĬR-RŬP'TĬǪN, *n.* An entrance by force; inroad.
ĬR-RŬP'TĬVE, *a.* Bursting forth; rushing in.
ĬŞ (ĭz). The third person singular of *to be.*
Ī'ŞĬN-GLĂSS (ī'zĭng-glȧs), *n.* A kind of glue
prepared from the intestines of certain fish:—
ĬŞ'LẠM-ĬŞM, *n.* Mahometanism.   [mica.
ĬSL'ẠND (ī'lạnd), *n.* A tract of land entirely sur-
rounded by water.   [island.
ĬSL'ẠND-ẸR (ī'lạnd-ẹr), *n.* An inhabitant of an
ĬSLE (ĭl), *n.* An island.
ĬSL'ẸT (ī'lẹt), *n.* A little isle or island.
Ī-SŎÇH'RǪ-NẠL, *a.* Having equal times.
Ī-SŎÇH'RǪ-NĬŞM, *n.* Equality of time. [time.
Ī-SŎÇH'RǪ-NOŬS, *a.* Having the same length of
ĬŞ'Ǫ-LĀTE, *v. a.* To detach; to insulate.
ĬŞ-Ǫ-LĀ'TĬǪN, *n.* Detached state; separation.
Ī-SŎS'CẸ-LĔŞ, *a.* Having two legs or sides equal.
ĬS-Ǫ-THĔR'MẠL, *a.* Having equal temperature.
ĬS'SŲ-Ạ-BLE (ĭsh'shụ-ạ-), *a.* That may be issued.
ĬS'SŲE (ĭsh'shū), *n.* Exit; egress:—event:—
termination:—progeny; offspring:—a vent.
ĬS'SŲE (ĭsh'shū), *v. n.* To come out; to proceed.
ĬS'SŲE (ĭsh'shū), *v. a.* To send out, send forth.
ĬS'SŲE-LĔSS (ĭsh'shụ-lĕs), *a.* Having no issue.
ĬSTH'MỤS (ĭst'mụs), *n.* A neck of land.
ĬT, *pr.* of the neuter gender, used for *thing.*
Ĭ-TĂL'IẠN (ĭ-tăl'yạn), *a.* Relating to Italy. [ian.
Ĭ-TĂL'IẠN-ĪZE (ĭ-tăl'yạn-īz), *v. a.* To make Ital-
Ĭ-TĂL'ĬC, *a.* Denoting a kind of leaning letters.
Ĭ-TĂL'Ĭ-CĬŞE, *v. a.* To represent in Italic letters.
Ĭ-TĂL'ĬCS, *n. pl.* Letters inclining or sloping to
the right, first used in Italy.
ĬTCH, *n.* A cutaneous disease:—teasing desire.
ĬTCH, *v. n.* To feel irritation in the skin:—to long.
Ī'TĔM, *n.* A new article; single entry:—a hint.
ĬT'ẸR-ĀTE, *v. a.* To repeat; to utter or do again.
ĬT-ẸR-Ā'TĬǪN, *n.* Repetition; recital again.
Ĭ-TĬN'ẸR-ẠNT, *a.* Travelling; wandering.
Ĭ-TĬN'ẸR-Ạ-RY, *n.* A book or account of travels.
Ĭ-TĬN'ẸR-ĀTE, *v. n.* To travel from place to place.
ĬT-SĔLF', *pr.* A neutral reciprocal pronoun.
Ī'VǪ-RY, *n.* The tusk of the elephant, &c.
Ī'VǪ-RY (ī'vǫ-rẹ), *a.* Made of, or like, ivory.
Ī'VY (ī'vẹ), *n.* An evergreen creeping plant.

J.

J͏, a consonant, has invariably the same sound with that of *g* in *ǵiant*; as, *jet*, *just*.

JĂB′BĔR, *v. n.* To talk idly; to chatter.

JĂB′BĔR, *n.* Idle, unmeaning talk; prate.

JĂB′BĔR-ĔR, *n.* One who talks inarticulately.

JĀ′CĔNT, *a.* Lying at length; extended.

JĀ′CĬNTH, *n.* A precious gem :—a plant.

JĀCK, *n.* An instrument to pull off boots :—an engine to turn a spit, &c. :—a young pike. [low.

JĂCK′-A̤-DĂN′DY̆, *n.* A little, impertinent fel-

JĂCK′ĂL, *n.* A small animal of the dog kind.

JĂCK′A̤-NĀPES, *n.* A monkey; an ape :—a cox-

JĂCK′ĂSS, *n.* The male of the ass. [comb; fop.

JĂCK′-BŎŎTS, *n. pl.* Boots which serve as ar-

JĂCK′DÂW, *n.* A species of crow; the daw. [mor.

JĂCK′ĔT, *n.* A short coat; a close waistcoat.

JĂCK′-PŬD′DĬNG, *n.* A zany; a merry-andrew.

JĂCK′SMĬTH, *n.* A maker of the engine jack.

JĂCK′-WĬŦH-A̤-LĂN′TĔRN, *n.* An ignis fatuus.

JĂC′O̤-BĬN, *n.* A gray or white friar :—a member of a French faction :—a sort of pigeon.

JĂC-O̤-BĬN′ĬC,) *a.* Partaking of the princi-
JĂC-O̤-BĬN′Ĭ-CA̤L,) ples of Jacobins.

JĂC′O̤-BĬN-ĬṢM, *n.* The principles of Jacobins.

JĂC′O̤-BĪTE, *n.* A partisan of James II., Eng-

JĂC-O̤-NĔT′, *n.* A kind of coarse muslin. [land.

JĂC-TĬ-TĀ′TĬON, *n.* A tossing :—vain boasting.

JĂC-Ṳ-LĀ′TĬON, *n.* Act of throwing weapons.

JĂC′Ṳ-LA̤-TO̤-RY̆, *a.* Throwing out; darting.

JĀDE, *n.* A worthless horse :—a sorry woman.

JĀDE, *v. a.* To tire; to weary; to ride down.

JĂD′ĬSH, *a.* Vicious; bad :—unchaste.

JĂG, *v. a.* To cut into indentures or teeth.

JĂG, JĂGG, *n.* A denticulation :—a small load.

JĂG′GĔD-NĔSS, *n.* State of being denticulated.

JĂG′GY̆, *a.* Uneven; denticulated; notched.

JĂG-Ṳ-ĂR′, *n.* The American tiger or panther.

JĀIL, *n.* Prison, place of confinement; gaol;— written both *jail* and *gaol*. See GAOL.

JĀIL′BĬRD, *n.* One who is or has been in jail.

JĀIL′ĔR, *n.* A keeper of a jail or prison.

JĂL′A̤P, *n.* A root used as a medicine.

JĂM, *n.* Conserve :—bed of stone :—child's frock.

JĂM, *v. a.* To squeeze closely; to press.

JĂMB (jăm), *n.* A side-piece of a fireplace, &c.

JĀNE, *n.* A kind of fustian :—a coin of Genoa.

JĂN′GLE, *v. n.* To prate; to quarrel; to bicker.

JĂN′GLE, *n.* Prate :—discordant sound; dispute.

JĂN′Ĭ-TOR, *n.* A door-keeper; a porter.

JĂN′Ĭ-ZA̤-RY̆, *n.* One of the Turkish guards.

JĂNT, JĂUNT, *n.* A ramble; excursion; flight.

JĂNT, *v. n.* To walk or ramble about. [tion.

JĂNT′Ĭ-NĔSS, *n.* Airiness; flutter; self-satisfac-

JĂN′TY̆, *a.* Showy; airy; fluttering; finical.

JĂN′Ṳ-A̤-RY̆, *n.* The first month of the year.

JA̤-PĂN′, *n.* A varnish, or work varnished.

JA̤-PĂN′, *v. a.* To varnish and embellish.

JA̤-PĂN′NĔR, *n.* One who japans.

JA̤-PĂN′NĬNG, *n.* Act or process of varnishing.

JĂR, *v. n. & a.* To clash; to quarrel; to shake.

JĂR, *n.* A vibration :—discord :—a vessel.

JĂRDĔṢ (järdz), *n. pl.* Callous tumors in horses.

JĂR′GŎN, *n.* Unintelligible talk; gibberish.

JĂS′MĬNE, JĔS′SA̤-MĬNE, *n.* A plant and flower.

JĂS′PĔR, *n.* A stone used in jewellery.

JĂUN′DĬCE (jän′dĭs), *n.* A disease by which the body becomes yellow. [—prejudiced.

JĂUN′DĬCED (jän′dĭst), *a.* Having the jaundice

JĂUNT (jänt), *v. n.* To ramble. See JANT.

JĂVE′LĬN (jăv′lĭn), *n.* A spear or half-pike.

JÂW, *n.* The bone of the mouth in which the teeth are fixed :—the mouth :—abuse.

JĀY (jā), *n.* A bird with gaudy feathers. [color.

JĀ′ZEL (jā′zl), *n.* A gem of an azure or blue

JĔAL′OŨS, *a.* Suspicious; emulous; cautious.

JĔAL′OŨS-Y̆ (jĕl′ŭs-ẹ), *n.* Suspicion in love; fear.

JĒĔR, *v. n. & a.* To scoff; to flout; to mock.

JĒĔR, *n.* A scoff; taunt; biting jest; flout; gibe.

JĒĔR′ĔR, *n.* A scoffer; a scorner; a mocker.

JĒĔR′ĬNG-LY̆, *ad.* Scornfully; contemptuously.

JE̤-HŌ′VA̤H, *n.* The Hebrew proper name of

JE̤-JŪNE′, *a.* Empty; vacant; dry; barren. [God.

JE̤-JŪNE′NĔSS, *n.* Penury; barrenness; dryness.

JĔL′LY̆, *n.* A kind of sweetmeat; gelly.

JĔN′NĔT, *n.* A Spanish horse. See GENET.

JĔN′NĔT-ĬNG, *n.* An apple ripe in June.

JĔOP′ARD (jĕp′pa̤rd), *v. a.* To hazard; to risk.

JĔOP′ARD-Y̆ (jĕp′pa̤r-dẹ), *n.* Hazard; danger.

JĔRK, *v. a. & n.* To thrust out; to throw; to pull

JĔRK, *n.* A lash; a sudden spring; a throw.

JĔR′KĬN, *n.* A jacket; a short coat, or close waistcoat :—a species of hawk.

JĔR′ṢEY̆ (jĕr′zẹ), *n.* Fine wool, or yarn of wool.

JĔS′SA̤-MĬNE, *n.* A fragrant flower. See JAS-

JĔST, *v. n.* To divert; to make sport. [MINE.

JĔST, *n.* Any thing ludicrous; laughing-stock.

JĔST′ĔR, *n.* One given to jesting or sport.

JĔST′ĬNG, *n.* Utterance of jests; sport.

JĔṢ′Ṳ-ĬT, *n.* One of the Society of Jesus.

JĔṢ-Ṳ-ĬT′ĬC,) *a.* Belonging to a Jesuit :—
JĔṢ-Ṳ-ĬT′Ĭ-CA̤L,) crafty; artful; deceitful.

JĔṢ-Ṳ-ĬT′Ĭ-CA̤L-LY̆, *ad.* Like a Jesuit.

JĔṢ′Ṳ-ĬT-ĬṢM, *n.* The principles of the Jesuits.

JĔT, *n.* A fine black fossil :—spout of water.

JĔT, *v. n.* To shoot forward; to project; to jut.

JĔT′SA̤M, *n.* Goods cast overboard in a storm.

JĔT′TY̆, *a.* Made of jet; black as jet.

JEW̄ (jū), *n.* A Hebrew; an Israelite :—a cheat.

JEW̄′ĔL (jū′ĕl), *n.* An ornament worn by ladies; a precious stone; a gem :—any thing precious. [precious.

JEW̄′ĔL-LĔR, *n.* A dealer in jewels.

JEW̄′ĔL-LĔR-Y̆,) *n.* Jewels collectively :—
JEW̄′ĔL-RY̆,) trade in jewels. [man.

JEW̄′ĔSS (jū′ĕs), *n.* A Hebrew or Jewish wo-

JEW̄′ĬSH (jū′ĭsh), *a.* Relating to the Jews.

JEW̄Ṣ′-HĂRP (jūz′härp), *n.* A musical instru-

JĬB, *n.* The foremost sail of a ship. [ment.

JĬB′-BŎŎM, *n.* A spar on a bowsprit.

JĬG, *n.* A light, careless dance or tune :—a trick.

JĬG′GĔR, *n.* A machine to hold on a cable.

JĬLL′-FLĬRT, *n.* A giddy or wanton woman.

JĬLT, *n.* A woman who deceives her lover.

JĬLT, *v. a. & n.* To trick or deceive in love.

JĬN′GLE, *v. n.* To sound with a sharp rattle.

JĬN′GLE, *v. a.* To cause to give a sharp sound.
JĬN′GLE, *n.* A rattling or clinking sound.
JŎB, *n.* A piece of chance work ; piece of labor.
JŎB, *v. a.* To strike or stab with a sharp instru-
JŎB, *v. n.* To buy and sell, as a broker. [ment.
JŎB′BER, *n.* One who does chance work, &c.
JŎCK′EY, *n.* One who rides or deals in horses.
JŎCK′EY (jŏk′ke), *v. a.* To cheat ; to trick.
JQ-CŌSE′, *a.* Merry ; waggish ; given to jest.
JQ-CŌSE′LY, *ad.* Waggishly ; in jest ; in game.
JŎC′U-LAR, *a.* Sportive ; merry ; jocose.
JŎC-U-LĂR′I-TY, *n.* Merriment ; disposition to
JŎC′U-LAR-LY, *ad.* In a jocose way. [jest.
JŎC′UND, *a.* Merry ; gay ; airy ; lively ; joyous.
JQ-CŬN′DI-TY, *n.* Gayety ; mirth ; joy.
JŎG, *v. a.* To push ; to give notice by a push.
JŎG, *v. n.* To move by jogs ; to travel leisurely.
JŎG, *n.* A push ; a slight shake ; a hint ; a stop.
JŎG′GER, *n.* One who moves heavily and dully.
JŎG′GLE, *v. a.* To push.—*v. n.* To shake.
JQ-HĂN′NĘŞ, *n.* A Portuguese gold coin of the
 value of 8 dollars ;—often contracted into *joe.*
JŌĬN, *v. a.* To couple ; to combine ; to unite.
JŌĬN, *v. n.* To adhere ; to close ; to unite with.
JŌĬN′DER, *n.* A conjunction ; act of joining.
JŌĬN′ĘR, *n.* One who joins :—a carpenter.
JŌĬN′ĘR-Y, *n.* Wood work ; carpentry.
JŌĬNT, *n.* An articulation of limbs :—a juncture.
JŌĬNT, *a.* Shared by two or more ; united.
JŌĬNT, *v. a.* To unite ; to divide a joint. [sures.
JŌĬNT′ĘD, *a.* Full of joints, knots, or commis-
JŌĬNT′ĘR, *n.* A sort of long plane :—a mason's
JŌĬNT′-HĒĬR (jōĭnt′âr), *n.* A co-heir. [tool.
JŌĬNT′LY, *ad.* Together ; not separately.
JŌĬNT′RĘSS, *n.* A woman having a jointure.
JŌĬNT′-STŎCK, *n.* Stock held in company.
JŌĬNT′-TĔN′AN-CY, *n.* A tenure by unity of title.
JŌĬNT′URE (jōĭnt′yur), *n.* An estate settled on
 a wife, to be enjoyed after her husband's death.
JŌĬNT′URE, *v. a.* To endow with a jointure.
JŌĬST, *n.* A small timber, as of a floor.
JŌKE, *n.* A jest ; something not serious ; fun.
JŌKE, *v. n.* To jest.—*v. a.* To cast jokes at.
JŌLE, *n.* The face or cheek :—head of a fish.
JŎL′LI-NĔSS, JŎL′LI-TY, *n.* Gayety; merriment.
JŎL′LY, *a.* Gay; merry ; airy; cheerful :—plump.
JŎL′LY-BŌAT (jŏl′le-bōt), *n.* A ship's small boat.
JŌLT, *v. n. & a.* To shake one, as a carriage.
JŌLT, *n.* A shock ; a shake ; a violent agitation.
JŌLT′-HĔAD (jōlt′hĕd), *n.* A great head ; dunce.
JŎN′QUIL, JŎN-QUĬLLE′, *n.* A kind of daffodil.
JŎS′TLE (jŏs′sl), *v. a.* To shake ; to justle.
JŎT, *n.* A point ; a tittle :—the least quantity.
JOŬR′NAL (jŭr′nal), *n.* A diary; a daily register.
JOŬR′NAL-ĬST (jŭr′nal-), *n.* A writer of journals.
JOŬR′NAL-ĪZE, *v. a.* To record in a journal.
JOŬR′NEY (jŭr′ne), *n.* Travel by land ; a pas-
 sage ; a tour ; an excursion.
JOŬR′NEY, *v. n.* To travel from place to place.
JOŬR′NEY-MAN, *n.* A hired workman.
JOŬST (jŭst), *n.* A tournament; a mock fight.
JOVE, *n.* Jupiter, an ancient heathen deity.
JŌ′VI-AL, *a.* Gay ; airy ; merry ; cheerful.
JŌ′VI-AL-LY, *ad.* Merrily ; gayly ; cheerfully.
JŌWL (jōl), *n.* The cheek ; jole. See JOLE.
JŌWL′ĘR or JŎWL′ĘR, *n.* A hunting dog.
JŌY, *n.* Gladness ; exultation ; festivity. [den.
JŌY, *v. n. & a.* To rejoice ; to be glad ; to glad-

JŌY′FÛL, *a.* Full of joy ; glad ; exulting.
JŌY′FÛL-LY, *ad.* With joy ; gladly ; exultingly.
JŌY′FÛL-NĔSS, *n.* Gladness ; joy ; exultation.
JŌY′LĘSS, *a.* Void of joy ; giving no pleasure.
JŌY′OŲS, *a.* Glad ; gay ; merry ; giving joy.
JŪ′BI-LANT, *a.* Rejoicing ; shouting for joy.
JŪ′BI-LĒĒ, *n.* A public festivity ; season of joy.
JU-CŬN′DI-TY, *n.* Pleasantness ; agreeableness.
JU-DĀ′I-CAL, *a.* Jewish ; belonging to Jews.
JŪ′DA-ĬŞM, *n.* The religious rites of the Jews.
JŪ′DA-ĪZE, *v. n.* To conform to the Jewish rites.
JUDGE, *n.* An officer who presides in a court
 of judicature :—one authorized to decide.
JŬDGE, *v. n. & a.* To discern ; to decide ; to
 determine :—to pass sentence as a judge.
JŬDGE′SHĬP, *n.* Office or dignity of a judge.
JŬDG′MENT, *n.* Act of judging ; decision ; sen-
 tence ; discernment ; criticism ; doom.
JŪ′DI-CA-TQ-RY, *n.* A court of justice ; tribunal.
JŪ′DI-CA-TŪRE, *n.* Power of distributing justice.
JU-DĬ′′CIAL (ju-dĭsh′al), *a.* Pertaining to courts
 of law, or the distribution of public justice.
JU-DĬ′′CIAL-LY (ju-dĭsh′al-e), *ad.* In form of law.
JU-DĬ′′CI-A-RY (ju-dĭsh′e-a-re), *a.* Relating to
 courts of judicature ; passing judgment upon.
JU-DĬ′′CI-A-RY, *n.* The power which dispenses
 justice ; judiciary power ; judicature.
JU-DĬ′′CIOŲS (ju-dĭsh′us), *a.* Prudent ; wise.
JU-DĬ′′CIOŲS-LY (ju-dĭsh′us-le), *ad.* Wisely.
JŬG, *n.* A vessel with a swelling belly. [tifice.
JŬG′GLE, *v. a.* To play tricks ; to practise ar-
JŬG′GLE, *n.* A trick ; an imposture ; deception.
JŬG′GLĘR, *n.* One who practises sleight of hand.
JŬG′GLING, *n.* Deception ; imposture ; trick.
JŪ′GU-LAR, *a.* Belonging to the throat.
JUICE (jūs), *n.* The sap in vegetables ; the
 water of fruit ; the fluid in animals.
JUICE′LĘSS (jūs′lĕs), *a.* Dry ; without moisture.
JŪI′CI-NĔSS (jū′se-nĕs), *n.* Plenty of juice.
JŪI′CY (jū′se), *a.* Moist ; abounding with juice.
JŪ′JUBE, *n.* A plant :—a kind of sweetmeat.
JŪ′LĘP, *n.* A pleasant liquid medicine.
JU-LY′, *n.* The seventh month in the year.
JŪ′MART, *n.* The offspring of a bull and a mare.
JŬM′BLE, *v. a.* To mix confusedly together.
JŬM′BLE, *n.* A confused mass or mixture.
JŬM′BLĘR, *n.* One who mixes things confusedly.
JŬMP, *v. n.* To leap ; to skip ; to bound.
JŬMP, *n.* A leap ; a skip ; a bound :—hazard.
JŬNC′TION, *n.* Union ; a joining ; a coalition.
JŬNCT′URE (jŭngkt′yur), *n.* A joint ; an articu-
 lation ; union ; unity ; a critical point of time.
JUNE, *n.* The sixth month of the year.
JŬN′GLE, *n.* A thick cluster of shrubs or rushes.
‖JŪN′IOR (jūn′yur *or* jū′ne-or), *a.* Younger.
‖JŪN′IOR, *n.* A person younger than another.
JŪ′NI-PĘR, *n.* A plant which bears a berry.
JŬNK, *n.* Pieces of old cable :—salt beef.
JŬNK′ĘT, *n.* A sweetmeat :—a stolen repast.
JŬNK′ĘT, *v. n.* To feast secretly or by stealth.
JŬN′TŌ, *n. ; pl.* JŬN′TŌŞ. A cabal ; a faction.
JŪ′PI-TĘR, *n.* Jove, a heathen deity :—a planet.
JU-RĬD′I-CAL, *a.* Used in courts of justice.
JU-RĬD′I-CAL-LY, *ad.* With legal authority. *
JŪ-RIS-CŌN′SULT, *n.* A counsellor at law ; jurist.
JŪ-RIS-DĬC′TION, *n.* Authority; extent of power.
JŪ-RIS-DĬC′TION-AL, *a.* Relating or according
 to jurisdiction or legal authority.

JŪ-RĬS-PRŪ′DĘNCE, *n.* The science of law.
JŪ′RĬST, *n.* One versed in civil law ; a civilian.
JŪ′RŎR, *n.* One that serves on a jury ; juryman.
JŪ′RY, *n.* A number of men sworn to inquire into and try any matter, and declare the truth on such evidence as may be delivered them.
JŪ′RY-MĄN, *n.* One who is impanelled on a jury.
JŪ′RY-MĀST, *n.* A mast erected to supply the place of one lost in a tempest, &c.
JŬST, *a.* Upright ; equitable ; honest ; exact.
JŬST, *ad.* Exactly ; merely ; barely ; almost.
JŬST, *n.* A mock fight ; tournament. See JOUST.
JŬS′TĬCE, *n.* Equity ; right ; law :—an officer.
JŬS′TĬCE-SHĬP, *n.* Rank or office of justice.
JⱯS-TĬ′′CĬ-Ą-RY (jⱯs-tĭsh′ę-a-rę), *n.* An administrator of justice ; a chief-justice. [son.
JŬS′TĬ-FĪ-Ą-BLE, *a.* Defensible by law or rea-
JŬS′TĬ-FĪ-Ą-BLE-NĔSS, *n.* The being justifiable.
JŬS′TĬ-FĪ-Ą-BLY, *ad.* So as to be justified.
JŬS-TĬ-FĬ-CĀ′TĬǪN, *n.* A defence ; vindication.
JŬS′TĬ-FĪ-ER, *n.* One who justifies. [dicate.
JŬS′TĬ-FỸ, *v. a.* To absolve ; to defend ; to vin-
JŬS′TLE (jŭs′sl), *v. a.* To joggle ; to push ; to shake ; to clash ; to jostle. [to shake.
JŬS′TLE (jŭs′sl), *v. n.* To encounter ; to clash ;
JŬS′TLE (jŭs′sl), *n.* A shock ; slight encounter.
JŬST′LY, *ad.* Uprightly ; honestly ; properly.
JŬST′NĘSS, *n.* Justice ; equity ; accuracy.
JŬT, *v. n.* To push or shoot out ; to butt.
JŬT′TY, *n.* A projection ; a pier ; a mole.
JŪ′VĘ-NĬLE, *a.* Young ; youthful ; frolicsome.
JŪ-VĘ-NĬL′Ĭ-TY, *n.* Youthfulness ; light manner.
JŬX-TĄ-PǪ-ŞĬ′′TĬǪN (jŭks-tạ-pǫ-zĭsh′Ɐn), *n.* A placing or being placed together ; apposition.

K.

K has, before all the vowels, one invariable sound, as in *keen, kill.*
KĀLE, *or* KĀIL, *n.* A kind of cabbage.
KĄ-LEĪ′DǪ-SCŌPE (kạ-lĬ′dǫ-skōp), *n.* An optical instrument exhibiting fine forms and colors.
KĂL′ĘN-DĄR, *n.* An account of time. See CAL-
KĂ′LĬ, *a.* A marine plant. [ENDAR.
KĂL′MĬ-Ą, *n.* An American evergreen shrub.
KĂN-GĄ-RŎŌ′ (kăn-gạ-rô′), *n.* A quadruped of New Holland, having short fore legs.
KÂW, *v. n.* To cry as a raven, crow, or rook.
KÂW, *n.* The cry of a raven or crow.
KĀYLE (kāl), *n.* A ninepin :—a kind of play.
KĔCK, *v. n.* To heave the stomach ; to retch.
KĔC′KLE, *v. a.* To defend with a rope, as a ca-
KĔCK′SY, *n.* A plant ; poisonous hemlock. [ble.
KĔDGE, *v. a.* To move with the tide, as a ship.
KĔDGE, KĔDG′ER, *n.* A small anchor.
KĔĒL, *n.* The lower timber of a ship.
KĔĒL′HÂUL, *v. a.* To drag under the keel.
KĔĒL′ĬNG, *n.* A name for the common codfish.
KĔEL′SǪN (kĕl′sⱯn), *n.* The piece of timber next above a ship's keel.
KĔĒN, *a.* Sharp ; acute ; severe ; piercing ; eager.
KĔĒN′LY, *ad.* Sharply ; eagerly ; bitterly.
KĔĒN′NĘSS, *n.* Sharpness ; asperity ; eagerness.
KĔĒP, *v. a.* [*imp. t. & pp.* kept.] To retain ; to preserve ; to hold :—to protect ; to guard.
KĔĒP, *v. n.* To remain ; to stay ; to last ; to lodge.
KĔĒP, *n.* Strongest part of a castle :—guard.
KĔĒP′ER, *n.* A defender :—one who keeps.
KĔĒP′ĬNG, *n.* Charge ; custody, guard ; support.
KĔĒP′SĀKE, *n.* A gift in token of regard.
KĔG, *n.* A small cask or barrel. See CAG.
KĔLP, *n.* Seaweed :—a salt from seaweed.
KĔL′TER, *n.* Order ; good condition. [know.
KĔN, *v. a.* To see at a distance ; to descry ; to
KĔN, *n.* View ; sight :—the reach of the sight.
KĔN′NĘL, *n.* A cot for dogs :—a watercourse.
KĔN′NĘL, *v. n.* To lie ; to dwell, as beasts.
KĔPT, *imp. t. & pp.* from *keep.* [a woman.
KĔR′CHĬEF (kĕr′chĭf), *n.* A head-dress, as for
KĔR′MĔŞ, *n. pl.* A substance used in dyeing.
KĔRN, *n.* An Irish foot-soldier :—a hand-mill.
KĔRN, *v. n.* To take the form of grains.
KĔR′NĘL, *n.* The edible substance in a shell.
KĔR′ŞEY, *n.* A kind of coarse cloth or stuff.
KĔR′ŞEY-MĒRE, *n.* A thin, twilled woollen cloth.
KĔS′TRĘL, *n.* A species of falcon ; windhover.
KĔTCH, *n.* A sea vessel with two masts.
KĔT′TLE, *n.* A vessel in which liquor is boiled.
KĔT′TLE-DRŬM, *n.* A drum with a body of
KĔT′TLE-PĬNŞ, *n. pl.* Ninepins ; skittles. [brass.
KĒY (kē), *n.* An instrument to fasten and open a lock, &c. :—a note in music :—index :—quay.
KĒY′AGE (kē′ạj), *n.* Money paid for wharfage.
KĒY′HŌLE (kē′hōl), *n.* A hole to put a key in.
KĒY′STŌNE, *n.* The middle stone of an arch.
KHÂN *or* KHĂN, *n.* In Asia, a ruler :—a sort of
KĪBE, *n.* A chilblain ; a chap in the heel. [inn.
KĬCK, *v. a. & n.* To strike or knock with the
KĬCK, *n.* A blow with the foot. [foot.
KĬCK′SHÂW, *n.* Something fantastical ; bawble.
KĬD, *n.* The young of a goat :—bundle of heath.
KĬD′NĂP, *v. a.* To steal, as a human being.
KĬD′NĂP-PER, *n.* One who steals human beings.
KĬD′NEY (kĭd′nę), *n.* One of two glands which secrete the urine :—kind ; humor ; habit. [ure.
KĬL′DER-KĬN, *n.* A small barrel :—liquid meas-
KĬLL, *v. a.* To deprive of life ; to destroy.
KĬLN (kĭl), *n.* An oven for burning bricks, &c.
KĬLN′DRỸ (kĭl′drī), *v. n.* To dry in a kiln.
KĬLT, *n.* A kind of short petticoat.
KĬM′BŌ, *a.* Crooked ; bent ; arched ; a-kimbo.
KĬN, *n.* A relation ; kindred ; relatives.
KĬND, *a.* Benevolent ; good ; favorable.
KĬND, *n.* Race ; generical class ; sort ; nature.
KĬND′-HEÄRT-ĘD (-härt-ĕd), *a.* Benevolent.
KĬN′DLE, *v. a. & n.* To set on fire ; to inflame.
KĬND′LĬ-NĔSS, *n.* Favor ; affection ; good will.
KĬND′LY, *a.* Congenial ; proper ; bland ; mild.
KĬND′LY, *ad.* Benevolently ; favorably ; fitly.
KĬND′NĘSS, *n.* Benevolence ; good-will ; favor.
KĬN′DRĘD, *n.* Relation ; affinity ; relatives.
KĬN′DRĘD, *a.* Congenial ; related ; cognate.
KĪNE, *n.* The plural of *cow.* [*Obsolescent.*]
KĬNG, *n.* A monarch ; a sovereign ; chief ruler.
KĬNG′CÛP, *n.* A plant and flower ; crowfoot.

ƙĬNG′DŎM, n. The dominion of a king :—class.
ƙĬNG′FĬSH-ĘR, n. A bird living on fishes, &c.
ƙĬNG′LỴ, a. Royal ; monarchical ; noble ; au-
ƙĬNG′Șʼ-Ē-VIL (kĭngzʼē-vl), n. Scrofula. [gust.
ƙĬNG′SHĬP, n. The office of a king ; royalty.
ƙĬNȘ′FŌLK (kĭnzʼfōk), n. Kindred ; relations.
ƙĬNȘ′MĄN, n. A man of the same race or family.
ƙĬNȘ′WOM-ĄN (kĭnzʼwûm-ąn), n. A female
ƙĬRK, n. A church, in Scotland. [relation.
ƙĬR′TLE (kĭrʼtl), n. An outer petticoat.
ƙĬSS, v. a. To touch with the lips ; to touch
ƙĬSS, n. A salute given by joining lips. [gently.
ƙĬSS′ĬNG–CŎM′FĬT, n. A perfumed sugar-plum.
ƙĬT, n. A small fiddle :—fish-tub :—a milk-pail.
ƙĬTCH′ĘN, n. A room for cooking provisions.
ƙĬTCH′ĘN-MĀID, n. A maid employed in a
   kitchen. [paper plaything.
ƙĪTE, n. A bird of prey of the hawk kind :—a
ƙĬT′LĬNG, n. A whelp :—a young cat ; kitten.
ƙĬT′TEN (kĭtʼtn), n. A young cat. [click.
ƙLĬCK, v. n. To make a small, sharp noise ; to
ƙLĬCK, ƙLĬCK′ĬNG, n. A small, sharp noise.
ƙNĂB (năb), v. a. To bite ; to catch ; to nab.
ƙNĂCK (năk), n. A toy :—readiness ; dexterity.
ƙNĂG (năg), n. A knot in wood ; a peg ; a shoot.
ƙNĂP (năp), n. A protuberance ; a swelling.
ƙNĂP (năp), v. a. To bite ; to break short.
ƙNĂP′SĂCK (năpʼsăk), n. A soldier's bag or sack.
ƙNĂR (năr), n. A hard knot in wood ; a knurl.
ƙNĂRLED (närld), a. Knotted ; gnarled.
ƙNĀVE (nāv), n. A rascal ; a scoundrel :—card.
ƙNĀV′ĘR-Ỵ (nāvʼer-ę), n. Dishonesty ; villany.
ƙNĀV′ĬSH (knāvʼĭsh), a. Dishonest ; fraudulent.
ƙNĀV′ĬSH-LỴ (nāvʼĭsh-lę), ad. Dishonestly.
ƙNĀV′ĬSH-NĔSS (nāvʼĭsh-nĕs), n. Knavery.
ƙNĔAD (nĕd), v. a. To work into a mass.
ƙNĔĒ (nē), n. The joint of the leg and thigh.
ƙNĔĒD (nĕd), a. Having knees ; having joints.
ƙNĔĒ′DĔĔP (nēʼdēp), a. Rising to the knees.
ƙNĔĒL (nĕl), v. n. [imp. t. & pp. kneeled or
   knelt.] To bend or rest on the knee. [knee.
ƙNĔĒ′PĂN (nēʼpán), n. A round bone on the
ƙNĔLL (nĕl), n. The sound of a funeral bell.
ƙNEW̄ (nū), imp. t. from know. [a gewgaw.
ƙNĬCK′KNĂCK (nĭkʼnăk), n. Any trifle or toy ;

KNĪFE (knīf), n. ; pl. KNĪVEȘ. A sharp instru-
   ment used for cutting. [a combatant.
KNĪGHT (nīt), n. A man of rank ; a champion ;
KNĪGHT (nīt), v. a. To create a knight.
KNĪGHT′-ĔR′RĄNT (nītʼ-), n. ; pl. KNĪGHTS′-
   ĔR′RĄNT. A wandering knight.
KNĪGHT′-ĔR′RĄNT-RỴ (nīt-ĕrʼrąnt-rę), n. The
   character, manners, or feats of a knight-errant.
KNĪGHT′HOOD (nītʼhûd), n. Dignity of a knight.
KNĪGHT′LỴ (nītʼlę), a. Pertaining to a knight.
KNĬT (nĭt), v. a. & n. [imp. t. & pp. knit or
   knitted.] To weave without a loom ; to unite.
KNĬT′TĘR, n. One who weaves or knits.
KNĬT′TĬNG–NĒĒ′DLE (nĭtʼtĭng-nēʼdl), n. A
   wire which is used in knitting. [a boss.
KNŎB (nŏb), n. A protuberance ; a hard bunch ;
KNŎBBED (nŏbd), a. Having protuberances.
KNŎB′BỴ (nŏbʼbę), a. Full of knobs ; hard.
KNŎCK (nŏk), v. a. & n. To strike, clash, beat.
KNŎCK (nŏk), n. A sudden stroke ; a blow.
KNŎCK′ĘR, n. A striker :—a door-hammer.
KNŌLL (nōl), v. a. & n. To ring, as a bell.
KNŌLL (nōl), n. A little round hill ; top of a hill.
KNŎT (nŏt), n. A tie ; a joint :—a knurl in
   wood :—difficulty :—a confederacy ; a cluster.
KNŎT (nŏt), v. a. & n. To tie ; to form knots ;
KNŎT′GRĂSS (nŏtʼgrăs), n. A plant. [to tangle.
KNŎT′TĘD (nŏtʼtęd), a. Full of knots ; uneven.
KNŎT′TĬ-NĔSS (nŏtʼ-), n. Fulness of knots.
KNŎT′TỴ (nŏtʼtę), a. Full of knots ; difficult.
KNŎŪT (nŏût), n. A Russian punishment.
KNŌW (nō), v. a. [imp. t. knew ; pp. known.]
   To perceive with certainty ; to recognize.
KNŌW (nō), v. n. To have certain perception.
KNŌW′ĬNG (nōʼĭng), a. Skilful ; intelligent.
KNŌW′ĬNG-LỴ (nōʼĭng-lę), ad. With knowledge.
KNŎWL′ĘDG̣E (nŏlʼlej), n. Certain perception ;
   science ; learning ; skill ; information.
KNŬC′KLE (nŭkʼkl), n. A joint of the finger.
KNŬC′KLE (nŭkʼkl), v. n. To submit.
KNŬR (nür), KNŬRL (nürl), n. A knot in wood.
KNŬRL′ĘD, KNŬRL′Ỵ, a. Full of knurls or
KŌ′PĔCK, n. A Russian copper coin. [knots.
KŌ′RĄN, n. Mahometan bible. See ALCORAN.
KŬ′MĮSS, KÔU′MĮS, n. Liquor from mares' milk.

L.

Ľ a liquid consonant, preserves always the
  same sound in English ; as in like, fall.
ĽÄ, n. A monosyllable or note in music.
ĽÄ (läw), interj. See ! look ! behold ! [dard.
ĽĂB′A-RŬM, n. [L.] The Roman imperial stan-
ĽĂB′DA-NŬM, n. A resin of a strong smell.
ĽÄ′BĘL, n. A name or title fixed to any thing ;
   a small slip or scrip of writing :—a brass rule.
ĽÄ′BĘL, v. a. To affix a label on.
ĽÄ′BĘNT, a. Sliding ; gliding ; slipping.
ĽÄ′BĮ-AL, a. Uttered by, or relating to, the lips.
ĽÄ′BĮ-AL, n. A letter pronounced by the lips.
ĽÄ′BĮ-ATE, LÄ′BĮ-ĀT-ĘD, a. Formed with lips.
ĽA-BĬM′E-TER, n. A surgical instrument.
ĽÄ-BĮ-O-DĔN′TĄL, a. Formed by the lips and
ĽÄ′BŎR, n. Pains ; toil ; work ; travail. [teeth.

LÄ′BŎR, v. n. To toil ; to do work :—to be in
   travail :—to move with difficulty.
LÄ′BŎR, v. a. To work at ; to beat ; to belabor.
LĂB′O-RA-TO-RỴ, n. A chemist's work-room.
LÄ′BŎR-ĘR, n. One who labors or does work.
LA-BŌ′RĮ-OŬS, a. Diligent ; assiduous ; tiresome.
LA-BŌ′RĮ-OŬS-LỴ, ad. With labor ; with toil.
LA-BŌ′RĮ-OŬS-NĔSS, n. Toilsomeness ; difficulty.
LA-BŬR′NŲM, n. A shrub of the cytisus genus.
LĂB′Ỵ-RĬNTH, n. A maze ; a place full of wind-
   ings ; perplexity ; intricacy. [rinth.
LĂB-Ỵ-RĬN′THĮ-AN, a. Winding ; like a laby-
LĂC, n. A concrete substance. See LACK.
LĀCE, n. Plaited cord ; ornaments of thread, &c.
LĀCE, v. a. To bind, as with a cord ; to adorn.
LĀCE′MĂN, n. One who deals in lace.

LĂÇ'ẸR-A-BLE, *a.* That may be torn or rent.
LĂÇ'ẸR-ĀTE, *v. a.* To tear; to rend; to mangle.
LĂÇ-ẸR-Ā'TIỌN, *n.* The act of tearing; breach.
LĂÇ'ẸR-A-TĬVE, *a.* Tearing; having power to
LĂ€H'RY-MẠL, *a.* Generating tears. [tear.
LĂ€H'RY-MẠ-RY, *a.* Used for containing tears.
LĂ€H'RY-MẠ-TỌ-RY, *n.* Vessel to preserve tears.
LĂCK, *v. a.* To want; to need; to be without.
LĂCK, *v. n.* To be in want; to be wanting.
LĂCK, *n.* Want; need :—100,000 rupees, &c.
LĂCK-A-DĀY' (lăk-a-dā'), *interj.* Implying *alas.*
LĂCK'BRĀIN (lăk'brān), *n.* One that lacks wit.
LĂCK'ẸR, *n.* One who lacks :—a varnish.
LĂCK'ẸR, *v. a.* To smear over with lacker.
LĂCK'EY (lăk'kẹ), *n.* A servant; a foot-boy.
LA-CŎN'ĬC, LA-CŎN'Ĭ-CẠL, *a.* Short; concise;
LA-CŎN'Ĭ-CẠL-LY, *ad.* Briefly; concisely. [brief.
LA-CŎN'Ĭ-CĬṢM, { *n.* A concise style :—a brief,
LĂC'Ọ-NĬṢM, } pithy phrase or expression.
LĂC'QUẸR, *n.* A varnish. See LACKER.
LĂC'TẠ-RY, *a.* Milky; full of juice like milk.
LĂC'TẸ-ẠL, *a.* Milky; conveying chyle.
LĂC'TẸ-ẠL, *n.* The vessel that conveys chyle.
LĂC'TẸ-OŬS, *a.* Milky; lacteal; conveying
LĂC-TĔS'CẸNCE, *n.* Tendency to milk. [chyle.
LĂC-TĔS'CẸNT, *a.* Producing milk.
LĂC'TĬC, *a.* Applied to the acid of sour milk.
LĂC-TĬF'ẸR-OŬS, *a.* That conveys or brings
LĂD, *n.* A boy; a young man; stripling. [milk.
LĂD'DẸR, *n.* A frame with steps for climbing.
LĀDE, *v. a.* [*imp. t.* laded ; *pp.* laden *or* laded.]
 To load; to freight :—to heave out.
LĀ'DEN (lā'dn), *pp.* from *lade* and *load.*
LĂD'ĬNG, *n.* Freight; weight; burden. [dle.
LĀ'DLE, *n.* A large spoon; a vessel with a han-
LĀ'DY, *n.* A well-bred woman; a title of respect.
LĀ'DY-BĬRD, LĀ'DY-FLỸ, *n.* A kind of insect.
LĀ'DY-DĀY, *n.* 25th March; the Annunciation.
LĀ'DY-LĪKE, *a.* Becoming a lady; soft; elegant.
LĀ'DY-LŎVE, *n.* A female sweetheart.
LĀ'DY-SHĬP, *n.* The title or state of a lady.
LĂG, *a.* Coming behind; sluggish; slow; tardy.
LĂG, *v. n.* To loiter; to stay behind.
LA-GŎÔN', *n.* A large, shallow pond or lake.
LĀ'ĬC, LĀ'Ĭ-CẠL, *a.* Belonging to the laity.
LĀ'ĬC, *n.* A layman ;—opposed to *clergyman.*
LĀID (lād), *imp. t.* & *pp.* from *lay.*
LĀIN (lān), *pp.* from *lie.* [beast.
LĀIR (lár), *n.* The couch of a boar or other wild
LĀIRD (lárd), *n.* The lord of a manor. [*Scot.*]
LĀ'Ĭ-TY, *n.* The people, distinct from the clergy.
LĀKE, *n.* A large extent of inland water :—a
 pigment of a reddish color. [See LLAMA.
LĀ'MẠ, *n.* The head of the Buddhist religion.
LA-MĂN'TĬNE, *n.* An animal; manatee or sea-
LĂMB (lăm), *n.* The young of a sheep. [cow.
LĂMB (lăm), *v. a.* To yean; to bring forth lambs.
LĂM'BẠ-TĬVE, *n.* & *a.* Medicine taken by licking.
LĂM'BẸNT, *a.* Playing about; gliding lightly
LĂMB'KĬN (lăm'kĭn), *n.* A little lamb. [over.
LĂMB'-LĪKE (lăm'lĭk), *a.* Mild; innocent.
LĀME, *a.* Crippled; disabled :—imperfect.
LĀME, *v. a.* To make lame; to cripple.
LĂM'ẸL-LẠR, *a.* Composed of scales or flakes.
LĂM'ẸL-LĂT-ẸD, *a.* Formed of plates; lamellar.
LĀME'LY, *ad.* Like a cripple :—imperfectly.
LĀME'NẸSS, *n.* State of a cripple; weakness.
LA-MĔNT', *v.* To bewail; to mourn; to grieve.

LA-MĔNT', *n.* Lamentation; expression of sor-
 row; a moaning. [ful; deplorable.
LĂM'ẸNT-A-BLE, *a.* To be lamented; mourn-
LĂM'ẸNT-A-BLY, *ad.* Mournfully; pitifully.
LĂM-ẸN-TĀ'TIỌN, *n.* An expression of sorrow.
LA-MĔNT'ẸR, *n.* One who mourns or laments.
LĂM'Ĭ-NẠ, *n.*; pl. LĂM'Ĭ-NÆ. [L.] A thin plate.
LĂM'Ĭ-NĀT-ẸD, *a.* Plated; consisting of plates.
LĂM'MẠS, *n.* The first day of August.
LĂMP, *n.* A vessel for producing light.
LĂM'PẠSS, *n.* A swelling in a horse's mouth.
LĂMP'BLĂCK, *n.* A fine soot from turpentine.
LĂM-PÔÔN', *n.* Personal satire; ridicule; abuse.
LĂM-PÔÔN', *v. a.* To abuse with personal satire.
LĂM-PÔÔN'ẸR, *n.* A scribbler of personal satire.
LĂM'PREY (lăm'prẹ), *n.* A fish like the eel.
LĂNCE, *n.* A long spear; a weapon of war.
LĂNCE, *v. a.* To pierce; to open with a lancet.
LĂN'CẸ-Ọ-LĀTE, *a.* Shaped like a lance-head.
LĂNÇ'ẸR, *n.* One armed with a lance. [ment.
LĂN'CẸT, *n.* A small, pointed surgical instru-
LĂNCH, *v. a.* To dart; to throw. See LAUNCH.
LĂND, *n.* A country; a region; earth; ground.
LĂND, *v. a.* & *n.* To set on shore; to come ashore.
LĂN-DÂU', *n.* A coach or pleasure-carriage.
LĂND'ẸD, *a.* Consisting of, or having, land.
LĂND'-FLOOD (lănd'flŭd), *n.* An inundation.
LĂND'-FŌR-CẸṢ, *n. pl.* Troops serving on land.
LĂND'GRĀVE, *n.* A German title of dominion.
LĂND-GRĀ'VĬ-ẠTE, *n.* Territory of a landgrave.
LĂND'HŌLD-ẸR, *n.* One who holds lands.
LĂND'ĬNG, *n.* A place to land at :—stair-top.
LĂND'JŎB-BẸR, *n.* One who buys and sells land.
LĂND'LĀ-DY, *n.* Mistress of an inn; a hostess.
LĂND'LẸSS, *a.* Having no property in land.
LĂND'LŎCKED (lănd'lŏkt), *a.* Enclosed with
LĂND'LŌRD, *n.* Master of an inn; a host. [land.
LĂNDS'MẠN, *n.* One who lives or serves on
LĂND'MĂRK, *n.* A mark of boundaries. [land.
LĂND'-ŎF-FĬCE, *n.* An office for the sale of land.
LĂND'SCĀPE, *n.* Prospect of a country; picture.
LĂND'-TĂX, *n.* A tax assessed upon land.
LĂND'-WĀIT-ẸR, *n.* An officer of the customs.
LĂND'WĂRD, *ad.* Towards the land.
LĀNE, *n.* A narrow street; an alley; a passage.
LĂN'GUẠGE (lăng'gwạj), *n.* Human speech:
 —speech peculiar to a nation :—style.
LĂN'GUĬD (lăng'gwĭd), *a.* Faint; weak; feeble.
LĂN'GUĬD-LY (lăng'gwĭd-lẹ), *ad.* Weakly; fee-
LĂN'GUĬD-NĔSS, *n.* Weakly; feebleness. [bly.
LĂN'GUĬSH (lăng'gwĭsh), *v. n.* To grow feeble.
LĂN'GUĬSH-ẸR, *n.* One who pines or languishes.
LĂN'GUĬSH-MĔNT, *n.* State of pining; softness.
LĂN'GUỌR (lăng'gwụr), *n.* Faintness; weakness.
LĀ'NĬ-ĀTE, *v. a.* To tear in pieces; to lacerate.
LA-NĬG'ẸR-OŬS, *a.* Bearing wool, as sheep.
LĂNK, *a.* Loose; lax; spare; slender; faint.
LĂNK'NẸSS, *n.* Want of plumpness; leanness.
LĂN'TẸRN, *n.* A case for a candle.—*a.* Thin.
LA-Nñ'GĬ-NOŬS, *a.* Downy; covered with soft
LĂN'YẠRD, *n.* A small rope or piece of cord. [hair.
LĂP, *n.* That part of a person sitting which
 reaches from the waist to the knees.
LĂP, *v. a.* To wrap or twist round :—to lick up.
LĂP, *v. n.* To be spread or turned over any thing.
LĂP'DŎG, *n.* A little dog fondled by ladies.
LA-PĔL', *n.* A part of a coat folding over.
LĂP'FŬL, *n.* As much as the lap can contain.

LĂP′Ĭ-DẠ-RŸ, n. One who cuts stones and gems.
LĂP′Ĭ-DẠ-RŸ, a. Monumental ; inscribed on
LĂP-Ĭ-DĔS′CẸNCE, n. Stony concretion. [stone.
LĂP-Ĭ-DĔS′CẸNT, a. Growing or turning to stone.
LĂP-Ĭ-DĬF′ĬC, a. Forming or turning into stone.
LẠ-PĬD′Ĭ-FȲ, v. a. & n. To turn into stone.
LĂP′Ĭ-DĬST, n. A dealer in stones or gems.
LĀ′PĬS LĂZ′Ụ-LĪ, n. A blue silicious stone.
LĂP′PẸT, n. A part of a dress that hangs loose.
LĂPSE, n. Flow ; fall ; glide :—petty error ;
slight fault ; mistake. [right.
LĂPSE, v. n. To glide ; to slip :—to fall from
LĂP′STŌNE, n. A stone used by a shoemaker.
LĂP′WĬNG, n. A noisy bird with long wings.
LĂR′BŌARD, n. The left-hand side of a ship.
LĂR′CẸ-NŸ, n. Theft ; robbery.
LĂRCH, n. A large coniferous tree.
LĂRD, n. The fat of swine melted. [grease.
LĂRD, v. a. To stuff with lard or bacon ; to
LĂRD′ẸR, n. A room where meats and other
provisions are kept for cooking.
LĂRGE, a. Big ; great ; wide ; liberal ; abundant.
LĂRGE′LŸ, ad. Widely ; amply ; liberally.
LĂRGE′NẸSS, n. Bigness ; liberality ; greatness.
LĂR′GẸSS, n. A present ; a gift ; a bounty.
LĂR′Ĭ-ĂT, n. A cord with a noose.
LĂRK, n. A small singing-bird :—a mad prank.
LĂRK′SPŬR, n. A plant and its flower. [ger.
LĂR′ỤM or LĂR′ỤM, n. Alarm ; noise noting dan-
LĂR′VẠ, n. ; pl. LĂR′VÆ. An insect in its
grub state :—reptile in stage of metamorphosis.
LĂR′ŸNX or LĀ′RŸNX, n. Upper part of the
trachea or windpipe ; Adam's apple. [India.
LẠS-CĂR′ or LĂS′CĂR, n. A native seaman of
LẠS-CĬV′Ĭ-OŬS, a. Lewd ; lustful ; wanton ; soft.
LẠS-CĬV′Ĭ-OŬS-LŸ, ad. Lewdly ; wantonly.
LẠS-CĬV′Ĭ-OŬS-NĔSS, n. Wantonness.
LĂSH, n. A stroke ; thong of a whip ; sarcasm.
LĂSH, v. a. & n. To strike ; to scourge ; to satirize.
LĂS′KẸTS, n. pl. Small lines or loops in tackling.
LĂSS, n. A girl ; a maid ; a young woman.
LĂS′SĬ-TŪDE, n. Weariness ; fatigue ; languor.
LĂSS′LÖRN, a. Forsaken by a mistress. [est.
LĂST, a. sup. Latest ; hindmost ; lowest ; mean-
LĂST, ad. The last time ; in conclusion.
LĂST, v. n. To endure ; to continue ; to remain.
LĂST, n. A mould to form shoes on :—a load.
LĂST′AGE, n. Tax for wares sold by the last.
LĂST′ĬNG, p. a. Continuing ; durable ; perpetual.
LĂST′LŸ, ad. In the last place ; at last ; finally.
LĂTCH, n. A fastening for a door, &c. :—snare.
LĂTCH, v. a. To catch ; to fasten ; to close.
LĂTCH′ẸT, n. The string that fastens a shoe.
LĀTE, a. [comp. later or latter ; superl. latest or
last.] Not early ; slow ; tardy ; deceased.
LĀTE, ad. Lately ; far in the day or night.
LĀTE′LŸ, ad. Not long ago ; recently ; of late.
LĀTE′NẸSS, n. Time far advanced ; recent time.
LĀ′TẸNT, a. Hidden ; concealed ; secret ; occult.
LĂT′ẸR-ẠL, a. Belonging to the side.
LĂT′ẸR-ẠL-LŸ, ad. By the side ; sidewise.
LĂT′ẸR-ẠN, n. The pope's palace at Rome.
LĂTH, n. ; pl. LĂTHS. A small, thin, long piece of
LĂTH, v. a. To fit up or cover with laths. [wood.
LĀTHE, n. A machine for turning wood or metals.
LĂTH′ẸR, v. a. To cover with foam of soap.
LĂTH′ẸR, n. Foam made of soap and water.
LĂTH′Ÿ, a. Thin or long as a lath.

LĂT′ĬN, a. Relating to the Latins ; Roman.
LĂT′ĬN, n. The Latin or Roman language.
LĂT′ĬN-ĬŞM, n. An idiom of the Latin tongue.
LĂT′ĬN-ĬST, n. One skilled in Latin.
LẠ-TĬN′Ĭ-TŸ, n. The style of the Latin language.
LĂT′ĬN-ĪZE, v. a. To translate into or make
LĂT′ĬSH, a. Somewhat late ; tardy. [Latin.
LĂT′Ĭ-TŪDE, n. Breadth ; width ; space ; extent :
—distance north or south from the equator.
LĂT-Ĭ-TŪ′DĬ-NẠL, a. Relating to latitude.
LĂT-Ĭ-TŪ-DĬ-NĀ′RĬ-ẠN, a. Not confined ; free.
LĂT-Ĭ-TŪ-DĬ-NĀ′RĬ-ẠN, n. One not rigidly or-
thodox. [itudinarians.
LĂT-Ĭ-TŪ-DĬ-NĀ′RĬ-ẠN-ĬŞM, n. Doctrine of lat-
LĀ′TRẠNT, a. Barking ; clamorous ; noisy.
LĂT′TẸN, n. Thin iron plate covered with tin.
LĂT′TẸR, a. Modern ; recent :—last of two or
LĂT′TẸR-LŸ, ad. Of late ; recently. [more.
LĂT′TĬCE (lăt′tĭs), n. Work like network.
LĂT′TĬCE (lăt′tĭs), v. a. To decussate ; to cross.
LÂUD, n. Praise.—v. a. To praise ; to extol.
LÂU′DẠ-BLE, a. Praiseworthy ; commendable.
LÂU′DẠ-BLE-NĔSS, n. Praiseworthiness.
LÂU′DẠ-BLŸ, ad. In a manner deserving praise.
LÂUD′Ạ-NŬM (or lŏd′dạ-nŭm), n. Any prepara-
tion of opium, especially the tincture or ex-
LÂU′DẠ-TỌ-RŸ, a. Bestowing praise. [tract.
LÂUGH (läf), v. n. To make that noise which
sudden merriment excites ; to appear gay.
LÂUGH (läf), v. a. To deride ; to ridicule.
LÂUGH (läf), n. A convulsion by merriment.
LÂUGH′Ạ-BLE (läf′ạ-bl), a. Exciting laughter.
LÂUGH′ĬNG-STŎCK (läf′ĭng-stŏk), n. An ob-
ject of ridicule ; a butt of jests.
LÂUGH′TẸR (läf′tẹr), n. Convulsive merriment.
LÂUNCH (länch), v. a. To push to sea ; to dart.
LÂUNCH (länch), n. Act of launching ; a boat.
LÂUN′DRẸSS (län′drẹs), n. A washer-woman.
LÂUN′DRŸ (län′drẹ), n. Washing ; washing-room.
LÂU′RẸ-ẠTE, a. Decked with laurel. [laureate.
LÂU′RẸ-ẠTE, n. One decked with laurel ; a poet-
LÂU′RẸL (lŏr′rẹl), n. An evergreen tree or shrub.
LÂU′RẸLLED (lŏr′rẹld), a. Crowned with laurel.
LĀ′VẠ or LĂ′VẠ, n. Matter discharged by volca-
LĂV′Ạ-TỌ-RŸ, n. A wash :—bathing-place. [noes.
LĀVE, v. a. & n. To wash ; to bathe.
LĂV′ẸN-DẸR, n. A sweet-scented plant used in
LĀ′VẸR, n. A washing-vessel. [medicine.
LĂV′ĬSH, a. Prodigal ; wasteful ; profuse ; wild.
LĂV′ĬSH, v. a. To scatter profusely ; to waste.
LĂV′ĬSH-LŸ, ad. Profusely ; prodigally.
LĂV′ĬSH-MĔNT, LĂV′ĬSH-NĔSS, n. Prodigality.
LÂW, n. A rule of action ; decree ; statute.
LÂW′-BREĀK-ẸR, n. One who violates a law.
LÂW′FŬL, a. Agreeable to law ; legal ; right.
LÂW′FŬL-LŸ, ad. Legally ; according to law.
LÂW′FŬL-NĔSS, n. Legality ; allowance of law.
LÂW′GĬV-ẸR, n. A legislator ; a maker of laws.
LÂW′LẸSS, a. Not restrained by law ; illegal.
LÂW′-MĀK-ẸR, n. One who makes laws.
LÂWN, n. Open space ; a plain :—fine linen.
LÂW′SŪIT (-sūt), n. Legal process ; a litigation.
LÂW′YẸR, n. A practitioner or professor of law.
LĂX, a. Loose ; vague ; not exact ; not strict.
LĂX-Ā′TĬỌN, n. The act of loosening ; looseness.
LĂX′Ạ-TĬVE, a. Relieving costiveness. [bowels.
LĂX′Ạ-TĬVE, n. A medicine that relaxes the
LĂX′Ĭ-TŸ, n. Looseness ; slackness ; openness.

LĂX′LY, *ad.* Loosely; without exactness.
LĂX′NĘSS, *n.* The state of being lax; laxity;
LĀY (lā), *imp. t.* from *lie.* [looseness.
LĀY (lā), *v. a.* [*imp. t.* & *pp.* laid.] To place; to
 put; to calm; to wager; to bring forth eggs.
LĀY (lā), *n.* A song; a poem; a row:—a meadow.
LĀY (lā), *a.* Relating to the laity; not clerical.
LĀY′ĘR, *n.* A stratum; a bed :—a twig. [age.
LĀY′MĄN, *n.* One of the laity; a laic :—an im-
LĀY′STÂLL (lā′stâwl), *n.* A heap of dung.
LĀ′ZĄR, *n.* One infected with filthy diseases.
LĀ′ZĄR-HÖÛSE, LĂZ-A-RĔT′TŌ, *n.* A hospital.
LĀ′ZĮ-LY, *ad.* Idly; sluggishly; heavily. [ness.
LĀ′ZĮ-NĔSS, *n.* Idleness; slothfulness; listless-
LĀ′ZY, *a.* Idle; sluggish; slothful; slow; tedious.
LĒA, LĒY (lē), *n.* Grass-land; a meadow.
LĒACH, *v. a.* To pass water through ashes. [ing.
LĒACH, *or* LĒACH′-TŬB, *n.* A vessel for leach-
LĔAD (lĕd), *n.* A heavy metal; a plummet.
LĔAD (lĕd), *v. a.* To fit with lead in any manner.
LĒAD (lēd), *v. a.* [*imp. t.* & *pp.* led.] To guide;
 to conduct; to show; to draw; to pass.
LĒAD (lēd), *v. n.* To go first and show the way.
LĒAD (lēd), *n.* Guidance :—the first place.
LĔAD′EN (lĕd′dn), *a.* Made of lead; heavy; dull.
LĒAD′ĘR, *n.* One that leads or conducts; captain.
LĒAF (lēf), *n.*; *pl.* LĒAVEŞ. Part of a plant; a
 petal :—part of a book, door, table, &c.
LĒAF (lēf), *v. n.* To bring leaves; to bear leaves.
LĒAF′LĘSS (lēf′lęs), *a.* Naked of leaves.
LĒAF′LĘT, *n.* Part of a compound leaf :—a small
LĒAF′Y (lē′fe), *a.* Full of leaves. [leaf.
LĒAGUE (lēg), *n.* A confederacy :—three miles.
LĒAGUE (lēg), *v. n.* To unite; to confederate.
LĒAGU′ĘR (lē′gẹr), *n.* One united in a league:
 —a camp. [or out.
LĒAK, *n.* A breach or hole which lets water in
LĒAK (lēk), *v. n.* To let water in or out.
LĒAK′AĢE, *n.* Allowance for accidental loss.
LĒAK′Y, *a.* Letting water in or out; loquacious.
LĒAN (lēn), *v. n.* To incline; to bend; to waver.
LĒAN, *a.* Not fat; thin; barren; poor; jejune.
LĒAN, *n.* The part of flesh distinct from fat.
LĒAN′NĘSS, *n.* Want of flesh; thinness; poverty.
LĒAP, *v. n.* To jump; to bound; to spring.
LĒAP, *v. a.* To pass over or into; to compress.
LĒAP, *n.* A bound; a jump; a sudden transition.
LĒAP′-FRŎG (lĕp′frŏg), *n.* A play of children.
LĒAP′-YĒAR, *n.* Every fourth year; bissextile.
LĔARN (lĕrn), *v. a.* & *n.* [*imp. t.* & *pp.* learned
 or learnt.] To gain knowledge or skill of.
LĔARN′ĘD (lĕr′nęd), *a.* Having learning.
LĔARN′ĘD-LY (lĕr′nęd-le),*ad.* With knowledge.
LĔARN′ĘR (lĕr′nẹr), *n.* One who learns.
LĔARN′ĮNG (lĕr′nịng), *n.* Literature; erudition.
LĒAS′A-BLE (lēs′a-bl), *a.* Capable of being
 leased or let to another.
LĒASE (lēs), *n.* A contract for a temporary pos-
 session of houses or lands :—any tenure.
LĒASE (lēs), *v. a.* To let by lease. [reapers.
LĒAŞE (lēz), *v. n.* To glean; to gather after
LĒASH, *n.* A thong; a band wherewith to tie.
†LĒAŞ′ĮNG (lēz′ịng), *n.* Lies; falsehood.
LĒAST (lēst), *a.* Superlative of *little;* smallest.
LĒAST, *ad.* In the smallest or lowest degree.
LĔATH′ĘR (lĕth′ẹr), *n.* Dressed hides of animals.
LĔATH′ĘR-DRĔSS′ĘR, *n.* One who dresses
 the skins of animals; a currier.

LĔATH′ĘRN (lĕth′ẹrn), *a.* Made of leather.
LĔATH′ĘR-SĔLL′ĘR, *n.* A dealer in leather.
LĔATH′ĘR-Y, *a.* Resembling leather; tough.
LĒAVE (lēv), *n.* Permission; license; farewell.
LĒAVE (lēv), *v. a.* [*imp. t.* & *pp.* left.] To quit;
 to forsake; to desert; to abandon; to bequeath.
LĒAVE (lēv), *v. n.* To cease; to desist.
LĒAVED (lēvd), *a.* Furnished with leaves; leafed.
LĔAV′EN (lĕv′vn), *n.* A fermenting mixture.
LĔAV′EN (lĕv′vn), *v. a.* To ferment; to imbue.
LĒAVEŞ (lēvz), *n.* The plural of leaf.
LĒAV′ĮNGŞ, *n. pl.* Remnant; relics; refuse.
LĔCH′ĘR, *n.* A debaucher; a lewd person.
LĔCH′ĘR-OŬS, *a.* Provoking lust; lewd; lustful.
LĔCH′ĘR-Y, *n.* Lewdness; lust; lasciviousness.
LĔC′TĮON, *n.* A reading; a variety in copies.
LĔCT′ŲRE (lĕkt′yụr), *n.* A discourse; a reproof.
LĔCT′ŲRE (lĕkt′yụr), *v. a.* To instruct; reprove.
LĔCT′ŲRE (lĕkt′yụr), *v. n.* To deliver lectures.
LĔCT′ŲR-ĘR (lĕkt′yụr-ẹr), *n.* One who lectures.
LĔCT′ŲRE-SHĮP, *n.* The office of a lecturer.
LĔD, *imp. t.* & *pp.* from *lead.* [of rock.
LĔDĢE, *n.* A row; a layer; a stratum; a ridge
LĔDĢ′ĘR, *n.* A merchant's account-book.
LĒĒ, *a.* Noting, or belonging to, the side oppo-
 site to the wind, as of a vessel.
LĒĒ, *n.* The side opposite to the wind.
LĒĒCH, *n.* A small bloodsucker :—a physician.
LĒĒK, *n.* A plant with a bulbous root.
LĒĒR, *n.* An oblique view or cast of the eye.
LĒĒR, *v. n.* To look obliquely; to look archly.
LĒĒR′ĮNG-LY, *ad.* With a kind of arch smile.
LĒĒŞ, *n. pl.* Dregs; sediment. [blows.
LĒĒ′-SHŌRE, *n.* The shore on which the wind
LĒĒT, *n.* A law-day; a court of jurisdiction.
LĒĒ′TĪDE, *n.* A tide running with the wind.
‖LĒĒ′WĀRD (lē′wụrd *or* lū′ụrd), *n.* Lee side.
‖LĒĒ′WĄRD, *ad.* From the wind; towards the lee.
LĒĒ′WĀY, *n.* Deviation by drifting to leeward.
LĔFT, *imp. t.* & *pp.* from *leave.*
LĔFT, *a.* Not right; sinistrous. [lucky.
LĔFT′-HĂND-ĘD, *a.* Using the left hand; un-
LĔG, *n.* The limb which one stands on.
LĔG′A-CY, *n.* A bequest or gift made by will.
LĒ′GĄL, *a.* Authorized by law; lawful.
LĘ-GĂL′Į-TY, LĒ′GĄL-NĔSS, *n.* Lawfulness.
LĒ′GĄL-ĪZE, *v. a.* To authorize; to make lawful.
LĒ′GĄL-LY, *ad.* Lawfully; according to law.
LĔG′A-TĄ-RY, *n.* One who has a legacy left.
LĔG′ATE, *n.* A deputy; an ambassador.
LĔG-A-TĒĒ′, *n.* One who has a legacy left him.
LĔG′A-TĪNE, *a.* Belonging to a legate.
LĘ-GĀ′TĮON, *n.* A deputation; an embassy.
LĘ-GĀ′TŌ. (*Mus.*) Smooth and gliding.
LĔG-A-TŌR′, *n.* One who leaves legacies. [ble.
LĒ′ĢEND *or* LĔĢ′END, *n.* A chronicle; a fa-
LĔĢ′ĘN-DA-RY, *a.* Fabulous; relating to legends.
LĔĢ′ĘN-DA-RY, *n.* A book or relator of legends.
LĔĢ′ĘR, *n.* A book of accounts. See LEDGER.
LĔĢ-ĘR-DĘ-MĀIN′, *n.* Sleight of hand; a juggle.
LĔĢ′ĢIN, LĔĢ′ĢĮNG, *n.* A covering for the leg.
LĔĢ-Į-BĬL′Į-TY, *n.* Capability of being read.
LĔĢ′Į-BLE, *a.* Capable of being read; apparent.
LĔĢ′Į-BLE-NĔSS, *n.* Quality of being legible.
LĔĢ′Į-BLY, *ad.* In a legible manner. [number.
LĒ′ĢION (lē′jụn), *n.* A body of soldiers :—a great
LĒ′ĢION-A-RY (lē′jụn-a-re), *a.* Relating to a le-
LĔĢ′ĮS-LĀTE, *v. n.* To make or enact laws.[gion.

LĔĢ-ĬS-LĀ′TĬǪN, n. The act of legislating; the making or enacting of laws.
LĔĢ′ĬS-LĀ-TĬVE, a. Giving laws; lawgiving.
LĔĢ′ĬS-LĀ-TǪR, n. One who makes laws.
LĔĢ′ĬS-LĀT-ŲRE (lĕd′jis-lāt-yŭr), n. The power or body that makes laws for a state.
LĘ-ĢĬT′Ĭ-MA-CY, n. Lawful birth; genuineness.
LĘ-ĢĬT′Ĭ-MĀTE, a. Born in marriage; lawful.
LĘ-ĢĬT′Ĭ-MĀTE, v. a. To make legitimate or lawful; to legalize. [genuinely.
LĘ-ĢĬT′Ĭ-MĀTE-LY, ad. Lawfully; legally;
LĘ-ĢĬT′Ĭ-MĀTE-NĔSS, n. Legality; lawfulness.
LĘ-ĢĬT-Ĭ-MĀ′TĬǪN, n. The act of legitimating.
LĔĢ′ŲME, LĘ-GŪ′MĔN, n. A pod:—pulse.
LĘ-GŪ′MĬ-NOŬS, a. Belonging to pulse.
‖LĒIṢ′ŲRE (lē′zhŭr or lĕzh′ŭr), n. Freedom from business or employment; vacancy.
‖LĒIṢ′ŲRE (lē′zhŭr), a. Convenient; unemployed; not occupied. [liberate.
‖LĒIṢ′ŲRE-LY (lē′zhŭr-lę), a. Not hasty; de-
‖LĒIṢ′ŲRE-LY (lē′zhŭr-lę), ad. At leisure.
LĔM′MA, n. A proposition previously assumed.
LĔM′ǪN, n. The fruit of the lemon-tree.
LĔM-ǪN-ĀDE′, n. Water, sugar, and lemon-juice.
LĔND, v. a. [imp. t. & pp. lent.] To afford or supply on condition of return or repayment.
LĔND′ĔR, n. One who lends any thing.
LĔNGTH, n. Extent from end to end; extension.
LĔNGTH′EN (lĕng′thn), v. a. & n. To extend; to protract; to prolong; to make or grow longer.
LĔNGTH′WĪṢE, ad. In direction of the length.
LĒ′NĬ-ĘNT, a. Assuasive; softening; mild.
LĔN′Ĭ-TĬVE, a. Assuasive; emollient. [tive.
LĔN′Ĭ-TĬVE, n. Any thing to ease pain; a pallia-
LĔN′Ĭ-TY, n. Mildness; mercy; tenderness.
LĔNṢ, n.; pl. LĔN′ṢEṢ. A piece of glass or transparent substance, so formed as to change the direction of the rays of light passing through
LĔNT, imp. t. & pp. from lend. [it.
LĔNT, n. The quadragesimal fast of 40 days.
LĔNT′EN (lĕnt′tn), a. Relating to Lent; meagre.
LĘN-TĬC′Ų-LAR, a. Doubly convex; lentiform.
LĔN′TĬ-FŌRM, a. Having the form of a lens.
LĔN′TĬL, n. A sort of pulse allied to the vetch.
LĔN′TĬSK, n. The mastic-tree; a fragrant wood.
LĔN′TǬR, n. [L.] Tenacity; vicosity; slowness.
LĔN′TOŬS, a. Viscous; viscid; tenacious. [diac.
LĒ′Ō, n. [L.] The Lion, the fifth sign of the zo-
LĒ′Ǫ-NĪNE, a. Belonging to a lion; lion-like.
LĔOP′ARD (lĕp′pard), n. A spotted beast of prey.
LĔP′ĔR, n. One infected with a leprosy.
LĔP′Ǫ-RĪNE, a. Belonging to, or like, a hare.
LĔP′RǬ-SY, n. A loathsome cutaneous disease.
LĔP′ROŬS, a. Infected with a leprosy.
LĔP′ROŬS-NĔSS, n. The state of being leprous.
LĔSS, a. The comparative of little; smaller.
LĔSS, ad. In a smaller or lower degree.
LĔS-SEĒ′, n. A person to whom a lease is given.
LĔSS′EN (lĕs′sn), v. a. & n. To make or grow
LĔSS′ĔR, a. Smaller; a corruption of less. [less.
LĔS′SǬN (lĕs′sn), n. A task to learn or read.
LĔS′SǬR, n. One who leases;—correlative of
LĔST, ad. That not; for fear that. [lessee.
LĔT, v. a. [imp. t. & pp. let.] To allow; to suffer; to permit; to lease; to put out to hire.
LĔT, v. a. To hinder; to obstruct. [Obs.]
LĔT, n. A hinderance; an obstacle; obstruction.
LĒ′THAL, a. Deadly; mortal; fatal.

LĘ-THÄR′ĢĬC, a. Sleepy by disease; drowsy.
LĔTH′AR-ĢY, n. A morbid drowsiness; sleepiness; torpor. [livion.
LĒ′THE, n. [Gr.] Oblivion; a draught of ob-
LĘ-THĒ′AN, a. Oblivious; causing oblivion.
LĘ-THĬF′ĔR-OŬS, a. Deadly; bringing death.
LĔT′TĘR, n. An alphabetic character:—a written message:—a printing type:—one who lets.
LĔT′TĘR, v. a. To stamp or mark with letters.
LĔT′TĘRED (lĕt′terd), a. Educated; learned.
LĔT′TĘR-FOŬND′ĘR, n. One who casts types.
LĔT′TĘR-PRĔSS, n. Print from types. [dition.
LĔT′TĘRṢ, n. pl. Learning; literature; eru-
LĔT′TUCE (lĕt′tis), n. A plant used for salad.
LĘ-VĂNT′, n. Eastern coasts of the Mediterra-
LĘ-VĂNT′ĔR, n. A strong easterly wind. [nean.
‖LĘ-VĂN′TĬNE or LĔV′AN-TĪNE, a. Of the le-
‖LĘ-VĂN′TĬNE, n. A kind of silk stuff. [vant.
LĔV′ĘE, n. Ceremonious visit or assemblage; a party or assembly:—an embankment.
LĔV′ĘL, a. Even; flat; smooth; plain; equal.
LĔV′ĘL, v. a. To make even; to lay flat; to aim.
LĔV′ĘL, v. n. To aim; to direct the view.
LĔV′ĘL, n. A plane; a standard; an instrument:
LĔV′ĘL-LĘR, n. One who levels. [—equality.
LĔV′ĘL-LĬNG, n. Art of finding a horizontal line.
LĔV′ĘL-NĔSS, n. Evenness; equality of surface.
LĔV′EN (lĕv′vn), n. Ferment. See LEAVEN.
LĒ′VĘR, n. A mechanical power or instrument.
LĔV′ĘR-ĘT, n. A hare in the first year.
LĔV′Ĭ-A-BLE, a. Capable of being levied. [Job.
LĘ-VĪ′A-THAN, n. A water animal mentioned in
LĔV′Ĭ-GĀTE, v. a. To polish; to plane; to pulver-
LĔV-Ĭ-GĀ′TĬǪN, n. The act of levigating. [ize.
LĒ′VĪTE, n. One of the tribe of Levi; a priest.
LĘ-VĬT′Ĭ-CAL, a. Relating to the Levites; priest-
LĘ-VĬT′Ĭ-CŬS, n. The third book of Moses. [ly.
LĔV′Ĭ-TY, n. Lightness; inconstancy; vanity.
LĔV′Y, v. a. To raise; to collect; to impose.
LĔV′Y, n. The act of raising money or men.
LEWD (lūd), a. Wanton; dissolute; libidinous.
LEWD′LY (lūd′lę), ad. Wantonly; lustfully.
LEWD′NĔSS, n. Lustful licentiousness. [aries.
LĔX-Ĭ-CŌG′RA-PHĘR, n. A writer of diction-
LĔX-Ĭ-CǪ-GRĂPH′Ĭ-CAL, a. Relating to, or partaking of, lexicography. [aries.
LĔX-Ĭ-CŌG′RA-PHY, n. The writing of diction-
LĔX′Ĭ-CǑN, n. A dictionary; a word-book.
LĔY (lē), n. A field. See LEA and LIE.
LĪ-A-BĬL′Ĭ-TY, n. The state of being liable.
LĪ′A-BLE, a. Obnoxious; not exempt; subject.
LĪ′A-BLE-NĔSS, n. The state of being liable.
LĪ′AR, n. One who tells lies or falsehoods.
LĪ-BĀ′TĬǪN, n. An offering made of wine, &c.
LĪ′BĘL, n. Defamation; a malicious satire.
LĪ′BĘL, v. a. To defame maliciously; to lampoon.
LĪ′BĘL-LĘR, n. One who libels or defames.
LĪ′BĘL-LOŬS, a. Defamatory; abusive.
LĬB′ĘR-AL, a. Generous; bountiful; free; candid.
LĬB′ĘR-ĂL′Ĭ-TY, n. Bounty; generosity; candor.
LĬB′ĘR-AL-ĪZE, v. a. To make liberal, catholic.
LĬB′ĘR-AL-LY, ad. Bountifully; largely; freely.
LĬB′ĘR-ĀTE, v. a. To free; to set free. [ance.
LĬB-ĘR-Ā′TĬǪN, n. Act of setting free; deliver-
LĬB′ĘR-Ā-TǬR, n. One who liberates. [rake.
LĬB′ĘR-TĪNE, n. One who lives dissolutely; a
LĬB′ĘR-TĪNE, a. Lax in morals; licentious; dissolute; immoral.

MÎEN, SÏR; MÔVE, NÖR, SǑN; BŬLL, BÜR, RÛLE.—Ç, Ǥ, soft; Ƈ, Ǥ, hard; Ṣ as Z; Ӿ as gz; ꞭHIS.

LĬB′ER-TĬN-ĬŞM, n. Licentiousness; dissoluteness; debauchery. [leave.
LĬB′ER-TỴ, n. Freedom; privilege; permission;
LĬ-BĬD′Ĭ-NOŬS, a. Lewd; lustful; licentious.
LĬ-BĬD′Ĭ-NOŬS-LỴ, ad. Lewdly; lustfully.
LĪ′BRẠ, n. [L.] Balance, 7th sign in the zodiac.
LĪ-BRĀ′RĬ-ẠN, n. One who has care of a library.
LĪ-BRĀ′RĬ-ẠN-SHĬP, n. The office of a librarian.
LĪ′BRẠ-RỴ, n. Collection of books; a book-room.
LĪ′BRĀTE, v. a. To poise; to hold in equipoise.
LĪ-BRĀ′TĬQN, n. The act of balancing; equipoise.
LĪ′BLẠ-TQ-RỴ, a. Balancing; playing or moving
LĪCE, n. The plural of louse. [like a balance.
LĬ′CẸNSE, n. Permission; liberty; excess.
LĬ′CẸNSE, v. a. To permit by a legal grant.
LĬ′CẸN-SẸR, n. A granter of permission.
LĬ-CĔN′TĬ-ẠTE (lĬ-sĕn′shẹ-ạt), n. One who has
a license to practise any profession. [dissolute.
LĬ-CĔN′TIOŲS (lĬ-sĕn′shŭs), a. Unrestrained;
LĬ-CĔN′TIOŲS-LỴ (-sĕn′shŭs-lẹ), ad. Disorderly.
LĬ-CĔN′TIOŲS-NĔSS (-sĕn′shŭs-nĕs), n. Excess.
LĪ′ℭHẸN, n. A plant of cellular structure.
LĬCK, v. a. To pass the tongue over; to lap.
LĬCK, n. A stroke with the tongue; a blow.
LĬCK′ER-ĬSH, a. Nice; fastidious:—greedy.
LĬC′Q-RĪCE, n. A plant; a sweet root.
LĬC′TQR, n. [L.] An officer among the Romans.
LĬD, n. A cover for a pan, box, &c. [line salt.
LĪE, or LỸE, n. Water impregnated with alka-
LĪE (lī), n. A criminal falsehood; a fiction.
LĪE (lī), v. n. To utter a criminal falsehood.
LĪE (lī), v. n. [imp. t. lay; pp. lain.] To rest
horizontally; to rest; to remain; to abide.
LIĒF (lĕf), ad. Willingly; gladly; freely.
LIĒGE (lēj), a. Bound by feudal tenure.; subject.
LIĒGE (lēj), n. A sovereign; a superior lord.
LIĒGE′MẠN (lēj′mạn), n. A subject; a vassal.
LĬ′ẸN, n. A legal claim on property. [rhœa.
LĬ′ẸN-TĔR-Ỵ, n. A particular kind of diar-
LĪ′ẸR, n. One that rests or lies down.
LIEŪ (lū), n. Place; room: (used with in.)
‖LIEU-TĔN′ĂN-CỴ, n. The office of a lieutenant.
▸‖LIEU-TĔN′ẠNT (lẹv-tĕn′ạnt or lū-tĕn′ạnt), n.
. A deputy; an officer second in rank.
LĪFE, n.; pl. LĪVEŞ. Vitality; animation; existence; spirit; vivacity; animal being.
LĪFE′-BLOOD (līf′blŭd), n. The vital blood.
LĪFE′-BŌAT (līf′bōt), n. A boat to preserve life.
LĪFE′-ẸS-TĀTE′, n. An estate held during life.
LĪFE′-ℊĬV-ĬNG, a. Imparting life; invigorating.
LĪFE′-GUĀRD (līf′gärd), n. The guard of a king,
LĪFE′LẸSS, a. Dead; deprived of life; dull. [&c.
LĪFE′TĪME, n. Continuance or duration of life.
LĬFT, v. a. To raise; to elevate; to exalt.
LĬFT, n. The act of lifting; effort; weight lifted.
LĬG′Ạ-MĔNT, n. A substance uniting bones.
LĬ-GĀ′TĬQN, n. The act of binding; confinement.
LĬG′Ạ-TŪRE, n. A bandage; a band; a cord.
LĪGHT (līt), n. The ethereal medium of sight;
illumination; knowledge:—a taper, &c.
LĪGHT (līt), a. Not heavy; active; slight; trifling; gay; airy:—bright; clear; not dark.
LĪGHT (līt), v. a. [imp. t. & pp. lighted; sometimes lit.] To kindle; to fill with light.
LĪGHT (līt), v. n. To fall; to dismount; to rest.
LĪGHT′ĀRMED (līt′ärmd), a. Not heavily armed.
LĪGHT′EN (lī′tn), v. n. To flash; to shine.
LĪGHT′EN (lī′tn), v. a. To illuminate:—to ease.
LĪGHT′ER (līt′er), n. One that lights; a boat.
LĪGHT′ER-MĂN, n. One who manages a lighter.
LĪGHT′-FĬN-ℊERED (līt′fĭng-ℊerd),a. Thievish.
LĪGHT′-HĔAD-ẸD (līt′hĕd-ẹd), a. Thoughtless.
LĪGHT′-HĔART-ẸD (līt′härt-ẹd), a. Gay; merry.
LĪGHT′-HŌŪSE (līt′hoŭs), n. A building with
a light or lights for guiding mariners.
LĪGHT′LỴ (līt′lẹ), ad. In a light manner.
LĪGHT′-MĪND-ẸD (līt′mīnd-ẹd), a. Unsteady.
LĪGHT′NẸSS (līt′nẹs), n. Levity; brightness.
LĪGHT′NĬNG (līt′nĭng), n. The electric flash
that attends thunder. [mal.
LĪGHTS (līts), n. pl. The lungs, as of an ani-
LĪGHT′SQME (līt′sŭm), a. Luminous; gay; airy.
LĬG′NẸ-OŬS, a. Made of wood; wooden.
LĬG′NĬ-FŌRM, a. Resembling wood. [wood.
LĬG′NŬM-VĪ′TÆ, n. [L.] A very hard and heavy
LĪ′GŪRE or LĬG′ŪRE, n. A precious stone.
LĪKE, a. Resembling; similar:—likely.
LĪKE, n. Similitude; a thing similar.
LĪKE, ad. In the same manner; likely.
LĪKE, v. a. To be pleased with; to approve.
LĪKE, v. n. To be pleased; to choose; to list.
LĪKE′LĬ-HOOD(līk′lẹ-hůd),n.Probability;show.
LĪKE′LĬ-NĔSS, n. The quality of being likely.
LĪKE′LỴ, a. Probable; such as may please.
LĪKE′LỴ, ad. Probably; with probability.
LĪ′KEN (lī′kn), v. a. To compare. [an image.
LĪKE′NẸSS, n. Resemblance; similitude; form;
LĪKE′WĬŞE, ad. In like manner; also; too.
LĬK′ĬNG, n. Inclination; desire; delight in.
LĪ′LẠC, n. An ornamental, deciduous shrub,
bearing purple or white flowers.
LĬL-Ĭ-Ā′CEOŲS (lĬl-ẹ-ā′shŭs), a. Like a lily.
LĬL′ĬED (lĬl′jd), a. Embellished with lilies.
LĬL′Ỵ (lĬl′ẹ), n. A plant and its flower.
LĪ′MẠ-TŪRE, n. Particles rubbed off by a file.
LĬMB (lĭm), n. A member:—a branch:—border.
LĬMB (lĭm), v. a. To tear; to dismember.
LĬM′BẸC, v. a. To strain. — n. A still; alembic.
LĬMBED (lĭmd), a. Formed with regard to limbs.
LĬM′BER, a. Flexible; easily bent; pliant.
LĬM′BER-NĔSS, n. Flexibility; pliancy. [limbs.
LĬMB′LẸSS, a. Wanting limbs; deprived of
LĬM′BŌ, n. A region bordering on hell; a prison.
LĪME, n. A viscous substance:—calcareous
earth:—the linden tree:—a kind of fruit.
LĪME, v. a. To insnare; to smear with lime.
LĪME′KĬLN (līm′kĬl), n. A furnace for lime.
LĪME′STONE, n. The stone of which lime is
made; carbonate of lime.
LĬM′ĬT, n. A bound; a border; utmost reach.
LĬM′ĬT, v. a. To confine; to restrain; to circum-
LĬM′ĬT-Ạ-BLE, a. That may be limited. [scribe.
LĬM′ĬT-Ạ-RỴ, a. Placed at the boundaries.
LĬM-Ĭ-TĀ′TĬQN, n. A restriction; a confinement.
LĬMN (lĭm), v. a. To draw; to plant.
LĬM′NER, n. A painter; a picture-maker.
LĬM′NĬNG, n. The art of painting in water-colors.
LĪ′MOŲS, a. Muddy; slimy; miry; boggy.
LĬMP, v. n. To halt; to walk lamely.
LĬMP, n. Halt in walking; the act of limping.
LĬMP′ER, n. One who limps in his walking.
LĬM′PET, n. A kind of mollusk shell-fish.
LĬM′PĬD, a. Clear; pure; transparent.
LĬM′PĬD-NĔSS, n. Clearness; purity. [lime.
LĪ′MỴ, a. Viscous; glutinous; containing or like
LĬN′Ạ-MĔNT, n. A tent made of lint for wounds.

LĬNCH'PĬN, *n.* The pin of an axle-tree.
LĬN'DĘN, *n.* A kind of tree ; the lime-tree.
LĪNE, *n.* A string ; delineation ; a verse ; a row ; a course ; a business ; a trench ; a limit ; the equator ; progeny :—one 10th or 12th of an inch.
LĪNE, *v. a.* To guard within ; to cover, double.
LĬN'Ę-AĢE, *n.* Race ; progeny ; family ; genealogy.
LĬN'E-AL, *a.* Descending in a line ; hereditary.
LĬN'E-AL-LỸ, *ad.* In a direct line of descent.
LĬN'E-A-MĔNT, *n.* A feature ; a form ; an outline.
LĬN'E-AR, *a.* Composed of lines ; having lines.
LĬN-E-Ā'TIǪN, *n.* A draught of a line or lines.
LĬN'ĘN, *n.* A stuff or cloth made of flax.
LĬN'ĘN, *a.* Made of linen ; resembling linen.
LĬN'ĘN-DRĀ'PĘR, *n.* One who deals in linen.
LĬNG, *n.* A grass :—a kind of sea-fish. [lay.
LĬN'ĢĘR (lǐng'ğẹr), *v. n.* To remain long ; to de-
LĬN'ĢĘT, *n.* A small mass of metal ; an ingot.
LĬN-GUA-DĔN'TAL (lǐng-gwạ-dĕn'tạl), *a.* Ut-tered by the joint action of the tongue and teeth.
LĬN'GUAL, *a.* Pertaining to the tongue. [guages.
LĬN'GUĬST (lǐng'gwĭst), *n.* A man skilful in lan-
LĬN'I-MĔNT, *n.* Ointment ; balsam ; unguent.
LĪN'ĮNG, *n.* The inner covering of any thing.
LĬNK, *n.* A single ring of a chain :—a torch.
LĬNK, *v. a.* To complicate ; to unite ; to join.
LĬNK'BŎỸ, *n.* A boy that carries a link or torch.
LĬN'NĘT, *n.* A small singing bird, of the finch
LĬN'SĒED, *n.* The seed of flax. [family.
LĬN-SEỸ-WOOL'SEỸ (lǐn'sẹ-wûl'sẹ), *n.* Stuff made of linen and wool mixed :—*a.* vile ; mean.
LĬNT, *n.* Flax ; linen scraped into soft substance.
LĬN'TĘL, *n.* The upper part of a door-frame.
LĬNT'STŎCK, *n.* A staff with a match at the end.
LĪ'ǪN, *n.* A fierce animal ; a sign in the zodiac.
LĪ'ǪN-ĔSS, *n.* A she-lion ; female of the lion.
LĬP, *n.* The border of the mouth :—the edge.
LĬ-PŎTH'Ỹ-MỸ, *n.* A swoon ; a fainting fit ;
LĬPPED (lǐpt), *a.* Having lips. [syncope.
LĬP'PĬ-TŪDE, *n.* Blearedness of eyes. [melted.
LĬQ'UA-BLE (lǐk'wạ-bl), *a.* Capable of being
LĬQ'UĀTE (lǐk'wāt), *v. n.* To melt ; to liquefy.
LĬ-QUĀ'TIǪN (lẹ-kwā'shụn), *n.* Act of melting.
LĬQ-UE-FĂC'TIǪN (lǐk-wẹ-făk'shụn), *n.* The act or process of melting. [able.
LĬQ'UE-FĪ-A-BLE (lǐk'wẹ-fī-ạ-bl), *a.* Dissolv-
LĬQ'UE-FỸ (lǐk'wẹ-fī), *v. a.* To melt ; to dissolve.
LĬQ'UE-FỸ (lǐk'wẹ-fī), *v. n.* To grow liquid.
LĬ-QUĔS'CĘN-CỸ, *n.* Aptness to melt or become
LĬ-QUĔS'CĘNT (-kwĕs'sẹnt), *a.* Melting. [liquid.
LĬQ'UĮD (lǐk'wĭd), *a.* Not solid ; fluid ; flowing.
LĬQ'UĮD (lǐk'wĭd), *n.* Liquid substance ; a fluid : —a kind of letter. [lessen.
LĬQ'UĮ-DĀTE (lǐk'wẹ-dāt), *v. a.* To clear ; to
LĬQ-UĮ-DĀ'TIǪN, *n.* The act of lessening debts.
LĬ-QUĬD'Į-TỸ, *n.* The state of being liquid.
LĬQ'UĮD-NĔSS (lǐk'wĭd-nĕs), *n.* Liquidity.
LĬQ'UǪR (lǐk'kụr), *n.* Any liquid ; strong drink.
LĬṢ'BǪN (lĭz'bụn), *n.* A kind of light wine.
LĬSP, *v. n. & a.* To speak with a lisp, like a child.
LĬSP, *n.* A defective speech or utterance.
LĬST, *n.* A catalogue ; a strip of cloth ; a border.
LĬST, *v. n.* To choose ; to desire ; to be disposed.
LĬST, *v. a.* To enlist ; to enroll ; to listen.
LĬS'TĘL, *n.* (*Arch.*) A narrow moulding ; a fillet.
LĬS'TEN (lĭs'sn), *v. n.* To hearken ; to attend.
LĬS'TEN-ER (lĭs'sn-ẹr), *n.* One that hearkens.
LĬST'LĘSS, *a.* Indifferent ; careless ; heedless.

LĬST'LĘSS-LỸ, *ad.* Carelessly ; without attention.
LĬST'LĘSS-NĔSS, *n.* Inattention ; want of desire.
LĬSTS, *n. pl.* A place enclosed for combats, &c.
LĬT'A-NỸ, *n.* A form of supplicatory prayer.
LĬT'ĘR-AL, *a.* According to the letter ; real.
LĬT'ĘR-AL-LỸ, *ad.* Not figuratively ; really.
LĬT'ĘR-A-RỸ, *a.* Relating to letters or literature.
LĬT'ĘR-ATE, *a.* Learned ; skilled in letters.
LĬT-ĘR-Ā'TĪ, *n. pl.* [L.] The learned ; men of learning ; literary persons.
LĬT-ĘR-Ā'TĬM, *ad.* [L.] Letter by letter ; literally.
LĬT'ĘR-A-TURE, *n.* Learning ; skill in letters.
LĬTH'ARĢE, *n.* Fused yellow protoxide of lead.
LĪTHE, *a.* Limber ; flexible ; soft ; pliant.
LĪTHE'NĘSS, *n.* Limberness ; flexibility.
LĪTHE'SǪME (lĭth'sụm), *a.* Pliant ; limber ; lithe.
LĬTH'Ǫ-GRĂPH, *n.* A lithographic engraving.
LĬTH'Ǫ-GRĂPH, *v. a.* To draw and etch on stone.
LĬ-THŎG'RA-PHĘR, *n.* One who practises li-thography ; an engraver on stone.
LĬTH-Ǫ-GRĂPH'ĬC, *a.* Relating to lithography.
LĬ-THŎG'RA-PHỸ, *n.* The art of engraving upon stone. [omy.
LĬ-THŎT'Ǫ-MĬST, *n.* One who performs lithot-
LĬ-THŎT'Ǫ-MỸ, *n.* Art of cutting for the stone.
LĬT'Į-GANT, *n.* One engaged in a suit of law.
LĬT'Į-GANT, *a.* Engaged in a juridical contest.
LĬT'Į-GĀTE, *v. a. & n.* To contest in law ; to dispute a case at law. [law.
LĬT-Į-GĀ'TIǪN, *n.* Judicial contest ; a suit of
LĬ-TĬĢ'IOŲS (lẹ-tĭd'jụs), *a.* Inclined to litigation.
LĬ-TĬĢ'IOŲS-LỸ (lẹ-tĭd'jụs-lẹ), *ad.* Wranglingly.
LĬ-TĬĢ'IOŲS-NĔSS (lẹ-tĭd'jụs-nĕs), *n.* Wrangling.
LĬT'TĘR, *n.* A carriage ; straw ; brood of pigs, &c.
LĬT'TĘR, *v. a.* To bring forth ; to scatter about.
LĬT'TLE, *a.* [*comp.* less *and* lesser ; *superl.* least.] Small ; diminutive ; not great ; not many.
LĬT'TLE, *n.* A slight affair ; not much.
LĬT'TLE, *ad.* In a small degree ; not much. [ness.
LĬT'TLE-NĔSS, *n.* Smallness of bulk :—mean-
LĬT'UR-ĢỸ, *n.* A formulary of public devotions.
LĬVE (lĭv), *v. n.* To be alive ; to dwell ; to feed.
LĪVE, *a.* Quick ; not dead ; active ; vivid.
LĪVE'LĮ-HOOD (līv'lẹ-hûd), *n.* Maintenance.
LĪVE'LĮ-NĔSS, *n.* Appearance of life ; vivacity.
LĪVE'LŎNG (lĭv'-), *a.* Tedious ; long in passing.
LĪVE'LỸ, *a.* Brisk ; vigorous ; sprightly ; gay.
LĬV'ĘR, *n.* One who lives :—one of the entrails.
LĬV'ĘR-CŎL'ǪR, *n.* Very dark red ; reddish-brown. [nunculaceous plant.
LĬV'ĘR-WORT (lĭv'ẹr-würt), *n.* A kind of ra-
LĬV'ĘR-Ỹ, *n.* A writ for possession :—a dress.
LĬV'ĘR-Ỹ, *v. a.* To clothe in a livery or dress.
LĬV'ĘR-Ỹ-MĂN, *n.* One who wears a livery.
LĬV'ĘR-Ỹ-STĀ'BLE, *n.* A stable where horses
LĬVEṢ (līvz), *n.* The plural of *life*. [are let.
LĬV'ĬD, *a.* Discolored ; black and blue ; lead-color.
LĬ-VĬD'Į-TỸ, LĬV'ĬD-NĔSS, *n.* Discoloration.
LĬV'ĬNG, *n.* Support ; maintenance ; livelihood.
LĪ'VRE (lī'vụr), *n.* [Fr.] A French coin.
LĬX-ĬV'Į-AL, *a.* Impregnated with lixivium.
LĬX-ĬV'Į-ŬM, *n.* [L.] Lie made of ashes, water, &c.
LĬZ'ARD, *n.* An animal resembling a serpent.
LŌ, *int.* Look ! see ! behold !
LŌACH (lōch), *n.* A small pale-yellow fish.
LŌAD (lōd), *n.* A burden ; a freight ; pressure.
LŌAD (lōd), *v. a.* [*imp. t.* loaded ; *pp.* loaded *or* laden.] To burden ; to freight ; to charge.

LŌAD'STÄR, *n.* The pole-star; the cynosure.
LŌAD'STŌNE (lŏd'stōn), *n.* Natural magnet.
LŌAF (lōf), *n.* ; pl. LŌAVEŞ. A mass of bread,&c.
LŌAM (lōm), *n.* Unctuous, rich earth; marl.
LŌAM'Y (lō'mẹ), *a.* Marly; smeared with loam.
LŌAN (lōn), *n.* Any thing lent:—act of lending.
LŌATH (lōth), *a.* Unwilling; disliking; reluctant.
LŌAᵺHE (lōth), *v. a. & n.* To hate; to nauseate.
LŌATH'FŮL (lōth'fůl), *a.* Hating; abhorring:—
  odious; hated; abhorred. [sion.
LŌAᵺH'ING, *n.* Disgust; disinclination; aver-
LOATH'NẸSS (lōth'nẹs), *n.* Unwillingness.
LŌAᵺH'SǪME (lōth'sųm), *a.* Disgusting; detes-
  table; offensive; foul. [gust.
LŌAᵺH'SǪME-NĔSS, *n.* Quality of raising dis-
LŌAVEŞ (lōvz), *n.* The plural of *loaf.*
LŎB, *n.* A clumsy person:—a worm:—a prison.
LŎB'BY, *n.* An opening before a room; small
LŌBE, *n.* Division or part of the lungs, &c. [hall.
LŎB'LŎL-LY, *n.* A kind of seafaring dish; a tree.
LŎB'STẸR, *n.* A well-known crustaceous fish.
LŌ'CĄL, *a.* Relating to, or being of, a place.
LǪ-CĂL'Ị-TY, *n.* Existence in place; position.
LŌ'CĄL-LY, *ad.* With respect to place.
LŌ'CĀTE, *v. a.* To place; to fix the place of.
LǪ-CĀ'TIǪN, *n.* Situation; the act of placing.
LŎℭH (lŏk), *n.* A lake or arm of the sea.
LOℭH, *or* LOOℭH, *n.* A medicine. [*Scotland.*]
LŎCK, *n.* An instrument to fasten doors, &c. :—
  part of a gun:—an enclosure in a canal to con-
  fine the water:—a tuft of hair. [close.
LŎCK, *v. a.* To shut or fasten with locks; to
LŎCK'ĄGE, *n.* Construction of locks. [drawer.
LŎCK'ẸR, *n.* Any thing closed with a lock; a
LŎCK'ẸT, *n.* A small lock; a catch or spring.
LŎCK'RĄM, *n.* A sort of coarse cloth. [locks.
LŎCK'SMĬTH, *n.* A man who makes and mends
LŌ-CǪ-MŌ'TIǪN, *n.* The power of changing place.
LŌ-CǪ-MŌ'TIVE, *a.* Able to change place.
LŌ'CŲST, *n.* A devouring insect :—a kind of tree.
LŌDE'STÄR, *n.* The pole-star. See LOADSTAR.
LŌDE'STŌNE, *n.* The magnet. See LOADSTONE.
LŎDGE, *v. a.* To afford a lodging; to place; to fix.
LŎDGE, *v. n.* To reside; to keep residence.
LŎDGE, *n.* A small house; a tenement; a society.
LŎDG'ẸR, *n.* One who lives at board, or lodges.
LŎDG'ING, *n.* A temporary abode; rooms hired.
LŎDGE'MẸNT, *n.* Collocation:—an encampment.
LŎFT, *n.* A floor; a high room or place.
LŎF'TĮ-LY, *ad.* On high; proudly; haughtily.
LŎF'TĮ-NÉSS, *n.* Elevation; sublimity; pride.
LŎF'TY, *a.* High; elevated; sublime; haughty.
LŎG, *n.* A bulky piece of wood :—a machine to
  measure the course of a ship at sea.
LŎG'Ą-RĬᵺHMS, *n. pl.* A series of numbers in
  arithmetical progression, corresponding to an-
  other series in geometrical progression. [way.
LŎG'-BOOK (lŏg'bůk), *n.* Register of a ship's
LŎG'ℊẸR-HĔAD, *n.* A dolt; a thickskull.
LŎGℊ'IC, *n.* The art of reasoning; dialectics.
LŎGℊ'Ị-CĄL, *a.* Pertaining to, or skilled in, logic.
LŎGℊ'Ị-CĄL-LY, *ad.* According to the laws of logic.
LǪ-ℊI''CIĄN (-jĭsh'ạn), *n.* A man versed in logic.
LŎG'-LĪNE, *n.* A line to measure a ship's way.
LǪ-GŌG'RĄ-PHY, *n.* A mode of printing.
LǪ-GŎM'Ą-ℭHĬST, *n.* A disputer about words.
LǪ-GŎM'Ą-ℭHY, *n.* A contention about words.
LŎG'WOOD (-wůd), *n.* A wood used in dyeing.

LŎÏN, *n.* The back of an animal; the reins.
LŎÏ'TẸR, *v. n. & a.* To linger; to be dilatory; to
LŎÏ'TẸR-ẸR, *n.* A lingerer; an idler. [idle.
LŎLL, *v. n.* To lean idly; to hang out the tongue.
LŌNE, *a.* Solitary; lonely; single; unmarried.
LŌNE'LĮ-NĔSS, *n.* Solitude; want of company.
LŌNE'LY, *a.* Solitary; addicted to solitude.
LŌNE'SǪME (lōn'sum), *a.* Solitary; dismal.
LŌNE'SǪME-LY, *ad.* In a solitary manner.
LŌNE'SǪME-NĔSS, *n.* Quality of being lonesome.
LŎNG, *a.* Not short; having length; extended.
LŎNG, *ad.* To a great extent :—not soon.
LŎNG, *v. n.* To wish or desire earnestly.
LŎN-GĄ-NĬM'Ị-TY, *n.* Forbearance; patience.
LŎNG'BŌAT (-bōt), *n.* The largest boat of a ship.
LŎNGE (lŭnj), *n.* [Fr.] A thrust in fencing.
LǪN-GĔV'Ị-TY, *n.* Length of life; long life.
LǪN-GĔ'VOŲS, *a.* Living long; longlived.
LŎNG'-HĔAD-ẸD, *a.* Having forecast; sagacious.
LǪN-GĬM'Ą-NOŬS, *a.* Having long hands.
LǪN-GĬM'Ẹ-TRY, *n.* Art of measuring distances.
LŎNG'ING, *n.* Earnest desire; continual wish.
LŎN'GỊ-TŪDE, *n.* Length :—distance of any part
  of the earth, east or west, from a meridian.
LŎN-GĬ-TŪ'DĮ-NĄL, *a.* Relating to longitude.
LŎNG'-LĪVED (lŏng'līvd), *a.* Having long life.
LŎNG-PRĬM'ẸR, *n.* A kind of printing type.
LŎNG-SŮF'FẸR-ĬNG, *a.* Patient; not easily pro-
  voked; forbearing. [forbearance.
LŎNG-SŮF'FẸR-ĬNG, *n.* Patience; clemency;
LŎNG-WĬND'ẸD, *a.* Long-breathed; tedious.
LŌÔ, *n.* A kind of game at cards. [game.
LŌÔ, *v. a.* To beat by winning every trick at a
LŌÔ'BY, *n.* A lubber; a clumsy clown. [seem.
LOOK (lůk), *v. n.* To direct the eye; to see; to
LOOK (lůk), *interj.* See! lo! behold! observe.
LOOK (lůk), *n.* Air of the face; mien; aspect.
LOOK'ẸR (lůk'ẹr), *n.* One that looks.
LOOK'ĬNG-GLĂSS (lůk'ĭng-glăs), *n.* A mirror.
LŌÔM, *n.* A frame for weaving cloth.
LŌÔM, *v. n.* To appear large at sea, as a ship.
LŌÔN, *n.* A scoundrel; a rascal :—a sea-fowl.
LŌÔP, *n.* A noose or double in a string or rope.
LŌÔP'HŌLE, *n.* An aperture; a shift; an evasion.
LŌÔSE, *v. a.* To unbind; to relax; to release.
LŌÔSE, *a.* Unbound; untied; not fast; not close;
  wanton; lax; vague; not strict; not rigid.
LŌÔSE'LY, *ad.* Not fast; not firmly; carelessly.
LŌÔS'EN (lô'sn), *v. n. & a.* To make loose;
  to relax :—to part; to separate.
LŌÔSE'NẸSS, *n.* Laxity; irregularity; a flux.
LŎP, *v. a.* To cut off; to bend; to let fall.
LŎP, *n.* That which is cut from trees.
LŎP'PĬNGŞ, *n. pl.* Tops of branches lopped off.
LǪ-QUĀ'CIOŲS (-kwā'shųs), *a.* Talkative; noisy.
LǪ-QUĂ''Ị-TY (-kwăs'se-tẹ), *n.* Too much talk.
LŌRD, *n.* A master; a husband :—a nobleman;
  a baron; a title :—the Supreme Being.
LŌRD, *v. n.* To domineer; to rule despotically.
LŌRD'LĮ-NĔSS, *n.* Dignity; pride; haughtiness.
LŌRD'LĬNG, *n.* A little or diminutive lord.
LŌRD'LY, *a.* Like a lord; haughty; imperious.
LŌRD'SHĬP, *n.* Dominion :—title given to lords.
LŌRE, *n.* Learning; doctrine; instruction.
LŌR'Ị-CĀTE, *v. a.* To plate over; to cover.
LŌR-Ị-CĀ'TIǪN, *n.* Act of loricating; a covering.
LŌR'Ị-MẸR, LŌR'Ị-NẸR, *n.* A bridle-maker.
LŌRN, *a.* Forsaken; lost; lonely; abandoned.

LÔ̩ṢE (lôz), *v. a.* [*imp. t. & pp.* lost.] To forfeit; to suffer loss of; to bewilder; to waste.

LÔ̩ṢE, *v. n.* Not to win; to decline; to fail.

LÔ̩Ṣ'ẸR (lôz'ẹr), *n.* One who loses or forfeits.

LŎSS, *n.* Damage; waste; forfeiture; puzzle.

LŎST, *imp. t. & pp.* from *lose.* [portion.

LŎT, *n.* Fortune; state assigned; chance; a

LŎT, *v. a.* To assign; to set apart; to sort.

LŌTH, *a.* Unwilling; averse. See LOATH.

LŌ'TIǪN (lō'shun), *n.* A medicinal wash.

LŌ'TǪS, LŌ'TŲS, *n.* A kind of plant.

LŎT'TẸR-Y̆,*n.* A distribution of prizes by chance.

LOŬD, *a.* Noisy; high-sounding; clamorous.

LOŬD'LY̆, *ad.* In a loud manner; clamorously.

LOŬD'NẸSS, *n.* Noise; force of sound; clamor.

LOUGH (lŏk), *n.* A lake. [*Ireland.*] [France.

LOUIS D'ŌR' (lô-e-dōr'), *n.* [Fr.] A gold coin of

LOŬNGE, *v. n.* To idle; to live lazily; to laze.

LOŬNG'ẸR, *n.* An idler; a loiterer. [insect.

LOŬṢE, *n.;* pl. LĪCE. A small, wingless, parasitic

LOŬṢ'Ĭ-NẸSS, *n.* State of abounding with lice.

LOŬṢ'Y̆, *a.* Infested with lice:—mean; low.

LOŬT, *n.* A mean, awkward fellow; a bumpkin.

LŎV'AGE, *n.* A deciduous, herbaceous plant.

LŎVE (lŭv), *v. a.* To regard with affection.

LŎVE (lŭv), *n.* Passion; affection; good-will: —courtship; fondness; the object beloved.

LŎVE'-KNŎT (lŭv'nŏt), *n.* A complicated knot.

LŎVE'-LĔT-TẸR, *n.* A letter of courtship.

LŎVE'-LĬ-NẸSS, *n.* Quality of being lovely.

LŎVE'-LŎRN (lŭv'-), *a.* Forsaken of one's love.

LŎVE'LY̆ (lŭv'le), *a.* Amiable; exciting love.

LŎV'ẸR, *n.* One who is in love; a friend.

LŎVE'SĬCK (lŭv'sĭk), *a.* Disordered with love.

LŎVE'SŎNG, *n.* A song expressive of love; am-

LŎVE'SŪIT (lŭv'sūt), *n.* Courtship. [orous song.

LŎVE'-TĀLE (lŭv'tāl), *n.* A narrative of love.

LŎVE'-TŌ-KEN (lŭv'tō-kn), *n.* A token of love.

LŎV'ĬNG–KĪND'NẸSS, *n.* Tenderness; mercy.

LOW (lō), *a.* Not high; humble; dejected; mean.

LOW (lō), *ad.* Not aloft; with a low voice.

LOW (lō *or* loŭ), *v. n.* To bellow as a cow.

LOW'ẸR (lō'ẹr), *v. a.* To bring low; to lessen.

LOW'ẸR (lō'ẹr), *v. n.* To grow less; to sink.

LOW'ẸR (loŭ'ẹr), *v. n.* To be clouded; to frown.

LOW'ẸR-ĬNG-LY̆,*ad.* With cloudiness; gloomily.

LOW'ẸR-MŌST, *a.* Lowest.

LOW'ĬNG (lō'ĭng), *n.* The bellowing of cattle.

LOW'LĂND (lō'lănd), *n.* Country that is low.

LOW'LĬ-NẸSS (lō'le-nĕs),*n.* Humility; meanness.

LOW'LY̆ (lō'le), *a.* Humble; meek; mild; mean.

LOW'LY̆ (lō'le), *ad.* Not highly; meanly; humbly.

LOW'NẸSS (lō'nẹs), *n.* State of being low.

LOW–SPĬR'ĬT-ẸD, *a.* Dejected; depressed; dull.

LŎY̆'ĂL, *a.* True to a prince, a lady, or a lover.

LŎY̆'ĂL-ĬST, *n.* One who adheres to his sover-

LŎY̆'ĂL-LY̆, *ad.* With fidelity or loyalty. [eign.

LŎY̆'ĂL-TY̆,*n.* Fidelity to a prince, lady, or lover.

LŎZ'ẸNGE, *n.* A form of medicine; ornament.

LŬB'BẸR, *n.* A sturdy drone; an idle clown.

LŬB'BẸR-LY̆, *a.* Lazy and bulky; clumsy.— *ad.* Awkwardly; clumsily.

LŪ'BRĬC, *a.* Slippery; smooth; wanton; lewd.

LŪ'BRĬ-CĂNT, *n.* Any thing which lubricates.

LŪ'BRĬ-CĀTE, *v. a.* To make smooth or slippery.

LỤ-BRĬÇ'Ĭ-TY̆, *n.* Slipperiness; smoothness.

LŪ'BRĬ-COŬS, *a.* Slippery; smooth; wanton.

LŪ'CẸNT, *a.* Shining; bright; splendid.

LŪ'CĔRN, *n.* A plant cultivated for fodder.

LŪ'CĬD, *a.* Shining; bright; clear; pellucid.

LŪ'CĬD-NẸSS, *n.* Transparency; clearness.

LŪ'CĬ-FẸR, *n.* The devil:—the morning star.

LỤ-CĬF'ẸR-OŬS, LỤ-CĬF'ĬC, *a.* Giving light.

LŪ'CĬ-FŎRM, *a.* Having the nature of light.

LŬCK, *n.* Chance; hap; fortune, good or bad.

LŬCK'Ĭ-LY̆, *ad.* Fortunately; by good hap.

LŬCK'Ĭ-NẸSS, *n.* Good fortune or chance.

LŬCK'LẸSS, *a.* Unfortunate; unhappy; unlucky.

LŬCK'Y̆, *a.* Fortunate; happy by chance.

LŪ'CRA-TĬVE, *a.* Gainful; profitable; beneficial.

LŪ'CRE (lū'kẹr), *n.* Gain; profit; advantage.

LỤC-TĀ'TIǪN, *n.* Struggle; effort; contest.

LŪ'CỤ-BRĀTE, *v. n.* To study by candle-light.

LŪ-CỤ-BRĀ'TIǪN, *n.* Nightly study or work.

LỤ-CŪ'BRA-TǪ-RY̆,*a.* Composed by candle-light.

LŪ'CỤ-LẸNT, *a.* Clear; transparent; evident.

LŪ'DĬ-CROŬS, *a.* Sportive; exciting laughter.

LŪ'DĬ-CROŬS-LY̆, *ad.* Sportively; in burlesque.

LŪ'DĬ-CROŬS-NẸSS,*n.* Burlesque; sportiveness.

LŬFF, *v. n.* To sail closer to the wind.

LŬFF, *n.* A sailing close to the wind.

LŬG, *v. a. & n.* To drag; to pull with violence.

LŬG'GAGE, *n.* Any thing cumbrous to be carried.

LỤ-GŪ'BRĬ-OŬS, *a.* Mournful; sorrowful.

LŪKE'WÂRM, *a.* Moderately warm; indifferent.

LŪKE'WÂRM-LY̆,*ad.* With lukewarmness.[ness.

LŪKE'WÂRM-NẸSS,*n.* Moderate warmth, cool-

LŬLL, *v. a.* To compose to sleep; to put to rest.

LŬL'LA-BY̆, *n.* A song to still babes.

LỤM-BĀ'GŌ, *n.* Pain about the lumbar regions.

LŬM'BAR, *n.* Pertaining to the loins.

LŬM'BẸR, *n.* Any thing cumbersome:—timber.

LŬM'BẸR, *v. a.* To heap together irregularly

LŬM'BRĬC, *n.* A worm. [or in disorder.

LŬM'BRĬ-CĂL, *a.* Noting certain small muscles.

LŪ'MĬ-NA-RY̆,*n.* Any body which gives light.

LŪ'MĬ-NOŬS, *a.* Shining; enlightened; bright.

LŪ'MĬ-NOŬS-LY̆, *ad.* In a shining manner.

LŪ'MĬ-NOŬS-NẸSS, *n.* Brightness; clearness.

LŬMP, *n.* A small or shapeless mass; the gross.

LŬMP, *v. a.* To unite or take in the gross.

LŬMP'ĬSH, *a.* Heavy; gross; dull; inactive.

LŪ'NA-CY̆, *n.* A kind of madness supposed to be influenced by the moon; madness in general.

LŪ'NAR, LŪ'NA-RY̆, *a.* Relating to the moon.

LỤ-NĀ'RĬ-ĂN, *n.* An inhabitant of the moon.

LŪ'NĀT-ẸD, *a.* Formed like a half moon.

LŪ'NA-TĬC, *n.* A madman.—*a.* Mad; insane.

LỤ-NĀ'TIǪN, *n.* The revolution of the moon.

LŬNCH, ⎫ *n.* Food between break-

LŬN'CHEǪN (-shun), ⎰ fast and dinner.

LŪNE, *n.* Any thing in the shape of a half moon.

LỤ-NĔT', LỤ-NĔTTE', *n.* A little moon. [tion.

LŬNGṢ, *n. pl.* The lights; the organs of respira-

LŪ-NĬ-SŌ'LAR, *a.* Relating to the sun and moon.

LŬNT.*n.* A match-cord with which guns are fired.

LŪ'NỤ-LAR, LŪ'NỤ-LĀTE, *a.* Like a new moon;

LŪ'PĬNE,*n.* A kind of pulse. [crescent-shaped.

LŪ'PỤ-LĬNE, *n.* The fine, yellow powder of hops.

LŬRCH, *n.* A forlorn or deserted condition.

LŬRCH, *v. n.* To shift; to play tricks; to lurk.

LŬRCH, *v. a.* To defeat; to disappoint; to steal.

LŪRE, *n.* An enticement; allurement. [tempt.

LŪRE,*v. a.* To attract; to entice; to draw; **to**

LŪ'RĬD, *a.* Pale; gloomy; dismal; ghastly.

LŬRK, *v. n.* To lie in wait; to lie hidden.

LŬRK′ẸR, *n.* One who lurks or lies in wait.
LŬRK′ĬNG–PLĀCE, *n.* A hiding-place.
LŬS′CIOŲS (lŭsh′ŭs), *a.* Too sweet; delicious.
LŬS′CIOŲS-LY (lŭsh′ŭs-lẹ), *ad.* Very sweetly.
LŬS′CIOŲS-NĔSS (lŭsh′ŭs-nĕs), *n.* Sweetness.
LŬSH, *a.* Juicy; full; succulent; deep-colored.
LŪ′SỌ-RY, *a.* Used in play; sportive; playful.
LŬST, *n.* Carnal desire; evil propensity.
LŬST, *v. n.* To desire carnally or vehemently.
LŬST′FŪL, *a.* Libidinous; having evil desires.
LŬST′FŪL-LY, *ad.* With sensual concupiscence.
LŬST′FŪL-NĔSS, *n.* Libidinousness; lust. [tle.
LŬST′Ĭ-LY, *ad.* Stoutly; with vigor; with met-
LŬST′Ĭ-NĔSS, *n.* Stoutness; vigor of body.
LŬS′TRẠL, *a.* Used in lustration or purification.
LŬS′TRĀTE, *v. a.* To purify; to cleanse.
LŬS-TRĀ′TIǪN, *n.* Purification by water. [nown.
LŬS′TRE (lŭs′tụr), *n.* Brightness; splendor; re-
LŬS′TRĬNG, *n.* A shining silk; lutestring.
LŬS′TROŲS, *a.* Bright; shining; luminous.
LŬS′TRŲM, *n.* [L.] A space of five years.
LŬS′TY, *a.* Stout; vigorous; healthy; large.
LŪ′TẠ-NĬST, *n.* One who plays upon the lute.
LŲ-TĀ′RĬ-OŬS, *a.* Living in mud :—like mud.
LŲ-TĀ′TIǪN, *n.* The act or process of luting.
LŪTE, *n.* A stringed instrument :—a cement.
LŪTE, *v. a.* To close or coat with lute.
LŪTE′STRĬNG, *n.* String of a lute :—lustring.
LŪ′THẸR-ẠN, *a.* Pertaining to Luther or to Lutheranism.

LŪ′THẸR-ẠN, *n.* A follower of Luther.
LŪ′THẸR-ẠN-ĬŞM, *n.* The doctrines of Luther.
LŪ′THẸRN, *n.* A sort of window on a roof.
LŪT′ĬNG, *n.* The coating of chemical vessels.
LŪ′TỤ-LĔNT, *a.* Muddy; thick; turbid.
LŬX, LŬX′ĀTE, *v. a.* To put out of joint.
LŲX-Ā′TIǪN, *n.* A disjointing; thing disjointed.
‖LŲX-Ū′RĬ-ẠNCE, *n.* Exuberance; rank growth.
‖LŲX-Ū′RĬ-ẠNT (lụg-zū′rẹ-ạnt), *a.* Exuberant.
‖LŲX-Ū′RĬ-ẠNT-LY, *ad.* Abundantly; plentifully.
‖LŲX-Ū′RĬ-ĀTE, *v. n.* To grow exuberantly.
‖LŲX-Ū′RĬ-OŬS (lụg-zū′rẹ-ŭs), *a.* Delighting in luxury; voluptuous; softening by pleasure.
‖LŲX-Ū′RĬ-OŬS-LY, *ad.* Deliciously; voluptu-
‖LŲX-Ū′RĬ-OŲS-NĔSS, *n.* Voluptuousness. [ously.
LŬX′Ų-RY (lŭk′shụ-rẹ), *n.* Delicious fare; a dainty; voluptuousness; devotion to pleasure.
LȲ-CĒ′ỤM, *n.*; pl. LȲ-CĒ′Ạ, *or* LȲ-CĒ′ỤMŞ. An academy; a literary association. [line salt.
LȲE, *or* LĪE, *n.* Water impregnated with alka-
LȲ′ĬNG, *p.* from *lie.—n.* The telling of lies.
LȲMPH (lĭmf), *n.* A pure, transparent fluid.
LYM-PHĂT′ĬC, *n.* A vessel containing lymph.
LYM-PHĂT′ĬC, *a.* Pertaining to lymph. [lymph.
LȲMPH′Ẹ-DŬCT, *n.* A vessel which conveys the
LȲNCH, *v. a.* To punish without trial.
LȲNX, *n.* A swift, sharp-sighted beast.
LȲRE, *n.* A harp; a musical instrument.
LȲR′ĬC, LȲR′Ĭ-CẠL, *a.* Pertaining to a lyre.
LȲ′RĬST, *n.* One who plays on a lyre or harp.

M.

M has, in English, one unvaried sound, formed by the compression of the lips; as, *mine, tame.*
MĂB, *n.* The queen of the fairies :—a slattern.
MĂC, in Irish and Scotch names, denotes *son.*
MĂC-Ạ-RŌ′NĬ, *n.* [It.] An edible paste :—a fop.
MĂC-Ạ-RŎN′ĬC, *a.* Relating to macaroni :—vain.
MĂC-Ạ-RŎÔN′, *n.* Macaroni; a cake :—a cox-
MẠ-CÂW′, *n.* A large species of parrot. [comb.
MĀCE, *n.* An ensign of authority :—a spice.
MĀCE′-BEẠR-ẸR, *n.* One who carries the mace.
MĂÇ′ẸR-ĀTE, *v. a.* To make lean :—to steep.
MĂÇ-ẸR-Ā′TIǪN, *n.* A making lean :—a steeping.
MĂ€H-Ĭ-Ạ-VĔL′ĬẠN (măk-kẹ-ạ-vĕl′yạn), *a.* Crafty
MĂ€H′Ĭ-NẠL, *a.* Relating to machines.
MĂ€H′Ĭ-NĀTE, *v. n.* To plan; to contrive.
MĂ€H-Ĭ-NĀ′TIǪN, *n.* An artifice; a contrivance.
MĂ€H′Ĭ-NĀ-TǪR, *n.* One who plots or contrives.
MẠ-ÇHĪNE′, *n.* Any complicated work; engine.
MẠ-ÇHĪN′ẸR-Y, *n.* Enginery; complicated work.
MẠ-ÇHĪN′ĬST, *n.* A constructor of machines.
MĂCK′ẸR-ẸL, *n.* A small sea-fish. [system.
MĀ′CRỌ-CŌŞM, *n.* The whole world or visible
MĂC-TĀ′TIǪN, *n.* Act of killing for sacrifice.
MĂC′Ų-LĀTE, *v. a.* To stain; to spot; to blotch.
MĂC-Ų-LĀ′TIǪN, *n.* A stain; a spot; a taint.
MĂD, *a.* Disordered in the mind :—furious.
MĂD′ẠM, *n.* A term of address to a lady.
MĂD′BRĀINED (măd′brānd), *a.* Hot-headed.
MĂD′CĂP, *n.* A wild, hot-brained fellow.
MĂD′DEN (măd′dn), *v. n. & a.* To become or make mad.

MĂD′DẸR, *n.* A perennial plant used for dyeing.
MĂDE, *imp. t. & pp.* from *make.*
MĂD-Ẹ-FĂC′TIǪN, *n.* The act of making wet.
MĂD′Ẹ-FȲ, *v. a.* To moisten; to make wet.
MẠ-DĒI′RẠ (mạ-dē′rạ), *n.* A rich wine.
MĂD′HÖÜSE, *n.* A house for lunatics.
MĂD′LY, *ad.* With madness; furiously; wildly.
MĂD′MĂN, *n.* A man void of reason; a maniac.
MĂD′NẸSS, *n.* Distraction; fury; wildness; rage.
MẠ-DŎN′NẠ, *n.* [It.] A picture of the Virgin Mary.
MĂD′RẸ-PŌRE, *n.* A worm; a kind of zoöphite.
MĂD′RĬ-GẠL, *n.* A pastoral or amorous poem.
MĂG-Ạ-ZÎNE′, *n.* A storehouse :—a pamphlet.
MĂG′GǪT, *n.* A small grub :—a whim; caprice.
MĂG′GǪT-Y, *a.* Full of maggots :—whimsical.
MĀ′GĪ, *n. pl.* [L.] Wise men of the East.
MĀ′GĬ-ẠN, *a.* Denoting the Magi of the East.
MĀ′GĬ-ẠN, *n.* One of the sect of the Magi.
MĂG′ĬC, MĂG′Ĭ-CẠL, *a.* Relating to magic.
MĂG′ĬC, *n.* Sorcery; enchantment; necromancy.
MĂG′Ĭ-CẠL-LY, *ad.* According to magic. [magic.
MẠ-GĬ″CIẠN (mạ-jĭsh′ạn), *n.* One skilled in
MĂG-ĬS-TĒ′RĬ-ẠL, *a.* Lofty; arrogant; imperious.
MĂG-ĬS-TĒ′RĬ-ẠL-LY, *ad.* Arrogantly; proudly.
MĂG-ĬS-TĒ′RĬ-ẠL-NĔSS, *n.* Imperiousness.
MĂG′ĬS-TRẠ-CY, *n.* The office of a magistrate.
MĂG′ĬS-TRĀTE, *n.* A public civil officer.
MĂG-NẠ-NĬM′Ĭ-TY, *n.* Greatness of mind; bravery.
MẠG-NĂN′Ĭ-MOŬS, *a.* Great of mind; brave.
MẠG-NĂN′Ĭ-MOŬS-LY, *ad.* With greatness of
MĂG′NĀTE, *n.* Man of rank; a grandee. [mind.

MĄG-NĒ′ṢĮ-Ą (mąg-nē′zhę-ą), *n.* Alkaline earth.
MĂG′NĘT, *n.* The loadstone, which attracts iron.
MĄG-NĔT′ĮC, *a.* Relating to the magnet,
MĄG-NĔT′Į-CĄL, or to magnetism; attractive.
MĄG-NĔT′Į-CĄL-LY, *ad.* By power of attraction.
MĂG′NĘT-ĪṢM, *n.* The science which treats of the properties of the magnet; power of attraction.
MĂG′NĘT-ĪZE, *v. a. & n.* To impart or receive the properties of magnetism; to become mag-
MĄG-NĬF′ĮC, *a.* Illustrious; grand. [netic.
MĄG-NĬF′Į-CĔNCE, *n.* Grandeur; showy splendor. [pous.
MĄG-NĬF′Į-CĔNT, *a.* Grand; splendid; pom-
MĄG-NĬF′Į-CĔNT-LY, *ad.* Splendidly; grandly.
MĂG′NĮ-FĪ-ĘR, *n.* He or that which magnifies.
MĂG′NĮ-FŸ, *v. a.* To make great, exalt, extol.
MĄG-NĬL′Q-QUĔNCE, *n.* Pompous language.
MĄG-NĬL′Q-QUĔNT, *a.* Speaking pompously.
MĂG′NĮ-TŪDE, *n.* Greatness; size; grandeur.
MĄG-NŌ′LĮ-Ą, *n.* The laurel-leafed tulip-tree.
MĂG′PĪE (măg′pī), *n.* A chattering bird.
MĄ-HŎG′Ą-NY, *n.* A valuable kind of wood.
MĄ-HŎM′Ę-DĄN, *n.* A mussulman; a profess-
MĄ-HŎM′Ę-TĄN, or of the religion of Mahomet; Mohammedan.
MĄ-HŎM′Ę-TĄN, *a.* Relating to Mahomet. [tans.
MĄ-HŎM′Ę-TĄN-ĪṢM, *n.* Religion of Mahome-
MĀID (mād), *n.* An unmarried woman;
MĀID′ĘN (mā′dn,) a virgin; woman-servant.
MĀID′ĘN (mā′dn), *a.* Fresh; new; unpolluted.
MĀID′ĘN-HĀIR (mā′dn-hår), *n.* A kind of fern.
MĀID′ĘN-HOOD (mā′dn-hûd), *n.* Virginity.
MĀID′ĘN-LĪKE (mā′dn-līk), *a.* Modest; decent.
MĀID′ĘN-LY (mā′dn-lę), *a.* Gentle; modest.
MĀID-MĀ′RĮ-ĄN (mād-mā′rĭ-ąn), *n.* A dance.
MĀID′SĔR-VĄNT, *n.* A female servant.
MĀIL, *n.* Armor:—a bag for letters, &c. [mail.
MĀIL, *v. a.* To arm defensively; to send by
MĀIL′-CŌACH, *n.* A coach that carries a mail.
MĀIM, *v. a.* To disable; to wound; to cripple.
MĀIM, *n.* A crippling; lameness; injury.
MĀIN, *a.* Principal; chief:—mighty; forcible.
MĀIN, *n.* The gross:—force; ocean; continent.
MĀIN′LĂND, *n.* The continent, not an island.
MĀIN′LY, *ad.* Chiefly; principally; greatly.
MĀIN′MĂST, *n.* The chief or middle mast.
MĀIN′SĀIL, *n.* The principal sail in a ship.
MĀIN′SHĔĔT, *n.* A rope fastening the mainsail.
MĄIN-TĀIN′ (męn-tān′), *v. a.* To preserve; to keep; to defend; to justify; to support.
MĄIN-TĀIN′Ą-BLE (męn-tān′ą-bl), *a.* Defensible.
MĀIN′TĘN-ĄNCE, *n.* Defence; sustenance.
MĀIN′-TŎP, *n.* The top of the mainmast.
MĀIN′-YĂRD, *n.* The yard of the mainmast.
MĀIZE, *n.* Indian corn, a plant and grain.
MĄ-JĔS′TĮC, *a.* Having majesty; stately;
MĄ-JĔS′TĮ-CĄL, august; grand. [ly.
MĄ-JĔS′TĮ-CĄL-LY, *ad.* With majesty; august-
MĄ-JĔS′TĮ-CĄL-NĔSS, *n.* Majesty; stateli-
MĄ-JĔS′TĮC-NĔSS, ness; grandeur.
MĂJ′ĘS-TY, *n.* Dignity; grandeur; a royal title.
MĀ′JQR, *a.* Greater; larger; senior; older.
MĀ′JQR, *n.* A military officer above a captain:—the first proposition of a syllogism. [age.
MĄ-JŎR′Į-TY, *n.* The greater number:—full
MĀKE, *v. a.* [*imp. t. & pp.* made.] To create, form, produce, compel, reach, gain, acquire.
MĀKE, *v. n.* To tend; to operate; to appear.

MĀKE, *n.* Form; structure; texture; nature.
MĀKE′PĒACE, *n.* A peace-maker; a reconciler.
MĀK′ĘR, *n.* The Creator:—one who makes.
MĀKE′WEIGHT (māk′wāt), *n.* Any small thing thrown in to make up weight. [make.
MĀK′ĮNG, *n.* Composition; structure; form;
MĂL′Ą-DY, *n.* A severe illness or indisposition; a disease; a distemper; a disorder.
MĂL′Ą-GĄ, *n.* A kind of wine from Malaga.
MĂL′Ą-PĔRT, *a.* Saucy; impudent; impertinent.
MĂL′Ą-PĔRT-NĘSS, *n.* Sprightly impudence.
MĄL-Ä′RĮ-Ą, *n.* [It.] Noxious vapor or exhala-
MĀLE, *a.* Of the male sex; masculine. [tion.
MĀLE, *n.* The he of any species. [ment.
‖MĀLE-ĂD-MĮN-ĮS-TRĀ′TIQN, *n.* Bad manage-
‖MĀLE′CQN-TĔNT, *n.* One who is dissatisfied.
‖MĀLE′CQN-TĔNT *or* MĀLE′CQN-TĔNT, *a.* Dissatisfied; discontented.
MĂL-Ę-DĬC′TIQN, *n.* A curse; an execration.
MĂL-Ę-FĂC′TQR, *n.* An offender; a criminal.
‖MĀLE-PRĂC′TĮCE,*n.* Practice contrary to rules.
MĄ-LĔV′Q-LĔNCE, *n.* Ill-will; malignity.
MĄ-LĔV′Q-LĔNT, *a.* Ill-disposed; malignant.
MĄ-LĔV′Q-LĔNT-LY, *ad.* Malignantly.
MĂL′ĮCE, *n.* Badness of design; malignity.
MĄ-LĬ″CIOŲS (mą-lĭsh′ŭs), *a.* Malignant.
MĄ-LĬ″CIOŲS-LY (-lĭsh′ŭs-lę), *ad.* With malice.
MĄ-LĬ″CIOŲS-NĔSS (mą-lĭsh′ŭs-), *n.* Malice.
MĄ-LĪGN′ (mą-līn′), *a.* Malicious; bad; fatal.
MĄ-LĪGN′ (mą-līn′), *v. a.* To revile; to defame.
MĄ-LĬG′NĄN-CY, *n.* Malevolence; malice.
MĄ-LĬG′NĄNT, *a.* Malicious; pernicious:—hostile to life; fatal.
MĄ-LĬG′NĄNT-LY, *ad.* With ill intention.
MĄ-LĪGN′ĘR (mą-līn′ęr), *n.* One who maligns.
MĄ-LĬG′NĮ-TY, *n.* Malice; maliciousness.
MĄ-LĪGN′LY (mą-līn′lę), *ad.* With ill will.
MĄ-LĬN′GĘR, *v. n.* To feign illness.
MĂL′KĮN (mâw′kĭn), *n.* A mop:—a vile servant.
MĂLL, *n.* A kind of beetle or hammer.
MÂLL, *v. a.* To beat or strike with a maul; to
MĂLL, *n.* A public walk. [maul.
MĂL′LĄRD, *n.* The drake of the wild duck:—the common wild duck. [l'eable.
MĂL-LĘ-Ą-BĬL′Į-TY, *n.* Quality of being mal-
MĂL′LĘ-Ą-BLE, *a.* That may be spread or drawn out by beating.
MĂL′LĘ-Ą-BLE-NĔSS, *n.* Malleability; ductility.
MĂL-LĘ-Ā′TIQN, *n.* The act of beating or ham-
MĂL′LĘT, *n.* A wooden hammer. [mering.
MĂL′LŌW, *n.* A mucilaginous plant. [wine.
MĂLM′ṢEY (măm′zę), *n.* A sort of grape and
MÂLT, *n.* Grain steeped in water and dried.
MÂLT, *v. a. & n.* To make, or be made, malt.
MĂLT′-FLŌOR, *n.* A floor to dry malt on.
MĂLT′MĄN, MĂLT′STĘR, *n.* A maker of malt.
MĂL-TRĒAT′ (mạl-trēt′), *v. a.* To treat ill.
MĄL-VĀ′CEOŲS (mạl-vā′shŭs), *a.* Relating to mallows. [fices.
MĂL-VĘR-SĀ′TIQN, *n.* Bad shifts; mean arti-
MĀM′Ę-LŪKE, *n.* One of a military people imported from Circassia into Egypt.
MĄM-MĀ′, *n.* A fond word for *mother.*
MĂM′MĄL, *n.* One of the mammalia.
MĄM-MĀ′LĮ-Ą, *n.* That class of warm-blooded animals which suckle their young.
MĂM′MĘT, *n.* A puppet; a figure dressed up.
MĄM-MĬF′ĘR-OŬS, *a.* Having breasts or paps.

MĂM′MĬ-FŎRM, _a._ Having the shape of breasts.
MĂM′MĬL-LĄ-RY̆, _a._ Belonging to the breasts.
MĂM′MQN, _n._ Riches ; the god of riches.
MĂM′MQTH, _n._ A huge quadruped, now extinct.
MĂN, _n. ;_ pl. MĔN. A human being ; a male.
MĂN, _v. a._ To furnish with men :—to fortify.
MĂN′Ą-CLE, _v. a._ To chain the hands of.[hands.
MĂN′Ą-CLE (măn′ną-kl), _n._ A shackle for the
MĂN′ĄĢE, _v. a._ To conduct ; to govern, direct.
MĂN′ĄĢE-Ą-BLE, _a._ Governable ; tractable.
MĂN′ĄĢE-MĔNT, _n._ Conduct ; administration.
MĂN′Ą-ĢĘR, _n._ A conductor :—a frugal person.
MĂN-Ą-TĒĒ′, ⎰ _n._ An herbivorous cetacean ;
MĄ-NĀ′TỤS, ⎱ the sea-cow.
MĂNCH-ĬN-ĒEL′, _n._ A tree of the West Indies.
MĂN′CĬ-PĀTE, _v. a._ To enslave ; to bind. [lege.
MĂN′CĬ-PLE, _n._ Steward or purveyor of a col-
MĄN-DĀ′MỤS, _n._ A writ from a superior court.
MĂN-DĄ-RĪN′, _n._ A Chinese magistrate. [sion.
MĂN′DĄTE, _n._ Command ; precept ; commis-
MĂN′DĄ-TQ-RY̆, _a._ Preceptive ; directory.
MĂN′DĬ-BLE, _n._ The jaw :—lower jaw of ani-
MĄN-DĬB′Ụ-LĄR, _a._ Belonging to the jaw.[mals.
MĂN′DRĀKE, _n._ An herbaceous venomous plant.
MĂN′DRĘL, _n._ Shank of a turner's lathe.
MĂN′DỤ-CĄ-BLE, _a._ That may be chewed or
MĂN′DỤ-CĀTE, _v. a._ To chew ; to eat. [eaten.
MĀNE, _n._ The hair on the neck of a horse, &c.
MĂN′-ĒAT-ĘR, _n._ One that eats human flesh.
MĄ-NEGE′ (mą-nāzh′), _n._ [Fr.] Horsemanship.
MĀ′NĒŞ, _n. pl._ [L.] A ghost ; a departed soul.
MĂN′FŬL, _a._ Bold ; stout ; noble ; valiant.
MĂN′FŬL-LY̆, _ad._ Boldly ; stoutly ; valiantly.
MĂN′FŬL-NĔSS, _n._ Stoutness ; boldness ; valor.
MĂN′GĄ-NĒSE, _n._ A grayish-white metal.
MĀNĢE, _n._ The itch or scab in dogs, &c.
MĂN′ĢĘR, _n._ A trough for animals to eat from.
MĂN′ĢĬ-NĔSS, _n._ Infection with the mange.
MĂN′GLE, _v. a._ To mutilate ; to lacerate ; to
maim :—to smooth, as linen.
MĂN′GLE, _n._ A calender for smoothing linen.
MĂN′GLĘR, _n._ One who mangles ; a hacker.
MĂN′GŌ (măng′gō), _n. ;_ pl. MĂN′GŌEŞ. A
fruit of the mango-tree ; a pickle.
MĂN′GRŌVE, _n._ A plant of the tropics.
MĂN′ĢY̆ (mān′ję), _a._ Infected with the mange.
MĂN′-HĀT-ĘR, _n._ One that hates mankind.
MĂN′HOOD (măn′hŭd), _n._ Man's estate ; cour-
MĀ′NĬ-Ą, _n._ Madness ; violent insanity. [age.
MĀ′NĬ-ĂC, ⎰ _a._ Affected with mania ; mad ;
MĄ-NĪ′Ą-CĄL, ⎱ raving ; insane.
MĀ′NĬ-ĂC, _n._ A mad person ; a lunatic.
MĂN′Ĭ-₵HŎRD, _n._ A sort of musical instrument.
MĂN′Ĭ-FĔST, _a._ Plain ; open ; evident ; appar-
ent ; clear ; obvious.
MĂN′Ĭ-FĔST, _n._ A list or invoice of a cargo.
MĂN′Ĭ-FĔST, _v. a._ To make appear ; to show.
MĂN-Ĭ-FĔS-TĀ′TIQN, _n._ Discovery ; exhibition.
MĂN′Ĭ-FĔST-LY̆, _ad._ Clearly ; evidently ; plainly.
MĂN-Ĭ-FĔS′TŌ, _n. ;_ pl. MĂN-Ĭ-FĔS′TŌEŞ. A
protestation or declaration of a government or
sovereign.
MĂN′Ĭ-FŌLD, _a._ Many in number.
MĂN′Ĭ-KĬN, _n._ A little man ; a dwarf :—appa-
ratus for showing the structure of the body.
MĀ′NĬ-ŎC, _n._ A kind of starch ; tapioca.
MĂN′Ĭ-PLE, _n._ A handful :—a band of soldiers.
MĄ-NĬP′Ụ-LĄR, _a._ Relating to a maniple.

MĄ-NĬP-Ụ-LĀ′TIQN, _n._ A manual operation.
MĂN-KĪND′, _n._ The human race or species.
MĂN′LĪKE, _a._ Like man ; becoming a man.
MĂN′LĬ-NĔSS, _n._ Dignity ; bravery ; stoutness.
MĂN′LY̆, _a._ Becoming a man ; firm ; brave.
MĂN′NĄ, _n._ A honey-like gum or juice.
MĂN′NĘR, _n._ Form ; custom ; habit ; kind ; mien.
MĂN′NĘR-ĬŞM, _n._ A uniformity of manner.
MĂN′NĘR-ĬST, _n._ An artist adhering to one
manner.
MĂN′NĘR-LĬ-NĔSS, _n._ Civility ; complaisance.
MĂN′NĘR-LY̆, _a._ Civil ; courteous ; complaisant.
MĂN′NĘRŞ, _n. pl._ Customary conduct ; habits ;
carriage ; polite behavior.
MĂN′NĬSH, _a._ Like a man ; bold ; masculine.
MĄ-NŒŬ′VRE (mą-nŭ′vụr), _n._ A stratagem ; a
dexterous movement ; skilful management.
MĄ-NŒŬ′VRE (mą-nŭ′vụr), _v. n._ To manage
with address, art, or stratagem ; to contrive.
MĂN′-QF-WÂR′, _n._ A public armed vessel.
MĂN′QR, _n._ The estate of a lord or great person-
MĄ-NŌ′RĬ-ĄL, _a._ Belonging to a manor. [age.
MĂNSE, _n._ A farm ; a house ; a parsonage.
MĂN′SIQN (măn′shụn), _n._ A house, residence.
MĂN′SLÂUGH-TĘR (măn′slâw-tẹr), _n._ The un-
lawful killing of a man, though without malice.
MĂN′SLĀY-ĘR, _n._ One that has killed another.
MĂN′-STĒAL-ĘR, _n._ One that steals and sells
men ; a kidnapper.
MĂN′-STĒAL-ĬNG, _n._ The act of stealing men.
MĂN′SUĘ-TŪDE (măn′swę-tūd), _n._ Mildness.
MĂN′TEL (măn′tl), _n._ Work before a chimney.
MĂN-TĘ-LĔT′, _n._ A small cloak :—a parapet.
MĂN′TLE, _n._ A kind of cloak or loose garment.
MĂN′TLE, _v. a._ To cloak ; to cover ; to disguise.
MĂN′TLE, _v. n._ To spread ; to revel ; to ferment.
MĂN′TỤ-Ą, _n._ A woman's gown or dress.
MĂN′TỤA-MĀK-ĘR (măn′tụ-mā-kẹr), _n._ One
who makes gowns for women ; a dress-maker.
MĂN′Ụ-ĄL (măn′yụ-ąl), _a._ Performed by hand.
MĂN′Ụ-ĄL, _n._ A small book :—a service-book.
MĂN-Ụ-FĂC′TQ-RY̆, _n._ A building or place
where a manufacture is carried on ; a factory.
MĂN-Ụ-FĂCT′ỤRE (măn-ụ-făkt′yụr), _n._ Prac-
tice of manufacturing :—any thing made by art.
MĂN-Ụ-FĂCT′ỤRE, _v. a._ To make or form by
art and labor.
MĂN-Ụ-FĂCT′ỤR-ĘR, _n._ An artificer ; a maker.
MĂN-Ụ-MĬS′SIQN (măn-ụ-mĭsh′ụn), _n._ The act
of giving liberty to slaves ; emancipation.
MĂN-Ụ-MĬT′, _v. a._ To release from slavery.
MĄ-NŪRE′, _v. a._ To fertilize with dung or
compost ; to enrich.
MĄ-NŪRE′, _n._ Any thing that fertilizes land.
MĂN′Ụ-SCRĬPT, _n._ A paper written ; a writing.
MAN′Y̆ (mĕn′nę), _a._ [_comp._ more ; _superl._ most.]
Consisting of a great number ; numerous.
MAN′Y̆ (mĕn′nę), _n._ A great number.
MAN′Y̆-TĪMEŞ (mĕn′nę-tīmz), _ad._ Frequently.
MĂP, _n._ A delineation of countries, &c. ; a
MĀ′PLE, _n._ A tree of many species. [chart.
MĂP′PĘR-Y̆, _n._ The art of designing maps.
MÄR, _v. a._ To injure ; to spoil ; to hurt, damage.
MĂR-Ą-NĂTH′Ą, _n._ A form of anathematizing.
MĄ-RĂŞ′MỤS, _n._ A wasting consumption.
MĄ-RÂU′DĘR, _n._ A plunderer ; a pillager.
MĄ-RÂUD′ĬNG, _a._ Plundering.—_n._ A robbing.
MĂR-Ą-VĒ′DĬ, _n._ A small Spanish copper coin.

MÄR′BLE, *n.* Stone susceptible of a bright polish.
MÄR′BLE, *a.* Made of, or like, marble. [ble.
MÄR′BLE, *v. a.* To variegate or vein like mar-
MÄR′CA-SĪTE, *n.* A variety of iron pyrites.
MÄRCH, *n.* The third month of the year :—a
movement of troops or of an army. [form.
MÄRCH, *v. n.* To move by steps or in military
MÄRCH, *v. a.* To cause to move, as an army.
MÄRCH′ES, *n. pl.* Limits of a country ; confines.
MÄR′ÇHION-ĔSS (mär′shun-ĕs), *n.* The wife of
a marquis ; a lady of the rank of a marquis.
MÄR′CID, *a.* Lean, withered ; faded ; rotten.
MARE, *n.* The female of a horse.
MÄR′GA-RĪTE, *n.* A pearl :—a mineral.
MÄR′GIN, *n.* The border ; the edge of a page.
MÄR′GIN-AL, *a.* Placed or written on the margin.
MÄR′GRÄVE, *n.* A title of nobility in Germany.
MAR-GRÄ′VI-ATE, *n.* Territory of a margrave.
MÄR-GRA-VĪNE′, *n.* The wife of a margrave.
MÄR′I-GŌLD, *n.* A kind of flowering plant.
MA-RÎNE′, *a.* Belonging to the sea ; maritime.
MA-RÎNE′, *n.* Sea-affairs ; shipping :—a sea-
MÄR′I-NER, *n.* A seaman ; a sailor. [soldier.
MÄR′I-TAL, *a.* Pertaining to a husband.
MÄR′I-TĪME, *a.* Marine ; relating to the sea.
MÄR′JO-RAM, *n.* A fragrant plant of many kinds.
MÄRK, *n.* A stamp ; a print ; a proof :—an ob-
ject to shoot at :—a silver coin.
MÄRK, *v. a.* To impress ; to stamp ; to note ; to
MÄRK, *v. n.* To note ; to take notice. [heed.
MÄR′KET, *n.* A place of sale ; sale. [sell.
MÄR′KET, *v. n.* To deal in market ; to buy or
MÄR′KET-A-BLE, *a.* Fit for sale in the market.
MÄR′KET-DĀY, *n.* The day of a public market.
MÄRKS′MAN, *n.* A man skilful to hit a mark.
MÄRL, *n.* A kind of fertilizing earth.
MÄRL, *v. a.* To manure with marl.
MÄR′LINE, *n.* A small cord of two strands.
MÄRL′-PĬT, *n.* A pit out of which marl is dug.
MÄRL′Y, *a.* Abounding with, or like, marl.
MÄR′MA-LĀDE, *n.* Fruit boiled with sugar.
MÄR-MO-ṢĔT′, *n.* A small monkey. [ruped.
MÄR′MOT *or* MAR-MÖT′, *n.* A rodent quad-
MÄRQUE (märk), *n.* [Fr.] A license or a ves-
sel for making reprisals on an enemy.
MAR-QUĒĒ′ (mar-kē′), *n.* [Fr.] A field-tent.
MÄR′QUESS, ⎱ *n.* One of the second order of
MÄR′QUIS, ⎰ nobility in England, next be-
low a duke. [quis.
MÄR′QUIS-ĀTE, *n.* Rank or seigniory of a mar-
MÄR′RIAGE (mär′rij), *n.* The act of uniting a
man and woman for life ; wedlock ; nuptials.
MÄR′RIAGE-A-BLE (mär′rij-),*a.*Fit for wedlock.
MÄR′RŌW (mär′rō), *n.* An oily substance in
bones :—the pith ; best part.
MÄR′ROW-BŌNE, *n.* A bone containing marrow.
MÄR′ROW-FÄT (mär′ro-fät), *n.* A kind of pea.
MÄR′ROW-LĔSS (mär′ro-lĕs), *a.* Void of marrow.
MÄR′ROW-Y (mär′ro-e), *a.* Pithy ; full of mar-
MÄR′RY, *v. a.* To join in marriage. [row.
MÄR′RY, *v. n.* To enter into the conjugal state.
MÄRS, *n.* The heathen god of war :—a planet.
MÄRSH, *n.* A swamp ; a watery tract of land.
MÄR′SHAL, *n.* An officer ; a military com-
mander in chief :—master of ceremonies.
MÄR′SHAL, *v. a.* To arrange ; to rank in order.
MÄR′SHAL-LER, *n.* One who marshals.
MÄR′SHAL-SHĬP, *n.* The office of a marshal.

MÄRSH′Y, *a.* Boggy ; wet ; fenny ; swampy.
MÄRT, *n.* Place of public traffic.—*v. n.* To trade.
MÄR′TEN, *n.* A large kind of weasel.
MÄR′TIAL (mär′shal), *a.* Warlike ; given to
war ; suiting war.
MÄR′TIN, *n.* A bird ; a species of swallow.
MÄR-TI-NĔT′, *or* MÄRT′LET, *n.* A kind of swal-
MÄR-TI-NĔT′, *n.* A severe disciplinarian. [low.
MÄR′TIN-GAL, *or* MÄR′TIN-GĀLE, *n.* Part of
harness.—(*Naut.*) A perpendicular spar. [11.
MÄR′TIN-MÄS, *n.* The feast of St. Martin, Nov.
MÄRT′NETS, *n. pl.* Lines fastened to the edge of
MÄR′TYR, *n.* One who dies for the truth.[a sail.
MÄR′TYR, *v. a.* To offer as a martyr ; to torture.
MÄR′TYR-DŌM, *n.* State or death of a martyr.
MÄR-TYR-O-LŎG′I-CAL, *a.* Relating to martyrs.
MÄR-TYR-ÖL′O-GIST, *n.* A writer of martyr-
ology.
MÄR-TYR-ÖL′O-GY, *n.* A register of martyrs.
MÄR′VEL, *n.* A wonder ; any thing astonishing.
MÄR′VEL, *v. n.* To wonder ; to be astonished.
MÄR′VEL-LOŬS, *a.* Wonderful ; astonishing.
MÄR′VEL-LOŬS-LY, *ad.* Wonderfully ; strange-
MÄR′VEL-LOŬS-NĔSS, *n.* Wonderfulness. [ly.
MÄS′CU-LĪNE, *a.* Male ; not female ; manly.
MÄS′CU-LĪNE-NĔSS, *n.* Resemblance of man.
MÄSH, *n.* A mixture ; a mass ; a mesh.
MÄSH, *v. a.* To beat into a mass ; to mix.
MÄSH′Y, *a.* Produced by crushing or pressure.
MÄSK, *n.* A disguise ; a visor ; a revel.
MÄSK, *v. a.* To disguise as with a mask ; to
MÄSK, *v. n.* To revel ; to be disguised. [cover.
MÄSK′ER, *n.* One who revels in a mask.
MĀ′SON (mā′sn), *n.* A builder ; a free-mason.
MA-SÖN′IC, *a.* Relating to masonry.
MĀ′SON-RY, *n.* The craft or work of a mason.
MÄS-QUER-ĀDE′ (mäs-ker-ād′), *n.* A diver-
sion in which the company is masked.
MÄS-QUER-ĀDE′, *v. n.* To assemble in masks.
MÄS-QUER-ĀD′ER, *n.* A person in a mask.
MÄSS, *n.* A body ; a lump ; bulk :—an assem-
blage :—the Catholic eucharistical service.
MÄS′SA-CRE (mäs′sa-ker), *n.* Butchery ; murder.
MÄS′SA-CRE (mäs′sa-ker), *v. a.* To butcher.
MÄS′SI-CÖT, *n.* A white oxide of lead.
MÄS′SI-NĔSS, MÄS′SIVE-NĔSS, *n.* Weight ; bulk.
MÄS′SIVE, MÄS′SY, *a.* Heavy ; weighty ; bulky.
MÄST, *n.* The elevated spar of a vessel :—a nut.
MÄST′ED, *a.* Furnished with masts.
MÄS′TER, *n.* One who has servants, persons,
or things in subjection ; a director ; a teacher.
MÄS′TER, *v. a.* To rule ; to govern, overpower.
MÄS′TER-KĔY, *n.* A key which opens many
locks :—a clew out of difficulties.
MÄS′TER-LY, *a.* Artful ; skilful ; magisterial.
MÄS′TER-PIÉCE, *n.* A capital performance ;
skill ; chief excellence. [ter.
MÄS′TER-SHĬP, *n.* Rule ; power :—office of mas-
MÄS′TER-STRŌKE, *n.* A capital performance.
MÄS′TER-Y, *n.* Dominion ; rule ; superiority.
MÄS′TIC, MÄS′TICH, *n.* The lentisk, a tree ; a
MÄS-TI-CĀ′TION, *n.* The act of chewing. [gum.
MÄS′TI-CA-TO-RY, *n.* A medicine to be chewed.
MÄS′TIFF, *n.* A large, fierce species of dog.
MÄST′LESS, *a.* Having or bearing no mast.
MÄS′TO-DÖN, *n.* A huge quadruped, allied to
the elephant, now extinct.
MÄT, *n.* A texture of sedge, flax, rushes, &c.

MĂT, *v. a.* To cover with mats; to twist. [bre.
MĂT-A-DŌRE', *n.* A term at quadrille and om-
MĂTCH, *n.* Any thing that catches fire :—a con-
test; an equal :—a union by marriage.
MĂTCH, *v. a.* To be equal to ; to suit; to marry.
MĂTCH, *v. n.* To be married ; to suit; to tally.
MĂTCH'A-BLE, *a.* Suitable; fit to be joined.
MĂTCH'LESS, *a.* Having no equal ; not alike.
MĂTCH'LESS-LY, *ad.* In a matchless manner.
MĂTCH'LESS-NĔSS, *n.* State of being matchless.
MĂTCH'LŎCK, *n.* A lock fired by a match.
MĂTCH'MĀK-ER, *n.* One who makes matches.
MĀTE, *n.* A companion ; an associate; second.
MĀTE, *v. n.* To match ; to marry ; to equal.
MĀTE'LESS, *a.* Having no mate or companion.
MA-TĒ'RI-AL, *a.* Consisting of matter ; corpo-
real ; not spiritual ; important ; essential.
MA-TĒ'RI-AL, *n.* That of which any thing is
made; substance. [rialists.
MA-TĒ'RI-AL-ĬSM, *n.* The doctrine of mate-
MA-TĒ'RI-AL-ĬST, *n.* One who denies the ex-
istence of spiritual substances. [istence.
MA-TĒ-RI-ĂL'I-TY, *n.* Corporeity ; material ex-
MA-TĒ'RI-AL-ĪZE, *v. a.* To form into matter.
MA-TĒ'RI-AL-LY, *ad.* In a material manner.
MA-TĒ'RI-AL-NĔSS, *n.* State of being material.
MA-TĔR'NAL, *a.* Motherly ; befitting a mother.
MA-TĔR'NI-TY, *n.* The relation of a mother.
MĂTH-E-MĂT'ĬC,   } *a.* Relating to mathe-
MĂTH-E-MĂT'I-CAL, } matics ; demonstrative.
MĂTH-E-MĂT'I-CAL-LY, *ad.* According to
mathematics.
MĂTH-E-MA-TĬ''CIAN (măth-e-ma-tĭsh'an), *n.*
A person versed in mathematics.
MĂTH-E-MĂT'ĬCS, *n. pl.* That science which
treats of whatever can be numbered or meas-
ured.
MA-THĒ'SIS, *n.* The doctrine of mathematics.
MĂT'ĬN, *a.* Relating to the morning.
MĂT'ĬNS, *n. pl.* Morning worship or service.
MĂT'RASS, *n.* An egg-shaped chemical glass
MĀ'TRICE, *n.* The womb :—a mould. [vessel.
MĂT'RI-CĪDE, *n.* The murder of a mother.
MA-TRĬC'U-LĀTE, *v. a.* To admit to a member-
MA-TRĬC'U-LATE, *n.* A man matriculated. [ship.
MA-TRĬC-U-LĀ'TION, *n.* Act of matriculating.
MĂT-RI-MŌ'NI-AL, *a.* Relating to marriage.
MĂT'RI-MO-NY, *n.* Marriage; the nuptial state.
MĀ'TRIX, *n.* [L.] Womb ; a mould ; a matrice.
MĀ'TRON, *n.* An elderly married woman.
MĂT'RO-NAL *or* MĀ'TRON-AL, *a.* Suitable to a
matron ; motherly. [matronal.
MĂT'RON-LY *or* MĀ'TRON-LY, *a.* Motherly ;
MA-TRŎSS', *n.* A sort of soldier of artillery.
MĂT'TER, *n.* Body; substance extended :—sub-
ject ; affair ; business :—importance :—pus.
MĂT'TER, *v. n.* To be of importance ; to import.
MĂT'TOCK, *n.* A tool of husbandry ; a pickaxe.
MĂT'TRESS, *n.* A quilted bed stuffed.
MĂT'U-RĀTE, *v. a. & n.* To ripen ; to grow ripe.
MĂT-U-RĀ'TION, *n.* The state of growing ripe.
MĂT'U-RA-TĬVE, *a.* Ripening ; growing ripe.
MA-TŪRE', *a.* Ripe ; complete ; well digested.
MA-TŪRE', *v. a. & n.* To ripen ; to advance to
ripeness ; to become ripe.
MA-TŪRE'LY, *ad.* Ripely ; completely ; early.
MA-TŪ'RI-TY, *n.* Ripeness ; completion.
MĂUD'LIN, *a.* Drunk ; fuddled.—*n.* A plant.

MÂU'GRE (mâw'ger), *ad.* In spite of.
MÂU'KIN, *n.* A drag to sweep an oven :—scare-
MÂUL, *n.* A heavy hammer. See MALL. [crow.
MÂUND *or* MÂUND, *n.* A hand-basket.
MÂUN'DER, *v. n.* To murmur ; to beg.
MÂUN-DY-THÛRS'DAY, *n.* Thursday before
Good Friday and Easter.
MÂU-SO-LĒ'UM, *n.* ; *pl.* MÂU-SO-LĒ'A. [L.] A
magnificent tomb or funeral monument.
MÂW, *n.* The stomach of animals ; craw.
MÂWK'ISH, *a.* Apt to give satiety ; insipid.
MÂWK'ISH-NĔSS, *n.* Aptness to cause loathing.
MÂW'-WORM, *n.* A worm in the stomach.
MĂX'IL-LA-RY, *a.* Belonging to the jaw-bone.
MĂX'IM, *n.* An axiom ; a general principle.
MĂX'I-MUM, *n.* [L.] The greatest quantity.
MĀY (mā), *aaxiliary verb.* [*imp. t.* might.] To
be permitted or allowed ; to be possible.
MĀY (mā), *n.* The fifth month of the year.
MĀY, *v. n.* To gather flowers on May morning.
MĀY'-DĀY (mā'dā), *n.* The first day of May.
MĀY'-FLŎW-ER, *n.* A flower that blossoms in
May.
MĀY'-GĀME, *n.* A diversion ; a sport; a play.
MĀY'ING, *n.* The gathering of flowers in May.
MĀY'OR, *n.* The chief magistrate of a city.
MĀY'OR-AL-TY, *n.* The office of a mayor.
MĀY'OR-ĔSS, *n.* The wife of a mayor.
MĀY'-PŌLE, *n.* A pole to be danced round on
May-day.
MĂZ'ARD, *n.* The head :—a sort of cherry.
MĀZE, *n.* A labyrinth ; uncertainty ; perplexity.
MĀZE, *v. a.* To bewilder ; to confuse; to amaze.
MA-ZŎL'O-GY, *n.* A branch of zoölogy which
treats of mammiferous animals.
MĀ'ZY, *a.* Perplexed with windings ; confused.
MĒ, *pron.* The objective case of *I.*
MĒAD, *n.* A drink made of water and honey.
MĒAD, MĒAD'ŌW, *n.* Grass land for mowing.
MĒA'GRE (mē'ger), *a.* Poor ; lean ; thin.
MĒA'GRE-LY (mē'ger-le), *ad.* Poorly ; thinly.
MĒA'GRE-NĔSS (mē'ger-nĕs), *n.* Leanness.
MĒAL, *n.* A repast :—the edible part of corn.
MĒAL'MĂN, *n.* One that deals in meal.
MĒAL'Y, *a.* Of the taste or softness of meal.
MĒAL'Y-MŌÛŦHED (mēl'e-mŏûthd), *a.* Bash-
ful or soft of speech ; not speaking freely.
MĒAN, *a.* Base ; low ; vile :—middle ; moderate.
MĒAN, *n.* A medium ; interval ; income.
MĒAN, *v. n.* To have in mind ; to purpose.
MĒAN, *v. a.* To purpose ; to intend ; to design.
ME-ĂN'DER, *n.* A maze ; a labyrinth ; winding.
ME-ĂN'DER, *v. n.* To run with a winding course.
ME-ĂN'DROUS, *a.* Winding ; meandering.
MĒAN'ING, *n.* Purpose ; intention ; the sense.
MĒAN'LY, *ad.* Moderately ; basely ; poorly.
MĒAN'NESS, *n.* Want of excellence ; baseness.
MĒANS, *n. sing.* Instrument ; as, *by* this means.
MĒANT (mĕnt), *imp. t. & pp.* from *mean.*
MĒAN'WHĪLE, *ad.* In the intervening time.
MĒA'SLES (mē'zlz), *n. pl.* A contagious cu-
taneous disease.
MĒA'SLY (mē'zle), *a.* Infected with measles.
MĒAS'U-RA-BLE (mĕzh'u-ra-bl), *a.* That may be
measured :—moderate ; in small quantity.
MĒAS'U-RA-BLY (mĕzh'u-ra-ble), *ad.* Moder-
ately.
MĒAS'URE (mĕzh'ur), *n.* That by which any

thing is measured ; proportion ; degree ; quantity :—musical time :—moderation ; limit :—metre.—*pl.* Proceedings.

MĔAŞ'ŲRE (mĕzh'ųr), *v. a.* To compute by rule ; to adjust ; to proportion ; to mark out ; to allot. [ble.

MĔAŞ'ŲRE-LĔSS (mĕzh'ur-lĕs), *a.* Immeasura-

MĔAŞ'ŲRE-MĔNT (mĕzh'ųr-mĕnt), *n.* Act of measuring ; mensuration. [ures.

MĔAŞ'ŲR-ĘR (mĕzh'ųr-ęr), *n.* One that meas-

MĔAT, *n.* Flesh to be eaten ; food in general.

MĘ-€HĂN'ĮC, *n.* A manufacturer ; an artificer.

MĘ-€HĂN'ĮC, } *a.* Relating to mechanism
MĘ-€HĂN'Į-CĄL, } or to mechanics ; servile.

MĘ-€HĂN'Į-CĄL-LȲ, *ad.* According to mechanism.

MĘ-€HĂN'Į-CĄL-NĔSS, *n.* Mechanical state.

MĔ€H-Ą-NĬ''CIĄN (mĕk-ạ-nĭsh'ạn), *n.* A mechanist ; a mechanical philosopher. [motion.

MĘ-€HĂN'ĮCS, *n. pl.* A science treating of

MĔ€H'ĄN-ĬŞM, *n.* Construction of a machine.

MĔ€H'ĄN-ĬST, *n.* A maker of machines.

MĔ€H'LĮN, *a.* Noting lace made at Mechlin.

MĔD'ĄL, *n.* An ancient coin :—a piece stamped in honor of some person or event.

MĘ-DĂL'LĮC, *a.* Pertaining to medals.

MĘ-DĂL'LIǪN (mę-dăl'yụn), *n.* A large medal or stamp :—a circular tablet.

MĔD'ĄL-LĬST, *n.* A man skilled in medals.

MĔD'DLE, *v. n.* To have to do ; to interpose.

MĔD'DLĘR, *n.* One who meddles ; a busybody.

MĔD'DLE-SŎME, *a.* Intermeddling ; officious.

MĔD-Į-ÆˊVĄL, *a.* Relating to the middle ages.

MĒ'DĮ-ĄL, *a.* Mean ; noting an average. [ties.

MĒ'DĮ-ĀTE, *v. n.* To interpose between two par-
MĒ'DĮ-ĄTE, *a.* Interposed ; intervening ; middle.

MĒ'DĮ-ĄTE-LȲ, *ad.* By a secondary cause.

MĒ-DĮ-Ā'TIǪN, *n.* Interposition ; intercession.

MĒ'DĮ-Ā-TǪR, *n.* An interposer ; an intercessor.

MĒ-DĮ-A-TŌ'RĮ-ĄL, *a.* Belonging to a mediator.

MĒ-DĮ-Ā'TǪR-SHĬP, *n.* The office of a mediator.

MĒ'DĮ-Ā-TRĬX, *n.* A female mediator.

MĔD'Į-CĄ-BLE, *a.* That may be healed ; curable.

MĔD'Į-CĄL, *a.* Relating to the art of healing.

MĔD'Į-CĄL-LȲ, *ad.* Physically ; medicinally.

MĔD'Į-CĄ-MĔNT, *n.* Any thing used in healing.

MĔD'Į-CĀTE, *v. a.* To tincture with medicine.

MĘ-DĬÇ'Į-NĄL, *a.* Healing ; belonging to physic.

MĘ-DĬÇ'Į-NĄL-LȲ, *ad.* In a medicinal manner.

MĔD'Į-CĬNE, *n.* Physic ; a remedy ; a drug.

MĒ'DĮ-Ō-CRE (mē'dę-ō-kųr), *a.* Middling.

MĒ-DĮ-ŎC'RĮ-TȲ, *n.* Moderate degree ; middle rate, state, or degree. [on.

MĔD'Į-TĀTE, *v. a.* To plan ; to scheme ; to think

MĔD'Į-TĀTE, *v. n.* To think ; to contemplate.

MĔD-Į-TĀ'TIǪN, *n.* Act of meditating ; deep thought ; contemplation. [flecting.

MĔD'Į-TĀ-TĮVE, *a.* Given to meditation ; re-

MĔD-Į-TĘR-RĀ'NĘ-ĄN, *a.* Encircled with land.

MĒ'DĮ-ŬM, *n.* ; pl. MĒ'DĮ-ŬMŞ *or* MĒ'DĮ-Ą. Space passed through ; middle state ; means.

MĔD'LĄR, *n.* A tree, and the fruit of the tree.

MĔD'LEȲ (mĕd'lę), *n.* A mixture ; mingled mass.

MĔD'LEȲ (mĕd'lę), *a.* Mingled ; confused.

MĘ-DŬL'LĄR, *a.* The same as *medullary.*

MĔD'ŲL-LĄ-RȲ, *a.* Pertaining to the marrow.

MĘ-DŬL'LĮNE, *n.* The pith of the sunflower, &c.

MĔED, *n.* A reward ; recompense :—desert.

MĔEK, *a.* Mild ; not proud ; soft ; gentle ; hum-

MĔEK'EN (mē'kn), *v. a.* To make meek. [ble.

MĔEK'LȲ, *ad.* Mildly ; gently ; humbly.

MĔEK'NĔSS, *n.* Gentleness ; mildness ; humility.

MĔET, *a.* Fit ; proper ; qualified ; seemly.

MĔET, *v. a.* [*imp. t. & pp.* met.] To come together ; to join ; to encounter ; to find ; to light

MĔET, *v. n.* To encounter ; to assemble. [on.

MĔET'ĮNG, *n.* An assembly ; interview ; a conflux.

MĔET'ĮNG-HŎÛSE, *n.* A house of public wor-

MĔET'LȲ, *ad.* Fitly ; properly ; suitably. [ship.

MĔET'NĔSS, *n.* Fitness ; propriety ; suitableness.

MĒ'GRĮM, *n.* Disorder of the head.—*pl.* Whims.

MĔL'ĄN-€HŎL-ĮC, *a.* Dejected ; gloomy ; dismal.

MĔL'ĄN-€HŎL-Į-NĔSS, *n.* Melancholy.

MĔL'ĄN-€HŎL-Ȳ, *n.* Gloom of mind ; sadness.

MĔL'ĄN-€HŎL-Ȳ, *a.* Gloomy ; dismal ; dejected.

MĔL'Į-LŎT, *n.* A plant ; a species of trifolium.

‖MĔL'IǪ-RĀTE (mĕl'yǫ-rāt *or* mē'lę-ǫ-rāt), *v. a.* To make better ; to ameliorate. [ment.

‖MĔL-IǪ-RĀ'TIǪN (mĕl-yǫ-rā'shụn), *n.* Improve-

MĔL-LĬF'ĘR-OŬS, *a.* Productive of honey.

MĔL-LĮ-FĮ-CĀ'TIǪN, *n.* Production of honey.

MĔL-LĬF'LŲ-ĘNCE, *n.* A flow of sweetness.

MĔL-LĬF'LŲ-ĘNT, MĔL-LĬF'LŲ-OŬS, *a.* Sweetly flowing, as with honey.

MĔL'LŌW (mĕl'lō), *a.* Soft ; fully ripe :—drunk.

MĔL'LŌW (mĕl'lō), *v. a. & n.* To ripen ; to soften.

MĔL'LŌW-NĔSS, *n.* Maturity ; ripeness ; softness.

MĘ-LŌ'DĮ-OŬS, *a.* Musical ; harmonious. [ly.

MĘ-LŌ'DĮ-OŬS-LȲ, *ad.* Musically ; harmonious-

MĘ-LŌ'DĮ-OŬS-NĔSS, *n.* Sweetness of sound.

MĔL-Ǫ-DRĄ-MĂT'ĮC, *a.* Relating to a melodrame.

MĔL'Ǫ-DRĀME, *n.* A dramatic performance with songs or music.

MĔL'Ǫ-DȲ, *n.* Music ; sweetness of sound.

MĔL'ǪN, *n.* A well-known plant and its fruit.

MĔLT, *v. a. & n.* To dissolve ; to become liquid.

MĔLT'ĮNG, *n.* Act of softening ; inteneration.

MĔM'BĘR, *n.* A limb ; a part ; a clause.

MĔM'BĘR-SHĬP, *n.* State of a member ; union.

MĔM-BRĄ-NĀ'CEOŬS (-shųs), MĘM-BRĀ'NĘ-OŬS, MĔM'BRĄ-NOŬS, *a.* Consisting of mem-

MĔM'BRĀNE, *n.* A supple, elastic web. [branes.

MĘ-MĔN'TŌ, *n.* ; pl. MĘ-MĔN'TŌEŞ. A memorial ; a notice ; a hint.

MĘ-MŎÏR' (mę-moïr' *or* mĕm'wâr), *n.* A history familiarly written ; a written account. [bered.

MĔM-Ǫ-RĄ-BĬL'Į-Ą, *n. pl.* Things to be remem-

MĔM'Ǫ-RĄ-BLE, *a.* Worthy of remembrance.

MĔM'Ǫ-RĄ-BLȲ, *ad.* In a memorable manner.

MĔM-Ǫ-RĂN'DŲM, *n.* ; pl. MĔM-Ǫ-RĂN'DĄ *and* MĔM-Ǫ-RĂN'DŲMŞ. [L.] A note to help the memory. [memory.

MĘ-MŌ'RĮ-ĄL, *a.* Preserving memory.

MĘ-MŌ'RĮ-ĄL, *n.* A monument ; record ; memorandum :—a written address.

MĘ-MŌ'RĮ-ĄL-ĬST, *n.* Presenter of a memorial.

MĔM'Ǫ-RȲ, *n.* The faculty of retaining or recollecting things past ; retention ; reminiscence.

MĔN, *n.* The plural of *man.*

MĔN'ACE, *v. a.* To threaten ; to threat ; to defy.

MĔN'ACE, *n.* Threat ; denunciation.

MĔN'Ą-CĘR, *n.* One who threatens. [animals.

MĘ-NĂGE' (mę-năzh'), *n.* [Fr.] A collection of

MĔN-Ä'GĘ-RIĔ (mę-nä'zhę-rē), MĔN-Ä'GĘ-RȲ, *n.* A collection of, or place for, animals.

MĔND, *v. a.* To repair ; to correct ; to improve.

MĔND, *v. n.* To grow better; to improve.
MĔND′A-BLE, *a.* Capable of being mended.
MĘN-DĀ′CIOŲS (mĕn-dā′shŭs), *a.* False; lying.
MĘN-DĂÇ′Į-TY, *n.* A falsehood; want of truth.
MĔN′DĮ-CĂN-CY, *n.* Beggary; mendicity.
MĔN′DĮ-CĂNT, *a.* Begging.—*n.* A beggar.
MĘN-DĬÇ′Į-TY, *n.* The life or state of a beggar.
MĚ′NĮ-ĄL, *a.* Belonging to servants; low; servile.
MĚ′NĮ-ĄL, *n.* A domestic or low servant.
MĘ-NŎL′Q-ĢY, *n.* A register of months.
MĔN′SĄL, *a.* Belonging to, or done at, the table.
MĔN′STRŲ-ĄL, *a.* Monthly; lasting a month.
MĔN′STRŲ-ŬM, *n.;* pl. MĔN′STRŲ-Ą. A sol-
  vent; a dissolving fluid. [mensurable.
MĔNS-Ų-RĄ-BĬL′Į-TY, *n.* The state of being
MĔNS′Ų-RĄ-BLE, *a.* That may be measured.
MĔNS-Ų-RĀ′TIQN, *n.* Act or art of measuring.
MĔN′TĄL, *a.* Intellectual; relating to the mind.
MĔN′TĄL-LY, *ad.* Intellectually; in the mind.
MĔN′TIQN, *n.* A recital, oral or written; a hint.
MĔN′TIQN, *v. a.* To name; to state; to express.
MĘ-PHĬT′ĮC, MĘ-PHĬT′Į-CĄL, *a.* Foul; noxious.
MĔR′CĄN-TĪLE, *a.* Trading; commercial.
MĔR′CĘ-NĄ-RĮ-NĔSS, *n.* Venality. [hireling.
MĔR′CĘ-NĄ-RY, *a.* Venal; hired; sold for money;
MĔR′CĘ-NĄ-RY, *n.* A hireling; one serving for
MĔR′CĘR, *n.* One who deals in silks. [pay.
MĔR′CĘR-Y, *n.* The trade or wares of mercers.
MĔR′CHĄN-DĪSE, *n.* Commerce; trade; wares.
MĔR′CHĄN-DĪSE, *v. n.* To trade; to traffic.
MĔR′GHĄNT, *n.* A trader or dealer by wholesale.
MĔR′CHĄNT-Ą-BLE, *a.* Fit to be bought and sold.
MĔR′CHĄNT-MĂN, *n.* A ship of trade.
MĔR′CĮ-FÛL, *a.* Compassionate; tender; ḳind.
MĔR′CĮ-FÛL-LY, *ad.* Tenderly; with pity.
MĔR′CĮ-FÛL-NĔSS, *n.* Tenderness; pity.
MĔR′CĮ-LĔSS, *a.* Void of mercy; pitiless; cruel.
MĔR′CĮ-LĔSS-LY, *ad.* In a manner void of pity.
MĔR′CĮ-LĘSS-NĔSS, *n.* Want of mercy or pity.
MĘR-CŪ′RĮ-ĄL, *a.* Containing mercury; active.
MĔR′CŲ-RY, *n.* A deity; a planet; quicksilver.
MĔR′CY, *n.* Tenderness; clemency; mildness.
MĔR′CY-SĒAT, *n.* The propitiatory of the Jews.
MĒRE, *a.* This or that only; absolute; bare.
MĒRE, *n.* A pool; a lake; a boundary; a ridge.
MĒRE′LY, *ad.* Simply; only; solely; absolutely.
MĔR-Ę-TRĬ′′CIOŲS (mĕr-ę-trĭsh′ŭs), *a.* Allur-
  ing by false show; lewd; false. [sink.
MĔRĢE, *v. a. & n.* To immerse; to plunge; to
MĘ-RĬD′Į-ĄN, *n.* Noon; midday; a great circle
  which the sun crosses at noon; highest point.
MĘ-RĬD′Į-ĄN, *a.* Relating to midday; highest.
MĘ-RĬD′Į-Q-NĄL, *a.* Southern; southerly.
MĔR′ĮT, *n.* Desert; due reward; claim; right.
MĔR′ĮT, *v. a.* To deserve; to have a right to; to
MĔR-Į-TŌ′RĮ-OŬS, *a.* Deserving reward. [earn.
MĔR-Į-TŌ′RĮ-OŬS-LY, *ad.* In a deserving manner.
MĔR-Į-TŌ′RĮ-OŲS-NĔSS, *n.* State of deserving
MĔR′LĮN, *n.* A kind of hawk or falcon. [well.
MĔR′MĀID, *n.* A sea woman; an animal fabled
  to have a woman's head and a fish's tail.
MĔR′RĮ-LY, *ad.* Gayly; cheerfully; with mirth.
MĔR′RĮ-MĔNT, *n.* Mirth; gayety; cheerfulness.
MĔR′RĮ-NĔSS, *n.* Mirth; merry disposition.
MĔR′RY, *a.* Gay; jovial; cheerful; laughing.
MĔR′RY-ĂN′DREW (mĕr′rę-ăn′drų), *n.* A buf-
  foon; a zany. [ing.
MĔR′RY-MĀK′ĮNG, *n.* A festival; a jovial meet-

MĔR′RY-THOUGHT (mĕr′rę-thâwt), *n.* A forked
  bone between the neck and breast of fowls.
MĘ-SĒĒMŞ′, *impersonal verb.* It seems to me.
MĔŞ-ĘN-TĔR′ĮC, *a.* Relating to the mesentery.
MĔŞ′ĘN-TĔR-Y, *n.* A membraṇe in the pelvis.
MĔSH, *n.* Space between the threads of a net.
MĔSH, *v. a.* To catch in a net; to insnare.
MĔSH′Y, *a.* Reticulated; like network.
MĔŞ′LĮN, *n.* A mixture of different kinds of grain.
MĔSNE (mēn), *a.* Middle; intermediate.
MĘ-SÖM′Ę-LĂS, *n.* A veined precious stone.
MĔŞS, *n.* A dish:—a medley:—a set or company.
MĔSS, *v. n.* To eat:—to feed together.
MĔS′SĄĢE, *n.* An errand; notice or advice sent.
MĔS′SĘN-ĢĘR, *n.* One who carries a message.
MĘS-SĪ′ĄH, *n.* Christ; the Saviour of the world.
MĘS-SĪ′ĄH-SHĬP, *n.* The office of Messiah.
MESSIEURS (mĕsh′ŭrz *or* mĕs′yęrs), *n. pl.* [Fr.]
  Sirs; gentlemen.
MĔSS′MĀTE, *n.* One who eats at the same table.
MĔS′SUĄĢE (mĕs′swạj), *n.* A dwelling-house
MĔT, *imp. t. & pp.* from *meet.* [with land, &c.
MĘ-TĂB′Q-LĄ, *n.* A change of time, air, or disease.
MĘ-TĂℂH′RQ-NĬŞM, *n.* A date too late in time.
MĔ′TAĢE, *n.* Measurement of coals.
MĔT′ĄL (mĕt′tl *or* mĕt′ạl), *n.* A heavy, hard
  substance, shining, opaque, and fusible by
  heat:—glass in a state of fusion. [metal.
MĘ-TĂL′LĮC, *a.* Relating to, or containing,
MĔT-ĄL-LĬF′ĘR-OŬS, *a.* Producing metals.
MĔT′ĄL-LĪNE, *a.* Consisting of metal; metal-
MĔT′ĄL-LĬST, *n.* A worker in metals. [lic.
MĔT-ĄL-LŎG′RĄ-PHY, *n.* Description of metals.
MĔT′ĄL-LÜR-ĢĬST, *n.* A worker in metals.
MĔT′ĄL-LÜR-ĢY, *n.* The art of working metals.
MĔT-Ą-MÖR′PHQSE, *v. a.* To change the form of.
MĔT-Ą-MÖR′PHQ-SĬS, *n.;* pl. MĔT-Ą-MÖR′PHQ-
  SĒŞ. Change of form or shape; transformation.
MĔT′Ą-PHQR, *n.* A figure of speech, a compari-
  son, or simile comprised in a word.
MĔT-Ą-PHŎR′ĮC, ⎰ *a.* Partaking of meta-
MĔT-Ą-PHŎR′Į-CĄL, ⎰ phor; figurative.
MĔT-Ą-PHŎR′Į-CĄL-LY, *ad.* Figuratively.
MĔT′Ą-PHRĀSE, *n.* A mere verbal translation.
MĔT′Ą-PHRĂST, *n.* A verbal or literal translator.
MĔT-Ą-PHRĂS′TĮC, *a.* Literal in interpretation.
MĔT-Ą-PHYŞ′ĮC, ⎰ *a.* Versed in metaphysics;
MĔT-Ą-PHYŞ′Į-CĄL, ⎰ relating to metaphysics.
MĔT-Ą-PHYŞ′Į-CĄL-LY, *ad.* By metaphysics.
MĔT-Ą-PHY-ŞĬ′′CIĄN (mĕt-ạ-fę-zĭsh′ạn), *n.* One
  versed in metaphysics. [psychology.
MĔT-Ą-PHYŞ′ĮCS, *n. pl.* The science of mind;
MĔT′Ą-PLĂŞM, *n.* Alteration of letters.
MĘ-TĂS′TĄ-SĬS, *n.* Change in seat of disease.
MĘ-TĂTH′Ę-SĬS, *n.* A transposition of letters, &c.
MĒTE, *v. a.* To measure; to reduce to measure.
MĒTE, *n.* A measure; a limit; a bound. [souls.
MĘ-TĔMP-SY-ℂHō′SĮS, *n.* Transmigration of
MĒ′TĘ-QR, *n.* A luminoŭs transient body rapid-
  ly moving in the atmosphere.
MĒ-TĘ-ŎR′ĮC, *a.* Relating to meteors or aerolites.
MĒ-TĘ-Q-RQ-LŎĢ′ĮC, ⎰ *a.* Relating to mete-
MĒ-TĘ-Q-RQ-LŎĢ′Į-CĄL, ⎰ orology. [teors.
MĒ-TĘ-Q-RŎL′Q-ĢĬST, *n.* A man skilled in me-
MĒ-TĘ-Q-RŎL′Q-ĢY, *n.* The doctrine of meteors.
MĘ-TĒ′Q-RQ-SCŌPE, *n.* An astronomical instru-
MĒ′TĘR, *n.* A measurer; as, a coal-*meter.* [ment.
MĒTE′WAND (mĕt′wŏnd), *n.* A measuring staff.

ME-THĔG′LĬN, *n.* Drink made of honey and water fermented; mead.
ME-THĬNKS′, *v. impers.* I think; it seems to me.
MĔTH′ǪD, *n.* A regular order; a manner; way.
ME-THŎD′ĬC, } *a.* Relating to method; ex-
ME-THŎD′Ĭ-CǍL, } act; regular.
ME-THŎD′Ĭ-CǍL-LỸ, *ad.* According to method.
MĔTH′ǪD-ĬŞM, *n.* The principles of Methodists.
MĔTH′ǪD-ĬST, *n.* One of a sect of Christians.
MĔTH-Ǫ-DĬS′TĬC, } *a.* Relating to the Meth-
MĔTH-Ǫ-DĬS′TĬ-CǍL, } odists. [order.
MĔTH′Ǫ-DĪZE, *v. a.* To regulate; to dispose in
ME-THOUGHT′ (me-thâwt′), *imp. t.* from *me-thinks.* I thought; it appeared to me.
MĔT-Ǫ-NỸM′Ĭ-CǍL, *a.* Put for something else.
ME-TŎN′Y-MY, *n.* A rhetorical figure by which one word is put for another. [my.
MĔT-Ǫ-PŎS′CǪ-PY, *n.* The study of physiogno-
MĒ′TRE (mē′tẹr), *n.* Verse; measure; numbers.
MĔT′RĬ-CǍL, *a.* Pertaining to metre or numbers.
ME-TRŎP′Ǫ-LĬS, *n.* The chief city of a country.
MĔT-RǪ-PŎL′Ĭ-TǍN, *n.* An archbishop.
MĔT-RǪ-PŎL′Ĭ-TǍN,*a.* Belonging to a metropolis.
MĔT′TLE (mĕt′tl), *n.* Substance; metal:—spirit; sprightliness; courage. [dor.
MĔT′TLED (mĕt′tld),*a.* Courageous; full of ar-
MĔT′TLE-SŎME (mĕt′tl-sŭm), *a.* Lively; brisk.
MEW (mū), *n.* A cage; an enclosure:—a sea-fowl:—*pl.* Buildings for horses; stables.
MEW (mū),*v. a.* To shut up; to confine; to shed.
MEW (mū), *v. n.* To change; to cry as a cat.
MEWL (mūl), *v. n.* To squall as a child.
MEWL′ẸR (mūl′ẹr),*n.* One who squalls or mewls.
ME-ZĒ′RẸ-ǪN, *n.* A flowering shrub.
MĔZ-ZǪ-TĬN′TŌ (mĕt-sǫ-tĬn′tō), *n.* A kind of engraving on copper. [miasma.
MĪ′ǍŞM, *n.* Noxious exhalation or effluvium;
MĬ-ǍŞ′MA, *n.;* pl. MĬ-ǍŞ′MA-TA. Noxious exha-lations or effluvia.
MĬ-ǍŞ-MĂT′ĬC, *a.* Noxious; infectious; tainted.
MĪ′CA, *n.* A shining mineral substance.
MĬ-CĀ′CEOUS (mĬ-kā′shụs), *a.* Relating to mica.
MĪCE, *n.* The plural of *mouse.* [chael, Sept. 29.
MĪCH′AẸL-MĂS (mĬk′ẹl-măs), *n.* Feast of St. Mi-
MĬC′KLE (mĬk′kl), *a.* Much; great. [*Scotland.*]
MĪ′CRǪ-CŎŞM, *n.* A little world; man′s body.
MĪ-CRǪ-CŎŞ′MĬC, } *a.* Relating to a micro-
MĪ-CRǪ-CŎŞ′MĬ-CǍL, } cosm. [jects.
MĪ-CRŎG′RA-PHY, *n.* Description of minute ob-
MĪ′CRǪ-SCŌPE, *n.* An optical instrument for viewing and examining the smallest objects.
MĪ-CRǪ-SCŎP′ĬC, } *a.* Relating to a micro-
MĪ-CRǪ-SCŎP′Ĭ-CǍL, } scope:—very minute.
MĬD, *a.* Middle; equally between two extremes.
MĬD′DĀY (mĬd′dā), *n.* Noon; meridian.
MĬD′DLE (mĬd′dl), *a.* Equally distant from the two extremes; intermediate; intervening.
MĬD′DLE, *n.* The part equidistant from two ex-tremes; centre; midst. [the middle of life.
MĬD′DLE-ĀGED (mĬd′dl-ājd), *a.* Being about
MĬD′DLĬNG,*a.* Of middle rank; moderate.
MĬD′LĂND, *a.* Surrounded by land; interior.
MĬD′LĔG, *n.* The middle of the leg. [night.
MĬD′NĪGHT (mĬd′nĬt), *n.* Twelve o′clock at
MĬD′NĪGHT, *a.* Being in the middle of the night.
MĬD′RĬFF, *n.* The diaphragm. [ship of war.
MĬD′SHĬP-MAN, *n.* An under officer on board a
MĬDST, *n.* The middle.—*a.* Midmost.

MĬDST, *prep.* Poetically used for *amidst.*
MĬD′STRĒAM, *n.* The middle of the stream.
MĬD′SŬM-MẸR, *n.* The summer solstice, June 21.
MĬD′WĀY, *n.* The middle of the way.
MĬD′WĀY, *ad.* In the middle of the passage.
MĬD′WĪFE, *n.* A woman who assists women in childbirth. [ing women in childbirth.
MĬD′WĪFE-RY (mĬd′wĬf-rẹ), *n.* The art of assist-
MĬD′WĬN-TẸR, *n.* The winter solstice, Dec. 21.
MIĒN (mēn), *n.* Air; look; manner; aspect.
MĬFF, *n.* A slight resentment. [*Colloquial.*]
MIGHT (mĬt), *imp. t.* from *may.*
MIGHT (mĬt), *n.* Power; strength; force; ability.
MIGHT′Ĭ-LY (mĬ′tẹ-lẹ), *ad.* Powerfully; strongly.
MIGHT′Ĭ-NĔSS (mĬ′tẹ-nĕs), *n.* Power; greatness.
MIGHT′Y (mĬ′tẹ), *a.* Strong; powerful; great.
MĬGN-Ǫ-NĔTTE′ (mĬn-yǫ-nĕt′), *n.* An annual plant and its flower.
MĪ′GRĀTE, *v. n.* To remove; to change place.
MĪ-GRĀ′TIǪN, *n.* Change of place; removal.
MĪ′GRA-TǪ-RY, *a.* Changing residence; wan-
MĬLCH (mĬlsh), *a.* Giving milk. [dering.
MĪLD, *a.* Kind; tender; soft; gentle; not acrid.
MĬL′DEW (mĬl′dụ), *n.* A disease in plants.
MĬL′DEW (mĬl′dū), *v. a.* To taint with mildew.
MĪLD′LY, *ad.* Tenderly; kindly; gently.
MĪLD′NẸSS, *n.* Gentleness; tenderness; mercy.
MĪLE, *n.* A measure of distance; 320 rods.
MĪLE′STŌNE, *n.* A stone set to mark the miles.
MĬL′FÖĬL, *n.* An herbaceous plant.
MĬL′IA-RY (mĬl′ya-rẹ),*a.* Small; like millet seed.
MĬL′Ĭ-TĂNT, *a.* Fighting; engaged in warfare.
MĬL′Ĭ-TA-RY, *a.* Relating to war; warlike.
MĬL′Ĭ-TA-RY, *n.* The soldiery; the army.
MĬL′Ĭ-TĀTE, *v. n.* To oppose; to operate against.
MĬ-LĬ″TIA (mĬ-lĬsh′ya), *n.* The enrolled soldiers.
MĬLK, *n.* Liquor with which females feed their young from the breast:—juice of plants.
MĬLK, *v. a.* To draw milk by the hand.
MĬLK′Ĭ-NĔSS,*n.* Resemblance of milk; softness.
MĬLK′MĀID,*n.* A woman employed in the dairy.
MĬLK′MĂN, *n.* A man who sells milk.
MĬLK′PĀIL, *n.* A pail for containing milk.
MĬLK′PĂN, *n.* A vessel in which milk is kept.
MĬLK-PŎR′RĬDGE, } *n.* Food made by boiling
MĬLK-PŎT′TAGE, } milk with water and meal or flour.
MĬLK′-SCŌRE, *n.* An account of milk owed for.
MĬLK′SŎP, *n.* A soft, simple, effeminate man.
MĬLK′-TÔÔTH, *n.* The first foretooth of a foal.
MĬLK′-WHĪTE, *a.* White as milk. [tender.
MĬLK′Y, *a.* Made of, or like, milk:—soft; gentle;
MĬLK′Y-WĀY (mĬlk′ẹ-wā), *n.* The galaxy.
MĬLL, *n.* An engine for grinding corn, &c.
MĬLL, *v. a.* To grind; to comminute; to stamp.
MĬLL′-CŎG, *n.* The tooth of a mill-wheel.
MĬLL′-DĂM, *n.* A dam for turning a mill.
MĬL′LE-NA-RY, *a.* Consisting of a thousand.
MĬL-LĔN′NĬ-AL, *a.* Pertaining to the millennium.
MĬL-LĔN′NĬ-ŬM, *n.* Christ′s reign of 1000 years.
MĬL′LE-PĔD, *n.* An insect; the wood-louse.
MĬL′LE-PŌRE, *n.* An animal that forms coral.
MĬL′LER, *n.* One who attends a mill:—a winged
MĬL-LĔS′Ĭ-MAL, *a.* Thousandth. [insect.
MĬL′LET, *n.* A plant and grain; a kind of fish.
MĬLL′-HŎRSE, *n.* A horse that turns a mill.
MĬL′LĬ-NẸR, *n.* One who makes bonnets for women.

MĬL'LĬ-NĔR-Y, _n._ Work or wares of milliners.
MĬL'LĬON (mĭl'yun), _n._ Ten hundred thousand.
MĬL'LĬONTH (mĭl'yunth),_a._Ordinal of a million.
MĬLL-RĒA', MĬLL-RĒĔ', _n._ A Portuguese coin.
MĬLL'STŌNE,_n._A stone by which corn is ground.
MĬLL'-TÔÔTH, _n._ A grinder ; a double tooth.
MĬLT, _n._ The sperm of the male fish :—spleen.
MĬLT'ER, _n._ The male of any fish.
MĬ-MĔT'ĬC, MĬ-MĔT'Ĭ-CAL,_a._ Imitative; apish.
MĬM'ĬC, _v. a._ [_imp. t. & pp._ mimicked.] To imitate for sport ; to ape ; to mock.
MĬM'ĬC, _n._ A ludicrous imitator ; a buffoon.
MĬM'ĬC, MĬM'Ĭ-CAL, _a._ Imitative ; apish.
MĬM'ĬC-RY, _n._ Burlesque or playful imitation.
MĬ-NĀ'CIOUS (mĭ-nā'shus), _a._ Full of threats.
MĬN'A-RĔT, _n._ Slender turret of a mosque.
MĬN'A-TO-RY, _a._ Threatening ; menacing.
MĬNCE, _v. a._ To cut into small parts ; to palliate.
MĬNCE, _v. n._ To walk or speak with affectation or affected nicety.
MĬNCE-PĪE' (mĭns-pī'), }_n._ A pie made of
MĬNCED-PĪE' (mĭnst-pī'), } minced meat, &c.
MĬN'CĬNG-LY, _ad._ In small parts ; affectedly.
MĪND, _n._ The intelligent or intellectual faculty in man ; the understanding ; choice ; opinion.
MĪND, _v. a._ To mark ; to attend ; to regard.
MĪND'ED, _a._ Disposed ; inclined ; affected.
MĪND'FÛL, _a._ Attentive ; heedful ; observant.
MĪND'FÛL-LY, _ad._ Attentively ; heedfully.
MĪND'FÛL-NĔSS, _n._ Attention ; regard.
MĪNE, _pr. poss._ from _I._ Belonging to me.
MĪNE, _n._ A place in the earth containing minerals or ores :—a cavern under a fortification.
MĪNE, _v. a. & n._ To sap ; to ruin by mines ; to
MĪN'ER, _n._ One that digs in mines. [dig.
MĬN'ER-AL, _n._ Matter dug out of mines ; a fossil.
MĬN'ER-AL, _a._ Consisting of fossil bodies.
MĬN'ER-AL-ĬST, _n._ One skilled in minerals.
MĬN'ER-AL-ĪZE, _v. a._ To combine with a mineral.
MĬN-ER-A-LŎG'Ĭ-CAL,_a._ Relating to mineralogy.
MĬN-ER-ĂL'O-GĬST, _n._ One versed in mineralogy.
MĬN-ER-ĂL'O-GY, _n._ The science of minerals.
MĬN'GLE, _v. a. & n._ To mix ; to join ; to be mixed.
MĬN'IA-TŪRE _or_ MĬN'Ĭ-A-TŪRE, _n._ A picture or representation in a small compass.
MĬN'ĬM, _n._ A dwarf :—a short note in music.
MĬN'Ĭ-MŬM, _n._ [L.] The smallest quantity.
MĬN'ION (mĭn'yun), _n._ A favorite ; a low, mean dependant :—a small printing type.
MĬN'ĬS-TER, _n._ An officer of the state or church ; an ambassador ; a delegate ; an agent.
MĬN'ĬS-TER, _v. a._ To give ; to supply ; to afford.
MĬN'ĬS-TER, _v. n._ To serve in any office.
MĬN-ĬS-TĒ'RĬ-AL, _a._ Relating to the ministry.
MĬN-ĬS-TĒ'RĬ-AL-LY, _ad._ In a ministerial manner. [mand.
MĬN'ĬS-TRĂNT, _a._ Attendant ; acting at com-
MĬN-ĬS-TRĀ'TION, _n._ Agency ; service ; office.
MĬN'ĬS-TRY, _n._ Office ; service ; agency :—ecclesiastical function :—the body of ministers.
MĬN'IUM _or_ MĬN'Ĭ-ŬM, _n._ [L.] Red lead.
MĬNK, _n._ A small animal valued for its fur.
MĬN'NŌW (mĭn'nŏ), _n._ A very small fish ; a pink.
MĪ'NQR, _a._ Inferior ; less ; smaller ; lower.
MĪ'NQR, _n._ One under age :—the second proposition in a syllogism. [the less number.
MĬ-NŎR'Ĭ-TY, _n._ The state of being under age ;
MĬN'O-TAUR, _n._ A fabulous monster.

MĬN'STER, _n._ A monastery ; a cathedral church.
MĬN'STREL, _n._ A singer ; a musician.
MĬN'STREL-SY, _n._ Music ; a band of musicians.
MĬNT, _n._ A place for coining money :—a plant.
MĬNT, _v. a._ To coin ; to stamp ; to invent.
MĬNT'AGE, _n._ Coinage ; the duty paid for coining.
MĬNT'ER, MĬNT'MAN, _n._ A maker of coins.
MĬNT'-MĂS-TER,_n._ One who presides in coinage.
MĬN'U-ĔT, _n._ A stately, regular dance.
MĬ-NŪTE', _a._ Very small ; exact ; trifling.
MĬN'UTE, _n._ The 60th part of an hour :—a note.
MĬN'UTE, _v. a._ To set down in short hints.
MĬN'UTE-BOOK (-bûk), _n._ A book of short hints.
MĬN'UTE-GLĂSS, _n._ A glass measuring minutes.
MĬN'UTE-GŬN,_n._ A gun discharged every minute.
MĬN'UTE-HĂND, _n._ A hand pointing to minutes.
MĬN'UTE-LY, _a._ Happening every minute.
MĬ-NŪTE'LY, _ad._ To a small point ; exactly ;
MĬ-NŪTE'NESS, _n._ Extreme smallness. [nicely.
MĬ-NŪ'TĬ-Æ (me-nū'she-ē), _n. pl._ [L.] Minute things ; the smallest particulars.
MĬNX, _n._ A pert, wanton girl :—a she puppy.
MĪ'NY, _a._ Relating to mines ; subterraneous.
MĬR'A-CLE, _n._ A wonder ; a supernatural event.
MĬ-RĂC'U-LOŬS, _a._ Done by miracle ; supernatural ; wonderful. [ner.
MĬ-RĂC'U-LOŬS-LY, _ad._ In a miraculous man-
MĬ-RĂC'U-LOŬS-NĔSS, _n._ State of being miracu-
MĬR-A-DŌR',_n._ [Sp.] A balcony or gallery. [lous.
MĬ-RĂGE' (me-räzh'), _n._ [Fr.] An optical illu-
MĪRE, _n._ Mud ; soft, wet earth. [sion.
MĪRE, _v. a._ To whelm in the mud ; to soil.
MĪR'Ĭ-NĔSS, _n._ Dirtiness ; fulness of mire.
MĬRK'Y, _a._ Dark ; wanting light ; gloomy.
MĬR'RQR, _n._ A looking-glass :—a pattern.
MĬR'RQR, _v. a._ To exhibit by use of a mirror.
MĬRTH, _n._ Merriment ; jollity ; gayety.
MĬRTH'FÛL, _a._ Merry ; gay ; joyful ; cheerful.
MĬRTH'FÛL-LY, _ad._ In a merry manner ; cheer-
MĬRTH'LESS, _a._ Joyless ; cheerless. [fully.
MĪR'Y, _a._ Deep in mud ; muddy ; full of mire.
MĬS. A prefix, denoting privation, or an ill sense.
MĬS-ĂC-CEP-TĀ'TION, _n._ A misunderstanding.
MĬS-AD-VĔNT'URE (mĭs-ad-vĕnt'yur), _n._ A misfortune ; mischance ; mishap.
MĬS-ĀIMED' (mĭs-āmd'), _a._ Not aimed rightly.
MĬS-AL-LĒGE', _v. a._ To cite falsely as a proof.
MĬS-AL-LĪ'ANCE, _n._ An improper association.
MĬS'AN-THRŌPE, _n._ A hater of mankind.
MĬS-AN-THRŎP'ĬC, }_a._ Relating to misan-
MĬS-AN-THRŎP'Ĭ-CAL, } thropy.
MĬS-ĂN'THRO-PĬST, _n._ A hater of mankind.
MĬS-ĂN'THRO-PY, _n._ Hatred of mankind.
MĬS-ĂP-PLĬ-CĀ'TION, _n._ Wrong application.
MĬS-AP-PLY', _v. a._ To apply to wrong purposes.
MĬS-ĂP-PRE-HĔND', _v. a._ To misunderstand.
MĬS-ĂP-PRE-HĔN'SION, _n._ A mistake.
MĬS-AS-CRĪBE', _v. a._ To ascribe falsely. [wrong.
MĬS-AS-SĪGN' (mĭs-as-sīn'), _v. a._ To assign
MĬS-BE-CŎME' (mĭs-be-kŭm'), _v. a._ To suit ill.
MĬS-BE-HĀVE', _v. n._ To act ill or improperly.
MĬS-BE-HĀVE', _v. a._ To conduct ill or improperly. [duct.
MĬS-BE-HĀV'IQR (mĭs-be-hāv'yur), _n._ Ill con-
MĬS-BE-LIĒF' (mĭs-be-lēf'), _n._ A wrong belief.
MĬS-BE-LIĔV'ER, _n._ One that believes wrong.
MĬS-BE-STŌW', _v. a._ To bestow wrong.
MĬS-CĂL'CU-LĀTE, _v. a._ To reckon wrong.

MĬS-CĂL-CŲ-LĀ'TIǪN, *n.* A wrong computation.
MĬS-CÂLL', *v. a.* To name improperly. [tion.
MĬS-CĂR'RĮAҼE (mĭs-kăr'rĭj), *n.* Failure; abor-
MĬS-CĂR'RY, *v. n.* To fail; to have an abortion.
MĬS-CĄST', *v. a.* To take a wrong account of.
MĬS-CĘL-LĀ'NĘ-OŬS, *a.* Composed of various
  kinds; diversified; various.
MĬS'CĘL-LA-NY, *n.* A mixture of various kinds.
MĬS-CHĂNCE', *n.* Ill luck; misfortune; mishap.
MĬS'CHĮEF (mĭs'chĭf), *n.* Harm; hurt; injury.
MĬS'CHĮEF-MĂK'ĘR, *n.* One who causes mis-
MĬS'CHĮEF-MĂK'ĬNG, *a.* Causing harm. [chief.
MĬS'CHIĘ-VOŬS (mĭs'chę-vŭs), *a.* Harmful;
  hurtful; injurious; wicked; noxious. [fully.
MĬS'CHIĘ-VOŬS-LY (mĭs'chę-vŭs-lę) *ad.* Hurt-
MĬS'CĮ-BLE, *a.* Possible to be mingled. [tion.
MĬS-CĪ-TĀ'TIǪN, *n.* An unfair or false quota-
MĬS-CĪTE', *v. a.* To cite or quote wrong.
MĬS-CLĀIM', *n.* A mistaken claim.
MĬS-CŎM-PŲ-TĀ'TIǪN, *n.* A false reckoning.
MĬS-CǪN-CĒIT', MĬS-CǪN-CĔP'TIǪN, *n.* False
  opinion, notion, or conception. [judge.
MĬS-CǪN-CĒIVE' (mĭs-kǫn-sēv'), *v. a.* To mis-
MĬS-CŎN'DŲCT, *n.* Ill behavior; ill manage-
MĬS-CǪN-DŬCT', *v. a.* To manage amiss. [ment.
MĬS-CǪN-JĔCT'ŲRE (-kǫn-jĕkt'yŭr), *n.* A wrong
  conjecture or guess.
MĬS-CǪN-JĔCT'ŲRE, *v. n.* To guess wrong.
MĬS-CǪN-STRŬC'TIǪN, *n.* A wrong interpreta-
MĬS-CǑN'STRŬE, *v. a.* To interpret wrong. [tion.
MĬS-CÖŬN'SĘL, *v. a.* To advise wrong.
MĬS-CÖŬNT', *v. a. & n.* To reckon wrong.
MĬS'CRĘ-ANT, *n.* An infidel:—a vile wretch.
MĬS-DĀTE', *v. a.* To date erroneously.
MĬS-DĒĒD', *n.* An evil action; a fault.
MĬS-DĒĒM', *v. a.* To judge ill of; to mistake.
MĬS-DĘ-MĒAN', *v. a.* To demean or behave ill.
MĬS-DĘ-MĒAN'ǬR (-dę-mē'nŭr), *n.* An offence.
MĬS-DĮ-RĔCT', *v. a.* To lead or guide amiss.
MĬS-DÔ', *v. a. & n.* To do wrong; to commit.
MĬS-DÔ'ĘR, *n.* An offender; a malefactor. [right.
MĬS-DÔ'ĬNG, *n.* An offence; deviation from
MĬS-ĘM-PLÖY', *v. a.* To use to wrong purposes.
MĬS-ĘM-PLÖY'MĘNT, *n.* Improper application.
MĬS-ĔN'TRY, *n.* A wrong entry.
MĪ'ṢĘR, *n.* A person excessively penurious. [less.
MĪṢ'ĘR-Ą-BLE, *a.* Unhappy; wretched; worth-
MĪṢ'ĘR-Ą-BLY, *ad.* Unhappily; wretchedly.
MĪ'ṢĘR-LY, *a.* Very avaricious; niggardly.
MĪṢ'Ę-RY, *n.* Wretchedness; misfortune.
MĬS-FĂSH'IǪN (-făsh'ŭn), *v. a.* To form wrong.
MĬS-FŎRM', *v. a.* To put in an ill form. [luck.
MĬS-FÖRT'ŲNE (mĭs-fört'yŭn), *n.* Calamity; ill
MĬS-ҼĪVE', *v. a.* To fill with doubt; to fail.
MĬS-ҼĪV'ĬNG, *n.* Doubt; distrust; hesitation.
MĬS-GŎV'ĘRN (-gŭv'ęrn), *v. a.* To govern ill.
MĬS-GŎV'ĘRN-MĔNT, *n.* Ill administration.
MĬS-GRÖŬND', *v. a.* To found falsely.
MĬS-GUĪD'ANCE (-ḡīd'ąns), *n.* False direction.
MĬS-GUĪDE' (mĭs-ḡīd'), *v. a.* To direct ill.
MĬS-HĂP', *n.* Ill chance; ill luck; a calamity.
MĬSH'MĂSH, *n.* A mixture; a hotchpotch.
MĬSH'NA, *n.* A collection of Jewish traditions.
MĬS-ĮN-FŎRM', *v. a.* To inform wrong; to de-
  ceive by false accounts.
MĬS-ĮN-FǪR-MĀ'TIǪN, *n.* False intelligence.
MĬS-ĮN-FŎRM'ĘR, *n.* One who misinforms.
MĬS-ĮN-STRŬCT', *v. a.* To instruct improperly.

MĬS-ĮN-STRŬC'TIǪN, *n.* Ill instruction.
MĬS-ĮN-TĔR'PRĘT, *v. a.* To explain wrong.
MĬS-ĮN-TĔR-PRĘ-TĀ'TIǪN, *n.* A wrong inter-
  pretation or explanation.
MĬS-JÖĬN', *v. a.* To join unfitly or improperly.
MĬS-JŬDҼE', *v. a. & n.* To judge wrong.
MĬS-LĀY', *v. a.* To lay in a wrong place. [place.
MĬS-LĀY'ĘR, *n.* One that puts in the wrong
MĬṢ'LE (mĭz'zl), *v. n.* To rain in minute drops.
MĬS-LĒAD', *v. a.* [*imp. t. & pp.* misled.] To guide
MĬS-LĒAD'ĘR, *n.* One that leads to ill. [wrong.
MĬṢ'LE-TŌE (mĭz'zl-tō), *n.* See MISTLETOE.
MĬS-LĪKE', *v. a. & n.* To disapprove; to dis-
MĬS-LĪKE', *n.* Disapprobation; dislike. [like.
MĬS-MĂN'ĄҼE, *v. a.* To manage ill. [conduct.
MĬS-MĂN'ĄҼE-MĔNT, *n.* Ill management; mis-
MĬS-MĂRK', *v. a.* To mark wrongly.
MĬS-MĂTCH', *v. a.* To match unsuitably.
MĬS-NĀME', *v. a.* To call by the wrong name.
MĮS-NŌ'MĘR, *n.* A wrong name; a misnaming.
MĬS-ǪB-ṢĔRVE', *v. a.* Not to observe accurately.
MĮ-SŎG'Ą-MĬST, *n.* A hater of marriage.
MĮ-SŎG'Y-NY, *n.* Hatred of women. [mislay.
MĬS-PLĀCE', *v. a.* To put in a wrong place; to
MĬS-PÖĬNT', *v. a.* To punctuate incorrectly.
MĬS-PRĬNT', *v. a.* To print wrong. [press.
MĬS-PRĬNT', *n.* Error in printing; error of the
MĬS-PRĬṢ'IǪN (mĭs-prĭzh'ŭn), *n.* (*Law.*) Neglect.
MĬS-PRǪ-NÖŬNCE', *v. a. & n.* To pronounce
  improperly or incorrectly. [metry.
MĬS-PRǪ-PÖR'TIǪN, *v. a.* To join without sym-
MĬS-QUŌTE' (mĭs-kwōt'), *v. a.* To quote falsely.
MĬS-RĘ-CĪ'TĄL, *n.* A wrong or incorrect recital.
MĬS-RĘ-CĪTE', *v. a.* To recite erroneously.
MĬS-RĔCK'ON (-rĕk'kn), *v. a.* To reckon wrong.
MĬS-RĘ-LĀTE', *v. a.* To relate inaccurately.
MĬS-RĘ-LĀ'TIǪN, *n.* An inaccurate narrative.
MĬS-RĘ-PÖRT', *v. a.* To give a false account of.
MĬS-RĘ-PÖRT', *n.* A false account or rumor.
MĬS-RĔP-RĘ-ṢĔNT', *v. a.* To represent wrong.
MĬS-RĔP-RĘ-ṢĔN-TĀ'TIǪN, *n.* A false account.
MĬS-RĔP-RĘ-ṢĔNT'ĘR, *n.* One who misrepre-
  sents.
MĬS-RŪLE', *n.* Tumult; confusion; disorder.
MĬSS, *n.* The title of a young unmarried woman.
MĬSS, *n.* Loss; want; mistake; omission.
MĬSS, *v. a.* Not to hit; to mistake; to omit.
MĬSS, *v. n.* Not to succeed; to fail; to mistake.
MĬS'SĄL, *n.* The Roman Catholic mass-book.
MĬS-SĔRVE', *v. a.* To serve unfaithfully.
MĬS-SHĀPE', *v. a.* [*imp. t.* misshaped; *pp.* mis-
  shaped *or* misshapen.] To shape ill; to de-
MĬS'SĮLE, *a.* That may be thrown. [form.
MĬS'SIǪN (mĭsh'ŭn), *n.* A commission; the act
  of sending; a delegation; persons sent. [gion.
MĬS'SIǪN-Ą-RY, *n.* One sent to propagate reli-
MĬS'SĮVE, *a.* Such as is sent; sent abroad.
MĬS'SĮVE, *n.* Letter sent:—messenger. [wrong.
MĬS-SPĒAK' (mĭs-spēk'), *v. a. & n.* To speak
MĬS-SPĔLL', *v. a.* To spell wrong. [waste.
MĬS-SPĔND', *v. a.* [*imp. t. & pp.* misspent.] To
MĬST, *n.* A small, thin rain; a fog; a haze.
MĬST, *v. a.* To cloud; to cover with a vapor.
MĬS-TĀKE', *v. a.* [*imp. t.* mistook; *pp.* mista-
  ken.] To conceive wrongly; to misapprehend.
MĬS-TĀKE', *v. n.* To err; not to judge right.—
  To be mistaken (mĭs-tā'kn), to err; to miscon-
MĬS-TĀKE', *n.* A misconception; an error. [ceive.

MĬS-STĀTE', *v. a.* To state wrong.
MĬS-STĀTE'MENT, *n.* A wrong statement.
MĬS-TĒACH' (mĭs-tēch'), *v. a.* To teach wrong.
MĬS-TĔLL', *v. a.* [*imp. t. & pp.* mistold.] To tell
MĬS-TĒRM', *v. a.* To term erroneously. [wrong.
MĬS-THĬNK', *v. a.* To think ill ; to think wrong.
MĬST'Ĭ-LY, *ad.* Darkly ; obscurely ; unintelligi-
MĬS-TĪME', *v. a. & n.* To time wrong. [bly.
MĬST'Ĭ-NĔSS, *n.* The state of being misty.
MĬS'TĬON, *n.* A mixture ; state of being mingled.
MĬS'TLE (mĭz'zl), *v. n.* To rain. See MIZZLE.
MĬS'TLE-TŌE (mĭz'zl-tō), *n.* A plant growing
MĬS-TŌLD', *imp. t. & pp.* of *mistell.* [on trees.
MĬS-TOOK' (mĭs-tŭk'), *imp. t.* of *mistake.*
MĬS-TRĀIN', *v. a.* To educate or train wrong.
MĬS-TRĄNS-LĀTE', *v. a.* To translate incor-
rectly. [tion.
MĬS-TRĄNS-LĀ'TION, *n.* An incorrect transla-
MĬS'TRĔSS, *n.* A woman who governs.
MĬS-TRŬST', *n.* Suspicion ; want of confidence.
MĬS-TRŬST', *v. a.* To suspect ; to doubt.
MĬS-TRŬST'FŬL, *a.* Diffident ; doubting.
MĬS-TRŬST'FŬL-NĔSS, *n.* Diffidence ; doubt.
MĬS-TŪNE', *v. a.* To tune amiss ; to put out of
tune. [scure.
MĬST'Y, *a.* Clouded ; filled with mists ; ob-
MĬS-ŬN-DER-STĂND', *v. a.* To misconceive.
MĬS-ŬN-DER-STĂND'ĬNG, *n.* Erroneous under-
standing ; an error :—dissension.
MĬS-ŪŞ'ĄĢE, *n.* Abuse ; ill use ; bad treatment.
MĬS-ŪŞE', *v. a.* To use improperly ; to abuse.
MĬS-ŪŞE', *n.* Wrong or erroneous use ; abuse.
MĬS-WRĪTE', (-rĭt'), *v. a.* To write incorrectly.
MĬS-WROUGHT' (-râwt'), *pp.* Badly worked.
MĪTE, *n.* A small insect :—any thing small.
MĬT'Ĭ-GĂNT, *a.* Lenient ; lenitive. [assuage.
MĬT'Ĭ-GĀTE, *v. a.* To temper ; to alleviate ; to
MĬT-Ĭ-GĀ'TION, *n.* Alleviation ; an assuaging.
MĪ'TRE (mī'ter), *n.* A kind of episcopal crown.
MĪ'TRED (mī'terd), *a.* Adorned with a mitre.
MĬT'TEN, *n.* A cover worn on the hand. [on.
MĬT'TĬ-MŬS, *n.* Warrant for committing to pris-
MĬX, *v. a.* [*imp. t. & pp.* mixed *or* mixt.] To
unite to something else ; to join ; to mingle.
MĬX'EN, *n.* A dunghill ; a laystall ; a compost-
MĬX'TION (mĭx'chun), *n.* A mixture. [heap.
MĬXT'ŲRE (mĭxt'yur), *n.* A mixing ; a mixed
MĬZ'MĀZE, *n.* A labyrinth ; a maze. [mass.
MĬZ'ZEN (mĭz'zn), *n.* The after mast of a ship.
MĬZ'ZLE, *v. n.* To misle ; to mistle ; drizzle.
MĬZ'ZLE, *n.* Small rain ; mist ; drizzle.
MNĘ-MŎN'ĬC (nę-mŏn'ĭk), } *a.* Assisting
MNĘ-MŎN'Ĭ-CĄL (nę-mŏn'ę-kąl), } the memory.
MNĘ-MŎN'ĬCS (-mŏn'ĭks), *n. pl.* Art of memory.
MŌAN (mōn), *v. a. & n.* To lament ; to grieve.
MŌAN, *n.* Lamentation ; audible sorrow. [ful.
MŌAN'FŬL, *a.* Sorrowful ; lamentable ; mourn-
MŌAT (mōt), *n.* A canal round a house or castle.
MŌAT (mōt), *v. a.* To surround with a moat.
MŎB, *n.* A crowd ; a rabble :—woman's cap.
MŎB, *v. a.* To harass ; to overbear by tumult.
MỌ-BĬL'Ĭ-TY, *n.* Activity ; fickleness.
MŎC'CĄ-SON (mŏk'kạ-sn), *n.* An Indian shoe.
MŎCK, *v. a.* To deride ; to ridicule ; to mimic.
MŎCK, *n.* Ridicule ; a fleer ; a sneer ; mimicry.
MŎCK, *a.* False ; counterfeit ; not real.
MŎCK'ER, *n.* One who mocks ; a scoffer. [show.
MŎCK'ER-Y, *n.* Scorn ; ridicule ; sport ; vain

MŎCK'ĬNG, *n.* Scorn ; derision ; an insult.
MŎCK'ĬNG-BĬRD, *n.* A bird which imitates oth-
MŌ'DĄL, *a.* Relating to the form or mode. [ers.
MỌ-DĂL'Ĭ-TY, *n.* Difference in mode or form.
MŌDE, *n.* Method ; form ; fashion ; state :—a silk.
MŎD'EL, *n.* A copy ; mould ; pattern ; standard.
MŎD'EL, *v. a.* To plan ; to shape, mould, form.
MŎD'EL-LER, *n.* Planner ; contriver ; former.
MŎD'ER-ĄTE, *a.* Not extreme ; middling ; tem-
perate ; not excessive ; mild. [still.
MŎD'ER-ĀTE, *v. a.* To regulate ; to restrain ; to
MŎD'ER-ĀTE, *v. n.* To become quiet ; to preside.
MŎD'ER-ĄTE-LY, *ad.* Temperately ; mildly.
MŎD'ER-ĄTE-NĔSS, *n.* Moderation. [gality.
MŎD-ER-Ā'TION, *n.* Calmness ; restraint ; fru-
MŎD'ER-Ā TOR, *n.* One who moderates or pre-
MŎD'ERN, *a.* Late ; recent ; not ancient. [sides.
MŎD'ERN-ĬSM, *n.* A modern practice or idiom.
MŎD'ERN-ĪZE, *v. a.* To render modern.
MŎD'ERN-NĔSS, *n.* Novelty ; recentness.
MŎD'ERNŞ, *n. pl.* Those who have lived lately.
MŎD'EST, *a.* Not arrogant ; diffident ; chaste.
MŎD'EST-LY, *ad.* Not arrogantly ; chastely.
MŎD'ES-TY, *n.* Moderation ; decency ; chastity.
MŎD'Ĭ-CŬM, *n.* [L.] A small portion ; a pittance.
MŎD'Ĭ-FĪ-Ą-BLE, *a.* That may be modified.
MŎD-Ĭ-FĬ-CĀ'TION, *n.* The act of modifying ;
MŎD'Ĭ-FĪ-ER, *n.* One that modifies. [form.
MŎD'Ĭ-FȲ, *v. a.* To qualify ; to shape ; to soften.
MỌ-DĬL'LION (mọ-dĭl'yun), *n.* (*Arch.*) An en-
riched block or horizontal bracket. [mode.
MŌ'DĬSH, *a.* Fashionable ; conformed to the
MŌ'DĬSH-LY, *ad.* Fashionably ; stylishly.
MŌ'DĬSH-NĔSS, *n.* An affectation of the fashion.
MŎD'Ų-LĀTE (mŏd'yu-lāt), *v. a.* To inflect or
adapt, as the voice or sounds ; to tune.
MŎD-Ų-LĀ'TION, *n.* Act of modulating ; melody.
MŎD'Ų-LĀ-TOR, *n.* One who modulates ; tuner.
MŎD'ŪLE (mŏd'yul), *n.* A model ; a measure.
MŌ'DŲS, *n.* [L.] A compensation for tithes.
MỌ-GŬL', *n.* The title of the chief of the Moguls.
MŌ'HĂIR, *n.* Stuff made of Angora wool.
MỌ-HĂM'MĘ-DĄN, *n.* See MAHOMETAN.
MŎÏ'DŌRE *or* MŎÏ-DŌRE', *n.* A Portuguese
coin, rated at about £1 7s. sterling.
MŎÏ'Ę-TY, *n.* Half ; one of two equal parts.
MŎÏL, *v. n.* To labor ; to toil ; to drudge.
MŎÏST, *a.* Moderately wet ; damp ; juicy. [wet.
MŎÏS'TEN (mŏï'sn), *v. a.* To make damp ; to
MŎÏST'NĔSS, *n.* Dampness ; moderate wetness.
MŎÏST'ŲRE (mŏïst'yur), *n.* Moderate wetness ;
MŌ'LĄR, *a.* Having power to grind. [dampness.
MỌ-LĂS'SĘŞ, *n.* A sirup which drains from su-
MŌLD, *n.* A form ; a matrix. See MOULD. [gar.
MŌLE, *n.* A spot ; a mark ; a mound ; an animal.
MŌLE'CĂST, *n.* A hillock cast up by a mole.
MŎL'Ę-CŪLE, *n.* A small mass ; minute particle.
MŌLE'HĬLL, *n.* A hillock thrown up by moles.
MỌ-LĔST', *v. a.* To disturb ; to trouble ; to vex.
MŎL-ĘS-TĀ'TION, *n.* Act of molesting ; a dis-
turbance ; a vexation.
MỌ-LĔST'ER, *n.* One who molests ; disturber.
MŌLE'-TRĂCK, *n.* The course of a mole under
ground. [ening.
MŎL'LIENT (mŏl'yent *or* mŏl'lę-ent), *a.* Soft-
MŎL'LĬ-FĪ-Ą-BLE, *a.* That may be softened.
MŎL-LĬ-FĬ-CĀ'TION, *n.* A softening ; mitiga-
tion.

MŎL′LĬ-FĪ-ẸR, *n.* He or that which softens.
MŎL′LĬ-FȲ, *v. a.* To soften; to assuage; to quiet.
MOL-LŬS′CẠ, *n.* A class of vermes or fishes.
MŎL′LŲSK, *n.* One of the mollusca.
MŎLT′ẸN, (mŏl′tn), *p. a.* Melted; made of metal.
MŎL-ȲB-DĒ′NŲM, *n.* A sort of brittle metal.
MŌ′MẸNT, *n.* Importance; force; an instant.
MŌ′MẸN-TẠ-RĬ-LY, *ad.* Every moment.
MŌ′MẸN-TẠ-RY, *a.* Lasting for a moment.
MỌ-MĔNT′OŲS, *a.* Important; weighty.
MỌ-MĔN′TŲM, *n.*; pl. MỌ-MĔN′TẠ. The force possessed by matter in motion; impetus.
MŎN′Ạ-ℂHĬŞM, *n.* State of monks; monastic life.
MŎN′ẠD, *n.* An atom; an indivisible particle.
MỌ-NĂD′ĬC, } *a.* Relating to, or composed of,
MỌ-NĂD′Ĭ-CẠL, } monads. [king.
MŎN′ARℂH, *n.* A sovereign: an emperor; a
MỌ-NĂRℂH′ẠL, *a.* Suiting a monarch; regal.
MỌ-NĂRℂH′ĬC, } *a.* Relating to monarchy;
MỌ-NĂRℂH′Ĭ-CẠL, } vested in a single ruler.
MŎN′ARℂH-ĬST, *n.* An advocate for monarchy.
MŎN′ARℂH-ĪZE, *v. n.* To play the monarch.
MŎN′ARℂH-Y, *n.* A kingly government; empire.
MŎN′ĂS-TĔR-Y, *n.* A convent; a cloister.
MỌ-NĂS′TĬC, } *a.* Religiously recluse; per-
MỌ-NĂS′TĬ-CẠL, } taining to monks or nuns.
MỌ-NĂS′TĬ-CẠL-LY, *ad.* In a monastic manner.
MỌ-NĂS′TĬ-CĬŞM, *n.* Monastic life or state.
MŎN′DAY (mŭn′dẹ), *n.* The 2d day of the week.
MŎN′Ẹ-TẠ-RY, *a.* Relating to money.
MŎN′EY (mŭn′nẹ), *n.* Metal coined for traffic; coin; bank-notes exchangeable for coin.
MŎN′EY-BĂG (mŭn′nẹ-băg), *n.* A large purse.
MŎN′EY-BRŌ-KẸR, *n.* A money-changer.
MŎN′EY-CHĂNG-ẸR, *n.* A broker in money.
MŎN′EYED (mŭn′nĭd), *a.* Rich in money.
MŎN′EY-LĔSS, *a.* Wanting money; penniless.
MŎN′EYŞ-WORTH (-würth), *n.* Full value.
MŎN′GẸR (mŭng′gẹr), *n.* A dealer; a seller.
MŎN′GRẸL (mŭng′grẹl), *a.* Of a mixed breed.
MŎN′GRẸL, *n.* Any thing of a mixed breed. [tion.
MỌ-NĬ″TIỌN (mọ-nĭsh′ụn), *n.* A hint; admoni-
MŎN′Ĭ-TỌR, *n.* One who admonishes or warns.
MŎN-Ĭ-TŌ′RĬ-ẠL, *a.* Relating to a monitor.
MŎN′Ĭ-TỌ-RY, *a.* Giving admonition or instruc-
MŎNK, *n.* One living in a monastery. [tion.
MŎNK′ẸR-Y, *n.* The life and state of monks.
MŎN′KEY (mŭng′kẹ), *n.* An ape; a baboon.
MŎNK′ĬSH, *a.* Monastic; pertaining to monks.
MŎN′Ọ-ℂHŎRD, *n.* An instrument of one string.
MỌ-NŎC′Ų-LẠR, MỌ-NŎC′Ų-LOŬS, *a.* One-eyed.
MŎN′Ọ-DĬST, *n.* A writer of monodies.
MŎN′Ọ-DŎN, *n.* The sea-unicorn; narwhal.
MŎN′Ọ-DY, *n.* A poem sung by one person only.
MỌ-NŎG′Ạ-MĬST, *n.* An adherent to monogamy.
MỌ-NŎG′Ạ-MY, *n.* Marriage of one wife only.
MŎN′Ọ-GRĂM, *n.* A cipher; a character.
MŎN′Ọ-GRĂPH, *n.* An account of a single thing.
MỌ-NŎG′RẠ-PHY, *n.* A description or representation drawn in lines without colors.
MŎN′Ọ-LŎGUE (mŏn′ọ-lŏg), *n.* A soliloquy.
MỌ-NŎM′Ạ-ℂHY, *n.* A duel; a single combat.
MŎN-Ọ-MĀ′NĬ-Ạ, *n.* Insanity on one subject.
MŎN-Ọ-MĀ′NĬ-ĂC, *n.* One having monomania.
MŎN-Ọ-PĔT′Ạ-LOŬS, *a.* Having but one leaf.
MỌ-NŎP′Ọ-LĬST, *n.* One who monopolizes.
MỌ-NŎP′Ọ-LĪZE, *v. a.* To engross so as to have the sole power of vending any commodity.

MỌ-NŎP′Ọ-LĪZ-ẸR, *n.* One who monopolizes.
MỌ-NŎP′Ọ-LY, *n.* An exclusive possession of a thing; sole privilege of selling.
MŎN′ỌP-TŌTE *or* MỌ-NŎP′TŌTE, *n.* A noun used only in one case. [seed; one-seeded.
MŎN-Ọ-SPĒR′MOŬS, *a.* (*Bot.*) Having only one
MŎN′Ọ-STĬℂH, *n.* A composition of one verse.
MŎN-Ọ-SYL-LĂB′Ĭ-CẠL, *a.* Of one syllable.
MŎN-Ọ-SȲL′LẠ-BLE, *n.* A word of only one syllable.
MŎN′Ọ-THĒ-ĬŞM, *n.* A belief in only one God.
MŎN′Ọ-TŌNE, *n.* Uniformity of sound.
MŎN-Ọ-TŎN′Ĭ-CẠL, *a.* Having an unvaried sound. [dence.
MỌ-NŎT′Ọ-NOŬS, *a.* Wanting variety in ca-
MỌ-NŎT′Ọ-NY, *n.* Uniformity of sound or tone.
MỌN-SŌŌN′, *n.* A periodical trade-wind.
MŎN′STẸR, *n.* Something unnatural or horrible.
MỌN-STRŎS′Ĭ-TY, *n.* State of being monstrous.
MŎN′STROŬS, *a.* Unnatural; strange; shocking.
MŎN′STROŬS-LY, *ad.* Shockingly; horribly.
MŎN′STROŬS-NĔSS, *n.* Monstrosity; enormity.
MŎN′TĔTH, *n.* A vessel to wash glasses in.
MŎNTH (mŭnth), *n.* One of the 12 divisions of the year; the space of four weeks.
MŎNTH′LY, *a.* Happening every month.
MŎNTH′LY, *ad.* Once in a month; every month.
MŎN′Ụ-MĔNT, *n.* A memorial; a tomb; a pillar.
MŎN-Ụ-MĔNT′ẠL, *a.* Memorial; commemorative; sepulchral.
MŌŌD, *n.* Temper; disposition; form; mode.
MŌŌD′Ĭ-NĔSS, *n.* Peevishness; vexation. [sive.
MŌŌD′Y, *a.* Out of humor; peevish; sad; pen-
MŌŌN, *n.* The luminary of the night:—a month.
MŌŌN′-BĒAM, *n.* A ray of lunar light.
MŌŌN′-CĂLF (mŏn′kăf), *n.* A monster:—a dolt.
MŌŌN′-EȲED (mŏn′īd), *a.* Dim-eyed; purblind.
MŌŌN′LĔSS, *a.* Not enlightened by the moon.
MŌŌN′LĪGHT (-līt), *n.* The light of the moon.
MŌŌN′LĪGHT, *a.* Illuminated by the moon.
MŌŌN′SHĪNE, *n.* The lustre of the moon.
MŌŌN′SHĬN-Y, *a.* Illuminated by the moon.
MŌŌN′STRŬCK, *a.* Affected by the moon.
MŌŌN′Y, *a.* Lunated; having a crescent.
MŌŌR, *n.* A tract of low land:—an African.
MŌŌR, *v. a. & n.* To fasten by anchors; to be
MŌŌR′CŎCK, *n.* The male of the moorhen. [fixed.
MŌŌR′GĀME, *n.* Red game; grouse.
MŌŌR′HĔN, *n.* A fowl that feeds in the fens.
MŌŌR′ING, *n.* Anchors, chains, &c., for securing a ship:—place for securing a ship by anchors.
MŌŌR′ISH, *a.* Marshy:—relating to Moors.
MŌŌR′LẠND, *n.* A marsh; a fen:—low ground.
MŌŌR′Y, *a.* Marshy; fenny; watery.
MŌŌSE, *n.* A large animal of the deer kind.
MŌŌT, *v. a.* To discuss; to plead in a mock cause.
MŌŌT, *a.* Disputable; unsettled; as, a *moot*
MŌŌT′ẸR, *n.* A disputer of moot points. [case.
MŎP, *n.* A utensil for cleaning floors, &c.
MŎP, *v. a.* To clean or rub with a mop.
MŌPE, *v. n.* To be stupid or dull; to drowse.
MŌPE, *n.* A drone; a stupid, spiritless person.
MŌ′PĬSH, *a.* Spiritless; inattentive; dejected.
MŌ′PĬSH-NĔSS, *n.* Dejection; inactivity. [girl.
MŎP′PĔT, MŎP′SEY, *n.* A puppet; a doll:—a
MŎR′ẠL, *a.* Relating to rational beings, and their duties to each other, as right or wrong; subject to a moral law:—probable:—virtuous.

MŎR′ĄL, *n.* The instruction of a fable, &c.
MŎR′ĄL-ĬST, *n.* A teacher of morals; a moral philosopher; a moral man. [ics.
MǪ-RĂL′Ĭ-TY, *n.* Doctrine of human duty; eth-
MŎR′ĄL-ĪZE, *v. a.* To apply in a moral sense.
MŎR′ĄL-ĪZE, *v. n.* To discourse on moral sub-
MŎR′ĄL-ĪZ-ĘR, *n.* One who moralizes. [jects.
MŎR′ĄL-LY, *ad.* In an ethical or moral manner.
MŎR′ĄLȘ, *n. pl.* The practice of the duties of life.
MǪ-RĂSS′, *n.* A fen; a bog; a moor; a marsh.
MǪ-RĂSS′Y, *a.* Moorish; marshy; fenny.
MǪ-RĀ′VĬ-ĄN, *n.* One of the United Brethren.
MŎR′BĮD, *a.* Diseased; sickly; unsound.
MŎR′BĮD-NĔSS, *n.* The state of being diseased.
MǪR-BĬF′ĬC, MǪR-BĬF′Ĭ-CĄL, *a.* Causing dis-
MǪR-BŌSE′, *a.* Proceeding from disease. [ease.
MǪR-DĀ′CIOŲS (-dā′shŭs), *a.* Biting; acrid. [ity.
MǪR-DĂC′Ĭ-TY, MŎR′DĮ-ÇĄN-CY, *n.* Biting qual-
MŎR′DĄNT, *n.* A substance to fix colors in cloth.
MŎR′DĮ-CĄNT, *a.* Biting; acrid; corrosive.
MŎR′DĮ-CĀ′TIǪN, *n.* The act of corroding.
MŌRE, *a.* [the comparative of *many* and *much.*] Greater in number or quantity. [ond time.
MŌRE, *ad.* To a greater degree; again; a sec-
MŌRE, *n.* A greater quantity or degree.
MǪ-RĒĔN′, *n.* A kind of stuff for curtains, &c.
MǪ-RĔL′, *n.* A plant:—a kind of cherry. [try.
MŌRE′LĄND, *n.* A mountainous or hilly coun-
MǪ-RĔL′LŌ, *n.* An acid, juicy cherry.
MŌRE-Ō′VĘR, *ad.* Besides; over and above.
MǪ-RĔSQUE′, *a.* After the manner of the Moors.
MŌ′RĮ-ǪN, *n.* A helmet; armor for the head.
MǪ-RĬS′CŌ, *n.* A Moorish dance or dancer.
MŎRN, *n.* The first part of the day; morning.
MŎRN′ĮNG, *n.* First part of the day:—early part.
MŎRN′ĮNG, *a.* Being in the early part of the day.
MŎRN′ĮNG-STÄR, *n.* The planet Venus; Luci-
MǪ-RŎC′CŌ, *n.* A fine sort of leather. [fer.
MǪ-RŌSE′, *a.* Sour of temper; peevish; sullen.
MǪ-RŌSE′LY, *ad.* Sourly; peevishly; sullenly.
MǪ-RŌSE′NĘSS, *n.* Sourness; peevishness.
MŎR′PHEW̄ (mŏr′fū), *n.* A scurf on the face.
MŎR′RŌW (mŏr′rō), *n.* The day after the pres-
MŎRSE, *n.* The sea-horse; the walrus. [ent.
MŎR′SĘL, *n.* A mouthful; a small quantity.
MŎRT, *n.* A tune at the death of game.
MŎR′TĄL, *a.* Subject to death; deadly; human.
MŎR′TĄL, *n.* A man; a human being.
MǪR-TĂL′Ĭ-TY, *n.* Subjection to death; death.
MŎR′TĄL-LY, *ad.* Irrecoverably; hopelessly.
MŎR′TĄR, *n.* Cement for building:—a vessel in which substances are pounded:—a cannon.
MŎRT′GĄ-ĢE (mŏr′gaj), *n.* A pledge; an estate.
MŎRT′GĄ-ĢE (mŏr′gaj), *v. a.* To pledge.
MŎRT-GĄ-ĢĒĔ′ (mǫr-gą-jē), *n.* One who takes or receives a mortgage.
MŎRT-GĄ-ĢE-ÖR′, *or* MŎRT-GĄĢ-ÖR′, *n.* (*Law.*) One who gives a mortgage. [a mortgage.
MŎRT′GĄ-ĢER (mŏr′gą-jęr), *n.* One who gives
MǪR-TĬF′ĘR-OŬS, *a.* Fatal; deadly. [tion.
MŎR-TĬ-FĬ-CĀ′TIǪN, *n.* A gangrene; humilia-
MŎR′TĮ-FĪ-ĘR, *n.* One who mortifies.
MŎR′TĮ-FY̆, *v. a.* To subdue, humble, depress.
MŎR′TĮ-FY̆, *v. n.* To gangrene:—to be subdued.
MŎR′TĮSE, *n.* A hole in wood for a tenon.
MŎR′TĮSE, *v. a.* To cut or make a mortise in.
MŎRT′MĀIN, *n.* An unalienable estate. [church.
MŎR′TŲ-Ą-RY, *n.* A burial-place:—gift left to a

MǪ-ȘĀ′ĮC, MǪ-ȘĀ′Ĭ-CĄL, *a.* Noting painting in small pebbles, cockles, &c.:—relating to Moses.
MǪ-ȘĀ′ĮC-WORK (-würk), *n.* An imitation of a painting in pebbles, marbles, tiles, or shells.
MŌSQUE (mŏsk), *n.* A Mahometan temple.
MǪS-QUÎ′TŌ (-kē′-), *n.* A troublesome insect.
MŎSS, *n.* A plant growing on trees, &c.
MŎSS, *v. a.* To cover with moss.
MŎSS′-GRŌWN (mŏs′grōn), *a.* Overgrown or covered with moss. [moss.
MŎS′SĮ-NĔSS, *n.* State of being covered with
MŎS′SY, *a.* Overgrown or covered with moss.
MŌST, *a.* [the superlative of *many* and *much.*] Greatest in number or quantity.
MŌST, *ad.* In the greatest or highest degree.
MŌST, *n.* The greatest number or quantity.
MŌST′LY, *ad.* For the greatest part; chiefly.
MŌTE, *n.* A small particle of matter; a spot.
MǪ-TĔT′, *n.* A kind of sacred air; a hymn.
MŎTH, *n.*; *pl.* MŎꝶHȘ. A small winged insect which eats cloth and furs.
MŎTH′-ĒAT-EN (-ē-tn), *a.* Eaten of moths.
MŎꝶH′ĘR (mŭth′ęr), *n.* A female parent:—a slimy substance in liquors. [mother.
MŎꝶH′ĘR-HOOD (mŭth′ęr-hŭd), *n.* State of a
MŎꝶH′ĘR-ĮN-LÂW′, *n.* The mother of a husband or wife.
MŎꝶH′ĘR-LĔSS, *a.* Destitute of a mother.
MŎꝶH′ĘR-LY, *a.* Relating to a mother; tender.
MŎꝶH′ĘR-ǪF-PĔARL, *n.* The internal layer of some shells, particularly of the pearl oyster.
MŎꝶH′ĘR-WĬT, *n.* Native wit; common sense.
MŎTH′Y, *a.* Full of or containing moths.
MŌ′TIǪN, *n.* The act of changing place; gait; action; movement:—a proposal or proposition made.
MŌ′TIǪN, *v. n.* To advise; to make proposal.
MŌ′TIǪN-LĔSS, *a.* Being without motion.
MŌ′TĮVE, *a.* Causing motion; tending to move.
MŌ′TĮVE, *n.* That which determines the choice.
MŎT′LEY (mŏt′lę), *a.* Mingled of various colors.
MŌ′TǪ-RY, *a.* Giving motion; moving.
MŎT′TŌ, *n.*; *pl.* MŎT′TŌEȘ. A sentence prefixed to a work, essay, &c.
MŌULD (mōld), *n.* Concreted matter; a spot; earth; soil:—a matrix; a cast; a form.
MŌULD (mōld), *v. n.* To gather mould; to rot.
MŌULD (mōld), *v. a.* To form; to shape.
MŌULD′ĘR, *v. n.* To be turned to dust; to waste.
MŌULD′Ĭ-NĔSS, *n.* The state of being mouldy.
MŌULD′ĮNG (mōld′ĭng), *n.* Ornament in wood,
MŌULD′WÂRP, *n.* A mole; a small animal. [&c.
MŌULD′Y, *a.* Overgrown with concretions.
MŌULT (mōlt), *v. n.* To shed the feathers, hair, &c.; to mew. [earth.
MŌŬND, *n.* A rampart; a fence; a bank of
MŎŬNT, *n.* A mountain; an artificial hill.
MŎŬNT, *v. a. & n.* To raise aloft, ascend, climb.
MŎŬNT′Ą-BLE, *a.* That may be ascended.
MŎŬN′TĄIN (mŏŭn′tįn), *n.* A very large hill.
MŎŬN′TĄIN, *a.* Relating to mountains. [tain.
MŎŬN-TĄIN-ĒĔR′, *n.* An inhabitant of a moun-
MŎŬN′TĄIN-OŬS (mŏŭn′tįn-ŭs), *a.* Hilly; full of mountains; large as mountains; huge.
MŎŬN′TĄIN-OŲS-NĔSS, *n.* The state of being mountainous. [tender.
MŎŬN′TE-BĂNK, *n.* A quack; a boastful pre-
MŎŬNT′ĮNG, *n.* An ascent; an embellishment.

MŌURN (mōrn), *v. a. & n.* To grieve for; to lament.
MŌURN'ẸR, *n.* One who mourns; a lamenter.
MŌURN'FŬL, *a.* Causing sorrow; sorrowful.
MŌURN'FŬL-LY, *ad.* Sorrowfully; with sorrow.
MŌURN'FŬL-NĔSS, *n.* Sorrow; show of grief.
MŌURN'ĮNG, *n.* Sorrow; the dress of sorrow.
MŎŬSE, *n.*; pl. MĪCE. A little animal.
MŎŬSE (mŏŭz), *v. n.* To catch mice, as a cat.
MŎŬSE'-HŌLE, *n.* A small hole made by mice.
MŎŬS'ẸR, *n.* One that catches mice.
MŎŬSE'-TRĂP, *n.* A trap for catching mice.
MŎŬS-TĂCHE', *n.* Mustache. See MUSTACHE.
MŎŬTH, *n.*; pl. MŎŬTHS. Aperture in the head
 at which the food is received:—an opening.
MŎŬTH, *v. a. & n.* To speak big or loud.
MŎŬTHED (mŏŭthd), *a.* Furnished with a mouth.
MŎŬTH'FŬL, *n.* What the mouth can hold.
MŎŬTH'PIECE, *n.* Part of an instrument for
 the mouth:—one who speaks for others.
MŌV'Ạ-BLE, *a.* That may be moved; not fixed.
MŌV'Ạ-BLE-NĔSS, *n.* Possibility to be moved.
MŌV'Ạ-BLEṢ, *n. pl.* Personal goods; furniture.
MŌV'Ạ-BLY, *ad.* So as it may be moved. [cite.
MŌVE, *v. a.* To put in motion; to propose; to in-
MŌVE, *v. n.* To change place; to walk; to stir.
MŌVE, *n.* The act of moving, as in chess.
MŌVE'MẸNT, *n.* A motion; a march; excitement.
MŌV'ẸR, *n.* The person or thing that moves.
MŌV'ĮNG, *p. a.* Pathetic; touching; affecting.
MŌW, *n.* A heap or mass of hay or corn.
MŌW (mō), *v. a.* [*imp. t.* mowed; *pp.* mowed *or*
 mown.] To cut with a scythe; to cut down.
MŌW'-BÜRN, *v. n.* To ferment in the mow.
MŌW'ẸR (mō'ẹr), *n.* One who cuts with a scythe.
MŌW'ĮNG, *n.* Act of cutting; land to be mowed.
MŌWN (mōn), *pp.* from *mow.* [gout, &c.
MŎX'Ạ, *n.* A cottony substance used for the
MŬCH, *a.* Large in quantity; long in time.
MŬCH, *ad.* In or to a great degree; by far; often.
MŬCH, *n.* A great deal; abundance.
MŪ'CĮD, *a.* Slimy; musty; mouldy.
MŪ'CĮD-NĔSS, *n.* Sliminess; mustiness.
MŪ'CĮL-ĄǴE, *n.* A slimy or viscous mass or body.
MŪ-CĮ-LĂǴ'I-NOŬS, *a.* Slimy; viscous; ropy.
MŬCK, *n.* Substance for manure; manure.
MŬCK, *v. a.* To manure with muck; to dung.
MŬCK'WORM (-würm), *n.* A worm bred in dung.
MŬCK'Y, *a.* Nasty; filthy; dirty; foul.
MŪ'COŬS (mū'kụs), *a.* Slimy; viscous.
MŪ'CRO̟-NĀT-ẸD, *a.* Narrowed to a sharp point.
MŪ'CỤ-LĔNT, *a.* Viscous; slimy; mucous.
MŪ'CỤS, *n.* [L.] Any slimy liquor or moisture.
MŬD, *n.* Dirt mixed with water; mire.
MŬD, *v. a.* To bury in mud; to pollute with dirt.
MŬD'DĮ-LY, *ad.* Turbidly; with foul mixture.
MŬD'DĮ-NĔSS, *n.* The state of being muddy.
MŬD'DLE, *v. a.* To make turbid; to foul; stupefy.
MŬD'DY, *a.* Turbid; foul with mud; dull.
MŬD'DY, *v. a.* To make muddy; to cloud.
MŬD'WĂLL, *n.* A wall built with mud.
MŪE (mū), *v. a.* To moult; to mew. See MEW.
MŬFF, *n.* A soft, warm cover for the hands.
MŬF'FĮN, *n.* A kind of light, spongy cake.
MŬF'FLE, *v. a.* To conceal; to wrap; to cover.
MŬF'FLE, *n.* A cover of a test or copper; a ves-
MŬF'FLẸR, *n.* A covering for the face. [sel.
MŬF'TĮ (mŭf'tẹ), *n.* A Mahometan high-priest.
MŬG, *n.* A cup or vessel to drink from.

MŬG'ĠY, MŬG'ĠĮSH, *a.* Moist; damp; close.
MỤ-LĂT'TŌ, *n.*; pl. MỤ-LĂT'TŌEṢ. One born
 of parents of whom one is white and the
 other black.
MŬL'BẸR-RY, *n.* A tree, and the fruit of the tree.
MŬLCT, *n.* A penalty; a pecuniary fine.
MŬLCT, *v. a.* To punish with fine or forfeiture.
MŬLC'TỤ-Ạ-RY, *a.* Punishing with fine.
MŪLE, *n.* An animal generated between a he-
 ass and a mare, or a horse and a she-ass.
MŪ-LẸ-TEÊR', *n.* A mule-driver. [feminality.
MŪ-LĮ-ĔB'RĮ-TY, *n.* Womanhood; softness;
MŪL'ĮSH, *a.* Like a mule; obstinate as a mule.
MŬLL, *v. a.* To soften and dispirit, as wine.
MŬL'LẸR, *n.* A stone or instrument for grinding.
MŬL'LẸT, *n.* A sea-fish having large scales.
MŬL'LĮ-GRŬBṢ, *n. pl.* A twisting of the intestines.
MŬL'LĮO̟N (mŭl'yụn), *n.* Part of a window-frame.
MŬLSE, *n.* Wine boiled with honey. [nal.
MỤLT-ĂNG'Ụ-LẠR, *a.* Many-cornered; polygo-
MŬL-TĮ-CĂP'SỤ-LẠR, *a.* Having many cells.
MŬL-TĮ-CĀ'VOŬS, *a.* Full of holes or cavities.
MŬL-TĮ-FĀ'RĮ-OŬS, *a.* Having great multiplicity.
MŬL-TĮ-FĀ'RĮ-OŬS-LY, *ad.* With multiplicity.
MŬL-TĮ-FĀ'RĮ-OŬS-NĔSS, *n.* Multiplied diversity.
MỤL'TĮF'Į-DOŬS, *n.* Divided into many parts.
MŬL'TĮ-FŌRM, *a.* Having various shapes or forms.
MŬL-TĮ-FŌRM'Į-TY, *n.* Diversity of shapes.
MŬL-TĮ-LĂT'ẸR-ẠL, *a.* Having many sides.
MŬL-TĮ-LĬN'Ẹ-ẠL, *a.* Having many lines.
MŬL-TĮ-NŌ'MĮ-ẠL, MŬL-TĮ-NŎM'Į-NẠL, MŬL-
 TĮ-NŎM'Į-NOŬS, *a.* Having many names.
MỤL-TĬP'Ạ-ROŬS, *a.* Bringing many at a birth.
MỤL-TĬP'ẠR-TĪTE, *a.* Divided into many parts.
MŬL'TĮ-PĔD, *n.* An insect with many feet.
MŬL'TĮ-PLE, *n.* A number which exactly con-
 tains another number several times or terms.
MŬL'TĮ-PLĪ-Ạ-BLE, *a.* Capable to be multiplied.
MŬL-TĮ-PLĮ-CĂND', *n.* The number to be mul-
 tiplied. [one.
MỤL-TĬP'LĮ-CẠTE, *a.* Consisting of more than
MŬL-TĮ-PLĮ-CĀ'TĮON, *n.* Act of multiplying.
MŬL'TĮ-PLĮ-CĀ-TO̟R, *n.* Number multiplied by.
MŬL-TĮ-PLĬÇ'Į-TY, *n.* Many; state of being many.
MŬL'TĮ-PLĪ-ẸR, *n.* One that multiplies.
MŬL'TĮ-PLY, *v. a. & n.* To increase in number.
MỤL-TĬP'O̟-TĔNT, *a.* Having manifold power.
MỤL-TĬS'O̟-NOŬS, *a.* Having many sounds.
MŬL'TĮ-TŪDE, *n.* Many; a crowd; the populace.
MŬL-TĮ-TŪ'DĮ-NOŬS, *a.* Numerous; manifold.
MỤL-TĬV'Į-OŬS, *a.* Having many ways.
MỤL-TŎC'Ụ-LẠR, *a.* Having more eyes than two.
MŬLT'ỤRE (mŭlt'yụr), *n.* A grist; toll for grind-
MŬM, *interj.* Silence; hush.—*a.* Silent. [ing.
MŬM, *n.* Ale brewed with meat. [mutter.
MŬM'BLE, *v. n. & a.* To speak inwardly; to
MŬM'BLẸR, *n.* One who mumbles; a mutterer.
MŬMM, *v. n.* To mask; to frolic in disguise.
MŬM'MẸR, *n.* A masker; a jester; a player.
MŬM'MẸR-Y, *n.* A masking; farcical show.
MŬM'MY, *n.* A dead body embalmed.
MŬMP, *v. a.* To nibble; to bite quick; to beg.
MŬMP'ĮSH, *a.* Sullen; obstinate.
MŬMPS, *n. pl.* Sullenness; a sort of quinsy. [ly.
MŬNCH, *v. a. & n.* To chew eagerly and greedi-
MŬN'DĀNE, *a.* Belonging to this world.
MŬN-DĮ-FĮ-CĀ'TĮON, *n.* The act of cleansing.
MŬN'DĮ-FŸ, *v. a.* To cleanse; to make clean.

MŲ-NĬÇ'Į-PĄL, *a.* Belonging to a municipality, city, or corporation.
MŲ-NĬÇ-Į-PĂL'Į-TY, *n.* A district or its people:—the government of a city, &c.
MŲ-NĬF'Į-CĔNCE,*n.* Liberality; the act of giving.
MŲ-NĬF'Į-CĔNT, *a.* Liberal; generous; bountiful.
MŲ-NĬF'Į-CĔNT-LY, *ad.* Liberally; generously.
MŪ'NĮ-MĔNT, *n.* A fortification; a support.
MŲ-NĬ''TĮON (-nĭsh'ųn), *n.* Materials for war.
MŪ'RĄL, *a.* Pertaining to, or like, a wall.
MŬR'DĘR, *n.* The act of killing a man unlawfully, and with premeditated malice.
MŬR'DĘ℞, *v. a.* To kill unlawfully, as a man.
MŬR'DĘR-ĘR, *n.* One who is guilty of murder.
MŬR'DĘR-OŬS, *a.* Bloody; guilty of murder.
MŬR'DĘR-OŬS-LY, *ad.* In a bloody manner.
MŪ'RĮ-ĄTE, *n.* A salt containing muriatic acid.
MŪ-RĮ-ĂT'ĮC, *a.* Noting a kind of acid.
MŪ'RĮNE, *a.* Of, or relating to, mice.
MŬRK'Y, *a.* Dark; cloudy; wanting light.
MŬR'MŲR, *n.* A low, shrill noise; a complaint.
MŬR'MŲR, *v. n.* To make a shrill noise; to grum-
MŬR'MŲR-ĘR, *n.* A grumbler; a repiner. [ble.
MŬR'MŲR-ĬNG, *n.* A low sound; a murmur.
MŬR'RAĮN, *n.* A plague among cattle.
MŬs'CĄ-DĔL, } *n.* A kind of sweet grape; a
MŬs'CĄ-DĪNE, } sweet wine:—a sweet pear.
MŬs'ÇLE (mŭs'sl), *n.* A fleshy fibre:—a mollusk.
MŬS-CŎ-VĀ'DŌ, *n.* A sort of unrefined sugar.
MŬS'CŲ-LĄR, *a.* Relating to muscles; strong.
MŬS-CŲ-LĂR'Į-TY, *n.* State of being muscular.
MŬS'CU-LOŬS, *a.* Full of muscles; brawny.
MŪ$E, *n.* One of nine ancient sister goddesses:—the power of poetry:—deep thought.
MŪ$E, *v. n.* To think.—*v. a.* To think on.
MŪ$'ĘR, *n.* One who muses; one absent of mind.
MŲ-$Ē'ŲM, *n.* ; pl. MŲ-$Ē'ŲM$, *or* MŲ-$Ē'Ą. A repository of curiosities.
MŬSH, *n.* Maize meal and water boiled.
MŬSH'RÔÔM, *n.* A spongy plant:—an upstart.
MŪ'$ĮC, *n.* The science of sounds; harmony.
MŪ'$Į-CĄL, *a.* Harmonious; melodious.
MŪ'$Į-CĄL-LY, *ad.* Harmoniously. [music.
MŲ-$Į''CIĄN (mų-zĭsh'ąn), *n.* One skilled in
MŪ'$ĮC-MĂS'TĘR, *n.* One who teaches music.
MŬSK, *n.* A strong perfume; a flower.
MŬSK, *v. a.* To perfume with musk.
MŬSK'-CĂT, *n.* The animal from which musk is obtained.
MŬS'KĘT, *n.* A soldier's hand-gun:—a hawk.
MŬS-KĘT-ĒĒR', *n.* A soldier armed with a mus-
MŬS-KĘ-TÔÔN', *n.* A small musket. [ket.
MŬS'KĮ-NĔSS, *n.* The scent of musk.
MŬSK'MĔL-ǪN, *n.* A species of melon. [mal.
MŬSK'-RĂT, MŬS'QUĂSH, *n.* An aquatic mam-
MŬSK'Y, *a.* Having the perfume of musk.
MŬ$'LĮN, *n.* Fine stuff made of cotton.
MŬ$'LĮN-ĔT, *n.* A kind of muslin.
MŲS-QUÎ'TŌ (mųs-kē'tō), *n.* An insect. See
MŬS'SŲL-MĂN, *n.* A Mahometan. [Mosquito.
MŬST, *v. auxiliary,* & *imp.* To be obliged.
MŬST, *v. a.* & *n.* To make or grow mouldy.

MŬST, *n.* New wine unfermented:—mustiness.
MŲS-TĂCHE' (mųs-täsh' *or* mųs-täsh'), *n.* Hair suffered to grow on the upper lip:—moustache.
MŬS'TĄRD, *n.* A plant and its seeds.
MŬS'TĘR, *v. a.* & *n.* To review; to assemble.
MŬS'TĘR, *n.* A review or a register of forces.
MŬS'TĘR-RŌLL, *n.* A register of forces.
MŬS'TĮ-NĔSS, *n.* Mould; damp foulness.
MŬS'TY, *a.* Mouldy; spoiled with damp or age.
MŪ-TĄ-BĬL'Į-TY, *n.* Changeableness; inconstancy:—mutableness.
MŪ'TĄ-BLE, *a.* Subject to change; inconstant.
MŪ'TĄ-BLE-NĔSS, *n.* Changeableness; insta-
MŲ-TĀ'TĮON, *n.* Change; alteration. [bility.
MŪTE, *a.* Silent; not speaking; not vocal.
MŪTE, *n.* A dumb person:—a letter not vocal.
MŪTE, *v. n.* To dung, as birds.—*n.* Dung of
MŪTE'LY, *ad.* Silently; not vocally. [birds.
MŪTE'NĔSS, *n.* Silence; aversion to speak.
MŪ'TĮ-LĀTE, *v. a.* To deprive of an essential part.
MŪ-TĮ-LĀ'TĮON, *n.* The deprivation of a limb,
MŪ'TĮ-LĀ-TǪR, *n.* One who mutilates. [&c.
MŪ-TĮ-NĒĒR', *n.* One guilty of mutiny.
MŪ'TĮ-NOŬS, *a.* Seditious; busy in insurrection.
MŪ'TĮ-NOŬS-LY, *ad.* Seditiously; turbulently.
MŪ'TĮ-NY, *v. n.* To rise against authority.
MŪ'TĮ-NY, *n.* An insurrection among seamen, &c.
MŬT'TĘR, *v. n.* To murmur.—*v. a.* To utter in-
MŬT'TĘR-ĘR, *n.* A murmurer. [distinctly.
MŬT'TON (mŭt'tn), *n.* Flesh of sheep; a sheep.
‖MŪT'Ų-ĄL (mŭt'yų-ąl), *a.* Reciprocal; each acting in return to the other; interchanged.
‖MŪT-Ų-ĂL'Į-TY, *n.* Reciprocation; interchange.
‖MŪT'Ų-ĄL-LY, *ad.* Reciprocally; in return.
MŬZ'ZLE, *n.* The mouth:—a fastening for the
MŬZ'ZLE, *v. a.* To bind the mouth. [mouth.
MȲ *or* MY, *pron. poss.* Belonging to me.
MȲ-ŎG'RĄ-PHY, *n.* A description of the muscles.
MȲ-ŎL'Ǫ-GY, *n.* The doctrine of the muscles.
MȲ'Ǫ-PY, *n.* Shortness or nearness of sight.
MȲR'Į-ĄD, *n.* Ten thousand:—a great number.
MȲR'MĮ-DǪN, *n.* A rough soldier:—a ruffian.
MY-RŎB'Ą-LĂN, *n.* A kind of dried fruit or plum.
MȲRRH, *n.* A strong aromatic gum-resin.
MȲR'TLE, *n.* A plant of many species.
MY-SĔLF', *pron.* I myself, not another.
MYS-TĒ'RĮ-OŬS, *a.* Full of mystery; obscure.
MYS-TĒ'RĮ-OŬS-LY, *ad.* Obscurely; enigmatically.
MYS-TĒ'RĮ-OŲS-NĔSS, *n.* Obscurity; perplexity.
MȲS'TĘ-RY, *n.* Something secret or unexplained.
MȲS'TĮC, *n.* One of a sect or class of Christians.
MȲS'TĮC, MȲS'TĮ-CĄL, *a.* Obscure; secret; dark.
MȲS'TĮ-CĄL-LY, *ad.* In a mystical manner.
MȲS'TĮ-CĄL-NĔSS, *n.* Quality of being mystical.
MȲS'TĮ-CĬ$M, *n.* The doctrine of the Mystics.
MȲS-TĮ-FĮ-CĀ'TĮON, *n.* Act of rendering mysterious.
MȲTH-Ǫ-LŎG'Į-CĄL, *a.* Relating to mythology.
MY-THŎL'Ǫ-GĬST, *n.* One versed in mythology.
MY-THŎL'Ǫ-GĪZE, *v. n.* To explain mythology.
MY-THŎL'Ǫ-GY, *n.* A system of fables; the fabulous history of the gods of the heathens.

N.

N, a semivowel, and a nasal letter, has in English an invariable sound ; as, *no, name, net*.
NĂB, *v. a.* To catch suddenly ; to seize.
NĂ′BŎB, *n.* The title of an Indian prince.
NĀ′DĬR, *n.* The point opposite to the zenith.
NĂG, *n.* A small horse ; a horse.
NĀ′ĬĂD (nā′yặd), *n.* A water-nymph.
NĀIL, *n.* A horny substance on the ends of the fingers and toes ; a claw :—an iron spike ; a stud or boss :—two inches and a quarter.
NĀIL (nāl), *v. a.* To fasten or stud with nails.
NĀIL′ĔR, *n.* A nail maker.
NĀIL′ĔR-Y, *n.* A manufactory for nails.
NAIVETE (nä′ev-tā′), *n.* [Fr.] Native simplicity.
NĀ′KĔD, *a.* Uncovered ; bare ; open ; plain.
NĀ′KĔD-LY, *ad.* Without covering ; simply.
NĀ′KĔD-NĔSS, *n.* Nudity ; want of covering.
NĀME, *n.* An appellation ; reputation ; fame.
NĀME, *v. a.* To give a name to ; to mention.
NĀME′LĔSS, *a.* Destitute of a name ; obscure.
NĀME′LY, *ad.* Particularly ; to mention by name.
NĀME′SĀKE, *n.* One that has the same name.
NĂN-KĒĔN′, *n.* A buff-colored cotton cloth.
NĂP, *n.* Slumber ; a short sleep :—down on cloth.
NĂP, *v. n.* To sleep ; to be drowsy or secure.
NĀPE, *n.* The joint of the neck behind.
NĂPH′THẶ (năp′thặ), *n.* A bituminous fluid.
NĂP′KĬN, *n.* A cloth to wipe the hands, &c.
NĂP′LĔSS, *a.* Wanting nap ; threadbare.
NĂP′PĬ-NĔSS, *n.* The quality of having a nap.
NĂP′PY, *a.* Frothy ; spumy ; hairy ; full of down.
NẶR-CĬS′SẶS, *n.* [L.] A daffodil ; a flower.
NẶR-CŎT′ĬC, *n.* A drug producing sleep.
NẶR-CŎT′ĬC, NẶR-CŎT′Ĭ-CẶL, *a.* Causing sleep.
NĂRD, *n.* An aromatic plant ; an ointment.
NĂR′RẶ-BLE, *a.* Capable of being told or related.
NĂR′RĀTE, *v. a.* To relate ; to tell ; to recite.
NẶR-RĀ′TĬǪN, *n.* An account ; a relation ; history.
NĂR′RẶ-TĬVE, *a.* Relating ; apt to relate or tell.
NĂR′RẶ-TĬVE, *n.* A relation ; an account ; a story.
NẶR-RĀ′TǪR, *n.* A teller ; a relator.
NĂR′RŌW (năr′rō), *a.* Not wide ; near ; covetous.
NĂR′RŌW (năr′rō), *v. a.* To contract ; to limit.
NĂR′RŌW, NĂR′RŌWS, *n.* A strait ; a sound.
NĂR′RǪW-LY, *ad.* Contractedly ; nearly.
NĂR′RǪW-MĬND′ĔD, *a.* Illiberal ; avaricious.
NĂR′RǪW-NĔSS, *n.* Want of extent ; poverty.
NĀ′SẶL, *a.* Belonging to the nose.
NĂS′CĔNT, *a.* Beginning to grow ; increasing.
NĂS′TĬ-LY, *ad.* Dirtily ; filthily ; nauseously.
NĂS′TĬ-NĔSS, *n.* Dirt ; filth ; grossness.
NĂS′TY, *a.* Dirty ; filthy ; sordid ; nauseous.
NĀ′TẶL, *a.* Native ; relating to nativity.
NĂT-Ặ-LĬ′′TĬOŲS (năt-ặ-lĭsh′ŭs), *a.* Relating to a birthday.
NĀ′TẶNT, *a.* Swimming ; floating.
NẶ-TĀ′TĬǪN, *n.* The act of swimming.
NĀ′TẶ-TǪ-RY, *a.* Enabling to swim ; swimming.
NĀ′TĬǪN, *n.* A people distinct from others.
NĀ′′TĬǪN-ẶL (năsh′ŭn-ặl), *a.* Relating to a nation ; general ; public ; not private.
NĂ-TĬǪN-ẶL′Ĭ-TY (năsh-ŭn-ăl′ọ-tọ), *n.* National character ; national bias or partiality.

NĀ′TĬVE, *a.* Produced by nature ; natural ; original.
NĀ′TĬVE, *n.* One born in any place. [nal.
NĀ′TĬVE-LY, *ad.* Naturally ; not artificially.
NẶ-TĬV′Ĭ-TY, *n.* Birth ; time or place of birth.
NĀ′TRǪN, *n.* A native carbonate of soda.
‖NĂT′Ų-RẶL (năt′yụ-rặl), *a.* Produced by nature ; tender ; unaffected ; illegitimate.
‖NĂT′Ų-RẶL, *n.* An idiot ; a fool ; a simpleton.
‖NĂT′Ų-RẶL-ĬSM, *n.* Mere state of nature. [ence.
‖NĂT′Ų-RẶL-ĬST, *n.* One versed in natural science.
‖NĂT-Ų-RẶL-Ĭ-ZĀ′TĬǪN, *n.* Act of naturalizing.
‖NĂT′Ų-RẶL-ĪZE, *v. a.* To adopt ; to invest with the privileges of a native citizen. [ly.
‖NĂT′Ų-RẶL-LY, *ad.* Unaffectedly ; spontaneously.
‖NĂT′Ų-RẶL-NĔSS, *n.* State of being natural.
NĀT′ŲRE (năt′yụr), *n.* The system of the world ; the universe ; visible creation ; natural affection ; disposition ; constitution ; sort ; birth.
NÂUGHT (nâwt), *a.* Bad ; corrupt ; worthless.
NÂUGHT (nâwt), *n.* Nothing ; erroneously *nought*.
NÂUGHT′Ĭ-LY (nâw′tĕ-lĕ), *ad.* Corruptly ; badly.
NÂUGHT′Ĭ-NĔSS (nâw′tĕ-nĕs), *n.* Wickedness.
NÂUGHT′Y (nâw′tĕ), *a.* Bad ; wicked ; corrupt.
NÂU′MẶ-CHY, *n.* A mock sea-fight. [stomach.
NÂU′SĔ-Ặ (nâw′shĕ-ặ), *n.* [L.] Sickness at the
NÂU′SĔ-ĀTE (nâw′shĕ-āt), *v. n.* To feel disgust.
NÂU′SĔ-ĀTE (nâw′shĕ-āt), *v. a.* To loathe. [ful.
NÂU′SEOŲS (nâw′shụs), *a.* Loathsome ; disgust-
NÂU′SEOŲS-LY (nâw′shụs-lĕ), *ad.* Loathsomely.
NÂU′SEOŲS-NĔSS (nâw′shụs-nĕs), *n.* Disgust.
NÂU′TĬC, NÂU′TĬ-CẶL, *a.* Relating to ships, sailors, navy, or navigation ; naval.
NÂU′TĬ-LŬS, *n.* ; pl. NÂU′TĬ-LĪ. [L.] A shell-fish furnished with something like oars and a sail.
NĀ′VẶL, *a.* Consisting of ships ; relating to ships.
NĀVE, *n.* Middle part of a wheel or of a church.
NĀ′VEL (nā′vl), *n.* Middle point of the belly.
NẶ-VĬC′Ų-LẶR, *a.* Relating to boats or vessels.
NĂV′Ĭ-GẶ-BLE, *a.* That may be navigated.
NĂV′Ĭ-GẶ-BLE-NĔSS, *n.* Capacity of navigation.
NĂV′Ĭ-GĀTE, *v. a. & n.* To pass by ships or boats.
NĂV-Ĭ-GĀ′TĬǪN, *n.* The act or art of navigating.
NĂV′Ĭ-GĀ-TǪR, *n.* One who navigates ; a seaman.
NĀ′VY, *n.* An assemblage of ships ; a fleet.
NĀY (nā), *ad.* No :—not only so, but more.
NĂZ-Ặ-RĒNE′, *n.* One of Nazareth ; a Christian.
NĂZ′Ặ-RĪTE, *n.* One devoted to religious duties.
NEAL, *v. a.* To temper by heat. See ANNEAL.
NĒAP (nĕp), *a.* Low ;—*used only of the tide*.
NĒAP, *n.* Draught-pole of a cart, &c. [*U. S.*]
NĒAP, *a.* Noting the lowest tides.
NĒ-Ặ-PŎL′Ĭ-TẶN (nĕ-ặ-pŏl′ĕ-tặn), *a.* Relating to Naples.
NĒAR (nĕr), *prep.* Close to ; nigh. [Naples.
NĒAR, *ad.* Almost ; not far off ; within a little.
NĒAR, *a.* Not distant ; close ; dear ; intimate.
NĒAR, *v. a. & n.* To approach ; to draw near.
NĒAR′LY, *ad.* At no great distance ; closely.
NĒAR′NĔSS, *n.* Closeness ; alliance :—avarice.
NĒAT, *n.* Oxen, cows, &c. ; a cow or ox.
NĒAT, *a.* Very clean ; cleanly ; nice ; pure.
NĒAT′HĔRD, *n.* One who has the care of cattle.
NĒAT′LY, *ad.* With neatness ; cleanlily.

NĒAT'NĘSS, n. Cleanliness ; pureness.
NĔB, n. Nose ; mouth ; bill of a bird. See NIB.
NĔB'Ų-LĄ, n. ; pl. NĔB'Ų-LÆ. [L.] A misty or cloudy appearance :—a film ; a spot.
NĔB'Ų-LOŬS, a. Misty ; cloudy.
NĔÇ-ĘS-SĀ'RĮ-ĄN, } n. An advocate for the
NĘ-CĔS-SĮ-TĀ'RĮ-ĄN, } doctrine of philosophical necessity. [necessary or needful.
NĔÇ'ĘS-SĄ-RIĘŞ (nĕs'ĕs-sĄ-rĕz), n. pl. Things
NĔÇ'ĘS-SĄ-RĮ-LỲ, ad. Inevitably ; by necessity.
NĔÇ'ĘS-SĄ-RỲ, a. Needful ; essential ; inevitable.
NĘ-CĔS'SĮ-TĀTE, v. a. To make necessary.
NĘ-CĔS'SĮ-TOŬS, a. Pressed with poverty ; needy.
NĘ-CĔS'SĮ-TỲ, n. Compulsion ; fatality ; state of being necessary :—want ; need ; poverty.
NĔCK, n. The part between the head and body.
NĔCK'CLŎTH, n. A cloth worn on the neck.
NĔCK'ĘR-CHIEF (nĕk'kĕr-chĭf), n. A cravat.
NĔCK'LĄCE, n. An ornament for the neck.
NĔC-RŲ-LŎG'Į-CĄL, a. Relating to necrology.
NĘ-CRŎL'Ų-ĢỲ, n. An obituary ; register of deaths.
NĔC'RŲ-MĂN-CĘR, n. A conjurer ; an enchanter.
NĔC'RŲ-MĂN-CỲ, n. Enchantment ; conjuration.
NĔC-RŲ-MĂN'TĮC, a. Relating to necromancy.
NĔC-RŲ-MĂN'TĮ-CĄL-LỲ, ad. By conjuration.
NĔC'TĄR, n. The feigned drink of the gods.
NĘC-TĀ'RĘ-ĄN, a. Like nectar ; nectareous.
NĔC'TĄRED (nĕk'tĄrd), a. Imbued with nectar,
NĘC-TĀ'RĘ-OŬS, a. Resembling nectar ; delicious.
NĔC'TĄ-kINE, a. Sweet as nectar.
NĔC'TĄ-RĪNE, n. A fruit of the peach kind.
NĔC'TĄR-OŬS, a. Sweet as nectar ; nectareous.
NĔC'TĄ-RỲ, n. The melliferous part of a flower.
NĒĒD, n. Exigency ; necessity ; want ; poverty.
NĒĒD, v. a. To want.—v. n. To be in want.
NĒĒD'FÛL, a. Necessary ; requisite ; needed.
NĒĒD'Į-LỲ, ad. In poverty ; poorly.
NĒĒD'Į-NĔSS, n. Want ; poverty ; need.
NĒĒ'DLE, n. A small instrument for sewing :—a steel pointer in the mariner's compass. [once.
NĒĒ'DLE-FÛL, n. Thread put into a needle at
NĒĒD'LĘSS, a. Unnecessary ; not requisite.
NĒĒD'LĘSS-LỲ, ad. Unnecessarily ; without need.
NĒĒD'LĘSS-NĔSS, n. Unnecessariness.
NĒĒDŞ, ad. Necessarily ; indispensably.
NĒĒD'Ỳ, a. Poor ; necessitous ; indigent.
NE'ER (nár), ad. A contraction for never.
NĘ-FĀ'RĮ-OŬS, a. Wicked ; abominable ; vile.
NĘ-FĀ'RĮ-OŬS-LỲ, ad. Abominably ; wickedly.
NĘ-GĀ'TIŲN, n. A denial ; an exclusion.
NĔG'Ą-TĬVE, a. Denying ; implying denial.
NĔG'Ą-TĬVE, n. A proposition or word that de-
NĔG'Ą-TĬVE, v. a. To reject by negation. [nies.
NĔG'Ą-TĬVE-LỲ, ad. With or by denial.
NĘG-LĔCT', v. a. To omit ; not to do ; to slight.
NĘG-LĔCT', n. Inattention ; slight ; negligence.
NĘG-LĔCT'FÛL, a. Heedless ; careless ; inattentive ; negligent. [attention.
NĘG-LĔCT'FÛL-LỲ, ad. With heedless in-
NEG-LĮ-ĢĒĒ', n. A sort of old-fashioned gown.
NĔG'LĮ-ĢENCE, n. Inattention ; carelessness.
NĔG'LĮ-ĢENT, a. Careless ; heedless ; inattentive.
NĔG'LĮ-ĢENT-LỲ, ad. Carelessly. [negotiated.
NĘ-GŌ'TĮ-Ą-BLE (-shĘ-Ą-bl), a. That may be
NĘ-GŌ'TĮ-ĀTE (-shĘ-āt), v. a. & n. To manage ; to traffic ; to conclude by treaty or agreement.
NĘ-GŌ-TĮ-Ā'TIŲN (nĘ-gō-she-ā'shŭn), n. Act of negotiating ; a treaty of business.

NĘ-GŌ'TĮ-Ā-TŲR (nĘ-gō'shĘ-ā-tŭr), n. One who negotiates.
NĒ'GRĘSS, n. A female of the black race of Africa ; a female negro. [black race.
NĒ'GRŌ, n. ; pl. NĒ'GRŌĘŞ. One of the African
NĒ'GŲS, n. A mixture of wine, water, sugar, &c.
NEIGH (nā), v. n. To utter the voice of a horse.
NEIGH (nā), n. The voice of a horse.
NEIGH'BŲR (nā'bur), n. One who lives near.
NEIGH'BŲR (nā'bur), v. a. To adjoin ; to confine
NEIGH'BŲR-HOOD (nā'bur-hûd), n. Vicinity. [on.
NEIGH'BŲR-ĬNG (nā'bur-ĭng), a. Being near.
NEIGH'BŲR-LĮ-NĔSS (nā'bur-lĘ-nĕs), n. Civility.
NEIGH'BŲR-LỲ (nā'bur-lĘ), a. Kind ; civil.
NĒI'THĘR, conj. Not either ; nor.
NĒI'THĘR, pron. Not either ; nor one nor other.
NĒ-Ų-LŎG'Į-CĄL, a. Relating to neology.
NĘ-ŎL'Ų-ĢĬSM, n. New words, terms, or doctrines ; neology. [&c.
NĘ-ŎL'Ų-ĢĬST, n. An introducer of new terms,
NĘ-ŎL'Ų-ĢỲ, n. A system of new words or doc-
NĒ'Ų-PHỸTE, n. A new convert ; tyro. [trines.
NĒ-Ų-TĔR'ĮC, n. One of modern times. [novel.
NĒ-Ų-TĔR'ĮC, NĒ-Ų-TĔR'Į-CĄL, a. Modern ;
NĔPH'EW (nĕv'vū), n. Son of a brother or sister.
NĘ-PHRĬT'ĮC, n. A medicine for the gravel.
NĘ-PHRĬT'ĮC, } a. Pertaining to the kidneys :
NĘ-PHRĬT'Į-CĄL, } —relieving disorders of the
NĔP'Ų-TĬSM, n. Fondness for nephews. [kidneys.
NĔP-TŪ'NĮ-ĄN, a. Relating to the ocean.
NĒ'RĘ-ĬD, n. A sea-nymph. [force ; courage.
NĔRVE (nĕrv), n. An organ of sensation :—
NĔRVE (nĕrv), v. a. To strengthen.
NĔRVE'LĘSS (nĕrv'lĘs), a. Without strength.
NĔR'VOŬS, a. Relating to the nerves :—strong ; vigorous :—having weak nerves.
NĔR'VOŬS-LỲ, ad. With strength ; with force.
NĔR'VOŬS-NĔSS, n. State of being nervous.
NĔS'CĮ-ĘNCE (nĕsh'ĘĘns), n. Ignorance.
NĔST, n. A bed of birds :—number of boxes, &c.
NĔST'-ĔGG, n. An egg left in the nest.
NĔS'TLE (nĕs'sl), v. n. To settle ; to lie close.
NĔST'LĮNG, n. A young bird in the nest.
NĔT, n. A texture woven with meshes ; a snare.
NĔT, a. Clear after deductions ; as, net weight.
NĔT, v. a. & n. To bring as clear produce ; to knit.
NĔTH'ĘR, a. Lower ; not upper ; infernal.
NĔTH'ĘR-MŌST, a. Lowest. [work.
NĔT'TĮNG, n. A reticulated piece of work ; net-
NĔT'TLE, n. A well-known stinging herb.
NĔT'TLE, v. a. To sting ; to irritate ; to provoke.
NĔT'TLER, n. One that nettles. [netting.
NĔT'WORK (nĕt'würk), n. Reticulated work ;
NEU-RŎL'Ų-ĢỲ, n. A description of the nerves.
NEU-RŎT'Ų-MỲ, n. The anatomy of the nerves.
NEŪ'TĘR (nū'tĘr), a. Of neither party ; neutral.
NEŪ'TĘR, n. One indifferent and unengaged.
NEŪ'TRĄL, a. Indifferent ; not on either side.
NEŪ'TRĄL, n. One who is not on either side.
NEU-TRĂL'Į-TỲ (nū-trăl'Ę-tĘ), n. A neutral state.
NEŪ'TRĄL-ĪZE, v. a. To render neutral.
NEŪ'TRĄL-LỲ, ad. Indifferently ; on neither part.
NĔV'ĘR, ad. Not ever ; at no time ; in no degree.
NĔV'ĘR-THĘ-LĔSS', ad. & c. However ; yet.
NEW (nū), a. Not old ; fresh ; novel ; modern.
NEW-FĂN'GLED (nū-făng'gld), a. New-made.
NEW-FĂSH'IŲNED (nū-făsh'ŭnd), a. Recently come into fashion.

NEW'ISH (nū'ish), *a.* Rather new.
NEW'LY (nū'le), *ad.* Freshly; lately; recently.
NEW'NESS, *n.* Freshness; recentness; novelty.
NEWS, *n. sing.* & *pl.* Fresh accounts; tidings.
NEWS'-MŎN-ĠER, *n.* One who deals in news.
NEWS'PA-PER, *n.* A print that conveys news.
NEWT (nŭt), *n.* An eft; a species of lizard.
NĔXT, *a.* Nearest in place, time, or order.
NĔXT, *ad.* At the time or turn nearest.
NIB, *n.* The bill of a bird:—point of a pen.
NIBBED (nĭbd), *a.* Having a nib. [bite as a fish.
NĬB'BLE, *v. a.* To eat slowly, or by nips; to
NĬB'BLE, *v. n.* To bite at by nips:—to carp.
NĬB'BLE, *n.* An act of a fish trying the bait.
NĬB'BLER, *n.* One that nibbles; a carper.
NICE, *a.* Exact; precise; delicate; fastidious.
NICE'LY, *ad.* Exactly; precisely; delicately.
NICE'NESS, *n.* Minute exactness; delicacy.
NI'CE-TY, *n.* Minuteness; accuracy; delicacy.
NICHE (nĭch), *n.* A hollow for a statue, &c.
NĬCK, *n.* Exact point of time; a notch; a score.
NĬCK, *v. a.* To hit; to cut in notches; to cozen.
NĬCK'EL, *n.* A metal of a whitish color.
NĬCK'NĀME, *n.* A name given in derision.
NĬCK'NĀME, *v. a.* To call by an opprobrious
NI-CO'TIAN, *a.* Relating to tobacco. [name.
NĬC'TĀTE, NĬC'TI-TĀTE, *v. n.* To wink.
NĬC-TĀ'TION, *n.* A winking of the eye.
NIDE, *n.* A brood; as, a *nide* of pheasants.
NĬD-I-FI-CĀ'TION, *n.* The act of building nests.
NI'DOR-OŬS, *a.* Smelling like roasted meat.
NĬD-U-LĀ'TION, *n.* Time of remaining in the
NI'DUS, *n.* [L.] A nest of birds, &c. [nest.
NIÈCE (nēs), *n.* Daughter of a brother or sister.
NĬG'GARD, *n.* A miser; a sordid fellow.
NĬG'GARD, *a.* Sordid; miserly. [mony.
NĬG'GARD-LI-NĔSS, *n.* Avarice; sordid parsi-
NĬG'GARD-LY, *a.* Avaricious; parsimonious.
NIGH (nī), *prep.* At no great distance from.
NIGH (nī), *ad.* Not far off; almost; nearly.
NIGH (nī), *a.* Near; not distant; not remote.
NIGH'NESS (nī'nes), *n.* Nearness; proximity.
NĪGHT (nīt), *n.* The time from sunset to sunrise.
NĪGHT'BORN (nīt'bŏrn), *a.* Produced in darkness.
NĪGHT'CĂP (nīt'kăp), *n.* A cap worn in bed.
NĪGHT'DEW (nīt'dū), *n.* Dew falling by night.
NĪGHT'DRĔSS, *n.* The dress worn at night.
NĪGHT'FĂLL, *n.* The close of day; evening.
NĪGHT'FĪRE, *n.* An ignis fatuus. [for undress.
NĪGHT'GŎWN, *n.* A loose gown used in bed, or
NĪGHT'HĂG, *n.* A witch wandering in the night.
NĪGHT'IN-GĀLE, *n.* A bird that sings at night.
NĪGHT'LY, *a.* Done by night; acting by night.
NĪGHT'LY (nīt'le), *ad.* By night; every night.
NĪGHT'MAN, *n.* One who removes filth by night.
NĪGHT'MĀRE, *n.* Morbid oppression during sleep.
NĪGHT'PIĒCE, *n.* A picture seen by candle-light.
NĪGHT'SHĀDE, *n.* A plant:—darkness of night.
NĪGHT'WATCH (nīt'wŏch), *n.* A watch by night.
NI-GRĔS'CENT, *a.* Growing black; blackish.
NI-HĬL'I-TY, *n.* Nothingness; non-existence.
NĬLL, *v. n.* Not to will; to refuse; to reject.
NĬM'BLE, *a.* Quick; active; ready; speedy.
NĬM'BLE-NĔSS, *n.* Quickness; activity.
NĬM'BLY, *ad.* Quickly; speedily; actively;
NINE, *a.* One more than eight. [briskly.
NINE'FŌLD, *a.* Repeated nine times.
NINE'HŌLES, *n.* A game requiring nine holes.

NINE'PĔNCE, *n.* A small silver coin. [wood.
NINE'PINS, *n.* A play with nine or ten pieces of
NINE'TĒĒN, *a.* Nine and ten.
NINE'TĒĒNTH, *a.* The ordinal of nineteen.
NINE'TI-ĔTH, *a.* The ordinal of ninety.
NINE'TY, *a.* Nine times ten. [pleton.
NĬN'NY, NĬN'NY-HĂM'MER, *n.* A fool; a sim-
NINTH, *a.* First after the 8th; the ordinal of 9.
NINTH'LY, *ad.* In the ninth place. [to destroy.
NĬP, *v. a.* To cut; to pinch; to bite; to blast;
NĬP, *n.* A pinch; a small cut; a blast.
NĬP'PERS (nĭp'perz), *n. pl.* Small pincers.
NĬP'PLE, *n.* A teat; a dug; pap; an orifice.
NĬs'AN, *n.* A Jewish month of spring.
NĬT, *n.* The egg of a louse or small insect.
NI'TEN-CY, *n.* Lustre; brightness; an endeavor.
NĬT'ID, *a.* Bright; shining; gay; spruce.
NI'TRĀTE, *n.* A chemical salt.
NI'TRE (nī'ter), *n.* Saltpetre; nitrate of potassa.
NI'TRIC, *a.* Relating to, or containing, nitre.
NI'TRO-ĠĒN, *n.* A kind of gas; azote.
NI'TROŬS, *a.* Impregnated with nitre.—*Nitrous
oxide,* an exhilarating gas.
NI'TRY, *a.* Nitrous; relating to nitre.
NĬT'TY, *a.* Abounding with the eggs of lice.
NI'VAL, *a.* Abounding with snow; snowy.
NĬV'E-OŬS, *a.* Snowy; resembling snow.
NŌ, *ad.* The word of refusal or denial.
NŌ, *a.* Not any; none.—*No one,* not any one.
NO-BĬL'I-TĀTE, *v. a.* To ennoble; to make noble.
NO-BĬL-I-TĀ'TION, *n.* The act of ennobling.
NO-BĬL'I-TY, *n.* Dignity; rank; people of rank.
NŌ'BLE, *a.* Exalted in rank; illustrious; liberal.
NŌ'BLE, *n.* One of high rank:—an ancient coin.
NŌ'BLE-MAN, *n.* One who is ennobled.
NŌ'BLE-NĔSS, *n.* Greatness; worth; dignity.
NO-BLĔSS', *n.* Nobility; noblemen collectively.
NŌ'BLY, *ad.* Greatly; illustriously; liberally.
NŌ'BŎD-Y, *n.* No one; not any one.
NO'CENT, *a.* Guilty; hurtful; mischievous.
NOC-TĂM-BU-LĀ'TION, *n.* Act of walking in
sleep; somnambulism; noctambulism.
NOC-TĂM'BU-LĬST, *n.* One who walks in sleep.
NOC-TĬV'A-GANT, *a.* Wandering in the night.
NŌC'TU-A-RY, *n.* Account of what passes by
night:—opposed to *diary.*
NOC-TŪR'NAL, *a.* Nightly; relating to night.
NOC-TŪR'NAL, *n.* An instrument formerly used
to view the stars.
NŌD, *v. n.* To bend the head; to be drowsy.
NŎD, *n.* A quick bend of the head; command.
NŎD'DER, *n.* One who nods; a drowsy person.
NŎD'DLE, *n.* The head;—*in contempt.*
NŎD'DY, *n.* A simpleton; an idiot; a fool.
NODE, *n.* A knob; a swelling; an intersection.
NO-DŌSE', NŌ'DOŬS, *a.* Knotty; full of knots.
NO-DŎS'I-TY, *n.* Complication; knottiness.
NŎD'U-LAR, *a.* Having the form of a nodule.
NŎD'ŪLE (nŏd'yūl), *n.* A small lump or knot.
NŎD'ŪLED (nŏd'yūld), *a.* Having nodules.
NŎG'ĠIN, *n.* A small mug or cup:—a gill.
NOĬSE, *n.* Any kind of sound; outcry; clamor.
NOĬSE, *v. a.* To spread by rumor or report.
NOĬSE'FŪL, *a.* Loud; clamorous; noisy.
NOĬSE'LESS, *a.* Silent; without sound; still.
NOĬ'SI-NĔSS, *n.* Loudness of sound; clamor.
NOĬ'SOME (noĭ'sum), *a.* Noxious; offensive.
NOĬ'SOME-LY (noĭ'sum-le), *ad.* Offensively.

NÖÏ'SǪME-NĔSS (nŏï'sum-nĕss), *n.* Offensive-
NÖÏ'SY, *a.* Sounding loud ; clamorous. [ness.
NǪ-LĬ''TIǪN (nǫ-lĭsh'un), *n.* Unwillingness.
NŎM'ĂD, *n.* One who leads a wandering life.
NǪ-MĂD'ĬC, *a.* Pastoral ; rude ; wandering.
NŎM'BLEṢ (nŭm'blz), *n.* The entrails of a deer.
NŌ'MĘN-CLĀ-TǪR, *n.* One who names.
NŌ'MĘN-CLĀT-ŲRE (nō'men-klāt-yur), *n.* A
glossary ; a dictionary ; a vocabulary.
NŎM'Ĭ-NĄL, *a.* Only in name ; not real ; titular.
NŎM'Ĭ-NĄL-ĬST, *n.* One of a school of philoso-
NŎM'Ĭ-NĄL-LY, *ad.* By name ; in name.[phers.
NŎM'Ĭ-NĀTE, *v. a.* To propose by name ; to
name ; to mention ; to appoint.
NŎM-Ĭ-NĀ'TIǪN, *n.* The act of nominating.
NŎM'Ĭ-NĄ-TĬVE, *a.* Applied to the first case of
NŎM'Ĭ-NĀ-TǪR, *n.* One that names. [nouns.
NŎM-Ĭ-NĔĒ', *n.* A person nominated to an office.
NŎN, *ad.* In composition, not.
NŎN'ĄǦE, *n.* Minority in age ; immaturity.
NŎN-ĄT-TĔND'ĄNCE, *n.* Want of attendance.
NŎN-ÇHĄ-LĂNCE', *n.* [Fr.] Indifference ; cool-
ness ; carelessness.
NŎN-CǪM-PLĬ'ĄNCE, *n.* A refusal to comply.
NŎN-CǪN-FÖRM'ĬST, *n.* One who does not
conform to the established religion.
NŎN-CǪN-FÖRM'Ĭ-TY, *n.* Want of conformity.
NŎN'DĘ-⸢CRĬPT, *a.* Not yet described.
NŎN'DĘ-SCRĬPT, *n.* A thing not yet described.
NŎNE (nŭn), *a.* Not one ; not any.
NŎN-ĔN'TĬ-TY, *n.* Non-existence ; an ideal
thing ; nothing.
NŎNE'SŬCH, *n.* An unequalled thing.
NŎN-ĔX-ĬST'ĘNCE, *n.* State of not existing.
NŎN-JŪR'ĬNG, *a.* Not swearing allegiance.
NŎN-JŪ'RǪR, *n.* One who refused to swear alle-
giance to the successors of James II.
NŎN-PĄ-RĔIL' (nŏn-pą-rĕl'), *n.* A kind of ap-
ple :—a printer's letter of a small size.
NŎN'PLŬS, *n.* A puzzle ; a great difficulty.
NŎN'PLŬS, *v. a.* To confound ; to puzzle.
NŎN-RĔṢ'Ĭ-DĔNCE, *n.* A failure of residence.
NŎN-RĔṢ'Ĭ-DĔNT, *n.* One who does not reside
in the place of his official duty.
NŎN-RĔṢ'Ĭ-DĔNT, *a.* Not residing ; absent.
NŎN-RĘ-ṢĬST'ĄNCE, *n.* Ready obedience.
NŎN-RĘ-ṢĬST'ĄNT, *a.* Not resisting ; unopposing.
NŎN'SĔNSE, *n.* Unmeaning language ; folly.
NŎN-SĔN'SĬ-CĄL, *a.* Unmeaning ; foolish.
NŎN-SĔN'SĬ-CĄL-LY, *ad.* Foolishly ; ridiculous-
NŎN-SĔN'SĬ-CĄL-NĔSS, *n.* Absurdity ; folly. [ly.
NŎN'SŪIT (nŏn'sūt), *n.* Stoppage of a lawsuit.
NŎN'SŪIT, *v. a.* To quash in a legal process.
NȎȎ'DLE, *n.* A fool ; a simpleton. [*Vulgar.*]
NȎȎK, *n.* A corner ; a narrow place ; a retreat.
NȎȎN, *n.* Midday ; twelve o'clock. [noon.
NȎȎN'DĀY, NȎȎN'TĬDE, *n.* Midday ; time of
NȎȎN'ĬNG, *n.* Repose or a repast at noon.
NȎȎṢE *or* NȎȎSE, *n.* A running knot. [entrap.
NȎȎṢE, *v. a.* To tie in a noose ; to catch ; to
NŌ'PĄL, *n.* A plant ; Indian fig. [*neither* or *not.*
NÖR, *conj.* A negative particle ; correlative to
NÖR'MĄL, *a.* Perpendicular ; regular.—*Normal
school*, a school for training school teachers.
NÖR'MĄN, *a.* Relating to Normandy, or to Nor-
mans.
NÖRTH, *n.* The point opposite to the south.
NÖRTH, *a.* Northern ; being in the north.

NÖRTH-ĒAST', *n.* The point between the north
and east. [point.
NÖRTH-ĒAST', *a.* Pertaining to the north-east
NÖRTH'ĘR-LY, *a.* Being towards or from the
NÖRTH'ĘRN, *a.* Being in the north. [north.
NÖRTH'-STĂR, *n.* The polestar ; the loadstar.
NÖRTH'WÂRD, *a.* Being towards the north.
NÖRTH'WĄRD, ⎱ *ad.* Towards the north.
NÖRTH'WĄRDṢ, ⎰
NÖRTH-WĔST', *n.* Point between the north
and west.
NÖRTH'-WĬND, *n.* The wind from the north.
NŌṢE, *n.* The prominence on the face :—scent.
NŌṢE, *v. a.* To scent ; to smell :—to face.
NŌṢE'GĀY (nōz'gā), *n.* A bunch of flowers.
NŌṢE'LĘSS, *a.* Destitute of a nose.
NŎS-Ǫ-LŎǦ'Ĭ-CĄL, *a.* Relating to nosology.
NǪ-SŎL'Ǫ-ǦY, *n.* The science of diseases.
NŎS'TRĬL, *n.* An aperture of the nose.
NŎS'TRŬM, *n.* [L.] A quack medicine.
NŎT, *ad.* A particle of negation or refusal.
NŎT'Ą-BLE, *a.* Industrious ; careful : bustling.
NŌT'Ą-BLE, *a.* Remarkable ; memorable.
NŎT'Ą-BLE-NĔSS, *n.* Carefulness ; industry
NŌT'Ą-BLE-NĔSS, *n.* Remarkableness.
NŎT'Ą-BLY, *ad.* Carefully ; with bustle.
NŌT'Ą-BLY, *ad.* Memorably ; remarkably.
NǪ-TĀ'RĬ-ĄL, *a.* Relating to, or by, a notary.
NŌ'TĄ-RY, *n.* An officer who attests contracts,
NǪ-TĀ'TIǪN, *n.* Act of noting or marking. [&c.
NŎTCH, *n.* A nick ; a hollow cut in any thing.
NŎTCH, *v. a.* To cut in small hollows.
NŌTE, *n.* A mark ; a notice ; a remark ; an ac-
count :—a tune ; a symbol :—a written paper.
NŌTE, *v. a.* To observe ; to remark ; to set down.
NŌTE'BOOK (-bûk), *n.* A book containing notes.
NŌT'ĘD, *p. a.* Remarkable ; eminent ; famous.
NŌT'ĘD-LY, *ad.* With observation ; with notice.
NŌT'ĘD-NĔSS, *n.* State of being noted ; celeb-
NŌT'ĘR, *n.* One who takes notice. [rity.
NŎTH'ĬNG (nŭth'ĭng), *n.* Nonentity ; negation.
NŎTH'ĬNG-NĔSS, *n.* Nihility ; non-existence.
NŌ'TĬCE, *n.* A remark ; heed ; observation ;
information.
NŌ'TĬCE, *v. a.* To note ; to heed ; to observe.
NŌ'TĬCE-Ą-BLE, *a.* Worthy of observation.
NŌ-TĬ-FĬ-CĀ'TIǪN, *n.* The act of notifying.
NŌ'TĬ-FY, *v. a.* To declare ; to make known.
NŌ'TIǪN, *n.* Thought ; idea ; image ; opinion.
NŌ'TIǪN-ĄL, *a.* Imaginary ; ideal ; visionary.
NŌ-TǪ-RĬ'Ę-TY, *n.* Public knowledge or ex-
posure ; notoriousness.
NǪ-TŌ'RĬ-OŬS, *a.* Publicly known ; infamous.
NǪ-TŌ'RĬ-OŬS-LY, *ad.* Publicly ; evidently.
NǪ-TŌ'RĬ-OŬS-NĔSS, *n.* Public fame ; notoriety.
NŌ'TŲS, *n.* [L.] The south wind.
NŎT-WĬTH-STĂND'ĬNG, *conj.* Nevertheless ;
however ; although.
NŎT-WĬTH-STĂND'ĬNG, *prep.* In spite of.
NOUGHT (nâwt), *n.* Nothing. See NAUGHT.
NOÛN, *n.* (*Gram.*) The name of any thing.
NOŬR'ĬSH (nŭr'rish), *v. a.* To support by food.
NOŬR'ĬSH-Ą-BLE, *a.* Susceptive of nourishment.
NOŬR'ĬSH-ĘR, *n.* One that nourishes.
NOŬR'ĬSH-MĔNT, *n.* Food ; sustenance ; nutri-
NŎV'ĘL, *a.* New ; not ancient ; unusual. [tion.
NŎV'ĔL, *n.* A fictitious tale in prose ; romance.
NŎV'ĔL-ĬST, *n.* A writer of novels.

Ā,Ē,Ī,Ō,Ū,Ȳ, *long;* Ă,Ĕ,Ĭ,Ŏ,Ŭ,Y̆, *short;* Ą,Ę,Ĭ,Ǫ,Ų,Y, *obscure.*—FĀRE,FÄR,FĂST,FÂLL ; HÊIR, HÈR ;

NŎV'ĔL-TY, n. Newness; innovation.
NỌ-VĔM'BĔR, n. The 11th month of the year.
NŎV'Ĕ-NẠ-RY, n. & a. Nine collectively.
NỌ-VĔN'NỊ-ẠL, a. Done every ninth year.
NỌ-VĔR'CẠL, a. Relating to a step-mother.
NŎV'ỊCE, n. One unskilled :—a probationer.
NỌ-VĬ''TỊ-ĀTE (nọ-vĭsh'ẹ-āt), n. State of a nov-
NŌW (nŏū), ad. At this time; at one time. [ice.
NŌW, n. The present time or moment.
NŌW'Ạ-DĀYṢ, ad. In the present age; now.
NŌ'WĀY, NŌ'WĀYṢ, ad. Not in any manner.
NŌ'WHĔRE, ad. Not in any place.   [gree.
NŌ'WĪṢE, ad. Not in any manner, or in any de-
NŎX'IOŲS (nŏk'shụs), a. Hurtful; harmful.
NŎX'IOŲS-LY (nŏk'shụs-lẹ), ad. Hurtfully.
NŎX'IOŲS-NĔSS (nŏk'shụs-nĕs), n. Hurtfulness.
NŎZ'LE, or NŎZ'ZLE (nŏz'zl), n. The nose.
NỤ-BĬF'ĔR-OŬS, a. Bringing or forming clouds.
NŪ'BỊLE, a. Marriageable; of an age fit for
NỤ-CĬF'ĔR-OŬS, a. Bearing nuts.   [marriage.
NŪ'CLẸ-ŬS, n.; pl. NŪ'CLẸ-Ī. [L.] That about
   which matter is accumulated.   [naked.
NỤ-DĀ'TIỌN, n. The act of making bare or
NŪDE, a. Bare; naked :—without force; void.
NŪ'DỊ-TY, n. Naked parts; nakedness.
NŪ'GẠ-TỌ-RY, a. Trifling; futile; insignificant.
NŪI'SẠNCE (nū'sạns), n. Something offensive.
NŬLL, a. Void; of no force; ineffectual.
NŬL'LỊ-FỸ, v. a. To annul; to make void.
NŬL'LỊ-TY, n. Want of force, or of existence.
NŬMB (nŭm), a. Torpid; chill; motionless.
NŬMB (nŭm), v. a. To make torpid; to stupefy.
NŬM'BĔR, v. a. To count; to tell; to reckon.
NŬM'BĔR, n. Any aggregate of units; many :—
   a figure.—pl. Harmony; verses; poetry.
NŬM'BĔR-ĔR, n. One who numbers.
NŬM'BĔR-LĔSS, a. More than can be counted.
NŬM'BĔRṢ, n. The fourth book in the Bible.
NŬMB'NĔSS (nŭm'nẹs), n. Torpor; deadness.
NŪ'MĔR-Ạ-BLE, a. Capable of being numbered.
NŪ'MĔR-ẠL, a. Relating to number.
NŪ'MĔR-ẠL, n. A numerical character or letter.
NŪ'MĔR-ẠL-LY, ad. According to number.
NŪ'MĔR-Ạ-RY, a. Relating to a certain number.
NŪ'MĔR-ĀTE, v. n. To reckon; to calculate.
NŪ-MĔR-Ā'TIỌN, n. Art of numbering; notation.
NŪ'MĔR-Ā-TỌR, n. One who numbers; a num-
   berer :—one of the terms of a fraction.
NỤ-MĔR'Ị-CẠL, a. Numeral; denoting number.

NỤ-MĔR'Ị-CẠL-LY, ad. With respect to number.
NŪ'MĔR-OŬS, a. Many; not few :—musical.
NŪ'MĔR-OŲS-NĔSS, n. The being numerous.
NŪ-MỊS-MĂT'Ị-CẠL, a. Relating to numismatics.
NŪ-MỊS-MĂT'ỊCS, n. The science of coins and
   medals; numismatology.
NỤ-MĬṢ-MẠ-TŎL'Ọ-ĢY, n. The science of coins.
NŬM'MẠ-RY,) a. Relating to coin or money.
NŬM'MỤ-LẠR,)
NŬM'SKŬLL, n. A dunce; a dolt; a blockhead.
NŬN, n. A woman who lives in a nunnery.
NŬN'CỊ-Ō (nŭn'shẹ-ō), n.; pl. NŬN'CỊ-ŌṢ. The
   pope's ambassador at a royal court.
NỤN-CŪ'PẠ-TĬVE,) a. Verbal; verbally pro-
NỤN-CŪ'PẠ-TỌ-RY,) nounced; not written.
NŬN'NĔR-Y, n. A house or convent of nuns.
NŬP'TIẠL (nŭp'shạl), a. Relating to marriage.
NŬP'TIẠLṢ (nŭp'shạlz), n. pl. Marriage.
NŬRSE, n. A woman that nurses or takes care
   of a child or a sick person.
NŬRSE, v. a. To bring up a child; to feed.
NŬRS'ĔR, n. One that nurses; a fomenter.
NŬRS'ĔR-Y, n. A plantation of young trees :—
   place where young children are nursed, taken
   care of, and brought up.
NŬRS'LỊNG, n. One nursed up; a fondling.
NŬRS'TLE, NŬS'TLE, v. a. To cherish; to fondle.
NŬRT'ỤRE (nürt'yụr), n. Food; diet; education.
NŬRT'ỤRE (nürt'yụr), v. a. To educate, train.
NŬT, n. A fruit :—a cylinder with teeth.
NỤ-TĀ'TIỌN, n. A kind of tremulous motion.
NŬT'-BRŌWN, a. Brown like a nut.   [nuts.
NŬT'-CRĂCK-ĔRṢ, n. pl. An instrument to break
NŬT'GÂLL, n. A hard excrescence of an oak.
NŬT'MĔG, n. A valuable species of spice.
NŪ'TRỊ-MĔNT, n. Nourishment; food; aliment.
NỤ-TRỊ-MĔNT'ẠL, a. Nourishing; alimental.
NŪ-TRĬ''TIỌN (nụ-trĭsh'ụn), n. Act of nourish-
NỤ-TRĬ''TIOŲS (nụ-trĭsh'ụs), a. Nourishing. [ing-
NŪ'TRỊ-TĬVE, a. Nourishing; nutrimental.
NŬT'-SHĔLL, n. The shell of a nut.
NŬT'-TREĒ, n. A tree that bears nuts. [nurstle.
NŬZ'ZLE, v. a. To hide the head; to nestle; to
NỸC'TẠ-LŌPS, n. One who sees best at night.
NỸC'TẠ-LŌ-PY, n. The seeing best in the night.
NỸMPH, n. A female deity :—pupa; nympha.
NỸM'PHẠ, n. [L.] The chrysalis of an insect.
NỸMPH'-LĪKE, a. Resembling a nymph.
NỸS'SẠ, n. A plant; sour gum-tree.

O.

O an English vowel, has several different
   sounds, as in note, not, more, nòr, come.
Ō, interj. Expressing a wish or exclamation.
ŌAF (ōf), n. A foolish child :—an idiot; a dolt.
ŌAF'ĬSH (ōf'ĭsh), a. Stupid; dull; doltish.
ŌAF'ĬSH-NĔSS, n. Stupidity; dulness; idiocy.
ŌAK (ōk), n. A forest tree and its wood. [oak.
ŌAK'-ĂP-PLE, n. A spongy excrescence on the
ŌAK'EN (ō'kn), a. Made of oak.   [hemp.
ŌAK'ỤM, n. Cords untwisted and reduced to
ŌAR (ōr), n. An instrument to row with.
ŌAR, v. a. To impel by rowing.—v. n. To row.

ŌAR'Y, a. Having the form or use of oars.
Ō'Ạ-SĬS, n.; pl. Ō'Ạ-SĒṢ. A fertile spot in an
   arid desert.   [ral.
ŌAT (ōt), n. A grain;—chiefly used in the plu-
ŌAT'CĂKE, n. A cake made of the meal of oats.
ŌAT'EN (ō'tn), a. Made of oats; bearing oats.
ŌATH (ōth), n. A solemn declaration, made
   with an appeal to God as a witness of its truth.
ŌAT'MĔAL, n. Flour made by grinding oats.
ŌATS (ōts), n. pl. A kind of grain for horses.
ỌB-DŪCE', v. a. To draw over, as a covering.
ỌB-DŬC'TIỌN, n. The act of covering.

MÎEN, SĬR; MỌVE, NŌR, SŎN; BŬLL, BÜR, RŪLE.—Ç, Ĝ, soft; Ɵ, Ǥ, hard; Ṣ as Z; Ӿ as GZ; ꞮHIS.

||ŎB′DŲ-RA-CY *or* ǪB-DŪ′RA-CY, *n.* Inflexible wickedness ; impenitence ; hardness of heart.
||ŎB′DŲ-RATE *or* ǪB-DŪ′RATE, *a.* Hard of heart ; obstinate ; stubborn : harsh ; unfeeling.
||ŎB′DŲ-RATE-LY, *ad.* Stubbornly.
||ŎB′DŲ-RATE-NĔSS *or* ǪB-DŪ′RATE-NĔSS, *n.* Stubbornness ; inflexibility ; obduracy.
Ǫ-BĒ′DĮ-ĘNCE, *n.* Act of obeying ; submission to authority.
Ǫ-BĒ′DĮ-ĘNT, *a.* Submissive to authority.
Ǫ-BĔ-DĮ-ĔN′TIAL, *a.* Relating to obedience.
Ǫ-BĔ′DĮ-ĔNT-LY, *ad.* With obedience.
Ǫ-BEI′SANCE (ǫ-bā′sans *or* ǫ-bē′sans), *n.* A bow ; a courtesy ; an act of reverence.
ŎB′Ę-LĬSK, *n.* A narrow column :—a mark [†].
Ǫ-BĒSE′, *a.* Corpulent ; very fat.
Ǫ-BĒSE′NĘSS, Ǫ-BĔS′Į-TY, *n.* Corpulence.
Ǫ-BEY′ (ǫ-bā′), *v. a.* To submit to ; to comply
Ǫ-BEY′ĘR (ǫ-bā′er), *n.* One who obeys. [with.
Ō′BĮT *or* ŎB′ĮT, *n.* Decease :—funeral solemni-
Ǫ-BĬT′Ų-A-RY, *a.* Relating to deaths. [ty.
Ǫ-BĬT′Ų-A-RY, *n.* A register or list of the dead.
ŎB′JĘCT, *n.* Design ; end ; ultimate purpose.
ǪB-JĔCT′, *v. a.* To oppose ; to urge against.
ǪB-JĔC′TIǪN, *n.* An adverse argument or reason ; opposition ; fault found.
ǪB-JĔC′TIǪN-A-BLE, *a.* Liable to objection.
ǪB-JĔC′TĮVE, *a.* Relating to the object, or to the object of thought ;—opposed to *subjective.*
ǪB-JĔC′TĮVE-LY, *ad.* In an objective manner.
ǪB-JĔCT′ǪR, *n.* One who offers objections.
ǪB-JŪR′GĀTE, *v. a.* To chide ; to reprove.
ŎB-JŪR-GĀ′TIǪN, *n.* A reproof ; reprehension.
ǪB-JŪR′GA-TǪ-RY, *a.* Reprehensive ; chiding.
ǪB-LĀTE′, *a.* Flattened at the poles.
ǪB-LĀ′TIǪN, *n.* An offering ; a sacrifice :—alms.
ŎB-LĔC-TĀ′TIǪN, *n.* Delight ; pleasure.
ŎB′LĮ-GĀTE, *v. a.* To bind by contract or duty.
ŎB-LĮ-GĀ′TIǪN, *n.* That which obligates ; binding power of an oath, vow, or duty ; contract.
ŎB′LĮ-GA-TǪ-RY, *a.* Imposing an obligation.
Ǫ-BLĪĢE′, *v. a.* To bind ; to impose obligations on ; to gratify ; to accommodate.
ŎB-LĮ-ĢĒĒ′, *n.* The person to whom another, called the *obligor,* is bound by a contract.
Ǫ-BLĪĢ′ĘR, *n.* One who obliges.
Ǫ-BLĪĢ′ĮNG, *p. a.* Accommodating ; friendly.
ŎB′LĮ-GÖR′, *n.* (*Law.*) One who binds himself to another ;—opposed to *obligee.*
ŎB-LĮ-QUĀ′TIǪN, *n.* Declination ; obliquity.
||ǪB-LÎQUE′ *or* ǪB-LĪQUE′, *a.* Not direct ; not perpendicular ; not parallel ; indirect.
||ǪB-LÎQUE′LY *or* ǪB-LĪQUE′LY,*ad.*Not directly.
||ǪB-LÎQUE′NĘSS, *n.* Obliquity.
||ǪB-LĬQ′UĮ-TY (ǫb-lĭk′wę-tę), *n.* A deviation from a right line, or from rectitude. [destroy.
ǪB-LĬT′ĘR-ĀTE, *v. a.* To efface ; to rub out ; to
ǪB-LĬT-ĘR-Ā′TIǪN, *n.* Effacement ; extinction.
ǪB-LĬV′Į-ǪN,*n.* Forgetfulness; amnesty; pardon.
ǪB-LĬV′Į-OŬS, *a.* Causing forgetfulness ; for-
ŎB′LŎNG, *a.* Longer than broad. [getful.
ŎB′LǪ-QUY, *n.* Censorious speech ; slander.
ŎB-MŲ-TĔS′CĘNCE, *n.* Silence ; loss of speech.
ǪB-NŎX′IOŲS (ǫb-nŏk′shŭs), *a.* Subject ; liable to punishment; exposed :—unpopular ; odious.
ǪB-NŎX′IOŲS-LY (ǫb-nŏk′shŭs-lę), *ad.* Liably.
ǪB-NŎX′IOŲS-NĔSS (ǫb-nŏk′shŭs-nĕs), *n.* Liableness ; liability :—unpopularity.

ŎB′ŌLE, *n.* (*Pharmacy.*) Twelve or ten grains.
ŎB-Ō′VATE, *a.* Having the shape of an egg.
ǪB-RĔP′TIǪN, *n.* The act of creeping secretly.
ǪB-SCĒNE′, *a.* Immodest ; offensive ; disgust-
ǪB-SCĒNE′LY, *ad.* In an obscene manner. [ing.
ǪB-SCĒNE′NĘSS, } *n.* Quality of being ob-
ǪB-SCĔN′Į-TY, } scene ; impurity ; lewdness.
ŎB-SCŲ-RĀ′TIǪN, *n.* Act of darkening.
ǪB-SCŪRE′, *a.* Dark ; gloomy ; abstruse ; un-
ǪB-SCŪRE′, *v. a.* To darken ; to conceal.[known.
ǪB-SCŪRE′LY, *ad.* Not brightly ; darkly ; dimly.
ǪB-SCŪ′RĮ-TY, *n.* Darkness ; privacy; perplexity.
ŎB′SĘ-CRĀTE, *v. a.* To beseech ; to entreat.
ŎB-SĘ-CRĀ′TIǪN, *n.* An entreaty; supplication.
ŎB′SĘ-QUĮĘS, *n. pl.* Funeral solemnities.
ǪB-SĒ′QUĮ-OŬS, *a.* Obedient ; compliant ; submissive ; meanly complying ; servile.
ǪB-SĒ′QUĮ-OŬS-LY, *ad.* Submissively.
ǪB-SĒ′QUĮ-OŬS-NĔSS,*n.* Obedience ; compliance.
ǪB-SĔRV′A-BLE,*a.* That may be observed.[note.
ǪB-SĔRV′A-BLY, *ad.* In a manner worthy of
ǪB-SĔR′VANCE, *n.* Respect ; reverence.
ǪB-SĔR′VANT,*a.*Attentive; watchful; respectful.
ŎB-SĘR-VĀ′TIǪN, *n.* Observance ; note ; remark.
ŎB-SĘR-VĀ′TǪR, *n.* An observer.
ǪB-SĔRV′A-TǪ-RY, *n.* A place for astronomical observations, &c.
ǪB-SĔRVE′, *v. a.* To watch, regard, note, obey.
ǪB-SĔRVE′, *v. n.* To be attentive ; to remark.
ǪB-SĔRV′ĘR, *n.* One who observes ; a remarker.
ǪB-SĔS′SIǪN (ǫb-sĕsh′ųn), *n.* Act of besieging.
ǪB-SĬD′Į-AN, *n.* A dark-colored mineral.
ǪB-SĬD′Į-Ǫ-NAL, *a.* Belonging to a siege.
ŎB-SǪ-LĔS′CĘNT, *a.* Growing out of use.
ŎB′SǪ-LĒTE, *a.* Gone out of use ; disused.
ŎB′SǪ-LĒTE-NĔSS, *n.* State of being out of use.
ŎB′STA-CLE, *n.* A hinderance ; an obstruction.
ǪB-STĔT′RĮC, *a.* Relating to obstetrics. [wifery.
ǪB-STĔT′RĮCS, *n. pl.* Science or art of mid-
ŎB′STĮ-NA-CY, *n.* Stubbornness ; contumacy.
ŎB′STĮ-NATE, *a.* Stubborn ; contumacious.
ŎB′STĮ-NATE-LY, *ad.* Stubbornly ; inflexibly.
ŎB′STĮ-NATE-NĔSS,*n.* Stubbornness ; obstina-
ŎB-STĮ-PĀ′TIǪN, *n.* Act of stopping up. [cy.
ǪB-STRĔP′ĘR-OŬS,*a.* Loud ; clamorous ; noisy.
ǪB-STRĔP′ĘR-OŬS-LY, *ad.* Loudly ; clamorous-
ǪB-STRĬC′TIǪN, *n.* An obligation ; a bond.[ly.
ǪB-STRŬCT′, *v. a.* To block up ; to bar, hinder.
ǪB-STRŬCT′ĘR, *n.* One that hinders or opposes.
ǪB-STRŬC′TIǪN, *n.* A hinderance ; an obstacle.
ǪB-STRŬC′TĮVE, *a.* Causing impediment.
ǪB-STRŬC′TĮVE,*n.* An impediment; an obsta-
ŎB′STRŲ-ĘNT, *a.* Hindering ; blocking up. [cle.
ǪB-TĀIN′, *v. a.* To gain ; to acquire ; to procure.
ǪB-TĀIN′, *v. n.* To get into use, prevail, succeed.
ǪB-TĀIN′A-BLE, *a.* That may be obtained.
ǪB-TĔND′, *v. a.* To oppose ; to continue against.
ǪB-TĔN-Ę-BRĀ′TIǪN, *n.* Darkness ; cloudiness.
ǪB-TĔST′, *v. a.* To beseech ; to supplicate.
ŎB-TĘS-TĀ′TIǪN, *n.* A supplication ; entreaty.
ǪB-TRŪDE′, *v. a.* To thrust into ; to urge upon.
ǪB-TRŪD′ĘR, *n.* One that obtrudes.
ǪB-TRŪ′SIǪN (-trū′zhųn), *n.* Act of obtruding.
ǪB-TRŪ′SĮVE, *a.* Inclined to obtrude.
ǪB-TŪND′, *v. a.* To blunt ; to dull ; to deaden.
ŎB-TŪS-ĂNG′Ų-LAR, *a.* Having obtuse angles.
ǪB-TŪSE′, *a.* Not pointed ; not acute :—dull.
ǪB-TŪSE′LY, *ad.* Without a point :—stupidly.

ǬB-TŪSE′NĔSS, *n.* Bluntness :—dulness.
ǬB-TŪ′ȘIǪN (ǫb-tū′zhųn), *n.* The act of dulling.
ǬB-ŬM′BRĀTE, *v. a.* To shade ; to cloud.
ŎB-ŬM-BRĀ′TIǪN, *n.* The act of darkening.
ǬB-VĒRSE′, *n.* The face of a coin ;—opposed to
ǬB-VĒRT′, *v. a.* To turn towards. [*reverse.*
ŎB′VĪ-ĀTE, *v. a.* To remove ; to prevent.
ŎB′VĬ-OŬS, *a.* Open ; exposed ; plain ; evident.
ŎB′VĬ-OŬS-LY̆, *ad.* Evidently ; apparently.
ŎB′VĬ-OŲS-NĔSS, *n.* The state of being evident.
ǪC-CĀ′ȘIǪN (ǫk-kā′zhųn), *n.* An occurrence ;
 a casualty ; opportunity ; need ; exigence.
ǪC-CĀ′ȘIǪN, *v. a.* To cause ; to produce, effect.
ǪC-CĀ′ȘIǪN-ĄL, *a.* Incidental ; casual ; acci-
 dental ; produced by some occurrence.
ǪC-CĀ′ȘIǪN-ĄL-LY̆, *ad.* Incidentally ; at times.
ǪC-CĀ′ȘIǪN-ĔR, *n.* One that causes or occasions.
ŎC′CĬ-DĔNT, *n.* The west. [posed to *oriental.*
ŎC-CĬ-DĔNT′ĄL, *a.* In the west ; western ;—op-
ǪC-CĬP′Ĭ-TĄL, *a.* Relating to the occiput.
ŎC′CĬ-PŬT, *n.* The hinder part of the head.
ǪC-CLŪ′ȘIǪN, *n.* The act of shutting up.
ǪC-CŬLT′, *a.* Secret ; hidden ; unknown.
ŎC-CŲL-TĀ′TIǪN, *n.* The act of concealment.
ŎC′CŲ-PĄN-CY̆, *n.* A holding ; a possession.
ŎC′CŲ-PĄNT, *n.* One who takes or has posses-
 sion ; an occupier. [*trade.*
ŎC-CŲ-PĀ′TIǪN, *n.* Possession ; business ;
ŎC′CŲ-PĪ-ĔR, *n.* One who occupies.
ŎC′CŲ-PY̆, *v. a.* To possess ; to keep ; to employ.
ǪC-CŬR′, *v. n.* To come ; to appear ; to happen.
ǪC-CŬR′RĔNCE, *n.* Any thing that occurs ; an
 incident ; accidental event.
Ō′CEĄN (ō′shạn), *n.* The vast body of salt wa-
 ter on the globe ; the great sea.
Ō-CE-ĂN′ĬC (ō-she-ăn′ĭk), *a.* Relating to the
 ocean.
Ǫ-CĔL′LĄT-ĔD, *a.* Having, or like, little eyes.
ŎCH′Ĭ-MY̆, *n.* A mixed, base metal.
ǪCH-LŎC′RĄ-CY̆, *n.* Government by the mul-
 titude ; mob-rule ; mobocracy.
Ō′CHRE (ō′kẹr), *n.* A species of colored earth.
Ō′CHRE-OŬS (ō′krẹ-ŭs), *a.* Consisting of ochre.
Ō′CHRE-Y̆ (ō′kẹr-ẹ), *a.* Partaking of ochre.
ŎC′TĄ-CHŎRD, *n.* A musical instrument.
ŎC′TĄ-GǑN, *n.* A plane figure of eight sides and
 eight angles. [*sides.*
ǪC-TĂG′Ǫ-NĄL, *a.* Having eight angles and
ǪC-TĂNG′Ų-LĄR, *a.* Having eight angles.
ŎC′TĀVE, *n.* An interval of eight sounds.
ǪC-TĀ′VǑ, *n.* ; *pl.* ǪC-TĀ′VǑŞ. A book hav-
 ing eight leaves to a sheet ;—used also as an
 adjective.
ǪC-TĔN′NĬ-ĄL, *a.* Happening every eighth year.
ǪC-TŌ′BĔR, *n.* The tenth month of the year.
ŎC-TǪ-GẸ-NĀ′RĬ-ĄN, *n.* A person 80 years old.
ǪC-TŎG′Ẹ-NĄ-RY̆ *or* ŎC′TǪ-GẸ-NĄ-RY̆, *a.* Of
 eighty years of age ;—used also as a noun.
ŎC-TǪ-PĔT′Ą-LOŬS, *a.* Having eight petals.
ŎC′TǪ-STY̆LE, *n.* A temple with eight columns.
ŎC-TǪ-SY̆L′LĄ-BLE, *n.* Word of eight syllables.
ŎC′Ų-LĄR, *a.* Relating to, or known by, the eye.
ŎC′Ų-LĄR-LY̆, *ad.* To the observation of the eye.
ŎC′Ų-LĬST, *n.* A surgeon skilled in diseases of
 the eyes. [*strange.*
ŎDD, *a.* Not even :—particular :—singular ;
ŎDD′Ĭ-TY̆, *n.* Singularity :—an odd person or
ŎDD′LY̆, *ad.* Not evenly :—strangely. [*thing.*

ŎDD′NĔSS, *n.* State of being odd ; strangeness.
ŎDDŞ (ŏdz), *n. sing. & pl.* Inequality ; dispute.
ŌDE, *n.* A short song ; a lyric poem.
‖Ō′DIOŬS (ōd′yŭs *or* ō′dẹ-ŭs), *a.* Hateful ; de-
 testable ; abominable ; invidious. [*vidiously.*
‖Ō′DIOŬS-LY̆ *or* Ō′DĬ-OŬS-LY̆, *ad.* Hatefully ; in-
Ō′DIOŬS-NĔSS, *n.* Hatefulness.
‖Ō′DĬŲM *or* Ō′DĬ-ŬM, *n.* Invidiousness ; hatred.
Ǫ-DŎM′Ẹ-TĔR, *n.* An instrument attached to
 a carriage-wheel for measuring distances.
Ō-DǪN-TĂL′GĬC, *a.* Pertaining to the toothache.
Ō′DǪR, *n.* Scent ; fragrance ; perfume.
Ō′DǪR-ĄTE, *a.* Scented ; having a strong scent.
Ō-DǪR-ĬF′ĔR-OŬS, *a.* Giving scent ; fragrant.
Ō′DǪR-OŬS, *a.* Fragrant ; sweet of scent.
Œ-CǪ-NŎM′ĬCS, *n.* Household affairs. See Eco-
Œ-DĒ′MĄ (ẹ-dē′mạ), *n.* A tumor. [NOMICS.
Œ-ĬL′IĄD (ẹ-ĭl′yạd), *n.* A glance ; a wink.
Ō′ER (ōr), *ad.* Contracted from *over.*
Œ-SŎPH′Ą-GŬS (ẹ-sŏf′fạ-gŭs), *n.* The gullet.
ŎF (ŏv), *prep.* From ; concerning ; noting the
 source, cause, or motion.
‖ŎFF (ŏf *or* âuf), *ad.* Noting departure or dis-
‖ŎFF, *interj.* Away ! begone ; depart ! [*tance.*
‖ŎFF, *prep.* Not on :—distant from. [*refuse.*
ŎF′FĄL, *n.* Waste meat ; carrion ; coarse flesh ;
ǪF-FĔNCE′, *n.* Any thing that offends ; crime ;
 injury ; anger ; displeasure. [*ure.*
ǪF-FĔNCE′FŪL, *a.* Injurious ; giving displeas-
ǪF-FĔNCE′LĔSS, *a.* Unoffending ; innocent.
ǪF-FĔND′, *v. a.* To displease ; to transgress.
ǪF-FĔND′, *v. n.* To be criminal ; to cause anger.
ǪF-FĔND′ĔR, *n.* A criminal ; a transgressor.
ǪF-FĔN′SĬVE, *a.* Displeasing ; making invasion.
ǪF-FĔN′SĬVE-LY̆, *ad.* Injuriously ; with offence.
ǪF-FĔN′SĬVE-NĔSS, *n.* Mischief ; cause of of-
 fence or disgust. [*pose.*
ŎF′FĔR, *v. a.* To present ; to sacrifice ; to pro-
ŎF′FĔR, *v. n.* To be present ; to be at hand.
ŎF′FĔR, *n.* A proposal ; price bid ; proffer.
ŎF′FĔR-ĔR, *n.* One who offers or sacrifices.
ŎF′FĔR-ĬNG, *n.* A sacrifice ; any thing offered.
ŎF′FĬCE, *n.* A public charge ; agency ; peculiar
 use ; business ; a place of business ; a room.
ŎF′FĬ-CĔR, *n.* A man in office ; a commander.
ŎF′FĬ-CĔRED (ŏf′fẹ-sẹrd), *a.* Commanded.
ǪF-FĬ″CIĄL (ǫf-fĭsh′ạl), *a.* Pertaining to office.
ǪF-FĬ″CIĄL-LY̆ (ǫf-fĭsh′ạl-ẹ), *ad.* By authority.
ǪF-FĬ″CĬ-ĀTE (ǫf-fĭsh′ẹ-āt), *v. n.* To discharge
 an office ; to perform an office for another.
ŎF-FĬ-CĪ′NĄL, *a.* Used in, or relating to, shops.
ǪF-FĬ″CIOŬS (ǫf-fĭsh′ŭs), *a.* Kind ; busy ; for-
 ward ; meddling ; meddlesome ; obtrusive.
ǪF-FĬ″CIOŬS-LY̆ (ǫf-fĭsh′ŭs-lẹ), *ad.* Busily.
ǪF-FĬ″CIOŬS-NĔSS (-fĭsh′ŭs-), *n.* Forwardness.
ŎFF′ĬNG, *n.* Deep water off the shore.
ŎFF′SCOÜR-ĬNG, *n.* Rejected matter ; refuse.
ŎFF′SCŬM, *n.* Refuse ; offscouring.
ŎFF′SĔT, *n.* A sprout :—a counterbalance.
ŎFF′SPRĬNG, *n.* Propagation ; a child ; children.
ǪF-FŬS′CĀTE, *v. a.* To dim ; to cloud, darken.
ŎFT (ŏft *or* âuft), *ad.* Often ; frequently.
ŎFT′EN (ŏf′fn), *ad.* Oft ; frequently ; many times.
ŎFT′EN-TĪMEŞ (ŏf′fn-tīmz), ŎFT′TĪMEŞ, *ad.*
 Often.
Ǫ-GĒĒ′, *n.* A sort of moulding in architecture.
Ō′GLE (ō′gl), *v. a.* To view with side glances.
Ō′GLĔR, *n.* A sly gazer ; one who ogles.

ŌH (ō), *interj*. Noting pain, sorrow, or surprise.
ŎÏL, *n*. A volatile or unctuous matter.
ŎÏL, *v. a*. To smear or lubricate with oil.
ŎÏL'-CŎL-ǪR (ŏïl'kŭl-lṳr), *n*. Color made by grinding coloring substances in oil.
ŎÏL'Ĭ-NĔSS, *n*. Unctuousness; greasiness.
ŎÏL'MẠN, *n*. One who trades in oils, pickles, &c.
ŎÏL'Ẏ, *a*. Like oil; containing oil; greasy.
ŎÏNT'MẸNT, *n*. An unguent; unctuous matter.
Ō'KRẠ, *n*. A tropical plant.
ŌLD, *a*. Not young; not new or fresh; ancient;
ŌLD'EN (ōld'dn), *a*. Old; ancient. [stale.
ŌLD'-FĂSH-ĮǪNED (-ụnd), *a*. Out of fashion.
ŌLD'NẸSS, *n*. Age; antiquity; not newness.
Ō-LẸ-ĂǦ'Ĭ-NOŬS (-ăd'jĭn-ŭs), *a*. Oily; unctuous.
Ō-LẸ-ĂS'TẸR, *n*. A plant bearing soft fruit.
ǪL-FĂC'TǪ-RẎ, *a*. Having the sense of smell.
ŎL-Ĭ-GĂR'ℭHĬ-CẠL, *a*. Relating to an oligarchy.
ŎL-Ĭ-GĂR-ℭHẎ, *n*. A species of aristocracy.
Ŏ'LĬ-Ō (ō'lẹ-ō *or* ōl'yō), *n.; pl*. Ō'LĬ-ŌṢ. A medley.
ŎL'Ĭ-TǪ-RẎ, *a*. Belonging to a kitchen-garden.
ŎL-Ĭ-VĂ'CEOŬS (ŏl-ẹ-vā'shụs), *a*. Relating to ol-
ŎL'ĮVE, *n*. An evergreen tree, and its fruit.[ives.
Ǫ-LẎM'PĬ-ẠD, *n*. A space of four years, from one celebration of the Olympic games to another.
Ǫ-LẎM'PĬC, *a*. Relating to games in Greece.
ŌM'BRE (ōm'bur), *n*. A game of cards. [bet.
Ǫ-MĒ'GẠ, *n*. The last letter of the Greek alpha-
ŎME'LẸT (ŏm'-), *n*. A pancake made with eggs.
Ō'MẸN, *n*. A sign, good or bad; a prognostic.
Ō'MẸNED (ō'mẹnd), *a*. Containing prognostics.
Ǫ-MĔN'TỤM, *n*. [L.] (*Anat*.) The call.
Ō'MẸR, *n*. A Hebrew measure.
ŎM'Ĭ-NOŬS, *a*. Foreboding; inauspicious.
ŎM'Ĭ-NOŬS-LẎ, *ad*. With good or bad omens.
Ǫ-MĬS'SĬǪN (ǫ-mĭsh{ụn), *n*. Neglect; a failure.
Ǫ-MĬT', *v. a*. To leave out; to pass by; to neglect.
ŎM'NĬ-BŬS, *n*. A long public carriage.
ŎM-NĬ-FĀ'RĬ-OŬS, *a*. Of all varieties or kinds.
ǪM-NĬF'ĬC, *a*. All-creating. [figure.
ŎM'NĬ-FŎRM, *a*. Having every shape, form, or
ŎM-NĬ-PER-CĬP'Ĭ-ẸNT, *a*. Perceiving every thing.
ǪM-NĬP'Ǫ-TĔNCE, } *n*. Almighty power; un-
ǪM-NĬP'Ǫ-TĔN-CẎ, } limited, infinite power.
ǪM-NĬP'Ǫ-TĔNT, *a*. Almighty; all-powerful.
ǪM-NĬP'Ǫ-TĔNT, *n*. The Almighty; one of the appellations of God. [limit.
ǪM-NĬP'Ǫ-TĔNT-LẎ, *ad*. Powerfully; without
ŎM-NĬ-PRĔS'ẸNCE, *n*. Presence in every place.
ŎM-NĬ-PRĔṢ'ẸNT, *a*. Present in every place.
||ǪM-NĬ''SCĬ-ENCE (ǫm-nĭsh'ẹ-ẹns *or* ǫm-nĭsh'-ẹns), *n*. Boundless knowledge. [ing.
||ǪM-NĬ''SCĬ-ENT (ǫm-nĭsh'ẹ-ẹnt), *a*. All-know-
ŎM'NĬ-ŬM, *n*. Aggregate of public stocks.
ǪM-NĬV'Ǫ-ROŬS, *a*. All-devouring. [upon.
ŎN, *prep*. Noting nearness of place or time;
ŎN, *ad*. Forward; onward; in succession.
ŎN, *interj*. Onward, expressing incitement.
ONCE (wŭns), *ad*. One time; formerly.
ONE (wŭn), *a*. Noting a single thing; any.
ONE (wŭn), *n*. A single person or thing.
Ǫ-NEĬ-RǪ-CRĬT'ĬC, *n*. An interpreter of dreams.
Ǫ-NEĬ-RǪ-CRĬT'ĬC, } *a*. Interpretative of
Ǫ-NEĬ-RǪ-CRĬT'Ĭ-CẠL, } dreams.
ONE'NẸSS (wŭn'nẹs), *n*. Unity; singleness.
ŎN'Ẹ-RẠ-RẎ, *a*. Relating to burdens; burdensome.
ŎN'ẸR-OŬS, *a*. Burdensome; oppressive.
ŎN'ĮǪN (ŭn'yụn), *n*. A bulbous plant and root.

ŎN'LẎ (ŏn'lẹ), *a*. Single; one and no more.
ŌN'LẎ, *ad*. Simply; singly; merely; barely.
ŎN'SẸT, *n*. An attack; an assault.
ŎN-TǪ-LŎǦ'ĬC, } *a*. Relating to ontology;
ŎN-TǪ-LŎǦ'Ĭ-CẠL, } metaphysical.
ǪN-TŎL'Ǫ-ǦĬST, *n*. One versed in ontology.
ǪN-TŎL'Ǫ-ǦẎ, *n*. The science of existence; meta-
ŎN'WẠRD, ŎN'WẠRDṢ, *ad*. Forward. [physics.
ŎN'WẠRD, *a*. Advanced; increased.
ŎN'Ẏ-ℭHẠ, *n*. An odoriferous shell :—the onyx.
Ō'NẎX (ō'nĭks), *n*. A semipellucid gem.
ÔÔZE, *n*. Soft mud; mire; slime :—soft flow.
ÔÔZE, *v. n*. To flow gently; to percolate.
ÔÔZ'Ẏ (ô'zẹ), *a*. Miry; muddy; slimy.
Ǫ-PĂC'Ĭ-TẎ, *n*. A state impervious to light.
Ǫ-PĀ'COŬS, *a*. Dark; obscure; not transparent.
Ǫ-PĀ'COŬS-NĔSS, *n*. The state of being opaque.
Ō'PẠL, *n*. A beautiful, precious stone. [opal.
Ō-PẠL-ĔS'CẸNCE, *n*. A shining like that of
Ō'PẠL-ĪNE, *a*. Relating to, or like, opal.
Ǫ-PĀQUE' (ǫ-pāk'), *a*. Dark; not transparent.
Ǫ-PĀQUE'NẸSS (ǫ-pāk'nẹs), *n*. Darkness.
ŌPE, *v. a. & n*. To open ;—*used in poetry*.
Ō'PEN (ō'pn), *v. a*. To unclose, unlock, show.
Ō'PEN (ō'pn), *v. n*. To unclose itself; to begin.
Ō'PEN (ō'pn), *a*. Unclosed; plain; clear; artless.
Ō'PEN-ẸR (ō'pn-ẹr), *n*. One that opens.
Ō'PEN-EẎED (ō'pn-īd), *a*. Vigilant; watchful.
Ō'PEN-HĂND'ẸD (ō'pn-hănd'ẹd), *a*. Liberal.
Ō'PEN-HEÄRT'ẸD (ō'pn-härt'ẹd), *a*. Generous.
Ō'PEN-ĬNG (ō'pn-), *n*. An aperture; a breach.
Ō'PEN-LẎ (ō'pn-lẹ), *ad*. Publicly; plainly.
Ō'PEN-NĔSS (ō'pn-nĕs), *n*. Plainness; clearness.
ŎP'Ẹ-RẠ, *n*. [It.] A musical entertainment.
ŎP'ẸR-ĀTE, *v. n*. To act; to produce effects.
ŎP-ẸR-Ā'TĬON, *n*. Agency; influence; action.
ŎP'ẸR-Ạ-TĬVE, *a*. Active; vigorous; efficacious.
ŎP'ẸR-Ạ-TĬVE, *n*. Mechanic laborer.
ŎP'ẸR-Ạ-TǪR, *n*. One that operates or performs.
ŎP-Ẹ-RŌSE', *a*. Laborious; full of labor; tedious.
Ō-PHĬ-ŎL'Ǫ-ǦĬST, *n*. One versed in ophiology.
Ō-PHĬ-ŎL'Ǫ-ǦẎ, *n*. The science of serpents.
||ǪPH-THĂL'MĬC (ǫp-thăl'mĭk *or* ǫf-thäl'mĭk), *a*. Relating to the eye. [mation of the eyes.
||ŎPH'THẠL-MY (ŏp'thạl-mẹ), *n*. (*Med*.) Inflam-
Ō'PĬ-ẠTE, *a*. Soporiferous; causing sleep.
Ō'PĬ-ẠTE, *n*. A medicine that causes sleep.
Ǫ-PĪNE', *v. n*. To think; to be of opinion. [ion.
Ǫ-PĬN'Ĭ-Ạ-TĬVE (ǫ-pĭn'yẹ-ạ-tĭv), *a*. Stiff in opin-
Ǫ-PĬN'ĮǪN (ǫ-pĭn'yụn), *n*. Judgment; notion.
Ǫ-PĬN'ĮǪN-ĂT-ẸD, *a*. Obstinate in opinion.
Ǫ-PĬN'ĮǪN-Ạ-TĬVE (-yụn-ạ-tĭv), *a*. Stubborn.
Ǫ-PĬN'ĮǪNED (-yụnd), *a*. Attached to opinion.
Ǫ-PĬN'ĮǪN-ĬST, *n*. One fond of his own notions.
Ō'PĬ-ŬM, *n*. The juice of the white poppy.
ŎP-Ǫ-DĔL'DǪC, *n*. A plaster :—a liniment.
Ǫ-PŎS'SỤM, *n*. An American quadruped.
ǪP-PŌ'NẸNT, *n*. An antagonist; an adversary.
ǪP-PŌ'NẸNT, *a*. Opposite; adverse; rival.
ŎP-PǪR-TŪNE', *a*. Seasonable; convenient; fit.
ŎP-PǪR-TŪNE'LẎ, *ad*. Seasonably; coveniently.
ŎP-PǪR-TŪ'NĬ-TẎ, *n*. A fit place; time; occasion.
ǪP-PŌṢE', *v.a*. To act against; to hinder; to resist.
ǪP-PŌṢE', *v. n*. To act adversely :—to object.
ǪP-PŌṢ'ẸR, *n*. One that opposes; an antagonist.
ŎP'PǪ-ṢĬTE, *a*. Placed in front; facing; adverse.
ŎP'PǪ-ṢĬTE-LẎ, *ad*. In an opposite manner.
ŎP'PǪ-ṢĬTE-NẸSS, *n*. State of being opposite.

ŎP-PǪ-ṢĬ''TIǪN (ŏp-pǫ-zĭsh'ǔn), *n.* Resistance ;
  contrariety :—party opposing.   [due.
ǪP-PRĔSS', *v. a.* To crush by hardship ; to sub-
ǪP-PRĔS'SIǪN (ǫp-prĕsh'ǔn), *n.* Act of oppress-
  ing ; extortion ; cruelty ; severity ; misery.
ǪP-PRĔS'SĮVE, *a.* Cruel ; inhuman ; heavy.
ǪP-PRĔS'SĮVE-LY, *ad.* In an oppressive manner.
ǪP-PRĔSS'ǪR, *n.* One who oppresses or harasses.
ǪP-PRŌ'BRĮ-OŬS, *a.*– Reproachful ; scurrilous.
ǪP-PRŌ'BRĮ-OŬS-LY,*ad.*Scurrilously ; abusively.
ǪP-PRŌ'BRĮ-OŲS-NĔSS, *n.* Reproachfulness.
ǪP-PRŌ'BRĮ-ŬM, *n.* Disgrace ; infamy.
ǪP-PŪGN' (ǫp-pūn'), *v. a.* To oppose ; to attack.
ǪP-PŪG'NĄN-CY, *n.* Opposition ; resistance.
ǪP-PŪGN'ĘR (ǫp-pūn'ęr), *n.* An assailer.
ŎP'TĄ-TĬVE, *a.* Expressive of desire.
ŎP'TĮC, *n.* An instrument or organ of sight.
ŎP'TĮC, ŎP'TĮ-CĄL, *a.* Relating to vision.
ǪP-TĬ''CIĄN (-tĭsh'ąn), *n.* One skilled in optics.
ŎP'TĮCS, *n.* The science of light and vision.
ŎP'TĮ-MĄ-CY, *n.* Nobility ; the body of nobles.
ŎP'TĮM-ĬṢM, *n.* The doctrine that every thing in
  nature is created and ordered for the best.
ŎP'TĮM-ĬST, *n.* One who believes in optimism.
ŎP'TIǪN, *n.* Choice ; the power of choosing.
ŎP'TIǪN-ĄL, *a.* Depending upon choice.
ŎP'Ų-LĔNCE, *n.* Great wealth ; affluence.
ŎP'Ų-LĔNT, *a.* Rich ; wealthy ; affluent. [native.
ŌR, *conj.* A disjunctive word, marking an alter-
ŌR, *n.* [Fr.] Gold ; a metal used in blazonry.
ŎR'Ą-CLE, *n.* Something delivered by supernat-
  ural wisdom :—one famed for wisdom. [cles.
Ǫ-RĂC'Ų-LĄR, Ǫ-RĂC'Ų-LOŬS, *a.* Uttering ora-
Ǫ-RĂC'Ų-LĄR-LY, *ad.* In the manner of an oracle.
Ō'RĄL, *a.* Delivered by mouth ; not written.
Ō'RĄL-LY, *ad.* By mouth ; without writing.
ŎR'ĄNĢE, *n.* A kind of tree, and its fruit.
ŎR'ĄNĢE, *a.* Relating to an orange,or to its color.
ŎR'ĄN-ĢĔR-Y, *n.* A plantation of orange-trees.
Ō-RĂNG'-ÔU-TĂNG', *n.* A large species of ape.
Ǫ-RĀ'TIǪN, *n.* A public speech ; a declamation.
ŎR'Ą-TǪR, *n.* An eloquent speaker :—petitioner.
ŎR-Ą-TŎR'Į-CĄL, *a.* Rhetorical ; eloquent.
ŎR-Ą-TŎR'Į-CĄL-LY, *ad.* In a rhetorical manner.
ŎR-Ą-TŌ'RĮ-Ō, *n.* [It.] A sacred musical drama.
ŎR'Ą-TǪ-RY, *n.* Eloquence :—place for worship.
ŎRB, *n.* A sphere ; a wheel ; a circle ; a globe.
ŎRB'ĘD (ŏrb'ĕd *or* ŏrbd), *a.* Round ; circular.
ǪR-BĬC'Ų-LĄR, *a.* Spherical ; circular ; globular.
ǪR-BĬC'Ų-LĄR-LY, *ad.* Spherically ; circularly.
ǪR-BĬC'Ų-LĄR-NĔSS, *n.* State of being orbicular.
ǪR-BĬC'Ų-LĀT-ĘD, *a.* Formed into an orb.
ŎR'BĮT, *n.* A line described by a revolving planet.
ŎR'BĮ-TY,   ⎫ *n.* Want or loss of parents or of
ŎR'BĮ-TŪDE, ⎭ children.
ŎRB'Y, *a.* Resembling an orb.   [trees.
ŎR'CHĄRD, *n.* A garden or enclosure of fruit-
ŎR'ȻHĘS-TRĄ *or* ǪR-ȻHĔS'TRĄ, *n.* [Gr.] A
  place for musicians ; a band of musicians.
ŎR'ȻHĘS-TRE (-tęr), *n.* A place for musicians ;
  a band of musicians ; orchestra.
ǪR-DĀIN', *v. a.* To appoint, decree, establish,
ŎR'DĘ-AL, *n.* A trial by fire or water :—test.
ŎR'DĘR, *n.* A method ; rule ; mandate ; class.
ŎR'DĘR, *v. a.* To regulate ; to manage ; to direct.
ŎR'DĘR-LĮ-NĔSS, *n.* Regularity ; method.
ŎR'DĘR-LY, *a.* Methodical ; regular ; quiet.

ŎR'DĮ-NĄL, *a.* Noting order; as, *second, third,* &c.
ŎR'DĮ-NĄL, *n.* A ritual ; a number noting order.
ŎR'DĮ-NĄNCE, *n.* A law ; a rule ; an appointment.
ŎR'DĮ-NĄ-RĮ-LY, *ad.* Commonly ; usually.
ŎR'DĮ-NĄ-RY, *a.* Common ; usual:—mean ; plain.
ŎR'DĮ-NĄ-RY, *n.* A judge :—a place of eating ;
  —*in the latter sense, also, pronounced* ŏrd'ną-rę.
ŎR'DĮ-NĄTE, *a.* Regular ; methodical ; orderly.
ŎR'DĮ-NĄTE, *n.* A geometrical distance or line.
ŎR'DĮ-NĄTE-LY, *ad.* In a regular manner.
ŎR-DĮ-NĀ'TIǪN, *n.* The act of ordaining ; institu-
ŌRD'NĄNCE, *n.* Cannon ; heavy artillery. [tion.
ŌRD'ŲRE (ŏrd'yųr), *n.* Dung ; filth ; excrement.
ŌRE, *n.* Metal yet in its mineral state.
Ō'RĘ-ĄD, *n.* A nymph of the mountains.
ŎR'GĄN, *n.* A natural or musical instrument.
ǪR-GĂN'ĮC,   ⎫ *a.* Instrumental ; acting as an
ǪR-GĂN'Į-CĄL, ⎭ instrument; respecting organs.
ǪR-GĂN'Į-CĄL-LY, *ad.* By means of organs.
ǪR-GĂN'Į-CĄL-NĔSS, *n.* State of being organical.
ŎR'GĄN-ĬṢM, *n.* Organical structure.
ŎR'GĄN-ĬST, *n.* One who plays on the organ.
ŎR-GĄN-Į-ZĀ'TIǪN,*n.*State of an organized body.
ŎR'GĄN-ĪZE, *v. a.* To construct ; to form.
ŎR'GĄN-LŎFT, *n.* Loft where an organ stands.
ŎR'GĄN-PĪPE, *n.* The pipe of a musical organ.
ŎR'GĂṢM, *n.* Immoderate excitement.
ŎR'GEĂT (ŏr'zhăt), *n.* Emulsion of almonds, &c.
ŎR'ĢĮĘṢ, *n. pl.* The rites of Bacchus ; frantic rev-
Ō'RĮ-ĘL, *n.* A sort of recess or window. [els.
Ō'RĮ-ĔNT, *a.* Rising, as the sun ; eastern ; bright.
Ō'RĮ-ĔNT, *n.* The east ; the part where the sun
  rises.
Ō-RĮ-ĔN'TĄL, *a.* · Eastern ; placed in the east.
Ō-RĮ-ĔN'TĄL, *n.* An inhabitant of the East.
Ō-RĮ-ĔN'TĄL-ĬṢM,*n.* An Eastern mode of speech.
Ō-RĮ-ĔN'TĄL-ĬST, *n.* An inhabitant of the East :
  —one versed in Oriental learning.
ŎR'Į-FĪCE, *n.* Any opening or perforation.
ŎR'Į-FLĂMB,   ⎫ (-ę-flăm), *n.* Ancient **regal**
ŎR'Į-FLĂMME, ⎭ standard of France.
ŎR'Į-ĢĬN, *n.* A beginning ; a source.
Ǫ-RĬĢ'Į-NĄL, *n.* Origin; first copy; an archetype.
Ǫ-RĬĢ'Į-NĄL, *a.* Pristine; first; having new ideas.
Ǫ-RĬĢ'Į-NĂL'Į-TY, *n.* State of being original.
Ǫ-RĬĢ'Į-NĄL-LY, *ad.* Primarily ; at first.
Ǫ-RĬĢ'Į-NĄL-NĔSS, *n.* State of being original.
Ǫ-RĬĢ-Į-NĀTE, *v. a.* To bring into existence.
Ǫ-RĬĢ'Į-NĀTE, *v. n.* To take existence.
Ǫ-RĬĢ-Į-NĀ'TIǪN, *n.* The act of originating.
Ǫ-RĪ'ǪN, *n.* One of the southern constellations.
ŎR'Į-ṢǪN, *n.* A prayer ; a supplication.
ŎR'NĄ-MĘNT, *n.* An embellishment; decoration.
ŎR'NĄ-MĘNT, *v. a.* To embellish ; to adorn.
ŎR-NĄ-MĔNT'ĄL, *a.* Giving embellishment.
ŎR-NĄ-MĔNT'ĄL-LY, *ad.* In an ornamental man-
ŎR'NĀTE, *a.* Bedecked ; decorated ; fine. [ner.
ŎR'NĀTE-LY, *ad.* Finely ; with decoration.
ŎR-NĮ-THǪ-LŎG'Į-CĄL, *a.* Relating to orni-
  thology.   [thology.
ŎR-NĮ-THŎL'Ǫ-GĬST, *n.* One versed in orni-
ŎR-NĮ-THŎL'Ǫ-ĢY, *n.* The science of birds.
ŎR'PHĄN, *n.* A child bereft of parents. [phan.
ŎR'PHĄN-AĢE, ŎR'PHĄN-ĬṢM, *n.* State of an or-
ŎR'PHĄNED (ŏr'fąnd), *a.* Bereft of parents.
ŎR'PĮ-MĔNT, *n.* Yellow sulphuret of arsenic.
ŎR'RĘ-RY, *n.* An instrument which represents
  the revolutions of the heavenly bodies.

Ŏr'thọ-dŏx, _a._ Sound in opinion and doctrine.
Ŏr'thọ-dŏx-lỵ, _ad._ With soundness of opinion.
Ŏr'thọ-dŏx-ỵ, _n._ Soundness in doctrine.
Ŏr-thọ-ĕp'ị-cạl, _a._ Relating to orthoepy.
Ŏr'thọ-ė-pĭst, _n._ One versed in orthoepy.
Ŏr'thọ-ė-pỵ, _n._ Art of pronouncing properly.
Ọr-thŏg'rạ-phẹr, _n._ One who is versed in orthography.
Ŏr-thọ-grăph'ị-cạl, _a._ Relating to spelling.
Ŏr-thọ-grăph'ị-cạl-lỵ, _ad._ According to rule.
Ọr-thŏg'rạ-phỵ, _n._ Art or mode of spelling.
Ọr-thŏl'ọ-gỵ, _n._ A right description of things.
Ŏr'tive, _a._ Rising; eastern.
Ŏr'tọ-lạn, _n._ A bird much esteemed for food.
Ŏrts, _n. pl._ Fragments; refuse; things left.
Ŏs'cịl-lāte, _v. n._ To move backward and forward, as a pendulum; to vibrate. [dulum.
Ŏs-cịl-lā'tiọn, _n._ The moving like a pen-
Ŏs'cịl-lạ-tọ-rỵ, _a._ Moving like a pendulum.
Ŏs'cị-tăn-cỵ, _n._ Act of yawning; sleepiness.
Ŏs'cị-tănt, _a._ Yawning; sleepy; sluggish.
Ŏs-cị-tā'tiọn, _n._ The act of yawning.
Ō'șịẹr (ō'zhẹr), _n._ A plant of the willow kind.
Ŏș'nạ-bŭrg, _n._ A coarse kind of linen.
Ŏs'prẹỵ, _n._ A large bird of prey. [knee.
Ŏs'sẹ-lĕt, _n._ A hard substance on a horse's
Ŏs'sẹ-oŭs, _a._ Bony; resembling a bone.
Ŏs'sị-cle (ŏs'sẹ-kl), _n._ A small bone.
Ọs-sĭf'ịc, _a._ Having power to ossify. [stance.
Ŏs-sị-fị-cā'tiọn, _n._ Change into bony sub-
Ŏs'sị-frāğe, _n._ A name of the sea-eagle.
Ŏs'sị-fỵ, _v. a. & n._ To change to bone.
Ŏs'sụ-ạ-rỵ (ŏsh'ụ-ạ-rẹ), _n._ A charnel-house.
Ọs-sĭv'ọ-roŭs, _a._ Devouring bones. [specious.
Ọs-tĕn'sị-ble, _a._ Held forth to view; apparent;
Ọs-tĕn-tā'tiọn, _n._ Show; ambitious display.
Ŏs-tĕn-tā'tioŭs, _a._ Boastful; fond of show.
Ŏs-tĕn-tā'tioŭs-lỵ, _ad._ Vainly; boastfully.
Ŏs-tĕn-tā'tioŭs-nĕss, _n._ Vanity; boastfulness.
Ŏs-tẹ-ŏl'ọ-ğer,) _n._ One versed in osteol-
Ŏs-tẹ-ŏl'ọ-ğĭst,) ogy.
Ŏs-tẹ-ŏl'ọ-ğỵ, _n._ A description of the bones.
Ŏs'tị-ạ-rỵ, _n._ Mouth of a river. [HOSTLER.
Ŏst'lẹr, _n._ A man who takes care of horses. See
Ŏs'trạ-cĭșm, _n._ A mode of banishment by ballot.
Ŏs'trạ-cīte, _n._ An oyster-shell in the fossil
Ŏs'trạ-cīze, _v. a._ To banish; to expel. [state.
Ŏs'trịch, _n._ A very large African bird. [ing.
Ŏt-ạ-coŭs'tịc, _n._ An instrument to assist hear-
Ŏth'ẹr (ŭth'ẹr), _pron. & a._ Not the same.
Ŏth'ẹr-wĭșe (ŭth'ẹr-wīz), _ad._ In a different manner.
Ŏt'tạr, Ŏt'tō, _n._ The essential oil of roses.
Ŏt'tẹr, _n._ An amphibious animal. [seat.
Ŏt'tọ-mạn, _n._ A Turk:—a kind of mat:—a
ought (âwt), _n._ Any thing. See AUGHT.
ought (âwt), _verb defective._ To be obliged.
oŭnce, _n._ A weight:—a kind of animal.
oŭr, oŭrș, _pron. poss._ Belonging to us.
oŭr-sĕlf', _pron. recip._ Used in the regal style.
oŭr-sĕlveș' (-sĕlvz'), _pron. pl._ We, not others.
ôu'șel, ôu'zel (ô'zl), _n._ A blackbird.
oŭst, _v. a._ To vacate; to deprive; to eject.
oŭst'ẹr, _v._ A dispossession; ejection.
oŭt, _ad._ Not within; not at home; loudly.
oŭt, _interj._ Expressing abhorrence or expulsion.
oŭt-ăct', _v. a._ To do or perform beyond.
oŭt-băl'ạnce, _v. a._ To outweigh.

oŭt-bĭd', _v. a._ To overpower by bidding.
oŭt'brēak, _n._ A breaking out; an eruption.
oŭt'brēak-ịng, _n._ That which breaks forth.
oŭt'căst, _p. a._ Thrown away; cast out.
oŭt'căst, _n._ An exile; one rejected or expelled.
oŭt'crỵ, _n._ A cry of distress; clamor; noise.
oŭt-dāre', _v. a._ To venture beyond. [surpass.
oŭt-dô', _v. a. [imp. t._ outdid; _pp._ outdone.] To
oŭt'ẹr, _a._ Being without; opposed to _inner._
oŭt'ẹr-mōst, _a._ Remotest from the midst.
oŭt-fāce', _v. a._ To brave; to stare down.
oŭt'fĭt, _n._ The equipment of a person or ship.
oŭt'gāte, _n._ An outlet; a passage outwards.
oŭt-ğĕn'ẹr-ạl, _v. a._ To excel in military skill.
oŭt-ğĭve', _v. a._ To surpass in giving.
oŭt-gō', _v. a. [imp. t._ outwent; _pp._ outgone.]
To surpass; to go beyond; to circumvent.
oŭt-gō'ịng, _n._ Egress; expenditure.
oŭt-grōw' (-grō'), _v. a._ To surpass in growth.
oŭt'-hoŭse, _n._ A barn, stable, coach-house, &c.
oŭt-lănd'ịsh, _a._ Not native; foreign.
oŭt-lăst', _v. a._ To surpass in duration.
oŭt'lâw, _n._ One deprived of the benefit of law.
oŭt'lâw, _v. a._ To deprive of the benefit of law.
oŭt'lâw-rỵ, _n._ An act of depriving of benefit
oŭt'lāy, _n._ Expense; expenditure. [of law.
oŭt'lẹt, _n._ A passage outwards; an egress.
oŭt'līne, _n._ Contour; an exterior line; a sketch.
oŭt-līve', _v. a._ To live beyond; to survive.
oŭt'mōst, _a._ Remotest from the middle.
oŭt-nŭm'bẹr, _v. a._ To exceed in number.
oŭt'pōrt, _n._ A port at a distance from a city.
oŭt'pōst, _n._ A station at a distance from the
oŭt-poŭr', _v. a._ To effuse; to emit. [army.
oŭt'rağe, _n._ Open violence; wanton abuse.
oŭt'rağe, _v. a._ To injure violently; to abuse.
oŭt-rā'ğeoŭs (oŭt-rā'jụs), _a._ Violent; furious.
oŭt-rā'ğeoŭs-lỵ (oŭt-rā'jụs-lẹ), _ad._ Violently.
oŭt-rīde', _v. a. & n._ To pass by riding; to
ride about. [once.
oŭt-rīght' (oŭt-rīt'), _ad._ Immediately; at
oŭt-rŭn', _v. a._ To leave behind; to exceed.
oŭt-sāil', _v. a._ To leave behind in sailing.
oŭt-sĕll', _v. a._ To sell at a higher rate.
oŭt'sĕt, _n._ An opening; a beginning.
oŭt-shīne', _v. a._ To excel in lustre.
oŭt'sīde, _n._ Surface; external part; the utmost.
oŭt'skĭrt, _n._ A suburb, border, outpost.
oŭt-stāre', _v. a._ To face down; to browbeat.
oŭt-strĭp', _v. a._ To outgo; to leave behind.
oŭt-tâlk' (oŭt-tâwk'), _v. a._ To exceed by talk.
oŭt-văl'ụe, _v. a._ To transcend in price.
oŭt-vīe' (oŭt-vī'), _v. a._ To exceed; to surpass.
oŭt-vōte', _v. a._ To conquer by suffrages. [ing.
oŭt-wâlk' (-wâwk'), _v. a._ To exceed in walk-
oŭt'wâll, _n._ An exterior wall. [eign.
oŭt'wạrd, _a._ External; exterior; visible; for-
oŭt'wạrd, oŭt'wạrdș, _ad._ To foreign parts.
oŭt'wạrd-lỵ, _ad._ Externally; in appearance.
oŭt-weigh' (-wā'), _v. a._ To exceed in gravity.
oŭt-wĭt', _v. a._ To overcome by stratagem.
oŭt'works, _n. pl._ External parts of a fortifica-
ôu'zel, _n._ A water-fowl; a blackbird. [tion.
ō'vạl, _a._ Oblong; shaped like an egg.
ō'vạl, _n._ A figure in the shape of an egg.
ọ-vā'rị-oŭs, _a._ Consisting of eggs.
ō'vạ-rỵ, _n._ The seat of eggs or impregnation.
ō'vāte, _a._ Of an oval figure; egg-shaped.

Ǫ-VĀ'TIǪN, n. In ancient Rome, a lesser triumph.
ŎV'EN (ŭv'vn), n. An arched cavity to bake in.
Ō'VẸR, prep. Above; across; upon; through.
Ō'VẸR, ad. Above the top; more; throughout.
Ō-VẸR-A-BŎŬND', v. n. To abound too much.
Ō-VẸR-ĂCT', v. a. & n. To act more than enough.
Ō'VẸR-ĂLLṢ, n. pl. A kind of loose trousers.
Ō-VẸR-ÄRCH', v. a. To cover as with an arch.
Ō-VẸR-ÂWE', v. a. To keep in awe; to terrify.
Ō-VẸR-BĂL'ANCE, v. a. To preponderate.
Ō-VẸR-BEÄR' (ō-vẹr-bår'), v. a. To bear down.
Ō'VẸR-BŌARD, ad. Off the ship; out of the ship.
Ō-VẸR-BÜR'DEN (-bür'dn), v. a. To overload.
Ō-VẸR-CĂST', v. a. [imp. t. & pp. overcast.] To
  cloud; to darken; to rate too high.   [high.
Ō-VẸR-CHÄRGE', v. a. To oppress; to rate too
Ō-VẸR-CLŎŬD', v. a. To cover with clouds.
Ō-VẸR-CŎME', v. a. [imp. t. overcame; pp. over-
  come.] To conquer; to surmount; to excel.
Ō-VẸR-DÔ', v. a. & n. To do more than enough.
Ō-VẸR-FLŌW', v. a. & n. To deluge; to inundate.
Ō'VẸR-FLŌW, n. An inundation; deluge.
Ō-VẸR-FLŌW'ING, n. Exuberance; copiousness.
Ō-VẸR-FREIGHT' (ō-vẹr-frāt'),v.a. To overload.
Ō-VẸR-GRŌW' (ō-vẹr-grō'), v. a. & n. To cover
  with growth; to grow beyond; to rise above.
Ō'VẸR-GRŌWTH, n. Exuberant growth. [over.
Ō-VẸR-HÄNG', v. a. & n. To jut over; to impend
Ō-VẸR-HÂUL', v. a. To spread over; to examine.
Ō-VẸR-HĔAD' (ō-vẹr-hĕd'), ad. Aloft; above.
Ō-VẸR-HEÄR', v. a. To hear privately or by
Ō-VẸR-HĔAT', v. a. To heat too much. [chance.
Ō-VẸR-JŎY', v. a. To transport; to ravish.
Ō-VẸR-LĀDE', v. a. To overload; to overburden.
Ō-VẸR-LĀY', v. a. To smother; to crush, cover.
Ō-VẸR-LEÄP', v. a. To pass over by a jump.
Ō-VẸR-LŌAD', v. a. To burden with too much.
Ō-VẸR-LOOK' (ō-vẹr-lŭk'), v. a. To oversee :—to
  inspect :—to peruse :—to excuse :—to neglect.
Ō-VẸR-MĂTCH', v. a. To be too powerful for.
Ō'VẸR-MĂTCH, n. One of superior powers.
Ō-VẸR-MĔAṢ'URE (-mĕzh'ụr), n. A surplus.
Ō-VẸR-MŬCH', a. Too much; more than enough.
Ō-VẸR-MŬCH', ad. In too great a degree.
Ō-VẸR-PĂSS', v. a. To cross; to overlook; to omit.
Ō'VẸR-PLŬS, n. A surplus; what remains.
Ō'VẸR-POÏṢE, n. A preponderant weight.
Ō-VẸR-PŎW'ER, v. a. To be too powerful for.
Ō-VẸR-PRĔSS', v. a. To overwhelm; to crush.
Ō-VẸR-RĀTE', v. a. To rate at too much.
Ō-VẸR-RĔACH', v. a. To deceive; to go beyond.
Ō-VẸR-RĪDE', v.a. To ride over; to ride too much.
Ō-VẸR-RŪLE', v. a. To control; to supersede.
Ō-VẸR-RŬN', v. a. To ravage; to overspread.
Ō-VẸR-SĒĒ', v. a. To superintend; to overlook.
Ō-VẸR-SĒ'ER,n. One who oversees; a supervisor.
Ō-VẸR-SĔT', v. a. & n. To turn bottom upwards.
Ō-VẸR-SHĀDE', v. a. To cover with darkness.
Ō-VẸR-SHĂD'ŌW (ō-vẹr-shăd'dō), v. a. To throw
  a shade over; to shelter; to protect.   [mark.
Ō-VẸR-SHÔÔT', v. a. & n. To shoot beyond the

Ō'VẸR-SĪGHT (ō'vẹr-sīt), n. Superintendence;
  a mistake; an error :—inattention.
Ō-VẸR-SPRĔAD' (-sprĕd'), v. a. To cover over.
Ō-VẸR-STŎCK', v. a. To fill too full; to crowd.
Ō-VẸR-STRĀIN', v. a. & n. To strain too far.
Ō'VẸRT, a. Open; public; apparent; manifest.
Ō-VẸR-TĀKE', v. a. To catch; to come up with.
Ō-VẸR-THRŌW', v. a. To overturn; to ruin; to
Ō-VẸR-THRŌW (-thrō), n. Ruin; defeat. [defeat.
Ō'VẸRT-LY, ad. Openly; manifestly.
Ō-VẸR-TŎP', v. a. To rise above; to surpass.
Ō'VẸR-TŪRE, n. A proposal; a flourish of music.
Ō-VẸR-TÜRN', v. a. To subvert; to overpower.
Ō'VẸR-TÜRN, n. A subversion; an overthrow.
Ō-VẸR-VĂL'ŲE, v. a. To rate at too high a price.
Ō-VẸR-WĒĒN', v. n. To think too highly.
Ō-VẸR-WĒĒN'ING, a. Vain; conceited; arrogant.
Ō-VẸR-WEIGH' (-wā'), v. a. To preponderate.
Ō'VẸR-WEĬGHT (ō'vẹr-wāt), n. Preponderance.
Ō-VẸR-WHĔLM', v. a. To immerse; to overcome.
Ō-VẸR-WORK' (-würk), v. n. To work too much.
Ō-VẸR-WROUGHT' (ō-vẹr-råwt'), pp. from over-
  work. Labored too much; worked all over.
Ō'VĮ-DŬCT, n. Tube which conducts the ovum.
Ǫ-VĬF'ẸR-OŬS, Ǫ-VĬG'ẸR-OŬS, a. Bearing eggs.
Ō'VĮ-FŌRM, a. Having the shape of an egg.
Ǫ-VĬP'A-ROŬS, a. Producing eggs.
Ō'VÖÏD, Ǫ-VÖÏD'AL, a. Egg-shaped.
Ō'VŪLE, n. A rudimentary seed.
Ō'VŲM, n.; pl. Ō'VA. [L.] An egg.
ŌWE (ō), v. a. To be indebted to or for. [ble to.
ŌW'ING (ō'ing), p. a. Due, as a debt :—imputa-
ŌWL, ŌWL'ẸT, n. A bird that flies by night.
ŌWL'ẸR, n. One who carries contraband goods.
ŌWL'ING, n. An offence against public trade.
ŌWL'ISH, a. Somewhat resembling an owl.
ŌWN (ōn), a. Belonging to; as, my own.
ŌWN (ōn), v. a. To possess by right :—to confess.
ŌWN'ẸR (ō'nẹr), n. The rightful proprietor.
ŌWN'ẸR-SHĬP (ō'nẹr-), n. Rightful possession.
ŎX, n.; pl. ŎX'EN. An animal of the bovine
  tribe; specifically, the castrated male.
ŎX'EȲE (ŏx'Ī), n. A plant of different genera.
ŎX'STĂLL, n. A stand for oxen.
ŎX'Į-DĀTE, v. a. To convert into an oxide.
ŎX'ĮDE (ŏks'ĭd), n. A combination, not acid,
  of a simple body with oxygen.
ŎX'Y-GẸN, n. A gas which generates acids,
  and forms the respirable or vital part of air.
ŎX'Y-GẸN-ĀTE, } v. a. To combine or impreg-
ŎX'Y-GẸN-ĪZE, }   nate with oxygen.
ŎX'Y-GŎN, n. An acute-angled triangle.
ŎX'Y-MĔL, n. A mixture of vinegar and honey.
ŎX'Y-TŌNE, n. Acute acent on the last syllable.
Ō'YER, n. Oyer and terminer, in Eng., the as-
  sizes; in the U. S., the highest criminal courts.
Ō-YĔS' [Fr. oyez.] Hear ye;—used by a sheriff
  or crier as an introduction to a proclamation.
ŌŸS'TẸR, n. A bivalve testaceous mollusk.
Ǫ-ZÆ'NA (ǫ-zē'na), n. An ulcer in the nostrils.
Ō'ZŌNE, n. A gaseous substance.

P.

P is a labial consonant, and has one uniform sound, as in *pelt*, *pull*, *cap*, &c.   [ment.

PĂB'Ṳ-LĂR, PĂB'Ṳ-LOŬS, *a.* Relating to ali-

PĂB'Ṳ-LŬM, *n.* [L.] Food; aliment; support.

PĀCE, *n.* A step:—gait:—a measure varying from 2½ to 5 feet:—⅕ of a rod:—degree of speed.

PĀCE, *v. n.* To move with a particular gait; to

PĀCE, *v. a.* To measure by paces or steps. [go.

PĀCED (pāst), *a.* Having a particular gait.

PĀÇ'ĘR, *n.* One that paces; a horse that paces.

PẠ-ÇHẶ', *n.* A Turkish governor; a bashaw.

PẠ-ÇHẶ'LĬC, *n.* The jurisdiction of a pacha.

PẠ-CĬF'ĬC, *a.* Promoting peace; mild; gentle.

PĂÇ-Ĭ-FĬ-CĀ'TIǪN, *n.* The act of making peace.

PĂÇ-Ĭ-FĬ-CĀ'TǪR, *n.* A peacemaker.

PẠ-CĬF'Ĭ-CẠ-TǪ-RẎ, *a.* Tending to make peace.

PĂÇ'Ĭ-FẎ, *v. a.* To appease; to quiet; to compose.

PĂCK, *n.* A bundle:—number of cards or hounds.

PĂCK, *v. a.* To bind up:—to send:—to sort.

PĂCK'AǴE, *n.* A bale; goods packed:—a charge.

PĂCK'CLŎTH, *n.* A cloth for packing goods in.

PĂCK'ĘT, *n.* A small pack; a mail of letters: —a vessel for despatches or passengers.

PĂCK'HŌRSE, *n.* A horse of burden.

PĂCK'-SĂD-DLE, *n.* A saddle to carry burdens.

PĂCK'STĂFF, *n.* A staff to support a pack.

PĂCK'THRĔAD (păk'thrĕd), *n.* Thread to tie up packs.

PĂCT, PĂC'TIǪN, *n.* A bargain; a covenant.

PĂD, *n.* An easy-paced horse:—a robber:—a sort of cushion or saddle.

PĂD, *v. n.* To travel gently:—to rob on foot.

PĂD, *v. a.* To walk in or on:—to stuff.

PĂD'DLE, *v. n.* To row; to play in the water.

PĂD'DLE, *v. a.* To touch gently:—to row.

PĂD'DLE, *n.* A short oar with a broad blade.

PĂD'DǬCK, *n.* A toad:—a small enclosure.

PĂD'LŎCK, *n.* A pendent or hanging lock.

PĂD-ṲA-SŎẎ' (păd-ṳ-sŏï'), *n.* A kind of silk.

PÆ'ẠN (pē'ạn), *n.* A song of triumph or praise.

PĀ'GẠN, *n.* A heathen; one not a Christian.

PĀ'GẠN, *a.* Relating to pagans; heathenish.

PĀ'GẠN-ĬSM, *n.* Pagan worship; heathenism.

PĀ'GẠN-ĪZE, *v. a.* To render heathenish.

PĀǴE, *n.* One side of a leaf:—a boy-servant.

PĀǴE, *v. a.* To mark the pages of a book.

‖PĂǴ'ĘANT *or* PĀ'ǴEANT, *n.* A statue in a show:—showy exhibition; a pompous show; a spectacle.

‖PĂǴ'ĘANT, *a.* Showy; pompous; ostentatious.

‖PĂǴ'ĘANT-RẎ, *n.* Pomp; show; a spectacle.

PĀ'GǪD, *n.* An East Indian idol.

PẠ-GŌ'DẠ, *n.* An East Indian idol and its temple:—an Indian coin.

PāID (pād), *imp. t.* & *pp.* from *pay*.

PāIL (pāl), *n.* An open vessel with a bail.

PāIL'FŬL, *n.* The quantity that a pail will hold.

PāIN, *n.* Penalty:—uneasy sensation:—*pl.* Travail; throes of childbirth.

PāIN, *v. a.* To afflict, torment, or make uneasy.

PāIN'FŬL, *a.* Full of pain; afflictive; difficult.

PāIN'FŬL-LẎ, *ad.* With great pain or affliction.

PāIN'FŬL-NĔSS, *n.* Affliction; suffering; distress.

PāIN'LĘSS, *a.* Free from pain; void of trouble.

PāINṢ, *n. sing.* or *pl.* Labor or care; trouble.

PāINṢ'TĂK-ĘR, *n.* One who takes pains or care.

PāINṢ'TĂK-ĬNG, *a.* Laborious; careful.

PāINT, *v. a.* To represent; to describe; to color.

PāINT (pānt), *v. n.* To lay colors on the face, &c.

PāINT, *n.* Color; a coloring substance. [rope.

PāINT'ĘR, *n.* One who practises painting:—a

PāINT'ĬNG, *n.* The art of representing objects by delineation and colors; a picture.

PÀIR (pår), *n.* Two things suited to each other; two of a sort; a couple; a brace.

PÀIR (pår), *v. n.* To be joined in pairs; to couple.

PÀIR, *v. a.* To join in couples; to unite.

PĂL'ACE, *n.* A royal or splendid house. [army.

PĂL'Ạ-DĬN, *n.* A chieftain in Charlemagne's

PĂL-ẠN-QUÎN' (păl-ạn-kēn'), *n.* A covered carriage in the East, borne by men.

PĂL'Ạ-TẠ-BLE, *a.* Pleasing to the taste.

PĂL'ẠTE, *n.* The organ of taste:—mental relish.

PẠ-LĀ'TIẠL, *a.* Like a palace; magnificent.

PĂL'Ạ-TĪNE, *n.* One invested with regal rights.

PĂL'Ạ-TĪNE, *a.* Possessing royal privileges.

PẠ-LĂ'VĘR, *n.* Superfluous talk; flattery.

PĀLE, *a.* Not ruddy; wan; whitish; pallid; dim.

PĀLE, *n.* A pointed stake:—an enclosure; a

PĀLE, *v. a.* To enclose with pales. [district.

PĀLE'EYED (pāl'īd), *a.* Having dim eyes.

PĀLE'FĀCED (pāl'fāst), *a.* Having the face wan.

PĀLE'LẎ, *ad.* Wanly; not freshly; not ruddily.

PĀLE'NĔSS, *n.* Wanness; sickly whiteness.

PĀ-LĘ-ŎG'RẠ-PHY, *n.* An ancient mode of writing; ancient writings collectively.

PĀ-LĘ-ŎL'Ǫ-ǴĬST, *n.* A writer on antiquity.

PĀ-LĘ-ŎL'Ǫ-ǴY, *n.* The science of antiquities.

PĀ'LĘ-OŬS, *a.* Husky; chaffy.

PẠ-LĔS'TRĬC,   } *a.* Belonging to the exercise

PẠ-LĔS'TRĬ-CẠL, }   of wrestling.

PĂL'ĘTTE (păl'let), *n.* A painter's board.

PÂL'FRĘY, *n.* A gentle horse for ladies.

PĀL'ĬNG, *n.* A fence made of pales.

PĂL-Ĭ-SĀDE', *n.* A fence or enclosure by pales.

PĂL-Ĭ-SĀDE', *v. a.* To enclose with palisades.

PÂLL, *n.* A cloak; a covering for the dead.

PÂLL, *v. a.* & *n.* To cloak; to cloy; to grow vapid.

PẠL-LĀ'DĬ-ŬM, *n.* [L.] Statue of Pallas:—safeguard; protection:—a whitish metal.

PĂL'LĘT, *n.* A small bed:—part of a watch, &c.

PĂL'LĬ-ĀTE, *v. a.* To extenuate; to soften; to ease.

PĂL-LĬ-Ā'TIǪN, *n.* An extenuation; a mitigation.

PĂL'LĬ-Ạ-TĬVE, *n.* Something mitigating.

PĂL'LĬD, *a.* Pale; not high-colored; not bright.

PĂL'LĬD-NĔSS, PĂL'LǪR, *n.* Paleness. [mallet.

PALL-MALL' (pĕl-mĕl'), *n.* A play with a ball and

PĂLM (päm), *n.* A tree:—victory; triumph:—the inner part of the hand; a measure of 3 inches.

PĂLM (päm), *v. a.* To conceal; to impose.

PĂL'MĂT-ĘD, *a.* Having the feet broad or webbed.

PĂLM'ĘR (päm'ęr), *n.* A pilgrim; a crusader.

PĂLM'ĘR-WORM (päm'ęr-würm), *n.* A worm.

PẠL-MĔT'TŌ, *n.* A species of the palm-tree.

Ā,Ē,Ī,Ō,Ū,Ῡ,*long*; Ă,Ĕ,Ĭ,Ŏ,Ŭ,Ῠ,*short*; Ạ,Ę,Ị,Ǫ,Ṳ,Ẏ,*obscure.*—FĀRE, FÄR, FĂST, FÂLL; HÊIR, HĔR;

PĂL'MĬ-PĔD, *a.* Web-footed ; fin-footed.
PĂL'MĬS-TĔR, *n.* One who deals in palmistry.
PĂL'MĬS-TRŸ, *n.* Fortune-telling by the palm.
PÁLM'Ÿ (pä'mẹ), *a.* Bearing palms ; flourishing.
PĂL-PĄ-BĬL'Ĭ-TŸ, *n.* Quality of being palpable.
PĂL'PĄ-BLE, *a.* That may be felt ; gross ; plain.
PĂL'PĄ-BLE-NĔSS, *n.* Quality of being palpable.
PĂL'PĄ-BLŸ, *ad.* In a palpable manner.
PĂL'PĬ-TÃTE,*v. a.*To beat as the heart ; to flutter.
PĂL-PĬ-TÃ'TĬQN, *n.* A throbbing of the heart.
PÂLS'GRÃVE, *n.* A count of the palace. [ic.
PÂL'SĬ-CĄL, *a.* Afflicted with the palsy; paralyt-
PÂL'SĬED (pâl'zįd), *a.* Diseased with palsy.
PÂL'SŸ, *n.* A privation of motion ; paralysis.
PÂL'TĔR, *v. n.* To shift ; to dodge ; to play tricks.
PÂL'TĔR-ĔR, *n.* One who palters ; a shifter.
PÂL'TRĬ-NĔSS, *n.* The state of being paltry.
PÂL'TRŸ, *a.* Sorry; worthless ; despicable ; mean.
PĂM, *n.* The knave of clubs.
PĂM'PĔR, *v. a.* To glut ; to feed luxuriously.
PĂM'PHLĔT (păm'flẹt), *n.* A small stitched book.
PĂM-PHLĔT-ÉĔR', *n.* A writer of small books.
PĂN, *n.* A vessel broad and shallow ; a hollow.
PĂN-Ą-CÉ'Ą, *n.* A universal remedy ; an herb.
PĄ-NÃ'DĄ, PĄ-NÃ'DŌ, *n.* Bread boiled in water.
PĂN'CĂKE, *n.* A cake fried in a pan.
PĄN-CRĂT'Ĭ-CĄL, *a.* Very strong ; athletic.
PĂN'CRĘ-ĂS (păng'krẹ-ăs), *n.* The sweetbread.
PĂN-CRĘ-ĂT'ĬC, *a.* Relating to the pancreas.
PĂN'DĘCT, *n.* A treatise ; a digest of law.
PĄN-DĔM'ĬC, *a.* Incident to a whole people.
PĂN'DĘR, *n.* A pimp ; a male bawd ; a procurer.
PĂN'DĘR, *v. n.* To be subservient to vice.
PĂN-DĬC-Ų-LÃ'TĬQN, *n.* Restlessness ; uneasi-
ness. [dore.
PĄN-DŌRE', *n.* A musical instrument ; a ban-
PÃNE, *n.* A square of glass ; a piece. [astic.
PĂN-Ę-GŸR'ĬC, PĂN-Ę-GŸR'Ĭ-CĄL, *a.* Encomi-
PĂN-Ę-GŸR'ĬC, *n.* A eulogy; encomiastic piece.
PĂN-Ę-GŸR'ĬST, *n.* A eulogist ; an encomiast.
PĂN'Ę-GŸR-ĪZE, *v. a.* To commend highly.
PĂN'ĘL, *n.* A square of wainscot :—a jury-roll.
PĂN'ĘL, *v. a.* To form into or with panels.
PĂNG, *n.* Extreme pain ; sudden anguish.
PĂN'ĬC, *n.* A sudden fright ; an alarm ; a plant.
PĂN'ĬC, *a.* Extreme ; sudden :—*applied to fear.*
PĂN'NĘL, *n.* A kind of rustic saddle.
PĂN'NIĘR (păn'yẹr *or* păn'nį-ẹr), *n.* A basket
carried on a horse, &c.
PĂN'Q-PLŸ, *n.* Complete armor for defence.
PĂN-Q-RÃ'MĄ *or* PĂN-Q-RÄ'MĄ, *n.* A large
PĂN'SŸ, *n.* A flower ; garden-violet. [painting.
PĂNT, *v. n.* To beat as the heart ; to long.
PĂNT, *n.* Palpitation ; a motion of the heart.
PĂN-TĄ-LŌŌN',*n.* A man's garment :—a buffoon.
PĂN'THĘ-ĬSM, *n.* The doctrine that nature or the
universe is God.
PĂN'THĘ-ĬST, *n.* A believer in pantheism.
PĂN-THĘ-ĬS'TĬC, *a.* Relating to pantheism.
PĄN-THĔ'QN, *n.* A temple dedicated to all the
PĂN'THĘR, *n.* A spotted wild beast. [gods.
PĂN'TĬLE, *n.* A tile with a hollow or incur-
vated surface ; pentile. See PENTILE.
PĄN-TŌ'FLE (pąn-tô'fl), *n.* A slipper for the foot.
PĂN'TQ-GRĂPH, *n.* A machine for copying.
PĄN-TŎM'Ę-TĔR, *n.* A measuring instrument.
PĂN'TQ-MĪME, *n.* A buffoon :—show :—a drama
exhibited only in gesture and dumb show.

PĂN-TQ-MĬM'ĬC, } *a.* Representing only by
PĂN-TQ-MĬM'Ĭ-CĄL, } gesture or dumb show.
PĂN'TRŸ, *n.* An apartment for provisions.
PĂP, *n.* A nipple :—food for infants :—pulp.
PĄ-PÄ', *n.* A fond name for *father.*
PÃ'PĄ-CŸ, *n.* The popedom ; papal authority.
PÃ'PĄL, *a.* Pertaining to the pope.
PĄ-PĂV'ĘR-OŬS, *a.* Pertaining to poppies.
PĄ-PÂW', *n.* A tropical tree and its fruit.
PÃ'PĘR, *n.* A thin substance to write on, &c.
PÃ'PĘR, *a.* Made of paper ; slight or thin.
PÃ'PĘR, *v. a.* To cover with paper. [of rooms.
PÃ'PĘR-HĂNG'ĬNGS,*n.pl.*Colored paper for walls
PÃ'PĘR-MĂK'ĘR, *n.* One who makes paper.
PÃ'PĘR-MĬLL, *n.* A mill for making paper.
PÃ'PĘR-MŎN'EŸ, *n.* Bank notes, or bills, &c.
PÃ'PĘR-STÃIN'ĘR, *n.* One who colors paper.
PĄ-PĔS'CĘNT, *a.* Containing pap ; like pap.
PĄ-PĬL-IQ-NÃ'CEOŲS (pą-pĭl-yǫ-nã'shųs), *a.* Re-
sembling a butterfly ; butterfly-shaped.
PĂP'ĬL-LĄ-RŸ, *a.* Having, or pertaining to,
PĄ-PĬL'LOŲS, *a.* Papillary. [nipples.
PÃ'PĬST, *n.* An adherent to the Catholic religion.
PĄ-PĬS'TĬC, PĄ-PĬS'TĬ-CĄL, *a.* Roman Catholic.
PÃ'PĬS-TRŸ, *n.* Roman Catholic doctrine.
PĄP-PŌŌSE', *n.* An Indian word for a child.
PĂP'POŲS, *a.* Having soft, light down.
PĂP'PŸ, *a.* Soft ; succulent ; resembling pap.
PĂP-Ų-LŌSE', PĂP'Ų-LOŬS, *a.* Having pimples.
PĄ-PŸ'RŲS, *n.* A rush, formerly used for paper.
PÄR, *n.* The state of equality ; equal value.
PĂR'Ą-BLE, *n.* A similitude ; an allegorical fable.
PĄ-RĂB'Q-LĄ, *n.* [L.] One of the conic sections.
PĂR-Ą-BŎL'ĬC, } *a.* Relating to a parable,
PĂR-Ą-BŎL'Ĭ-CĄL, } or to a parabola. [ner.
PĂR-Ą-BŎL'Ĭ-CĄL-LŸ, *ad.* In a parabolical man-
PĂR-Ą-BŎL'Ĭ-FŎRM, *a.* Formed like a parabola.
PĂR-Ą-CĔN'TRĬC, } *a.* Deviating from cir-
PĂR-Ą-CĔN'TRĬ-CĄL, } cularity.
PĄ-RĂCH'RQ-NĬSM, *n.* An error in chronology,
by placing an event later than it should be.
PĂR'Ą-CHŪTE, *n.* A machine to enable an aero-
naut to descend from his balloon.
PĂR'Ą-CLĔTE, *n.* An advocate ; the Holy Spirit.
PĄ-RÃDE', *n.* Show ; ostentation ; procession ;
military order ; a place where troops assemble.
PĄ-RÃDE', *v. a. & n.* To assemble ; to exhibit.
PĂR'Ą-DĬGM(păr'ą-dĭm),*n.*An example ; a model.
PĂR'Ą-DĪSE, *n.* Garden of Eden ; heaven.
PĂR-Ą-DĬ-SĪ'Ą-CĄL, *a.* Suiting, or like, paradise.
PĂR'Ą-DŎX, *n.* An opinion or assertion appar-
ently false or absurd, but not really so.
PĂR-Ą-DŎX'Ĭ-CĄL, *a.* Partaking of paradox.
PĂR-Ą-DŎX'Ĭ-CĄL-LŸ, *ad.* By way of paradox.
PĂR'Ą-DRŌME, *n.* An open gallery or space.
PĂR-Ą-GŌ'GĘ, *n.* A figure whereby a letter or
syllable is added at the end of a word.
PĂR'Ą-GŎN, *n.* A perfect model ; a pattern.
PĂR'Ą-GRĂM, *n.* A pun ; a play upon words.
PĂR'Ą-GRĂPH, *n.* A distinct part of a discourse.
PĂR-Ą-GRĂPH'Ĭ-CĄL, *a.* Relating to paragraphs.
PĂR-Ą-GRĂPH'Ĭ-CĄL-LŸ, *ad.* By paragraphs.
PĂR-ĄL-LĂC'TĬC, } *a.* Relating to a paral-
PĂR-ĄL-LĂC'TĬ-CĄL, } lax.
PĂR'ĄL-LĂX, *n.* Change of place or aspect ;
the distance between the true and apparent
place of the sun, or any star.
PĂR'ĄL-LĔL, *a.* In the same direction ; like.

PÄR'AL-LĚL, *n.* A line equidistant throughout from another line ; a line of latitude ; likeness.
PÄR'AL-LĚL, *v. a.* To make parallel ; to compare.
PÄR'AL-LĚL-ĬSM, *n.* The state of being parallel.
PÄR-AL-LĚL'Q-GRĂM, *n.* A quadrilateral figure whose opposite sides are parallel and equal.
PÄR-AL-LĚL-Q-PĪ'PĘD, } *n.* A prism whose
PÄR-AL-LĚL-Q-PĬP'Ę-DŎN, } base is a parallelogram.
PA-RĂL'Q-GĬSM, *n.* False reasoning ; paralogy.
PA-RĂL'Q-GY, *n.* False reasoning. [feeling.
PA-RĂL'Y-SĬS, *n.* A palsy ; loss of motion and
PÄR-A-LỸT'ĬC, *n.* One struck by palsy.
PÄR-A-LỸT'ĬC, } *a.* Pertaining to, or af-
PÄR-A-LỸT'Ĭ-CAL, } fected with, palsy.
PÄR'A-LỸZE, *v. a.* To affect as with palsy.
PÄR'A-MÖÜNT, *a.* Superior.—*n.* The chief.
PÄR'A-MÖUR (pär'a-môr), *n.* A lover ; a wooer.
PÄR'A-NỸMPH, *n.* A brideman :—a supporter.
PÄR'A-PĔGM (pär'a-pĕm), *n.* An ancient table.
PÄR'A-PĚT, *n.* (*Fort.*) A breastwork.
PÄR-A-PHĘR-NĀ'LĬ-A, *n. pl.* Goods at the wife's disposal :—ornaments ; appendages ; trappings.
PÄR'A-PHRĀ§E, *n.* A free and amplified translation ; a wordy or more ample explanation.
PÄR'A-PHRĀ§E, *v. a.* To explain in many words.
PÄR'A-PHRĂST, *n.* One who paraphrases.
PÄR-A-PHRĂS'TĬC, } *a.* Relating to para-
PÄR-A-PHRĂS'TĬ-CAL, } phrase ; diffuse.
PÄR-A-PHRĂS'TĬ-CAL-LY, *ad.* By paraphrase.
PÄR'A-SĂNG, *n.* A Persian measure of length.
PÄR-A-SĘ-LĒ'NĘ, *n.* [Gr.] A mock moon.
PÄR'A-SĪTE, *n.* A flatterer of rich men ; hanger-on.
PÄR-A-SĬT'ĬC, } *a.* Flattering :—growing on
PÄR-A-SĬT'Ĭ-CAL, } another tree, as plants.
PÄR-A-SĬT'Ĭ-CAL-LY, *ad.* In a flattering manner.
PÄR'A-SĬT-ĬSM, *n.* The behavior of a parasite.
PÄR'A-SŎL, *n.* A small canopy or umbrella.
PÄR'BÖĬL, *v. a.* To half boil ; to boil in part.
PÄR'CĘL, *n.* A small bundle or quantity.
PÄR'CĘL, *v. a.* To divide into portions.
PÄR'CĘN-A-RY, *n.* Joint inheritance.
PÄR'CĘN-ĘR, *n.* A coparcener.
PÄRCH, *v. a.* To burn slightly, scorch, dry up.
PÄRCH'MĘNT, *n.* Skin dressed for writing on.
PÄRD, *n.* The leopard ; a spotted animal.
PÄR'DON (pär'dn), *v. a.* To forgive ; to remit.
PÄR'DON (pär'dn), *n.* Forgiveness ; remission.
PÄR'DON-A-BLE (pär'dn-a-bl), *a.* That may be pardoned ; venial ; excusable.
PÄR'DON-A-BLY (pär'dn-a-ble), *ad.* Venially.
PÄR'DON-ĘR (pär'dn-ęr), *n.* One who pardons.
PÅRE, *v. a.* To cut off the surface of ; to dimin-
PÄR-Ę-GŎR'ĬC, *a.* Mollifying ; assuaging. [ish.
PÄR-Ę-GŎR'ĬC, *n.* An assuaging medicine.
PÄR-Ę-NĚT'ĬC, PÄR-Ę-NĚT'Ĭ-CAL, *a.* Hortatory.
PÅR'ĘNT (pår'ęnt), *n.* A father or mother.
PÅR'ĘNT-AGE *or* PÄR'ĘNT-AGE, *n.* Birth ; extraction ; descent.
PA-RĚNT'AL, *a.* Pertaining to parents ; tender.
PA-RĚN'THĘ-SĬS, *n.* ; *pl.* PA-RĚN'THĘ-SĒ§. A clause included in a sentence :—the mark thus [( )].
PÄR-ĘN-THĚT'ĬC, } *a.* Pertaining to, or in-
PÄR-ĘN-THĚT'Ĭ-CAL, } cluded in, a parenthesis.
PÄR-ĘN-THĚT'Ĭ-CAL-LY, *ad.* By parenthesis.
PÅR'ĘR, *n.* One that pares. [sun.
PAR-HĒ'LĬ-ON, *n.* ; *pl.* PAR-HĒ'LĬ-A. A mock

PA-RĪ'Ę-TAL, *a.* Of, or pertaining to, a wall.
PÄR'ĬNG, *n.* That which is pared off ; the rind.
PÄR'ĬSH, *n.* An ecclesiastical district.
PÄR'ĬSH, *a.* Belonging to a parish ; parochial.
PA-RĬSH'ĬON-ĘR, *n.* One that belongs to a parish.
PÄR-Ĭ-SYL-LĂB'ĬC, } *a.* Having equal sylla-
PÄR-Ĭ-SYL-LĂB'Ĭ-CAL, } bles.
PÄR'Ĭ-TOR, *n.* A beadle ; a summoner.
PÄR'Ĭ-TY, *n.* Equality ; resemblance ; likeness.
PÄRK, *n.* An enclosure of pasture or woodland.
PÄRK, *v. a.* To enclose as in a park.
PÄRK'ĘR, *n.* A keeper of a park.
PÄR'LANCE, *n.* Conversation ; discourse ; talk.
PÄR'LEY, *v. n.* To converse, discourse ; to talk.
PÄR'LEY, *n.* Oral treaty ; talk ; conference.
PÄR'LĬA-MĚNT (pär'lę-mĕnt), *n.* The British legislative assembly of lords and commons.
PÄR-LĬA-MĚNT'A-RY, *a.* Relating to parliament.
PÄR'LOR, *n.* A room ; a drawing-rocm.
PA-RŌ'ℂHĬ-AL, *a.* Belonging to a parish.
PÄR'Q-DY, *n.* A caricature of another's words.
PÄR'Q-DY, *v. a.* To copy by way of parody.
PÄR'OL, *a.* Oral ; by word of mouth ; verbal.
PA-RŌLE', *n.* Word given as an assurance.
PÄR'Q-QUĚT (pär'q-kĕt), *n.* A small kind of par-
PA-RŎT'ĬD, *a.* Relating to the parotis. [rot.
PA-RŎT'ĬD, PA-RŌ'TĬS, *n.* A salivary gland.
PÄR'QX-ỸSM, *n.* Exacerbation of a disease ; fit.
PÄR-RĬ-CĪ'DAL, *a.* Relating to parricide. [parent.
PÄR'RĬ-CĪDE, *n.* The murder, or murderer, of a
PÄR'ROT, *n.* A well-known bird. [to fence.
PÄR'RY, *v. a.* & *n.* To ward off thrusts or blows ;
PÄRSE, *v. a.* To resolve by grammatical rules.
PÄR-SĬ-MŌ'NĬ-OŬS, *a.* Covetous ; frugal ; sparing.
PÄR-SĬ-MŌ'NĬ-OŬS-LY, *ad.* Covetously ; sparingly.
PÄR-SĬ-MŌ'NĬ-OUS-NĚSS, *n.* A disposition to save.
PÄR'SĬ-MQ-NY, *n.* Covetousness ; niggardliness.
PÄRS'LEY (pärs'lę), *n.* A species of garden plant.
PÄRS'NĬP, *n.* A garden vegetable.
PÄR'SON (pär'sn), *n.* A priest ; a clergyman.
PÄR'SON-AGE (pär'sn-aj), *n.* A parson's house, &c.
PÄRT, *n.* A portion ; a member ; a division ; share ; concern ; side.—*pl.* Faculties :—regions. [rate.
PÄRT, *v. a.* & *n.* To divide ; to share ; to sepa-
PAR-TĀKE', *v. n.* & *a.* [*imp. t.* partook ; *pp.* partaken.] To take part in ; to participate.
PÄR-TERRE' (pär-târ'), *n.* [Fr.] A flower-garden.
PÄR'TIAL (pär'shal), *a.* Biassed to one party ; not impartial :—not total ; not general. [bias.
PÄR-TĬ-ĂL'Ĭ-TY (pär-she-ăl'ę-tę), *n.* An undue
PÄR'TIAL-LY, *ad.* With partiality :—in part.
PÄR-TĬ-BĬL'Ĭ-TY, *n.* Divisibility ; separability.
PÄR'TĬ-BLE, *a.* Divisible ; separable.
PAR-TĬℂ'Ĭ-PA-BLE, *a.* That may be participated.
PAR-TĬℂ'Ĭ-PĂNT, *a.* Sharing ; having part.
PAR-TĬℂ'Ĭ-PĂNT, } *n.* One who participates ;
PAR-TĬℂ'Ĭ-PĀ-TOR, } a partaker. [share.
PAR-TĬℂ'Ĭ-PĀTE, *v. n.* & *a.* To partake ; to have
PÄR-TĬℂ-Ĭ-PĀ'TION, *n.* Act of sharing ; division.
PÄR-TĬ-CĬP'Ĭ-AL, *a.* Of the nature of a participle.
PÄR-TĬ-CĬP'Ĭ-AL-LY, *ad.* In manner of a participle.
PÄR'TĬ-CĬ-PLE, *n.* One of the parts of speech.
PÄR'TĬ-CLE, *n.* A minute part ; an atom ; a jot ; a mote :—a word unvaried. [odd.
PAR-TĬC'U-LAR, *a.* Not general ; individual ;
PAR-TĬC'U-LAR, *n.* A single instance or point.
PAR-TĬC-U-LĂR'Ĭ-TY, *n.* Something particular.

PAR-TĬC′Ṳ-LАR-ĪZE, *v. a.* To mention distinctly.
PAR-TĬC′Ṳ-LАR-LY, *ad.* Distinctly; singly.
PÄRT′ING, *n.* A division; separation.
PÄR′TĪ-ŞĂN, *n.* An adherent to a party :—a pike.
PAR-TĬ′′TIǪN (par-tĭsh′ụn), *n.* A division; a part.
PAR-TĬ′′TIǪN, *v. a.* To divide into distinct parts.
PÄR′TĪ-TĬVE, *a.* (*Gram.*) Noting a part; distribu-
PÄRT′LY, *ad.* In some measure; in part. [tive.
PÄRT′NER, *n.* A partaker; a sharer; an associate.
PÄRT′NER-SHĬP, *n.* A joint interest or property.
PAR-TOOK′ (par-tûk′), *imp. t.* from *partake.*
PÄR′TRĬDǴE, *n.* A bird of game.
PAR-TŪ′RĬ-ĚNT, *a.* Bringing forth, or about to
    bring forth, young. [forth.
PÄR-TṲ-RĬ′′TIǪN (pär-tṳ-rĭsh′ụn), *n.* A bringing
PÄR′TY, *n.* A number of persons confederated; a
    faction; cause; a set :—one of two litigants.
PÄR′TY-CŎL′ǪRED, *a.* Having different colors.
PÄR′TY-MĂN, *n.* A man zealous for a party.
PÄR′TY-WÂLL, *n.* A wall separating two houses.
PĂS′ℂHĄL (päs′kạl), *a.* Relating to the passover.
PĄ-SHÂ′, *n.* A Turkish governor. See PACHA.
PĂS-QUĬN-ĀDE′, PĂS′QUĬN, *n.* A lampoon.
PĂS-QUĬN-ĀDE′, *v. a.* To lampoon.
PĂSS, *v. n.* To go; to proceed; to vanish; to
    occur; to be current; to be enacted.
PĂSS, *v. a.* To go beyond :—to spend :—to omit :
    —to enact :—to utter; to deliver :—to palm off.
PĂSS, *n.* A passage; license to go; push; state.
PĂSS′Ą-BLE, *a.* That may be passed; tolerable.
PĂSS′Ą-BLY, *ad.* Tolerably; moderately.
PĂS′SĄǴE, *n.* Act of passing; journey; road;
    way; occurrence; incident; part of a book.
PĂS′SEN-ǴER, *n.* A traveller; a wayfarer.
PĂSS′ER, *n.* One who passes; a passenger.
PĂS-SĪ-BĬL′Ī-TY, *n.* The quality of suffering.
PĂS′SĪ-BLE, *a.* That may feel or suffer.
PĂSS′ING, *p. a.* Surpassing.—*ad.* Exceedingly.
PĂSS′ING-BĔLL, *n.* The death-bell for a person.
PĂS′SIǪN (päsh′ụn), *n.* Anger; ardor; suffering.
PĂS′SIǪN-ĄTE (päsh′ụn-ạt), *a.* Moved by pas-
    sion; irascible; angry; hasty. [sion.
PĂS′SIǪN-ĄTE-LY (päsh′ụn-ạt-le), *ad.* With pas-
PĂS′SIǪN-ĄTE-NĔSS, *n.* Vehemence of mind.
PĂS′SIǪN-LĔSS, *a.* Cool; undisturbed; calm.
PĂS′SIǪN-WĔĒK, *n.* The week before Easter.
PĂS′SĪVE, *a.* Unresisting; suffering; not active.
PĂS′SĪVE-LY, *ad.* In a passive manner; inactive-
PĂS′SĪVE-NĔSS, *n.* Passibility; patience. [ly.
PĂSS′Ō-VER, *n.* A solemn festival of the Jews.
PĂSS′PŌRT, *n.* A permission of passage.
PĂST, *p. a.* from *pass.* Not present; gone by.
PĂST, *n.* The time gone by; past time.
PĂST, *prep.* Beyond or above; as, *past* age.
PĀSTE, *n.* A viscous, tenacious mixture; cement.
PĀSTE, *v. a.* To cement or fasten with paste.
PĀSTE′BŌARD (päst′bŏrd), *n.* A thick, stiff paper.
PĂS′TERN, *n.* The lowest part of a horse's leg.
PĂS′TĬL, *n.* [Fr. *pastille.*] A roll of paste for
    crayons or for fumigation :—a lozenge.
PĂS′TĪME, *n.* Sport; amusement; diversion.
PĂS′TǪR, *n.* A shepherd :—a clergyman.
PĂS′TǪ-RĄL, *a.* Rural; relating to a pastor.
PĂS′TǪ-RĄL, *n.* A rural poem; an idyl; a bucolic.
PĂS′TǪR-SHĬP, *n.* The office or rank of a pastor.
PĂS′TRY, *n.* Pies or baked paste. [pies, &c.
PĂS′TRY-COOK (päs′trẹ-kûk), *n.* One who makes
PĂST′ỤR-Ą-BLE (päst′ yụr-ạ-bl), *a.* Fit for pasture.

PĂST′ỤR-ĄǴE, *n.* Feed for cattle; grazing lands.
PĂST′ỤRE, *n.* Land on which cattle feed.
PĂST′ỤRE (päst′yụr), *v. a. & n.* To feed on grass.
PĂS′TY *or* PĀS′TY, *n.* A pie of meat without a
PĂT, *a.* Fit; convenient.—*ad.* Fitly. [dish.
PĂT, *v. a.* To strike lightly.—*n.* A light blow.
PĂTCH, *n.* A piece; a small spot; a parcel.
PĂTCH, *v. a.* To put patches on; to mend
PĂTCH′ER-Y, *n.* Botchery; bungling work.
PĂTCH′WORK (pätch′würk), *n.* Work composed
PĀTE, *n.* The head. [of pieces.
PĂT-Ē-FĂC′TIǪN, *n.* Act of opening; a declara-
    tion; revelation.
PĄ-TĔL′LĄ, *n.* Knee-pan :—a species of mollusk.
‖PĂT′ENT *or* PĀ′TENT, *a.* Open; public.
‖PĂT′ENT, *n.* An exclusive right or privilege.
PĂT-EN-TĒĒ′, *n.* One who has a patent.
PĄ-TĔR′NĄL, *a.* Fatherly; kind; hereditary.
PĄ-TĔR′NĪ-TY, *n.* The relation of a father.
PĂ′TER-NŎS′TER, *n.* [L.] The Lord's prayer.
PĂTH, *n.*; *pl.* PĂTHŞ. A way; a road; a track.
PĂTH, *v. a.* To go over; to make way for.
PĄ-THĔT′IC, ⎫ *a.* Affecting the passions;
PĄ-THĔT′Ī-CĄL, ⎭ tender; touching; moving.
PĄ-THĔT′Ī-CĄL-LY, *ad.* In an affecting manner.
PĄ-THĔT′Ī-CĄL-NĔSS, *n.* The being pathetic.
PĂTH′LESS, *a.* Untrodden; having no path.
PĂTH-Ǫ-LŎǴ′Ī-CĄL, *a.* Relating to pathology.
PĄ-THŎL′Ǫ-ǴY, *n.* That part of medicine which
    relates to diseases, their causes, nature, &c.
PĀ′THŎS, *n.* [Gr.] Passion; vehemence; warmth.
PĂTH′WĀY, *n.* A road; a narrow foot-way.
PĀ′TIENCE (pā′shens), *n.* A suffering without
    complaint; calm endurance; perseverance.
PĀ′TIENT (pā′shent), *a.* Calm; not hasty; dili-
PĀ′TIENT (pā′shent), *n.* A sick person. [gent.
PĀ′TIENT-LY (pā′shent-le), *ad.* With patience.
PĀ′TRĪ-ÄRℂH, *n.* A head of a family or church.
PĀ-TRĪ-ÄRℂH′ĄL, *a.* Belonging to patriarchs.
PĀ-TRĪ-ÄRℂH′ĀTE, ⎫ *n.* The office, rank, or
PĀ′TRĪ-ÄRℂH-SHĬP, ⎭ jurisdiction of a patri-
    arch; patriarchy. [arch.
PĀ′TRĪ-ÄRℂH-Y, *n.* The jurisdiction of a patri-
PĄ-TRĬ′′CIĄN (pạ-trĭsh′ạn), *a.* Noble; not plebe-
PĄ-TRĬ′′CIĄN (pạ-trĭsh′ạn), *n.* A nobleman. [ian.
PĂT-RĪ-MŌ′NĪ-ĄL, *a.* Possessed by inheritance.
PĂT-RĪ-MŌ′NĪ-ĄL-LY, *ad.* By inheritance.
PĂT′RĪ-MǪ-NY, *n.* A patrimonial, paternal, or
    hereditary estate :—a church-estate.
‖PĀ′TRĪ-ǪT, *n.* A lover of his country.
‖PĀ-TRĪ-ŎT′IC *or* PĂT-RĪ-ŎT′IC, *a.* Relating
    to, or actuated by, patriotism.
‖PĀ′TRĪ-ǪT-ĬŞM, *n.* Love of one's country.
PĄ-TRŌL′, *n.* A guard; a night watch; a round.
PĄ-TRŌL′, *v. n.* To go the rounds in a camp, &c.
PĀ′TRǪN, *n.* A supporter; a guardian; protector.
PĂT′RǪN-ĄǴE, *n.* Support; protection; favor.
PĂT′RǪ-NĄL, *a.* Protecting; supporting; guard-
PĀ′TRǪN-ĔSS, *n.* A female patron. [ing.
PĂT′RǪN-ĪZE, *v. a.* To protect; to support; to
    defend; to encourage. [porter.
PĂT′RǪN-ĪZ-ER, *n.* One who patronizes; a sup-
PĀ′TRǪN-LĔSS, *a.* Without a patron.
PĂT-RǪ-NȲM′IC, *n.* A name from a father, &c.
PĂT′TEN, *n.* A shoe of wood with an iron ring.
PĂT′TER, *v. n.* To make a noise like hail, &c.
PĂT′TERN, *n.* An archetype; exemplar; speci-
PĂT′TY, *n.* A pasty; as, a veal-*patty.* [men.

PĂT′TY-PĂN, *n.* A pan to bake patties in.
PÂU′CĮ-TY, *n.* Smallness of number or quantity.
PÄUNCH *or* PÂUNCH, *n.* The belly.
PÂU′PĘR, *n.* A poor person who receives alms.
PÂU′PĘR-ĬSM, *n.* The state of poverty.
PÂUŞE, *n.* A stop; suspense; doubt; break.
PÂUŞE, *v. n.* To wait; to stop; to deliberate.
PĀVE, *v. a.* To lay with stone, brick, &c.
PĀVE′MĘNT, *n.* A floor of stone, brick, &c.
PĀV′ĘR, PĀV′IĘR (pāv′yęr), *n.* One who paves.
PĄ-VĬL′IǪN (pą-vĭl′yun), *n.* A tent; a house.
PÂW, *n.* The foot of a beast :—the hand.
PÂW, *v. n.* To draw the foot along the ground.
PÂW, *v. a.* To handle roughly; to fawn.
PÂWN, *n.* Something given as security; pledge.
PÂWN, *v. a.* To pledge; to give in pledge.
PÂWN′BRŌ-KĘR, *n.* One who lends money on
PÂW-NĔĒ′, *n.* The receiver of a pawn. [pawns.
PĀY (pā), *v. a.* [*imp. t. & pp.* paid.] To dis-
charge, as a debt; to reward.—*v. n.* To suffer.
PĀY (pā), *n.* Wages; hire; money for service.
PĀY′Ą-BLE, *a.* Due; that is to be paid.
PĀY′DĀY (pā′dā), *n.* The day for payment.
PĀY-ĒĒ′, *n.* One to whom money is due.
PĀY′MĂS-TĘR, *n.* One who is to pay.
PĀY′MĘNT, *n.* Act of paying; money paid.
PĒA (pē), *n.; pl.* PĒAŞ, *or* PĒAŞE. A plant and
its fruit; a kind of pulse.
PĒACE (pēs), *n.* A respite from war; quiet; rest.
PĒACE (pēs), *interj.* Commanding silence.
PĒACE′Ą-BLE, *a.* Free from war; quiet; mild.
PĒACE′Ą-BLE-NĔSS, *n.* Quietness; tranquillity.
PĒACE′Ą-BLY, *ad.* Without war or tumult.
PĒACE′BREĂK-ĘR, *n.* A disturber of the peace.
PĒACE′FÛL, *a.* Quiet; pacific; mild; still.
PĒACE′FÛL-LY, *ad.* Without war; quietly.
PĒACE′FÛL-NĔSS, *n.* Quiet; freedom from war.
PĒACE′MĀ-KĘR, *n.* A promoter of peace.
PĒACE′-ŎF′FĘR-ĬNG, *n.* An offering to procure
peace.   [peace.
PĒACE′-ŎF′FĮ-CĘR, *n.* An officer to keep the
PĒACH (pēch), *n.* A kind of tree and its fruit.
PĒACH′-CŎL-ǪRED (pēch′kŭl-lęrd), *a.* Of a
color like a peach-blossom; of a rich pink color.
PĒA′CHĬCK (pē′chĭk), *n.* The chick of a peacock.
PĒA′CŎCK (pē′kŏk), *n.* A beautiful fowl.
PĒA′HĔN, *n.* The female of the peacock.
PĒA′-JĂCK-ĘT, *n.* A seaman's loose jacket.
PĒAK, *n.* Top of a hill or mountain :—a point.
PĒAL, *n.* A loud sound, as of bells, thunder, &c.
PĒAL, *v. n.* To play loud.—*v. a.* To assail.
PEÀR (pàr), *n.* A fruit of many varieties.
PĒARL (pĕrl), *n.* A precious substance; a film.
PĒARL′ĂSH, *n.* Purified potash.
PĒARLED (pĕrld), *a.* Adorned or set with pearls.
PĒARL′Y (pĕrl′ę), *a.* Abounding with pearls.
PEÀR-MĀIN′, *n.* A variety of the apple.
PEÀR′-TRĔĒ (pàr′trē), *n.* A tree that bears pears.
PĒAŞ′ĄNT (pĕz′ąnt), *n.* A laboring man; a rustic.
PĒAŞ′ĄNT-RY (pĕz′ąnt-rę), *n.* Peasants; rustics.
PĒAŞ′CŎD *or* PĒAS′CŎD, *n.* A pea-shell; a pea-
PĒAŞE (pēz), *n. pl.* Peas collectively.   [pod.
PĒA′-SHĔLL, *n.* The husk that contains peas.
PĒAT (pēt), *n.* A species of turf used for fire.
PĔB′BLE, *or* PĔB′BLE-STŌNE, *n.* A small stone.
PĔB′BLED (pĕb′bld), *a.* Abounding with pebbles.
PĔB′BLY, *a.* Full of, or resembling, pebbles.
PĘ-CĂN′, *n.* An American tree and its nut.

PĔC-CĄ-BĬL′Į-TY, *n.* State of being subject to
PĔC′CĄ-BLE, *a.* Liable to sin.   [sin.
PĔC-CĄ-DĬL′LŌ, *n.; pl.* PĔC-CĄ-DĬL′LŌEŞ. A
petty fault; a slight crime.
PĔC′CĄN-CY, *n.* A bad quality; an offence.
PĔC′CĄNT, *a.* Guilty; criminal; corrupt; bad.
PĔCK, *n.* The fourth part of a bushel.
PĔCK, *v. a.* To strike with the beak, as a bird.
PĔCK′ĘR, *n.* One that pecks :—a bird; the wood-
PĔC′TĮ-NĄL, *n.* A fish.—*a.* Like a comb. [pecker.
PĔC′TĮ-NĀT-ĘD, *a.* Formed like a comb.
PĔC′TǪ-RĄL, *a.* Belonging to the breast.
PĔC′TǪ-RĄL, *n.* A medicine :—a breastplate.
PĔC′Ų-LĀTE, *v. n.* To rob or defraud the public.
PĔC-Ų-LĀ′TIǪN, *n.* The theft of public money.
PĔC′Ų-LĀ-TǪR, *n.* A robber of the public.
‖PĘ-CŪL′IĄR *or* PĘ-CŪ′LĮ-ĄR, *a.* Belonging to
one only; particular; singular; appropriate.
‖PĘ-CŪL′IĄR, *n.* The exclusive property.
‖PĘ-CŪL-Į-ĂR′Į-TY (pę-kŭl-yę-är′ę-tę), *n.* Some-
thing peculiar; particularity.
‖PĘ-CŪL′IĄR-ĪZE, *v. a.* To make peculiar.
‖PĘ-CŪL′IĄR-LY, *ad.* Particularly; singularly.
‖PĘ-CŪN′IĄ-RY, *a.* Relating to, or consisting of,
money.   [master.
PĔD-Ą-GŎǴ′Į-CĄL, *a.* Belonging to a school-
PĔD′Ą-GŌGUE (pĕd′dą-gŏg), *n.* A schoolmaster.
PĒ′DĄL, PĔD′ĄL, *a.* Belonging to a foot. [foot.
PĔD′ĄL, *n.* A key of an organ, &c., moved by the
PĔD′ĄNT, *n.* A vain pretender to learning.
PĘ-DĂN′TĮC,   } *a.* Full of pedantry; osten-
PĘ-DĂN′TĮ-CĄL, } tatious of learning.
PĘ-DĂN′TĮ-CĄL-LY, *ad.* With pedantry.
PĔD′ĄN-TRY, *n.* Vain ostentation of learning.
PĔD′DLE, *v. n. & a.* To sell as a pedler.
PĔD′ES-TĄL, *n.* The basis of a pillar or statue.
PĘ-DĔS′TRĮ-ĄN, *a.* Going on foot :—prosy.
PĘ-DĔS′TRĮ-ĄN, *n.* One who journeys on foot.
PĘ-DĔS′TRĮ-OŬS, *a.* Going on foot; pedestrian.
PĔD′Į-CLE, *n.* The footstalk of a flower.
PĔD′Į-GRĔĒ, *n.* Genealogy; lineage; descent.
PĔD′Į-MĔNT, *n.* (*Arch.*) A triangular ornament.
PĔD′LĘR, *n.* One who peddles; a travelling
trader ;—written also *peddler* and *pedlar.*
PĔD′LĘR-Y, *n.* The business, or the wares, of
PĒ-DǪ-BĂP′TĬSM, *n.* Infant baptism. [pedlers.
PĒ-DǪ-BĂP′TĬST, *n.* One that holds to infant
baptism.   [ment.
PĘ-DŎM′Ę-TĘR, *n.* A mathematical instru-
PĒEL, *v. a.* To decorticate; to flay; to plunder.
PĒEL, *n.* A rind :—a baker's shovel.
PĒEL′ĘR, *n.* One who peels; a plunderer.
PĒEP, *v. n.* To begin to appear; to look slyly.
PĒEP, *n.* The first appearance; a sly look.
PĒEP′ĘR, *n.* One that peeps; a young chicken.
PĒER, *n.* An equal; an associate; a nobleman.
PĒER′AǴE, *n.* The state, rank, or dignity of a
peer; body of peers.
PĒER′ĘSS, *n.* The lady of a peer; a noble lady.
PĒER′LĘSS, *a.* Unequalled; having no peer.
PĒER′LĘSS-LY, *ad.* Without an equal.
PĒER′LĘSS-NĔSS, *n.* Universal superiority. [ful.
PĒEV′ĬSH, *a.* Petulant; easily offended; fret-
PĒEV′ĬSH-LY, *ad.* Petulantly; fretfully.
PĒEV′ĬSH-NĔSS, *n.* Querulousness; fretfulness.
PĒG, *n.* A wooden pin.—*v. a.* To fasten with a
PĔLF, *n.* Money; riches: *in a bad sense.* [peg.
PĔL′Į-CĂN, *n.* A large bird :—chemical vessel.

PĘ-LÎSSE' (pę-lēs'), n. [Fr.] A kind of coat or
PĔL'LĘT, n. A little ball :—a bullet. [robe.
PĔL'LĮ-CLE, n. A thin skin :—a saline crust.
PĔLL-MĔLL', ad. Confusedly ; tumultuously.
PĔLLS, n. pl. Parchment rolls of receipts and
  disbursements.
PĘL-LŪ'CĮD, a. Clear; transparent; not opaque.
PĔL-LŲ-CĬD'Į-TY,) n. Transparency; translu-
PĘL-LŪ'CĮD-NĔSS,) cency.
PĔLT, v. a. To strike with something thrown.
PĔLT, n. A skin ; a hide :—a blow ; a stroke.
PĔLT'-MŎN-ĢĘR, n. A dealer in pelts or skins.
PĔL'TRY, n. Pelts or skins in general.
PĔL'VĮS, n. The lower part of the belly. [sure.
PĔN, n. An instrument of writing :—an enclo-
PĔN, v. a. [imp. t. & pp. penned.] To write.
PĔN, v. a. [imp. t. & pp. pent or penned.] To shut
  up ; to incage. [ment.
PĒ'NĄL, a. Denouncing or incurring punish-
PĔN'ĄL-TY, n. Punishment ; censure ; forfeiture.
PĔN'ĄNCE, n. An infliction suffered for sin.
PĔNCE, n. The plural of penny.
PĔN'CĮL, n. A tool for painting, drawing, &c.
PĔN'CĮL, v. a. To paint ; to draw ; to write.
PĔN'DĄNT, n. An earring; an ornament; a flag.
PĔN'DĘNCE, n. Slopeness; inclination.
PĔN'DĘN-CY, n. Suspense; delay of decision.
PĔN'DĘNT, a. Hanging ; projecting ; jutting
PĔND'ĮNG, a. Depending ; yet undecided. [over.
PĔN-DŲ-LŎS'Į-TY,) n. The state of hanging ;
PĔN'DŲ-LOŬS-NĔSS,) suspension. [ed.
PĔN'DŲ-LOŬS, a. Hanging ; pendent ; suspend-
PĔN'DŲ-LŬM, n. A suspended, vibrating body.
PĔN-Ę-TRĄ-BĬL'Į-TY, n. The being penetrable.
PĔN'Ę-TRĄ-BLE, a. That may be penetrated.
PĔN'Ę-TRĂN-CY, n. The power of penetrating.
PĔN'Ę-TRĂNT, a. Penetrating ; sharp ; subtile.
PĔN'Ę-TRĀTE, v. a. To pierce ; to perforate :—
  to discern ; to understand.
PĔN'Ę-TRĀTE, v. n. To make way; to pass.
PĔN-Ę-TRĀ'TĮON, n. The act of entering :—
  discernment ; sagacity. [cious.
PĔN'Ę-TRĂ-TĮVE, a. Piercing ; acute ; saga-
PĔN'GUĮN (-gwĭn), n. A large bird :—a fruit.
PEN-ĬN'SŲ-LĄ, n. Land almost surrounded by
PĔN'Į-TĔNCE, n. Sorrow; contrition. [water.
PĔN'Į-TĔNT, a. Repentant; contrite for sin.
PĔN'Į-TĔNT, n. One contrite or sorrowful for
PĔN-Į-TĔN'TIĄL, a. Expressing penitence. [sin.
PĔN-Į-TĔN'TĮ-Ą-RY (pĕn-ę-tĕn'shę-ą-rę), n. One
  who does penance :—a house of correction.
PĔN-Į-TĔN'TĮ-Ą-RY, a. Relating to penance.
PĔN'Į-TĔNT-LY, ad. With repentance or sorrow.
PĔN'KNĪFE (pĕn'nĭf), n. A knife to cut pens.
PĔN'MĄN, n. One who writes :—an author.
PĔN'MĄN-SHĬP, n. The act or art of writing.
PĔN'NĄNT, n. A small flag, ensign, or colors.
PĔN'NĄTE, PĔN'NĀT-ĘD, a. Winged.
PĔN'NĮ-LĔSS, a. Moneyless ; poor ; destitute.
PĔN'NŎN, n. A flag; a banner; a streamer.
PĔN'NY, n.; pl. PĔNCE. One 12th of a shilling.
PĔN-NY-RÖŸ'AL, n. A well-known herb.
PĔN'NY-WEIGHT (pĕn'nę-wāt), n. A weight
  containing twenty-four grains troy. [gardly.
PĔN'NY-WĪSE, a. Saving small sums ; nig-
PĔN'NY-WORTH, n. A good bargain :—small
PĔN'SĮLE, a. Hanging ; suspended. [quantity.
PĔN'SĮON (pĕn'shŭn), n. A yearly allowance.

PĔN'SĮON, v. a. To support by an allowance.
PĔN'SĮON-Ą-RY, a. Maintained by a pension.
PĔN'SĮON-ĘR, n. One who receives a pension.
PĔN'SĮVE, a. Sorrowfully thoughtful ; serious.
PĔN'SĮVE-LY, ad. With melancholy ; seriously.
PĔN'SĮVE-NĔSS, n. Melancholy ; sorrowfulness.
PĔN'STŎCK, n. A sort of trough ; a sluice.
PĔNT, imp. t. & pp. from pen. Shut up.
PĔN-TĄ-CĂP'SŲ-LĄR, a. Having five capsules.
PĔN'TĄ-ℂHÖRD, n. A musical instrument with
  five strings.
PĔN'TĄ-GŎN, n. A figure with five angles.
PĘN-TĂG'Ǫ-NĄL, a. Having five angles.
PĔN'TĄ-GRĂPH, n. See PANTOGRAPH.
PĘN-TĂM'Ę-TĘR, n. A verse of five feet.
PĘN-TĂN'GŲ-LĄR, a. Having five angles.
PĔN-TĄ-PĔT'Ą-LOŬS, a. Having five petals.
PĔN'TĄ-STȲLE, n. A portico or building with
  five columns in front. [Moses.
PĔN'TĄ-TEŬℂH (-tūk), n. The five books of
PĔN'TĘ-CŎST, n. A feast among the Jews.
PĔN-TĘ-CŎST'ĄL, a. Belonging to pentecost.
PĔNT'HOŬSE, n. A sloping shed ; a lean-to.
PĔN'TĪLE, n. A tile with a hollow surface.
PĒ'NŬLT,) n. The last syllable of a word
PĘ-NŬL'TĮ-MĄ,) but one. [a word but one.
PĘ-NŬL'TĮ-MĀTE, a. Noting the last syllable of
PĘ-NŬM'BRĄ, n. An imperfect shadow.
PĘ-NŪ'RĮ-OŬS, a. Niggardly ; not liberal ; scant.
PĘ-NŪ'RĮ-OŬS-LY, ad. Sparingly ; parsimoni-
  ously. [mony.
PĘ-NŪ'RĮ-OŬS-NĔSS, n. Niggardliness ; parsi-
PĔN'Ų-RY, n. Extreme poverty ; indigence.
PĒ'Ǫ-NY, n. A plant with showy flowers.
PĒO'PLE (pē'pl), n. A nation ; body of persons.
PĒO'PLE, v. a. To stock with inhabitants.
PĔP'PĘR, n. An aromatic, pungent spice.
PĔP'PĘR, v. a. To sprinkle with pepper ; to beat.
PĔP'PĘR-BŎX, n. A box for holding pepper.
PĔP'PĘR-CÖRN, n. Any thing of trifling value.
PĔP'PĘR-MĬNT, n. An aromatic, pungent plant.
PĔP'TĮC, a. Promoting digestion.
PĘR-ĄD-VĔNT'ŲRE (-yŭr), ad. Perhaps. [survey.
PĘR-ĂM'BŲ-LĀTE, v. a. To walk through ; to
PĘR-ĂM-BŲ-LĀ'TĮON, n. A travelling survey.
PĘR-ĂM'BŲ-LĀ-TǪR, n. A measuring wheel.
PER-CĒIV'Ą-BLE (pęr-sēv'ą-bl), a. Perceptible.
PĘR-CĒIV'Ą-BLY (-sēv'ą-blę), ad. Perceptibly.
PĘR-CĒIVE' (pęr-sēv'), v. a. To see ; to know.
PĘR-CĔP-TĮ-BĬL'Į-TY, n. The being perceptible.
PĘR-CĔP'TĮ-BLE, a. That may be perceived.
PĘR-CĔP'TĮ-BLY, ad. In a perceptible manner.
PĘR-CĔP'TĮON, n. The power of perceiving ;
  discernment ; understanding ; idea. [ing.
PĘR-CĔP'TĮVE, a. Able to perceive ; perceiv-
PĔRCH, n. A measure of 5½ yards ; a pole :—
  something on which birds roost ; a small fish.
PĔRCH, v. a. & n. To roost or place on a perch.
PĘR-CHĂNCE', ad. Perhaps ; peradventure.
PĘR-CĬP'Į-ĔNT, a. Perceiving ; perceptive.
PĘR-CĬP'Į-ĔNT, n. One who is able to perceive.
PĔR'CǪ-LĀTE, v. To strain through ; to filter.
PĘR-CǪ-LĀ'TĮON, n. The act of percolating or
  straining ; filtration. [stroke.
PĘR-CŬS'SĮON (pęr-kŭsh'ŭn), n. A striking ;
PĘR-CŬS'SĮON-CĂP, n. A detonating copper
  cap, used with a percussion-lock.
PĘR-DĬ''TĮON, n. Destruction ; ruin ; death.

PĔR'E-GRĬ-NĀTE,*v.n.* To travel ; to live abroad.
PĔR-E-GRĬ-NĀ'TIQN, *n.* Travel ; foreign abode.
PĔR'E-GRĪNE, *a.* Foreign ; not native.   [ly.
PĔR'EMP-TQ-RĬ-LY, *ad.* Absolutely ; positive-
PĔR'EMP-TQ-RĬ-NĔSS,*n.* Positiveness ; decision.
PĔR'EMP-TQ-RY,*a.* Absolute ; decisive.
PER-ĔN'NĬ-AL, *a.* Lasting through the year :—
PER-ĔN'NĬ-AL, *n.* A durable plant. [perpetual.
PER-ĔN'NĬ-TY,*n.* Quality of lasting ; perpetuity.
PĔR'FECT, *a.* Possessing perfection ; faultless.
PĔR'FECT, *v. a.* To make perfect ; to finish.
PĔR'FECT-ER, *n.* One that makes perfect.
PER-FĔCT-Ĭ-BĬL'Ĭ-TY, *n.* Capacity of becoming
    perfect.   [fect.
PER-FĔCT'Ĭ-BLE, *a.* That may be made per-
PER-FĔC'TIQN, *n.* The state of being perfect.
PER-FĔC'TIQN-ĬST, *n.* One who holds to the
    possibility of attaining perfection.
PER-FĔC'TĬVE,*a.* Conducing to perfection. [ly.
PĔR'FECT-LY, *ad.* Totally ; completely ; exact-
PĔR'FECT-NĔSS, *n.* Completeness ; perfection.
‖PER-FĬD'Ĭ-OŬS *or* PER-FĬD'IOŲS, *a.* Guilty or
    partaking of perfidy ; treacherous.
‖PER-FĬD'Ĭ-OŬS-LY, *ad.* By breach of faith.
‖PER-FĬD'Ĭ-OŲS-NĔSS, *n.* The being perfidious.
PĔR'FĬ-DY, *n.* Treachery ; breach of faith.
PER-FLĀ'TIQN,*n.* The act of blowing through.
PĔR'FQ-RĀTE, *v. a.* To pierce through ; to bore.
PĔR-FQ-RĀ'TIQN, *n.* The act of piercing ; a hole.
PĔR'FQ-RĀ-TQR, *n.* An instrument for boring.
PER-FŌRCE', *ad.* By violence ; violently.
PER-FŌRM', *v. a.* To execute ; to do ; to ac-
    complish ; to effect ; to discharge.
PER-FŌRM'A-BLE, *a.* That may be done. [tion.
PER-FŌRM'ANCE, *n.* Execution ; a work ; an ac-
PER-FŌRM'ER, *n.* One that performs ; an actor.
PĔR'FŪME *or* PER-FŪME', *n.* Sweet odor ; fra-
    grance.
PER-FŪME', *v. a.* To impregnate with odor.
PER-FŪM'ER, *n.* One who deals in perfumes.
PER-FŪM'ER-Y, *n.* Perfumes in general.   [ent.
PER-FŬNC'TQ-RY, *a.* Slight ; careless ; indiffer-
PER-FŪSE', *v. a.* To tincture ; to overspread.
PER-HĂPS', *ad.* Peradventure ; it may be.
PĔR'Ĭ-ĂNTH, *n.* The leaves of a flower. [heart.
PĔR-Ĭ CĂR'DĬ-ŬM, *n.* A membrane enclosing the
PĔR'Ĭ-CĂRP, *n.* The seed-vessel of a plant.
PĔR-Ĭ-CRĀ'NĬ-ŬM, *n.* A membrane covering the
    skull.   [et wherein it is nearest the earth.
PĔR'Ĭ-ĠĒE, *n.* That point in the orbit of a plan-
PĔR-Ĭ-HĒL'Ĭ-QN, *n.* That point of a planet's
    orbit wherein it is nearest the sun.   [tion.
PĔR'ĬL, *n.* Danger ; hazard ; risk ; denuncia-
PĔR'ĬL-OŬS, *a.* Dangerous ; hazardous.
PĔR'ĬL-OŬS-LY,*ad.* Dangerously. [plane figure.
PE-RĬM'E-TER, *n.* The line which bounds a
PĒ'RĬ-QD, *n.* A circuit ; epoch ; series of years ;
    full stop ; end :—complete sentence. [periods.
PĒ-RĬ-ŎD'Ĭ-CAL, *a.* Stated ; regular ; relating to
PĒ-RĬ-ŎD'Ĭ-CAL-LY, *ad.* At stated periods.
PĔR'Ĭ-PA-TĔT'ĬC, *n.* A follower of Aristotle.
PĔR-Ĭ-PA-TĔT'ĬC, *a.* Belonging to the Peripa-
    tetics.   [&c.
PE-RĬPH'E-RY, *n.* Circumference of a circle,
PĔR'Ĭ-PHRĀSE, *v. a.* To express by circumlocu-
PE-RĬPH'RA-SĬS, *n.* A circumlocution.   [tion.
PĔR-Ĭ-PHRĂS'TĬ-CAL, *a.* Using many words.
PĔR-Ĭ-PHRĂS'TĬ-CAL-LY, *ad.* By periphrasis.

PĔR-Ĭ-PLEŬ-MŌ'NĬ-A, ⎰ *n.* Inflammation of the
PĔR-ĬP-NEŪ'MQ-NY, ⎱ lungs.
PĔR'ĬSH, *v. n.* To die ; to be destroyed ; to decay.
PĔR'ĬSH-A-BLE, *a.* Liable to perish or decay.
PĔR-Ĭ-STĂL'TĬC, *a.* Wormlike ; spiral.
PĔR'Ĭ-STȲLE, *n.* A circular range of pillars.
PĔR'Ĭ-WĬG, *n.* A wig ; a covering for the head.
PĔR'Ĭ-WĬG, *v. a.* To dress in false hair.
PĔR'Ĭ-WĬN-KLE, *n.* A small shell-fish.
PĔR'JŲRE, *v. a.* To forswear ; to swear falsely.
PĔR'JŲ-RER, *n.* One who swears falsely.
PĔR'JŲ-RY, *n.* The crime of swearing falsely.
PĔRK, *v. n. & a.* To hold up the head ; to dress.
PĔR'MA-NĔNCE, ⎰ *n.* State of being permanent ;
PĔR'MA-NĔN-CY, ⎱ durability ; duration.
PĔR'MA-NĔNT, *a.* Durable ; lasting ; not decay-
PĔR'MA-NĔNT-LY, *ad.* Durably ; lastingly. [ing.
PĔR-ME-A-BĬL'Ĭ-TY, *n.* The being permeable.
PĔR'ME-A-BLE, *a.* That may be passed through.
PER-MĬS'SĬ-BLE, *a.* That may be permitted.
PER-MĬS'SIQN (-mĭsh'ŭn), *n.* Allowance ; leave.
PER-MĬS'SĬVE, *a.* Granting liberty ; allowing.
PER-MĬS'SĬVE-LY, *ad.* By bare allowance.
PER-MĬT', *v. a.* To allow ; to suffer ; to give up.
PĔR'MĬT *or* PER-MĬT', *n.* License ; permission.
PER-MĬT'TANCE, *n.* Allowance ; permission.
PĔR-MŲ-TĀ'TIQN, *n.* Exchange ; change.
PER-NĬ''CIOŲS (-nĭsh'ŭs), *a.* Very mischievous.
PER-NĬ''CIOŲS-LY (-nĭsh'ŭs-le), *ad.* Ruinously.
PER-NĬ''CIOŲS-NĔSS, *n.* The being pernicious.
PĔR-Q-RĀ'TIQN, *n.* The conclusion of an ora-
PER-PĔND', *v. a.* To consider attentively. [tion.
PĔR-PEN-DĬC'Ų-LAR, *a.* Being at right angles.
PĔR-PEN-DĬC'Ų-LAR, *n.* A line crossing the
    plane of the horizon at right angles ; a plumb-
    line.   [pendicular.
PĔR-PEN-DĬC-Ų-LĂR'Ĭ-TY, *n.* The being per-
PĔR-PEN-DĬC'Ų-LAR-LY, *ad.* At right angles.
PĔR'PE-TRĀTE, *v. a.* To do or commit, as a
    crime.   [crime.
PĔR-PE-TRĀ'TIQN, *n.* The commission of a
‖PER-PĔT'Ų-AL (-yŲ-), *a.* Never ceasing. [ally.
‖PER-PĔT'Ų-AL-LY, *ad.* Constantly ; continu-
‖PER-PĔT'Ų-ĀTE, *v. a.* To make perpetual.
‖PER-PĔT-Ų-Ā'TIQN,*n.* Incessant continuance.
PĔR-PE-TŪ'Ĭ-TY, *n.* Duration to all futurity.
PER-PLĔX', *v. a.* To make anxious ; to embar-
    rass ; to distract ; to distress.   [lution.
PER-PLĔX'ED-LY, *ad.* Intricately ; with invo-
PER-PLĔX'ED-NĔSS, *n.* Anxiety ; difficulty.
PER-PLĔX'Ĭ-TY, *n.* Anxiety ; distraction of
    mind ; disturbance ; confusion.
PĔR'QUĬ-SĬTE, *n.* A fee or gift of office, &c.
PĔR'RY, *n.* A drink made of pears.   [malice.
PĔR'SE-CŪTE, *v. a.* To harass ; to pursue with
PĔR-SE-CŪ'TIQN, *n.* The act of persecuting.
PĔR'SE-CŪ-TQR, *n.* One who persecutes.
PĔR-SE-VĒR'ANCE, *n.* Persistence ; constancy.
PĔR-SE-VĒRE', *v. n.* To persist ; to be stead-
PER-SĬM'MQN, *n.* A tree and its fruit.   [fast.
PER-SĬST', *v. n.* To persevere ; to continue firm.
PER-SĬST'ENCE, *n.* Perseverance ; constancy.
PĔR'SON (për'sn), *n.* An individual ; a human
    being ; one :—the body ; exterior appearance.
PĔR'SQN-A-BLE, *a.* Handsome ; graceful.
PĔR'SQN-AĠE, *n.* A person of distinction.
PĔR'SQN-AL, *a.* Relating to a person ; peculiar.
PĔR-SQN-ĂL'Ĭ-TY, *n.* Individuality ; reflection.

PĔR'SŎN-ĂL-LȲ, *ad.* In person ; in presence.
PĔR'SŎN-ĂL-TȲ, *n.* Personal property. [feit.
PĔR'SŎN-ĀTE, *v. a.* To represent ; to counter-
PĔR-SŎN-Ā'TIǪN, *n.* The act of personating.
PĔR'SǪN-Ā-TǪR, *n.* One who personates.
PĔR-SŎN-Į-FĮ-CĀ'TIǪN, *n.* (*Rhet.*) The change
 of things to persons ; prosopopœia. [a person.
PĘR-SŎN'Į-FȲ, *v. a.* To change from a thing to
PĘR-SPĔC'TĮVE, *n.* A prospect :—the art of rep-
 resenting things on a plane surface ; repre-
 sentation.
PĘR-SPĔC'TĮVE, *a.* Relating to vision ; optical.
PĘR-SPĔC'TĮVE-LȲ, *ad.* Optically.
PĔR-SPĮ-CĀ'CIOŲS (për-spę-kā'shųs), *a.* Sharp
 of sight ; quick-sighted ; discerning ; acute.
PĔR-SPĮ-CĀ'CIOŲS-NĔSS, *n.* Quickness of sight.
PĔR-SPĮ-CĂÇ'Į-TȲ, *n.* Quickness of sight.
PĔR-SPĮ-CŪ'Į-TȲ, *n.* Easiness to be understood.
PĘR-SPĬC'Ų-OŬS, *a.* Clear ; easily understood.
PĘR-SPĬC'Ų-OŬS-LȲ, *ad.* Clearly ; not obscurely.
PĘR-SPĬC'Ų-OŲS-NĔSS, *n.* Perspicuity.
PĘR-SPĪR'Ą-BLE, *a.* That may be perspired.
PĔR-SPĮ-RĀ'TIǪN, *n.* Excretion by the pores.
PĘR-SPĪ'RĄ-TĬVE, *a.* Performing perspiration.
PĘR-SPĪRE', *v. n. & a.* To emit by the pores.
PĘR-SUĀD'Ą-BLE (-swä'dą-bl), *a.* Persuasible.
PĘR-SUĀDE' (pęr-swād'), *v. a.* To bring to a
 particular opinion ; to influence by argument.
PĘR-SUĀ-SĮ-BĬL'Į-TȲ, *n.* The being persuasible.
PĘR-SUĀ'SĮ-BLE, *a.* That may be persuaded.
PĘR-SUĀ'SĮǪN (-swā'zhųn), *n.* The act or art of
 persuading :—opinion ; creed ; belief.
PĘR-SUĀ'SĮVE, *a.* Having power to persuade.
PĘR-SUĀ'SĮVE, *n.* Exhortation ; argument.
PĘR-SUĀ'SĮVĘ-LȲ, *ad.* In a persuasive manner.
PĘR-SUĀ'SĮVE-NĔSS, *n.* Persuasive quality ; ex-
PĔRT, *a.* Lively ; saucy ; impudent. [hortation.
PĘR-TĀIN', *v. n.* To belong ; to relate.
PĔR-TĮ-NĀ'CIOŲS (-tę-nā'shųs), *a.* Perversely
 resolute ; stubborn ; obstinate.
PĔR-TĮ-NĀ'CIOŲS-LȲ, *ad.* Obstinately.
PĔR-TĮ-NĂÇ'Į-TȲ, *n.* Obstinacy ; constancy.
PĔR'TĮ-NĔNCE, } *n.* Appositeness ; fitness ;
PĔR'TĮ-NĔN-CȲ, } propriety ; relevancy.
PĔR'TĮ-NĔNT, *a.* Apt to the purpose ; apposite ;
 appropriate ; relevant.
PĔR'TĮ-NĔNT-LȲ, *ad.* To the purpose.
PĔRT'LȲ, *ad.* Smartly ; saucily ; petulantly.
PĔRT'NĘSS, *n.* Smartness ; sauciness.
PER-TŬRB', *v. a.* To disquiet, disturb.
PĔR-TŲR-BĀ'TIǪN, *n.* Disquiet of mind ; disor-
PER-TŪ'ŞĮǪN (-tū'zhųn), *n.* Perforation. [der.
PĔR'ŬKE, *n.* A cap of false hair ; a periwig.
PĘ-RŬ'ŞĄL, *n.* The act of perusing or reading ;
 examination.   [ine.
PĘ-RŬSE', *v. a.* To read ; to observe ; to exam-
PĘR-VĀDE', *v. a.* To pass through ; to permeate.
PĘR-VĀ'ŞĮǪN (-zhųn), *n.* Act of pervading.
PĘR-VĔRSE', *a.* Obstinate ; ill-disposed.
PĘR-VĔRSE'LȲ, *ad.* Stubbornly ; vexatiously.
PĘR-VĔRSE'NĘSS, *n.* Obstinacy ; petulance.
PĘR-VĔR'SIǪN, *n.* The act of perverting.
PĘR-VĔR'SĮ-TȲ, *n.* Perverseness ; ill disposi-
 tion ; frowardness. [right.
PĘR-VĔRT', *v. a.* To distort ; to turn from the
PĔR'VĔRT, *n.* One who is perverted.
PĘR-VĔRT'ĘR, *n.* One who perverts or distorts.
PĘR-VĔRT'Į-BLE, *a.* That may be perverted.

PĔR'VĮ-OŬS, *a.* Admitting passage ; permeable.
PĔR'VĮ-OŲS-NĔSS, *n.* The quality of being per-
PĔST, *n.* A plague ; pestilence ; mischief. [vious.
PĔS'TĘR, *v. a.* To disturb ; to perplex ; to
 harass ; to annoy. [sons.
PĔST'HŌŨSE, *n.* A hospital for infected per-
PĘS-TĬF'ĘR-OŬS, *a.* Destructive ; pestilential.
PĔS'TĮ-LĔNCE, *n.* A contagious or infectious
 distemper ; plague ; a pest. [nant.
PĔS'TĮ-LĔNT, *a.* Producing plagues ; malig-
PĔS-TĮ-LĔN'TIĄL, *a.* Pestilent ; destructive.
PĔŚ-TĮ-LĔN'TIĄL-LȲ, *ad.* By or with pesti-
 lence.   [tively.
PĔS'TĮ-LĔNT-LȲ, *ad.* Mischievously ; destruc-
PĔS'TLE (pĕs'sl), *n.* A tool to beat in a mortar.
PĔT, *n.* Slight anger :—a favorite ; a fondling.
PĔT, *v. a.* To treat as a pet ; to fondle ; to in-
PĔT'ĄL *or* PĒ'TĄL, *n.* A flower-leaf. [dulge.
PĔT'ĄL-OŬS, *a.* Having petals. [mortar.
PĘ-TĂR', PĘ-TĂRD', *n.* A kind of bell-shaped
PĘ-TĒ'ÇHĮ-ĄL, *a.* Pestilentially spotted.
PĒ'TĘR-PĔNCE, *n.* A tax paid to the pope.[leaf.
PĔT'Į-ŌLE, *n.* A leaf-stock ; a foot-stock of a
PĔT'ĮT (pĕt'tę), *a.* [Fr.] Small ; little ; petty.
PĘ-TĬ''TIǪN (-tĭsh'ųn), *n.* A request ; entreaty:
PĘ-TĬ''TIǪN, *v. a.* To solicit ; to supplicate.
PĘ-TĬ''TIǪN-Ą-RȲ, *a.* Supplicatory ; petitioning.
PĘ-TĬ''TIǪN-ĘR, *n.* One who offers a petition.
PĒ'TRE (pē'tęr), *n.* Nitre ; saltpetre.
PĘ-TRĔS'CĘNCE, *n.* The act of becoming stone.
PĘ-TRĔS'CĘNT, *a.* Turning to stone ; petrify-
 ing ; hardening. [stone.
PĔT RĮ-FĂC'TIǪN, *n.* The act of turning to
PĔT-RĮ-FĂC'TĮVE, *a.* Able to form stone.[stone.
PĘ-TRĬF'ĮC, *a.* Having power to change to
PĔT'RĮ-FȲ, *v. a.* To change to stone ; to harden.
PĔT'RĮ-FȲ, *v. n.* To become stone. [rock oil.
PĒ'TRǪL, PĘ-TRŌ'LĘ-ŬM, *n.* A brown bitumen;
PĔT'RǪ-NĔL, *n.* A horseman's pistol.
PĔT'TĮ-CŌAT, *n.* A woman's under garment.
PĔT'TĮ-FŎG-ĠER, *n.* A petty, small-rate law-
 yer.   [ger.
PĔT'TĮ-FŎG-ĠER-Ȳ, *n.* Practice of a pettifog-
PĔT'TĮ-NĔSS, *n.* Smallness ; littleness.
PĔT'TĮSH, *a.* Fretful ; peevish ; testy.
PĔT'TĮSH-LȲ, *ad.* In a pet ; fretfully.
PĔT'TĮSH-NĔSS, *n.* Fretfulness ; peevishness.
PĔT'TĮ-TŌEŞ, *n. pl.* The toes or feet of a pig.
PĔT'TŌ, *n.* [It.] The breast :—*figuratively*, pri-
PĔT'TȲ, *a.* Small ; inconsiderable ; little. [vacy.
PĔT'Ų-LĄNCE, *n.* Peevishness ; fretfulness.
PĔT'Ų-LĄNT, *a.* Fretful ; saucy ; peevish ; fro-
PĔT'Ų-LĄNT-LȲ, *ad.* With petulance. [ward.
PEW (pū), *n.* A seat enclosed in a church.
PĒ'WĮT, *n.* A bird ; the lapwing.
PEW'TER (pū'tęr), *n.* A compound metal.
PEW'TĘR-ĘR, *n.* A smith who works in pew-
PHĀ'Ę-TON (fā'ę-tn), *n.* A sort of carriage. [ter.
PHĀ'LĄNX *or* PHĂL'ĄNX, *n.* A troop of men.
PHĂN'TĄŞM, PHĄN-TĂŞ'MĄ, *n.* A spectre ;
 vision.   [vision.
PHĂN'TǪM, *n.* A spectre ; an apparition ; a
PHĂR-Į-SĀ'ĮC, } *a.* Relating to the Pharisees ;
PHĂR-Į-SĀ'Į-CĄL, } externally religious ; ritu-
PHĂR-Į-SĀ'Į-CĄL-NĔSS, *n.* Pharisaical show.[al.
PHĂR'Į-SA-ĮŞM, *n.* The conduct of a Pharisee.
PHĂR-Į-SĒ'ĄN, *a.* Resembling the Pharisees.
PHĂR'Į-SĒE, *n.* One of a strict Jewish sect.

PHÄR-MĄ-ÇEŪ'TĮC, *a.* Relating to pharmacy.
PHÄR-MĄ-CŎL'Ǫ-ǴĬST, *n.* A writer upon drugs.
PHÄR-MĄ-CŎL'Ǫ-ĢY, *n.* The knowledge of drugs ; pharmacy. [pensatory for medicines.
PHÄR-MĄ-CǪ-PŒ'IĄ (fär-mą-kǫ-pē'yą), *n.* A dis-
PHÄR'MĄ-CY, *n.* The trade of an apothecary or druggist.
PHĀ'RǪS, *n.* A light-house ; a watch-tower.
PHĄ̈E (fāz), *n.* Appearance, as of a planet.
PHĔAŞ'ĄNT (fĕz'ąnt), *n.* A sort of fowl.
PHĒ'NĬX, PHŒ'NĬX, *n.* A bird which is supposed to rise again from its own ashes.
PHĘ-NŎM'Ę-NŎN, *n.* ; pl. PHĘ-NŎM'Ę-NĄ. Appearance ; any thing remarkable.
PHĪ'ĄL, *n.* A small bottle ; a vial.
PHĬL-ĄN-THRŎP'ĬC,) *a.* Loving mankind.
PHĬL-ĄN-THRŎP'Į-CĄL,) [kind.
PHĮ-LĂN'THRǪ-PĬST, *n.* One who loves man-
PHĮ-LĂN'THRǪ-PY, *n.* Love of mankind. [kilt.
PHĬL'Į-BĔG, *n.* A kind of short petticoat :—a
PHĮ-LĬP'PĮC, *n.* A discourse full of invective.
PHĮ-LŎL'Ǫ-ǴER,) *n.* One versed in philology.
PHĮ-LŎL'Ǫ-ǴĬST,)
PHĬL-Ǫ-LŎǴ'ĮC,) *a.* Relating to philology ;
PHĬL-Ǫ-LŎǴ'Į-CĄL,) grammatical.
PHĮ-LŎL'Ǫ-ǴĪZE, *v. n.* To make criticisms.
PHĮ-LŎL'Ǫ-ĢY, *n.* The critical knowledge of languages ; criticism ; grammatical learning.
PHĬL'Ǫ-MĂTH, *n.* A lover of learning. [gale.
PHĬL'Ǫ-MĔL, PHĬL-Ǫ-MĒ'LĄ, *n.* The nightin-
PHĮ-LŎS'Ǫ-PHĘR, *n.* A man versed in philosophy.
PHĬL-Ǫ-SŎPH'ĮC,) *a.* Relating to philoso-
PHĬL-Ǫ-SŎPH'Į-CĄL,) phy ; rational ; calm.
PHĬL-Ǫ-SŎPH'Į-CĄL-LY, *ad.* Rationally.
PHĮ-LŎS'Ǫ-PHĬŞM, *n.* Sophistry ; false philosophy or reasoning. [phy.
PHĮ-LŎS'Ǫ-PHĬST, *n.* A pretender to philoso-
PHĮ-LŎS'Ǫ-PHĪZE, *v. n.* To reason ; to moralize.
PHĮ-LŎS'Ǫ-PHY, *n.* Knowledge, natural or moral ; an explanation of the reason of things.
PHĬL'TĘR, *n.* A love potion or charm.
PHĬL'TĘR, *v. a.* To charm to love.
PHĬZ, *n.* The face ; the visage : *in contempt.*
PHLĘ-BŎT'Ǫ-MĬST, *n.* One that lets blood.
PHLĘ-BŎT'Ǫ-MY, *n.* The act or art of blood-letting ; venesection. [ness.
PHLĔGM (flĕm), *n.* A watery humor :—cool-
PHLĘG-MĂT'ĮC *or* PHLĔG'MĄ-TĬC, *a.* Abounding in, or generating, phlegm :—dull ; cold ;
PHLĔG'MǪN, *n.* An inflamed tumor. [frigid.
PHLǪ-ǴĬS'TĮC, *a.* Partaking of phlogiston. [ity.
PHLǪ-ǴĬS'TǪN, *n.* The principle of inflammabil-
PHŎN'ĮCS, *n. pl.* The doctrine of sounds.
PHǪ-NŎG'RĄ-PHY, *n.* Kind of short-hand writ-
PHǪ-NŎL'Ǫ-ĢY, *n.* The doctrine of sounds. [ing.
PHŎS'PHǪ-RĂT-ĘD, *a.* Combined with phosphorus.
PHŎS-PHǪ-RĔSCE' (fŏs-fǫ-rĕs'), *v. n.* To shine as phosphorus ; to emit phosphoric light.
PHŎS-PHǪ-RĔS'CĘNCE, *n.* A faint light without heat.
PHŎS-PHǪ-RĔS'CĘNT, *a.* Shining ; luminous.
PHŎS'PHǪ-RŬS, *n.* A very combustible substance. [light.
PHǪ-TŎM'Ę-TĘR, *n.* An instrument to measure
PHǪ-TŎM'Ę-TRY, *n.* Measurement of light.
PHRĄ̈E, *n.* An expression ; a mode of speech.

PHRĄ̈E, *v. a.* To style ; to call ; to term.
PHRĀ-ŞĘ-Ǫ-LŎǴ'Į-CĄL, *a.* Relating to a phrase.
PHRĀ-ŞĘ-ŎL'Ǫ-ĢY, *n.* Manner of expression ; style ; diction ; phrase-book. [tic.
PHRĘ-NĔT'ĮC, *a.* Inflamed in the brain ; fran-
PHRĘ-NĔT'ĮC, *n.* A madman ; a frantic person.
PHRĘ-NĪ'TĮS, *n.* Inflammation of the brain.
PHRĔN-Ǫ-LŎǴ'Į-CĄL, *a.* Relating to phrenology.
PHRĘ-NŎL'Ǫ-ǴĬST, *n.* One versed in phrenology.
PHRĘ-NŎL'Ǫ-ĢY, *n.* The science which professes to determine the disposition and qualities of the mind by the form of the skull ; craniology.
PHRĔN'ŞY, *n.* Madness. See FRENZY.
PHTHĬŞ'ĮC (tĭz'ĭk), *n.* A difficulty in breathing.
PHTHĬŞ'Į-CĄL (tĭz'ę-kąl), *a.* Breathing hard.
PHY-LĂC'TĘR-Y, *n.* A bandage on which was inscribed some memorable sentence. [medicine.
PHYŞ'ĮC, *n.* The science of healing ; a purging
PHYŞ'ĮC, *v. a.* To purge ; to treat with physic.
PHYŞ'Į-CĄL, *a.* Natural ; not moral ; medicinal.
PHYŞ'Į-CĄL-LY, *ad.* According to nature. [ic.
PHY-ŞĬ''-CIĄN (fę-zĭsh'ąn), *n.* Professor of phys-
PHYŞ-Į-CŌ-THĘ-ŎL'Ǫ-ĢY, *n.* Natural theology.
PHYŞ'ĮCS, *n. pl.* Natural philosophy.
PHYŞ-Į-ŎG'NǪ-MER,) *n.* One who is versed in
PHYŞ-Į-ŎG'NǪ-MĬST,) physiognomy. [nomy.
PHYŞ-Į-ǪG-NŎM'Į-CĄL, *a.* Relating to physiog-
PHYŞ-Į-ŎG'NǪ-MY, *n.* The art of discovering the temper by the features of the face ; the face.
PHYŞ-Į-ŎL'Ǫ-ǴER, *n.* A physiologist.
PHYŞ-Į-Ǫ-LŎǴ'ĮC,) *a.* Relating to physiol-
PHYŞ-Į-Ǫ-LŎǴ'Į-CĄL,) ogy. [ogy.
PHYŞ-Į-ŎL'Ǫ-ǴĬST, *n.* One versed in physiol-
PHYŞ-Į-ŎL'Ǫ-ĢY, *n.* The science which treats of the life and organization of animals and plants.
PHY-TĬV'Ǫ-ROŬS, *a.* That eats vegetables.
PHY-TŎG'RĄ-PHY, *n.* A description of plants.
PHY-TŎL'Ǫ-ǴĬST, *n.* One skilled in phytology.
PHY-TŎL'Ǫ-ĢY, *n.* The doctrine of plants.
PĮ-ĂC'Ų-LĄR, *a.* Expiatory ; criminal.
PĬ'Ą-NĔT, *n.* A bird ; the lesser woodpecker.
PĮ-Ă'NĬST, *n.* A performer on the piano-forte.
PĮ-Ă'NǪ-FŌRTE *or* PĮ-ĂN'Ǫ-FŌRTE, *n.* A musical stringed instrument.
PĮ-ĂS'TĘR, *n.* A silver coin of variable value.
PĮ-ĂZ'ZĄ, *n.* A portico or covered walk.
PĪ'CĄ, *n.* A sort of printing type :—a bird.
PĬC-Ą-RÔÔN', *n.* A robber ; a plunderer.
PĬCK, *v. a.* To cull, select, glean, clean, open.
PĬCK, *v. n.* To eat slowly and by morsels.
PĬCK, *n.* A sharp-pointed, iron tool.
PĬCK'ĂXE, *n.* An axe with a sharp point.
PĬCK'ĘD, *a.* Pointed ; sharp ; smart ; spruce.
PĬCK'ĘD-NĔSS, *n.* The state of being picked.
PĬCK'ĘR, *n.* One who picks or culls ; a pickaxe.
PĬCK'ĘR-ĘL, *n.* A kind of fresh-water fish.
PĬCK'ĘT, *n.* A sharp stake :—a guard.
PĬCK'ĘT, *v. a.* To fasten to a picket. [condition.
PĬC'KLE, *n.* A salt liquor ; a thing picked ; state ;
PĬC'KLE, *v. a.* To preserve in pickle ; to season.
PĬCK'LŎCK, *n.* One that picks locks. [pocket.
PĬCK'PŎCK-ĘT, *n.* One who steals from the
PĬCK'THĂNK, *n.* A flatterer ; a parasite. [teeth.
PĬCK'TÔÔTH, *n.* Instrument for cleaning the
PĬC'NĬC, *n.* A sort of assembly or entertain-
PĬCT, *n.* A painted person. [ment.
PĮC-TŌ'RĮ-ĄL, *a.* Relating to pictures or painters.
PĬCT'ỤRE (pĭkt'yụr), *n.* A resemblance in colors.

PĬCT′ŲRE (pĭkt′yụr), *v. a.*To represent; to paint.
PĬCT-Ų-RĔSQUE′ (pĭkt-yụ-rĕsk′), *a.* Like a pic-
 ture; graphic; wild and beautiful; inartificial.
PĬD′DLE, *v. n.* To trifle :—to feed squeamishly.
PĬD′DLẸR, *n.* One who is busy about trifles.
PĪE (pī), *n.* An article of food:—a magpie.
PĪE′BÂLD (pī′bâld), *a.* Of various colors.
PIĔCE, *n.* A patch; a part; composition; a gun.
PIĔCE (pĕs), *v. a.* & *n.* To patch; to join.
PIĔCE′MĔAL, *ad.* In pieces; in fragments.
PIĔCE′MĔAL, *a.* Single; separate; divided.
PĪED (pīd), *a.* Variegated; party-colored.
PĪED′NẸSS (pīd′nẹs), *n.* Diversity of color.
PIĔR, *n.* A column to support an arch; a mole.
PIĔRCE, *v. a.* To penetrate; to enter :—to affect.
PIĔRCE, *v. n.* To make way by force; to enter.
PIĔRCE′Ạ-BLE, *a.* That may be penetrated.
PIĔR′CẸR, *n.* One that pierces.
PIĔR′CĮNG, *a.* Penetrating; keen; affecting.
PĪ′Ẹ-TĬŞM, *n.* Strict devotion or piety.
PĪ′Ẹ-TĬST, *n.* One who professes great purity.
PĪ′Ẹ-TY, *n.* Duty to God; duty to parents.
PĬG, *n.* The young of swine :—a mass of metal.
PĬG, *v. n.* To farrow; to bring forth pigs.
PĬG′EỌN (pĭd′jụn), *n.* A well-known bird.
PĬG′EỌN-HŌLE (pĭd′jụn-hōl), *n.* A cavity; a
 compartment for papers, &c.
PĬG′ẠIN, *n.* A small wooden vessel.
PĬG′MẸNT, *n.* Paint; color for painting.
PĬG′MY, *n.* A dwarf. See PYGMY.
PĬG′NŬT, *n.* An earth nut; a hog-nut.
PĬG′TÂIL, *n.* A cue; tie of hair; twisted tobacco.
PĪKE, *n.* A fish :—a lance :—a peak :—a fork.
PĬK′ẸD, *a.* Sharp; pointed. See PICKED.
PĪKE′MẠN, *n.* A soldier armed with a pike.
PĪKE′STÂFF, *n.* The staff or shaft of a pike.
PĮ-LĂS′TẸR, *n.* A square projecting pillar.
PĬLCH′ẠRD, *n.* A fish resembling a herring.
PĬLE, *n.* A piece of wood driven into the ground :
 —a heap :—an edifice.—*pl.* Hemorrhoids.
PĬLE, *v. a.* To heap; to accumulate. [theft.
PĬL′FẸR, *v. a.* & *n.* To steal; to practise petty
PĬL′FẸR-ẸR, *n.* One who steals petty things.
PĬL′GRĮM, *n.* One who travels to holy places.
PĬL′GRĮM-AǴE, *n.* A journey to a holy place.
PĬLL, *n.* A small ball or mass of medicine.
PĬLL, *v. a.* To strip; to rob; to plunder; to peel.
PĬL′LAǴE, *n.* Plunder.—*v. a.* To plunder; to
PĬL′LA-ǴER, *n.* A plunderer; a spoiler. [spoil.
PĬL′LẠR, *n.* A column; a supporter; a maintainer.
PĬL′LARED (pĭl′lạrd), *a.* Supported by columns.
PĬL-LÂU′, *n.* A Turkish dish of boiled rice, &c.
PĬLL′IỌN (pĭl′yụn), *n.* A woman's saddle; a pad.
PĬL′LỌ-RY, *n.* An instrument of punishment.
PĬL′LỌ-RY, *v. a.* To punish with the pillory.
PĬL′LŌW (pĭl′lō), *n.* A bag of feathers to sleep on.
PĬL′LŌW (pĭl′lō), *v. a.* To place on a pillow.
PĬL′LŌW-BEĔR, } *n.* The case or cover of a
PĬL′LŌW-CÂSE, } pillow.
PĪ′LỌT, *n.* One who steers a ship :—a guide.
PĪ′LỌT, *v. a.* To steer; to direct in the course.
PĪ′LỌT-AǴE, *n.* The office or the pay of a pilot.
PĪ′LOŲS, PĮ-LŌSE′, *a.* Hairy; full of hairs.
PĮ-MĔN′TẠ, PĮ-MĔN′TŌ, *n.* A kind of spice; all-
PĬMP, *n.* A procurer; a pander. [spice.
PĬMP, *v. n.* To pander; to act the pimp.
PĬM′PẸR-NĔL, *n.* A trailing or herbaceous plant.
PĬM′PLE, *n.* A small red pustule; a blotch.

PĬM′PLED (pĭm′pld), *a.* Full of pimples.
PĬN, *n.* A short, pointed wire; a peg; a bolt.
PĬN, *v. a.* To make fast; to join; to fix; to fasten.
PĬN′Ạ-FŌRE, *n.* A child's apron; an apron.
PĬN′CÂSE, *n.* A case for pins.
PĬN′CẸRŞ, *n. pl.* An instrument to draw nails, &c.
PĬNCH, *v. a.* To squeeze; to gripe; to straiten.
PĬNCH, *v. n.* To bear hard upon; to be frugal.
PĬNCH, *n.* A gripe; difficulty; distress.
PĬNCH′BĔCK, *n.* A mixed, gold-colored metal.
PĬNCH′ẸRŞ, *n. pl.* Pincers. See PINCERS.
PĬN′CŬSH-IỌN (pĭn′kûsh-ụn), *n.* A pad for pins.
PĬN-DĂR′ĮC, *a.* After the manner of Pindar; lofty.
PĪNE, *n.* An evergreen tree :—pineapple.
PĪNE, *v. n.* To languish; to waste away.
PĪNE′ĂP-PLE, *n.* The ananas, a fruit.
PĬN′ẸR-Y, *n.* A place where pineapples are raised.
PĬN′FĔATH-ẸR, *n.* Feather not fully grown.
PĬN′FŌLD, *n.* A place for confining beasts.
PĬN′HŌLE, *n.* A small hole or perforation.
PĬN′IỌN (pĭn′yụn), *n.* A wing :—a toothed wheel.
PĬN′IỌN (pĭn′yụn), *v. a.* To bind; to shackle.
PĬNK, *n.* A small, fragrant flower :—any thing
 supremely excellent :—a color :—a fish.
PĬNK, *v. a.* To work in eyelet-holes; to pierce.
PĬN′MĂ-KẸR, *n.* One who makes pins.
PĬN′MŎN-EY, *n.* A wife's pocket money.
PĬN′NẠCE, *n.* A small vessel :—a barge.
PĬN′NẠ-CLE, *n.* A pointed turret :—summit.
PĬN′NẠTE, PĬN′NĀT-ẸD, *a.* Formed like a wing.
PĬN′NẸR, *n.* Part of a head-dress :—a pinmaker.
PĬNT, *n.* Half a quart; one-eighth of a gallon.
PĬN′TLE, *n.* A long iron pin :—a bolt.
PĪ′NY, *a.* Abounding with pine-trees.
PĪ-Ọ-NEĔR′, *n.* A soldier who clears roads, &c.
PĪ′Ọ-NY, *n.* A large flower. See PEONY.
PĪ′OŲS, *a.* Revering God; godly; religious.
PĪ′OŲS-LY, *ad.* In a pious manner; religiously.
PĬP, *n.* A disease of fowls :—a seed of an apple.
PĬP, *v. n.* To chirp or cry as a bird; to peep.
PĪPE, *n.* A tube —:a tube for smoking :—an in-
 strument of music :—a cask for liquids.
PĪPE, *v. n.* & *a.* To play on the pipe; to whistle.
PĪP′ẸR, *n.* One who plays on the pipe.
PĪP′ĮNG, *a.* Weak; feeble :—hot; boiling.
PĬP′KĮN, *n.* A vessel; a small earthen boiler.
PĬP′PĮN, *n.* A kind of tart apple.
PĬQU′ẠN-CY (pĭk′ạn-sẹ), *n.* Sharpness; tartness.
PĬQU′ẠNT (pĭk′ạnt), *a.* Sharp; pungent; severe.
PĬQU′ẠNT-LY (pĭk′ạnt-lẹ), *ad.* Sharply; tartly.
PÎQUE (pēk), *n.* Ill-will; slight anger; grudge.
PÎQUE (pēk), *v. a.* To offend, irritate :—to value.
PĮ-QUĔT′ (pẹ-kĕt′), *n.* A game at cards.
PĪ′RẠ-CY, *n.* Robbery on the sea :—literary theft.
PĪ′RẠTE, *n.* A sea-robber :—a literary robber.
PĪ′RẠTE, *v. a.* & *n.* To rob; to take by robbery.
PĮ-RĂT′Į-CẠL, *a.* Predatory; practising robbery.
PĮ-RŌGUE′ (pẹ-rōg′), *n.* Canoe made of a tree.
PĬR-ÔU-ĔTTE′, *n.* A kind of step in dancing.
PĬS′CẠ-TỌ-RY, *a.* Relating to fishes. [zodiac.
PĬS′CĔŞ, *n. pl.* [L.] Fishes; 12th sign in the
PĮS-CĪV′Ọ-ROŬS, *a.* Fish-eating; living on fish.
PĬSH, *interj.* A contemptuous exclamation.
PĬŞ′MĪRE *or* PĬS′MĪRE, *n.* An ant; an emmet.
PĮS-TĂ′ÇHIŌ (pĭs-tā′shō), *n.* An oblong nut.
PĬS-TẠ-RĔEN′, *n.* A silver coin, value 17 cents.
PĬS′TĮL, *n.* Seed-organ of a flower.
PĬS′TỌL, *n.* A small fire-arm for the hand.

PĬS-TŌLE′, n. A gold coin of Spain, France, &c.
PĬS′TŎN, n. A cylinder used in pumps, &c.
PĬT, n. A hole, abyss; the grave; hollow part.
PĬT, v. a. To indent; to press into hollows.
PĬT′A-PĂT, n. A flutter.—ad. In a flutter.
PĬTCH, n. Residuum from boiling tar:—turpen-
   tine:—height:—angle of a roof.
PĬTCH, v. a. To fix; to plant; to cast; to smear.
PĬTCH, v. n. To light; to drop; to fall headlong.
PĬTCH′ER, n. A vessel for liquids.   [&c.
PĬTCH′FŎRK, n. A fork for pitching hay, corn,
PĬTCH′-PĪPE, n. An instrument to give the key.
PĬTCH′Y, a. Smeared with pitch; black; dark.
PĬT′CŌAL, n. Mineral coal.   [ate; tender.
PĬT′E-OŬS, a. Sorrowful; mournful; compassion-
PĬT′E-OŬS-LY, ad. In a piteous manner.
PĬT′E-OŬS-NĔSS, n. Sorrowfulness; tenderness.
PĬT′FĂLL, n. A covered or concealed pit.
PĬTH, n. A soft substance in plants; marrow:—
   chief part; force; energy; strength.
PĬTH′I-LY, ad. With strength; with force.
PĬTH′I-NĔSS, n. Energy; strength; force.
PĬTH′LESS, a. Wanting pith; wanting force.
PĬTH′Y, a. Abounding with pith; strong.
PĬT′I-A-BLE, a. Deserving pity; pitiful.
PĬT′I-A-BLE-NĔSS, n. The state of deserving pity.
PĬT′I-FŬL, a. Tender; pitiable:—mean; paltry.
PĬT′I-FŬL-LY, ad. With pity:—contemptibly.
PĬT′I-FŬL-NĔSS, n. Compassion:—despicable-
PĬT′I-LĔSS, a. Wanting pity; merciless. [ness.
PĬT′I-LĔSS-LY, ad. Without pity; mercilessly.
PĬT′MAN, n. One who works in a pit.
PĬT′SÂW, n. A large saw used by two men.
PĬT′TANCE, n. An allowance; a small portion.
PĬ-TŪ′I-TA-RY, a. Conducting phlegm or mucus.
PĬ-TŪ′I-TOŬS, a. Consisting of phlegm.
PĬT′Y, n. Compassion; sympathy with misery.
PĬT′Y, v. a. & n. To compassionate, sympathize.
PĬV′ŎT, n. A pin on which any thing turns.
PĬX, n. A box for the consecrated host; pyx.
PLĀ-CA-BĬL′I-TY, n. The quality of being placa-
PLĀ′CA-BLE, a. That may be appeased. [ble.
PLA-CÄRD′, n. A paper posted up; a card.
PLA-CÄRD′, v. a. To publish by posting; to post.
PLĀCE, n. Space; locality; room; rank; office.
PLĀCE, v. a. To put in place; to fix; to settle.
PLĀCE′MAN, n. One who fills a public station.
PLĂÇ′ĬD, a. Gentle; quiet; soft; kind; mild.
PLA-CĬD′I-TY, PLĂÇ′ĬD-NĔSS, n. Mildness; quiet.
PLĂÇ′ĬD-LY, ad. Mildly; gently; with quietness.
‖PLĀ′GI-A-RĬSM, n. Act of purloining the writ-
   ings of another; literary theft.
‖PLĀ′GI-A-RĬST, n. A thief in literature.
‖PLĀ′GI-A-RY or PLĀ′GIA-RY, n. One who
   commits plagiarism:—plagiarism.   [ble.
PLĀGUE (plāg), n. Pestilence; a disease; trou-
PLĀGUE (plāg), v. a. To infest; to tease; to vex.
PLĀ′GUY (plā′ge), a. Vexatious. [Vulgar.]
PLĀICE (plās), n. A species of flat-fish.
PLĂID (plăd), n. A striped or variegated cloth.
PLĀIN, a. Smooth; flat; clear; artless; homely.
PLĀIN, ad. Not obscurely; distinctly; simply.
PLĀIN, n. Level ground; an open or flat expanse.
PLĀIN, v. a. To level; to make plain. See PLANE.
PLĀIN′-DĒAL-ĬNG, n. Management void of art.
PLĀIN′-HEÄRT-ED, a. Frank; sincere; candid.
PLĀIN′LY, ad. Levelly; evidently; clearly.
PLĀIN′NESS, n. Flatness; want of show.

PLĀIN′-SPŌK-EN, a. Speaking frankly.
PLĀINT, n. Lamentation; complaint; lament.
PLĀIN′TĬFF, n. One who commences a lawsuit.
PLĀIN′TĬVE, a. Lamenting; complaining.
PLĀIN′TĬVE-LY, ad. In a plaintive manner.
PLĀIN′TĬVE-NĔSS, n. Quality of being plaintive.
PLĀIT, n. A fold; a double; a tress.
PLĀIT, v. a. To fold; to double; to braid.
PLĂN, n. A draught; a representation; a sketch;
   a scheme; a form; a model; a plot.
PLĂN, v. a. To scheme; to form in design.
PLĀNE, n. A level surface:—a joiner's tool.
PLĀNE, v. a. To level; to make smooth.
PLĀN′ER, n. One who smooths with a plane.
PLĂN′ET, n. A celestial body that revolves
   about another and larger body.
PLĂN′E-TA-RY, a. Pertaining to the planets.
PLĀNE′-TRĒĒ, n. A sort of tree. [blasted.
PLĂN′ET-STRŬCK, a. Affected by a planet;
PLĂN-I-FŌ′LI-OŬS, a. Consisting of plain leaves.
PLĂN-I-MĔT′RI-CAL, a. Relating to planimetry.
PLA-NĬM′E-TRY, n. Mensuration of plane sur-
   faces.   [leaves.
PLĂN-I-PĔT′A-LOŬS, a. Having flat petals or
PLĂN′ĬSH, v. a. To polish; to smooth. [plane.
PLĂN′I-SPHĒRE, n. A sphere projected on a
PLĂNK, n. A thick, strong sort of board.
PLĂNK, v. a. To cover or lay with planks.
PLĂN′NER, n. One who forms any plan.
PLĀ-NO-CŎN′I-CAL, } a. Flat on the one side
PLĀ-NO-CŎN′VĔX, } and convex on the other.
PLĂNT, n. Any vegetable production. [tle.
PLĂNT, v. a. To set; to cultivate; to fix; to set-
PLĂNT, v. n. To perform the act of planting.
PLĂN′TAIN (plăn′tin), n. An herb:—a tree.
PLĂN-TĀ′TION, n. A planting; a large farm:—
   a settlement; a colony.
PLĂNT′ER, n. One who plants; a cultivator.
PLĂSH, n. A small lake or puddle; a branch.
PLĂSH, v. a. To dash with water; to interweave.
PLĂSH′Y, a. Watery; filled with puddles.
PLĂSM, n. A mould; a matrix. [cement; stucco.
PLĂS′TER, n. Lime to cover walls; mortar;
PLĂS′TER, v. a. To overlay as with plaster.
PLĂS′TER-ER, n. One who plasters.
PLĂS′TER ĬNG, n. Work done in plaster.
PLĂS′TĬC, a. Giving form; fictile; soft.
PLĂS′TRON, n. A piece of leather stuffed.
PLĂT, v. a. To weave, to plait; to braid.
PLĂT, PLĂT′TĬNG, n. Work done by platting.
PLĂT, n. A small piece of ground, a plain.
PLĂT′ANE (plăt′an), n. The plane tree.
PLĀTE, n. Wrought silver or gold:—a dish.
PLĀTE, v. a. To cover with a coat of metal.
PLĀ-TEAU′ (plä-tō′), n. [Fr.] An elevated plain.
PLĂT′EN, n. The flat part of a printing-press.
PLĂT′FŌRM, n. A horizontal plain; a scheme.
PLĂT′I-NA, PLĂT′I-NŬM, n. A very heavy, hard
PLA-TŎN′ĬC, a. Relating to Plato; pure. [metal.
PLA-TŎÔN′, n. A body of soldiers.
PLĂT′TER, n. A large dish:—one who plats.
PLÂU′DĬT, n. Applause; loud praise.
PLÂUŞ-I-BĬL′I-TY, n. Appearance of right.
PLÂUŞ′I-BLE, a. Specious; right in appearance.
PLÂUŞ′I-BLE-NĔSS, n. Appearance of right.
PLÂUŞ′I-BLY, ad. With fair show; speciously.
PLĀY (plā), v. n. To sport; to game; to act.
PLĀY, v. a. To use; to perform; to exhibit; to act.

PLĀY, *n.* Amusement; sport; game; a drama.
PLĀY'-DAY, *n.* A day exempt from tasks or work.
PLĀY'ĘR, *n.* One who plays; an actor.
PLĀY'FĔL-LŌW, *n.* A companion in amusement.
PLĀY'FŬL, *a.* Sportive; full of play or levity.
PLĀY'FŬL-NĔSS, *n.* Sportiveness; levity.
PLĀY'GĀME, *n.* Amusement of children.
PLĀY'HŌŬSE, *n.* A house for dramatic performances; a theatre.
PLĀY'MĀTE, *n.* A companion in amusement.
PLĀY'THĬNG, *n.* A toy; a thing to play with.
PLĀY'WRĪGHT (plā'rīt), *n.* A maker of plays.
PLĒA (plē), *n.* A form of pleading; an apology.
PLĒAD (plēd), *v. n.* To argue; to urge.
PLĒAD, *v. a.* To discuss; to allege in pleading.
PLĒAD'A-BLE, *a.* Capable of being alleged in
PLĒAD'ĘR, *n.* One who pleads or argues. [plea.
PLĒAD'ĮNG, *n.* The act or form of pleading.
PLĔAŞ'ĄNT, *a.* That pleases; giving pleasure; delightful; grateful; gay; lively. [merrily.
PLĔAŞ'ĄNT-LỸ, *ad.* In a pleasant manner;
PLĔAŞ'ĄNT-NĔSS, *n.* Delightfulness; gayety.
PLĔAŞ'ĄNT-RỸ, *n.* Gayety; merriment; humor.
PLĔAŞE, *v. a.* To delight; to gratify; to humor.
PLĔAŞE, *v. n.* To choose; to like; to comply.
PLĔAŞ'ĮNG, *a.* Giving pleasure; agreeable.
PLĔAŞ'ŲR-A-BLE (plĕzh'ŭr-ạ-bl), *a.* Delightful.
PLĔAŞ'ŲR-Ạ-BLỸ, *ad.* With delight.
PLĔAŞ'ŲRE (plĕzh'ŭr), *n.* Delight; gratification.
‖PLĘ-BĒ'IĄN (plę-bē'yạn), *a.* Vulgar; common.
‖PLĘ-BĒ'IĄN, *n.* One of the lower people.
PLĔDGE, *n.* A pawn; a gage; a surety; a bail.
PLĔDGE, *v. a.* To pawn; to give as security.
PLĔDG-ĒĒ', *n.* One to whom a pledge is made.
PLĔDG'ĘR, *n.* One who offers a pledge. [&c.
PLĔDG'ĘT, *n.* Small mass of lint for wounds,
PLĒ'IĄ-DĒŞ, *n. pl.* The cluster of Seven Stars; the same as *pleiads*.
PLĒ'IĄDŞ (plē'yạdz), *n. pl.* The Seven Stars.
‖PLĔN'Ạ-RĮ-LỸ, *ad.* Fully; completely.
‖PLĔN'Ạ-RĮ-NĔSS, *n.* Fulness; completeness.
‖PLĔN'Ạ-RỸ *or* PLĒ'NẠ-RỸ, *a.* Full; complete.
PLĔN-Į-LŪ'NẠ-RỸ, *a.* Relating to the full moon.
PLĘ-NĬP'Q-TĔNCE, *n.* Fulness of power.
PLĘ-NĬP'Q-TĔNT, *a.* Invested with full power.
PLĔN-Į-PQ-TĔN'TĮ-Ạ-RỸ (plĕn-ę-pq-tĕn'shę-ạ-rę), *n.* A negotiator invested with full power.
PLĔN'Į-TŪDE, *n.* Fulness; repletion; abundance.
PLĔN'TĘ-OŬS, *a.* Copious; abundant; fertile.
PLĔN'TĘ-OŬS-LỸ, *ad.* Copiously; abundantly.
PLĔN'TĮ-FŬL, *a.* Copious; abundant; exuberant.
PLĔN'TĮ-FŬL-LỸ, *ad.* Copiously; abundantly.
PLĔN'TỸ, *n.* Abundance; exuberance.
PLĒ'Q-NĂŞM, *n.* A redundancy of words.
PLĒ-Q-NĂS'TĮC, *a.* Partaking of pleonasm;
PLĒ-Q-NĂS'TĮ-CAL, redundant. [blood.
PLĔTH'Q-RA, PLĔTH'Q-RỸ, *n.* A fulness of
PLĘ-THŎR'ĮC *or* PLĔTH'Q-RĬC, *a.* Of full habit.
PLEŪ'RA, *n.* [L.] A membrane within the thorax.
PLEŪ'RĮ-SỸ, *n.* An inflammation of the pleura.
PLEŪ-RĬT'ĮC, *a.* Relating to, or diseased
PLEŪ-RĬT'Į-CAL, with, pleurisy.
PLEŪ-RQ-PNEŪ-MŌ'NĮ-Ạ, *n.* Inflammation of the pleura and the lungs.
PLĪ-Ạ-BĬL'Į-TỸ, *n.* Flexibility; pliableness.
PLĪ'Ạ-BLE, *a.* Easy to be bent; flexible; pliant.
PLĪ'ĄN-CỸ, PLĪ'Ạ-BLE-NĔSS, *n.* Flexibility.
PLĪ'ĄNT, *a.* Bending; flexile; flexible; complying.

PLĪ'ĄNT-NĔSS, *n.* Flexibility; toughness.
PLĪ'CẠ, *n.* [L.] A Polish disease of the hair.
PLĮ-CĀ'TIQN, PLĬC'Ạ-TŪRE, *n.* A fold; a double.
PLĪ'ĘRŞ, *n. pl.* Pincers for bending wire, &c.
PLĪGHT (plīt), *v. a.* To pledge.—*n.* Condition.
PLĪGHT'ĘR (plīt'ęr), *n.* One that plights.
PLĬNTH, *n.* The lowermost part of a pillar.
PLŎD, *v. n.* To toil; to drudge; to study closely.
PLŎD'DĘR, *n.* A dull, heavy, laborious person.
PLŎT, *n.* A small extent of ground; a plat:—a scheme; a plan; a conspiracy; an intrigue.
PLŎT, *v. n.* To devise mischief; to contrive.
PLŎT'TĘR, *n.* A conspirator; a contriver.
PLŌŬGH (plŏŭ), *n.* An instrument of husbandry.
PLŌŬGH (plŏŭ), *v. n. & a.* To turn up the ground.
PLŌŬGH'BŌỸ (plŏŭ'bŏï), *n.* A boy that ploughs.
PLŌŬGH'MĄN (plŏŭ'mạn), *n.* One who ploughs.
PLŌŬGH'SHĂRE (plŏŭ'shăr), *n.* The iron of a plough.
PLŎV'ĘR, *n.* A lapwing; a bird.
PLŬCK, *v. a.* To snatch; to pull; to draw; to strip.
PLŬCK, *n.* A pull:—the liver, lights, &c.
PLŬG, *n.* A stopple.—*v. a.* To stop with a plug.
PLŬM, *n.* A fruit; a raisin:—sum of £100,000.
PLŪ'MĄGE, *n.* Feathers; suit of feathers.
‖PLŬMB (plŭm), *n.* A plummet; a leaden weight.
‖PLŬMB (plŭm), *ad.* Perpendicularly; directly.
‖PLŬMB (plŭm), *v. a.* To sound:—to adjust.
PLŲM-BĀ'GŌ, *n.* Graphite, or black lead; an ore.
‖PLŬMB'ĘR, *n.* One who works in lead.
‖PLŬMB'ĘR-Ỹ (plŭm'męr-ę), *n.* Works in lead.
PLŬM'-CĂKE, *n.* Cake made with raisins.
PLŪME, *n.* A feather:—pride:—a token of honor.
PLŪME, *v. a.* To strip; to feather, adorn, value.
PLŪ'MĮ-PĔD, *a.* Having feet covered with feathers.
PLŬM'MĘT, *n.* A weight of lead attached to a line:—pencil of lead.
PLŪ'MOŬS, *a.* Feathery; resembling feathers.
PLŪMP, *a.* Somewhat fat; not lean; sleek.
PLŬMP, *v. a.* To fatten; to swell; to make large.
PLŬMP, *ad.* With a sudden or heavy fall.
PLŬMP'ĘR, *n.* Something to dilate the cheeks.
PLŬMP'LỸ, *ad.* Roundly; fully; unreservedly.
PLŬMP'NĘSS, *n.* Fulness; distention.
PLŬM'-PŬD-DĮNG, *n.* Pudding made with plums.
PLŬM'-TRĔĒ, *n.* A tree that bears plums.
PLŪ'MỸ, *a.* Feathered; covered with feathers.
PLŬN'DĘR, *v. a.* To pillage; to rob; to strip.
PLŬN'DĘR, *n.* Pillage; spoils obtained in war.
PLŬN'DĘR-ER, *n.* A hostile pillager; a robber.
PLŬNGE, *v. a.* To thrust or immerse.
PLŬNGE, *v. n.* To sink suddenly; to rush.
PLŬNGE, *n.* Act of plunging; a strait; distress.
PLŪ'RAL, *a.* Implying more than one.
PLŪ'RAL-ĬST, *n.* A clergyman who holds more than one benefice, with cure of souls.
PLŲ-RĂL'Į-TỸ, *n.* A number more than one: —more cures of souls than one:—the greater
PLŪ'RAL-LỸ, *ad.* In a plural sense. [number.
PLŬSH, *n.* A kind of cloth with a nap or shag.
PLŪ'VĮ-AL, *a.* Rainy; relating to rain.
PLŪ-VĮ-ĂM'Ę-TĘR, *n.* A rain-gauge. [plait.
PLỸ, *n.* Bent; turn; bias; cast; form; fold;
PLỸ, *v. a. & n.* To work; to employ; to bend.
PNEŪ-MĂT'ĮC (nŭ-măt'ĭk), *a.* Relating
PNEŪ-MĂT'Į-CAL (nŭ-măt'ę-kạl), to air. [air.
PNEŪ-MĂT'ĮCS (nŭ-măt'ĭks), *n. pl.* Science of the
PNEŪ-MẠ-TŎL'Q-GỸ (nŭ-mạ-tŏl'q-ję), *n.* The doctrine of spiritual existence.

PŎACH (pōch), *v. a. & n.* To boil slightly :—to steal, as game.

PŎACH′ER (pōch′ẹr), *n.* One who steals game.

PŎCK, *n.* A pustule of the small-pox, &c.

PŎCK′ET, *n.* A small bag or pouch in a garment.

PŎCK′ET, *v. a.* To put in the pocket.

PŎCK′ET-BOOK (-bûk), *n.* A book for the pocket.

PŎCK′ET-GLĂSS, *n.* A glass for the pocket.

PŎCK′HŌLE, *n.* A scar made by the small-pox.

PŎCK′Y, *a.* Covered with pocks.

PŎD, *n.* A capsule of legumes ; a case of seeds.

PQ-DĂG′RĮ-CĄL, *a.* Relating to the gout.

PŌ′EM, *n.* The work of a poet ; a metrical composition ; a piece of poetry.

PŌ′E-SY, *n.* The art of writing poems ; poetry.

PŌ′ET, *n.* An author of poetry ; a writer of po-

PŌ′ET-ĂS-TER, *n.* A vile, petty poet. [ems.

PŌ′ET-ĔSS, *n.* A female poet.

PQ-ĔT′ĮC, *a.* Pertaining to, or expressed
PQ-ĔT′Į-CĄL, } in, or partaking of, poetry.

PQ-ĔT′Į-CĄL-LY, *ad.* In the manner of poetry.

PQ-ĔT′ĮCS, *n. pl.* The doctrine or theory of poetry.

PŌ′ET-LÂU′RE-ĄTE, *n.* Court-poet of England.

PŌ′ET-RY, *n.* Composition uniting fiction and metre ; metrical composition ; verse ; poems.

PŎÏG′NĄN-CY (pöï′nạn-sẹ), *n.* Point ; asperity.

PŎÏG′NĄNT (pöï′nạnt), *a.* Sharp ; severe ; keen.

PŎÏG′NĄNT-LY (pöï′nạnt-lẹ), *ad.* Sharply.

PŎÏNT, *n.* A sharp end :—a sting of an epigram : —state ; a stop ; an aim ; a degree :—a cape.

PŎÏNT, *v. a.* To sharpen ; to direct ; to distinguish ; to punctuate. [cate.

PŎÏNT, *v. n.* To note with the finger ; to indi-

PŎÏNT′AL, *n.* The pistil of a plant. [caĮ ; aimed.

PŎÏNT′ED, *p. a.* Sharp ; poignant ; epigrammati-

PŎÏNT′ED-LY, *ad.* In a pointed manner. [ness.

PŎÏNT′ED-NĔSS, *n.* Sharpness ; smartness ; keen-

PŎÏNT′EL, *n.* Something on a point :—a pencil.

PŎÏNT′ER, *n.* Any thing that points :—a dog.

PŎÏNT′LESS, *a.* Blunt ; not sharp ; obtuse.

PŎÏSE, *n.* Weight ; balance ; equipoise.

PŎÏSE, *v. a.* To balance ; to weigh ; to examine.

PŎÏ′SON (pöï′zn), *n.* What destroys life ; venom.

PŎÏ′SON (pöï′zn), *v. a.* To infect ; to corrupt.

PŎÏ′SON-ER (pöï′zn-ẹr), *n.* One who poisons.

PŎÏ′SON-OŬS (pöï′zn-ŭs), *a.* Containing poison.

PŎÏ′SON-OŬS-LY (pöï′zn-ŭs-lẹ), *ad.* Venomously.

PŎÏ′SON-OŬS-NĔSS, *n.* The quality of being poi-

PŌKE, *n.* A bag ; a sack ; a pouch. [sonous.

PŌKE, *v. a.* To feel in the dark :—to push or thrust.

PŌ′KER, *n.* An iron bar to stir the fire with.

PQ-LĂ′CRE (pq-lä′kẹr), *n.* A Levantine vessel.

PŌ′LAR, *a.* Relating to, or near, the pole.

PQ-LĂR′Į-TY, *n.* Tendency to the pole.

PŌLE, *n.* The extremity of the earth's axis ; a staff ; a slender piece of wood ; 5½ yards ; a

PŌLE, *v. a.* To furnish with poles. [rod.

PŌLE′ĂXE, *n.* An axe fixed to a long pole.

PŌLE′CĂT, *n.* An animal ; the minx or fitchet.

PQ-LĔM′ĮC, *n.* A disputant ; a controvertist.

PQ-LĔM′ĮC, PQ-LĔM′Į-CĄL, *a.* Controversial.

PŌLE′STĂR, *n.* A star near the pole :—any guide.

PQ-LÎCE′, *n.* The government of a city, &c.

PŎL′Į-CY, *n.* Art of government ; art ; prudence : —a warrant for money, &c. ; a ticket ; a writing.

PŎL′ĮSH, *v. a.* To smooth ; to brighten ; to refine.

PŎL′ĮSH, *n.* Artificial gloss ; elegance of manners.

PŎL′ĮSH-A-BLE, *a.* Capable of being polished.

PŎL′ĮSH-ER, *n.* One who, or that which, polishes.

PQ-LĪTE′, *a.* Refined or polished in manners ; well-bred ; civil ; courteous ; genteel.

PQ-LĪTE′LY, *ad.* With refinement ; genteelly.

PQ-LĪTE′NESS, *n.* Gentility ; good breeding.

PŎL′Į-TĬC, *a.* Wise ; prudent ; artful ; political.

PQ-LĬT′Į-CĄL, *a.* Relating to politics ; civil.

PQ-LĬT′Į-CĄL-LY, *ad.* With relation to politics.

PŎL-Į-TĬ″CIĄN (pŏl-lẹ-tĭsh′ạn), *n.* One skilled in

PŎL′Į-TĬC-LY, *ad.* Artfully ; cunningly. [politics.

PŎL′Į-TĬCS, *n. pl.* The science of government.

PŎL′Į-TY, *n.* A form of government ; policy.

PŎL′KA, *n.* A Hungarian dance.

PŎLL, *n.* The head ; a list of persons ; an election.

PŌLL, *v. a.* To lop the top of trees ; to clip short ; to shear ; to crop :—to take a list of.

PŎL′LĄRD, *n.* A tree lopped :—a sort of bran.

PŎL′LEN, *n.* (*Bot.*) A prolific farina or dust of

PŎLL′ER, *n.* One who votes or polls. [a flower.

PŎL′LOCK, PŎL′LĄCK, *n.* A fish of the cod kind.

PŎLL′TĂX, *n.* A tax levied on heads.

PQL-LŪTE′, *v. a.* To defile ; to taint ; to corrupt.

PQL-LŪT′ER, *n.* A defiler ; a corrupter.

PQL-LŪ′TIQN, *n.* Act of defiling ; defilement.

PŌ-LQ-NĀĮSE′ (pō-lq-nāz′), *n.* A robe :—a dance.

PQL-TRÔÔN′, *n.* A coward ; a scoundrel.

PŎL′Y, in compound words, signifies *many.*

PŎL-Y-ĂN′THUS, *n.* A plant ; a flower.

PQ-LYG′A-MĬST, *n.* An advocate for polygamy.

PQ-LYG′A-MY, *n.* A plurality of wives. [guages.

PŎL′Y-GLŎT, *n.* A book containing many lan-

PŎL′Y-GŎN, *n.* A figure of many angles.

PQ-LYG′Q-NĄL, *a.* Having many angles. [phers.

PQ-LYG′RĄ-PHY, *n.* The art of writing in ci-

PŎL-Y-HĒ′DRQN, *n.* A figure having many sides.

PŎL′Y-PE *or* PŎL′YPE, *n.* A radiate animal.

PŎL-Y-PĔT′A-LOŬS, *a.* Having many petals.

PQ-LYPH′Q-NĬSM, *n.* A multiplicity of sound.

PŎL′Y-PŬS, *n.* ; *pl.* PŎL′Y-PĪ. A disease or swelling in the nostrils, &c. :—an animal ; a polype.

PŎL′Y-SCŌPE, *n.* A multiplying glass.

PŎL-Y-SPĔR′MOŬS, *a.* Having many seeds.

PŎL-Y-SYL-LĂB′ĮC, *a.* Having many syllables.

PŎL′Y-SYL-LA-BLE, *n.* A word of many syllables.

PŎL-Y-TĔℂH′NĮC, *a.* Comprehending many arts.

PŎL′Y-THE-ĬSM, *n.* Doctrine of a plurality of gods.

PŎL′Y-THE-ĬST, *n.* Believer in a plurality of gods.

PŎL-Y-THE-Ĭs′TĮC, *a.* Relating to polytheism.

PŎM′ACE, *n.* The substance of apples ground.

PQ-MĀ′CEOŬS (pq-mā′shụs), *a.* Consisting of ap-

PQ-MĀDE′, *n.* An ointment ; pomatum. [ples.

PQ-MĀ′TUM, *n.* [L.] An ointment for the hair.

PŎME-CĬT′RQN, *n.* A fruit like a lemon.

PŎME-GRĂN′ATE, *n.* A tree and its fruit.

PŎM′MEL, *n.* A knob on a sword or saddle.

PŎM′MEL, *v. a.* To beat ; to bruise ; to punch.

PQ-MŎL′Q-GY, *n.* A treatise on fruit.

PŎMP, *n.* A grand procession ; show ; parade.

PŎM′PĮ-QN (pŭm′pẹ-ụn), *n.* A pumpkin.

PQM-PŎS′Į-TY, *n.* Ostentation ; boastfulness.

PŎM′POŬS, *a.* Splendid ; magnificent ; showy.

PŎM′POŬS-LY, *ad.* Magnificently ; splendidly.

PŎM′POŬS-NĔSS, *n.* Magnificence ; splendor.

PŎND, *n.* A small pool or lake ; a basin.

PŎN′DER, *v. a.* To weigh mentally ; to consider.

PŎN′DER-A-BLE, *a.* Capable of being weighed.

PŎN-DER-ŎS′Į-TY, *n.* Weight ; heaviness.

PŎN′DER-OŬS, *a.* Heavy ; weighty ; important.

Ă,Ē,Ī,Ō,Ū,Ȳ, *long ;* Ă,Ĕ,Ĭ,Ŏ,Ŭ,Y̆, *short ;* Ą,Ẹ,Į,Q,ỤY, *obscure.*—FĀRE, FÄR, FĂST, FÂLL ; HÊIR, HĔR ;

PŎN′DĔR-OŬS-LY, *ad.* With great weight. [ity.
PŎN′DĔR-OŲS-NĔSS,*n.*Heaviness; weight; grav-
PŎN′IARD (pŏn′yard), *n.* A dagger.—*v.a.*To stab.
PŎN′TAĢE, *n.* A duty for repairing bridges.
PŎN′TIFF, *n.* A priest; a high priest; the pope.
PǪN-TĬF′IC,   } *a.* Relating to a high priest,
PǪN-TĬF′I-CAL, } pontiff, or pope; popish.
PǪN-TĬF′I-CAL, *n.* A book of ecclesiastical rites.
 —*pl.* The dress of a bishop or priest.
PǪN-TĬF′I-CAL-LY, *ad.* In a pontifical manner.
PǪN-TĬF′I-CĀTE, *n.* The dignity of high priest,
 pontiff, or pope; papacy.   [bridge.
PǪN-TŌN′, PǪN-TŌŌN′, *n.* A floating vessel or
PŌ′NY, *n.* A small horse :—a translation. [*Cant.*]
PŎŌD, *n.* A Russian weight of 36 pounds.
PŌŌL, *n.* A small collection of water; a pond.
PŎŌP, *n.* The hindmost part of a ship.
PŎŌR, *a.* Not rich; indigent; paltry; lean.
PŎŌR′LY, *ad.* Without wealth or spirit; meanly.
PŎŌR′NĔSS, *n.* Poverty; meanness; sterility.
PŎŌR-SPĬR′IT-ĔD, *a.* Mean; cowardly; base.
PŎP, *n.* A small, smart, quick sound.
PŎP, *v. n.* To move or enter quickly or slyly.
PŎP, *v. a.* To put out or in suddenly; to shift.
PŎP, *ad.* Suddenly; unexpectedly. [fish.
PŌPE, *n.* The bishop of Rome :—a fresh-water
PŌPE′DǪM, *n.* The papacy; papal jurisdiction.
PŌPE–JŌAN′, (pōp jōn′), *n.* A game at cards.
PŌP′ĔR-Y, *n.* The religion of the church of Rome.
PŌPE′S′EȲE (pōps′ī), *n.* A gland in the thigh.
PŎP′GŬN, *n.* A tube for shooting pellets.
PŎP′IN-JĀY, *n.* A parrot; a woodpecker; a fop.
PŎP′ISH, *a.* Relating to the pope or popery.
PŎP′ISH-LY, *ad.* In a popish manner.
PŎP′LAR, *n.* A tree; tulip-tree or whitewood.
PŎP′LIN, *n.* A stuff made of silk and worsted.
PŎP′PY, *n.* A soporiferous plant and flower.
PŎP′Ų-LACE, *n.* The vulgar; the multitude.
PŎP′Ų-LAR, *a.* Beloved by the people; pleasing
 to the people; familiar; not critical; plain.
PŎP-Ų-LĂR′I-TY, *n.* The favor of the people.
PŎP′Ų-LAR-LY, *ad.* In a popular manner.
PŎP′Ų-LĀTE, *v. a.* To furnish with people.
PŎP-Ų-LĀ′TIǪN, *n.* Inhabitants of a country, &c.
PŎP′Ų-LOŬS, *a.* Full of inhabitants or people.
PŎP′Ų-LOŬS-NĔSS, *n.* State of being populous.
PŎR′CE-LAIN *or* PŎR′CE-LĀIN, *n.* Fine earth-
 en-ware; china-ware; china.
PŎRCH, *n.* An entrance with a roof; a portico.
PŎR′CŲ-PĪNE, *n.* A kind of large hedgehog.
PŌRE, *n.* A spiracle of the skin; a small hole.
PŌRE, *v. n.* To look or examine carefully.
PŌR′I-NĔSS, *n.* Fulness of pores.
PŎRK, *n.* Swine's flesh used for food.
PŎRK′ĔT, PŎRK′LING, *n.* A young hog.
PǪ-RŌS′I-TY, *n.* The quality of having pores.
PŌ′ROŲS, *a.* Having small spiracles or passages.
PŌ′ROŲS-NĔSS, *n.* The quality of having pores.
PŌR-PHY-RĬT′IC, *a.* Relating to porphyry.
PŌR′PHY-RY, *n.* A hard stone or mineral.
PŌR′PǪISE (pŏr′pus), PŌR′PŲS, *n.* The sea-hog.
PŎR′RIDGE, *n.* A kind of broth.   [in.
PŎR′RIDĢE-PŎT, *n.* A pot for boiling porridge
PŎR′RIN-GER, *n.* A vessel in which children eat.
PŌRT, *n.* A harbor; a haven :—a gate :—car-
 riage; air; mien :—a red wine.
PŌRT′A-BLE, *a.* That may be carried.
PŌRT′A-BLE-NĔSS, *n.* Quality of being portable.

PŌRT′AĢE, *n.* Carriage; a carrying-place.
PŌR′TAL, *n.* A gate; the arch of a gate; a door.
PŌRT-CŬL′LIS, *n.* A movable frame over a gate-
 way, to be let down at pleasure.
PŌRT-CŬL′LIS, *v. a.* To bar; to shut up.
PŌRTE, *n.* The Turkish or Ottoman court.
PǪR-TĔND′, *v. a.* To foretoken; to foreshow.
PǪR-TĔNT′,*n.*An omen of ill; ill-boding prodigy.
PǪR-TĔN′TOŲS, *a.* Foretokening ill; ominous.
PŌR′TĔR, *n.* A door-keeper; carrier :—a liquor.
PŌR′TĔR-AĢE, *n.* The hire of a porter; carriage.
PŌRT-FŌ′LI-Ō *or* PŌRT-FŎL′IŌ, *n.* ; pl. PŌRT-
 FŌ′LI-ŌŞ. Case like a book, for loose papers, &c.
PŌRT′HŌLE, *n.* A hole to point cannon through.
PŌR′TI-CŌ, *n.* : pl. PŌR′TI-CŌŞ. A covered walk.
PŌR′TIǪN, *n.* A part; allotment; a wife's fortune.
PŌR′TIǪN, *v. a.* To divide; to parcel; to endow.
PŌRT′LI-NĔSS, *n.* Dignity of mien; corpulency.
PŌRT′LY, *a.* Grand of mien; bulky; swelling.
PŌRT-MĂN′TEAU (-tō), *n.* A bag for clothes.
PŌR′TRAIT, *n.* A picture drawn from the life.
PŌR′TRAI-TŪRE (pŏr′tra-tūr), *n.* A picture; por-
PŌR-TRAY′, *v. a.* To paint; to describe. [trait.
PŌR′TRĔSS, *n.* A female guardian of a gate.
PŌRT′RĒĒVE, *n.* The bailiff of a port-town.
PŌR′Y, *a.* Full of pores; porous.
PŌŞE, *v. a.* To puzzle; to perplex; to stop.
PŌŞ′ĔR, *n.* One who poses; an examiner.
PǪ-ŞĬ′′TIǪN (pǫ-zĭsh′ŭn), *n.* Situation; attitude.
PŎŞ′I-TĬVE, *a.* Real; absolute; direct; certain.
PŎŞ′I-TĬVE-LY, *ad.* Absolutely; certainly.
PŎŞ′I-TĬVE-NĔSS, *n.* Actualness; confidence.
PǪŞ-ŞĔSS′, *v. a.* To have; to enjoy; to obtain.
PǪŞ-ŞĔS′SIǪN (pǫz-zĕsh′ŭn), *n.* The state of pos-
 sessing or having in one's power; property.
PǪŞ-ŞĔS′SIVE, *a.* Having or denoting possession.
PǪŞ-ŞĔSS′ǪR, *n.* An owner; a master; a proprie-
PǪŞ-ŞĔS′SǪ-RY, *a.* Having possession. [tor.
PŎŞ′SĔT, *n.* Milk curdled with wine, &c.
PŎS-SI-BĬL′I-TY, *n.* The power of being or doing.
PŎS′SI-BLE, *a.* That may be, or be done.
PŎS′SI-BLY, *ad.* By any power existing; perhaps.
PŌST, *n.* A messenger; a courier :—station; of-
 fice :—a piece of timber :—a French measure.
PŌST, *v. n.* To travel with speed. [to put.
PŌST, *v. a.* To fix on a post; to place; to station;
PŌST′AĢE, *n.* Money paid for conveying letters.
PŌST′BŎY, *n.* A courier; a boy that rides post.
PŌST′-ÇHĀIŞE, *n.* A travelling carriage.
PŌST′DĀTE, *v. a.*To date later than the real time.
PŌST-DI-LŪ′VI-AN, *a.* Posterior to the flood.
PŌST-DI-LŪ′VI-AN, *n.* One living, or one who
 lived since the flood.
PŌST′ĔR, *n.* A courier; one who travels hastily.
PǪS-TĒ′RI-ǪR, *a.* Subsequent; later; placed after.
PǪS-TĒ-RI-ŎR′I-TY, *n.* The state of being after.
PǪS-TĒ′RI-ǪRS, *n. pl.* The hinder parts.
PǪS-TĔR′I-TY, *n.* Succeeding generations; de-
PŎS′TĔRN, *n.* A small gate or door. [scendants.
PŌST′FĬX, *n.* A suffix; a letter or syllable added.
PŌST-FĬX′, *v. a.* To add or annex at the end.
PŌST-HĀSTE′, *n.* Haste like that of a courier.
PŌST′-HŌRSE, *n.* A horse for the use of couriers.
PŌST′-HOÛSE, *n.* A house with a post-office.
PŎST′HŲ-MOŬS, *a.* Being after one's death.
PŎST′HŲ-MOŬS-LY, *ad.* After one's death.
PŌS-TĬL′IǪN (pōs-tĭl′yŭn), *n.* One who guides
 the first pair of a set of horses in a coach.

PŌST′MĂN, n. A courier; a letter-carrier.
PŌST′-MÄRK, n. The mark or stamp of a post-office. [of a post-office.
PŌST′MĂS-TĘR, n. An officer who has charge
PŌST-MĘ-RĬD′Į-ĂN, a. Being in the afternoon.
PŌST′-NŌTE, n. A bank-note payable to order.
PŌST′-ŎF-FĮCE, n. Office for letters; post-house.
PŌST′PĀID, a. Having the postage paid.
PŌST-PŌNE′, v. a. To put off; to delay; to defer.
PŌST-PŌNE′MĘNT, n. A delay; act of putting off.
PŌST′SCRĬPT, n. A paragraph added to a letter.
PŌST′-TŌẄN, n. A town having a post-office.
PŎST′Ų-LĀTE (pŏst′yụ-lāt), v. a. To beg; to invite. [proof.
PŎST′Ų-LĀTE, n. Position assumed without
PŎST-Ų-LĀ′TIǪN, n. Supposition without proof.
PŎST′Ų-LĄ-TǪ-RỴ, a. Assumed without proof.
PŎST′ỤRE (pŏst′yụr), n. State; attitude.
PŎST′ỤRE-MĂS′TĘR, n. One who teaches postures or attitudes.
PŌ′ŞỴ, n. A motto on a ring :—a nosegay.
PŎT, n. A vessel to hold meat or liquids; a cup.
PŎT, v. a. To preserve or enclose in pots.
PŌ′TĄ-BLE, a. Such as may be drunk; drinkablę.
PŎT′ĂSH, n. A fixed alkali from wood.
PǪ-TĀ′TIǪN, n. A drinking-bout; a draught.
PǪ-TĀ′TŌ, n. A plant and tuber. [belly.
PŎT′-BĔL-LĮED (pŏt′bĕl-lįd), a. Having a large
PŌ′TĘN-CỴ, n. Power; efficacy; strength.
PŌ′TĘNT, a. Powerful; forcible; strong.
PŌ′TĘN-TĀTE, n. A monarch; a sovereign.
PǪ-TĔN′TĮĄL (pǫ-tĕn′shąl), a. Existing in possibility, not in act:—implying possibility, liberty, power, or obligation.
PǪ-TĔN-TĮ-ĂL′Į-TỴ, n. Possibility.
PǪ-TĔN′TIĄL-LỴ, ad. In possibility; in efficacy.
PŌ′TĘNT-LỴ, ad. Powerfully; forcibly.
PŎT′HĂNG-ĘR, n. A hook to hang a pot·on.
PŎTH′ĘR or PŎTH′ĘR, n. Bustle; tumult.
PŎT′HĔRB (pŏt′ĕrb), n. An herb fit for the pot.
PŎT′HOOK (pŏt′hŭk), n. A hook to hang pots on.
PŌ′TIǪN, n. A draught; a medical draught.
PŎT′LĬD, n. The lid or cover of a pot.
PŎT′SHĔRD, n. A fragment of a broken pot.
PŎT′TĄĢE, n. Any thing boiled for food.
PŎT′TĘR, n. A maker of earthen vessels.
PŎT′TĘR-Ỵ, n. Work, or wares, of a potter.
PŎT′TLE, n. A measure of four pints :—a basket.
PŎT-VĂL′IĄNT, a. Valiant by drink.
PŎÛCH, n. A purse; a pocket.—v. a. To pocket.
PŎU-ÇHŎŇG′, n. A species of black tea.
PŌUL′TĘR-ĘR (pōl′tęr-ęr), n. One who sells
PŌUL′TĮCE (pōl′tįs), n. A cataplasm. [fowls.
PŌUL′TĮCE (pōl′tįs), v. a. To apply a poultice to.
PŌUL′TRỴ (pōl′trę), n. Domestic fowls.
PŎÛNCE, n. The talon of a bird : — a powder.
PŎÛNCE, v. To pierce; to sprinkle; to seize.
PŎÛN′CĘT-BŎX, n. A small box perforated.
PŎÛND, n. A weight of 16 ounces avoirdupois, or of 12 ounces troy :—in money, 20 shillings : —a pinfold.
PŎÛND, v. a. To beat; to grind :—to shut up.
PŎÛND′AĢE, n. A sum deducted from a pound.
PŎÛND′ĘR, n. A gun of a certain bore; a pestle.
PŌUR (pōr), v. a. To send forth; to let out.
PŌUR (pōr), v. n. To stream; to flow; to rush.
PŎÛT, v. n. To look sullen; to shoot out.
PŎÛT, n. A fit of sullenness :—a fish :—a bird.

PŎV′ĘR-TỴ, n. Indigence; barrenness; defect.
PŎẄ′DĘR, n. Dust; gunpowder; hair-powder.
PŎẄ′DĘR, v. a. To reduce to dust; to sprinkle.
PŎẄ′DĘR-BŎX, n. A box for powder.
PŎẄ′DĘR-FLĂSK, ⎰ n. A case in which gun-
PŎẄ′DĘR-HÖRN, ⎱ powder is kept or carried.
PŎẄ′DĘR-MĬLL, n. A mill to make gunpowder
PŎẄ′DĘR-Ỵ, a. Like powder; dusty; friable. [in.
PŎẄ′ĘR, n. Command; authority; dominion; ability; force; strength; army; ruler; state.
PŎẄ′ĘR-FÛL, a. Having power; strong; potent; mighty; forcible; efficacious.
PŎẄ′ĘR-FÛL-LỴ, ad. Mightily; forcibly.
PŎẄ′ĘR-FÛL-NĔSS, n. Power; efficacy; might.
PŎẄ′ĘR-LĔSS, a. Weak; impotent; feeble.
PŎẄ′ĘR-LŎŌM, n. A loom worked by steam, &c.
PŎẄ′WŎẄ (pŏû′wŏû), n. An Indian dance or
PŎX, n. An eruptive disease; syphilis. [priest.
PRĂC-TĮ-CĄ-BĬL′Į-TY, ⎰ n. Possibility to be per-
PRĂC′TĮ-CĄ-BLE-NĔSS, ⎱ formed; feasibility.
PRĂC′TĮ-CĄ-BLE, a. That may be done or effected.
PRĂC′TĮ-CĄ-BLỴ, ad. In a practicable manner.
PRĂC′TĮ-CĄL, a. Relating to practice or use.
PRĂC′TĮ-CĄL-LỴ, ad. By practice; in real fact.
PRĂC′TĮ-CĄL-NĔSS, n. Quality of being practical.
PRĂC′TĮCE, n. Habit; use; performance; method.
PRĂC′TĮSE, v. a. To do habitually; to exercise.
PRĂC′TĮSE, v. n. To act; to exercise a profession.
PRĄC-TĮ′′TIǪN-ĘR, n. A practiser of any art.
PRÆ-TŌ′RĮ-ŬM, n. [L.] General's tent; palace.
PRĄG-MĂT′ĮC, ⎰ a. Impertinently busy; in-
PRĄG-MĂT′Į-CĄL, ⎱ termeddling; pedantic.
PRĄG-MĂT′Į-CĄL-LỴ, ad. Impertinently.
PRĄG-MĂT′Į-CĄL-NĔSS, n. Quality of meddling.
PRĀI′RIĘ (prā′rę), n. [Fr.] A large natural meadow, or tract of country, bare of trees.
PRĀIŞE, n. Renown; commendation; honor.
PRĀIŞE (prāz), v. a. To commend; to applaud.
PRĀIŞE′LĔSS, a. Wanting praise. [praise.
PRĀIŞE′WÖR-ŦHỴ (prāz′wür-thę), a. Deserving
PRĀNCE, v. n. To spring or bound, as a horse.
PRĂNK, v. a. To decorate; to dress showily.
PRĂNK, n. A frolic; a wild flight; a trick.
PRĀTE, v. n. To talk carelessly; to chatter.
PRĀTE, n. Tattle; idle talk; loquacity.
PRĀT′ĘR, n. An idle talker; a chatterer.
PRĂT′TLE, v. n. To talk lightly; to chatter.
PRĂT′TLE, n. Empty talk; trifling loquacity.
PRĂT′TLĘR, n. Trifling talker; a chatterer.
PRĂV′Į-TỴ, n. Corruption; badness; malignity.
PRĀWN, n. A small crustaceous fish.
PRĂX′ĮS, n. [L.] Use; practice :—example.
PRĀY (prā), v. n. To make petitions; to entreat.
PRĀY, v. a. To supplicate; to implore.
PRĀY′ĘR (prā′ęr), n. A petition to God; entreaty.
PRĀY′ĘR-BOOK (-bûk), n. Book of devotion.
PRĒACH, v. n. To discourse on the gospel, &c.
PRĒACH, v. a. To proclaim or publish; to teach.
PRĒACH′ĘR, n. One who preaches.
PRĒACH′ĮNG, n. A public, religious discourse.
PRĒ-ĄD-MŎN′ĮSH, v. a. To admonish beforehand.
PRĒ′ĂM-BLE, n. An introduction; a preface.
PRĘ-ĂM′BỤ-LĄ-TǪ-RỴ, a. Going before.
PRĘ-ÂU′DĮ-ĔNCE, n. Previous audience.
PRĔB′ĘND, n. A stipend in cathedral churches.
PRĘ-BĔN′DĄL, a. Of or belonging to a prebend.
PRĔB′ĘN-DĄ-RỴ, n. A stipendiary of a cathedral.
PRĘ-CĀ′RĮ-OÜS, a. Dependent; uncertain.

PRĘ-CĀ'RĮ-OŬS-LY, *ad.* Uncertainly.
PRĘ-CĀ'RĮ-OŬS-NĔSS, *n.* Doubt ; dependence.
PRĔC'A-TĬVE, PRĔC'A-TO-RY, *a.* Suppliant.
PRĘ-CÂU'TIǪN, *n.* A preservative caution.
PRĘ-CÂU'TIǪN-A-RY, *a.* Partaking of precaution ; preservative ; preventive.
PRĘ-CĒDE', *v. a.* To go before in rank or time.
PRĘ-CĒ'DĘNCE, } *n.* Act of going before ; pri-
PRĘ-CĒ'DĘN-CY,) ority :—the foremost place.
PRĘ-CĒ'DĘNT, *a.* Former ; going before.
PRĔÇ'Ę-DĔNT, *n.* Something done which is an example to be followed ; an example ; thing done before.
PRĔÇ'Ę-DĔNT-ĘD, *a.* Having a precedent.
PRĘ-CĒ'DĘNT-LY, *ad.* Beforehand. [er.
PRĘ-CĔN'TOR, *n.* A leader of a choir ; a chant-
PRĒ'CĘPT, *n.* A command ; order ; a mandate.
PRĘ-CĔP'TĮVE, *a.* Containing or giving precepts ; preceptory ; instructive.
PRĘ-CĔP'TOR, *n.* A head master :—a tutor.
PRĔÇ-ĘP-TŌ'RĮ-AL, *a.* Relating to a preceptor.
PRĔÇ'ĘP-TO-RY, *a.* Giving precepts ; preceptive.
PRĘ-CĔP'TRĘSS, *n.* A female preceptor or teacher.
PRĘ-CĔS'SIǪN (prę-sĕsh'ṷn), *n.* A going before.
PRĒ'CĮNCT *or* PRĘ-CĬNCT', *n.* A limit ; a boundary :—a district.
PRĒ''CIOŲS (prĕsh'ṷs), *a.* Of great price or value ; very valuable ; costly.
PRĒ''CIOŲS-NĔSS (prĕsh'ṷs-), *n.* Great worth.
PRĔÇ'Į-PĬCE, *n.* A headlong steep ; a cliff.
PRĘ-CĬP'Į-TANCE, } *n.* Rash haste ; precipita-
PRĘ-CĬP'Į-TAN-CY,) tion ; rashness. [rash.
PRĘ-CĬP'Į-TANT, *a.* Falling headlong ; hasty ;
PRĘ-CĬP'Į-TANT-LY, *ad.* In headlong haste.
PRĘ-CĬP'Į-TĀTE, *v. a.* To throw down ; hasten.
PRĘ-CĬP'Į-TATE, *a.* Steep ; hasty ; rash ; violent.
PRĘ-CĬP'Į-TATE, *n.* A term in chemistry.
PRĘ-CĬP'Į-TATE-LY, *ad.* Headlong ; rashly.
PRĘ-CĬP-Į-TĀ'TIǪN, *n.* Rashness ; rash haste.
PRĘ-CĬP'Į-TOŬS, *a.* Headlong ; steep ; hasty.
PRĘ-CĬP'Į-TOŬS-LY, *ad.* In a tumultuous hurry.
PRĘ-CĪSE', *a.* Exact ; strict ; nice ; formal.
PRĘ-CĪSE'LY, *ad.* Exactly ; with precision.
PRĘ-CĪSE'NĘSS, *n.* Exactness ; rigid nicety.
PRĘ-CĬ''ŞIAN (prę-sĭzh'an), *n.* One very exact.
PRĘ-CĬ''ŞIǪN (prę-sĭzh'ṷn), *n.* State of being precise ; exactness ; nicety.
PRĘ-CĪ'SĮVE, *a.* Cutting off ; exactly limiting.
PRĘ-CLŪDE', *v. a.* To shut out by anticipation.
PRĘ-CLŪ'ŞIǪN (prę-klū'zhṷn), *n.* Hinderance.
PRĘ-CLŪ'SĮVE, *a.* Hindering by some anticipation ; shutting out.
PRĘ-CŌ'CIOŲS (prę-kō'shṷs), *a.* Early ripe.
PRĘ-CŌ'CIOŲS-NĔSS (prę-kō'shṷs-nĕs), PRĘ-CŎÇ'Į-TY, *n.* Ripeness before the usual time.
PRĒ-COG-NĬ''TIǪN, *n.* Previous knowledge.
PRĒ-CǪN-CĒIVE', *v. a.* To imagine beforehand.
PRĒ-CǪN-CĔP'TIǪN, *n.* Opinion previously formed ; previous conception.
PRĒ-CǪN-CĔRT', *v. a.* To settle beforehand.
PRĒ-CŎN'TRACT, *n.* A previous contract.
PRĘ-CŬR'SOR, *n.* A forerunner ; a harbinger.
PRĘ-CŬR'SO-RY, *a.* Introductory ; previous.
PRĘ-DĀ'CEOŲS (prę-dā'shṷs), *a.* Living by prey.
PRĒ'DAL, *a.* Robbing ; practising plunder.
PRĔD'A-TO-RY, *a.* Practising rapine ; rapa-
PRĔD-Ę-CĔS'SOR, *n.* One going before. [cious.

PRĘ-DĔS-TĮ-NĀ'RĮ-AN, *n.* A believer in predestination. [tination.
PRĘ-DĔS-TĮ-NĀ'RĮ-AN, *a.* Relating to predes-
PRĘ-DĔS'TĮ-NĀTE, *v. a.* To predetermine ; to foreordain ; to predestine.
PRĘ-DĔS-TĮ-NĀ'TIǪN, *n.* Preordination.
PRĘ-DĔS'TĮ-NĀ-TOR, *n.* One who predestinates.
PRĘ-DĔS'TĮNE, *v. a.* To decree beforehand.
PRĒ-DĘ-TĔR-MĮ-NĀ'TIǪN, *n.* A previous decree.
PRĒ-DĘ-TĔR'MĮNE, *v. a.* To determine beforehand. [farms.
PRĒ'DĮ-AL, *a.* Consisting of, or relating to,
PRĔD-Į-CA-BĬL'Į-TY, *n.* The being predicable.
PRĔD'Į-CA-BLE, *a.* That may be predicated.
PRĘ-DĬC'A-MĔNT, *n.* A class ; state ; condition.
PRĔD'Į-CĀTE, *v. a. & n.* To affirm ; to declare.
PRĔD'Į-CATE, *n.* What is affirmed or denied.
PRĔD-Į-CĀ'TIǪN, *n.* An affirmation ; a declara-
PRĘ-DĬCT', *v. a.* To foretell ; to foreshow. [tion.
PRĘ-DĬC'TIǪN, *n.* Prophecy ; a foretelling.
PRĘ-DĬC'TĮVE, *a.* Prophetic ; foretelling.
PRĘ-DĬCT'OR, *n.* One who predicts ; foreteller.
PRĒ-DĮ-LĔC'TIǪN, *n.* A liking beforehand.
PRĒ-DĬS-PŌSE', *v. a.* To dispose previously.
PRĒ-DĬS-PǪ-ŞĬ''TIǪN (prē-dĭs-pǫ-zĭsh'ṷn), *n.* Previous inclination or adaptation.
PRĘ-DŎM'Į-NANCE, *n.* Prevalence ; ascendency.
PRĘ-DŎM'Į-NANT, *a.* Prevalent ; ascendent.
PRĘ-DŎM'Į-NANT-LY, *ad.* With superior influence ; prevailingly.
PRĘ-DŎM'Į-NĀTE, *v. n.* To prevail ; to abound.
PRĘ-DŎM-Į-NĀ'TIǪN, *n.* Superior influence.
PRĒ-ĔM'Į-NĔNCE, *n.* Superiority ; precedence.
PRĒ-ĔM'Į-NĔNT, *a.* Excellent above others.
PRĒ-ĔM'Į-NĔNT-LY, *ad.* In a preëminent manner. [others.
PRĒ-ĔMP'TIǪN, *n.* Right of buying before
PRĒĔN, *n.* A forked instrument of clothiers.
PRĒ-ĘN-GĀGE', *v. a.* To engage betorehand.
PRĒ-ĘN-GĀGE'MĘNT, *n.* Previous engagement.
PRĒ-ĘS-TĂB'LĮSH, *v. a.* To settle beforehand.
PRĒ-ĘS-TĂB'LĮSH-MĔNT, *n.* Settlement beforehand.
PRĒ-ĘX-ĬST', *v. n.* To exist beforehand.
PRĒ-ĘX-ĬST'ĘNCE, *n.* Previous existence.
PRĒ-ĘX-ĬST'ĘNT, *a.* Existing beforehand.
PRĔF'ACE, *n.* An introduction to a book, &c.
PRĔF'ACE, *v. a.* To introduce by something.
PRĔF'A-CĘR, *n.* The writer of a preface.
PRĔF'A-TO-RY, *a.* Introductory. [mander.
PRĒ'FĘCT, *n.* An officer ; a governor ; a com-
PRĔF'ĘC-TŪRE, *n.* Command ; office of prefect.
PRĘ-FĔR', *v. a.* To regard more ; to choose :
—to promote ; to advance ; to raise.
PRĔF'ER-A-BLE, *a.* Worthy of being preferred.
PRĔF'ER-A-BLE-NĔSS, *n.* State of being pref-
PRĔF'ER-A-BLY, *ad.* In preference. [erable.
PRĔF'ER-ĔNCE, *n.* Act of preferring ; choice.
PRĘ-FĔR'MĘNT, *n.* Advancement ; higher place.
PRĘ-FĬG-Ų-RĀ'TIǪN, *n.* Act of prefiguring ; antecedent representation. [ures.
PRĘ-FĬG'Ų-RA-TĮVE, *a.* Foreshowing by fig-
PRĘ-FĬG'ŲRE (prę-fĭg'yṷr), *v. a.* To exhibit by antecedent representation. [before.
PRĘ-FĬX', *v. a.* To appoint ; to settle ; to put
PRĒ'FĬX, *n.* A particle placed before a word.
PRĔG'NAN-CY, *n.* State of being with young.
PRĔG'NANT, *a.* Being with young ; fruitful ; full.

PRĔG′NĂNT-LY, *ad.* Fruitfully; fully.
PRĘ-HĔN′SĮLE,) *a.* Coiling around; grasp-
PRĘ-HĔN′SǪ-RY,) ing; taking hold.
PRĒ-JŬDĢE′, *v. a.* To determine beforehand.
PRĒ-JŬDĢ′MĘNT, *n.* Previous judgment.
PRĘ-JŪ′DĮ-CĀTE, *v. a. & n.* To prejudge.
PRĘ-JŪ-DĮ-CĀ′TIǪN, *n.* The act of prejudging.
PRĔJ′Ų-DĬCE (prĕd′jų-dĭs), *n.* Prepossession;
previous bias of the mind; mischief; injury.
PRĔJ′Ų-DĬCE, *v. a.* To fill with prejudice; to
hurt; to bias. [injurious.
PRĔJ-Ų-DĬ′′CIĄL (prĕd-ų-dĭsh′ąl), *a.* Hurtful;
PRĔJ-Ų-DĬ′′CIĄL-NĔSS, *n.* Mischievousness.
PRĔL′Ą-CY, *n.* The dignity or office of a prelate.
PRĔL′ĄTE, *n.* A bishop; a high ecclesiastic.
PRĘ-LĂT′ĮC,) *a.* Relating to prelacy or
PRĘ-LĂT′Į-CĄL,) prelates; haughty.
PRĘ-LĂT′Į-CĄL-LY, *ad.* With reference to prel-
PRĔL′Ą-TĬST, *n.* An advocate for prelacy. [ates.
PRĘ-LĔC′TIǪN, *n.* A reading; a lecture; a dis-
PRĘ-LĔC′TǪR, *n.* A reader; a lecturer. [course.
PRĒ-LĬ-BĀ′TIǪN, *n.* A previous taste; foretaste.
PRĘ-LĬM′Į-NĄ-RY, *a.* Previous; introductory.
PRĘ-LĬM′Į-NĄ-RY, *n.* First step; condition.
PRĔL′ŪDE, *n.* Flight or flourish of music be-
fore a full concert:—something introductory.
PRĘ LŪDE′, *v. n. & a.* To be previous; to in-
troduce; to precede.
PRĘ-LŪ′SĮVE, PRĘ-LŪ′SǪ-RY, *a.* Introductory.
PRĒ-MĄ-TŪRE′, *a.* Ripe too soon; too early.
PRĒ-MĄ-TŪRE′LY, *ad.* Too early; too soon.
PRĒ-MĄ-TŪRE′NĘSS,) *n.* Too great haste; un-
PRĒ-MĄ-TŪ′RĮ-TY,) seasonable earliness.
PRĘ-MĔD′Į-TĀTE, *v. a.* To contrive beforehand.
PRĘ-MĔD′Į-TĀTE, *v. n.* To think beforehand.
PRĒ-MĔD-Į-TĀ′TIǪN, *n.* Act of premeditating.
PRĔM′IĘR *or* PRĒ′MĮ-ĘR, *n.* A prime minister.
PRĘ-MĪSE′, *v. a.* To explain previously. [tions.
PRĘ-MĪSE′, *v. n.* To make previous proposi-
PRĔM′Į-SĘS, *n. pl.* (*Logic.*) The first two prop-
ositions of a syllogism.—(*Law.*) Houses or
lands:—statements before made.
PRĒ′MĮ-ŬM, *n.* A bounty; recompense; reward.
PRĒ-MŎN′ĮSH, *v. a.* To admonish beforehand.
PRĒ-MǪ-NĬ′′TIǪN, *n.* Previous intelligence.
PRĒ-MŎN′Į-TǪ-RY, *a.* Previously advising.
PRĒM-Ų-NĬ′RĘ, *n.* [L.] A writ; a penalty.
PRĒ-MŲ-NĬ′′TIǪN, *n.* Previous defence.
PRĒ-NŌ′TIǪN, *n.* Foreknowledge; prescience.
PRĒ-ŎC′CŲ-PĄN-CY, *n.* Previous possession.
PRĒ-ŎC-CŲ-PĀ′TIǪN, *n.* Prior occupation.
PRĒ-ŎC′CŲ-PȲ, *v. a.* To occupy previously.
PRĒ-ǪR-DĀIN′, *v. a.* To ordain beforehand.
PRĘ-ŎR′DĮ-NĂNCE, *n.* An antecedent decree.
PRĘ-ŎR DĮ-NĀ′TIǪN, *n.* Act of preordaining.
PRĔP-Ą-RĀ′TIǪN, *n.* Act of preparing; state
of being prepared; readiness. [ting.
PRĘ-PĂR′Ą-TĬVE, *a.* Tending to prepare; fit-
PRĘ-PĂR′Ą-TĬVE, *n.* That which prepares.
PRĘ-PĂR′Ą-TǪ-RY, *a.* Introductory; antecedent.
PRĘ-PĀRE′, *v. a.* To make ready, qualify, form.
PRĘ-PĀRE′, *v. n.* To take previous measures.
PRĘ-PĂR′ĘD-NĔSS, *n.* State of being prepared.
PRĒ-PĔNSE′, *a.* Preconceived; premeditated.
PRĘ-PŎN′DĘR-ANCE, *n.* Superiority of weight.
PRĘ-PŎN′DĘR-ANT, *a.* Outweighing.
PRĘ PŎN′DĘR-ĀTE, *v. a. & n.* To exceed in
weight; to outweigh.

PRĘ-PŎN-DĘR-Ā′TIǪN, *n.* Act of outweighing.
PRĔP-Ǫ-SĬ′′TIǪN (prĕp-ǫ-zĭsh′ųn), *n.* (*Gram.*)
A particle governing a noun or pronoun.
PRĘ-PŎS′Į-TǪR, *n.* A monitor; an inspector.
PRĘ-PǪS-SĔSS′, *v. a.* To preoccupy, prejudice.
PRĒ-PǪS-SĔS′SIǪN (prē-pǫz-zĕsh′ųn), *n.* Pre-
occupation; prejudice; preconceived opinion.
PRĒ-PǪS-SĔSS′ǪR, *n.* One that prepossesses.
PRĘ-PŎS′TĘR-OŬS, *a.* Distorted; reversed; per-
verted; wrong; absurd; foolish.
PRĘ-PŎS′TĘR-OŬS-LY, *ad.* Absurdly; foolishly.
PRĘ-PŎS′TĘR-OŬS-NĔSS, *n.* Absurdity.
PRĒ′PŪCE, *n.* The foreskin.
PRĒ-RĔQ′UĮ-SĮTE (prē-rĕk′wę-zĭt), *n.* Some-
thing previously required; requirement.
PRĒ-RĔQ′UĮ-SĮTE, *a.* Previously necessary.
PRĘ-RŎG′Ą-TĬVE, *n.* An exclusive privilege.
PRĘS′ĀĢE, *n.* Something that foreshows.
PRĘ-SĀĢE′, *v. a.* To forebode; to foreshow.
PRĔS′BY-TĘR, *n.* A member of a presbytery;
a priest; an elder. [rianism.
PRĔS-BY-TĒ′RĮ-AN, *a.* Relating to Presbyte-
PRĔS-BY-TĒ′RĮ-AN, *n.* One who holds to
church government by presbyteries.
PRĔS-BY-TĒ′RĮ-AN-ĬSM, *n.* Ecclesiastical gov-
ernment conducted by presbyters.
PRĔS′BY-TĘR-Y, *n.* A body of presbyters.
PRĒ′SCĮ-ĘNCE (prē′shę-ęns), *n.* Foreknowledge.
PRĒ′SCĮ-ĘNT (prē′shę-ęnt), *a.* Foreknowing.
PRĘ-SCRĪBE′, *v. a. & n.* To set down; to direct.
PRĒ′SCRĬPT, *n.* A direction; a precept; order.
PRĘ-SCRĬP′TIǪN, *n.* A custom long continued
till it has the force of law:—medical receipt.
PRĘ-SCRĬP′TĮVE, *a.* Established by custom.
PRĔS′ĘNCE, *n.* State of being present; port; air.
PRĔS′ĘNT, *a.* Now at hand; not absent; now
existing; not past; not future.
PRĔS′ĘNT, *n.* A gift; donative; present time.
PRĘ-SĘNT′, *v. a.* To exhibit, offer, give, prefer.
PRĘ-SĘNT′Ą-BLE, *a.* That may be presented.
PRĔS-ĘN-TĀ′NĘ-OŬS, *a.* Ready; quick.
PRĔS-ĘN-TĀ′TIǪN, *n.* Act of presenting; show.
PRĘ-SĔN′TA-TĬVE, *a.* Admitting presentations.
PRĔS-ĘN-TĒÉ′, *n.* One presented to a benefice.
PRĘ-SĘNT′ĘR, *n.* One that presents. [idea.
PRĒ-SĔNT′Į-MĔNT, *n.* A previous notion or
PRĔS′ĘNT-LY, *ad.* Immediately; soon after.
PRĘ-SĔNT′MĘNT, *n.* The act of presenting.
PRĘ-SĔRV′Ą-BLE, *a.* Capable of preservation.
PRĔS-ĘR-VĀ′TIǪN, *n.* The act of preserving.
PRĘ-SĔRV′Ą-TĬVE, *n.* That which preserves.
PRĘ-SĔRV′Ą-TĬVE, *a.* Tending to preserve.
PRĘ-SĔRV′Ą-TǪ-RY, *a.* Tending to preserve.
PRĘ-SĔRVE′, *v. a.* To shelter from harm; to
save; to keep:—to season, as fruit.
PRĘ-SĔRVE′, *n.* Fruit preserved in sugar.
PRĘ-SĔRV′ĘR, *n.* One who preserves.
PRĘ-SĪDE′, *v. n.* To be set over; to direct.
PRĔS′Į-DĔN-CY, *n.* The office of president;
superintendence; direction. [or state.
PRĔS′Į-DĔNT, *n.* One at the head of a society
PRĔS-Į-DĔN′TIĄL, *a.* Relating to a president.
PRĔS′Į-DĔNT-SHĬP, *n.* The office of president.
PRĘ-SĬD′Į-ĄL, *a.* Relating to a garrison. [son.
PRĘ-SĬD′Į-Ą-RY, *a.* Of, or relating to, a garri-
PRĔSS, *v. a.* To squeeze; to distress; to urge.
PRĔSS, *v. n.* To urge; to encroach; to crowd.
PRĔSS, *n.* An instrument for pressing or print-

ing :—the business of printing :—a crowd ; a throng :—case or frame for clothes.

PRĔSS′BĔD, *n.* A bed to be shut up in a case.

PRĔSS′GĂNG, *n.* A crew that impress men.

PRĔSS′MĂN, *n.* A printer who works at the press.

PRĔSS′-MŎN-EY (prĕs′mŭn-ę), *n.* Money given to a sailor when he is forced into the service.

PRĔSS′ŲRE (prĕsh′ur), *n.* Act of pressing ; force.

PRĘ-ṢŪM′A-BLE, *a.* That may be presumed.

PRĘ-ṢŪME′, *v. n.* To suppose, affirm, venture.

PRĘ-ṢŬMP′TIǪN (prę-zŭm′shun), *n.* Supposition ; strong probability ; arrogance ; boldness.

PRĘ-ṢŬMP′TĮVE, *a.* Probable ; supposed.

‖**PRĘ-ṢŬMPT′Ų-OŬS** (prę-zŭmt′yu-ŭs), *a.* Arrogant ; unreasonably confident ; bold. [dence.

‖**PRĘ-ṢŬMPT′Ų-OŬS-LY**, *ad.* With vain confi-

‖**PRĘ-ṢŬMPT′Ų-OŲS-NĔSS**, *n.* Vain confidence.

PRĒ-SŲP-PŌ′ṢAL, *n.* Previous supposition.

PRĒ-SŲP-PŌṢE′, *v. a.* To suppose beforehand.

PRĒ-SŲP-PǪ-ṢĬ′′TIǪN, *n.* Previous supposition.

PRĒ-SŲR-MĬṢE′, *n.* A surmise previously formed.

PRĘ-TĔNCE′, *n.* A pretext ; assumption ; show.

PRĘ-TĔND′, *v. a. & n.* To hold out an appearance of ; to simulate ; to allege falsely.

PRĘ-TĔND′ĘD-LY, *ad.* By false appearance.

PRĘ-TĔND′ĘR, *n.* One who pretends or claims.

PRĘ-TĔN′SIǪN, *n.* A claim ; a false appearance.

PRĒ′TĘR. A particle from the Latin, which signifies *beside* or *beyond.*

PRĒ-TĘR-ĮM-PĔR′FĘCT, *a.* Not perfectly past.

PRĔT′ĘR-ĬTE, *a.* (*Gram.*) Past or perfect.

PRĒ-TĘR-MĬS′SIǪN, *n.* The act of omitting.

PRĒ-TĘR-MĬT′, *v. a.* To pass by ; to neglect.

PRĒ-TĘR-NĂT′Ų-RAL (prē-tęr-năt′yu-ral), *a.* Different from what is natural ; unnatural.

PRĒ-TĘR-PĔR′FĘCT, *a.* (*Gram.*) Absolutely or perfectly past.

PRĒ-TĘR-PLŲ-PĔR′FĘCT, *a.* Past before another event. [false show.

PRĒ-TĔXT′ *or* **PRĒ′TĔXT**, *n.* A pretence ; a

PRĒ′TǪR, *n.* A chief judge in ancient Rome.

PRĘ-TŌ′RĮ-AL, } *a.* Relating to a pretor ; judicial.

PRĘ-TŌ′RĮ-AN, }

PRĒ′TǪR-SHĬP, *n.* The office of pretor.

PRĔT′TĮ-LY (prĭt′tę-lę), *ad.* Neatly ; pleasingly.

PRĔT′TĮ-NĔSS (prĭt′tę-nĕs), *n.* Beauty without dignity ; neatness ; neat elegance.

PRĔT′TY (prĭt′tę), *a.* Neat ; elegant ; pleasing.

PRĔT′TY (prĭt′tę), *ad.* In some degree ; moderately ; considerably.

PRĘ-VĀIL′, *v. n.* To be prevalent ; to overcome.

PRĘ-VĀIL′ĮNG, *a.* Predominant ; efficacious.

PRĔV′A-LĔNCE, *n.* Superiority; influence ;force.

PRĔV′A-LĔNT, *a.* Predominant ; efficacious.

PRĔV′A-LĔNT-LY, *ad.* Powerfully ; forcibly.

PRĘ-VĂR′Į-CĀTE, *v. n.* To evade the truth ; to equivocate ; to quibble ; to shuffle.

PRĘ-VĂR-Į-CĀ′TIǪN, *n.* A quibble ; a cavil.

PRĘ-VĂR′Į-CĀ-TǪR, *n.* A caviller ; a quibbler.

PRĘ-VĒ′NĮ-ĘNT, *a.* Preceding ; preventive.

PRĘ-VĔNT′, *v. a.* To hinder ; to obviate ; to stop.

PRĘ-VĔNT′A-BLE, *a.* That may be prevented.

PRĘ-VĔNT′ĘR, *n.* One that hinders.

PRĘ-VĔN′TIǪN, *n.* Hinderance ; obstruction.

PRĘ-VĔN′TĮVE, *a.* Preservative ; hindering.

PRĘ-VĔN′TĮVE, *n.* A preservative ; an antidote.

PRĘ-VĔN′TĮVE-LY, *ad.* In a preventive manner.

PRĒ′VĮ-OŬS, *a.* Antecedent ; going before ; prior.

PRĒ′VĮ-OŬS-LY, *ad.* Beforehand ; antecedently.

PRĒ′VĮ-OŲS-NĔSS, *n.* State of being previous.

PREY (prā), *n.* Rapine ; plunder ; ravage.

PREY (prā), *v. n.* To plunder ; to rob ; to waste.

PREY′ĘR (prā′ęr), *n.* A robber ; a devourer.

PRĪCE, *n.* Value ; estimation ; rate ; reward.

PRĬCK, *v. a.* To pierce, spur, mark, make acid.

PRĬCK, *n.* A point ; a spur ; a puncture ; pain.

PRĬCK′ĘR, *n.* A sharp-pointed instrument.

PRĬCK′ĘT, *n.* A buck in his second year.

PRĬCK′ĮNG, *n.* The sensation of being pricked.

PRĬC′KLE, *n.* A small, sharp point.

PRĬCK′LĮ-NĔSS, *n.* Fulness of sharp points.

PRĬCK′LY, *a.* Full of sharp points. [loftiness.

PRĪDE, *n.* Self-esteem ; vanity ; haughtiness ;

PRĪDE, *v. a.* To make proud ; to rate high.

PRĪ′ĘR, *n.* One who inquires narrowly.

PRIĔST (prēst), *n.* One who officiates in sacred offices ; a clergyman ; a minister. [priests.

PRIĔST′CRĂFT, *n.* Religious fraud ; fraud of

PRIĔST′ĔSS, *n.* A female priest. [of priests.

PRIĔST′HOOD (prēst′hûd), *n.* Office and order

PRIĔST′LĮ-NĔSS, *n.* The manner of a priest.

PRIĔST′LY, *a.* Becoming a priest ; sacerdotal.

PRIĔST′-RĬD-DEN, *a.* Governed by priests.

PRĬG, *n.* A pert, conceited little fellow.

PRĬG′ǴISH, *a.* Conceited ; pert. [*Colloquial.*]

PRĬM, *a.* Formal ; precise ; affectedly nice.

PRĬM, *v. a.* To deck up or form precisely.

PRĪ′MA-CY, *n.* The office or dignity of primate.

PRĪ′MAǴE, *n.* Charge in addition to freight.

PRĪ′MA-RĮ-LY, *ad.* Originally ; in the first place.

PRĪ′MA-RĮ-NĔSS, *n.* The state of being first.

PRĪ′MA-RY, *a.* First ; original ; chief ; principal.

PRĪ′MATE, *n.* The chief ecclesiastic in a church.

PRĪ′MATE-SHĬP, *n.* Dignity or office of primate.

PRĪME, *n.* The dawn :—the best part :—spring.

PRĪME, *a.* Early; principal ; first-rate ; excellent.

PRĪME, *v. a.* To put powder in the pan of a gun :—to lay the ground on a canvas for painting. [lence.

PRĪME′NĔSS, *n.* State of being first ; excel-

PRĬM′ĘR, *n.* A small book for children.

PRĮ-MĒ′VAL, *a.* Original ; first ; primitive.

PRĪM′ĮNG, *n.* Powder in the pan of a gun :— the first coat in painting.

PRĬM′Į-TĬVE, *a.* Original ; first ; primary.

PRĬM′Į-TĬVE, *n.* A primitive or original word,

PRĬM′Į-TĬVE-LY, *ad.* Originally ; at first.

PRĬM′NĔSS, *n.* Affected niceness or formality.

PRĪ-MǪ-ǴĒ′NĮ-AL, *a.* First-born ; primary.

PRĪ-MǪ-ǴĔN′Į-TǪR, *n.* A forefather ; ancestor.

PRĪ-MǪ-ǴĔN′Į-TŪRE, *n.* State of being first-

PRĪ-MÖR′DĮ-AL, *a.* Original ; first in order.[born.

PRĪ-MÖR′DĮ-AL, *n.* Origin ; first principle.

PRĬM′RŌṢE, *n.* A plant, and its flower.

PRĬNCE, *n.* A sovereign ; a ruler ; a king's son.

PRĬNCE′DŎM, *n.* State and power of a prince.

PRĬNCE′LĮ-NĔSS, *n.* State or dignity of a prince.

PRĬNCE′LY, *a.* Becoming a prince ; grand.

PRĬN′CE′Ṣ-FĔAŦH′ĘR, *n.* A plant and flower.

PRĬN′CĔSS, *n.* A sovereign or royal lady.

PRĬN′CĮ-PAL, *a.* Chief ; first ; capital ; essential.

PRĬN′CĮ-PAL, *n.* A head ; a chief ; a capital

PRĬN′CĮ-PĂL′Į-TY, *n.* A prince's domain. [sum.

PRĬN′CĮ-PAL-LY, *ad.* Chiefly ; above the rest.

PRĬN′CĮ-PLE, *n.* Constituent part ; cause :—a

fundamental truth ; an axiom :—ground of action ; motive :—doctrine ; tenet.
PRĬN′CĬ-PLE, *v. a.* To establish in principles.
PRĬNK, *v. a. & n.* To dress for show.
PRĬNT, *v. a. & n.* To mark any thing ; to imprint ; to impress words. [paper.
PRĬNT, *n.* A mark made by pressure :—a news-
PRĬNT′ER, *n.* One who prints books, &c. [raphy.
PRĬNT′ĬNG, *n.* Business of a printer ; typog-
PRĬNT′ĬNG-PRĔSS, *n.* A press used for printing.
PRĪ′OR, *a.* Former ; antecedent ; anterior.
PRĪ′OR, *n.* The head of a priory of monks.
PRĪ′OR-ĔSS, *n.* A superior of a convent of nuns.
PRĪ-ŎR′Ĭ-TY, *n.* State of being first ; precedence.
PRĪ′OR-Y, *n.* A convent inferior to an abbey.
PRĬSM, *n.* A sort of solid :—a sort of glass.
PRĬṢ-MĂT′ĬC, *a.* Formed as a prism.
PRĬṢ-MĂT′Ĭ-CĂL-LY, *ad.* In the form of a prism.
PRĬṢ′MÖÏD, *n.* A body somewhat like a prism.
PRĬṢ′ON (prĭz′zn), *n.* Place of confinement ; jail.
PRĬṢ′ON (prĭz′zn), *v. a.* To imprison ; to confine.
PRĬṢ′ON-BĀSE (prĭz′zn-bās), *n.* A rural play.
PRĬṢ′ON-ER (prĭz′zn-er), *n.* One who is confined in prison ; a captive ; one taken by an enemy. [hold.
PRĬṢ′ON-HÖÛSE (prĭz′zn-höûs), *n.* A jail ; a
PRĬS′TĬNE, *a.* First ; ancient ; original ; pri-
PRĬꞄH′EE. A corruption of *I pray thee.* [mary.
PRĪ′VA-CY, *n.* Secrecy ; retirement ; privity.
PRĪ′VATE, *a.* Not open ; secret ; alone ; not
PRĪ′VATE, *n.* A common soldier. [public.
PRĪ-VA-TĔĔR′, *n.* A private armed vessel.
PRĪ-VA-TĔĔR′, *v. n.* To fit out, or cruise in, privateers.
PRĪ′VATE-LY, *ad.* Secretly ; not openly. [ment.
PRĪ′VATE-NĔSS, *n.* Secrecy ; privacy ; retire-
PRĪ-VĀ′TĬON, *n.* The loss of any thing ; absence.
PRĬV′A-TĬVE, *a.* Causing privation ; not posi-
PRĬV′A-TĬVE, *n.* A negative property. [tive.
PRĬV′A-TĬVE-LY, *ad.* By privation ; negatively.
PRĬV′A-TĬVE-NĔSS, *n.* Notation of absence.
PRĬV′ET, *n.* A plant or shrub. [prerogative.
PRĬV′Ĭ-LEGE, *n.* A peculiar benefit ; immunity ;
PRĬV′Ĭ-LEGE, *v. a.* To grant a privilege ; to free.
PRĬV′Ĭ-LY, *ad.* Secretly ; privately ; clandestine-
PRĬV′Ĭ-TY, *n.* Private concurrence ; privacy. [ly.
PRĬV′Y, *a.* Secret ; private ; privately knowing.
PRĬV′Y, *n.* A partaker :—a necessary house.
PRĪZE, *n.* A reward gained by contest ; plunder.
PRĪZE, *v. a.* To raise with a lever. See PRY.
PRĪZE, *v. a.* To rate ; to esteem ; to value highly.
PRĪZE′-FĪGHT-ER, *n.* One that fights for a re-
PRĪZ′ER, *n.* One who prizes or values. [ward.
PRŌ. [L.] For ; *pro* and *con,* for and against.
PRŎB-A-BĬL′Ĭ-TY, *n.* State of being probable ; likelihood ; appearance of truth.
PRŎB′A-BLE, *a.* Likely ; having some evidence.
PRŎB′A-BLY, *ad.* Likely ; in likelihood. [proved.
PRŌ′BATE, *n.* Proof of a will :—copy of a will
PRO-BĀ′TĬON, *n.* Proof ; trial ; novitiate.
PRO-BĀ′TĬON-A-RY, *a.* Serving for trial.
PRO-BĀ′TĬON-ER, *n.* One upon probation.
PRŌ′BA-TO-RY, *a.* Serving for trial or proof.
PRŌBE, *n.* A surgeon's instrument.
PRŌBE, *v. a.* To search ; to try by a probe.
PRŌBE′-SCĬṢ-ṢORṢ, *n. pl.* A surgeon's scissors to open wounds.
PRŎB′Ĭ-TY, *n.* Honesty ; uprightness ; veracity.

PRŎB′LEM, *n.* A question proposed for solution.
PRŎB-LEM-ĂT′Ĭ-CAL, *a.* Uncertain ; disputable.
PRŎB-LEM-ĂT′Ĭ-CAL-LY, *ad.* Uncertainly.
PRO-BŎS′CĬS, *n.* The trunk of an elephant, &c.
PRO-CĒD′URE (pro-sēd′yur), *n.* Act of proceeding ; conduct ; process. [arise-
PRO-CĒĒD′, *v. n.* To go on ; to advance, issue,
PRO-CĒĒD′ER, *n.* One who proceeds.
PRO-CĒĒD′ĬNG, *n.* A transaction ; a procedure.
PRŌ′CĒĒDṢ *or* PRO-CĒĒDṢ′, *n. pl.* Produce ; income ; receipts ; rent.
PRO-CĒR′Ĭ-TY, *n.* Tallness ; height of stature.
PRŎC′ESS, *n.* A progress ; an order ; operation ; conduct :—course of law ; a suit.
PRO-CĔS′SĬON (pro-sĕsh′un), *n.* A train marching in ceremonious solemnity :—act of issuing.
PRO-CĔS′SĬON-AL, PRO-CĔS′SĬON-A-RY (pro-sĕs′shun-a-re), *a.* Relating to procession.
PRŌ′CHRO-NĬSM, *n.* The act of antedating, or of dating of a thing too early.
PRO-CLAĬM′, *v. a.* To promulgate ; to publish.
PRO-CLAĬM′ER, *n.* One who proclaims.
PRŎC-LA-MĀ′TĬON, *n.* A public, official notice.
PRO-CLĬV′Ĭ-TY, *n.* Tendency ; inclination.
PRO-CLĪ′VOUS, *a.* Inclined ; tending by nature.
PRO-CŌN′SUL, *n.* A Roman governor.
PRO-CŌN′SU-LAR, *a.* Belonging to a proconsul.
PRO-CŌN′SU-LATE, *n.* The office of proconsul.
PRO-CŌN′SUL-SHĬP, *n.* Office of a proconsul.
PRO-CRĂS′TĬ-NĀTE, *v. a. & n.* To put off from time to time ; to postpone ; to defer ; to delay.
PRO-CRĂS-TĬ-NĀ′TĬON, *n.* Delay ; dilatoriness.
PRO-CRĂS′TĬ-NĀ-TOR, *n.* A dilatory person.
PRŌ′CRE-ANT, *a.* Productive ; pregnant.
PRŌ′CRE-ĀTE, *v. a.* To generate ; to produce.
PRŌ-CRE-Ā′TĬON, *n.* Generation ; production.
PRŌ′CRE-Ā-TĬVE, *a.* Generative ; productive.
PRŌ′CRE-Ā-TĬVE-NĔSS, *n.* Power of generation.
PRŌ′CRE-Ā-TOR, *n.* A generator ; a begetter.
PRŎC′TOR, *n.* An advocate ; an attorney in a spiritual court :—an officer in a university.
PRŎC′TOR-SHĬP, *n.* Office or dignity of a proc-
PRO-CŬM′BENT, *a.* Lying down ; stooping. [tor.
PRO-CŪR′A-BLE, *a.* Obtainable ; acquirable.
PRŎC′U-RA-CY, *n.* The management of a thing.
PRŎC-U-RĀ′TĬON, *n.* Procurement ; manage-
PRŎC′U-RĀ-TOR, *n.* A manager ; agent. [ment.
PRŎC-U-RA-TŌ′RĬ-AL, *a.* Relating to, or done by, a procurator. [urator.
PRŎC-U-RĀ′TOR-SHĬP, *n.* The office of a proc-
PRO-CŪ′RA-TO-RY, *a.* Tending to procuration.
PRO-CŪRE′, *v. a.* To manage ; to obtain ; to acquire ; to gain ; to win ; to furnish.
PRO-CŪRE′MENT, *n.* The act of procuring.
PRO-CŪR′ER, *n.* One who procures ; obtainer.
PRO-CŪR′ESS, *n.* A bawd ; a seducing woman.
PRŎD′Ĭ-GAL, *a.* Profuse ; wasteful ; expensive.
PRŎD′Ĭ-GAL, *n.* A waster ; a spendthrift.
PRŎD-Ĭ-GĂL′Ĭ-TY, *n.* Extravagance ; profusion.
PRŎD′Ĭ-GAL-LY, *ad.* Profusely ; wastefully.
PRO-DĬG′ĬOUS (pro-dĭj′us), *a.* Amazing ; monstrous ; astonishing ; extraordinary.
PRO-DĬG′ĬOUS-LY (pro-dĭj′us-le), *ad.* Amazing-
PRO-DĬG′ĬOUS-NĔSS, *n.* Enormousness. [ly.
PRŎD′Ĭ-GY, *n.* A monster ; any thing astonishing.
PRO-DŪCE′, *v. a.* To bring forth, exhibit, cause.
PRŎD′ŪCE (prŏd′dūs), *n.* Product ; production.
PRO-DŪ′CER, *n.* One that generates or produces.

PRỌ-DŪ'ÇI-BLE, *a.* That may be produced.
PRŎD'ŲCT, *n.* A thing produced; produce; re-
PRỌ-DŬC'TILE, *a.* That may be drawn out.[sult.
PRỌ-DŬC'TIỌN, *n.* The act of producing; product.
PRỌ-DŬC'TIVE, *a.* That produces; fertile; gen-
erative; efficient. [ductive.
PRỌ-DŬC'TIVE-NĔSS, *n.* State of being pro-
PRŌ'ĔM, *n.* A preface; an introduction.
PRỌ-Ē'MI-ẠL, *a.* Introductory; prefatory.
PRŎF-Ạ-NĀ'TIỌN, *n.* Violation of things sacred.
PRỌ-FĀNE', *a.* Irreverent to things sacred; ir-
religious; impure; secular; not sacred.
PRỌ-FĀNE', *v. a.* To violate; to desecrate; to
put to wrong use. [edly.
PRỌ-FĀNE'LỰ, *ad.* With irreverence; wick-
PRỌ-FĀNE'NĔSS, *n.* Irreverence of what is sa-
cred; profanity.
PRỌ-FĀN'ER, *n.* One who profanes or pollutes.
PRỌ-FĂN'I-TỰ, *n.* Quality of being profane;
profaneness. [avow.
PRỌ-FĔSS', *v. a.* & *n.* To declare openly; to
PRỌ-FĔSS'ED-LỰ, *ad.* With open declaration.
PRỌ-FĔS'SIỌN (-fĕsh'ụn), *n.* A calling; a voca-
tion; an employment requiring a learned edu-
cation:—a declaration.
PRỌ-FĔS'SIỌN-ẠL, *a.* Relating to a profession.
PRỌ-FĔS'SIỌN-ẠL-LỰ, *ad.* By profession.
PRỌ-FĔSS'ỌR, *n.* One who professes or teaches.
PRŌ-FES-SŌ'RI-ẠL, *a.* Relating to a professor.
PRỌ-FĔSS'ỌR-SHIP, *n.* The office of a professor.
PRŎF'FER, *v. a.* To offer for acceptance; to pro-
pose; to attempt.
PRŎF'FER, *n.* An offer made; a proposal.
PRŎF'FER-ER, *n.* One who proffers; offerer.
PRỌ-FĬ''CIEN-CỰ (-fĭsh'ẹn-sẹ),*n.* Advancement.
PRỌ-FĬ''CIENT (prọ-fĭsh'ẹnt), *n.* One who has
made advances in any study or business.
PRŌ'FILE *or* PRỌ-FĪLE', *n.* The side-face; a
half face:—outline of a building.
PRŎF'IT, *n.* Gain; advantage; advancement.
PRŎF'IT, *v. a.* To benefit, advantage, advance.
PRŎF'IT, *v. n.* To gain advantage; to improve.
PRŎF'IT-Ạ-BLE, *a.* Gainful; lucrative; useful.
PRŎF'IT-Ạ-BLE-NĔSS, *n.* Gainfulness; useful-
ness. [ly.
PRŎF'IT-Ạ-BLỰ, *ad.* Gainfully; advantageous-
PRŎF'LI-GẠ-CỰ, *n.* Profligate or shameless con-
duct or vice; depravity. [ed.
PRŎF'LI-GẠTE, *a.* Abandoned to vice; wick-
PRŎF'LI-GẠTE, *n.* An abandoned wretch.
PRŎF'LI-GẠTE-LỰ, *ad.* With profligacy. [ness.
PRŎF'LI-GẠTE-NĔSS, *n.* Profligacy; dissolute-
PRỌ-FŌÛND', *a.* Deep; thorough; low; humble.
PRỌ-FŌÛND', *n.* The deep; the sea; the abyss.
PRỌ-FŌÛND'LỰ, *ad.* Deeply; thoroughly.
PRỌ-FŌÛND'NĔSS, *n.* Profundity; depth.
PRỌ-FŬN'DI-TỰ, *n.* Depth of place or knowledge.
PRỌ-FŪSE', *a.* Lavish; prodigal; overabounding.
PRỌ-FŪSE'LỰ, *ad.* Lavishly; with exuberance.
PRỌ-FŪSE'NĔSS, *n.* Lavishness; prodigality.
PRỌ-FŪ'ŞIỌN (prọ-fū'zhụn), *n.* Lavishness;
prodigality; extravagance; abundance.
PRỌ-GĔN'I-TỌR, *n.* A forefather; an ancestor.
PRŎG'E-NỰ, *n.* Offspring; descendants; race.
PRỌG-NŎS'TIC, *a.* Foretokening; foreshowing.
PRỌG-NŎS'TIC, *n.* That which foreshows; a
sign; a token; prediction. [show.
PRỌG-NŎS'TI-CĀTE, *v. a.* To foretell; to fore-

PRỌG-NŎS-TI-CĀ'TIỌN, *n.* Act of foretelling.
PRỌG-NŎS'TI-CĀ-TỌR, *n.* One who foretells.
PRŌ'GRĂM, } *n.* An outline or sketch of ex-
PRŌ'GRĂMME, } ercises.
PRŎG'RESS, *n.* A course; advancement.
PRỌ-GRĔSS', *v. n.* To proceed; to advance.
PRỌ-GRĔS'SIỌN (-grĕsh'ụn),*n.* Advance; course.
PRỌ-GRĔS'SIỌN-ẠL,*a.* Advancing; increasing.
PRỌ-GRĔS'SIVE,*a.* Going forward; advancing.
PRỌ-GRĔS'SIVE-LỰ,*ad.* By regular course.[cing.
PRỌ-GRĔS'SIVE-NĔSS, *n.* The state of advan-
PRỌ-HĬB'IT, *v. a.* To forbid, interdict, hinder.
PRỌ-HĬB'IT-ER, *n.* A forbidder; an interdicter.
PRŌ-HI-BĬ''TIỌN (-hẹ-bĭsh'ụn), *n.* An interdict.
PRỌ-HĬB'I-TỌ-RỰ, *a.* Forbidding; prohibiting.
PRỌ-JĔCT', *v. a.* To throw, scheme, contrive.
PRỌ-JĔCT', *v. n.* To jut out; to shoot forward.
PRŎJ'ECT, *n.* A scheme; a design; a contriv-
ance:—plan; device.
PRỌ-JĔC'TILE, *n.* A body projected in space.
PRỌ-JĔC'TILE, *a.* Impelling forward. [plan.
PRỌ-JĔC'TIỌN, *n.* The act of projecting:—a
PRỌ-JĔCT'ỌR, *n.* One who projects or designs.
PRỌ-JĔCT'ỤRE (prọ-jĕkt'yụr), *n.* A jutting out.
PRŌ'LĀTE, *a.* Extended beyond an exact sphere.
PRỌ-LĀ'TIỌN, *n.* Pronunciation; utterance.
PRỌ-LĔP'SIS, *n.* An anticipation; an anachro-
nism; prochronism.
PRỌ-LĔP'TIC, PRỌ-LĔP'TI-CẠL, *a.* Antecedent.
PRỌ-LĬF'IC, *a.* Fruitful; productive; fertile.
PRỌ-LĬF-I-CĀ'TIỌN, *n.* Generation; production.
PRỌ-LĬF'IC-NĔSS, *n.* The state of being prolific.
PRỌ-LĬX', *a.* Long; tedious; diffuse; wordy.
PRỌ-LĬX'I-TỰ, *n.* Tediousness; tiresome length.
PRỌ-LĬX'NESS, *n.* Tediousness; prolixity.
‖PRŎL-Ọ-CŪ'TỌR *or* PRỌ-LŎC'Ụ-TỌR, *n.* A
spokesman; the speaker of a convocation.
‖PRŎL-Ọ-CŪ'TỌR-SHIP, *n.* The office of prolo-
cutor. [tion.
PRŎL'ỌGUE (prŏl'ọg), *n.* A preface; introduc-
PRỌ-LŎNG', *v. a.* To lengthen out; to continue.
PRŌ-LỌN-GĀ'TIỌN, *n.* Act of lengthening; de-
PRỌ-LŎNG'ER, *n.* One that prolongs. .[lay.
PRŎM-E-NĀDE', *n.* [Fr.] A walk for pleasure;
a place of walking.
PRŎM-E-NĀDE', *v. n.* To take a walk.
PRŎM'I-NĔNCE, PRŎM'I-NĔN-CỰ, *n.* State of
being prominent; protuberance.
PRŎM'I-NĔNT, *a.* Conspicuous; protuberant.
PRŎM'I-NĔNT-LỰ, *ad.* With prominence.
PRỌ-MĬS'CỤ-OŬS, *a.* Mingled; confused; mixed.
PRỌ-MĬS'CỤ-OŬS-LỰ, *ad.* With confused mix-
ture. [cuous.
PRỌ-MĬS'CỤ-OỤS-NĔSS, *n.* The being promis-
PRŎM'ISE, *n.* An engagement to do some par-
ticular thing; a binding declaration; hopes.
PRŎM'ISE, *v. a.* & *n.* To assure by a promise.
PRŎM-I-SEĒ', *n.* One to whom a promise is
PRŎM'IS-ER, *n.* One who promises. [made.
PRŎM'IS-SỌ-RỰ, *a.* Containing a promise. [sea.
PRŎM'ỌN-TỌ-RỰ, *n.* High land jutting into the
PRỌ-MŌTE', *v. a.* To forward; advance; exalt.
PRỌ-MŌT'ER, *n.* One who promotes.
PRỌ-MŌ'TIỌN, *n.* Advancement; preferment.
PRỌ-MŌ'TIVE, *a.* Tending to promote; pro-
moting. [easy.
PRŎMPT (prŏmt), *a.* Quick; ready; acute;
PRŎMPT (prŏmt), *v. a.* To assist; to incite.

PRŎMPT'ER (prŏmt'er), *n.* One who prompts.
PRŎMP'TĬ-TŪDE, *n.* Readiness; quickness.
PRŎMPT'LY (prŏmt'le), *ad.* Readily; quickly.
PRŎMPT'NESS (prŏmt'nes), *n.* Readiness.
PRO-MŬL'GĀTE, *v. a.* To publish; to make known; to announce.
PRŎM-ŬL-GĀ'TIŎN, *n.* Act of promulgating; publication; exhibition.
PRŎM'ŬL-GĀ-TOR, *n.* A publisher.
PRO-MŬLGE', *v. a.* To promulgate; to publish.
PRO-MŬLG'ER, *n.* A publisher; a promulgator.
PRŌNE, *a.* Bending downward; inclined.
PRŌNE'NESS, *n.* The being prone; inclination.
PRŌNG, *n.* A spike or tine of a fork, &c.
PRO-NŎM'Ĭ-NAL, *a.* Relating to a pronoun.
PRŌ'NOUN, *n.* A word used instead of a noun.
PRO-NOUNCE', *v. a. & n.* To speak; to articulate; to utter; to declare. [nounced.
PRO-NOUNCE'A-BLE, *a.* That may be pro-
PRO-NOUNC'ER, *n.* One who pronounces.
PRO-NŬN-CĬ-Ā'TIŎN (pro-nŭn-she-ā'shun), *n.* The act or mode of pronouncing.
PRŎOF, *n.* Evidence; test; trial; impenetrability:—a rough sheet of print to be corrected.
PRŎOF, *a.* Impenetrable; able to resist.
PRŎP, *v. a.* To support; to sustain; to keep up.
PRŎP, *n.* A support; that which sustains.
PRŎP'A-GA-BLE, *a.* That may be propagated.
PRŎP'A-GĀTE, *v. a.* To extend, increase, spread.
PRŎP-A-GĀ'TIŎN, *n.* Act of propagating; generation; extension.
PRŎP'A-GĀ-TOR, *n.* One who propagates.
PRO-PĔL', *v. a.* To drive or urge forward. [lean.
PRO-PĔND', *v. n.* To incline to any part; to
PRO-PĔN'DEN-CY, *n.* Inclination or tendency.
PRO-PĔNSE', *a.* Leaning; inclined; disposed.
PRO-PĔNSE'NESS, *n.* A natural tendency.
PRO-PĔN'SIŎN, } *n.* Natural tendency, bent, or
PRO-PĔN'SĬ-TY, } inclination; bias.
PRŎP'ER, *a.* Peculiar; one's own; natural; fit.
PRŎP'ER-LY, *ad.* Fitly; in a strict sense.
PRŎP'ER-TY, *n.* A peculiar quality:—a possession; what one possesses; an estate; goods.
PRŎPH'E-CY, *n.* A foretelling; a prediction.
PRŎPH'E-SĪ-ER, *n.* One who prophesies.
PRŎPH'E-SY, *v. a. & n.* To predict; to foretell.
PRŎPH'ET, *n.* One who foretells; a predictor.
PRŎPH'ET-ĔSS, *n.* A female prophet.
PRO-PHĔT'ĬC, } *a.* Relating to a prophet;
PRO-PHĔT'Ĭ-CAL, } foretelling. [ecy.
PRO-PHĔT'Ĭ-CAL-LY, *ad.* In manner of a proph-
PRŎPH-Y̆-LĂC'TĬC, *n.* A preventive medicine.
PRŎPH-Y̆-LĂC'TĬC, } *a.* Preventing disease;
PRŎPH-Y̆-LĂC'TĬ-CAL, } preventive.
PRO-PĬN'QUĬ-TY, *n.* Nearness; kindred.
PRO-PĬ''TĬ-A-BLE (-pĭsh'e-a-bl), *a.* Placable.
PRO-PĬ''TĬ-ĀTE (-pĭsh'e-āt), *v. a.* To induce to favor; to conciliate; to make propitious.
PRO-PĬ-TĬ-Ā'TIŎN (-pĭsh-e-ā'shun), *n.* The act of making propitious; atonement. [peaser.
PRO-PĬ''TĬ-A-TOR (-pĭsh'e-a-tur), *n.* An ap-
PRO-PĬ''TĬ-A-TO-RY (-pĭsh'e-a-tur-e), *a.* Having the power to make propitious. [seat.
PRO-PĬ''TĬ-A-TO-RY, *n. Among the Jews,* mercy-
PRO-PĬ''TIOUS (-pĭsh'us), *a.* Favorable; kind.
PRO-PĬ''TIOUS-LY (pĭsh'us-le), *ad.* Favorably.
PRŌ'PO-LĬS, *n.* A red, resinous substance.
PRO-PŌ'NENT, *n.* One that makes a proposal.

PRO-PŌR'TIŎN, *n.* The comparative relation of one thing to another; symmetry; size; part.
PRO-PŌR'TIŎN, *v. a.* To adjust by comparative relation; to form symmetrically.
PRO-PŌR'TIŎN-A-BLE, *a.* That may be proportioned; proportional. [ble state.
PRO-PŌR'TIŎN-A-BLE-NĔSS, *n.* Proportiona-
PRO-PŌR'TIŎN-A-BLY, *ad.* By proportion.
PRO-PŌR'TIŎN-AL, *a.* Having due proportion.
PRO-PŌR-TIŎN-ĂL'Ĭ-TY, *n.* The quality of being proportional.
PRO-PŌR'TIŎN-AL-LY, *ad.* In a stated degree.
PRO-PŌR'TIŎN-ATE, *a.* Proportional.
PRO-PŌR'TIŎN-ATE, *v. a.* To make proportional; to equalize; to proportion.
PRO-PŌR'TIŎN-ATE-LY, *ad.* Proportionally.
PRO-PŌR'TIŎN-ATE-NĔSS, *n.* Proportionality.
PRO-PŌ'SAL, *n.* An offer; a proposition.
PRO-PŌSE', *v. a.* To offer for consideration.
PRO-PŌ'SER, *n.* One that proposes or offers.
PRŎP-O-ŞĬ''TIŎN (-zĭsh'un), *n.* A thing proposed or affirmed; a proposal. [ing.
PRŎP-O-ŞĬ''TIŎN-AL (-zĭsh'un-al), *a.* Propos-
PRO-POUND', *v. a.* To offer; to propose; to ex-
PRO-POUND'ER, *n.* One who propounds. [hibit.
PRO-PRĪ'E-TA-RY, *n.* A proprietor; an owner.
PRO-PRĪ'E-TA-RY, *a.* Belonging to a certain owner or proprietor. [right.
PRO-PRĪ'E-TOR, *n.* A possessor in his own
PRO-PRĪ'E-TRĔSS, *n.* A female proprietor.
PRO-PRĪ'E-TY, *n.* Fitness; justness; proper state.
PRO-PŬL'SIŎN, *n.* The act of driving forward.
PRŌ-RO-GĀ'TIŎN, *n.* Act of propagating; continuance; prolongation. [put off.
PRO-RŌGUE' (pro-rōg'), *v. a.* To protract; to
PRO-ŞĀ'ĬC, *a.* Belonging to prose; like prose.
PRO-SCRĪBE', *v. a.* To censure capitally; to condemn; to denounce; to interdict; to out-
PRO-SCRĪB'ER, *n.* One who proscribes. [law.
PRO-SCRĬP'TIŎN, *n.* Condemnation; outlawry.
PRO-SCRĬP'TĬVE, *a.* Proscribing. [ic measure.
PRŌSE, *n.* Discourse or language without poet-
PRŎS'E-CŪTE, *v. a.* To pursue; to continue; to carry on; to pursue by law; to sue. [suit.
PRŎS-E-CŪ'TIŎN, *n.* A pursuit; a criminal
PRŎS'E-CŪ-TOR, *n.* One who prosecutes.
PRŎS'E-LYTE, *n.* A convert to a new opinion.
PRŎS'E-LYTE, *v. a.* To make proselytes of; to convert.
PRŎS'E-LYT-ĬSM, *n.* Act of making proselytes.
PRŌŞ'ER, *n.* A writer of prose; a dull relater.
PRO-SŌ'DĬ-AN, *n.* One skilled in prosody.
PRO-SŎD'Ĭ-CAL, *a.* Of or relating to prosody.
PRŎS'O-DĬST, *n.* One who understands prosody.
PRŎS'O-DY, *n.* The laws of versification.
PRŎS-O-PO-PŒ'ĬA (prŏs-so-po-pē'ya), *n.* Personification. [of expectation.
PRŎS'PECT, *n.* A view; object of view; ground
PRO-SPĔC'TIŎN, *n.* A looking forward.
PRO-SPĔC'TĬVE, *a.* Looking forward; future.
PRO-SPĔC'TUS, *n.* The plan or outline of a literary work, &c. [vor.
PRŎS'PER, *v. a.* To make prosperous; to fa-
PRŎS'PER, *v. n.* To be prosperous; to thrive.
PROS-PĔR'Ĭ-TY, *n.* State of being prosperous; success; good fortune; welfare.
PRŎS'PER-OUS, *a.* Successful; fortunate; lucky.
PRŎS'PER-OUS-LY, *ad.* Successfully; fortunately.

PRŎS′PER-OŲS-NĔSS, *n.* Prosperity ; success.
PRŎS′TĮ-TŪTE, *v. a.* To sell to vile purposes.
PRŎS′TĮ-TŪTE, *a.* Vicious for hire ; sold to vice.
PRŎS′TĮ-TŪTE, *n.* A base hireling :—a public strumpet ; courtesan ; harlot. [ness.
PRŎS-TĮ-TŪ′TIQN, *n.* Act of prostituting ; lewd-
PRŎS′TĮ-TŪ-TQR, *n.* One who prostitutes.
PRŎS′TRĄTE, *a.* Lying at mercy ; thrown down.
PRŎS′TRĀTE, *v. a.* To lay flat ; to throw down.
PRQS-TRĀ′TIQN, *n.* Act of prostrating ; depres-
PRŌ′STȲLE, *n.* A range of pillars in front. [sion.
PRQ-TĔCT′, *v. a.* To defend ; to cover from evil.
PRQ-TĔC′TIQN, *n.* Defence ; a shelter ; a pass-
PRQ-TĔC′TĮVE, *a.* Defensive ; sheltering. [port.
PRQ-TĔCT′QR, *n.* One who protects ; a defend-er ; supporter ; guardian. [tector.
PRQ-TĔCT′Q-RĄTE, *n.* A government by a pro-
PRQ-TĔCT′QR-SHĮP, *n.* The office of a protector.
PRQ-TĔC′TRĘSS, *n.* A woman who protects.
PRQ-TĔND′, *v. a.* To hold out ; to stretch forth.
PRQ-TĔST′, *v. n.* To affirm with solemnity.
PRQ-TĔST′, *v. a.* To call as witness ; to affirm ; to assert :—to disown.
PRŌ′TEST *or* PRŎT′ĘST, *n.* A solemn declara-tion of opinion, as against something.
PRŎT′ĘS-TĂNT, *a.* Belonging to Protestants.
PRŎT′ĘS-TĂNT, *n.* One of the reformed religion.
PRŎT′ĘS-TĄNT-ĬSM, *n.* The reformed religion.
PRŎT-ĘS-TĀ′TIQN, *n.* A solemn declaration.
PRQ-TĔST′ĘR, *n.* One who protests.
PRQ-THŎN′Q-TĄ-RȲ, *n.* The head register or chief notary :—a chief clerk. [ing.
PRŌ′TQ-CŎL, *n.* The original copy of any writ-
PRŌ-TQ-MÄR′TȲR, *n.* The first martyr. [emplar.
PRŌ′TQ-TȲPE, *n.* The original of a copy ; an ex-
PRQ-TRĂCT′, *v. a.* To draw out ; delay ; lengthen.
PRQ-TRĂC′TIQN, *n.* The act of protracting.
PRQ-TRĂC′TĮVE, *a.* Dilatory ; prolonging.
PRQ-TRŪDE′, *v. a. & n.* To thrust or extend forward ; to jut out. [ward.
PRQ-TRŪ′SIQN, *n.* The act of thrusting for-
PRQ-TRŪ′SĮVE, *a.* Thrusting or pushing forward.
PRQ-TŪ′BĘR-ĄNCE, *n.* A prominence ; a bunch.
PRQ-TŪ′BĘR-ĄNT, *a.* Swelling ; prominent. [out.
PRQ-TŪ′BĘR-ĀTE, *v. n.* To bulge out ; to swell
PRQ-TŪ-BĘR-Ā′TIQN, *n.* The act of swelling out.
PRŎŬD, *a.* Possessing pride ; haughty ; high.
PRŎŬD′LȲ, *ad.* Arrogantly ; in a proud manner.
PRŎV′Ą-BLE, *a.* That may be proved. [dure.
PRÔVE, *v. a.* To evince ; to show ; to try ; to en-
PRÔVE, *v. n.* To make trial ; to succeed. [corn.
PRŎV′ĘN-DĘR, *n.* Food for brutes ; hay and
PRŎV′ĘRB, *n.* A common saying ; a maxim.
PRQ-VĔR′BĮ-ĄL, *a.* Mentioned in a proverb.
PRQ-VĔR′BĮ-ĄL-ĬST, *n.* One who uses proverbs.
PRQ-VĔR′BĮ-ĄL-LȲ, *ad.* In a proverb. [ply.
PRQ-VĪDE′, *v. a.* To procure ; to prepare ; to sup-
PRQ-VĪD′ĘD, *conj.* On condition that ; if.
PRŎV′Į-DĘNCE, *n.* The divine superintendence or government :—timely care ; foresight.
PRŎV′Į-DĔNT, *a.* Forecasting ; cautious ; prudent.
PRŎV-Į-DĔN′TIĄL, *a.* Effected by providence.
PRŎV-Į-DĔN′TIĄL-LȲ, *ad.* By providence.
PRŎV′Į-DĔNT-LȲ, *ad.* With wise precaution.
PRQ-VĪD′ĘR, *n.* One who provides or procures.
PRŎV′ĮNCE, *n.* A subject country ; region ; office.
PRQ-VĬN′CIĄL, *a.* Relating to a province ; rude.
PRQ-VĬN′CIĄL, *n.* A spiritual or chief governor.

PRQ-VĬN′CIĄL-ĬSM, *n.* A provincial idiom.
PRQ-VĬ′′ĮSIQN (-vĭzh′ụn), *n.* Act of providing ; preparation ; measures taken :—victuals ; food.
PRQ-VĬ′′ŞIQN, *v. a.* To supply with provisions.
PRQ-VĬ′′ŞIQN-ĄL, *a.* Temporarily established.
PRO-VĬ′′ŞIQN-ĄL-LȲ, *ad.* By way of provision.
PRQ-VĬ′′ŞIQN-Ą-RȲ, *a.* Making provision.
PRQ-VĬ′ŞŌ, *n.* [L.] Caution ; provisional condi-
PRQ-VĬ′ŞQR, *n.* A purveyor ; a steward. [tion.
PRQ-VĬ′ŞQ-RȲ, *a.* Conditional ; including a pro-viso :—provisional. [ment.
PRŎV-Q-CĀ′TIQN, *n.* A cause of anger ; incite-
PRQ-VŌ′CĄ-TĮVE, *a.* Stimulating ; inciting.
PRQ-VŌ′CĄ-TĮVE, *n.* Any thing that provokes or excites ; a stimulant. [tive.
PRQ-VŌ′CĄ-TĮVE-NĔSS, *n.* The being provoca-
PRQ-VŌKE′, *v. a.* To rouse, incite, enrage, offend.
PRQ-VŌK′ĘR, *n.* One who provokes ; an inciter.
PRŎV′QST, *n.* Chief of any body, as of a college.
PRQ-VŌST′ (-vō′), *n.* Executioner of an army.
PRŎV′QST-SHĮP, *n.* The office of a provost.
PRŎŴ, *n.* The head or forepart of a ship.
PRŎŴ′ĘSS, *n.* Bravery ; valor ; intrepidity.
PRŎŴL, *v. n.* To rove about ; to wander for
PRŎŴL, *n.* A ramble for plunder. [prey.
PRŎŴL′ĘR, *n.* One that roves about for prey.
PRŎX′Į-MĄTE, *a.* Next ; nearest ; immediate.
PRŎX′Į MĄTE-LȲ, *ad.* Immediately ; next.
PRQX-ĬM′Į-TȲ, *n.* Immediate nearness. [tute.
PRŎX′Ȳ, *n.* The agency of another ; a substi-
PRŪDE, *n.* A woman over-nice and scrupulous.
PRŪ′DĘNCE, *n.* Wisdom applied to practice ; caution ; discretion ; carefulness.
PRŪ′DĘNT, *a.* Practically wise ; discreet.
PRŪ-DĔN′TIĄL, *a.* Proceeding from prudence.
PRŲ-DĔN′TIĄL-LȲ, *ad.* According to prudence.
PRŲ-DĔN′TIĄLŞ, *n. pl.* Maxims of prudence.
PRŪ′DĘNT-LȲ, *ad.* Discreetly ; judiciously.
PRŪD′ĘR-Ȳ, *n.* Excessive nicety in conduct.
PRŪD′ĮSH, *a.* Affectedly precise or grave.
PRŪNE, *v. a.* To lop or cut off ; to trim.
PRŪNE, *n.* A dried plum. [stuff :—a plum.
PRŲ-NĔL′LŌ, *n.* A kind of woollen or mixed
PRŪN′ĘR, *n.* One that prunes or crops trees.
PRŲ-NĬF′ĘR-OŬS, *a.* Plum-bearing.
PRŪN′ĮNG-HOOK (-hŭk), *n.* A hook or knife
PRŪN′ĮNG-KNĬFE (-nīf), used in pruning.
PRŪ′RĮ-ĘN-CȲ, *n.* An itching desire.
PRŪ′RĮ-ĘNT, *a.* Itching ; uneasy with desire.
PRȲ *or* PRĪZE, *v. a.* To raise with a lever.
PRȲ, *v. n.* To inspect officiously or curiously.
PSĂLM (säm), *n.* A sacred song or hymn.
‖PSĂL′MĮST (săl′mĭst *or* säm′ĭst), *n.* A writer of psalms. [psalms.
‖PSĂL′MQ-DĬST (săl′mQ-dĭst), *n.* A singer of
‖PSĂL′MQ-DȲ (săl′mQ-dę), *n.* The practice or art of singing psalms.
PSĂL′TĘR (sâwl′tęr), *n.* The book of Psalms.
PSĂL′TĘR-Ȳ (sâwl′tęr-ę), *n.* A kind of harp.
PSEŪ′DŌ (sū′dō). A prefix, signifying *false.* [ing.
PSEŪ-DŎG′RĄ-PHȲ (sụ-dŏg′rạ-fę), *n.* False writ-
PSHÂW (shâw), *interj.* Expressing contempt.
PSȲ-ℂHŎL′Q-ĢȲ (sī-kŏl′Q-ję), *n.* The doctrine of the mind or soul ; intellectual philosophy.
PTÄR′MĮ-GĂN (tär′mę-), *n.* A bird ; the grouse.
PTĬS-ĂN′ (tĭz-zän′), *n.* A decoction of barley.
PTŎL-Ę-MĀ′ĮC (tŏl-ę-mā′ĭk), *a.* Belonging to the system of Ptolemy, the astronomer.

PTỸ'A-LĬṢM (tī'a-lĭzm), n. Salivation.
PŪ'BĔR-TY, n. The ripe age in mankind.
PŲ-BĔS'CENCE, n. State of puberty :—down.
PŲ-BĔS'CĔNT, a. Arriving at puberty :—downy.
PŬB'LĬC, a. Belonging to a state or nation ; not private ; common ; general ; open ; notorious.
PŬB'LĬC, n. The body of a nation ; the people.
PŬB'LĬ-CĂN, n. A Roman officer who was a collector of toll or tribute.
PŬB-LĬ-CĀ'TIŎN, n. The act of publishing ; a literary work. [and of nations.
PŬB'LĬ-CĬST, n. A writer on the laws of nature
PŲB-LĬÇ'Ĭ-TY, n. Notoriety.
PŬB'LĬC-LY, ad. In a public manner ; openly.
PŬB'LĬSH, v. a. To make public ; to put forth.
PŬB'LĬSH-ĔR, n. One who publishes books, &c.
PŬB'LĬSH-MĔNT, n. Public notice ; publication.
PŪ'CE-RŎN, n. The vine-fretter ; an insect.
PŬCK'ĔR, v. a. To gather into plaits or folds.
PŬCK'ĔR, n. A small fold or wrinkle. [mult.
PŬD'DĔR, n. A tumult.—v. n. To make a tu-
PŬD'DĬNG, n. A kind of food, baked or boiled.
PŬD'DLE, n. A small, muddy pool ; a dirty
PŲ-DĬÇ'Ĭ-TY, n. Modesty ; chastity. [plash.
PŪ'E-RĬLE, a. Childish ; boyish ; trifling.
PŪ-E-RĬL'Ĭ-TY, n. Childishness ; boyishness.
PŲ-ĔR'PE-RAL, a. Relating to childbirth.
PŬFF, n. A blast of wind ; a fungous ball ; praise.
PŬFF, v. n. To swell with wind, blow, pant.
PŬFF, v. a. To inflate ; to swell :—to praise.
PŬF'FĬN, n. A water-fowl :—a kind of fish.
PŬF'FY, a. Windy ; flatulent ; tumid ; turgid.
PŬG, n. A fondled dog :—a monkey.
PUGH (pô), interj. Expressing contempt.
PŪ'ĢĬL, n. A small handful. [the fist ; boxing.
PŪ'ĢĬL-ĬṢM, n. Art or practice of fighting with
PŪ'ĢĬL-ĬST, n. A fighter ; a boxer ; a prize-
PŪ-ĢĬL-ĬST'ĬC, a. Relating to pugilism. [fighter.
PŲG-NĀ'CIOŲS (-nā'shus), a. Fighting ; quarrel-
PŲG-NĂÇ'Ĭ-TY, n. Inclination to fight. [some.
PŪĬS'NE (pū'ne), a. Younger ; inferior ; small.
PŪ'ĬS-SĄNCE, n. Power ; strength ; force.
PŪ'ĬS-SĄNT, a. Powerful ; strong ; forcible.
PŪKE, n. An emetic ; a medicine causing vomit.
PŪKE, v. n. To spew ; to vomit. [ness.
PŬL'CHRĬ-TŪDE, n. Beauty ; grace ; comeli-
PŪLE, v. n. To cry ; to whine ; to whimper.
PŬLL, v. a. To draw forcibly ; to pluck ; to tear.
PŬLL, n. The act of pulling ; a contest ; a pluck.
PŬLL'ĔR, n. One that pulls ; an inciter.
PŬL'LĔT, n. A young hen. [elevating.
PŬL'LEY, n. A wheel turning on a pivot, for
PŬL'MŌ-NĄ-RY, } a. Belonging to, or affecting,
PŲL-MŎN'ĬC, } the lungs.
PŬLP, n. Any soft mass :—soft part of fruit.
PŬL'PĬT, n. An elevated place to speak in.
PŬLP'OŲS, PŬLP'Y, a. Soft ; pappy ; like pulp.
PŬL'SA-TĬLE, a. That may be struck or beaten.
PŲL-SĀ'TIŎN, n. The act of beating ; a throb-
PŲL-SĀ'TŎR, n. One who strikes ; a beater. [bing.
PŬL'SA-TO-RY, a. Beating like the pulse.
PŬLSE, n. The motion of an artery as the blood is driven through it ; a throb :—beans, &c.
PŬL'VER-A-BLE, a. That may be pulverized ; possible to be reduced to dust.
PŬL-VER-Ĭ-ZĀ'TIŎN, n. The act of pulverizing.
PŬL'VER-ĪZE, v. a. & n. To reduce or fall to
PŬL'VĬL, n. Sweet-scented powder. [powder.

PŪ'MĬCE or PŬM'ĬCE, n. Scoria from volca-
noes ; slug or cinder of a fossil.
PŬMP, n. Engine for drawing water :—a shoe.
PŬMP, v. n. To throw out water by a pump.
PŬMP, v. a. To raise out :—to examine artfully.
PŬMP'KĬN, n. The pompion, a plant and its fruit.
PŬN, n. A quibble ; a play upon words. [pun.
PŬN, v. n. To quibble.—v. a. To persuade by a
PŬNCH, v. a. To bore or perforate ; to push.
PŬNCH, n. An instrument ; a liquor ; a buffoon.
PŬNCH'-BŌWL, n. A bowl to hold punch.
PŬNCH'EŎN (pŭnch'un), n. A tool ; a cask.
PŬNCH'ĔR, n. One who punches ; a tool.
PŬN-CHĬ-NĔL'LŌ, n. A sort of buffoon ; a punch.
PŲNC-TĬL'IŌ (pųngk-tĭl'yō), n. ; pl. PŲNC-TĬL'-
IŌṢ. A small nicety of behavior ; a nice point.
PŲNC-TĬL'IOŲS (pųngk-tĭl'yus), a. Nice ; exact.
PŲNC-TĬL'IOŲS-LY (pųngk-tĭl'yus-le), ad. Ex-
actly ; scrupulously. [cing.
PŬNC'TŌ, n. ; pl. PŬNC'TŌEṢ. A point in fen-
PŬNCT'Ŭ-AL (pŭngkt'yu-al), a. Exact ; nice ; punctilious:—done at the precise time ; prompt.
PŬNCT-Ŭ-ĂL'Ĭ-TY, n. Scrupulous exactness.
PŬNCT'Ŭ-AL-LY, ad. Exactly ; nicely. [ing.
PŬNCT'Ŭ-ĀTE, v. a. To distinguish by point-
PŬNCT-Ŭ-Ā'TIŎN, n. Act or method of pointing.
PŬNCT'ŲRE (pŭngkt'yur), n. A small prick ; a
PŬNCT'ŲRE (pŭngkt'yur), v. a. To pierce. [point.
PŬN'DĬT, n. A learned Brahmin. [nancy.
PŬN'ĢEN-CY, n. A pricking ; sharpness ; poig-
PŬN'ĢENT, a. Pricking ; sharp ; acrid ; piercing.
PŪ'NĬ-NĔSS, n. Pettiness ; smallness.
PŬN'ĬSH, v. a. To chastise ; to afflict with pain.
PŬN'ĬSH-A-BLE, a. That may be punished.
PŬN'ĬSH-ĔR, n. One who punishes.
PŬN'ĬSH-MĔNT, n. Pain inflicted for a crime.
PŪ'NĬ-TĬVE, a. Pertaining to punishment.
PŪ'NĬ-TO-RY, a. Punishing ; tending to punish.
PŬNK, n. A common prostitute ; a strumpet.
PŬN'STĔR, n. One skilled in punning.
PŬNT, n. A flat-bottomed boat. [rate.
PŪ'NY, a. Petty ; inferior ; weak ; inferior in
PŬP, v. n. To bring forth puppies.
PŬP, n. A puppy :—a young seal. [ward.
PŪ'PĬL, n. Apple of the eye :—a scholar :—a
PŪ'PĬL-AĢE, n. State of a scholar ; wardship.
PŪ'PĬL-LA-RY, a. Pertaining to a pupil.
PŬP'PET, n. A small image to be moved.
PŬP'PY, n. A whelp ; the progeny of a bitch.
PŬP'PY-ĬṢM, n. Extreme affectation.
PŬR, PŬRR, n. A gentle noise made by a cat.
PŬR, v. n. To murmur as a cat or leopard.
PŬR'BLĪND, a. Near-sighted ; short-sighted.
PŬR'CHĄS-A-BLE, a. That may be purchased.
PŬR'CHĄSE, v. a. To buy for a price ; to obtain.
PŬR'CHĄSE, n. Any thing bought ; act of buying.
PŬR'CHĄS-ĔR, n. A buyer ; one that purchases.
PŪRE, a. Clear ; genuine ; uncorrupt ; chaste.
PŪRE'LY, ad. In a pure manner ; merely.
PŪRE'NESS, n. Clearness ; genuineness ; purity.
PŲR-GĀ'TIŎN, n. The act of cleansing or purify-
PŬR'GA-TĬVE, a. Cathartic ; cleansing. [ing.
PŬR'GA-TĬVE, n. A cathartic medicine.
PŬR-GA-TŌ'RĬ-AL, a. Relating to purgatory.
PŬR'GA-TO-RY, n. A place in which, according to Roman Catholics, souls are purged from im-
purities.
PŬRĢE, v. a. & n. To cleanse, clear, evacuate.

PŮRGE, *n.* A cathartic medicine; a purgative.
PŮRG′ER, *n.* One who purges:—a cathartic.
PŪ-RĬ-FĬ-CĀ′TIQN, *n.* Act of making pure; a rite.
PŪ′RĬ-FĬ-ER, *n.* A cleanser; a refiner.
PŪ′RĬ-FȲ, *v. a.* To make pure; to cleanse.
PŪ′RĬM, *n.* The Jewish feast of lots.
PŪ′RĬST, *n.* One over nice in the use of words.
PŪ′RĬ-TAN, *n.* An advocate for purity of religion.
PŪ′RĬ-TAN, *a.* Puritanical; strict; rigid.
PŪ-RĬ-TĂN′ĬC,   ⎫ *a.* Relating to the Puritans;
PŪ-RĬ-TĂN′Ĭ-CAL, ⎭   strict; rigid.
PŪ-RĬ-TĂN′Ĭ-CAL-LY, *ad.* Strictly; precisely.
PŪ′RĬ-TAN-ĬSM, *n* The notions of the Puritans.
PŪ′RĬ-TY, *n.* Cleanness; innocence; chastity.
PŮRL, *n.* A flow; a malt liquor; a lace.
PŮRL, *v. n.* To murmur; to flow gently.
PŮR′LIEŪ (pür′lü), *n.* Border; enclosure; district.
PŮRL′ĬNG, *n.* The gentle noise of a stream.
PŮR′LĬNȘ, *n. pl.* The inside braces to rafters.
PŲR-LÖÏN′, *v. a.* To steal; to take by theft.
PŲR-LÖÏN′ER, *n.* One that steals clandestinely.
PŮR′PLE, *a.* Red tinctured with blue.
PŮR′PLE, *n.* The purple color; a purple dress.
PŮR′PLE, *v a.* To make red; to color with purple.
PŮR′PLĬSH, *a* Somewhat purple; like purple.
PŮR′PŌRT, *n.* Design; meaning; tendency; aim.
PŮR′PŌRT, *v. n.* To intend; to tend to show.
PŮR′PQSE, *n.* Intention; design; aim; effect.
PŮR′PQSE, *v. a. & n.* To intend; to design.
PŮR′PQSE-LY, *ad.* By design; by intention.
PŮRSE, *n.* A small bag for money.
PŮRSE, *v. a.* To put into a purse, contract. [er.
PŮRSE′NĚT, *n.* A net with a mouth drawn togeth-
PŮRSE′-PRĬDE, *n.* Pride or insolence of wealth.
PŮRSE′-PROŬD, *a.* Puffed up with riches.
PŮR′SER, *n.* The paymaster of a ship.
PŮR′SĬ-NĔSS, *n.* Shortness of breath.
PŲR-SŪ′A-BLE, *a.* That may be pursued.
PŲR-SŪ′ANCE, *n.* A prosecution; a process.
PŲR-SŪ′ANT, *a.* Done in consequence.
PŲR-SŪE′ (pųr-sū′), *v. a.* To chase; to follow.
PŲR-SŪ′ER, *n.* One who pursues or follows.
PŲR-SŪIT′ (pųr-sūt′), *n.* A following; a chase.
PŮR′SUĬ-VĂNT (-swė-vănt), *n.* A messenger :—
PŮR′SY, *a.* Fat and short-breathed. [attendant.
PŮR′TE-NANCE, *n.* Appurtenance :—pluck.
PŪ′RŲ-LĔNCE, *n.* Pus, or the generation of pus.
PŪ′RŲ-LĔNT, *a.* Consisting of pus. [procure.
PŲR-VEY′ (pųr-vā′), *v. a. & n.* To provide; to
PŲR-VEY′ANCE (pųr-vā′ąns), *n.* Act of purvey-
ing; procurement; provision.
PŲR-VEY′QR (pųr-vā′ųr), *n.* One that purveys.
PŮR′VIEW (pür′vū), *n.* Sphere; limit; scope.
PŬS, *n.* A yellowish-white secretion; matter.
PŮSH, *v. a.* To thrust; to press forward.
PŮSH, *v. n.* To make a thrust; to burst out.
PŮSH, *n.* A thrust; an impulse; assault; attack.
PŮSH′PĬN, *n.* A child's play with pins.
PŪ-SĬL-LA-NĬM′Ĭ-TY, *n.* Cowardice; timidity.
PŪ-SĬL-LĂN′Ĭ-MOŬS, *a.* Cowardly; faint-hearted.

PŪ-SĬL-LĂN′Ĭ-MOŬS-LY, *ad.* With pusillanimity.
PŪ-SĬL-LĂN′Ĭ-MOŬS-NĔSS, *n.* Meanness of spirit.
PŬSS, *n.* A term for a cat, or for a hare.
PŬST′ŪLE (pŭst′yŭl *or* pŭs′tūl), *n.* A pimple.
PŬST′Ų-LOŬS, PŬST′Ų-LAR, *a.* Full of pustules.
PŬT, *v. a.* [*im. t. & pp.* put.] To lay; to place;
to apply; to propose; to state; to offer.
PŬT, *v. n.* To shoot or germinate; to bud.
PŬT, *n.* A rustic; a clown :—a game at cards.
PŬT′-ŎFF, *n.* A shift; an evasion; an excuse.
PŪ′TA-TĬVE, *a.* Supposed; reputed; not real.
PŪ′TRE-FĂC′TIQN, *n.* A growing rotten; rotten-
PŪ-TRE-FĂC′TĬVE, *a.* Making rotten.   [ness.
PŪ′TRE-FȲ, *v. a.* To make rotten.—*v. n.* To rot.
PŲ-TRĔS′CENCE, *n.* The state of rotting.
PŲ-TRĔS′CENT, *a.* Growing rotten or putrid.
PŪ′TRĬD, *a.* Rotten; corrupt; putrefied.
PŪ′TRĬD-NĔSS, PŲ-TRĬD′Ĭ-TY, *n.* Rottenness.
PŪ-TRĬ-FĬ-CĀ′TIQN, *n.* State of becoming rotten.
PŬT′TY, *n.* A kind of cement used by glaziers.
PŬZ′ZLE, *v. a.* To perplex; to confound.
PŬZ′ZLE, *n.* Embarrassment; perplexity :—a
PŬZ′ZLER, *n.* One who puzzles.   [riddle.
PȲE, *n.* Printing types mixed; pi. See PIE.
PȲ′GĂRG, *n.* A kind of eagle with a white tail.
PYG-MĒ′AN, *a.* Belonging to, or like, a pygmy.
PȲG′MY, *n.* A dwarf.—*a.* Small; little.
PY-LŌ′RŲS, *n.* The lower orifice of the stomach.
PȲR′A-CĂNTH, *n.* A plant; a kind of thorn.
PȲR′A-MĬD, *n.* A solid figure ending in a point.
PY-RĂM′Ĭ-DAL, *a.* Having the form of a pyramid.
PȲR-A-MĬD′ĬC,   ⎫ *a.* Relating to, or formed
PȲR-A-MĬD′Ĭ-CAL, ⎭   like, a pyramid.
PȲR-A-MĬD′Ĭ-CAL-LY, *ad.* In form of a pyramid.
PȲRE, *n.* A funeral pile; a pile to be burnt.
PY-RĪ′TĔS, *n.* A crystalline mineral ;—written
also *pȳr′ĭte.*
PY-RĬT′ĬC, PȲR′Ĭ-TOŬS, *a.* Relating to pyrites.
PȲR-Q-LĬG′NE-OŬS, ⎫ *a.* Obtained by the distil-
PȲR-Q-LĬG′NĬC,   ⎭   lation of wood in iron
PȲR′Q-MĂN-CY, *n.* Divination by fire. [retorts.
PȲR-Q-MĂN′TĬC, *a.* Divining by means of fire.
PY-RŌM′E-TER, *n.* An instrument to measure
very high degrees of heat.
PȲR-Q-TĔ€H′NĬC,   ⎫ *a.* Relating to fire-
PȲR-Q-TĔ€H′NĬ-CAL, ⎭   works.
PȲR-Q-TĔ€H′NĬCS, *n. pl.* Art of fireworks.
PȲR-Q-TĔ€H′NĬST, *n.* One skilful in pyro-
technics.
PȲR′Q-TĔ€H-NY, *n.* The art of making fire-
works for amusement or war.
PȲR′RHQ-NĬSM (pĭr′Q-nĭzm), *n.* Scepticism.
PȲR′RHQ-NĬST, *n.* A sceptic; a follower of
Pyrrho.   [oras.
PY-THĂG-Q-RĒ′AN, *n.* A follower of Pythag-
PY-THĂG-Q-RĒ′AN, *a.* Relating to Pythagoras.
PY-THĂG′Q-RĬSM, *n.* The doctrine of Pythag-
oras.
PȲTH′QN-ĔSS, *n.* A sort of witch.   [host.
PȲX, *n.* The box in which Catholics keep the

Q.

Q is a consonant followed by *u*. *Qu* is commonly pronounced like *kw*, as in *quail*.

QUĂCK, *v. n.* To cry like a duck :—to boast.
QUĂCK, *n.* A vain pretender to the science of medicine ; a charlatan ; an empiric.
QUĂCK, *a.* Falsely pretending to cure diseases.
QUĂCK'ER-Y, *n.* Act or pretensions of a quack.
QUĂCK'ISH, *a.* Boasting like a quack ; trickish.
QUAD-RĂ-ĢĔS'I-MĂL (kwŏd-), *a.* Lenten.
QUAD'RĂN-GLE (kwŏd'răng-gl), *n.* A figure with four angles :—a rectangular space.
QUĂ-DRĂN'ĢU-LAR, *a.* Having four angles.
QUAD'RANT (kwŏd'rant), *n.* A quarter of a circle :—an instrument for measuring angles.
QUĂ-DRĂNT'AL, *a.* In the fourth part of a circle.
||QUAD'RAT (kwŏd'rat), *n.* (*Printing.*) Piece of metal, used to fill up a space.
||QUA'DRATE, *a.* Square; having four equal sides.
||QUA'DRATE (kwŏd'rat), *n.* A square :—mathematical instrument. [square.
||QUA'DRATE, *v. n.* To suit ; to correspond ; to
QUĂ-DRĂT'IC, *a.* Pertaining to a square.
QUAD'RA-TURE (kwŏd'ra-tūr), *n.* The act of squaring :—a quadrate ; a square.
QUAD-RĔN'NI-AL, *a.* Happening every 4 years.
QUAD-RI-LĂT'ER-AL (kwŏd-), *a.* Having 4 sides.
QUĂ-DRĬLLE' (ka-drĭl'), *n.* A game at cards :—
QUĂ-DRĬP'AR-TĪTE, *a.* Having 4 parts. [a dance.
QUAD'RI-RĒME (kwŏd'rē-rēm), *n.* A Greek and Roman galley with four banks of oars.
QUAD-RI-SYL'LA-BLE (kwŏd-drē-sĭl'la-bl), *n.* A word of four syllables. [in a point.
QUĂ-DRĬV'I-AL, *a.* Having four ways meeting
QUAD'RU-PĔD (kwŏd'-), *n.* A four-footed animal.
QUAD'RU-PLE (kwŏd'ru-pl), *a.* Fourfold. [mal.
QUAD-RŬ'PLI-CATE, *v. a.* To double twice.
QUAD-RŬ-PLI-CA'TION (kwŏd-rŭ-plē-kā'shun), *n.* The taking of a thing four times.
QUÆ'RE (kwē'rē), *v.* [L.] Inquire. See QUERY.
QUĂFF, *v. a.* & *n.* To drink ; to swallow.
QUĂG'ĢY, *a.* Boggy ; soft ; marshy. [ing bog.
QUĂG'MĪRE, *n.* A shaking marsh ; a soft, yield-
QUĀIL (kwāl), *n.* A bird of game. [to quake.
QUĀIL, *v. n.* To languish; to sink into dejection;
QUĀIL, *v. a.* To crush ; to quell ; to depress.
QUĀINT, *a.* Pretty ; fine-spun ; odd ; affected.
QUĀINT'LY, *ad.* With petty elegance ; oddly.
QUĀINT'NESS, *n.* Petty elegance ; oddness.
QUĀKE, *v. n.* To shake with cold or fear, tremble.
QUĀKE, *n.* A shudder ; tremulous agitation.
QUĀ'KER, *n.* One of the Society of Friends.
QUĀ'KER-ĬSM, *n.* The principles of Quakers.
QUĀK'ING, *n.* Trepidation. [be qualified.
QUAL'I-FĪ-A-BLE (kwŏl'le-fī-a-bl), *a.* That may
QUAL-I-FI-CA'TION (kwŏl-le-fe-kā'shun), *n.* Accomplishment ; fitness :—abatement. [fies.
QUAL'I-FĪ-ER (kwŏl'e-fī-er), *n.* One that quali-
QUAL'I-FȲ (kwŏl'e-fī), *v. a.* To fit :—to abate ; to soften ; to modify :—to regulate ; to temper.
QUAL'I-TY (kwŏl'le-te), *n.* The nature of things relatively considered ; attribute ; property ; disposition ; temper ; rank.

||QUĂLM (kwäm *or* kwâm), *n.* Sudden seizure of sickly languor :—nausea :—scruple.
||QUĂLM'ISH (kwäm'ish), *a.* Seized with languor.
QUAN-DĀ'RY (kwọn-dā're *or* kwŏn'da-re), *n.* A doubt ; a difficulty ; a dilemma.
QUAN'TI-TY (kwŏn'te-te), *n.* Bulk ; weight :—a portion :—the measure of a syllable.
QUAN'TUM (kwŏn'tum), *n.* Quantity ; amount.
QUAR-AN-TÎNE' (kwŏr-an-tēn'), *n.* Prohibition from intercourse and commerce, imposed on vessels.
QUAR'REL (kwŏr'rel), *n.* A dispute ; a contest.
QUAR'REL (kwŏr'rel), *v. n.* To fight, disagree.
QUAR'REL-LER, *n.* One who quarrels. [tious.
QUAR'REL-SŎME (kwŏr'rel-sŭm), *a.* Conten-
QUAR'REL-SŎME-NĔSS (kwŏr'-), *n.* Petulance.
QUAR'RY (kwŏr're), *n.* A stone-pit :—prey.
QUAR'RY (kwŏr're), *v. a.* To dig out of a quarry.
QUÂRT, *n.* The fourth part of a gallon ; a vessel.
QUÂR'TAN, *n.* A fourth-day fever or ague.
QUÂR'TER, *n.* A fourth part :—a region :—mercy granted :—8 bushels.—*pl.* Stations for soldiers.
QUÂR'TER, *v. a.* To divide into four parts :—to station, as soldiers :—to lodge ; to diet.
QUÂR'TER-AĢE, *n.* A quarterly allowance.
QUÂR'TER-DAY, *n.* A day on which rent, &c., is
QUÂR'TER-DĔCK, *n.* Part of a ship's deck. [paid.
QUÂR'TER-LY, *a.* Occurring four times a year.
QUÂR'TER-LY, *ad.* Once in a quarter of a year.
QUÂR'TER-MĂS-TER, *n.* An officer in an army.
QUÂR'TERN, *n.* The fourth part of a pint. [law.
QUÂR'TER-SĔS'SIONS, *n. pl.* A kind of court of
QUÂR'TER-STĂFF, *n.* A staff of defence.
QUÂR'TILE, *n.* An aspect of two planets, when they are 90 degrees distant from each other.
QUÂR'TO, *n.* ; pl. QUÂR'TOS *or* QUÂR'TOES. A book in which every leaf is a quarter of a sheet.—*a.* Having four leaves in a sheet, as a
QUÂRTZ, *n.* A hard, silicious stone. [book.
QUÂRT'ZOSE, *a.* Containing, or like, quartz.
QUĂS, *n.* A mean fermented liquor in Russia.
QUASH (kwŏsh), *v. a.* To crush :—to annul.
QUAS'SI-A (kwŏsh'e-a), *n.* A tropical tree.
QUĀ'TER-COŬS'INS (kā'ter-kŭz'znz), *n. pl.* Those within the first four degrees of kindred.
QUĂ-TER'NA-RY, *a.* Consisting of four.
QUĂ-TER'NI-ON, *n.* Four ; a set of four.
QUĂ-TER'NI-TY, *n.* The number four.
QUÂ'TRAIN, *n.* Four lines rhyming alternately.
QUĀ'VER, *v. n.* To shake the voice ; to vibrate.
QUĀ'VER, *n.* A shake of the voice ; musical note.
QUAY (kē), *n.* A key ; a mole ; a wharf.
QUĒACH'Y, *a.* Shaking ; quaggy ; yielding.
QUĒAN (kwēn), *n.* A worthless woman.
QUĒAS'I-NĔSS, *n.* Sickness of the stomach.
QUĒAS'Y (kwē'ze), *a.* Sick with nausea ; squeamish ; fastidious. [ereign.
QUĒEN, *n.* The wife of a king :—a female sov-
QUĒER, *a.* Odd ; droll ; strange.
QUĒER'LY, *ad.* Strangely ; oddly ; singularly.
QUĒER'NESS, *n.* Oddness ; singularity. [kill.
QUĔLL, *v. a.* To crush ; to subdue ; to still ; to

Ā,Ē,Ī,Ō,Ū,Ȳ, *long* ; Ă,Ĕ,Ĭ,Ŏ,Ŭ,Y̆, *short* ; A,E,I,O,U,Y, *obscure.*—FÀRE,FÄR,FĂST,FÂLL; MÊIR,HÈR;

QUĔLL′ĘR, *n.* One that quells or subdues.
QUĔNCH, *v. a.* To extinguish; to still; to allay.
QUĔNCH′Ą-BLE, *a.* That may be quenched.
QUĔNCH′ĘR, *n.* One that quenches.
QUĔR-Į-MŌ′NĮ-OŬS, *a.* Querulous; complaining.
QUĒ′RĮST, *n.* One who inquires or asks questions.
QUĔRN, *n.* A hand-mill; mill for grinding grain.
QUĔR′PŌ, *n.* A close garment.
QUĔR′Ų-LOŬS, *a.* Repining; complaining.
QUĔR′Ų-LOŬS-LY, *ad.* In a complaining manner.
QUĔR′Ų-LOŲS-NĔSS, *n.* A habit of complaining.
QUĒ′RY, *n.* A question; an inquiry. [doubts.
QUĒ′RY, *v. n.* To ask questions; to express
QUĒ′RY, *v. a.* To examine by questions.
QUĔST, *n.* A search; the act of seeking.
QUĔS′TIǪN (kwĕst′yǫn), *n.* An interrogatory;
  an inquiry; a dispute; a doubt; a trial.
QUĔS′TIǪN (kwĕst′yǫn), *v. a. & n.* To examine
  one by questions; to doubt; to inquire.
QUĔS′TIǪN-Ą-BLE (kwĕst′yǫn-ạ-bl), *a.* Doubtful.
QUĔS′TIǪN-Ą-RY (kwĕst′yǫn-ạ-rẹ), *a.* Inquiring.
QUĔS′TIǪN-LĔSS, *ad.* Certainly; doubtless.
QUĔS′TǪR, *n.* A public treasurer in ancient Rome.
QUĔS′TǪR-SHĬP, *n.* The office of a questor.
QUĬB′BLE, *n.* A cavil; a low conceit; sort of pun.
QUĬB′BLE, *v. n.* To cavil; to equivocate; to pun.
QUĬB′BLĘR, *n.* One who quibbles; a punster.
QUĬCK, *a.* Living:—swift; nimble; speedy.
QUĬCK, *ad.* Nimbly; speedily; readily.
QUĬCK, *n.* The living flesh; the sensible part.
QUĬCK′EN (kwĭk′kn), *v. a.* To make alive:—to
  hasten; to accelerate; to excite. [ens.
QUĬCK′EN-ĘR (kwĭk′kn-ẹr), *n.* One who quick-
QUĬCK′LĪME, *n.* Fresh-burnt lime.
QUĬCK′LY, *ad.* Soon; speedily; without delay.
QUĬCK′NĘSS, *n.* Speed; activity; sharpness.
QUĬCK′SĂND, *n.* Moving sand; unsolid ground.
QUĬCK′SCĔNT-ĘD, *a.* Discovering by the smell.
QUĬCK′SĔT, *v. a.* To plant with living plants.
QUĬCK′SĔT, *n.* A living plant set to grow.
QUĬCK′-SĪGHT-ĘD, *a.* Having a sharp sight.
QUĬCK′-SĪGHT′ĘD-NĔSS, *n.* Sharpness of sight.
QUĬCK′SĬL-VĘR, *n.* Mercury; a fluid metal.
QUĬD, *n.* Something chewed; a cud. [*Low.*]
QUĬD′DĮ-TY, *n.* Essence; a trifling nicety; a cavil.
QUĬD′DLE, *v. n.* To busy one's self about trifles.
QUĬD′NŬNC, *n.* One curious to know every thing.
QUĬ-ĔS′CĘNCE, *n.* Rest; repose; quiet.
QUĬ-ĔS′CĘNT, *a.* Resting; not being in motion.
QUĪ′ĔT, *a.* Still; peaceable; smooth; not ruffled.
QUĪ′ĔT, *n.* Rest; repose; peace; stillness.
QUĪ′ĔT, *v. a.* To calm; to lull; to pacify; to still.
QUĪ′ĔT-ER, *n.* The person or thing that quiets.
QUĪ′ĔT-ĬSM, *n.* Tranquillity; system of the
QUĪ′ĔT-ĬST, *n.* One of a sect. [Quietists.
QUĪ′ĔT-LY, *ad.* Calmly; peaceably; at rest.

QUĪ′ĔT-NĔSS, *n.* State of being quiet; tranquil-
  lity; stillness; calmness.
QUĪ′Ę-TŪDE, *n.* Rest; repose; tranquillity.
QUĮ-Ē′TŲS, *n.* [L.] Final discharge; acquittance.
QUĬLL, *n.* A large feather of a goose, &c.
QUĬLL, *v. a.* To plait; to form in plaits, like
QUĬLT, *n.* A cover of a bed, &c. [quills.
QUĬLT, *v. a.* To stitch one cloth upon another.
QUĪ′NĄ-RY, *a.* Consisting of five.
QUĬNCE, *n.* A species of small tree and its fruit.
QUĬN′CŬNX, *n.* Trees, or any thing, formed with
  four in a square and one in the middle.
QUĬN′Į-Ą, QUĮ-NĪNE′, *n.* Medicinal substance.
QUĬN-QUĄ-ĢĔS′Į-MĄ, *n.* Shrove Sunday.
QUĬN-QUĂN′GỤ-LĄR, *a.* Having five corners.
QUĬN-QUĔN′NĮ-ĄL, *a.* Happening every five years.
QUĬN′SY, *n.* An inflammation in the throat.
QUĬNT, *n.* A set of five, as of cards.
QUĬN′TĄIN, *n.* A post set up for tilters.
QUĬN′TĄL, *n.* A hundred pounds avoirdupois.
QUĬN-TĔS′SĘNCE *or* QUĬN′TĘS-SĔNCE, *n.* The
  virtue or best part of any thing; essential part.
QUĬN′TĮLE, *n.* A certain aspect of the planets.
QUĬN′TỤ-PLE, *a.* Fivefold. [jeer; to mock.
QUĬP, *n.* A taunt; a sarcasm.—*v. a.* To taunt; to
QUĪRE, *n.* A chorus; a choir:—24 sheets of paper.
QUĪR′ĬS-TĘR, *n.* A chorister; leader of a choir.
QUĬRK, *n.* A smart taunt; a conceit; a quibble.
QUĬRK′ĬSH, *a.* Consisting of quirks, conceits, &c.
QUĬT, *v. a.* [*imp. t. & pp.* quit *or* quitted.] To
  leave; to forsake; to discharge; to repay.
QUĬT, *a.* Free; clear; discharged from.
QUĬT′CLĀIM, *n.* A release of claim by deed.
QUĪTE, *ad.* Completely; perfectly; totally.
QUĬT′RĔNT, *n.* A small rent reserved.
QUĬT′TĄNCE, *n.* A discharge; an acquittance.
QUĬV′ĘR, *n.* A case or sheath for arrows.
QUĬV′ĘR, *v. n.* To quake; to shiver; to shudder.
QUĬX-ŌT′ĬC, *a.* Like Don Quixote; absurd.
QUĬX′ǪT-ĬSM, *n.* Romantic and absurd notions.
QUĬZ, *n.* A hoax.—*v. a.* To puzzle; to hoax.
QUŎD′LĮ-BĔT, *n.* A nice point; a subtilty.
QUOĬF, *n.* A cap for the head. See COIF.
QUOĬN, *n.* A corner stone or brick; a corner.
QUOĬT, *n.* An iron, or flat stone, to pitch at a mark.
QUŎN′DĄM, *a.* Having been formerly; former.
QUŌ′RŲM, *n.* A bench of justices; such a num-
  ber of any persons as is sufficient to do busi-
QUŌ′TĄ, *n.* A share; a proportion. [ness.
QUǪ-TĀ′TIǪN, *n.* Citation; passage cited; price.
QUŌTE, *v. a.* To cite, as an author; to adduce.
QUOTH (kwōth *or* kwŭth), *v. def.* Used only in
  the imperfect tense; as, "*Quoth I*," said I.
QUǪ-TĬD′Į-ĄN, *a.* Daily; happening every day.
QUǪ-TĬD′Į-ĄN, *n.* A fever which returns daily.
QUŌ′TIĘNT, *n.* The result of dividing a number.

R.

R, a consonant, liquid, and semi-vowel, has a rough sound, as in *red, rose*. [other.

RĂB'BĔT, *v. a.* To fit pieces of wood to each

RĂB'BĔT, *n.* A groove in the edge of a board.

RĂB'BI *or* RĂB'BĪ, RĂB'BĬN, *n.* A Jewish doctor.

RAB-BĬN'I-CĂL, *a.* Relating to the rabbins.

RĂB'BĬT, *n.* A small quadruped. [ulace.

RĂB'BLE, *n.* A tumultuous crowd; a mob; pop-

RĂB'ĬD, *a.* Fierce; furious; mad; raging.

RĂB'ĬD-NĔSS, *n.* Fierceness; furiousness.

RĂB'I-NĔT, *n.* A kind of small ordnance.

RĀ'CA, *n.* [Syriac.] A miscreant; a wretch.

RAC-CÔÔN', *n.* An animal valued for its fur.

RĀCE, *n.* A family; breed:—contest in running.

RĀCE, *v. n.* To run swiftly, as in a race.

RĀCE'-HÖRSE, *n.* A horse bred to run for prizes.

RĂÇ-Ĕ-MĀ'TIŎN, *n.* A cluster, like that of grapes.

RĂÇ-Ĕ-MĬF'ĔR-O ŬS, *a.* Bearing clusters.

RĀ'CĔR, *n.* One that races; a horse that races.

RĀ'CI-NĔSS, *n.* The quality of being racy.

RĂCK, *n.* An engine of torture; extreme pain; a frame for hay; a grate; a liquor; a distaff.

RĂCK, *v. n.* To stream or fly, as vapor or clouds.

RĂCK, *v. a.* To torment; to harass; to strain:—to draw off from the lees, as liquor.

RĂCK'ĔT, *n.* A noise:—a thing to strike a ball.

RĂCK'-RĔNT, *n.* Rent raised to the utmost.

RĂCK'-RĔNT-ĔR, *n.* One who pays the rack-rent.

RĀ'CY, *a.* Strong; flavorous; tasting of the soil.

RĀ'DI-ANCE, RĀ'DI-AN-CY, *n.* Sparkling lustre.

RĀ'DI-ANT, *a.* Shining; emitting rays.

RĀ'DI-ANT-LY, *ad.* With sparkling lustre.

RĀ'DI-ĀTE, *v. n.* To emit rays; to shine.

RĀ'DI-ĀTE, *v. a.* To enlighten; to irradiate.

RĀ-DI-Ā'TIŎN, *n.* Lustre; an emission of rays.

RĂD'I-CĂL, *n.* Primitive word or letter; root.

RĂD'I-CĂL, *a.* Relating to the root; thorough; primitive; implanted by nature.

RĂD'I-CĂL-LY, *ad.* Originally; primitively.

RĂD'I-CĂL-NĔSS, *n.* The state of being radical.

RĂD'I-CĀTE, *v. a.* To root; to plant deeply.

RĂD-I-CĀ'TIŎN, *n.* The act of taking root.

RĂD'ĬSH, *n.* A root commonly eaten raw. [cle.

RĀ'DI-ŬS, *n.; pl.* RĀ'DI-Ī. Semi-diameter of a cir-

RĀ'DĬX, *n.; pl.* RA-DĪ'CĔS. [L.] The root.

RĂFF, *n.* A confused heap.—*Riff-raff*, the mob.

RĂF'FLE, *n.* A species of game or lottery.

RĂF'FLE, *v. n.* To cast dice for a prize.

RĂFT, *n.* A frame or float made of timber.

RĂF'TĔR, *n.* One of the timbers of a roof.

RĂG, *n.* A piece; a tatter.—*pl.* Worn-out clothes.

RĂG-A-MŬF'FĬN, *n.* A paltry, mean fellow.

RĀĢE, *n.* Violent anger; vehement fury.

RĀĢE, *v. n.* To be in anger; to exercise fury.

RĂG'ĢĔD, *a.* Dressed in rags; torn; rugged. [dish.

RĂG'MĂN, *n.* One who deals in rags.

RA-GÔÛT' (rä-gô'), *n.* [Fr.] A highly-seasoned

RĀIL, *n.* A bar of wood or iron:—a bird.

RĀIL, *v. a.* To enclose with rails:—to range.

RĀIL, *v. n.* To reproach; to utter reproaches.

RĀIL'ĔR, *n.* One who rails or defames.

RĀIL'ĬNG, *n.* Reproachful language:—a fence.

RĂIL'LĔR-Y (răl'lĕr-e), *n.* Slight satire; banter.

RĀIL'RŌAD, } *n.* A road constructed with rails

RĀIL'WĀY, } or tracks for the carriage-wheels.

RĀI'MĔNT, *n.* Vesture; vestment; dress.

RĀIN, *v. n.* To fall in drops.—*v. a.* To pour down.

RĀIN, *n.* Water falling from the clouds; shower.

RĀIN'BŌW (rān'bō), *n.* An arch formed by the refraction and reflection of the sun's rays.

RĀIN'GĀUĢE, *n.* An instrument for measuring

RĀIN'I-NĔSS, *n.* The state of being rainy. [rain.

RĀIN'Y, *a.* Abounding in rain; showery; wet.

RĀISE, *v. a.* To lift; to erect; to exalt:—to levy;

RĀI'SĬN (rā'zn), *n.* A dried grape. [to collect.

RĀ'JAH, *n.* A Hindoo chief or prince.

RĀKE, *n.* A tool with teeth:—a dissolute man.

RĀKE, *v. a.* To gather with a rake; to scour.

RĀK'ĬSH, *a.* Loose; lewd; dissolute.

RĂL'LY, *v. a.* To reunite; to treat jocosely.

RĂL'LY, *v. n.* To come into order:—to banter.

RĂL'LY, *n.* A bringing to order:—a banter.

RĂM, *n.* A male sheep:—Aries, the vernal sign.

RĂM, *v. a.* To drive with violence; to force in.

RĂM'A-DĂN, *n.* The Mahomedan lent or fast.

RĂM'BLE, *v. n.* To rove loosely; to wander.

RĂM'BLE, *n.* A roving; an irregular excursion.

RĂM'BLĔR, *n.* A rover; a wanderer.

RĂM-I-FI-CĀ'TIŎN, *n.* A branching:—a branch.

RĂM'I-FY, *v. a.* To separate into branches.

RĂM'I-FY, *v. n.* To be parted into branches.

RĂM'MĔR, *n.* One that rams:—a ramrod.

RĂM'MĬSH, *a.* Strong-scented; like a ram.

RĀ'MOŬS, *a.* Branchy; consisting of branches.

RĂMP, *v. n.* To sport; to play; to romp.

RĂMP, *n.* A leap; a spring; a bound.

RĂM'PAN-CY, *n.* Prevalence; exuberance.

RĂM'PANT, *a.* Exuberant; frisky; wanton.

RĂM'PĂRT, *n.* A bank round a fortified place.

RĂM'RŎD, *n.* The rammer of a gun.

RĂN, *imp. t.* from *run*.

RĂN'CHŌ, *n.* [Sp.] Hut:—hamlet:—farm.

RĂN'CĬD, *a.* Having a rank or strong smell; sour.

RĂN'CĬD-NĔSS, RĂN-CĬD'I-TY, *n.* Rank scent.

RĂN'CŎR (răng'kur), *n.* Malice; virulence. [ful.

RĂN'CŎR-OŬS (răng'kur-ŭs), *a.* Malignant; spite-

RĂN'CŎR-OŬS-LY, *ad.* Malignantly. [range.

RĂN'DŎM, *n.* Want of rule; chance; hazard:—

RĂN'DŎM, *a.* Done at hazard; chance.

RĂNG, *imp. t.* from *ring*. [rove over.

RĂNĢE, *v. a.* To place in order; to arrange; to

RĂNĢE, *v. n.* To be placed in order.

RĂNĢE, *n.* A rank; excursion; room:—a cooking apparatus or stove.

RĂNK, *a.* Strong; luxuriant; rancid; gross.

RĂNK, *n.* A row; class; order; degree; dignity.

RĂNK, *v. a.* To place abreast; to arrange.

RĂNK, *v. n.* To be ranged; to be placed.

RĂNK'ĔR, *n.* One who places or arranges.

RĂN'KLE, *v. n.* To fester; to be inflamed.

RĂNK'LY, *ad.* Luxuriantly; rancidly; grossly.

RĂNK'NĔSS, *n.* Exuberance; strong scent.

RĂN'SĂCK, *v. a.* To plunder; to search narrowly.

RĂN'SŎM, *n.* A price paid for redemption; release.

Ā,Ē,Ī,Ō,Ū,Ȳ, *long;* Ă,Ĕ,Ĭ,Ŏ,Ŭ,Y̆, *short;* A,E,I,O,U,Y, *obscure.*—FÀRE,FÄR,FÀST,FÂLL; HÊIR,HĔR;

RĂN'SǪM, *v. a.* To redeem from captivity, &c.
RĂN'SǪM-ĘR, *n.* One who ransoms or redeems.
RĂNT, *v. n.* To rave in violent language.
RĂNT, *n.* Extravagant declamation.
RĂNT'ĘR, *n.* One who rants; a noisy talker.
RĂNT'I-PŌLE, *a.* Wild; roving; rakish.
RA-NŬN'CŲ-LŬS, *n.; pl.* RA-NŬN'CŲ-LĪ. A plant and its flower; crow's-foot.
RĂP, *n.* A quick, smart blow:—counterfeit coin.
RĂP, *v. n.* To strike with a quick, smart blow.
RĂP, *v. a.* To strike; to transport; to seize.
RA-PĀ'CIOŲS (ra-pā'shus), *a.* Given to plunder.
RA-PĀ'CIOŲS-LY (ra-pā'shus-le), *ad.* By rapine.
RA-PĀ'CIOŲS-NĔSS (-shus-nĕs), *n.* Rapacity.
RA-PĂÇ'I-TY, *n.* Addictedness to plunder.
RĂPE, *n.* A violent defloration:—a plant.
RĂP'ID, *a.* Quick; swift; moving fast.
RĂP'ID, RĂP'IDŞ, *n.* Rapid currents in a river.
RA-PĬD'I-TY, *n.* Celerity; velocity; swiftness.
RĂP'ID-LY, *ad.* Swiftly; with quick motion.
RĂP'ID-NĔSS, *n.* Celerity; swiftness; speed.
RĀ'PI-ĘR, *n.* A sword used in thrusting.
RĂP'INE, *n.* Act of plundering; violence; force.
RĂP-PĒĒ', *n.* A coarse sort of black snuff.
RĂP'PĘR, *n.* A striker; knocker of a door.
RĂPT, *p. a.* Transported; being in a trance.
RĂPT'ŲRE (răpt'yur), *n.* Ecstasy; transport.
RĂPT'ŲR-OŬS, *a.* Ecstatic; transporting.
RĀRE, *a.* Scarce; excellent:—thin; subtile:—raw.
RĂR'ĘE-SHŌW, *n.* A show carried in a box.
RĂR-E-FĂC'TIǪN, *n.* The act of rarefying.
RĂR'Ę-FI-A-BLE, *a.* That may be rarefied.
RĂR'Ę-FȲ, *v. a. & n.* To make or become less dense.
RĀRE'LY, *ad.* Seldom; not often; finely.
RĀRE'NĔSS, *n.* Uncommonness:—thinness.
RĀRE'RĪPE, *n.* An early fruit; a peach. [ness.
RĂR'I-TY, *n.* Thinness; subtilty:—uncommon-
RĂS'CAL, *n.* A scoundrel; a knave; wretch.
RAS-CĂL'I-TY, *n.* Petty villany; knavery.
RAS-CĂLL'IǪN (ras-kăl'yun), *n.* A vile wretch.
RĂS'CAL-LY, *a.* Mean; sorry; base; worthless.
RĀŞE, *v. a.* To graze; to erase. See RAZE.
RĂSH, *a.* Hasty; violent; precipitate.
RĂSH, *n.* An efflorescence; a breaking out.
RĂSH, *v. a.* To cut into pieces; to divide.
RĂSH'ĘR, *n.* A thin slice of pork or bacon.
RĂSH'LY, *ad.* Hastily; without reflection.
RĂSH'NĔSS, *n.* Inconsiderate haste; temerity.
RĂSP, *n.* A large, coarse, rough file.
RĂSP, *v. a.* To rub or abrade with a rasp.
RĂS'PA-TǪ-RY, *n.* A surgeon's instrument.
RĂSP'BER-RY (răs'ber-e), *n.* A kind of berry.
RĂT, *n.* An animal of the mouse kind. [value.
RĀT'A-BLE, *a.* That may be set at a certain
RĀT'A-BLY, *ad.* By rate or proportion; propor-
RĂT-A-FĪ'A, *n.* A cordial liquor. [tionably.
RĂTCH, *n.* A sort of wheel; ratchet.
RĂTCH'ĘT, *n.* Arm of a ratchet-wheel.
RĂTCH'ĘT-WHEĒL, *n.* A wheel with teeth.
RĀTE, *n.* A price; degree; a portion; a tax.
RĀTE, *v. a.* To value at a price:—to chide, scold.
RĀT'ĘR, *n.* One who rates or estimates.
RĂTH'ĘR, *ad.* More willingly; preferably.
RĂT-I-FI-CĀ'TIǪN, *n.* The act of ratifying.
RĂT'I-FĪ-ĘR, *n.* The person or thing that ratifies.
RĂT'I-FȲ, *v. a.* To confirm; to settle; to establish.
RĀ'TI-Ō (-she-ō), *n.; pl.* RĀ'TI-ŌŞ. The relation which one thing has to another; proportion.

RĂ-TI-ŎÇ-I-NĀ'TIǪN (răsh-e-ŏs-e-nā'shun), *n.* The act, or the process, of reasoning.
RĀ'TIǪN, *n.* A certain allowance of food, &c.
RĂ''TIǪN-AL (răsh'un-al), *a.* Endowed with rea-son:—agreeable to reason; wise. [reasons.
RĂ-TI-Ǫ-NĀ'LE (răsh-e-ǫ-nā'le), *n.* A detail with
‖RĂ''TIǪN-AL-ĬŞM (răsh'un-al-ĭzm), *n.* Adher-ence to reason, as opposed to *supernaturalism.*
‖RĂ''TIǪN-AL-ĬST, *n.* Adherent to rationalism.
‖RĂ-TI-Ǫ-NĂL'I-TY (răsh-e-ǫ-năl'e-te), *n.* State of being rational. [son.
RĂ''TIǪN-AL-LY (răsh'un-al-le), *ad.* With rea-
RĂ''TIǪN-AL-NĔSS (răsh'un-al-nĕs), *n.* Rational-
RĂTS'BĀNE, *n.* A poison for rats; arsenic. [ity.
RĂT-TĂN', *n.* A small East Indian cane.
RĂT-TEĒN', *n.* A kind of woollen stuff. [scold.
RĂT'TLE, *v. n. & a.* To make a sharp noise:—to
RĂT'TLE, *n.* A quick noise; a plaything.—*pl.* The
RĂT'TLE-SNĀKE, *n.* A kind of serpent. [croup.
RĂT'TLING, *n.* A noise produced by wheels, &c.
RÂU'CI-TY, *n.* Hoarseness; a loud, rough noise.
RĂV'AGE, *v. a.* To lay waste; to sack; to pillage.
RĂV'AGE, *n.* Spoil; ruin; waste; desolation.
RĂV'A-GĘR, *n.* A plunderer; a spoiler.
RĀVE, *v. n.* To be furious or mad; to rage.
RĂV'EL (răv'vl), *v. a.* To entangle; to untwist.
RĂV'EL (răv'vl), *v. n.* To be unwoven.
RĂVE'LIN (răv'lin), *n.* Part of a fortification.
RĀ'VEN (rā'vn), *n.* A large black bird.
RĂV'EN (răv'vn), *v. a. & n.* To plunder; to prey.
RĂV'EN-ĘR (răv'vn-ęr), *n.* One that plunders.
RĂV'EN-OŬS (răv'vn-ŭs), *a.* Furiously voracious.
RĂV'EN-OŬS-LY (-vn-ŭs-le), *ad.* With voracity.
RĂV'EN-OŲS-NĔSS (răv'vn-us-nĕs), *n.* Voracity.
RĂV'IN, RĂV'ĘN, *n.* Prey; plunder. [low pass.
RA-VĪNE', *or* RĂV'INE, *n.* [Fr.] A hollow; a hol-
RĂV'ING, *n.* Madness.—*a.* Mad; furious.
RĂV'ISH, *v. a.* To deflower by violence; to take away by violence:—to delight; to transport.
RĂV'ISH-ĘR, *n.* One who ravishes. [transport.
RĂV'ISH-MĘNT, *n.* Violation:—rapture; ecstasy;
RÂW, *a.* Not subdued by the fire; crude:—sore; immature; unripe; new:—bleak; chill.
RÂW'BŌNED (râw'bōnd), *a.* Having little flesh.
RÂW'HĔAD (râw'hĕd), *n.* The name of a spectre.
RÂW'LY, *ad.* In a raw manner; unskilfully.
RÂW'NĔSS, *n.* The state of being raw.
RĀY (rā), *n.* A beam of light:—a fish:—an herb.
RĀY, *v. a.* To streak; to shoot forth:—to stripe.
RĀY'LĔSS, *a.* Dark; without rays of light.
RĀZE, *v. a.* To overthrow; to efface; to extirpate.
RA-ZEĒ', *n.* A ship of war made smaller.
RA-ZEĒ', *v. a.* To cut down, as a ship.
RĀ'ZǪR, *n.* A tool used in shaving:—a tusk.
RĀ'ZŲRE (rā'zhur), *n.* The act of erasing.
RĒ. A prefix denoting iteration or return.
RĒACH, *v. a.* To arrive at; to attain; to extend to.
RĒACH, *v. n.* To be extended; to penetrate.
RĒACH, *n.* Power; limit; extent:—fetch.
RĒ-ĂCT', *v. a. & n.* To act or do again.
RĒ-ĂC'TIǪN, *n.* A counteraction; resistance.
RĔAD, *v. a.* [*imp. t. & pp.* read (rĕd).] To peruse; to learn; to know or understand fully.
RĔAD, *v. n.* To peruse books; to tell; to declare.
RĔAD'A-BLE, *a.* That may be read; legible.
RĔAD'ĘR, *n.* One who reads or is studious.
RĔAD'ĘR-SHĬP, *n.* The office of reading prayers.
RĔAD'I-LY (rĕd'de-le), *ad.* With speed; quickly.

RĔAD'Ĭ-NĔSS (rĕd'de-nĕs), *n.* Promptitude.
RĔAD'ĬNG, *n.* Perusal of books; a lecture; a pre-lection; public recital :—a variation of copies.
RĒ-AD-MĬS'SION, *n.* Act of admitting again.
RĒ-AD-MĬT', *v. a.* To admit or let in again.
RĒ-AD-MĬT'TANCE, *n.* Act of readmitting; an allowance to enter again.
RĔAD'Y (rĕd'de), *a.* Prompt; prepared; willing.
RĒ-AF-FĪRM'ANCE, *n.* A second confirmation.
RĒ'AL, *a.* Relating to things; true; actual.
RĒ'AL, *n.* A Spanish and Mexican coin.
RĒ'AL-ĬSM, *n.* The doctrine of the realists ;—opposed to *nominalism.*
RĒ'AL-ĬST, *n.* One of a school of philosophers.
RE-ĂL'Ĭ-TY, *n.* Truth; fact; real existence.
RĒ-AL-I-ZĀ'TION, *n.* The act of realizing.
RĒ'AL-ĪZE, *v. a.* To bring into being or act.
RĒ'AL-LY, *ad.* With reality; in truth; truly.
RĔALM (rĕlm), *n.* A kingdom; an empire.
RĒ'AL-TY, *n.* Reality.—(*Law.*) Immobility.
RĒAM, *n.* Twenty quires of paper :—a strap.
RĒ-ĂN'Ĭ-MĀTE, *v. a.*To revive; to restore to life.
RĒ-AN-NĔX', *v. a.* To annex again.
RĒAP, *v. a.* To cut, as grain :—to obtain.
RĒAP, *v. n.* To cut grain; to harvest.
RĒAP'ER, *n.* One that cuts grain at harvest.
RĒ-AP-PEAR'ANCE, *n.* Act of appearing again.
RĒAR, *n.* The hinder troop, class, or part.
RĒAR, *v. a.* To raise up; to educate; to breed.
RĒAR'-ĂD'MĬ-RAL, *n.* In the English navy, an officer next in rank below a vice-admiral.
RĒAR'-GUĂRD, *n.* The guard that marches last.
RĒAR'-RĂNK, *n.* The last rank of a battalion.
RĒAR'WÂRD, *n.* Rear-guard :—end; latter part.
RĒ-AS-CĔND', *v.n.& a.*To climb or mount again.
RĒA'SON (rē'zn), *n.* The rational faculty :—absolute right; cause; motive; argument.
RĒA'SON (rē'zn), *v. n.* To argue rationally.
RĒA'SON (rē'zn), *v. a.* To examine rationally.
RĒA'SON-A-BLE (rē'zn-a-bl), *a.* Endued with reason :—just; rational; agreeable to reason.
RĒA'SON-A-BLE-NĔSS (rē'zn-a-bl-nĕs), *n.* Rationality; agreeableness to reason.
RĒA'SON-A-BLY (rē'zn-a-ble), *ad.* With reason.
RĒA'SON-ER (rē'zn-er), *n.* One who reasons.
RĒA'SON-ĬNG (rē'zn-ĭng), *n.* Argumentation.
RĒ-AS-SĔM'BLE, *v. a.* To assemble again.
RĒ-AS-SĔRT', *v. a.* To assert anew.
RĒ-AS-SŪME', *v. a.* To resume; to take again.
RĒ-AS-SŪRE' (rē-a-shŭr'), *v. a.* To assure again.
RĒ-BĀTE'MENT, *n.* A diminution.
RĒ'REC, *n.* A three-stringed instrument or fiddle.
RĔB'EL, *n.* One who resists lawful authority;
RĔB'EL, *a.* Rebellious. [a revolter.
RĒ-BĔL', *v. n.* To rise against lawful authority.
RĒ-BĔLL'ION (re-bĕl'yun), *n.* An insurrection.
RĒ-BĔLL'IOUS (re-bĕl'yus), *a.* Resisting authority; revolting; disobedient. [bellion.
RĒ-BĔLL'IOUS-LY (re-bĕl'yus-le), *ad.* By re-
RĒ-BŌUND', *v. n.* To spring or bound back.
RĒ-BŌUND', *v. a.* To reverberate; to beat back.
RĒ-BŌUND', *n.* Act of flying back; resilience.
RĒ-BŬFF', *n.* A repercussion :—sudden check.
RĒ-BŬFF', *v. a.* To beat back; to repel. [struct.
RĒ-BUILD' (re-bĭld'), *v. a.* To reëdify; to recon-
RĒ-BŪKE', *v. a.* To chide; to reprehend.
RĒ-BŪKE', *n.* A reprehension; an objurgation.
RĒ-BUR'Y (re-bĕr'e), *v. a.* To inter again.

RĒ'BUS, *n.* A sort of riddle or enigma.
RĒ-BŬT', *v. a.* To beat back; to repel.
RĒ-BŬT'TER, *n.* An answer to a rejoinder.
RĒ-CĀLL', *v. a.* To call back; to revoke.
RĒ-CĀLL', *n.* A revocation; act of calling back.
RĒ-CĂNT', *v. a.* To retract an opinion; to recall.
RĒ-CĂNT', *v. n.* To revoke what has been said.
RĒ-CAN-TĀ'TION, *n.* A recanting; a retraction.
RĒ-CĂNT'ER, *n.* One who recants. [stance of.
RĒ-CA-PĬT'U-LATE, *v. a.* To repeat the sub-
RĒ-CA-PĬT-U-LĀ'TION, *n.* A distinct repetition.
RĒ-CA-PĬT'U-LA-TO-RY, *a.* Repeating again.
RĒ-CĂP'TION, *n.* Act of retaking; reprisal.
RĒ-CĂPT'URE (rē-kăpt'yur), *v. a.* To retake.
RĒ-CĂST', *v. a.* To cast or throw again.
RĒ-CĒDE', *v. n.* To retreat; to relax any claim.
RĒ-CĒIPT' (re-sēt'), *n.* A reception :—a written acknowledgment of money, &c., received.
RĒ-CĒIPT' (re-sēt'), *v. a.* To give a receipt for.
RĒ-CĒIV'A-BLE, *a.* Capable of being received.
RĒ-CĒIVE', *v. a.* To take; to allow; to admit.
RĒ-CĒIV'ER, *n.* One that receives.
RĒ'CEN-CY, *n.* Newness; new state.
RĒ-CĔN'SION, *n.* An enumeration; a review.
RĒ'CENT, *a.* New; late; not antique; fresh.
RĒ'CENT-LY, *ad.* Lately; newly; freshly.
RĒ'CENT-NĔSS, *n.* Newness; freshness.
RĒ-CĔP'TA-CLE, *n.* A vessel or place into which any thing is received; a recipient.
RĒ-CĔP-TI-BĬL'I-TY, *n.* Possibility of receiving.
RĒ-CĔP'TION, *n.* Act of receiving; admission.
RĒ-CĔP'TIVE, *a.*Having the quality of admitting.
RĒC'EP-TO-RY *or* RĒ-CĔP'TO-RY, *a.* Received.
RĒ-CĔSS', *n.* Retirement; remission :—cavity.
RĒ-CĔS'SION (re-sĕsh'un), *n.* Act of retreating.
RĒ-CHĂRGE', *v. a.* To charge or attack anew.
RĒC'I-PĒ (rĕs'se-pē), *n.* A medical prescription.
RĒ-CĬP'I-ENT, *n.* A receiver; a vessel to receive.
RĒ-CĬP'RO-CAL, *a.* Alternate; interchangeable.
RĒ-CĬP'RO-CAL-LY, *ad.* Interchangeably.
RĒ-CĬP'RO-CAL-NĔSS, *n.* Mutual return.
RĒ-CĬP'RO-CĀTE, *v. n.* To act interchangeably.
RĒ-CĬP-RO-CĀ'TION, *n.* Action interchanged.
RĒC-I-PRŎC'I-TY, *n.* Reciprocal obligation.
RĒ-CĪ''SION (re-sĭzh'un), *n.* Act of cutting off.
RĒ-CĪ'TAL, *n.* A rehearsal; a narration.
RĒC-I-TĀ'TION, *n.* A repetition; a rehearsal.
RĒC-I-TA-TĪVE',) *n.* A kind of musical decla-
RĒC-I-TA-TĪ'VO.) mation used in operas.
RĒ-CĪTE', *v. a.* To rehearse; to repeat; tell over.
RĔCK'LESS, *a.* Careless; heedless; mindless.
RĔCK'LESS-NĔSS, *n.* Carelessness; negligence.
RĔCK'ON (rĕk'kn), *v. a.* To number; to esteem.
RĔCK'ON (rĕk'kn), *v. n.* To compute, calculate.
RĔCK'ON-ER (rĕk'kn-er), *n.* One who reckons.
RĔCK'ON-ĬNG (rĕk'kn-ĭng), *n.* Computation.
RĒ-CLAĪM', *v. a.* To reform; to recall; to tame.
RĒ-CLAĪM'A-BLE, *a.*Capable of being reclaimed.
RĒ-CLAĪM'ANT, *n.* One who reclaims.
RĒC-LI-NĀ'TION, *n.* Act of leaning or reclining.
RĒ-CLĪNE', *v. a. & n.* To lean back; to repose.
RĒ-CLŪSE', *n.* One shut up; a retired person.
RĒ-CLŪSE', *a.* Shut up; retired.
RĒ-CLŪ'SION (re-klū'zhun), *n.* State of a recluse.
RĒC-OG-NĪ''TION (rĕk-og-nĭsh'un), *n.* A renovation of knowledge; an acknowledgment.
RĒ-CŌG'NI-ZA-BLE *or* RĒC'OG-NI-ZA-BLE, *a.* That may be acknowledged.

RẸ-CŎG′NĮ-ZĄNCE, *n.* An acknowledgment; recognition :—obligation of record. [edge.
RĔC′ŎG-NIZE, *v. a.* To know again ; to acknowl-
RẸ-CŎG-NĮ-ZĔĒ′, *n.*One bound by recognizance.
RẸ-CŎG-NĮ-ZŌR′, *n.* Giver of a recognizance.
RẸ-CÖÏL′, *v. n.* To rush back ; to fall back.
RẸ-CÖÏL′, RẸ-CÖÏL′ĮNG, *n.* A falling back.
RẸ-CÖÏN′, *v. a.* To coin over again.
RẸ-CÖÏN′ĄĢE, *n.* The act of coining anew.
RĔC-ŎL-LĔCT′, *v. a.* To recall to mind ; to re-cover to memory ; to remember.
RĔC-ŎL-LĔC′TIǪN, *n.* Recovery to memory.
RĒ-CǪM-BĪNE′, *v. a.* To unite together again.
RĒ-CǪM-MĔNCE′, *v. a.* To begin anew.
RĔC-ǪM-MĔND′, *v. a.* To commend to another.
RĔC-ǪM-MĔND′Ą-BLE, *a.* Worthy of praise.
RĔC-ǪM-MĘN-DĀ′TIǪN,*n.*Act of recommending.
RĔC-ǪM-MĔN′DĄ-TǪ-RỾ, *a.* Conveying praise.
RĒ-CǪM-MĪT′, *v. a.* To commit anew.
RĔC′ǪM-PĔNSE, *v. a.* To repay ; to requite.
RĔC′ǪM-PĔNSE, *n.* A reward ; a compensation.
RĒ-CǪM-PŌSE′, *v. a.* To form or quiet anew.
RĔC-ǪN-CĪL′Ą-BLE, *a.* That may be reconciled.
RĔC′ǪN-CĪLE, *v. a.* To conciliate ; to adjust.
RĔC′ǪN-CĪLE-MĘNT, *n.* Reconciliation.
RĔC′ǪN-CĪL-ĘR, *n.* One who reconciles. [ship.
RĔC-ǪN-CĪL-Į-Ā′TIǪN, *n.* A renewal of friend-
RĔC′ǪN-DĪTE, *a.* Hidden ; secret ; abstruse.
RĒ-CǪN-DŬCT′, *v. a.* To conduct again.
RĔC-ǪN-NÖÏ′TRE (rĕk-Ǫn-nöï′tụr), *v. a.* To ex-amine ; to view, as for military purposes.
RĒ-CǪN-SĬD′ĘR, *v. a.* To consider again.
RĒ-CǪN-VEY′ (rē-kǪn-vā′),*v. a.*To convey again.
RẸ-CŌRD′, *v. a.* To register :—to celebrate.
RĔC′ǪRD, *n.* A register ; a memorial ; account.
RẸ-CŌRD′ĘR, *n.* One who records ; a registrar.
RẸ-CÖÜNT′, *v. a.* To relate in detail ; to tell.
RẸ-CŌURSE′ (rẹ-kōrs′), *n.* Application ; access.
RẸ-CŎV′ĘR, *v. a.* To restore ; to repair ; to regain.
RẸ-CŎV′ĘR, *v. n.* To grow well from a disease.
RẸ-CŎV′ĘR-Ą-BLE, *a.* That may be recovered.
RẸ-CŎV′ĘR-Ỿ, *n.* A restoration ; a regaining.
RĔC′RẸ-ĄNT, *a.* Cowardly; mean-spirited ; false.
RĒ-CRẸ-ĀTE′, *v. a.* To create anew.
RĔC′RẸ-ĀTE, *v. a.* To refresh ; to relieve :—to amuse ; to entertain ; to divert. [sion.
RĔC-RẸ-Ā′TIǪN, *n.* Relief ; refreshment ; diver-
RĒ-CRẸ-Ā′TIǪN, *n.* The act of creating anew.
RĔC′RẸ-Ā-TĮVE,*a.* Refreshing ; amusing ; divert-
RĔC′RẸ-MĔNT, *n.* Dross ; spume ; dregs. [ing.
RĔC-RẸ-MĔN′TAL, *a.* Consisting of rec-
RĔC-RẸ-MĘN-TĬ′′TIOỤS, *a.* rement ; drossy.
RẸ-CRĬM′Į-NĀTE, *v. n.* To return an accusation.
RẸ-CRĬM′Į-NĀTE, *v. a.* To accuse in return.
RẸ-CRĬM-Į-NĀ′TIǪN, *n.* Act of recriminating.
RẸ-CRĬM′Į-NĀ-TǪR, *n.* One who recriminates.
RẸ-CRĬM′Į-NĄ-TǪ-RỾ, *a.* Retorting accusation.
RẸ-CRÜIT′ (rẹ-krŭt′), *v. a.* To repair ; to supply.
RẸ-CRÜIT′ (rẹ-krŭt′), *v. n.* To raise new soldiers.
RẸ-CRÜIT′ (rẹ-krŭt′), *n.* A supply:—new soldier.
RĔC′TĂN-GLE, *n.* A right-angled parallelogram.
RẸC-TĂN′GỤ-LĄR, *a.* Having right angles.
RĔC′TĮ-FĪ-Ą-BLE, *a.* Capable of being rectified.
RĔC-TĮ-FĮ-CĀ′TIǪN, *n.* The act of rectifying.
RĔC′TĮ-FĪ-ĘR, *n.* One that rectifies.
RĔC′TĮ-FỾ, *v. a.* To make right, reform, refine.
RĔC′TĮ-LĬN′Ę-ĄR, *a.* Right-lined ; straight.
RĔC′TĮ-TŪDE, *n.* Uprightness ; equity ; rightness.

RĔC′TǪR, *n.* A ruler :—a pastor ; a clergyman.
RẸC-TŌ′RĮ-ĄL, *a.* Belonging to a rector.
RĔC′TǪR-SHĬP, *n.* The rank or office of rector.
RĔC′TǪ-RỾ, *n.* A parish church, parsonage, &c.
RẸ-CŬM′BĘNCE, *n.* Act or posture of lean-
RẸ-CŬM′BĘN-CỾ, *n.* ing ; rest ; repose.
RẸ-CŬM′BĘNT, *a.* Lying ; leaning ; reposing.
RẸ-CŪ′PĘR-Ą-TĬVE, *a.* Restorative ; restor-
RẸ-CŪ′PĘR-Ą-TǪ-RỾ, *a.* ing.
RẸ-CŬR′, *v. n.* To come back ; to return.
RẸ-CŬR′RĘNCE, RẸ-CŬR′RĘN-CỾ, *n.* A return.
RẸ-CŬR′RĘNT, *a.* Returning from time to time.
RĒ-CỤR-VĀ′TIǪN, *n.* A bending or flexure
RẸ-CŬR′VĮ-TỾ, backwards.
RẸ-CŬR′VOỤS, *a.* Bent backwards.
‖RẸ-CŪ′SĄN-CỾ, *n.* Non-conformity. [formist.
‖RẸ-CŪ′SĄNT *or* RĔC′Ụ-SĄNT, *n.* A non-con-
RĔD, *a.* Of the color of blood ; crimson.
RĔD, *n.* One of the primitive colors.—*pl.* Menses.
RĔD′BRĔAST (rĕd′brĕst), *n.* A kind of bird.
RĔD′-CHÂLK (-châwk), *n.* A red ore ; reddle.
RĔD′DEN, *v. a. & n.* To make or grow red.
RED-DĬ′′TIǪN (rẹd-dĭsh′ụn), *n.* A restitution.
RĔD′DĮ-TĬVE, *a.* Returning an answer.
RĔD′DLE, *n.* Red-chalk. See RED-CHALK.
RẸ-DĒĒM′, *v. a.* To deliver from captivity or punishment ; to ransom ; to rescue.
RẸ-DĒĒM′Ą-BLE, *a.* Capable of redemption.
RẸ-DĒĒM′ĘR, *n.* A ransomer :—Saviour of men.
RĒ-DẸ-LĬV′ĘR, *v. a.* To deliver back.
RĒ-DẸ-LĬV′ĘR-Ỿ, *n.* The act of delivering back.
RẸ-DĔMP′TIǪN, *n.* Act of redeeming ; ransom.
RẸ-DĔMP′TIǪN-ĘR,*n.*One who redeems himself
RĔD′-HŎT, *a.* Heated to redness. [by labor.
RẸ-DĬN′TẸ-GRĀTE, *v. a.* To restore. [tion.
RẸ-DĬN-TẸ-GRĀ′TIǪN, *n.* Renovation ; restora-
RĔD-LĒAD′ (rĕd-lĕd′), *n.* Minium ; red oxide of
RĔD′NESS, *n.* Quality of being red. [lead.
RĔD′Ǫ-LĘNCE, RĔD′Ǫ-LĘN-CỾ, *n.* Sweet scent.
RĔD′Ǫ-LĔNT, *a.* Diffusing fragrance ; fragrant.
RĒ-DOŬB′LE (rē-dŭb′bl), *v.* To double again.
RẸ-DÖÜBT′ (rẹ-döût′), *n.* (*Fort.*) An outwork.
RẸ-DÖÜBT′A-BLE (rẹ-döût′ạ-bl), *a.* Formidable.
RẸ-DÖÜND′, *v. n.* To conduce in the consequence.
RẸ-DRĔSS′, *v. a.* To set right ; to amend ; to ease.
RẸ-DRĔSS′, *n.* Amendment ; relief ; remedy.
RẸ-DRĔSS′ĘR, *n.* One who affords relief.
RĔD′STRĔAK, *n.* A species of apple. [subdue.
RẸ-DŪCE′, *v. a.* To restore ; to subjugate ; to
RẸ-DŪCE′MĘNT, *n.* A bringing back ; a reduc-
RẸ-DŪ′CĮ-BLE, *a.* Possible to be reduced. [tion.
RẸ-DŬC′TIǪN, *n.* Act of reducing ; conquest.
RẸ-DŬC′TĮVE, *a.* Having the power of reducing.
RẸ-DŬN′DĄNCE, *n.* State of being redundant ;
RẸ-DŬN′DĄN-CỾ, *n.* exuberance.
RẸ-DŬN′DĄNT, *a.* Superabundant ; superfluous.
RẸ-DŬN′DĄNT-LỾ, *ad.* Superabundantly.
RẸ-DŪ′PLĮ-CĀTE, *v. a.* To redouble ; to repeat.
RẸ-DŪ-PLĮ-CĀ′TIǪN, *n.* The act of doubling.
RĒ-ĔCH′Ǫ, *v. n.* To echo back ; to reverberate.
RĒĒD, *n.* A hollow, knotted stalk :—a pipe.
RẸ-ĔD′Į-FỾ, *v. a.* To rebuild ; to build again.
RĒĒD′Ỿ, *a.* Abounding with, or like, reeds.
RĒĒF, *n.* A portion of a sail :—a chain of rocks.
RĒĒF, *v. a.* To reduce the surface of a sail.
RĒĒK, *n.* Smoke ; steam ; vapor :—a rick.
RĒĒK, *v. n.* To smoke ; to steam ; to emit vapor.
RĒĒK′Ỿ, *a.* Smoky ; tanned ; black ; dark.

RĒĒL, *n.* A turning frame for yarn; a dance.
RĒĒL, *v. a.* To gather yarn off the spindle.
RĒĒL, *v. n.* To stagger; to totter in walking.
RĒ-ĘN-FŌRCE', *v. a.* To strengthen anew. [help.
RĒ-ĘN-FŌRCE'MĘNT, *n.* Fresh assistance; new
RĒ-ĘN'TĘR, *v. a.* To enter again; to enter anew.
RĒ-ĘS-TĂB'LĬSH, *v. a.* To establish anew.
RĒ-ĘS-TĂB'LĬSH-MĔNT,*n.*Act of reëstablishing.
RĒ-ĘX-ĂM'ĬNE, *v. a.* To examine anew.
RĘ-FĔC'TĬǪN, *n.* Refreshment; repast.
RĘ-FĔC'TǪ-RY, *n.* An eating-room. [to ascribe.
RĘ-FĔR', *v. a.* To direct to another; to submit;
RĘ-FĔR', *v. n.* To respect; to have relation.
RĔF'ĘR-A-BLE, *a.* That may be referred.
RĔF-ĘR-ĒĒ', *n.* One to whom some matter in
 dispute is referred.   [tion.
RĔF'ĘR-ĘNCE, *n.* Relation; respect; an arbitra-
RĘ-FĪNE', *v. a.* To purify; to clear from dross.
RĘ-FĪNE', *v. n.* To improve in accuracy, &c.
RĘ-FĪNE'MĘNT, *n.* Purity; polish; elegance.
RĘ-FĪN'ĘR, *n.* A purifier; one who refines.
RĘ-FĬT', *v. a.* To repair; to restore after damage.
RĘ-FLĔCT', *v. a.* To throw back; to cast back.
RĘ-FLĔCT', *v. n.* To throw back light; cast
 censure; to consider attentively; think.
RĘ-FLĔC'TĬǪN, *n.* The act of throwing back:
 —thought; attentive consideration; censure.
RĘ-FLĔC'TĬVE, *a.* Considering things past.
RĘ-FLĔCT'ǪR, *n.* One who, or that which, re-
 flects:—a reflecting surface. [ble.
RĘ-FLĔX-Ĭ-BĬL'Ĭ-TY, *n.* Quality of being reflexi-
RĘ-FLĔX'Ĭ-BLE, *a.* Capable of being reflected,
 or thrown back.
RĘ-FLĔX'ĬVE, *a.* Having respect to the past.
RĔF'LŬ-ĘN-CY, *n.* Quality of flowing back.
RĔF'LŬ-ĘNT, *a.* Running back; flowing back.
RĒ'FLŬX, *n.* The backward course of water.
RĘ-FŌRM', *v. a.* To form anew.
RĘ-FŌRM', *v. a. & n.* To change from worse to
 better; to correct; to restore; to amend.
RĘ-FŌRM', *n.* A reformation; an amendment.
RĔF-ǪR-MĀ'TĬǪN, *n.* A change from worse to
 better:—change in religion begun by Luther.
RĘ-FŌRM'A-TǪ-RY, *a.* Tending to reform.
RĘ-FŌRM'ĘR, *n.* One who reforms.
RĘ-FŌRM'ĬST, *n.* An adherent to reform.
RĘ-FRĂCT', *v. a.* To break the course of rays.
RĘ-FRĂC'TĬǪN, *n.* Deviation of rays of light.
RĘ-FRĂC'TĬVE, *a.* Having the power of refrac-
 tion; refracting.   [nacy.
RĘ-FRĂC'TǪ-RĬ-NĔSS, *n.* Stubbornness; obsti-
RĘ-FRĂC'TǪ-RY, *a.* Obstinate; contumacious.
RĔF'RA-GA-BLE, *a.* Capable of refutation.
RĘ-FRĀIN', *v. a.* To hold back; to keep from.
RĘ-FRĀIN', *v. n.* To forbear; to abstain.
RĘ-FRĀIN', *n.* The burden of a song; repetition.
RĘ-FRĀME', *v. a.* To put together again. [ble.
RĘ-FRĂN-ĢĬ-BĬL'Ĭ-TY, *n.* State of being refrangi-
RĘ-FRĂN'ĢĬ-BLE, *a.* Capable of being refracted.
RĘ-FRĔSH', *v. a.* To relieve; to revive; to cool.
RĘ-FRĔSH'ĘR, *n.* One that refreshes.
RĘ-FRĔSH'MĘNT,*n.*Relief after pain; food; rest.
RĘ-FRĬĢ'ĘR-ANT, *a.* Cooling; mitigating heat.
RĘ-FRĬĢ'ĘR-ĀTE, *v. a.* To cool; to allay heat of.
RĘ-FRĬĢ-ĘR-Ā'TĬǪN, *n.* The act of cooling.
RĘ-FRĬĢ'ĘR-Ā-TǪR, } *n.* A cooling vessel or
RĘ-FRĬĢ'ĘR-A-TǪ-RY, } apparatus.
RĔF'ŪĢE (rĕf'fūj), *n.* Shelter from danger.

RĔF-Ų-ĢĒĒ', *n.* One who flies for protection.
RĘ-FŬL'ĢĘNCE,RĘ-FŬL'ĢĘN-CY,*n.*Brightness.
RĘ-FŬL'ĢĘNT, *a.* Bright; shining; glittering.
RĘ-FŬL'ĢĘNT-LY, *ad.* In a shining manner.
RĘ-FŬND', *v. a.* To pour back; to repay; to re-
RĘ-FŪŞ'A-BLE, *a.* That may be refused. [store.
RĘ-FŪŞ'AL, *n.* A denial; right of choice; option.
RĘ-FŪŞE', *v. a.* To deny; to decline; to reject.
RĘ-FŪŞE', *v. n.* Not to accept; not to comply.
RĔF'ŲSE (rĕf'fųs), *a.* Left when the rest is taken.
RĔF'ŲSE, *n.* What remains; worthless matter;
RĘ-FŪT'A-BLE, *a.* That may be refuted. [dross.
RĘ-FŪT'AL, RĔF-Ų-TĀ'TĬǪN, *n.* Act of refuting.
RĘ-FŪTE', *v. a.* To prove false or erroneous.
RĒ-GĀIN', *v. a.* To recover; to gain anew.
RĒ'GAL, *a.* Pertaining to a king; royal; kingly.
RĘ-GĀLE', *v. a.* To refresh; to entertain; to feast.
RĘ-GĀLE', *n.* A sumptuous entertainment.
RĘ-GĀLE'MĘNT,*n.*Refreshment; entertainment.
RĘ-GĀ'LĬ-A,*n.pl.* [L.] Ensigns of royalty; badges,
RĘ-GĂL'Ĭ-TY, *n.* Royalty; sovereignty. [&c.
RĒ'GAL-LY, *ad.* In a regal manner; royally.
RĘ-GĂRD', *v. a.* To value; to observe; to respect.
RĘ-GĂRD', *n.* Attention; respect; reverence.
RĘ-GĂRD'A-BLE,*a.*Observable; worthy of notice.
RĘ-GĂRD'FŬL, *a.* Attentive; taking notice of.
RĘ-GĂRD'FŬL-LY, *ad.* Attentively; respectfully.
RĘ-GĂRD'LĘSS, *a.* Heedless; negligent; inatten-
RĘ-GĂRD'LĘSS-LY, *ad.* Without heed. [tive.
RĒ'GĘN-CY, *n.* Government by a regent; rule.
RĘ-ĢĔN'ĘR-A-CY, *n.* State of being regenerate.
RĘ-ĢĔN'ĘR-ĀTE, *v. a.* To cause to be born anew.
RĘ-ĢĔN'ĘR-ĀTE, *a.* Reproduced; born anew.
RĘ-ĢĔN'ĘR-ĀTE-NĔSS, *n.* Regeneracy.
RĒ-ĢĔN-ĘR-Ā'TĬǪN, *n.* Act of regenerating;
 renovation; new birth; birth by grace.
RĒ'GĘNT, *a.* Governing; exercising authority.
RĒ'GĘNT, *n.* A governor; a vicarious ruler.
RĒ'GĘNT-SHĬP, *n.* The office of a regent.
RĒ-ĢĔR-MĬ-NĀ'TĬǪN, *n.* Act of sprouting anew.
RĔĢ'Ĭ-CĪDE, *n.* A murderer or murder of a king.
RĔĢ'Ĭ-MĔN, *n.* Regulation of diet; government.
RĔĢ'Ĭ-MĔNT, *n.* A body of soldiers or troops
 commanded by a colonel.
RĔĢ-Ĭ-MĔNT'AL, *a.* Belonging to a regiment.
RĔĢ-Ĭ-MĔNT'ALŞ, *n. pl.* Military uniform.
RĒ'ĢĬǪN (rē'jųn), *n.* A country; a tract; a place.
RĔĢ'ĬS-TĘR, *n.* A list; a record:—a registrar.
RĔĢ'ĬS-TĘR,*v.a.*To record in a register; to enroll.
RĔĢ'ĬS-TĘR-SHĬP, *n.* The office of register.
RĔĢ'ĬS-TRĂR, *n.* A writer or keeper of records.
RĔĢ-ĬS-TRĀ'TĬǪN, *n.* The act of recording.
RĔĢ'ĬS-TRY, *n.* Act of recording:—a record.
RĔĢ'LĘT, *n.* Piece of wood used by printers, &c.
RĔĢ'NANT, *a.* Reigning; ruling; prevalent.
RĘ-GRĀTE', *v. a.* To engross; to forestall.
RĒ'GRĘSS, *n.* A passage back; a return.
RĘ-GRĔS'SĬǪN (rę-grĕsh'ųn), *n.* Act of returning.
RĘ-GRĔT', *n.* Grief for the past; sorrow.
RĘ-GRĔT', *v. a.* To grieve at; to mourn for.
RĘ-GRĔT'FŬL, *a.* Full of regret.; sorrowful.
RĔĢ'Ų-LAR, *a.* Agreeable to rule; orderly; exact.
RĔĢ'Ų-LAR, *n.* A priest:—a permanent soldier.
RĔĢ-Ų-LĂR'Ĭ-TY, *n.* Conformity to rule.
RĔĢ'Ų-LAR-LY, *ad.* In a regular manner.
RĔĢ'Ų-LĀTE, *v. a.* To adjust by rule; to direct.
RĔĢ-Ų-LĀ'TĬǪN, *n.* Act of regulating; method.
RĔĢ'Ų-LĀ-TǪR, *n.* One that regulates.

RE-GŬR'GĬ-TĀTE, *v. a.* To throw or pour back.
RĒ-HĒAR', *v. a.* To hear again.   [narration.
RE-HĒARS'AL (re-hër'sal),*n.* A repetition; recital;
RE-HĒARSE' (re-hërs'), *v. a.* To repeat; to recite.
RĒI'GLE, *n.* A groove for any thing to run in.
REIGN (rān), *v. n.* To rule as a king; to prevail.
REIGN (rān), *n.* Royal authority; sovereignty.
RĒ-ĬM-BŬRSE', *v. a.* To repay; to repair loss.
RĒ-ĬM-BŬRSE'MENT, *n.* Reparation; repayment.
REIN (rān), *n.* The strap of a bridle.   [strain.
REIN (rān), *v. a.* To govern by a bridle; to re-
REIN'DĒER (rān'dĕr), *n.* A northern deer.
REINS (rānz), *n. pl.* The kidneys :—the heart.
RĒ-ĬN-STȦLL', *v. a.* To install anew.
RĒ-ĬN-STĀTE', *v. a.* To put again in possession.
RĒ-ĬN-VĔST', *v. a.* To invest anew.
RE-ĬT'ER-ĀTE, *v. a.* To repeat again and again.
RE-ĬT'ER-Ā'TIQN, *n.* A repetition.   [to repel.
RE-JĔCT', *v. a.* To cast off; to refuse; to discard;
RE-JĔCT'ER, *n.* One who rejects; a refuser.
RE-JĔC'TIQN, *n.* Act of casting off; a refusal.
RE-JOÏCE', *v. n.* To be glad; to joy; to exult.
RE-JOÏCE', *v. a.* To exhilarate; to make joyful.
RE-JOÏ'CING, *n.* An expression or cause of joy.
RĒ-JOÏN', *v. a.* To join again; to meet one again.
RE-JOÏN', *v. n.* To answer to a reply.
RE-JOÏN'DER, *n.* An answer to a reply.
RĒ-KĬN'DLE, *v. a.* To set on fire again.
RE-LĂPSE', *v. n.* To slide or fall back.   [ness.
RE-LĂPSE', *n.* A falling back, as into vice or sick-
RE-LĀTE', *v. a.* To tell; to recite; to unfold.
RE-LĀTE', *v. n.* To have reference or relation.
RE-LĀT'ER, *n.* One who relates; a narrator.
RE-LĀ'TIQN, *n.* Reference; kindred; narrative.
RE-LĀ'TIQN-SHĬP, *n.* The state of being related.
RĔL'A-TĬVE, *a.* Having relation; respecting.
RĔL'A-TĬVE, *n.* A person related; a relation :
—a pronoun answering to an antecedent.
RĔL'A-TĬVE-LY, *ad.* In relation to something.
RE-LĂX', *v. a.* To slacken; to remit, ease, divert.
RE-LĂX', *v. n.* To be remiss; to be not rigorous.
RĔL-AX-Ā'TIQN, *n.* Act of relaxing; remission.
RE-LĀY', *n.* Horses kept to relieve others.
RE-LĒASE', *v. a.* To set free; to quit; to let go.
RE-LĒASE', *n.* Liberation; discharge; remission.
RE-LĒASE'MENT, *n.* The act of releasing.
RE-LĔNT', *v. n.* To yield; to soften; to grow tender.
RE-LĔNT'LESS, *a.* Unpitying; unmoved by pity.
RĔL'E-VAN-CY, *n.* The state of being relevant.
RĔL'E-VANT, *a.* Lending aid :—pertinent.
RE-LĪ'A-BLE, *a.* Trustworthy.   [*Modern.*]
RE-LĪ'ANCE, *n.* Trust; dependence; confidence.
RĔL'ĬC, *n.* That which remains :—a corpse.
RĔL'ĬCT, *n.* A woman whose husband is dead.
RE-LIĒF' (re-lēf'), *n.* Alleviation; succor; re-
dress :—the prominence of a figure.
RE-LIĒV'A-BLE (re-lēv'a-bl),*a.* Capable of relief.
RE-LIĒVE' (re-lēv'), *v. a.* To ease; to succor.
RE-LIĒ'VŌ,*n.* [It.] Prominence of a figure; relief.
RE-LĬG'IQN (re-lĭd'jun), *n.* Duty to God; practi-
cal piety :—a system of faith and worship.
RE-LĬG'IQN-ĬST; *n.* A devotee to any religion.
RE-LĬG'IOUS (re-lĭd'jus), *a.* Pious; holy; strict.
RE-LĬG'IOUS-LY (re-lĭd'jus-le), *ad.* Piously.
RE-LĬN'QUISH (re-lĭng'kwish), *v. a.* To forsake;
to abandon; to leave; to quit; to give up.
RE-LĬN'QUISH-ER, *n.* One who relinquishes.
RE-LĬN'QUISH-MENT, *n.* The act of forsaking.

RĔL'Ĭ-QUA-RY, *n.* A casket to keep relics in.
RĔL'ISH, *n.* Taste; liking; delight; flavor.
RĔL'ISH, *v. a.* To have a liking for; to taste of.
RĔL'ISH, *v. n.* To have a pleasing taste or flavor.
RĔL'ISH-A-BLE, *a.* Gustable; that may be rel-
RE-LŪ'CENT, *a.* Shining; transparent.   [ished.
RE-LŬC'TANCE, *n.* Unwillingness; repugnance.
RE-LŬC'TANT, *a.* Striving against; unwilling.
RE-LŬC'TANT-LY, *ad.* With unwillingness.
RE-LŪME', RE-LŪ'MINE, *v. a.* To light anew.
RE-LȲ', *v. n.* To trust; to confide; to depend.
RE-MĀIN', *v. a.* To continue, endure, be left.
RE-MĀIN'DER, *n.* What is left; a remnant.
RE-MĀINS', *n. pl.* Relics :—dead body.   [anew.
RĒ-MĀKE,' *v. a.* [*imp. t. & pp.* remade.] To make
RE-MĀND', *v. a.* To send or order back.
RE-MÄRK', *n.* Observation; note; notice taken.
RE-MÄRK', *v. a.* To note; to observe; to mark.
RE-MÄRK'A-BLE,*a.* Observable; worthy of note.
RE-MÄRK'A-BLY, *ad.* Observably; uncommonly.
RE-MÄRK'ER, *n.* An observer; one that remarks.
RĒ-MĂR'RY, *v. a.* To marry a second time.
RE-MĒ'DI-A-BLE, *a.* Capable of remedy; curable.
RE-MĒ'DI-AL, *a.* Affording remedy.
RĔM'E-DI-LĔSS, *a.* Not admitting remedy.
RĔM'E-DY, *n.* A medicine; a cure; reparation.
RĔM'E-DY, *v. a.* To cure; to heal; to repair.
RE-MĔM'BER, *v. a.* To bear in, or call to, mind.
RE-MĔM'BER-ER, *n.* One who remembers.
RE-MĔM'BRANCE, *n.* Retention in memory.
RE-MĔM'BRAN-CER, *n.* One that reminds.
RĔM'I-GRĀTE, *v. n.* To remove back again.
RĔM-I-GRĀ'TIQN, *n.* Removal back again.
RE-MĪND', *v. a.* To put in, or bring to, mind.
RĔM-I-NĬS'CENCE, *n.* Recollection.
RĔM-I-NĬS'CENT, *n.* One who calls to mind.
RE-MĬSS', *a.* Slack; careless; negligent.
RE-MĬS'SI-BLE, *a.* That may be remitted.   [don.
RE-MĬS'SIQN (re-mĭsh'un), *n.* Abatement; par-
RE-MĬSS'LY, *ad.* Carelessly; negligently.
RE-MĬSS'NESS, *n.* Carelessness; negligence.
RE-MĬT', *v. a.* To relax; to forgive; to pardon.
RE-MĬT', *v. n.* To slacken; to grow less intense.
RE-MĬT'TANCE, *n.* A sum sent or remitted.
RĔM'NANT, *n.* The residue; that which is left.
RE-MŎD'EL, *v. a.* To model anew.
RE-MŎN'STRANCE, *n.* A strong representation
against something; expostulation.
RE-MŎN'STRANT, *n.* One who remonstrates.
RE-MŎN'STRATE, *v. n.* To show reasons
against something; to expostulate.
RE-MŎN'STRA-TQR, *n.* One who remonstrates.
RĔM'Q-RA, *n.* [L.] A hinderance :—a fish.
RE-MŌRSE', *n.* The pain of guilt; compunction.
RE-MŌRSE'FŬL, *a.* Full of a sense of guilt.
RE-MŌRSE'LESS, *a.* Unpitying; cruel; savage.
RE-MŌRSE'LESS-LY, *ad.* Without remorse.
RE-MŌRSE'LESS-NĔSS, *n.* Savageness; cruelty.
RE-MŌTE', *a.* Distant; not near; foreign; alien.
RE-MŌTE'LY, *ad.* Not nearly; at a distance.
RE-MŌTE'NESS, *n.* The state of being remote;
RE-MŎÜNT', *v. n.* To mount again.   [distance.
RE-MŌV'A-BLE, *a.* That may be removed.
RE-MŌV'AL, *n.* Act of moving; a displacing.
RE-MŌVE', *v. a.* To cause to change place.
RE-MŌVE', *v. n.* To change place.   [distance.
RE-MŌVE', *n.* A change of place; a removal;
RE-MŪ'NER-A-BLE, *a.* Rewardable.

RĘ-MŪ′NĘR-ĀTE, *v. a.* To reward for service ; to recompense ; to requite. [pense.
RĘ-MŪ-NĘR-Ā′TIŅN, *n.* A reward ; a recom-
RĘ-MŪ′NĘR-A-TĬVE, *a.* Rewarding ; profitable.
RĒ′NĄL, *a.* Belonging to the reins or kidneys.
RĔN′ĄRD, *n.* The name of a fox in fable ; rey-
RĘ-NĂS′CĘNT, *a.* Rising again into being.[nard.
RĒ-NĂV′Ĭ-GĀTE, *v. a. & n.* To navigate again.
RĘN-CÖÛNT′ĘR, *n.* A personal opposition ; a combat ; an attack ; an encounter.
RĘN-CÖÛNT′ĘR, *v. a.* To attack hand to hand.
RĘN-CÖÛNT′ĘR, *v. n.* To encounter ; to fight.
RĔND, *v. a.* [*imp. t. & pp.* rent.] To tear or sever with violence ; to sunder ; to lacerate. [late.
RĔN′DĘR, *v. a.* To return ; to make ; to trans-
‖RĔN-DĘZ-V◊US′ (rĕn′dĘ-vô *or* rĕn-dĘ-vôz′), *n.* A place for the assembly of troops, &c.
‖RĔN-DĘZ-VÔUS′, *v. a. & n.* To meet. [sion.
RĘN-DĬ″TIŅN (-dĭsh′ųn), *n.* Surrender :—ver-
RĔN′Ę-GĀDE, ⎰ *n.* An apostate ; one who de-
RĔN-Ę-GĀ′DŌ, ⎱ serts to the enemy ; deserter.
RĘ-NEW̄′, *v. a.* To renovate ; to begin again.
RĘ-NEW̄′A-BLE, *a.* That may be renewed.
RĘ-NEW̄′ĄL, *n.* Act of renewing ; renovation.
RĘ-NĪ′TĘN-CỲ, *n.* Resistance to pressure.
RĘ-NĪ′TĘNT, *a.* Acting against impulse.
RĔN′NĘT, *n.* The prepared membrane of a calf's stomach ; runnet.
RĘ-NÖÛNCE′, *v. a.* To disown ; to disclaim.
RĘ-NÖÛNCE′MĘNT, *n.* Renunciation.
RĘ-NÖÛN′CĘR, *n.* One who renounces or denies.
RĔN′Ǫ-VĀTE, *v. a.* To renew ; to restore.
RĔN-Ǫ-VĀ′TIŅN, *n.* Renewal ; act of renewing.
RĘ-NŌŴN′, *n.* Fame ; celebrity ; distinction.
RĘ-NŌŴNED′ (rĘ-nöûnd′), *p. a.* Famous ; em-
RĔNT, *imp. t. & pp.* from *rend.* [inent.
RĔNT, *n.* Money paid for something held from another ; income :—a laceration ; fissure.
RĔNT, *v. a.* To lease :—to hold by lease.
RĔNT′A-BLE, *a.* That may be rented.
RĔNT′ĄL, *n.* A schedule or account of rent ; a
RĔNT′ĘR, *n.* One who rents. [rent-roll.
RĔNT′-RŌLL, *n.* An account or roll of rents.
RĘ-NŬN-CĬ-Ā′TIŅN (rĘ-nŭn-shĘ-ā′shųn), *n.* The act of renouncing ; abnegation ; recantation.
RĘ-PĀID′, *imp. t. & pp.* from *repay.*
RĘ-PÀIR′ (rĘ-pår′), *v. a.* To restore ; to amend.
RĘ-PÀIR′, *n.* Reparation ; restoration ; amends.
RĘ-PÀIR′, *v. n.* To go ; to betake one's self.
RĘ-PÀIR′A-BLE, *a.* That may be repaired.
RĘ-PÀIR′ĘR, *n.* One who repairs ; a restorer.
RĔP′AR-A-BLE, *a.* That may be repaired.
RĔP′A-RA-BLỲ, *ad.* In a reparable manner.
RĔP-A-RĀ′TIŅN, *n.* Act of repairing ; amends.
RĔP-AR-TĒĒ′, *n.* A smart, witty reply.
RĒ-PÀSS′, *v. a. & n.* To pass again ; to travel
RĘ-PÀST′, *n.* A meal :—food ; victuals. [back.
RĘ-PĀY′, *v. a.* [*imp. t. & pp.* repaid.] To pay back ; to recompense ; to reimburse.
RĒ-PĀY′MĘNT, *n.* The act of repaying. [voke.
RĘ-PĒAL′, *v. a.* To recall ; to abrogate ; to re-
RĘ-PĒAL′, *n.* A revocation ; an abrogation.
RĘ-PĒAL′A-BLE, *a.* That may be repealed.
RĘ-PĒAL′ĘR, *n.* One who repeals or abrogates.
RĘ-PĒAT′, *v. a.* To do again ; to rehearse.
RĘ-PĒAT′, *n.* A repetition ; a mark in music.
RĘ-PĒAT′ĘD-LỲ, *ad.* More than once. [watch.
RĘ-PĒAT′ĘR, *n.* One who repeats :—a kind of

RĘ-PĔL′, *v. a.* To drive back ; to resist.
RĘ-PĔL′LĘNT, *n.* A repelling medicine.
RĘ-PĔL′LĘNT, *a.* Having power to repel.
RĘ-PĔNT′, *v. n.* To have or exercise repentance.
RĘ-PĔNT′ANCE, *n.* Sorrow for sin ; penitence.
RĘ-PĔNT′ANT, *a.* Sorrowful for sin ; penitent.
RĒ-PĒO′PLE (rē-pē′pl), *v. a.* To people anew.
RĒ-PĘR-CŬS′SIŅN, *n.* Rebound ; reverberation.
RĒ-PĘR-CŬS′SĪVE, *a.* Driving back ; repellent.
RĔP′ĘR-TǪ-RỲ, *n.* A treasury ; book of records.
RĔP-Ę-TĬ″TIŅN (-tĭsh′ųn), *n.* Act of repeating.
RĔP-Ę-TĬ″TIŅN-ĄL, *a.* Containing repetitions.
RĘ-PĪNE′, *v. n.* To fret ; to be discontented.
RĘ-PĪN′ĘR, *n.* One that repines or murmurs.
RĘ-PLĔN′ĬSH, *v. a.* To stock ; to fill ; to supply.
RĘ-PLĒTE′, *a.* Full ; completely filled. [feit.
RĘ-PLĒ′TIŅN, *n.* The state of being full ; sur-
RĘ-PLĔV′Ĭ-A-BLE, *a.* That may be replevied.
RĘ-PLĔV′ĬN, *n.* (*Law.*) A recovery of goods.
RĘ-PLĔV′ĬN, RĘ-PLĔV′Ỳ, *v. a.* To take back by writ. [the defendant's plea.
RĔP-LĬ-CĀ′TIŅN, *n.* The plaintiff's answer to
RĘ-PLĪ′ĘR, *n.* One who replies or answers.
RĘ-PLỲ′, *v. n.* To answer ; to make a return.
RĘ-PLỲ′, *n.* An answer ; a return to an answer.
RĘ-PŌRT′, *v. a.* To relate ; to give account of.
RĘ-PŌRT′, *n.* A rumor :—account :—loud noise.
RĘ-PŌRT′ĘR, *n.* One who reports ; a relater.
RĘ-PŌ′ŞĄL, *n.* The act of reposing. [posit.
RĘ-PŌŞE′, *v. a.* To lay to rest ; to lodge ; to re-
RĘ-PŌŞE′, *v. n.* To sleep ; to be at rest ; to rest.
RĘ-PŌŞE′, *n.* Sleep ; rest ; quiet ; tranquillity.
RĘ-PŌŞ′ĬT, *v. a.* To lay up ; to lodge as for safety.
RĘ-PŌŞ′Ĭ-TǪ-RỲ, *n.* A place for laying up things.
RĒ-PǪŞ-ŞĔSS′, *v. a.* To possess again. [again.
RĒ-PǪŞ-ŞĔS′SIŅN, *n.* The act of possessing
RĔP-RĘ-HĔND′, *v. a.* To reprove ; to chide ; to blame ; to reproach ; to reprimand.
RĔP-RĘ-HĔND′ĘR, *n.* A blamer ; a censurer.
RĔP-RĘ-HĔN′SĬ-BLE, *a.* Blamable ; culpable.
RĔP-RĘ-HĔN′SĬ-BLE-NĔSS, *n.* Blamableness.
RĔP-RĘ-HĔN′SĬ-BLỲ, *ad.* Blamably ; culpably.
RĔP-RĘ-HĔN′SIŅN, *n.* Reproof ; open blame.
RĔP-RĘ-HĔN′SĪVE, ⎰ *a.* Containing reproof ;
RĔP-RĘ-HĔN′SǪ-RỲ, ⎱ reproving.
RĔP-RĘ-ŞĔNT′, *v. a.* To describe :—to act for.
RĔP-RĘ-ŞEN-TĀ′TIŅN, *n.* The act of repre-
senting ; exhibition :—body of representatives.
RĔP-RĘ-ŞĔN′TA-TĬVE, *a.* Bearing likeness.
RĔP-RĘ-ŞĔN′TA-TĬVE, *n.* One who represents ; a deputy ; a substitute ; agent. [tive.
RĔP-RĘ-ŞĔN′TA-TĬVE-LỲ, *ad.* By a representa-
RĔP-RĘ-ŞĔNT′ĘR, *n.* One who represents.
RĘ-PRĔSS′, *v. a.* To crush ; to quell ; to subdue.
RĘ-PRĔS′SIŅN (rĘ-prĕsh′ųn), *n.* Act of repress-
RĘ-PRĔS′SĪVE, *a.* Having power to repress.[ing.
RĘ-PRIĒVE′ (rĘ-prēv′), *v. a.* To respite.
RĘ-PRIĒVE′, *n.* A respite after sentence of death.
RĔP-RĬ-MĂND′, *v. a.* To chide, check, reprove.
RĔP′RĬ-MĂND, *n.* A reproof ; a reprehension.
RĒ-PRĬNT′, *v. a.* To print a new edition of.
RĒ′PRĬNT, *n.* A new impression. [tion.
RĘ-PRĪ′ŞĄL, *n.* A seizure by way of retalia-
RĘ-PRŌACH′ (rĘ-prōch′), *v. a.* To censure.
RĘ-PRŌACH′ (rĘ-prōch′), *n.* Censure ; shame.
RĘ-PRŌACH′A-BLE, *a.* Worthy of reproach.
RĘ-PRŌACH′FÛL, *a.* Scurrilous ; shameful ; vile.
RĘ-PRŌACH′FÛL-LỲ, *ad.* With reproach.

RĔP′RŌ-BĀTE, *a.* Lost to virtue; abandoned.
RĔP′RŌ-BĀTE, *n.* A man lost to virtue.
RĔP′RŌ-BĀTE, *v. a.* To disallow; to reject; to censure :—to abandon to hopeless ruin.
RĔP-RŌ-BĀ′TIŎN, *n.* The act of reprobating.
RĒ-PRŌ-DŪCE′, *v. a.* To produce again or anew.
RĒ-PRŌ-DŬC′TIŎN, *n.* Act of producing anew.
RĘ-PRÔÔF′, *n.* Blame to the face; a rebuke.
RĘ-PRÔV′Ā-BLE, *a.* Deserving reproof or blame.
RĘ-PRÔVE′, *v. a.* To blame; to chide; to rep-
RĔP′TĮLE, *a.* Creeping on the belly. [rehend.
RĔP′TĮLE, *n.* A creeping animal; a serpent, &c.
RĘ-PŬB′LĮC, *n.* A commonwealth; a free state.
RĘ-PŬB′LĮ-CĄN, *a.* Relating to a republic.
RĘ-PŬB′LĮ-CĄN, *n.* An advocate for republican government; a democrat.
RĘ-PŬB′LĮ-CĄN-ĮṢM, *n.* Republican principles.
RĒ-PŬB-LĮ-CĀ′TIŎN, *n.* A second publication.
RĒ-PŬB′LĮSH, *v. a.* To publish anew.
RĘ-PŪ′DĮ-ĀTE, *v. a.* To divorce; to reject.
RĘ-PŪ-DĮ-Ā′TIŎN, *n.* A divorce; a rejection.
RĘ-PŬG′NĄNCE, RĘ-PŬG′NĄN-CY, *n.* State of being repugnant; aversion; opposition.
RĘ-PŬG′NĄNT, *a.* Contrary; inconsistent.
RĘ-PŬG′NĄNT-LY, *ad.* Contradictorily.
RĘ-PŬLSE′, *n.* A rejection; a driving off.
RĘ-PŬLSE′, *v. a.* To beat back; to drive off.
RĘ-PŬL′SIŎN, *n.* The act or power of driving
RĘ-PŬL′SĮVE, *a.* Driving off; repelling. [off.
RĒ-PŬR′CHĄSE, *v. a.* To purchase again.
RĔP′Ų-TA-BLE, *a.* Honorable; of good repute.
RĔP′Ų-TĄ-BLE-NĔSS, *n.* Quality of being rep-
RĔP′Ų-TĄ-BLY, *ad.* With good repute. [utable.
RĔP-Ų-TĀ′TIŎN, *n.* Good repute; credit; honor.
RĘ-PŪTE′, *v. a.* To hold; to account; to think.
RĘ-PŪTE′, *n.* Character; reputation; credit.
RĘ-QUĔST′, *n.* A petition; an entreaty, demand.
RĘ-QUĔST′, *v. a.* To ask; to solicit; to entreat.
RĒ′QUĮ-ĘM *or* RĔQ′UĮ-ĘM, *n.* A hymn for the
RĘ-QUĪR′Ā-BLE, *a.* That may be required. [dead.
RĘ-QUĪRE′, *v. a.* To demand; to claim; to need.
RĘ-QUĪRE′MĘNT, *n.* A demand :—a thing required; requisition. [ful.
RĔQ′UĮ-ṢĮTE (rĕk′wę-zĭt), *a.* Necessary; need-
RĔQ′UĮ-ṢĮTE (rĕk′wę-zĭt), *n.* A thing necessary.
RĔQ′UĮ-ṢĮTE-NĔSS, *n.* Necessity.
RĔQ-UĮ-ṢĮ′′TIŎN (rĕk-wę-zĭsh′ųn), *n.* Demand.
RĘ-QUĪ′TĄL, *n.* A return; reward; recompense.
RĘ-QUĪTE′, *v. a.* To repay good or ill; to recom-
RĒ-SĀLE′, *n.* A sale at second hand. [pense.
RĘ-SCĬND′, *v. a.* To cut off; to abrogate a law.
RĘ-SCĬṢ′ṢIŎN (rę-sĭzh′ųn), *n.* An abrogation.
RĒ′SCRĬPT, *n.* An edict, or a public answer of an emperor or a pope.
RĔS′CŲE (rĕs′kų), *v. a.* To set free; to deliver.
RĔS′CŲE (rĕs′kų), *n.* A deliverance; liberation.
RĒ-SĔARCH′ (rę-sĕrch′), *n.* An inquiry; search.
RĒ-SĒIZ′ŲRE (rē-sē′zhųr), *n.* Repeated seizure.
RĘ-ṢĔM′BLĄNCE, *n.* A likeness; a similitude.
RĘ-ṢĔM′BLE, *v. a.* To compare :—to be like.
RĘ-ṢĔNT′, *v. a.* To take ill or as an affront.
RĘ-ṢĔNT′FŬL, *a.* Malignant; easily provoked.
RĘ-ṢĔNT′MĘNT, *n.* Deep sense of injury; anger.
RĔṢ-ĘR-VĀ′TIŎN, *n.* Act of reserving :—reserve; custody :—something held back.
RĘ-ṢĔRV′Ā-TŌ-RY, *n.* A repository.
RĘ-ṢĔRVE′, *v. a.* To keep or hold back; to keep in store; to retain; to lay up.

RĘ-ṢĔRVE′, *n.* A store kept untouched; an exception :—prohibition :—modesty; caution.
RĘ-ṢĔRVED′ (rę-zĕrvd′), *a.* Modest; not frank.
RĘ-ṢĔRV′ĘD-NĔSS, *n.* Want of frankness.
RĔṢ-ĘR-VOIR′ (rĕz-ęr-vwör′), *n.* A place where any thing is kept in store: a cistern; a tank.
RĒ-SĔT′, *v. a.* To set again, as a jewel.
RĒ-SĔT′TLE, *v. a.* To settle again.
RĒ-SĔT′TLE-MĔNT, *n.* Act of settling again.
RĘ-ṢĪDE′, *v. n.* To live in a place; to dwell.
RĔṢ′Į-DĔNCE, *n.* A place of abode; a dwelling.
RĔṢ′Į-DĔNT, *a.* Having abode in a place; fixed.
RĔṢ′Į-DĔNT, *n.* One who resides; an agent.
RĔṢ-Į-DĔN′TĮ-Ā-RY (-dĕn′shę-), *a.* Residing.
RĘ-ṢĬD′Ų-ĄL, *a.* Relating to the residue.
RĘ-ṢĬD′Ų-Ā-RY, *a.* Pertaining to the residue.
RĔṢ′Į-DŪE (rĕz′ę-dū), *n.* That which is left.
RĘ-ṢĬD′Ų-ŬM, *n.* [L.] The residue; remainder.
RĘ-ṢĪGN′ (rę-zīn′), *v. a.* To give up; to confide.
RĔṢ-ĮG-NĀ′TIŎN, *n.* Act of resigning :—state of being resigned; patience; submission.
RĘ-ṢĬL′Į-ĔNCE, RĘ-ṢĬL′Į-ĘN-CY, *n.* A rebound-
RĘ-ṢĬL′Į-ĔNT, *a.* Rebounding. [ing.
RĔṢ-Į-LĬ′′TIŎN (rĕz-ę-lĭsh′ųn), *n.* Resilience.
RĔṢ′ĮN, *n.* An inspissated juice of the pine, &c.
RĔṢ′ĮN-OŬS, *a.* Containing resin; like resin.
RĘ-ṢĬST′, *v. a. & n.* To oppose; to act against.
RĘ-ṢĬST′ĄNCE, *n.* Act of resisting; opposition.
RĘ-ṢĬST-Į-BĬL′Į-TY, *n.* Quality of being resisti-
RĘ-ṢĬST′Į-BLE, *a.* That may be resisted. [ble.
RĘ-ṢĬST′LĘSS, *a.* That cannot be resisted or opposed; irresistible. [solved.
RĔṢ′Ō-LŲ-BLE, *a.* That may be melted or dis-
RĔṢ′Ō-LŪTE, *a.* Determined; steady; firm; bold.
RĔṢ′Ō-LŪTE-LY, *ad.* Firmly; constantly.
RĔṢ′Ō-LŪTE-NĔSS, *n.* Unshaken firmness.
RĔṢ-Ō-LŪ′TIŎN, *n.* Act of resolving; decision; constancy; firmness :—analysis.
RĘ-ṢŎLV′Ā-BLE, *a.* That may be resolved.
RĘ-ṢŎLVE′ (rę-zŏlv′), *v. a.* To inform :—to solve; to clear; to melt; to dissolve, analyze.
RĘ-ṢŎLVE′, *v. n.* To determine; to decree.
RĘ-ṢŎLVE′, *n.* Resolution; fixed determination.
RĘ-ṢŎL′VĘNT, *n.* That which causes solution.
RĘ-ṢŎLV′ĘR, *n.* One that resolves.
RĔṢ′Ō-NĂNCE, *n.* Sound; a return of sound.
RĔṢ′Ō-NĂNT, *a.* Resounding; returning sound.
RĘ-ṢÖR′BĘNT, *a.* Swallowing up. [apply.
RĘ-ṢÖRT′, *v. n.* To have recourse; to repair; to
RĘ-ṢÖRT′, *n.* An assembly; a place of meeting.
RĘ-ṢÖRT′ĘR, *n.* One that frequents or visits.
RĘ-ṢÖŬND′, *v. a.* To echo; to reverberate; to sound; to celebrate. [turned.
RĘ-ṢÖŬND′, *v. n.* To be echoed back or re-
RĘ-SÖURCE′ (rę-sörs′), *n.* A resort; expedient.
RĘ-SPĔCT′, *v. a.* To regard; to have relation to; to think highly of; to esteem.
RĘ-SPĔCT′, *n.* Attention; honor; relation.
RĘ-SPĔC-TĄ-BĬL′Į-TY, *n.* The being respectable.
RĘ-SPĔC′TĄ-BLE, *a.* Worthy of respect; reputable; estimable; honorable.
RĘ-SPĔC′TĄ-BLY, *ad.* So as to merit respect.
RĘ-SPĔCT′FŬL, *a.* Ceremonious; full of respect.
RĘ-SPĔCT′FŬL-LY, *ad.* In a respectful manner.
RĘ-SPĔCT′FŬL-NĔSS, *n.* Quality of being respectful; civility; courtesy.
RĘ-SPĔC′TĮVE, *a.* Belonging to each; relative.
RĘ-SPĔC′TĮVE-LY, *ad.* As relating to each.

RE-SPĪR′A-BLE, *a.* That can respire :—that can be respired.

RĔS-PĮ-RĀ′TIQN, *n.* Act of breathing :—respite.

RE-SPĪRE′, *v. n.* To breathe :—to rest from toil.

RE-SPĪRE′, *v. a.* To breathe out ; to send out.

RĔS′PĮTE, *n.* Reprieve ; delay ; pause ; interval.

RĔS′PĮTE, *v. a.* To relieve ; to suspend ; to de-

RE-SPLĔN′DENCE, *n.* Lustre ; brightness. [lay.

RE-SPLĔN′DENT, *a.* Bright ; shining ; having lustre ; brilliant ; splendid.

RE-SPLĔN′DENT-LY, *ad.* With lustre ; brightly.

RE-SPŎND′, *v. n.* To answer ; to correspond.

RE-SPŎND′, *n.* A short anthem :—half-column.

RE-SPŎN′DENT, *n.* An answerer in a suit.

RE-SPŎNSE′, *n.* An alternate answer ; a reply.

RE-SPŎN-SĮ-BĬL′Į-TY, *n.* The state of being responsible ; accountability ; responsibleness.

RE-SPŎN′SĮ-BLE, *a.* Answerable ; accountable.

RE-SPŎN′SĮ-BLE-NĔSS, *n.* Responsibility.

RE-SPŎN′SĮVE, *a.* Answering ; making answer.

RĔST, *n.* Sleep ; repose ; support :—remainder.

RĔST, *v. n.* To sleep, die, be still, lean, remain.

RĔST, *v. a.* To lay or place, as on a support.

RĔS-TÂU-RĀ′TIQN, *n.* The act of recovering.

RĔS′TĮFF, *a.* Unwilling to stir ; obstinate ; res-

RĔS′TĮFF-NĔSS, *n.* Obstinate reluctance. [tive.

RĔST′ĮNG-PLĀCE, *n.* A place of rest.

RĔS-TĮ-TŪ′TIQN, *n.* The act of restoring.

RĔS′TĮVE, *a.* Unwilling to stir or go forward ; obstinate ; stubborn ; restiff.

RĔST′LESS, *a.* Being without rest ; unquiet.

RĔST′LESS-LY, *ad.* Without rest ; unquietly.

RĔST′LESS-NĔSS, *n.* Want of rest or quiet.

RE-STŌR′A-BLE, *a.* Capable of being restored.

RĔS-TQ-RĀ′TIQN, *n.* The act of restoring.

RE-STŌ′RA-TĬVE, *a.* Having power to restore.

RE-STŌ′RA-TĬVE, *n.* A medicine that restores.

RE-STŌRE′, *v. a.* To give back ; to return, as a thing taken ; to reinstate ; to cure ; to recover.

RE-STŌR′ER, *n.* One that restores or recovers.

RE-STRĀIN′, *v. a.* To withhold ; to repress ; to hold back ; to curb ; to check ; to limit.

RE-STRĀIN′A-BLE, *a.* Capable of being re-

RE-STRĀIN′ER, *n.* One that restrains. [strained.

RE-STRĀINT′, *n.* A holding back ; restriction.

RE-STRĬCT′, *v. a.* To limit ; to confine, restrain.

RE-STRĬC′TIQN, *n.* Confinement ; limitation.

RE-STRĬC′TĮVE, *a.* Causing restraint or limita-

RE-STRĬC′TĮVE-LY, *ad.* With limitation. [tion.

RE-STRĬNGE′, *v. a.* To contract ; to astringe.

RE-STRĬN′GEN-CY, *n.* Power of contracting.

RE-STRĬN′GENT, *n.* A restringent medicine.

RE-SŬLT′, *v. n.* To arise or proceed from.

RE-SŬLT′, *n.* Consequence ; effect ; decision.

RE-SŬME′A-BLE, *a.* That may be taken back.

RE-SŬME′, *v. a.* To take back ; to begin again.

RE-SŬMP′TIQN, *n.* The act of resuming.

RĔS-UR-RĔC′TIQN, *n.* Act of rising again, after death ; a revival from the dead.

RE-SŬS′CĮ-TĀTE, *v. a.* To stir up anew, revive.

RE-SŬS′CĮ-TĀTE, *v. n.* To awaken ; to revive.

RE-SŬS-CĮ-TĀ′TIQN, *n.* Act of resuscitating.

RE-TĀIL′, *v. a.* To sell in small quantities.

RĒ′TĀIL, *n.* Sale by small quantities.

RE-TĀIL′ER, *n.* One who retails. [to hire.

RE-TĀIN′, *v. a.* To keep ; to hold ; to preserve ;

RE-TĀIN′ER, *n.* One who retains :—a dependant :—a fee to retain a counsel.

RE-TĂL′Į-ĀTE, *v. a. & n.* To return like for like ; to repay ; to revenge.

RE-TĂL-Į-Ā′TIQN, *n.* The return of like for like.

RE-TĂL′Į-A-TQ-RY, *a.* Returning like for like.

RE-TĂRD′, *v. a.* To hinder ; to obstruct ; to de-

RĔTCH *or* RĔTCH, *v. n.* To try to vomit. [lay.

RE-TĔN′TIQN, *n.* Act of retaining :—memory.

RE-TĔN′TĮVE, *a.* Having power to retain. [tive.

RE-TĔN′TĮVE-NĔSS, *n.* Quality of being reten-

RĔT′Į-CLE (rĕt′e-kl), *n.* A small net ; reticule.

RE-TĬC′Ų-LAR, *a.* Having the form of a net.

RE-TĬC′Ų-LĀT-ED, *a.* Like net-work ; reticular.

RĔT′Į-CŪLE, *n.* A hand work-bag or case.

RĔT′Į-FŎRM, *a.* Having the form of a net.

RĔT′Į-NA, *n.* [L.] A membrane of the eye.

RĔT′Į-NŪE, *n.* A train of attendants ; a suite.

RE-TĪRE′, *v. n.* To retreat ; to withdraw.

RE-TĪRED′ (re-tīrd′), *p. a.* Private ; secluded.

RE-TĪRE′MENT, *n.* Private abode or way of life.

RE-TŎRT′, *v. a. & n.* To throw back ; to return.

RE-TŎRT′, *n.* Censure returned :—a glass vessel.

RĒ-TOŬCH′, *v. a.* To improve by new touches.

RĒ-TRĀCE′, *v. a.* To trace back ; to trace again.

RE-TRĂCT′, *v. a. & n.* To recall ; to recant.

RĒ-TRĂC-TĀ′TIQN, *n.* A recantation ; retraction.

RE-TRĂC′TIQN, *n.* Act of retracting or withdrawing ; recantation.

RE-TRĂC′TĮVE, *a.* Retracting ; withdrawing.

RE-TRĒAT′, *n.* Act of retreating :—retirement.

RE-TRĒAT′, *v. n.* To go back, retire, withdraw.

RE-TRĔNCH′, *v. a.* To cut off ; to lessen, reduce.

RE-TRĔNCH′MENT, *n.* A reduction of expense.

RE-TRĬB′UTE, *v. a.* To pay back ; to repay.

RĔT-RĮ-BŪ′TIQN, *n.* Repayment ; reward.

RE-TRĬB′Ų-TĬVE, } *a.* Making retribution ;

RE-TRĬB′Ų-TQ-RY, } repaying.

RE-TRIĔV′A-BLE, *a.* That may be retrieved.

RE-TRIĒVE′(re-trēv′), *v. a.* To recover ; to repair.

RĒ-TRQ-CĔS′SIQN (rē-trq-sĕsh′ụn), *n.* A going

RĔT-RQ-GRA-DĀ′TIQN, *n.* Retrogression. [back.

RĔT′RQ-GRĀDE, *a.* Going backward ; contrary.

RĔT′RQ-GRĀDE, *v. n.* To go backward.

RĔT′RQ-GRĔS′SIQN, *n.* Act of going backwards.

RĔT′RQ-SPĔCT, *n.* A review of things past.

RĔT-RQ-SPĔC′TIQN, *n.* Act of looking back, or on things past.

RĔT-RQ-SPĔC′TĮVE, *a.* Looking backwards.

RE-TŪRN′, *v. n.* To come or go back ; to respond.

RE-TŪRN′, *v. a.* To repay ; to give or send back.

RE-TŪRN′, *n.* The act of coming back :—repayment ; profit ; restitution ; relapse :—account.

RE-TŪRN′A-BLE, *a.* That may be returned.

RE-TŪRN′ER, *n.* One who pays or remits money.

RĒ-ŪN′IQN (rē-yūn′yụn), *n.* A second union.

RĒ-Ū-NĪTE′, *v. a. & n.* To unite again.

RE-VĒAL′, *v. a.* To show ; to discover ; to dis-

RE-VĒAL′ER, *n.* One who reveals. [close.

REVEILLE (re-vāl′ *or* re-vāl′yā), *n.* A beat of drums for awaking soldiers. [ment.

RĔV′EL, *v. n.* To feast with clamorous merri-

RĔV′EL, *n.* A feast with loose and noisy jollity.

RĔV-E-LĀ′TIQN, *n.* Act of revealing ; discovery :—communication of sacred truths by a teacher from heaven :—Apocalypse.

RĔV′EL-LER, *n.* One who revels.

RĔV′EL-RY, *n.* Loose jollity ; festive mirth.

RE-VĔNGE′ (re-vĕnj′), *v. a.* To return an injury.

RE-VĔNGE′, *n.* Return of an injury or affront.

RĘ-VĔNĢE′FŪL,.a. Vindictive ; full of revenge.
RĘ-VĔNĢE′FŪL-LY, ad. Vindictively.
RĘ-VĔNĢE′FŪL-NĔSS, n. Vindictiveness.
RĘ-VĔNĢ′ĘR, n. One who revenges. [profits.
RĔV′Ę-NŪE or RĘ-VĔN′ŲE, n. Income ; annual
RĘ-VĔR′BĘR-ANT, a. Resounding. [resound.
RĘ-VĔR′BĘR-ĀTE, v. a. & n. To beat back ; to
RĘ-VĔR-BĘR-Ā′TIǪN, n. Act of reverberating.
RĘ-VĔR′BĘR-A-TǪ-RY, a. Returning ; beating
back ; reverberating. [nace.
RĘ-VĔR′BĘR-A-TǪ-RY, n. A reverberating fur-
RĘ-VĒRE′, v. a. To reverence, honor, venerate.
RĔV′ĘR-ĘNCE, n. Veneration ; respect :—bow.
RĔV′ĘR-ĘNCE, v.a. To regard with reverence.
RĔV′ĘR-ĘN-CĘR, n. One who reverences.
RĔV′ĘR-ĘND, a. Deserving reverence ; a title.
RĔV′ĘR-ĘNT, a. Humble; expressing veneration.
RĔV-ĘR-ĚN′TIAL, a. Expressing reverence.
RĔV-ĘR-ĚN′TIAL-LY, ad. With show of rev-
erence ; reverently. [ence.
RĔV′ĘR-ĘNT-LY, ad. With awe ; with rever-
RĘ-VĔR′SAL, n. A change of sentence ; change.
RĘ-VĔRSE′, v. a. To overturn ; to subvert.
RĘ-VĔRSE′, n. Change ; a contrary ; an opposite.
RĘ-VĔRS′I-BLE, a. Capable of being reversed.
RĘ-VĔR′SIǪN, n. Act of reverting ; succession ;
right of succession. [cession.
RĘ-VĔR′SIǪN-A-RY, a. To be enjoyed in suc-
RĘ-VĔR′SIǪN-ĘR, n. One who has a reversion.
RĘ-VĔRT′, v. a. & n. To return ; to fall back.
RĘ-VĔRT′I-BLE, a. That may revert.
RĔV′Ę-RY, or RĔV-Ę-RIĒ′, n. A loose, wan-
dering, or deep musing ; a wild fancy.
RĘ-VIEW̄′ (rę-vū′), v. a. To see again :—to con-
sider again :—to survey ; to examine, inspect.
RĘ-VIEW̄′ (rę-vū′), n. Act of reviewing ; a re-
vision :—analysis of a book ; critique :—a pe-
riodical publication :—an inspection.
RĘ-VIEW̄′AL, n. A critical notice ; a review.
RĘ-VIEW̄′ĘR (rę-vū′ęr), n. One who reviews.
RĘ-VĪLE′, v. a. To reproach ; to vilify; to abuse.
RĘ-VĪL′ĘR, n. One who reviles. [guage.
RĘ-VĪL′ĮNG, n. Reproachful, contumelious lan-
RĘ-VĪ′SAL, n. A review ; a reëxamination.
RĘ-VĪSE′, v. a. To review ; to reëxamine.
RĘ-VĪSE′, n. A review :—a second proof-sheet.
RĘ-VĪS′ĘR, n. An examiner ; a superintendent.
RĘ-VĪ′′SIǪN (rę-vĭzh′ųn), n. A review ; revisal.
RĔ-VĪS′ĮT, v. a. To visit again. [awakening.
RĘ-VĪV′AL, n. A renewed life or activity ; an
RĘ-VĪ′VAL-ĬST, n. A promoter of revivals.
RĘ-VĪVE′, v. n. To return to life or vigor.
RĘ-VĪVE′, v. a. To bring to life, renew, rouse.
RĘ-VĪV′ĘR, n. He who, or that which, revives.
RĘ-VĬV-I-FĮ-CĀ′TIǪN, n. The act of recalling
RĘ-VĬV′I-FY, v. a. To recall to life. [to life.
RĔV′Ǫ-CA-BLE, a. That may be revoked.
RĔV-Ǫ-CĀ′TIǪN, n. Act of recalling ; a repeal.
RĘ-VǪKE′, v. a. To repeal ; to reverse ; to recall.
‖RĘ-VŌLT′ or RĘ-VŎLT′, v. n. To fall off ; to
renounce allegiance ; to desert ; to rebel ;
‖RĘ-VŌLT′, n. A desertion ; a change of sides.
‖RĘ-VŌLT′ĘR, n. One who revolts ; a deserter.
RĔV-Ǫ-LŪ′TIǪN, n. Rotation ; circular mo-
tion :—a change of a government in a country.
RĔV-Ǫ-LŪ′TIǪN-A-RY, a. Relating to or pro-
moting a revolution.
RĔV-Ǫ-LŪ′TIǪN-ĬST, n. A favorer of revolutions.

RĔV-Ǫ-LŪ′TIǪN-ĪZE, v. a. To cause a revolu-
tion in ; to remodel. [sider.
RĘ-VŎLVE′, v. n. & a. To roll round ; to con-
RĘ-VŬL′SIǪN, n. A turning or drawing back.
RĘ-VŬL′SĮVE, a. Having the power of revulsion.
RĘ-WÂRD′, v. a. To give in return ; to repay.
RĘ-WÂRD′, n. A recompense ; a compensation.
RĘ-WÂRD′ĘR, n. One that rewards. [ed.
RHAP-SŎD′I-CAL (rap-sŏd′ę-kạl), a. Unconnect-
RHĂP′SǪ-DĬST (răp′sǫ-dĭst), n. One who writes,
recites, or sings rhapsodies. [position.
RHĂP′SǪ-DY (răp′sǫ-dę), n. An irregular com-
RHĔT′Ǫ-RĬC (rĕt′ǫ-rĭk), n. The art of prose
composition :—oratory ; eloquence.
RHĘ-TŎR′I-CAL (rę-), a. Pertaining to rhetoric.
RHĘ-TŎR′I-CAL-LY, ad. In a rhetorical manner.
RHĔT-Ǫ-RĬ′′CIAN (rĕt ǫ-rĭsh′ạn), n. One who
teaches the science of rhetoric :—an orator.
RHEŬM (rŭm), n. A thin, watery humor.
RHEŬ-MĂT′ĮC (rŭ-măt′ĭk), a. Relating to, or
affected with, rheumatism.
RHEŬ′MA-TĬSM (rŭ′mạ-tĭzm), n. A painful dis-
temper affecting the muscles, joints, or limbs.
RHEŬ′MY (rŭ′mę), a. Affected with rheum.
RHĪ′NŌ (rī′nō), n. A cant word for money.
RHĮ-NŌÇ′Ę-RŎS (rĭ-nŏs′ę-rŏs), n. A quadruped.
RHŎD-Ǫ-DĔN′DRǪN (rŏd-ǫ-dĕn′drųn), n. A plant.
RHŎMB (rŭmb), n. A quadrilateral figure.
RHŎM′BĮC (rŭm′bĭk), a. Shaped like a rhomb.
RHŎM′BŎĬD (rŭm′bŏĭd), n. An oblique-angled
parallelogram.
RHŎM-BŎĬD′AL (rŭm-bŏĭd′ạl), a. Like a rhomb.
RHŪ′BÄRB (rŭ′bärb), n. A plant or root.
RHYME (rīm), n. An harmonical succession or
correspondence of sounds ; poetry ; a poem.
RHYME (rīm), v. n. To agree in sound ; to ver-
RHYME (rīm), v. a. To put into rhyme. [sify.
RHYM′ĘR, RHYME′STĘR, n. A maker of rhymes.
RHYTHM (rĭthm), n. Metre ; verse ; numbers.
RHYTH′MĮ-CAL (rĭth′mę-kạl), a. Harmonical.
RĪ′AL, n. A Spanish coin. See REAL.
RĬB, n. A bone :—a piece of timber :—a strip.
RĬB, v. a. To furnish with ribs ; to enclose.
RĬB′ALD, n. A low, mean wretch.—a. Vile.
RĬB′ALD-RY, n. Mean, lewd, or brutal language.
RĬB′BǪN, n. A strip or fillet of silk ; a slip of
silk :—written also riband.
RĬB′BǪN, v. a. To adorn with ribbons.
RĬBBED (rĭbd), a. Furnished with ribs.
RĬB′RŌAST (rĭb′rōst), v. a. To beat soundly. [Bur-
RĪCE, n. A cereal plant and its grain. [lesque.]
RĬCH, a. Wealthy ; opulent ; fertile ; fruitful.
RĬCH′ĘS, n. pl. Wealth ; opulence ; affluence.
RĬCH′LY, ad. With riches :—abundantly.
RĬCH′NĘSS, n. Opulence ; abundance ; fertility.
RĬCK, n. A pile of grain or hay.
RĬCK′ĘTS, n. pl. A disease in children.
RĬCK′ĘT-Y, a. Diseased with the rickets.
RĬD, v. a. [imp. t. & pp. rid.] To free ; to clear.
RĬD′DANCE, n. Deliverance ; disencumbrance.
RĬD′DEN (rĭd′dn), pp. from ride.
RĬD′DLE, n. An enigma ; problem :—coarse sieve.
RĬD′DLE, v. a. To solve ; to clear by a sieve.
RĪDE, v. n. [imp. t. rode ; pp. rode, ridden.] To
travel on horseback or in a vehicle ; to be
RĪDE, v. a. To sit on ; to manage at will. [borne.
RĪDE, n. An excursion in a vehicle, &c.
RĬD′ĘR, n. One who rides :—a clause annexed.

RĬDĢE, *n.* The top of the back, or of a slope.
RĬDĢE, *v. a.* To form, as a ridge; to wrinkle.
RĬDĢ'Y, *a.* Rising in, or consisting of, ridges.
RĬD'Ị-CŪLE, *n.* Wit that provokes laughter; derision; mockery. [deride.
RĬD'Ị-CŪLE, *v. a.* To expose to laughter; to
RỊ-DĬC'Ụ-LOŬS, *a.* Worthy of being laughed at.
RỊ-DĬC'Ụ-LOŬS-LY, *ad.* In a ridiculous manner.
RĬD'ĬNG–CŌAT, *n.* A coat used in riding.
RĬD'ĬNG–HĂB-ỊT, *n.* A riding dress for women.
RĬD'ĬNG–HOOD (-hûd), *n.* A hood for riding.
RỊ-DŎT'TŌ, *n.* [It.] A musical entertainment.
RĪFE, *a.* Prevalent; prevailing, as a disease.
RĪFE'LY, *ad.* Prevalently; abundantly.
RĪFE'NESS, *n.* Prevalence; abundance.
RĬFF'RĂFF, *n.* The refuse; sweepings; rabble.
RĪ'FLE, *v. a.* To rob; to pillage; to plunder.
RĪ'FLE, *n.* A sort of gun, grooved within.
RĪ'FLE-MĂN, *n.* One armed with a rifle.
RĪ'FLẸR, *n.* A robber; a plunderer; a pillager.
RĬFT, *n.* A cleft; a breach; an opening.
RĬG, *n.* A ridge; dress:—a frolic.
RĬG, *v. a.* To dress; to fit with tackling.
RĬG-Ạ-DÔÔN', *n.* A kind of gay, brisk dance.
RĬG'ĢẸR, *n.* One that rigs or dresses.
RĬG'ĢĮNG, *n.* The sails or tackling of a ship.
RĬG'GLE, *v. n.* To move backward and forward.
RĬGHT (rīt), *a.* True; not wrong; just; direct.
RĬGHT (rīt), *ad.* Properly; justly; truly; very.
RĬGHT (rīt), *n.* Conformity to the law of God, or of man; freedom from error or fault; equity; justice; just claim :—privilege.
RĬGHT (rīt), *v. a.* To free from wrong; rectify.
RĬGHT (rīt), *v. n.* To rise with masts erect.
RĪGHT'EOŲS (rī'chụs), *a.* Just; virtuous; up-
RĪGHT'EOŲS-LY (rī'chụs-lẹ), *ad.* Justly. [right.
RĪGHT'EOŲS-NĔSS (rī'chụs-nĕs), *n.* Justice.
RĪGHT'FŪL (rīt'fûl), *a.* Having right; lawful.
RĪGHT'FŪL-LY (rit'fûl-ẹ), *ad.* According to right.
RĪGHT'FŪL-NĔSS (rīt'fûl-nĕs), *n.* Rectitude.
RĪGHT'–HĂND (rīt'hănd), *n.* Not the left hand.
RĪGHT'LY (rīt'lẹ), *ad.* Properly; uprightly.
RĪGHT'NESS (rīt'-), *n.* Correctness; rectitude.
RĬĢ'ĮD, *a.* Stiff; severe; strict; sharp; cruel.
RỊ-ĢĬD'Ị-TY, *n.* Stiffness; severity; inflexibility.
RĬĢ'ĮD-LY, *ad.* Stiffly; severely; inflexibly. [ty.
RĬĢ'ĮD-NĔSS, *n.* Stiffness; severity; inflexibili-
RĬG'LET, *n.* A thin piece of wood. See REGLET.
RĬG'MẠ-RŌLE, *n.* A repetition of idle words.
RĬG'ŌR, *n.* Stiffness; severity; austerity.
RĬG'ŌR-OŬS, *a.* Severe; stern; harsh; exact.
RĬG'ŌR-OŬS-LY, *ad.* Severely; sternly; exactly.
RĬG'ŌR-OŲS-NĔSS, *n.* Severity; sternness.
RĬLL, *n.* A small brook; a streamlet.
RĬM, *n.* A border; a margin; an edge.
RĪME, *n.* Hoar frost; a hole; a chink.
RỊ-MŌSE', *or* RĪ'MOŲS, *a.* Full of chink
RĬM'PLE, *n.* A wrinkle; a fold; a ripple.
RĬM'PLE, *v. a.* To pucker; to wrinkle. [tion.
RĬM'PLĮNG, *n.* An uneven motion; an undula-
RĪ'MY, *a.* Steamy; foggy; full of frozen mist.
RĪND, *n.* Bark; husk; skin; coat; peel.
RĬNG, *n.* A circle; a circle of metal :—a sound.
RĬNG, *v. a. & n.* [*imp. t.* rung *or* rang; *pp.* rung.] To strike bells, &c.; to sound; to en-
RĬNG'DŎVE, *n.* A kind of pigeon. [circle.
RĬNG'LĔAD-ẸR, *n.* The head or leader of a ring or riotous body.

RĬNG'LET, *n.* A small ring :—a curl of hair.
RĬNG'STRĔAKED, *a.* Having circular streaks.
RĬNG'TĀIL, *n.* A kind of bird :—a sail.
RĬNG'WORM, *n.* A disease; a circular tetter.
RĬNSE, *v. a.* To wash; to cleanse by washing.
RĪ'ŎT, *n.* Noisy festivity :—a sedition; uproar.
RĪ'ŎT, *v. n.* To revel, banquet, raise an uproar.
RĪ'ŎT-ẸR, *n.* One who raises an uproar or riot.
RĪ'ŎT-OŬS, *a.* Wanton; seditious; turbulent.
RĪ'ŎT-OŬS-LY, *ad.* Seditiously; turbulently.
RĪ'ŎT-OŲS-NĔSS, *n.* The state of being riotous.
RĬP, *v. a.* To tear; to lacerate :—to disclose.
RĬP, *n.* A laceration :—a wicker fish-basket.
RĪPE, *a.* Mature; finished; complete; ready.
RĪPE'LY, *ad.* Maturely; at the fit time.
RĪP'EN (rī'pn); *v. n. & a.* To grow or make ripe.
RĪPE'NĔSS, *n.* State of being ripe; maturity.
RĬP'PLE, *v. n.* To fret on the surface, as water.
RĬP'PLE, *n.* Agitation of water; a little wave; a rimple :—a large flax-comb.
RĬP'PLĮNG, *n.* Ripples dashing on the shore.
RĪSE, *v. n.* [*imp. t.* rose; *pp.* risen.] To get up; to arise; to grow; to ascend; to increase.
RĪSE, *n.* Ascent; increase; beginning; eleva-
RĬŞ'EN (rĭz'zn), *pp.* from *rise.* [tion.
||RĬŞ-Ị-BĬL'Ị-TY, *n.* The quality of being risible.
||RĬŞ'Ị-BLE, *a.* Exciting laughter; laughable.
RĬŞ'ĮNG, *n.* The act of getting up; insurrection.
RĬSK, *n.* Hazard; danger; a chance of harm.
RĬSK, *v. a.* To hazard; to expose to danger.
RĪTE, *n.* A solemn act or ceremony of religion.
||RĬT'Ụ-ẠL (rĭt'yụ-ạl), *a.* Ceremonial.
||RĬT'Ụ-ẠL, *n.* A book of religious ceremonies.
||RĬT'Ụ-ẠL-LY, *ad.* According to the ritual.
RĪ'VẠL, *n.* A competitor; an antagonist.
RĪ'VẠL, *a.* Standing in competition; emulous.
RĪ'VẠL, *v. a.* To strive to excel; to emulate.
RĪ'VẠL-RY, *n.* Competition; emulation.
RĪ'VẠL-SHĬP, *n.* State or character of a rival.
RĪVE, *v. a.* [*imp. t.* rived; *pp.* riven.] To split; to cleave.
RĬV'EN (rĭv'vn), *pp.* from *rive.* [to cleave.
RĪV'ẸR, *n.* A large stream of water.
RĪV'ẸR, *n.* One who splits or cleaves.
RĪV'ẸR-DRĂG'ŌN, *n.* A crocodile. [ends.
RĬV'ẸT, *n.* A fastening pin clinched at both
RĬV'ẸT, *v. a.* To fasten strongly or with rivets.
RĬV'Ụ-LĔT, *n.* A small river; a brook.
RĬX'–DŎL-LẠR, *n.* A coin from 60 to 108 cents.
RŌACH (rōch), *n.* A fresh-water fish.
RŌAD (rōd), *n.* A broad way or passage; a path.
RŌAD'STĔAD, *n.* A place for ships to anchor in.
RŌAM, *v. n.* To wander; to ramble; to rove.
RŌAM'ẸR, *n.* A rover; a rambler; a vagrant.
RŌAN (rōn), *a.* Bay or sorrel :—black,with spots.
RŌAR (rōr), *v. n.* To cry; to make a loud noise.
RŌAR, *n.* The cry of a wild beast; a loud noise.
RŌAR'ĮNG, *n.* The cry of a lion, &c.; loud noise.
RŌAST (rōst), *v. a.* To cook, as meat; to heat.
RŌAST, *p. a.* [For *roasted.*] Roasted, as meat.
RŌAST, *n.* That which is roasted :—a banter.
RŌAST'ẸR, *n.* One who, or that which, roasts.
RŎB, *v. a.* To take without right; to plunder.
RŎB'BẸR, *n.* One that plunders by force; a thief.
RŎB'BẸR-Y, *n.* Theft by force or with privacy.
RŌBE, *n.* A gown of state; a dress of dignity.
RŌBE, *v. a.* To dress pompously; to invest.
RŎB'ĮN, RŎB'ĮN–RĔD'BRĔAST, *n.* An insessorial singing-bird.

RŎB′ĬN–GOOD–FĔL′LŌW (-gŭd-), *n.* A goblin.
RǪ-BŬST′, *a.* Strong; sinewy; vigorous; sturdy.
RǪ-BŬST′NĘSS, *n.* Strength; vigor.
RŎCK, *n.* A large mass of stone :—a defence.
RŎCK, *v. a.* & *n.* To shake; to move; to reel.
RŎCK′-CRŸS-TĄL, *n.* A silicious stone; quartz.
RŎCK′ĘR, *n.* One who, or that which, rocks.
RŎCK′ĘT, *n.* An artificial firework :—a plant.
RŎCK′Ĭ-NĔSS, *n.* The state of being rocky.
RŎCK′-RŬ-BY, *n.* A dark-red variety of garnet.
RŎCK′-SĄLT, *n.* Native common salt.
RŎCK′Y, *a.* Full of rocks; hard; stony.
RŎD, *n.* A twig; an instrument of correction; a switch; a wand :—sixteen and a half feet.
RŌDE, *imp. t.* & *pp.* from *ride.*
RŎD-Ǫ-MǪN-TĀDE′, *n.* Empty bluster; a rant.
RŌE (rō), *n.* Female of the hart :—eggs of fish.
RŌE′BŬCK, *n.* A small species of deer.
RǪ-GĀ′TIǪN, *n.* Litany; supplication.
RǪ-GĀ′TIǪN-WĒĒK, *n.* The second week before Whitsuntide.
RŌGUE (rōg), *n.* A knave; a villain :—a wag.
RŌGU′ĘR-Y (rō′gur-ę), *n.* Villany :—waggery.
RŌGU′ĬSH (rōg′ĭsh), *a.* Knavish; waggish.
RŌGU′ĬSH-LY (rōg′ĭsh-lę), *ad.* Like a rogue.
RŌGU′ĬSH-NĔSS (rōg′ĭsh-nĕs), *n.* Knavery.
RŌ̈ĬST, RŌ̈ĬST′ĘR, *v. n.* To bully; to bluster.
RŌLL, *v. a.* To move in a circle; to inwrap.
RŌLL, *v. n.* To run on wheels; to move round; to revolve; to rotate.
RŌLL, *n.* Act of rolling :—a mass made round; a roller; a register; a catalogue; a chronicle.
RŌLL′ĘR, *n.* A thing turning on its axis; fillet.
RŌLL′ĬNG-PĬN, *n.* A cylinder of wood.
RŌLL′ĬNG-PRĔSS, *n.* A sort of press.
RŌ′MĄN, *a.* Relating to Rome :—Roman Cath-
RǪ-MĂNCE′, *n.* A fable; a fiction. [olic.
RǪ-MĂNCE′, *v. n.* To lie; to forge stories, &c.
RǪ-MĂN′CĘR, *n.* A writer of romances or fables.
RŌ′MĄN-ĬSM, *n.* The tenets of the church of
RŌ′MĄN-ĬST, *n.* A Roman Catholic. [Rome.
RŌ′MĄN-ĪZE, *v. a.* To change to the Roman language, or to Romanism.
RǪ-MĂN′TĬC, *a.* Wild :—improbable; fanciful.
RǪ-MĂN′TĬ-CĄL-LY, *ad.* Wildly; extravagantly.
RǪ-MĂN′TĬC-NĔSS, *n.* State of being romantic.
RŌ′MĬSH, *a.* Relating to the church of Rome.
RŎMP, *n.* A rude, awkward girl :—rude play.
RŎMP, *v. n.* To play rudely and boisterously.
RŎMP′ĬSH, *a.* Inclined to rude or rough play.
RONDEAU (rŏn-dō′), *n.* [Fr.] A kind of poetry; an air ending with the first strain repeated.
RŎOD, *n.* Fourth part of an acre; a pole; a cross.
RŎOF, *n.* The cover of a house :—the palate.
RŎOF, *v. a.* To cover with a roof :—to enclose.
RŎOF′LĘSS, *a.* Wanting a roof; uncovered.
‖RŎOK (rŏk *or* rŭk), *n.* A bird allied to the crow :—a piece at chess :—a cheat.
‖RŎOK, *v. a.* & *n.* To cheat; to plunder.
‖RŎOK′ĘR-Y, *n.* A collection of rooks' nests.
RŎOM, *n.* Space; extent; stead; an apartment.
RŎOM′Ĭ-NĔSS, *n.* Space; quantity of extent.
RŎOM′Y, *a.* Spacious; wide; large.
RŎOST, *n.* That on which a bird sits to sleep.
RŎOST, *v. n.* To sleep as a bird :—to lodge.
RŎOT, *n.* That part of a plant which rests in the ground :—bottom; original; first cause.
RŎOT, *v. n.* To take root; to sink deep.

RŎOT, *v. a.* To fix deep; to radicate; to extir-
RŎOT′Y, *a.* Full of, or having, roots. *[pate.
RŌPE, *n.* A cord; a string; a halter; a cable.
RŌPE′-DĂN-CĘR, *n.* One who dances on a rope.
RŌPE′-MĂK-ĘR, *n.* One who makes ropes.
RŌPE′WĄLK (rōp′wȧk), *n.* A place or building where ropes are made.
RŌP′Ĭ-NĔSS, *n.* Viscosity; glutinousness.
RŌP′Y, *a.* Viscous; tenacious; glutinous.
RǪQ-UĘ-LAURE′ (rŏk-ę-lōr′), RŎQ′UĘ-LŌ (rŏk′-ę-lō), *n.* A kind of cloak or surtout.
RǪ-RĬF′ĘR-OŬS, *a.* Producing dew.
RŎS′CĬD, *a.* Dewy; abounding with dew.
RŌSĘ, *n.* A plant and flower :—knot of ribbons.
RŌSĘ-Ą-CĀ′CĬ-Ą, *n.* A flowering shrub.
RŌ′SA-RY, *n.* A series of prayers :—a chaplet: —a string of beads.
RŌSĘ, *imp. t.* from *rise.*
RŌ′SĘ-ATE (rō′zhę-ąt), *a.* Rosy; fragrant.
RŌSE′MĄ-RY, *n.* A sweet-smelling plant.
RŌ′SĘT, *n.* A red color used by painters.
RŌSĘ′-WĀ-TĘR, *n.* Water distilled from roses.
RŎS′ĬN, *n.* Inspissated turpentine. See RESIN.
RŎS′ĬN, *v. a.* To rub with rosin.
RŌ′SĬ-NĔSS, *n.* State or quality of being rosy.
RŎS′ĬN-Y, *a.* Resembling rosin; like rosin.
RŎS′TRĄL, *a.* Resembling a beak. [ship.
RŎS′TRAT-ĘD, *a.* Adorned with a beak, as a
RŎS′TRŲM, *n.* [L.] The beak of a bird or of a ship :—scaffold whence orators harangued.
RŌ′SY, *a.* Resembling a rose; blooming; red.
RŎT, *v. n.* To putrefy.—*v. a.* To make putrid.
RŎT, *n.* Distemper among sheep :—putrefaction.
RŌ′TĄ-RY, *a.* Turning on its axis, as a wheel.
RǪ-TĀ′TIǪN, *n.* A turning round; a succession.
RŌ′TĄ-TǪ-RY, *a.* Turning on its axis; whirl-
RŌTE, *n.* A mere repetition of words. [ing.
RŌTE, *v. n.* To go out by turn.
RŎT′TEN (rŏt′tn), *a.* Putrid; not firm or sound.
RŎT′TEN-NĔSS (rŏt′tn-nĕs), *n.* Putridness.
RǪ-TŬND′, *a.* Round; circular; spherical.
RǪ-TŬN′DĄ, *n.* A circular building.
RǪ-TŬN-DĬ-FŌ′LĬ-OŬS, *a.* Having round leaves.
RǪ-TŬN′DĬ-TY, *n.* Roundness; sphericity.
RǪ-TŬN′DŌ, *n.* A circular building.
ROUGE (rȯzh), *n.* [Fr.] Red paint for the face.
ROUGE (rȯzh), *v. a.* & *n.* To paint with rouge.
ROŬGH (rŭf), *a.* Not smooth; harsh; rude.
ROŬGH′CĂST (rŭf′kȧst), *v. a.* To form rudely.
ROŬGH′CĂST (rŭf′kȧst), *n.* A rude model.
ROŬGH′DRĂW (rŭf′drȧw), *v. a.* To trace coarse-
ROŬGH′EN (rŭf′fn), *v. a.* To make rough. [ly.
ROŬGH′EN (rŭf′fn), *v. n.* To grow rough.
ROŬGH-HEW′ (rŭf-hū′), *v. a.* To hew coarsely.
ROŬGH-HEWN′ (rŭf-hūn′), *p. a.* Unpolished.
ROŬGH′LY (rŭf′lę), *ad.* With roughness.
ROŬGH′NĘSS (rŭf′nes), *n.* Ruggedness.
ROŬGH′-RĪD-ĘR (rŭf′rīd-ęr), *n.* One that breaks refractory horses.
ROŬGH′-SHŎD (rŭf′shŏd), *a.* Having the feet fitted with calked or roughened shoes.
RŎŬND, *a.* Circular; spherical; full; plump.
RŎŬND, *n.* A circle; a sphere; a rundle; course.
RŎŬND, *ad.* Every way; on all sides.
RŎŬND, *prep.* On every side of; about; all over.
RŎŬND, *v. a.* & *n.* To make or go round.
RŎŬND′Ą-BŎŬT, *a.* Circuitous; indirect.
RŎŬN′DĘ-LĀY, *n.* A rondeau; a kind of poem.

RŎŬND′HĔAD, *n.* A term applied to a Puritan.
RŎŬND′HŎŬSE, *n.* A constable's prison :—cabin.
RŎŬND′ISH, *a.* Approaching to roundness.
RŎŬND′LY, *ad.* In a round form :—plainly.
RŎŬND′NĔSS, *n.* Rotundity; openness. [a circle.
RŎŬND′-RŎB-IN,*n.* A writing signed by names in
RŎŬSE, *v. a. & n.* To wake from rest ; to excite.
RŎŬT, *n.* A multitude ; a rabble ; a crowd ; com-
pany :—confusion of an army defeated.
RŎŬT, *v. a.* To put into confusion by defeat.
RÔUTE *or* RŎŬTE, *n.* [Fr.] A journey ; a way.
RÔU-TÎNE′, *n.* [Fr.] Regular course ; custom.
RŌVE, *v. n.* To ramble ; to range ; to wander.
RŌ′VĔR, *n.* A wanderer ; a ranger :—a robber.
RŌW (rō), *n.* A range of men or things ; a rank.
RŎW̑, *n.* A riotous disturbance ; brawl.
RŌW (rō), *v. n. & a.* To impel a vessel by oars.
RŌW̑′ĔL, *n.* The point of a spur :—a seton.
RŌW̑′ĔL, *v. a.* To pierce by a rowel.
RŌW′ĔR (rō′er), *n.* One that manages an oar.
RŎY̆′AL, *a.* Kingly ; regal :—noble ; illustrioṳs.
RŎY̆′AL, *n.* A kind of paper :—a light sail.
RŎY̆′AL-ĬST, *n.* An adherent to a king or royalty.
RŎY̆′AL-LY, *ad.* Regally ; as becomes a king.
RŎY̆′AL-TY, *n.* The office or state of a king.
RŬB, *v. a.* To scour ; to wipe ; to chafe.
RŬB, *v. n.* To fret ; to make a friction.
RŬB, *n.* Friction ; collision ; difficulty :—joke.
RŬB′BĔR, *n.* One that rubs :—a game.
RŬB′BISH, *n.* Ruins ; refuse ; fragments.
RṲ-BĔS′CĔNT, *a.* Tending to a red color.[white.
RṲ′BI-CĂN, *a.* Bay, sorrel, or black, with some
RṲ′BI-FŎRM, *a.* Having the form of red. [&c.
RṲ′BRIC, *n.* Directions printed in books of law,
RṲ′BY, *n.* A precious stone of a red color.
RṲ′BY, *a.* Of a red color ; like a ruby.
RṲC-TĀ′TIQN, *n.* The act of belching wind.
RŬD′DĔR,*n.* The instrument which steers a ship.
RŬD′DI-NĔSS, *n.* The quality of being ruddy.
RŬD′DLE, *n.* A species of chalk or red earth.
RŬD′DY, *a.* Approaching to redness ; florid.
RŬDE, *a.* Rough ; coarse ; harsh ; ignorant ; raw.
RŬDE′LY, *ad.* In a rude manner ; coarsely.
RŬDE′NĔSS, *n.* Coarseness ; incivility.
RṲ′DI-MĔNT, *n.* A first principle or element.
RṲ-DI-MĔNT′AL, *a.* Relating to first principles.
RŬE (rṳ), *v. a.* To grieve for.—*n.* A plant.
RŬE′FŬL (rṳ′fŭl), *a.* Mournful ; woful ; sorrowful.
RŬE′FŬL-LY, *ad.* Mournfully ; sorrowfully.
RŬE′FŬL-NĔSS,*n.* Sorrowfulness ; mournfulness.
RŬFF, *n.* A painted ornament ; a ruffle :—a bird.
RŬFF′IAN (rŭf′yan), *n.* A brutal fellow ; a rascal.
RŬFF′IAN (rŭf′yan), *a.* Brutal ; barbarous.
RŬF′FLE, *v. a.* To disorder, disturb :—to plait.
RŬF′FLE, *v. n.* To grow rough; to flutter; to jar.
RŬF′FLE, *n.* A linen ornament :—contention ; a
RŬG, *n.* A coarse, nappy, woollen cloth. [jar.
RŬG′ĠĔD, *a.* Rough ; uneven ; harsh ; rude.
RŬG′ĠĔD-LY, *ad.* In a rugged manner. [ness.
RŬG′ĠĔD-NĔSS, *n.* Roughness ; asperity ; rude-
RṲ′ĠINE (rṳ′jin), *n.* A surgeon's rasp.
RṲ-GŌSE′, RṲ′GOṲS, *a.* Full of wrinkles.
RṲ′IN, *n.* Destruction ; overthrow :—remains.
RṲ′IN, *v. a.* To subvert, demolish, destroy.
RṲ′IN-OŬS, *a.* Fallen to ruin :—pernicious.
RṲ′IN-OŬS-LY, *ad.* In a ruinous manner.
RŬLE, *n.* Government ; sway :—a standard ; a
canon ; a principle ; a mode :—an instrument.

RŬLE, *v. a.* To govern ; to control ; to manage.
RŬLE, *v. n.* To have power or command.
RŬL′ĔR, *n.* A governor :—an instrument.
RŬM, *n.* A spirit distilled from molasses.
RŬM′BLE, *v. n.* To make a hoarse, low noise.
RŬM′BLĔR, *n.* A person or thing that rumbles.
RŬM′BLING, *n.* A hoarse, low, continued noise.
RṲ′MI-NĂNT, *a.* Chewing the cud.
RṲ′MI-NĂNT, *n.* A ruminant animal.
RṲ′MI-NĀTE,*v. n.* To chew the cud; to muse.[on.
RṲ′MI-NĀTE, *v. a.* To chew over again ; to muse
RṲ-MI-NĀ′TIQN,*n.* Act of ruminating ; musing.
RŬM′MAĠE, *v. a. & n.* To search ; to examine.
RŬM′MAĠE, *n.* A search ; a bustle ; a tumult.
RṲ′MQR, *n.* A flying or popular report ; fame.
RṲ′MQR, *v. a.* To report abroad ; to bruit.
RŬMP, *n.* End of the backbone ; the buttock.
RŬM′PLE, *n.* A wrinkle ; a rude plait.
RŬM′PLE, *v. a.* To wrinkle ; to make uneven.
RŬN, *v. n.* [*imp. t.* ran ; *pp.* run.] To move swift-
ly ; to flee ; to go away ; to flow ; to melt.
RŬN, *v. a.* To pierce ; to fuse ; to incur.
RŬN, *n.* Course ; motion ; flow ; way ; stream.
RŬN′A-GĀTE, *n.* A fugitive ; rebel ; renegade.
RŬN′A-WĀY, *n.* One who deserts ; a fugitive.
RŬN′DLE, *n.* A round ; a step of a ladder.
RŬNG, *imp. t. & pp.* from *ring*. [of water.
RŬN′LĔT, RŬND′LĔT, *n.* A small cask or stream
RŬN′NĔL, *n.* A rivulet ; runlet.
RŬN′NĔR, *n.* One that runs ; a racer.
RŬN′NĔT, *n.* A liquor used to change milk to
curds and whey. See RENNET.
RŬNN′IQN (rŭn′yṇn), *n.* A paltry, scurvy wretch.
RŬNT, *n.* A small, stunted animal.
RṲ-PĔE′, *n.* A coin in British India.
RŬPT′ṲRE (rŭpt′yṳr), *n.* A breach :—hernia.
RŬPT′ṲRE (rŭpt′yṳr),*v. a.* To break ; to burst.
RṲ′RAL, *a.* Relating to the country ; pastoral.
RŬSH, *n.* A plant :—any thing worthless.
RŬSH, *v. n.* To move with violence or rapidity.
RŬSH, *n.* A violent motion or course.
RŬSH′I-NĔSS, *n.* The state of being full of rushes.
RŬSH′-LĪGHT, *n.* A small taper or candle.
RŬSH′Y, *a.* Abounding with, or made of, rushes.
RŬSK, *n.* A light, hard cake or bread.
RŬS′SĔT, *a.* Reddishly brown :—coarse ; rustic.
RŬS′SĔT, RŬS′SĔT-ING, *n.* A rough-skinned ap-
RŬST, *n.* A red crust on iron, &c. [ple.
RŬST, *v.* To make or become rusty. [clown.
RŬS′TIC, *n.* An inhabitant of the country ; a
RŬS′TIC, RŬS′TI-CAL, *a.* Rude ; rural ; plain.
RŬS′TI-CAL-LY, *ad.* Rudely ; inelegantly.
RŬS′TI-CAL-NĔSS, *n.* Quality of being rustical.
RŬS′TI-CĀTE, *v. n.* To reside in the country.
RŬS′TI-CĀTE,*v. a.* To banish into the country.
RŬS-TI-CĀ′TIQN, *n.* Exile into the country.
RṲS-TIÇ′I-TY, *n.* Rudeness ; rural appearance.
RŬST′I-NĔSS, *n.* The state of being rusty.
RŬS′TLE (rŭs′sl), *v. n.* To make a low noise.
RŬS′TLING, *n.* A succession of small sounds.
RŬST′Y, *a.* Covered with rust :—impaired.
RŬT, *n.* Copulation of deer :—track of a wheel.
RŬT, *v. n.* To desire to copulate, as a deer.
RŬTH′LĔSS, *a.* Cruel ; pitiless ; barbarous.
RŬTH′LĔSS-LY, *ad.* Without pity ; cruelly.
RŬTH′LĔSS-NĔSS, *n.* Want of pity ; cruelty.
RY̆′DĔR, *n.* A clause to a bill. See RIDER.
RY̆E (rī), *n.* An esculent grain.

S.

S has, in English, two sounds; first, its genuine sibilant or hissing sound, as in *son*; secondly, the sound of *z*, as in *wise*.

SĄ-BĀ′ŎTH *or* SĂB′Ą-ŎTH, *n.* Hosts; armies.
SĂB′BĄTH,*n.*The day of rest; Sunday; Lord's day.
SĂB′BĄTH–BREĀK-ĘR, *n.* A violator of the Sabbath.
SĄB-BĂT′I-CĄL, *a.* Belonging to the Sabbath.
SĂB′BĄ-TĬṢM,*n.* Rest; observance of the Sabbath.
SĀ′BĮ-ĄN-ĬṢM, *n.* The worship of the sun, moon,
SĂB′ĬNE, *n.* A plant; savin. [and stars.
SĀ′BLE, *n.* An animal and its fur.—*a.* Black.
SĀ′BRE (sā′bẹr), *n.* A cimeter; a falchion.
SĀ′BRE (-bẹr), *v. a.* To strike, or kill, with a sa-
SĂC-ℭHĄ-RĬF′ĘR-OŬS, *a.* Producing sugar. [bre.
SĂC′ℭHĄ-RĪNE, *a.* Having the qualities of sugar.
SĂℭ-ĘR-DŌ′TĄL, *a.* Belonging to the priesthood.
SĀ′CHĘM, *n.* An American Indian chief.
SĂCK, *n.* A bag :—a robe :—pillage :—a kind of
SĂCK, *v. a.* To put in bags; to pillage. [wine.
SĂCK′AĢE, SĂCK′ĬNG, *n.* Act of plundering;
SĂCK′BŬT, *n.* A kind of trumpet. [pillaging.
SĂCK′CLŎTH,*n.* Cloth of which sacks are made.
SĂCK′FŬL, *n.* As much as a sack will hold.
SĂCK–PŎS′SĘT, *n.* Drink made of milk,sack,&c.
SĂC′RĄ-MĔNT, *n.* Eucharist or Lord's supper.
SĂC-RĄ-MĔNT′AL, *a.* Pertaining to a sacrament.
SĂC-RĄ-MĔNT′AL-LY,*ad.* In a sacramental man-
SĄ′CRĘD, *a.* Holy; consecrated; inviolable. [ner.
SĀ′CRĘD-LY, *ad.* Inviolably; religiously.
SĀ′CRĘD-NĔSS, *n.* The state of being sacred.
SĂC′RĮ-FĪCE (săk′rẹ-fīz),*v. a.* To offer to Heaven; to immolate :—to destroy :—to devote.
SĂC′RĮ-FĪCE (săk′rẹ-fīz), *n.* An offering to God.
SĂC′RĮ-FĪ-CĘR (săk′rẹ-fī-zẹr), *n.* One who sacrifices. [or performing, sacrifice.
SĂC-RĮ-FĬ′′CIĄL (săk-rẹ-fĭsh′ạl), *a.* Relating to,
SĂC-RĮ-LĔĢE, *n.* A violation of things sacred.
SĂC-RĮ-LĒ′ĢIOŬS (săk-rẹ-lē′jụs), *a.* Violating things sacred; impious; irreverent.
SĂC-RĮ-LĒ′ĢIOŬS-LY, *ad.* With sacrilege.
SĂC′RĮS-TY, *n.* The vestry-room of a church.
SĂD, *a.* Sorrowful; heavy; gloomy; grave; bad.
SĂD′DEN (săd′dn),*v.a.* To make sad or sorrowful.
SĂD′DLE, *n.* A seat to put on a horse's back.
SĂD′DLE, *v. a.* To cover with a saddle :—to load.
SĂD′DLE-BŌW (săd′dl-bō), *n.* A bow of a saddle.
SĂD′DLĘR, *n.* One who makes saddles.
SĂD′DŲ-CĔE, *n.* One of an ancient Jewish sect.
SĂD′LY, *ad.* Sorrowfully; mournfully; gravely.
SĂD′NĘSS, *n.* Sorrowfulness; mournfulness.
SĀFE, *a.* Free from danger, hurt, or injury.
SĀFE, *n.* A buttery; a place of safety. [pass.
SĀFE–CŎN′DŲCT, *n.* Convoy; guard; warrant to
SĀFE′GUĂRD (sāf′gärd), *n.* A defence; a pass.
SĀFE′LY, *ad.* In a safe manner; without hurt.
SĀFE′NĘSS, *n.* Exemption from danger.
SĀFE′TY, *n.* Freedom from danger; security.
SĀFE′TY–VĂLVE, *n.* A valve opening outwards
SĂF′FRŎN (săf′fụrn), *n.* A plant. [from a boiler.
SĂF′FRŎN (săf′fụrn), *a.* Yellow; like saffron.
SĂG, *v. n.* To sink or hang down; to settle.

SĄ-GĀ′CIOŬS (sạ-gā′shụs), *a.* Discerning; acute.
SĄ-GĀ′CIOŬS-LY (-shụs-lẹ), *ad.* With sagacity.
SĄ-GĀ′CIOŬS-NĔSS,*n.*Quality of being sagacious.
SĄ-GĂÇ′Į-TY, *n.* Quick discernment; acuteness.
SĂG′Ą-MŌRE, *n.* A chief of an Indian tribe.
SĀĢE, *a.* Wise; grave; prudent; sagacious.
SĀĢE,*n.* A man of gravity and wisdom:—a plant
SĀĢE′LY, *ad.* Wisely; prudently. [or herb.
SĀĢE′NĘSS, *n.* Gravity; prudence.
SĂG′ĬT-TĄL, *a.* Belonging to an arrow. [zodiac.
SĂĢ-ĬT-TĀ′RĮ-ŬS, *n.* [L.] One of the signs of the
SĂĢ′ĬT-TĄ-RY, *a.* Belonging to an arrow.
SĀ′GŌ, *n.* A nutricious, granulated fecula or starch of East Indian plants.
SAID (sĕd), *imp. t. & pp.* from *say.* Mentioned.
SĀIL, *n.* An expanded sheet :—a ship; a vessel.
SĀIL, *v. n.* To move with sails; to pass by sea.
SĀIL′ĘR, *n.* A ship or vessel that sails.
SĀIL′ŎR, *n.* A seaman; a mariner. [tended.
SĀIL′–YĄRD, *n.* A pole on which a yard is ex-
SĀIN′FÖĬN *or* SĂIN′FÖĬN, *n.* A sort of plant.
SĀINT, *n.* A person eminent for piety. [canonize.
SĀINT, *v. a.* To number among the saints; to
SĀINT′ĘD, *a.* Holy; pious; virtuous; sacred.
SĀINT′LY, SĀINT′–LĪKE, *a.* Like a saint; pious.
SĀKE, *n.* Final cause; end; account; regard.
SĂL, *n.* [L.] Salt ;—a term used in chemistry.
SĂL′Ą-BLE, *a.* Fit for sale; marketable.
SĂL′Ą-BLE-NĔSS, *n.* State of being salable.
SĄ-LĀ′CIOŬS (sạ-lā′shụs), *a.* Lustful; lecherous.
SĂL′ĄD, *n.* Food of raw herbs, as lettuce.
SĂL′Ą-MĂN-DĘR, *n.* A batrachian reptile, fabled to live in fire. [der.
SĂL-Ą-MĂN′DRĮNE, *a.* Resembling a salaman-
SĂL′Ą-RY,*n.* A periodical payment for services.
SĀLE, *n.* Act of selling; vent; market; auction.
SĂL-Ę-RĀ′TŲS, *n.* A sort of refined pearlash.
SĀLEṢ′MĄN, *n.* One employed in selling.
SĀLE′WORK, *n.* Work made for sale.
SĂL′ĬC, *a.* Excluding females from the throne.
SĀ′LĮ-ĘNT, *a.* Leaping; bounding; darting.
SĂL′Į-FĪ-Ą-BLE, *a.* Capable of being salified.
SĂL′Į-FY, *v. a.* To change or form into salt.
SĂL-Į-NĀ′TIŎN, *n.* A washing with salt liquor.
SĄ-LINE′, *a.* Consisting of, or like, salt; briny.
SĄ-LĪ′VĄ, *n.* [L.] That which is spit up; spittle.
SĄ-LĪ′VĄL, *a.* Relating to saliva; salivary.
SĂL′Į-VĄ-RY, *a.* Relating to saliva. [glands.
SĂL′Į-VĀTE, *v. a.* To purge by the salivary
SĂL-Į-VĀ′TIŎN, *n.* The act of salivating.
SĄ-LĪ′VOŬS, *a.* Consisting of spittle; salivary.
SĂL′LŌW (săl′lō), *n.* A tree of the willow genus.
SĂL′LŌW (săl′lō), *a.* Sickly; yellow; pale.
SĂL′LŌW-NĔSS,*n.* Yellowness; sickly paleness.
SĂL′LY, *n.* A quick egress; a flight :—a frolic.
SĂL′LY, *v. n.* To make an eruption; to issue out.
SĂL′LY-PŌRT, *n.* A gate at which sallies are made; a postern gate.
SĂL-MĄ-GŬN′DĮ, *n.* A mixture of chopped meat, oil, vinegar, onions, &c. :—a medley.
SĂL′MŎN (săm′mụn), *n.* A delicious fish.
SĂL′MŎN-TRÖÛT′ (săm-mụn-trȫût′), *n.* A fish.

SẠ-LÔÔN', *n.* A spacious hall ; a drawing-room.
SẠL-SŪ'GỊ NOŬS, *a.* Saltish ; somewhat salt.
SÂLT, *n.* A substance used for seasoning :—a salt-cellar :—savor ; relish :—wit ; pungency.
SÂLT, *a.* Having the taste of salt ; briny.
SÂLT, *v. a.* To season or sprinkle with salt.
SẠL-TĀ'TIǪN, *n.* A jumping; a beat; palpitation.
SÂLT'-CĔL-LẠR,*n.*Small vessel for holding salt.
SÂLT'ẸR, *n.* One who salts ; one who sells salt.
SÂLT'ẸRN, *n.* A salt-work ; a place for making salt.
SÂLT'ĮSH, *a.* Somewhat salt. [salt.
SÂLT'NẸSS, *n.* The state of being salt. [salt.
SÂLT-PĒ'TRE (sâlt-pē'tẹr), *n.* Nitre ; a mineral
SÂLT'-PĬT, *n.* A pit where salt is procured.
SÂLT-RHEŬM', *n.* A disease in the skin ; herpes.
SẠ-LŪ'BRỊ-OŬS,*a.*Wholesome; promoting health.
SẠ-LŪ'BRỊ-OŬS-LỸ, *ad.* So as to promote health.
SẠ-LŪ'BRỊ-TỸ,*n.*Wholesomeness; healthfulness.
SĂL'Ụ-TẠ-RỊ-NĔSS, *n.* Wholesomeness. [geous.
SĂL'Ụ-TẠ-RỸ, *a.* Healthful; beneficial; advanta-
SĂL-Ụ-TĀ'TIǪN, *n.* Act of saluting ; a greeting.
SẠ-LŪ'TẠ-TǪ-RỸ, *a.* Containing salutations.
SẠ-LŪTE', *v. a.* To greet; to hail :—to kiss.
SẠ-LŪTE', *n.* A salutation ; a greeting:—a kiss.
SĂL-Ụ-TĬF'ẸR-OŬS, *a.* Wholesome ; bringing health.
SĂL-VẠ-BĬL'Į-TỸ, *n.* Possibility of being saved.
SĂL'VẠ-BLE, *a.* That may be saved.
SĂL'VẠǴE, *n.* A recompense for saving goods.
SẠL-VĀ'TIǪN, *n.* A deliverance from any evil.
SĂL'VẠ-TǪ-RỸ,*n.* A repository ; a conservatory.
SĂLVE (săv *or* sälv), *n.* An ointment ; a remedy.
SĂLVE (săv *or* sälv), *v. a.* To cure ; to remedy.
SĂL'VẸR, *n.* A plate to present any thing on.
SĂL'VŌ, *n.* An exception ; a reservation ; excuse.
SĀME, *a.* Identical ; not different or other.
SĀME'NẸSS,*n.* Identity; state of being the same.
SĀ'MĮ-ĔL,*n.* A destructive wind. See SIMOOM.
SĂMP, *n.* Food made of maize broken.
SĂM'PHĮRE, *n.* A plant used as a pickle, &c.
SĂM'PLE, *n.* A specimen ; a part to be shown.
SĂM'PLẸR, *n.* A piece of girl's needlework.
SĂN'Ạ-TĬVE, *a.* Powerful to cure ; healing.
SĂNC-TỊ-FĮ-CĀ'TIǪN, *n.* Act of making holy.
SĂNC'TỊ-FĬ-ẸR, *n.* One that sanctifies.
SĂNC'TỊ-FỸ, *v. a.* To make holy ; to purify.
SĂNC-TỊ-MŌ'NĮ-OŬS, *a.* Saintly ; appearing holy.
SĂNC-TỊ-MŌ'NĮ-OŬS-LỸ, *ad.* With sanctimony.
SĂNC'TỊ-MǪ-NỸ, *n.* Holiness ; austerity.
SĂNC'TIǪN, *n.* Confirmation; ratification. [firm.
SĂNC'TIǪN, *v. a.* To give a sanction to ; to con-
SĂNC'TỊ-TŪDE, *n.* Holiness ; saintliness.
SĂNC'TỊ-TỸ, *n.* Holiness ; purity ; godliness.
SĂNCT'Ụ-Ạ-RỸ (săngkt'yụ-ạ-rẹ),*n.* A holy place ; a temple ; a sacred asylum ; protection.
SĂND, *n.* Particles of stone.—*pl.* Barren land.
SĂND, *v. a.* To sprinkle or strew with sand.
SĂN'DẠL, *n.* A sort of slipper or loose shoe.
SĂN'DẠL-WOOD (-wûd), *n.* An aromatic wood.
SĂN'DẠ-RĂᴄH, *n.* A mineral :—a yellow resin.
SĂND'ẸD, *a.* Covered with sand ; barren.
SĂND'-ĒĔL, *n.* A kind of eel found in the sand.
SĂN'DỊ-VẸR, *n.* Dross separated from glass.
SĂND'Į-NĔSS, *n.* The state of being sandy.
SĂND'STŌNE, *n.* A loose and friable stone.
SĂND'Ỹ, *a.* Abounding with sand ; unsolid.
SĀNE, *a.* Sound in mind ; whole ; healthy.
SĂNG, *imp. t.* from *sing.*

SĂN'GỊ-ĂC, SĂN'JĂK, *n.* A Turkish governor.
SẠN-GUĬF'ẸR-OŬS, *a.* Conveying blood.
SĂN-GUĮ-FỊ-CĀ'TIǪN,*n.*The production of blood.
SĂN'GUĮ-FỸ, *v. n.* To produce blood.
SĂN'GUĮ-NẠ-RỸ, *a.* Cruel ; bloody ; murderous.
SĂN'GUĮNE (săng'gwĮn), *a.* Full of blood :—confi-
SĂN'GUĮNE-LỸ, *ad.* With sanguineness. [dent.
SĂN'GUĮNE-NĔSS, *n..* Ardor ; confidence.
SẠN-GUĬN'Ẹ-OŬS, *a.* Full of blood ; bloody.
SĂN'HẸ-DRĬM, *n.* Chief council of the Jews.
SĀ'NỊ-ĔŞ,*n.* [L.] Thin discharge from sores, &c.
SĀ'NỊ-OŬS,*a.*Relating to sanies; serous; ichorous.
SĂN'Į-TỸ, *n.* Soundness of mind.
SĂNK, *imp. t.* from *sink.* [*Obsolescent.*]
†SĂNŞ, *prep.* [Fr.] Without.
SĂN'SCRĮT, *n.* The ancient language of India.
SĂP, *n.* The vital juice of plants :—a trench.
SĂP, *v. a.* To undermine ; to subvert by digging.
SĂP, *v. n.* To proceed invisibly or by mine.
SĂP'ĮD, *a.* Tasteful ; palatable ; savory.
SĀ'PỊ-ẸNCE,*n.* Wisdom ; sageness ; knowledge.
SĀ'PỊ-ẸNT, *a.* Wise ; sage ; discerning.
SĂP'LẸSS, *a.* Wanting sap ; dry ; old ; husky.
SĂP'LĮNG, *n.* A young tree full of sap.
SĂP-Ǫ-NĀ'CEOŬS (-shụs),) *a.* Soapy ; resem-
SĂP'Ǫ-NẠ-RỸ,   ) bĮing soap. [ate.
SĀ'PǪR, *n.* [L.] Taste; power of affecting the pal-
SĂP-Ǫ-RĬF'ĮC,*a.* Having power to produce taste.
SĂP'PẸR, *n.* A kind of miner ; one who saps.
SĂP'PHĮC (săf'fĮk), *a.* Relating to Sappho :—de-
noting a kind of verse.
SĂP'PHĮRE (săf'fĮr), *n.* A precious stone or gem.
SĂP'PHĮR-ĪNE (săf'fĮr-Īn), *a.* Made of sapphire.
SĂP'PỊ-NĔSS, *n.* Succulence ; juiciness.
SĂP'PỸ,*a.* Abounding in sap ; juicy ; succulent.
SĂR'Ạ-BĂND, *n.* A Spanish dance. [the Saracens.
SĂR-Ạ-CĔN'ĮC, SĂR-Ạ-CĔN'Į-CẠL, *a.* Relating to
SĂR'CĂŞM, *n.* A keen reproach ; a scornful ex-
pression ; a gibe ; a taunt ; biting jest. [vere.
SẠR-CĂS'TĮC, SẠR-CĂS'TỊ-CẠL, *a.* Keen ; se-
SẠR-CĂS'TỊ-CẠL-LỸ, *ad.* Tauntingly ; severely.
SĂRCE'NẸT, *n.* A fine, thin-woven silk.
SẠR-CŎPH'Ạ-GOŬS, *a.* Feeding on flesh.
SẠR-CŎPH'Ạ-GŬS, *n.* ; *pl.* SẠR-CŎPH'Ạ-GĪ. [L.] A sort of stone coffin.
SẠR-CŎPH'Ạ-GỸ, *n.* The practice of eating flesh.
SĂR'DĮNE *or* SĂR'DĪNE, *n.* A kind of small fish.
SĂR'DǪ-NỸX, *n.* A precious stone. [fish.
SĂR-SẠ-PẠ-RĬL'LẠ,*n.* A plant and its root; smi-
SĂSH, *n.* A belt; a scarf:—a window-frame.[lax.
SĂS'SẠ-FRĂS, *n.* A tree with aromatic bark.
SĂT, *imp. t. & pp.* from *sit.*
SĀ'TẠN, *n.* The devil ; the arch-enemy.
SẠ-TĂN'ĮC, SẠ-TĂN'Į-CẠL, *a.* Devilish; infernal.
SẠ-TĂN'Į-CẠL-LỸ, *ad.*With malice; diabolically.
SĂTCH'ẸL,*n.* A little bag used by schoolboys,&c.
SĀTE, *v. a.* To satiate ; to glut ; to pall.
SĂT'ẸL-LĪTE (săt'tẹl-lĬt), *n.* A small planet re-
volving round a larger :—a follower.
SĂT-ẸL-LỸ''TIOŬS (săt-tẹl-lĬsh'ụs), *a.* Consist-
ing of satellites.
SĀ'TỊ-ĀTE (sā'shẹ-āt), *v. a.* To satisfy, fill, glut.
SĀ'TỊ-ẠTE (sā'shẹ-ạt), *a.* Glutted ; full to satiety.
SĀ-TỊ-Ā'TIǪN (sā-shẹ-ā'shụn), *n.* Fulness.
SẠ-TĪ'Ẹ-TỸ, *n.* State of being satiated ; reple-
tion ; fulness beyond desire ; excess.
SĂT'ĮN, *n.* A thick, close, and shining silk.
SĂT-Į-NĔT', *n.* Thin satin :—a twilled stuff.

SĂT'ĪRE, SĂT'ĬRE, *or* SĀ'TĬRE, *n.* A poem cen-
suring vice, folly, &c. ; a lampoon ; sarcasm.
SĄ-TĬR'ĬC, SĄ-TĬR'Ĭ-CĄL, *a.* Belonging to satire.
SĄ-TĬR'Ĭ-CĄL-LY, *ad.* With invective or satire.
SĂT'ĬR-ĬST, *n.* One who writes or uses satire.
SĂT'ĬR-ĪZE, *v. a.* To censure as in a satire.
SĂT-ĬS-FĂC'TĬQN, *n.* Act of satisfying ; content.
SĂT-ĬS-FĂC'TQ-RĬ-LY, *ad.* So as to content.
SĂT-ĬS-FĂC'TQ-RĬ-NĔSS, *n.* Power of satisfying.
SĂT-ĬS-FĂC'TQ-RY, *a.* Giving satisfaction.
SĂT'ĬS-FĪ-ĒR, *n.* One who makes satisfaction.
SĂT'ĬS-FȲ,*v.a.* To content; to please; to convince.
SĀ'TRĄP, *n.* A Persian governor or viceroy.
SĂT'RĄ-PY, *n.* The governor of a satrap.
SĂT'Ų-RĄ-BLE, *a.* That may be saturated.
SĂT'Ų-RĀTE, *v. a.* To impregnate fully.
SĂT-Ų-RĀ'TIQN, *n.* The act of saturating.
SĂT'ŲR-DAY, *n.* The last day of the week.
SĂT'ŲRN, *n.* A planet.—(*Alchemy.*) Lead.
SĄ-TŬR'NĬ-ĄN, *a.* Relating to Saturn :—happy.
SĂT'ŲR-NĪNE, *a.* Gloomy ; grave ; melancholy.
SĀ'TYR *or* SĂT'YR, *n.* A sylvan demigod.
SÂUCE, *n.* Something to give relish to food.
SÂUCE, *v. a.* To gratify with rich tastes.
SÂUCE'BŎX, *n.* An impertinent fellow.
SÂUCE'PĂN, *n.* A small skillet, or pan for sauce.
SÂU'CĔR, *n.* A small platter for a tea-cup, &c.
SÂU'CĬ-LY, *ad.* Impudently ; impertinently.
SÂU'CĬ-NĔSS, *n.* Impudence ; impertinence.
SÂU'CY, *a.* Insolent ; impudent ; impertinent.
‖SÄUN'TĔR *or* SÂUN'TĔR, *v. n.* To wander
about idly ; to loiter ; to linger. [idler.
‖SÄUN'TĔR-ĔR (sän'tĕr-ĕr), *n.* A rambler ; an
SÂU'SĄĢE,*n.* A composition of meat, spice, &c.
SĀV'Ą-BLE, *a.* Capable of being saved.
SĂV'ĄĢE, *a.* Cruel; uncivilized; barbarous; wild.
SĂV'ĄĢE, *n.* A man untaught and uncivilized.
SĂV'ĄĢE-NĔSS, *n.* Barbarousness ; cruelty.
SĂV'ĄĢE-RY,*n.*Cruelty; barbarity; wild growth.
SĄ-VĂN'NĄ,*n.* An open meadow without wood.
SAVANT (sä-väng'), *n.* [Fr.] A learned man.
SĀVE, *v. a.* To preserve from danger or death.
SĀVE, *prep.* Except; not including.
SĀVE'ĀLL, *n.* A pan to save the ends of candles.
SĂV'ĬN, *n.* An evergreen tree ; red-cedar.
SĀ'VĬNG, *a.* Frugal; parsimonious ; not lavish.
SĀV'ĬNG, *prep.* With exception in favor of.
SĀV'ĬNG, *n.* Any thing saved ; exception.
SĀV'ĬNGṢ-BĂNK, *n.* A bank in which small
sums or savings are deposited.
SĀV'IOŲR, *or* SĀV'IQR (säv'yŭr), *n.* One who
saves ; deliverer :—the Redeemer.
SĀ'VQR, *n.* A scent ; odor ; taste. [taste.
SĀ'VQR, *v. n. & a.* To have a smell or taste ; to
SĀ'VQ-RĬ-NĔSS, *n.* A pleasing taste or smell.
SĀ'VQ-RY, *a.* Pleasing to the smell or taste.
SĄ-VŌ�ў', *n.* A variety of the common cabbage.
SÂW, *imp. t.* from *see.* [a proverb.
SÂW, *n.* An instrument for cutting ;—a saying ;
SÂW, *v. a.* [*imp. t.* sawed ; *pp.* sawed *or* sawn.]
To cut timber, or other matter, with a saw.
SÂW'DŬST, *n.* Dust arising from sawing.
SÂW'ĔR, *or* SÂW'YĔR, *n.* One who saws. [horn.
SÂW'FĬSH, *n.* A fish with a sort of dentated
SÂW'PĬT, *n.* A pit where wood is sawed.
SĂX'Ĭ-FRĄĢE, *n.* An Alpine, medicinal plant.
SĄX-ĬF'RĄ-GOŬS, *a.* Dissolving the stone.
SĂX'QN, *a.* Belonging to the Saxons.

SĂX'QN-ĬṢM, *n.* An idiom of the Saxon language.
SĀY (sä), *v. a. & n.* [*imp. t. & pp.* said (sĕd).] To
speak ; to utter ; to tell ; to allege ; to declare.
SĀY (sä), *n.* A speech ; what one has to say.
SĀY'ĬNG, *n.* An expression ; opinion ; proverb.
SCĂB, *n.* An incrustation over a sore ; mange.
SCĂB'BĄRD, *n.* The sheath of a sword. [try.
SCĂB'BĔD (skăb'bĕd *or* skăbd), *a.* Scabby ; pal-
SCĂB'BĔD-NĔSS, *n.* The state of being scabbed.
SCĂB'BĬ-NĔSS, *n.* The quality of being scabby.
SCĂB'BY, *a.* Diseased with scabs ; scabbed.
SCĂ'BĬ-OŬS, *a.* Itchy ; leprous. [cal.
SCĂ'BROŲS,*a.* Rough ; rugged ; harsh ; unmusi-
SCĂF'FQLD, *n.* A temporary gallery or stage.
SCĂF'FQLD,*v.a.*To furnish with frames of timber.
SCĂF'FQLD-ĬNG, *n.* A temporary frame or stage.
SCĂL'Ą-BLE,*a.* That may be scaled with a ladder.
SCĄ-LĀDE', } *n.* An assault of a place, made by
SCĄ-LĀ'DŌ, } raising ladders against the walls.
SCĀLD, *v. a.* To burn with hot liquor.
SCĀLD, *n.* Scurf on the head ; a burn :—a poet.
SCĀLD'HĔAD, *n.* A disease of the scalp.
SCĀLD'ĬC, *a.* Relating to the poets called *scalds.*
SCĀLE, *n.* A balance ; sign *Libra* :—small shell
of a fish ; a lamina :—a ladder :—gradation ;
SCĀLE, *v. a.* To climb; to strip off scales. [gamut.
SCĀLE, *v. n.* To peel off in thin particles.
SCĀLED (skāld), *a.* Squamous ; having scales.
SCĄ-LĒNE', *a.* Having unequal sides ; oblique.
SCĀ'LĬ-NĔSS, *n.* The state of being scaly.
SCĂLL, *n.* A scab ; leprosy ; morbid baldness.
SCĂLL'IQN (skăl'yŭn), *n.* A kind of onion. [tion.
SCĂL'LQP (skŏl'lŏp), *n.* A shell-fish :—indenta-
SCĂL'LQP (skŏl'lŭp), *v. a.* To indent ; to notch.
SCĂLP, *n.* The skin of the top of the head.
SCĂLP, *v. a.* To deprive of the scalp.
SCĂL'PĔL, *n.* A surgical instrument.
SCĀ'LY, *a.* Covered with scales. [scramble.
SCĂM'BLE, *v. a. & n.* To mangle ; to stir ; to
SCĂM'MQ-NY, *n.* A plant :—a gum resin.
SCĂMP, *n.* A cheat ; a knave.
SCĂM'PĔR, *v. n.* To run with speed and fear.
SCĂN, *v. a.* To examine nicely ; to measure.
SCĂN'DĄL, *n.* An offence ; a reproach ; a censure.
SCĂN'DĄL-ĪZE,*v.a.* To offend, reproach, defame.
SCĂN'DĄL-OŬS,*a.* Opprobrious; shameful; vile.
SCĂN'DĄL-OŬS-LY,*ad.* Shamefully; opprobrious-
SCĂN'DĄL-OŬS-NĔSS, *n.* Public offence. [ly.
SCĂN'SIQN, *n.* The act of scanning a verse.
SCĂNT, *a.* Not plentiful ; scarce ; not liberal.
SCĂNT'Ĭ-LY, *ad.* Not plentifully ; sparingly.
SCĂNT'Ĭ-NĔSS, *n.* Want of space, compass, &c.
SCĂNT'LĬNG, *n.* Timber cut to a small size.
SCĂNT'LY, *ad.* Narrowly ; sparingly.
SCĂNT'NĔSS, *n.* Narrowness ; smallness.
SCĂNT'Y, *a.* Narrow ; small ; poor ; not ample.
SCĀPE, *n.* An escape ; a flight ; evasion ; freak.
SCĀPE'-GŌAT (skāp'gōt), *n.* A goat set at liberty
by the Jews on the day of solemn expiation.
SCĂP'Ų-LĄ, *n.* [L.] (*Anat.*) The shoulder-blade.
SCĂP'Ų-LĄ-RY, *a.* Relating to the shoulders.
SCĂP'Ų-LĄ-RY, *n.* Part of the habit of a friar.
SCĂR, *n.* A mark of a wound ; a cicatrix.
SCĂR, *v. a.* To mark as with a sore or wound.
SCĂR'Ą-BĔĔ, *n.* A kind of beetle ; an insect.
SCĂR'Ą-MŎŬCH, *n.* A buffoon in motley dress.
SCĀRCE, *a.* Not copious ; rare ; not common.
SCĀRCE, SCĀRCE'LY,*ad.*Hardly; with difficulty.

SCÀRCE'NESS, SCÀR'CI-TY, n. Want of plenty.
SCÀRE, v. a. To frighten ; to affright ; to terrify.
SCÀRE'CRŌW, n. An image to frighten birds.
SCÀRF, n. A garment worn on the shoulders.
SCÀRF, v. a. To dress in loose vesture, bind.
SCÀRF'ING, n. A junction of pieces of timber.
SCÀRF'SKĬN, n. The outer skin of the body.
SCÀR-I-FI-CĀ'TIQN, n. An incision of the skin.
SCÀR'I-FI-CĀ-TQR, n. An instrument for scari-
SCÀR'I-FI-ER, n. One that scarifies. [fying.
SCÀR'I-FȲ, v. a. To let blood by cutting the skin.
SCÀR-LA-TÏ'NA, n. The scarlet fever.
SCÀR'LET, n. A brilliant red color. [red.
SCÀR'LET, a. Of the color of scarlet ; brilliant
SCÀRP, n. The interior slope of a ditch ; escarp.
SCÀTE, n. A fish. See SKATE. [to destroy.
||SCÀTH, or SCÀTHE, v. a. To waste ; to damage ;
||†SCÀTH, n. Waste ; damage ; mischief.
SCÀT'TER, v. a. To disperse ; to spread thinly.
SCÀT'TER, v. n. To be dissipated or dispersed.
SCÀV'EN-GER, n. A cleaner of the streets.
SCĒNE (sēn), n. A stage ; an appearance :—part
of a play :—a curtain :—place of exhibition.
SCĒN'E-RY, n. Appearance ; a representation.
SCĔN'IC, SCĔN'I-CAL, a. Dramatic ; theatrical.
SCĔN-Q-GRĂPH'I-CAL, a. Drawn in perspective.
SCĔN-Q-GRĂPH'I-CAL-LY, ad. In perspective.
SCE-NŎG'RA-PHY, n. The art of perspective.
SCĔNT, n. Smell ; odor :—chase by the smell.
SCĔNT, v. a. To perceive by the nose ; to perfume.
SCĔNT'LESS, a. Inodorous ; having no smell.
||SCĔP'TIC (skĕp'tik), n. A doubter ; an infidel ;
a freethinker ;—written also skeptic.
||SCĔP'TI-CAL, a. Doubting ; not believing.
||SCĔP'TI-CAL-LY, ad. In a sceptical manner.
||SCĔP'TI-CĬSM, n. Doubt ; incredulity.
SCĔP'TRE (sĕp'ter), n. An ensign of royalty.
SCĔP'TRE (sĕp'ter), v. a. To invest with royalty.
SCĔP'TRED (sĕp'terd), a. Bearing a sceptre.
SCHĒD'ŪLE (skĕd'yūl, shĕd'yūl, or sĕd'yūl), n.
A small scroll ; an inventory ; a list.
SCHĒME, n. A plan ; a project ; a contrivance.
SCHĒME, v. a. & n. To plan ; to contrive.
SCHĒM'ER, SCHĒM'IST, n. A projector.
SCHĬR'RUS (skĭr'rus), n. See SCIRRHUS.
SCHĬSM (sĭzm), n. A division, as in the church.
SCHĬS'MA-TĬC (sĭz'ma-tĭk or sĭz-măt'ĭk), n. One
who promotes schism. [schism.
SCHĬS-MĂT'I-CAL (sĭz-măt'e-kal), a. Implying
SCHĬST (shĭst), n. A slaty rock.
SCHĬS'TŌSE (shĭs'tōs), a. Relating to schist.
SCHŎL'AR, n. A pupil :—a man of letters.
SCHŎL'AR-LĪKE,) a. Like or becoming a
SCHŎL'AR-LY,) scholar.
SCHŎL'AR-SHĬP, n. Learning ; literature.
SCHQ-LĂS'TĬC, n. An adherent of the schools.
SCHQ-LĂS'TĬC,) a. Belonging to a scholar
SCHQ-LĂS'TI-CAL,) or the schools ; pedantic.
SCHQ-LĂS'TI-CAL-LY, ad. As a scholastic.
SCHŌ'LĪ-ĂST, n. A writer of explanatory notes.
SCHŌ-LĪ-ĂS'TĬC, a. Pertaining to a scholiast.
SCHŌ'LĪ-ŬM (skō'le-ŭm), n. ; pl. SCHŌ'LĪ-A.
[L.] An annotation ; an explanatory note.
SCHŌŌL, n. A place of education ; a seminary.
SCHŌŌL, v. a. To instruct ; to train ; to teach.
SCHŌŌL'BŎY, n. A boy that attends school.
SCHŌŌL'DĀME, n. A schoolmistress. [dent.
SCHŌŌL'FĔL-LŌW (skŏl'fĕl-lō), n. A fellow-stu-

SCHŌŌL'-HŎÛSE, n. A house of instruction.
SCHŌŌL'ING, n. Instruction :—a reprimand.
SCHŌŌL'MAN, n. A scholastic divine.
SCHŌŌL'MĂS-TER, n. One who teaches a school.
SCHŌŌL'MĬS-TRESS, n. A female teacher.
SCHŌŌN'ER, n. A small vessel with two masts.
SCĪ-A-THĔR'I-CAL, a. Belonging to a sun-dial.
SCĪ-ĂT'ĬC, SCĪ-ĂT'I-CA, n. Neuralgia in the hip.
SCĪ-ĂT'I-CAL, a. Afflicting the hip.
SCĪ'ENCE, n. Knowledge :—a liberal art.
SCĪ-EN-TĬF'ĬC, a. Relating to, or versed in, science.
SCĪ-EN-TĬF'I-CAL-LY, ad. In a scientific manner.
SCĬM'I-TAR, n. A sword. See CIMETER.
SCĬN'TIL-LĂNT, a. Sparkling ; emitting sparks.
SCĬN'TIL-LĀTE, v. n. To sparkle ; to emit sparks.
SCĬN-TIL-LĀ'TIQN, n. Act of sparkling ; a spark.
SCĪ'Q-LĬSM, n. Superficial knowledge.
SCĪ'Q-LĬST, n. One of superficial knowledge.
SCĪ-ŎM'A-CHY, n. A battle with a shadow.
SCĪ'Q-MĂN-CY, n. Divination by shadows.
SCĪR-RHŎS'I-TY, n. Induration, as of a gland.
SCĪR'RHOUS (skĭr'rus), a. Indurated.
SCĪR'RHUS (skĭr'rus), n. Induration of a gland.
SCĬS'SI-BLE, SCĬS'SILE, a. Capable of being cut.
SCĬS'SIQN (sĭzh'un), n. The act of cutting.
SCĬS'SQRS (sĭz'zurz), n. pl. Small shears.
SCĬS'SURE (sĭzh'yur), n. A crack ; a fissure.
SCLE-RŎT'ĬC, n. A medicine which hardens.
SCŎFF, v. n. & a. To mock ; to deride ; ridicule.
SCŎFF, n. Derision ; mockery ; ridicule.
SCŎFF'ER, n. One who scoffs ; a scorner.
SCŎFF'ING-LY, ad. In contempt ; in ridicule.
SCŌLD, v. n. & a. To quarrel, brawl, chide, rate.
SCŌLD, n. A clamorous, rude, vulgar woman.
SCŌLD'ING, n. Clamorous, rude language.
SCŎL'LQP, n. A shell-fish. See SCALLOP.
SCŎL-Q-PĔN'DRA, n. A sort of insect :—an herb.
SCŎNCE, n. A branched candlestick :—a fixed
seat :—the head ; sense :—a mulct or fine.
SCŌŌP, n. A kind of large ladle ; a sweep.
SCŌŌP, v. a. To lade out ; to empty ; to cut hollow.
SCŌPE, n. Aim ; intention ; drift ; room ; space.
SCQR-BŪ'TĬC,) a. Relating to, or diseased
SCQR-BŪ'TI-CAL,) with, the scurvy.
SCŌRCH, v. a. To burn superficially.
SCŌRE, n. A notch ; a long incision ; a line
drawn :—account ; reason ; sake :—twenty.
SCŌRE, v. a. To cut ; to engrave ; to mark by a
line :—to note ; to change. [ment.
SCŌ'RI-A, n. ; pl. SCŌ'RI-Æ. [L.] Dross ; recre-
SCŌ-RI-FI-CĀ'TIQN, n. Reduction into scoria.
SCŌ'RI-FȲ, v. a. To reduce to scoria or dross.
SCŌ'RI-OUS, a. Drossy ; recrementitious.
SCŌRN, v. a. To despise ; to revile ; to contemn.
SCŌRN, n. Contempt ; scoff ; high disdain.
SCŌRN'ER, n. A contemner ; a despiser ; a scoffer.
SCŌRN'FÛL, a. Contemptuous ; disdainful.
SCŌRN'FÛL-LY, ad. Contemptuously ; insolently.
SCŌR'PI-QN, n. A reptile :—a sign of the zodiac.
SCŌR'TA-TQ-RY, a. Relating to lewdness.
SCŌT, n. A tax ; a payment ; a share.
SCŎTCH, v. a. To cut.—n. A slight cut.
SCŎTCH, v. a. To stop a wheel by a stone, &c.
SCŎT'-FRĒĒ, a. Without payment ; untaxed.
SCŎT'TI-CĬSM, n. A Scottish word or idiom.
SCOÛN'DREL, n. A mean rascal ; a petty villain.
SCOÛN'DREL, a. Base ; disgraceful ; mean.
SCOÛR, v. a. To purge, cleanse :—to range over.

SCÖÛR, *v. n.* To be purged :—to rove ; to scamper.
SCÖÛR'ẸR, *n.* One that scours :—a purge.
SCOÛRĢE (skürj), *n.* A whip ; a punishment.
SCOÛRĢE, *v. a.* To whip ; to punish.
SCÖÛT, *n.* One who is sent privily to observe the motions or state of an enemy.
SCÖÛT, *v. n. & a.* To act as a scout ; to ridicule.
SCÖŴL, *v. n.* To look angry, sour, or sullen.
SCÖŴL, *n.* A look of sullenness or discontent.
SCRĂB'BLE, *v. n.* To make irregular lines ; to scribble :—to struggle ; to scramble.
SCRĂG, *n.* Any thing thin or lean :—the neck.
SCRĂG'ĢẸD, *a.* Rough ; uneven ; full of points.
SCRĂG'ĢỊ-LY, *ad.* Meagrely ; leanly ; roughly.
SCRĂG'ĢY, *a.* Lean ; thin ; rough ; rugged.
SCRĂM'BLE, *v. n.* To catch eagerly; to struggle.
SCRĂM'BLE, *n.* Eager contest ; act of climbing.
SCRĂM'BLẸR, *n.* One who scrambles.
SCRĂNCH, *v. a.* To crush between the teeth.
SCRĂP, *n.* A particle ; a piece ; a fragment.
SCRĀPE, *v. a.* To pare lightly ; to rub ; to bow.
SCRĀPE, *n.* Difficulty ; perplexity ; distress.
SCRĀ'PẸR, *n.* An instrument; a fiddler ; a miser.
SCRĂTCH, *v. a.* To wound ; to tear with nails.
SCRĂTCH, *n.* A slight wound ; a rent :—a wig. *pl.* A disease in horses' feet.
SCRÂWL, *v. a. & n.* To draw or write clumsily.
SCRÂWL, *n.* Unskilful and inelegant writing.
SCRĒAK, *v. n.* To make a shrill or loud noise.
SCRĒAK (skrēk), *n.* A screech ; a shrill noise.
SCRĒAM, *v. n.* To cry out with a shrill voice.
SCRĒAM, *n.* A shrill, quick, loud cry.
SCRĒĒCH, *v. n.* To cry out as in terror.
SCRĒĒCH, *n.* A cry of horror and anguish.
SCRĒĒCH'-ÖŴL, *n.* An owl that hoots by night.
SCRĒĒN, *n.* Any thing that affords shelter.
SCRĒĒN, *v. a.* To shelter ; to hide ; to conceal.
SCREW (skrŭ), *n.* A cylinder grooved spirally.
SCREW (skrŭ), *v. a.* To turn by a screw ; to press.
SCRĬB'BLE, *n.* Worthless, careless writing.
SCRĬB'BLE, *v. a. & n.* To write carelessly.
SCRĬB'BLẸR, *n.* A worthless author or writer.
SCRĪBE, *n.* A writer; notary :—Jewish teacher.
SCRĬP, *n.* A small bag :—a schedule ; a small writing :—a certificate of stock. [cal.
SCRĬPT'Ụ-RẠL, *a.* Contained in the Bible ; bibli-
SCRĬPT'ỤRE (skrĭpt'yụr), *n.* The Bible.
SCRĬPT'Ụ-RĬST, *n.* One versed in the Scriptures.
SCRĪVE'NẸR, *n.* One who draws contracts, &c.
SCRŎF'Ụ-LẠ, *n.* A disease ; the king's evil.
SCRŎF'Ụ-LOŬS, *a.* Diseased with the scrofula.
SCRŌLL, *n.* A writing formed into a roll.
SCRŬB, *v. a.* To rub hard with something coarse.
SCRŬB, *n.* A mean drudge :—a worn-out broom.
SCRŬB'BY, *a.* Mean ; vile ; worthless ; dirty.
SCRŬ'PLE, *n.* A doubt :—a weight of 20 grains.
SCRŬ'PLE, *v. n.* To doubt ; to hesitate.
SCRŬ-PỤ-LŎS'Ị-TY, *n.* Doubt ; conscientiousness.
SCRŬ'PỤ-LOŬS, *a.* Nicely doubtful ; careful ; cautious ; exact ; conscientious.
SCRŬ'PỤ-LOŬS-LY, *ad.* Carefully ; anxiously.
SCRŬ'PỤ-LOŬS-NĔSS, *n.* State of being scrupulous ; scrupulosity.
SCRŬ'TẠ-BLE, *a.* That may be searched out.
SCRỤ-TĀ'TỌR, *n.* A searcher ; an examiner.
SCRỤ-TỊ-NĒĒR', *n.* A searcher ; an examiner.
SCRŬ'TỊ-NĪZE, *v. a.* To search ; to examine.
SCRŬ'TỊ-NOŬS, *a.* Captious ; full of inquiries.

SCRŬ'TỊ-NY, *n.* A strict search ; an examination.
SCRỤ-TOIRE' (skrŭ-twör'), *n.* A case for writing.
SCŬD, *v. n.* To flee ; to run away with speed.
SCŬD, *n.* A cloud swiftly driven by the wind.
SCŬD'DLE, *v. n.* To run with affected haste.
SCŬF'FLE, *n.* A confused quarrel ; a broil.
SCŬF'FLE, *v. n.* To strive or struggle roughly.
SCŬLK, *v. n.* To lurk secretly ; to lie close.
SCŬLK'ẸR, *n.* A lurker ; one who sculks.
SCŬLL, *n.* A small boat :—an oar :—the brainpan ; the cranium. See SKULL.
SCŬLL'ẸR, *n.* A cockboat :—one who sculls.
SCŬLL'ẸR-Y, *n.* A place to keep and clean dishes.
SCŬLL'IỌN (skŭl'yụn), *n.* A kitchen servant.
SCŬLP'TỌR, *n.* A carver of stone or wood.
SCŬLPT'ỤRE (skŭlpt'yụr), *n.* The art of carving and of engraving ; carved work.
SCŬLPT'ỤRE (skŭlpt'yụr), *v. a.* To carve.
SCŬM, *n.* What rises to the top of any liquor.
SCŬM, *v. a.* To clear off the scum of; to skim.
SCŬM'MẸR, *n.* A vessel. See SKIMMER.
SCŬM'MỊNGS, *n. pl.* Matter skimmed off.
SCŬP'PẸRS, *n. pl.* Small holes in a ship's sides.
SCŬRF, *n.* A kind of dry, miliary scab.
SCŬRF'Ị-NĔSS, *n.* The state of bring scurfy.
SCŬRF'Y, *a.* Having scurfs or scabs.
SCỤR-RĬL'Ị-TY, *n.* Vulgar or abusive language.
SCŬR'RỊ-LOŬS, *a.* Grossly opprobrious ; vile.
SCŬR'RỊ-LOŬS-LY, *ad.* With gross reproach.
SCŬR'RỊ-LOŬS-NĔSS, *n.* Scurrility ; vulgarity.
SCŬR'VỊ-LY, *ad.* Vilely ; basely ; coarsely.
SCŬR'VỊ-NĔSS, *n.* The state of being scurvy.
SCŬR'VY, *a.* Scabbed ; vile ; bad ; worthless.
SCŬR'VY, *n.* A disease incident to seamen, &c.
SCŬR'VY-GRĂSS, *n.* A plant ; spoonwort.
SCŬT, *n.* The tail of a hare, rabbit, &c.
SCŬTCH'EỌN (skŭch'ụn), *n.* See ESCUTCHEON.
SCŬ'TỊ-FÖRM, *a.* Shaped like a buckler.
SCŬT'TLE, *n.* A basket ; a grate ; a hole in a ship's deck, &c. :—a quick pace ; a short run.
SCŬT'TLE, *v. a.* To sink a ship by cutting holes in the bottom.
SCŬT'TLE, *v. n.* To run with haste. [grass.
SCȲTHE (sīth), *n.* An instrument for mowing
SĒA (sē), *n.* The ocean ; a body of water ; surge.
SĒA'-BĒAT (sē'bēt), } *a.* Dashed by the
SĒA'-BĒAT-EN (sē'bē-tn), } waves of the sea.
SĒA'-BÖRN, *a.* Produced on, or by, the sea.
SĒA'-BRĒACH (sē'brēch), *n.* Irruption of the sea.
SĒA'-BRĒĒZE, *n.* A wind blowing from the sea.
SĒA'-BUĬLT (sē'bĭlt), *a.* Built for, or on, the sea.
SĒA'-CĂLF (sē'kăf), *n.* The common seal.
SĒA'-CŌAL (sē'kōl), *n.* Coal brought by sea.
SĒA'-CŌAST (sē'kōst), *n.* Shore ; edge of the sea.
SĒA'-CÖŴ, *n.* A bulky animal ; the walrus.
SĒA'-FÀR-ẸR (sē'fàr-ẹr), *n.* A mariner.
SĒA'-FÀR-ỊNG (sē'fàr-ịng), *a.* Travelling by sea.
SĒA'-FĪGHT (sē'fīt), *n.* A battle on the sea.
SĒA'-FÖŴL (sē'föûl), *n.* A bird that lives at sea.
SĒA'-ĢĬRT (sē'ġïrt), *a.* Encircled by the sea.
SĒA'-GRĒĒN, *a.* Having the color of sea-water.
SĒA'-GŬLL, *n.* A bird common on sea-coasts.
SĒA'-HŎG (sē'hŏg), *n.* The porpoise.
SĒA'-HÖRSE (sē'hörs), *n.* The walrus. [tion.
SĒAL, *n.* A marine animal :—a stamp ; confirma-
SĒAL, *v. a.* To fasten with a seal, confirm, close.
SĒAL'ỊNG-WĂX, *n.* A wax used to seal letters, &c.
SĒAM, *n.* The suture of two edges :—a scar.

SĒAM, *v. a.* To join together :—to mark ; to scar.
SĒA'-MĀID, *n.* A mermaid ; a water-nymph.
SĒA'MĄN (sē'mąn), *n.* A sailor ; a mariner.
SĒA'MĄN-SHĬP, *n.* The skill of a good seaman.
SĒA'-MÄRK, *n.* A point or beacon at sea.
SĒA'-MEW̄, *n.* A fowl that frequents the sea.
SĒAM'LĘSS, *a.* Having no seam.
SĒA'-MŎN-STĘR, *n.* A strange animal of the sea.
SĒAM'STRĘSS *or* SĒAM'STRĘSS, *n.* A woman whose occupation it is to sew ; sempstress.
SĒAM'Y, *a.* Having a seam ; showing seams.
SĒA'-NȲMPH (sē'nĭmf), *n.* A goddess of the sea.
SĒA'-PIĒCE, *n.* Representation of any thing at
SĒA'PŌRT, *n.* A harbor or port for ships. [sea.
SĒAR, *a.* Dry ; withered ; no longer green.
SĒAR, *v. a.* To burn, cauterize, wither, dry.
SĒARCH (sërch), *v. a.* To examine, try, explore.
SĒARCH (sërch), *n.* Inquiry ; quest ; pursuit.
SĒARCH'ĘR, *n.* An examiner ; seeker ; inquirer.
SĒAR'CLŎTH, *n.* A plaster to cover a sore.
SĒAR'ĘD-NĔSS, *n.* The state of being seared.
SĒA'-RÔÔM, *n.* Open sea ; spacious main.
SĒA'-SĔR-VĮCE (sē'sër-vĭs), *n.* Naval service.
SĒA'-SHĔLL, *n.* A shell found in the sea.
SĒA'-SHŌRE (sē'shōr), *n.* The coast of the sea.
SĒA'SĬCK, *a.* Sick, as new voyagers on the sea.
SĒA'-SĪDE (sē'sĭd), *n.* The edge of the sea.
SĒA'ŞON (sē'zn), *n.* One of the four parts of the year :—a fit time. [imbue, dry, inure, fit.
SĒA'ŞON (sē'zn), *v. a.* To give a relish to ; to
SĒA'ŞON (sē'zn), *v. n.* To become mature or fit.
SĒA'ŞON-Ą-BLE (sē'zn-ą-bl), *a.* Done at the proper time ; opportune ; timely. [time.
SĒA'ŞON-Ą-BLE-NĔSS, *n.* Opportuneness of
SĒA'ŞON-Ą-BLY (sē'zn-ą-blę), *ad.* Opportunely.
SĒA'ŞON-ĬNG (sē'zn-ĭng), *n.* A condiment.
SĒAT, *n.* A chair ; mansion ; abode ; situation.
SĒAT, *v. a.* To place on seats ; to fix ; to settle.
SĒA'-TĔRM, *n.* A term used by seamen.
SĒA'-TŎST (sē'tŏst), *a.* Tossed by the sea.
SĒA'WĄRD, *a.* Directed towards the sea.
SĒA'WĄRD (sē'wąrd), *ad.* Towards the sea.
SĒA'-WÂ-TĘR, *n.* The salt water of the sea.
SĒA'-WĒED (sē'wēd), *n.* A marine plant.
SĒA'WOR-ᵵHY (sē'wür-ᵵhę), *a.* Fit to go to sea.
SĘ-BĀ'CEOŲS (sę-bā'shŭs), *a.* Relating to tallow.
SĒ'CĄNT, *n.* A line cutting another.—*a.* Cutting.
SĘ-CĒDE', *v. n.* To withdraw from fellowship.
SĘ-CĒD'ĘR, *n.* One who secedes.
SĘ-CĔS'SIQN (sę-sĕsh'ŭn), *n.* Act of seceding.
SĘ-CLŪDE', *v. a.* To shut up apart ; to separate.
SĘ-CLŪ'ŞIQN, *n.* A shutting out ; separation.
SĔC'QND, *a.* Next in order to the first ; inferior.
SĔC'QND, *n.* One who attends another in a duel : —a supporter :—a 60th part of a minute.
SĔC'QND, *v. a.* To support, assist, follow next.
SĔC'QND-Ą-RĮ-LY, *ad.* In the second order.
SĔC'QND-Ą-RĮ-NĔSS, *n.* State of being secondary.
SĔC'QND-Ą-RY, *a.* Not primary ; subordinate.
SĔC'QND-HÄND, *a.* Not original ; not new.
SĔC'QND-LY, *ad.* In the second place.
SĔC'QND-RĀTE, *n.* The second in order or worth.
SĔC'QND-RĀTE, *a.* Second in order or worth.
SĔC'QND-SĪGHT, *n.* Power of seeing things future.
SĒ'CRĘ-CY, *n.* Privacy ; solitude ; close silence.
SĒ'CRĘT, *a.* Kept hidden ; concealed ; private.
SĒ'CRĘT, *n.* A thing unknown or hidden; privacy.
SĔC'RĘ-TĄ-RY, *n.* An officer ; a writer ; a scribe.

SĔC'RĘ-TĄ-RY-SHĬP, *n.* The office of a secretary.
SĘ-CRĒTE', *v. a.* To hide ; to conceal ; to separate.
SĘ-CRĒ'TIQN, *n.* Act of secreting ; separation.
SĔC-RĘ-TĬ''TIOŲS (sĕk-rę-tĭsh'ŭs), *a.* Parted or separated by animal secretion.
SĒ'CRĘT-LY, *ad.* Privately; privily; not openly.
SĒ'CRĘT-NĔSS, *n.* State of being hidden ; privacy.
SĘ-CRĒ'TQ-RY *or* SĒ'CRĘ-TQ-RY, *a.* Performing secretion ; secreting.
SĔCT, *n.* A body of men united in tenets.
SĘC-TĀ'RĮ-ĄN, *n.* One of a sect or party.
SĘC-TĀ'RĮ-ĄN, *a.* Relating or adhering to a sect.
SĘC-TĀ'RĮ-ĄN-ĬŞM, *n.* Devotion to a sect.
SĔC'TĄ-RY, *n.* A follower of a particular sect.
SĔC'TIQN, *n.* The act of cutting ; part ; division.
SĔC'TQR, *n.* A mathematical instrument.
SĔC'Ų-LĄR, *a.* Not spiritual ; worldly.
SĔC'Ų-LĄR, *n.* A church officer ; a layman.
SĔC-Ų-LĂR'Į-TY, *n.* Worldliness.
SĔC'Ų-LĄR-ĪZE, *v. a.* To convert to secular use.
SĔC'Ų-LĄR-LY, *ad.* In a worldly manner.
SĔC'ŲN-DĪNE, *n.* The afterbirth ; placenta.
SĘ-CŪRE', *a.* Free from fear or danger ; safe.
SĘ-CŪRE', *v. a.* To make safe ; protect ; to insure.
SĘ-CŪRE'LY, *ad.* Without fear or danger ; safely.
SĘ-CŪRE'NĔSS, *n.* Want of vigilance or fear.
SĘ-CŪ'RĮ-TY, *n.* Protection ; safety ; certainty.
SĘ-DĂN', *n.* A portable chair for carriage. [rene.
SĘ-DĀTE', *a.* Calm ; quiet ; still ; unruffled ; se-
SĘ-DĀTE'LY, *ad.* Calmly; without disturbance.
SĘ-DĀTE'NĔSS, *n.* Calmness ; serenity.
SĔD'Ą-TĬVE, *a.* Assuaging ; composing.
SĔD'ĘN-TĄ-RĮ-NĔSS, *n.* State of being sedentary.
SĔD'ĘN-TĄ-RY, *a.* Sitting much :—inactive.
SĔDGE, *n.* A growth of narrow flags ; a flag.
SĔDG'Y, *a.* Overgrown with narrow flags.
SĔD'Į-MĔNT, *n.* That which settles at the bottom.
SĘ-DĬ''TIQN (sę-dĭsh'ŭn), *n.* Tumult ; rebellion.
SĘ-DĬ''TIOŲS (sę-dĭsh'ŭs), *a.* Factious ; turbulent.
SĘ-DĬ''TIOŲS-LY (sę-dĭsh'ŭs-lę), *ad.* Factiously.
SĘ-DŪCE', *v. a.* To entice ; to corrupt ; to mislead.
SĘ-DŪCE'MĘNT, *n.* Practice of seduction.
SĘ-DŪ'CĘR, *n.* One who seduces ; a corrupter.
SĘ-DŪ'CĮ-BLE, *a.* That may be seduced.
SĘ-DŬC'TIQN, *n.* Act of seducing ; corruption.
SĘ-DŬC'TĮVE, *a.* Tending to seduce or mislead.
SĘ-DŪ'LĮ-TY, *n.* Assiduity; industry; application.
SĔD'Ų-LOŬS, *a.* Assiduous ; industrious ; diligent.
SĔD'Ų-LOŬS-LY, *ad.* Assidulously; industriously.
SĔD'Ų-LOŬS-NĔSS, *n.* Assiduity; assiduousness.
SĒE, *n.* The seat or diocese of a bishop.
SĒE, *v. a.* [*imp. t.* saw ; *pp.* seen.] To perceive by the eye ; to observe ; to descry ; to discern.
SĒED, *n.* The substance from which plants and animals are generated :—offspring ; race.
SĒED, *v. n.* To bring forth seed ; to shed the seed.
SĒED'CĀKE, *n.* A sweet cake containing seeds.
SĒED'ĘD, *a.* Covered with, or bearing, seed.
SĒED'LĮNG, *n.* A plant or fruit from the seed.
SĒED'PLŎT, *n.* Ground on which seeds are sown.
SĒEDŞ'MĄN, *n.* A sower :—one that sells seeds.
SĒED'TĪME, *n.* The season of sowing.
SĒE'ĮNG, *n.* Sight ; vision.—*ad.* Since that.
SĒEK, *v. a. & n.* [*imp. t. & pp.* sought.] To look for ; to search for ; to solicit ; to endeavor.
SĒEK'ĘR, *n.* One that seeks ; an inquirer.
SĒEM, *v. n.* To appear ; to have semblance.
SĒEM'ĮNG, *n.* Appearance ; semblance.

Ā,Ē,Ī,Ō,Ū,Ȳ, *long* ; Ă,Ĕ,Ĭ,Ŏ,Ŭ,Y̆, *short* ; Ą,Ę,Į,Q,Ų,Y, *obscure.*—FÀRE, FÄR, FĂST, FÂLL ; HÊIR, HĔR ;

SĒĒM'ĬNG-LY, *ad.* In appearance; in show.
SĒĒM'ĬNG-NĔSS, *n.* Plausibility; appearance.
SĒĒM'LĬ-NĔSS, *n.* Decency; comeliness; grace.
SĒĒM'LY, *a.* Decent; becoming; proper; fit.
SĒĒN, *pp.* from *see.* Perceived; beheld.
SĒĒR, *n.* One who sees :—a prophet; a foreteller.
SĒĒ'SÂW, *n.* Reciprocating motion :—a play.
SĒĒ'SÂW, *v. n.* To move with a reciprocating motion up and down or to and fro.
SĒĒ̄THE, *v. a.* [*imp. t.* seethed *or* sod; *pp.* sodden.] To boil; to decoct in hot liquor.
SE-GÄR', *n.* A little roll of tobacco. See CIGAR.
SĔG'MENT, *n.* A part cut off; a section.
SĔG'RE-GĀTE, *v. a.* To set apart; to separate.
SĔG-RE-GĀ'TIQN, *n.* Separation from others.
SEIG-NEŪ'RĬ-ĄL (se-nū're-ąl), *a.* Invested with large powers; manorial; independent.
SĒIGN'IQR (sēn'yur), *n.* A lord; a title. [iory.
SĒIGN'IQR-ĄĢE (sēn'yur-ąj), *n.* Authority; seign-
SĒIGN'IQR-Y (sēn'yur-e), *n.* A lordship; a manor.
SĒINE (sēn), *n.* A kind of large fishing net.
SĒIŞ'ĬN, *or* SĒIZ'ĬN (sē'zįn), *n.* Possession.
SĒIZE (sēz), *v. a.* To grasp; to gripe; to take.
SĒIZ'ŲRE (sē'zhur), *n.* The act of seizing; gripe.
SĒ'LÄH. [Heb.] A word occurring in the Psalms.
SĔL'DQM, *ad.* Rarely; not frequently.
SE-LĔCT', *v. a.* To choose in preference to others.
SE-LĔCT', *a.* Nicely chosen; choice; culled.
SE-LĔC'TIQN, *n.* The act of selecting; choice.
SE-LĔCT'NESS, *n.* The state of being select.
SE-LĔCT'QR, *n.* One who selects; a chooser.
SĔL-E-NŎG'RĄ-PHY, *n.* (*Astron.*) A description of the moon.
SĔLF, *a.* or *pron.*; pl. SĔLVEŞ. Of one's own.
SĔLF-ĔV'Ĭ-DENT, *a.* Evident without proof.
SĔLF-EX-ĬST'ENCE, *n.* Existence in its own nature; underived existence.
SĔLF-EX-ĬST'ENT, *a.* Existing in its own nature.
SĔLF'ĬSH, *a.* Void of due regard for others.
SĔLF'ĬSH-LY, *ad.* In a selfish manner.
SĔLF'ĬSH-NĔSS, *n.* The quality of being selfish.
SĔLF'SĀME, *a.* Exactly the same; identical.
SĔLL, *v. a. & n.* [*imp. t. & pp.* sold.] To part with for a price; to vend; to exchange for money.
SĔL'VAĢE, *n.* The edge of cloth :—a kind of rope.
SĔLVEŞ (sĕlvz). The plural of *self.* See SELF.
SĔM'BLANCE, *n.* Likeness; resemblance; show.
SĔM'Ĭ (sĕm'e). [L.] A word used as a prefix, signifying *half.*
SĔM'Ĭ-ĂN-NŲ-ĄL, *a.* Happening every half year.
SĔM'Ĭ-BRĒVE, *n.* (*Mus.*) A note; half a breve.
SĔM'Ĭ-CĬR-CLE, *n.* A half of a circle.
SĔM-Ĭ-CĬR'CŲ-LĄR, *a.* Half round or circular.
SĔM-Ĭ-CŌ'LQN, *n.* A point made thus [;].
SĔM-Ĭ-DĬ-ĂM'E-TER, *n.* Half of a diameter.
SĔM-Ĭ-DĬ-ĂPH'Ą-NOŬS, *a.* Half transparent.
SĔM-Ĭ-FLŪ'ĬD, *a.* Imperfectly fluid.
SĔM-Ĭ-LŪ'NĄR, *a.* Resembling half a moon.
SĔM-Ĭ-MĔT'AL (sĕm-e-mĕt'tl), *n.* A half metal.
SĔM'Ĭ-NĄL, *a.* Belonging to seed :—original.
SĔM'Ĭ-NĄ-RĬST, *n.* A Roman Catholic priest.
SĔM'Ĭ-NĄ-RY, *n.* A school; a place of education.
SĔM-Ĭ-PEL-LŪ'CĬD, *a.* Imperfectly transparent.
SĔM'Ĭ-QUĀ-VER, *n.* (*Mus.*) A note; half a quaver.
SĔM'Ĭ-TŌNE, *n.* (*Mus.*) Half a tone.
SĔM'Ĭ-VŎW'-EL, *n.* A consonant which makes an imperfect sound, as, *f, h, l, m, n, r, s, y, w,* &c.
SĔM-PĬ-TĔR'NĄL, *a.* Eternal in futurity.

SĔM-PĬ-TĔR'NĬ-TY, *n.* Future endless duration.
SĔMP'STRESS, *n.* See SEAMSTRESS.
SĔN'Ą-RY, *a.* Belonging to, or containing, six.
SĔN'ĄTE, *n.* An assembly or a body of senators.
SĔN'ĄTE-HÖÛSE, *n.* The house of the senate.
SĔN'Ą-TQR, *n.* A counsellor; a legislator.
SĔN-Ą-TŌ'RĬ-ĄL, *a.* Belonging to a senator.
SĔN'Ą-TQR-SHĬP, *n.* The office of a senator.
SĔND, *v. a.* [*imp. t. & pp.* sent.] To transmit; to cause to go; to throw; to impel :—to bestow.
SE-NĔS'CENCE, *n.* The state of growing old.
SĔN'ES-ĊHĂL *or* SĔN'ES-ÇHĂL, *n.* A steward.
SĒ'NĪLE, *n.* Belonging to old age. [dotage.
SE-NĬL'Ĭ-TY, *n.* Old age; weakness of age;
SĒN'IQR (sēn'yur), *n.* One older than another.
SĒN'IQR (sēn'yur), *a.* Elder; older in office.
SĒN-IŌR'Ĭ-TY (sēn-yōr'e-te), *n.* Priority of birth.
SĔN'NĄ, *n.* A species of the cassia. [NIGHT.
SĔN'NĬGHT (sĕn'nįt), *n.* A week. See SEVEN-
SEN-SĀ'TIQN, *n.* Feeling :—excitement.
SĔNSE, *n.* Faculty by which external objects are perceived :—understanding :—meaning.
SĔNSE'LESS, *a.* Wanting sense; stupid; foolish.
SĔNSE'LESS-LY, *ad.* In a senseless manner.
SĔNSE'LESS-NĔSS, *n.* Folly; stupidity; absurdity.
SĔN-SĬ-BĬL'Ĭ-TY, *n.* Quick or delicate feeling.
SĔN'SĬ-BLE, *a.* Perceiving by, or perceptible by, the mind or senses :—discerning; judicious.
SĔN'SĬ-BLE-NĔSS, *n.* The quality of being sensi-
SĔN'SĬ-BLY, *ad.* In a sensible manner. [ble.
SĔN'SĬ-TĬVE, *a.* Having sense or quick feeling.
SĔN'SĬ-TĬVE-LY, *ad.* In a sensitive manner.
SEN-SŌ'RĬ-ŬM, SĔN'SQ-RY, *n.* Seat of sensation.
SĔNS'Ų-ĄL (sĕn'shu-ąl), *a.* Consisting in sense : —pleasing to the senses :—carnal. [appetite.
SĔNS'Ų-ĄL-ĬSM (sĕn'shu-ąl-ĭzm), *n.* Sensual
SĔNS'Ų-ĄL-ĬST (sĕn'shu-ąl-ĭst), *n.* One devoted to sensual pleasures; a voluptuary.
SĔNS-Ų-ĂL'Ĭ-TY (sĕn-shu-ăl'e-te), *n.* Devotedness to sensual pleasures. [sensual; to carnalize.
SĔNS'Ų-ĄL-ĪZE (sĕn'shu-ąl-īz), *v. a.* To make
SĔNS'Ų-ĄL-LY, *ad.* In a sensual manner.
SĔNT, *imp. t. & pp.* from *send.* [—a period.
SĔN'TENCE, *n.* Decision :—judgment; doom:
SĔN'TENCE, *v. a.* To judge; to condemn.
SEN-TĔN'TIĄL, *a.* Pertaining to sentences.
SEN-TĔN'TIOŲS, *a.* Pithy; pointed; terse.
SEN-TĔN'TIOŲS-LY, *ad.* Expressively; pithily.
SEN-TĔN'TIOŲS-NĔSS, *n.* Brevity with strength.
SĔN'TĬ-ENT (sĕn'she-ent), *a.* Having sensation.
SĔN'TĬ-ENT (sĕn'she-ent), *n.* One that perceives.
SĔN'TĬ-MĔNT, *n.* Thought; opinion :—feeling.
SĔN-TĬ-MĔN'TĄL, *a.* Having sentiment or feeling.
SĔN-TĬ-MĔN'TĄL-ĬST, *n.* One who affects feeling.
SĔN-TĬ-MEN-TĂL'Ĭ-TY, *n.* Affectation of feeling.
SĔN'TĬ-NĔL, *n.* A soldier on guard; a watch.
SĔN'TRY, *n.* A watch; a guard; a sentinel.
SĔN'TRY-BŎX, *n.* A shelter for a sentinel.
SĒ'PĄL, *n.* (*Bot.*) A leaf of a calyx.
SĔP-Ą-RĄ-BĬL'Ĭ-TY, *n.* State of being separable.
SĔP'Ą-RĄ-BLE, *a.* That may be separated.
SĔP'Ą-RĄ-BLE-NĔSS, *n.* Capacity of separation.
SĔP'Ą-RĀTE, *v. a.* To divide; to disunite; to dis-
SĔP'Ą-RĀTE, *v. n.* To part; to be disunited. [join.
SĔP'Ą-RĄTE, *a.* Divided; disjoined; disunited.
SĔP'Ą-RĄTE-LY, *ad.* Apart; singly; distinctly.
SĔP'Ą-RĄTE-NĔSS, *n.* State of being separate.
SĔP-Ą-RĀ'TIQN, *n.* Act of separating; disunion.

sĕp′ạ-rạ-tĭst, *n.* One who separates; a seceder.
sĕp′ạ-rā-tọr, *n.* One who divides; a divider.
sĕp′ạ-rạ-tọ-rў, *a.* Separating.—*n.* A vessel.
sē′pŏÿ, *n.* An East Indian native foot-soldier.
sĕpt, *n.* A clan; a family. [*Ireland.*]
sĕpt-ăn′gụ-lạr, *a.* Having seven angles.
sĕp-tĕm′bẹr, *n.* The ninth month of the year.
sĕp′tẹ-nạ-rў, *a.* Consisting of seven.
sĕp′tẹ-nạ-rў, *n.* The number seven.
sĕp-tĕn′nĭ-ạl, *a.* Lasting seven years.
sĕp-tĕn′trĭ-ọn, *n.* The north:—the Great
 Bear, or Charles's Wain.
sĕp-tĕn′trĭ-ọn-ạl, *a.* Northern.
sĕp′tĭc, sĕp′tĭ-cạl, *a.* Producing putrefaction.
sĕp-tĭ-lăt′ẹr-ạl, *a.* Having seven sides.
sĕp-tĭn′sụ-lạr, *a.* Consisting of seven islands.
sĕp-tụ-ăġ′ẹ-nạ-rў, *a.* Consisting of seventy.
sĕp-tụ-ạ-ġĕs′ĭ-mạ, *n.* 3d Sunday before Lent.
sĕp-tụ-ạ-ġĕs′ĭ-mạl, *a.* Consisting of seventy.
sĕp′tụ-ạ-ġĭnt, *n.* The version of the Old Testament from Hebrew into Greek.
sẹ-pŭl′chrạl, *a.* Relating to burial.
sĕp′ụl-chre (sĕp′ul-kẹr), *n.* A grave; a tomb.
sĕp′ụl-chre (sĕp′ul-kẹr), *v. a.* To bury.
sĕp′ụl-tūre, *n.* Interment; burial. [ant.
sẹ-quā′cioụs (sẹ-kwā′shụs), *a.* Following; pli-
sē′quẹl, *n.* Conclusion; succeeding part.
sē′quençe, *n.* Order of succession; succession.
sē′quẹnt, *a.* Following; succeeding. [apart.
sẹ-quĕs′tẹr, *v. a.* To seize and retain; to set
sẹ-quĕs′trạ-ble, *a.* That may be sequestered.
sẹ-quĕs′trāte, *v. n.* To sequester; to separate.
‖sĕq-uẹs-trā′tiọn, *n.* Deprivation of profits;
 the act of sequestering.
‖sĕq-uẹs-trā′tọr *or* sē-quẹs-trā′tọr, *n.*
 One who sequesters.
sẹ-răgl′ĭō (sẹ-răl′yō), *n.*; pl. sẹ-răgl′ĭōṣ.
 The palace of the Turkish sultan:—a house
 for concubines in the East; a harem.
sĕr′ạph, *n.*; pl. sĕr′ạphs, *or* sĕr′ạ-phĭm.
 An angel of the highest rank.
sẹ-răph′ĭc, sẹ-răph′ĭ-cạl, *a.* Angelic; pure.
sẹ-răs′kiẹr *or* sĕr-ạs-kiẹr′, *n.* A Turkish
 generalissimo.
sēre, *a.* Dry; withered; sear. See SEAR.
sĕr-ẹ-nāde′, *n.* Entertainment of music.
sĕr-ẹ-nāde′, *v. a.* To entertain with a serenade.
sĕr-ẹ-nāde′, *v. n.* To perform a serenade.
sẹ-rēne′, *a.* Calm; placid; quiet; unruffled.
sẹ-rēne′lў, *ad.* Calmly; quietly; coolly.
sẹ-rēne′nẹss, *n.* Serenity; calmness.
sẹ-rĕn′ĭ-tў, *n.* Calmness; peace; quietness.
sĕrf, *n.* A slave attached to the soil.
sĕrġe, *n.* A kind of twilled cloth.
sĕr′ġẹant (sär′jẹnt *or* sĕr′jẹnt), *n.* A petty
 officer in the army:—in England, a lawyer of
 high rank;—written also *serjeant.*
sē′rĭ-ẹṣ, *n.* A connected order or succession.
sē′rĭ-oŭs, *a.* Grave; solemn; earnest; impor-
sē′rĭ-oŭs-lў, *ad.* Gravely; in earnest. [tant.
sē′rĭ-oụs-nĕss, *n.* Gravity; solemnity.
sĕr′mọn, *n.* A discourse of a preacher.
sĕr′mọn-īze, *v. n.* To preach or write a sermon.
sẹ-rŏs′ĭ-tў, *n.* The state of being serous.
sē′roụs, *a.* Thin; watery; like serum.
sĕr′pẹnt, *n.* A snake:—a musical instrument.
sĕr′pẹn-tīne, *a.* Resembling a serpent; wind-
sĕr′pẹn-tīne, *n.* A magnesian stone. [ing.

sẹr-pĭġ′ĭ-noŭs, *a.* Diseased with serpigo.
sẹr-pī′ġọ *or* sẹr-pī′ġọ, *n.* A tetter; ringworm.
sĕr′rạte, sĕr′rāt-ẹd, *a.* Jagged like a saw.
sē′rụm, *n.* The watery part of the blood, &c.
sĕr′vạnt, *n.* One who serves another.
sĕrve, *v. a.* To attend at command, obey, assist.
sĕrve, *v. n.* To be a servant; to answer; to suit.
sĕr′vĭce, *n.* Office; duty; use; favor; course.
sĕr′vĭce-ạ-ble, *a.* Active; diligent; useful.
sĕr′vĭce-ạ-ble-nĕss, *n.* Activity; usefulness.
sĕr′vĭce-ạ-blў, *ad.* So as to be serviceable.
sĕr′vĭle, *a.* Slavish; dependent; fawning.
sĕr′vĭle-lў, *ad.* Meanly; slavishly.
sẹr-vĭl′ĭ-tў, *n.* Meanness; slavery.
sĕr′vĭ-tọr, *n.* A servant.—[*Oxford, Eng.*] A
 kind of student.
sĕr′vĭ-tūde, *n.* The state of a slave.
sĕs′ạ-mŭm, sĕs′ạ-mẹ, *n.* East Indian oily plant.
sẹs-quĭp′ẹ-dạl,   } *a.* Containing, or meas-
sĕs-quĭ-pẹ-dā′lĭ-ạn, } uring, a foot and a half.
sĕs′siọn (sĕsh′ụn), *n.* A sitting of a court, &c.
sĕss′-pôôl, *n.* A receptacle. See CESS-POOL.
sĕs′tẹrce, *n.* A Roman coin, value about 4 cents.
sĕt, *v. a.* [*imp. t. & pp.* set.] To place; to fix; to
 plant; to frame; to regulate; to adjust.
sĕt, *v. n.* To go down, as the sun; to be fixed.
sĕt, *p. a.* Regular; not lax; firm; stiff; fixed.
sĕt, *n.* A complete suit or assortment. [hairs.
sẹ-tā′ceoụs (sẹ-tā′shụs), *a.* Bristly; set with
sĕt′-ŏff, *n.* A decoration:—counter claim.
sē′tọn (sē′tn), *n.* A rowel:—an issue.
sẹt-tēē′, *n.* A large, long seat with a back.
sĕt′tẹr, *n.* One who sets:—a kind of dog.
sĕt′tĭng, *n.* The apparent fall of the sun, &c.
sĕt′tle, *n.* A seat; a bench with a high back.
sĕt′tle, *ι. a.* To fix; to establish; to determine.
sĕt′tle, *v. n.* To subside; to sink; to take rest.
sĕt′tle-mĕnt, *n.* Act of settling; adjustment:
 —a jointure; subsidence; a place settled.
sĕt′tlẹr, *n.* One who settles in a place.
sĕv′ẹn (sĕv′vn), *a.* Four and three.
sĕv′ẹn-fōld (sĕv′vn-fōld), *a.* Repeated 7 times.
sĕv′ẹn-nĭght (sĕn′nĭt), *n.* A week;—contracted to *sennight.* See SENNIGHT.
sĕv′ẹn-tēēn (sĕv′vn-tēn), *a.* Seven and ten.
sĕv′ẹn-tēēnth, *a.* The ordinal of seventeen.
sĕv′ẹnth (sĕv′vnth), *a.* The ordinal of seven.
sĕv′ẹnth-lў (sĕv′vnth-lẹ), *ad.* In the 7th place.
sĕv′ẹn-tĭ-ẹth, *a.* The ordinal of seventy.
sĕv′ẹn-tў (sĕv′vn-tẹ), *a.* & *n.* Seven times ten.
sĕv′ẹr, *v. a.* To force asunder; to disjoin.
sĕv′ẹr-ạl, *a.* Divers; many; distinct; different.
sĕv′ẹr-ạl-lў, *ad.* Distinctly; separately.
sĕv′ẹr-ạl-tў, *n.* A state of separation.
sĕv′ẹr-ạnce, *n.* Separation; partition. [ful.
sẹ-vēre′, *a.* Sharp; hard; rigid; austere; pain-
sẹ-vēre′lў, *ad.* Painfully; strictly; rigorously.
sẹ-vĕr′ĭ-tў, *n.* Strictness; rigor; austerity.
sew (sō), *v. n.* & *a.* To join with a needle.
sew′ẹr (sō′ẹr), *n.* One who sews.
sewer (sō′ẹr *or* shōr), *n.* A drain for water.
sew′ẹr-aġe (sō′ẹr-aj), *n.* Drainage by sewers.
sĕx, *n.* The distinction of male or female; wo-
sĕx-ăġ′ẹ-nạ-rў, *a.* Threescore. [mankind.
sĕx-ạ-ġĕs′ĭ-mạ, *n.* Second Sunday before Lent.
sĕx-ạ-ġĕs′ĭ-mạl, *a.* Sixtieth; pertaining to 60.
sĕx-ăn′gled, } *a.* Having six angles; hex-
sĕx-ăn′gu-lạr, } angular.

SEX-ĔN′NĬ-AL, *a.* Lasting six years.
SĔX′TAIN (sĕx′tạn), *n.* A stanza of six lines.
SĔX′TĄNT, *n.* The sixth part of a circle:—instrument for measuring angles. [grees apart.
SĔX′TĬLE, *n.* Aspect of two planets sixty de-
SĔX′TǪN, *n.* An under officer of the church.
SĔX′TǪN-SHĬP, *n.* The office of a sexton.
SĔX′TṲ-PLE, *a.* Sixfold; six times told. [sex.
SĔX′Ṳ-AL (sĕk′shṳ-ạl), *a.* Distinguishing the
SHĂB, *v. n.* To play mean tricks. [*Low.*]
SHĂB′BĬ-LY, *ad.* Meanly; despicably; basely.
SHĂB′BĬ-NĔSS, *n.* Meanness; paltriness.
SHĂB′BY, *a.* Mean; paltry; ragged; slovenly.
SHĂC′KLE, *v. a.* To chain; to fetter; to bind.
SHĂC′KLEṢ (shăk′klz), *n. pl.* Fetters; gyves.
SHĂD, *n.* A well-known fish, allied to the her-
SHĂD′DǪCK, *n.* A fruit like an orange. [ring.
SHADE, *n.* An interception of light; obscurity; a screen;.a shelter:—color:—shadow; a ghost.
SHADE, *v. a.* To cover from light or heat.
SHĀ′DĬ-NĔSS, *n.* The state of being shady.
SHĂD′ŌW (shăd′dō), *n.* A faint representation; a shade; a shelter:—a ghost; a spirit. [sent.
SHĂD′OW, *v. a.* To cloud; to darken; to repre-
SHĂD′ǪW-Y (shăd′dǫ-ẹ), *a.* Full of shade; dark.
SHĀ′DY, *a.* Secure from light or heat; cool.
SHĂFT, *n.* An arrow; deep pit; spire; handle.
SHĂG, *n.* Rough, woolly hair:—a kind of cloth;
SHĂG, *v. a.* To make shaggy or rough. [nap.
SHĂG′BÄRK, *n.* A kind of tree and its nut.
SHĂG′GᴇD, *or* SHĂG′GY, *a.* Rugged; hairy; rough with hair or wool. [ged.
SHĂG′GᴇD-NĔSS, *n.* The state of being shag-
SHĄ-GREEN′, *n.* A dried animal skin.
SHĀKE, *v. a.* [*imp. t.* shook; *pp.* shaken.] To agitate; to make to totter; to depress. [ble.
SHĀKE, *v. n.* To be agitated; to totter; to trem-
SHĀKE, *n.* A concussion; a vibratory motion.
SHĀK′ᴇR, *n.* The person or thing that shakes:—one of a religious denomination, called "The United Society."
SHĀK′ĬNG, *n.* A vibratory motion; concussion.
SHĀ′KY, *a.* Having fissures; unsound.
SHALE, *n.* A husk; a pod:—indurated clay.
SHĂLL, *v. auxiliary and defective.* It is used to form the future tense.
SHĄL-LÔÔN′, *n.* A slight woollen stuff.
SHĂL′LǪP, *n.* A large boat with two masts.
SHĄL-LŌT′, *n.* A plant. See ESCHALOT.
SHĂL′LŌW (-lō), *a.* Not deep:—futile; silly.
SHĂL′LŌW (-lō), *n.* A sand; a flat; a shoal.
SHĂL′LŌW (-lō), *v. a.* To make shallow. [ish.
SHĂL′LǪW-BRAINED (shăl′lǫ-brānd), *a.* Fool-
SHĂL′LǪW-NĔSS, *n.* Want of depth or thought.
SHĂLT. The second person singular of *Shall.*
SHĂM, *v. a.* To trick; to cheat; to delude.
SHĂM, *n.* A trick; false pretence; imposture.
SHĂM, *a.* False; counterfeit; fictitious.
SHĂM′BLEṢ, *n. pl.* A flesh-market; a butchery.
SHĂM′BLĬNG, *n.* The act of moving awkwardly.
SHĂM′BLĬNG, *a.* Moving awkwardly. [famy.
SHAME, *n.* Disgrace; ignominy; reproach; in-
SHAME, *v. a.* To make ashamed; to disgrace.
SHĀME′FĀCED (shām′fāst), *a.* Modest; bash-
SHĀME′FÛL, *a.* Disgraceful; ignominious. [ful.
SHĀME′FÛL-LY, *ad.* Disgracefully.
SHĀME′LᴇSS, *a.* Wanting shame; impudent.
SHĀME′LᴇSS-LY, *ad.* Without shame.
SHĀME′LᴇSS-NᴇSS, *n.* Impudence; immodesty.
SHĂM′OIS, SHĂM′MY (shäm′ẹ), *n.* Wash-leather.
SHĂM-PÔÔ′, *v. a.* To rub and press the limbs and muscles after warm bathing, &c. :—to rub
SHĂM′RǪCK, *n.* White clover. [the head.
SHĂNK, *n.* The leg from the knee to the ankle; large bone of the leg; long part of a thing.
SHĂNKED (shăngkt), *a.* Having a shank.[house.
SHĂN′TY, SHĂN′TEE, *n.* A tent, cabin, or mean
SHĀPE, *v. a.* [*imp. t.* shaped; *pp.* shaped *or* shapen.] To form; to mould; to adjust.
SHĀPE, *n.* Form; appearance; make; idea.
SHĀPE′LᴇSS, *a.* Wanting regularity of form.
SHĀPE′LĬ-NᴇSS, *n.* Beauty or proportion of form.
SHĀPE′LY, *a.* Symmetrical; well formed.
SHÄRD, *n.* A fragment of an earthen vessel.
SHÄRE, *v. a.* To divide; to partake with others.
SHÄRE, *v. n.* To have part; to have a dividend.
SHÄRE, *n.* Part; allotment; dividend obtained.
SHÄR′ᴇR, *n.* One who shares; a partaker.
SHÄRK, *n.* A voracious sea-fish; a sharper.
SHÄRK, *v. n. & a.* To cheat; to pick up slyly.
SHÄRP, *a.* Keen; piercing; acute; quick; sour.
SHÄRP, *v. a.* To make keen; to render quick.
SHÄR′PEN (shär′pn), *v. a.* To make sharp; to
SHÄR′PEN (shär′pn), *v. n.* To grow sharp. [edge.
SHÄRP′ᴇR, *n.* A tricking fellow; a cheat.[fully.
SHÄRP′LY, *ad.* Severely; keenly; acutely; pain-
SHÄRP′NᴇSS, *n.* Keenness; severity; ingenuity.
SHÄRP′SĔT, *a.* Hungry; ravenous; eager.
SHÄRP′-SĪGHT-ᴇD (-sī′tẹd), *a.* Seeing quick.
SHÄRP′-WĬT-TᴇD, *a.* Having an acute mind.
SHÄS′TᴇR, *n.* A Hindoo sacred book. [impair.
SHĂT′TᴇR, *v. a. & n.* To break into pieces:—to
SHĂT′TᴇRṢ, *n. pl.* Fragments; pieces.
SHĂT′TᴇR-Y, *a.* Not compact; loose of texture.
SHĀVE, *v. a.* [*imp. t.* shaved; *pp.* shaved *or* shaven.] To pare off; to cut:—to fleece.
SHĀVE′LĬNG, *n.* A man shaved; a friar.
SHĀV′ᴇR, *n.* One who shaves; a sharper.[thing.
SHĀV′ĬNG, *n.* A thin slice pared off from any
SHÂWL, *n.* A part of female dress.
SHÂWM, *or* SHÂLM (shâwm), *n.* A hautboy.
SHĒ, *pron. pers. fem.* The female.
SHEAF, *n.*; pl. SHEAVEṢ. A bundle of grain.
SHEAF (shĕf), *v. n.* To make sheaves.
SHEAR, *v. a.* [*imp. t.* sheared; *pp.* shŏrn *or* sheared.] To clip or cut off with shears.
SHEAR′ᴇR, *n.* One who shears; a reaper.
SHEARṢ, *n. pl.* An instrument with two blades.
SHEATH (shēth), *n.* A case; a scabbard.
SHEATHE, *v. a.* To put into a sheath.
SHEATH′Y (shēth′ẹ), *a.* Forming a sheath.
SHEAVE, *n.* The wheel of a block or pulley.
SHĔD, *v. a.* [*imp. t. & pp.* shed.] To spill; to
SHĔD, *n.* A slight building or covering. [let fall.
SHEEN, *a.* Bright; shiny.—*n.* Brightness.
SHEEP, *n. sing. & pl.* An animal bearing wool.
SHEEP′CŌT, *n.* An enclosure for sheep. [closed.
SHEEP′FŌLD, *n.* A place where sheep are en-
SHEEP′HOOK (shēp′hŭk), *n.* Shepherd's crook.
SHEEP′ĬSH, *a.* Bashful; meanly diffident.
SHEEP′ĬSH-LY, *ad.* With mean diffidence.[ness.
SHEEP′ĬSH-NᴇSS, *n.* Mean diffidence; bashful-
SHEEP′S′-EYE (shēps′ī), *n.* A loving, sly look.
SHEEP′S′-HEAD, *n.* A kind of fish:—a dunce.
SHEEP′SHEAR-ᴇR, *n.* One who shears sheep.
SHEEP′SHEAR-ĬNG, *n.* The shearing of sheep.

SHĒĒP′WÂLK (shēp′wâwk), *n.* A sheep pasture.
SHEER, *a.* Pure; clear; unmingled:—thin.
SHEER, *ad.* Clean; quick; at once.
SHEER, *v. n.* To deviate; to turn aside.
SHEET, *n.* Piece of linen or cotton for a bed:—
　any thing expanded:—rope of a sail. [like.
SHEET, *v. a.* To cover as with a sheet or the
SHEET′-ĂN-ÇHQR, *n.* The largest anchor:—
SHEET′ING, *n.* Cloth for sheets. [chief support.
SHEIK, *n.* A chief of a tribe of Arabs. [coin.
SHĚK′EL (shĕk′kl), *n.* A Jewish weight and
SHĚL′DRĀKE, *n.* A species of wild duck.
SHĔLF, *n.*; *pl.* SHĔLVEŞ. A board fixed against
　a supporter:—a bank or rock in the sea.
SHĔLF′Y, *a.* Full of shelves; shelvy.
SHĔLL, *n.* The hard covering of any thing.
SHĔLL, *v. a. & n.* To strip off or cast the shell.
SHĔLL′FĬSH, *n.* A fish invested with a shell.
SHĔLL′WORK (shĕl′wŭrk), *n.* Work made of
SHĔLL′Y, *a.* Abounding with shells. [shells.
SHĔL′TER, *n.* A cover; a harbor; protection.
SHĔL′TER, *v. a.* To cover; to defend; to pro-
SHĔL′TER-LĔSS, *a.* Destitute of shelter. [tect.
SHĔLVE, *v. n.* To overhang as a shelf; to slope.
SHĔLV′ING, *a.* Sloping; having declivity.
SHĔLV′Y, *a.* Full of shelves; shelfy.
SHE-MĬT′ĬC, *a.* Relating to Shem; semitic.
SHĔP′HERD (-ẹrd), *n.* One who tends sheep.
SHĔP′HERD-ĔSS, *n.* A female shepherd.
SHĔR′BET *or* SHẸR-BĔT′, *n.* A drink of wa-
　ter, raisins, lemons, rose-water, &c.
SHĔRD, *n.* An earthen fragment. See SHARD.
SHĔR′ĬFF, *n.* An executive county officer.
SHĔR′ĬFF-AL-TY, *n.* The office of a sheriff.
SHĔR′RY, SHĔR′RĬS, *n.* A rich, dry wine.
SHEW (shō), *v. a.* [*imp. t.* shewed; *pp.* shewn.]
　To exhibit; to prove; to direct. See SHOW.
SHEWN (shōn), *pp.* from *shew.* See SHOWN.
SHĬB′BQ-LĔTH, *n.* The criterion of a party; test.
SHIELD (shēld), *n.* A buckler:—protection.
SHIELD, *v a.* To defend; to protect; to secure.
SHĬFT, *v. n.* To change; to find means.
SHĬFT, *v. a.* To change; to alter; to transfer.
SHĬFT, *n.* An expedient; last resource:—fraud;
　artifice:—a woman's under garment or linen.
SHĬFT′ER, *n.* One who shifts or changes.
SHĬFT′LĔSS, *a.* Not using means to act or live.
SHĬL′LĬNG, *n.* A silver coin; twelve pence.
SHĪ′LY, *ad.* Not familiarly. See SHYLY.
SHĬN, *n.* The fore part of the leg.
SHINE, *v. n.* [*imp. t. & pp.* shone *or* shined.] To
　glisten; to be bright, gay, or splendid.
SHINE, *n.* Fair weather:—brightness; lustre.
SHĬN′GLE (shĭng′gl), *n.* A thin board to cover
　houses:—*pl.* a disease; a kind of tetter. [gles.
SHĬN′GLE (shĭng′gl), *v. a.* To cover with shin-
SHĪ′NY, *a.* Bright; splendid; luminous. [ship.
SHĬP. A termination, noting office, &c., as, lord-
SHĬP, *n.* A large sea vessel with three masts.
SHĬP, *v. a.* To put into a ship; to transport.
SHĬP′BŌARD, *ad.* On board or in a ship. [ship.
SHĬP′-MĂS-TER, *n.* A master or captain of a
SHĬP′MĀTE, *n.* One who serves in the same ship.
SHĬP′MENT, *n.* Act of shipping; goods shipped.
SHĬP′PĬNG, *n.* Vessels of navigation; a fleet.
SHĬP′WRĔCK (shĭp′rĕk), *n.* The loss of a ship.
SHĬP′WRĔCK (shĭp′rĕk), *v. a.* To destroy, as a
　ship, by dashing on rocks or shallows, &c.

SHĬP′WRĪGHT (shĭp′rīt), *n.* A builder or maker
SHÎRE *or* SHĪRE, *n.* A county. [of ships.
SHĬRK, *v. a. & n.* To procure by mean tricks;
　to shift.—*n.* A sharper; a shark.
SHĬRT, *n.* The under garment of a man.
SHĬRT, *v. a.* To cover; to clothe as in a shirt.
SHĪVE, *n.* A splinter or lamina:—piece.
SHĬV′ER, *v. a. & n.* To break into many parts.
SHĬV′ER, *v. n.* To quake; to tremble; to shud-
SHĬV′ER, *n.* A little piece:—a shaking fit. [der.
SHĬV′ER-ĬNG, *n.* The act of trembling; division.
SHĬV′ER-Y, *a.* Loose of coherence; incompact.
SHŌAL, *n.* A crowd; a shallow; a sandbank.
SHŌAL, *v. n.* To crowd; to throng; to grow shal-
SHŌAL, *a.* Shallow; obstructed by banks. [low.
SHŌAL′Ĭ-NĔSS, *n.* Frequency of shallow places.
SHŌAL′Y, *a.* Full of shoals or shallows.
SHŎCK, *n.* Conflict; concussion; offence; im-
　pression of disgust:—pile of sheaves of grain.
SHŎCK, *v. a.* To shake; to offend; to disgust.
SHŎCK′ĬNG, *a.* That shocks; dreadful. [ly.
SHŎCK′ĬNG-LY, *ad.* So as to disgust; offensive-
SHŎE (shô), *n.* A cover of the foot. [with shoes.
SHŎE (shô), *v. a.* [*imp. t. & pp.* shod.] To furnish
SHŎE′BLĂCK, *n.* One who cleans shoes.
SHŎE′MĀ-KER, *n.* One who makes shoes.
SHŎE′STRĬNG, *n.* A string to tie a shoe with.
SHŌNE *or* SHŎNE, *imp. t. & pp.* from *shine.*
SHOOK (shŭk), *imp. t. & pp.* from *shake.*
SHÔÔT, *v. a.* [*imp. t. & pp.* shot.] To discharge,
　as a gun, &c.; to let off; to strike; to emit.
SHÔÔT, *v. n.* To discharge a gun; to sprout.
SHÔÔT, *n.* A discharge; a young branch.
SHŎP, *n.* A place or a room for sale or for work.
SHŎP, *v. n.* To frequent shops; to purchase.
ṢHŎP′KEĒP-ER, *n.* A trader who sells in a shop.
SHŎP′LĬFT-ER, *n.* One who steals out of a shop.
SHŎP′LĬFT-ĬNG, *n.* The crime of a shoplifter.
SHŌRE, *n.* Coast of the sea:—a prop; a sup-
SHŌRE, *v. a.* To prop; to support. [port.
SHŌRL, *n.* A species of mineral. See SCHORL.
SHŌRN, *pp.* from *shear.* [brittle.
SHŎRT, *a.* Not long; brief; concise; scanty;
SHŎRT′EN (shör′tn), *v. a.* To make short; to lop.
SHŎRT′HĂND, *n.* Short writing; stenography.
SHŎRT′LĪVED (shört′lĭvd), *a.* Not living long.
SHŎRT′LY, *ad.* Quickly; soon; concisely; brief-
SHŎRT′NESS, *n.* The quality of being short. [ly.
SHŎRT′-SĪGHT-ĔD (-sī-tĕd), *a.* Not seeing far.
SHŎRT′-SĪGHT-ĔD-NĔSS, *n.* A defect of sight.
SHŎRT′-WĀIST-ĔD, *a.* Having a short body.
SHŎRT′-WĬND-ĔD, *a.* Short-breathed; asthmatic.
SHŎT, *imp. t. & pp.* from *shoot.* [let:—balls.
SHŎT, *n.* The act of shooting:—a ball or bul-
SHŌTE, *n.* A young hog:—a species of fish.
SHŎT′TEN (shŏt′tn), *a.* Having ejected spawn.
SHOUGH (shŏk), SHŎCK, *n.* A shaggy dog.
SHOUGH (shô), *interj.* Used in driving fowls.
SHOÛLD (shŭd), *v. auxiliary and defective.* Usu-
　ally denoting obligation or duty.
SHŌUL′DER (shōl′dẹr), *n.* The joint which con-
　nects the arm to the body:—a prominence.
SHŌUL′DER, *v. a.* To push; to take or put on
　the shoulder. [shoulder.
SHŌUL′DER-BĔLT, *n.* A belt crossing the
SHŌUL′DER-BLĀDE (shōl′dẹr-blād), *n.* The
　scapula, a bone of the shoulder. [let.
SHŌUL′DER-KNŎT (shōl′dẹr-nŏt), *n.* An epau-

SHŎŪT, n. A loud, vehement cry of triumph, &c.
SHŎŪT, v. n. To cry vehemently ; to exclaim.
SHŎVE (shŭv), v. a. To push ; to rush against.
SHŎVE (shŭv), n. The act of shoving ; a push.
SHŎV'EL (shŭv'vl), n. A tool for digging, &c.
SHŎV'EL (shŭv'vl), v. a. To throw with a shovel.
SHŌW (shō), v. a. [imp. t. showed ; pp. shown.]
To exhibit ; to make known ; to prove ; to
teach ; to direct ;—often written shew.
SHŌW (shō), v. n. To appear ; to look ; to seem.
SHŌW, n. A spectacle ; display ; exhibition.
SHŌW'BRĔAD (shō'brĕd), n. 12 loaves of un-
leavened bread, representing the 12 tribes of
Israel ;—written also shew-bread.
SHŌW'ER (shō'er), n. One who shows. [sion.
SHŎW'ER (shŏů'er), n. A fall of rain :—profu-
SHŎW'ER (shŏů'er), v. a. & n. To pour down.
SHŎW'ER-Y (shŏů'er-e), a. Raining in showers.
SHŌW'I-NĔSS, n. State of being showy.
SHŌWN (shōn), pp. from show. Exhibited. [tious.
SHŌW'Y (shō'e), a. Splendid ; gay ; ostenta-
SHRĂNK, imp. t. from shrink. [Obs.] [small pieces.
SHRĔD, v. a. [imp. t. & pp. shred.] To cut into
SHRĔD, n. A small piece cut off ; a strip.
SHREW (shrŭ), n. A peevish, brawling woman.
SHREWD (shrŭd), a. Sly ; cunning ; discerning.
SHREWD'LY (shrŭd'le), ad. Cunningly ; slyly.
SHREWD'NESS (shrŭd'nes), n. Sly cunning.
SHREW'ISH (shrŭ'ish), a. Froward ; clamorous.
SHREW'MÖŬSE (shrŭ'möůs), n. A small ani-
SHRIĔK (shrēk), v. n. To utter a sharp cry.[mal.
SHRIĔK (shrēk), n. A sharp cry ; a scream.
SHRĬLL, a. Sharp, piercing, tremulous, as sound.
SHRĬLL'NESS, n. The quality of being shrill.
SHRĬMP, n. A small crustacean :—a dwarf.
SHRĪNE, n. A case or box to hold things sacred.
SHRĬNK, v. n. [imp. t. & pp. shrunk.] To con-
tract itself ; to shrivel :—to fall back ; to recoil.
SHRĬNK, n. A corrugation :—a recoiling.
SHRĬV'EL (shrĭv'vl), v. a. & n. To contract or
be contracted into wrinkles ; to wither.
SHRŎŮD, n. Dress of the dead.
SHRŎŮD, v. a. To shelter ; to cover ; to dress.
SHRŎŮDS, n. pl. Large ropes of a ship.
SHRŌVE'TĪDE, SHRŌVE'-TŪES-DAY, n. Day
before Lent, preceding Ash-Wednesday.
SHRŬB, n. A bush :—spirit with acid and sugar.
SHRŬB'BER-Y, n. A plantation of shrubs.
SHRŬB'BY, a. Full of, or like, shrubs ; bushy.
SHRŬG, v. a. & n. To draw up the shoulders, &c.
SHRŬG, n. A contraction of the shoulders.
SHRŬNK, imp. t. & pp. from shrink.
SHRŬNK'EN (shrŭnk'kn), pp. from shrink.
SHŬD'DER, v. n. To quake with fear, &c.
SHŬD'DER, n. A tremor ; state of trembling.
SHŬF'FLE, v. a. & n. To throw into disorder :—
to play mean tricks :—to shove the feet.
SHŬF'FLE, n. The act of shuffling ; a trick.
SHŬF'FLER, n. One who shuffles or plays tricks.
SHŬF'FLING, n. Disorder :—artifice ; trick :—
an irregular gait. [clear of.
SHŬN, v. a. To avoid ; to decline ; to keep
SHŬT, v. a. & n. [imp. t. & pp. shut.] To close ;
to confine ; to bar ; to exclude ; to contract.
SHŬT'TER, n. One that shuts ; a cover ; a door.
SHŬT'TLE, n. An instrument used in weaving.
SHŬT'TLE-CŎCK, n. A cork stuck with feath-
ers, and beaten backward and forward.

SHȲ, a. Reserved ; coy ; cautious ; suspicious.
SHȲ'LY, ad. With shyness ; not familiarly.
SHȲ'NESS, n. Reservedness ; coyness.
SĬB'I-LANT, a. Hissing.—n. A hissing letter.
SĬB-I-LĀ'TION, n. A hissing sound.
SĬB'YL, n. A prophetess among the pagans.
SĬB'YL-LĪNE, a. Of or belonging to a sibyl.
SĬC'CI-TY, n. Dryness ; want of moisture.
SĬCE (sīz), n. The number six at dice.
SĬCK, a. Afflicted with disease ; ill ; disgusted.
SĬCK'EN (sĭk'kn), v. n. & a. To become or make
SĬCK'ISH, a. Somewhat sick ; nauseating. [sick.
SĬC'KLE, n. A hook with which grain is cut.
SĬCK'LI-NĔSS, n. The state of being sickly.
SĬCK'LY, a. Not healthy ; not sound ; weak.
SĬCK'NESS, n. Disease ; illness ; malady ; nausea.
SĪDE, n. The part of an animal fortified by the
ribs ; a part ; margin ; edge ; party ; interest.
SĪDE, a. Lateral ; oblique ; indirect ; long ; large.
SĪDE, v. n. To lean on one side ; to take a party.
SĪDE'BŌARD, n. A piece of furniture.
SĪDE'-BŎX, n. A seat on the side of a theatre.
SĪDE'LŎNG, a. Lateral ; oblique ; not direct.
SĪDE'LŎNG, ad. Laterally ; on the side.
SĬD'ER-AL, SĬ-DĒ'RE-AL, a. Starry ; relating to
SĬD'ER-ĪTE, n. A mineral :—a plant. [the stars.
SĬD-ER-O-GRĂPH'IC, | a. Relating to sider-
SĬD-ER-O-GRĂPH'I-CAL, | ography. [on steel.
SĬD-ER-ŎG'RA-PHY, n. The art of engraving
SĪDE'-SĂD-DLE, n. A woman's riding-saddle.
SĪDES'MAN, n. An assistant to a churchwarden.
SĪDE'WĀYS, SĪDE'WĪSE, ad. On one side.
SĪ'DLE, v. n. To go side foremost :—to saunter.
SIĒGE (sēj), n. Act of besetting a fortified place.
SĬ-ĔS'TA, n. [Sp.] An afternoon's nap.
SIĒVE (sĭv), n. A utensil for sifting.
SĬFT, v. a. To separate by a sieve ; to examine.
SĪGH (sī), v. n. To emit the breath audibly.
SĪGH (sī), n. A violent emission of the breath.
SĪGHT (sīt), n. The sense of seeing ; a show.
SĪGHT'LESS (sīt'les), a. Wanting sight ; blind.
SĪGHT'LI-NĔSS (sīt'le-nĕs), n. Comeliness. [ly.
SĪGHT'LY (sīt'le), a. Pleasing to the eye ; come-
SĪGN (sīn), n. A token ; an indication ; a mark :
—a miracle :—30 degrees in the zodiac.
SĪGN (sīn), v. a. To mark ; to show ; to ratify.
SĬG'NAL, n. A sign that gives notice ; a mark.
SĬG'NAL, a. Eminent ; memorable ; remarkable.
SĬG'NAL-ĪZE, v. a. To make remarkable.
SĬG'NAL-LY, ad. Remarkably ; memorably.
SĬG'NA-TŪRE, n. A sign :—a figure or
letter :—name of a person written.
SĪGN'ER (sīn'er), n. One that signs.
SĬG'NET, n. A seal ; particularly a king's seal.
SIG-NĬF'I-CANCE, | n. Power of signifying ;
SIG-NĬF'I-CAN-CY, | meaning ; force ; energy.
SIG-NĬF'I-CANT, a. Expressive ; important.
SIG-NĬF'I-CANT-LY, ad. With significance.
SĬG-NI-FI-CĀ'TION, n. Art of signifying ; ex-
pression :—meaning ; import ; sense.
SIG-NĬF'I-CA-TĪVE, a. Strongly expressive.
SĬG'NI-FY, v. a. To declare ; to mean ; to import.
SĬG'NI-FY, v. n. To express meaning with force.
SĪGN'IOR (sēn'yur), n. A title. See SEIGNIOR.
SĪGN'-MĂN'U-AL (sīn'-), n. The signature of a
king, written with his own hand. [hangs.
SĪGN'POST (sīn'-), n. A post on which a sign
SĪ'LENCE, n. Taciturnity ; secrecy ; stillness.

SĪ'LENCE, *interj.* Commanding silence.
SĪ'LENCE, *v. a.* To forbid to speak :—to still.
SĪ'LENT, *a.* Not speaking ; mute ; still ; quiet.
SĪ'LENT-LY, *ad.* Without speech or noise.
SĪ'LENT-NĔSS, *n.* State of being silent.
SĪ'LEX, *n.* Pure quartz or flint ; silica.
SĬL'I-CA, *n.* An earth of silex or flint.
SI-LĬ''CIOŲS (se-lĭsh'ŭs), *a.* Relating to silica.
SĬL-I-QUŌSE', SĬL'I-QUOŬS, *a.* Having a pod.
SĬLK, *n.* A fine, soft thread spun by silk-worms ;
stuff made of the thread :—style of maize.
SĬLK'EN (sĭlk'kn), *a.* Made of silk ; soft.
SĬLK'I-NĔSS, *n.* Softness ; smoothness.
SĬLK'-MĔR-CER, *n.* A dealer in silk.
SĬLK'-WĒAV-ER, *n.* One who weaves silk.
SĬLK'-WORM (-wŭrm), *n.* A worm that spins
SĬLK'Y, *a.* Made of silk :—soft ; tender. [silk.
SĬLL, *n.* A bottom piece of timber. [cider, &c.
SĬL'LA-BŬB, *n.* A liquor made of milk, wine,
SĬL'LI-NĔSS, *n.* Weakness ; harmless folly.
SĬL'LY, *a.* Stupid ; weak ; foolish ; witless.
SĬL'VAN, *a.* Woody ; full of woods. See SYL-
SĬL'VER, *n.* A white, hard metal :—money.[VAN.
SĬL'VER, *a.* Made of, or like, silver ; white ;
SĬL'VER, *v. a.* To cover with silver. [soft.
SĬL'VER-SMĬTH, *n.* One that works in silver.
SĬL'VER-Y, *a.* Besprinkled with, or like, silver.
SI-MÄR', *n.* A kind of long gown or robe.
SĬM'I-LAR, *a.* Having resemblance ; like.
SĬM-I-LĂR'I-TY, *n.* Likeness ; resemblance.
SĬM'I-LAR-LY, *ad.* With resemblance.
SĬM'I-LĔ, *n.* A comparison for illustration.
SI-MĬL'I-TŪDE, *n.* Resemblance ; comparison.
SĬM'MER, *v. n.* To boil gently with a hissing.
SI-MŌ'NI-ĂC, *n.* One who practises simony.
SĬM-O-NĪ'A-CAL, *a.* Relating to simony.
SĬM'O-NY, *n.* The crime of buying or selling
church preferment. [wind in Africa, &c.
SI-MŌÔM', *or* SI-MŌÔN', *n.* A hot, suffocating
SĬM'PER, *v. n.* To smile ; to smile foolishly.
SĬM'PER, *n.* A smile ; a foolish smile.
SĬM'PLE, *a.* Plain ; artless ; unmingled :—silly.
SĬM'PLE, *n.* Something unmixed :—plant.
SĬM'PLE-NĔSS, *n.* The quality of being simple.
SĬM'PLE-TON, *n.* A silly person ; a trifler.
SĬM-PLĬÇ'I-TY, *n.* State of being simple ; plain-
ness ; artlessness :—folly.
SĬM-PLI-FI-CĀ'TION, *n.* The act of simplifying.
SĬM'PLI-FY, *v. a.* To render simple or plain.
SĬM'PLIST, *n.* One skilled in simples or plants.
SĬM'PLY, *ad.* Plainly ; artlessly ; merely ; fool-
ishly.
SĬM'U-LĀTE, *v. a.* To feign ; to counterfeit.
SĬM-U-LĀ'TION, *n.* A dissembling ; a feigning.
SI-MŬL-TĀ'NE-OŬS, *a.* Acting or existing to-
gether or at the same time.
SI-MŬL-TĀ'NE-OŬS-LY, *ad.* At the same time.
SĬN, *n.* A violation of the laws of God ; iniqui-
SĬN, *v. n.* To violate the laws of God. [ty.
SĬN'A-PĬSM, *n.* A poultice of mustard-seed, &c.
SĬNCE, *conj.* Because that ; from the time that.
SĬNCE, *ad.* Ago ; before this :—from that time.
SĬNCE, *prep.* After ; from some time past.
SIN-CĒRE', *a.* Honest ; not feigned ; real ; pure.
SIN-CĒRE'LY, *ad.* Honestly ; without hypocrisy.
SIN-CĒRE'NESS, } *n.* Quality of being sincere ;
SIN-CĔR'I-TY,   }   candor ; honesty ; purity.
SĪNE, *n.* A sort of trigonometrical line.

SĪ'NE-CŪRE, *n.* An office without employment.
SĪ'NE-CŪ-RIST, *n.* One who holds a sinecure.
SĬN'EW (sĭn'nų), *n.* A tendon ; muscle ; nerve.
SĬN'EWED (sĭn'nūd), *a.* Having sinews ; firm.
SĬN'EW-LĔSS (sĭn'nų-lĕs), *a.* Having no sinews.
SĬN'EW-Y (sĭn'nų-e), *a.* Strong ; nervous.
SĬN'FŪL, *a.* Partaking of sin ; unholy ; iniqui-
tous ; impious ; wicked. [ly.
SĬN'FŪL-LY, *ad.* In a sinful manner ; wicked-
SĬN'FŪL-NĔSS, *n.* Iniquity ; wickedness.
SĬNG, *v. n.* [*imp. t.* sung *or* sang ; *pp.* sung.] To
form the voice to melody ; to carol. [brate.
SĬNG, *v. a.* To relate in poetry or song ; to cele-
SĬNĢE, *v. a.* To scorch ; to burn slightly.
SĬNG'ER, *n.* One who is skilled in singing.
SĬNG'ING, *n.* Art of one who sings ; the utter-
ance of melodious sounds. [sing.
SĬNG'ING-MĂS-TER, *n.* One who teaches to
SĬN'GLE (sĭng'gl), *a.* One ; not double :—par-
ticular ; individual ; pure :—unmarried.
SĬN'GLE, *v. a.* To select ; to choose from.
SĬN'GLE-NĔSS, *n.* Not duplicity ; sincerity.
SĬN'GLY, *ad.* Individually ; only ; by himself.
SĬNG'SŎNG, *n.* Bad singing ; bad intonation.
SĬN'GU-LAR (sĭng'gu-lar), *a.* Single ; only one ;
not plural ; particular ; rare ; unusual ; odd.
SĬN-GU-LĂR'I-TY, *n.* Peculiarity ; a curiosity.
SĬN'GU-LAR-LY, *ad.* Particularly ; strangely.
SĬN'IS-TER, *a.* Left ; corrupt ; unfair ; unlucky.
SĬN'IS-TROŬS, *a.* Perverse ; absurd ; wrong.
SĬNK, *v. n.* [*imp. t.* sunk *or* sank ; *pp.* sunk.] To
fall gradually ; not to swim ; to decline.
SĬNK, *v. a.* To immerse ; to delve ; to depress.
SĬNK, *n.* A drain :—a jakes ; a place of filth.
SĬNK'ING-FŬND, *n.* A fund to reduce a debt.
SĬN'LESS, *a.* Exempt from sin ; innocent.
SĬN'LESS-NĔSS, *n.* Exemption from sin.
SĬN'NER, *n.* One who sins or is irreligious.
SĬN'-ŎF-FER-ĬNG, *n.* A sacrifice for sin.
SĬN'O-PER, SĬN'O-PLE, *n.* A species of quartz.
SĬN'U-ĀTE (sĭn'yų-āt), *v. a.* To bend in and
SĬN-U-Ā'TION, *n.* A bending in and out. [out.
SĬN-U-ŎS'I-TY, *n.* The quality of being sinuous.
SĬN'U-OŬS, *a.* Bending in and out ; winding.
SĬP, *v. a. & n.* To drink by small draughts.
SĬP, *n.* A small draught with the lips. [liquid.
SĪ'PHON, *n.* A bent tube for decanting a
SĬP'PET, *n.* A small sop ; a sip.
SĬR, *n.* A word of respect ; a title of a knight.
SĪRE, *n.* A father ; a word of respect to a king.
SĪ'REN, *n.* A goddess or a sea-monster.
SĪ'REN, *a.* Alluring ; bewitching like a siren.
SI-RĪ'A-SĬS, *n.* (*Med.*) A stroke of the sun.
SĬR'I-ŬS, *n.* [L.] A bright star ; the dogstar.
SĬR'LOĬN, SŬR'LOĬN, *n.* The loin of beef.
SI-RŎC'CŌ, *n.* [It.] A periodical, relaxing south
wind in the south of Italy, Sicily, &c.
SĬR'RAH (săr'ra *or* sĬr'ra), *interj.* A term of re-
proach or insult.
SĬR'UP (sĬr'rup *or* sŭr'rup), *n.* Vegetable juice
boiled with sugar. [ents.
SĬS'TER, *n.* A woman born of the same par-
SĬS'TER-HOOD (-hŭd), *n.* A society of women.
SĬS'TER-IN-LÂW, *n.* A sister by marriage. [ter.
SĬS'TER-LY, *a.* Like a sister ; becoming a sis-
SĬT, *v. n.* [*imp. t. & pp.* sat.] To repose on a
seat :—to hold a session :—to incubate.
SĪTE, *n.* Situation ; local position ; locality.

SĪTHE, *n.* A scythe. See SCYTHE.
SĬT'TĬNG, *n.* Act of one that sits :—a session.
SĬT'Ŭ-ĀTE, SĬT'Ŭ-ĀT-ĘD, *p. a.* Placed ; seated.
SĬT-Ŭ-Ā'TIǪN, *n.* A position ; condition ; state.
SĬX, *a. & n.* Twice three ; one more than five.
SĬX'FŌLD, *a.* Six times told or repeated.
SĬX'PĘNCE, *n.* An English coin ; half a shilling.
SĬX'PĘN-NY, *a.* Worth or costing sixpence.
SĬX'TĒEN (sĭks'tĕn), *a.* Six and ten ; twice
SĬX'TĒENTH, *a.* The ordinal of sixteen. [eight.
SĬXTH, *a.* Next after the fifth.—*n.* A sixth part.
SĬXTH'LY, *ad.* In the sixth place.
SĬX'TĬ-ĘTH, *a.* The tenth six times repeated ;
 ordinal of sixty.
SĬX'TY, *a. & n.* Six times ten.   [large.
SĪZ'Ą-BLE, *a.* Of considerable or proper bulk ;
SĪ'ZĄR, *n.* A student of a low rank ; a servitor.
SĪZE, *n.* Bulk ; bigness :—a kind of glue.
SĪZE, *v. a.* To adjust :—to cover with size.
SĪ'ZĬ-NĔSS, *n.* Glutinousness ; viscosity.
SĪ'ZY, *a.* Viscous ; glutinous.
SKĀTE, *n.* An iron to slide with on ice :—a fish.
SKĀTE, *v. n.* To slide with skates on ice.
SKEIN (skān), *n.* A knot of thread, yarn, &c.
SKĔL'Ę-TǪN, *n.* The bones of the body in their
 natural situation :—sketch ; outline. [del.
SKĔP'TĬC, *or* SÇĔP'TĬC, *n.* A doubter ; an infi-
SKĔP'TĬ-CĄL, *a.* Doubting ; not believing ; scep-
 tical. See SCEPTICAL.   [cism.
SKĔP'TĬ-CĬSM, *n.* Doubt ; infidelity ; scepti-
SKĔTCH, *v. a.* To trace the outlines of ; to plan.
SKĔTCH, *n.* An outline ; a rough draught ; plan.
SKEW'ĘR, *n.* A wooden or iron pin for meat.
SKEW'ĘR, *v. a.* To fasten with skewers.
SKĬD, *n.* A piece of timber ; a slider.
SKIFF, *n.* A small, light boat ; a wherry.
SKĬL'FŬL, *a.* Knowing ; well versed ; able.
SKĬL'FŬL-LY, *ad.* With skill or dexterity.
SKĬL'FŬL-NĔSS, *n.* Art ; ability ; dexterity.
SKĬLL, *n.* Knowledge ; experience ; dexterity.
SKĬLLED (skĭld), *a.* Knowing ; versed.
SKĬL'LĘT, *n.* A small kettle or boiler.
SKĬM, *v. a.* To clear off :—to brush slightly.
SKĬM, *v. n.* To pass lightly ; to glide along.
SKĬM'MĘR, *n.* A shallow vessel ; one who skims.
SKĬM'-MĬLK, *n.* Milk deprived of the cream.
SKĬN, *n.* The natural covering of the flesh.
SKĬN, *v. a.* To flay ; to cover.—*v. n.* To become
SKĬN'FLĬNT, *n.* A miser. [skinned over.
SKĬN'NĘR, *n.* A dealer in skins or peltry.
SKĬN'NY, *a.* Consisting of skin ; wanting flesh.
SKĬP, *v. n.* To pass by quick leaps.—*v. a.* To
SKĬP, *n.* A light leap or bound ; a spring. [miss.
SKĬP'-JĂCK, *n.* An upstart :—a child's toy.
SKĬP'-KĔN-NĘL, *n.* A lackey ; a footboy.
SKĬP'PĘR, *n.* One that skips :—a ship-master.
SKĬR'MĬSH, *n.* A slight fight in war ; a contest.
SKĬR'MĬSH, *v. n.* To fight loosely or in parties.
SKĬR'MĬSH-ĘR, *n.* One who skirmishes.
SKĬRT, *n.* A loose edge ; a margin ; a border.
SKĬRT, *v. a.* To border ; to run along the edge.
SKĬT, *n.* A wanton wench :—a gibe ; a jeer.
SKĬT'TĬSH, *a.* Shy ; easily frighted .—fickle.
SKĬT'TĬSH-LY, *ad.* Shyly ; wantonly ; fickly.
SKĬT'TĬSH-NĔSS, *n.* Shyness ; fickleness.
SKĬT'TLEŞ (skĭt'tlz), *n. pl.* Ninepins.
SKĪ'VĘR, *n.* A split sheepskin.
SKŬLK, *v. n.* To hide ; to lurk in fear or malice.

SKŬLL, *n.* The cranium ; the brain-pan.
SKŬLL'-CĂP, *n.* A head-piece :—a plant.
SKŬNK, *n.* A fetid animal. [firmament.
SKY, *n.* The heavens ; the aerial region ; the
SKY'-CŎL-ǪR, *n.* The color of the sky , azure.
SKY'-CŎL-ǪRED (skī'kŭl-ųrd), *a.* Blue ; azure.
SKY'EY (skī'ę), *a.* Ethereal ; like the sky.
SKY'LĂRK, *n.* A lark that mounts and sings.
SKY'LĬGHT (skī'līt), *n.* A window in a roof.
SKY'-RŎCK-ĘT, *n.* A kind of rising firework.
SLĂB, *n.* A plane of stone :—an outside plank.
SLĂB'BĘR, *v. a.* To smear with spittle.
SLĂB'BĘR, *v. n.* To drivel ; to slaver.
SLĂB'BY, *a.* Thick ; viscous ; wet ; floody.
SLĂCK, *a.* Not tense ; loose ; remiss , not diligent.
SLĂCK, *v. a. & n.* To loosen ; to relax ; to flag.
SLĂCK, *n.* Coal broken in small pieces.
SLĂCK'EN (slăk'kn), *v. a. & n.* To slack ; to
 relax ; to abate ; to flag ; to be loosened.
SLĂCK'LY, *ad.* Loosely ; negligently ; remissly.
SLĂCK'NĘSS, *n.* Looseness ; remissness.
SLĂG, *n.* The dross or recrement of metal.
SLĀIN (slān), *pp.* from *slay.*   [lay.
SLĀKE, *v. a.* To quench ; to extinguish ; to al-
SLĂM, *v. a.* To shut hard ; to crush.—*n.* A bang.
SLĂN'DĘR, *v. a.* To censure falsely ; to defame.
SLĂN'DĘR, *n.* Defamation ; reproach ; ill name.
SLĂN'DĘR-ĘR, *n.* One who slanders. [ous.
SLĂN'DĘR-OŬS, *a.* Falsely abusive ; calumni-
SLĂN'DĘR-OŬS-LY, *ad.* With false reproach.
SLĂNG, *n.* Low, vulgar language ; ribaldry.
SLĂNG, *imp. t.* from *sling.* [*Obsolete.*]
SLĂNT, SLĂNT'ĬNG, *a.* Oblique ; sloping.
SLĂNT, *v. a.* To turn aslant or aside ; to slope.
SLĂP, *n.* A blow, as with the hand open.
SLĂP, *ad.* With a sudden and violent blow.
SLĂP, *v. a.* To strike with the open hand.
SLĂP'DĂSH, *ad.* All at once ; with hurry.
SLĂSH, *v. a. & n.* To cut long cuts ; to lash.
SLĂSH, *n.* A cut ; a wound ; a cut in cloth.
SLĂT, *n.* A narrow piece of timber ; sloat.
SLĀTE, *n.* A kind of stone ; a thin plate of slate.
SLĀTE, *v. a.* To cover with slate, as a roof.
SLĂT'TĘRN, *n.* A negligent, careless woman.
SLĂT'TĘRN-LY, *a.* Not clean ; slovenly.
SLĀ'TY, *a.* Having the nature of slate. [ery.
SLĂUGH'TĘR (slâw'tęr), *n.* Destruction ; butch-
SLĂUGH'TĘR (slâw'tęr), *v. a.* To slay ; to kill.
SLĂUGH'TĘR-HÖÜSE, *n.* A house for killing
 or butchering beasts.
SLĂUGH'TĘR-OŬS (slâw'tęr-ŭs), *a.* Destructive.
SLĀVE, *n.* One deprived of freedom ; a drudge.
SLĀVE, *v. n.* To drudge ; to moil ; to toil.
SLĂV'ĘR, *n.* A slave-ship.   [drivel.
SLĂV'ĘR, *n.* Spittle running from the mouth ;
SLĂV'ĘR, *v. n. & a.* To emit spittle ; to slabber.
SLĂV'ĘR-ĘR, *n.* A driveller ; an idiot.
SLĂV'ĘR-Y, *n.* Servitude ; the state of a slave.
SLĀVE'-TRĀDE, *n.* The traffic in slaves.
SLĂV'ĬSH, *a.* Servile ; mean ; base ; dependent.
SLĂV'ĬSH-LY, *ad.* Servilely ; meanly ; basely.
SLĂV'ĬSH-NĔSS, *n.* Servility ; meanness.
SLĄ-VŎN'ĬC, *a.* Relating to Slavonia.
SLĀY (slā), *v. a.* [*imp. t.* slew ; *pp.* slain.] To
 kill ; to destroy ; to butcher ; to slaughter.
SLĀY'ĘR (slā'ęr), *n.* A killer ; a destroyer.
SLĒAVE, *n.* Raw, untwisted silk.
SLĔD, *n.* A carriage drawn on runners.

SLĔDĢE, *n.* A large, heavy hammer :—a sled.
SLĒĒK, *a.* Smooth ; glossy ; not rough.
SLĒĒK, *v. a.* To render sleek, smooth, or glos-
SLĒĒK′LY, *ad.* Smoothly ; glossily. [sy.
SLĒĒK′NĘSS, *n.* Smoothness ; glossiness.
SLĒĒP, *v. n.* [*imp. t. & pp.* slept.] To take rest ;
 to slumber ; to nap ; to repose.
SLĒĒP, *n.* Repose ; rest ; slumber. [ber.
SLĒĒP′ĘR, *n.* One who sleeps :—a bottom tim-
SLĒĒP′Ĳ-LY, *ad.* Drowsily ; lazily ; stupidly.
SLĒĒP′Ĳ-NĔSS, *n.* Drowsiness ; desire to sleep.
SLĒĒP′LĘSS, *a.* Wanting sleep ; always awake.
SLĒĒP′LĘSS-NĔSS, *n.* State of being sleepless.
SLĒĒP′-WÂLK′ĘR, *n.* A somnambulist.
SLĒĒP′Y, *a.* Drowsy ; disposed to sleep ; dull.
SLĒĒT, *n.* Rain mixed with hail or snow.
SLĒĒT, *v. n.* To snow with a mixture of rain.
SLĒĒT′Y, *a.* Bringing, or consisting of, sleet.
SLĒĒVE, *n.* The dress that covers the arm.
SLĒĒVE′LĘSS, *a.* Having no sleeves.
SLEID (slād), *v. a.* To prepare for the sley.
SLEIGH (slā), *n.* A vehicle drawn on runners.
SLEIGH′ĲNG (slā′ĳng), *n.* The act of travelling
 or riding in a sleigh.
SLEĪGHT (slīt), *n.* Art ; trick ; dexterity.
SLĔN′DĘR, *a.* Thin ; not bulky ; slight ; weak.
SLĔN′DĘR-LY, *ad.* Without bulk ; slightly.
SLĔN′DĘR-NĔSS, *n.* Quality of being slender :
SLĔPT, *imp. t. & pp.* from *sleep.* [—littleness.
SLEW̄ (slū), *imp. t.* from *slay.*
SLEY (slā), *n.* A weaver's reed. [weavers.
SLEY (slā), *v. n.* To part or twist ; to sleid, as
SLĪCE, *v. a.* To cut into thin pieces ; to divide.
SLĪCE, *n.* A thin, broad piece cut off :—a fire-
SLĬD, *imp. t. & pp.* from *slide.* [shovel.
SLĬD′DEN (slĭd′dn), *pp.* from *slide.*
SLĪDE, *v. n. & a.* [*imp. t.* slid ; *pp.* slidden *or*
 slid.] To pass along smoothly ; to slip, glide.
SLĪDE, *n.* A smooth passage ; flow ; even course.
SLĪD′ĘR, *n.* One who, or that which, slides.
SLĪGHT (slīt), *a.* Small ; worthless ; weak.
SLĪGHT (slīt), *n.* Neglect ; contempt ; scorn.
SLĪGHT (slīt), *v. a.* To neglect ; to disregard.
SLĪGHT′LY (slīt′lę), *ad.* Without regard ; weakly.
SLĪGHT′NĘSS (slīt′nęs), *n.* Weakness ; neglect.
SLĪ′LY, *ad.* Cunningly ; with art. See SLYLY.
SLĬM, *a.* Weak ; slight ; slender ; thin of shape.
SLĪME, *n.* A viscous mire ; glutinous substance.
SLĪ′MĲ-NĔSS, *n.* Viscosity ; glutinous matter.
SLĬM′NĘSS, *n.* State or quality of being slim.
SLĬM′Y, *a.* Overspread with slime ; glutinous.
SLING, *n.* A missive weapon for throwing
 stones :—a throw ; a stroke.
SLING, *v. a.* To throw by a sling ; to cast.
SLING′ĘR, *n.* One who slings, or uses the sling.
SLĬNK, *v. n.* [*imp. t. & pp.* slunk.] To sneak ;
 to steal away.—*v. a.* To miscarry, as a mare.
SLĬP, *v. n.* To slide ; to glide ; to escape.
SLĬP, *v. a.* To convey secretly :—to let loose.
SLĬP, *n.* Act of slipping ; a slide ; a false step ;
 a mistake :—a twig :—an escape. [tied.
SLĬP′KNŎT, *n.* A bowknot ; a knot easily un-
SLĬP′PĘR, *n.* A light, loose shoe. [uncertainty.
SLĬP′PĘR-Ĳ-NĔSS, *n.* Smoothness, as of ice :—
SLĬP′PĘR-Y, *a.* Glib ; hard to hold ; uncertain.
SLĬP′SHŎD, *a.* Having the shoes not pulled up.
SLĬT, *v. a.* [*imp. t. & pp.* slit *or* slitted.] To cut
 lengthwise ; to divide by cutting ; to sunder.

SLĬT, *n.* A long cut or narrow opening.
SLĬT′TĲNG-MĬLL, *n.* A mill where iron plates
 or bars are cut into narrow rods.
SLĪVE, SLĪ′VĘR, *v. a.* To split ; to tear off.
SLĪ′VĘR *or* SLĬV′ĘR, *n.* A piece cut or torn off.
SLŎAT, *n.* A narrow piece of timber , a slat.
SLŎB′BĘR, *v. a.* To spill upon ; to slabber.
SLOE (slō), *n.* A thorny shrub, and its fruit.
SLŌŌP, *n.* A small vessel with one mast.
SLŎP, *v. a.* To drink hastily ; to dash with water.
SLŎP, *n.* Mean liquor ; liquid spilt.—*pl.* Ready-
 made clothing.
SLŌPE, *a.* Oblique ; not perpendicular.
SLŌPE, *n.* An oblique direction ; a declivity.
SLŌPE, *v. a.* To form to obliquity or declivity.
SLŌPE, *v. n.* To take an oblique direction.
SLŌPE′NĘSS, *n.* Obliquity ; declivity ; descent.
SLŌPE′WĪSE, *ad.* Obliquely ; not perpendicu-
SLŎP′PY, *a.* Miry and wet ; splashy. [larly.
SLŎP′SHŎP, *n.* A shop for ready-made clothes.
SLŎT, *n.* Track of a deer :—slit in a machine.
SLŌTH, *n.* Laziness :—an animal.
SLŌTH′FÛL, *a.* Idle ; lazy ; sluggish ; indolent.
SLŌTH′FÛL-LY, *ad.* Idly ; lazily ; with sloth.
SLŌTH′FÛL-NĔSS, *n.* Laziness ; sluggishness.
SLŎÛCH, *n.* A clown :—clownish gait or manner.
SLŎÛCH, *v. n.* To have a clownish manner.
SLOŬGH (slŭf), *n.* The cast skin of a serpent.
SLOŬGH (slŭf), *v. n.* To separate and come off.
SLOŬGH (slöŭ), *n.* A deep, miry place ; morass.
SLOŬGH′Y (slöŭ′e), *a.* Miry ; boggy ; muddy.
SLŎV′ĘN, *n.* One carelessly or dirtily dressed.
SLŎV′ĘN-LĲ-NĔSS, *n.* Negligence of dress, &c.
SLŎV′ĘN-LY, *a.* Indecently negligent of dress.
SLŌW (slō), *a.* Not swift ; late ; dull ; tardy.
SLŌW′LY (slō′lę), *ad.* Not swiftly ; not rashly.
SLŌW′NĘSS, *n.* Want of velocity ; delay.
SLŌW′-WORM (slō′würm), *n.* The blind worm.
SLŬB′BĘR, *v. a.* To stain ; to slobber ; to slaver ;
 to smear :—to do coarsely.
SLŬDĢE, *n.* Mire ; dirt mixed with water.
SLŪE (slū), *v. a.* To turn about its axis ; to turn.
SLŬG, *n.* A drone :—a hinderance :—a snail.
SLŬG′GĄRD, *n.* An idler ; an inactive, lazy,
 idle drone ; a lounger.
SLŬG′ĢĮSH, *a.* Dull ; lazy ; slothful ; idle ; slow.
SLŬG′ĢĮSH-LY, *ad.* Dully ; lazily ; idly ; slowly.
SLŬG′ĢĮSH-NĔSS, *n.* Dulness ; sloth ; laziness.
SLŪICE (slūs), *n.* A watergate ; a floodgate.
SLŪI′CY (slū′sę), *a.* Pouring as from a sluice.
SLŬM′BĘR, *v. n.* To sleep ; to repose ; to doze.
SLŬM′BĘR, *n.* Light sleep ; sleep ; repose.
SLŬM′BĘR-OŬS, SLŬM′BĘR-Y, *a.* Sleepy ; dozy.
SLŬMP, *v. n.* To sink in treading through snow,
SLŬNG, *imp. t. & pp.* from *sling.* [ice, &c.
SLŬNK, *imp. t. & pp.* from *slink.* [revile.
SLŬR, *v. a.* To sully ; to soil ; to reproach ; to
SLŬR, *n.* A slight reproach ; a trick :—a mark
 in music. [soft mud ; slosh.
SLŬSH, *n.* Snow in a state of liquefaction ;
SLŬT, *n.* A dirty woman.
SLŬT′TĘR-Y, *n.* The practice of a slut.
SLŬT′TĮSH, *a.* Nasty ; not nice ; not cleanly.
SLŬT′TĮSH-NĔSS, *n.* Nastiness ; dirtiness.
SLY, *a.* Meanly artful ; insidious ; cunning.
SLY′LY, *ad.* With secret artifice ; insidiously.
SLY′NĘSS, *n.* Artful secrecy ; art ; cunning.
SMACK, *v. n. & a.* To kiss :—to have a taste.

SMÁCK, *n.* Taste; savor; tincture:—a loud kiss :—a small sailing-vessel.
SMÂLL, *a.* Little; not great; slender; minute.
SMÂLL, *n.* The small or narrow part of any
SMÂLL'-BĒĒR, *n.* Beer of little strength.[thing.
SMÂLL'-CRĂFT, *n.* A vessel or vessels smaller than ships or brigs.
SMÂLL'NĘSS, *n.* Littleness; want of greatness.
SMÂLL-PŎX', *n.* An eruptive, malignant dis-
SMÂLT, *n.* A beautiful blue substance. [temper.
SMĄ-RĂG'DĮNE, *a.* Made of, or like, emerald.
SMĄRT, *n.* A quick, pungent, lively pain.
SMĄRT, *v. n.* To feel quick, lively pain.
SMĄRT, *a.* Pungent; sharp; quick; brisk; expert.
SMĄRT'LY, *ad.* Sharply; briskly; vigorously.
SMĄRT'NĘSS, *n.* Quickness; vigor; briskness.
SMĂSH, *v. a.* To break or dash in pieces.[rantly.
SMĂT'TĘR, *v. n.* To talk superficially or igno-
SMĂT'TĘR, *n.* Superficial or slight knowledge.
SMĂT'TĘR-ĘR, *n.* One who has a slight knowl-
SMĂT'TĘR-ĬNG, *n.* Superficial knowledge.[edge.
SMĒAR, *v. a.* To besmear; to soil; to daub.
SMĒAR, *n.* An ointment or any fat substance.
SMĒAR'Y, *a.* Dauby; adhesive.
SMĔLL, *v. a.* [*imp. t. & pp.* smelt.] To perceive by the nose. [smack.
SMĔLL, *v. n.* To perceive or emit smell; to
SMĔLL, *n.* The sense or power of smelling or perceiving by the nose :—scent; odor.
SMĔLT, *imp. t. & pp.* from *smell.* [food.
SMĔLT, *n.* A small fish much esteemed for
SMĔLT, *v. a.* To extract metal from, as from
SMĔLT'ĘR, *n.* One who melts ore. [ores.
SMĒRK, *v. n.* To smile pertly. See SMIRK.
SMĒRK, SMĒRK'Y, *a.* Nice; smart; janty.
SMĬCK'ĘR, *v. n.* To smirk; to look amorously.
SMĪLE, *v. n.* To express pleasure by the countenance :—to look gay :—to be propitious.
SMĪLE, *n.* A look of pleasure or kindness.
SMĪL'ĬNG-LY, *ad.* With a look of pleasure.
SMĬRCH, *v. a.* To cloud; to dusk; to soil.
SMĬRK, *v. n.* To smile affectedly; to smicker.
SMĪTE, *v. a.* [*imp. t.* smote; *pp.* smitten.] To strike; to kill; to destroy; to afflict; to blast.
SMĪTE, *v. n.* To strike; to collide. [man.
SMĬTH, *n.* One who works in metals :—a work-
SMĬTH'ĘR-Y, *n.* The shop, or work, of a smith.
SMĬTH'Y, *n.* The shop of a smith; smithery.
SMĬT'TEN (smĭt'tn), *pp.* from *smite.* Struck.
SMĬT'TLE, *v. a.* To infect.—*a.* Infectious.
SMŎCK, *n.* A woman's under garment; a shift.
SMŎCK'FRŎCK, *n.* A gabardine; a coarse frock.
SMŌKE, *n.* Sooty exhalation; sooty vapor.
SMŌKE, *v. n.* To emit smoke :—to use tobacco.
SMŌKE, *v. a.* To scent or dry by smoke :—to
SMŌK'ĘR, *n.* One that smokes. [find out.
SMŌK'Y, *a.* Emitting smoke; fumid :—obscure.
SMŌŌTH, *a.* Even; glossy; soft; bland; mild.
SMŌŌTH, *v. a.* To level; to make easy; to soften.
SMŌŌTH'LY, *ad.* Not roughly; evenly; mildly.
SMŌŌTH'NĘSS, *n.* Evenness of surface; softness.
SMŌTE, *imp. t.* from *smite.* [suppress.
SMŎTH'ĘR, *v. a.* To suffocate; to stifle; to
SMŎTH'ĘR, *v. n.* To be suffocated; to smoke.
SMŎTH'ĘR, *n.* Suppression; smoke; thick dust.
SMŌUL'DĘR-ĬNG,   ⎱ *a.* Burning and smok-
SMŌUL'DRY (smōl'drẹ), ⎰ ing without vent.
SMŬG, *a.* Nice; spruce; dressed with niceness.

SMŬG'GLE, *v. a.* To import or export secretly or without paying the duties.
SMŬG'GLĘR, *n.* One who smuggles.
SMŬG'GLĬNG, *n.* A secret importation of goods.
SMŬT, *n.* Spot with soot; mildew :—obscenity.
SMŬT, *v. a.* To mark with soot; to taint with
SMŬT, *v. n.* To gather smut. [mildew.
SMŬTCH, *v. a.* To blacken with smoke or soot.
SMŬT'TĮ-LY, *ad.* Blackly; smokily; obscenely.
SMŬT'TĮ-NĔSS, *n.* State of being smutty.
SMŬT'TY, *a.* Black with smoke :—obscene.
SNĂCK, *n.* A share; a part taken by compact.
SNĂF'FLE, *n.* A bridle which crosses the nose.
SNĂF'FLE, *v. a.* To bridle; to hold in a bridle.
SNĂG, *n.* A protuberance :—a tooth :—a branch : —a tree at the bottom of a river.
SNĂG'GĘD, SNĂG'GY, *a.* Full of snags; knotty.
SNĀIL, *n.* A slimy, testaceous animal.
SNĀKE, *n.* A serpent of the oviparous kind.
SNĀKE'RŌŌT, *n.* A medicinal plant.
SNĀK'Y, *a.* Serpentine; belonging to a snake.
SNĂP, *v. a.* To break short; to strike ；to bite.
SNĂP, *v. n.* To break short; to try to bite.
SNĂP, *n.* A quick breaking or bite; catch :—theft.
SNĂP'DRĂG-ǪN, *n.* A kind of play :—a plant.
SNĂP'PĬSH, *a.* Eager to bite; peevish; tart.
SNĂP'PĬSH-NĔSS, *n.* Peevishness; tartness.
SNĀRE, *n.* A gin; a net; a noose; a trap.
SNĀRE, *v. a.* To entrap; to ensnare.
SNĂRL, *v. n.* To growl; to speak roughly.
SNĂRL, *v. a.* To entangle; to embarrass.
SNĂRL'ĘR, *n.* One who snarls; a surly fellow.
SNĂR'Y, *a.* Entangling; insidious. [catch.
SNĂTCH, *v. a. & n.* To seize hastily; to bite or
SNĂTCH, *n.* A hasty catch; a broken part; a fit.
SNĂTH, *n.* The handle or pole of a scythe.
SNĒAK, *v. n.* To creep or withdraw slyly or
SNĒAK, *n.* A sneaking, mean fellow. [meanly.
SNĒAK'ĬNG, *p. a.* Servile; mean; low.
SNĒĘR, *v. n.* To show contempt by looks, &c.
SNĒĘR, *n.* A look of contempt; scorn; derision.
SNĒĘR'ĬNG-LY, *ad.* With a look of ludicrous scorn. [nose.
SNĒĒZE, *v. n.* To emit wind audibly by the
SNĒĒZE, *n.* An emission of wind by the nose.
SNĬCK'ĘR, SNĬG'GĘR, *v. n.* To laugh slyly.
SNĬP, *v. a.* To cut at once, as with scissors.
SNĬP, *n.* A chip; a shred; a share; a snack.
SNĪPE, *n.* A small fen fowl with a long bill.
SNĬP'SNĂP, *n.* A tart dialogue, with quick re-
SNĬV'EL (snĭv'vl), *n.* Mucus from the nose.[plies.
SNĬV'EL (snĭv'vl), *v. n.* To run at the nose :— to cry; to weep; to whine.
SNĬV'EL-LĬNG (snĭv'vl-), *a.* Whining; pitiful.
SNŌRE, *v. n.* To breathe with noise in sleep.
SNŌRE, *n.* A noise through the nose in sleep.
SNŌRT, *v. n.* To blow hard through the nose.
SNŎT, *n.* The mucus of the nose.
SNŎT'TY, *a.* Full of snot; foul; dirty.
SNŌŌT, *n.* The nose of a beast :—the nozzle.
SNŌW (snō), *n.* Vapor in flakes :—a vessel.
SNŌW (snō), *v. n.* To fall in flakes or snow.
SNŌW'BÂLL, *n.* A round lump of snow.
SNŌW'DRŎP, *n.* An early white flower.
SNŌW'Y (snō'ẹ), *a.* White like snow; pure.
SNŬB, *n.* A snag; a knot in wood :—a rebuke.
SNŬB, *v. a.* To check; to reprimand; to nip.
SNŬB'NŌṢED (snŭb'nōzd), *a.* Having a flat nose.

SNŬFF, *n.* Burnt candle-wick :—inhalation by the nose :—powdered tobacco.   [snuff.
SNŬFF, *v. a.* To inhale ; to smell ; to crop the
SNŬFF, *v. n.* To draw breath by the nose.
SNŬFF'BŎX, *n.* A box in which snuff is carried.
SNŬFF'ĘRṢ, *n. pl.* A utensil to snuff candles.
SNŬF'FLE, *v. n.* To speak through the nose.
SNŬG, *a.* Close ; concealed ; convenient ; neat.
SNŬG, SNŬG'GLE, *v. n.* To lie close, snug, or
SNŬG'LY, *ad.* Safely ; closely ; cosily. [warm.
SNŬG'NĘSS, *n.* Retiredness ; closeness.
SŌ, *ad.* In like manner ; thus ; therefore.
SŌAK (sōk), *v. a.* To steep.—*v. n.* To be steeped.
SŌAK'ĘR, *n.* One that soaks :—a great drinker.
SŌAP (sōp), *n.* A substance used in washing.
SŌAP'-BŎÏL-ĘR, *n.* One who makes soap.
SŌAP'STŌNE, *n.* A mineral ; a variety of steatite.
SŌAP'Y, *a.* Resembling, or pertaining to, soap ;
SŌAR (sōr), *n.* A towering flight.   [soft.
SŌAR, *v. n.* To fly aloft ; to tower ; to mount.
SŎB, *v. n.* To sigh with sorrow convulsively.
SŎB, *n.* A convulsive sigh ; audible grief.
SŌ'BĘR, *a.* Temperate ; regular ; calm ; serious.
SŌ'BĘR, *v. a.* To make sober or grave.
SŌ'BĘR-LY, *ad.* Temperately ; calmly ; seriously.
SŌ'BĘR-MIND'ĘD, *a.* Calm ; regular ; temperate.
SŌ'BĘR-NĔSS, *n.* Temperance ; calmness.
SǪ-BRĪ'Ę-TY, *n.* Temperance ; soberness ; calm-
SŎC'AǴE, *n.* An ancient tenure of lands. [ness.
SŌ-CĪ-A-BĬL'Ī-TY,   } *n.* The quality of being
SŌ'CĪ-A-BLE-NĔSS, }   sociable.
SŌ'CĪ-A-BLE (sō'shę-ą-bl), *a.* Familiar ; con-
versable ; inclined to company ; social.
SŌ'CĪ-A-BLE (sō'shę-ą-bl), *n.* A kind of phaeton.
SŌ'CĪ-A-BLY (sō'shę-ą-ble), *ad.* Companionably.
SŌ'CĪAL (sō'shąl), *a.* Relating to society ; com-
panionable ; familiar ; sociable.
SŌ'CĪAL-LY (sō'shąl-le), *ad.* In a social manner.
SŌ'CĪAL-NĔSS (sō'shąl-nĕs), *n.* The being social.
SǪ-CĪ'Ę-TY, *n.* Union of many in one interest ;
a community ; a company ; partnership.
SǪ-CĬN'Ī-ĄN, *n.* A follower of Socinus.
SǪ-CĬN'Ī-ĄN, *a.* Of, or belonging to, Socinianism.
SǪ-CĬN'Ī-ĄN-ĬŞM, *n.* The doctrines of Socinus.
SŎCK, *n.* Something put between the foot and
shoe :—shoe of the ancient comic actors.
SŎCK'ĘT, *n.* A hollow; the receptacle of the eye.
SŎD, *n.* A turf ; a clod.—*a.* Made of turf.
SŎD, *imp. t.* from *seethe.* Seethed.
SŌ'DA, *n.* (*Chem.*) A fixed mineral alkali.
SǪ-DĂL'Ī-TY, *n.* A fellowship ; a fraternity.
SŎD'DEN (sŏd'dn), *pp.* from *seethe.* Seethed.
SŎD'DY, *a.* Turfy ; covered with sods.   [DER.
SŎD'ĘR, *v. a.* To cement ; to solder. See SOL-
SŎD'ĘR, *n.* Metallic cement. See SOLDER.
SŌ'DĪ-ŬM, *n.* The metallic base of soda.
SŎD'Ǫ-MY, *n.* An unnatural crime ; buggery.
SǪ-ĔV'ĘR, *ad.* A word properly joined with a
pronoun or adverb, as *whosoever, howsoever.*
SŌ'FA, *n.* A long, easy, covered seat.
SŌF'FĬT, *n.* A sort of timber-ceiling.
‖SŎFT (sŏft *or* sȧuft), *a.* Not hard ; yielding.
‖SŎFT'EN (sŏf'fn), *v. a. & n.* To make or grow
‖SŎFT'-HEÄRT-ĘD, *a.* Kind-hearted ; gentle. [soft
‖SŎFT'LY, *ad.* Without hardness ; gently.
‖SŎFT'NĘSS, *n.* Quality of being soft ; mildness.
SŎG'ĠY, *a.* Moist ; damp ; soaked with water.
SǪ-HŌ', *interj.* A form of calling from a distance.

SŎÏL, *v. a.* To foul; to dirty ; to pollute.
SŎÏL, *n.* Ground ; earth ; dirt ; dung ; compost.
SŌ'JOŲRN, *v. n.* To dwell a while in a place.
SŌ'JOŲRN (sō'jųrn), *n.* A temporary residence.
SŌ'JOŲRN-ĘR, *n.* A temporary dweller.
SŌL, *n.* A French copper coin. See SOU.
SŌL, *n.* A note in music.   [to soothe.
SŎL'ACE, *v. a.* To comfort ; to cheer ; to amuse ;
SŎL'ACE, *n.* Comfort ; pleasure ; alleviation.
SŌ'LAND-GÔÔSE, SŌ'LĄN-GÔÔSE, *n.* An
aquatic fowl ; the gannet.
SǪ-LÄ'NŌ, *n.* A hot Mediterranean wind.
SŌ'LĄR, *a.* Relating to the sun ; sunny.
SŌLD, *imp. t. & pp.* from *sell.*
SŎL'DĘR, *v. a.* To unite or fasten surfaces of
metals with metallic cement ; to soder.
SŎL'DĘR, *n.* A metallic cement ; soder.
‖SŌLD'IĘR (sōl'jęr), *n.* A member of a military
company ; a warrior.   [warlike.
‖SŌLD'IĘR-LĪKE, SŌLD'IĘR-LY, *a.* Martial ;
‖SŌLD'IĘR-SHĬP, *n.* Martial qualities or skill.
‖SŌLD'IĘR-Y (sōl'jęr-ę), *n.* A body of soldiers.
SŌLE, *n.* Bottom of the foot or shoe :—a fish.
SŌLE, *v. a.* To furnish with soles, as shoes.
SŌLE, *a.* Single ; only.—(*Law.*) Not married.
SŌL'Ę-CĬŞM, *n.* Impropriety in language.
SŌLE'LY, *ad.* Singly ; only ; separately.
SŎL'ĘMN (sŏl'ęm), *a.* Anniversary :—religious-
ly grave ; awful ; formal ; ritual ; serious.
SǪ-LĔM'NĪ-TY, *n.* A ceremony ; a rite :—gravity.
SŎL-ĘM-NĪ-ZĀ'TIǪN, *n.* Act of solemnizing.
SŎL'ĘM-NĪZE, *v. a.* To celebrate in due form ;
to perform religiously :—to make solemn.
SŎL'ĘMN-LY, *ad.* In a solemn manner.
SŎL-FÄ', *v. n.* To pronounce the musical notes.
SǪ-LĬÇ'ĬT, *v. a.* To importune ; to entreat ; to ask.
SǪ-LĬÇ-Ī-TĀ'TIǪN, *n.* Importunity ; invitation.
SǪ-LĬÇ'ĬT-ǪR, *n.* One who solicits :—a lawyer.
SǪ-LĬÇ'ĬT-OŬS, *a.* Anxious ; careful ; concerned.
SǪ-LĬÇ'ĬT-OŬS-LY, *ad.* Anxiously ; carefully.
SǪ-LĬÇ'ĬT-RĔSS, *n.* A woman who solicits.
SǪ-LĬÇ'Ĭ-TŪDE, *n.* Mental disquietude ; anxi-
ety ; carefulness ; concern.   [grave.
SŎL'ĬD, *a.* Not fluid ; compact ; firm ; real ;
SŎL'ĬD, *n.* A solid or compact body or substance.
SǪ-LĬD'Ī-TY, *n.* Firmness ; compactness ; density.
SŎL'ĬD-LY, *ad.* Firmly ; densely ; compactly.
SŎL'ĬD-NĔSS, *n.* Solidity ; firmness ; density.
SŎL-Ī-DŬN'GŲ-LOŬS, *a.* Whole hoofed, as a
horse ; not cloven-footed.   [alone.
SŎL-Ī-FĬD'Ī-ĄN, *n.* One who rests on faith
SǪ-LĬL'Ǫ-QUY, *n.* A discourse to one's self.
SŎL'Ī-PĔD, *n.* An animal with hoofs not cloven.
SŎL-Ī-TÁIRE' (sŏl-ę-tȧr'), *n.* A recluse ; hermit.
SŎL'Ī-TĄR-Ī-LY, *ad.* In solitude ; with loneliness.
SŎL'Ī-TĄ-RĪ-NĔSS, *n.* Solitude ; retirement.
SŎL'Ī-TĄ-RY, *a.* Living alone ; retired ; single.
SŎL'Ī-TŪDE, *n.* A lonely life or place ; a desert.
SŌ'LŌ, *n. ; pl.* SŌ'LŌṢ. A tune for one person.
SŎL'STĬCE, *n.* The time when the sun is far-
thest from the equator either north or south.
SǪL-STĬ''TĬAL, *a.* Relating to the solstice.
SŌL-Ų-BĬL'Ī-TY, *n.* Susceptiveness of separation.
SŎL'Ų-BLE, *a.* Capable of dissolution ; relaxing.
SǪ-LŪ'TIǪN, *n.* A separation ; an explanation.
SŎLV'A-BLE, *a.* That may be solved or paid.
SŎLVE (sŏlv), *v. a.* To clear ; to explain, resolve.
SŎLV'ĘN-CY, *n.* Ability to pay all debts.

Ā,Ē,Ī,Ō,Ū,Ȳ, *long;* Ă,Ĕ,Ĭ,Ŏ,Ŭ,Ў, *short;* A,Ę,Ī,Ǫ,Ų,Y, *obscure.*—FȦRE,FÄR,FȦST,FȦLL ; HÊIR, HĔR ;

SŎL'VĘND, *n.* A substance to be dissolved.
SŎLV'ĘNT, *a.* Able to pay debts :—dissolving.
SŎLV'ĘNT, *n.* A fluid that dissolves.
SŎLV'ĘR, *n.* Whoever, or whatever, solves.
SŎM'BRE (sŏm'bẹr), *a.* Dark; gloomy.
SŎM'BROŲS *or* SŎM'BROŲS, *a.* Dark; sombre.
SŎME (sŭm), *a.* More or less; certain; any.
SŎME'BŎD-Ȳ, *n.* One; a person indeterminate.
SŎME'HŌW̆, *ad.* In one way or other.
SŎM'ĘR-SĔT, *n.* A leap with heels over head.
SŎME'THĬNG, *n.* A thing indeterminate.
SŎME'TĪME, *ad.* Once; formerly; at one time.
SŎME'TĪMEṢ, *ad.* Not never; now and then.
SŎME'WHAT (sŭm'hwŏt), *n.* Something; part.
SŎME'WHAT (sŭm'hwŏt), *ad.* In some degree.
SŎME'WHÊRE (sŭm'hwår), *ad.* In some place.
SŎM-NĂM'BŲ-LĬṢM, *n.* A walking in sleep.
SŎM-NĂM'BŲ-LĬST, *n.* One who walks in sleep.
SŎM-NĬF'ĘR-OŬS, *a.* Causing sleep; soporifer-
SŎM-NĬF'ĬC, *a.* Causing sleep; soporific. [ous.
SŎM'NŌ-LĔNCE, SŎM'NŌ-LĔN-CȲ,*n.*Sleepiness.
SŎN, *n.* Male child :—a native :—a male descend-
SŌ-NÄ'TA, *n.* [It.] Musical composition. [ant.
SŎNG, *n.* A ballad; a poem; a lay; a strain.
SŎNG'STĘR, *n.* A singer :—a singing bird.
SŎNG'STRĘSS, *n.* A female singer.
SŌ-NĬF'ĘR-OŬS, *a.* Giving or bringing sound.
SŎN'-ĬN-LÂW, *n.* The husband of a daughter.
SŎN'NĘT, *n.* A poem consisting of 14 lines.
SŎN-NĘT-ĒĒR', *n.* A small poet :—writer of son-
SŎN-Ọ-RĬF'ĬC, *a.* Producing sound. [nets.
SỌ-NŌ'ROŲS, *a.* Loud; shrill; high-sounding.
SỌ-NŌ'ROŲS-LȲ, *ad.* With high sound.
SỌ-NŌ'ROŲS-NĔSS, *n.* Quality of being sonorous.
SŎN'SHĬP, *n.* The relationship of a son.
SÔÔN, *ad.* Before long; shortly; early.
SOOT (sôt *or* sŭt), *n.* Condensed smoke.
SÔÔTH, *n.* Truth; reality; prognostication.
SÔÔTHE, *v. a.* To flatter; to calm; to mollify.
SÔÔTH'SĀY, *v. n.* To predict; to foretell.
SÔÔTH'SĀY-ĘR, *n.* A foreteller; a predicter.
SÔÔTH'SĀY-ĬNG, *n.* Prediction; a foretelling.
SOOT'Ĭ-NĔSS, *n.* State of being sooty.
SOOT'Ȳ (sôt'ẹ), *a.* Consisting of soot; black.
SŎP, *n.* Any thing steeped in liquor.
SŎP, *v. a.* To steep or soak in liquor.
SŌ'PHĬ (sō'fẹ), *n.* [Pers.] Monarch of Persia.
SŎPH'ĬṢM, *n.* A fallacious argument :—a fallacy.
SŎPH'ĬST, *n.* A captious or fallacious reasoner.
SŎPH'ĬS-TĘR, *n.* A sophist :—a sophomore.
SỌ-PHĬS'TĬC, *a.* Logically; deceitfully
SỌ-PHĬS'TĬ-CĄL, *a.* fallacious. [tilty
SỌ-PHĬS'TĬ-CĄL-LȲ, *ad.* With fallacious sub-
SỌ-PHĬS'TĬ-CĀTE,*v.a.* To adulterate; to pervert.
SỌ-PHĬS-TĬ-CĀ'TĬQN, *n.* Act of sophisticating.
SỌ-PHĬS'TĬ-CĀ-TQR, *n.* One who sophisticates.
SŎPH'ĬS-TRȲ, *n.* Fallacious reasoning.[ond year.
SŎPH'Ọ-MŌRE, *n.* A student in college in his sec-
SŎP-Ọ-RĬF'ĘR-OŬS, *a.* Causing sleep; somnifer-
SŎP-Ọ-RĬF'ĬC, *a.* Causing sleep; narcotic. [ous.
SŎR'CĘR-ĘR, *n.* A conjurer; a magician; wizard.
SŎR'CĘR-ĔSS,*n.*A female magician; enchantress.
SŎR'CĘR-Ȳ, *n.* Magic; enchantment; witchcraft.
SŎR'DĬD, *a.* Vile; base; covetous; niggardly.
SŎR'DĬD-LȲ, *ad.* Meanly; poorly; covetously.
SŎR'DĬD-NĔSS, *n.* Baseness; niggardliness.
SỌR-DĪNE', *n.* A small damper in a trumpet.
SŌRE, *n.* A place tender and painful; an ulcer.

SŌRE, *a.* Tender to the touch; painful; easily
SŌRE, *ad.* Intensely; in a great degree. [vexed.
SŌRE'LȲ, *ad.* With great pain or distress.
SŌRE'NĘSS, *n.* The tenderness of a hurt.
SỌ-RŎR'Ĭ-CĪDE, *n.* The murder of a sister.
SŎR'RĘL, *n.* A plant having an acid taste.
SŎR'RĘL, *a.* Reddish; somewhat red. [ly.
SŎR'RĬ-LȲ, *ad.* Meanly; despicably; wretched-
SŎR'RĬ-NĔSS, *n.* Meanness; wretchedness.
SŎR'RŌW (sŏr'rō), *v. n.* To grieve; to be sad.
SŎR'RŌW (sŏr'rō), *n.* Grief; sadness; regret.
SŎR'RQW-FŬL, *a.* Sad; mournful; grieving.
SŎR'RQW-FŬL-LȲ, *ad.* In a sorrowful manner.
SŎR'RQW-FŬL-NĔSS,*n.* State of being sorrowful.
SŎR'RȲ, *a.* Grieved; melancholy; dismal; vile.
SŌRT, *n.* A kind; species; manner; class; rank.
SŌRT, *v. a.* To separate; to conjoin; to cull.
SŎR-TÎE', *n.* [Fr.] A sudden attack; a sally.
SŎR'TĬ-LĔĢE, *n.* The act of drawing lots.
SŎR-TĬ''TĬQN (sọr-tĭsh'ụn), *n.* Selection by lot.
SŎT, *n.* An habitual drunkard :—a blockhead.
SŎT, *v. a.* To stupefy; to besot.—*v. n.* To tipple.
SŎT'TĬSH, *a.* Doltish; dull with intemperance.
SŎT'TĬSH-LȲ,*ad.* Stupidly; dully; senselessly.
SŎT'TĬSH-NĔSS, *n.* Dulness; drunken stupidity.
SŌU (sô), *n.; pl.* SŌUṢ. [Fr.] A French copper
SŌU-CHŎNG' (sô-shŏng'), *n.* A black tea. [coin.
SOŬGH (sŭf), *n.* A drain :—a whistling.
SOUGHT (sâwt), *imp. t. & pp.* from *seek.*
SŌUL (sōl), *n.* Immortal spirit of man; life; spirit.
SŌUL'LĔSS (sōl'lẹs),*a.*Without soul; mean; low.
SOŬND, *a.* Healthy; hearty; right; stout.
SOŬND, *n.* Noise; tone :—strait or narrow pas-
sage of the sea :—air-bladder of a fish.
SOŬND,*v. a.* To try depth; to examine; to cause
to make a noise.—*v. n.* To emit a noise.
SOŬND'BŌARD, *n.* Board which propagates
SOŬND'ĬNG,*a.* Sonorous; having sound.[sound.
SOŬND'ĬNGṢ, *n. pl.* Places fathomable at sea.
SOŬND'LȲ, *ad.* Heartily; stoutly; rightly; fast.
SOŬND'NĘSS, *n.* Health; heartiness; solidity.
SÔUP (sôp), *n.* A decoction of flesh for food.
SOŬR, *a.* Acid; crabbed; peevish; morose.
SOŬR, *v. a.* To make acid :—to make morose.
SOŬR, *v. n.* To become acid or peevish.
SŌURCE (sōrs), *n.* A spring; fountain; origin.
SOŬR'CROÛT, *n.* A German dish of cabbage.
SOŬR'LȲ, *ad.* With acidity; with acrimony.
SOŬR'NĔSS, *n.* Acidity; austereness; asperity.
SOŬSE, *n.* A plunge; pickle :—pigs' feet pickled.
SOŬSE (sôŭs), *v. a.* To pickle :—to plunge.
SOŬSE, *v. n.* To fall, as a bird on its prey.
SOŬTH, *n.* The part where the sun is to us at
SOŬTH, *a.* Southern; meridional. [noon.
SOŬTH, *ad.* Towards the south; from the south.
SOŬTH-ĒAST', *n.* Point between east and south.
SOŬTH'ĘR-LȲ,*a.* Lying towards the south. [nal.
SOŬTH'ĘRN, *a.* Belonging to the south; meridio-
SOŬTH'ĘRN-LȲ,*ad.*Towards, or from, the south.
SOŬTH'ĘRN-MŌST, *a.* Furthest towards the
south.
SOŬTH'ĬNG, *n.* Course or distance south.
SOŬTH'MŌST, *a.* Furthest towards the south.
SOŬTH'WĄRD *or* SOŬTH'WĄRD, *n.* Southern
parts or regions. [the south.
SOŬTH'WĄRD *or* SOŬTH'WĄRD, *ad.* Towards
SOŬTH-WĔST',*n.* Point between south and west.
SOŬTH-WĔST', *a.* Between the south and west.

SÔUVE′NÎR, *n.* [Fr.] A remembrancer.
SŎV′ẸR-EĬGN (sŭv′ẹr-ĭn), *a.* Supreme in power.
SŎV′ẸR-EĬGN (sŭv′ẹr-ĭn), *n.* A supreme ruler.
SŎV′ẸR-EĬGN-TY (sŭv′ẹr-ĭn-tẹ), *n.* Power or
state of a sovereign; supreme power.
SŎŴ, *n.* A female pig; the female of a boar.
SŌW (sŏ), *v. a. & n.* [*imp. t.* sowed; *pp.* sown *or*
sowed.] To scatter; to spread; to propagate.
SŌW′ẸR (sō′ẹr), *n.* One who sows; a scatterer.
SŌWN (sŏn), *pp.* from *sow.*   [China.
SŎY̆, *n.* A kind of sauce prepared in Japan and
SPĀCE, *n.* Room; extension; quantity of time.
SPĀ′CIOŲS (-shŭs), *a.* Wide; extensive; roomy.
SPĀ′CIOŲS-LY (spā′shŭs-lẹ), *ad.* Extensively.
SPĀ′CIOŲS-NĔSS (spā′shŭs-nĕs), *n.* Roominess.
SPĀDE, *n.* A sort of shovel:—a suit of cards.
SPĀDE′BŌNE, *n.* The shoulder-blade.   [color.
SPA-DĬ″CEOŲS (spạ-dĭsh′ŭs), *a.* Of a light red
SPĀKE, *imp. t.* from *speak.* [*Obs.*]
SPĂN, *n.* Nine inches; any short duration.
SPĂN, *v. a.* To measure by the hand extended.
SPĂN, *imp. t.* from *spin.* [*Obs.*]
SPĂN′GLE, *n.* A small piece of shining material.
SPĂN′GLE, *v. a.* To besprinkle with spangles.
SPĂN′IẸL (spăn′yẹl), *n.* A sporting dog.
SPĂN′ĬSH, *a.* Relating to Spain.
SPĂN′ĬSH-FLȲ′, *n.* A fly used to raise blisters.
SPĂNK, *v. a.* To strike with the open hand.
SPĂNK′ẸR, *n.* A coin:—any thing large:—a sail.
SPĂNK′ĮNG, *a.* Large; strong. [*Low.*]
SPĂR, *n.* A mineral:—a beam:—a mast, &c.
SPĂR, *v. n.* To fight; to box; to dispute.
SPĀRE, *v. a.* To save; to preserve:—to forbear:
—to do without:—to afford; to grant.
SPĀRE, *v. n.* To be frugal, tender, or merciful.
SPĀRE, *a.* Scanty; superfluous; lean; thin.
SPĀRE′RĬB, *n.* Ribs of pork with little flesh.
SPĂR′ĮNG, *a.* Frugal; scanty; parsimonious.
SPĂR′ĮNG-LY, *ad.* Not abundantly; frugally.
SPĂR′ĮNG-NĔSS, *n.* Parsimony:—caution.
SPĂRK, *n.* A particle of fire:—a beau; a lover.
SPĂRK′FÛL, SPĂRK′ĮSH, *a.* Airy; gay; showy.
SPĂR′KLE, *n.* A spark; a luminous particle.
SPĂR′KLE, *v. n.* To emit sparks; to shine, glit-
SPĂR′RŌW (spăr′rō), *n.* A small bird.   [ter.
SPĂR′RŌW-GRĂSS, *n.* Corrupted from *aspara-*
SPĂR′RŌW-HÂWK, *n.* A species of hawk. [*gus.*
SPĂR′RY, *a.* Consisting of, or resembling, spar.
SPĂRSE, *a.* Thinly scattered; set here and there.
SPĂṢM, *n.* A violent convulsion; cramp.
SPAṢ-MŎD′ĮC, *a.* Convulsive.
SPĂT, *i.* from *spit.* [*Nearly obsolete.*]
SPĂT′TẸR, *v. a.* To sprinkle; to throw; to asperse.
SPĂT′TẸR-DĂSH-EṢ, *n. pl.* Coverings for the legs.
SPĂT′TLE, SPĂT′Ų-LA, *n.* An apothecary's
SPĂV′ĮN, *n.* A disease in a horse's hock. [knife.
SPĂV′ĮNED (-vĭnd), *a.* Diseased with spavin.
SPÂWN, *n.* Eggs of fish or frogs:—offspring.
SPÂWN, *v. a. & n.* To produce, as fishes; to
SPÂWN′ẸR, *n.* The female fish.   [generate.
SPĀY, *v. a.* To castrate, as female animals.
SPĒAK (spĕk), *v. n.* [*imp. t.* spoke; *pp.* spoken.]
To utter words; to talk; to discourse. [claim.
SPĒAK, *v. a.* To utter; to pronounce; to pro-
SPĒAK′A-BLE, *a.* Possible to be spoken.
SPĒAK′ẸR, *n.* One who speaks:—the presiding
officer in a deliberative assembly.
SPĒAR, *n.* A long, pointed weapon; a lance.

SPĒAR, *v. a.* To kill or pierce.—*v. n.* To sprout.
SPĒAR′MAN, *n.* Soldier armed with a spear.
SPĒAR′MĬNT, *n.* A species of mint.   [chief.
SPĔ″CIAL (spĕsh′ạl), *a.* Particular; uncommon;
SPĔ″CIAL-TY (spĕsh′ạl-tẹ), *n.* Particularity:—
object of pursuit.—(*Law.*) Contract by deed.
SPĔ″CIAL-LY (spĕsh′ạl-ẹ), *ad.* Particularly.
SPĒ′CIẸ (spē′shẹ), *n.* Coin; gold and silver.
SPĒ′CIEṢ (spē′shẹz), *n.* A sort; a kind; a sub-
division; a class of nature; a single order.
SPẸ-CĬF′ĮC, *n.* An efficacious medicine.
SPẸ-CĬF′ĮC,   ) *a.* Distinguishing one from an-
SPẸ-CĬF′Į-CAL,) other:—specified; precise.
SPẸ-CĬF′Į-CAL-LY, *ad.* According to the species.
SPẸ-CĬF′Į-CĀTE, *v. a.* To discriminate; to specify.
SPĔÇ-Į-FĮ-CĀ′TIȮN, *n.* Act of specifying; dis-
tinct notation; mention.   [particularly.
SPĔÇ′Į-FȲ, *v. a.* To mention, name, or designate
SPĔÇ′Į-MĔN, *n.* A sample; a part. like the rest.
SPĒ′CIOŲS (spē′shŭs), *a.* Plausible; showy.
SPĒ′CIOŲS-LY (spē′shŭs-lẹ), *ad.* Plausibly.
SPĒ′CIOŲS-NĔSS, *n.* Quality of being specious.
SPĔCK, *n.* A small discoloration:—a spot.
SPĔCK, *v. a.* To spot; to mark in spots.
SPĔC′KLE (spĕk′kl), *n.* A small speck; a spot.
SPĔC′KLE, *v. a.* To mark with small spots.
SPĔC′KLED (spĕk′kld), *a.* Marked with spots.
SPĔC′TA-CLE, *n.* A show; an exhibition; a
gazing stock.—*pl.* Glasses to assist the sight.
SPĔC-TĂC′Ų-LAR, *a.* Relating to spectacles.
SPĔÇ-TĀ′TȮR, *n.* A looker on; a beholder.
SPĔÇ-TĀ′TȮR-SHĬP, *n.* Quality of a spectator.
SPĔC′TRE (spĕk′tẹr), *n.* An apparition; a ghost.
SPĔC′TRŲM, *n.* [L.] Image; appearance.
SPĔC′Ų-LAR, *a.* Relating to, or like, a mirror.
SPĔC′Ų-LĀTE, *v. n.* To meditate; to buy in
order to sell again; to traffic.
SPĔC-Ų-LĀ′TIȮN, *n.* Act of speculating; the-
ory; examination; contemplation; scheme.
SPĔC′Ų-LA-TĬST, *n.* A speculator; a theorizer.
SPĔC′Ų-LA-TĬVE, *a.* Contemplative; theoretical.
SPĔC′Ų-LA-TĬVE-LY, *ad.* Ideally; theoretically.
SPĔC′Ų-LA-TĬVE-NĔSS, *n.* The being speculative.
SPĔC′Ų-LĀ-TȮR, *n.* One who speculates.
SPĔC′Ų-LA-TO-RY, *a.* Exercising speculation.
SPĔC′Ų-LŬM, *n.* [L.] A mirror; a looking-glass.
SPĔD, *imp. t. & pp.* from *speed.*   [talk.
SPĒECH, *n.* Articulate utterance; language;
SPĒECH′LESS, *a.* Deprived of speech; dumb;
mute; silent.   [less.
SPĒECH′LESS-NĔSS, *n.* State of being speech-
SPĒED, *v. n.* [*imp. t. & pp.* sped.] To make haste;
to have success; to succeed; to prosper.
SPĒED, *v. a.* To hasten; to despatch; to assist.
SPĒED, *n.* Quickness; celerity; haste; despatch.
SPĒED′Į-LY, *ad.* With haste; quickly.
SPĒED′Į-NĔSS, *n.* The quality of being speedy.
SPĒED′Y, *a.* Quick; swift; nimble; not slow.
SPĔLL, *n.* A charm; a turn of work; relief.
SPĔLL, *v. a. & n.* [*imp. t. & pp.* spelled *or* spelt.]
To read; to discover by marks; to charm; to
SPĔLT, *n.* Kind of wheat. [form words of letters.
SPĔL′TẸR, *n.* Zinc; a kind of semi-metal.
SPĔN′CẸR, *n.* A garment; an outer jacket.
SPĔND, *v. a.* [*imp. t. & pp.* spent.] To consume;
to exhaust; to waste; to expend; to devote.
SPĔND, *v. n.* To make expense; to be lost.
SPĔND′THRĬFT, *n.* A prodigal; a lavisher.

SPĔRM, *n.* Animal seed ; spawn :—spermaceti.
SPĔR-MĄ-CĔ′TĮ, *n.* Fat from a whale's head.
SPĔR-MĂT′ĮC, SPĔR-MĂT′Į-CĄL, *a.* Seminal.
SPEW̄ (spū), *v. a.* To vomit ; to cast forth.
SPEW̄ (spū), *v. n.* To vomit ; to ease the stomach.
SPHĒRE (sfēr), *n.* A globe ; orb ; circuit. ·
SPHĔR′ĮC, SPHĔR′Į-CĄL, *a.* Round ; globular.
SPHĔR′Į-CĄL-LY, *ad.* In the form of a sphere.
SPHĔR′Į-CĄL-NĔSS, ⟩ *n.* State of being spher-
SPHĘ-RĬÇ′Į-TY,   ⟩ ical ; rotundity.
SPHĔR′ĮCS, *n. pl.* The doctrine of the sphere.
SPHĒ′ROÏD, *n.* A body like a sphere.
SPHĒ-ROÏD′ĄL, ⟩ *a.* Having the form of a
SPHĘ-ROÏD′Į-CĄL, ⟩ spheroid.
SPHĔR′ŪLE (sfēr′rūl), *n.* A little globe.
SPHĬNX, *n.* An Egyptian monster having the
 face of a woman and the body of a lion.
SPĪCE, *n.* Aromatic substance :—small quantity.
SPĪCE, *v. a.* To season with spice ; to tincture.
SPĪ′CĘR, *n.* One who deals in spice.
SPĪ′CĘR-Y, *n.* Spices ; a repository of spices.
SPĬC′Ų-LĄ, *n.; pl.* SPĬC′Ų-LÆ. [L.] Small spike.
SPĬC′Ų-LĄR, *a.* Resembling a dart ; pointed.
SPĬC′Ų-LĀTE, *v. a.* To make sharp at the point.
SPĪ′CY, *a.* Abounding in spice ; aromatic.
SPĪ′DĘR, *n.* An animal that spins a web for flies.
SPĬG′ŎT, *n.* A pin or peg to stop a vent.
SPĪKE, *n.* An ear of corn :—a large nail.
SPĪKE, *v. a.* To fasten, or set, with spikes, &c.
SPĪKE′NĄRD, *n.* A plant, and its oil or balsam.
SPĪ′KY, *a.* Having a sharp point or points.
SPĬLL, *v. a.* [*imp. t.* & *pp.* spilt *or* spilled.] To
 shed ; to lose by shedding.—*v. n.* To waste.
SPĬN, *v. a.* & *n.* [*imp. t.* & *pp.* spun.] To draw out
 into threads ; to form threads ; to twirl ; to
 protract ; to draw out.   [plant.
SPĬN′ĄCH, SPĬN′ĄGE, *n.* An esculent garden
SPĪ′NĄL, *a.* Belonging to the backbone.
SPĬN′DLE, *n.* A pin used in spinning :—a stalk.
SPĬN′DLE, *v. n.* To shoot into a slender stalk.
SPĬN′DLE-SHĂNKED (-shănkt), *a.* Having small
SPĪNE, *n.* The backbone :—a thorn.   [legs.
SPĪ′NĘL, SPĮ-NĔLLE′, *n.* A precious stone.
SPĬN′ET *or* SPĮ-NĔT′, *n.* A stringed instrument.
SPĮ-NĬF′ĘR-OŬS, *a.* Bearing spines or thorns.
SPĬN′NĮNG-JĔN′NY, *n.* A machine for spinning.
SPĬN′NĮNG-WHEĒL, *n.* A wheel for spinning.
SPĮ-NŎS′Į-TY, *n.* The state of being spinous.
SPĪ′NOŲS, *a.* Thorny ; full of thorns ; spiny.
SPĬN′STĘR, *n.* A woman that spins :—an un-
 married woman.
SPĬN′STRY, *n.* The work of spinning.
SPĪ′NY, *a.* Thorny ; spinous ;—perplexed.
SPĬR′Ą-CLE *or* SPĪ′RĄ-CLE, *n.* A breathing-
 hole ; a small aperture ; a vent.
SPĪ′RĄL, *a.* Winding, like a screw.—*n.* A curve.
SPĪ′RĄL-LY, *ad.* In a spiral form.
SPĪRE, *n.* A spiral :—a wreath :—a steeple.
SPĪRE, *v. n.* To shoot up pyramidically.
SPĬR′ĮT, *n.* An immaterial substance ; the soul ;
 a ghost :—vigor ; life :—strong liquor.
SPĬR′ĮT, *v. a.* To animate, encourage, excite.
SPĬR′ĮT-ĘD, *a.* Lively ; vivacious ; animated.
SPĬR′ĮT-LĔSS, *a.* Dejected ; low ; wanting courage.
SPĬR′ĮT-OŬS, *a.* Spirituous ; ardent ; active.
SPĬR′ĮTS, *n. pl.* Ardent spirits :—vivacity.
SPĬR′ĮT-Ų-ĄL (spĭr′ĭt-yų-al), *a.* Incorporeal ; re-
 lating to the spirit :—holy ; ecclesiastical.

SPĬR′ĮT-Ų-ĄL-ĬSM, *n.* Spiritual nature :—inter-
 course with departed spirits.
SPĬR-ĮT-Ų-ĂL′Į-TY, *n.* Spiritual nature ; devotion.
SPĬR′ĮT-Ų-ĄL-ĪZE, *v. a.* To refine ; to purify.
SPĬR′ĮT-Ų-ĄL-LY, *ad.* In a spiritual manner.
SPĬR′ĮT-Ų-OŬS (spĭr′ĭt-yų-ŭs), *a.* Having the
 quality of spirit ; active ; ardent ; alcoholic.
SPĬRT, *v. a.* & *n.* To throw out ; to stream.
SPĬRT, *n.* An injection ; a short effort. See *Spurt.*
SPĪ′RY, *a.* Pyramidal ; wreathed ; spiral.
SPĬS′SĮ-TŪDE, *n.* Grossness ; thickness.
SPĬT, *n.* A utensil for roasting meat :—spittle.
SPĬT, *v. a.* [*imp. t.* & *pp.* spitted.] To put on a spit.
SPĬT, *v. n.* & *a.* [*imp. t.* spit *or* spat ; *pp.* spit.]
 To throw out spittle from the mouth.
SPĪTE, *n.* Malice ; rancor ; hate ; malignity.
SPĪTE, *v. a.* To vex ; to thwart ; to offend.
SPĪTE′FŪL, *a.* Malicious ; malignant.
SPĪTE′FŪL-LY, *ad.* Maliciously ; malignantly.
SPĪTE′FŪL-NĔSS, *n.* Malice ; malignity.
SPĬT′TEN (spĭt′tn), *pp.* from *spit.* [*Obsolescent.*]
SPĬT′TĘR, *n.* One who spits :—a young deer.
SPĬT′TLE, *n.* Moisture of the mouth ; saliva.
SPLĂSH, *v. a.* To spatter with water or mud.
SPLĂSH, *n.* Water thrown up :—a puddle.
SPLĂSH′Y, *a.* Full of dirty water ; wet and muddy.
SPLĀY, *a.* Spread or turned outwards.
SPLĀY′FOOT (splā′fůt), ⟩ *a.* Having the foot
SPLĀY′FOOT-ĘD,   ⟩ turned outward.
SPLEĒN, *n.* The milt ; ill-will ; spite ; ill-humor.
SPLEĒN′FŪL, *a.* Peevish ; fretful ; melancholy.
SPLĔN′DĘNT, *a.* Shining ; glossy ; conspicuous.
SPLĔN′DĮD, *a.* Showy ; magnificent ; shining.
SPLĔN′DĬD-LY, *ad.* Magnificently ; pompously.
SPLĔN′DOR, *n.* Lustre ; magnificence ; show.
SPLĔN′Ę-TĬC, *a.* Fretful ; peevish ; morose.
SPLĔN′ĮC, *a.* Belonging to the spleen.
SPLĔNT, *n.* A kind of coal ; a splint. [knot.
SPLĪCE, *n.* The joining of two ropes without a
SPLĪCE, *v. a.* To join the ends of a rope, &c.
SPLĬNT, SPLĬNT′ĘR, *n.* Thin piece of wood, &c.
SPLĬNT, SPLĬNT′ĘR, *v. a.* To split ; to support.
SPLĬT, *v. a.* [*imp. t.* & *pp.* split.] To cleave ; to di-
SPLĬT, *v. n.* To burst in sunder ; to crack. [vide.
SPLŬT′TĘR, *n.* Bustle ; tumult ; stir. [*Vulgar.*]
SPLŬT′TĘR, *v. n.* To speak hastily and con-
 fusedly ; to stammer.   [mar.
SPOÏL, *v. a.* To plunder ; to rob ; to corrupt ; to
SPOÏL, *v. n.* To practise robbery ; to decay.
SPOÏL, *n.* Plunder ; pillage ; booty ; robbery.
SPOÏL′ĘR, *n.* One who spoils ; a plunderer.
SPŌKE, *n.* Bar of a wheel :—round of a ladder.
SPŌKE, *imp. t.* from *speak.*
SPŌ′KEN (spō′kn), *pp.* from *speak.* See SPEAK.
SPŌKES′MĄN, *n.* One who speaks for another.
SPŌ′LĮ-ĀTE, *v. a.* To rob ; to plunder ; to spoil.
SPŌ-LĮ-Ā′TIǪN, *n.* Act of robbery or privation.
SPǪN-DĀ′ĮC,   ⟩ *a.* Relating to, or consisting
SPǪN-DĀ′Į-CĄL, ⟩ of, spondees.
SPŎN′DEĒ, *n.* A foot of two long syllables.
SPŎNGE (spŭnj), *n.* A soft, porous substance.
SPŎNGE, *v. a.* To blot, wipe, squeeze, harass.
SPŎNGE, *v. n.* To live by mean arts ; to hang on.
SPŎN′GĘR, *n.* One who sponges ; a parasite.
SPŎN′GĮ-NĔSS, *n.* Quality of being spongy.
SPŎN′GĮNG-HOŪSE, *n.* A bailiff's house.
SPŎN′GY, *a.* Soft and full of small holes ; wet.
SPŎN′SĄL, *a.* Relating to marriage.

SPŎN′SIǪN, *n.* The act of becoming a surety.
SPŎN′SǪR, *n.* A surety:—godfather or god-
SPŎN-TA̧-NĒ′Į-TY, *n.* Voluntariness. [mother.
SPǪN-TĀ′NȨ-OŬS, *a.* Voluntary; acting of itself.
SPǪN-TĀ′NȨ-OŬS-LY, *ad,* Voluntarily.
SPŎN-TŌŎN′, *n.* A weapon; a kind of half-pike.
SPŎŎL, *n.* A weaver's quill.—*v. a.* To wind.
SPŎŎN, *n.* A utensil used in eating liquids.
SPŎŎN′BĬLL, *n.* A bird with a broad bill.
SPŎŎN′FŬL, *n.* As much as a spoon can hold.
SPŎŎN′-MĒAT, *n.* Food taken with a spoon.
SPǪ-RĂD′ĮC,   } *a.* Scattered; attacking few;
SPǪ-RĂD′Į-CA̧L, }   not epidemic.
SPŎRT, *n.* Diversion; frolic; mirth; hunting, &c.
SPŌRT, *v. a. & n.* To divert; to make merry.
SPŎRT′FŬL, *a.* Merry; ludicrous; done in jest.
SPŌR′TĮVE, *a.* Gay; merry; playful; ludicrous.
SPŎRTS′MA̧N, *n.* One who loves hunting, &c.
SPŎT, *n.* A blot; taint; disgrace:—a small place.
SPŎT, *v. a.* To maculate, corrupt, disgrace.
SPŎT′LȨSS, *a.* Free from spots; innocent; pure.
SPŎT′LȨSS-NĔSS, *n.* The state of being spotless.
SPŎT′TY, *a.* Full of spots; maculated.
SPŎŬ′SA̧L, *a.* Nuptial; matrimonial; conjugal.
SPŎŬ′SA̧L, *n.* Nuptials. See ESPOUSALS.
SPŎŬSȨ, *v. a.* To espouse; to wed. See ESPOUSE.
SPŎŬSȨ, *n.* A husband or wife; person married.
SPŎŬSȨ′LȨSS, *a.* Wanting a husband or wife.
SPŎŬT, *n.* A pipe; a wooden gutter; a cataract.
SPŎŬT, *v. a.* To pour with violence; to mouth.
SPŎŬT, *v. n.* To issue as from a spout.
SPRĀIN, *v. a.* To injure by straining. [cation.
SPRĀIN, *n.* A strain of ligaments without dislo-
SPRĂNG, *imp. t.* from *spring.* Sprung.
SPRĂT, *n.* A small fish. [about.
SPRÂWL, *v. n.* To spread the body or limbs
SPRĀY, *n.* The foam of the sea:—a twig.
SPRĔAD (sprĕd), *v. a. & n.* [*imp. t. & pp.* spread.]
   To diffuse; to expand; to divulge; to extend.
SPRĔAD (sprĕd), *n.* Extent; expansion.
SPRĔAD′ȨR (sprĕd′ȩr), *n.* One that spreads.
SPRĬG, *n.* A small branch; a twig; a spray.
SPRĬG, *v. a.* To mark or adorn with sprigs.
SPRĬG′ĢY, *a.* Full of sprigs or small branches.
SPRĪGHT (sprīt), *n.* A spirit; a shade; a ghost.
SPRĪGHT′FŬL (sprīt′fŭl), *a.* Lively; brisk; gay.
SPRĪGHT′FŬL-NĔSS, *n.* Sprightliness; gayety.
SPRĪGHT′LȨSS (sprīt′lȩs), *a.* Dull; sluggish.
SPRĪGHT′LĮ-NĔSS (sprīt′lȩ-nĕs), *n.* Vigor; gayety.
SPRĪGHT′LY (sprīt′lȩ), *a.* Gay; brisk; lively.
SPRĬNG, *v. n.* [*imp. t.* sprung *or* sprang; *pp.*
   sprung.] To begin to grow; to issue; to bound.
SPRĬNG, *v. a.* To start; to rouse:—to discharge.
SPRĬNG, *n.* The vernal season:—elastic force; a
   bound:—a fountain; a source; original.
SPRĬNĢȨ, *n.* A gin; a noose; a snare.
SPRĬNĢ′ȨR, *n.* One who springs; a young plant.
SPRĬNG′HÂLT, *n.* A lameness by which a horse
   twitches up his hind legs; stringhalt.
SPRĬNG′Į-NĔSS, *n.* Elasticity; wetness.
SPRĬNG′TĪDE, *n.* High tide at new and full moon.
SPRĬNĢ′Y, *a.* Full of springs and fountains:—
   that springs; elastic.
SPRĬN′KLE, *v. a.* To scatter; to besprinkle, wash.
SPRĬN′KLE, *v. n.* To scatter drops; to rain.
SPRĬN′KLE, *n.* A small quantity scattered.
SPRĬNK′LĮNG, *n.* A scattering in small drops.
SPRĪTE, *n.* A spirit. See SPRIGHT.

SPRŎŬT, *v. n.* To germinate; to shoot; to begin to
SPRŎŬT, *n.* A shoot of a plant; a germ. [grow.
SPRŬCE, *a.* Nice; trim; neat without elegance.
SPRŬCE, *v. a. & n.* To trim; to dress neatly.
SPRŬCE, *n.* An evergreen tree; sort of fir.
SPRŬCE′-BĒĒR, *n.* Beer tinctured with spruce.
SPRŬCE′NȨSS, *n.* Neatness; trimness; fineness.
SPRŬNG, *imp. t. & pp.* from *spring.*
SPRȲ, *a.* Nimble; active; lively. [*Colloquial.*]
SPŪME, *v. n.* To foam; to froth.—*n.* Foam; froth.
SPŪ′MOŲS, SPŪ′MY, *a.* Frothy; foamy.
SPŬN, *imp. t. & pp.* from *spin.*
SPŬNĢȨ, *n.* A soft substance. See SPONGE.
SPŬR, *n.* A sharp point; incitement:—snag.
SPŬR, *v. a.* To prick; to incite; to urge forward.
SPŬRĢȨ, *n.* A plant violently purgative.
SPŪ′RĮ-OŬS, *a.* Counterfeit; false; not legitimate.
SPŪ′RĮ-OŬS-LY, *ad.* Counterfeitly; falsely.
SPŪ′RĮ-OŲS-NĔSS, *n.* State of being spurious.
SPŬRN, *v. a.* To kick, reject, scorn, disdain.
SPŬRRED (spürd), *a.* Wearing spurs.
SPŬR′RĮ-ȨR, *n.* One who makes spurs. [fort.
SPŬRT, *n.* A sudden ejection; a jet; a short ef-
SPŬRT, *v. n. & a.* To fly or throw out.
SPŬT′TȨR, *v. n.* To speak hastily; to spit.
SPŬT′TȨR, *n.* Moisture thrown out in drops.
SPŬT′TȨR-ȨR, *n.* One that sputters.
SPȲ, *n.* One who watches another's motions;
   a secret emissary sent to an enemy.
SPȲ, *v. a.* To discover at a distance; to search.
SQUAB (skwŏb), *a.* Unfeathered; thick and stout.
SQUAB (skwŏb), *n.* A kind of sofa:—a pigeon.
SQUAB′BLE (skwŏb′bl), *v. n.* To quarrel; to fight.
SQUAB′BLE (skwŏb′bl), *n.* A low brawl; quarrel.
SQUAD (skwŏd), *n.* A small number of men.
SQUAD′RǬN (skwŏd′rṵn), *n.* A part of an army:
   —a part of a fleet.
SQUAL′ĮD (skwŏl′ĭd), *a.* Foul; nasty; filthy.
SQUAL′ĮD-NĔSS (skwŏl′ĭd-nĕs), *n.* Filthiness.
SQUÂLL, *v. n.* To scream out as a child; to yell.
SQUÂLL, *n.* A loud scream:—a gust of wind.
SQUÂLL′Y, *a.* Windy; gusty; stormy. [ness.
SQUĀ′LÖR, *n.* [L.] Coarseness; want of cleanli-
SQUĀ′MOŲS, *a.* Scaly; covered with scales.
SQUAN′DȨR (skwŏn′-), *v. a.* To spend profusely.
SQUAN′DȨR-ȨR (skwŏn′-), *n.* A spendthrift.
SQUĀRE, *a.* Having four right angles; equal.
SQUĀRE, *n.* A figure with four right angles and
   four equal sides:—a rule or instrument.
SQUĀRE, *v. a.* To form with right angles; to fit.
SQUASH (skwŏsh), *n.* A plant:—any thing soft.
SQUAT (skwŏt), *v. a.* To sit close to the ground.
SQUAT (skwŏt), *a.* Cowering; short and thick.
SQUAT (skwŏt), *n.* A lying close; a sudden fall.
SQUÂW, *n.* An Indian woman or wife.
SQUĒAK, *v. n.* To make a shrill noise; to cry out.
SQUĒAK, *n.* A cry of pain; a shrill, quick cry.
SQUĒAL, *v. n.* To cry with a shrill, sharp voice.
SQUĒAM′ĮSH, *a.* Fastidious; easily disgusted.
SQUĒAM′ĮSH-LY, *ad.* In a fastidious manner.
SQUĒAM′ĮSH-NĔSS, *n.* Niceness; fastidiousness.
SQUĒĒZE, *v. a.* To press; to oppress; to crush.
SQUĒĒZE, *v. n.* To urge one's way; to crowd.
SQUĒĒZE, *n.* A compression; a pressure.
SQUĬB, *n.* A little firework:—a flash.
SQUĬLL, *n.* A sea-onion:—a fish:—an insect.
SQUĬNT, *a.* Looking obliquely. [slope.
SQUĬNT, *v. n.* To look obliquely or awry:—to

Ā,Ē,Ī,Ō,Ū,Ȳ, *long;* Ă,Ĕ,Ĭ,Ŏ,Ŭ,Y̆, *short;* A̧,Ȩ,Į,Ǫ,Ṵ,Y̨, *obscure.*—FĀRE,FÄR,FĂST,FÂLL; HÊIR,HĒR;

SQUĬNT′-EȲED (skwĭnt′ĭd), *a.* Having eyes that squint; affected with strabismus.

SQUĪRE,*n.* A contraction of *esquire.* See ESQUIRE.

SQUĪRE, *v. a.* To attend; to wait on; to escort.

SQUĬRM, *v. n.* To wind or twist about.

SQUĬR′REL (skwĭr′rel, skwẽr′rel, *or* skwŭr′rel), *n.* A small, active, rodent animal.

SQUĬRT, *v. a.* To throw out in a quick stream.

SQUĬRT, *n.* A pipe to eject liquor:—a stream.

STĂB, *v. a.* To pierce; to wound mortally.

STĂB, *v. n.* To give a wound; to offer a stab.

STĂB, *n.* A wound with a sharp weapon; a blow.

STĂB′BER, *n.* One who stabs; a privy murderer.

STA-BĬL′I-MĔNT, *n.* Support; firmness; strength.

STA-BĬL′I-TY, *n.* Stableness; steadiness; firmness.

STĀ′BLE, *a.* Fixed; steady; constant; strong.

STĀ′BLE, *n.* A house or building for horses, &c.

STĀ′BLE, *v. a.* To put into a stable. [ity.

STĀ′BLE-NĔSS, *n.* Steadiness; constancy; stabil-

STĀ′BLING, *n.* A house or room for horses, &c.

†STĂB′LISH, *v. a.* To establish; to fix.

STĂCK, *n.* A pile of hay:—a number of chimneys.

STĂCK, *v. a.* To pile up in a stack or stacks.

STĂD′DLE (stăd′dl), *n.* A staff; a crutch; a tree.

STĀ′DI-ŬM, *n.*; *pl.* STĀ′DI-A. [L.] A race-ground; a race:—one eighth of a Roman mile.

STĂDT′HŌLD-ER (stăt′hŏld-er), *n.* Formerly, the chief magistrate of the Netherlands.

STĂFF, *n.*; *pl.* STĀVEŞ *or* STĀVES. A stick used in walking:—a prop; a support:—an ensign of office:—a body of officers.

STĂG, *n.* A male red deer:—a castrated bull.

STĀGE, *n.* A raised floor:—the theatre:—a place in which rest is taken on a journey:—a step in progress:—a stage-coach.

STĀGE′-CŌACH (stāj′kōch), *n.* A public coach.

STĀGE′-PLĀY, *n.* Theatrical entertainment.

STĀGE′-PLĀY-ER, *n.* An actor on the stage.

STĂG′GER, *v. n.* To reel; to faint:—to hesitate.

STĂG′GER, *v. a.* To make to reel; to alarm.

STĂG′GERŞ, *n. pl.* A kind of horse apoplexy.

STĂG′NAN-CY, *n.* The state of being stagnant.

STĂG′NANT, *a.* Motionless; still; not flowing.

STĂG′NĀTE, *v. n.* To cease to run or flow.

STAG-NĀ′TION, *n.* A cessation of running.

STĀID, *a.* Sober; grave; steady; not wild.

STĀID′NESS, *n.* Sobriety; gravity; regularity.

STĀIN, *v. a.* To blot, maculate, tinge, disgrace.

STĀIN, *n.* A blot; a spot; a taint of guilt; shame.

STĀIN′ER, *n.* One who stains; a dyer.

STĀIN′LESS, *a.* Free from stains:—unsullied.

STĀIR, *n.* A step.—*pl.* A series of steps.

STĀIR′CĀSE, *n.* A series of stairs.

STĀKE, *n.* A post:—a wager; a pledge; hazard.

STĀKE, *v. a.* To defend with stakes:—to wager.

STA-LĂC′TIC, } *a.* Pertaining to, or resem-
STA-LĂC′TI-CAL, } bling, a stalactite.

STA-LĂC′TITE, *n.* A pendent mass of limestone.

STĂL-AC-TĬT′IC, } *a.* Relating to stalac-
STĂL-AC-TĬT′I-CAL, } tites; stalactic. [stone.

STA-LĂG′MĪTE, *n.* A deposit or layer of lime-

STĀLE, *a.* Old; not fresh; flat; tasteless.

STĀLE, *n.* A long handle:—urine of beasts.

STĀLE, *v. n.* To make water, as a beast.

STĀLE′NESS, *n.* State of being stale.

STÂLK (stâwk), *v. n.* To walk with high steps.

STÂLK (stâwk), *n.* A stately step:—a stem.

STÂLK′ER (stâwk′er), *n.* One who stalks:—net.

STÂLK′ING-HŎRSE (stâwk′ing-hörs), *n.* A horse used by fowlers:—a mask; a pretence.

STÂLK′Y (stâwk′e), *a.* Hard like a stalk. [seat.

STÂLL, *n.* Place for horses, &c.:—a bench; a

STÂLL, *v. a.* To keep in a stall:—to install.

STĂLL′FĔD, *a.* Fed not with grass, but dry feed.

STĂLL′ION (stăl′yun), *n.* A horse not castrated.

STÂL′WART, STÂL′WORTH (-würth), *a.* Stout.

STĀ′MEN, *n.*; *pl.* STĀ′MENŞ. (*Bot.*) The filament, or stalk, and the anther of a flower.

STĂM′I-NA, *n. pl.* [L.] First principles of any thing:—solids of the body; strength.

STĂM′I-NAL, } *a.* Relating to, or having, sta-
STĂM′I-NATE, } mens.

STA-MĬN′E-OŬS, *a.* Consisting of stamens.

STĂM′MER, *v. n.* To falter in speaking; to stut-

STĂM′MER-ER, *n.* One who stammers. [ter.

STĂMP, *v. a.* To strike with the foot:—to mark.

STĂMP, *v. n.* To strike the foot downward.

STĂMP, *n.* An instrument for making an impression:—a mark; an impression; a cut.

STĂM-PĒDE′, *n.* Sudden or hurried flight.

STĂMP′ER, *n.* One who stamps:—stamp.

STĂNCH, *v. a.* To hinder from running.

STĂNCH, *v. n.* To cease to flow; to stop.

STĂNCH, *a.* Sound; firm; trusty; hearty.

STĂNCH′ER, *n.* One that stanches or stops.

STĂNCH′ION (stăn′shun), *n.* A prop; a support.

STĂND, *v. n.* [*imp. t. & pp.* stood.] To be upon the feet; to remain erect:—to halt; to persist.

STĂND, *v. a.* To endure; to abide; to suffer.

STĂND, *n.* A station; a halt; perplexity; a table.

STĂND′ARD, *n.* An ensign of war:—a rule; a rate.

STĂND′ARD, *a.* Affording a test to others.

STĂND′ARD-BEÀR′ER, *n.* A bearer of a standard.

STĂND′ING, *p. a.* Settled; lasting; stagnant.

STĂND′ING, *n.* Continuance; station; rank.

STĂND′ISH, *n.* A stand for pen and ink.

STĂNG, *n.* A long bar or pole; shaft of a cart.

STĂNK, *n.* A dam, or bank, to stop water.

†STĂNK, *imp. t.* from *stink.* Stunk.

STĂN′NA-RY, *n.* A tin-mine.—*a.* Relating to tin.

STĂN′ZA, *n.* A set of lines adjusted to each other.

STĀ′PLE, *n.* A mart; an emporium:—original or chief material:—fibre:—a loop of iron.

STĀ′PLE, *a.* Settled; established; principal.

STÄR, *n.* A luminous heavenly body:—asterisk.

STÄR′BOARD, *n.* The right hand side of a ship.

STÄRCH, *n.* A substance to stiffen linen with.

STÄRCH, *a.* Stiff; precise; rigid.

STÄRCH, *v. a.* To stiffen with starch.

STÄR′-CHĂM-BER, *n.* English criminal court.

STÄRCHED (stärcht), *p. a.* Stiffened; formal.

STÄRCH′ER, *n.* One who, or that which, starches.

STÄRCH′LY, *ad.* Stiffly; precisely.

STÄRCH′NESS, *n.* Stiffness; preciseness.

STÄRE, *v. n.* To look with fixed eyes.

STÄRE, *v. a.* To affect or influence by staring.

STÄRE, *n.* A fixed look:—a starling.

STÄR′ER, *n.* One who looks with fixed eyes.

STÄR′-GÄZ-ER, *n.* An astronomer, or astrologer.

STÄRK, *a.* Mere; simple; plain; gross.

STÄRK, *ad.* Wholly; in a high degree.

STÄR′LESS, *a.* Having no light of stars.

STÄR′LIGHT (stär′lît), *n.* The lustre of the stars.

STÄR′LING, *n.* A bird:—a defence to piers.

STÄRRED (stärd), *a.* Decorated with stars.

STÄR′RY, *a.* Consisting of, or like, stars; stellar.

STÄRT, *v. n.* To rise or move suddenly; to shrink.
STÄRT, *v. a.* To alarm, startle, rouse, produce.
STÄRT, *n.* A motion of terror; a quick spring.
STÄRT'ING-PŌST, *n.* A place to start from.
STÄR'TLE, *v. n.* To shrink with sudden fear.
STÄR'TLE, *v. a.* To fright; to shock; to deter.
STÄR'TLE, *n.* Sudden alarm; a shock; terror.
STÄR-VÄ'TIQN, *n.* Act of starving.
STÄRVE, *v. n.* To perish with hunger.
STÄRVE, *v. a.* To kill or oppress with hunger.
STÄRVE'LING, *n.* A lean, meagre animal.
STĀTE, *n.* Condition; pomp; dignity; a body politic; a kingdom or republic.—*pl.* Nobility.
STĀTE, *v. a.* To settle; to tell; to represent.
STĀT'ED, *p. a.* Settled; regular; fixed.
STĀT'ED-LY, *ad.* Regularly; not occasionally.
STĀTE'LI-NESS, *n.* Grandeur; pomp; majesty.
STĀTE'LY, *a.* Grand; lofty; majestic.
STĀTE'MENT, *n.* The act of stating; a recital.
STĀTE'-RŎŎM, *n.* A magnificent apartment; a small room in a steam-vessel, &c.
STĀTES'MAN, *n.* One versed in government.
STĂT'IC, STĂT'I-CAL, *a.* Relating to statics.
STĂT'ICS, *n. pl.* Science or art of weighing bodies.
STĀ'TIQN, *n.* Situation; post; office; state; rank.
STĀ'TIQN, *v. a.* To place in a certain post, &c.
STĀ'TIQN-A-RY, *a.* Fixed; not progressive.
STĀ'TIQN-ER, *n.* A dealer in paper, pens, &c.
STĀ'TIQN-ER-Y, *n.* Wares of a stationer.
STA-TIS'TIC, STA-TIS'TI-CAL, *a.* Relating to statistics. [statistics.
STĂT-IS-TI''CIAN (-tish'an), *n.* One versed in
STA-TIS'TICS, *n. pl.* Statement of national resources, population, agriculture, commerce, &c.
STĂT'U-A-RY, *n.* Art of making statues:—a' maker of statues:—a statue or statues.
STĂT'UE (stät'yu), *n.* An image in stone, &c.
STĂT'URE (stät'yur), *n.* The height of any ani-
STĂT'U-TA-BLE, *a.* According to statute. [mal.
STĂT'ŪTE (stät'yūt), *n.* A positive or written
STÄUNCH (stänch), *v. a.* See STANCH. [law.
STĀVE, *v. a.* To break in pieces; to push away.
STĀVE, *n.* A stanza; a verse:—a thin piece of timber for a cask.—(*Mus.*) Staff.
STĀVES *or* STĀVES, *n.* The plural of *staff.*
STĀY, *v. n.* [*imp. t.* & *pp.* staid *or* stayed.] To continue; to wait; to stop; to dwell.
STĀY, *v. a.* To stop; to restrain, prop, support.
STĀY, *n.* Continuance; a stop; a prop; a support.
STĀYED (stād), *p. a.* Fixed; serious; staid.
STĀY'-LĀCE, *n.* A lace to fasten stays with.
STĀY'-MĀK-ER, *n.* One who makes stays.
STĀYS, *n. pl.* Bodice or a waistcoat for women.
STĔAD (stĕd), *n.* Room; place:—bed-frame.
STĔAD'FAST (stĕd'fast), *a.* Firm; fixed; constant.
STĔAD'FAST-LY (stĕd'fast-le), *ad.* Firmly.
STĔAD'I-LY (stĕd'e-le), *ad.* With steadiness.
STĔAD'I-NĔSS (stĕd'e-nĕs), *n.* Constancy.
STĔAD'Y (stĕd'e), *a.* Firm; regular; constant.
STĔAD'Y (stĕd'e), *v. a.* To make steady.
STEĀK (stāk), *n.* A slice of beef, &c.; a collop.
STĒAL (stēl), *v. a.* [*imp. t.* stole; *pp.* stolen.] To take by theft; to withdraw privily. [theft.
STĒAL, *v. n.* To withdraw privily; to practise
STĔALTH (stĕlth), *n.* Theft; a secret act; privacy.
STĔALTH'Y (stĕlth'e), *a.* Performed by stealth;
STĒAM, *n.* The vapor of hot water. [sly.
STĒAM, *v. n.* To send up vapors; to fume.

STĒAM, *v. a.* To heat with, or expose to, steam.
STĒAM'-BŌAT, *n.* A vessel propelled by steam.
STĒAM-ĔN'GINE, *n.* An engine worked by steam.
STĒAM'ER,   } *n.* A vessel propelled by steam;
STĒAM'-SHĬP,   } a steam-boat.
STĒ'A-RĬNE, *n.* A white, crystalline fat.
STĒ'A-TĪTE, *n.* Soap-stone.
STĒĒD, *n.* A horse for state or war. [on.
STĒEL, *n.* Iron combined with carbon:—a weap-
STĒEL, *v. a.* To edge with steel; to make hard.
STĒEL, STĒEL'Y, *a.* Made of steel; hard; firm.
STĒEL'YARD, *n.* A kind of balance for weighing.
STĒĒP, *a.* Sloping headlong; precipitous.
STĒĒP, *n.* A precipice; a precipitous place.
STĒĒP, *v. a.* To soak; to macerate; to imbue.
STĒĒ'PLE, *n.* A tower of a church, &c.; a spire.
STĒĒ'PLED (stē'pld), *a.* Furnished with steeples.
STĒĒP'NESS, *n.* Precipitous declivity.
STĒĒR, *n.* A young bullock; a young ox.
STĒĒR, *v. a. & n.* To direct; to guide in a passage.
STĒĒR'AGE, *n.* Act of steering:—part in a ship.
STĒĒR'ER,   } *n.* One who steers a ship; a
STĒĒRS'MAN,   } pilot.
STĔG-A-NŎG'RA-PHY, *n.* Art of secret writing.
STĔL'LAR, STĔL'LA-RY, *a.* Relating to stars.
STĔL'LATE, STĔL'LĀT-ED, *a.* Pointed as a star.
STĔM, *n.* A stalk; twig; family; race:—a prow.
STĔM, *v. a.* To oppose, as a current; to stop.
STĔNCH, *n.* A stink; a bad smell.
STĔN'CIL, *n.* A piece of metal, leather, &c., perforated, used for marking. [hand.
STE-NŎG'RA-PHY, *n.* Art of writing in short
STEN-TO'RI-AN, *a.* Loud; vociferous. [walk.
STĔP, *v. n.* To move with the feet; to go; to
STĔP, *n.* A pace; footstep; a stair; a round of a ladder; a degree; an action; a proceeding.
—*Step* in composition denotes relationship by marriage, as *step*-father, *step*-son, &c.
STĔPPE, *n.* A vast plain. [*Russia.*]
STĔP'PING-STŌNE, *n.* A stone laid for the foot.
STĔR-E-Q-GRĂPH'IC, *a.* Relating to stereography.
STĔR-E-ŎG'RA-PHY, *n.* Delineation of solids.
STĔR-E-ŎM'E-TRY, *n.* Art of measuring solids.
STĔR'E-Q-SCŌPE, *n.* An optical instrument.
STĔR'E-Q-TYPE, *n.* A plate of fixed types.
STĔR'E-Q-TYPE, *a.* Made by fixed types.
STĔR'E-Q-TYPE, *v. a.* To cast, as stereotype plates; to print from stereotype plates.
STĔR'E-Q-TYP-ER, *n.* One who stereotypes. [ing.
STĔR-E-Q-TY-PŎG'RA-PHY, *n.* Stereotype print-
STĔR'ILE, *a.* Barren; unfruitful; not fertile.
STE-RĬL'I-TY, *n.* Barrenness; unfruitfulness.
STĔR'LING, *a.* Real:—noting English money.
STĔRN, *a.* Severe of look or manners; harsh.
STĔRN, *n.* The hind part of a ship, &c.
STĔRN'LY, *ad.* In a stern manner; severely.
STĔRN'NESS, *n.* Severity of look; harshness.
STĔR-NU-TĀ'TIQN, *n.* The act of sneezing.
STĔR-NŪ'TA-TĬVE, *a.* Provoking to sneeze.
STĔR-NŪ'TA-TO-RY, *n.* Substance for sneezing.
STĔTH'Q-SCŌPE, *n.* (*Med.*) An instrument for exploring the chest.
STĒ'VE-DŌRE, *n.* A loader or unloader of vessels.
STEW (stū), *v. a.* To boil slowly.
STEW (stū), *v. n.* To be boiled slowly.
STEW, *n.* A hot-house; a brothel; meat stewed.
STEW'ARD, *n.* A manager of another's affairs.
STEW'ARD-SHĬP, *n.* The office of a steward.

STEW′PĂN, *n.* A pan used for stewing.
STĬB′I-ĂL,*a.* Pertaining to antimony; antimonial.
STĬCK, *n.* A piece of wood ; a staff :—a stab.
STĬCK, *v. a.* [*imp. t. & pp.* stuck.] To fasten on ;
   to attach ; to fix :—to stab ; to pierce.
STĬCK, *v. n.* To adhere ; to stop :—to scruple.
STĬCK′I-NĔSS, *n.* Adhesive quality ; viscosity.
STĬC′KLE, *v. n.* To contest to altercate.
STĬCK′LĔR, *n.* An obstinate contender.
STĬCK′Y, *a.* Viscous ; adhesive ; glutinous.
STĬFF, *a.* Rigid ; inflexible ; stubborn ; formal.
STĬFF′EN (stĭf′fn),*v.a.& n.*To make or grow stiff.
STĬFF′LY, *ad.* Rigidly ; inflexibly ; stubbornly.
STĬFF′NĔCKED(stĭf′nĕkt),*a.*Stubborn;obstinate.
STĬFF′NĔSS, *n.* Inflexibility ; obstinacy.
STĪ′FLE, *v.a.* To suffocate, extinguish, suppress.
STĬG′MĄ, *n.* A brand ; a mark of infamy.
STĬG-MĂT′ĬC, *a.* Having a stigma ; marked.
STĬG′MĄ-TĪZE, *v. a.* To mark with infamy.
STĪ′LĄR, *a.* Belonging to the stile of a dial.
STĪLE, *n.* A set of steps :—dial-pin. See STYLE.
STĬ-LĔT′TŌ, *n.* [It.] A small dagger :—an in-
   strument to make eyelet-holes. [pease.
STĬLL, *v. a.* To make silent ; to quiet ; to ap-
STĬLL, *a.* Silent ; quiet ; calm ; motionless.
STĬLL, *ad.* Till now; nevertheless ; always ; ever.
STĬLL, *n.* A vessel for distillation ; an alembic.
STĬLL′BŎRN, *a.* Born lifeless ; dead at the birth.
STĬLL′NĔSS, *n.* Quietness ; silence ; taciturnity.
STĬL′LY, *ad.* Silently ; not loudly ; calmly.
STĬLTS, *n. pl.* Supports or props for walking.
STĬM′Ų-LĄNT, *a.* Stimulating ; exciting.
STĬM′Ų-LĄNT, *n.* A stimulating medicine.
STĬM′Ų-LĀTE, *v. a.* To excite ; to spur on ; to
   quicken.
STĬM-Ų-LĀ′TIŎN, *n.* Excitement ; pungency.
STĬM′Ų-LĄ-TĬVE, *a.* Stimulating ; exciting.
STĬM′Ų-LĀ-TŎR, *n.* One who stimulates.
STĬM′Ų-LŬS, *n.; pl.* STĬM′Ų-LĪ. [L.] That
   which stimulates ; a spur ; incitement.
STĬNG, *v. a.* [*imp. t. & pp.* stung.] To pierce or
   wound with a point or sting. [pain.
STĬNG, *n.* A sharp point ; any thing that gives
STĬNGₐ′ĔR, *n.* Whatever stings or vexes.
STĬN′GI-NĔSS, *n.* Covetousness ; niggardliness.
STĬN′GY, *a.* Covetous ; niggardly ; avaricious.
STĬNK, *v. n.* [*imp. t. & pp.* stunk.] To emit an
STĬNK, *n.* Offensive smell. [offensive smell.
STĬNT, *v. a.* To bound ; to limit, confine, stop.
STĬNT, *n.* A limit ; a bound :—quantity assigned.
STĬNT′ĔR, *n.* Whatever or whoever stints.
STĪ′PĔND, *n.* Wages ; a settled pay ; hire.
STĪ-PĔN′DĮ-Ą-RY, *a.* Receiving a stipend.
STĪ-PĔN′DĮ-Ą-RY,*n.*One who serves for a stipend.
STĬP′PLE, *v. n.* To engrave by means of dots.
STĬP′PLE, *n.* An instrument used in stippling.
STĬP′Ų-LĀTE, *v. n.* To contract ; to settle terms.
STĬP-Ų-LĀ′TIŎN, *n.* A contract ; a bargain.
STĬP′Ų-LĀ-TŎR, *n.* One who contracts or bar-
   gains. [iole.
STĬP′ŪLE, *n.* (*Bot.*) Scale at the base of a pet-
STĬR, *v. a.* To move ; to agitate ; to incite ; to
STĬR, *v. n.* To move ; to be in motion. [raise.
STĬR, *n.* Tumult ; commotion ; disturbance.
STĬR′Ą-BŎŬT, *n.* A dish of oatmeal boiled.
STĬR′RŬP (stŭr′rŭp *or* stŭr′rŭp), *n.* Iron for a
   horseman's foot to rest in.
STĬTCH, *v. a. & n.* To sew with a needle.

STĬTCH, *n.* A pass of a needle :—a sharp pain.
STĪVE, *v. a.* To stuff up close ; to make hot.
STĪ′VĔR, *n.* A Dutch copper coin.
STŌAT, *n.* An animal of the weasel kind.
STŎCK, *n.* Body of a plant ; a log :—a neck-cloth :
   —lineage :—cattle ; a store :—a fund of money.
STŎCK, *v. a.* To store ; to fill sufficiently.
STŎCK-ĀDE′, *n.* An enclosure of pointed stakes.
STŎCK-ĀDE′,*v. a.*To fortify with pointed stakes.
STŎCK′-BRŌ-KER, *n.* One who deals in stocks.
STŎCK′DŎVE (stŏk′dŭv), *n.* The wood-pigeon.
STŎCK′FĬSH, *n.* Codfish dried hard.
STŎCK′ĮNG, *n.* A covering for the leg. [stocks.
STŎCK′JŎB-BĔR, *n.* One who deals in funds or
STŎCK′JŎB-BĮNG, *n.* Speculation in stocks.
STŎCKS, *n. pl.* Frame for the legs ; public funds.
STŎCK′-STĬLL, *a.* Motionless as logs.
STŎCK′Y, *a.* Stout ; thick and firm ; stubbed.
STŌ′ĬC, *n.* A philosopher of the sect of Zeno.
STŌ′ĬC, STŌ′Į-CĄL,*a.*Relating to the Stoics ; cold.
STŌ′Į-CĄL-LY,*ad.* In a stoical manner ; austerely.
STŌ′Į-CĄL-NĔSS, *n.* The state of being stoical.
STŌ′Į-CĬṢM, *n.* System of the Stoics ; insensi-
STŌLE, *n.* A long vest ; a robe. [bility.
STŌLE, *imp. t.* from *steal.*
STŌLEN (stōln), *pp.* from *steal.* See STEAL.
STŎM′ĄℭH, *n.* The organ in which food is di-
   gested :—appetite :—anger ; temper :—pride.
STŎM′ĄℭH, *v. a.* To resent ; to brook.
STŎM′Ą-CHĔR, *n.* An ornament for the breast.
STŎ-MĂℭH′ĬC,   ) *a.* Relating to, or good for,
STŎ-MĂℭH′Į-CĄL,) the stomach.
STŌNE, *n.* A mineral ; a gem :—a concretion in
   the kidneys or bladder :—14 pounds :—a kernel.
STŌNE, *a.* Made of, or resembling, stone.
STŌNE, *v. a.* To beat or kill with stones.
STŌNE′-CŬT-TĔR, *n.* One who hews stones.
STŌNE′-FRŬIT, *n.* Peaches, plums, apricots, &c.
STŌNE′-PĬT, *n.* A pit where stones are dug.
STŌNE′-WORK, *n.* Work consisting of stone.
STŌN′Į-NĔSS, *n.* The state of being stony.
STŌN′Y, *a.* Made of, or full of, stones ; hard.
STOOD (stŭd), *imp. t. & pp.* from *stand.*
STŎŎK, *n.* A shock of corn of 12 sheaves.
STŎŎL, *n.* A seat without a back :—evacuation.
STŎŎP,*v. n.* To bend forward ; to lean ; to yield.
STŎŎP, *n.* The act of stooping :—a flagon.
STŎP, *v. a.* To hinder ; to obstruct ; to close up.
STŎP, *v. n.* To cease to proceed ; to desist.
STŎP, *n.* A pause ; a cessation ; obstruction.
STŎP′-CŎCK, *n.* A pipe made to let out liquor.
STŎP′PĄGE, *n.* Act of stopping ; an obstruction.
STŎP′PĔR,) *n.* That by which any hole, or the
STŎP′PLE,) mouth of any vessel, is filled up.
STŌ′RĂX, *n.* A plant :—a resinous gum.
STŌRE, *n.* A large quantity ; plenty ; a storehouse.
STŌRE, *v. a.* To furnish ; to lay up ; to hoard.
STŌRE′HŎŬSE, *n.* A magazine ; a warehouse.
STŎR′ĢE *or* STŎRĢE, *n.* Parental instinct.
STŌ′RĮED (stō′rįd), *a.* Furnished with stories ;
   adorned with historical pictures.
STŌRK, *n.* A large bird of passage. [tle.
STŎRM, *n.* A tempest ; an assault ; tumult ; bus-
STŎRM, *v. a.* To attack by open force.
STŎRM, *v. n.* To raise tempests ; to rage ; to blow.
STŎRM′Y, *a.* Tempestuous ; violent. [rooms.
STŌ′RY, *n.* A tale ; a narrative :—a loft ; a set of
STŌ′RY-TĔLL′ĔR, *n.* One who relates tales.

STŎŬT, *a.* Strong; lusty; valiant; brave; bold.
STŎŬT, *n.* A very strong kind of beer.
STŎŬT'LY, *ad.* Lustily; boldly; obstinately.
STŎŬT'NESS, *n.* Strength; valor; boldness.
STŌVE, *n.* A hot-house:—a place for a fire.
STŌVE, *v. a.* To keep warm in a house heated.
STŌ'VER, *n.* Fodder for cattle; hay; straw.
STŌW (stō), *v. a.* To lay up; to reposit in order.
STŌW'AGE, *n.* Room for laying up:—deposit.
STRĀ'BĬSM, STRA-BĬS'MŬS, *n.* A squinting.
STRĂD'DLE, *v. n.* To walk wide and awkwardly.
STRĂG'GLE, *v. n.* To wander; to rove; to ramble.
STRĂG'GLER, *n.* A wanderer; a rover.
STRĀIGHT (strāt), *a.* Not crooked; direct; right.
STRĀIGHT (strāt), *ad.* Immediately; directly.
STRĀIGHT'EN (strā'tn), *v. a.* To make straight.
STRĀIGHT'FÖR-WARD, *ad.* Directly.
STRĀIGHT'LY (strāt'le), *ad.* In a right line.
STRĀIGHT'NESS (strāt'nes), *n.* Rectitude.
STRĀIGHT'WAY (strāt'wā), *ad.* Immediately.
STRĀIN, *v. a.* To filter; to sprain; to stretch.
STRĀIN, *v. n.* To make violent efforts.
STRĀIN, *n.* A violent effort:—a style of speaking; a song; a note:—turn:—race.
STRĀIN'ER, *n.* An instrument of filtration.
STRĀIT, *a.* Narrow; close; strict; difficult.
STRĀIT, *n.* A narrow pass; distress; difficulty.
STRĀIT'EN (strā'tn), *v. a.* To make narrow; to contract; to confine; to distress.
STRĀIT'LĀCED (strāt'lāst), *a.* Stiff; strict.
STRĀIT'LY, *ad.* Narrowly; strictly; closely.
STRĀIT'NESS, *n.* Narrowness; rigor; distress.
STRĀKE, *n.* The iron band of a wheel; tire.
STRA-MĬN'E-OŬS, *a.* Strawy; light; chaffy.
STRĂND, *n.* The shore or beach, as of the sea.
STRĂND, *v. a.* To drive or force on the shallows.
STRĀNGE, *a.* Foreign; odd; unknown.
STRĀNGE'LY, *ad.* In a strange manner; oddly.
STRĀNGE'NESS, *n.* Quality of being strange.
STRĂN'GER, *n.* A foreigner; one unknown.
STRĂN'GLE, *v. a.* To choke; to suffocate.
STRĂN'GLES, *n. pl.* Swellings in a horse's throat.
STRĂN-GU-LĀ'TĬON, *n.* The act of strangling.
STRĂN'GU-RY, *n.* Difficulty in voiding urine.
STRĂP, *n.* A narrow, long slip of leather; thong.
STRĂP, *v. a.* To beat, or tie, with a strap.
STRĂP-PĀ'DŌ, *n.* A military punishment.
STRĂP'PĬNG, *a.* Vast; large; bulky. [*Low.*]
STRĀ'TA, *n. pl.* [L.] Beds; layers. See STRATUM.
STRĂT'A-GEM, *n.* An artifice in war; a trick.
STRĂT-Ĭ-FĬ-CĀ'TĬON, *n.* Arrangement in layers.
STRĂT'Ĭ-FY, *v. a.* To range in beds or layers.
STRA-TŎC'RA-CY, *n.* A military government.
STRĀ'TUM, *n.*; pl. STRĀ'TA. [L.] A layer or bed of gravel, earth, stone, or rocks.
STRĂW, *n.* The stalk on which grain grows.
STRĂW, *v. a.* To scatter. See STREW and STROW.
STRĂW'BER-RY, *n.* A plant and its fruit.
STRĂW'-BUĬLT (strâw'bĭlt), *a.* Made of straw.
STRĂW'-CÖL'ORED (strâw'kŭl'urd), *a.* Of the color of straw; light yellow.
STRĂW'Y, *a.* Made of straw; like straw; light.
STRĀY, *v. n.* To wander; to rove; to err; to devi-
STRĀY, *n.* An animal lost by wandering. [ate.
STRĒAK, *n.* A line of color; a stripe. [streaks.
STRĒAK, *v. a.* To stripe; to variegate with
STRĒAK'Y, *a.* Striped; variegated by streaks.
STRĒAM, *n.* A running water; a current; course.

STRĒAM, *v. n.* To flow; to run; to issue forth.
STRĒAM'ER, *n.* An ensign; a flag; a pennon.
STRĒAM'LET (strēm'let), *n.* A small stream.
STRĒAM'Y, *a.* Abounding in running water.
STRĒĒT, *n.* A way; a public way in a town, &c.
STRĒĒT'-WÂLK-ER, *n.* A prostitute.
STREIGHT (strāt), *n.* A passage. See STRAIT.
STRĔNGTH, *n.* Force; vigor; power; support.
STRĔNG'THEN (strĕng'thn), *v. a.* To make strong.
STRĔNG'THEN (strĕng'thn), *v. n.* To grow strong.
STRĔNG'THEN-ER, *n.* One that makes strong.
STRĔN'U-OŬS, *a.* Bold; active; ardent; zealous.
STRĔN'U-OŬS-LY, *ad.* Actively; zealously.
STRĔN'U-OŬS-NĔSS, *n.* State of being strenuous.
STRĔSS, *n.* Importance; weight; violence; force.
STRĔTCH, *v. a.* To extend; to expand; to draw out.
STRĔTCH, *v. n.* To be extended or drawn out.
STRĔTCH, *n.* Extension; reach; effort; extent.
STRĔTCH'ER, *n.* Any thing used for extension.
STREW (strō or strŭ), *v. a.* [*imp. t.* strewed; *pp.* strewed *or* strewn.] To spread; to scatter.
STRĪ'Æ, *n. pl.* Small channels or furrows.
STRĪ'ATE, STRĪ'A-TED, *a.* Formed in striæ.
STRĬC'KEN (strĭk'kn), *pp.* from *strike.* Afflicted; smitten:—advanced in years; far gone.
STRĬC'KLE, *n.* An instrument for whetting scythes:—a strike.
STRĬCT, *a.* Exact; severe; rigorous; confined.
STRĬCT'LY, *ad.* Exactly; rigorously; severely.
STRĬCT'NESS, *n.* Exactness; severity; rigor.
STRĬCT'URE (strĭkt'yur), *n.* Contraction:—a touch of criticism; a remark; censure.
STRĪDE, *n.* A long step; straddle.
STRĪDE, *v. n.* [*imp. t.* strode *or* strid; *pp.* stridden *or* strid.] To walk with long steps. [ing.
STRĬD'U-LOŬS, *a.* Making a small noise; creak-
STRĪFE, *n.* Contention; contest; discord.
STRĪFE'FŬL, *a.* Contentious; discordant.
STRĪKE, *v. a.* [*imp. t.* struck; *pp.* struck *or* stricken.] To hit with a blow; to impress; to inflict; to contract; to lower, as a flag.
STRĪKE, *v. n.* To make a blow; to collide.
STRĪKE, *n.* A dry measure:—a levelling instrument:—a revolt, as of workmen, in order to obtain higher wages.
STRĪK'ĬNG, *p. a.* Affecting; surprising.
STRĪK'ĬNG-LY, *ad.* So as to affect or surprise.
STRĬNG, *n.* A slender rope; cord; tendon; series.
STRĬNG, *v. a.* [*imp. t.* & *pp.* strung.] To furnish with strings; to put or place on a string.
STRĬNGED (strĭngd), *a.* Having strings. [ous.
STRĬN'GENT, *a.* Binding; contracting:—rigor-
STRĬNG'HÂLT, *n.* A disorder in horses; spring-
STRĬNG'Y, *a.* Fibrous; filamentous; ropy. [halt.
STRĬP, *v. a.* To make naked; to divest; to rob.
STRĬP, *n.* A narrow shred; a slip; a shred.
STRĪPE, *v. a.* To variegate with lines:—to beat.
STRĪPE, *n.* A colored streak:—a blow; a lash.
STRĪ'PED, *p. a.* Having stripes or colored streaks;
STRĬP'LĬNG, *n.* A youth; a lad. [streaked.
STRĬP'PĬNGS, *n. pl.* After-milkings.
STRĪVE, *v. n.* [*imp. t.* strove; *pp.* striven.] To struggle; to labor; to contend; to vie.
STRŌ'CLE, } *n.* An instrument, like a shovel,
STRŌ'KAL, } used by glass-makers.
STRŌKE, *n.* A blow:—affliction:—a touch.
STRŌKE, *v. a.* To rub gently; to soothe.
STRŌLL, *v. n.* To wander; to ramble; to rove.

STRŌLL, *n.* A ramble ; a wandering ; a roving.
STRŌLL'ER, *n.* A vagrant ; a wanderer.
STRŎNG, *a.* Vigorous ; powerful ; mighty ; hale.
STRŎNG'HŌLD, *n.* A fortress ; a fortified place.
STRŎNG'LY, *ad.* With strength ; powerfully ; [firmly.
STRŎNG'-WȦ-TER, *n.* Distilled spirit.
STRŎN'TĬ-Ą (strŏn'she-ą), *n.* An alkaline earth.
STRŎP, *n.* A piece of rope ; a razor-strop ; strap.
STRŌ'PHĘ, *n.* A stanza ; division of a poem.
STRŌVE, *imp. t.* from *strive.*
STRŌW (strō), *v. a.* [*imp. t.* strowed ; *pp.* strowed *or* strown.] To spread ; to scatter. See STREW.
STRŬCK, *imp. t.* & *pp.* from *strike.*
STRŬCT'ŲRE (strŭkt'yur), *n.* Form :—an edifice.
STRŬG'GLE, *v. n.* To labor ; to strive ; to contest.
STRŬG'GLE, *n.* Labor ; effort ; contest ; agony.
STRŬM'PĘT, *n.* A lewd woman ; a prostitute.
STRŬNG, *imp. t.* & *pp.* from *string.*
STRŬT, *v. n.* To walk with affected dignity.
STRŬT, *n.* An affected, stately walk.
STŬB, *n.* A thick, short stock ; a stump ; a log.
STŬB'BĘD, *a.* Truncated ; short and thick.
STŬB'BĘD-NĔSS,*n.* State of being short and thick.
STŬB'BLE, *n.* Stalks of corn after reaping.
STŬB'BORN, *a.* Obstinate ; inflexible ; stiff.
STŬB'BORN-LY, *ad.* Obstinately ; inflexibly.
STŬB'BORN-NĔSS, *n.* Obstinacy ; contumacy.
STŬB'BY, *a.* Short and thick ; short and strong.
STŬB'NAIL, *n.* A nail broken off ; a short nail.
STŬC'CŌ, *n.* [It.] A kind of fine plaster for walls.
STŬC'CŌ, *v. a.* To plaster walls with stucco.
STŬCK, *imp. t.* & *pp.* from *stick.* [mares.
STŬD, *n.* A post :—a knob :—a set of horses and
STŬD, *v. a.* To adorn with studs or knobs.
STŬ'DĘNT, *n.* One given to books ; a scholar.
STŬD'ĬED (stŭd'id), *a.* Learned ; versed in study.
STŬ'DĬ-OŬS, *a.* Given to study ; diligent ; careful.
STŬ'DĬ-OŬS-LY, *ad.* With study ; diligently.
STŬ'DĬ-OŬS-NĔSS, *n.* Application to study.
STŬD'Y, *n.* Application to books and learning ; attention ; meditation :—a room for study.
STŬD'Y, *v. n.* To think closely ; to muse.
STŬD'Y, *v. a.* To consider attentively ; to learn.
STŬFF, *n.* Any matter :—cloth :—furniture.
STŬFF, *v. a.* To fill very full ; to swell out.
STŬFF'ING, *n.* That by which any thing is filled.
STŬL'TĬ-FY, *v. a.* To make or prove foolish.
STŬM, *n.* Must ; wine unfermented. [err.
STŬM'BLE, *v. n.* To trip in walking ; to slip ; to
STŬM'BLE, *n.* A trip in walking ; a failure ; an
STŬM'BLER, *n.* One that stumbles. [error.
STŬM'BLĬNG-BLŎCK, } *n.* A cause of stum-
STŬM'BLĬNG-STŌNE, } bling, error, or offence.
STŬMP, *n.* The stub of a tree, &c.
STŬMP'Y, *a.* Full of stumps :—short ; stubby.
STŬN, *v. a.* To confound with noise or a blow ;
STŬNG, *imp. t.* & *pp.* from *sting.* [to stupefy.
STŬNK, *imp. t.* & *pp.* from *stink.*
STŬNT, *v. a.* To hinder from growth ; to stint.
STŪPE, *n.* Medicated cloth, &c., for a sore.
STŪPE, *v. a.* To foment ; to dress with stupes.
STŪ-PĘ-FĂC'TION, *n.* Insensibility ; stupidity.
STŪ-PĘ-FĂC'TĬVE, *a.* Causing insensibility.
STŪ'PĘ-FĪ-ER, *n.* One that stupefies.
STŪ'PĘ-FY, *v. a.* To make stupid ; to benumb.
STŲ-PĔN'DOŲS, *a.* Wonderful ; astonishing.
STŲ-PĔN'DOŲS-LY, *ad.* In a wonderful manner.
STŲ-PĔN'DOŲS-NĔSS, *n.* Wonderfulness.

STŬ'PĬD, *a.* Dull ; insensible ; sluggish.
STŲ-PĬD'Ĭ-TY, *n.* Dulness ; state of being stupid.
STŪ'PĬD-LY, *ad.* With stupidity ; dully.
STŪ'PĬD-NĔSS, *n.* Dulness ; stupidity.
STŪ'PÖR, *n.* [L.] Numbness ; insensibility.
STÜR'DĬ-LY, *ad.* Stoutly ; obstinately ; resolute-
STÜR'DĬ-NĔSS, *n.* Stoutness ; hardiness. [ly.
STÜR'DY, *a.* Hardy ; stout ; strong ; obstinate.
STÜR'GEON (stür'jun), *n.* A large fish.
STŬT'TER, *v. n.* To hesitate in speaking : to
STŬT'TER-ER, *n.* A stammerer. [stammer.
STY, *n.* A pen for swine :—a small tumor.
STŸG'Ĭ-ĄN, *a.* Pertaining to Styx ; infernal.
STŸLE, *n.* Manner of writing, speaking, &c. ; mode of painting :—mode of reckoning time : —title :—graver :—pin of a dial :—a filament.
STŸLE, *v. a.* To call ; to term ; to name.
STŸL'ĬSH, *a.* Showy ; modish ; fashionable.
STŸP'TĬC, STŸP'TĬ-CĄL, *a.* Checking bleeding.
STŸP-TĬÇ'Ĭ-TY, *n.* Power of stanching blood.
SUĀ'SĬ-BLE (swā'sę-bl), *a.* Easy to be persuaded.
SUĀ'ŞION (swā'zhun), *n.* Act of persuading.
SUĀ'SĬVE (swā'sĭv), *a.* Able to persuade.
SUĀ'SO-RY (swā'so-rę), *a.* Tending to persuade.
SUĂV'Ĭ-TY (swăv'ę-tę), *n.* Mildness ; softness.
SŬB, a prefix, signifies a subordinate degree.
SŬB-ĂÇ'ĬD, *a.* Sour in a small degree.
SŬB-ĂC'RĬD, *a.* Moderately acrid or sharp.
SŬB-ĂC'TION, *n.* The act of reducing.
SŬB-Ā'GĘNT, *n.* An agent of an agent.
SŬB'ĄL-TĔRN *or* SŲB-ÂL'TĘRN, *a.* Inferior ; subordinate. [officer,
SŬB'ĄL-TĔRN *or* SŲB-ÂL'TĘRN, *n.* A subaltern
SŬB-Ā'QUĘ-OŬS, *a.* Lying under water. [tee.
SŬB-CŎM-MĬT'TĘE, *n.* A subordinate commit-
SŬB-DĒA'CON (sŭb-dē'kn), *n.* An under-deacon.
SŬB-DĒAN', *n.* The vicegerent of a dean.
SŬB-DĬ-VĪDE', *v. a.* To divide what is divided.
SŬB-DĬ-VĬ''ŞION (-vĭzh'un), *n.* Division of a
SŲB-DŪ'Ą-BLE, *a.* That may be subdued. [part.
SŲB-DŪCE', SŲB-DŬCT', *v. a.* To take away.
SŲB-DŬC'TION, *n.* The act of taking away.
SŲB-DŪE' (sųb-dū'), *v. a.* To crush ; to conquer.
SŲB-JĀ'CĘNT, *a.* Lying under. [expose.
SŲB-JĔCT', *v. a.* To put under ; to enslave :—to
SŬB'JĘCT, *a.* Placed under ; exposed ; liable.
SŬB'JĘCT, *n.* One who lives under the domin- ion of another :—matter treated of ; theme.
SŲB-JĔC'TION, *n.* The act of subjecting ; state of being subject ; submission.
SŲB-JĔC'TĬVE, *a.* Relating to the subject ;— opposed to *objective.*
SŲB-JOĬN', *v. a.* To add to the end, or after.
SŬB'JŲ-GĀTE, *v. a.* To conquer ; to subdue.
SŬB-JŲ-GĀ'TION, *n.* The act of subduing.
SŬB-JŬNC'TION, *n.* The act of subjoining.
SŲB-JŬNC'TĬVE, *a.* Subjoined to something.
SŬB-LĬM'Ą-BLE, *a.* Possible to be sublimed.
SŬB'LĬ-MĀTE, *v. a.* To raise by heat :—to exalt.
SŬB'LĬ-MĀTE, *n.* A substance sublimated.
SŬB-LĬ-MĀ'TION, *n.* The art or process of sub- limating :—exaltation ; refinement. [grand.
SŲB-LĪME', *a.* High in place or style ; lofty ;
SŲB-LĪME', *n.* A grand or lofty style ; sublimity.
SŲB-LĪME', *v. a.* To raise by heat ; to sublimate.
SŲB-LĪME'LY, *ad.* In a sublime manner ; grandly.
SŲB-LĬM'Ĭ-TY, *n.* Quality of being sublime ; grandeur ; loftiness of style or sentiment.

SŬB-LŪ′NĄR, ⎫ *a.* Situated beneath the moon ;
SŬB′LŲ-NĄ-RY, ⎭ terrestrial ; of this world.
SŬB-MĄ-RÎNE′, *a.* Lying or acting under the sea.
SŲB-MĔRĢE′, *v. a.* To drown ; to put under
SŲB-MĔR′SIǪN, *n.* Act of submerging. [water.
SŲB-MĬS′SIǪN (sŭb-mĭsh′ŭn), *n.* The act of sub-
  mitting ; resignation ; obedience ; surrender.
SŲB-MĬS′SĮVE, *a.* Ready to yield or submit ;
  humble ; testifying submission.   [sion.
SŲB-MĬS′SĮVE-LY, *ad.* Humbly ; with submis-
SŲB-MĬS′SĮVE-NĔSS, *n.* Submissive disposition.
SŲB-MĬT′, *v. a.* To resign ; to yield ; to refer.
SŲB-MĬT′, *v. n.* To be subject ; to surrender.
SŲB-NĂS′CĘNT, *a.* Growing beneath something.
SŲB-ŎR′DĮ-NĄ-CY, *n.* The state of being subject.
SŲB-ŎR′DĮ-NĄTE, *a.* Inferior ; lower ; subject.
SŲB-ŎR′DĮ-NĄTE, *v. a.* To make subordinate.
SUB-ŎR′DĮ-NĄTE-LY, *ad.* In a subordinate man-
  ner.
SŲB-ŎR-DĮ-NĀ′TIǪN, *n.* Inferiority ; subjection.
SŲB-ŎRN′, *v. a.* To procure by collusion.
SŬB-ǪR-NĀ′TIǪN, *n.* The act of suborning.
SŲB-ŎRN′ĘR, *n.* One that suborns. [in court.
SŲB-PŒ′NĄ, *n.* A writ or summons for a witness
SŲB-PŒ′NĄ, *v. a.* To serve with a subpœna.
SŲB-SCRĪBE′, *v. a.* To sign, consent to, attest.
SŲB-SCRĪBE′, *v. n.* To give consent or promise.
SŲB-SCRĪB′ĘR, *n.* One who subscribes.
SŲB-SCRĬP′TIǪN, *n.* Act of subscribing :—a sig-
  nature ; attestation :—money subscribed.
SŬB′SĘ-QUĔNCE, *n.* The state of following.
SŬB′SĘ-QUĔNT, *a.* Following ; not preceding.
SŬB′SĘ-QUĔNT-LY, *ad.* At a later time.
SŲB-SĔRVE′, *v. a.* To serve instrumentally.
SŲB-SĔR′VĮ-ĘNCE, ⎫ *n.* Instrumental fitness of
SŲB-SĔR′VĮ-ĘN-CY, ⎭ use.   [conducive.
SŲB-SĔR′VĮ-ĘNT, *a.* Instrumental ; serviceable ;
SŲB-SĪDE′, *v. n.* To sink ; to tend downwards ;
SŲB-SĪ′DĘNCE, *n.* Act of sinking. [to abate.
SŲB-SĬD′Į-Ą-RY, *a.* Assistant ; brought in aid.
SŬB′SĮ-DĪZE, *v. a.* To grant a subsidy to.
SŬB′SĮ-DY, *n.* Aid in money to a foreign power
  to enable it to carry on a war ; a supply.
SŲB-SĬST′, *v. n.* To continue ; to have means of
SŲB-SĬST′, *v. a.* To feed ; to maintain. [living.
SŲB-SĬST′ĘNCE, *n.* Real being ; means of support.
SŲB-SĬST′ĘNT, *a.* Having real being ; inherent.
SŬB′STĄNCE, *n.* Something existing ; essential
  part ; something real ; body ; goods ; estate.
SŲB-STĂN′TIĄL (sŭb-stăn′shĄl), *a.* Real ; solid.
SŲB-STĂN-TĮ-ĂL′Į-TY (sŭb-stăn-shę-ăl′ę-tę), *n.*
  State of being substantial ; reality.
SŲB-STĂN′TIĄL-LY, *ad.* In substance ; truly.
SŲB-STĂN′TIĄL-NĔSS, *n.* State of being substan-
SŲB-STĂN′TIĄLṢ, *n. pl.* Essential parts. [tial.
SŲB-STĂN′TĮ-ĀTE (sŭb-stăn′shę-āt), *v. a.* To
  establish by evidence ; to prove ; to verify.
SŬB′STĄN-TĪVE, *n.* (*Gram.*) A noun.
SŬB′STĄN-TĪVE, *a.* Noting existence ; real.
SŬB′STĄN-TĪVE-LY, *ad.* As a substantive. [er.
SŬB′STĮ-TŪTE, *v. a.* To put in the place of anoth-
SŬB′STĮ-TŪTE, *n.* One acting in place of anoth-
  er ; a person or thing substituted.
SŬB-STĮ-TŪ′TIǪN, *n.* The act of substituting.
SŬB-STRĀ′TŲM, *n.* [L.] A stratum under anoth-
SŲB-TĔND′, *v. a.* To extend under.   [er.
SŲB-TĔNSE′, *n.* (*Geom.*) A chord of an arch.
SŬB′TĘR-FŪĢE, *n.* A shift ; an evasion ; a trick.

SUB-TĘR-RĀ′NĘ-ĄN, ⎫ *a.* Lying under the
SŬB-TĘR-RĀ′NĘ-OŬS, ⎭ earth ; placed below
  the surface of the earth ; underground.
SŬB′TĮLE, *a.* Thin ; rare ; not dense :—nice ;
  fine :—acute :—cunning. See SUBTLE.
SŬB′TĮLE-LY, *ad.* In a subtile manner ; thinly.
SŬB′TĮLE-NĔSS, *n.* Fineness ; rareness.
SŬB′TĮL-ĪZE, *v. a.* To make thin ; to refine.
SŬB′TĮL-TY, *n.* Thinness ; fineness ; subtlety.
SŬB′TLE (sŭt′tl), *a.* Sly ; artful ; acute ; cunning.
SŬB′TLE-TY (sŭt′tl-tę), *n.* Artfulness ; cunning.
SŬB′TLY (sŭt′tlę), *ad.* Slyly ; artfully ; cunningly.
SŲB-TRĂCT′, *v. a.* To withdraw from the rest.
SŲB-TRĂCT′ĘR, *n.* One that subtracts.
SŲB-TRĂC′TIǪN, *n.* Act of taking away a part.
SŬB′TRĄ-HĔND, *n.* The number to be subtracted.
SŬB′ÜRB, *n.* The outpart or confines of a city.
SŲB-ÜRB′ĄN, *a.* Inhabiting a suburb.
SŲB-VĔR′SIǪN, *n.* An overthrow ; destruction.
SŲB-VĔR′SĮVE, *a.* Having tendency to overturn.
SŲB-VĔRT′, *v. a.* To overthrow, overturn, ruin.
SŲB-VĔRT′ĘR, *n.* An overthrower ; a destroyer.
SŬC-CĘ-DĀ′NĘ-ŬM, *n.* [L.] A substitute.
SŲC-CĒĒD′, *v. a. & n.* To follow in order ; to
  come after or in place of ; to prosper.
SŲC-CĔSS′, *n.* Prosperity ; good fortune ; issue.
SŲC-CĔSS′FŬL, *a.* Prosperous ; fortunate.
SŲC-CĔSS′FŬL-LY, *ad.* Prosperously ; fortunately.
SŲC-CĔS′SIǪN (sŭk-sĕsh′ŭn), *n.* Order of events ;
  a series ; a lineage ; an order of descendants.
SŲC-CĔS′SĮVE, *a.* Following in order.
SŲC-CĔS′SĮVE-LY, *ad.* In succession or order.
SŲC-CĔS′SĮVE-NĔSS, *n.* State of being successive.
SŲC-CĔS′SǪR, *n.* One that follows another.
SŲC-CĬNCT′, *a.* Short ; concise ; brief ; laconic.
SŲC-CĬNCT′LY, *ad.* Briefly ; concisely.
SŲC-CĬNCT′NĘSS, *n.* Brevity ; conciseness.
SŬC′CǪR, *v. a.* To help ; to assist ; to relieve.
SŬC′CǪR, *n.* Aid ; assistance ; relief ; help.
SŬC′CǪR-ĘR, *n.* A helper ; an assistant.
SŬC′CǪ-TĂSH, *n.* Food made of unripe maize
  and beans boiled together.
SŬC′CŲ-LĔNCE, *n.* Quality of being succulent.
SŬC′CŲ-LĔNT, *a.* Juicy ; full of juice.
SŲC-CŪMB′, *v. n.* To yield ; to submit ; to sink.
SŲC-CŬS′SIǪN, *n.* The act of shaking ; shake.
SŬCH, *a.* Of that kind ; of the like kind. [bibe.
SŬCK, *v. a. & n.* To draw with the mouth ; to im-
SŬCK′ĘR, *n.* Whatever sucks :—a shoot of a plant.
SŬC′KLE, *v. a. & n.* To nurse at the breast.
SŬCK′LĬNG, *n.* A young creature fed by the pap.
SŬC′TIǪN, *n.* Act of sucking or drawing in.
SŲC-TŌ′RĮ-ĄL, *a.* Adapted to sucking.
SŪ′DĄ-TǪ-RY, *n.* A hot-house ; a sweating-bath.
SŬD′DĘN, *a.* Without notice ; hasty ; precipitate.
SŬD′DĘN-LY, *ad.* Without notice ; hastily.
SŬD′DĘN-NĔSS, *n.* The state of being sudden.
SŪ-DǪ-RĬF′ĮC, *a.* Promoting or causing sweat.
SŪ-DǪ-RĬF′ĮC, *n.* A medicine promoting sweat.
SŬDṢ, *n. pl.* Water impregnated with soap.
SUE (sū), *v. a.* To prosecute by law.
SUE, *v. n.* To beg ; to entreat ; to petition.
SŪ′ĘT, *n.* Hard fat about the loins and kidneys.
SŪ′ĘT-Y, *a.* Consisting of, or like, suet.
SŬF′FĘR, *v. a.* To bear ; to undergo ; to endure ;
  to sustain :—to permit ; to allow.
SŬF′FĘR, *v. n.* To endure pain of body or mind.
SŬF′FĘR-Ą-BLE, *a.* Tolerable ; that may be borne.

Ā,Ē,Ī,Ō,Ū,Ȳ, *long* ; Ă,Ĕ,Ĭ,Ŏ,Ŭ,Y̆, *short* ; Ą,Ę,Į,Ǫ,Ų,Y, *obscure.*—FȦRE,FÄR,FȦST,FÂLL ; HÊIR,HĔR ;

Sŭf′fẽr-ạ-ble-nĕss, *n.* Tolerableness.
Sŭf′fẽr-ạnce, *n.* Pain; patience:—permission.
Sŭf′fẽr-ẽr, *n.* One who suffers or endures.
Sŭf′fẽr-ĭng, *n.* Pain suffered; endurance.
Sụf-fīce′ (sụf-fīz′), *v. n.* To be sufficient.
Sụf-fīce′ (sụf-fīz′), *v. a.* To supply; to satisfy.
Sụf-fĭ′′ciẹn-cy (sụf-fĭsh′ẹn-sẹ),*n.*Competence.
Sụf-fĭ′′ciẹnt (-fĭsh′ẹnt), *a.* Equal to; enough.
Sụf-fĭ′′ciẹnt-ly (sụf-fĭsh′ẹnt-lẹ),*ad.* Enough.
Sŭf′fĭx, *n.* A letter or word annexed.
Sụf-fĭx′, *v. a.* To annex, as a letter or word.
Sŭf′fọ-cāte,*v. a.* To smother; to stifle, choke.
Sŭf-fọ-cā′tiọn, *n.* The act of choking.
Sŭf′fọ-cā-tĭve, *a.* Having the power to choke.
Sŭf′frạ-gắn,*n.*Subordinate or assistant bishop.
Sŭf′frạġe, *n.* A vote; voice given in election.
Sụf-fūṣe′, *v. a.* To spread over with something.
Sụf-fū′ṣiọn (sụf-fū′zhụn), *n.* An overspreading.
Sŭg′ạr (shŭg′ạr), *n.* A sweet substance.
Sŭg′ạr (shŭg′ạr), *v. a.* To sweeten. [died.
Sŭg′ạr-cằn′dy (shŭg′ạr-kăn′dẹ), *n.* Sugar can-
Sŭg′ạr-cāne (shŭg′ạr-kān), *n.* A cane or plant
   from the juice of which sugar is made.
Sŭg′ạr-plŭm (shŭg′ạr-plŭm), *n.* A sweatmeat.
Sŭg′ạr-y (shŭg′ạr-ẹ), *a.* Sweet; tasting of sugar.
Sụg-ġĕst′, *v. a.* To hint; to intimate.
Sụg-ġĕst′ẽr, *n.* One that suggests or hints.
Sụg-ġĕs′tiọn, *n.* Private hint; intimation.
Sū-ĭ-cī′dạl, *a.* Relating to suicide.
Sū′ĭ-cīde, *n.* Self-murder; a self-murderer.
Sūit (sūt), *n.* A set of the same kind, as clothes:
   a petition:—courtship:—prosecution:—retinue.
Sūit, *v. a. & n.* To fit; to adapt to; to agree.
Sūit′ạ-ble (sū′tạ-bl),*a.*Fitting; according with.
Sūit′ạ-ble-nĕss, *n.* Fitness; agreeableness.
Sūit′ạ-bly, *ad.* Agreeably; according to.
Suîte (swĕt), *n.* [Fr.] Retinue; train; a suit.
Sūit′ọr (sūt′ụr), *n.* One that sues:—a wooer.
Sŭl′cạte, sŭl′cāt-ẹd, *a.* Furrowed; grooved.
Sŭlk′ĭ-ly, *ad.* In the sulks; morosely.
Sŭlk′ĭ-nĕss, *n.* Sullenness; moroseness.
Sŭlk′y, *a.* Silently sullen; morose; sour; dull.
Sŭlk′y, *n.* A carriage for one person.
Sŭl′lẹn, *a.* Solitary; sour; gloomy; obstinate.
Sŭl′lẹn-ly, *ad.* Gloomily; intractably.
Sŭl′lẹn-nĕss, *n.* Moroseness; sluggish anger.
Sŭl′ly, *v. a.* To soil; to tarnish; to spot.
Sŭl′phạte, *n.* A substance formed of sulphuric
   acid and some other substance as a base.
Sŭl′phụr, *n.* A mineral substance; brimstone.
Sŭl′phụr-ạte, *a.* Of, or belonging to, sulphur.
Sŭl-phụr-ā′tiọn, *n.* Act of dressing or com-
   bining with sulphur.
Sụl-phū′rẹ-oŭs, } *a.* Containing, or impreg-
Sŭl′phụr-oŭs, } nated with, sulphur.
Sŭl′phụ-rĕt,*n.* A combination of sulphur with
   an alkali, earth, or metal.
Sụl-phū′rĭc, *a.* Relating to, or derived from,
   sulphur.—*Sulphuric acid,* a combination of sul-
   phur and oxygen; oil of vitriol.
Sŭl′phụr-y, *a.* Partaking of sulphur.
Sŭl′tạn, *n.* The Turkish sovereign.
Sụl-tā′nạ, *n.* The wife or consort of a sultan.
Sŭl′tạ-nĕss, *n.* The same as *sultana.*
Sŭl′trĭ-nĕss,*n.* State of being sultry. [moist.
Sŭl′try, *a.* Hot and close; hot, cloudy, and
Sŭm, *n.* The whole amount; quantity of money.
Sŭm, *v. a.* To compute; to cast up.

Sū′mạćh (shū′măk *or* sū′măk),*n.* A tree or shrub.
Sŭm′mạ-rĭ-ly, *ad.* Briefly; in the shortest way.
Sŭm′mạ-ry, *a.* Short; brief; compendious.
Sŭm′mạ-ry, *n.* A compendium; a synopsis.
Sŭm′mẽr, *n.* A season of the year:—a beam.
Sŭm′mẽr, *v. n.* To pass the summer.
Sŭm′mẽr-hȯüse, *n.* Country-house; an arbor.
Sŭm′mẽr-sĕt, *n.* A high leap. See SOMERSET.
Sŭm′mĭt, *n.* The top; the utmost height.
Sŭm′mọn, *v. a.* To call with authority; to cite.
Sŭm′mọn-ẽr, *n.* One who cites or summons.
Sŭm′mọnṣ, *n.* A call of authority; a citation.
Sŭmp′tẽr (sŭm′tẽr), *n.* A pack-horse or mule.
Sŭmpt′ụ-ạ-ry (sŭmt′yụ-ạ-rẹ), *a.* Relating to ex-
   pense:—regulating the expense of living.
Sŭmpt′ụ-oŭs (sŭmt′yụ-ŭs), *a.* Costly; splendid.
Sŭmpt′ụ-oŭs-ly, *ad.* Expensively; splendidly.
Sŭmpt′ụ-oŭs-nĕss,*n.*Expensiveness;costliness.
Sŭn, *n.* The luminary that makes the day.
Sŭn, *v. a.* To expose to, or warm in, the sun.
Sŭn′bēam (sŭn′bēm), *n.* A ray of the sun.
Sŭn′bēat, *p. a.* Shone on fiercely by the sun.
Sŭn′bŭrnt, *p. a.* Tanned; scorched by the sun.
Sŭn′day (sŭn′dẹ), *n.* The Christian Sabbath.
Sŭn′dẽr, *v. a.* To part; to separate; to divide.
Sŭn′dẽr, *n.* Two; two parts, as *in sunder.*
Sŭn′dī-ạl, *n.* A plate which shows the time.
Sŭn′-drīed (sŭn′drĭd), *p. a.* Dried by the sun.
Sŭn′drĭeṣ, *n. pl.* Sundry or several things.
Sŭn′dry, *a.* Several; various; more than one.
Sŭn′flȯw-ẽr, *n.* A plant and flower.
Sŭng, *imp. t. & pp.* from *sing.* See SING.
Sŭnk, *imp. t. & pp.* from *sink.* See SINK.
Sŭn′lẹss, *a.* Wanting sun; wanting warmth.
Sŭn′līght (sŭn′līt), *n.* The light of the sun.
Sŭn′ny, *a.* Bright; clear; exposed to the sun.
Sŭn′rīṣe, sŭn′rīṣ-ĭng, *n.* Morning; the east.
Sŭn′sĕt,*n.* Close of the day; evening:—the west.
Sŭn′shīne, *n.* The radiant light of the sun.
Sŭn′shīne, sŭn′shīn-y, *a.* Bright with the sun.
Sŭp, *v. a.* To drink by sups.—*v. n.* To eat supper.
Sŭp, *n.* A small draught of liquor; a sip.
Sū′pẽr, in composition, notes *excess* or *over.*
Sū′pẽr-ạ-ble, *a.* That may be conquered.
Sū-pẽr-ạ-bȯünd′, *v. n.* To be exuberant.
Sū-pẽr-ạ-bŭn′dạnce, *n.* More than enough.
Sū-pẽr-ạ-bŭn′dạnt, *a.* More than enough.
Sū-pẽr-ạ-bŭn′dạnt-ly, *ad.* Exuberantly.
Sū-pẽr-ădd′, *v. a.* To add over and above.
Sū-pẽr-ạd-dĭ′′tiọn, *n.* Act of superadding.
Sū-pẽr-ạn-ġĕl′ĭc, *a.* Superior to the angels.
Sū-pẽr-ăn′nụ-āte, *v. a.* To impair by age.
Sū-pẽr-ăn′nụ-āt-ẹd,*p. a.* Disqualified by age.
Sū-pẽr-ăn-nụ-ā′tiọn, *n.* State of being su-
   perannuated; disqualification by age.
Sụ-pẽrb′, *a.* Grand; pompous; august; stately.
Sụ-pẽrb′ly, *ad.* In a superb manner; grandly.
Sū-pẽr-cär′gō, *n.* An officer in a merchant ves-
   sel who manages the commercial transactions.
Sū-pẽr-cĭl′ĭ-oŭs, *a.* Haughty; dictatorial.
Sū-pẽr-cĭl′ĭ-oŭs-ly, *ad.* Haughtily.
Sū-pẽr-cĭl′ĭ-oŭs-nĕss,*n.* Haughtiness.
Sū-pẽr-ĕm′ĭ-nĕnce, *n.* Superior eminence.
Sū-pẽr-ĕm′ĭ-nĕnt,*a.* Eminent in a high degree.
Sū-pẽr-ĕm′ĭ-nĕnt-ly, *ad.* Very eminently.
Sū-pẽr-ĕr-ọ-gā′tiọn,*n.* Performance of more
   than duty or necessity requires.
Sū-pẽr-ĕr′ọ-gạ-tọ-ry, *a.* Exceeding duty.

SŪ-PĘR-ĔX′CĘL-LĔNT, *a.* Very excellent.
SŪ-PĘR-FĘ-TĀ′TIǪN, *n.* A second conception.
SŪ′PĘR-FĪCE, *n.* The outside; superficies.
SŪ-PĘR-FĬ″CIAL (sū-pęr-fĭsh′al), *a.* Being on the surface; shallow; not profound. [surface.
SŪ-PĘR-FĬ″CIAL-LY (-fĭsh′al-le), *ad.* On the
SŪ-PĘR-FĬ″CIAL-NĔSS, *n.* Shallowness. [face.
SŪ-PĘR-FĬ″CIĘS (-fĭsh′ęz), *n.* Outside; sur-
SŪ-PĘR-FĪNE′, *a.* Eminently fine; excellent.
SŪ-PĘR-FLŪ′I-TY, *n.* More than enough; excess.
SY-PĔR′FLU-OŬS, *a.* Exuberant; unnecessary.
SŪ-PĘR-HŪ′MAN, *a.* Above what is human.
SŪ-PĘR-ĮN-CŬM′BĘNT, *a.* Lying or resting on.
SŪ-PĘR-ĮN-DŪCE′, *v.a.* To bring in as an addition.
SŪ-PĘR-ĮN-DŬC′TIǪN, *n.* Act of superinducing.
SŪ-PĘR-ĮN-TĔND′, *v. a.* To oversee; to manage.
SŪ-PĘR-ĮN-TĔN′DĘNCE, *n.* Oversight; direction.
SŪ-PĘR-ĮN-TĔN′DĘNT, *n.* A director; overseer.
SY-PĒ′RĮ-ǪR, *a.* Higher; greater; preferable.
SY-PĒ′RĮ-ǪR, *n.* One who is above another.
SY-PĒ-RĮ-ŎR′I-TY, *n.* Preëminence; higher rank.
SY-PĔR′LA-TĬVE, *a.* Implying the highest degree.
SY-PĔR′LA-TĬVE-LY, *ad.* In the highest degree.
SY-PĔR′LA-TĬVE-NĔSS, *n.* Superlative quality.
SŪ-PĘR-LŪ′NAR, *a.* Above the moon; not
SŪ-PĘR-LŪ′NA-RY, ∫ of this world.
SY-PĔR′NAL, *a.* Placed above; celestial.
SŪ-PĘR-NĀ′TANT, *a.* Swimming on the top.
SŪ-PĘR-NĂT′Ụ-RAL, *a.* Being above nature.
SŪ-PĘR-NĂT′Ụ-RAL-LY, *ad.* Above nature's pow-
SŪ-PĘR-NŪ′MĘR-A-RY, *a.* More than enough. [er.
SŪ-PĘR-NŪ′MĘR-A-RY, *n.* A person or thing above the stated, required, or usual number.
SŪ-PĘR-SCRĪBE′, *v.a.* To write on the outside of.
SŪ-PĘR-SCRĬP′TIǪN, *n.* A writing on the outside.
SŪ-PĘR-SĒDE′, *v. a.* To make void; to set aside.
SŪ-PĘR-STĬ″TIǪN (sū-pęr-stĭsh′ụn), *n.* Spurious religion; false worship or devotion.
SŪ-PĘR-STĬ″TIOŲS (sū-pęr-stĭsh′ụs), *a.* Addicted to superstition:—weakly scrupulous.
SŪ-PĘR-STĬ″TIOŲS-LY, *ad.* With superstition.
SŪ-PĘR-STRŬC′TIǪN, *n.* An edifice raised on any thing.
SŪ-PĘR-STRŬCT′ỤRE (-strŭkt′yụr), *n.* That which is raised or built upon something else.
SŪ-PĘR-VĒNE′, *v. n.* To come in unexpectedly.
SŪ-PĘR-VĒ′NĮ-ĘNT, *a.* Added; additional.
SŪ-PĘR-VĔN′TIǪN, *n.* The act of supervening.
SŪ-PĘR-VĪSE′, *v. a.* To overlook; to superintend.
SŪ-PĘR-VĬ″ŞIǪN (-vĭzh′ụn), *n.* Inspection.
SŪ-PĘR-VĪ′ŞǪR, *n.* An overseer; an inspector.
SŪ-PĮ-NĀ′TIǪN, *n.* The state of being supine.
SY-PĪNE′, *a.* Lying with the face upward:—negligent; careless; indolent; drowsy.
SŪ′PĪNE, *n.* (*Gram.*) A kind of verbal noun.
SY-PĪNE′LY, *ad.* With the face upward; drowsily.
SY-PĪNE′NĔSS, *n.* The state of being supine.
SŬP′PĘR, *n.* The evening repast.
SŬP′PĘR-LĔSS, *a.* Destitute of supper.
SŬP-PLĂNT′, *v. a.* To displace by stratagem.
SŬP-PLĂNT′ĘR, *n.* One that supplants.
SŬP′PLE, *a.* Pliant; yielding; soft:—fawning.
SŬP′PLE, *v. n.* To grow soft; to grow pliant.
SŬP′PLE-MĔNT, *n.* An addition to supply defects.
SŬP-PLE-MĔNT′AL, ∫ *a.* Added for a supply;
SŬP-PLE-MĔNT′A-RY, ∫ additional.
SŬP′PLE-NĔSS, *n.* Pliantness; flexibility.
SŬP′PLE-TǪ-RY, *a.* Supplying deficiencies.

SŬP′PLĮ-ANT, *a.* Entreating; beseeching.
SŬP′PLĮ-ANT, *n.* A petitioner; a supplicant.
SŬP′PLĮ-ANT-LY, *ad.* In a submissive manner.
SŬP′PLĮ-CĂNT, *n.* One who supplicates.
SŬP′PLĮ-CĂNT, *a.* Entreating; petitioning.
SŬP′PLĮ-CĀTE, *v. n.* To implore; to entreat.
SŬP-PLĮ-CĀ′TIǪN, *n.* A humble petition; entreaty.
SŬP′PLĮ-CA-TǪ-RY, *a.* Petitionary; humble.
SYP-PLĪ′ĘR, *n.* One who supplies.
SYP-PLȲ′, *v. a.* To fill up; to afford; to furnish.
SYP-PLȲ′, *n.* Relief of want; sufficiency. [dure.
SYP-PŌRT′, *v. a.* To sustain; to bear up; to en-
SYP-PŌRT′, *n.* A prop; a maintenance; a supply.
SYP-PŌRT′A-BLE, *a.* Endurable; tolerable.
SYP-PŌRT′ĘR, *n.* One that supports; a sustainer.
SYP-PŌŞ′A-BLE, *a.* That may be supposed.
SYP-PŌŞE′, *v. a.* To assume or admit without proof; to imagine; to believe; to think.
SŬP-PǪ-ŞĬ″TIǪN (-zĭsh′ụn), *n.* An hypothesis.
SYP-PŎŞ-Į-TĪ″TIOŬS (sỵp-pŏz-ę-tĭsh′ụs), *a.* Not genuine; counterfeit; not real; spurious.
SYP-PŎŞ′Į-TĬVE, *a.* Implying supposition.
SYP-PŎŞ′Į-TĬVE-LY, *ad.* Upon supposition.
SYP PRĔSS′, *v. a.* To crush, subdue, conceal.
SYP-PRĔŞ′SIǪN (sỵp-prĕsh′ụn), *n.* The act of suppressing; concealment.
SYP-PRĔSS′ǪR, *n.* One that suppresses. [ter.
SŬP′PỤ-RĀTE, *v. a.* & *n.* To generate pus or mat-
SŬP-PỤ-RĀ′TIǪN, *n.* The act of suppurating.
SŬP′PỤ-RĀ-TĮVE, *a.* Promoting suppuration.
SŪ′PRA, in composition, signifies *above* or *before*.
SY-PRĔM′A-CY, *n.* Highest authority or power.
SY-PRĒME′, *a.* Highest in dignity and power.
SY-PRĒME′LY, *ad.* In the highest degree.
SŪR′BĀSE, *n.* Cornice above a pedestal.
SYR-CĒASE′, *v. n.* To be at an end; to cease.
SYR-CHĂRǴE′, *v. a.* To overload; to overburden.
SYR-CHĂRǴE′, *n.* An excessive load or charge.
SYR-CHĂRǴ′ĘR, *n.* One that overburdens.
SŪR′CĬN-GLE, *n.* A girth:—girdle of a cassock.
SŬR′CLE, *n.* A shoot; a twig; a sucker.
SŪR′CŌAT, *n.* A coat worn over the dress.
SŬRD, *a.* Incommensurable, as a number.
SŬRD, *n.* An incommensurable number.
SŬRE (shŭr), *a.* Certain; unfailing; infallible; confident; undoubting; safe; firm.
SŬRE (shŭr), *ad.* Certainly; without doubt.
SŬRE′FOOT-ĘD (shŭr′fŭt-ęd), *a.* Not stumbling.
SŬRE′LY (shŭr′le), *ad.* Certainly; without
SŬRE′NĔSS (shŭr′nęs), *n.* Certainty. [doubt.
SŬRE′TY (shŭr′te), *n.* Security, or one who gives security against loss or damage.
SŬRE′TY-SHĬP, *n.* The office or state of a surety.
SŬRF, *n.* The swell or dashing of the sea.
SŬR′FACE, *n.* The superficies; the outside.
SŬR′FEĮT (sŭr′fĭt), *v. a.* To feed to excess.
SŬR′FEĮT (sŭr′fĭt), *n.* Excess in eating.
SŬRǴE, *n.* A swelling sea; a wave; a billow.
SŬRǴE, *v. n.* To swell; to rise high, as waves.
SŬR′ǴEǪN (sŭr′jụn), *n.* A professor of surgery.
SŬR′ǴER-Y, *n.* Art of curing external injuries.
SŬR′ǴĮ-CAL, *a.* Pertaining to surgery.
SŬR′ǴY, *a.* Rising in billows; full of surges.
SŬR′LĮ-NĔSS, *n.* Moroseness; sour anger.
SŬR′LY, *a.* Morose; rough; uncivil; sour.
SYR-MĪŞE′, *v. a.* To suspect; to conjecture.
SYR-MĪŞE′, *n.* An imperfect notion; a suspicion.
SYR-MŌŬNT′, *v. a.* To conquer, surpass, exceed.

Ī,Ē,Ī,Ō,Ū,Ȳ, *long*; Ă,Ĕ,Ĭ,Ŏ,Ŭ,Y̆, *short*; A,E,I,Ǫ,Ụ,Y, *obscure.*—FĀRE,FÄR,FĂST,FÂLL; HÊIR,HĔR;

SŬR-MŎŬNT'A-BLE, a. Conquerable; superable.
SŬR'NĀME, n. A family name; an appellation.
SŬR-NĀME', v. a. To name by an appellation.
SŬR-PĂSS', v. a. To excel; to exceed; to transcend; to go beyond.
SŬR-PĂSS'A-BLE, a. That may be excelled.
SŬR-PĂSS'ING, p. a. Excellent in a high degree.
SŬR'PLĬCE, n. A clergyman's vestment.
SŬR'PLŬS, SŬR'PLŬS-AGE, n. An overplus.
SŬR-PRĪ'ṢAL, n. The act of taking unawares.
SŬR-PRĪŞE', n. Act of surprising; sudden confusion; astonishment; wonder. [ish.
SŬR-PRĪŞE', v. a. To take unawares; to astonish.
SŬR-PRĪŞ'ING, p. a. Wonderful; astonishing.
SŬR-PRĪŞ'ING-LY, ad. In a surprising manner.
SŬR-RE-BŬT'TER, n. (Law.) A plaintiff's answer to a defendant's rebutter. [der.
SŬR-RE-JŌĬN'DER, n. An answer to a rejoinder.
SŬR-RĔN'DER, v. a. & n. To render or deliver up; to relinquish; to yield.
SŬR-RĔN'DER, n. Act of yielding.
SŬR-RĔP'TIQN, n. A sudden invasion.
SŬR-REP-TĬ''TIOŲS (-rep-tĭsh'ŭs), a. Done by stealth; obtained or produced fraudulently.
SŬR-REP-TĬ''TIOŲS-LY, ad. By stealth; by stealth. [fraud.
SŬR'RO-GĀTE, n. A deputy; a delegate.
SŬR-RŎŬND', v. a. To encompass; to enclose.
SŬR-SŎL'ĬD, n. The fifth power of any number.
SŬR-TŌUT' (sụr-töt'), n. An outside coat.
SŬR-VEY' (sụr-vā'), v. a. To view; to oversee.
SŬR'VEY (sür'vā), n. View; prospect; retrospect:—inspection:—mensuration. [ing land.
SŬR-VEY'ING (sụr-vā'-), n. The art of measuring land.
SŬR-VEY'OR (-vā'ụr), n. An overseer:—a measurer of land. [of a surveyor.
SŬR-VEY'OR-SHĬP (-vā'ụr-shĭp), n. The office of a surveyor.
SŬR-VĪVE', v. a. & n. To live longer than; to outlive; to remain alive.
SŬR-VĪV'OR, n. One who outlives another.
SŬR-VĪV'OR-SHĬP, n. State of outliving another.
SŲS-CĔPT-Ĭ-BĬL'Ĭ-TY, n. The quality of admitting or being susceptible. [der.
SŲS-CĔPT'Ĭ-BLE, a. Capable of admitting; tender.
SŲS-CĔP'TĬVE, a. Susceptible; admitting.
SŲS-CĬP'Ĭ-ĔNT, a. Receiving; admitting.
SŲS-PĔCT', v. a. To mistrust; to think guilty.
SŲS-PĔND', v. a. To hang; to interrupt; to delay.
SŲS-PĔND'ER, n. One that suspends. [lay.
SŲS-PĔNSE', n. Uncertainty; indecision; a stop.
SŲS-PĔN'SIQN, n. A hanging up; a cessation.
SŲS-PĔN'SQ-RY, a. Suspending; doubtful.
SŲS-PĬ''CIQN (-pĭsh'ụn), n. Act of suspecting.
SŲS-PĬ''CIOŲS (-pĭsh'ŭs), a. Inclined to suspect; distrustful; jealous; causing suspicion.
SŲS-PĪ'RAL, n. A breathing hole; a ventiduct.
SŬS-PĮ-RĀ'TIQN, n. A sigh; the act of sighing.
SŲS-PĪRE', v. a. To sigh; to fetch a deep breath.
SŲS-TĀIN', v. a. To bear, support, maintain, help.
SŲS-TĀIN'A-BLE, a. Capable of being sustained.
SŲS-TĀIN'ER, n. One that sustains or supports.
SŬS'TE-NANCE, n. Maintenance; food; victuals.
SŬS-TEN-TĀ'TIQN, n. Support; maintenance.
SŬT'LER, n. A seller of victuals, &c., in a camp.
SŬT-TĒE', n. Self-immolation of a widow on the funeral pile of her deceased husband.
SŪT'ỤRE (sūt'yụr), n. A sewing:—a seam.
SWAB (swŏb), n. A kind of mop to clean floors.
SWAB (swŏb), v. a. To clean with a swab.

SWAD'DLE (swŏd'dl), v. a. To swathe; to bind.
SWAD'DLE (swŏd'dl), n. Clothes bound tight.
SWAD'DLING-BĂND, SWAD'DLING-CLŎTH (swŏd-), n. Cloth wrapped round an infant.
SWĂG, v. n. To sink down by its weight; to sag.
SWĂG'GER, v. n. To bluster; to bully; to brag.
SWĂG'GER-ER, n. A blusterer; a turbulent fellow.
SWĂG'GY, a. Hanging by its weight. [low.
SWĀIN, n. A young man; a pastoral youth.
SWĀLE, v. n. & a. To waste; to melt; to sweal.
SWAL'LŌW (swŏl'lō), n. A bird:—the throat.
SWAL'LŌW (swŏl'lō), v. a. To take down the throat; to absorb.
SWĂM, imp. t. from swim. [throat; to absorb.
SWAMP (swŏmp), n. A marsh; a bog; a fen.
SWAMP'Y (swŏm'pe), a. Boggy; fenny.
SWAN (swŏn), n. A handsome water-fowl.
SWAN'SKĬN (swŏn'skĭn), n. A soft flannel.
SWĀRD, n. The surface of the ground; turf.
†SWĀRE, the old pret. from swear.
SWÂRM, n. A multitude of bees, &c.; a crowd.
SWÂRM, v. n. & a. To raise as bees; to crowd.
SWÂRT, SWÂRTH, a. Black; brown; tawny.
SWÂRTH'I-LY, ad. Blackly; duskily; tawnily.
SWÂRTH'I-NĔSS, n. Darkness of complexion.
SWÂRTH'Y, a. Dark of complexion; black; tawny.
SWASH (swŏsh), n. A splashing of water. [ny.
SV.'ÂTH, n. A line of grass cut down by a mower.
SWĀTHE, v. a. To bind with bands; to confine.
SWĀY, v. a. & n. To wield; to bias; to govern.
SWĀY, n. Power; rule; influence; direction.
SWĒAL, v. a. To melt; to swale. See SWALE.
SWEAR (swâr), v. n. [imp. t. swore; pp. sworn.] To declare or promise upon oath.
SWEAR (swâr), v. a. To bind by an oath.
SWEAR'ER (swâr'er), n. One who swears.
SWEAR'ING, n. The act of declaring upon oath.
SWĔAT (swĕt), n. Fluid evacuated; labor; toil.
SWĔAT (swĕt), v. n. [imp. t. & pp. swĕat, swet, or sweated.] To emit moisture, perspire, toil.
SWĔAT (swĕt), v. a. To emit; to make to sweat.
SWĔAT'I-NĔSS, n. The state of being sweaty.
SWĔAT'Y (swĕt'e), a. Covered or moist with sweat.
SWĒ'DISH, a. Respecting the Swedes. [sweat.
SWEEP, v. a. [imp. t. & pp. swept.] To clean with a broom; to brush:—to drive off at once.
SWEEP, v. n. To pass with violence or pomp.
SWEEP, n. The act of sweeping:—one who sweeps.
SWEEP'ER, n. One that sweeps. [sweeps.
SWEEP'INGS, n. pl. Things swept away.
SWEEP'STAKES, n. One who wins all:—prize in a race, made up of several stakes.
SWEET, a. Pleasing to any sense; not sour; saccharine; luscious; fragrant; mild; grateful.
SWEET, n. Sweetness; something pleasing.
SWEET'BREAD, n. The pancreas of a calf, &c.
SWEET'BRĪ-ER, n. A fragrant shrub.
SWEET'EN (swēt'tn), v. a. & n. To make or grow sweet. [ens.
SWEET'EN-ER (swēt'tn-er), n. Whatever sweetens.
SWEET'HEART, n. A lover or mistress.
SWEET'ING, n. A sweet apple:—a darling.
SWEET'LY, ad. In a sweet manner; gently.
SWEET'MEAT, n. Fruit preserved with sugar.
SWEET'NESS, n. The quality of being sweet.
SWEET'WĬL-LIAM, n. A garden flower.
SWEET'WĬL-LŌW (swēt'wĭl-lō), n. A shrub.
SWELL, v. n. [imp. t. swelled; pp. swelled or swollen.] To grow larger or turgid; to tumefy.

SWĔLL, *v. a.* To make tumid; to heighten.
SWĔLL, *n.* An extension of bulk; an increase.
SWĔLL'ĬNG, *n.* Inflation:—a morbid tumor; a protuberance. [heat.
SWĔL'TĘR, *v. a. & n.* To melt or dry up with
SWĔL'TRY, *a.* Suffocating with heat; sultry.
SWĔPT, *imp. t. & pp.* from *sweep.* [to yield.
SWĔRVE, *v. n.* To wander; to deviate; to bend;
SWĔT, *imp. t. & pp.* from *sweat.* [ready.
SWĬFT, *a.* Quick; fleet; fast; nimble; rapid;
SWĬFT, *n.* A bird :—a newt:—a machine.
SWĬFT'LY, *ad.* Fleetly; rapidly; nimbly.
SWĬFT'NĘSS, *n.* Speed; nimbleness; celerity.
SWĬG, *v. n. & a.* To drink by large draughts.
SWĬLL, *v. a.* To drink grossly; to intoxicate.
SWĬLL, *n.* Liquid food given to swine.
SWĬLL'ĘR, *n.* A drunkard; one who swills.
SWĬM, *v. n. [imp. t.* swam *or* swum; *pp.* swum.] To float on water; to glide :—to be dizzy.
SWĬM, *v. a.* To pass by swimming.
SWĬM'MĘR, *n.* One who swims. [vertigo.
SWĬM'MĬNG, *n.* Act of floating on the water:—
SWĬM'MĬNG-LY, *ad.* Without obstruction.
SWĬN'DLE, *v. a.* To cheat; to defraud, cozen.
SWĬN'DLĘR, *n.* A sharper; a cheat; a rogue.
SWĪNE, *n. sing. & pl.* A hog; a pig.
SWĪNE'HĔRD, *n.* A keeper of hogs.
SWĪNE'-STY, *n.* A sty or pen for swine.
SWĬNG, *v. n. [imp. t. & pp.* swung.] To wave to and fro, hanging loosely; to vibrate.
SWĬNG, *v. a.* To make to play loosely.
SWĬNG, *n.* A waving motion :—free course. [ish.
SWĬNGE, *v. a.* To whip; to bastinade; to pun-
SWĬN'GĘL, *n.* The part of a flail which swings.
SWĬN'GLE, *v. a.* To beat and dress, as flax.— *v. n.* To dangle.
SWĬN'GLE, *n.* A wooden instrument for beating and dressing flax.
SWĬN'ĬSH, *a.* Befitting swine; gross; brutal.
SWĬSS, *a.* Of, or belonging to, Switzerland.
SWĬTCH, *n.* A small, flexible twig :—a contrivance on railroads. [track to another.
SWĬTCH, *v. a.* To lash :—to transfer from one
SWĬV'EL (swĭv'vl), *n.* A ring which turns upon a staple; a small cannon, turning on a pivot.
SWŌLLEN (swōln), *pp.* from *swell.*
SWŌÔN, *v. n.* To faint.—*n.* A fainting fit.
SWÔÔP, *v. a.* To seize at once; to catch up.
SWÔÔP, *n.* A seizing upon, as a bird of prey.
SWŎP, *v. a.* To exchange; to barter. [*Low.*]
SWŌRD (sōrd), *n.* A military weapon.
SWŌRD'ĘD (sōrd'ĕd), *a.* Girt with a sword.
SWŌRD'-KNŎT (sōrd'nŏt), *n.* A ribbon tied to the hilt of a sword.
SWŌRD'-PLĀY-ĘR (sōrd'plā-ẹr), *n.* A fencer.
SWŌRDṢ'MĄN (sōrdz'mạn), *n.* One who uses a sword.
SWŌRE, *imp. t,* from *swear.* [sword.
SWŌRN, *pp.* from *swear.*
SWŬM, *imp. t. & pp.* from *swim.*
SWŬNG, *imp. t. & pp.* from *swing.*
ṢȲC'Ą-MŌRE, *n.* A species of tree; the plane-tree.
ṢȲC'Ọ-PHĄN-CY, *n.* Mean flattery; servility.
ṢȲC'Ọ-PHĄNT, *n.* A parasite; a flatterer.
ṢȲC-Ọ-PHĂN'TĬC, *a.* Flattering; fawning
ṢȲC-Ọ-PHĂN'TĬ-CĄL, obsequiously.
SYL-LĂB'ĬC, *a.* Relating to syllables.
SYL-LĂB'Ĭ-CĄL-LY, *ad.* In a syllabical manner.
SYL-LĂB-Ĭ-CĀ'TĬQN, *n.* Formation of syllables.

SYL'LĄ-BLE, *n.* As much of a word as is uttered by the help of one vowel, or one articulation.
SYL'LĄ-BŬB, *n.* Milk mixed with wine or cider.
SYL'LĄ-BŬS, *n.* An abstract; a compendium.
SYL'LỌ-ĢĬṢM, *n.* An argument or form of reasoning consisting of three propositions.
SYL-LỌ-ĢĬS'TĬC, *a.* Relating to, or con-
SYL-LỌ-ĢĬS'TĬ-CĄL, sisting of, a syllogism.
SYL'LỌ-ĢĪZE, *v. n.* To reason by syllogism.
SYLPH, *n.* A fabled being of the air.
SYL'VĄ, *n.* [L.] A collection of poetical pieces : —trees of a country collectively.
SYL'VĄN, *a.* Woody; shady; relating to woods.
SYL'VĄN, *n.* A fabled deity of the woods; a satyr; a fawn. [creed.
SYM'BỌL, *n.* Type; emblem; abstract :—a
SYM-BŎL'ĬC, *a.* Serving as a symbol; typ-
SYM-BŎL'Ĭ-CĄL, ical; emblematical.
SYM-BŎL'Ĭ-CĄL-LY, *ad.* By representation.
SYM'BỌL-ĪZE, *v. n.* To have a resemblance.
SYM'BỌL-ĪZE, *v. a.* To cause to represent.
SYM-MĔT'RĬ-CĄL, *a.* Proportional in parts.
SYM'MĘ-TRĪZE, *v. a.* To make proportionate.
SYM'MĘ-TRY, *n.* A due proportion; harmony.
SYM-PĄ-THĔT'ĬC, *a.* Having mutual sen-
SYM-PĄ-THĔT'Ĭ-CĄL, sation; having a feeling in common.
SYM-PĄ-THĔT'Ĭ-CĄL-LY, *ad.* With sympathy.
SYM'PĄ-THĪZE, *v. n.* To feel with or for. another; to have sympathy.
SYM'PĄ-THY, *n.* Fellow-feeling; mutual sensibility; condolence; tenderness.
SYM-PHŌ'NĬ-OŬS, *a.* Harmonious; musical.
SYM'PHỌ-NY, *n.* Harmony of mingled sounds.
SYMP'TỌM, *n.* A sign; a token; an indication.
SYMP-TỌM-ĂT'ĬC, *a.* Relating to symp-
SYMP-TỌM-ĂT'Ĭ-CĄL, toms; indicating.
SYMP-TỌM-ĂT'Ĭ-CĄL-LY, *ad.* By symptom.
SYN'Ą-GŌGUE (sĭn'ą-gŏg), *n.* An assembly of Jews for worship; a Jewish house of worship.
SYN-Ą-LŒ'PHĄ, *n.* Contraction of a syllable.
SYN'ℭHRỌ-NĂL, *a.* Happening at the same time·
SYN-ℭHRŎN'Ĭ-CĄL, *a.* Happening together.
SYN'ℭHRỌ-NĬṢM, *n.* A concurrence of events.
SYN'ℭHRỌ-NĪZE, *v. n.* To agree in regard to time; to happen simultaneously. [time.
SYN'ℭHRỌ-NOŬS, *a.* Happening at the same
SYN'CỌ-PĀTE, SYN'CỌ-PĪZE, *v. a.* To contract.
SYN'CỌ-PĘ, *n.* A contraction of a word; fainting.
SYN'DĬC, *n.* A magistrate; an agent; a deputy.
SYN'DRQ-MĘ, *n.* Concurrence; concourse.
SY-NĔC'DQ-ℭHĘ, *n.* A figure by which a part is taken for the whole, or the whole for a part.
SYN'ỌD, *n.* An ecclesiastical assembly, meeting, or council. [synod.
SY-NŎD'ĬC, SY-NŎD'Ĭ-CĄL, *a.* Relating to a
SY-NŎN'Y-MĄ, *n. pl.* [L.] Synonymes.
SYN'Ọ-NYME, *n.* One of two or more words of the same language which have the same or similar meaning.
SY-NŎN'Y-MĪZE, *v. a.* To express or interpret by words of similar signification.
SY-NŎN'Y-MOŬS, *a.* Having the same meaning.
SY-NŎN'Y-MY, *n.* The quality of expressing by different words the same thing. [an epitome.
SY-NŎP'SĬS, *n.; pl.* SY-NŎP'SĒṢ. A general view;
SY-NŎP'TĬ-CĄL, *a.* Affording a general view.
SYN-TĂC'TĬ-CĄL, *a.* Pertaining to syntax.

SẎN′TĂX, *n.* The construction of sentences.
SẎN′THĘ-SĬS, *n.* Composition, or a putting to-
 gether;—opposed to *analysis.* [ing.
SYN-THĔT′ĬC, SYN-THĔT′Ĭ-CĄL, *a.* Compound-
SYN′THĔT′Ĭ-CĄL-LY, *ad.* By synthesis.
SẎPH′Ĭ-LĬS, *n.* The venereal disease.
SẎPH-Ĭ-LĬT′ĬC, *a.* Contaminated with syphilis.
SȲ′PHON, *n.* A tube. See SIPHON.
SẎR′Ĭ-ĂC, SẎR′Ĭ-ĄN, *a.* Relating to Syria.
SẎR′ĬNĢE, *n.* A pipe to squirt liquor with. [inge.
SẎR′ĬNĢE, *v. a.* To spout or wash with a syr-

SẎS′TĘM, *n.* A combination; a method; scheme.
SẎS-TĘM-ĂT′ĬC,   *a.* Partaking of system;
SẎS-TĘM-ĂT′Ĭ-CĄL,   methodical.
SẎS-TĘM-ĂT′Ĭ-CĄL-LY, *ad.* In form of a system.
SẎS′TĘM-Ą-TĬST,   *n.* One who reduces to
SẎS′TĘM-Ą-TĪZ-ĘR,   system.
SẎS′TĘM-Ą-TĪZE, *v. a.* To reduce to a system.
SẎS′TǪ-LĘ, *n.* The contraction of the heart·—
 the shortening of a long syllable.
SẎZ′Y-ĢY, *n.* Place of the moon or a planet, when
 in conjunction with, or opposition to, the sun.

T.

T, a mute consonant, at the beginning and end
 of words, has always the same sound.
TĂB′BY, *n.* A rich, watered silk.
TĂB′BY, *a.* Brinded; brindled; varied in color.
TĂB-E-FĂC′TĬON, *n.* The act of wasting away.
TĂB′Ę-FȲ, *v. n.* To waste; to emaciate. [ship.
TĂB′ĘR-NĄ-CLE, *n.* A tent; a place of wor-
TĂB′ĘR-NĄ-CLE, *v. n.* To dwell; to house.
TĂB′ĬD, *a.* Wasted by disease; consumptive.
TĂB′ĬD-NĔSS, *n.* Emaciation.
TĂB′LĄ-TŪRE, *n.* Painting on walls or ceilings.
TĀ′BLE, *n.* Any flat or level surface; a board;
 an index; a collection of heads; a catalogue.
TĀ′BLE, *v. n.* To board.—*v. a.* To set down.
TABLEAU (tăb-lō′), *n.*; pl. TABLEAUX (tăb-lōz′).
 [Fr.] A picture:—a list; a table.
TĀ′BLE-BĒĒR, *n.* Beer for the table.
TĀ′BLE-CLŎTH, *n.* Linen spread on a table.
TĀ′BLE-LĂND, *n.* Level, elevated·land.
TĀ′BLEṢ, *n. pl.* Draughts:—a tablet.
TĂB′LĘT, *n.* A small table; surface written on.
TĀ′BLE-TĂLK (tā′bl-tâwk), *n.* Discourse at ta-
TĄ-BŌŌ′, *v. a.* To interdict; to prohibit. [ble.
TĀ′BǪR, *n.* A drum beaten with one stick.
TĀ′BǪR-ĘR, *n.* One who beats the tabor.
TĀ′BǪR-ĔT, TĂB′RĘT, *n.* A small tabor.
TĂB′Ǫ-RÎNE, *n.* A tabor; a small drum. [ses.
TĂB′Ṳ-LĄR, *a.* In the form of tables or synop-
TĂB′Ṳ-LĀTE, *v. a.* To reduce to tables; to flat-
TĂB′Ṳ-LĀT-ĘD, *a.* Having a flat surface. [ten.
TĄ-ᴄHȲG′RĄ-PHY, *n.* The art of quick writing.
TĂÇ′ĬT, *a.* Silent:—implied; not expressed.
TĂÇ′ĬT-LY, *ad.* Silently; without words.
TĂÇ′Ĭ-TURN, *a.* Silent; uttering little. [serve.
TĂÇ-Ĭ-TURN′Ĭ-TY, *n.* Habitual silence or re-
TĂCK, *v. a.* To join; to unite; to fasten.
TĂCK, *v. n.* To turn about, as a ship. [ship.
TĂCK, *n.* A small nail:—rope:—turn of a
TĂCK′LE, *n.* A machine; rigging; an arrow.
TĂCK′LE, *v. a.* To supply with tackle.
TĂCK′LĮNG, *n.* Furniture of a mast, &c.
TĂCT, *n.* Skill; nice discernment; expertness.
TĂC′TĬC, TĂC′TĮ-CĄL, *a.* Relating to tactics.
TĄC-TĬ″CĬĄN (tąk-tĭsh′ąn), *n.* One skilled in
 tactics; an adroit manager. [battle.
TĂC′TĬCS, *n. pl.* The art of ranging men for
TĂC′TĬLE, *a.* Tangible; susceptible of touch.
TĄC-TĬL′Ĭ-TY, *n.* Perceptibility by the touch.
TĂC′TĬON, *n.* The act of touching.
TĂD′PŌLE, *n.* A young unformed frog, &c.

TĀ′EN (tān). A poetical contraction of *taken.*
TĂF′FĘ-TY, *n.* A thin, smooth, glossy silk.
TĂFF′RĄIL, *n.* Upper part of the stern of a ship.
TĂG, *n.* A metal, &c., at the end of a string.
TĂG, *v. a.* To fit any thing with an end; to join.
TĂG, *n.* A play:—a slight touch. See TĬG.
TAGLIA (tăl′yę-ą), *n.* [It.] A peculiar combi-
 nation of pulleys.
TĀIL, *n.* The hinder or lower part; the end.
TĀI′LǪR (tā′lųr), *n.* One who makes clothes.
TĀI′LǪR-ĬNG, *n.* The business of a tailor.
TĀI′LǪR-ĔSS, *n.* A female tailor. [corrupt.
TĀINT, *v. a.* To sully; to infect; to poison; to
TĀINT, *n.* A stain; infection; corruption, soil.
TĀKE, *v. a.* [*imp. t.* took; *pp.* taken.] To re-
 ceive; to seize; to catch; to copy; to bear; to
 admit; to suppose; to hire.
TĀKE, *v. n.* To incline:—to gain reception.
TĀ′KEN (tā′kn), *pp.* from *take.* [ing.
TĀK′ĬNG, *n.* A seizure:—vexation.—*a.* Allur-
TĂL′BǪT, *n.* A sort of hunting dog.
TĂL′BǪ-TȲPE, *n.* A photographic picture.
TĂLC, *n.* A magnesian mineral.
TĂL-CŌSE′, TĂLCK′Y, *a.* Of the nature of talc.
TĀLE, *n.* A narrative:—reckoning. [tale.
TĀLE′BEĂR-ĘR, *n.* An officious informer; tell-
TĀLE′BEĂR-ĬNG, *n.* The act of telling tales.
TĂL′ĘNT, *n.* A weight; sum:—a faculty; gift.
TĂL′ĘNT-ĘD, *a.* Possessing talents or abilities.
TĂL′ĬṢ-MĂN, *n.* A magical character or figure;
TĂL-ĬṢ-MĂN′ĬC, *a.* Magical. [a charm.
TÂLK (tâwk), *v. n.* To speak; to converse.
TÂLK (tâwk), *n.* Oral conversation:—rumor.
TÂLK′Ą-TĬVE (tâwk′ą-tĭv), *a.* Loquacious.
TÂLK′Ą-TĬVE-NĔSS (tâwk′-), *n.* Loquacity.
TÂLK′ĘR (tâwk′-), *n.* One who talks; a prat-
TÂLL, *a.* High in stature; high; lofty. [tler.
TĂL′LĄĢE, TĂIL′ĄĢE, *n.* An ancient impost.
TÂLL′NĘSS, *n.* Height of stature; loftiness.
TĂL′LŌW (tăl′lō), *n.* A sort of animal fat.
TĂL′LŌW, *v. a.* To smear with tallow.
TĂL′LǪW-CHĂND′LĘR, *n.* Maker of, or dealer
 in, tallow candles
TĂL′LǪW-ĬSH, TĂL′LǪW-Y, *a.* Like tallow.
TĂL′LY, *n.* A stick notched to keep accounts:
 —any thing made to suit another. [ble.
TĂL′LY, *v. a. & n.* To fit; to suit, to be suita-
TĂL′LY-MĂN, *n.* A dealer:—a keeper of a tally.
TĂL′MŲD, *n.* A book of Jewish laws.
TĂL′MŲD-ĬST, *n.* One versed in the Talmud

TĂL′ON, _n._ The claw of a bird of prey.
TĀ′LŬS, _n._ [L.] The ankle-bone :—a slope in a rampart or wall :—a heap of fragments at the foot of a great rock.
TĂM′A-BLE, _a._ That may be tamed.
TĂM′A-RĬND, _n._ A tree and its fruit.
TĂM′A-RĬSK, _n._ A flowering shrub.
TĂM′BOUR, _n._ [Fr.] A tambourine :—a frame.
TĂM-BOU-RÎNE′ (-bô-rēn′), _n._ A kind of drum.
TĀME, _a._ Not wild ; domestic ; subdued ; dull.
TĀME, _v. a._ To make gentle ; subdue ; crush.
TĀME′LY, _ad._ Not wildly ; meanly ; spiritless-
TĀME′NĘSS, _n._ The quality of being tame. [ly.
TĂM′Ĭ-NY, TĂM′MY, _n._ A thin, woollen stuff.
TĂM′PĘR, _v. n._ To meddle ; to practise secretly.
TĂN, _v. a._ To prepare skins :—to imbrown.
TĂN, _n._ The ground bark of the oak, &c.
TĂNG, _n._ A strong taste ; smack :—a sea-weed.
TĂN′ĢĘNT, _n._ A right line touching a curve.
TĂN-ĢĬ-BĬL′Ĭ-TY, _n._ The quality of being tangi-
TĂN′ĢĬ-BLE, _a._ Perceptible by the touch. [ble.
TĂN′ĢLE (tăng′gl), _v. a. & n._ To interweave ; to snarl ; to entangle ; to entrap.
TĂN′ĢLE, _n._ Any thing complicated ; a snarl.
TĂNK, _n._ A large cistern or basin.
TĂNK′ARD, _n._ A drinking vessel, with a cover.
TĂN′NĘR, _n._ One whose trade is to tan leath-
TĂN′NĘR-Y, _n._ A place for tanning hides. [er.
TĂN′NĬN, _n._ Substance which tans leather.
TĂN′NĬNG, _n._ The process of preparing leather.
TĂN′-PĬT, _n._ A pit where leather is impregnated.
TĂN′SY, _n._ An odorous plant. [tion.
TĂN′TA-LĬŞM, _n._ Act of tantalizing ; tantaliza-
TĂN-TA-LĬ-ZĀ′TĬON, _n._ Act of tantalizing.
TĂN′TA-LĪZE, _v. a._ To torment ; to torture.
TĂN′TA-MŎÛNT, _a._ Equivalent ; equal.
TĂN-TĬV′Y _or_ TĂN′TĬ-VY, _ad._ Swiftly.
TĂN′TRŬMŞ, _n. pl._ Freaks ; bursts of ill humor.
TĂP, _v. a._ To touch lightly :—to pierce; to broach.
TĂP, _n._ A gentle blow :—a pipe ; a spigot.
TĀPE, _n._ A narrow fillet or band of linen, &c.
TĀ′PĘR, _n._ A wax candle ; a small light.
TĀ′PĘR, _a._ Regularly narrowed ; conical.
TĀ′PĘR, _v. n. & a._ To grow or make taper or gradually smaller.
TĀ′PĘR-NĘSS, _n._ The state of being taper.
TĂP′ĘS-TRY, _n._ An ornamental cloth. [tailed.
TĂP′HŎÛSE, _n._ House where liquors are re-
TĂP-Ĭ-Ō′CA, _n._ A glutinous and nutritious substance from the root of the manioc plant.
TĀ′PĬR, _n._ An animal resembling the hog.
TĂPIS (tăp′ē), _n._ [Fr.] A carpet :—a table-cloth.
TĂP′-RŎÔT, _n._ The principal stem of a root.
TĂP′STĘR, _n._ One who draws beer, &c.
TĂR, _n._ A dark liquid pitch :—a sailor.
TĂR, _v. a._ To smear over with tar.
TA-RĂN′TU-LA, _n._ A venomous sort of spider.
TĂR′DĬ-LY, _ad._ Slowly ; sluggishly. [ness.
TĂR′DĬ-NĘSS, _n._ Slowness ; lateness ; dilatori-
TĂR′DY, _a._ Slow ; sluggish ; dilatory ; late.
TĂRE, _n._ A weed :—an allowance in weight.
†TĂRE, _imp. t._ from _tear._ Tore.
TĂR′ĢĘT, _n._ A shield :—a mark to be shot at.
TĂR-ĢĘT-IĔR′, _n._ One armed with a shield.
TĂR′GŬM, _n._ A Scripture paraphrase in Chal-
TĂR′ĬFF, _n._ A table of duties on goods. [dee.
TĂR′NĬSH, _v. a._ To sully ; to soil ; to stain.
TĂR′NĬSH, _v. n._ To lose lustre ; to be soiled.

TĂR-PÂUL′ĬNG, _n._ Tarred canvas :—a sailor.
TĂR′RY, _v. n._ To stay ; to delay ; to wait.
TĂR′RY, _a._ Consisting of tar ; resembling tar.
TĂRT, _a._ Sour ; acid ; sharp :—harsh ; severe.
TĂRT, _n._ A small pie of fruit or jelly.
TĂR′TAN, _n._ A checked cloth :—a vessel.
TĂR′TAR, _n._ A concrete salt :—a native of Tartary :—a person of irritable temper.
TĂR-TĀ′RĘ-AN, TĂR-TĀ′RĘ-OŬS, _a._ Infernal.
TĂR-TĀ′RĘ-OŬS, _a._ Consisting of tartar.
TĂR-TĂR′ĬC, _a._ Noting an acid from tartar.
TĂR′TAR-ĪZE, _v. a._ To impregnate with tartar.
TĂR′TAR-OŬS, _a._ Consisting of, or like, tartar.
TĂRT′LY, _ad._ Sharply ; sourly ; with acidity.
TĂRT′NĘSS, _n._ Sharpness ; sourness ; severity.
TĂR-TŬFFE′, _n._ A hypocrite.
TĂSK, _n._ Employment ; business imposed.
TĂSK, _v. a._ To impose or burden as with a task.
TĂSK′MĂS-TĘR, _n._ One who imposes tasks.
TĂS′SĘL, _n._ An ornamental bunch of silk, &c.
TĂS′SĘLLED (-sęld), _a._ Adorned with tassels.
TĂS′SĘŞ, _n. pl._ Armor for the thighs.
TĂST′A-BLE, _a._ That may be tasted ; savory.
TĀSTE, _v. a._ To perceive by the palate ; to relish.
TĀSTE, _v. n._ To have a relish or taste ; to eat.
TĀSTE, _n._ The act of tasting ; relish ; nice perception :—intellectual discernment or relish.
TĀSTE′FŬL, _a._ High relished ; savory :—tasty.
TĀSTE′LESS, _a._ Having no taste ; insipid.
TĀSTE′LĘSS-NĘSS, _n._ Insipidity ; want of taste.
TĀST′ĘR, _n._ One who tastes :—a dram-cup.
TĀST′Y, _a._ Having taste ; nice ; fine.
TĂT′TĘR, _v. a._ To tear ; to rend.—_n._ A rag.
TĂT-TĘR-DĘ-MĂL′ĬON (-yŭn), _n._ A ragged fel-
TĂT′TLE, _v. n._ To prate ; to talk idly. [low.
TĂT′TLE, _n._ Prate ; idle chat ; trifling talk.
TĂT′TLĘR, _n._ An idle talker ; a prater.
TĂT-TŎÔ′, _n._ A beat of drum :—a figure formed by punctures on the body. [tures and stains.
TĂT-TŎÔ′, _v. a._ To form figures on by punc-
TÂUGHT (tât), _imp. t. & pp._ from _teach._
‖TÂUNT (tänt _or_ tâwnt), _v. a._ To reproach ; to insult ; to revile ; to ridicule ; to upbraid.
‖TÂUNT (tänt), _n._ Insult ; sarcastic reproach.
‖TÂUNT′ĬNG-LY (tänt′ĭng-lę), _ad._ With insult.
TÂU′RŬS, _n._ [L.] The Bull ; the 2d sign in the zodiac. [thing.
TÂU-TO-LŎĢ′Ĭ-CAL, _a._ Repeating the same
TÂU-TŎL′O-ĢĬST, _n._ One who uses tautology.
TÂU-TŎL′O-ĢĪZE, _v. n._ To repeat the same thing in different words.
TÂU-TŎL′O-ĢY, _n._ A repetition of the same words, or of the same sense in different words.
TÂU-TŎPH′O-NY, _n._ A repetition of the same
TĂV′ĘRN, _n._ A public-house ; an inn. [sound.
TĂV′ĘRN-ĘR, _n._ One who keeps a
TĂV′ĘRN-KĒĔP-ĘR, tavern.
TÂW, _v. a._ To dress white or alum leather.
TÂW′DRĬ-LY, _ad._ In a tawdry manner.
TÂW′DRĬ-NĘSS, _n._ Gaudy or ostentatious finery.
TÂW′DRY, _a._ Very showy without elegance.
TÂW′ĘR-Y, _n._ The manufacture of white leather.
TÂW′NY, _a._ Dusky yellow, like things tanned.
TĂX, _n._ An impost ; a tribute ; charge ; censure.
TĂX, _v. a._ To load with imposts ; to charge :—to
TĂX′A-BLE, _a._ That may be taxed. [censure.
TĂX-Ā′TĬON, _n._ The act of taxing ; impost ; tax.
TĂX′Ĭ-DĔR-MĬST, _n._ One versed in taxidermy.

TĂX'Ĭ-DĔR-MŸ, *n.* Art of preserving skins.
TĒA (tē), *n.* A Chinese plant, or evergreen shrub :—a drink or liquor made of it.
TĒACH (tēch), *v. a.* [*imp. t.* & *pp.* taught.] To instruct; to inform; to show; to indicate.
TĒACH'Ａ-BLE, *a.* Willing or apt to learn; docile.
TĒACH'Ａ-BLE-NĔSS,*n.*Docility; aptness to learn.
TĒACH'ĘR, *n.* One who teaches; an instructor.
TĒA'CŬP, *n.* A cup to drink tea from.
TĒAK, *n.* A timber tree and its wood.
TĒAL, *n.* A wild fowl of the duck kind. [ing.
TĒAM, *n.* A number of horses or oxen for draw-
TĒAM'STĘR, *n.* A driver of a team.
TĒA'PŎT, *n.* A vessel in which tea is made.
TĒAR (tēr), *n.* Water from the eyes :—a drop.
TEĂR (tȧr), *v. a.* [*imp. t.* tore; *pp.* torn.] To pull in pieces; to rend; to laniate; to lacerate.
TEĂR (tȧr), *v. n.* To fume; to rave; to rant.
TEĂR (tȧr), *n.* A rent; a fissure; laceration.
TEĂR'ĘR (tȧr'ęr), *n.* One who rends or tears.
TĒAR'FŬL (tēr'fŭl), *a.* Weeping; full of tears.
TĒAR'LĘSS, *a.* Destitute of tears.
TĒAṢE (tēz), *v. a.* To comb; to scratch; to vex.
TĒA'ṢEL (tē'zl), *n.* A plant and its burr.
TĒAT (tēt), *n.* A dug; a pap; a nipple.
TĒA'ZLE, *v. a.* To raise a nap on cloth.
TĒA'ZLE, *n.* A prickly plant; teasel.
TĔCH'Ĭ-LŸ, *ad.* Peevishly; fretfully; frowardly.
TĔCH'Ĭ-NĔSS, *n.* Peevishness; fretfulness.
TĔƐH'NĬ-CＡL, *a.* Belonging to the arts.
TĔƐH'NĬ-CＡL-LŸ, *ad.* In a technical manner.
TĔƐH-NO-LŎǤ'Ĭ-CＡL, *a.* Relating to the arts.
TĔƐH-NŎL'O-ǤŸ, *n.* A description of the arts.
TĔCH'Ŷ, *a.* Peevish; fretful; irritable; touchy.
TĘC-TŎN'ĬC, *a.* Pertaining to building.
TĔD, *v. a.* To spread abroad new-mown grass.
TĔD'DĘR, *n.* & *v. a.* See TETHER.
TĒ DĒ'ŬM, *n.* [L.] A hymn sung in the church.
‖TĒ'DIOŲS (tē'dyụs *or* tē'dę-ŭs), *a.* Wearisome;
‖TĒ'DIOŲS-LŸ,*dd.*In a tedious manner.[irksome.
‖TĒ'DIOŲS-NĔSS, *n.* Wearisomeness; prolixity.
TĒ'DĬ-ŬM, *n.* Irksomeness; weariness.
TĒĒM, *v. n.* To bring young; to be pregnant.
TĒĒM, *v. a.* To bring forth; to produce.
TĒĒNṢ, *n. pl.* The years from 12 to 20.
TĒĒTH, *n.* The plural of *tooth.*
TĒĒTH, *v. n.* To breed teeth.
TĒĒ-TŌ'TＡL-ĘR, *n.* Advocate of teetotalism.
TĒĒ-TŌ'TＡL-Ĭ ṢM, *n.* Total abstinence.
TĒĒ-TŌ'TŬM, *n.* Sort of small top.
TĔG'Ụ-MĔNT, *n.* A cover; an envelope.
TĒ'HĒĒ, *v. n.* To laugh.—*n.* A laugh.
TĒIL, *n.* The lime or linden tree.
TĒ'LＡ-RŸ, *a.* Spinning webs, as a spider.
TĔL'Ę-GRĂM, *n.* A telegraphic message.
TĔL'Ę-GRĂPH, *n.* A machine or instrument to convey intelligence to a distance.
TĔL'Ę-GRĂPH, *v. a.* To convey by telegraph.
TĔL-Ę-GRĂPH'ĬC, *a.* Relating to a telegraph.
TĔL'Ę-SCŌPE, *n.* A glass used for distant views.
TĔL-Ę-SCŎP'ĬC, *a.* Belonging to a telescope.
TĔLL, *v. a.* [*imp. t.* & *pp.* told.] To utter; to express; to relate; to inform :—to count.
TĔLL, *v. n.* To give an account; to speak.
TĔLL'ĘR, *n.* One who tells, counts, or pays.
TĔLL'TĀLE, *n.* An officious tale-bearer.
TĔL-LŪ'RĬ-ŬM, *n.* A kind of white metal.
TĔM-Ę-RĀ'RĬ-OŬS,*a.* Rash; heady; adventurous.

TĘ-MĔR'Ĭ-TY, *n.* Rashness; extreme boldness.
TĔM'PĘR, *v. a.* To mingle; to modify; to soften.
TĔM'PĘR, *n.* Due mixture of contrary qualities:—disposition of mind; moderation :—irritation.
TĔM'PĘR-Ａ-MĔNT, *n.* Constitution; medium.
TĔM'PĘR-ＡNCE, *n.* Moderation; sobriety.
TĔM'PĘR-ＡTE,*a.* Not excessive; moderate; calm.
TĔM'PĘR-ＡTE-LŸ, *ad.* Moderately; calmly.
TĔM'PĘR-ＡTE-NĔSS, *n.* Freedom from excess.
TĔM'PĘR-Ａ-TŪRE, *n.* State of the air as to heat and cold; degree of heat.
TĔM'PĔST, *n.* A violent wind; a commotion.
TĔM'PĔST-TŎST, *a.* Driven about by storms.
TĘM-PĔST'Ụ-OŬS (tęm-pĕst'yụ-ŭs), *a.* Stormy.
TĘM-PĔST'Ụ-OŬS-LŸ, *ad.* Turbulently. [ous.
TĘM-PĔST'Ụ-OŲS-NĔSS, *n.* The being tempestu-
TĔM'PLＡR, *n.* A student in the law :—knight.
TĔM'PLE, *n.* An edifice :—side of the head.
TĔM'PLĘT, *n.* A piece of timber in a building.
TĔM'PO-RＡL, *a.* Measured by time; not eternal; secular; not spiritual; placed at the temples.
TĔM-PO-RĂL'Ĭ-TY, TĔM'PO-RＡLṢ, *n.* Secular rights or possessions.
TĔM'PO-RＡL-LŸ, *ad.* With respect to this life.
TĔM'PO-RＡL-NĔSS,*n.* Secularity; worldliness.
TĔM'PO-RＡL-TY, *n.* Temporality. [porary.
TĔM'PO-RＡ-RĬ-NĔSS, *a.* State of being tem-
TĔM'PO-RＡ-RŸ, *a.* Lasting only for a limited time; not permanent.
TĔM'PO-RĪZE,*v. n.* To comply with the times.
TĔM'PO-RĪZ-ĘR, *n.* A time-server; a trimmer.
TĔMPT (tĕmt), *v. a.* To entice to ill; to try.
TĔMPT'Ａ-BLE, *a.* Liable to temptation.
TĘMP-TĀ'TION (tęm-tā'shụn), *n.* Act of tempting; state of being tempted; enticement.
TĔMPT'ĘR (tĕm'tęr), *n.* One who entices to ill.
TĔN, *a.* & *n.* Twice five; the decimal number.
TĔN'Ａ-BLE, *a.* That may be held; defensible.
TĘ-NĀ'CIOŲS (tę-nā'shụs), *a.* Grasping hard; holding fast; retentive :—cohesive. [fast.
TĘ-NĀ'CIOŲS-LŸ, *ad.* With disposition to hold
TĘ-NĀ'CIOŲS-NĔSS (-shụs-nĕs), *n.* Tenacity.
TĘ-NĂ Ç'Ĭ-TY, *n.* The quality of being tenacious.
TĔN'ＡN-CY, *n.* The state of a tenant. [other.
TĔN'ＡNT, *n.* One that holds land, &c., of an
TĔN'ＡNT, *v. a.* To hold on certain conditions.
TĔN'ＡNT-Ａ-BLE, *a.* Fit to be tenanted.
TĔN'ＡNT-RY, *n.* A body of tenants.
TĔNCH, *n.* A fish allied to the carp.
TĔND, *v. a.* To watch; to guard; to attend.
TĔND, *v. n.* To move towards; to incline.
TĔN'DĘN-CY, *n.* Direction; course; drift. [cate.
TĔN'DĘR, *a.* Soft; kind; easily pained; deli-
TĔN'DĘR, *v. a.* To offer; to exhibit; to propose.
TĔN'DĘR, *n.* An offer; a proposal :—a vessel.
TĔN'DĘR-HEＡRT'ĘD,*a.* Compassionate; gentle.
TĔN'DĘR-LĬNG, *n.* First horn of a deer :—fond-
TĔN'DĘR-LOIN, *n.* A tender part of beef. [ling.
TĔN'DĘR-LŸ, *ad.* In a tender manner; gently.
TĔN'DĘR-NĔSS, *n.* The being tender; kindness.
TĔN'DĬ-NOŬS, *a.* Sinewy; containing tendons.
TĔN'DON, *n.* A sinew; a ligature of joints.
TĔN'DRĬL, *n.* The clasper of a vine, &c.
TĘ-NĒ'BRĬ-OŬS, TĔN'Ę-BROŬS,*a.*Dark; gloomy.
TĔN'Ę-MĔNT, *n.* A house; a habitation :—any thing held by a tenant, as a house, land, &c.
TĔN-Ę-MĔNT'ＡL, *a.* To be held by tenants.
TĔN'ĘT, *n.* A position; a principle; opinion.

TĔN′FŌLD, *a.* Ten times increased.
TĔN′NĬS, *n.* A play with a racket and ball.
TĔN′ǪN, *n.* End of a timber fitted to a mortise.
TĔN′ǪR, *n.* Mode; purport; drift:—the mean or middle part in music.
TĔNSE, *n.* A variation of the verb to denote time.
TĔNSE, *a.* Stretched; stiff; tight; not lax.
TĔNSE′NĔSS, *n.* State of being tense; tension.
TĔN′SĮ-BLE, TĔN′SĮLE, *a.* Capable of extension.
TĔN′SĮǪN, *n.* The act of stretching; distention.
TĔN′SĮVE, *a.* Giving a sensation of stiffness.
TĔNT, *n.* A soldier's movable lodge or pavilion: —a roll of lint:—a species of red wine.
TĔNT, *v. n.* To lodge.—*v. a.* To probe.
TĔN′TĄ-TĬVE, *a.* Trying; essaying; attempting.
TĔNT′ĘD, *a.* Covered with tents.
TĔNT′ĘR, *n.* Frame of hooks for stretching.
TĔNT′ĘR, *v. a.* To stretch or hang on tenters.
TĔNTH, *a.* First after the ninth; ordinal of ten.
TĔNTH, *n.* The tenth part:—a tithe.
TĔNTH′LY, *ad.* In the tenth place. [ness.
TĘ-NŪ′Į-TY, *n.* Thinness; slenderness; minute-
TĔN′U-OŬS, *a.* Thin; small; minute; slim.
TĔN′ŲRE (tĕn′yŭr *or* tē′nŭr), *n.* The manner or mode of holding lands or tenements.
TĔP-Ę-FĂC′TĬǪN, *n.* The act of making tepid.
TĔP′ĮD, *a.* Lukewarm; warm in small degree.
TĒ′PǪR, *n.* Lukewarmness; gentle heat.
TĔR′Ą-PHĬM, *n.* [Heb.] Idols, or lunar amulets.
TĔRCE, *n.* A vessel. See TIERCE.
TĔR′Ę-BĬNTH, *n.* The turpentine tree.
TĔR-Ę-BĬN′THĮNE, *a.* Relating to turpentine.
TĘR-GĔM′Į-NOŬS, *a.* Threefold. [change.
TĔR-GĮV-ĘR-SĀ′TĬǪN, *n.* A shift; evasion;
TĔRM, *n.* A limit; a boundary; a limited time: —a word; an expression.—*pl.* Conditions.
TĔRM, *v. a.* To name; to call; to denominate.
TĔR′MĄ-GĂN-CY, *n.* Turbulence; furiousness.
TĔR′MĄ-GĂNT, *a.* Turbulent; scolding; furious.
TĔR′MĄ-GĂNT, *n.* A scolding, brawling woman.
TĔRM′ĘR, *n.* One that holds for a term of years.
TĔR′MĮ-NĄ-BLE, *a.* Limitable; admitting bounds.
TĔR′MĮ-NĀTE, *v. a.* To limit; to put an end to.
TĔR′MĮ-NĀTE, *v. n.* To be limited; to end.
TĔR-MĮ-NĀ′TĬǪN, *n.* A bound; a limit; end.
TĔR-MĮ-NĀ′TĬǪN-ĄL, *a.* Relating to termination.
TĔR-MĮ-NŎL′Ǫ-GY, *n.* The explanation of terms.
TĔR′MĮ-NŬS, *n.;* pl. TĔR′MĮ-NĪ. [L.] A column;
TĔR′MĬTE, *n.* The white ant. [a bound.
TĔR′NĄ-RY, *a.* Relating to three.
TĔR′NĄ-RY, TĔR′NĮ-ǪN, *n.* The number three.
TĔR′RĄCE, *n.* Platform of earth:—balcony.
TĔR′RĄ-PĬN, *n.* A fresh-water tortoise.
TĔR′RĄ-CŎT′TĄ, *n.* [It.] Baked earth or clay.
TĘR-RĀ′QUE-OŬS, *a.* Composed of land and wa-
TĔR-RĒNE′, *a.* Earthy; earthly; terrestrial. [ter.
TĘR-RĔS′TRĮ-ĄL, *a.* Earthly; mundane. [ner.
TĘR-RĔS′TRĮ-ĄL-LY, *ad.* After an earthly man-
TĔR′RĮ-BLE, *a.* Dreadful; formidable; frightful.
TĔR′RĮ-BLE-NĔSS, *n.* Formidableness; dreadful-
TĔR′RĮ-BLY, *ad.* Dreadfully; formidably. [ness.
TĔR′RĮ-ĘR, *n.* A dog:—a survey of lands.
TĘR-RĬF′ĮC, *a.* Dreadful; causing terror.
TĔR′RĮ-FȲ, *v. a.* To fright; to shock with fear.
TĔR-RĮ-TŌ′RĮ-ĄL, *a.* Belonging to a territory.
TĔR′RĮ-TǪ-RY, *n.* Land; country; a district.
TĔR′RǪR, *n.* Great fear; dread; the cause of fear.
TĔRSE, *a.* Cleanly written; neat; sententious.

TĔRSE′LY, *ad.* With terseness; neatly.
TĔRSE′NĔSS, *n.* Smoothness or neatness of style.
TĔR′TĬĄN, *a.* Occurring every other day.
TĔR′TĬĄN, *n.* An ague intermitting but one day.
TĔR′TĮ-Ą-RY (tĕr′shę-ą-rę), *a.* Third. [time.
TĔR′TĮ-ĀTE (tĕr′shę-āt), *v. a.* To do for the third
TĔS′SĘL-LĀT-ĘD, *a.* Variegated by squares.
TĔST, *n.* Examination; trial; a standard.
TĔST, *v. a.* To try by a test; to prove.
TĘS-TĀ′CEĄN (tęs-tā′shun), *n.* A shell-fish.
TĘS-TĀ′CEOŲS (tęs-tā′shŭs), *a.* Having a shell.
TĔS′TĄ-MĔNT, *n.* A will:—name of each of the general divisions of the Holy Scriptures.
TĔS-TĄ-MĔNT′Ą-RY, *a.* Relating to, or given by,
TĔS′TĀTE, *a.* Having made a will. [will.
TĘS-TĀ′TǪR, *n.* One who makes or leaves a will.
TĘS-TĀ′TRĬX, *n.* A woman who leaves a will.
TĔST′ĘD, *p. a.* Tried by a test; witnessed.
TĔST′ĘR, *n.* A coin:—a cover of a bed.
TĔS′TĮ-CLE, *n.* An organ of seed in animals.
TĔS′TĮ-FĪ-ĘR, *n.* One who testifies. [certify.
TĔS′TĮ-FȲ, *v. n. & a.* To witness; to prove; to
TĔS′TĮ-LY, *ad.* Fretfully; peevishly; morosely.
TĔS-TĮ-MŌ′NĮ-ĄL, *n.* A certificate; attestation.
TĔS′TĮ-MǪ-NY, *n.* Evidence; proof; attestation.
TĔST′Į-NĔSS, *n.* Moroseness; peevishness.
TĔS-TŲ-DĬN′Ę-OŬS, *a.* Like the shell of a tortoise.
TĘS-TŪ′DǪ, *n.* [L.] A tortoise:—arched roof.
TĔST′Y, *a.* Fretful; peevish; apt to be angry.
TĘ-TÂUG′, *n.* A fish. See TAUTOG.
TĒTE-A-TETE (tāt′ą-tāt′), *ad.* [Fr.] Face to face.
TĔTH′ĘR, *n.* A restraint for horses, &c., at pas-
TĔTH′ĘR, *v. a.* To confine with a tether. [ture.
TĔT′RĄ-GŎN, *n.* A square; a four-sided figure.
TĘ-TRĂG′Ǫ-NĄL, *a.* Having four angles.
TĔ′TRĂM-Ę-TĘR, *a.* Having four metrical feet.
TĔT-RĄ-PĔT′Ą-LOŬS, *a.* Having four petals.
TĒ′TRĂRCH, *n.* A Roman governor or prince.
TĘ-TRĂRCH′ĀTE, *n.* Fourth part of a province.
TĘ-TRĂRCH′Į-CĄL, *a.* Belonging to a tetrarchy.
TĔT′RĄR-CHY, *n.* A tetrarchate. [verses.
TĘ-TRĂS′TĮCH, *n.* An epigram or stanza of four
TĔT′RĄ-STȲLE, *n.* A building with four columns or pillars in front. [lables.
TĔT-RĄ-SȲL′LĄ-BLE, *n.* A word of four syl-
TĔT′TER, *n.* A cutaneous disease; fret.
TEŪ-TŎN′ĮC, *a.* Relating to the Teutones.
TEW̄ (tū), *v. a.* To tease; to beat:—to pull.
TEW̄′ĘL (tū′ęl), *n.* An iron pipe in a forge.
TĔXT, *n.* An original writing; that on which a comment is written:—passage of Scripture.
TĔXT′-BOOK (tĕkst′bŭk), *n.* A book, or manual, of general principles used by students.
TĔXT′-HĂND, *n.* A kind of large handwriting.
TĔX′TĮLE, *a.* Woven; capable of being woven.
TĔXT′Ų-Ą-RY, TĔXT′Ų-ĄL, *a.* Serving as a text.
TĔXT′Ų-Ą-RY, *n.* One well versed in Scripture.
TĔXT′ŲRE (tĕkst′yŭr), *n.* A web:—manner of weaving:—combination of parts. [year.
THĂM′MŲZ, *n.* 10th month of the Jewish civil
THĂN, *conj.* A particle used in comparison.
THĀNE, *n.* An old English title of honor.
THĂNK, *v. a.* To express gratitude for a favor.
THĂNK′FŨL, *a.* Full of gratitude; grateful.
THĂNK′FŨL-LY, *ad.* With gratitude; gratefully.
THĂNK′FŨL-NĔSS, *n.* Gratitude.
THĂNK′LĔSS, *a.* Unthankful; ungrateful.
THĂNK′LĔSS-NĔSS, *n.* Ingratitude.

THANKS, n. pl. Expression of gratitude.
THANKS'GÏV-ER, n. A giver of thanks. [thanks.
THANKS'GÏV-ING, n. Act, or day, of giving
THANK'WÖR-THY, a. Meritorious.
THAT, pron. a. Not this, but the other.—pron.
  rel. Who or which, relating to an antecedent.
THAT, conj. Because; noting a consequence.
THATCH, n. Straw, &c., laid upon the top of a
THATCH, v. a. To cover with thatch. [house.
THATCH'ER, n. One who thatches.
THAW, v. n. & a. To grow liquid; to melt.
THAW, n. Liquefaction; a melting. [or thing.
THE or THE, article, noting a particular person
THE'A-TRE (-ter), n. A house for dramatic rep-
  resentations, shows, &c.; a play-house.
THE-ÄT'RIC, THE-ÄT'RI-CAL, a. Relating to a
  theatre; dramatic. [ner.
THE-ÄT'RI-CAL-LY, ad. In a theatrical man-
THEE, pron. Objective case singular of thou.
THEFT. The act of stealing; the thing stolen.
THEIR (thår), pron. a. Belonging to them.
THEIRS (thårz), pron. pos. from they.
THE'ISM, n. The belief in a God; deism.
THE'IST, n. One who believes in a God.
THE-IS'TIC, } a. Belonging to theism or
THE-IS'TI-CAL, } theists.
THEM, pron. The objective case of they. [tion.
THEME, n. A subject; a topic; a short disserta-
THEM-SELVES', pron. The very persons. [case.
THEN, ad. At that time; afterwards; in that
THENCE, ad. From that place; for that reason.
THENCE-FORTH', ad. From that time.
THENCE-FÖR'WARD, ad. On from that time.
THE-ÖC'RA-CY, n. Government immediately
  directed by God. [ing to a theocracy.
THE-O-CRÄT'IC, THE-O-CRÄT'I-CAL, a. Relat-
THE-ÖD'O-LÏTE, n. A mathematical instru-
  ment, used for heights and distances, &c. [gods.
THE-ÖG'O-NY, n. The generation of heathen
THE-O-LO'GI-AN, n. One versed in divinity.
THE-O-LÖG'IC, } a. Relating to theology;
THE-O-LÖG'I-CAL, } divine; sacred. [ogy.
THE-O-LÖG'I-CAL-LY, ad. According to theol-
THE-ÖL'O-GÏZE, v. a. To render theological.
THE-ÖL'O-GY, n. The science of divinity.
THE-ÖM'A-CHY, n. A fight against the gods.
THE-ÖR'BO, n. A musical instrument.
THE'O-REM, n. A position proposed to be
  proved; a proposition.
THE-O-RET'IC, } a. Relating to theory;
THE-O-RET'I-CAL, } speculative.
THE-O-RET'I-CAL-LY, ad. Speculatively.
THE'O-RIST, n. One who forms theories.
THE'O-RÏZE, v. n. To form theories. [tem.
THE'O-RY, n. A speculation; a scheme; a sys-
THER-A-PEU'TIC, } a. Relating to 'thera-
THER-A-PEU'TI-CAL, } peutics. [eases.
THER-A-PEU'TICS, n. pl. The art of curing dis-
THERE (thår), ad. In that place. [that place.
THERE'A-BOUT, THERE'A-BOUTS, ad. Near
THERE-ÄF'TER, ad. After that.
THERE-ÄT', ad. At that; at that place.
THERE-BY', ad. By that; near by.
THERE'FORE (thër'for or thår'for), ad. For
  that; for this reason; consequently; for that
THERE-FRÖM', ad. From that. [purpose.
THERE-IN', ad. In that; in this.
THERE-IN-TO', ad. Into that.

THERE-ÖF', ad. Of that; of this.
THERE-ÖN', ad. On that; on this.
THERE-ÖUT', ad. Out of that; therefrom.
THERE-TO', THERE-UN-TO', ad. To or unto
THERE-ÜN'DER, ad. Under that. [that.
THERE-UP-ÖN', ad. Upon that; upon this.
THERE-WITH', ad. With that; with this.
THE'RI-AC, THE-RI'A-CAL, a. Medicinal.
THER'MAL, a. Relating to warm baths; warm.
THER-MÖM'E-TER, n. An instrument to meas-
  ure the variations of heat. [mometer.
THER-MO-MET'RI-CAL, a. Relating to a ther-
THESE, pron. The plural of this. [theme.
THE'SIS, n.; pl. THE'SES. A proposition;
THE-ÜR'GIC, THE-ÜR'GI-CAL, a. Magical.
THE'UR-GY, n. Supernatural power; magic.
THEY (thä), pron. The plural of he, or she, or it.
THICK, a. Not thin; dense; gross; muddy;
THICK, n. The thickest part. [deep.
THICK, ad. Frequently; fast; closely. [thick.
THICK'EN (thik'kn), v. a. & n. To make or grow
THICK'ET, n. A close knot or cluster of trees.
THICK'LY, ad. Densely; deeply; closely.
THICK'NESS, n. State of being thick; density.
THICK'-SET, a. Close planted; thick.
THICK'-SKULL, n. A dolt; a blockhead; a fool.
THICK'-SKULLED (-skuld), a. Dull; stupid.
THIEF (thef), n.; pl. THIEVES. One guilty of
THIEVE, v. n. To practise theft. [theft.
THIEV'ER-Y, n. The practice of stealing; theft.
THIEV'ISH, a. Given to stealing; secret; sly.
THIEV'ISH-LY (thëv'ish-le), ad. Like a thief.
THIEV'ISH-NESS, n. Disposition to steal.
THIGH (thi), n. The leg above the knee.
THILL, n. Shaft of a wagon, &c.
THIM'BLE, n. A cap for the needle finger.
THIN, a. Not thick; rare; lean; slim; slender.
THIN, v. a. To make thin; to attenuate.
THINE, pron. pos. Belonging or relating to thee.
THING, n. Whatever is not a person.
THINK, v. n. [imp. t. & pp. thought.] To employ
  the mind; to reason; to cogitate; to esteem.
THINK, v. a. To imagine; to conceive; to believe.
THINK'ER, n. One who thinks; cogitator.
THIN'LY, ad. Not thickly; not closely.
THIN'NESS, n. Tenuity; scarcity; rareness.
THIRD, a. The first after the second. [ond.
THIRD, n. A third part:—60th part of a sec-
THIRD'LY, ad. In the third place.
THIRDS, n. pl. (Law.) A widow's portion of
  her deceased husband's estate. [sire.
THIRST, n. A painful want of drink; eager de-
THIRST, v. n. To feel want of drink; to be dry.
THIRST'I-NESS, n. The state of being thirsty.
THIRST'Y, a. Suffering want of drink; dry.
THIR'TEEN, a. Ten and three.
THIR'TEENTH, a. The third after the tenth.
THIR'TI-ETH, a. The ordinal of thirty.
THIR'TY, a. Thrice ten; five times six.
THIS, pron. The one which is present; not that.
THIS'TLE (this'sl), n. A prickly weed or plant.
THIS'TLY (this'le), a. Overgrown with thistles.
THITH'ER, ad. To that place or point.
THITH'ER-WARD, ad. Towards that place.
THOLE'-PIN, n. A pin set in a gunwale.
THONG, n. A strap or string of leather.
THO-RAC'IC, a. Pertaining to the thorax or
THO'RAL, a. Relating to a bed. [chest.

THŌ′RĂX, *n.* [L.] The breast; the chest.
THÖRN, *n.* A prickly plant; a spine:—trouble.
THÖRN′Y, *a.* Spiny; prickly:—perplexing.[fect.
THŎR′ŌUGH (thŭr′rō), *a.* Complete; full; per-
THŎR′OUGH-BĂSS, *n.* Science of harmony.
THŎR′OUGH-FARE (thŭr′rọ-fàr), *n.* A passage through; a place much passed through.
THŎR′OUGH-LY (thŭr′rọ-lẹ), *ad.* Completely.
THŎR′OUGH-PĀCED (thŭr′rọ-pāst), *a.* Complete.
THŎR′OUGH-WŎRT, *n.* A medicinal plant.
THŌṢE, *pron.* The plural of *that;* not these.
THŎŬ. The second pronoun personal.
THŌUGH (thō), *conj.* Although; in case that.
THŌUGHT (thâwt), *imp. t. & pp.* from *think.*
THŌUGHT (thâwt), *n.* Act of thinking; idea.
THŌUGHT′FŨL (thâwt′fũl), *a.* Full of thought.
THŌUGHT′FŨL-LY (thâwt′fũl-lẹ), *ad.* With thought. [ful.
THŌUGHT′FŨL-NĔSS, *n.* State of being thought-
THŌUGHT′LẸSS (thâwt′lẹs), *a.* Gay; careless.
THŌUGHT′LẸSS-LY, *ad.* Carelessly.
THŌUGHT′LẸSS-NĔSS, *n.* Want of thought.
THŎŬ′ṢĄND, *a.* or *n.* Ten hundred.
THŎŬ′ṢĄNDTH, *a.* The ordinal of a thousand.
THRĂL′DǪM, *n.* Slavery; servitude; bondage.
THRĂSH, *v. a.* To beat, as grain; to drub:— written also *thresh.*
THRĄ-SŎN′Į-CĄL, *a.* Boastful; bragging.
THRĔAD (thrĕd), *n.* A small twist of flax, silk, wool, &c.; any thing continued in a course.
THRĔAD (thrĕd), *v. a.* To pass through; to pierce.
THRĔAD′BÀRE, *a.* Deprived of the nap; trite.
THRĔAT (thrĕt), *n.* Menace; denunciation of ill.
THRĔAT′EN (thrĕt′tn), *v. a.* To menace; to de-
THRĔĒ, *a.* Two and one. [nounce evil upon.
THRĔĒ′FŌLD, *a.* Consisting of three.
THREE′PẸNCE (thrē′pẹns *or* thrĭp′ẹns), *n.* The sum of three pennies or pence. [pence.
THREE′PẸN-NY (thrĭp′ẹn-nẹ), *a.* Worth three-
THRĔĒ′SCŌRE, *a.* Thrice twenty; sixty.
THRĔSH, *v. a.* To beat, as grain; to thrash.
THRĔSH′ẸR, *n.* One who threshes:—a shark.
THRĔSH′ǪLD, *n.* A door-sill; an entrance; a
THREW (thrŭ), *imp. t.* from *throw.* [door.
THRĪCE, *ad.* Three times.
THRĬFT, *n.* Profit; frugality; good husbandry.
THRĬFT′Į-LY, *ad.* Frugally; prosperously.
THRĬFT′Į-NĔSS, *n.* Frugality; good husbandry.
THRĬFT′LẸSS, *a.* Profuse; extravagant.
THRĬF′TY, *a.* Frugal; sparing:—thriving.
THRĬLL, *v. a.* To pierce; to bore; to penetrate.
THRĬLL, *v. n.* To feel a sharp, tingling sensation.
THRĬLL, *n.* A breathing-hole; a sharp sound.
THRĪVE, *v. n.* [*imp. t.* throve; *pp.* thriven.] To prosper; to flourish; to grow rich.
THRŌAT (thrōt), *n.* The fore part of the neck.
THRŎB, *v. n.* To heave; to beat; to palpitate.
THRŎB, *n.* A beat; a strong pulsation.
THRŌE (thrō), *n.* The pain of travail; a pang.
THRŌNE, *n.* The seat of a king or of a bishop.
THRŌNE, *v. a.* To enthrone.
THRŎNG, *n.* A crowd; a great multitude.
THRŎNG, *v. n.* To crowd; to come in multi-
THRŎNG, *v. a.* To oppress with crowds. [tudes.
THRŎS′TLE (thrŏs′sl), *n.* The thrush; a bird.
THRŎT′TLE, *n.* The windpipe; the larynx.
THRŎT′TLE, *v. a.* To choke; to suffocate.
THROŬGH (thrŭ), *prep.* From end to end of.

THROŬGH (thrŭ), *ad.* From end to end; to the end.
THROŬGH′LY (thrŭ′lẹ), *ad.* Thoroughly. [*Obs.*]
THROŬGH-ÖŬT′ (thrŭ-), *prep.* Quite through.
THROŬGH-ÖŬT′ (thrŭ-), *ad.* In every part.
THRŌVE, *imp. t.* from *thrive.*
THRŌW (thrō), *v. a.* [*imp. t.* threw; *pp.* thrown.] To fling; to cast; to send; to toss; to drive.
THRŌW (thrō), *v. n.* To make a cast.
THRŌW (thrō), *n.* A cast:—a pang. See THROE.
THRŌW′ẸR, *n.* One that throws; a throwster.
THRŌWN (thrōn), *pp.* from *throw.*
THRŌW′STẸR, *n.* One who twists silk.
THRŬM, *n.* The end of weavers' threads. [play.
THRŬM, *v. a.* To weave; to knot; to grate; to
THRŬSH, *n.* A small singing bird. [drive.
THRŬST, *v. a.* [*imp. t. & pp.* thrust.] To push; to
THRŬST, *v. n.* To make a push; to press.
THRŬST, *n.* A hostile attack; an assault.
THŬMB (thŭm), *n.* The short, thick finger.
THŬMB (thŭm), *v. a.* To handle awkwardly.
THŬMP, *n.* A hard, heavy, dead, dull blow.
THŬMP, *v. a. & n.* To beat with heavy blows.
THŬMP′ĮNG, *a.* Great; huge. [*Vulgar.*] [air.
THŬN′DẸR, *n.* A loud rumbling noise in the
THŬN′DẸR, *v. n.* To discharge the electric flu- id; to make a loud or terrible noise.
THŬN′DẸR-BŌLT, *n.* Lightning; fulmination.
THŬN′DẸR-CLĂP, *n.* An explosion of thunder.
THŬN′DẸR-ẸR, *n.* One that thunders.
THŬN′DẸR-ĬNG, *a.* Loud; noisy; terrible.
THŬN′DẸR-SHŎW-ẸR, *n.* A rain with thunder.
THŬN′DẸR-STRŬCK, *p. a.* Astonished; amazed.
THŲ-RĬF′ẸR-OŬS, *a.* Bearing frankincense.
THŬRṢ′DAY, *n.* The fifth day of the week.
THŬS, *ad.* In this manner; to this degree.
THWĂCK, *v. a.* To strike; to thresh; to bang.
THWĂCK, *n.* A heavy, hard blow. [ient.
THWÂRT, *a.* Transverse; perverse; inconven-
THWÂRT, *v. a.* To cross; to oppose; to traverse.
THȲ, *pron.* Of thee; belonging to thee.
THȲME (tīm), *n.* A fragrant herb.
THȲ′MY (tī′mẹ), *a.* Abounding with thyme.
THȲ-SĔLF′, *pron. recip.* Used for emphasis.
TĪ-Ā′RĄ *or* TĪ-ÀR′Ą, *n.* High cap; mitre.
TĬB′Į-Ą, *n.* [L.] A pipe; bone of the leg.
TĬB′Į-ĄL, *a.* Relating to a pipe or the tibia.
TĬCK, *n.* A minute insect:—trust; score:— noise:—a case for a bed of feathers, &c.
TĬCK, *v. n.* To run on score; to trust; to beat.
TĬCK, *n.* The sound made in ticking.
TĬCK′EN, TĬCK′ĮNG, *n.* Cloth for a bed-case.
TĬCK′ẸT, *n.* A token of a right or privilege.
TĬCK′ẸT, *v. a.* To distinguish by a ticket.
TĬC′KLE, *v. a.* To cause to laugh; to please.
TĬCK′LĮSH, *a.* Easily tickled:—tottering.
TĬCK′LĮSH-NĔSS, *n.* State of being ticklish.
TĪ′DĄL, *a.* Relating to the tides.
TĬD′BĬT, *n.* A dainty; a delicate piece.
TĪDE, *n.* The ebb and flow of the sea; course.
TĪDE, *v. n.* To pour a flood; to be agitated.
TĪDE′-GĀTE, *n.* A gate for the tide to pass.
TĪDEṢ′MĄN, TĪDE′-WĂIT-ẸR, *n.* A custom-
TĪ′DĮ-LY, *ad.* Neatly; readily. [house officer.
TĪ′DĮ-NĔSS, *n.* Neatness; readiness.
TĪ′DĮNGṢ, *n. pl.* News; intelligence.
TĪ′DY, *a.* Neat; nice; spruce; ready.
TĪE (tī), *v. a.* To bind; to fasten; to confine.
TĪE (tī), *n.* A knot; a fastening; a bond.

TIĒR (tĕr), *n.* A row ; a rank.   [—a thrust.
‖TIERCE (tērs *or* tĕrs), *n.* A third part of a pipe :
‖TIĒR′CĘT (tēr′sęt), *n.* A triplet ; three lines.
TĬFF, *n.* Liquor ; drink :—a fit of peevishness.
TĬF′FA̤-NY̆, *n.* Gauzy or very thin silk.
TĬG, *n.* A play of children ;—called also *tag.*
TĪ′ĢĘR, *n.* A fierce animal of the feline genus.
TĪGHT (tīt), *a.*Tense ; close ; not loose ; not leaky.
TĪGHT′EN (tī′tn), *v. a.* To make tight.   [ly.
TĪGHT′LY̆ (tīt′lę), *ad.* Closely; not loosely; neat-
TĪGHT′NĘSS (tīt′nęs), *n.* Closeness ; neatness.
TĪ′GRĘSS, *n.* The female of the tiger.
TĪKE, *n.* A dog ; a cur :—a clown.   [&c.
TĪLE, *n.* A plate of burnt clay used for roofing,
TĪLE, *v. a.* To cover with tiles ; to cover as tiles.
TĪL′ĮNG, *n.* Tiles :—roof covered with tiles.
TĬLL, *n.* A money-box in a shop, &c.
TĬLL, *prep.* To the time of ; to ; until.
TĬLL, *ad.* or *conj.* To the time when ; until.
TĬLL, *v. a.* To cultivate ; to husband ; to prepare.
TĬL′LA̤-BLE, *a.* Arable ; fit for the plough.
•TĬL′LA̤ĢE, *n.* The art of tilling ; culture.
TĬL′LĘR, *n.* A ploughman :—handle of a rudder.
TĬLT, *n.* Canvas covering :—a military game.
TĬLT, *v. a.* To cover :—to point :—to turn up.
TĬLT, *v. n.* To fight ; to rush as in combat.
TĬLT′ĘR, *n.* One who tilts ; one who fights.
TĬLTH, *n.* Tilled land :—tillage.   [hammer.
TĬLT′-HĂM-MĘR, *n.* A large hammer ; trip-
TĬM′BĘR, *n.* Wood fit for building :—a beam.
TĬM′BĘR, *v. a.* To furnish with timber.
TĬM′BRĘL, *n.* A kind of musical instrument.
TĪME, *n.* The measure of duration ; a space of
   time ; season ; age ; interval :—repetition.
TĪME, *v. a.* To adapt to the time ; to regulate.
TĪME′KĒĒP-ĘR, ⎫ *n.* A watch or clock ; a
TĪME′PIĒCE,   ⎭   chronometer.
TĪME′LĘSS, *a.* Unseasonable :—endless.
TĪME′LY̆, *a.* Seasonable ; sufficiently early.
TĪME′SĔRV-ĘR, *n.* One who complies with the
TĪME′SĔRV-ĮNG, *a.* Servile ; selfish.   [times.
TĬM′ĮD, *a.* Fearful ; timorous ; not bold.
TĮ-MĬD′Į-TY̆, *n.* Fearfulness ; timorousness.
TĬM′QR-OŬS, *a.* Fearful ; full of fear and scruple.
TĬM′QR-OŬS-LY̆, *ad.* Fearfully; with much fear.
TĬM′QR-OŬS-NĔSS, *n.* Fearfulness ; timidity.
TĬN, *n.* A common, whitish metal :—tinned iron.
TĬN, *v. a.* To cover or overlay with tin.
TĬN′CA̤L (tĭng′kal), *n.* A mineral ; borax.
TĬNCT′URE (tĭngkt′yur), *n.* Color or taste super-
   added :—essence; extract of drugs.
TĬNCT′URE (tĭngkt′yur), *v. a.* To imbue, tinge.
TĬN′DĘR, *n.* An inflammable substance.
TĬN′DĘR-BŎX, *n.* A box for holding tinder.
TĪNE, *n.* The spike of a fork, harrow, &c.
TĬN′FŎĬL, *n.* Tin formed into a thin leaf.
TĬNG, *n.* A sharp sound, as of a bell.
TĬNĢE, *v. a.* To impregnate or imbue.
TĬN′GLE (tĭng′gl), *v. n.* To feel a quick pain.
TĬN′GLĮNG, *n.* A sharp, thrilling sensation.
TĬNK′ĘR, *n.* A mender of old metal ware.
TĬNK, TĬN′KLE, *v. n.* To make a sharp noise.
TĬNK′LĮNG, *n.* A small, quick, sharp noise.
TĬN′MA̤N, *n.* A manufacturer of, or dealer in, tin.
TĬN′NĘR, *n.* One who works in tin mines.
TĬN′NY̆, *a.* Abounding with, or like, tin.
TĬN′SĘL, *n.* Any thing showy and of little value.
TĬN′SĘL, *a.* Specious ; showy ; superficial.

TĬN′SĘL, *v. a.* To adorn with showy lustre.
TĬNT, *n.* A dye ; a color.—*v. a.* To tinge ; to color.
TĪ′NY̆, *a.* Little ; small ; puny.
TĬP, *n.* The top ; end ; point ; extremity.
TĬP, *v. a.* To top :—to cant :—to tap.
TĬP′PĘT, *n.* Something worn about the neck.
TĬP′PLE, *v.n.* & *a.*To drink to excess.—*n.* Drink.
TĬP′PLĘR, *n.* A drunkard ; a sot ; a toper.
TĬP′STA̤FF, *n.* An officer and his staff of justice.
TĬP′SY̆, *a.* Drunk ; overpowered with drink.
TĬP′TŌE (tĭp′tō), *n.* The end of the toe.
TĬP′TŎP, *n.* The highest point.   [sure.
TĮ-RĀDE′, *n.* [Fr.] A strain of invective :—cen-
TĪRE, *n.* Attire :—furniture :—hoop of a wheel.
TĪRE, *v. a.* To fatigue ; to make weary.
TĪRE, *v. n.* To fail with weariness.
TĪRE′SQME (tīr′sųm), *a.* Wearisome ; tedious.
TĪRE′-WOM-A̤N (tīr′wûm-a̤n), *n.* A milliner :—
   a dressing-woman of a theatre.
′TĬŞ (tĭz). Contracted for *it is.*   [or silver.
TĬS′SUE (tĭsh′u), *n.* Cloth interwoven with gold
TĬT, *n.* A small horse :—a titmouse ; tomtit.
TĮ-TĀ′NĮ-ŬM, *n.* A dark-colored metal.
TĬT′BĬT, *n.* A nice bit ; nice food ; tidbit.
TĪ╬H′A̤-BLE, *a.* Subject to the payment of tithes.
TĪ╬HE, *n.* A tenth :—a small part :—the tenth
   part of produce paid to the clergy.
TĪ╬HE, *v. a.* To tax ; to levy the tenth part.
TĪ╬HE′-FRĒĒ,*a.*Exempt from payment of tithes.
TĪ╬H′ĮNG, *n.* A decennary :—part of a parish.
TĪ╬H′ĮNG-MĂN, *n.* A parish or peace officer.
TĬT′ĮL-LĀTE, *v.* To tickle.   [pleasure.
TĬT-ĮL-LĀ′TIQN, *n.* Act of tickling ; slight
TĪ′TLE, *n.* An appellation of honor :—a name ;
   an inscription :—a claim of right.
TĪ′TLE, *v. a.* To entitle; to name ; to call.
TĪ′TLE-PĀĢE, *n.* The page of a book contain-
TĬT′MOŬSE, *n.* A small bird.   [ing the title.
TĬT′TĘR, *v. n.* To laugh with restraint.
TĬT′TĘR, *n.* A restrained laugh.
TĬT′TLE, *n.* A small particle ; a point ; a dot.
TĬT′TLE-TĂT′TLE, *n.* Idle talk ; prattle ; gabble.
TĬT′U-LA̤R, *a.* Existing only in name ; nominal.
TĬT′U-LA̤R-LY̆, *ad.* Nominally ; by title only.
TĬT′U-LA̤-RY̆, *a.* Relating to a title.   [mode.
TÔ, *ad.* A particle used before the infinitive
TÔ, *prep.* Noting motion towards ; in direction
   of ;—opposed to *from.*—*To-day, to-night,* **this**
   day, this night.
TŌAD (tōd), *n.* An animal resembling a frog.
TŌAD′ĒAT-ĘR, *n.* A servile sycophant.
TŌAD′STŌŌL, *n.* A plant like a mushroom. [to.
TŌAST, *v. a.* To dry at the fire :—to wish health
TŌAST (tōst), *n.* Bread toasted :—health pro-
   posed :—a female toasted or complimented.
TQ-BĂC′CŌ, *n.* A plant used for smoking, &c.
TQ-BĂC′CQ-NĬST, *n.* A dealer in tobacco.
TŎC′SĬN, *n.* An alarm-bell.
TŎD, *n.* Twenty-eight pounds of wool :—a fox.
TŎD′DLE, *v. n.* To walk feebly ; to tottle.
TŎD′DY̆, *n.* A juice :—a mixture of spirits and
TŌE (tō), *n.* An extremity of the foot. [water.
TŌFT, *n.* A place where a messuage has stood.
TŌ′GA̤-TĘD, TŌ′ǴĘD (tō′ǵęd *or* tōgd),*a.* Gowned.
TŎG′GLE (tŏg′gl), *n.* A pin :—a button.
TQ-ĢĔ╬H′ĘR, *ad.* In company ; not apart.
TÖĬL, *v. n.* To labor ; to work.
TÖĬL, *n.* Labor ; fatigue :—a net ; a snare.

TŎÏ'LĘT, n. [Fr. *toilette.*] Dressing-table :—dress.
TŎÏL'SǪME, a. Laborious ; weary.
TŎÏL'SǪME-NĔSS, n. Wearisomeness.
TŎÏSE, n. [Fr.] A measure of 6 French feet.
TǪ-KĀY' (tǫ-kā'), n. A kind of Hungarian wine.
TŌ'KEN (tō'kn), n. A sign ; a mark ; a memorial ;
TŌLD, i. & p. from *tell.* [a souvenir.
TŌLE, v. a. To draw or allure. See TOLL.
TǪ-LĒ'DŌ, n. A sword of fine temper. [ble.
TŎL'ĘR-A-BLE, a. That may be endured ; passa-
TŎL'ĘR-A-BLY, ad. Supportably ; passably.
TŎL'ĘR-ANCE, n. The power or act of enduring.
TŎL'ĘR-ANT, a. Enduring ; favoring toleration.
TŎL'ĘR-ĀTE, v. a. To suffer ; to permit ; to allow.
TŎL-ĘR-Ā'TIǪN, n. Act of tolerating ; allowance.
TŌLL, n. An excise of goods :—a sound.
TŌLL, v. n. To pay or take toll ; to sound as a bell.
TŌLL, v. a. To ring ; to take toll of :—tŏ allure.
TŌLL'BÔÔTH, n. A prison ; a jail.
TŌLL'DĬSH, n. A vessel in which toll is taken.
TŌLL'-GĂᵀH-ĘR-ĘR, n. A receiver of tolls.
TŎM'A-HÂWK, n. An Indian hatchet.
TǪ-MĀ'TŌ *or* TǪ-MÄ'TŌ, n. A plant and fruit.
TÔMB (tôm), n. A monument ; a grave.
TÔMB (tôm), v. a. To bury ; to entomb.
TÔMB'LĘSS (tôm'lĕs), a. Wanting a tomb.
TŎM'BŎY, n. A wild, coarse, romping girl.
TÔMB'STŌNE (tôm'stōn), n. A monument.
TŌME, n. [Fr.] One volume of many :—a book.
TǪ-MŎR'RŌW, n. The day after the present.
TǪ-MŎR'RŌW, ad. On the next day coming.
TŎM'RĬG, n. A rude, wanton girl ; a tomboy.
TŎM-TĬT', n. A titmouse ; a small bird.
TŎN, n. The weight of 20 hundred gross.
TŎN (tŏng), n. [Fr.] The prevailing fashion.
TŌNE, n. A note ; sound of the voice :—strength ;
TŌNED (tōnd), a. Having tone. [elasticity.
TŎNGŞ, n. pl. A utensil to take up fire, &c.
TŎNGUE (tŭng),n.The organ of speech :—speech ;
  a language :—point :—catch of a buckle, &c.
TŎNGUED (tŭngd), a. Having a tongue.
TŎNGUE'TIED (tŭng'tĭd), a. Unable to speak.
TŎN'ĬC,   } a. Increasing strength ; elastic :—
TŎN'Ĭ-CAL, }   relating to tones or sound.
TŎN'ĬCS, n. pl. Medicines which strengthen.
TŎN'NAĢE, n. The number of tons burden of
  a ship :—duty by the ton.
TŎN'SĬL, n. An oblong, suboval gland, situated
  at the base of the tongue.
TŎNS'ŲRE (tŏn'shựr), n. Act of clipping the hair.
TŎN-TÎNE', n. An annuity on survivorship.
TÔÔ, ad. Over ; overmuch :—likewise ; also.
TOOK (tûk), imp. t. from *take.*
TŌŌL, n. Any instrument :—a hireling. [tine.
TÔÔTH, n. ; pl. TĒĒTH. A bone in the jaw ; a
TÔÔTH, v. a. To furnish with teeth ; to indent.
TÔÔTH'ÅᴄHE, n. Ache or pain in the teeth.
TÔÔTH'DRÂW-ĘR, n. One who extracts teeth.
TÔÔTHED (tôtht), a. Having teeth ; sharp.
TÔÔTH'LĘSS, a. Wanting teeth ; deprived of
  teeth. [teeth.
TÔÔTH'PĬCK, n. An instrument for cleaning the
TÔÔTH'SǪME (tôth'sųm), a. Palatable.
TŎP, n. The highest part ; the summit ; surface.
TŎP, v. n. & a. To rise aloft ; to be eminent ; to
  excel ; to cover on the top ; to rise above ; to crop.
TŌ'PÄRᴄH, n. Chief ruler in a small state.
TŌ'PĂZ, n. A precious stone ; a gem.

TŌPE, v. n. To drink hard ; to drink to excess.
TŌ'PĘR, n. A drunkard ; a tippler. [mast.
TŎP'GĂL-LANT, a. Third above, as a sail or
TŎP'-HĔAV-Ŷ (tŏp'hĕv-ę), a. Heavy at the top.
TŌ'PHĘT, n. A polluted, unclean place near
  Jerusalem ;—*metaphorically,* hell.
TŎP'ĬC, n. A general head ; a subject ; matter.
TŎP'Ĭ-CAL, a. Relating to a place ; local.
TŎP'Ĭ-CAL-LY, ad. In a topical manner.
TŎP'KNŎT (tŏp'nŏt), n. A knot worn by women.
TŎP'MĂST, n. The 2d mast above the deck.
TŎP'MŌST, a. Uppermost ; highest.
TǪ-PŎG'RA-PHĘR, n. One versed in topography.
TŎP-Ǫ-GRĂPH'ĬC,   } a. Relating to topogra-
TŎP-Ǫ-GRĂPH'Ĭ-CAL, }   phy. [towns, &c.
TǪ-PŎG'RA-PHY, n. A description of cities,
TŎP'SÄIL, n. A sail extended on the topmast.
TŎP'SŶ-TŬR'VŶ, ad. With the bottom upwards.
TŎRCH, n. A flambeau ; a blazing brand.
TŎRCH'-BEÄR-ĘR, n. One who carries a torch.
TŎRCH'LĬGHT (tŏrch'lĭt), n. The light of a torch.
TŌRE, i. from *tear.* [vex, agonizeᵣ
TǪR-MĔNT', v. a. To put to pain, excruciate,
TŎR'MENT, n. Pain ; misery; anguish ; torture.
TǪR-MĔNT'ǪR, n. One who torments.
TŌRN, pp. from *tear.*
TǪR-NĀ'DŌ, n. A hurricane ; a whirlwind.
TǪR-PĒD'Ĭ-NAL, a. Relating to the torpedo.
TǪR-PĒ'DŌ, n. ; pl. TǪR-PĒ'DŌEŞ. A fish
  whose touch benumbs :—a machine for blow-
  ing up ships :—a small fire-work.
TǪR-PĔS'CĘNT, a. Becoming torpid.
TŎR'PĬD, a. Numbed ; motionless ; sluggish.
TǪR-PĬD'Ĭ-TY, n. Torpor ; state of being torpid.
TŎR'PĬD-NĔSS, n. The state of being torpid.
TŎR'PĬ-TŪDE, n. Numbness ; torpidness.
TŎR'PŎR, n. Numbness ; inability to move.
TŎR-RĘ-FĂC'TIǪN, n. Act of drying by the fire.
TŎR'RĘ-FŶ, v. a. To dry by the fire ; to roast.
TŎR'RENT, n. A rapid stream ; a violent current.
TŎR'RENT, a. Rolling in a rapid stream.
TŎR'RĬD, a. Parched ; burning ; violently hot.
TŎR'SĘL, n. Any thing in a twisted form.
TŎR'SIǪN, n. The act of twisting ; a flexure.
TŎR'SŌ, n. [It.] The trunk of a statue.
TŎRT, n. (*Law.*) A wrong ; mischief ; injury.
TŎR'TĬLE, TŎR'TĬVE, a. Twisted ; wreathed.
TŎR'TIOŲS (tŏr'shųs),a. Injurious ; doing wrong.
TŎR'TOISE (tŏr'tĭs), n. An animal covered with
  a hard shell, and of the genus *testudo.*
TŎRT'Ų-OŬS, a. Twisted ; wreathed ; winding.
TŎRT'ŲRE (tŏrt'yųr), n. Torment ; anguish.
TŎRT'ŲRE (tŏrt'yųr), v. a. To vex ; to torment.
TŎRT'ŲR-ĘR (tŏrt'yųr-ęr), n. One who tortures.
TŌ'RŶ, n. An English political partisan, opposed
TŌ'RŶ-ĬŞM, n. The notions of a Tory. [to *Whig.*
TŎSS, v. a. [imp. t. & pp. tossed *or* tost.] To
  throw ; to fling ; to agitate ; to disquiet.
TŎSS, v. n. To fling ; to winch ; to be tossed.
TŎSS, n. The act of tossing ; a cast ; a jerk.
TŎS'SĘL, n. A knot of ribbon. See TASSEL.
TŎSS'PŎT, n. A toper ; a tippler.
TŌ'TAL, a. Whole ; complete ; full ; not divided.
TǪ-TĂL'Ĭ-TY, n. The whole quantity or sum.
TŌ'TAL-LY, ad. Wholly ; fully ; completely.
TŌTE, v. a. To carry. [*Southern States.*]
TŎT'TĘR, v. n. To shake so as to threaten a fall.
TŎT'TĘR-ĬNG, a. Shaking ; threatening to fall.

TŎT'TLE, *v. n.* To totter; to toddle, as a child.
TOŬCH (tŭch), *v. a.* To perceive by the sense of feeling; to handle; to join; to affect. [a hint.
TOŬCH (tŭch), *n.* Contact; the sense of feeling;
TOŬCH'HŌLE (tŭch'hōl), *n.* A hole in a gun.
TOŬCH'I-NĔSS (tŭch'ę-nĕs), *n.* Peevishness.
TOŬCH'ĮNG (tŭch'ing), *prep.* With respect to.
TOŬCH'ĮNG (tŭch'ing), *a.* Pathetic; affecting.
TOŬCH'ĮNG-LY (tŭch'ing-lę), *ad.* With emotion.
TOŬCH'-MĘ-NŎT (tŭch'mę-nŏt), *n.* A plant.
TOŬCH'STŌNE (tŭch'stōn), *n.* A test; a criterion.
TOŬCH'WOOD (tŭch'wŭd), *n.* Rotten wood used to catch the fire struck from a flint.
TOŬCH'Y (tŭch'ę), *a.* Peevish; irritable; techy.
TOŬGH (tŭf), *a.* Not brittle; strong; firm; stiff.
TOŬGH'EN (tŭf'fn), *v. n. & a.* To grow or make
TOŬGH'NĘSS (tŭf'nęs), *n.* Tenacity. [tough.
TÔU-PĒĒ' (tô-pē'), *n.* A curl; a toupet.
TÔU-PET' (tô-pā', tô-pē', *or* tô-pĕt'), *n.* [Fr.] Artificial lock of hair; a curl.
TÔUR (tôr), *n.* A ramble; a roving journey.
TÔUR'ĮST (tôr'ist), *n.* One who makes a tour.
TÔUR'MA-LĪNE (tôr'ma-lĭn), *n.* A mineral.
TÔUR'NA-MĔNT (tôr'na-mĕnt), *n.* A tilt; a just; an equestrian mock encounter.
TÔUR'NEY *or* TOŬR'NEY, *n.* A tournament.
TOŬR'NĮ-QUĔT (tür'nę-kĕt), *n.* A bandage.
TOŬSE, *v. a.* To pull; to tear; to haul; to drag.
TOŬ'SLE (tŏŭ'zl), *v. a.* To tumble; to tangle.
TŌW (tō), *n.* The coarse part of flax or hemp.
TŌW (tō), *v. a.* To draw by a rope. [towing.
TŌW'AGE, *n.* Act of towing:—money paid for
TŌW'ARD, TŌW'ARDŞ, *prep.* In a direction to.
TŌW'ARD, *a.* Docile; apt; towardly.
TŌW'ARD-LĮ-NĔSS (tō'ard-lę-nĕs), *n.* Docility.
TŌW'ARD-LY (tō'ard-lę), *a.* Ready to do or learn.
TŌW'ARD-NĔSS (tō'ard-nĕs), *n.* Docility.
TŌW'EL, *n.* Cloth for wiping the hands, &c.
TŌW'ER, *n.* A high building:—a fortress.
TŌW'ER, *v. n.* To soar; to fly or rise high.
TŌW'ERED (tŏŭ'erd), *a.* Adorned by towers.
TŌW'ER-Y, *a.* Adorned or guarded with towers.
TŌW'-LĪNE, *n.* A rope or chain used in towing.
TŌWN, *n.* Any large collection of houses, or the inhabitants; a large village:—a city. [town.
TŌWN'-CLERK (tŏŭn'klärk), *n.* A register of a
TŌWN'-CRĪ-ER, *n.* A public crier of a town.
TŌWN'-HÔUSE, *n.* A hall for public business.
TŌWN'SHĮP, *n.* Corporation or district of a town.
TŌWNŞ'MAN, *n.* One of the same town.
TŌW'-RŌPE, *n.* A rope for towing; a tow-line.
TŎX-Į-CŎL'Ọ-GY, *n.* Science of poisons.
TŎY, *n.* A trifle; a plaything; a bawble; sport.
TŎY, *v. n.* To trifle; to dally; to play, sport.
TŎY'ĮSH, *a.* Trifling; wanton; sportive.
TŎY'MAN, *n.* One who deals in toys.
TŎY'SHŎP, *n.* A shop where toys are sold.
TRĀCE, *n.* A mark; footstep; track:—*pl.* Harness.
TRĀCE, *v. a.* To follow by the footsteps; to mark.
TRĀCE'A-BLE, *a.* That may be traced.
TRĀ'CER-Y, *n.* Ornamental stone-work. [path.
TRĂCK, *n.* A mark left by the foot; a road; a
TRĂCK, *v. a.* To follow by footsteps left.
TRĂCK'LESS, *a.* Untrodden; pathless.
TRĂCT, *n.* A region; a course:—a small book.
TRĂCT-A-BĬL'Į-TY, *n.* Manageableness. [ant.
TRĂCT'A-BLE, *a.* Manageable; docile; compli-
TRĂCT'A-BLE-NĔSS, *n.* Compliance; docility.

TRĂCT'A-BLY, *ad.* In a tractable manner.
TRĂC'TATE, *n.* A treatise; a tract; an essay.
TRĂC'TĮLE, *a.* That may be drawn out; ductile.
TRAC-TĬL'Į-TY, *n.* The quality of being tractile.
TRĂC'TĮON, *n.* The act of drawing; attraction.
TRĀDE, *n.* Traffic; commerce; occupation.
TRĀDE, *v. n.* To traffic; to deal; to barter.
TRĀ'DĘR, *n.* One engaged in trade or commerce.
TRĀDE'-SĀLE, *n.* A sale or auction by and for any particular trade, as that of booksellers.
TRĀDEŞ'MAN, *n.* A shopkeeper; a trader.
TRĀDE'-WĮND, *n.* Monsoon; a periodical wind.
TRA-DĬ''TĮON (tra-dĭsh'un), *n.* An oral account from age to age:—the act of giving up.
TRA-DĬ''TĮON-AL (tra-dĭsh'un-al), } *a.* Re-
TRA-DĬ''TĮON-A-RY (tra-dĭsh'un-a-rę), } lating to, or delivered by, tradition.
TRĀD'Į-TĪVE, *a.* Transmitted from age to age.
TRA-DŪCE', *v. a.* To censure; to calumniate.
TRA-DŪCE'MĘNT, *n.* Censure; obloquy.
TRA-DŪ'CER, *n.* A false censurer; a calumniator.
TRA-DŬC'TĮON, *n.* Propagation; conveyance.
TRA-DŬC'TĮVE, *a.* Derivable; deducible.
TRĂF'FĮC, *n.* Commerce; trade; barter.
TRĂF'FĮC, *v. n. & a.* [*imp. t. & pp.* trafficked.] To practise commerce; to trade; to exchange.
TRĂF'FĮCK-ER, *n.* A trader; a merchant.
TRĂG'A-CĂNTH, *n.* A concrete juice or gum.
TRA-GĒ'DĮ-AN, *n.* A writer or actor of tragedy.
TRĂG'Ę-DY, *n.* A dramatic representation of human passion and suffering:—dreadful event.
TRĂG'ĮC, } *a.* Relating to tragedy; mournful;
TRĂG'Į-CAL, } calamitous; sorrowful; dreadful.
TRĂG'Į-CAL-LY, *ad.* In a tragical manner.
TRĂG'Į-CAL-NĔSS, *n.* State of being tragical.
TRĂG-Į-CŎM'Ę-DY, *n.* A drama partaking both of tragedy and comedy.
TRĂG-Į-CŎM'ĮC, } *a.* Relating to, or partak-
TRĂG-Į-CŎM'Į-CAL, } ing of, tragicomedy.
TRĀIL, *v. a.* To hunt by track:—to draw along.
TRĀIL, *v. n.* To be drawn out or along.
TRĀIL, *n.* A track:—any thing drawn behind.
TRĀIN, *v. a.* To draw; to educate; to exercise.
TRĀIN, *n.* Artifice:—part of a gown drawn behind:—a process; method:—retinue; line.
TRĀIN'BĂND, *n.* A trained band; militia.
TRĀIN'BEAR-ER, *n.* One that holds up a train.
TRĀIN'ĮNG, *n.* Act of forming to any exercise.
TRĀIN'-ŎĮL, *n.* Oil from the fat of whales.
TRĀIPSE, *v. n.* To walk sluttishly or carelessly.
TRĀIT (trāt *or* trā), *n.* A stroke; touch; feature.
TRĀI'TOR, *n.* One who, being trusted, betrays.
TRĀI'TOR-OŬS, *a.* Treacherous; perfidious. [ly.
TRĀI'TOR-OŬS-LY, *ad.* Perfidiously; treacherous-
TRĀI'TOR-OŬS-NĔSS, *n.* Perfidiousness; treach-
TRĀI'TRESS, *n.* A woman who betrays. [ery.
TRA-JĔCT', *v. a.* To cast through; to throw.
TRA-JĔC'TĮON, *n.* A throwing; emission.
TRA-JĔC'TO-RY, *n.* The path or orbit of a comet.
TRĂL-A-TĬ''TĮOŬS, *a.* Metaphorical; not literal.
TRĂM, *n.* A small coal-wagon.
TRĂM'MEL, *n.* A net; shackle:—an iron hook.
TRĂM'MEL, *v. a.* To catch; to shackle.
TRA-MŎN'TANE, *a.* Beyond the mountains or Alps; ultramontane; foreign; barbarous.
TRĂMP, *v. a.* To tread.—*v. n.* To travel on foot.
TRĂM'PLE, *v. a. & n.* To tread under foot.
TRĂM'-RŌAD, TRĂM'-WĀY, *n.* A road for trams.

TRÄNCE, n. A temporary view of the spiritual world ; an ecstasy ; a rapture.

TRÄN'QUIL, a. Quiet ; peaceful ; undisturbed.

TRAN-QUIL'LI-TY, n. Quietness ; peace of mind.

TRÄN'QUIL-LIZE, v. a. To render tranquil ; to compose ; to render calm. [ner.

TRÄN'QUIL-LY, ad. In a tranquil state or man-

TRÄN'QUIL-NÈSS, n. The state of being tranquil.

TRÄNS-ÄCT', v. a. To manage ; to conduct ; to do.

TRÄNS-ÄCT', v. n. To conduct matters ; to treat.

TRÄNS-ÄC'TIQN, n. Dealing ; management.

TRÄNS-ÄCT'QR, n. One who transacts.

TRÄNS-ÄL'PINE, a. Situated beyond the Alps.

TRÄNS-AT-LÄN'TIC, a. Being beyond the At-lantic. [ceed.

TRÄN-SCÈND', v. a. To pass ; to surpass ; to ex-

TRÄN-SCÈND'ENCE, } n. Preëminence ; high
TRÄN-SCÈND'EN-CY, { excellence.

TRÄN-SCÈND'ENT, a. Excellent ; preëminent.

TRÄN-SCEN-DÈNT'AL, a. Supereminent ; very high :—beyond the bounds of experience.

TRÄN-SCEN-DÈN'TAL-ÏSM, n. Transcendental or abstruse metaphysics.

TRÄN-SCÈND'ENT-LY, ad. Supereminently.

TRÄN-SCÈND'ENT-NÈSS, n. Supereminence.

TRÄN-SCRIBE', v. a. To copy; to write a copy of.

TRÄN-SCRIB'ER, n. One who transcribes.

TRÄN'SCRIPT, n. A copy from an original.

TRÄN-SCRIP'TIQN, n. Act of copying. [copy.

TRÄN-SCRIP'TIVE-LY, ad. In the manner of a

TRÄN'SEPT, n. The cross part of a church.

TRÄNS-FÈR', v. a. To convey ; to make over.

TRÄNS'FER, n. A change of property.

TRÄNS-FÈR'A-BLE, a. That may be transferred.

TRÄNS-FÈR'RER, n. One who transfers.

TRÄNS-FIG-U-RÄ'TIQN, n. Change of form.

TRÄNS-FIG'URE (träns-fig'yur), v. a. To trans-

TRÄNS-FIX', v. a. To pierce through. [form.

TRÄNS-FÖRM', v. a. To change the form of.

TRÄNS-FQR-MÄ'TIQN, n. Change of form. [er.

TRÄNS-FÜSE', v. a. To pour out of one into anoth-

TRÄNS-FÜ'SI-BLE, a. That may be transfused.

TRÄNS-FÜ'SIQN, n. Act of transfusing. [break.

TRÄNS-GRÈSS', v. a. To pass over ; to violate ; to

TRÄNS-GRÈSS', v. n. To offend by violating a law.

TRÄNS-GRÈS'SIQN (träns-grèsh'un), n. Act of transgressing ; violation ; offence.

TRÄNS-GRÈSS'QR, n. One who transgresses.

TRÄN'SIENT (trän'shent), a. Short ; momentary.

TRÄN'SIENT-LY (trän'shent-le), ad. In passage.

TRÄN'SIENT-NÈSS, n. Short continuance.

TRÄN'SIT, n. Act of passing, as of a planet across the sun's disk, or as of goods through a country.

TRÄN-SÏ''TIQN (trän-sĭzh'un), n. Passage from one state to another ; change.

TRÄN'SI-TIVE, a. Passing.—(Gram.) Active.

TRÄN'SI-TQ-RI-LY, ad. With short continuance.

TRÄN'SI-TQ-RI-NÈSS, n. Speedy evanescence.

TRÄN'SI-TQ-RY, a. Fleeting ; quickly vanishing.

TRÄNS-LÄTE', v. a. To remove ; to transfer :—to interpret ; to change into another language.

TRÄNS-LÄ'TIQN, n. Act of translating ; version.

TRÄNS-LÄ'TQR, n. One who translates.

TRÄNS-LQ-CÄ'TIQN, n. A removal.

TRÄNS-LÜ'CEN-CY, n. Diaphaneity.

TRÄNS-LÜ'CENT, a. Transparent ; pellucid.

TRÄNS-MA-RÏNE', a. Lying or found beyond sea.

TRÄNS'MI-GRÄTE, v. n. To pass to another place.

TRÄNS-MI-GRÄ'TIQN, n. Passage from one state or place into another :—metempsychosis.

TRÄNS'MI-GRÄ-TQR, n. One who transmigrates.

TRÄNS-MÏS'SI-BLE, a. That may be transmitted.

TRÄNS-MÏS'SIQN (träns-mĭsh'un), n. A sending.

TRÄNS-MÏS'SIVE, a. Transmitted ; sent.

TRÄNS-MÏT', v. a. To send from one to another.

TRÄNS-MÏT'TAL, n. The act of transmitting.

TRÄNS-MÏT'TI-BLE, a. Transmissible.

TRÄNS-MÜT'A-BLE, a. Capable of change.

TRÄNS-MÜT'A-BLY, ad. With capacity of change.

TRÄNS-MU-TÄ'TIQN, n. A change ; alteration.

TRÄNS-MÜTE', v. a. To change from one nature, form, or substance, to another.

TRÄN'SQM, n. A beam :—a lintel over a door.

TRÄNS-PÄR'EN-CY, n. Clearness ; translucence.

TRÄNS-PÄR'ENT, a. Pervious to the light ; clear ; pellucid ; diaphanous ; translucent ; open.

TRÄNS-PÄR'ENT-LY, ad. With transparency.

TRÄNS-PÄR'ENT-NÈSS, n. Transparency.

TRÄN-SPÏC'U-OŬS, a. Transparent ; pellucid.

TRÄN-SPIERCE' (träns-pērs'), v. n. To pierce through ; to transfix ; to penetrate.

TRÄN-SPI-RÄ'TIQN, n. An emission in vapor.

TRÄN-SPIRE', v. n. To be emitted, as vapor :— to escape from secrecy to notice.

TRÄNS-PLÄCE', v. a. To put in a new place.

TRÄNS-PLÄNT', v. a. To plant in a new place.

TRÄNS-PLAN-TÄ'TIQN, n. Act of transplanting.

TRÄNS-PLÄNT'ER, n. One that transplants.

TRÄNS-PÖRT', v. a. To convey from place to place ; to banish : — to affect with passion or ecstasy ; to enrapture.

TRÄNS'PÖRT, n. Conveyance ; a vessel ; ecstasy.

TRÄNS-PQR-TÄ'TIQN, n. Conveyance ; banish-

TRÄNS-PÖRT'ER, n. One that transports. [ment.

TRÄNS-PÖŞ'AL, n. A transposition.

TRÄNS-PÖŞE', v. a. To put each in the place of the other ; to put out of place ; to remove.

TRÄNS-PQ-ŞÏ''TIQN (träns-pq-zĭsh'un), n. Act of putting one thing in the place of another.

TRÄNS-PQ-ŞÏ''TIQN-AL, a. Relating to transpo-sition ; reciprocally changing.

TRÄN-SUB-STÄN'TI-ÄTE (trän-sub-stän'she-āt), v. a. To change to another substance.

TRÄN-SUB-STÄN-TI-Ä'TIQN (trän-sub-stän-she-ä'shun), n. The change of bread and wine, in the eucharist, into the body and blood of Christ.

TRÄN-SU-DÄ'TIQN, n. The act of transuding.

TRÄN-SÜDE', v. n. To pass through in vapor.

TRÄNS-VÈR'SAL, a. Transverse ; crosswise.

TRÄNS-VÈRSE', v. a. To change ; to overturn.

TRÄNS-VÈRSE', a. Being in a cross direction.

TRÄNS-VÈRSE'LY, ad. In a cross direction.

TRÄP, n. A snare ; a stratagem :—a kind of rock.

TRÄP, v. a. To insnare ; to entrap.

TRA-PÄN', v. a. To insnare.—n. A cheat ; a snare.

TRÄP'-DÖOR (träp'dōr), n. A door in a floor, &c.

TRÄPE, v. n. To run about idly ; to traipse.

TRÄPES, n. An idle, slatternly woman.

TRA-PÈ'ZI-ŬM (tra-pē'zhe-ŭm), n. A quadri-lateral figure with no parallel sides.

TRÄP-E-ZÖÏD' or TRA-PÈ'ZÖÏD, n. A quadri-lateral figure with two parallel sides. [tion.

TRÄP'PINGS, n. pl. Ornaments ; dress ; decora-

TRÄSH'Y, a. Worthless ; vile ; useless.

TRÂU-MÄT'IC, a. Tending to heal wounds.

TRĂV'AĬL (trăv'ĭl), *v. n.* To toil; to be in labor.
TRĂV'AĬL, *n.* Toil:—labor in childbirth.
TRĂV'ĘL, *v. n.* To make a journey; to pass; to go.
TRĂV'ĘL, *v. a.* To pass; to journey over. [go.
TRĂV'ĘL, *n.* A journey.—*pl.* An account of travel.
TRĂV'ĘLLED (trăv'ęld), *a.* Having been abroad.
TRĂV'ĘL-LĘR, *n.* One who travels.
TRĂV'ĘRS-Ą-BLE, *a.* (*Law.*) Liable to objection.
TRĂV'ĘRSE, *ad.* Crosswise; athwart.
TRĂV'ĘRSE, *prep.* Through crosswise.
TRĂV'ĘRSE, *a.* Lying across.—*Traverse jury*, a jury for trying a disputed point.
TRĂV'ĘRSE, *n.* Any thing that thwarts or crosses.
TRĂV'ĘRSE, *v. a.* To cross; to survey; to oppose.
TRĂV'ĘRSE, *v. n.* To make opposition in fencing.
TRĂV'ĘS-TY, *n.* A burlesque translation.
TRĂV'ĘS-TY, *v. a.* To turn into burlesque.
TRÂWL'-NĔT, *n.* A kind of net dragged.
TRĀY (trā), *n.* A shallow wooden vessel.
TRĔACH'ĘR-OŬS (trĕch'ęr-ŭs), *a.* Partaking of treachery; faithless; perfidious.
TRĔACH'ĘR-OŬS-LY, *ad.* Faithlessly; perfidious-
TRĔACH'ĘR-OŬS-NĔSS, *n.* Perfidiousness. [ly.
TRĔACH'ĘR-Y (trĕch'ęr-ę), *n.* Perfidy; deceit.
TRĔA'CLE (trē'kl), *n.* Molasses; a sirup.
TRĔAD (trĕd), *v. n.* [*imp. t.* trod; *pp.* trodden.] To set the foot; to walk; to trample.
TRĔAD (trĕd), *v. a.* To walk on; to press; to beat.
TRĔAD (trĕd), *n.* A stepping; a step with the foot.
TRĔAD'LE (trĕd'dl), *n.* A part of a lathe, &c.
TRĔAD'-MĬLL (trĕd'mĭl), *n.* A mill kept in motion by persons treading on a wheel.
TRĔA'ŞON (trē'zn), *n.* The highest offence against a state or government; rebellion.
TRĔA'ŞON-Ą-BLE (trē'zn-ą-bl), *a.* Having the nature of treason; rebellious. [riches.
TRĔAŞ'URE (trĕzh'ur), *n.* Wealth hoarded;
TRĔAŞ'URE (trĕzh'ur), *v. a.* To hoard; to lay up.
TRĔAŞ'URE-HÖÜSE, *n.* A treasury.
TRĔAŞ'UR-ĘR (trĕzh'ur-ęr), *n.* One who has the care of the money of a state, corporation, &c.
TRĔAŞ'U-RY (trĕzh'u-rę), *n.* A place for money.
TRĔAT (trēt), *v. a.* To use; to handle; to manage.
TRĔAT, *v. n.* To discourse:—to make terms.
TRĔAT, *n.* An entertainment given; pleasure.
TRĔA'TĬSE, *n.* A discourse; dissertation.
TREAT'MĘNT, *n.* Usage; the manner of using.
TRĔA'TY (trē'tę), *n.* A negotiation; a compact.
TRĔB'LE (trĕb'bl), *a.* Triple; threefold.
TRĔB'LE (trĕb'bl), *v. a.* To multiply by three.
TRĔB'LE (trĕb'bl), *v. n.* To become threefold.
TRĔB'LE (trĕb'bl), *n.* (*Mus.*) The highest part.
TRĔB'LY (trĕb'ble), *ad.* In a threefold degree.
TRĔB'U-ÇHĔT, } *n.* A cucking-stool; a duck-
TRĔ'BUCK-ĘT, } ing-stool; a tumbrel.
TRĔE, *n.* The largest kind of vegetable.
TRĔE'NAIL (*often* trŭn'nęl), *n.* A wooden pin.
TRĔ'FÖĬL, *n.* A three-leaved plant; clover.
TRĔIL'LĄ GE (trĕl'yąj), *n.* [Fr.] A sort of rail-
TRĔL'LĬS, *n.* [Fr.] A sort of lattice-work. [work.
TRĔL'LĬSED (trĕl'lĭst), *a.* Having trellises. [der.
TRĔM'BLE, *v. n.* To shake; to quake; to shud-
TRĔM'BLING-LY, *ad.* So as to shake or quiver.
TRĘ-MĔN'DOUS, *a.* Dreadful; horrible; terrible.
TRĘ-MĔN'DOUS-LY, *ad.* Horribly; dreadfully.
TRĘ-MĔN'DOUS-NĔSS, *n.* Dread; horror.
TRĔ'MOR, *n.* State of trembling; a quivering.
TRĔM'U-LOŬS, *a.* Trembling; fearful; quivering.

TRĔM'U-LOŬS-LY, *ad.* With trepidation.
TRĔM'U-LOŬS-NĔSS, *n.* The state of quivering.
TRĔNCH, *v. a.* To cut; to ditch:—to fortify.
TRĔNCH, *v. n.* To encroach; to intrench.
TRĔNCH, *n.* A ditch; a defence for soldiers.
TRĔNCH'ANT, *a.* Cutting; sharp.
TRĔNCH'ĘR, *n.* A wooden plate; a platter:—
TRĔNCH'ĘR-MĂN, *n.* A feeder; an eater. [table.
TRĔND, *v. n.* To run; to tend; to stretch.
TRĘ-PĂN', *n.* A surgeon's instrument.
TRĘ-PĂN', *v. a.* To perforate with the trepan.
TRĘ-PHÎNE' *or* TRĘ-PHĬNE', *n.* Sort of trepan.
TRĔP-Į-DĀ'TĬON, *n.* State of trembling; terror.
TRĔS'PĄSS, *v. n.* To transgress, offend, intrude.
TRĔS'PĄSS, *n.* An offence; an unlawful en-
TRĔS'PĄSS-ĘR, *n.* One who trespasses. [trance.
TRĔSS, *n.* A lock; a ringlet; a curl of hair.
TRĔSS'ĘD, *a.* Knotted; curled; having tresses.
TRĔS'TLE (trĕs'sl), *n.* The frame of a table:— a support:—a three-legged stool.
TRĔT, *n.* An allowance in weight for waste.
TRĔV'ĘT, *n.* An iron stool with three legs;
TRĔY (trā), *n.* A three at cards or dice. [trivet.
TRĪ'A-BLE, *a.* Capable of trial or examination.
TRĪ'AD, *n.* Three united; union of three.
TRĪ'AL, *n.* A test; an examination; experiment.
TRĪ'ĂN-GLE (trī'ăng-gl), *n.* A figure of 3 angles.
TRĪ-ĂN'GU-LĄR, *a.* After the form of a triangle.
TRĪBE, *n.* A distinct body of people; a family.
TRĬB'LĘT, *n.* A tool for making rings with.
TRĬB-U-LĀ'TĬON, *n.* Distress; severe affliction.
TRĮ-BŪ'NĄL, *n.* A judge's seat; a court of jus-
TRĬB'ŪNE, *n.* An officer of ancient Rome. [tice.
TRĬB'ŪNE-SHĬP, *n.* Office of a tribune. [tribune.
TRĬB-U-NĬ''TĬAL (-nĭsh'ąl), *a.* Relating to a
TRĬB'U-TĄ-RY, *a.* Paying tribute; subject.
TRĬB'U-TĄ-RY, *n.* One who pays tribute.
TRĬB'UTE, *n.* A tax, or stated sum, paid in acknowledgment of subjection.
TRĪCE, *n.* A short time; an instant; a moment.
TRĬCK, *n.* A sly fraud; artifice; juggle; habit.
TRĬCK, *v. a.* To cheat; to defraud; to dress.
TRĬCK'ĘR-Y, *n.* The act of dressing up; artifice.
TRĬCK'ĬSH, *a.* Knavishly artful; cunning; sub-
TRĬC'KLE, *v. n.* To fall or run in drops. [tle.
TRĬCK'STĘR, *n.* One who practises tricks.
TRĪ-CÖR'PO-RĄL, *a.* Having three bodies.
TRĪ'DĘNT, *n.* Three-forked sceptre of Neptune.
TRĪ-ĔN'NĮ-ĄL, *a.* Happening every third year.
TRĪ'ĘR, *n.* One who tries; an attempter.
TRĪ'FĮD, *a.* Cut or divided into three parts.
TRĪ'FLE, *v. n.* To act with levity or folly.
TRĪ'FLE, *v. a.* To waste away; to dissipate.
TRĪ'FLE, *n.* A thing of no moment or value.
TRĪ'FLĘR, *n.* One who trifles or acts with levity.
TRĪ'FLĬNG, *a.* Wanting worth; unimportant.
TRĪ'FLĬNG-LY, *ad.* Without weight or impor-
TRĪ-FŌ'LĮ-ĄTE, *a.* Having three leaves. [tance.
TRĪ'FÖRM, *a.* Having a triple shape.
TRĬG'A-MY, *n.* The state of being thrice married, or of having three husbands or wives.
TRĬG'GĘR, *n.* A catch of a gun or wheel.
TRĪ'GLYPH, *n.* An ornament in a Doric frieze.
TRĬG'O-NĄL, *a.* Triangular; having three corners or angles. [onometry.
TRĬG-O-NO-MĔT'RĬ-CĄL, *a.* Relating to trig-
TRĬG-O-NO-MĔT'RĬ-CĄL-LY, *ad.* By, or according to, trigonometry.

TRĬG-Q-NŎM'Ḙ-TRY, *n.* Art of measuring trian-
TRĬ'GRĂPH, *n.* Three letters in one sound.[gles.
TRĪ-LĂT'ĔR-AL, *a.* Having three sides.
TRĪ-LĬT'ḘR-AL, *a.* Having three letters.
TRĬLL, *n.* A quaver; a tremulousness of music.
TRĬLL, *v. a.* To utter quavering; to shake.
TRĬLL, *v. n.* To trickle; to quaver.
TRĬLL'IQN (trĭl'yŭn), *n.* A million of millions.
TRĬM, *a.* Nice; snug; dressed up; spruce.
TRĬM, *n.* Dress; gear; ornaments; trimming.
TRĬM, *v. a.* To dress; to shave; to clip; to ad-
TRĬM, *v. n.* To fluctuate between parties. [just.
TRĬM'Ḙ-TḘR, *a.* Consisting of three poetical
TRĬM'LY, *ad.* Nicely; neatly; sprucely.[measures.
TRĬM'MḘR, *n.* One who trims; a timeserver.
TRĬM'MĬNG, *n.* Appendages to a coat, gown,
TRĬM'NḘSS, *n.* Neatness; petty elegance. [&c.
TRĪ'NAL, *a.* Threefold; trine.
TRĪNE, *n.* A certain aspect of planets.
TRĪNE, *a.* Threefold; thrice repeated.
TRĬN-Ḭ-TĀ'RḬ-AN, *n.* A believer of the doctrine
  of the Trinity. [the Godhead.
TRĬN'Ḭ-TY, *n.* The doctrine of three persons in
TRĬN'KḘT, *n.* A toy; ornament of dress; jewel.
TRĪ-NŌ'MḬ-AL, *a.* Containing three terms.
TRĪ'Ō, *n.* A piece of music for three voices or
  three instruments :—three united.
TRĬP, *v. a.* To supplant; to throw :—to detect.
TRĬP, *v. n.* To stumble :—to err :—to run.
TRĬP, *n.* A stumble; error :—a short voyage.
TRĬP'AR-TĪTE, *a.* Divided into three parts.
TRĬP-AR-TĬ''TIQN, *n.* A division into three parts.
TRĪPE, *n.* The entrails or stomach of the ox,
TRĬP'Ḙ-DAL, *a.* Having three feet. [&c.
TRĪ-PḘR'SQN-AL, *a.* Consisting of three persons.
TRĪ-PĔT'AL-OŬS, *a.* Having three flower-leaves.
TRĬP'-HĂM-MḘR, *n.* A tilt-hammer.
TRĬPH'THŎNG (trĭp'thŏng), *n.* A union of three
TRĬP'LE, *a.* Threefold; treble. [vowels.
TRĬP'LE, *v. a.* To treble; to make threefold.
TRĬP'LḘT, *n.* Three of a kind; three lines
  rhyming together.
TRĬP'LḬ-CATE, *a.* Made thrice as much.
TRĬP'LḬ-CATE, *n.* A third of the same kind.
TRĬP-LḬ-CĀ'TIQN, *n.* The act of trebling.
TRĪ-PLĬÇ'Ḭ-TY, *n.* The state of being threefold.
TRĪ'PQD, *n.* A seat, &c., with three feet.
TRĬP'PĬNG, *a.* Quick; nimble :—stumbling.
TRĬP'PĬNG, *n.* A stumbling :—a light dance.
TRĬP'PĬNG-LY, *ad.* With agility.
TRĬP'TŌTE, *n.* A noun used but in three cases.
TRĪ'RĒME, *n.* A galley with three tiers of oars.
TRĪ-SĔC'TIQN, *n.* A division into three equal
  parts. [lables.
TRĬS-YL-LĂB'Ḭ-CAL, *a.* Consisting of three syl-
TRĬS'YL-LA-BLE, *n.* A word of three syllables.
TRĪTE, *a.* Worn out; stale; common; not new.
TRĪTE'LY, *ad.* In a trite or common way.
TRĪTE'NḘSS, *n.* Staleness; commonness.
TRĪ'THḘ-ĬSM, *n.* The doctrine of three Gods.
TRĪ'THḘ-ĬST, *n.* A believer in tritheism.
TRĪ-THḘ-ĬS'TĬC, *a.* Relating to tritheism.
TRĬT'U-RA-BLE, *a.* That may be triturated.
TRĬT'U-RĀTE, *v. a.* To pulverize; to pound.
TRĬT-U-RĀ'TIQN, *n.* Reduction to powder.
TRĪ'UMPH, *n.* Pomp for victory; conquest; joy.
TRĪ'UMPH, *v. n.* To rejoice at victory; to exult.
TRĪ-ŬM'PHAL, *a.* Used in celebrating victory.

TRĪ-ŬM'PHANT, *a.* Celebrating victory; vic-
  torious; exulting. [ner.
TRĪ-ŬM'PHANT-LY, *ad.* In a triumphant man-
TRĪ'UMPH-ḘR, *n.* One who triumphs.
TRĪ-ŬM'VĬR, *n.; pl.* TRĪ-ŬM'VḬ-RĪ. [L.] One
  of three men united in the same office.
TRĪ-ŬM'VḬ-RATE, *n.* Government by three men.
TRĪ'ŪNE, *a.* Being at once three and one.
TRĪ-Ū'NḬ-TY, *n.* The state of being triune.
TRĬV'ḘT, *n.* A stool with three legs; trevet.
  See TREVET.
TRĬV'Ḭ-AL *or* TRĬV'IAL, *a.* Vile; light; trifling.
TRĬV'Ḭ-AL-LY, *ad.* Vulgarly; lightly.
TRĬV'Ḭ-AL-NĔSS, *n.* Worthlessness.
TRŌ'CAR, *n.* A surgical instrument.
TRQ-ℭHĀ'ĬC, } *a.* Relating to, or consisting
TRQ-ℭHĀ'Ḭ-CAL, } of, troches.
TRŌ'ℭHE, *n.* A kind of lozenge, or solid medi-
  cine ;—written also *troch.*
TRŌ'ℭHĒĔ, *n.* In prosody, a foot, consisting
  of a long and a short syllable. [motion.
TRQ-ℭHĬL'ĬCS, *n. pl.* The science of rotary
TRŎD, *imp. t. & pp.* from *tread.*
TRŎD'DEN (trŏd'dn), *pp.* from *tread.*
TRŎG'LQ-DȲTE, *n.* One who inhabits caves.
TRŌLL, *v. a. & n.* To move circularly; to roll.
TRŎL'LQP, *n.* A slattern; a slovenly woman.
TRŎM-BŌ'NḘ *or* TRŎM'BŌNE, *n.* A long, very
  sonorous, brass musical instrument.
TRÔÔP, *n.* A company; a body of soldiers.
TRÔÔP, *v. n.* To march in a body, or in haste.
TRÔÔP'ḘR, *n.* A horse soldier; a horseman.
TRŌPE, *n.* A figure of speech which changes a
  word from its original signification.
TRŌ'PHIED (trō'fĭd), *a.* Adorned with trophies.
TRŌ'PHY, *n.* Something taken in battle.
TRŎP'ĬC, *n.* A line at which the sun turns back.
TRŎP'Ḭ-CAL, *a.* Figurative :—within the tropics.
TRŎP'Ḭ-CAL-LY, *ad.* Figuratively; not literally.
TRŎP-Q-LŎG'Ḭ-CAL, *a.* Varied by tropes.
TRQ-PŎL'Q-ĠY, *n.* A tropical mode of speech.
TRŎT, *v. n.* To move with a high, jolting pace.
TRŎT, *n.* The jolting, high pace of a horse, &c.
TRŎTH, *n.* Faith; fidelity; truth; verity.
TRŌTH'PLĪGHT (trŏth'plīt), *n.* A betrothing.
TRŎT'TḘR, *n.* One that trots :—a sheep's foot.
TROÙ'BA-DOÙR, *n.* [Fr.] An early poet of
  Provence, or the south of France. [vex.
TROÙB'LE (trŭb'bl), *v. a.* To disturb, afflict,
TROÙB'LE (trŭb'bl), *n.* Disturbance; affliction.
TROÙB'LḘR (trŭb'blḙr), *n.* A disturber.
TROÙB'LE-SŎME (trŭb'blḙ-sŭm), *a.* Vexatious;
  teasing; tiresome; harassing; perplexing.
TROÙB'LOŲS (trŭb'blŭs), *a.* Confused; disor-
TRŌÙGH (trŏf), *n.* A long, hollow vessel. [dered.
TROÙNCE, *v. a.* To punish; to beat severely.
TROÙ'SḘRS, *n. pl.* Long, loose pantaloons.
TROÙT, *n.* A delicate, spotted fish.
TRŌ'VḘR, *n.* (*Law.*) An action for goods found
  and not delivered to the owner on demand.
†TRŌW, *v. n.* To think; to believe.
TRŌŴ'ḘL, *n.* A tool used by bricklayers.
TRŌȲ'-WEIGHT (trŏȳ'wāt), *n.* A kind of
  weight with twelve ounces in a pound. [duty.
TRÙ'ANT, *n.* An idler; one who neglects his
TRÙ'ANT, *a.* Idle; wandering from school, &c.
TRŬCE, *n.* A temporary peace; a short quiet.
TRŬCE'-BREĀK-ḘR, *n.* A violator of a covenant.

TRŬCK, *v. n.* & *a.* To traffic, exchange, barter.
TRŬCK, *n.* Traffic by exchange:—sort of cart.
TRŬCK′ẸR, *n.* One who traffics by exchange.
TRŬC′KLE, *v. n.* To be in subjection; to yield.
TRŬC′KLE-BĔD, *n.* A bed that runs on wheels.
TRŬ′CỤ-LĔNCE, TRŬ′CỤ-LĔN-CỶ, *n.* Fierceness.
TRŬ′CỤ-LĔNT, *a.* Savage; barbarous; cruel.
TRŬDĢE, *v. n.* To travel laboriously; to jog on.
TRŬE (trŭ), *a.* Not false; veracious; genuine; real; faithful; steady; honest; exact.
TRŬE′-BŎRN, *a.* Having a right by birth; gen- [uine.
TRŬE′-HEÄRT-ẸD, *a.* Honest; faithful.
TRŬE′-LŎVE-KNŎT, *n.* Particular kind of knot.
TRŬE′NẸSS, *n.* Sincerity; faithfulness.
TRŬE′PĔN-NỶ, *n.* An honest person or fellow.
TRŬF′FLE (trŭ′fl), *n.* A subterraneous fungus.
TRŬG, *n.* A hod for coals, mortar, &c.
TRŬ′ĬṢM, *n.* A self-evident and undeniable truth.
TRŬLL, *n.* A wench; a vagrant strumpet.
TRŬ′LỶ, *ad.* According to truth; really; exact-
TRŬMP, *n.* A trumpet:—a winning card. [ly.
TRŬMP, *v. a.* To win with a trump; to devise.
TRŬMP, *v. n.* To play a trump card; to sound.
TRŬMP′ẸR-Ỷ, *n.* Empty talk; worthless trash.
TRŬM′PẸT, *n.* An instrument of martial music.
TRŬM′PẸT, *v. a.* To publish aloud; to proclaim.
TRŬM′PẸT-ẸR, *n.* One who trumpets.
TRŬN′CĀTE, *v. a.* To maim; to lop; to cut short.
TRŬN-CĀ′TIǪN, *n.* Act of lopping or maiming.
TRŬN′CHEǪN (trŭn′shụn), *n.* A staff; a cudgel.
TRŬN′DLE, *v. n.* & *a.* To roll; to bowl along.
TRŬN′DLE, *n.* Any round, rolling thing.
TRŬN′DLE-BĔD, *n.* A bed on trundles; truc-kle-bed. See TRUCKLE-BED.
TRŬNK, *n.* The body of any thing:—a chest for clothes:—proboscis of an elephant, &c.
TRŬNK′-HŌṢE, *n.* Large breeches formerly worn.
TRŬNN′IǪNS (-yụnz), *n. pl.* Knobs of cannon.
TRŬ′ṢIǪN (trŭ′zhụn), *n.* The act of thrusting.
TRŬSS, *n.* A bandage for ruptures:—a bundle.
TRŬSS, *v. a.* To pack up close together.
TRŬST, *n.* Confidence; reliance; charge; credit.
TRŬST, *v. a.* To confide in; to believe; to credit.
TRŬST, *v. n.* To have confidence, rely, expect.
TRŬS-TEĒ′, *n.* One intrusted with any thing.
TRŬST′Ị-LỶ, *ad.* Honestly; faithfully. [ness.
TRŬST′Ị-NĔSS, *n.* Honesty; fidelity; faithful-
TRŬST′Ỷ, *a.* Honest; faithful; fit to be trusted.
TRŬTH, *n.* Conformity to fact or reality; ve-racity; fidelity; honesty; virtue; integrity.
TRỸ, *v. a.* To examine; to prove, essay, attempt.
TRỸ, *v. n.* To endeavor; to make an essay.
TRỸ′ĬNG, *p. a.* Bringing to trial; severe.
TŬB, *n.* A large, open vessel of wood.
TŪBE, *n.* A pipe; a siphon; a long, hollow body.
TŪ′BẸR, *n.* A vegetable root, as a potato.
TŪ′BẸR-CLE, *n.* Tumor in an organ; a pimple.
TỤ-BĔR′CỤ-LẠR, *a.* Full of tubercles.
TŪBE′RŌṢE *or* TŪ′BẸR-ŌṢE, *n.* A tuberous
TŪ′BẸR-OŬS, *a.* Full of tubers or knobs. [plant.
TŪ′BỤ-LẠR, *a.* Long and hollow; fistular.
TŪ′BỤ-LĀT-ẸD, TŪ′BỤ-LOŬS, *a.* Long and hol-
TŬCK, *n.* A small sword; a net:—a fold. [low.
TŬCK, *v. a.* To compress; to enclose under.
TŬCK′ẸR, *n.* A piece of linen for the breast.
TŪEṢ′DAỶ (tūz′dẹ), *n.* Third day of the week.
TŪ′FẠ, TŬFF, *n.* A volcanic earth.
TỶ-FÔON′, *n.* A tempest. See TYPHOON.

TŬFT, *n.* A cluster of hair, grass, ribbons, &c.
TŬFT, *v. a.* To form into or adorn with a tuft.
TŬFT′ẸD, *a.* Growing in tufts or clusters.
TŬFT′Ỷ, *a.* Adorned with tufts.
TŬG, *v.* To pull with great effort; to draw.
TŬG, *n.* A long, hard pull; a great effort.
TŬG′ĢẸR, *n.* One that tugs or pulls hard.
TỤ-Ĭ″TIǪN (tụ-ĭsh′ụn), *n.* Guardianship; in-
TŪ′LĬP, *n.* A plant and its flower. [struction.
TŬM′BLE, *v. n.* To fall suddenly; to roll about.
TŬM′BLE, *v. a.* To turn over; to throw about.
TŬM′BLE, *n.* Act of tumbling; a fall.
TŬM′BLẸR, *n.* One who tumbles, or who shows feats of activity:—a drinking glass.
TŬM′BRẸL, *n.* A dung cart:—a ducking-stool.
TŪ-MẸ-FĂC′TIǪN, *n.* A swelling; a tumor.
TŪ′MẸ-FỸ, *v. a.* To swell; to make to swell.
TŪ′MĬD, *a.* Swelled; puffed up; pompous.
TŪ′MǪR, *n.* A morbid swelling; affected pomp.
TŪ′MǪR-OŬS, *a.* Swelling; protuberant.
TŪ-MỤ-LŌSE′, *a.* Formed in heaps; full of
TŪ′MỤ-LOŬS, heaps or mounds.
TŪ′MỤ-LŬS, *n.*; *pl.* TŪ′MỤ-LĬ. [L.] A mound.
TŪ′MULT, *n.* A wild commotion; a stir; bustle.
TỤ-MŬLT′Ụ-Ạ-RĬ-LỶ, *ad.* In a tumultuary man-
TỤ-MŬLT′Ụ-Ạ-RỶ, *a.* Disorderly; confused. [ner.
TỤ-MŬLT′Ụ-OŬS (tụ-mŭlt′yụ-ŭs), *a.* Disorderly; turbulent; violent; full of tumults. [violence.
TỤ-MŬLT′Ụ-OŬS-LỶ, *ad.* With confusion and
TỤ-MŬLT′Ụ-OŬS-NĔSS, *n.* Disorder; violence.
TŬN, *n.* A large cask:—20 cwt. See TON.
TŪN′Ạ-BLE, *a.* That may be tuned; harmonious.
TŪN′Ạ-BLE-NĔSS, *n.* Harmony; melodiousness.
TŪN′Ạ-BLỶ, *ad.* Harmoniously; melodiously.
TŪNE, *n.* A series of notes; harmony; order.
TŪNE, *v. a.* To put into a musical state; to
TŪNE′FÛL, *a.* Musical; harmonious. [sing.
TŬNG′STẸN, *n.* A hard, brittle metal. [nicle.
TŪ′NĬC, *n.* A Roman garment:—a covering; tu-
TŪ′NĬ-CLE, *n.* A natural covering; integument.
TŪN′ĬNG, *n.* Act of singing in concert.
TŬN′NẸL, *n.* A shaft of a chimney, &c.; a fun-nel:—a conical vessel with a wide mouth:—a subterranean passage for a canal or a road.
TŬR′BẠN, *n.* The Turkish cover for the head.
TŬR′BẠNED (tŭr′bạnd), *a.* Wearing a turban.
TŬR′BĬD, *a.* Thick; muddy; not clear.
TŬR′BĬD-NĔSS, *n.* Muddiness; thickness.
TŬR′BĬ-NĀT-ẸD, *a.* Twisted; spiral; conical.
TŬR-BĬ-NĀ′TIǪN, *n.* Act of spinning like a top.
TŬR′BǪT, *n.* A delicate flat fish. [der.
TŬR′BỤ-LĔNCE, *n.* Tumult; confusion; disor-
TŬR′BỤ-LĔNT, *a.* Disorderly; tumultuous.
TŬR′BỤ-LĔNT-LỶ, *ad.* Tumultuously; violent-
TŬR′CĬṢM, *n.* The religion of the Turks. [ly.
TỤ-REĒN′, *n.* A deep vessel for soups, &c.
TŬRF, *n.* A clod covered with grass; peat:—a
TŬRF, *v. a.* To cover with turfs. [race-ground.
TŬRF′Ị-NĔSS, *n.* State of abounding with turfs.
TŬRF′Ỷ, *a.* Full of turfs; covered with turf.
TŬR′GẸNT, *a.* Swelling; tumid; pompous.
TỤR-GĔS′CẸNCE, *n.* Act of swelling; tur-
TỤR-GĔS′CẸN-CỶ, gidity. [mid.
TŬR′GĬD, *a.* Swelling; bloated; pompous; tu-
TỤR-GĬD′Ị-TỶ, *n.* The state of being swollen.
TŬR′GĬD-NĔSS, *n.* State of being turgid.
TŬR′KEỶ (tŭr′kẹ), *n.* A large domestic fowl.
TŬR′KOÎṢ *or* TỤR-KÖĬṢ′, *n.* A mineral.

TŬR′MĚ-RĬC, *n.* An Indian plant or root.
TŬR′MOÏL, *n.* Trouble ; disturbance.
TŲR-MOÏL′, *v. a.* To harass ; to weary.
TŲR-MOÏL′, *v. n.* To be in a state of commotion.
TŬRN, *v. a. & n.* To move round ; to revolve ;
 to change ; to transform ; to alter ; to return.
TŬRN, *n.* Act of turning ; change ; vicissitude.
TŬRN′CŌAT (-kōt), *n.* A renegade ; an apostate.
TŬRN′ĚR, *n.* One who turns in a lathe.
TŬRN′ĚR-Y, *n.* Art of turning ; things turned.
TŬRN′ĮNG, *n.* A flexure ; a winding ; a mean-
TŬR′NĮP, *n.* A white esculent root. [der.
TŬRN′KĔY (-kē), *n.* A keeper of prison-doors.
TŬRN′PĪKE, *n.* A gate on a road ; a toll-gate.
TŬRN′PĪKE-RŌAD, *n.* A road on which turn-
 pikes are erected and tolls are paid.
TŬRN′SŌLE, *n.* The heliotrope ; a plant.
TŬRN′SPĬT, *n.* One that turns the spit ; a dog.
TŬRN′STĪLE, *n.* A turnpike in a footpath.
TŬR′PĔN-TĪNE, *n.* Resin from the pine, &c.
TŬR′PĮ-TŪDE, *n.* Inherent vileness ; wicked-
TŬR′RĔT, *n.* A small tower or eminence. [ness.
TŬR′RĔT-ĔD, *a.* Furnished with turrets.
TŬR′TLE, *n.* A species of dove :—a sea-tortoise.
TŬS′CĄN, *a.* Noting an order of architecture.
TŬSH, TŬT, *interj.* Expressing check or rebuke.
TŬSK, *n.* A long, pointed tooth ; a fang.
TŬSK′ĔD, TŬSK′Y, *a.* Having tusks.
TŬS′SLE (tŭs′sl), *n.* A struggle. [*Vulgar.*]
TŪ′TĔ-LĄGE, *n.* Guardianship ; protection ; care.
TŪ′TĔ-LĄR, ⎫
TŪ′TĔ-LĄ-RY, ⎬ *a.* Protecting ; guarding.
TŪ′TŎR, *n.* One who instructs ; a preceptor.
TŪ′TŎR, *v. a.* To instruct ; to teach ; to discipline.
TŪ′TŎR-ĄGE, *n.* The office of tutor ; instruction.
TŪ′TŎR-ĔSS, *n.* An instructress ; a governess.
TŬT′TY, *n.* An impure oxide of zinc.
TWAD′DLE (twŏd′dl), *n.* Idle talk ; nonsense.
TWĀIN, *a. & n.* Two ; twice one. [noise.
TWĂNG, *v. n.* To sound with a quick, sharp
TWĂNG, *v. a.* To make to sound sharply.
TWĂNG, *n.* A sharp, quick sound ; a relish.
TWAT′TLE (twŏt′tl), *v. n.* To prate ; to chatter.
TWĒĒ′DLE, *v. a.* To handle lightly or softly.
TWĒĒ′ZĔRṢ, *n. pl.* Small pincers to pluck with.
TWĔLFTH, *a.* Second after the tenth.
TWĔLFTH′TĪDE, *n.* Twelfth day after Christ-
TWĔLVE, *a.* Two and ten ; twice six. [mas.
TWĔLVE′MŎNTH (*or* twĕl′mŭnth), *n.* A year.
TWĔLVE′PĔNCE, *n.* A shilling.
TWĔLVE′-PĔN-NY, *a.* Sold for a shilling. [ty.
TWĔN′TĮ-ĔTH, *a.* Twice tenth ; ordinal of twen-
TWĔN′TY, *a. & n.* Twice ten ; a score.
TWĪ′BĬLL, *n.* A halberd :—a pavier's tool.
TWĪCE, *ad.* Two times ; doubly.
TWĬG, *n.* A small shoot ; a little branch. [twigs.
TWĬG′GĔN, TWĬG′GY, *a.* Made of or full of
TWĪ′LĬGHT (twī′līt), *n.* The faint light before
 sunrise and after sunset : obscure light.
TWĪ′LĬGHT (twī′līt), *a.* Obscure ; shaded.
TWĬLL, *v. a.* To weave in ribs ; to quilt.

TWĬN, *n.* One of two children born at the same
 birth.—*pl.* The *Gemini*, a sign of the zodiac.
TWĬN′-BŎRN, *a.* Born at the same birth.
TWĪNE, *v. a.* To twist ; to wind ; to cling to.
TWĪNE, *v. n.* To convolve itself ; to wind.
TWĪNE, *n.* A twisted thread ; twist :—embrace.
TWĬNGE, *v. a.* To torment ; to pinch ; to tweak.
TWĬNGE, *n.* A short, sudden, sharp pain ; pinch.
TWĬN′KLE, *v. n.* To sparkle ; to flash ; to quiver.
TWĬN′KLE, ⎫ *n.* A sparkling light ; a motion
TWĬNK′LĬNG, ⎬ of the eye :—a moment.
TWĬN′LĬNG, *n.* A twin lamb. [whirl.
TWÏRL, *v. a. & n.* To turn round ; to revolve ; to
TWÏRL, *n.* Rotation ; a circular motion ; twist.
TWĬST, *v. a.* To form by complication ; to wind.
TWĬST, *v. n.* To be contorted or convolved.
TWĬST, *n.* A sewing silk ; cord :—contortion.
TWĬT, *v. a.* To upbraid ; to flout ; to reproach.
TWĬTCH, *v. a.* To pluck forcibly ; to snatch.
TWĬTCH, *n.* A quick pull ; a sudden contraction.
TWĬT′TĔR, *v. n.* To make a noise, as swallows.
TWĬT′TĔR, *n.* A small noise :—sort of laughter.
TWÔ (tô), *a.* One and one ;—*used in composition.*
TWÔ′-ĔDGED (tô′ĕdjd), *a.* Having two edges.
TWÔ′FŌLD (tô′fōld), *a.* Double ; two.—*ad.* Doubly.
TWÔ′-HĂND-ĔD, *a.* Employing both hands ; large.
TWO′PĔNCE (tô′pĕns *or* tŭp′pĕns), *n.* Two
 pennies :—a small coin.
‖TWOPENNY (tô′pĕn-ę *or* tŭp′pĕn-ę), *a.* Worth
 twopence.
TŸM′BĄL, *n.* A kind of kettle-drum.
TŸM′PĄN, *n.* A drum ; tympanum :—a panel :
 —the frame of a printing-press.
TŸM′PĄ-NŬM, *n.* [L.] Drum of the ear.
TŸM′PĄ-NY, *n.* A flatulence ; the wind dropsy.
TŸPE, *n.* A symbol, figure, or emblem :—a
 model ; a pattern :—a metallic printing letter.
TŸ-PHÔÔN′, *n.* A violent wind ; hurricane.
TŸ′PHŲS, *n.* A debilitating or nervous fever.
TŸ′PHOÏD, *a.* Relating to, or like, a typhus.
TŸP′ĮC, TŸP′Į-CĄL, *a.* Emblematical ; figura-
TŸP′Į-CĄL-LY, *ad.* In a typical manner. [tive.
TŸP′Į-CĄL-NĔSS, *n.* State of being typical.
TŸP′Į-FY, *v. a.* To figure ; to show in emblem.
‖TŸ-PŎG′RA-PHĔR, *n.* A printer.
‖TŸ-PO-GRĂPH′ĮC, *a.* Relating to printing.
‖TŸ-PO-GRĂPH′Į-CĄL *or* TŸP-O-GRĂPH′Į-CĄL,
 a. Relating to printing :—emblematical.
‖TŸ-PO-GRĂPH′Į-CĄL-LY, *ad.* By means of types.
‖TŸ-PŎG′RA-PHY, *n.* The art of printing.
TŸ-RĂN′NĮC, ⎫ *a.* Relating to, or like, a ty-
TŸ-RĂN′NĮ-CĄL, ⎬ rant ; cruel ; despotic.
TŸ-RĂN′NĮ-CĄL-LY, *ad.* In the manner of a
 tyrant ; despotically.
TŸ-RĂN′NĮ-CĪDE, *n.* Act of killing a tyrant.
TŸR′AN-NĪZE, *v. n.* To play or act the tyrant.
TŸR′AN-NY, *n.* The government of a tyrant ;
 cruel government ; rigor ; severity.
TŸ′RANT, *n.* A cruel, despotic ruler or master.
TŸ′RŌ, *n. ;* pl. TŸ′RŌṢ. A beginner ; a student.
TZÄR (zär), *n.* The czar. See CZAR.

U.

U, the fifth English vowel, was formerly the same letter as the consonant V. But the consonant and vowel are now different characters.

Ū′BĘR-OŬS (yū′bẹr-ŭs), *a.* Fruitful; abundant.
Ū′BĘR-TY, *n.* Abundance; fruitfulness.
Ū-BĪ′Ę-TY, *n.* Existence in some place.
Ū-BĬQ′UĮ-TĄ-RY (yū-bĭk′wẹ-tạ-rẹ), *a.* Existing every where.
Ū-BĬQ′UĮ-TY (yū-bĭk′wẹ-tẹ), *n.* Omnipresence.
ŬD′DĘR, *n.* The breast or dugs of a cow, &c.
ŬG′LĮ-LY, *ad.* With deformity or vileness.
ŬG′LĮ-NĔSS, *n.* Deformity; turpitude.
ŬG′LY, *a.* Deformed; offensive to the sight.
Ū-KĀSE′, *n.* *In Russia,* a proclamation or edict.
ŬL′CĘR, *n.* A running sore of continuance.
ŬL′CĘR-ĀTE, *v. n. & a.* To turn to an ulcer.
ŬL-CĘR-Ā′TIǪN, *n.* The act of ulcerating; a sore.
ŬL′CĘRED (-sẹrd), *a.* Grown to an ulcer.
ŬL′CĘR-OŬS, *a.* Afflicted with ulcers. [ous.
ŬL′CĘR-OǓS-NĔSS, *n.* The state of being ulcer-
Ū-LĒ′MĄ, *n.* College of the Turkish hierarchy.
Ū-LĬG′Į-NOǓS, *a.* Slimy; muddy; oozy.
ŬL′LAGE, *n.* What a cask wants of being full.
ŬL-TĒ′RĮ-ǪR, *a.* Lying beyond; further.
ŬL′TĮ-MĄTE, *a.* Last; final; furthest; extreme.
ŬL′TĮ-MĄTE-LY, *ad.* In the last consequence.
ŬL-TĮ-MĀ′TUM, *n.* [L.] Last offer; the final proposition.
ŬL-TRĄ-MĄ-RÎNE′, *n.* A very beautiful blue.
ŬL-TRĄ-MĄ-RÎNE′, *a.* Being beyond sea; foreign. [tains.
ŬL-TRĄ-MǑN′TĄNE, *a.* Being beyond the moun-
ŬL-TRĄ-MǓN′DĄNE, *a.* Being beyond the world.
ŬL′U-LĀTE, *v. n.* To howl; to wail.
ŬM′BĘL, *n.* A form of inflorescence. [liferous.
ŬM′BĘL-LĄTE, ŬM′BĘL-LĀT-ĘD, *a.* Umbel-
ŬM-BĘL-LĬF′ĘR-OǓS, *a.* Bearing umbels.
ŬM′BĘR, *n.* A brown ore, used as a pigment.
ŬM-BĬL′Į-CĄL, *a.* Belonging to the navel.
ŬM′BLEŞ (-blz), *n. pl.* A deer's entrails.
ŬM′BRAGE, *n.* Shade; resentment; an affront.
ŬM-BRĀ′GE-OǓS, *a.* Shady; yielding shade.
ŬM-BRĔL′LĄ, *n.* A screen from the sun or rain.
ŬM′PĮ-RAGE, *n.* Arbitration; friendly decision.
ŬM′PĪRE, *n.* One who settles disputes.
ŬN. A prefix implying *negation.* It is prefixed chiefly to adjectives, participles, and adverbs, and almost at pleasure. *Un* and *in* are, in many cases, used indifferently; as, *un*expert or *in*expert; *un*constant, or *in*constant.
ŬN-Ā′BLE, *a.* Not able; not having ability. [ble.
ŬN-ĄC-CĔPT′Ą-BLE, *a.* Not pleasing; disagreea-
ŬN-ĄC-CǑM′PĄ-NĮED (ŭn-ạk-kŭm′pạ-nįd), *a.* Alone; solitary. [complete.
ŬN-ĄC-CǑM′PLĮSHED (-ạk-kǒm′plįsht), *a.* In-
ŬN-ĄC-COǓNT′Ą-BLE, *ad.* Not accountable;
ŬN-ĄC-COǓNT′Ą-BLY, *ad.* Strangely. [strange.
ŬN-ĄC-CŬS′TǪMED (-ạk-kŭs′tụmd), *a.* Not accustomed; not usual; new. [owned.
ŬN-ĄC-KNǑWL′ĘDGED (ŭn-ạk-nǒl′ẹjd), *a.* Not
ŬN-ĄC-QUĀINT′ĘD, *a.* Not known; unusual.

ŬN-Ą-DÖRNED′ (-dörnd′), *a.* Not decorated.
ŬN-ĄD-VĪŞ′Ą-BLE, *a.* Not to be advised.
ŬN-ĄD-VĪŞED′ (-vīzd′), *a.* Indiscreet; rash.
ŬN-ĄD-VĪŞ′ĘD-LY (-vī′zẹd-lẹ), *ad.* Indiscreetly.
ŬN-ĄD-VĪŞ′ĘD-NĔSS, *n.* Imprudence.
ŬN-ĄF-FĔCT′ĘD, *a.* Real; sincere; not moved.
ŬN-ĄF-FĔCT′ĘD-LY, *ad.* Really; sincerely.
ŬN-ĀID′ĘD, *a.* Not assisted; not helped. [ble.
ŬN-ÂL′TĘR-Ą-BLE, *a.* Unchangeable; immuta-
ŬN-ÂL′TĘR-Ą-BLY, *ad.* Unchangeably.
ŬN-Ā′MĮ-Ą-BLE, *a.* Not amiable; not lovely.
Ū-NĄ-NĬM′Į-TY (yū-nạ-nĭm′ẹ-tẹ), *n.* State of being unanimous; harmony; agreement.
Ū-NĂN′Į-MOŬS (yū-năn′ẹ-mŭs), *a.* Being of one mind; agreeing in design or opinion.
Ū-NĂN′Į-MOǓS-LY, *ad.* With one mind. [mous.
Ū-NĂN′Į-MOǓS-NĔSS, *n.* State of being unani-
ŬN-ĂN′SWĘR-Ą-BLE (ŭn-ăn′sẹr-ạ-bl), *a.* Not to be answered or refuted; irrefutable.
ŬN-ĂN′SWĘR-Ą-BLY, *ad.* Beyond confutation.
ŬN-ĂN′SWĘRED (-sẹrd), *a.* Not answered.
ŬN-ĂPT′, *a.* Not apt; dull; unfit; improper.
ŬN-ĂPT′NĘSS, *n.* Unfitness :—dulness.
ŬN-ÄRMED′ (-ärmd′), *a.* Having no arms.
ŬN-AR-RĀYED′ (-rād′), *a.* Not arrayed.
ŬN-ĂSKED′ (-ăskt′), *a.* Not asked or sought.
ŬN-ĄS-SĀIL′Ą-BLE, *a.* Exempt from assault.
ŬN-ĄT-TĀIN′Ą-BLE, *a.* Not to be attained.
ŬN-ĄT-TĔMPT′ĘD, *a.* Untried; not assayed.
ŬN-ĄT-TĔND′ĘD, *a.* Having no attendants.
ŬN-ÂU′THǪR-ĪZED (-âw′thụr-īzd), *a.* Not authorized.
ŬN-Ą-VĀIL′Ą-BLE, *a.* Useless; vain. [thorized.
ŬN-Ą-VĀIL′ĮNG, *a.* Ineffectual. [ble.
ŬN-Ą-VÖĬD′Ą-BLE, *a.* Inevitable; not avoida-
ŬN-Ą-WÀRE′, *a.* Without thought; inattentive.
ŬN-Ą-WÀREŞ′, *ad.* When not thought of; suddenly; unexpectedly.
ŬN-ÂWED′ (-âwd′), *a.* Unrestrained by fear.
ŬN-BĄP-TĪZED′ (-tīzd′), *a.* Not baptized.
ŬN-BÄR′, *v. a.* To remove a bar from. [fit.
ŬN-BĘ-CǑM′ĮNG, *a.* Indecent; indecorous; un-
ŬN-BĘ-CǑM′ĮNG-LY, *ad.* Not becomingly.
ŬN-BĘ-LĪĔF′, *n.* Incredulity; infidelity.
ŬN-BĘ-LIĒV′ĘR, *n.* An infidel; a sceptic.
ŬN-BĔND′, *v. a.* To straighten; to relax; to re-
ŬN-BĔND′ĮNG, *a.* Not yielding; resolute. [mit.
ŬN-BĔNT′, *a.* Unshrunk; unsubdued; relaxed.
ŬN-BĘ-SĒĔM′ĮNG, *a.* Unbecoming; unfit.
ŬN-BĘ-WĀILED′ (-wāld′), *a.* Not lamented.
ŬN-BĪ′ĄS, *v. a.* To free from bias or prejudice.
ŬN-BĬD′DEN (ŭn-bĭd′dn), *a.* Not invited.
ŬN-BĪND′, *v. a.* To loose; to untie.
ŬN-BĬT′, *v. a.* To free the bit from.
ŬN-BLĀM′Ą-BLE, *a.* Not culpable; innocent.
ŬN-BLĔM′ĮSHED (-ĭsht), *a.* Not stained.
ŬN-BŌLT′, *v. a.* To set open; to unbar.
ŬN-BÖRN′, *a.* Not yet brought into life; future.
ŬN-BO′ŞǪM (-bûz′ụm), *v. a.* To reveal, disclose.
ŬN-BOUGHT′ (-bâwt′), *a.* Not purchased.
ŬN-BOÛND′ĘD, *a.* Unlimited; unrestrained.
ŬN-BRĪ′DLED (-dld), *a.* Loose; licentious.
ŬN-BRǑ′KEN (-brō′kn), *a.* Not broken or tamed.

ŬN-BŬC′KLE, *v. a.* To loose from buckles.
ŬN-BÙR′DEN (-bür′dn), *v. a.* To rid of a load.
ŬN-BUR′ĮED (ŭn-bĕr′rĭd), *a.* Not interred.
ŬN-CÂLLED′ (-kâwld′), *a.* Not summoned.
ŬN-CĄ-NŎN′Į-CĄL, *a.* Not agreeable to the can-
ŬN-CÂUGHT′ (-kâwt′), *a.* Not yet taken. [ons.
ŬN-CĔR-Ę-MŌ′NĮ-OŬS, *a.* Not ceremonious.
ŬN-CĔR′TAĮN, *a.* Doubtful ; unsettled.
ŬN-CĔR′TAĮN-TY, *n.* Want of certainty ; doubt.
ŬN-CHĀIN′, *v. a.* To free from chains.
ŬN-CHĀNǴE′Ą-BLE, *a.* Not subject to change.
ŬN-CHĀNǴ′ĮNG, *a.* Suffering no alteration.
ŬN-CHĂR′Į-TĄ-BLE, *a.* Wanting charity.
ŬN-CHĂR′Į-TĄ-BLE-NĔSS, *n.* Want of charity.
ŬN-CHĂR′Į-TĄ-BLY, *ad.* Without charity.
ŬN-CHĀSTE′, *a.* Lewd ; not chaste ; not pure.
ŬN-CHĔCKED′ (-chĕkt′), *a.* Unrestrained.
ŬN-ℭHRĬS′TIĄN, (-krĭst′yąn), *a.* Not Christian.
ŬN-ℭHÜRCH′, *v. a.* To deprive of the rights or
  privileges of a church.   [in ancient MSS.
ŬN′CIĄL, *a.* Noting letters of large size, used
ŬN-CĬR′CŲM-CĪŞED (ŭn-sër′kųm-sīzd), *a.* Not
  circumcised.   [want of circumcision.
ŬN-CĬR-CŲM-CĬ″ŞIǪN (-sër-kųm-sĭzh′ųn), *n.* A
ŬN-CĬV′ĮL, *a.* Unpolite ; rude ; not courteous.
ŬN-CĬV′ĮL-ĪZED (ŭn-sĭv′ĭl-īzd), *a.* Barbarous.
ŬN-CLĂSP′, *v. a.* To open the clasp of.
ŬN-CLĂS′SĮC, ŬN-CLĂS′SĮ-CĄL, *a.* Not classic.
ŬN′CLE (ŭng′kl), *n.* A father's or mother's broth-
ŬN-CLĒAN′, *a.* Foul ; dirty ; filthy :—lewd. [er.
ŬN-CLĒAN′LY (-klĕn′lę), *a.* Foul ; filthy.
ŬN-CLĬNCH′, *v. a.* To open, as the closed hand.
ŬN-CLŎG′, *v. a.* To free from impediment.
ŬN-CLŌŞE′, *v. a.* To open ; to disclose.
ŬN-CLŌ̂THE′, *v. a.* To strip ; to make naked.
ŬN-CLŌ̂ÛD′, *v. a.* To unveil ; to clear from obscu-
ŬN-CŎL′ǪRED (-kŭl′lųrd), *a.* Not colored. [rity.
ŬN-CŎME′LY, *a.* Not comely ; wanting grace.
ŬN-CŎM′FǪRT-Ą-BLE, *a.* Not comfortable ;
  wanting comfort ; dismal.
ŬN-CŎM′FǪRT-Ą-BLY, *ad.* Without comfort.
ŬN-CŎM′MǪN, *a.* Not frequent ; rare ; unusual.
ŬN-CŎM-PLAĮ-ŞĂNT′, *a.* Not civil ; not obliging.
ŬN-CǪM-PÖÛND′ĘD, *a.* Simple ; not mixed.
ŬN-CǪN-CĒIVED′ (-kǫn-sēvd′), *a.* Not thought.
ŬN-CǪN-CĔRN′, *n.* Want of concern.   [lute.
ŬN-CǪN-DĬ″TIǪN-ĄL (-kǫn-dĭsh′ųn-), *a.* Abso-
ŬN-CǪN-NĔCT′ĘD, *a.* Not coherent ; lax ; loose.
ŬN-CŎN′QUĘR-Ą-BLE (-kŏng′kęr-ą-bl), *a.* Insu-
  perable ; not to be overcome ; invincible.
ŬN-CŎN′SCIǪN-Ą-BLE   (ŭn-kŏn′shųn-ą-bl), *a.*
  Unreasonable ; unjust ; enormous ; vast.
ŬN-CŎN′SCIǪN-Ą-BLY, *ad.* Unreasonably.
ŬN-CŎN′SCIǪŲS (-kŏn′shųs), *a.* Not couscious.
ŬN-CǪN-TRŌL′LĄ-BLE, *a.* Not to be controlled.
ŬN-CǪN-TRŌLLED′ (-kǫn-trōld′), *a.* Not con-
  trolled or restrained.
ŬN-CǪR-RŬPT′, *a.* Honest ; upright ; incorrupt.
ŬN-COÛP′LE (-kŭp′pl), *v. a.* To set loose.
ŬN-CÔUTH′ (-kôth′), *a.* Odd ; strange.
ŬN-CÔUTH′LY (-kôth′lę), *ad.* Oddly ; strangely.
ŬN-CÔUTH′NĘSS (-kôth′nęs), *n.* Strangeness.
ŬN-CŎV′ĘR, *v. a.* To divest of a covering.
ŬN-CRŌ̂WN′, *v. a.* To deprive of a crown.
ŬNC′TIǪN (ŭngk′shųn), *n.* Ointment ; warmth
  of devotion ; that which melts to devotion.
ŬNC-TŲ-ŎS′Į-TY, *n.* Fatness ; oiliness.
ŬNC′TŲ-OŬS, *a.* Fat ; clammy ; oily ; greasy.

ŬNC′TŲ-OŲS-NĔSS, *n.* Oiliness ; greasiness.
ŬN-CŬL′TĮ-VĀT-ĘD, *a.* Not cultivated ; ùn-
  tilled :—rude ; rough.   [lets.
ŬN-CÜRL′, *v. a. & n.* To loose or fall from ring-
ŬN-DĂUNT′ĘD (-dänt′ęd), *a.* Not daunted.
ŬN-DĔC′Ą-GǑN, *n.* A figure of eleven angles.
ŬN-DĘ-CĀYED′ (-kād′), *a.* Not impaired.
ŬN-DĘ-CĒIVE′, *v. a.* To free from deception.
ŬN-DĘ-CĪD′ĘD, *a.* Not determined ; not settled.
ŬN-DĔCK′, *v. a.* To deprive of ornaments.
ŬN-DĘ-FĪLED′ (-fīld′), *a.* Not polluted.
ŬN-DĘ-FĪNED′ (-fīnd′), *a.* Not explained.
ŬN-DĘ-NĪ′Ą-BLE, *a.* That cannot be denied.
ŬN-DĘ-NĪ′Ą-BLY, *ad.* Indisputably ; plainly.
ŬN-DĘ-PRĀVED′ (-prāvd′), *a.* Not corrupted.
ŬN′DĘR, *prep.* Not over ; below ; beneath.
ŬN′DĘR, *ad.* Below ; not above ; less ; not more.
ŬN′DĘR, *a.* Inferior ; subject ; subordinate.
ŬN-DĘR-ĂC′TIǪN, *n.* A subordinate action.
ŬN-DĘR-Ā′ǴENT, *n.* A subordinate agent.
ŬN-DĘR-BĬD′, *v. a.* To bid or offer less for.
ŬN′DĘR-BRŬSH, *n.* Undergrowth.
ŬN-DĘR-GŌ′, *v. a.* [*imp. t.* underwent ; *pp.* un-
  dergone.] To suffer ; to sustain ; to endure.
ŬN′DĘR-GRĂD′Ų-ĄTE, *n.* A student, in a col-
  lege or university, not graduated.
ŬN-DĘR-GRÖÛND′, *n.* Subterraneous space.—
  a. Being below the surface.   [derbrush.
ŬN′DĘR-GRŎWTH, *n.* Shrubs under trees ; un-
ŬN-DĘR-HĂND′, *a.* Secret ; clandestine ; sly.
ŬN-DĘR-LĀY′, *v. a.* To lay under ; to support.
ŬN-DĘR-LĔT′, *v. a.* To let below the value :—
  to let, as a tenant or lessee.
ŬN-DĘR-LĪNE′, *v. a.* To draw a line under. [low.
ŬN′DĘR-LĬNG, *n.* An inferior agent ; a sorry fel-
ŬN′DĘR-MĂS′TĘR, *n.* A subordinate master.
ŬN-DĘR-MĪNE′, *v. a.* To sap :—to injure secretly.
ŬN-DĘR-MĪN′ĘR, *n.* One who undermines.
ŬN′DĘR-MŌST, *a.* Lowest in place or condition.
ŬN-DĘR-NĒAℱH′, *ad.* In the lower place.—*prep.*
ŬN-DĘR-PĬN′, *v. a.* To prop ; to support. [Under.
ŬN-DĘR-PĬN′NĮNG, *n.* Stones under a building.
ŬN′DĘR-PLŎT, *n.* A plot subservient to the
  main plot ; a secret plot.
ŬN-DĘR-PRŎP′, *v. a.* To support ; to sustain.
ŬN-DĘR-RĀTE′, *v. a.* To rate or value too low.
ŬN-DĘR-SCŌRE′, *v. a.* To line or mark under.
ŬN′DĘR-SĔC′RĘ-TĄ-RY, *n.* A subordinate or
  inferior secretary.
ŬN-DĘR-SĔLL′, *v. a.* To sell cheaper than.
ŬN′DĘR-SĔR′VĄNT, *n.* A servant of the lower
  class ; one under another servant.
ŬN′DĘR-SHĔR′ĮFF, *n.* The deputy of a sheriff.
ŬN-DĘR-STĂND′, *v. a.* [*imp. t. & pp.* understood.]
  To comprehend ; to know the meaning of.
ŬN-DĘR-STĂND′, *v. n.* To have understanding.
ŬN-DĘR-STĂND′ĮNG, *n.* The faculties of the
  mind ; skill ; sense ; intelligence ; agreement.
ŬN-DĘR-STĂND′ĮNG, *a.* Knowing ; skilful.
ŬN-DĘR-STOOD′ (-stûd′), *i. & p.* from *understand.*
  See UNDERSTAND.   [person.
ŬN′DĘR-STRĂP-PĘR, *n.* An inferior agent or
ŬN-DĘR-TĀKE′, *v. a.* [*imp. t.* undertook ; *pp.* un-
  dertaken.] To attempt ; to engage in.
ŬN-DĘR-TĀKE′, *v. n.* To assume any business.
ŬN-DĘR-TĀ′KEN (-tā′kn), *pp.* from *undertake.*
ŬN-DĘR-TĀK′ĘR, *n.* One who undertakes :—
  one who manages funerals.

ŬN-DĘR-TĀK′ĮNG, n. An enterprise.
ŬN-DĘR-TOOK′ (-tûk′), imp. t. from *undertake.*
ŬN-DĘR-VĂL-Ų-Ā′TIǪN, n. Act of undervaluing; a rate below the worth.
ŬN-DĘR-VĂL′ŲE (-văl′yụ), v. a. To rate low.
ŬN-DĘR-WĔNT′, imp. t. from *undergo.* [shrubs.
ŬN′DĘR-WOOD (ŭn′dęr-wûd), n. Small trees or
ŬN-DĘR-WORK′ (-würk′), v. a. & n. [imp. t. & pp. underworked *or* underwrought.] To labor or polish less than enough:—work for less than others.
ŬN-DĘR-WORK′MĄN, n. A subordinate laborer.
ŬN-DĘR-WRĪTE′ (-rīt′), v. a. To write under; to subscribe:—to insure.
ŬN-DĘR-WRĪT′ĘR, n. One who underwrites.
ŬN-DĒ′VĮ-ĀT-ĮNG, a. Not deviating; regular.
ŬN-DĬD′, imp. t. from *undo.*
ŬN-DĬS-CŎV′ĘRED (-ęrd), a. Not discovered.
ŬN-DĬS-TĬN′GUĬSHED (-tĭng′gwĭsht), a. Not distinguished; not discriminated.
ŬN-DŌ′, v. a. [imp. t. undid; pp. undone.] To ruin; to destroy:—to loose:—to reverse.
ŬN-DŌ′ĮNG, n. Ruin; destruction:—reversal.
ŬN-DŎNE′, pp. from *undo;* not done:—ruined.
ŬN-DŎÛBT′ĘD-LY (-döût′ęd-le),ad. Indubitably.
ŬN-DRĔSS′, v. a. To divest of clothes; to strip.
ŬN′DRĔSS, n. A loose or negligent dress.
ŬN-DŪE′, a. Not due; unfit; excessive.
ŬN′DŲ-LĄ-RY, a. Playing like waves. [as waves.
ŬN′DŲ-LĀTE, v. a. & n. To play or make to play,
ŬN′DŲ-LĀT-ĘD, a. Having undulations.
ŬN-DŲ-LĀ′TIǪN, n. A notion like that of waves.
ŬN′DŲ-LĄ-TǪ-RY, a. Moving like waves.
ŬN-DŪ′LY, ad. Not properly; not duly.
ŬN-DŪ′TĮ-FŮL, a. Not dutiful; disobedient.
ŬN-ĒA′ŞY (ŭn-ē′zę), a. Not easy; disturbed.
ŬN-Ē′QUĄL, a. Not equal; not just; inferior.
ŬN-ĘX-CĔP′TIǪN-Ą-BLE, a. Not liable to objec-
ŬN-FĀIR′, a. Disingenuous; not honest. [tion.
ŬN-FĀITH′FŮL, a. Not faithful; treacherous.
ŬN-FĂSH′IǪN-Ą-BLE (ŭn-făsh′ụn-ą-bl), a. Not fashionable; not according to fashion.
ŬN-FĂS′TEN (-făs′sn), v. a. To loose; to unfix.
ŬN-FĀ′VǪR-Ą-BLE, a. Not favorable; unkind.
ŬN-FĒĒL′ĮNG, a. Insensible; void of feeling.
ŬN-FEIGNED′ (ŭn-fānd′), a. Real; sincere.
ŬN-FĔT′TĘR, v. a. To free from shackles.
ŬN-FĬT′, a. Unsuitable.—v. a. To disqualify.
ŬN-FĬX′, v. a. To loosen; to make less fast.
ŬN-FLĔDǴED′ (-flĕjd′), a. Without feathers.
ŬN-FŌLD′, v. a. To expand, discover, display.
ŬN-FŎRT′Ų-NĄTE, a. Not fortunate; unhappy.
ŬN-FŎÛND′ĘD, a. Void of foundation; false.
ŬN-FRIĔND′LY, a. Not friendly; hostile.
ŬN-FRŬIT′FŮL, a. Not fruitful; not prolific.
ŬN-FŪRL′, v. a. To expand; to unfold; to open.
ŬN-FÛR′NĬSH, v. a. To deprive; to strip; to divest. [pert.
ŬN-GĀIN′LY, a. Awkward; uncouth; not ex-
ŬN-GĔN′ĘR-OŬS, a. Not noble; illiberal. [ture.
ŬN-ĢĒ′NĮ-ĄL, a. Not kind or favorable to na-
ŬN-ĢĔN′TLE-MĄN-LĪKE, \ a. Illiberal; not be-
ŬN-ĢĔN′TLE-MĄN-LY, / coming a gentle-
ŬN-ĢĬRD′, v. a. To loose from a girdle. [man.
ŬN-GLŪE′, v. a. To loosen any thing glued.
ŬN-GŎD′LĮ-NĔSS, n. Impiety; wickedness.
ŬN-GŎD′LY, a. Wicked; impious; profane.
ŬN-GRĀCE′FŮL, a. Not graceful; awkward.

ŬN-GRĀ′CIOŬS (-shụs), a. Odious; offensive.
ŬN-GRĀTE′FŮL, a. Unthankful; unacceptable.
ŬN′GUĘNT (ŭng′gwęnt), n. An ointment.
ŬN-HĂL′LŌW (-hăl′lō), v. a. To profane.
ŬN-HĂND′SǪME (-hăn′sụm), a. Not handsome.
ŬN-HĂP′PĮ-NĔSS, n. Infelicity; misfortune.
ŬN-HĂP′PY, a. Miserable; unfortunate; unlucky.
ŬN-HĔALTH′Y, a. Sickly; wanting health.
ŬN-HĬNǴE′, v. a. To take from hinges; to loose.
ŬN-HŌ′LY, a. Not holy; profane; impious.
ŬN-HOOP′ (-hûp′), v. a. To divest of hoops.
ŬN-HŎRSE′, v. a. To throw from a horse.
Ū′NĮ-CÖRN (yū′nę-körn), n. A beast or quadruped that has only one horn:—a bird:—a fish.
Ū′NĮ-FÖRM (yū′nę-förm), a. Unvaried in form; alike; equable; even; regular; constant.
Ū′NĮ-FÖRM (yū′nę-förm), n. A like dress; the regimental dress of a soldier.
Ū-NĮ-FÖR′MĮ-TY, n. The state of being uniform.
Ū′NĮ-FÖRM-LY, ad. Without variation.
Ū-NĮ-ĢĒN′Į-TŪRE, n. Singleness of birth.
ŬN-ĮM-PÖR′TĄNT, a. Not important; trifling.
ŬN-ĮN-TĔL′LĮ-ĢĮ-BLE, a. Not to be understood.
ŬN-ĬN′TĘR-ĔST-ĘD, a. Not having interest.
ŬN-ĬN′TĘR-ĔST-ĮNG, a. Exciting no interest.
ŬN′IǪN (yūn′yụn), n. Act of joining; concord:—upper inner corner of an ensign.
Ū-NĪQUE′ (yū-nēk′), a. [Fr.] Sole; without an equal or another of the same kind.
Ū′NĮ-SǪN, n. Accordance of sounds; agreement.
Ū′NĮT (yū′nĭt), n. One; the least number.
Ū-NĮ-TĀ′RĮ-AN, n. A believer in God as existing in one person only; an anti-Trinitarian.
Ū-NĮ-TĀ′RĮ-AN-ĬSM, n. The doctrines of Unitari-
Ū-NĪTE′ (yū-nīt′), v. a. To join together. [ans.
Ū-NĪTE′, v. n. To join; to concur; to coalesce.
Ū-NĪ′′TIǪN (yū-nĭsh′ụn), n. The act of uniting.
Ū′NĮ-TY, n. The state of being one:—concord.
Ū′NĮ-VĂLVE, n. A shell with but one valve.
Ū-NĮ-VĔR′SĄL, a. Total; whole; comprising all.
Ū-NĮ-VĔR′SĄL, n. The whole:—a general proposition in logic. [salvation of all men.
Ū-NĮ-VĔR′SĄL-ĬST, n. One who believes in the
Ū-NĮ-VĘR-SĂL′Į-TY, n. Extension to the whole.
Ū-NĮ-VĔR′SĄL-LY, ad. Throughout the whole.
Ū′NĮ-VĔRSE, n. The whole creation.
Ū-NĮ-VĔR′SĮ-TY, n. A school where all the arts and sciences are taught and studied. [certain.
Ū-NĬV′Ǫ-CĄL, a. Having only one meaning:—
ŬN-JŬST′, a. Iniquitous; contrary to justice.
ŬN-KĔN′NĘL, v. a. To drive from a kennel.
ŬN-KĪND′, a. Not favorable; not benevolent.
ŬN-KNĬT′ (-nĭt′), v. a. To unweave; to open.
ŬN-LĀCE′, v. a. To loosen the laces of. [sel.
ŬN-LĀDE′, v. a. To empty or remove from a ves-
ŬN-LĂTCH′, v. a. To open by lifting up the
ŬN-LĂW′FŮL, a. Contrary to law; illegal. [latch.
ŬN-LĔARN′, v. a. To forget or lose what has been learned.
ŬN-LĔAV′ENED (-lĕv′vnd), a. Not leavened.
ŬN-LĔSS′, conj. Except; if not; supposing not.
ŬN-LĪKE′, a. Dissimilar; having no likeness.
ŬN-LĪKE′LY, a. Improbable.—ad. Improbably.
ŬN-LŌAD′ (-lōd′), v. a. To free from load.
ŬN-LŎCK′, v. a. To open or unfasten what is shut:—to solve. [pieces.
ŬN-LŌÔSE′, v. a. To loose.—v. n. To fall in
ŬN-LŬCK′Y, a. Unfortunate; not successful.

ŬN-MĀKE′, *v. a.* To deprive of qualities ; to ruin.
ŬN-MĂN′, *v. a.* To deprive of manly qualities.
ŬN-MĂN′NER-LY, *a.* Ill-bred ; not complaisant.
ŬN-MĂR′RY, *v. a.* To separate ; to divorce.
ŬN-MĂSK′, *v. a. & n.* To strip of a mask or dis-
ŬN-MĒAN′ING, *a.* Having no meaning. [guise.
ŬN-MĔR′CI-FŬL, *a.* Not merciful ; cruel ; severe.
ŬN-MĬND′FŬL, *a.* Careless ; inattentive.
ŬN-MĬN′GLE, *v. a.* To separate things mixed.
ŬN-MŎŎR′, *v. a.* To loose from anchorage.
ŬN-MŬF′FLE, *v. a.* To remove a muffle from.
ŬN-MŬZ′ZLE, *v. a.* To loose from a muzzle.
ŬN-NĂT′U-RĄL, *a.* Contrary to nature ; affected.
ŬN-NĂT′U-RĄL-ĪZE, *v. a.* To divest of nature.
ŬN-NĔÇ′ĘS-SĄ-RY, *a.* Not necessary ; needless.
ŬN-NĔRVE′, *v. a.* To weaken ; to enfeeble.
ŬN-ǪB-JĔC′TIǪN-Ą-BLE, *a.* Not liable to objec-
tion ; unexceptionable.
ŬN-ǪF-FĔND′ĮNG, *a.* Harmless ; innocent ; pure.
ŬN-ŎS-TĘN-TĀ′TIOŲS, *a.* Not boastful ; modest.
ŬN-PĂCK′, *v. a.* To open, as things packed.
ŬN-PĂL′ĄT-Ą-BLE, *a.* Not palatable ; nauseous.
ŬN-PĂR′ĄL-LĔLED (ŭn-păr′ąl-lĕld), *a.* Having
no parallel or equal ; unequalled.
ŬN-PĂR′DON-Ą-BLE, *a.* Not to be pardoned.
ŬN-PĂR-LĮA-MĔNT′Ą-RY (ŭn-păr-lę-mĕnt′ą-rę),
a. Contrary to the rules of parliament.
ŬN-PĔG′, *v. a.* To loose from pegs.
ŬN-PĒO′PLE (ŭn-pē′pl), *v. a.* To depopulate.
ŬN-PĘR-PLĔX′, *v. a.* To relieve from perplexity.
ŬN-PHĬL-O-ŞŎPH′Į-CĄL, *a.* Not philosophical.
ŬN-PĬN′, *v. a.* To open what is fastened with a pin.
ŬN-PLĔAṢ′ĄNT (ŭn-plĕz′ąnt), *a.* Disagreeable.
ŬN-PLĔDGED′ (ŭn-plĕjd′), *a.* Not bound ; free.
ŬN-PLŪME′, *v. a.* To strip of plumes ; to degrade.
ŬN-PǪ-ĔT′ĮC, ŬN-PǪ-ĔT′Į-CĄL, *a.* Not poetical.
ŬN-PŎL′ĮSHED (ŭn-pŏl′ĭsht), *a.* Not polished.
ŬN-PǪL-LŪT′ĘD, *a.* Not corrupted ; not defiled.
ŬN-PŎP′U-LAR, *a.* Not having the public favor.
ŬN-PŎP-U-LĂR′Į-TY, *n.* Want of popularity.
ŬN-PRĔÇ′Ę-DĔNT-ĘD, *a.* Unexampled.
ŬN-PRĔJ′U-DĬCED (ŭn-prĕd′ju-dĭst), *a.* Free from
prejudice ; free from prepossession.
ŬN-PRĘ-TĔND′ING, *a.* Not pretending ; modest.
ŬN-PRĬNCE′LY, *a.* Unsuitable to a prince.
ŬN-PRĬN′CĮ-PLED (ŭn-prĭn′sę-pld), *a.* Devoid
of principle ; wicked :—not settled in tenets.
ŬN-PRŎF′ĮT-Ą-BLE, *a.* Affording no profit ; use-
ŬN-PRŎF′ĮT-Ą-BLE-NĔSS, *n.* Uselessness. [less.
ŬN-PRŎF′ĮT-Ą-BLY, *ad.* Without advantage.
ŬN-PRŎM′ĮS-ING, *a.* Not promising good.
ŬN-PRǪ-PĮ′′TIOŲS (ŭn-prǫ-pĭsh′ŭs), *a.* Not pro-
pitious ; inauspicious.
ŬN-PŬB′LĮSHED (ŭn-pŭb′lĭsht), *a.* Not published.
ŬN-QUAL′Į-FĪED (ŭn-kwŏl′ę-fīd), *a.* Not quali-
fied ; not fit :—not softened ; not abated.
ŬN-QUĔNCH′Ą-BLE, *a.* Not to be extinguished.
ŬN-QUĔS′TIǪN-Ą-BLE, *a.* Not to be doubted.
ŬN-QUĔS′TIǪN-Ą-BLY, *ad.* Without doubt.
ŬN-RĂV′EL (ŭn-răv′vl), *v. a.* To disentangle ; to
unknit ; to ravel :—to clear ; to explain.
ŬN-RĂV′EL (ŭn-răv′vl), *v. n.* To be unfolded.
ŬN-RĒ′ĄL, *a.* Not real ; vain ; unsubstantial.
ŬN-RĒA′ŞON-Ą-BLE (ŭn-rē′zn-ą-bl), *a.* Not
agreeable to reason ; irrational :—exorbitant.
ŬN-RĒA′ŞON-Ą-BLE-NĔSS (ŭn-rē′zn-ą-bl-nĕs), *n.*
Inconsistency with reason :—exorbitance.
ŬN-RĒA′ŞON-Ą-BLY, *ad.* Without reason.

ŬN-RĔC-ǪN-CĪL′Ą-BLE, *a.* Not to be reconciled.
ŬN-RĘ-GĔN′ĘR-Ą-CY, *n.* An unregenerate state.
ŬN-RĘ-GĔN′ĘR-ĄTE, *a.* Not regenerate.
ŬN-RĘ-LĔNT′ĮNG, *a.* Hard ; cruel ; feeling no pity.
ŬN-RĘ-LIĔVED′ (ŭn-rę-lēvd′), *a.* Not relieved.
ŬN-RĘ-MĒ′DĮ-Ą-BLE, *a.* Admitting no remedy.
ŬN-RĘ-ṢĔRVED′ (ŭn-rę-zĕrvd′), *a.* Open ; frank.
ŬN-RĬD′DLE, *v. a.* To solve ; to explain.
ŬN-RĬG′, *v. a.* To strip off the rigging of.
ŬN-RĬGHT′EOŲS (ŭn-rī′chŭs), *a.* Unjust ; wicked.
ŬN-RĪPE′, *a.* Not ripe ; green ; immature.
ŬN-RĪ′VĄLLED (ŭn-rī′vąld), *a.* Having no rival.
ŬN-RĬV′ĘT, *v. a.* To unfasten the rivets of.
ŬN-RŌBE′, *v. a.* To undress ; to disrobe.
ŬN-RŌLL′, *v. a.* To open what is rolled or con-
ŬN-RŎŎF′, *v. a.* To strip off the roof of. [volved.
ŬN-RŎŎT′, *v. a.* To tear from roots ; to extirpate.
ŬN-RŬF′FLE, *v. n.* To cease from commotion.
ŬN-RŪ′LY, *a.* Turbulent ; ungovernable.
ŬN-SĂD′DLE, *v. a.* To take off the saddle from.
ŬN-SĀFE′, *a.* Not safe ; hazardous ; dangerous.
ŬN-SĂT-ĮS-FĂC′TǪ-RY, *a.* Not giving satisfaction.
ŬN-SĀ′VǪR-Y, *a.* Tasteless ; insipid ; disgusting.
ŬN-SĀY′, *v. a.* [*imp. t. & pp.* unsaid.] To retract.
ŬN-SCREW′ (ŭn-skrŭ′), *v. a.* To loosen, unfasten.
ŬN-SCRĬPT′U-RĄL, *a.* Not agreeable to Scripture.
ŬN-SCRŪ′PU-LOŬS, *a.* Not scrupulous.
ŬN-SĒAL′, *v. a.* To open, as any thing sealed.
ŬN-SĒAM′, *v. a.* To rip ; to cut open. [ble.
ŬN-SĒARCH′Ą-BLE (ŭn-sĕrch′ą-bl), *a.* Inscruta-
ŬN-SĒA′ŞON-Ą-BLE (ŭn-sē′zn-ą-bl), *a.* Ill-timed.
ŬN-SĒAT′, *v. a.* To throw from the seat.
ŬN-SĒĒM′LY, *a.* Indecent ; uncomely ; improper.
ŬN-SĔT′TLE, *v. a.* To make unsettled.
ŬN-SĔX′, *v. a.* To deprive of sex.
ŬN-SHĂC′KLE, *v. a.* To loose from bonds.
ŬN-SHĒATHE′, *v. a.* To draw from the scabbard.
ŬN-SHĬP′, *v. a.* To take out of a ship.
ŬN-SĪGHT′LY (ŭn-sīt′lę), *a.* Ugly ; deformed.
ŬN-SKĬL′FŬL, *a.* Wanting skill or knowledge.
ŬN-SKĬL′FŬL-LY, *ad.* Without knowledge.
ŬN-SŌ′CĮ-Ą-BLE (ŭn-sō′shę-ą-bl), *a.* Not sociable.
ŬN-SŌ′CĮ-Ą-BLY, *ad.* With reserve.
ŬN-SǪ-PHĬS′TĮ-CĀT-ĘD, *a.* Not sophisticated.
ŬN-SPĒAK′Ą-BLE, *a.* Not to be expressed ; inex-
pressible ; unutterable ; ineffable.
ŬN-SPĒAK′Ą-BLY, *ad.* Inexpressibly ; ineffably.
ŬN-SPHĒRE′, *v. a.* To remove from a sphere. [ity.
ŬN-SPĬR′ĮT-U-ĄL-ĪZE, *v. a.* To deprive of spiritual-
ŬN-SPŎT′TĘD, *a.* Not spotted ; immaculate.
ŬN-STĀ′BLE, *a.* Not fixed ; inconstant. [ble.
ŬN-STĒAD′Y (ŭn-stĕd′dę), *a.* Inconstant ; muta-
ŬN-STŬD′ĮED (ŭn-stŭd′įd), *a.* Not premeditated.
ŬN-SŪIT′Ą-BLE, *a.* Unfit ; not adapted ; not equal.
ŬN-SŬL′LĮED (ŭn-sŭl′lįd), *a.* Not stained ; pure.
ŬN-TĒACH′, *v. a.* To cause to forget.
ŬN-TĔN′Ą-BLE, *a.* Not capable of defence.
ŬN-THĂNK′FŬL, *a.* Not thankful ; ungrateful.
ŬN-THĂNK′FŬL-NĔSS, *n.* Ingratitude.
ŬN-THĬNK′ĮNG, *a.* Thoughtless ; inconsiderate.
ŬN-THRŌNE′, *v. a.* To pull down from a throne.
ŬN-TĪE′, *v. a.* To unbind ; to loose, as a knot.
ŬN-TĬL′, *ad.* To the time that ; till.
ŬN-TĬL′, *prep.* To ; till ;—*used of time.*
ŬN-TĪME′LY, *a.* Premature ; unseasonable.
ŬN′TǪ, *prep.* To. " Come *unto* me."
ŬN-TŌW′ĄRD, *a.* Froward ; perverse ; awkward.
ŬN-TŌW′ĄRD-LY, *ad.* Awkwardly ; perversely.

ŬN-TRẴCT′Ạ-BLE, *a.* Not governable ; not docile.
ŬN-TRŬE′, *a.* Not true ; false ; not faithful.
ŬN-TRŬTH′, *n.* A falsehood ; a false assertion.
ŬN-TŪNE′, *v. a.* To put out of tune ; to disorder.
ŬN-TWĪNE′, *v. a.* To untwist ; to unwind.
ŬN-TWĬST′, *v. a.* To untwine ; to disentangle.
ŬN-Ū′ṢỤ-ẠL (ŭn-yū′zhụ-ạl), *a.* Not common.
ŬN-VĀIL′, *v. a.* To uncover ; to unveil.
ŬN-VĀ′RỊED (ŭn-vā′rịd), *a.* Not diversified.
ŬN-VĀ′RNỊSHED (ŭn-vär′nịsht), *a.* Not adorned.
ŬN-VĀ′RỴ-ING, *a.* Not liable to change.
ŬN-VEIL′ (ŭn-vāl′), *v. a.* To uncover ; to divest.
ŬN-VŌTE′, *v. a.* To annul, as a former vote.
ŬN-WẴRP′, *v. a.* To reduce from a warped state.
ŬN-WẴR′RẠNT-Ạ-BLE (ŭn-wŏr′rạnt-ạ-bl), *a.* Not
  defensible ; not to be justified ; not allowed.
ŬN-WẴR′Ỵ, *a.* Wanting caution ; imprudent.
ŬN-WEĀ′RỊED (ŭn-wē′rịd), *a.* Indefatigable.
ŬN-WEAVE′ (ŭn-wēv′), *v. a.* [*imp. t.* ụnwove ;
  pp. unwoven.] To unfold ; to undo. [ceived.
ŬN-WĚL′CỌME, *a.* Not pleasing ; not well re-
ŬN-WĚLL′, *a.* Not well ; slightly indisposed.
ŬN-WIĒLD′Ỵ, *a.* Unmanageable ; bulky ; weighty.
ŬN-WĬLL′ING, *a.* Not inclined ; not willing.
ŬN-WĪND′, *v. a.* [*imp. t.* & *pp.* unwound.] To
ŬN-WĪND′, *v. n.* To be unwound. [untwist.
ŬN-WĪṢE′, *a.* Weak ; defective in wisdom.
ŬN-WĬT′TING-LỴ, *ad.* Without knowledge.
ŬN-WOR′THỊ-NĚSS, *n.* Want of worth or merit.
ŬN-WOR′THỴ (ŭn-wür′thẹ), *a.* Not deserving ;
  wanting merit ; mean ; worthless ; contemptible.
ŬN-WOÛND′, *pp.* from *unwind.* Untwisted.
ŬN-YŌKE′, *v. a.* To loose from the yoke.
ŬP, *ad.* Aloft ; above ; not down :—out of bed.
ŬP, *prep.* From a lower to a higher part.
ŬP-BEẴR′ (ŭp-bår′), *v. a.* [*imp. t.* upbore ; *pp.* up-
  borne.] To sustain aloft ; to raise ; to support
ŬP-BRẴID′, *v. a.* To chide ; to reproach.
ŬP-BRẴID′ĘR, *n.* One that reproaches.
ŬP-CẴST′, *p. a.* Thrown upwards.
ŬP′CẴST, *n.* A throw ;—*a term of bowling.*
ŬP′HĘR, *n.* A pole used in scaffolding.
ŬP′HĬLL, *a.* Difficult ; laborious :—ascending.
ŬP-HŌLD′, *v. a.* [*imp. t.* & *pp.* upheld.] To lift
  on high ; to support ; to sustain ; to defend.
ŬP-HŌLD′ĘR, *n.* A supporter ; an undertaker.
ŬP-HŌL′STĘR-ĘR, *n.* One who furnishes houses.
ŬP-HŌL′STĘR-Ỵ, *n.* Furniture for houses.
ŬP′LẠND, *n.* High land.—*a.* High ; lofty.
ŬP-LĬFT′, *v. a.* To raise aloft ; to elevate.
ŬP-ŎN′, *prep.* Not under ; on ; relating to.
ŬP′PĘR, *a.* Higher in place. [power.
ŬP′PĘR-MŌST, *a.* Highest in place, rank, or
ŬP′PỊSH, *a.* Proud ; pettish. [*Low.*]
ŬP-RĀIṢE′, *v. a.* To raise up ; to exalt.
ŬP-REẴR′, *v. a.* To rear or raise on high.
ŬP′RĪGHT (ŭp′rīt), *a.* Straight up ; perpendicu-
  lar :—equitable ; honest ; just.
ŬP′RĪGHT (ŭp′rīt), *n.* Something erect.
ŬP′RĪGHT-LỴ (ŭp′rīt-lẹ), *ad.* With uprightness.
ŬP′RĪGHT-NĚSS (ŭp′rīt-nĕs), *n.* Honesty. [rise.
ŬP-RĪṢE′, *v. n.* [*imp. t.* uprose ; *pp.* uprisen.] To
ŬP′ROẴR, *n.* A tumult ; bustle ; confusion.
ŬP-RÔÔT′, *v. a.* To tear up by the root.
ŬP-SĚT′, *v. a.* To overturn ; to overthrow.
ŬP′SHŎT, *n.* Conclusion ; the end ; final event.
ŬP′SĪDE, *n.* The upper side ; upper part.
ŬP′SĪDE-DŌWN′, *ad.* In complete disorder.

ŬP′STẴRT, *n.* One suddenly raised to power, &c.
ŬP′STẴRT, *a.* Suddenly raised ; insolent.
ŬP-TÜRN′, *v. a.* To throw up ; to furrow.
ŬP′WẠRD, *a.* Directed to a higher part.
ŬP′WẠRD, } *ad.* Towards a higher place ;—
ŬP′WẠRDṢ, } opposed to *downwards.*
ŬP-WĪND′, *v. a.* [*imp. t.* & *pp.* upwound.] To
  wind up ; to convolve.
Ū-RẴ′NỊ-ŬM, *n.* A sort of metal. [ens.
Ū-RẠN-ÖL′Ọ-GỴ, *n.* The description of the heav-
Ū′RẠ-NŬS, *n.* A planet ;—once called *Herschel* and
  Georgium Sidus ; discovered by Dr. Herschel in
ÜR′BẠN, *a.* Of, or pertaining to, a city. [1781.
ỤR-BĀNE′, *a.* Civil ; courteous ; elegant.
ỤR-BĂN′Ị-TỴ, *n.* Civility ; elegance ; politeness.
ÜR′CHỊN, *n.* A hedgehog :—a brat ; a child.
Ū′RẸ-TĘR (yū′rẹ-tẹr), *n.* A urinary tube. [der.
Ū-RĒ′THRẠ, *n.* Passage for urine from the blad-
ÜRGE, *v. a.* To incite ; to push ; to press ; to solicit.
ÜR′GẸN-CỴ, *n.* Pressure of difficulty ; entreaty.
ÜR′GẸNT, *a.* Cogent ; pressing ; importunate.
ÜR′GẸNT-LỴ, *ad.* Cogently ; importunately.
ÜRG′ĘR, *n.* One who presses ; an importuner.
Ū′RỊM, *n.* An ornament in the breastplate of
  the Jewish high-priest.
Ū′RỊ-NẠL, *n.* A vessel for holding urine.
Ū′RỊ-NẠ-RỴ (yū′rẹ-nạ-rẹ), *a.* Relating to urine.
Ū′RỊ-NĂ-TOR, *n.* One who searches under water.
Ū′RỊNE (yū′rịn), *n.* Water from animals.
Ū′RỊ-NOŬS (yū′rẹ-nŭs), *a.* Partaking of urine.
ÜRN, *n.* A vase :—a water-pot :—a vessel in
  which the ashes of burnt bodies were put.
ÜR′SẠ, *n.* [L.] The Bear ; a constellation.
ÜR′SỊNE, *a.* Relating to, or like, a bear.
ÜR′SỤ-LĬNE, *a.* Denoting an order of nuns.
Ū′RỤS, *n.* European wild ox.
Ŭs, *pron. pl.* The objective case of *we.*
ŪṢ′AGE (yūz′ạj), *n.* Treatment ; custom ; practice.
ŪṢ′ẠNCE, *n.* Use ; usury ; interest for money.
ŪSE (yūs), *n.* The act of using ; need ; useful-
  ness ; usage ; habit ; custom ; profit.
ŪṢE (yūz), *v. a.* To employ, accustom, treat.
ŪṢE, *v. n.* To be accustomed ; to frequent.
ŪSE′FÛL (yūs′fûl), *a.* Serviceable ; profitable.
ŪSE′FÛL-LỴ, *ad.* In a useful manner.
ŪSE′FÛL-NĚSS, *n.* The quality of being useful.
ŪSE′LẸSS, *a.* Answering no purpose or end.
ŪSE′LẸSS-NĚSS, *n.* Unfitness to any end.
ŬSH′ĘR, *n.* An under-teacher :—an introducer.
ŬSH′ĘR, *v. a.* To introduce ; to forerun. [spirit.
ŬS-QUẸ-BÂUGH′ (ŭs-kwẹ-bâw′), *n.* A distilled
Ū′ṢỤ-ẠL (yū′zhụ-ạl), *a.* Common ; customary.
Ū′ṢỤ-ẠL-LỴ (yū′zhụ-ạl-lẹ), *ad.* Commonly.
Ū′ṢỤ-ẠL-NĚSS (yū′zhụ-ạl-nĕs), *n.* Commonness.
Ū′ṢỤ-FRŬCT (yū′zhụ-frŭkt), *n.* Temporary use.
Ū-ṢỤ-FRŬC′TỤ-Ạ-RỴ, *n.* One that has usufruct.
Ū′ṢỤ-RĘR (yū′zhụ-rẹr), *n.* One who receives usury.
Ū-ṢŪ′RỊ-OŬS, *a.* Given to the practice of usury.
Ū-ṢÜRP′, *v. a.* To seize or possess without right.
Ū-ṢỤR-PĀ′TỊON, *n.* Illegal seizure or possession.
Ū-ṢÜRP′ĘR (yū-zürp′ẹr), *n.* One who usurps.
Ū′ṢỤ-RỴ (yū′zhụ-rẹ), *n.* Illegal interest.
Ū-TĚN′SỊL *or* Ū′TẸN-SỊL, *n.* An instrument.
Ū′TĘR-ĪNE (yū′tẹr-īn), *a.* Belonging to the
  womb :—born of the same mother.
Ū′TẸ-RŬS, *n.* [L.] The womb.
Ū-TĬL′Ị-TỴ, *n.* Usefulness ; profit ; convenience.
ŬT′MŌST, *a.* Extreme ; furthest ; highest.

ŬT'MŌST, *n.* The greatest quantity or degree.
Ū-TŌ'PĬ-ĄN, *a.* Fanciful ; chimerical ; ideal.
ŬT'TĘR, *a.* Extreme ; excessive ; complete.
ŬT'TĘR, *v. a.* To speak ; to publish ; to sell.
ŬT'TĘR-Ą-BLE, *a.* That may be told or uttered.
ŬT'TĘR-ĄNCE, *n.* Pronunciation ; delivery.

ŬT'TĘR-LY, *ad.* Fully ; completely ; perfectly.
ŬT'TĘR-MŌST, *a.* Extreme ; most remote.
ŬT'TĘR-MŌST, *n.* The greatest degree.
Ū'VĘ-OŬS, *a.* Resembling a grape.
ŬX-Ō'RĬ-OŬS, *a.* Submissively fond of a wife.
ŬX-Ō'RĬ-OŲS-NĔSS, *n.* Fond submission to a wife.

V.

V, an English consonant, has but one sound,
 and is nearly allied to *f.*
VĀ'CĄN-CY, *n.* Empty space ; vacuity; a chasm.
VĀ'CĄNT, *a.* Empty; void ; free ; disengaged.
VĀ'CĀTE, *v. a.* To annul ; to make vacant.
VĄ-CĀ'TIǪN, *n.* A suspension of studies, &c. ;
 an intermission ; a recess ; leisure.
VĂC'CĬ-NĀTE, *v. a.* To inoculate with vaccine
 matter for the cow-pox.
VĂC-CĬ-NĀ'TIǪN, *n.* Inoculation for the cow-pox.
VĂC'CĪNE *or* VĂC'CĬNE, *a.* Belonging to a
 cow :—relating to vaccination.
VĂÇ'ĬL-LĂN-CY, *n.* A wavering ; inconstancy.
VĂÇ'ĬL-LĀTE, *v. n.* To waver ; to be inconstant.
VĂÇ-ĬL-LĀ'TIǪN, *n.* A reeling ; a staggering.
VĂC'Ų-ĬST, *n.* One who holds to a vacuum.
VĄ-CŪ'Ĭ-TY, *n.* Emptiness ; space unfilled ; inan-
VĂC'Ų-OŬS, *n.* Empty; unfilled ; vacant. [ity.
VĂC'Ų-OŲS-NĔSS, *n.* The state of being empty.
VĂC'Ų-ŬM, *n.* Space unoccupied by matter.
VĀ'DE-MĒ'CŲM, *n.* [L.] A book to be carried
VĂG'Ą-BǑND, *a.* Wandering ; vagrant. [about.
VĂG'Ą-BǑND, *n.* A vagrant ; a wanderer ; a beg-
VĂG'Ą-BǑND-RY, *n.* Beggary; knavery. [gąr.
VĄ-GĀ'RY, *n.* A wild freak or fancy ; a whim.
VĂG'Ĭ-NĄL *or* VĄ-GĪ'NĄL, *a.* Relating to a sheath.
VĀ'GRĄN-CY, *n.* A state of wandering.
VĀ'GRĄNT, *a.* Wandering ; unsettled ; vagabond.
VĀ'GRĄNT, *n.* A beggar ; wanderer ; a vagabond.
VĀGUE (vāg), *a.* Unfixed ; unsettled ; uncertain.
VĀIL, *n.* A curtain ; a cover ; veil. See VEIL.
VĀILŞ, *n. pl.* Money given to servants ; vales.
VĀIN, *a.* Fruitless ; unreal ; meanly proud ;
 conceited :—idle.—*In vain,* to no purpose. [it.
VĀIN-GLŌ'RĬ-OŬS, *a.* Vain or proud without mer-
VĀIN-GLŌ'RY, *n.* Empty pride ; vain boasting.
VĀIN'LY, *ad.* Without effect ; idly ; foolishly.
VĀI'VŌDE, *n.* A prince in the Dacian provinces.
VĂL'ĄNCE, *n.* Drapery hanging round a bedstead.
VĂL'ĄNCE, *v. a.* To decorate with drapery.
VĀLE, *n.* A space between hills ; a valley.
VĂL-E-DĬC'TIǪN, *n.* A farewell ; an adieu.
VĂL-E-DĬC'TǪ-RY, *a.* Bidding farewell.
VĂL'ĘN-TĪNE, *n.* A sweetheart chosen on Valen-
VĄ-LĒ'RĬ-ĄN, *n.* A plant. [tine's Day; a letter.
VĂL'ĘT, *n.* A waiting-servant.
VĂL-E-TŪ-DĬ-NĀ'RĬ-ĄN, *n.* One who is sickly.
VĂL-E-TŪ-DĬ-NĀ'RĬ-ĄN,) *a.* Weakly ; sickly ;
VĂL-E-TŪ'DĬ-NĄ-RY,)   infirm of health.
VĂL'ĬĄNT (văl'yąnt), *a.* Stout ; heroic ; brave.
VĂL'ĬĄNT-LY (văl'yąnt-lę), *ad.* Stoutly ; bravely.
VĂL'ĬĄNT-NĔSS (văl'yąnt-nĕs), *n.* Valor.
VĂL'ĬD, *a.* Efficacious ; weighty ; conclusive.
VĄ-LĬD'Ĭ-TY, *n.* Force to convince ; strength.
VĄ-LĪSE' *or* VĄ-LÎSE', *n.* A bag for clothes.

VĄL-LĀ'TIǪN, *n.* An intrenchment ; a rampart.
VĂL'LĘY (văl'lę), *n.* A hollow between hills.
VĂL'ǪR, *n.* Personal bravery; prowess ; courage.
VĂL'ǪR-OŬS, *a.* Brave ; stout ; valiant.
VĂL'ǪR-OŬS-LY, *ad.* In a brave manner. [value.
VĂL'Ų-Ą-BLE (văl'yu-ą-bl), *a.* Precious ; having
VĂL-Ų-Ā'TIǪN, *n.* An appraisement ; a set value.
VĂL'Ų-Ā-TǪR, *n.* One who sets a price.
VĂL'ŲE (văl'yu), *n.* Price ; worth ; rate. [mate.
VĂL'ŲE, *v. a.* To rate highly; to appraise ; to esti-
VĂL'ŲE-LĔSS (văl'yu-lĕs), *a.* Being of no value.
VĂL'Ų-ĘR (văl'yu-ęr), *n.* One that values.
VĂLVE, *n.* A folding door ; a lid ; a cover ; a
VĂL'VŪLE, *n.* A small valve. [shell.
VĂMP, *n.* The upper leather of a shoe.
VĂMP, *v. a.* To mend, as with a vamp.
VĂM'PĪRE, *n.* A pretended demon :—a large bat.
VĂN, *n.* Front of an army:—a fan :—a light wagon.
VĂN-CÔU'RIER (văn-kô'rēr), *n.* Avant-courier.
VĂN'DĄL-ĬŞM, *n.* Barbarity; ferocity. [neck.
VĂN-DȲKE', *n.* A kind of handkerchief for the
VĀNE, *n.* A weathercock.
VĂNG, *n.* (*Naut.*) A steadying rope. [army.
VĂN'GUĂRD (văn'gärd), *n.* The first line of an
VĄ-NĬL'LĄ, *n.* A climbing, fragrant plant.
VĂN'ĬSH, *v. n.* To disappear ; to pass away.
VĂN'Ĭ-TY, *n.* Emptiness ; inanity ; falsehood ;
 arrogance ; idle show ; empty, vain pride.
VĂN'QUĬSH (văng'kwĭsh), *v. a.* To conquer.
VĂN'QUĬSH-Ą-BLE, *a.* That may be overcome.
VĂN'QUĬSH-ĘR, *n.* A conqueror ; a subduer.
VĂN'TĄĢE, *n.* Superiority; advantageous state.
VĂN'TĄĢE-GRŌŬND, *n.* Superiority of state.
VĂP'ĬD, *a.* Dead ; spiritless ; mawkish ; flat.
VĂP'ĬD-NĔSS, *n.* State of being vapid or spiritless.
VĀ'PǪR, *n.* An exhalation ; fume ; steam ; wind.
 —*pl.* Hysteric fits ; whims ; spleen.
VĀ'PǪR, *v. n.* To emit vapor : — to bully, brag.
VĂP-Q-RĀ'TIǪN, *n.* Evaporation.
VĀ'PǪR-BĀTH, *n.* A bath of vapor or steam.
VĀ'PǪR-ĘR, *n.* A boaster ; a braggart.
VĀ'PǪR-ĬNG-LY, *ad.* In a boasting manner.
VĀ'PǪR-ĬSH, *a.* Vaporous :—peevish.
VĂP-Q-RĬ-ZĀ'TIǪN, *n.* Conversion into vapor.
VĂP'Q-RĪZE, *v. a.* To convert into vapor.
VĀ'PǪR-OŬS, *a.* Full of vapors ; windy.
VĀ'PǪR-Y, *a.* Vaporous :—peevish ; splenetic.
VĀ'RĬ-Ą-BLE, *a.* Liable to vary or change ;
 changeable ; mutable ; inconstant.
VĀ'RĬ-Ą-BLE-NĔSS, *n.* Mutability; inconstancy.
VĀ'RĬ-Ą-BLY, *ad.* Changeably ; inconstantly.
VĀ'RĬ-ĄNCE, *n.* Discord ; difference ; dissension.
VĀ-RĬ-Ā'TIǪN, *n.* A change ; difference ; devia-
VĂR'Ĭ-CŌSE, *a.* Swelled, as a vein. [tion.
VĀ'RĬ-E-GĀTE, *v. a.* To diversify with colors.

Ā,Ē,Ī,Ō,Ū,Ȳ,*long* ; Ă,Ĕ,Ĭ,Ŏ,Ŭ,Ў,*short* ; Ą,Ę,Į,Ǫ,Ų,Y,*obscure.*—FĀRE, FÄR, FĀST, FÀLL ; HÊIR, HËR ;

VĂ-RĮ-Ẹ-GĀ′TIǪN, *n.* Act of variegating.
VẠ-RĪ′Ẹ-TY, *n.* Change ; intermixture ; diversity.
VĂ′RĮ-Ǫ-LOÏD *or* VẠ-RĪ′Ǫ-LOÏD, *n.* An eruptive disease ; small-pox modified by vaccination.
VẠ-RĪ′Ǫ-LOŬS, *a.* Relating to the small-pox.
VĂ′RĮ-OŬS, *a.* Different ; manifold ; changeable.
VĂ′RĮ-OŬS-LY, *ad.* In a various manner.
VĂR′LẸT, *n.* A scoundrel :—*anciently*, a valet.
VĂR′NĮSH,*n.* A shining liquid substance :—cover.
VĂR′NĮSH, *v. a.* To cover with varnish.
VĂR′NĮSH-ẸR, *n.* One who varnishes.
VĂR′VẸLS, *n. pl.* Silver rings on a hawk's leg.
VĀ′RY, *v. a.* To change, diversify, variegate.
VĀ′RY, *v. n.* To be unlike ; to deviate, disagree.
VĂS′CŲ-LAR, *a.* Relating to, or full of, vessels.
VĀSE *or* VĀSE, *n.* A vessel :—an ornament.
VĂS′SAL, *n.* A subject ; a feudatory ; a slave.
VĂS′SAL, *v. a.* To subject ; to enslave.
VĂS′SAL-AĢE, *n.* State of a vassal ; slavery.
VĂST, *a.* Very large ; great ; enormous.
VĂS-TĀ′TIǪN, *n.* Waste ; devastation.
VĂST′LY, *ad.* Greatly ; to a great degree.
VĂST′NẸSS, *n.* Immensity; enormous greatness.
VĂST′Y, *a.* Large ; enormously great.
VĂT, *n.* A cistern of tanners, brewers, &c.
VĂT′Į-CĂN, *n.* A palace of the pope at Rome.
VĂT′Į-CĪDE, *n.* The murder of a prophet.
VẠ-TĬÇ′Į-NAL, *a.* Containing predictions.
VẠ-TĬÇ′Į-NĀTE, *v. n.* To prophesy ; to foretell.
VẠ-TĬÇ-Į-NĀ′TIǪN, *n.* Prediction ; prophecy.
VAUDE′VĬLLE, VAUDE′VĬL (vŏd′vĭl), *n.* A light song :—comic drama with songs.
VÂULT, *n.* An arch ; a cave :—tomb :—leap.
VÂULT, *v. a.* To arch ; to shape to a vault.
VÂULT, *v. n.* To leap ; to jump ; to tumble.
VÂULT′ẸR, *n.* A leaper ; a jumper ; a tumbler.
VÂUNT *or* VÀUNT, *v. a.* & *n.* To boast ; to brag.
VÂUNT *or* VÀUNT, *n.* A brag ; a boast.
VÂUNT′ẸR *or* VÀUNT′ẸR, *n.* One who vaunts.
VÂUNT′ĮNG-LY *or* VÀUNT′ĮNG-LY,*ad.*Boastfully.
VĒAL (vēl), *n.* The flesh of a calf for the table.
VĒ′DÄ *or* VẸ-DÄ′, *n.* A Hindoo sacred book.
VẸ-DĔTTE′, *n.* [Fr.] A sentinel on horseback.
VĒĒR, *v. a.* & *n.* To turn ; to change direction.
VĒĒR′ĮNG, *n.* The act of turning or changing.
VĔĢ′Ẹ-TẠ-BLE, *n.* A plant :—an esculent plant.
VĔĢ′Ẹ-TẠ-BLE, *a.* Belonging to plants.
VĔĢ′Ẹ-TAL, *a.* Vital, as common to plants and animals.
VĔĢ-Ẹ-TĀ′RĮ-AN,*n.*One who lives on vegetables.
VĔĢ′Ẹ-TĀTE, *v. n.* To grow, as plants ; to shoot.
VĔĢ-Ẹ-TĀ′TIǪN, *n.* The growth of plants.
VĔĢ′Ẹ-TĀ-TĮVE, *a.* Growing, as plants.
VĔĢ′Ẹ-TĀ-TĮVE-NĔSS, *n.* Vegetative quality.
VĒ′HẸ-MĔNCE,*n.*Violence ; force ; ardor ; fervor.
VĒ′HẸ-MĔNT, *a.*Violent ; ardent ; eager ; fervent.
VĒ′HẸ-MĔNT-LY,*ad.*Eagerly ; ardently ; urgently.
VĒ′HĮ-CLE (vē′hẹ-kl),*n.* A carriage ; conveyance.
VẸ-HĬC′U-LAR, *a.* Belonging to a vehicle.
VEIL (vāl), *n.* A cover ; a curtain :—a disguise.
VEIL (vāl), *v. a.* To cover ; to hide ; to conceal.
VEIN (vān), *n.* A tube conveying blood :—course of metal in mines :—turn of mind :—humor ; propensity :—a streak :—a current.
VEINED (vānd), VEIN′Y (vā′nẹ), *a.* Full of veins.
VẸ-LĬF′ẸR-OŬS, *a.* Carrying sails.
VĔL-LĒ′Į-TY, *n.* The lowest degree of desire.
VĔL′LĮ-CĀTE, *v. a.* To twitch, pluck, stimulate.

VĔL-LĮ-CĀ′TIǪN, *n.* A twitching ; stimulation.
VĔL′LŲM, *n.* A fine kind of parchment.
VẸ-LŎÇ′Į-TY,*n.* Speed ; swiftness ; quick motion.
VĔL′VẸT, *n.* A stuff with a nap or pile upon it.
VĔL′VẸT, *a.* Made of velvet ; soft ; velvety.
VĔL′VẸT-ĒĒN, *n.* A kind of stuff like velvet.
VĔL′VẸT-Y, *a.* Made of, or like, velvet.
VĒ′NAL, *a.* Mercenary ; base :—venous.
VẸ-NĂL′Į-TY, *n.* Mercenariness ; prostitution.
VẸ-NĀ′TIǪN, *n.* The veining of leaves.
VĔND, *v. a.* To sell ; to transfer for money.
VẸN-DĒĒ′, *n.* One to whom any thing is sold.
VĔND′ẸR, *n.* One who vends ; a seller.
VĔND′Į-BLE, *a.* Salable ; that may be sold.
VĔND′Į-BLE-NĔSS, *n.* State of being salable.
VẸN-DĬ″TIǪN, *n.* Sale ; the act of selling.
VẸN-DŪE′, *n.* An auction ; a public sale.
VẸ-NĒĒR′, *n.* A thin piece of wood.
VẸ-NĒĒR′, *v. a.* To cover with thin wood, &c.
VĔN-Ẹ-FĬ″CIAL (vĕn-ẹ-fĭsh′ạl), *a.* Acting by poi-
VĔN′ẸR-Ạ-BLE, *a.* Worthy of reverence. [son.
VĔN′ẸR-Ạ-BLE-NĔSS,*n.* State of being venerable.
VĔN′ẸR-Ạ-BLY, *ad.* With veneration.
VĔN′ẸR-ĀTE, *v. a.* To treat with veneration.
VĔN′ẸR-Ā′TIǪN, *n.* Reverence ; awful respect.
VĔN′ẸR-Ā-TǪR, *n.* A reverencer ; a reverer.
VẸ-NĒ′RẸ-AL, *a.* Relating to lust ; syphilitic.
VĔN′Ẹ-RY, *n.* Hunting :—sexual intercourse.
VĒ-NẸ-SĔC′TIǪN,*n.* Blood-letting ; phlebotomy.
VĔN′ĢEANCE (vĕn′jạns), *n.* Penal retribution.
VĔNĢE′FŬL, *a.* Vindictive ; revengeful.
VĒ′NĮ-AL, *a.* Pardonable ; excusable ; allowed.
VĒ′NĮ-AL-NĔSS, *n.* The state of being venial.
VĔN′ĮSǪN (vĕn′zn *or* vĕn′ẹ-zn), *n.* The flesh of
VĔN′ǪM, *n.* Poison ; poisonous matter. [deer.
VĔN′ǪM, *v. a.* To infect ; to poison ; to envenom.
VĔN′ǪM-OŬS, *a.* Poisonous ; malignant.
VĔN′ǪM-OŬS-LY, *ad.* Poisonously ; malignantly.
VĔN′ǪM-OŲS-NĔSS,*n.*Poisonousness ; malignity.
VĒ′NOŲS, *a.* Relating to the veins :—veined.
VĔNT,*n.* An aperture ; a hole :—discharge :—sale.
VĔNT, *v. a.* To let out ; to emit, publish, sell.
VĔN′TAIL (vĕn′tạl), *n.* Visor of a helmet.
VĔN′TẸR, *n.* [L.] The abdomen :—the womb.
VĔN′TĮ-DŬCT, *n.* A passage for the wind or air.
VĔN′TĮ-LĀTE, *v. a.* To fan, refresh, or purify with wind :—to fan, as grain ; to winnow.
VĔN-TĮ-LĀ′TIǪN, *n.* Act of fanning or ventilat-
VĔN′TĮ-LĀ-TǪR,*n.* A ventilating machine. [ing.
VĔN′TRAL, *a.* Belonging to the venter or belly.
VĔN′TRĮ-CLE, *n.* A small cavity in an animal body, particularly of the heart.
VẸN-TRĬL′Ǫ-QUĬSM, } *n.* The act or art of
VẸN-TRĬL′Ǫ-QUY, } speaking inwardly.
VẸN-TRĬL′Ǫ-QUĬST, *n.* One who speaks so that the sound seems not to issue from himself.
VẸN-TRĬL′Ǫ-QUOŬS, *a.* Like a ventriloquist.
VĔNT′ŪRE (vĕnt′yŭr), *n.* A hazard ; chance ; hap.
VĔNT′ŪRE (vĕnt′yŭr), *v. n.* & *a.*To dare ; to risk.
VĔNT′ŪR-ẸR (vĕnt′yŭr-ẹr), *n.* One who ventures.
VĔNT′ŪRE-SǑME(vĕnt′yŭr-sŭm),*a.*Bold ; daring.
VĔNT′ŪR-OŬS (vĕnt′yŭr-ŭs), *a.* Daring ; bold.
VĔN′ŪE (vĕn′u), *n.* (*Law.*) A neighborhood.
VĒ′NŲS, *n.* [L.] Goddess of love :—a planet.
VẸ-RĀ′CIOŲS (vẹ-rā′shụs), *a.* Observant of truth.
VẸ-RĂÇ′Į-TY, *n.* Truth ; observance of truth.
VẸ-RĂN′DA, *n.* A kind of open portico.
VẸ-RĀ′TRĮ-Ạ, *n.* A vegetable alkaloid.

VĔRB, *n.* (*Gram.*) A part of speech which sig-
nifies to be, to act, or to be acted upon.
VĔR′BAL, *a.* Oral; uttered by the mouth; literal.
VĔR′BAL-LY, *ad.* In or by words; orally.
VER-BĀ′TIM, *ad.* [L.] Word for word. [ing.
VĔR-BER-Ā′TION, *n.* Infliction of blows; a beat-
VĔR′BI-AGE, *n.* Verbosity; empty discourse.
VER-BŌSE′, *a.* Exuberant in words; prolix.
VER-BŌS′I-TY, *n.* Exuberance of words.
VĔR′DANT, *a.* Green; fresh; flourishing.
VĔR′DER-ER, *n.* An officer of the forest.
VĔR′DICT, *n.* The decision of a jury; judgment.
VĔR′DI-GRÎS, *n.* The greenish rust of copper.
VĔRD′URE (vĕrd′yur), *n.* Greenness or fresh-
ness of grass; green.
VĔRD′UR-OŬS (vĕrd′yur-ŭs), *a.* Green; fresh.
VĔRGE, *n.* A rod; a mace :—brink; edge; border.
VĔRGE, *v. n.* To tend :—to incline; to slope.
VĔRG′ER, *n.* A mace-bearer in cathedrals, &c.
VĔR′I-FĪ-A-BLE, *a.* That may be verified.
VĔR′I-FI-CĀ′TION, *n.* Confirmation; proof.
VĔR′I-FĪ-ER, *n.* One who verifies. [fulfil.
VĔR′I-FY, *v. a.* To confirm; to prove true; to
VĔR′I-LY, *ad.* In truth; certainly; really.
VĔR-I-SĬM′I-LAR, *a.* Probable; likely.
VĔR-I-SI-MĬL′I-TŪDE, *n.* Probability; likelihood.
VĔR′I-TA-BLE, *a.* True; agreeable to fact.
VĔR′I-TA-BLY, *ad.* In a true manner; truly.
VĔR′I-TY, *n.* Truth; reality:—a true assertion.
VĔR′JUICE, *n.* Liquor from crab apples, &c.
VĔR′MES, *n. pl.* [L.] (*Ent.*) Worms.
VĔR-MI-CĔL′LI (vĕr-me-chĕl′e), *n.* [It.] A paste
in the form of worms or small pipes.
VER-MĬC′U-LAR, *a.* Acting like a worm; spiral.
VER-MĬC′U-LĀTE, *v. a.* To inlay so as to re-
semble the track of worms.
VĔR′MI-CŪLE, *n.* A little grub or worm. [grubs.
VER-MĬC′U-LOŬS, *a.* Full of grubs; resembling
VĔR′MI-FŌRM, *a.* Having the shape of a worm.
VĔR′MI-FŪGE, *n.* Medicine that expels worms.
VER-MĬL′ION (ver-mĭl′yun), *n.* The red sul-
phuret of mercury :—a beautiful red color.
VĔR′MIN, *n.* Any small, noxious animal.
VĔR-MI-NĀ′TION, *n.* Generation of vermin.
VĔR′MIN-OŬS, *a.* Tending to breed vermin.
VER-MĬP′A-ROŬS, *a.* Producing worms.
VER-MĬV′O-ROŬS, *a.* Feeding on worms. [try.
VER-NĂC′U-LAR, *a.* Native; of one's own coun-
VĔR′NAL, *a.* Belonging to the spring.
VĔR′NI-ER, *n.* Movable scale of a quadrant, &c.
VE-RŎN′I-CA, *n.* A napkin with the figure of
Christ's face :—speedwell, a plant. [able.
VĔR′SA-TILE, *a.* Turning round; changing; vari-
VĔR′SA-TILE-NĔSS,) *n.* Quality of being ver-
VĔR-SA-TĬL′I-TY,) satile; variableness.
VĔRSE, *n.* A measured line; poetry; a paragraph.
VĔRSED (vĕrst), *p. a.* Skilled in; knowing.
VĔR-SI-FI-CĀ′TION, *n.* Art of making verses.
VĔR′SI-FĪ-ER, *n.* A maker of verses.
VĔR′SI-FY, *v. n. & a.* To make or relate in verse.
VĔR′SION, *n.* A translation; act of translating.
VĔRST, *n.* A Russian measure; 3501 feet.
VĔR′SUS, *prep.* [L.] (*Law.*) Against.
VĔRT, *n.* Any green tree :—green color.
VĔR′TE-BRA, *n.*; *pl.* VĔR′TE-BRÆ. [L.] A
joint of the spine; vertebre. [spine.
VĔR′TE-BRAL, *a.* Relating to the joints of the
VĔR′TE-BRE (vĕr′te-ber), *n.* Joint of the spine.

VĔR′TEX, *n.*; *pl.* VĔR′TI-CĒS. [L.] The ze-
nith :—the top or summit of any thing. [ular.
VĔR′TI-CAL, *a.* Placed in the vertex; perpendic-
VĔR′TI-CAL-LY, *ad.* In a vertical manner.
VĔR′TI-CAL-NĔSS, *n.* State of being vertical.
VER-TĬÇ′IL-LATE *or* VĔR-TI-CĬL′LATE, *a.*
Having leaves in a circle on one joint of a stem.
VER-TĬÇ′I-TY, *n.* Power of turning; rotation.
VĔR′TI-CLE, *n.* An axis; a hinge; a joint.
VER-TĬG′I-NOŬS, *a.* Turning round; giddy.
VĔR′TI-GŌ, VER-TĪ′GŌ, *or* VER-TĬ′GŌ, *n.* Gid-
VĔR′VAIN *or* VĔR′VĀIN, *n.* A plant. [diness.
VĔR′Y, *a.* True; real.—*ad.* In a great degree.
VĔS′I-CĀTE, *v. a.* To raise blisters on.
VĔS-I-CĀ′TION, *n.* The act of blistering.
VE-SĬC′A-TO-RY, *n.* A blistering plaster.
VĔS′I-CLE, *n.* A small elevation of the cuticle
containing lymph :—a little cell or bladder.
VE-SĬC′U-LAR, *a.* Hollow; containing vesicles.
VĔS′PER, *n.* [L.] The evening star; Venus.
VĔS′PERS, *n. pl.* Catholic evening service.
VĔS′PER-TĪNE, *a.* Pertaining to the evening.
VĔS′SEL, *n.* A cask or utensil for holding liquids,
&c. :—a ship; a bark :—a tube; a pipe.
VĔST, *n.* An outer garment :—a waistcoat.
VĔST, *v. a.* To dress; to clothe; to invest with.
VĔS′TAL, *n.* A virgin consecrated to Vesta.
VĔS′TAL, *a.* Denoting virginity; pure; chaste.
VĔST′ED, *a.* Fixed; established; not contingent.
VĔS′TI-BULE, *n.* The porch or entrance of a house.
VĔS′TIGE, *n.* A footstep; a trace; a mark.
VĔST′MENT, *n.* A garment; part of dress.
VĔS′TRY, *n.* A room in or adjoining a church :
—assembly for parochial purposes.
VĔST′URE (vĕst′yur), *n.* A garment; robe; dress.
VĔTCH, *n.* A leguminous, climbing plant.
VĔTCH′Y, *a.* Made of, or abounding in, vetches.
VĔT′ER-AN, *n.* An old soldier; one long practised.
VĔT′ER-AN, *a.* Long practised or experienced.
VĔT-ER-I-NĀ′RI-AN, *n.* One skilled in the dis-
eases of horses and cattle; a horse-doctor.
VĔT′ER-I-NA-RY, *a.* Pertaining to farriery, or
to the healing of diseases of horses and cattle.
VĒ′TŌ, *n.* [L.] A prohibition. [disquiet.
VĔX, *v. a.* To plague; to torment; to harass; to
VEX-Ā′TION, *n.* Act of vexing; trouble; plague.
VEX-Ā′TIOUS, *a.* Afflictive; troublesome.
VEX-Ā′TIOUS-LY, *ad.* Troublesomely; uneasily.
VĪ′A. [L., *a way.*] By the way of.
VĪ′A-DŬCT, *n.* Elevated construction of arches,
VĪ′AL, *n.* A small bottle; a phial. [&c.
VĪ′AND, *n.* Food; victuals;—commonly in *pl.*
VI-ĂT′I-CŬM, *n.* [L.] Provision for a journey.
VĪ′BRĀTE, *v. a. & n.* To brandish; to move to
and fro, as a pendulum; to oscillate.
VĪ-BRĀ′TION, *n.* A moving with quick return.
VĪ′BRA-TO-RY, *a.* Vibrating; causing to vibrate.
VĬC′AR, *n.* The priest of a parish :—a substitute.
VĬC′AR-AGE, *n.* Benefice or residence of a vicar.
VI-CĀ′RI-AL, *a.* Belonging to a vicar; vicarious.
VI-CĀ′RI-OŬS, *a.* Delegated; substituted.
VI-CĀ′RI-OŬS-LY, *ad.* In the place of another.
VĬC′AR-SHIP, *n.* The office of a vicar.
VĪ′CE. [L.] In room of; instead of.
VĪCE. A prefix denoting acting instead or sec-
ond in rank, as *vice*-president.
VĪCE, *n.* Depravity; wickedness; immorality:—
a griping or holding machine.

VĪCE-ĂD′MĬ-RĄL, n.   An English naval officer in rank next below the admiral.
VĪCE-ĂD′MĬ-RĄL-TY, n.   Office of a vice-admi-
VĪCE-Ā′ĢENT, n.   An assistant agent.   [ral.
VĪCE-CHĂN′CEL-LQR, n. A judge in a chancery court:—2d magistrate of an English university.
VĪCE-ĢĒ′REN-CY, n.   Office of a vicegerent.
VĪCE-ĢĒ′RENT, n.   A lieutenant; a deputy.
VĪCE′RÖŸ,n.One who governs in place of a king.
VĪCE-RÖŸ′AL-TY, n.   The dignity of a viceroy.
VĪCE′RÖŸ-SHĬP, n.   The office of a viceroy.
VĬÇ′ĬN-AĢE, n.   A neighborhood; a vicinity.
VĬÇ′Ĭ-NĄL or VĬ-CĪ′NĄL, a.   Neighboring.
VĬ-CĬN′Ĭ-TY, n.   Nearness; a neighborhood.
VĪ′′CIOŲS (vĭsh′ŭs), a. Devoted to vice; wicked.
VĪ′′CIOŲS-LY (vĭsh′ŭs-), ad. Corruptly; sinfully.
VĪ′′CIOŲS-NĔSS (vĭsh′ŭs-nĕs), n. Corruptness.
VĬ-CĬS′SĬ-TŪDE, n. A regular change; recipro-cal succession; interchange; revolution.
VĬC′TĬM, n. A sacrifice:—something destroyed.
VĬC′TQR, n.   A conqueror; a vanquisher.
VĬC′TQR-ĔSS, n.   A female that conquers.
VĬC-TŌ′RĬ-OŬS, a.   Conquering; triumphant.
VĬC-TŌ′RĬ-OŬS-LY, ad. With victory.   [rious.
VĬC-TŌ′RĬ-OŲS-NĔSS, n.   State of being victo-
VĬC′TQ-RY, n.   Conquest; success; a triumph.
VĬCT′UAL (vĭt′tl), v. a.   To supply with food.
VĬCT′UAL-LER, n.   A provider of victuals.
VĬCT′UALȘ (vĭt′tlz), n. pl.   Food; provision.
VĬ-CŪ′NĄ (vē-kûn′yą), n.   A sort of llama.
VĬD′Ų-ĄL, a. Belonging to the state of a widow.
VĪE (vī), v. n.   To contest; to contend; to strive.
VIEW̄ (vū), v. a.   To survey; to look on; to see.
VIEW̄ (vū), n.   Prospect; sight; survey; show.
VIEW̄′ER (vū′er), n.   One who views.
VIEW̄′LESS (vū′les), a.   Unseen; not discernible.
VĬĢ′ĬL, n.   A watch:—devotion:—a fast.
VĬĢ′Ĭ-LANCE, n.   Watchfulness; care; guard.
VĬĢ′Ĭ-LANT, a.   Watchful; diligent; attentive.
VĬĢ′Ĭ-LANT-LY, ad.   Watchfully; attentively.
VĬGN-ĔTTE′ (vĭn-yĕt′ or vĭn′yĕt), n.   An or-namental carving; a picture of leaves and flowers :—print on the title-page of a book.
VĬG′QR, n.   Force; strength; energy; efficacy.
VĬG′QR-OŬS, a. Strong; full of strength and life.
VĬG′QR-OŬS-LY, ad.   With force or strength.
VĬG′QR-OŲS-NĔSS, n.   Force; strength.
VĪLE, a. Base; mean; worthless; sordid; wick-
VĪLE′LY, ad. Basely; meanly; shamefully.[ed.
VĪLE′NESS, n.   Baseness; meanness.
VĬL′Ĭ-FĪ-ER, n.   One that vilifies; a defamer.
VĬL′Ĭ-FȲ, v. a.   To debase; to defame; to abuse.
VĬL′LĄ, n.   A country-seat; a manor.
VĬL′LAĢE, n.   A small collection of houses.
VĬL′LĄ-ĢER, n.   An inhabitant of a village.
VĬL′LAĬN (vĭl′lịn), n.   One who held by a base tenure; a villein :—a vile person; a knave.
VĬL′LĄ-NAĢE, n.   State of a villain; baseness.
VĬL′LĄ-NOŬS, a.   Base; vile; wicked; sorry.
VĬL′LĄ-NOŬS-LY, ad.   Wickedly; basely.
VĬL′LĄ-NOŲS-NĔSS, n.   Baseness; wickedness.
VĬL′LĄ-NY, n. Wickedness; baseness; a crime.
VĬL-LÕSE′, VĬL′LOŲS, a.   Shaggy; rough.
VĬM′Ĭ-NĄL, a. Relating to, or producing, twigs.
VĬ-MĬN′E-OŬS, a. Made of twigs.   [winy.
VĬ-NĀ′CEOŲS (vī-nā′shŭs), a. Relating to wine;
VĬN′CĬ-BLE, a.   Conquerable; superable.
VĬN′CĬ-BLE-NĔSS, n. Liableness to be overcome.

VĮN-DĒ′MĬ-ĄL, a.   Belonging to a vintage.
VĬN′DĮ-CĀTE, v. a. To justify; to support, clear.
VĬN-DĮ-CĀ′TIQN, n.   A defence; a justification.
VĬN′DĮ-CĀ-TĮVE or VĮN-DĬC′Ą-TĮVE, a. Tend-ing to vindicate or justify; vindicatory.
VĬN′DĮ-CĀ-TQR, n.   One who vindicates.
VĬN′DĮ-CĄ-TQ-RY, a.   Exculpatory; defensory.
VĮN-DĬC′TĬVE, a.   Given to revenge; revenge-
VĮN-DĬC′TĬVE-LY, ad.   Revengefully.   [ful.
VĮN-DĬC′TĬVE-NĔSS, n.   A revengeful temper.
VĪNE, n. The plant that bears the grape :—stem.
VĪNE′-DRĔSS-ER, n.   One who cultivates vines.
VĪNE′-FRĔT-TER, n.   The plant-louse; an in-
VĬN′E-GĄR, n.   An acid liquor.   [sect.
VĪNE′YĄRD, n.   A ground planted with grape-
VĪ′NOŲS, a. Having the qualities of wine. [vines.
VĬNT′AĢE, n.   The time of making wine; grapes.
VĬN′TĄ-ĢER, n.   One who gathers the vintage.
VĬNT′NER, n.   One who sells wine.
VĬNT′RY, n.   A place where wine is sold.
VĪ′NY, a.   Belonging to, or yielding, vines.
VĪ′QL, n.   A stringed instrument of music.
VĪ′Q-LĄ-BLE, a.   That may be violated or hurt.
VĬ-Q-LĀ′CEOŲS (vī-ǫ-lā′shŭs), a.   Like violets.
VĪ′Q-LĀTE, v. a.   To injure; to break; to ravish.
VĬ-Q-LĀ′TIQN, n.   Infringement; a deflowering.
VĪ′Q-LĄ-TQR, n.   One who violates or injures.
VĪ′Q-LĔNCE, n.   Force; outrage; vehemence.
VĪ′Q-LĔNT, a.   Forcible; vehement; extorted.
VĪ′Q-LĔNT-LY, ad.   With force; vehemently.
VĪ′Q-LĔT, n.   A plant and flower:—a color.
VĬ-Q-LĬN′, n.   A fiddle; a stringed instrument.
VĬ-Q-LĬN′ĬST, VĪ′QL-ĬST, n. A player on the viol.
VĬ-Q-LQN-CĔL′LÕ (vē-ǫ-lǫn-chĕl′lõ or vē-ǫ-lǫn-sĕl′lõ), n.   [It.] A kind of bass violin.
VĪ′PER, n.   A venomous serpent.
VĪ′PER-ĪNE, a.   Belonging to a viper; viperous.
VĪ′PER-OŬS, a.   Having the qualities of a viper.
VĬ-RĀ′GQ or VĬ-RĀ′GÕ, n.   A female warrior :—a termagant :—a turbulent woman.
VĬR′ĢĬN, n.   A maid; a woman not a mother.
VĬR′ĢĬN, a. Befitting a virgin; maidenly; pure.
VĬR′ĢĬN-ĄL, a.   Maidenly; relating to a virgin.
VĬR′ĢĬN-ĄL, n.   A musical instrument.   [gin.
VĬR-ĢĬN′Ĭ-TY, n.   Maidenhood; state of a vir-
VĬR′ĢÕ, n.   [L.]   The Virgin; sixth sign in the
VĬ-RĬD′Ĭ-TY, n.   Greenness.   [zodiac.
VĪ′RĬLE, a.   Belonging to man; manly; bold.
VĬ-RĬL′Ĭ-TY, n.   Manhood; character of man.
VIRTU (vĭr-tû′), n. [It.] A love of the fine arts :—objects of art; curiosities, &c.
VĬRT′Ų-AL (vĭrt′yu-ąl), a.   Being in essense or effect, though not in fact; efficacious.
VĬRT′Ų-AL-LY, ad.   In effect, or efficaciously.
VĬRT′ŪE (vĭrt′yū), n. Moral goodness; efficacy.
VĬR-TŲ-Õ′SQ, n.   [It.]   It. pl. VĬR-TŲ-Õ′SĮ; Eng. VĬR-TŲ-Õ′SÕS.   One skilled in paint-ings, medals, antiques, curiosities, &c.
VĬRT′Ų-OŬS (vĭrt′yu-ŭs), a.   Morally good; up-right; honest :—efficacious; powerful.
VĬRT′Ų-OŬS-LY, ad.   In a virtuous manner.
VĬRT′Ų-OŲS-NĔSS, n.   State of being virtuous.
VĬR′Ų-LĔNCE, n.   Quality of being virulent; malignity; acrimony; bitterness.
VĬR′Ų-LĔNT, a.   Venomous; bitter; malignant.
VĬR′Ų-LĔNT-LY, ad.   Malignantly; with bitter-
VĪ′RŲS, n.   [L.] Purulent matter; poison. [ness.
VĬŞ′AĢE, n.   The face; the countenance; look.

VĬṢ'AGED (vĭz'ajd), *a.* Having a face or visage.
VIS-A-VIS (vĭz'ạ-vē'), *n.* [Fr.] A carriage which holds only two persons, who sit face to face.
VĬS'CE-RẠ, *n. pl.* [L.] The entrails or intestines.
VĬS'CER-AL, *a.* Relating to the viscera.
VĬS'CĮD, *a.* Glutinous; viscous. [tenacity.
VĮS-CĬD'Į-TY, VĮS-CŎS'Į-TY, *n.* Glutinousness;
VĬS'CÖÛNT (vī'köûnt), *n.* A degree of nobility next below an earl. [a viscount.
VĮS'CÖÛNT-ĘSS (vī'köûnt-ęs), *n.* The lady of a viscount.
VĬS'COŲS, *a.* Glutinous; sticky; tenacious.
VĪSE, *n.* A griping machine. See VICE.
VĬSH'NŲ, *n.* The name of a Hindoo deity.
VĬṢ-Į-BĬL'Į-TY, *n.* The quality of being visible.
VĬṢ'Į-BLE, *a.* Perceptible by the eye; apparent.
VĬṢ'Į-BLE-NĔSS, *n.* The state of being visible.
VĬṢ'Į-BLY, *ad.* In a perceptible manner.
VĬ''ṢĮON (vĭzh'ụn), *n.* Sight; phantom; dream.
VĬ''ṢĮON-Ạ-RY (vĭzh'ụn-ạ-rẹ), *a.* Fanciful; not real; ideal; imaginative; fantastic.
VĬ''ṢĮON-Ạ-RY, *n.* A dreamer; a wild schemer.
VĬṢ'ĮT, *v. a.* To go to see; to attend; to inflict.
VĬṢ'ĮT, *n.* The act of going to see another.
VĬṢ'ĮT-Ạ-BLE, *a.* Liable to be visited.
VĬṢ'Į-TĄNT, *n.* One who visits; a visitor.
VĬṢ-Į-TĀ'TĮON, *n.* Act of visiting:—infliction: —a judicial examination. [visitor.
VĬṢ-Į-TĄ-TŌ'RĮ-ĄL, *a.* Relating to a judicial
VĬṢ'ĮT-QR, *n.* One who visits:—an inspector.
VĬṢ'QR, *n.* A mask:—a part of a helmet.
VĬṢ'QRED (vĭz'ụrd), *a.* Masked. [avenue.
VĬS'TẠ, *n.* [It.] A view; prospect through an
VĬṢ'Ų-ĄL (vĭzh'ụ-ạl), *a.* Used in or aiding sight.
VĪ'TĄL, *a.* Necessary to life; having life; living; indispensable; essential.
VĮ-TĂL'Į-TY, *n.* The power of subsisting in life.
VĪ'TĄL-LY, *ad.* In such a manner as to give life.
VĪ'TĄLS, *n. pl.* The parts essential to life.
VĬ''TĮ-ĀTE (vĭsh'ẹ-āt), *v. a.* To make vicious; to corrupt; to deprave; to spoil.
VĬ-TĮ-Ā'TĮON (vĭsh-ẹ-ā'shụn), *n.* Depravation.
VĬ-TĮ-ŎS'Į-TY (vĭsh-ẹ-ŏs'ẹ-tẹ), *n.* Depravity.
VĬ''TĮOŲS (vĭsh'ụs), *a.* Corrupt. See VICIOUS.
VĬT'RĘ-OŬS, *a.* Glassy; resembling glass.
VĬT'RĘ-OŲS-NĔSS, *n.* State of being vitreous.
VĬT-RĮ-FĂC'TĮON, *n.* Act of vitrifying.
VĬT-RĮ-FĮ-CĀ'TĮON, *n.* Vitrifaction.
VĬT'RĮ-FȲ, *v. a. & n.* To convert into glass.
VĬT'RĮ-QL, *n.* A compound mineral salt.
VĬT-RĮ-ŎL'ĮC, *a.* Containing vitriol.
VĬT'Ų-LĪNE, *a.* Relating to a calf or to veal.
VĬ-TŬ'PĘR-ĀTE, *v. a.* To blame; to censure.
VĬ-TŬ-PĘR-Ā'TĮON, *n.* Blame; censure.
VĬ-TŬ'PĘR-Ạ-TĬVE, *a.* Containing censure.
VĬ-VĀ'CĮOŲS (vī-vā'shụs), *a.* Gay; active; lively.
VĬ-VĂÇ'Į-TY, *n.* Liveliness; sprightliness. [ly.
VĪ'VẠ-RY, *n.* A place for keeping live fish, &c.
VĪV'ĮD, *a.* Lively; quick; sprightly:—clear.
VĪV'ĮD-LY, *ad.* With life; with quickness.
VĪV'ĮD-NĔSS, *n.* Life; vigor; quickness.
VĬ-VĬF'ĮC, VĬ-VĬF'Į-CĄL, *a.* Giving life.
VĬ-VĬF'Į-CĀTE, *v. a.* To make alive; to animate.
VĬV-Į-FĮ-CĀ'TĮON, *n.* Act of giving life. [mate.
VĬV'Į-FȲ, *v. a.* To make alive; to animate.
VĬ-VĬP'Ạ-ROŬS, *a.* Bringing forth young alive.
VĬX'EN (vĭk'sn), *n.* A scolding woman.
VĬX'EN-LY, *a.* Having the qualities of a vixen.
VĬZ, *ad.* [A contraction of *videlicet.*] Namely.

VĬZ'IĘR (vĭz'yẹr *or* vĭz'yĕr), *n.* A Turkish minister.
VŌ'CẠ-BLE, *n.* A word; a name; a term. [ister.
VQ-CĂB'Ų-LẠ-RY, *n.* A dictionary; list of words.
VŌ'CĄL, *a.* Having a voice; uttered by the voice.
VQ-CĂL'Į-TY, *n.* The state of being vocal.
VŌ'CĄL-ĪZE, *v. a.* To make vocal.
VŌ'CĄL-LY, *ad.* In words; articulately.
VQ-CĀ'TĮON, *n.* A calling; trade; employment.
VŎC'Ạ-TĬVE, *a.* Denoting a grammatical case.
VQ-CĬF'ĘR-ĀTE, *v. n.* To cry out loudly; to clamor; to make outcries.
VQ-CĬF-ĘR-Ā'TĮON, *n.* A clamor; an outcry.
VQ-CĬF'ĘR-OŬS, *a.* Clamorous; noisy.
VŌGŪE (vōg), *n.* Fashion; mode; custom.
VÖÏCE (vöïs), *n.* Sound emitted by the mouth: —a vote; suffrage; opinion expressed.
VÖÏCED (vöïst), *a.* Furnished with a voice.
VÖÏD, *a.* Empty; vain; null; free; destitute.
VÖÏD, *n.* An empty space; vacuum; vacancy.
VÖÏD, *v. a.* To emit; to vacate; to annul.
VÖÏD'Ạ-BLE, *a.* That may be voided.
VÖÏD'ẠNCE, *n.* An emptying; ejection; vacancy.
VÖÏD'ĘR, *n.* One who voids:—a basket or tray.
VÖÏD'NĔSS, *n.* Emptiness; vacuity; inefficacy.
VŎL'Ạ-TĬLE, *a.* Flying; fickle; evaporating.
VŎL'Ạ-TĬLE-NĔSS, } *n.* The quality of being
VŎL-Ạ-TĬL'Į-TY, } volatile, or of flying away by evaporation:—levity. [volatile.
VŎL-Ạ-TĬL-Į-ZĀ'TĮON, *n.* The act of making
VŎL'Ạ-TĬL-ĪZE, *v. a.* To make volatile; to subtilize to a high degree.
VQL-CĂN'ĮC, *a.* Relating to a volcano; produced by, or issuing from, a volcano.
VŎL'CẠ-NĬST, *n.* One versed in volcanoes.
VQL-CĀ'NŌ, *n.; pl.* VQL-CĀ'NŌEṢ. A mountain ejecting fire, smoke, and lava; a burning mountain.
VŎL-Į-TĀ'TĮON, *n.* The act or power of flying.
VQ-LĬ''TĮON (vọ-lĭsh'ụn), *n.* The act of willing; the power of willing or choosing.
VŎL'Į-TĬVE, *a.* Having the power to will.
VŎL'LEY (vŏl'lẹ), *n.* A flight of shot:—a burst.
VŎL'LEY, *v. a. & n.* To throw out at once.
VQL-TĀ'ĮC, *a.* Relating to Volta or voltaism.
VŎL'TẠ-ĮSM, *n.* A branch of electricity. [bility.
VŎL-Ų-BĬL'Į-TY, *n.* Fluency of speech; muta-
VŎL'Ų-BLE, *a.* Rolling; active; fluent of words.
VŎL'Ų-BLY, *ad.* In a voluble manner. [pass.
VŎL'ŲME (vŏl'yụm), *n.* A book; a roll; com-
VQ-LŬ'MĮ-NOŬS, *a.* Consisting of many volumes.
VQ-LŬ'MĮ-NOŬS-LY, *ad.* In many volumes.
VQ-LŬ'MĮ-NOŲS-NĔSS, *n.* State of being voluminous.
VŎL'ŲN-TẠ-RĮ-LY, *ad.* Of one's own accord.
VŎL'ŲN-TẠ-RĮ-NĔSS, *n.* State of being voluntary.
VŎL'ŲN-TẠ-RY, *a.* Acting without compulsion. or by choice; spontaneous. [will.
VŎL'ŲN-TẠ RY, *n.* An air or music played at
VŎL-ŲN-TĒÊR', *n.* A person, as a soldier, who serves of his own accord.
VŎL-ŲN-TĒÊR', *v. n. & a.* To engage in service voluntarily; to act or offer voluntarily.
VQ-LŬP'TŲ-Ạ-RY, *n.* A man given up to pleasure; a sensualist; an epicure. [rious.
VQ-LŬP'TŲ-OŬS, *a.* Given to pleasure; luxu-
VQ-LŬP'TŲ-OŬS-LY, *ad.* In a voluptuous manner.
VQ-LŬP'TŲ-OŲS-NĔSS, *n.* Love of pleasure. [ner.
VQ-LŪTE', *n.* A member of a column.

VŎM'IT, v. a. & n. To throw up from the stomach.
VŎM'IT, n. Matter thrown up:—an emetic.
VQ-MĬ''TIQN (vq-mǐsh'un), n. Act of vomiting.
VŎM'I-TĬVE, a. Emetic; causing vomits.
VŎM'I-TQ-RY, a. Procuring vomits; emetic.
VQ-RĀ'CIOUS (vq-rā'shus), a. Greedy; ravenous.
VQ-RĀ'CIOUS-LY, ad. Greedily; ravenously.
VQ-RĀ'CIOUS-NĔSS, VQ-RĂÇ'I-TY, n. Greediness.
VQ-RĂG'I-NOŬS, a. Full of gulfs or whirlpools.
VŎR'TĔX, n. [L.] pl. VŎR'TI-CĔS. A whirlpool; a whirl:—a whirlwind.
VŎR'TI-CAL, a. Having a whirling motion.
VŌ'TA-RĔSS, n. A female votary.
VŌ'TA-RY, n. One devoted to any service, &c.
VŌ'TA-RY, a. Consequent to a vow; devoted.
VŌTE, n. A suffrage; a ballot; a voice given.
VŌTE, v. a. & n. To choose by suffrage; to ballot.
VŌT'ER, n. One who votes or has a right to vote.
VŌ'TIVE, a. Given by vow.
VŎUCH, v. a. To obtest; to attest; to declare.
VŎUCH, v. n. To bear witness; to testify.
VŎUCH, n. A warrant; an attestation.
VŎUCH'ER, n. One who, or that which, vouches.

VŎUCH-SĀFE', v. a. & n. To condescend; to grant.
VŎW, n. A solemn, religious promise. [grant.
VŎW, v. a. To consecrate; to devote.
VŎW, v. n. To make vows or solemn promises.
VŎW'EL, n. A letter which can be uttered by itself alone; as a, e, i, o, u.
VŎW'ELLED (vŏŭ'eld), a. Furnished with vowels.
VŎY'AGE, n. A passing or journey by sea. [els.
VŎY'AGE, v. n. To travel by sea.
VŎY'A-GER, n. One who travels by sea.
VŬL'CAN-ĪZE, v. a. To combine with sulphur by heat, as caoutchouc.
VŬL'GAR, a. Common; mean; low; rustic; rude.
VŬL'GAR, n. The common people. [rude.
VŬL'GAR-ĬSM, n. A vulgar phrase or expression.
VUL-GĂR'I-TY, n. Grossness; rudeness of manners.
VŬL'GAR-LY, ad. Commonly; rudely. [ners.
VŬL'GATE, n. Ancient Latin version of the Bible.
VŬL'NER-A-BLE, a. That may be wounded. [ble.
VŬL'NER-A-RY, a. Useful in the cure of wounds.
VŬL'PINE, a. Belonging to a fox; crafty.
VŬLT'URE (vŭlt'yur), n. A large bird of prey.
VŬLT'U-RINE, a. Belonging to a vulture.
VŬLT'U-ROŬS, a. Like a vulture; rapacious.

W.

W is sometimes used in diphthongs as a vowel, for u, as in view, strew. The sound of w consonant is uniform. [side.
WAB'BLE (wŏb'bl), v. n. To move from side to
WĂCKE (wăk'e or wăk), n. A kind of rock.
WAD (wŏd), n. A little mass of tow, paper, &c.
WAD (wŏd), v. a. To stuff with a wad or wadding.
WAD'DING (wŏd'ding), n. A soft stuffing for garments:—any thing stuffed in; wad.
WAD'DLE (wŏd'dl), v. n. To walk like a duck.
WĀDE, v. n. To walk, as through water.
WĀ'FER, n. A thin cake:—a paste for sealing
WAF'FLE (wŏf'fl), n. A sort of thin cake. [letters.
WĂFT, v. a. To carry through; to buoy.
WĂFT, v. n. To float; to swim; to fly.
WĂFT, n. A floating body:—motion of a flag.
WĂFT'ER, n. A passage-boat:—one who wafts.
WĂG, v. a. To move lightly; to shake slightly.
WĂG, v. n. To be in motion; to go; to pack off.
WĂG, n. One full of low humor; a humorist.
WĂGE, v. a. To make; to carry on; to stake.
WĀ'GER, n. A bet; pledge; any thing pledged:—an offer to make oath.
WĀ'GER, v. a. & n. To lay; to pledge as a bet.
WĀ'GER-ER, n. One who bets; one who wagers.
WĀ'GES, n. pl. Hire or reward paid for services.
WĂG'GER-Y, n. Mischievous merriment; sport.
WĂG'GISH, a. Merrily mischievous; frolicsome.
WĂG'GISH-LY, ad. In a waggish manner.
WĂG'GISH-NĔSS, n. Merry mischief.
WĂG'GLE, v. n. To move from side to side.
||WĂG'ON, or WĂG'GON, n. A four-wheeled carriage or vehicle.
||WĂG'ON-AGE, n. Money paid for carriage.
||WĂG'ON-ER, n. One who drives a wagon.
WĂG'TAIL, n. A sort of bird. [owner.
WĀIF, n. Any thing found astray without an

WĀIL, v. a. & n. To lament; to grieve.
WĀIL, WĀIL'ING, n. Audible sorrow; lamentation.
WĀIL'FŬL, a. Sorrowful; mournful. [tation.
WĀIN, n. A carriage; a sort of wagon.
WĀIN'RŌPE, n. A large cord; a cart-rope.
WĀIN'SCOT, n. The inner covering of a room.
WĀIN'SCOT, v. a. To line walls with boards.
WĀIST, n. The middle part of the body. [&c.
WĀIST'BAND, n. The upper part of the breeches,
WĀIST'COAT (wās'kot or wĕs'kot), n. An inner garment; a part of a man's dress; a vest.
WĀIT, v. n. & a. To expect, stay, attend, watch.
WĀIT, n. Ambush; as, to lie in wait.
WĀIT'ER, n. An attendant; a servant:—a tray.
WĀIT'ING-MĀID, n. A female attendant.
WĀIVE, v. a. To put off; to defer; to forego.
WĀKE, v. n. To watch; to cease to sleep.
WĀKE, v. a. To rouse from sleep; to excite.
WĀKE, n. A feast; watch; vigils:—track in
WĀKE'FŬL, a. Not sleeping; vigilant. [water.
WĀKE'FŬL-NĔSS, n. Forbearance of sleep.
WĀ'KEN (wā'kn), v. a. & n. To rouse; to wake.
WĀLE, n. A ridge; streak; mark of a stripe.
WÂLK (wâwk), v. n. To go on foot; to move.
WÂLK (wâwk), v. a. To pass through; to lead.
WÂLK (wâwk), n. Act of walking; gait; way.
WÂLK'ER (wâwk'er), n. One that walks.
WÂLL, n. A series of brick or stone raised up for an enclosure:—side of a room.
WÂLL, v. a. To enclose with a wall; to defend.
WAL'LET (wŏl'let), n. A bag:—a knapsack.
WÂLL'-EYE (wâl'ī), n. A disease of the eye.
WÂLL'-EYED (wâl'īd), a. Having white eyes.
WÂLL'-FLŎW-ER, n. An ornamental plant.
WÂLL'-FRŬIT, n. Fruit planted against a wall.
WAL'LOP (wŏl'lup), v. n. To boil:—to beat.
WAL'LOW (wŏl'lō), v. n. & a. To roll in mire, &c.

WAL'LŌW (wŏl'lō), *n.* A kind of rolling walk.
WÅLL'WORT (wâl'würt), *n.* The dwarf elder.
WÅL'NŲT, *n.* A tree, and its fruit.
WÅL'RŲS, *n.* The morse or sea-horse.
WALTZ (wŏltz), *n.* A sort of German dance.
WAM'BLE (wŏm'bl), *v. n.* To roll with nausea.
WÂM'PŲM, *n.* Shells or strings of shells used by the American Indians for money.
WAN (wŏn), *a.* Pale and sickly; languid of look.
WAND (wŏnd), *n.* A stick; a long rod; a staff.
WAN'DĘR (wŏn'dęr), *v. n.* To rove; to ramble.
WAN'DĘR-ĘR (wŏn'dęr-), *n.* A rover; rambler.
WAN'DĘR-ĬNG (wŏn'dęr-ĭng), *n.* Aberration.
WĀNE, *v. n.* To grow less; to decrease.
WĀNE, *n.* The decrease of the moon; decline.
WAN'NĘSS (wŏn'nęs), *n.* Paleness; languor.
WANT (wŏnt), *v. a.* Not to have; to need, wish.
WANT (wŏnt), *v. n.* To lack; to be deficient.
WANT (wŏnt), *n.* Need; deficiency; poverty.
WAN'TǪN (wŏn'tųn), *a.* Licentious; gay; airy.
WAN'TǪN (wŏn'tųn), *n.* A strumpet:—a trifler.
WAN'TǪN (wŏn'tųn), *v. n.* To play; to revel.
WAN'TǪN-LY (wŏn'tųn-lę), *ad.* In a wanton manner; gayly; sportively. [ness.
WAN'TǪN-NĚSS (wŏn'tųn-nĕs), *n.* Sportive-
WÂR, *n.* Open hostility between nations.
WÂR, *v. n.* To make war; to contend. [sing.
WÂR'BLE, *v. a. & n.* To quaver; to carol; to
WÂR'BLE, *n.* A song; the singing of birds :—a tumor in the hide of oxen, &c.
WÂR'BLĘR, *n.* A singer; a songster.
WÂRD, *v. a.* To guard; to watch; to defend.
WÂRD, *v. n.* To be vigilant; to keep guard.
WÂRD, *n.* A garrison; a fortress; a district of a town :—custody :—one under a guardian.
WÂR'DEN (wâr'dn), *n.* A keeper; a guardian.
WÂR'DEN-SHĬP, *n.* The office of a warden.
WÂRD'ĘR, *n.* A keeper; a guard :—truncheon.
WÂRD'RŌBE, *n.* A room where clothes are kept :—clothes; garments; wearing apparel.
WÂRD'-RŌÔM, *n.* A room in ships of war.
WÂRD'SHĬP, *n.* Guardianship; pupilage.
WÂRE, *n.* Commodity; something to be sold.
WÂRE'HŌÛSE, *n.* A storehouse for merchandise.
WÂR'FÂRE, *n.* Military service; strife. [dently.
WÂR'Ĭ-LY *or* WĀ'RĬ-LY, *ad.* Cautiously; pru-
WÂR'LĪKE, *a.* Military; relating to war.
WÂRM, *a.* Not cold; zealous; ardent; keen.
WÂRM, *v. a. & n.* To heat moderately.
WÂRM'ĬNG-PĂN, *n.* A pan for warming a bed.
WÂRM'LY, *ad.* With gentle heat; ardently.
WÂRMTH, *n.* Gentle heat; ardor; zeal.
WÂRN, *v. a.* To caution; to admonish.
WÂRN'ĬNG, *n.* A caution; a previous notice.
WÂRP, *n.* Thread that crosses the woof :—a rope.
WÂRP, *v. a. & n.* To contract; to shrivel :—to
WÂR'-PRŌÔF, *n.* Valor proved by war. [turn.
WAR'RĄNT (wŏr'rąnt), *v. n.* To support; to authorize; to justify; to secure.
WAR'RĄNT (wŏr'rąnt), *n.* A commission; a grant; authority :—a writ for arrest.
WAR'RĄNT-Ą-BLE (wŏr'rąnt-ą-bl), *a.* Justifiable.
WAR'RĄNT-Ą-BLE-NĔSS, *n.* Justifiableness.
WAR'RĄNT-Ą-BLY (wŏr'rąnt-ą-blę), *ad.* Justi-fiably. [a warranty is given.
WAR-RĄNT-ĒĒ' (wŏr-rąnt-ē'), *n.* One to whom
WAR'RĄNT-ĘR (wŏr'rąnt-ęr), WAR-RĄNT-ÖR', *n.* One who warrants.

WAR'RĄN-TY (wŏr'rąn-tę), *n.* Deed of security.
WAR'RĘN (wŏr'ręn), *n.* An enclosure for rabbits.
WAR'RĘN-ĘR (wŏr'ręn-ęr), *n.* The keeper of a warren. [man.
WÂR'RIǪR (wâr'yųr), *n.* A soldier; a military
WÂRT, *n.* A small protuberance on the flesh.
WÂRT'Y, *a.* Grown over with, or like, warts.
WÂR'-WHÔÔP, *n.* An Indian yell of war.
WÂR'WŌRN, *a.* Worn with war.
WÂR'Y *or* WĀ'RY, *a.* Cautious; scrupulous;
WAȘ (wŏz), *i.* from *be.* [prudent.
WASH (wŏsh), *v. a.* To cleanse with water, &c. :—to moisten :—to color superficially.
WASH (wŏsh), *v. n.* To perform ablution.
WASH (wŏsh), *n.* Alluvion; a marsh; a fen; a lotion :—feed of hogs :—the act of washing.
WASH'BÅLL (wŏsh'bâl), *n.* A ball of soap.
WASH'ĘR (wŏsh'ęr), *n.* One that washes :—a movable ring on the axis of a wheel.
WASH'ĘR-WOM'ĄN (wŏsh'ęr-wûm'ąn), *n.* A woman who washes clothes.
WASH'PǑT (wŏsh'pǒt), *n.* A vessel for washing.
WASH'Y (wŏsh'ę), *a.* Watery; damp; weak.
WASP (wŏsp), *n.* A stinging insect.
WASP'ĬSH (wŏsp'ĭsh), *a.* Peevish; petulant.
WASP'ĬSH-LY (wŏ·p'ĭsh-lę), *ad.* Peevishly.
WASP'ĬSH-NĚSS (wŏsp'ĭsh-nĕs), *n.* Peevishness.
WAS'SAĬL (wŏs'sĭl), *v. n.* To drink; to carouse.
WAS'SAĬL (wŏs'sĭl), *n.* Liquor made of apples and ale :—a carousal :—a song.
WAS'SAĬL-ĘR (wŏs'sĭl-ęr), *n.* A carouser.
WAST (wŏst). Second person singular of *was.*
WĀSTE, *v. a.* To diminish; to squander.
WĀSTE, *v. n.* To dwindle; to be consumed.
WĀSTE, *a.* Desolate; uncultivated; worthless.
WĀSTE, *n.* Loss; useless expense; desolate tract.
WĀSTE'FÛL, *a.* Destructive; lavish; prodigal.
WĀSTE'FÛL-LY, *ad.* With useless comsumption.
WĀSTE'FÛL-NĔSS, *n.* Prodigality; extravagance.
WATCH (wŏch), *n.* Attention; guard :—a period of the night :—a pocket timepiece.
WATCH (wŏch), *v. n.* To wake; to keep guard.
WATCH (wŏch), *v. a.* To guard; to observe.
WATCH'ĘR (wŏch'ęr), *n.* One who watches.
WATCH'FÛL (wŏch'fûl), *a.* Vigilant; attentive.
WATCH'FÛL-LY (wŏch'fûl-lę), *ad.* Vigilantly.
WATCH'FÛL-NĔSS (wŏch'fûl-nĕs), *n.* Vigilance.
WATCH'-HŌÛSE (wŏch'hŏûs), *n.* A place where a watch or guard is set :—a lock-up.
WATCH'-MĀK-ĘR (wŏch'māk-ęr), *n.* A maker of watches :—a repairer of watches.
WATCH'MĄN (wŏch'mąn), *n.* A guard; sentinel.
WATCH'-TŌW-ĘR (wŏch'tŏû-ęr), *n.* A tower on which a sentinel is placed to keep guard.
WATCH'WORD (wŏch'würd), *n.* The word given to sentinels to know their friends.[mond.
WÂ'TĘR, *n.* A fluid; the sea :—lustre of a dia-
WÂ'TĘR, *v. a.* To irrigate; to supply with water.
WÂ'TĘR, *v. n.* To shed moisture; to take in wa-
WÂ'TĘR-BEÂR'ĘR, *n.* The sign *Aquarius.* [ter.
WÂ'TĘR-CǑL'ǪR, *n.* Color mixed with gum-
WÂ'TĘR-CŌURSE, *n.* Channel for water.[water.
WÂ'TĘR-CRĔSS, *n.* A plant used as a salad.
WÂ'TĘR-FÅLL, *n.* A cataract; a cascade.
WÂ'TĘR-FÖWL, *n.* A fowl that frequents water.
WÂ'TĘR-GÂUĢE, *n.* An instrument to measure water. [in water.
WÂ'TĘR-GRÙ'ĘL, *n.* Food made of meal boiled

WÂ′TĘR-Į-NĔSS, *n.* Humidity; moisture.
WÂ′TĘR-ĬNG-PLĀCE, *n.* A place resorted to on account of mineral water or for pleasure.
WÂ′TĘR-ĬSH, *a.* Resembling water; watery.
WÂ′TĘR-LĪNE, *n.* A line distinguishing that part of a ship under water from that which is above.
WÂ′TĘR-LŎGGED (-lŏgd), *a.* (*Naut.*) Noting a vessel when leaky and unmanageable.
WÂ′TĘR-MĂN, *n.* A ferryman; a boatman.
WÂ′TĘR-MĂRK, *n.* Mark of the rise of water: —a manufacturer's mark on paper.
WÂ′TĘR-MĔL-ǪN, *n.* A plant, and its fruit.
WÂ′TĘR-MĬLL, *n.* A mill turned by water.
WÂ′TĘR-RĂM, *n.* A machine for raising water.
WÂ′TĘR-SHĔD, *n.* An elevated line or ridge of land between two river-basins.
WÂ′TĘR-SPŎŪT, *n.* An aqueous meteor. [ter.
WÂ′TĘR-TĪGHT (wâ′tęr-tīt), *a.* Excluding wa-
WÂ′TĘR-WHĒĔL, *n.* A wheel turned by water.
WÂ′TĘR-WŎRKS, *n. pl.* Hydraulic engines or structures:—artificial spouts of water.
WÂ′TĘR-Y, *a.* Thin; liquid; like water; wet.
WAT′TLE (wŏt′tl), *n.* A barb; a twig; a hurdle.
WAT′TLE (wŏt′tl), *v. a.* To bind with twigs.
WĀVE, *n.* A billow; swell of water; inequality.
WĀVE, *v. n.* To play loosely; to float, undulate.
WĀVE, *v. a.* To make uneven; to waft; to put
WĀVE′LĘSS, *a.* Smooth; without waves. [off.
WĀ′VĘR, *v. n.* To be unsettled; to fluctuate.
WĀ′VĘR-ĘR, *n.* One who wavers.
WĀ′VY, *a.* Rising in waves; playing to and fro.
WÂWL, WÂUL, *v. n.* To cry; to howl.
WĂX, *n.* A thick, tenacious substance.
WĂX, *v. a.* To smear or to join with wax.
WĂX, *v. n.* [*imp. t.* waxed; *pp.* waxen *or* waxed.] To grow; to increase; to become.
WĂX′EN (wăk′sn), *a.* Made of wax.
WĂX′WORK (-würk), *n.* Figures formed of wax.
WĂX′Y, *a.* Soft like wax; yielding.
WĂY, *n.* A road; a passage:—course; direction:—room:—manner:—means; method.
WĀY′FĂR-ĘR, *n.* A passenger; a traveller. [ney.
WĀY′FĂR-ĬNG, *a.* Travelling; being on a jour-
WĀY′LĀY *or* WĀY-LĀY′, *v. a.* To beset by the
WĀY′LĘSS, *a.* Pathless; untracked. [way.
WĀY′WĄRD, *a.* Froward; liking one's own way.
WĀY′WĄRD-LY, *ad.* Frowardly; perversely.
WĀY′WĄRD-NĔSS, *n.* Frowardness; perverse-
WĒ, *pron.* The plural of *I.* [ness.
WĒAK, *a.* Having little strength; feeble; not strong; infirm; pliant; indiscreet; simple.
WĒAK′EN (wē′kn), *v. a.* To make weak.
WĒAK′EN (wē′kn), *v. n.* To become weak.
WĒAK′EN-ĘR (wē′kn-ęr), *n.* One that weakens.
WĒAK′LĬNG, *n.* A feeble creature.
WĒAK′LY, *ad.* Feebly; faintly:—indiscreetly.
WĒAK′LY, *a.* Not strong; not healthy; feeble.
WĒAK′NĔSS, *n.* Feebleness; infirmity; defect.
WĒAK′-SĪDE, *n.* A foible; failing; infirmity.
WĒAL, *n.* Happiness; prosperity; welfare:— a mark; a stripe; wale.
WĔALTH (wĕlth), *n.* Riches; opulence.
WĔALTH′Į-LY (wĕlth′ę-lę), *ad.* Richly.
WĔALTH′Į-NĔSS (wĕlth′ę-nĕs), *n.* Richness.
WĔALTH′Y, *a.* Rich; opulent; abundant.
WĒAN, *v. a.* To put from the breast; to detach.
WĒAN′LĬNG, *n.* A child newly weaned.

WĔAP′ǪN (wĕp′pn), *n.* An instrument of offence or defence; a sword, musket, &c.
WĔAP′ǪN-LĔSS (wĕp′pn-lĕs), *a.* Unarmed.
WEĂR (wår), *v. a.* [*imp. t.* wore; *pp.* worn.] To waste; to consume:—to carry on the body.
WEĂR (wår), *v. n.* To be wasted or consumed.
WEĂR (wår), *n.* Act of wearing:—a dam; a net.
WĒA′RĮ-NĔSS (wē′rę-nĕs), *n.* Lassitude; fatigue.
WĒA′RĮ-SŎME (wē′rę-sŭm), *a.* Tedious; tiresome; troublesome. [ly.
WĒA′RĮ-SŎME-LY (wē′rę-sŭm-lę), *ad.* Tedious-
WĒA′RĮ-SŎME-NĔSS, *n.* Tiresomeness.
WĒA′RY (wē′rę), *a.* Subdued by fatigue; tired.
WĒA′RY (wē′rę), *v. a.* To tire; to fatigue.
WĒA′SAND (wē′znd), *n.* The windpipe.
WĒA′SEL (wē′zl), *n.* An animal that kills mice.
WĔATH′ĘR (wĕth′ęr), *n.* The state of the air with respect to heat, cold, dryness, rain, &c.
WĔATH′ĘR, *v. a.* To pass through; to endure.
WĔATH′ĘR-BĔAT′EN (wĕth′ęr-bē′tn), *a.* Harassed, seasoned, or tarnished by hard weather.
WĔATH′ĘR-CŎCK, *n.* A vane:—a fickle person.
WĔATH′ĘR-GĀGE, *n.* The advantage of the wind:—advantage of position. [mometer.
WĔATH′ĘR-GLĂSS, *n.* A barometer; a ther-
WĔATH′ĘR-WĪSE, *a.* Skilful in the weather.
WĔAVE, *v. a.* [*imp. t.* wove *or* weaved; *pp.* woven *or* weaved.] To form by texture; to in-
WĔAVE, *v. n.* To work with a loom. [sert.
WĔAV′ĘR, *n.* One who weaves.
WĔB, *n.* Any thing woven:—a film; a membrane.
WĔBBED (wĕbd), *a.* Joined by a web. [brane.
WĔB′-FOOT-ĘD (wĕb′fŭt-ęd), *a.* Palmiped.
WĔD, *v. a. & n.* To marry; to join in marriage.
WĔD′DĘD, *a.* Belonging to matrimony. [riage.
WĔD′DĬNG, *n.* A marriage; nuptial ceremony.
WĔDGE, *n.* A body with an edge:—a mass.
WĔDGE, *v. a.* To fasten by wedges:—to force.
WĔD′LŎCK, *n.* State of marriage; matrimony.
WĔDNĔS′DAY (wĕnz′dę), *n.* 4th day of the week.
WĒED, *n.* A noxious plant:—mourning dress.
WĒED, *v. a.* To rid of weeds:—to root out.
WĒED′Y, *a.* Abounding with or having weeds.
WĒEK, *n.* The space of seven days.
WĒEK′DAY, *n.* Any day not Sunday.
WĒEK′LY, *a.* Happening or done once a week.
WĒEK′LY, *ad.* Once a week.
WĒEN, *v. n.* To think; to imagine; to fancy.
WĒEP, *v. n.* [*imp. t. & pp.* wept.] To shed tears; to lament; to bewail; to bemoan.
WĒEP, *v. a.* To lament; to bemoan.
WĒEP′ĘR, *n.* One who weeps.
WĒE′VIL (wē′vl), *n.* An insect injurious to grain.
WĔFT, *n.* The woof of cloth. [grain.
WEIGH (wā), *v. a.* To examine by balance; to raise; to balance:—to ponder; to consider.
WEIGH (wā), *v. n.* To have weight; to press.
WEIGH′ĘR (wā′ęr), *n.* One who weighs.
WEIGHT (wāt), *n.* The heaviness of any thing; a ponderous mass; gravity; importance.
WEIGHT′Į-LY (wā′tę-lę), *ad.* With weight.
WEIGHT′Į-NĔSS (wā′tę-nĕs), *n.* Ponderosity.
WEIGHT′Y (wā′tę), *a.* Heavy:—important.
WĒIRD (wērd), *a.* Skilled in witchcraft.
WĔL′CǪME (wĕl′kųm), *a.* Admitted willingly.
WĔL′CǪME, *interj.* A form of salutation.
WĔL′CǪME, *n.* Kind reception of a guest.
WĔL′CǪME, *v. a.* To salute with kindness.

WĔL′COM-ĘR, *n.* One who welcomes.
WĔLD, *v. a.* To beat into firm union.
WĔL′FÀRE, *n.* Happiness; success; prosperity.
WĔL′KĮN, *n.* The visible regions of the air.
WĔLL, *n.* A deep, narrow pit of water:—foun-
WĔLL, *v. n.* To spring; to issue forth. [tain.
WĔLL, *a.* Being in health; fortunate; happy.
WĔLL, *ad.* Not ill; properly; not amiss.
WĔLL′Ą-DĀY, *interj.* Expressing grief; alas!
WĔLL′-BĒ-ĮNG, *n.* Happiness; prosperity.
WĔLL′-BÖRN, *a.* Not meanly descended.
WĔLL′-BRĔD, *a.* Elegant of manners; polite.
WĔLL-DŌNE′,*interj.*Denoting praise or surprise.
WĔLL-FĀ′VQRED (wĕl-fā′vurd), *a.* Beautiful.
WĔLL-MĒAN′ĮNG,*a.* Having a good intention.
WĔLL-MĔT′, *interj.* A term of salutation.
WĔLL′-NĪGH (wĕl′nī), *ad.* Almost; nearly.
WĔLL′-SPĔNT, *a.* Passed with virtue or benefit.
WĔLL-SPŌ′KEN (wĕl-spō′kn), *a.* Speaking well.
WĔLL′SPRĬNG, *n.* A fountain; a source.
WĔLL-WĬSH′ĘR, *n.* One who wishes good.
WĔLSH, *a.* Relating to Wales or the people of
  Wales.   [people of Wales.
WĔLSH, *n.* The language of Wales.—*pl.* The
WĔLT, *n.* A border; a guard; an edging.
WĔLT, *v. a.* To sew any thing with a border.
WĔL′TĘR, *v. n.* To roll in blood, water, or mire.
WĔN, *n.* A fleshy or callous excrescence.
WĔNCH, *n.* A young woman:—a strumpet.
WĔNCH, *v. n.* To frequent loose women.
WĔN′NY, *a.* Having the nature of a wen.
WĔNT, *imp. t.* from *go.*
WĔPT, *imp. t. & pp.* from *weep.*
WĒRE (wẽr), *imp. t. pl.* from *be.*
WĔRT, the second person singular of the sub-
  junctive imperfect from *be.*
WĔST, *n.* The region where the sun sets.
WĔST, *a.* Being towards or coming from the
WĔST′ĘR-LY, *a.* Being towards the west. [west.
WĔST′ĘRN, *a.* Being in or towards the west.
WĔST′WĄRD, *ad.* Towards the west.
WĔST′WĄRD-LY,*ad.* With tendency to the west.
WĔT, *n.* Water; humidity:—rainy weather.
WĔT, *a.* Humid; moist; rainy; watery.
WĔT, *v. a.* [*imp. t. & pp.* wet *or* wetted.] To
WĔTH′ĘR, *n.* A castrated ram.   [moisten.
WĔT′NĘSS,*n.* The state of being wet; humidity.
WHĀLE, *n.* The largest of marine animals.
WHĀLE′BŌNE (hwāl′bōn), *n.* The horny, elastic
  substance in the jaw of the whale.   [large.
WHAP′PĘR (hwŏp′per), *n.* Something very
WHÂRF, *n.; pl.* WHÂRFS *or* WHÂRVĘṢ. A
  place to land goods at; a sort of quay.
WHÂRF′AĢE, *n.* Fee for landing at a wharf.
WHÂRF′ĮN-ĢĘR,*n.* One who attends a wharf.
WHAT (hwŏt),*pron.* That which; which part.
WHAT-ĔV′ĘR   } (hwŏt-), *pron.* Being this
WHAT-SQ-ĔV′ĘR, } or that.
WHĔAL, *n.* A pustule; a pimple.
WHĔAT, *n.* The finest kind of grain.
WHĔAT′EN (hwē′tn), *a.* Made of wheat. [ter.
WHĒĒ′DLE,*v. a.* To entice by soft words; to flat-
WHĒĒL, *n.* A circular body; a circle.
WHĒĒL,*v. n.* To move on wheels; to turn round.
WHĒĒL, *v. a.* To move on wheels; to roll.
WHĒĒL′BĂR-RŌW,*n.* Carriage with one wheel.
WHĒĒL′WRĬGHT (-rīt), *n.* A maker of wheels.
WHĒĒL′Y, *a.* Circular; suitable to rotation.

WHĒĒZE, *v. n.* To breathe with noise.
WHĔLK, *n.* A stripe; a pustule:—a mollusk.
WHĔLM,*v. a.* To cover with water; to immerse.
WHĔLP, *n.* The young of a dog, lion, &c.
WHĔLP, *v. n.* To bring young, as beasts.
WHĔN, *ad.* At the time that; at what time.
WHĔNCE, *ad.* From what place, source, &c.
WHĔNCE-SQ-ĔV′ĘR,*ad.*From what place soever.
WHĔN-ĔV′ĘR,   } *ad.* At whatever time.
WHĔN-SQ-ĔV′ĘR, }
WHĒRE (hwâr), *ad.* At which or what place.
WHÊRE′Ą-BÖÛT, } *ad.* Near what or which
WHÊRE′Ą-BÖÛTS, } place.
WHÊRE-ĂṢ′, *ad.* The thing being so that.
WHÊRE-ĂT′, *ad.* At which; at what.
WHÊRE-BȲ′, *ad.* By which; by what.
WHÊRE′FŌRE, *ad.* For which reason; why.
WHÊRE-ĬN′, *ad.* In which; in what.
WHÊRE-ĮN-TÔ′, *ad.* Into which.
WHÊRE-ŌF′, *ad.* Of which; of what. [upon.
WHÊRE-ŎN′, *ad.* On which; on what; where-
WHÊRE-SQ-ĔV′ĘR, *ad.* In what place soever.
WHÊRE-TÔ′, WHÊRE-ŲN-TÔ′, *ad.* To which.
WHÊRE-ŲP-ŎN′, *ad.* Upon which; whereon.
WHÊR-ĔV′ĘR, *ad.* At whatever place. [which.
WHÊRE-WĬTH′, WHÊRE-WĬTH-ÂL′, *ad.* With
WHĔR′RY, *n.* A light boat used on rivers, &c.
WHĔT, *v. a.* To sharpen; to edge; to provoke.
WHĔT, *n.* Act of sharpening; what makes hun-
WHĔTH′ĘR,*conj.* A particle answered by *or.*[gry.
WHĔTH′ĘR, *pron.* Which of two.
WHĔT′STŌNE, *n.* A sharpening stone.
WHEY (hwā), *n.* The thin part of milk. [whey.
WHEY′EY (hwā′e), WHEY′ĬSH (hwā′-), *a.* Like
WHĬCH, *pron. rel.* Relating to things.   [er.
WHĬCH-SQ-ĔV′ĘR,*pron.*Whether one or the oth-
WHĬFF, *n.* A blast; a puff of wind or smoke.
WHĬF′FLE,*v.n.*To move inconstantly; to shuffle.
WHĬF′FLE-TRĒĒ, *n.* See WHIPPLETREE.
WHĬG, *n.* One of the party opposed to Tory.
WHĬG′ĢĘR-Y, *n.* The principles of the Whigs.
WHĬG′ĢĬSH, *a.* Relating to the whigs.
WHĬG′ĢĬSM, *n.* Whiggery.
WHĪLE, *n.* A time; a space of time.
WHĪLE, *v. n.* To loiter.—*v. a.* To draw out.
WHĪLE, WHĪLST, *ad.* During the time.
†WHĪ′LQM, *ad.* Formerly; once; of old.
WHĬM, *n.* A freak; an odd fancy; a caprice.
WHĬM′PĘR, *v. n.* To cry without any loud noise.
WHĬM′PĘR-ĬNG, *n.* A small cry; a squeak.
WHĬM′ṢEY (hwĭm′ze), *n.* A freak; a whim.
WHĬM′ṢĮ-CĄL, *a.* Freakish; oddly fanciful.
WHĬM′ṢĮ-CĄL-LY, *ad.* So as to be oddly fanciful.
WHĬM′ṢĮ-CĄL-NĔSS,*n.* State of being whimsical.
WHĬM′WHĂM, *n.* A gewgaw; a trifle; a freak.
WHĬN, *n.* Furze; gorse:—whinstone.
WHĪNE, *v. n.* To lament plaintively; to moan.
WHĪNE, *n.* A plaintive noise; mean complaint.
WHĪN′ĘR,*n.* One who whines; a grumbler.
WHĬN′NY, *v. n.* To make a noise like a horse.
WHĬN′STŌNE, *n.* Trap-rock.
WHĬP, *v. a.* To strike with a lash:—to sew.
WHĬP, *v. n.* To move nimbly; to run.
WHĬP, *n.* An instrument of correction; a lash.
WHĬP′CÖRD, *n.* Cord of which lashes are made.
WHĬP′HĂND, *n.* An advantage over another.
WHĬP′LĂSH,*n.* The lash or small end of a whip.
WHĬP′PĘR, *n.*One who punishes with whipping.

WHĬP′PĬNG, *n.* Correction with a whip. [inals.
WHĬP′PĬNG-PŌST, *n.* A post for whipping crim-
WHĬP′PLE-TREĒ, *n.* A bar to which the traces
   of a harness are fastened.
WHĬP′PÔÔR-WĬLL, *n.* A species of bird.
WHĬP′SÂW, *n.* A large saw used by two persons.
WHĬP′STĘR, *n.* A nimble fellow; a sharper.
WHĬP′STŎCK, *n.* The handle of a whip. [hurry.
WHĬR, *v. n.* To fly or turn rapidly.—*v. a.* To
WHĬRL, *v. a.* & *n.* To turn round rapidly.
WHĬRL, *n.* A quick rotation; a circular motion.
WHĬRL′BŌNE, *n.* The patella; the kneepan.
WHĬRL′Ị-GĬG, *n.* A toy which children spin
   round.   [vortex.
WHĬRL′PÔÔL, *n.*   Water moving circularly;
WHĬRL′WĬND, *n.* Stormy wind, moving circular-
WHĬR′RĬNG, *n.* Noise made by a bird's wing. [ly.
WHĬSK, *n.* A small brush or broom:—a sweep-
   ing motion:—a cooper's plane.
WHĬSK, *v. a.* & *n.* To sweep; to move nimbly.
WHĬS′KĘR, *n.* Hair growing on the cheek.
WHĬS′KĘRED (hwĭs′kerd), *a.* Having whiskers.
WHĬS′KEY, *n.* A spirit distilled from grain.
WHĬS′PĘR, *v. n.* To speak with a low voice.
WHĬS′PĘR, *v. a.* To utter in a low voice.
WHĬS′PĘR, *n.* A low voice; cautious speech.
WHĬS′PĘR-ĘR, *n.* One that whispers; a tattler.
WHĬS′PĘR-ĬNG, *n.* A backbiting; speaking low.
WHĬST, *n.* A game at cards.—*a.* Silent.—*interj.*
   Be still.   [sical sound by the breath; to blow.
WHĬS′TLE (hwĭs′sl), *v. n.* To form a kind of mu-
WHĬS′TLE (hwĭs′sl), *n.* A sound made by the
   breath, &c.:—a small wind instrument.
WHĬS′TLĘR (hwĭs′sler), *n.* One who whistles.
WHĬT, *n.* A point; a jot; a small part.
WHĪTE, *a.* Having the color of snow; pale; pure.
WHĪTE, *n.* Whiteness; any thing white.
WHĪTE-LĔAD′ (hwīt-lĕd′), *n.* Carbonate of lead.
WHĪTE′-LĬV-ĘRED (hwīt′lĭv-ęrd), *a.* Cowardly.
WHĪTE′MĒAT, *n.* Food of milk, butter, eggs, &c.
WHĪ′TEN (hwī′tn), *v. a.* To make white.
WHĪ′TEN (hwī′tn), *v. n.* To grow white.
WHĪ′TEN-ĘR (hwī′tn-er), *n.* One who whitens.
WHĪTE′NĘSS, *n.* State of being white; purity.
WHĪTE′SMĬTH, *n.* A worker in white iron.
WHĪTE′THŌRN, *n.* Common hawthorn.
WHĪTE′WASH, (-wŏsh), *n.* A wash for whitening.
WHĪTE′WASH (hwīt′wŏsh), *v. a.* To cover with
WHĬTH′ĘR, *ad.* To what place.   [whitewash.
WHĬTH-ĘR-SŌ-ĔV′ĘR, *ad.* To whatsoever place.
WHĪT′ĬNG, *n.* A sea-fish:—a soft chalk.
WHĪT′ĬSH, *a.* Somewhat white.   [um.
WHĬT′LĔATH-ĘR, *n.* Leather dressed with al-
WHĬT′LŌW, *n.* A tumor on a finger or toe.
WHĬT′SŬN-DAY,) *n.* The 7th Sunday after
WHĬT′SŬN-TĪDE,)   Easter, answering to Pen-
WHĬT′TLE, *n.* A sort of knife.   [tecost.
WHĬT′TLE, *v. a.* To cut with a knife.
WHĬZ, *v. n.* To make a loud, hissing noise.
WHĬZ, *n.* A loud humming or hissing noise.
WHŌ (hô), *pron. rel.* Applied to persons.
WHŌ-ĔV′ĘR (hô-ĕv′ęr), *pron.* Any one.
WHŌLE (hōl), *a.* All; total; complete; sound.
WHŌLE (hōl), *n.* The total; all of a thing.
WHŌLE′SĀLE, *n.* Sale in large quantities.
WHŌLE′SĀLE, *a.* Buying or selling in the lump.
WHŌLE′SǪME (hōl′sum), *a.* Sound; salutary.
WHŌLE′SǪME-LY, *ad.* Salubriously.

WHŌL′LY (hōl′le), *ad.* Completely; totally.
WHŌM (hôm). The objective case of *who.* [ever.
WHÔM-SǪ-ĔV′ĘR, *pron.* The objective of *whoso-*
WHÔÔP (hôp), *n.* A shout of pursuit.
WHÔÔT (hôt), *v. a.* To insult. See HOOT.
‖WHŌRE (hōr), *n.* A prostitute; a strumpet.
‖WHŌRE (hōr), *v. n.* To practise whoredom.
‖WHŌRE′DǪM (hōr′dųm), *n.* Fornication.
‖WHŌRE′MĀS-TĘR, WHŌRE′MŎN-ĢĘR, *n.* A
   lewd or licentious man; a fornicator.
‖WHŌR′ĬSH (hōr′ĭsh), *a.* Unchaste; incontinent.
WHŎR′TLE-BĔR-RY, *n.* A shrub and its fruit.
WHÔSE (hôz), *pron.* Possessive of *who* and *which.*
WHÔ-SǪ-ĔV′ĘR (hô-sǫ-ĕv′ęr), *pron.* Whoever.
WHŬR, *v. n.* To pronounce the letter *r* roughly.
WHȲ (hwī), *ad.* For what reason; for which.
WĬCK, *n.* The cotton of a candle or lamp.
WĬCK′ĘD, *a.* Given to vice; sinful; flagitious.
WĬCK′ĘD-LY, *ad.* Criminally; corruptly; badly.
WĬCK′ĘD-NĔSS, *n.* Sin; vice; guilt; moral ill.
WĬCK′ĘR, *a.* Made of small twigs or sticks.
WĬCK′ĘT, *n.* A small gate; door in a gate.
WĪDE, *a.* Broad; extended far each way; remote.
WĪDE, *ad.* At a distance; with great extent.
WĪDE′LY, *ad.* With great extent; remotely; far.
WĪ′DEN (-dn), *v. a.* & *n.* To make or grow wide.
WĪDE′NĘSS, *n.* Breadth; extent each way.
WĬD′ĢEON (wĭdj′ịn), *n.* A water-fowl.
WĬD′ŌW, *n.* A woman whose husband is dead.
WĬD′ŌW (wĭd′ō), *v. a.* To deprive of a husband.
WĬD′ŌW-ĘR, *n.* A man whose wife is dead.
WĬD′ǪW-HOOD (-ǫ-hûd), *n.* State of a widow.
WĬD′ǪW-WĀIL, *n.* A low, yellowish shrub.
WĬDTH, *n.* Breadth; wideness; broadness.
WIELD (wēld), *v. a.* To use with full power.
WIELD′Y (wēl′de), *a.* Manageable.
WĪFE, *n.*; *pl.* WĪVĘS. A married woman.
WĬG, *n.* False hair worn on the head:—a cake.
WĬGHT (wĭt), *n.* A person; a being.
WĬG′WÂM, *n.* An Indian's cabin or hut.
WĪLD, *a.* Not tame; desert; loose; disorderly.
WĪLD, *n.* A desert; a tract uncultivated.
WĬL′DĘR, *v. a.* To lose or puzzle; to bewilder.
WĬL′DĘR-NĔSS, *n.* A desert; a tract of solitude.
WĪLD′FĪRE, *n.* An inflammable composition.
WĪLD′FŎŴL, *n.* A fowl or bird of the forest.
WĪLD′GÔÔSE-CHĀSE′, *n.* A vain, foolish pur-
WĪLD′ĬNG, *n.* A wild, sour apple.   • [suit.
WĪLD′LY, *ad.* In a wild manner; disorderly.
WĪLD′NĔSS, *n.* State of being wild; rudeness.
WĪLE, *n.* A deceit; fraud; trick; stratagem.
WĬL′FŬL, *a.* Stubborn; obstinate; perverse.
WĬL′FŬL-LY, *ad.* Obstinately; by design.
WĬL′FŬL-NĔSS, *n.* Obstinacy; perverseness.
WĬ′LĮ-LY, *ad.* By stratagem; fradulently.
WĬ′LĮ-NĔSS, *n.* Cunning; guile; craftiness.
WĬLL, *n.* Faculty of choosing to do or forbear
   an action; choice:—command:—a testament.
WĬLL, *v. a.* To desire; to direct; to enjoin.
WĬLL, *v. auxiliary.* Used to form the future tense.
WĬLL′ĬNG, *a.* Inclined to any thing; desirous.
WĬLL′ĬNG-LY, *ad.* With one's own consent.
WĬLL′ĬNG-NĔSS, *n.* Consent; ready compliance.
WĬL′LŌW (wĭl′lō), *n.* A species of tree. [lows.
WĬL′LǪW-Y (wĭl′lǫ-e), *a.* Abounding with wil-
WĬLT, *v. n.* To wither; to droop.   [tle.
WĬ′LY, *a.* Cunning; sly; insidious; artful; sub-
WĬM′BLE, *n.* An instrument to bore holes.

MÎEN, SĬR; MÔVE, NŎR, SǪN; BŬLL, BÜR, RÛLE.—Ç, Ģ, *soft;* Ꝯ, Ꝣ, *hard;* Ş *as* Z; X *as* GZ; ꞦHIꜱ

WĬN, *v. a.* [*imp. t. & pp.* won.] To gain by conquest, play, &c.; to obtain; to procure. [back.
WĬNCE, WĬNCH, *v. a. & n.* To shrink or start
WĬNCH, *n.* A handle to turn a nut or screw.
WĬND, *n.* Air in motion :—breath.
WĬND, *v. a.* [*imp. t. & pp.* winded.] To ventilate.
WĪND, *v. a.* [*imp. t. & pp.* wound.] To turn; to twist :—to regulate in motion :—to embrace.
WĪND, *v. n.* To turn; to change; to move round.
WĬND'ĄGE, *n.* The difference between the diameter of the bore of a gun and that of the ball.
WĬND'BŎÛND, *a.* Confined by contrary winds.
WĬND'-ĔGG, *n.* An egg not impregnated.
WĬND'ĘR, *n.* He or that which winds. [tree.
WĬND'FÂLL, *n.* Fruit blown down from the
WĬND'FLŎW-ĘR, *n.* The anemone; a flower.
WĬND'GÂLL, *n.* A tumor on a horse's leg.
WĬND'-GŬN, *n.* A gun discharged by air; air-gun.
WĬND'Ĭ-NĔSS, *n.* The state of being full of wind.
WĪND'ĬNG, *n.* A flexure; a meander.
WĪND'ĬNG-SHĒĔT, *n.* A shroud for the dead.
WĬND'LĄSS, *n.* A machine for raising, &c.
WĬND'MĬLL, *n.* A mill turned by the wind.
WĬN'DŌW, *n.* An aperture in a building by which air and light are admitted. [the breath.
WĬND'PĪPE *or* WĪND'PĪPE, *n.* The passage for
WĬND'WĄRD, *a.* Lying towards the wind.
WĬND'WĄRD, *n.* The point towards the wind.
WĬND'Y, *a.* Consisting-of wind; stormy; airy.
WĪNE, *n.* The fermented juice of the grape.
WĪNE'-BĬB-BĘR, *n.* A great drinker of wine.
WĬNG, *n.* The limb of a bird used in flying :—a fan to winnow :—flight; side of an army.
WĬNG, *v. a.* To furnish with wings; to fly.
WĬNGED (wĭngd *or* wĭng'ĕd), *a.* Having wings.
WĬNG'-SHĔLL, *n.* A shell covering the wings of
WĬNG'Y, *a.* Having wings; swift. [insects.
WĬNK, *v. n.* To shut the eyes; to connive.
WĬNK, *n.* The act of closing the eye :—a hint.
WĬN'NĘR, *n.* One who wins.
WĬN'NĬNG, *p. a.* Attractive; charming.
WĬN'NŌW (wĭn'nō), *v. a.* To fan :—to separate.
WĬN'TĘR, *n.* The cold season of the year.
WĬN'TĘR, *v. n.* To pass the winter.
WĬN'TĘR, *v. a.* To feed or keep in the winter.
WĬN'TĘR-KĬLL, *v. a.* To kill by cold of winter.
WĬN'TĘR-LY, *a.* Suitable to winter; wintry.
WĬN'TRY, *a.* Brumal; cold; suitable to winter.
WĪ'NY, *a,* Having the taste or qualities of wine.
WĪPE, *v. a.* To cleanse by rubbing; to clear.
WĪPE, *n.* Act of wiping :—a blow :—a jeer.
WĪRE, *n.* Metal drawn into a thread.
WĪRE'DRÂW, *v. a.* To spin or draw into wire.
WĪR'Y, *a.* Made of wire; like wire.
†WĬS, *v. a.* [*imp. t. & pp.* wist.] To think.
WĬŞ'DQM, *n.* Quality of being wise; knowledge rightly used; sapience; prudence; sagacity.
WĪŞE, *a.* Having wisdom; judicious; prudent.
WĪŞE, *n.* Manner; the way of being or acting.
WĪŞE'Ą-CRE (wĭz'ą-kęr), *n.* A fool; a dunce.
WĪŞE'LY, *ad.* With wisdom; prudently.
WĬSH, *v. a. & n.* To desire; to long for; to long.
WĬSH, *n.* A longing desire; a thing desired.
WĬSH'FÛL, *a.* Longing; showing desire; eager.
WĬSP, *n.* A small bundle, as of hay or straw.
WĬST'FÛL, *a.* Attentive; full of thought; eager.
WĬT, *v. n.* To know; to be known :—now only used in the phrase *to wit*; that is to say.

WĬT, *n.* Intellect; humor; invention; quickness of fancy :—a man of humor or genius.
WĬTCH, *n.* A woman who practises sorcery.
WĬTCH, *v. a.* To bewitch; to enchant.
WĬTCH'CRÄFT, *n.* The practice of witches;
WĬTCH'-ĔLM, *n.* A species of elm. [sorcery.
WĬTCH'ĘR-Y, *n.* Enchantment; sorcery.
WĬTH, *prep.* By; noting cause or means.
WĬTH-ÂL', *ad.* Along with the rest; likewise.
WĬTH-DRÂW', *v. a. & n.* To take back; to retire.
WĬTH-DRÂW'ĬNG-RŎÔM, *n.* Room for retirement.
WĬTH, WĬTHE, *n.* A twig; an osier. [stroy.
WĬTH'ĘR, *v. n. & a.* To fade; to dry up; to de-
WĬTH'ĘR-BĂND, *n.* An iron under a saddle.
WĬTH'ĘRŞ, *n. pl.* The elevated ridge near the bottom of a horse's neck.
WĬTH-HŌLD', *v. a.* [*imp. t. & pp.* withheld.] To restrain; to hold back; to hinder; to refuse.
WĬTH-HŌL'DEN, *pp.* from *withhold.* [*Rare.*]
WĬTH-ĬN', *prep.* In the inner part of; not beyond.
WĬTH-ĬN', *ad.* In the inner parts; inwardly.
WĬTH-ÖÛT', *prep.* Not within; not with.
WĬTH-ÖÛT', *ad.* Not on the inside; out of doors.
WĬTH-ÖÛT', *conj.* Unless; if not; except.
WĬTH-STĂND', *v. a.* [*imp. t. & pp.* withstood.] To oppose; to resist; to stand against.
WĬTH'Y, *n.* A willow tree.—*a.* Made of withes.
WĬT'LĘSS, *a.* Wanting wit or understanding.
WĬT'LĬNG, *n.* A pretty pretender to wit.
WĬT'NĘSS, *n.* Testimony; a bearer of testimony.
WĬT'NĘSS, *v. a. & n.* To attest; to see.
WĬT'-SNĂP-PĘR, *n.* One who affects repartee.
WĬT'TĘD, *a.* Having wit ;—*used in composition.*
WĬT'TĬ-CĬŞM, *n.* Attempt at wit; a conceit.
WĬT'TĬ-LY, *ad.* Ingeniously; cunningly; artfully.
WĬT'TĬ-NĔSS, *n.* The quality of being witty.
WĬT'TY, *a.* Ingenious; full of wit; sarcastic.
WĪVE, *v. a. & n.* To match to a wife; to marry,
WĪVEŞ, *n.* The plural of *wife.* [as a man.
WĬZ'ĄRD, *n.* A conjurer; a sorcerer; enchanter.
WĬZ'ĄRD, *a.* Enchanting; haunted by wizards.
WĬZ'EN (wĭz'zn), *v. n.* To wither; to become
WŌAD (wōd), *n.* A plant used in dyeing. [dry.
WŌE (wō), *n.* Grief; sorrow; misery; calamity.
WŌ'FÛL, *a.* Sorrowful; calamitous; wretched.
WŌ'FÛL-LY, *ad.* Sorrowfully; wretchedly.
WOLF (wûlf), *n.;* pl. WOLVEŞ. A beast of prey.
WOLF'DŎG (wûlf'dŏg), *n.* A species of dog.
WOLF'ĬSH (wûlf'ĭsh), *a.* Resembling a wolf.
WOLF'S'BÂNE (wûlfs'bān), *n.* Poisonous plant.
WOM'ĄN (wûm'ąn), *n.;* pl. WOMEN. An adult female of the human race. [woman.
WOM'ĄN-HOOD (wûm'ąn-hûd), *n.* State of
WOM'ĄN-ĬSH (wûm'ąn-ĭsh), *a.* Like a woman.
WOM'ĄN-KĪND (wûm'ąn-kīnd), *n.* Female sex.
WOM'ĄN-LY (wûm'ąn-le), *a.* Becoming a woman.
WOMB (wôm), *n.* Place of the fœtus :—a cavity.
WOM'ĘN (wĭm'męn), *n.* The plural of *woman.*
WŎN (wŭn), *i. & p.* from *win.*
WŎN'DĘR, *v. n.* To be surprised or astonished.
WŎN'DĘR, *n.* Admiration; amazement; surprise.
WŎN'DĘR-ĘR, *n.* One who wonders. [ishing.
WŎN'DĘR-FÛL, *a.* Admirable; strange; aston-
WŎN'DĘR-FÛL-LY, *ad.* In a wonderful manner.
WŎN'DĘR-MĔNT, *n.* Astonishment; amazement.
WŎN'DĘR-WORK'ĬNG, *a.* Doing wonders.
WŎN'DROŲS, *a.* Admirable; marvellous; strange.
WŎN'DROŲS-LY, *ad.* In a wonderful manner.

WŎNT, *v. n.* To be accustomed; to use.
WŎN'T *or* WŎN'T. A contraction used for *will not.*
WŎNT'ĘD, *p. a.* Accustomed; used; usual.
wôô, *v. a. & n.* To court; to sue; to make love.
WOOD (wûd), *n.* A large collection of trees; a forest:—the substance of trees; timber.
WOOD'BĪNE (wûd'bīn), *n.* The honeysuckle.
WOOD'CHŬCK (wûd'-), *n.* A quadruped of the marmot family; ground-hog.
WOOD'CŎCK (wûd'kŏk), *n.* A kind of bird.
WOOD'CŬT, *n.* An engraving on wood.
WOOD'ĘD (wûd'ęd), *a.* Supplied with wood.
WOOD'EN (wûd'dn), *a.* Ligneous; made of wood.
WOOD'FRĔT-TĘR (wûd'frĕt-ęr), *n.* An insect.
WOOD'LĂND (wûd'lănd), *n.* Woods; a forest.
WOOD'LĂND (wûd'-), *a.* Belonging to woods.
WOOD'-LÖÛSE (wûd'-), *n.* An insect. [cutter.
WOOD'MĄN (wûd'-), *n.* A sportsman:—timber-
WOOD'-NŌTE (wûd'nŏt), *n.* Wild music. [woods.
WOOD'-NŸMPH (wûd'nĭmf), *n.* A nymph of the
WOOD'PĔCK-ĘR (wûd'pĕk-kęr), *n.* A bird.
WOOD'PĬG-EON (wûd'pĭd-jụn), *n.* Ring-dove.
WOOD'WORM (wûd'wûrm), *n.* A worm in wood.
WOOD'Ÿ (wûd'ę), *a.* Abounding with wood.
WÔÔ'ĘR, *n.* One who courts a woman.
WÔÔF, *n.* Threads that cross the warp; weft.
WOOL (wûl), *n.* Fleece of sheep:—short hair.
WOOL'-CŌMB-ĘR(-kŏm-ęr), *n.* A comber of wool.
WOOL'FĘL (wûl'fęl), *n.* A skin with the wool on
WOOL'LĘN (wûl'lęn), *a.* Made of wool. [it.
WOOL'LĘN (wûl'lęn), *n.* Cloth made of wool.
WOOL'LĘN-DRĀ'PĘR, *n.* A dealer in woollen goods. [wool.
WOOL'LŸ (wûl'lę), *a.* Consisting of, or like,
WOOL'SĂCK (wûl'săk), *n.* A sack of wool.
WOOL'-STĀ-PLĘR (wûl'-), *n.* A dealer in wool.
WORD (wûrd), *n.* A single part of speech; an articulate sound:—a promise:—token:—message.
WORD (wûrd), *v. a.* To express in words.
WORD'Ĭ-NĔSS (wûrd'ę-nĕs), *n.* Verbosity.
WORD'Ÿ (wûrd'ę), *a.* Verbose; full of words.
WŌRE, *imp. t.* from *wear.* See WEAR.
WORK (wûrk), *v. n.* [*imp. t. & pp.* wrought *or* worked.] To labor; to toil; to act:—to ferment.
WORK (wûrk), *v. a.* To form by labor; to effect.
WORK (wûrk), *n.* Toil; labor; a performance.
WORK'FĔL-LŌW, *n.* A fellow-laborer.
WORK'HÖÛSE (wûrk'höûs), *n.* A poor-house.
WORK'MĄN (wûrk'mąn), *n.* An artificer.
WORK'MĄN-LĪKE (wûrk'mąn-līk), *a.* Skilful.
WORK'MĄN-SHĬP (wûrk'mąn-shĭp), *n.* Skill; art.
WORK'SHŎP (wûrk'shŏp), *n.* A place for work.
WORLD (wûrld), *n.* The system of beings; earth; terraqueous globe :—a secular life :—mankind.
WORLD'LĬ-NĔSS (wûrld'-), *n.* Worldly state.
WORLD'LĬNG (wûrld'lĭng), *n.* One devoted to worldly gain and pleasure. [earthly.
WORLD'LŸ (wûrld'lę), *a.* Relating to this world;
WORM (wûrm), *n.* An insect; any thing spiral.
WORM (wûrm), *v. n.* To work imperceptibly.
WORM (wûrm), *v. a.* To force by secret means.
WORM'-ĔAT-EN(wûrm'ē-tn), *a.* Eaten by worms.
WORM'WOOD (wûrm'wûd), *n.* A bitter plant.
WORM'Ÿ (wûrm'ę), *a.* Full of worms :—grov-
WŌRN, *pp.* from *wear.* [elling.
WŎR'RŸ, *v. a.* To tear; to harass; to tease.
WORSE (wûrs), *a.; compar.* of *bad.* More bad.
WORSE (wûrs), *ad.* In a manner more bad.

WOR'SHĬP (wür'shĭp), *n.* Dignity; honor; a title of honor :—adoration; religious reverence.
WOR'SHĬP (wür'shĭp), *v. a.* To adore; to honor.
WOR'SHĬP (wür'shĭp), *v. n.* To perform adoration.
WOR'SHĬP-FŬL (wür'shĭp-fûl), *a.* Claiming respect; entitled to respect; venerable.
WOR'SHĬP-PĘR (wür'shĭp-pęr), *n.* An adorer.
WORST (würst), *a.; superlative* of *bad.* Most bad.
WORST (würst), *v. a.* To defeat; to overthrow.
WÔRS'TĘD (wôrs'tĕd), *n.* A kind of woollen yarn.
WORT (würt), *n.* An herb :—new beer or ale.
†WORTH (würth), *v. a.* To betide.
WORTH (würth), *n.* Price; value; importance.
WORTH (würth), *a.* Equal in value to; deserving.
WOR'THĬ-LŸ (wür'thę-lę), *ad.* Suitably; justly.
WOR'THĬ-NĔSS (wür'thę-nĕs), *n.* Desert; merit.
WORTH'LESS (würth'lęs), *a.* Having no value.
WOR'THŸ (wür'thę), *a.* Deserving; meritorious.
WOR'THŸ (wür'thę), *n.* A man of merit.
†WŎT, †WŌTE, *v. n.* To know; to be aware.
WOÛLD (wûd), *v. auxiliary* of *will.*
WÔUND (wônd *or* wöûnd), *n.* A hurt; an injury.
WÔUND *or* WÖÛND, *v. a.* To hurt by violence.
WÖÛND (wöûnd), *imp. t. & pp.* from *wind.*
WŌVE, *imp. t.* from *weave.*
WŌ'VEN (wō'vn), *pp.* from *weave.*
WRĂCK (răk), *n.* Ruin; destruction. See WRECK.
WRĂN'GLE (răng'gl), *v. n.* To dispute; to quarrel.
WRĂN'GLE (răng'gl), *n.* A quarrel; a dispute.
WRĂN'GLĘR (răng'glęr), *n.* An angry disputant.
WRĂP (răp), *v. a.* [*imp. t. & pp.* wrapped, wrapt.] To roll together; to involve; to cover.
WRĂP'PĘR, *n.* One that wraps :—a cover.
WRĂP'PĬNG, *n.* A covering; a wrapper.
WRĂP'RĂS-CĄL, *n.* A kind of coarse upper coat.
WRĂTH (răth), *n.* Anger; fury; rage.
WRĂTH'FŬL, *a.* Angry; furious; raging. [heed.
WRĔAK (rĕk), *v. a.* To execute; to inflict; to
WRĔATH (rēth), *n.; pl.* WRĔATHŞ. A garland.
WRĔATHE (rēth), *v. a.* [*imp. t.* wreathed; *pp.* wreathed, wreathen.] To twist; to interweave.
WRĔATHE (rēth), *v. n.* To be interwoven.
WRĔATH'Ÿ (rē'thę), *a.* Spiral; curled; twisted.
WRĔCK (rĕk), *n.* Destruction by sea :—ruin.
WRĔCK (rĕk), *v. a.* To strand :—to ruin.
WRĔCK'ĘR, *n.* A plunderer of wrecked vessels.
WRĔN (rĕn), *n.* A small bird.
WRĔNCH (rĕnch), *v. a.* To pull; to sprain.
WRĔNCH (rĕnch), *n.* A pull; a sprain.
WRĔST (rĕst), *v. a.* To extort; to distort; to force.
WRĔST (rĕst), *n.* Distortion; violence.
WRĔS'TLE (rĕs'sl), *v. n.* To contend; to struggle.
WRĔST'LĘR (rĕs'lęr), *n.* One who wrestles.
WRĔST'LĬNG (rĕs'lĭng), *n.* An exercise; a struggle.
WRĔTCH (rĕch), *n.* A miserable mortal; knave.
WRĔTCH'ĘD (rĕch'ęd), *a.* Miserable; worthless.
WRĔTCH'ĘD-LŸ, *ad.* Miserably; despicably.
WRĬG'GLE (rĭg'gl), *v. n.* To move to and fro.
WRĬG'GLE (rĭg'gl), *v. a.* To make to wriggle.
WRĬGHT (rīt), *n.* A workman; an artificer.
WRĬNG (rĭng), *v. a.* [*imp. t. & pp.* wrung *or* wringed.] To twist, turn, press, extort, harass.
WRĬN'KLE (rĭng'kl), *n.* A corrugation; a crease.
WRĬN'KLE (rĭng'kl), *v. a.* To make uneven.
WRĬST (rĭst), *n.* The joint or part between the fore-arm and the hand.
WRĬST'BĄND (rĭst'bąnd), *n.* A band or fastening about the wrist.

WRĬT (rĭt), *n.* Scripture :—a judicial instrument.
†WRĬT (rĭt), *imp. t.* & *pp.* from *write.*
WRĪTE (rīt), *v. a.* [*imp. t.* wrote; *pp.* written.] To express by letters ; to engrave.
WRĪTE (rīt), *v. n.* To perform the act of writing.
WRĪT′ẸR (rīt′ẹr), *n.* One who writes ; an author.
WRĪTHE (rīth), *v. a.* To distort ; to twist.
WRĪTHE (rīth), *v. n.* To be distorted with agony.
WRĪT′ỊNG (rīt′ịng), *n.* Any thing written.
WRĪT′ỊNG-MÄS′TẸR, *n.* One who teaches to write.
WRĬT′TEN (rĭt′tn), *pp.* from *write.*
WRŎNG (rŏng), *n.* An injury ; injustice ; error.
WRŎNG (rŏng), *a.* Not right ; not just ; unfit.
WRŎNG (rŏng), *ad.* Not rightly ; amiss.
WRŎNG (rŏng), *v. a.* To injure ; to use unjustly.
WRŎNG′-DÔ-ẸR, *n.* An injurious person.
WRŎNG′FÛL (rŏng′fûl), *a.* Injurious ; unjust.
WRŎNG′-HĔAD-ẸD (rŏng′hĕd-ẹd), *a.* Perverse.
WRŎNG′LỴ (rŏng′lẹ), *ad.* Unjustly ; amiss.
WRŎNG′NẸSS (rŏng′nẹs), *n.* Error ; evil.
WRŌTE (rōt), *imp. t.* from *write.*
WROTH (râwth *or* rŏth), *a.* Angry; exasperated ; irate.
WROUGHT (râwt), *imp. t.* & *pp.* from *work.* Performed ; labored ; manufactured.
WRŬNG (rŭng), *imp. t.* & *pp.* from *wring.*
WRȲ (rī), *a.* Crooked ; distorted ; wrested.
WRȲ′NĔCK, *n.* A distorted neck :—a bird.
WRȲ′NẸSS (rī′nẹs), *n.* The state of being wry.

X.

X is a letter which begins no word purely English. In the middle and end of words, it sounds like *ks*, and at the beginning like *z*.
XĂN′THỊC, *a.* Of a yellowish color.
XĒ′BĔC, *n.* A small, three-masted vessel.
XĒ-RỌ-CỌL-LȲR′Ị-ŬM, *n.* A salve for sore eyes.
XẸ-RŌ′DĒṢ (zẹ-rō′dēz), *n.* A dry tumor.
XĔR-Ọ-MȲ′RỤM (zĕr-ọ-mī′rụm), *n.* An ointment.
XẸ-RŌ′TĒṢ (zẹ-rō′tēz), *n.* A dry habit of body.
XĬPH′Ị-ẠS (zĭf′ẹ-ạs), *n.* The sword-fish.
XỊ-PHŎĬ′DĒṢ (zẹ-fŏĭ′dēz), *n.* The pointed, sword-like cartilage or gristle of the breast-bone.
XȲ-LỌ-BĂL′SẠ-MŬM, *n.* Wood of the balsam-tree.
XȲ-LŎG′RẠ-PHỴ, *n.* Art of engraving on wood.
XȲ-LŎPH′Ạ-GĂN, *n.* A wood-eating insect.
XȲS′TẸR (zĭs′tẹr), *n.* A surgeon's instrument.

Y.

Y at the beginning of words is a consonant ; at the end of words, and when it follows a consonant, it is a vowel, and has the sound of *i.*
YACHT (yŏt), *n.* A vessel of state or pleasure.
YĂM, *n.* A large esculent root.
YĂN′KẸE (yăng′kẹ), *n.* A native or an inhabitant of New England. [*Cant.*]
YÄRD, *n.* Enclosure :—measure of three feet.
YÄRD′-ÄRM, *n.* End of a ship's yard.
YÄRD′STĬCK, *n.* A stick a yard long.
YÄRD′WAND (yärd′wŏnd), *n.* Measure of a yard.
YÄRN, *n.* Spun wool ; thread of wool, &c.
YĂR′RŌW (yăr′rō), *n.* A plant ; the milfoil.
YÂWL, *n.* A boat belonging to a ship.
YÂWN, *v. n.* To gape ; to open wide.—*n.* A gape.
†Ỵ-CLĔPED′ (ẹ-klĕpt′), *pp.* Called ; termed.
YĒ, *pron.* The nominative plural of *thou ;* you.
YEA (yā *or* yē), *ad.* Yes ; a particle of affirmation.
YĒAN, *v. n.* To bring young, as sheep.
YĒAN′LỊNG, *n.* The young of sheep.
YĒAR, *n.* Twelve calendar months ; 365 days.
YĒAR′-BOOK (yēr′bûk), *n.* A book of annual reports.
YĒAR′LỊNG, *a.* Being a year old.
YĒAR′LỊNG, *n.* An animal one year old.
YĒAR′LỴ, *a.* Annual.—*ad.* Annually.
YËARN (yërn), *v. n.* To feel pain, desire, or pity.
YËARN′ỊNG, *n.* Longing ; strong desire.
YĒAST, *n.* Barm used in leavening bread ; leaven ; yest.
YĒAST′Ỵ, *a.* Containing yeast ; foamy.
YĔLK, *n.* The yellow part of an egg ; yolk.
YĔLL, *v. n.* To cry out.—*n.* A cry of horror.
YĔL′LŌW (yĕl′lō), *a.* Being of a gold color.
YĔL′LŌW, *n.* Yellow color.
YĔL′LỌW-FĒ′VẸR, *n.* A malignant fever.
YĔL′LỌW-HĂM′MẸR (yĕl′lọ-hăm′ẹr), *n.* A bird.
YĔL′LỌW-ĬSH (yĕl′lọ-ĭsh), *a.* Approaching to yellow.
YĔL′LŌWṢ (yĕl′lōz), *n. pl.* A disease in horses ; jaundice.
YĔLP, *v. n.* To bark as a dog.
YEŌ′MẠN (yō′mạn), *n.* A farmer ; a freeholder.
YEŌ′MẠN-RỴ (yō′mạn-rẹ), *n.* The body of yeomen.
YËRK, *v. a.* To throw out ; to kick ; to strike.
YĔS (yĕs *or* yĭs), *ad.* Yea ; truly; opposed to *no.*
YĔST, *n.* The foam of beer ; barm ; yeast.
YĔS′TẸR, *a.* Being before the present day.
YĔS′TẸR-DĀY, *n.* The day next before to-day.
YĔT, *conj.* Nevertheless ; notwithstanding.
YĔT, *ad.* Beside ; still ; at least ; hitherto.
YEW (yṻ), *n.* A tree of tough wood.
YEW′ẸN (yṻ′ẹn), *a.* Made of the wood of yew.
YĔX, *v. n.* To hiccough.—*n.* The hiccough.
YIĒLD (yēld), *v. a.* To produce, give, afford.
YIĒLD (yēld), *v. n.* To give up ; to submit.
YŌKE, *n.* A bandage for the neck ; a mark of servitude :—a chain ; a bond :—a couple ; a pair.
YŌKE, *v. a.* To bind by a yoke ; to couple.
YŌKE′-FĔL-LŌW, *n.* A companion.
YŌLK (yōk), *n.* Yellow part of an egg ; yelk.
YŎN, YŎN′DẸR, *a.* Distant, but within view.
YŎN, YŎN′DẸR, *ad.* At a distance within view.
YŌRE, *ad.* Long since ; of old time.—*In days of yore,* in time past ; formerly.
YOṺ (yṻ), *personal pron.* Plural of *thou.*

YOŬNG (yŭng), *a.* Not old ; youthful :—ignorant.
YOŬNG (yŭng), *n.* The offspring of animals.
YOŬNG'ISH (yŭng'ish), *a.* Somewhat young.
YOŬNG'LING (yŭng'ling), *n.* A young animal.
YOŬNG'STER, YOŬNK'ER, *n.* A young person.
YOŬR (yŭr), *pron.* Belonging to you.
YOŬR-SĚLF' (yŭr-sĕlf'), *pron.* You ; even you.

YOŬTH (yŭth), *n.* The part of life succeeding to childhood :—a young man ; young persons.
YOŬTH'FŬL (yŭth'fŭl), *a.* Young ; vigorous.
YOŬTH'FŬL-LY, *ad.* In a youthful manner.
ŸT'TRI-A, *n.* A very rare kind of earth.
YŬC'CA, *n.* An American tree, and its fruit.
YŪLE, *n.* Time of Christmas and of Lammas.

Z.

Z, a consonant, has, in English, the same sound as the soft or vocal *s.*
ZĂ℄'℄HŌ, *n.* The lowest part of a pedestal.
ZĂF'FRE, *n.* An oxide of cobalt ; a mineral.
ZĂM'BŌ, *n.* Offspring of an Indian and negro.
ZĀ'NY, *n.* A merry-andrew ; a buffoon.
ZĂR'NI℄H, *n.* Name of a kind of minerals.
ZĂX, *n.* A tool for cutting slates.
ZĒAL, *n.* Passionate ardor ; earnestness ; warmth.
ZĔAL'OT (zĕl'ut), *n.* A person full of zeal.
ZĔAL'OUS (zĕl'lus), *a.* Ardent ; passionate.
ZĔAL'OUS-LY, *ad.* With passionate ardor.
ZĒ'BRA, *n.* An African animal like an ass.
ZĒ'BU, *n.* A species of ox found in India.
ZĒ'℄HIN *or* ZE-℄HÎN', *n.* An Italian gold coin.
ZĔD, *n.* A name of the letter Z.
ZĔM-IN-DÀR', *n.* A landholder in India.
ZĔM'IN-DA-RY, *n.* Possession of a zemindar.
ZĒ'NITH, *n.* The point overhead, opposite to the ZĒ'O-LĪTE, *n.* A kind of mineral. [nadir.
ZĔPH'YR, *n.* The west wind :—a soft wind.
ZĒ'RŌ, *n.* The point from which a thermometer is graduated :—the arithmetical cipher.
ZĔST, *n.* A relish ; a taste added ; gusto.
ZĒ'TA, *n.* A Greek letter ; a dining room ; a closet.

ZEŪG'MA, *n.* A figure in grammar ; ellipsis.
ZĬG'ZĂG, *a.* Having sharp and quick turns.
ZĬNC, *n.* A bluish-white metal.
ZĬR'CŌN, *n.* A crystalline mineral.
ZŌ'CLE, *n.* A sort of stand or pedestal supporting a column ; socle.
ZŌ'DI-ĂC, *n.* A broad circle of the heavens, containing the 12 signs and the sun's path.
ZO-DĪ'A-CAL, *a.* Relating to the zodiac.
ZŌNE, *n.* A girdle :—a division of the earth.
ZŌNE'LESS, *a.* Having no zone or girdle.
ZO-ŎG'RA-PHER, *n.* One who describes animals.
ZO-ŎG'RA-PHY, *n.* A description of animals.
ZŌ-O-LŎG'I-CAL, *a.* Describing living creatures.
ZO-ŎL'O-GĬST, *n.* One who is versed in zoölogy.
ZO-ŎL'O-GY, *n.* The science of animals.
ZŌ'O-PHYTE, *n.* A substance which partakes of the nature both of vegetables and animals.
ZO-ŎT'O-MĬST, *n.* One versed in zoötomy.
ZO-ŎT'O-MY, *n.* Dissection of the bodies of beasts.
ZȲ-MŎL'O-GY, *n.* The doctrine of fermentation.
ZȲ-MO-SĬM'E-TER, *n.* An instrument for measuring the degree of fermentation.
ZȲ-MŎT'IC, *a.* Applied to epidemic, endemic, and contagious diseases.

MÎEN, SÏR ; MÔVE, NÖR, SÖN ; BŪLL, BŬR, RŪLE.—Ç, Ǥ, *soft;* ℄, Ǥ, *hard;* Ş *as* Z ; Ҳ *as* gz ; ҬHIS.

WORDS AND PHRASES

FROM

FOREIGN LANGUAGES.

In the preceding part of this Dictionary, some words from foreign languages are inserted, which are but partially Anglicized; and most of the words and phrases which here follow are still less Anglicized.

ABBREVIATIONS. — L. *Latin;* Gr. *Greek;,* It. *Italian;* Fr. *French;* Sp. *Spanish.*

Ab extra. [L.] From without.
Ab incunabulis. [L.] From the cradle.
Ab initio. [L.] From the beginning.
Ab origine. [L.] From the origin.
Ab ovo. [L.] From the egg.
Absence d'esprit. [Fr.] Absence of mind.
Absit invidia. [L.] Envy apart.
Absque ullâ conditione. [L.] Unconditionally.
Ab urbe conditâ. [L.] From the building of the city, i. e. Rome.
A capite ad calcem. [L.] From head to heel.
Accessit. [L.] He came nearly up to.
Actionnaire. [Fr.] Shareholder.
Ad arbitrium. [L.] At discretion.
Ad captandum. [L.] To attract.
Addendum (pl. addenda), [L.] An addition; an appendix.
Ad eundem. [L.] To the same.
Ad finem. [L.] To the end.
Ad hominem. [L.] Personal; to the individual.
Ad infinitum. [L.] To infinity; without end.
Ad interim. [L.] In the mean while.
Ad libitum. [L.] At pleasure.
Ad nauseam usque. [L.] To satiety or disgust.
Ad quod damnum. [L.] To what damage.
Ad referendum. [L.] For further consideration.
Adscriptus glebæ. [L.] Attached to the soil.
Ad unguem. [L.] To the touch of the nails.
Ad utrumque paratus. [L.] Prepared for either event.
Ad valorem. [L.] According to the value.
Adversaria. [L.] A commonplace-book.
Ægloga. [L.] An eclogue, idyl, *or* bucolic.
Æquanimiter. [L.] With equanimity.
Æquo animo. [L.] With equanimity.
Ætatis suæ. [L.] Of his or her age.
Affaire d'amour. [Fr.] A love affair.
Affaire d'honneur. [Fr.] An affair of honor.
Affaire du cœur. [Fr.] An affair of the heart.
Affettuoso. [It.] (*Music.*) Denoting what is to be sung or played tenderly.
Affirmatim. [L.] Affirmatively.
A fin de. [Fr.] To the end that.
A fortiori. [L.] With stronger reason.
Agapæ. [L.] Feasts of charity or love.
Agenda. [L. pl., *things to be done.*] Business to be done; a memorandum-book; a ritual or service-book.
Agnus Dei. [L.] Lamb of God.
A grands frais. [Fr.] At great expense.
Ajutage. [Fr.] A pipe to water-works.
A l'abandon. [Fr.] At random.
A la bonne heure. [Fr.] At an early hour.
A l'abri. [Fr.] Under shelter.
A la dérobée. [Fr.] By stealth.
A la Française. [Fr.] After the French manner.
Alamire. [It.] A note in music.
A l'Anglaise. [Fr.] After the English manner.
Albugo. [L.] A disease in the eye.
A l'improviste. [Fr.] On a sudden; unawares.
Allemande. [Fr.] A German dance.
Alma mater. [L.] Kind or benign mother.
Almacantar. [Ar.] A circle parallel to the horizon.
A l'outrance. [Fr.] To the very death.
Alter ego. [L.] My other self.
Alter idem. [L.] Another exactly similar.
Alto-rilievo. [It.] That kind of relief in sculpture which projects as much as the life.
A main armée. [Fr.] With force of arms.
Amende honorable. [Fr.] An infamous punishment: — an apology for an injury.
A mensâ et thoro. [L.] From bed and board.
A merveille. [Fr.] To a wonder; marvellously.
Amicus curiæ. [L.] A friend of the court.
Ami de court. [Fr.] A court friend.
Amo. [L.] I love.
Amor nummi. [L.] Love of money.
Amor patriæ. [L.] Patriotism.
Amour propre. [Fr.] Self-love; vanity..
Amphiscii. [L.] People who inhabit the torrid zone, whose shadows fall both ways.
Amuck, or *Amock.* An East Indian term for slaughter.
Ana. [Gr.] A word used in the prescriptions of physicians, importing *in the like quantity, equally.*
Ana. A termination annexed to the names of authors to denote a collection of their memorable sayings; as, *Johnsoni-ana.*
Anadiplosis. [Gr.] Repetition of a word.
Anaphora. [Gr.] (*Rhet.*) A figure which begins several clauses of a sentence with the same word.

Anglicè. [L.] In English.
Anguis in herbâ. [L.] A snake in the grass.
Animo et fide. [L.] By courage and faith.
Animus. [L.] Mind ; intention.
Animus furandi. [L.] The intention of stealing.
Animus imponentis. [L.] The intention of the imposer.
Anno Christi. [L.] In the year of Christ.
Anno Domini. [L.] In the year of our Lord.
Anno mundi. [L.] In the year of the world.
Annus mirabilis. [L.] The year of wonders.
Antanaclasis. [Gr.] (*Rhet.*) A figure by which the same word is repeated in a different sense.
Ante bellum. [L.] Before the war.
Ante lucem. [L.] Before daylight.
Ante meridiem. [L.] Before noon.
Anti. [Gr.] Against.
Antiperistasis. [Gr.] The opposition of a contrary quality, by which the quality opposed gains strength.
Antiphrasis. [Gr.] (*Rhet.*) The use of wórds in a sense opposite to their proper meaning.
Antiptosis. [Gr.] (*Gram.*) The putting of one case for another.
Antiscii. [L.] The people who, inhabiting on different sides of the equator, at noon have their shadows projected opposite ways.
Antispasis. [Gr.] (*Med.*) Revulsion of a humor.
Antœci. [Gr.] Those inhabitants of the earth who live under the same longitude and latitude, but in different hemispheres.
Antonomasia. [Gr.] (*Rhet.*) A form of speech in which the name of some office or dignity is used instead of the proper name.
Aparithmesis. [Gr.] (*Rhet.*) Enumeration.
A parte ante. [L.] Of the preceding part.
Aperçu. [Fr.] A sketch; summary.
A perte de vue. [Fr.] Beyond one's view.
Aphœresis. [Gr.] The taking of a letter or syllable from the beginning of a word.
Apodixis. [L.] Evident demonstration.
Apodosis. [Gr.] Application of a similitude.
Aponeurosis. [Gr.] Extension of a nerve.
Apophasis. [Gr.] A figure by which the orator seems to waive what he would plainly insinuate.
Apophyge. [Gr.] The spring of a column.
A posteriori. [L.] From the latter; from the effect to the cause.
Apparatus belli. [L.] Materials for war.
Appoggiatura. [It.] (*Music.*) A note directing an easy and graceful movement.
Appui. [Fr.] Point of support; purchase.
A prima vista. [It.] At first sight.
A priori. [L.] From the cause to the effect.
Apropos. [Fr.] Opportunely.
A propos de rien. [Fr.] Apropos to nothing.
Arcana cœlestia. [L.] Heavenly secrets.
Ardentia verba. [L.] Words that burn.
A rez de chaussée. [Fr.] Even with the ground.
Argent comptant. [Fr.] Ready money.
Argumentum ad crumenam. [L.] An argument to the purse.
Argumentum ad hominem. [L.] An argument to the man.
Argumentum ad ignorantiam. [L.] An argument to ignorance, or founded on an adversary's ignorance of facts.
Argumentum ad judicium. [L.] An argument to the judgment.

Argumentum ad verecundiam. [L.] An argument to modesty.
Arietta. [It.] A short air, song, or tune.
Arioso. [It.] A movement of a common air.
Arpeggio. [It.] (*Music.*) The distinct sound of the notes of an instrumental chord, accompanying the voice.
Arrectis auribus. [L.] With attentive ears.
Artes honorabit. [L.] He will honor the arts.
Arthritis. [Gr.] (*Med.*) The gout.
Ascii. [L.] Those people who, at certain times of the year, have no shadow at noon.
Assumpsit. [L.] (*Law.*) A voluntary promise or undertaking ; a species of action.
Asymptote. [Gr.] (*Geom.*) A line which approaches nearer and nearer to some curve, but never meets it.
Asyndeton. [Gr.] (*Rhet.*) A figure which omits the conjunction ; as, *veni, vidi, vici.*
A tâtons. [Fr.] Groping.
A teneris annis. [L.] From earliest years.
A tort et à travers. [Fr.] At random.
A toute force. [Fr.] With all one's might.
Attaché. [Fr.] A person belonging or attached to another person or company.
Au bon droit. [Fr.] To the just right.
Audacter et sincerè. [L.] Boldly and sincerely.
Audax at cautus. [L.] Bold but wary.
Aude sapere. [L.] Dare to be wise.
Au désespoir. [Fr.] In despair.
Audi alteram partem. [L.] Hear the other side.
Au fait. [Fr.] Skilful ; expert.
Au fond. [Fr.] To the bottom.
Augustana Confessio. [L.] The Augsburg Confession.
Au pis aller. [Fr.] At the worst.
Aura popularis. [L.] The popular breeze.
Aurea mediocritas. [L.] The golden mean.
Auri sacra fames. [L.] The accursed appetite for gold.
Aurum potabile. [L.] Potable gold.
Aut Cæsar, aut nullus. [L.] Either Cæsar, or nobody.
Auto de fe. [Sp., *act of faith.*] A sentence of the Inquisition for burning a heretic.
Autrefois acquit. [Fr.] Formerly acquitted.
Aux armes. [Fr.] To arms.
Auxilium ab alto. [L.] Help is from on high.
Avant-courier. [Fr.] One who is despatched before the rest to notify approach.
Ave. [L.] An address to the Virgin, so called from the first words, *Ave, Maria.*
Avec permission. [Fr.] With permission.
A verbis ad verbera. [L.] From words to blows.
A vinculo matrimonii. [L.] From the bond of matrimony.
Avise la fin. [Fr.] Consider the end.
A vostra salute. [It.]
A votre santé. [Fr.] } To your health.
A vuestra salud. [Sp.]

B.

Badinage. [Fr.] Light or playful discourse.
Ballista. [L.] An ancient warlike machine for throwing heavy stones, &c.
Banco regis. [L.] On the king's bench.
Bas bleu. [Fr.] Blue-stocking ; a literary woman.

Basso-rilievo. [It.] See BASS-RELIEF.
Beau idéal. [Fr.] A species of beauty created by fancy, or existing only in the imagination.
Beau-monde. [Fr.] The gay world.
Beaux-esprits. [Fr.] Men of wit.
Bel esprit. [Fr.] A brilliant mind.
Bella! horrida bella! [L.] War! horrid war!
Bellum lethale. [L.] A deadly war.
Ben trovato. [It.] Well-invented.
Bibliomania. [L.] The rage for possessing scarce or curious books ; book-madness.
Bijou. [Fr.] A jewel; a trinket.
Billet doux. [Fr.] A love-letter.
Bis. [L.] Twice, or repeated.
Bizarre. [Fr.] Odd ; strange ; fantastical.
Bona fide. [L.] In good faith ; really.
Bon gré. [Fr.] With a good grace.
Bon gré, mal gré. [Fr.] With good or ill grace.
Bonhomie. [Fr.] Good-natured simplicity.
Bonis avibus. [L.] With good omens.
Bon-mot. [Fr.] A jest; a witty repartee.
Bonne. [Fr.] A governess ; a lady's maid.
Bonne bouche. [Fr.] A delicate bit.
Bon-ton. [Fr.] Fashion.
Boudoir. [Fr.] A small private apartment.
Bouillon. [Fr.] Broth ; soup.
Bourse. [Fr.] An exchange.
Boutez en avant. [Fr.] Push forward.
Brevet d'invention. [Fr.] A patent.
Breveté. [Fr.] Patented.
Brevi manu. [L.] With a short hand ; off-hand.
Brutum fulmen. [L.] A harmless thunderbolt.
Buona mano. [It.] A slight present.
Burletta. [It.] A comic or farcical opera.

C.

Cache. [Fr.] A hole dug in the ground for concealing and preserving goods or luggage.
Cachet. [Fr.] A seal ; a private state letter.
Cacoëthes. [L.] An evil custom ; a bad habit.
Cacoëthes carpendi. [L.] A rage for finding fault or carping.
Cacoëthes loquendi. [L.] A rage for speaking.
Cacoëthes scribendi. [L.] A rage for writing.
Cadenza. [It.] (*Music.*) The fall or modulation of the voice.
Caduceus. [L.] Mercury's wand.
Cæca invidia est. [L.] Envy is blind.
Cætera desunt. [L.] The remainder is wanting.
Cæteris paribus. [L.] Other things being equal.
Café. [Fr.] A coffee-house.
Caique. [Fr.] A skiff of a galley.
Calotte. [Fr.] A cap or coif of hair.
Caloyers. Monks of the Greek church.
Campus Martius. [L.] A place for military exercises.
Candida pax. [L.] White-robed peace.
Cantate Domino. [L.] Sing to the Lord.
Capias. [L.] (*Law.*) A sort of writ or process.
Capitulum, or *Caput.* [L.] Section ; chapter.
Caponnière. [Fr.] (*Fort.*) A covered lodgement, with a little parapet.
Capot. [Fr.] A winning at the game of piquet.
Capriccio. [It.] (*Music.*) A loose, irregular species of composition.
Capriccioso. [It.] (*Music.*) A term to express a fantastic, free style.

Caput mortuum. [L.] Worthless remains.
Caret (pl. *carent*). [L.] It is wanting.
Carpe diem. [L.] Improve time ; embrace the opportunity.
Carte blanche. [Fr.] A blank paper to be filled up with such conditions as the person to whom it is sent thinks proper ; unconditional terms.
Casus belli. [L.] A cause for war.
Catalogue raisonné. [Fr.] A catalogue of books arranged according to subjects.
Cavatina. [It.] (*Music.*) A short air.
Caveat actor. [L.] Let the doer beware.
Caveat emptor. [L.] Let the buyer beware.
Cavendo tutus. [L.] Safe through caution.
Cavin. [Fr.] A hollow, fit to cover troops.
Centum. [L.] A hundred.
Centumviri. [L.] The hundred Roman judges.
Certiorari. [L.] To be made more certain.
Cessor. [L.] (*Law.*) He that ceases so long to perform a duty as to incur danger.
Champs Elysées. [Fr.] Elysian fields.
Chapeau de bras. [Fr.] A military cocked hat.
Chargé d'affaires. [Fr.] An ambassador or public minister of secondary rank.
Châteaux en Espagne. [Fr.] Castles in the air.
Chef d'œuvre. [Fr.] A masterpiece.
Chère amie. [Fr.] A mistress.
Cheval de bataille. [Fr.] A war-horse.
Chevaux-de-frise. [Fr.] A military fence, or piece of timber used in defending a passage ; a kind of trimming.
Chevisance. [Fr.] Enterprise ; bargain.
Chevron. [Fr.] An honorable ordinary.
Clarum et venerabile nomen. [L.] An illustrious and venerable name.
Classes aisées. [Fr.] Classes having a competence.
Cognoscente (pl. *cognoscenti*). [It.] One who is well versed in any thing; a connoisseur.
Cognovit. [L.] (*Law.*) An acknowledgment by the defendant of the plaintiff's cause.
Comitas inter gentes. [L.] Comity between nations.
Comitia. [L.] Popular assemblies of the Romans.
Comme il faut. [Fr.] As it should be.
Commissariat. [Fr.] A body of officers who provide provisions, &c., for an army.
Commune bonum. [L.] A common good.
Communibus annis. [L.] One year with another.
Communi consensu. [L.] By common consent.
Componere lites. [L.] To settle disputes.
Compos mentis. [L.] Of sound mind.
Compte rendu. [Fr.] A report or account.
Con amore. [It.] With love or inclination.
Concio ad clerum. [L.] A sermon or address to the clergy.
Concordia discors. [L.] Discordant concord.
Congé d'élire. [Fr.] The king's permission to a dean and chapter to choose a bishop.
Contra bonos mores. [L.] Against good manners or morals.
Conversazione. [It.] A meeting of company.
Copula. [L.] (*Logic.*) The word which unites the subject and predicate of a proposition.
Coram nobis. [L.] Before us.
Cordon sanitaire. [Fr.] A line of guards against contagion or pestilence.
Corpus delicti. [L.] The main offence.
Corrigenda. [L.] Words to be altered.

Corruptio optimi pessima. [L.] The corruption of the best becomes the worst.
Cortége. [Fr.] A train of attendants.
Cor unum, via una. [L.] One heart, one way.
Couleur de rose. [Fr.] Rose color; flattering hue.
Coup de grace. [Fr.] The mercy-stroke; finishing stroke.
Coup de main. [Fr.] A bold effort or attack.
Coup de plume. [Fr.] A literary attack or contest.
Coup de soleil. [Fr.] Sun-stroke.
Coup d'essai. [Fr.] First attempt.
Coup de théâtre. [Fr.] Theatrical effect.
Coup d'état. [Fr.] A stroke of policy in state affairs.
Coup d'œil. [Fr.] A slight view; a glance.
Coupée. [Fr.] A motion in dancing.
Coupons. [Fr.] Dividend-warrants; papers, or parts of a commercial instrument bearing interest, of which a part is cut off as it falls due.
Courage sans peur. [Fr.] Courage without fear.
Coureurs des bois. [Fr.] Forest-runners.
Coûte que coûte. [Fr.] Let it cost what it may.
Cranium. [L.] The skull.
Credenda. [L.] Things to be believed.
Credo quia impossibile est. [L.] I believe because it is impossible.
Crescit eundo. [L.] It increases in its course.
Crux criticorum. [L.] The puzzle of critics.
Crux medicorum. [L.] The puzzle of physicians.
Crux mathematicorum. [L.] The puzzle of mathematicians.
Cuerpo. [Sp.] The body. — *To be in cuerpo,* is to be without full dress.
Cui bono? [L.] For whose benefit?
Cum grano salis. [L.] With a grain of salt; with some allowance.
Cum privilegio. [L.] With privilege or license.
Curiosa felicitas. [L.] A felicitous tact.
Curioso. [It.] A curious person; a virtuoso.
Currente calamo. [L.] With a rapid pen.
Custos morum. [L.] The guardian of morals.
Custos rotulorum. [L.] The keeper of the rolls.

D.

Da capo. [It.] (*Music.*) Signifying that the first part of a tune should be repeated.
D'accord. [Fr.] Agreed; in tune.
Dado. [It.] Plain part of a column; the die.
Dames de la halle. [Fr.] Market-women.
Data. [L.] Things granted; premises.
De bonne grace. [Fr.] Willingly and kindly.
Debouchure. [Fr.] The mouth of a river or strait.
Débris. [Fr.] Fragments; ruins.
Début. [Fr.] The beginning or opening of a discourse, or any design; first appearance.
Deceptio visûs. [L.] Optical illusion.
Decimo-sexto. [L.] A book is a *decimo-sexto* when a sheet is folded into 16 leaves.
Decrevi. [L.] I have determined.
De die in diem. [L.] From day to day.
De facto. [L.] In fact; in reality.
De gustibus non disputandum. [L.] There is no disputing about tastes.
Déjeûner. [Fr.] A breakfast.
Déjeûner à la fourchette. [Fr.] A meat breakfast.

De jure. [L.] By or of right; by law.
Delirium tremens. [L.] The drunkard's madness.
De minimis non curatur. [L.] No notice is taken of trifles.
Dénouement. [Fr.] The discovery of the plot of a drama; catastrophe; a finishing.
De novo. [L.] Anew; from the beginning.
Deo favente. [L.] Providence favoring.
Deo gratias. [L.] Thanks to God.
Deo juvante. [L.] With God's help.
Deo monente. [L.] Providence warning.
Deo volente. [L.] If God will.
De profundis. [L.] Out of the depths.
Desideratum. [L.] A thing desired.
Desunt cætera. [L.] The remainder is wanting.
Detur digniori. [L.] Let it be given to the more worthy.
Deus vobiscum. [L.] God be with you.
Dextro tempore. [L.] At a propitious time.
Dictum (pl. *dicta*). [L.] A positive assertion.
Dies faustus. [L.] A lucky day.
Dies infaustus. [L.] An unlucky day.
Dies iræ. [L.] Day of wrath.
Dies non. [L.] No day in court.
Dieu défend le droit. [Fr.] God defends the right.
Dieu et mon droit. [Fr.] God and my right.
Dii majorum gentium. [L.] The twelve superior gods.
Dii penates. [L.] Household gods.
Dilettante (pl. *dilettanti*). [It.] One who delights in cultivating or promoting the fine arts.
Dirigo. [L.] I guide.
Disjecta membra. [L.] Scattered remains.
Divide et impera. [L.] Divide and govern.
Docendo discimus. [L.] We learn by teaching.
Dolce. [It.] Same as *Dolcemente.*
Dolcemente. [It.] (*Music.*) In a soft, agreeable manner.
Doloroso. [It.] (*Music.*) Soft and pathetic.
Dorer la pilule. [Fr.] To gild the pill.
Dos d'âne. [Fr.] A shelving ridge.
Double entendre. [Fr.] Double meaning.
Double entente. [Fr.] Double signification.
Doux yeux. [Fr.] Soft glances.
Dramatis personæ. [L.] Characters of the drama; characters represented.
Droit des gens. [Fr.] The law of nations.
Droit et avant. [Fr.] Right and forward.
Duello. [It.] The duel; the rule of duelling.
Dulia. [Gr.] An inferior kind of worship.
Dum vivimus, vivamus. [L.] While we live, let us live.
Dura mater. [L.] A membrane covering the brain.
Durante beneplacito. [L.] During our good pleasure.
Durante vitâ. [L.] During life.

E.

Eau de Cologne. [Fr.] Cologne water.
Eau de vie. [Fr.] Brandy.
Ecce homo. [L.] Behold the man.
Ecce signum. [L.] Behold the sign, or badge.
Echelon. [Fr.] (*Mil.*) A movement of an army in the form of steps.
E contra. [L.] On the other hand.

E contrario. [L.] On the contrary.
Editio princeps. [L.] The first edition.
Elapso tempore. [L.] The time having elapsed.
Elegit. [L.] A writ of execution.
Elève. [Fr.] A pupil.
Elite. [Fr.] The flower of an army.
Eloignement. [Fr.] Estrangement.
Embonpoint. [Fr.] Good plight of body; plumpness.
Embouchure. [Fr.] The aperture of a flute, &c.; the mouth of a river.
Emeritus. [L.] An epithet applied to one who is discharged from further public duty.
Empressement. [Fr.] Eagerness; haste; zeal.
Enceinte. [Fr.] Ground enclosed; — pregnant; being with child.
En famille. [Fr.] In a family way.
Enfans de famille. [Fr.] Children of the family.
Enfant gâté. [Fr.] A spoiled child.
Enfant trouvé. [Fr.] A foundling.
En fin. [Fr.] At length; at last.
En masse. [Fr.] In a mass or body.
Ennui. [Fr.] Wearisomeness; disgust.
En passant. [Fr.] In passing; by the way.
En plein jour. [Fr.] In broad day.
En revanche. [Fr.] In return; as a requital.
En route. [Fr.] On the way or road.
Ensemble. [Fr.] One with another; a relative proportion of parts to the whole.
Entre deux vins. [Fr.] Neither drunk nor sober.
Entremets. [Fr.] Dainties between the courses.
Entre nous. [Fr.] Between ourselves.
Entresol. [Fr.] A low-studded story between the basement and second story.
Eo nomine. [L.] By that name.
Epicedium. [L.] An elegy; a funeral poem.
Epigeum, Epigee. That part of the orbit in which a planet comes nearest to the earth.
Epiglottis. A cartilage of the larynx.
Epiphonema. (*Rhet.*) An exclamation.
Epiploce. (*Rhet.*) A sort of climax.
E pluribus unum. [L.] One of many. — The motto of the United States. — *The allusion is to the formation of one federal government out of several independent States.*
Equanimiter. [L.] With equanimity.
Ergo. [L.] Therefore; — *a term in logic.*
Errare humanum est. [L.] To err is human.
Espérance et Dieu. [Fr.] Hope and God.
Esprit de corps. [Fr.] The spirit of the body.
Esprit fort. [Fr.] A freethinker.
Essayez. [Fr.] Try; attempt.
Est modus in rebus. [L.] There is a medium in all things.
Esto perpetua. [L.] Let it endure forever.
Et cætera. [L.] And the rest.
Et sequentia. [L.] And what follows.
Et sic de cæteris. [L.] And so of the rest.
Et sic de similibus. [L.] And so of the like.
Et tu, Brute. [L.] And even you, Brutus.
Euphorbium. [L.] A medicinal gum resin.
Ex abrupto. [L.] Abruptly.
Ex abundantiâ. [L.] Out of the abundance.
Ex animo. [L.] Heartily; sincerely.
Ex beneplacito. [L.] At pleasure.
Ex cathedra. [L.] From the chair or pulpit; from high authority.
Excelsior. [L.] Higher; more elevated.
Exceptis excipiendis. [L.] The proper exceptions being made.

Excerpta. [L.] Extracts.
Ex concesso. [L.] From what has been admitted.
Excudit. [L.] He fashioned or made it.
Ex curiâ. [L.] Out of court.
Ex delicto. [L.] From the crime.
Ex dono. [L.] By the gift of.
Exempli gratia. [L.] For example; for instance.
Exeunt. [L.] They go out.
Exeunt omnes. [L.] All go out.
Exigeant. [Fr.] Requiring too much.
Ex merâ gratiâ. [L.] From mere favor.
Ex mero motu. [L.] From a mere motion.
Ex officio. [L.] By virtue of his office.
Ex opere operato. [L.] By external works.
Ex parte. [L.] On one part or side.
Experimentum crucis. [L.] The experiment of the cross: — a decisive experiment.
Expertus. [L.] An experienced person.
Ex post facto. [L.] After the deed is done.
Expressis verbis. [L.] In express terms.
Expressivo. [It.] (*Music.*) With expression.
Ex professo. [L.] By profession.
Ex tempore. [L.] Off-hand; on the spur of the moment: — extemporaneously.
Ex uno disce omnes. [L.] From one learn all.
Exuviæ. [L.] Cast skins; cast shells; whatever is shed by animals.

F.

Facile princeps. [L.] The admitted chief.
Fac totum. [L.] A man of all work.
Fæx populi. [L.] The dregs of the people.
Faire bonne mine. [Fr.] To put a good face on.
Faire mon devoir. [Fr.] To do my duty.
Faire sans dire. [Fr.] To do, not say.
Fait accompli. [Fr.] A thing already done.
Falsetto. [It.] (*Music.*) A feigned voice.
Fama clamosa. [L.] Public scandal.
Famille, En famille. [Fr.] In a family way; domestically.
Fantasia. [It.] (*Music.*) A kind of air.
Fasces. [L.] Rods anciently carried before the Roman consuls as a mark of authority.
Fascine. [Fr.] A fagot.
Fasti et nefasti dies. [L.] Lucky and unlucky days.
Fata obstant. [L.] The Fates oppose.
Faux pas. [Fr.] A false step.
Feme covert. [Fr.] A married woman.
Feme sole. [Fr.] A single woman.
Femme de chambre. [Fr.] A chamber-maid.
Femme de charge. [Fr.] A housekeeper.
Feræ naturæ. [L.] Of a wild nature.
Ferme ornée. [Fr.] An ornamented farm.
Fête. [Fr.] A feast; a festival day.
Fête champêtre. [Fr.] A rural feast celebrated out of doors.
Feu du joie. [Fr.] A bonfire.
Feuillemort. [Fr.] Color of a faded leaf.
Feuilleton. [Fr.] A small leaf; a supplement to, or the bottom of a page of, a newspaper.
Feuilletoniste. [Fr.] A writer of *feuilletons.*
Fiat lux. [L.] Let light be.
Fide et amore. [L.] By faith and love.
Fide et fiduciâ. [L.] By fidelity and confidence.
Fide et fortitudine. [L.] By faith and fortitude.

Fidei defensor. [L.] Defender of the faith.
Fidelis ad urnam. [L.] Faithful unto death.
Fideliter. [L.] Faithfully.
Fide, non armis. [L.] By faith, not arms.
Fides Punica. [L.] Punic faith: — treachery.
Fidus Achates. [L.] Faithful Achates.
Fidus et audax. [L.] Faithful and daring.
Fieri facias. [L.] (*Law.*) A kind of judicial writ.
Filius nullius. [L.] A son of nobody.
Filius populi. [L.] A son of the people.
Filius terræ. [L.] A son of the earth. — (*Oxford, Eng.*) a student of low birth.
Fille de chambre. [Fr.] A chamber-maid.
Fille de joie. [Fr.] A prostitute.
Finem respice. [L.] Look to the end.
Finis coronat opus. [L.] The end crowns the work.
Flagrante bello. [L.] While the war was raging.
Flagrante delicto. [L.] In the actual commission of the crime.
Flebile ludibrium. [L.] A sad mockery.
Flota. [Sp.] A fleet of ships.
Forma pauperis. [L.] In the character of a pauper.
Forte. [It.] (*Music.*) Loudly, with strength and spirit.
Fortes fortuna juvat. [L.] Fortune favors the brave.
Fortissimo. [It.] (*Music.*) Very loud.
Fortiter et recte. [L.] With fortitude and rectitude.
Fortiter in re. [L.] With firmness in action.
Friseur. [Fr.] A hair-dresser.
Front à front. [Fr.] Face to face.
Fugit hora. [L.] The hour flies.
Fuit Ilium. [L.] Troy *has* been.
Fulmen brutum. [L.] A harmless thunderbolt.
Functus officio. [L.] Having discharged his office.
Furor loquendi. [L.] A rage for speaking.
Furor scribendi. [L.] A rage for writing.
Furor poëticus. [L.] Poetic rage or fire.

G.

Gallicè. [L.] In French.
Garde à cheval. [Fr.] A mounted guard.
Garde de corps. [Fr.] A body-guard.
Garde mobile. [Fr.] Guards liable to general service.
Gardez bien. [Fr.] Guard well; take care.
Gendarme. [Fr.] A military man. — The *gendarmes, gens d'armes,* or *gendarmerie,* are a select body of troops in France, employed by the police.
Genius loci. [L.] The genius of the place.
Gens de condition. [Fr.] People of rank.
Gens d'église. [Fr.] Churchmen.
Gens de guerre. [Fr.] The military.
Gens de langues. [Fr.] Linguists.
Gens de lettres. [Fr.] The literati.
Gens de peu. [Fr.] The meaner sort.
Gens togata. [L.] Gownsmen; civilians.
Genus irritabile vatum. [L.] The irritable race of poets.
Georgium Sidus. [L.] A planet, called also *Herschel* and *Uranus.*
Germanicè. [L.] In German.

Glebæ ascriptus. [L.] A servant belonging to the soil.
Gloria in excelsis. [L.] Glory to God in the highest.
Gloria Patri. [L.] Glory be to the Father.
Goutte à goutte. [Fr.] Drop by drop.
Gradus ad Parnassum. [L.] An aid to writing Latin and Greek poetry.
Grande parure. [Fr.] Full dress.
Gratia placendi. [L.] The delight of pleasing.
Gratis dictum. [L.] Mere assertion.
Grex venalium. [L.] A venal throng.
Grisette. [Fr.] The wife or daughter of a French tradesman.
Guerra al cuchillo. [Sp.] War to the knife.
Guerre à l'outrance. [Fr.] War to the knife.
Guerre à mort. [Fr.] War to the death.

H.

Habeas corpus. [L.] A writ for delivering a person from false imprisonment, &c.
Hagiographa. [L.] Sacred writings.
Haro. [Fr.] Hue and cry.
Haud passibus æquis. [L.] With unequal steps.
Haut et bon. [Fr.] Lofty and good.
Hauteur. [Fr.] Haughtiness.
Haut-goût. [Fr.] A strong relish.
Heurēka (εὕρηκα). [Gr.] I have found it.
Hic et ubique. [L.] Here and every where.
Hic jacet. [L.] Here lies; — *sepultus,* buried.
Hinc illæ lachrymæ. [L.] Hence these tears.
Hoc loco. [L.] In this place.
Hoc saxum posuit. [L.] He placed this stone.
Hoc tempore. [L.] At this time.
Hoi polloi (οἱ πολλοί). [Gr.] The many.
Hominis est errare. [L.] To err is human.
Homme de robe. [Fr.] A man in civil office.
Homme des affaires. [Fr.] A man of business.
Homme d'esprit. [Fr.] A man of wit or talent.
Homo sui juris. [L.] One who is his own master.
Honor est a Nilo. [L.] Honor is from the Nile. *An anagram on "Horatio Nelson."*
Honos alit artes. [L.] Honor cherishes the arts.
Hookah. A sort of tobacco-pipe in the East.
Hora è sempre. [It.] It is always time.
Hora fugit. [L.] The hour flies.
Horresco referens. [L.] I shudder as I relate.
Hors de combat. [Fr.] Not in a condition to fight.
Hospitium. [L.] An inn.
Hôtel des Invalides. [Fr.] A hospital in Paris for wounded soldiers, &c.
Hôtel de ville. [Fr.] Town-hall; city-hall.
Hôtel Dieu. [Fr.] A hospital.
Huissier. [Fr.] Door-keeper; usher.
Humanum est errare. [L.] To err is human.
Hysteron proteron. A rhetorical figure, when that which was done first is last mentioned.

I.

Ibidem. [L.] In the same place.
Ich dien. [German.] I serve.
Idem. [L.] The same.
Idem sonans. [L.] Signifying the same.

Id est. [L.] That is.
Id genus omne. [L.] All persons of that description.
Ignis fatuus. [L.] Will o' the Wisp.
Illuminati, or *Illuminees.* Members of associations in modern Europe, hostile to the existing religious institutions.
Il sent le fagot. [Fr.] He smells of the fagot.
Imo pectore. [L.] From the bottom of the heart.
Imperium in imperio. [L.] A state within a state.
In æquilibrio. [L.] In equilibrium.
In articulo mortis. [L.] At the point of death.
In capite. [L.] In chief.
In cælo quies. [L.] There is rest in heaven.
In commendam. [L.] In recommendation.
In curià. [L.] In court.
Inde iræ. [L.] Hence these resentments.
Index expurgatorius. [L.] A purifying index; a list of prohibited books.
In dubiis. [L.] In matters of doubt.
In equilibrio. [L.] In an even poise.
In esse. [L.] In actual being.
In extenso. [L.] In full; at large.
In extremis. [L.] At the point of death.
Infanta. (*Spain and Portugal.*) A princess of royal blood.
Infante. (*Spain and Portugal.*) A prince of the royal blood.
In formâ pauperis. [L.] As a poor man.
In foro conscientiæ. [L.] Before the tribunal of conscience.
Infra dignitatem. [L.] Below one's dignity.
In futuro. [L.] In future.
In limine. [L.] At the threshold.
In loco. [L.] In the proper place.
In loco parentis. [L.] In place of a parent.
In medias res. [L.] Into the midst of affairs.
In memoriam. [L.] In memory.
In nubibus. [L.] In the clouds.
In partibus infidelium. [L.] In infidel [i. e. not *Catholic*] countries.
In petto. [It.] In reserve or secrecy.
In posse. [L.] In possible being.
In præsenti. [L.] At the present time.
In propriâ personâ. [L.] In person.
In puris naturalibus. [L.] Stark naked.
In re. [L.] In the act; in reality.
In sæcula sæculorum. [L.] For ages on ages.
Insculpsit. [L.] He engraved it.
In situ. [L.] In the natural situation.
Inspeximus. [L., *we have inspected:* the first word in ancient charters, &c.] An exemplification.
Instar omnium. [L.] An example which may suffice for all.
In statu quo. [L.] In the former state.
Intaglio. [It.] A precious stone having a head or some figure engraved on it.
Inter alia. [L.] Among other things.
Inter nos. [L.] Between ourselves.
Inter pocula. [L.] In his cups.
In terrorem. [L.] In terror; by way of warning.
Inter se. [L.] Among themselves.
Inter parietes. [L.] Within walls; in private.
In toto. [L.] In the whole; entirely.
In transitu. [L.] In the passage; in passing.
In usum Delphini. [L.] For the use of the Dauphin.
In vacuo. [L.] In a vacuum.
In vino veritas. [L.] There is truth in wine.

Invitâ Minervâ. [L.] Without capacity or genius.
Ipse dixit. [L.] He himself said it.
Ipsissima verba. [L.] The very words.
Ipsissimis verbis. [L.] In the very words.
Ipso facto. [L.] By the act itself.
Ipso jure. [L.] By the law itself.
Italicè. [L.] In Italian.
Item. [L.] Also.

J.

Jacta est alea. [L.] The die is cast.
Januis clausis. [L.] With closed doors.
Je ne sais quoi. [Fr.] I know not what.
Je suis prêt. [Fr.] I am ready.
Jet d'eau. [Fr.] A water pipe or spout.
Jeu de mots. [Fr.] A play upon words.
Jeu d'esprit. [Fr.] A display of wit; a witticism.
Jeu de théâtre. [Fr.] A stage-trick; a claptrap.
Jubilate Deo. [L.] Be joyful in the Lord.
Judicium Dei. [L.] The judgment of God.
Juncta juvant. [L.] United, they assist.
Juniores ad labores. [L.] Young men for labor.
Jupiter tonans. [L.] The Thunderer, Jove.
Jure divino. [L.] By the divine law.
Jure humano. [L.] By human law.
Juris utriusque doctor. [L.] Doctor of both laws (civil and canonical).
Jus civile. [L.] The civil law.
Jus divinum. [L.] Divine right.
Jus et norma loquendi. [L.] The rule and law of speech.
Jus gentium. [L.] The law of nations.
Jus possessionis. [L.] The right of possession.
Jus proprietatis. [L.] The right of property.
Juste milieu. [Fr.] The golden mean.

L.

Labore et honore. [L.] By labor and honor.
Labor ipse voluptas. [L.] Labor itself is a pleasure.
Labor omnia vincit. [L.] Labor conquers all things.
Laisser faire. [Fr.] To let alone; to leave matters to their natural course.
Laissez nous faire. [Fr.] Let us act for ourselves.
La maladie sans maladie. [Fr.] Hypochondria.
Lapsus calami. [L.] A slip of the pen.
Lapsus linguæ. [L.] A slip of the tongue.
Lar (pl. *lares*). [L.] A household god.
Lares et penates. [L.] Household gods: — home.
L'argent. [Fr.] Silver; money.
Largo,) [It.] (*Music.*) Terms denoting a
Larghetto.) slow movement.
Latinè dictum. [L.] Said in Latin.
Latitat. [L.] A writ of summons.
Latria. [L.] The highest kind of worship.
Laudari a viro laudato. [L.] To be praised by a man who is himself praised.
Laus Deo. [L.] Praise be to God.
Lector benevole. [L.] Gentle reader.
Legatus a latere. [L.] A papal ambassador extraordinary.
Le grand monarque. [Fr.] The great monarch.

Le grand œuvre. [Fr.] The great work.
L'empire des lettres. [Fr.] The republic of letters.
Le point du jour. [Fr.] Daybreak.
Le roi et l'état. [Fr.] The king and the state.
Le roi le veut. [Fr.] The king wills it.
Les extrêmes se touchent. [Fr.] Extremes meet.
Lettre de marque. [Fr.] A letter of marque or reprisal.
Lettres de cachet. [Fr.] Sealed letters of the king, containing private orders.
Lex loci. [L.] The law of the place.
Lex terræ. [L.] The law of the land.
Lex non scripta. [L.] The unwritten law; the common law.
Lex scripta. [L.] The written or statute law.
Lex talionis. [L.] The law of retaliation.
Libretto. [It.] A little book; a pamphlet.
Licentia vatum. [L.] Poetical license.
Limæ labor. [L.] The labor of the file.
L'inconnu. [Fr.] The unknown.
L'incroyable. [Fr.] The incredible.
Lis litem generat. [L.] Strife begets strife.
Lis sub judice. [L.] A case not yet decided.
Lite pendente. [L.] During the trial.
Literatim. [L.] Letter by letter; literally.
Littérateur. [Fr.] A literary man.
Loci communes. [L.] Commonplaces; topics.
Loco citato. [L.] In the place before cited.
Locum tenens. [L.] A substitute; a proxy.
Locus criminis. [L.] The place of the crime.
Locus in quo. [L.] The place in which.
Locus penitentiæ. [L.] Place for repentance.
Locus sigilli. [L.] The place of the seal.
Longo intervallo. [L.] With a long interval.
Loyal en tout. [Fr.] Loyal in every thing.
Loyauté m'oblige. [Fr.] Loyalty binds me.
Lucidus ordo. [L.] A lucid arrangement.
Lupus in fabulâ. [L.] The wolf in the fable.
Lusus naturæ. [L.] A freak of nature; a monster.

M.

Macte virtute. [L.] Go on increasing in virtue.
Mademoiselle. [Fr.] A miss; a young girl.
Maestoso. [It.] (*Music.*) A term directing the part to be played with grandeur.
Magna charta. [L.] The great charter of English liberty.
Magna est veritas, et prævalebit. [L.] Truth is powerful, and will prevail.
Magnifico. [It.] A grandee of Venice.
Magni nominis umbra. [L.] The shadow of a great name.
Magnum bonum. [L.] A great good.
Magnum opus. [L.] A great work.
Magnus Apollo. [L.] Great Apollo: — a great oracle or authority.
Maintien le droit. [Fr.] Maintain the right.
Maison de campagne. [Fr.] A country-house.
Maison de ville. [Fr.] A town-house.
Maître d'hôtel. [Fr.] A steward.
Maladie du pays. [Fr.] Homesickness.
Malâ fide. [L.] In bad faith; treacherously.
Mal à propos. [Fr.] Out of place; unseasonable.
Malis avibus. [L.] With bad omens.
Malum in se. [L.] A thing wrong in itself.
Malum prohibitum. [L.] A thing wrong because forbidden.

Mania a potu. [L.] Madness from drink; delirium tremens.
Manu forti. [L.] With a strong hand.
Manu propria. [L.] With one's own hand.
Masorah. A Hebrew work on the Bible.
Materia medica. [L.] Substance used in medicine.
Mauvais goût. [Fr.] Bad taste.
Mauvaise honte. [Fr.] Extreme bashfulness.
Maximus in minimis. [L.] Very great in very little things.
Mediocria firma. [L.] The middle station is safest.
Memento mori. [L.] Be mindful of death.
Memor et fidelis. [L.] Mindful and faithful.
Memoriâ in æternâ. [L.] In eternal remembrance.
Memoriter. [L.] By rote.
Mens divinior. [L.] Inspired mind of the poet.
Mens sana in corpore sano. [L.] A sound mind in a sound body.
Meo periculo. [L.] At my own risk.
Meum et tuum. [L.] Mine and thine: — property.
Mezzo termine. [It.] A middle course.
Minutiæ. [L.] Trifles; minute points.
Mirabile dictu. [L.] Wonderful to relate.
Mirabile visu. [L.] Wonderful to see.
Mobile perpetuum. [L.] Perpetual motion.
Modo et formâ. [L.] In manner and form.
Modus operandi. [L.] The mode of operation.
Mollia tempora fandi. [L.] The favorable moments for speaking.
Monsieur. [Fr.] Sir: *the title of the French king's eldest brother.*
Morceau (pl. morceaux). [Fr.] A small piece.
More majorum. [L.] After the manner of our ancestors.
Mot du guet. [Fr.] A watchword.
Moto proprio. [L.] Of his own accord.
Mots d'usage. [Fr.] Phrases in common use.
Multum in parvo. [L.] Much in a little space.
Mutatis mutandis. [L.] The necessary changes being made.

N.

Natale solum. [L.] Natal soil.
Ne cede malis. [L.] Yield not to misfortunes.
Necessitas non habet legem. [L.] Necessity has no law.
Nefasti dies. [L.] Unlucky days.
Nem. con. [L., for *nemine contradicente.*] No one opposing.
Nenia. [Gr.] A funeral song; an elegy.
Ne plus ultra. [L.] The utmost limit.
Ne quid nimis. [L.] Do not take too much of any thing: — avoid extremes.
Ne vile velis. [L.] Desire nothing base.
Nil desperandum. [L.] Never despair.
N'importe. [Fr.] It matters not.
Nisi prius. [L.] (*Law.*) A judicial writ.
Nolens volens. [L.] Willing or unwilling.
Noli me tangere. [L.] Touch me not.
Nolle prosequi. [L.] (*Law.*) An agreement by the plaintiff that he will not further prosecute his suit.
Nolo episcopari. [L.] I wish not to be made bishop.

Nom de guerre. [Fr.] A war name ; — an assumed travelling title.
Nom de plume. [Fr.] An assumed name of a writer.
Non assumpsit. [L.] (*Law.*) He did not assume ; — a plea in personal actions.
Non compos mentis. [L.] Not of sound mind.
Non constat. [L.] It does not appear.
Non est inventus. [L.] He has not been found.
Non libet. [L.] It does not please me.
Non mi ricordo. [It.] I do not remember.
Non nobis solum. [L.] Not to us alone.
Non obstante. [L.] Notwithstanding any thing to the contrary.
Non sequitur. [L.] It does not follow : — an unwarranted conclusion.
Nosce teipsum. [L.] Know thyself.
Nota bene. [L.] Take notice.
N'oubliez pas. [Fr.] Forget not.
Nous verrons. [Fr.] We shall see.
Nouvellette. [Fr.] A tale ; a short novel.
Novus homo. [L.] A new man.
Nudis verbis. [L.] In plain words.
Nudum pactum. [L.] A bare contract.
Nugæ canoræ. [L.] Melodious trifles.
Nullius filius. [L.] A son of nobody.
Nunc aut nunquam. [L.] Now or never.
Nunquam non paratus. [L.] Never unprepared.

O.

Obiter dictum. [L.] A thing said by the way.
Observanda. [L.] Things to be observed.
Occurrent nubes. [L.] Clouds will intervene.
Odium theologicum. [L.] The hatred of theologians.
Œil de bœuf. [Fr.] Bull's eye.
Officina gentium. [L.] The workshop of nations.
Ohe! jam satis. [L.] O! there is now enough.
Olla podrida. [Sp.] A heterogeneous mixture.
Omnia mutantur, et nos mutamur in illis. [L.] All things change, and we change with them.
Omnia vincit labor. [L.] Labor overcomes all obstacles.
On dit. [Fr., *it is said.*] A loose report.
Onomatopœia. (*Rhet.*) A figure, when the sound of the word corresponds to the thing signified.
Onus probandi. [L.] The burden of proof.
Operæ pretium est. [L.] It is worth while.
Opera illius mea sunt. [L.] His works are mine.
Optimates. [L.] The chief men in a state.
Opus operatum. [L.] A mere outward work.
Ora e sempre. [It.] Now and always.
Ora et labora. [L.] Pray and labor.
Ora pro nobis. [L.] Pray for us.
Ore rotundo. [L.] With a full, round voice.
Ore tenus. [L.] From the mouth.
Origo mali. [L.] The origin of the evil.
O, si sic omnia! [L.] O that he had always spoken or acted thus !
Os rotundum. [L.] A round mouth ; — a flowing and eloquent delivery.
O tempora, O mores! [L.] O the times and the manners !
Otia dant vitia. [L.] Idleness leads to vice.
Otium cum dignitate. [L.] Leisure with dignity.

27

Outre. [Fr.] Extravagant ; out of the common limits ; overstrained.
Ouvrier. [Fr.] An artisan ; workman.

P.

Pacta conventa. [L.] Conditions agreed upon.
Pallida mors. [L.] Pale death.
Pandemonium. The great hall or council chamber of the fallen angels.
Par excellence. [Fr.] By way of eminence.
Pari passu. [L.] With equal pace.
Par nobile fratrum. [L.] A noble pair of brothers.
Paronomasia. ⎫ A play upon words ; a pun.
Paronomasy. ⎭
Particeps criminis. [L.] An accomplice in the crime.
Parturiunt montes. [L.] The mountain is in labor.
Passe-partout. [Fr.] A master-key.
Passim. [L.] Every where.
Paterfamilias. [L.] The father of a family.
Pater patriæ. [L.] The father of his country.
Pathopœia. An address to the passions.
Patois. [Fr.] A corrupt speech or dialect.
Patriis virtutibus. [L.] By hereditary virtue.
Penchant. [Fr.] Inclination ; — propensity.
Pendente lite. [L.] While the suit is pending.
Per. [L.] By ; as, *per* day, i. e. by the day.
Per annum. [L.] By the year ; yearly.
Per capita. [L.] By the head ; singly.
Per centum. [L.] By the hundred.
Per diem. [L.] By the day.
Père de famille. [Fr.] The father of a family.
Per fas et nefas. [L.] Through right and wrong.
Per saltum. [L.] By a leap : — by fits and starts.
Per se. [L.] By itself ; for its own sake.
Petitio principii. [L.] A begging of the question.
Petit maître. [Fr.] A fop ; a coxcomb.
Pia mater. [L.] A membrane covering the brain.
Pillau. ⎫ A Turkish dish made of boiled rice and
Pillaw. ⎭ mutton fat or juice.
Pis aller. [Fr.] The worst or last shift.
Poco á poco. [Sp.] Little by little ; — softly.
Point d'appui. [Fr.] Point of support.
Pons asinorum. [L.] The bridge of asses.
Posse comitatus. [L.] The power of the county ; an armed body.
Post mortem. [L.] After death.
Post nubila jubila. [L.] After sorrow, joy.
Post obitum. [L.] After death.
Postulatum. [L.] A thing required ; an assumed position.
Pour prendre congé. [Fr.] To take leave.
Præcipe. (*Law.*) A kind of writ.
Præcognita. [L.] Things previously known.
Præmonitus, præmunitus. [L.] Forewarned, forearmed.
Primæ viæ. [L.] The first passages.
Prima facie. [L.] On the first face or view.
Primum mobile. [L.] First impulse ; that which puts every thing in motion.
Primus inter pares. [L.] The first among equals.
Principiis obsta. [L.] Resist the first beginnings.
Privatim. [L.] Privately ; in secret.
Probatum est. [L.] It is tried and proved.

Pro bono publico. [L.] For the public good.
Pro confesso. [L.] As if conceded.
Pro Deo et ecc.esiâ. [L.] For God and the church.
Pro et con. [L.] For and against.
Profanum vulgus. [L.] The profane vulgar.
Pro formâ. [L.] For form's sake.
Pro hac vice. [L.] For this time.
Proh pudor. [L.] O, for shame !
Projet de loi. [Fr.] A legislative bill or draft.
Prolegomena. [Gr.] Introductory remarks ; a preface.
Proœmium. [L.] A preface ; an introduction.
Pro ratâ. [L.] In proportion.
Pro re natâ. [L.] For a special purpose.
Pro tanto. [L.] For so much ; — as far as it goes.
Protégé. [Fr.] A person protected and patronized.
Pro tempore. [L.] For the time ; temporarily.
Proteus. [L.] One who assumes any shape.
Publicè. [L.] Publicly ; in public.
Punica fides. [L.] Punic faith ; — treachery.

Q.

Qualis rex, talis grex. [L.] Like king, like people.
Quamdiu se bene gesserit. [L.] As long as he shall conduct himself properly ; — during good behavior.
Quanti est sapere ! [L.] How valuable is wisdom !
Quantum libet. [L.] As much as you please.
Quantum sufficit. [L.] Enough.
Quid nunc ? [L.] What now ? what news ?
Quid pro quo. [L.] One thing for another ; — an equivalent.
Quid rides ? [L.] Why do you laugh ?
Qui vive ? [Fr.] "Who goes there ?" On the alert.
Quo ad hoc. [L.] As to this ; to this extent.
Quo animo. [L.] With what intention.
Quocunque nomine. [L.] Under whatever name.
Quod avertat Deus. [L.] Which may God avert.
Quod erat demonstrandum. [L.] Which was to be demonstrated.
Quod erat fuciendum. [L.] Which was to be done.
Quo jure. [L.] By what right.
Quot homines, tot sententiœ. [L.] Many men, many minds.
Quo warranto. [L.] A kind of writ.

R.

Raison d'état. [Fr.] A reason of state.
Rara avis. [L.] A rare bird.
Ratione soli. [L.] In respect of the soil.
Rectè et suaviter. [L.] Justly and mildly.
Rectus in curiâ. [L.] Upright in the court ; with clean hands.
Reductio ad absurdum. [L.] A reduction to an absurdity.
Regatta. [It.] A kind of boat race.
Regium donum. [L.] Royal gift.

Re infectâ. [L.] The business being unfinished.
Reis effendi. A Turkish state minister.
Religio loci. [L.] The spirit of the place.
Remis velisque. [L.] With oars and sails.
Renascentur. [L.] They will be born to another life.
Renovate animos. [L.] Renew your courage.
Rentes. [Fr.] Funds bearing interest ; stocks.
Requiescat in pace. [L.] May he rest in peace.
Res angusta domi. [L.] Narrow circumstances.
Respice finem. [L.] Look to the end.
Respublica. [L.] The republic.
Resurgam. [L.] I shall rise again.
Ride si sapis. [L.] Laugh if you are wise.
Rire sous cape. [Fr.] To laugh in one's sleeve.
Ritornello. [It.] The repeat or burden of a song.
Rota. [L.] A list of persons ; a court.
Ruat cœlum. [L.] Let the heavens fall.
Ruit mole suâ. [L.] It falls to ruin by its own weight.
Ruse. [Fr.] Cunning ; artifice ; fraud ; deceit.
Ruse contre ruse. [Fr.] Trick against trick.
Ruse de guerre. [Fr.] A stratagem of war.
Rus in urbe. [L.] The country in the city.

S.

Sal Atticum. [L.] Attic salt ; wit.
Salvo jure. [L.] Without detriment to the right.
Salvo pudore. [L.] Without offence to modesty.
Sanctum sanctorum. [L.] The holy of holies.
Sang-froid. [Fr.] Coolness ; indifference ; freedom from agitation.
Sans cérémonie. [Fr.] Without ceremony.
Sans culotte. [Fr.] A man without breeches ; raganuffin.
Sans rime et sans raison. [Fr.] Without rhyme or reason.
Sans souci. [Fr.] Without care.
Sans tache. [Fr.] Without spot.
Sapere aude. [L.] Dare to be wise.
Sartor resartus. [L.] The cobbler mended.
Satis verborum. [L.] Enough of words.
Savant (pl. savans). [Fr.] A learned man.
Savior-vivre. [Fr.] Good breeding, or behavior.
Savoir-faire. [Fr.] Tact ; skill ; industry.
Scandalum magnatum. [L.] (*Law.*) Scandal or opprobrium done to any high personage.
Scire facias. [L.] (*Law.*) A kind of judicial writ.
Secundum artem. [L.] According to art.
Secundum usum. [L.] According to custom
Semel et simul. [L.] Once and together.
Semper fidelis. [L.] Always faithful.
Semper idem. [L.] Always the same.
Semper paratus. [L.] Always prepared.
Senatûs-consultum. [L.] A decree of the senate.
Senex, bis puer. [L.] Once a man, twice a boy.
Separatio a mensâ et thoro. [L.] (*Law.*) Separation from bed and board.
Seriatim. [L.] In regular order.
Servare modum. [L.] To keep within bounds.
Sesquipedalia verba. [L.] Words a foot and a half long.
Sic passim. [L.] So every where.
Similia similibus curantur. [L.] Like is cured by like. [The principle of homœopathy.]

Simplex munditiis. [L.] Of simple elegance.
Sine curâ. [L.] Without care.
Sine die. [L.] Without naming a day.
Sine invidiâ. [L.] Without envy.
Sine odio. [L.] Without hatred.
Sine quâ non. [L.] Without which, not; an indispensable condition.
Siquis. [L.] A notification.
Siste, viator. [L.] Stop, traveller.
Soi-disant. [Fr.] Self-called; pretended.
Soirée. [Fr.] An evening party.
Soli Deo gloria. [L.] To God alone be glory.
Solvuntur tabulæ. [L.] (*Law.*) The bills are dismissed: — the defendant is acquitted.
Sortie. [Fr.] A sally; a going out.
Sotto voce. [It.] In an under-tone or whisper.
Spero meliora. [L.] I hope for better things.
Spolia opima. [L.] The richest booty.
Status quo. [L.] The state in which.
Stet. [L.] Let it stand.
Suaviter in modo, fortiter in re. [L.] Gentle in manner, forcible in execution.
Sub colore juris. [L.] Under color of law.
Sub judice lis est. [L.] The cause is yet before the judge.
Sub rosâ. [L.] Under the rose; privately.
Sub silentio. [L.] In silence.
Sui generis. [L.] Of a peculiar kind.
Summum bonum. [L.] The greatest good.
Suo jure. [L.] By his own right.
Suo Marte. [L.] By his own prowess.
Supersedeas. [L.] (*Law.*) A writ to stay proceedings.
Suppressio veri. [L.] The suppression of the truth.
Suum cuique. [L.] Let every one have his own.

T.

Table d'hôte. [Fr.] An ordinary.
Tædium vitæ. [L.] Weariness of life.
Tangere vulnus. [L.] To touch a sore place.
Tant mieux. [Fr.] So much the better.
Tant pis. [Fr.] So much the worse.
Tempora mutantur, et nos mutamur in illis. [L.] Times change, and we change with them.
Tempus fugit. [L.] Time flies.
Tenax propositi. [L.] Tenacious of his purpose.
Terra firma. [L.] Solid land; the continent.
Terra incognita. [L.] An unknown land.
Tertium quid. [L.] A third something.
Tic douloureux. [Fr.] A painful affection of the nerves, mostly in the face.
Toga virilis. [L.] The Roman gown of manhood.
To kalon (τὸ καλόν). [Gr.] The beautiful; the chief good.
To prepon (τὸ πρέπον). [Gr.] The becoming; the proper.
Totidem verbis. [L.] In so many words.
Toties quoties. [L.] As often as.
Totis viribus. [L.] With all his might.
Toto cœlo. [L.] By the whole heavens.
Toujours prêt. [Fr.] Always ready.
Toujours propice. [Fr.] Always propitious.
Tourner casaque. [Fr.] To turn the coat.
Tous frais faits. [Fr.] All expenses paid.
Tout au contraire. [Fr.] Just the contrary.

Tout ensemble. [Fr.] The whole taken together.
Tria juncta in uno. [L.] Three joined in one.
Troja fuit. [L.] Troy was — [is no more.]
Tuum est. [L.] It is thine own.

U.

Uberrima fides. [L.] A superabundant faith.
Ubi supra. [L.] Where above mentioned.
Ultima ratio. [L.] The last reasoning.
Ultimus, or *Ultimo.* [L.] The last; — often contracted to *Ult.*
Unâ voce. [L.] With one voice.
Usque ad aras. [L.] To the very altars.
Usque ad nauseam. [L.] So as to disgust.
Usus loquendi. [L.] Usage in speaking.
Utile dulci. [L.] The useful with the agreeable.
Ut infra. [L.] As stated or cited below.
Uti possidetis. [L.] As you possess: — let each party keep what is in his possession.
Ut supra. [L.] As above stated, or cited.

V.

Vade in pace. [L.] Go in peace.
Vade mecum. [L.] A book or manual that a person always carries with him.
Væ victis. [L.] Woe to the vanquished.
Valet anchora virtus. [L.] Virtue is an anchor.
Valet de chambre. [Fr.] A valet; a body servant.
Valete et plaudite. [L.] Farewell and applaud.
Variæ lectiones. [L.] Various readings.
Variorum. [L.] *Variorum editions* are editions of works in which the notes of various commentators are inserted.
Variorum notæ. [L.] The notes of various editors.
Velis et remis. [L.] With sails and oars.
Venire facias. [L.] You shall cause to come.
Veni, vidi, vici. [L.] I came, I saw, I conquered.
Ventis secundis. [L.] With favorable winds.
Verbatim et literatim. [L.] Word for word, and letter for letter.
Veritas prævalebit. [L.] Truth will prevail.
Veritas vincit. [L.] Truth conquers.
Vérité sans peur. [Fr.] Truth without fear.
Vetturino. [It.] An owner or driver of a *vettura,* an Italian travelling carriage.
Vexata quæstio. [L.] A question much disputed; a vexed question.
Via media. [L.] A middle way or course.
Via militaris. [L.] A military way.
Vice. [L.] In the room of.
Vice versâ. [L.] The terms being reversed.
Vide. [L.] See.
Videlicet. [L.] To wit; namely; that is. *This word is generally written* viz.
Vide ut supra. [L.] See the preceding.
Vi et armis. [L.] By force of arms; by violence.
Vigilate et orate. [L.] Watch and pray.
Vigueur de dessus. [Fr.] Strength is from above.
Vinculum matrimonii. [L.] Bond of matrimony.
Virtus sola nobilitat. [L.] Virtue alone ennobles.
Virtute et fide. [L.] By virtue and faith.
Virtute et labore. [L.] By virtue and toil.
Virtute et operâ. [L.] By virtue and industry.

Virtute, non astutiâ. [L.] By virtue, not by craft.
Virtute, non verbis. [L.] By virtue, not by words.
Virtute officii. [L.] By virtue of his office.
Virtute securus. [L.] Safe through virtue.
Virtutis amore. [L.] Through the love of virtue.
Viser à deux buts. [Fr.] To aim at two marks.
Vis inertiæ. [L.] The power of inertness.
Vis medicatrix naturæ. [L.] The healing power of nature.
Vis poetica. [L.] Poetic genius.
Vis vitæ. [L.] The power or vigor of life.
Vita brevis, ars longa. [L.] Life is short, and art is long.
Vitæ via virtus. [L.] Virtue is the way of life.
Vivat respublica. [L.] Long live the republic.
Vivat regina. [L.] Long live the queen.
Vivat rex. [L.] Long live the king.
Vivâ voce. [L.] By the living voice; by word of mouth.
Vive la bagatelle. [Fr.] Success to trifles.

Vive la république. [Fr.] Long live the republic.
Vive le roi. [Fr.] Long live the king.
Vive, vale. [L.] Live, and be well.
Viz (a contraction of *videlicet*). Namely.
Volo, non valeo. [L.] I am willing, but not able.
Voltigeur. [Fr.] A light horseman.
Vota vita mea. [L.] My life is devoted.
Vox et præterea nihil. [L.] Voice and nothing more; sound without sense.
Vox populi. [L.] The voice of the people.
Vulgò. [L.] Commonly.
Vulnus immedicabile. [L.] An incurable wound.

Z.

Zonam perdidit. [L.] He has lost his purse.
Zonam solvere. [L.] To unloose the virgin zone.

PRONUNCIATION

OF

GREEK AND LATIN PROPER NAMES.

PREFACE AND REMARKS.

NEARLY two thirds of the Proper Names contained in the following Vocabulary have been taken from Walker's "Key to the Classical Pronunciation of Greek, Latin, and Scripture Proper Names;" and the Names here inserted, which are not found in Walker's Key, have been derived from the works of various other authors, the principal of which are those of Carr, Sharpe, Trollope, Pauly, and Smith.

The following rules and observations relating to the pronunciation of Greek and Latin Proper Names are in general accordance with the principles of Walker; but as the system of notation used in this Dictionary is applied to these names in the Vocabulary, and as all the words are divided into syllables, some of his rules for their pronunciation are here omitted as unnecessary.

1. Greek and Latin names introduced into modern languages naturally acquire, in sound and rhythm, the main characteristics of the different languages which receive them. That which is chiefly attended to and sought after, in classical names, is the seat of the accent; and when the seat of the accent and the syllabication are determined, these names are pronounced, in the English language, according to the powers of the letters in common English words.

2. In Greek and Latin names, the accent is always placed on either the second or the third syllable from the end of the word. In words of more than two syllables, if the penult is long in quantity, it is accented; if short, the antepenult receives the accent.

3. The vowel of the penult before *x*, *z*, *j*, or any two consonants except a mute followed by a liquid, as *l* or *r*, is long by *position*. In other cases its quantity must be determined by poetic usage, etymology, or the mode in which the word is written in Greek. The digraphs *ch*, *ph*, *rh*, and *th* are to be regarded as single consonants.

27*

4. An accented vowel in the penultimate syllable, when followed by a single consonant, by *j* or *z*, or by a mute with *l* or *r*, has the long sound; as, *A'bas*, *A'cra*; otherwise, it is short; as, *Abăn'tis*. This pronunciation, in cases like the first and last of these examples, is so obvious, that it has not been deemed necessary to include such words in the Vocabulary.

Exception. — Before *gl* and *tl*, the vowel of the penult, unless it be *u*, has the short sound; as *Ægle* (ĕg'le), *Atlas* (ăt'las).

5. The final *e* is always sounded; as in *Bereni'ce*. This remark, of course, does not apply to Anglicized forms; as, *Pros'er-pine*, for *Proserpina*.

6. In Greek and Latin names, the letter *g* has its soft sound before the vowels *e*, *i*, and *y*, and before the diphthongs *æ* and *œ*; but in most Scripture names, it has its hard sound before these vowels.

7. The digraph *ch*, in Greek and Latin names, and likewise in almost all Hebrew names, is sounded hard, like *k*.

8. Every final *i*, though unaccented, has its long open sound, as in *Abolani*. But when *i*, or its equivalent *y*, ends an unaccented first syllable of a word, it has, in some cases, its long sound, as in *Bianor*; in some, it takes the indistinct sound of *e*, as in *Cilicia*; and in some it is difficult to determine which of these sounds is to be preferred, as there is a want of agreement with respect to them both among orthoepists and good speakers.

9. The termination *es* is pronounced like the English word *ease*; as, *Achilles* (a-kil'lēz).

10. The terminations *aus* and *ous* are always pronounced in two syllables; as, *Men-e-la'us*, *An-tin'o-us*.

11. The termination *eus* in proper names which in Greek end in ευς, as *Orpheus*, *Prometheus*, is to be pronounced as one syllable, the *eu* being a diphthong. Walker, following Labbe

(317)

generally separates the vowels in pronunciation. But the diphthong is never resolved in Greek; and very rarely, if ever, in Latin poetry of the golden or the silver age. But in the termination *eus* in adjectives, *eu* is not a diphthong.

12. There is a class of proper names ending in *ia*, which, in their classical pronunciation, have the accent on the penultimate; as, *Alexandri'a*, *Cassandri'a*, *Deidami'a*, *Philadelphi'a*, *Samari'a*, &c. The English analogy strongly favors the antepenultimate accent in the pronunciation of this class of words; and Walker countenances this accent in relation to a part of them, especially such as are much used in English, and have consequently become, in a measure, Anglicized. The following words, namely, *Alexandria*, *Philadelphia*, and *Samaria*, are so much An-

glicized, that it would seem pedantic, in reading or speaking English, to pronounce them otherwise than with the antepenultimate accent. But such of these names as are scarcely at all Anglicized, as *Antiochia*, *Deidamia*, *Laomedia*, &c., may very properly be allowed to retain their classical accentuation.

13. There are some other classical names which have become more or less Anglicized, and which have, in consequence, had their pronunciation, in a greater or less degree, changed from the classical standard. Thus, *Arius*, the name of the celebrated heretic, is pronounced *A'rius* in English, though the penult is long in Greek; and the usage of the English poets has substituted *Hype'rion* for *Hyperi'on*.

The following Rules of Pronunciation are referred to by Figures in the following Vocabulary.

RULE 1. — The consonants *c*, *s*, and *t*, immediately preceded by the accent, and standing before *i*, followed by another vowel, commonly have the sound of *sh ;* as in *Pho'cion* (fō'shĕ-ŏn), *Ac'cius* (ăk'she-ŭs), *Al'sium* (ăl'she-ŭm), *Helve'tii* (hel-vē'she-ī). — *C*, following an accented syllable, has also the same sound before *eu* and *yo*, as in *Cadu'ceus* (ka-dū'she-ŭs), *Si''cyon* (sĭsh'e-ŏn).

Exceptions. — *T*, when preceded by *s* or *x*, has its hard sound, as in *Sestius*, *Sextius*. — When *si* or *zi*, immediately preceded by an accented vowel, is followed by a vowel, the *s* or *z* generally takes the sound of *zh ;* as, *Mœ'sia* (mē'zhe-a), *He'siod* (hē'zhe-ŏd), *Ely''sium* (e-lĭzh'e-ŭm), *Saba'zius*, (sa-bā'zhe-ŭs). According to Walker, the words *Asia*, *Sosia*, and *Theodosia* are the only exceptions; but to these a few others should perhaps be added, as *Lysias*, *Tysias*.

X, ending an accented syllable, and standing before *i* followed by a vowel, has the sound of *ksh ;* as in *Alex'ia* (a-lĕk'she-a).

RULE 2. — In some proper names, *t* preserves its true sound; as, *Ætion*, *Amphictyon*, *Androtion*, *Eurytion*, *Gration*, *Harpocration*, *Hippotion*, *Iphition*, *Metion*, *Ornytion*, *Pallantion*, *Philistion*, *Polytion*, *Sotion*, *Stration*, and a few others; but *Hephæstion* and *Theodotion* are Anglicized, the last syllable being pronounced like the last syllable in *question*, *commotion*. In the words *Æsion*, *Dionysion*, and *Iasion*, the *s* takes the sound of *z*, but not of *zh*.

RULE 3. — In words ending in *eia*, *eii*, *eium*, and *eius*, with the accent on the *e*, the *i* following the accent is to be understood as articulating the following vowel like *y* consonant; as, *Elege'ia* (el-e-jē'ya), *Pompe'ii* (pom-pē'yi), *Pompe'ium* (pom-pē'yum), *Pompe'ius* (pom-pē'yus). The same rule also applies to words ending in *ia*, preceded by *a* or *o* having the accent upon it, as *Acha'ia* (a-kā'ya), *Lato'ia* (la-tō'ya), and likewise to words having the accent on a vowel, followed by *ia*, though they may not end the word, as *Ple'iades* (plē'ya-dēz).

The digraph *yi*, followed by a vowel, generally represents the Greek diphthong *υι*, and forms but one syllable; as, *Harpyia*, pronounced *Harpy'ya*, or, as some prefer, *Har-pwy'a*.

RULE 4. — The diphthongs *æ* and *œ*, ending a syllable with the accent on it, are pronounced like long *e*, as in *Cæ'sar* (sē'zar) ; but when followed by a consonant in the same syllable, like short *e*, as in *Dæd'alus* (dĕd'a-lŭs).

RULE 5. — In Greek and Latin words which begin with uncombinable consonants, the first letter is silent; thus, *C* in *Cneus* and *Ctesiphon*, *M* in *Mneus*, *P* in *Psyche* and *Ptolemy*, *Ph* in *Phthia*, and *T* in *Tmolus*, are not sounded.

RULE 6. — The termination *eus* in most *Greek* proper names corresponds to *εύς*, and is then to be pronounced in one syllable ; as, *Æ'geus*, *Or'pheus*, used as nouns; but *Æ-ge'us*, *Or-phe'us*, as adjectives.

GREEK AND LATIN PROPER NAMES.

The *figures* annexed to the words refer to the *Six Rules of Pronunciation*, on page 318. Thus the figure 1, annexed to *Abantias*, refers to Rule 1, which shows that the word is pronounced *Ạ-băn'-shẹ-ăs*.

The words in *Italics* are the preceding words *Anglicized*. Thus the Latin word *Adrianus* is changed, in English, into *Adrian*.

Ā'bạ, *and* Ā'bæ
Ăb'ạ-ạ
Ăb'ạ-bạ
Ăb-ạ-cæ'nụm
Ăb-ạ-cē'nẹ
A-bæ'ạ
Ăb'ạ-gạ
Ạ-bág'ạ-rŭs
Ăb'ạ-lạ
Ăb'ạ-lŭs
A-băn'tēş
Ăb-ạn-tī'ạ-dēş
Ạ-băn'tị-ás 1
Ạ-băn'tị-däs
Ăb-ạr-bā'rẹ-ạ
Ăb'ạ-rī
Ạ-băr'ị-mŏn, *or*
  Ăb-ạ-rī'mọn
Ăb'ạ-rĭs
Ăb'ạ-rŭs, *or*
  Ạ-bā'rụs
Ăb'ạ-sạ, *or*
  Ạ-bā'sạ
Ăb-ạ-sī'tịs
Ăb-ạs-sē'nạ
Ăb-ạs-sē'nī
Ăb'ạ-tŏs
Ăb-dạ-lŏn'ị-mŭs, *or*
  Ăb-dạ-lŏn'y-mŭs
Ab-dē'rạ
Ạb-dē'rị-ạ
Ăb-dẹ-rī'tēş
Ab-dē'rụs
Ăb-dọ-lŏn'ị-mŭs
Ā-bẹ-ā'tæ
Ăb-ẹl-lā'nī
Ăb-ẹl-lī'nụm
Ạ-bĕl'lụs
Ā'bẹl
Ăb'ẹ-lŭx
Ạ-bĕr'cị-ŭs 1
Ăb'gạ-rŭs
Ā'bị-ạ
Ā-bị-ā'nụs
Ā'bị-ī
Ăb-ị-lē'nẹ
Ạ-bĭs'ạ-rēş
Ạ-bĭs'ạ-rĭs
Ăb-ị-sŏn'tēş
Ạ-bĭ-tị-ā'nụs 1
Ạ-blā'bị-ŭs
Ạ-blā'vị-ŭs
Ạ-blē'rụs

Ạ-blē'tēş
Ăb'nọ-bạ
Ăb-ọ-brī'cạ
Ạ-bō'bụs
Ăb-ọ-dī'ạ-cŭm
Ạ-bœc'rị-tŭs 4
Ăb-ọ-lā'nī
Ăb'ọ-lŭs
Ạ-bŏn-ị-teī'chọs
Ăb-ọ-rā'cạ
Ạ-bō'rạs
Ăb-ọ-rĭg'ị-nēş
Ăb'ọ-tĭs
Ăb-rạ-dā'tạs, *or*
  Ạ-brád'ạ-tás
Ăb-rạ-dā'tēş
Ạ-brā'hạ-mŭs
Ạ-brĕn'tị-ŭs 1
Ăb-rẹt-tē'nẹ
Ăb-rẹt-tē'nụs
Ạ-brŏc'ọ-mäs
Ạ-brŏc'ọ-mēş
Ạ-brŏd-ị-æ'tụs
Ạ-brō'nị-ŭs
Ạ-brŏn'y-chŭs
Ạ-brō'tạ
Ạ-brŏt'ọ-nŭm
Ạ-brŭ'pọ-lĭs
Ạ-brўp'ọ-lĭs
Ăb'sạ-rŭs, *or*
  Ăb-sā'rụs
Ab-sē'ụs
Ăb-sĭm'ạ-rŭs
Ăb-sĭn'thị-ī
Ăb'sọ-rŭs
Ạb-sўr'tị-dēş
Ăb'ụ-lạ
Ăb-ụ-lī'tēş
Ăb-ụn-dăn'tị-ŭs 1
Ạ-bū'rị-ŭs
Ăb-ụ-sē'nạ, *or*
  Ăb-ụ-sī'nạ
Ăb-y-dē'nī
Ăb-y-dē'nụs
Ạ-bў'dī
Ạ-bў'dọs
Ạ-bў'dụs ·
Ăb'y-lạ
Ăb'y-lŏn
Ăb-ys-sī'nī
Ăc-ạ-căl'lịs
Ăc-ạ-cē'şị-ŭm 1
Ăc-ạ-cē'şị-ŭs 1

Ăc-ạ-cē'tēş
Ạ-cā'cị-ŭs 1
Ăc'ạ-cŭs
Ăc-ạ-dẹ-mī'a, *or*
  Ăc-ạ-dē'mị-ạ
Ăc-ạ-dē'mụs
Ăc-ạ-dē'rạ
Ăc-ạ-dī'rạ
Ăc-ạ-lăn'drụs
Ăc'ạ-lē
Ăc-ạ-mär'chịs
Ăc'ạ-mäs
Ạ-căn'thị-nē
Ạ-căn'thị-ō
Ăc'ạ-rạ
Ạ-cā'rị-ạ
Ăc-ạr-nā'nēş
Ăc-ạr-nā'nị-ạ
Ăc-ạ-thăn'tụs
Ăc'ạ-tŏn
Ăc'bạ-rŭs
Ăc'cị-ạ 1
Ăc'cị-lạ
Ăc'cị-ŏn 1
Ăc'cị-ŭs 1
Ăc'cụ-ạ
Ăç-ẹ-dī'cī
Ăç'ẹ-lạ
Ăç'ẹ-lē
Ăç'ẹ-lŭm
Ạ-cĕph'ạ-lī
Ạ-cĕr'ạ-tŭs
Ăç-ẹ-rī'nạ
Ăç-ẹr-rō'nị-ạ
Ăç-ẹr-rō'nị-ŭs
Ăç-ẹr-sĕc'ọ-mēş
Ăç-ẹ-săm'ẹ-nŭs
Ăç'ẹ-säs
Ạ-cē'şị-ạ 1
Ạ-cē'şị-ás 1
Ăç-ẹ-sī'nēş
Ăç-ẹ-sī'nụs
Ạ-cē'şị-ŭs 1
Ạ-cĕs'tēş
Ạ-cĕs'tị-ŭm 1
Ạ-cĕs-tọ-dō'rụs
Ăç-ẹs-tŏr'ị-dēş
Ạ-cē'tēş
Ăch-ạ-bў'tọs
Ạ-chæ'ạ
Ạ-chæ'ī
Ạ-chæ'ị-ŭm
Ạ-chæm'ẹ-nēş 4

Ăch-æ-mē'nị-ạ
Ăch-æ-mĕn'ị-dēş
Ạ-chæ'tụs
Ạ-chæ'ụs
Ạ-chā'ị-ạ 3
Ạ-chā'ị-äs 3
Ạ-chā'ị-cŭs
Ạ-chā'ịs
Ăch'ạ-lē
Ăch'ạ-rạ
Ạ-chär'ạ-cạ
Ăch-ạ-rĕn'sēş
Ạ-chär'næ
Ạ-chā'tēş
Ăch-ẹ-lō'ị-dēş
Ăch-ẹ-lō'ịs
Ăch-ẹ-lō'rị-ŭm
Ăch-ẹ-lō'ụs
Ạ-chē'lụs
Ăch-ẹ-mĕn'ị-dēş
Ạ-chē'rạs
Ạ-chĕr'dụs
Ăch-ẹ-rŏ'nī
Ăch'ẹ-rŏn
Ăch-ẹ-rón'tị-ạ 1
Ạ-chĕr'rạs
Ăch'ẹ-rŭnş
Ăch-ẹ-rŭ'şị-ạ 1
Ăch-ẹ-rŭ'şị-äs 1
Ăch-ẹ-rŭ'sịs
Ạ-chē'tụs
Ạ-chī'lạs
Ạ-chĭl'lạs
Ăch-ịl-lē'ạ
Ạ-chĭl-lẹi-ĕn'sēş
Ăch-ịl-lē'ịs
Ạ-chĭl'lēş
Ăch-ịl-lē'ụm
Ạ-chĭl'leūs (*n.*) 6
Ăch-ịl-lē'ụs (*a.*)
Ăch-ịl-lī'dēş
Ạ-chī'vī
Ăch-lạ-dæ'ụs
Ăch'ọ-lạ
Ăch-ọ-lā'ī
Ạ-chō'lị-ŭs
Ạ-chŏl'ọ-ē, *or*
  Ăch-ọ-lō'ẹ
Ạ-chō'reūs 6
Ạ-chō'rụs
Ăch-rạ-dī'nạ
Ăch'rạ-dŭs
Ăç-ị-chō'rị-ŭs

Ăç-ị-dā'lị-ạ
Ăç-ị-dā'sạ
Ăç-ị-dī'nụs
Ạ-cī'lạ, *W.*
  Ăç'ị-lạ, *S.*
Ạ-cĭl'ị-ạ
Ạ-cĭl-ị-ā'nụs
Ăç-ị-lĭg'ẹ-nạ
Ạ-cĭl'ị-ŭs
Ạ-cĭl'lạ
Ăç-ịn-dў'nụs, *and*
  Ạ-cĭn'dy-nŭs
Ăç-ị-nī'pō
Ăç'ị-rĭs
Ā'cị-ŭm 1
Ạc-mē'nēş
Ạc-mō'nị-ạ
Ạc-mŏn'ị-dēş
Ăç-œ-mē'tæ
Ăç-œ-nŏn-ọ-ē'tụs
Ạ-cœ'tēş
Ăc-ọ-lў'tī
Ăc-ọ-mĭn'ạ-tŭs
Ăc'ọ-næ
Ạ-cŏn'tēş
Ạ-cŏn'teūs 6
Ạ-cŏn'tị-ŭs 1
Ăc-ọn-tŏb'ọ-lī
Ạ-cŏn-tọ-bū'lụs
Ăc'ọ-rŭs
Ā'crạ
Ăc-rạ-dī'nạ
Ạ-cræ'ạ
Ạ-cræ'pheūs 6
Ạ-cræ'phị-ạ
Ạ-cræph'nị-ạ 4
Ăc-rạ-gạl-lī'dæ
Ăc'rạ-gäs
Ăc-rạ-tŏph'ọ-rŭs
Ăc-rạ-tŏp'ọ-tēş
Ạ-crā'tụs
Ā'crị-æ
Ā'crị-äs
Ăc-rị-dŏph'ạ-gī
Ạ-crī'ọn
Ạ-crī''sẹ-ŭs 1
Ạ-crĭs-ị-ō'nẹ
Ạ-crĭs-ị-ọ-nē'ịs
Ạ-crĭs-ị-ọ-nē'ụs
Ạ-crĭs-ị-ọ-nī'ạ-dēş
Ạ-crĭ''sị-ŭs 1
Ạ-crī'tạs
Ạ-crō'ạ-thŏn

Ăc-rọ-cẹ-râu'nị-ạ
Ăc-rọ-cẹ-râu'nị-ŭm
Ăc-rọ-cẹ-rē'tēş
Ăc-rọ-cọ-rĭn'thụs
Ạ-crŏ'mạ
Ăc-rọ-pā'tọs, *or*
  Ạ-crŏp'ạ-tŏs
Ạ-crŏp'ọ-lĭs
Ạ-crŏp-ọ-lĭs'tịs
Ạ-crŏp-ọ-lī'tạ
Ăc-rọ-rē'ạ
Ăc-rọ-rē'ī
Ăc'rọ-tạ
Ạ-crŏt'ạ-tŭs
Ăc-rọ-tẹ-leū'tị-ŭm l
Ăc-rọ-thō'ọn
Ăc-rọ-thō'ụm
Ạc-tæ'ạ
Ạc-tæ'ọn
Ăc'tị-ạ 1
Ạc-tī'ạ-cŭs
Ạc-tĭs'ạ-nēş, *or*
  Ăc-tị-sā'nēş
Ăc'tị-ŭm 1
Ăc'tị-ŭs 1
Ạc-tŏr'ị-dēş
Ạc-tō'rị-ŏn
Ăc'tọ-rĭs
Ạc-tō'rị-ŭs
Ăc-tụ-ā'rị-ŭs
Ạ-cū'lẹ-ō
Ạ-cū'mẹ-nŭs
Ạ-cū-sị-lā'ụs
Ạ-cū'tị-cŭs
Ạ-cū'tị-ŭs l
Ạ-cȳ'rụs
Ăç'y-tŭs
Ăd'ạ-dạ
Ăd-ạ-măn-tæ'ạ
Ăd-ạ-măn'tị-ŭs l
Ăd'ạ-măs
Ạ-dā'mụs
Ăd'ạ-nạ
Ăd'ạ-thạ
Ăd-dẹ-phā'ģị-ạ
Ăd'dụ-ạ
Ạ-dĕl'phị-ŭs
Ạ-dē'mọn
Ạ-dĕph'ạ-gŭs
Ā'dēş, *or* Hā'dēş
Ăd-gạn-dĕs'trị-ŭs
Ā-dị-ạ-bē'nẹ
Ā-dị-ăt'ọ-rĭx
Ăd-ị-măn'tụs
Ăd-ị-mē'tẹ
Ăd-mē'tạ, *or* -tẹ
Ăd-mē'tụs
Ạ-dō'nị-ạ
Ạ-dō'neūs 6, *and*
  Ạ-dŏ'nẹ-ŭs (*n.*)
Ăd-ọ-nē'ụs (*a.*)
Ạ-dŏn'ị-cŭs
Ạ-dō'nịs
Ăd'rạ-ạ
Ăd-rạ-mī'tæ
Ăd-rạ-mȳt'tị-ŭm
Ạ-drā'nạ, *or*
  Ăd'rạ-nạ
Ạ-drā'nẹ
Ạ-drā'nụm

A-drā'nụs
Ăd-rạs-tē'ạ, *or* -tī'ạ
Ăd-rạs-tī'nẹ
A-drē'nẹ
Ā-drị-ạn-ŏp'ọ-lĭs
Ā-drị-ā'nụm
Ā-drị-ā'nụs
Ā'drị-ạn
Ā-drị-ăt'ị-cŭm
Ăd-ry-mē'tụm
Ăd-ụ-ăt'ị-cạ
Ăd-ụ-ăt'ị-cī
Ạ-dū'lạ, *or* -lẹ
Ạ-dū'lạs
Ạ-dū'lịs
Ăd-ụ-lī'tæ
Ăd-ụ-lī'tọn
Ạ-dū'sị-ŭs l
Ăd'vọ-lănş
Ăd-yr-măch'ị-dæ,
Æ-ạ-cē'ạ
Æ'ạ-cēş
Æ-ăç'ị-dăs
Æ-ăç'ị-dēş
Æ-ạ-cī'ụm
Æ'ạ-cŭs
Æ-ạ-mē'nẹ
Æ-ạn-tē'ụm
Æ-ăn'tị-dēş
Æ-ăn'tịs
Æ'ạ-tŭs
Æ-bū'tị-ŭs l
Æ-bū'rạ
Æ-çhī'ọn
Æch-măg'ọ-răs
Æçh'mịs 4
Æc-lā'nụm
Æc-ụ-lā'nụm
Æ-dĕp'sụs
Æ-dē'sị-ạ ī
Æ-dē'sị-ŭs l
Æ-dĕs'sạ
Æd'ị-lạ 4
Æ-dī'lēş
Æd'ị-lŭs 4
Æ-dĭp'sụs
Ạ-ē'dọn
Ā-ẹ-dō'nịs
Æd'ụ-ēş 4
Æd'ụ-ī 4
Æ-ē'tạ
Æ-ē'tēş
Æ-ē'tị-ăs l
Æ-ẹ-tī'nẹ
Æ-ē'tịs
Æ-gā'lẹ-ŏs
Æ-gā'lẹ-ŭm
Æ-gā'tēş
Æ'ģẹ-ăs, *or*
  Æ-ģē'ạs
Æ-ģẹ-ā'tēş
Æ-ģē'lẹ-ŏn
Æ-ģē'rị-ạ
Æ-ģē'tī
Æ'ģeūs (*n.*) 6
Æ-ģē'ụs (*a.*)
Æ'ģị-æ, *or* Æ-ģī'æ
Æ-ģī'ạ-lē
Æ-ģị-ạ-lē'ạ
Æ-ģī'ạ-leūs 6

Æ-ģị-ạ-lī'ạ
Æ-ģī'ạ-lŭs
Æ-ģĭc'ọ-rēş
Æģ'ị-dạ 4
Æ-ģī'dēş
Æ-ģīd'ị-ŭs
Æģ'ị-lạ 4
Æ-ģĭl'ị-ạ
Æģ'ị-lĭps 4
Æ-ģĭm'ị-ŭs
Æ-ģĭm'ọ-rŭs
Æ-ģĭm'ụ-rŭs, *or*
  Æģ-ị-mū'rụs 4
Æģ'ị-mŭs 4
Æ-ģī'nạ
Æģ-ị-nē'tạ 4
Æģ-ị-nē'tēş 4
Æ-ģĭn'ị-ŭm
Æ-ģī'ọ-çhŭs
Æ'ģị-ŏn
Æģ'ị-păn 4
Æģ-ị-pā'nēş 4
Æ-ģī'rạ
Æ-ģĭr-ọ-ĕs'sạ
Æg-ị-rū'sạ 4
Æ-ģĭs'thụs
Æ-ģī''tị-ŭm l
Æ'ģị-ŭm
Æģ'lẹ 4
Æg-lē'ịs 4
Æg'lēş 4
Æg-lē'tēş 4
Æg'lọ-ģē 4
Æ-gŏb'ọ-lŭs
Æ-gŏç'ẹ-rŏs
Æ-gō'nẹ
Æg-ọ-nē'ạ 4
Æ-gō'nēş
Æ-gŏph'ạ-gŭs
Æ-gŏs'ạ-ģœ
Æ'gọs Pŏt'ạ-mī, *or*
  Pŏt'ạ-mŏs
Æ-gŏs'thẹ-nạ
Æ-gū'sạ
Æģ'y-lạ 4
Æģ-y-pā'nēş 4
Æ-ģȳp'sọs
Æ-ģȳp'sụs
Æ-ģȳp'tị-ī 1
Æ-ģȳp'tị-ŭm l
Æ-ģȳp'tụs
Æ-lā'nạ
Æ'lị-ạ
Æ-lị-ā'nụs
Æ'li-ạn
Æl'ị-nŏn 4
Æl'ị-nŏs 4
Æ'lị-ŭs
Ạ-ĕl'lọ-pŭs
Æ-lū'rụs
Æ-mā'thị-ạ
Æ-mĭl'ị-ạ
Æ-mĭl-ị-ā'nụs
Æ-mĭl'ị-ŭs
Æm-nĕs'tụs 4
Æm'ọ-dæ 4
Æ'mọn
Æ-mō'nạ
Æ-mō'nị-ạ
Æ-mŏn'ị-dēş

Æm'ọ-nĭs 4
Æ-mȳl'ị-ạ
Æ-mȳl-ị-ā'nụs
Æ-mȳl'ị-ī
Æ-mȳl'ị-ŭs
Æ-năn'tị-ŏn 2
Æ-nā'rị-ạ
Æ-nā'sị-ŭs l
Æ-nē'ạ
Æ-nē'ạ-dæ
Æ-nē'ạ-dēş
Æ'nẹ-ăs, *and*
  Æ-nē'ạs
Æ-nē'ạs Gạ-zæ'ụs
Æ-nē'ạs Tăc'tị-cŭs
Æ-nē'ịs
Æ-nē'id
Æ-nĕs-ị-dē'mụs
Æ-nē'sị-ŭs l
Æ-nē'tẹ
Æ-nē'tụs
Æ'neūs 6
Æ-nī'ạ, *and*
  Æ'nị-ạ
Æ-nī'ạ-cŭs
Æ-nị-ā'nēş
Æn'ị-cŭs 4
Æ-nī'dæ
Æ-nī'ọ-çhī
Æn-ọ-bär'bụs 4
Æn'ọ-clēş 4
Æ-nō'nēş
Æ-nȳ'rạ
Æ'ọ-lēş
Æ-ō'lị-ạ
Æ-ō'lị-æ
Æ-ŏl'ị-dạ
Æ-ŏl'ị-dēş
Æ'ọ-lĭs
Æ'ọ-lŭs
Æ-ō'nị-ạ
Æ-ō'rạ
Æ-pā'lị-ŭs
Æ-pē'ạ
Æp'ụ-lō 4
Æp'y-tŭs 4
Æ-quā'nạ
Æ-quā'nụs
Æ-quĭc'ọ-lạ
Æ-quĭc'ọ-lī
Æ-quĭc'ọ-lŭs
Æ-quĭc'ụ-lī
Æq-uị-mē'lị-ŭm 4
Ạ-ē'rị-ạ
Ạ-ē'rị-ŭs
Ạ-ĕr'ọ-pē
Ạ-ĕr'ọ-pŭs
Æs'ạ-cŭs 4
Æ-sā'ģẹ-ạ
Æ-sā'pụs
Æs'ạ-rạ 4
Æ-sā'rụs, *and*
  Æs'ạ-rŭs 4
Æs'çhị-nēş 4
Æs'çhị-nŭs
Æs'çhị-rŏn 4
Æs-chrọ-dō'rạ 4
Æs-çhȳl'ị-dēş 4
Æs'çhy-lŭs 4
Æs-cụ-lā'pị-ŭs 4

Æ-sē'pụs
Æ-sër'nị-ạ
Æs-ẹr-nī'nụs 4
Æ'sị-ŏn 2
Æ-sī'tæ
Æ-sō'nịs
Æ-sŏn'ị-dēş
Æs-ọ-pē'ụs 4
Æ-sō'pụs
Æ'sọp
Æs'trị-ạ 4
Æs'tụ-ī 4
Æs'ụ-ạ 4
Æs'ụ-lạ 4
Æs'ụ-læ 4
Æ-sȳ'ẹ-tēş 1
Æ-sȳ'mẹ
Æs-ym-nē'tœ 4
Æs-ym-nē'tēş 4
Æ-sȳm'nụs
Æth'ạ-lē 4
Æth-ạ-lē'ạ 4
Æ-thăl'ị-dēş
Æ-thā'lị-ŏn
Æ-thā'lị-ŏs
Æ-thē'rị-ē
Æ-thī'cēş
Æth'ị-cŭs 4
Æ-thĭl'lạ
Æ-thī'ọn
Æ-thī'ọ-pēş
Æ-thị-ō'pi-ạ
Æ'thị-ŏps
Ạ-ĕth'lị-ŭs 4
Æ-thū'sạ
Æ-thȳ'ıạ 3
Æ'tị-ạ l
Ạ-ē'tị-ŏn 2
Æ-tị-ọ-nē'ạ l
Æ-tī'tēş
Ạ-ē'tị-ŭs l
Æt'nạ 4
Æt-næ'ụs 4
Æ-tō'lẹ
Æ-tō'lị-ạ
Æ-tō'lịs
Æ-tō'lụs
Æx (ĕks) 4
Æx-ō'nẹ
Ā'frạ
Ạ-frā'nị-ạ
Ạ-frā'nị-ŭs
Ăf'rị-cạ
Ăf-rị-cā'nụs
Ăf'rị-cŭm
Ăf'rị-cŭs
Ăg'ạ-bŭs
Ạ-găc'ly-tŭs
Ạ-găg-rị-ā'næ
Ăg-ạ-lăs'sēş
Ăg'ạ-mē
Ăg-ạ-mē'dẹ
Ăg-ạ-mē'dēş
Ăg-ạ-mĕm'nọn
Ăg-ạ-mĕm-nŏn'ị-
  dēş
Ăg-ạ-mĕm-nŏ'nị-ŭs
Ăg-ạ-mē'tọr
Ạ-găm'mạ-tæ
Ăg-ạm-nĕs'tọr

Ăg'ạ-mŭs
Ăg-ạ-nī'cẹ
Ăg-ạ-nĭp'pẹ
Ăg-ạn-ĭp-pē'ŭs
Ăg-ạ-nĭp'pị-dēṣ ·
Ạ-găn'zạ-gạ
Ăg'ạ-pæ
Ăg-ạ-pē'nọr
Ăg-ạ-pē'tụs
Ạ-gā'pị-ŭs
Ăg'ạ-rạ
Ăg-ạ-rē'nī
Ăg'ạ-rī
Ăg-ạ-rĭs'tạ
Ạ-gā'sị-ăs 1
Ạ-găs'ị-clēṣ
Ạ-gā'sō
Ạ-găs'sæ
Ạ-găs'thẹ-nēṣ
Ạ-găs'trọ-phŭs
Ăg'ạ-sŭs
Ăg'ạ-thạ
Ăg-ạ-thạ-gē'tụs
Ăg-ạ-thăn'gẹ-lŭs
Ăg-ạ-thär'chị-dăs
Ăg-ạ-thär'chị-dēṣ
Ăg-ạ-thär'chụs
Ăg-ạ-thĕm'ẹ-rŭs
Ăg-ạ-thī'ạ
Ạ-gā'thị-ăs, or
  Ăg-ạ-thī'ạs
Ăg-ạ-thī'nụs
Ăg-ạ-thọ-clē'ạ
Ạ-găth'ọ-clēṣ
Ăg-ạ-thọ-dæ'mọn
Ăg'ạ-thŏn
Ăg-ạ-thŏn'y-mŭs
Ạ-găth'ọ-pŭs
Ăg-ạ-thŏs'thẹ-nēṣ
Ăg-ạ-thŏt'y-chŭs
Ăg-ạ-thŷr'nạ
Ăg-ạ-thŷr'nụm
Ăg-ạ-thŷr'nụs
Ăg-ạ-thŷr'sī
Ạ-gâu'ī
Ạ-gā've
Ăg-băt'ạ-nạ
Ă-gẹ-ē'nạ
Ăg-ẹ-lā'dạs
Ăg-ẹ-lā'dēṣ
Ăg-ẹ-lăs'tụs
Ăg-ẹ-lā'ụs
Ăg-ẹ-lē'ạ
Ăg-ẹ-lē'ịs
Ăg'ẹ-lēṣ
Ạ-gĕn'ạ-thạ
Ạ-gĕn'dị-cŭm, or
  Ăg-ẹn-dī'cụm
Ạ-gē'nọr
Ăg-ẹ-nŏr'ị-dēṣ
Ạ-gĕp'ọ-lĭs
Ăg-ẹ-rī'nụs
Ăg-ẹ-rō'nạ
Ăg-ẹ-săn'der
Ăg-ẹ-săn'drị-dăs
Ăg-ẹ-sī'ạ-năx
Ạ-gē'sị-ăs 1
Ạ-gēs'ị-clēṣ
Ạ-gēs-ị-dā'mụs
Ạ-gĕs-ị-lā'ụs

Ăg-ẹ-sĭm'brọ-tŭs
Ăg-ẹ-sĭp'ọ-lĭs
Ăg-ẹ-sĭs'trạ-tạ
Ăg-ẹ-sĭs'trạ-tŭs
Ạ-gē'tạs
Ăg-gē'nụs (ăj-ē'-
  nụs)
Ạg-grī'næ
Ā'gị-ăs
Ăg'ị-dæ
Ăg-ị-lā'ụs
Ạ-gīn'nụm
Ăg-lā'ị-ạ 4
Ăg-lā'ị-ē 4
Ăg-lạ-ọ-nī'cẹ
Ăg-lā'ọ-pē
Ăg-lā'ọ-pēṣ
Ăg-lạ-ọ-phē'mẹ
Ăg-lā'ọ-phŏn
Ăg-lạ-ŏs'thẹ-nēṣ
Ăg-lâu'rọs
Ăg'lạ-ŭs, or
  Ăg-lā'ụs
Ăg-nā'lị-ạ
Ăg'nị-ŭs
Ăg-nọ-nī'ạ
Ăg-nŏn'ị-dēṣ
Ăg-nō'tēṣ
Ăg-nŏth'ẹ-tæ
Ăg-ọ-nā'lị-ạ
Ạ-gŏ'nị-ạ
Ạ-gŏ'nēṣ
Ạ-gŏ'nịs
Ạ-gŏ'nị-ŭs
Ạ-gŏ'nụs
Ăg'ọ-rạ
Ăg-ọ-răc'rị-tŭs
Ăg-ọ-ræ'ạ
Ăg-ọ-rā'nịs
Ăg-ọ-răn'ọ-mī
Ăg-ọ-răs'tọ-clēṣ
Ạ-græ'ạ
Ạ-græ'ī
Ạ-græ'ụs
Ăg'rạ-găs
Ạ-grâu'lẹ
Ạ-grâu'lị-ạ
Ạ-grâu'lọs
Ạ-grâu-ọ-nī'tæ
Ā'grẹ-ēṣ
Ạ-grē'nī
Ā'greŭs 6
Ā-grị-ā'nēṣ
Ạ-grĭc'ọ-lạ
Ăg-rĭ''cị-ŭs 1
Ăg-rị-gen-tī'nụs
Ăg-rị-gĕn'tụm
Ạ-grĭn'ị-ŭm
Ạ-grī'ọ-dŏs
Ā-grị-ō'nị-ạ
Ạ-grī'ọ-păs
Ạ-grī'ọ-pē
Ā-grị-ŏph'ạ-gī
Ăg-rị-ọp-pē'ụm
Ăg-rị-pī'nạ
Ăg-rị-pī'nụs
Ạ-grĭs'ọ-pē
Ā'grị-ŭs
Ạ-græ'cị-ŭs 1

Ạ-græ'tạs
Ăg'rọ-lăs
Ạ-grō'tạs
Ạ-grŏt'ẹ-rạ
Ạ-gȳ'ieūs 3 6
Ăg-yl-læ'ụs
Ạ-gȳl'lẹ
Ạ-gȳl'leūs 6
Ạ-gȳr'ị-ŭm
Ạ-gȳr'ị-ŭs
Ạ-gȳr'rhị-ŭs
Ạ-gȳr'tēṣ
Ạ-gȳ'rụs
Ạ-hā'lạ
Ă-ị-dō'neūs 6
Ạ-ī'lạ
Ạ-ĭm'y-lŭs
Ā'ị-ŭs Lọ-cū'tị-ŭs 1
Ăl-ạ-băn'dạ
Ăl-ạ-băn'dị-cŭs
Ăl'ạ-bĭs
Ăl'ạ-bŭs
Ạ-læ'ī
Ạ-læ'sụs
Ạ-læ'ụs
Ăl-ạ-gō'nị-ạ
Ạ-lā'lạ
Ăl-ạl-cŏm'ẹ-næ
Ạ-lăl-cọm-ẹ-nē'ịs
Ăl-ạl-cŏm'ẹ-nēṣ
Ạ-lăl-cọ-mē'nị-ạ
Ạ-lā'lị-ạ
Ăl-ạ-mā'nēṣ
Ăl-ạ-măn'nī
Ạ-lā'nī
Ạ-lā'nụs
Ăl'ạ-rēṣ
Ăl-ạ-rī'cụs
Ăl'ạ-rĭc
Ăl-ạ-rō'dị-ī
Ạ-lăs'tọ-rēṣ
Ăl-ạs-tŏr'ị-dēṣ
Ăl-ạ-thē'ụs
Ạ-lā'threŭs 6
Ạ-lâu'dæ
Ạ-lā'zọn
Ăl-ạ-zō'nēṣ
Ạl-bā'nī
Ạl-bā'nị-ạ
Ạl-bā'nụs
Ăl'bạ Sȳl'vị-ŭs
Ăl-bĕn'sēṣ
Ăl-bẹ-rī'cụs
Ăl'bị-ạ Tẹ-rĕn'tị-ạ 1
Ạl-bī'cī
Ăl-bị-ē'tæ
Ăl-bị-gâu'nụm
Ạl-bī'nạ
Ạl-bĭn'ị-ŭs
Ăl-bī-nọ-vā'nụs
Ạl-bĭn-tẹ-mē'lị-ŭm
Ạl-bī'nụs
Ăl'bị-ŏn
Ạl-bī'ọ-nēṣ
Ạl-bū'cị-ŭs 1
Ăl'bụ-lạ
Ạl-bū'nạ
Ạl-bū'nẹ-ạ
Ạl-bū'tị-ŭs 1
Ạl-cæn'ẹ-tŭs 4

Ạl-cæ'ụs
Ạl-căm'ẹ-nēṣ
Ạl-cā'nọr
Ạl-căth'ọ-ē
Ạl-căth'ọ-ŭs
Ăl-cẹ-dō'nị-ạ
Ạl-cē'nọr
Ăl-cẹs-ị-mär'chụs
Ạl-cĕs'ị-mŭs
Ạl-cĕs'tẹ
Ạl-cĕs'tịs
Ăl'cẹ-tăs
Ăl'chị-dăs
Ăl-cị-bī'ạ-dēṣ
Ạl-cī'dæ
Ạl-cĭd'ạ-măs
Ăl-cị-dạ-mē'ạ
Ăl-cị-dăm'ị-dăs
Ăl-cị-dā'mụs
Ạl-cī'dēṣ
Ạl-cĭd'ị-cē
Ạl-cĭd'ọ-cŭs
Ạl-cĭm'ạ-chŭs
Ạl-cĭm'ẹ-dē
Ạl-cĭm'ẹ-dŏn
Ạl-cĭm'ẹ-nēṣ
Ăl'cị-mŭs
Ạl-cĭn'ọ-ē
Ăl'cị-nör
Ạl-cĭn'ọ-ŭs
Ạl-cī'ọ-pŭs
Ăl'cị-phrŏn
Ạl-cĭs'thẹ-nē
Ạl-cĭth'ọ-ē
Ạlc-mæ'ọn
Ălc-mæ-ŏn'ị-dæ
Ạlc-mē'nạ, or -nẹ
Ạl-cŏm'ẹ-næ
Ăl'cọ-nē
Ạl-cȳ'ọ-nạ
Ạl-cȳ'ọ-nē
Ạl-cȳ'ọ-neŭs 6
Ăl-cy-ŏn'ị-dēṣ 1
Ạl-dū'ạ-bĭs
Ā'lẹ-ạ
Ạ-lē'bạs
Ạ-lē'bị-ŏn
Ạ-lē'bụs
Ạ-lĕc'try-ŏn
Ạ-lē'ị-ŭs Căm'pụs 3
Ăl-ẹ-măn'nī
Ăl-ẹ-mā'nụs
Ạ-lē'mọn
Ăl-ẹ-mŏn'ị-dēṣ
Ăl-ẹ-mū'sị-ī 1
Ā'lẹ-ŏn
Ạ-lē'rị-ạ
Ạ-lē'rịs
Ạ-lē'sạ
Ạ-lē'sị-ạ 1
Ạ-lē'sị-ŭs 1
Ạ-lē'sụs
Ạ-lē'tēṣ
Ạ-lē'thēṣ
Ạ-lē'thị-ạ
Ạ-lē'thị-ŭs
Ạ-lĕt'ị-dăs
Ạ-lē'tịs
Ăl-ẹ-trị-nā'tēṣ
Ạ-lē'trị-ŭm

Ạ-lē'tụm
Ạ-leū'ạ-dæ
Ā'lẹ-ŭs
Ạ-lē'vạs
Ăl-ẹx-ăm'ẹ-nŭs
Ăl-ẹx-ạn'drạ
Ăl-ẹx-ạn-drē'ạ
Ăl-ẹx-ạn-drī'ạ
Ăl-ẹx-ăn'drị-ạ
Ăl-ẹx-ăn'drị-dēṣ
Ăl-ẹx-ạn-drī'nạ
Ăl-ẹx-ạn-drī'nụs
Ăl-ẹx-ạn-drŏp'ọ-lịs
Ăl-ẹx-ā'nọr
Ăl-ẹx-är'chụs
Ạ-lĕx'ị-ạ 1
Ăl-ẹx-ī'ạ-rēṣ
Ăl-ẹx-ĭc'ạ-cŭs
Ạ-lĕx'ị-clēṣ
Ăl-ẹx-ĭc'rạ-tēṣ
Ạ-lĕx'ị-dạ
Ăl-ẹx-ī'nụs
Ạ-lĕx'ị-ō 1
Ăl-ẹx-ĭp'pụs
Ăl-ẹx-īr'họ-ē
Ạ-lĕx'ị-ŭs 1
Ăl-fạ-tër'nạ
Ăl-fē'nụs
Ăl'fị-ŭs
Ăl'gị-dŭs
Ạl-gō'nụm
Ā-lị-ăc'mọn
Ā-lị-är'tụm
Ăl-ị-bī'dạ
Ăl'ị-cĭs
Ā-lị-ē'nụs
Ạ-lī'fæ
Ăl-ị-læ'ī
Ăl-ị-mĕn'ị-dēṣ
Ăl-ị-mĕn'tụs
Ạ-lĭm'ẹ-nŏs
Ăl-ịn-dō'ị-ạ 3
Ạ-lī'phæ
Ăl-ị-phā'nụs
Ăl-ị-phē'rạ
Ăl-ị-phē'rị-ạ
Ăl-ị-phē'rụs
Ăl-ịr-rō'thị-ŭs
Ăl-ị-sŏn'tị-ạ 1
Ạ-lī'sụm
Ạl-lē'dị-ŭs
Ăl'lị-ạ
Ăl-lị-ē'nụs
Ạl-lī'fæ
Ăl-lị-fā'nụs
Ăl'lị-ŭs
Ạl-lŏb'rọ-gēṣ
Ăl'lọ-brŏx
Ạl-lŏb'ry-gēṣ
Ăl-lọ-phȳ'lụs
Ạl-lŏt'rị-gēṣ
Ạl-lū'tị-ŭs 1
Ạl-mē'nẹ
Ạl-mō'pēṣ
Ăl-my-rō'dẹ
Ạ-lō'ạ
Ạ-lō'eŭs 6
Ăl-ọ-ī'dæ
Ăl-ọ-ī'dēṣ
Ạ-lō'ịs

Ạ-lō'ne
Ạ-lō'nịs
Ăl'ọ-pē
Ạ-lŏp'ẹ-cạ
Ăl-ọ-pē'cẹ-ạ
Ạ-lŏp'ẹ-cēş
Ạ-lō'pị-ŭs
Ạ-lō'rụs
Ạ-lō'tị-ạ 1
Ạl-pē'nụs
Ăl'pēş
Ălps
Ạl-phæ'ạ 3
Ạl-phē'ạ
Ạl-phē'ị-ăs 3
Ạl-phē'nọr
Ạl-phē'nụs
Ạl-phĕs-ị-bœ'ụs
Ạl-phē'ụs
Ạl-phī'ọn
Ăl'phị-ŭs
Ạl-pī'nụs
Ạl-pō'nụs
Ăl-sị-ẹ-tī'nụs 1
Ăl'sị-ŭm 1
Ạl-thæ'ạ
Ạl-thæm'ẹ-nēş 4
Ạl-thĕm'ẹ-nēş
Ạl-thē'pụs
Ạl-tị'nụm
Ạ-lŭn'tị-ŭm 1
Ā-ly-ăt'tēş
Ăl'y-bạ
Ăl-y-bī'dạ
Ăl-y-cæ'ạ
Ăl-y-cæ'ụs
Ạ-lȳ'mọn
Ạ-lȳp'ị-ŭs
Ạ-lȳ'pụs
Ăl-yx-ŏth'ọ-ē
Ăl-y-zē'ạ
Ạ-lȳ'zeūs 6
Ạ-măd'ọ-cī
Ạ-măd'ọ-cŭs
Ạ-mæ'şị-ạ 1
Ăm'ạ-ḡē
Ăm-ạl-thæ'ạ
Ăm-ạl-thē'ạ
Ăm-ạl-thē'ụm
Ạ-măn'ị-cæ
Ạ-măn'ị-dēş
Ạ-măn'tị-ạ 1
Ăm-ạn-tī'nī
Ạ-mā'nụs
Ạ-măr'ạ-cŭs
Ăm-ạ-rȳl'lịs
Ăm-ạ-rȳn'ceūs 6
Ăm-ạ-rȳn'thị-ạ
Ăm-ạ-rȳn'thụs
Ăm-ạ-rȳ''şị-ạ 1
Ăm-ạ-sē'ạ
Ăm-ạ-sē'nụs
Ăm-ạ-sī'ạ
Ạ-mā'sịs
Ạ-mā'tạ
Ăm-ạ-thē'ạ
Ăm'ạ-thŭs
Ạ-măx-ạm-pē'ụs
Ạ-măx-ạn-tī'ạ
Ạ-măx'ị-ạ 1

Ạ-măx'ị-tạ
Ăm-ạx-ŏb'ị-ī
Ăm-ạ-zē'nēş
Ạ-mā'zọn
Ăm'ạ-zŏn
Ạ-măz'ọ-nēş
Ăm'ạ-żŏnş
Ăm-ạ-zŏn'ị-cŭs
Ăm-ạ-zŏn'ị-dēş
Ăm-ạ-zō'nị-ŭm
Ăm-ạ-zō'nị-ŭs
Ăm-bạr-vā'lēş
Ăm-bạr-vā'lị-ạ
Ăm-bā'tæ
Ăm'bẹ-nŭs
Ăm-bị-ạ-lī'tēş
Ăm-bị-ā'nụm
Ăm-bị-ạ-tī'nụm
Ăm-bị-băr'ẹ-tī
Ăm-bị-gā'tụs
Ăm-bī'ọ-rīx
Ăm'blạ-dạ
Ăm-bọ-lọ-ḡē'rạ
Ăm-brā'cị-ạ 1
Ăm-brạ-cị-ō'tæ 1
Ăm-brā'cị-ŭs 1
Ăm-brō'dạx
Ăm-brō'nēş
Ăm-brō'şị-ŭs 1
Ăm'brōse
Ăm-brȳl'lịs
Ăm'brȳ-ŏn, *or*
 Ăm-brȳ'ọn
Ăm-brȳ'sụs
Ăm-bu-bā'jị-æ, *or*
 Ăm-bu-bā'jæ
Ăm'bu-lī
Ăm'ẹ-lēş
Ạ-mē'lị-ŭs
Ăm-ẹ-nā'nụs
Ăm-ẹ-nī'dēş
Ạ-mĕn'ọ-clēş
Ăm-ẹ-nō'phịs
Ạ-mē'rị-ạ
Ạ-mē'rị-ăs
Ăm-ẹ-rī'nụs
Ăm-ẹ-rī'ọ-lạ
Ạ-mĕs'ẹ-lŭm
Ạ-mĕs'trạ-tŭs
Ạ-mĕs'trị-ŭs
Ā-mị-ā'nụs
Ăm-ị-clæ'ụs
Ạ-mī'clạs
Ăm-ịc-tæ'ụs
Ăm'ị-dạ, *or*
 Ạ-mī'dạ
Ăm'ị-lŏs
Ăm-ị-mō'nẹ, *or*
 Ăm-y-mō'nẹ
Ạ-mĭn'ị-ŭs
Ạ-mĭn'ọ-clēş
Ạ-mĭp'sị-ăs 1
Ăm-ị-sē'nạ
Ạ-mī''şị-ạ 1
Ạ-mī''şị-ŭs 1
Ăm-ị-sŏd'ạ-rŭs
Ạ-mī'sụs
Ăm-ị-tēr'nụm
Ăm-ị-thā'ọn, *or*
 Ăm-y-thā'ọn

Ăm-ị-tī'nụm
Ạm-mā'lō
Ăm-mị-ā'nụs
Ăm-mọ-chŏs'tọs
Ăm-mọ-mē'tụs
Ạm-mō'nạs
Ăm-mọ-nị-ā'nụs
Ạm-mō'nị-ī
Ạm-mō'nị-ŭs
Ạm-mō'thẹ-ạ
Ạm-nĕm'ọ-nēş
Ăm'nị-ăs
Ạm-nī'sụs
Ạm-nī'tēş
Ăm-œ-bæ'ụs
Ạ-mœ'beūs 6
Ạ-mœ'nụs
Ăm-ọ-mē'tụs
Ăm-ọm-phăr'ẹ-
Ạ-mör'ḡēş
Ạm-pē'lị-ŭs
Ăm'pẹ-lŏs, *or* -lŭs
Ăm-pẹ-lū'sị-ạ 1
Ăm-phạx-ī'tịs
Ạm-phē'ạ
Ăm-phị-ạ-lā'ụs
Ạm-phị'ạ-lŭs
Ăm-phị-ăr-ạ-ē'ụm
Ăm-phị-ăr-ạ-ī'dēş
Ăm-phị-ạ-rā'ụs
Ăm-phị-clē'ạ
Ạm-phĭc'ty-ŏn 2
Ăm-phịc-tȳ'ọ-nēş
Ăm'phị-cŭs
Ăm-phĭd'ạ-măs
Ăm-phị-dā'mụs
Ạm-phĭd'ị-cŭs
Ăm-phĭd'ọ-lī
Ăm-phị-drō'mị-ạ
Ăm-phị-ḡẹ-nī'ạ
Ăm-phị-ḡē'nị-ạ
Ăm-phị-lō'chị-ŭs
Ăm-phị-lŏch'ị-cŭm
Ạm-phīl'y-tŭs
Ăm-phĭm'ạ-chŭs
Ăm-phĭm'ẹ-dŏn
Ăm-phĭn'ọ-mē
Ăm-phī'ọn
Ăm-phĭp'ạ-gŭs
Ăm-phĭp'ọ-lēş
Ăm-phĭp'ọ-lịs
Ăm-phĭp'y-rŏs
Ăm-phị-rē'tụs
Ạm-phĭr'ọ-ē
Ạm-phī'sạ
Ăm-phịs-bæ'nạ
Ăm-phịs-sē'nẹ
Ăm-phịs'thẹ-nēş
Ăm-phịs-tī'dēş
Ăm-phĭs'trạ-tŭs
Ạm-phī'sụs
Ạm-phīth'ẹ-ạ
Ăm-phị-thẹ-ā'trụm
Ạm-phĭth'ẹ-mịs
Ạm-phĭth'ọ-ē
Ăm-phị-trī'tẹ
Ạm-phīt'rụ-ō [dēş
Ạm-phīt-ry-ọ-nī'ạ-

Ăm'phị-tŭs
Ạm-phī'ụs
Ạm-phŏt'ẹ-rŭs
Ạm-phŏt-ry-ọ-nī'ạ-
 dēş
Ạm-phrȳ'sọs
Ạm-phrȳ'sụs
Ămp'sạ-gạ, *or*
 Ạmp-sā'gạ
Ămp-sị-gū'rạ
Ăm-pȳç'ị-dēş
Ạ-mū'lị-ŭs
Ạ-mȳ'clạ
Ăm-y-clæ'ụs
Ạ-mȳ'clạs
Ạ-mȳ'clẹ
Ăm-y-clī'dēş
Ăm'y-cŭs
Ăm'y-dŏn
Ăm-y-mō'nẹ
Ăm-y-nŏm'ạ-chŭs
Ăm-yn-tī'ạ-dēş
Ạ-mȳn-tị-ā'nụs 1
Ăm-yn-tŏr'ị-dēş
Ăm-y-rī'cụs
Ăm'y-rịs
Ạ-mȳr'ị-ŭs
Ăm-y-thā'ọn
Ăm-y-thạ-ō'nị-ŭs
Ạ-năb'ạ-sịs
Ạ-năb'ạ-tæ
Ăn-ạ-cē'ạ
Ăn'ạ-cēş
Ăn-ạ-cē'ụm, *or*
 Ăn-ạ-cī'ụm
Ăn-ạ-chăr'sịs
Ăn-ạ-clē'tụs
Ạ-năc'rẹ-ŏn, *or*
 Ạ-nā'crẹ-ŏn
Ăn-ạc-tō'rị-ạ
Ăn-ạc-tō'rị-ē
Ăn-ạc-tō'rị-ŭm
Ạ-năc'tọ-rŭm
Ăn-ạ-dy-ŏm'ẹ-nē
Ạ-năg'nị-ạ
Ăn-ạ-ḡy-rŏn'tụm
Ạ-năg'y-rŭs
Ăn-ạ-ī'tịs
Ạ-nā'nị-ŭs
Ăn-ạ-phlȳs'tụs
Ạ-nā'pị-ŭs
Ạ-nā'pụs
Ạ-năr'ḡy-rī
Ăn-ạs-tā'şị-ạ 1
Ăn-ạs-tā'şị-ŭs 1
Ạ-năt'ọ-lē
Ăn-ạ-tō'lị-ŭs
Ạ-nâu'chị-dás
Ạ-nâu'rụs
Ạ-nâu'sịs
Ăn-ạx-ăg'ọ-răs
Ăn-ạx-ăn'dẹr
Ăn-ạx-ăn'drị-dēş
Ăn-ạx-ăr'chụs
Ăn-ạx-ăr'ẹ-tē
Ăn-ạx-ē'nọr
Ạ-năx'ị-ăs 1
Ăn-ạx-ĭb'ị-ạ
Ăn-ạx-ĭb'ị-ŭs
Ăn-ạx-ĭc'rạ-tēş

Ạ-năx-ị-dā'mụs
Ạ-năx-ị-lā'ụs
Ăn-ạx-ĭl'ị-dēş
Ạ-năx-ị-măn'dẹr
Ăn-ạx-īm'ẹ-nēş
Ăn-ạx-ĭp'ọ-lịs
Ăn-ạx-ĭp'pụs
Ăn-ạx-īr'rhọ-ē
Ăn-cạ-lī'tēş
Ăn-cā'rị-ŭs
Ăn-chā'rēş
Ăn-chā'rị-ạ
Ăn-chā'rị-ŭs
Ăn-chā'tēş
Ăn-chĕm'ọ-lŭs
Ăn-chẹ-sī'tēş
Ăn-chĕs'mụs
Ăn-chī'ạ-lạ
Ăn-chị-ạ-lē'ạ
Ăn-chị-ạ-lī'ạ
Ăn-chī'ạ-lŭs
Ăn-chị-mō'lị-ŭs
Ăn-chīn'ọ-ē
Ăn-chī'sạ
Ăn-chī'sēş
Ăn-chī''şị-ạ 1
Ăn-chị-sī'ạ-dēş
Ăn-chị-sī'tēş
Ăn'chọ-ē
Ăn'chọ-rạ
Ăn-chū'rụs
Ăn-cī'lẹ
Ăn-cō'nạ
Ăn'cụs Măr'tị-ŭs 1
Ăn-cȳ'lẹ
Ăn-cȳ'rạ
Ăn-cy-rā'nụs
Ăn-cȳ'rọn
Ăn-dăb'ạ-tæ
Ăn-dā'nạ
Ăn-dā'nị-ạ
Ăn-dẹ-cā'ọ-nēş
Ăn-dẹ-cā'vị-ạ
Ăn-dẹ-gā'vụm
Ăn-dē'rạ
Ăn-dŏç'ị-dēş
Ăn-dŏin'ạ-tịs
Ăn-dræ'mọn
Ăn-drạ-gā'thị-ŭs
Ăn-drăg'ạ-thụs
Ăn-drăg'ọ-răs
Ăn-drăm'y-tēş
Ăn-drạ-nọ-dō'rụs
Ăn'drẹ-ăs
Ăn'drew
Ăn-drē'mọn
Ăn'dreūs 6
Ăn'drị-ạ
Ăn-drī'ạ-cạ
Ăn'drị-clŭs
Ăn'drị-ŏn
Ăn-drō'bị-ŭs
Ăn-drọ-bū'lụs
Ăn-drọ-clē'ạ
Ăn'drọ-clēş
Ăn-drọ-clī'dēş
Ăn'drọ-clŭs, *or*
 Ạn-drō'clŭs
Ăn-drọ-cȳ'dēş
Ạn-drŏd'ạ-mǎs

An-drŏ'dus
An-drŏ'ge-ŭs
An-drŏg'y-nŭs
An-drŏm'a-chē
An-drŏm'a-dăs
An-drŏm'e-da
An-drŏm'e-dēs, or
  Ăn-dro-mē'dēs
Ăn-dro-nī'cus
An-drŏn'i-dăs
An-drŏph'a-ği
An-drŏp'o-lĭs
An-drŏs'the-nēs
An-drŏ'ti-ŏn 2
Ăn-e-lŏn'tis
Ăn-e-mo-lī'a
Ăn-e-mo-rī'a
Ăn-e-mŏ'sa
Ăn-e-mū'ri-ŭm
Ăn-e-răs'tus
A-nē'tor
Ăn'gā-rī
An-ğē'li-a
Ăn'ğe-lŭs
Ăn-ğe-rŏ'na
An-ğī'tēs
Ăn-ğī''ti-a 1
Ăn'gli-a
An-guī''ti-a 1
Ā-ni-ā'nus
Ăn-i-cē'tus
A-nī''ci-ŭm 1
A-nī''ci-ŭs Găl'lus 1
Ā'ni-ĕn
Ā-ni-e-nīc'o-la
Ā-ni-ē'nus
A-nī'grus
Ăn-i-nē'tum
Ăn-i-tŏr'ğis
Ā'ni-ŭs
Ăn'na Com-nē'na
An-næ'us
Ăn-nā'lis
Ăn-nī'a-dæ
Ăn-ni-ā'nus
Ăn'ni-băl
Ăn'ni-bĭ
An-nīç'e-rĭs
Ăn-ni-chŏ'rī
Ăn'ni-ŭs Scăp'u-la
A-nŏ'lus
Ăn'o-nŭs
Ăn-si-bā'ri-ī
Ăn-tæ-ŏp'o-lĭs
An-tăg'o-răs
Ăn-tăl'ci-dăs
Ăn-tăr'a-dŭs
An-tē'a
An tĕc'a-nĭs
Ăn-tē'i-ŭs 3
An-tē'nor
Ăn-te-nŏr'i-dæ
Ăn-te-nŏr'i-dēs
Ăn-te-răs'ti-lĭs
Ăn-ter-brŏ'ği-ŭs
Ăn'te-rŏs
Ăn'te-rŭs
Ăn-thē'a
Ăn'the-ăs
Ăn-thē'don

An-thē'la
Ăn'the-mĭs
An-thē'mi-ŭs
Ăn'the-mŏn
An-the-mŏn'i-dēs
Ăn'the-mŭs
Ăn-the-mū'si-a 1
An-thē'ne
An-thē'rus
Ăn-thes-phŏ'ri-a
Ăn-thes-tē'ri-a
Ăn'theus 6
An-thī'a
Ăn-thi-ā'nus
Ăn'thi-ăs
Ăn'thi-mŭs
Ăn'thi-næ
Ăn'thi-ŭm
Ăn-tho-lŏ'ği-a
An-thŏ'rēs
An-thrā'ci-a 1
An-thrŏp'i-nŭs
An-thrŏ-po-mor-
  phī'tæ
Ăn-thro-pŏph'a-ği
An-tī'a
Ăn-ti-a-nī'ra 1
Ăn'ti-as 1
Ăn-ti-bac-chī'us
An-tĭc'a-tō
An-tĭch'tho-nēs
An-tĭç-i-nŏ'lis
Ăn-ti-clē'a
Ăn'ti-clēs
Ăn-ti-clī'dēs
An-tĭc'ra-gus
An-tĭc'ra-tēs
An-tĭç'y-ra
An-tĭd'a-măs
An-tĭd'o-mŭs
Ăn-ti-dŏ'rus
An-tĭd'o-tŭs
An-tĭğ'e-nēs
Ăn-ti-ğe-nī'das, or
  Ăn-ti-ğĕn'i-dăs
An-tĭg'o-na
An-tĭg'o-nē
Ăn-ti-go-nī'a, or
  Ăn-ti-gŏ'ni-a
An-tĭg'o-nŭs
An-tĭl'e-ŏn
Ăn-ti-lĭb'a-nŭs
An-tĭl'o-chŭs
Ăn-ti-măch'i-dēs
Ăn-tĭm'a-chŭs
Ăn-tĭm'e-nēs
Ăn-ti-mĕn'i-dăs
An-tĭn'o-ē
An-tĭn-o-ē'a
An-tĭn'o-ŭs
An-tī'num
Ăn-ti-o-chē'nus
An-ti-o-chī'a
Ăn'ti-ŏch
An-tī'o-chĭs
An-tī'o-chŭs
An-tī'o-pa, or -pē
Ăn-ti-ŏ'rus
An-tĭp'a-rŏs
Ăn'ti-păs

An-tĭp'a-ter
Ăn-ti-pā'tri-a, or
  Ăn-ti-pa-trī'a
Ăn-ti-păt'ri-dăs
An-tĭp'a-trĭs
Ăn-tĭph'a-tēs
Ăn-ti-phē'mus
An-tĭph'i-lŭs
Ăn'ti-phŏu
An-tĭph'o-nŭs
Ăn'ti-phŭs
An-tĭp'o-dēs
Ăn-ti-pœ'nus
An-tĭp'o-lĭs
An-tĭr'rhi-ŭm
An-tĭr'rho-dŏs
An-tĭs'the-nēs
An-tĭs'ti-ŭs
An-tĭth'e-ŭs
Ăn'ti-ŭs 1
An-tŏm'e-nēs
An-tŏ'ni-a
An-tŏ'ni-ī
Ăn-to-nī'na
Ăn-to-nī'nus
Au-tō-ni-ŏp'o-lĭs
An-tŏ'ni-ŭs
Ăn'to-ny
An-tŏ'rēs
An-tŏr'i-dēs
A-nū'bis
Ăn-u-lī'nus
Anx-ā'num
Ănx'i-ŭs 1
Ănx'u-rŭs
Ăn'y-sĭs
Ăn'y-ta, or -tē
Ăn'y-tŭs
An-zā'be
Ā-o-brī'ga
Ā-ŏl'li-ŭs
Ā'o-nēs
A-ō'ni-a
A-ŏn'i-dēs
Ā'o-rĭs
A-ō'rus
A-ō'tĭ
A-ō'us
A-pā'me
Ăp-a-mē'a
Ăp-a-mē'ne
Ăp-a-mī'a
Ăp-an-chŏm'e-nē
Ăp-a-tū'ri-a
Ăp-a-tū'rum
Ā-pe-âu'ros
A-pe-li-ō'tēs
A-pĕl'lēs
Ăp-el-lē'us
Ăp-en-nī-nĭc'o-la
Ăp-en-nī-nĭg'e-na
Ăp-e-ran-tī'a
Ăp-e-rŏ'pi-a
Ăp'e-sŭs
Ăph-a-cī'tis
Ăph-a-rē'tus
Ăph'a-reūs 6
A-phĕp'si-ŏn 1

Ăph'e-săs
Ăph'e-tæ
A-phē'tor
A-phī'das
Ăph-nē'um
Ăph-nī'tis
Ăph-œ-bē'tus
A-phrī'cēs
Ăph-ro-dī''se-ŭs 1
Ăph-ro-dī''si-a 1
Ăph-ro-dī-si-ā'nus 1
Ăph-ro-dī''si-ăs 1
Ăph-ro-dī''si-ŭm 1
Ăph-ro-dī'te
Ăph-ro-dī-tŏp'o-lĭs
Aph-thī'tēs
Aph-thō'ni-ŭs
Ăph'y-tē, or
  A-phȳ'te
Ăph'y-tĭs
Ā-pi-ā'nus
Ăp-i-cā'ta
A-pĭ''ci-ŭs 1
A-pĭd'a-nŭs
A-pĭd'o-nēs
Ăp'i-na
A-pī'o-læ
Ā'pi-ŏn
Ăp-i-sā'on
A-pĭ''ti-ŭs 1
A-pŏc'o-pa
Ăp-o-dō'tī, or
  A-pŏd'o-tī
A-pœç'i-dēs
A-pŏl-li-nā'rēs
A-pŏl-li-nā'ris
Ăp-ol-lĭn'i-dēs
A-pŏl'li-nĭs
Ăp-ol-lĭn'e-ŭs
A-pŏl-li-nŏp'o-lĭs
Ăp-ol-lŏc'ra-tēs
A-pŏl-lo-dō'rus
Ăp-ol-lō'ni-a
A-pŏl-lo-nī'a-dēs
Ăp-ol-lō'ni-ăs
Ăp-ol-lō-ni-ā'tis
Ăp-ol-lŏn'i-dăs
Ăp-ol-lŏn'i-dēs
Ăp-ol-lō'nĭs
Ăp-ol-lō'ni-ŭs
Ăp-ol-lŏph'a-nēs
Ăp-ol-lŏth'e-mĭs
A-pŏl'ly-ŏn
Ăp-o-mȳ'ios 3
A-pō-ni-ā'na
A-pō'ni-ŭs
Ăp'o-nŭs
Ăp-os-trŏ'phi-a
Ăp-o-tro-pæ'ī
Ăp-o-the-ō'sis
Ăp-o-thē'o-sĭs
Ap-pī'a-dēs
Ăp·pi-ā'nus
Ăp'pi-an
Ăp'pi-ăs
Ăp'pi-a Vī'a
Ăp'pi-ī Fŏ'rum
Ăp'pi-ŭs
Ăp'pu-la
Ăp-pu-lē'i-ŭs 3

Ā'pri-ēs
A-prī'lis
Ā'pri-ŭs
A-prŏ-ni-ā'nus
Ăp'sa-rŭs, or
  Ap-sā'rus
Ap-sĭn'thi-ī
Ăp'si-nēs
Ăp'so-rŭs
Ăp'te-ra
Ăp-u-ā'nī
Ăp-u-lē'i-a 3
Ăp-u-lē'i-ŭs 3
Ăp'u-lŭs
A-pŭs'ti-ŭs
Ăp'y-rī
A-quā'ri-ŭs
A-quĭc'o-lŭs
Ăq'ui-la (ăk'we-la)
Ăq-ui-lā'ri-a
Ăq-ui-lē'i-a 3
Ăq-ui-lī'na
Ăq-ui-lī'nus
A-quĭl'li-a
Ăq'ui-lō
Ăq-ui-lō'ni-a
Ăq-ui-lo-nĭğ'e-na
A-quī'nas
A-quĭn'i-ŭs
A-quī'num
A-quī'nus
Ăq-ui-tā'ni-a
Ăq-ui-tăn'i-cŭs
Ăq-ui-tā'nus
Ăq'ui-tēs (ăk'we-
  tēz)
Ăr-a-băr'chēs
Ăr'a-bēs
A-rā-bi-ā'nus
A-răb'i-cŭs
Ăr'a-bĭs
Ăr-a-brī'ca
Ăr'a-bŭs
Ăr-a-cē'lī
A-răch'ne
Ăr-ach-nē'a
Ăr-a-chŏ'si-a 1
Ăr-a-chŏ'tæ
Ăr-a-chŏ'tus
Ăr-a-cĭl'lum
Ăr-a-cŏ'si-ī 1
A-răc'thi-ăs
Ăr'a-cŭs
Ăr-a-cȳn'thus
Ăr'a-dŏs, or -dŭs
Ăr-æ-thȳr'e-a
Ăr-a-phī'a
Ăr'a-rĭs
A-rā'ros, or -rus
  poet.
Ăr'a-rŭs, river.
Ăr-a-tē'us
A-rā'tus
A-râu'ri-cŭs
A-rā'vus
Ăr-ax-ē'nus
A-răx'ēs
Ăr'ba-cēs, or
  Ar-bā'cēs
Ăr'ba-cŭs

Ar-bē'la, *and*
  Är'be-la
Ar-bē'lus
Ar-bŏc'a-la, *or*
  Är-bo-cā'la
Ar-bō'na
Ar-bō'rj-ŭs
Ar-bŭs'cu-la
Är'ca-dēs
Ar-cā'dj-a
Ar-cā'num
Ar-cā'thj-ăs
Ar-cē'o-phŏn
Ar-cēs'j-lăs
Ar-cĕs-j-lā'us
Ar-cē'sj-ŭs 1
Är-chæ-ăt'j-dăs
Är-chæ-ŏp'o-lĭs
Ar-chăg'a-thŭs
Ar-chăn'der
Är-chan-drŏp'o-lĭs
Ar-chăn'dros
Är-che-bū'lus
Ar-chĕd'j-cŭs
Ar-chĕg'e-tēs
Är-che-lā'js
Är-che-lā'us
Ar-chĕm'a-chŭs
Ar-chĕm'o-rŭs
Ar-chĕp'o-lĭs
Är-chep-tŏl'e-mŭs
Ar-chĕs'tra-ta
Ar-chĕs'tra-tŭs
Är-che-tī'mus
Ar-chē'tjus 1
Är'chj-a
Är-chj-bī'a-dēs
Ar-chĭb'j-ŭs
Är-chj-bū'lus
Ar-chĭd'a-măs
Är-chj-dā'mj-a, *or*
  Är-chj-da-mī'a
Är-chj-dā'mus
Är'chj-dăs
Är-chj-dĕm'j-dēs
Är-chj-dē'mus
Är-chj-dē'us
Ar-chĭd'j-cē
Ar-chĭd'j-ŭm
Är-chj-găl'lus
Är-chĭg'e-nēs
Ar-chĭl'o-chŭs
Är-chj-mē'dēs
Är-chj-mē'lus
Ar-chī'nus
Är-chj-pĕl'a-gŭs
Ar-chĭp'o-lĭs
Ar-chĭt'e-lēs
Ar-chī'tjs
Ar-chŏn'j-dēs
Ar-chŏn'tēs
Är'chy-lŭs
Ar-chȳ'tas
Ar-cĭt'e-nĕns
Ar-co-brī'ca
Ar-con-nē'sus
Arc-tī'nus
Arc-tŏph'y-lăx
Arc-tū'rus
Är'da-lŭs

Ar-dā'nj-a
Är-dax-ā'nus
Är'de-a
Är-de-ā'tēs
Är-dj-æ'ī
Är'dj-cēs
Är·ao-nē
Ar-dŏ'ne-a
Är-du-ī'ne
Är-dy-ĕn'sēs
A-rē'a
Ā-re-ăç'j-dæ
Ā're-ăs
A-rē'gon
A-rēg'o-nĭs
Ā-re-ĭth'o-ŭs
Är'e-lăs
Är-e-lā'tus
A-rĕl'lj-ŭs
Är-e-mŏr'j-ca
A-rē'na
Är-e-nā'cum, *or*
  A-rĕn'a-cŭm
A-rē'næ
A-rē'ne
Ā-re-ŏp-a-gī'tæ
Ā-re-ŏp'a-gŭs
A-rē'os
Är'e-săs
A-rĕs'tæ
A-rĕs'tha-năs, *or*
  Är-es-thā'nas
Ar-es-tŏr'j-dēs
Är'e-ta
Är-e-tā'dēs
Är-e-tæ'us
Är-e-tăph'j-la
A-rē'te, *and*
  Är'e-tē
Är'e-tēs
Är'e-thăs
Är'e-thŏn
Är-e-thū'sa
Är-e-thū'sjs
Är-e-thū'sj-ŭs 1
A-rē'tj-ăs 1
Är-e-tī'nī
Är-e-tī'num
Är-e-tī'nus
A-rē'tj-ŭs 1
Är-e-tŭl'la
A-rē'tus
Ā'reūs (*n.*) 6
A-rē'us (*a.*)
Är'e-va
A-rĕv'a-cī
Är'ga-lŭs
Är-gan-thō'na
Är-gan-thō'nj-ŭs
Ar-găr'j-cŭs
Är-gē'a
Är-ge-ā'thæ
Är-gē'ī
Är-gĕn'num
Är-gen-nū'sa
Är-gen-tā'rj-ŭs
Är-gĕn'te-ŭs
Är-gen-tī'na
Är-gĕn-to-rā'tum
Är-gĕs'tēs

Ar-gĕs'tra-tŭs
Ar-gē'us
Ar-gī'a
Är'gj-ăs
Ar-gī''cj-ŭs 1
Ar-gĭl-e-ō'nĭs
Är-gj-lē'tum
Ar-gĭl'j-ŭs
Är'gj-lŭs
Ar-gī'nus
Är-gj-nū'sæ
Ar-gī'o-pē
Är-gj-phŏn'tēs
Ar-gĭth'e-a
Är'gj-ŭs, *and*
  Ar-gī'us
Ar-gī'va
Är-gī'vī
Är'gīves
Ar-gō'da
Är·gŏl'j-cŭs
Är'go-lĭs
Är-go-nâu'tæ
Ar-gō'us
Är-gū'ra
Ar-gўn'nis
Ar-gўn'nus
Är'gy-ra
Är-gy-răs'pj-dēs
Är-gy-rī'nī
Är-gy-rĭp'pa, *or*
  Ar-gўr'j-pa
Är-gy-rŏp'o-lĭs
Är'gy-rŭs
Ā'rj-a, *or* A-rī'a
Ā-rj-ăd'na
Ā-rj-ăd'ne
Ā-rj-æ'us
Ā-rj-ăm'e-nēs
Ā-rj-ăm'nēs
Ā-rj-ā'na
Ā-rj-ā'nī, *or*
  Ā-rj-ē'nī
Ā-rj-ăn'tas
Ā-rj-ā'nus
Ā-rj-ăr-a-thē'a, *or*
  -thī'a
Ā-rj-a-rā'thēs
A-rī'as
Ā-rj-ăs'me-nŭs
Är'j-bæ
Är-j-bæ'us
Är'j-bēs
A-rī''cj-a 1
Är-j-cī'na
Är-j-cī'nus
Är-j-dō'ljs
Ā-rj-ē'nī
Ā-rj-ē'njs
Ā'rj-ēs
A-rī'e-tĭs, Frŏns
Är-jg-nō'tus
Ā'rj-ī, *or* A-rī'ī
Är'j-ma
Är-j-măs'pī
Är-j-măs'pj-ăs
Är-j-măs'thæ
Är-j-ma-thē'a, *or*
  -thī'a
Är-j-mā'zēs

Är'j-mī
A-rĭm'j-nŭs
Är-jm-phæ'ī
Är'j-mŭs
Är-jn-thæ'us
Ā-rj-o-bar-zā'nēs
Ā-rj-o-măn'dēs
Ā-rj-o-măr'dus
Ā-rj-o-mē'dēs
A-rī'on
Ā-rj-o-vĭs'tus
Är-j-pē'thēs
Är'j-phrŏn
Är-js-tæn'e-tŭs 4
Är-js-tæ'us
Är-js-tăg'o-ra
Är-js-tăg'o-răs
Är-js-tăn'der
Är-js-tăn'dros
Är-js-tär'che
Är-js-tär'chus
Är-js-ta-zā'nēs
A-rĭs'te-ăs
A-rĭs'te-ræ
A-rĭs'teūs 6
A-rĭs'the-nēs
A-rĭs'tj-ăs
Är-js-tī'bus
Är-js-tī'dēs
A-rĭs'tj-ŏn
Är-js-tĭp'pus
A-rĭs'tj-ŭs
Är-js-to-bū'la
Är-js-to-bū'lus
Är-js-to-clĕ'a
A-rĭs'to-clēs
Är-js-to-clī'das
Är-js-to-clī'dēs
Är-js-tŏc'ra-tēs
Är-js-tŏc're-ŏn
Är-js-tŏc'rj-tŭs
Är-js-to-dā'ma
Är-js-to-dē'mus
Är-js-tŏd'j-cŭs
Är-js-tŏg'e-nēs
Är-js-to-gī'ton
Är-js-to-lā'us
Är-js-tŏl'o-chŭs
Är-js-tŏm'a-chē
Är-js-tŏm'a-chŭs
Är-js-to-mē'dēs
Är-js-tŏm'e-dŏn
Är-js-tŏm'e-nēs
Är-js-to-nī'cus
Är-js-tŏn'j-dēs
Är-js-tŏn'o-ŭs
A-rĭs'to-nŭs
Är-js-tŏn'y-mŭs
Är-js-tŏph'a-nēs
Är-js-tŏph'j-lī
Är-js-to-phĭl'j-dēs
Är-js-tŏph'j-lŭs
Är-js-to-phŏn'tēs
Är-js-to-phȳ'lī
Är-js-tŏr'j-dēs
Är-js-tŏt'e-lēs
Är'js-tŏ-tle
Är-js-to-tī'mus
Är-js-tŏx'e-nŭs
Är-js-tȳl'lus

Ā'rj-ŭs, *or* A-rī'us
Är'me-nē
Ar-mē'nj-a
Är-men-tā'rj-ŭs
Är-mjl-lā'tus
Är-mj-lŭs'trj-ŭm
Ar-mĭn'j-ŭs
Ar-mŏr'j-cī
Ar-mŏs'a-ta, *or*
  Är·mo-sā'ta
Ar-mŏs'o-ta
Ar-mō'zon
Är'ne-æ
Är-nj-ĕn'sēs
Ar-nō'bj-ŭs
Är'o-a, *or* Är'o-ē
A-rō'ma, *and*
  Är'o-ma
A-rŏm'a-ta
A-rŏm'a-tŭm
Är'o-sĭs
Ar-pā'nī
Ar-pī'nas
Ar-quĭ''tj-ŭs 1
Är'quj-tŭs
Är-ra-bō'na
Är-ra-chī'on
Är-rhj-bæ'us
Är-rhj-dæ'us
Ar-rē'chī
Ar-rē'tj-ŭm 1
Är-rj-ā'nus
Är'ri-an
Är'rj-ŭs
Ar-rŭn'tj-ŭs 1
Ar-sā'bēs
Är'sa-cēs, *or*
  Ar-sā'cēs
Ar-sā'cj-a 1
Ar-săç'j-dæ
Ar-săm'e-nēs
Ar-sā'mēs
Ar-săm'e-tēs
Är-sa-mŏs'a-ta, *or*
  Är-sa-mo-sā'ta
Är-sa-mŏs'o-ta
Ar-sā'nēs
Ar-sā'nj-ăs
Ar-sē'na
Är-se-nā'rj-a
Ar-sē'nj-ŭs
Ar-sē'sa
Är'sj-a 1
Ar-sĭn'o-ē
Ar-sī'tēs
Är-ta-bā'nus
Är-ta-ba-zā'nēs
Är'ta-brī
Är-ta-brī'tæ
Är'ta-cē
Är-ta-cē'na
Ar-tā'cj-a 1
Ar-tā'cj-ē 1
Är-tæ'ī
Är-ta-gē'ra, *or* -ræ
Ar-tăm'e-nēs
Är'ta-mō
Ar-tā'nēs
Ar-tā'nus
Är-ta-ō'zus

Är-tạ-pā'nụs
Ạr-tā'tụs
Är-tạ-văs'dēṣ
Är-tạx-äs'ạ-tạ
Ar-täx'ạ-tạ
Är-tạx-ërx'ēṣ
Ar-täx'j-äs 1
Är-tạ-ÿc'tēṣ
Är-tạ-ÿn'tēṣ
Är'tẹ-mäs
Ạr-tĕm'bạ-rēṣ
Ạr-tĕm-j-dō'rụs
Är'tẹ-mïs
Är-tẹ-mï''ṣi-ạ 1
Är-tẹ-mï''ṣi-ŭm 1
Är-tẹ-mī'tạ
Är'tẹ-mŏn
Är-tẹ-mō'nạ
Ạr-tē'nạ
Ärth'mj-ŭs
Ạr-tïm'pạ-sạ
Är-tạ-bạr-zā'nēṣ
Ạr-tō'cēṣ
Ạr-tŏch'mēṣ
Ạr-tō'nạ
Ạr-tō'nj-ŭs
Ạr-tō'rj-ŭs
Är-tạ-trō'gụs
Ạr-tŏx'ạ-rēṣ
Ạr-tū'rj-ŭs
Ạr-tȳ'nēṣ
Ạr-tȳn'j-ạ
Är-tys-tō'nạ
Är'ụ-æ
Ạ-rŭ'cī
Är-ụ-ē'rjs
Är-ụ-lē'nụs
Ạ-rŭn'tj-ŭs 1
Är-ụ-pī'nụm
Är-ụ-pī'nụs
Ạ-rŭ-ṣj-ā'nụs 1
Är-ụ-sī'nī
Ạr-vī'nạ
Ạr-vïr'ạ-gŭs
Ạr-vï''ṣj-ŭm 1
Ạr-vī'sụs
Ärx'ạ-tạ
Är'y-băs
Ä-ry-ē'njs
Ạ-rÿx'ạ-tạ
Är-zạ-nē'nẹ
Äs-bạ-mē'ạ
Äs'bọ-lŭs
Ạs-bō'tụs
Ạs-bū'tēṣ
Ạs-bȳ'tẹ
Ạs-căl'ạ-bŭs
Ạs-căl'ạ-phŭs
Äs'cạ-lŏn
Ạs-cā'nj-ạ
Ạs-cā'nj-ŭs
Äs'cạ-rŭs
Ạs-chē'ụm
Äs'chẹ-tŏs
Äs'chẹ-tŭs
Äs-cj-bür'gj-ŭm
Äs'cj-ī 1
Ạs-clē-pj-ē'ạ
Äs-clẹ-pī'ạ-dēṣ
Ạs-clē-pj-ọ-dō'rụs

Ạs-clē-pj-ŏd'ọ-tŭs
Ạs-clē'pj-ŭs
Äs-clẹ-tā'rj-ŏn
Ạs-cō'lj-ạ
Ạs-cō'nj-ŭs Lā'bẹ-ō
Äs'cụ-lŭm
Äs'drụ-băl
Ā'sẹ-ạ
Ạ-sĕl'lj-ō
Ạ-sē'ụs
Ā'sj-ạ 1
Ā-sj-ăǵ'ẹ-nēṣ 1
Ā-sj-ăt'j-cŭs 1
Ạ-sī'dō
Ạ-sī'lụs
Äs'j-nạ
Äs-j-nā'rj-ạ
Äs-j-nā'rj-ŭs
Äs'j-nē
Ạ-sĭn'j-ŭs
Ạ-sĭ''ṣj-ŭm 1
Ä'sj-ŭs 1
Ạṣ-nā'ụs
Ạ-sō'pj-ạ
Äs-ọ-pī'ạ-dēṣ
Ạ-sō'pjs
Ạ-sō'pj-ŭs
Ạ-sō'pọs
Ạ-sō'pụs
Äs-pạ-bō'tạ
As-pál-ạ-thī'ạ
As-păl'ạ-thŏs
Äs'pạ-lïs
As-păm'j-thrēṣ
Äs-pạ-rā'ǵj-ŭm
As-pā'ṣj-ạ 1
Äs-pạ-sī'rụs
As-pā'ṣj-ŭs 1
Äs-pạ-thī'nēṣ
Äs-pạ-thī'sjs
Äs-phạl-tī'tēṣ
As-plē'dọn
Äs-pọ-rē'nụs
As-prē'nạs
Ạs-pür-ǵj-ā'nī
Äs-sạ-bī'nụs
Äs-sạ-cā'nī, or -cē'nī
Ạs-săǵ'ẹ-tēṣ
Ạs-săr'ạ-cŭs
Ạs-sē'rạ
Äs-sẹ-rī'nī
Ạs-sē'sụs
Ạs-sō'rụm
Äs-sụ-ē'rụs
As-sū'ræ
Äs-tạ-cē'nī
As-tăç'j-dēṣ
Äs'tạ-cŭs
Äs-tạ-ǵē'nī
Äs'tạ-pạ
As-tā'phj-ŭm
Äs'tạ-pŭs
As-tĕl'ẹ-bē
Ạs-tĕl'ẹ-phŭs
Ạs-tē'rj-ạ
Ạs-tē'rj-ē
Ạs-tē'rj-ŏn
Äs'tẹ-rïs
Äs-tẹ-rō'dj-ạ
28

Ạs-tĕr-ọ-pæ'ụs
Äs-tĕr'ọ-pē
Äs-tĕr-ọ-pē'ạ
Äs-tẹ-rū'ṣj-ŭs 1
As-tī'ǵī
Äs'tj-lŭs
As-tïn'ọ-mē
As-tī'ọ-chŭs
Äs'tọ-mī
As-trăb'ạ-cŭs
As-træ'ạ
Äs-trạm-psȳ'çhụs
Äs'treūs 6
Äs'tụ-rạ
Äs'tụ-rēṣ
As-tū'rj-ạ
As-tū'rj-cŭs
As-tȳ'ạ-ǵē
As-tȳ'ạ-ǵēṣ
As-tȳ'ạ-lŭs
As-tȳ'ạ-näx
Äs-ty-crạ-tē'ạ, or
  -tī'ạ
As-tȳd'ạ-mäs
Äs-ty-dạ-mī'ạ
As-tȳl'j-dēṣ
Äs'ty-lŏs, and
  As-tȳ!lọs
Äs-ty-mē'dēṣ
As-tȳm-ẹ-dū'sạ
As-tȳn'ọ-mŭs
As-tȳn'ọ-ŭs
As-tȳ'ọ-chē
Äs-ty-ọ-çhī'ạ
As-tȳ'ọ-çhŭs
As-tȳph'j-lŭs
Äs'ty-rạ
Äs'ty-rŏn
Äs'y-chïs
Ạ-sȳ'lụs
Ạ-sȳn'crj-tŭs
Ạ-tăb'ụ-lŭs
Ạ-tăb'y-rïs
Ät-ạ-by-rī'tẹ
Ät-ạ-bȳr'j-ŭm
Ät'ạ-cē
Ät-ạ-cī'nụs, Vär'rō
Ät-ạ-lăn'tạ
Ät-ạ-lạn-tī'ạ-dēṣ
Ät-ạ-lȳ'dạ
Ät-ạr-bē'çhjs
Ạ-tär'gạ-tïs
Ạ-tär'nẹ-ạ
Ạ-tär'neūs 6
Ät-ạr-nī'tēṣ
Ạ-tē'j-ŭs 3
Ạ-tē'nạ, or -nẹ
Ät-ẹ-nọ-mā'rụs
Ạ-tër'gạ-tïs
Ạ-tē'rj-ŭs
Ạ-tē-rj-ā'nụs
Äth-ạ-mā'nēṣ
Äth-ạ-mā'njs
Äth-ạ-mā'nịs
Äth-ạ-mạn-tī'ạ-dēṣ
Äth'ạ-mäs
Ạ-thán-ạ rī'cụs
Ạ-thän'ạ-ric
Äth-ạ-nā'ṣj-ŭs 1
Ạ-thän'ạ-tī

Äth'ạ-nïs
Ä'thẹ-äs
Ạ-thē'nạ
Ạ-thē'næ
Äth-ẹ-næ'ạ
Äth-ẹ-næ'ụm
Äth-ẹ-năǵ'ọ-răs
Äth-ẹ-nā'js
Ạ-thē'nẹ
Ạ-thē-nj-ĕn'sjs
Ạ-thē'nj-ŏn
Ạ-thĕn'ọ-clēṣ
Ạ-thĕn-ọ-dō'rụs
Äth-ẹ-nŏǵ'ẹ-nēṣ
Äth'ẹ-sïs
Äth'lj-bïs
Äth'mọ-nŭm
Ạ-thō'ụs
Äth'rj-bïs
Ath-rŭl'lạ
Ạ-thȳm'brạ
Äth'y-räs
Ā'tj-ạ 1
Ạ-tïd'j-ŭs
Ạ-tïl'j-ạ
Ạ-tïl-j-cī'nụs
Ạ-tïl'j-ŭs
Ät-j-mē'tụs
Ạ-tī'nạ
Ạ-tïn'j-ạ
Ät-jn-tā'nēṣ
Ā'tj-ŭs 1
Ät-lạn-tē'ạ, or -tī'ạ
Ät-lạn-tē'ụs
Ät-lăn'tj-cŭs
Ät-lạn-tī'ạ-dēṣ
Ät-lăn'tj-dēṣ
Ät-lăn'tj-äs 1
Ät'mọ-nī
Ät'rạ-cēṣ
Ạ-trăc'j-dēṣ
Ät'rạ-cïs
Ät-rạ-mī'tæ
Ät-rạ-mÿt'tj-ŭm 2
Ät'rạ-pēṣ
Ät-rạ-tī'nụs
Ạ-trĕb'ạ-tēṣ, or -tī
Ät-rẹ-bā'tēṣ
Ạ-trē'nī
Ä'treūs (n.) 6
Ạ-trē'ụs (a.)
Ạ-trī'dæ
Ạ-trī'dēṣ
Ät-rọ-mē'tụs
Ạ-trō'nj-ŭs
Ät-rọ-pạ-tē'nī
Ạ-trŏp'ạ-tēṣ
Ät-rọ-pā'tj-ạ 1
Ạ-trŏp'ạ-tŭs
Ät'rọ-pŏs
Ät-tạ-gŭs
Ạ-tăc'ọ-ræ, or -rī
Ät-tạ-gī'nụs
Ät-tạ-lī'ạ
Ät-tă-lj-ā'tạ, or -tēṣ
Ät-tā-lj-ō'tạ, or -tēṣ
Ät-tĕg'ụ-a
Ạ-tē'j-ŭs Căp'j-tō
Ät-tj-ā'nụs
Ät'tj-cạ

Ät-tj-cïl'lạ
Ät'tj-cŭs
Ät-tïd-j-ā'tēṣ
Ät'tj-lạ
Ät-tïl-j-ā'nụs
Ät-tïl'j-ŭs
Ät-tī'nạs
Ät'tj-ŭs
Ạt-tū'dạ
Ạt-tū'ṣj-ạ 1
Ät-ụ-ăt'j-cī
Ät'ụ-bī
Ät'ụ-rŭs
Ạ-tū'sạ
Ạ-tȳ'ạ-dæ
Ạ-tȳm'nj-ŭs
Âu-chā'tæ
Âu-chā'tēṣ
Âu-dē'nạ
Âu-dĕn'tj-ŭs
Âu-dō'lẹ-ŏn
Âu-fē'j-ạ Ā'quạ 3
Âu-fj-dē'nạ
Âu-fïd'j-ạ
Âu-fïd'j-ŭs
Âu'fj-dŭs
Âu-fj-lē'nạ
Âu-fj-lē'nụs
Âu'gạ-rŭs
Âu-ǵē'ạ
Âu-ǵē'æ
Âu-ǵē'ạs, and
  Âu'gẹ-äs
Âu-ǵē'ụs
Âu-ǵī'ạs
Âu'ǵj-læ
Âu-ǵī'nụs
Âu'gụ-rēṣ
Âu-gụ-rī'nụs
Âu-gụs-tā'lj-ạ
Âu-gụs-tī'nụs
Âu-gŭs'tine
Âu-gŭs-tọ-brī'gạ
Âu-gŭs-tọ-dū'nụm
Âu-gŭs-tọ-nĕm'ẹ-
  tŭm
Âu-gŭs'tụ-lŭs
Âu-lēs'tēṣ
Âu-lē'tēṣ
Âu-lọ-crē'nẹ
Âu-lō'nj-ŭs
Âu-rạ-nī'tjs
Âu-rā'ṣj-ŭs 1
Âu-rē'lj-ạ
Âu-rē-lj-ā'nụs
Âu-rē'li-an
Âu-rē'lj-ŭs
Âu-rē'ọ-lŭs
Âu-rī'gạ
Âu-rïn'j-ạ
Âu'rj-ŭs
Âu-rō'rạ
Âu-rŭn'cạ
Âu-rŭn'cẹ
Âu-rŭn-cụ-lē'j-ạ 3
Âu-rŭn-cụ-lē'j-ŭs 3
Âus-chī'sæ
Âus'cī
Âu'sẹ-rïs
Âu-sẹ-tā'nī

Âu-sī'tæ
Âu'sǫ-nēş
Âu-sō'nǐ-ǎ
Âu-sŏn'ǐ-dæ
Âu-sō'nǐ-ǔs
Âu'spǐ-cēş
Âus-tǎ-ģē'nǎ
Âus'tęr
Âus-tē'şǐ-ŏn 1
Âus-trā'lǐs
Âus-trī'nǔs
Âu-tǎ-nī'tǐs
Âu-tā-rǐ-ā'tæ
Âu-tǎr'ǐ-tǔs
Âu-tē-şǐ-ǫ-dū'rǔm 1
Âu-tē'şǐ-ŏn 1
Âu-tǫ-bū'lǔs
Âu-tŏc'ǎ-nēş
Âu-tŏch'thǫ-nēş
Âu'tǫ-clēş
Âu-tŏc'rǎ-tēş
Âu-tǫ-crē'nę
Âu-tŏl'ę-mǔs
Âu-tō'lę-ŏn
Âu-tŏl'ǫ-læ
Âu-tŏl'ǫ-lēş
Âu-tŏl'y-cǔs
Âu-tŏm'ǎ-tē
Âu-tŏm'ę-dŏn
Âu-tǫ-mę-dū'sǎ
Âu-tŏm'ę-nēş
Âu-tŏm'ǫ-lī
Âu-tŏn'ǫ-ē
Âu-tŏn'ǫ-ǔs
Âu-tŏph-rǎ-dā'tēş
Âu'trǐ-cǔm, or
   Âu-trī'cǔm
Âu-trǐg'ǫ-nēş
Âu-tū'rǎ
Âux-ē'şǐ-ǎ 1
Âux'ǐ-mŏn
Âux-ū'mę
Ạ-vǎr'ǐ-cǔm, or
   Ăv-ǎ-rī'cǔm
Ạ-vǎr'ǐ-cǔs
Ăv'ǎ-sēş
Ạ-vē'ǐ-ǎ 3
Ăv'ę-lǐs
Ạ-vē'nǐ-ō
Ạ-vĕn'tǐ-cǔm
Ăv-ęn-tī'nǔs
Ā-vǐ-ā'nǔs
Ạ-vǐd-ǐ-ē'nǔs
Ạ-vǐd'ǐ-ǔs
Ā-vǐ-ē'nǔs
Ạ-vī'ǫ-lǎ
Ạ-vǐ-tǐ-ā'nǔs 1
Ạ-vī'tǔs
Ā'vǐ-ǔm
Ăx'ę-nǔs
Ạx-ǐ'ę-rŏs
Ạx-ǐ'ǫ-chǔs
Ạx-ǐ'ǫn
Ăx-ǐ-ǫ-nī'cǔs 1
Ăx-ǐ-ō'tæ 1
Ăx-ǐ-ō'thę-ǎ 1
Ăx'ǫ-nǎ
Ạx-ō'nēş, people.
Ăx'ǫ-nēş, tablets.
Ạx-ū'mę

Ăx'y-lǔs, country.
Ăx-ў'lǔs, man.
Ạ-zǎm'ǫ-rǎ
Ạ-zā'nī
Ạ-zē'cǎ
Ā'zeǔs 6
Ạ-zī'dēş
Ạ-zī'rǐs
Ăz'ǫ-nǎx
Ạ-zō'tǔs

B.

Bǎ-bǐl'ǐ-ǔs
Bǎb'ǐ-lǔs
Bā'brǐ-ǔs
Bǎb'y-lō
Bǎb'y-lŏn
Bǎb-y-lō'nǐ-ǎ
Bǎ-bўt'ǎ-cē
Bǎc-ǎ-bā'sǔs
Bǎc'cǎ-rǎ
Bǎc'chæ
Bǎc-chā'nǎl
Bǎc'chǎ-nǎl
Bǎc-chǎ-nā'lǐ-ǎ
Bǎc-chǎn'tēş
Bǎc-chē'ǔs
Bǎc-chī'ǎ-dæ
Bǎc-chī'dǎs
Bǎc'chǐ-dēş
Bǎc-chī'ǔm
Bǎc-chī'ǔs, author.
Bǎc'chǐ-ǔs (in Hor.)
Bǎc-chўl'ǐ-dēş
Bǎc'chy-lǔs
Bǎ-cē'nǐs
Bā-chǐ-ā'rǐ-ǔs
Bǎc'ǫ-rǐs
Bǎc-trǐ-ā'nǎ
Bǎc-trǐ-ā'nī
Bǎc-ǔ-ā'tæ
Bǎ-cǔn'tǐ-ǔs 1
Bǎd'ǎ-cǎ
Bǎ-dī'ǎ, or Bā'dǐ-ǎ
Bā'dǐ-ǔs
Bǎd-ǔ-hĕn'næ
Bæc'ǔ-lǎ 4
Bæç'y-lǎ 4
Bæ-thō'rǫn
Bæt'ǐ-cǎ 4
Bæt'ǐ-cǔs 4
Bæt'ǔ-lō
Bæ-tū'rǐ-ǎ
Bæt'y-lǔs 4
Bǎ-gā'cǔm, or
   Bǎg'ǎ-cǔm
Bǎg-ǎ-dā'ǫ-nēş
Bǎ-ģē'sǔs
Bǎ-ģǐs'tǎ-mē
Bǎ-ģǐs'tǎ-nǎ
Bǎ-ģǐs'tǎ-nēş
Bǎ-ģǐs'tǎ-nǔs
Bǎ-gō'ǎs
Bǎ-gō'sǎs
Bǎg-ǫ-dā'rēş
Bǎ-gǒph'ǎ-nēş
Bǎ-gō'ǔs

Bǎg'rǎ-dǎ
Bā'ǐ-æ 3
Bā-ǐ-ǫ-cǎs'sæ
Bā'ǐ-ǔs
Bǎl'ǎ-crǔs
Bǎl-ǎ-nā'græ
Bǎl'ǎ-nǔs
Bǎl'ǎ-rī, or Bǎ-lā'rī
Bǎl'ǎ-rǔs
Bǎl'ǎ-trō
Bǎl-bǐ'nǔs
Bǎl-bū'rǎ
Bǎl-cē'ǎ
Bǎl-dǔ-ǐ'nǔs
Bâld'win
Bā-lę-ā'rēş
Bǎ-lē'tǔs
Bǎl-ǐs-bē'gǎ
Bā'lǐ-ǔs
Bǎl'lǐ-ō
Bǎl-lŏn'ǫ-tī
Bǔl'sǎ-mŏn
Bǎl-vĕn'tǐ-ǔs 1
Bǎl'y-rǎ
Bǎl'y-rǎs
Bǎm-bў'cę
Bǎn-dū'sǐ-ǎ 1
Bū-nǐ-ū'ræ, or -rī
Bǎn-ǐ-zŏm'ę-nēş
Bǎn'tǐ-ǎ 1
Bǎn'tǐ-æ 1
Bǎn-tī'nǎ
Bǎn'tǐ-ǔs 1
Bǎ-nū'bǎ-rī
Bǎph'y-rǔs
Bǎr'ǎ-dō
Bǎr'ǎ-thrǔm
Bǎr'bǎ-rī
Bǎr-bā'rǐ-ǎ
Bǎr-bā'tǐ-ō 1
Bǎr-bā'tǐ-ǔs 1
Bǎr-bā'tǔs
Bǎr-bĕs'ǔ-lǎ
Bǎr-bŏs'thę-nēş
Bǎr-bўth'ǎ-cē
Bǎr-cæ'ī, or Bǎr-cī'tæ
Bǎr'cǐ-nō
Bǎr-cī'nǔs
Bǎr-dā'nēş
Bǎr-dę-sā'nēş
Bǎr-dī'nǎ
Bā'rę-ǎ, man.
Bǎ-rē'ǎ, town.
Bā'rę-ǎs Sǫ-rā'nǔs
Bǎr'gǫ-sǎ
Bǎr-gū'sǐ-ī 1
Bǎr-gўl'ǐ-ǎ
Bǎr'gy-lǔs
Bǎ-rī'nę
Bǎr'ǐ-sǎs
Bā'rǐ-ǔm
Bǎr-sī'nę, and
   Bǎr-sē'nę
Bǎr-zǎ-ĕn'tēş
Bǎr-zā'nēş
Bǎs-ǎ-nī'tēş
Bǎ-sē'rǎ
Bǎs-ǐ-lē'ǎ
Bǎs-ǐ-lī'ǎ

Bǎ-sǐl-ǐ-ā'nǔs
Bǎ-sǐl'ǐ-cǎs
Bǎ-sǐl'ǐ-cǔs
Bǎs-ǐ-lī'dæ
Bǎs-ǐ-lī'dēş
Bǎs-ǐ-lī'ī
Bǎs-ǐ-lī'nǎ
Bǎ-sǐl-ǐ-ǫ-pŏt'ǎ-mǒs
Bǎs'ǐ-lǐs
Bǎ-sǐl'ǐ-ǔs, man.
Bǎş'il
Bǎs-ǐ-lī'ǔs, river.
Bǎs'ǐ-lǔs
Bǎs-sā'nǐ-ǎ
Bǎs'sǎ-reǔs 6
Bǎs-sǎr'ǐ-dēş
Bǎs'sǎ-rǐs
Bǎs-sǐ-ā'nǔs 1
Bǎs-sī'nǔs
Bǎs-tǎr'næ
Bǎs-tę-tā'nī
Bǎs-tĕr'næ
Bǎs'tǐ-ǎ 1
Bǎt'ǎ-lǔs
Bǎt-ǎ-nō'chǔs
Bǎ-tā'vī, or
   Bǎt'ǎ-vī
Bǎ-tā'vǐ-ǎ
Bǎt-ǎ-vǫ-dū'rǔm
Bǎ-tā'vǔs, or
   Bǎt'ǎ-vǔs
Bǎ-tē'ǎ
Bǎth-ǎ-nā'tǐ-ǔs 1
Bǎth'y-clēş
Bǎ-tī'ǎ
Bā-tǐ-ā'tǔs 1
Bā-tǐ-ē'ǎ 1
Bǎ-tī'nī
Bǎt-rǎ-chō-my-ǫ-
   mā'chǐ-ǎ
Bǎt'rǎ-chǔs
Bǎt'tǎ-rǔs
Bǎt-tī'ǎ-dēş
Bǎt'ǔ-lǔm
Bǎt'ǔ-lǔs
Bā'vǐ-ǔs
Bǎv'ǫ-tǎ
Bǎz-ǎ-ĕn'tēş
Bǎz-ǎ-ǐ'rǎ
Bǎ-zī'rǎ
Bę-ā'trǐx
Bē'bǐ-ǔs
Bę-brī'ǎ-cǔm
Bĕb'ry-cē
Bĕb'ry-cēş, and
   Bę-brў'cēş
Bǎ-brў''cǐ-ǎ 1
Bę-brў''cǐ-ī 1
Bę-chī'rēş, or -rī
Bę-drī'ǎ-cǔm
Bĕl'ǎ-tēş
Bĕl-bī'nǎ

Bĕl'ģǐ-ǔs
Bē'lǐ-ǎs
Bĕl'ǐ-dēş, pl.
Bę-lī'dēş, sing.
Bę-lǐs'ǎ-mǎ
Bĕl-ǐ-sā'rǐ-ǔs
Bę-lǐs'tǐ-chē
Bę-lī'tæ ·
Bĕl-lā'ǐ-nēş
Bĕl-lĕr'ǫ-phŏn
Bĕl'lę-rǔs
Bĕl-lǐ-ē'nǔs
Bĕl-lō'nǎ
Bĕl-lǫ-nā'rǐ-ī
Bĕl-lŏv'ǎ-cī, or
   Bĕl-lǫ-vā'cī
Bĕl-lŏv'ǎ-cǔm, or
   Bĕl-lǫ-vā'cǔm
Bĕl-lǫ-vē'sǔs
Bĕl-mī'nǎ
Bĕl'phę-gŏr
Bęl-sī'nǔm
Bę-lū'nǔm
Bęm-bī'nǎ
Bę-nā'cǔs
Bĕn-dǐ-dī'ǎ
Bĕn-dǐ-dī'ǔm
Bĕn-ę-vĕn'tǔm
Bęn-thĕs-ǐ-cў'mę
Bę-pŏl-ǐ-tā'nǔs
Bĕr'bǐ-cæ
Bĕr-ę-cўn'thǐ-ǎ
Bĕr-ę-cўn'thǔs
Bĕr-ę-cyn-tī'ǎ-dēş
Bĕr-ę-nī'cę
Bĕr-ę-nī'cǐs
Bĕr'ģǐ-nē
Bĕr'ģǐ-ŏn
Bĕr-ģǐs-tā'nī
Bĕr'gǫ-mǔm
Bĕr'ǫ-ē
Bę-rō'nēş
Bĕr-ǫ-nī'cę
Bę-rō'sǔs
Bę-rō'thǎ
Bē'ry-ǎs
Bę-rўb'rǎ-cēş
Bę-rў'tǔs, and
   Bĕr'y-tǔs
Bĕs-ǎn-tī'nǔs
Bĕs'ǎ-rǎ
Bĕs'bǐ-cǔs
Bę-sǐd'ǐ-æ
Bę-sī'lǔs
Bĕs'tǐ-ǎ
Bĕs'tǐ-ǔs
Bĕs-yn-ģē'tī
Bę-tǎr'mǫ-nēş
Bĕt'ǎ-sī
Bę-thō'rǫn
Bĕt'ǐ-rǎ
Bę-tū'rǐ-ǎ
Bī-ā'nǫr
Bǐ-bǎc'ǔ-lǔs
Bǐb'ǎ-gǎ
Bǐb'lǐ-ǎ, and
Bīl'lǐ-ǎ
Bǐb'lǐ-nǎ
Bǐb'ǔ-lǎ
Bǐb'ǔ-lǔs

Bī-cŏr'nĭ-ġẹr
Bī-ē'phĭ
Bī-ġĕr-rĭ-ō'nĕş
Bĭl'bĭ-lĭs
Bī-mā'tẹr
Bīn'ġĭ-ŭm
Bī'ọ-neŭs (n.)
Bī-ọ-nē'ụs (a.)
Bīr'rĭ-ŭs
Bĭ-săl'tæ
Bĭs'sụ-lạ
Bĭs'tọ-nĕş
Bĭs-tō'nĭ-ạ
Bĭs-tŏn'ĭ-dĕş
Bĭs'tọ-nĭs, and
  Bĭs-tō'nĭs
Bĭth'y-æ
Bĭ-thȳ'nĭ
Bĭ-thȳn'ĭ-ạ
Bĭ-thȳn'ĭ-cŭs
Bĭ-thȳn'ĭ-ŭm
Bĭ''tĭ-ăs 1
Bĭt-ụ-ī'tụs, or
  Bĭ-tū'ĭ-tŭs
Bĭ-tū'rĭ-cŭm
Bĭ-tū'rĭ-gĕş
Bĭt'ụ-rĭx
Bĭ''zĭ-ạ 1
Bĭ-zō'nẹ
Bĭ''zy-ạ 1
Blạ-ē'nẹ
Blæ'şĭ-ī 1
Blăn-dẹ-nō'nạ
Blạn-dō'nạ
Blạn-dū'şĭ-ạ 1
Blā'şĭ-ō 1
Blā'şĭ-ŭs 1
Blăs'tạ-rĕş
Blăs-tọ-phœ-nī cĕş
Blā'vĭ-ạ
Blĕm'my-ĕş
Blē'my-æ
Blē'my-ī
Blẹ-nī'nạ
Blĕph'ạ-rō
Blĭ''tĭ-ŭs 1
Blō'şĭ-ŭs
Blū'cĭ-ŭm 1
Bọ-ăd-ĭ-cē'ạ, or
  Bō-ạ-dĭç'ẹ-ạ
Bō'æ, and Bœ'ạ
Bọ-ā'grĭ-ŭs
Bŏb-ẹ-nē'ạ
Bọ-cā'lĭ-ăs
Bŏc'chọ-rĭs
Bọ-dū-ag-nā'tụs
Bọ-dū'nī
Bœ-bē'ĭs
Bœ'bĭ-ạ
Bŏ-ẹ-drō'mĭ-ạ
Bœ-ọ-tär'çhæ
Bœ-ō'tĭ-ạ 1
Bœ-ō'tĭ-ŭs 1
Bœ-ō'tụs
Bœr-ẹ-bĭs'tạs 4
Bọ-ē'thĭ-ŭs
Bọ-ē'thus
Bọ-ē'tĭ-ŭs 1
Bŏ'ĭ-ạ 3
Bŏ'ĭ-ī 3

Bọ-jŏc'ạ-lŭs
Bŏj'ọ-rĭx
Bọ-lā'nụs
Bọl-bē'nẹ
Bŏl-bĭ-tī'nẹ
Bŏl-bĭ-tī'nụm
Bŏl'ġĭ-ŭs
Bọ-lē'rĭ-ŭm
Bọ-lī'nạ, or
  Bŏl'ĭ-nạ
Bŏl-ĭ-næ'ụs
Bọl-lā'nụs
Bọm-bȳ'cẹ
Bŏ-mĭ-ĕn'sĕş
Bŏm-ọ-nī'cæ
Bŏn-ĭ-fā'cĭ-ŭs 1
Bọ-nō'nĭ-ạ
Bọ-nō'şĭ-ŭs 1
Bọ-nō'şụs
Bō-ọ-sū'rạ
Bọ-ō'tĕş
Bọ-ō'tụs, and
  Bœ-ō'tụs
Bör-bẹ-tŏm'ạ-gŭs
Bŏ'rẹ-ạ
Bọ-rē'ạ-dĕş
Bō-rẹ-ā'lĭs
Bŏ'rẹ-ăs
Bŏ-rẹ-ăs'mĭ
Bọ-rē'ọn
Bọr-gŏ'dĭ
Bọ-rī'ọn
Bọ-rī'nụs
Bọ-rȳs'thẹ-nĕş
Bŏs'phọ-rŭs
Bŏs'pọ-rŏs
Bŏs'pọ-rŭs
Bọs-trē'nụs
Bọ-tā-nĭ-ā'tĕş
Bọ-thrŏ'dụs
Bọ-trŏ'dụs
Bŏt'tĭ-ạ
Bō-vĭ-ā'nụm
Brăc'ạ-nạ
Brạc-cā'tĭ
Brạch-mā'nĕş
Brạch-mā'nĭ
Brạ-çhō'dĕş
Bræ'şĭ-ạ 1
Brạn-chī'ạ-dĕş
Brăn'çhĭ-dæ
Brăn'çhụs
Brạn-chȳl'lĭ-dĕş
Brā'şĭ-æ 1
Brăs'ĭ-dăs
Brăs-ĭ-dē'ạ, or -dĭ'ạ
Brăs'ĭ-lăs
Brău-rō'nĭ-ạ
Brẹ-ġæ'tĭ-ŭm 1
Brĕn'nī, and
  Breŭ'nī
Brĕs'cĭ-ạ 1
Brĕt'tĭ-ī 2
Breŭ'cụs
Brĭ-ā'rẹ-ŭs, or
  Brī'ạ-reŭs 6
Brĭ-găn'tĕş
Brĭ-găn'tĭ-ạ 1
Brĭ-găn'tĭ-cŭs
Brĭg-an-tī'nụs

Brĭ-găn'tĭ-ŭm 1
Brĭ-sē'ĭs
Brī'sĕş
Brī'seŭs 6
Brĭ-tăn'nĭ-ạ
Brĭ-tăn'nĭ-cŭs
Brĭt-ọ-mär'tĭs
Brĭt-ọ-mā'rụs, or
  -rĭs, or
  Brĭ-tŏm'ạ-rŭs
Brĭt'ọ-nĕş, and
  Brĭ-tō'nĕş
Brī-ū'lạ
Brĭx'ĭ-ạ 1
Brĭx'ĭ-nō
Brŏc-ụ-bē'lụs
Brọ-ġĭt'ạ-rŭs
Brō'mĭ-ạ
Brŏn'tĕş
Brọn-tī'nụs
Brŏ'tĕş
Brŏ'tẹ-ăs
Brŏ'thẹ-ŭs
Brŭc'tẹ-rī
Brŭc'tẹ-rŭs
Brụ-mā'lĭ-ạ
Brụn-dĭ''şĭ-ŭm 1
Brụn-dū'şĭ-ŭm 1
Brŭ-tĭ-ā'nụs 1
Brụ-tĭd'ĭ-ŭs
Brŭ'tĭ-ī 1
Brŭt'tĭ-ī
Brŭt'tĭ-ŭm
Brŭ'tụ-lŭs
Brȳ-ĕn'nĭ-ŭs
Brȳ'ġĕş
Brȳs'ẹ-ạ
Brȳs'ẹ-æ, and
  Bry-sē'æ
Bū-bạ-cē'nẹ
Bụ-bā'cĕş
Bū'bạ-rĭs
Bū-bạs-tī'ạ-cŭs
Bū'bạ-sŭs
Bụ-bō'nạ
Bū'cĕş
Bụ-cĕph-ạ-lī'ạ
Bụ-cĕph'ạ-lŭs
Bụ-chæ'tĭ-ŭm 1
Bū'çhẹ-tạ
Bụ-cĭl-ĭ-ā'nụs
Bụ-cŏl'ĭ-cạ
Bụ-cŏl'ĭ-cŭm
Bụ-cō'lĭ-ŏn
Bū'cọ-lŭs
Bụ-dē'ạ
Bū'dĭ-ī
Bụ-dī'nī
Bụ-dŏ'rĭs
Bū'dọ-rŭm, or
  Bụ-dō'rụm
Bụ-dŏ'rụs
Bū'ġẹ-nĕş
Bụ-lăg'ọ-răs
Bụ-lĭm'ẹ-ī
Bụl-lā'tĭ-ŭs 1
Bụl-lī'ọ-nĕş
Bụ-mā'dụs
Bụ-mŏ'dụs
Bụ-nī'mạ

Bū-nọ-mē'ạ
Bū'pạ-lŭs
Bū'phạ-gŭs
Bụ-phō'nĭ-ạ
Bụ-prā'şĭ-ŭm 1
Bụ-rā'ĭ-cŭs
Bụr-dĭg'ạ-lạ
Bụr-gŭn-dĭ-ō'nĕş
Bū'rĭ-çhŭs
Bŭr-rĭ-ē'nụs
Bür'sĭ-ạ 1
Bụ-sī'rĭs
Bū-sĭ-rī'tĕş
Bū'tạ-dæ
Bū'tẹ-ō
Bū'tĕş
Bū'thọ-ē
Bụ-thrŏ'tọs
Bụ-thrŏ'tụm
Bụ-thrŏ'tụs
Bụ-thȳr'ẹ-ŭs
Bū'tọ-ạ
Bū'tọ-nĕş
Bụ-tŏr'ĭ-dĕş
Bū'trạ
Bụ-trŏ'tụs
Bụ-zē'rī
Bū'zy-ġĕş
By-băs'sĭ-ạ 1
Byb-lē'şĭ-ạ 1
Bȳb'lĭ-ạ
Bȳb'lĭ-ī
Bȳb'lĭs
Bȳb'lụs
Bȳ'cẹ
Bȳl-ạ-zō'rạ
Byl-lī'ọ-nĕş
Bȳr'rhĭ-ạ
By-zā'cĭ-ŭm 1
Bȳz-ạn-tī'ạ-cŭs
Bȳz-ạn-tī'nụs
By-zăn'tĭ-ŏn 2
By-zăn'tĭ-ŭm 1
By-zăn'tĭ-ŭs 1
By-zē'nụs
By-zē'rĕş
Bȳ''zĭ-ạ 1

C.

Căb'ạ-dĕş
Căb'ạ-lạ
Cạ-băl'ạ-cạ
Căb'ạ-lēş
Cạ-bā'lĭ-ī
Căb-ạ-lī'nụs
Cạ-bā'lĭs
Căb-ạl-lī'nụm
Cạ-băl'lĭ-ō
Căb'ạ-sạ
Cạ-băs'ĭ-lăs
Cạ-bē'lēş
Cạ-bē'sụs
Căb-ĭl-lō'nụm
Cạ-bī'rạ
Cạ-bĭr'ĭ-ạ
Cạ-bū'rạ
Căb'ụ-rŭs

Căb'y-lē
Căch'ạ-lēş
Căc-ọ-dæm'ọ-nĕş 4
Cạ-cū'thĭs
Cạ-cȳp'ạ-rĭs
Cạ-dē'nạ
Cạd-mē'ạ
Cạd-mē'ụs
Cạd-mī'lụs
Cád'rẹ-ma
Cạ-dū'cẹ-ŭs 1
Cạ-dū'sī
Cạ-dū'şĭ-ī 1
Cád'y-tĭs
Cæ-cē'tĭ-ŭs 1
Cæ'cĭ-ăs 1
Cæ-cĭl'ĭ-ạ
Cæ-cĭl-ĭ-ā'nụs
Cæ-cĭl'ĭ-ŭs
Cæç'ĭ-lŭs 4
Cæ-cī'nụs
Cæc'ụ-bŭm 4
Cæc'ụ-bŭs 4
Cæc'ụ-lŭs 4
Cæ-dĭ''cĭ-ŭs 1
Cæd'ĭ-cŭs 4
Cæ-dĭ-tĭ-ā'nụs 1
Cæ-dĭ''tĭ-ŭs 1
Cæ'lĭ-ạ
Cæl'ĭ-nŭs 4
Cæ-lĭ-ō-mọn-tā'nụs
Cæ'lĭ-ŭs
Cæm'ạ-rō 4
Cæ'neŭs 6
Cæ-nī'dĕş
Cæ-nī'nạ
Cæ-nŏt'rọ-pæ
Cæ-pā'rĭ-ŭs
Cæ-pā'şĭ-ŭs 1
Cæ-rā'tụs
Cæ're, or Cæ'rĕş
Cæ-rĕl'lĭ-ạ
Cær'ẹ-sī 4
Cær'ĭ-tĕş 4
Cær'ụ-lŭs 4
Cæ'şạr
Cæs-ạ-rē'ạ 4
Cæ-sā'rĭ-ŏn
Cæ-sā'rĭ-ŭs
Cæs-ạ-rọ-dū'nụm 4
Cæs-ạ-rŏm'ạ-gŭs 4
Cæ-sē'nạ
Cæ-sĕn'nĭ-ăs
Cæ-sē'tĭ-ŭs 1
Cæ'şĭ-ạ 1
Cæ'şĭ-ŭs 1
Cæ-sō'nĭ-ạ
Cæs-ọ-nī'nụs 4
Cæ-sō'nĭ-ŭs
Cæs-ụ-lē'nụs 4
Cæt'ọ-brĭx 4
Cæ-trŏ'nĭ-ŭs
Cæt'ụ-lŭm 4
Cạ-gā'cō
Cā-ĭ-cī'nụs
Cạ-ī'cụs
Cā-ĭ-ē'tạ
Cā-ĭ-ẹ-tā'nụs
Cạ-ī'ọ-lŭs
Cā'ĭ-phăs

Cā'i-ŭs, *and*
  Cā'i-ą 3
Cą ̇ŭ'tą
Cāl'ą-bẹr, Quĭn'tụs
Cą-lā'brị-ą
Cāl'ą-brŭs
Cal-ą-çhē'nẹ
Cal-ac-tī'nụs
Cāl-ą-gŏr'rịs
Cāl-ą-gŭ'rịs
Cāl-ą-gŭr-rị-tā'nī
Cāl'ą-ĭs
Cāl'ą-mĭs
Cāl-ą-mī'są
Cāl-ą-mī'tēş
Cāl'ą-mŭs
Cą-lā'nų
Cāl'ą-ŏn
Cą-lāph'ą-tēş
Cą-lā'rụs
Cāl'ą-tēş
Cāl-ą-thā'ną
Cą-lā'thị-ŏn
Cāl'ą-thŭs
Cą-lā'tị-ą 1
Cāl-ą-tī'nụs
Cāl-âu-rē'ą
Cą-lâu'rị-ą, *or*
  Cāl-âu-rī'ą
Cą-lā'vị-ī
Cą-lā'vị-ŭs
Cāl'cą-gŭs
Cāl-chẹ-dŏ'nị-ą
Cąl-c̄hĭn'į-ą
Cą-lē'cąs
Cą-lēd'ǫ-nēş
Cāl-ẹ-dŏ'nị-ą
Cą-lē'lą
Cą-lē'nụs
Cą-lē'rụs
Cą-lē'şị-ŭs 1
Cą-lē'tæ
Cāl'ẹ-tī
Cą-lē'tọr
Cāl'gą-cŭs
Cā-lị-ăd'nẹ
Cāl-ị-cē'nī
Cą-lĭd'į-ŭs
Cāl-ị-dŏ'rụs
Cāl'ị-dŭs
Cāl'ị-gą
Cą-lĭg'ụ-lą
Cāl'ị-pŭs
Cąl-læs'çhrŭs•4
Cąl-lā'ị-cī
Cąl-lā'į-nŭs
Cāl-lą-tē'bụs
Cąl-lā-tị-ā'nụs 1
Cąl-lā'tịs
Cāl-lē'nī
Cāl-lẹ-tē'rị-ą
Cāl'lị-ą
Cąl-lī'ą-dēş
Cąl-lī'ą-năx
Cāl-lị-ą-nī'rą
Cąl-lī'ą-rŭs
Cāl'lị-ăs
Cąl-lĭb'į-ŭs
Cāl-lị-cē'rụs
Cąl-lĭçh'ǫ-rŭs

Cąl-lĭ''cį-ăs 1
Cāl'lị-clēş
Cāl-lị-cǫ-lŏ'ną
Cāl-lị-crą-tē'ą
Cą-lĭc'rą-tēş
Cāl-lị-crăt'į-dăs
Cąl-lĭc'rị-tŭs
Cāl-lị-dăm'ą-tēş
Cāl-lị-dē'mụs
Cāl-lị-dĕm'į-dēş
Cąl-lĭd'į-ŭs
Cąl-lĭd'rǫ-mŭs
Cąl-lĭģ'ẹ-nēş
Cāl-lị-ģē'tụs
Cāl-lị-ģī'tụs
Cąl-lĭm'ą-çhŭs
Cāl-lị-măr'çhụs
Cāl-lị-mē'dēş
Cąl-lĭm'ẹ-dŏn
Cāl-lị-nī'cụm
Cāl-lị-nī'cụs
Cąl-lī'nụs
Cąl-lĭn'ǫ-ŭs
Cāl-lị-ǫ-dŏ'rụs
Cąl-lī'ǫ-pē
Cāl-lị-ŏ'pị-ŭs
Cāl-lị-pą-tī'rą
Cāl'lị-phŏn
Cąl-lĭp'į-dæ
Cąl-lĭp'į-dēş
Cāl'lị-pŭs
Cāl-lị-pȳ'ģēş
Cāl-lị-pȳ'gǫs
Cą-lĭr'rhǫ-ē
Cāl-lịs-tē'ą
Cąl-lĭs'thẹ-nēş
Cāl-lịs-tī'ą
Cąl-lĭs-tǫ-nī'cụs
Cąl-lĭs'trą-tŭs
Cąl-lĭx'ẹ-ną
Cąl-lĭx'ẹ-nŭs
Cāl-ǫ-cĭs'sụs
Cāl-ǫ-cȳ'rụs
Cāl-ǫ-ģē'rụs
Cāl'ǫ-pŭs
Cāl-pẹ-tā'nụs
Cāl-pẹ-tị-ā'nụs 1
Cāl'pẹ-tŭs
Cąl-phŭr'nị-ą
Cąl-phŭr'nị-ŭs
Cąl-pŭr'nị-ą
Cąl-pŭr'nị-ŭs
Cāl-ụ-cŏ'nēş
Cāl-ụ-sĭd'į-ŭs
Cą-lū'şị-ŭm 1
Cąl-vē'ną
Cąl-vĕn'tị-ŭs 1
Cāl'vị-ą
Cąl-vī'ną
Cąl-vī'nụs
Cąl-vĭ''şị-ŭs 1
Cāl'y-bē
Cāl-y-bī'tą
Cāl-y-căd'nụs
Cāl'y-cē
Cą-lȳd'į-ŭm
Cāl'y-dŏn
Cāl-y-dŏ'nịs
Cāl-y-dŏ'nị-ŭs
Căm-ą-lǫ-dū'nụm

Cą-măn'tị-ŭm 1
Căm-ą-rā'cụm, *or*
  Cą-măr'ą-cŭm
Căm-ą-rī'ną
Căm-ą-tē'rụs
Cąm-bâu'lēş
Căm'bēş
Căm-bǫ-rī'tụm
Cąm-bū'nī
Cąm-bȳ'lụs
Căm-by-sē'nẹ
Cąm-bȳ'sēş
Căm-ẹ-lā'nī
Căm-ẹ-lī'tæ
Căm-ẹl-ǫ-dū'nụm
Cą-mē'ną
Cą-mē-nị-ā'tą
Căm'ẹ-rą
Căm-ẹ-rā'cụm. *See*
  Camaracum
Căm-ẹ-rī'nụm, *and*
  Cą-mē'rị-ŭm
Căm-ẹ-rī'nụs
Cą-mē'rị-ŭs
Cą-mër'tị-ŭm 1
Căm'ị-cŭs, *or*
  Cą-mī'cụs
Cą-mī'rą
Cą-mī'rụs
Căm-ị-sē'nẹ
Căm-ịs-sā'rēş
Cą-mŏ'nị-ŭs
Cąm-pā'ną Lĕx
Cąm-pā'nị-ą
Cąm-pā'nụs
Căm'pẹ-sŭs
Căm-pǫ-dū'nụm
Căm'pụs Măr'tị-ŭs 1
Căm-ụ-lǫ-ģī'nụs
Cą-mū'nī
Căn'ą-cē
Căn'ą-chē
Căn-ą-çhŭs
Cā'næ
Cą-nā'nụs
Cą-nā'rị-ą
Cą-nā'rị-ī
Căn'ą-thŭs
Căn'dą-cē
Cąn-dâu'lēş
Cąn-dā'vị-ą
Căn'dị-dŭs
Cąn-dī'ǫ-pē
Căn'dy-bą
Căn-ẹ-phŏ'rị-ą
Cą-nĕ'thụs
Cą-nĭc'ụ-lą
Cą-nĭc-ụ-lā'rēş
  Dī'ēş
Cą-nĭd'į-ŭs
Cą-nĭn-ẹ-fā'tēş
Cą-nĭn'į-ŭs
Cą-nĭs'tị-ŭs
Cā'nị-ŭs
Cą-nŏ'bụs
Cą-nŏp'į-cŭm
Cą-nŏ'pụs
Căn'tą-bẹr
Căn'tą-brą
Căn'tą-brĭ

Cąn-tā'brị-ą
Cąn-tā'brị-æ
Căn-tą-cụ-zē'nụs
Căn'thą-rą
Căn-thą-rŏl'ẹ-thrŏn
Căn'thą-rŭs
Cąn-thē'lą
Căn'tị-ŭm 1
Căn-ụ-lē'į-ą 3
Căn·ụ-lē'į-ŭs 3
Cą-nū'lị-ą
Cą-nū'şị-ŭm 1
Cą-nū'şị-ŭs 1
Cą-nū'tị-ŭs 1
Căp'ą-neūs (*n.*)
Căp-ą-nē'ụs (*a.*)
Căp'ą-rą
Cą-pā-tị-ā'ną 1
Cą-pē'ną
Cą-pē'nī
Cą-pē'nụs
Căp'ẹ-tŭs
Cą-phā'reūs (*n.*) 6
Căph-ą-rē'ụs, *or*
  Cą-phā'rẹ-ŭs (*a.*)
Cą-phē'reūs 6
Cą-phē'rịs
Cą-phī'rą
Cā'phy-æ
Cā'phy-ē
Cā'pị-ō
Căp-ịs-sē'nẹ
Căp'į-tō
Căp-ị-tǫ-lī'nụs
Căp-ị-tō'lị-ŭm
Cąp-nŏb'ą-tæ
Cąp-păd'ǫ-cēş
Căp-pą-dŏ'cị-ą 1
Căp'pą-dŏx
Cą-prā'rị-ą
Cą-prā'şị-ą 1
Cā'prẹ-æ, *or*
  Cā'prẹ-ą
Cą-prē'ǫ-lŭs
Căp-rị-fĭ-cị-ā'lịs 1
Cą-prī'mą
Cą-prī'ną
Cą-prĭp'ẹ-dēş
Cā'prị-ŭs
Căp-rǫ-tī'ną
Căp'są-ģē
Căp'ụ-ą
Căr-ą-băc'trą
Căr'ą-bĭs
Căr-ą-căl'lą
Căr-ą-cā'tēş, *or*
  Cą-răc'ą-tēş
Cą-răc'tą-cŭs
Căr'ą-lĭs
Căr-ą-mā'lụs
Căr-ą-nī'tịs
Cą-rān'tǫ-nŭs
Căr'ą-nŭs, *or*
  Cą-rā'nụs
Cą-râu'şị-ŭs 1
Căr-bō'nēş
Căr'bụ-lą
Căr-çhē'dǫn
Căr'cị-ną

Căr'cị-nŭş
Cąr-dā'cēş
Căr-dą-mē'nẹ
Cąr-dăm'y-lē
Căr'dẹ-ą
Cąr-dē'sụs
Căr'dị-ą
Cąr-dĭn'ẹ-ą
Căr'dụ-æ
Cąr-dū'çhī
Căr-dȳ'tụs
Cą-rē'nēş
Căr'ẹ-są
Cą-rē'sụs
Cąr-fĭn'į-ą
Cā'rị-ą, Cā'rị-ăs
Cā-rị-ā'tæ
Cą-rī'ną
Căr'į-nē
Cą-rī'nụs
Cā'rị-ō
Cą-rī'ǫn
Cą-rĭs'są-nŭm
Cą-rĭs'tị-ą
Cąr-mā'nī
Cąr-mā'nị-ą
Cąr-mā'nǫr
Cąr-mē'į-ŭs 3
Cąr-mē'lụs
Căr'mẹl
Cąr-mē'nị-ŏn
Căr-mẹn-tā'lēş
Căr'mị-dēş
Cąr-nā'şị-ŭs 1
Cąr-nē'ą
Cąr-nē'ą-dēş
Cąr-nē'ụs
Cąr-nī'ǫn
Căr'nǫ-nēş
Cąr-nū'tēş
Cąr-nū'tụs
Căr'ǫ-lŭs
Chărlẹş
Căr-ǫs-cē'pī
Cąr-pā'şị-ą 1
Cąr-pā'şị-ŭm 1
Cąr-pā'tēş, *or*
  Căr'pą-tēş
Cąr-pā'thị-ŭs
Căr'pą-thŭs
Cąr-pē'į-ą 3
Cąr-pẹ-tā'nī
Cąr-phȳl'lị-dēş
Cąr-pī'ą
Căr-pŏc'rą-tēş
Cąr-pŏph'ǫ-rą
Căr'ræ, *and*
  Căr'rhæ
Cąr-rī'nąs
Căr-rị-nā'tēş
Cąr-rǔ'cą
Cąr-sē'ǫ-lī
Căr'sụ-læ
Cąr-tā'lị-ăs
Căr'tą-rē
Cąr-tē'į-ą 3
Căr'tẹ-nŭs
Căr'tẹ-rŏn
Căr-thą-ģĭn-ị-ĕn'sĭ
Cąr-thā'gō

Cär'thaġe
Cär'tha-lō
Cär'tha-sĭs
Car-thē'ạ
Car-tĭl'i-ŭs
Cạ-rŭ'rạ
Cạ-rŭ'sạ
Car-vĭl'i-ŭs
Cā'ry-ạ
Cā'ry-æ
Cā-ry-ā'tæ
Cā-ry-ăt'i-dēş
Cā-ry-ā'tis
Cạ-rȳ'ọ-nēş
Căr-ys-tē'us
Cạ-rȳs'ti-ŭs
Cā'ry-ŭm
Cạ-sā'le
Cạs-cĕl'li-ŭs
Căs-i-lī'nụm
Căs'i-nạ
Cạ-sī'nụm
Cā-sị-ō'tis 1
Cā'si-ŭs 1
Căs'me-nạ
Cạs-pē'ri-ạ
Cạs-pĕr'u-lạ
Cạs-pī'ạ-dæ
Căs-pi-ā'nạ
Căs'pi-ī
Cạs-pī'rạ
Căs'pi-ŭm Mā're
Căs-san-dā'ne
Căs-san-drē'ạ
Cạs-său'dreŭs 6
Căs-san-drī'ạ
Căs'si-ạ 1
Căs-si-ā'nụs 1
Căs'si-ạn
Căs-si-e-pē'i-ạ 1, 3
Căs-si-ọ-dō'rụs 1
Cạs-sī'ọ-pē
Căs-si-ọ-pē'ạ 1
Căs-si-ō'tis 1
Cạs-sĭt'e-rạ
Căs-si-tĕr'i-dēş
Căs'si-ŭs 1
Căs-si-ve-lāu'nụs
Cạs-sō'pe
Căs'sọ-tĭs
Cạs-tăb'ạ-lạ
Căs'tạ-bŭs
Cạs-tā'li-ạ
Cạs-tăl'i-dēş
Căs'tạ-lĭs
Cạs-tā'li-ŭs Fŏnş
Cạs-thē'nēş
Căs-ti-ạ-nī'rạ
Căs'ti-cŭs
Cạs-tō'lụs
Căs'tọ-rēs, *pl.*
Cạs-trā'ti-ŭs 1
Căs'tri-cŭs
Căs'tu-lō
Căt-ạ-bā'nụs
Căt-ạ-ce-cāu'me-nē
Căt-ạ-clō'thēş
Căt-ạ-ġe-lăs'i-mŭs
Căt-ạ-man-tăl'e-dēş
Căt-ạ-mĕn'te-lēş

Căt'ạ-nạ, *or* -nē
Căt-ạ-ō'ni-ạ
Căt-ạ-phrō'ni-ạ
Cạ-tăph'ry-ġēş
Căt-ạ-răc'tạ
Căt-ar-rhăc'tēş
Cạ-tăr'rhy-tŭs
Cạ-tē'nạ
Căt'e-nēş
Cạ-thæ'ạ
Căth'ạ-rī
Cā'ti-ạ 1
Cā-ti-ā'nụs 1
Cā-ti-ē'nạ 1
Cā-ti-ē'nụs 1
Căt-i-lī'nạ
Căt'i-līne
Cạ-tĭl'i-ŭs
Căt'i-lŭs
Căt'i-nạ
Cā'ti-ŭs 1
Cạ-tī'zī
Căt-ọ-brī'gạ
Cā'treŭs 6
Căt-ụg-nā'tụs
Cạ-tū-li-ā'nạ
Căt'u-lŭs
Cạ-tū'ri-ġēş
Câu'cạ-sŭs
Câu-cọ-nē'ạ
Câu-cō'nēş
Câu-dī'nụs
Câu'di-ŭm
Câu'lọn
Câu-lō'ni-ạ
Câu'ni-ī
Câu'ni-ŭs
Câu'nụs
Câu'rọs
Câu'rụs
Căv'ạ-rēş
Căv-ạ-rĭl'lụs
Căv-ạ-rī'nụs
Căv'ạ-rŭs
Cā'vi-ī
Cạ-ȳ'cī
Cạ-ȳ'cụs
Cē'ạ-dēş
Cĕb-ạl-lī'nụs
Cĕb-ạ-rĕn'sēş
Cẹ-bĕn'næ
Cē'brẹn
Cẹ-brē'nẹ
Cẹ-brē'ni-ạ
Cẹ-brē'nis
Cẹ-brī'ọ-nēş
Cẹ-cī'dēş
Cẹ-cĭl'i-ŭs
Cẹ-cī'nạ
Cẹ-crō'pi-ạ
Cẹ-crŏp'i-dæ
Cẹ-crŏp'i-dēş
Cĕc'rọ-pĭs
Cē'crŏps
Cẹ-crȳph-ạ-lē'ạ
Cē'dre-æ, *or*
Cẹ-drē'æ
Cē-dre-ā'tis
Cẹ-drē'nụs

Cẹ-drŭ'si-ī 1
Ceg-lū'sạ
Cẹ-lē'i-ạ 3
Cĕl'ạ-dŏn
Cĕl'ạ-dŭs
Cẹ-læ'nạ
Cẹ-læ'næ
Cẹ-læ'nō
Cē'le-æ
Cĕl-e-lā'tēş
Cẹ-lĕn'de-rĭs
Cẹ-lē'neŭs 6
Cĕl'e-rēş
Cĕl-e-rī'nạ
Cĕl-e-rī'nụs
Cĕl'e-trŭm
Cē'le-ŭs
Cẹ-lō'nēş
Cĕl'ti-bẹr
Cĕl-ti-bē'rēş
Cĕl-ti-bē'rī
Cĕl-ti-bē'ri-ạ
Cĕl'ti-cạ
Cĕl-tọ-găl'ạ-tæ
Cẹl-tō'ri-ī
Cẹl-tŏs'cy-thæ
Cĕm'me-nŭs
Cĕn'ạ-bŭm. *See* Genabum.
Cẹ-næ'ụm
Cĕn'chre-æ
Cen-chrē'ụs
Cĕn'chri-ŭs
Cẹ-nēs'pọ-lĭs
Cẹ-nē'ti-ŭm 1
Cĕn-i-măg'nī
Cẹ-nī'nạ
Cĕn-ọ-mā'nī
Cen-sō'rēş
Cĕn-sọ-rī'nụs
Cĕn-tạ-rē'tụs
Cen-tâu'ri-cŭs
Cen-tâu'rụs
Cen-tē'ni-ŭs
Cen-tĭm'ạ-nŭs
Cĕn-tọ-brī'cạ
Cĕn'tọ-rēş
Cen-tŏr'i-pạ
Cen-trī'tēş
Cen-trō'nēş
Cen-trō'ni-ŭs
Cen-tŭm'vi-rī
Cen-tū'ri-ạ
Cen-tū'ri-pạ
Cen-tū'ri-pæ
Cen-tū'ri-pē
Cĕph'ạ-læ
Cĕph-ạ-lás
Cĕph-ạ-lē'nạ
Cĕph-ạ-lē'næ
Cĕph-ạ-lē'nēş
Cĕph-ạ-lē'nī
Cĕph-ạ-lē'ni-ạ
Cĕph'ạ-lō
Cĕph-ạ-lœ'di-ăs
Cĕph-ạ-lœ'dis
Cĕph-ạ-lœ'di-ŭm
Cĕph'ạ-lŏn
Cĕph-ạ-lŏt'ọ-mī

Cĕph-ạ-lū'di-ŭm
Cĕph'ạ-lŭs
Cẹ-phē'is
Cẹ-phē'nēş
Cē'pheŭs (*n.*) 6
Cẹ-phē'ụs (*a.*)
Cẹ-phī''si-ạ 1
Cĕph-i-sī'ạ-dēş
Cẹ-phīş'i-ăs 1
Cẹ-phī''si-ŏn 1
Cẹ-phī'sis
Cẹ-phĭs-ọ-dō'rụs
Cĕph-i-sŏd'ọ-tŭs
Cẹ-phī'sụs
Cē'phrẹn
Cē'pi-ō
Cĕr'ạ-cạ
Cẹ-răc'ạ-tēş
Cĕr'ạ-meūs 6
Cĕr-ạ-mī'cụs
Cẹ-rā'mi-ŭm
Cĕr'ạ-mŭs
Cĕr'ạ-sŭs
Cĕr'ạ-tạ
Cẹ-rā'thụs
Cẹ-rā'tọn
Cẹ-rā'tụs
Cẹ-râu'ni-ạ
Cẹ-râu'ni-ī
Cẹ-râu'si-ŭs 1
Cer-bē'ri-ŏn
Cĕr'be-rŏs
Cĕr'be-rŭs
Cĕr'cạ-phŭs
Cĕr-cạ-sō'rụm
Cer-cē'is
Cer-cē'ne
Cĕr-cēs'tēş
Cĕr'ce-tæ
Cĕr'ci-dás
Cĕr'ci-dēş
Cĕr'ci-ī 1
Cer-cī'nạ
Cĕr-ci-nī'tis
Cĕr-cĭn'i-ŭm
Cĕr'ci-ŭs 1
Cer-cọ-bū'lụs
Cĕr-cọ-nī'cụs
Cĕr-cō'pēş
Cĕr'cy-ŏn 1
Cĕr-cȳ'ọ-nēş
Cĕr-cȳph'ạ-læ
Cĕr-cȳ'rạ
Cĕr-dō'us
Cĕr-dȳl'i-ŭm
Cē-rẹ-ā'li-ạ
Cē-rẹ-ā'lis
Cē-rẹ-ā'li-ŭs
Cĕr'ẹ-tæ
Cẹ-rē'tēş
Cē'reŭs 6
Cē-ri-ā'lis
Cē'ri-ī .
Cẹ-rĭl'læ
Cĕr'i-tēş
Cer-mā'nụs
Cer-nē'ạ
Cĕr-ọ-păs'tạ-dēş
Cĕr'phẹ-rēş
Cĕr-rẹ-tā'nī

Cer-rhæ'ī
Cĕr-sọ-blĕp'tēş
Cĕr'ti-mạ
Cẹr-tō'ni-ŭm
Cẹr-tō'nụs
Cẹr-vā'ri-ŭs
Cĕr'vi-ŭs
Cẹ-rȳ'cēş
Cẹ-rȳ''ci-ŭs 1
Cĕr-y-mī'cạ
Cĕr-y-nē'ạ, *or* -nī'ạ
Cĕr-y-nī'tēş
Cẹ-sĕl'li-ŭs
Cẹ-sĕn'ni-ạ
Cĕs'ti-ŭs
Cẹs-trī'nạ
Cẹs-trī'nụs
Cẹ-tē'ī
Cẹ-thē'gụs
Cē'ti-ī 1
Cē'ti-ŭs 1
Cẹ-trō'ni-ŭs
Cē'ụs, *and* Cæ'ụs
Chạ-bē'rụs
Chā'bēş
Chạ-bī'nụs
Chạ-blā'si-ī 1
Chạ-bō'rạs
Chā'bri-ạ
Chā'bri-ăs
Chā'bry-ĭs
Chạ-dĭ''si-ŭs 1
Chæ-ạ-nī'tæ
Chæ're-ạ
Chæ're-ăs
Chæ-rĕc'rạ-tēş
Chær-ẹ-dē'mụs 4
Chæ-rē'mọn
Chær'ẹ-phŏn 4
Chæ-rĕs'trạ-tē
Chæ-rĕs'trạ-tŭs
Chær-i-bū'lụs 4
Chæ-rĭn'thụs
Chæ-rĭp'pụs
Chær-ọ-nē'ạ 4
Chær-ọ-nī'ạ 4
Chạl-cæ'ạ
Chạl-cē'ạ
Chạl-cē'dọn
Chạl-ce-dō'ni-ạ
Chạl-cĕt'ọ-rēş
Chăl-ci-dē'ne
Chăl-ci-dĕn'sēş
Chăl'ci-deūs 6
Chạl-cĭd'i-cē
Chạl-cĭd'i-cŭs
Chạl-cĭd'i-ŭs
Chăl-ci-œ'cụs
Chạl-cī'ọ-pē
Chạl-cī'tis
Chăl-cọ-cŏn'dy-lēş
Chạl-cō'dọn
Chăl'cọn
Chạl-cŏn'dy-lēş
Chạl-cŏs'thẹ-nēş
Chăl'cụs
Chạl-dæ'ạ
Chạl-dæ'ī
Chạ-lĕs'trạ
Chăl'ẹ-tŏs

Chăl'e-tŭs
Chăl-ĭ-nī'tĭs
Cha-lī'nŭs
Chăl-ọ-nī'tạ
Chăl-ọ-nī'tĭs
Chăl'y-bēş
Chăl'y-bŏn
Chăl-y-bọ-nī'tĭs
Chā'lybş
Cha-mā'nī
Cha-mā'vī
Chā'ọn
Chā'ọ-nēş
Cha-ō'nĭ-ạ
Chā-ọ-nī'tĭs
Chā'ŏs
Chăr-ạc-mō'bạ
Chăr-ạ-cō'mạ
Chăr'ạ-drạ, or
  Cha-rā'drạ
Chăr'ạ-drŏs, or
  Cha-rā'drọs
Chăr'ạ-drŭs
Cha-ræ'ạ-dăs
Chăr-ạn-dæ'ī
Cha-răx'ụs
Chăr'ị-clēş
Chăr-ị-clī'dēş
Chăr-ị-clī'tŭs
Chăr'ị-clō, or
  Cha-rī'clō
Chăr-ị-dē'mŭs
Chăr'ị-lạ
Chăr-ị-lā'ụs
Cha-rī'nī
Cha-rī'nŭs
Chā-rị-ọ-mē'rŭs
Chā'rĭs
Cha-rĭ''şị-ạ 1
Cha-rĭ-şị-ā'nŭs 1
Cha-rĭ''şị-ŭs 1
Cha-rĭs'tị-ạ
Chăr'ị-tēş
Chăr'ị-tŏn
Chạr-mā'dạs
Chăr'me
Chăr'mị-dăs
Chăr'mị-dēş
Chạr-mī'nŭs
Chạr-mī'ọ-nē
Chăr'mĭs
Chạr-mŏs'y-nạ
Chăr'mọ-tăs
Chăr'mŭs
Cha-rœ'ạ-dēş
Chā'rọn
Cha-rŏn'dạs
Chăr-ọ-nē'ạ
Chăr-ọ-nī'ụm
Chăr-ọ-pī'nŭs
Chā'rŏps
Chăr'ọ-pŭs
Cha-rўb'dĭs
Chăt'rạ-mĭs
Chăt-rạ-mī'tæ
Chau'bī, and
  Chau'cī
Chau'lạ
Chau-lā'şị-ī 1
Chau'rụs

Chăv'ọ-nēş
Cha-ў'cī
Cha-zē'ne
Chē'ạ
Chē'læ
Che-lī'dọn
Chĕl-ị-dŏ'nị-ạ
Chĕl-ị-dŏ'nị-æ
Chĕl-ị-dŏ'nịs
Che-lĭd-ọ-nī'sụm
Chĕl-ọ-nā'tạs
Che-lŏ'ne
Che-lŏ'nịs
Chĕl-ọ-nŏph'ạ-ģī
Chĕl-y-dŏ're-ạ
Chē'lys
Chĕm'mịs
Chē'næ
Chē'nị-ŏn
Chē'nị-ŭs
Chē'ŏps
Chĕr-e-mŏc'rạ-tēş
Che-rĭs'ọ-phŭs
Chĕr'ọ-phŏn
Chĕr-rọ-nē'ạ
Chĕr'sị-ăs 1
Chĕr-sĭd'ạ-măs
Chĕr'sị-phrō
Chĕr-sō'nạ
Chĕr-sọ-nē'sụs
Che-rŭs'cī
Chị-dō'rụs
Chī'ē
Chĭl-ị-är'çhụs
Chĭl'ị-ŭs, and
  Chĭl'e-ŭs
Chị-lō'nịs
Chị-mæ'rạ
Chĭm'ạ-rŭs
Chĭm'e-rạ
Chị-mē'rị-ŭm
Chĭn'ạ-lăph
Chī-ŏm'ạ-rạ
Chī'ọn
Chī'ọ-nē
Chī-ŏn'ị-dēş
Chī'ọ-nĭs
Chī'ŏs
Chī-rĭs'ọ-phŭs
Chī'rọn
Chị-tō'ne
Chĭt'rị-ŭm
Chlæ'ne-ăs
Chlī'de
Chlō'e
Chlō'reūs 6
Chō-ạ-rē'ne
Chō-ạ-rī'nạ
Chọ-ăs'pēş
Chŏ'ạ-træ, or
  Chọ-ā'træ
Chō'bus
Chœr'ạ-dēş 4
Chœ're-æ
Chœr'ị-lŭs 4
Chŏl-ọn-tī'çhụs
Chọ-mā-tị-ā'nụs 1
Chōn'nị-dăs
Chọ-nū'phịs

Chọ-rā'gụs
Chọ-răs'mī
Chọ-rĭ''cị-ŭs 1
Chŏr-ị-nē'ụs
Chŏr-ọm-næ'ī
Chọr-zē'ne
Chŏs'rọ-ēş
Chrĕm'e-tēş
Chrĕs'ị-phŏn
Chres-phŏn'tēş
Chrĭs-tị-ā'nụs
Chrīs'tian
Chrĭs-tọ-dō'rụs
Chrịs-tŏph'ọ-rŭs
Chrĭs'tọ-pher
Chrọ-mā'tị-ŭs 1
Chrŏ'mị-ạ
Chrŏ'mị-ŭs
Chrŏ'nị-ŭs
Chrȳ'ạ-sŭs
Chrўs'ạ-lŭs
Chrўs'ạ-mē
Chry-săn'thị-ŭs
Chry-sā'ọr
Chry-sā'ọ-reūs 6
Chry-sā'ọ-rĭs
Chry-săs'pị-dēş
Chry-sē'ịs
Chrўs'e-rŭs
Chrȳ'seūs 6
Chrўs-ọ-ăs'pị-dēş
Chrўs-ọ-cĕph'ạ-lŭs
Chry-sŏç'e-rŏs
Chrўs'ọ-chïr
Chry-sŏch'ọ-ŭs
Chry-sō'dị-ŭm
Chry-sŏg'ọ-nŭs
Chrўs-ọ-lā'ụs
Chry-sŏl'ọ-gŭs
Chrўs-ọ-lō'rạs
Chry-sŏp'ọ-lĭs
Chry-sŏr'rhọ-æ
Chry-sŏr'rhọ-ăs
Chry-sŏs'tọ-mŭs
Chrўs'ọs-tọm
Chry-sŏth'e-mĭs
Chthō'nị-ạ 5
Chthō'nị-ŭs 5
Chthŏn-ọ-phў'le 5
Chў'trụm
Cī-ạ-ģị'sī
Cī-ā'nụs
Cĭb'ạ-læ, or -lĭs
Cĭb-ạ-rī'tịs
Cị-bō'tụs
Cĭb'y-rạ
Cīç'e-rō
Cĭc'ọ-nēş
Cị-cū'tạ
Cĭç-y-nē'thụs
Cĭl-bị-ā'nī
Cĭl-bị-cē'nī
Cĭl'ị-cēş
Cị-lĭ''cị-ạ 1
Cĭl-ị-cọn-nē'sụs
Cĭl-nị-ā'nạ
Cĭl'nị-ŭs
Cĭm-bē'rị-ŭs
Cĭm'brị-cŭm
Cĭm'brị-cŭs

Cĭm-ị-nī'ce
Cĭm'ị-nŭs
Cịm-mē'rị-ī
Cĭm'me-rĭs
Cịm-mē'rị-ŭm
Cị-mō'lụs
Cĭn'ạ-dŏn
Cĭn'ạ-rạ
Cị-năr'ạ-dăs
Cĭn'ạ-rŭs
Cĭn'cị-ạ 1
Cĭn-cịn-nā'tụs
Cĭn'cị-ŭs 1
Cĭn'e-ăs
Cị-nē'şị-ăs 1
Cịn-ģĕt'ọ-rĭx
Cĭn-gụ-lā'nī
Cĭn'gụ-lŭm
Cĭn-ị-ā'tạ
Cị-nĭth'ị-ī
Cĭn'nạ-dŏn
Cĭn'nạ-mŭs
Cĭn-nị-ā'nạ
Cĭnx'ị-ạ 1
Cị-nō'lịs
Cị-nō'rụs
Cĭn'y-phŭs
Cĭn'y-răs
Cĭn-y-rī'ạ
Cị-pē'rụs
Cïr'ce
Cịr-cē'ị-ī 3
Cịr-cē'şị-ŭm 1
Cïr'cị-ŭs 1
Cĭs-ạl-pī'nạ Găl'-
  lị-ạ
Cĭs'sạ-mŭs
Cịs-sē'ịs
Cĭs'seūs 6
Cĭs'sị-ạ 1
Cĭs'sị-æ 1
Cĭs'sị-dăs
Cĭs'sị-dēş
Cĭs-sọ-ĕs'sạ
Cịs-sū'sạ
Cịs-tē'næ
Cịs-thē'ne
Cĭs-tọ-bō'cī
Cị-tē'rị-ŭs
Cị-thæ'rọn
Cĭth-ạ-rĭs'tạ
Cĭth-ạ-rĭs'tị-ŭm
Cị-thē'lạs
Cĭth'e-rŏn
Cĭ''tị-ŭm 1
Cị-vī'lịs
Cĭz'y-cŭm
Clăd'ạ-ŭs
Clā'de-ŭs
Clā'nị-ŭs
Clạ-rā'nụs
Clạ-rĕn'tị-ŭs 1
Clăs'sị-cŭs
Clăs'sị-ŭs 1
Clás-tĭd'ị-ŭm
Clau'dị-ạ
Clau-dị-ā'nụs
Clau'di-an
Clau-dị-ŏp'ọ-lĭs
Clau'dị-ŭs

Clâu'sụs
Clā-vị-ē'nụs
Clăv'ị-ģer
Clạ-zŏm'e-næ
Clē'ạ-dăs
Cle-æn'e-tŭs 4
Cle-ær'e-tạ 4
Cle-än'drị-dăs
Cle-ā'nọr
Cle-är'çhụs
Cle-är'ị-dăs
Clē'menş
Clĕm'ent
Cle-mĕn'tị-ạ 1
Clĕm-en-tī'nụs
Clē'ọ-bĭs
Clē-ọ-bū'lạ
Cle-ŏb-u-lī'nạ
Clē-ọ-bū'lụs
Cle-ŏch'ạ-rēş
Cle-ŏch-ạ-rī'ạ
Cle-ŏc'rị-tŭs
Cle-ŏd'ạ-măs
Clē-ọ-dä'mụs
Clē-ọ-dē'mụs
Clē-ọ-dō'rạ
Cle-ŏg'e-nēş
Clē-ọ-lā'ụs
Cle-ŏm'ạ-chŭs
Cle-ŏm'brọ-tŭs
Clē-ọ-mē'dēş
Cle-ŏm'e-nēş
Cle-ō'nạ
Cle-ō'næ
Cle-ō'ne
Clē-ọ-nī'cạ
Clē-ọ-nī'cụs
Cle-ŏn'y-mŭs
Clē'ọ-păs
Cle-ŏp'ạ-ter
Clē-ọ-pā'trạ
Cle-ŏp'ạ-trĭs
Cle-ŏph'ạ-nēş
Clē'ọ-phĭs
Cle-ŏph'ọ-lŭs
Clē'ọ-phŏn
Clē-ọ-phў'lụs
Clē-ọp-tŏl'e-mŭs
Clē'ọ-pŭs
Cle-ō'rạ
Cle-ŏs'the-nēş
Cle-ŏs''trạ-tạ
Cle-ŏs'trạ-tŭs
Clē-ọ-tī'mụs
Cle-ŏx'e-nŭs
Clĕp'sy-drạ, or
  Clep-sў'drạ
Clĕs'ị-dēş
Clĕt-ạ-bē'nī
Clĭb'ạ-nŭs
Clị-dē'mụs
Clĭg'e-nēş
Clĭm'ạ-cŭs
Clĭm'e-nŭs
Clị-nī'ạ-dēş
Clĭn'ị-ăs
Clị-nĭp'pị-dēş
Clị-nŏm'ạ-chŭs
Clĭs-ị-thē'rạ
Clĭs'the-nēş

Clĭ-tär'chu̧s
Clī'te̞
Clĭ-tër'nĭ-a̧
Clit'ĭ-phō
Clĭt-o̧-dē'mu̧s
Clĭ-tŏm'a̧-chŭs
Cl.t'o̧-phŏn
Clĭ-tō'rĭ-a̧
Clo̧-ā'ca̧
Clŏ-a̧-cī'na̧
Clŏ'dĭ-a̧
Clŏ-dĭ-ā'nu̧s
Clŏ'dĭ-ŭs
Clœ'lĭ-a̧
Clœ'lĭ-ŭs
Clŏn'dĭ-cŭs
Clŏ'nĭ-ŭs
Clū-a̧-cī'na̧
Clu̧-ĕn'tĭ-ŭs 1
Clŭ'pe̞-a̧
Clū'sĭ-a̧ 1
Clu̧-sī'nĭ Fŏn'tēs̞
Clu̧-sī'o̧-lŭm
Clū'sĭ-ŭs 1
Clŭ'vĭ-a̧
Clū-vĭ-ē'nu̧s
Clū-vĭ-ŭs
Clȳm'e̞-nē
Clȳm-e̞-nē'ĭ-dēs̞
Clȳm-e̞-nē'ĭs
Clȳm'e̞-nŭs
Clȳp'e̞-a̧
Cly-sŏn'y-mŭs
Clȳt-e̞m-nēs'tra̧
Clȳ''tĭ-a̧, *or*
  Clȳ''tĭ-ē 1
Clȳ''tĭ-ŭs 1
Clȳt-o̧-mē'dēs̞
Clȳt-o̧-nē'u̧s
Cna̧-cā'dĭ ŭm 5
Cnăc'a̧-lĭs 5
Cnăc'a̧-lŭs 5
Cnæ'u̧s, *or*
  Cnē'u̧s 5
Cnā'ḡĭ-a̧ 5
Cnā'pheu̧s, Pē'-
  tru̧s 5
Cne̞-mī'dēs̞ 5
Cnē'mu̧s 5
Cnĭ-dĭn'ĭ-ŭm 5
Cnī'du̧s 5 .
Cnŏ'pu̧s 5
Cnŏs'sĭ-a̧ 1, 5
Cnŏs'su̧s 5
Cŏ-a̧-mā'nĭ
Co̧-ā'træ
Cŏb'a̧-rēs̞
Co̧-cál'ĭ-dēs̞
Cŏc'a̧-lŭs
Cŏc-ce̞-ĭ-ā'nu̧s 3
Co̧c-cē'ĭ-ŭs 3
Co̧c-cȳḡ'ĭ-ŭs
Cŏ'clēs̞
Cŏc'lĭ-tēs̞
Cŏc-o̧-sā'tēs̞
Cŏc'tĭ-æ 1
Co̧-cū'su̧s
Co̧-cȳ'to̧s, *or* -tu̧s
Co̧-dā'nu̧s Sī'nu̧s
Co̧-dĭ'nu̧s

Cŏd-o̧-män'nu̧s
Cŏd'rĭ-dæ
Cœ-cĭl'ĭ-ŭs
Cœl-a̧-lē'tæ 4
Cœl-e̞-sȳr'ĭ-a̧, *and*
  Cœl-o̧-sȳr'ĭ-a̧ 4
Cœ-lē'tæ
Cœ'lĭ-a̧
Cœ-lĭ-o̧-brī'ga̧
Cœ'lĭ-ŭs
Cœr'a̧-nŏs, *or* -nŭs 4
Cœ-rät'a̧-dās̞
Cŏ'ēs̞
Cœs'y-ra̧ 4
Cŏ-ḡæ-ŏ'nu̧m
Cŏg'a̧-mŭs
Cŏg-ĭ-dū'nu̧s
Cŏ'hĭ-bŭs
Cŏl-a̧-cē'a̧
Co̧-län'co̧-rŭm
Cŏl'a̧-phŭs
Cŏl'a̧-pĭs
Co̧-läx'a̧-ĭs
Co̧-läx'ēs̞
Cŏl'chī
Cŏl'chĭ-cŭs
Cŏl'chĭs, *and*
  Cŏl'cho̧s
Cŏ'lĭ-ăs
Cŏl'ĭ-chăs
Co̧-lī'nu̧s
Cŏl'la̧-bŭs
Co̧l-lā'tĭ-a̧ 1
Cŏl-la̧-tī'nu̧s
Co̧l-lī'na̧
Co̧l-lū'cĭ-a̧ 1
Co̧l-lū'thu̧s
Cŏl'ly-tŭs
Cŏl'o̧-bī
Cŏl'o̧-ē
Co̧-lŏ'næ, *or* -ne̞
Co̧-lŏ'neu̧s 6
Co̧-lŏ'nĭ-a̧
Co̧-lŏn'ĭ-dēs̞
Co̧-lŏ'nĭs
Co̧-lŏ'no̧s, *or* -nu̧s
Cŏl-o̧-pē'ne̞
Cŏl'o̧-phŏn
Co̧-lŏs'se̞
Co̧-lŏ'tēs̞
Co̧l-thē'ne̞
Cŏl-u̧-brā'rĭ-a̧
Co̧-lŭm'næ Hër'-
  cu̧-lĭs
Cŏl-u̧-mĕl'la̧
Co̧-lū'thu̧s
Co̧-mæ'thō
Cŏm-a̧-ḡē'na̧
Cŏm-a̧-ḡē'nĭ
Co̧-mā'nĭ-a̧
Co̧-mā'nu̧s
Cŏm'a̧-rī
Cŏm'a̧-rĭ-a̧
Cŏm'a̧-rŭs
Co̧-mā'ta̧
Co̧-mā'zo̧n
Co̧m-ba̧'bu̧s
Cŏm'be̞
Co̧m-brē'a̧
Cŏm'bu̧-tĭs

Co̧-mē'dæ
Co̧-mē'tēs̞
Co̧-mĭn'ĭ-ŭs
Co̧-mĭ''tĭ-a̧ 1
Cŏ'mĭ-ŭs
Cŏm-ma̧-ḡē'ne̞
Co̧m-mĭn-ĭ-ā'nu̧s
Co̧m-mŏ-dĭ-ā'nu̧s
Cŏm'mo̧-dŭs
Co̧m-nē'nu̧s
Cŏm-pĭ-tā'lĭ-a̧
Co̧m-plū'tu̧m
Cŏmp'sa̧-tŭs
Co̧m-pū'sa̧
Cŏn'ca̧-nī
Cŏn'ca̧-nŭs
Co̧n-cör'dĭ-a̧
Co̧n-cör'dĭ-ŭs
Cŏn'da̧-lŭs
Co̧n-dā'te̞
Cŏn-dĭ-ā'nu̧s
Cŏn-do̧-chā'tēs̞
Co̧n-drū'sī
Co̧n-dȳl'e̞-a̧
Cŏn'dy-lŭs
Cŏn-e̞m-brī'ca̧
Cŏn-e̞-to̧-dū'nu̧s
Co̧n-fū'cĭ-ŭs 1
Co̧n-ḡē'du̧s, *or*
  Cŏn'ḡe̞-dŭs
Cŏn'grĭ-ō
Co̧-nī'a̧-cī
Cŏ'nĭ-ī
Cŏn-ĭm-brī'ca̧
Co̧-nĭs'a̧-lŭs
Cŏn'nĭ-dăs, *or*
  Co̧n-nī'dăs
Co̧-nŏ'neu̧s 6
Co̧-nŏ'pe̞
Cŏn-o̧-pē'u̧m, *and*
  Co̧-nŏ'pe̞-ŭm
Co̧n-sĕn'tēs̞
Co̧n-sĕn'tĭ-a̧ 1
Co̧n-sĕn'tĭ-ŭs 1
Co̧n-sĭd'ĭ-ŭs
Cŏn-sĭ-lī'nu̧m
Co̧n-stăn'tĭ-a̧ 1
Cŏn-sta̧n-tī'a̧
Cŏn-sta̧n-tī'na̧ [lĭs
Co̧n-stăn-tĭ-nŏp'o̧-
Cŏn-sta̧n-tī'nu̧s
Cŏn'stan-tīne
Co̧n-stăn'tĭ-ŭs 1
Cŏn'su̧-lēs̞
Cŏn-tes-tā'nī
Cŏn-to̧-po̧-rī'a̧
Co̧n-tū'bĭ-a̧
Cŏn've̞-næ
Cŏ'o̧n
Cŏ'ŏs, *and* Cŏs
Co̧-pā'ĭs
Cŏ'phēs̞
Cŏ'pĭ-a̧
Co̧-pŏ'nĭ-ŭs
Co̧-prā'tēs̞, *or*
  Cŏp'ra̧-tēs̞
Cŏ'preu̧s 6
Co̧-prŏn'y-mŭs
Cŏr-a̧-cē'sĭ-ŭm 1, *or*
  Cŏr-a̧-cĕn'sĭ-ŭm 1

Cŏr-a̧-cī'nu̧s
Cŏr-a̧-co̧-nā'su̧s
Co̧-rál'e̞-tæ
Co̧-rā'nu̧s
Cŏr'be̞-ŭs
Cŏr-bĭ-ā'ne̞
Cŏr'bu̧-lō
Cŏr'co̧-ba̧
Cŏr'co̧-răs̞
Cŏr'cu̧-lŭm
Co̧r-cȳ'ra̧
Co̧r-dā'lĭ-ō
Cŏr'da̧-lŭs
Cŏr'du̧-ba̧
Cŏr-du̧-ē'ne̞
Co̧r-dȳ'la̧
Cŏ're̞
Cŏr'e̞-sŭs, *man.*
Co̧-rē'su̧s, *mountain*
Co̧-rē'ta̧s
Co̧-rē'tu̧s
Cŏr-fĭd'ĭ-ŭs
Cŏr-fĭn'ĭ-ŭm
Co̧-rī'a̧
Co̧-rī'clēs̞
Co̧-rĭn'e̞-ŭm
Cŏr-ĭn-thī'a̧-cŭs
Cŏ-rĭ-o̧-lā'nu̧s
Co̧-rī'o̧-lī, *and*
  Cŏ-rĭ-ŏl'la̧
Co̧-rī'tha̧
Cŏr'ĭ-tŭs, *or*
  Cŏr'y-thŭs
Cŏr'ma̧-sa̧
Co̧r-nē'lĭ-a̧
Co̧r-nē-lĭ-ā'nu̧s
Co̧r-nē'lĭ-ī
Co̧r-nĭc'u̧-lŭm
Cŏr-nĭ-fĭ''cĭ-ŭs 1
Cŏr'nĭ-ḡer
Co̧r-nū'tu̧s
Co̧-rŏ'bĭ-ŭs
Co̧-rŏ'na̧
Cŏr-o̧-nā'tu̧s
Co̧-rŏ'ne̞
Cŏr-o̧-nē'a̧
Co̧-rŏ'neu̧s 6
Cŏr-o̧-nī'a̧
Cŏr-o̧-nī'dēs̞
Co̧-rŏ'nĭs
Cŏr'o̧-pē, *or*
  Co̧-rŏ'pe̞
Co̧r-rhā'ḡĭ-ŭm
Co̧r-sē'a̧, *or* -sī'a̧
Cŏr'sĭ-æ 1
Cŏr'sĭ-ca̧
Co̧r-sō'te̞
Co̧r-sū'ra̧
Co̧r-tō'na̧
Co̧r-tȳ'na̧
Cŏr-u̧n-cā'nĭ-ŭs
Cŏr-u̧n-cā'nu̧s
Co̧r-vī'nu̧s
Cŏr-y-băn'tēs̞
Cŏr'y-băs̞
Cŏr'y-bŭs
Co̧-rȳ''cĭ-a̧ 1
Co̧-rȳç'ĭ-dēs̞
Co̧-rȳ''cĭ-ŭs 1
Cŏr'y-cŭs

Cŏr'y-dŏn
Cŏr'y-läs̞
Cŏr-y-lē'u̧m
Co̧-rȳm'bĭ-fer
Cŏr'y-na̧
Cŏr-y-nē'ta̧, *and*
  Cŏr-y-nē'tēs̞
Cŏr-y-phā'sĭ-ŭm 1
Cŏr'y-phē
Co̧-rȳ'tha̧
Cŏr-y-thĕn'sēs̞
Cŏr'y-thŭs
Co̧-rȳ'tu̧s
Co̧s-cō'nĭ-a̧
Co̧s-cō'nĭ-ŭs
Co̧s-sæ'a̧, *and*
  Cŏs'se̞-a̧
Co̧s-sĭn'ĭ-ŭs
Cŏs'sĭ-ō 1
Co̧s-sū-tĭ-ā'nu̧s 1
Co̧s-sū'tĭ-ŭs 1
Co̧s-sȳ'ra̧
Cós-to̧-bō'cī
Cŏ'tēs̞, *and*
  Cŏt'tēs̞
Co̧-thŏ'ne̞-a̧, *or*
  Cŏth-o̧-nē'a̧
Cŏ-tĭ-a̧-ē'u̧m 1
Cŏt'ĭ-lŭs
Cŏt-ĭ-nū'sa̧
Cŏt'ĭ-sō
Co̧-tō'nĭs
Cŏt'tĭ-æ Ăl'pēs̞
Cŏt-tĭ-ā'nu̧s
Cŏt'tĭ-ŭs
Co̧t-tō'nĭs
Cŏ-ty-a̧-ē'u̧m 1
Cŏ-ty-a̧-ī'o̧n 1
Cŏt'y-la̧
Co̧-tȳl'ĭ-ŭs
Cŏ-ty-ō'ra̧ 1
Cŏ-ty-ō'ru̧s 1
Co̧-tȳ'tō
Co̧-tȳt'tĭ-a̧
Co̧-tȳt'tō
Cra̧m-bū'sa̧
Crăn'a̧-ē
Crăn'a̧-ī
Crăn'a̧-ŭs
Cra̧'ne̞
Cra̧-nē'a̧, *or* -nī'a̧
Cra̧-nē'u̧m
Crăp'a̧-thŭs
Crás-pe̞-dī'tēs̞
  Sī'nu̧s
Cra̧s-sī'nu̧s
Crás'sĭ-pēs̞
Cra̧s-sĭ''tĭ-ŭs 1
Crás'tĭ-nŭs
Cra̧-tæ'ĭs
Cra̧-tæm'e̞-nēs̞
Cra̧-tŏ'a̧
Crā'te̞-ăs̞
Crát'e̞-rŭs
Crā'tēs̞
Cra̧-tēs-ĭ-clē'a̧
Crăt-e̞-sĭp'pĭ-dăs̞
Cra̧-teū'as̞
Cra̧-tē'vas̞
Cra̧-tī'nu̧s ·

Crą-tĭs'thę-nēş
Crăt'y-lŭs
Crâu'sị-æ 1
Crâux'ị-dăs
Crę-mē'dǫn
Crĕm'ę-rą
Crĕm-ę-tā'ǫn
Crĕm'my-ŏn
Crę-mō'ną
Crę-mū'tị-ŭs 1
Crę-nā'cŭs
Crĕn'ị-dēş
Crē-ǫn-tī'ą-dēş
Crę-ŏph'ą-ǵī
Crę-ŏph'ị-lŭs
Crē-ǫ-phȳ'lŭs
Crē-ǫ-pō'lŭs
Crĕp-ę-rē'ị-ŭs 3
Crę-pē'rị-ŭs
Crĕph-ą-ǵę-nē'tŭs
Crĕs'ị-lăs
Crē'sị-ŭs 1
Cręs-phŏn'tēş
Crĕs'sị-ŭs 1
Cręs-tō'nę
Crę-tæ'ŭs
Crē'tę
Crēte
Crē'tę-ą
Crē'tēş
Crē'teŭs 6
Crē'thę-ĭs
Crē'theŭs 6
Crę-thī'dēş
Crĕt'ị-cŭs
Crę-ū'są
Creŭ'sịs
Crī'ą-sŭs
Crị-mī'są
Crị-mī'sŭs
Crị-năg'ǫ-răs
Crị-nī'sŭs
Crị-nī'tŭs
Crị-ō'ą
Crịs-pī'ną
Crịs-pī'nŭs
Crị-thē'ịs
Crị-thō'tę
Crĭ''tị-ăs 1
Crĭt-ǫ-bū'lŭs
Crĭt-ǫ-dē'mŭs
Crĭt-ǫg-nā'tŭs
Crĭt-ǫ-lā'ŭs
Crị-tō'nị-ŭs
Crī'u Mę-tō'pǫn
Crǫ-bī'ą-lŏn
Crǫ-bī'ą-lŭs
Crŏb'y-lŭs
Crǫ-bȳ'zī
Crŏc'ą-lē
Crō'cę-æ
Crŏc-ǫ-dī'lǫn
Crŏc-ǫ-dī-lŏp'ǫ-lĭs
Crŏc-ǫ-dī'lŭs
Crǫ-cō'tị-ŭm 1
Crŏç-y-lē'ą
Crǫ-ī'tēş
Crǫ-mī'tịs
Crŏm'my-ŏn, or
　Crō'my-ŏn

Crō'nị-ą
Crŏn'ị-dēş
Crǫ-nī'ǫn, *and*
　Crō'nị-ŏn, *or* -ŭm
Crō'nị-ŭs
Crŏt'ą-lŭs
Crǫ-tō'ną
Crǫ-tō-nị-ā'tæ
Crŏt-ǫ-pī'ą-dēş
Crǫ-tō'pị-ăs
Crǫ-tō'pŭs
Crŭs-tū'mę-rī
Crŭs-tu-mē'rị-ą
Crŭs-tu-mē'rị-ŭm
Crŭs-tu-mī'nŭm
Crŭs-tū'mị-ŭm
Crŭs-tū'nŭs
Crŭs-tur-nē'nị-ŭs
Cryp-tē'ą
Ctē'ą-tŭs 5
Ctĕm'ę-nē 5
Ctē'sị-ăs 1, 5
Ctę-sĭb'ị-ŭs 5
Ctĕs'ị-clēş 5
Ctę-sĭl'ǫ-chŭs 5
Ctĕs'ị-phŏn 5
Ctę-sĭp'pŭs 5
Ctē'sị-ŭs 5
Ctĭm'ę-nē 5
Cū'cu-făs
Cū'lą-rō
Cŭl'lę-ō
Cul-lē'ǫ-lŭs
Cu-mā'nŭs
Cu-nī'ną
Cu-pā'vō
Cu-pī'dō
Cū'pid
Cū-pị-ĕn'nị-ŭs
Cur-cū'lị-ō
Cū'rēş
Cu-rē'tēş
Cu-rē'tịs
Cu-rē'tị-ŭs 1
Cū'rị-ą
Cū-rị-ā'tị-ī 1
Cū-rị-ā'tị-ŭs 1
Cu-rĭc'tæ
Cū'rị-ō
Cū-rị-ō'nēş
Cū-rị-ŏs-ǫ-lī'tæ, *or*
　Cū-rị-ŏs-ǫ-lī'tēş
Cu-rī'tịs
Cū'rị-ŭm
Cū'rị-ŭs
Cū-rǫ-pą-lā'tēş
Cür'tị-ą 1
Cür'tị-ŭs 1
Cu-rū'lịs
Cŭs'pị-ŭs
Cu-tĭl'ị-æ
Cȳ-ą-mī'tēş
Cȳ-ăm-ǫ-sō'rŭs
Cȳ'ą-mŭs
Cȳ'ą-nē
Cȳ-ā'nę-ą
Cȳ-ā'nę-ē
Cȳ-ā'nę-ŭs
Cȳ-ą-răx'ēş, *or*
　Cȳ-ăx'ą-rēş

Cȳ'ą-thŭs
Cȳb'ą-lē
Cy-bē'bę
Cȳb'ę-lą
Cȳb'ę-lŭs
Cȳb'ị-rą, *or.*
　Cĭb'y-rą
Cy-bĭs'trị-ą
Cy-cē'sị-ŭm 1
Cȳ'chreŭs (*n.*) 6
Cy-çhrē'ŭs (*a.*)
Cȳc'lą-dēş
Cy-clī'ą-dăs
Cy-clŏb'ǫ-rŭs
Cȳc'lị-cī
Cy-clō'pēş
Cȳ' clŏps
Cȳd'ị-ăs
Cȳd'ị-mŏs
Cȳd-ǫ-nē'ą
Cy-dō'nēş
Cy-dō'nị-ą
Cy-dō'nị-ŭs
Cȳd'rą-rą, *or*
　Cy-drā'rą
Cy-drē'lŭs
Cȳd-rǫ-lā'ŭs
Cȳ'drŭs
Cȳl'ą-bŭs
Cȳl-bị-ā'nī
Cȳl'ị-cēş
Cyl-lăb'ą-rŭs
Cȳl'lą-rŭs
Cyl-lē'nę
Cȳl-le-nē'ŭs
Cyl-lē'nị-ŭs
Cyl-lē'nŭs
Cyl-lȳr'ị-ī
Cȳl-ǫ-nē'ŭs, *or*
　Cȳl-ǫ-nī'ŭs
Cȳ'mą, *or* Cȳ'mæ
Cȳ'mę
Cy-mē'lŭs
Cy-mŏd'ǫ-cē
Cy-mŏd-ǫ-cē'ą
Cy-mŏd-ǫ-cē'ąs
Cy-mō'lŭs, *and*
　Cị-mō'lŭs
Cȳm-ǫ-pǫ-lī'ą
Cy-mŏth'ǫ-ē
Cȳn-æ-ǵī'rŭs
Cy-næ'thị-ŭm
Cy-næ'thŭs
Cy-nā'nę
Cy-nā'pēş
Cȳn'ą-rą
Cȳn'ę-ăs
Cy-nĕǵ'ę-tæ
Cȳn-ę-ǵī'rŭs
Cy-nē'sị-ī 1
Cy-nē'tæ
Cȳn-ę-tē'ą
Cy-nē'tēş
Cȳn'ị-ą
Cȳn'ị-cē
Cȳn'ị-cī
Cȳn'ị-cŭs
Cȳn-ǫ-cĕph'ą-lī
Cȳn-ǫ-phŏn'tịs
Cy-nŏr'tị-ŏn 2

Cȳn-ǫ-săr'ǵēş
Cy-nŏs'pǫ-lĭs
Cȳn-ǫs-sē'mą
Cȳn-ǫ-sū'rą
Cȳn'ǫ-sūre
Cȳn'thị-ą
Cy-nū'rị-ą
Cȳp-ą-rĭs'sī
Cȳp-ą-rĭs'sị-ą 1
Cȳph'ą-rą
Cȳp-rị-ā'nŭs
Cȳp'rị-ąn
Cȳ'prŭs
Cȳp'sę-lą
Cyp-sĕl'ị-dēş
Cȳp'sę-lŭs
Cy-râu'nịs
Cȳ'rę
Cy-rē'næ
Cyr-ę-nā'ị-cą
Cȳr-ę-nā'ị-cī
Cy-rē'nę
Cy-rĕs'chą-tą
Cy-rē'tị-æ 1
Cy-rī'ą-dēş
Cy-rĭl'lŭs
Cȳr'il
Cy-rī'nŭs
Cȳ-rǫ-pæ-dī'ą
Cy-rŏp'ǫ-lĭs
Cȳr'rha-dæ
Cȳr'rhēş
Cyr-rhĕs'tị-cą
Cȳr-rị-ā'ną
Cȳr'sị-lŭs
Cyr-tō'ną
Cyr-tō'nēş
Cy-thē'rą
Cy-thē'rę
Cȳth-ę-rē'ą
Cȳth-ę-rē'ịs
Cy-thē'rịs
Cy-thē'rị-ŭs
Cy-thē'rǫn
Cy-thē'rŭs
Cy-tĭn'ị-ŭm
Cȳt-ịs-sō'rŭs
Cy-tō'rŭs
Cȳz-ị-cē'nī
Cȳz'ị-cŏs
Cȳz'ị-cŭm
Cȳz'ị-cŭs

D.

Dā'æ, *or* Dā'hæ
Dā'cī, *and* Dā'cæ
Dā'cị-ą 1
Dā'cị-ŭs 1
Dăc'ty-lī
Dăd-ąs-tā'ną
Dăd'ị-cæ
Dą-dū'chŭs
Dæd'ą-lą 4
Dæd-ą-lē'ą 4
Dæd'ą-lŭs 4
Dæm'ǫ-nēş 4

Dăg-ą-sī'rą
Dā'ī
Dā'ị-clēş
Dā'ị-dēş
Dą-ĭm'ą-chŭs
Dą-ĭm'ę-nēş
Dā'ị-phrŏn
Dą-ī'rą
Dăl'dị-ą
Dăl'mą-tą
Dăl'mą-tæ
Dąl-mā'tị-ą 1
Dąl-mā'tị-ŭs 1
Dăl'mị-ŭm
Dăm-ą-ǵē'tŭs
Dăm'ą-lĭs
Dăm-ąs-cē'ną
Dăm-ąs-cē'nŭs
Dą-măs'cị-ŭs 1
Dą-mā'sị-ą 1
Dăm-ą-sĭp'pŭs
Dăm-ą-sĭs'trą-tŭs
Dăm-ą-sị-thȳ'mŭs
Dăm-ą-sī'tǫn
Dăm'ą-sŭs
Dā'mę-ăs
Dā'mị-ą
Dā-mị-ā'nŭs
Dąm-nō'nị-ī
Dăm'nǫ-rĭx
Dą-mŏch'ą-rĭs
Dăm'ǫ-clēş
Dą-mŏc'rą-tēş
Dą-mŏc'rị-tą
Dą-mŏc'rị-tŭs
Dą-mœ'tąs
Dą-mŏǵ'ę-rŏn
Dą-mŏm'ę-lēş
Dăm-ǫ-nī'cŭs
Dăm-ǫ-phăn'tŭs
Dą-mŏph'ị-lą
Dą-mŏph'ị-lŭs
Dăm'ǫ-phŏn
Dą-mŏs'trą-tŭs
Dą-mŏt'ę-lēş
Dą-mŏx'ę-nŭs
Dą-mȳr'ị-ăs
Dăn'ą-ē
Dăn'ą-ī
Dą-nā'ị-dæ, *and*
　Dąn-dăr'ị-dæ
Dą-nū'bị-ŭs
Dăn'ube
Dā'ǫ-chŭs
Dā'ǫ-nēş
Dăph'ị-tăs, *or*
　Dą-phī'tąs
Dăph'neūs 6
Dăph-nę-phŏ'rị-ą
Daph-nŏp'ą-tēş
Dăr'ą-bą
Dăr'ą-bēş
Dăr'ą-dăx
Dăr-ąn-tā'sị-ą 1
Dąr-dā'nę-ī
Dăr'dą-nī

Dạr-dā'nị-ạ
Dạr-dăn'ị-dæ
Dạr-dăn'ị-dēş
Där'dạ-nĭs
Där'dạ-nŭs
Dạ-rē'ị-ŭm 3
Dạ-rē'tịs
Dạ-rē'ŭs
Dạ-rī'ạ
Dạ-rī'cụs
Dā-rị-ē'cēş
Dạ-rī'tæ
Dạ-rī'ŭs
Dạs-cū'sạ
Dăs-cy-lē'ụm
Dạs-cўl'ị-ŭm
Dăs'cy-lŭs
Dā'sẹ-ạ
Dā'şị-ŭs 1
Dăs-sạ-rē'tæ
Dăs-sạ-rē'nĭ
Dăs-sạ-rī'tæ
Dăs-sạ-rī''tị-I]
Dạs-tī'rạ
Dăt'ạ-mēş
Dăt-ạ-phĕr'nēş
Dâu'lịs
Dâu'nị-ạ
Dâu'nụs
Dâu'rị-fẹr
Dâu'rị-sēş
Dăv'ạ-rạ
Dăx-ị-mọ-nī'tịs
Dĕb'ọ-rŭs
Dĕc-ạ-dū'chī
Dẹ-cæ'nẹ-ŭs
Dẹ-căp'ọ-lĭs
Dẹ-cĕb'ạ-lŭs
Dĕç-ẹ-lē'ạ, or -lī'ạ
Dĕç-ẹ-lē'ụm
Dĕç-ẹ-lī'cụm
Dĕç'ẹ-lŭs
Dẹ-cĕm'vị-rī
Dẹ-cĕn'tị-ŭs 1
Dẹ-cē'tị-ạ 1
Dē-cị-ā'nụs 1
Dē-cị-ā'tēş 1
Dē-cị-ā'tụm 1
Dẹ-cĭd'ị-ŭs Săx'ạ
Dẹ-cĭm'ị-ŭs
Dĕç'ị*mŭs
Dẹ-cĭn'ẹ-ŭs
Dē'cị-ō 1
Dē'cị-ŭs 1
Dĕc'ụ-lạ
Dĕc'ụ-mạ
Dĕc-ụ-mā'tēş
Dẹ-cū'rị-ō
Dĕd-ị-tăm'ẹ-nēş
Dē-ị-ạ-nī'rạ 3
Dẹ-ĭc'ọ-ŏn
Dẹ-ĭd-ạ-mī'ạ
Dẹ-ĭl'ẹ-ŏn
Dẹ-ĭl'ọ-chŭs
Dẹ-ĭm'ạ-chŭs
Dẹ-ī'ọ-cēş
Dẹ-ī'ọ-chŭs
Dẹ-ī'ọ-nē
Dē-ị-ŏn'ị-dēş
Dẹ-ī'ọ-neŭs 6

Dẹ-I-ọ-pē'ạ
Dē-ị-ọ-pī'tēş
Dē-ị-ŏt'ạ-rŭs
Dẹ-ĭph'ị-lạ
Dẹ-ĭph'ọ-bē
Dẹ-ĭph'ọ-bŭs
Dē'ị-phŏn
Dẹ-ĭp'y-lē
Dẹ-ĭp'y-lŭs
Dẹ-ĭp'y-rŭs
Dĕj-ạ-nī'rạ
Dĕj'ọ-cēş
Dẹ-jŏt'ạ-rŭs
Dē'lị-ạ
Dẹ-lī'ạ-dēş
Dē'lị-ŭs
Dĕl'lị-ŭs
Dẹl-mā'tị-ŭs 1
Dẹl-mĭn'ị-ŭm
Dẹl-phĭc'ọ-lạ
Dĕl'phị-cŭs
Dẹl-phĭd'ị-ŭs
Dẹl-phī'nēş
Dẹl-phĭn'ị-ạ
Dẹl-phĭn'ị-ŭm
Dẹl-phī'nụs
Dĕl'phị-ŭm
Dẹl-phў'nẹ
Dẹl-tō'tọn
Dẹ-mā'dēş
Dẹ-mæn'ẹ-tŭs 4
Dẹ-măg'ọ-răs
Dĕm-ạ-rā'tạ
Dĕm-ạ-rā'tụs
Dẹ-măr'ẹ-tē
Dẹ-măr'ẹ-tēş
Dĕm-ạ-rĭs'tẹ
Dẹ-mā'trị-ạ
Dē'mẹ-ạ
Dẹ-mē'tẹr
Dẹ-mē'trị-ạ
Dẹ-mē'trị-ŭs
Dĕm'ị-phŏ
Dĕm-ọ-ạ-năs'sạ
Dĕm-ọ-cē'dēş
Dẹ-mŏch'ạ-rēş
Dĕm'ọ-clēş
Dẹ-mŏc'ọ-ŏn
Dẹ-mŏc'rạ-tēş
Dẹ-mŏc'rị-tŭs
Dẹ-mŏd'ạ-măs
Dẹ-mŏd'ị-cē
Dẹ-mŏd'ọ-cŭs
Dẹ-mŏ'lẹ-ŏn
Dẹ-mŏ'lẹ-ŭs
Dẹ-mŏ'năx
Dĕm-ọ-nē'sụs
Dĕm-ọ-nī'cạ
Dĕm-ọ-nī'cụs
Dẹ-mŏph'ạ-nēş
Dẹ-mŏph'ị-lŭs
Dĕm'ọ-phŏn
Dẹ-mŏph'ọ-ŏn
Dẹ-mŏp'ọ-lĭs
Dĕm-ọp-tŏl'ẹ-mŭs
Dẹ-mŏs'the-nēş
Dẹ-mŏs'trạ-tŭs
Dĕm-ọ-tī'mụs
Dẹ-mū'chụs
Dĕm'y-lŭs

Dẹn-drī'tịs
Dĕn-sẹ-lē'tæ
Dẹn-tā'tụs
Dĕn-thẹ-lē'tæ
Dē-ọ-brī'gạ
Dẹ-ŏd'ạ-tŭs
Dẹ-ō'ịs
Dĕr'bị-cēş, or
   Dẹr-bī'cēş
Dĕr'cẹ
Dẹr-cē'bị-ī
Dĕr'cẹ-tŏ, and -tĭs
Dẹr-cўl'lị-dăs
Dĕr'cy-lĕs
Dĕr'cy-nŭs
Dẹr-thō'nạ
Dẹr-tō'nạ
Dẹr-tō'sạ
Dĕs-ị-dē'rị-ŭs
Dĕs-ị-lā'ụs
Dĕs'pọ-tạ
Dẹ-sū'dạ-bạ
Deŭ-cā'lị-ŏn
Deŭ-cē'tị-ŭs 1
Deŭ'dọ-rīx
Deŭ-rī'ọ-pŭs
Dĕv'ọ-nạ
Dẹx-ăm'ẹ-nē
Dẹx-ăm'ẹ-nŭs
Dẹx-ĭc'rẹ-ŏn
Dẹx-ĭth'ẹ-ạ
Dĕx'ị-ŭs 1
Dī-ăb'ọ-lŭs
Dī-ăc'ọ-nŭs
Dī-ăc-ọ-pē'nạ
Dī-ạ-crē'ạ
Dī'ạ-crĭs
Dī-ạc-tŏr'ị-dēş
Dī-ăd'ọ-chŭs
Dī-ạ-dū-mẹ-nị-ā'nụs
Dī-ạ-dū'mẹ-nŭs
Dī'ạ-gŏn, and
   Dī'ạ-gŭm
Dī-ăg'ọ-răs
Dī-ā'lịs
Dī-ạ-măs-tị-gō'sịs
Dī-ā'nạ
Dī'ạn (in poetry)
Dī-ā'nạs
Dī-ăn'ạ-sạ
Dī-ā'nị-ŭm
Dī-ăph'ạ-nēş
Dī-ạ-pŏn'tị-ŭs 1
Dī-ā'sị-ạ 1
Dī-âu'lụs
Dĭb'ị-ō
Dị-bū'tạ-dēş, or
   Dĭb-ụ-tā'dēş
Dī-cæ-ạr-chī'ạ
Dī-cär'chụs
Dī'cẹ
Dĭç-ẹ-är'chụs
Dī-cē'nẹ-ŭs
Dĭç'ẹ-tăs
Dĭc'ọ-măs
Dịc-tā'tọr
Dịc-tĭd-ị-ĕn'sēş
Dịc-tī'nạ
Dĭd'ị-ŭs
Dĭd'y-mạ

Dĭd'y-mæ
Dĭd-y-mā'ọn
Dĭd'y-mē
Dĭd'y-mŭm
Dĭd'y-mŭs
Dī-ĕn'ẹ-cēş
Dī-ĕs'pị-tẹr
Dī-ģē'nạ
Dī-ģĕn'tị-ạ 1
Dī-ģē'rī
Dī-ģĭ''tị-ŭs
Dī-ị-pọ-lī'ạ
Dī-ĭt'rẹ-phēş
Dī-nā'cị-ŭm 1
Dī-năr'chụs
Dĭn'dy-mạ
Dĭn-dy-mē'nẹ
Dĭn'dy-mŏs
Dĭn'dy-mŭm
Dĭn'dy-mŭs
Dĭn'ị-ạ
Dĭn'ị-æ
Dĭn'ị-ăs
Dĭn'ị-chē
Dī-nŏch'ạ-rēş
Dī-nŏc'rạ-tēş
Dī-nŏd'ọ-chŭs
Dī-nŏģ-ẹ-tī'ạ
Dī-nŏl'ọ-chŭs
Dī-nŏm'ạ-chē
Dī-nŏm'ạ-chŭs
Dī-nŏm'ẹ-nēş
Dī-nŏs'the-nēş
Dī-nŏs'trạ-tŭs
Dī-ọ-cæs-ạ-rē'ạ
Dī-ō'clẹ-ạ, town.
Dī-ọ-clē'ạ, festival.
Dī'ọ-clēş
Dī-ọ-clē-tị-ā'nụs 1
Dī-ọ-clī'dēş
Dī-ọ-dō'rụs
Dī-ŏd'ọ-tŭs
Dī-ŏģ'ẹ-nēş
Dī-ŏģ-ẹ-nī'ạ
Dī-ọ-ģē-nị-ā'nụs
Dī-ŏģ'ẹ-nŭs
Dī-ọg-nē'tụs
Dī-ọ-mē'ạ
Dī-ọ-mē'dạ
Dī-ŏm-ẹ-dē'ạ
Dī-ŏm-ẹ-dē'æ
Dī-ọ-mē'dēş
Dī'ọ-mĕd
Dī-ŏm'ẹ-dŏn
Dī'ọ-mŭs
Dī-ō'nẹ
Dī-ọ-nў''sị-ạ 1
Dī-ọ-ny-sī'ạ-dēş
Dī-ọ-nў''sị-ăs 1
Dī-ọ-nўs'ị-dēş
Dī-ọ-nў-sị-ọ-dō'rụs 1
Dī-ọ-nў''sị-ŏn 2
Dī-ọ-ny-sĭp'ọ-lĭs
Dī-ọ-nў''sị-ŭs 1
Dī-ọ-nўs-ọ-dō'rụs
Dī-ọ-ny-sŏp'ọ-lĭc
Dī-ọ-nȳ'sọs
Dī-ọ-nȳ'sụs
Dī-ŏph'ạ-nēş

Dī-ọ-pī'thēş
Dī-ọ-pœ'nụs
Dī-ŏp'ọ-lĭs
Dī-ō'rēş
Dī-ọs-cŏr'ị-dēş
Dī-ŏs'cọ-rŭm
Dī-ŏs'cọ-rŭs
Dī-ọs-cū'rī
Dī-ọs-cū'rị-dēş
Dī-ŏs-cụ-rī'ụm
Dī-ŏs'pạ-ģē
Dī-ŏs'pọ-lĭs
Dī-ọ-tī'mẹ
Dī-ọ-tī'mụs
Dī-ọ-tŏģ'ẹ-nēş
Dī-ŏt'rẹ-phēş
Dī-pæ'æ
Dĭph'ị-lăs
Dĭph'ị-lŭs
Dī-phŏr'ị-dăs
Dĭph'rị-dăs
Dĭph'ry-ģēş
Dī-pœ'næ
Dĭp'ọ-lĭs
Dĭp'y-lŭm
Dī'ræ
Dĭr'cẹ
Dĭr'cẹ-tĭs
Dĭr'phy-ạ
Dịs-cŏr'dị-ạ
Dĭs'cọ-rŭm
Dĭs'ọ-ræ
Dĭth-y-răm'bụs
Dī-tị-ō'nēş 1
Dĭv'ị-cō
Dĭv-ị-tī'ạ-cŭs
Dĭv-ọ-dū'nụm
Dĭv-ọ-dū'rụm
Dĭv'ọ-nạ
Dī'vụs Fĭd'ị-ŭs
Dī-zē'rụs
Dọ-bē'rēş
Dọ-bē'rụs
Dŏç'ị-lĭs
Dŏç-ị-mē'ụm
Dŏç'ị-mŭs
Dō'clẹ-ạ
Dọ-dō'nạ
Dŏd-ọ-næ'ụs
Dọ-dō'nẹ
Dọ-dŏn'ị-dēş
Dō'ī
Dŏl-ạ-bĕl'lạ
Dŏl-ị-chā'ọn
Dŏl'ị-chē
Dŏl'ị-chŏs
Dọ-lī'ọn
Dọ-lī'ọ-nēş
Dọ-lī'ọ-nĭs
Dō'lị-ŭs
Dŏl-ọ-mē'nạ
Dŏl-ọ-mē'nẹ
Dŏl'ọ-pēş
Dọ-lō'pị-ạ
Dŏl-ọ-pī'ọn
Dŏm-ị-dū'cụs
Dọ-mĭn'ị-cạ
Dọ-mĭ''tị-ạ 1
Dọ-mĭ-tị-ā'nụs 1
Dọ-mĭ''tị-ạn

Do̧-mĭ''ti̧-ŭs 1
Do̧m-nī'nu̧s
Do̧m-nŏt'o̧-nŭm
Dŏn'a̧-cē
Do̧-nā'tu̧s
Dŏn-i̧-lā'u̧s
Do̧-nū'ca̧
Do̧-nū'sa̧
Do̧-nȳ'sa̧
Do̧r-cē'a̧
Dŏr'ceūs 6
Dŏr'ci̧-ŭm 1
Dŏr'da̧-lŭs
Dō'rēṣ
Dō'ri̧-ăs
Dŏr'i̧-ca̧
Dŏr'i̧-cŭs
Dŏr'i̧-dăs
Dō-ri̧-ĕn'sēṣ
Dō'ri̧-eūs 6
Dŏr'i̧-lăs
Dŏr-i̧-lā'u̧s
Do̧-rĭm'a̧-chŭs
Dō'ri̧-ō
Dō'ri̧-ŭm
Dō'ri̧-ŭs
Do̧-rŏs'to̧-lŭm
Do̧-rŏs'to̧-rŭm
Do̧-rō'thȩ-ŭs
Dŏr-o̧x-ā'ni̧-ŭm
Do̧-rȳ'a̧-sŭs
Dŏr'y-clŭs, or
  Do̧-rȳ'clu̧s
Dŏr-y-læ'u̧m
Dŏr'y-lăs
Dŏr-y-lā'u̧s
Do̧-rȳph'o̧-rī
Do̧-rȳph'o̧-rŭs
Do̧-sī'a̧-dăs
Do̧-sī'a̧-dēṣ
Do̧-sĭth'ȩ-ŭs
Do̧-sĭth'o̧-ē
Do̧s-sē'nu̧s
Dŏt'a̧-dăs
Dō'ti̧-ŏn 2
Do̧x-ăp'a̧-tȩr
Do̧x-īp'a̧-tȩr
Drăc'a̧-nŭs
Dra̧-cŏn'ti̧-dēṣ
Dra̧-cŏn'ti̧-ŭs 1
Drăc'o̧-nŭm
Drăg'a̧-nī
Dra̧-hō'nu̧s
Drăn'cēṣ
Drăn-gi̧-ā'na̧
Drā'pēṣ
Drĕp'a̧-na̧, and
  Drĕp'a̧-nŭm
Drĕp'a̧-nē
Drȩ-pā'ni̧-ŭs
Drĭm'a̧-chŭs
Drī-ŏd'o̧-nēṣ
Drī-ŏp'i̧-dēṣ
Drŏ'ī
Dro̧-măch'ȩ-tŏs
Drŏ'meūs 6
Drŏm-o̧-clī'dēṣ
Drŏp'i̧-cī
Drŏ'pi̧-ŏn
Dru̧-ĕn'ti̧-a̧ 1

Dru̧-ĕn'ti̧-ŭs 1
Dru̧-gē'rī, or
  Drū'gȩ-rī
Drū'i̧-dæ
Dru'ĭdṣ
Drȳ'a̧-dēṣ
Drȳ'a̧dṣ
Drȳ-ā'di̧-a̧
Drȳ-a̧n-tī'a̧-dēṣ
Drȳ-a̧n-tī'dēṣ
Drȳ-mō'dēṣ
Drȳ-mū'sa̧
Drȳ-mæm'ȩ-tŭm 4
Drȳ'o̧-pē
Drȳ-o̧-pē'i̧-a̧ 3
Drȳ'o̧-pēṣ
Drȳ-ŏp'i̧-da̧
Drȳp'ȩ-tĭs, or
  Dry-pē'ti̧s
Dū'bi̧-ŭs
Du̧-cā'ri̧-ŭs
Du̧-cē'ti̧-ŭs 1
Du̧-cŏr'to̧-rŭm
Du̧-ĭl'li̧-a̧
Du̧-ĭl'li̧-ŭs Nē'pŏs
Du̧-lĭch'i̧a̧
Du̧-lĭch'i̧-ŭm
Du̧-lŏp'o̧-lĭs
Du̧m-nō'ni̧-ī
Dŭm'no̧-rĭx
Du̧-rā'ni̧-ŭs
Dū'ra̧-nŭs
Du̧-rā'ti̧-ŭs 1
Dū'ra̧-tō
Dū'ri̧-a̧
Dū'ri̧-ŭs
Dū-ro̧-brī'væ
Dū-ro̧-cŏr'to̧-rŭm
Du̧-rō'ni̧-a̧
Du̧-rō'ni̧-ŭs
Dū-ro̧-vёr'nu̧m
Dū-sa̧-rē'nī
Du̧-ŭm'vi̧-rī
Dȳ-a̧r-dĕn'sēṣ
Dȳ'mȩ
Dȳ-năm'ȩ-nē
Dȳ-nā'mi̧-ŭs
Dyr-rā'chi̧-ŭm
Dȳs-ci̧-nē'tu̧s
Dȳs'co̧-lŏs
Dȳs-ni̧-cē'tu̧s
Dȳ-sō'ru̧m
Dȳ-sō'ru̧s
Dys-pŏn'teūs 6
Dys-pŏn'ti̧-ī 1

E.

Ē'a̧-nēṣ, or
  Æ'a̧-nēṣ
Ē-ā'nu̧s
Ē-ăr'i̧-nŭs
Ē-ā'si̧-ŭm 1
Ēb'do̧-mē
Æ' oj-ŏn
Ēb'o̧-da̧
Ȩ-blā'na̧
Ēb'o̧-ra̧

Ēb-o̧-rā'cu̧m, or
  Ȩ-bŏr'a̧-cu̧m
Ēb'o̧-rēṣ
Ēb'o̧-rŭm
Ȩ-bō'si̧-a̧ 1
Ēb-ro̧-dū'nu̧m
Ēb-ro̧-ī'cēṣ
Ȩ-bū'dæ
Ēb'u̧-rō
Ēb-u̧-ro̧-dū'nu̧m
Ēb-u̧-rō'nēṣ
Ēb-u̧-ro̧-vī'cēṣ
Ēb'u̧-sŭs
Ēc-a̧-mē'da̧
Ēc-băt'a̧-na̧
Ēc-dē'mu̧s
Ēc'di̧-cŭs
Ēc-ȩ-chĭr'i̧-a̧
Ēç'ȩ-tra̧
Ȩ-chē'æ
Ȩ-chĕc'ra̧-tēṣ
Ēch'ȩ-dæ
Ēch-ȩ-da̧-mī'a̧
Ēch-ȩ-dē'mu̧s
Ēch-ȩ-dō'ru̧s
Ȩ-chēl'a̧-tŭs
Ēch'ȩ-lŭs
Ȩ-chĕm'bro̧-tŭs
Ȩ-chĕm'ȩ-nēṣ
Ȩ-chē'mon
Ēch'ȩ-mŭs
Ēch-ȩ-nē'u̧s
Ēch-ȩ-phrŏn
Ēch-ȩ-pō'lu̧s
Ēch-ȩ-tī'mu̧s
Ēch'ȩ-tra̧
Ēch'ȩ-tŭs
Ȩ-chĕv-ȩ-thĕn'sēṣ
Ēch-i̧-dō'ru̧s
Ȩ-chĭn'a̧-dēṣ
Ēch-i̧-nē'i̧s
Ȩ-chī'nos, or -nu̧s
Ēch i̧-nŭs'sa̧
Ȩ-chī'on
Ēch-i̧-ŏn'i̧-dēṣ
Ēch-i̧-ō'ni̧-ŭs
Ē'chi̧-ŭs
Ē'chō
Ēc'no̧-mŏs, or -mŭs
Ēc-phăn'ti̧-dēṣ
Ēd'ȩ-cŏn
Ȩ-dē'ta̧
Ēd'ga̧-rŭs, *L.*
Ēd'gar
Ēd'i̧-tha̧, *L.*
Ē'dith
Ȩ-dō'nēṣ, and
  Ēd'o̧-nēṣ
Ȩ-dō'nu̧s
Ȩ-dū'sa̧
Ēd-vī'nu̧s
Ēd'win
Ȩ-dȳl'i̧-ŭs
Ȩ-ē'ti̧-ŏn 2
Ȩ-gā'lȩ-ŏs
Ȩ-gĕl'i̧-dŭs
Ȩ-gē'ri̧-a̧
Ȩ-gēs-a̧-rē'tu̧s
Ēg-ȩ-sī'nu̧s
Ȩ-gē'ta̧

Ēg-nā'ti̧-a̧ 1
Ēg-nā'ti̧-ŭs 1
Ēg-năt-u̧-lē'i̧-ŭs 3
Ē-ī'o̧n
Ē-ī'o̧-nēṣ
Ē-ī'o̧-neūs 6
Ēī-zē'lu̧s
Ȩ-læ'u̧s
Ȩ-læ-u̧-tī'chu̧s
Ēl-a̧-găb'a̧-lŭs, or
  Ēl-a̧-ga̧-bā'lu̧s
Ȩ-lā'i̧s
Ēl-a̧-ī'tēṣ
Ȩ-lā'i̧-ŭs 3
Ēl-a̧-phȩ-bō'li̧-a̧
Ēl'a̧-phŭs
Ēl-a̧p-tō'ni̧-ŭs
Ēl'a̧-ra̧
Ēl'a̧-sŭs
Ēl'a̧-tē'a̧
Ēl'a̧-tī'a̧
Ēl'a̧-treūs 6
Ēl'a̧-tŭs
Ȩ-lā'vȩr, or
  Ēl'a̧-vȩr
Ē'lȩ-a̧
Ē-lȩ-ā'tēṣ
Ȩ-lĕc'tri̧-dēṣ
Ȩ-lĕc'tri̧-ŭs
Ȩ-lĕc'try-ŏn
Ȩ-lĕc-try-ō'nȩ
Ēl-ȩ-gē'i̧-a̧ 3
Ēl-ȩ-gī'a̧
Ȩ-lē'ī
Ēl-ȩ-lē'i̧-dēṣ
Ēl'ȩ-leūs 6
Ē'lȩ-ŏn
Ȩ-leu̧-chī'a̧
Ē'lȩ-u̧s (*n.*)
Ȩ-lē'u̧s (*a.*)
Ēl-eu̧-sĭn'i̧-a̧
Ēl-eu̧-sī'nu̧s
Ēl-eu̧-sĭp'o̧-lĭs
Ȩ-leū'si̧s
Ȩ-leū'si̧-ŭm 1
Ȩ-leū'thȩ-ræ
Ēl-eu̧-thē'ri̧-a̧
Ȩ-leū-thȩ-ro̧-cĭl'i̧-
  cēṣ
Ȩ-leū-thȩ-rō-la̧-cō'-
Ȩ-leū'thȩ-rŏs [nēṣ
Ȩ-lī'a̧-ca̧
Ȩ-lī''ci̧-ŭs 1
Ȩ-li̧-ŏn'si̧s
Ēl-i̧-mē'a̧
Ȩ-lī'sa̧
Ēl-i̧s-phā'si̧-ī 1
Ȩ-lō'pi̧-a̧
Ȩ-lō'ru̧s
Ēl-pē'no̧r
Ēl-pĭd'i̧-ŭs
Ēl-pi̧-nī'cē

Ēl-u̧-ī'na̧
Ēl'u̧-sa̧
Ēl'y-cēṣ
Ēl-y-mā'i̧s
Ēl'y-mī
Ēl'y-mŭs
Ēl'y-rŭs
Ȩ-lȳ''si̧-ŭm 1
Ȩ-mā'thi̧-a̧
Ȩ-mā'thi̧-ŏn
Ēm'a̧-thŭs
Ēm'ba̧-tŭm
Ēm-bŏl'i̧-ma̧
Ēm'bo̧-lŭs
Ȩ-mĕr'i̧-ta̧
Ēm'ȩ-sa̧
Ēm'ȩ-sŭs
Ēm-i̧-sē'nu̧s
Ēm-mē'li̧-ŭs
Ēm-mĕn'i̧-dæ
Ȩ-mō'da̧
Ȩ-mō'dī Mŏn'tēṣ
Ȩ-mō'du̧s
Ēm-pĕd'o̧-clēṣ
Ēm'pȩ-dŭs
Ēm-pȩ-rā'mu̧s
Ēm-pō'clu̧s
Ēm-pō'ri̧-a̧
Ēm-pō'ri̧-æ
Ēm-pŏr'i̧-cŭs
Ēm-pō'ri̧-ŭs
Ēm-pū'sa̧
Ēm-pȳr'i̧-ŭm
Ȩ-næs'i̧-mŭs 4
Ēn'a̧-lŭs
Ēn-a̧-rĕph'o̧-rŭs
Ȩ-năr'ȩ-tē
Ēn-cĕl'a̧-dŭs
Ēn-chē'lȩ-æ
Ēn-dē'i̧s
Ēn'dȩ-ra̧
Ēn-dē'ru̧m
Ēn'di̧-ŭs
Ēn-dȳm'i̧-ŏn
Ēn'ȩ-tī
Ēn-gŏn'a̧-sī
Ēn-gŏn'a̧-sĭs
Ēn'gui̧-ŏn
Ēn'ğy-ŭm
Ȩ-năn-ti̧-ŏph'a̧-nēṣ
Ē-nī'o̧-peūs θ
Ēn-ī'peūs 6
Ēn-nȩ-a̧-crū'nos
Ēn'ni̧-ŭs
Ēn-nō'di̧-ŭs
Ēn'no̧-mŏs, or
  Ēn'no̧-mŭs
Ēn-nŏs-i̧-ğæ'u̧s
Ēn'o̧-pē
Ēn-o̧-sĭch'thon
Ȩ-nŏt-o̧-cœ'tæ
Ēn-tō'ri̧-a̧
Ē-ny-ā'li̧-ŭs
Ē-nȳ'eūs 6
Ȩ-nȳ'ō
Ē'o̧-nē
Ȩ-ō'u̧s
Ȩ-pæn'ȩ-tŭs 4
Ȩ-păg'a̧-thŭs
Ȩ-pā'gri̧s

Ĕp-ą-măn-dŭ-ọ-dū'-rŭm [rŭm
Ĕp-ą-măn-tą-dū'-
Ĕ-păm-ı-nŏn'dąs
Ĕp-ąn-tē'lı-ī
Ĕ-păph-rọ-dī'tŭs
Ĕp'ą-phŭs
Ĕ-pĕb'ọ-lŭs
Ĕ-pē'ī
Ĕ-pĕr'ą-tŭs
Ĕp-ę-trī'mī
Ĕ-pē'ŭm, or
  Ē'pĭ-ŭm
Ĕ-pē'ŭs
Ĕ-phē'bī
Ĕ-phē'şı-ŭs 1
Ĕph'ę-sŏs
Ĕph'ę-sŭs
Ĕph'ę-tæ
Ĕph'ọ-rī
Ĕph'ọ-rŭs
Ē'phrą-ĕm
Ĕph'rą-tą
Ĕph'y-rą, or -rē
Ĕph-y-rę-ī'ą-dĕş
Ĕp-ĭ-căs'tę
Ĕp-ĭ-cĕr'dĕş
Ĕp-ĭ-chā'ĭ-dĕş
Ĕ-pĭch'ą-rĭs
Ĕp'ĭ-clĕş
Ĕp-ĭ-clī'dĕş
Ĕp-ĭc-nę-mĭd'ĭ-ī
Ĕp-ĭ-crā'nę
Ĕ-pĭc'rą-tĕş
Ĕp-ĭ-crē'nę
Ĕp-ĭc-tē'tŭs
Ĕp-ĭ-cŭ-rē'ī
Ĕp-i-cu-rē'ąnş
Ĕp-ĭ-cū'rŭs
Ĕp-ĭ-cȳ'dĕş
Ĕp-ĭ-cy-dī'dĕş
Ĕp-ĭ-dăm'nĭ-ŭm
Ĕp-ĭ-dăm'nŭs
Ĕp-ĭ-dăph'nę
Ĕp-ĭ-dâu'rŭs
Ĕp-ĭ-dē'lĭ-ŭm
Ĕ-pĭd'ı-cŭs
Ĕ-pĭd'ĭ-ŭs
Ĕp-ĭ-dō'tĕş
Ĕ-pĭd'ọ-tŭs
Ĕ-pĭg'ę-nĕş
Ĕ-pī'ğeūs 6
Ĕp-ĭg-nō'mŭs
Ĕ-pĭg'ọ-nī
Ĕ-pĭg'ọ-nŭs
Ĕ-pī'ī, and Ĕ-pē'ī
Ĕp-ĭ-lā'ıs
Ĕ-pĭl'y-cŭs
Ĕ-pĭm'ą-nĕş
Ĕp-ĭ-mē'dĕş
Ĕp-ĭ-mĕl'ĭ-dĕş
Ĕp-ĭ-mĭm'ę-nĕş
Ĕp-ĭ-mĕn'ĭ-dĕş
Ĕp-ĭ-mē'theūs 6
Ĕp-ĭ-mē'thĭs
Ĕp-ĭ-nī'cŭs
Ĕ-pī'ọ-chŭs
Ĕ-pī'ọ-nē
Ĕp-ĭ-phą-nē'ą
Ĕ-pĭph'ą-nĕş

Ĕp-ĭ-phā'nĭ-ą, *wo-man.*
Ĕp-ĭ-phā-nī'ą, *city.*
Ĕp-ĭ-phā'nĭ-ŭs
Ĕ-pīp'ọ-lē
Ĕ-pī'rọs
Ĕ-pī'rŭs
Ĕ-pĭs'thę-nĕş
Ĕ-pīt'ą-dĕş
Ĕp-ĭ-tā'lĭ-ŭm
Ĕp-ĭ-thē'rąs
Ĕp'ĭ-tŏs
Ĕ-pĭt'y-rŭs
Ē'pĭ-ŭm, or
  Ĕ-pī'ŭm
Ĕp'ọ-ną
Ĕ-pōn'y-mŭs
Ĕ-pō'pę
Ĕ-pō'peūs 6
Ĕ-pōp'sĭ-ŭs 1
Ĕp-ọ-rē'dĭ-ą
Ĕp-ọ-rēd'ọ-rĭx
Ĕp'pĭ-ŭs
Ĕp'ŭ-lō
Ĕ-pȳt'ĭ-dĕş
Ĕp'y-tŭs
Ē-quą-jŭs'tą
Ĕ-quĭc'ọ-lŭs
Ĕ-quīr'ĭ-ą
Ĕ-quī''tĭ-ŭs 1
Ĕq'uĭ-tĕş
Ē-quọ-tū'tĭ-cŭs
Ĕr'ą-cŏn
Ĕr-ą-sĭn'ĭ-dĕş
Ĕr-ą-sī'nŭs
Ĕr-ą-sĭp'pŭs
Ĕr-ą-sīs'trą-tŭs
Ĕ-răt'ĭ-dæ
Ĕr'ą-tō
Ĕr-ą-tŏs'thę-nĕş
Ĕr-ą-tŏs'trą-tŭs
Ĕr'ą-tŭs
Ĕr-chī'ą
Ĕr'ę-bŭs
Ĕr-ęch-thē'ŭm
Ĕ-rĕch'theūs (*n.*)
Ĕr-ęch-thē'ŭs (*a.*)
Ĕr-ęch-thī'dæ
Ĕ-rē'mŭs
Ĕr-ę-nē'ą
Ĕr'ę-sŭs
Ĕ-rē'trĭ-ą
Ĕ-rē'tŭm
Ĕr-eu-thā'lĭ-ŏn
Ĕr-găm'ę-nĕş
Ĕr'gą-nę
Ĕr-găn'ĭ-cą
Ĕr-ğē'tĭ-ŭm 1
Ĕr-ğē'tŭm
Ĕr'ğĭ-ăs
Ĕr-ğī'nŭs
Ĕr-ĭ-bō'tĕş
Ĕr-ĭ-cā'tĕş
Ĕr-ĭ-cē'ą
Ĕr-ĭ-cē'tĕş
Ĕr-ĭch-thō'nĭ-ŭs
Ĕr-ĭ-cĭn'ĭ-ŭm
Ĕ-rī'cŭs
Ē'ric, Hĕn'ry
Ĕr-ĭ-cū'są

Ĕ-rĭd'ą-nŭs
Ĕ-rĭg'ę-ną
Ĕr-ĭg-dū'pŭs
Ĕr'ĭ-gŏn
Ĕ-rĭg'ọ-nē
Ĕr-ĭ-gō'nē'ĭ-ŭs 3
Ĕr-ĭ-gō'nŭs, *river.*
Ĕr-ĭg'ọ-nĕş, *painter.*
Ĕr-ĭ-ğȳ'ĭŭs
Ĕ-rĭn'dĕş
Ĕ-rĭn'ę-ŏs
Ĕ-rĭn'ny-ĕş
Ē-rĭ-ō'pĭs
Ĕ-rĭph'ą-nĭs
Ĕ-rĭph'ĭ-däs
Ĕr'ĭ-phŭs
Ĕr-ĭ-phȳ'lę
Ĕr-ĭ-sīch'thọn
Ĕr'ĭ-thŏs
Ĕr'ĭ-thŭs
Ĕ-rō'chŭs
Ĕ-rŏph'ĭ-lŭs
Ĕ-rŏs'trą-tŭs
Ĕ-rō'tĭ-ą 1
Ĕ-rō-tĭ-ā'nŭs 1
Ĕ-rō'tĭ-ŏn 2
Ĕ-rō'tĭ-ŭm 1
Ĕr-rŭ'cą
Ĕr'sę
Ĕ-rŭ'brŭs
Ĕ-rŭ'cĭ-ŭs 1
Ĕrx'ĭ-ăs 1
Ĕ-rȳ'ą-lŭs
Ĕ-rȳb'ĭ-ŭm
Ĕr-y-cī'ną
Ĕ-rȳ''cĭ-ŭs 1
Ĕr-yg-dū'pŭs
Ĕr-y-măn'thŭs
Ĕr'y-măs
Ĕ-rȳm'næ
Ĕ-rȳm'neūs 6
Ĕr'y-mŭs
Ĕr-y-thē'ą
Ĕr-y-thē'ŭm
Ĕr-y-thī'ą
Ĕr'y-thī'nī
Ĕr'y-thrą
Ĕ-rȳth-rą-bō'lŭs
Ĕr'y-thræ
Ĕ-rȳth'rĭ-ŏn
Ĕr-yx-īm'ą-chŭs
Ĕ-sā'ĭ-ăs
Ĕs-quĭl'ĭ-æ
Ĕs-quĭ-lī'nŭs
Ĕs-drą-ē'lọn
Ĕs-sēd'ọ-nĕş
Ĕs'su-ī
Ĕs-tĭ-ō'nĕş
Ĕs'u-lą
Ĕ-sū'rĭ-ō
Ĕ-tē'ą
Ĕ-tē'ọ-clĕş
Ĕ-tē'ọ-clŭs
Ē-tę-ō'neūs 6
Ē-tę-ọ-nī'cŭs
Ē-tę-ō'nŭs
Ĕ-tē'şĭ-æ 1
Ĕ-thā'lĭ-ŏn
Ĕ-thē'clŭs
Ĕ-thē'lę-ŭm

Ĕ-thē'lŭs
Ĕ-thē'mọn
Ē-thę-ō'nọs
Ĕth-ọ-dā'ĭ-ą
Ē'tĭ-ăs 1
Ĕt-mā'nę-ı
Ĕ-trǎ'rĭ-ą
Ĕ-trǎç'ĭ-dĕş
Ĕt'y-lŭs
Ĕ-tȳm'ọ-clĕş
Eū-æn'ę-tŭs 4
Eū'ą-ğĕş
Eū'ą-gŏn
Eū-ăg'ọ-räs
Eū-ā'grĭ-ŭs
Eū'ą-grŏs, or
  Eū-ā'grọs
Eū-ăn'ğę-lŭs
Eū-ą-nŏr'ĭ-däs
Eū'bą-ğĕş, or
  Eū'hą-ğĕş
Eū'bą-tŏs
Eū'bĭ-ŭs
Eū-bœ'ą
Eū bō'ĭ-cŭs
Eū'bọ-ĭs
Eū-bō'tąs
Eū-bō'tę
Eū-bō'tĕş
Eū-bū'lę
Eū-bū'leūs 6
Eū-bū'lĭ-dĕş
Eū-bū'lŭs
Eū-căm'pĭ-däs
Eū-cē'rŭs
Eū-çhē'nọr
Eū-çhē'rĭ-ą
Eū-çhē'rĭ-ŭs
Eū'çhĭ-dĕş
Eū-clē'ą, or -clī'ę
Eū-clī'dĕş
Eū'clid
Eū'clĭ-ō
Eū'crą-tē
Eū-crăt'ĭ-dĕş
Eū'crĭ-tŭs
Eūc-tē'mọn
Eūc-trē'şĭ-ī 1
Eū-dăm'ĭ-däs
Eū-dā'mŭs
Eū-dē'mŭs
Eū'dĭ-cŭs
Eū-dō'cĭ-ą 1
Eū-dŏç'ĭ-mŭs
Eū-dō'rŭs
Eū-dŏx'ĭ-ą 1
Eū-dŏx'ĭ-ŭs 1
Eū-ęl-ğē'ą
Eū-ĕl'pĭ-dĕş
Eū-ę-mĕr'ĭ-däs
Eū-ĕm'ę-rŭs
Eū-ē'nĭ-ŭs
Eū-ē'nọr
Eū-ē'nŭs
Eū-ĕph'ę-nŭs
Eū-ē'rĕş
Eū-ĕr'ğę-tæ
Eū-ęs-pĕr'ĭ-dĕş
Eū'ę-tĕş
Eū-gā'nę-ı

Eū'ğę-nĕş
Eū-ğē'nĭ-ą
Eū-ğĕn'ĭ-cŭs
Eū-ğō'nĭ-ŭm
Eū-ğē'nĭ-ŭs
Eū'ğę-ŏn
Eū-ğī'ą
Eū'ğĭ-ŏn
Eū'hą-ğĕş
Eū-hĕm'ę-rŭs
Eū'họ-dŭs
Eū'hy-drą
Eū'hy-drŭm
Eū'hy-ŭs
Eū'ĭ-ăs
Eū'ĭ-ŏs, or -ŭs
Eū-ĭp'pę
Eū-lā'lĭ-ą
Eū-lā'lĭ-ŭs
Eū-lĭm'ę-nē
Eū-lō'ğĭ-ŭs
Eū'lọ-gŭs
Eū-mā'chĭ-ŭs
Eū'mą-chŭs
Eū-mā'rąs
Eū-mē'cĕş
Eū-mē'dą
Eū-mē'dĕş
Eū-mē'lĭs
Eū-mē'lŭs
Eū'mę-nĕş
Eū-mę-nī'ą, or
  Eū-mē'nĭ-ą
Eū-mĕn'ĭ-dĕş
Eū-mē'nĭ-ŭs
Eū-mŏl'pĭ-dæ
Eū-mŏn'ĭ-dĕş
Eū-nā'pĭ-ŭs
Eū-nē'ọs, *Homer.*
Eū'nę-ŏs, *Strabo.*
Eū-nī'cę
Eū-nī'cŭs
Eū-nō'mĭ-ą
Eū-nō'mĭ-ŭs
Eū'nọ-mŭs
Eū-nō'nĕş
Eū-nū'chŭş
Eū'ny-mŏs
Eū'ọ-dŭs
Eū-ŏn'y-mŭs
Eū'ọ-räs
Eū-pā'ğĭ-ŭm
Eū-păl'ą-mŏn
Eū-păl'ą-mŏs, or
  Eū-păl'ą-mŭs
Eū-pā'lĭ-ŭm
Eū'pą-tŏr
Eū-pą-tō'rĭ-ą
Eū-păt'ọ-rĭs
Eū-peī'thĕş
Eū'phą-ĕş
Eū-phē'mę
Eū-phē'mĭ-ą
Eū-phē'mŭs
Eū-phŏ'rĭ-ŏn
Eū-phrā'nọr
Eū-phrā'tĕş
Eū-phrŏs'y-nē
Eū-pī'thĕş
Eū-pĭth'ĭ-ŭs

Eū-plœ'a
Eū-pŏl'e-mŭs
Eū'po-lĭs
Eū-pŏ'lŭs
Eū'pre-pēṣ
Eū-rĭ-a-nǎs'sa
Eū-rĭp'ĭ-dēṣ
Eū-rī'pŭs
Eū-ro-ǎq'uĭ-lō
Eū-rŏc'ly-dŏn
Eū-rō'mŭs
Eū-rō'nĭ-ŭs
Eū-rŏn'o-tŭs
Eū-rō'pa
Eū-rō'pŭs
Eū-rō'tas
Eū-rō'tō
Eū-rȳ'a-lē
Eū-rȳ'a-lŭs
Eū-rȳ'a-nǎx
Eū-rȳb'a-tēṣ
Eū-rȳb'a-tŭs
Eū-rȳb'ĭ-a
Eū-ry-bī'a-dēṣ
Eū-rȳb'ĭ-ŭs
Eū-ry-bō'tas
Eū-rȳb'o-tŭs
Eū-ry-clē'a
Eū'ry-clēṣ
Eū-ry-clī'dēṣ
Eū-rȳc'ra-tēṣ
Eū-ry-crǎt'ĭ-dǎs
Eū-ry-cȳ'de
Eū-rȳd'a-mǎs
Eū-rȳd'a-mē
Eū-ry-dǎm'ĭ-dǎs
Eū-rȳd'ĭ-cē
Eū-ry-ē'lŭs
Eū-ry-ga-nī'a
Eū-rȳl'e-ŏn
Eū-rȳl'o-çhŭs
Eū-rȳm'e-dē, and
  Eū-ry-mē'de
Eū-rȳm'e-dŏn
Eū-rȳm'e-nēṣ
Eū-rȳm'ĭ-dēṣ
Eū-rȳn'o-mē
Eū-rȳ'o-nē
Eū-ry-phā'mŭs
Eū'ry-phŏn
Eū-ry-pŏn'tĭ-dæ
Eū-ryp-tŏl'e-mŭs
Eū-rȳp'y-lŭs
Eū-rȳs'a-cēṣ
Eū-rȳs'the-nēṣ
Eū-rys-thĕn'ĭ-dæ
Eū-rȳs'theūs (n.) 6
Eū-rys-thē'ŭs (a.)
Eū-ry-tā'nēṣ
Eū'ry-tē
Eū-rȳt'e-æ, or
  Eū-ry-tē'æ
Eū-rȳt'e-lē
Eū-rȳth'e-mĭs
Eū-rȳt'ĭ-ŏn 2
Eū'ry-tĭs
Eū'ry-tŭs
Eū'se-bēṣ
Eū-sē'bĭ-a, woman.

Eū-se-bī'a, city.
Eū-sē'bĭ-ŭs
Eū-sĕm'a-ta
Eū-sē'ne
Eū-stā'thĭ-ŭs
Eū'stace
Eū-stŏ'chĭ-ŭs
Eū-stŏ'lĭ-ŭs
Eū-strā'tĭ-ŭs 1
Eū-tĕl'ĭ-dǎs
Eū-thā'lĭ-a
Eū-thā'lĭ-ŭs
Eū-thē'næ
Eū'thy-clēṣ
Eū-thȳc'ra-tēṣ
Eū-thy-dē'mŭs
Eū-thȳm'ĭ-dǎs
Eū-thȳm'ĭ-ŭs
Eū-thȳ'mŭs
Eū-thy-nī'cŭs
Eū-thȳn'o-ŭs
Eū'thy-phrŏn
Eū-tŏ'cĭ-ŭs 1
Eū-tŏl'mĭ-ŭs
Eū-trǎp'e-lŭs
Eū-trē'sĭs
Eū-trō'pĭ-a
Eū-trō'pĭ-ŭs
Eū'ty-çhēṣ
Eū-tȳçh-ĭ-ā'nŭs
Eū-tȳçh'ĭ-dē
Eū-tȳçh'ĭ-dēṣ
Eū-tȳçh'ĭ-ŭs
Eū'ty-çhŭs
Eūx-ǎn'thĭ-ŭs
Eūx-ĕn'ĭ-dæ
Eūx'e-nŭs
Eūx-ī'nŭs Pŏn'tŭs
Eūx-ĭp'pe
Eūx-ĭth'e-ŭs
Eūx-ŏm'a-tæ
Eūx-ȳn'the-tŭs
Ev-. See Eu-.
Ēv'a-ġēṣ
Ē-vǎg'o-rǎs
Ē-vā'grĭ-ŭs
Ēv'a-grŭs, or
  Ē-vā'grus
Ē-vǎn'ġe-lŭs
Ēv-a-nŏr'ĭ-dǎs
Ē-vǎn'thēṣ
Ē-vĕm'e-rŭs, or
  Eū-hĕm'e-rŭs
Ē-vē'nor
Ē-vē'nos, or -nŭs
Ē-vĕph'e-nŭs
Ē-vē'rēṣ
Ē-vēr'ġe-tēṣ
Ēv-es-pĕr'ĭ-dēṣ
Ē'vĭ-ǎs
Ē'vĭ-ŏs, or -ŭs
Ē-vō'dĭ-ŭs
Ēv'o-dŭs
Ēv'o-rǎs
Ex-ā'dĭ-ŭs
Ex-ǽn'e-tŭs 4
Ex-æ-rǎm'bŭs
Ex-æ'thrēṣ
Ex-ǎg'o-nŭs
Ex-ŏm'a-tæ

Ex-quĭl'ĭ-æ
Ex-sū-pe-rǎn'tĭ-ŭs 1
Ex-u-pē'rĭ-ŭs
E-zē-çhĭ-ē'lŭs

F.

Fa-bā'rĭ-a
Fǎb'a-rĭs
Fa-bā'tŭs
Fa-bē'rĭ-ŭs
Fā'bĭ-a
Fā-bĭ-ā'nī
Fā-bĭ-ā'nŭs
Fā'bĭ-ŭs
Fǎb-ra-tē'rĭ-a
Fa-brī''cĭ-ŭs 1
Fǎb-ul-lī'nŭs
Fǎç-e-lī'na
Fā'dĭ-ŭs
Fæ-sĭd'ĭ-ŭs
Fæs'u-læ 4
Fǎl-a-crī'ne, or
  Fǎl-a-crī'num
Fa-lā'nĭ-ŭs
Fal-cĭd'ĭ-a
Fal-cō'nĭ-a
Fǎl'cu-la
Fa-lē'rĭ-a
Fa-lē'rĭ-ī
Fǎl-e-rī'na
Fǎn'nĭ-a
Fǎn'nĭ-ī
Fǎn'nĭ-ŭs
Fǎr'fa-rŭs
Fǎr'sĭ-na
Fǎs-cĕl'lĭ-na
Fǎs'cĭ-nŭs
Fǎs-tĭd'ĭ-ŭs
Fāu'cĭ-ŭs 1
Fāu'cu-la
Fāu-nā'lĭ-a
Fāu'nī
Fāu-nĭġ'e-na
Fāu'nus
Fāu-stī'na
Fāus-tĭ-nŏp'o-lĭs
Fāu-stī'nŭs
Fāu'stĭ-tǎs
Fāu'stu-lŭs
Fāu'stŭs
Fā've-a
Fa-vĕn'tĭ-a 1
Fǎv-en-tī'nŭs
Fa-vē'rĭ-a
Fa-vō'nĭ-ŭs
Fǎv-o-rī'nŭs
Fĕb'ru-a
Fĕb-ru-ā'rĭ-ŭs
Fĕb'ru-ŭs
Fē-cĭ-ā'lēṣ 1
Fĕl'ġĭ-nǎs
Fe-lĭç'ĭ-tǎs
Fēl'sĭ-na
Fēn-es-tĕl'la
Fe-rā'lĭ-a
Fĕr-en-tā'num
Fĕr-en-tī'num

Fe-rē'trĭ-ŭs
Fe-rō'nĭ-a
Fer-rē'o-lŭs
Fes-cĕn'nĭ-a
Fĕs-cen-nī'nŭs
Fes-cĕn'nĭ-ŭm
Fēs'u-læ
Fē-tĭ-ā'lēṣ 1
Fī-brē'nŭs
Fī-cē'lĭ-æ
Fī-cŭl'ne-a
Fī-dē'na
Fĭd-e-nā'tēṣ
Fī-dĕn'tĭ-a 1
Fĭd-en-tī'nŭs
Fī'dēṣ
Fī-dĭc'u-læ
Fĭd'ĭ-ŭs
Fĭg'u-lŭs
Fĭm'brĭ-a
Fĭr-mā'nŭs
Fĭr-mĭ-ā'nŭs
Fĭr'mĭ-cŭs
Fĭr'mĭ-ŭs
Flǎc-cĭ-nā'tor
Flǎm'ĭ-nēṣ
Fla-mĭn'ĭ-a
Flǎm-ĭ-nī'nŭs
Fla-mĭn'ĭ-ŭs
Fla-nǎt'ĭ-cŭs
Fla-nō'na
Flā'vĭ-a
Flā-vĭ-ā'nŭs
Flā'vĭ-an
Fla-vī'na
Fla-vĭn'ĭ-ŭs
Flā-vĭ-o-brī'ga
Flā'vĭ-ŭs
Fla-vō'na
Flo-rā'lĭ-a
Flo-rĕn'tĭ-a 1
Flŏr'ence
Flŏr-en-tī'nŭs
Flo-rĕn'tĭ-ŭs
Flō-rĭ-ā'nŭs
Flu-ō'nĭ-a
Fœ'nĭ-ŭs
Fō'lĭ-a
Fŏn-tā'nŭs
Fon-tē'ĭ-a 3
Fon-tē'ĭ-ŭs 3
Fŏn-tĭ-nā'lĭs
Fŏr'mĭ-æ
Fŏr-mĭ-ā'num
Fŏr'mĭ-ō
Fŏr-na-cā'lĭ-a
Fŏr-tū'na
Fŏr-tu-nā'tæ Ĭn'su-læ
Fŏr-tu-nā-tĭ-ā'nŭs 1
Fŏr-tu-nā'tŭs
Fŏr'u-lī
Frǎn'cĭ-a 1
Frĕd-e-rī'cŭs
Frĕd'er-ĭc
Fre-ġē'næ
Fren-tā'nī
Frĭd-e-rī'cŭs
Frĕd'er-ĭc
Frĭd-o-lī'nŭs
Frĭd'o-lĭn

Frĭg'ĭ-dŭs
Frĭ''sĭ-ī 1
Fron-tī'nŭs
Frŭ'sĭ-nō
Fu-cī'na
Fū'cĭ-nŭs
Fŭf-fī''tĭ-ŭs 1
Fŭ'fĭ-ŭs
Fu-gā'lĭ-a
Fŭl-cĭn'ĭ-ŭs
Fŭl-ġĕn'tĭ-ŭs 1
Fŭl-ġĭ-nā'tēṣ
Fŭl-ġĭn'ĭ-a
Fŭl'ġĭ-nŭm
Fŭl-ġī'nŭs
Fŭl'lĭ-nŭm
Fŭl'vĭ-a
Fŭl'vĭ-ŭs
Fŭn-dā'nĭ-ŭs
Fŭn-dā'nŭs
Fŭn'du-lŭs
Fū'rĭ-a
Fū'rĭ-ī
Fu-rī'na
Fū'rĭ-ŭs
Für'nĭ-ŭs
Fŭs-cĭ-cu-lē'nŭs
Fŭs-cī'na
Fŭs-cī'nŭs
Fū'sĭ-a 1
Fū'sĭ-ŭs 1

G.

Gǎb'a-la
Gǎb'a-lēṣ
Gǎb'a-lŭs
Gǎb'a-rŭs
Ga-bā'za
Ga-bē'ne
Gā-bĭ-ē'ne
Gā-bĭ-ē'nŭs
Gā'bĭ-ī
Ga-bī'na
Ga-bĭn-ĭ-ā'nŭs
Ga-bĭn'ĭ-ŭs
Ga-bī'nŭs
Ga-brē'ta Sĭl'va
Gā-brĭ-ē'lĭ-ŭs
Gǎd'a-ra
Ga-dē'nī
Ga-dī'ra
Gǎd-ĭ-tā'num Frē-
  tum
Gǎd-ĭ-tā'nŭs
Gæ-sā'tæ
Gæ-tū'lī
Gæ-tū'lĭ-a
Gæ-tū'lĭ-cŭs
Gā'ĭ-ŭs
Ga-lā'brĭ-ī
Gǎl-ac-tŏph'a-ġī
Gǎl'a-ta
Gǎl'a-tæ
Gǎl-a-tæ'a
Gǎl-a-tē'a
Ga-lā'tĭ-a 1
Gǎl'a-tŏn

Gą-läx'j-ą 1
Găl'bu-lą
Gą-lē'nŭs
Gā'len
Gā-lę-ō'tæ
Gą-lē'rj-ą
Gą-lē-rj-ā'nŭs
Gą-lē'rj-ŭs
Gą-lē'sŭs
Gā'lę-ŭs
Gąl-frī'dus
Gĕof'frey, Jĕf'frey
Găl-i-læ'ą
Gą-lĭn-thj-ā'dj-ą
Gą-lĭn'thj-äs
Gąl-læ'cj-ą 1
Găl'lj-ą
Găl'lj-cā'nŭs
Gąl-lĭç'j-nŭs
Găl'lj-cŭs
Găl-lj-ē'nŭs
Gąl-lī'ną
Găl-lj-nā'rj-ą
Găl'lj-ō
Gąl-lī'tą
Găl'lj-ŭs
Găl-lo-græ'cj-ą 1
Gąl-lō'nj-ŭs
Găm'ą-lą
Gąm-brē'um
Gą-mē'lj-ą
Găn-dą-rī'tæ
Găn'gą-mą
Gąn-gär'j-dæ
Gán'ĝeş
Gąn-ĝē'tjs
Găn-y-mē'dę
Găn-y-mē'dĕş
Găn'y-mēde
Gą-ræ'j-cŭm
Gär'ą-dŭs
Gär-ą-män'tjs
Gár'ą-mäs
Gā-rę-ā'tæ
Gā-rę-äth'y-rą
Gär'j-däs
Gąr-gā'nŭs
Gąr-gā'phj-ą
Gąr-gā'phj-ē
Gär'gą-rą
Gąr-gär'j-dæ
Gär'gą-rŭs
Gąr-ĝē'nŭs
Gąr-ĝĕt'tŭs
Gąr-ĝĭl-j-ā'nŭs
Gąr-ĝĭl'j-ŭs
Gąr-ĝĭt'tj-ŭs
Gąr-gō'nj-ŭs
Gą-rĭl'j-ŭs
Gą-rī'tĕş
Gär'rj-cŭs
Gą-sō'rŭs
Gā'thę-æ
Gā-thę-ā'tąs, *or*
  Gą-thē'ą-tás
Gâu-dĕn'tj-ŭs 1
Gâu-gą-mē'lą
Gâu-lą-nī'tis
Gâu'lŭs, Gâu'lę-ŏn
Gâu'rą-däs

Gâu-rā'nŭs
Gâu'rŭs
Gā'ŭs, *or* Gā'os
Gā'vj-ŭs
Gā-zj-ū'rą
Gą-zō'rŭs
Gĕb-ą-lē'nę
Gę-dĭp'pą
Gę-drō'sī
Gę-drō'sj-ą 1
Gę-gā'nj-ī
Gē'lą
Gę-lā'nor
Gē'las
Gę-läs'j-mŭs
Gę-lā'sj-ŭs 1
Gĕl'bis
Gĕl'du-bą
Gē'lī
Gĕl'lj-ą
Gĕl-lj-ā'nŭs
Gĕl'lj-äs
Gĕl'lj-ŭs
Gē'lō, Gē'lon
Gę-lō'ī
Gę-lō'nĕş, Gę-lō'nī
Gē'los
Gĕm'j-ną
Gĕm'j-nī
Gę-mĭn'j-ŭs
Gĕm'j nŭs
Gĕn'ą-bŭm, *or*
  Gę-nā'bum
Gę-nâu'nī
Gę-nē'sj-ŭs 1
Gę-nē'tæ
Gę-nē'tĕş
Gę-nē'vą
Gĕn'j-sŭs, *or*
  Gĕn'y-sŭs
Gē'nj-ŭs
Gęn-nā'dj-ŭs
Gęn-nā'j-dĕş
Gę-nō'nī
Gĕn-o-vē'fą, *or* -vą
gĕn'ę-viĕve
Gĕn-sę-rī'cŭs
gĕn'ser-ĭc
Gĕn'tj-ŭs 1
Gĕn'u-ą
Gę-nū'cj-ŭs 1
Gĕn'u-sŭs
Gę-nū'tj-ą 1
Gĕn'y-sŭs
Gę-ŏm'o-rī
Gē-o-pŏn'j-cą
Gę-ŏr'ĝj-cą
gĕŭr'ĝics
Gę-ŏr'ĝj-ŭs
gĕŭrĝe
Gĕph-j-rō'tę
Gę-phŷ'rą
Gĕph-y-ræ'ī
Gę-phŷ'rĕş
Gĕp'j-dæ
Gĕr-ą-nē'ą
Gĕr'ą-są
Gę-rē'ą
Gę-rē'nj-ą

Gę-rĕs'tj-cŭs
Gęr-ĝī'thą
Gęr-ĝĭth'j-ŭm
Gęr-gō'vj-ą
Gē'rj-ŏn
Gęr-mā'nj-ą
Gęr-män-j-cī'ą
Gęr-män'j-cŭs
Gęr-mā'nj-ī
Gęr-mā'nŭs
Gęr-mī'nŭs
Gē'ron
Gĕr-on-tē'um
Gę-rŏn'tj-ŭs 1
Gę-rŏs'trą-tŭs
Gęr-trū'dis
Gĕr'trude
Gę-rū'nj-ŭm
Gē'rŭs, *and*
  Gĕr'rhŭs
Gē'ry-ŏn
Gę-rŷ'o-nēş
Gē'rys
Gę-sän'dęr
Gę-sĭth'o-ŭs
Gĕs-o-rī'ą-cŭm
Gęs-sā'tæ
Gē'tą
Gē'tæ
Gę-thŏs'y-nē
Gĕt'j-cŭs
Gę-tū'lj-ą
Gĭd-dę-nē'mę
Gī-găn'tĕş
Gī-gąn-tē'ŭs
Gī'gas
Gī'ĝjs
Gī-gō'nŭs
Gĭl'lō
Gįn-dā'nēş
Gĭn'dēş
Gĭn'ĝe
Gįn-gū'num
Gĭp'pj-ŭs
Gĭs'çhą-lą
Gĭs'cō, *or* Gĭs'gō
Gj-tī'ą-däs
Glā'brj-ō
Glā-dj-ą-tō'rj-ī
Glăn-do-mē'rum
Glăph'y-rą
Glăph'y-ræ
Glăph'y-rŭs
Glâu'cę
Glâu'cj-ą 1
Glâu'cj-äs 1
Glâu'cj-dēş
Glâu-cĭp'pę
Glâu-cĭp'pŭs
Glâu'cjs
Glâu'con
Glâu-cŏn'o-mē
Glâu-cō'pjs
Glâu'cŭs
Glâu-gą-nī'cæ
Glâu'tj-äs 1
Glŏb'u-lŭs
Glŷç'ę-rą
Gly-cē'rj-ŭm
Gly-cē'rj-ŭs

Glŷm'pĕş
Glŷm'pi-cŭs
Gnā'pheūs, Pē'-
  trŭs 5, 6
Gnā'thō 5
Gnā'tj-ą 5, 1
Gnĭ'dos, *or* -dŭs 5
Gnō'sos 5
Gnŏs'sj-ą 5, 1
Gnŏs'sjs 5
Gnŏs'sŭs 5
Gŏb-ą-nĭ''tj-ō 1
Gŏb'ą-rĕş
Gō'bry-äs
Gŏd-ę-frī'dus
Gŏd'frey, Gĕof'frey
Gŏg-ą-rē'nę
Gōl'ĝī
Gŏm'o-rą
Go-nā'tąs
Gŏn'ĝy-lŭs
Go-nī'ą-dĕş
Gŏr-dj-ā'nŭs
Gŏr-dj-ē'um
Gŏr-dj-tā'nŭm
Gŏr-dj-ŭ-cō'mon
Gŏr'dj-ŭs
Gŏr-dj-ŭ-tī'çhus
Gor-dū'nī
Gŏr'gą-sŭs
Gŏr'ĝe
Gŏr'ĝj-äs
Gŏr'ĝj-däs
Gŏr'ĝj-ŏn
Gŏr'go-nĕş
Gor-gō'nj-ą
Gor-gō'nj-ŭs
Gor-gŏph'o-rą
Gor-gō'pąs
Gor-gō'pjs
Gor-gŷth'j-ŏn
Gŏr'tŭ-æ
Gor-tŷ'ną
Gor-tŷn'j-ą
Gŏth-o-frē'dus
Gŏd'frey, Gĕof'frey
Go-thō'nĕş
Grąc-chā'nŭs
Grą-dī'vus
Græ'cī
Græ'cj-ą 1
Græ-cī'nus
Græ-cŏs'tą-sĭs
Græ'cus
Grā'j-ŭs 3
Grą-jŏç'ę-lī
Grą-jū'ĝę-næ
Grā'nę
Grą-nī'cus
Grā'nj-ŭs
Grą-tē'æ Ĭn'sŭ-læ
Grā'tj-ą 1
Grā'tj-æ 1
Grā'ces
Grā-tj-ąn-ŏp'o-lĭs 1
Grā-tj-ā'nŭs 1
Grā'ti-ąn
Grą-tĭd'j-ą
Grą-tĭd-j-ā'nŭs

Grą-tĭd'j-ŭs
Grā'tj-ŏn 2
Grā'tj-ŭs 1
Grā'vj-ī
Grā'vj-ŭs
Grę-ĝĕn'tj-ŭs 1
Grĕg'o-räs
Grę-gō-rj-ā'nŭs
Grę-gō'rj-ŭs
Grĕg'o-ry
Gro-nē'ą
Grŭ'mj-ō
Grų-thŭn'ĝī
Grŷ-nē'um
Grŷ'neūs (*n.*) 6
Grŷ-nē'ŭs (*a.*)
Gry-nī'um
Guąl-tē'rŭs
Wâl'ter
Guĭl-j-ĕl'mŭs, Guĭl-
  lĕl'mŭs, Guĭl-lër'-
  mŭs, *or* Gū-lj-ĕl'-
  mŭs
Wĭl'liam
Gū'neūs 6
Gųn-thē'rŭs, *L.*
Gŷ'ą-rą
Gŷ'ą-reūs 6
Gŷ'ą-rī
Gŷ'ą-rŏs, *and*
  Gŷ'ą-rŭs
Gŷ'as
Gŷ'ēş
Gŷ'ĝe
Gŷ'ĝēş
Gŷl-ą-cē'ą
Gym-nā'sj-ą 1
Gym-nā'sj-ŭm 1
Gym-nē'sj-ą 1
Gym-nē'sj-æ 1
Gym-nē'tĕş
Gym-no-pæ-dī'ą
Gym-nŏs-o-phĭs'tæ
gym-nŏs'o-phĭsts
Gŷ-næ'cę-äs
Gŷn-æ-co-thœ'nąs
Gŷn'dēş
Gyr-tō'ną
Gŷ-thē'um, *or*
  Gŷth'j-ŭm

H.

Hą-drā'num
Hā'drj-ą
Hā-drj-ą-nŏp'o-lĭs
Hā-drj-ā'nī
Hā-drj-ā'nŭs
Hā'dri-ąn
Hā-drj-ăt'j-cŭm
Hăd-rŭ-mē'tum
Hăd-y-lē'um
Hæ-mō'nj-ą
Hæ-mŏn'j-dĕş
Hæm'o-nis 4
Hæ'mus
Hā-ĝi-ŏp-o-lī'tą
Hąg-nág'o-rą

Hag-nī'a-dēs
Ha læ'sa
Ha-lā'la, or A-lā'la
Ha-lē'sus
Hal-cȳ'o-nē
Hal-cȳ'o-neūs 6
Hā'lēs
Ha-lē'sa, or
　Häl'e-sa
Ha-lē'si-ŭs 1
Ha-lē'sus
Hā'li-a, a Nereid.
Ha-lī'a, or Hā'li-a,
　a festival.
Hā-li-ăc'mon
Hā-li-är'tos, or -tus
Hā'li-äs
Hál-i-car-näs'seūs 6
Hăl-i-car-näs'sus
Ha-lī''cy-æ 1
Hā'li eïs
Hál-i-mē'de
Hăl-i-jr rhō'thi-ŭs 1
Häl-i-thër'sus
Ha-lī'um
Hā'li-ŭs
Hál-i-zō'nēs
Hal-mō'nēs
Hăl'my-rïs
Hăl'my-rō'tēs
Ha-lō'a
Ha-lō'ne
Häl-on-nē'sus
Ha-lō'ti a 1
Ha-lō'tus
Hál'y-cŭs
Ha-lȳ''zi-a 1
Häm-a-drȳ'a-dēs
Häm'a-dry-ads
Ha-mā'dry-äs
Häm-ar-tò'lus
Ha-mäx'i-a 1
Ha-mäx'i-tŭs
Häm-ax-ŏb'i-ī
Hamp-säg'o-räs
Hämp'si-cŭs
Hän'ni-bäl
Hän-ni-bäl-li-ā'nus
Här'ca-lō, or
　Cär'tha-lō
Har-mā'ni-a
Här-ma-tē'li-a
Här'ma-tŭs
Här-me-no-pū'lus
Har-mŏd'i-ŭs
Har-mō'ni-a
Har-mŏn'i-dēs
Har-mō'ni-ŭs
Har-mŏs'y-nī
Har-mō'zon
Har-mū'za
Har-pā'gi-a, or
　Här-pa-gī'a
Har-păg'i-dēs
Här'pa-gŭs
Har-pál'i-cē
Har-pā'li-ŏn
Här'pa-lŏs, or -lŭs
Har-păl'y-cŭs
Här'pa-sa

Här'pa-sŭs
Här'po-cräs
Har-pŏc'ra-tēs
Här-po-crā'ti-ŏn 1
Har-pȳ'ia 3
Har-pȳ'iæ 3
Här'pies
Ha-rū'dēs
Has-bȳ'te
Häs'dru-bäl
Ha-tē'ri-ŭs
Hâu'sta-nēs
Hē-âu-tŏn-ti-mo-
　rū'me-nŏs
Hĕb-do mäg'e-tēs
Hĕb'do-mē
Hē'be
Hē'brus
He-bū'dēs
Hĕc'a-bē
Hĕc-a-ër'ģe
Hĕc'a-lē
Hĕc-a-lē'si-a 1
Hĕc-a-mē'de
Hĕc-a-tæ'us
Hĕc'a-tē
Hĕc-a-tē'si-a 1
Hĕc'a-tō
Hĕc-a-to-dō'rus
Hĕc-a-tom-phō'ni-a
Hĕc-a-tŏm'po-lïs
Hĕc-a-ton-nē'sī
Hĕc'u-ba
Hĕç'y-ra
Hĕd'i-la
Hĕd'u-ēs
Hĕd'u-ī
Hĕd'y-lē
Hĕd-y-lē'um, or
　He-dȳl'i-ŭm
Hĕd'y-lŭs
He-dȳm'e-lēs
Hĕd'y-phŏu
He-ģēl'o-chŭs
He-ģē'mon, and
　Hĕģ'e-mon
He-ģĕm'o-nē
Hĕģ-e-sän'dri-däs
Hĕģ-e-sī'a-näx
He-ģē'si-äs 1
Hĕģ-e-sī'o-chŭs
Hĕģ-e-sïn'o-ŭs
Hĕģ-e-sī'nus
Hĕģ-e-sïp'y-lē
Hĕģ-e-sïs'tra-tŭs
He-ģē'tor
Hĕģ-e-tŏr'i-dēs
Hē'ģi-äs
Hē'ģi-ō
Hĕl'a-ra
Hĕl-cē'bus
Hĕl'e-na
He lē'ni-a
Hĕl-e-nī'us
He-lē'nor
Hĕl'e-nŭs
Hē'le-ŏn
He-lī'a-dēs
Hĕl-i-cā'on

Hĕl'i-cē
Hĕl'i-cŏn
Hĕl-i-co-nī'a-dēs
Hĕl-i-cō'nis
Hĕl-i-mē'na
Hĕl'i-mŭs
He-lī'o-clēs
Hē-li-o-dō'rus
Hē-li-o-găb'a-lŭs, or
　Hē-li-o-ga-bā'lus
Hē-li-ŏp'o-lïs
Hē'li-ŏs
Hē'li-ŭs
Hel-lā'di-ŭs
Hĕl-la nī'ce
Hĕl-la nī'cus, some-
　times Hel-lán'i-
　cŭs
Hĕl-la-nŏc'ra-tēs
Hĕl-la-nŏd'i-cæ
Hĕl'le
Hel-lē'nēs
Hĕl-le-nŏp'o-lïs
Hel-lō'pi-a
Hel-lō'ti-a 1
Hel-lō'tis
He-lō'ris
He-lō'rum
He-lō'rus
He-lō'tæ
He-lō'tēs
Hel-pïd'i-ŭs
Hel-vē'ti-a 1
Hel-vē'ti-ī 1
Hel-vē'tum
Hĕl'vi-a
Hel-vïd'i-ŭs
Hĕl'vi-ī
Hel-vī'na
Hĕl'vi-ŭs
Hĕl'y-mŭs
He-mā'thi-ŏn
Hĕm-e rŏs-co pī'um
He-mïç'y-nēs
He-mïth'e-a
He-mō'dus
He-mō'na
Hĕn'e-tī
He-nī'o-chē
Hē-ni-o-chī'a
He nī'o-chŭs
Hen-rī'cus
Hĕn'ry
He-phæs'ti-a, city.
Hĕph-æs-tī'a, festi-
　val.
Hĕph-æs-tī'a-dēs
He-phæs'ti-ī 4
He-phæs'ti-ō 4
He-phæs'ti-ŏn 2, 4
He-phæs'tion 2, 4
He-phæs'tus 4
Hep-tăn'o-mïs
Hĕp-ta-phō'nos
Hep-tăp'o-lïs
Hep-tăp'o-rŭs
Hĕp-tăp'y-lŏs
Hĕp-ta-ȳd'a-ta
Hĕr'a-clás
Hĕr-a-clē'a

He-răc'le-ŏn
He-răc-le-ō'nas
He-răc-le-ō'tēs
Hĕr'a-clēs
Hĕr-a-clē'um
He-răc-li-ā'nus
Hĕr-a-clī'dæ
Hĕr-a-clī'dēs
Hĕr-a-clī'dis
Hĕr-a-clī'tus
Hĕr-a-clī'us
He-ræ'eūs 6
Her-bē'sos, or
　Her-bē'sus
Hĕr'bi-ta
Her-cē'us
Hĕr-cu-lā'ne-ŭm
Hĕr-cu-lā'nus
Hĕr'cu-lēs
Her-cū'le-ŭm
Her-cū'le-ŭs
Her-cȳ'na
Her-cȳn'i-a
Her-cȳn'i-ŭs
Her-dō'ni-a
Her-dō'ni-ŭs
Hē're-äs
Hĕr'i-lŭs
Hē'ri-ŭs, or
　He-rī'us
Hĕr'ma-chŭs, prop-
　erly Her-mär'-
　chus
Hĕr'mæ
Her-mæ'um
Her-măg'o-räs
Her-măn'di-ca
Her-ma-nū'bis
Her-mäph-ro-dī'tus
Her-mär'chus
Hĕr'me-äs, or
　Hĕr'mēs
Her-mē'as, or
　Her-mī'as
Hĕr'me-rŏs
Hĕr'mēs
Hĕr-me-sī'a-näx
Her-mī'as, and
　Hĕr'mi-äs
Her-mïn'i-ŭs
Her-mī'nus
Her-mī'o-nē
Hĕr-mi-o-nē'a, or
　Hĕr-mi-o-nī'a
Hĕr-mi-ŏn'i-cŭs
　Sī'nus
Her-mī'o-nïs
Her-mŏc're-ŏn
Hĕr-mo-dō'rus
Her-mo-ģē-ni-ā'nus
Hĕr-mŏģ'e-nēs
Hĕr-mo-lā'us
Her-mō'näx
Her-mŏp'o-lïs
Hĕr-mo-tī'mus
Her-mŭn'du-rī, or
　Her-mun-dū'rī
Hĕr'ni-cī
He-rō'dēs
Hĕr'od

He-rō-di-ā'nus
He-rō'di-an
He-rŏd'i-cŭs
Hĕr-o-dī'um
Hĕr-o-dō'rus
He-rŏd'o-tŭs
Hĕr-o-dū'lus
He-rō'ēs
He-rō'īs
Hē-ro-ŏp'o-lïs
He-rŏph'i-lŭs
He-rŏs'tra-tŭs
Hĕr'se
Her-sïl'i-a
Hĕr'u-lī
Hĕr'u-lŭs
He-sī'o-dŭs
Hē'si-od
He-sī'o-na, or nĕ
He-sī'o-nēs
Hĕs-pē'ri-a
Hĕs-pĕr'i-dēs
Hĕs-pē'ri-ē
Hĕs'pe-rïs
Hĕs-pe-rī'tæ
Hĕs-pē'ri-ŭs
Hĕs-pe-rŭ'gō
Hĕs'pe-rŭs
Hĕs'ti-a
Hĕs-ti-æ-ō'tis
Hĕs-ti-ō'nēs
He-sȳch'i-ŭs
He-trïc'u-lŭm
He-trŭ'ri-a
Hex-ăp'y-lŭm
Hī-bē'ri-a
Hī-bër'ni-a
Hī-bē'rus
Hī-cē'si-ŭs 1
Hïc-e-tā'on
Hïç'e-täs
Hī-däs'me-nŭs
Hïd'ri-eūs 6
Hī'e-ra
Hī-e-ra-cō'me
Hī-e-rā'con
Hī-e-răm'e-nēs
Hī-e-răp'o-lïs
Hī'e-räs
Hī'e-räx
Hī'e-rī
Hī ĕr'i-chŭs
Jĕr'i-chō, formerly
　Hī-ĕr'i-chō
Hī'e-rō
Hī-e-ro-cæs-a-rē'a
Hī-e-ro-cē'pi-a
Hī-e-ro-cē'pis
Hī-e-ro-cē'rix
Hī-ĕr'o-clēs
Hī-e-ro dū'lum
Hī-e-rom-nē'mon
Hī-e-ro-nē'sos
Hī-e-rŏn'i-ca, Lĕx
Hī-e-ro-nī'cæ
Hī-e-ro-nī'cēs
Hī-e-rŏn'i-cŭs (a.)
Hī-e-rŏn'y mŭs
Jĕr'ome, formerly
　Hī'e-rōme

Hī-ẹ-rọ-sŏl'y-mạ
Jẹ-ru'sạ-lĕm, for-
  merly Hī-ẹ-ru'sạ-
  lĕm
Hī-ẹ-rō'thẹ-ŭs
Hī'ẹ-rŭs
Hī-ġī'nụs
Hịg-nā'tị-ạ, or
  Ĕg-nā'tị-ạ Vī'ạ 1
Hĭl-ạ-ī'rạ
Hī-lā'rị-ạ
Hī-lā-rị-ā'nụs
Hī-lā'rị-ŭs
Hĭl'ạ-ry
Hĭl'ạ-rŭs
Hĭm-ạn-tŏp'ọ-dēṣ
Hĭm'ẹ-rạ
Hī-mē'rị-ŭs
Hĭm'ẹ-rŭs
Hī-phĭn'ọ-ŭs
Hịp-pág'ọ-răs
Hịp-pág'rẹ-tŭs
Hịp-pál'cị-mŭs
Hịp-pär'chị-ạ
Hịp-pär'chụs
Hĭp-pạ-rī'nụs
Hịp-pā'rị-ŏn
Hĭp'pạ-rịs
Hịp-pás'ị-dēṣ
Hĭp'pạ-sŭs
Hĭp-pẹ-mŏl'ġī
Hĭp'pẹūs 6
Hĭp'pị-ạ
Hĭp'pị-ŭs
Hịp-pŏb'ọ-tŭs
Hĭp-pọ-cẹn-tâu'rī
Hịp-pọ-clī'dēṣ
Hĭp'pọ-clŭs
Hịp-pŏc'ọ-ŏn
Hĭp-pọ-cọ-rȳs'tēṣ
Hịp-pŏc'rạ-tēṣ
Hịp-pŏc-rạ-tī'ạ, or
  Hịp-pŏc-rạ-tē'ạ
Hịp-pọ-crē'nẹ
Hĭp'pọ-crēne
Hịp-pŏd'ạ-măs
Hịp-pŏd-ạ-mī'ạ
Hịp-pŏd'ạ-mŭs
Hịp-pŏd'ị-cē
Hịp-pŏd'rọ-mŭs
Hĭp'pọ-lạ
Hịp-pŏl'ọ-chŭs
Hịp-pŏl'y-tē
Hịp-pŏm'ạ-chŭs
Hịp-pŏm'ẹ-dŏn
Hịp-pŏm-ẹ-dū'sạ
Hịp-pŏm'ẹ-nē
Hịp-pŏm'ẹ-nēṣ
Hịp-pō'nạ
Hịp-pō'năx
Hịp-pō-nị-ā'tēṣ
Hĭp-pọ-nī'cụs
Hĭp-pọ-nī'tịs
Hịp-pō'nị-ŭm
Hịp-pŏn'ọ-ŭs
Hịp-pŏp'ọ-dēṣ
Hịp-pŏs'trạ-tŭs
Hịp-pŏt'ạ-dēṣ
Hĭp'pọ-tăs
Hĭp'pọ-tēṣ

Hịp-pŏth'ọ-ē
Hịp-pŏth'ọ-ŏn
Hịp-pŏth-ọ-ŏn'tịs
Hịp-pŏth'ọ-ŏs, or
Hịp-pŏth'ọ-ŭs
Hịp-pō'tị-ŏn 2
Hịp-pọ-tŏx'ọ-tæ
Hịp-pū'rịs
Hĭp'sị-dēṣ
Hịr-pī'nī
Hịr-pī'nụs
Hĭr'tị-ạ 1
Hĭr'tị-ŭs 1
Hĭr-tụ-lē'ị-ŭs 3
Hĭs'pạ-lạ
Hĭs'pạ-lĭs
Hịs-pā'nị-ạ
Hịs-pā'nụs
Hịs-tăs'pēṣ
Hĭs-tị-æ'ạ
Hĭs-tị-æ-ō'tịs
Hĭs'tọ-rĭs
Hĭs'trị-ạ
Hō'dị-ŭs
Hœ'dụs
Họl-mō'nēṣ
Hŏl'ọ-crŏn, or
  Ŏl'ọ-crŭs
Họ-mĕr'ị-dæ
Hŏm-ẹ-rī'tæ [ġēṣ
Họ-mē-rọ-mạs-tī'-
Hŏm-ẹ-rŏn'ị-dæ
Họ-mē'rụs
Hō'mẹr
Họ-mī'læ, L.
Hŏm'ọ-lē
Họ-mō'lị-ŭm
Hŏm-ọ-lō'ị-dēṣ
Họ-mŏn-ạ-dĕn'sēṣ
Hŏm-ọ-tī'mī
Hō'nŏr
Hŏn-ọ-rā'tụs
Họ-nō'rị-ạ
Hŏn-ọ-rī'ạ-dēṣ
Họ-nō'rị-ŭs
Họp-lē'tēṣ
Hŏp'lẹūs 6
Họp-lī'tæ
Hŏr-ạ-cī'tæ
Hō'ræ
Họ-rā'tị-ạ 1
Họ-rā'tị-ŭs 1
Hŏr'ạce
Họ-rā'tụs
Hŏr'cị-ăs 1
Hŏr-ọ-lō'ġị-ŭm
Hŏr'tạ-lŭs
Họr-tā'nụm
Họr-tĕn'sị-ạ 1
Họr-tĕn'sị-ŭs 1
Họr-tī'nụs (a.)
Họr-tō'nạ, or
  Ọr-tō'nạ
Họ-sĭd'ị-ŭs 1
Fŏ'sị-ŭs 1
Hŏs-pị-tā'lịs
Họs-tī'lị-ạ
Họs-tĭl-ị-ā'nụs
Họs-tĭl'ị-ŭs
Hŏs'tị-ŭs

Hụm-frē'dụs. or
  Hụm-frī'dụs
Hŭm'phrẹy
Hŭn-nẹ-rī'cụs
Hŭn'nẹr-ĭc
Hụn-nī'ạ-dēṣ
Hȳ-ạ-cĭn'thị-ạ
Hȳ'ạ-dēṣ
Hȳ'ạ-lạ
Hȳ-ạ-mē'ạ, or
  Hy-ā'mị-ạ
Hȳ-ạm-pē'ạ
Hȳ-ăm'pọ-lĭs
Hȳ-ăn'thēṣ
Hȳ-ạ-pē'ạ
Hȳ-ạr-bī'tạ
Hy̆b'ẹ-lạ
Hȳ-bër'nị-ạ
Hy̆b'lạ
Hy̆b'rẹ-ăs
Hy̆b-rị-ā'nēṣ
Hy̆b'rị-ăs
Hy̆c'cạ-rạ
Hȳ'dạ, and Hȳ'dẹ
Hy̆d'ạ-rạ
Hȳ-dăs'pēṣ
Hȳ'drạ
Hȳ-drā'mị-ạ
Hȳ-drạ-ō'tēṣ
Hy̆d'rẹ-ạ
Hȳ-drē'lụs
Hȳ-drŏch'ọ-ŭs
Hȳ-drọ-phō'rị-ạ
Hȳ'drụs
Hȳ-drŭ'sạ
Hȳ'ẹ-lē
Hȳ-ġē'ạ
Hȳ-ġẹ-ī'ạ
Hȳ-ġī'ạ-nạ
Hȳ-ġī'nụs
Hȳ-lăç'ị-dēṣ
Hȳ'læ
Hȳ'lēṣ
Hȳ'lẹūs 6
Hȳ-lē'ụs, or
  Hȳ-læ'ụs
Hy̆l'ị-ăs
Hy̆l'ị-cạ, or -cē
Hyl-lā'ị-cŭs
Hy̆l'lị-cŭs
Hȳ-lŏn'ọ-mē
Hy̆m'ẹ-ăs
Hȳ-ō'pẹ
Hȳ-pæ'sị-ạ 1
Hy̆p'ạ-nĭs
Hy̆p-ạ-rī'nụs
Hy̆p'ạ-sĭs
Hy̆p'ạ-tạ
Hȳ-pā'tēṣ
Hy̆p'ạ-thạ
Hȳ-pā'tị-ạ 1
Hȳ-pā'tị-ŭs 1
Hy̆p'ạ-tŭs
Hȳ-pē'nọr
Hy̆p-ẹ-rā'ọn
Hȳ-për'bạ-tŭs
Hȳ-për'bị-ŭs
Hȳ-për'bọ-lŭs
Hy̆p-ẹr-bō'rẹ-ī
Hy̆p-ẹ-rē'ạ

Hy̆p-ẹ-rē'chị-ŭs
Hy̆p-ẹ-rē'nọr
Hy̆p-ẹ-rī'ạ
Hy̆p-ẹ-rē'sị-ạ 1
Hy̆p-ẹ-rī'dēṣ
Hy̆p-ẹ-rī'ọn
Hȳ-pē'rị-ọn
Hy̆p-ẹrm-nĕs'trạ
Hȳ-pĕr'ọ-chē
Hy̆p-ẹ-rŏch'ị-dēṣ
Hȳ-pĕr'ọ-chŭs
Hy̆p-ẹ-tā'ọn
Hy̆ph-ạn-tē'ọn
Hy̆ph'ạ-sĭs
Hȳ-pĭr'ọ-chŭs
Hy̆p-ọ-thē'bạ
Hy̆p-ọ-thē'cæ
Hyp-sē'ạ
Hyp-sē'lạ, or -lịs
Hyp-sē'nọr
Hy̆p'sẹūs 6
Hy̆p'sị-clēṣ
Hy̆p-sị-crạ-tē'ạ
Hyp-sĭc'rạ-tēṣ
Hyr-cā'nị-ạ
Hyr-cā'nụm Mā'rẹ
Hyr-cā'nụs
Hy̆r'ị-ạ
Hy̆r'ị-ẹūs 6
Hy̆r'ị-ŭm
Hyr-mī'nạ
Hyr-nē'thọ
Hyr-nīth'ị-ŭm
Hyr-tăç'ị-dēṣ
Hy̆r-tạ-cī'nạ
Hy̆r'tạ-cŭs
Hy̆''sị-ạ, or -æ 1
Hys-tăs'pēṣ
Hy̆s-tị-ē'ụs

I.

I-ăc'chụs
I'ạ-chŏn
I-ā'dẹr
I-ăd'ẹ-rạ
I-ăl'ẹ-mŭs
I-ăl'mẹ-nŭs
I-ăl'y-sŭs
I-ăm'bẹ
I-ăm'blị-chŭs
I-ạm-bū'lụs
I-ăm'ẹ-nŭs
I-ăm'ị-dæ
I'ạ-mŭs
I-ạ-nī'rạ
I-ăn'thẹ
I-ăn'thịs
I-ā'ọn
I-ā'ọ-nēṣ
I-ạ-pĕt'ị-dēṣ
I-ạ-pĕt-ị-ŏn'ị-dēṣ
I-ăp'ẹ-tŭs
I-ā'pịs
I-ăp'ọ-dēṣ
I-ăp'y-dēṣ
I-ạ-py̆d'ị-ạ
I-ăp'y-ġēṣ, or

I-ạ-py̆'ġēṣ
I-ạ-py̆ġ'ị-ạ
I-ā'pyx
I-är'bạ
I-ạr-bī'tạ
I-är'chạs
I-är'dạ-nŭs
I-ăs'ị-dēṣ
I-ā'sị-ŏn 2
I-ā'sị-ŭs 1
I'ạ-sĭs
I-ā'sọn
I-ạ-sŏn'ị-dēṣ
I'ạ-sŭs
I-ạx-ăm'ạ-tæ
I-ạx-är'tæ
I-ăx'ạr-tēṣ
I-ăz'y-ġēṣ
I-ā'zyx
I-bē'rī
I-bē'rị-ạ
Ib-ẹ-rī'nạ
I-bē'rụs
Ib'y-cŭs
I-cā'rị-ạ
I-cā'rị-ŭs
Ic'ạ-rŭs
Ic'cị-ŭs 1
Iç'ẹ-lŭs
I-cē'nī
Iç'ẹ-tăs
Iċh-nŏb'ạ-tēṣ
Iċh-nū'sạ
Iċh-ọ-nū'phịs
Iċh'thys
I-cĭl'ị-ŭs
I''cị-ŭs 1
I-cō'nị-ŭm
I-cō'sị-ŭm 1
Ic-tị-mŭ'lī
Ic-tī'nụs
I-dā'cị-ŭs 1
I-dæ'ạ
I-dā'lị-ạ
I-dā'lị-ē
Id'ạ-lĭs
I-dā'lị-ŭm
Id'ạ-lŭs
I-där'nēṣ
I-dā'tị-ŭs 1
I'dẹ
Id'ẹ-ạ
I-dē'rạ
I-dĭs-tạ-vī'sụs
I-dĭt-ạ-rī'sụs
I-dŏm'ẹ-nē
I-dŏm'ẹ-nẹūs 6
I-dō'thẹ-ē
Id'rị-ẹūs 6 *
I'drụs
I-dū'bẹ-dạ
I-dū'mẹ
Id-u-mē'ạ
I-dy̆'ị-ạ 3
I-ër'nẹ
I-ē'tæ, and I'ẹ-tæ
I-ē'tạs
I-ġē'nī, or I-cē'nī
I-ġĭl'ị-ŭm
Ig-nā'tị-ŭs 1

Ig-nē'tēş
Ig-u-vī'nī
Ī-gū'vį-ŭm
Īl-ạ-ī'rạ
Īl-ạ-ī'rī
Īl-ẹ-ā'tēş
Īl-ẹr-cā'ọ-nēş
Ī-lẽr'dēş
Īl-ẹr-gā'ọ-nēş
Ị-lẽr'ġẹ-tæ, *Strabo.*
Īl-ẹr-ġẽ'tēş
Ī-lẽr'tēş
Ī'leūs 6
Īl'į-ạ
Ị-lǐ'ạ-cī Lū'dī
Ị-lǐ'ạ-cŭs
Ị-lǐ'ạ-dēş
Īl'į-ăs
Īl'į-cī
Īl'į-ŏn
Ị-lǐ'ọ-nạ
Ị-lǐ'ọ-neūs 6
Īl'į-ŏs
Īl'į-pạ
Īl-į-thȳ'įạ 3
Īl'į-ŭm, *or* Īl'į-ŏn
Īl-lǐb'ạ-nŭs
Īl-lǐb'ẹ-rǐs
Īl-lǐp'u-lạ
Īl-lį-tür'ġis
Īl-lȳr'į-cŭm
Īl-lȳr'į-cŭs Sī'nus
Īl'ly-rǐs
Īl-lȳr'į-ạ
Īl-lȳr'į-ŭm
Īl-lȳr'į-ŭs
Īl-ur-ġẽ'ạ
Il-vā'tēş
Ī-lȳr'ġis
Ī-măn-u-ĕn'tį-ŭs 1
Ī-mā'ọn
Īm'ạ-ŭs, *or* Į-mā'ŭs
Īm'bạ-rŭs
Įm-brăs'į-dēş
Īm'brạ-sŭs
Īm'breūs 6
Īm'brį-ŭs
Įm-brǐv'į-ŭm
Īn'ạ-chī
Ī-nā'chį-ạ
Ī-năch'į-dēş
Īn'ạ-chǐs
Ī-nā'chį-ŭm
Īn'ạ-çhŭs
Ī-năm'ạ-mēş
Ī-năr'į-mē
Īn'ạ-rŭs
Īn-cį-tā'tus
Īn'dį-ạ
Īn'dį-cŭs
Īn-dīġ'ẹ-tēş, *gods.*
Īn-dį-ġẽ'tēş, *a peo-*
Īn'fẹ-rī   [*ple.*
Įn-gæv'ọ-nēş 4, *or*
  Īn-gæ-vō'nēş
Īn-guį-ọ-mē'rus
Īn-nē'sạ
Īn-nọ-cĕn'tį-ŭs 1
Ī-nō'ạ
Ī-nō'pus

Ī-nō'ŭs
Įn-stăn'tį-ŭs 1
Īn'su-brēş
Įn-sū'brį-ạ
Īn-tẹ-mē'lį-ŭm
Īn-tẹr-cā'tį-ạ 1
Īn'u-ŭs
Īn'y-cŭm, *or* -cŭs,
  Į-nȳ'cus
Į-ŏb'ạ-tēş, *and*
  Jŏb'ạ-tēş
Ī'ọ-bēş
Ī-ŏd-ạ-mī'ạ
Ī-ọ-lā'į-ạ 3
Ī'ọ-lăs, *or* Ī-ọ-lā'ŭs
Ī-ŏl'chọs
Ī'ọ-lē
Ī'ọ-nē, *a Nereid.*
Ī-ō'nẹ, *a city.*
Ī-ō'nēş
Ī-ō'nį-ạ
Ī-ŏn'į-cŭs
Ī-ō'pạs
Ī'ọ-pē
Ī'ọ-phŏn
Īph'į-ăs
Īph'į-clēş, *or*
  Į-phī'clēş
Īph'į-clŭs, *or*
  Į-phī'clus
Ī-phīc'rạ-tēş
Īph-į-crăt'į-dēş
Ī-phīd'ạ-măs
Īph-į-dẹ-mī'ạ
Īph-į-ġẹ-nī'ạ
Īph-į-mẹ-dī'ạ
Ī-phīm'ẹ-dŏn
Ī-phīn'ọ-ē
Ī-phīn'ọ-ŭs
Ī'phįs
Ī-phǐt'į-ŏn 2
Īph'į-tŭs
Īph-thī'mẹ
Īp-sē'ạ
Ī-rā'įs, *L.*
Īr-ạ-phį-ō'tēş
Īr'ạ-sạ
Ī-rē'nẹ
Īr-ẹ-nŏp'ọ-lǐs
Įr-pī'nus
Ī-sā'cus
Īs'ạ-dăs
Ī-sæ'us
Ī-săg'ọ-răs
Ī-săl'cēş
Īs'ạ-mŭs
Ī-sā'nọr
Ī-sā'pįs
Īs'ạ-rạ
Īs'ạ-rŭs
Ī-sâu'rį-ạ
Ī-sâu'rį-cŭs
Ī-sâu'rus
Īs-çhăg'ọ-răs
Īs-çhē'nį-ạ
Īs'çhẹ-nŭs
Īs-çhọ-lā'ŭs
Įs-çhŏm'ạ-çhē
Įs-çhŏm'ạ-çhŭs

Īs-chŏp'ọ-lǐs
Įs-çhȳ'rạs, *L.*
Īs-dẹ-ġër'dēş
Ī·sē'ạ
Ī-sē'pus
Į-sī'ạ
Į-sī'ạ-cī
Į-sī'ạ-cŭs
Įs-į-dō'rus
Is'i-dōre
Ī-sǐg'ọ-nŭs
Īs-mạ-ē'lạ
Īs'mạ-rŭs
Īs-mē'nẹ
Īs-mē'nį-ăs
Īs-mĕn'į-dēş
Īs-mē'nus
Ī-sŏc'rạ-tēş
Īs-sē'dọn
Īs-sĕd'ọ-nēş
Īs'sį cŭs
Īs-tæv'ọ-nēş 4, *or*
  Īs-tæ-vō'nēş
Īst'hmį-ŭs
Īs-tį-æ-ō'tįs, *prop-*
  erly Hīs-tį-æ-ō'tįs
Įs-tō'nẹ
Īs'trį-ạ
Īs-trŏp'ọ-lǐs
Ī-tā'lį-ạ
Ĭt'ạ-ly
Ī-tăl'į-cạ
Ī-tăl'į-cŭs
Īt'ạ-lŭs
Īt'ẹ-ạ
Ī-tĕm'ạ-lēş
Īth'ạ-cạ
Ī-thē'mọn
Ī-thŏb'ạ-lŭs
Īth-ọ-mā'tạs
Ī-thō'mẹ
Ī-thō'mus
Ī-thō'nẹ
Ī-tō'nį-ạ
Ī-tō'nus
Ī-tū'nạ, *or* Īt'u-nạ
Ī-tū'rį-ŭs
Īt'y-lŭs
Ī-ū'lįs
Ī-ū'lus
Įx-ĭb'ạ-tæ
Įx-ī'ọn
Īx-į-ŏn'į-dēş

J.

Jăc-cẹ-tā'nī
Jạ-cō'bus
Jāmeş
Jăd'ẹ-rạ
Jăl'y-sŭs
Jăm'nį-ạ, *or*
  Jam-nī'ạ
Jạ-nīc'u-lŭm
Jăn-ọ-pū'lus
Jăn-u-ā'rį-ŭs
Jạ-pĕt'į-dēş
Jăp'ẹ-tŭs

Jạ-sō'nį-ŭm
Jăv-ọ-lē'nus
Jăx-ăm'ạ-tæ
Jăz'y-ġēş
Jĕn'y-sŭs
Jẹ-rō'mus
Jẹ-rŏn'y-mŭs
Jọ-ăn'nēş, *or*
  Jọ-hăn'nēş
Jŏhn
Jŏb'ạ-tēş
Jọr-dā'nēş, *and*
  Jör'dạ-nēş
Jọ-sē'phus
Jọ-tăp'ạ-tạ
Jŏt'ạ-pē
Jō-vį-ā'nus
Jŏ'vi-ạn
Jọ-vĭn-į-ā'nus
Jọ-vĭn'i-ạn
Jọ-vī'nus
Jū-dạ-cǐl'į-ŭs
Ju-dæ'ạ
Ju-gā'lįs
Ju-gā'rį-ŭs
Jū'gu-læ
Jū-gur-thī'nus
Jū'lį-ạ
Ju-lī'ạ-cŭm
Ju-lī'ạ dēş
Jū-lį-ā'nus
Jū'li-ạn
Jū'lį-ī
Jū-lį-ŏb'ọ-nạ
Jū-lį-ọ-brī'gạ
Jū-lį-ŏm'ạ-gŭs
Jū-lį-ŏp'ọ-lǐs
Jū'lį-ŭs Cæ'şar
Jū'nį-ạ
Ju-nī'ạ-dēş
Ju-nĭl'į-ŭs
Jū'nį-ŭs
Jū-nọ-nā'lį-ạ
Ju-nō'nēş
Ju-nō'nį-ạ
Ju-nō'nįs
Jū-nọ-pū'lus
Jū'pį-tẹr
Jus-tī'nạ
Jus-tĭn-į-ā'nus
Jus-tĭn'i-ạn
Jus-tī'nus
Jŭs'tin
Jus-tĭ''tį-ạ 1
Jū-vẹ-nā'lįs
Jū've-nạl
Jū-vẹn-tī'nus
Ju-vĕn'tį-ŭs 1

L.

Lăb'ạ-næ Ā'quæ
Lăb'ạ-rǐs
Lăb'ạ-rŭm
Lăb'ạ-rŭs
Lăb'dạ-cŭs
Lăb'dạ-lŏn
Lā-bẹ-ā'tæ, *or* -tēş

Lā-bẹ-ā'tįs
Lā'bẹ-ō
Lạ-bē'rį-ŭs
Lạ-bē'rus
Lăb-į-cā'nạ
Lạ±bī'cī
Lạ-bī'cus
Lā-bį-ē'nus
Lăb-į-nē'tus
Lạ-bō'bį-ŭs
Lăb-ọ-rī'nī Căm'pī
Lạ-bō'tạs, *man.*
Lăb'ọ-tăs, *river.*
Lạ-brăn'deūs 6
Lā'brăx
Lā'brọn
Lạ-bȳ'cạs
Lăb-y-nē'tus
Lăb-y-rǐn'thus
Lăc-ạ-nī'tįs
Lăç-ẹ-dæ'mọn
Lăç-ẹ-dæm'ọ-nēş 4
Lăç-ẹ-dẹ-mō'ni-ạnş
Lăç-ẹ-dæ-mŏn'į cŭs
Lăç-ẹ-dæ-mō'nį-ī
Lạ-cē'dạs
Lăç-ẹ-dẹ-mō'nį-ŭs
Lăç-ẹ-rē'ạ, *or* -rī'ạ
Lăç-ẹ-tā'nī
Lăç-ẹ-tā'nį-ạ
Lạ-çhā'nį-ŭs
Lăch'ạ-rēş
Lā'chēş
Lăch'ẹ-sǐs
Lạ-çhī'sạ
Lăç'į-dăs
Lạ-cī'dēş
Lạ-cĭn'į-ạ
Lạ-cĭn-į-ĕn'sēş
Lạ-cĭn'į-ŭs
Lạ-cō'nēş
Lạ-cō'nį-ạ, *and*
  Lạ-cŏn'į-cạ
Lăc'rạ-tēş
Lăc-rạ-tī'dēş
Lăc'rį-nēş
Lạc-tăn'tį-ŭs 1
Lạ-cȳ'dēş
Lā'dẹ
Lā'dēş
Lăd-ọ-cē'ạ
Lạ-ē'ạ
Læ'cạ
Læ'lăps
Læ'lį-ạ
Læ-lį-ā'nus
Læ'lį-ŭs
Læ'nạ, *and*
  Lẹ-æ'nạ
Læ'nẹ-ŭs
Læ'nį-ŭs
Læ'pạ Măg'nạ
Lạ-ër'tēş
Lā-ẹr-tī'ạ-dēş
Lạ-ẽr'tį-ŭs 1
Læs-pō'dį-ăs 2
Læs-trȳ'gọn 2
Læs-trȳg'ọ-nēş 2
Læ'tạ
Læ-tī''tį-ạ 1

Læ-tō'rĭ-ạ
Læ-tō'rĭ-ŭs
Læ'tụs
Læ'vī
Læ·vī'nạ
Læ·vī'nụs
Læ'vĭ-ŭs
Lạ-gā'rĭ-ạ
Lā'ġĭ-ạ
Lăġ'ĭ-dēṣ
Lăġ-ĭ-nī'ạ, and
  Lạ-gĭn'ĭ-ạ
Lăg'ọ-rās
Lạ-gū'sạ
Lạ-gȳ'rạ, or
  Lăg'y-rạ
Lạ-ī'ạ-dēṣ
Lā'ĭ-ás 3
Lā'ĭs
Lā'ĭ-ŭs 3
Lăl'ạ-gē
Lăl-ẹ-tā'nĭ-ạ
Lăm'ạ-çhŭs
Lạm-bē'çạ
Lạm-bē'sẹ
Lạm-brā'nī
Lăm'ẹ-dŏn
Lạ-mē'tụs
Lā'mĭ-ạ
Lạ-mī'ạ-cŭm Bĕl'-
  lum
Lā'mĭ-æ
Lā'mĭ-ás, Æ'lĭ-ŭs
Lạ-mī'rụs
Lạ-mō'tĭs
Lạm-pā'dĭ-ō
Lạm-pā'dĭ-ŭs
Lăm-pẹ-tī'ạ, city.
Lạm-pē'tĭ-ạ 1, wo-
  man.
Lạm-pē'tĭ-ē 1
Lạm-pē'ụs, and
  Lạm-pī'ạ
Lăm'pĭ-dō
Lăm-pọ-nē'ạ
Lăm-pō'nĭ-ạ, or
  Lăm-pọ-nī'ạ
Lạm-pō'nĭ-ŭs
Lăm'prĭ-ás
Lạm-prĭd'ĭ-ŭs
Lăm'prọ-clēṣ
Lămp'sạ-cŏs, or
  Lămp'sạ-cŭs
Lạmp-tē'rĭ-ạ
Lăm'y-rŏs
Lăm'y-rŭs
Lạ-nā'tụs
Lạn-cē'ạ, or -cī'ạ,
  fountain.
Lăn'cĭ-ạ 1, town.
Lăn'dĭ-ạ
Lăn'gạ-rŭs
Lạn-ġī'ạ
Lạ-nī'cẹ
Lạ-nū'vĭ-ŭm
Lā-ọ-bŏ'tạs
Lạ-ŏc'ọ-ŏn
Lạ-ŏd-ạ-mās
Lạ-ŏd-ạ-mī'ạ
Lạ-ŏd'ĭ-cẹ

Lạ-ŏd-ĭ-cē'ạ
Lạ-ŏd'ọ-cŭs
Lạ-ŏg'ọ-nŭs
Lạ-ŏg'ọ-räs
Lạ-ŏg'ọ-rē
Lạ-ŏm-ẹ-dī'ạ
Lạ-ŏm'ẹ-dŏn
Lạ-ŏm-ẹ-dọn-tē'-
  ụs (a.) [dæ
Lạ-ŏm-ẹ-dọn-tĭ'ạ-
Lạ-ŏm-ẹ-dọn-tĭ'ạ-
Lā-ọ-nī'cus [dēṣ
Lạ-ŏn'ọ-mē
Lạ-ŏn-ọ-mē'nẹ
Lạ-ŏth'ọ-ē
Lā'ọ-ŭs
Lăp'ạ-thŭs
Lạ-pē'thŭs
Lā'phrĭ-ạ
Lạ-phȳs'tĭ-ŭm
Lạ-pĭd'ẹ-ī
Lạ-pĭd'ẹ-ŭs
Lăp'ĭ-thæ
Lăp'ĭ-thō
Lăp'ĭ-thŭs
Lăr-ẹn-tā'lĭ-ạ
Lạ-rĕn'tĭ-ạ 1, and
  Lâu-rĕn'tĭ-ạ 1
Lạ-rī'dēṣ
Lạ-rī'nạ
Lạ-rī'nụm
Lā'rĭ-ŭs
Lạ-rŏ'nĭ-ŭs
Lär'tĭ-ŭs 1
Lär-tọ-læ-ē'tæ
Lạ-rȳ''ṣĭ-ŭm 1
Lăs'cạ-rĭs
Lăs'sĭ-ạ 1
Lăs'thẹ-nēṣ
Lạs-thē'nĭ-ạ, or
  Lăs-thẹ-nī'ạ
Lăt'ạ-gŭs
Lăt-ẹ-rā'nụs
Lạ-tē'rĭ-ŭm
Lăth'u-rŭs
Lā-tĭ-ā'lĭs 1
Lā-tĭ-ā'rĭs 1
Lạ-tī'nī
Lạ-tĭn'ĭ-ŭs
Lạ-tī'nụs
Lā'tĭ-ŭm 1
Lā'tĭ-ŭs 1
Lạ-tō'bĭ-ŭs
Lăt-ọ-brī'ġī. or
  Lạ-tŏb'rĭ-ġī
Lạ-tō'ĭ-ạ 3
Lạ-tō'ĭ-dēṣ
Lạ-tō'ĭs
Lạ-tō'mĭ-æ
Lạ-tō'nạ
Lăt-ọ-rē'ạ
Lạ-tō'ụs
Lā'treŭs 6
Lā'trĭs
Lạ-tū'mĭ-æ
Lâu'cọ-ŏn
Lâu-dạ-mī'ạ
Lâu-dō'nĭ-ạ
Lâu-fē'ĭ-ạ 3

Lâu'rạ, Lâu'rẹ-ạ
Lâu-rē'ạ-cŭm
Lâu-rẹn-tā'lĭ-ạ
Lâu-rĕn'tēṣ Ā'grī
Lâu-rĕn'tĭ-ạ 1
Lâu-rẹn-tī'nī
Lâu-rĕn'tĭ-ŭs 1
Lâu'rẹnce
Lọ-rĕn'zō
Lâu-rē'ọ-lŭs
Lâu'rĭ-ŏn, or
  Lâu-rī'ọn
Lâu'rụs
Lā'ụs, river.
Lâuṣ Pọm-pē'ĭ-ạ 3
Lâu'tĭ-ŭm 1
Lâu'tụ-læ
Lạ-vër'nĭ-ŭm
Lā-vĭ-ā'nạ
Lạ-vī'cụm
Lạ-vĭn'ĭ-ạ
Lạ-vĭn'ĭ-ŭm, or
  Lạ-vī'nụm
Lạ-vī'nụs
Lē'ạ-dēṣ
Lẹ-æ'ī
Lẹ-än'drĭ-ás
Lē-ạ-nī'tæ
Lĕb-ạ-dē'ạ, or
  Lĕb-ạ-dī'ạ
Lĕb'ẹ-dŏs, or -dŭs
Lẹ-bē'nạ
Lẹ-cā'nĭ-ạ
Lẹ-cā'nĭ-ŭs
Lĕc-ạ-pē'nụs
Lĕc'tĭ-ŭs 1
Lẹc-tō'rĭ-ạ
Lĕç'y-thŭs
Lē'ġĭ-ō
Lē'ĭ-tŭs
Lĕl'ẹ-ġēṣ
Lẹ-mā'nụs
Lĕm-nĭ-sẹ-lē'nẹ
Lĕm-ọ-vī'cēṣ
Lẹ-mō'vĭ-ī
Lĕm'u-rēṣ
Lẹ-mū'rĭ-ạ
Lĕm-u-rā'lĭ-ạ
Lẹn-tĭd'ĭ-ŭs
Lẹn-tī'nụs
Lĕn'tu-lŭs
Lẹ-ŏb'ạ-tēṣ
Lē-ọ-bō'tēṣ
Lē-ọ-cē'dēṣ
Lẹ-ŏch'ạ-rēṣ
Lē-ọ-cō'rĭ-ŏn
Lẹ-ŏc'rạ-tēṣ
Lẹ-ŏc'rĭ-tŭs
Lẹ-ŏd'ạ-mās
Lẹ-ŏd'ọ-cŭs
Lẹ-ō'dēṣ
Lẹ-ŏg'ọ-räs
Lẹ-ō'nạ
Lē-ọ-nā'tụs
Lẹ-ŏn'ĭ-dás
Lē-ọn-nā'tụs
Lẹ-ŏn'teŭs 6
Lē-ọn-tī'ạ-dēṣ
Lē-ọn-tī'nī
Lẹ-ŏn'tĭ-ŭm 1

Lẹ-ŏn'tĭ-ŭs 1
Lẹ-ŏn-tọ cĕph'ạ-lŭs
Lē-ọn-tŏd'ạ-mē
Lē-ọn-tȳçh'ĭ-dēṣ
Lẹ-ŏph'ạ-nēṣ
Lẹ-ŏph'ọ-rạ
Lẹ-ō'phrọn
Lẹ-ŏp're-pēṣ
Lē-ọ-prĕp'ĭ-dēṣ
Lẹ-ŏs'thẹ-nēṣ
Lē-ọ-trŏph'ĭ-dēṣ
Lē-ọ-tȳçh'ĭ-dēṣ
Lẹ-phȳr'ĭ-ŭm
Lĕp'ĭ-dạ
Lĕp'ĭ-dŭs
Lẹ-pī'nụs
Lẹ-pŏn'tĭ-cŭs
Lẹ-pŏn'tĭ-ī 1
Lẹ-pō'rĭ-ŭs
Lē'prẹ-ŏs
Lē'prẹ-ŭm, or
  Lē'prĭ-ŭm
Lĕp'tĭ-nēṣ
Lē'rĭ-ạ
Lẹ-rī'nạ
Lĕs'bĭ-ŭs
Lĕs'bọ-clēṣ
Lĕs-bọ-nī'cụs
Lẹs-bō'năx
Lĕs'çhēṣ
Lĕs'ọ-rạ
Lẹs-trȳg'ọ-nēṣ
Lĕs'u-rạ
Lẹ-tā'nụm
Lẹ-thæ'ụs
Lē'thẹ
Lẹ-tō'ĭs
Lẹ-trī'nī
Leu-cā'dĭ-ạ
Leu-cā'dĭ-ŭs
Leu-cā'nī
Leu-cā'ṣĭ-ŏn 2
Leu-cā'tēṣ
Leū'cẹ
Leu-cĭp'pĭ-dēṣ
Leū-cọ-ġæ'ī Fŏn'-
  tēṣ
Leū'cọ-lạ
Leu-cō'nẹ
Leu-cō'nēṣ
Leu-cŏn'ĭ-cŭs
Leu-cŏn'ọ-ē
Leu-cŏn'ọ-tŭs
Leu-cŏp'ẹ-trạ
Leū-cọ-phrȳ'nẹ
Leū'cọ-phrȳs
Leu-cŏp'ọ-lĭs
Leu-cō'ṣĭ-ạ 1
Leū-cọ-sȳr'ĭ-ī
Leu-cŏs'y-rī
Leu-cŏth'ọ-ē, or
  Leu-cō'thẹ-ạ
Leū-cy-ā'nĭ-äs 1
Leu-tȳçh'ĭ-dēṣ
Lẹ-vā'nạ
Lẹ-vī'nụs
Lẹx-ā'nọr
Lẹx-ĭph'ạ-nēṣ
Lẹx-ō'vĭ-ī
Lĭb'ạ-næ

Lĭ-bā'nĭ-ŭs
Lĭb'ạ-nŭs
Lĭb-ẹn-tī'nạ
Lĭb'ẹ-rạ
Lĭb-ẹr-ā'lĭ-ạ
Lĭb-ẹr-ā'lĭs
Lĭ-bē'thrạ
Lĭ-bĕth'rĭ-dēṣ
Lĭb'ĭ cī, Lĭ-bē'cĭ-ī 1
Lĭb-ĭ-tī'nạ
Lĭb'ĭ-ŭs Sẹ-vē'rụs
Lĭ-bŏn'ọ-tụs
Lĭb-ọ-phœ-nī'cēṣ
Lī'brạ
Lī'brī
Lĭ-bür'nĭ-ạ
Lĭ-bür'nĭ-dēṣ
Lĭb'y-ạ
Lĭb'y-cŭm Mā'rẹ
Lĭb'y-cŭs
Lĭb-y-phœ-nī'cēṣ
Lĭb-ys-tī'nụs
Lĭc'ạ-tēṣ
Lĭ'chạ
Lĭch'ạ-dēṣ
Lĭ'chạs
Lĭ-cĭ-ā'nụs 1
Lĭ-cĭn'ĭ-ạ
Lĭ-cĭn-ĭ-ā'nụs
Lĭ-cĭn'ĭ-ŭs
Lĭç'ĭ-nŭs
Lĭ-cȳm'nĭ-ŭs
Lĭ'dẹ
Lĭ-gā'rĭ-ŭs
Lĭ-gē'ạ
Lĭ'ger
Lĭ'ger, or Lĭg'ẹ-rĭs
Lĭg'ọ-rās
Lĭ-gū'rĭ-ạ
Lĭg-u-rī'nụs
Lĭ-gŭs'tĭ-cŭm Mā'-
Lĭg'y-ēṣ [rẹ
Lĭ-gȳr'gụm
Lĭ-læ'ụs
Lĭl'y-bē
Lĭ-mæ'ạ
Lĭ-mē'nĭ-ạ
Lĭm-ẹn-tī'nụs
Lĭ-mē'rạ
Lĭm-ẹ-tā'nụs
Lĭm'næ
Lịm-nā'tẹ
Lĭm-nạ-tĭd'ĭ-ạ
Lịm-nī'ạ-cē
Lĭm-nī'ạ-dēṣ
Lĭm-nĭ-ŏ'tæ
Lịm-nŏ'nĭ-ạ
Lĭm-nọ-rē'ạ
Lĭ-mō'nẹ
Lĭm'ọ-nŭm, or
  Lĭ-mō'nụm
Lĭm'y-rạ
Lịn-cā'ṣị-ī 1
Lĭn'gọ-nēṣ
Lịn-gŏn'ĭ-cŭs
Lī'ọ-dēṣ
Lĭp'ạ-rĭs
Lĭp'ạ-rō
Lĭp-ọ-dō'rụs
Lĭ-quĕn'tĭ-ạ 1

Lį-rī'ǫ-pĕ
Lī-sĭn'į-ăs
Lĭt'a-brŭm
Lį-tā'nạ
Lī tăv'į-cŭs
Lĭth-ǫ-bō'lį-ạ
Lī-tō'rį-ŭs
Lī-tū'bį-ŭm
Lĭv'į-ạ
Lĭv-į-nē'į-ŭs 3
Lĭv'į-ŭs
Lĭv'y
Lō'cę-ŭs 1
Lō'chạ
Lǫ-chā'gus
Lō'chį-ăs
Lǫ-cō'zụs
Lō'crī
Lǫ-cŭ'tį-ŭs 1
Lǫ-ģī'um
Lǫ-gŏth'ę-tạ
Lŏl-lį-ā'nụs
Lŏl'lį-ŭs
Lǫn-dĭn'į-ŭm
Lǫn-dī'nụm
Lon'dǫn
Lŏn-gạ-rē'nụs
Lǫn-ģĭm'ạ-nŭs
Lǫn-ģī'nụs
Lǫn-gō'nē
Lŏn'gụ-lạ
Lǫn-gŭn'tį-cạ
Lŏr'y-mạ
Lō'ụs, *or* Ā'ǫ-ŭs
Lŏx'į-ăs 1
Lū'cạ-gŭs
Lụ-cā'nī
Lụ-cā'nį-ạ
Lū-cạ-nī'ạ-cŭs
Lụ-căn'į-cŭs
Lụ-cā'nį-ŭs
Lụ-cā'nụs
Lū'cạn
Lụ-cā'rį-ạ, *or*
   Lụ-cē'rį-ạ
Lục-cē'į-ŭs 3
Lū'cę-rēş
Lụ-cē'rį-ŭs
Lụ-cē'tį-ŭs 1
Lū'cį-ạ 1
Lū-cį-ā'nụs 1
Lū'ci-ạn
Lū'cį-fer
Lụ-cĭl'į-ŭs
Lụ-cĭl'lį-ŭs
Lụ-cī'nạ
Lụ-cī'ǫ-lŭs
Lū'cį-ŭs 1
Lụ-crē'tį-ạ 1
Lụ-crĕt'į-lĭs
Lụ-crē'tį-ŭs 1
Lụ-crī'nụs
Lū'crįs
Lục-tā'tį-ŭs 1
Lục-tē'rį-ŭs
Lū'cụ-mō
Lū-cụ-mō'nį-ŭs
Lū-dǫ-vī'cụs
Lū'dǫ-vĭc, Lĕw'ịs,
   Lŏu'ịs

Lū-ęn-tī'nụm
Lụg-dū'nụm
Lụ-pēr'cạl
Lū'pęr-cǎl, Shak.
Lū-pęr-cā'lį-ạ
Lū'pį-ăs, *or*
   Lū'pį-ạ
Lū-pǫ-dū'nụm
Lụs-cī'nụs
Lū-sį-tā'nį-ạ
Lū-sį-tā'nụs
Lū'sį-ŭs 1
Lụ-sō'nēş
Lŭs'trį-cŭs
Lụ-tā'tį-ŭs 1
Lụ-tē'rį-ŭs
Lụ-tē'tį-ạ 1
Lụ-tē'vạ
Lụ-tō'rį-ŭs
Lụx-ō'rį-ŭs
Lȳ-bō'tụs
Lȳc'ạ-băs
Lȳc-ạ-bē'tụs
Lȳ-cæ'ạ
Lȳ-cæ'ụm
Lȳ-cā'ǫn
Lȳc-ạ-ō'nį-ạ
Lȳc-ạ-rē'tụs
Lȳ'cę
Lȳç'ę-ăs
Lȳ'cēş
Lȳ-cē'tụs
Lȳ-cē'ụm
Lȳch'nį-dŭs
Lȳch-nī'tįs
Lȳ''cį-ạ 1
Lȳç'į-dăs
Lȳ-cĭm'nį-ạ
Ly-cī'nụs
Lȳ''cį-ŭs 1, *or*
   Ly-cī'ụs (*a.*)
Lȳc'ǫ-ạ
Lȳ-cō'lę-ŏn
Lȳc-ǫ-mē'dēş
Lȳc-ǫ-mē'dį-ŭs
Lȳ-cō'nę
Lȳc-ǫ-nē'sụs
Lȳ-cŏn'į-dēş
Lȳ-cō'pēş
Lȳc'ǫ-phrŏn
Lȳ-cŏp'ǫ-lĭs
Lȳc-ǫ-pǫ-lī'tēş
Lȳ-cō'pụs
Lȳc-ǫ-rē'ạ
Lȳ-cō'reūs 6
Lȳ-cō'rį-ăs
Lȳ-cō'rįs
Lȳc-ǫ-sū'rạ
Lȳ-cō'tạs
Lȳc-ụr-ģī'dēş
Lȳ'dę
Lȳd'į-ạ
Ly-dī'ạ-dēş
Lȳd'į-ŭs
Lȳg'dạ-mŭs
Lȳm'į-rĕ
Lyn-cēs'tæ

Lyn-cĕs'tį-ŭs
Lȳn'ceūs (*n.*) 6
Lyn-cē'ụs (*a.*)
Lyn-cī'dæ
Lyn-cī'dēş
Lyn-cæ'ụs
Lyr-cæ'ǫs
Lyr-cē'ạ, *or* -ŭm
Lyr-cē'ụs, *or* -cī'ụs
Lȳr'į-cē
Lȳr'ǫ-pē
Lȳ-sā'nį-ăs
Lȳs-ạ-nŏr'į-dăs
Lȳ'sę
Ly-sī'ạ-dēş
Ly-sī'ạ-năx
Lȳ''sį-ăs 1
Lȳs'į-clēş
Lȳ-sĭc'rạ-tēş
Lȳ-sĭd'į-cē
Lȳ-sĭm'ạ-chē
Lȳs-į-mā'chį-ạ
Lȳs-į-măch'į-dēş
Lȳ-sĭm'ạ-chŭs
Lȳs-į-mę-lī'ạ
Lȳ-sĭn'ǫ-ē
Lȳ-sĭs'trạ-tŭs
Lȳ-sĭt'ę-lēş
Lȳs-į-thī'dēş
Lȳ-sĭth'ǫ-ŭs
Lȳ''sį-ŭs 1
Lȳs'trạ
Lyx-ē'ạ
Ly-zā'nį-ăs

M.

Mā'cæ
Măc-ạ-rē'įs
Măc'ạ-reūs 6
Mạ-cā'rį-ạ
Măc'ạ-rĭs
Mạ-cā'rį-ŭs
Măc'ạ-rŏn
Mạ-cär'tạ-tŭs
Mạ-cā'tụs
Măc'cį-ŭs 1
Măc'ę-dō
Măc-ę-dō'nį-ạ
Măc-ę-dŏn'į-cŭs
Măc-ę-dō'nį-ŭs
Mạ-sō'rįs
Măc-ę-rī'nụs
Măc'ę-tạ
Măc'ę-tæ
Mạ-chæ'reūs 6
Mạ-chæ'rį-ō
Mạ-chæ'rụs
Mạ-chăn'į-dăs
Mạ-chā'ǫn
Mạ-chā'ǫ-nēş
Mạ-chā'tạs
Măch-ę-lō'nēş
Mạ-chē'rụs
Măch-ę-tē'ģĭ
Mạ-cĭl-į-ā'nụs
Mạ-cŏr'ạ-bạ, *or*
   Măc-ǫ-rā'bạ
Mæ'crạ
Mā-crį-ā'nụs
Mā'crįs
Măc'rį-tŭs
Mā'crŏ
Mạ-crō'bį-ī
Mạ-crō'bį-ŭs
Măc'rǫ-chĭr
Mạ-crō'nēş
Măc-rǫ-tī'chụs
Măc-rǫ-pǫ-gō'nēş
Măc-ry-nē'ạ
Mạc-tō'rį-ŭm
Măc'ụ-lạ
Măc-ụ-lō'nụs
Mạ-dē'tēş
Mā-dį-ạ-nī'tæ
Mạ-drē'nī
Măd-ụ-ạ-tē'nī
Mā'dy-ēş
Măd'y-tụs
Mæ-ăn'der
Mæ-ăn'drị-ạ
Mæ-ăn'drị-ŭs
Mæ-cē'nạs
Mæ'cį-ŭs 1
Mæd-ǫ-bị-thȳ'nī 4
Mæ'lį-ŭs
Mæm-ạc-tē'rį-ạ 4
Mæn'ạ-dēş 4
Mæn'ạ-lạ 4
Mæ-năl'į-dēş
Mæn'ạ-lŏs 4
Mæn'ạ-lŭs 4
Mæ'nį-ŭs
Mæn'ǫ-bạ 4
Mæn-ǫ-bō'rạ 4
Mæ'nạs
Mæ-nŏm'ę-nạ
Mæ'nǫn
Mæ'nụs
Mæ'ǫn
Mæ'ǫ-nēş
Mæ-ō'nị-ạ
Mæ-ŏn'į-dæ
Mæ-ŏn'į-dēş
Mæ'ǫ-nĭs
Mæ-ō'tæ
Mæ-ō'tį-ạ 1
Mæ-ŏt'į-cŭs
Mæ-ŏt'į-dēş
Mæ-ō'tịs Pā'lụs
Mæ'sị-ạ Sȳl'vạ 1
Mæ-sō'lụs
Mæt'ǫ-nạ 4
Mæ'vį-ạ
Mæ'vį-ŭs
Măg'ạ-bạ
Măg-ạ-dā'tēş
Măg'dǫ-lŭm, *or*
   Mạg-dō'lụm
Mạ-ģĕl'lạ
Măģ'ę-tæ
Măģ-ę-tō'brị-ạ
Mā'ģī
Mā'ģį-ŭs
Măg'nạ Græ'cį-ạ 1
Măg-nĕn'tị-ŭs 1
Măg-nē'şį-ạ 1
Măg-nē'tēş

Măg-nŏp'ǫ-lĭs
Măg-ǫn-tī'ạ-cŭm
Mạ-hăl'cēş
Mā'į-ạ 3
Mā-į-ū'mạ, *or* -mạs
Mạ-jō-rį-ā'nụs
Mạ-jō'rį-ạn
Mạ-jū'mạ, *or* -mạs
Măl'ạ-cạ
Măl'ạ-chạ
Măl-ạch-bē'lụs
Mā'lạ For-tū'nạ
Măl'ạ-lăs
Măl'chį-ŏn
Mā'lę-ạ, *or* Mạ-lē'ạ
Mạ-lē'bạ
Măl'ę-lăs
Mạ-lē'nę
Măl-ę-vĕn'tụm
Mā'lį-ạ
Mạ-lī'ạ-cŭs
Mā'lį-ī
Mạ-lĭ-şį-ā'nụs 1
Mạl-lē'ǫ-lŭs
Măl'lį-ŭs
Mạl-lŏph'ǫ-rạ
Mạ-lō'dēş
Măl'thạ-cē
Mạl-thī'nụs
Mạ-lū'chạ
Mạl-vā'nạ
Mạ-mā'ụs
Măm-ęr-cī'nụs
Mā'męrş
Mạ-mĕr'thēş
Măm-ęr-tī'nạ
Măm-ęr-tī'nī
Măm-ęr-tī'nụs
Mạ-mĭl'į-ạ
Mạ-mĭl'į-ŭs
Mạm-mō'nạs
Mạ-mū-rį-ā'nụs
Mạ-mū'rį-ŭs
Mạ-næ'thǫn
Mạ-năs'tạ-băl
Mạn-cī'nụs
Mạn-dā'nę, *or*
   Măn'dạ-nē
Mạn-dā'nēş
Mạn-dē'lạ
Mạn-dō'nį-ŭs
Măn'drǫ-clēş
Măn-drǫ-clī'dạs
Mạn-dū'bị-ī
Măn-dụ-brā'tį-ŭs 1
Mạn-dū'rį-ạ
Măn'ę-rŏs
Mā'nēş
Măn'ę-thō
Mā'nį-ạ
Mạ-nĭl'į-ạ
Mạ-nĭl'į-ŭs
Măn'į-mī
Mā'nį-ŭs
Măn'lį-ạ
Măn-lį-ā'nạ
Măn'lį-ŭs
Mạn-nē'į-ạ 3
Mạn-nē'į-ŭs 3
Mạn-suē'tụs

Măn-tē'um
Măn-ti-ā'na 1
Măn-ti-nē'a
Măn'ti-neūs 6
Măn'ti-ŭs 1
Măn'tu-a
Măn-tu-ā'nus
Măr-a-căn'da
Măr'a-tha
Măr'a-thŏn
Măr'a-thŭs
Măr-cel-lī'nus
Măr'ci-a 1
Măr-ci-ā'na 1
Măr-ci-ā'nus 1
Măr'ci-an
Măr-cīl-i-ā'nus
Măr-cīl'i-ŭs
Măr'ci-ŏn 1
Măr'ci-ŭs 1
Măr-cŏ-măn'nī, *or*
　Măr-cŏm'a-nī
Măr-cŏm'e-rēş
Măr'di-a
Măr'do-nēş
Măr-dŏ'ni-ŭs
Mā-re-ŏt'i-cŭs
Mā-re-ō'tis
Măr-ga-rī'ta
Măr-gi-ā'na
Măr-gĭn'i-a
Măr-gī'tēş
Mā'ri-a, *and*
　Ma-rī'a
Ma-rī'a-ba
Mā-ri-ā'na
Mā-ri-ā'næ Fŏs'sæ
Mā-ri-an-dȳ'nī
Mā-ri-an-dȳ'num
Mā-ri-ā'num
Mā-ri-ā'nus
Ma-rī'ca
Ma-rī'cī
Măr'i-cŭs
Măr-i-dū'num
Ma-rī'na
Ma-rī'nus
Mā'ri-ŏn
Măr'i-sŭs
Ma-rī'ta
Ma-rĭt'i-ma
Mā'ri-ŭs
Măr'ma-cŭs
Măr-măr'i-ca
Măr-măr'i-dæ
Măr-mā'ri-ŏn
Măr-o-bŏd'u-ī
Măr-o-bū'du-ī
Măr-o-bū'dum
Măr-o-nē'ĭ
Măr-o-nīl'lus
Măr-pē'şi-a 1
Măr-pē'sus
Măr-rŭ'bi-ī
Măr-ru-cī'nī
Măr-rŭ'vi-ŭm, *or*
　Măr-rŭ'bi-ŭm
Măr'sa-la
Măr'se
Mărş'pi-ter

Măr'sy-a 1
Măr-sȳ'a-ba
Măr'sy-ăs 1
Măr'ti-a 1
Măr-ti-ā'lis 1
Măr'tial
Măr-ti-ā'nus 1
Măr-tĭǵ'e-na
Măr-tī'na
Măr-tĭn-i-ā'nus 1
Măr-tī'nus
Măr'ti-ŭs 1
Măr-ty-rŏp'o-lĭs
Mā'ry-ŏn
Măs-æ-sȳ'lī
Măs-æ-sȳl'i-ī
Mas-cē'zel
Măs'cli-ŏn
Măs-i-ǵī'ton
Ma-sīs'ti-ŭs
Mā'si-ŭs Mŏnş 1
Măs'sa-ga
Mas-săǵ'e-tæ
Mas-sā'na
Mas-sā'nī
Măs'si-cŭs
Mas-sĭl'i-a
Mas-sī'ra
Mas-sȳ'la
Mas-sȳ'lī
Mas-trăm'e-la
Mas-tū'şi-a 1
Măs'u-lūs
Ma-sū'ri-ŭs
Ma-tër-ni-ā'nus
Ma-thī'on
Ma-tĭd'i-a
Mā-ti-ē'nī 1
Ma-tĭn'i-ŭs
Ma-tī'nus
Mā'ti-ŭs 1
Ma-trā'li-a
Mā'tre-ăs
Ma-trīn'i-a
Ma-trĭn'i-ŭs
Ma-trī'nus
Ma-trō'na
Măt'ro-na, *river.*
Măt-ro-nā'li-a
Măt-tī'a-cī
Ma-tū'ce-tæ
Ma-tū'rus
Ma-tū'ta
Măt-u-tī'nus
Mâu'ra
Mâu-rī-ci-ā'nus 1
Mâu-rī''ci-ŭs 1
Mâu'rice
Mâu-rī'cus (*n.*)
Mâu'ri-cŭs (*a.*)
Mâu-ri-tā'ni-a 1
Mâu-rī''ti-ŭs 1
Mâu-rŭ'şi-a 1
Mâu-rŭ'şi-ī 1
Mâu-so-lē'um
Mâu-sō'lī
Mâu-sō'lus
Ma-vŏr'ti-a 1
Ma-vŏr'ti-ŭs

Măx-ĕn'ti-ŭs 1
Măx-ē'ra, *or* -ras
Măx-ē'ræ
Măx-ĭm-i-ā'nus
Măx-ĭm'i-an
Măx-i-mĭl-i-ā'na
Măx-i-mī'na
Măx-i-mī'nus
Măx'i-mɩn
Măx'i-mŭs
Măz'a-ca
Măz'a-cēş
Ma-zā'rēş, *or*
　Măz'a-rŭş
Măz'e-răs
Măz'i-cēş
Măz'y-ǵēş
Mē'a-rŭs
Mĕch'a-neūs 6
Me-cĭs'teūs 6
Me-cœ'nas, *or*
　Me-cæ'nas
Mĕç-œ-nā'tēş
Mĕc'ri-da
Me-dē'a
Mē'de-ŏn
Mē'di-a
Mē'di-ăs
Mĕd'i-cŭs
Mē-di-o-lā'num
Me-dī'o-lŭm
Mē-di-ō-ma-trī'cēş,
　or Mē-di-o-măt'-
　ri-cēş, *or* -cī
Mē'di-ŏn
Mē-di-ŏx'u-mī
Mĕd-i-trī'na
Me-dō'a-cŭs, *or*
　Me-dū'a-cŭs
Mĕd-o-bi-thȳ'nī
Mĕd-o-brī'ga
Mĕd'o-cŭs
Me-dŏn'ti-ăs 1
Me-dō'rēş
Mĕd-u-ā'na
Mĕd'u-lī
Mĕd-ul-lī'na
Mĕd-ul-lī'nus
Me-dū'sa
Mĕg-a-bȳ'zī
Mĕg-a-bȳ'zus
Mĕg'a-clēş
Mĕg-a-clī'dēş
Mĕg-a-dō'rus
Mĕg'a-lē
Me-gā'le-ăs
Mĕg-a-lē'şi-a 1
Me-gā'li-a
Mĕg-a-lŏp'o-lĭs
Mĕg-a-mē'de
Mĕg-a-nī'ra
Mĕg'a-ra
Mĕg'a-reūs (*n.*) 6
Măg-a-rē'us (*a.*)
Mĕg'a-rĭs
Mĕg-a-rŏn'i-dēş
Me-găs'the-nēş
Mĕg-a-tī'çhus
Mē'ǵēş
Me-ǵĭs'ta

Me-ǵĭs'ti-a
Me-ǵĭs'ti-äs
Me-ǵĭs'to-nŭs
Mă-her-dā'tēş
Me-læ'næ
Mĕl-am-pē'a
Mĕl-am-pȳ'gus
Mĕl-an-çhlæ'nī
Me-lăn'co-măs
Mĕl'a-nē
Mĕl'a-nēş
Mĕl'a-neūs 6
Me-lā'ni-a
Me-lā'ni-ŏn
Mĕl-a-nĭp'pi-dēş
Mĕl-a-nĭp'pus
Mĕl-a-nō'pus
Mĕl-a-nŏs'y-rī
Me-lăn'theūs 6
Me-lăn'thi-ī
Me-lăn'thi-ŏn
Me-lăn'thi-ŭs
Mē-le-ā'ǵer
Mē-le-ăg'ri-dēş
Mē-le-ā'gros
Mē'lēş
Mĕl'e-sē
Me-lē'şi-ăs 1
Mĕl-e-sĭǵ'e-nēş, *or*
　Mĕl-e-sĭǵ'e-na
Mĕl'e-tē
Me-lē'ti-ŭs 1
Me-lē'tus
Mē'li-a
Me-lĭb'o-cŭs
Mĕl-i-bœ'a
Mĕl-i-bœ'us
Mĕl'i-çhŭs
Mē'li-ē
Mĕl-i-gū'nis
Me-lī'na
Mē'li-ör
Mĕl'i-sa, *or* -sē
Mĕl-is-sē'nus
Me-lĭs'seūs 6
Mĕl'i-ta
Mĕl'i-tē
Mĕl-i-tē'na, *or* -ne
Mĕl'i-teūs 6
Mĕl'i-tō
Me-lī'tus, *or*
　Me-lē'tus
Mē'li-ŭs
Me-lō'bi-ŭs
Me-lŏb'o-sĭs
Mĕl-o-dū'num
Mel-lō'na
Mel-pī'a
Mel-pŏm'e-nē
Me-măç'e-nī
Mĕm'mi-a
Mem-mī'a-dēş
Mĕm'mi-ŭs
Mem-nŏn'i-dēş
Mĕm-no-nī'um
Mem-phī'tis
Mĕn'a-cē
Me-næch'mus 4
Mĕn'a-lăs
Me-năl'ci-dăs

Mĕn-a-lĭp'pus
Me-năn'der
Mĕn'a-pī
Me-nā'pi-ī
Mĕn'a-pĭs
Men-çhē'rēş
Mĕn'dēş
Mĕn'e-clēş
Mĕn-e-clī'dēş
Mĕn-e-cō'lus
Me-nĕc'ra-tēş
Mĕn-e-dē'mus
Me-nĕǵ'e-tăs, *or*
　Me-nĕǵ'e-tēş
Mĕn-e-la-ī'a
Mĕn-e-lā'us
Me-nĕm'a-çhŭs
Me-nē'ni-ŭs
Mĕn'e-phrŏn
Mē'nēş
Me-nĕs'theūs, *or*
　Mnĕs'theūs 6
Me-nĕs'the-ī Pŏr'-
　tus
Me-nĕs'thi-ŭs
Me-nĕs'tra-tŭs
Mĕn'e-tăs
Me-nĕx'e-nŭs
Me-nĭp'pi-dēş
Mē'ni-ŭs
Me-nŏçh'a-rēş
Mĕn-o-dō'rus
Me-nŏd'o-tŭs
Me-nœ'ceūs (*n.*) 6
Mĕn-œ-cē'us (*a.*)
Mĕn-œ-tī'a-dēş
Me-nœ'ti-ŭs 1
Me-nŏǵ'e-nēş
Me-nŏph'i-lŭs
Mĕn'to-rēş
Me-phī'tis
Mer-cā'tör
Mer-cū'ri-ŭs
Mĕr'cu-ry
Me-rī'o-nēş
Mĕr'me-rŏs, *or*
　Mĕr'me-rŭs
Mĕrm'na-dæ
Mĕr'mo-dăs
Mĕr-o-brī'ca
Mĕr'o-ē
Mĕr'o-pē
Mĕr'o-pĭs
Mĕr'u-la
Ma-săb'a-tēş
Me-sā'bi-ŭs
Mĕs-a-nī'tēş
Me-sā'pi-a
Me-sĕm'bri-a
Me-sē'ne
Mĕs'o-a
Mĕs-o-mē'dēş
Mĕs-o-po-tā'mi-a
Mĕs'pi-la
Mes-săb'a-tæ
Mes-sā'la
Mĕs-sa-lī'na
Mĕs-sa-lī'nus
Mĕs-sā'na
Mĕs-sā'pus

Měs'sa-tǐs
Mes-sē'is
Mes-sē'ne, *or*
  Mes-sē'na
Mes-sē'ni-a
Mes-sē'ni-ō
Mes-sē'nus
Měs'si-ŭs 1
Mes-sō'ġis
Me-sū'la
Mět'a-bŭs
Mět-a-ġǐt'ni-a
Mět'a-gŏn
Mět-a-go-nī'tis
Mět-a-mor-phō'sis
Mět-a-nœ'a
Mět-a-nī'ra
Mět-a-pon-tī'nī
Mět-a-pŏn'tum
Me-tâu'rus
Me-tē'lis
Mět-el-lī'num
Mět-e-rē'a
Me-thā'na, *or*
  Měth'a-na
Me-thā'pus
Me-thī'on
Me-thō'di-ŭs
Me-thō'ne
Měth'o-ra
Me-thū'ri-dēs
Me-thўd'ri-ŭm
Mē-ti-a-cū'sa 1
Me-tǐl'i-a
Me-tǐl'i-ī
Me-tī'lis
Me-tǐl'i-ŭs
Me-tī'o-chŭs
Me-tī'on
Mē'ti-ŭs 1
Mět-o-chī'ta
Me-tœ'ci-a 1
Me-tō'pus
Mět'o-rēs
Mē'tra
Me-trō'a
Me-trō'bi-ŭs
Mět'ro-clēs
Mět-ro-dō'rus
Me-trŏp'o-lǐs
Me-trō'um
Mět'ti-ŭs
Me-tū'lum
Me-vā'ni-a
Mē'vi-ŭs
Me-zěn'ti-ŭs 1
Měz-e-tū'lus
Mī-a-cō'rus
Mī-cē'a
Mī-cē'læ
Mī'cha-ěl
Mī'ci-ō 1
Mǐç'i-tē
Mǐç'y-thŭs
Mǐd-a-ē'um, *or*
  Mǐd-a-ī'on
Mī'de
Mī-dē'a, *nymph.*
Mī-dē'a, *or*
  Mǐd'e-a, *city.*

Mǐd'i-ǎs
Mī-ē'za
Mī-lā'ni-ŏn
Mī-lē'si-ī 1
Mī-lē'si-ŭs 1
Mī-lē'ti-a 1
Mī-lē'ti-ŭm 1
Mī-lē'tos, *or* -tus
Mǐl'i-ǎs
Mi-lī'nus
Mǐl-i-ō'ni-a
Mǐl-i-ō'ni-ŭs
Mi-lǐz-i-ġē'ris
Mī-lō'ni-ŭs
Mǐl'phi-ō
Mil-tī'a-dēs
Mǐl'vi-ŭs
Mǐl'y-ǎs
Mim-nē'dus
Mǐn'ci-ŭs 1
Mǐn'da-rŭs
Mī-nē'i-dēs
Mī-nēr'va
Mǐn-er-vā'li-a
Mī-nēr'vi-ŭs
Mǐn-er-vī'na
Mǐn'i-ō
Mī-nō'a
Mī-nō'i-dēs
Mī-nō'is
Mǐn-o-tâu'rus
Mǐn'the
Mịn-tür'næ
Mī-nū-ci-ā'nus 1
Mī-nū'ci-ŭs 1
Mī-nū'ti-a 1
Mī-nū'ti-ŭs 1
Mǐn'y-æ
Mǐn'y-ǎs
Mǐn'y-cŭs
Mǐn-y-ī'a
Mǐn'y-tus
Mǐr'a-cēs
Mǐr-o-brī'ga
Mī-sāg'e-nēs
Mǐs-ar-ġўr'i-dēs
Mǐs'ce-ra
Mī-sē'num
Mī-sē'nus
Mịs-ġē'tēs
Mī-sīth'e-ŭs
Mǐth-ra-dā'tēs
Mī'thras
Mī-thrē'nēs
Mǐth-ri-dā'tēs
Mǐth-ri-dăt'i-cŭs
Mǐth-ri-dā'tis
Mǐth-ro-bar-zā'nēs
Mǐt-y-lē'næ
Mǐt-y-lē'ne
Mna-sē'as 5
Mnā'se-ǎs 5
Mnā'si-ǎs 1, 5
Mnǎs'i-clēs 5
Mna-sī'lo-chŭs 5
Mna-sǐp'pi-dǎs 5
Mna-sīth'e-ŭs 5
Mnǎs-i-tī'mus 5
Mna-sў'lus 5
Mna-sўr'i-ŭm 5

Mne-mī'um 5
Mne-mŏn'i-dēs 5
Mne-mŏs'y-nē 5
Mněs-i-bū'lus 5
Mněs'i-clēs 5
Mněs-i-dā'mus 5
Mněs-i-dē'mus 5
Mněs-i-lā'us 5
Mne-sǐl'o-chŭs 5
Mne-sīm'a-chē 5
Mne-sīm'a-chŭs 5
Mne-sīph'i-lŭs 5
Mne-sīth'e-ŭs 5
Mněs'the-ŭs 5, 6
Mněs'thi-ŭs 5
Mněs'ti-a 5
Mō-a-bī'tæ
Mo-ǎġ'e-tēs
Mo-cŏr'e-tæ
Mŏd-es-tī'nus
Mō'di-a
Mŏd'o-nŭs
Mœ'ci-a 1
Mœ'nus
Mœ'on
Mœ-ŏn'i-dēs
Mœ-rǎġ'e-nēs
Mœ-rǎġ'e-tēs
Mœ'ris
Mœr'o-clēs 4
Mœ'si-a 1
Mo-gŭn'ti-a 1
Mŏg-ụn-tī'a-cŭm
Mo-ġў'nī
Mo-lī'a, *or* -lē'a
Mo-lī'on
Mo-lī'o-nē
Mo-lī'o-nēs
Mo-lŏs'si-a 1
Mol-pā'di-a
Mol-păg'o-rǎs
Mŏl'peŭs 6
Mŏl-y-crē'um
Mo-lўc'ri-a
Mo-lўc'ri-ŏn
Mo-lў'rus
Mo-nā'chi-ŭm
Mŏn'a-chŭs
Mo-næ'sus
Mo-nē'sēs
Mo-nē'sus
Mo-nē'ta
Mŏn'i-ca
Mŏn'i-ma
Mŏn'i-mŭs
Mŏn-o-bā'zus
Mŏn-o-dǎc'ty-lŭs
Mŏn'o-dŭs
Mo-nœ'cus
Mo-nō'le-ŭs
Mŏn'o-mŭs
Mo-nŏph'a-ġē
Mo-nŏph'i-lŭs
Mo-nŏs'ce-lī
Mo-nŏth-e-lī'tæ
Mon-tā'nus
Mŏn'y-chŭs
Mŏn'y-mŭs
Mŏp'si-ŭm 1
Mop-sō'pi-a

Mŏp'so-pŭs
Mŏp-su-crē'ne
Mŏp-su-ěs'ti-a 1
Mor-găn'ti-ŭm 1
Mor-ġěn'ti-a 1
Mor-ġē'tēs
Mŏr-i-mē'ne
Mŏr'i-nī
Mŏr'i-nŭs
Mŏr-i-tǎs'gus
Mō'ri-ŭs
Mŏr'pheŭs 6
Mŏr'si-mŭs
Mŏr'y-chŭs
Mŏs'cha
Mŏs'chi-cī Mŏn'tēs
Mŏs'chi-ŏn
Mŏs-cho-pū'lus
Mŏs'chus
Mō'ses
Mŏs-sy-nœ'cī
Mos-tē'nī
Mo-sў'chlus
Mŏs-y-nœ'cī
Mo-sў'nī
Mo-thō'ne
Mō-ti-ē'nī 1
Mō'ty-a, *or* Mo-tў'a
Mŏx-o-ē'ne
Mō'y-sēs
Mū-ci-ā'nus 1
Mū'ci-ŭs 1
Mū-ġil-lā'nus
Mŭl'ci-ber
Mū'lu-cha, *or*
  Mu-lū'cha
Mŭl'vi-ŭs Pŏns
Mu-nā'ti-ŭs 1
Mu-nī'tus
Mu-nўch'i-a
Mū'ny-chŭs
Mu-ræ'na
Mur-cǐb'i-ī
Mu-rē'na
Mu-rē'tus
Mū-ri-dū'num
Mur-găn'ti-a 1
Mur-rā'nus
Mur-rhē'nus
Mur-rhī'na
Mür'ti-a 1
Mū'sa, An-tō'ni-ŭs
Mū'sæ
Mu-săġ'e-tēs
Mu-sē'a
Mu-sē'um
Mū-si-cā'nus
Mu-sō-ni-ā'nus
Mu-sō'ni-ŭs Rŭ'fus
Mus-tē'la
Mū'te
Mū'ti-a 1
Mu-tī'ca
Mū'ti-lŭs
Mū'ti-na
Mu-tī'nus
Mū'ti-ŭs 1
Mu-tū'nus
Mu-tŭs'cæ

Mū'ty-cē
Mu-zē'ris
Mўc'a-lē
Mў-cē'na
Mў-cē'næ
Mў-cē'ne
Mў-cē'neŭs 6
Mўç-e-rī'nus
Mўç-i-bër'na
Mўç'i-thŭs
Mўc'o-nē
Mўc'o-nŏs
Mў-ěc'pho-rǐs
Mў-ē'nus
Mўg'a-lē
Mўg'do-nēs
Myg-dō'ni-a
Myg-dŏn'i-dēs
Mўg'do-nŭs
Mў'ia-grŭs
Mў-iō'dēs
Mўl'a-sa
Mў'lēs
Mў'leŭs 6
Mўn'do-nēs
Mў'nēs
Mўn'i-æ
Mў'o-nēs
Mў-o-nē'sus
Mў-ō'ni-a
Mўr'a-cē
Mўr'a-cēs
Myr-cī'nus
Mўr'ġe-tæ
My-rī'ca
My-rī'ce
My-rī'cus
My-rī'na
Mўr'i-nŭs (*n.*)
My-rī'nus (*a.*)
Mўr'i-œ
Mўr-i-ŏn'y-ma
Myr-lē'a
Myr-měç'i-dēs
Myr-mē'ci-ŭm 1
Mўr'mi-dŏn
Myr-mǐd'o-nēs
My-rō-ni-ā'nus
Mў-rŏn'i-dēs
Mў-rō'nus
Mўr'rhi-nŭs
Mўr'si-lŭs
Mўr'si-nŭs
Mўr'ta-lē
Mўr'te-a, *Venus*
Myr-tē'a, *city.*
Mўr'ti-lŭs
Mўr'ti-ŭm 1
Myr-tō'um Mā're
Myr-tō'us
Myr-tŭn'ti-ŭm
Myr-tū'sa
Mўs'ce-lŏs
Mў''si-ŭs 1
Mўs-o-ma-cěd'o-
  nēs
Mys-tǎl'i-dēs
Mўs'tēs
Mўth'e-cŭs
Mў-thǐd'i-ca

Mўt-ĭ-lē'nẹ
Mÿ-tĭs'trạ-tŭs

N.

Năb-ạr-zā'nēş
Năb-ạ-tæ'ĭ
Năb'ạ-thēş
Năc'cạ-ræ
Năc'ọ-lē
Năc-ọ-lē'ạ, or -lĭ'ạ
Năc'ọ-nē
Năc'rạ-sạ
Nạ-dăg'ạ-rạ
Næ'nĭ-ạ
Næ'vĭ-ạ
Næ'vĭ-ŭs
Næv'ọ-lŭs 4
Năg'ạ-rạ
Nạ-ĝē'rĭ, or -ĝĭ'rĭ
Nạ-hăn-ạr-vā'lĭ,
  Nā-hạr-vā'lĭ, or
  Nạ-hár'vạ-lĭ
Nạ-ĭ'ạ-dēş
Nā'ĭ-as 3
Nạ-mū'sạ
Năm-nē'tēş
Năn-ạ-gū'nạ
Năn-nē'ĭ-ŭs 3
Năn-nē'tēş
Năn-tụ-ā'tēş, or -tæ
Năp'ạ-rĭs
Nạ-pā'tạ
Nā'pẹ
Nạ-pē'gus
Năph'ĭ-lŭs
Nạ-pō'cạ
Nạ-răg'ạ-rạ
Nạ-rā'vạs
Nạr-bō'nạ
Nạr-cæ'ụs
Năr'gạ-rạ
Nár'nĭ-ạ
Nạ-rō'nạ
Nạr-thē'cĭs
Nạ-rÿ''cĭ-ạ 1
Nár'y-cŭs
Năs'ạ-mŏn
Năs-ạ-mō'nēş
Năs'cĭ-ŏ 1, or
  Nā'tĭ-ŏ 1
Nạ-sī'cạ
Nạ-sĭd-ĭ-ē'nụs
Nạ-sĭd'ĭ-ŭs
Năs'ụ-ạ
Nạ-tā'lĭ-ạ
Nạ-tā'lĭs
Nâu-bŏl'ĭ-dēş
Nâu'bọ-lŭs
Nâu-clĭ'dēş
Nâu'cọ-lŭs
Nâu'crạ-tēş
Nâu'crạ-tĭs
Nâu-cÿ'dēş
Nâu'lọ-chạ
Nâu'lọ-chŭm
Nâu'lọ-chŭs
Nâu-păc'tụs

Nâu'plĭ-ạ
Nâu-plĭ'ạ-dēş
Nâu'plĭ-ŏs
Nâu'plĭ-ŭs
Nâu-pör'tụs
Nâu'rạ
Nâu-sĭc'ạ-ạ
Nâu-sĭc'ạ-ē
Nâu'sĭ-clēş
Nâu-sĭm'ẹ-nēş
Nâu-sĭ-nī'cụs
Nâu-sĭph'ạ-nēş
Nâu-sĭs'trạ-tạ
Nâu-sĭth'ọ-ŭs
Nâus'tạ-lŏ
Nâu'tēş
Nā'vĭ-ŭs
Nạ-zā'rĭ-ŭs
Nā-zĭ-ạn-zē'nụs 1
Nẹ-æ'rạ
Nẹ-ăl'cẹ
Nẹ-ăl'cēş
Nē-ạn-drī'ạ
Nẹ-ăp'ạ-phŏs
Nẹ-ăp'ọ-lĭs
Nẹ-ăr'chụs
Nẹ-brŏ'dēş
Nẹ-brŏph'ọ-nŏs
Nĕb'ụ-lạ
Nẹ-cĕs'sĭ-tăs
Nē'chŏs
Nẹ-crŏp'ọ-lĭs
Nẹc-tăn'ạ-bĭs
Nẹc-tăn'ẹ-bŭs
Nẹc-tā'rĭ-ŭs
Nĕc-tĭ-bē'rēş
Nẹ-cÿ''şĭ-ạ 1
Nẹ-ĭ'tæ
Nē'leūs (n.) 6
Nẹ-lē'ụs (a.)
Nẹ-lī'dēş
Nē'mẹ-ạ, city.
Nẹ-mē'ạ, or
  Nē'mẹ-ạ, games.
Nē'mēş
Nĕm'ẹ-sạ
Nẹ-mē-şĭ-ā'nụs 1
Nĕm'ẹ-sĭs
Nẹ-mē'şĭ-ŭs 1
Nẹ-mē'tēş
Nẹ-mē'ụs (a.)
Nēm-ọ-rā'lĭ-ạ
Nē-ọ-bū'lẹ
Nē-ọ-cæs-ạ-rē'ạ 4
Nē-ọ-chŏ'rụs
Nē'ọ-clēş
Nē-ọ-clĭ'dēş
Nẹ-ŏc'ọ-rŏs, or
  Nẹ-ŏc'ọ-rŭs
Nẹ-ŏg'ẹ-nēş
Nẹ-ọ-lā'ụs
Nẹ-ŏm'ạ-gŭs
Nē-ọ-mē'nĭ-ạ
Nē-ọ-mē'rĭs
Nē-ọn-tī'chọs
Nē'ọ-phrŏn
Nẹ-ŏph'y-tŭs
Nẹ-ŏp-tŏl'ẹ-mŭs
Nē'ọ-rĭs

Nẹ-ō'thẹ-ŭs
Nē'pẹ
Nĕp'ẹ-tē
Nẹ-phā'lĭ-ạ
Nĕph'ẹ-lē
Nĕph-ẹ-lē'ĭs
Nĕph'ẹ-lĭs
Nĕph-ẹ-rī'tēş
Nẹ-pī'ạ
Nẹ-pō-tĭ-ā'nụs 1
Nĕp-tụ-nā'lĭ-ạ
Nẹp-tū'nĭ-ạ
Nĕp-tụ-nī'nẹ
Nẹp-tū'nĭ-ŭm
Nẹp-tū'nĭ-ŭs
Nẹp-tū'nụs
Nĕp'tūne
Nẹ-rā'tĭ-ŭs 1
Nẹ-rē'ĭ-dēş
Nē're̦-ĭdş
Nē-rẹ-ĭ'nẹ
Nẹ-rē'ĭs, or
  Nē'rẹ-ĭs
Nẹ-rē'ĭ-ŭs 3
Nẹ-rē'tụm
Nē'reūs (n.) 6
Nẹ-rē'ụs (a.)
Nĕr'ĭ-cŭm, or -cŭs
Nē-rĭ-ē'nẹ
Nẹ-rī'nẹ
Nē'rĭ-ō
Nĕr'ĭ-phŭs
Nẹ-rī'tæ
Nĕr'ĭ-tŏs, or -tŭs
Nĕr'ĭ-tŭm
Nē'rĭ-ŭm
Nē'rĭ-ŭs
Nẹ-rō'nĭ-ạ
Nĕr-ụ-lī'nụs
Nĕr'ụ-lŭm
Nĕr'vĭ-ī
Nĕr'vĭ-ŭs
Nẹs-ăc'tĭ-ŭm 1
Nẹ-sī'dēş
Nẹ-sĭm'ạ-chŭs
Nē-şĭ-ō'pẹ 1
Nē-şĭ-ō'tēş 1
Nẹ-sō'pẹ
Nĕs'pẹ-tŏs
Nẹs-sō'nĭs
Nĕs'tọ-clēş
Nẹs-tŏr'ĭ-dēş
Nẹs-tō'rĭ-ŭs
Neū'rī
Nĭ-cæn'ẹ-tŭs 4
Nĭ-căg'ọ-răs
Nĭ-cā'nọr
Nĭ-căr'chụs
Nĭ-căr'ẹ-tē
Nĭc-ạr-thī'dēş
Nĭ-cā'tọr
Nĭ-căt'ọ-rĭs
Nĭ'cẹ
Nĭç'ẹ-ạ
Nĭç-ẹ-phŏ'rĭ-ŭs
Nĭ-cĕph'ọ-rŭs
Nĭ-cĕr'ạ-tŭs
Nĭç'ẹ-rŏs
Nĭ-cē'tạs
Nĭ-cē'tēş

Nĭç-ẹ-tē'rĭ-ạ
Nĭ''cĭ-ạ 1
Nĭ-cī'ạ-dēş
Nĭ''cĭ-ăs 1
Nĭc-ọ-bū'lẹ
Nĭc-ọ-bū'lụs
Nĭ-cŏch'ạ-rēş
Nĭc'ọ-clēş
Nĭ-cŏc'rạ-tēş
Nĭ-cō'crẹ-ŏn
Nĭc-ọ-dā'mụs
Nĭc-ọ-dē'mụs
Nĭc-ọ-dō'rụs
Nĭ-cŏd'rọ-mŭs
Nĭc-ọ-lā'ụs
Nĭ-cō'lẹ-ŏs
Nĭ-cŏl'ọ-chŭs
Nĭ-cŏm'ạ-chạ
Nĭc-ọ-măch'ĭ-dēş
Nĭ-cŏm'ạ-chŭs
Nĭc-ọ-mē'dēş
Nĭc-ọ-mẹ-dī'ạ
Nĭc-ọ-mē'di-ạ
Nĭ-cō'nĭ-ạ, or -ŭm
Nĭ-cŏph'ạ-nēş
Nĭc'ọ-phŏn
Nĭc'ọ-phrŏn
Nĭ-cŏp'ọ-lĭs
Nĭ-cŏs'thẹ-nēş
Nĭ-cŏs'trạ-tŭs
Nĭ-cŏt-ẹ-lē'ạ
Nĭ-cŏt'ẹ-lēş
Nĭ-cŏth'ọ-ē
Nī'ĝẹr
Nī-ĝĭd'ĭ-ŭs
Nĭ-ĝī'rạ
Nĭ-grē'tēş
Nĭ-grī'nụs
Nĭ-grī'tæ
Nĭ-lā'mọn
Nī'leūs 6
Nĭ-lō'tēş
Nĭ-lŏx'ẹ-nŭs
Nĭn'ẹ-vē
Nĭn'ĭ-ăs, or
  Nĭn'y-ăs
Nĭn'nĭ-ŭs
Nĭn'ọ-ē
Nĭn'y-ăs
Nī'ọ-bē
Nĭ-phā'tēş
Nī'phẹ
Nī'reūs 6
Nĭ-sæ'ạ
Nĭ-sæ'ụs
Nĭ-sē'ĭ-ạ 3
Nĭ-sē'ĭs
Nĭs-ĭ-bē'nụs
Nĭs'ĭ-bĭs
Nĭ-sō'pẹ
Nĭ-sÿ'rọs, or -rụs
Nĭ-tē'tĭs
Nĭ-tĭ-ŏb'rĭ-gēs, or
  Nĭ-tĭ-ọ-brī'gēs
Nĭ-tō'crĭs
Nĭt'rĭ-ạ
Mĭ-vā'rĭ-ạ
Nĭ-vŏm'ạ-gŭs
Nọ-bĭl'ĭ-ör
Nŏc-tĭ-lū'cạ

Nŏc-tụ-ĭ'nụs
Nọ-dī'nụs
Nọ-dō'tụs
Nọ-ē'mọn
Nọ-ē'tụs
Nọ-lā'nụs
Nŏm'ạ-dēş
Nō'mæ
Nŏm-ẹn-tā'nụs
Nō'mĭ-ĭ
Nọ-mī'ọn
Nō'mĭ-ŭs
Nọ-mŏph'y-lăx
Nŏn-ạ-crī'nụs
Nọ-nā'crĭs, or
  Nŏn'ạ-crĭs
Nō'næ
Nō-nĭ-ā'nụs
Nō'nĭ-ŭs
Nŏn'nĭ-ŭs
Nŏn'nọ-sŭs
Nō'pĭ-ạ, or
  Cnō'pĭ-ạ 5
Nọr-bā'nạ
Nọr-bā'nụs
Nọ-rĭ''cĭ-ī 1
Nŏr'ĭ-cŭm
Nŏr'tĭ-ạ 1
Nŏs-ọ-cọ-mī'ụm
Nŭs'ọ-rạ
Nō'tĭ-ŭm 1
Nọ-vā'rĭ-ạ
Nọ-vā-tĭ-ā'nụs 1
Nọ-vā'tiạn
Nọ-vā'tụs
Nō-vẹm-pā'ĝī
Nō-vẹm-pŏp'ụ-lĭs
Nŏv'ẹ-rŭs
Nọ-vē'şĭ-ŭm 1
Nō-vĭ-ọ-dū'nụm
Nō-vĭ-ŏm'ạ-gŭm
Nō-vĭ-ŏm'ạ-gŭs
Nō'vĭ-ŭs
Nŏv-ọ-cō'mụm
Nọ-vŏm'ạ-gŭs
Nū'bæ
Nụ-cē'rĭ-ạ
Nū'cĭ-ŭs 1
Nū'cræ
Nụ-ĭth'ọ-nēş, or
  Nū-ĭ-thō'nēş
Nụ-mā'nạ
Nụ-măn'tĭ-ạ 1
Nū-mạn-tī'nạ
Nū-mạn-tī'nụs
Nụ-mā'nụs Rĕm'ụ-
  lŭs   [ŭs
Nū'mạ Pọm-pĭl'ĭ-
Nū'mẹ-nēş
Nụ-mē'nĭ-ạ, or
  Nē-ọ-mē'nĭ-ạ
Nụ-mē'nĭ-ŭs
Nū'mĭ-dạ
Nụ-mĭd'ĭ-ạ
Nụ-mĭd'ĭ-cŭs

Nu-mĭd'ĭ-ŭs
Nu-mĭ-sĭ-ā'nus
Nu-mĭ''sĭ-ŭs 1
Nū'mĭ-tŏr
Nū-mĭ-tō'rĭ-ŭs
Nu-mō'nĭ-ŭs
Nun cō're-ŭs
Nŭn'dĭ-na
Nŭn'dĭ-næ
Nūr'sĭ-a 1
Nū'trĭ-a
Nyc-tē'ĭs
Nyc-tē'lĭ-a
Nyc-tē'lĭ-ŭs
Nўc'teūs 6
Nўc'tĭ-lŏs
Nўc'tĭ-lŭs
Nyc-tĭm'e-nē
Nўc'tĭ-mŭs
Nym-bæ'um
Nўm'phæ
Nymphs
Nym-phæ'us
Nym-phĭd-ĭ-ā'nus
Nym-phĭd'ĭ-ŭs
Nўm-pho-dō'rus
Nўm-pho-lĕp'tēs
Nym-phŏm'a-nēs
Nўp'sĭ-ŭs 1
Nȳ-sæ'us
Nў-sē'ĭ-ŭs 3
Nȳ-sē'on, *or* -um
Nȳ'seūs 6
Ny-sī'a-dēs
Nȳ''sĭ-æ Pŏr'tæ 1
Nȳ''sĭ-ăs 1
Ny-sī'ros
Nȳ''sĭ-ŭs 1
Nys-sē'nus
Nÿs'sen

O.

Ō'a-nŭs
O-ā'rĭ-on
Ō-är'sēs
Ō'a-rŭs
Ō'a-sĭs
O-äx'ēs
Ŏb'o-da
Ŏb'o-dăs
Ŏb'rĭ-măs
Ŏb'rĭ-mō
Ŏb'rĭ-mŭs
Ŏb'se-quĕns
Ŏb-ul-trō'nĭ-ŭs
O-cā'le-a, *or*
  Ŏc-a-lī'a
O-cā'le-æ
Ŏc-cā'sĭ-ō 1
O-cē'a-na
Ō-ce-ăn'ĭ-dēs, *and*
  Ō-ce-a-nĭt'ĭ-dēs 1
Ō-ce-a-nī'ne 1
Ō-ce-a-nī'tĭs 1
Ō-cē'a-nŭs
Ō-cē'ĭ-a 3
Ō-cē'lĭs

O-cĕl-lo-dū'rum
Ŏç'e-lŭm
O-chē'nĭ-ŭs
Ō-chē'sĭ-ŭs 1
Ŏch'ĭ-mŭs
Ŏch'ro-na
Ō'chus
Ŏch-y-rō'ma
O-cō'lum
Ō-crē'sĭ-a 1
Ō-crĭc'o-la
O-crĭd'ĭ-ŏn
Ō-crĭ''sĭ-a 1
Ŏc-ta-cĭl'ĭ-ŭs
Ŏc-ta-vē'nus
Oc-tā'vĭ-a
Ŏc-tā-vĭ-ā'nus
Ŏc-tā'vĭ-ŭs
Ŏc-to-dū'rus
Ŏc-to-gē'sa
O-cȳ'a-lŭs
Ō-cȳp'e-tē
Ō-cȳr'o-ē
Ŏd'a-tĭs
Ŏd-e-nā'tus
O-dē'um
Ō-dī'nus
Ō-dī'tēs
Ō'dĭ-ŭs
Ŏd-o-ā'cer, *or*
  Ō-dō'a-cer
O-dō'ca
Ŏd-o-măn'tī
Ŏd'o-nēs
Ŏd'ry-sæ
Ŏd-ys-sē'a
Ŏd'ys-sey
Ŏd-ys-sē'um
O-dȳs'seūs 6
Œ'a-ger
Œ'a-grŭs, *or*
  Œ-ā'grus
Œ-ăn'the, *and*
  Œ-an-thī'a
Œ-an-thē'a
Œ-ăn'the-æ
Œ'a-sō
Œ-bā'lĭ-a
Œ-băl'ĭ-dēs
Œb'a-lŭs 4
Œb'a-rēs 4
Œb'a-sŭs 4
Œ-bō'tas
Œ'breūs 6
Œ-chā'lĭ-a
Œ'cleūs 6
Œ-clī'dēs 4
Ō-ē'clus
Œc-u-mē'nĭ-ŭs 4
Œ-dĭp'o-dēs
Œd-ĭ-pō'dĭ-a 4
Œd-ĭ-po-dī'on 4
Œd-ĭ-pŏd-ĭ-ŏn'ĭ-
Œd'ĭ-pŭs 4   [dēs 4
Œ-năn'thēs
Œ'ne-a
Œn-e-ō'ne 4
Œ'neūs (*n.*) 6
Œ-nē'us (*a.*)
Œ-nī'a-dæ

Œ-nī'dēs
Œn'o-ē 4
Œ-nŏm'a-ŭs
Œ-nō'ne, *or* -na
Œ-nŏph'y-ta
Œ-nō'pĭ-a
Œ-nŏp'ĭ-dēs
Œ-nō'pĭ-ŏn
Œ-nō'trī
Œ-nō'trĭ-a
Œ-nŏt'rĭ-dēs
Œ-nŏt'ro-pæ
Œ-nō'trus
Œ-nū'sæ
Œ-o-bā'zus
Œ-ŏl'y-cŭs
Œ-ō'nus
O-ĕr'o-ē
Œ-sȳ'me
Œ'ta
Œt'y-lŭs, *or*
  Œt'y-lŭm 4
O-fĭl'lĭ-ŭs
Ŏg-dŏl'a-pĭs
Ŏg-dō'rus
Ŏg'e-nŏs
Ŏg-lō'sa
Ŏg'mĭ-ŭs
O-gō'a
Ō-gŭl'nĭ-a
Ō-gŭl'nĭ-ŭs
Ŏg'y-gēs
Ō-gȳg'ĭ-a
Ō-gȳg'ĭ-dæ
Ŏg'y-rĭs
Ō'ĭ-clēs
Ō'ĭ-cleūs 6
Ō-ī'leūs 6
Ō-ĭ-lī'a-dēs
Ō-ĭ-lī'dēs
Ŏl'a-nē
O-lā'nus
Ŏl'ba-sa
Ol-bē'lus
Ŏl'bĭ-a
Ŏl'bĭ-ŭs
Ŏl'ca-dēs
Ŏl-cha-chī'tēs
Ŏl-chīn'ĭ-ŭm
O-lē'a-rŏs, *or*
  O-lī'a-rŏs
O-lĕn'ĭ-dēs
O-lē'nĭ-ē
Ŏl'e-nŏs
Ŏl'e-nŭm
Ŏl'e-nŭs
Ŏl'e-rŭs
Ō'le-ŭm
O-lĭn'ĭ-æ
Ŏl-ĭ-sī'pō, *or*
  Ŏl-y-sĭp'pō
O-lī'zon
Ŏl'lĭ-ŭs
Ŏl-lŏv'ĭ-cō
Ŏl'mĭ-æ
Ŏl-mī'us, *or*
  Ŏl-mē'us
Ŏl-mō'nēs
Ŏl'o-crŭs

Ŏl'o-rŭs
O-lū'rus
Ō-lȳb'rĭ-ŭs
Ŏl-ym-pē'ne
O-lȳm'pĭ-a
Ŏl-ym-pī'a-dēs
O-lȳm'pĭ-ăs
O-lȳm'pĭ-cŭs
O-lȳm'pĭ-ē'um
O-lȳm-pĭ-o-dō'rus
O-lȳm-pĭ-o-nī'cēs
O-lȳm-pĭ-ŏs'the-nēs
O-lȳm'pĭ-ŭs
Ŏl-ym-pū'sa
O-lȳ'ras
O-lȳ'zon
O-mā'rĭ-ŭs
Ŏm'brĭ-cī
Ŏm'brĭ-ŏs
Om-brō'nēs
Ŏm'o-lē, *or*
  Hŏm'o-lē
Ŏm-o-phā'ġĭ-a
Ŏm'pha-cē
Ŏm'pha-lē
Om-phā'lĭ-ŏn
Ŏm'pha-lŏs
O-næ'um, *or*
  O-æ'ne-ŭm
Ŏn'a-ger
Ŏn'a-rŭs, *or*
  O-nā'rus
O-năs'ĭ-mŭs
Ŏn'a-sŭs
O-nā'tas
Ou-cē'um
Ŏn ches-mī'tēs
Ŏn'cheūs 6
Ŏn'cho-ē
O-nē'um
Ŏn-e-sĭc'rĭ-tŭs
O-nĕs'ĭ-mŭs
O-nē'sĭ-ŭs 1
O-nē'tor
Ŏn-e-tŏr'ĭ-dēs
O-nī'on
O-nī'um
Ŏn'o-ba
O-nŏb'a-lăs
Ŏn-o-chō'nus
Ŏn-o-măc'rĭ-tŭs
Ŏn-o-mas-tŏr'ĭ-dēs
Ŏn-o-măs'tus
Ŏn'o-phăs
Ŏn'o-phĭs
Ŏn-o-săn'der
O-nŭg'na-thŭs
O-nū'phĭs
O nȳ'tēs
O-nȳ'thēs
O-pā'lĭ-a
O-pĕl'ĭ-cŭs
Ŏph'e-lăs
O-phē'lĭ-ŏn
O-phĕl'tēs
Ō'phĭ-a
O-phī'a-dēs
Ō-phĭ-ā'nus
Ō'phĭ-ăs
Ō-phĭ-ō'dēs

O-phī'on
O-phī'o-nēs
O-phī'o-neūs 6
Ō-phĭ-ŏn'ĭ-dēs
Ō'phĭs
Ŏph-ĭ-tō'a
O-phī'tēs
O-phĭ-ū'chus
Ō-phĭ-ū'sa
Ŏph-ry-nē'um
Ŏp'ĭ-cī
O-pĭġ'e-na
O-pĭl'ĭ-ŭs
O-pī'ma Spō'lĭ-a
O-pĭm-ĭ-ā'nus
O-pĭm'ĭ-ŭs
Ŏp'ĭ-ter
Ŏp-ĭ-ter-ġī'nī
O-pī'tēs
Ŏp'o-ĭs
O-pō'ne
O-pō'peūs 6
O-pŏr'ĭ-nŭs
Ŏp'pĭ-a
Ŏp-pĭ-ăn'ĭ-cŭs
Ŏp-pĭ-ā'nus
Ŏp'pĭ-an
Op-pĭd'ĭ-ŭs
Ŏp'pĭ-dŭm Nō'vum
Op-tā'tus
Ŏp'tĭ-mŭs
O-pŭn'tĭ-a 1
O-răc'u-lŭm
Ŏr'a-sŭs
O-rā'ta
Or-bē'lus
Or-bĭ''cĭ-ŭs
Ŏr'bĭ-ŭs
Or-bō'na
Ŏr'ca-dēs
Or-chā'lĭs
Ŏr'cha-mŭs
Or-chĭs-tē'ne
Or-chŏm'e-nŭm
Or-chŏm'e-nŭs
Or-cī'nus
Or-cȳn'ĭ-a.
Or-dē'sus
Or-do-vī'cēs
O-rē'a-dēs
Ō're-ăds
O-rē'as, *nymph.*
Ō're-ăs, *man.*
Ō're-ŏs
Or-e-sĭt'ro-phŭs
O-rēs'tæ
O-rĕs'tēs
Or-es-tē'um
O-rĕs'theūs 6
Or-es-tī'dæ
Or-es-tī'dēs, *and*
  O-rĕs'tĭ-dēs
Ŏr're-tæ
Or-e-tā'nī
Or-e-tĭl'ĭ-a
O-rē'tum
Ō're-ŭs
Ŏr'fĭ-tŭs
Ŏr'ga-na
Or-ġĕt'o-rĭx

Ŏr'ġi-ạ
Ŏr-ị-bā'şi-ŭs 1
O-rĭb'ạ-sŭs
Ŏr'ị-cŏs
Ŏr'ị-cŭm, *or*
　Ŏr'ị-cŭs
Ō'rị-ĕnş
O-rĭġ'ę-nēş
Ŏr'i-ġĕn
O-rī'gō
O-rī'nę
O-rī'nus
Ŏ-rị-ŏb'ạ-tēş
O-rī'ọn
O-rī'ọs
Ŏr-i-sŭl'lạ Lĭv'ị-ạ
O-rī'tæ
O-rīth'ị-ăs
Ŏr-ị-thȳ'iạ
Ŏr-ị-thȳ'ọs
O-rī''tị-ăs 1
O-rī'ụs
Ŏr'mę-nĭs
Ŏr'mę-nŭs
Ŏr'nę-æ, *or*
　Qr-nē'æ
Ŏr-nę-ā'tæ
Ŏr'neūs 6, *man.*
Qr-nē'ụs, *a Centaur.*
Ŏr-nī'thọn
Ŏr'nị-thŭs
Ŏr'nị-tŭs
Qr-nŏs'pạ-dēş
Ŏr-nȳt'ị-ŏn 2
Ŏr'ny-tŭs
Ŏr'ọ-bạ
Q-rō'bị-ạ
Q-rō'bị-ī
Ŏr'ọ-bis
Q-rō'dēş
Q-ræ'tēş
Q-rŏm'ę-dŏn
Ŏr-ọn-tē'ụs (*a.*)
Ŏr-ọ-phër'nēş
Q-rō'pụs
Ŏr'ọ-sạ
Q-rō'şị-ŭs.1
Q-rŏs'pę-dạ
Qr-tō'nạ
Ŏr'pheūs (*n.*) 6
Qr-phē'ụs (*a.*)
Ŏr'phị-tŭs
Orph-næ'ụs
Ŏr-sŏd'ị-cē
Ŏr-sē'ịs
Ŏr'sị-nēş
Ŏr'tạ-lŭs
Qr-thæ'ạ
Ŏr-thăġ'ọ-răs
Ŏr'the
Ŏr'thị-ạ
Qr-thō'şị-ạ 1
Qr-thō'sịs
Qr-tō'nạ
Ŏr-tȳġ'ị-ạ
Ŏr-tȳġ'ị-ŭs
Ŏ-rị-ăn'dẹr
Q-rȳ'ụs
Ŏs'ạ-cēş
Ŏs-çhọ-phō'rị-ạ

Ŏs'cị-ŭs 1
Q-sĭn'ị-ŭs
Q-sī'rịs
Q-sĭs'mị-ī
Ŏs'phạ-gŭs
Ŏs-rhọ-ē'nę
Qs-sŏn'ọ-bạ
Ŏs-tę-ō'dēş
Ŏs'tị-ạ
Qs-tō'rị-ŭs
Ŏs-trạ-cī'nę
Qs-trŏg'ọ-thī
Ŏs-y-mán'dị-ăs
Ŏt'ạ-cēş
Ŏt-ạ-cĭl'ị-ŭs
Q-tā'nēş
Q-tăx'ēş
Ŏth'mạ-rŭs
Q-thrō'nụs
Q-thrȳ'ạ-dēş
Q-thrȳ'ọ-neūs 6
Q-thrȳ''şị-ŭs 1
Q-trē'rạ
Ŏ'treūs 6
Q-trī'ạ-dēş
Ŏt-ryn-tī'dēş
Ŏt-tọ-rŏc'ọ-ræ
Q-vĭd'ị-ŭs
ŏv'id
Q-vĭn'ị-ạ
Q-vĭn'ị-ŭs
Ŏx'ạ-thrēş
Qx-ī'æ
Ŏx'ị-mēş
Qx-ī'ọ-næ
Ŏx-ȳ'ạ-rēş
Ŏx-y-cā'nụs
Ŏx-y-dā'tēş
Qx-ȳd'rạ-cæ
Ŏx'y-lŭs
Ŏx-y-nē'ạ
Ŏx-y-ō'pụm
Qx-ȳp'ọ-rŭs
Ŏx-y-ryn-çhī'tæ
Qx-ȳth'ę-mĭs
Q-zē'nę
Q-zī'nēş
Ŏz'ọ-læ, *or* Ŏz'ọ-lī

P.

Pạ-cā'rị-ŭs
Pạ-cā-tị-ā'nụs 1
Pạ-cā'tụs
Păc'cị-ŭs 1
Pạ-çhī'nụs
Pạ-çhō'mị-ŭs
Pạ-çhȳm'ę-rēş
Pạ-çhȳ'nọs, *or* -nụs
Pā-cị-ā'nụs 1
Pā'ci-an
Pạ-cĭf'ị-cŭs
Pạ-cĭl'ị-ŭs
Páç'ị lŭs
Pạ-cō-nị-ā'nụs
Pạ-cō'nị-ŭs
Páç'ọ-rŭs
Păc'tị-ạ 1

Pạc-tō'lụs
Păc-tụ-mē'ị-ŭs 3
Păc'ty-ăs
Păc'ty-ēş
Pạ-cū'vị-ŭs
Pạ-dæ'ī
Pád'u-ạ
Pạ-dū'sạ
Pæ'ạn
Pæ-ā'nēş
Pæ-dăr'ị-tŭs
Pæd'ạ-sŭs 4
Pæ'dị-ŭs
Pæg'nị-ŭm 4
Pæ-mā'nī
Pæ'ọn
Pæ'ọ-nēş
Pæ-ō'ni-ạ
Pæ-ŏn'ị-dēş
Pæ-ō'nị-ŭs
Pæ'ọ-plæ
Pæ-rĭs'ạ-dēş
Pæ'sọs
Pæs'tụm 4
Pæ-tā'nị-ŭm
Pæ-tī'nụs
Pæ-tō'vị-ŭm
Pạ-gā'nī
Pág'ạ-sæ, *or*
　Pág'ạ-sạ
Pág'ạ sŭs
Pạ-lā'cị-ŭm, *or*
　Pạ-lā'tị-ŭm 1
Pā-læ-ăp'ọ-lĭs
Pạ-læb'y-blŭs 4
Pạ-læ'mọn
Pā-læ-ŏl'ọ-gŭs
Pạ-læp'ạ-phŏs 4
Pál-æ-phạr-sā'lụs
Pạ-læph'ạ-tŭs 4
Pạ-læp'ọ-lĭs 4
Pál-æs-tī'nạ
Pál-æs-tī'nụs
Pạ-læs'trạ 4
Pạ-læs'trị-ō 4
Pạ-læt'y-rŭs 4
Pál'ạ-mäs
Pál-ạ-mē'dēş
Pál-ạ-tī'nụs
Pạ-lā'tị-ŭm 1
Pạ-lē'ạ
Pạ-lē'mọn
Pál-fụ-rị-ā'nạ
Pál-fū'rị-ŭs Sū'rạ
Pál-ị-bō'thrạ, *or*
　Pạ-lĭb'ọ-thrạ
Pál-ị-bọ-thrē'nī
Pál-ị-cā'nụs
Pạ-lī'cī
Pạ-lī'cụs
Pạ-lĭl'ị-ạ
Pạ-lī'lịs
Pạ-lĭn'drọ-mŏs
Pál-ị-nū'rụs
Pā-lị-ū'rụs
Pạl-lác'ọ-păs
Pál'lạ-däs
Pál'lạ-dēş
Pạl-lā'dị-ŭm
Pạl-lā'num

Pál-lạn-tē'ụm
Pạl-lán'tị-ăs 1
Pạl-lán'tị-dēş
Pál-lán'tị-ŏn 2
Pạl-lē'nạ
Pạl-lē'neūs 6
Pạl-mī'sọs
Pạl-mȳ'rạ
Pál-my-rē'nę
Pál'pę-tŭs
Pạl-phū'rị-ŭs
Pál-ụm-bī'nụm
Pạm-bō'tịs
Pạ-mī'sụs
Pám'mạ-çhŭs
Pám'mę-nēş
Pám'phạ-gŭs
Pám'phị-lạ
Pạm-phĭl'ị-dăs
Pám'phị-lŭs
Pạm-phȳ'lạ, *or* -lē
Pạm-phȳ'lịs
Pạm-phȳ'lụs
Pạm-prē'pị-ŭs
Pán-ạ-cē'ạ
Pán'ạ-crạ
Pạ-næ'tị-ŭs 1
Pán-æ-tō'lụs
Pán'ạ-rụs
Pạ-năr'ę-tŭs
Pán-ạ-rĭs'tę
Pạ-năth-ę-næ'ạ
Pạn-çhæ'ạ
Pạn-çhā'ị-ạ 3
Pạn-çhā'tēş
Pán'crạ-tēş
Pán'crạ-tĭs
Pạn-crā'tị-ŭm 1
Pạn-dæ'ạ
Pạn-dā'rę-ŏs
Pạn-dā'rị-ạ
Pán'dạ-rŭs
Pán-dạ-tā'rị-ạ
Pạn-dā'tēş
Pạn-dē'mị-ạ
Pạn-dē'mụs
Pạn-dī'ạ
Pạn-dī'ọn
Pạn-dī'ọ-nĭs
Pán-dọ-çhī'ụm
Pạn-dō'rạ
Pạn-dō'şị-ạ 1
Pán'drọ-sŏs
Pā'nę-ăs
Pạ-nĕġ'y-rĭs
Pán'ę-lŭs
Pán'ę-mŭs, *month.*
Pạ-nē'mụs, *man.*
Pạ-nē'ụm
Pạn-ġæ'ụs
Pán-hęl-lē'nēş
Pā'nị-ạ
Pạ-nī'ạ-sĭs
Pán-ị-ġē'rịs
Pā-nị-ō'nị-ŭm
Pā'nị-ŭs
Pán'nị-cŭs
Pán'nọ-nēş
Pạn-nō'nị-ạ
Pán-ọ-dō'rụs

Păn'ọ-pē
Pán-ọ-pē'ạ
Pạ-nō'pę-æ
Pán'ọ-pēş
Pán'ọ-peŭs 6
Pạ-nō'pi-ŏn
Pán'ọ-pĭs
Pạ-nŏp'ọ-lĭs
Pán'tạ-clēş
Pạn-tæn'ę-tŭs 4
Pạn-tæ'nụs
Pạn-tăġ'ạ-thŭs
Pạn-tā'ġi-ạ
Pạn-tā'ġị-ăs
Pạn-tā'lę-ŏn
Pạn-tâu'chụs
Pạn-tē'lę-ŭs
Pán'teŭs 6
Pạn-thē'ạ
Pán'thę-ŏn, *or*
　Pạn-thē'ọn
Pán'thę-ŭs
Pạn-thō'ị-dēş
Pán'thọ-ŭs
Pạn-tĭc'ạ-pēş
Pạn-tĭch'ị-ŭm
Pạn-tŏl'ạ-bŭs
Pạ-nȳ'ạ-sĭs
Pạ-nȳ'ạ-sŭs
Pạ-phā'ġēş
Pā'phị-ạ
Pā'phị-ē
Pā'phị-ŭs
Páph'lạ-gŏn
Paph-lăġ'ọ-nēş
Páph-lạ-gō'nị-ạ
Pā-pị-ā'nụs
Pā'pị-ăs
Páp'ị-lŭs
Pạ-pĭn-ị-ā'nụs
Pạ-pĭn'i-an
Pạ-pĭn'ị-ŭs
Pạ-pĭr'ị-ạ
Pạ-pĭr-ị-ā'nụs
Pạ-pĭr'ị-ŭs
Pā'pị-ŭs
Pạ-prē'mịs
Pạ-pȳr'ị-ŭs
Pár-ạ-bȳs'tọn
Pár-ạ-çhĕl-ọ-ī'tæ
Pár-ạ-clē'tụs, *or*
　Pár-ạ-clī'tụs
Pár-ạ-dī'sụs
Pạ-ræt'ạ-cæ 4
Pạ-ræt-ạ-cē'nę 4
Pár-æ-tō'nị-ī
Pár-æ-tō'nị-ŭm
Pár'ạ-lī
Pár-ạ-lị-pŏm'ę-nạ
Pár'ạ-lŭs
Pár-ạ-pọ-tā'mị-ạ
Pạ-rā'şị-ạ 1
Pạ-rā'şị-ŭs 1
Pár'ę-ạ
Pár'ẹ-drī
Pár-ẹn-tā'lị-ạ
Pár'ịs
Pạ-rĭs'ạ-dēş
Pạ-rĭ''şị-ī 1
Pár'ị-sŭs

Pā'rĭ-ŭm
Pā'rĭ-ŭs
Păr'me-năs
Par-měn'ĭ-děs
Par-mē'nĭ-ō
Păr'me-nō
Par-nā'sŭs
Păr-o-päin'ĭ-sŭs, *or*
  Pár-o-pa-mī'sŭs
Pa-rō'pŭs
Păr-o-rē'a, *or* -rī'a
Par-pā'ne-ŭs
Par-rhā'sĭ-a 1
Păr'rha-sĭs
Par-rhā'sĭ-ŭs 1
Pär-tha-mīs'ĭ-rĭs
Par-thā'on
Pär-tha-ŏn'ĭ-děs
Par-thē'nĭ-a
Par-thē'nĭ-ē
Par-thē'nĭ-ī
Par-thěn'ĭ-cē
Par-thē'nĭ-ŭs
Pär'the-nŏn
Par-thěn'o-pē
Pär'the-nŏs
Pär'thĭ-a
Par-thī'nī
Pär-thy-ē'ne
Par-tĭc'u-lō
Pa-rȳ'a-drēs
Pā-ry-ē'tæ
Pa-rȳs'a-děs
Pa-rȳs'a-tĭs, *or*
  Pár-y-sā'tĭs
Pa-sär'ga-da, *or*
  Pa-sär'ga-dæ
Pas-chā'sĭ-ŭs 1
Pā'se-äs
Păs-ĭ-bū'la
Păs'ĭ-clēs
Păs-ĭ-cŏmp'sa
Păs-ĭ-mē'lus
Păs-ĭ-pē'da
Pa-sĭph'a-ē
Pa-sĭph'ĭ-lē
Pa-sĭph'ĭ-lŭs
Pa-sĭt'e-lēs
Pa-sĭth'o-ē
Pa-sĭt'ĭ-grĭs
Păs'sa-rŏn
Păs-se-rī'nŭs
Păs-sĭ-ē'nŭs 1
Păt'a-ġē
Păt-a-lē'ne
Păt'a-lŭs
Păt'a-ra
Păt'a-reūs 6
Păt-a-vī'nŭs
Pa-tā'vĭ-ŭm
Pa-tē'ra
Pa-tēr'cu-lŭs
Păt-ĭ-zī'thēs
Pa-trī''cĭ-ŭs 1
Pát'rick
Pā'trō
Păt'ro-băs
Pa-trō'clēs, *or*
  Păt'ro-clēs
Pa-trō'clī

Păt-ro-clī'děs
Pa-trō'clŭs
Pā'tron
Pa-trō'us
Păt'ta-la
Păt-ta-lē'ne
Pa-tŭl'cĭ-ŭs 1
Pa-tū'mŭs
Pâu'la
Pâu-lī'na
Pâu-lī'nŭs
Pâu'lŭs
Pâu-sā'nĭ-äs
Pâu'sĭ-äs 1
Pâu-sĭ-lī'pon
Pâu-sĭ-lȳ'pŭs
Pâu-sĭm'a-chŭs
Păx'a-mŭs
Pěc'tĭ-ŭs 1
Pe-dā'cĭ-a 1
Pe-dā'lĭ-ŭm
Pe-dā'nī
Pe-dā'nĭ-ŭs
Pěd'a-sa, *or* -sŭs
Pe-dī'a-dĭs
Pē-dĭ-ā'nŭs
Pē-dĭ-ā'tĭ-a
Pē-dĭ-ē'a
Pē'dĭ-ŭs
Pe-gäs'ĭ-děs
Pěg'a-sĭs
Pěg'a-sŭs
Pe-lā'ġĭ-a
Pe-lā'ġĭ-ŭs
Pěl'a-gŏn
Pe-lăg'o-nēs
Pěl-a-gō'nĭ-ŭs
Pe-lās'ġī
Pe-lās'ġĭ-a
Pe-lās'ġĭ-cŭs
Pe-lās-ġĭ-ō'tĭs
Pěl'a-tēs
Pěl'e-căs
Pe-lē'cēs
Pe-lēn'do-nēs
Pěl-e-thrō'nĭ-ī
Pe-lět'ro-nēs
Pē'leūs 6
Pē'lĭ-a
Pa-lī'a-děs
Pē'lĭ-äs
Pe-lī'děs
Pěl-ĭ-næ'um
Pěl-ĭ-næ'ŭs
Pē'lĭ-ŏn
Pē'lĭ-ŭm
Pel-lā'na
Pel-lē'ne
Pěl'lĭ-ō
Pe-lō'děs
Pěl'o-pē
Pěl-o-pē'a
Pěl-o-pī'a
Pe-lō'pĭ-ŭs (*a.*)
Pěl-o-pon-nē'sŭs

Pe-lō'rĭs
Pe-lō'rŭm, *or*
  Pe-lō'rŭs
Pe-lū-sĭ-ō'ta 1
Pe-lū'sĭ-ŭm 1
Pěm'pe-lŭs
Pe-nā'tēs
Pen-dā'lĭ-ŭm
Pe-nē'ĭ-a 3
Pe-nē'ĭs
Pe-nē'le-ŭs
Pe-někl'o-pē
Pe-nē'os
Pe-nē'ŭs
Pe-nĭc'u-lŭs
Pěn'ĭ-däs
Pē'nĭ-ŭs
Pen-nī'næ
Pen-tăp'y-lŏn
Pěn-te-dăc'ty-lŏn
Pěn'te-lē
Pen-těl'ĭ-cŭs
Pěn-te-lī'um
Pěn-the-sĭ-lē'a
Pěn'theūs (*n.*)
Pen-thē'ŭs (*a.*)
Pen-thī'děs
Pěn'thĭ-lŭs
Pěp-a-gŏm'e-nŭs
Pěp-a-rē'thos
Pe-phrē'dō
Pěr'a-tŭs
Per-cěn'nĭ-ŭs
Per-cō'pe
Per-cō'sĭ-a 1
Per-cō'sĭ-ŭs 1
Per-cō'te
Pěr-e-grī'na
Pěr-e-grī'nŭs
Pē'reūs 6
Pěr'ga-mŏs
Pěr'ga-mŭs
Pěr'ga-sē
Pěr'ġe
Pěr-ĭ-ăn'der
Pěr-ĭ-är'chŭs
Pěr-ĭ-bœ'a[7]
Pěr-ĭ-bō'mĭ-ŭs
Pěr'ĭ-clēs
Pěr-ĭ-clȳm'e-nŭs
Pěr-ĭc-tī'o-nē
Pěr-ĭ-dī'a
Pe-rī-e-ġē'tēs
Pěr-ĭ-ē'rēs
Pe-rĭġ'e-nēs
Pěr-ĭ-gū'ne
Pěr-ĭ-lā'ŭs
Pe-rīl'e-ŏs
Pe-rīl'lĭ-ŭs
Pěr-ĭ-mē'de
Pěr-ĭ-mē'děs
Pěr-ĭ-mē'la, *or* -le
Pěr-ĭ-měl'ĭ-děs
Pěr-ĭ-pa-tět'ĭ-cī
Pěr-i-pa-tět'ics
Pe-rĭp'a-tŭs
Pe-rĭph'a-nēs
Pěr'ĭ-phăs
Pěr-ĭ-phē'mŭs
Pěr-ĭ-phē'tēs

Pěr-ĭ-pho-rē'tŭs
Per-ĭ-plec-tŏm'e-
Pe-rĭs'a-děs [nēs
Pe-rĭs'te-rē
Pe-rĭs'the-nēs
Pěr-ĭ-stȳ'lum, *and*
  Pe-rĭs'ty-lŭm
Pe-rīt'a-nŭs
Pe-rī'tŭs
Pěr-ĭ-tō'nĭ-ŭm
Pē'rō, *or* Pěr'o-nē
Pěr'o-ē
Pěr'o-la
Per-pe-rē'ne
Per-pho-rē'tŭs
Per-sa-bō'ra
Per-sē'a
Per-sē'ĭs
Per-sěp'o-lĭs
Pěr'sēs
Pěr'seūs (*n.*) 6
Per-sē'ŭs (*a.*)
Pěr'sĭ-a 1
Pěr'sĭ-cŭs
Pěr'sĭ-ŭs Flăc'cŭs 1
Pěr'tĭ-năx
Per-tū'sa
Pe-rū'sĭ-a 1
Pěr-u-sī'nŭs
Pes-cěn'nĭ-ŭs
Pěs'sĭ-nŭs, *or*
  Pes-sī'nŭs
Pět'a-lē
Pe-tā'lĭ-a
Pět'a-lŭs
Pět'a-sŏs
Pe-tē'lĭ-a
Pět-e-lī'nŭs
Pē'te-ŏn
Pět'e-rŏs
Pē'te-ŭs
Pět'ĭ-cŭs
Pe-tĭl'ĭ-a
Pe-tĭl'ĭ-ī
Pe-tĭl'ĭ-ŭs
Pět-o-sī'rĭs
Pē'tra
Pe-træ'a
Pe-trē'ĭ-ŭs 3
Pe-trī'num
Pět-ro-cō'rĭ-ī
Pe-trō'nĭ-a
Pe-trō'nĭ-ŭs
Pět'ta-lŭs
Pět'tĭ-ŭs
Pe-tū'sĭ-a 1
Peu-cā'le-ī
Peū'ce
Peu-cěd'a-nŏs
Peū'ce-la
Peu-cěs'tēs
Peu-cē'tĭ-a 1
Peu-cē'tĭ-ī 1
Peu-cī'nĭ
Peū-co-lā'ŭs
Pěx-o-dō'rŭs
Pha-cū'sa
Phæ-ā'cēs
Phæ-ā'cĭ-a 1
Phæ-bā'dĭ-ŭs

Phæd'ĭ-ma 4
Phæd'ĭ-mŭs 4
Phæ'don
Phæ'dra
Phæ'drĭ-a
Phæ-drī'a-děs
Phæd'ro-mŭs 4
Phæd'y-ma 4
Phæ-mŏn'o-ē
Phæ-năg'o-rē
Phæ-năr'e-tē
Phæ'nĭ-äs
Phæn-o-mē'rĭs 4
Phæ'non
Phæ-ŏc'o-měs
Phæs'a-na 4
Phæs'tus 4
Phā'e-thŏn
Phā-e-thon-tī'a-děs
Phā-e-thŏn'tĭ-děs
Phā-e-thū'sa
Phæ'ŭs
Pha-ġē'sĭ-a 1
Phā'ĭ-nŭs
Phăl-a-crī'ne
Pha-læ'cĭ-ŭs 1
Pha-læ'cŭs
Pha-læ'sĭ-a, *or* -æ 1
Pha-lā'ra, *or*
  Phăl'a-ra
Phăl'a-rĭs
Pha-lā'rus
Phăl'cĭ-dŏn
Phā'le-äs
Pha-lē'reūs 6, *or*
  Pha-lē're-ŭs
Pha-lē'rĭ-a
Phăl'e-rĭs
Pha-lē'rum
Pha-lē'rus
Phā'lĭ-äs
Pha-lī'nŭs
Phăl'lĭ-ca
Pha-lō're
Pha-lȳ''sĭ-ŭs 1
Phā'me-äs
Pha-nā'cēs
Pha-næ'ŭs
Pha-năg'o-ra
Phā'nēs
Phā'nĭ-a
Phā'nĭ-äs
Phā'nĭ-ŭm
Phăn'o-clēs
Pha-nŏc'ra-tēs
Phăn-o-dē'mus
Pha-nŏd'ĭ-cŭs
Pha-nŏm'a-chŭs
Pha-nŏs'the-nēs
Phăn'o-tē
Phăn'o-teūs 6
Pha-nō'the-a
Phăn'o-tĭs
Phan-tā'sĭ-a 1
Phăn'ta-sŏs
Pha-răç'ĭ-děs
Phā'ræ, *or* Phē'ræ
Phăr-an-dā'tēs
Phā'ra-ō
Pha-răs'ma-nēs

Phạr-bē′lụs
Phạr-cē′dọn
Phā′rị-ŭs
Phär-mạ-cē′ạ, or
  Phär-mạ-cī′ạ
Phär-mạ-cū′sạ
Phär-nạ-bā′zụs
Phạr-nā′cẹ-ạ
Phär′nạ-cēş
Phạr-nā′cị-ạ 1
Phär-nạ-pā′tēş
Phạr-nū′chụs
Phạr-sā′lị-ạ
Phạr-sā′lọs
Phạr-sā′lụs
Phạ-rū′şị-ī 1
Phär′y-bŭs
Phạ-rўc′ạ-dŏn
Phär′y-ġæ
Phăs-ạ-ē′lịs
Phạ-sē′lịs
Phạ-sī′ạ-dēş
Phā-şị-ā′nạ 1
Phā′şị-ăs 1
Phâu-rū′şị-ī 1
Phăv-ọ-rī′nụs
Phạ-zē′mọn
Phē′ạ, or Phē′ị-ạ 4
Phẹ-cā′dụm
Phē′ġeūs 6
Phĕl′lị-ạ
Phĕl′lọ-ē
Phē′mị-æ
Phē′mị-ŭs
Phẹ-mŏn′ọ-ē
Phĕn-ẹ-bē′thịs
Phē′nẹ-ŏs
Phē′nẹ-ŭm
Phē′nẹ-ŭs
Phē′ræ
Phẹ-ræ′ạ
Phĕr′ẹ-clŭs
Phẹ-rĕc′rạ-tēş
Phĕr-ẹ-cȳ′ạ-dæ
Phĕr-ẹ-cȳ′dēş
Phĕr-ẹn-dā′tēş
Phĕr-ẹ-nī′cẹ
Phĕr-ẹ-nī′cụs
Phẹ-rĕph′ạ-tē
Phē′rēş
Phĕr-ẹ-tı′ạ-dēş
Phẹ-rē′tị-ăs 1
Phĕr-ẹ-tī′mạ
Phĕr′ị-nŭm
Phẹ-rū′sạ
Phī′ạ-lē
Phī-ā′lị-ạ, or
  Phị-gā′lị-ạ
Phī′ạ-lŭs
Phị-cē′ọn
Phĭc′ọ-rēş
Phĭd′ị-ăs
Phĭd′ị-lē
Phị-dĭp′pị-dēş
Phị-dĭ′′tị-ạ 1
Phị-dō′lạs
Phĭd′y-lē
Phĭg-ạ-lē′ạ, or
  Phị-gā′lị-ạ
Phĭl-ạ-dĕl-phī′ạ

Phĭl-ạ-dĕl′phị-ạ
Phĭl-ạ-dĕl′phụs
Phī′læ
Phị-læ′nịs
Phị-læ′ụs
Phị-lā′grị-ŭs
Phĭl-ạ-lē′thēş
Phị-lā′mọn
Phị-lär′ẹ-tŭs
Phị-lär′ġy-rŭs
Phĭl′ẹ-ăs
Phị-lē′bụs
Phĭl-ẹ-mā′tị-ŭm 1
Phị-lĕm′ẹ-nŭs
Phị-lē′mọn
Phị-lē′nẹ
Phị-lē′nị-ŭm
Phĭl′ẹ-rŏs
Phị-lē′şị-ŭs 1
Phị-lē′tạs
Phị-lē′tị-ŭs 1
Phị-lē′tọr
Phị-lē′tụs
Phĭl′ẹ-ŭs
Phị-lī′ạ-dăs
Phị-lī′ạ-dēş
Phĭl′ị-dás
Phĭl′ị-dēş
Phị-lī′nẹ
Phị-lī′nụs
Phĭl-ịp-pē′ī
Phĭl-ịp-pē′ụs
Phị-lĭp′pị-cŭs
Phĭl-ịp-pŏp′ọ-lĭs
Phĭl-ịs-tī′dēş
Phị-lĭs′tị-ō
Phị-lĭs′tị-ŏn 2
Phị-lўr′ị-dēş
Phĭl-ọ bœ-ō′tụs
Phĭl-ọ-cạ-lē′ạ, or
  Phĭl-ọ-cạ-lī′ạ
Phĭl-ọ-chär′ị-dăs
Phị-lŏch′ọ-rŭs
Phĭl′ọ-clēş   [ŭm 1
Phĭl-ọ-cọ-mā′şị-
Phị-lŏc′rạ-tēş
Phĭl-ọc-tē′tēş
Phĭl-ọ-cȳ′prụs
Phĭl-ọ-dạ-mē′ạ, or
  Phĭl-ọ-dạ-mī′ạ
Phĭl-ọ-dā′mụs
Phĭl-ọ-dē′mụs
Phị-lŏd′ị-cē
Phị-lœ′tị-ŭs 1
Phĭl-ọ-dū′lụs
Phị-lŏġ′ẹ-nēş
Phị-lŏl′ạ-chēş
Phĭl-ọ-lā′ụs
Phị-lŏl′ọ-gŭs
Phị-lŏm′ạ-chē
Phị-lŏm′brọ-tŭs
Phĭl-ọ-mē′dị-ạ
Phĭl-ọ-mē′dụs
Phĭl-ọ-mē′lạ
Phĭl-ọ-mẹ-lī′dēş
Phĭl-ọ-mē′lị-ŭm
Phĭl-ọ-mē′lụs
Phĭl-ọ-mē′tọr
Phĭl-ọ-mū′sụs
Phị-lō′nị-ạ

Phị-lŏn′ị-dēş
Phị-lō′nịs
Phị-lŏn′ọ-ē
Phị-lŏn′ọ-mŭs
Phị-lō′nụs
Phị-lŏp′ạ-tör
Phị-lō′phị-ŏn
Phĭl′ọ-phrŏn
Phĭl′ọ-pŏl′ẹ-mŭs
Phị-lŏp′ọ-nŭs
Phĭl′ọ-rō′mụs
Phĭl′ọ-stĕph′ạ-nŭs
Phị-lŏs′trạ-tŭs
Phị-lō′tạs
Phị-lŏt′ẹ-rạ
Phị-lō′thẹ-ạ
Phĭl′ọ-thē′rụs
Phị-lō′thẹ-ŭs
Phĭl′ọ-tī′mụs
Phị-lō′tị-ŭm 1
Phị-lō′tịs
Phĭl′tẹ-rē
Phị-lū′mẹ-nạ
Phị-lū′mẹ-nŭs
Phĭl′y-rạ
Phĭl′y-rē′ịs
Phĭl′y-rēş
Phị-nē′ụm
Phī′neūs (n.) 6
Phị-nē′ụs (a.)
Phị-nī′dēş
Phĭn′tị-ạ 1
Phĭn′tị-ăs 1
Phlĕġ′ẹ-lăs
Phlĕġ′ẹ-thŏn
Phlē′ġị-ăs
Phlē′grạ
Phlẹ-græ′ọs
Phlē′ġy-æ
Phlē′ġy-ăs
Phlī-ā′şị-ạ 1
Phlī-ā′şị-ŭs 1
Phlœ′ụs
Phlō′ġịs
Phlō′ġị-ŭs
Phlȳ′eūs 6
Phọ-bē′tọr
Phọ-cā′ị-cŭs
Phŏc′ạ-ĭs
Phō′cẹ
Phọ-cĕn′sēş
Phō′ceūs (n.) 6
Phọ-cē′ụs (a.)
Phō′cị-cī
Phō′cị-ŏn 1
Phọ-cū′sæ
Phọ-cȳl′ị-dēş
Phœ-bā′dị-ŭs
Phœ′bạs
Phœ′bẹ
Phœ-bē′ụm
Phœ-bē′ụs
Phœ-bĭ′′cị-ŭs 1
Phœb′ị-dăs 4
Phœ-bĭġ′ẹ-nạ
Phœ′bụs
Phœ′mọs
Phœ-nī′cẹ
Phœ-nī′cēş
Phœ-nī′′cẹ-ŭs 1

Phœ-nī′′cị-ạ 1
Phœ-nĭç′ị-dēş
Phœ-nī′′cị-ŭm 1
Phœ-nī′cụs
Phœn-ị-cū′sạ 4
Phœ′nịx
Phœ′tị-ŭm
Phŏl′ọ-ē
Phọ-mō′thịs
Phŏn-ọ-lĕn′ị-dēş
Phör′cy-dēş
Phör′mị-ō
Phọ-rō′neūs (n.) 6
Phŏr-ọ-nē′ụs (a.)
Phór-ọ-nī′dæ
Phọ-rō′nịs
Phŏs′phọ-rŏs
Phŏs′phọ-rŭs
Phọ-tī′nụs
Phō′tị-ŭs 1
Phrạ-ā′tēş
Phrạ-ät′ị-cēş
Phrạ-dā′tēş
Phrạ-hā′tēş
Phrạ-nĭc′ạ-tēş
Phrás′ị-clēş
Phrás′ị-mŭs
Phrā′şị-ŭs 1
Phrät-ạ-phĕr′nēş
Phrẹ-ġē′nạ
Phrī-ạ-pā′tị-ŭs 1
Phrī′′cị-ŏn 1
Phrọ-nē′şị-ŭm 1
Phrŏn′ị-mạ
Phrặ-gụn-dī′ọ-nēş
Phrȳ′ġēş
Phrȳġ′ị-ạ
Phrȳġ′ị-ŭs
Phrȳ′nẹ
Phrȳn′ị-chŭs
Phryx-ē′ụs (a.)
Phthī′ạ 5
Phthī′ạs 5
Phthī-ō′tēş 5
Phthī-ō′tịs 5
Phthī-rŏph′ạ-ġī 5
Phụr-nū′tụs
Phȳ-ā′cēş
Phȳġ′ẹ-lạ
Phȳl′ạ-cē
Phȳl′ạ-cŭs
Phȳ′lẹ
Phȳ-lē′ịs
Phȳ′leūs 6
Phy-lī′dēş
Phȳl′ị-rạ
Phȳl′ị-rēş
Phyl-láç′ị-dēş
Phyl-lā′lị-ạ
Phyl-lē′ị-ŭs 3
Phȳl′leūs (n.) 6
Phyl-lē′ụs (a.)
Phȳl′lị-dăs
Phȳl′lị-ŭs
Phyl-lŏd′ọ-cē
Phy-rī′tēş
Phy-rŏm′ạ-chŭs
Phȳs′cọ-ạ
Phȳş-ị-ọg-nō′mọn

Phy-tăl′ị-dēş
Phȳt′ạ-lŭs
Phy-tē′ụm
Phȳ′′tị-ạ 1
Phȳx′ị-ŭm 1
Pī-ā′lị-ạ
Pī′ạ-sŭs
Pī-cā′nụs
Pī-cē′næ
Pī-cē′nī
Pī-cĕn′tị-ạ 1
Pĭç-ẹn-tī′nī
Pĭç-ẹu-tī′nụs
Pī-cē′nụm
Pī′crạ
Pịc-tā′vī, or
  Pĭc′tọ-nēş
Pịc-tā′vị-ŭm
Pī-dō′rụs
Pị-dȳ′tēş
Pī′ẹ-lŭs
Pī′ẹ-rạ
Pī′ẹ-rēş
Pī-ē′rị-ạ
Pī-ĕr′ị-dēş
Pī′ẹ-rĭs
Pī′ẹ-rŏs, or -rŭs
Pī′ẹ-tás
Pī′grēş
Pī-lē′sụs
Pĭl′ị-ạ
Pī-lō′rụs
Pịm-plē′ạ
Pịm-plō′ị-dēş
Pịm-plē′ịs
Pịm-prä′mạ
Pĭn′ạ-rạ
Pī-nā′rị-ŭs
Pĭn′ạ-rŭs
Pĭn′dạ-rŭs
Pĭn′dạ-sŭs
Pī-nē′tụs
Pĭn′thị-ạ
Pĭn′thị-ăs
Pĭn′y-tŭs
Pī′ọ-nē
Pī′ọ-nịs
Pī-ræ′eūs 6
Pī-rē′nẹ
Pị-rī′cụs
Pī-rĭth′ọ-ŭs
Pī-rŏ′mịs
Pĭr′ọ-ŭs 6
Pī-rŭs′tæ
Pī′sæ
Pī-sæ′ụs
Pī-sā′nụs
Pī-sā′tēş
Pī-sâu′rụm
Pī-sâu′rụs
Pī-sē′nọr
Pīs′ẹ-ŭs
Pī′′sị-ăs 1
Pīs′ị-dæ
Pī-sĭd′ị-ạ
Pī-sĭd′ị-cē
Pīs-ịs-trät′ị-dæ
Pīs-ịs-trät′ị-dēş
Pī-sĭs′trạ-tụs

Pī-sō'nēs
Pī-sō'nįs
Pĭs'sį-rŭs
Pĭs-tǫ-clē'rįs
Pįs-tō'rį-ą
Pĭs'ty-rŭs
Pĭt'ą-nē
Pį-thăg'ǫ-rás
Pī-thē'cį-ŭm 1
Pī-thē'cǫn Cŏl'pŏs
Pĭth-ē-cū'są, or
  Pĭth-ē-cū'sæ
Pĭth-ǫ-lā'ŭs
Pį-thŏ'lē-ŏn
Pĭt-į-ū'sæ
Pĭt'thę-ą
Pįt-thē'įs
Pĭt'theŭs (n.)6
Pįt-thē'ŭs (a.)
Pĭt-ŭ-ā'nį-ŭs
Pĭt-ŭ-lā'nī
Pĭt'y-ą
Pĭt-y-ĕ'ą, or -ī'ą
Pĭt-y-ǫ-nē'sŭs
Pĭt'y-ŭs
Pĭt-y-ū'są
Pĭt-y-ū'sæ
Pįx-ŏd'ą-rŭs
Plą-cĕn'tį-ą 1
Pláç-į-dē-į-ā'nŭs
Plą-cĭd'į-ą
Pláç'į-dŭs
Plăç'į-tŭs
Plœ-tō'rį-ŭs
Plą-nā'sį-ą 1
Pląn-cī'ną
Plăn'cį-ŭs 1
Plą-nē'sį-ŭm 1
Plą-nū'dēs
Plą-tæ'ą
Plát'ą-gō
Plą-tăg-į dō'rŭs
Plăt-ą-mō'dēs
Plăt'ą-mŏn
Plą-tā'nį-ŭs
Plát'ą-nŭs
Plā'tę-ą, or
  Plą-tē'ą
Plą-tē'æ
Plą-tŏn'į-cī
Plą-tō'nį-ŭs
Plâu'tį-ą 1
Plâu-tį-ā'nŭs 1
Plâu-tĭl'lą
Plâu'tį-ŭs 1
Plâu'tŭs
Plē'ią-dēs, 3, and
  Plę-ī'ą-dēs
Plē'į-ăs 3
Plę-ī'ǫ-nē
Plę-mĭn'į-ŭs
Pleu-mŏx'į-ī 1
Pleu-rā'tŭs
Pleū'rǫn
Pleu-rŏ'nį-ą
Pleū'sį-dēs
Pleū-sį-dĭp'pŭs
Plĭn'į-ŭs
Plĭn'y
Plįn-thī'nę, or

Plĭn'thį-nē
Plĭn-thį-nē'tēs
Plįs-tär'çhŭs
Plĭs'thą-nŭs
Plįs-thĕn'į-dēs
Plĭs'thę-nēs
Plįs-tī'nŭs
Plįs-tō'ą-năx
Plĭs-tǫ-nī'cēs
Plĭs-tǫ-nī'cŭs
Plįs-tō'rŭs
Plǫ-thē'ą
Plŏ'tį-ą
Plǫ-tī'ną
Plǫ-tī'nŭs
Plŏ'tį-ŭs 1
Plŭ-tär'çhŭs
Plŭ'tärçh
Plū'tį-ą 1
Plŭ-tō'nį-ŭm
Plū'vį-ŭs
Plyn-tē'rį-ą
Pnĕb'ę-bĭs 5
Pnī'ǵeŭs 5, 6
Pnȳ-tág'ǫ-rás 5
Pnȳx 5
Pǫb-lĭ''cį-ŭs 1
Pŏd-ą-lē'ą
Pŏd-ą-lĭr'į-ŭs
Pǫ-där'cēs
Pǫ-dā'rēs
Pǫ-där'ǵę
Pǫ-dō'cą
Pœ-ąn-tī'ą-dēs
Pœ'ąs
Pœç'į-lē 4
Pœm-ą-nē'nŭs 4
Pœm'ę-nĭs 4
Pœ'nī
Pœ'ǫn
Pœ-ō'nį-ą
Pœ'ŭs
Póg-ǫ-nā'tŭs
Pŏl-ę-mǫ-crā'tį-ą 1
Pŏl'ę-mŏn
Pŏl-ę-mŏ'nį-ŭm
Pǫ-lē'nǫr
Pō'lį-ăs
Pō-lį-ē'į-ą 3
Pō-lį-ē'ŭm
Pō'lį-eūs 6
Pō-lį-ǫr-cē'tēs
Pǫ-lĭs'trą-tŭs
Pŏl-į-tē'ą
Pǫ-lī'tēs
Pŏl-į-tō'rį-ŭm
Pō-lį-ū'çhǫs
Pǫl-lĕn'tį-ą 1
Pŏl-lį-ā'nŭs
Pŏl'lį-ō
Pǫl-lī'tą
Pŏl'lį-ŭs
Pǫl-lū'cēs
Pǫl-lū'tį-ą 1
Pō-ly-æ-mŏn'į-dēs
Pō-ly-æ'nŭs
Pō-ly-ą-rā'tŭs
Pō-ly-är'çhŭs
Pŏl-y-bī'ą-dēs
Pǫ-lȳb'į-ŭs

Pŏl-y-bœ'ą
Pŏl-y-bō'tēs
Pǫ-lȳb'ǫ-tŭm
Pŏl'y-bŭs
Pŏl-y-cā'ǫn
Pŏl-y-cär'pŭs
Pŏl'y-cärp
Pŏl-y-cäs'tę
Pǫ-lȳçh'ą-rēs
Pŏl-y-clē'ą
Pŏl'y-clēs·
Pŏl-y-clē'tŭs
Pǫ-lȳc'rą-tēs
Pŏl-y-crē'tą, or
  Pŏl-y-crī'tą
Pǫ-lȳc'rį-tŭs
Pǫ-lȳd'ą-mãs
Pŏl-y-dăm'ną
Pŏl-y-deu-cē'ą
Pŏl-y-dō'rą
Pŏl-y-dō'rŭs
Pŏl-y-ǵī'tǫn
Pǫ-lȳǵ'į-ŭm
Pǫ-lȳǵ'į-ŭs
Pŏl-y-gnō'tŭs
Pǫ-lȳg'ǫ-nŭs
Pŏl-y-hȳm'nį-ą
Pŏl-y-ĭd'į-ŭs
Pŏl-y-ī'dŭs
Pŏl-y-lā'ŭs
Pŏl-y-mē'dę
Pǫ-lȳm'ę-dón
Pŏl-y-mē'lą, or -lę
Pǫ-lȳm'ę-nēs
Pŏl-ym-nĕs'tǫr
Pǫ-lȳm'nį-ą
Pŏl-y-nē'ŭs
Pŏl-y-nī'cēs
Pǫ-lȳn'ǫ-ē
Pŏl-y-pā'ŭs
Pŏl-y-pē'mǫn
Pŏl-y-pēr'çhǫn
Pŏl-y-phē'mŭs
Pŏl'y-phēme
Pŏl-y-phē'tēs
Pŏl-y-phī'dēs
Pŏl-y-phŏn'tēs
Pŏl'y-phrŏn
Pŏl-y-pœ'tēs
Pŏl-yr-rhē'nį-ą
Pŏl-y-stĕph'ą-nŭs
Pǫ-lȳs'trą-tŭs
Pŏl-y-tĕçh'nŭs
Pǫ-lȳ'tēs
Pŏl-y-tį-mē'tŭs
Pŏl-y-tī'mŭs
Pǫ-lȳt'į-ŏn 2
Pǫ-lȳt'rǫ-pŭs
Pǫ-lȳx'ę-ną
Pŏl-yx-ĕn'į-dăs
Pǫ-lȳx'ę-nŭs
Pŏl-y-zē'lŭs
Pǫ-mē'tį-ą 1
Pǫ-mē'tį-ī 1
Pŏm-ę-tī'ną
Pǫ-mŏ'ną
Pǫm-pē'į-ą 3
Pŏm-pę-į-ā'nŭs
Pǫm-pē'į-ī 3, or
  Pǫm-pē'į-ŭm 3

Pǫm-pē-į-ŏp'ǫ-lĭs
Pǫm-pē'į-ŭs 3
Pŏm'pęy
Pŏm'pę-lŏn
Pŏm-pę-lō'ną
Pǫm-pĭl'į-ą
Pǫm-pĭl'į-ŭs
Pǫm-pī'lŭs
Pǫm-pō'nį-ŭs
Pǫm-pō-sį-ā'nŭs 1
Pǫmp-tī'næ
Pǫmp-tī'nŭs
Pŏn'tį-ą 1
Pŏn'tį-cŭm Mā'rę
Pŏn'tį-cŭs
Pǫn-tĭd'į-ŭs
Pǫn-tĭl-į-ā'nŭs
Pǫn-tī'ną
Pǫn-tī'nŭs
Pŏn'tį-ŭs 1
Pŏn-tǫ-pǫ-rī'ą
Pŏn'tŭs Eūx-ī'nŭs
Pǫ-pĭl'į-ŭs Læ'nąs
Pǫp-lĭc'ǫ-lą
Pǫp-pæ'ą Są-bī'ną
Pŏp-ŭ-lō'nį-ą, or
  Pŏp-ŭ-lō'nį-ŭm
Pŏr'ą-tą
Pŏr'cį-ą 1
Pŏr'cį-ŭs 1
Pŏr-dǫ-sę-lē'nę
Pǫ-rĕd'ǫ-răx
Pǫ-rī'ną
Pŏr-ǫ-sę-lē'nę
Pǫr-phȳr'į-ŏn
Pǫr-phȳr'į-ŭs
Pŏr'phy-ry
Pŏr-phy-rǫ-ǵĕn'į-
  tŭs   [tŭs
Pŏr-phy-rŏǵ-ęn-nē'-
Pŏr'rį-mą
Pǫr-sē'ną, or
  Pŏr'sę-ną
Pǫr-thā'ǫn
Pŏr'tį-ą 1
Pŏr'tį-ŭs 1
Pŏr-tŭm-nā'lį-ą
Pǫr-tū'nŭs
Pǫ-sĭd'ę-ŏn
Pǫ-sī'dēs
Pŏs-į-dē'ŭm
Pǫ-sĭd'į-ŭm, or
  Pŏs-į-dī'ŭm
Pǫ-sĭd'į-ŭs
Pǫ-sī'dǫn
Pŏs-į-dŏ'nį-ą
Pŏs-į-dŏ'nį-ŭm
Pŏs-į-dŏ'nį-ŭs
Pō'sį-ō 1
Pǫst-hū'mį-ą
Pǫst-hū'mį-ŭs
Pŏst'hŭ-mŭs
Pŏs-tŭ-mį-ā'nŭs
Pŏs-tū'mį-ŭs
Pŏs'tŭ-mŭs
Pǫ-tăm'į-dēs
Pǫ-tā'mį-ŭs
Pŏt'ą-mŏn
Pŏt'ą-mŭs
Pǫ-tĕn'tį-ą 1

Pǫ-thī'nŭs
Pǫ-tī'ną
Pǫ-tī''tį-ŭs 1
Pǫ-tī'tŭs
Pǫt-nī'ą-dēs
Pŏt'nį-æ
Prác'tį-ŭm 1
Prăc'tį-ŭs 1
Præ'cį-ą 1
Præn-ęs-tī'nī 4
Præs'tī 4
Præt-ęx-tā'tŭs 4
Præ'tǫr
Præ-tō'rį-ŭs
Præ-tū'tį-ŭm 1
Prăm'nį-ŭm, or
  Pram-nī'ŭm Vī'-
Prā'sį-ą 1   [nŭm
Prā'sį-æ 1
Prā'sį-ī 1
Prăs'į-nŭs
Prăt'į-nás
Präx'į-ăs 1
Prăx-į-bū'lŭs
Prąx-ĭd'ą-măs
Prąx-ĭd'į-cē
Präx'į-lą
Prąx-ĭph'ą-nēs
Prąx-ĭt'ę-lēs
Prąx-ĭth'ę-ą
Prē'lį-ás
Preū'ǵe-nēs
Prī-ăm'į-dēs
Prī-ą-mē'įs
Prī'ą-mŭs
Prī-ą-pē'į-ą 3
Prī-ā'pŭs
Prī-ē'nę
Prīm-į-pī'lŭs
Prī'ǫ-lą
Prī-ŏn'ǫ-tŭs
Prĭs-cį-ā'nŭs 1
Prĭs'cį-ąn
Prŏ-æ-rē'sį-ŭs 1
Prŏ-bį-ā'nŭs
Prǫ-bī'nŭs
Prŏçh'ǫ-rŭs
Prŏçh'y-tą
Prǫ-cĭl'į-ŭs
Prǫ-clē'ą
Prŏ'clēs
Prǫ-clī'dæ
Prŏc-ǫn-nē'sŭs
Prǫ-cō'pį-ŭs
Prŏ'crįs
Prŏc'ŭ-lą
Prŏc-ŭ-lē'į-ą 3
Prŏc-ŭ-lē'į-ŭs 3
Prŏc-ŭ-lī'ną
Prŏc'ŭ-lŭs
Prŏ'cy-ŏn 1
Prŏd'į-cŭs
Prŏd'rǫ-mŭs
Prŏ'ę-drī
Prœt'į-dēs 4
Prǫ-lā'ŭs
Prŏm'ą-chŭs
Prǫ-măth'į-dăs
Prǫ-mā'thį-ŏn
Prŏm'ę-dŏn

Prŏm-e-nē'a
Prọ-mē'thẹ-ī
Prọ-mē'theūs (n.) 6
Prŏm e-thē'ụs (a.)
Prŏm-e-thī'dēş
Prọ-mē'thịs
Prọ-mē'thụs
Prŏm'ọ-lŭs
Prŏm'ọ-na
Prọ-mō'tụs
Prŏm'ụ-lŭs
Prọ-năp'ị-dēş
Prŏn'ọ-ē
Prŏn'ọ-mŭs
Prŏn'ọ-ŭs, or
  Prō'nụs
Prŏn'ụ-ba
Prọ-për'tị-ŭs 1
Prọ-pœt'ị-dēş 4
Prọs-clȳs'tị-ŭs
Prŏs-e-lē'nī
Prọ-sër'pị-na
Prŏs'er-pīne
Prọ-sō'pịs
Prŏs-ọ-pī'tịs
Prọ-tā'dị-ŭs
Prọ-tăg'ọ-răs
Prŏt-a-gŏr'ị-dēş
Prō'tẹ-ăs
Prō'tẹ-ī Cọ-lŭm'næ
Prọ-tē'nọr
Prọ-tĕs-ị-lā'ụs
Prō'teūs 6
Prŏth-ọ-ē'nọr
Prŏth'ọ-ŭs
Prọ-tŏg-ẹ-nē'a
Prọ-tŏg-ẹ-nī'a
Prọ-tŏm-e-dī'a
Prọ-tŏm-e-dū'sa
Prō-try-gē'a
Prŏx'ẹ-nŭs
Prŏx'ị-mŭs
Prụ-dĕn'tị-ŭs 1
Prŭm'nị-dēş
Prū'sị-ăs 1
Prym-nē'şị-a
Prȳt'a-nēş
Prȳt-a-nē'ụm
Prȳt'a-nĭs
Psăm'a-thē 5
Psăm'a-thŏs 5
Psăm-me-nī'tụs 5
Psam-mĕt'ị-chŭs 5
Psẹ-bō'a 5
Psẹ-nē'rụs 5
Pseū-dọ-cē'lịs 5
Pseū'dọ-lŭs 5
Pseū-dọ-man-tī'a
Pseụ-dŏs'tọ-ma 5
Psĭt'ta-cē 5
Psĭt'ta-cŭs 5
Psȳ'chẹ 5
Psȳ-chọ-man-tē'ụm
Psȳt-ta-lē'a, or
  Psȳt-ta-lī'a 5
Ptē'lẹ-ŏn 5
Ptē'lẹ-ŏs 5
Ptē'lẹ-ŭm 5
Ptĕr'ẹ-la 5
Ptĕr'ẹ-lăs 5

Ptē'rị-a 5
Ptē'rị-ŏn 5
Ptọ-chī'ụm 5
Ptŏl-e-mæ'ụm 5
Ptŏl-e-mæ'ụs 5
Ptŏl'e-my
Ptŏl-e-mā'ịs 5
Ptŏl-e-mọ-crā'tị-a 1
Ptŏl'ị-chŭs 5
Pụb-lĭ''cị-a 1
Pụb-lĭ''cị-ŭs 1
Pụb-lĭc'ọ-la
Pụb-lĭl'ị-ŭs
Pŭb'lị-ŭs
Pụ-dī'ca
Pū-dị-cĭ''tị-a 1
Pụl-chē'rị-a
Pŭl'fị-ō
Pū'nị-cụm Bĕl'lụm
Pū-pị-ē'nụs
Pū'pị-ŭs
Pū'tẹ-ăl
Pụ-tē'ọ-lī
Pȳ-a-nĕp'sị-a 1
Pȳg'e-la
Pyg-mā'lị-ŏn
Pȳl'a-dēş
Pȳ-læm'ẹ-nēş 4
Pȳ-lăg'ọ-ræ
Pȳ-lăg'ọ-răs
Pȳ-lā'ọn
Pȳ-lär'tēş
Pȳ-lē'nẹ
Pȳl'e-ŭs
Pȳl'lẹ-ŏn
Pȳ-lō'rụs
Pȳm'a-tŭs
Py-ræch'mēş 4
Py-răm'ị-dēş
Pȳr'a-mŭs
Pȳr'a-sŭs
Py-rē'ị-cŭs
Py-rē'nẹ
Py-rē'neūs 6
Pȳr'ẹ-tŭs, river.
Py-rē'tụs, man.
Pȳr'ġī
Pȳr'ġị-ŏn
Pȳr-gọ-pŏl-ị-nī'cēş
Pyr-gŏt'ẹ-lēş
Pȳr-ị-phlĕġ'ẹ-thŏn
Py-rĭp'pẹ
Py-rŏm'a-chŭs
Py-rō'dēş
Pȳr'ọ-eīs
Pȳr'ọ-ĭs
Py-rō'nị-a
Pyr-rhē'nēş
Pȳr'rhị-a
Pȳr'rhị-ăs
Pȳr'rhị-cha
Pȳr'rhị-chŭs
Pȳr'rhị-dæ
Pȳs'tẹ
Py-thæn'ẹ-tụs 4
Py-thăg'ọ-răs
Py-thăg-ọ-rē'ī
Py-thăg-ọ-rē'ạns
Py-thăn'ġẹ-lŭs
Pȳth-a-rā'tụs

Pȳth'e-ăs
Pȳ'thēş
Pȳth'e-ŭs
Pȳth'ị-a
Pȳth'ị-ăs
Pȳth'ị-cŭm
Pȳth'ị-ŏn, or
  Pȳth'ị-ŭm
Pȳth-ị-ọ-nī'cēş
Pȳth'ị-ŭs
Py-thŏch'a-rĭs
Pȳth'ọ-clēş
Pȳth-ọ-clī'dēş
Py-thŏc'rị-tŭs
Pȳth-ọ-dē'lụs
Pȳth-ọ-dō'rụs
Pȳth-ọ-lā'ụs
Py-thō'nēş
Pȳth-ọ-nī'cē
Py-thŏn'ị-cī
Pȳth-ọ-nī'cụs
Pȳt'ta-lŭs

Q.

Quạ-drā'ta
Quạ-drā'tụs
Quăd'rị-frŏnş, or
  Quăd'rị-cĕps
Quæs-tō'rēş
Quā'rị-ŭs
Quar-tī'nụs
Quī-ē'tụs
Quĭnc-tị-ā'nụs 1
Quịnc-tĭl'ị-a
Quĭnc'tị-ŭs 1
Quĭn-dẹ-cĭm'vị-rī
Quịn-quā'trị-a
Quịn-quā'trụs
Quĭn-quẹn-nā'lēş
Quịn-quĕv'ị-rī
Quĭn'tị-a 1
Quĭn-tị-ā'nụs 1
Quịn-tĭl'ị-a
Quin-tĭl'ị-ăn
Quịn-tī'lịs
Quịn-tĭl'ị-ŭs
Quĭn'tị-ŭs 1
Quĭr-ị-nā'lị-a
Quĭr-ị-nā'lịs
Quị-rīn'ị-ŭs
Quị-rī'nụs
Quị-rī'tēş

R.

Rạ-bīr'ị-ŭs
Rạ-cĭl'ị-ŭs
Rạ-cō'tēş, or -tĭs
Ræ-sā'cēş
Rā'tị-a 1
Rạ-mī'sēş
Răm'nēş
Ramp-sĭn'ị-tụs

Rạ-tū'mẹ-na
Râu'rạ-cī, or
  Râu-rā'cī
Râu-rī'cī
Răv'ị-dŭs
Răv'ọ-la
Rẹ-ā'tẹ
Rĕb'ị-lŭs
Rẹ-dĭc'ụ-lŭs
Rĕd'ọ-nēş
Rẹ-ġĭl-ị-fū'ġị-ŭm
Rẹ-ġĭl-lị-ā'nụs
Rẹ-ġī'na
Rẹ-ġī'nụm
Rẹ-ġī'nụs
Rĕġ'ụ-lŭs
Rĕm'ụ-lŭs
Rẹ-mū'rị-a
Rĕp-ẹn-tī'nụs
Rẹ-pō-sị-ā'nụs 1
Rĕs'tị-ō
Rĕs-tị-tū'tụs
Rẹ-tī'na
Rhạb-dū'chī
Rhạ-cē'lụs
Rhā'cị-a 1
Rhā'cị-ŭs 1
Rhạ-cō'tēş, or -tĭs
Rhăd-a-mán'thụs
Rhăd'ị-nē
Rhā'dị-ŭs
Rhæs'ẹ-na 4
Rhæ'tī, or Rǣ'tī
Rhæ'tị-a 1
Rhạ-ġē'a
Rhạ-mē'lụs
Rhăm'nēş
Rhăm'phị-ăs
Rhạm-nū'sị-a
Rhạmp-sĭn'ị-tụs, or
  Rhămp-sị-nī'tụs
Rhạ-phē'a, or
  Rhạ-phī'a
Rhạp-sō'dī
Rhā'rị-ŭs
Rhạs-cū'pọ-rĭs
Rhạ-tō'ụs
Rhĕd'ọ-nēş
Rhē'ġị-ŏn
Rhē'ġị-ŭm
Rhẹ-nē'a
Rhē-ọ-mī'thrēş
Rhẹ-tē'nọr
Rhĕt'ị-cō
Rhẹ-tŏġ'ẹ-nēş
Rhẹ-ū'nụs
Rhẹx-ē'nọr
Rhẹx-ĭb'ị-ŭs
Rhī-ā'nụs
Rhĭd'a-gō
Rhị-mŏt'a-clēş
Rhị-nŏc-ọ-lū'ra
Rhị-nŏc-ọ-rū'ra
Rhĭn-ọt-mē'tụs
Rhī'peūs 6
Rhī'pheūs 6
Rhọ-bē'a
Rhŏd'a-lŭs
Rhŏd'a-nŭs
Rhō'dẹ

Rhọ-dī'a, a nymph.
Rhō'dị-a, town.
Rhō'dị-ī
Rhŏd-ọ-ġȳ'nẹ
Rhŏd'ọ-pē
Rhŏd'ọ-phŏn
Rhọ-dō'pịs
Rhœ'bụs
Rhœ-tē'ụm
Rhœ'teūs (n.) 6
Rhœ-tē'ụs (a.)
Rhœ'tị-ŏn 2
Rhœ'tụs
Rhọm-bī'tēş
Rhọ-sā'cēş
Rhọx-ā'nī
Rhŭn'da-cŭs
Rhụ-tē'nī
Rhụ-thē'nī
Rhȳn'da-cŭs
Rhȳ''tị-ŭs 1
Rĭc'ị-mer
Rī'ġæ
Rĭġ-e-bē'lụs
Rī-gŏm'a-gŭs
Rĭn-ġị-bē'rī
Rī'pheūs 6
Rīx'a-mæ
Rịx-ăm'a-ræ
Rọ-bī'gō
Rọ-bī'gụs
Rŏd-e-rī'cụs
Rŏd'er-ĭc
Rọ-mā'nī
Rọ-mā'nụs
Rọ-mē'chị-ŭm
Rọ-mĭl'ị-ŭs
Rŏm'ụ-la
Rọ-mū'lị-dæ
Rŏm'ụ-lŭs
Rŏs'chị-nŭs
Rŏs'cị-ŭs 1
Rŏ'sị-ŭs 1
Rŏs-ụ-lā'nụs (a.)
Rọ-tŏm'a-gŭs
Rŏx-ā'na
Rŏx-ọ-lā'nī
Rụ-bĕl'lị-ŭs
Rū'bị-cŏn
Rū-bị-ē'nụs Lăp'pa
Rụ-bī'gō
Rū'bra Săx'a
Rŭ'bræ
Rụ-brē'nụs
Rŭ'brị-ŭs
Rŭc'cị-nō
Rŭ'dị-æ
Rụf-frī'nụs
Rụ-fī'na
Rụ-fīn-ị-ā'nụs
Rụ-fī'nụs
Rŭ'fị-ŭs
Rŭ'fụ-lŭs
Rŭ'ġị-ī
Rụ-mī'na
Rụ-mī'nụs, or
  Rŭ'mị-nŭs
Rụn-cī'na
Rụ-pĭl'ị-ŭs
Rŭs'cị-ŭs 1

Rus-cō'nj-a
Rŭs'pj-na
Rŭs'tj-cŭs
Ru-tē'nī
Ru-thē'nī
Rŭ'tj-la
Rŭ'tj-lŭs
Rŭ'tu-ba
Rŭ'tu-bĭs
Rŭ'tu-lī
Rŭ'tu-pæ
Rŭ-tu-pī'nus

S.

Săb'a-chŭs
Săb'a-cŏn
Sā'bæ
Sa-bæ'ī
Sa-bā'rj-a
Sa-bā'ta
Sa-bā'tha
Săb'a-thæ
Săb-a-tī'nus
Sa-bā'zj-ŭs 1
Săb'ba-tha
Sa-bĕl'lj-ŭs
Sa-bĭd'j-ŭs
Sa-bī'na
Săb-j-næ'us
Sa-bī'nī
Sa-bĭn-j-ā'nus
Sa-bī'nus
Sa-bī'ra
Sa-bō'cī
Sa-bō'tha
Săb'ra-cæ
Săb'ra-ta
Săb'ra-tha
Sa-brī'na
Săb'u-ra
Săb-u-rā'nus
Săc'a-dăs
Sā'cæ
Săc-a-pē'ne
Săch-a-lī'tĕş
Sa-crā'nī
Sa-crăt'j-vjr
Sa-crā'tor
Săc'ro-nē
Săd'a-lĕş
Săd'o-cŭs
Sā-dy-ā'tĕs
Sæǵ-j-mē'rus 4
Sæ'nj-ŭs
Sæ-pī'num
Sæt'a-bĕş 4
Sæt'a-bĭs 4
Săg'a-na
Săg-a-rī'nus
Săg'a-rĭs
Săg-a-rĭs'tj-ō
Săg-a-rī'tjs
Săg-jt-tā'rj-ŭs
Sa-ǵĭt'tj-ǵer
Săǵ-jt-tīp'o-tĕnş
Săg-un-tī'nus
Sa-ī'tæ

Sa-ī'tjs
Sa-lā'cj-a 1
Săl'a-cŏn
Săl-a-ǵī'sa
Săl-a-mī'na
Săl-a-mĭn'j-a
Săl'a-mĭs
Sa-lā'nus
Săl'a-ra
Sa-lā'rj-a
Sa-lăr'j-ca
Săl'du-ba
Sa-lĕ-j-ā'nus 3
Sa-lĕ'j-ŭs 3
Sa-lĕ'nī
Săl-en-tī'nī
Sal-gā'ne-a
Săl'ga-neŭs 6
Sā-lj-ā'rjs
Săl'j-cĕş, Xd
Sā-lj-ē'nus
Sa-lī'næ
Săl-j-nā'tor
Săl-j-sŭb'su-lī
Sā'lj-ŭs
Sal-lŭs'tj-ŭs
Săl'lust
Săl'ma-cĭs
Sal-măn'tj-ca
Sal-mō'na
Sal-mō'neŭs 6
Sal-mō'njs
Săl-o-dū'rum
Sa-lō'me
Săl'o-mŏn
Sa-lō'na, or
   Sa-lō'næ
Săl-o-nē'a
Sa-lō'nj-a
Săl-o-nī'na
Săl-o-nī'nus
Sa-lō'nj-ŭs
Săl-pj-nā'tĕş
Săl'pj-ŏn
Săl'su-læ
Sa-lŭs'tj-ŭs
Săl-vj-ā'nus
Săl'vi-an
Sal-vĭd-j-ē'nus
Săl'vj-ŭs
Sā'ly-ĕş, or
   Sā'ly-ī
Sa-lỹn'thj-ŭs
Săm-a-rī'a
Sa-mā'ri-a
Săm-a-rī'ta
Săm-a-ro-brī'va
Săm'a-tæ
Sam-bū'los
Sā'me, or Sā'mos
Sa-mē'nī
Sā'mj-a
Săm'j-cŭm
Sā'mj-ŭs
Sam-nī'tæ
Sam-nī'tĕş
Săm'nītes
Săm'nj-ŭm
Săm-o-cho-nī'tĕş
Săm'o-lăs

Sa-mō'nj-ŭm
Sa-mŏs'a-ta
Săm-o-thrā'ce
Săm-o-thrā'cj-a 1
Sa-mỹl'j-a
Săn'a-ŏs
Săn-cho-nī'a-thŏn
San-dā'ce, or
   San-dâu'ce
San-dā-lj-ō'tjs
San-dā'lj-ŭm
Săn'da-nŭs
Săn-dī'on
San-dō'cĕş
Săn'ga-la
San-gā'rj-ō
San-gā'rj-ŭs
Săn'ga-rĭs
San-guĭn'j-ŭs
Săn'nj-ō
Săn-nỹr'j-ŏn
Săn'to-næ
Săn'to-nĕş, or -nī
Săn'to-nŭs
Sa-ō'ce
Sa-ŏc'o-răs
Sa-ō'tĕş
Săph'a-rŭs
Sā'phō (să'fō)
Săp-j-rē'ne
Sa-pī'rĕş
Sa-pō'rĕş
Săp'phō (sŭf f̄.)
Săp'tj-ne
Săr-a-cē'ne
Săr-a-cē'nī
Sa-răc'o-rī
Săr-a-mē'ne
Sa-răn'gĕş
Săr-an-tē'nus
Săr-a-pā'nī
Săr'a-pŭs
Săr'a-sa
Sa-răs'pa-dĕş
Sa-rā'vus
Sar-dăn-a-pā'lus
Săr-dē'ne
Săr'dĕş
Săr'dj-ca
Sar-dĭn'j-a
Săr'do-nĕş
Săr-dōn'j-cŭs
Sar-dō'nyx
Săr-dŏp'a-trĭs
Săr-dō'us
Săr'ma-tæ
Sar-mā'tj-a 1
Săr-măt'j-cŭs
Săr-mj-zĕǵ-e-thū'sa
Săr'nj-ŭs
Sa-rón'j-cŭs Sī'nus
Sa-rō'njs
Săr-pē'don
Săr-rā'nus
Săr'ra-pĭs
Săr-răs'tĕş
Săr'sj-na
Săs'o-nĕş
Săs-pī'rĕş, or -rī
Săs'sj-na

Săs-sj-nā'tĕş
Săt-a-ǵỹ'tæ
Săt'a-la
Săt'a-năs
Sa-tā'nĕş, pl.
Sa-tär'chæ
Sa-tăs'pĕş
Sā'tj-æ 1
Săt-j-bar-zā'nĕş
Sa-tĭc'u-la
Sa-tĭc'u-lŭs
Sa-trā'j-dæ
Săt-ra-pē'nī
Săt'ra-pĕş
Săt'rj-cŭs
Săt'rj-cŭm, or
   Sa-trī'cum
Sa-trŏp'a-cĕş
Săt'u-ra
Săt-u-rē'j-ŭm 3
Sa-tū're-ŭm
Săt-u-rē'j-ŭs 3
Sa-tū'rj-ō
Sa-tū'rj-ŭs
Săt-ur-nā'lj-a
Sa-tür'nj-a
Săt-ur-nĭǵ'e-na
Săt-ur-nī'nus
Sa-tür'nj-ŭs
Săt'u-rŭm
Săt'y-rī
Săt'y-rŭs
Sa-vĕr'rj-ō
Sâu-fē'j-a 3
Sâu-fē'j-ŭs 3
Sâu're-a
Sâu-rŏm'a-tæ
Sa-vē'ra
Sa-vō'na
Săx'o-nĕş
Săz'j-chĕş
Sçæ'a (sē'a)
Sçæ'va (sē'va)
Sçæ-vī'nus
Sçæv'o-la 4
Scăl'a-bĭs
Scăl'pj-ŭm
Sca-măn'drj-ŭs
Scan-dā'rj-a
Scan-dē'a
Scăn-dj-nā'vj·a
Scan-tĭn'j-ŭs
Scap-tĕn'su-la
Scap-tĕs'y-lē
Scăp'tj-a 1
Scăp'tj-ŭs 1
Scăp'u-la
Scăr'dj-ī
Scar-dō'na
Scar-phē'a, or
   Scar-phī'a
Scâu'rus
Sçĕd'a-sŭs
Sçĕl'e-drŭs
Sçĕl-e-rā'tus
Sçe-nī'tæ
Schē'dj-a
Schē'dj-ŭs
Schē'rj-a
Schœ-nē'js

Sçhœ'neŭs 6
Sçhœ'nus
Sçī-ăp'o-dĕş
Sçï'a-thŏs
Sçī'dros
Sçī-ŏ'ne
Sçj-pī'a-dæ
Sçj-pī'a-dĕş
Sçĭp'j-ō
Sçī-rā'dj-ŭm
Sçj-rī'tæ
Sçj-rī'tjs
Sçī-rŏn'j-dĕş
Scō'drī
Scŏl'o-tī
Sco-pē-lj-ā'nus
Scŏp'e-lŏs
Scō'pj-ŭm
Scor-dĭs'cæ
Scör'pj-ŏs, or -ŭs
Sco-tī'nus
Scrī-bō'nj-a
Scrī-bō-nj-ā'nus
Scrī-bō'nj-ŭs
Sçỹl'a-cē
Sçỹl-a-cē'j-ŏn 3
Sçỹl-a-cē'um
Sçỹl'la
Sçỹl'lj-ăs
Sçy-lū'rus
Sçỹp'pj-ŭm
Sçy-rī'a-dĕş
Sçỹr'pj-ŭm
Sçỹt'a-lē
Sçỹ'thæ
Sçy-thē'nī
Sçỹ'thĕş, or
   Sçỹ'tha
Sçỹth'j-a
Sçỹth-j-ā'nus
Sçỹth'j-dĕş
Sçy-thī'nus
Sçy-thŏp'o-lĭs
Sĕb-as-tē'a
Sĕb-as-tē'nī
Se-băs'tj-a, or
   Sĕb-as-tī'a
Sĕb-as-tŏp'o-lĭs
Sĕb'e-da
Sĕb-en-nỹ'tus
Se-bē'thjs
Se-bē'tos
Se-bē'tus
Se-bī'nus
Se-bō'sus
Se-bū-sj-ā'nī 1
Sĕç'e-la
Sec-tā'nus
Sĕc-un-dĭl'la
Sĕc-un-dī'nus
Se-dā'tus
Se-dĭǵ'j-tŭs
Sĕd-j-tā'nī
Se-dū'lj-ŭs
Se-dū'nī
Se-dū'sī-ī 1
Se-ǵē'tj-a
Sĕǵ-j-mē'rus
Sĕg-o-brī'ga
Sĕg-o-dū'num

Sĕg'ọ-năx
Sẹ-gŏn'tj-ạ 1
Sĕg-ọn-tī'ạ-cī
Sẹ-gō'vj-ạ
Sẹ-gŭn'tj-ạ 1
Sẹ-gŭn'tj-ŭm 1
Sẹ-gū-ṣj-ā'nī
Seī-sạch-thī'ạ
Sē'j-ŭs, *or* Sē'jụ
Sẹ-jā'nụs, Æ'lj-ŭs
Sẹl-dō'mụs
Sẹ-lē'nẹ
Sĕl-eụ-cē'na
Sĕl-eụ-cī'ạ
Se-leŭ'ci-ạ 1
Sẹ-leū'cj-dæ
Sẹ-leŭ-cọ-bē'lụs
Sẹ-leŭ'cụs
Sẹ-lī''cj-ŭs 1
Sẹ-lī'nụnṣ, *or*
  Sẹ-lī'nụs
Sē'lj-ŭs
Sẹl-lā'ṣj-ạ 1
Sẹl-lē'js
Sẹ-lўm'brj-ạ
Sẹm-brī'tæ
Sĕm'ẹ-lạ
Sĕm'ẹ-lē
Sẹ-mĭd'ẹ-ī
Sĕm-j-ġẹr-mā'nī
Sĕm-j-gŭn'tụs
Sẹ-mĭr'ạ-mĭs
Sĕm'nọ-nēṣ
Sẹm-nŏ'thẹ-ī
Sẹ-mō'nēṣ
Sẹm-prō'nj-ạ
Sẹm-prō'nj-ŭs
Sẹ-mū'rj-ŭm
Sẹ-nā'tụs
Sĕn'ẹ-cạ
Sẹ-nē'cj-ō 1
Sē'nj-ạ
Sĕn'ọ-nēṣ, *and*
  Sẹ-nō'nēṣ
Sẹn-tī'nụm
Sĕn'tj-ŭs 1
Sē'pj-ás
Sē'pj-ŭs
Sẹ-plā'ṣj-ạ 1 *[ris)*
Sẹp-phō'rjs (*sẹf-fō'-*
Sẹp-tĕm'pẹ-dạ
Sẹp-tĕm'trj-ō
Sẹp-tē'rj-ŏn
Sẹp-tĭ-cj-ā'nụs 1
Sẹp-tī''cj-ŭs 1
Sẹp-tĭm-j-ā'nụs
Sẹp-tĭm'j-ŭs
Sĕp-tj-mụ-lē'j-ŭs 3
Sĕp'y-rạ
Sĕq'uạ-na
Sĕq'uạ-nī
Sẹ-quăn'j-cŭs
Sẹ-quĭn'j-ŭs
Sẹ-rā'pēṣ
Sĕr-ạ-pē'ụm
Sẹ-rā'pj-ō
Sẹ-rā'pjs
Sẹr-bō'njs
Sĕr'dj-cạ
Sẹ-rē'nạ

Sẹ-rē-nj-ā'nụs
Sẹ-rē'nụs
Sẹr'ġj-ạ
Sẹr-ġī'ọ-lŭs
Sēr'ġj-ŭs
Sĕr'j-cạ
Sĕr'j-cŭs
Sẹ-rī'phụs
Sĕr'my-lạ
Sẹr-rē'ụm
Sẹr-tō'rj-ŭs
Sẹr-væ'ụs
Sĕr-vj-ā'nụs
Sẹr-vĭl'j-ạ
Sẹr-vĭl-j-ā'nụs
Sẹr-vĭl'j-ŭs
Sĕr'vj-ŭs
Sĕs-ạ-mē'nī
Sĕs'ạ-mŭm
Sĕs'ạ-rạ
Sĕs-ạ-rē'thụs
Sĕs-ọ-ō'sjs
Sĕs'tj-ás
Sẹs-tī'nụm
Sĕs'tj-ŭs
Sẹ-sū'vj-ī
Sĕt'ạ-bĭs
Sē'tj-ạ 1
Sē'tj-ŭs 1
Sẹ-vē'rạ
Sẹ-vē-rj-ā'nụs
Sĕv-ẹ-rī'nạ
Sẹ-vē'rụs
Sĕx'tj-ạ
Sẹx-tĭl-j-ā'nụs
Sẹx-tī'ljs
Sẹx-tĭl'j-ŭs
Sĕx'tj-ŭs
Sj-bī'nī
Sĭb'ọ-tēṣ
Sj-bū'rj-ŭs
Sĭb-yl-lī'nụs
Sj-bўn'tj-ŭs 1
Sj-bўr'tj-ŭs 1
Sī-căm'brj-ạ
Sī-cā'nī
Sī-cā'nj-ạ
Sī-cā'nụs
Sj-cĕl'j-dēṣ
Sīc'ẹ-lĭs
Sj-cē'mụs
Sj-cē'nụs
Sj-çhæ'ụs
Sj-cīl'j-ạ
Sīc'j-nŭs
Sīc'ọ-rĭs
Sīc'ọ-rŭs
Sīc'ụ-lī
Sīc'ụ-lŭm Frē'tụm
Sīc'ụ-lŭs
Sī''cy-ŏn 1
Sī-cy-ō'nj-ạ 1
Sīd-ạ-cē'nẹ
Sī-dē'lẹ
Sī-dē'nẹ
Sī-dē'nụs
Sī-dē'rō
Sī-dē'rụs
Sī-dē'tēṣ

Sĭd-j-cī'nī
Sĭd'ọ-nĭs, *or*
  Sī-dō'njs
Sī-dō'nj-ŭs
Sĭd'y-mạ
Sī-ġæ'um, *or*
  Sī-ġē'um
Sī-gā'lj-ŏn
Sī-ġē'ọn
Sī-ġē'rj-ŭs
Sĭg'nj-ạ
Sjg-nī'nụs
Sĭg-ọ-vĕs'sụs
Sj-ġȳ'nī
Sī-lā'ī
Sī-lā'nạ
Sī-lā'nj-ŏn
Sī-lā'nụs
Sĭl'ạ-rĭs
Sĭl'ạ-rŭs
Sī-lē'nī
Sī-lē'nj-ŭm
Sī-lĕn-tj-ā'rj-ŭs 1
Sī-lē'nụs
Sĭl-j-cĕn'sẹ
Sj-lĭ''cj-ŭs 1
Sĭl'j-ŭs I-tăl'j-cŭs
Sĭl'phj-ŭm
Sĭl'pj-ạ
Sĭl'ụ-rēṣ
Sjl-vā'nụs
Sĭl'vj-ạ
Sjl-vī'nụs
Sĭl'vj-ŭs
Sī-mā'lj-ō
Sj-măn'ġẹ-lŭs
Sjm-brĭv'j-ŭs
Sjm-brū'vj-ŭs
Sī-mē'rạ
Sī-mē'thjs
Sī-mē'thụs
Sĭm'j-ạ
Sĭm'j-læ
Sĭm'j-lĭs
Sĭm'mj-ăs
Sĭm'ọ-eīs
Sĭm'ọ-ĭs
Sĭm-ọ-ĭ''sj-ŭs 1
Sī-mŏn'j-dēṣ
Sjm-plĭ''cj-ŭs 1
Sĭm'ụ-lŭs
Sĭm'y-rạ
Sĭn-ạ-ī'tạ
Sī-nē'rạ
Sĭn'gạ-rạ
Sĭn-ġj-dū'nụm
Sĭn'gụ-lĭs
Sĭn-gụ-lō'nēs
Sĭn'nạ-cēṣ
Sĭn'nạ-çhạ
Sĭn'ọ-ē
Sī-nō'pẹ
Sī-nō'peūs 6
Sĭn'ọ-rĭx
Sĭn'tj-cē
Sĭn'tj-ī 1
Sĭn-ụ-ẹs-sā'nụs
Sī-ō'pẹ
Sĭp'y-lŭs
Sjr-bō'njs

Sī-rĕd'ọ-nēṣ
Sī-rē'nēṣ
Sī'rẹnṣ
Sĭr-ẹ-nū'sæ
Sĭr'j-ŭs
Sĭr'mj-ŭm
Sī-rō'mụs
Sĭr-ọ-pæ'ọ-nēṣ
Sĭr'ọ-pŭm
Sĭs'ạ-phō
Sĭs'ạ-pŏn
Sĭs-ạ-pō'nẹ
Sĭs'ạ-rạ
Sĭs'cj-ạ 1
Sĭs'j-nēṣ
Sĭs-ọ-cŏs'tụs
Sj-sū'rụs
Sj-sўph'j-dēṣ
Sĭs'y-phŭs
Sī-tăl'cēṣ
Sī-thē'nī
Sĭth'nj-dēṣ
Sĭth'ọ-nēṣ
Sī-thō'nj-ạ
Sĭth'ọ-nĭs
Sĭ''tj-ŭs 1
Sī-tŏm'ạ-gŭs
Sĭt'ọ-nēṣ
Sĭt'tạ-cē
Sĭt-tạ-cē'nẹ
Sĭt-tẹ-bē'rjs
Sĭz'y-ġēṣ
Smẹr-dŏm'ẹ-nēṣ
Smjn-dўr'j-dēṣ
Smĭn'theūs 6
Sọ-æ'mj-ăs
Sọ-ā'nạ
Sọ-ā'nēṣ
Sŏc'rạ-tēṣ
Sọ-crā'tj-ŏn 2
Sŏd'ọ-mạ
Sọ-ē'mjs
Sŏg-dj-ā'nạ
Sŏg-dj-ā'nụs
Sọ-lā'nụs
Sŏl'ẹ-nŭs
Sọ-lī'nụs
Sọl-lē'ụm
Sō'lœ, *or* Sō'lī
Sŏl'ọ-eīs
Sŏl'ọ-ĭs
Sọ-lō'nj-ŭm
Sŏl-y-ġē'ạ, *or*
  Sŏl-y-ġī'ạ
Sŏl'y-mạ
Sŏl'y-mæ
Sŏl'y-mī
Sŏl'y-mŭs
Sŏn'çhjs
Sŏn-tj-ā'tēṣ 1
Sŏn'tj-ŭs 1
Sŏp'ạ-tẹr
Sọ-phæn'ẹ-tŭs 4
Sọ-phăg-ạ-sē'nụs
Sọ-phē'nẹ
Sō'phj-ạ
Sō-phj-ā'nụs
Sŏph'j-lŭs
Sŏph'ọ-clēṣ
Sọ-phō'nj-äs

Sō'phrọn
Sŏph'rọ-na
Sọ-phrō'nj-ạ
Sọ-phrŏn'j-cŭs
Sŏph-rọ-nīs'cụs
Sọ-phrō'nj-ŭs
Sọ-phrŏs'y-nē
Sọ-pī'thēṣ
Sŏp'ọ-lĭs
Sọ-răc'tẹ
Sọ-rū'nụs
Sör-bj-ọ-dū'nụm
Sör'dj-cē
Sọ-rī''tj-ạ 1
Sō'sj-ạ Gál'lạ 1
Sō-sj-ā'nụs 1
Sō'sj-ăs
Sọ-sĭb-j-ā'nụs
Sọ-sĭb'j-ŭs
Sŏs'j-clēṣ
Sọ-sĭc'rạ-tēṣ
Sọ-sĭġ'ẹ-nēṣ
Sō'sj-ī 1
Sŏs'j-lŭs
Sọ-sī'nụs
Sọ-sĭp'ạ-tẹr
Sọ-sĭph'ạ-nēṣ
Sọ-sĭp'ọ-lĭs
Sọ-sĭs'trạ-tŭs
Sọ-sĭth'ẹ-ŭs
Sō'sj-ŭs 1
Sŏs'pj-tạ
Sŏs'thẹ-nēṣ
Sŏs'trạ-tạ
Sŏs'trạ-tŭs
Sŏsx'ẹ-trạ
Sŏt'ạ-dēṣ
Sọ-tā'rēṣ
Sọ-tē'rj-ạ
Sọ-tĕr'j-çhŭs
Sọ-tĕr'j-cŭs
Sọ-tĕr'j-dás
Sō-tj-ā'tēṣ 1
Sō'tj-ŏn 2
Sọ-tī'rạ
Sō'tj-ŭs 1
Sŏx'ọ-tæ
Sọ-zŏm'ẹ-nŭs
Sŏz'ọ-mĕn
Spăl'ẹ-thrạ
Spā'nj-ŭs
Spär-gạ-pī'thēṣ
Spär'tạ-cŭs
Spar-tā'nī, *or*
  Spär-tj-ā'tæ 1
Spar-tā'rj-ŭs
Spar-tā'nụs
Spär-tj-ā'nụs 1
Spär-tj-ā'tēṣ 1
Spär'tọ-cŭs
Spar-tō'lụs
Spát'ạ-lē
Spē'çhj-ạ
Spĕn'dj-ŭs
Spẹ-rā'tụs
Spẹr-çhē'js
Spẹr-çhī'ạ
Spĕr-çhj-ŏn'j-dēṣ
Spẹr-çhī'ọs
Spẹr-çhī'ụs

Spër·ma-tŏph'a-ǧī
Spēş
Sphac-tē'rj-a
Sphe-cē'a
Sphŏ'drj-ăs
Sphra-ǧĭd'j-ŭm
Sphra-ǧĭt'j-sēş
Spin'tha-rŭs
Spĭ-rĭd'j-ŏn
Spĭ-tăm'e-nēş
Spĭ-thŏb'a-tēş
Spĭth-rj-dā'tēş
Spo-lē'tj-ŭm 1
Spo-lē'tum
Spŏr'a-dēş
Spu-rī'na
Spu-rī'nus
Spŭ'rj-ŭs
Sta-bē'rj-ŭs
Stā'bj-æ
Stăb'u-lŭm
Sta-ǧī'ra, or -rus
Stā-j-ē'nus 3
Stā'j-ŭs 3
Stăm'e-nē
Stăph'y-la
Sta-phўl'j-ŭs
Stăph'y-lŭs
Sta-sā'nŏr
Stā'se-ăs
Sta-sĭl'e-ŭs
Stăs'j-mŭs
Sta-sī'nus
Sta-tē'nus
Stā-tj-ā'nus 1
Sta-tĭl'j-a
Stăt'j-næ
Sta-tī'nus
Sta-tī'ra
Stā'tj-ŭs 1
Sta-tŏ'rj-ŭs
Stâu-rā'cj-ŭs 1
Stĕg'a-nŏs
Stel-lā'tēş
Stĕl'lj-ō
Stĕn-o-bœ'a
Ste-nŏc'ra-tēş
Stĕn'to-rĭs
Stĕn-y-clē'rus
Stĕph'a-na, or -nē
Ste-phā'nj-ō
Stĕph-a-njs-cĭd'j-
Ste-phā'nj-ŭm [ŭm
Stĕph'a-nŭs
Stĕr'o-pē
Stĕr'o-pēş
Ster-tĭn'j-ŭs
Ste-săg'o-răs
Ste-sē'nor
Stĕs'j-clēş
Stĕs-j-lā'us
Stĕs-j-lē'a
Ste-sĭm'bro-tŭs
Sthĕn-e-lā'j-dăs
Sthĕn'e-lē
Sthĕn-e-lē'js
Sthĕn'e-lŭs
Sthē'nj-ŭs
Stĭch'j-ŭs
Stĭl'be, or Stĭl'bj-a

Stĭl'j-chō
Stĭm'j-cŏn
Stĭm'u-la
Stĭph'e-lŭs
Stĭph'j-lŭs
Stj-rī'tæ
Stœch'a-dēş 4
Stœ'chas
Stŏ'j-cī
Stŏ'ics
Sto-ĭç'j-da
Stŏ'j-cŭs
Stra-tē'gus
Strā'tj-ē 1
Strā'tj-ŏn 2
Strāt-j-ŏt'j-cŭs
Strā'tj-ŭs 1
Străt'o-clēş
Străt-o-clī'a
Străt'o-lăs
Străt-o-nī'ce
Stra-tŏn-j-cē'a
Străt-o-nī'cus
Stra-tŏ'njs Tŭr'rjs
Stra-tŏph'a-nēş
Stro-bī'lus
Stro-gŏ'la
Strom-bĭch'j-dēş
Strŏn'ǧy-lē, or
  Strŏn'ǧy-lŏs
Stron-ǧўl'j-ŏn
Strŏph'a-dēş
Strŏ'phj-ŭs
Stru-thī'a
Stru-thŏph'a-ǧī
Stry-mŏn'j cŭs
Strўm'o-nĭs
Stu-dī'ta
Stu-dī'tēş
Stўǧ'j-ŭs
Sty-lī'tēş
Sty-lŏb'a-tēş
Stym-phā'la
Stym-phā'lj-a, or
  Stym-phā'ljs
Stym-phā'lus
Suā'da
Sua-dē'la
Su-ăǧ'e-la
Su-ā'na
Sū-ar-dō'nēş
Su-bā'trj-ī
Sŭb-al-pī'nus
Sŭb'la-cŭm
Sub-mā'nus
Sŭb-mon-tō'rj-ŭm
Sū'bo-ta
Su-bū'ra
Sū'cu-rŏ
Su-dē'tī
Su-ē'bī
Su-ē'bus
Suĕs'sa
Sues-sā'nus
Suĕs-se-tā'nī
Sues-sī'o-nēş
Sues-sŏ'nēş
Sue-tō'nj-ŭs
Suē'vī
Suē'vj-ŭs

Su-fē'nas
Suf-fē'nus
Suf-fē'tēş
Suf-fē'tj-ŭs 1, or
  Su-fē'tj-ŭs 1
Sŭg'dj-ăs
Sū'j-dăs
Suĭl-lā'rēş
Suĭl'lj-ŭs
Suĭ'o-nēş
Sŭl'cj-ŭs 1
Sŭl'mo-na
Sul-pĭ''cj-a 1
Sul-pĭ-cj-ā'nus 1
Sul-pĭ''tj-a 1
Sul-pĭ''tj-ŭs 1
Sum-mā'nus
Sum-mœ'nj-ŭm
Sū'nj-ăs
Sū'nj-cī
Sū'nj-dēş
Sū'nj-ŏn
Sū'nj-ŭm
Su-ŏd'a-na
Su-ō-ve-tâu-rĭl'j-a
Sū'pe-rŭm Mā're
Sur-dī'nus
Su-rē'na
Su-rē'nas
Sū'rj-a
Sū'rj-ŭm
Sū'sa-na
Su-sā'rj-ŏn
Sū-sj-ā'na 1
Sū'trj-ŭm
Sў'a-ǧer
Sy-ā'grj-ŭs
Sy-ā'grus, or
  Sў'a-grŭs
Sўb-a-rī'ta
Sўb'a-rīte
Sўb-a-rī'tjs
Sўb'e-rŭs
Sўb'o-ta
Sўb'o-tăs
Sў-căm'j-na
Sў-chæ'us
Sўc-o-la-trŏn'j-dæ
Sў'e-dra
Sў-ē'ne
Sў-e-nē'sj-ŭs 1
Sў-e-nī'tēş
Sў-ĕn'ne-sĭs
Sўg'a-rŏs
Sўl'e-a
Sy-lē'um
Sў'leūs 6
Sy-lī'o-nēş
Sўl'o-sŏu
Syl-vā'nus
Sўl'vj-a
Sўl'vj-ŭs
Sўm'bo-la
Sўm'bo-lī
Sўm'bo-lŭm
Sy-mæ'thus
Sўm'e-ŏn
Sўm'ma-chŭs
Sўm-pho-rō'sa
Sym-plĕg'a-dēş

Sym-plē'gas
Sym-pō'sj-ŭs 1
Sўn'e-drī
Sўn-e-phē'bī
Sў-nē'sj-ŭs 1
Sўn'ǧe-lŭs
Sўn'ha-lŭs
Sўn'na-da
Sўn'no-ŏn
Sўn'o-dŭs
Sў-nō'pe
Sўn'tj-păs
Sўn'tj-chē
Sўr'a-cēş
Sўr-a-cō'sj-a 1
Sўr-a-cū'sæ
Sўr'a-cūse
Sўr'j-a
Sўr-j-ā'nus
Sўr'ma-tæ
Syr-nē'thō
Sўr-o-cĭl'j-cēş
Sўr-o-mē'dj-a
Sўr-o phœ-nī'cēş
Sўr'tēş
Sўr'tj-cŭs
Sўs-j-găm'bjs
Sy-sĭm'e-thrēş
Sўs'j-năs

T.

Ta-âu'tēş
Tăb'a-lŭs
Ta-bā'nus, or
  Tăb'a-nŭs
Ta-bē'nī
Tăb'ra-ca
Ta-bū'da
Tăc'a-pē
Tăc-a-phŏ'rjs
Tăc-fa-rī'nas
Ta-chŏmp'sō
Tăch'o-rī
Tā'chŏs, or
  Tā'chus
Tăç'j-ta
Tăç'j-tŭs
Ta-cō'la
Tā'dj-ŭs
Tæ'dj-a
Tæ-dĭf'e-ra
Tæn'a-ra 4
Tæn'a-rŏs 4
Tæn'a-rŭs 4
Tæ'nj-ăs
Ta-ē'pa
Ta-gŏ'nj-ŭs
Tăl-a-ī-ŏn'j-dēş
Tăl-a-ŏn'j-dēş
Ta-lā'sj-ŭs 1
Tăl'a-ŭs
Tăl'e-tŭm
Ta-lī'dēş
Tal-thўb'j-ŭs
Ta-lĭ''sj-ŭs 1
Tăm'a-rē
Tăm'a-rŭs

Tăm'a-sŭs
Tăm'e-sĭs
Tăm'phj-lŭs
Tăm'pj-ŭs
Tăm'y-næ
Tăm'y-răs
Tăm'y-rĭs
Tăn'a-ǧer
Tăn'a-gra, or
  Ta-nā'gru
Tăn'a-grŭs
Tăn'a-ĭs
Tăn'a-quĭl
Ta-nē'tum
Tan-tā'le-ŭs
Tăn'ta-lŭs
Ta-nū'sj-ŭs 1
Tā'o-cē
Ta-ō'cī
Tā'o-chī
Tā'phj-æ
Tā-phj-ăs'sus
Tā'phj-ī
Tā'phj-ŭs
Tā'phros
Tăp'o-rī
Tăp-o-sī'rjs
Tăp'pu-lŭs
Ta-prŏb'a-nē
Tăp'y-rī
Tăr'a-nĭs
Ta-rā'sj-ŭs 1
Tăr-a-tăl'la
Tar-bĕl'lj-cŭs
Tar-chē'tj-ŭs 1
Tăr'chj-a
Tăr-chon-dĭm'o-tŭs
Tăr-en-tī'nus
Tar-ǧĭb'j-lŭs
Tăr-j-chē'a
Ta-rĭch'e-æ
Tā'rj-ŭs
Tăr'næ
Tar-pē'j-a 3
Tar-pē'j-ŭs 3
Tar-quĭn'j-a
Tar-quĭn'j-ī
Tar-quĭn'j-ŭs
Tăr'quin
Tar-quĭ''tj-ŭs 1
Tăr'quj-tŭs
Tăr-ra-cī'na
Tăr'ra-cŏ
Tar-rŭ'tj-ŭs 1
Tăr'sj-ŭs 1
Tar-tē'sus
Ta-rŭn'tj-ŭs 1
Tăr-u-sā'tēş
Tas-ǧē'tj-ŭs 1
Tăs'sj-tō
Tā-tj-ā'nus 1
Tā'tian
Tā'tj-ī 1
Tā'tj-ŭs 1
Tâu-chī'ra
Tâu-lăn'tj-ī 1
Tâu'las
Tâu'nus
Tâu-rā'nj-a
Tâu-rā'nus

Tâu-răn'tēṣ
Tâu're-ạ
Tâu'rī
Tâu-rī'ạ
Tâu'rị-cạ
Tâu-rī'nī
Tâu-rī'nụm
Tâu-rī'nụs
Tâu'rị-ŏn
Tâu-rị-ō'nẹ
Tâu-rĭs'cī
Tâu'rị-ŭm
Tâu'rị-ŭs
Tâu-rŏb'ọ-lŭs
Tâu-rọ-cĕph'ạ-lŭs
Tâu'rọ-ĭs
Tâu-rŏm'ẹ-nŏs
Tâu-rọ-mĭn'ị-ŭm
Tâu-rŏ'pọs
Tâu-rọ-pọ-lī'ạ
Tâu-rŏp'ọ-lĭs
Tâu-rŏp'ọ-lŭs
Tâu-rụ'bụ-læ
Tâu'rụs
Táx'ị-lạ
Táx'ị-lī
Táx'ị-lŭs, or
　Táx'ị-lēṣ
Táx-ị-măg'ụ-lŭs
Tạ-ȳ́ǵ'ẹ-tē
Tạ-ȳ́ǵ'ẹ-tŭs, or
　Tạ-ȳ́g'ẹ-tạ
Te-ā'nụm
Tē'ạ-rŭs
Tẹ-ā'tẹ
Tē'chēṣ
Tĕch'nạ-tĭs
Tĕc'tạ-mŭs
Tẹc-tŏs'ạ-ǵēṣ, or
　Tẹc-tŏs'ạ-ǵæ
Tẹc-tŏs'ạ-ǵī
Tĕc'tọ-sáx
Tē'ǵẹ-ạ, or
　Tẹ-ǵǽ'ạ
Tē-ǵẹ-ā'tēṣ
Tĕg'ụ-lạ
Tĕǵ'y-rạ
Tē'ị-ạ 3
Tē'ị-ŏs 3
Tē'ị-ŭm 3
Tē'ị-ŭs 3 .
Tĕl'ạ-mŏn
Tĕl-ạ-mọ-nī'ạ-dēṣ
Tĕl'chịn
Tẹl-chī'nēṣ
Tẹl-chĭn'ị-ŭs
Tẹ-lē'ạ, or -lī'ạ
Tẹ-lĕb'ọ-æ, or
　Tẹ-lĕb'ọ-ēṣ
Tĕl-ẹ-bō'ị-dēṣ
Tĕl'ẹ-clēṣ
Tĕl'ẹ-clŭs
Tĕl-ẹ-clī'dēṣ
Tẹ-lĕc'ọ-ŏn
Tĕl-ẹ-dā'mụs
Tẹ-lĕg'ọ-nŭs
Tĕl'ẹ-mŭs
Tĕl-ẹ-nī'cụs
Tẹ-lĕph'ạ-nēṣ
Tĕl'ẹ-phŭs

Tĕl-ẹ-sär'chị-dēṣ
Tẹ-lē'sị-ạ 1
Tẹ-lē'sị-ăs 1
Tẹ-lĕs'ị-clēṣ
Tĕl-ẹ-sĭl'lạ
Tẹ-lĕs-ị-nī'cụs
Tĕl-ẹ-sī'nụs
Tẹ-lĕs'phọ-rŭs
Tĕl-ẹ-stäg'ọ-răs
Tẹ-lĕs'tēṣ
Tĕl'ẹ-tē
Tĕl'ẹ-thŭs
Tĕl-ẹ-thū'sạ
Tẹ-leū'rị-ăs
Tẹ-leū'tẹ
Tẹ-leū'tị-ăs 1
Tĕl'ị-nēṣ
Tẹl-lē'næ
Tĕl'lị-ăs
Tĕl'mẹ-rạ
Tẹl-phū'sạ
Tẹ-mā'thị-ạ
Tĕm'brị-ŭm
Tĕm-ẹ-nī'ạ
Tĕm-ẹ-nī'tēṣ
Tẹ-mē'nị-ŭm
Tĕm'ẹ-nŏs
Tĕm'ẹ-nŭs
Tĕm-ẹ-rĭn'dạ
Tĕm'ẹ-sạ
Tĕm'ẹ-sæ
Tĕm'ẹ-sē
Tĕm'ị-sŭs
Tẹm-mī'cēṣ
Tẹm-pā'nị-ŭs
Tĕm'pẹ
Tĕm'pẹ-ạ
Tẹm-pȳ'rạ
Tĕnch'tẹ-rī, or
　Tĕnch-tē'rī
Tē'nẹ-ạ
Tẹ-nē'æ
Tĕn'ẹ-dŏs
Tĕn'ẹ-rŭs
Tē'nēṣ
Tĕn'ẹ-sĭs
Tẹ-nē'ụm
Tĕn'ty-rạ
Tẹ-rē'dọn
Tẹ-rē'ị-dēṣ
Tẹ-rĕn'tị-ạ 1
Tẹ-rĕn-tị-ā'nụs 1
Tĕr-ẹn-tī'nụs
Tẹ-rĕn'tị-ŭs 1
Tĕr'ence
Tē'reūs 6
Tẹr-ǵĕm'ị-nŭs
Tĕr-ǵes-tī'nụs
Tē'rị-ás
Tĕr-ị-bā'zụs
Tẹ-rĭd'ạ-ē
Tĕr-ị-dā'tēṣ
Tĕr'ị-gŭm
Tẹ-rī'nạ
Tẹr-măn'tị-ạ 1
Tĕr'mẹ-rạ
Tĕr'mẹ-rŭs
Tĕr-mē'sụs
Tĕr-mị-nā'lị-ạ
Tĕr-mị-nā'lịs

Tër'mị-nŭs
Tër'mị-sŭs
Tẹrp-sĭch'ọ-rē
Tĕrp'sị-ŏn
Tĕr-rạ-cī'nạ
Tĕr-rạ-sĭd'ị-ŭs
Tĕr'tị-ạ 1
Tĕr'tị-ŭs 1
Tẹr-tŭl-lị-ā'nụs
Tẹr-tŭl'lị-ạn
Tĕs'tị-lŭs
Tĕs'tị-ŭs
Tĕt-rạ-cō'mụm
Tẹ-trā'dị-ŭs
Tĕt-rạ-gō'nịs
Tĕt'rị-cạ
Tĕt'rị-cŭs
Tĕt'tị-ŭs
Teū'cer
Teū-chī'rạ
Teū'crī
Teū'crị-ạ
Teū-mē'sọs
Teū-ō'chịs
Teū'tạ
Teū-tág'ọ-nŭs
Teū'tạ-lŭs
Teū-tā'mị-ăs, or
　Teū'tạ-mĭs
Teū'tạ-mŭs
Teū'tạs, or
　Teū-tā'tēṣ
Teū-thrā'nị-ạ
Teū'thrạs
Teū-thrō'nẹ
Teū-tī'ạ-plŭs
Teū-tŏm'ạ-tŭs
Teū'tọ-nēṣ, and
　Teū'tọ-nī
Teū-tŏn'ị-cŭs
Thăc'cọ-nạ
Thăl'ạ-mæ
Thăl'ạ-mŭs
Thạ-lás'sị-ō 1
Thạ-lăs'sị-ŭs 1
Thā'lēṣ
Thạ-lĕs'trị-ạ
Thạ-lē'tạs
Thạ-lī'ạ
Thā-lị-är'chụs
Thā'lị-ŭs
Thăl'pị-ŭs
Thăm'ụ-dạ
Thăm'y-rĭs
Thăm'y-rŭs
Thăn'ạ-tŏs
Thăp'sạ-cŭs
Thạr-ǵē'lị-ạ
Thạ-rī'ạ-dēṣ
Thā'sị-ŭs 1, or
　Thrā'sị-ŭs 1
Thâu'mạ-cī
Thâu-mā'cị-ạ 1
Thạu-măn'tị-ăs 1
Thâu'mạs
Thâu-mā'sị-ŭs 1
Thâu-măs-tọ-rī'tēṣ
Thē-æ-tē'tụs
Thẹ-ắǵ'ẹ-nēṣ
Thẹ-ā'ǵēṣ, or

Thē'ạ-ǵēṣ
Thẹ-ā'nō
Thẹ-ăr'ị-dăs
Thē'bæ
Thēbeṣ
Thĕb'ạ-ĭs
Thẹ-bā'nụs
Thē'be, *or* Thē'bạ
Thē'clạ
Thē'ị-ạ 3
Thē'ị-ăs 3
Thĕl-ạ-ī'rạ
Thĕl-ạ-phăs'sạ
Thĕl-ẹ-sī'nạ
Thĕl-ẹ-sī'nụs
Thĕl'ị-nē
Thẹl-pū'sạ
Thẹlx-ĭn'ọ-ē
Thẹlx-ī'ọn
Thẹlx-ī'ọ-pē
Thĕm'ẹ-nŭs
Thẹ-mē'sị-ŏn 1
Thĕm-ịs-cȳ'rạ
Thĕm'ị-sŏn
Thĕm-ịs-tī'ạ-dēṣ
Thẹ-mĭs'tị-ŭs
Thẹ-mĭs'tọ-clēṣ
Thĕm-ị-stŏǵ'ẹ-nēṣ
Thē-ọ-clē'ạ
Thē'ọ-clēṣ
Thē'ọ-clŭs
Thē-ọ-clȳm'ẹ-nŭs
Thẹ-ŏc'ly-tŭs
Thẹ-ŏc'rị-nēṣ
Thẹ-ŏc'rị-tŭs
Thẹ-ŏd'ạ-măs, *or*
　Thī-ŏd'ạ-măs
Thē-ọ-dā'mụs
Thē'ọ-dás
Thẹ-ŏd'ạ-tŭs
Thē-ọ-dĕc'tēṣ
Thẹ-ŏd-ẹ-rī'cụs
Thẹ-ŏd'ọ-cŭs
Thē-ọ-dō'nịs Vĭl'lạ
Thē-ọ-dō'rạ
Thẹ-ŏd-ọ-rē'tụs
Thẹ-ŏd'ọ-rĕt
Thẹ-ŏd-ọ-rī'cụs
Thẹ-ŏd'ọ-rĭc
Thẹ-ŏd-ọ-rī'tụs
Thẹ-ŏd-ọ-rọ-mē'dēṣ
Thē-ọ-dō'rụs
Thē'ọ-dōre
Thē-ọ-dō'sị-ạ 1
Thē-ọ-dō'sị-ŭs 1
Thẹ-ŏd'ọ-tạ, *or*
　Thẹ-ŏd'ọ-tē
Thē-ọ-dō'tịọn 2
Thẹ-ŏd'ọ-tŭs
Thē-ọ-dū'lụs
Thē-ọ-ǵī'tọn
Thē-ọg-nē'tụs
Thẹ-ŏl'y-tŭs
Thẹ-ŏm'ẹ-dŏn
Thẹ-ō'nạs
Thē-ọ-nī'cụs
Thē-ọ-nī'nụs
Thẹ-ŏn'ọ-ē
Thē'ọ-pē
Thẹ-ŏph'ạ-nē

Thẹ-ŏph'ạ-nēṣ
Thē-ọ-phā'nị-ạ, *or*
　Thẹ-ŏph-ạ-nī'ạ
Thẹ-ŏph'ị-lạ
Thẹ-ŏph'ị-lŭs
Thē-ọ-phy-lăc'tụs
Thẹ-ŏph'y-lăct
Thē-ọ-pŏl'ẹ-mŭs
Thẹ-ŏp'rọ-pŭs
Thẹ-ō'rịs
Thẹ-ō'rị-ŭs
Thē-ọ-tī'mụs
Thẹ-ŏx'ẹ-nạ
Thē-ọx-ē'nị-ạ
Thē-ọx-ē'nị-ŭs
Thẹ-ŏx'ẹ-nŭs
Thẹ-răp'næ [nŭs
Thĕr-ạ-pọn-tĭg'ọ-
Thẹ-rā'sị-ạ 1
Thĕr'ị-clēṣ
Thẹ-rĭd'ạ-măs
Thẹ-rĭm'ạ-chŭs
Thĕr'ị-nŭs
Thẹ-rĭp'pị-dăs
Thẹ-rī'tạs
Thĕr'mæ
Thẹr-mā'ị-cŭs
Thẹr-măn'tị-ạ 1
Thẹr-mō'dọn
Thẹ-rŏd'ạ-măs
Thẹ-rŏm'ẹ-dŏn
Thĕr-ọ-nī'cẹ
Thẹr-sĭl'ọ-chŭs
Thẹr-sī'tēṣ
Thẹ-rū'chụs
Thẹs-bī'tēṣ
Thĕs'cẹ-lŭs
Thẹ-sē'ạ
Thẹ-sē'ịs
Thẹ-sē'ụm
Thē'seūs (*n.*) 6
Thẹ-sē'ụs (*a.*)
Thẹ-sī'dæ
Thẹ-sī'dēṣ
Thĕs-mọ-phō'rị-ạ
Thẹs-mŏph'ọ-rŏs
Thẹs-mŏth'ẹ-tæ
Thẹs-pē'ạ, *or*
　Thẹs-pī'ạ
Thẹs-pī'ạ-dæ
Thẹs-pī'ạ-dēṣ
Thĕs'pị-æ
Thĕs'pị-ŭs
Thĕs'prị-ō
Thẹs-prō'tī
Thẹs-prō'tị-ạ 1
Thẹs-prō'tịs
Thẹs-sā'lị-ạ
Thẹs-sā'lị-ŏn
Thẹs-sā-lị-ō'tịs
Thĕs'sạ-lĭs
Thĕs-sạ-lọ-nī'cạ
Thĕs'sạ-lŭs
Thĕs'tạ-lŭs
Thĕs'tị-ạ
Thẹs-tī'ạ-dæ, *and*
　Thẹs-tī'ạ-dēṣ
Thĕs'tị-ăs
Thĕs-tị-dī'ụm
Thĕs'tị-ŭs

Thęs-tŏr′ǐ-dēş
Thĕs′ty-lǐs
Thĕs′ty-lŏs
Thĕs′ty-lŭs
Theū-dō′şǐ-ŭs 1
Theū′dǫ-tŭs
Theū-rŏp′ǐ-dēş
Theū-tā′tēş
Theū′tǐs, *or*
  Teū′thǐs
Thī′ạ
Thī-ạl-lē′lạ
Thī-ŏd′ạ-mãs
Thïr′mǐ-dạ
Thǐs′bę
Thī″şǐ-ăs 1
Thǐs′ǫ-ạ
Thŏ-ạn-tē′ạ
Thǫ-ăn′tǐ-ăs 1
Thǫ-ăn′tǐ-ŭm 1
Thŏm′y-rǐs
Thǫ-nī′tēş
Thǫ-nī′tǐs
Thō′ǫn
Thǫ-ō′sạ
Thǫ-ō′tēş
Thǫ-rā′nǐ-ŭs
Thō′rǐ-ạ
Thŏr′ǐ-cŭs
Thō′rǐ-ŭs
Thǫs-pī′tēş
Thō′ŭs
Thrā′cę
Thrā′cǐ-ạ 1
Thrāce
Thrãç′ǐ-dæ
Thrā′sę-ạ
Thrā′sę-ăs
Thrạ-sǐd′ę-ŭs
Thrā′şǐ-ŭs 1
Thrạ-sŏn′ǐ-dēş
Thrā′sy-ăs
Thrăs-y-bū′lŭs
Thrạ-sȳl′ǫ-chŭs
Thrạ-sȳm′ạ-chŭs
Thrăs-y-mē′dēş
Thrăs-y-mē′lŭs
Thrăs-y-mē′nŭs
Thrē′cę
Thrę-ǐ″cǐ-ŭs 1
Thrō′nǐ-ŭm
Thrō′nǐ-ŭs
Thụ-dē′mŭs
Thụ-ğĕn′ǐ-dēş
Thū′lę
Thū′rǐ-ạ
Thū′rǐ-æ
Thū′rǐ-ī, *or*
  Thū′rǐ-ŭm
Thụ-rī′nŭs
Thū′rǐ-ŭs
Thŭs′cǐ-ạ 1
Thȳ′ạ-dēş
Thȳ-ā′mǐ-ạ, *or*
  Thȳ-ạ-mī′ạ
Thȳ′ạ-mŭs
Thȳ-ạ-tī′rạ
Thȳ-ē′nę
Thȳ-ĕs′tēş
Thȳ-ęs-tē′ŭs

Thȳ-ęs-tī′ạ-dēş
Thȳ′ǐạ
Thȳ′ǐạ-dēş
Thȳ′ǐạs
Thym-bræ′ŭs
Thȳm′brǐ-ạ
Thȳm′brǐ-ŭm
Thȳm′brǐ-ŭs
Thȳm′ę-lē
Thȳ-mē′nạ
Thy-mŏch′ạ-rēş
Thȳm′ǫ-clēş
Thȳn′ǐ-ạ
Thȳn′ǐ-ăs
Thȳ-ō′nę
Thȳ-ō′neūs 6
Thȳ-ō′tēş
Thȳ-ræ′ŭs
Thȳ′rę
Thȳr′ę-ạ
Thȳr-ę-ā′tæ
Thȳr-ę-ā′tǐs
Thȳ′reūs 6
Thȳr′ǐ-dēş
Thȳr′ǐ-ŏn
Thȳr′ǐ-ŭs
Thyr-sãg′ę-tēş
Tī-ā′rạ
Tī′ạ-sạ, *or* Tī-ā′sạ
Tǐb-ạ-rē′nī
Tī-bē′rǐ-ăs
Tǐb-ę-rǐn′ǐ-dēş
Tǐb-ę-rī′nŭs
Tǐb′ę-rǐs
Tī-bē′rǐ-ŭs
Tī-bē′rŭs
Tī-bē′sǐs
Tǐb-ǐ-sē′nŭs
Tī′brǐs
Tǐb′ụ-lạ
Tǐb-ụr-tī′nŭs
Tī-bür′tǐ-ŭs 1
Tī′chǐs
Tǐch′ǐ-ŭs
Tī-chō′nǐ-ŭs
Tǐç′ǐ-dạ
Tǐ-cī′nŭm
Tǐ-cī′nŭs, *river.*
Tǐç′ǐ-nŭs, *man.*
Tǐd′ǐ-ŭs
Tī-fā′tạ
Tǐg′ạ-sǐs
Tǐğ-ęl-lī′nŭs
Tǐ-grā-nǫ-cër′tạ
Tī′grēş
Tī′grǐs
Tǐg-ụ-rī′nī
Tǐl-ạ-tæ′ī
Tǐl-ạ-vĕmp′tŭs
Tǐl′lǐ-ŭs
Tǐl-phū′sạ
Tī-mæ′ạ
Tī-mæn′ę-tŭs 4
Tī-mãg′ę-nēş
Tǐm-ạ-ğĕn′ǐ-dēş
Tǐm-ạ-ğē′tēş
Tī-mãg′ǫ-rãs
Tī-măn′drǐ-dēş
Tī-măn′ğę-lŭs
Tī-măn′thēş

Tī-mär′chǐ-dēş
Tī-mär′ę-tạ, *or*
  Tī-mär′ę-tę
Tī-mā′şǐ-ŏn 1
Tǐm-ạ-sǐth′ę-ŭs
Tī-mā′şǐ-ŭs 1
Tī-mā′vụs
Tǐm′ę-ăs
Tī-mē′şǐ-ăs 1
Tī-mē′şǐ-ŭs 1
Tī-mŏch′ạ-rēş
Tǐm-ǫ-clē′ạ
Tǐm′ǫ-clēş
Tǐm-ǫ-clī′dạs
Tī-mŏc′rạ-tēş
Tī-mō′crę-ŏn
Tǐm-ǫ-dē′mŭs
Tǐm-ǫ-lā′ŭs
Tī-mō′lę-ŏn
Tī-mō′lŭs
Tī-mŏm′ạ-chŭs
Tī-mō′năx
Tī-mŏn′ǐ-dēş
Tī-mŏs′the-nēş
Tī-mō′the-ŭs
Tī-mŏx′ę-nŭs
Tǐn′ğǐs
Tǐn′ǐ-ạ
Tǐph′y-sạ
Tī-rē′şǐ-ăs 1
Tǐr-ǐ-bā′sēş
Tǐr-ǐ-bā′zụs
Tǐr-ǐ-dā′tēş
Tī-rȳn′thǐ-ạ
Tī-sãg′ǫ-rãs
Tī-săm′ę-nēş
Tī-săm′ę-nŭs
Tī″şǐ-ăs 1
Tī-sǐc′rạ-tēş
Tī-şǐ-ē′nŭs 1
Tī-sǐph′ǫ-nē
Tī-sǐph′ǫ-nŭs
Tǐs′ǫ-bǐs
Tǐs-săm′ę-nŭs
Tǐs-sạ-phër′nēş
Tī-tæ′ạ
Tī′tạn, *or*
  Tī-tā′nŭs
Tǐt′ạ-nạ, *or* -nę
Tī-tā′nēş
Tī′tạnş
Tǐt-ạ-nē′ŭs
Tī-tā′nǐ-ạ
Tī-tăn′ǐ-dēş
Tī-tā′nǐ-ŭs
Tī-tā′nŭs, *giant.*
Tǐt′ạ-nŭs, *river.*
Tǐt-ạ-rē′şǐ-ŭs 1
Tǐt-ạ-rē′sụs
Tī-tē′nŭs
Tī-thō′nǐs
Tī-thō′nŭs
Tī-thō′rę-ạ
Tī-thrō′nǐ-ŭm
Tī″tǐ-ạ 1
Tī-tǐ-ā′nạ 1
Tī-tǐ-ā′nŭs 1
Tī″tǐ-ēş 1
Tī″tǐ-ī 1
Tī-tǐn′ǐ-ŭs

Tī″tǐ-ŭs 1
Tǐt-thē′ŭm
Tī-tū′rǐ-ŭs
Tǐt′y-ŏs
Tǐt′y-rŭs
Tǐt′y-ŭs
Tlę-pŏl′ę-mŭs
Tmā′rǫs 5
Tmā′rŭs 5
Tmō′lŭs 5
Tŏch′ạ-rī
Tœs′ǫ-bǐs 4
Tǫ-gā′tạ
Tŏl-ęn-tī′nŭm
Tǫ-lē′nŭs
Tŏl-ę-tā′nŭs
Tǫ-lē′tŭm
Tŏl-ǐs-tō′bǐ-ī
Tŏl′mǐ-dēş
Tŏl′ǫ-phŏn
Tǫ-lō′sạ
Tǫ-lŭm′nǐ-ŭs
Tǫ-mæ′ŭm
Tŏm′ạ-rŭs, *or*
  Tǫ-mā′rŭs
Tǫ-mē′rŭs
Tŏm′ǐ-sạ
Tǫ-mī′tæ
Tŏm′ǫ-rī
Tŏm′y-rǐs
Tǫn-dō′tạ
Tō′nę-ạ
Tǫn-ğǐl-ǐ-ā′nŭs
Tǫn-ğǐl′ǐ-ŭs
Tǫ-pā′zǫs
Tǫ-pā′zụs
Tǫ-pī′rǐs, *or* -rụs, *or*
  Tŏp′ǐ-rǐs
Tǫ-rā′nǐ-ŭs
Tō-rę-ā′tæ
Tŏr′ę-tæ
Tŏr′ǐ-nī
Tǫ-rŏ′nę
Tǫr-quā′tụs
Tǫ-rȳ′nę
Tŏx-ạ-rǐd′ǐ-ạ
Tŏx′eūs 6
Tǫx-ǐc′rạ-tē
Tŏx′ǐ-lī
Tŏx′ǐ-lŭs
Trā′bę-ạ
Trạ-chā′lǐ-ŏ
Trăch′ạ-lŭs
Trā′chạs
Trạ-chē′ạ
Trā′chǐn
Trăch-ǫ-nī′tǐs
Trạ-ğœ′dǐ-ạ
Trạ-gū′rǐ-ŭm
Trăj-ạ-nŏp′ǫ-lǐs
Trạ-jā′nŭs
Trā′jạn
Trăl′lēş
Trăl-lǐ-ā′nŭs
Trạm-bē′lŭs
Trā′nǐ-ō, *or* -ŭs
Trăns-ạl-pī′nŭs
Trăns-pạ-dā′nŭs
Trăns-tǐb-ę-rī′nạ
Trăns-tǐb-ę-rī′nŭs

Trạ-pē′zạ
Trạ-pē′zǫu
Trạ-pē′zụs
Trạ-phē′ạ
Trăs-ǐ-mē′nŭs
Trâu′şǐ-ŭs 1
Trę-bā′tǐ-ŭs 1
Trę-bĕl-lǐ-ā′nŭs
Trę-bĕl-lǐ-ē′nŭs
Trę-bĕl′lǐ-ŭs
Trĕ′bǐ-ŭs
Trę-bō′nǐ-ạ
Trę-bō-nǐ-ā′nŭs
Trę-bō′nǐ-ŭs
Trĕb′ụ-lạ
Trę-mĕl′lǐ-ŭs
Trĕm′ụ-lŭs
Trēş′vǐ-rī
Trĕv′ǐ-rī
Trī-ā′rǐ-ạ
Trī-ā′rǐ-ŭs
Trī-bō-nǐ-ā′nŭs
Trǐb′ǫ-cī
Trī-bū′nī
Trī-bū′nŭs
Trǐc-ạ-rā′nạ, *or*
  Trǐc-ạ-rā′nŭm
Trǐc-ạs-tī′nī
Trǐc′cæ (*trǐk′sē*)
Trǐc-cǐ-ā′nŭs 1
Trǐch′ǐ-năs
Trī-chō′nǐs
Trī-chō′nǐ-ŭm
Trǐç-ǐp-tī′nŭs
Trī-clā′rǐ-ạ
Trǐc-ǫ-lō′nī
Trī-crā′nạ
Trī-crē′nạ
Trǐd-ęn-tī′nī
Trī-ē′rēş, *or* -rǐs
Trī-ę-tĕr′ǐ-cạ
Trǐf-ǫ-lī′nŭs
Trī-ğĕm′ǐ-nŭs
Trī-gō′nŭm
Trī-gō′nŭs
Trǐn′ạ-crǐs
Trī-nā′crǐ-ŭs
Trī-nā′sụs
Trǐn′ę-meǐs
Trǐn-ę-mī′ạ
Trī-ŏc′ạ-lạ
Trī′ǫ-clạ
Trī′ǫ-dŭs
Trī-ō′nēş
Trī′ǫ-păs
Trī-ǫ-pē′ǐ-ŭs 3
Trī-ǫ-pē′ǐs
Trī-ō′pǐ-ŭm
Trǐ-phȳ′lǐs
Trǐ-phȳ′lŭs
Trǐp′ǫ-dī
Trǐp′ǫ-lǐs
Trǐp-tŏl′ę-mŭs
Trǐq′uę-trạ
Trī-tē′ạ, *or*
  Trī-tī′ạ
Trǐ″tǐ-ạ 1, *or*
  Trǐt′tǐ-ạ
Trǐ″tǐ-ŭm 1
Trǐt-ǫ-ğę-nī′ạ

Trĭ-tō′nĕş
Trĭ-tō′nịs
Trĭ-tō′nụs
Trĭ-ŭm-pị-lĭ′nĭ
Trĭ-ŭm′vị-rĭ
Trĭv′ị-ạ
Trĭv′ị-æ Ăn′trụm
Trĭv′ị-æ Lū′cụs
Trị-vī′cụm
Trŏ′ạ-dĕş
Trŏch′ạ-rĭ
Trŏch′ọ-ĭs
Trœ-zē′nẹ
Trọ-ǵĭl′ị-ŭm
Trŏǵ′ị-lŭs
Trọg-lŏd′y-tæ
Trọg-lŏd′y-tēş
Trŏ′ị-lŏs
Trŏ′ị-lŭs
Trọ-jū′ǵẹ-næ
Trŏm-ẹn-tī′nạ
Trŏph′ị-lŭs
Trŏph′ị-mŭs
Trŏs′sụ-lĭ
Trŏs′sụ-lŭm
Trŏs′sụ-lŭs
Trŏt′ị-lŭm
Trŭ-ẹn-tī′nụm
Trўg-ọ-dæm′ọ-nĕş 4
Trўph′ẹ-rŭs
Trўph-ị-ọ-dō′rụs
Trўph-ọ-nī′nụs
Tū′bẹ-rō
Tū-bị-lŭs′trị-ạ
Tū′bụ-lŭs
Tŭc′cị-ạ 1
Tŭc-cị-tō′rạ
Tŭc′cị-ŭs 1
Tū′cị-ạ 1
Tụ-dĕr′tị-ạ 1
Tū-dị-tā′nụs
Tū′drĭ
Tụ-ĕr′ọ-bĭs
Tū′ǵẹ-nĭ
Tū-gụ-rī′nụs
Tŭl′lị-ạ
Tŭl-lị-ā′nụm
Tụl-lī′ọ-lạ
Tŭl′lị-ŭs
Tụ-nē′tạ
Tụ-rā′nị-ŭs
Tụr-bā′lị-ō
Tür-dẹ-tā′nĭ
Tür′dụ-lĭ
Tụ-rē′sịş
Tū′rị-ạ
Tū-rị-ā′sō
Tū′rị-cŭm
Tū′rị-ŭs
Tū′rọ-nĕş
Tū′rọ-nĭ, *Gaul.*
Tụ-rō′nĭ, *Ger.*
Tụr-pĭl′ị-ạ
Tụr-pĭl-ị-ā′nụs
Tür′pị-ō
Tụr-rā′nị-ŭs
Tür-rị-ā′nụs
Tụr-rī′nụs
Tụ-rŭl′lị-ŭs
Tụs-cā′nị-ạ

Tŭs′cĭ
Tŭs′cị-ạ 1
Tŭs-cụ-lā′nụm
Tŭs′cụ-lŭm
Tụ-tā′nụs
Tụ-tē′lạ
Tū-tẹ-lī′nạ
Tū′thọ-ạ
Tū′tị-ạ 1
Tū-tị-cā′nụs
Tū′tị-cŭm
Tū-tị-lī′nạ
Tȳ′ạ-nạ
Tȳ-ạ-nē′ị-ŭs 3
Tȳ-ạ-næ′ụs
Tȳ′ạ-neūs 6
Tȳ-ạ-nī′tịs
Tȳ′chẹ
Tȳch′ị-cŭs
Tȳch′ị-ŭs
Tȳ-chō′nị-ŭs
Tȳ′dẹ
Tȳ′deūs 6
Ty-dī′dĕş
Tȳ-ē′nịs
Tȳ-lăn′ǵị-ĭ
Tym-brē′nụs
Tȳ-mō′lụs
Tym-pā′nị-ạ
Tyn-dā′rẹ-ŏs
Tyn-dā′rẹ-ŭs
Tyn-dăr′ị-dæ
Tyn-dăr′ị-dĕş
Tȳn′dạ-rĭs
Tȳn′dạ-rŭs
Tȳn′nị-chŭs
Tȳ-pā′nẹ-æ
Tȳ-phā′ọn
Tȳ-phō′eūs 6
Tȳ-phō′ị-ŭs, *or*
  Tȳ-phō′ẹ-ŭs (*a.*)
Tȳ-phō′nịs
Tȳr-ạ-cī′næ
Tȳ-răǵ′ẹ-tæ
Tȳr-ạn-ǵī′tæ, *or*
  Tȳ-răn′ǵẹ-tæ
Tȳ′rēş
Tȳr-ị-dā′tēş
Tȳr′ị-ĭ
Ty-rī′ọ-tēş
Tȳr′ị-ŭs
Tȳ-rŏǵ′ly-phŭs
Tyr-rhē′nĭ
Tyr-rhē′nị-ạ
Tyr-rhē′nụm
Tyr-rhē′nụs
Tyr′rheūs 6
Tyr-rhī′dæ
Tyr-rhĭǵ′ẹ-næ
Tyr-sē′tạ
Tȳ′′sị-ăs 1
Tzăc′ọ-nĕş 5
Tzĕt′zēş 5

U.

Ū′bị-ĭ
Ū′cụ-bĭs

Ul-rī′cụs
Ŭl′ric
Ū-fẹn-tī′nạ
Ū-lĭx′ēş
Ū-lĭx′eūs 6
Ŭl-pị-ā′nụs
Ŭl′pị-ạn
Ŭl′pị-ŭs
Ū′lụ-bræ
Ū-lȳs′sēş
Ụm-brē′nụs
Ŭm′brị-ạ
Ụm-brĭ′′cị-ŭs 1
Ụm-mĭd′ị-ŭs
Ŭn-dẹ-cĕm′vị-rĭ
Ū′nị-cŭs
Ŭnx′ị-ạ 1
Ụp-sā′lụm
Ŭ-rā′cạ
Ū-rā′gụs
Ū-rā′nị-ạ, *or* -ē
Ū-rā′nị-ī, *or*
  Ū′rị-ī
Ū-rā′nị-ŭs
Ū′rạ-nŭs
Ụr-bā′nụs
Ŭr′bị-cạ
Ŭr′bị-cŭs
Ụr-bĭǵ′ẹ-nŭs
Ụr-bī′nụm
Ŭ-rē′ụm
Ŭr′ǵẹ-nŭm
Ụr-gụ-lā′nị-ạ
Ū′rị-ạ
Ū-rī′ọn
Ū-rī′tēş
Ụr-sĭd′ị-ŭs
Ụr-sī′nụs
Ŭr′sụ-lŭs
Ụs-cā′nạ
Ŭs′cẹ-nŭm
Ū-sĭp′ị-ī
Ụs-tī′cạ
Ŭ′tị-cạ
Ŭx′ạ-mạ
Ŭx-ẹl-lọ-dū′nụm
Ŭx′ị-ī 1
Ụx-ĭs′ạ-mạ
Ū-zī′tạ

V.

Vạ-cū′nạ
Vạ-dăv′ẹ-rō
Văd-ị-mō′nịs Lā′-cụs
Văǵ-ẹ-drŭ′sạ
Vạ-ǵē′nĭ
Vạ-ǵĕn′nĭ
Vạ-ǵē′sụs
Vā′hạ-lĭs
Vạ-ī′cụs
Văl-ạ-mī′rụs
Vạ-lĕn′tị-ạ 1
Văl-ẹn-tĭn-ị-ā′nụs
Văl-ẹn-tĭn′ị-ạn
Văl-ẹn-tī′nụs
Vạ-lē′rị-ạ

Vạ-lē-rị-ā′nụs
Vạ-lē′rị-ạn
Vạ-lē′rị-ŭs
Văl′ẹ-rŭs
Văl′ǵị-ŭs
Vạl-lā′tạ
Vạl-lā′tụm
Văn′dạ-lĭ
Vạn-dā′lị-ī
Vạn-ǵī′ọ-nĕş
Văn′nị-ŭs
Vạ-rā′nĕş
Vạ-rē′nụs
Văr-gụn-tē′ị-ŭs 3
Vā′rị-ạ
Văr′ị-cŭs
Vạ-rĭn′ị-ŭs
Vạ-rī′nĭ
Vä′rị-ŭs
Vạ-sā′tæ
Vạ-sā′tēş
Văs′cọ-nĕş
Vạs-cŏn′ị-cŭs
Vā′tị-ạ 1
Văt-ị-cā′nụs
Vā-tị-ē′nụs 1
Vạ-tĭn′ị-ŭs
Vạ-trē′nụs
Vẹ-chī′rēş
Vẹc-tĭd′ị-ŭs
Vĕc′tị-ŭs 1
Vẹc-tō′nĕş
Vẹ-dī′ụs, *Pluto*
Vē′dị-ŭs Pŏl′lị-ō
Vẹ-ǵē′tị-ŭs 1
Vē′ị-ạ 3
Vē-ị-ā′nị-ŭs
Vē-ị-ā′nụs 3
Vē-ị-ĕn′tēş 3
Vē-ị-ĕn′tō 3
Vē′ị-ī 3
Vĕj′ọ-vĭs
Vẹ-lā′brụm
Vẹ-lā′nị-ŭs
Vĕl′ẹ-dạ
Vẹ-lē′ị-ạ 3
Vē′lị-ạ
Vẹ-lĭb′ọ-rī
Vĕl′ị-cạ
Vẹ-lī′nạ
Vẹ-lī′nụm
Vẹ-lī′nụs
Vĕl-ị-tèr′nụs
Vĕl′ị-tēş
Vĕl′ị-træ, *or*
  Vẹ-lī′træ
Vē′lị-ŭs
Vĕl′lạ-vī
Vĕl′lẹ-dạ
Vẹl-lē′ị-ŭs 3
Vẹ-năn′tị-ŭs 1
Vĕn′ẹ-dæ
Vĕn′ẹ-dī
Vẹ-nĕd′ị-cŭs Sī′- [nụs
Vĕn′ẹ-lī
Vẹ-nē′rị-ạ
Vĕn′ẹ-tī
Vẹ-nē′tị-ạ 1
Vĕn′ịce
Vĕn′ẹ-tŭs

Vĕn′nọ-nĕş, *or*
  Vẹn-nō′nĕş
Vẹn-nō′nị-ŭs
Vẹn-tĭd′ị-ŭs
Vĕn-ụ-lē′ị-ŭs 3
Vĕn′ụ-lŭs
Vẹ-nū′şị-ạ 1, *or*
  Vẹ-nū′şị-ŭm 1
Vẹ-pī′cụs
Vĕr′ạ-grĭ, *or*
  Vẹ-rā′grĭ
Vẹ-rā′nị-ạ
Vẹ-rā′nị-ŭs
Vĕr-ạn-nī′ọ-lŭs
Vẹr-bā′nụs Lā′cụs
Vẹr-bĭǵ′ẹ-nŭs
Vĕr-cịn-ǵĕt′ọ-rĭx
Vẹ-rē′nạ
Vẹ-rē′tụm
Vē′rị-ạ
Vẹr-ǵĭl′ị-ạ
Vẹr-ǵĭl′ị-æ
Vẹr-ǵĭl′ị-ŭs
Vẹr-ǵĭn′ị-ŭs
Vĕr′ǵị-ŭm
Vẹr-gŏb′rẹ-tŭs
Vẹ-rī′nạ
Vĕr′ị-tăs
Vĕr-ọ-dŏc′tị-ŭs 1
Vĕr-ọ-măn′dụ-ī
Vẹ-rō′nạ
Vẹ-rō′nĕş
Vĕr-ọ-nī′cạ
Vĕr-rẹ-ǵị′nụm
Vĕr′rēş
Vĕr′rị-tŭs
Vĕr′rị-ŭs Flăc′cụs
Vẹr-rŭ′gō
Vĕr′tạ gụs
Vĕr′tị-cō
Vĕr′ụ-læ
Vĕr-ụ-lā′mị-ŭm
Vĕr-ụ-lā′nụs
Vĕs′ạ-gụs
Vĕs′bị-ŭs, *or*
  Vẹ-sū′bị-ŭs
Vĕs′cị-ạ 1
Vĕs-cị-ā′nụm 1
Vĕs-cụ-lā′rị-ŭs
Vẹ-sē′vị-ŭs, *and*
  Vẹ-sē′vụs
Vẹ-sŏn′tị-ō 1
Vĕs-pā-şị-ā′nụs 1
Vĕs-pā′şị-ạn
Vĕs-pẹ-rŭ′gō
Vẹs-tā′lị-ạ
Vẹs-tā′lịs
Vẹs-tĭ′′cị-ŭs 1
Vẹs-tĭl′ị-ŭs
Vẹs-tī′nī
Vẹs-tĭ′nụs
Vẹs-tō′rị-ŭs
Vẹs-trĭ′′cị-ŭs 1
Vĕs′ụ-lŭs
Vẹ-sū′vị-ŭs
Vĕs′vị-ŭs
Vẹ-trā′nị-ō
Vĕt-tị-ē′nụs
Vĕt′tị-ŭs
Vẹt-tō′nĕş

Vĕt-ṳ-lō′nį-ą
Vẹ-tū′rį-ą
Vẹ-tū′rį-ŭs
Vī′ą-dŭs, or
　Vī′ą-drŭs, or
　Vī-ā′drṳs
Vī-ā′lįs
Vī-bĕn′nį-ŭs
Vī-bĭd′į-ą
Vī-bĭd′į-ŭs
Vĭb-į-ē′nṳs
Vĭb-į-ō′nēş
Vĭb′į-ŭs
Vĭb-ṳ-lā′nṳs
Vĭb-ṳ-lē′nṳs
Vī-bŭl′lį-ŭs
Vī-căp′ọ-tą, or
　Vī′cą Pō′tą
Vī-cĕn′tį-ą 1
Vī-cē′tį-ą 1
Vįc-tō′rį-ą
Vĭc-tọ-rī′ną
Vĭc-tọ-rī′nṳs
Vįc tō′rį-ŭs
Vįc-tŭm′vį-æ
Vĭl′lį-ą
Vĭl′lį-ŭs
Vĭm-į-nā′cį-ŭm 1
Vĭm-į·nā′lįs
Vī-nā′lį-ą
Vįn-cĕn′tį-ŭs 1
Vĭn′cį-ŭs 1
Vįn-dĕl′į-cī
Vĭn-dẹ-lĭ′′cį-ą 1
Vįn-dē-mį-ā′tọr
Vįn-dĕm′į-tŏr
Vįn-dĭ-cį-ā′nṳs 1
Vįn-dĭ′′cį-ŭs 1
Vĭn′dį-lī
Vĭn-dọ-bō′ną, or
　Vįn-dŏb′ọ-ną
Vį-nĭ-cį-ā′nṳs 1
Vī-nĭd′į-ŭs
Vĭn′į-ŭs
Vĭn′nį-ŭs
Vįp-sā′nį-ą
Vįp-sā′nį-ŭs
Vį-rā′gō
Vĭr′bį-ŭs
Vįr-dū′mą-rŭs
Vįr-ġĭl′į-ŭs
Vĭr′ġįl
Vįr-ġĭn′į-ą
Vįr-ġĭn′į-ŭs

Vĭr-į-ā′thṳs
Vĭr-į-dóm′ą-rŭs
Vī-rĭd′ọ-vĭx
Vĭr-į-plā′cą
Vĭr-ọ-dū′nṳm
Vĭr′rį-ŭs
Vī-rŭ′nṳm
Vĭs-cẹl-lī′nṳs
Vī-sĕl′lį-ŭs
Vĭs′tṳ-lą
Vī-tā-lį-ā′nṳs
Vī-tĕl′lį-ą
Vī-tĕl-lį-ā′nṳs
Vī-tĕl′lį-ŭs
Vĭ′′tį-ą 1
Vī-tĭs′ą-tŏr
Vĭt-ọ-dū′rṳm
Vĭt′rį-cŭs
Vį-trŭ′vį-ŭs
Vĭt′ṳ-lą
Vĭt′ṳ-lŭs
Vĭv-į-ā′nṳs
Vọ-cō′nį-ą
Vọ-cō′nį-ŭs
Vọ-cŏn′tį-ą 1
Vọ-cŏn′tį-ī 1
Vŏc′ṳ-lą
Vŏġ′ẹ-sŭs
Vŏl-ą nē′rį-ŭs
Vọ-lā′ną
Vŏl-ą-tĕr′rą
Vŏl′cæ, or
　Vŏl′ġæ
Vọl-cā′tį-ŭs 1
Vŏl′ẹ-sŭs
Vọ-lŏġ′ẹ-sēş
Vọ-lŏġ′ẹ-sŭs, or
　Vŏl-ọ-ġē′sṳs
Vọl-sĭn′į-ī
Vọl-sĭn′į-ŭm
Vọl-tĭn′į-ą
Vọl-tür′cį-ŭs 1
Vṳ-lū′bį-lĭs
Vọ lŭm′næ Fā′nṳm
Vọ-lŭm′nį-ą
Vọ-lŭm′nį-ŭs
Vọ-lū′pį-ą
Vŏl-ṳ-sē′nṳs
Vọ-lū-şį-ā′nṳs 1
Vọ-lū′şį-ŭs 1
Vŏl′ṳ-sŭs
Vŏl-ṳ-tī′ną
Vọ-mā′nṳs
Vọ-nō′nēş

Vọ-rā′nṳs
Vŏs′ẹ-gŭs
Vŏ-tį-ē′nṳs 1
Vŭl-cą-nā′lį-ą
Vṳl-cā′nĭ
Vṳl-cā′nį-ŭs
Vṳl-cā′nṳs
Vŭl′cąn
Vṳl-cā′tį-ŭs 1
Vṳl-fē′nį-ŭs
Vṳl-ġĭv′ą-gą
Vṳl-tē′į-ṳs 3
Vŭl-tṳ-rē′į-ŭs 3
Vṳl-tū′rį-ŭs
Vṳl-tür′cį-üs 1

X.

Xăn′thį-ą
Xăn′thį-ăs
Xăn′thį-cą
Xăn′thį-clēş
Xąn-thĭp′pę
Xăn-thọ-pū′lṳs
Xăn′tį-clēş
Xąn-tĭp′pę
Xẹ-năg′ọ-răs
Xĕn′ẹ-rēş
Xĕn′ẹ-tŭs
Xē′nẹ-ŭs
Xẹ-nī′ą-dēş
Xē′nį-ăs
Xē′nį-ŭs
Xĕn-ọ-clē′ą
Xĕn′ọ-clēş
Xĕn-ọ-clī′dēş
Xẹ-nŏc′rą-tēş
Xẹ-nŏc′rį-tē
Xẹ-nŏc′rį-tŭs
Xĕn-ọ-dā′mṳs
Xĕn-ọ-dē′mṳs
Xẹ-nŏd′į-cē
Xĕn-ọ-dō′rṳs
Xĕn-ọ-dō′tēş
Xẹ-nŏd′ọ-tŭs
Xẹ-nœ′tąs
Xĕn-ọ-mē′dēş
Xẹ-nŏph′ą-nēş
Xẹ-nŏph′į-lŭs
Xĕn′ọ-phŏn
Xĕn-ọ-phọn-tī′ŭs
Xĕn-ọ-pį-thē′ą, or

Xĕn-ọ-pį-thī′ą
Xĕr-ọ-lўb′į-ą
Xẹrx-ē′nę
Xĕrx′ēş
Xī-mē′nę
Xī-phē′nę
Xīph-į-lī′nṳs
Xȳ′çhṳs
Xȳn′į-ą
Xȳn′į-ăs
Xȳn-œ′cį-ą 1
Xȳp′ẹ-tē
Xȳs′tį-cī
Xȳs′tį-lĭs

Z.

Zăb′ą-tŭs
Zăb-dį-cē′nę
Zăb′ṳ-lŭs, or
　Zăb′ọ-lŭs
Zą-chā′rį-ăs
Zăc′ọ-rŭs
Zą-gō′rṳs
Zą-græ′ṳs
Zā′greŭs 6
Zăl′ą-tēş
Zą-lē′cṳs
Zā′mẹ-ĭs
Zăn′clę
Zăr-bį-ē′nṳs
Ząr-dō′cēş
Zăr′ẹ-tæ
Zā-rį-ā′drēş
Zā-rį-ăs′pēş
Zăr-mą-nọ-çhē′gąs
Zā′tēş
Zā′thēş
Zâu-ē′cēş, or
　Zą-vē′cēş
Zẹ-bī′ną
Zẹ-lē′ą
Zē′lēş
Zẹ-lī′ą
Zẹ-lō′tṳs
Zẹ-nō′bį-ą
Zẹ-nō′bį-ī
Zẹ-nō′bį-ŭs
Zĕn′ọ-clēş
Zĕn-ọ-clī′dēş
Zĕn-ọ-dō′rṳs
Zĕn-ọ-dō′tį-ą, or

Zĕn-ọ-dō′tį-ŭm 1
Zẹ-nŏd′ọ-tŭs
Zẹ-nŏph′ą-nēş
Zĕn-ọ-pọ-sī′dọn
Zẹ-nŏth′ẹ-mĭs
Zĕph′y-rĭs
Zĕph-y-rī′tįs
Zẹ-phȳr′į-ŭm
Zĕph′y-rŭm
Zĕph′y-rŭs
Zē′tēş
Zē′thēş
Zeŭ-ġį-tā′ną
Zeŭg′mą
Zeŭs 6
Zeŭx-į-dā′mṳs
Zeŭx′į-dás
Zeŭx-ĭp′pę
Zeŭx′įs
Zeŭx′ō
Zī-ē′lą
Zĭg-ą-bē′nṳs
Zį-ġĭ′rą
Zĭl′į-ą
Zĭm′ą-rą
Zį-mȳ′rī
Zī-ŏb′ẹ-rĭs
Zī-phē′nę
Zmĭl′ą-cēş
Zọ-dį′ą-cŭs
Zō′į-lŭs
Zœ-tē′ŭm
Zŏn′ą-răs, or
　Zọ-nā′rąs
Zŏph′ọ-rŭs
Zọ-pȳr′į-ō
Zọ-pȳr′į-ŏn
Zŏp′y-rŭs
Zŏr-ọ-ăs′ter
Zŏr-ọ-ăs-trē′ṳs (a.)
Zŏs′į-mŭs
Zŏs′į-nē
Zọs-tē′rį-ą
Zŏt′į-cŭs
Zṳ-phō′nēş
Zȳ-drē′tæ
Zȳ-găn′tēş
Zȳġ′ẹ-ną
Zȳġ′į-ą
Zȳġ′į-ī
Zȳ-gŏm′ą-lą
Zȳ-grī′tæ
Zȳ-mē′thṳs

PRONUNCIATION
OF
SCRIPTURE PROPER NAMES.

RULES OF PRONUNCIATION.

1. ONE of the principal differences between the pronunciation of the Hebrew proper names and that of the Greek and Latin, relates to the sound of the letter *g*, which, in Greek and Latin names, is soft before *e*, *i*, and *y*; as, *Gellius, Gippius, Gyas*; but in Hebrew names it is hard; as, *Gerizim, Gideon*; except *Bethphage*, which, by passing through the Greek of the New Testament, has become conformed to the rule relating to words from the Greek.

2. The digraph *ch*, in Hebrew names, is sounded hard, like *k*; as, *Chebar, Enoch*; but the words *Rachel, Cherubim*, also *Cherub* (an angel), are Anglicized in their pronunciation, the *ch* being sounded like *ch* in *cheer*; but *Cherub*, a city, is pronounced *ke'rub*.

3. Every final *i*, forming a distinct syllable, though unaccented, is pronounced with its long sound; as, *A'ī, Aris'a-ī*.

4. The two vowels *ai* are sometimes pronounced in one syllable; as, *Mor'de-cai*; and sometimes in two, as, *Hag'ga-i*.

5. The two vowels *ia*, when preceded by another vowel, are sometimes pronounced in one syllable, and sometimes in two. When pronounced in one syllable, the *i* is sounded like *y* consonant; as, *Benaiah* (be-na'yah), *Isaiah* (i-sa'-yah). When pronounced in two syllables, the accent is on the *i*; as, *Ad-a-i'ah*.

6. The diphthong *ei* is pronounced, according to Walker, like *ee*, *Ceilan* (sē'lan). When *ei* is followed by a vowel, the *i* is usually sounded like *y* consonant; as, *Iphideiah* (if-e-dē'yah), *Sameius* (sa-mē'yus).

7. Gentile names ending in *ene*, *ine*, and *ite*, with their plurals, being Anglicized, are pronounced like English formatives; as, *Nazarene', Philis'tine, Gad'ites, Am'monite, Ish'maëlites*; except *Magdale'ne*. Words of this class ending in *ite* have the accent on the same syllable as their primitives.

8. The consonants *c*, *s*, and *t*, before *ia* and *iu*, preceded by the accent, in a number of Scripture names, take the sound of *sh*; as, *Cappadocia, Asia, Galatia, Tertius*. See Pronunciation of Greek and Latin Proper Names, Rule 1.

SCRIPTURE PROPER NAMES.

The following Vocabulary contains all the *Scripture Proper Names* that are found in Walker's "Vocabulary of Scripture Proper Names," together with more than 700 proper names found in the Bible, though not given by Walker.

With respect to pronunciation, Walker has been followed in relation to the words found in his Vocabulary; and when a diversity is exhibited, his pronunciation is placed first, and such deviations from him as are deemed worthy of attention, by the following orthoepists, Oliver, Perry, Smart, Carr, and Taylor, are noted. There are some cases in which the mode adopted by the other orthoepists is doubtless to be preferred to that of Walker.

The abbreviation *C.* stands for *Carr*, *O.* for *Oliver*, *P.* for *Perry*, *Sm.* for *Smart*, *T.* for *Taylor*, and *W.* for *Walker*.

Ā'a-lär	Ăb'a-cŭc	A-băg'tha	Ăb'a-rĭm	Ăb'ba
Aå'ron (ar'on)	A-băd'don	Ăb'a-na	A-bā'rim, *P.*	Ăb'da
Aå'ron-ītes	Ăb-a-dī'as	A-bā'na, *P.*	Ăb'a-rŏn	Ăb'de-el

Ăb'dĭ
Ab-dī'as
Ăb'dĭ-el
Ăb'don
A-bĕd'ne-gō
Ā'bel
Ā'bel Bĕth-mā'a-chäh
Ā'bel Mā'ĭm
Ā'bel Me-hō'lah
Ā'bel Mĭz'ra-ĭm
Ā'bel Shĭt'tĭm
Ā'bez
Ā'bĭ
A-bī'a
A-bī'ah
Ā-bĭ-ăl'bon
A-bī'a-säph
A-bī'a-thär
Ā'bĭb
A-bī'da
A-bī'dah
Ăb'ĭ-dăn
  A-bī'dan, P.
Ā'bĭ-el
  A-bī'el, P.
Ā-bĭ-ē'zer
Ā-bĭ-ĕz'rīte
Ăb'ĭ-gail
Ăb-ĭ-hā'ĭl
A-bī'hu
A-bī'hud
A-bī'jah
A-bī'jam
Ăb-ĭ-lē'ne
A-bĭm'a-el
A-bĭm'e-lĕch
A-bĭn'a-däb
Ăb'ĭ-ner
A-bĭn'o-ăm
A-bī'ram
A-bī'ron
Ăb-ĭ-sē'ī
Ăb'ĭ-shäg
  A-bī'shăg, P.
A-bĭsh'a-ī
  A-bī'sha-ī, P.
A-bĭsh'a-lŏm
  A-bī'sha-lŏm, P.
  Ăb-ĭ-shā'lom, C.
A-bĭsh'u-a
  A-bī'shu-a, P.
  Ăb-ĭ-shū'a, C.
Ăb'ĭ-shür
A-bī'shur, P.
Ăb'ĭ-sŭm
Ăb'ĭ-tăl
  A-bī'tal, P.
Ăb'ĭ-tŭb
A-bī'ud
Ăb'ner
Ā'bram
Ā'bra-ham
Ăb'sa-lom
Ăb'sa-lŏn
A-bū'bus
Ăc'a-tăn
Ăc'cad
Ăc'ca-rŏn
Ăc'chŏ

Ăc'cŏs
Ăc'cŏz
A-cĕl'da-ma
A-chā'ĭ-a (a-kā'ya)
A-chā'ĭ-cŭs
Ā'chän
Ā'chär
Ā'chăz
Ăch'bör
Ā-chĭ-ăch'a-rŭs
A-chī'as
Ā'chĭm
Ā'chĭ-ör
Ā'chĭsh
Ăch'ĭ-tŏb
A-chĭt'o-phĕl,
Ăch'me-tha
  Ăch-mē'tha, P.
Ā'chör
Ăch'sa
Ăch'sah
Ăch'shaph
Ăch'zĭb
Ă'çĭ-pha (ăs'e-fa)
Ăç'ĭ-thō
A-cū'a
Ā'cub
Ăd'a-däh
  A-dā'dah, O. P.
Ā'dah
Ăd-a-ī'ah
Ăd-a-lī'a
Ăd'am
Ăd'a-mäh
  A-dā'mah, P.
Ăd'a-mī
  A-dā'mī, P.
Ā'där
Ăd'a-sa
Ăd'be-el
  Ăd'bĕĕl, P.
  Ad-bē'el, T.
Ăd'dan
Ăd'dar
Ăd'dī
Ăd'dŏ
Ăd'don
Ăd'dus
Ā'der
Ăd'ĭ-da
Ā'dĭ-el
  Ăd'ĭ-el, T.
  A-dī'el, P.
Ā'dĭn
Ăd'ĭ-na
  A-dī'na, O. P T.
Ăd'ĭ-nŏ
  A-dī'nŏ, O. P.
Ăd'ĭ-nŭs
  A-dī'nus, O.
Ăd-ĭ-thā'ĭm
Ăd'la-ī
Ăd'mah
Ăd'ma-tha
Ăd'na

Ăd'o-nī'jah
  A-dŏn'ĭ-jäh, P.
A-dŏn'ĭ-kăm
Ā-do-nī'kam, T.
Ăd-on-ī'ram
A-dŏn-ĭ-zē'dek
A-dō'ra
Ăd-o-rā'ĭm
A-dō'ram
A-drăm'me-lĕch
Ăd-ra-mȳt'tĭ-ŭm
Ā'drĭ-a
Ā'drĭ-el
Ā'dū'el
Ăd'u-el, C.
A-dŭl'lam
A-dŭl'lam-īte
A-dŭm'mĭm
Ā-e-dī'as
Æ-nē'as, Virgil.
Æ'ne-ăs, Acts.
Æ'nŏn
Ăg'a-ba
Ăg'a-bŭs
Ā'gag
Ā'gag-īte
Ā'gar
Ăg-a-rēnes'
Ăg̃'e-ē
  Ā'g̃ee, P.
Ag-g̃ē'us
A-grĭp'pa
Ā'gur
Ā'hăb
A-här'ah
A-här'hel
A-hăs'a-ī
A-hăs'ba-ī
A-hăs-u-ē'rus
A-hā'va
Ā'häz
Ā-ha-zī'ah
Äh'ban
Ā'her
Ā'hī
A-hī'ah
A-hī'am
A-hī'an
Ā-hĭ-ē'zer
A-hī'hud
A-hī'jah
A-hī'kam
A-hī'lud
A-hīm'a-ăz
A-hī'man
A-hīm'e-lĕch
A-hī'moth
A-hĭn'a-däb
A-hĭn'o-ăm
A-hī'ō
A-hī'ra
A-hī'ram
A-hī'ram-ītes
A-hĭs'a-mäch
A-hĭsh'a-här
A-hī'shar
A-hĭth'o-phĕl
A-hī'tub
Äh'läb
Äh'laī

Ah-lā'ī, P.
A-hō'ah
A-hō'hīte
A-hō'lah
A-hō'lĭ-ăb
A-hŏl'ĭ-bäh
Ā-ho-lĭb'a-mäh
A-hū'ma-ī
A-hū'zam
A-hŭz'zath
Ā'ī
A-ī'ah, or Ā'jah
A-ī'ath
A-ī'ja
Ăij'a-lŏn (ăd'ja-)
Ăij'e-lĕth Shā'har
Ā'ĭn
A-ī'rus
Ăj'a-lŏn
Ā'kän
Ăk'kub
Ăk-ra-bat-tī'ne
A-kräb'bĭm
Ăl'a-mĕth
A-läm'me-lĕch
Ăl'a-mŏth
  A-lā'mŏth, O.
Ăl'cĭ-mŭs
Ăl'e-ma
A-lē'meth
  Ăl'e-mĕth, T.
Ăl-ex-ăn'der
Ăl-ex-ăn'drĭ-a
Ăl-ex-ăn'drĭ-ans
A-lī'ah
A-lī'an
  Ăl'ĭ-an, T.
Ăl'lom
Ăl'lon
Ăl'lon Băch'uth
Al-mŏ'dăd
  Ăl'mo-dăd, P.
Ăl'mon
Ăl'mon Dĭb-la-thā'ĭm
Ăl'na-thän
Ā'lŏth
Ăl'pha
Al-phæ'us, or
  Al-phē'us
Ăl-ta-nē'us
Al-tăs'chĭth
Ā'lush
Ăl'vah
Ăl'van
Ā'mad
A-măd'a-tha
A-măd'a-thŭs
Ā'mal
Ăm'a-lĕk
Ăm'a-lĕk-ītes
  A-măl'e-kītes, P
Ā'mam
Ā'man
Ăm'a-na
  A-mā'na, T.
Ăm-a-rī'ah
Ăm-a-rī'as
A-mā'sa, or
  Ăm'a-sa

A-măs'a-ī
A-măsh'a-ī
Ăm-a-sī'ah
Ăm-a-thē'ĭs
Ăm'a-thĭs
Ăm-a-zī'ah
A-mĕd'a-tha
Ā'mĕn'
Ā'mī
A-mĭn'a-däb
A-mĭt'taī
  A-mĭt'ta-ī, P.
A-mĭz'a-bäd
Ăm'mah
Am-mĕd'a-tha
Ăm'mī
Am-mĭd'ĭ-öī
Ăm'mĭ-el
  Am-mī'el, P.
Am-mī'hud
  Ăm'mĭ-hŭd, O.
Am-mĭn'a-däb
Am-mĭn'a-dĭb
Ăm-mĭ-shăd'da-ī
Am-mĭz'a-bäd
Ăm'mon
Ăm'mon-īte
Ăm'mo-nī-tess
Ăm'non
Ā'mok
Ā'mon
Ăm'o-rīte
Ā'mos
Ā'mŏz
Am-phĭp'o-lĭs
Ăm'plĭ-äs
Ăm'ram
Ăm'ram-ītes
Ăm'ra-phĕl
  Am-rā'phel; P.
Ăm'zī
Ā'näb
Ăn'a-el
Ā'nah
Ăn-a-hā'rath
Ăn-a-ī'ah
Ā'năk
Ăn'a-kĭms
A-năm'me-lĕch
Ăn'a-mĭm
  A-nā'mĭm, P.
Ā'nan
A-nā'nī
Ăn-a-nī'ah
Ăn-a-nī'as
A-năn'ĭ-el
  Ăn-a-nī'el, O.
Ā'nath
Ăn'a-thŏth
Ăn'drew̄
Ăn-dro-nī'cus
Ā'nem, or Ā'nen
Ā'ner
Ăn'e-thŏth-īte
A-nĕth'o-thīte, O. P. T.
Ăn'e-tŏth-īte
Ā'nĭ-äm
A-nī'am, T.
Ā'nĭm

Ăn'nạ
Ăn'nạ-ăs
Ăn'nạs
Ạn-nū'ụs
  Ăn'nụ-ŭs, C.
Ā'nọs
Ăn'tị-çhrĭst
Ăn-tị-lĭb'ạ-nŭs
Ăn-tị-ọ-chī'ạ
Ăn'ti-ŏçh
Ăn-tị-ō'çhị-ạnş
Ạn-tī'ọ-çhĭs
Ạn-tī'ọ-çhŭs
Ăn'tị-păs
Ạn-tĭp'ạ-tẹr
  Ăn-tị-pā'tẹr, T.
Ạn-tĭp'ạ-trĭs
  Ăn-tị-pā'trịs, T.
Ạn-tọ'nị-ạ
Ăn-tọ-thī'jah
  Ạn-tŏth'ị-jäh, P.
Ăn'tọth-īte
Ā'nụb
Ā'nụs
Ạ-pā'ınẹ
Ạ-pĕl'lēş
Ạ-phär'sạch-ītes
Ạ-phär'sặth-çhītes
Ạ-phär'sītes
Ā'phẹk
Ạ-phē'kạh
  Ăph'ẹ-käh, P.
Ạ-phĕr'ẹ-mạ
Ạ-phĕr'rạ
Ạ-phī'ạh
Ā'phịk
Ăph'rạh
Ăph'sēş
Ăp-ọl-lō'nị-ạ
Ăp-ọl-lō'nị-ŭs
Ăp-ọl-lŏph'ạ-nēş
Ạ-pŏl'lọs
Ạ-pŏl'ly-ŏn
Ạ-pŏl'yọn
Ăp'pạ-ĭm
  Ạp-pā'ịm, T.
Ăp'phị-ạ (ăf'fẹ-ạ)
Ăp'phụs (ăf'fụs)
Ăp'pị-ī Fō'rụm
Ăq'uị-lạ
  Ạ-quĭl'ạ, P.
Ăr
Ā'rạ
Ā'rạb
  Ăr'ạb, P. Sm.
Ăr'ạ-bäh
Ăr-ạ-bạt-thā'nẹ
Ăr-ạ-bạt-tī'nẹ, or
  Ăr-ạ-băt'tị-nē
Ạ-rā'bị-ạ
Ạ-rā'bị-ạn
Ā'răd
Ăr'ạ-dŭs
Ā'rạh
Ā'rạm
Ā'rạm-ī-tẹss [ịm
Ā'rạm-Nā-hạ-rā'-
Ā'rạm-Zō'bạh
Ā'rạn
Ăr'ạ-răt

Ăr'ạ-răth
Ạ-rā'thēş
Ạ-râu'nạh
Ăr-ạ-ū'nạh, P.
Ăr'bạ, or Ăr'bạh
Ăr'bạth-īte
Ạr-băt'tịs
Ạr-bē'lạ, Syria.
Ăr'bīte
Ạr-bō'nạ-ī
Ạr-çhẹ-lā'ụs
Ăr'çhẹ-vītes
Ăr'çhī
Ạr-çhĭp'pụs
Ărçh'ītes
Ạrc-tū'rụs
Ărd
Ăr'dăth
Ărd'ītes
Ăr'dọn
Ạ-rē'lī
Ạ-rē'lītes
Ăr-ẹ-ŏp'ạ-ġīte
Ăr-ẹ-ŏp'ạ-gŭs
Ā'rēş
Ạ-rē'tạs
  Ăr'ẹ-täs, O. P.
Ạ-rē'ụs
Ā-rị-ạ-rā'thēş
Ăr'gŏb
Ạ-rīd'ạ-ī
Ạ-rīd'ạ-thạ
Ạ-rī'ẹh
Ā'rị-ẹl
Ăr-ị-mạ-thæ'ạ
  Ăr-ị-mạ-thē'ạ
Ā'rị-ŏçh
Ạ-rĭs'ạ-ī
Ăr-ịs-tär'çhụs
Ăr-ịs-tọ-bū'lụs
Ărk'ītes
Ăr-mạ-ġĕd'dọn
Ạr-mē'nị-ạ
Ạr-mō'nī
Ăr'nạ
Ăr'nŏn
Ā'rọd
Ăr'ọ-dī
  Ạ-rō'dī, O. T.
Ā'rọd-ītes
Ăr'ọ-ẹr
  Ạ-rō'ẹr, P. T.
Ăr'ọ-ẹr-īte, or
  Ạ-rō'ẹr-īte
Ā'rọm
Ăr'păd
Ăr'phăd
Ạr-phăx'ạd
Ăr'sạ-cēş
Ăr'sạ-rĕth
Ăr-tạx-ёrx'ēş
Ăr'tẹ-mạs
Ăr'ụ-bŏth
Ạ-rü'mạh
  Ăr'ụ-mäh, P.
Ăr'văd
Ăr'vạd-ītes
Ăr'zạ
Ā'sạ

Ăs-ạ-dī'ạs
Ăs'ạ-ẹl
Ăs'ạ-hĕl
  Ạ-sā'hẹl, O. P.
Ăs-ạ-hī'ạh
Ăs-ạ-ī'ạh
Ăs'ạ-nạ
Ā'sạph
Ạ-săr'ạ-ẹl
Ạ-săr'ẹ-ẹl
  Ăs-ạ-rē'ẹl, O. T.
Ăs-ạ-rĕ'lạh
As-băz'ạ-rĕth
Ăs'cạ-lŏn
Ạ-sē'ạs
Ạ-sĕb-ẹ-bī'ạ
Ăs-ẹ-bī'ạ
Ăs'ẹ-năth
Ā'sẹr
Ạ-sē'rẹr
Ăsh-ạ-bī'ạh
Ā'shạn
Ăsh'bẹ-ạ
  Ash-bē'ạ, P.
Ăsh'bẹl
Ăsh'bẹl-ītes
Ăsh'çhẹ-năz
Ăsh'dŏd
Ăsh'dọd-ītes
Ăsh'dọth-ītes
Ăsh'dọth Pĭş'gạh
Ăsh'ẹr
Ăsh'ẹr-ītes
Ăsh'ị-mạ
Ăsh'kẹ-lŏn
Ăsh'kẹ-năz
Ăsh'nạh
Ăsh'pẹ-năz
Ăsh'rị-ẹl
Ăsh'tạ-rŏth
Ăsh'tẹ-mōh
Ăsh'tẹ-rạth-īte
Ăsh'tọ-rĕth
Ăsh'ụr
Ăsh'ụr-ītes
Ăsh'văth
Ā'sị-ạ (ā'shẹ-ạ)
Ăs-ị-bī'ạs
Ā'sị-ẹl
  Ạ-sī'ẹl, P.
Ăs'ị-phạ
Ăs'kẹ-lŏn
Ăs'mạ-dāi
Ăs'mạ-vĕth
Ăs-mọ-dē'ụs
Ăs-mọ-nē'ạnş
Ăs'nạh
Ạs-năp'pẹr
Ạ-sō'çhịs
Ā'sọm
Ăs'pạ-thạ
Ăs'phạr
Ạs-phăr'ạ-sŭs
Ăs'rị-ẹl
Ăs'rị-ẹl-ītes
Ăs-sạ-bī'ạs
Ạs-săl'ị-mŏth
Ăs-sạ-nī'ạs
Ăs-sạ-rē'mọth
Ăs'shụr

Ạs-shū'rịm
Ăs-sị-dē'ạnş
Ăs'sịr
Ăs'sọs
Ăs-sụ-ē'rụs
Ăs'sụr
Ạs-sўr'ị-ạ
Ạs-sўr'ị-ạn
Ăs'tạ-rŏth
Ăs'tăth
Ạs-tў'ạ-ġēş
Ạ-sŭp'pịm
Ạ-sўn'crị-tŭs
Ā'tăd
Ăt'ạ-răh
Ạ-tär'gạ-tĭs
Ăt'ạ-rŏth
Ăt'ạ-rŏth–Ā'dạr
Ăt'ạ-rŏth–Ăd'dạr
Ā'tẹr
Ăt-ẹ-rẹ-zī'ạs
Ā'thăçh
Ăth-ạ-ī'ạh
Ăth-ạ-lī'ạh
Ăth-ạ-rī'ạs
Ạ-thē'nị-ạnş
Ăth-ẹ-nō'bị-ŭs
Ăth'ẹnş
Ăth'lại
  Ath-lā'ī, P.
Ăt'ị-phạ
Ăt'rŏth
Ăt'tại
  Ăt'tạ-ī, P.
Ăt-tạ-lī'ạ
Ăt'tạ-lŭs
Ạt-thăr'ạ-tēş
Âu'ġị-ạ
Âu-gŭs'tụs
Âu-rā'nụs
Âu-tē'ạs
  Âu'tẹ-ăs, C.
Ā'vạ
Ăv'ạ-răn
Ăv'ạ-rŏn
Ā'vẹn
Ā'vịm
Ā'vịmş
Ā'vītes
Ā'vịth
Ăz'ạ-ẹl
Ăz-ạ-ē'lụs
Ā'zạh
Ā'zạl
Ăz-ạ-lī'ạh
Ăz-ạ-nī'ạh
Ạ-zā'phị-ŏn
Ăz'ạ-rạ
Ạ-zăr'ạ-ẹl
Ạ-zā'rẹ-ẹl
  Ăz'ạ-rēēl, O. P.
  Ăz-ạ-rē'ẹl, T.
Ăz-ạ-rī'ạh
Ăz-ạ-rī'ạs
Ā'zăz
Ạ-zā'zẹl
Ăz-ạ-zī'ạh
Ạz-băz'ạ-rĕth
Ăz'buk
Ạ-zē'kạh

Ā'zẹl
Ā'zẹm
Ăz-ẹ-phū'rịth
Ạ-zē'tạs
Ăz'găd
Ạ-zī'ạ
Ạ-zī'ẹ-ī
Ā'zị-ẹl
  Ạ-zī'ẹl, P.
Ạ-zī'zạ
Ăz'mạ-vĕth
  Ạz-mā'vẹth, P.
Ăz'mọn
Ăz'nọth Tā'bọr
Ā'zör
Ạ-zō'tụs
Ăz'rị-ẹl
Ăz'rị-kăm
  Ạz-rī'kạm, T.
Ạ-zū'bạh
  Ăz'ụ-bäh, P.
Ā'zụr
Ăz'ụ-răn
Ăz'zạh
Ăz'zạn
Ăz'zụr

B.

Bā'ạl, or Bĕl
Bā'ạ-läh
  Bạ-ā'lạh, P.
Bā'ạl-ăth
  Bạ-ā'lạth, P.
Bā'ạl-ăth Bē'ẹr
Bā'ạl Bē'rịth
Bā'ạ-lē
Bā'ạl Găd
Bā'ạl Hā'mọn
Bā'ạl Hā'nạn
Bā'ạl Hā'zọr
Bā'ạl Hёr'mọn
Bā'ạl-ī
  Bạ-ā'lī, P.
Bā'ạl-ĭm
  Bạ-ā'lịm, P.
Bā'ạ-lĭs
Bā'ạl Mē'ọn
Bā'ạl Pē'ọr
Bā'ạl Pĕr'ạ-zĭm
Bā'ạl Shăl'ị-shạ
  Shạ-lī'shạ, O. P.
Bā'ạl Tā'mạr
Bā'ạl Zē'bub
Bā'ạl Zē'phọn
Bā'ạ-nạ
Bā'ạ-näh
  Bạ-ā'nạh, P. T.
Bā-ạ-nī'ạs
Bā'ạ-rạ
  Bạ-ā'rạ, P. T.
Bā'ạ-shạ
  Bạ-ā'shạ, P. T.
Bā-ạ-sē'iạh
  Bā-ạ-seī'ạh, T,
Bā-ạ-sī'ạh
Bā'bẹl
Bā'bī

Băb'y-lọn
Băb-y-lō'nĭ-ạns
Băb-y-lō'nĭsh
Bā'cạ
Băc'chĭ-dēş
Băc'chụs
Bạ-cē'nọr
Bạc-chū'rụs
Băch-ī'rītes
Băch'ụth Ăl'lọn
Bā'gō
Bạ-gō'ạs
Băg'ọ-ī
Bạ-hā'rụm-īte
Bạ-hū'mụs
Bạ-hū'rịm
Bā'jith
Băk-băk'kạr
Băk'bŭk
Băk-bŭk-ī'ạh
Bā'laam (bā'lạm)
Bā'lạc
Băl'ạ-dăn
Bā'lạh
Bā'lạk
Băl'ạ-mō
Bạ-lăs'ạ-mŭs
Bạl-nū'ụs
Bạl-thā'sạr
Bā'mạh
Bā'mọth
Bā'mọth Bā'ạl
Băn
Băn-ạ-ī'ạs
Bā'nī
Bā'nĭd
Bạn-nā'ịạ
Băn'nụs
Băn'ụ-ăs
Bạ-răb'bạs
Băr'ạ-chĕl
　Bạ-rā'chẹl, P.
Băr-ạ-chī'ạh
Băr-ạ-chī'ạs
Bā'rak
Bạr-hū'mītes
　Băr'hụ-mītes, P.
Bạ-rī'ạh
Băr-jē'sụs
Băr-jō'nạ
Băr'kŏs
Băr'nạ-bạs
Bạ-rō'dịs
Băr'sạ-bạs
Băr'tạ-cŭs
Bạr-thŏl'ọ-mew
Băr-tĭ-mæ'ụs, or
　Bär-tĭ-mē'ụs
Bā'rụch
Bạr-zĕl'ạ-ī
Bạr-zĭl'lạ-ī
Băs'ạ-lŏth
Băs'cạ-mạ
Bā'shạn, or
　Bás'sạn
Bā'shạn Hā'vọth
　Jā'ir

Băsh'ẹ-măth
　Bạ-shē'mạth, P.
Băs'ĭ-lŭs
Băs'lĭth
Băs'mạth
Băs'sạ
Băs'tạ-ī
Bạth-răb'bĭm
Băth'shẹ-bạ
　Bạth-shē'bạ, P.
Băth'shụ-ạ
　Bạth-shū'ạ, P.
Băth-zăch-ạ-rī'ạs
Băv'ạ-ī
　Bạ-vā'ī, P.
Băz'lĭth
Băz'lụth
Bē-ạ-lī'ạh
Bē'ạ-lŏth
　Bẹ-ā'lŏth, P. T.
Bē'ạn
Bĕb'ạ-ī
　Bẹ-bā'ī, P.
Bē'cher
Bẹ-chō'rạth
　Bĕch'ọ-răth, P.
Bĕc'tĭ-lĕth
Bē'dăd
Bĕd-ạ-ī'ạh
Bē'dạn
Bẹ-dē'iạh
　Bĕd-ẹ-ī'ạh, P.
Bē-el-ī'ạ-dạ
Bẹ-ĕl'sạ-rŭs
Bē-el-tĕth'mụs
Bẹ-ĕl'ze-bŭb
　Bēĕl'ze-bŭb, P.
Bē'er
Bẹ-ē'rạ
Bẹ-ē'rạh, or
　Bē'rạh
Bē-er-ē'lịm
　Bẹ-ĕr'ẹ-lĭm, T.
Bẹ-ē'rī
Bē-er-lạ-hā'ĭ-rŏĭ
　Bē-er-lạ-hāi'rŏĭ,
Bẹ-ē'rọth　[O.
　Bē'ẹ-rŏth, P.
Bẹ-ē'rọth-ītes
Bẹ-ĕr'shẹ-bạ
　Bē-er-shē'bạ, T.
Bẹ-ĕsh'tẹ-räh
Bē'hẹ-mŏth
　Bẹ-hē'mọth, P.
Bē'kạh
Bĕl
Bē'lạ, or Bē'lạh
Bē'lạ-ītes
Bĕl'ẹ-mŭs
Bē'lĭ-ạl
Bĕl'mạ-ĭm
Bĕl'men
Bĕl-shăz'zạr
Bĕl-tẹ-shăz'zạr
Bĕn
Bẹ-nā'iạh (-yạ)
　Bĕn-ạ-ī'ạh, P.

Bẹn-ăm'mī
Bẹn-ĕb'ẹ-răk
Bĕn-e-jā'ạ-kăn
Bĕn'hạ-dăd
　Bẹn-hā'dạd, P. T.
Bẹn-hā'il
Bẹn-hā'nạn
Bĕn'ĭ-nū
　Bẹn-ī'nū, O. T.
Bĕn'jạ-mĭn
Bĕn'jạ-mīte
Bē'nō
Bẹ-nō'nī
Bẹ-nū'ī
　Bĕn'ụ-ī, C.
Bẹn-zō'heth
Bē'ọn
Bē'ọr
Bē'rạ
Bĕr'ạ-chäh
　Bẹ-rā'chạh, P.T.
Bĕr-ạ-chī'ạh
Bĕr-ạ-ī'ạh
Bē'rẹ-ạ, 1 Macc.
Bẹ-rē'ạ, or
　Bẹ-rœ'ạ
Bĕr-e-chī'ạh
Bē'red
Bē'rī
Bẹ-rī'ạh
Bẹ-rī'ītes
Bē'rītes
Bē'rịth
Bẹr-nī'cẹ
　Bër'nịce, P.
Bẹ-rō'dạch Băl'ạ-
　dăn
　Bĕr'ọ-dăch Băl'ạ-
　dăn, P.
Bē'rŏth
Bĕr'ọ-thāi
　Bẹ-rō'thạ-ī, P.
　Bẹ-rō'thại, O. T.
Bẹ-rō'thạh
Bē'rọth-īte
Bẹr-rē'thō
Bẹr-zē'lụs
Bē'sại
Bĕs-ọ-dē'iạh
　Bĕs-ọ-deī'ạh, T.
　Bẹ-sō-dẹ-ī'ạh, P.
Bē'sör
Bē'tạh
Bĕt'ạ-nē
Bē'tẹn
Bĕth-ăb'ạ-rạ
Bĕth'ạ-năth
　Bĕth-ā'nạth, P.
Bĕth'ạ-nŏth
　Bĕth-ā'nọth, P.
Bĕth'ạ-ny
Bĕth-ăr'ạ-bäh
Bĕth-ā'rạm, O.P.
Bĕth-är'bẹl
Bĕth-ā'vẹn
Bĕth-ăz'mạ-vĕth

Bĕth-bā-ạl-mē'ọn
Bĕth-bā'rạh
　Bĕth'bạ-räh, P.
Bĕth'bạ-sī
Bĕth-bĭr'ẹ-ī
Bĕth'cạr
Bĕth-dā'gŏn
Bĕth-dĭb-lạ-thā'ịm
Bĕth-ē'dẹn
Bĕth'ẹl
Bĕth'ẹl-īte
Bĕth-ē'mẹk
Bē'thẹr
Bẹ-thĕs'dạ
Bĕth-ē'zẹl
Bĕth-gā'dẹr
Bĕth-gā'mụl
Bĕth-hăc'çẹ-rĕm
Bĕth-hā'rạn
Bĕth-hŏg'lạh
Bĕth-hō'rọn
Bĕth-jĕsh'ĭ-mŏth
Bĕth-jĕs'ĭ-mŏth
Bĕth-lĕb'ạ-ŏth
Bĕth'lẹ-hĕm
Bĕth'lẹ-hĕm Ĕph'-
　rạ-täh
Bĕth'lẹ-hem-īte
Bĕth'lẹ-hĕm Jū'-
　dạh
Bĕth-lō'mọn
Bĕth-mā'ạ-chäh
Bĕth-mär'cạ-bŏth
Bĕth-mē'ọn
Bĕth-nĭm'rạh
Bĕth-ō'rọn
Bĕth-pā'lẹt
Bĕth-päz'zẹz
Bĕth-pē'ọr
Bĕth'phạ-ġē *
　Bĕth'phạġe, P.
　Bĕth-phā'ġe, T.
Bĕth'phẹ-lĕt
　Bĕth-phē'lẹt, P.
Bĕth'rạ-phạ
　Bĕth-rā'phạ, P.
Bĕth'rẹ-hŏb
　Bĕth-rē'họb, O.
Bĕth-sā'ĭ-dạ
　Bĕth-sāi'dạ, P. T.
Bĕth'sạ-mŏs
Bĕth'sạn
Bĕth'shạn
Bĕth-shē'ạn
Bĕth'shẹ-mĕsh
　Bĕth-shē'mẹsh,
　　T.
Bĕth'shẹm-īte
Bĕth-shĭt'tạh
Bĕth-sū'rạ
Bĕth-tăp'pụ-ạh
Bẹ-thū'ẹl
Bĕth'ụ-ẹl, C.
Bē'thụl
Bĕth-ụ-lī'ạ
Bĕth'zụr
Bẹ-tō'lĭ-ŭs

Bĕt-ọ-măs'thẹm, &
　Bĕt-ọ-mĕs'thạm
Bĕt'ọ-nĭm
　Bẹ-tō'nịm, P.
Bẹ-ū'lạh
　Beū'lạh, P. T.
Bē'zại
Bẹ-zăl'ẹ-ẹl
　Bĕz-ạ-lē'ẹl, T.
Bē'zẹk
Bē'zẹr
Bē'zẹth
Bī'ạ-tăs
Bĭch'rī
Bĭd'kạr
Bĭg'thạ
Bĭg'thạn
Bĭg'thạ-nạ
Bĭg'vạ-ī
　Bĭg-vā'ī, O. T.
Bĭl'dăd
Bĭl'ẹ-ăm
　Bī-lē'ạm, P.
Bĭl'gạh
Bĭl'gạ-ī
　Bjl-gā'ī, O. T.
Bĭl'hạ, or Bĭl'hạh
Bĭl'hăn
Bĭl'shăn
Bĭm'hăl
Bĭn'ẹ-ạ
　Bī-nē'ạ, P.
Bĭn'nụ-ī
　Bịn-nū'ī, O. P.
Bĭr'shạ
Bĭr'zạ-vĭth
　Bịr-zā'vịth, T.
Bĭsh'läm
Bị-thī'ạh
Bĭth'rọn
Bị-thy̆n'ị-ạ
Bịz-jŏth'jạh
Bĭz'thạ
Blăs'tụs
Bō-ạ-nër'ġēş
Bō'ạz, or Bō'ŏz
Bŏc'cạs
Bŏch'ẹ-rŭ
　Bọ-chē'rụ, P.
Bō'chịm
Bō'hăn
Bō'rịth
Bŏs'cạth
Bō'sọr
Bŏş'ọ-rạ
Bŏş'rạh
Bŏz'kạth
Bŏz'rạh
Bŭk'kī
Bụk-kī'ạh
Bŭl
Bū'nạh
Bŭn'nī
Bŭz
Bū'zī
Bŭz'īte

---

* *Bethphage.* — "This word is generally pronounced, by the illiterate, in two syllables, and without the second *h*, as if written *Beth'page.*" — WALKER.

C.

Căb'bon
Cā'bul
Căd'dis
Cā'dĕş
Cā'dĕş Bär'ne
Cā'desh
Căd'mi-el
Cæ'şar
Cæs-a-rē'a (sĕs-)
Cæs-a-rē'a Phi-lĭp'pī
Cā'ia-phăs (kā'ya-)
  Ca-ī'a-phăs, O.
Cāin
Ca-ī'nan
  Cāi'nan, P. T.
Cā'lah
Căl-a-mŏl'a-lŭs
Căl'cōl
Cal-dē'a
Cal-dē'anş
Cal-dēēş'
Cā'leb
Cā'leb Ĕph'ra-täh
Căl'i-täs
Cal-lĭs'the-nĕş
Căl'neh
Căl'nŏ
Căl'phī
Căl'va-ry
Cā'mon
Cā'na
Cā'naan (kā'nan)
  Cā'na-an, O.
Cā'naan-ītes
  Cā'na-an-ītes, O.
Cā'naan-i-tess
Cā'naan-i-tish
Căn'da-cē
  Can-dā'ce, T. P.
Căn'neh
Ca-për'na-ŭm
Căph-ar-săl'a-ma
Ca-phĕn'a-tha
Ca-phī'ra
Căph'tho-rĭm
Căph'tör
Căph'to-rĭm
Căph'to-rĭmş
Căp-pa-dō'ci-a 8
Căr-a-bā'şi-on
Căr'cas
Căr'cha-mĭs
Căr'che-mish
  Car-che'mish, P.
Ca-rē'ah
Cā'ri-a
Car-mā'ni-anş
Cär'me
Cär'mel
Cär'mel-īte
Cär'mel-i-tess
Cär'mī
Cär'mītes
Cär'na-ĭm
Cär'ni-ŏn
Cär-pha-săl'a-ma

Cär'pus
Car-shē'na
Ca-sīph'i-a
Căs-i-phī'a, T.
Căs'leu
Căs'lu-hĭm
  Cas-lū'him, O.
Căs'phon, or
  Căs'phor
Căs'pis
Căs'tor
Ca-thū'a
Cē'dron
Cēi'lan (sē'lan)
Cēl-o-sўr'i-a
Cĕn'chre-a
  Cen-chrē'a, T.
Cĕn-de-bē'ŭs
Cē'phas
Cē'ras
Cē'şar, or Cæ'şar
Cĕs-a-rē'a
Cĕs-a-rē'a Phi-lĭp'- [pī
Cē'tab
Chā'bris
Chā'di-ăs
Chæ're-ăs
Chăl'cōl
Chal-dē'a
Chal-dē'an
Chăl-dēēş'
Chā'naan, or
  Cā'naan
Chā'naan-īte, or
  Cā'naan-īte
Chăn-nu-nē'ŭs
Chär-a-ăth'a-lär
Chär'a-ca
Chär'a-shĭm, or
  Chär'a-sĭm
Chär'che-mĭsh
Chär'cus
Chā're-a
Chär'mis
Chär'ran
Chăs'e-ba
Chē'bar
Chĕd-or-lā'o-mer
  Chĕd-or-la-ō'-mer, P. T.
Chē'lal
Chĕl'ci-ăs
Chĕl'li-anş
Chĕl'luh
Chĕl'lus
Chē'lŏd
Chē'lub
Che-lū'bai
Chĕm'a-rĭmş
Chē'mŏsh
Che-nā'a-näh
  Che-nāa'nah, P.
Chĕn'a-nī
Chĕn-a-nī'ah
Chē'phar Ha-ăm'-mo-nāi
Che-phī'rah
Chē'ran
Chē're-ăs
Chĕr'eth-ĭmş

Chĕr'eth-ītes
Chē'rith, or
  Chē'rish
Chē'rub, city.
Chĕs'a-lŏn
Chē'sed
Chē'sil
Che-sŭl'loth
Che-thī'im
Chet-tī'im
Chē'zib
Chī'don
Chĭl'e-äb
Chi-lī'on
  Chĭl'i-ŏn, P. T.
Chĭl'mad
Chĭm'häm
Chĭn'ne-rĕth, or
  Cĭn'ne-rĕth
  Chĭn'ne-rĕth, T.
Chĭn'ne-rŏth, or
  Cĭn'ne-rŏth
Chī'os
Chĭs'leu
  Chis-lē'u, P.
Chĭs'lon
Chĭs'loth Tā'bör
Chĭt'tim
  Chĭt'tim, T.
Chī'un
Chlō'e
Chŏb'a, or
  Chōb'a-ī
Cho-rā'shan
Cho-rā'zin
Chŏs-a-mē'ŭs
Cho-zē'ba
CHRĪST
Chrĭst'ian
Chŭb
Chūn
Chū'za
Chŭsh'an Rĭsh-a-thā'im
  Chū'shan Rĭsh-a-thā'im, P.
Chū'sī
Cj-lĭ''ci-a
Cĭn'ne-rĕth, or
  Cĭn'ne-rŏth
Cĭr'a-ma
Cĭs
Cī'sai
Cĭt'imş
Clau'da
Clau'di-a
Clau'di-ŭs
Clĕm'ent
Clē'o-păs, O.
Clē-o-pā'tra
Clē'o-phăs
Clō'e
Clō'pas
Cnī'dus (nī'dus)
Cœl-o-sўr'i-a
Cō'la
Col-hō'zeh
Cō'li-ŭs
Co-lŏs'se

Co-lŏs'si-anş (ko-lŏsh'e-anz)
Co-nī'ah
Cŏn-o-nī'ah
Cō'os
Cör'be
Cō're
Cör'inth
Co-rĭn'thi-anş
Co-rĭn'thus
Cor-nē'li-ŭs
Cŏs
Cō'sam
Cöû'tha
Cŏz
Cŏz'bī
Crā'tĕş
Crĕs'cenş
Crēte
Crētes
Crē'ti-anş (krē'she-anz)
Crĭs'pus
Cŭsh
Cū'shan
Cū'shan Rĭsh-a-thā'im
  Cŭsh'an Rĭsh-a-thā'im, T.
Cū'shī
Cŭth
Cŭth'ah
  Cū'thah, O. P.
Cȳ'a-mŏn
Cўp'ri-anş
Cȳ'prus
Cȳr'a-ma, or
  Cĭr'a-ma
Cȳ-rē'ne
Cȳ-rē'ni-an
Cȳ-rē'ni-ŭs
Cȳ'rus

D.

Dăb'a-rēh
Dăb'ba-shĕth
Dăb'e-răth
Dā'bri-a
Da-cō'bī
Dad-dē'ŭs
Dā'gon
Dāi'săn
Dăl-a-ī'ah
Dal-mā'ti-a 8
Dăl-ma-nū'tha
Dăl'phon
Dăm'a-rĭs
Dăm-a-scēneş'
Da-măs'cus
Dăn
Dăn'i-el
Dăn'ītes
Dan-jā'an
Dăn'nah
Dăph'ne
Dā'ra
Där'da
Dā'ri-an

Da-rī'us
Där'kon
Dā'than
Dăth'e-ma
Dā'vid
Dē'bir
Dĕb'o-ra
Dĕb'o-räh
De-căp'o-lĭs
Dē'dan
Dĕd'a-nĭm
  De-dā'nĭm, T.
De-hā'vītes
  Dē'ha-vītes, T.
Dē'kar
Dĕl-a-ī'ah
Dĕl'i-läh
  De-lī'lah, P.
Dē'lus
Dē'mas
De-mē'tri-ŭs
Dĕm'o-phŏn
Dër'be
Dĕs'sau, or
  Dĕs'sa-ū
De-ū'el
  Deū'el, P.
Deū-ter-ŏn'o-my
Dī-ā'na, or Dī-ăn'a
Dĭb'la-ĭm
  Dib-lā'im, P. T.
Dĭb'lath
Dĭb-la-thā'im
Dī'bon
Dī'bon Găd
Dĭb'rī
Dĭd'y-mŭs
Dĭk'lah
Dĭl'e-ăn
  Dī-lē'an, P.
  Dī'le-ăn, O. Sm.
Dĭm'nah
Dī'mon
Di-mō'nah
Dī'nah
Dī'na-ītes
Dĭn'ha-bäh
  Din-hā'bah, P. T.
Dī-o-nў''si-ŭs
Dī-ŏs-co-rĭn'thi-ŭs
Dī-ŏt're-phĕş
  Dī-o-trē'phĕş, P
Dī'shan
Dī'shŏn
Dĭz'a-häb
Dō'cus
Dŏd'a-ī
  Do-dā'ī, P. T.
Dŏd'a-nĭm
  Do-dā'nim, P. T.
Dŏd'a-väh
  Do-dā'vah, P. T.
Dō'dō
Dō'eg
Dŏph'kah
Dör
Dō'ra
Dör'cas
Do-rўm'e-neş
Do-sĭth'e-ŭs

Dō-sį-thē'ụs, T.
Dō'tha-ĭm, or
  Dō'than
Dọ-thā'ĭm, T.
Drụ-sĭl'lạ
Dū'mah
Dū'rạ

E.

Ē'ạ-nēṣ
  Ē-ā'nēṣ, O.
Ē'bạl
Ē'bẹd
Ẹ-bĕd'mẹ-lĕch
  Ē'bẹd-mē'lẹch,
Ēb-ẹn-ē'zẹr [T.
Ē'bẹr
Ẹ-bī'ạ-săph
Ẹ-brŏ'nah
Ẹ-cā'nụs
Ẹc-băt'ạ-nạ, or -nē
Ẹc-clē-şį-ăs'tēṣ
Ẹc-clē-şį-ăs'tį-cŭs
Ĕd
Ē'dạr
Ẹd-dī'ạs
Ē'dẹn
Ē'dẹr
Ē'dĕṣ
Ĕd'nạ
Ē'dọm
Ē'dọm-ītes
Ĕd'rẹ-ī
Ĕg'lah
Ĕg'lạ-ĭm
  Ĕg-lā'ĭm, T.
Ĕg'lọn
Ē'ġypt
Ẹ-ġy̆p'tiạn
Ē'hī
Ē'hŭd
Ē'kẹr
Ĕk'rẹ-bĕl
Ĕk'rọn
Ĕk'rọn-ītes
Ē'lạ
Ĕl'ạ-däh
  Ẹ-lā'dah, P. T.
Ē'lah
Ē'lăm
Ē'lạm-ītes
Ĕl'ạ-säh
  Ẹ-lā'sah, O. T.
Ē'lăth
Ĕl-bĕth'ẹl
Ĕl'cį-ạ 8
Ĕl'dạ-äh
  Ẹl-dā'ah, P. T.
Ĕl'dăd
Ē'lẹ-ăd
  Ẹ-lē'ad, P.
Ē-lẹ-ā'lẹh
Ẹ-lē'ạ-sạ
Ẹ-lē'ạ-säh
  Ē-lẹ-ā'sah, O. P.
Ē-lẹ-ā'zạr
Ē-lẹ-ạ-zū'rụs

Ĕl-ẹ-lŏ'hẹ Ĭṣ'rạ-ẹl
  Ẹl-ĕl'ọ-hē, T.
Ē'lẹph
Ẹ-leū'thẹ-rŭs
Ĕl-eụ-zā'ī, or
  Ẹ-leū'zạ-ī
Ẹl-hā'nạn
Ē'lī
Ẹ-lī'ạb
Ẹ-lī'ạ-dạ
Ẹ-lī'ạ-däh
Ẹ-lī'ạ-dăs
Ẹ-lī'ạ-dŭn
Ẹ-lī'ah
Ẹ-lī'ah-bạ
Ẹ-lī'ạ-kĭm
Ẹ-lī'ạ-lī
Ẹ-lī'ạm
Ẹ-lī-ạ-ọ-nī'ạs
Ẹ-lī'ạs
Ẹ-lī'ạ-săph
Ẹ-lī'ạ-shĭb
Ẹ-lī'ạ-sĭb
Ẹ-lī'ạ-sĭs
Ẹ-lī'ạ-thạ, or -thäh
Ẹ-lī'dạd
Ē'lį-ẹl
Ē-lį-ē'nạ-ī
Ē-lį-ē'zẹr
Ẹ-lī'hạ-bạ
Ĕl-į-họ-ē'nạ-ī
Ĕl-į-hŏ'rẹph
Ẹ-lī'hụ
Ẹẹlī'jah
Ĕl'į-kạ
  Ẹ-lī'kạ, P. T.
Ē'lįm
Ẹ-lĭm'ẹ-lĕch
Ē-lį-œ'nạ-ī
  Ē-lį-ọ-ē'nạ-ī, P.
Ē-lį-ŏ'nạs
Ĕl'į-phăl
  Ẹ-lī'phạl
Ẹ-lĭph'ạ-lät
Ẹ-lĭph'ạ-lēh
Ẹ-lĭph'ạ-lĕt
Ĕl'į-phăz
  Ẹ-lĭph'ạz, P.
Ẹ-lĭph'ẹ-lēh
Ẹ-lĭph'ẹ-lĕt
Ẹl-lĭş'ạ-bĕth
Ĕl-į-sæ'us, or
  Ĕl-į-sē'ụs
Ẹ-lī'shạ
Ẹ-lī'shah
Ẹ-lĭsh'ạ-mạ, or
  Ẹ-lĭsh'ạ-mäh
Ẹ-lĭsh'ạ-phăt
Ẹ-lĭsh'ẹ-bạ
Ẹ-lį-shū'ạ
  Ẹ-lĭsh'ụ-ạ, C.
Ẹ-lĭs'į-mŭs
Ẹ-lī'ụ
Ẹ-lī'ụd
Ẹ-lī'z'ạ-phăn
Ĕl-į-zē'ụs
Ẹ-lī'zụr
Ĕl'kạ-näh
  Ẹl-kā'nah, P. T.
Ĕl'kọ-shīte

Ĕl'lạ-săr
  Ẹl-lā'sạr, T.
Ĕl'mọ-dăm
  Ẹl-mŏ'dạm, O. T.
Ĕl'nạ-ăm
  Ẹl-nā'ạm, P.
Ĕl'nạ-thăn
  Ẹl-nā'thạn, P. T.
Ĕl'ọ-hĭm
Ẹ-lŏ'ī
Ē'lŏn
Ē'lŏn Bĕth'hạ-năn
  Ē'lŏn Bĕth-hā'-
    nạn, P.
Ē'lọn-ītes
Ē'lŏth
Ĕl'pạ-ăl
  Ẹl-pā'ạl, P. T.
Ĕl'pạ-lĕt
  Ẹl-pā'lẹt, P. T.
Ẹl-pā'rạn
Ĕl'tẹ-kēh
  Ẹl-tē'kẹh, P. T.
Ĕl'tẹ-kŏn
  Ẹl-tē'kọn, P.
Ĕl'tọ-läd •
  Ẹl-tŏ'lạd, O. P. T.
Ē'lŭl
Ẹ-lū'zạ-ī
  Ĕl-ụ-zā'ī, O.
Ĕl-y-mā'įs
Ĕl'y-măs
  Ẹ-lȳ'mạs, P.
Ĕl-y-mē'ạnṣ
Ĕl'zạ-băd
  Ẹl-zā'băd, P.
Ĕl'zạ-phăn·
  Ẹl-zā'phạn, T.
Ẹm-măn'ụ-ĕl
Ē'mĭmṣ
Ĕm'mạ-ŭs
Ĕm'mẹr
Ĕm'mŏr
Ē'năm
Ē'năn
Ẹ-năs'į-bŭs
Ĕn'dör
Ē'nẹ-ăs
  Ẹ-nē'ạs, P. T.
Ĕn-ẹg-lā'įm
  Ẹn-ĕg'lạ-ĭm, O.
Ĕn-ẹ-mĕs'sạr
Ẹ-nē'nį-ŭs
Ẹn-găd'dī
Ẹn-găn'nįm
Ĕn'ġẹ-dī
  Ẹn-ġē'dī, P. T.
Ẹn-hăd'dạh
Ẹn-hăk'kọ-rē
  Ẹn-hăk'kōre, P.
Ẹn-hā'zọr
Ẹn-mĭsh'pạt
Ē'nọch (ē'nọk)
Ē'nŏn, or Æ'nŏn
Ē'nọs
Ē'nŏsh
Ẹn-rĭm'mọn
Ẹn-rō'ġẹl
Ĕn'shẹ-mĕsh
  Ẹn-shē'mẹsh, O.

Ẹn-tăp'pụ-äh
Ĕp'ạ-phrăs
Ẹ-păph-rọ-dī'tụs
Ẹ-pĕn'ẹ-tŭs
  Ĕp-ẹ-nē'tụs, T.
Ē'phah
Ē'phai
  Ē'phạ-ī, P.
Ē'phẹr
Ē-phẹs-dăm'mįm
Ẹ-phē'şį-ạnṣ (ẹ-fē'-
    zhẹ-ạnz)
Ĕph'ẹ-sŭs
Ĕph'įạl
Ĕph'phạ-thạ
Ē'phrạ-ĭm
Ē'phrạ-įm-īte
Ē'phrạ-ĭn
Ĕph'rạ-täh
  Ẹ-phrā'tạh, P.
Ĕph'rạth
Ĕph'rạth-īte
Ē'phrọn
Ẹp-į-cụ-rē'ạnṣ
Ẹ-pĭph'ạ-nēṣ
Ẹr
Ē'răn
Ē'rạn-ītes
Ẹ-răs'tụs
Ē'rĕch
Ē'rī
Ē'rītes
Ẹ-şā'iạs (ẹ-zā'yạs)
Ē-sạr-hăd'dọn
Ē'sâu
Ē'şāy
Ĕs-drạ-ē'lọn, or
  Ĕs-drạ-ē'lọm
Ĕs'drạs
Ẹs-drē'lọn
Ĕs'ẹ-bŏn
Ẹ-sē'brį-ăs
  Ĕs-ẹ-brī'ạs, O.
Ē'sẹk
Ĕsh'bā-ạl
  Ĕsh-bā'ạl, T.
Ĕsh'băn
Ĕsh'cŏl
Ē'shẹ-ạn
  Ĕsh'ẹ-ạn, O. T.
Ẹ-shē'ạn, P.
Ē'shẹk
Ĕsh'kạ-lọn-ītes
Ĕsh'tạ-ŏl
Ĕsh'tâu-lītes, or
  Ĕsh'tạ-ụl-ītes
Ẹsh-tĕm'ọ-ạ
  Ĕsh-tẹ-mŏ'ạ, P.
Ĕsh'tẹ-mōh
Ĕsh'tọn
Ĕs'lī
Ẹ-sŏ'rạ
Ĕs'rįl
Ĕs'rọm
Ĕst'hạ-ŏl
Ĕs'thẹr (ĕs'tẹr)
Ē'tạm
Ē'thạm
Ē'thạn
Ĕth'ạ-nĭm

Ĕth'bā-ạl
  Ĕth-bā'ạl, T.
Ē'thẹr
Ē-thį-ō'pį-ạ
Ē-thį-ō'pį-ạn
Ĕth'mạ
Ĕth'năn
Ĕth'nī
Eū-bū'lụs
  Eū'bụ-lŭs, P.
Eū-ër'ġẹ-tēṣ
Eū'mẹ-nēṣ
Eū'nạ-tăn
Eū-nī'cẹ
  Eū'nįce, Jones.
Eū-ŏ'dį-ăs
Eū'pạ-tör
Eū-phrā'tēṣ
Eū-pŏl'ẹ-mŭs
Eū-rŏc'ly-dŏn
Eū'ty-çhŭs
Ēve
Ē'vī
Ē'vįl Mẹ-rŏ'dăch
  Ē'vįl Mĕr'ọ-
    dăch, P.
Ĕx'ọ-dŭs
Ē'zạr
Ĕz'bạ-ī
  Ĕz-bā'ī, P.
Ĕz'bŏn
Ĕz-ẹ-çhī'ạs
Ĕz-ẹ-cī'ạs
Ĕz-ẹ-kī'ạs
Ẹ-zē'kį-ẹl
Ē'zẹl
Ē'zẹm
Ē'zẹr
Ĕz-ẹ-rī'ạs
Ẹ-zī'ạs
Ē'zį-ọn Gā'bẹr, or
  Ē'zį-ọn-ġē'bẹr
Ĕz'nīte
Ĕz'rạ
Ĕz'rạ-hīte
Ĕz'rī
Ĕz'rįl
Ĕz'rọn, or Hĕz'rọn

F.

Fē'lįx
Fĕs'tụs
Fŏr-tụ-nā'tụs

G.

Gā'ạl
Gā'ash
Gā'bạ
Găb'ạ-ẹl
Găb'ạ-thạ
Găb'bạ-ī
  Găb'baį, O. T.
Găb'bạ-thạ
Găb'dẹṣ

Gā'brĭ-ăs
Gā'brĭ-ĕl
Găd
Găd'ạ-rạ
Găd-ạ-rĕnĕṣ'
Găd'dĕṣ
Găd'dī
Găd'dĭ-ĕl
Gạd-dī'ĕl, P.
Gā'dī
Găd'ītes
Gā'hăm
Gā'här
Gā'iụs (gā'yụs)
Găl'ạ-ăd
Gā'lăl
Gạ-lā'tĭ-ạ
Gạ-lā'tĭ-ạnṣ
Găl'e-ĕd
Găl'gạ-lạ
Găl-ĭ-læ'ạn, or
Găl-ĭ-lē'ạn
Găl'ĭ-lēe
Găl'lĭm
Găl'lĭ-ō
Găm'ạ-el
Gạ-mā'lĭ-ĕl
Găm'mạ-dĭmṣ
Gā'mul
Gär
Gā'rĕb
Gär'ĭ-zĭm
Gär'mīte
Găsh'mụ
Gā'tạm
Găth
Găth Hē'phẹr
Găth Rĭm'mọn
Gā'zạ
Gạ-zā'rạ
Gā'zạth-ītes
Gā'zer
Gạ-zē'rạ
Gā'zez
Găz'ītes
Gā'zītes, P.
Găz'zạm
Gē'bạ
Gē'bạl
Gē'bẹr
Gē'bĭm
Gĕd-ạ-lī'ạh
Gĕd'dụr
Gĕd'ẹ-ọn
Gē'dẹr
Gẹ-dē'rạh
Gĕd'ẹ-räh, P.
Gĕd'ẹ-rạth-īte
Gẹ-dē'rạth īte, O.
Gẹ-dĕr'ạth-īte, P.
Gĕd'ẹ-rīte
Gẹ-dē'rọth
Gĕd'ẹ-rŏth, P.
Gĕd-e-rọth-ā'ịm
Gē'dör
Gẹ-hā'zĭ
Gẹ-hĕn'nạ, Milton.
Gĕl'ĭ-lŏth
Gẹ-lī'lọth, P.
Gẹ-măl'lĭ

Gĕm-ạ-rī'ạh
Gẹ-nĕs'ạ-rĕth
Gẹ-nĕs'ạ-rĕth, P.
Gĕn'ẹ-sĭs
Gẹ-nē'zạr
Gĕn-nē'sạr
Gĕn-nĕs'ạ-rĕt
Gĕn-nē'ụs
Gĕn'tīle
Gẹ-nū'bạth
Gĕn'ụ-băth, T.
Gē'ọn
Gē'rạ
Gē'rạh
Gē'rạr
Gĕr-gē-sēnẹṣ'
Gĕr'gē-sītes
Gĕr'ĭ-zĭm
Gẹ-rĭz'ĭm, O.
Gĕr-rhē'nĭ-ạnṣ
Gĕr'shọm
Gĕr-shọn
Gĕr'shọn-īte
Gĕr'sọn
Gē'sem
Gē'shạm
Gē'shem
Gē'shụr
Gĕsh'ụ-rī
Gĕsh'ụ-rītes
Gĕth-sĕm'ạ-nẹ
Gē'thẹr
Gẹ-ū'ĕl
Gĕū'ĕl, P.
Gē'ụ-ĕl, C.
Gē'zer
Gĕz'rītes
Gī'ạh
Gĭb'bạr
Gĭb'bẹ-thŏn
Gĭb'ẹ-ạ
Gĭb'ẹ-äh
Gĭb'ẹ-äth
Gĭb'ẹ-ạth-īte
Gĭb'ẹ-ọn
Gĭb'ẹ-ọn-īte
Gĭb'lītes
Gĭd-dăl'tī
Gĭd'dĕl
Gĭd'ẹ-ọn
Gĭd-ẹ-ō'nī
Gī'dŏm
Gī'hŏn
Gīl'ạ-lāi
Gĭ-lā'lạ-ī, P.
Gĭl-ạ-lā'ī, T.
Gīl'bọ-ạ
Gĭl-bō'ạ, O. T.
Gīl'ẹ-ad
Gīl'ẹ-ad-īte
Gīl'găl
Gī'lōh
Gī'lọ-nīte
Gīm'zō
Gī'nạth
Gĭn'nẹ-thō
Gĭn-nē'thō, P.
Gĭn'nẹ-thŏn
Gĭn-nē'thọn, P.
Gīr'gạ-shīte
31*

Gĭr'gạ-sīte
Gĭs'pạ
Gĭt'tạh Hē'phẹr
Gĭt'tạ-ĭm
Gĭt-tā'ịm, P. T.
Gĭt'tīte
Gĭt'tĭth
Gī'zọ-nīte
Gīz'rītes
Gnī'dụs (nī'dụs)
Gō'ạth
Gōb
Gōg
Gō'lạn
Gŏl'gọ-thạ
Gọ-lī'ạth
Gō'mer
Gọ-mŏr'rạh, or
Gọ-mŏr'rhạ
Gör'gĭ-ăs
Gör'ty-nạ
Gọr-tȳ'nạ, C. Sm.
Gō'shẹn
Gŏth-ọ-lī'ạs
Gọ-thŏn'ĭ-ĕl
Gō'zăn
Grā'bạ
Grē'cĭ-ạ
Grē'cĭ-ạn
Grēēce
Grēēk
Grēēk'ĭsh
Gŭd'gọ-däh
Gụd-gō'dạh, P.
Gū'nī
Gū'nītes
Gür
Gụr-bā'ạl

H.

Hā-ạ-häsh'tạ-rĭ
Hạ-ăm'mọ-näi
Hạ-bā'ịah (hạ-bā'-yạh)
Hā-bạ-ī'ạh, P.
Hăb'ak-kŭk
Hạ-băk'kuk, O.
Hăb-ạ-zĭ-nī'ạh
Hăb'bạ-cŭc
Hā'bör
Hăch-ạ-lī'ạh
Hăch'ĭ-läh
Hăch'mọ-nĭ
Hạch-mō'nĭ, T.
Hăch'mọ-nīte
Hā'dăd
Hăd-ạd-ē'zer
Hā'dạd Rĭm'mọn
Hā'dạr
Hăd-ạr-ē'zer
Hăd'ạ-shäh
Hạ-dā'shạh, P. T.
Hạ-dăs'sạh
Hạ-dăt'tạh
Hā'dĭd
Hăd'lạ-ī
Hạ-dō'rạm

Hā'drạch
Hā'găb
Hăg'ạ-bạ
Hăg'ạ-bäh
Hā'gạr
Hā-gạr-ēnẹṣ'
Hā'gạr-īte
Hăg'gạ-ī *
Hăg'gẹ-rī
Hăg'gī
Hạg-gī'ạh
Hăg'gītes
Hăg'gĭth
Hā'gĭ-ạ
Hā'ī
Hăk'kạ-tăn
Hăk'kŏz
Hạ-kū'phạ
Hăk'ụ-phạ, P.
Hā'lạh
Hā'lăk
Hā'lī
Hăl-ĭ-cạr-năs'sụs
Hăl'hŭl
Hạl-lō'esh, or
Hạl-lō'hẹsh
Hăm
Hā'mạn
Hā'mạth
Hā'mạth-īte
Hā'mạth Zō'bạh
Hăm'ĭ-tăl
Hăm-mạh-lē'kọth
Hăm'mạth
Hạm-mĕd'ạ-thạ
Hăm'mẹ-lĕch
Hạm-mŏl'ẹ-kĕth
Hăm'mọn
Hăm'mọth Dör
Hăm'mọ-näh
Hạ-mō'nạh, O. T.
Hā'mọn Gŏg
Hā'mör
Hā'mọth
Hạ-mū'ĕl
Hăm'ụ-ĕl, P. C.
Hā'mul
Hā'mul-ītes
Hạ-mū'tạl
Hăm'ụ-tăl, P.
Hạ-năm'ẹ-ĕl
Hăn'ạ-mēĕl, P.
Hā'nạn
Hạ-năn'ẹ-ĕl
Hăn'ạ-nēĕl, P.
Hăn'ạ-nĭ
Hạ-nā'nĭ, P. T.
Hăn-ạ-nī'ạh
Hā'nĕṣ
Hăn'ĭ-ĕl
Hạ-nī'ĕl, P.
Hăn'nạh
Hăn'nạ-thŏn
Hăn'nĭ-ĕl
Hā'nọch
Hā'nọch-ītes
Hā'nụn
Hăph-ạ-rā'ịm, or
Hạph-rā'ịm
Hā'rạ

Hăr'ạ-däh
Hā'rạn
Hā'rạ-rīte
Hạr-bō'nạ
Hạr-bō'nạh
Hā'rẹph
Hā'rẹth
Här-hạ-ī'ạh
Hạ-rā'ịah, O.
Här'hạs
Här'hụr
Hā'rĭm
Hā'rĭph
Här'nẹ-phẹr
Hạr-nē'phẹr, P.
Hā'rọd
Hā'rọd-īte
Här'ọ-ēh
Hạ-rō'ẹh, P.
Hā'rọ-rīte
Här'ọ-shĕth
Här'shạ
Hā'rum
Hạ-rū'mạph
Här'ụ-măph, P.
Hạ-rū'phīte
Här'ụ-phīte, P.
Hā'rụz
Hăs-ạ-dī'ạh
Hăs-ẹ-nū'ạh
Hạ-sĕn'ụ-äh, C.
Hăsh-ạ-bī'ạh
Hạ-shăb'nạh
Hăsh-ạb-nī'ạh
Hạsh-băd'ạ-nạ
Hā'shẹm
Hạsh-mō'nạh
Hăsh'mọ-näh, P.
Hā'shụb
Hạ-shū'bạh
Hā'shụm
Hạ-shū'phạ
Hăs'rạh
Hăs-sẹ-nā'ạh
Hăs'shụb
Hạ-sū'phạ
Hā'tạch
Hā'thăth
Hạ-tī'phạ
Hăt'ĭ-phạ, P. T.
Hăt'ĭ-tạ
Hạ-tī'tạ, O.
Hạt-tā'ạ-văh
Hăt'tĭ-cŏn
Hăt'tĭl
Hăt'tụsh
Hâu'rạn
Hăv'ĭ-läh
Hạ-vĭl'ạh, P.
Hā'vọth Jā'ịr
Hăz'ạ-ĕl
Hạ-zā'ĕl, P.
Hạ-zā'ịah (hạ-zā'-yạh)
Hā-zạ-ī'ạh, P.
Hā'zạr Ăd'dạr
Hā'zạr Ē'nạn
Hā'zạr Găd'dạh
Hā'zạr Hăt'tĭ-cŏn
Hā'zạr Mā'vẹth

Hā′zạr Shū′ạl
Hā′zạr Sū′sạh
Hā′zạr Sū′sịm
Hăz′ạ-zŏn Tā′mạr
Hā′zẹl Ẹl-pō′nī
Hạ-zē′rịm
  Hăz′ẹ-rĭm, P.
Hạ-zē′rọth
  Hăz′ẹ-rŏth, P.
Hăz′ẹ-zŏn Tā′mạr
Hā′zị-ẹl
  Hạ-zī′ẹl, P.
Hā′zō
Hā′zör
Hăz′ụ-băh
Hăz′zụ-rĭm
Hē′bẹr
Hē′bẹr-ītes
Hē′brew (-brŭ)
Hē′brew-ĕss
Hē′brọn
Hē′brọn-ītes
Hĕg′ạ-ī
  Hẹ-gā′ī, T.
Hē′ğẹ
Hē′lạh
Hē′lạm
Hĕl′bạh
Hĕl′bŏn
Hẹl-chī′ạh
Hĕl′dạ-ī
  Hẹl-dā′ī, P.
Hē′lẹb
Hē′lẹd
Hē′lẹk
Hē′lẹk-ītes
Hē′lẹm
Hē′lẹph
Hē′lẹz
Hē′lị
Hẹ-lī′ạs
Hē-lị-ọ-dō′rụs
Hĕl′kạ-ī
  Hẹl-kā′ī, P.
Hĕl′kạth
Hĕl′kạth Hăz′zụ-
Hẹl-kī′ạs   [rĭm
Hē′lọn
Hē′mạm
Hē′mạn
Hē′mạth
Hĕm′dạn
Hĕn
Hē′nạ
Hĕn′ạ-dăd
  Hẹ-nā′dăd, P.
Hē′nọch
Hē′phẹr
Hē′phẹr-ītes
Hĕph′zị-băh
Hĕr′cụ-lēş
Hē′rēş
Hē′rẹsh
Hĕr′mạs
Hĕr′mēş
Hẹr-mŏğ′ẹ-nēş
Hĕr′mọn
Hĕr′mọn-ītes
Hĕr′ọd
Hẹ-rō′dị-ạnş

Hẹ-rō′dị-ạs
Hẹ-rō′dị-ŏn
Hē′sẹd
Hĕsh′bŏn
Hĕsh′mŏn
Hĕs′rụn, or
  Hĕz′rọn
Hĕs′rọn-ītes
Hĕth
Hĕth′lọn
Hĕz′ẹ-kī
Hĕz-ẹ-kī′ạh
Hē′zịr
Hē′zị-ŏn
  Hĕz′ị-ŏn, O. P.
Hĕz′rạ-ī
Hĕz′rō
Hĕz′rọn
Hĕz′rọn-ītes
Hĭd′dạ-ī
  Hịd-dā′ī, P.
Hĭd′dẹ-kĕl
Hī′ẹl
Hī-ẹ-răp′ọ-lĭs
Hī-ĕr′ẹ-ẹl
Hī-ĕr′ẹ-mŏth
Hī-ĕr-ị-ē′lụs
Hī-ĕr′mạs
Hī-ẹ-rŏn′y-mŭs
Hī-ẹ-rŭ′sạ-lĕm
Hịg-gā′iọn (hig-
Hī′lẹn   [gā′yọn)
Hịl-kī′ạh
Hĭl′lẹl
Hĭn′nọm
Hī′rạh
Hī′rạm
Hịr-cā′nụs
Hĭt′tīte

Hŏr′ọ-nīte
Hō′rọ-nīte, P.
Hō′sạ, or Hō′sạh
Họ-sē′ạ (họ-zē′ạ)
Hōsh-ạ-ī′ạh
Hōsh′ạ-mạ
  Họ-shā′mạ, P.
Họ-shē′ạ
Hō′thạm
Hō′thạn
Hō′thịr
Hū′kọk
Hŭk′kọk
Hŭl
Hŭl′dạh
Hŭm′tạh
Hū′phạm
Hū′phạm-ītes
Hŭp′pạh
Hŭp′pịm
Hür
Hū′rại
Hū′rạ-ī, P.
Hū′rạm
Hū′rī
Hū′shại
Hū′shạ-ī, P.
Hū′shạm
Hū′shạth-īte
Hū′shịm
Hŭz
Hū′zŏth
Hŭz′zạb
Hȳ-däs′pēş
Hȳ-mẹ-næ′ụs, or
  Hȳ-mẹ-nē′ụs

I.

Ĭb′hạr
Ĭb′lẹ-ăm
  Ịb-lē′ạm, P.
Ịb-nē′iạh
  Ịb-neī′ạh, T.
  Ĭb-nẹ-ī′ạh, P.
Ịb-nī′jạh
Ĭb′rī
Ĭb′zăn
Ĭch′ạ-bọd
  Ị-chā′bọd, P.
Ī-cō′nị-ŭm
Ĭd′ạ-läh
  Ị-dā′lạh, P. T.
Ĭd′băsh
Ĭd′dō
Ĭd′ụ-ẹl
Ĭd-ụ-mæ′ạ, or
  Ĭd-ụ-mē′ạ
  Ī-dụ-mē′ạ, P.
Ĭd-ụ-mæ′ạnş, or
  Ĭd-ụ-mē′ạnş
Ī′gạl
Ĭg-dạ-lī′ạh
Ĭğ′ẹ-ạl
  Ị-ğē′ạl, O. T.
Ī′ịm
Ĭj-ẹ-ăb′ạ-rĭm

Ī′jŏn
Ĭk′kẹsh
Ī′lại
  Ị-lā′ī, P.
Ịl-lȳr′ị-cŭm
Ĭm′lạ, or Ĭm′lạh
Ĭm′mạh
Ịm-măn′ụ-ẹl
Ĭm′mẹr
Ĭm′nạ, or
  Ĭm′nạh
Ĭm′rạh
Ĭm′rī
Ị-rī′jạh
Ĭr′nạ-hăsh
  Ịr-nā′hăsh, T.
Ī′rọn
Ĭr′pẹ-ẹl
  Ịr-pē′ẹl, T.
Ịr-shē′mẹsh
  Ĭr′shẹ-mĕsh, O.
Ī′rụ
Ī′şaac (ī′zạk)
Ī-şā′iạh (ī-zā′yạh)
Ĭs′cạh
Ịs-căr′ị-ọt
Ĭs′dạ-ẹl
Ĭsh′bạh
Ĭsh′băk
Ĭsh′bī Bē′nọb
Ĭsh′bọ-shĕth
  Ịsh-bō′shẹth, T.
Ī′shī
Ị-shī′ạh
Ị-shī′jạh
Ĭsh′mạ
Ĭsh′mạ-ẹl
Ĭsh′mạ-ẹl-ītes
Ĭsh′mạ-ī′ạh
  Ịsh-mā′iạh, T.
Ĭsh′mẹ-ẹl-ītes
Ĭsh′mẹ-rāi
  Ĭsh′mẹ-rā′ī, P.
Ī′shọd
Ĭsh′păn
Ĭsh′tŏb
Ĭsh′ụ-äh
Ĭsh′ụ-āi
Ĭsh′ụ-ī
Ĭs-mạ-chī′ạh
Ĭs′mạ-ẹl
Ĭs-mạ-ī′ạh
Ĭs′pạh
Ĭş′rạ-ẹl
Ĭş′rạ-ẹl-īte
Ĭş′rạ-ẹl-ī-tịsh
Ĭs′sạ-chạr
Ĭs-shī′ạh
Ĭs-tạl-cū′rụs
Ĭs′ụ-äh
Ĭs′ụ-ī

Ĭs′ụ-ītes
Ị-tăl′iạn
Ĭt′ạ-ly
Ĭth′ạ-ī, or Ĭt′tạ-ī
Ĭth′ạ-mär
Ĭth′ị-ẹl
Ĭth′mạh
Ĭth′năn
Ĭth′rạ
Ĭth′răn
Ĭth′rẹ-ăm
Ĭth′rīte
Ĭt′tạh Kā′zịn
Ĭt′tạ-ī
  Ịt-tā′ī, P.
Ĭt-ụ-rē′ạ
Ī′vạh
Ĭz′ẹ-här
Ĭz′e-hạr-ītes
Ĭz′här
Ĭz′hạr-ītes
Ĭz-rạ-hī′ạh
Ĭz′rạ-hīte
Ĭz′rẹ-ẹl
Ĭz′rī

J.

Jā′ạ-kăn
Jạ-ăk′ọ-băh
  Jaa-kō′bạh, P.
Jạ-ā′lạ, or -läh
Jạ-ā′lạm
Jā′ạ-nāi
  Jạ-ā′nại, C. T.
Jạ-ăr-ẹ-ŏr′ẹ-ğĭm
Jā′ạ-sạu
  Jạ-ā′sạu, T.
Jạ-ā′sị-ẹl
Jạ-ăz-ạ-nī′ạh
Jạ-ā′zẹr
Jā-ạ-zī′ạh
Jạ-ā′zị-ẹl
Jā′bạl
Jăb′bọk
Jā′bẹsh
Jā′bẹz
Jā′bịn
Jăb′nẹ-ẹl
Jăb′neh
Jā′chạn
Jā′chịn
Jā′chịn-ītes
Jā′cọb
Jạ-cū′bụs
Jā′dạ
Jạ-dā′ū
Jạd-dū′ạ
Jā′dŏn
Jā′ẹl
Jā′gụr
JÄH
Jạ-hăl′ẹ-lĕl
Jā′hăth
Jā′hăz
Jạ-hā′zạ
Jạ-hā′zạh
Jā-hạ-zī′ạh

Ja-hā'zi-el
   Ja-hăz'i-el, *T.*
Jäh'da-ī
   Jah-dā'ī, *P. T.*
Jäh'di-el
   Jah-dī'el, *P.*
Jäh'dō
Jäh'le-el
   Jäh'lēēl, *O.*
Jäh'le-el-ītes
Jäh'ma-ī
   Jah-mā'ī, *T.*
Jäh'zah
Jäh'ze-el
   Jāh'zēēl, *P.*
Jäh'ze-el-ītes
Jäh'ze-räh
   Jah-zē'rah, *P.*
Jäh'zi-el
Jā'ir
Jā'i-rīte
Jā'i-rŭs
   Ja-ī'rus, *C. O.*
Jā'kan
Jā'keh
Jā'kim
Jā'lon
Jăm'brēs
Jăm'brī
Jāmes
Jā'min
Jā'min-ites
Jăm'lech
Jam-nī'a
Jăm'nītes
Jän'na
Jän'nēs
Ja-nō'ah
Ja-nō'hah
Jā'num
Jā'pheth
Ja-phī'a
Jăph'let
Jăph'le-tī
   Japh-lē'tī, *T.*
Jā'phō
Jā'rah
Jā'reb
Jā'red
Jär-e-sī'ah
Jär'ha
Jā'rib
Jär'i-mŏth
Jär'muth
Ja-rō'ah
Jás'a-el
Jā'shen
Jā'sher
Ja-shō'be-ăm
Jäsh'ub
   Jā'shub, *P. T.*
Jäsh'u-bī Lē'hem
Jäsh'ub-ītes
Jā'si-el
   Ja-sī'el, *P.*
Jā'son
Ja-sŭ'bus
Jā'tal
Jäth'ni-el
Jăt'tir

Jā'van
Jā'zar
Jā'zer
Jā'zi-el
Jā'ziz
Jē'a-rim
   Je-ā'rim, *P.*
Je-ät'e-rāi
Je-bĕr-e-chī'ah
Jē'bus
Je-bū'sī
   Jĕb'u-sī, *P.*
Jĕb'u-sīte
Jĕc-a-mī'ah
Jĕch-o-lī'ah
Jĕch-o-nī'as
Jĕc-o-lī'ah
Jĕc-o-nī'ah
Jĕc-o-nī'as
Je-dā'iah
   Jĕd-a-ī'ah, *P.*
Jĕd'du
Je-dē'iah
Je-dē'us
Je-dī'a-el
Jĕd'i-däh
   Je-dī'dah, *O.*
Jĕd-i-dī'ah
Jē'di-el
   Jĕd'i-el, *O. T.*
Jĕd'u-thŭn
   Je-dū'thun, *T.*
Je-ē'lī
Je-ē'lus
Je-ē'zer
Je-ē'zer-ītes
Jē'gar Sā-ha-dū'- [tha
   Je-hā'le-el
   Je-hăl'e-el, *O.*
Je-hăl'e-lĕl
Jē-ha-lē'le-el
   Je-hăl'e-lēēl, *P.*
Jeh-dē'iah
   Jeh-deī'ah, *T.*
   Jēh-de-ī'ah, *P.*
Je-hĕz'e-kĕl
Je-hī'ah
Je-hī'el
Je-hī'e-lī
Jē-hiz-kī'ah
Je-hō'a-däh
Jē-ho-ăd'dan
Je-hō'a-häz
Je-hō'ash
Je-hō'ha-nän
   Jē-ho-hā'nan, *T.*
Je-hōï'a-chĭn
Je-hōï'a-da
Je-hōï'a-kĭm
Je-hōï'a-rĭb
Je-hŏn'a-däb
Je-hŏn'a-than
Je-hō'ram
Jē-ho-shăb'e-ăth
Je-hŏsh'a-phăt
Je-hŏsh'e-ba
Je-hŏsh'u-a
JE-HŌ'VAH
Je-hō'vah Jī'reh
Je-hō'vah Nĭs'sī

Je-hō'vah Shā'lom
Je-hō'vah Shăm'- [mah
Je-hō'vah Tsïd'ke- [nū
Je-hŏz'a-băd
Je-hŏz'a-dăk
Jē'hū
Je-hŭb'bah
Jē'hu-căl,
   Je-hū'cal, *O. P.*
Jē'hŭd
Je-hū'dī
Jē-hu-dī'jah
Jē'hŭsh
Je-ī'el
Je-käb'ze-el
Jĕk-a-mē'am
Jĕk-a-mī'ah
Je-kū'thi-el
Jĕm'i-ma
   Je-mī'ma, *O. P.*
Jĕm'na-an
Je-mū'el
Jĕm'u-el, *C. T.*
Jĕph'thæ
Jĕph'thah
Je-phŭn'ne
Je-phŭn'neh
Jē'rah
Je-räh'me-el
   Jĕr-ah-mē'el, *T.*
Je-räh'me-el-ītes 8
Jĕr'e-chŭs
Jē'red
Jĕr'e-mäi
Jĕr-e-mī'ah
Jĕr-e-mī'as
Jĕr'e-mŏth
Jĕr'e-my
Je-rī'ah
Jĕr'i-bāi
Jĕr'i-chō
Jē'ri-el
   Je-rī'el, *P. T.*
Je-rī'jah
Jĕr'i-mŏth
Jē'ri-ōth
   Jĕr'i-ŏth, *P. T.*
Jĕr-o-bō'am
Jĕr'o-häm
   Je-rō'ham, *T.*
Je-rŭb'ba-al
   Jē-rub-bā'al, *T.*
Je-rŭb'e-shĕth
   Jē-rub-ĕsh'eth, *T.*
Jĕr'u-el
   Je-rū'el, *P. T.*
Je-rū'sa-lĕm
Je-rū'sha, *or*
   Je-rū'shah
Je-sā'iah
   Jĕs-a-ī'ah, *P.*
Je-shā'iah, *or*
   Jĕsh-a-ī'ah
Jĕsh'a-näh
   Je-shā'nah, *T.*
Jĕsh-är'e-läh
Je-shĕb'e-ăb
Jē'sher
Jĕsh'i-mŏn

Je-shïsh'a-ī
Jĕsh-o-ha-ī'ah
Jĕsh'u-a, *or* -äh
Jĕsh'u-rŭn
Je-sī'ah
Je-sïm'i-el
Jĕs'se
Jĕs'su-ē
Jē'sū
Jĕs'u-ī
Jĕs'u-ītes
Jĕs'u-rŭn
JĒ'SŲS
Jē'ther
Jē'theth
Jĕth'lah
Jē'thrō
Jē'tur
Jē'u-ĕl
Jeū'el, *P.*
Jē'ush
Jē'uz
Jew
Jew'ess
Jew'ish
Jew'ry
Jĕz-a-nī'ah
Jĕz'e-bĕl
Je-zē'lus
Jē'zer
Jē'zer-ītes
Je-zī'ah
Jē'zi-el
   Je-zī'el, *P.*
Jez-lī'ah
Jĕz'o-är
   Je-zō'ar, *P.*
Jĕz-ra-hī'ah
Jĕz're-el
   Jĕz'rēēl, *P.*
Jĕz're-el-īte
Jĕz're-el-ī-tess
Jĭb'sam
Jĭd'laph
Jĭm'nah
Jĭm'nītes
Jĭph'tah
Jĭph'thah-ĕl
Jō'ab
Jō'a-chäz
Jō'a-chĭm
Jō'a-cĭm
Jō-a-dā'nus
Jō'ah
Jō'a-häz
   Jo-ā'häz, *P. T.*
Jō'a-kĭm
Jo-ā'nan
Jo-ăn'na
Jo-ăn'nan
Jō'a-rĭb
Jō'ash
Jō'a-thäm
Jō-a-zäb'dus
Jōb
Jō'băb
Jŏch'e-bĕd
Jō'da
Jō'ed
Jō'el

Jo-ē'lah
Jo-ē'zer
Jŏg'be-häh
Jŏg'lī
Jō'ha
Jo-hā'nan
Jo-hän'nĕs
Jŏhn (*jŏn*)
Jōï'a-da
   Jo-ī'a-da, *Sm.*
Jōï'a-kĭm
   Jo-ī'a-kĭm, *Sm.*
Jōï'a-rĭb
   Jo-ī'a-rĭb, *Sm.*
Jŏk'de-ăm
   Jok-dē'am, *T.*
Jō'kim
Jŏk'me-ăm
   Jok-mē'am, *T.*
Jŏk'ne-ăm
   Jok-nē'am, *P.*
Jŏk'shan
Jŏk'tan
Jŏk'the-el
   Jŏk'thēēl, *T.*
Jō'na
Jŏn'a-däb
Jō'nah
Jō'nan
Jō'nas
Jŏn'a-than
Jŏn'a-thäs
Jō'nath Ē'lem Re-chō'kim
Jŏp'pa, *or* Jŏp'pe
Jō'ra-ī
   Jo-rā'ī, *P.*
Jō'rah
Jō'ram
Jŏr'dan
Jŏr'i-bäs
Jŏr'i-bŭs
Jō'rim
Jŏr'ko-am
   Jor-kō'ăm, *T.*
Jōs'a-bäd
Jōs'a-phăt
Jōs-a-phī'as
Jō'se
Jŏs'e-dĕc
Jŏs'e-dĕch
Jō'seph
Jo-sē'phus
Jō'sēs
Jŏsh'a-bäd
Jō'shah
Jŏsh'a-phăt
Jŏsh-a-vī'ah
Josh-bĕk'a-shäh
Jŏsh'u-a
Jo-sī'ah
Jo-sī'as
Jŏs-i-bī'ah
Jŏs-i-phī'ah
Jŏt'bah
Jŏt'bath
Jŏt'ba-thäh
   Jot-bā'thah, *P.*
Jō'tham
Jŏz'a-bäd

Jŏz'ạ-chär
  Jọ-zā'chạr, P.
Jŏz'ạ-dăk
Jū'bạl
Jū'cạl
Jū'dạ
Jụ-dæ'ạ, or
  Jụ-dē'ạ
Jū'dạh
Jū'dạ-ĭṣm
Jū'dạs
Jūde
Jū'dịth
Jū'el
Jū'lị-ạ
Jū'lị-ŭs
Jū'nị-ạ
Jū'pị-tẹr
Jụ-shăb'hẹ-sĕd
Jŭs'tụs
Jŭt'tạh

K.

Kăb'zẹ-ẹl
Kā'dēṣ
Kā'dẹsh, or
  Cā'dẹsh
Kā'dẹsh Bär'nẹ-ạ
  Bạr-nē'ạ, O.
Kăd'mị-ẹl
Kăd'mọn-ītes
Kăl'lạ-ī
Kā'nạh
Kạ-rē'ạh
Kär'kạ-ạ
Kär'kọr
Kär'nạ-ĭm
  Kạr-nā'ịm, T.
Kär'tạh
Kär'tạn
Kăt'tạth
Kē'dạr
Kĕd'ẹ-mäh
  Kẹ-dē'mạh, P.
Kĕd'ẹ-mŏth
  Kẹ-dē'mọth, P.
Kē'dẹsh
Kẹ-hĕl'ạ-thäh
Kēi'lạh
  Keï'lạh, T.
Kẹ-lā'iạh
Kĕl'ị-tạ
Kẹ-mū'ẹl
  Kĕm'ụ-ẹl, C.
Kē'nạn
Kē'nạth
Kē'năz
Kĕn'ẹz-īte
Kĕn'ītes
  Kē'nītes, P. T.
Kĕn'ịz-zītes
Kĕr-ẹn-hăp'pụch
Kē'rị-ŏth
  Kẹ-rī'ọth, P.
Kē'rŏs
Kẹ-tū'rạh
Kẹ-zī'ạ

Kĕ'zịz　　[väh
Kĭb'rọth Hạt-tā'ạ-
Kĭb'zạ-ĭm
  Kĭb-zā'ịm, T.
Kĭd'rọn
  Kī'drọn, P.
Kī'nạh
Kïr
Kịr-här'ạ-sĕth
Kịr-här'ẹ-sĕth
Kïr'hạ-rĕsh
  Kịr-hā'rẹsh, T.
Kïr'hẹ-rĕsh
  Kịr-hē'rẹsh, O.
Kïr'ị-ăth, or
  Kïr'jạth
Kïr-ị-ạ-thā'ịm
Kïr-ị-ăth-ị-ā'rị-ŭs
Kïr'ị-ŏth
Kïr'jạth Ā'ịm
Kïr'jạth Är'bạ
Kïr'jạth Ā'rịm
Kïr'jạth Bā'ạl
Kïr'jạth Hū'zọth
Kïr'jạth Jē'ạ-rïm
Kïr'jạth Săn'nạh
Kïr'jạth Sē'phẹr
Kïsh
Kïsh'ī
Kïsh'ị-ŏn
Kī'shọn, or
  Kī'sọn
Kïth'lịsh
Kït'rọn
  Kī'trọn, P.
Kït'tịm
Kō'ạ
Kō'hạth
Kō'hạth-ītes
Kŏl-ạ-ī'ạh
Kō'rạh
Kō'rạh-ītes
Kō'rạth-ītes
Kō'rẹ
Kör'hīte
Kör'hītes
Kōz
Kush-ā'iạh
  Kū-shạ-ī'ạh, P.

L.

Lā'ạ-däh
Lā'ạ-dăn
  Lạ-ā'dạn, T.
Lā'bạn
Lăb'ạ-nạ
  Lạ-bā'nạ, T.
Lăc-ẹ-dẹ-mō'nị-ạnş
Lā'chịsh
Lạ-cū'nụs
Lā'dạn
Lā'ẹl
Lā'hăd
Lạ-hāi'röï
Lăh'mạm
Lăh'mī
Lā'ịsh

Lā'kụm
Lā'mẹch
Lạ-ŏd-ị-cē'ạ
Lạ-ŏd-ị-cē'ạnş
Lăp'ị-dŏth
Lạ-sē'ạ
Lā'shạ
Lạ-shā'rọn
  Lăsh'ạ-rŏn, P.
Lăs'thẹ-nēş
Lăt'ịn
Lăz'ạ-rŭs
Lē'ạh
Lẹ-ăn'nọth
Lĕb'ạ-näh
Lĕb'ạ-nọn
Lĕb'ạ-ŏth
Lẹ-bā'ọth, T.
Lẹb-bæ'ụs, or
  Lẹb-bē'ụs
Lẹ-bō'nạh
Lē'cạh
Lē'hạ-bïm
  Lẹ-hā'bịm, T.
Lē'hī
Lĕm'ụ-ẹl
Lē'shẹm
Lĕt'tụs
Lẹ-tū'shịm
Lẹ-ŭm'mịm
Lē'vī
Lẹ-vī'ạ-thạn
Lē'vịs
Lē'vīte
Lẹ-vĭt'ị-cạl
Lẹ-vĭt'ị-cŭs
Lïb'ạ-nŭs
Lïb'ẹr-tïneş
Lïb'nạh
Lïb'nī
Lïb'nītes
Lïb'y-ạ
Lïb'y-ạnş
Lïk'hī
Lī'nụs
Lọ-ăm'mī
Lŏd
Lŏd'ẹ-bär
  Lọ-dē'bạr, T.
Lō'ịs
Lō Rụ'hạ-mäh
  Lō Rụ-hā'mạh, O.
Lŏt
Lō'tạn
Lŏth-ạ-sū'bụs
Lō'zọn
Lū'bịm
Lū'bịmş
Lū'cạs
Lū'cị-fẹr
Lū'cị-ŭs
Lŭd
Lū'dịm
Lū'hịth
Lūke
Lŭz
Lўc-ạ-ō'nị-ạ
Lў''cị-ạ
Lўd'dạ
Lўd'ị-ạ

Lўd'ị-anş
Ly-sā'nị-as
Lў''sị-as (lĭsh'ẹ-ạs)
Lў-sïm'ạ-chŭs
Lўs'trạ

M.

Mā'ạ-chäh
  Mạ-ā'chạh, T.
Mạ-ăch'ạ-thīte
Mạ-ăd'ai
  Mā-ạ-dā'ī, O.
Mā-ạ-dī'ạh
Mạ-ā'ī
Mạ-äl'ẹh Ạ-crăb'-
  bịm
Mā'ạ-nī
Mā'ạ-räth
Mā-ạ-sē'ịạh
  Mā-ạ-seī'ạh, T.
Mạ-ăs'ị-āi
Mā-ạ-sī'ạs
Mā'ạth
Mā'ạz
Mā-ạ-zī'ạh
Măb'dạ-ī
Măc'ạ-lŏn
Măc-cạ-bæ'ụs, or
  Măc-cạ-bē'ụs
Măc'cạ-bēēş
Măç-ẹ-dō'nị-ạ
Măç-ẹ-dō'nị-ạn
Măch'bạ-nāi
  Mạch-bā'nại, T.
Măch'bẹ-näh
  Mạch-bē'nạh, T.
Mā'chī
Mā'chịr
Mā'chịr-ītes
Măch'mạs
Măch-nạ-dē'bại
Măch-pē'lạh
  Măch'pẹ-läh, P.
Mā'crọn
Măd'ạ-ī
  Mạ-dā'ī, P.
Mạ-dī'ạ-bŭn
Mạ-dī'ạh
Mā'dị-an
Măd-măn'nạh
Măd'mẹn
Măd-mē'nạh
Mā'dọn
Mạ-ē'lụs
Măg'bịsh
Măg'dạ-lạ
Măg'dạ-lĕn
Măg-dạ-lē'nẹ
  Măg'dạ-lēne, P.
Măg'dị-ẹl
Mā'gẹd
Mạ-gĭd'dō
Mā'gŏg
Mā'gọr Mïs'sạ-bïb
Măg'pị-ăsh
Mā'hạ-läh
  Mạ-hā'lạh, T.

Mạ-hạ-lā'lẹ-ẹl
  Mạ-hăl'ạ-lēēl, P.
Mā'hạ-lăth
Mā'hạ-lăth Lẹ-ăn'-
  nọth
Mā'hạ-lăth Măs'-
  chịl
Mạ-hā'lẹ-ẹl
Mā'hạ-lī
Mā-hạ-nā'ịm
Mā'hạ-nēh Dăn
  Mạ-hā'nẹh, T.
Mạ-här'ạ-ī
Mā'hạth
Mā'hạ-vīte
Mạ-hā'zị-ŏth
Mā'hẹr-shăl'ạl-
  hăsh'bạz
  Mạ-hër'shạ-lạl-
  hăsh'băz, P.
Măh'lạh
Măh'lī
Măh'lītes
Măh'lọn
Mā'hŏl
Mại-ăn'ẹ-ăs
Mā'kăz
Mā'kẹd
Mạk-hē'lọth
  Măk'hẹ-lŏth, P.
Mạk-kē'dạh
  Măk'kẹ-däh, P.
Măk'tẹsh
Măl'ạ-chī
Măl'chạm
Mạl-chī'ạh
Măl'chị-ẹl
  Mạl-chī'el, P.
Măl-chị-ẹl-ītes
Mạl-chī'jạh
Mạl-chī'rạm
Măl-chị-shū'ạ
  Mạl-chĭsh'ụ-ạ, P.
Măl'chụs
Mạ-lē'lẹ-ĕl
Măl'lọs
Măl'lọ-thī
Măl'lụch
Mạ-mā'ịas (mạ-
  mā'yạs)
Măm'mọn
Măm-nị-tạ-nāi'mụs
Măm're
Mạ-mū'chụs
Măn'ạ-ĕn
  Mạ-nā'ẹn, T.
Măn'ạ-häth
  Mạ-nā'hạth, P.
Măn-as-sē'ạs
Mạ-năs'sẹh
Mạ-năs'sēş
Mạ-năs'sītes
Mā'nẹh
Mā'nī
Măn'lị-ŭs
Mạ-nō'ạh
Mā'ọch
Mā'ọn
Mā'ọn-ītes

Mā'ra
Mā'rah
Mär'a-läh
Mär-a-näth'a
  Mär-an-ā'tha, *P.*
Mär'cus
Mär-do-chē'us
Ma-rē'shah
  Mär'e-shäh, *T.*
Märk
Mär'i-sa
  Ma-rī'sa, *T.*
Mär'i-möth
Mär'moth
Mā'roth
Mär'se-na
  Mar-sē'na, *T.*
Märs' Hĭll
Mär'tha
Mā'ry
Mäs'a-lŏth
Mäs'chĭl
Mäsh
Mā'shal
Ma-sī'as
Mäs'man
Mäs'pha
Mäs're-käh
Mäs'sa
Mäs'sah
Mas-sī'as
Mäth-a-nī'as
Ma-thū'sa-la
Mät-tha-nī'as
Mā'tred
Mā'trī
Mät'tan
Mät'ta-näh
Mät-ta-nī'ah
Mät'ta-tha
Mät'ta-thäh
Mät-ta-thī'as
Mät-te-nā'ī
Mät'than
Mät'that
Mat-thē'las [*thu*)
Mät'thew (*măth'*-
Mat-thī'as
Mät-ti-thī'ah
Mäz-i-tī'as
Mäz'za-rŏth
Me'ah
Me-ā'nī
Me-ā'rah
Me-bŭn'nai
Mĕch'e-rath-īte
Mĕd'a-ba
Mē'dad
Mē'dan
Mĕd'e-ba
Mēde
Mē'di-a
Mē'di-an
Me-ē'da
Me-ğĭd'dō, *or*
  Me-ğĭd'don
Me-hĕt'a-bēel
Me-hĕt'a-bĕl
Me-hī'da
Mē'hir

Me-hō'lah
Me-hŏl'ath-īte
Me-hū'ja-el
Me-hū'man
Me-hū'nim
Me-hū'nims
Me-jär'kon
Mĕk'o-näh
  Me-kō'nah, *T.*
Mĕl-a-tī'ah
Mĕl'chī
Mĕl-chī'ah
Mĕl-chī'as
Mĕl'chi-el
Mĕl-chĭş'e-dĕc
Mĕl-chĭz'e-dĕk
Mĕl-chi-shū'a
  Mĕl-chĭsh'u-a, *P.*
Mē'le-a, *or*
  Me-lē'a
Mē'lech
Mĕl'i-cū
Mĕl'i-ta
Mĕl'zar
Mĕm'mi-ŭs
Mĕm'phis
Me-mū'can
Mĕn'a-hĕm
  Me-nā'hem, *O.*
Mē'nan
Mē'ne
Mĕn-e-lā'us
Me-nĕs'theus
Me-ŏn'e-nĭm
  Mē-o-nē'nim, *P.*
Me-ŏn'o-thai
Mĕph'a-äth
  Me-phā'ath, *T.*
Me-phĭb'o-shĕth
Mē'rab
Mĕr-a-ī'ah
Me-rā'ioth (-*yoth*)
Mē'ran
Mĕr'a-rī
  Me-rā'rī, *O. T.*
Mĕr'a-rītes
Mĕr-a-thā'im
Mer-cū'ri-ŭs
Mē'red
Mĕr'e-mŏth
Mē'res
Mĕr'i-bäh
Mĕr'i-bäh Kā'desh
Me-rĭb'ba-al
  Mĕr-ib-bā'al, *P.*
Me-rō'dach
  Mĕr'o-dăch, *P.*
Me-rō'dach Băl'a-
Mē'rom   [dän
Me-rŏn'o-thīte
Mē'röz
Mē'ruth
Mē'sech
Mē'sha
Mē'shach
Mē'shech
Me-shĕl-e-mī'ah
Me-shĕz'a-bēel
Me-shĕz'a-bĕl
Me-shĭl'le-mĭth

Me-shĭl'le-mŏth
Me-shō'bab
Me-shŭl'lam
Me-shŭl'le-mĕth
Mĕs'o-ba-īte
  Mĕs-o-bā'īte, *T.*
Mĕs-o-po-tā'mi-a
Mĕs-sī'ah
Mĕs-sī'as
Me-tē'rus
Mē'theg Ăm'mah
Mĕth'o-är
Me-thū'sa-el
Me-thū'se-läh
Me-ū'nim
Mĕz'a-häb
  Me-zā'hab, *P.*
Mī'a-mĭn
Mĭb'har
Mĭb'sam
Mĭb'zar
Mī'cah
Mī-cā'iah (-*yah*)
Mī'cha
Mī'cha-el
Mī'chah
Mī-chā'iah (-*yah*)
Mī'chal
Mī-chē'as
Mĭch'mas
Mĭch'mash
Mĭch'me-thäh
Mĭch'rī
Mĭch'tam
Mĭd'din
Mĭd'i-an
Mĭd'i-an-īte
Mĭd'i-an-ī-tish
Mĭg'da-lĕl
  Mĭg-dā'lel, *P.*
Mĭg'dal Găd
Mĭg'dol
Mĭg'ron
Mĭj'a-mĭn
  Mi-jā'min, *P.*
Mĭk'loth
Mĭk-nē'iah
  Mĭk-nei'ah, *T.*
Mĭl-a-lā'ī
  Mi-lā'la-ī, *P.*
Mĭl'cah
Mĭl'com
Mī-lē'tum
Mī-lē'tus
Mĭl'lō
Mi-nī'a-mĭn
Mĭn'nī
Mĭn'nith
Mĭph'kad
Mĭr'i-am
Mĭr'ma
Mĭs'a-el
Mĭs'gab
Mĭsh'a-el
Mī'sha-el, *P*
Mī-shā'el, *T.*
Mī'shal
Mī'sham
Mī'she-al
Mī-shē'al, *T.*

Mĭsh'ma
Mĭsh-măn'nah
Mĭsh'ra-ītes
Mĭs'par
Mĭs'pe-rĕth
  Mĭs-pē'reth, *T.*
Mĭs're-phŏth-mā'-
Mĭs'sa-bĭb   [im
Mĭth'cah
Mĭth'nīte
Mĭth're-dăth
Mĭth-ri-dā'tēş
Mĭt-y-lē'ne
Mī'zar
Mĭz'pah
Mĭz'peh
Mĭz'ra-ĭm
  Mĭz-rā'im, *T.*
Mĭz'zah
Mnā'son (*nā'son*)
Mō'ab
Mō'ab-īte
Mō'ab-ī-tess
Mō'ab-ī-tish
Mō-a-dī'ah
Mŏch'mur
Mō'din
Mō'eth
Mŏl'a-däh
  Mo-lā'dah, *P.*
Mō'lech
Mō'lī
Mō'lid
Mō'lŏch
Mŏm'dis
Mō-o-sī'as
Mō'ras-thīte
Mör'de-cāi
Mō'reh
Mŏr'esh-ĕth Găth
Mo-rī'ah
Mo-sē'ra
Mo-sē'roth
Mō'şeş
Mo-sŏl'lam
Mo-sŏl'la-mŏn
Mō'za
Mō'zah
Mŭp'pim
Mū'shī
Mū'shītes
Muth-lăb'ben
Mўn'dus
Mȳ'ra
Mў''şi-a

N.

Nā'am
Nā'a-mäh
  Na-ā'mah, *P.*
Nā'a-man
  Na-ā'man, *P*
Nā'a-ma-thīte
  Na-ā'ma-thīte, *P.*
Nā'a-mītes
Nā'a-räh
Nā'a-rai
Nā'a-răn
Nā'a-răth
Na-ăsh'on
Na-ăs'son
Nā'a-thŭs
Nā'bal
Năb-a-rī'as
Năb-a-thē'ans
Nā'bath-ītes
Nā'bŏth
Năb u-cho-dŏn'o-sör
Nā'chön
Nā'chör
Nā'dăb
Na-däb'a-tha
Năg'ğe
Na-hā'li-el
Nā'ha-läl
Na-hăl'lal
Nā'ha-lŏl
Nā'ham
Na-hăm'a-nī
Na-hăr'a-ī
Nā-ha-rā'im
Nā'ha-rī
Nā'häsh
Nā'häth
Năh'bī
Nā'hör
Năh'shon
Nā'hum
Nā'i-dŭs
Nā'in
Nā'ioth (-*yoth*)
Na-nē'a
Nā'o-mī
  Na-ō'mi, *T.*
Nā'phish
Năph'i-sī
Năph'ta-lī
Năph'thar
Năph'tu-hĭm
Nar-cĭs'sus
Năs'bas
Nā'shon
Nā'sith
Nā'sör
Nā'than
Na-thăn'a-el
Năth-a-nī'as
Nā'than Mē'lech
Nā'um
Nā've
Năz-a-rēne'
Năz'a-rĕth
Năz'a-rīte
Nē'ah
Ne-ăp'o-lĭs
Nē-a-rī'ah
Nĕb'a-ī
  Ne-bā'ī, *T.*
Ne-bā'ioth (-*yoth*)
Ne-bā'joth
  Nĕb'a-jŏth, *P.*
Ne-băl'lat
Nē'băt
Nē'bō
Nĕb-u-chad-nĕz'zar
Nĕb-u-chad-rĕz'zar
Nĕb-u-shăs'ban

Nĕb-u-zăr'ạ-dăn
Nĕb-u-zạ-rā'dạn, [P.
Nē'çhō
Ne-cō'dạn
Nĕd-ạ-bī'ạh
Nĕ-e-mī'as
Nĕg̟'j-nŏth
Ne-hĕl'ạ-mīte
Nĕ-he-mī'ạh
Nĕ-he-mī'as
Nĕ'hj-lŏth
Nē'hụm
Ne-hŭsh'tạ
Ne-hŭsh'tạn
Nē'j-ẹl
Nẹ-ī'ẹl, P.
Nē'kẹb
Ne-kŏ'dạ
Nĕk'ọ-dạ, P.
Ne-mū'ẹl
Ne-mū'ẹl-ītes
Nē'phẹg
Nē'phī
Nē'phjs
Nē'phjsh
Ne-phĭsh'ẹ-sĭm
Nĕph'thạ-lī
Nĕph'thạ-lĭm
Nĕph'tọ-äh
Neph-tō'ạh, T.
Ne-phŭ'sjm
Nēr
Nē'reŭs, or
Nē'rẹ-ŭs
Nĕr'gạl
Nĕr'gạl Shạ-rē'zẹr
Nē'rī
Ne-rī'ạh
Ne-rī'as
Nē'rō
Ne-thăn'ẹ-ẹl
Nĕth-ạ-nī'ạh
Nĕth'j-nīmṣ
Ne-tō'phạh
Ne-tŏph'ạ-thī
Ne-tŏph'ạ-thīte
Ne-zī'ạh
Nē'zjb
Nĭb'hăz
Nĭb'shăn
Nĭ-cā'nọr
Nĭc-ọ-dē'mụs
Nĭc-ọ-lā'j-tạnṣ
Nĭc'ọ-las
Nĭ-cŏp'ọ-lĭs
Nī'ger
Nĭm'rạh
Nĭm'rjm
Nĭm'rŏd
Nĭm'shī
Nĭn'ẹ-vẹ
Nĭn'ẹ-vẹh
Nĭn'ẹ-vītes
Nī'sạn
Nĭs'rŏçh
Nō, or Nō Ā'mọn
Nō-ạ-dī'ạh
Nō'ạh, or Nō'ẹ
Nŏb
Nō'bạh

Nŏd
Nō'dăb
Nō'ẹ-bạ
Nō'gạ, or
Nō'gạh
Nō'hạh
Nŏm'ạ-dēṣ
Nŏn
Nŏph (nŏf)
Nō'phạh
Nụ-mē'nj-ŭs
Nŭn
Nўm'phạs

O.

Ŏb-ạ-dī'ạh
Ō-bạ-dī'ạh, T.
Ō'bạl
Ọb-dī'ạ
Ō'bẹd
Ō'bẹd Ē'dọm
Ō'beth
Ō'bjl
Ō'bọth
Ō'çhj-ẹl
Ŏç-j-dē'lụs
Ŏç'j-nạ
Ŏc'rạn
Ō'dẹd
Ọ-dŏl'lạm
Ŏd-ọn-är'kĕṣ
Ŏg
Ō'hạd
Ō'hẹl
Ōl'ạ-mŭs
Ōl'j-vĕt
Ŏl-ọ-fër'nĕṣ
Ọ-lўm'pạs
Ọ-lўm'pj-ŭs
Ŏm-ạ-ē'rụs
Ō'mạr
Ọ-mē'gạ
Ō'mẹ-gạ, O. Sm.
Ŏm'rī
Ŏn
Ō'nạm
Ō'nạn
Ọ-nĕs'j-mŭs
Ŏn-e-sĭph'ọ-rŭs
Ọ-nī'ạ-rēṣ
Ọ-nī'as
Ō'nō
Ō'nụs
Ō'phẹl
Ō'phjr
Ŏph'nī
Ŏph'rạh
Ō'rẹb
Ō'rẹn, or Ō'rạn
Ọ-rī'ọn
Ŏr'nạn
Ŏr'pạh
Ŏr-thọ-sī'as
Ọ-ṣā'iạs (ọ-zā'yạs)
Ọ-ṣē'ạ
Ọ-ṣē'as
Ō'ṣẹe

Ō'shẹ-ạ
Ọ-shē'ạ, O. P.
Ŏth'nī
Ŏth'nj-ẹl
Ŏth-ọ-nī'as
Ŏx
Ō'zẹm
Ọ-zī'as
Ō'zj-ẹl
Ŏz'nī
Ŏz'nītes
Ọ-zō'rạ

P.

Pā'ạ-rāi
Pā-ạ-rā'ī, P.
Pā'dạn
Pā'dạn Ā'rạm
Pā'dọn
Pā'g̟j-ẹl
Pạ-g̟ī'ẹl, O. C.
Pā'hạth Mō'ạb
Pā'ī
Pā'lạl
Păl-ẹs-tī'nạ
Păl'ẹs-tīne
Păl'lụ
Păl'lụ-ītes
Păl'tī
Păl'tj-ẹl
Pạl-tī'ẹl, P. T.
Păl'tīte
Pạm-phўl'j-ạ
Păn'nạg
Pā'phọs
Pär'ạ-dīse
Pā'rạh
Pā'rạn
Pär'bạr
Pạr-mäsh'tạ
Pär'mẹ-năs
Pär'nạch
Pā'rŏsh
Pạr-shăn'dạ-thạ
Pär-shạn-dā'thạ, [P.
Pär'thj-ạnṣ
Pär'ụ-äh
Pạ-rū'ạh, P.
Pạr-vā'jm
Pär'vạ-īm, C.
Pā'sạch
Pạs-dăm'mjm
Pạ-sē'ạh
Păsh'ụr
Pā'shụr, P.
Păt'ạ-rạ
Pạ-thē'ụs
Păth'rọs
Pā'thrọs, P. T.
Pạth-rū'sjm
Păt'mọs
Păt'rọ-băs
Pạ-trŏ'bạs, T.
Pạ-trŏ'clụs
Pā'ụ
Pâul
Pâu'lụs

Pĕd'ạ-hĕl
Pẹ-dā'hẹl, O. P.
Pĕd'ạh-zür
Pẹ-däh'zụr, O. T.
Pẹ-dā'iạh
Pē-dạ-ī'ạh, O. P.
Pē'kạh
Pĕk-ạ-hī'ạh
Pē'kọd
Pĕl-ạ-ī'ạh
Pĕl-ạ-lī'ạh
Pĕl-ạ-tī'ạh
Pē'lẹg
Pē'lẹt
Pē'lẹth
Pē'lẹth-ītes
Pẹ-lī'as
Pĕl'ọ-nīte
Pẹ-nī'ẹl
Pẹ-nĭn'nạh
Pẹn-tăp'ọ-lĭs
Pẹ-nū'ẹl
Pē'ọr
Pĕr'ạ-zĭm
Pẹ-rā'zjm, P.
Pē'rẹsh
Pē'rẹz
Pē'rẹz Ŭz'zạh
Për'gạ
Për'gạ-mŏs
Pẹ-rī'dạ
Pĕr'jz-zītes
Për'mẹ-năs, or
Pär'mẹ-năs
Pẹr-sĕp'ọ-lĭs
Për'seŭs
Për'sj-ạ
Për'sj-ạn
Për'sjs
Pẹ-rŭ'dạ
Pē'tẹr
Pĕth-ạ-hī'ạh
Pē'thör
Pẹ-thū'ẹl
Pẹ-ŭl'thại
Phā'ạth Mō'ạb
Phăc'ạ-rĕth
Phāi'sụr
Phạl-dā'iụs (-yụs)
Phạ-lē'ạs
Phā'lẹc, or
Phā'lẹg
Phăl'lụ
Phăl'tī
Phăl'tj-ẹl
Phạ-nū'ẹl
Phăr'ạ-cĭm
Phā'raōh (fā'rō)
Phā'rạ-ōh, O.
Phā'raōh Hŏph'rạ
Phā'raōh Nē'çhōh
Phăr-ạ-thō'nī
Phā'rēṣ
Phā'rez
Phā'rez-ītes
Phạ-rī'rạ
Phär'j-sēē
Phä'rŏsh
Phär'par
Phär'zītes

Phā'sẹ-ặ
Phạ-sē'ạh, O.
Phạ-sē'ljs
Phăs'j-rŏn
Phäs'sạ-rŏn
Phē'bẹ
Phe-nī'cẹ
Phē'njce, P.
Phẹ-nĭ''cj-ạ
Phĕr'ẹ-sītes
Phĕr'ẹ-zīte
Phĭb'ẹ-sĕth
Phī'çhọl
Phĭl-ạ-dẹl-phī'ạ
Phĭl-ạ-dĕl'phj-ạ
Phj-lär'çhēṣ
Phī-lē'mọn
Phī-lē'tụs
Phĭl'jp
Phj-lĭp'pī
Phj-lĭp'pj-ạnṣ
Phj-lĭs'tj-ạ
Phj-lĭs'tjm
Phj-lĭs'tjne
Phj-lŏl'ọ-gŭs
Phĭl-ọ-mē'tọr
Phĭn'ẹ-ạs
Phĭn'ẹ-ĕs
Phĭn'ẹ-hăs
Phī'sọn
Phlē'gọn
Phō'rọs
Phrўg'j-ạ
Phrўg'j-ạn
Phŭd
Phū'rạh
Phū'rjm
Phŭt
Phū'vạh
Phy-gĕl'lụs
Phў'sọn
Pĭb'ẹ-sĕth, or
Pī-bē'sẹth
Pī-hạ-hī'rọth
Pī'lạte
Pĭl'dăsh
Pĭl'ẹ-hạ
Pj-lē'ṣẹr
Pjl-nē'ṣẹr
Pĭl'tại
Pjl-tā'ī, P.
Pī'nọn
Pī'rạ
Pī'rạm
Pĭr'ạ-thŏn
Pĭr'ạ-thọn-īte
Pĭṣ'gạh
Pī-sĭd'j-ạ
Pī'sọn
Pĭs'pạh
Pī'thọm
Pī'thọn
Plē'iạ-dēṣ
Pleī'ạ-dēṣ, T.
Pŏçh'ẹ-rĕth
Pŏn'tj-ŭs Pī'lạte
(pŏn'shẹ-ŭs)
Pŏn'tụs
Pŏr'ạ-thạ
Pọ-rā'thạ, P.

Pör'ci-ŭs
Pŏs-i-dō'ni-ŭs
Pŏt'i-phar
Po-tīph'e-räh
Pót-i-phē'rah, *T.*
Prĭs'ca
Prĭs-cĭl'la
Prŏch'o-rŭs
Pro-chō'rus, *P.*
Ptŏl-e-mā'is (*tŏl-*)
Ptŏl'e-mēē (*tŏl-*)
Ptŏl-e-mē'us (*tŏl-*)
Pū'a, *or* Pū'ah
Pŭb'li-ŭs
Pū'dens
Pū'hītes
Pŭl
Pū'nītes
Pū'non
Pür, *or* Pū'rim
Pŭt
Pu-tē'o-lī
Pū'ti-el

Q.

Quār'tus [ŭs
Quĭn'tus Mĕm'mi-

R.

Rā'a-mäh
Rāa'mah, *P.*
Rā-a-mī'ah
Ra-ăm'sēş
Răb'bah
Răb'bath
Răb'bī
Răb'bith
Rab-bō'nī
Răb'măg
Răb'sa-cēş
Răb'sa-rĭs
Răb'sha-kĕh
Rā'ca, *or* Rā'cha
Rā'chäb
Rā'chäl
Rā'chel
Răd'da-ī
Rā'gau
Rā'gēş
Ra-gu'el
Rā'häb
Rā'häm
Rā'hel
Rā'kem
Răk'kath
Răk'kon
Răm
Rā'ma, *or* Rā'mah
Rā'math
Rā-math-ā'im
Răm'a-thĕm
Rā'math-īte
Rā'math Lē'hī
Rā'math Mĭz'peh

Ra-mē'sēş
Răm'e-sēş, *T.*
Ra-mī'ah
Rā'moth
Rā'moth Gĭl'e-ad
Rā'pha
Rā'pha-el
Rā'phael, *C.*
Răph'a-ĭm
Rā'pha-ĭm, *O.*
Rā'phon
Rā'phu
Răs'sēş, *or* Răs'sĭs
Răth'u-mus
Rā'zĭs
Rē-a-ī'a, *or* -ah
Re-ā'iah, *T.*
Rē'ba
Re-bĕc'ca
Re-bĕk'ah
Rē'chäb
Rē'chab-ītes 7
Rē'chah
Rē-el-ā'iah
Re-ĕl'i-ŭs
Rēē-sā'ias
Rē'ġem
Re-ġĕm'me-lĕch
Re-ha-bī'ah
Rē'hob
Rē-ho-bō'am
Re-hŏb'o-am, *O.*
Re-hō'both
Rē'ho-bŏth, *T.*
Rē'hu, *or* Rē'u
Rē'hum
Rē'ī
Rē'kem
Rĕm-a-lī'ah
Rē'meth
Rĕm'mon [är
Rĕm'mon Mĕth'o-
　Me-thō'ar, *T*
Rĕm'phan
Rē'pha-el
Rē'phah
Rĕph-a-ī'ah
Re-phā'iah, *T.*
Rĕph'a-ĭm
Re-phā'im, *T.*
Rĕph'a-ĭms
Rĕph'i-dĭm
Re-phĭd'im, *T.*
Rē'sen
Rē'sheph
Rē'u
Reŭ'ben
Reŭ'ben-ītes
Re-ū'el
Reŭ'el, *P.*
Reŭ'mah
Rē'zeph
Re-zī'a
Rē'zin
Rē'zon
Rhē'ġi-ŭm
Rhē'sa
Rhō'da
Rhōdeş
Rhŏd'o-cŭs

Rhō'dus
Rī'bai
Rĭb'lah
Rĭm'mon
Rĭm'mon Pā'rez
Rĭn'nah
Rī'phăth
Rĭs'sah
Rĭth'mah
Rĭz'pah
Rŏb'o-am
Ro-bō'am, *P.*
Ro-ġē'lim
Rōh'gah
Rō'i-mŭs
Ro-măm-ti-ē'zer
Rō'man
Rōme
Rŏsh
Rŭ'fus
Rŭ'ha-mäh
Ru-hā'mah, *O.*
Rŭ'mah
Rŭth

S.

Sā-bach-thā'nī
Săb'a-ŏth
Sa-bā'oth, *Sm.*
Sā'bat
Săb-a-tē'us, *or* -as
Săb'a-tŭs
Săb'ban
Săb-ba-thē'us
Sab-bē'us
Săb'dī, *or* Zăb'dī
Sa-bē'ans
Sā'bī, *or* Sā'bi-ē
Săb'ta, *or* Săb'tah
Săb'te-cha
Săb'te-chäh
Sā'car
Săd-a-mī'as
Sā'das
Sad-dē'us
Săd'duc
Săd'du-cēēş
Sā'dŏc
Sā-ha-dū'tha
Sā'la
Sā'lah
Săl'a-mĭs
Săl-a-săd'a-ī
Sa-lā'thi-el
Săl'cah, *or*
　Săl'chah
Sā'lem
Sā'lim
Săl'la-ī
Săl'lu
Săl'lum, *or*
　Shăl'lum
Sal-lū'mus
Săl'ma, *or*
　Săl'mah
Săl-man-ā'sar
Săl'mon

Săl-mō'ne
Sā'lom
Sa-lō'me
Sā'lu
Sā'lum
Săm'a-el
Sa-mā'ias (-*yas*)
Sa-mā'ri-a
Sa-măr'i-tan
Săm'a-tŭs
Sa-mē'ius
Săm'gar Nē'bō
Sā'mī
Sā'mis
Săm'lah
Săm'mus
Sā'mos
Săm-o-thrā'ci-a
Sămp'sa-mēş
Săm'son
Săm'u-el
Săn-a-băs'sar
Săn-a-băs'sa-rŭs
Săn'a-sĭb
Sañ-băl'lat
San-săn'nah
Săph
Sā'phat
Săph-a-tī'as
Sā'pheth
Săph'ir [ra)
Sap-phī'ra (*saf-fī'-*
Sā'ra, *or* Sā'rai
Săr-a-bī'as
Sā'rah
Săr-a-ī'a, *or* -ah
Sa-rā'ias (-*yas*)
Săr'a-mĕl
Sā'raph
Sar-chĕd'o-nŭs
Sar-dē'us
Săr'dis
Săr'dītes
Sā're-a
Sa-rĕp'ta
Săr'gon
Sā'rid
Sā'ron
Sa-rō'thī, *or* -thie
Sar-sē'chim
　Săr'se-chĭm, *P.*
Sā'ruch
Sā'tan
Săth-ra-bu-zā'nēş
Sâul
Săv'a-răn
Sā'vi-ăs
　Sa-vī'as, *O.*
Scē'va (*sē'va*)
Scyth'i-an
Scy-thŏp'o-lĭs
Scyth-o-pŏl'i-tanş
Sē'ba
Sē'băt
Sĕc'a-cäh
　Se-cā'cah, *T.*
Sĕch-e-nī'as
Sē'chu
Se-cŭn'dus
Sĕd-e-cī'as

Sē'gub
Sē'ir
Sē'i-räth
　Se-ī'rath, *P.*
Sē'la
Sē'lah
Sē'la Hăm'mah-
　lē'koth
Sē'led
Sĕl-e-mī'a, *or*
　Sĕl-e-mī'as
Sĕl-eu-cī'a
Se-leū'ci-a
Se-leū'cus
Sĕm
Sĕm-a-chī'ah
Sĕm-a-ī'ah
Sĕm'e-ī
Se-mĕl'li-ŭs
Sĕn'a-äh
　Se-nä'ah, *T.*
Sē'neh
Sē'nir
Sĕn-na-chē'rib
　Sen-näch'e-rib,
　P. T. Sm.
Sĕn'u-äh
　Se-nū'ah, *P.*
Se-ō'rim
Sē'phar
Sĕph'a-räd
Sĕph-ar-vā'im
Sē'phar-vītes
Se-phē'la
Sē'rah
Sĕr-a-ī'ah
Sē'red
Sĕr'ġi-ŭs
Sē'ron
Sē'rug
Sē'sis
Sĕs'thel
Sĕth
Sē'thur
Shā-al-ăb'bin
Sha-ăl'bim
Sha-ăl'bo-nīte
Shā'aph
Shā-a-rā'im
Sha-äsh'gäz
Shab-bĕth'a-ī
Shăch'i-a
　Sha-chī'a, *T.*
Shăd'da-ī
Shā'drach
Shā'ġe
Shā-ha-rā'im
Sha-hăz'i-măth
Shā'lem
Shā'lim
Shăl'i-sha
Shăl'le-chĕth
Shăl'lum
Shăl'lun
Shăl'ma-ī
　Shăl'mai, *T.*
Shăl'man
Shăl-ma-nē'şer
Shā'ma
Shăm-a-rī'ah

Shā'med
Shā'mer
Shăm'gar
Shăm'huth
Shā'mir
Shăm'ma
Shăm'mah
Shăm'ma-ī
Shăm'moth
Sham-mū'a, *or*
  Sham-mū'ah
Shăm-she-rā'ī
Shā'pham
Shā'phan
Shā'phat
Shā'pher
Shăr'a-ī
  Sha-rā'ī, *P. T.*
Shăr'a-ĭm
  Sha-rā'ĭm, *T.*
Shā'rar
Sha-rē'zer
Shå'ron
Shå'ron-īte
Sha-rū'hen
  Shăr'u-hĕn, *P.*
Shăsh'a-ī
Shā'shăk
Shā'ul
Shā'ul-ītes
Shā'veh
Shăv'sha
Shē'al
She-ăl'tĭ-el
Shē-a-rī'ah
Shē ar-jā'shub
Shē'ba, *or*
  Shē'bah
Shē'bam
Shĕb-a-nī'ah
Shĕb'a-rĭm
Shē'ber
Shĕb'na
Shĕb'u-el
Shĕch-a-nī'ah
Shē'chem
Shē'chem-ītes
Shĕd'e-ür
Shē-ha-rī'ah
Shē'lah
Shē'lan-ītes
Shĕl-e-mī'ah
Shē'leph
Shē'lesh
Shĕl'o-mī
  She-lō'mī, *T.*
Shĕl'o-mĭth
Shĕl'o-mŏth
She-lū'mj-el

Shĕm
Shē'ma
Shĕm'a-äh
Shĕm-a-ī'ah
Shĕm-a-rī'ah
Shĕm'e-ber
  She-mē'ber, *T.*
Shē'mer
She-mī'da
She-mī'da-ītes
Shĕm'i-nĭth
She-mĭr'a-mŏth
She-mū'el
Shĕn
She-nā'zar
Shē'nir
Shē'pham
Shĕph-a-tī'ah
Shē'phī
Shē'phō
She-phū'phan
Shē'rah
Shĕr-e-bī'ah
Shē'resh
She-rē'zer
Shē'shăch
Shē'shai
Shē'shan
Shesh-băz'zar
Shĕth
Shē'thar
Shē'thar Bŏz'na-ī
Shē'va
Shĭb'bo-lĕth
Shĭb'mah
Shī'cron
Shĭg-gā'ion (-yon)
Shĭ-gī'o-nŏth
Shī'hon
Shī'hör
Shī'hör Lĭb'nath
Shĭl'hī
Shĭl'hĭm
Shĭl'lem
Shĭl'lem-ītes
Shĭ-lō'ah
Shī'lōh, *or* Shī'lō
Shĭ-lō'nī
Shĭ-lō'nīte
Shĭl'shah
Shĭm'e-a
Shĭm'e-äh
Shĭm'e-ăm
Shĭm'e-ăth
Shĭm'e-ăth-ītes
Shĭm'e-ī
Shĭm'e-on
Shĭm'hī
Shī'mī

Shĭm'ītes
Shĭm'ma
Shī'mon
Shĭm'rath
Shĭm'rī
Shĭm'rith
Shĭm'ron, *or*
  Shĭm'rom
Shĭm'ron-ītes
Shĭm'ron Mē'ron
Shĭm'shai
  Shĭm'sha-ī, *P.*
Shī'năb
Shī'nar
Shī'on
Shī'phī
Shĭph'mīte
Shĭph'rah
Shĭph'tan
Shī'sha
Shī'shăk
Shĭt'ra-ī
  Shi-trā'ī, *P.*
Shĭt'tah
Shĭt'tim
Shī'za
Shō'a, *or* Shō'ah
Shō'băb
Shō'băch
Shō'ba-ī
  Sho-bā'ī, *P. T.*
Shō'bal
Shō'bek
Shō'bī
Shō'chō, *or*
  Shō'chōh
Shō'cō
Shō'ham
Shō'mer
Shō'phăch
Shō'phan
Sho-shăn'nim
Sho-shăn'nim
  Ē'duth
Shū'a
Shū'ah
Shū'al
Shū'ba-el
  Shu-bā'el, *P.*
Shū'ham
Shū'ham-ītes
Shū'hīte
Shū'lam-īte
Shū'math-ītes
Shū'nam-īte
Shū'nem
Shū'nī
Shū'nītes
Shū'pham

Shū'pham īte
Shŭp'pim
Shür
Shū'shan
Shū'shan Ē'duth
Shū'thal-hītes
Shū'the-läh
Sī'a
Sī'a-ha
Sī'ba, *or* Sē'ba
Sĭb'be-chāi
  Sĭb-be-chā'ī, *P.*
Sĭb'bo-lĕth
Sĭb'mah
Sĭb'ra-ĭm
  Sib-rā'ĭm, *T.*
Sī'chem
Sī''cy-on (-she-)
Sĭd'dim
Sī'de
Sī'don
Sī-dō'nj-an
Sj-gī'o-nŏth
Sī'hon
Sī'hör
Sī'las
Sĭl'la
Sj-lō'ah,* *O. P.*
  Sĭl'o-äh, *C. T. W.*
Sj-lō'am,* *O. P.*
  Sĭl'o-ăm, *C. W.*
Sj-lō'e,* *O.*
  Sĭl'o-ē, *C. Sm. W.*
Sjl-vā'nus
Sī-mal-cū'e
Sĭm'e-on
Sĭm'e-on-ītes
Sī'mon
Sĭm'rī
Sĭn
Sī'na
Sī'nai
  Sī'na-ī, *P.*
Sī'nim
Sĭn'īte
Sī'on
Sĭph'mŏth
Sĭp'pai
  Sĭp'pa-ī, *P.*
Sī'rach
Sī'rah
Sĭr'i-on
Sj-săm'a-ī
Sĭs'e-ra
Sj-sĭn'nĕs
Sĭt'nah
Sī'van
Smÿr'na
Sō

Sō'chō, *or*
  Sō'chōh
Sō'cōh
Sō'dī
Sŏd'om
Sŏd'o-ma
Sŏd'om-ītes
Sŏd-o-mī'tjsh
Sŏl'o-mon
Sŏp'a-ter
Sŏph'e-rĕth
  So-phē'reth, *T.*
Sŏph-o-nī'as
Sō'rek
So-sĭp'a-ter
Sŏs'the-nĕs
Sŏs'tra-tŭs
Sō'ta-ī
Spāin
Spär'ta
Stā'chys (*stā'kĭs*)
Stĕph'a-năs
Stē'phen (*stē'vn*)
Stō'ĭcs
Sū'ah
Sū'ba
Sū'ba-ī
Sū'chath-ītes
Sŭc'coth
Sŭc'coth Bē'noth
Sŭd
Sū'di-ăs
Sŭk'kj-īms
Sür
Sū'sa
Sū'san-chītes
Su-săn'na
Sū'sī
Sÿ'char
Sÿ'chem
Sÿ'chem-īte
Sÿ-ē'lus
Sÿ-ē'ne
Sÿn'ty-chē
Sÿr'a-cūse
Sÿr'i-a
Sÿr'i-ăc
Sÿr'i-an
Sÿr'i-ŏn
Sÿ-ro-phe-nĭ''cj-an

T.

Tā'a-năch
  Ta-ā'nach, *T.*
Tā'a-näth Shī'lōh
Tăb'a-ŏth

---

* *Silo'ah, Silo'am, Silo'e.* — Walker, in his note on the name *Siloa*, admits that " this word, according to the present general rule of pronouncing these words, ought to have the accent on the second syllable, as it is Græcized by Σιλωά ;" but he defers to the authority of Milton, who accents it on the antepenultima. But *Shiloah*, which is merely a variation of the same word, is accented by Walker and all the other orthoepists on the second syllable, in accordance with its accent in Hebrew, and the analogy of *Manoah, Tekoah, Zanoah.* The more common form *Siloam* is Σιλωάμ in the Greek of the New Testament and of Josephus. Such being the case, the fact that Milton in a single passage (*Par. Lost*, i. 11) accents *Siloa* on the first syllable does not seem to justify us in deserting a general rule. If the usage of the poets is appealed to, the familiar hymn of Bishop Heber may be cited : " By cool *Silo'am's* shady rill," &c.

Tăb′ba-ŏth
Tăb′bath
Tā′be-al
Ta-bē′al, T.
Tā′be-el
Ta-bĕl′li-ŭs
Tăb′e-räh
Ta-bē′rah, T.
Tăb′i-tha
Tā′bŏr
Tăb′ri-mŏn
Tăch′mo-nīte
Tăd′mŏr
Tā′hän
Tā′han-ītes
Ta-hăp′a-nēṣ
Tā′hăth
Tăh′pan-hēṣ
Tăh′pe-nēṣ
Tăh′re-a
Tăh′tim Hŏd′shī
Tăl′i-tha Cū′mī
Tăl′mai
Tal-mā′ī, P.
Tăl′mon
Tăl′sas
Tā′mah
Tā′mar
Tăm′muz
Tā′nach
Tăn′hu-mĕth
Tan-hū′meth, T.
Tā′nis
Tā′phath
Tăph′nēṣ
Tā′phon
Tăp′pu-äh
Tā′rah
Tăr′a-läh
Tā′re-a
Tăr′pel-ītes
Tăr′shis
Tăr′shish
Tăr′sus
Tăr′tăk
Tär′tan
Tăt′na-ī
Tăt′nai, T.
Tē′bah
Tĕb-a-lī′ah
Tē′beth
Te-hăph′ne-hēṣ
Te-hĭn′nah
Tē′kel
Te-kō′a, or
Te-kō′ah
Te-kō′ite
Tĕl′a-bĭb
Te-lā′bĭb, O.
Tē′lah

Tĕl′a-ĭm
Te-lā′ĭm, T
Te-lăs′sar
Tē′lem
Tĕl-ha-rē′sha
Tel-här′sa
Tĕl′me-la
Tĕl′me-läh
Tel-mē′lah, T.
Tē′ma
Tē′man
Tĕm′a-nī
Tē′ma-nī, Sm.
Tĕm′an-īte, P.
Tĕm′e-nī
Tē′me-nī, Sm.
Tē′rah
Tĕr′a-phĭm
Tē′resh
Tĕr′ti-ŭs
Ter-tŭl′lus
Tē′ta
Thad-dē′us *
Thā′hash
Thā′mah
Thā′mar
Thăm′na-tha
Thā′ra
Thär′ra
Thär′shish
Thär′sus
Thăs′sī
Thē′bez
The-cō′e
The-lā′sar
The-lēr′sas
Thē′man
The-ŏc′a-nŭs
The-ŏd′o-tŭs
The-ŏph′i-lŭs
Thē′ras
Thĕr′me-lĕth
Thĕs-sa-lō′ni-ans
Thĕs-sa-lo-nī′ca
Theū′das
Thĭm′na-thäh
Thĭs′be
Thŏm′as (tŏm′as)
Thŏm′o-ī
Thrā′ci-a
Thra-sē′as
Thŭm′mim
Thy̆-a-tī′ra
Ti-bē′ri-as
Ti-bē′ri-ŭs
Tĭb′hath
Tĭb′nī
Tī′dal
Tĭg′lath Pi-lē′ser

Tī′gris
Tĭk′vah
Tĭk′vath
Tĭl′gath Pĭl-nē′ṣer
Tī′lon
Ti-mæ′us, or
Tī-mē′us
Tĭm′na
Tĭm′nah
Tĭm′nath
Tĭm′na-thäh
Tĭm′nath Hē′rēṣ
Tĭm′nath Sē′rah
Tĭm′nīte
Tī′mon
Ti-mō′the-ŭs
Tĭm′o-thy
Tĭph′sah
Tī′ras
Tī′rath-ītes
Tĭr′ha-käh
Tir-hā′kah, T
Tĭr′ha-näh
Tir-hā′nah, T.
Tĭr′i-a
Tĭr′sha-tha
Tĭr′zah
Tĭsh′bīte
Tī′tans
Tī′tus
Tī′zīte
Tō′ah
Tŏb
Tŏb-Ăd-o-nī′jah
To-bī′ah
To-bī′as
Tō′bie
Tō′bi-el
To-bī′jah
Tō′bit
Tō′chen
To-gär′mah
Tō′hu
Tō′ī
Tō′la
Tō′lad
Tō′la-ītes
Tŏl′ba-nēṣ
Tō′phel
Tō′phet, or
Tō′pheth
Tō′ū
Trăch-o-nī′tis
Trĭp′o-lĭs
Trō′as
Tro-gy̆l′li-ŭm
Trŏph′i-mŭs
Try̆-phē′na
Try̆′phon
Try̆-phō′sa

Tū′bal
Tū′bal Cā′in
Tū′bal Cāin, P.
Tū-bi-ē′nī
Ty̆ch′i-cŭs
Ty̆-răn′nŭs
Ty̆re
Ty̆r′i-anṣ
Ty̆′rŭs

U.

Ū′cal
Ū′el
Ū′la-ī,
U-lā′ī, P.
Ū′lam
Ŭl′la
Ŭm′mah
Ŭn′nī
Ū-phär′sin
Ū′phăz
Ŭr
Ŭr′bāne, properly
Ŭr′ban †
Ŭr′ba-ne, Sm. W.
Ur-bā′ne, O. P.
Ū′rī
U-rī′ah
U-rī′as
Ū′ri-el
U-rī′el, P.
U-rī′jah
Ū′rim
Ū′ta
Ū′tha-ī
Ū′thī
Ŭz
Ū′za-ī
Ū′zal
Ŭz′za
Ŭz′zah
Ŭz′zen Shē′rah
Ŭz′zī
Uz-zī′a
Uz-zī′ah
Uz-zī′el
Uz-zī′el-ītes

V.

Va-jĕz′a-tha
Va-nī′ah
Väsh′nī
Väsh′tī
Vŏph′sī

X.

Xăn′thi-cŭs

Z.

Zā-a-nā′ĭm
Zā′a-năn
Zā-a-năn′nĭm
Zā′a-văn
Zā′băd
Zăb-a-dæ′anṣ, or
Zăb-a-dē′anṣ
Zăb-a-dā′ias (-yạs)
Zăb′bai
Zăb′bud
Zab-dē′us
Zăb′dī
Zăb′di-el
Zā′bud
Zăb′u-lon
Zăc′ca-ī
Zac-chæ′us, or
Zac-chē′us
Zăc′cur
Zăch-a-rī′ah, or
Zăch-a-rī′as
Zăch′a-ry
Zā′cher
Zā′dok
Zā′häm
Zā′ir
Zā′laph
Zăl′mon
Zal-mō′nah
Zal-mŭn′na
Zăm′bis
Zăm′brī
Zā′moth
Zam-zŭm′mims
Za-nō′ah
Zăph′nath-pā-a-
Zā′phon   [nē′ah
Zā′ra
Zär′a-cēṣ
Zā′rah
Zär-a-ī′as
Zā′re-äh
Za-rē′ah, P. T.
Zā′re-ath-ītes
Zā′red
Zär′e-phăth
Zär′e-tăn
Zā′reth Shā′har
Zär′hītes
Zär′ta-näh
Zar-tā′nah, T.

---

* *Thadde′us.* — All the orthoepists agree in accenting this word on the penultimate; but when it is used as a Christian name, the accent, in this country at least, is usually placed on the first syllable.

† *Urban.* — "So it ought to be printed in our modern Bibles, not 'Urbane,' which is now deceptive, though it was not so according to the orthography of 1611; it suggests a trisyllable, and the termination of a female name. It is Οὐρβανόν in the original." (Rom. xvi. 9.) — TRENCH, *On the Authorized Version*, &c., p. 60, note, Amer. edition.

The word is spelt *Urban* in the translations of Wickliffe, Tyndale, and Cranmer. The Genevan version and the Roman Catholic translation retain the Latin form, *Urbanus*.

32

Zär'thạn
Zăth'ọ-ē
Zăth'thū
Zạ-thū'ī
Zăt'tū
Zā'vạn
Zā'zạ
Zĕb-ạ-dī'ạh
Zĕ'bạh
Zẹ-bā'ịm
Zĕb'ẹ-dēe
Zẹ-bī'nạ
Zẹ-bō'ịm
Zẹ-böï'ịm
Zẹ-bū'dạh
  Zĕb'ụ-däh, *P.*
Zĕ'bụl
Zĕb'ụ-lọn-īte
Zĕb'ụ-lŭn
Zĕb'ụ-lụn-īte
Zĕch-ạ-rī'ạh
Zĕ'dăd
Zĕd-ẹ-chī'ạs
Zĕd-ẹ-kī'ạh
Zēĕb
  Zē'ẹb, *Sm. T.*

Zē'lạh
Zē'lẹk
Zẹ-lō'phẹ-hăd
Zẹ-lō'tĕṣ
Zĕl'zạh
Zĕm-ạ-rā'ịm
Zĕm'ạ-rīte
Zẹ-mī'rạ
Zē'nạn
Zē'nạs
Zĕph-ạ-nī'ạh
Zē'phạth
Zĕph'ạ-thäh
  Zẹ-phā'thạh, *P.*
Zē'phī, *or*
  Zē'phō
Zē'phọn
Zĕph'ọn-ītes
Zĕr
Zē'rạh
Zĕr-ạ-hī'ạh
Zĕr-ạ-ī'ạh
Zē'rĕd
  Zẹ-rē'dạ, *P.*
Zẹ-rĕd'ạ-thäh

Zĕr'ẹ-răth
  Zẹ-rē'rạth, *T.*
Zē'rĕsh
Zē'rẹth
Zē'rī
Zē'rör
Zẹ-rŭ'ạh
Zẹ-rŭb'bạ-bĕl
Zĕr-ụ-ī'ạh
Zē'thạm
Zē'thạn
Zē'thạr
Zī'ạ
Zī'bạ
Zīb'ẹ-ọn
Zīb'ị-ạ
Zīb'ị-äh
  Zị-bī'ạh, *T.*
Zīch'rī (*zĭk'rī*)
Zīd'dịm
Zịd-kī'jạh
Zī'dọn, *or* Sī'dọn
Zī-dō'nị-ạnṣ
Zīf
Zī'hạ
Zīk'lăg

Zīl'lạh
Zīl'pạh
Zīl'thại
Zīm'mạh
Zīm'răm, *or*
  Zīm'răn
Zīm'rī
Zīn
Zī'nạ
Zī'ọn, *or*
  Sī'ọn
Zī'ọr
Zīph
Zī'phạh
Zīph'ịmṣ
Zīph'ị-ọn
Zīph'ītes
Zī'phrọn
  Zīph'rọn, *T.*
Zīp'pör
Zịp-pō'rạh
  Zīp'pọ-răh, *P.*
Zīth'rī
Zīz
Zī'zạ
Zī'zạh

Zō'ạn
Zō'ạr
Zō'bạ, *or*
  Zō'bạh
Zọ-bē'bạh
Zō'hạr
Zō'hẹ-lĕth
  Zọ-hē'lẹth, *P.*
Zō'hĕth
Zō'phạh
Zō'phại
Zō'phạr
Zō'phịm
Zō'rạh
Zō'rạth-ītes
Zō'rẹ-äh
  Zọ-rē'ạh, *T.*
Zō'rītes
Zọ-rŏb'ạ-bĕl
Zū'ạr
Zŭph
Zūr
Zū'rị-ẹl
  Zụ-rī'ẹl, *P.*
Zū-rị-shăd'dạ-ī
Zū'zịmṣ

PRONUNCIATION

OF

MODERN GEOGRAPHICAL NAMES.

REMARKS.

THE pronunciation of geographical names is a very difficult branch of orthoepy. These names pertain to all parts of the globe; their vernacular or native pronunciation is regulated or affected by every variety of language; and it would be impossible to represent, in all cases, the native pronunciation by any combination of English letters.

There are a great many names, respecting the pronunciation of which it is difficult to determine how far the English analogy should be allowed to prevail over the analogy of the languages to which the words respectively belong. If we look for authorities for the pronunciation of these names, we find comparatively few; and most of such authorities as exist embrace but a small part of the words of this class; and there is also much disagreement among orthoepists with respect to the pronunciation of such of these names as they undertake to pronounce.

With regard to the geographical names which pertain to all the countries in which the English language is spoken, including the British empire in Europe, the United States, and the British provinces generally, their pronunciation is, of course, conformed, for the most part, to the analogy of the English language. In addition to these, all the geographical names which belong to other parts of the globe, but which have become Anglicized by having changed their native form and assumed an English orthography, are also conformed to the general principles of English pronunciation. The most common geographical names, such as those which relate to the great divisions of the globe, the names of the countries, kingdoms, states, principal cities, &c., are differently written, as well as differently pronounced, in different languages.

All the common geographical names, such as are familiar to all intelligent persons, have be-

(375)

come more or less Anglicized, and their pronunciation is more or less conformed to the English analogy. Many of these words may be considered as perfectly Anglicized, and they are accordingly pronounced as common English words; but there are many that are only partially Anglicized, and with regard to such it is often difficult to determine how far, in pronouncing them, the English analogy should be allowed to prevail over that of the language to which the words properly belong.

Some foreign geographical names are introduced into the English language without changing their orthography; but their pronunciation is, nevertheless, conformed to the English analogy. The word *Paris*, for example, an Englishman or an Anglo-American, in speaking his own language, would pronounce, in conformity to it, *Par'is*; though, if he were speaking French, he would pronounce it *pä're*, in conformity with the French language.

With respect to the class of words which are partially Anglicized, there is a great diversity in the manner of pronouncing them. Some respectable speakers incline to pronounce them, for the most part, according to the English analogy, while others aspire to pronounce them as they are pronounced in the several languages to which they appertain; and there are many cases in which it is difficult to determine which is to be the more approved, the English or the foreign method. A person conversant with foreign languages will be likely to pronounce such words in the foreign manner; while a mere English scholar may be naturally expected, and may be permitted, to incline more strongly to the English mode. It may be often desirable to know what the native mode of pronouncing such words is, though it may not be advisable, in common use, to adopt it.

PRONUNCIATION OF SEVERAL EUROPEAN LANGUAGES.

The following rules, respecting the pronunciation of certain letters in the principal modern languages of Continental Europe, may be of some use in relation to the pronunciation of names pertaining to the several countries where these languages are spoken, and which are not included in the present Vocabulary. Yet it may be advisable for a mere English scholar to make but a partial application of them in practice.

VOWELS.

A. — The vowel *a*, in situations in which the analogy of the English language would naturally give it the sound of long *a*, has, in most of the languages of the Continent of Europe, what is called the *Italian* sound, that is, the sound of *a* in *far* and *farther*. In other situations, its sound approaches nearly to its short English sound, as in *man, fat*.

E. — In these languages, the sound of the vowel *e*, at the end of an accented syllable, is generally the same as that of the English long *a* in *fate, name*. In other situations, it has the sound of the English short *e*, as in *met, men*, or of *e* in *there, where*.

I. — The long sound of *i*, in these languages, is the same as in the English word *marine*, being the same as the English long sound of *e* in *mete, seen*. The short sound is the same as its English short sound, as in *pin*.

O. — The vowel *o* has the same sounds that it has in English in the words *note, not*, and *nor*.

U. — The vowel *u*, in most of these languages, has the same sound that it has in English in the word *rule*, being the same as *oo* in *fool, moon*, and, when short, it has the sound of *u* in *bull*, or of *oo* in *good*. The sound of *u* in the French language, and also in the Dutch, has no equivalent sound in English; and it can be learned only by oral instruction. It may be regarded as intermediate between the sound of long *e* and *oo*, partaking of both.

Y. — The vowel *y* has, in most of these languages, the same sound as *i*, that is, of long *e*, as in *me*; but in the Dutch language (in which it is now written *ij*), it has the sound of the English long *i*, as in *pine*. In Danish and Swedish, it is like the French and Dutch *u*.

DIPHTHONGS.

AE or *Ä*. — The sound of the diphthong *ae*, in Dutch, is like the English sound of *a* in *far*; in German, the sound of *ae* or *ä* is like that of the English long *a*, as in *fate*.

AI. — The sound of the diphthong *ai*, in French, is like that of the English long *a*, as in *fate*; in the other languages, like that of the English long *i*, as in *pine*.

AU and *EAU*. — The diphthong *au*, and the triphthong *eau*, in French, have the sound of the English long *o*, as in *note ;* as *Chaumont* (shō-mōng'), *Beauvais* (bō-vā'). In German, Dutch, Danish, Italian, Spanish, and Portuguese, the diphthong *au* has nearly the English sound of *ow* in *now* ; as, *Austerlitz* (ôûs'ter-lĭts). The German diphthong *äu*, or *aeu*, has a sound like that of the English diphthong *oi* in *toil* ; as, *Stäudlin* (stöĭt'lĭn).

EI and *EY*. — The diphthong *ei*, in French, sounds like the English long *a* in *fate*. In German, the diphthongs *ei* and *ey* have a sound similar to the English sound of long *i*, as in *pine* ; as, *Heĭ'del-berg*.

EU. — The French diphthong *eu* has a sound similar to the English sound of *e* in *her*, or *u* in *fur*. The German diphthong *eu* has a sound similar to that of the English diphthong *oi* in *toil* ; as, *Neustadt* (nöĭ'stät).

IE. — The diphthong *ie*, in French, German, Dutch, &c., has the sound of the English long *e*, as in *mete* ; as, *Wiē'land*.

OE or *Ö*. — The sound of the German, Danish, and Swedish diphthong *oe* or *ö* resembles that of the French *eu*. It has no equivalent sound in English, and is not easily explained. It may be conceived as intermediate between the long English sounds of *a* and *o*, and resulting from an attempt to utter them simultaneously. It may be approximately represented in English by *ĕh*, as in the name of Goethe or Göthe (pronounced g̃ĕh'tā).

OO. — The diphthong *oo*, in German, Dutch, and Danish, has the sound of *oo* in the English word *door*, or of *o* in *note*.

OU. — The French diphthong *ou* has the sound of the English *oo* in *tool* ; as, *Toulouse'* (tô-lôz'.)

UE or *Ü*. The sound of the German, Dutch, and Danish diphthong *ue* or *ü*, is like that of the French *u*.

CONSONANTS.

The sounds of most of the consonants, in the Continental languages, are the same as in English. Some of the principal exceptions are the following : —

B. — The sound of *b*, in German, at the end of a syllable, is like that of the English *p* ; — in Spanish, between two vowels, similar to *v*.

C. — The sound of *c*, in German, before *e*, *i*, and *y*, is like that of *ts* in English ; — in Italian, before *e* and *i*, like that of *ch* in the English word *chill* ; in Spanish, before *e* and *i*, like that of *th* in *thin*.

D. — The sound of *d*, in German and Dutch, at the end of a syllable, is like that of *t* in English ; — in Danish and Spanish, between two vowels or at the end of a syllable, like that of *th* in *this*.

G. — The sound of *g* in French, before *e*, *i*, and *y*, is like that of *zh* in English, or of *s* in *pleasure* ; — in Spanish, before *e* and *i*, the same as the Spanish *j* ; — in Italian, before *e* and *i*, like that of *g* in the English word *gem*, or *j* in *jet* ; — in Dutch, its sound is that of a strongly aspirated *h* ; — in German, at the beginning of words, it is hard, like *g* in *get* ; at the end of a syllable, or between vowels, it has a peculiar sound intermediate between those of consonant *y* and of *g* in *get* ; following *n*, it combines with it in a nasal sound, as in English, — and in words ending in *ngen*, it is thrown back on the penultimate syllable ; as, *Hech'ing-en*.

H. — This letter is mute in French, Spanish, and Italian ; — in Portuguese, when it follows *l* or *n*, it takes the sound of consonant *y*, or serves as a sign that the *l* has a liquid sound ; as, *Minho* (mēn'yō).

J. — The sound of *j*, in French and Portuguese, is like that of *zh* in English ; — in Spanish, it is like that of *h* strongly aspirated ; — in Italian, and also in Hungarian when not preceded by *d*, *g*, or *t*, it is like the long English *e* in *me* ; — in the remaining languages, it is like that of consonant *y*.

M. — This letter, in French, when preceded by a vowel, and followed by any other consonant except *m*, serves to mark the vowel as nasal. It is represented, in English, by *ng*.

N. — The letter *n*, in French, when preceded by a vowel, and followed by any other conso-

nant except *n*, also serves as a sign that the preceding vowel is nasal : — in Spanish, *ñ* has a liquid sound, like that of *n* in the English word *name*, blended with the sound of consonant *y*.

V. — The sound of *v*, in German, is the same as that of *f* in English.

W. — The sound of *w*, in the German and Dutch languages, is similar to that of *v* in English.

X. — The sound of *x*, in Spanish, is like that of *h* strongly aspirated, being the same as that of the Spanish *j*, and also of *g* before *e* and *i* ; — in Portuguese, it is like *sh* in the English word *shall*.

Z. — The sound of *z* in German, and most generally in Italian, is like that of *ts* in English ; — in Spanish, like *th* in the English word *thin* ; — *zz* in Italian, like *ts*.

DIGRAPHS.

CH. — The sound of the digraph *ch*, in French and Portuguese, is the same as the English *sh*, or of *ch* in *chaise* ; — in Spanish, the same as *ch* in the English word *chill* ; — in Italian (as in words from the ancient languages, Hebrew, Greek, and Latin), like that of *k*. — In German and Dutch, it has a hard, guttural sound, not easily represented in English, but resembling that of *h* strongly aspirated. It is represented in this Vocabulary, as it is in others, by the letter *k*.

GL. — This digraph, in Italian, blends the sounds of *l* and consonant *y*.

GN. — This digraph, in French and Italian, sounds like the Spanish *ñ*, or like the letters *ni* in the English word *onion*.

LL. — The sound of *ll*, in Spanish, is like that of *gl* in Italian, or that of the letters *lli* in the English word *million*.

SC. — This digraph, in Italian, before *e* and *i*, is sounded like *sh* in the English word *shell*.

SCH. — The sound of *sch*, in German, is the same as that of *sh* in the English word *shell* ; — in Italian, before *e* and *i*, and also in Dutch, like that of *sk* in the English word *skill*.

TH. — The digraph *th*, in these languages, has the sound of *t* ; as, *Theis* (tīs).

32*

MODERN GEOGRAPHICAL NAMES.

Aä'chen (ä'ken)
Aâl'börg (âl'börg)
Aär (är)
Aär'gau (är'göû)
Aâr'hûus
Aäth (ät)
Ăb'a-cō
Ăb-a-kăn'
Ăb-a-kănsk'
Ăb-an-caȳ' (ăb-an-kī')
Ạ-bä'nō
Ạ-băs'cj-a (a-băsh'e-a)
Ăbbe-vĭlle', (Fr.)
Ăb'be-vĭlle, (S. C.)
Ăb-er-brŏth'ock
Ăb-er-brŏth'wjck (-jk)
Ăb-er-dēēn'
Ăb-er-ga-vĕn'ny, (or ăb-er-ġĕn'e)
Ăb-er-nĕth'y
Ăb-er-ȳst'wjth
Ăb'jng-don
Ă'bō, or Ā'bō
Abomey (ăb-ǫ-mā')
Ăb-ôo-shêhr' (-shár')
Ăb-ôu-kîr'
Ăb-ôu-sîr'
Ăb-ôu-tîġe'
Ạb-răn'tes
Ạ-brōl'hōs (-yōs)
Abruzzo (a-brŭt'sō)
Ạb-sē'com
Ăb-û-tîġe'
Ăb-ys-sĭn'j-a
Ạ-cā'dj-a
Ăc-a-pûl'cō
Ăc-cǫ-măc'
A-chēēn'
Ăch'jll
Ăch-mîm'
Ăc-ǫn-că'gua (-gwa)
Ạcqs (ăks)
Ăc'quj (ăk'kwe)
Acre (ā'ker, or ä'ker)
Ạ-dáir'
Ạ-dā'lj-a, or Ạ-dä'lj-a
Ăd'a-nä, or Ä-dä'nä
A-dĕl', or Ä'del
Ä'den, or Ā'den
Ăd'j-ġe, or Ăd'jġe
Ăd-i-rŏn'dack
Ăd'ler-bërg
Ạ-dôur'
Ä-dō'wăh, or Ăd'ǫ-wăh
Ăd-ra-mî'tj
Ä'drj-a

Ā-drj-an-ō'ple
Ā-drj-ät'jc
Æ-ġē'an
Æ-ġī'na, or Æġ'j-na
Æröe (ā'rǫ-ē)
Af-ghän-js-tän'
Äf-j-ôum'
Äf-ra-gō'la
Ăg'a-dēs
Ăgde (ăgd)
Agen (ä-zhäng')
Ăg'ġer-hûus
Âgh'rjm (âwg'rjm)
Ăg'jn-cōurt, (or ăd'jjn-kôr)
Agnadello (än-ya-dĕl'lō)
Agnone (an-yō'nä)
Ā-gua-dîl'la (ä-gwa-dēl'-ya)
A-guaȳ'ō (a-gwī'ō)
A-gûl'has (-yas)
Äh-mĕd-a-băd'
Äh-med-nûg'gur
Äh-wás'
Aïch'städt (īk'stät)
Āi'gle
Ain (äng)
Aïu-täb'
Aisne (ān)
Āix (āks, or ās)
Aix-la-Cha-pelle' (äks-la-sha-pĕl')
Ajaccio (a-yät'chō)
A-jän'
A-jäs-a-lŭck'
Aj-mēēr'
Ăk'a-bä
Ak-bär-a-băd'
Ăk-er-mǎn'
Ak-hjs-sär'
Ak-mîm'
Ak-shêhr'
Ăl-a-bä'ma
A-lăch'u-a
Ăl-a-dŭ'lj-a
Ăl-a-gō'as
A-läis' (a-lā')
Ăl-a-me'da (-mā'-)
Ăl'a-mō
Ăl'a-mōs
A-lăp-a-hä'
Ăl'a-quâ
Ăl-a-shêhr' (-shár')
Xla-ta-ma-hâ'
Albacete (äl-ba-thā'tä)
Ạl-bä'nō

Albegna (al-bān'ya)
Ăl-be-märle'
Ăl-bu-fe'ra (-fā'-)
Ăl-bu-quër'que (ăl-bu-kër'ka, or äl'bô-kërk)
Ăl-ca-lä'
Ăl'ca-mō
Al-căn'ta-rä
Ăl-ca-rí'a
Ăl'ces-ter (or âwl'ster)
Ălc-mâer'
Al-cō'na
Ạl-cō'y
âl-dän'
âl'der-ney
A-lĕn'çon, (or äl-äng-sōng')
Alentejo (äl-eng-tā'zhō)
Ăl-e-rî'a, or
   Ạ-le'rj-a (-lā'-)
Ăl-es-săn'drj-a
A-leū'tian
Ăl-ex-an-drĕt'ta
Ăl-ex-än'drj-a
Ăl-gär've
Ăl-ġe-zî'ras
Ăl'go-a, or Ạl-gō'a
Ạl-gō'ma
Ạl-hä'ma, (or ä-lä'mä)
Ăl-j-cănt'
Ăl-j-căn'te
Ăl-j-cä'ta
Ăl-j-cŭ'dj
Ălk-mâar'
Ăl-la-ha-băd'
Ăl'lah-shêhr (-shár)
Ăl'le-ghä-ny
Ăl'lo-wāy
Ăl-ma-dĕn'
Ạl-me'j-dä (al-mā'e-dä)
Ăl-me-rî'a
Ăl-mj-răn'te
Ạl-mō'rah
Almuñecar (al-mŭn-ya-kär')
Alnwick (ăn'njk)
Ạl-pē'na
Ạl-sáce'
Ạl-taī'
Ăl-ta-ma-hâ'
Ăl-ta-mî'ra
Ăl-ta-mŭ'ra
Ăl'ten-bŭrg
Ăl'to-nä
Ălt'zeȳ (ält'sī)

Ạ-lŭ'ta
Ăl-va-rá'dō
Ăm'a-ġer
A-mäl'fj
Ăm-a-pä'la
Ăm-a-răn'te
Ăm-a-ra-pû'ra
A-mä'se-rä
Ăm-a-tîque'
A-mäx'j-chî
Ăm'ble-sīde
Amboise (äng-bwäz')
A-mĕd-a-bäd'
Ăm-ed-nä'gur
Ăm'e-länd
X'mers-fört
Ăm'er-shäm
Am-hä'ra
Ăm'j-ĕns, (or äm-e-äng')
A-mîte'
Amlwch (ăm'lôk)
Ăm-mǫ-nôô'suc
Ăm-os-kĕag'
Ăm'phj-lä
Ăm-ret-sîr'
Ăn-a-dîr'
Anahuac (än-a-wăk')
Ăn'a-pä, or A-nä'pa
Ăn-a-tōl'j-cō
Ăn-da-lŭ'sj-a
Ăn-da-män'
Ăn-de-räb'
Ăn'der-nách
Ăn-dŭ'jar (an-dŭ'har)
Ăn-dŭx'ar (an-dŭ'har)
Ăn-e-gā'da
Ăn-ga-rä', or Ăn-gä'rä
Ănġ-er-mann-länd'
Ăn'gle-sey
Ăn-gos-tū'ra
Angoulême (äng-gô-läm')
An-guïl'la (-gwïl'-)
Ăn'gus (äng'gus)
Ăn-j-bä'
Ăn'jôu, (or äng-zhô')
Ạn-kō'ber
Ạn-nägh' (an-nä')
Ăn-na-môô'ka
Ănn Ạ-rŭn'del
Ăn'ne-cy, (or än'sē')
Ăn-no-bŏn'
Ăn-no näy'
Ăns'pách
Ạn-tä'lō
Ăn-te-que'ra (-kā'ra)

Antibes (äng-tēb')
An-tiē'tam
An-tî'gua (-ga)
An-tîlleş' (an-tēlz'), or An-tîl'leş
Ăn-tị-ọ-quî'ạ (-kē'ạ)
An-tîp'ạ-rŏs
Ăn-tị-sä'nạ
Ăn-tị-vä'rị
An-zî'cō
Ánzin (äng-zäng')
Ăn-zụ-än'
Ạ-pä'chẹ
Ăp-pạ-lăch'ẹe
Ăp-pạ-lăch-ị-cō'lạ
Ăp-pẹn-zĕll'
Ăp-pọ-mät'tọx
Ạ-pŭ're (ạ-pŭ'rä)
Ạ-pŭ'rị-mäc
Ă'quị (ä'kwẹ)
Ăq'uị-lạ (äk'wẹ-lä)
Aquileia (äk-wẹ-lä'yä)
Aquin (ä-käng')
Ạ-quî'nō
Ăr-ạ-guȳ'
Ạ-räiçhe', Ĕl
Ăr'ạl, or Ạ-räl'
Ăr-ạn-juez' (-hwĕth')
Ạ-rau' (ạ-röŭ')
Ăr-brŏath'
Ărçh-än'ǵel
Ărçh-ị-pĕl'ạ-gō
Ạr-cō'lạ
Ăr'dẹ-bîl
Ar-dèche' (ạr-dāsh')
Ăr-dẹ-län'
Ardennes (är-dĕn')
Ăr-ẹ-cî'vō
Ăr-ẹ-quî'pạ (-kē'pạ)
Ạ-rĕz'zō (ạ-rĕt'sō)
Ăr-gen-tän' (är-zhän-täng')
Ăr-ǵẹn-tä'rō
Argenteuil (är-zhän-tŭl')
Ăr'ǵen-tīne
Ăr-gŏs'tọ-lị
Ạr-ǵȳle', or Ăr'ǵȳle
Ăr'ǵy-rō Cás'trō
A-rî'çạ
Ariège (ä'rẹ-äzh')
Ạ-rîn'hŏs (-yōs)
Ạ-rîs'pẹ
Ạr-kän'sạs
Ar-kî'kō
Ărleş, (or ärl)
Ạr-mägh' (ạr-mä'), or Ăr'mạgh (-nạ)
Armagnac (är-män-yäk')
Ărn'heïm
Ărn'städt (ärn'stät)
Ăr'ọ-ĕ, or Ạ-rōe'
Ạ-rôôs'tôôk
Ạr-pî'nō
Ărques (ärk)
Ăr-rạ-cän'
Arriège (ä-rẹ-äzh')
Artois (är-twä')
Ăr'ụn-dĕl, (Eng.)

Ạ-rŭn'dẹl, (U. S.)
Ăs-çhäf'fẹn-bürg
Ăsçh-ẹrş-le'bẹn (äsh-ẹrz-lä'bẹn)
Ăs'cọ-lị
Ăsh-ạn-tēĕ', or Ạ-shăn'-tẹe
Ăsh-mŭ-neïn'
Ăsh'ọ-vẹr
Ăsh-tạ-bū'lạ
Ăsh'uẹ-lŏt (-wẹ-)
Ā'sị-ạ (ā'shẹ-ạ)
Ạs-pĕrn'
Ăs-phạl-tī'tĕş
Ăs-prọ-pŏt'ạ-mō
As-sĭn'nị-böïn
Ăs-sî'sị
Ăs-sou-än'
Ăs-tẹr-ạ-bäd'
Ăs-trạ-çhän'
Ạs-tŭ'rị-ạs
Ăt-ạ-cä'mạ
Ăt-au-aī' (ăt-öû-ī')
Ăt'bạ-rä
Ătch-ạ-fạ-laȳ'ạ
At-chēēn'
Ạt-fe' (ạt-fā')
Ăth-ạ-pĕs'cōw
Ath-lōne'
Ăth'ọl, or Ā'thŏl
Ạ-thȳ', or Ăth'y
Ạ-tî'nạ
Ăt-ôô-ī', or Ạ-tôô'ị
A-trä'tō
Ăt'tạ-lä, or Ạt-tä'lạ
Attigny (ạt-tēn'yẹ)
Ăt-ū-ī', or Ạ-tŭ'ị
Aube (ōb)
Aubigny (ō-bēn'yẹ)
Aubusson (ō-bŭs-sŏng')
Auch (ōsh)
Aude (ōd)
Au'ẹr-bäçh (öû'ẹr-bäk)
Au'ẹr-städt (öû'ẹr-stät)
Âu'ǵẹ-lä
Au'rịch (öû'rịk)
Aurillac (ō-rēl'yäk)
Âu-rŭng-ạ-bäd'
Âus'tẹr-lïtz (or öûs'tẹr-lïts)
Au-tŭn' (ō-tŭn')
Auvergne (ō-várn')
Aux Cayes (ō-käz)
Auxerre (ō-sár')
Âux-ŏnne', (or ō-sŏn')
Ăv'ạ-lŏn
Ạ-väts'çhạ
Ạ-ve'ị-rō (ạ-vā'ẹ-rō)
Ăv-ẹl-lî'nō
Avenches (ạ-vänsh')
Avesnes (ạ-vān')
Aveyron (ä-vā-rōng')
Avezzano (ä-vẹt-sä'nō)
Avignon (äv-ēn-yōng')
Ăv'ị-lä
Ạv-lō'nạ
Ạ-vō'çạ
Ā'vọn
Ăv-öȳ-ĕlleş'
Avranches (äv-ränsh')

Ax-ăm', or Ăx'ụm
Aȳ-ạ-cŭ'chō
Aȳ-ạ-mŏn'te (ī-ạ-mŏn'tā)
Āyleş'bụ-ry
Ayr'shîre
A-zër-bị-jän' or Ăz-ẹr-baī'jän
Ăz'ọf, or Ăz'ọph
Ạ-zōreş', or Ạ-zō'rĕş

B.

Bacchiglione (băk-kēi-yō'nä)
Băch-ị-ăn'
Bạ-däg'ry
Băd-ạ-jōs' (băd-ạ-hōs')
Băd-ạk-shän'
Bä-dẹn-weï'ler
Baeza (bä-ā'thạ)
Băg-dád', or Băg'dăd
Bagnara (bạn-yä'rạ)
Bagnères (bän-yár')
Bagnarea (bän-yạ-rā'ạ)
Bagnols (bän-yōl')
Bạ-hā'mạ
Bảh-î'ạ (bä-ē'ạ)
Bạ-hî'rẹh
Băh'lịng-ẹn
Băhr-ĕl-Ăb'ị-ăd
Băhr-ĕl-Ăz'rẹk
Baī'käl
Baī'reŭth (bī'rŭt)
Baja (bä'yä)
Băkh'tẹ-gän
Bä'kŭ, or Bạ-kŭ'
Băl-ạ-ghâut'
Băl-ạ-klä'vạ
Bä'lạ-rŭc'
Băl-ạ-sōre'
Băl'ạ-tŏn
Băl'bĕc, or Băl-bĕc'
Bâle (bäl), or Bä'şel
Băl-ẹ-är'ịc
Băl-fụ-rōsh'
Bạ-lîze'
Băl-kän'
Băl-lị-nä'
Băl-lị-nạ-slōe'
Bâlls'tọn-spä
Băl-ly-shän'nọn
Băm-bôuk'
Băm-ị-ăn'
Băm-mạ-kôô'
Bạ-nät'
Băn'çạ (băng'kạ)
Bạn-căl'lạ-ry
Băn-côut'
Bănff (bämf)
Băn-gạ-lōre' (băng-)
Băn-kŏk'
Băn-tăm', or Băn'tạm
Bapaume (bạ-pōm')
Băr'ạ-bä
Băr-ạ-cō'ạ
Bạ-räiche'
Bạr-bä'dọeş
Bär-cẹ-lō'nạ

Bạ-reil'ly (bạ-rā'lẹ)
Bạ-rî'tạ
Bär-lẹ-dŭc'
Barnaul (bär-nöûl')
Bạ-rōach' (bạ-rōch')
Bạ-rō'dạ
Bär'ọ-mĕtz (-mĕts)
Barraux (bär-rō')
Barrèges (bär-räzh')
Bä'şẹl, or Bâle (bäl)
Bạs-män'
Basques (bäsk)
Bạs-sä'nō
Basse Terre (bäs-tár')
Bäs'sọ-rä, or Bạs-sō'rạ
Bäs-tän'
Bạs-tî'ạ
Bastogne (bäs-tōн')
Bạ-tä'vị-ạ
Băth
Băt-ịs-căn'
Baton Rouge (bä-tn-rōzh')
Battaglia (bạt-täl'yạ)
Bát-tị-cạ-lō'ạ
Bausset (bō'sā)
Bautzen (böût'sẹn)
Baux (bō)
Baȳ-ạ-zîd'
Bayeux (bä-yŭ')
Bä-yŏnne'
Baȳ'ôu (bī'ô)
Baȳ'reŭth (bī'rôt)
Bäz-tän'
Bēa'mịn-stẹr
Béarn (bā-ärn')
Beaucaire (bō-kár')
Beaū'fŏrt (S. C.)
Beau'fŏrt (bō'fŏrt) (Af.)
Beau'lẹy (bō'lẹ)
Beau-mä'rịs (bō-)
Beaune (bŏn)
Beauvais (bō-vā')
Bĕc'clẹş (bĕk'klz)
Bĕd-nōre'
Bĕd-ŏu-înş'
Bĕd-ọ-wēēn'
Béfort (bā-fŏr')
Beira (bā'ẹ-rä)
Beï'rôut, (or bä'rôt)
Bēith
Beja (bä-zhä')
Bē-jạ-pôur'
Bẹ-lĕd'-ẹl-Jẹ-rîd'
Bĕl-fâst', or Bĕl'fâst
Belfort (bĕl-fŏr')
Bĕl-grāde'
Bĕlle-fọn-tāine'
Bĕlle-fŏnte'
Bĕlle-mŏnte'
Bĕlle'vîlle
Bĕl-lịn-zō'nạ
Bĕl-lŭ'nō
Bẹ-lôô-chịs-tän'
Bē'lụr-tăg
Bĕl-vị-dēre'
Belvoir (bē'vụr)
Bẹ-nä'reş
Bĕn-côô'lẹn
Bĕnd-ẹ-mîr'

Běn-e-věn'tŏ
Běn-gâl'
Ben-gä'zi
Běn-gue'la (běn-gä'la)
Be-nîn'
Běn-i-suěf'
Běn-Lō'mond
Ben-sā'lem
Běns'heĩm
Bentevoglio (běn-te-vōl'yō)
Běn'theĩm (běn'tīm)
Be-rär'
Be-rät'
Ber-bîce'
Běr-e-zî'na
Běr-e-zŏf'
Bër'ga-mō
Bërg'en
Bërg'en-hŭus
Bërg'en-ŏp-Zôôm'
Bër-ham-pōre'
Ber-lĭn', or Bër'lĭn
Ber-mŭ'das
Bër'ri-ěn
Ber-tič'
Bër'wick, (or bër'rĭk)
Besançon (bä-zäng'-sŏng')
Běs-sa-rä'bi-a
Be-thäb'a-ra
Běth'le-hem
Běv-e-rěn'
Bexar (bā-här')
Beyra (bā'e-rä)
Beȳ'rôôt, (or bā'rôt)
Bhät-gŏng' (bät-)
Bhürt-pōre' (bürt-)
Bî-ăl'ys-tŏk, or Bî-a-lȳs'tŏk
Bĭd-as-sō'a
Biěl'e-fěld (-fělt)
Biěl'go-rŏd, or Bî-ěl-go-rŏd'
Bj-ěnne'
Bjl-bä'ō
Bjl-bō'a
Bĭl-e-dŭl'ge-rîd
Bĭl'ler-j-ca
Bjn-gä'zi
Bĭng'en
Bĭng'ham-ton
Bî'ō-bî-ō
Bïr'ket-ěl-Ke-rôun'
Bïr'ket-ěl-Măr-j-ôut'
Bïr'ming-häm
Bïs-na-gär'
Bjs-sä'gōs
Bïs'tj-neau (bïs'te-nō)
Blănk'en-bŭrg
Blěch'ing-ley
Bleī'bërg
Blěn'heĩm, or Blěn'-heĩm
Blois (blwä, or blöï)
Bocage (bō-käzh')
Bō'den-sēē'
Bœuf (bŭf)
Bœuf-Baȳ'ôu (bŭf-)
Boglio (bōl'yō)

Bŏg-lj-pōre'
Bō-go-tä'
Bōh'mer-wâld
Bois-le-Duc (bwä-le-dŭk')
Bŏk-hä'ra
Bŏl-běc'
Bo-lî'var, or Bŏl'j-vär
Bologna (bo-lōn'yä)
Bŏl-se'nä (bŏl-sä'nä)
Bŏl'so-ver
Bōl'ton
Bol-zä'nō
Bō'mar-sŭnd
Bŏm-bāy'
Bō-nâir'
Bō-na-ven-tŭ'ra
Bō'na Vïs'ta
Bŏn-dôu'
Bo-něss'
Bŏn-j-fä'ciō (-chō)
Bo-nîn'
Bōom (bōm)
Bôô-tän'
Bō-paul'
Bŏr-deaux' (bŏr-dō')
Borgne (börn)
Börn'hōlm
Bŏr-nôu'
Bŏr-o-dî'nō
Bŏsh-u-än'as
Bŏs'na-Se-raī'
Bŏs'na-Se-rä'jō
Bŏs'pho-rŭs
Bŏt'e-toürt
Bŏt'zen (-sen)
Bôuches'-dŭ-Rhōne' (bôsh'-)
Bouillon (bōl-yōng')
Boŭ-je'iäh (bō-jä'yä)
Boulogne (bô-lōn')
Bourbonnes-les-Bains (bôr-bōn'-lä-bäng')
Bourdeaux (bôr-dō')
Bourges (bôrzh)
Bôu-tón'
Bovines (bō-vēn')
Bōw'doin (bō'dn)
Bo-yä'ca
Bozzolo (bŏt'so-lō)
Brä'bänt, or Bra-bänt'
Brä'hj-lōw
Bräh'ma-pôô'tra
Brauns'bërg (bröûns'-bërg)
Bra-zîl'
Bra-zō'rj-a
Brăz'os
Brazza (brăt'sä)
Bread-ăl'bane
Brě'da, or Bre-dä'
Brěg'ěntz (-ěnts)
Breī'sach
Bre-neau' (bre-nō')
Brěs'cia (brěsh'a)
Brěs'lâu, (or brěs'löû)
Bretagne (bre-tän')
Brē'ton, (or brět'on)
Briançon(brē-äng'sōng')

Brî-åre'
Bridlington (bür'ling-ton)
Briēg (brēg)
Briēl
Brî-enne'
Brî-ěntz' (-ěnts')
Brî-eûx' (brē-û')
Brīgh'ton (brī'tn)
Brĭn'dj-sî
Brî-ôude'
Brĭs'äch
Brĭs'gau (brĭs'göû)
Brôek (brŭk)
Brŏm'ley
Brŏmp'ton
Brŏn'do-lō
Brough (brŭf)
Brŭch'säl
Brŭ'ges
Brŭhl (brŭl)
Brŭnn
Brŭs'sels
Brzesc (zěsk)
Bŭch'an
Bŭ-cha-rěst'
Bu-chä'rj-a
Bŭd'weïs
Bue-nåire' (bwä-når')
Buěn Aȳ're (bwěn-ī'rä)
Bue-na-ven-tŭ'ra (bwä-)
Buenos Ayres (bwä'nos-ī'res, or bō'nos-år'ez)
Buïlth (bïlth)
Bŭ-ja-län'ce
Bŭk-hä'rj-a
Bŭ'läch
Bŭlkh
Bŭn'combe (bŭng'kum)
Bŭn-del-cŭnd'
Bŭn'der A-bäs'sj
Bŭntz'lâu, (or bŭnts'-löû)
Bŭr-ham-pôur'
Bŭr-ram-pôô'ter
Bŭr'scheĩd (bŭr'shīt)
Bury (běr'e)
Bŭ-sä'cō
Bŭ-shîre'
Bŭtte (bŭt)
Bŭt'ter-mēre
Bŭ-trjn-tō', or Bŭ-trĭn'tō
By-rä'ghur, or Bȳ-ra-ghür'

C.

Căb'ell
Ca-bre'ra (ka-brä'ra)
Cä-bŭl', or Cä-bôul'
Ca-bŭ-ljs-tän'
Caceres (kä'tha-rěs)
Cac-hä'ō, or Căch'aō [rä]
Cachoeira (kä-shō-ā'e-
Ca-cŏn'gō
Ca-dō're (-rä)

Cä'ĕn, (or käng)
Căer-lē'on
Căer-mär'then
Căer-när'von
Căer-phĭl'ly
Căf'fres (käf'ferz)
Căf-j-rjs-tän'
Cagliari (käl'yä-re⸲
Ca-hâw'ba
Cä'hïr, (or kår)
Ca-hôôs'
Cahors (ka-hör')
Caī'cōs (kī'kōs)
Căirn-görm'
Caī'rō (Egypt)
Cāi'rō (U. S.)
Căl-a-bär'
Căl-a-hŏr'ra
Căl'ais (käl'js)
Căl-a-mä'ta
Căl-a-mj-ä'něs
Căl-a-ta-yŭd'
Căl-a-trä'va
Căl-a-ve'ras (-vä'-)
Căl'ca-sieû (käl'ka-shô)
Căl'der
Căl'en-bërg
Cal-lä'ō, (or kal-yä'ō)
Căl-la-pôô'ya
Calne (kâwn)
Căl-ta-gj-rō'ne
Căl-ta-nj-sět'ta
Cal-vä'dōs
Căl'vërt
Ca-män'che
Căm-a-rō'nes
Căm-ba-hēē'
Cam-bāy'
Cam-bō'dj-a
Căm-bōge'
Căm'bräy, or Căm-bräy'
Cām'bridge
Cä-mîn'ha (ka-mēn'ya)
Campagna(kam-pän'ya)
Cămp'bell (käm'el)
Cam-pēach'y
Căm'pō Bäs'sō
Căn-a-jo-här'ie
Căn-an-dāi'gua (-gwa⸲
Căn-a-nōre'
Ca-nā'ra, or Căn'a-rä
Ca-nā'rjes
Căn-a-sâu'ga
Căn-a-stō'ta
Ca-ñäv'e-ral
Căn-da-här'
Can-dēish'
Ca-nē'a
Căn-js-tē'ō
Ca-nŏn'j-cŭt
Cannes (kän)
Can-nôu'chee
Căn'tal, or Can-täl'
Căn'ter-bu-ry (-běr-e)
Căn'ton
Can-tȳre'
Cāpe Brět'on, or Bre-tôn'
Cāpe Gĭr'ar-deau (jĭr'ar-dō)

Cāpe Haī'tī-ẹn
Cāp-ı-tạ nä'tạ
Cȧ'pō d'îs'trī-ạ
Cȧ'prı
Cȧp'ụ-ạ
Cär'ạ-män
Cär-ạ-mä'nı-ạ
Cär-cạ-sŏnne'
Cär'dẹ-näs
Cär'dı-gän
Cạr-dō'nạ
Cär-ı-ä'cō
Cär-ıb-bē'ạn
Cär-ıb-bēē'
Cär līsle' (kär·līl')
Car'lọ·wītz
Cärlş'bäd
Cärlş·crō'nạ, or Cärlş-crō'nạ
Cärlş'rŭhe (kärlz'rô)
Cärl'städt (-stät)
Carmagnola (kär-mạn-yō'lạ)
Cạr-mō'nạ
Cạr-nät'ıc
Cạr-nâul'
Cär-nı-ō'lạ
Cär-ọ-lī'nạ
Cä·rọ-nī'
Cạr-pā'thı-ạn
Cär-pẹn-tä'rı-ạ
Cär-pẹn-träs', (or kär-päng·trä')
Cạr-rä'rạ
Cär-rıck-fẹr'gụs
Carshalton (käs-hör'tn)
Cạr-tä'gō
Cär-tạ-ḡē'nạ
Cär'tẹr-ĕt
Cär-thạ-ḡē'nạ
Cär-ụ pä'nō
Cạ-säc', or Cā'sạc
Cạ-sạl'
Cạ-sä'le (-lä)
Cäs-ạ-nä'nạ
Cäs'bın, or Cäs-bîn'
Cäsçh'au (käsh'öû)
Cạ-shän'
Cäsh'ell
Cäsh'gär, or Cạsh-gär'
Cäsh-mēre', or Cäsh'mēre
Cạs-sî'nạ
Cäs-sı-quı-ä'rı
Cäs-tẹl-nau'dạ-ry' (käs-tẹl-nō'dạ-rē')
Cạs-tĕl' Ve-trä'nō (-vä-)
Castiglione (käs-tēl-yō'nä)
Cạs-tīle'   [nä]
Castillon (käs-tēl-yŏng')
Cạs-tîne'
Cäs'tle-bär' (käs'sl-bär')
Castres (käs'tr)
Cäs'trọ Ḡīō-vän'nı
Cät-ạ-bäm'bạ
Cät-ạ-hôu'lạ
Cät-ạ-lō'nı-ạ
Cạ-tä'nı-ạ, or Cạ-tä'nı-ạ
Cä-tạn-zä'rō

Cateau Cambresis (kạ-tō' käm·brẹ-zē')
Cäth-ạ-rî'nẹn-städt (-stät)
Cạt-män'dôô, or Cät-mạn-dôô'
Cạ-tör'cẹ, (or kạ-tōr'thä)
Cät-tạ-râu'gụs
Cạt-tä'rō, or Cät'tạ-rō
Câu-bŭl'
Câu'cạ, (or köû'kạ)
Câu'cạ-sụs
Câugh nạ-wâ'gạ (kâw-)
Caune (kōn)
Câu'vẹr y
Cäv'ạ·lä
Cäv'ạn
Cȧ'vẹr-y
Câwn-pōre'
Cäx-ạ-mär'cạ
Caxias (kạ-shē'ạs)
Caxoeira (kä-shọ-ā'ẹ-rạ)
Caÿ'cōs (kī'kōs)
Caÿ-ẹnne' (kī-ĕn')
Caÿ-män', or Cäy'mạn
Cạ-yūse'
Cäz-ẹ-nō'vı-ạ
Ce-ạ-rä' (sä-)
Cē-bû'
Cĕç'ıl, or Cē'çıl
Cĕf'ạ-lŭ
Cẹ-lä'nō
Cĕl'ẹ-bĕş
Cĕl'ıẹ
Cĕn'ıs, (or sẹ-nē')
Cĕph-ạ-lō'nı-ạ, or Cĕph-ạ-lọ-nî'ạ
Cẹ-räm'
Cerignola (sĕr-ın-yō'lạ)
Cĕr'ı-gō, or Cẹ-rî'gō
Cer-ve'rä (sẹr-vā'rä)
Cĕr'vı-ä (chĕr've-ạ)
Cĕr'vın, (or sĕr-väng')
Ce-se'nä (chä-sā'nä)
Ceū'tạ, (or sä'ụ-tä)
Cévennes (sä-vĕn')
Cẹy-lōu', or Cēy'lọu
Cha-cä'ō
Chä'cō
Chạ-gäing'
Chä'gre (shä'gụr)
Chä'grĕs
Chä-leûr'
Châlons (shä-lōng')
Chäm'bẹr-ry
Chäm'bẹrş-bürg
Chäm-bĭēē'
Châmouni (shä'mô-nē', or shä-mô'nẹ)
Champagne (shäm-pän'-yä)
Chäm-pāign' (-pān')
Chäm-plāin'
Chän'dẹ-leûr'
Chän-dẹr-nạ-gōre'
Chän-tîl'ly (shän-tēl'yē)
Chạ-pä'lạ
Charente (shä-rängt')
Chär'ı-tŏn
Çhär'kŏv

Çhärle'mŏnt, or
  Çhär'le-mŏnt
Charleroi (shȧrl-rwä',
  or shȧr-lẹ-röï')
Çhärle'vïlle
Çhär'lẹ-voıx' (shär'lẹ-
  vwä')
Chartres (shär'tr)
Châteaubriant (shä-tō'-
  brẹ-äng')
Châteaudun (shä-tō·
  dŭn')
Château-Gonthier (shä-
  tō-gōn'tẹ-ā)   [gā']
Châteauguay (shä-tō-
Châteauroux (shä-tō-rô')
Châtellerault (shä-tĕl-
Chät-tạ-hôô'chẹe   [rō']
Chạt-tôô'gạ
Chaudière (shō-dẹ-ȧr')
Chaumont (shō-mông')
  (Fr.)
Chaumont (shō-mō')
  (U. S.)
Çhau-tâu'quạ
Çhazy (shạ-zē')
Chẹ-bŭc'tō
Chĕl'ı-cŭt
Chĕlmş'fọrd (chĕmz'-
  fọrd)
Chĕl'tẹn-häm, (or
  chĕlt'nạm)
Ȼhĕm'nïtz (-nïts)
Chẹ-mŭng'
Chẹ-nän'gō
Chen-yäng'
Chẹ-päch'ẹt
Cher (shȧr)
Ȼhẹ-räs'cō
Çhër'bourg
Ȼhër'sō
Ȼhër'sọn
Ȼhër-sọ-nēse'
Chĕrt'sẹy, (or chĕs'sẹ)
Chĕs'ạ-pēake
Chẹ-sŭn'côôk
Chĕt-ı-mäch'ẹş
Chĕv'ı-ọt
Ȼhî-ä'nä
Chî-ä'pä
Ȼhî-ä'rı
Ȼhî-ä'vạ-rî, or
  Ȼhî-ạ-vä'rî
Ȼhî-ạ-vĕn'nạ
Chị-câ'gō
Chĭch'eş•ter
Chĭck-ạ-hŏm'ı-ny
Chĭck-ạ-mäg'gạ
Chĭck'ạ-pēē
Chicot (shē'kō)
Ȼhî'em-sēē
Çhî-ĕnne'
Chieti (kẹ-ā'tẹ)
Chĭg-nĕc'tō
Chị-huä'huä (-wä'wä)
Chị-kāi'lıs
Chî'lı, or Chĭl'ı
Chĭl-lı-cō'thẹ
Chĭm-bọ-rä'zō
Chĭn'sụ-rä, or

Chịn-sŭ'rạ
Chĭn-yäng'
Ȼhî'ōs
Chĭp'pẹn-häm, (or chĭp'-
  nạm)
Chĭp'pẹ-wāy
Chị-pụs-cō'ạ
Chị-quî'tōs (chẹ-kē'tōs)
Chĭş'wıck (chĭz'ık)
Chĭt-ạ-gŏng'
Chĭt-töre'
Ȼhŏc'zım
Cholmondely (chŭm'lẹ)
Chọ-lŭ'lä
Ȼhō-rạ-sän', or Ȼhọ-
  räs'sạn
Chọ-wân'
Ȼhrïs-tı-ā'nạ
Ȼhrïs-tı-ä'nı-ạ
Ȼhrïs'tıạn-sänd
Ȼhrïs'tıạn-städt (-stät)
Chū-lạ-hō'mạ
Chŭm'bŭl
Chŭm'leigh (chŭm'lẹ)
Chŭ-quı-sä'cạ (chŭ-kẹ-
  sä'kạ)
Ȼhŭr (kôr)
Cîc-ạ-côle'
Cî-ẹn-fue'gōs (sē-ẹn-
  fwä'gōs)
Cïm-ạr-rōn'
Cïn-ạ-lō'ạ
Cïn-cın-nä'tı
Cịr-cäs'sı-ạ (sịr-käsh'-
  ẹ-ạ)
Cï'rẹn-cĕs-tẹr, (or sĭs'-
  ẹ-tẹr)
Cïrk'nïtz (-nïts)
Cĭt-tạ-dĕl'lạ (chĭt-)
Cî-ú-däd' Re-äl' (-rä-äl')
Civita Vĕç'chı-ä (chē'-
  vẹ-tä-vĕk'kẹ-ä)
Clȧc-män'nạn
Clä'ḡẹn-fŭrth (-fŭrt)
Clāi'bọrne
Cläme-cy' (kläm-sē')
Clär'ẹ-mŏnt, or Clȧre'-
  mŏnt
Clau'sẹn-bŭrg (klöû'-)
Clausthal (klöûs'täl)
Clẹr-mŏnt', or
  Clĕr'mŏnt
Clēve'lạnd
Clēveş
Clīth'ẹ-rōe
Clŏg'hẹr, (or klō'hẹr)
Clŏn-ạ-kĭl'ty
Clŏn-mĕll'
Cō-ạ-hō'mạ
Cō-ạ-huî'lä (-wē'lä)
Cō-än'gō (-äng'-)
Cọ-bî'jä (-hä)
Cŏb'lĕntz (-lĕnts)
Cŏch-ạ-bäm'bạ
Codogno (kọ-dōn'yō)
Cọ-dō'rụs
Côev'ọr-dẹn
Coeymans (kwē'mạnz)
Cognac (kŏn-yäk')
Cohahuila (kō-ạ-wē'lä)

Cǫ-hōeş'
Cǫ-ĭm-ba-tôôr'
Cǫ-ĭm'bra
Coire (kwär)
Cōl'ches-ter
Cōle-rāine'
Cǫ-lî'ma
Cǫl-mär'
Coln (kōn, or köün)
Cologna (kǫ-lōn'yä)
Cologne (kǫ-lōn')
Cǫ-lŏm'bj-a
Cǫ-lŏm'bō
Cŏl'ǫn-sāy, or
  Cǫ-lŏn'sāy
Cŏl-ǫ-rä'dō
Cǫ-lŭm-bj-ăn'a
Cǫ-măc'
Cǫ-măn'cheş
Cǫ-mär'gō
Cō-maȳ-ä'gua
Cŏm'ber-mēre
Comines (kǫ-mēn')
Cŏm'ǫ-rĭn
Cǫ-mörn'
Cŏm'ǫ-rō
Compiègne (kŏm-pē-än')
Cŏm-pǫs-tĕl'la
Cǫn-cän', or
  Cŏn'can
Cŏn'cǫrd (kŏng'-)
Condé (kŏn'dā)
Cǫ-nē'cuh
Cŏn'e-mâugh (-mâw)
Cŏn-es-tō'ga
Cǫ-nē'sus
Cŏn-ga-rēē' (kŏng-)
Cŏn'gle-tǫn
Cŏn'nâught, or Cŏn-
  nâught'
Cŏn-ne-cǫ-chēague'
Cǫn-nĕct'j-cŭt (-nĕt'-)
Cŏn-stan-tî'na
Cŏn-stăn-tj-nō'ple
Côô-mas-siē'
Cǫ-ŏs'
Côô-saw-hătch'ie
Cǫ-pī'ah
Cō-pj-ä'pō, or Cō-pj-a-pō'
Cǫ-pĭm'es-câw
Cŏqu'et (kŏk'et)
Cǫ-quîm'bō (-kēm'-)
Cŏr-a-chiē'
Cŏr'bäch
Cŏr-beau' (-bō')
Cŏr-beil' (kör-bāl')
Cǫr-dĭl'le-ras, (or kör-
  dēl-yā'ras)
Cŏr'dǫ-vä
Cǫ-rē'a
Cǫr-fü', or Cŏr'fu
Cŏr'jnth
Cŏr-ǫ-măn'del
Cǫ-rō'ne
Corrèze (kŏr-rāz')
Cŏr-rj-ĕn'tes
Cŏr'sj-ca
Corté (kŏr'tā)
Cǫr-tō'na
Cǫ-rŭn'na

Cŏr'y-dǫn
Cǫ-shŏc'tǫn
Cosne (kōn)
Cǫs-sêir'
Cŏs-sĭm-ba-zär'
Cŏs'ta Rî'ca
Cō-ta-gaȳ'a
Côte d'Or (kōt-dör')
Cotignola (kō-tēn-yō'lä)
Cō-tǫ-päx'ị
Cŏtt'bŭs
Côu-län'
Côur'land
Côur-trāy'
Coutances (kó-täns')
Cŏv'en-try
Cŏv'ĭng-tǫn
Cŏweş (kŏüz)
Cŏŵ-ē'ta
Crā'cōw
Crécy (krĕs'e)
Cre'fĕld (krä'fĕlt)
Crĕm'nĭtz (-nĭts)
Cre-mō'na
Crĕv'ĕlt
Crĭ-mē'a
Crǫ-ä'tj-a (krǫ-ä'she-a)
Crŏm'ar-ty, or Crǫ-mär'-
Crŏn'städt (-stät)   [ty
Csongrád (chŏn-gräd')
Cŭ-bä'gua (-gwä)
Cu-bän'
Cŭd-da-lōre'
Cud-dä'päh, or
  Cŭd'da-päh
Cuĕn'çä (kwĕn'sä)
Cuj-ä'ba (kwe-ä'ba)
Culhuacan (kôl-wa-
  kän')
Cŭ-lî-a-căn'
Cul-lō'den
Cŭl-rŏss', (or kô'rŏs)
Cŭ-ma-nä'
Cu-mä'nj-a
Cŭm-ma-zēē'
Cŭ-ra-çōa' (-sō')
Cŭ-ra-raȳ'
Cŭr-dis-tän'
Cŭr-zō'lä
Cut-täck'
Cŭx-hä'ven
Cŭ-yä'bä, or
  Cŭ-yä-bä'
Cuȳ-a-hō'ga (kî-a-hō'ga)
Cŭz'cō
Cȳc'la-dēş
Czaslau (zäs-löû')
Czernowitz (chĕr'nǫ-
  vĭts)
Czirknicz (tsĕrk'nĭts)

D.

Da-cō'täh
Dăg-hes-tän'
Däh'ǫ-mey (-mä)

Dăl-a-gō'a
Dä-le-cär'li-a
Dal-hôu'şie
Dál-kēith'
Dälleş
Dăm-a-rjs-cŏt'ta
Dän'âw
Dăn-ne-mō'ra
Dänt'zịc (-sịk)
Dän'ŭbe
Där-da-nĕlleş'
Dar-fôur'
Dä'rj-ĕn
Därm'städt (-stät)
Dauphiné (dō-fē-nä')
Dâu'phj-ny
De-brĕc'zịn
De-brĕt'zịn (-sịn)
De-cä'tur
Dĕc'can, or Dec-cän'
De-cîze'
Dĕl-a-gō'a
Dĕlf'zȳl
Del-gä'da
Dĕl'hj (dĕl'le)
Dĕl'hî (U. S.)
Del-vî'nō
Dĕm-e-rä'ra
Dem-bē'a
De-mō'na
Dĕn'bịgh (dĕn'be)
Dĕn'de-räh
Dĕn-der-mŏnd'
De-peȳs'ter
Dĕpt'fǫrd (dĕt'furd)
Der-bĕnd'
Dërne
De-Ruȳ'ter
Dĕs-a-guä-de'rō (gwä-
  dä'-)
Dĕs-cŏn-ǫ-cî'da
Dĕs-e-ä'da
Dĕş-e-rĕt'
De-shä'
Des Moines (dĕ-moin')
Dĕs-pǫ-blä'dō
Dĕs'sâu, (or dĕs'söû)
Dĕt'tịng-en
Deutz (döïts)
Deux–Ponts' (dŭ-pŏnts')
De-vĕn'ter
De-vī'zeş
Dha-wâl-a-ghî'rị (da-
  wâl-a-gē're)
Dj-är-be-kîr'
Diě'men's Länd
Diĕp'hŏlz (-hōlts)
Dî-ĕppe'
Diĕst
Diĕtz (dēts)
Dîgne (dēn)
Dî'jŏn' (dē'zhōng')
Dil'lịng-en
Dĭn-age-pōre'
Dî-nän' (dē-näng')
Dî-nänt'
Dīx-än'
Dīx-mŭde'
Djŏl'j-bä
Dniĕ'per (nē'per)

Dniĕs'ter (nĕs'ter)
Dô-äb'
Dŏf·re-fj-ĕld'.   [le)
Dŏl-ğĕl'ly, (or dŏl-ğĕth'-
Dŏl-lärt'   [j-ca
Dŏm-j-nî'ca, or Dǫ-mĭn'-
Dŏm-j-nìque' (Fr.)
Dŏn-äg-ha-dēē'
Dŏn'e-gäl
Dŏn'gǫ-lä (dŏng'-)
Dŏn'na-ghüe
Dŏn-naī'
Dôô-shäk'
Dordogne (dör-dōn')
Dordrecht (dör'drĕkt)
Dör'nŏçh
Dör-pät', or Dör'pat
Dôu'äy (dô'ä)
Dôu'rō (dô'rō)
Dŏv-re-fj-ĕld'
Dŏŵ-le-ta-bäd'
Draguignan (drä-ğĕn-
  yäng')
Dräve, or Dräve
Drenthe (drĕnt, or
  drĕn'te)
Drĕş'den, or Drĕs'den
Dreux (drŭ)
Drî'nō
Drŏgh'e-da (drŏg'-)
Drō'hǫ-bĭcz (-bĭch)
Dröït'wịch (dröït'ịch)
Drǫ-mōre', or
  Drō'mōre
Drŏn'theīm (drŏn'tīm)
Du-äneş'bürg
Du-bŭque' (-bôk')
Duero (dŭ-ä'rō)
Dŭ'ịs-bŭrg
Duiveland (döï've-länt)
Dulcigno (dŭl-chēn'yō)
Dulwich (dŭl'jj)
Dŭm-blāne'
Dŭm-frieş'
Dŭn-bär'
Dŭn-dâlk' (dŭn-dâwk')
Dŭn-däs'
Dŭn-dēē'
Dŭn-fĕrm'line, (or dŭn-
  fĕr'lịn)
Dŭn-găn'nǫn
Dŭn-gär'van
Dŭn-ğe nĕss'
Dŭn-kĕld'
Dŭn-kïrk'
Dŭn-ôôn'
Dŭn-sĭn'nane, or
  Dŭn-sịn-nāne'
Dunwich (dŭn'jj)
Duquesne (dŭ-kān')
Dŭ-rance'
Dŭ-răn'gō (-răng'-)
Dŭ-răz'zō, (or dŭ-răt'sō)
Dŭr'ham (dŭr'am)
Dŭr'läch
Dŭs'şel-dörf
Dŭt'lịng-en
Du-vâl'
Dwa-rä'cä
Dwî'na, or Dwî'nä

E.

Ĕb-säm′bṳl, or Ĕb-sạm-
　bṳl′
Ĕch′tẹr-näch
Ĕç′i-jä, (or ä′thẹ-hä)
Ĕckmühl (ĕk′mṳl)
Ĕc-uạ-dŏr′ (ĕk-wạ-dŏr′)
Ĕdge′cọmbe (ĕj′kṳn)
E-dĭ′nạ
Edinburgh (ĕd′ịn-bŭr-rọ,
　or ĕd′ịn-bürg)
Ĕd′ịs-tō
Ĕf′fịng-häm
Ĕg′ẹr
E-ġĭ′nạ, or Ĕġ′ị-nä
Ĕg′rị-pō, or E-grĭ′pō (ä-)
Ĕh-rẹn-breĭt′steĭn
Eĭch′städt (ĭk′stät)
Eĭ′lẹn-bŭrg
Eĭm′bĕck
Eĭ′mẹ-ō
Eĭ′sẹ-näch
Eĭs′lẹ-bĕn
E-kät-ẹ-rĭ′nẹn-bŭrg
E-kät-ẹ-rĭ′nọ-gräd
E-kät-ẹ-rĭ′nọ-släv
Ĕl A-räịche′
Ĕl′bẹr-fĕld
Ĕl-beŭf′, or Ĕl-bœŭf′
Ĕl′che (ĕl′chä)
Ĕl Dọ-rä′dō
Ĕl-ẹ-phän′tạ
Ĕl-ẹ-phän-tĭ′nạ
E-leū′thẹ-rạ
Ĕl′ġịn
E-lĭs′ạ-bĕth-gräd′
Ĕl-lōre′
Ĕl-mĭ′nạ
Ĕl-mĭ′rạ
Ĕl-sị-nōre′, or Ĕl-sị-neŭr′
Ĕl′wạng-ẹn
Ĕm′mẹr-ịch
E-nä′rẹ
Ĕn-ga-dîne′
Enghien (än-ġē′äng)
England (ĭng′glạnd)
Ĕn-ị-sēi′
Ĕnk-hui′zẹn (ẹnk-höĭ′-
　zẹn)
Ĕn-nịs-cör′thy
Ĕn-nịs-kĭl′lẹn
Ĕn′tre-Rĭ′ōs
E-pĕr′ị-ĕs
Ĕp-er-näy′
Ĕp′ị-näl
Ĕr′bäch
Ĕr′fŭrt
Ĕr′ịcht
Ĕr-ị-vän′
Ĕr′lạng-en
Ĕr′lau (ĕr′löŭ)
ĕr-mẹ-nĕk′
Ĕr′zẹ-rŭm, or
　Ĕrz-rôôm′
Ĕrz-ġẹ-bîr′ġe
Ĕs-cäm′bị-ạ
Ĕs-cū′rị-ạl
E-sō′pṳs

Esquimaux (ĕs′kẹ-mō)
Ĕs-sẹ-quî′bō (-kē′-)
Ĕss′lịng-ẹn
Ĕs-thō′nị-ạ
Ĕs-trẹ-mạ-dŭ′rạ
Ĕs′trẹ-mōz′
Ĕs′zẹk (ĕs′sẹk)
Étampes (ä-tämp′)
Ĕt′ọ-wäh
Ĕtsẹch (ĕtsh)
Eū (yŭ)
Eupen (öĭ′pẹn)
Eūre (yūr)
Eutin (öĭ-tēn′)
Eūx′ịne
Ēveṣ′häm
Ĕv′ọ-rä, or E-vō′rạ
Évreux (ĕv-rŭ′)
Eў′ạ-lĕt
Eў′lâu, (or ĭ′löû)

F.

Fạ-ĕn′zạ
Fäh′lŭn
Faĭ-ôum′
Fä-läịẹe′
Fäl′kĭrk, or Fäl-kĭrk′
Falkland (fäwk′lạnd)
Fä′nō, or Fä-nō′
Fä′rŏe, or Fä′rọ-ē
Fär-sịs-tän′
Fâu-quĭẹr′ (fâw-kēr′)
Fäv′ẹrsh-ạm
Faў-âl′
Fạy-ĕtte′
Fäy′ẹtte-vĭlle
Faў-ôum′
Fēē′ġẹe
Fĕh-rạ-bäd′
Fĕl-ạn-î′che
Fẹ-lĭ-cị-ä′nạ
Fĕm′ẹrn
Fē-ọ-dō′sị-ạ (-dō′zhẹ-ạ)
Fẹr-mä′nạgh (fẹr-mä′-
Fẹr-möў′　　　[nạ)
Fẹr-rä′rä
Fĕr′rọl, or Fẹr-rōl′
Fäv′ẹrsh-ạm
Fẹz-zän′
Fĭch-tĕl-ġẹ-bîr′ġe
Fĭ′-ĕs′ọ-le (-lä)
Figeac (fĭzh′äk′)
Figueras (fẹ-gä′rạs)
Fĭn-ịs-tĕrre′
Fismes (fēm)
Fiume (fẹ-ŭ′mä)
Flèche, La (lä flĕsh)
Flĕnṣ′börg
Foggia (fŏd′jä)
Foglia (fŏl′yạ)
Foix (fwä)
Foligno (fọ-lēn′yō)
Fontainebleau (fŏn-tän-
　blō′)
Fŏn-tạ-rä′bị-ạ
Fontenay-le-Compte
　(fŏnt-nä′lẹ-kōngt′)

Fŏn-tẹ-nöў′
Fontevrault (fŏn-tẹv-rō′)
För′lî, or Fọr-lî′
För′mẹn-te′rä (-tä′-)
Fọr-mō′sạ
För-sÿth′
För-tẹ-vẹn-tŭ′rạ
Fọs-sä′nō
Fōth′ẹr-ịn-gāy
Fôu′dî
Fougères (fō-zhår′)
Fôu′lähṣ
Foŭrche
Foў′ẹrṣ (fî′ẹrz)
Franche Comté (fränsh
　kōng′tä)
François (frän′swä)
Frän′ẹ-kẹr
Fränk′ẹn-steĭn′
Fränk′ẹn-thäl (-täl)
Frạs-cä′tị
Frau′ẹn-bŭrg (frôŭ′-)
Frau′städt (frôŭ′stät)
Frĕd′ẹr-ịcks-hâll
Freĭ′bŭrg
Freĭ′sịng
Freĭ′sịng-ẹn
Freĭ′städt (-stät)
Fréjus (frä-zhŭs′)
Freў′bürg
Freў′städt (-stät)
Frî′bürg
Fried′lạnd
Frîsche′häff
Frieṣ′lạnd
Frî′ō
Frị-ŭ′lị, or Frî′ụ-lî
Frŏdṣ′häm
Frọn-te′rạ (-tä′-)
Frontignac (frŏn-tēn-
　yäk′)
Fuẹr-tä-vẹn-tŭ′rạ
Fŭl′dä
Fünch′ạl, or Fŭn-çhäl′
Fŭnf-kîrch′ẹn
Furnes (fŭrn)
Fŭr-rŭck-ạ-bäd′
Fürth (fŭrt)
Fÿz-ạ-bäd′

G.

Gạ-dä′mịs
Gä-e′tä (gä-ä′tä)
Gaillac (gäl-yäk′)
Gaillon (gäl-yōng′)
Gåir′lŏch
Gạ-läp′ạ-gōṣ, or
　Gäl-lị-pä′gōṣ
Gäl-ạ-shiĕlṣ′
Gạ-lätz′ (-lätṣ′)
Gäl-lĭp′ọ-lị
Gäl′lị-pọ-lĭs′
Gäl′lọ-wāy
Gäl′vẹs-tọn
Gål′wāy
Gän′ġēṣ
Gän-jäm′

Gärd′inẹr (gärd′nẹr)
Gär-dŏn′
Gär-gä′nō
Gạ-rŏnne′
Gäs-cọn-äde′
Gäs′cọ-ny
Gaspé (gäs′pẹ)
Gẹ-âu′gạ
Ġēel, (or gäl)
Ġĕf′le (ġĕf′fl)
Ġēn-ẹ-sē′ō
Ġēn′ẹ-viēve
Genévois (zhĕn-ẹ-vwä′)
Ġēn′ọ-ạ
Gera (gä′rä)
Ġẹ-rō′nä, (or hä-rō′nä)
Gers (zhår)
Gex (zhĕx)
Ġeў′sẹrṣ
Ghạ-dä′mịs
Ghâuts (gâwts)
Gheel (ġēl, or gäl)
Ghĕnt, (or gŏng)
Ġhẹr-gŏng′
Ġhị-län′
Gịb-rål′tạr
Ġiĕs′sẹn (ġēs′sẹn)
Gijon (hē-hōn′)
Ġî′lạ, (or hē′lạ)
Ġị-lō′lō
Ġịr′ġẹ
Ġịr-ġĕn′tị
Gironde (zhẹ-rōnd′)
Ġî′zẹh, or Ġî′zẹh
Glạ-mör′gạn
Gläṣ′gōw, or Gläṣ′gō
Glauchau (glöû′köû)
Glẹ-nĕlg′
Glō′gau (glō′göû)
Glọ-gâw′
Gloŭces′tẹr (glŏs′tẹr)
Glückstadt (glŭk′stät)
Gmünd (gmŭnt)
Gnesen (gnä′zẹn)
Gnĕs′nạ (nĕs′nạ)
Gọ-däv′ẹ-ry
Goes (hôs)
Gọ-jäm′
Gö-lị-äd′
Gŏm-brôôn′
Gọ-me′rạ (-mä′-)
Gọ-naīveṣ′
Gọ-näve′
Gön-zä′lẹs
Gọ-rēē′
Görlitz (gür′lịts)
Görtz (gürts)
Gōṣ′bẹr-tọn
Gō′thạ, (or gō′tä)
Gŏt′tẹn-bürg
Göttengen (gĕt′ịng-ẹn)
Gôu′dä
Gôur (gôr)
Gō-yäz′
Goz′zo (gŏt′sō)
Grä′cị-äs ä Dî′ōs
Grä-cị-ō′sạ
Gräm-mŏnt′
Grạ-nä′dạ
Gränt′häm

Grăn'vĭlle (U. S.)
Grăn-vĭlle' (Fr.)
Gratiot (grăsh'ẹ-ŏt)
Grätz (grĕts)
Graudenz (grŏû'dẹnts)
Gravelines (grăv'lĕn')
Grēē'nọck
Grēēn'wĭch (grĕn'ĭj)
Greīfs-wâl'dẹ
Grẹ-nä'dạ
Grĕn-ō'ble
Grĭn'dẹl-wâld
Grĭ'sọnş, (or grē-zōng')
Grŏn'ing-ẹn
Grōss-wár'deīn
Grŏt'on (grŏt'tn)
Grünberg (grün'bërg)
Gruyères (grü-yár')
Guä-dạ-lá'vĭ-är, or
  Guä-dạ-lạ-vî'är
Guä-dạ-lạx-ä'rạ, (or
  gwä-dạ-lạ-hä'rạ)
Guä-dạ-lû'pẹ, or Guä-dạ-
  lûpe' (gâw-)
Guä-dạl-quĭv'ịr, or Guä-
  dạl-quị-vîr'
Guä-dẹ-lôupe' (gâw-dẹ-
  lôp')
Guä-dj-ä'nạ
Guä-män'gạ
Guä-nạ-hä'nị
Guä-nä're (rä)
Guä-nạ-juä'tō, or Guä-
  nạ-xuä'tō (-hwä'tō)
Guän'cạ Vẹ-lî'cä
Guär'dạ (gwär'dạ)
Guär-dạf-uî' (gär-dạf-
  wē')
Guä-tị-mä'lạ
Guạx-a'cạ, (or gwä-hä'-   [kä]
Guaȳ-ä'mạ
Guaȳ-ạ-quîl' (gwī-ạ-
  kēl')
Guaȳ'mạs
Guäz-ạ-cuäl'cō
Guebres (ğē'berz)
Guëlph (gwĕlf)
Guéret (gā-rā')
Güern'şey
Guer-re'rō (ğer-rā'rō)
Guî-ä'nạ (ğē-ä'nạ)
Guĭc'ọ-wạr (gwĭk'-)
Guî-ĕnne' (ğē-ĕn')
Guĭn'ẹa (ğĭn'ẹ)
Guingamp (găng-găng')
Guî-pûs'cọ-ä (ğē-)
Guĭş'bör-ọugh (ğĭz'-)
Guîşe (ğēz)
Gŭm-bĭn'nẹn
Gŭnd-wä'nạh
Gŭntz'bûrg (gŭnts'bûrg)
Gŭr-wâl', or
  Gür'wäl
Guy-ä'nä (ğē-)
Guȳ-ạn-dŏtte' (ğī-)
Gŭ-zẹl-hĭs'şạr
Gŭ'zẹ-rät'
Gwä'lị-ör
Gwĭn-nĕtt'
Ġyŭ'lạ (jŭ'lạ)

H.

Hăd'leigh (hăd'lẹ)
Hăd-rạ-mâut'
Häer'lẹm (här'lẹm)
Hāgue (hāg)
Haguenau (äg-nō')
Haī-nän'
Hainault (hā'nō, or hĭ'-
  nöûlt)
Hä-jy-pôôr'
Häl'bẹr-städṭ (-stät)
Häleş-ōw'ẹn
Häl'lẹ
Häl'leīn
Hallowell (hŏl'lọ-ẹl)
Häm-ạ-dän'
Häm'ọ-ạze
Hä'nau (hä'nöû)
Häng-tcheôu'
Hän'ọ-ver
Här-fleŭr'
Här'lịng-ẹn
Här'tle-pôôl (här'tl-pôl)
Härtz, or Härz (härts)
Här'wịch (här'ịj)
Häş'le-mēre (-zl-)
Häş'lịng=dĕn
Hät'tẹ-räs
Haute (hōt)
Häv'ẹr-fọrd-wĕst'
Häv'ẹr-hĭll (-ĭl) (Eng.)
Hā'vẹr-hĭll (-ĭl) (U. S.)
Hâvre (hä'vr)
Hâvre-de-Grace (hăv'vr-
  dẹ-gräs')
Hạ-waī'ị (hạ-wī'ẹ)
Hâw'ịck, or Hâ'wịck
Hāy'tị
Häze'broûck (äz'brûk)
Hĕb'rị-dēş
Hĕch'ịng-ẹn
Hĕd-jäz'
Heī'dẹl-bërg
Heīl'brŏnn
Hĕl'gọ-länd
Hĕl'ị-gọ-länd
Hĕl'leş-pônt
Helmstädt (hĕlm'stät)
Hĕl-mûnd'
Hĕl'sịng-förş
Hẹl-vĕl'lyn
Hĕl'voet-slŭys, (or slöīs)
Hẹn-lō'pẹn
Hẹn-rī'cō
Hĕr-ạ-clē'ạ
Hẹ-rät', or Hē'rät
Hérault (hā-rō', or hä'-   [rō]
Hĕr'ẹ-fọrd
Hĕr'mạn-städt (hĕr'-
  mạn-stät)
Hernösand (hĕr'nọ-
  sänd)
Hĕrrn'hŭt
Hertford (här'fọrd)
  (Eng.)
Hërt'fọrd (U. S.)
Hĕr-zẹ-gọ-vî'nạ
Hĕsse Căs'sẹl

Ḣeuseden (höĭs'dẹn)
Heyts'bụ-ry (hāts'-)
Hịères (hē-ár')
Hĭld-bûrg-hau'sẹn (hĭlt-
  bûrg-höû'zẹn)
Hĭl'dẹs-heīm
Hĭm-ạ-laȳ'ạ, or Hịm-
  mä'lẹh
Hĭn-dọs-tän'
Hîrsçh'bërg
Hĭs-pạn-ị-ō'lạ
Ḣī-was'sẹe (hī-wŏs'ẹ)
Hō-ạng-hō', or
  Họ-ăng'hō
Họ-bō'kẹn
Hŏçh'heīm
Họ-deī'dä
Hōgue (hōg)
Hō-hẹn-lĭn'dẹn
Hō'hẹn-lō'he
Hō-hẹn-zŏl'lẹrn (hō-ẹn-
  (tsŏl'lẹrn)
Hō-kị-ĕn'
Holmes (hōmz)
Hŏl'steīn
Hŏl'y-hĕad
Hō'ly-ōke, or
  Hŏl'yōke
Hŏl'y-wĕll
Họ-nän', or Hō'nạn
Họn-dû'rạs
Hŏn'fleŭr
Hŏn'ị-tọn
Hŏn-ọ-lû'lû
Hôôğ'ẹ-vēēn
Hôôgh'ly (hôg'lẹ)
Hōorn
Hoŭgh'ạm (hŭf'ạm)
Hōugh'tọn (hō'tọn)
Hôu-quăng'
Hôu-sạ-tŏn'ịc
Höûs'sạ
Hôus'tọn
Hŭ-ạ-heī'nẹ
Huä-sạ-cuäl'cō
Huäs'cō, (or wäs'kō)
Hué (hû-ã', or hwā)
Huĕl'vä, (or wĕl'vä)
Huĕs'kä, (or wĕs'kä)
Huĭl-quịl-e'mŭ (hwĭl-
  kwịl-ā'mŭ)
Hulme (hôm)
Hürd'wär
Huy (höĭ)
Hvēēn (vēn, or vän)
Hȳ'dẹr-ạ-bäd'
Hȳ'drạ, (or hē'drạ)
Hȳ-drạ-bäd'

I.

Ĭb'ẹr-vĭlle
Ĭb-rạ-î'lạ
Ī'cọlm-kĭll (-kọm-)
Ị-gle'sị-äs (-glä'-)
Ĭg'lau (ĭg'löû)
î-guạ-lä'dä (-gwạ-)
Ĭl'chẹs-tẹr
Ĭl'frạ-combe (-kŭịn)
îl'ha Grăn'dẹ (ēl'yạ)
Ĭl'kẹs-tọn
Illimani (ĕl-yẹ-mä'nẹ)
Ĭl-lị-nöĭs', (or Ĭl-lẹ-nöī'}
Ĭl-lȳr'ị-ạ
Ĭl'mịn-stẹr
Ĭm-ẹ-rĭ''tị-ạ (-rĭsh'ẹ-ạ)
Ĭm'ọ-lä
Ĭn'dị-ạ, (or Ĭn'jẹ-ạ)
Ĭn-dị-ăn'ạ (ĭn-jẹ-ăn'ạ)
Ĭn-dịạn-ăp'ọ-lĭs
Ĭn'dịeş, (or Ĭn'jịz)
Ĭn-dōre'
Ĭn-dôur'
Indre (äng'dr)
Ĭn'gọl-städt (ĭng'gọl-
  stät)
Ĭnk-er-män'
Ĭnns'prûck
Ĭn-vẹ-rā'ry
Ĭn-vẹr-kēith'ịng
Ĭn-vẹr-lŏçh'y
Ĭn-vẹr-nĕss'
Ĭn-vẹ-rŭ'ry
Ī-ō'nạ
Ī'ọ-wạ
Ĭps'wịch, (or ĭp'sịj)
Ị-quî'que (ẹ-kē'kä)
Ị-räk' Ăd'jẹ-mî
Ị-räk' Ăr'ạ-bị
Ĭr-kôutsk'
Ĭr-ọ-quöĭs'
Ĭr-rạ-wâd'dy
Ĭs'çhị-ạ
Ĭsçh'ịm
Ị-se'ō (ẹ-sā'ō)
î'şẹr (ē'zẹr)
Isère (ẹ-zár')
î'şẹr-lōhn (ē'zẹr-lōn')
Isla (ī'lạ)
Ịs-lăm-ạ-bäd'
Islay (ī'lā)
Ĭş'lịng-tọn
Ĭs-mạ-îl', or Ĭs'māil
î'sọ-lä
Ĭs-pạ-hăn'
Ĭs-sạ-quē'nạ
Issoire (ĭs-swär')
Ĭs-sôu-dŭn'
Ĭt-ạ-pî-cụ-rŭ'
Ĭt-ạ-wâm'bạ
Ĭth'ạ-cạ
Ị-vî'çä, or Ĭv'ị-çä
Ĭv-re'ạ (-rā'-)

J.

Jaca (hä'kạ)
Jăc-mĕl' (zhăk-mĕl')
Jăcque-mĕl' (zhăk-mĕl')
Jaen (hä-ĕn')
Jăf'fạ, (or yäf'fạ)
Jăf-nạ-pạ-täm'
Jä'guạ (hä'gwạ)
Jäl-ôô-ăn'
Jạ-lôun'
Jạ-mäi'cạ

Jạ-nei'rō (jạ-nā'rō)
Jä'nị-nä (yä'nẹ-nä)
Jạ-lä'pạ (hạ-lä'pä)
Jạ-lĭs'cō (hạ-lĭs'kō)
Jạ-pän'
Jăque-mĕl'
Jär-năc' (zhär-näk')
Jär'ọ-släv (yär'ọ-släv)
Jäs'sy (yäs'sẹ)
Jauer (yöû'ẹr)
Jä'vạ, or Jä'vạ
Jĕd'dō, (or yĕd'dō)
Jĕl-ạ-lạ-bäd'
Jē'nạ, (or yä'nạ)
Jerez (hä-rĕth')
Jesi (yā'sẹ)
Jĕs'sō, (or yĕs'sō)
Jĕs-sụl-mēēr'
Jeȳ-pōre'
Jî-jō'nạ (hē-hō'nạ)
Jọ-än'nị-nä, or
  Jō-ạn-nî'nạ
Jŏl'ị-bä
Jĕn'kiọ-pĭng
Jọ-rŭl'lō (họ-rŭl'yō)
Jôud-pōre'
Joux (zhô)
Jū'ạn Fẹr-năn'dẹz
Jŭg'ḡẹr-nåuth (-nåut)
Jujuy (hŭ-hwē')
Juliers (zhŭ'lẹ-ä)
Jŭl'lịn-dẹr
Jungfrau (yŭng'frôû)
Jū-nị-ät'ạ

K.

Käar'tạ
Kaïr-wän'
Kaï-sạ-rî'ẹh
Käl-ạ-mạ-zôô'
Käl'ịsçh
Kạ-lŭ'gä
Käm'ị-niēc
Kä-mîn'iĕtz (-yĕts)
Käm-tchät'kạ
Kạ-nä'whạ (kạ-nåw'wạ)
Kän-dạ-här'
Kạn-kâ'kẹe
Kạ-rä'hịs-sär', or
  Kä-rạ-hîs'sạr
Kä-rạ-mä'nị-ạ
Kär'ạ-sŭ, or
  Kạ-rä'sŭ
Käsh-gär'
Kạs-kăs'kị-ạ
Kạ-täh'dịn
Kä'trịne, or Kät'rịne
Kạ-zän'
Kehl (kāl)
Keighley (kēth'lẹ)
Kẹ-lăt'
Kẹ-nä'whạ (kẹ-nåw'wạ)
Kē'ōgh (kē'ō)
Kē'ọ-kŭk
Kërgue'lẹn'ṣ Länd
Kër-mạn-shåw'
Kẹr-shåw'

Kĕṣ'wịck, (or kĕz'ịk)
Kĕts'kẹ-mĕt
Khä-mîl'
Khạ-räṣm'
Khär-kôf'
Khî'vạ
Khọ-känd'
Khō-rạs-sän'
Khŭ-zịs-tän'
Kị-äkh'tạ
Kî-ạn-kŭ'
Kĭck-ạ-pôô'
Kĭd'dẹr-mĭn-stẹr
Kị-ĕf', or Kî-ĕv'
Kiĕl
Kĭl-dåre'
Kịl-kĕn'ny
Kịl-lä'lạ
Kịl-lä'lōe, or
  Kĭl-lạ-lōe'
Kịn-cär'dịne
Kĭng-Kî-Tä'ō
Kịn-rŏss'
Kịn-säle'
Kịn-tōre'
Kịn-tȳre'
Kî'ọ-wäy
Kịr-kâl'dy
Kirkcudbright (kĭrk-kô'brẹ)
Kĭr-mạn-shâh'
Kĭr-riẹ-müir'
Kĭs-kị-mĭn'ẹ-täs
Kĭt-tän'nịng
Kĭt-tạ-tĭn'ny
Kî-ŭ'sị-ŭ
Kî-ụ-tä'jạh
Kĭz'ịl Ir'mạk
Klä'ḡẹn-fŭrth (-fŭrt)
Klät'tau (-töû)
Klau'sẹn-bŭrg (klöû'-)
Knĭs'tẹ-neau (nĭs'tẹ-nō)
Kō-lîn'
Kŏl-y-văn'
Kō'nị-ẹh
Kŏn'jgṣ-bërg
Kôôs-kôôs'kẹ
Kôô-tạ-naï'
Kō-rạs-sän'
Kör-dọ-fän'
Kŏs-cị-ŭs'kō
Kôu-bän'
Kôursk
Kŏw'nō (kŏv'nō)
Krás-nọ-yärsk'
Kreuznach (kröïts'näk)
Kŭr-dịs-tän'
Kŭr-rẹe-chäne'
Kū-taï'yẹh
Kụt-tōre'

L.

Läa'lạnd
Läb-rạ-dōr'
Läc'cạ-dīveṣ
Läch-ạ-wäx'ẹn
Lä-Chîne'

Läch'sä
Läck-ạ-wän'nạ
Lạ-drōneṣ'
Lä-fạy-ĕtte'
Lä-Fôurçhe'
Lä Guaȳ'rä
Lạ-gŭ'nä
Lạ-Hōgue'
Lạ-hōre'
Lạ-hôu' (lạ-hô')
Lä Män'chä
Lạ-mär'
Lä Märçhe
Lăm-bạ-ye'que (yä'kä)
Lä-me'gō (-mä'-)
Läm'mẹr-mŭir
Lạ-Möïlle'
Läm'sạ-kî
Lä-naï'
Län'ạrk, or Lạ-närk'
Län-cẹ-rō'tạ
Län-däff'
Län-dẹr-neau' (-nō'-)
Landes (längd)
Län'drẹ-cy
Ländṣ'crọ-nä, or
  Ländṣ-crō'nạ
Ländṣ'hŭt
Län-geäc' (län-zhäk')
Läng'ẹ-länd
Läng-ẹn-säl'zạ (-tsạ)
Läng'hoĭm (läng'ụm)
Län'gres (läng'gr)
Län-guẹ-dŏc' (läng-ḡẹ-dŏk')
Lạ-nî'cạ
Lä Plä'tạ
Lä-räçhe' (lä-räsh')
Lạ-re'dō (lạ-rä'dō)
Lär-ịs-tän'
Lär'nị-kä
Lä-Sälle'
Lät-ạ-cŭn'gä
Lät-ạ-kî'ạ
Lät-tạ-kôô'
Lau'bän (löû'bän)
Lâu'ẹn-bürg, (or löû'-
  ẹn-bürg)
Lau-ṣănne' (lō-zăn')
Lauterbourg (lō-tẹr-bôr')
Lau'tẹr-brŭnn (löû'-)
Lä-väl'
Lä-vaur' (lä-vōr')
Lä-vō'rō
Laȳ'băçh
Lĕam'ịng-tọn
Lebrija (lä-brē'hä)
Lĕc'ce (lĕt'chä)
Lĕçh
Lĕc-tôure'
Lee'wạrd (lē'wạrd, or
  lŭ'ụrd)
Lĕg-hörn', or Lĕg'hörn
Legnano (lĕn-yä'nō)
Lē'hīgh (lē'hī)
Lĕices'tẹr (lĕs'tẹr)
Leigh (lĕ)
Leigh'lịn (lĕk'lin)
  Lēigh'lịn (lē'lịn)
Lēigh'tọn (lĕ'tụn)

Leï'nịng-ẹn
Leïn'stẹr, or Lēin'stẹr
Leïp'sịc
Leï-rì'ạ
Lēith (lēth)
Leït'mẹ-rĭtz (-rĭts)
Leït'rịm, or Lēi'trịm
Lẹ-năp'ẹ
Lĕn'ạ-wēē
Lĕn'nị-Lẹn-năp'pẹ
Lẹ-nōir' (lẹ-nōr')
Lẹn-tî'nä
Le-ọ-gäne' (lä-)
Lĕom'ịn-stẹr (U. S.)
Leominster (lĕm'stẹr)
  (Eng.)
Lẹ-ŏn', or Lē'ọn
Lē-ọ-nî'dị
Lē-ọn-tî'nị
Lẹ-ō'pọld-städt (-stät)
Lẹ-pän'tō
Le Puy (lẹ-pwē')
Lĕr'ị-cî, (or lĕr'ẹ-chē)
Lĕr'ị-dä
Lĕr'wịck (lĕr'ịk)
Lĕs'ị-nä
Leuçh'tẹn-bŭrg (löïk'-)
Leuk (löïk)
Leut'mạ-rĭtz (löït'mạ-
  rĭts)
Leutschau (löït'shöû)
Lẹ-vänt'
Lĕv'ẹn, or Lē'vẹn
Lẹ-wâr'dẹn, or Leeû'-
  wạr-dĕn
Leū'ịs-hăm, or
  Leū'ịsh-ạm
Lĕx'ịng-tọn
Leyden (lī'dn, or lä'dn)
Lēy'lạnd
Lî-bôurne'
Lĭch'tẹ-nau (-nöû)
Lĭch'tẹn-fĕlṣ
Lĭch'tẹn-steïn
Liēḡe, (or lē-äzh')
Liēg'nĭtz (-nĭts)
Lî-êrre'
Lîlle, or Lîsle (lĕl)
Lî'mä, or Lī'mạ
Lĭm-ōḡes' (lĭm-ōzh')
Lî-môu-ṣin' (lē-mô-
  zäng')
Lî-môux' (lē-mô')
Lị-nä'rẹs
Lĭn'cọln (lĭng'kụn)
Lĭn'dâu, (or lĭn'döû)
Lĭng'ẹn
Lĭn'kiọ-pĭng
Lịn-lĭth'gōw
Lĭp'ạ-rị
Lĭp'pẹ-Dĕt'mōld
Lî-ṣị-eŭx' (lē-zẹ-ŭ')
Lĭth-ụ-ä'nị-ạ
Lĭt'ịz
Lĭt-tọ-rä'lẹ
Lị-vä'dị-ạ, or Lĭv-ạ-dî'ạ
Ljŭs'ne (lyôs'nä)
Llän-däff'
Llạn-gŏl'lẹn, (or lạn-
  gŏth'lẹn)

Llăn'ĭd-loĕs (lăn'ĭd-lĕs)
Llá'nŏs (lyä'nŏs)
Llanrwst (lăn-rôst')
Llerena (lyạ-rā'nä)
Lọ-ăn'gō (lọ-äng'gō)
Lọ-cär'nō
Lọch-ä'bẹr
Loches (lōsh)
Lŏch Lĕv'ẹn
Lŏch Lō'mọnd
Lŏch-mā'bẹn
Lŏch'y
Lodève (lŏ-dāv')
Lō'dĭ (lō'dē)
Lọ-fŏ'dẹn
Logroño (lọ-grŏn'yŏ)
Loire (lwär)
Loiret (lwä-rā')
Loja (lō'hä)
Lō'kẹr-ĕn
Lọm-bŏk'
Lō'mọnd
Lôô-chôô'
Lọ-rāin' (Ohio)
Lọ-rĕt'tō
L'Orient (lō-rẹ-äng')
Lŏr-rāine' (Fr.)
Lŏs Ăn'gẹ-lĕs
Lŏst-wĭth'iel
Löû'don
Lôu'dọun
Loŭgh'bŏr-ọugh (lŭf'-bŭr-ọ)
Lough Erne (lŏk'ĕrn')
Lough Neagh (lŏk'nē', or lŏk'nē'ạ)
Lough-reā' (lŏk-rā')
Lôu-î'sạ
Lôu-ĭs-bürg
Lôu-ĭs-äde'
Lôu-ĭs-i-ä'nạ
Lôu'ĭs-vĭlle, (or lô'ẹ-vĭl)
Lôu-väin'
Louviers (lô'vẹ-ä)
Lôu'vō
Lŏw'ẹll
Lŏwĕṣ'tŏft
Lowositz (lō'vọ-sĭts)
Lozère (lō-zár')
Lụ-bĕck', or Lạ'bĕck
Lụ-cā'yạ, (or lụ-kī'ạ)
Lŭc'cạ, or Lŭc'cä
Lŭ-ce'nä (lŭ-thā'nä)
Lŭ-ce'rä (lŭ-chā'rä)
Lŭ-cẽrne'
Lụ-çŏn', (or lụ-sŏng')
Lŭ-dạ-mär'
Lŭd'wĭgṣ-bŭrg
Lŭd'wĭgṣ-lŭst
Lụ-gā'nō
Lŭnd
Lŭ'nẹ-bụrg
Lŭ-nĕl'
Lŭ'nẹ-vĭlle'
Lụ-pä'tạ
Lụ-sä'tĭ-ạ (lụ-sā'shẹ-ạ)
Lŭt'zẹn (-sẹn)
Lŭx'ẹm-bürg
Lụ-zẽrne'
Lụ-zŏn'

Ly-cŏm'ĭng
Lȳm'fĭ-ōrd
Lyonnais (lē-ọn-nā')
Lȳ'ọnṣ (lī'ọnz)

M.

Mäas
Mạ-cä'ŏ, (or mạ-köû')
Măc-ạ-pä'
Măc'clẹṣ-fiĕld (-klz-)
Măç-ẹ-dō'nị-ạ
Măc-ẹ-rä'tä (mäch-)
Mạ-chī'ạs
Măck-i-nâw'
Mạc-leän'
Mạ-cômb' (-kôm')
Mạ-côu'pĭn
Mạ-crôôm'
Măc-quar'rẹe (-kwŏr'-)
Măd-ạ-gäs'cạr
Măd-ạ-wâs'cạ
Măd-dạ-lō'nị
Mạ-dẽi'rạ, (or mạ-dā'rạ)
Mạ-dräs'
Mạ-drîd', or Măd'rĭd
Mạ-dŭ'rạ
Mäel'strôm
Mäeṣe (mäz)
Maĕs'trĭcht (mĕs'trĭkt)
Măg-ạ-dŏx'ạ
Măg-dạ-lē'nạ, (or -lā'nạ)
Mạ-gĕl'lạn, or Măg-ẹl-län'
Măg-ẹ-rōe'
Măg-ġiō'rẹ (mạ-jō'rä)
Mạ-gĭn-dạ-nä'ŏ
Măg-nî'ṣạ
Magny (män'yẹ)
Mä-hä-nŭd'dy
Mạ-hōn', or Mạ-hôn'
Mạ-hō'nịng
Măh-rät'tạ
Mä'j-dä
Maī-hịd-pōre'
Mä'j-nä
Mạ-kō'quẹ-tạ (-kẹ-)
Măl-ạ-bär'
Măl'ạ-gạ
Mạ-läi'sị-ạ (mạ-lä'shẹ-ạ)
Mälar (mä'lạr)
Mälaren (mä'lạr-ẹn)
Mạ-läy'
Mạ-lä'yạ
Măl-dîvẹṣ', or Măl'dīvẹṣ
Malheur (mạ-lôr')
Malines (mä-lēn')
Măl'mẹ-dy
Mălmeṣ'bụ-ry (mämz'-)
Malplaquet (măl-pläk'ä)
Măl'strôm
Măl-vạ-sî'ạ, or Mạl-vä'sị-ạ
Măl'vẹrn, or Mäl'vẹrn
Mäl'wäh
Mạ-mär'ọ-nĕck

Mạ-näar'
Măn-ạ-gŭnk'
Mänçhe
Mạn-dä'rạ
Măn-dạ-vēē'
Mạn-dĭn'gō (-dĭng'-)
Mä'nẹ
Măn-frẹ-dō'nị-ạ
Măn-gạ-lōre'
Măn'heīm
Măn-ị-tôu-wŏc'
Männ'hạrụs-bẽrg
Man-re'sä (-rā'sä)
Mäns, Lẹ (lẹ-mäng')
Mạn-sôu'rä
Mạn-tchôô'rị-ạ
Măn'tọ-vä
Măn-zạ-nä'rẹs, (or män-thä-nä'rẹs)
Măn-zạ-nîl'lō (-yō)
Măr-ạ-caȳ'bō (-kī'bō)
Măr-ạm-baȳ'ạ
Măr'ạ-mĕc
Măr-ạn-hăm'
Marañon (măr'ạ-nŏn, or măr-ạn-yōn')
Mạ-rä'vị
Märçhe
Măr-che'nạ (-chā'-)
Măr-dîn'
Măr-gạ-rî'tạ
Măr-ị-ä'nạ
Măr-iē-Gạ-länte'
Mä-rị-ĕl'
Mạ-rî'ẹn-băd
Mạ-rî'ẹn-bürg
Mạ-rî-ẹn-wẽr'dẹr
Mạ-rî-ẹn-zĕll' (-tsĕl')
Mạ-rîn'
Mā'rị-ọn, or Măr'ị-ọn
Mạ-rĭt'zä (-sä)
Märl'bŏr-ọugh
Măr'mọ-rạ
Măr-ọ-nî', or Mạ-rō'nî
Mä-rŏsçh' (-rŏsh')
Mạ-rŏss'
Mạr-que'sạṣ (mạr-kä'-sạz)
Mạr-sä'lä
Marseilles (mär-sälz')
Măr-tạ-bän'
Măr-tị-nî'cō
Măr'tị-nîque'
Mạr-wâr'
Mā'ry-lẹ-bōne, (or măr'-ẹ-bọn) [rō)
Masafuero (măs-ạ-fwä'-
Măs'cạ-lî
Mạs-cä'lî
Măs'hạm (măs'ạm)
Mạs-kē'gọn
Măs-sạ-chŭ'sẹtts
Măs'sọ-wäh
Măs'ụ-äh
Mạ-sŭ-lị-pạ-tăm'
Măt-ạ-mō'rạs
Mạ-tăn'zạs
Mät-ạ-păn'
Mạt-tăp'ọ-ny
Măt-ạ-rî'ạ

Măt-ạ-rŏ'
Mạ-te'rä (-tā'-)
Măts'maī
Măt'ụ-rä, or Mạ-tŭ'rä
Mâuch Chŭnk
Mâuch'lịne
Mâu'î
Mâu-mēē'
Mau-rẹ-päs' (mŏ-rẹ-pä')
Mâu-rĭ''tị-ŭs (-rĭsh'ẹ-
Maȳ-ä'cọ　　　　[ŭs)
Maȳ-ạ-guä'nạ
Mayence (mä-yäns')
Maȳ-ĕnne'
Mayne (män, or mīn)
Māy-nôôth'
Mạ-zăn-dẹ-răn'
Măz-ạt-län'
Mạz-zä'rä (mạt-sä'rä)
Mẹ-ä'cō
Meaux (mō)
Mĕch'lịn
Mẹ-chō-ạ-căn'
Mĕck'lẹn-bürg
Mẹ-cŏn'
Mĕc-răn'
Mẹ-dî'nạ, or Mẹ-dī'nạ (Ar.)
Mẹ-dī'nạ (Ohio)
Mĕd-ị-tẹr-rā'nẹ-ạn
Mee-rŭt'
Mĕigṣ (mĕgz)
Meī-kŏng'
Meī'nịng-ẹn
Meīs'sẹn (mī'sẹn)
Mẹ-jẽr'däh
Mĕk-ị-nĕz'
Melazzo (mä-lăt'sō)
Mĕl'bọurne
Mẹ-lĭn'dạ
Mĕl-rōṣe'
Mĕl'tọn-Mōw'brạy
Mẹ-lŭn'
Mĕm'ẹl
Mĕm'mịng-ẹn
Mĕm-phrẹ-mā'gŏg
Mẹ-näi', or Mĕn'aī
Mẹ-naī'nạ
Mẹ-năn'
Mẹ-närd'
Mendaña (-dän'yạ)
Mende (mängd)
Mĕn-dọ-cî'nō
Mẹn-dō'zạ
Mẹ-nin' (mẹ-năng')
Mẹn-nŏm'ọ-niẹ
Mĕntz (mĕnts)
Mẹ-nŭf'
Mẹn-zä'lẹh
Mĕq'uị-nĕz (mĕk'ẹ-nĕz)
Mẹr-dîn'
Mẹr-guî' (mẹr-ġē')
Mĕr'ị-dä
Mĕr-ị-mạ-chî'
Mĕr'ị-ọ-nĕth
Mĕr-mẹn-tau' (-tō')
Mĕr'ọ-ē
Mĕr'sẹ-bürg
Mĕr'thyr Tȳd'vịl
Mĕṣ'chĭd

Mĕsh'ĕd
Mĕs-ọ-lŏn'g̃ị
Mẹs-sî'nạ
Mĕs-ụ-rä'dō
Mĕs-ụ-ra'tä
Mĕt'ẹ-lïn
Metz (mĕts, or mäs)
Meurthe (mŭrt)
Meŭṣe (mūz)
Mézières (mĕz-yàr')
Mî-ä'cō
Mĭ-ăm'ị
Mî-ä'vä
Mĭçh'ị-gän
Mĭçh-ịl-ị-măck'ị-năc, (or măk-ẹ-nâw')
Mî-chō-ạ-căn'
Mĭd'del-bürg
Mĭd'dle-bŏr-ọugh
Mĭd'dle-bu-ry (-bĕr-ẹ)
Mĭl'ạn, or Mị-lán'
Milhau (mē-lō')
Mĭl'lẹdge-vĭlle
Mî'lō
Mĭl-wâu'kiẹ
Mĭn'ciō (mĭn'chō)
Mĭn-dạ-nä'ō
Mịn-dō'rō
Mịn-grē'lị-ạ
Mĭn'hō, (or mēn'yō)
Mĭn-nẹ-sō'tạ
Mĭn-nẹ-tär'ee
Miño (mēn'yō)
Mĭq-uẹ-lŏn' (-ẹ-)
Mĭr-ạ-mị-çhî'
Mị-răn'dọ-lä
Mî-rẹ-côurt' (-kôr')
Mırepoix (mēr-pwä')
Mĭs'ị-trä
Mıskolcz (mĭsh-kōlts')
Mịs-sĭs'quẹ (-kẹ)
Mĭs-sịs-sĭp'pị
Mĭs-sọ-lŏn'g̃hị
Mịs-sôu'rị (mịs⁴sô'rẹ)
Mịs-träs'
Mĭt'tau (mĭt'töû)
Mọ-bîle'
Mō-cạ-răn'gạ (-răng'-)
Mō'çhạ
Mō'dẹ-nä
Mŏd'ị-cä
Mŏg-ạ-dōre'
Mohacs (mō-häch')
Mō'hâwk
Mọ-hē'gạn
Mō-hị-lĕv', or Mọ-hí'lẹv
Moıssac (mwạ-säk')
Mŏl'dau (-döû)
Mọl-dạ vị-ạ
Mọl-fĕt'tä
Mọ-lîse', or Mọ-lî'se (-sä)
Mō-lọ-kaī'
Mŏm-bäs'
Mŏm-bä'zạ
Mŏm'pŏx (or mŏm-pō')
Mŏn'ạ-cō
Mŏn'ạ-ghăn (-găn)
Mŏn-ạs-tîr'

Mŏn-chạ-bôô'
Mŏn-de'gō (-dā'gō)
Mondoñedo (mŏn-dọn-yā'dō)
Mŏn-dọ-vî'
Mọ-nĕm-bạ-sî'ạ
Mŏn'fạ-lôut
Mŏn-fẹr-rä'tō
Mŏn-ghîr'
Mọn-gō'lị-ạ
Mŏn-ị-teau' (-tō')
Mŏn-ọ-mọ-tä'pạ
Mọ-nŏn-gạ-hē'lạ
Mō-nọn-gā'lị-ạ
Mọ-nŏp'ọ-lị
Mŏn-re-ä'le (-lä)
Mọn-rō'vị-ạ
Mons (mōngs)
Mŏn'tạ-gūe
Montauban (mōng-tō-bäng')
Montbéliard (mōng-bā-lẹ-är')
Mŏnt-cälm' (-käm')
Mŏn'tẹ-çhî-ä'rō
Mŏn-tē'gō
Mŏn-tēith'
Mŏn-tẹ-lō'vẹz (-vẹs)
Mŏn-tẹ-ne'grō (-nā'-)
Mŏn-tẹ-reau' (-rō')
Mŏn-tẹ-rey' (-rā')
Mŏn'tẹ Vĭd'ẹ-ō, (or mŏn'tẹ-vẹ-dā'ō)
Mŏnt-fẹr-rät'
Mŏnt-gŏm'ẹr-y
Montilla (mŏn-tēl'yä)
Mŏnt-märtre' (mōng-märtr')
Mŏnt-mọ-rĕn'cy
Mŏnt-pēl'iẹr (-yẹr)
Mŏnt-pĕl'lị-ẹr, (or mŏng-pĕl'ẹ-ä)
Mŏn-trōṣe'
Mŏnt-sẹr-rät'
Môôr-shĕd-ạ-băd'
Mọ-quĕl'ụm-nẹ
Mọ-răd-ạ-băd'
Mọ-rä'vä
Mŏr'ay (mŭr'rẹ)
Mŏr-bị-hän'
Mọ-rē'ạ
Mọ-re'nä (mọ-rä'nä)
Mọr-lä'çhị-ạ
Morlaix (mŏr-lä')
Mọ-rōn'
Mŏr-tägne' (mŏr-tän')
Mŏr-tä'rạ
Mörte-mär'
Mŏs'chō
Mŏs'cōw
Mọ-ṣĕlle'
Mọs-quî'tō (-kē'tō)
Mō'sŭl
Mọ-tä'lạ, or Mô'tạ-lä
Mọ-tä'pạ
Mọ-trîl'
Moulins (mô-läng')
Môul-tän'
Mōul'triẹ

Möünt De-ṣërt'
Môur-zôuk'
Möÿ-ạ-mĕn'sịng
Mō-zạm-bîque'
Mŭhl (môl)
Mŭh'lẹn-bûrg
Mühlheim (môl-hīm')
Mŭhr (môr)
Mŭl'dẹ
Mŭl-lịn-gär'
Mŭ'nịch
Mür'çị-ạ (mür'shẹ-ạ)
Mür'freẹṣ-bŏr-ọugh
Mür'rum-bĭd-gee
Mür-vị-e'drō (mŭr-vẹ-ā'-drō)
Mŭs-cät'
Mŭs-cạ-tîne'
Mus-cō'g̃ee
Mŭs'cọ-vy
Mus-kĭn'gum
Mŭs'sel-bürgh (-bürg, or -bŭr-ọ)
Mўc'ọ-nî
Mўc'ọ-nŏs
Mў-sōre'
Mўt'ị-lē

N.

Nā'ạs
Nä-bạ-jō'ä (-hō'ä)
Näc-ọg-dō'cheṣ
Nạg-pôôr'
Nạ-hänt'
Nạ-mä'quạs
Nä'mụr, or Nä-mŭr'
Nän-gạ-sä'kị
Nän-kîn'
Nän'sẹ-mŏnd
Näntes
Nän'tị-cōke
Nänt'wịch (nänt'ịch)
Nä'pleṣ (nä'plz)
Näp'lôus
Näp'ọ-lị
Nạr-bŏnne'
Nạ-mä'dä
Nä'rọ-vä, or Nạ-rō'vä
Nāṣe'by
Nạ-shō'bạ
Näs'sâu, (or näs'söû)
Nä'tạl, or Nạ-täl'
Nätch-ị-tŏch'eṣ, (or näk'ẹ-tŏsh)
Nạ-tō'lị-ạ
Nạt-tōre'
Nâu'gạ-tŭck
Nâup'lị-ạ
Näv'ạn
Näv'ạ-rîn
Näv-ạ-rî'nō
Nạ värre'
Näv-ị-dăd'
Neagh, (nä, or nē'ạ)
Nĕdj'ẹd
Nẹ-ĕm-bụ-cŭ'
Nĕg-ạ-pạ-täm'

Nĕg'rọ-pŏnte
Nĕïl-ghĕr'ry
Neïs'sẹ (nī'sẹ)
Nejin (nä-zhĕn')
Nẹl-lōre'
Nemours (nẹ-môr')
Nenagh (nẹ-nä')
Nẹ-pâul'
Nĕp'ịs-sïng
Nérac (nä-räk')
Nërt'sçhïnsk
Nĕs'cọ-pĕc
Nẹ-thôu' (nẹ-tô')
Neŭ'bürg, (or nöï'bûrg)
Neufchâtel (nŭf-shạ-tĕl')
Neusatz (nöï'säts)
Neŭse (nŭs)
Neŭ'sōhl, (or nöï'zōl)
Neŭ'städt, (or nöï'stät)
Nĕ'vạ, (or nä-vä')
Nẹ-vä'dä
Nevers (nẹ-vàr')
Nĕv'ẹr-sïnk
New-cäs'tle, or New'cäs-tle
New E-chō'tạ
New'found-länd
New Gre-nä'dạ .
New Ör'lẹ-ạnṣ
Ngami ('n-gä'mẹ)
Nī-äg'ạ-rạ
Nïc-ạ-rä'guä (-gwä)
Nîce (nēs)
Nïc-ọ-bär'
Nïc-ọ-let' (-lä')
Nị-cŏp'ọ-lị
Nị-cō'sị-ạ, or Nî-cọ-sî'ạ
Nïc-ọ-te'rạ (-tä'-), *P. T.*
Nî-cō'te-rä (-tä-), *M.*
Niē'men
Nieŭ'pört
Nièvre (nē-ā'vr)
Nī'g̃er
Nijni (nïzh'nẹ)
Nïk-ọ-laï'ẹf
Nïl-cŭnd'
Nïm'ẹ-guĕn (-g̃ĕn)
Nịm-we'g̃ĕn (-wä'-)
Nî'ört (nē'ör)
Nị'phọn, or Nī'phọn
Nïp'ịs-sïng
Nïsh-ạ-pôur·
Nismes, or Nîmes (nēmz, or nēm)
Nïs-sị-bîn'
Nïtch-ẹ-guŏn' (-gwŏn')
Nî vĕlles' (nẹ-vĕl')
Nọ-ce'rä (nọ-chä'rä)
Nord-hau'sen (nört-höû'-zen)
Nordköping (nört'kọ-pïng) [ẹn]
Nördlingen (nört'lịng-)
Nör'fọlk, (or nör'fọk)
Nör'rịdge-wŏck
Nör-thŭm'ber-länd
Nör'wịch (nör'rịj)
Nŏt'tịng-häm
Nọ vä'rä

Nŏv-gọ-rŏd', *or* Nŏv-ọ-
   gọ-rŏd'
Nŏx'ụ-bēē
Noyon (nwạ-yŏng')
Nŭ-e'ceş (nŭ-ā'seş)
Nuc-vî'tạs (nwā-)
Nŭ-kạ-kî'vạ
Nŭ'rẹm-bërg
Nyköping (nẹ-kö'pịng)

O.

Oahu (wä'hô)
Oajaca (wä-hä'kä)
Ọ-beid' (ọ-bäd')
Ŏ'bẹr-lïn
Ocaña (ọ-kän'yä)
Ŏc-cọ-quân'
Ō-cẹ-än'ạ (ō-shẹ-än'ạ)
Ŏc-ẹ-ō'lạ
Ō'chil
Ŏck-lọ-kō'nẹe
Oc-mŭl'ġee
Ọ-cō'nẹe
Ŏ'crạ-cōke
Ŏc-tọ-rä'rạ
Ō'dẹn-sēē
Ō-dẹy-pōre'
ôe'lạnd (ô'lạnd)
Oels (ĕls)
ôe'rẹ-brō
ôe'sẹl (ô'sẹl)
Oët'tịng-ẹn
Ŏf'fẹn-bäch
Ŏg'dẹnş-bürg
Ọ-ġēē'chẹe
Ŏ'gle-thörpe (-gl-)
Oglio (ōl'yō)
Oise (wáz)
Ō-kạ-näg'ạr
Ŏk-hôtsk'
Ŏk-tïb'bẹ-hâ
Ŏl'dẹn-bürg
Ō-lẹ-än'
Oleggio (ọ-lĕd'jō)
Ō-lẹ-ō'nä
Oléron (ō-lä-rōng')
Ŏl-ị-vĕn'zä
Olmütz (ŏl'mŭts)
Ŏl'ọ-nĕtz, *or*
   Ọ-lō'nẹtz (-nẹts)
Ọ-lŏt'
Ŏm-ạ-hâ'
Ọ-män'
Ọ-mō'ạ
Ọm-pŏm-pọ-nôô'sục
Ọ-nē'gạ
Oneglia (ọ-nāl'yä)
Ọ-neï'dạ
Ŏn-ọn-dä'gạ
Ọn-tä'rị-ō
Ŏô-jeïn'
Oô-nạ-läs'kạ
Oôr'fä
Oô-rôo-mēē'ạ
Oôs-tạ-nâu'lẹe
Ôôs'tẹr-höût

Ŏp-ẹ-lôu'sạs
Ŏp'pẹn-heïm
Ọ-rän', *or* Ō'rạn
Ŏrebro (ŏr'ẹ-brō)
Ŏr'ẹ-gŏn
Ō'rẹl, *or* Ọ-rĕl'
Ō-rẹl-lä'nä, (*or* ō-rẹl-
   yä'nä)
Ō'rẹn-bürg
Ọ-rĕn'se (-sä)
Ō-rị-hue'lä (ō-rẹ-wä'lä)
Ō-rị-nō'cō
Ọ-rïs'kạ-ny
Ō-rịs-tä'nō
Ŏr-ị-zä'bä
ŏr'lẹ-ạnş
ŏr-lôf'
Ŏr-ọ-pe'sạ (-pä'-)
ŏr'sọ-vä
ŏr'tẹ-gäl
Orthèz (ŏr-tä')
Ọ-rŭ'bä
Ō-rŭ'rō
ŏr-vj-e'tō (-ä'-)
Ọ-sāġe'
Ọs-cẹ-ō'lạ
Ŏsh'kŏsh
Ŏsh-môô-naỹn'
Ŏş'ị-mō
Ŏş'nạ-bürg
Ŏş-sạ-bâw'
Ŏş'sị-pēē
Ŏş'sọ-lä
Ŏş'sọ-ry
Ọs-sŭ'nä
Ọş-tĕnd'
Ŏş'tị-äks
Ọş-trä'sị-ạ (-shẹ-ạ)
Ŏş-wẹ-gätch'iẹ
Ọş-wē'gō
Ŏş'wẹs-try
Ŏt-ạ-bä'lō
Ō'tạ-heïte, *or*
   Ō-tạ-heï'te
Ọt-chä'kọv, *or*
   Ŏt-chạ-kŏv'
Ọ-trän'tō, *or* Ō'trạn-tō
Ọt-sē'gō
Ŏt'tạ-wâ
Ouach-ị-tâ' (wŏsh-)
ôude (ôd)   [när'dä]
ôude'närde, (*or* ŏû-dẹ-
ôu'fä (ò'fä)
Oŭn'dle (ŭn'dl)
ôu'rạl, *or* Ôu-räl'
ôu-rälsk'
ôu-rî'que (-kä)
ôur'fä (ôr'fä)
ôur'gä (ôr'gä)
ôur-mî'äh
Ourthe (ôrt)
ôuşe (ôz, *or* öûz)
ôu-tchạng-fôu'
ôuz-bĕks'
Ō-vẹr-ỹs'sẹl
Ō-vị-e'dō (-ä'-)
Ọ-vō'cä
Ọ-wâs'cō
Ọ-wē'gō
Ọ-whỹ'hēē

Ō-yạ-pŏc'
Ọ-zärk'

P.

Pạ-chŭ'cä
Păc'ọ-lĕt
Pạ-däng'
Păd'ẹr-börn
Păd'ọ-vä
Păd'ụ-ạ
Paglia (päl'yä)
Pāiş'lẹy
Pạ-lăt'ị-nāte
Păl'ạ-tïne
Păl-ạ-wăn'
Păl-ẹm-băng'
Pạ-lĕn'cị-ạ
Pạ-lĕn'que (-kä)
Pạ-lër'mō
Păl'ẹs-tïne
Păl-ẹs-trî'nä
Păl-hạn-pôôr'
Păl-ị-câud-çhĕr'ry
Păl'lị-sẹr
Păl-mî'rạs
Păl-mỹ'rạ
Păm'lị-cō
Păm-pẹ-lŭ'nä
Păm-plō'nä
Păn-ạ-mä'
Pạ-naỹ' (pạ-nï')
Pạ-nō'lä
Pạ-nŭ'cō
Pä'ọ-lä
Păp'ụ-ä
Pä-rä'
Păr-ạ-guāy', *or*
   Pär-ạ-guaỹ'
Păr-ạ-î'bä
Păr-ạ-măr'ị-bō, *or*
   Pä-rạ-mạ-rî'bō
Păr-ạ-nä'
Pä-rạ-nạ-guä'
Păr-ạ-nạ-î'bä
Păr-ạ-tî'
Pạ-rĕc'çhị-ä
Pä'rị-ä
Pạ-rî'mä
Păr-ị-nä'
Pär-mẹ-şăn'
Pär-räl'
Păs-cạ-gôu'lạ
Pạs-cuä'rō
Păs-quọ-tänk'
Pạs-sā'ịc
Păs-sạ-mạ-quŏd'dy
Păs-sạ-rôô-wăn'
Passau (päs'söû)
Pạs-sy' (pạs-sē')
Păt-ạ-gō'nị-ạ
Pạ-tāy'
Păt'ẹ-rä
Pạ-träs'
Pau (pō)
Pä-vî'ä
Pâw'cạ-tŭck
Pâw-tŭck'ẹt

Paỹ'tạ
Pēē'bleş (pē'blz)
Peï'hō, (*or* pä'hō)
Peï'pụs, (*or* pä'ẹ-pŭs)
Pē-kïng', *or* Pē-kïn'
Pẹ-lew̄'
Pĕm'bị-nä
Pĕm-ị-ġẹ-was'sẹt (pĕm-
   ẹ-jẹ-wŏs'sẹt)
Pẹ-năng'
Pĕnn-syl-vā'nị-ạ
Pĕn-rỹn', *or* Pĕn'rỹn
Pĕn-sạ-cō'lạ
Pẹn-zănce'
Pẹ-ō'rị-ạ
Pẹr-dî'dō
Pĕr-ẹ-slävl'
Për'gọ-lạ
Périgord (pĕr'ẹ-gör')
Périgueux (pĕr'ẹ-gŭ')
Pẹr-nä'guạ
Pér-nạm-bŭ'cō
Pér'nau (pér'nöû)
Pe-rō'te (pä-rō'tä)
Perpignan (për-pēn-
   yáng')
Pẹr-quïm'ạnş
Për'sị-ạ (për'shẹ-ạ)
Pẹ-rŭ'
Pẹ-rŭ'ġị-ạ
Pe'sạ-rō (pä'-)
Pĕs-çhị-e'rä (-ä'-)
Pẹ-shä'wụr
Pĕsth (pĕst)
Pē-tchẹe-lēē'
Pē'tẹr-bör-ọugh
Pē'tẹrş-bürg
Pē-tẹr-wâr'deïn
Pẹ-trō-zạ-vŏdsk'
Pẹt-sçhö'rä
Phïl-ạ-dĕl'phị-ạ
Phị-lïp'pịneş
Phïl-ịp-pŏp'ọ-lị
Pî-ạ-cĕn'zä (pē-ạ-chĕnt'-
Pị-ä've (-vä)   [sä
Pïc'ạr-dy
Pị-chïn'chạ
Pî'cō
Pïc-tôu' (pïk-tô')
Piēd'mŏnt
Pị-ĕn'zä (pẹ-ĕnt'sä)
Pî-e'tọ-lä (-ä'-)
Pignerol (pïn-yạ-rōl')
Pïl-cọ-mä'yō
Pïl'lau (pïl'löû)
Pïn-ẹ-rō'lō
Pî-ọm-bî'nō
Pïq'uạ (pïk'wạ)
Pïr'mạ-sĕns
Pî'şä
Pịs-căt'ạ-quạ
Pịs-căt'ạ-quïs
Pïs-tō'jä (pïs-tō'yä)
Pït'cāith-ly
Pî'tẹ-ä
Plạ-cĕn'cị-ạ
Placer (plä-thër')
   Plạ-cêr'
Plăque-mîne'
Plä'tä, Lä

Plau'en (plöû'en)
Pleïs'se (plĭ'se) [ár']
Plombières (plŏm-be-
Pŏ-co-mōke'
Pọd-gör'zä
Pŏd-lä'chị-ä
Pọ-dō'lị-ạ
Pöïnt Côu-pēē'
Poitiers (pöï-tērz', or
    pwä'tẹ-ā)
Pọl-tä'vä
Pŏl-y-nē'sị-ạ
Pŏm-ẹ-rä'nị-ạ
Pọm-pē'ị-ī,
Pŏn-dị-chĕr'ry
Pŏnt-chạr-träin'
Pontefract (pŏm'fret)
Pŏn-tẹ-ve'drä (-vä'-)
Pŏn'tị-ăc
Pŏn'tọ-tŏc
Pôô'näh
Pō-pạ-yăn'
Pō-pẹr-ïng'ẹn
Pŏp-ọ-cä'tạ-pĕtl
Pŏrt'-au-Prïnce' (-ō-)
Pör'tị-cî, (or pör'tẹ-chē)
Pōrt Mạ-hōn'
Pōr'tō Praȳ'ä
Pōr'tō-Prĭn'cị-pē
Pōr'tō Rî'cō
Pōrt'ụ-gạl
Pō'ṣen
Pō-sị-lĭp'pō
Pọ-tĕn'zä (pọ-tĕnt'sä)
Pọ-tō'mạc
Pŏ-tọ-sî', or Pọ-tō'sị
Pŏts'däm
Pŏt-tạ-wât'ọ-mịeṣ
Pọugh-kĕep'sịẹ
Pōul'tọn
Pöŵ-hạt-tän'
Pō-yäng'
Pŏz-zụ-ō'lō (pŏt-sụ-ō'lō)
Prāgue (präg)
Prāi-rịe-dụ-Chïen'
Preble (prĕb'bl)
Prĕğ'ẹl
Prĕnz'löŵ (prĕnts'löû)
Presque Isle (prĕsk-ēl')
Prĕs'tēigne (-tēn)
Prĕs-tọn-pänṣ'
Prĕv'ẹ-sä
Prïĕg'nĭtz (-nĭts)
Prĭn-cị-pä'tō (-chẹ-)
Prî-väs'
Prō'cị-dä (prō'chẹ-dä)
Provence (prŏv-vänṣ')
Prussịa (prŭsh'ạ, or prŭ'-
    shạ)
Prŭth (prŭt)
Przemysl (zhĕm'ịzl)
Pskov (skŏf)
Puebla (pwä'blä, or pŭ-
    ä'blä)
Pŭ-ĕr'tō Rî'cō
Puglia (pŭl'yä)
Puy-de-Dôme (pwĕ'dẹ-
    dōm')
Pwllheli (pôl-hĕl'ẹ
Pỹr'ẹ-nēēṣ

Q.

Quẹ-bĕc'
Quĕd'lịn-bürg
Quĕl'päert
Que-rä'tạ-rō (kä-)
Quesnoy (kĕn·wä')
Quiberon (kĕ-brŏng')
Quĭl-ẹ-mä'nẹ (kĭl-)
Quî-lị-ä'nō (kwē-)
Quĭl-ị-män'cy
Quî'lọ-ä (kē'-)
Quimper (kăm-pår')
Quĭn'ẹ-bâug
Quĭr'ị-nạl
Quî'tō (kē'tō)

R.

Raab (räb)
Rạ-bät'
Rạ-cîne'
Răc-ọ-nî'ğị
Răd'ạ-mä
Rạ-gụ'sä
Râh'wäy
Rāi'ṣịn
Rä-jạ-mŭn'dry
Räj-pôô-tä'nä
Râ'lẹigh (râw'lẹ) [yä']
Rambouillet (räm-bôl-
Räm-ị-lies'
Räm'lẹ-äh
Rạm-pôôr'
Rạn-cä'guä
Rạ-pîdes' (-pēd')
Răp-pạ-hăn'nọck
Rär'ị-tän
Räs'tädt (-stät)
Räth-keäle'
Rät'ị-bör
Rät'ịs-bŏn
Răv'enṣ-bĕrg
Răv'ẹn-steɪn
Rĕad'ịng
Re-cạ-nä'tị (rä-)
Re-cî'fe (rä-sē'fä)
Re'ğen (rä'-)
Re'ğenṣ-bûrg (rä'-)
Reggio (rĕd'jō)
Rẹ-hō'both
Reï'chẹn-au (-öû)
Reï'chẹn-bäch
Reï'chẹn-bĕrg
Reïch'städt (-stät)
Reï'gäte
Reï'kị-ạ-vĭk
Rĕimṣ
Re-ị-nō'sạ (rä-)
Renaix (rẹ-nä')
Rĕn'frew (-frŭ)
Rennes (rĕn)
Rĕns'sẹ-laẹr
Requeña (rä-kän'yä)
Rẹ-sä'cä
Re-sî'nä (rä-)
Re'ûs (rä'ûs) (Sp.)

Reûs, (or röïs) (Ger.)
Reut'lịng-ẹn (röït'-)
Rĕv'ẹl
Re-vîl'lạ (-vēl'yạ)
Rhe (rä)
Rheä (rä)
Rhēimṣ (rēmz, rĕmz,
    or rängz)
Rheïn'thäl (rïn'täl)
Rhōdeṣ (rōdz)
Rhodez (rō-dä'), or
    Rhodez (rō-däs')
Rî-ạ-zän'
Rïc-cạ-rēēṣ'
Rîche'lieû, (or rēsh'ẹ-lŭ)
Rideau (rē-dō')
Riẽ'ṣẹn-ğẹ-bïrğ'ẹ
Rị-e'tị (rẹ-ä'tẹ)
Rî'gä, or Rï'gạ
Rïg'ọ-lĕt
Rïm'ị-nî
Rî-ọ-băm'bä
Rî'ō Brä'vō
Rî'ō Cŏl-ọ-rä'dō
Rī'ō dĕl Nörte
Rî'ō Dŭl'ce (-sä)
Rī'ō Grände, or
    Grän'de (-dä)
Rio Janeiro (rē'ō-jạ-nä'-
    rō, or rī'ō-jạ-nē'rō)
Rî-ōm' (rē-ōng')
Rî'ō Sạ-lä'dō
Rî'ō Tî'grẹ
Rî'ō Vĕr'dẹ
Rî'pẹn
Rïs-tọ-gôuche'
Rĭv'ọ-lî
Rōane (rōn)
Rọ-ănne'
Rō-ạn-ōke'
Rŏch'däle
Rŏche'fôrt
Rochefoucault (rōsh'fô-
Rọ-chĕlle'   [kō']
Rôer
Rôer-mŏn'dẹ
Rō'gạ-ṣĕn
Rō-hịl-cŭnd'
Romagna (rọ-män'yä)
Rọ-mä'nị-ạ, or
    Rō-mạ-nî'ä
Rŏm'fọrd
Rŏn-cẹs-väl'lẹs
Rŏs'băch
Rọs-cŏm'mọn
Rŏs-creä'
Rọ-ṣĕt'tạ
Rọs-sä'nō
Rō'thẹn-bûrg (rō'tẹn-
    bûrg)
Rŏth'ẹr-hạm
Rŏthe-säy'
Rŏt'ter-däm
Roubaix (rô-bä')
Rôu'ẹn, (or rô-äng')
Roulers (rô-lår')
Roussillon (rô-sïl'-
    yöng')
Rō-vẹ-re'dō
Rovigno (rọ-vēn'yō)

Rọ-vî'gō
Rōw-ăn'
Rŭ'dọl-städt (-stät)
Rügen (rŭ'ğẹn)
Rŭ-mē'lị-ạ, or
    Rŭ-mẹ-lî'ạ
Rŭp-pîn'
Russia (rŭsh'ạ, or rŭ'-
    shạ)
Rŭst'ṣchŭck
Rŭth'ẹr-fôrd
Rŭ-thẹr-glĕn'

S.

Säade (säd)
Sääl'(säl)
Säa'le
Säal'fĕld (-fĕlt)
Saarbrück (sär'brŭk)
Säar-lôu'ịs
Säatz (säts)
Sạ-bî'nạ
Sạ-bîne'
Sä-ble-stän'
Säck-ạ-tôô'
Sâ'cō
Sâcs, or Sâuks
Säg-ạ-dạ-hŏc'
Säg-hạ-lî'ẹn, or
    Sạ-ghä'lị-ẹn
Säg'ị-nâw
Sägue'näy (säg'nä)
Säh'ạ-rä, or Sạ-hä'rạ
Säh-rụn-pōre'
Saïd (sīd)
Saï'dä
Sä'ịdè
Saï-gŏn'
St. Âl'bạnṣ, (or âw'-
    bụnz)
St. Ä'mänd (sănt-)
St. Äṣ'ạph
St. Âu-gụs-tîne'
St. Âus'tle
St. Brieux (säng-brẹ-ŭ')
St. Clöûd, (or säng'klô')
St. Cŏl'ụmb
St. Croix (-krŏïx, or
    -krwä)
St. Cyr (säng'sēr')
St. Dĕn'ịs, (or säng-dẹ-
    nē')
St. Dïz'ị-ẹr (säng-dïz'-
    ẹ-ā)
Saintes (sängt)
St. Etienne (ĕt-ẹ-ĕn')
St. Eụ-stä'tị-ạ (-shẹ-ạ)
St. Fe-lî'pe (-fä-lē'pä)
St. Flôur
St. Ğĕn-ẹ-viẽve'
St. Ğër'mạin, (or säng-
    zher-mäng')
St. Ğiör'ğiō (-jör'jō)
St. Ğiọ-vän'nị
St. Ğŏt'hạrd
St. Hẹ-lē'nạ
St. Hĕl'ị-ẹr

St. Ĭl-dẹ-fŏn'sō
St. Jā'gō, (or -yä'gō)
St. Jēan, (or säng-
    zhäng')
St. Lôu'ịs, (or -lô'ẹ)
St. Lū'cị-ạ, (or -lụ-sē')
St. Mä'lō
St. Mī'chạ-ẹl, (or -mī'-
    kẹl)
St. Mĭg'uẹl (-mĭg'wẹl,
    or mẹ-g̅ĕl')
St. Neots (-nôts, or
    nöuts)
  St. Neots (sẹnt-nēts')
St. Ō'mẹr, (or -ō-màr')
Saintonge (säng-tŏnzh')
St. Pĭērre, (or säng-pē-
    àr')
St. Pölton (sänt pōl'tọn)
St. Quĕn'tịn, (or säng-
    kän-täng')
St. Săl-vạ-dōr'
St. Sẹ-bäs'tịan (-sẹ-bäst'-
    yạn)
St. Sẹr-vän' (-väng')
St. Sĕv-ẹr-î'nạ
St. Yrieix (-ē'rẹ-ā)
Säk'kạ-rä
Sạ-lä'dō
Säl-ạ-mọ-nĭē'
Säl'fọrd, or
  Sâl'fọrd
Sạ-lî'nä (Italy)
Sạ-lī'nạ (U. S.)
Sạ-līne', or
  Sạ-lîne'
Sâliṣ'bụ-ry
Sạl-lēē'
Sạl-lîl'lō (-yō)
Sạ-lō'nä
Säl-ọ-nî'cạ
Säl'ọp, or Sā'lọp
Sạl-sĕtte'
Sä-lū'dä
Sä-lûz'zō (sä-lût'sō)
Säl-vạ-dōr'
Säl-wĭn'
Sälz'bürg
Sälz'we-dĕl (sälts'wä-
    dĕl)
Sạ-mä'nä, or
  Sä-mạ-nä'
Sạ-mär'
Säm-ạ-räng'
Säm-ạr-cänd'
Säm'bre (säm'br)
Säm-ọ-ģĭ'tị-ạ
Säm-ọ-thrä'kị
Säm-öў-ēdeṣ'
Sạm-sôôn'
Sä'nä, or
  Sä-nä'
Săn Âu-gụs-tîne'
Săn Dị-e'gō (-ä'-)
Săn-dọ-mîr'
Sänd'wịch, (or -wịj)
Săn Frạn-cĭs'cō
Sạn-gä'ị
Săn'gạ-mŏn
Săn-ị-läc'

Săn Joaquin (hō-ạ-kēn')
Săn José (-hō-sā')
Săn Jŭ'ạn, (or -hô-än')
Săn Mạ-rî'nō
Sanquhar (săn-kwär')
Sạn-săn'dịng
Săn'tạ Crŭz (-krŭs)
Săn'tạ Fé (-fē, or -fä')
Săn'tạ Mạ-rî'ạ
Sạn-tän'dẹr
Săn'tạ-rĕm
Săn'tạ Rō-sạ-lî'ạ
Săn-tị-ä'gō
Săn-tịl-lä'nä (săn-tịl-
    yä'nä)
Săn-tọ-rî'nị
Saône (sōn)
Sär'ạ-bät
Sär-ạ-gŏs'sạ
Sär-ạ-năc'
Sär-ạ-töf'
Sär-ạ-wäk'
Sär-ạ-wän'
Sạ-raỹ-ạ-cû'
Sä-rēē', or Sä-rî'
Sä'rös
Särre
Särthe (särt)
Säs-kạ-shâw'ịn, or
    Sạs-kätch'ạ-wân
Säs'sạ-rî
Sät-ạ-dôô'
Sạ-tä'lị-ạ, or
  Sä-tạ-lî'ä
Sạ-tä'räh
Sâu-gür'
Sault (sô) St. Mä'ry
Saumur (sō-mûr')
Säve, or Säve
Säve-näy'
Savigliano (säv-ēl-
    yä'nō)
Savigny (sạ-vēn'yẹ)
Säv'ọ-läx
Sạ-vō'nä
Sạ-vöỹ', or Säv'öỹ
Säxe-Äl'tẹn-bürg
Säxe-Weī'mạr
Saỹn (sīn)
Scâ-fĕll'
Scăn-dẹ-rôôn'
Scăn-dị-nä'vị-ạ
Seär'bŏr-ọugh (-bŭr-rọ)
Scär'pạn-tō
Sçhäff-hau'ṣen (-höû'-)
Sçhätt'-ẹl-Är'ạb
Sçhau'ẹn-bürg (shöû'-)
Sçhĕldt, or Sçhĕldt
    (skĕlt, or shĕlt)
Sçhĕl-ẹs-tädt' (shĕl-ẹs-
    tät')
Sçhĕl'lịng
Sçhĕm'nĭtz
Sçhẹ-nĕc'tạ-dy
Sçhĭē-däm'
Sçhị-räz', or Sçhî'rạz
Schönbrunn (shĕn'-
    brŭn)
Sçhö'nẹn

Sçhôô'dịc
Sçhôôl'ẹy's (Mt.)
Sçhôû'wẹn
Sçhûm'lä
Sçhuỹ'lẹr (skī'lẹr)
Sçhûỹl'kĭll (skŭl'kĭl)
Sçhwä'bäçh
Sçhwârt'zẹn-bürg
Sçhwärz'bürg
    (shwärts'-)
Sçhwârz'wâld
    (shwärts'-)
Sçhweīd'nĭtz (shwīt'-
    nĭts)
Sçhweīn'fûrt
Sçhweītz (shwīts)
Sçhwĕr'ịn, or
    Sçhwẹ-rîn'
Scigliano (shịl-yä'nō)
Sçĭl'ly
Sçĭnde
Sçī'ō, (or shē'ō)
Sçī-ō'tō
Sçĭt'u-āte
Sçlạ-vō'nị-ạ
Scŭ'tạ-rî, or
    Scŭ-tä'rị
Sẹ-ä'rä
Sẹ-bā'gō
Sẹ-bäs'tọ-pŏl, or
    Sĕb-ạs-tō'pọl
Sẹ-bĕn'ị-cō
Sĕc'çhị-ä
Sẹ-cŭn-dẹr-ạ-bäd'
Sẹ-dän'
Sĕg-ẹs-tän'
Segni (sān'yē)
Sẹ-gör'bẹ
Sọ-gō'vị-ạ
Seine (sān, or sĕn)
Sĕis-tän'
Sẹ-lĕf'kẹh
Sĕl-ẹn-g̅ĭnsk'
Sĕm'ị-nōleṣ
Sĕm'lịn, or
    Sẹm-lîn'
Sĕm'päçh
Sĕn'ẹ-cạ
Sĕn'ẹ-gâl
Sĕn-ẹ-gäm'bị-ạ
Sẹn-naär'
Sĕr-ạm-pōrẹ'
Sĕr'ẹs
Sereth (sä-rĕt')
Sĕr-ị-nä'gụr
Sẹ-rîng-ạ-pạ-täm'
Sẹr-phän'tō
Se'sị-ä (sā'-)
Sĕt'lĕdje
Sẹ-tû'bäl
Sẹ-väs'tọ-pŏl, or
    Sĕv-ạs-tō'pọl
Sẹ-vĭēr'
Sĕv'ịlle, or Sẹ-vĭlle'
Sêvre (sävr)
Sêvres (sävr)
Sē-wịs-tän'
Sey-çhĕlleṣ' (sā-shĕlz')
Seyne (sān)
Shäh-ạ-bäd'

Shä'mō
Shäng-haī'
Shät-ụl-Är'ạb
Shawangunk (shŏng'-
    gụm)
Shâw'nẹe-töŵn
Shẹ-böỹ'gạn
Shēēr-nĕss'
Shĕn-ạn-dō'äh
Shër-shĕll'
Shī-ạ-was'sẹe (-wŏs'-)
Shị-räz', or Shî'räz
Shịr-vän'
Shọ-shō'nēēṣ
Shrewṣ'bụ-ry (shrŭz'-
    bẹr-ẹ)
Shûm'lä
Sī-ăm', or Sī'ạm
Sî-cŭl-iä'nō (-yä'nō)
Sĭēg'bërg
Sĭē'g̅ĕn
Sị-ĕr'rạ Lẹ-ō'nẹ
Sị-ĕr'rạ Nẹ-vä'dä
Sĭg'mạ-rĭng-ẹn
Sị-guĕn'zạ
Sị-kŏkf', or Sịt-kŏkf'
Sịl-hĕt'
Sị-lĭs'trị-ạ
Sĭm-bïrsk'
Sĭm-fẹ-rō'pọl, or
    Sîm-fe-rọ-pōl' (-fä-)
Sĭm'plŏn, (or säng'-
    plōng')
Sĭn-cạ-pōre'
Sịn-gän'
Sĭn-gạ-pōre' (sĭng-)
Sinigaglia (sĭn-ẹ-gäl'yä)
Sĭn'ọb
Sĭn'ọ-pē, or
    Sị-nō'pẹ
Sioux (sẹ-ô', or sô)
Sịr-hĭnd'
Sị-säl'
Sịs-tō'vä
Sị-ût'
Sị-väs'
Sị-wäh'
Skäg'ẹr Räck
Skĕn-ẹ-ăt'ẹ-les
Skĭb-bẹ-rēēn'
Slĕs'wịck
Slĭēb-blôôm'
Sluys (slôs, or slöïs)
Smäl'cạl-dĕn
Smọ-lĕnsk'
Snẹe-hät'tạn
Snōw'dọn
Sōane
Sŏc-ọ-nûs'cō
Sọ-cō'trä, or
    Sŏc'ọ-trä
Sọ-fä'lä
Soignies (söïng'nēs, or
    swän-yē')
Soissons (swäs'sōng')
Sọ-leûre'
Sŏl-fạ-tä'rä
Sŏl-fẹ-rî'nō
Sŏm'ẹr-sĕt
Sŏm'ẹrṣ (Isles)

Sŏmme
Sŏm-nâuth' (-nâwt')
Sŏn'der-hau'şen (-hŏû'-)
Sǫ-nō'rä
Sŏô-lôô'
Sǫ-phî'ạ
Sǫ-rä̈tä
Sǫ-rĕlle', or Sŏr'ĕl
Sǫ-rō'rạ
Sǫr-rĕn'tō, or
  Sŏr'rĕn-tō
Sôu-dän'
Sôu-rạ-baȳ'ạ
Southwark (sŭtħ'ạrk)
Sôu-zĕl'
Spä, or Spâ
Spạ-lä'trō
Spän'dau (spän'dŏû)
Spey (spā)
Speȳ'ĕr
Spezia (spĕd'zę-ä)
Spezzia (spĕt'sę-ä)
Spïtz-bĕrğ'ęn
Splügen (splü'ğen)
Spǫ-le'tō (spǫ-lä'tō)
Spŏr'ạ-dĕş
Squâm
Squïl-lä'ce (skwïl-lä'-chä)
Stä'brôek (stä'brôk)
Stạ-ğî'rạ
Stäïneş
Stäl-į-me'ne (-mä'nä)
Stäm-bôul'
Stäm-pạ-lî'ạ
Stän-ǫ-vŏï'
Stär'gärd (-gärt)
Stät'en Ïs'land
Stäun'tǫn
Stạ-vän'ğęr (-väng'-)
Stäv'ĕr-ęn
Stēĕn'bĕrg-ęn
Stĕt-tîn', or Stĕt'tįn
Steū'bĕn, or Steū-bĕn'
Steū'bęn-vïlle
Steȳ'ĕr
Stey'nįng (stä'-)
Stŏck'hôlm
Stôur
Stoür'brïdğe
Strạ-bäne', or
  Strạ-bäne'
Sträl'sŭnd
Strän'râ-ęr, or
  Strạn-râer'
Sträth-ä'ven
Strau'bįng (strŏû'bįng)
Strĕl'įtz (-ïts)
Strïv'ạ-lî, or
  Strî-vä'lî
Strŏm'bǫ-lî
Stür'mįn-stęr
Stŭtt'gärd
Suä'bį-ạ
Suä'kęm
Sŭb'lĕttes
Sŭ-der-mä'nį-ạ
Sụ-dĕ'tĕş
Sŭ'ez
Sŭf'fǫlk, (or sŭf'fǫk)

Sŭ-gụl-mĕs'sạ
Suî'rä (swē'rä)
Sụl-mō'nä
Sụ-mä'trạ
Sụm-bä'wạ
Sụ-rät'
Sür-į-näm'
Sŭ-säm'
Sụ-wâ'nęe
Sve'ạ-börg (svä'-)
Swäff'hạm, (or swŏf'-ạm)
Swân'sęa
Swē'den
Swinemünde (swē-nạ-mǔn'dä)
Switz'ĕr-land
Sȳ-ē'nę
Szär-väs' (zär-)
Szĕg-ę-dîn' (zĕg-)

T.

Täb-ạ-rēĕ'hä
Tạ-brîz', or Tạ-brēĕz'
Tạ-cä'mes
Tác-ạ-rî'guä
Tạ-cäz'zę, (or tạ-kät'sä)
Tạ-cŏn'nęt
Tạ-cō'ny
Tác-ụ-baȳ'ạ
Täd'cạs-ter
Täd-ôu-säc'
Täf'į-lĕt
Täg'ạn-rŏck, or
  Täg'ạn-rŏg
Tạ-gäz'zę
Tagliamento (täl-yạ-mĕn'tō)
Tạ-hî'tį
Taī-wän'
Täl-ạ-ve'rạ (-vä'-)
Täl'bǫt
Täl-cạ-huä'nä
Taliaferro (tŏl'ę-vęr)
Täl-lạ-dē'gạ
Täl-lạ-hätch'ię
Täl-lạ-pôô'sạ
Tạm-â'quạ
Täm-ạ-rä'cä
Täm'ạ-täve
Täm-âu-lî'pạs
Tạm-bō'rä
Tạ-mîşe'
Täm-pî'cō
Tạ-nän-ạ-rî'vôô, or
  Tä-nạ-nä-rį-vôô'
Tạ-nä'rō, or
  Tä'nạ-rō
Tä'ney
Tän-ğiēr'
Tän-jŏre'
Tạn-näs'sę-rïm
Tän-nę-sär'
Tä-ǫr-mî'nä
Tạ-pä'jŏs (-yŏs)
Täp-pạ-hän'nŏck
Täp-tēĕ'

Tär-ạ-kaī'
Tär'ạn-tō
Tạ-räre'
Tä-räs-cōn' (-kŏng')
Tär-bạg-taī'
Tärbes (tärb)
Tạ-rî'fä
Tạ-rî'jạ (tạ-rē'hạ)
Tär'nǫ-pŏl, or
  Tạr-nō'pǫl
Tär'pǫr-ley
Tär-rạ-gō'nä
Tär'ụ-dänt
Täsh-kĕnd'
Täsh-kŭnd'
Tạş-mä'nį-ạ
Täs-sį-sǔ'dǫn
Tau'ber (tŏû'-)
Tâu'dę-ny
Täun'tǫn
Tâu'rį-dä
Täv'ạst-hǔus
Täv'ạst-länd
Tạ-vî'rä
Täv'įs-tŏck
Taȳ-ä'bạs
Täze'węll
Tchä'ny
Tchër'nį-gŏf
Tchǔdş'kōe
Tcį-nän'
Tę-ä'kį
Tĕçhe (tĕsh)
Tēĕm-bôô'
Tĕf'lįs
Tę-hä'mä
Tē-hę-rän', or
  Tęh-râun'
Tę-huän'tę-pĕc
Teign (tïn, or tän)
Teign'mouth (tïn'-)
Tę-jǔ'cō (tę-hǔ'cō)
Tĕl-įn-gä'nä
Tĕl-lį-chĕr'ry
Tĕl'lį-cō
Tĕm-ęs-vär'
Tĕm-ple-mōre'
Tę-näs'sę-rïm
Tĕn'ę-rïffe
Tĕn-nęs-sēĕ'
Tĕn'tęr-dĕn
Tĕp-ę-ä'cä
Tę-pîc'
Tę-pŏz-cǫ-lǔ'lạ
Tę-quĕn-dạ-mä', or
  Tĕq-uęn-dä'mä
Tĕr'ạ-mō
Tęr-ce'į-rä (tęr-sä'ę-rä)
Tęr-ce'rä (-sä'rä)
Tę-rĕk'
Tĕr-gǫ-vïs'tạ
Tĕr'mį-nî
Tĕr'mǫ-lî
Tĕr-näte', or Tĕr'näte
Tĕr-rạ-cî'nạ, (or tĕr-rạ-chē'nä)
Tĕr'rạ dĕl Fue'gō
  (-fwä'gō)
Tĕr'rạ dî Lạ-vō'rō
Tĕr-rạ-nō'vạ

Terre Bonne (tår-bŏn')
Terre Haute (tår-hōt', or
  tĕr'ę-hōt)
Tĕsçh'en (tĕsh'en)
Tęs-sîn', or Tĕs'sįn
Tĕt-ụ-än'
Tĕv-ę-rō'nę
Tĕv'į-ǫt, (or tïv'į-ǫt)
Tewks'bụ-ry
Tĕx'ạs
Teȳn (tīn)
Tęz-cǔ'cō
Thame (tām)
Thames (tĕmz)
Thän'et
Thę-ä'kį
Thē'bạ-ïd
Thēbeş
Theïss (tīs)
Theresienstadt (tạ-rā'-
  zę-ęn-stät')
Thiagur (tę-ä'gụr), or
  Thî-ạ-gür' (tē-)
Thıbet (tę-bĕt')
Thibodeauxville (tïb-ǫ-
  dō'vïl)
Thiel (tēl)
Thielt (tēlt)
Thiers (tē-år')
Thî'vä (tē'vä)
Thō'len (tō'len)
Thō'mạr (tō'mạr)
Thörn, (or törn)
Thun (tǔn)
Thurgau (tǔr'gŏû)
Thụr-gō'vį-ạ
Thụ-rïn'ğį-ạ
Thürleş
Tïb'bō, or Tïb-bôô'
Tï'ber
Tį-bĕt', or Tïb'ęt
Tïçh'vîn
Tį-cî'nō, (or tę-chĕ'nō)
Tï-cŏn'dę-rō'gạ
Tį-dōre'
Tiël (tēl)
Tî-en-tsîn'
Tïf'lįs
Tî'gre (tē'grä)
Tî'grįs
Tį-lä'pä
Tïl-lạ-tō'bä
Tïl'sįt
Tįm-bǔc'tôô, or
  Tïm-bục-tôô'
Tï'mör, or
  Tį-mör'
Tïm-ǫr-lâut'
Tïm-pạ-nō'gŏs
Tïn'į-än
Tïn-nę-vĕl'ly
Tï-ō'gạ
Tį-ōugh-nį-ō'gạ (tę-ō-)
Tïp'ę-rä
Tïp-pę-cạ-nôe'
Tïp-pę-rä'ry
Tïr-ēĕ'
Tïrle-mŏnt'
Tïsh-ę-mïn'gō
Tït-į-cä'cä

Tĭt'tḙ-riĕ
Tĭv'ẹr-tọn
Tĭv'ọ-lị
Tlăl-păn'
Tlĕm-săn'
Tọ-bā'gŏ
Tọ-hŏl'
Tọ-bŏlsk'
Tọ-bŏ'sŏ
Tŏ-cạn-tĭnŝ'
Tọ-căt'
Tọ-caȳ'ä
Tọ-cŭ'yŏ
Tŏd'mör-dẹn
Töplitz (tĕp'lĭts)
Tọ-kāy'
Tọ-lē'dŏ
Tŏ-lẹn-tî'nŏ
Tọ-lŏ'sä
Tọ-lŭ'cä
Tŏm-bĕck'bẹe
Tŏm-bĭg'bẹe
Tŏm-bŭc'tôô
Tŏng-ạ-tä'bôô
Tŏn-kîn'
Tŏn-nêrre'
Tŏn-nẹ-wân'tạ
Tŏn'nịng-ẹn
Tŏn-quîn' (tŏn-kĕn')
Tôôm-bŭd'drä
Topayos (tọ-pī'yŏs)
Tọ-pē'käh
Tör-bāy', or Tör'bāy
Tör'gâu, (or tör'göu)
Tọ-rî'nŏ
Tör'mẹs
Tör'nẹ-ạ
Tọ-rŏn'tŏ
Tör'ọn-täl
Torquay (tör-kē')
Torriglia (tọr-rēl'yä)
Tör-rịs-däl'
Tọr-tō'lä, or Tör'tọ-lä
Tọr-tō'nä
Tọr-tō'sä
Tọr-tŭ'gạ
Tọ-tä'nä
Tŏt-nĕss', or Tŏt'nẹss
Tôul (tôl)
Tôu-lŏn' (tô-lŏng')
Tôu-lôuṣe' (tô-lôz')
Touraine (tô-rān')
Tôur-nạ-ghâut'
Tôur-nāy'
Tours (tôr, or tôrz)
Towcester (tŏûs'tẹr)
Trăf-ạl-gär', or
  Trạ-fál'gạr
Trăj-ạn-ŏp'ọ-lị
Trạ-lēē'
Trạ-môre'
Trä'nî
Trăn-quẹ-bär'
Trăn-syl-vā'nị-ạ
Trăp'ạ-nị
Trăv-ạn-côre'
Trăv'ịs
Trăz-ŏs-mŏn'tẹs
Trĕb-ị-ṣŏnd'
Trĕd'ẹ-gär

Treī'sạm
Trĕm'ẹ-cĕn
Trĕm'ị-tî
Trẹ-mŏnt'
Trēveṣ, (or trāv)
Tre-vî'gî (trā-)
Treviglio (trā-vĕl'yŏ)
Tre-vî'ṣŏ (trā-)
Trî'cạ-lä
Trĭch-ị-nŏp'ọ-ly
Trị-ĕste'
Trĭnc-ọ-mạ-lēē'
Trĭn-ị-dăd'
Trĭn-ọ-mạ-lēē'
Trĭp'ọ-lị
Trĭp'ọ-lĭs
Trĭp-ọ-lĭz'zạ
Trŏl-hæt'tạ
Trŏnd'hjẹm (-yẹm)
Trŏp'pau (trŏp'pöû)
Trŏs'ạchs
Trŏw'brịdge
Troyes (trwä)
Truxillo (trŭ-hēl'yŏ)
Tschẹr-käsk'
Tsị-äm'pä
Tū'ạm
Tŭ'ạ-rĭck
Tŭ-ät', (or twăt)
Tŭ-băc'
Tübingen (tŭ'bịng-ẹn)
Tŭ-cụ-män'
Tŭ-de'lä (tŭ-dā'lä)
Tū-gạ-lôô'
Tụ-lä'rẹ
Tŭ'lẹ
Tŭl-lạ-môre'
Tŭlle
Tŭm'bẹz (-bẹs)
Tŭn-gụ-rä'guä
Tŭn'gụ-sĕṣ, or
  Tŭn-gŭ'sẹṣ
Tū'nị-cạ
Tuŏl'ụm-nẹ (twŏl'-)
Turcoing (tŭr-kwäng')
Tür-cọ-mā'nị-ạ
Tŭr'cọ-mănṣ
Tŭ'rịn, or Tŭ-rĭn'
Tŭr-kẹs-tän'
Tŭrn-höût'
Tụ-rŏn'
Tŭr-shēēz'
Tŭ-rụ-chănsk'
Tŭs-cạ-lôô'sạ
Tŭs-cạ-râw'ạs
Tŭs-cạ-rō'rạ
Tuy (twē)
Tvër (vër)
Twēē'dạle
Tȳne'mouth
Tȳr'nau (tër'nöû)
Tȳr'ọl, or Ty-rŏl')
Ty-rōne'

U.

Ŭ-be'dä (-bā'-)
Ŭ-caȳ-ä'le (-lä)

Ŭ'dị-ne (-nä)
Udvarhely (ôd-vạr-hāl')
Uist (wĭst)
Ūi'tẹn-hāğe
Ū'krāine, (or ô-krān')
Ŭ'lẹ-ạ-börg
Ū-liẹ-tē'ạ
Ulm (ŭlm, or ûlm)
Ŭlṣ'wâ-tẹr
Ŭm'bạ-gŏg
Ŭ'mẹ-ạ
Ŭm-mẹ-rạ-pôô'rä
Ŭmp'quâ
Ŭn-dẹr-wâl'dẹn
Ŭn'strŭt
Ŭn-tẹr-wâl'dẹn
Ŭ-pọ-lŭ'
Ŭp'sạl, or Ụp-sä'lä
Ŭp-sạl-lä'tä
Ū'răl, (or ô-răl')
Ŭ-rälsk'
Ụr-bā'nạ
Ŭr-bî'nŏ
Ŭr'fä
Ŭr-mî'ä
Ŭr'sẹ-rĕn
Ŭ-rụ-guāy' (-gwā'), or
  Ŭ-rụ-guaȳ' (-gwī')
Ŭ-rụ-mî'äh
Ŭ'sẹ-dŏm
Ŭsh'ạnt, (or ûsh-äng')
Ŭs'tị-ûg
Ū'täh
Ŭ'tạ-wâs
Ū'trĕcht
Ŭ-tre'rä (-trā'-)
Ụt-tŏx'ẹ-tẹr, (or ŭx'ẹ-
  ter)
Uwchlan (yûk'lạn)
Ŭx-mäl'
Ŭz-bĕcks'
Uzès (ô-zās')
Ŭz'näch (ôts'näk)

V.

Vaī'gạts
Valais (vä-lā')
Văl'dāi, or Văl'daī
Valdepeñas (văl-dẹ-
  pān'yạs)
Vạl-dĭv'ị-ạ
Valence (văl-äns')
Vạ-lĕn'cị-ạ (-shẹ-ạ)
Vạ-lĕn-cị-ä'nä
Valenciennes (văl-än-
  sẹ-ĕn')
Vạ-lĕn'tị-ạ (-shẹ-ạ)
Văl-lạ-dọ-lîd'
Vallejo (vạl-yä'hŏ)
Văl-lọm-brō'sä
Valois (văl-wä')
Văl-pạ-raī'sŏ
Văl'tẹ-lîne
Văl-tẹl-lî'nä
Văn-côu'vẹr
Vạn-dä'lị-ạ
Văn Diē'mẹn'ṣ Länd

Văn-ị-kŏ'rŏ
Vännes (vän)
Vạ-rî'nạs
Văs-ạr-hē'ly
Văs-ịl-ị-pŏt'ạ-mŏ
Văs'sạl-bŏr-ọugh
Văs-sy' (-sē')
Vau-clûṣe' (vŏ-klŭz')
Vaud (vŏ)
Vau-dreûil' (vŏ-drôl')
Veglia (vĕl'yä)
Vẹ-lāy'
Vē'lẹz, (or vā'lẹth)
Vẹ-lî'nŏ
Vẹl-le'trị (vẹl-lā'trẹ)
Vẹl-lōre'
Venaissin (vĕn-ās-säng')
Vẹ-năn'gŏ (-năng'-)
Vendée (vän-dā')
Vendôme (vän-dōm')
Vĕn-ẹ-zuē'lä, (or -zwä'-)
Vĕn'ịce
Vẹn-lôô'
Vē'rạ Crŭz', (or vā'rä-
  krŭs')
Vē'rạ Päz'
Vẹ-rä'guä
Vẹr-cĕl'lị (vẹr-chĕl lẹ)
Vẹr-dŭn'
Vẹr-ğĕnneṣ'
Vermejo (vẹr-mā'hŏ)
Vẹr-mĭl'iọn
Vẹr-mŏnt'
Vẹ-rō'nä
Vẹr-sāilleṣ'
Vẹr-sĕtz' (-sĕts')
Verviers (vër'vẹ-ā)
Vẹ-ṣôul' (vẹ-zôl')
Vẹ-sū'vị-ŭs
Vẹ-vāy'
Vị-ä'nä
Vị-äṣ'mä
Vị-ät'kä
Vî'börg
Vị-cĕn'zä, (or vẹ-chĕn'-
Vîch (vēk)   [zä)
Vĭcks'bürg
Vị-dîn'
Vị-ĕnne'
Vî'gŏ
Vị-lāine'
Vịl-lăch'
Vĭl'lä Re-äl' (-rä-)
Vĭl'lä Rî'cä
Vĭlle-frănçhe'
Vĭlle-neûve'
Vịl-lĕtte'
Vịl-vŏor'dẹn
Vịn-cĕnneṣ'
Vĭnd'hyä (vĭnd'yä)
Vintimiglia (vĭn-tẹ-
  mēl'yä)
Vî'que (vē'kä)
Vîre (vër)
Vị-se'û (vẹ-sä'ô), or
  Vî'se-û (-sä-)
Vĭs'tụ-lạ
Vị-tĕpsk'
Vị-tër'bŏ
Vitre (vĕtr)

Vį-tîm′
Vįt-tō′rį-ạ
Viviers (vĭv′ę-ā)
Vĭz-ạ-găp-ạ-tăm′
Vlăd-į-mîr′
Vŏ′g̈ęlṣ-bĕrg
Voghera (vo-gā′rä)
Voiron (vwä-rōng′)
Vŏl-hȳn′į-ạ
Vǫ-lŏg′dä
Vŏl-tür′nō
Vǫr-ärl′bĕrg
Vŏr′ǫ-nĕtz (-nĕts)
Vosges (vōzh)
Vŭ′kǫ-vär
Vŭ-ŏx′ęn

W.

Wäag (wäg)
Wäal (wäl)
Wä′băsh
Wä′daȳ
Wăd′y
Wä′grạm
Waït′zẹn (-sẹn)
Wạl-äh′mụtte
Wäl′chẹ-rẹn
Wäl′dĕck
Wäl-dĕn′sĕṣ
Wäl′dǫ-bŏr-ǫugh
Wạl-lä′chį-ạ
Wäl′lạ-Wäl′lạ
Wäl′lẹn-städt (-stät)
Wäl′lįng-fōrd
Wäl′sạll
Wält′hạm (Eng.)
Wäl′thạm (U. S.)
Wäl′tǫn
Wạn-chöŵ′
Wandṣ′worth (wŏnz′-würth)
Wạn-gä′rä
Wăn-lǫck-hĕad′
Wạ-pĕl′lō
Wăp-sį-pĭn′ę-cŏn
War′ạ-deïn (wŏr′-)
War′ạs-dĭn (wŏr′-)
Wär′mįn-stẹr
War′rẹn (wŏr′rẹn)
Wär′wịch, (or wŏr′įk)
Wash′įng-tǫn (wŏsh′-įng-tǫn)
Wash-į-tä′ (wŏsh-ę-täw′)
Wash′tẹ-nâw (wŏsh′-)
Wạ-tâu′gạ
Wä-tẹr-ē̂′
Wä′tẹr-fǫrd
Wä′tẹr-lôô
Wä′tẹr-vĭlle
Wä-tẹr-vlĭĕt′
Wâu-kē′gạn
Wâu′kẹ-shä

Wavertree (wä′trẹ)
Wavre (wä′vr)
Wĕar′mǫuth
Wednes′bu-ry (wĕnz′-bẹr-ẹ)
Wednesfield (wĕnz′fĕld)
Weïch′sẹl-bŭrg
Weï′mạr
Weïn′heïm
Weïs′sẹn-bôurg
Weïs′sẹn-fĕls
Wemyss (wĕmz)
Wĕn′dǫ-vẹr
Weô′blẹy (wô′blẹ)
Wẹr-nį-g̈ẹ-rō′dẹ
Wĕrt′heïm
Wĕs′tẹr-äs
Wĕs′tẹr-wäld
Wĕst′mạn-länd
Wĕst-mēath′
Wĕst′mįn-stẹr
Wĕst′mǫre-länd
Wĕst-phä′lį-ạ
Wĕt-tẹ-rä′vį-ạ
Wexiö (wĕk′shö)
Wey (wä)
Weȳ′ẹr
Wey′mǫuth (wä′mụth)
Whäl′lẹy
Whĭd′äh
Wię-lĭcz′kä (wę-lĭch′-kä)
Wĭĕ′sẹl-bŭrg [kä]
Wĭĕ′sẹn
Wĭg′ạn
Wĭlkes′bär-rẹ
Wįl-läm′mẹtte
Wĭl′mįng-tǫn
Wĭl′nạ
Wĭn′andẹr-mēre, or Wĭn′dẹr-mēre
Wĭn′chẹl-sēa
Wĭn′chẹs-tẹr
Wĭnd′ṣǫr (wĭn′zǫr)
Wĭn-nẹ-bä′gō
Wĭn′nį-pĕg
Winnipiseogee (wĭn-ę-pẹ-sâw′kẹ)
Wịs-bä′dẹn, or Wĭs′bạ-dĕn
Wĭṣ′beach (wĭz′bịch)
Wịs-căs′sẹt
Wịs-cŏn′sịn
Wĭs′mạr
Wĭt′g̈ẹn-steïn
Wĭth′ạm
Wĭt′tẹn-bĕrg
Wō-ạ-hôô′
Wô′burn
Wolfenbüttel (wŏl′fẹn-bŭt′tẹl)
Wŏll′steïn
Wol-vẹr-hämp′tǫn (wûl-)
Wol′vẹr-lẹy (wûl′-)
Woolwich (wûl′ịj)
Wôôn-sŏck′ẹt

Wooton (wût′tn)
Worcester (wûs′tẹr)
Worstead (wôrs′tẹd)
Wotton–under–Edge (wô-tn-ŭn′drịj)
Wor′thịng (wür′-)
Wrăg′by (răg′bẹ)
Wrĕx′hạm (rĕx′ạm)
Wür′tẹm-bĕrg
Würzburg (würts′bürg)
Wȳ-ạn-dŏt′
Wȳ′börg
Wȳ′cǫmbe (wī′kǫm), or Wȳc′ǫmbe (wĭk′ụm)
Wȳ-ō′mĭng

X.

Xä-lä′pä (hä-lä′pä)
Xauxa (höû′hä)
Xē′nį-ạ (zē′-)
Xenil (hä-nēl′)
Xeres (hä-rĕs′)
Xį-cō′cō (zę-kō′kō)
Xî′mō (zē′mō)
Xĭn-gü′ (shĭn-gü′)
Xî-xō′nä (hē-hō′nä)
Xō′ạ (shō′ạ)
Xō-chį-mĭl′cō (hō-)
Xŭl′lä (zŭl′lä)
Xuxuy (hŭ-hwē′)

Y.

Yăk′ę-mä
Yä-kôutsk′
Yäl-ạ-bŭ′shạ
Yạ-mäs′kạ
Yăm-pạ-rä′ẹs
Yäng-tcheôu′
Yäng′tsẹ-kį-ăng′
Yä′nį-nä
Yä-ǫ-tcheôu′
Yä-quî′ (yä-kē′), or Y-ä′quį (-kẹ)
Yạr-kŭnd′
Yär′ǫ-släf
Yär′rį-bä
Yạ-zôô′
Yĕd′dō
Yẹ-kät-ẹ-rî′nẹn-bŭrg
Yẹ-kät-ẹ-rî′nǫ-grăd
Yẹ-kät-ẹ-rî′nǫ-släv
Yĕm′ẹn, or Yē′men
Yĕn-į-kä′le (-lä)
Yĕn-į-sēi, (or yĕn-ę-sä′ę)
Yĕn-į-sēisk′, (or yĕn-ę-sā′ịsk)
Yeô′vịl
Yĕth′ǫlm (yĕth′ǫm)
Yeyd (yäd)

Youghall (yŏ′âwl, or yâwl)
Youghiogeny (yŏk-ę-gä′nę)
Ypres (ē′pr)
Ȳp-sį-lăn′tį
Ȳs′sẹl (ĭs′sẹl)
Ȳs′tädt (ĭs′tät)
Ȳth′ạn (ĭth′ạn)
Yŭ-cạ-tän′
Yŭn-năn′
Yu-rŭ′pä
Yŭz-gät′
Ȳv-ẹr-dŭn′
Yvetot (ēv-tō′)

Z.

Zaab (zäb)
Zäan-däm′
Zä′ạ-rä, or Zạ-ä′rä
Zăc-ạ-lŭ′lä
Zăc-ạ-te′cạs (-tä′-)
Zạ-gräb′
Zä-îre′
Zạm-bēze′
Zạ-mō′rä (thạ-mō′rä)
Zạm-pä′lä
Zăn-guę-bär′
Zän′tẹ
Zăn-zį-bär′
Zēa′lạnd
Zẹ-bîd′
Zẹ-bŭ′
Zĕg̈′ę-dîn
Zei′lä (zä′lä)
Zei-tün′ (zä-tün′)
Zeïtz (tsïts)
Zĕl′le (tsĕl′lä)
Zĕrbst (tsĕrpst)
Zî′ä
Zıē-g̈ẹn-haȳn′ (tsē-)
Zįm-bä′ō
Zĭrk′nĭtz (tsïrk′nĭts)
Zittau (tsĭt′töû)
Zlŏck′zöŵ
Znä′ym, or Znaȳm
Zŏll′vẹr-eïn
Zôu-wän′
Zŭf-fẹr-ạ-băd′
Zŭg (tsŭg)
Zŭ′lį-ä (sŭ′-)
Zŭl′pịch (tsŭl′pĭk)
Zuñi (zŭn′yę)
Zŭ′rịch
Zŭt′phẹn
Zuȳ′dẹr Zēē′
Zweibrücken (tswī′brŭk-kẹn)
Zwĕl′lẹn-däm
Zwĭck′au (tswĭk′öû)
Zwŏll (tswŏl)
Zwör′nîk
Zȳt′ǫ-miĕrṣ

SIGNS.

SIGNS OF THE PLANETS.

⊙ The Sun.
☿ Mercury.
♀ Venus.
⊕ The Earth.
●) ○ (The Moon.

♂ Mars.
⚶ Vesta.
⚵ Juno.
⚴ Pallas.
⚳ Ceres.

♃ Jupiter.
♄ Saturn.
⛢ Uranus.
♆ Neptune.

SIGNS OF THE ASPECTS.

☌ Conjunction, i. e. in the same degree.
✶ Sextile, 60 degrees.
□ Quartile, 90 degrees.
△ Trine, 120 degrees.
☍ Opposition, 180 degrees.
☊ Dragon's Head, *or* ascending node.

☋ Dragon's Tail, *or* descending node.
☽ The Moon in its first quarter.
⊙ The Sun.   ○ The full Moon.
☽ *or* ● The new Moon.
☾ The Moon in its last quarter.
✶ A Star.

SIGNS OF THE ZODIAC.

Spring signs.
1. ♈ Aries, the Ram.
2. ♉ Taurus, the Bull.
3. ♊ Gemini, the Twins.

Summer signs.
4. ♋ Cancer, the Crab.
5. ♌ Leo, the Lion.
6. ♍ Virgo, the Virgin.

Autumn signs.
7. ♎ Libra, the Balance.
8. ♏ Scorpio, the Scorpion.
9. ♐ Sagittarius, the Archer.

Winter signs.
10. ♑ Capricornus, the Goat.
11. ♒ Aquarius, the Waterman.
12. ♓ Pisces, the Fishes.

MISCELLANEOUS SIGNS.

☞ An index.
¶ A paragraph.
§ A section.
? Interrogation ; query.
∧ Caret, is wanting.
= Equal to.
— Minus, less, *or* take away.
+ Plus, *or* add.
÷ Divided by.
× Multiplied by.
x The unknown quantity required.

√ Root of.
′ Minutes.
″ Seconds.
° Degrees.
℔ By the.
$ Dollars.
£ Pounds sterling.
℥ Ounces. ℥j One ounce.
ʒ Drams.   ʒiij Three drams.
℈ Scruples.

ABBREVIATIONS

USED IN

WRITING AND PRINTING.

A. Answer. — Acre. — Adjective. — Afternoon.

A. A. P. S. American Association for the Promotion of Science.

A. A. S. (*Academiæ Americanæ Socius.*) Fellow of the American Academy.

A. A. S. S. (*Academiæ Antiquarianæ Societatis Socius.*) Member of the American Antiquarian Society.

A. B. (*Artium Baccalaureus.*) Bachelor of Arts.

A. B. C. F. M. American Board of Commissioners for Foreign Missions.

Abp. Archbishop.

A. B. S. American Bible Society.

A. C. (*Ante Christum.*) Before Christ.

Acct. Account.

A. C. S. American Colonization Society.

A. D. (*Anno Domini.*) In the Year of our Lord.

Ad., or Adv. Adverb.

Adj. Adjective.

Adjt. Adjutant.

Adjt. Gen. Adjutant-General.

Ad lib. (*Ad libitum.*) At pleasure.

Admr. Administrator.

Admx. Administratrix.

Adv. (*Ad valorem.*) At the value. — Advent. — Advocate.

Æt., or Æ. (*Ætatis.*) Of age, aged.

A. & F. B. S. American and Foreign Bible Society.

A. F., or A. fir. Firkin of Ale.

Af. Africa.

A. H. (*Anno Hegiræ.*) In the Year of the Hegira.

A. H. M. S. American Home Missionary Society.

Al., or Ala. Alabama.

Ald. Alderman.

Alex. Alexander.

Alt. Altitude.

A. M. (*Artium Magister.*) Master of Arts.

A. M. (*Ante Meridiem.*) Before noon.

A. M. (*Anno Mundi.*) In the Year of the World.

Am., or Amer. American.

Amb. Ambassador.

Amt. Amount.

An. (*Anno.*) In the Year.

An., or Ans. Answer.

Ana. (*Medicine.*) In like quantity.

Anat. Anatomy.

Ang. Sax. Anglo-Saxon.

Anon. Anonymous.

Ant., or Antiq. Antiquities.

A. O. S. S. (*Americanæ Orientalis Societatis Socius.*) Member of the American Oriental Society.

Ap., Apr., or Apl. April.

Ap. Apostle.

Apo. Apogee.

Apoc. Apocalypse.

Ar., or Arab. Arabic.

Arch. Architecture.

Arith. Arithmetic.

Ark. Arkansas.

A. R. S. S. (*Antiquariorum Regiæ Societatis Socius.*) Fellow of the Royal Society of Antiquaries.

Art. Article.

A. S. A. S. Member of the American Statistical Association.

A. S., or A. Sax. Anglo-Saxon.

A. S. S. U. American Sunday School Union.

Astrol. Astrology.

Astron. Astronomy.

A. T. S. American Tract Society. — American Temperance Society.

Att., or Atty. Attorney.

Atty. Gen. Attorney-General.

A. U. A. American Unitarian Association.

A. U. C. (*Anno Urbis Conditæ.*) In the Year from the Building of the City [Rome].

Aug. August.

Av. Average. — Avenue.

Avoir. Avoirdupois.

B.

B. (*Basso.*) Bass, in Music.

B., or Bk. Book. — b. Born.

B. A. Bachelor of Arts. — British America.

Bal. Balance.

Bar. Barrel. — Barleycorn.

Bart., or Bt. Baronet.

Bbl., or Bl. Barrel.

B. C. Before Christ.

B. C. L. Bachelor of Civil Law.

B. D. Bachelor of Divinity.

Bd. Bound.

Bds. Bound in boards.

Belg. Belgic.

Benj. Benjamin.

B. F., or B. fir. Firkin of Beer.

Bib. Bible. — Biblical.

Bk. Bank. — Book.

B. L. (*Baccalaureus Legum.*) Bachelor of Laws.

B. M. (*Baccalaureus Medicinæ.*) Bachelor of Medicine.

Bot. Botany.

Bp. Bishop.

Br., or Bro. Brother.

Brig. Brigade. — Brigadier.

Brig. Gen. Brigadier-General.

Brit. Britain. — British.

Bu., or Bush. Bushel.

B. V. (*Beata Virgo.*) Blessed Virgin.

B. V. (*Bene Vale.*) Farewell.

C.

C. (*Centum.*) A hundred. — Cent. — Congress.

C., or Cap. (*Caput.*) Chapter.

Cal. California. — Calends.

Cant. Canticles.

Cap. Capital. — Caps. Capitals.

Capt. Captain.

Car. Carpentry. — Carat.

C. A. S. (*Connecticuttensis Academiæ Socius.*) Fellow of the Connecticut Academy.

Cash. Cashier.

Cath. Catholic. — Catherine.

C. B. Cape Breton.

C. C. County Court. — County Commissioner.

C. C. (*Compte Courant.*) Account Current.

C. C. P. Court of Common Pleas.

C. E. Civil Engineer. — Canada East.

Celt. Celtic.

Cent., or Ct. (*Centum.*) A hundred.

C. H. Court-House.
Ch., *or* C. Church.
Chal., *or* Ch. Chaldron.
Chal. Chaldee. — Chaldaic.
Chap., *or* Ch. Chapter.
Chem. Chemistry. [ogy.
Chron. Chronicles. — Chronol-
C. J. Chief Justice.
Cl. Clerk. — Clergyman.
Co. County. — Company.
Col. Colonel. — Colossians.
Coll. College. — Collector.
Com. Commissioner. — Com-
modore. — Commentary. —
Commerce. — Committee.
Comp. Comparison.
Con. (*Contra.*) Against, or in
opposition.
Conch. Conchology.
Con. Cr., *or* C. C. Contra Credit.
Cong., *or* C. Congress.
Conj., *or* c. Conjunction.
Conn., *or* Ct. Connecticut.
Cons., *or* Const. Constable.
Cor. Corinthians.
Cor. Sec. Corresponding Sec-
retary.
C. P. Common Pleas. — Court
of Probate.
C. P. S. (*Custos Privati Sigilli.*)
Keeper of the Privy Seal.
Cr. Credit. — Creditor.
Crim. Con. Criminal Conver-
sation, *or* Adultery.
Crystal. Crystallography.
C. S. (*Custos Sigilli.*) Keeper
of the Seal. — Court of Ses-
sions.
Ct. Cent. — Count. — Court. —
Connecticut.
Cur. Current, *or* This month.
C. W. Canada West.
Cwt. (*Centum* and *weight.*)
Hundred-weight.
Cyc. Cyclopædia.

D.

D., *or* d. (*Denarius.*) Penny.
D., *or* d. Day. — Died. — Dime.
Dan. Daniel. — Danish.
Dat. Dative.
D. C. District of Columbia.
D. C. L. Doctor of Civil Law.
D. D. (*Divinitatis Doctor.*) Doc-
tor of Divinity.
Dea. Deacon.
Dec. December. — Declination.
Deg. Degree, *or* Degrees.
Del. Delaware. — Delegate.
Del. (*Delineavit.*) He drew it ;
— placed on a copperplate
with the name of the drafts-
man.
Den. Denmark.
Dep., *or* Dept. Department.
Dep. Deputy.
Dept., *or* Dpt. Deponent.

Deut. Deuteronomy.
D. F. Defender of the Faith. —
Dean of the Faculty.
Dft., *or* Deft. Defendant.
D. G. (*Dei Gratiâ.*) By the
Grace of God.
Diam. Diameter.
Dict. Dictator. — Dictionary.
Dim. Diminutive.
Dis., Disc., *or* Disct. Discount.
Dist. District.
Dist. Atty. District-Attorney.
Div. Divided. — Division.
D. M. Doctor of Music.
Do. (*Ditto.*) The same ; as
aforesaid.
Dols., *or* $. Dollars.
Doz. Dozen.
D. P. Doctor of Philosophy.
Dr. Doctor. — Debtor. — Dram.
Dut. Dutch.
D. V. (*Deo Volente.*) God will-
ing.
Dwt. (*Denarius* and *weight.*)
Pennyweight.

E.

E. East. — Earl. — Eagle.
Ecc., *or* Eccles. Ecclesiastical.
Eccl. Ecclesiastes. — Ecclesi-
astical.
Eccl. Hist. Ecclesiastical His-
tory.
Ecclus. Ecclesiasticus.
Ed. Edition. — Editor.
E. E. Errors excepted. — Eng-
lish Ells.
E. Fl. Ells Flemish.
E. Fr. Ells French.
E. G., *or* e. g. (*Exempli Gratiâ.*)
For example.
E. I. East Indies, *or* East India.
E. I. C. East India Company.
Elec. Electricity.
E. Lon. East Longitude.
Emp. Emperor. — Empress.
Ency., *or* Encyc. Encyclopædia.
E. N. E. East-north-east.
Eng. England. — English.
Ent. Entomology.
Env. Ext. Envoy Extraordinary.
Ep. Epistle.
Eph. Ephesians. — Ephraim.
E. S. Ells Scotch.
E. S. E. East-south-east.
Esq., *or* Esqr. Esquire.
E. T. English Translation.
Et al. (*Et alii.*) And others.
Et al. (*Et alibi.*) And elsewhere.
Etc., *or* &c. (*Et cætera.*) And
others ; and so forth.
Eth. Ethiopic.
Ex. Example. — Exodus.
Exc. Excellency. — Exception.
Exch. Exchequer.
Exod. Exodus.
Exon. (*Exonia.*) Exeter.

Exr. Executor.
Ezek. Ezekiel.

F.

F., *or* f. Franc. — Feminine.
— Florin.
Fahr. Fahrenheit.
Far. Farthing. — Farriery.
F. A. S. Fellow of the Society
of Arts.
F. D. (*Fidei Defensor,* or *De-
fensatrix.*) Defender of the
Faith.
F. E., *or* Fl. E. Flemish Ell.
Feb. February.
Fem. Feminine.
F. E. S. Fellow of the Ento-
mological Society.
F. G. S. Fellow of the Geo-
logical Society.
F. H. S. Fellow of the Horti-
cultural Society.
Fig. Figure. — Figurative.
Fir. Firkin.
Fl., Flor., *or* Fa. Florida.
Fl. Flemish.
Fl., *or* fl. Flourished. — Florin.
Fl. E. Flemish Ell.
F. L. S. Fellow of the Linnæ-
an Society.
Fo., *or* Fol. Folio.
Fort. Fortification.
Fr. France. — French. — Fran-
cis.
F. R. A. S. Fellow of the Royal
Astronomical Society.
Fr. E. French Ell.
Freq. Frequentative.
F. R. G. S. Fellow of the Royal
Geographical Society.
F. R. S. Fellow of the Royal
Society.
Frs. Friesic, Frisian.
F. R. S. E. Fellow of the Royal
Society, Edinburgh.
F. R. S. L. Fellow of the Royal
Society of Literature.
F. S. A. Fellow of the Society
of Antiquaries. — Fellow of
the Society of Arts.
F. S. A. E. Fellow of the So-
ciety of Antiquaries, Edin-
burgh.
Ft. Foot, *or* Feet. — Fort.
Fth. Fathom.
Fur. Furlong.
F. Z. S. Fellow of the Zoölogi-
cal Society.

G.

Ga., *or* Geo. Georgia.
Gael. Gaelic.
Gal. Galatians. — Gallon.
G. B. Great Britain.

Gen. General. — Genitive. — Genesis.
Gent. Gentleman.
Geo. George. — Georgia.
Geog. Geography.
Geol. Geology.
Geom. Geometry.
Ger. German. — Germany.
Goth., or Go. Gothic.
Gov. Governor.
Gov. Gen. Governor-General.
G. R. (*Georgius Rex.*) King George.
Gram. Grammar.
Guin. Guinea, guineas.

H.

H., h., or hr. Hour.
Hab. Habakkuk.
Hag. Haggai.
H. B. C. Hudson's Bay Company.
H. B. M. His, or Her, Britannic Majesty.
Heb. Hebrews. — Hebrew.
H. E. I. C. Honorable East India Company.
Her. Heraldry.
Herp. Herpetology.
Hf. bd. Half-bound.
Hhd. Hogshead.
Hil. Hilary.
Hin. Hindoo. — Hindostan. — Hindostanee.
Hist. History.
H. M. His, or Her, Majesty.
H. M. S. His, or Her, Majesty's Ship, or Service.
Hon. Honorable.
Hon'd. Honored.
Hort. Horticulture.
H. P. Half-pay.
H. R. House of Representatives.
H. R. H. His, or Her, Royal Highness.
H. S. (*Hic situs.*) Here lies.
H. S. S. Fellow of the Historical Society.
Hun. Hungary. — Hungarian.
Hund. Hundred.
Hyd. Hydrostatics.

I.

I., or Isl. Island.
Ia. Indiana.
Ib., or Ibid. (*Ibidem.*) In the same place.
Icel. Iceland. — Icelandic.
Ich. Ichthyology.
Id. (*Idem.*) The same.
I. e., or i. e. (*Id est.*) That is.
I. H. S. (*Jesus Hominum Salvator.*) Jesus the Saviour of Men.
Ill. Illinois.

Imp. Imperial. — Imperative. — Imperfect.
In. Inch, inches.
Inc., or Incor. Incorporated.
Incog. (*Incognito.*) Unknown.
Ind. India. — Indian. — Indiana.
Ind. Ter. Indian Territory.
Infin. Infinitive.
In loc. (*In loco.*) In the place.
Inst. Instant, or Of the present month.
Int. Interest.
Interj., or Int. Interjection.
In trans. (*In transitu.*) On the passage.
Io. Iowa.
I. O. O. F. Independent Order of Odd Fellows.
Ipecac. Ipecacuanha.
Ir. Ireland. — Irish. — Iridium.
Isa. Isaiah.
I. t., or imp. t. Imperfect tense.
I. T. Indian Territory.
It. Italy. — Italian. — Italic.
Itin. Itinerary.

J.

J Judge.
J. A. Judge Advocate.
Ja., or Jas. James.
Jac. Jacob.
Jam. Jamaica.
Jan. January.
J. C. D. Doctor of Civil Law.
J. D. (*Jurum Doctor.*) Doctor of Laws.
Jer. Jeremiah.
J. H. S. (*Jesus Hominum Salvator.*) Jesus the Saviour of Men.
Jno. John.
Jona. Jonathan.
Jos. Joseph.
Josh. Joshua.
Jour. Journal.
J. P. Justice of the Peace.
J. Prob. Judge of Probate.
J. R. (*Jacobus Rex.*) King James.
Jr., or Jun. Junior.
J. U. D. (*Juris utriusque Doctor.*) Doctor of both Laws; i. e. the Canon and the Civil Law.
Judg. Judges.
Jul. July. — Julius.
Jul. Per. Julian Period.
Jus. P. Justice of the Peace.

K.

K. King.
Kan. Kansas.
K. B. Knight of the Bath.
K. B. King's Bench.
K. C. King's Council.
K. C. B. Knight Commander of the Bath.

Ken., or Ky. Kentucky.
K. G. Knight of the Garter.
K. G. C. Knight of the Grand Cross.
K. G. C. B. Knight of the Grand Cross of the Bath.
Kil. Kilderkin.
Kingd., or Km. Kingdom.
Knt., Kt., or K. Knight.
K. T. Knight of the Thistle.
Ky. Kentucky.

L.

L. Lord. — Lady. — Latin.
L., or Lib. (*Liber.*) Book.
L., Lib., lb., or ℔. (*Libra.*) Pound in weight.
L., l., or £. Pound sterling.
La., or Lou. Louisiana.
Lam. Lamentations.
Lat. Latitude. — Latin.
Lb., or ℔. Pound in weight.
L. C. Lord Chancellor. — Lower Canada.
L. C., or l. c. (*Loco citato.*) In the place cited.
L. C. J. Lord Chief Justice.
Ld., or L. Lord.
Ldp., or Lp. Lordship.
Lea. League.
Leg., or Legis. Legislature.
Lev. Leviticus.
L. I. Long Island.
Lib. Librarian.
Lib., or L. (*Liber.*) Book.
Lieut., or Lt. Lieutenant.
Lieut. Col. Lieutenant-Colonel.
Lieut. Gen. Lieutenant-General.
Lieut. Gov. Lieutenant-Governor.
Lit. Literature. — Literary.
Lit., or lit. Literally.
Liv., or liv. Livre.
LL. B. (*Legum Baccalaureus.*) Bachelor of Laws.
LL. D. (*Legum Doctor.*) Doctor of Laws.
Lon., or Long. Longitude.
Lond. London.
Lou., or La. Louisiana.
Low L. Low Latin.
L. S. (*Locus Sigilli.*) Place of the Seal.
L. S. D., or l. s. d. Pounds, shillings, pence.

M.

M. Marquis. — Masculine. — Monsieur, Sir, or Mister. — Morning. — Month. — Minute. — Mile. — Married.
M. (*Mille.*) A thousand.

M. (*Meridies.*) Meridian, Mid-day, *or* Noon.
M., Mon., *or* Mond. Monday.
M. A. Master of Arts. — Military Academy.
Ma., *or* Minn. Minnesota.
Mac., *or* Macc. Maccabees.
Mad., *or* Madm. Madam.
Mag. Magazine.
Maj. Major.
Maj. Gen. Major-General.
Mal. Malachi.
Man. Manege, *or* Horsemanship.
Mar. March.
March. Marchioness.
Marq. Marquis, *or* Marquess.
Mas., *or* Masc. Masculine.
Mass., *or* Ms. Massachusetts.
Math. Mathematics. — Mathematicians.
Matt. Matthew.
M. B. (*Medicinæ Baccalaureus.*) Bachelor of Medicine.
M. B. (*Musicæ Baccalaureus*). Bachelor of Music.
M. C. Member of Congress. — Master Commandant.
M. D. (*Medicinæ Doctor.*) Doctor of Medicine.
Md. Maryland.
Me. Maine.
M. E. Methodist Episcopal.
Mech. Mechanics.
Med. Medicine.
Mem. (*Memento.*) Remember.
Mem. Memorandum.
Messrs., *or* MM. (*Messieurs.*) Gentlemen. — Sirs.
Met. Metaphysics.
Meteor. Meteorology.
Meth. Methodist.
Mex. Mexico, *or* Mexican.
M. Goth. Mœso-Gothic.
M. H. S. Massachusetts Historical Society. — Member of the Historical Society.
Mic. Micah.
Mich. Michigan.—Michaelmas.
Mid. Midshipman.
Mil. Military.
Min. Mineralogy.
Min., *or* min. Minute, minutes.
Minn. Minnesota.
Min. Plen. Minister Plenipotentiary.
Miss., *or* Mi. Mississippi.
Mlle. Mademoiselle.
MM. Messieurs. — Gentlemen.
M. M. S. Moravian Missionary Society.
M. M. S. S. (*Massachusettensis Medicinæ Societatis Socius.*) Member of the Massachusetts Medical Society.
Mo. Missouri. — Month.
Mod. Modern.
Mon., *or* Mond. Monday.
Mons. Monsieur, *or* Sir.

M. P. Member of Parliament. — Member of Police.
M. P. C. Member of Parliament in Canada.
Mr. Mister, *or* Master.
M. R. A. S. Member of the Royal Asiatic Society.
M. R. C. S. Member of the Royal College of Surgeons.
M. R. I. Member of the Royal Institution.
M. R. I. A. Member of the Royal Irish Academy.
Mrs. Mistress (*pron.* Missis.)
M. R. S. L. Member of the Royal Society of Literature.
M. S. (*Memoriæ Sacrum.*) Sacred to the Memory.
MS. Manuscript.
MSS. Manuscripts.
Mt. Mount, *or* Mountain.
Mus. Music. — Museum.
Mus. D. Doctor of Music.
M. W. S. Member of the Wernerian Society.
Myth. Mythology.

N.

N. North. — Note. — Number. — Nail. — Nitrogen.
N., *or* n. Noun. — Name.
N. A. North America. — North American.
Nat. National. — Natural.
Nath. Nathaniel, *or* Nathanael.
Nat. Hist. Natural History.
Nat. Phil. Natural Philosophy.
Naut. Nautical.
N. B. (*Nota bene.*) Mark well; take notice.
N. B. New Brunswick. — North Britain.
N. C. North Carolina. [east.
N. E. New England. — North-
Neb. Nebraska.
Neh. Nehemiah.
Nem. con. (*Nemine contradicente.*) No one contradicting; unanimously.
Nem. diss. (*Nemine dissentiente.*) No one dissenting; unanimously.
Neth. Netherlands.
Neut. Neuter.
N. F. Newfoundland.
New Test., *or* N. T. New Testament.
N. H. New Hampshire.
N. H. H. S. New Hampshire Historical Society.
N. J. New Jersey. [tude.
N. Lat., *or* N. L. North Lati-
N. M. New Mexico.
N. N. E. North-north-east.
N. N. W. North-north-west.
No. (*Numero.*) Number.
Nom. Nominative.

Non pros. (*Non prosequitur.*) He does not prosecute.
Norm. Norman.
Norm. Fr. Norman French.
Norw. Norway. — Norwegian.
Nov. November.
N. P. Notary Public. — New Providence.
N. P. D. North Polar Distance.
N. S. New Style (after 1752).
N. S. Nova Scotia.
N. T. New Testament.
Num., *or* Numb. Numbers.
N. W. North-west.
N. W. T. North-west Territory.
N. Y. New York.
N. Y. H. S. New York Historical Society.

O.

O. Ohio. — Oxygen.
Ob. (*Obiit.*) He, *or* she, died.
Obj. Objection. — Objective.
Obs. Observation. — Observatory. — Obsolete.
Obt. Obedient.
Oct. October.
O. F. Odd Fellows.
Olym. Olympiad. [ment.
Old Test., *or* O. T. Old Testa-
Opt. Optics.
Or. Oregon.
Ord. Ordinary. — Ordnance.
Ornith. Ornithology.
O. S. Old Style (before 1752).
O. T. Old Testament.
Oxon. (*Oxonia.*) Oxford.
Oz., *or* oz. Ounce, *or* ounces.

P.

P., *or* p. Page. — Participle. — Pole. — Pint. — Pipe.
Pa., *or* Penn. Pennsylvania.
P. a., *or* p. a. Participial adjective.
Pal. Paleontology.
Parl. Parliament.
Part., *or* p. Participle.
Payt. Payment.
P. C. Privy Councillor.
Pd. Paid. — Palladium.
P. E. Protestant Episcopal.
P. E. I. Prince Edward's Island.
Penn. Pennsylvania.
Per. Persia. — Persian.
P., p., *or* ℔. (*Per.*) By the.
Per an. (*Per annum.*) By the Year.
Per cent., *or* Per ct. (*Per centum.*) By the Hundred.
Perf. Perfect.
Peri. Perigee.
Persp. Perspective.
Pet. Peter.

Phar. Pharmacy.
Ph. D., *or* P. D. (*Philosophiæ Doctor.*) Doctor of Philosophy.
Phil. Philip. — Philippians. — Philosophy. — Philosopher. — Philosophical.
Phila. Philadelphia.
Philom. (*Philomathes.*) Lover of Learning.
Philomath. (*Philomathematicus.*) A lover of Mathematics.
Phon. Phonography.
Phren. Phrenology.
P. H. S. Pennsylvania Historical Society.
Phys. Physics. — Physiology.
Pinx., *or* pxt. (*Pinxit.*) He, *or* she, painted it.
Pk. Peck.
Pl. Plural. — Place. — Plate.
P. M. (*Post Meridiem.*) Afternoon.
P. M. Postmaster. — Passed Midshipman.
P. M. G. Postmaster-General.
P. O. Post-Office.
Pol. Polish. — Poland.
Pop. Population.
Port. Portugal. — Portuguese.
Pos. Possessive.
Pp. Past participle.
Pp., *or* pp. Participles.—Pages.
P. P. C. (*Pour prendre congé.*) To take leave.
P. R. Porto Rico.
Pr. Preposition. — (*Per.*) By, *or* by the.
P. R. A. President of the Royal Academy.
Prep., *or* Pre. Preposition.
Pres. Present. — President.
Pret. Preterite.
Priv. Privative.
Prob. Problem.
Prof. Professor. [noun.
Pron., *or* pr. Pronounced; pro-
Pron. a. Pronominal adjective.
Prop. Proposition.
Pros. Prosody.
Prot. Protestant. [the time.
Pro tem. (*Pro tempore.*) For
Prov. Proverbs. — Provost. — Province.
Prox. (*Proximo.*) Next, *or* Of the next Month.
P. R. S. President of the Royal Society.
Prus. Prussia. — Prussian.
P. S. Privy Seal. — (*Post Scriptum.*) Postscript.
Ps. Psalm, *or* Psalms.
Pt. Pint. — Payment.
P. t. Post-town.
Pub. Published. — Publisher.
Pub. Doc. Public Document
Pun. Puncheon.
P. v. Post village.
Pwt. Pennyweight.

Q.

Q., *or* Qu. Question. — Queen.
Q., *or* q. (*Quadrans.*) Farthing.
Q. B. Queen's Bench.
Q. C. Queen's Council.
Q. D., *or* q. d. (*Quasi dicat.*) As if he should say.
Q. E. (*Quod est.*) Which is.
Q. E. D. (*Quod erat demonstrandum.*) Which was to be demonstrated.
Q. E. F. (*Quod erat faciendum.*) Which was to be done.
Q. L., *or* q. l. (*Quantum libet.*) As much as you please.
Q. P., *or* q. pl. (*Quantum placet.*) As much as you please.
Qr., *or* qrs. Quarter, *or* Quarters. — Farthings.
Q. S. Quarter Section.
Q. S., *or* q. s. (*Quantum sufficit.*) A sufficient quantity.
Qt., *or* qt. Quart. — Quantity.
Qu., Qy., *or* q. (*Quære.*) Query.
Ques. Question.
Q. V., *or* q. v. (*Quod vide.*) Which see.
Q. V., *or* q. v. (*Quantum vis.*) As much as you please.

R.

R. (*Rex.*) King. — (*Regina.*) Queen.
R., *or* r. Rood. — Rod. — Rises. — River. — Rare.
R. A. Royal Academy. — Royal Academician. — Royal Artillery. — Rear Admiral. — Right Ascension.
Rad. Radical.
R. E. Royal Engineers.
Rec. Recipe.
Recd. Received.
Recpt. Receipt.
Rec. Sec. Recording Secretary.
Rect. Rector.
Ref. Reformed. — Reference.
Ref. Ch. Reformed Church.
Reg. Prof. Regius Professor.
Regr., *or* Reg. Register. — Registrar.
Regt. Regiment.
Rel. Pron. Relative Pronoun.
Rep. Representative. — Reporter.
Rep., *or* Repub. Republic.
Rev. Reverend. — Revelation. — Review.
Rhet. Rhetoric.
R. I. Rhode Island.
R. I. H. S. Rhode Island Historical Society.
R. M. Royal Marines.
R. M. S. Royal Mail Steamer.

R. N. Royal Navy.
Ro. (*Recto.*) Right-hand Page.
Robt. Robert.
Rom. Romans.
Rom. Cath. Roman Catholic.
R. R. Railroad.
Rt. Hon. Right Honorable.
Rt. Rev. Right Reverend.
Rt. Wpful. Right Worshipful.
Rus. Russia. — Russian.

S.

S. South. — Shilling. — Second. — Sign. — Sunday. — Scribe.
S., *or* St. Saint.
S. A. South America.
Sam. Samuel. — Samaritan.
Sans., *or* Sansc. Sanscrit.
S. A. S. (*Societatis Antiquariorum Socius.*) Fellow of the Society of Antiquaries.
Sat. Saturday.
Sax. Saxon. — Saxony.
S. C. South Carolina.
Sc., *or* Sculp. (*Sculpsit.*) He, *or* she, engraved it.
S. caps. Small capitals.
Sch. (*Scholium.*) A note.
Scil., *or* Sc. (*Scilicet.*) To wit.
Sclav. Sclavonic. [tish.
Scot. Scotland, Scotch, *or* Scot-
Sculp. Sculpture.
Sculp. (*Sculpsit.*) He, *or* she, engraved it.
S. E. South-east.
Sec. Secretary. — Section. — Second.
Sec. Leg. Secretary of Legation.
Sect. Section. [ator.
Sen. Senior. — Senate. — Sen-
Sep., *or* Sept. September.
Sept. Septuagint.
Serg., *or* Serj. Sergeant, *or* Serjeant.
Servt. Servant.
Sh., *or* S. Shilling.
S. H. S. (*Societatis Historiæ Socius.*) Fellow of the Historical Society.
Sing. Singular.
S. J. C. Supreme Judicial Court.
S. Lat., *or* S. L. South Latitude.
Slav. Slavonic.
S. L. Solicitor at Law.
Sol. Solomon. — Solution.
Sol. Gen. Solicitor-General.
Sp. Spain. — Spanish.
S. P. A. S. (*Societatis Philosophicæ Americanæ Socius.*) Member of the American Philosophical Society.
S. P. G. Society for the Propagation of the Gospel.
S. P. Q. R. (*Senatus Populusque Romanus.*) The Senate and the Roman People.

Sq., *or* Sqr. Square.
Sq. ft. Square feet.
Sq. in. Square inches.
Sq. m. Square miles.
Sq. r. Square roods.
Sq. yd. Square yards.
SS., *or* ss. (*Scilicet.*) To wit; namely.
S. S. E. South-south-east.
S. S. W. South-south-west.
St. Saint. — Street. — Stone.
S. T. D. (*Sacræ Theologiæ Doctor.*) Doctor of Divinity.
Ster., *or* Stg. Sterling.
S. T. P. (*Sacræ Theologiæ Professor.*) Professor of Theology.
Su. Goth. Suio-Gothic, *or* Norse.
Sup., *or* Supp. Supplement.
Sup., *or* Super. Superior. — Superfine.
Supt. Superintendent.
Surg. Surgeon. — Surgery.
Surg. Gen. Surgeon-General.
Surv. Gen. Surveyor-General.
S. W. South-west.
Sw. Sweden. — Swedish.
Switz. Switzerland.
Syn. Synonyme.
Syr. Syria. — Syriac.

T.

T., *or* t. Town, *or* township.
T. E. Topographical Engineers.
Tenn. Tennessee.
Tex. Texas.
Text. Rec. (*Textus Receptus.*) Received Text.
Theo. Theodore.
Theol. Theology.
Theoph. Theophilus.
Theor. Theorem.
Thess. Thessalonians.
Thos. Thomas.
Thurs. Thursday.
Tier. Tierce.
Tim. Timothy.
T. O. Turn over.
Tr. Translator. — Translation. — Treasurer. — Trustee.

Trans. Translation. — Translator. — Translated.
Trin. Trinity.
Tues., *or* Tu. Tuesday.
Turk. Turkey. — Turkish.
Typ. Typographer.

U.

U. C. Upper Canada.
U. E. I. C. United East India Company.
Ult. (*Ultimo.*) Last, *or* Of the last month.
Univ. University.
U. S., *or* u. s. (*Ut*, or *uti, supra.*) As above.
U. S. United States.
U. S. A. United States Army. — United States of America.
U. S. M. United States Mail. — United States Marine.
U. S. N. United States Navy.
U. S. S. United States Ship.
U. T. Utah Territory.

V.

V. Verb. — Verse.
V., Vi., *or* Vid. (*Vide.*) See.
V., *or* vs. (*Versus.*) Against.
Va. Virginia.
V. A., *or* v. a. Verb Active.
V. C. Vice-Chancellor.
V. D. M. (*Verbi Dei Minister.*) Minister of God's Word.
Vis., *or* V. Viscount.
Viz. (*Videlicet.*) To wit; namely.
V. N., *or* v. n. Verb Neuter.
Vol. Volume. — Vols. Volumes.
V. P. Vice-President.
V. R. (*Victoria Regina.*) Queen Victoria.
Vs., *or* V. (*Versus.*) Against.
V. t., *or* V. tr. Verb transitive.
Vt. Vermont.
Vul. Vulgate.

W.

W. Welsh. — West.
W., *or* Wed. Wednesday.
W., *or* Wk. Week.
W. I. West India. — West Indies.
Wis., *or* Wisc. Wisconsin.
Wk. Week.
W. Lon. West Longitude.
Wm. William.
W. M. S. Wesleyan Missionary Society.
W. N. W. West-north-west.
Wp. Worship.
Wpful. Worshipful.
W. S. Writer to the Signet.
W. S. W. West-south-west.
W. T. Washington Territory.
Wt. Weight.

X.

Xmas., *or* Xm. Christmas.
Xn., *or* Xtian. Christian.
Xnty., *or* Xty. Christianity.
Xper., *or* Xr. Christopher.
Xt. Christ.

Y.

Y., *or* Yr. Year.
Y. B., *or* Yr. B. Year-Book.
Yd. Yard. — Yds. Yards.
Ye. The.
Ym. Them.
Yn. Then.
Yr. Your.
Yrs. Yours.
Ys. This.
Yt. That.

Z.

Zech. Zechariah.
Zeph. Zephaniah.
Zoöl. Zoölogy.

Printed in the USA
CPSIA information can be obtained
at www.ICGtesting.com
CBHW060858041223
2314CB00009BA/651